ENCARTA® BOOK OF QUOTATIONS

ENCARTA® BOOK OF QUOTATIONS

FOREWORD

ANNE H. SOUKHANOV

EDITOR

BILL SWAINSON

St. Martin's Press 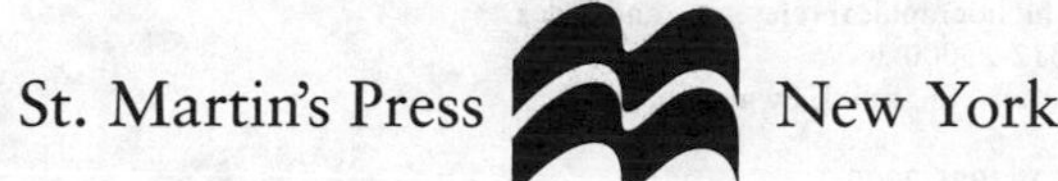 New York

A BLOOMSBURY REFERENCE BOOK
Created from the Bloomsbury Database of Quotations

First published in the United States of America in 2000 by
St. Martin's Press
175 Fifth Avenue
New York, NY 10010

Library of Congress Cataloging-in-Publication Data

Encarta book of quotations: / edited by Bill Swainson; foreword by Anne Soukhanov.

p. cm.
Includes bibliographical references and index.
ISBN 0-312-23000-1
1. Quotations, English. I. Swainson, Bill.

PN6081. W5985 2000
082--dc21

00-033263
CIP

Typeset by Selwood Systems, Midsomer Norton, Bath
Printed in the United States of America

Contents

QUOTATIONS DATABASE

Editor
Bill Swainson

Database Manager
Edmund Wright

Managing Editor
Sarah Waldram

Project Manager
Katy McAdam

Production Editor
Nicky Thompson

Project Coordinator
Alasdair MacLean

Database Administrator
Peter Hosking

Output Technician
Melanie Tate

EDITORIAL CONSULTANTS

Vastiana Belfon
Researcher in African, Afro-Caribbean, and African American culture

David Bellos
Princeton University

John Caley
Han Shan Tang Books, London

Katherine Darton
MIND, London

John Durant
Science Museum, London

Douglas Houston
Poet and author

Michael Hulse
Translator and poet

John Wyse Jackson
Editor, author, and bookseller

Dr. Catriona Kelly
New College, Oxford

Alberto Manguel
Author

Susan North
Victoria and Albert Museum, London

Neil Powell
Author and critic

Ramesh Rajballie
Historian

Dr. Joseph Rhymer
Writer and theologian

Dr. R. M. Youngson
Consultant ophthalmologist and medical writer

Zhou Xun
School of Oriental and African Studies, London

CONTRIBUTORS AND EDITORS

Contributors
Paul Binding
Edward Butcher
Robert Clarke
Julia Cresswell
Steve Eddy
Laura Lawrie
Tina Persaud
Jeffrey Petts
Peter Porter
Eva Salzman
Jo Shapcott
Snezana Vujovic
Heather Wardle

Vetting Editor
Jenny Parrott

Contributing Editors
Stephen Adamson
Mark Crean
Sheila Dallas
Dominique Enright
Stan Kurzban
David Milsted
Lisa Nave
James Randall
Pauline Sidey
Susan Turner
Richard Tyrrell
Kamala Wickramasinghe
Sarah Yates

Editors
Claire Ellerton
Kathy Fahey
Hannah Griffiths
Andrew McAllister
Molly McGrann
Vanessa Mitchell
Sandra Scott
Eleanor Stanley
Pamela White
Emily Young

PROJECT ASSISTANTS

Charlotte Adams
Holger Becker
Diana de Bellaigue
Jonathan Butler
Roland Chambers
Kristine Coco
Jonathan Collins
Bernadette Crowley
Barry Day
Menal Elamin
Michael Fox
Roya Ireland
Andy Lacey
Victoria Le Fevre
Colin Midson
Sarah Mulligan
Ceri Prenter
Ben Wardle

PROOFREADERS

Stuart Fortey
Margaret Hill
Ruth Hillmore
Irene Lakhani
Mark Miller
Margaret Mullen

BLOOMSBURY REFERENCE

U.S. General Editor
Encarta® World English Dictionary
Anne H. Soukhanov

Editor-in-Chief
Dr. Kathy Rooney

Publisher
Nigel Newton

Production Director
Penny Edwards

Design Director
William Webb

Production Manager
Polly Napper

Frontmatter Designer
Simon Mercer

Foreword

Anne H. Soukhanov, General Editor
Encarta® World English Dictionary

> *Every quotation contributes something to the stability or enlargement of the language.*
>
> SAMUEL JOHNSON (1709–84)
> Preface, *A Dictionary of the English Language* (1755)

THE BOOK THAT YOU ARE READING is the first 21st-century collection of memorable quotations spanning the centuries, reflecting the voices of people worldwide, many quoted here for the first time. It is an original work, derived from the Bloomsbury Quotations Database, created expressly for this purpose. This book contains 25,000 entries representing the thoughts of over 6,200 writers and speakers, from a statement by the 18th-century B.C. Babylonian ruler Hammurabi to January 2000 quotations by Tony Blair, Al Gore, and George W. Bush.

The quotations focus on the major themes informing our lives—politics, law, religion, science, technology, medicine, business, communications, the arts, sports, entertainment, literature, and history. In reading through this collection, one is instantly impressed with the way the words of different personages are invested with the history of the times in which they live or lived—with the way their respective words resonate or clash. Take the words of Nelson Mandela, uttered on December 31, 1999, "The freedom flame can never be put down by anybody." Then review the words of Martin Luther King, Jr., uttered on August 28, 1963, "I have a dream that one day this nation will rise up, live out the true meaning of its creed: we hold these truths to be self-evident, that all men are created equal."

Recall Boris Yeltsin's remarks on December 31, 1999, the occasion of his retirement as President of Russia, "I ask you to forgive me for not fulfilling some hopes of those people who believed that we would be able to jump from the totalitarian past into a bright, rich, and civilized future in one go." His words, expressive of his nation's latest time of troubles, coexist within this volume with the words of another Russian, Tsar Ivan IV ("Ivan the Terrible"), in a letter dated September 1577, "Did I ascend the throne by robbery or armed bloodshed? I was born to rule."

From the words of ancients such as Archimedes, Plutarch, Socrates, and Julius Caesar, to those of moderns such as Umberto Eco, Buchi Emecheta, Ruth Bader Ginsburg, and Barbara Jordan, this collection affords a sharply delineated sense of history in terms of our transactions as a global people, recently unfettered from old borders slowing or restricting communication. Careful reading of these quotations—many of them translations into English from other tongues—can perhaps draw us closer together, even contributing to the stability of the world and the enlargement of our understanding of the past so that together we can create a better future. And if history is, in words attributed to Konrad Adenauer, "the sum total of the things that could have been avoided," then, as Maya Angelou expressed it during the January 20, 1993, U.S. presidential inauguration:

> History, despite its
> wrenching pain,
> Cannot be unlived, but if
> faced with courage, need not be
> lived again.

Thus, the words we speak are redolent of the human condition, whether good or evil, beautiful or ugly, right or wrong, violent or peaceful, brilliant or stupid, sad or funny. And so if "laughter is the best medicine" in an increasingly complex world, this book is laced with trenchant, humorous observations and opinions, themselves expressive of this human condition: "If you want to know where the apathy is, you're probably sitting on it" (Florynce R. Kennedy), "I don't believe in God, but I'm afraid of Him" (Gabriel García Márquez), "Going to trial with a lawyer who considers your life-style a Crime in Progress is not a happy prospect" (Hunter S. Thompson), "Get mad, then get over it" (Colin Powell), "In these days of computer viruses, asking if you may put your disk into someone's computer is the technological equivalent of unsafe sex" (Ruth Dudley Edwards), "War is the best university" (Samora Machel), "The one thing that doesn't abide by majority rule is a person's conscience" (Harper Lee), "Never judge a cover by its book" (Fran Lebowitz), "A good newspaper is never nearly good enough but a lousy newspaper is a joy forever" (Garrison Keillor), "Media is a word that has come to mean bad journalism" (Graham Greene), "The difference between us is that my family begins with me, whereas yours ends with you" (Iphicrates), "I guess I should warn you. If I turn out to be particularly clear, you've probably misunderstood what I've said" (Alan Greenspan), "The American dream is not dead. True, it is gasping for breath but it is not dead" (Barbara Jordan), "The wrong sort of people are always in power because they would not be in power if they were not the wrong sort of people" (Jon Wynne-Tyson), "There are three things you just can't do in life. You can't beat the phone company, you can't make a waiter see you until he is ready to see you, and you can't go home again" (Bill Bryson).

This book illustrates how today, as in Shakespeare's time, "Brevity is the soul of wit."

Introduction

Bill Swainson, Editor

I quote from others only the better to express myself.

MONTAIGNE

THIS BOOK CONTAINS 25,000 quotations by more than 6,200 authors drawn from earliest times to the present. Truly international in scope, it is also completely up to date, with approximately half the quotations being taken from the last 100 years, and two-thirds from the last 200 years.

Like the editors of the *Encarta® World English Dictionary,* we have taken inspiration from the fact that, in the last 50 years, wherever we live, our awareness of and participation in the rest of the world are greater than ever before. Also, in that same period English has become the main international language, with one in five people speaking it as their first language, and 375 million using it as their second language. In addition, English is the main international language of business, pop music, sports, advertising, academic conferences, diplomacy, science, and technology. The Bloomsbury Quotations Database from which this book is derived has been created for use by people living and working in this new, much wider world, and we hope that the range of languages and cultures from which the quotations in the book are drawn reflect this change. Taken together they amount to a portrait of our common humanity.

The quotations and their authors

In compiling this book we have done our utmost to ensure that the quotations we have chosen are drawn from and reflect the new wider world we all inhabit. Many of them will be genuinely familiar, others will not, but a surprising number will seem as if we have known them all our lives, like

> The breeze of love blows for an hour
> and makes amends for the ill winds
> of the whole of a lifetime.

from the great Egyptian novelist Naguib Mahfouz's *Echoes of an Autobiography* (1994).

But while this collection contains much that is new, it also contains quotations from all ages that have stood the test of time. So the user will find both Shakespeare's timeless "A rose by any other name would smell as sweet" from *Romeo and Juliet* (1595) and Gertrude Stein's "Rose is a rose is a rose is a rose" from *Sacred Emily* (1913); both "Be not forgetful to entertain strangers: for thereby some have entertained angels unawares" from the Bible (Hebrews 13:1–2) and Tennessee Williams's "I have always depended on the kindness of strangers" from *A Streetcar Named Desire* (1947); and both Aristotle's general statement that "poetry is something more philosophical and more worthy of serious attention than history" and Theodor Adorno's assertion, pinned precisely to its time, that "To write poetry after Auschwitz is barbaric," a cry of outrage, whose pain we can still feel, even if we disagree with it.

Included in this book are sayings by or about people who have achieved national or international stature as historical figures, politicians, thinkers, writers, artists, musicians, scientists, celebrities, and pioneers of all kinds, together with figures (real and fictional) from popular culture. The range of contemporary authors includes Chinua Achebe, Kofi Annan, Margaret Atwood, Paul Auster, Joseph Brodsky, Raymond Carver, Bill Clinton, Kurt Cobain, the Dalai Lama, Roddy Doyle, Umberto Eco, Alan Greenspan, Seamus Heaney, Chrissie Hynde, Lee Iacocca, C. L. R. James, Michael Jordan, Spike Lee, Naguib Mahfouz, Malcolm X, Nelson Mandela, Armistead Maupin, Toni Morrison, Walter Mosley, Michael Ondaatje, Camille Paglia, Salman Rushdie, Edward Said, Matt Groening's *The Simpsons*, Will Smith, Steven Spielberg, Gloria Steinem, Quentin Tarantino, Alice Walker, Oprah Winfrey, and Boris Yeltsin.

One of the incidentally fascinating things about quotations is how modern the great writers of ancient times can sound, as, for example, in Horace's line "We are just statistics, born to consume resources" from *Epistles*, bk. 1, no. 2 (20? B.C.) and how timeless our contemporaries can sound, as in the African American writer Maya Angelou's observation that "Human beings are more alike than unalike, and what is true anywhere is true everywhere, yet I encourage travel to as many destinations as possible for the sake of education as well as pleasure" from "Passports to Understanding," *Wouldn't Take Nothing for My Journey Now* (1993).

Subject areas

"In the dying world I come from," wrote Evelyn Waugh in his late novel *The Loved One* (1948), "quotation is a national vice. It used to be the classics, now it's lyric verse." More than fifty years later, at the beginning of a new millennium, we would want to redefine quotation again as any memorable saying that is or could be, and in some cases, perhaps, should be, part of common international currency, whether culled from the classics or lyric verse, a media soundbite, or the words of a song.

So, while gathering together the widest possible range of quotations by the widest possible range of authors to create an international collection of familiar sayings, we have also sought to cover subject areas that have been underrepresented or overlooked. Thus there are, for example, substantial numbers of quotations from African, Afro-Caribbean, and African American sources, as well as from China, Russia, the Indian sub-continent, Asia, the American continents, and Europe. How could a book of quotations be complete without, for example, quotations such as these from an African American, a Kenyan, a Palestinian, and a Tibetan:

Hope I lives till I get home
I'm tired of eatin'
What they eats in Rome.
Mari Evans

White people have often confused the symbol of our poverty with our culture.
Tom Mboya

Why did my country become a gateway
to hell? Since when are apples bitter?
When did moonlight stop bathing orchards?
Fadwa Tuqan

No matter what part of the world we come from, we are all basically the same human beings. We all seek happiness and try to avoid suffering.
Dalai Lama

We have drawn many of the quotations from the sacred texts and commentaries on the world's great religions:

O ye who believe!
Cancel not your charity by reminders of your generosity.
Koran

The whole worth of a kind deed lies in the love that inspires it.
Talmud

And many from science and technology:

One never notices what has been done; one can only see what remains to be done.
Marie Curie

We have discovered the secret of life!
On entering a Cambridge pub with James Watson to celebrate the fact that they had unraveled the structure of DNA.
Francis Crick

Even if there is only one possible unified theory, it is just a set of rules and equations. What is it that breathes fire into the equations and makes a universe for them to describe?
Stephen Hawking

And psychology and medicine:

As far as we can discern, the sole purpose of human existence is to kindle a light in the darkness of mere being.
Carl Gustav Jung

Logical activity is not the whole of intelligence. One can be intelligent without being particularly logical.
Jean Piaget

As well as business, money, and management:

Develop the business around the people; build it, don't buy it; and, then, be the best.
Richard Branson

In the end, all business operations can be reduced to three words: people, product, and profits.

Lee Iacocca

Money, it turned out, was exactly like sex, you thought of nothing else if you didn't have it and thought of other things if you did.

James Baldwin

Money has no smell.

Answering Titus's objection to a tax on public lavatories.

Vespasian

Sports:

Baseball—with its lore and legends, its cultural power, its seasonal associations...its mythic transformation of the immediate—was the literature of my boyhood.

Philip Roth

Talent wins games, but teamwork wins championships.

Michael Jordan

And popular culture:

I frequently hear music in the heart of noise.

George Gershwin

Nobody loves me but my mother,
And she could be jiving, too.

B. B. King

People on people

There are many remarkably astute, acerbic, heartfelt, witty, or downright scurrilous quotations by the famous on the famous or the infamous (and vice versa), from Cicero on Socrates to Gore Vidal on Andy Warhol, and all reveal something about the subject and the author. It is a special feature of this book that such quotations have been gathered under the subject, rather than the author, of the quotation, with the great advantage that this gives a good idea of what a speaker or writer's contemporaries and successors thought of his or her life and works. Here Descartes' idea of reading as "a conversation with the finest men of past centuries" comes vividly to life as writers, politicians, artists, and celebrities comment freely on one another's strengths and weaknesses.

Among such quotations can be found the great Russian poet Anna Akhmatova's view of Tolstoy's hidden agenda in *Anna Karenina* as expressed to her close friend the diarist Lydia Chukovskaya, on May 18, 1939:

> You must have noticed that the main idea of that great work is this: if a woman leaves her lawful husband to live with another man, this inevitably makes her a prostitute. Don't argue! That's exactly what it is.

And among many more and some less edifying examples is Byron's opinion of Wordsworth:

We learn from Horace, "Homer sometimes sleeps";
We feel without him, Wordsworth sometimes wakes.

An anonymous report on Fred Astaire's first screen test:

Can't act. Can't sing. Slightly bald. Can dance a little.

Albert Einstein's assessment of Marie Curie:

Of all celebrated beings, the only one whom fame has not corrupted.

William Faulkner's of Ernest Hemingway:

He has never been known to use a word that might send the reader to the dictionary.

Adlai Stevenson's of Richard Nixon:

Nixon is the kind of politician who would cut down a redwood tree and then mount the stump for a conservation speech.

And finally, it allows us to include what must be one of the briefest and happiest exchanges between author and publisher. To the question "?" which was the entire contents of a telegram sent by Victor Hugo to his publishers asking after the sales of *Les Misérables*, the cheerful reply came back:

!

How the information is set out

This book is organized in alphabetical order by author for ease of reference. At the head of each entry appears the name by which a quoted author made his or her reputation and is best known. Immediately after in brackets appears that author's real or full name and life dates. Then follow nationality and designation:

Main name, Other names (Real name; Dates)
Nationality and designation

Each quotation by a particular author is numbered. The text of the quotation is then followed by the date of composition, if known and if earlier than the source used, and then, where necessary, a context note. The quotation is completed by the source information, usually, but not always, a printed source.

1 Quotation
Quote date. Context note
Source information

The whole quotation is then set out like this:

Calder, Nigel (Nigel David Ritchie Calder; b.1931) British science writer and broadcaster

1 In a sense human flesh is made of stardust. Every atom in the human body, excluding only the primordial hydrogen atoms, was fashioned in stars that formed, grew old and exploded most violently before the Sun and Earth came into being.
January 27, 1977. Originally broadcast. *The Key to the Universe: a Report on the New Physics* (1977)

Anonymous quotations are dealt with slightly differently. For example, sacred texts generally appear under the title of the work in question. Thus, for example, the Bible will appear under "B," the Koran under "K," and the Talmud under "T." In addition, clear-cut groups of anonymous quotes have been collected so that, for example, "Epitaphs" appear under "E" and Children's Verse under "C." A substantial selection of proverbs, the anonymous folk wisdom of the world, has been grouped under "P," including examples ancient:

> If you chase two hares, one will escape.
>
> African (Shona) proverb

And modern:

> Capitalism is the exploitation of man by man.
> Communism is the complete opposite.

With so many current and familiar quotations coming from films and television we have decided generally to include quotations under the actor, director, or screenwriter most closely associated with them. Thus quotes from films made famous by Mae West appear under her entry alongside her own original contributions, including the exquisite line:

> I used to be Snow White...but I drifted.

The indexes

There are two indexes: the keyword index and the thematic index. The keyword index offers an easy way to track down a half-remembered quotation or a quotation that contains a specific word. Every quotation has been indexed by a keyword. Each entry in the keyword index gives a short phrase in which the keyword is abbreviated, followed by the main name of the author and the number of the quotation:

> **love**
>
> We must l. one another or die AUDEN, W. H., 38
>
> L. that dare not speak its name DOUGLAS, ALFRED, 2
>
> How alike are the groans of l. to those of the dying LOWRY, MALCOLM, 3
>
> **loves**
>
> A woman must marry the man who l. her BÂ, MARIAMA, 1

The thematic index is a helpful tool for gathering quotations on a particular theme—for an essay, or a presentation or a speech—and enables the user to find quotations that do not actually include a specific word, for example, Ambition, Architecture, Leadership, or Love. Every quotation in this book has been indexed according to one of over 1,250 themes. In the thematic index, all quotations appropriate to a specific theme are listed in alphabetical order by author name, followed by the relevant quotation number. A reader browsing for quotations about

Ambition, Architecture, Leadership, or Love, would find among them the following:

Ambition Keats, John, 47; White, Patrick, 4

I would sooner fail than not be among the greatest.
John Keats

Well, good luck to you, kid! I'm going to write the Great Australian Novel.
Patrick White

Architecture Le Corbusier, 1; Mies van der Rohe, Ludwig, 1

A house is a machine for living in.
Le Corbusier

Less is more.
Ludwig Mies van der Rohe

Love Jerrold, Douglas, 3; Labé, Louise, 1

The surest way to hit a woman's heart is to take aim kneeling.
Douglas Jerrold

A woman's heart always has a burned mark.
Louise Labé

Leadership Marx, Groucho, 33; Meir, Golda, 6

Only one man in a thousand is a leader of men—the other 999 follow women.
Groucho Marx

A leader who doesn't hesitate before he sends his nation into battle is not fit to be a leader.
Golda Meir

We hope that every one of the quotations in this book is a succinct, memorable saying that exemplifies an event or an age, provides an evocative or witty expression of a sensation or emotion, or a pithy summation of an ethical, philosophical, scientific, religious, or political point of view. And we also hope that having whetted the user's appetite, this book will satisfy it each time, for as the *Talmud* says:

A quotation at the right moment is like bread to the famished.

Aa

Aaron, Hank (Henry Lewis Aaron, "The Hammer"; b.1934) U.S. baseball player

1 I've got a bat...I let the fellow with the ball do the fretting.
Quoted in *Baseball* (Geoffrey C. Ward and Ken Burns; 1994)

Abakanowicz, Magdalena (b.1930) Polish sculptor and graphic artist

1 Art will remain the most astonishing activity of mankind born out of struggle between wisdom and madness, between dream and reality in our mind.
Quoted in *Magdalena Abakanowicz* (Barbara Rose, ed.; 1993)

Abbott, Berenice (1898–1991) U.S. photographer

1 Photography can never grow up if it imitates some other medium. It has to walk alone; it has to be itself.
"It Has to Walk Alone," *Infinity* (1951)

Abbott, George (George Francis Abbott; 1887–1995) U.S. director, producer, playwright, and actor

1 Very few plays are any good and *no* first plays are any good.
Saturday Evening Post (1955)

2 If you have a good part in a hit, your whole life will change, you will become a success, and you will pay a price for that success. You will play the same part all the rest of your life under different names.
Quoted in *Tumultuous Merriment* (Heywood Hale Broun; 1979)

Abel, Niels Henrik (1802–29) Norwegian mathematician

1 By studying the masters—not their pupils.
1825? When asked how he had become a great mathematician so quickly. Quoted in *Men of Mathematics* (E. T. Bell; 1937)

Abelard, Peter (1079–1142?) French theologian and philosopher

1 It is vicious to give in to our desires; but not to have any desires at all is impossible for our weak nature.
Abailard's Ethics (J. Ramsey McCallum, tr.; 1935)

2 We call the intention good which is right in itself, but the action is good, not because it contains within it some good, but because it issued from a good intention.
Abailard's Ethics (J. Ramsey McCallum, tr.; 1935)

3 Against the disease of writing one must take special precautions, since it is a dangerous and contagious disease.
The Letters of Abelard and Heloise (C. K. Scott Moncrieff, tr.; 1942), no. 8

Abernethy, John (1764–1831) British surgeon

1 "Pray, Mr. Abernethy, what is a cure for gout?" was the question of an indolent and luxurious citizen.
"Live upon sixpence a day—and earn it," was the cogent reply.
Quoted in *Medical Portrait Gallery* (Thomas J. Pettigrew; 1840), vol. 2

2 Private patients, if they do not like me, can go elsewhere; but the poor devils in the hospital I am bound to take care of.
Quoted in *Memoirs of John Abernethy* (George Macilwain; 1853), ch. 5

3 Why, Madam, do you know there are upward of thirty yards of bowels squeezed underneath that girdle of your daughter's? Go home and cut it; let Nature have fair play, and you will have no need of my advice.
Advice to a woman who took her tightly laced daughter to him. Quoted in *Memoirs of John Abernethy* (George Macilwain; 1853), ch. 33

Abrahams, Peter (Peter Henry Abrahams; b.1919) South African-born novelist, journalist, and political commentator

1 The eyes of a lover tell lies.
Mine Boy (1946)

2 The Negro is not free. He is not free on any level of living. But the fact that he is not free does not make him morally infallible.
Return to Goli (1953)

3 All my life had been dominated by a sign, often invisible but no less real for that, which said: RESERVED FOR EUROPEANS ONLY.
Tell Freedom (1954)

4 Whatever they say, most men want the woman of their choice also to be the mother of their children: a sort of visible and outward symbol of commitment and surrender.
The View From Coyaba (1985)

Abse, Dannie (b.1923) Welsh poet and physician

1 "Most Welshmen are worthless,
an inferior breed, doctor."
He did not know I was Welsh.
Then he praised the architects
of the German death-camps—
did not know I was a Jew.
White Coat, Purple Coat: Collected Poems, 1948–1988 (1989), quoted in *Twentieth-Century Anglo-Welsh Poetry* (Dannie Abse, ed.; 1997)

Abubaker Haddad, Y. (Abubaker Y. Al-Shingety) Sudanese academic and author

1 Perhaps, for the first time since the demise of the Nazis...America found an absolute other in the Nation of Islam.
Quoted in *The Muslims of America* (Yvonne Y. Haddad, ed.; 1991)

Abzug, Bella (originally Bella Savitzky; 1920–98) U.S. lawyer, politician, and campaigner

1 They call me Battling Bella, Mother Courage, and a Jewish mother with more complaints than Portnoy...But whatever I am—and this ought to be made very clear—I am a very serious woman.
Abzug was a member of the House of Representatives when she said this. *Bella!* (1972)

2 Richard Nixon self-impeached...gave us Gerald Ford as his revenge.
Rolling Stone (December 2, 1976)

Ace, Goodman (1899–1982) U.S. radio and TV writer and comedian

1 TV...is our latest medium—we call it a medium because nothing's well done.
Letter to Groucho Marx (1954), quoted in *The Groucho Letters* (Groucho Marx; 1967)

Achard, Marcel (Marcel-Auguste Ferreol; 1899–1974) French playwright

1 To come up with a witticism, I'd kill father and mother. Luckily, I'm an orphan.
"La Table ronde," *Patate* (1957), epigraph

Achebe, Chinua (Albert Chinualumogu Achebe; b.1930) Nigerian novelist, poet, and essayist

1 An angry man is always a stupid man.
Anthills of the Savannah (1987)

2 Contradictions if well understood and managed can spark off the fires of invention. Orthodoxy whether of the right or of the left is the graveyard of creativity.
Anthills of the Savannah (1987)

3 I have never seen the sense in *sleeping* with people. A man should wake up in his own bed. A woman likewise. Whatever they choose to do prior to sleeping is no reason to deny them that right.
Anthills of the Savannah (1987)

4 The most awful thing about power is not that it corrupts absolutely but that it makes people so utterly boring, so predictable.
Anthills of the Savannah (1987)

5 Writers don't give prescriptions. They give headaches!
Anthills of the Savannah (1987)

6 A debt may get mouldy, but it never decays.
No Longer At Ease (1960)

7 Real tragedy is never resolved. It goes on hopelessly for ever.
No Longer At Ease (1960)

8 Okonkwo's fear ... was not external but lay deep within himself. It was the fear of himself, lest he should be found to resemble his father.
Things Fall Apart (1958)

Acheson, Dean (Dean Gooderham Acheson; 1893–1971) U.S. lawyer and statesman

1 Great Britain has lost an Empire and has not yet found a role.
Speech, West Point Military Academy (December 5, 1962)

2 I will undoubtedly have to seek what is happily known as gainful employment, which I am glad to say does not describe holding public office.
1952. Remark made on leaving his position as secretary of state. He subsequently returned to private legal practice. *Time* (December 22, 1952)

3 A memorandum is written not to inform the reader but to protect the writer.
Wall Street Journal (September 8, 1977)

4 It is worse than immoral, it's a mistake.
Describing the Vietnam war. Reported in "Letter from America" (Alistair Cooke), BBC radio

5 The manner in which one endures what must be endured is more important than the thing that must be endured.
Quoted in *Plain Speaking: An Oral Biography of Harry S. Truman* (Merle Miller; 1974)

6 Washington is like a self-sealing tank on a military aircraft. When a bullet passes through, it closes up.
Quoted in *The Wise Men* (Walter Isaacson and Evan Thomas; 1986)

Ackerley, J. R. (Joseph Randolph Ackerley; 1896–1967) British writer

1 I was born in 1896, and my parents were married in 1919.
The opening words of the book. *My Father and Myself* (1968)

Acland, Richard, Sir (Richard Thomas Dyke Acland; 1906–90) British politician and writer

1 Publication is the male equivalent of childbirth.
Observer, London (May 19, 1974), "Sayings of the Week"

Acton, Lord, 1st Baron Acton of Aldenham (John Emerich Edward Dalberg Acton; 1834–1902) British historian

Quotations about Acton

1 Power corrupts, but lack of power corrupts absolutely.
Adlai Stevenson (1900–65) U.S. statesman. Parody of a remark by Lord Acton. *Observer*, London (January 1963)

Quotations by Acton

2 Power tends to corrupt, and absolute power corrupts absolutely. Great men are almost always bad men...There is no worse heresy than that the office sanctifies the holder of it.
Often misquoted as "Power corrupts..." Letter to Bishop Mandell Creighton (April 3, 1887), quoted in *The Life and Letters of Mandell Creighton* (Louise Creighton; 1904), vol. 1, ch. 13

3 The danger is not that a particular class is unfit to govern. Every class is unfit to govern.
Letter to Mary Gladstone (1881)

4 The one pervading evil of democracy is the tyranny of the majority.
The History of Freedom (John Figgis and Reginald Laurence, eds.; 1907)

Adamov, Arthur (1908–70) Russian-born French playwright

1 The reason why Absurdist plays take place in No Man's Land with only two characters is primarily financial.
Speech to the Edinburgh International Drama Conference (September 13, 1963)

Adams, Abigail (originally Abigail Smith; 1744–1818) U.S. feminist

1 I arrived about one o'clock at this place known by the name of "the city," and the Name is all you can call so!...a new country with Houses scattered over a space of ten miles, and trees and stumps in plenty, with a castle of a House.
Her first impressions on arriving in Washington, D.C., to take up residence in the still incomplete White House with her husband, President John Adams. Letter (1801), quoted in *A History of the United States* (R. B. Nye and J. E. Morpurgo; 1965), vol. 1

2 A habit the pleasure of which increases with practice, but becomes more irksome with neglect.
Referring to writing letters. Letter to her daughter (May 8, 1808)

3 The natural tenderness and delicacy of our constitution, added to the many dangers we are subject to from your sex, renders it almost impossible for a single lady to travel without injury to her character.
Letter to Isaac Smith, Jr. (April 20, 1771)

4 I am more and more convinced that man is a dangerous creature and that power, whether vested in many or a few, is ever grasping, and like the grave, cries "Give, give."
Letter to John Adams (November 17, 1775)

5 If perticuliar care and attention is not paid to the Ladies we are determined to foment a Rebelion, and will not hold ourselves bound by any Laws in which we have no voice, or Representation.
Letter to John Adams (March 31, 1776)

6 If you complain of neglect of education in sons, what shall I say with regard to daughters...I most sincerely wish...that our new Constitution may be distinguished for encouraging learning and virtue. If we mean to have heroes, statesmen, and philosophers, we should have learned women.
Letter to John Adams (September 24, 1774)

7 Men of all senses in all ages abhor these customs which treat us only as the vassals of your sex.
Letter to John Adams (March 31, 1776)

8 That your sex are naturally tyrannical is a truth so thoroughly established as to admit of no dispute; but such of you as wish to be happy, willingly give up the harsh title of master for the more tender and endearing one of friend.
Letter to John Adams (March 3, 1776)

9 Whilst you are proclaiming peace and good will to men, emancipating all nations, you insist upon retaining absolute power over your wives. But you must remember that arbitrary power is most like other things which are very hard, very liable to be broken.
Written less than two months before the Declaration of Independence. Letter to John Adams (May 7, 1776)

Adams, Ansel (Ansel Easton Adams; 1902–84) U.S. photographer

1 A photograph is not an accident, it is a concept. It exists at, or before, the moment of exposure of the negative. From that point on to the final print, the process is chiefly one of *craft*.
"A Personal Credo," *The American Annual of Photography* (1944), vol. 58

Adams, Douglas (Douglas Noel Adams; b.1952) British writer

1 "Its all right, it's just a horse in the bathroom," he said quietly.
Dirk Gently's Holistic Detective Agency (1993), ch. 8

2 The idea of walking through walls frankly revolted him. It was something he had been trying strenuously to avoid all night.
Dirk Gently's Holistic Detective Agency (1993), ch. 15

3 Anything that, in happening, causes itself to happen, happens again.
Mostly Harmless (1992)

4 Life, the Universe and Everything.
The Ultimate Question, which the Earth was constructed to solve. *The Hitch Hiker's Guide to the Galaxy* (1979)

5 "Good grief," said Arthur, "is this really the interior of a flying saucer?"
The Hitch Hiker's Guide to the Galaxy (1979), ch. 5

6 Mostly harmless.
Description of planet Earth. *The Hitch Hiker's Guide to the Galaxy* (1979), ch. 6

7 Space...is big. Really big. You just won't believe how vastly hugely mindbogglingly big it is. I mean you may think it's a long way down the road to the chemist, but that's just peanuts to space.
"Chemist" means drugstore. *The Hitch Hiker's Guide to the Galaxy* (1979), ch. 8

8 Here I am, brain the size of a planet and they ask me to take you down the bridge.
A typical complaint from Marvin the computer. *The Hitch Hiker's Guide to the Galaxy* (1979), ch. 11

9 "Forty-two," said Deep Thought, with infinite majesty and calm.
Answering the question: "What is the meaning of Life, the Universe and Everything?" *The Hitch Hiker's Guide to the Galaxy* (1979), ch. 27

10 What god would be hanging around Terminal Two of Heathrow Airport trying to catch the 15.37 flight to Oslo?
The Long Dark Tea-Time of the Soul (1988), ch. 6

11 I don't go to mythical places with strange men.
The Long Dark Tea-Time of the Soul (1988), ch. 22

12 There is a theory which states that if ever anyone discovers exactly what the Universe is for and why it is here, it will instantly disappear and be replaced by something even more bizarre and inexplicable.
The Restaurant at the End of the Universe (1980), First Epigraph

13 There was an accident with a contraceptive and a time machine.
Zaphod Beeblebrox's explanation of how his father came to be Zaphod Beeblebrox the Second and his great-grandfather Zaphod Beeblebrox the Fourth. *The Restaurant at the End of the Universe* (1980), ch. 3

14 He's spending a year dead for tax reasons.
The Restaurant at the End of the Universe (1979), ch. 17

Adams, Franklin P. (Franklin Pierce Adams, "F. P. A."; 1881–1960) U.S. journalist

1 When the political columnists say "Every thinking man" they mean themselves and when the candidates appeal to "Every intelligent voter" they mean everybody who is going to vote for them.
Nods And Becks (1944)

2 Years ago we discovered the exact point the dead center of middle age. It occurs when you are too young to take up golf and too old to rush up to the net.
Nods and Becks (1944)

3 As I have often said, I am easily influenced. Compared with me a weather vane is Gibraltar.
Quoted in *Wit's End* (Robert E. Drennan; 1973)

Adams, Frederick Upham (1859–1921) U.S. inventor and writer

1 The fact that a thing is old makes me suspicious of it. I believe in the present. I have no veneration for the past and study it only to avoid mistakes.
President John Smith (1896)

Adams, Gerry (Gerald Adams; b.1948) Northern Irish politician

1 We must develop our popular strength in the Twenty-six Counties to complement the struggle in the Six County area. This means armed struggle in the Six Counties and political struggle in the Twenty-six Counties.
Articulating what was to become Sinn Fein's "gun-and-ballot-box" strategy in Northern Ireland. The 26 counties refers to the Irish Republic and the 6 counties to Northern Ireland. Speech to Sinn Féin Árd Fheis (November 2, 1980), quoted in *Phrases Make History Here* (Conor O'Clery; 1986)

2 Peace cannot be built on exclusion. That has been the price of the past 30 years.
Referring to Northern Ireland. *Daily Telegraph*, London (April 11, 1998)

3 Think of someone visiting a prison for the past 19 years or of someone visiting a grave for the past 19 years. Without being too overburdeningly morbid about it, it's a very abnormal way to spend your life.
Referring to the long-running Northern Ireland conflict and the way in which the abnormal has become normalized. *Guardian*, London (September 22, 1996)

4 It's like stew—you can have all the right ingredients but you have to cook it properly.
Referring to all-party negotiations on the political future of Northern Ireland. Interview, *The World at One*, BBC radio (April 7, 1998)

5 It's my view that the peace process will be irreversible and for good.
October 7, 1994. Referring to John Major's Anglo-Irish peace initiative. *Times*, London (October 8, 1994)

Adams, Henry (Henry Brooks Adams; 1838–1918) U.S. historian

1 I have no object but a superficial one as far as history is concerned. To me, accuracy is relative. I care very little whether my details are exact, if only my *ensemble* is in scale.
Letter to Henry Osborn Taylor (Undated)

2 Science will be the master of man. The engines he will have invented will be beyond his strength to control. Some day science shall have the existence of mankind in its power, and the human race commit suicide by blowing up the world.
Letter to his brother (April 11, 1862)

3 American society is a sort of flat, freshwater pond which absorbs silently, without reaction, anything which is thrown into it.
Letter to Royal Cortissoz (September 20, 1911)

4 Young man, I have lived in this house many years and have seen the occupants of the White House...come and go, and nothing you minor officials or the occupant of that house can do will affect the history of the world for long.
Said to Franklin D. Roosevelt when he was assistant secretary of the U.S. Navy. Remark (1913), quoted in *This is My Story* (Eleanor Roosevelt; 1937)

5 A friend in power is a friend lost.
The Education of Henry Adams (1907)

6 A teacher affects eternity.
The Education of Henry Adams (1907)

7 For history, international relations are the only sure standards of movement; the only foundation for a map.
The Education of Henry Adams (1907)

8 History is a tangled skein that one may take up at any point, and break when one has unravelled enough.
The Education of Henry Adams (1907)

9 Nothing is easier to teach than historical method, but, when learned, it has little use.
The Education of Henry Adams (1907)

10 Politics, as a practice, whatever its professions, has always been the systematic organization of hatreds.
The Education of Henry Adams (1907)

11 Practical politics consists in ignoring facts.
1904. *The Education of Henry Adams* (1907)

12 The chief wonder of education is that it does not ruin everybody concerned in it, teachers and taught.
The Education of Henry Adams (1907)

13 The historian must not try to know what is truth, if he values his honesty; for if he cares for his truths, he is certain to falsify his facts.
The Education of Henry Adams (1907)

14 The laws of history only repeat the lines of force or thought.
The Education of Henry Adams (1907)

15 The study of history is useful to the historian by teaching him his ignorance of women; and the mass of this ignorance crushes one who is familiar enough with what are called historical sources to realize how few women have ever been known.
The Education of Henry Adams (1907)

16 They know enough who know how to learn.
1904. *The Education of Henry Adams* (1907)

17 To historians, the single interest is the law of reaction between force and force—between mind and nature—the law of progress.
The Education of Henry Adams (1907)

18 When the historian never fully realizes his ignorance—which sometimes happens to Americans—he becomes even more tiresome to himself than to others, because his naiveté is irrepressible.
The Education of Henry Adams (1907)

19 I want to look like an American Voltaire or Gibbon, but am slowly settling down to be a third-rate Boswell hunting for a Dr. Johnson.
Quoted in *Henry Adams: The Major Phase* (Ernest Samuels; 1964)

20 History is incoherent and immoral.
1907. Quoted in *History and the Social Sciences* (Mark Krug; 1967)

Adams, James (James Truslow Adams; 1879–1949) U.S. historian and editor

1 All history must necessarily have reference to the existence and condition of *Man*. History is a memorial of the succession of time; and in the created universe, man is the only being known to man to whom the succession of Time is an object of perception.
"Society and Civilization," *American Review* (July 1945)

Adams, Joey (b.1911) U.S. actor

1 Worrying about the past is like trying to make birth control pills retroactive.
Attrib.

Adams, John (1735–1826) U.S. president

Quotations about Adams

1 An imagination sublimated and eccentric, propitious neither to the regular display of sound judgment nor to steady perseverance in a systematic plan of conduct.
Alexander Hamilton (1757–1804) U.S. president. Quoted in *John Adams, 1784–1826* (Page Smith; 1962)

2 He is vain, irritable, and a bad calculator of the force and probable effect of the motives which govern men. This is the ill which can possibly be said of him. He is as disinterested as the Being who made him.
Thomas Jefferson (1743–1826) U.S. president. Letter to James Madison (1787)

Quotations by Adams

3 The history of our revolution will be one continued lie from one end to the other.
Letter to Dr. Benjamin Rush (April 4, 1790)

4 The second day of July 1776 will be the most memorable epoch in the history of America...It ought to be solemnized with pomp and parade, with shows, games, sports, guns, bells, bonfires and illuminations from one end of this continent to the other, from this time forward, forevermore.
The Continental Congress voted for independence from Britain on July 2, 1776, but July 4 was chosen as the commemorative date. Letter to his wife, Abigail Adams (July 2, 1776), quoted in *The Adams Family Correspondence* (L. H. Butterfield, ed.; 1963), vol. 2

5 English is destined to be in the next and succeeding centuries more generally the language of the world than Latin was in the last or French is in the present age.
1780. Quoted in *Speaking Freely* (Stuart Berg Flexner and Anne H. Soukhanov; 1997)

Adams, John Quincy (1767–1848) U.S. president

Quotations about Adams

1 He is no literary old gentleman, but a bruiser, and loves the melee.
Ralph Waldo Emerson (1803–82) U.S. poet and essayist. Journal (19th century)

2 He is like one of those old cardinals, who as quick as he is chosen Pope, throws away his crutches and his crookedness, and is as straight as a boy. He is an old roué, who cannot live on slops, but must have sulfuric acid in his tea.
Ralph Waldo Emerson (1803–82) U.S. poet and essayist. Quoted in *Journals* (Edward Waldo Emerson and Waldo Emerson Forbes, eds.; 1909–14)

Quotations by Adams

3 I am a man of reserved, cold, austere, and forbidding manners: my political adversaries say, a gloomy misanthropist, and my personal enemies, an unsocial savage.
Diary (June 4, 1819)

4 The public history of all countries, and all ages, is but a sort of mask, richly colored. The interior working of the machinery must be foul.
Diary (November 9, 1822)

5 The great object of the institution of civil government is the improvement of those who are parties to the social compact.
First Message to Congress (1825)

6 I take it for granted that the present question is a mere preamble—a title-page to a great tragic volume.
Referring to the Missouri Compromise—a measure in the U.S. Congress allowing Missouri to be admitted as the 24th state of the Union. At the time Congress was equally divided between "slave states" and "free states." Missouri applied for admission as a slave state, and the North feared that this would upset the balance of power. The compromise involved the admission of Maine as a free state. Remark (March 1820)

7 Think of your forefathers! Think of your posterity!
Speech, Plymouth, Massachusetts (December 22, 1802)

8 The doughty knight of the stuffed cravat.
Referring to the U.S. statesman Thomas Hart Benton. Quoted in *The First Ten* (Alfred Steinberg; 1967)

9 I inhabit a weak, frail, decayed tenement; battered by the winds and broken in on by the storms, and, from all I can learn, the landlord does not intend to repair.
1848. Said during his last illness. Attrib.

Adams, Richard (Richard George Adams; b.1920) British novelist

1 Many human beings say that they enjoy the winter, but what they really enjoy is feeling proof against it.
"Feeling proof against" means "armed against." *Watership Down* (1972), ch. 50

Adams, Samuel (1722–1803) American revolutionary leader

Quotations about Adams

1 Truly the man of the Revolution.
Thomas Jefferson (1743–1826) U.S. president. Quoted in *Sam Adams: Pioneer in Propaganda* (John C. Miller; 1936)

2 He commanded the most profound attention whenever he arose in an assembly by which the froth of declamation was heard with the most sovereign contempt.
Thomas Jefferson (1743–1826) U.S. president. Referring to Samuel Adams. Quoted in *Samuel Adams: The Fateful Years, 1764–1776* (Stewart Beach; 1965)

Quotations by Adams

3 A nation of shop-keepers are very seldom so disinterested.
Referring to Britain, following the Declaration of Independence, July 4, 1776. Speech, Philadelphia (August 1, 1776)

Adams, Samuel Hopkins (1871–1958) U.S. journalist

1 Medicine would be the ideal profession if it did not involve giving pain.
The Health Master (1913), ch. 3

Adams, Sarah Flower (Sarah Fuller Flower Adams; 1805–48) British poet and hymnwriter

1 Nearer, my God, to thee,
Nearer to thee!
"Nearer, My God, to Thee" (1840), st. 1

Adams, Scott (b.1957) U.S. cartoonist

1 A consultant is a person who takes your money and annoys your employees while tirelessly searching for the best way to extend the consulting contract.
The Dilbert Principle (1996)

2 Nothing defines human beings better than their willingness to do irrational things in the pursuit of phenomenally unlikely payoffs.
The Dilbert Principle (1996)

3 The biggest change in the workplace of the future will be the widespread realization that having one idiot boss is a much higher risk than having many idiot clients.
The Dilbert Principle (1996)

Adams, William (b.1934) U.S. business executive

1 A company's ethical conduct is something like a big flywheel. It might have a lot of momentum, but it will eventually slow down and stop unless you add energy.
Quoted in *Managing Corporate Ethics* (Francis J. Aguilar; 1994)

Adamson, Harold (Harold Campbell Adamson; 1906–80) U.S. lyricist

1 Comin' in on a Wing and a Prayer
Film and song title based on the words of a war pilot from a disabled plane to ground control. "Comin' in on a Wing and a Prayer" (1943)

Addams, Jane (1860–1935) U.S. social reformer and feminist

Quotations about Addams

1 She simply inhabits reality, and everything she says necessarily expresses its nature. *She can't help writing truth.*
William James (1842–1910) U.S. psychologist and philosopher. *American Journal of Sociology* (1909)

2 She had compassion without condescension. She had pity without retreat into vulgarity. She had infinite sympathy for common things without forgetfulness of those that are uncommon...those who have known her say she was not only good, but great.
Walter Lippmann (1889–1974) U.S. writer and editor. Remark (May 23, 1935), quoted in *American Heroine: The Life and Legend of Jane Addams* (Allen Freeman Davis; 1973)

Quotations by Addams

3 Civilization is a method of living, an attitude of equal respect for all men.
Speech, Honolulu (1933)

4 Old-fashioned ways which no longer apply to changed conditions are a snare in which the feet of women have always become readily entangled.
"Utilization of Women in City Government," *Newer Ideals of Peace* (1907)

5 In his own way each man must struggle, lest the moral law become a far-off abstraction utterly separated from his active life.
Twenty Years at Hull House (1910)

Addams Family, The U.S. television series

1 They're creepy and they're kooky
mysterious and spooky
and not a little loopy
the Addams family.
Signature song lyric. *The Addams Family* (1960s)

Addison, Joseph (1672–1719) English essayist, poet, and statesman

Quotations about Addison

1 Whoever wishes to attain an English style, familiar but not coarse and elegant but not ostentatious, must give his days and nights to the volumes of Addison.
Samuel Johnson (1709–84) British lexicographer and writer. "Addison," *Lives of the English Poets* (1779–81)

2 Damn with faint praise, assent with civil leer,
And, without sneering, teach the rest to sneer.
Alexander Pope (1688–1744) English poet. *Epistle to Dr. Arbuthnot* (1735), l. 201

Quotations by Addison

3 Music, the greatest good that mortals know,
And all of heaven we have below.
"A Song for St. Cecilia's Day" (1694), st. 3

4 A day, an hour, of virtuous liberty
Is worth a whole eternity in bondage.
Cato (1713), Act 1, Scene 2

5 'Tis not in mortals to command success,
But we'll do more, Sempronius; we'll deserve it.
Cato (1713), Act 1, Scene 2

6 And if the following day, he chance to find
A new repast, or an untasted spring,
Blesses his stars, and thinks it luxury.
Cato (1713), Act 1, Scene 4

7 Content thyself to be obscurely good.
When vice prevails, and impious men bear sway,
The post of honour is a private station.
Cato (1713), Act 4, Scene 1

8 The woman that deliberates is lost.
Cato (1713), Act 4, Scene 1

9 What pity is it
That we can die but once to serve our country!
Cato (1713), Act 4, Scene 1

10 Sweet are the slumbers of the virtuous man.
Cato (1713), Act 5, Scene 4

11 A reader seldom peruses a book with pleasure until he knows whether the writer of it be a black man or a fair man, of a mild or choleric disposition, married or a bachelor.
Spectator, London (March 1, 1711), no. 1

12 Thus I live in the world rather as a Spectator of mankind, than as one of the species, by which means I have made myself a speculative statesman, soldier, merchant, and artisan, without ever meddling with any practical part of life.
Spectator, London (March 1, 1711), no. 1

13 Nothing is capable of being well set to music that is not nonsense.
Spectator, London (1711), no. 18

14 The infusion of a China plant sweetened with the pith of an Indian cane.
Referring to tea with sugar. *Spectator,* London (1711), no. 69

15 Sir Roger told them, with the air of a man who would not give his judgment rashly, that "much might be said on both sides".
Sir Roger de Coverley was a fictional archetype of the old-fashioned and eccentric English country squire. *Spectator,* London (July 20, 1711), no. 122

16 I have often thought, says Sir Roger, it happens very well that Christmas should fall out in the Middle of Winter.
Sir Roger de Coverley was a fictional archetype of the old-fashioned and eccentric English country squire. *Spectator,* London (January 8, 1712), no. 269

17 Health and cheerfulness mutually beget each other.
Spectator, London (May 24, 1712), no. 387

18 Our sight is the most perfect and most delightful of all our senses. It fills the mind with the largest variety of ideas, converses with its objects at the greatest distance, and continues the longest in action without being tired or satiated with its proper enjoyments.
Spectator, London (June 21, 1712), no. 411

19 The Hand that made us is divine.
Spectator, London (August 23, 1712), no. 465

20 A woman seldom asks advice until she has bought her wedding clothes.
Spectator, London (September 4, 1712), no. 475

21 We are always doing something for posterity, but I would fain see posterity do something for us.
Spectator, London (August 20, 1714), no. 583

22 See in what peace a Christian can die.
1719. Last words, to his stepson Lord Warwick. *Conjectures on Original Composition* (Edward Young; 1759)

23 I have but ninepence in ready money, but I can draw for a thousand pounds.
Comparing his ability to make conversation with his ability to write. Reply to a woman who complained "of his having talked little in company." Quoted in *Life of Samuel Johnson* (James Boswell; 1791), May 7, 1773

24 It is very wonderful to see persons of the best sense passing away a dozen hours together in shuffling and dividing a pack of cards, with...no other ideas but those of black or red spots ranged together in different figures.
Attrib.

Ade, George (1866–1944) U.S. playwright, journalist, author, and humorist

1 The time to enjoy a European tour is about three weeks after you unpack.
1899. *Forty Modern Fables* (1901)

2 "Whom are you?" said he, for he had been to night school.
"The Steel Box," *The Chicago Record* (March 16, 1898)

3 The music teacher came twice each week to bridge the awful gap between Dorothy and Chopin.
Attrib. *Dictionary of Humorous Quotations* (Evan Esar, ed.; 1949)

4 If it were not for the presents, an elopement would be preferable.
Attrib.

Adenauer, Konrad (1876–1967) West German chancellor

1 I do not know what will become of Germany when I am no longer on hand unless we can still manage to create Europe in time.
Remark to Paul Henri Spaak (September 1954)

2 The countries of western Europe are no longer in a position to protect themselves individually.
Speech (May 1953)

3 We must free ourselves from thinking in terms of nation states.
Speech (May 1953)

4 History is the sum total of the things that could have been avoided.
Attrib.

5 I haven't asked you to make me young again. All I want is to go on getting older.
Replying to his doctor. Attrib.

Adler, Alfred (1870–1937) Austrian psychiatrist

1 It lies in the nature of a neurotic to wish to diminish the feeling of inferiority by constant proofs of his superiority.
1912. *The Neurotic Constitution* (1921)

2 Religious insanity, fantasies and hallucinations of God, heaven,

and the saints, as well as the feeling of being crushed are to be understood as infantile megalomaniac ideas.
1912. *The Neurotic Constitution* (1921)

3 The neurotic individual is the typical killjoy and peace destroyer. He is misled by his megalomaniac ideal...and is always busy trying to hypostasize and deify his own guiding line, and to cross those of others.
1912. *The Neurotic Constitution* (1921)

4 The Messalina is to be compared with Don Juan, a nymphomaniac who always imagines herself unsatiated and belittled because in this neurotic form real possibilities for gratification are unattainable.
1912. Referring to pyschological "types" named after figures of literature and history. Valeria Messalina (22?–48?), the third wife of the Emperor Claudius, was known for her cruelty and lust. Don Juan was a promiscuous hero in folklore traditions originating from Spain. *The Neurotic Constitution* (1921)

5 The craving for security...leads him to seek the protection of the father, mother, God, alcoholism, or an idea.
1912. Referring to the behavior of the neurotic. *The Neurotic Constitution* (1921)

6 I heard a patient laugh aloud when told of the Messina earthquake. He suffered from severe masochistic attacks.
1912. Referring to the earthquake in Messina, Italy (1908), that claimed 84,000 lives. *The Neurotic Constitution* (1921)

7 It is easier to fight for one's principles than to live up to them.
1927? Quoted in *Alfred Adler: Apostle of Freedom* (Phyllis Bottome; 1939), ch. 5

8 Each generation has its few great mathematicians, and mathematics would not even notice the absence of the others. They are useful as teachers, and their research harms no one, but it is of no importance at all. A mathematician is great or he is nothing.
Quoted in "Mathematics and Creativity," *New Yorker* (February 19, 1972)

9 The mathematical life of a mathematician is short. Work rarely improves after the age of twenty-five or thirty. If little has been accomplished by then, little will ever be accomplished.
Quoted in "Mathematics and Creativity," *New Yorker* (February 19, 1972)

10 Against whom?
Said when he heard that an egocentric had fallen in love. "Exponent of the Soul," *Some of My Best Friends* (J. Bishop; 1920)

Adler, Freda (b.1934) U.S. educator

1 But there is another side to chivalry. If it dispenses leniency, it may with equal justification invoke control.
Sisters in Crime (1975), ch. 4

2 It is little wonder that rape is one of the least-reported crimes. Perhaps it is the only crime in which the victim becomes the accused and, in reality, it is she who must prove her good reputation, her mental soundness, and her impeccable propriety.
Sisters in Crime (1975), ch. 9

Adler, Larry (Lawrence Cecil Adler; b.1914) U.S. harmonica player and composer

1 Vasectomy means not ever having to say you're sorry.
Referring to a line about love in the movie *Love Story.* Attrib.

Adler, Polly (Pearl Adler; 1900?–62) Russian-born U.S. madam and author

1 A House Is Not a Home
Title of her memoirs. *A House is Not a Home* (1953)

Adler, Viktor (1852–1918) Austrian politician

1 The Austrian government...is a system of despotism tempered by casualness.
Speech, International Socialist Congress, Paris (July 17, 1889)

Adonis (formerly 'Ali Ahmad Sa'id; b.1929) Syrian poet

1 I live between the fire and the plague
with my language—with this mute universe.
"The Fall" (1961), quoted in *When the Words Burn* (John Mikhail Asfour, ed., tr.; 1988)

2 The sky opens,
the soil turns into books
and in every book is God. Awakened,
the sleep of stone is gone from my face,
and no mirage is now in my eye.
"The Days of the Hawk," *When the Words Burn* (John Mikhail Asfour, ed., tr.; 1988)

Adorno, Theodor (1903–69) German philosopher, sociologist, and musicologist

1 A German is someone who cannot tell a lie without believing it himself.
Minima Moralia (E. F. N. Jephcott, tr.; 1951)

2 Much knowledge if out of proportion to the disposition of forces, is invalid, however formally correct it may be.
Minima Moralia (E. F. N. Jephcott, tr.; 1951)

3 The demand for intellectual honesty is itself dishonest.
Minima Moralia (E. F. N. Jephcott, tr.; 1951)

4 The lie has long since lost its honest function of misrepresenting reality. Nobody believes anybody, everyone is in the know. Lies are told only to convey to someone that one has no need either of him or his good opinion.
Minima Moralia (E. F. N. Jephcott, tr.; 1951)

5 There is nothing innocuous left...Even the blossoming tree lies the moment its bloom is seen without the shadow of terror; even the innocent "How lovely!" becomes an excuse for an existence outrageously unlovely.
Minima Moralia (E. F. N. Jephcott, tr.; 1951)

6 To write poetry after Auschwitz is barbaric.
Prisms (Samuel and Sherry Weber, trs.; 1967)

7 Skepticism about what is unproven can easily turn into a prohibition upon thinking.
Quoted in *Critical Models: Inventions and Catchwords* (Henry Pickford, tr.; 1998)

8 Of the world as it exists, one cannot be enough afraid.
Attrib.

Advertisements

1 It beats as it sweeps as it cleans.
1919? Advertising slogan for the Hoover vacuum cleaner.

2 At sixty miles an hour the loudest noise in this new Rolls-Royce comes from the electric clock.
1950s. U.S. advertisement for Rolls-Royce cars (from 1958); from a car test by the technical editor of the magazine *Motor*. *Motor* (1958)

3 Archeologists dig up dirt on each other.
September 23, 1986. Advertisement on CBS television.

4 I'll bet he drinks Carling Black Label.
Advertising slogan for Carling Black Label. (1990s)

5 Probably the best lager in the world.
1970s. Advertising slogan for Carlsberg lager.

6 You too can have a body like mine.
1920s. Advertising slogan for Charles Atlas.

7 I'd like to teach the world to sing.
Advertising slogan for Coca-Cola. (1970s)

8 It's the real thing.
Advertising slogan for Coca-Cola. (1960s)

9 I'm only here for the beer.
1971. Advertising slogan for Double Diamond beer.

10 Put a tiger in your tank.
1964. Advertising slogan for Exxon.

11 Heineken refreshes the parts other beers cannot reach.
Advertising slogan for Heineken. (1975)

12 Beanz Meanz Heinz.
1967. Advertising slogan for Heinz baked beans.

13 Never knowingly undersold.
1920s. Advertising slogan for John Lewis stores in Britain.

14 It's finger-lickin' good.
Advertising slogan for Kentucky Fried Chicken. (1958)

15 Blondes have more fun.
1957. Advertising slogan for Lady Clairol.

16 Come to Marlboro country.
1970s. Advertising slogan for Marlboro cigarettes.

17 A Mars a day helps you work, rest and play.
Advertising slogan for Mars candy bar first used in the 1960s.

18 It's the right one.
1970s. Advertising slogan for Martini.

19 Real people wear fake fur.
1980s. Advertising slogan for People for Ethical Treatment of Animals.

20 Schhh... you know who.
Advertising slogan for Schweppes. (1970s)

21 It could be you!
1995. Advertising slogan for the British National Lottery.

22 The bank that likes to say yes.
Advertising slogan for Trustee Savings Bank. (1980s)

23 You've come a long way, baby.
1968. Advertising slogan for Virginia Slims cigarettes. The first cigarette advertisement aimed specifically at women.

24 The breakfast of champions.
1950. Advertising slogan for Wheaties breakfast cereal.

25 Garbo Talks!
Promotional slogan for the motion picture *Anna Christie* (1930).

Ady, Thomas (*fl.* 17th century) British poet

1 Matthew, Mark, Luke and John,
The Bed be blest that I lie on.
A Candle in the Dark (1662)

Æ (George William Russell; 1867–1935) Irish poet

1 No, thank you, I was born intoxicated.
Refusing a drink that was offered him. Quoted in *10,000 Jokes, Toasts, and Stories* (L. Copeland)

2 A literary movement: five or six people who live in the same town and hate each other.
Attrib.

Aeschylus (525?–456 B.C.) Greek tragedian and dramatist

1 Hold him alone truly fortunate who has ended his life in happy well-being.
Agamemnon (458 B.C.), l. 928

2 Home from Troy refined by fire
Sends back to friends the dust
That is heavy with tears, stowing
A man's worth of ashes
In an easily handled jar.
Referring to Greek losses in the Trojan War. *Agamemnon* (458 B.C.), ll. 440–444

3 It is always the season for the old to learn.
Fragments (5th century? B.C.)

4 Fortune is for all; judgment is theirs who have won it for themselves.
Fragments (5th century B.C.), fragment 217

5 Words are the physicians of a mind diseased.
Prometheus Bound (5th century B.C.), l. 378

6 He does not wish to appear the best, but to be it.
Seven Against Thebes (467 B.C.), l. 592

7 Obedience is the mother of success and the wife of safety.
The Libation Bearers (458 B.C.)

8 Success is man's god.
The Libation Bearers (458 B.C.)

Aesop (620?–560 B.C.) Greek writer

1 The gods help them that help themselves.
"Hercules and the Waggoner," *Aesop's Fables* (6th century B.C.)

2 Beware that you do not lose the substance by grasping at the shadow.
"The Dog and the Shadow," *Aesop's Fables* (6th century B.C.)

3 I am sure the grapes are sour.
"The Fox and the Grapes," *Aesop's Fables* (6th century B.C.)

4 Thinking to get at once all the gold that the goose could give, he killed it, and opened it only to find—nothing.
"The Goose with the Golden Eggs," *Aesop's Fables* (6th century B.C.)

5 It is not only fine feathers that make fine birds.
"The Jay and the Peacock," *Aesop's Fables* (6th century B.C.)

Ai Qing (also known as Ai Ch'ing; b.1910) Chinese poet

1 Echo...call her and she will call you
Curse her and you she will curse
You can't win if you argue
The last word's always hers.
"Echo" (1950s), quoted in *The Red Azalea* (Edward Morin, ed.; 1990)

2 Hope...Go after her—she'll fly away
Ignore her—she'll chase you
She'll always keep you company
Until your breathing stops.
"Hope" (1950s), quoted in *The Red Azalea* (Edward Morin, ed.; 1990)

3 Liquor, she is lovely
With a personality of fire
And a shape like water
...She can make bright people clever
And fools ever more foolish.
"Liquor" (1950s), quoted in *The Red Azalea* (Edward Morin, ed.; 1990)

4 I love this sad land of my country,
The expanse of boundless desert
Arouses my respect—I see
Our ancestors
Leading flocks of sheep
Blowing on their pipes
Sink into the dust of this big desert.
"The North" (Tao Tao Sanders, tr.), quoted in *Anthology of Chinese Literature* (Cyril Birch, ed.; 1972), vol. 2

5 The North is sad
and the endless Yellow River
Churning turbulent waves
Has poured down upon the broad North
Disasters and misfortunes, and the frost of years
Has carved into the broad North
Poverty and hunger.
"The North" (Tao Tao Sanders, tr.), quoted in *Anthology of Chinese Literature* (Cyril Birch, ed.; 1972), vol. 2

Airey, Lawrence, Sir (b.1926) British tax official

1 The only way to get your windows cleaned these days is to give the man cash and not ask if he is reporting it to the revenue.
Daily Express, London (May 7, 1981)

Akhmatova, Anna (originally Anna Andreyevna Gorenko; 1888–1966) Russian poet

Quotations about Akhmatova

1 I honor it as a memorial to all the victims of the years of terror. It's so simply written, without any melodrama. Melodrama would have ruined it.
1971–75
Dmitri Shostakovich (1906–75) Russian composer. Referring to Anna Akhmatova's poem *Requiem* (1938). *Testimony: The Memoirs of Shostakovich* (Solomon Volkov, ed., Antonina W. Bouis, tr.; 1979), ch. 8

2 O Muse of weeping, most magnificent of muses!
O you chance progeny of a white night!
You send down upon Russia a black blizzard,
And your wailing pierces us like arrows.
Marina Tsvetaeva (1892–1941) Russian poet. The first of a cycle of eleven poems addressed to the poet Anna Akhmatova. "O Muse of weeping, most magnificent of muses" (1916), quoted in *Tsvetaeva* (Viktoria Schweitzer; Peter Norman, tr., 1992)

Quotations by Akhmatova

3 I am not one of those who left their land
For enemies to tear apart.
"I am not one of those who left their land..." (Peter Norman, tr.; June 22, 1939), quoted in *The Akhmatova Journals: 1938–1941* (Lydia Chukovskaya, ed.; 1989), no. 41

4 Things in poetry should, I think,
Be out of place, not tidy, everyday.
"I have no need for a host of odes..." (Peter Norman, tr.; January 21, 1940), quoted in *The Akhmatova Journals: 1938–1941* (Lydia Chukovskaya, ed.; 1989), no. 11

5 And the stone word fell
Upon my still living breast.
Never mind, I was prepared for this.
Somehow, I shall stand the test.
"The Sentence" (Peter Norman, tr.; June 22, 1939), quoted in *The Akhmatova Journals: 1938–1941* (Lydia Chukovskaya, ed.; 1989), no. 3

6 Time is now writing the twenty-fourth drama
Of Shakespeare with a passionless hand.
Addressed to Londoners during the Blitz. "To Londoners" (Peter Norman, tr.; 1940), quoted in *The Akhmatova Journals: 1938–1941* (Lydia Chukovskaya, ed.; 1989), no. 51

7 Theater is spectacle. Whereas Chekhov's plays epitomize the disintegration of theater. But that's not the point. I don't like him because all his people are pathetic, they know nothing of heroic deeds.
Referring to Anton Chekhov. (Milena Michalski and Sylva Rubashova, trs.; October 17, 1940), quoted in *The Akhmatova Journals: 1938–1941* (Lydia Chukovskaya, ed.; 1989)

8 A wonderful book. A great book...Hemingway, Dos Passos descended from him. They all fed on crumbs from his table.
Referring to James Joyce's novel *Ulysses* (1922). (Milena Michalski and Sylva Rubashova, trs.; October 17, 1940), quoted in *The Akhmatova Journals: 1938–1941* (Lydia Chukovskaya, ed.; 1989)

9 You must have noticed that the main idea of that great work is this: if a woman leaves her lawful husband to live with another man, this inevitably makes her a prostitute. Don't argue! That's exactly what it is.
Referring to Leo Tolstoy's novel *Anna Karenina* (1875–77). (Milena Michalski and Sylva Rubashova, trs.; May 18, 1939), quoted in *The Akhmatova Journals: 1938–1941* (Lydia Chukovskaya, ed.; 1989)

Akhtar-ul-Iman Indian poet

1 I hate her, she despises me.
But when we meet
in the loneliness, the darkness,
we become one whole, like a lump of kneaded clay,
hatred leaves, silence stays,
the silence that covered the earth after it was created,
and we go on breaking
like branches.
"Compromise," *The Oxford Anthology of Modern Indian Poetry* (Viany Dharwadker and A. K. Ramanujan, eds.; 1994)

Akhter, Farida Bangladeshi academic

1 The consumption explosion in the West, specially in the United

States, is much more dangerous than the population "explosion" in terms of putting pressure on natural resources...and yet the poor of developing countries...are now being blamed for the destruction of the environment.
Depopulating Bangladesh (1992)

Akins, Zoë (1886–1958) U.S. playwright

1 The Greeks Had a Word for It
Play title. *The Greeks Had a Word for It* (1930)

Alain (Émile-Auguste Chartier; 1868–1951) French philosopher and essayist

1 Nothing is more dangerous than an idea, when you have only one idea.
Propos sur la religion (1908–19), no. 74

Alain-Fournier (Henri-Alban Fournier; 1886–1914) French writer and journalist

1 How can a man who has once strayed into Heaven ever hope to make terms with the earth?
Le Grand Meaulnes (1913), pt. 3, ch. 4

Alba, Duke of, Third Duke of Alba (Fernando Álvarez de Toledo; 1507–82) Spanish soldier

1 I have tamed men of iron and why, then, shall I not be able to tame these men of butter?
Reply to Philip II of Spain on his appointment as captain-general of the Netherlands. Attrib.

Albee, Edward (Edward Franklin Albee III; b.1928) U.S. playwright

1 Nobody hears old people complain because people think that's all old people do. And that's because old people are gnarled and sagged and twisted into the shape of a complaint.
The American Dream (1961)

2 When you're a kid you use the cards as a substitute for a real experience, and when you're older you use real experience as a substitute for the fantasy.
Said by Jerry, referring to pornographic playing cards. *The Zoo Story* (1958)

3 I'll tell you what game we'll play. We're done with Humiliate the Host...and we don't want to play Hump the Hostess...We'll play a round of Get the Guests.
Who's Afraid of Virginia Woolf? (1962)

4 You asked me if I knew women. Well, one of the things I do not know about them is what they talk about while the men are talking. I must find out some time.
Who's Afraid of Virginia Woolf? (1962)

5 Who's Afraid of Virginia Woolf?
Play title. *Who's afraid of Virginia Woolf?* (1962)

6 I have a fine sense of the ridiculous, but no sense of humor.
Who's Afraid of Virginia Woolf? (1962), Act 1

7 You gotta have a swine to show you where the truffles are.
Who's Afraid of Virginia Woolf? (1962), Act 1

Al-Biruni (Abu ar-Rayhan Muhammad ibn Ahmad al-Biruni; 973–1048) Arab scientist and scholar

1 The sciences were transmitted into the Arabic language from different parts of the world; by it they were embellished and penetrated the hearts of men, while the beauties of the language flowed in their veins and arteries.
Kitab al-Saydala (11th century)

Albo, Joseph (1380?–1444?) Spanish philosopher of Judaism

1 To know God's nature one would have to be God Himself.
Sefer ha-Ikkarim (Louis Jacobs, tr.; 1485)

Alcala Galiano, Juan Valera Spanish writer

1 The French took three years of struggle and shed oceans of blood to win their liberty. All we have needed in Spain have been two days of explanation and one of rejoicing.
1870. Commenting on the revolution of 1868, that restored the constitution after a period of absolutist rule. Quoted in *The Spanish Labyrinth* (Gerald Brenan; 1943)

Alcott, Bronson (Amos Bronson Alcott; 1799–1888) U.S. teacher and philosopher

1 The true teacher defends his pupils against his own personal influence.
"The Teacher," *Orphic Sayings From The Dial* (July 1840)

Alcott, Louisa May (1832–88) U.S. novelist

1 Women have been called queens for a long time, but the kingdom given them isn't worth ruling.
An Old-Fashioned Girl (1869)

2 Housekeeping ain't no joke.
Little Women (1868–69), pt. 1

3 When women are the advisers, the lords of creation don't take the advice till they have persuaded themselves that it is just what they intended to do; then they act upon it, and if it succeeds, they give the weaker vessel half the credit of it; if it fails, they generously give her the whole.
Little Women (1868–69), pt.1

4 Girls are so queer you never know what they mean. They say No when they mean Yes, and drive a man out of his wits for the fun of it.
Little Women (1868–69), pt. 2

5 It takes people a long time to learn the difference between talent and genius, especially ambitious young men and women.
Little Women (1868–69), pt. 2

6 She had a womanly instinct that clothes possess an influence more powerful over many than the worth of character or the magic of manners.
Little Women (1868–69), pt. 2

Alcuin (also known as Albinus; 735–804) English cleric, theologian, and scholar

1 Happy is the people for whom divine mercy has provided so good and wise a ruler.
Referring to Charlemagne, who had been crowned Emperor of the Romans by Pope Leo III on Christmas Day, 800. Letter to Charlemagne (September–October 801)

2 The voice of the people is the voice of God.
Letter to Charlemagne (800), quoted in *Works* (1863), vol. 1

3 If many people follow your enthusiastic endeavours, perhaps a new Athens might be created in the land of the Franks, or rather a much better one.
799. Attrib.

4 But above all things I strive to train them to be useful to the Holy Church of God and for the glory of your kingdom.
796. Referring to his pupils at his school at Tours. Attrib.

Aldiss, Brian (Brian Wilson Aldiss; b.1925) British science-fiction writer

1 Keep violence in the mind where it belongs.
"Charteris," *Barefoot in the Head* (1969)

2 Science fiction is no more written for scientists than ghost stories are written for ghosts.
"Introduction," *Penguin Science Fiction* (1973)

3 Science fiction is the search for a definition of mankind and his status in the universe which will stand in our advanced but confused state of knowledge (science), and is characteristically cast in the Gothic or post-Gothic mode.
Trillion Year Spree (1986), ch. 1

Aldrich, Henry (1647–1710) English cleric and scholar

1 If all be true that I do think,
There are five reasons we should drink;
Good wine—a friend—or being dry—
Or lest we should be by and by—
Or any other reason why.
Reasons for Drinking (1689)

Aldrich, Thomas Bailey (1836–1907) U.S. writer and editor

1 We vivisect the nightingale
To probe the secret of his note.
"Realism," *The Poems of Thomas Bailey Aldrich* (1907)

2 Though I am not genuine Boston, I am Boston-plated.
Quoted in *The Life of Thomas Bailey Aldrich* (Ferris Greenslet; 1908)

Aldrin, Buzz (Edwin Eugene Aldrin, Jr.; b.1930) U.S. astronaut

1 Beautiful! Beautiful! Magnificent desolation!
Said on joining Neil Armstrong for the first moon walk. Remark (July 20, 1969)

Alegre, Costa (1864–90) São Tomé poet

1 My color is black, It stands for mourning and sorrow; White is your race You are full of grace.
Voices from an Empire: A History of Afro-Portuguese Literature (Russell G. Hamilton; 1975)

Alembert, Jean le Rond d' (1717–83) French scientist, mathematician, and philosopher

1 The imagination in a mathematician who creates makes no less difference than in a poet who invents...Of all the great men of antiquity, Archimedes may be the one who most deserves to be placed beside Homer.
Discours preliminaire de l'encyclopédie (1751)

2 The true system of the World has been recognized, developed and perfected...Everything has been discussed and analysed, or at least mentioned.
Referring to the *Encyclopédie* (1751–80), which he helped to edit. *Elements of Philosophy* (1759)

3 Just go on...and faith will soon return.
Said to a friend, referring to infinitesimals. Quoted in *The Mathematical Experience* (P. J. Davis and R. Hersh; 1981)

Alençon, Sophie-Charlotte, Duchesse d' (d.1897) Bavarian-born duchess

1 Because of my title, I was the first to enter here. I shall be the last to go out.
May 4, 1897. Refusing help during a fire, May 4, 1897, at a charity bazaar in Paris. She died along with 120 others. Attrib.

Alexander, C. F. (originally Cecil Frances Humphreys; 1818–95) Irish poet and hymnwriter

1 All things bright and beautiful,
All creatures great and small,
All things wise and wonderful,
The Lord God made them all.
Hymn. "All Things Bright and Beautiful," *Hymns for Little Children* (1848)

2 The rich man in his castle,
The poor man at his gate,
God made them, high or lowly,
And ordered their estate.
Hymn. "All Things Bright and Beautiful," *Hymns for Little Children* (1848)

3 Once in royal David's city
Stood a lowly cattle shed,
Where a Mother laid her Baby
In a manger for His bed:
Mary was that Mother mild,
Jesus Christ her little Child.
"Once in Royal David's City," *Hymns for Little Children* (1848)

4 There is a green hill far away,
Without a city wall,
Where the dear Lord was crucified,
Who died to save us all.
"There is a Green Hill Far Away," *Hymns for Little Children* (1848)

Alexander I, Tsar (Aleksandr Pavlovich; 1777–1825) Russian monarch

1 Napoleon thinks I am a fool, but he who laughs last laughs longest.
Said after meeting Napoleon I at Erfurt, Germany. Letter to his sister, Catherine (October 8, 1808)

2 It is enough for people to know that the Emperor of Russia and his army have crossed over the bridge.
Said after the Russian army's entrance to Paris, when asked if he wished to change the name of the Pont d'Austerlitz (which commemorated a battle against Napoleon I in which Russia and its allies had been defeated). Remark to French officials (April 1814)

Alexander II, Tsar (Aleksandr Nikolayevich; 1818–81) Russian monarch

1 A constitution or national army is totally out of the question.

I will allow neither one nor the other in any form.
Referring to Poland, during a period of demonstrations and uprisings demanding independence from Russia. Letter to Grand Duke Constantine, Viceroy of Poland (June 10, 1862)

2 It is better to begin to abolish serfdom from above than to wait for it to abolish itself from below.
Remark (March 30, 1856)

Alexander the Great, King of Macedonia (Alexander III of Macedon; 356–323 B.C.) Macedonian monarch

Quotations about Alexander the Great

1 He...said: "This is the House of God whose like is not to be found in the world." And the king brought forth vessels of silver and gold and precious stone in great profusion and gave them to the treasure of the House of God.
Micha Joseph Bin Gorion (1865–1921) Russian writer and collector of Jewish folktales. Quoted in *Mimekor Yisrael* (I. M. Lask, tr.; Emanuel bin Gorin, ed.; 1976), vol. 1

2 Your memorial will be that all the children of the priests who will be born during this year in the whole of Judah and Jerusalem will be given your name Alexander.
Micha Joseph Bin Gorion (1865–1921) Russian writer and collector of Jewish folktales. Referring to the reward offered to Alexander the Great by a priest of the Second Temple in return for a donation of gold. Quoted in *Mimekor Yisrael* (I. M. Lask, tr.; Emanuel bin Gorion, ed.; 1976), vol. 1

3 The known world was too small for Alexander; the eaves of a roof are infinity for a swallow.
Joaquim Maria Machado de Assis (1839–1908) Brazilian novelist and short-story writer. *Epitaph of a Small Winner* (1880)

4 Alexander wept when he heard from Anaxarchus that there was an infinite number of worlds..."Do you not think it a matter worthy of lamentation that when there is such a vast multitude of them, we have not yet conquered one?"
Plutarch (46?–120?) Greek biographer and philosopher. "On the Tranquillity of the Mind" (1st–2nd century)

Quotations by Alexander the Great

5 If I were not Alexander, I would be Diogenes.
Attrib. "Alexander," *Parallel Lives* (Plutarch; 120?), ch. 14, section 3

6 I am dying with the help of too many physicians.
323 B.C. Attrib.

Alexandra, Empress (Alexandra Feodorovna; 1872–1918) German-born Russian empress

1 Be the Emperor, be Peter the Great, John the Terrible, the Emperor Paul—crush them all under you—Now don't you laugh, naughty one—but I long to see you so with those men who try to govern *you*.
Letter to her husband, Tsar Nicholas II (December 27, 1916)

al-Fayed, Mohamed (b.1933) Egyptian businessman

1 The dog barks but the caravan passes on.
Referring to his critics. Interview, *Daily Express*, London (March 14, 1990)

2 Some of our customers have asked if they can be buried with me. Certainly, but space is limited. It will cost £10 million per person, mummification £1 million extra, and you must be prepared to rest for eternity standing up.
1990. Attrib.

Alfieri, Vittorio, Conte (1749–1803) Italian poet and dramatist

1 Heaven takes care that no man secures happiness by crime.
Oreste (1787–89), Act I, Scene 2

Alfonso X, King of Léon and Castile (called Alfonso the Wise, Alfonso the Astronomer; 1221–84) Spanish monarch

1 Had I been present at the Creation, I would have given some useful hints for the better ordering of the universe.
Referring to the complicated Ptolemaic model of the universe. Often quoted as, "Had I been consulted I would have recommended something simpler." Attrib.

Alfonso XIII, King of Spain (1886–1941) Spanish monarch

1 You can measure the social caste of a person by the distance between the husband's and wife's apartments.
Attrib.

Alfred, King of Wessex (called Alfred the Great; 849–899) English monarch

1 All the youth now in England of free men, who are rich enough to be able to devote themselves to it, be set to learn as long as they are not fit for any other occupation, until they are able to read English writing well.
Preface to *Cura Pastoralis* by Pope Gregory I (890?)

al-Ghazali (Abu Hamid Muhammad ibn Muhammad at-Tusi al-Ghazali, "Algazel"; 1058–1111) Islamic philosopher and theologian

1 Adam...is the divine handwriting, which is not in characters and letters (for His handwriting transcends both characters and letters, even as His word transcends sound and syllables, and His pen transcends reed and steel, and His hand transcends flesh and bone).
The Niche for Lights (11th–12th century), quoted in *Four Sufi Classics* (Idris Shah, ed., 1980)

2 If the Prophet was Allah's hearing and vision and tongue, then Allah and He alone is the Hearer, the Seer, the Speaker.
The Niche for Lights (11th–12th century), quoted in *Four Sufi Classics* (Idris Shah, ed.; 1980)

3 The Prophet said to Gabriel..."Has the sun moved?" And Gabriel answered: "No—Yes." "How so?" asked he; and the other replied: "Between my saying No and Yes it has moved a distance equal to five hundred years."
The Niche for Lights (11th–12th century), quoted in *Four Sufi Classics* (Idris Shah, ed.; 1980)

4 The verses of the Koran, in relation to intelligence, have the value of sunlight in relation to the eyesight, to wit, it is by this sunlight that the act of seeing is accomplished.
The Niche for Lights (11th–12th century), quoted in *Four Sufi Classics* (Idris Shah, ed.; 1980)

Algren, Nelson (Nelson Ahlgren Abraham; 1909–81) U.S. novelist and short-story writer

1 Never eat at a place called Mom's. Never play cards with a man called Doc. Never go to bed with a woman whose troubles are greater than your own.
A Walk on the Wild Side (1956)

2 It is a joint where the bulls and the foxes live well and the lambs wind up head-down from the hook.
Referring to Chicago, Illinois. *Chicago: City on the Make* (1951)

3 A Walk on the Wild Side
1956. Novel title.

4 The Man with the Golden Arm
1949. Novel title. It was made into a motion picture (1955), starring Frank Sinatra.

Alhegelan, Nouha Saudi Arabian writer

1 In almost all Arab countries the veil has been abolished, but not by force or by occidental criticism. It has been abolished by the women who decided one day that they did not want it any more.
"Women in the Arab World", *Irish Arab World* (1978)

Ali ('Ali ibn-Abi-Talib; 600?–661) Arab caliph and son-in-law of Muhammad

1 Question me before you lose me, for I have the knowledge of those who came earlier and those who will come later...By God, I know the Qur'an and its interpretation better than anyone who claims knowledge of it.
Quoted in "The Life of the Commander of the Faithful," *The Book of Guidance into the Lives of the Twelve Imams* (Abu al-Mufid; 10th century)

Ali, Muhammad (Cassius Marcellus Clay, Jr.; b.1942) U.S. boxer

1 I'm so fast I could hit you before God gets the news.
New York Times (June 29, 1975)

2 It's just a job. Grass grows, birds fly, waves pound the sand. I beat people up.
New York Times (April 6, 1977)

3 I want to get out with my greatness intact.
Announcing his retirement. *Observer,* London (July 4, 1974)

4 You know I hate fighting. If I knew how to make a living some other way, I would.
Observer, London (November 21, 1971), "Sayings of the Week"

5 The man who views the world at 50 the same as he did at 20 has wasted 30 years of his life.
Interview, *Playboy* (November 1975)

6 How could they say that my religion, Islam, was a "race hate" religion after all the plunder and enslavement and domination of my people by white Christians in the name of white supremacy?
The Greatest: My Own Story (co-written with Richard Durham; 1976)

7 Keep asking me, no matter how long
On the war in Viet Nam, I sing this song
I ain't got no quarrel with the Viet Cong.
February 1966. *The Greatest: My Own Story* (co-written with Richard Durham; 1976)

8 Sugar Ray Robinson warned me that my career would be wrecked if I became a "Black Muslim."
The Greatest: My Own Story (co-written with Richard Durham; 1976)

9 I was a Muslim...I didn't hate nobody. I ain't preached no violence but I couldn't take that army step.
Referring to his refusal to be drafted into the U.S. Army in 1967, for which he was stripped of his world heavyweight title. *The Greatest: My Own Story* (co-written with Richard Durham; 1976)

10 "The odds are against you Joe," I tell him. "In a fight with me, nobody's gonna bet on a Baptist beating a Muslim."
Said to Joe Frazier, who lost to Ali in a return match in 1974; he had previously beaten Ali in a championship bout in 1971. *The Greatest: My Own Story* (co-written with Richard Durham; 1976)

11 Nobody heard of Vietnam until there was a war. Nobody heard of Korea until there was a war. Nobody heard of Zaire until I fought there, and paying me is a whole lot cheaper than fighting a war.
Muhammad Ali: His Life and Times (Thomas Hauser; 1991)

12 Float like a butterfly
Sting like a bee.
Describing his boxing style, devised by aide Drew "Bundini" Brown. *The Cassius Clay Story* (G. Sullivan; 1964), ch. 8

13 I'm the greatest!
Remark often said before, during, and after his fights.

14 When you're as great as I am, it's hard to be humble.
Attrib.

15 You don't want no pie in the sky when you die. You want something here on the ground while you're still around.
Attrib.

Ali, Zeenat Arab historian

1 The Prophet Mohammad wanted equality for women. But when Islam went from the desert to the palaces, men put in certain loopholes.
Independent, London (September 16, 1993)

Alibhai-Brown, Yasmin British writer and broadcaster

1 Anyone who pushes for equality, or criticises the male Anglo-Saxon world, is declared "PC" and thereby discredited and silenced. McCarthyism to counteract imagined totalitarianism. Where have we seen that before?
Independent, London (August 11, 1993)

Alison, Richard (b. 1606) English poet

1 There cherries grow, that none can buy
Till cherry ripe themselves do cry.
An Hour's Recreation in Music (1606)

2 There is a garden in her face,
Where roses and white lilies grow.
An Hour's Recreation in Music (1606)

Al-Khansa (Tumadir bint 'Amr ibn al-Harith ibn ash-Sharid; 575–646) Arab poet

1 My eye cried and woke me.
The night was pain.
"The Night" (7th century)

Allainval, Abbé d' (Léonor Jean Christine Soulas; 1700–53) French playwright

1 A Superfluity of Good Things
Play title, also translated as *An Embarrassment of Riches*. *A Superfluity of Good Things* (1726)

Allen, Ethan (1738–89) U.S. soldier and revolutionary

1 In the name of the Great Jehovah and the Continental Congress.
Allen's reply when asked on whose authority he demanded the surrender of the British forces holding Fort Ticonderoga. Speech (May 10, 1775)

Allen, Fred (John Florence Sullivan; 1894–1956) U.S. comedian

1 I have just returned from Boston. It is the only thing to do if you find yourself up there.
Letter to Groucho Marx (June 12, 1953)

2 The vaudeville actor was part gypsy and part suitcase.
Much Ado About Me (1956)

3 A celebrity is a person who works hard all his life to become known, then wears dark glasses to avoid being recognized.
Treadmill to Oblivion (1954)

4 Hollywood is the place where people from Iowa mistake each other for stars.
Quoted in *Filmgoer's Book of Quotes* (Leslie Halliwell; 1973)

5 The average vice-president is a form of executive fungus that attaches itself to a desk. On a boat this growth would be called a barnacle.
Quoted in *The American Treasury 1455–1955* (Clifton Fadiman; 1955)

6 After quitting radio I was able to live on the money I saved on aspirins.
Attrib.

7 Committee—a group of men who individually can do nothing but as a group decide that nothing can be done.
Attrib.

8 Executive: an ulcer with authority.
Attrib.

9 California is a great place—if you happen to be an orange.
Also attributed to Orson Welles. Attrib.

10 Where were you fellows when the paper was blank?
Remark to writers who heavily edited one of his scripts. Attrib.

Allen, James (1864–1912) U.S. theologian and author

1 Purpose is the keystone in the temple of achievement.
The Master of Destiny (1909)

Allen, William (1803–79) U.S. politician

1 Fifty-four forty or fight!
Referring to the northern boundary of Oregon, which was disputed with Britain. The 49th parallel was agreed as the frontier in 1846. Attrib.

Allen, Woody (Allen Stewart Konigsberg; b.1935) U.S. film actor and director

Quotations about Allen

1 Woody makes a movie as if he were lighting 10,000 safety matches to illuminate a city. Each one is a little epiphany: topical, ethnic, or political.
Gene Wilder (b.1935) U.S. actor and director. *New Yorker* (1978), quoted in *Chambers Film Quotes* (Tony Crawley, ed.; 1991)

Quotations by Allen

2 Don't knock it, it's sex with someone you love.
Referring to masturbation. *Annie Hall* (1977)

3 It was the most fun I ever had without laughing.
Referring to sex. *Annie Hall* (1977)

4 Is sex dirty? Only if it's done right.
Everything You Always Wanted to Know About Sex (1972)

5 Not only is there no God, but try getting a plumber on weekends.
"My Philosophy," *Getting Even* (1971)

6 WOMAN You are the greatest lover I have ever known.
ALLEN Well, I practice a lot when I'm on my own.
Love and Death (1975)

7 I can't listen to that much Wagner. I start getting the urge to conquer Poland.
Manhattan Murder Mystery (1993)

8 I'm short enough and ugly enough to succeed on my own.
Play It Again, Sam (1972)

9 I'm really a timid person—I was beaten up by Quakers.
Sleeper (1973)

10 My brain? It's my second favorite organ.
Sleeper (1973)

11 I think crime pays. The hours are good, you travel a lot.
Take the Money and Run (1969)

12 I don't watch funny movies. I watch Ingmar Bergman. He's concerned with the silence of God and in some small way, so am I.
Time (July 3, 1972)

13 I don't believe in an afterlife, although I am bringing a change of underwear.
Without Feathers (1976)

14 Money is better than poverty, if only for financial reasons.
Without Feathers (1976)

15 It's not that I'm afraid to die. I just don't want to be there when it happens.
"Death (A Play)," *Without Feathers* (1976)

16 How can I believe in God when just last week I got my tongue caught in the roller of an electric typewriter?
1975. "Selections from the Allen Notebooks," *Without Feathers* (1976)

17 The thing to remember is that each time of life has its appropriate rewards, whereas when you're dead it's hard to find the light switch.
"The Early Essays," *Without Feathers* (1976)

18 The lion and the calf shall lie down together but the calf won't get much sleep.
"The Scrolls," *Without Feathers* (1976)

19 And my parents finally realize that I'm kidnapped and they snap into action immediately: they rent out my room.
Woody Allen and His Comedy (Eric Lax; 1975)

20 Death is an acquired trait.
Woody Allen and His Comedy (Eric Lax; 1975)

21 I don't want to achieve immortality through my work...I want to achieve it through not dying.
Woody Allen and His Comedy (Eric Lax; 1975)

22 Play It Again, Sam
1969. Motion-picture title, based on Ingrid Bergman's often-misquoted request to "Play it, Sam" in the motion picture *Casablanca* (1942).

23 Eighty percent of success is showing up.
Attrib.

24 I want to tell you a terrific story about oral contraception. I asked this girl to sleep with me and she said "no."
Attrib.

25 Sex between a man and a woman can be wonderful—provided you get between the right man and the right woman.
Attrib.

Alliluyeva, Svetlana (originally Svetlana Iosifovna Stalin; b.1926) Russian-born U.S. writer

1 God grants an easy death only to the just.
Twenty Letters to a Friend (1967)

Allingham, William (1824–89) Irish poet

1 Up the airy mountain,
Down the rushy glen,
We daren't go a-hunting,
For fear of little men.
"The Fairies" (1850)

al-Mufid, Abu Abdullah Muhammad al-Harithi al-Baghdadi, Sheikh (*fl.* 10th century) Iraqi scholar and jurist

1 Be happy with what you have and make provision for the day of your return to God...The journey is long, the appointment is on the day of the Resurrection, the destiny is Heaven or the fire of Hell.
10th century. "The Life of the Commander of the Faithful," *The Book of Guidance into the Lives of the Twelve Imams* (I. K. A. Howard, tr.; 1981)

2 Go forward into battle and do not shrink away since there is no escape from death...By God, in Whose hands is the life of Ali, a thousand sword blows on the head is easier than death in bed.
10th century. "The Life of the Commander of the Faithful," *The Book of Guidance into the Lives of the Twelve Imams* (I. K. A. Howard, tr.; 1981)

3 No tool is more beneficial than intelligence. No enemy is more harmful than ignorance.
10th century. "The Life of the Commander of the Faithful," *The Book of Guidance into the Lives of the Twelve Imams* (I. K. A. Howard, tr.; 1981)

4 Often a mighty man is the humblest of creatures and a humble man is the mightiest of creatures.
10th century. "The Life of the Commander of the Faithful," *The Book of Guidance Into the Lives of the Twelve Imams* (I. K. A. Howard, tr.; 1981)

5 The drinker of wine...becomes drunk. When he becomes drunk, he talks nonsense. When he talks nonsense, he spreads calumnies.
10th century. "The Life of the Commander of the Faithful," *The Book of Guidance into the Lives of the Twelve Imams* (I. K. A. Howard, tr.; 1981)

6 When a man dies, the angels ask about what he brought while the people ask about what he has left behind.
10th century. "The Life of the Commander of the Faithful," *The Book of Guidance Into the Lives of the Twelve Imams* (I. K. A. Howard, tr.; 1981)

7 I heard the Apostle of God, may God bless him and his family, say: "I am the city of knowledge and Ali is its gate."
10th century. Referring to Ali ibn Abi Talib, Muhammad's companion, cousin, and son-in-law, whose military prowess earned him the name "Commander of the Faithful." "The Life of the Commander of the Faithful," *The Book of Guidance Into the Lives of the Twelve Imams* (I. K. A. Howard, tr.; 1981)

8 He freed a thousand slaves with his own money in his desire to seek the face of God and to escape the fire of Hell, money which he had labored for with his own hands and for which his own brow had sweated.
10th century. Referring to Husain, grandson of Muhammad and younger son of Ali ibn Abi Talib. "The Lives of the Other Imams: Imam Ali ben al-Husayn," *The Book of Guidance Into the Lives of the Twelve Imams* (I. K. A. Howard, tr.; 1981)

9 God endowed him with wisdom and the distinction of speech...He made him an Imam while still in the state of apparent childhood just as He made Jesus, son of Mary, a prophet in the cradle.
10th century. Referring to Imam Mohammed al-Mahdi, known as the Twelfth Imam to Shiite Muslims. "The Lives of the Other Imams: The Twelfth Imam," *The Book of Guidance Into the Lives of the Twelve Imams* (I. K. A. Howard, tr.; 1981)

10 God will bring forth the flesh and bodies of the believers in the graves. It is as if I could see them advancing from Juhayna shaking off the soil from their hair.
10th century. Referring to the time of the return of Imam Mohammed al-Mahdi, the Twelfth Imam of Shi'ite Muslims. "The Lives of the Other Imams: The Twelfth Imam," *The Book of Guidance Into the Lives of the Twelve Imams* (I. K. A. Howard, tr.; 1981)

al-Nawawi, Muhyid-Din Abu Zakariyya ibn Sharaf, Imam (1233–77) Syrian Islamic scholar

1 The intelligent man...must not exert himself except for three things: taking provision for the Final Abode, taking some trouble to earn a living, and pleasure in something which is not haram.
13th century. From the proverbs of the prophet Ibrahim (Abraham), as quoted by Muhammad. The word "haram" designates that which is forbidden. *The Complete Forty Hadith* (Abdassamad Clarke, tr.; 1988), 12th Hadith

2 Intention is the measure for rendering actions true, so that where intention is sound action is sound, and where it is corrupt then action is corrupt.
13th century. *The Complete Forty Hadith* (Abdassamad Clarke, tr.; 1988), 1st Hadith

3 Know that the appetite for sexual intercourse is one which the prophets and people of right action love...for it softens the heart.
13th century. *The Complete Forty Hadith* (Abdassamad Clarke, tr.; 1988), 25th Hadith

4 Adam...said "If you want to do something, then if your hearts are agitated, do not do it, for when I drew near to eating from the tree my heart was agitated at eating."
13th century. From Adam's last words to his sons. *The Complete Forty Hadith* (Abdassamad Clarke, tr.; 1988), 27th Hadith

5 Acts of disobedience are the postal service of disbelief.
13th century. *The Complete Forty Hadith* (Abdassamad Clarke, tr.; 1988), 6th Hadith

6 Anger is a policeman and a foul cunning slave who assumes the aspect of a counselor, but whose advice is deadly poison.
13th century. *The Complete Forty Hadith* (Abdassamad Clarke, tr.; 1988), 6th Hadith

7 The people of knowledge said that "The body is the kingdom of the self and its city."
13th century. *The Complete Forty Hadith* (Abdassamad Clarke, tr.; 1988), 6th Hadith

Al-Razi (Abu Bakr Muhammad ibn Zakariya al-Razi, also known as Rhazes; 865?–928?) Persian physician and philosopher

1 Truth in medicine is an unattainable goal, and the art as described in books is far beneath the knowledge of an experienced and thoughtful physician.
Quoted in *History of Medicine* (Max Neuburger; 1910)

2 In treating a patient, let your first thought be to strengthen his natural vitality.
Attrib.

Alsop, Joseph (Joseph Wright Alsop, Jr.; 1910–89) U.S. journalist

1 Gratitude, like love, is never a dependable international emotion.
Observer, London (November, 1952)

al-Takriti, Barzan (Barzan Ibrahim Hassan al-Takriti) Iraqi ambassador

1 I think the Kuwaitis enjoy a crisis now and again. It brings them world attention.
Referring to reports that Iraq might be about to re-invade Kuwait. *Times*, London (December 5, 1994)

Altgeld, John Peter (1847–1902) German-born U.S. lawyer and politician

1 No community can be said to possess local self-government if the executive can, at his pleasure, send military forces to patrol its streets under pretense of enforcing some law.
Protesting at the use of federal troops to break a strike by employees of the Pullman railroad car company. Letter to President Grover Cleveland (July 6, 1894)

Alther, Lisa (b.1944) U.S. writer

1 If this was adulthood the only improvement she could detect in her situation was that she could now eat dessert without eating her vegetables.
Kinflicks (1976)

Al-Tirmidhi (Abu Isa Muhammad ibn Isa ibn Sawrah ibn Shaddad Al-Tirmidhi; 824–892?) Islamic scholar

1 The grave is either like a ditch from the ditches of Hell, or like a luxuriant garden from the luxuriant gardens of Paradise.
Sunan of Al-Tirmidhi (9th century), quoted in *Salvation of the Soul and Islamic Devotions* (Muhammad Abul Quasem; 1983)

Altman, Robert (b.1925) U.S. film director

Quotations about Altman

1 People say that Bob allows you the most enormous freedom and that they're creating their own part, which is an enormous lie. Everyone's lining up in the exact direction he wants them to go...you're the same marionette you are with other directors.
Geraldine Chaplin (b.1944) U.S. actor. Interview, *Crowdaddy* (July 1976), quoted in *Filmmakers Speak* (Jay Leyda, ed.; 1977)

Quotations by Altman

2 What's a cult? It just means not enough people to make a minority.
An interview. *Observer*, London (April 11, 1981)

Amagat, Emile Hilaire (1841–1915) French physicist

1 Women cannot be part of the Institute of France.
Referring to Marie Curie's rejection by the Académie des Sciences, for which she had been nominated in 1910. She was rejected by one vote and then refused to let her name be submitted again. For ten years, she would not let the Académie publish her work. Remark (1910)

Ambrose, Saint (339?–397) German-born Roman Doctor of the Church

1 When in Rome, live as the Romans do: when elsewhere, live as they live elsewhere.
Advice given to Saint Augustine. Attrib.

Amergin (also spelled Amorgen; *fl.* 1268 B.C.) Irish mythical poet

1 I am a stag: *of seven tines*
I am a flood: *across a plain*
I am a wind: *on a deep lake*
I am a tear: *the Sun lets fall.*
13th century. Quoted in "The Alphabet Calendar of Amergin" (Robert Graves, tr.), *The Faber Book of Irish Verse* (John Montague, ed.; 1974)

American Museum of Natural History U.S. museum

1 A zebra is a light-colored animal with dark stripes, not a dark one with light stripes.
Newsweek (December 30, 1957)

Amery, Julian (Harold Julian Amery; b.1919) British Conservative politician

1 We have suffered the inevitable consequences of a combination of unpreparedness and feeble counsel.
Referring to Argentina's seizure of the Falkland Islands (Islas Malvinas). Speech to the British Parliament (April 3, 1982)

Ames, Fisher (1758–1808) U.S. politician

1 A monarchy is a merchantman which sails well, but will sometimes strike a rock, and go to the bottom; whilst a republic is a raft which would never sink, but then your feet are always in the water.
1795. Quoted in *Essays*, 2nd series (R. W. Emerson; 1844), no. 7

Amichai, Yehuda (b.1924) German-born Israeli poet

1 I found myself
Suddenly, and too early in life,

Like the inner wall of a house
Which has become an outside wall after wars and devastations.
"Like the Inner Wall of a House," *Amen* (1978), ll. 1–4

2 Hebrew and Arabic,
which are like stones on the tongue and sand on the throat,
have softened for tourists like oil.
"Patriotic Songs," *Amen* (1978), ll. 5–7

3 Knowledge of peace
passes from country to country,
like children's games,
which are so much alike, everywhere.
"Patriotic Songs," *Amen* (1978), no. 15, ll. 7–10

4 There is a dark memory on which the noise of
Playing children is scattered like powdered sugar.
"Sadness of the Eyes and Descriptions of a Journey," *Amen* (1978), ll. 1–2

5 When a man is abandoned by
his love, an empty round space
expands inside him like a cave
for wonderful stalagmites.
"Song," *Amen* (1978), ll. 1–4

6 God has pity on kindergarten children.
He has less pity on schoolchildren.
And on grownups he has no pity at all.
"God Has Pity on Kindergarten Children," *Voices of Israel* (Joseph Cohen, ed.; 1990)

7 Look, we too are going in the reverse-flower-way:
to begin with a calyx exulting towards the light
...and to end as a root, in the darkness, in the deep womb.
"Look: Thoughts and Dreams," *Voices of Israel* (Joseph Cohen, ed.; 1990)

8 Extreme pacifism...amounts only to sitting back and getting yourself slaughtered.
April 10, 1984. Quoted in Interview, *Voices of Israel* (Joseph Cohen, ed.; 1990)

Amiel, Henri Frédéric (1821–81) Swiss writer and philosopher

1 Health is the first of all liberties, and happiness gives us the energy which is the basis of health.
1865. *Journal intime* (1883–84)

2 There is no curing a sick man who believes himself in health.
1877. *Journal intime* (1883–84)

Amies, Hardy, Sir (Edwin Hardy Amies; b.1909) British couturier

1 To dismiss the English style by saying that the key is understatement is to overlook an air of nonchalance which is habitual and comes from an innate sense of security.
The Englishman's Suit (1994), ch. 12

Amin, Idi (b.1925) Ugandan soldier and politician

1 Your experience will be a lesson to all of us men to be careful not to marry ladies in very high positions.
Message to Lord Snowdon, on the break-up of his marriage to Princess Margaret. Quoted in *International Gossip* (Andrew Barrow; 1978)

2 In any country there must be people who have to die. They are the sacrifices any nation has to make to achieve law and order.
1976. Quoted in *The Cynic's Lexicon* (Jonathon Green, ed.; 1984)

Amis, Kingsley, Sir (1922–95) British novelist

1 Women are really much nicer than men:
No wonder we like them.
"A Bookshop Idyll" (1956)

2 Death has got something to be said for it:
There's no need to get out of bed for it;
Wherever you may be,
They bring it to you, free.
1976. "Delivery Guaranteed" (1979)

3 I wish I could have a little tape-and-loudspeaker arrangement sewn into the binding of this magazine, to be triggered off by the light reflected from the reader's eyes on to this part of the page, and set to bawl out at several bels: MORE WILL MEAN WORSE.
Referring to what he described as "the delusion that there are thousands of young people who are capable of benefiting from university training but have somehow failed to find their way there." *Encounter* (July 1960)

4 Outside every fat man there is an even fatter man trying to close in.
One Fat Englishman (1963), ch. 3

5 He was of the faith chiefly in the sense that the church he currently did not attend was Catholic.
One Fat Englishman (1963), ch. 8

6 It was no wonder that people were so horrible when they started life as children.
One Fat Englishman (1963), ch. 14

7 These days, for a quid pro quo,
Ralph's chum does what, and with which;
Buck's playmates, family men,
Eye a Boy Scout now and then.
Sex is a momentary itch,
Love never lets you go.
"An Ever-Fixed Mark," *The Penguin Book of Homosexual Verse* (Stephen Coote, ed.; 1983)

Amis, Martin (b.1949) British writer

1 The surest guarantee of sexual success is sexual success (you can't have one without the other and you can't have the other without the one).
Success (1978)

2 Novelist, essayist, dramatist, epigrammist, television polemicist, controversialist, pansexualist, socialist and socialite: if there is a key to Gore Vidal's public character it has something to do with his towering immodesty, the enjoyable superbity of his self love.
The Moronic Inferno (1986)

3 When it comes to flying, I am a nervous passenger but a confident drinker and Valium-swallower.
"Emergency Landing," *Worst Journeys* (Keath Fraser, ed.; 1991)

Ammons, A. R. (Archie Randolph Ammons; b.1926) U.S. poet

1 I have a life that did not become,
that turned aside and stopped,
astonished.

"Easter Morning" (1981), quoted in *The Norton Anthology of American Literature* (Nina Baym, ed.; 1998), vol. 2

2 I would as soon believe
in paradise as in
nothing.

"The Dwelling" (1987), quoted in *The Norton Anthology of American Literature* (Nina Baym, ed.; 1998), vol. 2

3 One must write and
rewrite till one writes it right.

Garbage (1993)

Ampère, Jean-Jaques (Jean-Jaques Antoine Ampère; 1800–64) French writer and historian

1 Books create eras and nations, just as eras and nations create books.

"De l'histoire de la littérature Française," *Mélanges d'histoire littéraire et de littérature* (1876)

2 The future, gentlemen, is the faith of our age: it is the torch of the past, the guiding star of the present.

"Les Renaissances," *Mélanges d'histoire littéraire et de littérature* (1876)

Amr ibn al-'As (d. 664) Arab soldier

1 As Amr lay on his death-bed a friend said to him: "You have often remarked that you would like to find an intelligent man at the point of death, and to ask him what his feelings were. Now I ask you."

The Harvest of a Quiet Eye (Alan L. Mackay; 1977)

Anaxagoras (500?–428? B.C.) Greek philosopher

1 In everything there is a portion of everything except Mind.

Quoted in *The Presocratic Philosophers* (G. S. Kirk, J. E. Raven, and M. Schofield; 1983)

2 Neither is there a smallest part of what is small, but there is always a smaller (for it is impossible that what is should cease to be). Likewise there is always something larger than what is large.

5th century B.C. Attrib.

Andersch, Alfred (1914–80) German experimental writer

1 History tells how it was. A story how it might have been.

Winterspelt (1974)

Andersen, Hans Christian (1805–75) Danish writer

1 None of the Emperor's clothes had ever had such a success before. "But, Daddy, he's got nothing on!" piped up a small child.

1837. The emperor has been sold an "invisible" costume, which in reality does not exist. "The Emperor's New Clothes," *Fairy Tales* (L. W. Kingsland, tr.; 1959–61)

2 And so they could see she was a real princess, because she had felt the pea through twenty mattresses and twenty eiderdowns. No one but a real princess could possibly be so sensitive.

The princess proves she is a princess by being sensitive to a pea placed under 20 mattresses on her bed. "The Princess and the Pea," *Fairy Tales* (L. W. Kingsland, tr.; 1959–61)

3 It doesn't matter about being born in a duckyard, as long as you're hatched from a swan's egg.

"The Ugly Duckling," *Fairy Tales* (L. W. Kingsland, tr.; 1959–61)

4 The Ugly Duckling

Story title. *Tales, Told for Children* (1843)

5 Most of the people who will walk after me will be children, so make the beat keep time with short steps.

Planning the music for his funeral. *Hans Christian Andersen* (Rumer Godden; 1955)

Anderson, Elizabeth Garrett (1836–1917) British physician

1 Because I prefer to earn a thousand rather than twenty pounds a year.

Reply when asked why she did not train to be a nurse. *Dr. Elizabeth Garrett Anderson* (Louisa Garrett Anderson; 1939)

Anderson, Eric (William Eric Kinloch Anderson; b.1936) British teacher

1 The most insidious influence on the young is not violence, drugs, tobacco, drink or sexual perversion, but our pursuit of the trivial and our tolerance of the third rate.

Observer, London (June 12, 1994), "Sayings of the Week"

Anderson, John B. (b.1922) U.S. journalist

1 George Bush is just a tweedier version of Ronald Reagan.

New York Times Magazine (February 17, 1980)

Anderson, Kye U.S. business executive

1 Pushing a new enterprise past all the barriers to success takes learnable skills...but it also takes a tenacious inner passion bordering on monomania. This combination is what I call leadership.

Harvard Business Review (May–June 1992)

Anderson, Laurie (b.1947) U.S. performance artist

1 I think a Benedictine convent is very close to the art world in a lot of ways. The nuns are isolated, but these are people who think and feel and have a relationship to—to a kind of ideal, a spiritual or intellectual ideal.

1990. Quoted in "Laurie Anderson," *View* (Robin White (interviewer); January 1990)

Anderson, Marian (1897–1993) U.S. opera singer

1 Sometimes, it's like a hair across your cheek. You can't see it, you can't find it with your fingers, but you keep brushing at it because the feel of it is irritating.

Referring to racial prejudice. *Ladies Home Journal* (September 1960)

2 Where there is money, there is fighting.

1931. *Marian Anderson, a Portrait* (Kosti Vehanen; 1941)

Anderson, Maxwell (James Maxwell Anderson; 1888–1959) U.S. playwright

1 Virginity is rather a state of mind.
Elizabeth the Queen (1930), Act 2, Scene 3

2 What price Glory?
Play title. *What Price Glory?* (co-written with Laurence Stallings; 1924)

Anderson, Poul (Poul William Anderson; b.1926) U.S. writer

1 I have yet to see any problem, however complicated, which, when looked at in the right way, did not become still more complicated.
New Scientist (1969)

Anderson, P. W. (Philip Warren Anderson; 1923–95) U.S. physicist

1 You never understand everything. When one understands everything, one has gone crazy.
Attrib.

Anderson, Sherwood (Sherwood Berton Anderson; 1876–1941) U.S. novelist and short-story writer

1 The most materialistic age in the history of the world, when wars would be fought without patriotism, when men would forget God and only pay attention to moral standards...was telling its story.
1919. Referring to the early 20th century. "Godliness," *Winesburg, Ohio* (Malcolm Cowley, ed.; 1960)

2 Everyone knows of the talking artists...They talk of art and are passionately, almost feverishly, in earnest about it. They think it matters much more than it does.
1919. "Loneliness," *Winesburg, Ohio* (Malcolm Cowley, ed.; 1960)

3 An American town worked terribly at the task of amusing itself.
1919. Referring to Winesburg, Ohio. "Sophistication," *Winesburg, Ohio* (Malcolm Cowley, ed.; 1960)

4 Most boys have seasons of wishing they could die gloriously instead of just being grocery clerks and going on with their humdrum lives.
1919. "The Untold Lie," *Winesburg, Ohio* (Malcolm Cowley, ed.; 1960)

5 I do not want attention centered on me. If I could work the rest of my life unknown, unnoticed by those who make current opinion, I would be happier.
1930. Quoted in "Fame is No Good, Take It from Me," *No Heroics, Please* (Raymond Carver; 1991)

6 Fame is no good, my dear. Take it from me.
1927. Letter to a schoolteacher from Washington, D.C., who had asked Sherwood Anderson to read and comment on two of her stories. Quoted in "Fame is No Good, Take It from Me," *No Heroics, Please* (Raymond Carver; 1991)

7 When an American stays away from New York too long something happens to him. Perhaps he becomes a little provincial, a little dead and afraid.
Quoted in *Selected Letters of Sherwood Anderson* (Charles E. Modin; 1984)

Andersson, Benny Swedish singer

1 Knowing me, knowing you
There is nothing we can do
Knowing me, knowing you
We just have to face it
This time we're through.
Song lyric. "Knowing Me, Knowing You" (co-written with Stig Andersson and Bjorn Ulvaeus; 1977)

Andrewes, Lancelot (1555–1626) English prelate

1 A cold coming they had of it, at this time of the year; just, the worst time of the year, to take a journey, and specially a long journey, in. The ways deep, the weather sharp, the days short, the sun farthest off *in solstitio brumali*, the very dead of Winter.
"Sermon Twelve," *Of the Nativity* (1618)

Andropov, Yuri (Yuri Vladimirovich Andropov; 1914–84) Russian-born Soviet head of state

1 Let no one expect us to disarm unilaterally. We are not a naive people.
Speech to the Central Committee of the Soviet Communist Party (November 22, 1982)

Angelou, Maya (originally Marguerite Johnson; b.1928) U.S. writer

1 History, despite its
wrenching pain,
Cannot be unlived, but if
faced with courage, need not be
lived again.
Read at the inauguration of President Bill Clinton. "On the Pulse of Morning" (January 20, 1993)

2 We were Black Americans in West Africa, where for the first time in our lives the color of our skin was accepted as correct and normal.
All God's Children Need Travelling Shoes (1986)

3 You may write me down in history
With your bitter, twisted lies,
You may trod me in the very dirt
But still, like dust, I'll rise.
"Still I Rise," *And Still I Rise* (1976)

4 Self-pity in its early stages is as snug as a feather mattress. Only when it hardens does it become uncomfortable.
Gather Together in My Name (1974)

5 But what mother and daughter understand each other, or even have the sympathy for each other's lack of understanding.
I Know Why The Caged Bird Sings (1970)

6 Children's talent to endure stems from their ignorance of alternatives.
I Know Why The Caged Bird Sings (1970)

7 My life has been one great big joke,
A dance that's walked
A song that's spoke,
I laugh so hard I almost choke
When I think about myself.
"When I Think About Myself," *Just Give Me a Cool Drink of Water 'fore I Die* (1971)

8 Your skin like dawn

Mine like dusk.
One paints the beginning
of a certain end.
The other, the end of a
sure beginning.
"Passing Time," *Maya Angelou: Poems* (1986)

9 Death to the young is more than that undiscovered country; despite its inevitability, it is a place having reality only in song or in other people's grief.
Singin' and Swingin' and Gettin' Merry Like Christmas (1976)

10 If one is lucky, a solitary fantasy can totally transform one million realities.
The Heart of a Woman (1981)

11 Youthful cynicism is sad to observe, because it indicates not so much knowledge learned from bitter experiences as insufficient trust even to attempt the future.
The Heart of a Woman (1981)

12 The Midwesterner in Kansas, the black American in Durham—both are certain they are the real America. And Boston just *knows* it is.
Time (April 24, 1978)

13 Now, after years of observation and enough courage to admit what I have observed, I try to plant peace if I do not want discord; to plant loyalty and honesty if I want to avoid betrayal and lies.
"At Harvest Time," *Wouldn't Take Nothing for my Journey Now* (1993)

14 Jealousy in romance is like salt in food. A little can enhance the savor, but too much can spoil the pleasure and, under certain circumstances, can be life-threatening.
"Jealousy," *Wouldn't Take Nothing for my Journey Now* (1993)

15 Human beings are more alike than unalike, and what is true anywhere is true everywhere, yet I encourage travel to as many destinations as possible for the sake of education as well as pleasure.
"Passports to Understanding," *Wouldn't Take Nothing for my Journey Now* (1993)

16 Curious, but we have come to a place, a time, when virtue is no longer considered a virtue. The mention of virtue is ridiculed, and even the word itself has fallen out of favor.
"When Virtue Becomes Redundant," *Wouldn't Take Nothing for my Journey Now* (1993)

17 The very idea that African-American language is...separate and apart is very threatening, because it can encourage young men and women not to learn standard English.
Referring to Ebonics. Quoted in *Wichita Eagle* (December 22, 1996)

18 Bitterness is like cancer. It eats upon the host. But anger is like fire. It burns all clean.
Writing Lives: Conversations Between Women Writers (Mary Chamberlain, ed.; 1988)

Angelus Silesius (pen name of Johannes Scheffler; 1624–77) Silesian poet and mystic

1 Abandonment ensnares God, but to abandon even God is an abandonment which few men can comprehend.
"Mystical Abandonment" (1657?), quoted in *The Penguin Book of German Verse* (Leonard Foster, ed.; 1957)

2 It is not the world that confines you, you yourself are the World, which holds you so fast a prisoner with yourself in yourself.
"You Are Your Own Prison" (1657?), quoted in *The Penguin Book of German Verse* (Leonard Foster, ed.; 1957)

3 Become the essence, man, for when this world shall wane, All chance will fall away, but essence will remain.
1657? One of his epigrams, on the essential and the accidental. "Chance and Essence," *A German Treasury* (Stanley Mason, tr.; 1993)

4 Time is as Eternity is, and Eternity as Time, only if you yourself make no difference between them.
1657? "Time is Eternity," *The Penguin Book of German Verse* (Leonard Foster, ed., 1957)

Anglo-Saxon Chronicle

1 In this king's time there was nothing but disturbance and wickedness and robbery, for forthwith the powerful men who were traitors rose against him.
Referring to the reign of Stephen, king of England (1135–54). *Anglo-Saxon Chronicle* (874–1154)

Anka, Paul (Paul Albert Anka; b.1941) U.S. singer and songwriter

1 I did it my way.
Based on the Claude François original, "Comme d'habitude." "My Way" (1969)

2 It was three o'clock in the morning in New York. It was pouring with rain, and it came to me..."And now the end is near and so I face the final curtain"...And I said wow that's it, that's for Sinatra...and then I cried.
Remark on completing the English lyrics of "My Way", based on the Claude François original, "Comme d'habitude." Attrib.

Anna Comnena (1083–1148?) Byzantine historian and princess

1 The mounted Kelt is irresistible, he would bore his way through the walls of Babylon.
Kelt is an alternative spelling of Celt, derived from the Greek *Keltoi*. *Alexiad* (1137–48?), quoted in *The Alexiad of Anna Comnena* (E. R. A. Sewter, tr.; 1969)

Annan, Kofi (b.1938) Ghanaian UN secretary-general

1 The best way of using force is to show it in order not to have to use it.
Attrib.

Anne, Queen of Great Britain and Ireland (1665–1714) British monarch

1 I have changed my ministers, but I have not changed my measures; I am still for moderation and will govern by it.
Remark (January 1711)

Anne, Princess, The Princess Royal (Anne Elizabeth Alice Louise; b.1950) British princess

1 It's a very boring time. I am not particularly maternal—it's an occupational hazard of being a wife.
Referring to being pregnant. *Daily Express*, London (April 14, 1981)

2 When I appear in public people expect me to neigh, grind my

teeth, paw the ground and swish my tail—none of which is easy.

Observer, London (May 22, 1977), "Sayings of the Week"

Anonymous

1 Love makes time pass. Time makes love pass.

French sundial motto

2 The insane, the mad, the frenzied, and others residing in the same places, who are there lodged and cared for with great diligence and attention.

Referring to England's first insane asylum, the Hospital of St. Mary of Bethlehem (commonly corrupted to "Bedlam"), in London; now called Bethlem Royal Hospital and resited to Beckenham, Kent. Fund-raising document for Bethlem Hospital (1519), quoted in *Bethlem Hospital 1247–1997, A Pictorial Record* (Patricia Allderidge; 1997)

3 Hail Mary, full of grace, the Lord is with thee: Blessed art thou among women, and blessed is the fruit of thy womb, Jesus.

"Hail Mary" (11th century)

4 Valor gave them a common death, history a common fame, posterity a common monument.

The monument stands on the Plains of Abraham, the site of the Battle of Québec (September 13, 1759), and commemorates the deaths of General James Wolfe and Marquis Louis Joseph de Montcalm de Saint-Veran. Inscription on monument (1828)

5 If the circumstances stand so with your Highness, that you believe you can get here time enough, in a condition to give assistance this year...we, who subscribe this, will not fail to attend your Highness upon your landing.

Fearful that James II's policies were directed towards the restoration of the Roman Catholic Church, seven English "notables" invited the Protestant William of Orange (1650–1702) to bring an army of liberation to England. He landed in Torbay on November 17, 1688, and was crowned King of England the following year. Letter from seven English notables to William of Orange (July 10, 1688)

6 Shame be to him who evil thinks.

The original French is "Honi soit qui mal y pense." The Order of the Garter is the senior order of British knighthood, founded by Edward III (1327–77), of which the badge is a garter of dark blue velvet. Motto of the Order of the Garter (April 23, 1348)

7 A cat loves fish, but hates to get his fur wet.

MS. Trinity College, Cambridge (1250?)

8 Labor relations have to be war; and their end result cannot be "harmony"; it must be victory for one side and defeat for the other. The best you can hope for are rules of civilized warfare and armistice long enough for each side to bury its dead.

Remark by a member of the National Labor Relations Board (1940s), quoted in *Mary Parker Follett: Prophet of Management* (Pauline Graham, ed.; 1995)

9 Today we were unlucky. But remember, we have only to be lucky once. You will have to be lucky always.

Issued by the Provisional IRA after their bombing of the Grand Hotel, Brighton, failed to kill Margaret Thatcher. Statement (Irish Republican Army; October 1984)

10 Lord, I have set my hopes in thee, I shall not be destroyed for ever.

"Te Deum" (Saints Ambrose and Augustine; 87) Attrib.

11 TO HELL WITH YOU. OFFENSIVE LETTER FOLLOWS.

Telegram to Sir Alec Douglas-Home

12 I met wid Napper Tandy, and he took me by the hand,
And he said, "How's poor ould Ireland, and how does she stand?"
She's the most disthressful country that iver yet was seen,
For they're hangin' men an' women there for the wearin' o' the Green.

Green is the color of Irish Nationalism. "The Wearin' o' the Green" (1795?)

13 The two governments of Ireland...affirm that any change in the status of Northern Ireland would only come about with the consent of a majority of the people of Northern Ireland.

The agreement on security cooperation between the Irish Republic and the United Kingdom, signed by Garrett Fitzgerald and Margaret Thatcher. *Anglo-Irish Agreement* (November 15, 1985), article 1

14 Marconi's most cherished possession was a gold tablet presented to him by 600 survivors of the *Titanic* who had been saved by the fact that the ship's wireless transmitter had been able to call ships from hundreds of miles away to pick up survivors.

Referring to Marchese Marconi (1874–1937), inventor of the first practical radio-signaling system. Obituary, *Daily Herald* (July 21, 1937)

15 Establish such a politie of civil and military power and create and secure such a large revenue...as may be the foundation of a large, well-grounded sure English dominion in India for all time to come.

Mid 18th century. *Dispatch from the East India Company to its chief executive in Surat* (mid–18th century)

16 We present you with this Book, the most valuable thing that this world affords. Here is wisdom; this is the royal Law; these are the lively Oracles of God.

The Presenting of the Holy Bible at the Coronation. *English Coronation Records* (G. Wickham Legge; 1901)

17 John Wayne is dead.
The hell I am.

Inscription on a wall in Bermondsey Antique Market, London, together with a ghostly denial. *Evening Standard,* London (1980)

18 So passes the glory of the world.

Referring to the large number of ruined castles in England, Normandy, and Anjou, which had been demolished after the rebellion (1173–74) against Henry II. *Histoire de Guillaume le Maréchal* (Paul Meyer, ed.; 1891–1901)

19 God blew and they were scattered.

Referring to the defeat of the Spanish Armada (1588). Inscription on a medallion (1588)

20 Here on 11 November 1918 succumbed the criminal pride of the German Reich, vanquished by the free peoples which it tried to enslave.

Referring to the signing of the Armistice at the end of World War I (November 11, 1918). Inscription on a monument in the forest of Compiègne, France (1919?)

21 If you're so smart, why aren't you rich?

"The American Question," *Intellectual Capital* (Thomas A. Stewart; 1997)

22 Superman, disguised as Clark Kent, mild-mannered reporter for a great metropolitan newspaper, fights a never-ending battle for truth, justice, and the American way.

Hence the catchphrase "Mild-mannered Clark Kent." Introduction to U.S. radio series (1950s)

23 These are the duties of a physician: First...to heal his mind and to give help to himself before giving it to anyone else.

Journal of the American Medical Association (1964), 189:989

24 One physician cures you of the colic; two physicians cure you of the medicine.

Journal of the American Medical Association (Vincent J. Derbes; 1964), 190:765

25 All present and correct.
Report by the British Army orderly sergeant to the officer of the day. *King's Regulations*

26 A rich man is one who isn't afraid to ask the salesman to show him something cheaper.
Ladies' Home Journal (January 1946)

27 We have ways of making men talk.
Film catch phrase, often repeated as "We have ways of making you talk." *Lives of a Bengal Lancer* (co-writers Waldemar Young, John L. Balderston, Achmed Abdullah, Grover Jones, and William Slavens McNutt; 1934)

28 "This is the tobacco he kills with," whispered Wind to the boys. The Sun Bearer held the pipe up to the sun that hung on the wall, lit it, and gave it to the boys to smoke...They said it tasted sweet, but it did them no harm.
Describing the Hero Twins' meeting with the Navajo sun god. "Changing Woman and the Hero Twins," *Navajo Legends* (Washington Matthews; 1897), quoted in *The Heath Anthology of American Literature* (Paul Lauter, ed.; 1998), vol. 1

29 We want and deserve tin-can architecture in a tin-horn culture. And we will probably be judged not by the monuments we build but by those we have destroyed.
Referring to the demolition of Pennsylvania Station, New York. *New York Times* (October 30, 1960), editorial

30 In our country one finds harmony between God and man. When we compare this with the relationship between God and man in Western countries, we notice a great difference.
From the Japanese *Kokutai ni Hongi*. "Harmony Between Humankind and Nature," *Sacred Texts of the World* (Ninian Smart and Richard D. Hecht, eds.; 1982)

31 Living beings of sinful actions, who are born again and again in ever-recurring births, are not disgusted with the round of rebirth, but they are like warriors, never tired of the battle of life.
From the Jaina sutras. "Living Beings and the Round of Rebirth," *Sacred Texts of the World* (Ninian Smart and Richard D. Hecht, eds.; 1982), doctrine 1

32 You've got an arm like a leg.
Heckler to a relief pitcher. *Sport* (September 1963)

33 Most Gracious Queen, we thee implore
To go away and sin no more,
But if that effort be too great,
To go away at any rate.
Queen Caroline (1768–1821), the wife of King George IV, was accused of adultery and tried by the House of Lords. The trial was abandoned because of public support for her. King George would not be reconciled with her, and she was prevented from attending his coronation in 1821. She died shortly afterward. Epigram on Queen Caroline, *The Diary of Lord Colchester* (November 15, 1820)

34 Once I am sure a patient has terminal cancer I tell them straight, I say, "It's time to go visit with the grandchildren." They seem to appreciate it.
Said by a doctor from New Mexico. *The Encyclopedia of Alternative Medicine and Self-Help* (Malcolm Hulke, ed.; 1978)

35 And yet there is only
One great thing.
The only thing:
To live to see in huts and on journeys
The great day that dawns
And the light that fills the world.
"Song," *The Mackenzie Eskimo. Report of the Fifth Thule Expedition, 1921–1924* (Knud Rasmussen (H. Ostermann, ed.); 1942), quoted in *The Heath Anthology of American Literature* (Paul Lauter, ed.; 1998), vol. 1

36 My name is George Nathaniel Curzon,
I am a most superior person.
My face is pink, my hair is sleek,
I dine at Blenheim once a week.
Blenheim Palace, near Oxford, England was the family home of the politically powerful Churchill family. *The Masque of Balliol* (1870?)

37 Fascism is the open, terrorist dictatorship of the most reactionary, most chauvinist, and most imperialist elements of finance capital.
Theses and Decisions of the Third Plenum of the Executive Committee of the Communist International (1934)

38 And as we stand on the edge of darkness
Let our chant fill the void
That others may know
In the land of the night
The ship of the sun
Is drawn by
The grateful dead.
Tibetan Book of the Dead (4000? B.C.)

39 You pays your money and you takes your choice.
Peepshow rhyme. Collectanea, *V.S. Lean* (1902–04)

40 Be frank and explicit with your lawyer...it is his business to confuse the issue afterwards.
Quoted in *A Cynic's Breviary* (J. R. Solly; 1925)

41 No one should be judge in his own cause.
Legal maxim. Quoted in *A Cynic's Breviary* (J. R. Solly; 1925)

42 A neighborhood is where, when you go out of it, you get beat up.
Quoted in "Group Dynamics," *America Comes of Middle Age* (Murray Kempton; 1963)

43 Who lives medically lives miserably.
Anatomy of Melancholy (Robert Burton; 1624)

44 Any officer who shall behave in a scandalous manner, unbecoming the character of an officer and a gentleman shall...be cashiered.
The words "conduct unbecoming the character of an officer" are a direct quotation from the British Naval Discipline Act (August 10, 1860), Article 24. "79: Disgraceful Conduct," *Articles of War* (1872)

45 Only You Can Prevent Forests.
Sign in the quarters of U.S. airmen spraying defoliants during the Vietnam War. Quoted in *A Soldier Reports* (William C. Westmoreland; 1976)

46 Life in the home is indeed attended by a great many faults and calamities.
Quoted in *Buddhist Scriptures* (Edward Conze, ed., tr.; 1959), pt. 1, ch. 1

47 As an artist becomes enamored of a woman he has himself painted, so the affection, which a person has for another with whom he feels at home, is entirely of his own making.
Quoted in *Buddhist Scriptures* (Edward Conze, ed., tr.; 1959), pt. 2, ch. 3

48 Delusion injures others, brings hardship to oneself, soils the mind, and may well lead to hell.
Quoted in *Buddhist Scriptures* (Edward Conze, ed., tr.; 1959), pt. 2, ch. 3

49 Do not make a fetish of truffles as the bourgeois do. Truffles are excellent, but they are not sublime.
Quoted in *Clarisse or The Old Cook* (Elise Vallée, tr.; 1926)

50 Leave no stone unturned.
Response of the Delphic oracle to Polycrates, as the best way to find treasure buried by Xerxes' general, Mardonius, on the field of Plataea. The oracle replied, "Turn every stone." *Corpus Paroemiographorum Graecorum* (E. L. von Leutsch and F. G. Schneidewin, eds.; 1839–51)

51 I spent all my Golden Money
on a pair of Silver Shoes.
Graffiti in toilet. Quoted in *Evening Standard Magazine,* London (March 6, 1998)

52 If the end be well, all is well. All's well that ends well.
Quoted in *Gesta Romanorum* (1824), Tale lxvii

53 Even if someone throws a stone at you, respond with food.
Independent, London (November 29, 1993)

54 Farewell, father and mother, forgive us that we're being unfaithful as your children; we must be faithful first to our country.
May 1989. Part of a declaration of Chinese students about to embark on a hunger strike, in support of democratic reforms. Quoted in *June Four: A Chronicle of the Chinese Democratic Uprising* (Zi Jin and Qin Zhou, trs.; 1989)

55 Social event as an extension of business, politics, or work is essentially a white phenomenon.
Said by an African American social theorist in the *New York Times.* Quoted in *Miss Manners Rescues Civilization* (Judith Martin; 1996)

56 Raise the stone, and there thou shalt find me, cleave the wood and there am I.
Quoted in "Sayings of Our Lord," *Oxyrhynchus Papyri Logion* (Bernard P. Grenfell and Arthur S. Hunt, eds.; 1898)

57 Let him who is without sin jail the first Stone.
1967. Popular poster displayed during the trial of The Rolling Stones for drug possession. Quoted in *Rock 'n' Roll Babylon* (Gary Herman; 1994)

58 Would you not say that any young woman who seeks to contact a member of a rock 'n' roll group in order to procure sexual intercourse, that such a young woman is in a very sorry state?
1975. Said by counsel during a court case brought by Frank Zappa against the Albert Hall, London, for cancelling his concerts on the grounds of obscenity. Quoted in *Rock 'n' Roll Babylon* (Gary Herman; 1994)

59 We voted to die with dignity.
Said by a reporter on *The Buffalo Courier Express,* whose unions had refused to accept the scale of cuts Rupert Murdoch demanded to buy the paper. The paper shut down when the deal fell through. Quoted in *Rupert Murdoch: Ringmaster of the Information Circus* (William Shawcross; 1993)

60 Originally, at the creation, the earth was pure. The lump flung by God was of pure clay. But the offense of the jackal defiled the earth and upset the world-order. That is why the Nummo came down to reorganize it.
From the tradition of the Dogon people of Mali, West Africa. The Nummo is a god. Quoted in "Ogotemmeli Narrates the Descent of the Cosmic Granary," *Sacred Texts of the World* (Ninian Smart and Richard D. Hecht, eds.; 1982)

61 Wakan comes from the wakan beings. These wakan beings are greater than mankind in the same way that mankind is greater than animals. They are never born and never die.
Wakan, or Wakan Tanka, is the omnipotent supreme being of the Sioux Native Americans. Quoted in "Sioux Song," *Sacred Texts of the World* (Ninian Smart and Richard D. Hecht, eds.; 1982)

62 Then a song of power came to me and I sang it there in the midst of that terrible place where I was...
A good nation I will make live.
This the nation above has said.
They have given me the power to make over.
From the tradition of the Oglala Sioux of the North American plains. Quoted in "The Great Vision of Black Elk," *Sacred Texts of the World* (Ninian Smart and Richard D. Hecht, eds.; 1982)

63 If you borrow $2000 dollars from a bank and can't pay it back, you have a problem, but if you borrow a million and can't repay, they have a problem.
Quoted in *The Art of Getting Your Own Sweet Way* (Philip B. Crosby; 1981)

64 Could Job have been thinking of Chicago when he wrote: Here are men that alter their neighbor's landmark...shoulder the poor aside, conspire to oppress the friendless.
Written by a group of Chicago clergymen appalled by the impact of modernization on local neighborhoods. Quoted in *The Death and Life of Great American Cities: The Failure of Town Planning* (Jane Jacobs; 1961)

65 The French may not wish to talk about their Arab clients, but they're even shakier about the South Americans. All those drug baronesses. Without cocaine, half a dozen couture houses would have gone to the wall. But they won't talk about that.
Quoted in *The Fashion Conspiracy* (Nicholas Coleridge; 1989), ch. 8

66 When your neighbor loses his job, it's a slowdown; when you lose your job, it's a recession; when an economist loses his job, it's a depression.
Ronald Reagan said something similar in 1980. Quoted in *The Financial Times Guide to Using the Financial Pages* (Romesh Vaitlingam; 1996)

67 Some years after his death it was decided by a popular vote conducted in his country that Louis Pasteur was the greatest Frenchman of all time. The success of his method might be explained as being due to the exercise of three fundamental rules, keen observation, precise tests, and the drawing of irrefutable conclusions from critical premises.
Attrib. *The Genius of Louis Pasteur* (Piers Compton; 1932)

68 Laws of thermodynamics. 1) You cannot win. 2) You cannot break even. 3) You cannot get out of the game.
Quoted in *The Harvest of a Quiet Eye* (Alan L. Macky, ed.; 1977)

69 In my happier days I used to remark on the aptitude of the saying, "When in life we are in the midst of death." I have since learned that it's more apt to say, "When in death we are in the midst of life."
Said by a survivor from Belsen. *The Oxford Book of Death* (D. J. Enright, ed.; 1983)

70 A friend...told me of a method to counter the increasing doses of insulin, but this involved the eating of chocolate at a certain time, and, rationing being still in force, I knew I could not do this indefinitely.
1940s–1950s. Referring to the treatment of the mentally sick with insulin shock therapy. During World War II (1939–45) rationing was introduced in the United Kingdom to regulate the distribution of items in short supply. Quoted in *The Plea for the Silent* (D. McIntosh Johnson and Norman Dodds, eds.; 1957)

71 They did not, in all their sailing round about England, so much as sink or take one ship, bark, pinnace, or cockboat of ours, or even burn so much as one sheepcote in this land.
Referring to the Spanish Armada. Quoted in *The Reign of Elizabeth, 1558–1603* (John B. Black; 1936), ch. 10

72 This is a rotten argument, but it should be good enough for their lordships on a hot summer afternoon.
A note on a ministerial brief read out by mistake in the upper chamber of the British Parliament, the House of Lords. *The Way the Wind Blows* (Lord Home; 1976)

73 We set ourselves to bite the hand that feeds us.
Quoted in *Thoughts on the Cause of the Present Discontents* (Edmund Burke; 1770), vol. 1

74 Say it ain't so, Joe.
1920. A boy's plea to baseball player Shoeless Joe Jackson at the time of the "Black Sox" scandal in which Chicago White Sox players were accused of receiving money to lose the 1919 world series.

75 Begin low, speak slow; take fire, rise higher; when most impressed be self-possessed; at the end wax warm, and sit down in a storm.
Advice to public speakers.

76 Anyone for tennis?
Allegedly the first line ever spoken by Humphrey Bogart as a professional actor.

77 It pays to advertise.
Already current by 1912? when Cole Porter used it as the title of an early song.

78 Oh, my dear fellow, the noise...and the people!
A soldier describing battle conditions; variously attributed, often to a Captain Strahan at the Battle of Bastogne (1944), but almost certainly dates from Dunkirk (1940).

79 Oh no, thank you, I only smoke on special occasions.
British Labour minister dining with King George VI, when offered a cigar.

80 Take me to your leader.
Customary line spoken by fictional alien invaders.

81 Hail Caesar; those who are about to die salute you.
Gladiators' greeting to the Roman Emperor.

82 Nostalgia isn't what it used to be.
Graffiti.

83 Nothing in excess.
Inscribed on the Temple of Apollo at Delphi.

84 The King over the Water.
Early 18th century. Jacobite toast. Referring to James II's son, James Edward Stuart (1688–1766), who was exiled in France in 1715 after leading a failed uprising in Scotland.

85 There is no such thing as a free lunch.
Often attributed to Milton Friedman.

86 A stage between infancy and adultery.
On youth.

87 More to the point, would you allow your gamekeeper to read it?
1960. Referring to Mervyn Griffiths-Jones' remark, "Is it a book you would...wish your wife or your servants to read?", during the *Lady Chatterley's Lover* obscenity trial (1960). Lady Chatterley's lover is her husband's gamekeeper.

88 It isn't the ecstatic leap across that I deplore, it's the weary trudge home.
Referring to single beds.

89 Anyone who isn't confused here doesn't really understand what's going on.
Referring to the sectarian problems in Northern Ireland.

90 Has anyone here been raped and speaks English?
Said to have been shouted by a television journalist to a group of Belgian civilians waiting to be evacuated from the Congo in 1960 (since 1997 Democratic Republic of the Congo).

91 You're phony. Everything about you is phony. Even your hair—which looks false—is real.
U.S. diplomat to the British politician Brendan Bracken during World War II. (1942?)

92 Don't tell my mother I'm in politics—she thinks I play the piano in a whorehouse.
U.S. saying.

93 Where did you get that hat?
1885? Vaudeville song title.

Anouilh, Jean (1910–87) French playwright

1 Nothing is true except what is not said.
Antigone (1942)

2 It takes a certain courage and a certain greatness even to be truly base.
Ardèle (1948)

3 Love is, above all, the gift of oneself.
Ardèle (1948)

4 Oh, love is real enough, you will find it some day, but it has one arch-enemy—and that is life.
Ardèle (1948)

5 Saintliness is also a temptation.
Becket (1959)

6 There will always be a lost dog somewhere that will prevent me from being happy.
La Sauvage (1938), Act 3

7 What fun it would be to be poor, as long as one was *excessively* poor! Anything in excess is most exhilarating.
Ring Round the Moon (1947)

8 Dying, dying...dying is nothing. So start by living. It's less fun and it lasts longer.
Typifying his technique of ironic reversal. *Roméo et Jeannette* (1947), Act 3

9 Every man thinks God is on his side. The rich and powerful know that he is.
The Lark (1953)

10 Have you noticed that life, real honest to goodness life, with murders and catastrophes and fabulous inheritances, happens almost exclusively in newspapers?
The Rehearsal (1950)

11 When you are forty, half of you belongs to the past...And when you are seventy, nearly all of you.
Attrib.

Anselm, Saint, Archbishop of Canterbury (Saint Anselm of Canterbury; 1033–1109) Italian-born philosopher and prelate

1 The truth of a proposition should be sought only in the proposition itself.
De Veritate (1080)

2 Unless I am mistaken therefore, we can define "truth" as "rightness" perceptible by the mind alone.
De Veritate (1080)

3 I do not seek to understand so that I may believe, but I believe so that I may understand.
Proslogion (1078)

4 Something than which nothing greater can be thought so truly

exists that it is not possible to think of it as not existing.
Proslogion (1078)

Ansoff, Igor (b.1918) U.S. author and academic

1 For many firms periodic, or even continual, strategic repositioning must become a way of life.
Implanting Strategic Management (1984)

Ant, Adam (Stuart Leslie Goddard; b.1954) British pop singer and songwriter

1 The time to worry is when everybody likes you. When everybody likes you you've had it.
Quoted in *The Wit and Wisdom of Rock and Roll* (Maxim Jabukowski, ed.; 1983)

Antall, Jozsef (1932–93) Hungarian prime minister

1 We all know the Iron Curtain has been demolished, but in its place an economic and social curtain might come down.
Independent, London (October 29, 1992)

Antar ('Antarah Ibn Shaddad al-'Absi; 550?–615) Arab warrior and poet

1 In blackness there is some virtue, if you observe its beauty well.
A Bedoueen Romance (Terrick Hamilton, tr.; 1819), vol. 1

Anthony, Susan B. (Susan Brownell Anthony; 1820–1906) U.S. social reformer

Quotations about Anthony

1 We touch our caps, and place tonight
The visitor's wreath upon her,
The woman who outranks us all
In courage and honor.
Ida Husted Harper, U.S. writer and lecturer. Susan B. Anthony (1820–1906) was the leader of the U.S. woman suffrage movement. *The Life and Work of Susan B. Anthony* (1899), vol. 1

2 Who does not feel sympathy for Susan Anthony? She has striven long and earnestly to become a man. She has met with some rebuffs, but has never succumbed. She has never done any good in the world, but then she doesn't think so.
Ida Husted Harper, U.S. writer and lecturer. Susan B. Anthony (1820–1906) was the leader of the U.S. woman suffrage movement. *The Life and Work of Susan B. Anthony* (1899), vol. 1

Quotations by Anthony

3 And yet, in the schoolroom more than any other place, does the difference of sex, if there is any, need to be forgotten.
Elizabeth Cady Stanton (Theodore Stanton and Harriot Stanton Blatch, ed.; 1890?), vol. 2

4 And I shall earnestly and persistently continue to urge all women to the practical recognition of the old Revolutionary maxim, "Resistance to tyranny is obedience to God."
Speech made in court (June 18, 1873), quoted in *Jailed for Freedom* (Doris Stevens)

5 There never will be complete equality until women themselves help to make laws and elect lawmakers.
"The Status of Women, Past, Present and Future," *The Arena* (May 1897)

6 The true republic: men their rights and nothing more; women their rights and nothing less.
Motto printed on the front of her newspaper, *The Revolution* (1868–70).

7 So long as society says a woman is incompetent to be a lawyer, minister or doctor, but has ample ability to be a teacher...every man of you who chooses this profession tacitly acknowledges that he has no more brains than a woman?
1881. Attrib.

8 Woman must not depend on the protection of man, but must be taught to protect herself.
1871. Attrib.

Antiphon (*fl.* 5th century B.C.) Greek philosopher

1 Many dues imposed by law are hostile to nature.
Quoted in *The Presocratics* (Edward Hussey; 1972)

Antonioni, Michelangelo (b.1912) Italian filmmaker

1 One can almost trick an actor by demanding one thing and obtaining another. The director must know how to demand, and how to distinguish what is good and bad, useful and superfluous, in everything the actor offers.
March 16, 1961. *Film Culture* (Spring 1962), quoted in *Film-makers Speak* (Jay Leyda, ed.; 1977)

2 I don't work from a written script. My work begins when I look through the viewfinder of the camera—that for me is the moment of creation.
Interview, *Times*, London (November 29, 1960), quoted in *Film-makers Speak* (Jay Leyda, ed.; 1977)

3 I feel like a father towards my old films. You bring children into the world, then they grow up and go off on their own. From time to time you get together and it's always a pleasure to see them again.
Quoted in *Halliwell's Filmgoer's Companion* (Leslie Halliwell; 1993)

Antrim, Minna (originally Minna Thomas (b.1856) U.S. writer

1 A fool bolts pleasure, then complains of moral indigestion.
Naked Truth and Veiled Allusions (1902)

2 Experience is a good teacher, but she sends in terrific bills.
Naked Truth and Veiled Allusions (1902)

3 The "Green-Eyed Monster" causes much woe, but the absence of this ugly serpent argues the presence of a corpse whose name is Eros.
Naked Truth and Veiled Allusions (1902)

4 To be loved is to be fortunate, but to be hated is to achieve distinction.
Naked Truth and Veiled Allusions (1902)

Apicius, Marcus Gavius (*fl.* 1st century) Roman gastronome and epicure

1 Stuff the dormice with minced pork, the minced meat of whole dormice, pounded with pepper, pine-kernels, asafoetida, and *liquamen*. Sew up, place on a tile, put in the oven, or cook, stuffed, in a small oven.
1st century. Quoted in *The Roman Cookery Book* (Barbara Flower and Elizabeth Rosenbaum, trs.; 1958)

Apollinaire, Guillaume (Wilhelm Apollinaris de Kostrowitzky; 1880–1918) Italian-born French poet

1 One can't carry one's father's corpse about everywhere.
Referring to the need for a clean break between the old (the impressionists) and the new (the cubists). "Sur la peinture," *Méditations esthétiques: Les Peintres cubistes* (1913), pt. 1

2 A structure becomes architecture and not sculpture when its elements no longer have their justification in nature.
1913. Quoted in *The Cubist Painters* (1944)

Appelfield, Aharon (b.1932) Israeli writer

1 All the good things that we have been led to believe existed only in Socialism and in Marxism, and in Communism, too, we found to exist in our own tradition and at a more refined, civilized level.
September 25, 1986. Comparing the virtues of Communism, Socialism, and Marxism with those of the Jewish tradition. Quoted in Interview, *Voices of Israel* (Joseph Cohen; 1990)

Appleton, Edward Victor, Sir (1892–1965) British physicist

1 I do not mind what language an opera is sung in so long as it is a language I don't understand.
Attrib. *Observer*, London (August 28, 1955), "Sayings of the Week"

Appleton, Thomas Gold (1812–84) U.S. writer and artist

1 Good Americans, when they die, go to Paris.
Quoted in *The Autocrat of the Breakfast Table* (Oliver Wendell Holmes; 1856), ch. 6

2 A Boston man is the east wind made flesh.
Attrib.

Aptheker, Herbert (b.1915) U.S. historian

1 It is what the masses endure, how they resist, how they struggle that forms the body of true history. It is the coming into being, the bringing forth of the new...that is the heart of true history.
A Documentary History of the Negro People in the United States (1951)

2 Their history demonstrates that no matter what the despoilers of humanity may do—enslave, segregate, torture, lynch—they cannot destroy the people's will to freedom, their urge towards equality, justice, and dignity.
Referring to African Americans. *A Documentary History of the Negro People in the United States* (1951)

3 The history of anti-slavery begins with the first slave; similarly the history of anti-racism begins with the original object of scorn, derision, and insult.
"The History of Anti-Racism in the United States," *Black Scholar* (January–February 1975)

Aquinas, Thomas, Saint (1225–74) Italian theologian and philosopher

Quotations about Aquinas

1 This dumb ox will fill the whole world with his bellowing.
Albertus Magnus (1200?–80?) German scholar. Referring to his pupil Thomas Aquinas, whose nickname was "The Dumb Ox." Quoted in *Aquinas* (Anthony Kenny; 1969)

Quotations by Aquinas

2 Human law is law only by virtue of its accordance with right reason, and by this means it is clear that it flows from Eternal law. In so far as it deviates from right reason it is called an Unjust law; and in such a case, it is no law at all, but rather an assertion of violence.
Summa Theologica (1266–73)

3 Justice is a certain rectitude of mind whereby a man does what he ought to do in the circumstances confronting him.
Summa Theologica (1266–73)

4 The error of Jovian consisted in holding virginity not to be preferable to marriage. This error is refuted above all by the example of Christ Who both chose a virgin for His mother and remained Himself a virgin.
Summa Theologica (1266–73)

5 Future contingents cannot be certain to us...only to God whose understanding is in eternity above time...The man who sees the whole road from a height sees simultaneously all those who are going along the road.
Summa Theologica (1266–73), I, pt. 1

6 It is necessary to assume something which is necessary of itself, and has no cause of its necessity outside itself but is rather the cause of necessity in other things. And this all men call God.
Summa Theologica (1266–73), I, pt. 1

7 Since we cannot know what God is, but only what He is not, we must consider the ways in which He is not rather than the ways in which He is.
Summa Theologica (1266–73), I, pt. 1

8 Whatever is in motion must be moved by something else. Moreover, this something else...must itself be moved by something else, and that in turn by yet another thing...So we reach a first mover which is not moved by anything. And this all men think of as God.
Summa Theologica (1266–73), I, pt. 1

9 Law...is nothing else than an ordinance of reason for the common good.
Summa Theologica (1266–73), I, pt. 1.2

10 Laws can be unjust because they are contrary to the divine good...In no way is it permissible to observe them.
Summa Theologica (1266–73), I, pt. 1.2

11 Evil denotes the absence of Good. But it is not every absence of good that is called evil.
Summa Theologica (1266–73), I, pt. 1a

Aquino, Corazon (b.1933) Filipino president

1 It wasn't until we got over the self pity that we were able to accept suffering as part of our life with Christ. A man or woman reaches this plane only when he or she ceases to be the hero.
Referring to imprisonment of both herself and her husband. Speech (1984)

Arabian Nights, The

1 Who will change old lamps for new ones?...new lamps for old ones?
1500? The *Arabian Nights* derives from a sequence of Persian tales, translated into Arabic (850?), and later from Arabic into English. *Arabian Nights* (early 15th century), "The History of Aladdin"

2 Open Sesame!
1500? The *Arabian Nights* derives from a sequence of Persian tales, translated into Arabic (850?), and later from Arabic into English. *Arabian Nights* (early 15th century), "The History of Ali Baba"

Arabin, William St. Julien (1773?–1841) British judge

1 Prisoner, God has given you good abilities, instead of which you go about the country stealing ducks.
Quoted in *Arabinesque at Law* (Sir R. Megarry; 1830?)

Arafat, Yasir (Muhammad Abed Ar'ouf Arafat; b.1929) Palestinian political and military leader

1 Beirut will be the Hanoi and Stalingrad of the Israeli army.
Referring to the Israeli invasion of Lebanon and the encirclement of Beirut. Drawing a comparison with Soviet defeat at the Battle of Stalingrad (1942–43) during World War II, and the resistance of Hanoi to the U.S. army during the Vietnam War (1959–75). Radio broadcast (1982), quoted in *Arafat: From Defender to Dictator* (Saïd Aburish; 1998)

2 If I fall take my place.
1968. Said after a battle with Israel at Karameh, after which Yasir Arafat led his Fatah group into the Palestine Liberation Organization (PLO), taking over the leadership in 1969. This phrase subsequently became a slogan of the PLO. Quoted in *Arafat: From Defender to Dictator* (Saïd K. Aburish; 1998)

Aragon, Louis (1897–1982) French writer

1 Speech was not given to man: he took it.
Le Libertinage (1924)

2 The function of genius is to furnish cretins with ideas twenty years later.
"La Porte-plume," *Traité du style* (1928)

Arbus, Diane (originally Diane Nemerov; 1923–71) U.S. photographer

1 There are things nobody would see if I didn't photograph them.
Quoted in *Diane Arbus* (1972)

Arbuthnot, John (1667–1735) Scottish writer and physician

1 The first Care in building of Cities, is to make them airy and well perflated; infectious Distempers must necessarily be propagated amongst Mankind living close together.
"An Essay Concerning the Effects of Air on Human Bodies" (1732)

2 There are very few things which we know, which are not capable of being reduc'd to a Mathematical Reasoning; and when they cannot it's a sign our knowledge of them is very small and confus'd.
Of the Laws of Chance (1692)

3 He warns the heads of parties against believing their own lies.
The Art of Political Lying (1712)

Archer, Gilbert Scottish business executive

1 Paddy Ashdown is the first trained killer to be a party leader...Mrs Thatcher being self-taught.
Paddy Ashdown, leader of the Liberal Democrat Party (1988–99), was previously a member of the Royal Marines. Remark (1992)

Archer, Jeffrey, Baron Archer of Weston-super-Mare (b.1940) British politician and author

1 Pull off a coup and you're a national hero, fail and you're an evil criminal; in business it's the same difference between bankruptcy and making a fortune.
"The Coup," *A Quiver Full of Arrows* (1980)

2 One lesson a man learns in the Harvard Business School is that an executive is only as good as his health.
Not a Penny More, Not a Penny Less (1976)

3 I was unemployed with debts of £400,000. I know what unemployment is like and a lot of it is getting off your backside and finding a job.
Referring to a period before he became a best-selling novelist. *Observer*, London (October 13, 1985), "Sayings of the Week"

Archer, John Richard (1863–1932) British councillor and mayor

1 The people in this country are sadly ignorant with reference to the darker races, and our object is to show to them that we have given up the idea of becoming hewers of wood and drawers of water, that we claim our rightful place within this Empire...if we are good enough to be brought to fight the wars of the country we are good enough to receive the benefits of the country.
Address to the inaugural meeting of the African Progress Union (1918), quoted in *Staying Power: The History of Black People in Britain* (Peter Fryer; 1984)

Archilochus (Archilochus of Paros; 680? B.C.–640? B.C.) Greek poet

1 The fox knows many things—the hedgehog knows one *big* thing.
Attrib.

Archimedes (287?–212 B.C.) Sicilian-born Greek mathematician and inventor

Quotations about Archimedes

1 Who would not rather have the fame of Archimedes than that of his conqueror Marcellus?
Sir William Rowan Hamilton (1805–65) Irish mathematician. Quoted in *Mathematical Circles Revisited* (H. Eves; 1971)

2 And Archimedes, as he was washing, thought of a manner of computing the proportion of gold in King Hiero's crown by seeing the water flowing over the bathing-stool. He leaped up as one possessed or inspired, crying, "I have found it! Eureka!"
Plutarch (46?–120?) Greek biographer and philosopher. "Pleasure not Attainable according to Epicurus" (1st–2nd century)

3 Being perpetually charmed by...his geometry, he neglected to eat and drink and took no care of his person...he was often carried by force to the baths, and when there he would trace geometrical figures in the ashes of the fire...being in a state of great ecstasy and divinely possessed by his science.
Plutarch (46?–120?) Greek biographer and philosopher. *Parallel Lives* (1st century)

Quotations by Archimedes

4 *Eureka!*
I have found it!
An exclamation of joy supposedly uttered as, stepping into a bath and noticing the water overflowing,

he saw the answer to a problem and began the train of thought that led to his principle of buoyancy.
De Architectura (220? B.C.), bk. 8, preface, section 10

5 Give me a firm place to stand, and I will move the earth.
On the action of a lever. *Synagoge* (220? B.C.), bk. 8, proposition 10, section 11

Arden, Elizabeth (originally Florence Nightingale Graham; 1884–1966) Canadian-born U.S. beauty expert and business executive

1 Nothing that costs only a dollar is worth having.
Quoted in *In Cosmetics the Old Mystique is No Longer Enough* (Eleanore Carruth; 1973)

Arendt, Hannah (1906–75) German-born U.S. philosopher and historian

1 In the modern age history emerged as something it never had been before...a man-made process, the only all comprehending process which owed its existence exclusively to the human race.
Between Past and Future: Six Exercises in Political Thought (1961)

2 The connection between history and nature is by no means an opposition. History receives into its remembrance those mortals who through deed and word have proved themselves worthy of nature, and their everlasting fame means that they...may remain in the company of the things that last forever.
Between Past and Future: Six Exercises in Political Thought (1961)

3 Immortality is what nature possesses without effort and without anybody's assistance, and immortality is what the mortals must therefore try to achieve if they want to live up to the world in which they were born.
Between Past and Future: Six Exercises in Political Thought (1961), ch. 2

4 Promises are the uniquely human way of ordering the future, making it predictable and reliable to the extent that this is humanly possible.
"Civil Disobedience," *Crises of the Republic* (1972)

5 The defiance of established authority, religious and secular, social and political, as a world-wide phenomenon may well one day be accounted the outstanding event of the last decade.
"Civil Disobedience," *Crises of the Republic* (1972)

6 Power and violence are opposites; where the one rules absolutely, the other is absent. Violence appears where the power is in jeopardy, but left to its own cause it ends in power's disappearance.
"On Violence," *Crises of the Republic* (1972)

7 The Third World is not a reality but an ideology.
"On Violence," *Crises of the Republic* (1972)

8 What really distinguishes this generation in all countries from earlier generations...is its determination to act, its joy in action, the assurance of being able to change things by one's own efforts.
"Thought on Politics and Revolution," *Crises of the Republic* (1972)

9 The fearsome word-and-thought-defying banality of evil.
Eichmann in Jerusalem (1963)

10 It is quite gratifying to feel guilty if you haven't done anything wrong: how noble! Whereas it is rather hard and certainly depressing to admit guilt and to repent.
Eichmann in Jerusalem (1963), ch. 15

11 No punishment has ever possessed enough power of deterrence to prevent the commission of crimes. On the contrary, whatever the punishment, once a specific crime has appeared for the first time, its reappearance is more likely than its initial emergence could ever have been.
Eichmann in Jerusalem (1963), epilogue

12 The good things in history are usually of very short duration, but afterwards have a decisive influence over what happens over long periods of time.
"Authority," *Nomos I* (Carl J. Friedrich and John W. Chapman, eds.; 1963)

13 Only crime and the criminal, it is true, confront us with the perplexity of radical evil; but only the hypocrite is really rotten to the core.
On Revolution (1963), ch. 2

14 Economic growth may one day turn out to be a curse rather than a good, and under no conditions can it either lead into freedom or constitute a proof for its existence.
On Revolution (1963), ch. 6

15 No cause is left but the most ancient of all, the one, in fact, that from the beginning of our history has determined the very existence of politics, the cause of freedom versus tyranny.
On Revolution (1963), introduction

16 A complete victory of society will always produce some sort of "communistic fiction," whose outstanding characteristic is that it is indeed ruled by an "invisible hand," namely, by nobody.
The Human Condition (1958)

17 We have almost succeeded in leveling all human activities to the common denominator of securing the necessities of life and providing for their abundance.
The Human Condition (1958), pt. 3, ch. 17

18 The new always happens against the overwhelming odds of statistical laws and their probability...the new therefore always appears in the guise of a miracle.
The Human Condition (1958), pt. 5, ch. 24

19 Love, by its very nature, is unworldly, and it is for this reason rather than its rarity that it is not only apolitical but antipolitical, perhaps the most powerful of all antipolitical human forces.
The Human Condition (1958), pt. 5, ch. 33

20 The act of forgiving can never be predicted: it is the only reaction that acts in an unexpected way and thus retains, though being a reaction, something of the original character of action.
"Action," *The Human Condition* (1958), ch. 33

21 The human condition is such that pain and effort are not just symptoms which can be removed without changing life itself...For mortals, the "easy life of the gods" would be a lifeless one.
"Labor," *The Human Condition* (1958), ch. 16

22 Total loyalty is possible only when fidelity is emptied of all

concrete content, from which changes of mind might naturally arise.
The Origins of Totalitarianism (1951), ch. 10, sect. 1

23 The concentration camps, by making death itself anonymous (making it impossible to tell whether a prisoner is dead or alive), robbed death of its meaning as the end of a fulfilled life.
The Origins of Totalitarianism (1951), ch. 12, sect. 3

24 Under conditions of tyranny it is easier to act than think.
Quoted in *A Certain World* (W. H. Auden; 1970)

25 With the loss of tradition we have lost the thread which safely guided us through the vast realms of the past, but this thread was also the chain fettering each successive generation to a predetermined aspect of the past.
Quoted in *New York Review of Books* (1971)

26 In other words, it is quite true that the past *haunts* us; it is the past's function to haunt us who are present and wish to live in the world as it really is, that is, *become* what it is now.
Quoted in *The Meaning of History* (N. Gordon and Joyce Carper; 1991)

Argyll, 12th Duke of (Ian Campbell; b.1937) British aristocrat

1 There are only two kinds of people in the world. Those who are nice to their servants and those who aren't.
Attrib.

Argyris, Chris (Christopher Argyris; b.1923) U.S. industrial psychologist

1 The human mind is finite though managers sometimes act as if it wasn't.
Quoted in *Key Management Ideas* (Stuart Crainer; 1996)

Ariosto, Ludovico (1474–1533) Italian poet

1 Nature made him, and then broke the mold.
Referring to Charlemagne's paladin, Roland. *Orlando Furioso* (1532), can. 10, st. 84

Aristophanes (448? B.C.–385? B.C.) Greek playwright

1 LYSISTRATA Woman, stick to your spinning
or I shall make your pretty little headikins weep and wail
War is the business of the male!
Lysistrata quotes men's reactions to women in politics. *Lysistrata* (Leo Aylen, tr.; 411 B.C.), ll. 520- 522

2 Old men are children for a second time.
The Clouds (423 B.C.)

Aristotle (384 B.C.–322 B.C.) Greek philosopher

Quotations about Aristotle

1 Our tradition of political thought had its definite beginning in the teachings of Plato and Aristotle. I believe it came to no less of a definite end in the theories of Karl Marx.
Hannah Arendt (1906–75) German-born U.S. philosopher and historian. *Between Past and Future* (1961), ch. 1

2 Aristotle maintained that women have fewer teeth than men; although he was twice married, it never occurred to him to verify this statement by examining his wives' mouths.
Bertrand Russell (1872–1970) British philosopher and mathematician. *The Impact of Science on Society* (1952)

3 An Aristotle was but the rubbish of an Adam, and Athens but the rudiments of Paradise.
Robert South (1634–1716) English theologian. *Twelve Sermons* (1692), vol. 1, sermon 2

Quotations by Aristotle

4 The soul is characterized by these capacities: self-nutrition, sensation, thinking, and movement.
De Anima (4th century B.C.), 413b

5 Everything necessarily is or is not, and will be or will not be; but one cannot divide and say that one or the other is necessary.
De Interpretatione (4th century B.C.), 19a

6 Cratylus...reproached Heraclitus for saying that you cannot step into the same river twice—for he himself thought you could not do so even once.
Metaphysics (4th century B.C.), 1010a

7 We must say that the same opinions have arisen among men in cycles, not once, twice, nor a few times, but infinitely often.
Meteorologica (335–322? B.C.)

8 It is better to pay a creditor than to give to a friend.
Nicomachean Ethics (4th century B.C.)

9 Watch the costs and the profits will take care of themselves.
Nicomachean Ethics (4th century B.C.)

10 Piety requires us to honor truth over our friends.
Nicomachean Ethics (4th century B.C.), 1096a

11 Is it likely that whereas joiners and shoemakers have certain functions or activities, man as such has none, but has been left by nature a functionless being.
Nicomachean Ethics (4th century B.C.), 1097b

12 Intellectual virtue owes both its birth and its growth to teaching...while moral growth comes about as a result of habit.
Nicomachean Ethics (4th century B.C.), 1103a

13 Men are good in one way, but bad in many.
Nicomachean Ethics (4th century B.C.), 1106b

14 The origin of action—its efficient, not its final cause—is choice, and that of choice is desire and reasoning with a view to an end.
Nicomachean Ethics (4th century B.C.), 1139a

15 The good person is related to his friend as to himself (for his friend is another self).
Nicomachean Ethics (4th century B.C.), 1166a

16 What we have to learn to do, we learn by doing.
Nicomachean Ethics (4th century B.C.), bk. 2

17 To run away from trouble is a form of cowardice and, while it is true that the suicide braves death, he does it not for some noble object but to escape some ill.
Nicomachean Ethics (4th century B.C.), bk. 3

18 The man who gets angry at the right things and with the right people, and in the right way and at the right time and for the right length of time, is commended.
Nicomachean Ethics (4th century B.C.), bk. 4

19 It is absurd to suppose that purpose is not present because we do not observe the agent deliberating...The best illustration is a doctor doctoring himself.
Physics (4th century B.C.), 199b

20 Motion being eternal, the first mover, if there is but one, will be eternal also.
Physics (4th century B.C.), 259a

21 Now a whole is that which has a beginning, a middle, and an end.
Referring specifically to the dramatic form of tragedy. *Poetics* (335–322? B.C.), ch. 7

22 For this reason poetry is something more philosophical and more worthy of serious attention than history.
Poetics (335–322? B.C.), ch. 9

23 Probable impossibilities are to be preferred to improbable possibilities.
Poetics (335–322? B.C.), ch. 24

24 Music has the power of producing a certain effect on the moral character of the soul, and if it has the power to do this, it is clear that the young must be directed to music and must be educated in it.
Politics (335–322? B.C.)

25 It is thus clear that, just as some are by nature free, others are by nature slaves, and for these latter the condition of slavery is both beneficial and just.
Politics (335–322? B.C.), 1255a

26 That form of government is best in which every man, whoever he is, can act best and live happily.
Politics (335–322? B.C.), 1324a

27 Man is by nature a political animal.
Politics (335–322? B.C.), bk. 1

28 Man, when perfected, is the best of animals, but, when separated from law and justice, he is the worst of all.
Politics (335–322? B.C.), bk. 1

29 Where some people are very wealthy and others have nothing the result will be either extreme democracy or absolute oligarchy, or despotism will come from either of those excesses.
Politics (335–322? B.C.), bk. 4

30 Inferiors revolt in order that they may be equal and equals that they may be superior. Such is the state of mind which creates revolutions.
Politics (335–322? B.C.), bk. 5

31 Law is a form of order and good law must necessarily mean good order.
Politics (335–322? B.C.), bk. 7, ch. 4, sect. 5

32 A deduction is an argument in which, certain things being laid down, something other than these necessarily comes about through them.
Topics (4th century B.C.), 100a

33 Plato is dear to me, but dearer still is truth.
Attrib. (330? B.C.)

Arlen, Michael (Dikran Kouyoumdjian; 1895–1956) Bulgarian-born British novelist

Quotations about Arlen

1 Every other inch a gentleman.
Rebecca West (1892–1983) Irish-born British novelist, critic, and journalist. Quoted in *Rebecca West* (Victoria Glendinning; 1987), pt. 3, ch. 5

Quotations by Arlen

2 It is amazing how nice people are to you when they know you are going away.
Attrib.

Arlington, Henry Bennet, 1st Earl of (1618–85) English statesman

1 Our business is to break with them and yet to lay the breache at their door.
Referring to the diplomacy that preceded the third Dutch War (1672–74). *Henry Bennet, Earl of Arlington* (Violet Barbour; 1914)

Armah, Ayi Kwei (b.1939) Ghanaian writer and educator

1 Each thing that goes away returns and nothing in the end is lost.
Fragments (1969)

2 It doesn't hurt an artist to taste a bit of madness.
Fragments (1969)

3 It is so surprising, is it not, how even the worst happenings of the past acquire a sweetness in the memory. Old harsh distresses are now merely pictures and tastes which hurt no more, like itching scars which can only give pleasure now.
The Beautyful Ones Are Not Yet Born (1968)

4 The whole world is covered over with the hell of Europe.
Referring to European imperialism. *Why Are We So Blest?* (1972)

Armani, Giorgio (b.1934) Italian fashion designer

1 I design for women who are content not to overstate their importance in the world or pose as princesses or ball-breakers.
Sunday Times, London (February 1989), magazine, quoted in *Sultans of Swing* (Georgina Howell; 1990), ch. 18

2 I realized that fashion was moving in a very brutal, nostalgic and sometimes vulgar direction, and I refused it.
The Fashion Conspiracy (1989)

3 Modern fashion is about freedom, democracy and individualism, and this is a development that I, for one, welcome.
Quoted in "Style or Fashion? Top Designers go to War," *Guardian*, London (Susannah Frankel; September 12, 1996)

Armistead, Lewis Addison (1817–63) U.S. Confederate general

1 Give them the cold steel, boys!
1863. Exhortation given to his troops during the U.S. Civil War. Attrib.

Armour, Philip D. (Philip Danforth Armour; 1832–1901) U.S. business executive

1 I do not love the money. What I do love is the getting of

it...What other interest can you suggest to me? I do not read. I do not take part in politics. What can I do?
Quoted in *Forbes* (October 26, 1987)

Armstrong, John (1709?–79) Scottish physician and poet

1 For want of timely care
Millions have died of medicable wounds.
The Art of Preserving Health (1744)

2 'Tis not too late to-morrow to be brave.
The Art of Preserving Health (1744)

Armstrong, Louis (Louis Daniel Armstrong, "Satchmo"; 1901–71) U.S. jazz trumpeter

Quotations about Armstrong

1 The heroines of her lyrics are Amazonian and Junoesque, indefatigably sexual; her voice and Louis' trumpet exchange brazen and derisive comment.
Elaine Feinstein (b.1930) British poet and novelist. Referring to Bessie Smith's performances with Louis Armstrong. *Bessie Smith: Empress of the Blues* (1985), ch. 1

2 Bessie was original in the way Armstrong was. She shaped old melodies to the phrases of her own thought. In "Careless Love", his cornet and her voice respond to one another with joyous virtuosity.
Elaine Feinstein (b.1930) British poet and novelist. Referring to Bessie Smith and Louis Armstrong. *Bessie Smith: Empress of the Blues* (1985), ch. 12

3 George V...must have felt a twinge of astonishment when, at a Command Performance, young Louis Armstrong unleashed a red-hot trumpet solo at him with the words "This one's for you, Rex!"
Humphrey Lyttelton (b.1921) British jazz trumpeter. *Take It From the Top* (1975), pt. 3, ch. 1

4 Bessie Smith shared with Louis Armstrong a sort of built-in musical radar which steered her away from approaching symmetry.
Humphrey Lyttelton (b.1921) British jazz trumpeter. *The Best of Jazz* (1978), ch. 5

5 A lot of people, mostly white, took plenty of advantage of Louis' good heart, but he never once came up evil about it. He was a prince. Hell, he was king of the tribe.
Mezz Mezzrow (1899–1972) U.S. jazz musician. *Really the Blues* (1946), ch. 12

Quotations by Armstrong

6 Musicians don't retire; they stop when there's no more music in them.
Observer, London (April 21, 1968), "Sayings of the Week"

7 Things were hard in New Orleans in those days and we were lucky if we ate, let alone paid for lessons. In order to carry on at all we had to have love of music in our bones.
Satchmo: My Life in New Orleans (1955), ch. 11

8 I thought I was hot stuff when the gals argued over me...I was too interested in my music to pay attention to that sort of jive. To most of it anyway.
Satchmo: My Life in New Orleans (1955), ch. 12

9 I had hit the big time. I was up North with the greats. I was playing with my idol, the King, Joe Oliver. My boyhood dream had come true at last.
Closing sentences of the book, following his move from New Orleans to Chicago. Referring to U.S. jazz cornetist, band leader, and composer, Joe Oliver. *Satchmo: My Life in New Orleans* (1955), ch. 14

10 As far as Religion, I'm a Baptist *and* a good friend of the Pope, and I always wear a Jewish Star for luck.
Louis (Max Jones and John Chilton; 1975)

11 What d'you expect me to do—go back on that cart sellin' coal with that ol' mule fartin' in my face?
Referring to his first job when asked if he intended retiring. Quoted in *Take It From the Top* (Humphrey Lyttelton; 1975), pt. 3, ch. 8

12 That's a good horn...but you need to put some of that hot water through it...get rid of all them newts and saveloys!
Said on returning a trumpet borrowed from British jazz musician Spike MacIntosh. Quoted in *Take It From the Top* (Humphrey Lyttelton; 1975), pt. 3, ch. 8

13 Folk music? Why, daddy, I don't know no other kind of music *but* folk music. I ain't never heard a horse sing a song.
The Jazz Book (Joachim E. Berendt; 1983)

14 A lotta cats copy the Mona Lisa, but people still line up to see the original.
When asked whether he objected to people copying his style. Attrib.

Armstrong, Michael U.S. business executive

1 America was never intended to be a nation of the government, by the government, and for the government.
Speech (November 9, 1993)

2 If self-interest is the irreversible force behind the markets' opening, self-interest can also be short-sighted—clinging to small but immediate advantages and ignoring the long-term opportunities of a truly level playing field.
Speech (January 15, 1997)

3 Sanctions are the ultimate "feel-good" foreign policy.
Speech (January 15, 1997)

4 The ancient Romans had a tradition: whenever one of their engineers constructed an arch, as the capstone was hoisted into place, the engineer assumed accountability for his work in the most profound way possible: he stood under the arch.
Speech (May 9, 1995)

5 Today there are more Chinese studying English than there are Americans.
Speech (February 11, 1997)

6 While we may need a balanced budget to discipline our politicians, what we need for export growth is a balanced economy.
Speech (May 9, 1995)

Armstrong, Neil (Neil Alden Armstrong; b.1930) U.S. astronaut

1 Tranquillity Base here—the Eagle has landed.
The words spoken on the touchdown of the first lunar-landing space module, as part of the Apollo 11 mission. Remark (July 21, 1969)

2 No matter when you had been to this spot before, a thousand years ago or a hundred thousand years ago, or if you came back to it a million years from now, you would see some

different things each time, but the scene would be generally the same.
Referring to the topography of the Moon. *First on the Moon* (co-written with Grace Farmer and Dora Jane Hamblin; 1970)

3 That's one small step for man, one giant leap for mankind.
Remark after having stepped onto the moon. Armstrong later claimed that he had said, "small step for a man...," but that the "a" had been lost in the radio transmission. *New York Times* (July 21, 1969)

Arnauld, Antoine (1612–94) French philosopher, lawyer, mathematician, and priest

1 I call the soul or mind thinking substance. Thinking, knowing, and perceiving are all the same thing. I also take the idea of an object and the perception of an object to be the same thing.
Des vraies et fausses idées (1683), 38

Arnim-Boytzenburg, Adolf Heinrich von, Count (1803–68) German statesman

1 The government must always be in advance of the public opinion.
Speech (April 2, 1848)

Arno, Peter (Curtis Arnoux Peters; 1904–68) U.S. cartoonist

1 Tell me about yourself—your struggles, your dreams, your telephone number.
Caption to a cartoon of a man talking to a woman. *New Yorker*

2 Well, back to the old drawing board.
Caption to a cartoon of people leaving a crashed plane. *New Yorker*

Arnold, George (1834–65) U.S. poet and humorist

1 Life for the living, and rest for the dead.
"The Jolly Old Pedagogue" (1866), st. 2

2 The living need charity more than the dead.
"The Jolly Old Pedagogue," *Collected Poems* (1866)

Arnold, Matthew (1822–88) British poet and critic

Quotations about Arnold

1 He is not as handsome as his photographs—or his poetry.
March 31, 1873
Henry James (1843–1916) U.S.-born British writer and critic. Attrib.

Quotations by Arnold

2 And we are here as on a darkling plain
Swept with confused alarms of struggle and flight,
Where ignorant armies clash by night.
"Dover Beach" (1867)

3 Is it so small a thing
To have enjoy'd the sun,
To have lived light in the spring,
To have loved, to have thought, to have done?
"Empedocles on Etna" (1852), Act 1, Scene 2, l. 397

4 I am past thirty, and three parts iced over.
Letter to Arthur Hugh Clough (February 12, 1853), quoted in *The Life and Correspondence of Thomas Arnold* (Penrhyn Stanley; 1844), vol. 1

5 Time may restore us in his course
Goethe's sage mind and Byron's force:
But where will Europe's latter hour
Again find Wordsworth's healing power?
"Memorial Verses" (1852)

6 When Byron's eyes were shut in death,
We bow'd our head and held our breath.
He taught us little: but our soul
Had *felt* him like the thunder's roll.
"Memorial Verses" (1852)

7 He will find one English book and one only, where, as in the *Iliad* itself, perfect plainness of speech is allied with perfect nobleness; and that book is the Bible.
"On Translating Homer" (1861)

8 Cruel, but composed and bland,
Dumb, inscrutable and grand,
So Tiberius might have sat,
Had Tiberius been a cat.
"Poor Matthias" (1885), l. 40

9 Resolve to be thyself: and know, that he
Who finds himself, loses his misery.
"Self-Dependence" (1852), l. 31

10 Truth sits upon the lips of dying men.
"Sohrab and Rustum" (1853), l. 656

11 Wandering between two worlds, one dead,
The other powerless to be born.
"Stanzas from the Grande Chartreuse" (1855)

12 She left lonely for ever
The kings of the sea.
"The Forsaken Merman" (1849)

13 Before this strange disease of modern life,
With its sick hurry, its divided aims.
"The Scholar-Gipsy" (1853)

14 Tired of knocking at Preferment's door.
"The Scholar-Gipsy" (1853)

15 And sigh that one thing only has been lent
To youth and age in common—discontent.
"Youth's Agitations" (1852)

16 The pursuit of perfection, then, is the pursuit of sweetness and light....He who works for sweetness and light united, works to make reason and the will of God prevail.
Culture and Anarchy (1869), ch. 1

17 Our society distributes itself into Barbarians, Philistines, and Populace; and America is just ourselves, with the Barbarians quite left out, and the Populace nearly.
Culture and Anarchy (1869), Preface

18 I am bound by my own definition of criticism: a disinterested endeavour to learn and propagate the best that is known and thought in the world.
"Functions of Criticism at the Present Time," *Essays in Criticism, First Series* (1865)

19 A criticism of life under the conditions fixed for such a criticism by the laws of poetic truth and poetic beauty.
"The Study of Poetry," *Essays in Criticism, Second Series* (1888)

20 The difference between genuine poetry and the poetry of

Dryden, Pope, and all their school, is briefly this: their poetry is conceived and composed in their wits, genuine poetry is conceived and composed in the soul.
"Thomas Gray," *Essays in Criticism, Second Series* (1888)

21 The true meaning of religion is thus not simply morality, but morality touched by emotion.
Literature and Dogma (1873), ch. 1

22 The eternal *not ourselves* that makes for righteousness.
Literature and Dogma (1873), ch. 8

23 Culture is the passion for sweetness and light, and (what is more) the passion for making them prevail.
Literature and Dogma (1873), Preface

24 Culture, the acquainting ourselves with the best that has been known and said in the world, and thus with the history of the human spirit.
Literature and Dogma (1873), Preface

Arnold, Thomas (1795–1842) British educator

1 As for rioting, the old Roman way of dealing with that is always the right one; flog the rank and file, and fling the ringleaders from the Tarpeian rock.
From an unpublished letter from Thomas Arnold written before 1828. Quoted in "Anarchy and Authority," *Cornhill Magazine* (Matthew Arnold; August 7, 1868)

2 What we must look for here is, first, religious and moral principles; secondly, gentlemanly conduct; thirdly, intellectual ability.
1835. Address to the scholars of Rugby, *The Life and Correspondence of Thomas Arnold* (Penrhyn Stanley; 1844), vol. 1, ch. 1

Aron, Raymond (Raymond Claude Ferdinand; 1905–83) French writer

1 Man has truly a past only when he is conscious of having one, for this consciousness alone introduces the possibility of dialogue and choice.
Dimensions de la conscience historique (1962), pt. 1, ch. 1

2 Political thought in France is either nostalgic or utopian.
L'Opium des intellectuels (1957)

Arp, Jean (Hans Arp; 1887–1966) German-born French sculptor

1 The important thing about Dada, it seems to me, is that Dadaists despised what is commonly regarded as art, but put the whole universe on the lofty throne of art.
"Looking," *Arp* (James Thrall Soby, ed.; 1958)

2 I love nature but not its substitutes. Naturalistic, illusionistic art is a substitute.
Quoted in *On My Way, Poetry and Essays. 1912...1947* (Ralph Manheim, tr.; 1948)

3 Sometimes her work has been described as applied art. Stupidity as well as malice inspire such a remark. Art can be expressed just as well by means of wool, paper, ivory, ceramics, glass as by painting, stone, wood, clay.
Referring to Jean Arp's artist wife, Sophie Taeuber-Arp (1889–1943). Quoted in *The Art of Jean Arp* (Herbert Read; 1968)

Arran, 9th Earl of (Arthur Desmond Colquhoun Gore; b.1938) British publisher

1 Life is much easier, being an Earl. It has changed me a lot. I'm much nastier now.
Sunday Times, London (January 15, 1967)

Artemisia, Queen of Halicarnassus (480 B.C.–425 B.C.) Carian monarch and military leader

1 Spare your ships, and do not fight at sea; for the Greeks are far superior to us in naval matters, as men are to women.
The Carians had been driven from their native islands in the Aegean Sea by invading Greeks, to what became the independent province of Caria, now the Gulf of Gökora in southwest Turkey. *The Histories* (Herodotus; 446? B.C.), bk. 8

Asaf, George (George H. Powell; 1880–1951) British songwriter

1 What's the use of worrying?
It never was worth while,
So, pack up your troubles in your old kit-bag,
And smile, smile, smile.
Popular with British soldiers in World War I. "Pack up Your Troubles in Your Old Kit Bag" (1915)

Ascham, Roger (1515–68) English humanist and scholar

1 I remember when I was young, in the north, they went to the grammar school little children: they came from thence great lubbers: always learning, and little profiting: learning without book everything, understanding within the book little or nothing.
The Scholemaster (1570)

2 There is no such whetstone, to sharpen a good wit and encourage a will to learning, as is praise.
The Scholemaster (1570)

3 Mark all mathematical heads which be wholly and only bent on these sciences, how solitary they be themselves, how unfit to live with others, how unapt to serve the world.
Quoted in *Mathematical Practitioners of Tudor and Stuart England* (E. G. R. Taylor; 1954)

Ascherson, Neal (Charles Neal Ascherson; b.1932) British journalist and author

1 The trouble with a free market economy is that it requires so many policemen to make it work.
Observer, London (May 26, 1985)

2 Work is a dull way to get rich.
Observer, London (October 20, 1985)

Ashbery, John (John Lawrence Ashbery; b.1927) U.S. poet and critic

1 How much longer will I be able to inhabit the divine sepulcher
Of life, my great love? Do dolphins plunge bottomward
To find the light? Or is rock
that is searched? Unrelentingly? Huh.
"How Much Longer Will I Be Able to Inhabit the Divine Sepulcher...," *The Tennis Court Oath* (1959), quoted in *The Penguin Book of American Verse* (Geoffrey Moore, ed.; 1977)

Ashby, Eric, Baron Ashby of Brandon (1904–92) English botanist and educator

1 The habit of apprehending a technology in its completeness: this is the essence of technological humanism, and this is what we should expect education in higher technology to achieve...the path to culture should be through a man's specialism, not by-passing it.
1958. Quoted in *The Jingle Bell Principle* (Miroslav Holub; 1992)

Ashcroft, John (b.1948) British business executive

1 Every manager is a sales manager.
Financial Times, London (January 24, 1990)

2 One man's definition of excessive is another's derisory sum.
Financial Times, London (December 24, 1987), "Quotes of the Year"

3 Management democracy is everybody agreeing to do what the leader wants.
Sunday Telegraph, London (June 5, 1988), magazine

4 The worst mistake a boss can make is not to say "well done".
Sunday Telegraph, London (June 5, 1988), magazine

Ashe, Arthur (Arthur Robert Ashe, Jr.; 1943–93) U.S. tennis player

1 I began to have a sense in reading many of the letters and the essays on me in newspapers and magazines that I was reading my obituary, but I could not say, as Mark Twain did, that the reports of my death are greatly exaggerated. Exaggerated, but not greatly.
Days of Grace: A Memoir (1993)

Asher, Richard (Richard Alan John Asher; 1912–69) British psychiatrist

1 The difference between the maniac and the schizophrenic laugh is—mania and the world laughs with you, schizophrenia and you smile alone.
Quoted in *A Sense of Asher* (Ruth Holland, ed.; 1984)

Ashrawi, Hanan (Hanan Mikhail Ashrawi; b.1946) Palestinian politician

1 It's not good enough to have just any old state, a replica of a Third World state, an instrument of Israeli domination.
Referring to the establishment of a Palestinian state. *Independent*, London (May 31, 1995)

Asimov, Isaac (1920–92) Russian-born U.S. writer

1 A candy store is a good thing in some ways. You work for yourself and the work is steady. The profits are small but they're there, and we went through the entire period of the Great Depression without missing a meal.
Before the Golden Age (1974), pt. 2

2 Things called Stars appeared, which robbed men of their souls and left them unreasoning brutes, so that they destroyed the civilization they themselves had built up.
On the fictional world of Lagash, night comes once every 2049 years. *Nightfall* (1970)

3 At two-tenths the speed of light, dust and atoms might not do significant damage...but the faster you go, the worse it is...So 60,000 kilometers per second may be the *practical* speed limit for space travel.
The Relativity of Wrong (1996)

4 When people thought the Earth was flat, they were wrong. When people thought the world was spherical, they were wrong. But if you think that thinking that the Earth is spherical is just as wrong as thinking that the Earth is flat, then your view is wronger than both of them put together.
The Relativity of Wrong (1996)

Asquith, Herbert Henry (1852–1928) British prime minister

1 One to mislead the public, another to mislead the Cabinet, and the third to mislead itself.
Explaining why the War Office kept three sets of figures. Quoted in *The Price of Glory* (Alastair Horne; 1962), ch. 2

Asquith, Margot (originally Emma Alice Margaret Tennant; 1865–1945) British political hostess and writer

1 An imitation rough diamond.
Referring to an American general. *As I Remember* (1922)

2 Rich men's houses are seldom beautiful, rarely comfortable, and never original. It is a constant source of surprise to people of moderate means to observe how little a big fortune contributes to Beauty.
As I Remember (1922), ch. 17

3 To marry a man out of pity is folly...One can only influence the strong characters in life, not the weak; and it is the height of vanity to suppose that you can make an honest man of anyone.
The Autobiography of Margot Asquith (1922), ch. 6

4 No. The "t" is silent—as in "Harlow."
When Jean Harlow asked whether the "t" was pronounced in "Margot." Quoted in *Great Tom* (T. S. Matthews; 1973), ch. 7

5 Lloyd George could not see a belt without hitting below it.
1936. Quoted in "Margot Oxford," *Listener*, London (Lady Violet Bonham Carter; June 11, 1953)

6 She tells enough white lies to ice a wedding cake.
Referring to Lady Desborough. Quoted in "Margot Oxford," *Listener*, London (Lady Violet Bonham Carter; June 11, 1953)

Asser (d.909?) Welsh monk, bishop, and chronicler

1 He often affirmed with frequent laments and sighs...that among all his difficulties and hindrances in this present life this was the greatest...when he had youth and leisure and aptitude for learning, he had no teachers.
Referring to Alfred the Great. *De Rebus Gestis Aelfredi Magni* (893)

2 Many Franks, Gauls, Pagans, Britons, Scots and Armoricans, nobles and poor men alike, submitted voluntarily to his dominion; all of whom he ruled, loved, honoured and enriched as if they were his own people.
Referring to Alfred the Great. *De Rebus Gestis Aelfredi Magni* (893)

Astaire, Fred (Fred Austerlitz; 1899–1987) U.S. dancer and actor

on a square of ivory. She is a miniaturist, but never two-dimensional. All her characters are round, or capable of rotundity.
E. M. Forster (1879–1970) British novelist. Referring to Sir Walter Scott's opinion of Jane Austen. *Aspects of the Novel* (1927)

4 Nothing very much happens in her books, and yet, when you come to the bottom of a page, you eagerly turn it to learn what will happen next...The novelist who has the power to achieve this has the most precious gift a novelist can possess.
Somerset Maugham (1874–1965) British writer. *Ten Novels and Their Authors* (1958)

5 I have discovered that our great favourite, Miss Austen, is my countrywoman...with whom mamma before her marriage was acquainted. Mamma says that she was then the prettiest, silliest, most affected, husband-hunting butterfly she ever remembers.
Mary Russell Mitford (1787–1855) British writer. Letter to Sir William Elford (April 3, 1815)

6 Jane Austen's books, too, are absent from this library. Just that one omission alone would make a fairly good library out of a library that hadn't a book in it.
Mark Twain (1835–1910) U.S. writer and humorist. *Following the Equator* (1897), pt. 2

Quotations by Austen

7 I do not want people to be very agreeable, as it saves me the trouble of liking them a great deal.
Letter (December 24, 1798)

8 Mrs. Hall of Sherbourne was brought to bed yesterday of a dead child, some weeks before she expected, owing to a fright. I suppose she happened unawares to look at her husband.
Letter (October 27, 1798), quoted in *Jane Austen's Letters* (R. W. Chapman, ed.; 1952)

9 We met...Dr. Hall in such very deep mourning that either his mother, his wife, or himself must be dead.
Letter (May 17, 1799), quoted in *Jane Austen's Letters* (R. W. Chapman, ed.; 1952)

10 What dreadful hot weather we have! It keeps me in a continual state of inelegance.
Letter (September 18, 1796), quoted in *Jane Austen's Letters* (R. W. Chapman, ed.; 1952)

11 One of Edward's mistresses was Jane Shore, who has had a play written about her, but it is a tragedy and therefore not worth reading.
This early work, written when the author was fifteen, was subtitled "by a partial, ignorant and prejudiced historian." Jane Shore (d.1527?) was mistress to Edward IV (1442–83). *A History of England* (1791)

12 One half of the world cannot understand the pleasures of the other.
Emma (1816), ch. 9

13 Nobody is healthy in London, nobody can be.
Emma (1816), ch. 12

14 Human nature is so well disposed towards those who are in interesting situations, that a young person, who either marries or dies, is sure to be kindly spoken of.
Emma (1816), ch. 22

15 The sooner every party breaks up the better.
Emma (1816), ch. 25

16 Business, you know, may bring money, but friendship hardly ever does.
Emma (1816), ch. 34

17 Young ladies should take care of themselves. Young ladies are delicate plants. They should take care of their health and their complexion. My dear, did you change your stockings?
The valeditudinarian Mr. Woodhouse to Jane Fairfax on hearing she had been walking in the rain. *Emma* (1816), ch. 34

18 What did she say? Just what she ought, of course. A lady always does.
Emma (1816), ch. 49

19 She was nothing more than a mere good-tempered, civil, and obliging young woman; as such we could scarcely dislike her—she was only an object of contempt.
"Letter the 13th," *Love and Friendship* (1790)

20 There certainly are not so many men of large fortune in the world, as there are pretty women to deserve them.
Mansfield Park (1814), ch. 1

21 Certainly, my home at my uncle's brought me acquainted with a circle of admirals. Of *Rears* and *Vices*, I saw enough. Now, do not be suspecting me of a pun, I entreat.
Mansfield Park (1814), ch. 6

22 Let other pens dwell on guilt and misery. I quit such odious subjects as soon as I can.
Mansfield Park (1814), ch. 48

23 And it was not very wonderful that Catherine, who by nature had nothing very heroic about her, should prefer cricket, baseball, riding on horseback, and running about the country, at the age of fourteen, to books.
Northanger Abbey (1818), ch. 3

24 But are they all horrid, are you sure they are all horrid?
Referring to Gothic novels, fashionable in England at the beginning of the 19th century, but frowned upon in polite society. *Northanger Abbey* (1818), ch. 6

25 A woman, especially if she have the misfortune of knowing anything, should conceal it as well as she can.
Northanger Abbey (1818), ch. 14

26 "My idea of good company, Mr. Elliot, is the company of clever, well-informed people, who have a great deal of conversation; that is what I call good company."
"You are mistaken," said he gently, "that is not good company, that is the best."
Persuasion (1818), ch. 16

27 One does not love a place the less for having suffered in it unless it has all been suffering, nothing but suffering.
Persuasion (1818), ch. 20

28 All the privilege I claim for my own sex (it is not a very enviable one, you need not covet it) is that of loving longest, when existence or when hope is gone.
Anne Elliott to Captain Wentworth. *Persuasion* (1818), ch. 23

29 She was a woman of mean understanding, little information, and uncertain temper.
Pride and Prejudice (1813), ch. 1

30 It is a truth universally acknowledged, that a single man in

possession of a good fortune must be in want of a wife.
The opening words of the book. *Pride and Prejudice* (1813), ch. 1

31 A lady's imagination is very rapid; it jumps from admiration to love, from love to matrimony in a moment.
Pride and Prejudice (1813), ch. 6

32 Happiness in marriage is entirely a matter of chance.
Pride and Prejudice (1813), ch. 6

33 It is happy for you that you possess the talent of flattering with delicacy. May I ask whether these pleasing attentions proceed from the impulse of the moment, or are the result of previous study?
Pride and Prejudice (1813), ch. 14

34 Next to being married, a girl likes to be crossed in love a little now and then.
Pride and Prejudice (1813), ch. 24

35 One cannot be always laughing at a man without now and then stumbling on something witty.
Pride and Prejudice (1813), ch. 40

36 Loss of virtue in a female is irretrievable...one false step involves her in endless ruin...her reputation is no less brittle than it is beautiful, and...she cannot be too much guarded in her behavior toward the undeserving of the other sex.
Mary Bennet to her sister Elizabeth, after hearing of Lydia's elopement with Wickham. *Pride and Prejudice* (1813), ch. 47

37 For what do we live, but to make sport for our neighbors, and laugh at them in our turn?
Pride and Prejudice (1813), ch. 57

Auster, Paul (b.1947) U.S. writer

1 Becoming a writer is not a "career decision" like becoming a doctor or a policeman. You don't choose it so much as get chosen, and...you have to be prepared to walk a long, hard road for the rest of your days.
Hand to Mouth (1997)

2 Money, of course, is never just money. It's always something else, and it's always something more, and it always has the last word.
Hand to Mouth (1997)

3 For nothing is really itself anymore. There are pieces of this and pieces of that, but none of it fits together...Everything falls apart, but not every part of everything, at least not at the same time.
In the Country of Last Things (1987)

4 Memory is not an act of will, after all. It is something that happens in spite of oneself, and when too much is changing all the time...things are bound to slip through it.
In the Country of Last Things (1987)

5 The stomach is a bottomless pit, a hole as big as the world...No, there is nothing people will not do, and the sooner you learn that, the better off you will be.
In the Country of Last Things (1987)

6 Someone started talking about the moon landing, and then someone else declared that it had never really happened. The whole thing was a hoax, he said, a television extravaganza staged by the government to get our minds off the war.
Moon Palace (1989)

7 To what extent would people tolerate blasphemies if they gave them amusement?
"City of Glass," *New York Trilogy* (1987)

Austin, Alfred (1835–1913) British poet

1 I dare not alter these things; they come to me from above.
1900? When accused of writing ungrammatical verse. *A Number of People: A Book of Reminiscences* (Edward Marsh; 1939)

2 Across the wires the electric message came:
"He is no better, he is much the same."
Referring to the illness of Edward, Prince of Wales. Generally attributed to Austin but there is no definite evidence that he wrote it. Attrib.

Austin, Mary (originally Mary Hunter; 1868–1934) U.S. novelist

1 It grew upon me finally that there is a male incapacity for re-patterning the personal life which is insuperable.
Referring to her reasons for divorcing her husband. "Earth Horizon: an Autobiography" (1932), quoted in *A Mary Austin Reader* (E. F. Lanigan, ed.; 1996)

2 In America for a man to become a university professor means that he is too early removed from the necessity of making good on his own among equals.
Referring to President Woodrow Wilson, formerly a professor of jurisprudence at Princeton. Letter to H. G. Wells (January 24, 1917), quoted in *Literary America, 1903–1934: The Mary Austin Letters* (T. M. Pearce, ed.; 1979)

3 After the first shock and surprise of the war, you could feel all over America, like the tightening of a ship's cordage in the rain, the common consciousness of the Power overseas.
Referring to World War I. Letter to H.G. Wells (January 24, 1917), quoted in *Literary America, 1903–1934: the Mary Austin Letters* (T. M. Pearce, ed.; 1979)

4 *You* let this thing happen, you people over there. Was it apathy or idealism that kept you sunning yourself on the doorstep with your dog scratching fleas, while a basilisk hatched under your walls?
Referring to World War I and Europeans at the point of U.S. entry into the war. Letter to H. G. Wells (January 24, 1917), quoted in *Literary America, 1903–1934: the Mary Austin Letters* (T. M. Pearce, ed.; 1979)

5 I know I'm feminine, damnably feminine, and not ashamed of it, but I'm not ladyish. You can count on my behaving like a gentleman.
Referring to possible literary collaboration with Sinclair Lewis. Letter to Sinclair Lewis (February 28, 1931), quoted in *Literary America, 1903–1934: the Mary Austin Letters* (T. M. Pearce, ed.; 1979)

6 The love life of the average middle class American...is thin rather than vicious.
"Sex in American Literature" (1923), quoted in *A Mary Austin Reader* (E. F. Lanigan, ed.; 1996)

7 The Puritans...ceased to need or to find pleasure in ritual and symbol or any representative art; their religious mysticism was reduced to a pale phosphorescence of renunciation.
"Sex in American Literature" (1923), quoted in *A Mary Austin Reader* (E. F. Lanigan, ed.; 1996)

8 Come away, you who are obsessed with your own importance in the scheme of things...come away by the brown valleys and

full-bosomed hills to the even-breathing days, to the kindliness, earthiness, ease of El Pueblo de Las Uvas.
"The Land of Little Rain" (1903), quoted in *A Mary Austin Reader* (E. F. Lanigan, ed.; 1996)

9 For all the toll the desert takes of man, it gives compensation, deep breaths, deep sleep, and the communion of the stars. It comes upon one with new force in the pauses of the night that the Chaldeans were a desert-bred people.
"The Land of Little Rain" (1903), quoted in *A Mary Austin Reader* (E. F. Lanigan, ed.; 1996)

10 I have made a practice of standing out against male assumption of every sort, especially their assumption of the importance of masculine disapproval.
"Woman Alone" (1927), quoted in *A Mary Austin Reader* (E. F. Lanigan, ed.; 1996)

Austin, Warren Robinson (1877–1962) U.S. diplomat

1 The Jews and Arabs should sit down and settle their differences like good Christians.
1948. Referring to the Arab-Israeli conflict. Attrib.

2 It is better for aged diplomats to be bored than for young men to die.
Response when asked if he got tired during long debates at the UN. Attrib.

Avedon, Richard (b.1923) U.S. fashion and portrait photographer

1 Beauty can be as isolating as genius, or deformity. I have always been aware of a relationship between madness and beauty.
Quoted in *Model: The Ugly Business of Beautiful Women* (Michael Gross; 1995)

Avery, Oswald Theodore (1877–1955) Canadian-born U.S. physician and bacteriologist

1 Whenever you fall, pick up something.
Attrib.

Avicenna (Abu Ali al-Hussain ibn Abdallah ibn Sina; 980–1037) Persian philosopher and physician

1 Writing about erotics is a perfectly respectable function of medicine, and about the ways to make the woman enjoy sex; these are an important part of reproductive physiology.
Sex in Society (Alex Comfort; 1964)

2 That disease is called Incubus in which, when a person gets to sleep, he seems to have a heavy weight pressing on him, spirit oppressed, voice abolished, power to move impeded, throat obstructed almost to strangulation.
Many ancient texts on mental health refer to incubus in a similar vein. An incubus was also the term for the notion of a demon that has sex with a sleeping person. Attrib.

Awolowo, Obafemi, Chief (1909–87) Nigerian lawyer and politician

1 There is radiance in the darkness, if we could but see. To be able to see this radiance, all you need do is to cultivate the courage to look.
June 30, 1967. *Voice of Courage: Selected Speeches of Chief Obafemi Awolowo* (1981), vol. 2

2 It will, I believe, be generally agreed that ERADICATION OF CORRUPTION from any society is not just a difficult task: *it is without dispute, an impossible objective.*
August 18, 1975. *Voice of Courage: Selected Speeches of Chief Obafemi Awolowo* (1981), vol. 2

3 In honest hands, literacy is the surest and the most effective means to true education. In dishonest hands, it may be a most dangerous, in fact a suicidal, acquisition.
Voice of Reason: Selected Speeches of Chief Obafemi Awolowo (1981), vol. 1

Axelrod, George (b.1922) U.S. screenwriter

1 The Seven Year Itch
1955. Play and film title.

Ayala, Francisco Spanish writer

1 The smallest and thinnest roots of the industrial world insert themselves deep in the healthy flesh of the country and sensitize its neutral volume.
"Hunter in the Dawn" (1929)

2 The minute frames of celluloid coined by its machines are currency of excellent circulation among the children of every corner of the Earth; the only currency universally accepted.
Referring to movies. *Investigation into the Cinema* (1929)

Ayckbourn, Alan (b.1939) British playwright and director

1 I've never to this day really known what most women think about anything.
1973. *Absurd Person Singular* (1974), Act 3

2 My mother used to say, Delia, if S-E-X ever rears its ugly head, close your eyes before you see the rest of it.
Bedroom Farce (1975), Act 2

3 The greatest feeling in the world...Revenge. Pure, unadulterated revenge. Not weedy little jealousy. Not some piddling little envy. But good, old-fashioned, bloodcurdling revenge.
Revengers' Comedies (1991), Act 2, Scene 1

4 When you've been married a few years—you can't help window shopping.
Round and Round the Garden (1973), Act 1, Scene 1

5 If you gave Ruth a rose, she'd peel all the petals off to make sure there weren't any greenfly. And when she'd done that, she'd turn round and say, do you call that a rose? Look at it, it's all in bits.
Table Manners (1975), Act 2, Scene 1

6 Few women care to be laughed at and men not at all, except for large sums of money.
The Norman Conquests (1974), preface

7 Nevertheless—you know, in life, you get moments—just occasionally which you can positively identify as being among the happy moments.
Time of My Life (1993), Act 2

Ayer, A. J., Sir (Alfred Jules Ayer; 1910–89) British philosopher

1 Sentences which simply express moral judgements do not say anything. They are pure expressions of feeling and as such do

not come under the category of truth and falsehood.
Language, Truth and Logic (1936)

2 Theism is so confused and the sentences in which "God" appears so incoherent and so incapable of verification or falsification that to speak of belief or unbelief, faith or unfaith, is logically impossible.
Language, Truth and Logic (1936)

3 The principles of logic and metaphysics are true simply because we never allow them to be anything else.
Language, Truth and Logic (1936)

4 In nature one thing just happens after another. Cause and effect have their place only in our imaginative arrangements and extensions of these primary facts.
The Central Questions of Philosophy (1973)

5 I conclude then that the necessary and sufficient conditions for knowing that something is the case are first that what one is said to know be true, secondly that one be sure of it, and thirdly that one should have the right to be sure.
The Problem of Knowledge (1956)

Aymé, Marcel (1902–67) French writer

1 When Paris has a sniffle, the whole of France blows her nose.
Silhouette du scandale (1938)

Ayres, Pam (b.1947) British poet

1 Medicinal discovery,
It moves in mighty leaps,
It leapt straight past the common cold
And gave it us for keeps.
"Oh No, I Got a Cold," *Some of Me Poetry* (1976)

Azikiwe, Nnamdi (1904–96) Nigerian president, newspaper editor, and financier

1 Originality is the essence of true scholarship. Creativity is the soul of the true scholar.
Speech to Methodist Boy's High School, Lagos (November 11, 1934), quoted in *Zik: A Selection from the Speeches of Nnamdi Azikiwe* (1961)

Bb

Bâ, Mariama (1929–81) Senegalese novelist and campaigner for women's rights

1 A woman must marry the man who loves her but never the one she loves; that is the secret of lasting happiness.
So Long a Letter (1979)

2 Friendship has splendors that love knows not. It grows stronger when crossed, whereas obstacles kill love. Friendship resists time, which wearies and severs couples. It has heights unknown to love.
So Long a Letter (1979)

3 Man is one: greatness and animal fused together. None of his acts is pure charity. None is pure bestiality.
So Long a Letter (1979)

Babeuf, François Noël (pen name Gracchus Babeuf; 1760–97) French revolutionary

1 The French Revolution is merely the herald of a far greater and much more solemn revolution, which will be the last...The hour has come for founding the Republic of Equals, that great refuge open to every man.
Conjuration des Égaux (1796)

Bacall, Lauren (Betty Joan Perske; b.1924) U.S. stage and film actor

1 I think your whole life shows in your face and you should be proud of that.
Remark (1988)

2 VIVIAN A lot depends who's in the saddle.
Responding to the words "Speaking of horses, you've got a touch of class, but I don't know how far you can go," said by private detective Philip Marlowe played by Humphrey Bogart. *The Big Sleep* (William Faulkner, Leigh Brackett, Jules Furthman, and Raymond Chandler; 1946)

3 You know you don't have to act with me, Steve. You don't have to say anything, and you don't have to do anything. Not a thing. Oh, maybe just whistle. You know how to whistle, don't you, Steve? You just put your lips together and blow.
Lauren Bacall's coolly provocative lines as Slim to Steve (Humphrey Bogart) in the film of Ernest Hemingway's novel. *To Have and Have Not* (1945)

Bach, Edward (1880–1936) British physician and microbiologist

1 Disease is in essence the result of conflict between soul and mind—So long as our souls and personalities are in harmony all is joy and peace, happiness and health. It is when our personalities are led astray from the path laid down by the soul, either by our own worldly desires or by the persuasion of others, that a conflict arises.
The Alternative Health Guide (Brian Inglis and Ruth West; 1989)

Bacon, Francis, 1st Baron Verulam and Viscount Saint Albans (1561–1626) English philosopher, statesman, and lawyer

Quotations about Bacon

1 In his adversity I ever prayed, that God would give him strength; for greatness he could not want.
Ben Jonson (1572–1637) English playwright and poet. *Timber, or Discoveries Made upon Men and Matter* (1640)

Quotations by Bacon

2 I have taken all knowledge to be my province.
Letter to Lord Burghley (1592)

3 Alonso of Aragon was wont to say in commendation of age, that age appears to be best in four things—old wood best to burn, old wine to drink, old friends to trust, and old authors to read.
Apothegms (1624)

4 Cosmus, Duke of Florence, was wont to say of perfidious friends, that "We read that we ought to forgive our enemies; but we do not read that we ought to forgive our friends."
Apothegms (1624)

5 Hope is a good breakfast, but it is a bad supper.
Apothegms (1624)

6 One of the Seven was wont to say: "That laws were like cobwebs; where the small flies were caught, and the great brake through."
Referring to the Seven Sages of the ancient world. *Apothegms* (1624)

7 Like strawberry wives, that laid two or three great strawberries at the mouth of their pot, and all the rest were little ones.
Describing the tactics of the Commission of Sales in their dealings with Elizabeth I. *Apothegms New and Old* (1625)

8 Riches are a good handmaid, but the worst mistress.
De Dignitate et Augmentis Scientiarum (Gilbert Watts, tr.; 1640), Antitheta, 6; bk. 1, ch. 6, sect. 3

9 The worst solitude is to be destitute of sincere friendship.
De Dignitate et Augmentis Scientiarum (Gilbert Watts, tr.; 1640), Antitheta, 37; bk. 1, ch. 7, sect. 81

10 Prosperity doth best discover vice; but adversity doth best discover virtue.
"Of Adversity," *Essays* (1625)

11 Prosperity is the blessing of the Old Testament, adversity is the blessing of the New.
"Of Adversity," *Essays* (1625)

12 Virtue is like precious odours—most fragrant when they are incensed or crushed.
"Of Adversity," *Essays* (1625)

13 For none deny there is a God, but those for whom it maketh that there were no God.
"Of Atheism," *Essays* (1625)

14 I had rather believe all the fables in the legend, and the Talmud, and the Alcoran, than that this universal frame is without a mind.
"Of Atheism," *Essays* (1625)

15 There is no excellent beauty that hath not some strangeness in the proportion.
"Of Beauty," *Essays* (1625)

16 Virtue is like a rich stone, best plain set.
"Of Beauty," *Essays* (1625)

17 There is in human nature generally more of the fool than of the wise.
"Of Boldness," *Essays* (1625)

18 Mahomet made the people believe that he would call a hill to him...when the hill stood still, he was never a whit abashed, but said, "If the hill will not come to Mahomet, Mahomet will go to the hill."
Often misquoted as "If the mountain will not come to Mohammed..." "Of Boldness," *Essays* (1625)

19 Houses are built to live in and not to look on; therefore let use be preferred before uniformity, except where both may be had.
"Of Building," *Essays* (1625)

20 A wise man will make more opportunities than he finds.
"Of Ceremonies and Respects," *Essays* (1625)

21 I knew one that when he wrote a letter, he would put that which was most material in the postscript, as if it had been a by-matter.
"Of Cunning," *Essays* (1625)

22 Men fear death, as children fear to go in the dark; and as that natural fear in children is increased with tales, so is the other.
"Of Death," *Essays* (1625)

23 To choose time is to save time.
"Of Dispatch," *Essays* (1625)

24 It is a miserable state of mind to have few things to desire and many things to fear.
"Of Empire," *Essays* (1625)

25 Nothing destroyeth authority so much as the unequal and untimely interchange of power pressed too far, and relaxed too much.
"Of Empire," *Essays* (1625)

26 Riches are for spending.
"Of Expense," *Essays* (1625)

27 If a man look sharply, and attentively, he shall see Fortune: for though she be blind, yet she is not invisible.
"Of Fortune," *Essays* (1625)

28 A crowd is not company, and faces are but a gallery of pictures, and talk but a tinkling cymbal, where there is no love.
"Of Friendship," *Essays* (1625)

29 It redoubleth joys, and cutteth griefs in halves.
"Of Friendship," *Essays* (1625)

30 Whosoever is delighted in solitude is either a wild beast or a god.
"Of Friendship," *Essays* (1625)

31 God Almighty first planted a garden. And indeed it is the purest of human pleasures.
"Of Gardens," *Essays* (1625)

32 If a man be gracious and courteous to strangers, it shows he is a citizen of the world.
"Of Goodness and Goodness of Nature," *Essays* (1625)

33 In charity there is no excess.
"Of Goodness and Goodness of Nature," *Essays* (1625)

34 The inclination to goodness is imprinted deeply in the nature of man: insomuch, that if it issue not towards men, it will take unto other living creatures.
"Of Goodness and Goodness of Nature," *Essays* (1625)

35 It is a strange desire to seek power and to lose liberty.
"Of Great Place," *Essays* (1625)

36 Set it down to thyself, as well to create good precedents as to follow them.
"Of Great Place," *Essays* (1625)

37 As the births of living creatures at first are ill-shapen, so are all innovations, which are the births of time.
"Of Innovations," *Essays* (1625)

38 He that will not apply new remedies must expect new evils: for time is the greatest innovator.
"Of Innovations," *Essays* (1625)

39 The place of justice is a hallowed place.
"Of Judicature," *Essays* (1625)

40 It is impossible to love and be wise.
"Of Love," *Essays* (1625)

41 Nuptial love maketh mankind; friendly love perfecteth it; but wanton love corrupteth and embaseth it.
"Of Love," *Essays* (1625)

42 A single life doth well with churchmen, for charity will hardly water the ground where it must first fill a pool.
"Of Marriage and the Single Life," *Essays* (1625)

43 He that hath wife and children hath given hostages to fortune; for they are impediments to great enterprises, either of virtue or mischief.
"Of Marriage and the Single Life," *Essays* (1625)

44 He was reputed one of the wise men, that made answer to the question, when a man should marry? A young man not yet, an elder man not at all.
"Of Marriage and the Single Life," *Essays* (1625)

45 Wives are young men's mistresses, companions for middle age, and old men's nurses.
"Of Marriage and the Single Life," *Essays* (1625)

46 A man's nature runs either to herbs, or to weeds; therefore let him seasonably water the one, and destroy the other.
"Of Nature in Men," *Essays* (1625)

47 Nature is often hidden, sometimes overcome, seldom extinguished.
"Of Nature in Men," *Essays* (1625)

48 It is generally better to deal by speech than by letter.
"Of Negotiating," *Essays* (1625)

49 New nobility is but the act of power, but ancient nobility is the act of time.
"Of Nobility," *Essays* (1625)

50 Nobility of birth commonly abateth industry.
"Of Nobility," *Essays* (1625)

51 Children sweeten labours, but they make misfortunes more bitter.
"Of Parents and Children," *Essays* (1625)

52 The joys of parents are secret, and so are their griefs and fears.
"Of Parents and Children," *Essays* (1625)

53 Age will not be defied.
"Of Regiment of Health," *Essays* (1625)

54 There is a wisdom in this beyond the rules of physic. A man's own observation, what he finds good of and what he finds hurt of, is the best physic to preserve health.
"Of Regiment of Health," *Essays* (1625)

55 A man that studieth revenge keeps his own wounds green.
"Of Revenge," *Essays* (1625)

56 Revenge is a kind of wild justice; which the more man's nature runs to, the more ought law to weed it out.
"Of Revenge," *Essays* (1625)

57 Why should I be angry with a man for loving himself better than me?
"Of Revenge," *Essays* (1625)

58 Money is like muck, not good except it be spread.
"Of Seditions and Troubles," *Essays* (1625)

59 The four pillars of government...(which are religion, justice, counsel, and treasure).
"Of Seditions and Troubles," *Essays* (1625)

60 The remedy is worse than the disease.
"Of Seditions and Troubles," *Essays* (1625)

61 The surest way to prevent seditions (if the times do bear it) is to take away the matter of them.
"Of Seditions and Troubles," *Essays* (1625)

62 Histories make men wise; poets, witty; the mathematics, subtile; natural philosophy, deep; moral, grave; logic and rhetoric, able to contend.
"Of Studies," *Essays* (1625)

63 Reading maketh a full man; conference a ready man; and writing an exact man.
"Of Studies," *Essays* (1625)

64 Read not to contradict and confute, nor to believe and take for granted, nor to find talk and discourse, but to weigh and consider.
"Of Studies," *Essays* (1625)

65 Some books are to be tasted, others to be swallowed, and some few to be chewed and digested.
"Of Studies," *Essays* (1625)

66 Studies serve for delight, for ornament, and for ability.
"Of Studies," *Essays* (1625)

67 They perfect nature and are perfected by experience.
"Of Studies," *Essays* (1625)

68 It were better to have no opinion of God at all, than such an opinion as is unworthy of him.
"Of Superstition," *Essays* (1625)

69 There is a superstition in avoiding superstition.
"Of Superstition," *Essays* (1625)

70 Travel, in the younger sort, is a part of education; in the elder, a part of experience. He that travelleth into a country before he hath some entrance into the language, goeth to school, and not to travel.
"Of Travel," *Essays* (1625)

71 A mixture of a lie doth ever add pleasure.
"Of Truth," *Essays* (1625)

72 It is not the lie that passeth through the mind, but the lie that sinketh in, and settleth in it, that doth the hurt.
"Of Truth," *Essays* (1625)

73 No pleasure is comparable to the standing upon the vantage-ground of truth...and to see the errors, and wanderings, and mists, and tempests, in the vale below.
"Of Truth," *Essays* (1625)

74 What is truth said jesting Pilate, and would not stay for an answer.
"Of Truth," *Essays* (1625)

75 All colours will agree in the dark.
"Of Unity in Religion," *Essays* (1625)

76 It was prettily devised of Aesop, "The fly sat upon the axletree of the chariot-wheel and said, what a dust do I raise."
"Of Vain-Glory," *Essays* (1625)

77 In the youth of a state arms do flourish; in the middle age of a state, learning; and then both of them together for a time; in the declining age of a state, mechanical arts and merchandise.
"Of Vicissitude of Things," *Essays* (1625)

78 The greatest vicissitude of things amongst men is the vicissitude of sects and religions.
"Of Vicissitude of Things," *Essays* (1625)

79 Be so true to thyself, as thou be not false to others.
"Of Wisdom for a Man's Self," *Essays* (1625)

80 A man that is young in years may be old in hours, if he have lost no time.
"Of Youth and Age," *Essays* (1625)

81 For my name and memory, I leave it to men's charitable

speeches, and to foreign nations, and the next ages.
Final will and testament (December 19, 1625), quoted in *The Letters and Life of Francis Bacon* (J. Spedding, ed.; 1874), vol. 7

82 Knowledge itself is power.
"De Haresibus" ("Of Heresies"), *Meditationes Sacrae,* Religious Meditations (1597)

83 Nature, to be commanded, must be obeyed.
Novum Organum (1620), aphorism 129

84 For what a man would like to be true, that he more readily believes.
Novum Organum (1620), aphorism 49

85 Celsus...tells us that the experimental part of medicine was first discovered, and that afterwards men philosophized about it; and hunted for and assigned causes; and not by an inverse process that philosophy and the knowledge of causes led to the discovery and development of the experimental part.
Novum Organum (1620), aphorism 73

86 That great mother of sciences.
Referring to natural philosophy. *Novum Organum* (1620), aphorism 80

87 Books must follow sciences, and not sciences books.
"A Proposition...Touching Amendment of the Laws of England," *Resuscitatio* (1657)

88 Just as it is always said of slander that something always sticks when people boldly slander, so it might be said of self-praise (if it is not entirely shameful and ridiculous) that if we praise ourselves fearlessly, something will always stick.
The Advancement of Learning (1605)

89 We are much beholden to Machiavel and others, that write what men do, and not what they ought to do.
The Advancement of Learning (1605)

90 If a man will begin with certainties, he shall end in doubts; but if he will be content to begin with doubts, he shall end in certainties.
The Advancement of Learning (1605), bk. 1

91 So let great authors have their due, as time, which is the author of authors, be not deprived of his due, which is further and further to discover truth.
The Advancement of Learning (1605), bk. 1

92 A dance is a measured pace, as a verse is a measured speech.
The Advancement of Learning (1605), bk. 2

93 But men must know, that in this theatre of man's life it is reserved only for God and angels to be lookers on.
The Advancement of Learning (1605), bk. 2

94 For man seeketh in society comfort, use, and protection.
The Advancement of Learning (1605), bk. 2

95 States as great engines move slowly.
The Advancement of Learning (1605), bk. 2

96 The poets did well to conjoin Music and Medicine in Apollo, because the office of Medicine is but to tune this curious harp of man's body and to reduce it to harmony.
The Advancement of Learning (1605), bk. 2

97 They are ill discoverers that think there is no land, when they can see nothing but sea.
The Advancement of Learning (1605), bk. 2

98 Words are the tokens current and accepted for conceits, as moneys are for values.
The Advancement of Learning (1605), bk. 2

99 It was ever holden that honours in free monarchies and commonwealths had a sweetness more than in tyrannies; because the commandment extendeth more over the wills of men, and not only over their deeds and services.
The Advancement of Learning (1605), bk. 2, ch. 8

100 Lucid intervals and happy pauses.
The Life of Henry VII (1622)

101 I do not believe that any man fears to be dead, but only the stroke of death.
"An Essay on Death," *The Remaines of the Right Honourable Francis Lord Verulam* (1648)

102 Universities incline wits to sophistry and affectation.
1603. *Valerius Terminus,* quoted in *Letters and Remains of the Lord Chancellor Bacon* (Robert Stephens, ed.; 1734), ch. 26

103 If a man have not a friend he may quit the stage.
Quoted in *Homosexuality: A History* (Colin Spencer; 1995)

104 Opportunity makes a thief.
1598. "A Letter of Advice to the Earl of Essex...," *The Letters and Life of Francis Bacon* (J. Spedding, ed.; 1861), vol. 1

Bacon, Francis (1909–92) Irish-born British artist

1 How can I take an interest in my work when I don't like it?
From an exhibition catalog. *Francis Bacon* (Sir John Rothenstein, ed.; 1962)

2 When talking about the violence of paint, it's nothing to do with the violence of war. It's to do with an attempt to remake the violence of reality itself.
1971. Quoted in *Interviews with Francis Bacon* (David Sylvester; 1980), interview 3

Bacon, Roger ("Doctor Mirabilis"; 1220?–92) English monk, philosopher, and scientist

1 Experimental science is the mistress of the speculative sciences, it alone is able to give us important truths within the confines of the other sciences, which those sciences can learn in no other way.
Opus Majus (1266–67)

2 Reasoning draws a conclusion and makes us grant the conclusion, but does not make the conclusion certain, nor does it remove doubt.
Opus Majus (1266–67)

3 All science requires mathematics.
Opus Majus (1266–67), pt. 4

4 For the things of this world cannot be made known without a knowledge of mathematics.
"Distincta Prima," *Opus Majus* (1266–67), pt. 4

Baden-Powell, Robert, 1st Baron Baden-Powell of Gilwell (Robert Stephenson Smyth Baden-Powell; 1857–1941) British soldier and founder of the Boy Scout movement

1 A scout smiles and whistles under all circumstances.
Scouting for Boys (1908)

2 Be Prepared...the meaning of the motto is that a scout must

prepare himself by previous thinking out and practising how to act on any accident or emergency so that he is never taken by surprise; he knows exactly what to do when anything unexpected happens.
Motto of the Boy Scout movement. *Scouting for Boys* (1908)

3 It is called in our schools "beastliness", and this is about the best name for it...should it become a habit it quickly destroys both health and spirits; he becomes feeble in body and mind, and often ends in a lunatic asylum.
Referring to masturbation. *Scouting for Boys* (1908)

4 On my honour I promise that I will do my best...to do my duty to God and the King...to help other people at all times...to obey the Scout Law.
The Boy Scout's promise. *Scouting for Boys* (1908)

Bader, Douglas, Sir (Douglas Robert Stuart Bader; 1910–82) British aviator and social reformer

1 Don't listen to anyone who tells you that you can't do this or that. That's nonsense. Make up your mind you'll never use crutches or a stick, then have a go at everything...never, never let them persuade you that things are too difficult or impossible.
Speaking to a 14-year-old boy who had had a leg amputated after a car crash. *Flying Colours* (Laddie Lucas; 1980)

Baedeker, Karl (1801–59) German publisher

1 Oxford is on the whole more attractive than Cambridge to the ordinary visitor; and the traveler is therefore recommended to visit Cambridge first, or to omit it altogether if he cannot visit both.
"From London to Oxford," *Baedeker's Great Britain* (1887)

2 The traveler need have no scruple in limiting his donations to the smallest possible sums, as liberality frequently becomes a source of annoyance and embarrassment.
"Gratuities," *Northern Italy* (1895)

Baer, George Frederick (1842–1914) U.S. lawyer and industrialist

1 The rights and interests of the laboring man will be protected and cared for, not by the labor agitators, but by the Christian men to whom God in His infinite wisdom has given control of the property interests of the country.
Written during the Pennsylvania miners' strike. Open letter to the press (October 1902)

Baez, Joan (Joan Chandos Baez; b.1941) U.S. folksinger and human-rights activist

1 You don't get to choose how you're going to die. Or when. You can only decide how you're going to live. Now.
Daybreak (1970)

Bagehot, Walter (1826–77) British economist and journalist

1 Writers, like teeth, are divided into incisors and grinders.
"The First Edinburgh Reviewers," *Estimates of Some Englishmen and Scotchmen* (1858)

2 It has been said that England invented the phrase, "Her Majesty's Opposition"; that it was the first government which made a criticism of administration as much a part of the policy as administration itself. This critical opposition is the consequence of cabinet government.
"The Cabinet," *The English Constitution* (1867)

3 The mystic reverence, the religious allegiance, which are essential to a true monarchy, are imaginative sentiments that no legislature can manufacture in any people.
"The Cabinet," *The English Constitution* (1867)

4 It has been said, not truly, but with a possible approximation to truth, "that in 1802 every hereditary monarch was insane".
"The House of Lords," *The English Constitution* (1867)

5 Nations touch at their summits.
"The House of Lords," *The English Constitution* (1867)

6 The best reason why Monarchy is a strong government is that it is an intelligible government. The mass of mankind understand it, and they hardly anywhere in the world understand any other.
"The Monarchy," *The English Constitution* (1867)

7 The characteristic of the English Monarchy is that it retains the feelings by which the heroic kings governed their rude age, and has added the feeling by which the constitutions of later Greece ruled in more refined ages.
"The Monarchy," *The English Constitution* (1867)

8 The Sovereign has, under a constitutional monarchy such as ours, three rights—the right to be consulted, the right to encourage, the right to warn.
"The Monarchy," *The English Constitution* (1867)

9 Throughout the greater part of his life George III was a kind of "consecrated obstruction".
"The Monarchy," *The English Constitution* (1867)

10 Women—one half the human race at least—care fifty times more for a marriage than a ministry.
"The Monarchy," *The English Constitution* (1867)

11 A schoolmaster should have an atmosphere of awe, and walk wonderingly, as if he was amazed at being himself.
Quoted in *Literary Studies* (Hartley Coleridge; 1878), vol. 1

12 Poverty is an anomaly to rich people. It is very difficult to make out why people who want dinner do not ring the bell.
Quoted in *Literary Studies* (Hartley Coleridge; 1879), vol. 2

13 Life is a school of probability.
Quoted in *The World of Mathematics* (J. R. Newman, ed.; 1956)

Bagnold, Enid (1889–1981) British author and playwright

1 Hanging head downwards between cliffs of bone, was the baby, its arms all but clasped about its neck, its face aslant upon its arms, hair painted upon its skull, closed, secret eyes, a diver poised in albumen, ancient and epic, shot with delicate spasms, as old as a Pharaoh in its tomb.
The Door of Life (1938), ch. 2

Bai Fengxi (b.1932?) Chinese writer

1 If a woman is strong there will be no peace in the house.
Return of an Old Friend on a Stormy Night (1983)

2 Women are not the moon. Emit your own light.
Return of an Old Friend on a Stormy Night (1983)

Bai Juyi (also known as Po Chü-i; 772–846) Chinese poet

1 Each morning I lamented the hairs that had fallen;
each evening I lamented the hairs that had fallen.
When all had fallen—that was truly lamentable!
But now that they're gone, it isn't so bad.
"Lamenting My Falling Hairs" (8th–9th century), quoted in *China's Imperial Past* (Charles O. Hucker; 1975)

2 The tailor has given me comfort for life,
But should I alone be treated so well?
How could one get such a gown so immense
As to wholly enclose every corner of the earth.
"My New Quilted Gown" (8th–9th century), quoted in *China's Imperial Past* (Charles O. Hucker; 1975)

3 With their arrogant manner, they fill up the road;
The horses they ride glisten in the dust.
Expressing a Confucian concern that the ruling class conduct themselves responsibly. "The Frivolous Rich" (8th–9th century), quoted in *China's Imperial Past* (Charles O. Hucker; 1975)

Bailey, David (David Royston Bailey; b.1938) British fashion photographer

1 The only reason I ever did fashion was because of the girls. It was the gates of heaven. But I only wanted to photograph girls I liked.
Sunday Times, London (March 1989), magazine, quoted in *Sultans of Style* (Georgina Howell; 1990), ch. 2

Bailey, Pearl (Pearl Mae Bailey; 1918–90) U.S. singer and actor

1 Children, you must remember something. A man without ambition is dead. A man with ambition but no love is dead. A man with ambition and love for his blessings here on earth is ever so alive. Having been alive, it won't be hard in the end to lie down and rest.
Talking to Myself (1971)

2 Everybody wants to do something to help, but nobody wants to be the first.
The Raw Pearl (1968)

3 There's a period of life when we swallow a knowledge of ourselves, and it becomes either good or sour inside.
The Raw Pearl (1968)

Bailey, Thomas A. (Thomas Andrew Bailey; 1902–83) U.S. historian

1 History does repeat itself, with variations, and the price seems to go up each time.
"The Mythmakers of American History," *Journal of American History* (June 1968)

2 One is tempted to say that old myths never die; they just become embedded in the textbooks.
"The Mythmakers of American History," *Journal of American History* (June 1968)

3 The historian who attempts to interpret the past in terms of present-day values often undertakes the almost impossible task of serving two masters of trying to be both a chronicler and a chameleon.
"The Mythmakers of American History," *Journal of American History* (June 1968)

4 Too many historical writers are the votaries of cults, which, by definition are dedicated to whitewashing warts and hanging halos.
"The Mythmakers of American History," *Journal of American History* (June 1968)

5 We Americans seem not to realize that impermanence is one of the most permanent features of history, and that victory does not keep.
"The Mythmakers of American History," *Journal of American History* (June 1968)

6 Too many so-called historians are really "hysterians"; their thinking is more visceral than cerebral. When their duties as citizens clash with their responsibilities as scholars, Clio frequently takes a back seat.
Clio was the muse of history. "The Mythmakers of American History," *Journal of American History* (June 1968)

Bailly, Jean Sylvain (1736–93) French astronomer, historian, and revolutionary

1 It's time for me to enjoy another pinch of snuff. Tomorrow my hands will be bound, so as to make it impossible.
Said on the evening before his execution. *Anekdotenschatz* (H. Hoffmeister; 1793)

Bailyn, Bernard (b.1922) U.S. historian

1 For the essence and drama of history lie precisely in the active and continuous relationship between the underlying conditions that set the boundaries of human existence and the everyday problems with which people consciously struggle.
"The Challenge of Modern Historiography," *American Historical Review* (February 1982)

2 No effective historian of the future can be innocent of statistics, and indeed he or she should probably be a literate amateur economist, psychologist, anthropologist, sociologist, and geographer.
"The Challenge of Modern Historiography," *American Historical Review* (February 1982)

3 The drama of people struggling with the conditions that confine them through the cycles of limited life spans is the heart of all living history, and the development of that drama itself, not a metahistorical scheme of classifying events, must provide the framework for any effective interpretation of history.
"The Challenge of Modern Historiography," *American Historical Review* (February 1982)

4 The historian must re-tell, with a new richness, the story of what some one of the worlds of the past was, how it ceased to be what it was, how it faded and blended into new configurations, how at every stage what was, was the product of what had been, and developed into what no one could have anticipated.
"The Challenge of Modern Historiography," *American Historical Review* (February 1982)

Bainbridge, Beryl (Beryl Margaret Bainbridge; b.1934) British author and journalist

1 Clothes do matter.
Another Part of the Wood (1968)

2 He is, after all, the reflection of the tenderness I bear for myself. It is always ourselves we love.
"Maggie," *A Weekend with Claud* (1967)

3 Prejudice is planted in childhood, learnt like table manners and cadences of speech, nurtured through fictions like *Uncle Tom's Cabin* and *Gone With the Wind*.
Forever England North and South (1987)

4 She supposed that basically she was an unhappy person who was happy.
Forever England North and South (1987)

5 Time was when you could go on an outing to a town barely thirty miles distant from your own and it was like visiting another country.
Forever England North and South (1987)

6 I like funerals. All those flowers—a full life coming to a close.
The Bottle Factory Outing (1974), ch. 1

Bainbridge, Kenneth T. (Kenneth Tompkins Bainbridge; 1904–96) U.S. physicist

1 Now we are all sons of bitches.
July 16, 1945. After the first atomic bomb test near Alamogordo, New Mexico, on July 16, 1945. *The Decision to Drop the Atomic Bomb* (Dennis D. Wainstock; 1996)

Bainville, Jacques (1879–1936) French journalist and historian

1 We're dying from not knowing and not understanding our past.
Journal (August 18, 1916)

2 The old repeat themselves and the young have nothing to say. The boredom is mutual.
Lecture, "Le Charme de la conversation" (1937)

Bairnsfather, Bruce (Charles Bruce Bairnsfather; 1888–1959) Indian-born British cartoonist

1 Well, if you knows of a better 'ole, go to it.
Caption to a cartoon about trench warfare. *Fragments from France* (1915)

Baker, Josephine (Freda Josephine McDonald; 1906–75) U.S.-born French singer and dancer

1 A violinist had his violin, a painter his palette. All I had was myself. *I* was the instrument that I must care for.
Josephine (co-written with Jo Bouillon; 1976)

2 If only statesmen had hearts as sincere as their words!
Josephine (co-written with Jo Bouillon; 1976)

3 My face and rump were famous! I could honestly say that I'd been blessed with an "intelligent" derrière. Most people's were only good to sit on!
Josephine (co-written with Jo Bouillon; 1976)

4 The stage is my best medicine.
Josephine (co-written with Jo Bouillon; 1976)

5 I like Frenchmen very much, because even when they insult you they do so nicely.
Quoted in *The New Quotable Woman* (Elaine Partnow, ed.; 1993)

6 It's far easier to become a star again than become one.
Quoted in *What Am I Doing Here* (Bruce Chatwin; 1989)

Baker, Russell (Russell Wayne Baker; b.1925) U.S. journalist

1 In today's highly complex society it takes years of training in rationalization, accommodation, and compromise to qualify for the good jobs with the really big payoffs you need to retain a first-rate psychiatrist in today's world.
New York Times (March 21, 1968)

Bakunin, Mikhail (Mikhail Aleksandrovich Bakunin; 1814–76) Russian-born anarchist

1 The urge for destruction is also a creative urge!
Under pseudonym "Jules Elysard." "Die Reaktion in Deutschland," *Jahrbuch für Wissenschaft und Kunst* (1842)

2 God, or rather the fiction of God, is the consecration and the intellectual and moral source of all slavery...and the freedom of mankind will never be complete until the disastrous and insidious fiction of a heavenly master is annihilated.
Quoted in *Bakunin on Anarchy* (Sam Dolgoff, ed.; 1973)

3 The privileged man, whether politically or economically, is a man depraved in mind and heart. That is a social law which admits of no exception, and it is applicable to entire nations as to classes, corporations, and individuals.
Quoted in *Bakunin on Anarchy* (Sam Dolgoff, ed.; 1973)

Balanchine, George (1904–83) Russian-born U.S. choreographer

Quotations about Balanchine

1 As a choreographer, Balanchine was more in control, more the center of attention than he would have been as a dancer. It was a question of ego. And, of course, he liked to make ballets for the women he loved.
Mikhail Baryshnikov (b.1948) Latvian-born U.S. dancer. Quoted in *George Balanchine* (Richard Buckle; 1988)

2 He wanted a landing so soft that it wouldn't break eggs. It did not matter how high you jumped so long as you landed "like a bird" or "like a pussycat."
Richard Buckle (b.1916) British ballet critic. Quoting George Balanchine on technique. *George Balanchine* (1988)

3 As you know, the company really has only one star and that is Balanchine.
André Yevgenyevich Eglevsky (1917–77) Russian-born U.S. ballet dancer. Referring to George Balanchine and the New York City Ballet's democratic policy of program billing. Quoted in *George Balanchine* (Don McDonagh; 1983)

4 I had an encounter with Mr. B in class which underscored his demand for starvation...With his knuckles, he thumped on my

sternum and down my rib cage...remarking: "Must see the bones." I was less than a hundred pounds even then...He did not merely say "Eat less." He said repeatedly, "Eat nothing."
Gelsey Kirkland (b.1952) U.S. ballet dancer. *Dancing on my Grave* (co-written with Greg Lawrence; 1986)

Quotations by Balanchine

5 Choreography is like cooking or gardening. Not like painting because painting stays. Dancing disintegrates. Like a garden. Lots of roses come up, and in the evening they're gone.
Quoted in *Portrait of Mr. B* (Lincoln Kirstein; 1984)

6 Dance has to look like the music. If you see music simply as an accompaniment, then you don't hear it. I occupy myself with how not to interfere with the music.
Quoted in *Portrait of Mr. B* (Lincoln Kirstein; 1984)

Baldwin, James (James Arthur Baldwin; 1924–87) U.S. writer and civil-rights activist

1 Children have never been very good at listening to their elders, but they have never failed to imitate them.
Esquire (1960)

2 Women are like water. They are tempting like that, and they can be treacherous, and they can seem to be that bottomless.
Giovanni's Room (1956)

3 It is rare that one *likes* a world-famous man—by the time they become world-famous they rarely like themselves.
"The Dangerous Road Before Martin Luther King," *Harper's Magazine* (February 1961)

4 Money, it turned out, was exactly like sex, you thought of nothing else if you didn't have it and thought of other things if you did.
Nobody Knows My Name (1961)

5 Perhaps the master who had coupled with his slave saw his guilt in his wife's pale eyes in the morning. And the wife saw his children in the slave quarters.
Nobody Knows My Name (1961)

6 The most dangerous creation of any society is that man who has nothing to lose, for his purity, by definition, is unassailable.
Nobody Knows My Name (1961)

7 The price one pays for pursuing any profession or calling is an intimate knowledge of its ugly side.
Nobody Knows My Name (1961)

8 Nothing is more desirable than to be released from an affliction, but nothing is more frightening than to be divested of a crutch.
Nobody Knows My Name (1961), introduction

9 The future is like heaven—everyone exalts it but no one wants to go there now.
"A Fly in Buttermilk," *Nobody Knows My Name* (1961)

10 There is never a time in the future in which we will work out our salvation. The challenge is in the moment, the time is always now.
"Faulkner and Desegregation," *Nobody Knows My Name* (1961)

11 A ghetto can be improved in one way only: out of existence.
"Fifth Avenue, Uptown," *Nobody Knows My Name* (1961)

12 Freedom is not something that anybody can be given; freedom is something people take and people are as free as they want to be.
"Notes for a Hypothetical Novel," *Nobody Knows My Name* (1961)

13 I am certainly convinced that it is one of the greatest impulses of mankind to arrive at something higher than a natural state.
"The Male Prison," *Nobody Knows My Name* (1961)

14 All art is a kind of confession, more or less oblique. All artists, if they are to survive are forced, at last, to tell the whole story, to vomit the anguish up.
"The Northern Protestant," *Nobody Knows My Name* (1961)

15 At the root of the American Negro problem is the necessity of the American white man to find a way of living with the Negro in order to be able to live with himself.
"Stranger in the Village", *Notes of a Native Son* (1955)

16 It is only in his music, which Americans are able to admire because a protective sentimentality limits their understanding of it, that the Negro in America has been able to tell his story.
"Many Thousands Gone," *Notes of a Native Son* (1955)

17 People are trapped in history and history is trapped in them.
"Stranger in the Village," *Notes of a Native Son* (1955)

18 People who shut their eyes to reality simply invite their own destruction, and anyone who insists on remaining in a state of innocence long after that innocence is dead turns himself into a monster.
"Stranger in the Village," *Notes of a Native Son* (1955)

19 Rage can only with difficulty, and never entirely, be brought under the domination of the intelligence and is therefore not susceptible to any arguments whatever.
"Stranger in the Village," *Notes of a Native Son* (1955)

20 The future is...black.
Observer, London (August 25, 1963), "Sayings of the Week"

21 If the concept of God has any validity or use, it can only be to make us larger, freer, and more loving. If God cannot do this, then it is time we got rid of Him.
The Fire Next Time (1963)

22 If we do not now dare everything, the fulfillment of that prophecy, re-created from the Bible in song by a slave, is upon us: God gave Noah the rainbow sign, No more water, the fire next time!
The Fire Next Time (1963)

23 In the end, it is the threat of universal extinction hanging over all the world today that changes, totally and forever, the nature of reality and brings into devastating question the true meaning of man's history.
The Fire Next Time (1963)

24 To accept one's past—one's history—is not the same thing as drowning in it; it is learning how to use it. An uninvented past can never be used; it cracks and crumbles under the pressures of life like clay in a season of drought.
The Fire Next Time (1963)

25 Do I really *want* to be integrated into a burning house?
"Down at the Cross—Letter from a Region in My Mind," *The Fire Next Time* (1963)

26 The only thing white people have that black people need, or should want, is power—and no one holds power for ever.
"Down at the Cross—Letter from a Region in My Mind," *The Fire Next Time* (1963)

27 It comes as a great shock around the age of five, six or seven to discover that the flag to which you have pledged allegiance...has not pledged allegiance to you...to see Gary Cooper killing off the Indians, and, although you are rooting for Gary Cooper...the Indians are you.
February 1965. Speech at Cambridge Union Society, *The Price of the Ticket* (1985)

28 History, I contend, is the present.
Quoted in *Emerge* (January 1990)

29 To be black and conscious in America is to be in a constant state of rage.
Quoted in *The White Album* (Joan Didion; 1979)

30 The trick is to love somebody...If you love one person, you see everybody else differently.
Attrib.

Baldwin, Stanley, 1st Earl Baldwin of Bewdley (1867–1947) British prime minister

Quotations about Baldwin

1 Not even a public figure. A man of no experience. And of the utmost insignificance.
George Nathaniel Curzon (1859–1925) British statesman. Referring to Stanley Baldwin on his appointment as Prime Minister. *Curzon: The Last Phase* (Harold Nicolson; 1924)

Quotations by Baldwin

2 You will find in politics that you are much exposed to the attribution of false motives. Never complain and never explain.
Quoting Benjamin Disraeli, British prime minister (1864; 1874–80), himself quoted in J. Morley, *Life of William Ewart Gladstone* (1903, vol. 1). Remark to Harold Nicolson (July 21, 1943)

3 There is a wind of nationalism and freedom blowing round the world, and blowing as strongly in Asia as elsewhere.
Speech, London (December 4, 1934)

4 Our attempt to lead the world towards disarmament by unilateral example has failed.
1935. Referring to the introduction of conscription in Germany. Speech to the British Parliament (March 4, 1935)

5 The only defence is in offence, which means that you have to kill more women and children more quickly than the enemy if you want to save yourselves.
Speech, *Hansard* (November 1932)

6 I think it is well also for the man in the street to realise that there is no power on earth that can protect him from being bombed. Whatever people may tell him, the bomber will always get through.
Speech to the British Parliament, *Hansard* (November 10, 1932)

7 A platitude is simply a truth repeated till people get tired of hearing it.
Speech to the British Parliament, *Hansard* (May 29, 1924), col. 727

8 The intelligent are to the intelligentsia what a man is to a gent.
Attrib. *Stanley Baldwin* (G. M. Young; 1952)

9 He spent his whole life in plastering together the true and the false and therefrom extracting the plausible.
The Fine Art of Political Wit (Leon A. Harris; 1965)

10 What the proprietorship of these papers is aiming at is power, and power without responsibility—the prerogative of the harlot through the ages.
Speech at election rally, March 18, 1931, attacking the English press barons Lords Rothermere and Beaverbrook. (March 18, 1931)

11 I would rather be an opportunist and float than go to the bottom with my principles round my neck.
Attrib.

12 There are three groups that no British Prime Minister should provoke: the Vatican, the Treasury, and the miners.
A similar remark is often attributed to Harold Macmillan, British prime minister (1957–63). Attrib.

Balenciaga, Cristóbal (1895–1972) Spanish fashion designer

1 Why do you want me to carry on? There is no one left to dress.
1968. Referring to his retirement. Quoted in *Sultans of Style* (Georgina Howell; 1990), ch. 1

2 I will not prostitute myself.
1964. When asked if he would design ready-to-wear clothes. Quoted in *Sultans of Style* (Georgina Howell; 1990), ch. 1

Balfour, Arthur, 1st Earl of Balfour (Arthur James Balfour; 1848–1930) British prime minister

1 His Majesty's Government views with favour the establishment in Palestine of a national home for the Jewish people.
The so-called "Balfour Declaration." Letter to Lionel Walter, Lord Rothschild (November 2, 1917)

2 It is unfortunate, considering that enthusiasm moves the world, that so few enthusiasts can be trusted to speak the truth.
Letter to Mrs. Drew (May 19, 1891), quoted in *Some Hawarden Letters* (L. March-Phillips and B. Christian, eds.; 1917), ch. 7

3 I look forward to a time when Irish patriotism will as easily combine with British patriotism as Scottish patriotism combines now.
Speech, Glasgow, Scotland (December 1889)

4 Science is the great instrument of social change...the most vital of all revolutions which have marked the development of modern civilization.
Speech, London (1908)

5 He has only half learned the art of reading who has not added to it the even more refined accomplishments of skipping and skimming.
Mr. Balfour (E. T. Raymond; 1920)

6 History does not repeat itself. Historians repeat each other.
Attrib.

7 Nothing matters very much, and very few things matter at all.
Attrib.

Ball, John (1338?–81) English priest and rebel

1 From the beginning all were created equal by nature, slavery was introduced through the unjust oppression of worthless men, against the will of God; for, if God had wanted to create slaves, he would surely have decided at the beginning of the world who was to be slave and who master.
Sermon, Blackheath, near London (1381)

2 When Adam delved and Eve span,
Who was then the gentleman?
Sermon on the day before the Peasants' Revolt (June 12, 1381), quoted in *The Later Middle Ages, 1272–1485* (George Holmes; 1962)

Ball, Lucille (Lucille Désirée Ball; 1911–89) U.S. film and television actor and comedian

1 The secret of staying young is to live honestly, eat slowly, and lie about your age.
Quoted in *Esquire* (February 1993)

2 I think knowing what you *cannot* do is more important than knowing what you can do. In fact, that's good taste.
Quoted in *The Real Story of Lucille Ball* (Eleanor Harris; 1954)

3 Luck? I don't know anything about luck. I've never banked on it, and I'm afraid of people who do. Luck to me is something else: hard work and realizing what is opportunity and what isn't.
Quoted in *The Real Story of Lucille Ball* (Eleanor Harris; 1954)

Balladur, Édouard (b.1929) Turkish-born French prime minister

1 I cannot believe that the great British people, in order to protect their identity, would now be cowering on the very island from which they set sail to travel the world.
May 1994. On British suspicion of the European Union. *Observer*, London (May 8, 1994), "Sayings of the Week"

Ballard, J. G. (James Graham Ballard; b.1930) Chinese-born British writer

1 In a totally sane society, madness is the only freedom.
Running Wild (1988)

Balliett, Whitney (b.1926) U.S. jazz critic

1 A critic is a bunch of biases held loosely together by a sense of taste.
Dinosaurs in the Morning (1962), introductory note

2 The Sound of Surprise
1959. Book title. Referring to jazz.

Balmain, Pierre (Pierre Alexandre Claudius Balmain; 1914–82) French couturier

1 The trick of wearing mink is to look as though you are wearing a cloth coat. The trick of wearing a cloth coat is to look as though you are wearing mink.
Observer, London (December 24, 1955)

Balzac, Honoré de (1799–1850) French writer

1 "I shan't take Your Lordship there," he said, "for that's the *queens*' quarters..." "Really!" said Lord Durham, "and what are they?" "That's the third sex, my lord."
Referring to homosexuality. *A Harlot High and Low* (1838–47), quoted in *A History of Gay Literature* (Gregory Woods; 1998)

2 Irony is the very substance of Providence.
Eugénie Grandet (1833)

3 Man is neither good nor bad; he is born with instincts and abilities.
La Comédie humaine (1842), vol. 1, foreword

4 Equality may perhaps be a right, but no power on earth can ever turn it into a fact.
La Duchesse de Langeais (1834)

5 There is no such thing as a great talent without great willpower.
La Muse du département (1843)

6 The response that man has the greatest difficulty in tolerating is pity, especially if he warrants it. Hatred is a tonic, it makes one live, it inspires vengeance; but pity kills, it makes our weakness weaker.
La Peau de chagrin (1831), ch. 1

7 Despotism accomplishes great things illegally; liberty doesn't even go to the trouble of accomplishing small things legally.
La Peau de chagrin (1831), ch. 3

8 No man should marry until he has studied anatomy and dissected at least one woman.
La Physiologie du mariage (1829)

9 Physically, a man is a man for a much longer time than a woman is a woman.
La Physiologie du mariage (1829)

10 The majority of husbands remind me of an orangutan trying to play the violin.
La Physiologie du mariage (1829)

11 I prefer thought to action, ideas to events, meditation to movement.
Louis Lambert (1832)

12 I should like one of these days to be so well known, so popular, so celebrated, so famous, that it would permit me...to break wind in society, and society would think it a most natural thing.
Attrib.

13 It is easier to be a lover than a husband, for the same reason that it is more difficult to show a ready wit all day long than to produce an occasional *bon mot*.
Attrib.

14 I am laughing to think what risks you take to try to find money in a desk by night where the legal owner can never find any by day.
Said on waking to find a robber in the room. Attrib.

Bambara, Toni Cade (1939–95) U.S. novelist, short-story writer, and educator

1 And what is religion, you might ask. It's a technology of living.
The Salt Eaters (1980)

2 Take away the miseries and you take away some folks' reason for living. Their conversation piece anyway.
The Salt Eaters (1980)

3 The dream is real, my friends. The failure to make it work is the unreality.
The Salt Eaters (1980)

4 The story is a piece of work. The novel is a way of life.
"What It Is I Think I'm Doing Anyhow," *The Writer on Her Work* (Janet Sternburg, ed.; 1981), vol. 1

Banchao (32–102) Chinese diplomat and military leader

1 How can one catch tiger cubs without entering the tiger's lair?
Quoted in *History of the Later Han* (Fan Ye; 398–445?)

Bancroft, George (1800–91) U.S. historian and diplomat

Quotations about Bancroft

1 He needs a great deal of cutting and pruning, but we think him an infant Hercules.
Ralph Waldo Emerson (1803–82) U.S. poet and essayist. Quoted in *New England Quarterly* (Michael Kraus; December 1934)

Quotations by Bancroft

2 It established a religion without a prelate, a government without a king.
Referring to Calvinism in Switzerland. *History of the United States* (1855), vol. 3

Banda, Hastings (Hastings Kamuzu Banda; 1902?–97) Malawian president

1 I wish I could bring Stonehenge to Nyasaland to show there was a time when Britain had a savage culture.
1963. *Observer,* London (March 10, 1963), "Sayings of the Week"

Bandyopadhyay, Pranab Indian poet and writer

1 Give the naked child a piece of cloth.
Viet Nam is bombed, Bangladesh bleeds,
rival nuclear revels rumble round the globe:
the child is innocent of them all.
Give him a piece of cloth.
"The Child," *The Voice of the Indian Poets* (Pranab Bandyopadhyay, ed.; 1975)

Banerjee, Sudhansu Mohan Indian civil servant and academic

1 A city of teeming millions and multi-millionaires.
of beggars, lepers, haves and have-nots
of dug-up trenches pavements and roads;
oh, is the pattern of developing Calcutta—
...a city battered, shattered and shivering,
maimed, mauled and man handled.
"Long Live Calcutta," *The Voice of the Indian Poets* (Pranab Bandyopadhyay, ed.; 1975)

Bangs, Edward (*fl.* 18th century) U.S. songwriter

1 Yankee Doodle came to town
Riding on a pony;
Stuck a feather in his cap
And called it Macaroni.
"Yankee Doodle; or Father's Return to Camp" (1775)

Banham, John, Sir (John Michael Middlecott Banham; b.1940) British business executive

1 As well as good academic records I look for people who've climbed mountains or been captain of the tiddlywinks team at university. People who other people will follow.
1990. Referring to recruitment. *Independent,* London (October 11, 1990)

Bankhead, Tallulah (Tallulah Brockman Bankhead; 1903–68) U.S. actor

Quotations about Bankhead

1 More of an act than an actress.
Anonymous

Quotations by Bankhead

2 It's one of the tragic ironies of the theater that only one man in it can count on steady work—the night watchman.
Tallulah (1952)

3 I have three phobias which, could I mute them, would make my life as slick as a sonnet, but as dull as ditch water: I hate to go to bed, I hate to get up, and I hate to be alone.
Tallulah (1952), ch. 1

4 I've been called many things, but never an intellectual.
Tallulah (1952), ch. 15

5 Dear God, please don't let me make a fool of myself tonight.
Prayer before a first night. Quoted in *No People Like Show People* (Maurice Zolotow; 1951)

6 I'm as pure as the driven slush.
Observer, London (February 24, 1957), "Sayings of the Week"

7 There is less in this than meets the eye.
Referring to the play *Aglavaine and Selysette* (1896) by Maurice Maeterlinck, said to Alexander Woollcott. "Capsule Criticism," *Shouts and Murmurs* (A. Woollcott; 1922)

8 I'll come and make love to you at five o'clock. If I'm late start without me.
Somerset Maugham (E. Morgan; 1980)

9 Cocaine isn't habit-forming—I should know I've been using it for years.
Tallulah (1952), ch. 4

10 The only thing I regret about my past life is the length of it. If I had my past life over again I'd make all the same mistakes only sooner.
Times, London (July 28, 1981)

11 Don't bother to thank me. I know what a perfectly ghastly season it's been for you Spanish dancers.
Said on dropping $50 into a tambourine held out by a Salvation Army collector. *With Malice Toward All* (Dorothy Hermann; 1982)

12 Only good girls keep diaries. Bad girls don't have the time.
Attrib.

13 I thought I told you to wait in the car.
When greeted by a former admirer after many years. Attrib.

Banks, Ernie (Ernest Banks; b.1931) U.S. baseball player

1 I like my players to be married and in debt. That's the way you motivate them.
April 11, 1976. Comment made as a minor league instructor for the Chicago Cubs. *New York Times*

2 It's a great day for a ballgame; let's play two.
1998. This catchphrase summed up his attitude to baseball. Attrib.

Banks, Iain (Iain Menzies Banks; b.1954) Scottish writer

1 That's my score to date. Three. I haven't killed anybody for years, and don't intend to ever again.
It was just a stage I was going through.
The opening words of the novel spoken by the narrator, a murderer. *The Wasp Factory* (1984)

Banks, Joseph, Sir (1743–1820) British naturalist

1 Upon the whole New Holland, tho' in every respect the most barren country I have seen, is not so bad that between the products of sea and land, a company of people who should have the misfortune of being shipwrecked upon it might not support themselves.
On leaving New South Wales, Australia. Banks was a participant in Captain Cook's circumnavigation of the world (1768–71). *Note* (August 1770)

Banks, Russell (b.1940) U.S. novelist

1 Facts do not make history; facts do not even make events...a fact is an isolated particle of experience, is reflected light without a source, planet with no sun, star without constellation, constellation beyond galaxy, galaxy outside the universe—fact is nothing.
Affliction (1989)

2 Identify with the victims and you become one yourself. Victims make lousy litigators.
The Sweet Hereafter (1991)

3 Significant pain isolates you...but under certain circumstances, it may be all you've got, and after great loss, you must use whatever's left, even if it isolates you from anyone else.
The Sweet Hereafter (1991)

Banks-Smith, Nancy British journalist

1 In my experience, if you have to keep the lavatory door shut by extending your left leg, it's modern architecture.
Guardian, London (February 20, 1979)

Banville, Théodore de (Étienne Claude Jean Baptiste Théodore Faullain de Banville; 1823–91) French poet and playwright

1 Poetic license. There's no such thing.
Petit traité de poésie française (1872)

Bara, Theda (Theodosia Goodman, "The Vamp"; 1890–1955) U.S. actor

1 There is a little bit of the vampire instinct in every woman.
Referring to her success in early movies. Remark (April 2, 1955)

Baraka, Imamu Amiri (originally Everett LeRoi Jones; b.1934) U.S. author, editor, playwright, and political activist

1 "Bad taste"...has been the one factor that has kept the best Negro music from slipping sterilely into the echo chambers of middle brow American culture.
1963. "Jazz and the White Critic," *Black Music* (1969), ch. 1

2 Jazz...and its sources were *secret* as far as the rest of America was concerned, in much the same sense that the actual life of the black man in America was secret to the white American.
1963. Referring to the emergence of jazz in the United States at the turn of the 20th century. "Jazz and the White Critic," *Black Music* (1969), ch. 1

3 There are so many hobbyists, social workers, and men-whose-best-friends-are-X's connected in one way or another with the music...But what can you say of a society that sends Benny Goodman and Robert Frost to Russia as cultural savants?
1962. Referring to jazz. "Present Perfect (Cecil Taylor)," *Black Music* (1969), ch. 15

4 Knowing how to play an instrument is the barest superficiality if one is thinking of becoming a musician. It is the ideas that one utilizes *instinctively* that determine the degree of profundity any artist reaches.
1961. "The Jazz Avant-Garde," *Black Music* (1969), ch. 10

5 "Culture" is simply how one lives, and is connected to history by habit.
Blues People: Negro Music in White America (1963)

6 If you are black, the only roads into the mainland of American life are through subservience, cowardice, and loss of manhood. These are the white man's roads. It is time we built our own.
"'Black' is a Country," *Home: Social Essays* (1966)

7 If we live all our lives under lies, it becomes difficult to see *anything* if it does not have anything to do with these lies.
"Cuba Libre," *Home: Social Essays* (1966)

8 God is man idealized.
"The Legacy of Malcolm X, and the Coming of the Black Nation," *Home: Social Essays* (1966)

9 The landscape should belong to the people who see it all the time.
"The Legacy of Malcolm X, and the Coming of the Black Nation," *Home: Social Essays* (1966)

10 A man is either free or he is not. There cannot be any apprenticeship for freedom.
"Tokenism: 300 Years for Five Cents," *Home: Social Essays* (1966)

11 A rich man told me recently that a liberal is a man who tells other people what to do with their money.
"Tokenism: 300 Years for Five Cents," *Home: Social Essays* (1966)

12 God has been replaced, as he has all over the West, with respectability and air conditioning.
"What does Nonviolence Mean?," *Home: Social Essays* (1966)

13 We'll pretend the people cannot see you. That is, the citizens. And that you are free of your own history. And I am free of my history. We'll pretend that we are both anonymous beauties smashing along through the city's entrails.
The Dutchman (1964), Scene 1

14 Plantations didn't have any wire. Plantations were big open whitewashed places like heaven, and everybody on 'em was grooved to be there. Just strummin' and hummin' all day. And that's how the blues was born.
The Dutchman (1964), Scene 2

Barbellion, W. N. P. (Bruce Frederick Cummings; 1889–1919) British naturalist

1 How I hate the man who talks about the "brute creation", with an ugly emphasis on *brute*. Only Christians are capable of it.
June 22, 1910. *Journal of a Disappointed Man* (1919)

2 In the enfranchised mind of the scientific naturalist, the usual feelings of repugnance simply do not exist. Curiosity conquers prejudice.
August 16, 1915. *Journal of a Disappointed Man* (1919)

3 Palæontology...has relieved me of the harassing desire to live, I feel content to live dangerously, indifferent to my fate...For nothing can alter the fact that I *have* lived; I *have been I*, if for ever so short a time.
December 22, 1912. *Journal of a Disappointed Man* (1919)

Barber, Samuel (1910–81) U.S. composer

1 I have always believed that I need a circumference of silence. As to what happens when I compose, I really haven't the faintest idea.
Quoted in *American Composers* (David Ewen; 1982)

Barbey d'Aurevilly, Jules-Amédée (1808–89) French novelist and critic

1 The crimes of extreme civilization are certainly worse than those of extreme barbarism.
"La vengeance d'une femme," *Les Diaboliques* (1874)

2 Happy beings are grave. They carry their happiness cautiously, as they would a glass filled to the brim which the slightest movement could cause to spill over, or break.
"Le bonheur dans le crime," *Les Diaboliques* (1874)

3 Equality, this chimera of the peasantry, exists only among noblemen.
"Le dessous de cartes," *Les Diaboliques* (1874)

4 Passions are less mischievous than boredom, for passions tend to diminish, boredom to increase.
Une vieille maîtresse (1851), ch. 2

Barbour, John (also John Barbere or John Barbier; 1316?–95) Scottish poet and cleric

1 Storys to rede ar delitabill,
Suppos that thai be nocht bot fabill.
The Brus (1375), bk. 1

2 A! fredome is a noble thing!
Fredome mayse man to haiff liking.
The Brus (1375), bk. 1

Bardot, Brigitte (originally Camille Javal; b.1934) French film actor and animal-rights activist

1 We must fight against animal overpopulation. I call on all cat and dog owners to have their pets sterilized.
France-Soir (June 1991)

2 I gave my beauty and my youth to men. I am going to give my wisdom and experience to animals.
Referring to her animal-rights campaign. *Guardian*, London (1987)

3 It is better to be unfaithful than faithful without wanting to be.
Observer, London (February 18, 1968), "Sayings of the Week"

Barger, Sonny U.S. Hell's Angel

1 I'm no peace-creep in any sense of the word. If a man don't want to be my friend, I'm going to hurt him and he's going to hurt me.
1969. Referring to the killing of an audience member by Hell's Angels at a Rolling Stones concert in Altamont, California. Quoted in *Rock 'n' Roll Babylon* (Gary Herman; 1994)

Barham, Richard Harris (pen name Thomas Ingoldsby; 1788–1845) British cleric and humorist

1 They were a little less than "kin", and rather more than "kind".
Nelly Cook's observation on the canon and his "niece." "Nell Cook," *The Ingoldsby Legends* (1840)

2 A servant's too often a negligent elf;
If it's business of consequence, DO IT YOURSELF!
"The Ingoldsby Penance!—Moral," *The Ingoldsby Legends* (1842)

Baring, Maurice (1874–1945) British writer and journalist

1 If you would know what the Lord God thinks of money, you have only to look at those to whom He gives it.
Attrib.

Baring-Gould, Sabine (1834–1924) British author, cleric, and hymnwriter

1 Onward, Christian soldiers,
Marching as to war,
With the Cross of Jesus
Going on before.
"Onward Christian Soldiers" (1864)

2 Now the day is over,
Night is drawing nigh,
Shadows of the evening
Steal across the sky.
"The Evening Hymn" (1865)

3 Through the night of doubt and sorrow
Onward goes the pilgrim band,
Singing songs of expectation,
Marching to the Promised Land.
Translated from the Danish of B. S. Ingermann (1789–1862). "Through the Night of Doubt and Sorrow" (1867)

Barker, George (George Granville Barker; 1913–91) British poet

1 Outside the huge negations pass

Like whirlwinds writing on the grass
Inscriptions teaching us that all
The lessons are ephemeral.
"Verses for the Sixtieth Birthday of T. S. Eliot" (1948)

Barker, Howard (b.1946) British playwright

1 A characteristic of Thatcherism is a reversion to the idea of nature, irreparable in its forces. Poverty and sickness are seen as part of an order.
Times, London (January 3, 1990)

2 The artist who makes himself accessible is self-destructive.
Times, London (January 3, 1990)

3 The complexities of poetry are destroyed by the media. In the theatre, spoken language can be defended and expanded.
Times, London (January 3, 1990)

Barker, Ronnie (Ronald William George Barker; b.1929) British comic actor

1 The marvellous thing about a joke with a double meaning is that it can only mean one thing.
"Daddie's Sauce," *Sauce* (1977)

Barlow, Joel (1754–1812) U.S. poet and diplomat

1 I sing the sweets I know, the charms I feel,
My morning incense, and my evening meal,
The sweets of Hasty-Pudding.
Come, dear bowl,
Glide o'er my palate, and inspire my soul.
Hasty-pudding is a dish of boiled corn. "Hasty-Pudding" (1796)

Barnard, Charlotte Alington (pen name "Claribel"; 1830–69) British poet and composer

1 I cannot sing the old songs
I sang long years ago,
For heart and voice would fail me,
And foolish tears would flow.
"The Old Songs," *Fireside Thoughts* (1865)

Barnard, Christiaan (Christiaan Neethling Barnard; b.1922) South African surgeon

1 The prime goal is to alleviate suffering, and not to prolong life. And if your treatment does not alleviate suffering, but only prolongs life, that treatment should be stopped.
Attrib.

Barnes, Clive (Clive Alexander Barnes; b.1927) British-born theater and ballet critic

1 This is the kind of show that gives pornography a bad name.
Review of *Oh, Calcutta!* Attrib.

Barnes, Djuna (pen name Linda Steptoe; 1892–1982) U.S. writer and illustrator

1 Life, the permission to know death.
Nightwood (1936)

2 No man needs curing of his individual sickness; his universal malady is what he should look to.
Nightwood (1936)

3 Sanity is an unknown room: a known room is always smaller than an unknown.
Nightwood (1936)

4 She wanted to be the reason for everything and so was the cause of nothing.
Nightwood (1936)

5 Those who love everything are despised by everything, as those that love a city in its profoundest sense, become the shame of that city...their good is incommunicable, outwitted, being the rudiment of a life that has developed, as in a man's body are evidences of lost needs.
Nightwood (1936)

6 When a Jew dies on a Christian bosom he dies impaled.
Nightwood (1936)

7 Nicknames...give away the whole drama of man. They fall into many classes; the three most current are: those we invent to make a person what he should be...those we invent to make him appear what he is not...and those we invent to more tightly wrap him in that which he is.
"The Psychology of Nicknames," *Ryder* (1928), ch. 29

Barnes, Ernest William (1874–1953) British prelate and mathematician

1 From the point of view of sexual morality the aeroplane is valuable in war in that it destroys men and women in equal numbers.
Rise of Christianity (1947)

Barnes, Julian (Julian Patrick Barnes; b.1946) British writer

1 I wonder why happiness is despised nowadays: dismissively confused with comfort or complacency, judged an enemy of social—even technological—progress.
Metroland (1980)

2 One cathedral is worth a hundred theologians capable of proving the existence of God by logic.
Staring at the Sun (1988)

3 The mind longs for certainty, and perhaps it longs most for a certainty which clubs it down. What the mind can understand, what it can ploddingly prove and approve, might be what it most despises.
Staring at the Sun (1988)

4 You grew old first not in your own eyes, but in other people's eyes; then, slowly, you agreed with their opinion of you.
Staring at the Sun (1988)

5 Love is just a system for getting someone to call you darling after sex.
Talking It Over (1991), ch. 16

Barnes, Peter (b.1931) British playwright and director

1 I know I am God because when I pray to him I find I'm talking to myself.
The Ruling Class (1968)

Barnes, Stuart British rugby player

1 I don't think sportsmen can use "sports and politics don't mix" as an excuse. I didn't want to represent 50 million English people touring a country where the regime was abhorrent.
Referring to his refusal to tour South Africa in 1984. *Independent,* London (May 11, 1994)

Barnes, William (1801–86) British poet, philologist, and cleric

1 My love is the maïd ov all maïdens,
Though all maïd be comely.
"In the Spring," *Pentridge by the River* (1859)

Barnevik, Percy U.S. business executive

1 I believe you can go into any traditionally centralized corporation and cut its headquarters staff by 90 percent in one year.
Interview, *Harvard Business Review* (March–April, 1991)

2 We can't wait for the region to stabilize. We want to create a home market there now.
Referring to the post-Communist countries of Eastern Europe. Quoted in *Fortune* (May 16, 1994)

3 You shouldn't mix up the long-term business opportunities with the occasional shoot-out. These things will happen.
Said after the October 1993 uprising against the government of President Boris Yeltsin, when conservative forces occupied Russia's Parliament. Quoted in *Fortune* (November 1, 1993)

Barney, Natalie Clifford (1876–1972) U.S. writer and literary hostess

1 If we keep an open mind, too much is likely to fall into it.
"Adam" (1962), no. 299

2 Why grab possessions like thieves, or divide them like socialists, when you can ignore them like wise men?
"Adam" (1962), no. 299

Barney, Sydney D. British tailor and gentleman's outfitter

1 Slide fasteners are recommended for all trousers. Fly fronts with buttons and buttonholes not only protrude but create weal, friction, loss of buttons and encourage a degree of forgetfulness.
Clothes and the Man: A Guide to Correct Dress for All Occasions (1962), ch. 6

Barnfield, Richard (1574–1627) English poet

1 The waters were his winding sheet, the sea was made his tomb;
Yet for his fame the ocean sea, was not sufficient room.
Referring to Sir John Hawkins (1532–95), second in command to Drake on the expedition to the Caribbean (1567). He died at sea off Puerto Rico. "Epitaph on Hawkins" (1595)

2 If music and sweet poetry agree,
As they must needs (the sister and the brother),
Then must the love be great 'twixt thee and me,
Because thou lov'st the one, and I the other.
"To His Friend Master R.L..." (1598?), quoted in *The Penguin Book of Elizabethan Verse* (Edward Lucie-Smith, ed.; 1965)

3 Love I did the fairest boy,
That these fields did ere enjoy.
"Sonnet 12," *A History of Gay Literature* (Gregory Woods; 1998)

4 My flocks feed not,
My ewes breed not,
My rams speed not,
All is amiss.
Love is dying,
Faith's defying,
Heart's denying,
Causer of this.
"The Unknown Shepherd's Complaint," *England's Helicon* (Nicholas Ling, ed.; 1600)

5 As it fell upon a day
In the merry month of May...
Everything did banish moan,
Save the nightingale alone
She, poor bird, as all forlorn,
Lean'd her breast up-till a thorn,
And there sung the dolefull'st ditty
That to hear it was great pity.
Also attributed to William Shakespeare. "An Ode: Address to the Nightingale," *Poems in Divers Humours* (1598)

6 If it be sin to love a lovely lad,
Oh then sin I, for whom my soul is sad.
"The Affectionate Shepherd," *The Affectionate Shepherd* (1594), quoted in *New Oxford Book of Sixteenth-Century Verse* (Emrys Jones, ed.; 1991)

7 Scarce had the morning star hid from the light
Heaven's crimson canopy with stars bespangled,
But I began to rue th'unhappy sight
Of that fair boy that had my heart entangled;
Cursing the time, the place, the sense, the sin;
I came, I saw, I viewed, I slipped in.
"The Affectionate Shepherd," *The Affectionate Shepherd* (1594), quoted in *New Oxford Book of Sixteenth-Century Verse* (Emrys Jones, ed.; 1991)

8 Sometimes I wish that I his pillow were,
So might I steale a kisse, and yet not seene,
So might I gaze upon his sleeping eine,
Although I did it with a panting feare.
"Sonnet 8," *The Name of Love* (Michael Lassell, ed.; 1995)

Barnum, P. T. (Phineas Taylor Barnum; 1810–91) U.S. impresario

1 There's a sucker born every minute.
Attrib.

2 How were the receipts today in Madison Square Garden?
1891. Last words. Attrib.

Baroja, Pío (1872–1956) Basque writer

1 Sublime moments, heroic acts, are rather the deeds of an exalted intelligence than of the will.
The Quest (Isaac Goldberg, tr.; 1922)

2 Justice is a human illusion: essentially everything is destruction and creation.
The Tree of Knowledge (1911)

3 One may be quixotic in an anomalous case, but to be so as a general rule is absurd.
The Tree of Knowledge (1911)

4 An indifferent spectator like myself watches the hyena, the spider, and the tree and understands them; a man with a sense of justice shoots the hyena, crushes the spider under his foot, and sits down under the shade of the tree, imagining that he has done a good deed.
Said by Iturrioz. *The Tree of Knowledge* (1911)

5 In the novel as in literature as a whole, the problem is how to invent; above all how to invent characters who have life.
Quoted in *The Spanish Avant-Garde* (Derek Harris; 1995)

Barrault, Jean-Louis (1910–94) French actor, director, and producer

1 Theater is the first serum to be invented by mankind against that malady, anguish.
1959. "Comment le théâtre naît en nous," *Nouvelles réflexions sur le théâtre* (Joseph Chiari, tr.; 1961)

Barrès, Maurice (Auguste Maurice Barrès; 1862–1923) French politician and novelist

1 The politician is an acrobat. He keeps his balance by saying the opposite of what he does.
Mes Cahiers 1896–1963 (1963)

Barrie, J. M., Sir (James Matthew Barrie; 1860–1937) British playwright and novelist

1 God gave us our memories so that we might have roses in December.
Rectorial address, St. Andrews University (May 3, 1922)

2 It is not real work unless you would rather be doing something else.
Rectorial address, St. Andrews University (May 3, 1922)

3 Never ascribe to an opponent motives meaner than your own.
Rectorial address, St. Andrews University (May 3, 1922)

4 Times have changed since a certain author was executed for murdering his publisher. They say that when the author was on the scaffold he said goodbye to the minister and to the reporters, and then he saw some publishers sitting in the front row below, and to them he did not say goodbye. He said instead, "I'll see you later."
Speech, New York (November 5, 1896)

5 The Elizabethan age might be better named the beginning of the smoking era.
My Lady Nicotine (1890)

6 I know I'm not clever but I'm always right.
Peter Pan (1904)

7 Second to the right, and straight on till morning.
Peter's directions, navigating by the stars, for how to get to Never Never Land. *Peter Pan* (1904)

8 Every time a child says "I don't believe in fairies" there is a little fairy somewhere that falls down dead.
Peter Pan (1904), Act 1

9 When the first baby laughed for the first time, the laugh broke into a thousand pieces and they all went skipping about, and that was the beginning of fairies.
Peter Pan (1904), Act 1

10 To die will be an awfully big adventure.
Peter Pan (1904), Act 3

11 Do you believe in fairies? Say quick that you believe. If you believe, clap your hands!
Peter Pan (1904), Act 4

12 What is algebra exactly; is it those three-cornered things?
Quality Street (1901), Act 2, Scene 1

13 Oh the gladness of her gladness when she's glad,
And the sadness of her sadness when she's sad,
But the gladness of her gladness
And the sadness of her sadness
Are as nothing, Charles,
To the badness of her badness when she's bad.
Rosalind (1914)

14 His Lordship may compel us to be equal upstairs, but there will never be equality in the servants' hall.
The Admirable Crichton (1902), Act 1

15 It's grand, and ye canna expect to be baith grand and comfortable.
The Little Minister (1891), ch. 10

16 One's religion is whatever he is most interested in, and yours is Success.
The Twelve-Pound Look (1914)

17 It's a sort of bloom on a woman. If you have it, you don't need to have anything else; and if you don't have it, it doesn't much matter what else you have.
Referring to charm. *What Every Woman Knows* (1908), Act 1

18 You've forgotten the grandest moral attribute of a Scotsman, Maggie, that he'll do nothing which might damage his career.
What Every Woman Knows (1908), Act 2

19 I have always found that the man whose second thoughts are good is worth watching.
What Every Woman Knows (1908), Act 3

20 Every man who is high up likes to feel that he has done it himself; and the wife smiles, and lets it go at that. It's our only joke. Every woman knows that.
What Every Woman Knows (1908), Act 4

21 It is all very well to be able to write books, but can you waggle your ears?
Said to H. G. Wells. *Barrie: The Story of A Genius* (J. A. Hammerton; 1929)

22 Some of my plays peter out, and some pan out.
Attrib.

Barrow, Isaac (1630–77) English mathematician and cleric

1 Smiling always with a never fading serenity of countenance, and flourishing in an immortal youth.
"Duty of Thanksgiving," *The Works of the Learned Isaac Barrow* (Rev. Dr. Tillotson, ed.; 1683), vol. 1

Barry, Dave (b.1947) U.S. humorist

1 The sink is the great symbol of the bloodiness of family life. All life is bad, but family life is worse.
As Far as You Can Go (1963), pt. I, ch. 1

2 Americans would rather live next to a pervert heroin addict Communist pornographer than a person with an unkempt lawn.
The Taming of the Screw (1983)

3 I believe that if God had wanted us to share our homes with insects, He would not have made them so unattractive.
The Taming of the Screw (1983)

4 Interior decorators are people who have spent years studying the principles of color, shape, and texture, until they have reached the point where they would rather die than agree with an ordinary person such as yourself on a matter of taste.
The Taming of the Screw (1983)

Barrymore, Ethel (originally Ethel May Blythe; 1879–1959) U.S. actor

1 The people are unreal. The flowers are unreal, they don't smell. The fruit is unreal, it doesn't taste of anything. The whole place is a glaring, gaudy, nightmarish set, built up in the desert.
1923. Referring to Hollywood. Quoted in *Filmgoer's Book of Quotes* (Leslie Halliwell; 1973)

2 For an actress to be a success she must have the face of Venus, the brains of Minerva, the grace of Terpsichore, the memory of Macaulay, the figure of Juno, and the hide of a rhinoceros.
The Theater in the Fifties (George Jean Nathan; 1953)

Barrymore, John (originally John Blythe, "The Great Profile"; 1882–1942) U.S. actor

1 Audiences? No, the plural is impossible. Whether it be in Butte, Montana, or Broadway, it's an audience. The same great hulking monster with four thousand eyes and forty thousand teeth.
Letter to playwright Ashton Stevens (April 1906), quoted in *Good Night, Sweet Prince* (Gene Fowler; 1943)

Barrymore, Lionel (originally Lionel Blythe; 1878–1954) U.S. actor

Quotations about Barrymore

1 Lionel Barrymore first played my grandfather, later my father, and finally, he played my husband. If he'd lived, I'm sure I'd have played his mother. That's the way it is in Hollywood. The men get younger and the women get older.
Lillian Gish (1893–1993) U.S. actor. Quoted in *Film Yearbook 1984* (1984)

Quotations by Barrymore

2 I've played everything but the harp.
When asked what words he would like engraved on his tombstone. Attrib.

Bart, Lionel (1930–1999) British composer and lyricist

1 Got myself a crying, walking, sleeping, talking, living doll.
Song lyric. The song was the first British top twenty hit for Cliff Richard. "Living Doll" (1959)

Barth, Karl (1886–1968) Swiss theologian

1 Men have never been good, they are not good, they never will be good.
Time (April 12, 1954)

2 The dreams are over, the constructions have been shattered, with which Christian Germans in particular have distorted and ultimately denied the gospel for so long.
1945. Letter to German theologians in prisoner-of-war camps. Quoted in "Modern German History and Protestant Theology," *A Requiem for Hitler* (Klaus Scholder; 1989)

Barthelme, Donald (1931–89) U.S. novelist and short-story writer

1 The distinction between children and adults...is at bottom a specious one, I feel. There are only individual egos, crazy for love.
"Me and Mrs. Mandible," *Come Back, Dr. Caligari* (1964)

2 Doubt is a necessary precondition to meaningful action. Fear is the great mover in the end.
"The Rise of Capitalism," *Sadness* (1972)

3 Endings are elusive, middles are nowhere to be found, but worst of all is to begin, to begin, to begin.
"The Dolt," *Unspeakable Practices, Unnatural Acts* (1968)

Barthes, Roland (1915–80) French philosopher and writer

1 It would seem that we are condemned for some time always to speak *excessively* of reality.
Mythologies (1957)

2 I think that cars today are almost the exact equivalent of the great Gothic cathedrals...the supreme creation of an era, conceived with passion by unknown artists.
"La nouvelle Citroën," *Mythologies* (1957)

3 Our literature is characterized by the pitiless divorce between the producer of the text and its user, between its owner and its customer, between its author and its reader.
S/Z (Richard Miller, tr.; 1990)

4 We know now that a text consists not of a line of words, releasing a single "theological" meaning (the "message" of the Author-God), but of a multi-dimensional space in which are married and contested several writings.
Posthumously published. *The Rustle of Language* (Richard Howard, tr.; 1984)

Bartholomaeus Anglicus ("Bartholomew the Englishman"; *fl.* 1230–50) English theologian and friar

1 Melancholy is a humour, boystrous & thycke, and is bredde of troubled drastes of blode; & hath his name of melon—that

is black, & colim, that is humor: wherupon it is called melancolia, as it were a black humor.
De Proprietatibus Rerum (1483)

Bartlett, Christopher A. (b.1943) U.S. business and management writer

1 A company's ability to innovate is rapidly becoming the primary source of competitive success.
Managing Across Borders: The Transnational Solution (co-written with Sumantra Ghoshal; 1989)

2 By legitimizing the diversity of a multidimensional organization, management creates the core of an organization flexible enough to respond to environmental change.
Managing Across Borders: The Transnational Solution (co-written with Sumantra Ghoshal; 1989)

3 The strategic challenge for the transnational corporation is the simultaneous achievement of efficiency, flexible responsiveness, and worldwide learning and innovation.
Managing Across Borders: The Transnational Solution (co-written with Sumantra Ghoshal; 1989)

Barton, Bruce (Bruce Fairchild Barton; 1886–1967) U.S. business executive, author, and politician

1 What we ought to do is to send up a flight of a thousand B-29s and drop a million Sears Roebuck catalogs all over Russia.
Remark (1940s), quoted in *America* (Alistair Cooke; 1973)

2 Jesus picked up twelve men from the bottom ranks of business and forged them into an organization that conquered the world.
The Man Nobody Knows: A Discovery of the Real Jesus (1925)

3 When you're through changing, you're through.
Attrib.

Barton, Clara (Clarissa Harlowe Barton; 1821–1912) U.S. humanitarian and writer

1 An institution or reform movement that is not selfish, must originate in the recognition of some evil that is adding to the sum of human suffering...I suppose it is a philanthropic movement to try to reverse the process.
The Red Cross (1898)

2 It is wise statesmanship that suggests that in time of peace we must prepare for war, and it is no less a wise benevolence that makes preparation in the hour of peace for assuaging the ills that are sure to accompany war.
Possibly referring to the words of the 3rd-century military writer, Vegetius Renatus: "Let him who desires peace be prepared for war." (Compare Aristotle: "We make war that we may live in peace," and an old inscription in a Venetian armory: "Happy is that city which in time of peace thinks of war.") *The Red Cross* (1898)

Barton, John (b.1928) British theater director

1 It's the fusion of poetry, truth and character that is refined in Shakespeare.
Referring to William Shakespeare. *Playing Shakespeare* (1995)

Baruch, Bernard Mannes (1870–1965) U.S. financier, statesman, and philanthropist

1 There are no such things as incurable, there are only things for which man has not found a cure.
Speech, President's Committee on Employment of the Physically Handicapped (April 30, 1954)

2 Let us not be deceived—we are today in the midst of a cold war.
Speech to the South Carolina legislature (April 16, 1947)

3 I'm not smart. I try to observe. Millions saw the apple fall but Newton was the one who asked why.
New York Post (June 24, 1965)

4 I will never be an old man. To me, old age is always fifteen years older than I am.
Observer, London (August 21, 1955), "Sayings of the Week"

5 We can't always cross a bridge until we come to it; but I always like to lay down a pontoon ahead of time.
Quoted in *The Home Book of Humorous Quotations* (A. K. Adams, ed.; 1969)

6 A speculator is a man who observes the future, and acts before it occurs.
Attrib.

Baryshnikov, Mikhail (Mikhail Nikolayevich Baryshnikov; b.1948) Latvian-born U.S. dancer

1 He was desperate to catch up...Because he had so little training, he had lots of technical problems and this made him furious.
Referring to Rudolf Nureyev's late start, at age 17. Reported in "Triumph of a Star's Charisma," *Times*, London (Nadine Meisner; April 8, 1998)

Barzani, Mustafa (1903–79) Kurdish political and military leader

1 Our movement and people are being destroyed in an unbelievable way with silence from everyone.
Message to Henry Kissinger, U.S. Secretary of State (March 10, 1975), quoted in *Kurdistan* (Jonathan C. Randal; 1998)

2 Have the Kurdish people committed such crimes that every nation in the world should be against them?
Remark (1975), quoted in *Kurdistan* (Jonathan C. Randal; 1998)

Barzun, Jacques (Jacques Martin Barzun; b.1907) French-born U.S. writer, cultural critic, and educator

1 All periods of history show a strain of madness and all are chaotic.
Lecture at Columbia University, New York (January 29, 1973)

2 There can be no history without the gift of knowing what to leave out.
"History: The Muse and Her Doctors," *American Historical Review* (February 1972)

3 What, then, are the criteria of history? There are four: Narrative, Chronology, Concreteness, and Memorability.
"History: The Muse and Her Doctors," *American Historical Review* (February 1972)

4 Whereas there is one natural science, there are endless histories, overlapping and contradicting, argumentative and detached,

biased and ambiguous. It is in these very ways that they truly render the past of mankind.
"History: The Muse and Her Doctors," *American Historical Review* (February 1972)

5 History, like a vast river, propels logs, vegetation, rafts, and debris; it is full of live and dead things, some destined for resurrection; it mingles many waters and holds in solution invisible substances stolen from distant soils.
Clio and the Doctors (1974)

6 That is the triumph of history—truth absolute is not at hand; the original with which to match the copy does not exist.
Clio and the Doctors (1974)

7 Whoever wants to know the heart and mind of America had better learn baseball, the rules and realities of the game—and do it by watching first some high school or small-town teams.
God's Country and Mine (1954)

8 The intellectuals' chief cause of anguish are one another's works.
The House of Intellect (1959)

Bashkirtseff, Marie (Marie Konstantinovna Bashkirtseff; 1860–84) Russian painter and diarist

1 If I had been born a man, I would have conquered Europe. As I was born a woman, I exhausted my energy in tirades against fate, and in eccentricities.
The Journal of a Young Artist (June 25, 1884)

Basie, Count (William Basie; 1904–84) U.S. jazz musician and bandleader

1 I don't think that a band can really swing on just a kick-off, you know; I think you've got to set the tempo first. If you can do it the other way, that's something else...Anyway we do it our way.
Referring to jazz. Quoted in *Count Basie* (Alun Morgan; 1984)

2 I love the road. It may be a little tough on my wife and kid, never seeing their father and husband until Birdland comes around, but it has been and will remain a great thrill and challenge to me.
Referring to touring. Quoted in *Count Basie* (Alun Morgan; 1984)

Basil the Great, Saint (329?–379?) Greek father of the Church

1 Drunkenness, the ruin of reason, the destruction of strength, premature old age, momentary death.
Homilies (4th century), no. 14, ch. 7

Bastard, Thomas (1566–1618) English poet and cleric

1 Age is deformed, youth unkind,
We scorn their bodies, they our mind.
Chrestoleros (1598), bk. 7, epigram 9

Bateman, Edgar (*fl.* 1894) British songwriter

1 Wiv a ladder and some glasses,
You could see to 'Ackney Marshes,
If it wasn't for the 'ouses in between.
"If it wasn't for the 'ouses in between" (co-written with George Le Brunn; 1894)

Bates, Katharine Lee (1859–1929) U.S. writer and educator

1 O beautiful for spacious skies,
For amber waves of grain,
For purple mountain majesties
Above the fruited plain!
America! America!
God shed His grace on thee
And crown thy good with brotherhood
From sea to shining sea!
"America the Beautiful" (1893)

Bateson, Dingwall, Sir (Dingwall Latham Bateson; 1898–1967) British lawyer

1 A solicitor is a man who calls in a person he doesn't know to sign a contract he hasn't seen to buy property he doesn't want with money he hasn't got.
Attrib.

Bateson, Gregory (1904–80) British-born U.S. anthropologist

1 In the transmission of human culture, people always attempt to replicate, to pass on to the next generation the skills and values of the parents, but the attempt always fails because cultural transmission is geared to learning, not DNA.
Mind and Nature (1978)

Battiscombe, Georgina (originally Esther Georgina Harwood; b.1905) British author

1 A picnic is the Englishman's grand gesture, his final defiance flung in the face of fate. No climate in the world is less propitious to picnics than the climate of England, yet with a recklessness which is almost sublime the English rush out of doors to eat a meal on every possible and impossible occasion.
English Picnics (1951)

Baudelaire, Charles (Charles Pierre Baudelaire; 1821–67) French poet

1 A man who drinks only water has a secret to hide from his fellows.
Du vin et du haschisch (1851)

2 Sexuality is the lyricism of the masses.
Journaux intimes (1887)

3 Whenever you receive a letter from a creditor write fifty lines upon some extraterrestrial subject, and you will be saved.
Journaux intimes (1887)

4 God is the only being who, to rule, doesn't even need to exist.
"Fusées," *Journaux intimes* (1887)

5 No task is a long one but the task on which one dare not start. It becomes a nightmare.
"Mon Coeur mis à nu," *Journaux intimes* (1887)

6 I am bored with France, particularly as everybody here resembles Voltaire.
"Mon Coeur mis à nu," *Journaux intimes* (1887)

7 One shouldn't believe that the Devil only tempts men of genius.
"Mon Coeur mis à nu," *Journaux intimes* (1887)

8 There are in every man, at every hour, two simultaneous postulations, one towards God, the other towards Satan.
"Mon Coeur mis à nu," *Journaux intimes* (1887)

9 There exist only three beings worthy of respect: the priest, the soldier, the poet. To know, to kill, to create.
"Mon Coeur mis à nu," *Journaux intimes* (1887)

10 To be a great man and a saint to oneself, that is the one important thing.
"Mon Coeur mis à nu," *Journaux intimes* (1887)

11 Hypocrite reader—my likeness—my brother.
"Au Lecteur," *Les Fleurs du mal* (1857)

12 The poet is like the prince of the clouds,
Who rides out the tempest and laughs at the archer.
But when he is exiled on the ground, amidst the clamor,
His giant's wings prevent him from walking.
"L'Albatross," *Les Fleurs du mal* (1857)

13 Everything there is nothing but order and beauty,
Luxury, peace and sensual indulgence.
"L'invitation au voyage," *Les Fleurs du mal* (1857), refrain

14 Here is the charming evening, the criminal's friend;
It comes like an accomplice, with stealthy tread.
"Tableaux parisiens," *Les Fleurs du mal* (1857), no. 95, "Le Crépuscule du soir"

15 What do I care that you are good? Be beautiful! and be sad!
"Madrigal triste," *Nouvelles fleurs du mal* (1868), st.1

16 I have more memories than if I were a thousand years old.
Spleen (1869)

Baudouin I, King of the Belgians (1930–93) Belgian monarch

1 It takes twenty years or more of peace to make a man, it takes only twenty seconds of war to destroy him.
Address to U.S. Congress (May 12, 1959)

Baudrillard, Jean French cultural critic

1 Executives are like joggers. If you stop a jogger, he goes on running on the spot. If you drag an executive away from business, he goes on running on the spot, pawing the ground, talking business.
Cool Memories (1987)

Baum, L. Frank (Lyman Frank Baum; 1856–1919) U.S. writer

1 This doesn't look like Kansas, Toto.
Dorothy's remark to her dog Toto on first arriving in the land of Oz, later made famous by the hugely successful musical film *The Wizard of Oz* (1939), starring Judy Garland. *The Wonderful Wizard of Oz* (1900)

2 The road to the City of Emeralds is paved with yellow brick.
The sentence in the original novel that led to the song "Follow the Yellow Brick Road" in the film, *The Wizard of Oz* (1939). *The Wonderful Wizard of Oz* (1900), ch. 2

3 I'm really a very good man; but I'm a very bad Wizard.
Said by the Wizard of Oz. *The Wonderful Wizard of Oz* (1900), ch. 15

Baum, Vicki (originally Hedvig Baum; 1888–1960) Austrian-born U.S. writer

1 Marriage always demands the greatest understanding of the art of insincerity possible between two human beings.
And Life Goes On (1932)

2 To be a Jew is a destiny.
And Life Goes On (1932)

3 A woman who is loved always has success.
Grand Hotel (1931)

Bax, Arnold, Sir (Arnold Edward Trevor Bax; 1883–1953) British composer

1 One should try everything once, except incest and folk-dancing.
Farewell to My Youth (1943)

Baxter, Richard (1615–91) English cleric and scholar

1 I preached as never sure to preach again,
And as a dying man to dying men.
Love Breathing Thank and Praise (1681)

Bayle, Pierre (1647–1706) French philosopher and critic

1 If an historian were to relate truthfully all the crimes, weaknesses, and disorders of mankind, his readers would take his work for satire rather than for history.
Historical and Critical Dictionary (1697)

Bayly, Thomas Haynes (1797–1839) British writer

1 It was a dream of perfect bliss,
Too beautiful to last.
"It Was a Dream," *Songs, Ballads, and Other Poems* (1844), st. 1, ll. 1–2

2 Tell me the tales that to me were so dear,
Long, long ago, long, long ago.
"Long, Long Ago," *Songs, Ballads, and Other Poems* (1844), st. 1, ll. 1–2

3 She wore a wreath of roses,
The night that first we met.
"She Wore a Wreath of Roses," *Songs, Ballads, and Other Poems* (1844)

4 Friends depart, and memory takes them
To her caverns, pure and deep.
"Teach Me To Forget," *Songs, Ballads, and Other Poems* (1844), st. 1, ll. 1–2

5 Fear not, but trust in Providence,
Wherever thou may'st be.
"The Pilot," *Songs, Ballads, and Other Poems* (1844)

6 The rose that all are praising
Is not the rose for me.
"The Rose That All Are Praising," *Songs, Ballads, and Other Poems* (1844)

7 Why don't the men propose, Mamma?
Why don't the men propose?
"Why Don't the Men Propose?," *Songs, Ballads, and Other Poems* (1844)

Bazaine, Achille-François (1811–88) French military leader

1 We are in the chamber pot, and tomorrow we shall be covered in shit.
August 1870. Said at Sedan, on the eve of certain defeat at the hands of the German army during the Franco-Prussian War (1870–71). Quoted in *Europe: A History* (Norman Davies; 1996), ch. 10

Beale, Betty U.S. journalist

1 Until that day when women, and only women, shall determine which American males must, by law, have vasectomies, then—and only then—will you or any man have the right to determine which American women can have abortions.
Ms (March 1982)

Beard, Charles (Charles Austin Beard; 1874–1948) U.S. historian

1 History, like science and literature, belongs to the republic of letters which knows no political boundaries, tariffs, and embargoes. Historians, to be sure, have their locus in space and time but history as thought transcends these particular considerations.
"The Historian and Society," *Canadian Historical Review* (March 1933)

2 It is by becoming unmoral that history serves the highest morality.
"The Historian and Society," *Canadian Historical Review* (March 1933)

3 If the history of a people is a philosophy of the whole social organism in process of becoming, then it ought to furnish material with which discernment can be whetted.
The Rise of American Civilization (1927)

4 The history of a civilization, if intelligently conceived, may be an instrument of civilization.
The Rise of American Civilization (1927)

5 When absolutes in history are rejected, the absolutism of relativity is also rejected.
Attrib. *The Law of Civilization and Decay* (Brooks Adams; 1895), introduction

6 If all historical conceptions are merely relative to passing events, to transitory phases of ideas and interests, then the conception of relativity is itself relative.
Quoted in *The Law of Civilization and Decay* (Brooks Adams; 1895), introduction

7 The historian who writes history therefore, consciously or unconsciously performs an act of faith...His faith is at bottom a conviction that something true can be known about the movement of history and his conviction is a subjective decision, not a purely objective discovery.
Quoted in *The Law of Civilization and Decay* (Brooks Adams; 1895), introduction

Beard, James (1903–85) U.S. chef and author

1 Food is our common ground, a universal experience.
Beard on Food (1974)

Beard, Mary Ritter (1876–1958) U.S. historian

1 In their quest for rights they have naturally placed emphasis on their wrongs, rather than their achievements and possessions, and have retold history as a story of their long Martyrdom.
Referring to women. *On Understanding Women* (1931)

2 History has been conceived—and with high justification in the records—as the human struggle for civilization against barbarism in different ages and places, from the beginning of human societies.
Women as a Force in History (1946)

3 The dogma of women's complete historical subjugation to men must be rated as one of the most fantastic myths ever created by the human mind.
Women as a Force in History (1946)

Beardsley, Aubrey (Aubrey Vincent Beardsley; 1872–98) British artist and illustrator

1 Really I believe I'm so affected, even my lungs are affected.
Attrib. "Noble Essences," *Left Hand, Right Hand!* (Sir Osbert Sitwell; 1950), vol. 5, ch. 6

Beaton, Cecil, Sir (Cecil Walter Hardy Beaton; 1904–80) British photographer and theatrical designer

1 San Francisco is perhaps the most European of all American cities.
It Gives Me Great Pleasure (1955)

2 Previous to Chanel, clothes were designed for mature women, the social and cultural leaders of fashion. With Chanel's advent they were all designed for youth; or, if not for young women, were designed to make mature women look young.
The Glass of Fashion (1954), ch. 9

Beattie, Ann (b.1947) U.S. writer and art critic

1 There are things that get whispered about that writers are there to overhear.
Referring to *Best American Short Stories*. *New York Times* (November 1, 1987)

Beattie, James (1735–1803) Scottish poet and philosopher

1 Old age comes on apace to ravage all the clime.
The Minstrel (1771), bk. 1, st. 25

Beatty, David, 1st Earl Beatty, Viscount Borodale of Wexford, and Baron Beatty of the North Sea and of Brooksby (1871–1936) British admiral

1 There's something wrong with our bloody ships today, Chatfield.
May 30, 1916. Remark during the Battle of Jutland, World War I. Attrib.

Beaumarchais, Pierre-Augustin Caron de (1732–99) French playwright

1 I make myself laugh at everything, so that I do not weep.
The Barber of Seville (1775), Act 1, Scene 2

2 Today, if something is not worth saying, people sing it.
The Barber of Seville (1775), Act 1, Scene 2

3 Slander away, slander away; something will always stick.
The Barber of Seville (1775), Act 3, Scene 13

4 Because you are a great lord, you believe yourself to be a great genius! You took the trouble to be born, but no more.
The Marriage of Figaro (1778), Act 2, Scene 21

5 Drinking when we are not thirsty and making love all year round, madam; that is all there is to distinguish us from other animals.
The Marriage of Figaro (1778), Act 2, Scene 21

6 How many idiots go to make up a public?
Quoted in *Behind the Scenes of the Comédie-Française* (A. Houssaye; 1889)

Beaumont & Fletcher (Francis Beaumont 1584–1616, and John Fletcher 1579–1625) English playwrights

1 As cold as cucumbers.
Cupid's Revenge (1615), Act 1, Scene 1

2 Calamity is man's true touchstone.
Four Plays in One: The Triumph of Honour (performed 1647), Scene 1

3 As men
Do walk a mile, women should talk an hour,
After supper. 'Tis their exercise.
Philaster (1609), Act 2, Scene 4

4 PHILASTER Oh, but thou dost not know
What 'tis to die.
BELLARIO Yes, I do know, my Lord:
'Tis less than to be born; a lasting sleep;
A quiet resting from all jealousy,
A thing we all pursue; I know besides,
It is but giving over of a game,
That must be lost.
Philaster (1609), Act 3, Scene 1

5 You are no better than you should be.
The Coxcomb (1610), Act 4, Scene 3

6 But what is past my help is past my care.
The Double Marriage (1621), Act 1, Scene 2

7 From the crown of the head to the sole of the foot.
The Honest Man's Fortune (1625?), Act 2, Scene 2

8 Let's meet, and either do, or die.
The Island Princess (1621), Act 2, Scene 2

9 Upon my buried body lay
Lightly gently earth.
The Maid's Tragedy (1611), Act 2, Scene 1

10 Those have most power to hurt us that we love.
The Maid's Tragedy (1611), Act 5, Scene 6

11 Kiss till the cow comes home.
The Scornful Lady (1616), Act 2, Scene 2

12 There is no other purgatory but a woman.
The Scornful Lady (1616), Act 3, Scene 1

13 It would talk:
Lord how it talk't!
The Scornful Lady (1616), Act 4

14 Beggars can't be choosers.
The Scornful Lady (1616), Act 5, Scene 3

15 My dancing days are done.
The Scornful Lady (1616), Act 5, Scene 3

16 Vow me no vows.
Wit Without Money (1614), Act 4, Scene 4

17 Whistle and she'll come to you.
Wit Without Money (1614), Act 4, Scene 4

18 Charity and beating begins at home.
Wit Without Money (1614), Act 5, Scene 2

19 The fit's upon me now!
Come quickly, gentle lady;
The fit's upon me now.
Wit Without Money (1614), Act 5, Scene 4

Beaumont, Francis (1584–1616) English playwright

1 What things have we seen
Done at the Mermaid! heard words that have been
So nimble and so full of subtile flame.
As if that every one from whence they came
Had meant to put his whole wit in a jest,
And resolved to live a fool the rest
Of his dull life.
Letter to Ben Jonson (1605)

2 I'll have a fling.
Rule a Wife and Have a Wife (performed 1624), Act 3, Scene 5

3 Nose, nose, jolly red nose,
Who gave thee this jolly red nose?
Nutmegs and ginger, cinnamon and cloves,
And they gave me this jolly red nose.
The Knight of the Burning Pestle (1607), Act 1

4 This is a pretty flim-flam.
The Knight of the Burning Pestle (1607), Act 2, Scene 3

5 Plot me no plots.
The Knight of the Burning Pestle (1607), Act 2, Scene 5

6 The sturdy steed now goes to grass and up they hang his saddle.
The Knight of the Burning Pestle (1607), Act 4, interlude

7 I'll put a spoke among your wheels.
The Mad Lover (1616), Act 3, Scene 6

8 Nothing's so dainty sweet as lovely melancholy.
The Nice Valour (1616?), Act 3, Scene 3

9 All your better deeds
Shall be in water writ, but this in marble.
The Nice Valour (1616?), Act 5, Scene 5

Beaumont, William (1785–1853) U.S. physician

1 Of all the lessons which a young man entering upon the profession of medicine needs to learn, this is perhaps the first—that he should resist the fascination of doctrines and hypotheses till he has won the privilege of such studies by honest labor and faithful pursuit of real and useful knowledge.
Notebook (1833?)

Beauvoir, Simone de (1908–86) French writer and feminist theorist

1 If you live long enough, you'll see that every victory turns into a defeat.
All Men Are Mortal (1946)

2 I tore myself away from the safe comfort of certainties through my love for truth; and truth rewarded me.
All Said and Done (1974)

3 I cannot be angry at God, in whom I do not believe.
Observer, London (January 7, 1979)

4 If you haven't been happy very young, you can still be happy later on, but it's much harder. You need more luck.
Observer, London (May 19, 1975), "Sayings of the Week"

5 Any man who has known real loves, real revolts, real desires, and real will knows quite well that he has no need of any guarantee to be sure of his goals; their certitude comes from his own drive.
The Ethics of Ambiguity (1948)

6 Is this kind of ethics individualistic or not? Yes, if one means by that that it accords to the individual an absolute value and that it recognizes in him alone the power of laying the foundations of his own existence.
Referring to an existentialist ethics. *The Ethics of Ambiguity* (1948)

7 A man would never get the notion of writing a book on the peculiar situation of the human male.
The Second Sex (1949)

8 Between women love is contemplative. There is no struggle, no victory, no defeat; in exact reciprocity each is at once subject and object, sovereign and slave; duality becomes mutuality.
The Second Sex (1949)

9 Buying is a profound pleasure.
The Second Sex (1949)

10 For him she is sex—absolute sex, no less. She is defined and differentiated with reference to man and not he with reference to her; she is the incidental, the inessential as opposed to the essential. He is the Subject, he is the Absolute—she is the Other.
The Second Sex (1949)

11 Man is defined as a human being and woman as a female—whenever she behaves as a human being she is said to imitate the male.
The Second Sex (1949)

12 One is not born a woman, one becomes one.
The Second Sex (1949)

13 Refusal to make herself the object is not always what turns women to homosexuality; most lesbians, on the contrary, seek to cultivate the treasures of their femininity.
The Second Sex (1949)

14 Society, being codified by man, decrees that woman is inferior; she can do away with this inferiority only by destroying the male's superiority.
The Second Sex (1949)

15 The most mediocre of males feels himself a demigod as compared with women.
The Second Sex (1949)

16 There is an absolute human type, the masculine...Man superbly ignores the fact that his anatomy also includes glands, such as the testicles, and that they secrete hormones...He believes he apprehends objectivity.
The Second Sex (1949)

17 To be a woman, if not a defect, is at least a peculiarity.
The Second Sex (1949)

18 What is an adult? A child blown up by age.
1967. *The Woman Destroyed* (Patrick O'Brien, tr.; 1971)

19 It is in great part the anxiety of being a woman that devastates the feminine body.
Quoted in *Womansize* (Kim Chernin; 1983)

Beaverbrook, Max Aitken, Lord, 1st Baron Beaverbrook of Beaverbrook and of Cerkley (William Maxwell Aitken; 1879–1964) Canadian-born British newspaper owner and politician

1 The people have lost confidence in themselves, and they turn to the Government, looking for a restoration of that confidence. It is the task of the Government to supply it.
Remark made after the fall of Singapore during World War II. Letter to Winston Churchill (February 17, 1942)

2 Let me say that the credit belongs to the boys in the back rooms. It isn't the man who sits in the limelight like me who should have the praise. It is not the men who sit in prominent places. It is the men in the back rooms.
From the song "The Boys in the Back Room," sung by Marlene Dietrich in the film *Destry Rides Again.* *Listener,* London (March 27, 1941)

3 With the publication of his Private Papers in 1952, he committed suicide 25 years after his death.
Referring to Earl Haig. *Men and Power* (1956)

4 If you want to make mischief come and work on my papers.
Inviting the journalist Anthony Howard to join his staff. *Radio Times,* London (June 27, 1981)

5 I am the cat that walks alone.
Alluding to the "Just So" story by Rudyard Kipling. *Beaverbrook* (A. J. P. Taylor; 1972)

6 Go out and speak for the inarticulate and the submerged.
Said to Godfrey Winn. Quoted in *Somerset Maugham* (E. Morgan; 1980)

7 Buy old masters. They fetch a better price than old mistresses.
Attrib.

8 Because he shakes hands with people's hearts.
Referring to being asked why Godfrey Winn was paid so much. Attrib.

Bechet, Sidney (Sidney Joseph Bechet; 1897–1959) U.S. jazz musician

1 After emancipation...all those people who had been slaves, they needed the music more than ever now; it was like they were trying to find out in this music what they were supposed to do with this freedom.
Referring to jazz. *Treat It Gentle* (1960)

Beck, Earl R. (Earl Ray Beck; b.1916) U.S. historian

1 History is not a pie to be sliced into clear and well-defined pieces; it is rather a great river with the changes in the course and rapidity of the current sometimes abrupt, sometimes almost imperceptible.
Attrib.

2 History itself is virtually indefinable, its scope unlimited, its depth unfathomable.
Attrib.

3 No one can really *know* the life of his own day, let alone that of times long past. Always the historian sees as in a mirror darkly, the reds and golds rendered drab by the shadows of time.
Attrib.

Becker, Boris (b.1967) German tennis player

1 It's all about self-belief and a sense of proportion. I say to myself that the worst thing that I can do is lose a tennis match.
1989. *Daily Telegraph*, London (November 4, 1989)

Becker, Carl (Carl Lotus Becker; 1873–1945) U.S. historian

1 History is the artificial extension of social memory.
"Everyman His Own Historian," *American Historical Review* (January 1932)

2 Let us admit that there are two histories, the actual series of events that once occurred; and the ideal series that we affirm and hold in memory.
"Everyman His Own Historian," *American Historical Review* (January 1932)

3 The history that lies inert in unread books does no work in the world. The history that does work in the world, the history that influences the course of history, is living history, that pattern of remembered events whether true or false, that enlarges and enriches the collective specious present...of Mr. Everyman.
"Everyman His Own Historian," *American Historical Review* (January 1932)

4 It is rather an imaginative creation, a personal possession which each one of us, Mr. Everyman, fashions out of his individual experience, adapts to his practical or emotional needs, and adorns as well as may be to suit his aesthetic tastes.
Referring to history. "Everyman His Own Historian," *American Historical Review* (January 1932)

5 If the historian could indeed separate himself from the process which he describes...his greatest success should be with those periods that differ most from the one in which he lives. But he has, in fact, most success with those periods in which men's habitual modes of thought and action most resemble his own.
"Detachment and the Writing of History," *Atlantic Monthly* (October 1910)

6 If we cannot be on familiar terms with our past, it is no good. We must have a past that is the product of all the present.
"Detachment and the Writing of History," *Atlantic Monthly* (October 1910)

7 The "facts" of history do not exist for any historian until he creates them, and into every fact he creates some part of his individual experience must enter.
"Detachment and the Writing of History," *Atlantic Monthly* (October 1910)

8 The historical reality is continuous, and infinitely complex; and the cold hard facts into which it is said to be analyzed are not concrete portions of the reality, but only aspects of it.
"Detachment and the Writing of History," *Atlantic Monthly* (October 1910)

9 The modern historian admits that there were lies, but denies that there were miracles.
"Detachment and the Writing of History," *Atlantic Monthly* (October 1910)

10 The past is a kind of screen upon which we project our vision of the future; and it is indeed a moving picture, borrowing much of its form and color from our fears and aspirations.
"Detachment and the Writing of History," *Atlantic Monthly* (October 1910)

11 The past will provide humanity with any fate you like to imagine. O History, how many truths have been committed in thy name.
"Mr. Wells and the New History," *Everyman His Own Historian* (1935)

12 The significance of man is that he is that part of the universe that asks the question, What is the significance of Man?
Progress and Power (1936), ch. 3

Beckett, Samuel (Samuel Barclay Beckett; 1906–89) Irish playwright, novelist, and poet

1 That's what hell will be like, small chat to the babbling of Lethe about the good old days when we wished we were dead.
Embers (1959)

2 Can there be misery—(*he yawns*)—loftier than mine?
Endgame (1958)

3 CLOV Do you believe in the life to come?
HAMM Mine was always that.
Endgame (1958)

4 HAMM What time is it?
CLOV The same as usual.
1957. *Endgame* (1958)

5 All those lips that had kissed me, those hearts that had loved me (it is with the heart one loves, is it not, or am I confusing it with something else?).
1946. *First Love* (1973)

6 Personally I have no bone to pick with graveyards, I take the air there willingly, perhaps more willingly than elsewhere, when take the air I must.
1946. *First Love* (1973)

7 What constitutes the charm of our country, apart of course from the scant population, and this without help of the meanest contraceptive, is that it is all derelict.
1946. Referring to Ireland. *First Love* (1973)

8 WINNIE Oh, this *is* a happy day, this will have been another happy day! (*Pause.*) After all. (*Pause.*) So far.
Happy Days (1961), Act 2

9 Caught by the rain far from shelter Macmann stopped and lay down, saying, The surface thus pressed against the ground

will remain dry, whereas standing I would get uniformly wet all over.
Malone Dies (1951)

10 If I had the use of my body I would throw it out of the window.
Malone Dies (1951)

11 Let me say before I go any further that I forgive nobody. I wish them all an atrocious life and then the fires and ice of hell and in the execrable generations to come an honoured name.
Malone Dies (1951)

12 The sun shone, having no alternative, on the nothing new.
Murphy (1938), ch. 1

13 No love...spared that...no love such as normally vented on the speechless infant...in the home...no...nor indeed for that matter any of any kind...no love of any kind...at any subsequent stage.
Not I (1973)

14 I don't know when I died. It always seemed to me I died old, about ninety years old, and what years.
1946. "The Calmative," *The Expelled and Other Novellas* (1980)

15 It took three women to put on my trousers. They didn't seem to take much interest in my private parts which to tell the truth were nothing to write home about, I didn't take much interest in them myself.
1946. "The End," *The Expelled and Other Novellas* (1980)

16 The memory came faint and cold of the story I might have told, a story in the likeness of my life, I mean without the courage to end or the strength to go on.
1946. "The End," *The Expelled and Other Novellas* (1980)

17 They never lynch children, babies, no matter what they do they are whitewashed in advance.
1946. "The Expelled," *The Expelled and Other Novellas* (1980)

18 It will be silence, where I am, I don't know, I'll never know, in the silence you don't know, you must go on, I can't go on, I'll go on.
The Unnamable (1958)

19 Where now? Who now? When now? Unquestioning. I, say I. Unbelieving. Questions, hypotheses, call them that. Keep going, going on, call that going, call that on.
The Unnamable (1958)

20 He can't think without his hat.
Waiting for Godot (1954), Act 1

21 Nothing happens, nobody comes, nobody goes, it's awful!
Waiting for Godot (1954), Act 1

22 VLADIMIR That passed the time.
ESTRAGON It would have passed in any case.
VLADIMIR Yes, but not so rapidly.
Waiting for Godot (1954), Act 1

23 VLADIMIR You should have been a poet.
ESTRAGON I was. (*Gestures towards his rags.*) Isn't that obvious.
Waiting for Godot (1954), Act 1

24 ESTRAGON Let's go.
VLADIMIR We can't.
ESTRAGON Why not?
VLADIMIR We're waiting for Godot.
Waiting for Godot (1954), Act 1, passim

25 Habit is a great deadener.
Waiting for Godot (1954), Act 2

26 One day we were born, one day we shall die, the same day, the same second, is that not enough for you? (*Calmer.*) They give birth astride of a grave.
Waiting for Godot (1954), Act 2

27 One of the thieves was saved. (*Pause.*) It's a reasonable percentage.
Waiting for Godot (1954), Act 2

28 We all are born mad. Some remain so.
Waiting for Godot (1954), Act 2

29 We always find something, eh, Didi, to give us the impression that we exist?
Waiting for Godot (1954), Act 2

30 VLADIMIR Well, shall we go?
ESTRAGON Yes, let's go.
They do not move.
The final words of the play. *Waiting for Godot* (1954), Act 2

31 Or was it not perhaps something that was not Watt, nor of Watt, but behind Watt, or beside Watt, or before Watt, or beneath Watt, or above Watt, or about Watt, a shade uncast, a light unshed, or the grey air aswirl with vain entelechies?
Watt (1953)

Beckett, Terence, Sir (b.1923) British business executive

1 We may be a hobbled tiger, but we do not intend to be a lame duck.
Referring to ignoring government wage restraints at Ford Motor Company. Remark (1978)

Beckford, William (William Thomas Beckford; 1759–1844) British writer and art collector

1 He did not think, with the Caliph Omar Ben Adalaziz, that it was necessary to make a hell of this world to enjoy paradise in the next.
Vathek (1782)

2 Your presence I condescend to accept; but beg you will let me be quiet; for, I am not over-fond of resisting temptation.
Vathek (1782)

Becon, Thomas (1512–67) English cleric

1 For when the wine is in, the wit is out.
Catechism (1560), no. 375

Becque, Henry (Henry François Becque; 1837–99) French playwright

1 What makes equality such a difficult business is that we only want it with our superiors.
Querelles littéraires (1890)

Bede ("The Venerable Bede"; 673?–735) English monk and scholar

1 For if history relates good things of good men, the attentive hearer is excited to imitate that which is good; or if it mentions evil things of wicked persons, nevertheless the religious and pious hearer or reader...is the more earnestly excited to perform those things which he knows to be good and worthy of God.
Ecclesiastical History (731)

2 They answered that they were called Angles. "It is well," he said, "for they have the faces of angels, and such should be the co-heirs of the angels of heaven."
Referring to Pope Gregory I, who saw fair-complexioned slaves in Rome, and was inspired to send a mission to England to convert the Angles to Christianity. *Ecclesiastical History* (731)

3 They came from three very powerful nations of the Germans; that is, from the *Saxones*, *Angli*, and *Iutae*.
Referring to the Anglo-Saxon invaders of England. *Ecclesiastical History* (731)

Bee, Barnard (Barnard Elliot Bee; 1824–61) U.S. Confederate soldier

1 There is Jackson with his Virginians, standing like a stone wall. Let us determine to die here, and we will conquer.
July 21, 1861. Said at the First Battle of Bull Run. Hence General Thomas Jackson's nickname, "Stonewall Jackson." *Reminiscences of Sixty Years in the National Metropolis* (Benjamin Perley Poore; 1886), ch. 2

Beecham, Thomas, Sir (1879–1961) British conductor and impresario

1 I have recently been all round the world and have formed a very poor opinion of it.
Speech at the Savoy, *News Review* (August 22, 1946)

2 A musicologist is a man who can read music but can't hear it.
Quoted in *Beecham Remembered* (Humphrey Procter-Gregg; 1976)

3 There are two golden rules for an orchestra: start together and finish together. The public doesn't give a damn what goes on in between.
Beecham Stories (H. Atkins and A. Newman; 1993)

4 This god-forsaken city, with a climate so evil that no self-respecting singer would ever set foot in it! It is a catarrhal place that has been the cause through the centuries of the nasal Liverpool accent.
Beecham Stories (H. Atkins and A. Newman; 1993)

5 Well, I think we have successfully paved the way this afternoon for another quarter of a century of German music.
Said after conducting an all British program at Covent Garden during World War I. Quoted in *Farewell My Youth* (Arnold Bax; 1943)

6 The English may not like music—but they absolutely love the noise it makes.
The Wit of Music (L. Ayre; 1966)

7 All festivals are bunk. They are for the purpose of attracting trade to the town. What that has to do with music, I don't know.
Attrib.

8 Brass bands are all very well in their place—outdoors and several miles away.
Attrib.

9 The sound of the harpsichord resembles that of a bird-cage played with toasting-forks.
Attrib.

10 When we sing "All we, like sheep, have gone astray", might we please have a little more regret and a little less satisfaction?
Said to a choir rehearsing Handel's *Messiah*. Attrib.

11 I don't like your Christian name. I'd like to change it.
Said to his future wife. She replied, "You can't, but you can change my surname." Attrib.

12 Certainly not—if you don't object if I'm sick.
When asked whether he minded if someone smoked in a non-smoking compartment. Attrib.

Beecher, Henry Ward (1813–87) U.S. cleric and abolitionist

1 Law represents the effort of men to organize Society; government, the efforts of selfishness to overthrow liberty.
American Rebellion: Report of Speeches Delivered in England (1864)

2 Laws and institutions are constantly tending to gravitate. Like clocks, they must be occasionally cleansed, and wound up, and set to true time.
Life Thoughts (1863)

3 Not that which men do worthily, but that which they do successfully, is what history makes haste to record.
Life Thoughts (1863)

4 Laws are not masters but servants, and he rules them who obeys them.
Proverbs from Plymouth Pulpit (1887)

5 Riches without law are more dangerous than is poverty without law.
Proverbs from Plymouth Pulpit (1887)

6 I have known many an instance of a man writing a letter and forgetting to sign his name, but this is the only instance I have ever known of a man signing his name and forgetting to write the letter.
Said on receiving a note containing the single word "Fool." Attrib.

Beeching, H. C. (Henry Charles Beeching; 1859–1919) British cleric and writer

1 First come I; my name is Jowett.
There's no knowledge but I know it.
I am Master of this college:
What I don't know isn't knowledge.
Referring to Benjamin Jowett, master of Balliol College, Oxford. *The Masque of Balliol* (1870s)

Beefheart, Captain (Don Van Vliet; b.1941) U.S. singer and songwriter

1 I just wanna raise the art and culture to where I can sit at the same table.
Quoted in *The Wit and Wisdom of Rock and Roll* (Maxim Jabukowski, ed.; 1983)

2 I'm a genius and there's nothing I can do about it.
Quoted in *The Wit and Wisdom of Rock and Roll* (Maxim Jabukowski, ed.; 1983)

Beer, Thomas (1888?–1940) U.S. author

1 I agree with one of your reputable critics that a taste for

drawing rooms has spoiled more poets than ever did a taste for gutters.
The Mauve Decade (1926)

Beerbohm, Max, Sir (Henry Maximilian Beerbohm, "The Incomparable Max"; 1872–1956) British essayist, critic, and caricaturist

Quotations about Beerbohm

1 The Incomparable Max.
George Bernard Shaw (1856–1950) Irish playwright. *Dramatic Opinions and Essays* (1907), vol. 2

Quotations by Beerbohm

2 What were they going to do with the Grail when they found it, Mr Rossetti?
Referring to Rossetti's painting of the Arthurian legend. Cartoon caption

3 It is a fact that not once in all my life have I gone out for a walk. I have been taken out for walks; but that is another matter.
"Going Out for a Walk" (1918)

4 I believe the twenty-four hour day has come to stay.
"Perkins and Mankind," *A Christmas Garland* (1912)

5 "After all," as a pretty girl once said to me, "women are a sex by themselves, so to speak."
"The Pervasion of Rouge," *A Defence of Cosmetics* (1896)

6 Great men are but life-sized. Most of them, indeed, are rather short.
And Even Now (1921)

7 I maintain that though you would often in the fifteenth century have heard the snobbish Roman say, in a would-be off-hand tone, "I am dining with the Borgias to-night," no Roman ever was able to say, "I dined last night with the Borgias."
Hosts and Guests (1920)

8 Mankind is divisible into two great classes: hosts and guests.
Hosts and Guests (1920)

9 Anything that is worth doing has been done frequently. Things hitherto undone should be given, I suspect, a wide berth.
Mainly on the Air (1946)

10 The lower one's vitality, the more sensitive one is to great art.
Seven Men (1919), "Enoch Soames"

11 Most women are not so young as they are painted.
The Yellow Book (1894)

12 To give an accurate and exhaustive account of that period would need a far less brilliant pen than mine.
The Yellow Book (1895), vol. IV, "1880"

13 Americans have a perfect right to exist. But he did often find himself wishing Mr. Rhodes had not enabled them to exercise that right at Oxford.
Zuleika Dobson (1911)

14 The dullard's envy of brilliant men is always assuaged by the suspicion that they will come to a bad end.
Zuleika Dobson (1911)

15 The loveliest face in all the world will not please you if you see it suddenly eye to eye, at a distance of half an inch from your own.
Zuleika Dobson (1911)

16 Zuleika, on a desert island, would have spent most of her time in looking for a man's foot-print.
Zuleika Dobson (1911), ch. 2

17 It needs no dictionary of quotations to remind me that the eyes are the windows of the soul.
Zuleika Dobson (1911), ch. 4

18 Women who love the same man have a kind of bitter freemasonry.
Zuleika Dobson (1911), ch. 4

19 You will find that the woman who is really kind to dogs is always one who has failed to inspire sympathy in men.
Zuleika Dobson (1911), ch. 6

20 Beauty and the lust for learning have yet to be allied.
Zuleika Dobson (1911), ch. 7

21 You cannot make a man by standing a sheep on its hind legs. But by standing a flock of sheep in that position you can make a crowd of men.
Zuleika Dobson (1911), ch. 9

22 Only mediocrity can be trusted to be always at its best.
Conversations with Max (S. N. Behrman; 1960)

23 Only the insane take themselves quite seriously.
Max: A Biography (D. Cecil; 1964)

24 They were a tense and peculiar family, the Oedipuses, weren't they?
Max: A Biography (D. Cecil; 1965)

25 Old friends are generally the refuge of unsociable persons.
The Incomparable Max (C. S. Roberts, ed.; 1962)

26 I am a Tory Anarchist, I should like everyone to go about doing just as he pleased—short of altering any of the things to which I have grown accustomed.
Attrib.

Beers, Ethel Lynn (1827–79) U.S. poet

1 All quiet along the Potomac to-night,
No sound save the rush of the river,
While soft falls the dew on the face of the dead
The picket's off duty forever.
"All Quiet Along the Potomac," *Harper's Magazine* (1861)

Beethoven, Ludwig van (1770–1827) German composer

Quotations about Beethoven

1 What can you do with it?—it's like a lot of yaks jumping about.
Thomas Beecham (1879–1961) British conductor and impresario. Referring to Beethoven's 7th symphony. *Beecham Stories* (H. Atkins and A. Newman; 1993)

2 There's no denying...that Beethoven came with music in his soul, Picasso was drawing like an angel in the crib. You're born with it.
Louise Nevelson (1900–88) Russian-born U.S. sculptor. Referring to Ludwig van Beethoven and Pablo Picasso. *Dawns and Dusks* (1976)

3 This is not Beethoven lying here.
1828
Franz Peter Schubert (1797–1828) Austrian composer. Last words. Attrib.

Quotations by Beethoven

4 I used to be able to make all my other circumstances subservient to my art. I admit, however, that by so doing I became a bit crazy.
Letter (February 1818), quoted in *The Letters of Beethoven* (E. Anderson, ed., tr.; 1961), no. 894

5 In the world of art, as in the whole world of creation, freedom and progress are the main objectives.
Letter (July 29, 1819), quoted in *The Letters of Beethoven* (E. Anderson, ed., tr.; 1961), no. 955

6 Only art and science can raise men to the level of God.
Letter, *The Letters of Beethoven* (E. Anderson, ed., tr.; July 17, 1812), no. 376

7 Between ourselves the best thing of all is a combination of the surprising and the beautiful.
Letter, *The Letters of Beethoven* (E. Anderson, ed., tr.; July 16, 1823), no. 1209

8 Off with you! You're a happy fellow, for you'll give happiness and joy to many other people. There is nothing better or greater than that!
1822. Said to Franz Liszt when Liszt, aged 11, had visited Beethoven and played for him. Quoted in *Beethoven: Letters, Journals and Conversations* (Michael Hamburger, ed.; 1952)

9 When I composed that, I was conscious of being inspired by God Almighty. Do you think I can consider your puny little fiddle when He speaks to me?
Said when a violinist complained that a passage was unplayable. *Music All Around Me* (Anthony Hopkins; 1967)

10 Do not let that trouble Your Excellency; perhaps the greetings are intended for me.
Said when walking with Goethe, when Goethe complained about greetings from passers-by. *Thayer's Life of Beethoven* (Elliot Forbes, ed.; 1967)

Behan, Brendan (1923–64) Irish playwright and author

1 If my aunt had bollocks she'd be me uncle.
Richard's Cork Leg (1972), Act 1

2 I think weddings is sadder than funerals, because they remind you of your own wedding. You can't be reminded of your own funeral because it hasn't happened. But weddings always makes me cry.
Richard's Cork Leg (Alan Simpson, ed.; 1973), Act 1

3 Other people have a nationality. The Irish and the Jews have a psychosis.
Richard's Cork Leg (Alan Simpson, ed.; 1973), Act 1

4 The English and Americans dislike only *some* Irish—the same Irish that the Irish themselves detest, Irish writers the ones that *think*.
Richard's Cork Leg (Alan Simpson, ed.; 1973), Act 1

5 They say this is one of the healthiest graveyards in Dublin. Set on the shore of Dublin Bay. The sea air is very healthy...the ozoon, you know.
Richard's Cork Leg (1972), Act 1

6 He was born an Englishman and remained one for years.
The Hostage (1958), Act 1

7 WOMEN Never throw stones at your mother,
You'll be sorry for it when she's dead.
MEN Never throw stones at your mother,
Throw bricks at your father instead.
The Hostage (1958), Act 1

8 I am a sociable worker.
The Hostage (1958), Act 2

9 I wish I'd been a mixed infant.
The Hostage (1958), Act 2

10 When I came back to Dublin, I was courtmartialled in my absence and sentenced to death in my absence, so I said they could shoot me in my absence.
The Hostage (1958), Act 2

11 Communism will not come terrible like an army with banners, but like a Corporation dustman carting off the rubbish of the ages.
1950. "Dustman" means garbage collector. Attrib. *Dead As Doornails* (Anthony Cronin; 1976), ch. 3

12 Come in, you Anglo-Saxon swine
And drink of my Algerian wine.
'Twill turn your eyeballs black and blue,
And damn well good enough for you.
Painted as an advertisement on the window of a Paris café, the owner of which could not speak English. *My Brother Brendan* (Dominic Behan; 1965)

13 There's no such thing as bad publicity except your own obituary.
Quoted in *My Brother Brendan* (Dominic Behan; 1965)

14 A bit of shooting takes your mind off your troubles—it makes you forget the cost of living.
1958. Attrib.

15 I am married to Beatrice Salkeld, a painter. We have no children, except me.
1961. Attrib.

16 I have never seen a situation so dismal that a policeman couldn't make it worse.
Attrib.

17 I'm a Communist by day and a Catholic as soon as it gets dark.
Attrib.

18 Thank you, sister. May you be the mother of a bishop!
1964. Said to a nun nursing him on his deathbed. Attrib.

Behn, Aphra (1640?–89) English novelist and playwright

Quotations about Behn

1 Mrs. Behn is still to be found here and there in the dusty worm eaten libraries of old country houses, but as a rule we imagine she has been ejected from all *decent* society for more than a generation or two.
Anonymous. "Literary Garbage," *Saturday Review* (January 27, 1862)

2 She was involved in an insurrection of slaves, thus going one better than Harriet Beecher Stowe, who merely preached abolitionism.
Anthony Burgess (1917–93) British writer and critic. *Observer*, London (December 30, 1980)

3 Mrs. Behn was the first woman in history to earn her living as an author and her remains were appropriately entombed in the cloisters of Westminster Abbey.
Frank Muir (1920–98) British writer and broadcaster. *The Frank Muir Book: An Irreverent Companion to Social History* (1976)

Quotations by Behn

4 Since Man with that inconstancy was born,
To love the absent, and the present scorn,
Why do we deck, why do we dress
For a short-liv'd happiness?
"To Alexis, in Answer to His Poem Against Fruition," *Lycidus* (1688)

5 Of all that writ, he was the wisest bard, who spoke this mighty truth.
He that knew all that ever learning writ,
Knew only this—that he knew nothing yet.
The Emperor of the Moon (1687), Act 1, Scene 3

6 Who is't that to women's beauty would submit,
And yet refuse the fetters of their wit?
The Forced Marriage (1670), prologue

7 Love ceases to be a pleasure, when it ceases to be a secret.
"Four O'clock. General Conversation," *The Lover's Watch* (1686)

8 Faith, Sir, we are here to-day, and gone tomorrow.
The Lucky Chance (1686)

9 I owe a duty, where I cannot love.
The Moor's Revenge (1677), Act 2, Scene 3

10 A brave world, Sir, full of religion, knavery, and change: we shall shortly see better days.
The Roundheads (1682), Act 1, Scene 1

11 In short, the only Wit that's now in Fashion
Is but the Gleanings of good Conversation.
1677. *The Rover* (1678), prologue

12 Come away; poverty's catching.
The Rover (1678), pt. 2, Act 1

13 Variety is the soul of pleasure.
The Rover (1678), pt. 2, Act 1

14 Money speaks sense in a language all nations understand.
The Rover (1678), pt. 2, Act 3, Scene 1

15 The Devil's in her tongue, and so 'tis in most women's of her age; for when it has quitted the tail, it repairs to the upper tier.
The Town Fop (1677)

16 "Sure, I rose the wrong way to-day, I have had such damn'd ill luck every way."
The Town Fop (1677), Act 5, Scene 1

Behrman, S. N. (Samuel Nathaniel Behrman; 1893–1973) U.S. playwright and screenwriter

1 Early in life, Duveen...noticed that Europe had plenty of art and America had plenty of money, and his entire astonishing career was the product of that simple observation.
Joseph Duveen was a British art dealer. *Duveen* (1952)

Bell, Alexander Graham (1847–1922) Scottish-born U.S. inventor and educator

1 Mr Watson, come here; I want you.
March 10, 1876. The first telephone conversation in Boston. Attrib.

Bell, Clive (Arthur Clive Heward Bell; 1881–1964) British art critic

1 It would follow that "significant form" was form behind which we catch a sense of ultimate reality.
Art (1914), pt. 1, ch. 3

2 Only reason can convince us of those three fundamental truths without a recognition of which there can be no effective liberty: that what we believe is not necessarily true; that what we like is not necessarily good; and that all questions are open.
Civilization (1928), ch. 5

Bell, Eric Temple (1883–1960) Scottish-born U.S. mathematician

1 The longer mathematics lives the more abstract—and therefore, possibly also the more practical—it becomes.
Quoted in *The Mathematical Intelligencer* (1991), vol. 13

Bell, Martin (b.1938) British journalist and politician

1 I knew that politics would bring many strange experiences, but nothing in life can prepare a man to make small talk to a transsexual bird cage.
Referring to Miss Moneypenny, a 7-ft transsexual election candidate who wore a bird cage on her head. *Independent*, London (May 10, 1997)

Bell, Ronald (1914–82) British politician

1 The connection between humbug and politics is too long established to be challenged.
Remark (December 5, 1979)

Bell, T. British doctor

1 Although it is true that the hymen is often relaxed in virgins, or broken and diminished by accidents independent of all coition, such accidents are very rare, and the absence of the hymen is assuredly a good ground of strong suspicion.
Kalogynomia (1821)

Bellamy, Edward (1850–98) U.S. essayist and journalist

1 We hold the period of youth sacred to education, and the period of maturity, when the physical forces begin to flag, equally sacred to ease and agreeable relaxation.
Looking Backward, 2000–1887 (1888), ch. 6

2 The nation guarantees the nurture, education, and comfortable maintenance of every citizen from the cradle to the grave.
Looking Backward, 2000–1887 (1888), ch. 9

3 An American credit card is just as good as American gold used to be.
Looking Backward, 2000–1887 (1888), ch. 13

4 Equal wealth and opportunities of culture...have simply made us all members of one class.
Looking Backward, 2000–1887 (1888), ch. 14

Belli, Melvin (Melvin Mouron Belli, "The King of Torts"; 1907–96) U.S. lawyer

1 If you can tell...and show...let them see and feel...taste or smell the evidence, then you will reach the jury.
Quoted in *Celebrity Register* (Earl Blackwell; 1990)

Belloc, Hilaire (Joseph-Pierre Hilaire Belloc; 1870–1953) French-born British writer

1 I'm tired of Love: I'm still more tired of Rhyme.
But Money gives me pleasure all the Time.
"Fatigued" (1923)

2 I always like to associate with a lot of priests because it makes me understand anti-clerical things so well.
Letter to E. S. P. Haynes (November 9, 1909)

3 Of all the politicians I ever saw
The least significant was Bonar Law.
Unless it was MacDonald, by the way:
Or Baldwin—it's impossible to say.
"Of All the Politicians I Ever Saw" (1988), quoted in *The Faber Book of English History in Verse* (Kenneth Baker, ed.; 1988)

4 The fleas that tease in the high Pyrenees.
"Tarantella" (1923)

5 I shoot the Hippopotamus
With bullets made of platinum,
Because if I use leaden ones
His hide is sure to flatten 'em.
"The Hippopotamus," *A Bad Child's Book of Beasts* (1896)

6 Alas! That such affected tricks
Should flourish in a child of six!
"Godolphin Horne," *Cautionary Tales* (1907)

7 "Oh, my Friends, be warned by me,
That Breakfast, Dinner, Lunch and Tea
Are all the Human Frame requires..."
With that the Wretched Child expires.
"Henry King," *Cautionary Tales* (1907)

8 The Chief Defect of Henry King
Was chewing little bits of String.
"Henry King," *Cautionary Tales* (1907)

9 They answered, as they took their fees,
"There is no cure for this disease."
"Henry King," *Cautionary Tales* (1907)

10 A trick that everyone abhors
In little girls is slamming doors.
"Rebecca," *Cautionary Tales* (1907)

11 The nicest child I ever knew
Was Charles Augustus Fortescue.
"Charles Augustus Fortescue," *Cautionary Tales for Children* (1907), quoted in *Complete Verse* (1991)

12 Godolphin Horne was Nobly Born;
He held the Human race in Scorn.
"Godolphin Horne," *Cautionary Tales for Children* (1907), quoted in *Complete Verse* (1991)

13 Always keep a-hold of Nurse
For fear of finding something worse.
"Jim," *Cautionary Tales for Children* (1907), quoted in *Complete Verse* (1991)

14 For every time She shouted "Fire!"
They only answered "Little Liar!"
And therefore when her Aunt returned,
Matilda, and the House, were burned.
"Matilda," *Cautionary Tales for Children* (1907), quoted in *Complete Verse* (1991)

15 Matilda told such Dreadful Lies
It made one Gasp and Stretch one's Eyes.
"Matilda," *Cautionary Tales for Children* (1907), quoted in *Complete Verse* (1991)

16 Whatever happens, we have got
The Maxim Gun, and they have not.
1898. From a semi-allegorical satire on the arrogance of the white man in Africa. Said by Captain Blood, friend of Commander Sin, referring to African mutineers. "The Modern Traveller," *Complete Verse* (1991), pt. 6

17 The accursed power which stands on Privilege
(And goes with Women, and Champagne, and Bridge)
Broke—and Democracy resumed her reign:
(Which goes with Bridge, and Women and Champagne).
"On a Great Election," *Epigrams* (1923)

18 When I am dead, I hope it may be said:
"His sins were scarlet, but his books were read."
"On His Books," *Epigrams* (1923)

19 He therefore was at strenuous pains
To atrophy his puny brains
And registered success in this
Beyond the dreams of avarice,
Till, when he had at last become
Blind, paralytic, deaf and dumb,
Insensible and cretinous
He was admitted ONE OF US.
"The Statesman," *Ladies and Gentlemen* (1932), quoted in *Complete Verse* (1991)

20 The Llama is a woolly sort of fleecy hairy goat,
With an indolent expression and an undulating throat
Like an unsuccessful literary man.
"The Llama," *More Beasts for Worse Children* (1897)

21 Oh! let us never, never doubt
What nobody is sure about!
"The Microbe," *More Beasts for Worse Children* (1897)

22 The Microbe is so very small
You cannot make him out at all.
"The Microbe," *More Beasts for Worse Children* (1897)

23 I had an aunt in Yucatan
Who bought a Python from a man
And kept it for a pet.
She died, because she never knew
These simple little rules and few—
The Snake is living yet.
"The Python," *More Beasts for Worse Children* (1897), quoted in *Complete Verse* (1991)

24 Lord Finchley tried to mend the Electric Light
Himself. It struck him dead: And serve him right!

It is the business of the wealthy man
To give employment to the artisan.
"Lord Finchley," *More Peers* (1911), quoted in *Complete Verse* (1991)

25 Like many of the upper class
He liked the sound of broken glass.
"About John," *New Cautionary Tales* (1930), quoted in *Complete Verse* (1991)

26 A committee is a cul-de-sac down which ideas are lured and then quietly strangled.
New Scientist (1973)

27 I am a sundial, and I make a botch
Of what is done far better by a watch.
"On Another," *Sonnets and Verse* (1923), quoted in *Complete Verse* (1991)

28 The Devil, having nothing else to do,
Went off to tempt My Lady Poltagrue.
My Lady, tempted by a private whim,
To his extreme annoyance, tempted him.
"On Lady Poltagrue, a Public Peril," *Sonnets and Verse* (1923), quoted in *Complete Verse* (1991)

29 I call you bad, my little child,
Upon the title page,
Because a manner rude and wild
Is common at your age.
"Introduction," *The Bad Child's Book of Beasts* (1896), quoted in *Complete Verse* (1991)

30 The nuisance of the tropics is
The sheer necessity of fizz.
"The Modern Traveller," *The Modern Traveller* (1898), pt. 4, st. 4, quoted in *Complete Verse* (1991)

31 Of Courtesy, it is much less
Than Courage of Heart or Holiness;
Yet in my Walks it seems to me
That the Grace of God is in Courtesy.
"Courtesy," *Verses* (1910), quoted in *Complete Verse* (1991)

32 From quiet homes and first beginning,
Out to the undiscovered ends,
There's nothing worth the wear of winning,
But laughter and the love of friends.
"Dedicatory Ode," *Verses* (1910), quoted in *Complete Verse* (1991)

33 Child! do not throw this book about!
Refrain from the unholy pleasure
Of cutting all the pictures out!
Preserve it as your chiefest treasure.
1896. "On the Gift of a Book to a Child," *Verses* (1910), quoted in *Complete Verse* (1991)

34 I am a Catholic. As far as possible I go to Mass every day. As far as possible I kneel down and tell these beads every day. If you reject me on account of my religion, I shall thank God that he has spared me the indignity of being your representative.
Speech to the voters of South Salford. (1906), quoted in *Life of Hilaire Belloc* (R. Speight; 1957), ch. 10

35 If I had known there was no Latin word for tea I would have let the vulgar stuff alone.
Attrib.

36 Candidates should not attempt more than six of these.
Suggested addition to the Ten Commandments. Attrib.

Bellori, Giovanni Pietro (1615–96) Italian art theorist and antiquarian

1 Noble Painters and Sculptors, imitating that first maker, also form in their minds an example of superior beauty, and in beholding it they emend nature with faultless color or line.
Quoted in Bellori's "Idea," *Idea, A Concept in Art Theory* (Erwin Panofsky, ed., J. S. Peake, tr.; 1968)

2 Painters and Sculptors, choosing the most elegant natural beauties, perfect the Idea, and their works exceed and remain superior to nature—which is the ultimate value of the arts.
Quoted in Bellori's "Idea," *Idea, A Concept in Art Theory* (Erwin Panofsky, ed., J. S. Peake, tr.; 1968)

Bellow, Saul (b.1915) Canadian-born U.S. writer

1 Where is the Proust of Papua? When the Zulus have a Tolstoy, we will read him.
Harper's Magazine, November 1994

2 Of course, in an age of madness, to expect to be untouched by madness is a form of madness. But the pursuit of sanity can be a form of madness, too.
Henderson, The Rain King (1959)

3 A man may say, "From now on I'm going to speak the truth." But the truth hears him and hides before he's done speaking.
Herzog (1964)

4 One lover is always more moved than the other.
Herzog (1964)

5 Will never understand what women want. What do they want? They eat green salad and drink human blood.
Herzog (1964)

6 If I'm out of my mind, it's all right with me, thought Moses Herzog.
Opening words. *Herzog* (1964)

7 America should thank God for its gangsters. The Mafia at least makes sense. These political guys don't know what the hell they're doing.
Humboldt's Gift (1975)

8 I went to the Village at night and listened to the finest talkers in New York...But Humboldt was the best of them all. He was simply the Mozart of conversation.
Humboldt's Gift (1975)

9 Modern poets had more wonderful material than Homer or Dante. What they didn't have was a sane and steady idealization. To be Christian was impossible, to be pagan also. That left you-know-what.
Humboldt's Gift (1975)

10 Real questions to the dead...must pass through the heart to be transmitted. The time to ask the dead something is in the last instant of consciousness before sleeping.
Humboldt's Gift (1975)

11 Socially, psychologically, politically, the very essence of human

institutions was an extract of what we assumed about death.
Humboldt's Gift (1975)

12 The temptation to lie down is very great. Humboldt was a weakening entity. Poets have to dream, and dreaming in America is no cinch.
Humboldt's Gift (1975)

13 Under Nixon the great corporations became drunk with immunity. The good old bourgeois virtues, even as window dressing, are gone forever.
Humboldt's Gift (1975)

14 When Napoleon gave the French intellectuals ribbons stars and baubles, he knew what he was doing...From the time of Richelieu and earlier, the French had been big in the culture business.
Humboldt's Gift (1975)

15 I knew that what you needed in a big American city was a deep no-affect belt, a critical mass of indifference...But now the moronic inferno had caught up with me.
Source of the title of Martin Amis's book on contemporary America, *Moronic Inferno* (1986).
Humboldt's Gift (1975)

16 Erotic practices have been diversified. Sex used to be a single-crop farming, like cotton or wheat, now people raise all sorts of things.
More Die of Heartbreak (1987)

17 The secret motive of the absent-minded is to be innocent while guilty. Absent-mindedness is spurious innocence.
More Die of Heartbreak (1987)

18 There ain't no little ways to make things better, the only big thing is money. That's the only sunbeams, money. Nothing is black where it shines, and the only place where you see black is where it ain't shining. What we colored have to have is our own rich.
1951. "Looking for Mr. Green," *Mosby's Memoirs and Other Stories* (1968)

19 New York makes one think of the collapse of civilization, about Sodom and Gomorrah, the end of the world. The end wouldn't come as a surprise here. Many people already bank on it.
Mr. Sammler's Planet (1970), pt. 1

20 How they love money, thought Wilhelm. They adore money! Holy money! Beautiful money! It was getting so that people were feeble-minded about everything except money.
Seize the Day (1956), ch. 2

21 The real universe. That's the present moment. The past is no good to us. The future is full of anxiety. Only the present is real—the here-and-now. Seize the day.
Seize the Day (1956), ch. 4

22 Commodities all the way to the horizon. There's enough of everything for everybody. That's how productive and rich the social order is. The whole process began with the proposition that the conquest of nature was going to be the top job of the modern age.
The Actual (1997)

23 Retirement is an illusion. Not a reward but a mantrap. The bankrupt underside of success. A shortcut to death. Golf courses are too much like cemeteries.
The Actual (1997)

24 Everyone knows that there is no fineness or accuracy of suppression. If you hold down one thing you hold down the adjoining.
The Adventures of Augie March (1953), ch. 1

25 Don't bother me with this ephemeral stuff—wives, kids, diapers, death.
The Dean's December (1982)

26 First man conquers nature, and then he learns that conquered nature has lost its purity and he's very upset by this loss. But it's not science that's to blame, it's technocrats and politicians. They've misused science.
The Dean's December (1982)

27 I imagine, sometimes, that if a film could be made of one's life, every other frame would be death. It goes so fast we're not aware of it.
The Dean's December (1982)

28 Perhaps only poetry had the strength to rival the attractions of narcotics, the magnetism of TV, the excitements of sex, or the ecstasies of destruction.
The Dean's December (1982)

29 What is barely hinted at in other American cities is condensed and enlarged in New York.
Quoted in *New York* (Mike Marquese and Bill Harris; 1985)

Belushi, John (1949–82) U.S. actor and comedian

1 It's 106 miles to Chicago, we got a full tank of gas, half a pack of cigarettes. It's dark and we're wearing sunglasses. Hit it.
As Jake Blues. *The Blues Brothers* (Dan Aykroyd and John Landis; 1980)

2 In your 20s, you feel like you're indestructible...In your 30s, you think...I'll be around here a little longer, so I'm going to take better care of myself.
1982. Belushi died of a drug overdose two months later. Quoted in *Rolling Stone* (January 21, 1982)

Benchley, Robert (Robert Charles Benchley; 1889–1945) U.S. humorist, writer, editor, and critic

1 Even nowadays a man can't step up and kill a woman without feeling just a bit unchivalrous.
"Down in Front," *Chips off the Old Benchley* (1949)

2 A great many people have come up to me and asked how I manage to get so much work done and still keep looking so dissipated.
"How to Get Things Done," *Chips off the Old Benchley* (1949)

3 I have been told by hospital authorities that more copies of my works are left behind by departing patients than those of any other author.
"Why Does Nobody Collect Me?," *Chips off the Old Benchley* (1949)

4 If you think that you have caught a cold, call in a good doctor. Call in three good doctors and play bridge.
"How to Avoid Colds," *From Bed to Worse* (1934)

5 In America, there are two classes of travel—first class, and with children.
Pluck and Luck (1926)

6 If Mr. Einstein doesn't like the natural laws of the universe, let him go back to where he came from.
1921. Quoted in *American Chronicle* (Lois and Alan Gordon; 1987)

7 Streets full of water. Please advise.
Telegram sent to his editor on arriving in Venice. *Wits End* (R. E. Drennan; 1973), "Robert Benchley"

8 I do most of my work sitting down; that's where I shine.
Attrib.

9 I don't trust a bank that would lend money to such a poor risk.
Addressed to a bank that granted his request for a loan. Attrib.

10 See Hebrews 13:8.
Criticism of a long-running play. Hebrews 13:8 reads: "Jesus Christ the same yesterday, and today, and for ever." Attrib.

11 She sleeps alone at last.
Suggested epitaph for an actor. Attrib.

12 So who's in a hurry?
When asked whether he knew that drinking was a slow death. Attrib.

Benda, Julien (1867–1956) French philosopher and essayist

1 Our age is the age of the nationalization of intellect in political hatreds.
La Trahison des clercs (1927)

2 The Intellectuals' Betrayal
Book title. *La Trahison des clercs* (1927)

Benedict, Ruth (originally Ruth Fulton; 1887–1948) U.S. anthropologist

1 The trouble with life isn't that there is no answer, it's that there are so many answers.
Journal entry (January 7, 1913), quoted in *An Anthropologist at Work* (Margaret Mead; 1959)

2 No man ever looks at the world with pristine eyes. He sees it edited by a definite set of customs and institutions and ways of thinking.
Patterns of Culture (1934)

3 If we justify war, it is because all peoples always justify the traits of which they find themselves possessed, not because war will bear an objective examination of its merits.
Patterns of Culture (1934), ch. 1

4 Racism is an *ism* to which everyone in the world today is exposed; for or against, we must take sides. And the history of the future will differ accordingly to the decision which we make.
Race: Science and Politics (1940), ch. 1

5 A man's indebtedness...is not virtue; his repayment is. Virtue begins when he dedicates himself actively to the job of gratitude.
The Chrysanthemum and the Sword (1946), ch. 6

6 I have always used the world of make-believe with a certain desperation.
Quoted in *An Anthropologist at Work* (Margaret Mead; 1959)

Benét, Stephen Vincent (1898–1943) U.S. poet and novelist

1 I have fallen in love with American names,
The sharp names that never get fat,
The snakeskin-titles of mining-claims,
The plumed war-bonnet of Medicine Hat,
Tucson and Deadwood and Lost Mule Flat.
"American Names" (1927)

2 I shall not rest quiet in Montparnasse
I shall not lie easy at Winchelsea
You may bury my body in Sussex grass,
You may bury my tongue at Champmédy
I shall not be there, I shall rise and pass
Bury my heart at Wounded Knee.
Also the source of the title of Dee Brown's celebrated book about Native Americans, *Bury My Heart at Wounded Knee* (1971). "American Names" (1927)

3 Don't eat too many almonds; they add weight to the breasts.
Gigi (1943)

Benjamin, Judah (Judah Philip Benjamin; 1811–84) Caribbean-born Confederate statesman and lawyer

Quotations about Benjamin

1 Mr. Benjamin was a brilliant lawyer, but he knew as much about war as an Arab knows of the Sermon on the Mount.
Anonymous. Quoted in *Johnny Reb and Billy Yank* (Alexander Hunter; 1905)

Quotations by Benjamin

2 The gentleman will please remember that when his half-civilized ancestors were hunting the wild boar in Silesia, mine were princes of the earth.
Replying to a U.S. senator of Germanic origin who had made an anti-Semitic remark. Attrib.

Benkert, Karoly Maria Hungarian physician

1 In addition to the normal sexual urge in men and women, Nature in her sovereign mood had endowed at birth certain male and female individuals with the homosexual urge.
1869. One of the first uses of the term "homosexual." Quoted in *Homosexuality: A History* (Colin Spencer; 1995)

Benn, Ernest, Sir (Ernest John Oickstone Benn; 1875–1954) British publisher

1 The art of looking for trouble, finding it whether it exists or not, diagnosing it incorrectly, and applying the wrong remedy.
Defining the art of politics. Attrib.

Benn, Tony (Anthony Neil Wedgwood Benn; b.1925) British politician and author

1 We are not just here to manage capitalism but to change society and to define its finer values.
Speech at the British Labour Party Conference (October 1, 1975)

2 Broadcasting is really too important to be left to the broadcasters and somehow we must find some new way of

using radio and television to allow us to talk to each other.
Similar remarks were made by Georges Clemenceau and Charles de Gaulle. Speech, Bristol (October 18, 1968)

3 The Marxist analysis has got nothing to do with what happened in Stalin's Russia; it's like blaming Jesus Christ for the Inquisition in Spain.
Observer, London (April 27, 1980)

4 If I rescued a child from drowning, the Press would no doubt headline the story "Benn grabs child".
Observer, London (March 2, 1975), "Sayings of the Week"

5 Most things in life are moments of pleasure and a lifetime of embarrassment; photography is a moment of embarrassment and a lifetime of pleasure.
Sunday Times, London (December 3, 1989)

6 I am on the right wing of the middle of the road and with a strong radical bias.
Attrib.

Bennett, Alan (b.1934) British playwright, actor, and director

1 Life is rather like a tin of sardines—we're all of us looking for the key.
Beyond the Fringe (1960)

2 Why is it always the intelligent people who are socialists?
Forty Years On (1969)

3 Tidy the old into tall flats. Desolation at fourteen storeys becomes a view.
An apartment block is sometimes referred to as "flats." *Forty Years On* (1969)

4 It's the one species I wouldn't mind seeing vanish from the face of the earth. I wish they were like the White Rhino—six of them left in the Serengeti National Park, and all males.
Referring to dogs. *Getting On* (1971), Act 1

5 Drama is the back-stairs of the intellect. Philosophers and historians go in by the front door, but playwrights and novelists sneak up the back stairs with their more disreputable luggage.
Sunday Times, London (November 24, 1991)

6 I'm not good at precise, coherent argument. But plays are suited to incoherent argument, put into the mouths of fallible people.
Sunday Times, London (November 24, 1991)

7 There are more microbes *per person* than the entire population of the world. Imagine that. Per person. This means that if the time scale is diminished in proportion to that of space it would be quite possible for the whole story of Greece and Rome to be played out between farts.
The Old Country (1978), Act 2

8 Sapper, Buchan, Dornford Yates, practitioners in that school of Snobbery with Violence that runs like a thread of good-class tweed through twentieth-century literature.
Times, London (January 21, 1983)

Bennett, Arnold (Enoch Arnold Bennett; 1867–1931) British writer

1 The people who live in the past must yield to the people who live in the future. Otherwise the world would begin to turn the other way round.
Milestones (1912)

2 Good taste is better than bad taste, but bad taste is better than no taste.
Observer, London (August 24, 1930), "Sayings of the Week"

3 "Ye can call it influenza if ye like," said Mrs Machin. "There was no influenza in my young days. We called a cold a cold."
The Card (1911), ch. 8

4 A cause is like champagne and high heels—one must be prepared to suffer for it.
The Title (1918)

5 Being a husband is a whole-time job. That is why so many husbands fail. They cannot give their entire attention to it.
The Title (1918)

6 Journalists say a thing that they know isn't true, in the hope that if they keep on saying it long enough it will be true.
The Title (1918)

7 Mother is far too clever to understand anything she does not like.
The Title (1918)

8 Well, my deliberate opinion is—it's a jolly strange world.
The Title (1918)

9 Mr Lloyd George spoke for a hundred and seventeen minutes, in which period he was detected only once in the use of an argument.
"After the March Offensive," *Things That Have Interested Me* (1921)

10 Pessimism, when you get used to it, is just as agreeable as optimism.
"The Slump in Pessimism," *Things That Have Interested Me* (1921)

11 A man of sixty has spent twenty years in bed and over three years eating.
Bartlett's Unfamiliar Quotations (Leonard Louis Levinson; 1972)

Bennett, Edward W. U.S. historian

1 History does offer some lessons, and it strikes me that one thing that it can teach...is to ask how those unlike ourselves can act the way we do.
"Intelligence and History from the Other Side of the Hill," *Journal of Modern History* (June 1988)

2 History, too, has its uses, such as the provision of a "usable" past.
"Intelligence and History from the Other Side of the Hill," *Journal of Modern History* (June 1988)

3 Wide agreement now exists that history is not confined to studying the outlooks or intentions of people. But, in practice, historians still very often deal with these matters, assessing them as typical for classes or groups, if not individuals.
"Intelligence and History from the Other Side of the Hill," *Journal of Modern History* (June 1988)

Bennett, Gwendolyn (1902–81) U.S. journalist, poet, and teacher

1 Oh little brown girl, born for sorrow's mate,
Keep all you have of queenliness,

Forgetting that you once were slave,
And let your full lips laugh at Fate!
"To a Dark Girl" (1922)

Bennett, James Gordon, Jr. (1841–1918) U.S. newspaper owner and editor

1 Deleted by French censor.
Used to fill empty spaces in his papers during World War I when news was lacking. *Americans in Paris* (Brian Morton; 1984)

Bennett, Lerone, Jr. (b.1928) U.S. journalist, historian, and poet

1 I woke up this morning
Just befo' the break of day.
I was bitter, blue and black, Lawd.
There ain't nothing else to say.
"Blues and Bitterness" (1964)

2 Black America in the nineties was a symphony of contradictions in search of a theme and creative conductors.
The Shaping of Black America (1975)

Bennis, Warren (b.1925) U.S. educationalist and writer

1 Economic activity should not only be efficient in its use of resources but should also be socially just, and environmentally and ecologically sustainable.
Beyond Leadership: Balancing Economics, Ethics and Ecology (co-written with Jagdish Parikh and Ronnie Lessem; 1994)

2 In order to serve its purpose, a vision has to be a shared vision.
Beyond Leadership: Balancing Economics, Ethics and Ecology (co-written with Jagdish Parikh and Ronnie Lessem; 1994)

3 Just as the human body can crave more and more of a drug that is actually poisoning it, so a society can crave lethal weapons, cadavers, or human organs which if freely traded, would inflict social damage.
Beyond Leadership: Balancing Economics, Ethics and Ecology (co-written with Jagdish Parikh and Ronnie Lessem; 1994)

4 Many Anglo-Saxons have a love affair with the manipulative ethos.
Beyond Leadership: Balancing Economics, Ethics and Ecology (co-written with Jagdish Parikh and Ronnie Lessem; 1994)

5 Successful executives are great askers.
Beyond Leadership: Balancing Economics, Ethics and Ecology (co-written with Jagdish Parikh and Ronnie Lessem; 1994)

6 Sustainable development challenges the entire industrial and commercial system to restructure itself.
Beyond Leadership: Balancing Economics, Ethics and Ecology (co-written with Jagdish Parikh and Ronnie Lessem; 1994)

7 The extraordinary manager operates on the emotional and spiritual resources of the organization, on its values, commitment, and aspirations.
Beyond Leadership: Balancing Economics, Ethics and Ecology (co-written with Jagdish Parikh and Ronnie Lessem; 1994)

8 With a vision, the executive provides the all-important bridge from the present to the future of the organization.
Beyond Leadership: Balancing Economics, Ethics and Ecology (co-written with Jagdish Parikh and Ronnie Lessem; 1994)

9 If there is a spark of genius in the leadership function at all, it must lie in this transcending ability...to assemble...a clearly articulated vision of the future that is at once simple, easily understood, clearly desirable, and energizing.
Leaders (co-written with Burt Nanus; 1985)

10 Managers have their eyes on the bottom line; leaders have their eyes on the horizon.
"On Becoming a Leader," *Leadership* (June 9, 1992)

11 Executive compensation should go far toward salving the pricked ego of the leader whose followers speak their minds.
"Thoughts on the Essentials of Leadership," *Mary Parker Follett: Prophet of Management* (Pauline Graham, ed.; 1995)

12 Leaders learn by leading, and they learn best by leading in the face of obstacles. As weather shapes mountains, problems shape leaders.
On Becoming a Leader (1988)

13 The problem facing almost all leaders in the future will be how to develop their organizations' social architecture so that it actually generates intellectual capital.
Strategy and Business (1997), "Noteworthy Quotes"

14 Lots of people in organizations may have vision, but there's absolutely zero meaning to what they're doing. They've actually forgotten why they are there, which is why bureaucracies become stodgy and obsolete and filled with inertia.
Interview, *Strategy and Business* (1997)

15 Managers do right things. Leaders do things right.
Technology Review, M.I.T. (April 1979)

16 Failing organizations are usually over-managed and under-led.
Why Leaders Can't Lead (1989)

17 My discovery was this: I had become the victim of a vast, amorphous, unwitting, unconscious conspiracy to prevent me from doing anything whatever to change the university's status quo.
Referring to university bureaucracy. Quoted in *How to Get Ahead in Business* (Tom Cannon, ed.; 1993)

Benny, Jack (Benjamin Kubelsky; 1894–1974) U.S. actor and comedian

Quotations about Benny

1 This was some great act this guy had; Jack Benny carried a violin he didn't play, a cigar he didn't smoke, and he was funniest when he said nothing.
George Burns (1896–1996) U.S. comedian and actor. *All My Best Friends* (1989)

2 Why didn't you hit a home run like I told you to? If you're not going to do what I tell you, what's the use of my being a manager?
Groucho Marx (1895–1977) U.S. comedian and film actor. Said to Jack Benny after he struck out in a charity game. *Baseball* (September 1948)

Quotations by Benny

3 Give me my golf clubs, fresh air and a beautiful partner, and you can keep my golf clubs and the fresh air.
Attrib.

4 I don't deserve this, but I have arthritis, and I don't deserve that either.
Said when accepting an award. Attrib.

Benson, A. C. (Arthur Christopher Benson; 1862–1925) British writer

1 Land of Hope and Glory, Mother of the Free,
How shall we extol thee, who are born of thee?
Wider still and wider shall thy bounds be set;
God who made thee mighty, make thee mightier yet.
Written to be sung as the Finale to Elgar's *Coronation Ode.* "Land of Hope and Glory" (1902)

Benson, E. F. (Edward Frederic Benson; 1867–1940) British novelist

1 There is no surer way of calling the worst out of anyone than that of taking their worst as being their true selves; no surer way of bringing out the best than by only accepting that as being true of them.
Rex (1925)

Benson, Lee (b.1922) U.S. historian

1 That generations of historians have resorted to what might be called "proof by haphazard quotation" does not make the procedure valid or reliable; it only makes it traditional.
Toward the Scientific Study of History (1972)

Bentham, Jeremy (1748–1832) British philosopher, economist, jurist, and social reformer

1 A full-grown horse or dog is beyond comparison a more rational, as well as a more conversable animal, than an infant of a day, or a week, or even a month, old. But suppose that the case were otherwise, what would it avail? The question is not, Can they *reason*? nor, Can they *talk*? but, Can they *suffer*?
An Introduction to the Principles of Morals and Legislation (1789)

2 Nature has placed mankind under the governance of two sovereign masters, *pain* and *pleasure*. It is for them alone to point out what we ought to do, as well as to determine what we shall do.
An Introduction to the Principles of Morals and Legislation (1789)

3 All punishment is mischief: all punishment in itself is evil.
An Introduction to the Principles of Morals and Legislation (1789), ch. 13

4 Every law is an evil, for every law is an infraction of liberty.
An Introduction to the Principles of Morals and Legislation (1789), introduction

5 When security and equality are in conflict, it will not do to hesitate a moment. Equality must yield.
An Introduction to the Principles of Morals and Legislation (1789), introduction

6 All inequality that has no special utility to justify it is injustice.
"Supply Without Burthen or Escheat Vice Taxation," *Jeremy Bentham's Economic Writings* (W. Stark, ed.; 1952)

7 He rather hated the ruling few than loved the suffering many.
Referring to James Mill. *Memories of Old Friends, being Extracts from the Journals and Letters of Caroline Fox* (H. N. Pym, ed.; 1882)

8 Lawyers are the only persons in whom ignorance of the law is not punished.
Attrib.

9 Liberty then is neither more nor less than the absence of coercion...It exists without Law, and not by means of Law.
Attrib.

Bentley, Edmund Clerihew (1875–1956) British writer and journalist

1 When their lordships asked Bacon
How many bribes he had taken
He had at least the grace
To get very red in the face.
Referring to Sir Francis Bacon. "Bacon," *Baseless Biography* (1939)

2 The Art of Biography
Is different from Geography.
Geography is about Maps,
But Biography is about Chaps.
Biography for Beginners (1905), Introduction

3 Sir Christopher Wren
Said, "I am going to dine with some men.
If anybody calls
Say I am designing St Paul's."
"Sir Christopher Wren," *Biography for Beginners* (1905)

4 Sir Humphry Davy
Abominated gravy.
He lived in the odium
Of having discovered Sodium.
"Sir Humphry Davy," *Biography for Beginners* (1905)

5 George the Third
Ought never to have occurred
One can only wonder
At so grotesque a blunder.
Referring to George III. "George the Third," *More Biography* (1929)

Bentley, Nicolas (Nicolas Clerihew Bentley; 1907–78) British cartoonist and writer

1 No news is good news; no journalists is even better.
Attrib.

2 One should not exaggerate the importance of trifles. Life, for instance, is much too short to be taken seriously.
Attrib.

Bentley, Richard (1662–1742) English classical scholar

1 It would be port if it could.
Comment on claret. *Bentley* (R. C. Jebb; 1902), ch. 12

Benton, Thomas Hart ("Old Bullion"; 1782–1858) U.S. politician

Quotations about Benton

1 A liar of magnitude.
John Quincy Adams (1767–1848) U.S. president. Quoted in *The President Who Wouldn't Retire* (Leonard Falkner; 1967)

Quotations by Benton

2 Mr. President, sir...I never quarrel, sir. But sometimes I fight, sir; and whenever I fight, sir, a funeral follows, sir.
Quoted in *Profiles in Courage* (John F. Kennedy; 1956)

Berdyaev, Nikolai (Nikolai Alexandrovich Berdyaev; 1874–1948) Ukrainian philosopher

1 In art there is liberation. The essential in artistic creativity is victory over the burden of necessity.
The Meaning of the Creative Act (Donald A. Lowrie, tr.; 1916)

2 Man is not only of this world but of another world, not only of necessity, but of freedom.
The Meaning of the Creative Act (Donald A. Lowrie, tr.; 1916)

3 The human spirit is in prison. Prison is what I call this world, the given world of necessity.
The Meaning of the Creative Act (Donald A. Lowrie, tr.; 1916)

Berenson, Bernard (1865–1959) Lithuanian-born U.S. art historian

1 Between truth and the search for truth, I opt for the second.
Essays in Appreciation (1958)

2 Psychoanalysts are not occupied with the minds of their patients; they do not believe in the mind but in a cerebral intestine.
Conversations with Berenson (Umberto Morra; 1963)

3 I wanted to become a work of art myself, and not an artist.
Quoted in *Sunset and Twilight: Diaries 1947–1958* (N. Mariano, ed.; 1964)

Beresford, Charles William de la Poer, 1st Baron (1846–1919) Irish-born British naval officer and author

1 Very sorry can't come. Lie follows by post.
Reply, by telegram, to a dinner invitation at short notice from Edward, Prince of Wales. *The World of Fashion 1837–1922* (R. Nevill; 1923), ch. 5

Berger, John (John Peter Berger; b.1926) British novelist, essayist, and art critic

1 The economic and military unification of the world has not brought peace but genocide.
1999. *Pig Earth* (1999 edition), introduction

2 The historic role of capitalism...to destroy history, to sever every link with the past and to orientate all effort and imagination to that which is about to occur.
1999. *Pig Earth* (1999 edition), introduction

3 The twentieth-century struggle between capitalism and socialism is, at an ideological level, a fight about the content of progress.
1999. *Pig Earth* (1999 edition), introduction

Bergman, Ingmar (b.1918) Swedish film and stage director

Quotations about Bergman

1 Bergman taught me how little you can do, rather than how much.
Liv Ullmann (b.1939) Japanese-born Norwegian actor and director. *Time* (December 4, 1972), quoted in *Chambers Film Quotes* (Tony Crawley, ed.; 1991)

Quotations by Bergman

2 A film for me begins with something very vague—a chance remark or a bit of conversation, a hazy but agreeable event unrelated to any particular situation. It can be a few bars of music, a shaft of light across the street.
Bergman Discusses Film-Making (Lars Malmström and David Kushner, trs.; 1960)

3 My professor told me when I started in the 40s that a director should listen and keep his mouth shut. Took me a long time to understand I talked too much. Now I know you should listen with your ears—and your heart.
Paris Passion (December 1989), quoted in *Chambers Film Quotes* (Tony Crawley, ed.; 1991)

4 Eight hours of hard work each day to get 3 minutes of film. And during those eight hours there are maybe only 10 or 12 minutes if you're lucky, of real creation...Everything and everyone on a movie set must be attuned to finding those minutes of creativity.
Interview, *Playboy* (June 1964), quoted in *Film-makers Speak* (Jay Leyda, ed.; 1977)

5 My sexuality struck me like a clap of thunder, incomprehensible, hostile, and tormenting.
The Magic Lantern (Joan Tate, tr.; 1988)

6 Sometimes I have to console myself with the fact that he who has lived a lie loves the truth.
The Magic Lantern (Joan Tate, tr.; 1988)

7 To me it was the beginning. I was overcome with a fever that has never left me. The silent shadows turned their pale faces towards me and spoke in inaudible voices to my most secret feelings. Sixty years have gone by and nothing has changed; the fever is the same.
Referring to seeing his first film. *The Magic Lantern* (Joan Tate, tr.; 1988)

8 KNIGHT God, You who are somewhere, who must be somewhere, have mercy upon us.
Set in the 14th century, the movie *The Seventh Seal* is a morality tale about a knight who plays a game of chess with Death. *The Seventh Seal* (1956)

9 The theater is like a faithful wife. The film is the great adventure—the costly, exacting mistress.
Quoted in *Halliwell's Filmgoer's Companion* (Leslie Halliwell; 1993)

Bergman, Ingrid (1915–82) Swedish actor

1 There is a kind of acting in the United States, especially in the movies, where the personality remains the same in every part. I like changing as much as possible. The Swedish idea of acting is that you do change; you play another person each time. To me, doing that is natural.
Interview, *The Player* (1962), quoted in *Film-makers Speak* (Jay Leyda, ed.; 1977)

2 I have no regrets. I wouldn't have lived my life the way I did if I was going to worry about what people were going to say.
Attrib.

3 It's not whether you really cry. It's whether the audience thinks you are crying.
Attrib.

Bergson, Henri-Louis (1859–1941) French philosopher

1 The present contains nothing more than the past, and what is found in the effect was already in the cause.
Creative Evolution (1907), ch. 1

2 Intelligence is characterized by a natural incomprehension of life.
Creative Evolution (1907), ch. 2

3 The fundamental law of life is the complete negation of repetition.
Laughter (1900)

4 The universe is a machine for creating gods.
Two Sources for Morality and Religion (1932)

Berkeley, Bishop (George Berkeley; 1685–1753) Irish prelate and philosopher

1 We see only the appearances, and not the real qualities of things...for aught we know, all we see, hear, and feel may be only phantom and vain chimera, and not all agree with the real things, existing in *rerum natura*.
A Treatise Concerning the Principles of Human Knowledge (1710)

2 Their *esse* is *percipi*, nor is it possible that they should have any existence, out of the minds of thinking things which perceive them.
Referring to inanimate objects. *A Treatise Concerning the Principles of Human Knowledge* (1710)

3 We have first raised a dust and then complain we cannot see.
A Treatise Concerning the Principles of Human Knowledge (1710), introduction

4 It is impossible that a man who is false to his friends and neighbours should be true to the public.
Maxims Concerning Patriotism (1750)

Berkhofer, Robert Frederick, Jr. (b.1931) U.S. historian

1 The historian is merely trying to do in time what the anthropologist does in space.
A Behavioral Approach to Historical Analysis (1969)

Berkman, Alexander (1870–1936) Lithuanian-born U.S. writer and anarchist

1 Government is the common enemy. All weapons are justifiable in the noble struggle against this terrible curse.
Prison Memoirs of an Anarchist (1912)

Berlin, Irving (Israel Baline; 1888–1989) Russian-born U.S. composer and lyricist

Quotations about Berlin

1 Irving Berlin *is* American music.
Jerome Kern (1885–1945) U.S. composer. Quoted in *Guardian*, London (September 25, 1989)

Quotations by Berlin

2 There's No Business Like Show Business
Song title. "Annie Get Your Gun" (1946)

3 Got no check books, got no banks.
Still I'd like to express my thanks—
I got the sun in the mornin' and the moon at night.
"I Got the Sun in the Mornin'," *Annie Get Your Gun* (1946)

4 We joined the Navy to see the world,
And what did we see? We saw the sea.
"We Saw the Sea," *Follow the Fleet* (1936)

5 I'm dreaming of a white Christmas.
"White Christmas," *Holiday Inn* (1942)

Berlin, Isaiah, Sir (1909–97) Latvian-born British philosopher and historian of ideas

1 "Every man to count for one and no one to count for more than one"...appears, more than any other formula, to constitute the irreducible minimum of the ideal of equality.
Concepts and Categories (1978)

2 Men cannot live without seeking to describe and explain the universe to themselves.
Concepts and Categories (1978)

3 The goal of philosophy is always the same, to assist men to understand themselves and thus operate in the open, and not wildly, in the dark.
Concepts and Categories (1978)

4 Injustice, poverty, slavery, ignorance—these may be cured by reform or revolution. But men do not live only by fighting evils. They live by positive goals, individual and collective, a vast variety of them, seldom predictable, at times incompatible.
"Political Ideas in the Twentieth Century," *Four Essays on Liberty* (1969)

Berlioz, Hector (Louis Hector Berlioz; 1803–69) French composer

1 Time is a great teacher, but unfortunately it kills all its pupils.
Attrib.

Bernal, John Desmond (1901–71) Irish crystallographer

1 Life is a partial, continuous, progressive, multiform and conditionally interactive self-realization of the potentialities of atomic electron states.
The Origin of Life (1967)

Bernanos, Georges (1888–1948) French novelist and essayist

1 Hell, madame, is to love no more.
Journal d'un curé de campagne (1936), ch. 2

Bernard, Claude (1813–78) French physiologist

1 Man can learn nothing except by going from the known to the unknown.
An Introduction to the Study of Experimental Medicine (1865), ch. 2

Bernard, Tristan (Paul Bernard; 1866–1947) French novelist and dramatist

1 In the theater the audience want to be surprised—but by things that they expect.
Contes, Répliques et Bon Mots (1964)

Bernard, W. B. (William Bayle Bernard; 1807–75) British playwright

1 A Storm in a Teacup
Play title. *A Storm in a Teacup* (1854)

Bernard of Chartres (d.1130?) French humanist and philosopher

1 We are like dwarfs on the shoulders of giants, so that we can see more than they, and things at a greater distance, not by virtue of any sharpness of sight on our part, or any physical distinction, but because we are carried high and raised up by their giant size.
The Metalogicon (John of Salisbury; 1159), bk. 3, ch. 4

Bernard of Clairvaux, Saint ("The Mellifluous Doctor"; 1090–1153) French monk, mystic, theologian, and religious reformer

1 I have freed my soul.
Epistles (1481), no. 371

2 O mighty soldier, O man of war, at last you have a cause for which you can fight without endangering your soul; a cause in which to win is glorious and for which to die is but gain...Take the sign of the cross. At once you will have an indulgence for all the sins which you confess with a contrite heart.
12th century. Sermon given at Vézelay referring in particular to the Second Crusade (1147–48). Quoted in *Richard the Lionheart* (J. Gillingham; 1989), ch. 6

3 The Christian glories in the death of a pagan because thereby Christ himself is glorified.
12th century. *Richard the Lionheart* (J. Gillingham; 1989), ch. 9

Bernbach, William (1911–82) U.S. advertising executive

1 In communications, familiarity breeds apathy.
Bill Bernbach Said... (1989)

2 Nobody counts the number of ads you run; they just remember the impression you make.
Bill Bernbach Said... (1989)

3 Properly practiced creativity can make one ad do the work of ten.
Bill Bernbach Said... (1989)

4 Today's smartest advertising style is tomorrow's corn.
Bill Bernbach Said... (1989)

5 Advertising isn't a science. It's persuasion. And persuasion is an art.
Quoted in *Speaking Freely* (Stuart Berg Flexner and Anne H. Soukhanov; 1997)

6 A logo is like a man's name. When I mention a certain man you know well, everything about that man jumps into your mind...A logo does the same thing for a product.
Quoted in "William Bernbach," *The Art of Writing Advertising* (Denis Higgins; 1965)

7 The most important element of success in ad writing is the product itself.
Quoted in "William Bernbach," *The Art of Writing Advertising* (Denis Higgins; 1965)

8 Those who are going to be in business tomorrow are those who understand that the future, as always, belongs to the brave.
Attrib.

Berne, Eric (Eric Leonard Berne; 1910–70) U.S. psychiatrist

1 Human life is mainly a process of filling in time until the arrival of death, or Santa Claus, with very little choice, if any, of what kind of business one is going to transact during the long wait.
Games People Play (1964), ch. 18

2 Games People Play
1964. Book title.

3 No man is a hero to his wife's psychiatrist.
Attrib.

Bernhardt, Sarah (Sarah-Marie-Henrietta-Rosine Bernard, "The Divine Sarah"; 1844–1923) French actor and theater manager

1 For the theatre one needs long arms; it is better to have them too long than too short. An *artiste* with short arms can never, never make a fine gesture.
Memories of My Life (1907), ch. 6

2 I do love cricket—it's so very English.
On seeing a game of soccer. *Nijinsky* (R. Buckle; 1975)

Bernoulli, Daniel (1700–82) Dutch-born Swiss scientist

1 It would be better for the true physics if there were no mathematicians on earth.
Quoted in *The Mathematical Intelligencer* (1991), vol. 13, no. 1

Bernstein, Leonard (1918–90) U.S. composer, conductor, and pianist

1 It would be nice to hear someone accidentally whistle something of mine, somewhere, just once.
The Joy of Music (1959)

2 Ma, I want lessons!
Recalling his inheritance, aged ten, of his aunt's piano. Quoted in *Simpson's Contemporary Quotations* (James B. Simpson; 1997)

Berra, Yogi (Lawrence Peter Berra; b.1925) U.S. baseball player, manager, and coach

1 It ain't over 'til it's over.
Said at the time of the 1973 pennant race, when Berra's team the Mets were being notoriously inconsistent. Remark (1973)

2 Baseball is ninety percent mental. The other half is physical.
Yogi: It Ain't Over... (co-written with Tom Horton; 1989)

3 How can you think and hit at the same time?
Attrib.

4 It was déjà vu all over again.
Attrib.

5 When you come to a fork in the road, take it.
Attrib.

Berry, Chuck (Charles Edward Anderson Berry; b.1926) U.S. pop singer and composer

1 Though I play from desire, I feel I should be paid for the hire.
Chuck Berry: The Autobiography (1988)

Berry, Wendell (Wendell Erdman Berry; b.1934) U.S. poet, novelist, and essayist

1 The fault of a colonial economy is that it is dishonest: it misrepresents reality. In practice it is simply a way of keeping costs off the books of an exploitative interest.
1986. Referring to his view that the U.S. economy "preys on its internal colonies." "Does Community Have a Value?," *The Landscape of Harmony* (1987)

2 Alone, practicality becomes dangerous; spirituality, alone, becomes feeble and pointless. Alone, either becomes dull. Each is the other's discipline, in a sense, and in good work the two are joined.
1985. "Preserving Wildness," *The Landscape of Harmony* (1987)

3 Nature is not easy to live with. It is hard to have rain on your cut hay, or floodwater over your cropland, or coyotes in your sheep...nature does not respect your intentions.
1985. "Preserving Wildness," *The Landscape of Harmony* (1987)

4 Our present economy...does not account for affection at all, which is to say that it does not account for value. It is simply a description of the career of money as it preys upon both nature and human society.
1985. "Preserving Wildness," *The Landscape of Harmony* (1987)

5 The good worker loves the board before it becomes a table, loves the tree before it yields the board, loves the forest before it gives up the tree.
1985. "Preserving Wildness," *The Landscape of Harmony* (1987)

Berryman, John (John McAlpin Berryman; 1914–72) U.S. poet

1 Our Sunday morning when dawn-priests were applying
Wafer and wine to the human wound, we laid
Ourselves to cure ourselves down.
1952. *Berryman's Sonnets* (1967), no. 71, quoted in *Selected Poems 1938–1968* (1972)

2 I am a maid of shots & pills
swivel the lights of Beverly Hills.
"American Lights Seen from Off Abroad," *His Thoughts Made Pockets as the Plane Buckt* (1958), ll. 15–16

3 I am all satisfied love & chalk
mutter the great lights of New York.
"American Lights Seen from Off Abroad," *His Thoughts Made Pockets as the Plane Buckt* (1958), ll. 17–18

4 Your first day in Dublin is always your worst.
"The Dream Songs," *His Toy, His Dream, His Rest* (1968), l. 299

5 We must travel in the direction of our fear.
"A Point of Age," *Poems* (1942)

6 Am I a bad man? Am I a good man?
—Hard to say, Brother Bones. Maybe you both,
like most of we.
The Dream Songs (1968)

7 Fan-mail from foreign countries, is that fame?
The Dream Songs (1968)

8 Filling her compact & delicious body
with chicken paprika, she glanced at me
twice.
The Dream Songs (1968)

9 I don't operate often. When I do,
persons take note.
The Dream Songs (1968)

10 It takes me so long to read the 'paper
said to me one day a novelist hot as a firecracker,
because I have to identify myself with everyone in it,
including the corpses, pal.
The Dream Songs (1968)

11 Life, friends, is boring. We must not say so.
The Dream Songs (1968)

12 Literature bores me, especially great literature.
The Dream Songs (1968)

13 Where did it all go wrong? There ought to be a law against
Henry.
—Mr. Bones: there is.
The Dream Songs (1968)

Bertalanffy, Ludwig von German scientist

1 What is called human progress is a purely intellectual affair...not much development, however, is seen on the moral side. It is doubtful whether the methods of modern warfare are preferable to the big stones used for cracking the skull of the fellow-Neanderthaler.
Scientific Monthly (1956)

Bertolucci, Bernardo (b.1940) Italian film director

1 I don't know how to use the camera. But I know what I want. I want each take to be a film in itself. I am against editing. I would like to make a film of one long take. I feel that editing renders films all alike, gives them the brushing of conventionality.
Interview, *Newsweek* (February 12, 1973), quoted in *Film-makers Speak* (Jay Leyda, ed.; 1977)

2 Having no children had been a kind of choice up to the moment when, from a choice, it became a sadness.
Observer, London (May 1, 1994), "Sayings of the Week"

Bethmann Hollweg, Theobald von (1856–1921) German chancellor

1 Just for the word "neutrality," a word which in wartime has so often been disregarded—just for a scrap of paper, Great Britain is going to make war on a kindred nation who desires nothing better than to be friends with her.
Said to Sir Edward Goschen. Remark (1914), quoted in "British Documents," *Origins of the War 1898–1914* (1926), vol. 11

2 To rattle the saber at every diplomatic entanglement...is not only blind but criminal.
Remark to Crown Prince Wilhelm of Germany (November 15, 1913), quoted in *Europe: A History* (Norman Davies; 1996), ch. 10

3 The future belongs to Russia, which grows and grows, looming above us as an increasingly terrifying nightmare.
Referring to Bethmann Hollweg's fear of the increasing threat posed by Russia, Serbia's ally, on the eve of World War I. Remark to his personal assistant (July 8, 1914), quoted in *Europe: A History* (Norman Davies; 1996), ch. 10

4 This war is only turning into an unlimited world catastrophe through England's participation. It was in London's hands to curb French revanchism and pan-Slav chauvinism. Whitehall has not done so...And why? For Belgian neutrality...We enter the war with a clear conscience.
Referring to World War I. Remark to Sir Edward Goschen, British ambassador to Germany (August 4, 1914), quoted in *Europe: A History* (Norman Davies; 1996), ch. 10

5 Russia has thrown a firebrand into our house.
Blaming Russia for the outbreak of a European-wide war. Speech, Reichstag, Berlin (August 3, 1914), quoted in *Europe: A History* (Norman Davies; 1996)

Bethune, Mary McLeod (1875–1955) U.S. educator and human-rights activist

1 The true worth of a race must be measured by the character of its womanhood.
Address to Chicago Women's Federation (June 30, 1933), quoted in *Black Women in White America* (Gerda Lerner; 1972)

2 Without faith nothing is possible. With it, nothing is impossible.
"My Last Will and Testament" (1975)

3 I believe, first of all, in God, and next to all, in Mary McLeod Bethune.
Quoted in *Mary McLeod Bethune* (Emma Gelders Steine; 1957)

4 I don't mind being different. I don't want to be Jim-Crowed to a back seat because I'm black and I don't want to be ushered to a front seat because I'm not white so they can "palaver" over me.
Quoted in *Mary McLeod Bethune* (Emma Gelders Steine; 1957)

Betjeman, John, Sir (1906–84) British poet and broadcaster

1 And girls in slacks remember Dad,
And oafish louts remember Mum,
And sleepless children's hearts are glad,
And Christmas morning bells say "Come!"
Even to shining ones who dwell
Safe in the Dorchester Hotel.
"Christmas," *A Few Late Chrysanthemums* (1954)

2 Are the requisites all in the toilet?
The frills round the cutlets can wait
Till the girl has replenished the cruets
And switched on the logs in the grate.
"How to Get On in Society," *A Few Late Chrysanthemums* (1954)

3 Phone for the fish knives Norman,
As Cook is a little unnerved;
You kiddies have crumpled the serviettes
And I must have things daintily served.
Satirizing the social pretensions of the English middle classes. "Serviettes" means "(table) napkins." "How to Get On in Society," *A Few Late Chrysanthemums* (1954)

4 There was sun enough for lazing upon beaches,
There was fun enough for far into the night
But I'm dying now and done for,
What on earth was all the fun for?
For I'm old and ill and terrified and tight.
"Sun and Fun," *A Few Late Chrysanthemums* (1954), st. 5

5 Dear Mary,
...Yes, it will be bliss
To go with you by train to Diss,
Your walking shoes upon your feet;
We'll meet, my sweet, at Liverpool Street.
1974. Addressed to Lady Wilson, wife of Harold Wilson. "A Mind's Journey to Diss," *John Betjeman's Collected Poems* (1979), ll. 1–5

6 Love-thirty, love-forty, oh! weakness of joy,
The speed of a swallow, the grace of a boy,
With carefullest carelessness, gaily you won,
I am weak from your loveliness, Joan Hunter Dunn.
1945. A subaltern was an officer of junior rank in the British army. "A Subaltern's Love Song," *John Betjeman's Collected Poems* (1958)

7 And is it true? And is it true,
This most tremendous tale of all,
Seen in a stained-glass window's hue,
A Baby in an ox's stall?
1954. "Christmas," *John Betjeman's Collected Poems* (1958)

8 It's awf'lly bad luck on Diana,
Her ponies have swallowed their bits;
She fished down their throats with a spanner
And frightened them all into fits.
1954. "Spanner" means wrench. "Hunter Trials," *John Betjeman's Collected Poems* (1958)

9 Gracious Lord, oh bomb the Germans
Spare their women for Thy Sake,
And if that is not too easy
We will pardon Thy Mistake
But, gracious Lord, whate'er shall be,
Don't let anyone bomb me.
1940. "In Westminster Abbey," *John Betjeman's Collected Poems* (1958)

10 Think of what our Nation stands for,
Books from Boots' and country lanes,
Free speech, free passes, class distinction,
Democracy and proper drains.
"In Westminster Abbey," *John Betjeman's Collected Poems* (1958)

11 Come, friendly bombs, and fall on Slough
It isn't fit for humans now.
There isn't grass to graze a cow
Swarm over, Death!
...
Come, friendly bombs, and fall on Slough
To get it ready for the plough.
The cabbages are coming now:
The earth exhales.
1937. "Slough," *John Betjeman's Collected Poems* (1958)

12 Business men with awkward hips
And dirty jokes upon their lips,
And large behinds and jingling chains,
And riddled teeth and riddling brains.
"The City," *John Betjeman's Collected Poems* (1958)

13 Oh! chintzy, chintzy cheeriness,
Half dead and half alive!
1931. "Chintz" means brightly printed (often floral) material for covering furniture, originally imported from India. "Death in Leamington," *Mount Zion* (1932)

14 One cannot assess in terms of cash or exports and imports an imponderable thing like the turn of a lane or an inn or a church tower or a familiar skyline.
July 1969. On hearing that a new London airport might be sited at the Buckinghamshire village of Wing. *Observer*, London (July 20, 1969), "Sayings of the Week"

15 Too many people in the modern world view poetry as a luxury, not a necessity like petrol. But to me it's the oil of life.
Observer, London (1974), "Sayings of the Year"

16 Lord, put beneath Thy special care
One-eighty-nine Cadogan Square.
"In Westminster Abbey," *Old Lights for New Chancels* (1940)

17 Oh would I could subdue the flesh
Which sadly troubles me!
And then perhaps could view the flesh
As though I never knew the flesh
And merry misery.
"Senex," *Old Lights for New Chancels* (1940), st. 1

18 The dread of beatings! Dread of being late!
And greatest dread of all, the dread of games!
"Marlborough," *Summoned by Bells* (1960), ch. 7

Bettelheim, Bruno (1903–90) Austrian-born U.S. psychoanalyst

1 No longer can we be satisfied with a life where the heart has its reasons which reason cannot know. Our hearts must know the world of reason, and reason must be guided by an informed heart.
Guardian, London (March 15, 1990)

2 Fairy tales unconsciously understand, and...offer examples of both temporary and permanent solutions to pressing difficulties.
The Uses of Enchantment (1976)

Betti, Ugo (1892–1953) Italian playwright and poet

1 Memories are like stones, time and distance erode them like acid.
Goat Island (1946)

2 We wander but in the end there is always a certain peace in being what one is, in being that completely. The condemned man has that joy.
Goat Island (1946)

3 "Mad" is a term we use to describe a man who is obsessed with one idea and nothing else.
Struggle Till Dawn (G. H. McWilliam, tr.; 1949)

4 Murderers, in general, are people who are consistent, people who are obsessed with one idea and nothing else.
Struggle Till Dawn (G. H. McWilliam, tr.; 1949)

5 We cannot bear to regard ourselves simply as playthings of blind chance; we cannot admit to feeling ourselves abandoned.
Struggle Till Dawn (G. H. McWilliam, tr.; 1949)

6 When a man prays, do you know what he's doing?...He's saying to himself: "Keep calm, everything's all right, it's all right."
Struggle Till Dawn (G. H. McWilliam, tr.; 1949)

7 All of us are mad. If it weren't for the fact every one of us is slightly abnormal, there wouldn't be any point in giving each person a separate name.
The Fugitive (G. H. McWilliam, tr.; 1953)

8 Nobody is bound by obligation unless it has first been freely accepted.
The Fugitive (G. H. McWilliam, tr.; 1953)

9 Perhaps there is nothing in the whole of creation that knows the meaning of peace. For is the soil not restless compared to the unyielding rock?
The Fugitive (G. H. McWilliam, tr.; 1953)

10 Justice! Custodian of the world! But since the world errs, justice must be the custodian of the world's errors.
The Gambler (Gino Rizzo, tr.; 1950)

11 At a given moment I open my eyes and exist. And before that, during all eternity, what was there? Nothing.
The Inquiry (Gino Rizzo, tr.; 1944–45)

12 I think the family is the place where the most ridiculous and least respectable things in the world go on.
The Inquiry (Gino Rizzo, tr.; 1944–45)

13 We play make believe, pretend to take ourselves and each other seriously—to love each other, hate each other but then—it isn't true! It isn't true, we don't care at all.
The Inquiry (Gino Rizzo, tr.; 1944–45)

14 Who cares about great marks left behind? We have one life, rigidly defined. Just one. One life. We have nothing else.
The Inquiry (Gino Rizzo, tr.; 1944–45)

Beugnot, Count French aristocrat

1 We seemed to be saying to all those flunkies: you will kill us when you will, but you will not prevent us from being pleasant.
A typical aristocratic response to the prospect of execution during the French Revolution (1789–99). Quoted in *Last Letters: Prisons and Prisoners of the French Revolution 1793–1794* (Olivier Blanc, ed.; 1987)

Bevan, Aneurin (called Nye Bevan; 1897–1960) Welsh politician

Quotations about Bevan

1 Not while I'm alive, he ain't.
Ernest Bevin (1881–1951) British labor leader and statesman. Remark on being told that Aneurin Bevan was "his own worst enemy." Also attributed to others. Quoted in *Aneurin Bevan* (Michael Foot; 1973)

2 He was the only man I knew who could make a curse sound like a caress.
Michael Foot (b.1913) British politician and writer. *Aneurin Bevan 1897–1945* (1962), vol. 1

Quotations by Bevan

3 This island is almost made of coal and surrounded by fish. Only an organizing genius could produce a shortage of coal and fish in Great Britain at the same time.
Speech at the British Labour Party Conference, Blackpool (May 18, 1945)

4 It is not possible to create peace in the Middle East by jeopardising the peace of the world.
Remark made at a rally protesting against Britain's armed intervention in the Suez dispute. Speech, Trafalgar Square, London (November 4, 1956)

5 If you carry this resolution and follow out all its implications and do not run away from it, you will send a Foreign Secretary, whoever he may be, naked into the conference chamber.
October 2, 1957. Opposing unilateral disarmament by the United Kingdom. Speech at the British Labour Party Conference, *Daily Herald* (October 4, 1957)

6 In Place of Fear
Title of a book about disarmament. *In Place of Fear* (1952)

7 We know what happens to people who stay in the middle of the road. They get run down.
Observer, London (December 9, 1953)

8 The language of priorities is the religion of Socialism.
June 8, 1949. *Report of the 48th Annual Conference of the British Labour Party* (1949)

9 I read the newspapers avidly. It is my one form of continuous fiction.
Times, London (March 29, 1960)

10 Righteous people terrify me...Virtue is its own punishment.
Quoted in *Aneurin Bevan* (Michael Foot; 1973)

11 Politics is a blood sport.
1950s. *My Life with Nye* (Jennie Lee; 1980)

12 Fascism is not itself a new order of society. It is the future refusing to be born.
Attrib.

13 I stuffed their mouths with gold!
Explaining how he persuaded British doctors not to oppose the introduction of the National Health Service. Attrib.

Beveridge, Albert J. (Albert Jeremiah Beveridge; 1862–1927) U.S. politician and historian

1 It has been charged that our conduct of the war has been cruel...Senators must remember that we are not dealing with Americans or Europeans. We are dealing with Orientals.
Referring to the crushing of rebellion in the Philippines. Speech, U.S. Senate (January 9, 1900)

Beveridge, William Henry, 1st Baron Beveridge of Tuggal (1879–1963) British economist and social reformer

1 Ignorance is an evil weed, which dictators may cultivate among their dupes, but which no democracy can afford among its citizens.
Full Employment in a Free Society (1944), pt. 4

2 Scratch a pessimist, and you find often a defender of privilege.
Observer, London (December 17, 1943), "Sayings of the Week"

3 The trouble in modern democracy is that men do not approach to leadership until they have lost the desire to lead anyone.
Observer, London (April 15, 1934), "Sayings of the Week"

4 The object of government in peace and in war is not the glory of rulers or of races, but the happiness of the common man.
Social Insurance and Allied Services (1942), pt. 7

Bevin, Ernest (1881–1951) British labor leader and statesman

1 I deny Hitler's right, I deny any state's right, to put a limitation on the progress of the human mind.
Speech, Swansea, Wales (November 1, 1941)

2 There never has been a war yet which, if the facts had been put calmly before the ordinary folk, could not have been prevented...The common man, I think, is the great protection against war.
Speech to the British Parliament (November 23, 1945), House of Commons

3 If you open that Pandora's Box you never know what Trojan 'orses will jump out.
Referring to the Council of Europe. *Ernest Bevin and the Foreign Office* (Sir Roderick Barclay; 1975), ch. 3

Bhabha, Homi British writer and academic

1 If hybridity is heresy, to blaspheme is to dream.
The Location of Culture (1994)

Bhagavad-Gita

1 Hell has three gates: lust, anger, and greed.
The Bhagavad-Gita

Bhutto, Benazir (b.1953) Pakistani stateswoman

1 What is not recorded is not remembered.
Daughter of Destiny (1989)

2 You cannot be fuelled by bitterness. It can eat you up but it cannot drive you.
Daughter of Zulfikar Ali Bhutto, prime minister of Pakistan (1971–77) who was unseated by a military coup, Benazir Bhutto herself was twice prime minister (1988–90, 1993–96), both times being dismissed by the president amid allegations of corruption. Attrib.

Bibescu, Elizabeth Charlotte Lucy, Princess (1897–1945) British writer

1 It is never any good dwelling on goodbyes. It is not the being together that it prolongs, it is the parting.
Attrib.

Bible

1 And when he had spoken these things, while they beheld, he was taken up; and a cloud received him out of their sight.
Acts, *King James Bible* (1611), 1:9

2 This man purchased a field with the reward of iniquity; and falling headlong, he burst asunder in the midst, and all his bowels gushed out.
The death of Judas Iscariot, who betrayed Jesus Christ. It differs from Matthew's Gospel which states that Judas returned the money to the Jewish authorities and then hanged himself (27:3–5). Acts, *King James Bible* (1611), 1:18

3 Let his habitation be desolate, and let no man dwell therein: and his bishoprick let another take.
The decision by the remaining apostles to replace Judas Iscariot. Acts, *King James Bible* (1611), 1:20

4 And when the day of Pentecost was fully come, they were all with one accord in one place.
And suddenly there came a sound from heaven as of a rushing mighty wind...
And they were all filled with the Holy Ghost, and began to speak with other tongues, as the Spirit gave them utterance.
Acts, *King James Bible* (1611), 2:1–4

5 Others mocking said, These men are full of new wine.
Referring to the "gift of tongues." Acts, *King James Bible* (1611), 2:13

6 All that believed were together, and had all things in common; and sold their possessions and goods, and parted them to all men, as every man had need.
Acts, *King James Bible* (1611), 2:44–45

7 Then Peter said, Silver and gold have I none; but such as I have give I thee: In the name of Jesus Christ of Nazareth rise up and walk.
Acts, *King James Bible* (1611), 3:6

8 This is the stone which was set at nought of you builders, which is become the head of the corner.
Part of Peter's defense before the Jewish council when ordered to stop preaching. Acts, *King James Bible* (1611), 4:11

9 Refrain from these men, and let them alone: for if this counsel or this work be of men, it will come to nought: but if it be of God, ye cannot overthrow it; lest haply ye be found even to fight against God.
Comment by Gamaliel, a noted Jewish theologian who taught Paul, at the trial of Peter and the other apostles. Acts, *King James Bible* (1611), 5:38–39

10 When they heard these things, they were cut to the heart, and they gnashed on him with their teeth.
Acts, *King James Bible* (1611), 7:54

11 And as he journeyed, he came near Damascus: and suddenly there shined round about him a light from heaven:
And he fell to the earth, and heard a voice saying unto him, Saul, Saul, why persecutest thou me?
And he said, Who art thou, Lord? And the Lord said, I am Jesus whom thou persecutest: it is hard for thee to kick against the pricks.
Acts, *King James Bible* (1611), 9:3–5

12 And the Lord said unto him, Arise, and go into the street which is called Straight, and enquire in the house of Judas for one called Saul, of Tarsus: for, behold, he prayeth.
Acts, *King James Bible* (1611), 9:11

13 But the Lord said unto him, Go thy way: for he is a chosen vessel unto me, to bear my name before the Gentiles, and kings, and the children of Israel.
Acts, *King James Bible* (1611), 9:15

14 But Peter took him up, saying, Stand up; I myself also am a man.
Acts, *King James Bible* (1611), 10:26

15 Then Peter opened his mouth, and said, Of a truth I perceive that God is no respecter of persons.
Acts, *King James Bible* (1611), 10:34

16 And the people gave a shout, saying, It is the voice of a god, and not of a man.
And immediately the angel of the Lord smote him, because he gave not God the glory: and he was eaten of worms, and gave up the ghost.
Acts, *King James Bible* (1611), 12:22–23

17 They shook off the dust of their feet against them.
Referring to Paul and Barnabas when they were expelled from Pisidian Antioch. Acts, *King James Bible* (1611), 13:51

18 God that made the world and all things therein, seeing that he is Lord of heaven and earth, dwelleth not in temples made with hands.
Acts, *King James Bible* (1611), 17:24

19 For in him we live, and move, and have our being; as certain also of your own poets have said, For we are also his offspring.
Acts, *King James Bible* (1611), 17:28

20 And now, behold, I go bound in the spirit unto Jerusalem, not knowing the things that shall befall me there.
Acts, *King James Bible* (1611), 20:22

21 And the chief captain answered, With a great sum obtained I this freedom. And Paul said, But I was free born.
Acts, *King James Bible* (1611), 22:28

22 Seek him that maketh the seven stars and Orion, and turneth the shadow of death into the morning, and maketh the day dark with night: that calleth for the waters of the sea, and poureth them out upon the face of the earth: The Lord is his name.
Amos, *King James Bible* (1611), 5:8

23 Beware lest any man spoil you through philosophy and vain deceit, after the tradition of men, after the rudiments of the world, and not after Christ.
Colossians, *King James Bible* (1611), 2:8

24 Where there is neither Greek nor Jew, circumcision nor uncircumcision, Barbarian, Scythian, bond nor free; but Christ is all, and in all.
Colossians, *King James Bible* (1611), 3:11

25 Husbands, love your wives, and be not bitter against them.
Colossians, *King James Bible* (1611), 3:19

26 Fathers, provoke not your children to anger, lest they be discouraged.
Colossians, *King James Bible* (1611), 3:21

27 Let your speech be alway with grace, seasoned with salt, that ye may know how ye ought to answer every man.
Colossians, *King James Bible* (1611), 4:6

28 That at what time ye hear the sound of...all kinds of musick, ye fall down and worship the golden image that Nebuchadnezzar the king hath set up:
And whoso falleth not down and worshippeth shall the same hour be cast into the midst of a burning fiery furnace.
Daniel, *King James Bible* (1611), 3:5–6

29 Then was Nebuchadnezzar full of fury, and the form of his visage was changed against Shadrach, Meshach, and Abed-nego: therefore he spake, and commanded that they should heat the furnace one seven times more than it was wont to be heated.
Daniel, *King James Bible* (1611), 3:19

30 The same hour was the thing fulfilled upon Nebuchadnezzar: and he was driven from men, and did eat grass as oxen, and his body was wet with the dew of heaven, till his hairs were grown like eagles' feathers, and his nails like birds' claws.
Daniel, *King James Bible* (1611), 4:33

31 In the same hour came forth fingers of a man's hand, and wrote over against the candlestick upon the plaister of the wall of the king's palace: and the king saw the part of the hand that wrote.
Daniel, *King James Bible* (1611), 5:5

32 And this is the writing that was written, MENE, MENE, TEKEL, UPHARSIN.
This is the interpretation of the thing: MENE; God hath numbered thy kingdom, and finished it.
TEKEL; Thou art weighed in the balances, and art found wanting.
PERES; Thy kingdom is divided, and given to the Medes and Persians.
Daniel, *King James Bible* (1611), 5:25–28

33 Then the king commanded, and they brought Daniel, and cast him into the den of lions. Now the king spake and said unto Daniel, Thy God whom thou servest continually, he will deliver thee.
Daniel, *King James Bible* (1611), 6:16

34 When thy son asketh thee in time to come, saying, What mean the testimonies, and the statutes, and the judgements, which the Lord our God hath commanded you? Then thou shalt say unto thy son, We were Pharaoh's bondmen in Egypt; and the Lord brought us out of Egypt with a mighty hand.
Deuteronomy, *King James Bible* (1611), 6:20–21

35 For the Lord thy God bringeth thee into a good land...
A land wherein thou shalt eat bread without scarceness...
When thou hast eaten and art full, then thou shalt bless the Lord thy God for the good land which he hath given thee.
Deuteronomy, *King James Bible* (1611), 8:7–10

36 Take heed to yourselves, that your heart be not deceived, and ye turn aside, and serve other gods, and worship them.
Deuteronomy, *King James Bible* (1611), 11:16

37 Thou shalt not hearken unto the words of that prophet, or that dreamer of dreams.
Deuteronomy, *King James Bible* (1611), 13:3

38 I call heaven and earth to record this day against you, that I have set before you life and death, blessing and cursing: therefore choose life, that both thou and thy seed may live.
Deuteronomy, *King James Bible* (1611), 30:19

39 Be strong and of a good courage, fear not, nor be afraid of them: for the Lord thy God, he it is that doth go with thee; he will not fail thee, nor forsake thee.
Deuteronomy, *King James Bible* (1611), 31:6

40 He found him in a desert land, and in the waste howling wilderness; he led him about, he instructed him, he kept him as the apple of his eye.
Deuteronomy, *King James Bible* (1611), 32:10

41 And there arose not a prophet since in Israel like unto Moses, whom the Lord knew face to face.
Deuteronomy, *King James Bible* (1611), 34:10

42 Vanity of vanities, saith the Preacher, vanity of vanities; all is vanity.
What profit hath a man of all his labour which he taketh under the sun?
One generation passeth away, and another generation cometh: but the earth abideth for ever.
Ecclesiastes, *King James Bible* (1611), 1:2–4

43 All things are full of labour; man cannot utter it: the eye is not satisfied with seeing, nor the ear filled with hearing.
The thing that hath been, it is that which shall be; and that which is done is that which shall be done: and there is no new thing under the sun.
Ecclesiastes, *King James Bible* (1611), 1:8–9

44 There is no remembrance of former things; neither shall there be any remembrance of things that are to come with those that shall come after.
Ecclesiastes, *King James Bible* (1611), 1:11

45 And I gave my heart to seek and search out by wisdom concerning all things that are done under heaven: this sore travail hath God given to the sons of man to be exercised therewith.
I have seen all the works that are done under the sun; and, behold, all is vanity and vexation of spirit.
Ecclesiastes, *King James Bible* (1611), 1:13–14

46 For in much wisdom is much grief: and he that increaseth knowledge increaseth sorrow.
Ecclesiastes, *King James Bible* (1611), 1:18

47 The wise man's eyes are in his head; but the fool walketh in darkness: and I myself perceived also that one event happeneth to them all.
Ecclesiastes, *King James Bible* (1611), 2:14

48 To every thing there is a season, and a time to every purpose under the heaven:
A time to be born, and a time to die; a time to plant, and a time to pluck up that which is planted;
A time to kill, and a time to heal; a time to break down, and a time to build up;
A time to weep, and a time to laugh; a time to mourn, and a time to dance.
Ecclesiastes, *King James Bible* (1611), 3:1–3

49 Wherefore I praised the dead which are already dead more than the living which are yet alive.
Yea, better is he than both they, which hath not yet been, who hath not seen the evil work that is done under the sun.
Ecclesiastes, *King James Bible* (1611), 4:2–3

50 Two are better than one; because they have a good reward for their labour.
For if they fall, the one will lift up his fellow: but woe to him that is alone when he falleth; for he hath not another to help him up.
Ecclesiastes, *King James Bible* (1611), 4:9–10

51 And if one prevail against him, two shall withstand him; and a threefold cord is not quickly broken.
Ecclesiastes, *King James Bible* (1611), 4:12

52 Better is a poor and a wise child than an old and foolish king, who will no more be admonished.
Ecclesiastes, *King James Bible* (1611), 4:13

53 Then I commended mirth, because a man hath no better thing under the sun, than to eat, and to drink, and to be merry: for that shall abide with him of his labour the days of his life, which God giveth him under the sun.
Ecclesiastes, *King James Bible* (1611), 8:15

54 Whatsoever thy hand findeth to do, do it with thy might; for there is no work, nor device, nor knowledge, nor wisdom, in the grave, whither thou goest.
Ecclesiastes, *King James Bible* (1611), 9:10

55 I returned, and saw under the sun, that the race is not to the swift, nor the battle to the strong, neither yet bread to the wise, nor yet riches to men of understanding, nor yet favour to men of skill; but time and chance happeneth to them all.
Ecclesiastes, *King James Bible* (1611), 9:11

56 The words of wise men are heard in quiet more than the cry of him that ruleth among fools.
Ecclesiastes, *King James Bible* (1611), 9:17

57 A feast is made for laughter, and wine maketh merry: but money answereth all things.
Ecclesiastes, *King James Bible* (1611), 10:19

58 Cast thy bread upon the waters: for thou shalt find it after many days.
Ecclesiastes, *King James Bible* (1611), 11:1

59 And further, by these, my son, be admonished: of making many books there is no end; and much study is a weariness of the flesh.
Ecclesiastes, *King James Bible* (1611), 12:12

60 Let us hear the conclusion of the whole matter: Fear God, and keep his commandments: for this is the whole duty of man.
Ecclesiastes, *King James Bible* (1611), 12:13

61 By grace are ye saved through faith; and that not of yourselves: it is the gift of God: not of works, lest any man should boast.
Ephesians, *King James Bible* (1611), 2:8–9

62 Wherefore putting away lying, speak every man truth with his neighbour...let not the sun go down upon your wrath:
Neither give place to the devil.
Let him that stole steal no more: but rather let him labour, working with his hands the thing which is good.
Ephesians, *King James Bible* (1611), 4:25–28

63 Children, obey your parents in the Lord: for this is right.
Ephesians, *King James Bible* (1611), 6:1

64 Put on the whole armour of God, that ye may be able to stand against the wiles of the devil.
For we wrestle not against flesh and blood, but against principalities, against powers, against the rulers of the darkness of this world, against spiritual wickedness in high places.
Ephesians, *King James Bible* (1611), 6:11–12

65 And the king loved Esther above all the women, and she obtained grace and favour in his sight more than all the virgins; so that he set the royal crown upon her head, and made her queen instead of Vashti.
Esther, *King James Bible* (1611), 2:17

66 Now there arose up a new king over Egypt, which knew not Joseph.
Exodus, *King James Bible* (1611), 1:8

67 And when she could not longer hide him, she took for him an ark of bulrushes, and daubed it with slime and with pitch, and put the child therein; and she laid it in the flags by the river's brink.
Exodus, *King James Bible* (1611), 2:3

68 He called his name Gershom: for he said, I have been a stranger in a strange land.
Exodus, *King James Bible* (1611), 2:22

69 And the angel of the Lord appeared unto him in a flame of fire out of the midst of a bush: and he looked, and, behold, the bush burned with fire, and the bush was not consumed.
Exodus, *King James Bible* (1611), 3:2

70 And I am come down to deliver them out of the hand of the Egyptians, and to bring them up out of that land unto a good land and a large, unto a land flowing with milk and honey; unto the place of the Canaanites, and the Hittites, and the Amorites, and the Perizzites, and the Hivites, and the Jebusites.
Exodus, *King James Bible* (1611), 3:8

71 And God said unto Moses, I AM THAT I AM: and he said, Thus shalt thou say unto the children of Israel, I AM hath sent me unto you.
Exodus, *King James Bible* (1611), 3:14

72 For they cast down every man his rod, and they became serpents: but Aaron's rod swallowed up their rods.
Exodus, *King James Bible* (1611), 7:12

73 Your lamb shall be without blemish, a male of the first year: ye shall take it out from the sheep, or from the goats.
Exodus, *King James Bible* (1611), 12:5

74 And thus shall ye eat it; with your loins girded, your shoes on your feet, and your staff in your hand; and ye shall eat it in haste: it is the Lord's passover.
For I will pass through the land of Egypt this night, and will smite all the firstborn in the land of Egypt, both man and beast.
Exodus, *King James Bible* (1611), 12:11–12

75 And the Lord went before them by day in a pillar of a cloud, to lead them the way; and by night in a pillar of fire, to give them light; to go by day and night.
Exodus, *King James Bible* (1611), 13:21

76 And the children of Israel went into the midst of the sea upon the dry ground: and the waters were a wall unto them on their right hand, and on their left.
Exodus, *King James Bible* (1611), 14:22

77 The Lord is a man of war: the Lord is his name.
Exodus, *King James Bible* (1611), 15:3

78 Now therefore, if ye will obey my voice indeed, and keep my covenant, then ye shall be a peculiar treasure unto me above all people: for all the earth is mine: and ye shall be unto me a kingdom of priests, and an holy nation.
The main reference for the promise by God to the Hebrews at Mount Sinai that they would be his chosen people. Exodus, *King James Bible* (1611), 19:5–6

79 And mount Sinai was altogether on a smoke, because the Lord descended upon it in fire: and the smoke thereof ascended as the smoke of a furnace, and the whole mount quaked greatly.
Exodus, *King James Bible* (1611), 19:18

80 For in six days the Lord made heaven and earth, the sea, and all that in them is, and rested the seventh day: wherefore the Lord blessed the sabbath day, and hallowed it.
Honour thy father and thy mother: that thy days may be long upon the land which the Lord thy God giveth thee.
Exodus, *King James Bible* (1611), 20:11–12

81 And if any mischief follow, then thou shalt give life for life,
Eye for eye, tooth for tooth, hand for hand, foot for foot,
Burning for burning, wound for wound, stripe for stripe.
Exodus, *King James Bible* (1611), 21:23–25

82 Thou shalt not suffer a witch to live.
Exodus, *King James Bible* (1611), 22:18

83 The first of the firstfruits of thy land thou shalt bring into the house of the Lord thy God. Thou shalt not seethe a kid in his mother's milk.
Exodus, *King James Bible* (1611), 23:19

84 I will set thy bounds from the Red sea even unto the sea of the Philistines, and from the desert unto the river: for I will deliver the inhabitants of the land into your hand; and thou shalt drive them out before thee.
One of a series of promises by God, in this case to Moses, setting out the boundaries of the "Promised Land" after the escape of the Hebrews from Egypt. Some interpret this passage as the justification for the territorial claims of the modern State of Israel. Exodus, *King James Bible* (1611), 23:31

85 And the Lord said unto Moses, Come up to me into the mount, and be there: and I will give thee tables of stone, and a law, and commandments which I have written; that thou mayest teach them.
Exodus, *King James Bible* (1611), 24:12

86 They shall make an ark of shittim wood: two cubits and a half shall be the length thereof, and a cubit and a half the breadth thereof, and a cubit and a half the height thereof. And they shall overlay it with pure gold...and shalt make upon it a crown of gold round about.
The Ark of the Covenant, the portable shrine which was the most important focus for Hebrew worship. It had its own tent until King Solomon built the temple in Jerusalem to house it. Exodus, *King James Bible* (1611), 25:10–11

87 And he received them at their hand, and fashioned it with a graving tool, after he had made it a molten calf: and they said, These be thy gods, O Israel, which brought thee up out of the land of Egypt.
Exodus, *King James Bible* (1611), 32:4

88 And he said, Thou canst not see my face: for there shall no man see me, and live.
Exodus, *King James Bible* (1611), 33:20

89 And it shall come to pass, while my glory passeth by, that I will put thee in a cleft of the rock, and will cover thee with my hand while I pass by.
Exodus, *King James Bible* (1611), 33:22

90 And thou, son of man, be not afraid of them, neither be afraid of their words, though briers and thorns be with thee, and thou dost dwell among scorpions: be not afraid of their words, nor be dismayed at their looks, though they be a rebellious house.
Ezekiel, *King James Bible* (1611), 2:6

91 Son of man, I have made thee a watchman unto the house of Israel: therefore hear the word at my mouth, and give them warning from me.
The definition of the prophet Ezekiel's role among the Hebrews in exile in Babylonia after the destruction of Jerusalem. Ezekiel, *King James Bible* (1611), 4:17

92 Son of man, thou dwellest in the midst of a rebellious house, which have eyes to see, and see not; they have ears to hear, and hear not: for they are a rebellious house.
Ezekiel, *King James Bible* (1611), 12:2

93 And he said unto me, Son of man, can these bones live? And I answered, O Lord God, thou knowest.
Again he said unto me, Prophesy upon these bones, and say unto them, O ye dry bones, hear the word of the Lord.
Ezekiel, *King James Bible* (1611), 37:3–4

94 So I prophesied as I was commanded: and as I prophesied, there was a noise, and behold a shaking, and the bones came together, bone to his bone.
Ezekiel, *King James Bible* (1611), 37:7

95 By the river upon the bank thereof...shall grow all trees for meat, whose leaf shall not fade, neither shall the fruit thereof be consumed: it shall bring forth new fruit according to his months...and the fruit thereof shall be for meat, and the leaf thereof for medicine.
From Ezekiel's vision of the new Jerusalem. Ezekiel, *King James Bible* (1611), 47:12

96 The people could not discern the noise of the shout of joy from the noise of the weeping of the people: for the people shouted with a loud shout, and the noise was heard afar off.
Ezra, *King James Bible* (1611), 3:13

97 But Jerusalem which is above is free, which is the mother of us all.
Galatians, *King James Bible* (1611), 4:26

98 For the flesh lusteth against the Spirit, and the Spirit against the flesh: and these are contrary the one to the other: so that ye cannot do the things that ye would.
Galatians, *King James Bible* (1611), 5:17

99 But the fruit of the Spirit is love, joy, peace, longsuffering, gentleness, goodness, faith,
Meekness, temperance: against such there is no law.
Galatians, *King James Bible* (1611), 5:22–23

100 Be not deceived: God is not mocked: for whatsoever a man soweth, that shall he also reap.
Galatians, *King James Bible* (1611), 6:7

101 And God said, Let there be light: and there was light.
And God saw the light, that it was good: and God divided the light from the darkness.
And God called the light Day, and the darkness he called Night. And the evening and the morning were the first day.
Genesis, *King James Bible* (1611), 1:3–5

102 And God called the dry land Earth; and the gathering together of the waters called he Seas: and God saw that it was good.
And God said, Let the earth bring forth grass, the herb yielding

seed, and the fruit tree yielding fruit after his kind, whose seed is in itself, upon the earth: and it was so.
Genesis, *King James Bible* (1611), 1:10–11

103 And God made two great lights: the greater light to rule the day, and the lesser light to rule the night: he made the stars also.
Genesis, *King James Bible* (1611), 1:16

104 And God said, Let the earth bring forth the living creature after his kind, cattle, and creeping thing, and beast of the earth after his kind: and it was so.
Genesis, *King James Bible* (1611), 1:24

105 God created man in his own image, in the image of God created he him; male and female created he them...God said unto them, Be fruitful, and multiply, and replenish the earth, and subdue it: and have dominion over...every living thing that moveth upon the earth.
Genesis, *King James Bible* (1611), 1:27–28

106 And on the seventh day God ended his work which he had made; and he rested on the seventh day from all his work which he had made.
Genesis, *King James Bible* (1611), 2:2

107 And the Lord God formed man of the dust of the ground, and breathed into his nostrils the breath of life; and man became a living soul.
And the Lord God planted a garden eastward in Eden; and there he put the man whom he had formed.
Genesis, *King James Bible* (1611), 2:7–8

108 And the Lord God took the man, and put him into the garden of Eden...
And the Lord God commanded the man, saying, Of every tree of the garden thou mayest freely eat:
But of the tree of the knowledge of good and evil, thou shalt not eat of it: for in the day that thou eatest thereof thou shalt surely die.
Genesis, *King James Bible* (1611), 2:15–17

109 And the Lord God said, It is not good that the man should be alone; I will make him an helpmeet for him.
And out of the ground the Lord God formed every beast of the field, and every fowl of the air; and brought them unto Adam to see what he would call them.
Genesis, *King James Bible* (1611), 2:18–19

110 And the Lord God caused a deep sleep to fall upon Adam, and he slept: and he took one of his ribs, and closed up the flesh instead thereof;
And the rib, which the Lord God had taken from man, made he a woman, and brought her unto the man.
And Adam said, This is now bone of my bones, and flesh of my flesh: she shall be called Woman, because she was taken out of Man.
Genesis, *King James Bible* (1611), 2:21–23

111 Now the serpent was more subtil than any beast of the field which the Lord God had made.
Genesis, *King James Bible* (1611), 3:1

112 And when the woman saw that the tree was good for food, and that it was pleasant to the eyes, and a tree to be desired to make one wise, she took of the fruit thereof, and did eat, and gave also unto her husband with her; and he did eat.
And the eyes of them both were opened, and they knew that they were naked; and they sewed fig leaves together; and made themselves aprons.
Genesis, *King James Bible* (1611), 3:6–7

113 In the sweat of thy face shalt thou eat bread, till thou return unto the ground; for out of it wast thou taken: for dust thou art and unto dust shalt thou return.
And Adam called his wife's name Eve; because she was the mother of all living.
Genesis, *King James Bible* (1611), 3:19–20

114 Abel was a keeper of sheep, but Cain was a tiller of the ground.
Genesis, *King James Bible* (1611), 4:2

115 And all the days of Methuselah were nine hundred sixty and nine years: and he died.
Genesis, *King James Bible* (1611), 5:27

116 And it repented the Lord that he had made man on the earth, and it grieved him at his heart.
Genesis, *King James Bible* (1611), 6:6

117 And they went in unto Noah into the ark, two and two of all flesh, wherein is the breath of life...
And the flood was forty days upon the earth; and the waters increased, and bare up the ark, and it was lifted up above the earth.
Genesis, *King James Bible* (1611), 7:15–17

118 Who so sheddeth man's blood, by man shall his blood be shed: for in the image of God made he man.
Genesis, *King James Bible* (1611), 9:6

119 I do set my bow in the cloud, and it shall be for a token of a covenant between me and the earth.
Genesis, *King James Bible* (1611), 9:13

120 He was a mighty hunter before the Lord: wherefore it is said, Even as Nimrod the mighty hunter before the Lord.
Genesis, *King James Bible* (1611), 10:9

121 And the whole earth was of one language, and of one speech.
Genesis, *King James Bible* (1611), 11:1

122 Therefore is the name of it called Babel; because the Lord did there confound the language of all the earth: and from thence did the Lord scatter them abroad upon the face of all the earth.
Genesis, *King James Bible* (1611), 11:9

123 Now the Lord had said unto Abram, Get thee out of thy country...unto a land that I will shew thee:
And I will make of thee a great nation, and I will bless thee, and make thy name great; and thou shalt be a blessing.
Genesis, *King James Bible* (1611), 12:1–2

124 But the men of Sodom were wicked and sinners before the Lord exceedingly.
Genesis, *King James Bible* (1611), 13:13

125 Then the Lord rained upon Sodom and upon Gomorrah brimstone and fire from the Lord out of heaven.
Genesis, *King James Bible* (1611), 19:24

126 But his wife looked back from behind him, and she became a pillar of salt.
Genesis, *King James Bible* (1611), 19:26

127 And Abraham said, My son, God will provide himself a lamb for a burnt offering: so they went both of them together.
Genesis, *King James Bible* (1611), 22:8

128 And Abraham lifted up his eyes, and looked, and behold behind him a ram caught in a thicket by his horns: and Abraham went and took the ram, and offered him up for a burnt offering in the stead of his son.
Genesis, *King James Bible* (1611), 22:13

129 And Jacob said to Rebekah his mother, Behold, Esau my brother is a hairy man, and I am a smooth man.
Genesis, *King James Bible* (1611), 27:11

130 And he dreamed, and behold a ladder set up on the earth, and the top of it reached to heaven: and behold the angels of God ascending and descending on it.
Genesis, *King James Bible* (1611), 28:12

131 Leah was tender eyed; but Rachel was beautiful and well favoured.
Genesis, *King James Bible* (1611), 29:17

132 Now Israel loved Joseph more than all his children, because he was the son of his old age: and he made him a coat of many colours.
Genesis, *King James Bible* (1611), 37:3

133 And they said one to another, Behold, this dreamer cometh.
Come now therefore, and let us slay him, and cast him into some pit, and we will say, Some evil beast hath devoured him: and we shall see what will become of his dreams.
Genesis, *King James Bible* (1611), 37:19–20

134 And all his sons and all his daughters rose up to comfort him; but he refused to be comforted; and he said, For I will go down into the grave unto my son mourning. Thus his father wept for him.
Genesis, *King James Bible* (1611), 37:35

135 And Judah said unto Onan, Go in unto thy brother's wife, and marry her, and raise up seed to thy brother.
And Onan knew that the seed should not be his; and it came to pass, when he went in unto his brother's wife, that he spilled it on the ground, lest that he should give seed to his brother.
Genesis, *King James Bible* (1611), 38:8–9

136 And the seven thin ears devoured the seven rank and full ears. And Pharaoh awoke, and, behold, it was a dream.
Genesis, *King James Bible* (1611), 41:7

137 And the famine was sore in the land.
Genesis, *King James Bible* (1611), 43:1

138 And take your father and your households, and come unto me: and I will give you the good of the land of Egypt, and ye shall eat the fat of the land.
Genesis, *King James Bible* (1611), 45:18

139 But the Lord is in his holy temple: let all the earth keep silence before him.
Habakkuk, *King James Bible* (1611), 2:20

140 Now therefore thus saith the Lord of hosts; Consider your ways.
Ye have sown much, and bring in little; ye eat, but ye have not enough; ye drink, but ye are not filled with drink; ye clothe you, but there is none warm; and he that earneth wages earneth wages to put it into a bag with holes.
Haggai, *King James Bible* (1611), 1:5–6

141 For the word of God is quick, and powerful, and sharper than any two-edged sword, piercing even to the dividing asunder of soul and spirit, and of the joints and marrow, and is a discerner of the thoughts and intents of the heart.
Hebrews, *King James Bible* (1611), 4:12

142 And almost all things are by the law purged with blood; and without shedding of blood is no remission.
Hebrews, *King James Bible* (1611), 9:22

143 It is a fearful thing to fall into the hands of the living God.
Hebrews, *King James Bible* (1611), 10:31

144 Now faith is the substance of things hoped for, the evidence of things not seen.
Hebrews, *King James Bible* (1611), 11:1

145 By faith the walls of Jericho fell down, after they were compassed about seven days.
Hebrews, *King James Bible* (1611), 11:30

146 Let brotherly love continue.
Be not forgetful to entertain strangers: for thereby some have entertained angels unawares.
Hebrews, *King James Bible* (1611), 13:1–2

147 Jesus Christ the same yesterday, and today, and for ever.
Hebrews, *King James Bible* (1611), 13:8

148 Here we have no continuing city, but we seek one to come.
Hebrews, *King James Bible* (1611), 13:14

149 I will betroth thee unto me for ever; yea, I will betroth thee unto me in righteousness, and in judgement, and in lovingkindness, and in mercies. I will even betroth thee unto me in faithfulness: and thou shalt know the Lord.
Hosea, *King James Bible* (1611), 2:19–20

150 For they have sown the wind, and they shall reap the whirlwind: it hath no stalk: the bud shall yield no meal: if so be it yield, the strangers shall swallow it up.
Hosea, *King James Bible* (1611), 8:7

151 For after that in the wisdom of God the world by wisdom knew not God, it pleased God by the foolishness of preaching to save them that believe.
For the Jews require a sign, and the Greeks seek after wisdom:
But we preach Christ crucified, unto the Jews a stumblingblock, and unto the Greeks foolishness.
I Corinthians, *King James Bible* (1611), 1:21–23

152 But as it is written, Eye hath not seen, nor ear heard, neither have entered into the heart of man, the things which God hath prepared for them that love him.
I Corinthians, *King James Bible* (1611), 2:9

153 For the kingdom of God is not in word, but in power.
I Corinthians, *King James Bible* (1611), 4:20

154 Meats for the belly, and the belly for meats: but God shall destroy both it and them. Now the body is not for fornication, but for the Lord; and the Lord for the body.
I Corinthians, *King James Bible* (1611), 6:13

155 But if they cannot contain, let them marry: for it is better to marry than to burn.
I Corinthians, *King James Bible* (1611), 7:9

156 But he that is married careth for the things that are of the world, how he may please his wife.
I Corinthians, *King James Bible* (1611), 7:33

157 Now as touching things offered unto idols, we know that we all have knowledge. Knowledge puffeth up, but charity edifieth.
I Corinthians, *King James Bible* (1611), 8:1

158 Know ye not that they which run in a race run all, but one receiveth the prize? So run, that ye may obtain.
And every man that striveth for the mastery is temperate in all things. Now they do it to obtain a corruptible crown; but we an incorruptible.
I Corinthians, *King James Bible* (1611), 9:24–25

159 All things are lawful for me, but all things are not expedient: all things are lawful for me, but all things edify not.
I Corinthians, *King James Bible* (1611), 10:23

160 For the earth is the Lord's, and the fullness thereof.
I Corinthians, *King James Bible* (1611), 10:26

161 When I was a child, I spake as a child, I understood as a child, I thought as a child: but when I became a man, I put away childish things.
For now we see through a glass, darkly; but then face to face: now I know in part; but then shall I know even as also I am known.
And now abideth faith, hope, charity, these three; but the greatest of these is charity.
I Corinthians, *King James Bible* (1611), 13:11–13

162 If after the manner of men I have fought with beasts at Ephesus, what advantageth it me, if the dead rise not? Let us eat and drink; for tomorrow we die.
Be not deceived: evil communications corrupt good manners.
I Corinthians, *King James Bible* (1611), 15:32–33

163 There is one glory of the sun, and another glory of the moon, and another glory of the stars: for one star differeth from another star in glory.
So also is the resurrection of the dead. It is sown in corruption; it is raised in incorruption.
I Corinthians, *King James Bible* (1611), 15:41–42

164 For we walk by faith, not by sight.
II Corinthians, *King James Bible* (1611), 5:7

165 Every man according as he purposeth in his heart, so let him give; not grudgingly, or of necessity: for God loveth a cheerful giver.
II Corinthians, *King James Bible* (1611), 9:7

166 His letters, say they, are weighty and powerful; but his bodily presence is weak, and his speech contemptible.
II Corinthians, *King James Bible* (1611), 10:10

167 For ye suffer fools gladly, seeing ye yourselves are wise.
II Corinthians, *King James Bible* (1611), 11:19

168 And lest I should be exalted above measure through the abundance of the revelations, there was given to me a thorn in the flesh, the messenger of Satan to buffet me, lest I should be exalted above measure.
II Corinthians, *King James Bible* (1611), 12:7

169 The grace of the Lord Jesus Christ, and the love of God, and the communion of the Holy Ghost be with you all.
II Corinthians, *King James Bible* (1611), 13:14

170 And...as they still went on...there appeared a chariot of fire, and horses of fire, and parted them both asunder; and Elijah went up by a whirlwind into heaven.
And Elisha saw it, and he cried, My father, my father, the chariot of Israel, and the horsemen thereof. And he saw him no more.
II Kings, *King James Bible* (1611), 2:11–12

171 And when Jehu was come to Jezreel, Jezebel heard of it; and she painted her face, and tired her head, and looked out at a window.
II Kings, *King James Bible* (1611), 9:30

172 And they went to bury her: but they found no more of her than the skull, and the feet, and the palms of her hands.
II Kings, *King James Bible* (1611), 9:35

173 In those days was Hezekiah sick unto death. And the prophet Isaiah the son of Amoz came to him, and said unto him, Thus saith the Lord, Set thine house in order; for thou shalt die, and not live.
Then he turned his face to the wall.
II Kings, *King James Bible* (1611), 20:1–2

174 All the army of the Chaldees, that were with the captain of the guard, brake down the walls of Jerusalem round about.
Now the rest of the people that were left in the city, and the fugitives that fell away to the king of Babylon, with the remnant of the multitude, did Nebuzaradan the captain of the guard carry away.
The destruction of Jerusalem by the Babylonians and the beginning of the 48-year Hebrew exile in Babylonia. II Kings, *King James Bible* (1611), 25:10–11

175 Saul and Jonathan were lovely and pleasant in their lives, and in their death they were not divided: they were swifter than eagles, they were stronger than lions.
II Samuel, *King James Bible* (1611), 1:23–24

176 David danced before the Lord with all his might; and David was girded with a linen ephod. So David and all the house of Israel brought up the ark of the Lord with shouting, and with the sound of the trumpet.
II Samuel, *King James Bible* (1611), 6:14–15

177 Thine house and thy kingdom shall be established for ever before thee: thy throne shall be established for ever.
One of the main sources for the belief that the Messiah would be a king descended from David. II Samuel, *King James Bible* (1611), 7:16

178 For even when we were with you, this we commanded you, that if any would not work, neither should he eat.
II Thessalonians, *King James Bible* (1611), 3:10

179 But evil men and seducers shall wax worse and worse, deceiving, and being deceived.
II Timothy, *King James Bible* (1611), 3:13

180 If we say that we have no sin, we deceive ourselves, and the truth is not in us.
If we confess our sins, he is faithful and just to forgive us our sins, and to cleanse us from all unrighteousness.
I John, *King James Bible* (1611), 1:8–9

181 Whoso hath this world's good, and seeth his brother have need, and shutteth up his bowels of compassion from him, how dwelleth the love of God in him?
I John, *King James Bible* (1611), 3:17

182 Beloved, let us love one another: for love is of God; and every one that loveth is born of God, and knoweth God.
He that loveth not knoweth not God; for God is love.
I John, *King James Bible* (1611), 4:7–8

183 There is no fear in love; but perfect love casteth out fear: because fear hath torment. He that feareth is not made perfect in love.
I John, *King James Bible* (1611), 4:18

184 Zadok the priest took an horn of oil out of the tabernacle, and anointed Solomon. And they blew the trumpet; and all the people said, God save king Solomon.
Referring to the coronation of King Solomon. It is also used in the text of an anthem sung at the coronation of British monarchs. I Kings, *King James Bible* (1611), 1:39

185 So David slept with his fathers, and was buried in the city of David.
I Kings, *King James Bible* (1611), 2:10

186 Then the king answered and said, Give her the living child, and in no wise slay it: she is the mother thereof.
And all Israel heard of the judgment which the king had judged; and they feared the king: for they saw that the wisdom of God was in him, to do judgment.
I Kings, *King James Bible* (1611), 3:27–28

187 The priests brought in the ark of the covenant of the Lord unto his place, into the oracle of the house, to the most holy place.
The installation of the Hebrews' sacred portable shrine in the temple of Jerusalem newly built by King Solomon. I Kings, *King James Bible* (1611), 8:6

188 And when the queen of Sheba heard of the fame of Solomon concerning the name of the Lord, she came to prove him with hard questions.
I Kings, *King James Bible* (1611), 10:1

189 When the queen of Sheba had seen all Solomon's wisdom, and the house that he had built, and the meat of his table, and the sitting of his servants, and the attendance of his ministers, and their apparel, and his cupbearers, and his ascent by which he went up unto the house of the Lord; there was no more spirit in her.
I Kings, *King James Bible* (1611), 10:4–5

190 And, behold, the Lord passed by, and a great and strong wind rent the mountains...but the Lord was not in the wind: and after the wind an earthquake; but the Lord was not in the earthquake:
And after the earthquake a fire; but the Lord was not in the fire: and after the fire a still small voice.
I Kings, *King James Bible* (1611), 19:11–12

191 Being born again, not of corruptible seed, but of incorruptible, by the word of God, which liveth and abideth for ever.
For all flesh is as grass, and all the glory of man as the flower of grass. The grass withereth, and the flower thereof falleth away.
I Peter, *King James Bible* (1611), 1:23–24

192 Ye are a chosen generation, a royal priesthood, an holy nation, a peculiar people.
This echoes the main Old Testament covenant passage at Mount Sinai (Exodus 19:5–6). I Peter, *King James Bible* (1611), 2:9

193 Honour all men. Love the brotherhood. Fear God. Honour the king.
I Peter, *King James Bible* (1611), 2:17

194 Even as Sara obeyed Abraham, calling him lord...
Likewise, ye husbands, dwell with them according to knowledge, giving honour unto the wife, as unto the weaker vessel, and as being heirs together of the grace of life; that your prayers be not hindered.
I Peter, *King James Bible* (1611), 3:6–7

195 Come now, and let us reason together, saith the Lord: though your sins be as scarlet, they shall be as white as snow; though they be red like crimson, they shall be as wool.
Isaiah, *King James Bible* (1611), 1:18

196 How is the faithful city become an harlot! it was full of judgment; righteousness lodged in it; but now murderers.
Isaiah, *King James Bible* (1611), 1:21

197 And it shall come to pass in the last days, that the mountain of the Lord's house shall be established in the top of the mountains, and shall be exalted above the hills; and all nations shall flow unto it.
Isaiah, *King James Bible* (1611), 2:2

198 And he shall judge among the nations, and shall rebuke many people: and they shall beat their swords into plowshares, and their spears into pruning-hooks: nation shall not lift up sword against nation, neither shall they learn war any more.
Isaiah, *King James Bible* (1611), 2:4

199 Therefore the Lord himself shall give you a sign; Behold, a virgin shall conceive, and bear a son, and shall call his name Immanuel.
Butter and honey shall he eat, that he may know to refuse the evil, and choose the good.
Isaiah, *King James Bible* (1611), 7:14–15

200 The people that walked in darkness have seen a great light: they that dwell in the land of the shadow of death, upon them hath the light shined.
Isaiah, *King James Bible* (1611), 9:2

201 For unto us a child is born, unto us a son is given: and the government shall be upon his shoulder: and his name shall be called Wonderful, Counsellor, The mighty God, The everlasting Father, The Prince of Peace.
Isaiah, *King James Bible* (1611), 9:6

202 And there shall come forth a rod out of the stem of Jesse, and a Branch shall grow out of his roots:
And the spirit of the Lord shall rest upon him, the spirit of wisdom and understanding, the spirit of counsel and might, the spirit of knowledge and of the fear of the Lord.
Isaiah, *King James Bible* (1611), 11:1–2

203 The wolf also shall dwell with the lamb, and the leopard shall lie down with the kid; and the calf and the young lion and the fatling together: and a little child shall lead them...
They shall not hurt nor destroy in all my holy mountain: for the earth shall be full of the knowledge of the Lord, as the waters cover the sea.
Isaiah, *King James Bible* (1611), 11:6–9

204 The Lord shall give thee rest from thy sorrow, and from thy fear, and from the hard bondage wherein thou wast made to serve.
Isaiah, *King James Bible* (1611), 14:3

205 And behold joy and gladness, slaying oxen, and killing sheep, eating flesh, and drinking wine: let us eat and drink; for tomorrow we shall die.
Isaiah, *King James Bible* (1611), 22:13

206 Take an harp, go about the city, thou harlot that hast been forgotten; make sweet melody, sing many songs, that thou mayest be remembered.
Isaiah, *King James Bible* (1611), 23:16

207 They shall not drink wine with a song; strong drink shall be bitter to them that drink it.
Isaiah, *King James Bible* (1611), 24:9

208 In that day the Lord with his sore and great and strong sword shall punish leviathan the piercing serpent, even leviathan that crooked serpent; and he shall slay the dragon that is in the sea.
Isaiah, *King James Bible* (1611), 27:1

209 For precept must be upon precept, precept upon precept; line upon line, line upon line; here a little, and there a little.
Isaiah, *King James Bible* (1611), 28:10

210 Write it before them in a table, and note it in a book, that it may be for the time to come for ever and ever.
Isaiah, *King James Bible* (1611), 30:8

211 Then the eyes of the blind shall be opened, and the ears of the deaf shall be unstopped.
Then shall the lame man leap as an hart, and the tongue of the dumb sing: for in the wilderness shall waters break out, and streams in the desert.
Isaiah, *King James Bible* (1611), 35:5–6

212 Comfort ye, comfort ye my people, saith your God. Speak ye comfortably to Jerusalem, and cry unto her, that her warfare is accomplished, that her iniquity is pardoned: for she hath received of the Lord's hand double for all her sins.
Isaiah, *King James Bible* (1611), 40:1–2

213 The voice of him that crieth in the wilderness, Prepare ye the way of the Lord, make straight in the desert a highway for our God.
Every valley shall be exalted, and every mountain and hill shall be made low: and the crooked shall be made straight, and the rough places plain.
Isaiah, *King James Bible* (1611), 40:3–4

214 He shall feed his flock like a shepherd: he shall gather the lambs with his arm, and carry them in his bosom, and shall gently lead those that are with young.
Isaiah, *King James Bible* (1611), 40:11

215 The isles saw it, and feared; the ends of the earth were afraid, drew near, and came.
They helped every one his neighbour; and every one said to his brother, Be of good courage.
Isaiah, *King James Bible* (1611), 41:5–6

216 Behold my servant, whom I uphold; mine elect, in whom my soul delighteth; I have put my spirit upon him: he shall bring forth judgement to the Gentiles... He shall not fail nor be discouraged, till he have set judgement in the earth: and the isles shall wait for his law.
From the first of four poems in Isaiah about a servant who suffers for his loyalty to God. They are often interpreted as prophecies about Jesus. Isaiah, *King James Bible* (1611), 42:1–4

217 There is no peace, saith the Lord, unto the wicked.
Isaiah, *King James Bible* (1611), 48:22

218 He hath made my mouth like a sharp sword; in the shadow of his hand hath he hid me, and made me a polished shaft, in his quiver hath he hid me; and said unto me, Thou art my servant, O Israel, in whom I will be glorified.
From the second of four poems in Isaiah about a suffering servant. They are often interpreted as prophecies about Jesus. Isaiah, *King James Bible* (1611), 49:2–3

219 Awake, awake; put on thy strength, O Zion; put on thy beautiful garments, O Jerusalem, the holy city: for henceforth there shall no more come into thee the uncircumcised and the unclean.
Isaiah, *King James Bible* (1611), 52:1

220 He is despised and rejected of men; a man of sorrows, and acquainted with grief: and we hid as it were our faces from him; he was despised, and we esteemed him not. Surely he hath borne our griefs, and carried our sorrows.
From the fourth poem in Isaiah about a suffering servant. They are often interpreted as prophecies about Jesus. Isaiah, *King James Bible* (1611), 53:3–5

221 All we like sheep have gone astray; we have turned every one to his own way; and the Lord hath laid on him the iniquity of us all.
He was oppressed, and he was afflicted, yet he opened not his mouth: he is brought as a lamb to the slaughter, and as a sheep before her shearers is dumb, so he openeth not his mouth.
Isaiah, *King James Bible* (1611), 53:6–7

222 The righteous perisheth, and no man layeth it to heart: and merciful men are taken away, none considering that the righteous is taken away from the evil to come.
Isaiah, *King James Bible* (1611), 57:1

223 Gentiles shall come to thy light, and kings to the brightness of thy rising.
Origin of the belief that the wise men who brought gifts to the infant Jesus (Matthew 2) were kings. Isaiah, *King James Bible* (1611), 60:3

224 The spirit of the Lord God is upon me; because the Lord hath anointed me to preach good tidings unto the meek; he hath

sent me to bind up the brokenhearted, to proclaim liberty to the captives, and the opening of the prison to them that are bound.
Quoted by Jesus at the opening of his public ministry (Luke 4:18). Isaiah, *King James Bible* (1611), 61:1

225 But now thy kingdom shall not continue: the Lord hath sought him a man after his own heart, and the Lord hath commanded him to be captain over his people, because thou hast not kept that which the Lord commanded thee.
I Samuel, *King James Bible* (1611), 13:14

226 And the people said unto Saul, Shall Jonathan die, who hath wrought this great salvation in Israel? God forbid: as the Lord liveth, there shall not one hair of his head fall to the ground; for he hath wrought with God this day. So the people rescued Jonathan, that he died not.
I Samuel, *King James Bible* (1611), 14:45

227 The Lord said unto Samuel, look not on his countenance, or on the height of his stature; because I have refused him: for the Lord seeth not as man seeth; for man looketh on the outward appearance, but the Lord looketh on the heart.
Instructions to Samuel about the choice of a Hebrew king to succeed Saul; David was chosen. I Samuel, *King James Bible* (1611), 16:7

228 And he took his staff in his hand, and chose him five smooth stones out of the brook, and put them in a shepherd's bag which he had, even in a scrip; and his sling was in his hand: and he drew near to the Philistine.
I Samuel, *King James Bible* (1611), 17:40

229 David put his hand in his bag, and took thence a stone, and slang it, and smote the Philistine in his forehead; and he fell upon his face to the earth.
The young David's defeat of the Philistine champion, Goliath. I Samuel, *King James Bible* (1611), 17:49

230 And the women answered one another as they played, and said, Saul hath slain his thousands, and David his ten thousands.
I Samuel, *King James Bible* (1611), 18:7

231 Remembering without ceasing your work of faith, and labour of love, and patience of hope in our Lord Jesus Christ, in the sight of God and our Father.
I Thessalonians, *King James Bible* (1611), 1:3

232 For yourselves know perfectly that the day of the Lord so cometh as a thief in the night.
I Thessalonians, *King James Bible* (1611), 5:2

233 Prove all things; hold fast that which is good.
I Thessalonians, *King James Bible* (1611), 5:21

234 This is a faithful saying, and worthy of all acceptation, that Christ Jesus came into the world to save sinners; of whom I am chief.
I Timothy, *King James Bible* (1611), 1:15

235 This is a true saying, If a man desire the office of a bishop, he desireth a good work.
A bishop then must be blameless, the husband of one wife, vigilant, sober, of good behaviour, given to hospitality, apt to teach;
Not given to wine, no striker, not greedy of filthy lucre; but patient, not a brawler, not covetous.
I Timothy, *King James Bible* (1611), 3:1–3

236 For every creature of God is good, and nothing to be refused, if it be received with thanksgiving.
I Timothy, *King James Bible* (1611), 4:4

237 Drink no longer water, but use a little wine for thy stomach's sake and thine often infirmities.
I Timothy, *King James Bible* (1611), 5:23

238 For we brought nothing into this world, and it is certain we carry nothing out.
I Timothy, *King James Bible* (1611), 6:7

239 For the love of money is the root of all evil: which while some coveted after, they have erred from the faith, and pierced themselves through with many sorrows.
I Timothy, *King James Bible* (1611), 6:10

240 Fight the good fight of faith, lay hold on eternal life, whereunto thou art also called, and hast professed a good profession before many witnesses.
I Timothy, *King James Bible* (1611), 6:12

241 Blessed is the man that endureth temptation: for when he is tried, he shall receive the crown of life, which the Lord hath promised to them that love him.
James, *King James Bible* (1611), 1:12

242 Wherefore, my beloved brethren, let every man be swift to hear, slow to speak, slow to wrath:
For the wrath of man worketh not the righteousness of God.
James, *King James Bible* (1611), 1:19–20

243 Submit yourselves therefore to God. Resist the devil, and he will flee from you.
Draw nigh to God, and he will draw nigh to you. Cleanse your hands, ye sinners; and purify your hearts, ye double minded.
James, *King James Bible* (1611), 4:7–8

244 Grudge not one against another, brethren, lest ye be condemned: behold, the judge standeth before the door.
James, *King James Bible* (1611), 5:9

245 Let him know, that he which converteth the sinner from the error of his way shall save a soul from death, and shall hide a multitude of sins.
James, *King James Bible* (1611), 5:20

246 I cannot hold my peace, because thou hast heard, O my soul, the sound of the trumpet, the alarm of war.
Jeremiah, *King James Bible* (1611), 4:19

247 Is this house, which is called by my name, become a den of robbers in your eyes? Behold, even I have seen it, saith the Lord.
Quoted by Jesus as he drove the money changers out of the temple in Jerusalem (Matthew 21:13). Jeremiah, *King James Bible* (1611), 7:11

248 The harvest is past, the summer is ended, and we are not saved.
Jeremiah, *King James Bible* (1611), 8:20

249 Can the Ethiopian change his skin, or the leopard his spots?

then may ye also do good, that are accustomed to do evil.
Jeremiah, *King James Bible* (1611), 13:23

250 The heart is deceitful above all things, and desperately wicked: who can know it?
Jeremiah, *King James Bible* (1611), 17:9

251 A voice was heard in Ramah, lamentation and bitter weeping; Rachel weeping for her children refused to be comforted for her children, because they were not.
Originally referring to an invasion by Assyrians or Babylonians, this verse is quoted in Matthew's Gospel at Herod's slaughter of the children following Jesus's birth. Jeremiah, *King James Bible* (1611), 31:15

252 I will make a new covenant with the house of Israel, and with the house of Judah...I will put my law in their inward parts, and write it in their hearts; and will be their God, and they shall be my people.
Originally a message of hope as the Babylonians destroyed Jerusalem, it is alluded to by Jesus at the last supper (Luke 22:20). Jeremiah, *King James Bible* (1611), 31:31, 33

253 And the Lord said unto Satan, Hast thou considered my servant Job, that there is none like him in the earth, a perfect and an upright man, one that feareth God, and escheweth evil?
Then Satan answered the Lord, and said, Doth Job fear God for nought?
Job, *King James Bible* (1611), 1:8–9

254 Naked came I out of my mother's womb, and naked shall I return thither: the Lord gave, and the Lord hath taken away; blessed be the name of the Lord.
Job, *King James Bible* (1611), 1:21

255 Then said his wife unto him, Dost thou still retain thine integrity? curse God, and die.
Job, *King James Bible* (1611), 2:9

256 Let the day perish wherein I was born, and the night in which it was said, There is a man child conceived.
Job, *King James Bible* (1611), 3:3

257 The eye of him that hath seen me shall see me no more: thine eyes are upon me, and I am not.
Job, *King James Bible* (1611), 7:8

258 They grope in the dark without light, and he maketh them to stagger like a drunken man.
Job, *King James Bible* (1611), 12:25

259 Man that is born of a woman is of few days, and full of trouble.
Job, *King James Bible* (1611), 14:1

260 Then Job answered and said, I have heard many such things: miserable comforters are ye all.
Job, *King James Bible* (1611), 16:1–2

261 I have said to corruption, Thou art my father: to the worm, Thou art my mother, and my sister.
Job, *King James Bible* (1611), 17:14

262 For I know that my redeemer liveth, and that he shall stand at the latter day upon the earth:
And though after my skin worms destroy this body, yet in my flesh shall I see God.
Job, *King James Bible* (1611), 19:25–26

263 No mention shall be made of coral, or of pearls: for the price of wisdom is above rubies.
Job, *King James Bible* (1611), 28:18

264 I was eyes to the blind, and feet was I to the lame.
Job, *King James Bible* (1611), 29:15

265 The mountains shall drop down new wine, and the hills shall flow with milk, and all the rivers of Judah shall flow with waters, and a fountain shall come forth of the house of the Lord.
Joel, *King James Bible* (1611), 3:18

266 In the beginning was the Word, and the Word was with God, and the Word was God.
The same was in the beginning with God.
All things were made by him; and without him was not any thing made that was made.
In him was life; and the life was the light of men.
John, *King James Bible* (1611), 1:1–4

267 The Word was made flesh, and dwelt among us.
John, *King James Bible* (1611), 1:14

268 The next day John seeth Jesus coming unto him, and saith, Behold the Lamb of God, which taketh away the sin of the world.
John, *King James Bible* (1611), 1:29

269 Jesus saith unto her, Woman, what have I to do with thee? mine hour is not yet come.
John, *King James Bible* (1611), 2:4

270 When the ruler of the feast had tasted the water that was made wine...the governor of the feast called the bridegroom,
And saith unto him, Every man at the beginning doth set forth good wine; and when men have well drunk, then that which is worse: but thou hast kept the good wine until now.
John, *King James Bible* (1611), 2:9–10

271 Jesus answered and said unto him, Verily, verily, I say unto thee, Except a man be born again, he cannot see the kingdom of God.
John, *King James Bible* (1611), 3:3

272 Jesus answered, Verily, verily, I say unto thee, Except a man be born of water and of the Spirit, he cannot enter into the kingdom of God.
That which is born of the flesh is flesh; and that which is born of the Spirit is spirit.
John, *King James Bible* (1611), 3:5–6

273 For God so loved the world, that he gave his only begotten Son, that whosoever believeth in him should not perish, but have everlasting life.
John, *King James Bible* (1611), 3:16

274 And this is the condemnation, that light is come into the world, and men loved darkness rather than light, because their deeds were evil.
John, *King James Bible* (1611), 3:19

275 My meat is to do the will of him that sent me, and to finish his work.
John, *King James Bible* (1611), 4:34

276 Afterward Jesus findeth him in the temple, and said unto him, Behold, thou art made whole: sin no more, lest a worse thing come unto thee.
John, *King James Bible* (1611), 5:14

277 Verily, verily, I say unto you, He that heareth my word, and believeth on him that sent me, hath everlasting life, and shall not come into condemnation; but is passed from death unto life.
Verily, verily, I say unto you, The hour is coming, and now is, when the dead shall hear the voice of the Son of God: and they that hear shall live.
John, *King James Bible* (1611), 5:24–25

278 There is a lad here, which hath five barley loaves, and two small fishes: but what are they among so many?
And Jesus said, Make the men sit down. Now there was much grass in the place. So the men sat down, in number about five thousand.
John, *King James Bible* (1611), 6:9–10

279 And Jesus said unto them, I am the bread of life: he that cometh to me shall never hunger; and he that believeth on me shall never thirst.
John, *King James Bible* (1611), 6:35

280 So when they continued asking him, he lifted up himself, and said unto them, He that is without sin among you, let him first cast a stone at her.
John, *King James Bible* (1611), 8:7

281 She said, No man, Lord. And Jesus said unto her, Neither do I condemn thee: go, and sin no more.
John, *King James Bible* (1611), 8:11

282 Then spake Jesus again unto them, saying, I am the light of the world: he that followeth me shall not walk in darkness, but shall have the light of life.
John, *King James Bible* (1611), 8:12

283 And ye shall know the truth, and the truth shall make you free.
John, *King James Bible* (1611), 8:32

284 He answered and said, Whether he be a sinner or no, I know not: one thing I know, that, whereas I was blind, now I see.
John, *King James Bible* (1611), 9:25

285 For judgement I am come into this world, that they which see not might see; and that they which see might be made blind.
John, *King James Bible* (1611), 9:39

286 Jesus said unto her, I am the resurrection, and the life: he that believeth in me, though he were dead, yet shall he live.
John, *King James Bible* (1611), 11:25

287 When Jesus therefore saw her weeping, and the Jews also weeping which came with her, he groaned in the spirit, and was troubled,
And said, Where have ye laid him? They said unto him, Lord, come and see.
Jesus wept.
John, *King James Bible* (1611), 11:33–35

288 If I then, your Lord and Master, have washed your feet; ye also ought to wash one another's feet.
John, *King James Bible* (1611), 13:14

289 By this shall all men know that ye are my disciples, if ye have love one to another.
John, *King James Bible* (1611), 13:35

290 In my Father's house are many mansions: if it were not so, I would have told you. I go to prepare a place for you.
John, *King James Bible* (1611), 14:2

291 Jesus saith unto him, I am the way, the truth, and the life: no man cometh unto the Father, but by me.
John, *King James Bible* (1611), 14:6

292 I am the vine, ye are the branches: he that abideth in me, and I in him, the same bringeth forth much fruit: for without me ye can do nothing.
John, *King James Bible* (1611), 15:5

293 Greater love hath no man than this, that a man lay down his life for his friends.
John, *King James Bible* (1611), 15:13

294 Now Caiaphas was he, which gave counsel to the Jews, that it was expedient that one man should die for the people.
John, *King James Bible* (1611), 18:14

295 Pilate saith unto him, What is truth? And when he had said this, he went out again unto the Jews, and saith unto them, I find in him no fault at all.
John, *King James Bible* (1611), 18:38

296 Then cried they all again, saying, Not this man, but Barabbas. Now Barabbas was a robber.
John, *King James Bible* (1611), 18:40

297 Pilate answered, What I have written I have written.
John, *King James Bible* (1611), 19:22

298 When Jesus therefore saw his mother, and the disciple standing by, whom he loved, he saith unto his mother, Woman, behold thy son!
Then saith he to the disciple, Behold thy mother! And from that hour that disciple took her unto his own home.
John, *King James Bible* (1611), 19:26–27

299 When Jesus therefore had received the vinegar, he said, It is finished: and he bowed his head, and gave up the ghost.
John, *King James Bible* (1611), 19:30

300 Now in the place where he was crucified there was a garden; and in the garden a new sepulchre, wherein was never man yet laid.
John, *King James Bible* (1611), 19:41

301 The first day of the week cometh Mary Magdalene early, when it was yet dark, unto the sepulchre, and seeth the stone taken away from the sepulchre.
Then she runneth, and cometh to Simon Peter, and to the other disciple...and saith unto them, They have taken the Lord out of the sepulchre, and we know not where they have laid him.
John, *King James Bible* (1611), 20:1–2

302 Jesus saith unto her, Woman, why weepest thou? whom seekest

thou? She, supposing him to be the gardener, saith unto him, Sir, if thou have borne him hence, tell me where thou hast laid him, and I will take him away...
Jesus saith unto her, Touch me not; for I am not yet ascended to my Father: but go to my brethren, and say unto them, I ascend unto my Father, and your Father; and to my God, and your God.
John, *King James Bible* (1611), 20:15–17

303 The other disciples therefore said unto him, We have seen the Lord. But he said unto them, Except I shall see in his hands the print of the nails, and put my finger into the print of the nails, and thrust my hand into his side, I will not believe.
John, *King James Bible* (1611), 20:25

304 Then saith he to Thomas, Reach hither thy finger, and behold my hands; and reach hither thy hand, and thrust it into my side: and be not faithless, but believing.
And Thomas answered and said unto him, My Lord and my God.
John, *King James Bible* (1611), 20:27–28

305 He saith unto him the third time, Simon, son of Jonas, lovest thou me? Peter was grieved because he said unto him the third time, Lovest thou me? And he said unto him, Lord, thou knowest all things; thou knowest that I love thee. Jesus saith unto him, Feed my sheep.
John, *King James Bible* (1611), 21:17

306 Now the Lord had prepared a great fish to swallow up Jonah. And Jonah was in the belly of the fish three days and three nights.
Jonah, *King James Bible* (1611), 1:17

307 And the priests that bare the ark of the covenant of the Lord stood firm on dry ground in the midst of Jordan, and all the Israelites passed over on dry ground, until all the people were passed clean over Jordan.
Joshua, *King James Bible* (1611), 3:17

308 So the people shouted when the priests blew with the trumpets: and it came to pass, when the people heard the sound of the trumpet, and the people shouted with a great shout, that the wall fell down flat, so that the people went up into the city, every man straight before him, and they took the city.
Joshua, *King James Bible* (1611), 6:20

309 And the princes said unto them, Let them live; but let them be hewers of wood and drawers of water unto all the congregation; as the princes had promised them.
Joshua, *King James Bible* (1611), 9:21

310 Mercy unto you, and peace, and love, be multiplied.
Jude, *King James Bible* (1611), 1:2

311 And when he shewed them the entrance into the city, they smote the city with the edge of the sword; but they let go the man and all his family.
Judges, *King James Bible* (1611), 1:25

312 They fought from heaven; the stars in their courses fought against Sisera.
Judges, *King James Bible* (1611), 5:20

313 And the men of the city said unto him on the seventh day before the sun went down, What is sweeter than honey? and what is stronger than a lion? And he said unto them, If ye had not plowed with my heifer, ye had not found out my riddle.
Judges, *King James Bible* (1611), 14:18

314 In those days there was no king in Israel, but every man did that which was right in his own eyes.
Judges, *King James Bible* (1611), 17:6

315 And I said, My strength and my hope is perished from the Lord:
Remembering mine affliction and my misery, the wormwood and the gall.
Lamentations, *King James Bible* (1611), 3:18–19

316 It is good for a man that he bear the yoke in his youth.
Lamentations, *King James Bible* (1611), 3:27

317 Waters flowed over mine head; then I said, I am cut off.
Lamentations, *King James Bible* (1611), 3:54

318 And the angel came in unto her, and said, Hail, thou that art highly favoured, the Lord is with thee: blessed art thou among women.
And when she saw him, she was troubled at his saying, and cast in her mind what manner of salutation this should be.
Luke, *King James Bible* (1611), 1:28–29

319 And Mary said, My soul doth magnify the Lord,
And my spirit hath rejoiced in God my Saviour.
For he hath regarded the low estate of his handmaiden: for, behold, from henceforth all generations shall call me blessed.
Luke, *King James Bible* (1611), 1:46–48

320 He hath shewed strength with his arm; he hath scattered the proud in the imagination of their hearts.
He hath put down the mighty from their seats, and exalted them of low degree.
He hath filled the hungry with good things; and the rich he hath sent empty away.
Luke, *King James Bible* (1611), 1:51–53

321 And the child grew, and waxed strong in spirit, and was in the deserts till the day of his shewing unto Israel.
Luke, *King James Bible* (1611), 1:80

322 And it came to pass in those days, that there went out a decree from Caesar Augustus, that all the world should be taxed.
Luke, *King James Bible* (1611), 2:1

323 And she brought forth her firstborn son, and wrapped him in swaddling clothes, and laid him in a manger; because there was no room for them in the inn.
Luke, *King James Bible* (1611), 2:7

324 And there were in the same country shepherds abiding in the field, keeping watch over their flock by night.
And, lo, the angel of the Lord came upon them, and the glory of the Lord shone round about them.
Luke, *King James Bible* (1611), 2:8–9

325 Glory to God in the highest, and on earth peace, good will toward men.
Luke, *King James Bible* (1611), 2:14

326 But Mary kept all these things, and pondered them in her heart.
Luke, *King James Bible* (1611), 2:19

327 Lord, now lettest thou thy servant depart in peace, according to thy word:
For mine eyes have seen thy salvation,
Which thou hast prepared before the face of all people;
A light to lighten the Gentiles, and the glory of thy people Israel.
Luke, *King James Bible* (1611), 2:29–32

328 And it came to pass, that after three days they found him in the temple, sitting in the midst of the doctors, both hearing them, and asking them questions.
And all that heard him were astonished at his understanding and answers.
Luke, *King James Bible* (1611), 2:46–47

329 And the devil, taking him up into an high mountain, shewed unto him all the kingdoms of the world in a moment of time.
Luke, *King James Bible* (1611), 4:5

330 And he said unto them, Ye will surely say unto me this proverb, Physician, heal thyself: whatsoever we have heard done in Capernaum, do also here in thy country.
Luke, *King James Bible* (1611), 4:23

331 No man also having drunk old wine straightway desireth new: for he saith, The old is better.
Luke, *King James Bible* (1611), 5:39

332 And he said to the woman, Thy faith hath saved thee; go in peace.
Luke, *King James Bible* (1611), 7:50

333 When the time was come that he should be received up, he steadfastly set his face to go to Jerusalem.
The start of the last journey of Jesus and his disciples. Luke, *King James Bible* (1611), 9:51

334 Go your ways: behold, I send you forth as lambs among wolves.
Carry neither purse, nor scrip, nor shoes: and salute no man by the way.
And into whatsoever house ye enter, first say, Peace be to this house.
Luke, *King James Bible* (1611), 10:3–5

335 And Jesus answering said, A certain man went down from Jerusalem to Jericho, and fell among thieves, which stripped him of his raiment, and wounded him, and departed, leaving him half dead.
And by chance there came down a certain priest that way: and when he saw him, he passed by on the other side.
Luke, *King James Bible* (1611), 10:30–31

336 But a certain Samaritan, as he journeyed...had compassion on him...and bound up his wounds...and brought him to an inn, and took care of him.
And on the morrow when he departed, he took out two pence, and gave them to the host, and said unto him, Take care of him; and whatsoever thou spendest more...I will repay thee.
Luke, *King James Bible* (1611), 10:33–35

337 And he said, He that shewed mercy on him. Then said Jesus unto him, Go, and do thou likewise.
Luke, *King James Bible* (1611), 10:37

338 Woe unto you, lawyers! for ye have taken away the key of knowledge: ye entered not in yourselves, and them that were entering in ye hindered.
Luke, *King James Bible* (1611), 11:52

339 What man of you, having an hundred sheep, if he lose one of them, doth not leave the ninety and nine in the wilderness, and go after that which is lost until he find it?...
I say unto you, that likewise joy shall be in heaven over one sinner that repenteth, more than over ninety and nine just persons, which need no repentance.
Luke, *King James Bible* (1611), 15:4–7

340 I will arise and go to my father, and will say unto him, Father, I have sinned against heaven, and before thee,
And am no more worthy to be called thy son: make me as one of thy hired servants.
And he arose, and came to his father. But when he was yet a great way off, his father saw him, and had compassion, and ran, and fell on his neck, and kissed him.
Luke, *King James Bible* (1611), 15:18–20

341 And bring hither the fatted calf, and kill it; and let us eat, and be merry:
For this my son was dead, and is alive again; he was lost, and is found. And they began to be merry.
Luke, *King James Bible* (1611), 15:23–24

342 There was a certain rich man, which was clothed in purple and fine linen, and fared sumptuously every day:
And there was a certain beggar named Lazarus, which was laid at his gate, full of sores...
And it came to pass, that the beggar died, and was carried by the angels into Abraham's bosom: the rich man also died, and was buried.
Luke, *King James Bible* (1611), 16:19–22

343 And when he was demanded of the Pharisees, when the kingdom of God should come, he answered them and said, The kingdom of God cometh not with observation:
Neither shall they say, Lo here! or, lo there! for, behold, the kingdom of God is within you.
Luke, *King James Bible* (1611), 17:20–21

344 Remember Lot's wife.
Luke, *King James Bible* (1611), 17:32

345 And he answered and said unto them, I tell you that, if these should hold their peace, the stones would immediately cry out.
Luke, *King James Bible* (1611), 19:40

346 And when they were come to the place, which is called Calvary, there they crucified him, and the malefactors, one on the right hand, and the other on the left.
Luke, *King James Bible* (1611), 23:33

347 Then said Jesus, Father, forgive them; for they know not what they do. And they parted his raiment, and cast lots.
Luke, *King James Bible* (1611), 23:34

348 And when Jesus had cried with a loud voice, he said, Father, into thy hands I commend my spirit: and having said thus, he gave up the ghost.
Luke, *King James Bible* (1611), 23:46

349 I will send you Elijah the prophet before the coming of the great and dreadful day of the Lord: and he shall turn the heart of the fathers to the children, and the heart of the children to their fathers.
The prophet Elijah was taken to heaven in a chariot of fire (II Kings 2) and was expected to return as herald of the Messiah. Some believed that John the Baptist was the reincarnation of Elijah (Matthew 11:10; John 1:21). Malachi, *King James Bible* (1611), 4:5–6

350 And he said unto them, The sabbath was made for man, and not man for the sabbath: Therefore the Son of man is Lord also of the sabbath.
Mark, *King James Bible* (1611), 2:27–28

351 He ordained twelve, that they should be with him, and that he might send them forth to preach, and to have power to heal sicknesses, and to cast out devils.
Mark, *King James Bible* (1611), 3:14–15

352 If a kingdom be divided against itself, that kingdom cannot stand. And if a house be divided against itself, that house cannot stand.
Mark, *King James Bible* (1611), 3:24–25

353 All sins shall be forgiven unto the sons of men, and blasphemies wherewith soever they shall blaspheme: but he that blasphemeth against the Holy Ghost hath never forgiveness, but is in danger of eternal damnation.
Mark, *King James Bible* (1611), 3:28–29

354 And he asked him, What is thy name? And he answered, saying, My name is Legion: for we are many.
Mark, *King James Bible* (1611), 5:9

355 And forthwith Jesus gave them leave. And the unclean spirits went out, and entered into the swine: and the herd ran violently down a steep place into the sea (they were about two thousand); and were choked in the sea.
Mark, *King James Bible* (1611), 5:13

356 Whosoever shall not receive you, nor hear you, when ye depart thence, shake off the dust under your feet as a testimony against them.
Mark, *King James Bible* (1611), 6:11

357 There is nothing from without a man, that entering into him can defile him: but the things which come out of him, those are they that defile the man.
Mark, *King James Bible* (1611), 7:15

358 He rebuked Peter, saying, Get thee behind me, Satan: for thou savourest not the things that be of God, but the things that be of men.
Mark, *King James Bible* (1611), 8:33

359 For what shall it profit a man, if he shall gain the whole world, and lose his own soul? Or what shall a man give in exchange for his soul?
Mark, *King James Bible* (1611), 8:36–37

360 If thou canst believe, all things are possible to him that believeth. And straightway the father of the child cried out, and said with tears, Lord, I believe; help thou mine unbelief.
Mark, *King James Bible* (1611), 9:23–24

361 Is it not written, My house shall be called of all nations the house of prayer? but ye have made it a den of thieves.
Said by Jesus, as he cleared the money changers from the temple. The quotation is drawn from Isaiah 56:7 and Jeremiah 7:11. Mark, *King James Bible* (1611), 11:17

362 And there came a certain poor widow, and she threw in two mites, which make a farthing. And he called unto him his disciples, and saith unto them, Verily I say unto you, That this poor widow hath cast more in, than all they which have cast into the treasury: For all they did cast in of their abundance; but she of her want did cast in all that she had, even all her living.
Mark, *King James Bible* (1611), 12:42–44

363 Father, all things are possible unto thee; take away this cup from me: nevertheless not what I will, but what thou wilt.
Prayer of Jesus in the Garden of Gethsemane immediately before his arrest. Mark, *King James Bible* (1611), 14:36

364 Art thou the Christ, the Son of the Blessed? And Jesus said, I am: and ye shall see the Son of man sitting on the right hand of power, and coming in the clouds of heaven.
Jesus's quotation from Daniel 7:13–14 convicted him of blasphemy. Mark, *King James Bible* (1611), 14:61–62

365 Ye seek Jesus of Nazareth, which was crucified: he is risen; he is not here: behold the place where they laid him.
Mark, *King James Bible* (1611), 16:6

366 And he said unto them, Go ye into all the world, and preach the gospel to every creature.
Mark, *King James Bible* (1611), 16:15

367 Now when Jesus was born in Bethlehem of Judaea in the days of Herod the king, behold, there came wise men from the east to Jerusalem,
Saying, Where is he that is born King of the Jews? for we have seen his star in the east, and are come to worship him.
Matthew, *King James Bible* (1611), 2:1–2

368 And when they were come into the house, they saw the young child with Mary his mother, and fell down, and worshipped him: and when they had opened their treasures, they presented unto him gifts; gold, and frankincense, and myrrh.
And being warned of God in a dream...they departed into their own country another way.
Matthew, *King James Bible* (1611), 2:11–12

369 Herod, when he saw that he was mocked of the wise men, was exceeding wroth, and sent forth, and slew all the children that were in Bethlehem, and in all the coasts thereof, from two years old and under, according to the time which he had diligently inquired of the wise men.
Matthew, *King James Bible* (1611), 2:16

370 For this is he that was spoken of by the prophet Esaias, saying, The voice of one crying in the wilderness, Prepare ye the way of the Lord, make his paths straight.
And the same John had his raiment of camel's hair, and a leathern girdle about his loins; and his meat was locusts and wild honey.
Matthew, *King James Bible* (1611), 3:3–4

371 Then was Jesus led up of the Spirit into the wilderness to be tempted of the devil.
And when he had fasted forty days and forty nights, he was afterward an hungred.
And when the tempter came to him, he said, If thou be the Son of God, command that these stones be made bread.
But he answered...Man shall not live by bread alone, but by every word that proceedeth out of the mouth of God.
Matthew, *King James Bible* (1611), 4:1–4

372 Jesus said unto him, It is written again, Thou shalt not tempt the Lord thy God.
Again, the devil taketh him up into an exceeding high mountain, and sheweth him all the kingdoms of the world, and the glory of them.
Matthew, *King James Bible* (1611), 4:7–8

373 From that time Jesus began to preach, and to say, Repent: for the kingdom of heaven is at hand.
Matthew, *King James Bible* (1611), 4:17

374 And he saith unto them, Follow me, and I will make you fishers of men.
Matthew, *King James Bible* (1611), 4:19

375 Blessed are the meek: for they shall inherit the earth.
Blessed are they which do hunger and thirst after righteousness: for they shall be filled.
Blessed are the merciful: for they shall obtain mercy.
Blessed are the pure in heart: for they shall see God.
Matthew, *King James Bible* (1611), 5:5–8

376 Let your light so shine before men, that they may see your good works, and glorify your Father which is in heaven.
Matthew, *King James Bible* (1611), 5:16

377 For verily I say unto you, Till heaven and earth pass, one jot or one tittle shall in no wise pass from the law, till all be fulfilled.
Matthew, *King James Bible* (1611), 5:18

378 And if thy right eye offend thee, pluck it out, and cast it from thee: for it is profitable for thee that one of thy members should perish, and not that thy whole body should be cast into hell.
Matthew, *King James Bible* (1611), 5:29

379 But I say unto you, That ye resist not evil: but whosoever shall smite thee on thy right cheek, turn to him the other also.
And if any man will sue thee at the law, and take away thy coat, let him have thy cloke also.
And whosoever shall compel thee to go a mile, go with him twain.
Matthew, *King James Bible* (1611), 5:39–41

380 When thou doest alms, let not thy left hand know what thy right hand doeth.
Matthew, *King James Bible* (1611), 6:3

381 But when ye pray, use not vain repetitions, as the heathen do: for they think that they shall be heard for their much speaking.
Be not ye therefore like unto them: for your Father knoweth what things ye have need of, before ye ask him.
Matthew, *King James Bible* (1611), 6:7–8

382 Lay not up for yourselves treasures upon earth, where moth and rust doth corrupt, and where thieves break through and steal:
But lay up for yourselves treasures in heaven, where neither moth nor rust doth corrupt, and where thieves do not break through nor steal:
For where your treasure is, there will your heart be also.
Matthew, *King James Bible* (1611), 6:19–21

383 No man can serve two masters: for either he will hate the one, and love the other; or else he will hold to the one, and despise the other. Ye cannot serve God and mammon.
Matthew, *King James Bible* (1611), 6:24

384 Judge not, that ye be not judged.
Matthew, *King James Bible* (1611), 7:1

385 Ask, and it shall be given you; seek, and ye shall find; knock, and it shall be opened unto you:
For every one that asketh receiveth; and he that seeketh findeth; and to him that knocketh it shall be opened.
Matthew, *King James Bible* (1611), 7:7–8

386 Beware of false prophets, which come to you in sheep's clothing, but inwardly they are ravening wolves.
Matthew, *King James Bible* (1611), 7:15

387 Even so every good tree bringeth forth good fruit; but a corrupt tree bringeth forth evil fruit.
A good tree cannot bring forth evil fruit, neither can a corrupt tree bring forth good fruit.
Every tree that bringeth not forth good fruit is hewn down, and cast into the fire.
Wherefore by their fruits ye shall know them.
Matthew, *King James Bible* (1611), 7:17–20

388 Therefore whosoever heareth these sayings of mine, and doeth them, I will liken him unto a wise man, which built his house upon a rock:
And the rain descended, and the floods came, and the winds blew, and beat upon that house; and it fell not: for it was founded upon a rock.
Matthew, *King James Bible* (1611), 7:24–25

389 Lord, I am not worthy that thou shouldest come under my roof: but speak the word only, and my servant shall be healed.
The Roman centurion's reply when Jesus offered to go to his house. Matthew, *King James Bible* (1611), 8:8

390 But the children of the kingdom shall be cast out into outer darkness: there shall be weeping and gnashing of teeth.
Matthew, *King James Bible* (1611), 8:12

391 But Jesus said unto him, Follow me; and let the dead bury their dead.
Matthew, *King James Bible* (1611), 8:22

392 They that be whole need not a physician, but they that are sick.
Matthew, *King James Bible* (1611), 9:12

393 Heal the sick, cleanse the lepers, raise the dead, cast out devils: freely ye have received, freely give.
Matthew, *King James Bible* (1611), 10:8

394 And ye shall be hated of all men for my name's sake: but he that endureth to the end shall be saved.
Matthew, *King James Bible* (1611), 10:22

395 The disciple is not above his master, nor the servant above his lord.
Matthew, *King James Bible* (1611), 10:24

396 Think not that I am come to send peace on earth: I came not to send peace, but a sword.
Matthew, *King James Bible* (1611), 10:34

397 Whosover shall give to drink unto one of these little ones a cup of cold water only in the name of a disciple, verily I say unto you, he shall in no wise lose his reward.
Matthew, *King James Bible* (1611), 10:42

398 Go and shew John again those things which ye do hear and see: the blind receive their sight, and the lame walk, the lepers are cleansed, and the deaf hear, the dead are raised up, and the poor have the gospel preached to them.
Jesus's reply to the messengers sent by his cousin, John the Baptist, to ask if he really was the Messiah. Jesus alludes to a number of messianic passages in Isaiah, including 26:19 and 29:18.
Matthew, *King James Bible* (1611), 11:4–5

399 He that hath ears to hear, let him hear.
Matthew, *King James Bible* (1611), 11:15

400 O generation of vipers, how can ye, being evil, speak good things? for out of the abundance of the heart the mouth speaketh.
Matthew, *King James Bible* (1611), 12:34

401 For whosoever shall do the will of my Father which is in heaven, the same is my brother, and sister, and mother.
Matthew, *King James Bible* (1611), 12:50

402 And he spake many things unto them in parables, saying, Behold, a sower went forth to sow;
And when he sowed, some seeds fell by the way side, and the fowls came and devoured them up:
Some fell upon stony places, where they had not much earth...
But others fell into good ground, and brought forth fruit, some an hundredfold, some sixtyfold, some thirtyfold.
Matthew, *King James Bible* (1611), 13:3–8

403 And they were offended in him. But Jesus said unto them, A prophet is not without honour, save in his own country, and in his own house.
Matthew, *King James Bible* (1611), 13:57

404 But when Herod's birthday was kept, the daughter of Herodias danced before them, and pleased Herod.
Whereupon he promised with an oath to give her whatsoever she would ask.
And she, being before instructed of her mother, said, Give me John Baptist's head in a charger.
Matthew, *King James Bible* (1611), 14:6–8

405 And in the fourth watch of the night Jesus went unto them, walking on the sea.
And when the disciples saw him walking on the sea, they were troubled, saying, It is a spirit; and they cried out for fear.
But straightway Jesus spake unto them, saying, Be of good cheer; it is I; be not afraid.
Matthew, *King James Bible* (1611), 14:25–27

406 If the blind lead the blind, both shall fall into the ditch.
Matthew, *King James Bible* (1611), 15:14

407 And I say also unto thee, That thou art Peter, and upon this rock I will build my church; and the gates of hell shall not prevail against it.
And I will give unto thee the keys of the kingdom of heaven.
Matthew, *King James Bible* (1611), 16:18–19

408 Then said Jesus unto his disciples, If any man will come after me, let him deny himself, and take up his cross, and follow me.
Matthew, *King James Bible* (1611), 16:24

409 If ye have faith as a grain of mustard seed, ye shall say unto this mountain, Remove hence to yonder place; and it shall remove; and nothing shall be impossible unto you.
Matthew, *King James Bible* (1611), 17:20

410 And said, Verily I say unto you, Except ye be converted, and become as little children, ye shall not enter into the kingdom of heaven.
Matthew, *King James Bible* (1611), 18:3

411 And whoso shall receive one such little child in my name receiveth me.
But whoso shall offend one of these little ones which believe in me, it were better for him that a millstone were hanged about his neck, and that he were drowned in the depth of the sea.
Matthew, *King James Bible* (1611), 18:5–6

412 For where two or three are gathered together in my name, there am I in the midst of them.
Matthew, *King James Bible* (1611), 18:20

413 Then came Peter to him, and said, Lord, how oft shall my brother sin against me, and I forgive him? till seven times?
Jesus saith unto him, I say not unto thee, Until seven times: but, Until seventy times seven.
Matthew, *King James Bible* (1611), 18:21–22

414 Wherefore they are no more twain, but one flesh. What therefore God hath joined together, let not man put asunder.
Matthew, *King James Bible* (1611), 19:6

415 Whosoever shall put away his wife, except it be for fornication, and shall marry another, committeth adultery: and whoso marrieth her which is put away doth commit adultery.
Matthew, *King James Bible* (1611), 19:9

416 Jesus said unto him, If thou wilt be perfect, go and sell that thou hast, and give to the poor, and thou shalt have treasure in heaven: and come and follow me.
But when the young man heard that saying, he went away sorrowful: for he had great possessions.
Matthew, *King James Bible* (1611), 19:21–22

417 Then said Jesus unto his disciples, Verily I say unto you, That a rich man shall hardly enter into the kingdom of heaven.
And again I say unto you, It is easier for a camel to go through the eye of a needle, than for a rich man to enter into the kingdom of God.
Matthew, *King James Bible* (1611), 19:23–24

418 But many that are first shall be last; and the last shall be first.
Matthew, *King James Bible* (1611), 19:30

419 And a very great multitude spread their garments in the way; others cut down branches from the trees, and strewed them in the way.
And the multitudes that went before, and that followed, cried, saying, Hosanna to the Son of David: Blessed is he that cometh in the name of the Lord.
Matthew, *King James Bible* (1611), 21:8–9

420 For many are called, but few are chosen.
Matthew, *King James Bible* (1611), 22:14

421 And he saith unto them, Whose is this image and superscription?
They say unto him, Caesar's. Then saith he unto them, Render therefore unto Caesar the things which are Caesar's; and unto God the things that are God's.
Matthew, *King James Bible* (1611), 22:20–21

422 Jesus said unto him, Thou shalt love the Lord thy God with all thy heart, and with all thy soul, and with all thy mind.
This is the first and great commandment.
And the second is like unto it, Thou shalt love thy neighbour as thyself.
On these two commandments hang all the law and the prophets.
Matthew, *King James Bible* (1611), 22:37–40

423 Woe unto you, scribes and Pharisees, hypocrites! for ye are like unto whited sepulchres, which indeed appear beautiful outward, but are within full of dead men's bones, and of all uncleanness.
Matthew, *King James Bible* (1611), 23:27

424 And ye shall hear of wars and rumours of wars: see that ye be not troubled: for all these things must come to pass, but the end is not yet.
For nation shall rise against nation, and kingdom against kingdom: and there shall be famines, and pestilences, and earthquakes, in divers places.
All these are the beginning of sorrows.
Matthew, *King James Bible* (1611), 24:6–8

425 Immediately after the tribulation of those days shall the sun be darkened, and the moon shall not give her light, and the stars shall fall from heaven, and the powers of the heavens shall be shaken:
And then shall appear the sign of the Son of man in heaven: and then shall all the tribes of the earth mourn, and they shall see the Son of man coming in the clouds of heaven with power and great glory.
Matthew, *King James Bible* (1611), 24:29–30

426 Heaven and earth shall pass away, but my words shall not pass away.
Matthew, *King James Bible* (1611), 24:35

427 And unto one he gave five talents, to another two, and to another one; to every man according to his several ability; and straightway took his journey.
Matthew, *King James Bible* (1611), 25:15

428 His lord said unto him, Well done, thou good and faithful servant: thou hast been faithful over a few things, I will make thee ruler over many things: enter thou into the joy of thy lord.
Matthew, *King James Bible* (1611), 25:21

429 For unto every one that hath shall be given, and he shall have abundance: but from him that hath not shall be taken away even that which he hath.
And cast ye the unprofitable servant into outer darkness: there shall be weeping and gnashing of teeth.
Matthew, *King James Bible* (1611), 25:29–30

430 And before him shall be gathered all nations: and he shall separate them one from another, as a shepherd divideth his sheep from the goats:
And he shall set the sheep on his right hand, but the goats on the left.
Matthew, *King James Bible* (1611), 25:32–33

431 For I was an hungred, and ye gave me meat: I was thirsty, and ye gave me drink: I was a stranger, and ye took me in:
Naked, and ye clothed me: I was sick, and ye visited me: I was in prison, and ye came unto me.
Matthew, *King James Bible* (1611), 25:35–36

432 And the King shall answer and say unto them, Verily I say unto you, Inasmuch as ye have done it unto one of the least of these my brethren, ye have done it unto me.
Matthew, *King James Bible* (1611), 25:40

433 What will ye give me, and I will deliver him unto you? And they covenanted with him for thirty pieces of silver.
Judas Iscariot's agreement with the chief priests for the betrayal of Jesus. Judas returned the money after the condemnation of Jesus (Matthew 27:3–5). Matthew, *King James Bible* (1611), 26:15

434 And he answered and said, He that dippeth his hand with me in the dish, the same shall betray me...
Then Judas, which betrayed him, answered and said, Master, is it I? He said unto him, Thou hast said.
Matthew, *King James Bible* (1611), 26:23–25

435 And as they were eating, Jesus took bread, and blessed it, and brake it, and gave it to the disciples, and said, Take, eat; this is my body.
And he took the cup, and gave thanks, and gave it to them, saying, Drink ye all of it;
For this is my blood of the new testament, which is shed for many for the remission of sins.
Matthew, *King James Bible* (1611), 26:26–28

436 Jesus said unto him, Verily I say unto thee, That this night, before the cock crow, thou shalt deny me thrice.
Matthew, *King James Bible* (1611), 26:34

437 Watch and pray, that ye enter not into temptation: the spirit indeed is willing, but the flesh is weak.
Matthew, *King James Bible* (1611), 26:41

438 And forthwith he came to Jesus, and said, Hail, master; and kissed him.
And Jesus said unto him, Friend, wherefore art thou come? Then came they, and laid hands on Jesus, and took him.
Matthew, *King James Bible* (1611), 26:49–50

439 Then said Jesus unto him, Put up again thy sword into his

place: for all they that take the sword shall perish with the sword.
Matthew, *King James Bible* (1611), 26:52

440 Then Judas...brought again the thirty pieces of silver to the chief priests and elders, saying, I have sinned in that I have betrayed the innocent blood. And they said, What is that to us? see thou to that. And he cast down the pieces of silver in the temple, and departed, and hanged himself.
Matthew, *King James Bible* (1611), 27:3–5

441 When Pilate saw that he could prevail nothing, but that rather a tumult was made, he took water, and washed his hands before the multitude, saying, I am innocent of the blood of this just person: see ye to it.
Then answered all the people, and said, His blood be on us, and on our children.
Matthew, *King James Bible* (1611), 27:24–25

442 Teaching them to observe all things whatsoever I have commanded you: and, lo, I am with you alway, even unto the end of the world. Amen.
Matthew, *King James Bible* (1611), 28:20

443 They shall beat their swords into plowshares and their spears into pruning hooks: nation shall not lift up a sword against nation, neither shall they learn war any more. But they shall sit every man under his vine and under his fig tree; and none shall make them afraid.
Micah, *King James Bible* (1611), 4:3–4

444 Thou, Bethlehem Ephratah, though thou be little among the thousands of Judah, yet out of thee shall he come forth unto me that is to be ruler in Israel; whose goings forth have been from of old, from everlasting.
King David was born in Bethlehem and now, three centuries later at a time of foreign occupation, Micah foretells a time when another like David will free the people and rule them. Matthew's Gospel applies the prophecy to the birth of Jesus (2:6). Micah, *King James Bible* (1611), 5:2

445 Trust ye not in a friend, put ye not confidence in a guide: keep the doors of thy mouth from her that lieth in thy bosom.
Micah, *King James Bible* (1611), 7:5

446 Woe to the bloody city!...the prey departeth not...The horseman lifteth up both the bright sword and the glittering spear; and there is a multitude of slain, and a great number of carcases; and there is none end of their corpses; they stumble over their corpses.
The prophet revels in the destruction of Assyria's capital Nineveh by the Babylonians after a century of ruthless Assyrian domination of the Hebrews and the other conquered peoples. Nahum, *King James Bible* (1611), 3:1–3

447 And I said, Should such a man as I flee? and who is there, that, being as I am, would go into the temple to save his life? I will not go in.
Nehemiah, *King James Bible* (1611), 6:11

448 The Lord bless thee, and keep thee:
The Lord make his face shine upon thee, and be gracious unto thee:
The Lord lift up his countenance upon thee, and give thee peace.
Numbers, *King James Bible* (1611), 6:24–26

449 And Moses lifted up his hand, and with his rod he smote the rock twice: and the water came out abundantly, and the congregation drank, and their beasts also.
Numbers, *King James Bible* (1611), 20:11

450 That at the name of Jesus every knee should bow, of things in heaven, and things in earth, and things under the earth.
Philippians, *King James Bible* (1611), 2:10

451 Rejoice in the Lord alway: and again I say, Rejoice.
Philippians, *King James Bible* (1611), 4:4

452 And the peace of God, which passeth all understanding, shall keep your hearts and minds through Christ Jesus.
Philippians, *King James Bible* (1611), 4:7

453 Finally, brethren, whatsoever things are true, whatsoever things are honest, whatsoever things are just, whatsoever things are pure, whatsoever things are lovely, whatsoever things are of good report; if there be any virtue; and if there be any praise, think on these things.
Philippians, *King James Bible* (1611), 4:8

454 For the lips of a strange woman drop as an honeycomb, and her mouth is smoother than oil:
But her end is bitter as wormwood, sharp as a two-edged sword.
Proverbs, *King James Bible* (1611), 5:3–4

455 Wisdom hath builded her house, she hath hewn out her seven pillars.
Proverbs, *King James Bible* (1611), 9:1

456 Stolen waters are sweet, and bread eaten in secret is pleasant.
Proverbs, *King James Bible* (1611), 9:17

457 He that spareth his rod hateth his son: but he that loveth him chasteneth him betimes.
Proverbs, *King James Bible* (1611), 13:24

458 Pride goeth before destruction, and an haughty spirit before a fall.
Proverbs, *King James Bible* (1611), 16:18

459 He that is slow to anger is better than the mighty; and he that ruleth his spirit than he that taketh a city.
Proverbs, *King James Bible* (1611), 16:32

460 As cold waters to a thirsty soul, so is good news from a far country.
Proverbs, *King James Bible* (1611), 25:25

461 Answer a fool according to his folly, lest he be wise in his own conceit.
Proverbs, *King James Bible* (1611), 26:5

462 Boast not thyself of tomorrow; for thou knowest not what a day may bring forth.
Proverbs, *King James Bible* (1611), 27:1

463 Who can find a virtuous woman? for her price is far above rubies
The heart of her husband doth safely trust in her, so that he shall have no need of spoil.
She will do him good and not evil all the days of her life.
Proverbs, *King James Bible* (1611), 31:10–12

464 Behold, he cometh with clouds; and every eye shall see him, and they also which pierced him: and all kindreds of the earth

shall wail because of him. Even so, Amen.
I am Alpha and Omega, the beginning and the ending, saith the Lord, which is, and which was, and which is to come, the Almighty.
Revelation, *King James Bible* (1611), 1:7–8

465 Behold, I stand at the door and knock: if any man hear my voice, and open the door, I will come to him, and will sup with him, and he with me.
Revelation, *King James Bible* (1611), 3:20

466 And I looked, and behold a pale horse: and his name that sat on him was Death, and Hell followed with him. And power was given unto them over the fourth part of the earth, to kill with sword, and with hunger, and with death, and with the beasts of the earth.
Revelation, *King James Bible* (1611), 6:8

467 And one of the elders answered, saying unto me, What are these which are arrayed in white robes...And he said to me, These are they which came out of great tribulation, and have washed their robes, and made them white in the blood of the Lamb.
Revelation, *King James Bible* (1611), 7:13–14

468 And there was war in heaven...
And the great dragon was cast out, that old serpent, called the Devil, and Satan, which deceiveth the whole world: he was cast out into the earth, and his angels were cast out with him.
Revelation, *King James Bible* (1611), 12:7–9

469 And that no man might buy or sell, save he that had the mark, or the name of the beast, or the number of his name.
Here is wisdom. Let him that hath understanding count the number of the beast: for it is the number of a man; and his number is Six hundred threescore and six.
Revelation, *King James Bible* (1611), 13:17–18

470 Behold, I come as a thief. Blessed is he that watcheth, and keepeth his garments, lest he walk naked, and they see his shame.
And he gathered them together into a place called in the Hebrew tongue Armageddon.
Revelation, *King James Bible* (1611), 16:15–16

471 And there came one of the seven angels which had the seven vials, and talked with me, saying unto me, Come hither; I will shew unto thee the judgement of the great whore that sitteth upon many waters.
Revelation, *King James Bible* (1611), 17:1

472 And upon her forehead was a name written, MYSTERY, BABYLON THE GREAT, THE MOTHER OF HARLOTS AND ABOMINATIONS OF THE EARTH.
And I saw the woman drunken with the blood of the saints, and with the blood of the martyrs of Jesus: and when I saw her, I wondered with great admiration.
Revelation, *King James Bible* (1611), 17:5–6

473 And I saw heaven opened, and behold a white horse; and he that sat upon him was called Faithful and True, and in righteousness he doth judge and make war.
Revelation, *King James Bible* (1611), 19:11

474 Blessed and holy is he that hath part in the first resurrection: on such the second death hath no power, but they shall be priests of God and of Christ, and shall reign with him a thousand years.
And when the thousand years are expired, Satan shall be loosed out of his prison,
And shall go out to deceive the nations which are in the four quarters of the earth.
Revelation, *King James Bible* (1611), 20:6–8

475 And I saw the dead, small and great, stand before God; and the books were opened: and another book was opened, which is the book of life: and the dead were judged out of those things which were written in the books, according to their works.
Revelation, *King James Bible* (1611), 20:12

476 And I saw a new heaven and a new earth: for the first heaven and the first earth were passed away; and there was no more sea.
And I John saw the holy city, new Jerusalem, coming down from God out of heaven, prepared as a bride adorned for her husband.
Revelation, *King James Bible* (1611), 21:1–2

477 And he shewed me a pure river of water of life, clear as crystal, proceeding out of the throne of God and of the Lamb.
In the midst of the street of it, and on either side of the river, was there the tree of life, which bare twelve manner of fruits, and yielded her fruit every month: and the leaves of the tree were for the healing of the nations.
Revelation, *King James Bible* (1611), 22:1–2

478 There is no respect of persons with God.
Romans, *King James Bible* (1611), 2:11

479 When the Gentiles, which have not the law, do by nature the things contained in the law, these, having not the law, they are a law unto themselves.
Romans, *King James Bible* (1611), 2:14

480 Being justified by faith, we have peace with God.
Romans, *King James Bible* (1611), 5:1

481 The wages of sin is death; but the gift of God is eternal life through Jesus Christ our Lord.
Romans, *King James Bible* (1611), 6:23

482 All things work together for good to them that love God.
Romans, *King James Bible* (1611), 8:28

483 We are accounted as sheep for the slaughter.
Romans, *King James Bible* (1611), 8:36

484 There is no power but of God: the powers that be are ordained of God.
Paul makes it clear that he means government officials. Romans, *King James Bible* (1611), 13:1

485 Render therefore to all their dues: tribute to whom tribute is due; custom to whom custom; fear to whom fear; honour to whom honour.
Romans, *King James Bible* (1611), 13:7

486 Owe no man anything, but to love one another: for he that loveth another hath fulfilled the law.
Romans, *King James Bible* (1611), 13:8

487 Whatsoever things were written aforetime were written for our learning, that we through patience and comfort of the scriptures might have hope.
Romans, *King James Bible* (1611), 15:4

488 And Ruth said, Intreat me not to leave thee, or to return from following after thee: for whither thou goest, I will go; and where thou lodgest, I will lodge: thy people shall be my people, and thy God my God.
Ruth, *King James Bible* (1611), 1:16–17

489 And he shall be unto thee a restorer of thy life and a nourisher of thine old age: for thy daughter in law, which loveth thee, which is better to thee than seven sons, hath born him.
Ruth, *King James Bible* (1611), 4:15

490 He brought me to the banqueting house, and his banner over me was love.
Stay me with flagons, comfort me with apples: for I am sick of love.
His left hand is under my head, and his right hand doth embrace me.
Song of Solomon, *King James Bible* (1611), 2:4–6

491 The voice of my beloved! behold, he cometh leaping upon the mountains, skipping upon the hills.
Song of Solomon, *King James Bible* (1611), 2:8

492 My beloved spake, and said unto me, Rise up, my love, my fair one, and come away.
For, lo, the winter is past, the rain is over and gone;
The flowers appear on the earth; the time of the singing of birds is come, and the voice of the turtle is heard in our land.
Song of Solomon, *King James Bible* (1611), 2:10–12

493 Take us the foxes, the little foxes, that spoil the vines: for our vines have tender grapes.
Song of Solomon, *King James Bible* (1611), 2:15

494 My beloved is mine, and I am his: he feedeth among the lilies. Until the day break, and the shadows flee away, turn, my beloved, and be thou like a roe or a young hart upon the mountains of Bether.
Song of Solomon, *King James Bible* (1611), 2:16–17

495 A fountain of gardens, a well of living waters, and streams from Lebanon.
Song of Solomon, *King James Bible* (1611), 4:15

496 I sleep, but my heart waketh: it is the voice of my beloved that knocketh, saying, Open to me, my sister, my love, my dove, my undefiled: for my head is filled with dew, and my locks with the drops of the night.
Song of Solomon, *King James Bible* (1611), 5:2

497 My beloved is gone down into his garden, to the beds of spices, to feed in the gardens, and to gather lilies.
Song of Solomon, *King James Bible* (1611), 6:2–3

498 Make haste, my beloved, and be thou like to a roe or to a young hart upon the mountains of spices.
Song of Solomon, *King James Bible* (1611), 8:14

499 Unto the pure all things are pure: but unto them that are defiled and unbelieving is nothing pure; but even their mind and conscience is defiled.
Titus, *King James Bible* (1611), 1:15

500 Rejoice greatly, O daughter of Zion; shout, O daughter of Jerusalem: behold, thy King cometh unto thee: he is just, and having salvation; lowly, and riding upon an ass, and upon a colt the foal of an ass.
A messianic prophecy whose symbolism Jesus used when he entered Jerusalem riding on a donkey (Matthew 21:2–11). Zephaniah, *King James Bible* (1611), 9:9

501 Let there be light.
Genesis, *Vulgate* (404?), 1:3

502 It is finished.
John, *Vulgate* (404?), 19:30

Bichat, Marie François (Marie François Xavier Bichat; 1771–1802) French anatomist and physiologist

1 Life is the ensemble of functions that resist death.
Recherches physiologiques sur la vie et la mort (1800)

Bickerstaffe, Isaac (1735?–1812?) Irish playwright

1 Perhaps it was right to dissemble your love,
But why did you kick me downstairs?
An Expostulation (1789)

2 And this the burthen of his song,
For ever us'd to be,
I care for nobody, not I,
If no one cares for me.
Love in a Village (1762), Act 1, Scene 2

3 We all love a pretty girl under the rose.
Love in a Village (1762), Act 2, Scene 2

4 Young fellows will be young fellows.
Love in a Village (1762), Act 2, Scene 2

5 Ay, do despise me! I'm the prouder for it; I like to be despised.
The Hypocrite (1768), Act 5, Scene 1

6 In every port he finds a wife.
Thomas and Sally (1761)

Bidault, Georges (Georges Augustin Bidault; 1899–1983) French statesman

1 The weak have one weapon: the errors of those who think they are strong.
1962. *Observer*, London (15 July, 1962)

Bierce, Ambrose (Ambrose Gwinett Bierce; 1842–1914?) U.S. writer and journalist

1 What this country needs—what every country needs occasionally—is a good hard bloody war to revive the vice of patriotism on which its existence as a nation depends.
Referring to the United States. Letter (February 15, 1911)

2 CORPORATION, n. An ingenious device for securing individual profit without individual responsibility.
The Cynic's Word Book (1906)

3 FINANCE, n. The art or science of managing revenues and resources for the best advantage of the manager. The pronunciation of this word with the i long and the accent on the first syllable is one of America's most precious discoveries and possessions.
The Cynic's Word Book (1906)

4 ACCIDENT, n. An inevitable occurrence due to the action of immutable natural laws.
The Devil's Dictionary (1911)

5 ALLIANCE, n. In international politics, the union of two thieves who have their hands so deeply inserted in each other's pockets that they cannot separately plunder a third.
The Devil's Dictionary (1911)

6 An inventor is a person who makes an ingenious arrangement of wheels, levers, and springs, and believes it civilization.
The Devil's Dictionary (1911)

7 ARCHITECT: one who drafts a plan of your house, and plans a draft of your money.
The Devil's Dictionary (1911)

8 AUTOMOBILE, n. A four-wheeled vehicle that runs up hills and down pedestrians.
The Devil's Dictionary (1911)

9 BORE, n. A person who talks when you wish him to listen.
The Devil's Dictionary (1911)

10 BRAIN, n. An apparatus with which we think that we think.
The Devil's Dictionary (1911)

11 BRIDE, n. A woman with a fine prospect of happiness behind her.
The Devil's Dictionary (1911)

12 Calamities are of two kinds: misfortune to ourselves, and good fortune to others.
The Devil's Dictionary (1911)

13 CARTESIAN, adj. Relating to Descartes, a famous philosopher, author of the celebrated dictum, *Cogito ergo sum*—whereby he was pleased to suppose he demonstrated the reality of human existence. The dictum might be improved, however, thus: *Cogito cogito ergo cogito sum*—"I think that I think, therefore I think that I am"; as close an approach to certainty as any philosopher has yet made.
The Devil's Dictionary (1911)

14 CHILDHOOD, n. The period of human life intermediate between the idiocy of infancy and the folly of youth—two removes from the sin of manhood and three from the remorse of age.
The Devil's Dictionary (1911)

15 CHRISTIAN, n. One who believes that the New Testament is a divinely inspired book admirably suited to the spiritual needs of his neighbor. One who follows the teachings of Christ in so far as they are not inconsistent with a life of sin.
The Devil's Dictionary (1911)

16 COMMERCE, n. A kind of transaction in which A plunders from B the goods of C, and for compensation B picks the pocket of D of money belonging to E.
The Devil's Dictionary (1911)

17 CONSERVATIVE, n. A statesman who is enamored of existing evils, as distinguished from the Liberal, who wishes to replace them with others.
The Devil's Dictionary (1911)

18 DEBAUCHEE, n. One who has so earnestly pursued pleasure that he has had the misfortune to overtake it.
The Devil's Dictionary (1911)

19 DENTIST, n. A prestidigitator who, putting metal into your mouth, pulls coins out of your pocket.
The Devil's Dictionary (1911)

20 DIAGNOSIS, n. A physician's forecast of disease by the patient's pulse and purse.
The Devil's Dictionary (1911)

21 ECONOMY, n. Purchasing the barrel of whiskey that you do not need for the price of the cow that you cannot afford.
The Devil's Dictionary (1911)

22 EGOIST, n. A person of low taste, more interested in himself than in me.
The Devil's Dictionary (1911)

23 FUTURE, n. That period of time in which our affairs prosper, our friends are true and our happiness is assured.
The Devil's Dictionary (1911)

24 GRAVE, n. A place in which the dead are laid to await the coming of the medical student.
The Devil's Dictionary (1911)

25 HISTORY, n. An account, mostly false, of events, mostly unimportant, which are brought about by rulers, mostly knaves, and soldiers, mostly fools.
The Devil's Dictionary (1911)

26 HOMEOPATHY, n. A school of medicine midway between Allopathy and Christian Science. To the last both the others are distinctly inferior, for Christian Science will cure imaginary diseases, and they can not.
The Devil's Dictionary (1911)

27 IGNORAMUS, n. A person unacquainted with certain kinds of knowledge familiar to yourself, and having certain other kinds that you know nothing about.
The Devil's Dictionary (1911)

28 IMPIETY, n. Your irreverence toward my deity.
The Devil's Dictionary (1911)

29 INFANCY, n. The period of our lives when, according to Wordsworth, "Heaven lies about us." The world begins lying about us pretty soon afterwards.
The Devil's Dictionary (1911)

30 INSURANCE, n. An ingenious modern game of chance in which the player is permitted to enjoy the comfortable conviction that he is beating the man who keeps the table.
The Devil's Dictionary (1911)

31 KING, n. A male person commonly known in America as a "crowned head," although he never wears a crown and has usually no head to speak of.
The Devil's Dictionary (1911)

32 LOGIC, n. The art of thinking and reasoning in strict accordance

with the limitations and incapacities of the human understanding.
The Devil's Dictionary (1911)

33 LONGEVITY, n. Uncommon extension of the fear of death.
The Devil's Dictionary (1911)

34 MAN, n. An animal so lost in rapturous contemplation of what he thinks he is as to overlook what he indubitably ought to be.
The Devil's Dictionary (1911)

35 MARRIAGE, n. The state or condition of a community consisting of a master, a mistress and two slaves, making in all two.
The Devil's Dictionary (1911)

36 MAUSOLEUM, n. The final and funniest folly of the rich.
The Devil's Dictionary (1911)

37 PAINTING, n. The art of protecting flat surfaces from the weather and exposing them to the critic.
The Devil's Dictionary (1911)

38 PATIENCE, n. A minor form of despair, disguised as a virtue.
The Devil's Dictionary (1911)

39 PEACE, n. In international affairs, a period of cheating between two periods of fighting.
The Devil's Dictionary (1911)

40 PHYSICIAN, n. One upon whom we set our hopes when ill and our dogs when well.
The Devil's Dictionary (1911)

41 POSITIVE, adj. Mistaken at the top of one's voice.
The Devil's Dictionary (1911)

42 PRAY, v. To ask that the rules of the universe be annulled on behalf of a single petitioner, confessedly unworthy.
The Devil's Dictionary (1911)

43 PRESENT, n. That part of eternity dividing the domain of disappointment from the realm of hope.
The Devil's Dictionary (1911)

44 RADICALISM, n. The conservatism of to-morrow injected into the affairs of to-day.
The Devil's Dictionary (1911)

45 REFERENDUM, n. A law for submission of proposed legislation to a popular vote to learn the nonsensus of public opinion.
The Devil's Dictionary (1911)

46 SAINT, n. A dead sinner revised and edited.
The Devil's Dictionary (1911)

47 SELFISH, adj. Devoid of consideration for the selfishness of others.
The Devil's Dictionary (1911)

48 SPECIALIST, n. One who knows everything about something and nothing about anything else.
The Devil's Dictionary (1911)

49 All are lunatics, but he who can analyze his delusion is called a philosopher.
Epigram. Attrib.

Biermann, Wolf (b.1936) German poet

1 Our life goes at such a fearful pace
—a few years full of youth and grace
and then you fall flat on your face
before world history.
"Balance-sheet Ballad at Thirty" (Steve Gooch, tr.; 1966)

Biggers, Earl Derr (1884–1933) U.S. novelist and playwright

1 Theory like mist on eyeglasses. Obscure facts.
Charlie Chan in Egypt (1935)

Biko, Stephen (1946–77) South African political leader

1 We have set out on a quest for true humanity, and somewhere on the distant horizon we can see the glittering prize...In time we shall be in a position to bestow upon South Africa the greatest gift possible—a more human face.
1973. "Black Consciousness and the Quest for a True Humanity," *Steve Biko: I Write What I Like* (Aeelred Stubbs, ed.; 1978)

2 It would seem that the greatest waste of time in South Africa is to try and find logic in why the white government does certain things.
1971. "Fear—An Important Determinant in South African Politics," *Steve Biko: I Write What I Like* (Aeelred Stubbs, ed.; 1978)

3 I would like to remind the black ministry, and indeed all black people that God is not in the habit of coming down from heaven to solve people's problems on earth.
May 1972. "The Church as Seen by a Young Layman," *Steve Biko: I Write What I Like* (Aeelred Stubbs, ed.; 1978)

4 Being black is not a matter of pigmentation—being black is a reflection of a mental attitude.
1971. "The Definition of Black Consciousness," *Steve Biko: I Write What I Like* (Aeelred Stubbs, ed.; 1978)

5 Ground for a revolution is always fertile in the presence of absolute destitution.
1970. "We Blacks," *Steve Biko: I Write What I Like* (Aeelred Stubbs, ed.; 1978)

6 The biggest mistake the black world ever made was to assume that whoever opposed apartheid was an ally.
January 1971. "White Racism and Black Consciousness," *Steve Biko: I Write What I Like* (Aeelred Stubbs, ed.; 1978)

Billings, John Shaw (1838–1913) U.S. physician and librarian

1 The education of the doctor which goes on after he has his degree is, after all, the most important part of his education.
Boston Medical and Surgical Journal (1894)

2 It has been considered from the point of view of the hygienist, the physician, the architect, the tax-payer, the superintendent, and the nurse, but of the several hundred books, pamphlets, and articles on the subject with which I am acquainted, I do not remember to have seen one from the point of view of the patient.
1870s. *Public Health Reports* (1874–75)

Billings, Josh (Henry Wheeler Shaw; 1818–85) U.S. humorist

1 A sekret ceases tew be a sekret if it iz once confided—it iz like

a dollar bill, once broken, it iz never a dollar agin.
"Affurisms," *Josh Billings: His Sayings* (1865)

2 Poverty iz the stepmother ov genius.
"Affurisms," *Josh Billings: His Sayings* (1865)

3 Love iz like the meazles; we kant have it bad but onst, and the latter in life we hav it the tuffer it goes with us.
Josh Billings' Wit and Wisdom (1874)

4 I have finally come to the conclusion that a good reliable set of bowels is worth more to a man than any quantity of brains.
Bartlett's Unfamiliar Quotations (Leonard Louis Levinson, ed.; 1972)

Billings, Victoria (b.1945) U.S. journalist and writer

1 The best thing that could happen to motherhood already has. Fewer women are going into it.
"Meeting Your Personal Needs," *Womansbook* (1974)

Billson, Christine British writer

1 I am admired because I do things well. I cook, sew, knit, talk, work and make love very well. So I am a valuable item.
You Can Touch Me (1961)

Binchy, Maeve (b.1940) Irish novelist, playwright, and short-story writer

1 It's not perfect, but to me on balance Right Now is a lot better than the Good Old Days.
Referring to modern Ireland. *Irish Times,* Dublin (November 15, 1997)

Bing, Siegfried (1838–1905) German-born French writer and art dealer

1 If the painter's task is limited to giving shape to the content of his imagination, the mission of decorative art is to adapt itself to the taste and habit of others.
1898. *Artistic America* (B. Eisler, tr.; 1977)

Bingen, Hildegard of (1098–1179) German abbess, mystic, and composer

1 Man rushes to woman like the stag to the spring, and the woman to him like the threshing floor of the barn, shaken and heated by the many blows of the flail when the grain is threshed.
Quoted in *Women in the Middle Ages* (Sibylle Harksen; 1975)

Bin Gorion, Micha Joseph (1865–1921) Russian writer and collector of Jewish folktales

1 Yet wine is mightier than the king. For great and true...though the king may be, yet when he drinks the wine rules over him.
Referring to Nebuchadnezzar. Quoted in *Mimekor Yisrael* (Emanuel bin Gorion, ed.; I. M. Lask, tr.; 1976), vol. 1

2 And when the priests and Levites saw that the Temple was destroyed, they took their lyres and trumpets and fell into the fire and were burned.
Referring to the destruction of Solomon's Temple by Nebuchadnezzar. Quoted in *Mimekor Yisrael* (Emanuel bin Gorion, ed., I. M. Lask, tr.; 1976), vol. 1

Bing Xin (Xie Wanying; b.1900) Chinese writer

1 More anniversaries of national humiliation than any other festivals, that...was China when I was young.
"Because We Are Still Young" (1973), quoted in *Literature of the People's Republic of China* (Kai-yu Hsu, ed.; 1980)

2 Yesterday you told me the world is joyful, yet today you tell me the world is disappointing.
"Myriad Stars" (1923), quoted in *Anthology of Modern Chinese Poetry* (Michelle Yeh, ed., tr.; 1992)

Binyon, Laurence (Robert Laurence Binyon; 1869–1943) British poet and art historian

1 With proud thanksgiving, a mother for her children,
England mourns for her dead across the sea.
In response to the slaughter of World War I. "For the Fallen," *Poems for the Fallen* (1914), ll. 1–2

2 They shall grow not old, as we that are left grow old:
Age shall not weary them, nor the years condemn.
At the going down of the sun and in the morning
We will remember them.
In response to the slaughter of World War I. "For the Fallen," *Poems for the Fallen* (1914), ll. 13–14

3 Now is the time for the burning of the leaves.
"The Ruins," *The Burning of the Leaves* (1942)

Bird, Caroline (b.1915) U.S. writer

1 A career woman who has survived the hurdle of marriage and maternity encounters a new obstacle: the hostility of men.
Born Female (1968), ch. 3

2 The contraceptive pill may reduce the importance of sex not only as a basis for the division of labor, but as a guideline in developing talents and interests.
Born Female (1968), foreword

Bird, Frederick Bruce (b.1938) U.S. author

1 An organization can develop a strong and vibrant voice of conscience only by finding ways to harmonize its multiple voices of conscience.
The Muted Conscience (1996)

2 Businessman and businesswoman are mute not only when they fail to speak up about flagrant abuse they become aware of...but also when they fail to speak up for causes or projects that they judge to be morally valuable.
The Muted Conscience (1996)

Birnbach, Lisa (b.1957) U.S. writer

1 Even if they've never been near a duck blind or gone beagling, Preppies are dressed for it. Rugged outerwear (snakeproof boots, jackets that will keep you warm at 60 degrees below zero) and hearty innerwear (fisherman's sweaters and flannel-lined khakis) are de rigueur in even the most sophisticated suburbs.
The Official Preppy Handbook (1980), ch. 4

Birrell, Augustine (1850–1933) British statesman and writer

1 That great dust-heap called "history".
Obiter Dicta (1884), "Carlyle"

2 It is not an Irish rebellion. It would be a pity if ex post facto it became one, and was added to the long and melancholy list of Irish rebellions.
April 30, 1916. From his last report before resigning as chief secretary for Ireland, referring to the uprising of Easter 1916 that led to Irish independence. Quoted in *Ourselves Alone* (Robert Kee; 1976)

Birt, John, Sir (b.1944) British broadcasting executive

1 There is a bias in television journalism. It is not against any particular party or point of view—it is a bias against *understanding*.
This launched a series of articles written jointly with Peter Jay. *Times*, London (February 28, 1975)

Bishop, Elizabeth (1911–79) U.S. poet

1 The doctor procured for me a hypodermic syringe of my own, a very flashing one, all red and chromium, and I play with it every now and then, feeling too decadent for words.
Referring to an attack of flu and asthma. Letter to Frani Blough (January 1, 1935), quoted in *One Art: The Selected Letters of Elizabeth Bishop* (Robert Giroux, ed.; 1994)

2 The "samambaia"...is a giant fern, big as a tree, and there are toads as big as your hat and snails as big as bread & butter plates, and during this month butterflies the color of this page and sometimes almost as big flopping about.
Referring to her surroundings in Petropolis, Brazil, where she lived for 15 years. Letter to James Merrill (March 1, 1955), quoted in *One Art: The Selected Letters of Elizabeth Bishop* (Robert Giroux, ed.; 1994)

3 Undoubtedly gender does play an important part in the making of any art, but art is art and to separate writings, paintings, musical compositions, etc., into two sexes is to emphasize values in them that are not art.
Letter to Joan Keele (June 8, 1977)

4 I have that continuous uncomfortable feeling of "things" in the head, like icebergs or rocks or awkwardly placed pieces of furniture. It's as if all the nouns were there but the verbs were lacking.
Referring to difficulties in writing. Letter to Marianne Moore (September 11, 1940), quoted in *One Art: The Selected Letters of Elizabeth Bishop* (Robert Giroux, ed.; 1994)

5 The art of losing isn't hard to master;
so many things seem filled with the intent
to be lost that their loss is no disaster.
"One Art," *Geography III* (1976)

6 The state with the prettiest name,
the state that floats in brackish water,
held together by mangrove roots.
1939. Referring to Florida. "Florida," *North and South* (1946), ll. 1–3

7 I caught a tremendous fish
and held him beside the boat
half out of water, with my hook
fast in a corner of his mouth.
"The Fish," *North and South* (1946), ll. 1–4

8 I stared and stared
and victory filled up
the little rented boat.
"The Fish," *North and South* (1946), ll. 65–67

9 My grandfather said to me
as we sat on the wagon seat,
"Be sure to remember to always
speak to everyone you meet."
"Manners," *Questions of Travel* (1965)

10 Is it lack of imagination that makes us come
to imagined places, not just stay at home?
"Questions of Travel," *Questions of Travel* (1965)

Bishop, Isabella (originally Isabella Lucy Bird; 1831–1904) British traveler and author

1 The worst part of the climb, one slip, and a breathing, thinking, human being would lie 3000 feet below, a shapeless, bloody heap!
A Lady's Life in the Rocky Mountains (1879)

2 It is my practice in travelling to make my arrangements very carefully, to attend personally to every detail, and to give other people as little trouble as possible.
Letter, *Journeys in Persia and Kurdistan* (1891), no. 25

Bismarck, Prince Otto von, Duke of Lauenburg (Otto Edward Leopold von Bismarck, "The Iron Chancellor"; 1815–98) German chancellor

Quotations about Bismarck

1 "Are there German philosophers? Are there German writers? Are there good German books?" people ask me when I am abroad. I blush; but, with that gallantry of which I am capable in hopeless situations, I answer, "Yes! Bismarck!"
Friedrich Wilhelm Nietzsche (1844–1900) German philosopher and poet. *Twilight of the Gods* (1888)

Quotations by Bismarck

2 The Russians do not possess the kind of self-restraint that would make it possible for us to live alone with them and France on the continent.
Letter to his son, Herbert (October 1886), quoted in *Germany, 1866–1945* (Gordon A. Craig; 1978)

3 We do not live alone in Europe but with three other Powers that hate and envy us.
Referring to Prussia's victory over Austria-Hungary at Königgrätz. Letter to his wife (July 9, 1866), quoted in *Germany, 1866–1945* (Gordon A. Craig; 1978)

4 Any war that breaks out must place the survival of the European order in jeopardy.
Letter to the German ambassador in Vienna (November 1883), quoted in *Germany, 1866–1945* (Gordon A. Craig; 1978)

5 I always hear the word "Europe" on the lips of politicians who seek from other posers what they dare not demand in their own name.
Remark (January 9, 1871)

6 The ability to wait while conditions develop is a requisite of practical policy.
Remark (February 1869), quoted in *Germany, 1866–1945* (Gordon A. Craig; 1978), ch. 1

7 At the moment of decision the masses will stand on the side of kingship, regardless of whether the latter happens to follow a liberal or a conservative tendency.
Remark (1866), quoted in *Germany, 1866–1945* (Gordon A. Craig; 1978), ch. 2

8 If there is ever another war in Europe, it will come out of some damned silly thing in the Balkans.
Remark to Ballen, shortly before Bismarck's death. Attrib.

9 In Prussia it is only the kings who make revolution.
Remark to Napoleon III (1862)

10 All politics reduce themselves to this formula: to try to be one of three, as long as the world is governed by an unstable equilibrium of five powers.
Remark to the Russian ambassador to Germany (January 1880), quoted in *Germany, 1866–1945* (Gordon A. Craig; 1978), ch. 4

11 We will not go to Canossa.
Refers to submission of Emperor Henry IV to Pope Gregory VII at Canossa, northern Italy, in 1077. Speech declaring his anti-Roman Catholic policy (May 14, 1872)

12 The great questions of our day cannot be solved by speeches and majority votes...but by iron and blood.
Often misquoted as "blood and iron." Speech given in Prussian Parliament (September 30, 1862)

13 Politics is not an exact science.
Speech in the Prussian Parliament (December 19, 1863)

14 Anyone who has ever looked into the glazed eyes of a soldier will think hard before starting a war.
Speech, Reichstag, Berlin (August 1867)

15 I am supposed to have said that in the whole of the Orient there is no interest worth the revenues of a single Pomeranian manor. That is incorrect...What I said was that I will not advise the active participation of Germany in these things so long as I see no interest in it which...would be worth the healthy bones of a single Pomeranian grenadier.
Speech, Reichstag, Berlin (December 5, 1876)

16 That the state should concern itself with those of its citizens who need help to a greater degree than hitherto, is...a conservative policy which has as its goal to encourage the view among the unpropertied classes of the population...that the state is not only a necessary institution but also a beneficent one.
Speech, Reichstag, Berlin (1884)

17 We Germans fear God and nothing else on earth; and it is the fear of God, and nothing else, that makes us love and cherish peace.
Speech, Reichstag, Berlin (February 6, 1888)

18 Gentlemen, let us work speedily! Let us put Germany, so to speak, in the saddle. You will see, well enough, that she can ride.
Speech to constituent assembly of the North German Confederation, Berlin (March 11, 1867)

19 Politics is not a science...but an art.
Speech to the Reichstag (March 15, 1884)

20 An honest broker.
Referring to his professed role in the diplomacy of 1878, including the Congress of Berlin. Speech to the Reichstag (February 19, 1878)

21 Politics is the art of the possible.
August 11, 1867. Remark to Meyer von Waldeck. *Bismarck-Worte* (H. Amelung; 1918)

22 You can do everything with bayonets except sit on them.
Attrib. *Europe: A History* (Norman Davies; 1996), ch. 10

23 When you say that you agree to a thing in principle you mean that you have not the slightest intention of carrying it out in practice.
Attrib.

24 You can do anything with children if you only play with them.
Attrib.

Bjelke-Petersen, Johannes, Sir (b.1911) New Zealand-born Australian politician

1 A strike has to reach a climax before it gets better, just like a boil.
Sydney Morning Herald (September 7, 1985)

2 It is better to tax 25 per cent of something rather than 60 per cent of nothing.
Sydney Morning Herald (July 6, 1985), "Sayings of the Week"

Black, Hugo LaFayette (1886–1971) U.S. judge and politician

1 In revealing the workings of government that led to the Vietnam War, the newspapers nobly did precisely that which the Founders hoped and trusted they would do.
Concurring in the Supreme Court's decision to overturn government attempts to prevent publication of the Pentagon Papers (classified Defense Department documents on the Vietnam War). Speech (June 30, 1971), quoted in *Simpson's Contemporary Quotations* (James B. Simpson; 1997)

2 Sex is a fact of life...and while it may lead to abuses...no words need be spoken...for people to know that the subject is one pleasantly interwoven in all human activities and involves the very substance of creation itself.
Dissenting from the Supreme Court ruling that "titillating" advertising could be deemed obscene and upholding the criminal conviction of a publisher of erotic literature. Speech (March 21, 1966), quoted in *Simpson's Contemporary Quotations* (James B. Simpson; 1997)

3 No higher duty, or more solemn responsibility rests upon this Court than that of translating into living law and maintaining this constitutional shield...for the benefit of every human being subject to our Constitution—of whatever race, creed, or persuasion.
Speech in a law suit (1940)

Black, Shirley Temple (b.1928) U.S. politician and former child actor

1 I stopped believing in Santa Claus at an early age. Mother took me to see him in a department store and he asked me for my autograph.
Attrib.

Black Elk (Hehaka Sapa; 1863–1950) Native American Sioux leader and mystic

1 Everything an Indian does is in a circle...In the old days when we were a strong and happy people, all our power came to

us from the sacred hoop of the nation, and so long as the hoop was unbroken, the people flourished.
Quoted in *Black Elk Speaks, Being the Life Story of a Holy Man of the Oglala Sioux* (John G. Neihardt; 1961)

Blacker, Valentine (1778–1823) British soldier

1 Put your trust in God, my boys, and keep your powder dry.
Phrase often attributed to Oliver Cromwell. *Ballads of Ireland* (1856), vol. 1

Blackett, Patrick M. S. (Patrick Maynard Stuart Blackett; 1897–1974) British physicist

1 A first-rate laboratory is one in which mediocre scientists can produce outstanding work.
Attrib.

Black Hawk, Chief (Ma-ka-tae-mish-kia-kiak; 1767–1838) Native American leader

1 His heart is dead, and no longer beats quick in his bosom. He is now a prisoner to the white men; they will do with him as they wish. But he can stand torture and is not afraid of death. He is no coward. Black Hawk is an Indian.
Referring to himself, at his surrender after the Bad Axe Massacre. Remark (August 1832), quoted in *Touch the Earth* (T. C. McLuhan; 1971)

2 May the Great Spirit shed light on yours—and that you may never experience the humility that the power of the American government has reduced me to, is the wish of him, who, in his native forests, was once as proud and bold as yourself.
Referring to the massacre of Native Americans by U.S. army forces. Remark to General Henry Atkinson (1833), quoted in *Touch the Earth* (T. C. McLuhan; 1971)

Blackmore, R. D. (Richard Doddridge Blackmore; 1825–1900) British novelist

1 Women, who are, beyond all doubt, the mothers of all mischief, also nurse that babe to sleep when he is too noisy.
Lorna Doone (1869)

2 Here was I, a yeoman's boy, a yeoman every inch of me, even where I was naked; and there was she, a lady born, and thoroughly aware of it, and dressed by people of rank and taste, who took pride in her beauty, and set it to advantage.
Lorna Doone (1869), ch. 8

3 However, for a moralist I never set up, and never shall, while common sense abides with me. Such a man must be truly wretched, in this pure dearth of morality; like a fisherman where no fish be; and most of us have enough to do, to attend to our own morals.
Lorna Doone (1869), ch. 69

4 I was launched into this vale of tears on the 7th of June 1825, at Longworth in Berkshire. Before I was four months old, my mother was taken to a better world, and so I started crookedly.
Lorna Doone (1869), Introduction

Blackmun, Harry A. (Harry Andrew Blackmun; 1908–99) U.S. associate justice of the Supreme Court

1 This right of privacy...is broad enough to encompass a woman's decision whether or not to terminate her pregnancy.
Said during a Supreme Court decision in the *Roe v. Wade* case concerning the right to abortion, ruling that a woman's right to abortion was constitutionally protected. Majority opinion of the Supreme Court (1973)

Blackstone, William, Sir (1723–80) British jurist

1 No vote can be given by lunatics, idiots, minors, aliens, females, persons convicted of perjury, subornation of perjury, bribery treating or undue influence, or by those tainted of felony or outlawed in a criminal suit.
Commentaries on the Laws of England (1765–69)

2 The king never dies.
Commentaries on the Laws of England (1765–69), bk. 1, ch. 7

3 The royal navy of England hath ever been its greatest defence and ornament; it is its ancient and natural strength, the floating bulwark of the island.
Commentaries on the Laws of England (1765–69), bk. 1, ch. 13

4 That the king can do no wrong, is a necessary and fundamental principle of the English constitution.
Commentaries on the Laws of England (1765–69), bk. 3, ch. 17

5 It is better that ten guilty persons escape than one innocent suffer.
Commentaries on the Laws of England (1765–69), bk. 4, ch. 27

6 Man was formed for society.
Commentaries on the Laws of England (1765–69), Introduction, pt. 2

Blackwell, Antoinette Louisa (Antoinette Louisa Brown Blackwell; 1825–1921) U.S. Unitarian minister, feminist and abolitionist

1 Conventionality has indeed curtailed feminine force by hindering healthful and varied activity.
The Sexes Throughout Nature (1875)

2 Mr. Darwin...has failed to hold definitely before his mind the principle that the difference of sex, whatever it may consist in, must itself be subject to natural selection and to evolution.
The Sexes Throughout Nature (1875)

Blackwell, Elizabeth (1821–1910) British-born U.S. physician

1 Social intercourse—a very limited thing in a half civilized country becomes in our centers of civilization a great power.
Medicine as a Profession for Women (co-written with Emily Blackwell; 1860), quoted in *The New Quotable Woman* (Elaine Partnow, ed.; 1993)

2 This failure to recognize the equivalent value of internal with external structure has led to as crude a fallacy as a comparison of the penis with such a vestige as the clitoris, while failing to recognize that vast amount of erectile tissue, mostly internal, in the female, which is the direct seat of sexual spasm.
The Human Element in Sex (1894)

3 The total deprivation of it produces irritability.
Referring to sex. *The Human Element in Sex* (1894)

Blackwell, Otis U.S. lyricist

1 Great Balls of Fire
1957. Song title. One of the biggest hits of Jerry Lee Lewis, co-written with Jack Hammer.

Blair, Robert (1699–1746) Scottish preacher and poet

1 The School-Boy, with his Satchel in his Hand,
Whistling aloud to bear his Courage up.
The Grave (1743), ll. 58–59

2 Of joys departed,
Not to return, how painful the remembrance!
The Grave (1743), ll. 109–110

3 The *Good* he scorn'd
Retir'd reluctant, like an ill-us'd ghost,
Not to return; or if it did, its visits
Like those of *Angels*, short, and far between.
The Grave (1743), ll. 586–589

Blair, Tony (Anthony Charles Lynton Blair; b.1953) British prime minister

Quotations about Blair

1 We want him to be the last British Prime Minister with jurisdiction in Ireland.
Gerry Adams (b.1948) Northern Irish politician. *Irish Times,* Dublin (October 18, 1997)

Quotations by Blair

2 Entrepreneurship will become a core skill which all our young people will need to exploit the opportunities emerging from science and technology, culture and communications.
Lecture to the Fabian Society, London (1998)

3 Government intervention is necessary to protect the weak and ensure that all gain some of the benefit of economic progress.
Lecture to the Fabian Society, London (1998)

4 Modern companies collaborate to compete.
Lecture to the Fabian Society, London (1998)

5 My vision for the 21st century is of a popular politics reconciling themes which in the past have wrongly been viewed as antagonistic—patriotism and internationalism; rights and responsibilities; the promotion of enterprise and the attack on poverty and discrimination.
Lecture to the Fabian Society, London (1998)

6 The successful economies of the future will excel at generating and disseminating knowledge, and commercially exploiting it.
Lecture to the Fabian Society, London (1998)

7 This is not the time for soundbites. I can feel the hand of history on our shoulders.
Referring to the constitutional talks in Northern Ireland. *Daily Telegraph,* London (April 8, 1998)

8 We are the party of the individual because we are the party of the community.
Independent, London (October 5, 1994)

9 We must do more than attack the scourge of unemployment. We should also get rid of dead-end, low-paid work with no prospects.
Independent, London (June 14, 1994)

10 The art of leadership is saying no, not yes. It is very easy to say yes.
Mail on Sunday, London (October 2, 1994)

11 What struck me both last night and again today is this real sense of confidence and optimism. You just want to bottle it and keep it.
January 1, 2000. Referring to the mood in the United Kingdom at the dawn of the new millennium. *Observer,* London (January 2, 2000)

Blake, Charles Dupee (1846–1903) British writer of nursery rhymes

1 Rock-a-bye baby on the tree top,
When the wind blows the cradle will rock,
When the bough bends the cradle will fall,
Down comes the baby, cradle and all.
Attrib.

Blake, Edward (1833–1912) Canadian statesman

1 The history of the diplomatic service of England, as far as Canada is concerned, has been a history of error, wrong, and concession.
Speech to the Canadian Parliament (1882)

Blake, Eubie (James Hubert Blake; 1883–1983) U.S. pianist and composer

1 If I'd known I was gonna live this long, I'd have taken better care of myself.
Observer, London (February 13, 1983), "Sayings of the Week"

2 Down South where I come from you don't go around hitting too many white keys.
1983. When asked why his compositions contained so many sharps and flats. Attrib.

Blake, William (1757–1827) British poet, painter, engraver, and mystic

Quotations about Blake

1 Blake...presents only the essential, only, in fact, what can be presented, and need not be explained...He approached everything with a mind unclouded by current opinions. There was nothing of the superior person about him. This makes him terrifying.
T. S. Eliot (1888–1965) U.S.-born British poet and playwright. *The Sacred Wood* (1920)

2 He has no sense of the ludicrous, and, as to God, a worm crawling in a privy is as worthy an object as any other, all being to him indifferent. So to Blake the Chimney Sweeper etc. He is ruined by vain struggles to get rid of what presses on his brain—he attempts impossibles.
William Hazlitt (1778–1830) British essayist and critic. Quoted in *Diary, Reminiscences, and Correspondence of H. C. Robinson* (Henry Crabb Robinson; 1869)

Quotations by Blake

3 To see a World in a Grain of Sand
And a Heaven in a Wild Flower,
Hold Infinity in the palm of your hand
And Eternity in an hour.
"Auguries of Innocence" (1803?), ll. 1–4, quoted in *The Poetry and Prose of William Blake* (David V. Erdman, ed.; 1965)

4 A Robin Red breast in a Cage
Puts all Heaven in a Rage.
"Auguries of Innocence" (1803?), ll. 5–6, quoted in *The Poetry and Prose of William Blake* (David V. Erdman, ed.; 1965)

5 A dog starv'd at his Master's Gate
Predicts the ruin of the State.
"Auguries of Innocence" (1803?), ll. 9–10, quoted in *The Poetry and Prose of William Blake* (David V. Erdman, ed.; 1965)

6 A truth that's told with bad intent
Beats all the Lies you can invent.
"Auguries of Innocence" (1803?), ll. 53–54, quoted in *The Poetry and Prose of William Blake* (David V. Erdman, ed.; 1965)

7 He who shall teach the Child to Doubt
The rotting Grave shall ne'er get out.
"Auguries of Innocence" (1803?), ll. 63–64, quoted in *The Poetry and Prose of William Blake* (David V. Erdman, ed.; 1965)

8 The Strongest Poison ever known
Came from Caesar's Laurel Crown.
"Auguries of Innocence" (1803?), ll. 103–104, quoted in *The Poetry and Prose of William Blake* (David V. Erdman, ed.; 1965)

9 When I tell any Truth it is not for the sake of convincing those who do not know it, but for the sake of defending those who do.
Public Address (1810?), quoted in *Complete Writings* (Geoffrey Keynes, ed.; 1957)

10 For everything that lives is holy, life delights in life.
America: A Prophecy (1793), pt. 8, l. 13

11 There can be no Good Will. Will is always Evil; it is persecution to others or selfishness.
Annotations to Swedenborg (1788)

12 He who would do good to another, must do it in Minute Particulars:
General Good is the plea of the scoundrel, hypocrite & flatterer:
For Art & Science cannot exist but in minutely organized Particulars.
Jerusalem (1804–20), ch. 3, pl. 55, ll. 60–62, quoted in *The Poetry and Prose of William Blake* (David V. Erdman, ed.; 1965)

13 "I care not whether a Man is Good or Evil; all that I care
"Is whether he is a Wise Man or a Fool. Go! put off Holiness,
"And put on Intellect."
Jerusalem (1804–20), ch. 4, pl. 91, ll. 55–57, quoted in *The Poetry and Prose of William Blake* (David V. Erdman, ed.; 1965)

14 O ye Religious, discountenance every one among you who shall pretend to despise Art and Science!
"To the Christians," *Jerusalem* (1804–20), pl. 77, quoted in *The Poetry and Prose of William Blake* (David V. Erdman, ed.; 1965)

15 Mock on, Mock on, Voltaire, Rousseau:
Mock on, Mock on: 'tis all in vain!
You throw the sand against the wind,
And the wind blows it back again.
Manuscript Notebooks (1811), no. 4

16 He who binds to himself a joy
Doth the winged life destroy;
But he who kisses the joy as it flies
Lives in Eternity's sunrise.
Manuscript Notebooks (1811), no. 59

17 The Errors of a Wise Man make your Rule,
Rather than the Perfections of a Fool.
Manuscript Notebooks (1811), no. 61

18 And did those feet in ancient time
Walk upon England's mountains green?
And was the holy Lamb of God
On England's pleasant pastures seen?
...
I will not cease from Mental Fight,
Nor shall my Sword sleep in my hand,
Till we have built Jerusalem
In England's green and pleasant Land.
1804–08. Better known as the hymn "Jerusalem," with music by Sir Hubert Parry; not to be confused with Blake's longer poem *Jerusalem*. *Milton: A Poem in Two Books* (1804), no. 1, preface, ll.1–4, 13–16, quoted in *The Poetry and Prose of William Blake* (David V. Erdman, ed.; 1965)

19 God forbid that Truth should be confined to Mathematical Demonstration!
Notes on Reynold's Discourses (1808?)

20 Children of the future Age
Reading this indignant page:
Know that in a former time
Love!, sweet Love!, was thought a crime.
"A Little Girl Lost," *Songs of Experience* (1789–94), ll. 1–4

21 I was angry with my friend:
I told my wrath, my wrath did end.
I was angry with my foe:
I told it not, my wrath did grow.
"A Poison Tree," *Songs of Experience* (1789–94), ll. 1–4

22 "Love seeketh not itself to please,
"Nor for itself hath any care,
"But for another gives its ease,
"And builds a Heaven in Hell's despair."
"The Clod & the Pebble," *Songs of Experience* (1789–94), ll. 1–4

23 "Love seeketh only Self to please,
"To bind another to Its delight,
"Joys in another's loss of ease,
"And builds a Hell in Heaven's despite."
"The Clod & the Pebble," *Songs of Experience* (1789–94), ll. 9–12

24 Then the Parson might preach, & drink, & sing,
And we'd be as happy as birds in the spring;
And modest dame Lurch, who is always at Church,
Would not have bandy children, nor fasting, nor birch.
"The Little Vagabond," *Songs of Experience* (1789–94), ll. 9–12

25 O Rose, thou art sick!
The invisible worm
That flies in the night,
In the howling storm,

Has found out thy bed
Of crimson joy:
And his dark secret love
Does thy life destroy.
"The Sick Rose," *Songs of Experience* (1789–94), ll. 1–8

26 Tyger! Tyger! burning bright
In the forests of the night,

What immortal hand or eye
Could frame thy fearful symmetry?
"The Tyger," *Songs of Experience* (1789–94), ll. 1–4

27 And what shoulder & what art,
Could twist the sinews of thy heart?
And, when thy heart began to beat,
What dread hand? & what dread feet?
"The Tyger," *Songs of Experience* (1789–94), ll. 9–12

28 When the stars threw down their spears,
And water'd heaven with their tears,
Did he smile his work to see?
Did he who made the Lamb make thee?
"The Tyger," *Songs of Experience* (1789–94), ll. 17–20

29 Then cherish pity, lest you drive an angel from your door.
"Holy Thursday," *Songs of Innocence* (1789), l. 12

30 When the green woods laugh with the voice of joy.
"Laughing Song," *Songs of Innocence* (1789), l. 1

31 When the voices of children are heard on the green,
And laughing is heard on the hill.
"Nurse's Song," *Songs of Innocence* (1789), ll. 1–2

32 Can I see another's woe,
And not be in sorrow too?
Can I see another's grief,
And not seek for kind relief?
"On Another's Sorrow," *Songs of Innocence* (1789), ll. 1–4

33 For Mercy has a human heart,
Pity a human face,
And Love, the human form divine,
And Peace, the human dress.
"The Divine Image," *Songs of Innocence* (1789), ll. 9–12

34 Little Lamb, who made thee?
Dost thou know who made thee?
"The Lamb," *Songs of Innocence* (1789), ll. 1–2

35 Both read the Bible day & night
But thou read'st black where I read white.
The Everlasting Gospel (1818?), ll. 13–14, quoted in *The Poetry and Prose of William Blake* (David V. Erdman, ed.; 1965)

36 Mutual Forgiveness of each Vice
Such are the Gates of Paradise.
The Gates of Paradise (1793–1818), prologue, ll. 1–2, quoted in *The Poetry and Prose of William Blake* (David V. Erdman, ed.; 1965)

37 If the doors of perception were cleansed every thing would appear to man as it is, infinite.
"A Memorable Fancy," *The Marriage of Heaven and Hell* (1790–93), pl. 14

38 In seed time learn, in harvest teach, in winter enjoy.
"Proverbs of Hell," *The Marriage of Heaven and Hell* (1790–93), l. 1

39 The road of excess leads to the palace of wisdom.
"Proverbs of Hell," *The Marriage of Heaven and Hell* (1790–93), l. 3

40 He who desires but acts not, breeds pestilence.
"Proverbs of Hell," *The Marriage of Heaven and Hell* (1790–93), l. 5

41 The cut worm forgives the plow.
"Proverbs of Hell," *The Marriage of Heaven and Hell* (1790–93), l. 6

42 A fool sees not the same tree that a wise man sees.
"Proverbs of Hell," *The Marriage of Heaven and Hell* (1790–93), l. 8

43 Prisons are built with stones of Law, Brothels with bricks of Religion.
"Proverbs of Hell," *The Marriage of Heaven and Hell* (1790–93), pl. 8, l. 1

44 What is now proved was once, only imagin'd.
"Proverbs of Hell," *The Marriage of Heaven and Hell* (1790–93), pl. 8, l. 13

45 Damn braces: Bless relaxes.
"Proverbs of Hell," *The Marriage of Heaven and Hell* (1790–93), pl. 9, l. 18

46 Exuberance is Beauty.
"Proverbs of Hell," *The Marriage of Heaven and Hell* (1790–93), pl. 10, l. 4

47 Sooner murder an infant in its cradle than nurse unacted desires.
"Proverbs of Hell," *The Marriage of Heaven and Hell* (1790–93), pl. 10, l. 7

48 Without Contraries is no progression. Attraction and Repulsion, Reason and Energy, Love and Hate, are necessary to Human existence.
"The Argument," *The Marriage of Heaven and Hell* (1790–93), pl. 3

49 Energy is Eternal Delight.
"The Voice of the Devil," *The Marriage of Heaven and Hell* (1790–93), pl. 4

50 Those who restrain desire, do so because theirs is weak enough to be restrained.
"The Voice of the Devil," *The Marriage of Heaven and Hell* (1790–93), pls. 5–6

51 The Desire of Man being Infinite, the possession is Infinite, and himself Infinite.
There is no Natural Religion (1788)

52 To generalize is to be an idiot.
1808? Annotation written on a copy of Sir Joshua Reynolds's *Discourses*. Quoted in *Life of Blake* (Alexander Gilchrist; 1863)

Blanchflower, Danny (Robert Dennis Blanchflower; 1926–93) Northern Irish soccer player

1 The great fallacy is that the game is first and last about winning. It's nothing of the kind. The game is about glory. It's about doing things in style, with a flourish, about going out and beating the other lot, not waiting for them to die of boredom.
Quoted in *The Glory Game* (Hunter Davies; 1985)

Bland, James A. (1854–1911) U.S. entertainer and composer

1 There's where I labor'd all day in the cotton
There's where I worked in the fields of yellow corn
No place on earth do I love more sincerely
Than old Virginny, the state where I was born.
Carry Me Back to Old Virginny

Bleasdale, Alan (b.1946) British playwright

1 All the names under the sun and my mother picked Doreen. I mean, how can you go to a Hunt Ball or a dinner at the Town Hall and be announced as..."Doreen".
Having a Ball (1986), Act 1

2 Oh dear, not another Greta Garbo, that'll be four we've got now.
It's a Madhouse (1976), Act 2

3 Seen better heads on a mop.
It's a Madhouse (1976), Act 2

Bliss, Philip Paul (1838–76) U.S. hymnwriter

1 Hold the fort, for I am coming
Ho, My Comrades, See the Signal!
Suggested by a flag message from General W. T. Sherman near Atlanta, October 1864. "The Charm," *Gospel Hymns and Sacred Songs* (1875)

Bloch, Marc (1886–1944) French historian

1 The reactionaries of 1815 hid their faces at the very name of revolution; those of 1940 used it to camouflage their seizure of power.
Referring to France. In 1815, the French monarchy was restored after the defeat of Napoleon at Waterloo. In 1940, after the defeat of France by Germany, the collaborationist Vichy government was formed, with many French politicians taking high office. *Apologie pour l'histoire, ou métier d'historien* (1949)

Blok, Aleksandr (Aleksandr Aleksandrovich Blok; 1880–1921) Russian poet

1 How often we sit weeping—you
and I—over the life we lead!
My friends, if you only knew
the darkness of the days ahead!
"A Voice from the Chorus" (June 6, 1910), quoted in *Selected Poems: Alexander Blok* (Jon Stallworthy and Peter France, trs.; 1974)

2 Russia is a sphinx. Grieving, jubilant,
and covering herself with blood
she looks, she looks, she looks at you her slant
eyes lit with hatred and with love.
"The Scythians" (January 30, 1918), sect. 1, quoted in *Selected Poems: Alexander Blok* (Jon Stallworthy and Peter France, trs.; 1974)

3 You cannot stand upright
for the wind: the wind
scouring God's world.
Referring to the Russian Revolution (1917). "The Twelve" (January 1918), sect. 1, quoted in *Selected Poems: Alexander Blok* (Jon Stallworthy and Peter France, trs.; 1974)

4 The wind plays up; snow flutters down.
Twelve men are marching through the town.
Referring to the Red Army. "The Twelve" (January 1918), sect. 2, quoted in *Selected Poems: Alexander Blok* (Jon Stallworthy and Peter France, trs.; 1974)

5 The brain is not an organ to be relied upon. It is developing monstrously. It is swelling like a goiter.
Attrib.

Bloom, Allan (Allan David Bloom; 1930–92) U.S. philosopher

1 Economists tell us how to make money; psychiatrists give us a place to spend it.
The Closing of the American Mind (1987)

Bloomberg, Michael (Michael Rubens Bloomberg; b.1942) U.S. business executive

1 Central planning didn't work for Stalin or Mao, and it won't work for an entrepreneur either.
Bloomberg on Bloomberg (co-written with Matthew Winkler; 1997)

2 After hard work, the biggest determinant is being in the right place at the right time.
Referring to business success. *Newsweek* (August 4, 1997)

Bloomer, Amelia Jenks (1818–94) U.S. social reformer

1 We all felt that the dress was drawing attention from what we thought to be of far greater importance...In the minds of some people the short dress and woman's rights were inseparably connected. With us, the dress was but an incident, and we were not willing to sacrifice greater questions to it.
Quoted in *The Bloomer Girls* (Charles N. Gattey; 1968)

Blücher, Gebhard Leberecht von, Prince of Wahlstadt ("Marshal Forward"; 1742–1819) Prussian field marshal

1 What rubbish!
1814. Referring to London, as seen from the Monument; often misquoted as *"Was für plündern!"* ("What a place to plunder!"). Quoted in *Memoirs* (Evelyn, Princess Blücher; 1932)

Blue, Lionel, Rabbi (b.1930) British rabbi, author, and broadcaster

1 It is not possible to meet with Jewish spirituality without meeting Jews, and Jews may not be immediately likeable.
To Heaven with Scribes and Pharisees (1975)

2 Over the concentration camp entrance the Nazis hung a sign, *Arbeit macht Frei* (work makes free). This was terrible because it distorted a truth which is one of the deepest in Jewish experience—the salvation, to which work, honestly done, is the door.
To Heaven with Scribes and Pharisees (1975)

Blue, Vida (Vida Rochelle Blue; b.1949) U.S. baseball player

1 I just pick it up and throw it. He hit it. They scored. We didn't. That's it. It's over. It's history. OK?
Quoted in *Vida: His Own Story* (co-written with Bill Libby; 1972)

Blum, Léon (1872–1950) French statesman, lawyer, and critic

1 A French Jew, of a long line of French ancestors, speaking only the language of my country, mainly nourished by its culture, refusing to leave at a moment when I faced the greatest dangers.
Referring to his decision to remain in France during World War II. Quoted in *Europe Since 1870* (James Joll; 1973), ch. 4

Blume, Judy (originally Judy Sussman; b.1938) U.S. author

1 Are you there God? It's me, Margaret. I just told my mother I want a bra. Please help me grow God. You know where. I want to be like everyone else.
Are You There God? It's Me, Margaret (1970)

Blunden, Edmund (Edmund Charles Blunden; 1896–1974) British poet and scholar

1 I have been young, and now am not too old;
And I have seen the righteous forsaken,
His health, his honour and his quality taken
...This is not what we formerly were told.
"Report on Experience," *Near and Far* (1929), st. 1

Bly, Robert (b.1926) U.S. poet, translator, and writer

1 Terror just before death,
Shoulders torn, shot
...the boy
Tortured with the telephone generator,
"I felt sorry for him
And blew his head off with a shotgun."
...Our own gaiety
Will end up
in Asia, and in your cup you will look down
And see
Black Starfighters.
We were the ones we intended to bomb!
"Driving Through Minnesota During the Hanoi Bombings" (1968)

2 Alive, we are like a sleek black water beetle.
Skating across still water in any direction
We choose, and soon to be swallowed
Suddenly from beneath.
"Night" (1962)

Blyden, Edward Wilmot (1832–1912) Liberian educator, statesman, and diplomat

1 A man without common sense, without tact, as a mechanic or agriculturist or trader, can do far less harm to the public than the man without common sense who has had the opportunity of becoming, and has had the reputation of being, a scholar.
Christianity, Islam and the Negro Race (1888)

2 If you are not yourself, if you surrender your personality, you have nothing left to give the world. You have no pleasure, no use, nothing which will attract and charm me, for by the suppression of your individuality, you lose your distinctive character.
Sierra Leone Times (May 27, 1893)

Blythe, Ronald (Ronald George Blythe; b.1922) British writer

1 As for the British churchman, he goes to church as he goes to the bathroom, with the minimum of fuss and no explanation if he can help it.
The Age of Illusion (1963), ch. 12

2 Old age is...a lot of crossed off names in an address book.
The View in Winter (1979)

3 To be old is to be part of a huge and ordinary multitude...the reason why old age was venerated in the past was because it was extraordinary.
The View in Winter (1979)

Boas, Franz (1858–1942) German-born U.S. anthropologist

1 Much of what we ascribe to human nature is no more than a reaction to the restraints put upon us by our civilization.
Quoted in *Coming of Age in Samoa* (Margaret Mead; 1928)

Boccaccio, Giovanni (1313–75) Italian writer and humanist

1 It is annoying and impossible to suffer proud women, because in general Nature has given men proud and high spirits, while it has made women humble in character and submissive, more apt for delicate things than for ruling.
"Niobe," *Concerning Famous Women* (1360–74)

2 It often happens, that he who endeavors to ridicule other people, especially in things of a serious nature, becomes himself a jest, and frequently to his great cost.
Decameron (1353), "The Second Day"

3 Although love dwells in gorgeous palaces, and sumptuous apartments, more willingly than in miserable and desolate cottages, it cannot be denied but that he sometimes causes his power to be felt in the gloomy recesses of forests, among the most bleak and rugged mountains, and in the dreary caves of a desert.
Decameron (1353), "The Third Day"

4 There are some people so indiscreet in appearing to know what they had better be unacquainted with, that they think, by reproving other people's inadvertencies, to lessen their own shame: whereas they make that vastly greater.
Decameron (1353), "The Third Day"

5 Whoever rightly considers the order of things may plainly see the whole race of woman-kind is...made subject to man, to be governed according to his discretion: therefore it is the duty of every one of us...to be humble, patient, and obedient, as well as chaste.
Decameron (1353), "The Ninth Day"

Boesak, Allan (Allan Aubrey Boesak; b.1945) South African cleric and political leader

1 One of the problems I have with the Christian Church is that we do not get angry enough. There is not enough rage in us.
July 1984. *If This is Treason I Am Guilty* (1987)

Boesky, Ivan (Ivan Frederick Boesky; b.1937) U.S. financier

1 Greed is all right...Greed is healthy. You can be greedy and still feel good about yourself.
Ivan Boesky was later charged with fraud and jailed. Commencement address, Berkeley, California (May 18, 1986)

2 I'm the boss. I'm allowed to yell.
Quoted in *Den of Thieves* (James B. Stewart; 1991)

3 What good is the moon if you cannot buy it or sell it?
Said to his wife, referring to the beauty of the moon. Quoted in *Times*, London (1986)

4 My advice to this investor is the same that I give to the young investors in my classes...Devote the same earnest attention to investing that $50,000 as you devoted to earning it.
Quoted in *Wall Street Journal* (January 2, 1985)

Boethius (Anicius Manlius Severinus Boethius; 480?–524?) Roman philosopher and statesman

1 We have found the definition of "person," namely, "an individual substance of a rational nature."
Contra Eutychen (524?)

2 If chance is defined as an event produced by random motion without any causal nexus, I would say there is no such thing as chance.
The Consolation of Philosophy (523?)

3 In every adversity of fortune the most unhappy sort of misfortune is to have been happy.
The Consolation of Philosophy (523?)

4 "There is nothing that an omnipotent God could not do." "No." "Then, can God do evil?" "No." "So that evil is nothing, since that is what He cannot do who can do anything."
The Consolation of Philosophy (523?)

Bogan, Louise (1897–1970) U.S. poet and critic

1 Women have no wilderness in them,
They are provident instead,
Content in the tight hot cell of their hearts
To eat dusty bread.
"Women" (1923), st. 1

2 It is not possible for a poet...to protect himself from the tragic elements in human life...Illness, old age, and death—subjects as ancient as humanity—these are the subjects that the poet must speak of very nearly from the first moment that he begins to speak.
Selected Criticism (1958)

Bogarde, Dirk, Sir (Dereck Niven Van Den Bogaerde; 1921–99) British actor and novelist

1 I am an orderly man. I say this with no sense of false modesty, or of conceit...Being orderly, as a matter of fact, can be excessively tiresome and it often irritates me greatly, but I cannot pull away.
An Orderly Man (1983), ch. 1

2 My idea of hell. You see all the people you thought were dead and all the people who deserve to be dead. After a while, you start to think you might be dead too.
Referring to the Cannes film festival. *Films Illustrated* (July 1975), quoted in *Chambers Film Quotes* (Tony Crawley, ed.; 1991)

3 I love the camera and it loves me. Well, not very much sometimes. But we're good friends.
Attrib.

Bogart, Humphrey (Humphrey DeForest Bogart; 1899–1957) U.S. actor

Quotations about Bogart

1 Humphrey Bogart was a brilliant smoker. He taught generations how to hold a cigarette, how to inhale, how to squint through the smoke. But as a kisser, Bogart set an awful example. His mouth addressed a woman's lips with the quivering nibble of a horse closing in on an apple.
Lance Morrow U.S. journalist. "Changing the Gestures of Passion," *Fishing in the Tiber* (1988)

Quotations by Bogart

2 Play it, Sam. Play "As Time Goes By."
Often misquoted as "Play it again, Sam." Also said by Ingrid Bergman in the character of Ilsa Lund. *Casablanca* (Julius J. Epstein, Philip G. Epstein, Howard Koch; 1942)

3 If she can stand it I can. Play it!
Said as Rick. *Casablanca* (Julius J. Epstein, Philip G. Epstein, Howard Koch; 1942)

4 Of all the gin joints in all the towns in all the world, she walks into mine!
Said as Rick. *Casablanca* (Julius J. Epstein, Philip G. Epstein, Howard Koch; 1942)

5 Here's looking at you, kid.
Said as Rick to Ingrid Bergman as Ilsa. *Casablanca* (Julius J. Epstein, Philip G. Epstein, Howard Koch; 1942)

6 Louis, I think this is the beginning of a beautiful friendship.
Said as Rick to the policeman, Louis. The last words of the movie. *Casablanca* (Julius J. Epstein, Philip G. Epstein, Howard Koch; 1942)

7 I was born when she kissed me. I died when she left me. For a few weeks I was alive while she loved me.
Said as Dixon Steele. *In a Lonely Place* (Andrew Salt; 1950)

8 I don't mind if you don't like my manners. I don't like 'em myself. They're pretty bad. I grieve over 'em on long winter evenings.
Said as private detective Philip Marlowe. *The Big Sleep* (William Faulkner, Leigh Brackett, Jules Furthman, and Raymond Chandler; 1946)

9 My, my, my. Such a lot of guns around and so few brains.
Said as private detective Philip Marlowe. *The Big Sleep* (William Faulkner, Leigh Brackett, Jules Furthman, and Raymond Chandler; 1946)

10 Any little pinhead who makes one picture is called a "star."
"Picture" in this context refers to a motion picture. Attrib. *The Stars* (Richard Schickel; 1962)

11 The only thing you owe the public is a good performance.
Attrib. *The Wit and Wisdom of Hollywood* (Max Wilk; 1971)

Bogart, John B. (1845–1921) U.S. journalist

1 When a dog bites a man that is not news, but when a man bites a dog that is news.
1882. Sometimes attributed to Charles Dana and Amos Cummings. Quoted in *The Story of the Sun New York, 1833–1918* (Frank M. O'Brien; 1918), ch. 10

Bohm, David (David Joseph Bohm; 1917–92) U.S. physicist

1 There are no things, only processes.
Attrib.

Bohn, Henry George (1796–1884) British publisher

1 The longest way round is the shortest way home.
A Polyglott of Foreign Proverbs (1857)

Bohr, Niels (Niels Henrik David Bohr; 1885–1962) Danish physicist

1 An expert is a man who has made all the mistakes which can be made in a very narrow field.
Attrib.

2 Of course I don't believe in it. But I understand that it brings you luck whether you believe in it or not.
When asked why he had a horseshoe on his wall. Attrib.

Boileau, Nicolas (Nicolas Boileau-Despréaux; 1636–1711) French poet and critic

1 The dreadful burden of having nothing to do.
Épitres (1690?), no. 11

2 A fool always finds a greater fool to admire him.
L'Art poétique (1674), pt. 1

3 No one who cannot limit himself has ever been able to write.
L'Art poétique (1674), pt. 1

4 Often the fear of one evil leads us into a worse.
L'Art poétique (1674), pt. 1

5 Let a single completed action, all in one place, all in one day, keep the theater packed to the end of your play.
L'Art poétique (1674), pt. 1

6 Happy who in his verse can gently steer
From grave to light, from pleasant to severe.
L'Art poétique (1674), pt. 1

7 Of every four words I write, I strike out three.
Satires (1666)

Bo Juyi (also known as Po Chü-I; 772–846) Chinese poet and government official

1 "Those who speak know nothing;
Those who know are silent."
These words, as I am told,
Were spoken by Lao-Tze.
If we are to believe that Lao-Tze
Was himself one who knew,
How comes it that he wrote a book
Of five thousand words?
Quoted in *The Jingle Bell Principle* (Miroslav Holub; 1992)

Boland, Eavan (Eavan Aisling Boland; b.1944) Irish poet, journalist, and lecturer

1 That the science of cartography is limited
—and not simply by the fact that this shading of
forest cannot show the fragrance of balsam,
the gloom of cypresses,
is what I wish to prove.
"That the Science of Cartography is Limited," *Collected Poems* (1995)

Boleyn, Anne (also Anne Bullen; 1507?–36) English queen

1 The king has been very good to me. He promoted me from a simple maid to be a marchioness. Then he raised me to be a queen. Now he will raise me to be a martyr.
1536. Said before her execution. Attrib. *Notable Women in History* (W. Abbot; 1913)

Bolingbroke, Henry St. John, 1st Viscount (1678–1751) English statesman

1 Whilst I loved much, I never loved long, but was inconstant to them all for the sake of all.
Letter to Charles Wyndham (December 26, 1735)

2 Nations, like men, have their infancy.
Letters on the Study and Use of History (1752), Letter 4

3 The dignity of history.
Letters on the Study and Use of History (1752), Letter 5

4 Faction is to party what the superlative is to the positive: party is a political evil and faction is the worst of all parties.
The Idea of a Patriot King (1738)

Bolitho, William (1890–1930) British writer

1 The shortest way out of Manchester is notoriously a bottle of Gordon's gin.
Attrib.

Böll, Heinrich (1917–85) German novelist

1 One should leave moments alone, never repeat them.
1963. *The Clown* (Leila Vennewitz, tr.; 1965), ch. 19

2 Strangely enough I like the kind to which I belong: people.
1963. *The Clown* (Leila Vennewitz, tr.; 1965), ch. 23

Bolt, Robert (Robert Oxton Bolt; 1924–95) British playwright

1 Morality's not practical. Morality's a gesture. A complicated gesture learnt from books.
A Man for All Seasons (1960)

2 The nobility of England, my lord, would have snored through the Sermon on the Mount.
A Man for All Seasons (1960)

Boltanski, Christian (b.1944) French artist

1 I belong to the young tradition of Central Europe, but my real country is painting.
Quoted in *Flash Art* (Démosthènes Davvetas, interviewer; October–November 1985), no. 124

Bolyai, Farkas (1775–1856) Hungarian mathematician

1 For God's sake, please give it up. Fear it no less than the sensual passion, because it, too, may take up all your time and deprive you of your health, peace of mind and happiness in life.
Letter to his son, János, attempting to dissuade him from his pursuit of non-Euclidean geometry, which Bolyai created and developed. Quoted in *The Mathematical Experience* (P. Davis and R. Hersh; 1981)

Bolyai, János (1802–60) Hungarian mathematician

1 Out of nothing I have created a strange new universe.
Referring to non-Euclidean geometry. Attrib.

Bombeck, Erma (originally Erma Louise Fiste; 1927–96) U.S. journalist

1 I worry about scientists discovering that lettuce has been fattening all along.
If Life is a Bowl of Cherries What am I Doing in the Pits? (1978)

2 You hear a lot of dialogue on the death of the American family. Families aren't dying. They are merging into big conglomerates.
"Empty Fridge, Empty Nest," *San Francisco Examiner* (October 1, 1978)

Bond, Alan (b.1938) Australian business executive

1 Get me inside any boardroom and I'll get any decision.
Daily Telegraph, London (June 27, 1989)

2 I cannot tolerate strikes. What would my workers say if I go on strike and say I'm not going to sign any more cheques today?
Financial Times, London (September 5, 1981)

3 When I'm older I'm going to buy and sell people like you.
Said as a boy to one of his teachers. *Sunday Telegraph*, London (June 2, 1989)

Bonham-Carter, Lady Violet, Baroness Asquith of Yarnbury (1887–1969) British politician and publicist

1 Outer space is no place for a person of breeding.
Attrib.

Bonheur, Rosa (1822–99) French painter

1 Remember that at a certain period I spent whole days in the slaughterhouses. Indeed, you have to love your art in order to live in pools of blood...I had no alternative but to realize that the garments of my own sex were a total nuisance...the costume I am wearing is my working outfit, nothing else.
Quoted in "Rosa Bonheur," *Art and Sexual Politics* (Lind Nochlin, 1973)

Bonhoeffer, Dietrich (1906–45) German theologian

1 A God who let us prove his existence would be an idol.
"If you believe it, you have it." An Attempt at a Lutheran Catechism (1931), quoted in *No Rusty Swords* (E. Robinson and J. Bowden, eds.; 1965)

2 Death is the supreme festival on the road to freedom.
1943–44. *Letters and Papers from Prison* (Eberhard Bethge, ed.; 1981)

3 It is infinitely easier to suffer in obedience to a human command than to accept suffering as free, responsible men.
1943–44. *Letters and Papers from Prison* (Eberhard Bethge, ed.; 1981)

4 The essence of chastity is not the suppression of lust, but the total orientation of one's life towards a goal.
1943–44. *Letters and Papers from Prison* (Eberhard Bethge, ed.; 1981)

5 If you board the wrong train, it is no use running along the corridor in the other direction.
The Way to Freedom: Letters, Lectures and Notes (1935–39)

6 Man has learned to cope with all questions of importance without recourse to God as a working hypothesis.
June 8, 1944. *Letters and Papers from Prison* (Eberhard Bethge, ed.; 1981)

7 No actions are bad in themselves, even murder can be justified.
1928–36. Quoted in *No Rusty Swords* (Edwin H. Rosenbaum, ed.; 1970)

8 Would it not be a blasphemous frivolity to think that the devil could be exorcised with the cry "No more war" and with a new organization?
1928–36. Quoted in *No Rusty Swords* (Edwin H. Rosenbaum, ed.; 1970)

Bonner, Marita (Marita Odette Bonner Occomy; 1899–1971) U.S. short-story writer and essayist

1 Women were not supposed to be so soft. Supposed to be soft, but not so soft you could knock a rock through them without their saying a word.
"The Prison-Bound" (1987)

2 At least you know what you want life to give you. A career as fixed and as calmly brilliant as the North Star. The one real thing that money buys. Time.
On Being Young—A Woman—and Colored (1925)

3 People like to place you and your desires and tastes where they think your particular color and hirsute growth belong.
"One True Love," *Frye Street and Environs* (Joyce Flynn and Joyce Occomy Stricklin, eds.; 1987)

4 What's the need of working if it doesn't get you anywhere? What's the use of boring around in the same hole like a worm? Making the hole bigger to stay in?
"The Purple Flower," *Frye Street and Environs* (Joyce Flynn and Joyce Occomy Stricklin, eds.; 1987)

Bontemps, Arna (Arna Wendell Bontemps; 1902–73) U.S. writer

1 Yet what I sowed and what the orchard yields
My brother's sons are gathering stalk and root,
Small wonder then my children glean in fields
They have not sown, and feed on bitter fruit.
"A Black Man Talks of Reaping" (1963), st. 3

2 Yet would we die as some have done:
Beating a way for the rising sun.
"The Daybreakers" (1963)

Bookchin, Murray (b.1921) U.S. historian and social ecologist

1 To speak of limits to growth under a capitalistic market economy is as meaningless as to speak of limits of warfare under a warrior society.
Remaking Society (1990)

Book of Common Prayer

1 O all ye Works of the Lord, bless ye the Lord.
Benedicite (1662)

2 In the midst of life we are in death.
Burial of the Dead (1662), First anthem

3 Man that is born of a woman hath but a short time to live, and is full of misery.
Burial of the Dead (1662), First anthem

4 Almighty God, give us the grace that we may cast away the works of darkness, and put upon us the armour of light, now in the time of this mortal life.
Collect, 1st Sunday in Advent (1662)

5 Grant that those things which we ask faithfully we may obtain effectually.
Collect, 23rd Sunday after Trinity (1662)

6 Read, mark, learn and inwardly digest.
Collect, 2nd Sunday in Advent (1662)

7 Increase and multiply upon us thy mercy; that, thou being our ruler and guide, we may so pass through things temporal, that we finally lose not the things eternal.
Collect, 4th Sunday after Trinity (1662)

8 All our doings without charity are nothing worth.
Collect, Quinquagesima Sunday (1662)

9 Lighten our darkness, we beseech thee, O Lord; and by thy great mercy defend us from all perils and dangers of this night.
Evening Prayer, Third Collect (1662)

10 The blessing of God Almighty, the Father, the Son, and the Holy Ghost, be amongst you and remain with you always.
Holy Communion (1662), "The Blessing"

11 Ye that do truly and earnestly repent you of your sins, and are in love and charity with your neighbours, and intend to lead a new life, following the commandments of God, and walking from henceforth in his holy ways.
Holy Communion (1662), "The Invitation"

12 Grant that this day we fall into no sin, neither run into any kind of danger.
Morning Prayer (1662), Third Collect, for Grace

13 We have erred, and strayed from thy ways like lost sheep.
Morning Prayer (1662), "General Confession"

14 We have left undone those things which we ought to have done; and we have done those things we ought not to have done.
Morning Prayer (1662), "General Confession"

15 As it was in the beginning, is now, and ever shall be: world without end.
Morning Prayer (1662), "Gloria"

16 When two or three are gathered together in thy Name thou wilt grant their requests.
Morning Prayer (1662), "Prayer of St. Chrysostom"

17 Being now come to the years of discretion.
Order of Confirmation (1662)

18 Defend, O Lord, this thy Child with thy heavenly grace, that he may continue thine for ever; and daily increase in thy holy Spirit more and more, until he come unto thy everlasting kingdom.
Order of Confirmation (1662)

19 Renounce the devil and all his works.
Public Baptism of Infants (1662)

20 O merciful God, grant that the old Adam in this Child may be so buried, that the new man may be raised up in him.
Invocation of blessing on the child. Public Baptism of Infants (1662)

21 To have and to hold from this day forward, for better for worse, for richer for poorer, in sickness and in health, to love and to cherish, till death us do part.
Solemnization of Matrimony (1662), "Betrothal"

22 Wilt thou love her, comfort her, honour, and keep her in sickness and in health; and, forsaking all other, keep thee only unto her, so long as ye both shall live?
Solemnization of Matrimony (1662), "Betrothal"

23 First, It was ordained for the procreation of children, to be brought up in the fear and nurture of the Lord, and to the praise of his holy Name.
Solemnization of Matrimony (1662), "Exhortation"

24 Therefore if any man can show any just cause, why they may not lawfully be joined together, let him now speak, or else hereafter for ever hold his peace.
Solemnization of Matrimony (1662), "Exhortation"

25 If any of you know cause, or just impediment, why these two persons should not be joined together in holy Matrimony, ye are to declare it.
Solemnization of Matrimony (1662), "The Banns"

26 Those whom God hath joined together let no man put asunder.
Solemnization of Matrimony (1662), "Wedding"

27 With this Ring I thee wed, with my body I thee worship, and with all my worldly goods I thee endow.
Solemnization of Matrimony (1662), "Wedding"

28 All the deceits of the world, the flesh, and the devil.
The Litany (1662)

29 In the hour of death, and in the day of judgement.
The Litany (1662)

Book of Lord Shang

1 Neither in high or low grades should there be hereditary succession to the offices, ranks, lands, or emoluments of officials.
The Book of Lord Shang is a Chinese compilation of writings of the Legalist school, a philosophy that stressed the rule of law. *Book of Lord Shang* (11th century–3rd century B.C.), quoted in *The Chinese Experience* (Raymond Dawson; 1978)

Boone, Daniel (1734–1820) American pioneer

1 I can't say I was ever lost, but I was bewildered once for three days.
Reply when asked if he had ever been lost. Attrib.

Boorde, Andrew (also Andrew Borde; 1490?–1549) English physician, writer, and monk

1 There be iiii kyndes of madness...thinking themselves to conjure, to create, to make things that no man can do, but God. Melancholia—ever in feare and drede, thinking that thei shall never do well.
Frenesis—they do rave and speke, and cannot tell what they saye.
Demoniachus—these be ever possessed of the devil.
The Breviary of Healthe (1597)

2 There is another kinde of madnesse named lunaticus, the whiche is madnesse that dothe infest a man ones in a mone, the whiche doth cause one to be geryshe changeable and waveringe witted, not constant, but fantasticall.
The Breviary of Healthe (1597)

Boorman, John (b.1933) British film director

1 Movie-making is the process of turning money into light. All they have at the end of the day is images flickering on a wall.
Quoted in *The Oxford Book of Money* (Kevin Jackson, ed.; 1995)

Boorstin, Daniel J. (Daniel Joseph Boorstin; b.1914) U.S. historian and librarian

1 Nothing is real unless it happens on television.
New York Times (February 19, 1978)

2 Never have people been more the masters of their environment. Yet never has a people felt more deceived and disappointed. For never has a people expected so much more than the world could offer.
The Image (1961), introduction

3 The celebrity is a person who is known for his well-knownness.
"From Hero to Celebrity: The Human Pseudo-event," *The Image* (1961)

4 A best-seller was a book which somehow sold well simply because it was selling well.
"From Shapes to Shadows: Dissolving Forms," *The Image* (1961)

5 If history cannot give us panaceas, it is the best possible cure of the yen for panaceas. And the only proven antidote for utopianism.
Quoted in *Newsweek* (July 6, 1970)

Booth, Barton (1681–1733) English tragic actor

1 True as the needle to the pole,
Or as the dial to the sun.
"Song" (18th century), quoted in *The Oxford Book of Eighteenth Century Verse* (David Nichol Smith, ed.; 1926)

Booth, Charles (1840–1916) British shipowner, statistician, and social reformer

1 While there is more drinking, there is less drunkenness than formerly, and that the increase in drinking is to be laid mainly to the account of the female sex. This latter phase seems to be one of the unexpected results of the emancipation of women.
Life and Labour of the People in London, 17 vols. (1891–1903)

Booth, John Wilkes (1839–65) U.S. actor and assassin

1 I have too great a soul to die like a criminal.
John Wilkes Booth assassinated President Abraham Lincoln on April 14, 1865. He died resisting arrest 12 days later. Attrib.

Boothby, Frances (*fl.* 1669) English poet and playwright

1 I'm hither come, but what d'ye think to say?
A Woman's Pen present you with a Play:
Who smiling told me I'd be sure to see,
That once confirm'd the House would empty be,
Not one yet gone!
Prologue to a play. *Marcelia, or The Treacherous Friend* (1669)

Boothroyd, Betty (b.1929) British stateswoman

1 Good temper and moderation are the characteristics of parliamentary language.
Independent, London (February 9, 1995)

Borah, William E. (William Edgar Borah; 1865–1940) U.S. politician

1 We do not want the racial antipathies or national antagonisms of the Old World translated to this continent, as they will should we become a part of European politics. The people of this country are overwhelmingly for a policy of neutrality.
Radio broadcast (February 22, 1936)

Boren, David L. (b.1941) U.S. politician

1 Those who mill around at the crossroads of history do so at their own peril.
Chicago Tribune (January 5, 1990)

Borges, Jorge Luis (1899–1986) Argentinian writer and poet

1 The original is unfaithful to the translation.
Referring to Henley's translation of *Vathek: An Arabian Tale* (1786) by the British writer William Beckford. "Sobre el 'Vathek' de William Beckford" (1943)

2 Gertrude Stein...is perhaps less important for her work, unreadable at times and intentionally obscure, than for her personal influence and her curious literary theories.
An Introduction to American Literature (1967), ch. 9

3 I have known uncertainty: a state unknown to the Greeks.
"The Babylonian Lottery," *Ficciones* (1945)

4 To die for a religion is easier than to live it absolutely.
1953? *Labyrinths* (1962), quoted in *Labyrinths: Selected Stories and Other Writings* (Donald A. Yates and James E. Irby, eds.; 1962)

5 There is no point in being overwhelmed by the appalling total of human suffering; such a total does not exist. Neither poverty nor pain is accumulable.
"A New Refutation of Time," *Other Inquisitions, 1937–1952* (1952)

6 The Falklands thing was a fight between two bald men over a comb.
Referring to the war with the United Kingdom over the Falkland Islands, 1982. *Time* (February 14, 1983)

7 We have stopped believing in progress. What progress that is!
Attrib.

Borman, Frank (b.1928) U.S. astronaut and business executive

1 Capitalism without bankruptcy is like Christianity without hell.
Observer, London (1986)

Born, Bertran de (1140–1209?) French soldier and troubadour

1 I love the gay Eastertide, which brings forth leaves and flowers; and I love the joyous song of the birds, re-echoing through the copse. But I also love to see, amidst the meadows, tents and pavilions spread; it gives me great joy to see, drawn up on the field, knights and horses in battle array.
Early 13th century

Born, Max (1882–1970) German physicist

1 Only two possibilities exist: either one must believe in determinism and regard free-will as a subjective illusion, or one must become a mystic, and regard the discovery of natural laws as a meaningless illusion.
Bulletin of Atomic Scientists (1957)

2 The human race has today the means for annihilating itself—either in a fit of complete lunacy, i.e., in a big war, by a brief

fit of destruction, or by careless handling of atomic technology, through a slow process of poisoning and of deterioration in its genetic structure.
Bulletin of Atomic Scientists (1957)

Borrow, George Henry (1803–81) British writer and traveler

1 If you must commit suicide...always contrive to do it as decorously as possible; the decencies, whether of life or of death, should never be lost sight of.
Lavengro (1851), ch. 23

2 A losing trade, I assure you, sir: literature is a drug.
Lavengro (1851), ch. 30

3 Youth will be served, every dog has his day, and mine has been a fine one.
Lavengro (1851), ch. 92

4 My favourite, I might say, my only study, is man.
The Bible in Spain (1843), ch. 5

5 Fear God, and take your own part.
The Romany Rye (1857), ch. 16

Boschini, Marco (1613–1705) Italian art theorist

1 Invention, treasure conserved in the jewel box of fantasy, power of the soul, that lifts up the images and, guided by a fine understanding, consigns them to the governing hand that transmutes them into practice...This is the most essential part of painting.
Rich Mines of Venetian Painting (1676)

Bosquet, Pierre (Pierre Joseph François Bosquet; 1810–61) French army officer

1 It is magnificent, but it is not war.
October 25, 1854. Referring to the Charge of the Light Brigade at the Battle of Balaclava. Attrib.

Bossidy, John Collins (1860–1928) U.S. writer

1 And this is good old Boston,
The home of the bean and the cod,
Where the Lowells talk only to Cabots,
And the Cabots talk only to God.
Toast at the Holy Cross College alumni dinner. *Springfield Sunday Republican* (December 14, 1910)

Bossuet, Jacques-Bénigne (1627–1704) French preacher and bishop

1 I do not flatter myself that I can make you understand France. I don't know that I understand her myself. I don't try to understand her, for she doesn't give me the time to do so as she whisks me along with her on her grand adventure.
Lettres aux Anglais (17th century?)

2 The heretic, that is to say, he who has a particular opinion.
L'Histoire des variations des églises protestantes (1688), preface

3 England, ah, faithless England, which the protection afforded by its seas rendered inaccessible to the Romans, the faith of the Savior spread even there.
Premier Sermon pour La Fête de la Circoncision de Notre Seigneur (1816), vol. 11

Boswell, James (1740–95) Scottish lawyer and biographer

1 Men know that women are an overmatch for them, and therefore they choose the weakest or the most ignorant. If they did not think so, they never could be afraid of women knowing as much as themselves.
Journal of a Tour to the Hebrides (1785)

2 Talking of ghosts, he said, "It is wonderful that five thousand years have now elapsed since the creation of the world, and still it is undecided whether or not there has ever been an instance of the spirit of any person appearing after death. All argument is against it, but all belief is for it."
1778. *Life of Samuel Johnson* (1791)

3 A man, indeed, is not genteel when he gets drunk; but most vices may be committed very genteelly: a man may debauch his friend's wife genteelly: he may cheat at cards genteelly.
1775. *The Life of Samuel Johnson* (1791)

4 There are two things which I am confident I can do very well: one is an introduction to any literary work, stating what it is to contain, and how it should be executed in the most perfect manner.
1775. *The Life of Samuel Johnson* (1791)

Botha, Elize (?–1997) South African wife of P. W. Botha

1 People think we do not understand our black and colored countrymen. But there is a special relationship between us.
Remark (1987)

Botha, P. W. (Pieter Willem Botha; b.1916) South African prime minister

1 South Africa will not allow the double standards and hypocrisy of the Western world, even in the application of legal principles, to stand in the way of our responsibility to protect our country.
Speech (1986)

2 You won't force South Africans to commit national suicide.
Speech (1996)

3 My feelings are that for the first time we are participating in an election that will have legitimacy. Now we can go to the polling booth without a bad conscience.
Referring to the first free elections to be held in South Africa after the collapse of apartheid. *Independent*, London (April 28, 1994)

Botham, Ian (b.1955) British cricketer

1 I'm a bit like an old, battered Escort. You might find one panel that's original. I've had about ten operations—back, shoulder, wrist, knee, cheek.
Referring to his retirement from professional cricket. An Escort is a popular make of Ford automobile. *Times*, London (December 30, 1993)

Bottomley, Gordon (1874–1948) British poet and playwright

1 When you destroy a blade of grass
You poison England at her roots:
Remember no man's foot can pass
Where evermore no green life shoots.
"To Ironfounders and Others" (1912)

Boucicault, Dion (Dionysius Lardner Boursiquot; 1820–90) Irish-born U.S. actor and playwright

1 The fire and energy that consist of dancing around the stage in an expletive manner, and indulging in ridiculous capers and extravagancies of language and gesture, form the materials of a clowning character, known as "the stage Irishman," which it has been my vocation, as an artist and as a dramatist, to abolish.
Letter to a Christchurch newspaper (1885), quoted in *A Book of Irish Quotations* (Sean McMahon, ed.; 1984)

2 The girl I love is beautiful, she's fairer than the dawn:
She lives in Garryowen, and she's called the Colleen Bawn.
"The Colleen Bawn" (1860)

3 Men talk of killing time, while time quietly kills them.
London Assurance (1841), Act 2, Scene 1

4 Nature did me that honour.
19th century. Reply on being asked if he were an Irishman. Attrib.

Boulay de La Meurthe, Antoine (1761–1840) French politician

1 It is worse than a crime, it is a blunder.
Referring to the summary execution of the Duc d'Enghien by Napoleon (1804). Attrib.

Boulton, Harold Edwin (1859–1935) Scottish songwriter

1 Speed, bonny boat, like a bird on the wing;
"Onward", the sailors cry;
Carry the lad that's born to be king
Over the sea to Skye.
Song lyric. "Skye Boat Song" (1908)

Boulton, Matthew (1728–1809) British engineer

1 I sell here, Sir, what all the world desires to have—power.
March 22, 1775. Said to James Boswell, on his engineering works. Quoted in *The Life of Samuel Johnson* (James Boswell; 1791), vol. 2

Bourassa, Henri (Joseph Napoléon Henri Bourassa; 1868–1952) Canadian politician and journalist

1 I am a liberal of the British school. I am a disciple of Burke, Fox, Bright, Gladstone, and of the other Little Englanders who made Great Britain and its possessions what they are.
Speech to the Canadian Parliament (March 13, 1900)

2 There is no greater farce than to talk of democracy. To begin with, it is a lie; it has never existed in any great country.
Le Devoir (February 11, 1943)

Bourdillon, Francis William (1852–1921) British writer

1 The night has a thousand eyes,
And the day but one;
Yet the light of the bright world dies,
With the dying sun.

The mind has a thousand eyes,
And the heart but one;
Yet the light of a whole life dies,
When love is done.
"The Night Has a Thousand Eyes," *Among the Flowers* (1878)

Bourgeois, Louise (originally Louise Goldwater; b.1911) French-born U.S. sculptor

1 Art is a way of recognizing oneself, which is why it will always be modern.
Quoted in *Bourgeois* (Donald Kuspit; 1988)

2 What modern art means is that you have to keep finding new ways to express yourself, to express the problems, that there are no settled ways, no fixed approach.
Quoted in *Bourgeois* (Donald Kuspit; 1988)

3 You do not make sculpture because you like wood. That is absurd. You make sculpture because the wood allows you to express something that another material does not allow you to do.
Quoted in *Bourgeois* (Donald Kuspit; 1988)

Bourke-White, Margaret (originally Margaret White; 1906–71) U.S. photographer and photojournalist

1 Work to me is a sacred thing.
Portrait of Myself (1963)

2 Nothing attracts me like a closed door. I cannot let my camera rest until I have pried it open, and I wanted to be first.
Referring to her pioneering work in industrial photography. *Portrait of Myself* (1963)

Bourne, Randolph S. (Randolph Silliman Bourne; 1886–1918) U.S. essayist and critic

1 We have constantly to check ourselves in reading history with the remembrance that, to the actors in the drama, events appeared very different from the way they appear to us. We know what they were doing far better than they knew themselves.
Youth and Life (1913)

Bowen, Charles, Baron (Charles Synge Christopher Bowen; 1835–94) British judge

1 The rain it raineth on the just
And also on the unjust fella:
But chiefly on the just, because
The unjust steals the just's umbrella.
19th century. Quoted in *Sands of Time* (Walter Sichel; 1923)

2 A blind man in a dark room—looking for a black hat—which isn't there.
Characterization of a metaphysician. Attrib.

Bowen, Elizabeth (Elizabeth Dorothea Cole; 1899–1973) Irish novelist and short-story writer

1 I could wish that the English kept history in mind more, that the Irish kept it in mind less.
"Notes on Eire" (November 9, 1949)

2 Experience isn't interesting till it begins to repeat itself—in fact, till it does that, it hardly *is* experience.
The Death of the Heart (1938)

3 Intimacies between women often go backwards, beginning in revelations and ending in small talk without loss of esteem.
The Death of the Heart (1938)

4 Art is the only thing that can go on mattering once it has stopped hurting.
The Heat of the Day (1949)

5 One can live in the shadow of an idea without grasping it.
The Heat of the Day (1949)

6 Silences have a climax, when you have got to speak.
The Heat of the Day (1949)

7 Nobody speaks the truth when there's something they must have.
The House in Paris (1935)

8 No, it is not only our fate but our business to lose innocence, and once we have lost that, it is futile to attempt a picnic in Eden.
"Out of a Book" *Orion III* (Rosamund Lehmann et al, eds.; 1946)

Bowie, David (David Robert Jones; b.1947) British pop singer

1 There's a streak of madness in the family. I've a horrible fear it's genetic. One of the reasons I've never been in analysis is I've always been afraid of what I might find out.
Photoplay (September 1983)

2 I never will consent to having my name or my face used in any merchandizing context beyond advertising the actual artistic work I've done. I have said no even when I was tempted with regular earnings for Ziggy Stardust dolls.
Variety (May 17, 1983)

3 It's true—I am bisexual. But I can't deny I've used the fact very well. I suppose it's the best thing that ever happened to me.
Quoted in *Rock 'n' Roll Babylon* (Gary Herman; 1994)

4 I decided to use the masks so I didn't have the humiliation of going on stage and being myself.
Referring to his use of stage personae in his concert performances. Quoted in *Rock 'n' Roll Babylon* (Gary Herman; 1994)

Bowles, Paul (b.1910) U.S. writer and composer

1 He awoke, opened his eyes. The room meant very little to him; he was deeply immersed in the non-being from which he had just come...there was the certitude of an infinite sadness at the core of his consciousness, but the sadness was reassuring, because alone it was familiar.
The Sheltering Sky (1948)

2 One year was like another year. Eventually everything would happen.
The Sheltering Sky (1948)

Bowles, William Lisle (1762–1850) British clergyman and poet

1 The cause of Freedom is the cause of God!
"A Political Address to the Right Honourable Edmund Burke" (1791), l. 78

Bowra, Maurice (1898–1971) British scholar and classicist

1 Any amusing deaths lately?
Attrib.

2 Splendid couple—slept with both of them.
Referring to a well-known literary couple. Attrib.

Box-Car Bertha (Bertha Thompson) U.S. author and hobo

1 I don't ever remember anyone telling me a real fairy story...but the tales of the gandy dancers, and of the bundle stiffs, of their jobs in the wheatfields of Minnesota...the breathtaking yarns of mushing in Alaska, or getting pinched in San Francisco... were thrillers I remember to this day.
Referring to her childhood on the road. *Sister of the Road: The Autobiography of Box-Car Bertha* (as told to Dr. Ben L. Reitman; 1937)

Bo Yang (Guo Yidong; b.1920) Taiwanese writer

1 On the Chinese mainland, the Anti-Rightist campaign was followed by the Cultural Revolution, an earthshaking disaster without precedent in the history of human civilization.
Speech, Iowa University (September 24, 1984)

Boyer, Charles (1897–1978) French film actor

1 Come with me to the Casbah.
Often quoted as if said by Charles Boyer, but not actually in the film. *Algiers* (1938)

Boyle, Robert (1627–91) Irish-born scientist

1 It seems to me...highly dishonourable for a Reasonable Soul to live in so Divinely built a Mansion, as the Body she resides in, altogether unacquainted with the exquisite Structure of it.
Some Considerations Touching the Usefulness of Natural Philosophy (1663), pt. 1

2 It is my intent to beget a good understanding between the chymists and the mechanical philosophers who have hitherto been too little acquainted with one another's learning.
The Sceptical Chymist (1661)

Brabazon, Derek (Derek Charles Moore-Brabazon; 1910–64) British business executive

1 I take the view, and always have done, that if you cannot say what you have to say in twenty minutes, you should go away and write a book about it.
1955. Attrib.

Bracken, Brendan (1901–58) British newspaper publisher and politician

1 It's a good deed to forget a poor joke.
Observer, London (October 17, 1943), "Sayings of the Week"

Bracken, Peg (b.1918) U.S. writer and humorist

1 Unnecessary dieting is because everything from television and fashion ads have made it seem wicked to cast a shadow. This wild, emaciated look appeals to some women, though not to many men, who are seldom seen pinning up a *Vogue* illustration in a machine shop.
The I Hate to Cook Book (1960)

Brackett, Anna C. (Anna Callender Brackett; 1836–1911) U.S. writer

1 The more we reduce ourselves to machines in the lower things, the more force we shall set free to use in the higher.
The Technique of the Rest (1892)

Bradbury, Malcolm (Malcolm Stanley Bradbury; b.1932) British academic, novelist, and critic

1 Sympathy—for all these people, for being foreigners—lay over the gathering like a woolly blanket; and no one was enjoying it at all.
Eating People is Wrong (1959), ch. 2

2 I like the English. They have the most rigid code of immorality in the world.
Eating People is Wrong (1959), ch. 5

3 Reading someone else's newspaper is like sleeping with someone else's wife. Nothing seems to be precisely in the right place, and when you find what you are looking for, it is not clear then how to respond to it.
Stepping Westward (1965), bk. 1, ch. 1

4 My experience of ships is that on them one makes an interesting discovery about the world. One finds one can do without it completely.
Stepping Westward (1965), bk. 1, ch. 2

5 The English are polite by telling lies. The Americans are polite by telling the truth.
Stepping Westward (1965), bk. 2, ch. 5

6 You Liberals think that goats are just sheep from broken homes.
Three plays for television. *The After Dinner Game* (1982)

7 He goes from the light and air of humanities to the dark mass of social science.
The History Man (1975)

8 "We stay together, but we distrust one another."
"Ah, yes...but isn't that a definition of marriage?"
Howard Kirk to his lover Flora Beniform. *The History Man* (1975), ch. 3

9 I've noticed your hostility towards him...I ought to have guessed you were friends.
The History Man (1975), ch. 7

10 If God had meant us to have group sex, I guess he'd have given us all more organs.
"A Very Hospitable Person," *Who Do You Think You Are?* (1987)

Bradbury, Ray (Ray Douglas Bradbury; b.1920) U.S. science-fiction writer

1 You have to know how to accept rejection and reject acceptance.
April 5, 1995. WAMU radio station, Washington, D.C.

2 Where robot mice and robot men, I said, run round in robot towns.
"Where Robot Mice and Robot Men Run Round in Robot Towns" (1977), prologue

3 Touch a scientist and you touch a child.
Los Angeles Times (August 9, 1976)

Bradford, Bobby U.S. jazz trumpeter

1 It's pretty stupid to put people down without even knowing what they're doing. I'll tell you, if a guy came along playing a coke bottle, I'd wait until I heard him before I laughed.
1962. Quoted in *Black Music* (Amiri Bakara; 1969), ch. 14

Bradford, John (1510?–55) British Protestant martyr

1 There, but for the grace of God, goes John Bradford.
1550s. Said on seeing some criminals being led to execution. Quoted in *Dictionary of National Biography* (1917)

Bradford, William (1590–1657) English-born American religious leader and colonist

1 And the season it was winter, and they that know the winters of that country know them to be sharp and violent, and subject to cruel and fierce storms, dangerous to travel to known places, much more to search an unknown coast.
History of Plimouth Plantation, 1620–1647 (1856), ch. 7

2 Behold, now, another providence of God. A ship comes into the harbor.
History of Plimouth Plantation, 1620–1647 (1856), ch. 7

3 Being thus arrived in a good harbor, and brought safe to land, they fell upon their knees and blessed the God of Heaven who had brought them over the vast and furious ocean.
History of Plimouth Plantation, 1620–1647 (1856), ch. 7

4 So they left the goodly and pleasant city, which had been their resting-place near twelve years; they knew they were pilgrims, and looked not much on those things, but lift up their eyes to the heavens, their dearest country, and quieted their spirits.
Describing the departure of some of the Pilgrim Fathers from Leiden, the Netherlands, to join the *Mayflower* at Plymouth. *History of Plimouth Plantation, 1620–1647* (1856), ch. 7

5 For summer being done, all things stand upon them with a weather-beaten face, and the whole country, full of woods and thickets, represented a wild and savage hue.
History of Plimouth Plantation, 1620–1647 (1856), ch. 9

6 So they committed themselves to the will of God and resolved to proceed.
History of Plimouth Plantation, 1620–1647 (1856), ch. 9

7 May not and ought not the children of these fathers rightly say: "Our fathers were Englishmen which came over this great ocean, and were ready to perish in this wilderness."
Referring to the Pilgrims, after their arrival at Cape Cod. *History of Plimouth Plantation, 1620–1647* (1856), ch. 10

Bradley, Bill (William Warren Bradley; b.1943) U.S. senator and basketball player

1 There has never been a great athlete who died not knowing what pain is.
Quoted in *A Sense of Where You Are* (John McPhee; 1965)

Bradley, F. H. (Francis Herbert Bradley; 1846–1924) British philosopher

1 If "Christianity" is to mean the taking the Gospels as our rule of life, then we none of us are Christians and, no matter what we say, we all know we ought not to be.
Unpublished essay on Christian morality (undated), quoted in *A Dictionary of Philosophical Quotations* (A. J. Ayer and Jane O'Grady, eds.; 1992)

2 It is monstrous to say that for us man has no more right than lower animals or inanimate nature. It is also monstrous to say that these have no right as against him. The covering of a hideous world with the greatest possible number of inferior

beings so long as they are human is not the end—even for us.
Unpublished essay on Christian morality (undated), quoted in *A Dictionary of Philosophical Quotations* (A. J. Ayer and Jane O'Grady, eds.; 1992)

3 Our pleasure in any one who in some way resembles those we love should warn us that love is in its essence not individual.
Aphorisms (1930)

4 The propriety of some persons seems to consist in having improper thoughts about their neighbours.
Aphorisms (1930)

5 The secret of happiness is to admire without desiring. And that is not happiness.
Aphorisms (1930)

6 Metaphysics is the finding of bad reasons for what we believe upon instinct; but to find these reasons is no less an instinct.
Appearance and Reality (1893), Preface

7 His mind is open; yes, it is so open that nothing is retained; ideas simply pass through him.
Attrib.

Bradley, Omar (Omar Nelson Bradley; 1893–1981) U.S. general

1 With the monstrous weapons man already has, humanity is in danger of being trapped in this world by its moral adolescents. Our knowledge of science has already outstripped our capacity to control it. We have many men of science, too few men of God.
Address, Boston, Massachusetts (November 10, 1948)

2 The wrong war, at the wrong place, at the wrong time, and with the wrong enemy.
Concerning a proposal by Douglas MacArthur, commander of United Nations forces in Korea, that the Korean War should be extended into China. Said in evidence to a U.S. Senate inquiry (May 1951)

3 The way to win an atomic war is to make certain it never starts.
Observer, London (April 20, 1952), "Sayings of the Week"

Bradstreet, Anne (1612–72) British-born U.S. poet

1 I am obnoxious to each carping tongue,
Who sayes my hand a needle better fits,
A Poet's Pen, all scorne, I should thus wrong;
For such despight they cast on female wits:
If what I doe prove well, it won't advance,
They'll say it's stolne, or else, it was by chance.
"The Prologue," *The Tenth Muse Lately Sprung up in America* (1650)

2 Let Greeks be Greeks, and Women what they are,
Men have precedency, and still excell
This meane and unrefined stuffe of mine,
Will make your glistering gold but more to shine.
"The Prologue," *The Tenth Muse Lately Sprung up in America* (1650)

Bragg, Melvyn, Lord (b.1939) British writer and broadcaster

1 Patriotism is seen not only as the last refuge of the scoundrel but as the first bolt-hole of the hypocrite.
Speak for England (1979), Introduction

Brahms, Johannes (1833–97) German composer

Quotations about Brahms

1 If you're not able to do the music of our day well, you're certainly not able to do the music of the past. I'm not interested in people who do Brahms without knowing Schoenberg. You cannot read Dostoyevsky without knowing Proust.
Christoph von Dohnányi (b.1929) German musician. *Independent*, London (April 29, 1994)

2 Brahms is just like Tennyson, an extraordinary musician with the brains of a third-rate village policeman.
April 4, 1893
George Bernard Shaw (1856–1950) Irish playwright. Attrib.

Quotations by Brahms

3 If there is anyone here whom I have not insulted, I beg his pardon.
Said on leaving a gathering of friends. Attrib.

Braine, John (1922–86) British novelist

1 Most married couples in the end arrive at tolerable arrangements for living—arrangements that may strike others as odd, but which suit them very well.
Remark (1970)

2 Pleasant people are just as real as horrible people.
Remark (1983)

3 Time, like a loan from the bank, is something you're only given when you possess so much that you don't need it.
Room at the Top (1957), ch. 15

Braithwaite, Edward R. (b.1920) Guyanese novelist and educator

1 I did not become a teacher out of any sense of vocation; mine was no considered decision in the interests of youthful humanity or the spread of planned education. It was a decision forced on me by the very urgent need to eat.
To Sir, With Love (1959)

2 Yes, it is wonderful to be British—until one comes to Britain.
To Sir, With Love (1959)

Bramah, Ernest (Ernest Bramah Smith; 1868–1942) British writer

1 One cannot live for ever by ignoring the price of coffins.
Kai Lung Unrolls His Mat (1923)

2 There are those who collect the refuse of the public streets, but in order to be received into the band it is necessary to have been born one of the Hereditary Confederacy of Superfluity Removers and Abandoned Oddment Gatherers.
Kai Lung Unrolls His Mat (1923)

3 Although there exist many thousand subjects for elegant conversation, there are persons who cannot meet a cripple without talking about feet.
The Wallet of Kai Lung (1900)

Brancusi, Constantin (1876–1957) Romanian-born French sculptor

1 Nothing grows well in the shade of a big tree.
Refusing Rodin's invitation to work in his studio. Quoted in *Compton's Encyclopedia* (1992)

2 Architecture is inhabited sculpture.
Quoted in *Themes and Episodes* (Igor Stravinsky; 1966)

Brand, Jo (b.1958) British comic

1 I take a different approach to the "fat is sexy" view. I would rather people just left us alone.
Observer, London (April 10, 1994)

2 It's sad that women are encouraged to be obsessed with the triviality of their appearance. There are more important things in life than appearance.
Observer, London (April 10, 1994)

3 I would be quite happy for men to hit women if there was a law saying that women could carry guns. Because then, if a man hit you, you could shoot him.
Q (June 1994)

Brandeis, Louis D. (Louis Dembitz Brandeis; 1856–1941) U.S. judge

1 Neither the common law nor the Fourteenth Amendment confers the absolute right to strike.
Supreme Court opinion, Dorchy v. Kansas (1926)

2 The right to be let alone—the most comprehensive of rights and the most valued by civilized men.
Supreme Court opinion, Olmstead v. United States (1928)

3 Experience should teach us to be most on our guard to protect liberty when the Government's purposes are beneficent.
Olmstead vs. United States (1928)

4 A lawyer who has not studied economics and sociology is very apt to become a public enemy.
Referring to himself. Quoted in *The Legacy of Holmes and Brandeis* (Samuel J. Konefsky; 1956)

5 History is not life. But since only life makes history the union of the two is obvious.
Attrib. *The Words of Justice Brandeis* (Solomon Goldman, ed.; 1953)

6 The federal Constitution is perhaps the greatest of human experiments.
Quoted in *The Words of Justice Brandeis* (Solomon Goldman, ed.; 1953)

Brando, Marlon (b.1924) U.S. actor

Quotations about Brando

1 Whether the film is good or bad Brando is always compulsive viewing, like Sydney Greenstreet, the vulgarian of all time, or Peter Lorre, or even Bette Davis daring to do *Baby Jane*.
Anthony Hopkins (b.1937) Welsh stage and film actor. Attrib.

Quotations by Brando

2 The subtlest acting I've ever seen is by ordinary people trying to show they feel something they don't or trying to hide something. It's something everyone learns at an early age.
Newsweek, BBC radio (March 13, 1972), quoted in *Chambers Film Quotes* (Tony Crawley, ed.; 1991)

3 An actor's a guy who, if you ain't talking about him, ain't listening.
1955. *Observer,* London (January 1956), "Sayings of the Year"

4 I could've been a contender. I could've had class and been somebody. Real class. Instead of a bum. It was you Charlie.
Said as Terry Malloy in the film directed by Elia Kazan. *On the Waterfront* (Budd Schulberg; 1954)

5 The most repulsive thing you could ever imagine is the inside of a camel's mouth. That and watching a girl eat octopus or squid.
Playboy Magazine (January 1979)

6 A man who doesn't spend time with his family can never be a real man.
Said as Vittorio Corleone. *The Godfather* (Francis Ford Coppola and Mario Puzo; 1972)

7 Acting is the expression of a neurotic impulse. It's a bum's life. Quitting acting, that's the sign of maturity.
Quoted in *Halliwell's Filmgoer's and Video Viewer's Companion* (1990)

8 I'm not interested in making an assessment of myself and stripping myself for the general public to view.
Quoted in *Halliwell's Filmgoer's and Video Viewer's Companion* (1990)

Brandt, Willy (Herbert Ernest Karl Frahm; 1913–92) German statesman

1 A Europe living in peace calls for its members to be willing to listen to the arguments of the others, for the struggle of convictions and interests will continue. Europe needs tolerance. It needs freedom of thought, not moral indifference.
Address given on the presentation of a Nobel Prize in peace (December 11, 1971), quoted in *Willy Brandt, Peace* (Klaus Reiff, ed.; 1971)

2 A good German cannot be a nationalist. A good German knows that he cannot refuse a European calling. Through Europe, Germany returns to itself and to the constructive forces of its history.
Address given on the presentation of a Nobel Prize in peace (December 11, 1971), quoted in *Willy Brandt, Peace* (Klaus Reiff, ed.; 1971)

3 Peace, like freedom, is no original state which existed from the start; we shall have to make it, in the truest sense of the word.
Address given on the presentation of a Nobel Prize in peace (December 11, 1971), quoted in *Willy Brandt, Peace* (Klaus Reiff, ed.; 1971)

4 A nation must be willing to look dispassionately at its own history.
Declaration on the 25th anniversary of the end of World War II (May 8, 1970), quoted in *Willy Brandt, Peace* (Klaus Reiff, ed.; 1971)

5 Europe should not unite against something, but for something, namely for the betterment of the European nations and for their constructive role in the world.
Lecture, Düsseldorf (November 30, 1967), "Permanent Peace in Europe as the Goal," quoted in *Willy Brandt, Peace* (Klaus Reiff, ed.; 1971)

6 The struggle for peace and the struggle for human rights are inseparable.
Speech, Stockholm, the day after receiving a Nobel Prize in peace (December 12, 1971), quoted in *Willy Brandt, Peace* (Klaus Reiff, ed.; 1971)

Branscomb, Lew (Lewis McAdory Branscomb; b.1926?) U.S. physicist and executive

1 Science is some kind of cosmic apple juice from the Garden of Eden. Those of it are doomed to carry the burden of original sin.
News Summaries (April 9, 1971)

Branson, Richard (b.1950) British entrepreneur and publicist

1 I believe in benevolent dictatorship provided I am the dictator.
Remark (1984)

2 A well-run business must have high and consistent standards of ethics.
Speech to the Institute of Directors, London (May 1993)

3 Develop the business around the people; build it, don't buy it; and, then, be the best.
Speech to the Institute of Directors, London (May 1993)

4 Growth does not always lead a business to build on success. All too often it converts a highly successful business into a mediocre large business.
Speech to the Institute of Directors, London (May 1993)

5 Our education system has largely failed to adapt to the fact that our prosperity and its very fabric has always been dependent on the market economy.
Speech to the Institute of Directors, London (May 1993)

6 What you do is begin as a billionaire. Then you go into the airline business.
Advice on becoming a millionaire. Speech to the Institute of Directors, London (May 1993)

7 I started fresh—a "virgin"—in the mail order record business, on the back of the abolition of retail price maintenance.
Quoted in *How to Get Ahead in Business* (Tom Cannon, ed.; 1993)

Braque, Georges (1882–1963) French painter and sculptor

1 Art is meant to disturb, science reassures.
Le Jour et la nuit: Cahiers 1917–1952 (1952)

2 Truth exists; only lies are invented.
Le Jour et la nuit: Cahiers 1917–1952 (1952)

3 I am far more concerned about being in tune with nature than copying it.
Quoted in "Late Lyrics: Braque," *Art in America* (Jed Perl; February 1983), vol. 71

4 The painting is finished when it has blotted out the idea.
Quoted in "Late Lyrics: Braque," *Art in America* (Jed Perl; February 1983), vol. 71

Brassaï (Gyula Halasz; 1889–1984) Hungarian-born French photographer

1 For me, there is only one criterion for a good photograph: that it be unforgettable.
1982. Quoted in "Guest Speaker: Brassaï. The Three Faces of Paris," *Architectural Digest* (Avis Berman; July 1984)

Brathwaite, Edward Kamau (b.1930) Barbadian poet, playwright, and historian

1 It is not
it is not
it is not enough
to be pause, to be hole
to be void, to be silent
to be semicolon, to be semicolony.
"Negus," *The Arrivants* (1973)

2 This isn't no time for playin'
the fool nor makin' no sport; this is cricket!
"Rites," *The Arrivants* (1973)

3 Never seen
a man
travel more
seen more
lands
than this poor
path-
less harbor-
less spade.
"The Journeys," *The Arrivants* (1973)

Brathwaite, Richard (1588?–1673) English poet

1 To Banbury came I, O profane one!
Where I saw a Puritane-one
Hanging of his cat on Monday
For killing of a mouse on Sunday.
Barnabee's Journal (1638), pt. 1, st. 4

Braudel, Fernand (1902–85) French historian

1 Is not artificial wealth a masterpiece of human achievement?
Quoted in *Intellectual Capital* (Thomas A. Stewart; 1997)

Brautigan, Richard (1935?–84) U.S. novelist and poet

1 In Watermelon Sugar the deeds were done and done again as my life is done in watermelon sugar. I'll tell you about it because I am here and you are distant.
Opening words of the novel. *In Watermelon Sugar* (1968)

2 During all the time that was his life, Mr. Hayman never had a cup of coffee, a smoke, a drink, or a woman and thought he'd be a fool if he did.
Trout Fishing in America (1967)

3 Far away now in the mountains...a photograph guards the memory of a man. The photograph is all alone out there. The snow is falling eighteen years after his death. It covers up the door.
Trout Fishing in America (1967)

4 Go on ahead and try for him. He'll hit a couple of times more, but you won't catch him. He's not a particularly smart fish. Just lucky. Sometimes that's all you need.
Trout Fishing in America (1967)

5 "Sir," the salesman said, "I wouldn't want you to think that we would ever sell a murky trout stream here. We always make sure they're running crystal clear before we even think about moving them."
Trout Fishing in America (1967)

6 Trout Fishing in America Shorty...would stop children on the

street and say to them, "I ain't got no legs. The trout chopped my legs off in Fort Lauderdale. You kids got legs...Wheel me into that store over there."

Trout Fishing in America (1967)

7 Some towns are known as the peach capital of America, or the cherry capital or the oyster capital...Mooresville, Indiana, is the John Dillinger capital of America.

John Dillinger was a gangster in Indiana. He was held responsible by the FBI for 16 killings, and was eventually shot dead by them. *Trout Fishing in America* (1967), prologue to "Girder Creek"

Brecht, Bertolt (1898–1956) German playwright and poet

Quotations about Brecht

1 "I have known three great poets, each one a prize son of a bitch." I: "Who?" He: "Yeats, Frost, Bert Brecht." (Now about Brecht he was wrong: Brecht wasn't a great poet.)

Joseph Brodsky (1940–96) Russian-born U.S. poet and writer. From a conversation with W. H. Auden. "To Please a Shadow," *Less Than One* (1986)

Quotations by Brecht

2 And I always thought: the very simplest words
Must be enough. When I say what things are like
Everyone's heart must be torn to shreds.

"And I Always Thought" (Michael Hamburger, tr.; 1953–56)

3 Love is also like a coconut which is good while it is fresh, but you have to spit it out when the juice is gone, what's left tastes bitter.

Baal (1922)

4 It isn't important to come out on top; what matters is to come out alive.

Jungle of Cities and Other Plays (1966)

5 She's not so pretty anyone would want to ruin her.

Mother Courage and Her Children (1941)

6 What they could do with around here is a good war.

Mother Courage and Her Children (1941), Scene 1

7 Whenever there are tremendous virtues it's a sure sign something's wrong.

Mother Courage and Her Children (1941), Scene 2

8 When he told men to love their neighbor, their bellies were full. Nowadays things are different.

Mother Courage and Her Children (1941), Scene 2

9 I don't trust him. We're friends.

Mother Courage and Her Children (1941), Scene 3

10 A war of which we could say it left nothing to be desired will probably never exist.

Mother Courage and Her Children (1941), Scene 6

11 The finest plans have always been spoiled by the littleness of those that should carry them out. Even emperors can't do it all by themselves.

Mother Courage and Her Children (1941), Scene 6

12 War is like love, it always finds a way.

Mother Courage and Her Children (1941), Scene 6

13 What happens to the hole when the cheese is gone?

Mother Courage and Her Children (1941), Scene 6

14 Don't tell me peace has broken out.

Mother Courage and Her Children (1941), Scene 8

15 I love the people with their straightforward minds. It's just that their smell brings on my migraine.

The Caucasian Chalk Circle (1948)

16 You want justice, but do you want to pay for it, hm? When you go to a butcher you know you have to pay, but you people go to a judge as if you were off to a funeral supper.

The Caucasian Chalk Circle (1948), Act 4

17 Those who have had no share in the good fortunes of the mighty often have a share in their misfortunes.

The Caucasian Chalk Circle (1948), Scene 1

18 It is my will to go with the man I love. I do not wish to count the cost. I do not wish to consider whether it is good. I do not wish to know whether he loves me. It is my will to go with him whom I love.

The Good Person of Szechwan (1943)

19 You can only help one of your luckless brothers by trampling down a dozen others.

The Good Person of Szechwan (1943)

20 ANDREA Unhappy the land that has no heroes.
GALILEO No, unhappy the land that needs heroes.

The Life of Galileo (1938–39), Scene 13

21 If there are obstacles, the shortest line between two points may be the crooked one.

The Life of Galileo (1938–39), Scene 13

22 Life is short and so is money.

The Threepenny Opera (1929)

23 The wickedness of the world is so great you have to run your legs off to avoid having them stolen from under you.

The Threepenny Opera (1929)

24 What's breaking into a bank compared with founding a bank?

The Threepenny Opera (1929)

25 First comes the grub, then comes the morals.

"Ballad about the Question: 'What Keeps a Man Alive?'," *The Threepenny Opera* (1929)

26 Oh, the shark has pretty teeth, dear,
And he shows them pearly white.
Just a jack-knife has Macheath, dear
And he keeps it out of sight.

"The Ballad of Mack the Knife," *The Threepenny Opera* (1929), prologue

Breggin, Peter R. (Peter Roger Breggin; b.1936) U.S. psychiatrist and author

1 A caring, understanding relationship—made safe by professional ethics and restraint—is the essence of psychotherapy.

Toxic Psychiatry (1991)

2 I am in favor of holding psychiatry responsible for the damage it inflicts on its patients.

Toxic Psychiatry (1991)

3 Psychiatry will fight to the bitter end against any kind of reform. To this day, it resists even the slightest control over its most obviously abusive practices, such as state mental

hospitals, involuntary drugging, electroshock, and lobotomy, and it fights every attempt to increase patients' rights.
Toxic Psychiatry (1991)

Brel, Jacques (Jacques Romain Brel; 1929–78) Belgian singer and songwriter

1 In this job, you tell of who you are...me, I work for myself...if you sing to please someone other than yourself, you cannot...but feel that you are prostituting yourself.
Interview, *Le Parisien libre* (1963), quoted in *Jacques Brel* (Alan Clayson; 1996), prologue

2 I'm obsessed by those things that are ugly and sordid, that people don't want to talk about.
Quoted in *Jacques Brel* (Alan Clayson; 1996), prologue

Brenan, Gerald (Edward Fitz-Gerald Brenan; 1894–1987) Maltese-born British writer and novelist

1 Spain, since the loss of its Catholic faith, has been above everything else a country in search of an ideology.
The Spanish Labyrinth (1943)

2 In a happy marriage it is the wife who provides the climate, the husband the landscape.
Thoughts in a Dry Season (1978)

3 We are closer to the ants than to the butterflies. Very few people can endure much leisure.
Thoughts in a Dry Season (1978)

4 We confess our bad qualities to others out of fear of appearing naive or ridiculous by not being aware of them.
Thoughts in a Dry Season (1978)

5 When we attend the funerals of our friends we grieve for them, but when we go to those of other people it is chiefly our own deaths that we mourn for.
"Death," *Thoughts in a Dry Season* (1978)

6 Intellectuals are people who believe that ideas are of more importance than values. That is to say, their own ideas and other people's values.
"Life," *Thoughts in a Dry Season* (1978)

7 Old age takes away from us what we have inherited and gives us what we have earned.
"Life," *Thoughts in a Dry Season* (1978)

8 The cliché is dead poetry. English, being the language of an imaginative race, abounds in clichés, so that English literature is always in danger of being poisoned by its own secretions.
"Literature," *Thoughts in a Dry Season* (1978)

Brennan, William J. (William Joseph Brennan, Jr.; 1906–97) U.S. Supreme Court justice

1 Clerks get into the damnedest wrangles—which is the way they help me.
Referring to clerks serving justices. *Life* (February 1987)

2 Capital punishment...treats members of the human race...as objects to be toyed with and discarded.
Address, University of California, Hastings College of Law, *Los Angeles Times* (November 19, 1985)

3 Five votes! Five votes can do anything around here.
The U.S. Supreme Court has nine members, so five votes are a majority. Quoted in *Simpson's Contemporary Quotations* (James B. Simpson; 1997)

Brentano, Franz (1838–1917) German philosopher

1 Every mental act is conscious; it includes within it a consciousness of itself.
Psychology from an Empirical Standpoint (1874)

Bresson, Robert (1907–1999) French filmmaker

1 I never use professional actors nowadays...For in my opinion the moment actors assume certain expressions, the result cannot be true cinema, only filmed theater.
Interview, *Montreal Star* (July 16, 1966), quoted in *Film-makers Speak* (Jay Leyda, ed.; 1977)

Breton, André (1896–1966) French writer

1 Subjectivity and objectivity commit a series of assaults on each other during a human life out of which the first one suffers the worse beating.
Nadja (1928), preface

Breton, Nicholas (1555?–1626?) English writer

1 I wish my deadly foe, no worse
Than want of friends, and empty purse.
"A Farewell to Town" (1577)

2 Come little babe, come silly soul,
thy father's shame, thy mother's grief,
Born as I doubt to all our dole,
And to thy self unhappy chief:
Sing lullaby and lap it warm,
Poor soul that thinks no creature harm.
"A Sweet Lullaby" (1597)

3 We rise with the lark and go to bed with the lamb.
The Court and Country (1618)

Bretonneau, Pierre (1778–1862) French physician

1 I only take money from sick people.
19th century. Comment to a hypochondriac. *Bulletin of the New York Academy of Medicine*, 5: 154

Brezhnev, Leonid (Leonid Ilyich Brezhnev; 1906–82) Soviet president

1 When internal and external forces that are hostile to socialism try to turn the development of some socialist country towards the restoration of a capitalist regime, then socialism in that country and the socialist community as a whole is threatened.
1968. The "Brezhnev doctrine," used to justify the Warsaw Pact's invasion of Czechoslovakia (1968), asserted the right of pact states to intervene in each other's internal affairs.

Briand, Aristide (1862–1932) French statesman

Quotations about Briand

1 This devil of a man is the opposite of Briand: the latter knows nothing and understands everything; the other knows

everything and understands nothing.
Georges Clemenceau (1841–1929) French prime minister and journalist. Referring to Raymond Poincaré, five times prime minister of France and French president (1913–20), and French statesman Aristide Briand. Attrib.

Quotations by Briand

2 Draw back the rifles, draw back the machine guns, draw back the cannons—trust in conciliation, in arbitration, in peace!...A country grows in history not only because of the heroism of its troops on the field of battle, it grows also when it turns to justice and to right for the conservation of its interests.
Referring to Germany's admission to membership of the League of Nations. Speech, Geneva, Switzerland (September 10, 1926)

Brice, Fanny (Fannie Borach; 1891–1951) U.S. entertainer

1 Your audience gives you everything you need; there is no director who can direct you like an audience.
Quoted in *The Fabulous Fanny* (Norman Katlov; 1953)

Bridget of Sweden, Saint (originally Birgitta Persson; 1303–73) Swedish visionary

1 Some women behave like harlots; when they feel the life of a child in their wombs, they induce herbs or other means to cause miscarriage, only to perpetuate their amusement and unchastity. Therefore I shall deprive them from everlasting life and send them to everlasting death.
Revelations (14th century), vol. 7

Brien, Alan (b.1925) British critic and journalist

1 I have done almost every human activity inside a taxi which does not require main drainage.
Punch, London (July 5, 1972)

2 Violence is the repartee of the illiterate.
Punch, London (February 7, 1973)

Bright, John (1811–89) British politician

1 England is the mother of parliaments.
January 18, 1865. *Times*, London (January 19, 1865)

2 Force is not a remedy.
November 16, 1880. *Times*, London (November 17, 1880)

Brillat-Savarin, Anthelme (1755–1826) French politician, gastronome, and writer

1 Tell me what you eat and I will tell you what you are.
"Aphorismes, pour servir de prolégomènes," *Physiologie du Goût* (1825), no. 4

Brinton, Crane (Clarence Crane Brinton; 1898–1968) U.S. historian

1 The writing of history is, like the preaching of a sermon, an art, and its success is to be measured less by its conformity with rules established by the critics than by its effect on its audience.
"The New History: Twenty-five Years After," *Journal of Social Philosophy* (January 1936)

Brinton, Thomas (also spelled Thomas Brunton; 1320?–89?) English bishop

1 It is neither fitting nor safe that all the keys should hang from the belt of one woman.
Criticizing the influence of Alice Perrers over the ageing Edward III. Sermon, Westminster Abbey (May 18, 1376)

Bristow, Alan (b.1923) British business executive

1 I believe in industry. I believe in the Queen. I believe in God. But most of all, I believe in Alan Bristow.
Daily Express, London (January 14, 1986)

Brittain, Vera (1893–1970) British writer and feminist

Quotations about Brittain

1 And in retrospect, my mother was not essentially a novelist, but a chronicler of her times...a promoter of causes rather than a woman of creative imagination.
John Catlin (b.1947) British solicitor. Referring to Vera Brittain. *Family Quartet* (1987)

Quotations by Brittain

2 It is probably true to say that the largest scope for change still lies in men's attitude to women, and in women's attitude to themselves.
Lady into Woman (1953), ch. 15

3 The idea that it is necessary to go to a university in order to become a successful writer, or even a man or woman of letters (which is by no means the same thing), is one of those phantasies that surround authorship.
On Being an Author (1948), ch. 2

4 Meek wifehood is no part of my profession;
I am your friend, but never your possession.
"Married Love," *Poems of the War and After* (1934)

5 Politics are usually the executive expression of human immaturity.
The Rebel Passion (1964)

Broca, Paul (Pierre Broca; 1824–80) French surgeon and anthropologist

1 Private practice and marriage—those twin extinguishers of science.
Letter (April 10, 1851)

Brodsky, Joseph (Joseph Alexandrovich Brodsky; 1940–96) Russian-born U.S. poet and writer

1 So long had life together been that now
the second of January fell again
on Tuesday, making her astonished brow
lift like a windshield wiper in the rain.
"Six Years Later" (Richard Wilbur, tr.; 1969), ll. 1–4

2 I was born and brought up in the Baltic marshland
by zinc-gray breakers that always marched on
in twos. Hence all rhymes, hence that wan, flat voice.
"A Part of Speech," *A Part of Speech* (Joseph Brodsky, tr.; 1969)

3 Life—the way it really is—is a battle not between Bad and Good, but between Bad and Worse.
New York Times (October 1, 1972)

4 Always pick a house with baby-clothes hanging out in the yard. Deal only with the over-fifty crowd.
"Advice to a Traveller," *Worst Journeys* (Keath Fraser, ed.; 1991)

5 If somebody yells "Hey stranger!" don't answer. Play deaf and dumb.
"Advice to a Traveller," *Worst Journeys* (Keath Fraser, ed.; 1991)

6 When you halt in the desert make an arrow from pebbles, so, if suddenly woken up, you'll grasp which way to go.
"Advice to a Traveller," *Worst Journeys* (Keath Fraser, ed.; 1991)

Brome, Alexander (1620–66) English poet

1 I have been in love, and in debt, and in drink,
This many and many a year.
"The Mad Lover," *Songs and Other Poems* (1664)

Brome, Richard (1590?–1652) English playwright

1 I am a gentleman, though spoiled i' the breeding. The Buzzards are all gentlemen. We came in with the Conqueror.
English Moor (1637), Act 2, Scene 2

2 You rose o' the wrong side to-day.
The Court Beggar (1632), Act 2

Bronowski, Jacob (1908–74) Polish-born British mathematician, poet, and humanist

1 Every animal leaves traces of what it was; man alone leaves traces of what he created.
The Ascent of Man (1973), ch. 1

2 That is the essence of science: ask an impertinent question, and you are on the way to the pertinent answer.
The Ascent of Man (1973), ch. 4

3 Physics becomes in those years the greatest collective work of science—no, more than that, the great collective work of art of the twentieth century.
Referring to the period around the turn of the century marked by the elucidation of atomic structure and the development of the quantum theory. *The Ascent of Man* (1973), ch. 10

4 The wish to hurt, the momentary intoxication with pain, is the loophole through which the pervert climbs into the minds of ordinary men.
The Face of Violence (1954), ch. 5

5 The world is made of people who never quite get into the first team and who just miss the prizes at the flower show.
The Face of Violence (1954), ch. 6

6 Science has nothing to be ashamed of, even in the ruins of Nagasaki.
Lecture at Massachusetts Institute of Technology. "The Sense of Human Dignity" (March 19, 1953)

Brontë, Anne (1820–49) British novelist and poet

1 What is it that constitutes virtue, Mrs. Graham? Is it the circumstance of being able and willing to resist temptation; or that of having no temptations to resist.
The Tenant of Wildfell Hall (1848), ch. 3

Brontë, Charlotte (1816–55) British novelist

Quotations about Brontë

1 Girls, do you know Charlotte has been writing a book, and it is much better than likely?
Patrick Brontë (1777–1861) British cleric. Quoted in *The Life of Charlotte Brontë* (Elizabeth Gaskell; 1857), ch. 16

2 Trivial personalities decomposing in the eternity of print.
Virginia Woolf (1882–1941) British novelist and critic. Referring to *Jane Eyre* by Charlotte Brontë. "Jane Eyre," *The Common Reader: First Series* (1925)

Quotations by Brontë

3 Dread remorse when you are tempted to err, Miss Eyre: remorse is the poison of life.
Jane Eyre (1847), ch. 14

4 I grant an ugly *woman* is a blot on the fair face of creation; but as to the *gentlemen*, let them be solicitous to possess only strength and valour: let their motto be: Hunt, shoot, and fight: the rest is not worth a fillip.
Jane Eyre (1847), ch. 17

5 The soul fortunately, has an interpreter—often an unconscious, but still a truthful interpreter—in the eye.
Jane Eyre (1847), ch. 28

6 Reader, I married him.
Jane Eyre (1847), ch. 38

7 Conventionality is not morality. Self-righteousness is not religion. To attack the first is not to assail the last. To pluck the mask from the face of the Pharisee, is not to lift an impious hand to the Crown of Thorns.
Jane Eyre (1847), preface to the 2nd ed.

8 An abundant shower of curates has fallen upon the north of England.
Shirley (1849), ch. 1

9 Misery generates hate; these sufferers hated the machines which they believed took their bread from them; they hated the buildings which contained these machines; they hated the manufacturers who owned those buildings.
Referring to the effect of the introduction of knitting frames into northern England. *Shirley* (1849), ch. 2

Brontë, Emily (Emily Jane Brontë; 1818–48) British poet and novelist

1 No coward soul is mine,
No trembler in the world's storm-troubled sphere:
I see Heaven's glories shine,
And faith shines equal, arming me from fear.
"No Coward Soul Is Mine" (1846)

2 A good heart will help you to a bonny face, my lad...and a bad one will turn the bonniest into something worse than ugly.
Wuthering Heights (1847), ch. 7

3 If all else perished, and he remained, I should still continue to be; and if all else remained, and he were annihilated, the universe would turn to a mighty stranger: I should not seem a part of it.
Wuthering Heights (1847), ch. 9

4 My love for Linton is like the foliage in the woods: time will change it, I'm well aware, as winter changes the trees. My love for Heathcliff resembles the eternal rocks beneath: a source of little visible delight, but necessary. Nelly, I *am* Heathcliff!
Wuthering Heights (1847), ch. 9

Brooke, Rupert (Rupert Chawner Brooke; 1887–1915) British poet

Quotations about Brooke

1 A young Apollo, golden-haired,
Stands dreaming on the verge of strife,
Magnificently unprepared
For the long littleness of life.
1910
Frances Cornford (1886–1960) British poet. "Youth," *Collected Poems* (1954)

2 Brooke got perhaps a certain amount of vivid poetry in life and then went off to associate with literary hen-coops like Lascelles Abercrombie in his writings.
1915
Ezra Pound (1885–1972) U.S. poet, translator, and critic. Referring to Rupert Brooke shortly after his death in 1915. Letter to Harriet Monroe (December 12, 1915), quoted in *The Selected Letters of Ezra Pound, 1907–1941* (D. D. Paige, ed.; 1950)

Quotations by Brooke

3 Now, God be thanked who has matched us with His hour,
And caught our youth, and wakened us from sleeping.
"Peace" (1914), quoted in *The Poetical Works of Rupert Brooke* (Geoffrey Keynes, ed.; 1970)

4 These laid the world away; poured out the red
Sweet wine of youth; gave up the years to be
Of work and joy, and that unhoped serene,
That men call age; and those who would have been,
Their sons, they gave, their immortality.
"The Dead" (1914), quoted in *The Poetical Works of Rupert Brooke* (Geoffrey Keynes, ed.; 1970)

5 Stands the Church clock at ten to three?
And is there honey still for tea?
"The Old Vicarage, Grantchester" (1912), quoted in *The Poetical Works of Rupert Brooke* (Geoffrey Keynes, ed.; 1970)

6 Unkempt about those hedges blows
An unofficial English rose.
"The Old Vicarage, Grantchester" (1912), quoted in *The Poetical Works of Rupert Brooke* (Geoffrey Keynes, ed.; 1970)

7 If I should die, think only this of me:
That there's some corner of a foreign field
That is forever England.
"The Soldier" (1914), quoted in *The Poetical Works of Rupert Brooke* (Geoffrey Keynes, ed.; 1970)

8 There is excitement in the game, but little beauty except in the long-limbed "pitcher," whose duty it is to hurl the ball rather further than the length of a cricket-pitch, as bewilderingly as possible. In his efforts to combine speed, mystery and curve, he gets into attitudes of a very novel and fantastic, but quite obvious beauty.
Referring to baseball. *Letters from America* (1916)

Brookner, Anita (b.1928) British novelist and art historian

1 It was clear that wealth had rendered her helpless.
A Misalliance (1986), ch. 9

2 I see that if a woman has it in mind to bring a man to heel she may have to play a part which runs counter to her own instincts.
Brief Lives (1990), ch. 4

3 In real life, of course, it is the hare who wins. Every time. Look around you. And in any case it is my contention that Aesop was writing for the tortoise market...Hares have no time to read. They are too busy winning the game.
Hotel du Lac (1984)

4 The company of their own sex, Edith reflected, was what drove many women into marriage.
Hotel du Lac (1984)

Brooks, Gwendolyn (b.1917) U.S. poet and novelist

1 Abortions will not let you forget.
You remember the children you got that you did not get.
"The Mother," *A Street in Bronzeville* (1945), st. 1

2 we are each other's
business:
we are each other's
magnitude and bond.
"Paul Robeson," *Family Pictures* (1970)

3 There can be no whiter whiteness than this one:
An insurance man's shirt on its morning run.
"Mrs Small," *The Bean Eaters* (1960)

4 We real cool.
We
Left school. We
Lurk late. We
Strike straight. We
Sing sin. We
Thin gin. We
Jazz June. We
Die soon.
"We Real Cool," *The Bean Eaters* (1960)

5 This is the urgency: Live!
and have your blooming in the noise of the whirlwind.
"The Second Sermon on the Warpland," *The Mecca* (1968)

6 The Ladies from the Ladies' Betterment League
Arrive in the afternoon, the late light slanting
In diluted gold bars across the boulevard, brag
Of proud, seamed faces with mercy and murder hinting
Here, there, interrupting, all deep and debonair,
The pink paint on the innocence of fear.
"The Lovers of the Poor," *The World of Gwendolyn Brooks* (1960), quoted in *The Penguin Book of American Verse* (Geoffrey Moore, ed.; 1977)

7 Their League is allotting largesse to the Lost.
Referring to the "Ladies' Betterment League." "The Lovers of the Poor," *The World of Gwendolyn Brooks* (1960), quoted in *The Penguin Book of American Verse* (Geoffrey Moore, ed.; 1977)

8 I tell poets that when a line just floats into your head, don't pay attention 'cause it probably has floated into somebody else's head.
I Dream a World: Portraits of Black Women Who Changed America (Brian Lanker; 1989)

Brooks, John U.S. business executive

1 For almost a generation, from the 1929 crash to the bull market of the 1950s, young men of talent and ambition grew up thinking of Wall Street as anathema and did not go to work there.
The Go-Go Years (1973)

2 The hedge funds of 1965...were Wall Street's last bastions of secrecy, mystery, exclusivity, and privilege. They were the parlor cars of the new gravy train.
The Go-Go Years (1973)

3 Wall Street in 1965...stood out as a last bastion of all-but-unchallenged male supremacy. It thought working women ought to be office drudges or sex objects, or both.
The Go-Go Years (1973)

Brooks, Mel (Melvin Kaminsky; b.1926) U.S. film actor and director

1 Tragedy is if I cut my finger. Comedy is if I walk into an open sewer and die.
New Yorker (October 30, 1978)

2 I love gentiles. In fact, one of my favorite activities is Protestant spotting.
Interview. *Playboy Magazine* (October 1966)

3 That's it, baby, if you've got it, flaunt it.
The Producers (1968)

Brooks, Phillips (1835–93) U.S. Episcopal bishop and evangelist

1 O little town of Bethlehem,
How still we see thee lie;
Above thy deep and dreamless sleep
The silent stars go by.
Christmas carol. "O Little Town of Bethlehem" (1868), verse 1

Brooks, Thomas (1608–80) English cleric

1 For great is truth, and shall prevail.
The Crown and Glory of Christianity (1662)

Brophy, Brigid (Brigid Antonia Brooks; 1929–95) British novelist and critic

1 To defend society from sex is no one's business. To defend it from officiousness is the duty of everyone who values freedom—or sex.
Observer, London (August 9, 1970), "Sayings of the Week"

Brougham, Henry Peter, Baron (1778–1868) British lawyer and politician

1 The great Unwashed.
Attrib.

Broun, Heywood (1888–1939) U.S. journalist

1 Posterity is as likely to be wrong as anybody else.
Sitting on the World (1924)

2 Obscenity is such a tiny kingdom that a single tour covers it completely.
Quoted in *Shake Well Before Using* (Bennett Cerf; 1948)

3 Repartee is what you wish you'd said.
Quoted in *The Algonquin Wits* (Robert E. Drennan; 1968)

Brown, George (1818–80) Scottish-born Canadian journalist and politician

1 I have no fear that the people of Upper Canada would ever desire to become the fag-end of the neighbouring republic.
Upper Canada refers to what is now Ontario Province. Speech, Reform Party Convention, Toronto (November 10, 1859)

2 Those who seek to change an established government by force of arms assume a fearful responsibility—a responsibility which nothing but the clearest and most intolerable injustice will acquit them for assuming.
Speech, Toronto (1863)

Brown, George Mackay (1921–96) Scottish poet and novelist

1 Beast, what is love?
Phallus, rut, spasm

Peasant what is love?
Plough, furrow, seed

Priest, what is love?
Prophecy, event, ritual.
"Lord of the Mirrors," *Poems New and Selected* (1971)

2 An angel, are you?
Mister, let me tell you
The magistrates
Want no comic-singers in town this winter.
The poem is an ironic treatment of the Christmas story. "The Keeper of the Midnight Gate," *Winterfold* (1976)

Brown, Helen Gurley (b.1922) U.S. journalist

1 Good girls go to heaven, bad girls go everywhere.
Slogan. Attrib. *Cosmopolitan*

Brown, H. Rap (Jamil Abdullah al-Amin; b.1943) U.S. civil rights campaigner

1 America is the ultimate denial of the theory of man's continuous evolution.
Die Nigger Die! (1969)

2 Justice means "just-us-white-folks."
Die Nigger Die! (1969)

3 The fight is for freedom, not whiteness.
Die Nigger Die! (1969)

4 Violence is as American as cherry pie.
Die Nigger Die! (1969)

Brown, James (b.1928) U.S. singer, songwriter, and producer

1 Sometimes I look back on my life and wonder just how one man could achieve all I've done.
Quoted in *The Wit and Wisdom of Rock and Roll* (Maxim Jabukowski, ed.; 1983)

Brown, John (1800–59) U.S. abolitionist

Quotations about Brown

1 Let no man pray that Brown be spared. Let Virginia make him a martyr. Now, he has only blundered. His soul was noble: his work was miserable. But a cord and a gibbet would redeem all that, and round up Brown's failure with a heroic success.
Henry Ward Beecher (1813–87) U.S. cleric and abolitionist. Quoted in *John Brown* (Oswald G. Villard; 1910)

2 When John Brown stretched forth his arm the sky was cleared —the armed hosts of freedom stood face to face over the chasm of a broken union, and the clash of arms was at hand.
Frederick Douglass (1817–95) U.S. abolitionist, writer, and orator. Speech, Storer College, Harpers Ferry, West Virginia (May 1882)

3 That new saint, than whom nothing purer or more brave was ever led by love of men into conflict and death...will make the gallows glorious like the cross.
December 1859
Ralph Waldo Emerson (1803–82) U.S. poet and essayist. Referring to John Brown's execution. Attrib.

Quotations by Brown

4 I am as content to die for God's eternal truth on the scaffold as in any other way.
Said on the day before his execution. Remark (December 2, 1859)

5 I am fully persuaded that I am worth inconceivably more to hang than for any other purpose.
Said before his execution. Remark (November 2, 1859), quoted in *The Home Book of Quotations* (Burton Stevenson; 1984)

6 I, John Brown, am now quite certain that the crimes of this guilty land will never be purged away but with blood.
December 2, 1859. Last statement at his trial before execution. Quoted in *John Brown and His Men* (Richard Josiah Hinton; 1894)

Brown, John Mason (1900–69) U.S. journalist

1 Some television programs are so much chewing gum for the eyes.
Interview (July 28, 1955)

2 Tallulah Bankhead barged down the Nile last night and sank. As the Serpent of the Nile she proves to be no more dangerous than a garter snake.
Referring to her performance as Shakespeare's Cleopatra. *New York Evening Post* (November 11, 1937)

Brown, Lew (Louis Brownstein; 1893–1958) U.S. songwriter

1 Keep your sunny side up.
Song lyric. "Sunny Side Up" (co-written with Buddy De Silva; 1929)

2 Life is Just a Bowl of Cherries
1931. Song title.

Brown, Norman O. (Norman Oliver Brown; b.1913) U.S. writer and educator

1 History is shaped, beyond our conscious wills, not by the cunning of Reason but by the cunning of Desire.
Life Against Death (1959)

2 Psychoanalysis can provide a theory of "progress," but only by viewing history as a neurosis.
Life Against Death (1959)

3 The riddle of history is not in Reason but in Desire; not in labor, but in love.
Life Against Death (1959)

Brown, Pat (b.1905) U.S. politician

1 When a man throws an empty cigarette package from an automobile, he is liable to a fine of $50. When a man throws a billboard across a view, he is richly rewarded.
Ogilvy on Advertising (1985)

Brown, Sterling (1901–89) U.S. poet, critic, and teacher

1 *One thing they cannot prohibit*
The strong men...coming on,
The strong men gittin' stronger.
Strong men...
Stronger...
"Strong Men," *Southern Road* (1932)

Brown, Thomas (1663–1704) English satirist and translator

1 I do not love thee, Doctor Fell,
The reason why I cannot tell;
But this alone I know full well,
I do not love thee, Doctor Fell.
1700. Referring to Doctor John Fell (1625–86), dean of Christ Church, Oxford, Bishop of Oxford, and champion of Oxford University Press. Translation of Martial's *Epigrams*, Book 1, no. 32, quoted in *Amusements Serious and Comical by Tom Brown* (A. L. Heyward, ed.; 1927)

2 In the reign of King Charles the Second, a certain worthy Divine...address'd himself to the auditory...: "In short, if you don't live up to the precepts of the Gospel, but abandon your selves to your irregular appetites, you must expect to receive your reward in a certain place, which 'tis not good manners to mention here."
Laconics (1707)

3 To treat a poor wretch with a bottle of Burgundy, and fill his snuff-box, is like giving a pair of laced ruffles to a man that has never a shirt on his back.
Laconics (1707)

Brown, Thomas Edward (1830–97) British school teacher and poet

1 A garden is a lovesome thing, God wot!
"My Garden" (1893)

2 A rich man's joke is always funny.
"The Doctor" (1887)

Brown, William Wells (1814?–84) U.S. writer and abolitionist

1 We may search in history in vain to find a people who have sunk themselves as low, and made themselves appear as infamous by their treatment of their fellow men, as have the people of the United States.
Letter to Wendell Phillips (November 22, 1849), quoted in *A Documentary History of the Negro People in the United States* (Herbert Aptheker; 1951), vol. 1

2 I will not yield to you in affection for America, but I hate her institution of slavery. I love her, because I am identified with her enslaved millions by every tie that should bind man to his fellow-man.
Letter to Wendell Phillips (November 22, 1849), quoted in *A Documentary History of the Negro People in the United States* (Herbert Aptheker; 1951), vol. 1

3 When will Americans learn, that if they would encourage liberty in other countries, they must practice it at home?
Quoted in *Here I Stand* (Paul Robeson; 1958)

Browne, Cecil (b.1932) U.S. business executive

1 But not so odd
As those who choose
A Jewish God,
But spurn the Jews.
Replying to William Norman Ewer.

Browne, Thomas (1605–82) English physician and writer

Quotations about Browne

1 Who would not be curious to see the lineaments of a man who, having himself been twice married wished that mankind were propagated like trees.
Charles Lamb (1775–1834) British essayist. *New Monthly Magazine* (January 1826)

Quotations by Browne

2 Half our days we pass in the shadow of the earth; and the brother of death exacteth a third part of our lives.
The opening sentence of this posthumously published essay. "On Dreams" (1716), quoted in *Sir Thomas Browne's Works* (S. Wilkin, ed.; 1836), vol. 4

3 That children dream not in the first half year, that men dream not in some countries, are to me sick men's dreams, dreams out of the ivory gate, and visions before midnight.
This essay was published posthumously. "On Dreams" (1716), quoted in *Sir Thomas Browne's Works* (S. Wilkin, ed.; 1836), vol. 4

4 He who discommendeth others obliquely commendeth himself.
This essay was published posthumously. *Christian Morals* (1716), pt. 1

5 They do most by Books, who could do much without them, and he that chiefly owes himself unto himself, is the substantial Man.
This essay was published posthumously. *Christian Morals* (1716), pt. 2

6 With what shift and pains we come into the World we remember not; but 'tis commonly found no easy matter to get out of it.
This essay was published posthumously. *Christian Morals* (1716), pt. 2

7 There is another man within me, that's angry with me, rebukes, commands, and dastards me.
Religio Medici (1642)

8 We all labour against our own cure, for death is the cure of all diseases.
Religio Medici (1642)

9 For my part, I have ever believed, and do now know, that there are witches.
Religio Medici (1642), pt. 1

10 I dare, without usurpation, assume the honourable style of a Christian.
Religio Medici (1642), pt. 1, sect. 1

11 A man may be in as just possession of truth as of a city, and yet be forced to surrender.
Religio Medici (1642), pt. 1, sect. 6

12 I could never divide my self from any man upon the difference of an opinion, or be angry with his judgment for not agreeing with me in that, from which perhaps within a few days I should dissent my self.
Religio Medici (1642), pt. 1, sect. 6

13 As for those wingy mysteries in divinity, and airy subtleties in religion, which have unhinged the brains of better heads, they never stretched the *pia mater* of mine; methinks there be not impossibilities enough in Religion for an active faith.
Religio Medici (1642), pt. 1, sect. 9

14 Who can speak of eternity without a solecism, or think thereof without an ecstasy? Time we may comprehend, 'tis but five days elder than ourselves.
Religio Medici (1642), pt. 1, sect. 11

15 We carry within us the wonders we seek without us: There is all Africa and her prodigies in us.
Religio Medici (1642), pt. 1, sect. 15

16 All things are artificial, for nature is the art of God.
Religio Medici (1642), pt. 1, sect. 16

17 God is like a skilful Geometrician.
Religio Medici (1642), pt. 1, sect. 16

18 Persecution is a bad and indirect way to plant religion. There are many (questionless) canonized on earth, that shall never be Saints in Heaven.
Religio Medici (1642), pt. 1, sect. 26

19 And, considering the thousand doors that lead to death, do thank my God that we can die but once.
Religio Medici (1642), pt. I, sect. 44

20 I am not so much afraid of death, as ashamed thereof; 'tis the very disgrace and ignominy of our natures, that in a moment can so disfigure us that our nearest friends, wife, and children, stand afraid and start at us.
Religio Medici (1642), pt. 1, sect. 44

21 I have tried if I could reach that great resolution of his to be honest without a thought of heaven or hell.
Referring to Seneca. *Religio Medici* (1642), pt. 1, sect. 47

22 To believe only possibilities, is not faith, but mere Philosophy.
Religio Medici (1642), pt. 1, sect. 48

23 The heart of man is the place the Devil's in: I feel sometimes a hell within myself.
Religio Medici (1642), pt. 1, sect. 51

24 There is no road or ready way to virtue.
Religio Medici (1642), pt. 1, sect. 55

25 For the world, I count it not an inn, but an hospital, and a place, not to live, but to die in.
Religio Medici (1642), pt. 2

26 It is the common wonder of all men, how among so many million of faces, there should be none alike.
Religio Medici (1642), pt. 2

27 Lord, deliver me from myself.
Religio Medici (1642), pt. 2

28 No man can justly censure or condemn another, because indeed no man truly knows another.
Religio Medici (1642), pt. 2

29 There is surely a piece of divinity in us, something that was before the elements, and owes no homage unto the sun.
Religio Medici (1642), pt. 2

30 I feel not in myself those common antipathies that I can discover in others: those national repugnances do not touch me, nor do I behold with prejudice the French, Italian, Spaniard, or Dutch; but where I find their actions in balance with my countrymen's, I honour, love and embrace them in the same degree.
Religio Medici (1642), pt. 2, sect. 1

31 Charity begins at home, is the voice of the world.
Religio Medici (1642), pt. 2, sect. 4

32 I could be content that we might procreate like trees, without conjunction, or that there were any way to perpetuate the World without this trivial and vulgar way of coition: it is the foolishest act a wise man commits in all his life.
Religio Medici (1642), pt. 2, sect. 9

33 Sleep is a death;—O make me try
By sleeping, what it is to die!
And as gently lay my head
On my grave, as now my bed.
Religio Medici (1642), pt. 2, sect. 12

34 Life itself is but the shadow of death, and souls but the shadows of the living. All things fall under this name. The sun itself is but the dark *simulacrum*, and light but the shadow of God.
The Garden of Cyrus (1658), ch. 4

35 All things began in order, so shall they end, and so shall they begin again; according to the ordainer of order and mystical mathematics of the city of heaven.
The Garden of Cyrus (1658), ch. 5

36 Men have lost their reason in nothing so much as their religion, wherein stones and clouts make martyrs.
Urn Burial (1658), ch. 4

37 Were the happiness of the next world as closely apprehended as the felicities of this, it were a martyrdom to live.
Urn Burial (1658), ch. 4

38 Man is a noble animal, splendid in ashes, and pompous in the grave.
Urn Burial (1658), ch. 5

39 The long habit of living indisposeth us for dying.
Urn Burial (1658), ch. 5

40 No one should approach the temple of science with the soul of a money changer.
Sir Thomas Browne's Works (S. Wilkin, ed.; 1835)

Browne, William (1591?–1645?) English poet

1 Underneath this sable hearse
Lies the subject of all verse,
Sidney's sister, Pembroke's mother;
Death! ere thou hast slain another,
Fair and learn'd, and good as she,
Time shall throw a dart at thee.
Epitaph. "On the Countess of Pembroke" (1623)

2 Well-languaged Daniel.
Britannia's Pastorals (1616), bk. 2, song 2

Browning, Elizabeth Barrett (1806–61) British poet

1 Do ye hear the children weeping, O my brothers,
Ere the sorrow comes with years?
"The Cry of the Children" (1844), st. 1

2 And that dismal cry rose slowly
And sank slowly through the air,
Full of spirit's melancholy
And eternity's despair!
And they heard the words it said
Pan is dead! great Pan is dead!
Pan, Pan is dead!
"The Dead Pan," st. 26

3 "Yes," I answered you last night;
"No," this morning, sir, I say
Colours seen by candle-light
Will not look the same by day.
"The Lady's Yes" (1844)

4 Since when was genius found respectable?
Aurora Leigh (1856), bk. 6

5 The devil's most devilish when respectable.
Aurora Leigh (1856), bk. 7

6 If thou must love me, let it be for naught
Except for love's sake only.
No. 14, *Sonnets from the Portuguese* (1850)

7 God's gifts put man's best gifts to shame.
No. 26, *Sonnets from the Portuguese* (1850)

8 How do I love thee? Let me count the ways.
I love thee to the depth and breadth and height
My soul can reach, when feeling out of sight
For the ends of Being and idea Grace.
No. 43, *Sonnets from the Portuguese* (1850)

9 I love thee with a love I seemed to lose

With my lost saints—I love thee with the breath,
Smiles, tears, of all my life!—and, if God choose,
I shall but love thee better after death.
No. 43, *Sonnets from the Portuguese* (1850)

Browning, Robert (1812–89) British poet

Quotations about Browning

1 As Browning is a man with a moderate gift passionately desiring movement and fullness, and obtaining but a confused multitudinousness, so Keats with a very high gift, is yet also consumed with this desire: and cannot produce the truly living and moving, as his conscience keeps telling him.
Matthew Arnold (1822–88) British poet and critic. Referring to Robert Browning and John Keats. Letter to A. H. Clough (1848)

Quotations by Browning

2 A minute's success pays the failure of years.
"Apollo and the Fates" (1886), st. 42

3 What Youth deemed crystal, Age finds out was dew.
"Jochanan Hakkadosh," st. 101, l. 302, quoted in *The Poetical Works of Robert Browning* (1888–94)

4 Solomon of saloons
And philosophic diner-out.
"Mr. Sludge, 'The Medium'" (1864)

5 But, thanks to wine-lees and democracy,
We've still our stage where truth calls spade a spade!
Aristophanes' Apology (1875)

6 Ignorance is not innocence but sin.
"The Inn Album," *Aristophanes' Apology* (1875)

7 Womanliness means only motherhood;
All love begins and ends there.
"The Inn Album," *Aristophanes' Apology* (1875)

8 How very hard it is
To be a Christian!
Christmas-Eve and Easter-Day (1850)

9 In the natural fog of the good man's mind.
Christmas-Eve and Easter-Day (1850), l. 226

10 "'Tis well averred,
A scientific faith's absurd."
Christmas-Eve and Easter-Day (1850), pt. 6

11 When is man strong until he feels alone?
Colombe's Birthday (1889), Act 3

12 Boot, saddle, to horse, and away!
"Cavalier Tunes," *Dramatic Lyrics* (1842), "Boot and Saddle"

13 "You're wounded!" "Nay," the soldier's pride
Touched to the quick, he said:
"I'm killed, Sire!" And his chief beside
Smiling the boy fell dead.
"Incident of the French Camp," *Dramatic Lyrics* (1842), st. 5

14 She had a heart how shall I say? too soon made glad,
Too easily impressed.
"My Last Duchess," *Dramatic Lyrics* (1842)

15 That's my last Duchess painted on the wall,
Looking as if she were alive.
Opening lines. "My Last Duchess," *Dramatic Lyrics* (1842), ll. 1–2

16 The rain set early in to-night
All her hair
In one long yellow string I wound
Three times her little throat around,
And strangled her. No pain felt she;
I am quite sure she felt no pain
And all night long we have not stirred,
And yet God has not said a word!
"Porphyria's Lover," *Dramatic Lyrics* (1842)

17 Hamelin Town's in Brunswick,
By famous Hanover city;
The river Weser, deep and wide,
Washes its wall on the southern side;
A pleasanter spot you never spied.
"The Pied Piper of Hamelin," *Dramatic Lyrics* (1842)

18 And the muttering grew to a grumbling;
And the grumbling grew to a mighty rumbling;
And out of the houses the rats came tumbling.
The poem tells the legend of the Pied Piper of Hamelin, according to which a rat-catcher played on his pipe in order to rid Hamelin, a German town, of rats. The legend says that as he left Hamelin, still playing the pipe, the town's children followed him as the rats had done. "The Pied Piper of Hamelin," *Dramatic Lyrics* (1842)

19 Rats!
They fought the dogs and killed the cats,
And bit the babies in the cradles.
"The Pied Piper of Hamelin," *Dramatic Lyrics* (1842), st. 2

20 When at noon his paunch grew mutinous
For a plate of turtle green and glutinous.
"The Pied Piper of Hamelin," *Dramatic Lyrics* (1842), st. 4

21 Anything like the sound of a rat
Makes my heart go pit-a-pat!
"Come in!" the Mayor cried, looking bigger:
And in did come the strangest figure!
"The Pied Piper of Hamelin," *Dramatic Lyrics* (1842), st. 5

22 So munch on, crunch on, take your nuncheon,
Breakfast, supper, dinner, luncheon.
"The Pied Piper of Hamelin," *Dramatic Lyrics* (1842), st. 7

23 And after April, when May follows,
And the whitethroat builds, and all the swallows!
"Home-Thoughts, from Abroad," *Dramatic Romances and Lyrics* (1845)

24 Oh, to be in England!
Now that April's there.
"Home-Thoughts, from Abroad," *Dramatic Romances and Lyrics* (1845)

25 That's the wise thrush; he sings each song twice over,
Lest you should think he never could recapture
The first fine careless rapture!
"Home-Thoughts, from Abroad," *Dramatic Romances and Lyrics* (1845)

26 Ah, thought which saddens while it soothes!
"Pictor Ignotus," *Dramatic Romances and Lyrics* (1845)

27 I feel for the common chord again.
The C Major of this life.
"Abt Vogler," *Dramatis Personae* (1864), st. 12

28 Stung by the splendour of a sudden thought.
"A Death in the Desert," *Dramatis Personae* (1864), l. 59

29 Such ever was love's way; to rise, it stoops.
"A Death in the Desert," *Dramatis Personae* (1864), l. 134

30 It's wiser being good than bad;
It's safer being meek than fierce;
It's fitter being sane than mad.
My own hope is, a sun will pierce
The thickest cloud earth ever stretched;
That after Last returns the First,
Though a wide compass round be fetched;
That what began best can't end worst,
Nor what God blessed once prove accurst.
"Apparent Failure," *Dramatis Personae* (1864), st. 7

31 What is he buzzing in my ears?
"Now that I come to die,
Do I view the world as a vale of tears?"
Ah, reverend sir, not I!
"Confessions," *Dramatis Personae* (1864), st. 1

32 How sad and bad and mad it was!
But then, how it was sweet!
"Confessions," *Dramatis Personae* (1864), st. 9

33 Grow old along with me!
The best is yet to be,
The last of life, for which the first was made:
Our times are in His hand
Who saith, "A whole I planned,
Youth shows but half; trust God: see all, nor be afraid!"
"Rabbi Ben Ezra," *Dramatis Personae* (1864), st. 1

34 Therefore I summon age
To grant youth's heritage.
"Rabbi Ben Ezra," *Dramatis Personae* (1864), st. 13

35 Ten men love what I hate,
Shun what I follow, slight what I receive;
Ten, who in ears and eyes
Match me: we all surmise,
They this thing, and I that: whom shall my soul believe?
"Rabbi Ben Ezra," *Dramatis Personae* (1864), st. 22

36 Time's wheel runs back or stops: potter and clay endure.
"Rabbi Ben Ezra," *Dramatis Personae* (1864), st. 27

37 Let age approve of youth, and death complete the same!
"Rabbi Ben Ezra," *Dramatis Personae* (1864), st. 32

38 Good, to forgive;
Best, to forget!
Living, we fret;
Dying, we live.
La Saisiaz (1878), Prologue

39 Oppression makes the wise man mad.
Luria (1846), Act 4, Scene 16

40 A people is but the attempt of many
To rise to the completer life of one;
And those who live as models for the mass
Are singly of more value than they all.
Luria, A Tragedy (1846), Act 5, ll. 299–302, quoted in *The Poetical Works of Robert Browning* (1888–94)

41 So, I gave her eyes my own eyes to take,
My hand sought hers as in earnest need,
And round she turned for my noble sake,
And gave me herself indeed.
"A Light Woman," *Men and Women* (1855)

42 Tis an awkward thing to play with souls,
And matter enough to save one's own.
"A Light Woman," *Men and Women* (1855), st. 12

43 So free we seem, so fettered fast we are!
"Andrea del Sarto," *Men and Women* (1855)

44 Ah, but a man's reach should exceed his grasp,
Or what's a heaven for?
"Andrea del Sarto," *Men and Women* (1855), ll. 97–8

45 It all comes to the same thing at the end.
"Any Wife to Any Husband," *Men and Women* (1855), st. 16

46 What of soul was left, I wonder, when the kissing had to stop?
"A Toccata of Galuppi's," *Men and Women* (1855), st. 14

47 Best be yourself, imperial, plain and true!
"Bishop Blougram's Apology," *Men and Women* (1855)

48 We mortals cross the ocean of this world
Each in his average cabin of a life.
"Bishop Blougram's Apology," *Men and Women* (1855)

49 The grand Perhaps!
"Bishop Blougram's Apology," *Men and Women* (1855), l. 182

50 All we have gained then by our unbelief
Is a life of doubt diversified by faith,
For one of faith diversified by doubt:
We called the chess-board white—we call it black.
"Bishop Blougram's Apology," *Men and Women* (1855), ll. 209–12

51 How you'd exult if I could put you back
Six hundred years, blot out cosmogony,
Geology, ethnology, what not.
...
And set you square with Genesis again.
"Bishop Blougram's Apology," *Men and Women* (1855), from l. 678

52 No, when the fight begins within himself,
A man's worth something.
"Bishop Blougram's Apology," *Men and Women* (1855), ll. 693–4

53 He said true things, but called them by wrong names.
"Bishop Blougram's Apology," *Men and Women* (1855), l. 996

54 And I have written three books on the soul,
proving absurd all written hitherto,
And putting us to ignorance again.
"Cleon," *Men and Women* (1855), ll. 57–9

55 If you get simple beauty and nought else,
You get about the best thing God invents.
"Fra Lippo Lippi," *Men and Women* (1855), ll. 217–8

56 A man can have but one life and one death,
One heaven, one hell.
"In a Balcony," *Men and Women* (1855), ll. 13–4

57 Do I carry the moon in my pocket?
"Master Hugues of Saxe-Gotha," *Men and Women* (1855), st. 29

58 Suddenly, as rare things will, it vanished.
"One Word More," *Men and Women* (1855), st. 4

59 Dante, who loved well because he hated,
Hated wickedness that hinders loving.
Referring to Dante. "One Word More," *Men and Women* (1855), st. 5

60 Who knows but the world may end to-night?
"The Last Ride Together," *Men and Women* (1855), st. 2

61 It was roses, roses, all the way.
"The Patriot," *Men and Women* (1855), st. 1

62 Progress is
The law of life, man is not man as yet.
Paracelsus (1835)

63 PARACELSUS
I am he that aspired to KNOW: and thou?
APRILE
I would LOVE infinitely, and be loved!
Paracelsus (1835), pt. 2, ll. 384–5

64 God is the perfect poet,
Who in his person acts his own creations.
Paracelsus (1835), pt. 2, ll. 648–9

65 Measure your mind's height by the shade it casts!
Paracelsus (1835), pt. 3, l. 821

66 I give the fight up: let there be an end,
A privacy, an obscure nook for me
I want to be forgotten even by God.
Paracelsus (1835), pt. 5, ll. 363–5

67 All service ranks the same with God—
With God, whose puppets, best and worst,
Are we: there is no last or first.
Pippa Passes (1841), Epilogue

68 The year's at the spring,
And day's at the morn;
Morning's at seven;
The hill-side's dew-pearled;
The lark's on the wing;
The snail's on the thorn;
God's in His heaven—
All's right with the world.
Pippa Passes (1841), pt. 1, ll. 221–8

69 God must be glad one loves His world so much!
Pippa Passes (1841), pt. 3, l. 73

70 Any nose
May ravage with impunity a rose.
Sordello (1840), bk. 6, l. 881

71 But facts are facts and flinch not.
1868. *The Ring and the Book* (1868–69), bk. 2, l. 1049

72 'T was a thief said the last kind word to Christ:
Christ took the kindness and forgave the theft.
1869. *The Ring and the Book* (1868–69), bk. 6, ll. 869–70

73 Faultless to a fault.
1868. *The Ring and the Book* (1868–69), bk. 9, l. 1175

74 White shall not neutralize the black, nor good
Compensate bad in man, absolve him so:
Life's business being just the terrible choice.
1868. *The Ring and the Book* (1868–69), bk. 10, ll. 1235–7

75 There's a new tribunal now
Higher than God's – the educated man's!
1868. *The Ring and the Book* (1868–69), bk. 10, ll. 1975–6

Brownmiller, Susan (b.1935) U.S. journalist and writer

1 A ballerina must not be overly tall, or else she might tower over her male partner on pointe. Her breasts and hips cannot be large, for this would spoil the sylphlike illusion.
Femininity (1986)

2 The idealization of gender-related movement is romantically expressed in the pas de deux of classic ballet...A male dancer proudly exhibits his upper body strength for lifting, catching, and steadying his partner...A female dancer...an illusion of exquisite, unearthly fragility.
Femininity (1986)

Brubeck, Dave (David Warren Brubeck; b.1920) U.S. jazz pianist, composer, and bandleader

1 Jazz is about the only form of art existing today in which there is freedom of the individual without the loss of group contact.
Quoted in *The Jazz Book* (Joachim Berendt; 1982)

Bruce, Lenny (Leonard Alfred Schneider; 1925–66) U.S. comedian

1 Every day people are straying away from the church and going back to God. Really.
1960s. "Religions Inc.," quoted in *The Essential Lenny Bruce* (John Cohen, ed.; 1967)

2 It was one of those parties, got out of hand, you know.
Referring to the Crucifixion. *Guardian*, London (May 10, 1979)

3 I'm Super-Jew!
Jumping from a window, he got away with a broken leg. *Observer*, London (August 21, 1966)

4 In the Halls of Justice the only justice is in the halls.
Quoted in *The Cynic's Lexicon* (Jonathon Green, ed.; 1984)

5 But I'm not original. The only way I could say I was original is if I created the English language. I did, man, but they don't believe me.
1960? Quoted in *The Essential Lenny Bruce* (John Cohen, ed.; 1967)

6 In fact, when you really hate, what's the vernacular we use? "*Screw* you, mister!" If we were taught it was a sweet Christian act of procreation, it was the nicest thing we can do for each other, you'd use the term correctly and say, "*Un*screw you, mister."
1960? Quoted in *The Essential Lenny Bruce* (John Cohen, ed.; 1967)

7 I'll die young, but it's like kissing God.
Referring to his drug addiction. Attrib.

Brugha, Cathal (1874–1922) Irish politician

1 Don't you realize that, if you sign this thing, you will split Ireland from top to bottom?
Referring to the treaty establishing the Irish Free State, after which civil war did indeed follow. Comment to Eamon de Valera (December 1921), quoted in *Erskine Childers* (Jim Ring; 1996)

Brummell, "Beau" (George Bryan Brummell; 1778–1840) British dandy

1 No perfumes, but very fine linen, plenty of it, and country washing.
Memoirs (Harriette Wilson, ed.; 1825), vol. 1

2 Shut the door, Wales.
Said to the Prince of Wales. Attrib.

Brundtland, Gro Harlem (b.1939) Norwegian prime minister

1 There is resentment against the "minimum gender" rule. There are so many jobs. It is a question of power.
Referring to the minimum percentage of posts in the Norwegian government reserved for women. *Seattle Times* (May 14, 1989)

Bruno, Frank (Franklin Roy Bruno; b.1961) British boxer

1 Boxing's just showbusiness with blood.
Observer, London (December 29, 1991)

Bruno, Giordano (Filippo Bruno, "Il Nolano"; 1548?–1600) Italian philosopher and poet

1 Perhaps your fear in passing judgment is greater than mine in receiving it.
Said to the cardinals who excommunicated him. Attrib.

Bruyn, Severyn (Severyn Ten Haut Bruyn; b.1927) U.S. author

1 When local communities are losing their capacity for self reliance...small, democratic firms offer a spark of hope. They are seeding themselves slowly in the territories of nation-states to provide a new path towards a humanized economy.
Quoted in "A New Direction for Community Development in the United States," *Real-Life Economics* (Paul Ekins and Manfred Max-Neef, eds.; 1992)

2 While the oppressive conditions of feudalism led to a quest for freedom and individuality, the conditions of capitalism have led to a quest for community and social justice.
Quoted in "A New Direction for Community Development in the United States," *Real-Life Economics* (Paul Ekins and Manfred Max-Neef, eds.; 1992)

Bryan, Mary E. (1838–1913) U.S. writer

1 Women are learning that genius has no sex. How should a woman write? I answer, as men, as all should write to whom the power of expression has been given—honestly and without fear.
How Should Women Write? (1860)

Bryan, William Jennings ("The Great Commoner"; 1860–1925) U.S. politician and lawyer

Quotations about Bryan

1 With him, words take the place of actions. He thinks that to say something is to do something, which is an imperfect view of administration.
Henry Cabot Lodge (1850–1924) U.S. politician. Letter to Sturgis Bigelow (May 23, 1913)

2 His mind was like a soup dish, wide and shallow; it could hold a small amount of nearly anything, but the slightest jarring spilled the soup into somebody's lap.
Irving Stone (1903–89) U.S. novelist and playwright. *They Also Ran* (1945)

3 He is *absolutely* sincere. That is what makes him dangerous.
Woodrow Wilson (1856–1924) U.S. president. Attrib. *Defender of the Faith: William Jennings Bryan, the Last Decade, 1915–1925* (L. W. Levine; 1965)

Quotations by Bryan

4 There is no more reason to believe that man descended from some inferior animal than there is to believe that a stately mansion has descended from a small cottage.
Biology teacher John Scopes was prosecuted for violating Tennessee's Butler Act, which forbade the teaching of the theory of evolution in public schools because it contradicted the Biblical account of creation. Prosecution speech, trial of John Scopes, Dayton, Tennessee (July 28, 1925)

5 One miracle is just as easy to believe as another.
Said during the trial of John Scopes for teaching evolution in Tennessee. Remark (July 21, 1925)

6 The burning issue of imperialism growing out of the Spanish War involves the very existence of the Republic and the destruction of our free institutions.
Referring to the Spanish-American War (1898). Speech, Democratic National Convention (July 5, 1900)

7 The humblest citizen of all the land, when clad in the armor of a righteous cause, is stronger than all the hosts of error.
The First Battle: A Story of the Campaign of 1896 (1896), vol. 1, ch. 10

Bryant, William Cullen (1794–1878) U.S. poet and journalist

1 Loveliest of lovely things are they
On earth that soonest pass away.
The rose that lives its little hour
Is prized beyond the sculptured flower.
"A Scene on the Banks of the Hudson" (1828), st. 3

2 The hills,
Rock-ribbed, and ancient as the sun.
"Thanatopsis" (1817), l. 37

3 Go forth under the open sky, and list
To Nature's teachings.
"Thanatopsis" (1817), ll. 14–15

4 Truth crushed to earth shall rise again,
The eternal years of God are hers;
But Error, wounded, writhes with pain,
And dies among his worshippers.
"The Battle-Field" (1839), st. 9

5 The melancholy days are come, the saddest of the year,
Of wailing winds and naked woods and meadows brown and sear.
"The Death of the Flowers" (1832), st. 1

6 These are the gardens of the Desert, these
The unshorn fields, boundless and beautiful,
For which the speech of England has no name—
The Prairies.

"The Prairies," *Poems* (1834), quoted in *The Penguin Book of American Verse* (Geoffrey Moore, ed.; 1977)

7 To fling
Ossa upon Olympus, and to pile
Pelion with all its growth of leafy woods
On Ossa.

The Odyssey (1872), bk. 11

Bryce, James (1838–1922) British politician, jurist, and historian

1 Medicine...the only profession that labours incessantly to destroy the reason for its own existence.

Speech (March 23, 1914)

2 California, more than any other part of the Union, is a country by itself, and San Francisco a capital.

The American Commonwealth (1901)

3 There is a hearty Puritanism in the view of human nature which pervades the instrument of 1787. It is the work of men who believed in original sin, and were determined to leave open for transgressors no door which they could possibly shut.

Referring to the U.S. Constitution. *The American Commonwealth* (1901)

Bryson, Bill (William Bryson; b.1951) U.S. writer

1 It sometimes occurs to me that the British have more heritage than is good for them.

Notes From a Small Island (1995)

2 Here are instructions for being a pigeon: 1. Walk around aimlessly for a while, pecking at cigarette butts and other inappropriate items. 2. Take fright at someone walking along the platform and fly off to a girder. 3. Have a shit. 4. Repeat.

Notes From a Small Island (1995), ch. 10

3 I have a small, tattered clipping that I sometimes carry with me and pull out for purposes of private amusement. It's a weather forecast from the *Western Daily Mail* and it says, in toto: "Outlook: Dry and warm, but cooler with some rain."

Referring to his experiences in Britain. *Notes From a Small Island* (1995), ch. 23

4 Here is a country that fought and won a noble war, dismantled a mighty empire in a generally benign and enlightened way, created a far-seeing welfare state—in short, did nearly everything right—and then spent the rest of the century looking on itself as a dismal failure.

Referring to his experiences in Britain. *Notes From a Small Island* (1995), ch. 29

5 I come from Des Moines. Somebody had to.

Opening words. *The Lost Continent* (1989)

6 My mother only ever said two things. She said, "I don't know, dear." And she said, "Can I get you a sandwich, honey?"

The Lost Continent (1989), ch. 1

7 Stand on two phone books almost anywhere in Iowa and you get a view.

The Lost Continent (1989), ch. 2

8 There are three things you just can't do in life. You can't beat the phone company, you can't make a waiter see you until he is ready to see you, and you can't go home again.

The Lost Continent (1989), ch. 2

9 I mused for a few moments on the question of which was worse, to lead a life so boring that you are easily enchanted or a life so full of stimulus that you are easily bored.

The Lost Continent (1989), ch. 4

10 It struck me as notably ironic that Southerners could despise blacks so bitterly and yet live comfortably alongside them, while in the North people by and large did not mind blacks, even respected them as humans and wished them every success, just so long as they didn't have to mingle with them too freely.

The Lost Continent (1989), ch. 6

11 The people named the town after Oxford in England in the hope that this would persuade the state to build the university there, and the state did. This tells you most of what you need to know about the workings of the Southern mind.

Referring to Oxford, Mississippi. *The Lost Continent* (1989), ch. 6

12 Have you ever watched an infant at play and said to yourself, "I wonder what goes on in his little head?" Well, watch *Grand Ole Opry* for five minutes sometime and you will begin to have an idea.

The Lost Continent (1989), ch. 9

13 I had read so much for so long about murders and street crime that I felt a personal gratitude to anyone who left me alone. I wanted to hand out cards that said, "Thank you for not killing me."

The Lost Continent (1989), ch. 14

14 People in New York go to Calcutta to get some relief from begging.

The Lost Continent (1989), ch. 14

15 Michigan is shaped like an oven mitt and is often about as exciting.

The Lost Continent (1989), ch. 18

16 I was headed for Nebraska. Now there's a sentence you don't want to have to say too often if you can possibly help it.

The Lost Continent (1989), ch. 20

Brzezinski, Zbigniew (b.1928) Polish-born U.S. political scientist and politician

1 The notion that our only strategic choice is MAD—mutually assured destruction—which means nothing less than an unstable pact to commit instant and total mutual suicide in the event of war—is irrational, immoral, and unnecessary.

"Entering the Age of Defense," *Washington Post* (October 2, 1988)

Buber, Martin (1878–1965) Austrian-born Israeli philosopher of religion and Zionist

1 All men, somewhere, in some loneliness of their pain or of their thought, come close to God; there is no invulnerable heathen.

1923. Quoted in *On Judaism* (N. H. Glazer, ed., Eva Jose et al., trs.; 1967)

2 For Judaism, God is not a Kantian idea but an elementally

present spiritual reality—neither something conceived by pure reason nor something postulated by practical reason, but emanating from the immediacy of existence as such.
1923. Quoted in *On Judaism* (N. H. Glazer, ed., Eva Jose et al., trs.; 1967)

3 For the Jew of antiquity, the world is not divided. Nor is man divided; he is, rather, separated; he has fallen, he has become inadequate and unlike God.
1923. Quoted in *On Judaism* (N. H. Glazer, ed., Eva Jose et al., trs.; 1967)

4 God does not want to be believed in, to be debated and defended by us, but simply to be realized through us.
1923. Quoted in *On Judaism* (N. H. Glazer, ed., Eva Jose et al., trs.; 1967)

5 If there were no religious reality, if God were only a fiction, it would be mankind's duty to demolish it.
1923. Quoted in *On Judaism* (N. H. Glazer, ed., Eva Jose et al., trs.; 1967)

6 If the Spirit of Israel is no more to us than the synthetic personality of our nation...then we are indeed like unto all the nations; and we are drinking together with them from the cup that inebriates.
1923. Quoted in *On Judaism* (N. H. Glazer, ed., Eva Jose et al., trs.; 1967)

7 It is this striving for unity that makes Judaism a phenomenon of mankind, that transforms the Jewish question into a human question.
1923. Quoted in *On Judaism* (N. H. Glazer, ed., Eva Jose et al., trs.; 1967)

8 Messianism is Judaism's most profoundly original idea.
1923. Quoted in *On Judaism* (N. H. Glazer, ed., Eva Jose et al., trs.; 1967)

9 My soul is not by the side of my people; my people *is* my soul.
1923. Quoted in *On Judaism* (N. H. Glazer, ed., Eva Jose et al., trs.; 1967)

10 Socialism is a diminution, a narrowing, a finitizing of the Messianic ideal.
1923. Quoted in *On Judaism* (N. H. Glazer, ed., Eva Jose et al., trs.; 1967)

11 The Jew is the most obvious antithesis of the Greek. The Greek wants to master the world, the Jew to perfect it. For the Greek the world exists; for the Jew, it becomes. The Greek confronts it, the Jew is involved with it.
1923. Quoted in *On Judaism* (N. H. Glazer, ed., Eva Jose et al., trs.; 1967)

12 The Jew...sees the forest more truly than the trees, the sea more truly than the wave, the community more truly than the individual.
1923. Quoted in *On Judaism* (N. H. Glazer, ed., Eva Jose et al., trs.; 1967)

13 The Jews were...the mythless people, and as such were either glorified or held in contempt.
1923. Quoted in *On Judaism* (N. H. Glazer, ed., Eva Jose et al., trs.; 1967)

14 There is religious reality, and...it has become manifest in and through Judaism; in fact, Judaism exists for the sake of this reality.
1923. Quoted in *On Judaism* (N. H. Glazer, ed., Eva Jose et al., trs.; 1967)

15 This knowledge...—that the world is a devastated house that must be restored for the spirit; and that so long as this remains unaccomplished, the spirit has no dwelling place—is Jesus' most deep-seated Judaism.
1923. Quoted in *On Judaism* (N. H. Glazer, ed., Eva Jose et al., trs.; 1967)

16 We Jews need to know that our being and our character have been formed not solely by the nature of our fathers but also by their fate, and by their pain, their misery, and their humiliation.
1923. Quoted in *On Judaism* (N. H. Glazer, ed., Eva Jose et al., trs.; 1967)

Buchanan, James (1791–1868) U.S. president

1 If you are as happy, my dear sir, on entering this house as I am in leaving it and returning home, you are the happiest man in the country.
Referring to his departure from the White House at the end of his presidency, and the arrival of his successor, Abraham Lincoln. Remark to Abraham Lincoln (March 4, 1861)

Buchanan, Robert Williams (1841–1901) British poet, novelist, and playwright

1 She just wore
Enough for modesty—no more.
"White Rose and Red" (1873), pt. 1, sect. 5, l. 60

2 The Fleshly School of Poetry.
Referring to Algernon Charles Swinburne, William Morris, Dante Gabriel Rossetti, and others. *Contemporary Review* (October 1871)

Büchner, Georg (Karl Georg Büchner; 1813–37) German dramatist

1 The revolution is like Saturn, it devours its own children.
Referring to the French Revolution (1789–99). *Danton's Death* (1835), Act 1, Scene 5, quoted in *Complete Plays, Lenz and Other Writings* (John Reddick, tr.; 1993)

2 We didn't make the revolution, the revolution made us.
Referring to the French Revolution (1789–99). *Danton's Death* (1835), Act 2, Scene 1, quoted in *Complete Plays, Lenz and Other Writings* (John Reddick, tr.; 1993)

3 Can you take your country with you on the soles of your shoes?
Danton's Death (1835), Act 3, Scene 1, quoted in *Complete Plays, Lenz and Other Writings* (John Reddick, tr.; 1993)

4 That is the rock of atheism. The tiniest spasm of pain, be it in a single atom, and divine creation is utterly torn asunder.
Danton's Death (1835), Act 3, Scene 1, quoted in *Complete Plays, Lenz and Other Writings* (John Reddick, tr.; 1993)

5 It frightens me when I think about the world—when I think about eternity. Busyness, Woyzeck, busyness! That's the eternal, that is eternal, that's eternal. That you can understand.
1836. *Woyzeck* (1879), Scene 1

6 Every man's a chasm. It makes you dizzy when you look down it.
1836. *Woyzeck* (1879), Scene 10

7 The world is out of order!
1836. *Woyzeck* (1879), Scene 12

8 Except for Shakespeare, all writers are made to look like schoolboys by history and nature.
February 21, 1835. Quoted in *Complete Plays, Lenz and Other Writings* (John Reddick, tr.; 1993)

9 I believe that in social matters one must start from an absolute principle of *justice*, seek the development of a new life and spirit in the *people*, and let the decrepit society of today go to the devil.
1836. Quoted in *Complete Plays, Lenz and Other Writings* (John Reddick, tr.; 1993)

10 If we could only imagine that the holes in our trousers were palace windows, we could live like kings; as it is, we're miserably cold.
1835. Quoted in *Complete Plays, Lenz and Other Writings* (John Reddick, tr.; 1993)

11 The relation between the poor and the rich is the only revolutionary element in the world.
1835. Quoted in *Complete Plays, Lenz and Other Writings* (John Reddick, tr.; 1993)

12 What is it in man that lies, murders, steals?
1834. Quoted in *Complete Plays, Lenz and Other Writings* (John Reddick, tr.; 1993)

Buchwald, Art (b.1925) U.S. humorist

1 An economist is a man who knows 100 ways of making love but doesn't know any women.
Attrib.

Buck, Pearl (1892–1973) U.S. novelist

1 In this unbelievable universe in which we live there are no absolutes. Even parallel lines, reaching into infinity, meet somewhere yonder.
A Bridge for Passing (1962)

2 The American woman, when she is an unmarried mother, simply disappears for a while from her community and then comes back, childless, her secret hidden for life.
Children for Adoption (1964), ch. 1

3 Nothing and no one can destroy the Chinese people. They are relentless survivors. They are the oldest civilized people on earth. Their civilization passes through phases but its basic characteristics remain the same. They yield, they bend to the wind, but they never break.
China, Past and Present (1972), ch. 1

4 Ah well, perhaps one has to be very old before one learns how to be amused rather than shocked.
China, Past and Present (1972), ch. 6

5 I feel no need for any other faith than my faith in human beings.
I Believe (1939)

6 Euthanasia is a long, smooth-sounding word, and it conceals its danger as long, smooth words do, but the danger is there, nevertheless.
The Child Who Never Grew (1950), ch. 2

7 No one really understood music unless he was a scientist, her father had declared, and not just a scientist, either, oh, no, only the real ones, the theoreticians, whose language was mathematics.
The Goddess Abides (1972), pt. I

8 It is better to be first with an ugly woman than the hundredth with a beauty.
The Good Earth (1931), ch. 1

9 It takes a brave man to face a brave woman, and man's fear of women's creative energy has never found expression more clear than in the old German clamor, renewed by the Nazis, of "Kinder, Küche und Kirche" for women.
To My Daughters with Love (1967)

Buckingham, Duke of (George Villiers; 1628–87) English statesman

1 The world is made up for the most part of fools and knaves, both irreconcilable foes to truth.
"To Mr Clifford On His Humane Reason" (Dramatic Works; 1715), vol. 2

2 Ay, now the plot thickens very much upon us.
The Rehearsal (1671), Act 2, Scene 2

Buckle, Henry Thomas (1821–62) British historian

1 Among the arts, medicine, on account of its eminent utility, must always hold the highest place.
Miscellaneous and Posthumous Works (Helen Taylor, ed.; 1872), vol. 2

Buckle, Richard (b.1916) British ballet critic

1 She paints all the shyness, doubts and delicate hesitations of first love...Her dancing is exquisite: her feet are as precise as pens, yet delicate as feathers.
Referring to Galina Ulanova. Quoted in "Glory in the Garden," *Guardian*, London (Mary Clarke; March 23, 1998), obituary of Galina Ulanova

Buckley, William F., Jr. (William Frank Buckley, Jr.; b.1925) U.S. writer

1 The most casual student of history knows that, as a matter of fact, truth does *not* necessarily vanquish...The cause of truth must be championed, and it must be championed dynamically.
God and Man at Yale (1951)

Buddha (Gautama Siddhartha; 563?–483? B.C.) Nepalese-born founder of Buddhism

1 All things, oh priests, are on fire...The eye is on fire; forms are on fire; eye-consciousness is on fire; impressions received by the eye are on fire.
The Fire Sermon (528? B.C.)

2 I do not fight with the world but the world fights with me.
Quoted in *Buddhism* (Edward Conze; 1951)

3 I have never yet met with anything that was dearer to anyone than his own self. Since to others, to each one for himself, the self is dear, therefore let him who desires his own advantage not harm another.
Quoted in *Buddhism* (Edward Conze; 1951)

4 This Aryan Eightfold Path, that is to say: Right view, right aim, right speech, right action, right living, right effort, right mindfulness, right contemplation.
5th century B.C. Quoted in *Some Sayings of the Buddha* (F. L. Woodward, ed.; 1974)

5 Ye must leave righteous ways behind, not to speak of unrighteous ways.
5th century B.C. Quoted in *Some Sayings of the Buddha* (F. L. Woodward, ed.; 1974)

Budgell, Eustace (1686–1737) English writer

1 What Cato did, and Addison approved
Cannot be wrong.
May 4, 1737. Lines found on his desk after his suicide. Quoted in "Life of Eustace Budgell," *Lives of the Poets* (Colley Cibber; 1753), vol. 5

Buffalo Bill (William Frederick Cody; 1846–1917) U.S. guide, scout, and showman

1 True to friend and foe.
Quoted by the announcer prior to Buffalo Bill's entrance in his touring Wild West Show (1883–1901). Personal motto (1883), quoted in *American Heritage Dictionary of American Quotations* (Margaret Miner and Hugh Rawson, eds.; 1997)

Buffett, Warren (Warren Edward Buffett; b.1930) U.S. financier

1 Buy stocks like you buy your groceries, not like you buy your perfume.
Fortune (March 9, 1992)

2 Wall Street is the only place people ride to in a Rolls-Royce to get advice from people who take the subway.
New York Newsday (August 25, 1991)

3 At too many companies, the boss shoots the arrow of managerial performance, and then hastily paints the bullseye around the spot where it lands.
Shareholder (June 1989)

4 A public-opinion poll is no substitute for thought.
"Noteworthy Quotes," *Strategy and Business* (1998)

5 I don't look to jump over 7-foot bars: I look around for 1-foot bars that I can step over.
Attrib.

6 It takes 20 years to build a reputation and five minutes to ruin it. If you think about that, you'll do things differently.
Attrib.

Buffon, Comte de (George-Louis Leclerc; 1707–88) French naturalist

1 Style is the man himself.
Speech given on his reception to the French Academy. "Discourse on Style" (August 25, 1753)

2 Genius is only a greater aptitude for patience.
Quoted in *Voyage à Montbar* (Herault de Sechelles; 1803)

Bugs Bunny U.S. cartoon character

1 What's up, Doc?
Used in "Bugs Bunny" cartoons (1937–63).

Bukovsky, Vladimir (b.1942) Russian writer and scientist

1 The pessimist is the man who believes things couldn't possibly be worse, to which the optimist replies "Oh yes they could."
Guardian Weekly, London (July 10, 1977)

2 Whether he wants it or not, a Soviet citizen is in a state of permanent inner dialogue with the official propaganda.
Attrib.

Bukowski, Charles (1920–94) German-born U.S. writer

1 If you have the ability to love
love yourself first
but always be aware of the possibility of
total defeat
whether the reason for that defeat
seems right or wrong.
"How To Be a Great Writer," *Love is Dog from Hell* (1977)

2 Almost everyone is born a genius and buried an idiot.
Notes of a Dirty Old Man (1969)

3 An intellectual is a man who says a simple thing in a difficult way; an artist is a man who says a difficult thing in a simple way.
Notes of a Dirty Old Man (1969)

4 Beautiful thoughts, and beautiful women never last.
Notes of a Dirty Old Man (1969)

5 If you want to know where God is, ask a drunk.
Notes of a Dirty Old Man (1969)

6 If you want to know who your friends are, get yourself a jail sentence.
Notes of a Dirty Old Man (1969)

7 The difference between art and life is that art is more bearable.
Notes of a Dirty Old Man (1969)

8 There is nothing as boring as the truth.
Notes of a Dirty Old Man (1969)

9 We have wasted History like a bunch of drunks shooting dice back in the men's crapper of the local bar.
Notes of a Dirty Old Man (1969)

10 Yeah sure, I'll be in unless I'm out.
"don't come round but if you do...," *The Penguin Book of American Verse* (Geoffrey Moore, ed.; 1977)

Bulgakov, Mikhail (Mikhail Afanasievich Bulgakov; 1891–1940) Russian novelist and playwright

Quotations about Bulgakov

1 You lived aloof, maintaining to the end
your magnificent disdain.
Anna Akhmatova (1888–1966) Russian poet. "In Memory of M. B." (Stanley Kunitz and Max Hayward, trs.; 1940), quoted in *Anna Akhmatova: Selected Poems* (Stanley Kunitz and Max Hayward, trs.; 1973)

2 No, don't suppress. What shall we get by suppression? That such literature will be distributed around the corner and read with such satisfaction, as I have a couple of hundred times read in manuscript form poems by Yesenin.
Vladimir Mayakovsky (1893–1930) Russian poet and playwright. Referring to the proposed suppression of Mikhail Bulgakov's play based on his novel, *The White Guard* (1925), and also Sergey Yesenin. Speech at discussion on "Theatre Politics of the Soviet Government" (October 2, 1926), quoted in *Mayakovsky* (H. Marshall, ed., tr.; 1965), introduction

Quotations by Bulgakov

3 ANY SATIRIST IN THE SOVIET UNION MUST QUESTION THE SOVIET SYSTEM.
Am I conceivable in the USSR?
Letter to the USSR government (March 28, 1930), quoted in *The KGB's Literary Archive* (John Crowfoot, ed., tr.; 1993), ch. 3

4 Love leaped out at us like a murderer jumping out of a dark alley. It shocked us both—the shock of a stroke of lightning, the shock of a flick-knife.
1929–40. *The Master and Margarita* (Michael Glenny, tr.; 1966), ch. 1

5 "And the devil doesn't exist either, I suppose?"
1929–40. Said by the Devil to one who has denied the historical existence of Jesus. *The Master and Margarita* (Michael Glenny, tr.; 1966), ch. 3

6 The third member of the company was a cat the size of a pig, black as soot and with luxuriant cavalry officer's whiskers.
1929–40. Description of Behemoth, the Devil's cat. *The Master and Margarita* (Michael Glenny, tr.; 1966), ch. 4

7 Who told you there was no such thing as real, true, eternal love? Cut out his lying tongue!
1929–40. *The Master and Margarita* (Michael Glenny, tr.; 1966), ch. 19

8 Forgive me and forget me as soon as you can. I am leaving you forever. Don't look for me, it will be useless. Misery and unhappiness have turned me into a witch. It is time for me to go.
1929–40. Margarita's farewell note to her husband. *The Master and Margarita* (Michael Glenny, tr.; 1966), ch. 20

9 I was speaking of compassion...Sometimes it creeps in through the narrowest cracks. That is why I suggested using rags to block them up.
1929–40. *The Master and Margarita* (Michael Glenny, tr.; 1966), ch. 24

10 Manuscripts don't burn.
1929–40. *The Master and Margarita* (Michael Glenny, tr.; 1966), ch. 24

11 Remove the document—and you remove the man.
1929–40. *The Master and Margarita* (Michael Glenny, tr.; 1966), ch. 24

12 The stars will still remain when the shadows of our presence and our deeds have vanished from the earth. There is no man who does not know that. Why, then, will we not turn our eyes towards the stars? Why?
The last words of the novel. *The White Guard* (Michael Glenny, tr.; 1925)

13 Great and terrible was the year of Our Lord 1918, of the Revolution the second.
The opening sentence of the novel. *The White Guard* (Michael Glenny, tr.; 1925)

Buller, Arthur Henry Reginald (1874–1944) British botanist and mycologist

1 There was a young lady named Bright,
Whose speed was far faster than light;
She set out one day
In a relative way,
And returned home the previous night.
"Relativity," *Punch*, London (December 19, 1923)

Bullock, Alan (Alan Louis Charles Bullock; b.1914) British academic and historian

1 The people Hitler never understood, and whose actions continued to exasperate him to the end of his life, were the British.
Hitler, A Study in Tyranny (1952), ch. 8

2 Hitler showed surprising loyalty to Mussolini, but it never extended to trusting him.
Hitler, A Study in Tyranny (1952), ch. 11

Bulmer-Thomas, Ivor (1905–93) British writer and politician

1 If ever he went to school without any boots it was because he was too big for them.
Referring to Harold Wilson. Conservative Party Conference (1949)

Bülow, Bernhard von, Prince (Bernhard Heinrich von Bülow; 1849–1929) German statesman

1 In a word, we desire to throw no one into the shade, but we also demand our own place in the sun.
1897. Referring to Germany's Far East ambitions. Speech to the Reichstag (December 6, 1897)

Bunch, Charlotte (b.1944) U.S. editor

1 Feminism is an entire world view or gestalt, not just a laundry list of "women's issues."
New Directions for Women (September 1981)

Bunin, Ivan (Ivan Alekseyevich Bunin; 1870–1953) Russian novelist and poet

1 Does it really matter whose story this is? Every creature on earth deserves to have its story told.
"Chang's Dreams" (Sophie Lund, tr.; 1916)

Bunner, Henry Cuyler (1855–96) U.S. writer

1 The Doctor fared even better. The fame of his new case spread far and wide. People seemed to think that if he could cure an elephant he could cure anything.
"The Infidelity of Zenobia," *Short Sixes* (1891)

Bunting, Basil (1900–85) British poet

1 Brag, sweet tenor bull,
descant on Rawthey's madrigal,
each pebble its part
for the fells' late spring.
Briggflatts (1966), ll. 1–4

Buñuel, Luis (1900–83) Spanish film director

Quotations about Buñuel

1 When Buñuel was casting *Viridiana* he wanted me: "I saw him as a corpse in a film and he was wonderful." So Buñuellian!
Fernando Rey (1915–94) Spanish film actor. *Knave* (August 1986), quoted in *Chambers Film Quotes* (Tony Crawley, ed.; 1991)

Quotations by Buñuel

2 Shooting is really a bore. What is important is the writing of the script and the editing of the footage...Images come to me spontaneously, sometimes completely unrelated to the story line, and I incorporate them into the script. Then I follow my screenplay practically without deviating from it.
Interview, *Action* (November–December 1974), quoted in *Film-makers Speak* (Jay Leyda, ed.; 1977)

3 I have a horror of posed shots, and I detest unusual angles. Sometimes I work out with my cameraman what we think is a superbly clever perspective...and then when the time comes for

shooting, we...throw the whole plan out, and simply shoot with no special camera effects.
Interview, *Arts* (July 21, 1955), quoted in *Film-makers Speak* (Jay Leyda, ed.; 1977)

4 I am an atheist still, thank God.
Le Monde (December 16, 1959)

5 If alcohol is Queen, then tobacco is her consort. It's a fond companion for all occasions, a loyal friend through fair weather and foul.
My Last Breath (1983)

6 Nothing would disgust me more morally than winning an Oscar.
Variety (1971), quoted in *Chambers Film Quotes* (Tony Crawley, ed.; 1991)

Bunyan, John (1628–88) English preacher and writer

Quotations about Bunyan

1 Was there ever yet anything written by mere man that was wished longer by its readers, excepting *Don Quixote*, *Robinson Crusoe*, and the *Pilgrim's Progress*?
Samuel Johnson (1709–84) British lexicographer and writer. Quoted in *Anecdotes of the Late Samuel Johnson* (Hester Lynch Piozzi; 1786)

2 My word, Bunyan, you're a lucky fellow. You've got a window out of which you can look, see the sky, and here I am in a dark room.
1991
Terry Waite (b.1939) British religious adviser. Writing about his experiences in captivity. *Times*, London (November 21, 1991)

Quotations by Bunyan

3 I could also have stepped into a style much higher than this... but I dare not. God did not play in convincing of me...neither did I play...when the pangs of hell caught hold upon me; wherefore I may not play...but be plain and simple, and lay down the thing as it was.
Referring to literary style. *Grace Abounding to the Chief of Sinners* (1666), Preface

4 A castle called Doubting Castle, the owner whereof was Giant Despair.
The Pilgrim's Progress (1678), pt. 1

5 A very stately palace before him, the name of which was Beautiful.
The Pilgrim's Progress (1678), pt. 1

6 Dark as pitch.
The Pilgrim's Progress (1678), pt. 1

7 Hanging is too good for him, said Mr. Cruelty.
The Pilgrim's Progress (1678), pt. 1

8 It beareth the name of Vanity Fair, because the town where 'tis kept is lighter than vanity.
The Pilgrim's Progress (1678), pt. 1

9 Now Giant Despair had a wife, and her name was Diffidence.
The Pilgrim's Progress (1678), pt. 1

10 So I awoke, and behold it was a dream.
The Pilgrim's Progress (1678), pt. 1

11 Some said, "John, print it;" others said, "Not so."
Some said, "It might do good;" others said, "No."
The Pilgrim's Progress (1678), pt. 1

12 So soon as the man overtook me, he was but a word and a blow.
The Pilgrim's Progress (1678), pt. 1

13 The name of the slough was Despond.
The Pilgrim's Progress (1678), pt. 1

14 As I walked through the wilderness of this world.
Opening words. *The Pilgrim's Progress* (1678), pt. 1

15 A man that could look no way but downwards, with a muckrake in his hand.
The Pilgrim's Progress (1684), pt. 2

16 A man there was, tho' some did count him mad,
The more he cast away, the more he had.
The Pilgrim's Progress (1684), pt. 2

17 An ornament to her profession.
The Pilgrim's Progress (1684), pt. 2

18 A very zealous man.... difficulties, lions, or Vanity-Fair he feared not at all; 'Twas only Sin, Death, and Hell that was to him a terror.
The Pilgrim's Progress (1684), pt. 2

19 One leak will sink a ship, and one sin will destroy a sinner.
The Pilgrim's Progress (1684), pt. 2

20 Some things are of that nature as to make
One's fancy chuckle, while his heart doth ache.
The Pilgrim's Progress (1684), pt. 2

21 Who so beset him round
With dismal stories,
Do but themselves confound
His strength the more is.
The Pilgrim's Progress (1684), pt. 2

22 Who would true valour see,
Let him come hither;
One here will constant be,
Come wind, come weather
There's no discouragement
Shall make him once relent
His first avow'd intent
To be a pilgrim.
The Pilgrim's Progress (1684), pt. 2

23 I have formerly lived by hearsay, and faith, but now I go where I shall live by sight, and shall be with Him in whose company I delight myself.
Referring to Mr. Standfast. *The Pilgrim's Progress* (1684), pt. 2

24 He that is down needs fear no fall;
He that is low, no pride.
Shepherd boy's song. *The Pilgrim's Progress* (1684), pt. 2

25 I do not repent me of all the trouble I have been at to arrive where I am. My sword, I give to him that shall succeed me...My marks and scars I carry with me, to be a witness for me, that I have ... fought His battles, who will now be my rewarder. So he passed over.
The death of Mr. Valiant-for-Truth. *The Pilgrim's Progress* (1684), pt. 2

Burbank, Luther (1849–1926) U.S. botanist

1 As a scientist, I cannot help feeling that all religions are on a tottering foundation. None is perfect or inspired.
"I'm an Infidel, Declares Burbank, Casting Doubt on Soul Immortality Theory," *San Francisco Bulletin* (January 22, 1926)

2 I do not believe what has been served to me to believe. I am a doubter, a questioner, a skeptic. When it can be proved to me that there is immortality, that there is resurrection beyond the gates of death, then will I believe. Until then, no.
"I'm an Infidel, Declares Burbank, Casting Doubt on Soul Immortality Theory," *San Francisco Bulletin* (January 22, 1926)

3 I believe in the immortality of influence.
The Harvest of the Years (co-written with Wilbur Hale; 1927)

4 Science...has opened our eyes to the vastness of the universe and given us light, truth, and freedom from fear where once was darkness, ignorance, and superstition.
The Harvest of the Years (co-written with Wilbur Hale; 1927)

5 Science, unlike theology, never leads to insanity.
The Harvest of the Years (co-written with Wilbur Hale; 1927)

6 The clear light of science teaches us that we must be our own saviors, if we are to be found worth saving.
The Harvest of the Years (co-written with Wilbur Hale; 1927)

7 The scientist is a lover of truth for the very love of truth itself, wherever it may lead.
The Harvest of the Years (co-written with Wilbur Hale; 1927)

Burchard, Samuel Dickinson (1812–91) U.S. Presbyterian minister and politician

1 We are Republicans and don't propose to leave our party and identify ourselves with the party whose antecedents are rum, Romanism, and rebellion.
Addressing a meeting with James Blaine, Republican nominee in the 1884 presidential election. Speech, New York City (October 1884)

Burchfield, Robert (Robert William Burchfield; b.1923) New Zealand-born British lexicographer and scholar

1 To finish is both a relief and a release from an extraordinarily pleasant prison.
On completing the supplements to the Oxford English Dictionary. *Observer,* London (September 11, 1986), "Sayings of the Week"

Buren, Daniel (b.1938) French painter

1 In art, banality soon becomes extraordinary. The instances are numerous.
Quoted in "Beware," *Conceptual Art* (Ursula Meyer; 1972)

Bürger, Gottfried August (1747–94) German poet

1 An emperor's word may no man wrest, nor garble.
Die Weiber von Weinsberg (1774), st. 11

Burgess, Anthony (John Anthony Burgess Wilson; 1917–93) British writer and critic

1 Do they merit vitriol, even a drop of it? Yes, because they corrupt the young, persuading them that the mature world, which produced Beethoven and Schweitzer, sets an even higher value on the transient anodynes of youth than does youth itself...They are the Hollow Men. They are electronic lice.
Referring to disc jockeys. *Punch*, London (September 20, 1967)

2 A perverse nature can be stimulated by anything. Any book can be used as a pornographic instrument, even a great work of literature if the mind that so uses it is off-balance. I once found a small boy masturbating in the presence of the Victorian steel-engraving in a family Bible.
A Clockwork Orange (1962)

3 Not a future. At least not in Europe. America's different, of course, but America's really only a kind of Russia. You've no idea how pleasant it is not to have any future. It's like having a totally efficient contraceptive.
Honey for the Bears (1963), pt. 2, ch. 6

4 Bath twice a day to be really clean, once a day to be passably clean, once a week to avoid being a public menace.
Inside Mr. Enderby (1963)

5 He said it was artificial respiration but now I find I'm to have his child.
Inside Mr. Enderby (1963)

6 Laugh and the world laughs with you; snore and you sleep alone.
Inside Mr. Enderby (1963)

7 The possession of a book becomes a substitute for reading it.
New York Times Book Review (1966)

8 Without class differences, England would cease to be the living theatre it is.
Observer, London (May 26, 1985), "Sayings of the Week"

9 Death comes along like a gas bill one can't pay.
Interview, *Playboy Magazine* (September 1974)

Burgess, Gelett (Frank Gelett Burgess; 1866–1951) U.S. humorist

1 Ah, yes, I wrote the "Purple Cow"—
I'm sorry, now, I wrote it!
But I can tell you, anyhow,
I'll kill you if you quote it.
"Cinq Ans Après" (1914)

2 I never saw a purple cow,
I never hope to see one;
But I can tell you, anyhow,
I'd rather see than be one.
"The Purple Cow" (1895)

Burgoyne, John, Sir (1722–92) British general and playwright

1 After a fatal procrastination...we took a step as decisive as the passage of the Rubicon, and now find ourselves plunged at once in a most serious war without a single requisition, gunpowder excepted, for carrying it on.
Said after the Battle of Lexington, the first military clash in the American Revolution. Letter from Boston (April 1775)

Burke, Billie (1886–1970) U.S. actor

1 To survive there, you need the ambition of a Latin-American

revolutionary, the ego of a grand opera tenor, and the physical stamina of a cow pony.
Referring to Hollywood. Quoted in *Filmgoer's Book of Quotes* (Leslie Halliwell; 1973)

Burke, Edmund (1729–97) Irish-born British statesman and political philosopher

Quotations about Burke

1 Burke said that there were Three Estates in Parliament; but, in the Reporters' Gallery yonder, there sat a *Fourth Estate*, more important far than they all.
Thomas Carlyle (1795–1881) Scottish historian and essayist. "The Hero as Man of Letters," *On Heroes, Hero-Worship, and the Heroic in History* (1841)

2 If a man were to go by chance at the same time with Burke under a shed, to shun a shower, he would say "this is an extraordinary man".
May 15, 1784
Samuel Johnson (1709–84) British lexicographer and writer. *Life of Samuel Johnson* (James Boswell; 1791)

Quotations by Burke

3 To innovate is not to reform.
Letter to a Noble Lord (1796)

4 The king, and his faithful subjects, the lords and commons of this realm, the triple cord, which no man can break.
Referring to the House of Lords and the House of Commons (the upper and lower houses of the British Parliament). Letter to a Noble Lord (1796)

5 People crushed by law have no hopes but from power. If laws are their enemies, they will be enemies to laws; and those, who have much to hope and nothing to lose, will always be dangerous, more or less.
Letter to Charles James Fox (October 8, 1777)

6 The arrogance of age must submit to be taught by youth.
Letter to Fanny Burney (July 29, 1782)

7 Between craft and credulity, the voice of reason is stifled.
Letter to the Sheriffs of Bristol (1777)

8 If any ask me what a free government is, I answer, that for any practical purpose, it is what the people think so. Liberty, too, must be limited in order to be possessed.
Letter to the Sheriffs of Bristol (1777)

9 I know many have been taught to think that moderation, in a case like this, is a sort of treason.
Letter to the Sheriffs of Bristol (1777)

10 Nothing in progression can rest on its original plan. We may as well think of rocking a grown man in the cradle of an infant.
Letter to the Sheriffs of Bristol (1777)

11 Nothing is so fatal to religion as indifference, which is, at least, half infidelity.
Letter to William Smith (January 29, 1795)

12 Somebody had said, that a king may make a nobleman, but he cannot make a gentleman.
Letter to William Smith (January 29, 1795)

13 It is a general popular error to imagine the loudest complainers for the public to be the most anxious for its welfare.
"Observations on a Publication, 'The Present State of the Nation'" (1793)

14 There is a limit at which forbearance ceases to be a virtue.
"Observations on a Publication, 'The Present State of the Nation'" (1793)

15 Individuals pass like shadows; but the commonwealth is fixed and stable.
Remark (February 11, 1780)

16 The people never give up their liberties but under some delusion.
"Except" is sometimes substituted for "but." Speech at a county meeting, Buckinghamshire, England (1784)

17 In doing good, we are generally cold, and languid, and sluggish; and of all things afraid of being too much in the right. But the works of malice and injustice are quite in another style. They are finished with a bold, masterly hand.
Speech, Bristol, England (1780), quoted in *The Writings and Speeches of Edmund Burke* (H. G. Bohn; 1855)

18 A thing may look specious in theory, and yet be ruinous in practice; a thing may look evil in theory, and yet be in practice excellent.
Speech for the prosecution at the impeachment of Warren Hastings, former governor-general of India (February 19, 1788)

19 Religious persecution may shield itself under the guise of a mistaken and over-zealous piety.
Speech for the prosecution at the impeachment of Warren Hastings, former governor-general of India (February 18, 1788), quoted in *Speeches...in the Trial of Warren Hastings* (E. A. Bond; 1859), vol. 1

20 The only liberty I mean, is a liberty connected with order; that not only exists along with order and virtue, but which cannot exist at all without them.
Edmund Burke was elected MP (Member of Parliament) for Bristol in 1774. Speech on his arrival at Bristol (1774)

21 Dangers by being despised grow great.
Speech to the British Parliament (May 11, 1792)

22 Magnanimity in politics is not seldom the truest wisdom; and a great empire and little minds go ill together.
Speech to the British Parliament (March 22, 1775)

23 The greater the power, the more dangerous the abuse.
Speech to the British Parliament (February 7, 1771)

24 He has put to hazard his ease, his security, his interest, his power, even his darling popularity, for the benefit of a people whom he has never seen.
Referring to Charles Fox's East India Bill (1783). Speech to the British Parliament (1783)

25 Your governor stimulates a rapacious and licentious soldiery to the personal search of women, lest these unhappy creatures should avail themselves of the protection of their sex to secure any supply for their necessities.
Referring to Charles Fox's East India Bill, and referring to Warren Hastings, first governor-general of India. Speech to the British Parliament (1783)

26 All government, indeed every human benefit and enjoyment, every virtue, and every prudent act, is founded on compromise and barter.
Referring to "Conciliation with America." Speech to the British Parliament (March 22, 1775)

27 The concessions of the weak are the concessions of fear.
Referring to "Conciliation with America." Speech to the British Parliament (March 22, 1775)

28 The use of force alone is but *temporary*. It may subdue for a moment; but it does not remove the necessity of subduing again: and a nation is not governed, which is perpetually to be conquered.
Referring to "Conciliation with America." Speech to the British Parliament (March 22, 1775)

29 The people are the masters.
Speech to the British Parliament, "On the Economical Reform" (February 11, 1780)

30 Parliament is not a congress of ambassadors from different and hostile interests; which interests each must maintain...but parliament is a deliberative assembly of one nation, with one interest, that of the whole; where, not local purposes...ought to guide, but the general good, resulting from the general reason of the whole.
Edmund Burke was elected Member of Parliament for Bristol in 1774. Speech to the electors of Bristol (November 3, 1774)

31 Your representative owes you, not his industry only, but his judgement; and he betrays instead of serving you if he sacrifices it to your opinion.
Edmund Burke was elected Member of Parliament for Bristol in 1774. Speech to the electors of Bristol (November 3, 1774)

32 I am convinced that we have a degree of delight, and that no small one, in the real misfortunes and pains of others.
A Philosophical Inquiry into the Origin of Our Ideas of the Sublime and Beautiful (1757), pt. 1

33 Beauty in distress is much the most affecting beauty.
A Philosophical Inquiry into the Origin of Our Ideas of the Sublime and Beautiful (1757), pt. 3

34 The fabric of superstition has in our age and nation received much ruder shocks than it had ever felt before; and through the chinks and breaches of our prison we see such glimmerings of light, and feel such refreshing airs of liberty, as daily raise our ardour for more.
A Vindication of Natural Society (1756)

35 The writers against religion, whilst they oppose every system, are wisely careful never to set up any of their own.
A Vindication of Natural Society (1756), preface

36 All men that are ruined are ruined on the side of their natural propensities.
Letters on a Regicide Peace (1796), no. 1

37 A state without the means of some change is without the means of its conservation.
Reflections on the Revolution in France (1790)

38 But the age of chivalry is gone. That of sophisters, economists, and calculators, has succeeded; and the glory of Europe is extinguished for ever.
Reflections on the Revolution in France (1790)

39 Good order is the foundation of all good things.
Reflections on the Revolution in France (1790)

40 Government is a contrivance of human wisdom to provide for human wants. Men have a right that these wants should be provided for by this wisdom.
Reflections on the Revolution in France (1790)

41 I flatter myself that I love a manly, moral, regulated liberty as well as any gentleman.
Reflections on the Revolution in France (1790)

42 In the groves of their academy, at the end of every vista, you see nothing but the gallows.
Reflections on the Revolution in France (1790)

43 Kings will be tyrants from policy when subjects are rebels from principle.
Reflections on the Revolution in France (1790)

44 Learning will be cast into the mire and trodden down under the hoofs of a swinish multitude.
Reflections on the Revolution in France (1790)

45 Make the Revolution a parent of settlement, and not a nursery of future revolutions.
Reflections on the Revolution in France (1790)

46 Man is by his constitution a religious animal. A perfect democracy is therefore the most shameless thing in the world.
Reflections on the Revolution in France (1790)

47 Nobility is a graceful ornament to the civil order. It is the Corinthian capital of polished society.
Reflections on the Revolution in France (1790)

48 No man can mortgage his injustice as a pawn for his fidelity.
Reflections on the Revolution in France (1790)

49 People will not look forward to posterity, who never look backward to their ancestors
Reflections on the Revolution in France (1790)

50 Superstition is the religion of feeble minds.
Reflections on the Revolution in France (1790)

51 Whenever our neighbour's house is on fire, it cannot be amiss for the engines to play a little on our own.
Reflections on the Revolution in France (1790)

52 And having looked to government for bread, on the very first scarcity they will turn and bite the hand that fed them.
Thoughts and Details on Scarcity (1797)

53 I am not one of those who think that the people are never in the wrong. They have been so, frequently and outrageously, both in other countries and in this. But I do say, that in all disputes between them and their rulers, the presumption is at least upon a par in favour of the people.
Thoughts on the Cause of the Present Discontents (1770)

54 To complain of the age we live in, to murmur at the present possessors of power, to lament the past, to conceive extravagant hopes of the future, are the common dispositions of the greatest part of mankind.
Thoughts on the Cause of the Present Discontents (1770)

55 We must soften into a credulity below the milkiness of infancy to think all men virtuous. We must be tainted with a malignity truly diabolical, to believe all the world to be equally wicked and corrupt.
Thoughts on the Cause of the Present Discontents (1770)

56 When bad men combine, the good must associate; else they

will fall one by one, an unpitied sacrifice in a contemptible struggle.
Thoughts on the Cause of the Present Discontents (1770)

57 The cold neutrality of an impartial judge.
"Translator's Preface," *To His Constituents* (J. P. Brissot; 1794)

58 Laws, like houses, lean on one another.
Published posthumously (1812). *Tracts on the Popery Laws* (1765?), ch. 3, pt. 1

59 There is but one law for all, namely that law which governs all law, the law of our Creator, the law of humanity, justice, equity—the law of nature and of nations.
1788. Opening speech for the prosecution at the impeachment of Warren Hastings, who was tried for alleged "high crimes and misdemeanors" committed while governor-general of India. Quoted in "Ninth and Eleventh Reports of Committee on Indian Affairs, Charges Against Warren Hastings," *The Writings and Speeches of Edmund Burke* (H. G. Bohn; 1855), vol. 4

60 Bad laws are the worst sort of tyranny.
1780. Speech at Bristol previous to the 1780 election when he lost his parliamentary seat; he had been Member of Parliament for Bristol since 1774.

61 An event has happened, upon which it is difficult to speak, and impossible to be silent.
May 5, 1789. Speech for the prosecution at the impeachment of Warren Hastings, former governor-general of India.

62 To tax and to please, no more than to love and to be wise, is not given to men.
Referring to Charles Townshend. Attrib.

Burke, Johnny (1908–64) U.S. songwriter

1 Don't you know each cloud contains
Pennies from Heaven?
"Pennies from Heaven" (1936)

2 Like Webster's Dictionary
We're Morocco bound.
Song lyric. "Road to Morocco," *The Road to Morocco* (1942)

Burke, Thomas (1886–1945) Scottish-born British writer

1 Watch how a man takes praise and there you have the measure of him.
T. P.'s Weekly (June 8, 1928)

Burnet, Gilbert (1643–1715) Scottish bishop and historian

1 He said once to myself that he was no atheist but he could not think God would make a man miserable only for taking a little pleasure out of the way.
Referring to Charles II. *The History of My Own Times*, 2 vols. (1724, 1734)

2 A great error to waste young gentlemen's years so long in learning Latin by so tedious a grammar.
Quoted in *The Later Stuarts* (Sir George Clark; 1934)

Burnett, Leo (1891–1971) U.S. advertising executive

1 If you don't get noticed, you don't have anything. You just have to be noticed, but the art is in getting noticed naturally, without screaming or without tricks.
Quoted in "Leo Burnett," *The Art of Writing Advertising* (Denis Higgins; 1965)

Burney, Fanny (Frances Burney d'Arblay; 1752–1840) British novelist and diarist

1 Indeed, the freedom with which Dr. Johnson condemns whatever he disapproves is astonishing.
Diary (August 23, 1778)

2 Travelling is the ruin of all happiness! There's no looking at a building here after seeing Italy.
Cecilia (1782), bk. 4, ch. 2

3 Now I am ashamed of confessing that I have nothing to confess.
Evelina (1778), Letter 59

Burns, George (Nathan Birnbaum; 1896–1996) U.S. comedian and actor

1 Happiness? A good cigar, a good meal, a good cigar, a good woman—or a bad woman; it depends how much happiness you can handle.
Interview on NBC television (October 16, 1984)

2 If it's a good script, I'll do it. And if it's a bad script, and they pay me enough, I'll do it.
Remark (November 1988)

3 I was brought up to respect my elders and now I don't have to respect *anybody*.
Remark at the age of 87 (1983)

4 When Jack Benny has a party, you not only bring your own scotch, you bring your own rocks.
Living It Up; Or, They Still Love Me in Altoona! (1976)

5 I smoke 10 to 15 cigars a day, at my age I have to hold on to something.
Attrib.

6 The secret of acting is sincerity. If you can fake that, you've got it made.
1986. Attrib.

7 Too bad all the people who know how to run the country are busy driving cabs and cutting hair.
Attrib.

8 Why shouldn't I play God? Anything I do at my age is a miracle.
Referring to winning the title role in the musical *Oh God!* at the age of 98. Attrib.

Burns, Ken (Kenneth Lauren Burns; b.1953) U.S. filmmaker and historian

1 History in this country has become castor oil for people.
"History, Humanities and Media: An Address," *Discourse* (June–July 1989)

Burns, Robert (1759–96) Scottish poet and songwriter

Quotations about Burns

1 "Looks like he had a boil on his neck," says Ellen in front of the statue of Burns. "Ah," whispers Harry Goldweiser with a fat-throated sigh, "but he was a great poet."
John Dos Passos (1896–1970) U.S. novelist. *Manhattan Transfer* (1925), pt. 2

2 If you can imagine a Scotch commercial traveller in a Scotch

commercial hotel leaning on the bar and calling the barmaid "Dearie" then you will know the keynote of Burns' verse.
A. E. Housman (1859–1936) British poet and classicist. Quoted in *Electric Delights* (William Plomer; 1978), "A. E. Housman"

3 It is the fine humanity, the muscular sense, and the generous humor of Burns which save him from being merely Scotch.
James Russell Lowell (1819–91) U.S. poet, editor, essayist, and diplomat. "Nationality in Literature" (1849), quoted in *The Great Critics* (James Harry Smith and Edd Winfield Parks, eds.; 1951)

Quotations by Burns

4 While quacks of State must each produce his plan,
And even children lisp the Rights of Man;
Amid this mighty fuss just let me mention,
The Rights of Woman merit some attention.
"Address on the Rights of Woman" (November 26, 1792)

5 Ae fond kiss, and then we sever;
Ae fareweel, and then for ever!
"Ae Fond Kiss" (1792)

6 Had we never loved sae kindly,
Had we never loved sae blindly!
Never met or never parted,
We had ne'er been broken-hearted.
"Ae Fond Kiss" (1792)

7 Flow gently, sweet Afton, among thy green braes;
Flow gently, I'll sing thee a song in thy praise.
My Mary's asleep by thy murmuring stream,
Flow gently, sweet Afton, disturb not her dream.
"Afton Water" (1792)

8 My luve's like a red red rose
That's newly sprung in June:
My luve's like the melodie
That's sweetly play'd in tune.
Derived from many folk songs. "A Red Red Rose" (1796)

9 Should auld acquaintance be forgot,
And never brought to min'?
"Auld Lang Syne" (1796)

10 We'll tak a cup o' kindness yet,
For auld lang syne.
"Auld Lang Syne" (1796)

11 We twa hae run about the braes,
And pu'd the gowans fine.
"Auld Lang Syne" (1796)

12 O saw ye bonnie Lesley
As she gaed o'er the border?
She's gane, like Alexander,
To spread her conquests farther

To see her is to love her,
And love but her for ever,
For Nature made her what she is,
And ne'er made anither!
"Bonnie Lesley" (1798)

13 Gin a body meet a body
Coming thro' the rye;
Gin a body kiss a body,
Need a body cry?
"Coming Thro' the Rye" (1796)

14 Some books are lies frae end to end.
"Death and Doctor Hornbook" (1787)

15 To make a happy fire-side clime
To weans and wife,
That's the true pathos and sublime
Of human life.
1789. "Epistle to Dr. Blacklock" (1796), st. 9, ll. 4–7, quoted in *The Poetry of Robert Burns* (William Ernett Henely and Thomas F. Henderson, eds.; 1896)

16 Just now I've taen the fit o' rhyme,
My barmie noddle's working prime.
"Epistle to James Smith" (1786), st. 4, ll.1–2, quoted in *The Poetry of Robert Burns* (William Ernett Henely and Thomas F. Henderson, eds.; 1896)

17 A prince can make a belted knight,
A marquis, duke, and a' that;
But an honest man's aboon his might,
Guid faith, he maunna fa' that.
"For a' That an a' That" (1790), st. 4

18 The rank is but the guinea's stamp,
The man's the gowd for a' that!
For a' that and a' that
A man's a man for a' that.
"For a' That and a' That" (1790)

19 Auld Nature swears, the lovely dears
Her noblest work she classes, O;
Her 'prentice han' she tried on man,
And then she made the lasses, O!
"Green Grow the Rashes" (1787)

20 Green grow the rashes O,
Green grow the rashes O,
The sweetest hours that e'er I spend,
Are spent amang the lasses O!
"Green Grow the Rashes" (1787)

21 O, gie me the lass that has acres o' charms,
O, gie me the lass wi' the weel-stockit farms.
"Hey for a Lass wi' a Tocher" (1799)

22 John Anderson, my jo, John,
When we were first acquent,
Your locks were like the raven,
Your bonnie brow was brent.
"John Anderson, My Jo" (1790)

23 There were three kings into the east,
Three kings both great and high;
And they hae sworn a solemn oath
John Barleycorn should die.
Barley is used in the brewing of ale and the distilling of whiskey. "John Barleycorn" (1787)

24 Man's inhumanity to man
Makes countless thousands mourn!
"Man Was Made to Mourn" (1786)

25 Nature's law,
That man was made to mourn!
"Man Was Made to Mourn" (1786)

26 O Death, the poor man's dearest friend,
The kindest and the best!
"Man Was Made to Mourn" (1786)

27 Farewell to the Highlands, farewell to the North,
The birth-place of valour, the country of worth.
"My Heart's in the Highlands" (1790)

28 My heart's in the Highlands, my heart is not here;
My heart's in the Highlands a-chasing the deer;
Chasing the wild deer, and following the roe,
My heart's in the Highlands, wherever I go.
"My Heart's in the Highlands" (1790)

29 The minister kiss'd the fiddler's wife,
An' could na preach for thinkin' o't.
"My Love She's but a Lassie Yet" (1790)

30 Liberty's in every blow!
Let us do or die!
Also known as "Robert Bruce's March to Bannockburn." "Scots, Wha Hae" (1799)

31 Scots, wha hae wi' Wallace bled,
Scots, wham Bruce has aften led,
Welcome to your gory bed,
Or to victorie.
Also known as "Robert Bruce's March to Bannockburn." "Scots, Wha Hae" (1799)

32 For thus the royal mandate ran,
When first the human race began,
"The social friendly, honest man,
Whate'er he be,
'Tis he fulfils great Nature's plan,
And none but he!"
"Second Epistle to John Lapraik" (1786), st. 15

33 Nae man can tether time or tide.
"Tam o' Shanter" (1791)

34 Inspiring bold John Barleycorn!
What dangers thou canst make us scorn!
Wi' tippenny, we fear nae evil;
Wi' usquebae, we'll face the devil!
Barley is used in the brewing of ale and the distilling of whiskey. "Tippeny" is Scots dialect for "ale"; "usquebae" for whiskey (from the Scottish Gaelic *uisge beatha*, "water of life"). "Tam o' Shanter" (1791)

35 Freedom and Whisky gang tegither!
"The Author's Earnest Cry and Prayer" (1786), l. 185

36 Thou minds me o' departed joys,
Departed never to return
And my fause lover stole my rose,
But ah! he left the thorn wi' me.
"The Banks o' Doon" (1792)

37 Ye banks and braes o' bonnie Doon,
How can ye bloom sae fresh and fair?
How can ye chant, ye little birds,
And I sae weary fu' o' care?
"The Banks o' Doon" (1792)

38 From scenes like these old Scotia's grandeur springs,
That makes her loved at home, revered abroad:
Princes and Lords are but the breath of kings,
"An honest man's the noblest work of God."
"The Cotter's Saturday Night" (1786), st. 19

39 A fig for those by law protected!
Liberty's a glorious feast!
Courts for cowards were erected,
Churches built to please the priest.
Also known as "Love and Liberty—a Cantata." "The Jolly Beggars" (1799)

40 Let them cant about decorum
Who have characters to lose.
Also known as "Love and Liberty—a Cantata." "The Jolly Beggars" (1799)

41 I once was a maid, tho' I cannot tell when,
And still my delight is in proper young men.
Also known as "Love and Liberty—a Cantata." "The Jolly Beggars" (1799), ll. 57–58

42 Partly wi' love o'ercome sae sair,
And partly she was drunk.
Also known as "Love and Liberty—a Cantata." "The Jolly Beggars" (1799), ll. 183–184

43 A man may drink and no be drunk;
A man may fight and no be slain;
A man may kiss a bonnie lass,
And aye be welcome back again.
"There Was a Lass, They Ca'd Her Meg" (1788)

44 We labour soon, we labour late,
To feed the titled knave, man,
And a' the comfort we're to get,
Is that ayont the grave, man.
Posthumously published. "The Tree of Liberty" (1838)

45 But yet the light that led astray
Was light from Heaven.
"The Vision" (1785)

46 Deil tak the hindmost.
"To a Haggis" (1786)

47 O wad some Pow'r the giftie gie us
To see oursels as others see us!
It wad frae mony a blunder free us,
And foolish notion.
"To a Louse" (1786)

48 I'm truly sorry Man's dominion
Has broken Nature's social union,
An' justifies th' ill opinion
Which makes thee startle
At me, thy poor, earth-born companion
An' fellow-mortal!
"To a Mouse" (1786)

49 The best laid schemes o' mice an' men
Gang aft a-gley,
An' lea'e us nought but grief an' pain
For promis'd joy.
"To a Mouse" (1786)

50 Wee, sleekit, cow'rin', tim'rous beastie,
O what a panic's in thy breastie!
"To a Mouse" (1786)

51 What can a young lassie, what shall a young lassie,
What can a young lassie do wi' an auld man?
"What Can a Young Lassie Do wi an Auld Man" (1792)

52 No churchman am I for to rail and to write,
No statesman nor soldier to plot or to fight,
No sly man of business contriving a snare,
For a big-belly'd bottle's the whole of my care.
1782. "No Churchman Am I," *Poems and Songs of Robert Burns* (J. Barke, ed.; 1955)

53 O Scotia! my dear, my native soil!
For whom my warmest wish to Heaven is sent!
Long may thy hardy sons of rustic toil
Be blest with health, and peace and sweet content!
And O! may heaven their simple lives prevent
From Luxury's contagion, weak and vile!
1785. "The Cotter's Saturday Night," *Poems and Songs of Robert Burns* (J. Barke, ed.; 1955), st. 20

54 Don't let the awkward squad fire over me.
1796. Said shortly before his death. Quoted in *Works of Burns; With his Life* (A. Cunningham; 1834), vol. 1

55 Critics!...Those cut-throat bandits in the paths of fame.
Attrib.

Burroughs, Edgar Rice (1875–1950) U.S. novelist

1 Me Tarzan.
The famous line "Me Tarzan, you Jane" does not appear in either the book or the original film (1932). *Tarzan of the Apes* (1914)

Burroughs, John (1837–1921) U.S. naturalist and writer

1 To treat your facts with imagination is one thing, to imagine your facts is another.
The Heart of Burroughs Journals (C. Barrus, ed.; 1967)

2 If we take science as our sole guide, if we accept and hold fast that alone which is verifiable, the old theology must go.
The Light of Day (1900)

Burroughs, Nannie Helen (1883–1961) U.S. journalist

1 This nation openly endorses, tolerates, and legalizes the very abuses against which she originally waged a bloody revolution.
Referring to rioting in Harlem, New York City. *The Afro-American* (April 13, 1935)

Burroughs, William S. (William Seward Burroughs; 1914–97) U.S. writer

Quotations about Burroughs

1 The method must be purest meat,
and no symbolic dressing,
actual visions & actual prisons
as seen then and now.
1954
Allen Ginsberg (1926–97) U.S. poet. "On Burroughs' Work," *The Green Automobile* (1961), quoted in *The Penguin Book of American Verse* (Geoffrey Moore, ed.; 1977)

Quotations by Burroughs

2 I am neither a Moslem nor a Christian, but I owe a great deal to Islam and could never have made my connection with God ANYWHERE EXCEPT HERE.
Referring to Morocco. Letter to Allen Ginsberg (1957), quoted in *The Letters of William S. Burroughs* (Oliver Harris, ed.; 1993)

3 Nothing is true.
Cities of the Red Night (1981), introduction

4 I should have been more alert, of course, but I never could mix vigilance and sex.
Originally published under the pseudonym William Lee. *Junkie* (1953), ch. 9

5 Criminal law is one of the few professions where the client buys someone else's luck.
Originally published under the pseudonym William Lee. *Junkie* (1953), ch. 11

6 Kick is seeing things from a special angle. Kick is momentary freedom from the claims of the ageing, cautious, nagging, frightened flesh.
Originally published under the pseudonym William Lee. *Junkie* (1953), ch. 15

7 America is not a young land: it is old and dirty and evil before the settlers, before the Indians. The evil is there waiting.
Naked Lunch (1959)

8 Writers live the sad truth just like everyone else. The only difference is, they file reports.
Naked Lunch (1959)

9 Junk is the ideal product...the ultimate merchandise. No sales talk necessary. The client will crawl through a sewer and beg to buy.
Naked Lunch (1959), introduction

10 The face of "evil" is always the face of total need.
Naked Lunch (1959), introduction

11 The title means exactly what the words say: NAKED Lunch—a frozen moment when everyone sees what is on the end of every fork.
Naked Lunch (1959), introduction

12 In the U.S. you have to be a deviant or exist in extreme boredom...Make no mistake; all intellectuals are deviants in the U.S.
Yage Letters (co-written with Allen Ginsberg; 1963)

13 I was very drunk. I suddenly said, "It's time for our William Tell act. Put a glass on your head."
Before accidentally killing his wife, by shooting a bullet through her head in a drunken party game. Quoted in *The Life and Legacy of William Burroughs: The Priest They Called Him* (Graham Caveney; 1998)

Burton, Richard (Richard Walter Jenkins; 1925–84) British actor

1 An actor is something less than a man while an actress is something more than a woman.
Halliwell's Filmgoer's and Video Viewer's Companion 8th ed. (Leslie Halliwell; 1990)

2 The Welsh are all actors. It's only the bad ones who become professionals.
Quoted in *Listener*, London (January 9, 1986), "Langham Diary"

Burton, Robert (1577–1640) English scholar and churchman

1 If there is a hell upon earth, it is to be found in a melancholy man's heart.
The Anatomy of Melancholy (1621), pt. I

2 A nightingale dies for shame if another bird sings better.
The Anatomy of Melancholy (1621), pt.1, sect. 2

3 From this it is clear how much more cruel the pen is than the sword.
The Anatomy of Melancholy (1621), pt. 1, sect. 2

4 I may not here omit those two main plagues, and common dotages of human kind, wine and women, which have infatuated and besotted myriads of people. They go commonly together.
The Anatomy of Melancholy (1621), pt.1, sect. 2

5 See one promontory (said Socrates of old), one mountain, one sea, one river, and see all.
The Anatomy of Melancholy (1621), pt. 1, sect. 2

6 They are proud in humility; proud in that they are not proud.
The Anatomy of Melancholy (1621), pt. 1, sect. 2

7 Were it not that they are loath to lay out money on a rope, they would be hanged forthwith, and sometimes die to save charges.
The Anatomy of Melancholy (1621), pt. 1, sect. 2

8 Christ himself was poor...And as he was himself, so he informed his apostles and disciples, they were all poor, prophets poor, apostles poor.
The Anatomy of Melancholy (1621), pt. 2, sect. 2

9 Many things happen between the cup and the lip.
The Anatomy of Melancholy (1621), pt. 2, sect. 2

10 Tobacco, divine, rare, superexcellent tobacco, which goes far beyond all their panaceas...a sovereign remedy to all diseases. But, as it is commonly abused by most men...'tis a plague, a mischief, a violent purger of goods, lands, health, hellish, devilish, and damned tobacco, the ruin and overthrow of body and soul.
The Anatomy of Melancholy (1621), pt. 2, sect. 4

11 Birds of a feather will gather together.
The Anatomy of Melancholy (1621), pt. 3, sect. 1

12 Every man for himself, his own ends, the Devil for all.
The Anatomy of Melancholy (1621), pt. 3, sect. 1

13 Health indeed is a precious thing, to recover and preserve which, we undergo any misery, drink bitter potions, freely give our goods: restore a man to his health, his purse lies open to thee.
The Anatomy of Melancholy (1621), pt. 3, sect. 1

14 Going as if he trod upon eggs.
The Anatomy of Melancholy (1621), pt. 3, sect. 2

15 Jupiter himself was turned into a satyr, a shepherd, a bull, a swan, a golden shower, and what not for love.
The Anatomy of Melancholy (1621), pt. 3, sect. 2

16 Marriage and hanging go by destiny; matches are made in heaven.
The Anatomy of Melancholy (1621), pt. 3, sect. 2

17 No cord nor cable can so forcibly draw, or hold so fast, as love can do with a twined thread.
The Anatomy of Melancholy (1621), pt. 3, sect. 2

18 As clear and as manifest as the nose in a man's face.
The Anatomy of Melancholy (1621), pt. 3, sect. 3

19 Make a virtue of necessity.
The Anatomy of Melancholy (1621), pt. 3, sect. 3

20 For "ignorance is the mother of devotion," as all the world knows.
The Anatomy of Melancholy (1621), pt. 3, sect. 4

21 One religion is as true as another.
The Anatomy of Melancholy (1621), pt. 3, sect. 4

22 The Devil himself, which is the author of confusion and lies.
The Anatomy of Melancholy (1621), pt. 3, sect. 4

23 When they are at Rome, they do there as they see done.
The Anatomy of Melancholy (1621), pt. 3, sect. 4

24 Where God hath a temple, the Devil will have a chapel.
The Anatomy of Melancholy (1621), pt. 3, sect. 4

25 All my joys to this are folly,
Naught so sweet as Melancholy.
"Author's Abstract of Melancholy," *The Anatomy of Melancholy* (1621)

26 All poets are mad
"Democritus to the Reader," *The Anatomy of Melancholy* (1621)

27 I say with Didacus Stella, a dwarf standing on the shoulders of a giant may see farther than a giant himself.
"Democritus to the Reader," *The Anatomy of Melancholy* (1621)

28 Rob Peter, and pay Paul.
"Democritus to the Reader," *The Anatomy of Melancholy* (1621)

29 They lard their lean books with the fat of others' works.
"Democritus to the Reader," *The Anatomy of Melancholy* (1621)

30 We can say nothing but what hath been said. Our poets steal from Homer.... Our story-dressers do as much; he that comes last is commonly best.
"Democritus to the Reader," *The Anatomy of Melancholy* (1621)

Bush, George (George Herbert Walker Bush; b.1924) U.S. president

Quotations about Bush

1 Reagan can portray a real macho guy. Bush can't. He comes off looking like Liberace.
Carl Parker U.S. senator. Referring to Ronald Reagan and George Bush. Attrib.

2 Bush had two faults. He didn't care for domestic politics, and he didn't care for people.
Charles Wheeler (b.1923) British journalist and broadcaster. Remark made on BBC television (1992)

Quotations by Bush

3 Learning is good in and of itself...the mothers of the Jewish ghettoes of the east would pour honey on a book so the

children would know that learning is sweet. And the parents who settled hungry Kansas would take their children in from the fields when a teacher came.
Accepting his nomination as presidential candidate. Acceptance speech, Republican Party Convention, New Orleans (August 18, 1988)

4 The Congress will push me to raise taxes and I'll say no, and they'll push, and I'll say no, and they'll push again. And I'll say to them, read my lips: no new taxes.
Accepting his nomination as presidential candidate. Acceptance speech, Republican Party Convention, New Orleans (August 18, 1988), quoted in *New York Times* (August 19, 1988)

5 A time of historic change is no time for recklessness.
Address on national television (November 22, 1990)

6 When America is stronger, the world is safer.
Address to Congress (February 9, 1989)

7 A new breeze is blowing—and a nation refreshed by freedom stands ready to push on: there is new ground to be broken, and new action to be taken.
Inaugural address (January 20, 1989)

8 But I see history as a book with many pages—and each day we fill a page with acts of hopefulness and meaning.
Inaugural address (January 20, 1989)

9 The United States is the best and fairest and most decent nation on the face of the earth.
Remark (May 1988)

10 I know what I've told you I'm going to say, I'm going to say. And what else I say, well, I'll take some time to figure out—figure that out.
Remark at a press conference (December 4, 1990)

11 I will draw a line in the sand.
Referring to the defense of Saudi Arabia by U.S. forces following the Iraqi invasion of Kuwait. Remark at a press conference (1990)

12 America's freedom is the example to which the world expires.
Speech, Detroit (1988)

13 I don't know that atheists should be considered citizens, nor should they be considered patriots. This is one nation under God.
Free Inquiry, magazine (1988)

14 The war wasn't fought about democracy in Kuwait.
Referring to the Gulf War (1991). *Observer*, London (July 14, 1991)

15 War is never cheap or easy.
Referring to the Gulf War (1991). *Observer*, London (January 20, 1991)

16 It's not whether people like you but whether they share the bright dreams...and understand the heartbeat of the country.
Sunday Times, London (October 16, 1988), "Sayings of the Week"

17 Our goal is not the conquest of Iraq. It is the liberation of Kuwait.
Referring to the Gulf War (1991). *Times*, London (January 16, 1991)

18 I have opinions of my—own strong opinions—but I don't always agree with them.
Attrib.

Bush, George W. (b.1948) U.S. politician

1 I would hope our country would get beyond group thought and we'd herald each individual, regardless of their heritage and regardless of their background.
January 26, 2000. Republican debate in New Hampshire, *New York Times* (January 27, 2000)

Bush, Vannevar (1890–1974) U.S. engineer and government official

1 Science has a simple faith, which transcends utility. Nearly all men of science, all men of learning for that matter, and men of simple ways too, have it in some form and in some degree. It is the faith that it is the privilege of man to understand, and that this is his mission.
"The Search for Understanding," *Science Is Not Enough* (1967)

Bushnell, Horace (1802–76) U.S. minister and theologian

1 Let him think to gain many to Christ imperceptibly, by keeping alive the interest in God's truth, and letting it distill upon the hearers as a dew.
1861. Written in opposition to Christians such as Jonathan Edwards who insisted on the need for a conversion experience. *Christian Nurture* (1967)

Bussy-Rabutin (Roger de Rabutin; 1618–93) French soldier and writer

1 Absence is to love what wind is to fire; it extinguishes the small, it inflames the great.
Histoire Amoureuse des Gaules (1665)

2 Love comes from blindness, friendship from knowledge.
"Maximes d'Amour," *Histoire Amoureuse des Gaules* (1665)

Busta, Christine (b.1915) Austrian writer

1 Nothing can still or staunch.
Throw earth into my mouth
and I'll sing you grass.
"Epitaph" (1965), quoted in *German Poetry 1910–1975* (Michael Hamburger, ed., tr.; 1977)

Butler, Joseph (1692–1752) English philosopher and theologian

1 Conscience and self-love, if we understand our true happiness, always lead us the same way.
Fifteen Sermons (1726), no. 3

2 Things and actions are what they are, and the consequences of them will be what they will be: why then should we desire to be deceived?
Fifteen Sermons (1726), no. 7

3 Every work both of nature and of art, is a system: and...every particular thing, both natural and artificial, is for some use or purpose out of and beyond itself.
Fifteen Sermons (1726), preface

4 That which is the foundation of all our hopes and of all our fears; all our hopes and fears which are of any consideration: I mean a Future Life.
The Analogy of Religion (1736), introduction

5 Sir, the pretending to extraordinary revelations and gifts of the

Holy Ghost is a horrid thing, a very horrid thing.
Said to John Wesley. Quoted in *Works*, vol. 13

Butler, Nicholas Murray (1862–1947) U.S. educator

1 A society like ours, of which it is truly said to be often but three generations "from shirt-sleeves to shirt-sleeves."
Referring to the United States. *True and False Democracy* (1907)

2 An expert is one who knows more and more about less and less.
1901. Commencement address, Columbia University. Attrib.

Butler, Rab, Baron (Richard Austen Butler, "Rab"; 1902–82) British politician

1 Mr. Macmillan is the best prime minister we have.
Often quoted in the form above. In fact, Butler simply answered "Yes" to the question "Would you say that this is the best prime minister we have?" Press interview, London Airport (1955)

Butler, Samuel (1612–80) English satirist

1 *Diseases* of their own Accord,
But *Cures* come difficult and hard.
"Satyr upon the Weakness and Misery of Man," quoted in *Satires and Miscellaneous Poetry and Prose* (René Lamar; 1928)

2 For every why he had a wherefore.
Hudibras (1663), pt. 1, can. 1, l. 132

3 He could distinguish and divide
A hair 'twixt south and southwest side.
Hudibras (1663), pt. 1, can. 1, ll. 67–8

4 For rhetoric he could not ope
His mouth, but out there flew a trope.
Hudibras (1663), pt. 1, can. 1, ll. 81–2

5 A Babylonish dialect
Which learned pedants much affect.
Hudibras (1663), pt. 1, can. 1, ll. 93–4

6 And wisely tell what hour o' the day
The clock does strike, by algebra.
Hudibras (1663), pt. 1, can. 1, ll. 125–6

7 He ne'er consider'd it, as loth
To look a gift-horse in the mouth.
Hudibras (1663), pt. 1, can. 1, ll. 483–4

8 Great actions are not always true sons
Of great and mighty resolutions.
Hudibras (1663), pt. 1, can. 1, ll. 885–6

9 Cleric before, and Lay behind;
A lawless linsy-woolsy brother,
Half of one order, half another.
Hudibras (1663), pt. 1, can. 1, ll. 1226–8

10 As if religion was intended
For nothing else but to be mended.
Hudibras (1663), pt. 1, can. 1, ll. 202–203

11 Through perils both of wind and limb,
Through thick and thin she follow'd him.
Hudibras (1663), pt.1, can.2

12 I am not now in fortune's power:
He that is down can fall no lower.
Hudibras (1663), pt. 1, can. 3, ll. 877–8

13 Cause grace and virtue are within
Prohibited degrees of kin;
And therefore no true saint allows
They shall be suffer'd to espouse.
Hudibras (1663), pt. 1, can. 3, ll. 1047–50

14 Learning, that cobweb of the brain,
Profane, erroneous, and vain.
Hudibras (1663), pt. 1, can. 3, ll. 1339–40

15 To swallow gudgeons ere they're catched,
And count their chickens ere they're hatched.
Hudibras (1664), pt. 2

16 For truth is precious and divine,
Too rich a pearl for carnal swine.
Hudibras (1664), pt. 2, can. 2

17 Oaths are but words, and words but wind.
Hudibras (1664), pt. 2, can. 2, l. 107

18 Love is a boy, by poets styl'd,
Then spare the rod, and spoil the child.
Hudibras (1664), pt. 2, can. 2, ll. 843–4

19 Why should not *Conscience* have *Vacation*
As well as other Courts o' th' Nation?
Hudibras (1664), pt. 2, can. 2, ll. 323–324

20 But *Hudibras* gave him a twitch
As quick as Lightning in the Breech,
Just in the place where *Honour's* lodg'd,
As wise Philosophers have judg'd;
Because a kick in that part more
Hurts *honour* than deep wounds before.
Hudibras (1664), pt. 2, can. 3, ll. 1073–78

21 What makes all doctrines plain and clear?
About two hundred pounds a year.
And that which was prov'd true before
Prove false again? Two hundred more.
Hudibras (1678), pt. 3, can. 1, ll. 1277–80

22 With Crosses, Relics, Crucifixes,
Beads, Pictures, Rosaries, and Pixes,
The Tools of working out Salvation
By meer mechanick operation.
Hudibras (1678), pt. 3, can. 1, ll. 1495–98

23 He that complies against his will,
Is of his own opinion still.
Hudibras (1678), pt. 3, can. 2

24 For those that fly may fight again,
Which he can never do that's slain.
Hudibras (1678), pt. 3, can. 3, ll. 243–4

25 For Justice, though she's painted blind,
Is to the weaker side inclin'd.
Hudibras (1678), pt. 3, can. 3, ll. 709–10

26 A client is fain to hire a lawyer to keep from the injury of other lawyers—as Christians that travel in Turkey are forced

to hire Janissaries, to protect them from the insolencies of other Turks.
Prose Observations (1660–80)

Butler, Samuel (1835–1902) British writer and composer

1 Exploring is delightful to look forward to and back upon, but it is not comfortable at the time, unless it be of such an easy nature as not to deserve the name.
Erewhon (1872)

2 While to deny the existence of an unseen kingdom is bad, to pretend that we know more about it than its bare existence is no better.
Erewhon (1872), ch. 15

3 An art can only be learned in the workshop of those who are winning their bread by it.
Erewhon (1872), ch. 20

4 It has been said that the love of money is the root of all evil. The want of money is so quite as truly.
Erewhon (1872), ch. 20

5 The wish to spread those opinions that we hold conducive to our own welfare is so deeply rooted in the English character that few of us can escape its influence.
Erewhon (1872), ch. 20

6 An honest God's the noblest work of man.
Further Extracts from the Note Books (1934)

7 A hen is only an egg's way of making another egg.
Life and Habit (1878)

8 I keep my books at the British Museum and at Mudie's.
The British Museum was, until 1998, the home of the British Library, and Mudie's was one of the main British subscription lending libraries toward the end of the 19th century. *The Humour of Homer, And Other Essays* (1913), "Ramblings in Cheapside"

9 Half the vices which the world condemns most loudly have seeds of good in them and require moderate use rather than total abstinence.
The Way of All Flesh (1903)

10 Every man's work, whether it be literature or music or pictures or architecture or anything else, is always a portrait of himself.
The Way of All Flesh (1903), ch. 14

11 They would have been equally horrified at hearing the Christian religion doubted, and at seeing it practised.
The Way of All Flesh (1903), ch. 15

12 Pleasure after all is a safer guide than either right or duty.
The Way of All Flesh (1903), ch. 19

13 That vice pays homage to virtue is notorious; we call it hypocrisy.
The Way of All Flesh (1903), ch. 19

14 The advantage of doing one's praising for oneself is that one can lay it on so thick and exactly in the right places.
The Way of All Flesh (1903), ch. 34

15 'Tis better to have loved and lost than never to have lost at all.
The Way of All Flesh (1903), ch. 77

16 I reckon being ill as one of the greatest pleasures of life, provided one is not too ill and is not obliged to work till one is better.
The Way of All Flesh (1903), ch. 80

17 I know no exception to the rule that it is cheaper to buy milk than to keep a cow.
The Way of All Flesh (1903), ch. 86

18 X-RAYS Their moral is this—that a right way of looking at things will see through almost anything.
Quoted in *Note Books* (H. Festing Jones, ed.; 1912)

19 All progress is based upon a universal innate desire on the part of every organism to live beyond its income.
Quoted in *Note Books* (H. Festing Jones, ed.; 1912)

20 An apology for the Devil—it must be remembered that we have only heard one side of the case. God has written all the books.
Quoted in *Note Books* (H. Festing Jones, ed.; 1912)

21 God is Love I dare say. But what a mischievous devil Love is!
Quoted in *Note Books* (H. Festing Jones, ed.; 1912)

22 Is life worth living? This is a question for an embryo, not for a man.
Quoted in *Note Books* (H. Festing Jones, ed.; 1912)

23 It does not matter much what a man hates, provided he hates something.
Quoted in *Note Books* (H. Festing Jones, ed.; 1912)

24 It is the function of vice to keep virtue within reasonable bounds.
Quoted in *Note Books* (H. Festing Jones, ed.; 1912)

25 Justice is being allowed to do whatever I like. Injustice is whatever prevents my doing it.
Quoted in *Note Books* (H. Festing Jones, ed.; 1912)

26 Life is one long process of getting tired.
Quoted in *Note Books* (H. Festing Jones, ed.; 1912)

27 Life is the art of drawing sufficient conclusions from insufficient premises.
Quoted in *Note Books* (H. Festing Jones, ed.; 1912)

28 Man is the only animal that can remain on friendly terms with the victims he intends to eat until he eats them.
Quoted in *Note Books* (H. Festing Jones, ed.; 1912)

29 Marriage is distinctly and repeatedly excluded from heaven. Is this because it is thought likely to mar the general felicity?
Quoted in *Note Books* (H. Festing Jones, ed.; 1912)

30 Parents are the last people on earth who ought to have children.
Quoted in *Note Books* (H. Festing Jones, ed.; 1912)

31 Some men love truth so much that they seem to be in continual fear lest she should catch a cold on overexposure.
Quoted in *Note Books* (H. Festing Jones, ed.; 1912)

32 The great pleasure of a dog is that you may make a fool of yourself with him and not only will he not scold you, he will make a fool of himself too.
Quoted in *Note Books* (H. Festing Jones, ed.; 1912)

33 The public buys its opinions as it buys its meat, or takes in its milk, on the principle that it is cheaper to do this than to

keep a cow. So it is, but the milk is more likely to be watered.
Quoted in *Note Books* (H. Festing Jones, ed.; 1912)

34 Though analogy is often misleading, it is the least misleading thing we have.
Quoted in *Note Books* (H. Festing Jones, ed.; 1912)

35 To live is like love, all reason is against it, and all healthy instinct for it.
Quoted in *Note Books* (H. Festing Jones, ed.; 1912)

36 Vaccination is the medical sacrament corresponding to baptism.
Quoted in *Note Books* (H. Festing Jones, ed.; 1912)

37 When a man is in doubt about this or that in his writing, it will often guide him if he asks himself how it will tell a hundred years hence.
Quoted in *Note Books* (H. Festing Jones, ed.; 1912)

38 When you have told anyone you have left him a legacy the only decent thing to do is to die at once.
Quoted in *Samuel Butler: A Memoir* (H. Festing Jones, ed.; 1920), vol. 2

39 Brigands demand your money or your life; women require both.
Attrib.

Butlin, Billy, Sir (William Heygate Edmund Colborne Butlin; 1899–1980) South African-born British entertainment entrepreneur

1 On my retirement I became a consultant to the company—but nobody consulted me.
The Billy Butlin Story (1982), ch. 17

Butz, Earl (b.1909) U.S. politician

1 He no play-a da game. He no make-a da rules!
Referring to the Pope's strictures against contraception. Remark (1974)

Byatt, A. S. (originally Antonia Susan Drabble; b.1936) British novelist and academic

1 Motherhood meant I have written four fewer books, but I know more about life.
Sunday Times, London (October 21, 1990)

Byng, George, 1st Viscount Torrington (1663–1733) English admiral

1 Most men were in fear that the French would invade, but I was always of another opinion, for I always said that, whilst we had a fleet in being, they would not dare to make an attempt.
Justifying his refusal to give battle to a numerically superior French fleet; when subsequently ordered to do so, he was defeated off Beachy Head (July 10, 1690). *The Later Stuarts* (Sir George Clark; July 10, 1690)

Byrne, David (b.1952) U.S. musician

1 It's assumed that a lot of musicians are speaking for someone else—speaking for the steelworkers or for the underprivileged—whereas a lot of musicians are privileged people.
Interview, *New Musical Express,* London (December 8, 1984), quoted in *Shots from the Hip* (Charles Shaar Murray; 1993)

Byron, Henry James (1834–84) British playwright and actor

1 Life's too short for chess.
Our Boys (1875), Act 1

Byron, Lord, 6th Baron Byron of Rochdale (George Gordon Noel Byron; 1788–1824) British poet

Quotations about Byron

1 If they had said the sun and the moon was gone out of the heavens, it could not have struck me with the idea of a more awful and dreary blank in creation than the words: "Byron is dead."
Jane Carlyle (1801–66) Scottish diarist. Letter to her future husband, Thomas Carlyle (May 20, 1824), quoted in *Collected Letters of Thomas and Jane Welsh Carlyle* (C. R. Sanders et al., eds.; 1970)

2 Lord Byron is a poet whose fervent mind penetrates with unequalled acuity into things past and present, and anticipates future events that may result from them.
Johann Wolfgang von Goethe (1749–1832) German poet, playwright, and scientist. "On Byron's Cain" (1824)

3 Mad, bad, and dangerous to know.
Caroline Lamb (1785–1828) British novelist. Her impression of Lord Byron when first meeting him in March 1812. *Journal* (1812)

4 From the poetry of Lord Byron they drew a system of ethics, compounded of misanthropy and voluptuousness, a system in which the two great commandments were, to hate your neighbour, and to love your neighbour's wife.
1830
Thomas Babington Macaulay (1800–59) British politician, historian, and writer. "On Moore's *Life of Lord Byron,*" *Essays Contributed to the Edinburgh Review* (1843)

5 Byron's technique is rotten.
1916
Ezra Pound (1885–1972) U.S. poet, translator, and critic. Letter to Iris Barry (July 27, 1916), quoted in *The Selected Letters of Ezra Pound, 1907–1941* (D. D. Paige, ed.; 1950)

Quotations by Byron

6 And wilt thou weep when I am low?
"And Wilt Thou Weep When I Am Low?" (1808)

7 The glory and the nothing of a name.
"Churchill's Grave" (1816), l. 43

8 The world is a bundle of hay,
Mankind are the asses who pull;
Each tugs it a different way,
And the greatest of all is John Bull.
"Epigram" (1820)

9 With death doomed to grapple,
Beneath this cold slab, he
Who lied in the chapel
Now lies in the Abbey.
Epitaph for William Pitt (January 1820)

10 Friendship is Love without his wings!
"L'Amitié est l'Amour sans Ailes" (1831)

11 Maid of Athens, ere we part,
Give, oh give me back my heart!

Or, since that has left my breast,
Keep it now, and take the rest!
"Maid of Athens, Ere We Part" (1810)

12 'Tis done—but yesterday a King!
And arm'd with Kings to strive
And now thou art a nameless thing:
So abject—yet alive!
"Ode to Napoleon Bonaparte" (1814), st. 1

13 She walks in beauty, like the night
Of cloudless climes and starry skies;
And all that's best of dark and bright
Meet in her aspect and her eyes.
"She Walks in Beauty" (1815)

14 Never under the most despotic of infidel governments did I behold such squalid wretchedness as I have seen since my return in the very heart of a Christian country.
Speaking against the death penalty for machine wrecking. Speech to the House of Lords, the upper house of the British Parliament (February 27, 1812)

15 I am ashes where once I was fire.
"To the Countess of Blessington" (1823)

16 So, we'll go no more a roving
So late into the night,
Though the heart be still as loving,
And the moon be still as bright.
"We'll Go No More A-roving" (1817)

17 Though the night was made for loving,
And the day returns too soon,
Yet we'll go no more a roving
By the light of the moon.
"We'll Go No More A-roving" (1817)

18 If I should meet thee
After long years,
How should I greet thee?
With silence and tears.
"When We Two Parted" (1816)

19 I like the weather, when it is not rainy,
That is, I like two months of every year.
Beppo (1818)

20 In short, he was a perfect cavaliero,
And to his very valet seem'd a hero.
Beppo (1818)

21 In hope to merit Heaven by making earth a Hell.
Childe Harold's Pilgrimage (1812–18), can. 1, l. 305

22 Had sigh'd to many, though he loved but one.
Childe Harold's Pilgrimage (1812–18), can. 1, st. 5

23 Maidens, like moths, are ever caught by glare,
And Mammon wins his way where Seraphs might despair.
Childe Harold's Pilgrimage (1812–18), can. 1, st. 9

24 "All that we know is, nothing can be known."
Childe Harold's Pilgrimage (1812–18), can. 2, st. 7

25 Fair Greece! sad relic of departed worth!
Immortal, though no more! though fallen, great!
Childe Harold's Pilgrimage (1812–18), can. 2, st. 73

26 Hereditary bondsmen! know ye not
Who would be free themselves must strike the blow?
Childe Harold's Pilgrimage (1812–18), can. 2, st. 76

27 A thousand years scarce serve to form a state:
An hour may lay it in the dust.
Childe Harold's Pilgrimage (1812–18), can. 2, st. 84

28 Land of lost gods and godlike men.
Childe Harold's Pilgrimage (1812–18), can. 2, st. 85

29 What is the worst of woes that wait on age?
What stamps the wrinkle deeper on the brow?
To view each loved one blotted from life's page,
And be alone on earth, as I am now.
1812. *Childe Harold's Pilgrimage* (1812–18), can. 2, st. 98

30 What deep wounds ever closed without a scar?
Childe Harold's Pilgrimage (1812–18), can. 3, l. 787

31 The self-torturing sophist, wild Rousseau.
Childe Harold's Pilgrimage (1812–18), can. 3, st. 77

32 I have not loved the world, nor the world me;
I have not flatter'd its rank breath, nor bow'd
To its idolatries a patient knee.
Childe Harold's Pilgrimage (1812–18), can. 3, st. 113

33 There are some feelings time cannot benumb,
Nor torture shake, or mine would now be cold and dumb.
Childe Harold's Pilgrimage (1812–18), can. 4, st. 19

34 Then farewell, Horace; whom I hated so,
Not for thy faults, but mine.
Childe Harold's Pilgrimage (1812–18), can. 4, st. 77

35 While stands the Coliseum, Rome shall stand;
When falls the Coliseum, Rome shall fall;
And when Rome falls—the World.
Childe Harold's Pilgrimage (1812–18), can. 4, st. 145

36 Oh that the desert were my dwelling-place,
With one fair spirit for my minister,
That I might all forget the human race,
And hating no one, love but only her!
Childe Harold's Pilgrimage (1812–18), can. 4, st. 177

37 There is a pleasure in the pathless woods,
There is a rapture on the lonely shore,
There is society, where none intrudes,
By the deep Sea, and music in its roar:
I love not Man the less, but Nature more.
Childe Harold's Pilgrimage (1812–18), can. 4, st. 178

38 What is writ is writ;
Would it were worthier!
Childe Harold's Pilgrimage (1812–18), can. 4, st. 185

39 She,
Was married, charming, chaste, and twenty-three.
Don Juan (1819–24), can. 1, st. 59

40 What men call gallantry, and gods adultery,
Is much more common where the climate's sultry.
Don Juan (1819–24), can. 1, st. 63

41 Christians have burnt each other, quite persuaded

That all the Apostles would have done as they did.
Don Juan (1819–24), can. 1, st. 83

42 A little still she strove, and much repented,
And whispering "I will ne'er consent"—consented.
Don Juan (1819–24), can. 1, st. 117

43 Sweet is revenge—especially to women.
Don Juan (1819–24), can. 1, st. 124

44 Pleasure's a sin, and sometimes sin's a pleasure.
Don Juan (1819–24), can. 1, st. 133

45 Man's love is of man's life a thing apart,
'Tis woman's whole existence.
Don Juan (1819–24), can. 1, st. 194

46 What is the end of fame? 'Tis but to fill
A certain portion of uncertain paper.
Don Juan (1819–24), can. 1, st. 218

47 There's nought, no doubt, so much the spirit calms
As rum and true religion.
Don Juan (1819–24), can. 2, st. 15

48 All who joy would win
Must share it,—Happiness was born a twin.
Don Juan (1819–24), can. 2, st. 172

49 Let us have wine and women, mirth and laughter,
Sermons and soda-water the day after.
Don Juan (1819–24), can. 2, st. 178

50 Man, being reasonable, must get drunk;
The best of life is but intoxication.
Don Juan (1819–24), can. 2, st. 179

51 And thus they form a group that's quite antique,
Half naked, loving, natural, and Greek.
Don Juan (1819–24), can. 2, st. 194

52 Agree to a short armistice with truth.
Don Juan (1819–24), can. 3

53 Cost his enemies a long repentance,
And made him a good friend, but bad acquaintance.
Don Juan (1819–24), can. 3

54 In her first passion woman loves her lover,
In all the others all she loves is love.
Don Juan (1819–24), can. 3, st. 3

55 'Tis melancholy, and a fearful sign
Of human frailty, folly, also crime,
That love and marriage rarely can combine,
Although they both are born in the same clime;
Marriage from love, like vinegar from wine
A sad, sour, sober beverage—by time
Is sharpen'd from its high celestial flavour,
Down to a very homely household savour.
Don Juan (1819–24), can. 3, st. 5

56 Romances paint at full length people's wooings,
But only give a bust of marriages:
For no one cares for matrimonial cooings,
There's nothing wrong in a connubial kiss:
Think you, if Laura had been Petrarch's wife,
He would have written sonnets all his life?
Don Juan (1819–24), can. 3, st. 8

57 All tragedies are finish'd by a death,
All comedies are ended by a marriage.
The future states of both are left to faith.
Don Juan (1819–24), can. 3, st. 9

58 Dreading that climax of all human ills,
The inflammation of his weekly bills.
Don Juan (1819–24), can. 3, st. 35

59 Though sages may pour out their wisdom's treasure,
There is no sterner moralist than Pleasure.
Don Juan (1819–24), can. 3, st. 65

60 The mountains look on Marathon—
And Marathon looks on the sea:
And musing there an hour alone,
I dream'd that Greece might still be free.
Don Juan (1819–24), can. 3, st. 86

61 But words are things, and a small drop of ink,
Falling like dew upon a thought, produces
That which makes thousands, perhaps millions, think.
Don Juan (1819–24), can. 3, st. 88

62 Milton the prince of poets—so we say;
A little heavy, but no less divine:
An independent being in his day—
Learn'd, pious, temperate in love and wine.
Don Juan (1819–24), can 3, st. 91

63 Ah! surely nothing dies but something mourns!
Don Juan (1819–24), can. 3, st. 108

64 Nothing so difficult as a beginning
In poesy, unless perhaps the end.
Don Juan (1819–24), can. 4

65 And if I laugh at any mortal thing,
Tis that I may not weep.
Don Juan (1819–24), can. 4, st. 4

66 The precious porcelain of human clay.
Don Juan (1819–24), can. 4, st. 11

67 The women pardoned all except her face.
Don Juan (1819–24), can. 5

68 I have a passion for the name of "Mary",
For once it was a magic sound to me:
And still it half calls up the realms of fairy
Where I beheld what never was to be.
Don Juan (1819–24), can. 5, st. 4

69 Why don't they knead two virtuous souls for life
Into that moral centaur, man and wife?
Don Juan (1819–24), can. 5, st. 158

70 There is a tide in the affairs of women,
Which, taken at the flood, leads God knows where.
Alluding to *Julius Caesar*, Act 4, Scene 3, ll. 217–218. *Don Juan* (1819–24), can. 6, st. 2

71 A lady of a "certain age", which means
Certainly aged.
Don Juan (1819–24), can. 6, st. 69

72 When Bishop Berkeley said "there was no matter",
And proved it—'twas no matter what he said.
Don Juan (1819–24), can. 11, st. 1

73 Nought's permanent among the human race,
Except the Whigs *not* getting into place.
Don Juan (1819–24), can. 11, st. 82

74 Merely innocent flirtation,
Not quite adultery, but adulteration.
Don Juan (1819–24), can. 12, st. 63

75 Now hatred is by far the longest pleasure;
Men love in haste, but they detest at leisure.
Don Juan (1819–24), can. 13, st. 4

76 Of all tales 'tis the saddest—and more sad,
Because it makes us smile.
Don Juan (1819–24), can. 13, st. 9

77 I hate to hunt down a tired metaphor.
Don Juan (1819–24), can. 13, st. 36

78 The English winter—ending in July,
To recommence in August.
Don Juan (1819–24), can. 13, st. 42

79 Society is now one polish'd horde,
Form'd of two mighty tribes, the *Bores* and *Bored*.
Don Juan (1819–24), can. 13, st. 95

80 All human history attests
That happiness for man,—the hungry sinner!—
Since Eve ate apples, much depends on dinner.
Don Juan (1819–24), can. 13, st. 99

81 I for one venerate a petticoat.
Don Juan (1819–24), can. 14, st. 26

82 Of all the horrid, hideous notes of woe,
Sadder than owl-songs or the midnight blast,
Is that portentous phrase, "I told you so."
Don Juan (1819–24), can. 14, st. 50

83 'Tis strange—but true; for truth is always strange;
Stranger than fiction: if it could be told,
How much would novels gain by the exchange!
Don Juan (1819–24), can. 14, st. 101

84 I'll publish, right or wrong:
Fools are my theme, let satire be my song.
English Bards and Scotch Reviewers (1809)

85 'Tis pleasant, sure, to see one's name in print;
A book's a book, although there's nothing in't.
English Bards and Scotch Reviewers (1809)

86 A man must serve his time to every trade
Save censure—critics all are ready made
Take hackney'd jokes from Miller, got by rote,
With just enough of learning to misquote.
English Bards and Scotch Reviewers (1809), ll. 63–6

87 Be warm, but pure: be amorous, but be chaste.
English Bards and Scotch Reviewers (1809), l. 306

88 The petrifactions of a plodding brain.
English Bards and Scotch Reviewers (1809), l. 416

89 As soon
Seek roses in December—ice in June;
Hope constancy in wind, or corn in chaff;
Believe a woman or an epitaph,
Or any other thing that's false, before
You trust in critics.
English Bards and Scotch Reviewers (1809), ll. 76–80

90 I awoke one morning and found myself famous.
Remark made after the publication of the first canto of *Childe Harold's Pilgrimage* (1812). Entry in *Memoranda* (1812)

91 They never fail who die
In a great cause.
Marino Faliero, Act 2, Scene 2, ll. 93–94, quoted in *The Works of Lord Byron*, 13 vols. (Ernest Hartley Coleridge and R. E. Prothero, eds.; 1898–1904)

92 All farewells should be sudden.
Sardanapalus (1821), Act 5

93 The "good old times"—all times when old are good—
Are gone.
The Age of Bronze (1823), st. 1, ll. 1–2

94 For what were all these country patriots born?
To hunt, and vote, and raise the price of corn?
The Age of Bronze (1823), st. 14

95 The spirit burning but unbent,
May writhe, rebel—the weak alone repent!
The Corsair (1814), can. 2, st. 10

96 Oh! too convincing—dangerously dear
In woman's eye the unanswerable tear!
The Corsair (1814), can. 2, st. 15

97 Ten thousand schemes of petulance and pride
Despatch her scheming children far and wide:
Some east, some west, some everywhere but north,
In quest of lawless gain, they issue forth.
And thus—accursed be the day and year!
She sent a Pict to play the felon here.
1811. Referring in general to Britain and in particular to Lord Elgin (the "Pict"), who removed the marble sculptures from the Parthenon and shipped them to London, where they have been kept (since 1816) in the British Museum. *The Curse of Minerva* (1812)

98 And lovelier things have mercy shown
To every failing but their own;
And every woe a tear can claim,
Except an erring sister's shame.
The Giaour (1813), ll. 418–21

99 A better farmer ne'er brushed dew from lawn,
A worse king never left a realm undone!
Referring to George III. *The Vision of Judgment* (1822), st. 8

100 And when the tumult dwindled to a calm,
I left him practising the hundredth psalm.
The Vision of Judgment (1822), st. 106

Cabell, James Branch (1879–1958) U.S. novelist and journalist

1 I am willing to taste any drink once.
Jurgen (1919)

2 The religion of Hell is patriotism and the government is an enlightened democracy.
Jurgen (1919)

3 The optimist proclaims that we live in the best of all possible worlds; and the pessimist fears this is true.
The Silver Stallion (1926), bk. 4, ch. 26

Cabellero, Francisco Largo Spanish politician

1 The only hope of the masses now is in social revolution. It alone can save Spain from Fascism.
February 1934. In response to Republican unwillingness to take agrarian reform seriously. Remark, quoted in *The Spanish Labyrinth* (Gerald Brenan; 1943)

Cabot, Richard Clarke (1868–1939) U.S. physician

1 Ethics and Science need to shake hands.
The Meaning of Right and Wrong (1933), Introduction

2 Before you tell the "truth" to the patient, be sure you know the "truth," and that the patient wants to hear it.
Journal of Chronic Diseases (1963), 16:443

Cabral, Amilcar (1921–73) Guinean revolutionary leader and freedom fighter

1 Hide nothing from the masses of our people. Tell no lies. Expose lies whenever they are told. Mask no difficulties, mistakes, failures. Claim no easy victories.
Party directive (1965), quoted in *Revolution in Guinea: An African People's Struggle, Selected Texts by Amilcar Cabral* (Richard Handyside, ed.; 1969)

Cadogan, William (1711–97) British physician

1 Children, in general, are overclothed and overfed. To these causes, I impute most of their diseases.
Essays upon Nursing and Management of Children (1748)

Caesar, Julius (Gaius Julius Caesar; 100–44 B.C.) Roman general and statesman

Quotations about Caesar

1 A man of great common sense and good taste,—meaning thereby a man without originality or moral courage.
George Bernard Shaw (1856–1950) Irish playwright. *Caesar and Cleopatra* (1901), Notes

Quotations by Caesar

2 The die is cast.
Said on crossing the River Rubicon, in Northern Italy, at the start of the civil war against Pompey (49 B.C.). Remark, quoted in *The Twelve Caesars* (Suetonius; A.D. 121?)

3 All Gaul is divided into three parts.
The Gallic Wars (51? B.C.), vol. 1, ch. 1

4 Caesar's wife must be above suspicion.
Said in justification of his divorce from Pompeia, after she was unwittingly involved in a scandal. *Lives* (Plutarch; 62? B.C.)

5 I came, I saw, I conquered.
48 B.C. Inscription used in Caesar's triumph of 48 B.C. to celebrate his victory over Pompey at Pharsalia, and referring to his characteristically swift and ruthless tactics. Quoted in *The Twelve Caesars* (Suetonius; A.D. 121?)

6 You too, Brutus?
44 B.C. Last words. Quoted in *The Twelve Caesars* (Suetonius; A.D. 121?)

Cage, John (John Milton Cage, Jr.; 1912–92) U.S. composer

1 Any training in art is at least a partial training in anarchy.
International Dance Course for Professional Choreographers and Composers, Surrey University, Guildford, England (August 1981)

2 A composer knows his work as a woodsman knows a path he has traced and retraced, while a listener is confronted by the same work as one is in the woods by a plant he has never seen before.
Silence (1961)

3 And what is the purpose of writing music...simply a way to wake up to the very life we're living, which is so excellent once one gets one's mind and one's desires out of its way and lets it act of its own accord.
Silence (1961)

4 Composing's one thing, performing's another, listening's a third. What can they have to do with one another?
Silence (1961)

5 It is better to make a piece of music than to perform one, better to perform one than to listen to one, better to listen to one than to misuse it as a means of distraction, entertainment, or acquisition of "culture."
Silence (1961)

6 Music is edifying, for from time to time it sets the soul in operation.
Silence (1961)

7 New music, new listening. Not an attempt to understand something that is being said, for, if something were being

said, the sounds would be given in the shapes of words. Just an attention to the activity of sounds.
Silence (1961)

8 Try as we may to make a silence, we cannot.
Silence (1961)

9 Until I die there will be sounds. And they will continue following after my death. One need not fear about the future of music.
Silence (1961)

10 I was asked by Syvilla Fort...to write music...evocative of her African heritage...Nothing satisfied me until finally, realizing that it was the sound of the piano itself that was objectionable, I decided to change that sound by placing objects on and between the strings.
Quoted in *John Cage, Writer: Previously Uncollected Pieces* (Richard Kostelanetz, ed.; 1993)

11 I have nothing to say, I am saying it, and that is poetry.
Sunday Times, London (quoted by Cyril Connolly; September 10, 1972)

Cage, Nicolas (Nicholas Coppola; b.1964) U.S. actor

1 Did I ever tell you this snakeskin jacket is a symbol of my individuality and belief in personal freedom?
As Sailor on marrying Lulu (played by Laura Dern). *Wild at Heart* (1990)

Cagney, James (1899–1986) U.S. actor

1 You dirty double-crossing rat!
Usually misquoted by impressionists as "You dirty rat." *Blonde Crazy* (1931)

2 A song-and-dance man...is what I am basically...I think dancing is a primal urge coming to life at the first moment we need to express joy.
Cagney by Cagney (1976)

3 Dancing, if done consistently and as part of a measured regimen is a form of health insurance...one must never surprise the heart.
Cagney by Cagney (1976)

4 I couldn't dance at all except for that marvelously intricate step, the Peabody, named I think after its inventor, a Boston cop.
Cagney by Cagney (1976)

5 It was a female impersonation act, I found to my great surprise. Six guys in skirts serving basically as a chorus line and one of the "girls" was quitting...And that is how I began to learn dancing—as a chorus girl.
Cagney by Cagney (1976)

6 I went into show business strictly from hunger. Starvation helps to turn you into a good actor, I guess.
Quoted in *Film-makers Speak* (Jay Leyda, ed.; 1977)

Cahn, Sammy (Samuel Cohen; 1913–93) U.S. songwriter

1 Love and marriage, love and marriage,
Go together like a horse and carriage.
Song lyric. "Love and Marriage," *Our Town* (1955)

Cain, James M. (James Mallahan Cain; 1892–1977) U.S. novelist and screenwriter

1 The Postman Always Rings Twice
1934. Book title.

Caine, Michael (b.1933) British actor

1 To qualify for a Los Angelean, you need three things: (a) a driver's licence; (b) your own tennis court; (c) a preference for snorting cocaine.
Photoplay (February 1984)

2 When you reach the top, that's when the climb begins.
Attrib.

3 Not many people know that.
Caine's catch phrase, which was made the title of his memoirs, is said to have been his comment when habitually offering information garnered from *The Guinness Book of Records.* Attrib.

Cai Qijiao (also known as Ts'ai Ch'i-chiao; b.1918) Chinese poet

1 To search the heart is poetry's lifeblood.
"Poetry" (1976), quoted in *The Red Azalea* (Edward Morin, ed.; 1990)

Caird, Edward (1835–1908) British philosopher and theologian

1 When you have learnt all that Oxford can teach you, go and discover why, with so much wealth in Britain, there continues to be so much poverty and how poverty can be cured.
Said to Lord Beveridge. Attrib.

Calder, Alexander (1898–1976) U.S. sculptor

1 The sense of motion in painting has long been considered one of the primary elements of composition...Just as one can compose colors, or forms, so I can compose motions.
1933. "Alexander Calder: Cosmic Imagery and the use of Scientific Instruments," *October Arts* (Joan M. Marter; 1978), vol. 53, no.2

Calder, Nigel (Nigel David Ritchie Calder; b.1931) British science writer and broadcaster

1 In a sense human flesh is made of stardust. Every atom in the human body, excluding only the primordial hydrogen atoms, was fashioned in stars that formed, grew old and exploded most violently before the Sun and Earth came into being.
January 27, 1977. Originally broadcast. *The Key to the Universe: a Report on the New Physics* (1977)

Calder, Ritchie, Baron (Peter Ritchie-Calder; 1906–82) Scottish educator and writer

1 That is how the atom is split. But what does it mean? To us who think in terms of practical use it means—Nothing!
Daily Herald (June 27, 1932)

Calderón de la Barca, Pedro (1600–81) Spanish playwright and poet

1 For man's greatest crime is to have been born.
Life is a Dream (1635), Act 1

2 What mazed confusion!
It is a labyrinth wherein the reason
Can find no clue.
Life is a Dream (1635), Act 1

3 Even in dreams good works are not wasted.
Life is a Dream (1635), Act 2

4 For I see now that I am asleep that I dream when I am awake.
Life is a Dream (1635), Act 2

5 He dreams who thrives and prospers in this life.
He dreams who toils and strives. He dreams who injures,
Offends, and insults. So that in this world
Everyone dreams the thing he is, though no one
Can understand it.
Life is a Dream (1635), Act 2

6 How seldom does prediction fail, when evil!
How oft, foretelling good!
Life is a Dream (1635), Act 2

7 What is life? A frenzy. What is life? An illusion, a shadow, a fiction, and the greatest good is worth little; since all of life is a dream, and dreams are dreams.
Life is a Dream (1635), Act 2

8 Pleasure is a lovely flame
That's soon converted into dust and ashes
By any wind that blows it.
Life is a Dream (1635), Act 3

9 Fame, like water, bears up the lighter things, and lets the weighty sink.
Attrib.

Calderone, Mary (1904–98) U.S. physician and sex educator

1 SIECUS was founded in 1964, when one in two marriages was warped by sexual problems. Sex had to be brought out of the Victorian closet—freed from the guilt and fear, bigotry and misconceptions...if America was to recover from its deep-rooted sexual trouble.
SIECUS is an acronym for Sex Information and Education Council of the United States. Interview (1979)

Caldwell, Erskine (Erskine Preston Caldwell; 1903–87) U.S. novelist and short-story writer

1 Here is hard-core unemployment, widespread and chronic; here is a region of shacks...In this region of steep mountains, a person is exceptionally fortunate if he is able to hack out two or three ten-foot rows of land for potatoes or beans.
Referring to poverty-stricken sharecroppers in rural Georgia. *Around About America* (1964)

Caldwell, Sarah (b.1924) U.S. opera director and conductor

1 If you approach an opera as though it were something that always went the same way, that's what you get. I approach an opera as if I didn't know it.
Quoted in "Sarah Caldwell: The Flamboyant of the Opera," *MS* (Jane Scovell Appleton; May 1975)

2 We must continuously discipline ourselves to remember how it felt the first moment.
Referring to music. Quoted in "Sarah Caldwell: The Flamboyant of the Opera," *MS* (Jane Scovell Appleton; May 1975)

Calhoun, John C. (John Caldwell Calhoun; 1782–1850) U.S. statesman

1 We are not a nation, but a union, a confederacy of equal and sovereign states.
Letter to Oliver Dyer (January 1, 1849)

2 History furnishes many instances of similar struggles, where the love of liberty has prevailed against power under every disadvantage, and among them few more striking than that of our own Revolution.
Speech championing states' rights (February 15, 1833)

3 I have, Senators, believed from the first that the agitation of the subject of slavery would, if not prevented by some timely and effective measure, end in disunion.
Speech to the Senate (March 4, 1840)

4 The government of the absolute majority instead of the government of the people is but the government of the strongest interests; and when not efficiently checked, it is the most tyrannical and oppressive that can be devised.
Speech to the Senate (February 15, 1833)

Caligula (Gaius Julius Caesar Germanicus; 12–41) Roman emperor

1 Would that the Roman people had but one neck!
Attrib. *Life of Caligula* (Suetonius; 121?), ch. 30

Call, Frank Oliver (1878–1956) Canadian poet and linguist

1 The soul of Canada is a dual personality, and must remain only half revealed to those who know only one language.
Referring to the two main languages spoken in Canada, French and English. *The Spell of French Canada* (1926)

Callaghan, Jim, Baron Callaghan of Cardiff (Leonard James Callaghan; b.1912) British prime minister

1 You know, Mr Paisley, we are the children of God.
Ian Paisley is a Unionist politician and Protestant cleric in Northern Ireland. He responded "No, we are not, Mr Callaghan. We are the children of wrath." Quoted in *A House Divided* (James Callaghan; 1973)

2 Either back us or sack us.
Speech at Labour Party Conference, Brighton (October 5, 1977)

3 We used to think that you could spend your way out of a recession...that option no longer exists.
Speech, Labour Party Conference (September 28, 1976)

4 A lie can be half-way round the world before the truth has got its boots on.
Speech to the British Parliament (November 1, 1976)

5 Britain has lived for too long on borrowed time, borrowed money and even borrowed ideas.
Observer, London (October 3, 1976), "Sayings of the Week"

Callas, Maria (Maria Anna Sofia Cecilia Meneghini (born Kalogeropoulos); 1923–77) U.S. soprano

1 He did not marry for love and I do not think that his wife did either.
Referring to the marriage of Jacqueline Kennedy to Aristotle Onassis, Maria Callas's ex-lover. Quoted in *Maria Callas: Sacred Monster* (Stelios Galatopoulos; 1998)

Callcott, George H. (George Hardy Callcott; b.1929) U.S. historian

1 In history, as in art, man sees himself. Seeing himself, he understands the past.
History in the United States 1800–1860 (1970)

2 In the Romantic age, history, like art and poetry, was more real than reality, more trustworthy than science. It was a noble definition of history; but then history was a noble subject.
History in the United States 1800–1860 (1970)

Callimachus (*fl.* 5th century B.C.) Greek sculptor

1 Say not that the good die.
Epigram 10

Calment, Jeanne (1875–1997) French citizen

1 God has forgotten me.
Referring to her long life (she was 120 at the time). *Daily Telegraph*, London (October 1995)

Calverley, C. S. (Charles Stuart Calverley; 1831–84) British poet and parodist

1 The heart which grief hath cankered
Hath one unfailing remedy—the Tankard.
"Beer" (1861)

2 Yet it is better to drop thy friends,
O my daughter, than to drop thy "H's".
"Of Friendship," *The Complete Works of C. S. Calverley. With A Biographical Note by Sir Walter J. Sendall* (1901), st. 1, ll. 3–4

Calvin, John (1509–64) French church reformer

1 It is a mockery to allow women to baptise. Even the Virgin Mary was not allowed this.
Christianae Religionis Institutio (1536)

Calvino, Italo (1923–85) Cuban-born Italian novelist and short-story writer

1 Writing always means hiding something in such a way that it is then discovered.
If on a Winter's Night a Traveller (William Weaver, tr.; 1979), ch. 8

2 But perhaps it is this distrust of our senses that prevents us from feeling comfortable in the universe.
Mr. Palomar (William Weaver, tr.; 1983)

3 I have tried to remove weight, sometimes from people, sometimes from heavenly bodies, sometimes from cities; above all I have tried to remove weight from the structure of stories and from language.
Six Memos for the Next Millennium (Patrick Creagh, tr.; 1992)

4 The word connects the visible trace with the invisible thing, the absent thing, the thing that is desired or feared, like a frail emergency bridge flung over an abyss.
1985. "Exactitude," *Six Memos for the Next Millennium* (Patrick Creagh, tr.; 1992)

5 A child's pleasure in listening to stories lies partly in waiting for things he expects to be repeated: situations, phrases, formulas.
1985. "Quickness," *Six Memos for the Next Millennium* (Patrick Creagh, tr.; 1992)

6 My work as a writer has from the beginning aimed at tracing the lightning flashes of the mental circuits that capture and link points distant from each other in time and space.
1985. "Quickness," *Six Memos for the Next Millennium* (Patrick Creagh, tr.; 1992)

7 We are bombarded today by such a quantity of images that we can no longer distinguish direct experience from what we have seen for a few seconds on television. The memory is littered with bits and pieces of images, like a rubbish dump.
1985. "Visibility," *Six Memos for the Next Millennium* (Patrick Creagh, tr.; 1992)

Calvo Sotelo, José (?–1936) Spanish politician

1 I prefer a Red Spain to a broken Spain.
Referring to the perceived threat to Spain's unity by Basque and Galician nationalists. He was a politician of the extreme right. Quoted in *The Spanish Labyrinth* (Gerald Brenan; 1943)

Cambó, Francisco, General, Spanish banker, industrialist, and political leader

1 During a whole century, Spain has lived under the appearance of a constitutional democratic regime, without the people having ever, directly or indirectly, had the least share in the Government.
Quoted in *The Spanish Labyrinth* (Gerald Brenan; 1943)

2 Considering the circumstances in which the country finds itself, the most conservative thing is to be a revolutionary.
As the leader of the Catalan Conservatives, Francisco Cambó supported Catalonian independence. Many so-called revolutionaries were in favour of a united Spanish republic, which he thought posed a threat to the independence of Catalonia. Quoted in *The Spanish Labyrinth* (Gerald Brenan; 1943)

Cambridge, Godfrey (1933–78) U.S. comedian, actor, and civil rights advocate

1 Middle income, that means, if you steal, you can pay the rent.
"Laugh at this Negro, but Darkly," *Esquire* (November 1964)

Cambridge Rape Crisis Centre British organization

1 Words such as "beast," "monster" and "sex fiend" are commonly used to describe the rapist. Yet we rarely see the simple word "man," which the rapist invariably is.
Out of Focus

Camden, William (1551–1623) English antiquary and historian

1 My friend, judge not me,
Thou seest I judge not thee.
Betwixt the stirrup and the ground
Mercy I asked, mercy I found.
"Epitaphs," *Remains Concerning Britain* (1605)

Cameron, James (James Mark Cameron; 1911–85) British journalist and broadcaster

1 It was long ago in my life as a simple reporter that I decided that facts must never get in the way of truth.
Attrib.

Campbell, Glen (b.1934) U.S. singer

1 The reason there's so much smog in L.A. is so God can't see what they're doing down there.
Quoted in *The Wit and Wisdom of Rock and Roll* (Maxim Jabukowski, ed.; 1983)

Campbell, James (b.1951) Scottish writer

1 When Goebbels decreed that the "Judeo-Negroid" swing sounds were potentially harmful to the master race...Skvorecky...transformed "St Louis Blues" into "The Song of Resetova Lhota" ("I'm on my way to see my Aryan folk...") and carried on playing.
Referring to Czech novelist and jazz saxophonist, Josef Skvorecky, during the Nazi occupation of his country. *The Picador Book of Blues and Jazz* (1995), introduction

2 There is no more potent example of the equation between jazz and freedom in modern European history than...the ghetto Swingers and the Killer Drillers—which played in the concentration camps, where several of their members perished.
Referring to the Nazi concentration camps during the German occupation of Czechoslovakia at the time of World War II. *The Picador Book of Blues and Jazz* (1995), introduction

Campbell, Joseph (1904–87) U.S. writer, editor, and teacher

1 Follow your bliss.
1987. Motto. Published the year after Campbell's death. *The Power of Myth* (1988)

Campbell, Mrs. Patrick (Beatrice Stella Tanner; 1865–1940) British actor

1 Do you know why God withheld the sense of humour from women? That we may love you instead of laughing at you.
Quoted in *Mrs. Pat: the Life of Mrs Patrick Campbell* (Margot Peters; 1984)

2 It doesn't matter what you do in the bedroom as long as you don't do it in the street and frighten the horses.
1910? *The Duchess of Jermyn Street* (Daphne Fielding; 1964), ch. 2

3 Marriage is a result of the longing for the deep, deep peace of the double bed after the hurly-burly of the chaise-longue.
Referring to her recent marriage. Quoted in *While Rome Burns* (Alexander Woollcott; 1934), "The First Mrs Tanqueray"

Campbell, Naomi (b.1970) British model

1 I'm not what you'd call true to type—the typical English rose!
You Magazine (June 28, 1992)

2 You've got to understand, this business is about selling, and blonde and blue-eyed girls are what sells.
Quoted in *Guardian*, London (Alison Daniels; April 11, 1997)

3 And I don't like the word supermodel. I'm not as marketable as the other top models because I'm black. You can't sell white cosmetics on black skin, and there aren't any big companies out there who cater for ethnic women.
Quoted in "Life can be tough on only £10,000 a day," *Times*, London (Kate Muir; October 18, 1991)

Campbell, Patrick (Patrick Gordon Campbell; 1913–80) British humorous writer and editor

1 Journalism is the only job that requires no degrees, no diplomas and no specialised knowledge of any kind.
My Life and Easy Times (1967)

Campbell, Roy (1901–57) South African-born poet, translator, and journalist

1 South Africa, renowned both far and wide
For politics and little else beside.
1928. "The Wayzgoose," *Collected Poems of Roy Campbell* (1949), pt. 1, ll. 3–4

Campbell, Susan M. (b.1941) U.S. lecturer and author

1 Teamwork is a constant balancing act between self-interest and group interest.
From Chaos to Confidence (1995)

Campbell, Thomas (1777–1844) Scottish poet

1 To-morrow let us do or die!
"Gertrude of Wyoming" (1809), pt. 3, st. 37

2 'Tis distance lends enchantment to the view,
And robes the mountain in its azure hue.
"Pleasures of Hope" (1799), pt. 1, l. 7

3 What millions died—that Caesar might be great!
"Pleasures of Hope" (1799), pt. 2

4 O star-eyed Science! hast thou wandered there,
To waft us home the message of despair?
"Pleasures of Hope" (1799), pt. 2, l. 325

5 Truth, ever lovely, since the world began
The foe of tyrants, and the friend of man.
"Pleasures of Hope" (1799), pt. 2, l. 347

6 O leave this barren spot to me!
Spare, woodman, spare the beechen tree.
"The Beech-Tree's Petition" (1809?), st. 1–2

7 Better be courted and jilted
Than never be courted at all.
"The Jilted Nymph" (1843), ll. 19–20

8 An original something, fair maid, you would win me
To write—but how shall I begin?
For I fear I have nothing original in me—
Excepting Original Sin.
"To a Young Lady, Who Asked Me to Write Something Original for Her Album" (1843)

9 To live in hearts we leave behind
Is not to die.
Hallowed Ground (1825)

10 Now Barabbas was a publisher.
A Publisher and his Friends: Memoir and Correspondence of the late John Murray (1891), vol. 1, ch. 14

11 Gentlemen, you must not mistake me. I admit that he is the sworn foe of our nation, and, if you will, of the whole human

race. But, gentlemen, we must be just to our enemy. We must not forget that he once shot a bookseller.
1832. Excusing himself in proposing a toast to Napoleon at a literary dinner. *The Life and Letters of Lord Macaulay* (G. O. Trevelyan; 1876)

Campion, Thomas (1567–1620) English poet, composer, and physician

1 The man of life upright,
Whose guiltless heart is free
From all dishonest deeds
Or thought of vanity.
"The Man of Life Upright" (1614)

2 When to her lute Corinna sings,
Her voice revives the leaden strings,
And both in highest notes appear,
As any challenged echo clear.
But when she doth of mourning speak,
Ev'n with her sighs the strings do break.
A Book of Airs (1601), no. 6

3 Good thoughts his only friends,
His wealth a well-spent age,
The earth his sober inn
And quiet pilgrimage.
A Book of Airs (1601), no. 18

4 Follow thy fair sun, unhappy shadow.
Follow Thy Fair Sun (1614)

5 There is a garden in her face,
Where roses and white lilies grow;
A heav'nly paradise is that place,
Wherein all pleasant fruits do flow.
There cherries grow, which none may buy
Till "Cherry ripe" themselves do cry.
Fourth Book of Airs (1617), no. 7, st. 1

6 Those cherries fairly do enclose
Of orient pearl a double row,
Which when her lovely laughter shows,
They look like rosebuds fill'd with snow.
Fourth Book of Airs (1617), no. 7, st. 1

7 The Summer hath his joys,
And Winter his delights.
Though Love and all his pleasures are but toys,
They shorten tedious nights.
Third Book of Airs (1617?), no. 12

Camus, Albert (1913–60) Algerian-born French novelist, essayist, and playwright

1 An intellectual is someone whose mind watches itself.
Notebooks (1935–42)

2 As soon as one does not kill oneself, one must keep silent about life.
Notebooks (1935–42)

3 It is a kind of spiritual snobbery that makes people think that they can be happy without money.
Notebooks (1935–42)

4 Politics and the fate of mankind are shaped by men without ideas and without greatness. Men who have greatness within them don't go in for politics.
Notebooks (1935–42)

5 Real nobility is based on scorn, courage, and profound indifference.
Notebooks (1935–42)

6 The need to be right—the sign of a vulgar mind.
Notebooks (1935–42)

7 There is dignity in work only when it is work freely accepted.
Notebooks (1935–42)

8 Alas, after a certain age every man is responsible for his face.
The Fall (1956)

9 A single sentence will suffice for modern man: he fornicated and read the papers.
The Fall (1956)

10 Don't wait for the Last Judgement. It takes place every day.
The Fall (1956)

11 No man is a hypocrite in his pleasures.
The Fall (1956)

12 Style, like sheer silk, too often hides eczema.
The Fall (1956)

13 A world that can be explained even with bad reasons is a familiar world. But in a universe suddenly divested of illusions and lights, man feels an alien, a stranger.
The Myth of Sisyphus (1942)

14 If God exists, all depends on him and we can do nothing against his will. If he does not exist, everything depends on us.
The Myth of Sisyphus (1942)

15 Man stands face to face with the irrational. He feels within him the longing for happiness and for reason. The absurd is born of the confrontation between the human need and the unreasonable silence of the world.
The Myth of Sisyphus (1942)

16 There is but one truly serious philosophical problem, and that is suicide. Judging whether life is, or is not worth living amounts to answering the fundamental question of philosophy.
The Myth of Sisyphus (1942)

17 Since the order of the world is shaped by death, mightn't it be better for God if we refuse to believe in Him, and struggle with all our might against death without raising our eyes towards the heaven where He sits in silence?
The Plague (1947)

18 When a war breaks out, people say, It's too stupid; it can't last long. But though a war may well be too stupid, that doesn't prevent its lasting. Stupidity has a knack of getting its way.
The Plague (1947)

19 All modern revolutions have ended in a reinforcement of the power of the State.
The Rebel (1951)

20 He who despairs over an event is a coward, but he who holds hopes for the human condition is a fool.
The Rebel (1951)

21 I am not made for politics because I am incapable of wishing for, or accepting the death of my adversary.
The Rebel (1951)

22 I proclaim that I believe in nothing and that everything is absurd, but I cannot doubt the validity of my own proclamation and I am compelled to believe, at least, in my own protest. The first and only datum...within absurdist experience, is rebellion.
The Rebel (1951)

23 One cannot be a part-time nihilist.
The Rebel (1951)

24 The future is the only kind of property that the masters willingly concede to slaves.
The Rebel (1951)

25 The slave begins by demanding justice and ends by wanting to wear a crown. He must dominate in his turn.
The Rebel (1951)

26 What is a rebel? A man who says no: but whose refusal does not imply a renunciation.
The Rebel (1951)

27 We have chosen to accept human justice with its terrible imperfections, careful only to correct it through a desperately maintained honesty.
1944. Article in the wartime French resistance movement newspaper *Combat,* which Camus joined in 1943. Quoted in *Camus, a Biography* (H. R. Lottman, 1979), "First Combats"

Canby, Henry S. (Henry Seidel Canby; 1878–1961) U.S. historian

1 History is not only becoming, it is also being.
American Memoir (1947)

Candid Camera U.S. television series

1 Smile, you're on Candid Camera.
Catchphrase from the U.S. and British television series. *Candid Camera* (1950s–1960s)

Canetti, Elias (1905–94) Bulgarian-born writer

1 Killing is the lowest form of survival.
Crowds and Power (1960)

2 A country in which the people go around stark naked and only cover their ears. In that land all shame resides in the ears.
The Agony of Flies (1992)

3 All literature wavers between nature and paradise and loves to mistake one for the other.
The Agony of Flies (1992)

4 A person often falls very ill in order to become someone else and then returns to health much disappointed.
The Agony of Flies (1992)

5 God made a mistake in his calculations at the Tower of Babel: nowadays everybody speaks the same technology.
The Agony of Flies (1992)

6 It serves no purpose to tell oneself the truth and nothing but the truth. The only truth that does not transform itself into nothing is horror and annihilation.
The Agony of Flies (1992)

7 One can write history as if it had always looked the way it does today. But then why write history at all?
The Agony of Flies (1992)

8 The act of naming is the great and solemn consolation of mankind.
The Agony of Flies (1992)

9 The historians of facts who omit the most interesting thing about history—namely, its invention.
The Agony of Flies (1992)

10 The poet lives by exaggeration and makes himself known through misunderstandings.
The Agony of Flies (1992)

11 The power of dreams...is tied to the multiformity of animals: with their disappearance one may soon expect the dreams to dry up as well.
The Agony of Flies (1992)

12 It is important what you still have planned at the end. It shows the extent of injustice in your death.
The Human Province (1973)

13 The great aphorists read as if they had all known each other well.
The Human Province (1973)

14 Whenever you observe an animal closely, you feel as if a human being sitting inside were making fun of you.
The Human Province (1973)

Canning, George (1770–1827) British prime minister

1 A steady patriot of the world alone,
The friend of every country but his own.
Referring to the Jacobin. "New Morality," *The Anti-Jacobin* (1821)

2 And finds, with keen discriminating sight,
Black's not so black; nor white so very white.
"New Morality," *The Anti-Jacobin* (1821), l. 199

3 Give me the avowed, erect and manly foe;
Firm I can meet, perhaps return the blow;
But of all plagues, good Heaven, thy wrath can send,
Save me, oh, save me, from the candid friend.
"New Morality," *The Anti-Jacobin* (1821), l. 207

4 I called the New World into existence to redress the balance of the Old.
The King's Message (December 12, 1826)

5 Things are getting back to a wholesome state. Every nation for itself, and God for us all.
George Canning supported nationalist movements in South America and Europe. Quoted in *Europe: A History* (Norman Davies; 1996), ch. 10

Cannon, Walter Bradford (1871–1945) U.S. physiologist

1 My first article of belief is based on the observation, almost

universally confirmed in present knowledge, that what happens in our bodies is directed toward a useful end.
"Some Working Principles," *The Way of an Investigator* (1973)

Cánovas del Castillo, Antonio, Don, Spanish politician

1 I come to galvanize the political corpse of Spain.
He came to power after the failure of the 1868 revolution. Quoted in *The Spanish Labyrinth* (Gerald Brenan; 1943)

2 Spaniards are those people who can't be anything else.
Response when asked, for the purpose of some clause of the Constitution, to define the limits of Spanish nationality. Quoted in *The Spanish Labyrinth* (Gerald Brenan; 1943)

Cantona, Eric (b.1966) French soccer player

1 The quest for spontaneity is fundamental in art and football expresses it best.

Cantor, Eddie (1892–1964) U.S. entertainer

1 Love isn't like a reservoir. You'll never drain it dry. It's much more like a natural spring. The longer and the farther it flows, the stronger and the deeper and the clearer it becomes.
The Way I See It (Phyllis Rosenteur, ed.; 1959)

Cao Xueqin (also known as Ts'ao Hsüeh-ch'in; 1715–63) Chinese novelist

1 I suddenly recalled all the girls I had known, considering each in turn, and it dawned on me that all of them surpassed me in behavior and understanding; that I, shameful to say, for all my masculine dignity, fell short of the gentler sex.
A Dream of Red Mansions (with Gao E; 18th century), vol. 1, ch. 1

Cao Yu (also known as Ts'ao Yü; 1910–97) Chinese playwright

1 FAN What I've done I've done on my own responsibility. Not that I'm like your grandfather, or your great-uncle, or your dear father himself—doing the most atrocious things in private, and wearing a mask of morality in public.
Thunderstorm (Wang Tso-Liang and A. C. Barnes, trs.; 1933), Act 2

Capone, Al (Alphonse Capone; 1899–1947) Italian-born U.S. gangster

1 They can't collect legal taxes from illegal money.
1930. Objecting to the U.S. Bureau of Internal Revenue claiming large sums in unpaid back tax. *Capone* (J. Kobler; 1971)

2 I've been accused of every death except the casualty list of the World War.
The Bootleggers (Kenneth Allsop; 1961), ch. 11

3 This is virgin territory for whorehouses.
Talking about suburban Chicago. *The Bootleggers* (Kenneth Allsop; 1961), ch. 16

4 I don't even know what street Canada is on.
Attrib.

Capote, Truman (Truman Streckfus Persons; 1924–84) U.S. novelist

Quotations about Capote

1 The book, when it came out in 1965, was considered an instant classic, largely because Capote told everyone it was.
Bill Bryson (b.1951) U.S. writer. Referring to Truman Capote's *In Cold Blood* (1965). *The Lost Continent* (1989), ch. 20

Quotations by Capote

2 I didn't want to harm the man. I thought he was a very nice gentleman. Soft-spoken. I thought so right up to the moment I cut his throat.
In Cold Blood (1966)

3 The most dangerous thing in the world is to make a friend of an Englishman, because he'll come sleep in your closet rather than spend 10 shillings on a hotel.
Observer, London (March 24, 1968), "Sayings of the Week"

4 Venice is like eating an entire box of chocolate liqueurs at one go.
Observer, London (November 26, 1961), "Sayings of the Week,"

5 Breakfast At Tiffany's
1958. Book title.

6 Other Voices, Other Rooms
1948. Book title.

7 That's not writing, that's typing.
Referring to Jack Kerouac's novel *On The Road*. Attrib.

Capra, Frank (1897–1991) Italian-born U.S. film director

1 I made mistakes in drama. I thought drama was when actors cried. But drama is when the audience cries.
Cinemas No 12, Antenne 2, French television (February 1983), quoted in *Chambers Film Quotes* (Tony Crawley, ed.; 1991)

Caracciolo, Francesco, Duke of Brienza (1752–99) Neapolitan diplomat and admiral

1 In England there are sixty different religions, and only one sauce.
18th century. *Notes and Queries* (December 1968)

Cardin, Pierre (b.1922) Italian-born French fashion designer

1 I do not believe there has ever been a name as important as Pierre Cardin in the general history of couture.
Sunday Times, London (October 21, 1990)

Cardozo, Benjamin (Benjamin Nathan Cardozo; 1870–1938) U.S. Supreme Court justice

1 Justice is not to be taken by storm. She is to be wooed by slow advances.
The Growth of the Law (1924)

Carducho, Vicente (1570 or 1576–1638) Italian-born Spanish painter and theorist

1 Each artist has a tendency to reproduce or imitate his own likeness...And so you will see that if a painter is choleric he will show anger in his works; if phlegmatic, mildness; if devout, religion; if lustful, sensuality.
1633. *Dialogues on Painting* (D. G. Cruzada Villaamil, ed.; 1865)

2 I don't know which is more ennobling; generosity or the possession and appreciation of a beautiful object. For sometimes such objects bring renown and esteem to an entire nation.
1633. *Dialogues on Painting* (D.G. Cruzada Villaamil, ed.; 1865)

Carew, Jan (b.1922) Guyanese-born novelist, actor, and newspaper editor

1 Learning had made us not more human, but less so. Learning had not increased our knowledge of good and evil, but intensified and made more rational and deadly our greed for gain.
Black Midas (1969)

2 The Caribbean writer today is a creature balanced between limbo and nothingness, exile abroad and homelessness at home.
Fulcrums of Change (1988)

Carew, Thomas (1595?–1639?) English poet and diplomat

1 He that loves a rosy cheek,
Or a coral lip admires,
Or, from star-like eyes, doth seek
Fuel to maintain his fires;
As old Time makes these decay,
So his flames must waste away.
"Disdain Returned" (1640)

Carey, George, Archbishop (George Leonard Carey; b.1935) British Anglican bishop

1 My fear will be that in 15 years' time Jerusalem, Bethlehem, once centres of strong Christian presence, might become a kind of Walt Disney Theme Park.
Observer, London (January 12, 1992)

2 The idea that only a male can represent Christ at the altar is a most serious heresy.
Reader's Digest (April 1991)

3 I see it as an elderly lady, who mutters away to herself in a corner, ignored most of the time.
Referring to the Church of England. *Reader's Digest* (March 1991)

Carey, Henry (1687?–1743) English poet and composer

1 Confound their politics,
Frustrate their knavish tricks.
British national anthem. "God Save the King" (1740?)

2 God save our Gracious King,
Long live our noble King,
God save the King.
Send him victorious,
Happy and glorious.
British national anthem. "God Save the King" (1740?)

3 Of all the days that's in the week
I dearly love but one day—
And that's the day that comes betwixt
A Saturday and Monday.
Song lyric. "Sally in our Alley" (1737)

4 Of all the girls that are so smart
There's none like pretty Sally;
She is the darling of my heart
And she lives in our alley.
Song lyric. "Sally in our Alley" (1737)

5 Genteel in personage,
Conduct, and equipage;
Noble by heritage,
Generous and free.
The Contrivances (1715), Act 1, Scene 2

Carey, Michael S., Very Reverend (1913–85) British churchman

1 The use of the birch is not to be deplored. All the best men in the country have been beaten, archbishops, bishops and even deans. Without sensible correction they could not be the men they are today.
Attrib.

Carey, Robert, Sir (1560?–1639) English courtier

1 By putting her hand to her head, when the King of Scots was named to succeed her, they all knew he was the man she desired should reign after her.
Referring to the death of Elizabeth I, and the succession of James VI of Scotland as James I of England. *Memoirs of the Life of Robert Carey, Baron of Leppington and Earl of Monmouth* (John Earl of Corke and Orrery, ed.; 1759)

Carkesse, James British clerk

1 Who e're is mad, he first had Wit to lose;
Betwixt Fool and Physitian wink and chuse.
Lucida Intervalla: containing divers Miscellaneous poems written at Finsbury and Bethlem by the Doctors Patient Extraordinary (1679)

Carlos I, Juan, King (b.1938) Spanish monarch

1 I am very close to youth. I admire and share their desire to seek a better, more genuine world. I know that in the rebelliousness that worries so many people there can be found the great generosity of those who want open horizons.
Said after the ceremony in which he had been named as successor to Francisco Franco. Speech, Madrid (1969), quoted in *The Spaniards* (John Hooper; 1986)

2 A soldier, an army, which loses its sense of discipline ceases to be an army.
Quoted in *Spain: Dictatorship to Democracy* (Raymond Carr and Juan Pablo Fusi Aizpurna; 1979)

Carlyle, Jane (originally Jane Baillie Welsh; 1801–66) Scottish diarist

1 I am not at all the sort of person you and I took me for.
Letter to Thomas Carlyle (May 7, 1822), quoted in *Collected Letters of Thomas and Jane Welsh Carlyle* (C. R. Sanders et al., eds.; 1970), vol. 2

2 Medical men all over the world having merely entered into a tacit agreement to call all sorts of maladies people are liable to, in cold weather, by one name; so that one sort of treatment may serve for all, and their practice thereby be greatly simplified.
Journal (March 4, 1837)

3 When one has been threatened with a great injustice, one accepts a smaller as a favour.
Journal (November 21, 1855)

Carlyle, Thomas (1795–1881) Scottish historian and essayist

Quotations about Carlyle

1 It was very good of God to let Carlyle and Mrs Carlyle marry one another and so make only two people miserable instead of four, besides being very amusing.
Samuel Butler (1835–1902) British writer and composer. Referring to Thomas Carlyle. Letter to Miss Savage (November 21, 1884), quoted in *Letters Between Samuel Butler and Miss E. M. A. Savage* (1935)

2 He has his talents, his vast and cultivated mind, his vivid imagination, his independence of soul and his high-souled principles of honour. But then—ah, these Buts! Saint Preux never kicked the fireirons, nor made puddings in his tea cup.
Jane Carlyle (1801–66) Scottish diarist. Referring to her husband, Thomas Carlyle. *Journal* (July 1821)

Quotations by Carlyle

3 The crash of the whole solar and stellar systems could only kill you once.
Letter to John Carlyle (1831)

4 I never heard tell of any clever man that came of entirely stupid people.
Speech, Edinburgh (April 2, 1886)

5 Work is the grand cure of all the maladies and miseries that ever beset mankind.
Speech, Edinburgh (April 2, 1876)

6 Self-contemplation is infallibly the symptom of disease.
Characteristics (1877)

7 A man willing to work, and unable to find work, is perhaps the saddest sight that fortune's inequality exhibits under the sun.
Chartism (1839)

8 A poet without love were a physical and metaphysical impossibility.
"Burns," *Critical and Miscellaneous Essays* (1838)

9 A witty statesman said, you might prove anything by figures.
"Chartism," *Critical and Miscellaneous Essays* (1838)

10 All reform except a moral one will prove unavailing.
"Corn Law Rhymes," *Critical and Miscellaneous Essays* (1838)

11 History is the essence of innumerable biographies.
"History," *Critical and Miscellaneous Essays* (1838)

12 The great law of culture is: Let each become all that he was created capable of becoming.
"Jean Paul Friedrich Richter," *Critical and Miscellaneous Essays* (1838)

13 A well-written Life is almost as rare as a well-spent one.
"Richter," *Critical and Miscellaneous Essays* (1838)

14 Literary men are...a perpetual priesthood
"The State of German Literature," *Critical and Miscellaneous Essays* (1838)

15 The three great elements of modern civilization, Gunpowder, Printing, and the Protestant Religion.
"The State of German Literature," *Critical and Miscellaneous Essays* (1838)

16 How does the poet speak to men with power, but by being still more a man than they?
"Burns," *Edinburgh Review* (1828)

17 Clever men are good, but they are not the best.
"Goethe," *Edinburgh Review* (1828)

18 We are firm believers in the maxim that for all right judgment of any man or thing it is useful, nay, essential, to see his good qualities before pronouncing on his bad.
"Goethe," *Edinburgh Review* (1828)

19 Genius (which means transcendent capacity of taking trouble, first of all).
Frederick the Great (1858), vol. 4, ch. 3

20 The Public is an old woman. Let her maunder and mumble.
Journal (1835)

21 Respectable Professors of the Dismal Science.
Referring to economics. *Latter-Day Pamphlets* (1850), 1

22 Nature admits no lie.
Latter-Day Pamphlets (1850), 5

23 Happy the people whose annals are blank in history-books!
Life of Frederick the Great (1858–65), bk. 16, ch. 1

24 Blessed is the healthy nature; it is the coherent, sweetly co-operative, not incoherent, self-distracting, self-destructive one!
"Sir Walter Scott," *London and Westminster Review* (1838)

25 No great man lives in vain. The history of the world is but the biography of great men.
"The Hero as a Divinity," *On Heroes, Hero-Worship, and the Heroic in History* (1841)

26 The true University of these days is a collection of books.
"The Hero as a Man of Letters," *On Heroes, Hero-Worship, and the Heroic in History* (1841)

27 The Hero can be Poet, Prophet, King, Priest or what you will, according to the kind of world he finds himself born into.
"The Hero as Poet," *On Heroes, Hero-Worship, and the Heroic in History* (1841)

28 Captains of industry.
Past and Present (1843), bk. 4, ch. 4

29 It is a mathematical fact that the casting of this pebble from my hand alters the centre of gravity of the universe.
Sartor Resartus (1833–34)

30 No man who has once heartily and wholly laughed can be altogether irreclaimably bad.
Sartor Resartus (1833–34), bk. 1, ch. 4

31 Man is a tool-using animal...Without tools he is nothing, with tools he is all.
Sartor Resartus (1833–34), bk. 1, ch. 5

32 Be not the slave of Words.
Sartor Resartus (1833–34), bk. 1, ch. 8

33 Lives there the man that can figure a naked Duke of Windlestraw addressing a naked House of Lords?
Sartor Resartus (1833–34), bk. 1, ch. 9

34 Language is called the garment of thought: however, it should rather be, language is the flesh-garment, the body, of thought.
Sartor Resartus (1833–34), bk. 1, ch. 11

35 Sarcasm I now see to be, in general, the language of the devil.
Sartor Resartus (1833–34), bk. 2, ch. 4

36 "Do the duty which lies nearest thee," which thou knowest to be a duty! Thy second duty will already have become clearer.
Sartor Resartus (1833–34), bk. 2, ch.9

37 France was a long despotism tempered by epigrams.
The French Revolution (1837), pt. 1, bk. 1, ch. 1

38 To a shower of gold most things are penetrable.
The French Revolution (1837), pt. 1, bk. 3, ch. 7

39 A whiff of grapeshot.
Describing how Napoleon, early in his career, quelled a minor riot in Paris. *The French Revolution* (1837), pt.1, bk. 5, ch. 3

40 History a distillation of rumour.
The French Revolution (1837), pt. 1, bk. 7, ch. 5

41 The difference between Orthodoxy or My-doxy and Heterodoxy or Thy-doxy.
The French Revolution (1837), pt. 2, bk. 4, ch. 2

42 The seagreen Incorruptible.
Referring to Robespierre. *The French Revolution* (1837), pt. 2, bk. 4, ch. 4

43 Music is well said to be the speech of angels.
The Opera (1852)

44 A good book is the purest essence of a human soul.
Speech made in support of the London Library. *Carlyle and the London Library* (F. Harrison; 1840)

45 If Jesus Christ were to come to-day, people would not even crucify him. They would ask him to dinner, and hear what he had to say, and make fun of it.
Carlyle at his Zenith (D. A. Wilson; 1927)

46 MARGARET FULLER I accept the universe.
CARLYLE Gad! she'd better!
Attrib. *Varieties of Religious Experience* (William James; 1902)

47 I don't pretend to understand the Universe—it's a great deal bigger than I am...People ought to be modester.
Attrib.

48 There they are cutting each other's throats, because one half of them prefer hiring their servants for life, and the other by the hour.
Referring to the American Civil War (1861–65). Attrib.

Carman, Bliss (William Bliss Carman; 1861–1929) Canadian poet

1 The scarlet of the maples can shake me like a cry
Of bugles going by.
And my lonely spirit thrills
To see the frosty asters like a smoke upon the hills.
"A Vagabond Song," *Songs in Vagabondia* (co-written with Richard Hovey; 1894), st. 2

Carnap, Rudolf (1891–1970) German philosopher

1 Logic is the last scientific ingredient of Philosophy; its extraction leaves behind only a confusion of non-scientific, pseudo problems.
The Unity of Science (M. Black, tr.; 1934)

2 Science is a system of statements based on direct experience, and controlled by experimental verification. Verification in science is not, however, of single statements but of the entire system or a sub-system of such statements.
The Unity of Science (M. Black, tr.; 1934)

Carnegie, Andrew (1835–1919) Scottish-born U.S. industrialist and philanthropist

Quotations about Carnegie

1 Businesses can be misread: Witness the European reporter who, after being sent to this country to profile Andrew Carnegie, cabled his editor, "My God, you'll never believe the sort of money there is in running libraries."
Warren Buffett (b.1930) U.S. financier. Berkshire Hathaway Annual Report (1988)

Quotations by Carnegie

2 As an end, the acquisition of wealth is ignoble in the extreme; I assume that you save and long for wealth only as a means of enabling you the better to do some good in your day and generation.
Speech, Curry Commercial College, Pittsburgh (June 23, 1885), "The Road to Business Success"

3 Boss your boss just as soon as you can; try it on early. There is nothing he will like so well if he is the right kind of boss.
Speech, Curry Commercial College, Pittsburgh (June 23, 1885), "The Road to Business Success"

4 Concentrate your energy, thought and capital exclusively upon the business in which you are engaged..."Don't put all your eggs in one basket" is all wrong. I tell you "put all your eggs in one basket, and then watch that basket."
Speech, Curry Commercial College, Pittsburgh (June 23, 1885), "The Road to Business Success"

5 Instead of the question "What must I do for my employer?" substitute "What can I do?"
Speech, Curry Commercial College, Pittsburgh (June 23, 1885), "The Road to Business Success"

6 There is no business in America...which will not yield a fair profit if it receive the unremitting, exclusive attention, and all the capital of capable and industrious men.
Speech, Curry Commercial College, Pittsburgh (June 23, 1885), "The Road to Business Success"

7 The vast majority of the sons of rich men are unable to resist the temptations which wealth subjects them to, and sink to unworthy lives.
Speech, Curry Commercial College, Pittsburgh (June 23, 1885), "The Road to Business Success"

8 The only irreplaceable capital an organization possesses is the knowledge and ability of its people. The productivity of that capital depends on how effectively people share their competence with those who can use it.
Quoted in *Intellectual Capital* (Thomas A. Stewart; 1997)

9 No man will make a great leader who wants to do it all himself, or to get all the credit for doing it.
Quoted in "Noteworthy Quotes," *Strategy and Business* (1999)

10 Concentration is my motto—first honesty, then industry, then concentration.
Attrib.

11 The surest foundation of a manufacturing concern is quality. After that, and a long way, comes cost.
Attrib.

12 Beyond this never earn, make no effort to increase fortune, but spend the surplus each year for benevolent purposes.
1868. Referring to earning $50,000 a year. Attrib.

Carnegie, Dale (Dale Carnagey; 1888–1955) U.S. writer and speaker

1 There is only one way under high heaven to get the best of an argument and that is to avoid it.
Dale Carnegie's Scrapbook (Dorothy Carnegie, ed.; 1959)

2 When dealing with people, let us remember we are not dealing with creatures of logic. We are dealing with creatures of emotion, creatures bristling with prejudices and motivated by pride and vanity.
Dale Carnegie's Scrapbook (Dorothy Carnegie, ed.; 1959)

3 How to Win Friends and Influence People
Book title. (1936)

Carr, John Dickson (1906–77) U.S. detective-fiction author

1 Facts are piffle.
The Crooked Hinge (1938)

Carrel, Alexis (1873–1944) French biologist and surgeon

1 Intelligence is almost useless to the person whose only quality it is.
Man, the Unknown (1935)

Carriera, Rosalba (Rosalba Giovanna Carriera; 1675–1757) Italian painter

1 I see but as one sees after an operation, that is to say very dimly. Even this is a blessing for one who has had the misfortune to become blind. When I was sightless I cared for nothing, now I want to see everything.
Letter (August 23, 1749)

Carrington, Lord, 6th Baron Carrington (Peter Alexander Rupert Carrington; b.1919) British politician

1 Detente is like the race in *Alice in Wonderland* where everyone had to have a prize.
Speech (March, 1980)

2 It is, of course, a bit of a drawback that science was invented after I left school.
Observer, London (January 23, 1983)

Carroll, Lewis (Charles Lutwidge Dodgson; 1832–98) British writer and mathematician

1 I am fond of children (except boys).
Letter to Kathleen Eschwege (1879), quoted in *The Life and Letters of Lewis Carroll* (S. D. Collingwood; 1898)

2 "What is the use of a book", thought Alice, "without pictures or conversations?"
Alice's Adventures in Wonderland (1865), ch. 1

3 "Curiouser and curiouser!" cried Alice.
Alice's Adventures in Wonderland (1865), ch. 2

4 How doth the little crocodile
Improve his shining tail,
And pour the waters of the Nile
On every golden scale!
Alice's Adventures in Wonderland (1865), ch. 2

5 "You are old, Father William," the young man said,
"And your hair has become very white;
And yet you incessantly stand on your head—
Do you think at your age, it is right?"
Alice's Adventures in Wonderland (1865), ch. 5

6 "In my youth," Father William replied to his son,
"I feared it might injure the brain;
But now that I'm perfectly sure I have none,
Why, I do it again and again."
Replying to the young man who asked Father William if he thought it was right to stand on his head at his great age. *Alice's Adventures in Wonderland* (1865), ch. 5

7 "If everybody minded their own business," the Duchess said in a hoarse growl, "the world would go round a deal faster than it does."
Alice's Adventures in Wonderland (1865), ch. 6

8 "I never ask advice about growing," Alice said indignantly.
"Too proud?" the other enquired.
Alice felt even more indignant at this suggestion. "I mean," she said, "that one can't help growing older."
"One can't, perhaps," said Humpty Dumpty; "but Two can."
Alice's Adventures in Wonderland (1865), ch. 6

9 Speak roughly to your little boy,
And beat him when he sneezes:
He only does it to annoy,
Because he knows it teases.
Alice's Adventures in Wonderland (1865), ch. 6

10 "Would you tell me, please, which way I ought to go from here?"
"That depends a good deal on where you want to get to," said the Cat.
Alice's Adventures in Wonderland (1865), ch. 6

11 This time it vanished quite slowly, beginning with the end of the tail, and ending with the grin, which remained some time after the rest of it had gone.
Describing the Cheshire Cat. *Alice's Adventures in Wonderland* (1865), ch. 6

12 "Take some more tea," the March Hare said to Alice, very earnestly.
"I've had nothing yet," Alice replied in an offended tone, "so I can't take more."

"You mean you can't take *less*," said the Hatter: "it's very easy to take *more* than nothing."
Alice's Adventures in Wonderland (1865), ch. 7

13 "Then you should say what you mean," the March Hare went on. "I do," Alice hastily replied; "at least—at least I mean what I say—that's the same thing, you know."
"Not the same thing a bit!" said the Hatter. "Why, you might just as well say that 'I see what I eat' is the same thing as 'I eat what I see'!"
Alice's Adventures in Wonderland (1865), ch. 7

14 Twinkle, twinkle, little bat!
How I wonder what you're at!
Up above the world you fly!
Like a teatray in the sky.
Alice's Adventures in Wonderland (1865), ch. 7

15 "Off with his head!"
Alice's Adventures in Wonderland (1865), ch. 8

16 Everything's got a moral, if only you can find it.
Alice's Adventures in Wonderland (1865), ch. 9

17 "Reeling and Writhing, of course, to begin with," the Mock Turtle replied; "and then the different branches of Arithmetic—Ambition, Distraction, Uglification, and Derision."
Alice's Adventures in Wonderland (1865), ch. 9

18 Take care of the sense, and the sounds will take care of themselves.
Alice's Adventures in Wonderland (1865), ch. 9

19 "Will you walk a little faster?" said a whiting to a snail, "There's a porpoise close behind us, and he's treading on my tail."
Alice's Adventures in Wonderland (1865), ch. 10

20 Will you, won't you, will you, won't you, will you join the dance?
Alice's Adventures in Wonderland (1865), ch. 10

21 Soup of the evening, beautiful Soup!
Said by the Mock Turtle. *Alice's Adventures in Wonderland* (1865), ch. 10

22 The Queen of Hearts, she made some tarts,
All on a summer day:
The Knave of Hearts, he stole those tarts,
And took them quite away!
Alice's Adventures in Wonderland (1865), ch. 11

23 "Where shall I begin, please your Majesty?" he asked.
"Begin at the beginning" the King said, gravely, "and go on till you come to the end: then stop."
Alice's Adventures in Wonderland (1865), ch. 11

24 "No, no!" said the Queen. "Sentence first—verdict afterwards."
Alice's Adventures in Wonderland (1865), ch. 12

25 "That's not a regular rule: you invented it just now." "It's the oldest rule in the book," said the King. "Then it ought to be Number One," said Alice.
Alice's Adventures in Wonderland (1865), ch. 12

26 For the Snark *was* a Boojum, you see.
The Hunting of the Snark (1876)

27 What I tell you three times is true.
The Hunting of the Snark (1876)

28 "I don't know what you mean by 'glory'," Alice said. Humpty Dumpty smiled contemptuously. "Of course you don't—till I tell you. I meant 'there's a nice knock-down argument for you'!" "But glory doesn't mean 'a nice knock-down argument'," Alice objected.
Through the Looking-Glass and What Alice Found There (1871)

29 "And hast thou slain the Jabberwock?
Come to my arms, my beamish boy!
O frabjous day! Callooh! Callay!"
He chortled in his joy.
Through the Looking-Glass and What Alice Found There (1871), ch. 1

30 'Twas brillig, and the slithy toves
Did gyre and gimble in the wabe;
All mimsy were the borogoves,
And the mome raths outgrabe.

"Beware the Jabberwock, my son!
The jaws that bite, the claws that catch!"
Through the Looking-Glass and What Alice Found There (1871), ch. 1

31 Now, *here,* you see, it takes all the running *you* can do, to keep in the same place. If you want to get somewhere else, you must run at least twice as fast as that!
Through the Looking-Glass and What Alice Found There (1871), ch. 2

32 Speak in French when you can't think of the English for a thing.
Through the Looking-Glass and What Alice Found There (1871), ch. 2

33 Tweedledum and Tweedledee
Agreed to have a battle;
For Tweedledum said Tweedledee
Had spoiled his nice new rattle.
Through the Looking-Glass and What Alice Found There (1871), ch. 2

34 But answer came there none—
And this was scarcely odd because
They'd eaten every one.
Through the Looking-Glass and What Alice Found There (1871), ch. 4

35 "Contrariwise," continued Tweedledee, "if it was so, it might be; and if it were so, it would be: but as it isn't, it ain't. That's logic."
Through the Looking-Glass and What Alice Found There (1871), ch. 4

36 "I weep for you," the Walrus said:
"I deeply sympathize."
With sobs and tears he sorted out
Those of the largest size,
Holding his pocket-handkerchief
Before his streaming eyes.
Through the Looking-Glass and What Alice Found There (1871), ch. 4

37 "The time has come," the Walrus said,
"To talk of many things:
Of shoes—and ships—and scaling-wax—
Of cabbages—and kings—
And why the sea is boiling hot—
And whether pigs have wings."
Through the Looking-Glass and What Alice Found There (1871), ch. 4

38 The Walrus and the Carpenter
Were walking close at hand;
They wept like anything to see
Such quantities of sand:
'If this were only cleared away,'
They said, 'it *would* be grand!'
Through the Looking-Glass and What Alice Found There (1871), ch. 4

39 "I'm very brave generally," he went on in a low voice: "only to-day I happen to have a headache."
The White Knight. *Through the Looking-Glass and What Alice Found There* (1871), ch. 4

40 The rule is, jam tomorrow and jam yesterday—but never jam today.
Through the Looking-Glass and What Alice Found There (1871), ch. 5

41 Why, sometimes I've believed as many as six impossible things before breakfast.
Through the Looking-Glass and What Alice Found There (1871), ch. 5

42 I can explain all the poems that ever were invented—and a good many that haven't been invented just yet.
Through the Looking-Glass and What Alice Found There (1871), ch. 6

43 "They gave it me," Humpty Dumpty continued thoughtfully,..."for an un-birthday present."
Through the Looking-Glass and What Alice Found There (1871), ch. 6

44 "When *I* use a word," Humpty Dumpty said in rather a scornful tone, "it means just what I choose it to mean—neither more nor less."
Through the Looking-Glass and What Alice Found There (1871), ch. 6

45 With a name like yours, you might be any shape, almost.
Said by Humpty Dumpty to Alice. *Through the Looking-Glass and What Alice Found There* (1871), ch. 6

46 If you'll believe in me, I'll believe in you.
Through the Looking-Glass and What Alice Found There (1871), ch. 7

47 "I'm sure nobody walks much faster than I do!" "He can't do that," said the King, "or else he'd have been here first."
Through the Looking-Glass and What Alice Found There (1871), ch. 7

48 It's as large as life, and twice as natural!
Through the Looking-Glass and What Alice Found There (1871), ch. 7

49 The Lion looked at Alice wearily. "Are you animal—or vegetable—or mineral?" he said, yawning at every other word.
Through the Looking-Glass and What Alice Found There (1871), ch. 7

50 "Speak when you're spoken to!" the Red Queen sharply interrupted her.
Through the Looking-Glass and What Alice Found There (1871), ch. 9

Carson, Edward, Sir (Edward Henry Carson; 1854–1935) Northern Irish politician and jurist

1 We do not want a sentence of death with a stay of execution for six years.
Dismissing the suggestion that the Home Rule Bill should exclude Northern Ireland for six years. Speech (March 1914)

2 Ulster is not asking for concessions. Ulster is asking to be let alone.
Rejecting the possibility of Home Rule in Ireland. Speech to the British Parliament (February 11, 1914)

Carson, George Nathaniel (1859–1925) British politician

1 The British flag has never flown over a more powerful or a more united empire...Never did our voice count for more in the councils of nations; or in determining the future destinies of mankind.
Speech to the House of Lords, the upper house of the British Parliament (November 18, 1918)

Carson, Rachel (Rachel Louise Carson; 1907–64) U.S. ecologist

1 The ocean is a place of paradoxes.
"Under Sea," *Atlantic Monthly* (September 1937)

2 As crude a weapon as the cave man's club, the chemical barrage has been hurled against the fabric of life.
Silent Spring (1962)

3 Over increasingly large areas of the United States, spring now comes unheralded by the return of the birds, and the early mornings are strangely silent where once they were filled with the beauty of bird song.
Silent Spring (1962)

4 The "control of nature" is a phrase conceived in arrogance, born of the Neanderthal age of biology and the convenience of man.
Silent Spring (1962)

5 For all at last return to the sea—to Oceanus, the ocean river, like the ever-flowing stream of time, the beginning and the end.
The closing words of the book. *The Sea Around Us* (1951)

Carter, Angela (originally Angela Olive Stalker; 1940–92) British novelist, essayist, and short-story writer

1 I believe that all myths are products of the human mind and reflect only aspects of material human practice. I'm in the demythologising business.
"Notes From the Front Line," *Shaking A Leg: Journalism and Writings* (1983)

2 The desert, the abode of enforced sterility, the dehydrated sea of infertility, the post-menopausal part of the earth.
The Passion of New Eve (1977), ch. 3

3 Solitude and melancholy, that is a woman's life.
The Passion of New Eve (1977), ch. 9

4 The destination of all journeys is their beginning.
The Passion of New Eve (1977), ch. 11

5 Pornographers are the enemies of women only because our contemporary ideology of pornography does not encompass the possibility of change.
The Sadeian Woman (1979), ch. 1

6 My anatomy is only part of an infinitely complex organisation, my self.
"Polemical Preface," *The Sadeian Woman* (1979)

7 Myth deals in false universals, to dull the pain of particular circumstances.
"Polemical Preface," *The Sadeian Woman* (1979)

8 But you have no silver linings without a cloud.
Wise Children (1991)

9 Comedy is tragedy that happens to other people.
Wise Children (1991)

10 "If the child is father of the man," she asked, "then who is the mother of the woman?"
Wise Children (1991)

11 She had, I kid you not, left lipstick on every pair of underpants further up the hierarchy than assistant director on her way to the top.
Wise Children (1991)

12 She never had the looks to lose so she never lost them.
Wise Children (1991)

13 There was a house we all had in common and it was called the past.
Wise Children (1991)

14 They call it "serial monogamy".
Wise Children (1991)

15 Welcome to the wrong side of the tracks.
Wise Children (1991)

Carter, Jimmy (James Earl Carter; b.1924) U.S. president

Quotations about Carter

1 He is the only man, since my dear husband died, to have the effrontery to kiss me on the lips.
Elizabeth (b.1900) British queen consort. Referring to President Jimmy Carter. Attrib.

2 Like the sorry tapping of Neville Chamberlain's umbrella on the cobblestones of Munich.
Ronald Reagan (b.1911) U.S. president and actor. Referring to President Jimmy Carter's foreign policy. Attrib.

Quotations by Carter

3 A simple and proper function of government is just to make it easy for us to do good and difficult for us to do wrong.
Acceptance speech, Democrat National Convention, New York City (July 15, 1976)

4 History teaches perhaps few lessons. But surely one such lesson learned by the world at great cost is that aggression unopposed becomes a dangerous disease.
Address to the nation (January 4, 1980)

5 We become not a melting pot but a beautiful mosaic. Different people, different beliefs, different yearnings, different hopes, different dreams.
Speech, Pittsburgh, Pennsylvania (October 27, 1976)

6 I have looked on a lot of women with lust. I've committed adultery in my heart many times. God forgives me for it.
Interview. *Playboy* (October 1976)

7 I'm surprised that a government organization could do it that quickly.
During a visit to Egypt, after being told that it took twenty years to build the Great Pyramid. Remark, *Time* (March 1979)

8 Whatever starts in California unfortunately has an inclination to spread.
Quoted in *Promises to Keep: Carter's First 100 Days* (Robert Shogan; 1977)

Carter, Lillian (originally Bessie Lillian Gordy; 1898–1983) U.S. nurse and mother of Jimmy Carter

1 I love all my children, but some of them I don't like.
Woman (April 9, 1977)

2 Sometimes when I look at my children I say to myself, "Lillian, you should have stayed a virgin."
1980. Attrib.

Cartier, George-Étienne, Sir (1814–73) Canadian statesman

1 If today Canada is a portion of the British Empire, it is due to the conservatism of the French-Canadian clergy.
Confederation Debates (February 7, 1865)

Cartier-Bresson, Henri (b.1908) French photographer, painter, and writer

1 For me the camera is a sketchbook, an instrument of intuition and spontaneity, the master of the instant which—in visual terms—questions and decides simultaneously.
Aperture (1976)

2 In order to "give a meaning" to the world, one has to feel oneself involved in what he frames through the viewfinder.
Aperture (1976)

3 In a portrait, I'm looking for the silence in somebody.
Observer, London (May 15, 1994), "Sayings of the Week"

Cartland, Barbara, Dame (Mary Barbara Hamilton Cartland; 1901–2000) British novelist

Quotations about Cartland

1 I think of the postmodern attitude as that of a man who loves a very cultivated woman and knows he cannot say to her, "I love you madly," because he knows that she knows (and that she knows that he knows) that these words have already been used by Barbara Cartland.
Umberto Eco (b.1932) Italian writer and literary scholar. Barbara Cartland is the highly prolific author of romance novels. "Postmodernism, Irony, the Enjoyable," *Reflections on the Name of the Rose* (William Weaver, tr.; 1983)

Quotations by Cartland

2 I answer 20,000 letters a year and so many couples are having problems because they are not getting the right proteins and vitamins.
Observer, London (August 31, 1986), "Sayings of the Week"

3 I'll wager you that in 10 years it will be fashionable again to be a virgin.
Observer, London (June 20, 1976), "Sayings of the Week"

4 I said 10 years ago that in 10 years time it would be smart to be a virgin. Now everyone is back to virgins again.
Observer, London (July 12, 1987), "Sayings of the Week"

5 I always say what I think and feel—it's got me into a lot of trouble but only with women. I've never had a cross word with a man for speaking frankly but women don't like it—I can't think why, unless it's natural love of subterfuge and intrigue.
The Isthmus Years (1942), ch. 1

6 Of course they have, or I wouldn't be sitting here talking to someone like you.
When asked in a radio interview whether she thought that British class barriers had broken down. *Class* (J. Cooper; 1978)

Cartwright, John ("The Father of Reform"; 1740–1824) British politician and reformer

1 One man shall have one vote.
People's Barrier Against Undue Influence (1780), ch. 1

Cartwright, Richard, Sir (Richard John Cartwright; 1835–1912) Canadian statesman

1 All that Canada owes to Great Britain is a great deal of Christian forgiveness.
Attrib.

Carver, George Washington (1864–1943) U.S. inventor and horticulturist

1 When you can do the common things of life in an uncommon way you'll command the attention of the world.
World's Great Men of Color (Joel Augustus Rogers; 1947), vol. 2

Carver, Raymond (Raymond Clevie Carver, Jr.; 1938–88) U.S. poet, short-story writer, and essayist

1 He had a necessary trade. He was a baker. He was glad he wasn't a florist. It was better to be feeding people. This was a better smell anytime than flowers.
"A Small, Good Thing," *Cathedral* (1983), quoted in *The Heath Anthology of American Literature* (Paul Lauter, ed.; 1998), vol. 2

2 So far, he had kept away from any real harm, from those forces he knew existed and that could cripple or bring down a man if the luck went bad, if things suddenly turned.
"A Small, Good Thing," *Cathedral* (1983), quoted in *The Heath Anthology of American Literature* (Paul Lauter, ed.; 1998), vol. 2

3 At night the salmon move
out from the river and into the town.
"At Night the Salmon Move," *Fires: Essays, Stories and Poems* (1983)

4 They had leaned on each other and laughed until the tears had come, while everything else—the cold and where he'd go in it—was outside, for a while anyway.
"Distance," *Fires: Essays, Stories and Poems* (1983)

5 Surely we have diminished one another.
"Morning, Thinking of Empire," *Fires: Essays, Stories and Poems* (1983)

6 Two things are certain: 1) people no longer care what happens to other people; and 2) nothing makes any real difference any longer.
"So Much Water, So Close to Home," *Fires: Essays, Stories and Poems* (1983)

7 She had money and she had connections. Connections were more important than money. But money and connections both—that was unbeatable.
"The Pheasant," *Fires: Essays, Stories and Poems* (1983)

8 She should have stayed in Hollywood. She didn't like people who were forever trying to find themselves, the brooding, introspective bit.
"The Pheasant," *Fires: Essays, Stories and Poems* (1983)

9 There was a time when I thought I loved my first wife more than life itself. But now I hate her guts. I do. How do you explain that? What happened to that love?
"What We Talk about When We Talk about Love," *What We Talk about When We Talk about Love* (1981)

10 Autobiography is the poor man's history.
"Blackbird Pie," *Where I'm Calling from* (1988)

Carville, James (Chester James Carville, Jr.; b.1944) U.S. political advisor

1 I used to think that if there was reincarnation, I wanted to come back as the president or the pope. But now I want to be the bond market: you can intimidate everybody.
Quoted in *The Financial Times Guide to Using the Financial Pages* (Romesh Vaitilingam; 1996)

Cary, Joyce (Arthur Joyce Lunel Cary; 1888–1957) Irish-born British novelist

1 Sara could commit adultery at one end and weep for her sins at the other, and enjoy both operations at once.
The Horse's Mouth (1944), ch. 8

2 Remember I'm an artist. And you know what that means in a court of law. Next worst to an actress.
The Horse's Mouth (1944), ch. 14

3 It is the misfortune of an old man that though he can put things out of his head he can't put them out of his feelings.
To be a Pilgrim (1942), ch. 8

4 I wanted the experience of war. I thought there would be no more wars.
Reason for going to the Balkan War in 1912. Attrib.

Casals, Pablo (Pau Casals; 1876–1973) Catalan cellist, conductor, and composer

1 The heart of the melody can never be put down on paper.
Conversations (1955)

2 The art of interpretation is not to play what is written.
Letter, *Times*, London (December 29, 1946), quoted in *The Song of the Birds* (Julian Lloyd Webber, ed.; 1985)

3 Beauty is all about us, but how many are blind! They look at the wonder of this earth and seem to see nothing. People move hectically but give little thought to where they are going. They seek excitement...as if they were lost and desperate.
Quoted in *Joys and Sorrows* (Julian Lloyd Webber, ed.; 1970)

4 The love of one's country is a natural thing. But why should love stop at the border?
Quoted in *Joys and Sorrows* (Julian Lloyd Webber, ed.; 1970)

5 Let us not forget that the greatest composers were also the greatest thieves. They stole from everyone and everywhere.
Quoted in *The Song of the Birds* (Julian Lloyd Webber, ed.; 1985)

6 The most perfect technique is that which is not noticed at all.
Quoted in *The Song of the Birds* (Julian Lloyd Webber, ed.; 1985)

Casanova, Giovanni Giacomo, Chevalier de Seingalt (1725–98) Italian adventurer

1 This dance is the expression of love from beginning to end, from the sigh of desire to the ecstasy of enjoyment. It seemed to me impossible that after such a dance the girl could refuse anything to her partner.
1767. Describing the *fandango* in Madrid. Quoted in *World History of Dance* (Curt Sachs; 1937)

Casely-Hayford, Joseph Ephraim (1865–1930) Ghanaian journalist, lawyer, and nationalist

1 Reform never comes to a class or a people unless and until those concerned have worked out their own salvation.
Ethiopia Unbound: Studies in Race Emancipation (1911), p. 169

2 The time is past when the African can be expected to continue to be the burden-bearer of the world.
African Aims and Attitudes (Martin Minogue and Judith Molloy, eds.; 1979), p.18

Casement, Roger, Sir (Roger David Casement; 1864–1916) Irish nationalist

1 In Ireland alone, in this twentieth century, is loyalty held to be a crime.
Speech, after being found guilty of treason (1916)

2 Ireland is being treated today among the nations of the world as if she were a convicted criminal.
Speech, after being found guilty of treason (1916)

3 The government of Ireland by England rests on restraint, and not on law; and since it demands no love it can evoke no loyalty.
Speech, after being found guilty of treason (1916)

4 Ireland has no blood to give to any land, to any cause, but Ireland.
October 5, 1914. Quoted in *Phrases Make History Here* (Conor O'Clery; 1986)

Cash, Johnny ("The Man in Black"; b.1932) U.S. country music singer-songwriter and guitarist

1 Convicts are the best audience I ever played for.
Attrib.

Cassavetes, John (1929–89) U.S. filmmaker, actor, and screenwriter

1 I don't look at a script during the actual filming. I'm not really listening to dialogue...I'm just watching a conversation. You're not aware of exactly what people are saying. You're aware of what they're intending and what kind of feeling is going on in that scene.
Interview, *The Film Director as Superstar* (Joseph Gelmis; 1970)

Casson, Hugh, Sir (Hugh Maxwell Casson; b.1910) British architect

1 The British love permanence more than they love beauty.
Observer, London (June 14, 1964), "Sayings of the Week"

Castellani, Maria (b.1930) Italian educator and writer

1 Fascism recognizes women as part of the life force of the country, laying down a division of duties between the two sexes.
Italian Women Past and Present (1937)

Castillejo, José Spanish writer

1 The Anarchists have destroyed many churches, but the clergy had first destroyed the Church.
Referring to anarchist bombing campaigns against churches in Spain, particularly in Barcelona, in the first decade of the 20th century. The Church was perceived to be intolerant and abusive of power in matters of education and religious jurisdiction. Quoted in *The Spanish Labyrinth* (Gerald Brenan; 1943)

Castle, Barbara, Baroness (originally Barbara Anne Betts; b.1911) British politician

1 I never doubted I couldn't enter into any marriage that denied me my career. But equally I never doubted that my husband was of very great importance to me...My femininity is big enough to embrace everything. That's to me the richness of life.
Guardian, London (June 1993)

Castle, Irene (Irene Foote; 1893–1969) U.S. ballroom dancer

1 The one big target for the crusaders was the tango. I suppose its opponents objected to the man bending the woman over backwards and peering into her eyes with a smouldering passionate look.
Castles in the Air (1958)

Castlereagh, Lord, Viscount Castlereagh (Robert Stewart; 1769–1822) Irish-born British politician

Quotations about Castlereagh

1 I met Murder on the way—
He had a mask like Castlereagh.
Percy Bysshe Shelley (1792–1822) English poet. Viscount Castlereagh (1769–1822) was British foreign secretary (1812–22). He was highly unpopular and became identified with such controversial events as the Peterloo massacre of 1819. "The Masque of Anarchy" (1819), st. 2 (Leigh Hunt, ed.; 1832)

Quotations by Castlereagh

2 I understand that you are inclined to hold the insurrection cheap. Rely upon it, there never was in any country so formidable an effort on the part of the people.
Referring to the 1798 rebellion in Ireland. Letter to Thomas Pelham (1798), quoted in *Citizen Lord: Edward Fitzgerald, 1763–1798* (Stella Tillyard; 1997)

Castro, Fidel (Fidel Alejandro Castro Ruz; b.1927) Cuban leader

1 A revolution is not a bed of roses. A revolution is a struggle to the death between the future and the past.
Second anniversary of the Cuban revolution. Speech, Havana (January 1961)

2 I was a man who was lucky enough to have discovered a political theory, a man who was caught up in the whirlpool of Cuba's political crisis long before becoming a fully fledged Communist... Discovering Marxism...was like finding a map in the forest.
Chile (November 18, 1971)

3 I believe that all of us ought to retire relatively young.
Interview, *Playboy* (January 1967)

Cather, Willa (Willa Sibert Cather; 1873–1947) U.S. novelist, poet, and journalist

1 From the flat red sea of sand rose great rock mesas, generally Gothic in outline, resembling vast cathedrals...This plain might once have been an enormous city, all the smaller quarters destroyed by time, only the great public buildings left—piles of architecture that were like mountains.
Referring to the landscape of Acoma, New Mexico. Founded about 1075, it is the oldest continuously inhabited settlement in the United States and a National Historic Landmark. *Death Comes for the Archbishop* (1927), ch. 3

2 The mesa plain had an appearance of great antiquity, and of incompleteness; as if with all the materials for world-making assembled, the Creator had...gone away and left everything...The country was still waiting to be made into a landscape.
Referring to the landscape of Acoma, New Mexico. Founded about 1075, it is the oldest continuously inhabited settlement in the United States and a National Historic Landmark. *Death Comes for the Archbishop* (1927), ch. 3

3 July came in with that breathless, brilliant heat which makes the plains of Kansas and Nebraska the best corn country in the world. It seems as if we could hear the corn growing in the night.
My Ántonia (1918), ch. 19

4 The history of every country begins in the heart of a man or woman.
O Pioneers! (1913), pt. 2, ch.4

5 Only solitary men know the full joys of friendship. Others have their family but to a solitary and an exile his friends are everything.
Shadows on the Rock (1931), bk. 3, ch. 5

6 It's good for one's soul to sit there all the day through...then, as Daudet said, one becomes a part of the foam that drifts, of the wind that blows, and of the pines that answer.
"Le Lavandou," *Virago Book of Women Travellers* (Mary Morris, ed.; 1996)

7 One cannot divine nor forecast the conditions that will make happiness; one only stumbles upon them by chance, in a lucky hour, at the world's end somewhere.
"Le Lavandou," *Virago Book of Women Travellers* (Mary Morris, ed.; 1996)

8 Out of every wandering in which people and places come and go in long successions, there is always one place remembered above the rest.
"Le Lavandou," *Virago Book of Women Travellers* (Mary Morris, ed.; 1996)

Catherine of Aragón, Queen (1485–1536) Spanish-born English queen consort

1 I came not into this realm as merchandise, nor yet to be married to any merchant.
Replying to the request that she acquiesce to the marriage of Henry VIII and Anne Boleyn. Letter (1533)

Catherine the Great (1729–96) German-born Russian empress

1 I must rule after my own fashion.
Said soon after her accession, following the deposition of her husband, Tsar Peter III. Speech to the Russian Senate, St. Petersburg (June 1762)

2 The intention of autocracy is the glory of the citizen, the state, and the sovereign.
1767. *The Nakaz, the draft instructions for a legal code* (Nikolai Chechulin, ed.; 1907)

3 The sovereign is absolute; for, in a state whose expanse is so vast, there can be no other appropriate authority except that which is concentrated in him.
1767. *The Nakaz, the draft instructions for a legal code* (Nikolai Chechulin, ed.; 1907)

4 I shall be an autocrat: that's my trade. And the good Lord will forgive me: that's his.
Attrib.

Catherwood, Mary (originally Mary Hartwell; 1847–1902) U.S. writer

1 Two may talk together under the same roof for many years, yet never really meet; and two others at first speech are old friends.
"Marianson," *Mackinac and Lake Stories* (1899)

Cato the Elder (Marcius Porcius Cato, "Cato the Censor"; 234 – 149 B.C.) Roman statesman, orator, and writer

1 Carthage must be destroyed.
After visiting Carthage (175 B.C.), he was reputed to have ended each speech to the senate with these words. Carthage was destroyed by Rome, following the third Punic war (146 B.C.). *Naturalis Historia* (Pliny the Elder; 77), bk. 15, ch. 74

Catt, Carrie Chapman (originally Carrie Clinton Lane; 1859–1947) U.S. woman suffrage leader and pacifist

1 There are two kinds of restrictions upon human liberty—the restraint of law and that of custom. No written law has ever been more binding than unwritten custom supported by popular opinion.
Speech (February 1900), quoted in *History of Woman Suffrage* (Elizabeth C. Stanton, Susan B. Anthony, and Matilda J. Gage, eds.; 1902), vol. 4

2 Once, this movement represented the scattered and disconnected protests of individual women...Happily those days are past...there has emerged a present-day movement possessing a clear understanding and a definite, positive purpose.
Referring to the Woman Suffrage movement. Speech, Stockholm, Sweden (1911)

3 When a just cause reaches its flood-tide, as ours has done in that country, whatever stands in the way must fall before its overwhelming power.
Referring to the Woman Suffrage movement. Speech, Stockholm, Sweden (1911)

Catullus (Gaius Valerius Catullus; 84? –54? B.C.) Roman poet

1 For you used to think my trifles were worth something.
Carmina (60? B.C.), 1

2 For the godly poet must be chaste himself, but there is no need for his verses to be so.
Carmina (60? B.C.), 16

3 Ah, what is more blessed than to put cares away, when the mind lays by its burden, and tired with labor of far travel we have come to our own home and rest on the couch we have longed for?
Carmina (60? B.C.), 31

4 For there is nothing sillier than a silly laugh.
Carmina (60? B.C.), 39

5 I hate and love.
Carmina (60? B.C.), 85

6 And for ever, brother, hail and farewell!
Carmina (60? B.C.), 101

7 Wandering through many countries and over many seas, I come, my brother, to these sorrowful obsequies, to present you with the last guerdon of death, and speak, though in vain, to your silent ashes.
Carmina (60? B.C.), 101

8 It is difficult suddenly to lay aside a long-cherished love.
Of Arrius (60? B.C.)

Cavafy, Constantine (Konstantine Petrou Kavafis; 1863–1933) Egyptian-born Greek poet

1 The consummation of their lawless pleasure
Was done. They rose up from the mattress;
And hurriedly they dress themselves without speaking.
"Their Beginning" (1921), quoted in *Poems by C. P. Cavafy* (John Mavrogordato, tr.; 1951)

2 And now, what will become of us without the barbarians?
Those people were a kind of solution.
Waiting for the Barbarians (1904)

Cavell, Edith (Edith Louisa Cavell; 1865–1915) British nurse

1 Standing, as I do, in view of God and eternity, I realize that patriotism is not enough. I must have no hatred or bitterness towards anyone.
October 12, 1915. World War I nurse, before her execution by German firing squad; to the chaplain who attended her. *Times*, London (October 23, 1915)

Cavendish, Spencer Compton, 8th Duke of Devonshire (1833–1908) British statesman

1 I dreamt that I was making a speech in the House. I woke up, and by Jove I was!
1895? *Thought and Adventures* (W. S. Churchill; 1932)

Cavour, Camillo Benso, Conte di (1810–61) Italian statesman

1 We are ready to proclaim throughout Italy this great principle: a free church in a free state.
March 27, 1861. Speech, quoted in *Reminiscences of the Life and Character of Count Cavour* (William de la Rive; 1862), ch. 13

2 Rome must be the capital of Italy because without Rome Italy cannot be constituted.
Speech, Turin (March 25, 1861)

Cawein, Madison (Madison Julius Cawein; 1865–1914) U.S. poet

1 An old Spanish saying is that "a kiss without a moustache is like an egg without salt."
Nature-Notes (1906)

Caxton, William (1422?–91) English printer

1 I, according to my copy, have done set it in imprint, to the intent that noble men may see and learn the noble acts of chivalry, the gentle and virtuous deeds that some knights used in those days.
Le Morte D'Arthur (Thomas Malory; 1485), Original Preface

Cayley, Arthur (1821–95) British mathematician

1 As for everything else, so for a mathematical theory: beauty can be perceived but not explained.
Quoted in *The World of Mathematics* (J. R. Newman, ed.; 1956)

Cecil, David (Edward Christian David Gascoyne Cecil; 1902–86) British academic, writer, and critic

1 It does not matter that Dickens' world is not life-like; it is alive.
Early Victorian Novelists (1934)

Cecil, Robert, 1st Viscount Cecil of Chelwood (1864–1958) British statesman

1 Virtue consisted in avoiding scandal and venereal disease.
Life in Edwardian England (1969)

2 They improvidentially piped growing volumes of sewage into the sea, the healing virtues of which were advertised on every railway station.
Referring to seaside resorts. *Life in Edwardian England* (1969)

Cecil, William, Baron Burghley or Burchleigh (1520–98) English statesman

1 Soldiers in peace are like chimneys in summer.
Attrib.

2 That realm cannot be rich whose coin is poor or base.
Referring to Elizabeth I's reform of coinage. Attrib.

Cela, Camilo José (b.1916) Spanish writer

1 Things are always best seen when they are a trifle mixed-up, a trifle disordered; the chilly administrative neatness of museums and filing cases, of statistics and cemeteries, is an inhuman and antinatural kind of order; it is, in a word, disorder. True order belongs to Nature, which never yet has produced two identical trees or mountains or horses.
Journey to the Alcarria (1948)

2 When debts are not paid because they cannot be paid, the best thing to do is not to talk about them, and shuffle the cards again.
Journey to the Alcarria (1948)

Céline, Louis-Ferdinand (Louis-Ferdinand Destouches; 1894–1961) French novelist and physician

1 Music, Beauty, are within us...great works are those that awaken our spirit, great men are those who give them form.
Semmelweis (1936)

2 Those who talk about the future are scoundrels. It is the present that matters. To evoke one's posterity is to make a speech to maggots.
Voyage au bout de la nuit (1932)

3 Truth is a never-ending agony. The truth of this world is death. One must choose—die or lie. I've never been able to kill myself.
Voyage au bout de la nuit (1932)

4 When one has no imagination, dying doesn't mean much, when one has, dying means too much.
Voyage au bout de la nuit (1932)

Celtis, Conrad (Conrad Pickel; 1459–1508) German humanist and poet

1 O free, strong people, O noble, brave race, clearly worthy of the Roman Empire; the Pole and the Dane hold our famous harbor and the gateway to the sea! On the east our most powerful peoples are enslaved, Bohemians, Moravians, Slovaks, and Silesians; they live like limbs cut from the body of our Germany.
Inaugural address, University of Ingolstadt, Bavaria (1492)

Centlivre, Susannah (Susannah Freeman; 1667?–1723?) English playwright and actor

1 Nothing melts a Woman's heart like gold.
The Basset-Table (1705), Act 4

Cervantes, Miguel de (Miguel de Cervantes Saavedra; 1547–1616) Spanish novelist and playwright

Quotations about Cervantes

1 The mass of mankind is divided into two classes, the Sancho Panzas who have a sense for reality, but no ideals, and the Don Quixotes with a sense for ideals, but mad.
George Santayana (1863–1952) Spanish-born U.S. philosopher, poet, and novelist. Referring to characters in *Don Quixote* (1605, 1615), by Miguel de Cervantes. Quoted in *Interpretations of Poetry and Religion* (William G. Holzberger and Herman J. Saatkaup, Jr.; 1989), preface

2 Cervantes laughed chivalry out of fashion.
Horace Walpole (1717–97) British writer. Letter to Sir Horace Mann (July 19, 1774)

Quotations by Cervantes

3 That which costs little is less valued.
Don Quixote (1605–15)

4 The painter Orbaneja of Ubeda, if he chanced to draw a cock, he wrote under it, "This is a cock," lest the people should take it for a fox.
Don Quixote (1605–15)

5 Too much sanity may be madness. And maddest of all, to see life as it is and not as it should be!
Don Quixote (1605–15)

6 They can expect nothing but their labour for their pains.
From old proverb "Nothing is gotten without pains (labor)." *Don Quixote* (1605–15), Author's Preface

7 Too much of a good thing.
Don Quixote (1605–15), pt. 1, bk. 1, ch. 6

8 I find my familiarity with thee has bred contempt.
Don Quixote (1605–15), pt. 1, bk. 3, ch. 6

9 Ill-luck, you know, seldom comes alone.
Don Quixote (1605–15), pt. 1, bk. 3, ch. 6

10 I am almost frighted out of my seven senses.
Don Quixote (1605–15), pt. 1, bk. 3, ch. 9

11 A closed mouth catches no flies.
Don Quixote (1605–15), pt. 1, bk. 3, ch. 11

12 I never thrust my nose into other men's porridge. It is no bread and butter of mine; every man for himself, and God for us all.
Don Quixote (1605–15), pt. 1, bk. 3, ch. 11

13 Let us make hay while the sun shines.
Don Quixote (1605–15), pt. 1, bk. 3, ch. 11

14 Delay always breeds danger.
Don Quixote (1605–15), pt. 1, bk. 4, ch. 2

15 They must needs go whom the Devil drives.
Don Quixote (1605–15), pt. 1, bk. 4, ch. 4

16 I can tell where my own shoe pinches me; and you must not think, sir, to catch old birds with chaff.
Don Quixote (1605–15), pt. 1, bk. 4, ch. 5

17 Every tooth in a man's head is more valuable than a diamond.
Don Quixote (1605–15), pt. 1, ch. 4

18 Take care, your worship, those things over there are not giants but windmills.
Don Quixote (1605–15), pt. 1, ch. 8

19 Didn't I tell you, Don Quixote, sir, to turn back, for they were not armies you were going to attack, but flocks of sheep?
Don Quixote (1605–15), pt. 1, ch. 18

20 The Knight of the Doleful Countenance.
Sancho Panza describing Don Quixote; sometimes translated as "The Knight of the Sad Countenance." *Don Quixote* (1605–15), pt. 1, ch. 19

21 Fear has many eyes and can see things underground.
Don Quixote (1605–15), pt. 1, ch. 20

22 A leap over the hedge is better than good men's prayers.
Don Quixote (1605–15), pt. 1, ch. 21

23 I have always heard, Sancho, that doing good to base fellows is like throwing water into the sea.
Don Quixote (1605–15), pt. 1, ch. 23

24 A knight errant who turns mad for a reason deserves neither merit nor thanks. The thing is to do it without cause.
Don Quixote (1605–15), pt. 1, ch. 25

25 Let them eat the lie and swallow it with their bread. Whether the two were lovers or no, they'll have accounted to God for it by now. I have my own fish to fry.
Don Quixote (1605–15), pt. 1, ch. 25

26 One shouldn't talk of halters in the hanged man's house.
Don Quixote (1605–15), pt. 1, ch. 25

27 In me the need to talk is a primary impulse, and I can't help saying right off what comes to my tongue.
Don Quixote (1605–15), pt. 1, ch. 30

28 She isn't a bad bit of goods, the Queen! I wish all the fleas in my bed were as good.
Don Quixote (1605–15), pt. 1, ch. 30

29 When the head aches, all the members partake of the pain.
Don Quixote (1605–15), pt. 2, ch. 2

30 Every man is as Heaven made him, and sometimes a great deal worse.
Don Quixote (1605–15), pt. 2, ch. 4

31 We cannot all be friars, and many are the ways by which God leads his own to eternal life. Religion is knight-errantry.
Sancho asks if we should all become monks to get to heaven. *Don Quixote* (1605–15), pt. 2, ch. 8

32 Well, now, there's a remedy for everything except death.
Don Quixote (1605–15), pt. 2, ch. 10

33 The pen is the tongue of the mind.
Don Quixote (1605–15), pt. 2, ch. 16

34 He's a muddle-headed fool, with frequent lucid intervals.
Sancho Panza describing Don Quixote. *Don Quixote* (1605–15), pt. 2, ch. 18

35 There are only two families in the world, my old grandmother used to say, The *Haves* and the *Have-Nots*.
Don Quixote (1605–15), pt. 2, ch. 20

36 A private sin is not so prejudicial in the world as a public indecency.
Don Quixote (1605–15), pt. 2, ch. 22

37 He has an oar in every man's boat, and a finger in every pie.
Don Quixote (1605–15), pt. 2, ch. 22

38 Tell me what company thou keepest, and I'll tell thee what thou art.
Don Quixote (1605–15), pt. 2, ch. 23

39 A good name is better than riches.
Don Quixote (1605–15), pt. 2, ch. 33

40 He is as mad as a March hare.
Don Quixote (1605–15), pt. 2, ch. 33

41 I drink when I have occasion, and sometimes when I have no occasion.
Don Quixote (1605–15), pt. 2, ch. 33

42 Many go out for wool, and come home shorn themselves.
Don Quixote (1605–15), pt. 2, ch. 37

43 You may as well expect pears from an elm.
Don Quixote (1605–15), pt. 2, ch. 40

44 The pot calls the kettle black.
Don Quixote (1605–15), pt. 2, ch. 43

45 When thou art at Rome, do as they do at Rome.
Don Quixote (1605–15), pt. 2, ch. 54

46 Many count their chickens before they are hatched; and where they expect bacon, meet with broken bones.
Don Quixote (1605–15), pt. 2, ch. 55

47 My thoughts ran a wool-gathering; and I did like the countryman who looked for his ass while he was mounted on his back.
Don Quixote (1605–15), pt. 2, ch. 58

48 I shall be as secret as the grave.
Don Quixote (1605–15), pt. 2, ch. 62

49 Blessings on him who invented sleep, the mantle that covers all human thoughts, the food that satisfies hunger, the drink that slakes thirst, the fire that warms cold.
Don Quixote (1605–15), pt. 2, ch. 68

50 Never look for birds of this year in the nests of the last.
Don Quixote (1605–15), pt. 2, ch. 74

51 Fortune leaves always some door open to come at a remedy.
Don Quixote (1605–15), pt. 3, ch. 1

52 Journey all over the universe in a map, without the expense and fatigue of traveling, without suffering the inconveniences of heat, cold, hunger, and thirst.
Don Quixote (1605–15), pt. 3, ch. 6

53 Good painters imitate nature, bad ones spew it up.
El Licenciado Vidriera (1613)

54 A silly remark can be made in Latin as well as in Spanish.
The Dialogue of the Dogs (1613)

55 Don't put too fine a point to your wit for fear it should get blunted.
The Little Gypsy (1605)

Césaire, Aimé (Aimé Fernand Césaire; b.1913) Martiniquan poet, teacher, and political leader

1 A civilization that proves incapable of solving the problems it creates is a decadent civilization.
Discourse on Colonialism (1955)

2 They talk to me about civilization, I talk about proletarianization and mystification.
Discourse on Colonialism (1955)

3 It is not by hatred of other races that I prosecute for mine.
Return to My Native Land (C. L. R. James, tr.; 1947)

4 The work of man is only just beginning
and it remains to conquer
all the violence entrenched
in the recesses of his passion.
No race holds the monopoly of beauty, of intelligence, of strength
and there is place for all at the rendezvous of victory.
Return to My Native Land (C. L. R. James, tr.; 1947)

5 What I desire is that Marxism and communism should serve the black people, not that the black people should serve Marxism and communism. Doctrines and movements must be for men, and not men for doctrines and movements.
Communism and the French Intellectuals, 1914–1960 (David Caute; 1964)

Cézanne, Paul (1839–1906) French painter

1 Taste is the best judge. It is rare. Art addresses itself only to an excessively limited number of individuals.
Letter to Emile Bernard (1904), quoted in *Letters of Paul Cézanne* (John Rewald, ed.; 1976)

2 The artist...must beware of the literary spirit which so often causes the painter to deviate from his true path—the concrete study of nature—to lose himself too long in intangible speculation.
Letter to Emile Bernard (1904), quoted in *Letters of Paul Cézanne* (John Rewald, ed.; 1976)

3 The artist must scorn all judgment that is not based on an intelligent observation of character.
Letter to Emile Bernard (1904), quoted in *Letters of Paul Cézanne* (John Rewald, ed.; 1976)

4 To paint well is to express one's own time where it is most progressive, to stand on the summit of the world, on the heights of humanity.
Quoted in *Joachim Gasquet's Cézanne: A Memoir with Conversations* (Christopher Pemberton, tr.; 1991)

5 The day is coming when a single carrot, freshly observed, will set off a revolution.
Attrib.

Chabrol, Claude (b.1930) French film director and screenwriter

1 What I like is what people are at the beginning of a scene and what they are at the end of a scene. I'm primarily interested in their relationships, and the plot is just a means to get at the behavior of the characters.
Interview, *Times,* London (May 13, 1972), quoted in *Film-makers Speak* (Jay Leyda, ed.; 1977)

Chagall, Marc (1887–1985) Russian-born French painter and designer

1 Art seems to me above all a state of soul.
Quoted in *My Life* (Elizabeth Abbott, tr.; 1922)

2 People have reproached me for putting poetry into my pictures. It is true that there are other things to be required of the art of painting. But show me a single great work that does not have its portion of poetry.
Quoted in *The World of Marc Chagall* (Roy McMullen; 1968)

3 You might say that in my mother's womb I had already noticed the purity of the colors of the flowers...I don't know if color chose me or I chose color, but since childhood I've been married to color in its pure state.
Quoted in *The World of Marc Chagall* (Roy McMullen; 1968)

Chalkhill, John (1600?–42) English poet

1 Oh, the gallant fisher's life!
It is the best of any
'Tis full of pleasure, void of strife,
And 'tis beloved of many.
"Piscator's Song," *The Compleat Angler* (Izaak Walton; 1653–75)

Chamberlain, Joseph (1836–1914) British statesman

1 The day of small nations has long passed away. The day of Empires has come.
May 12, 1904. Speech, Birmingham, *Times,* London (May 13, 1904)

Chamberlain, Neville (Arthur Neville Chamberlain; 1869–1940) British prime minister

Quotations about Chamberlain

1 Listening to a speech by Chamberlain is like paying a visit to Woolworths; everything in its place and nothing over sixpence.
1937
Aneurin Bevan (1897–1960) Welsh politician. *Aneurin Bevan* (Michael Foot; 1973), vol. 1, ch. 8

2 Well, he seemed such a nice old gentleman, I thought I would give him my autograph as a souvenir.
Adolf Hitler (1889–1945) Austrian-born German political and military leader. Referring to Neville Chamberlain. Attrib.

Quotations by Chamberlain

3 In war, whichever side may call itself the victor, there are no winners, but all are losers.
Speech, Kettering (July 3, 1938)

4 This morning the British Ambassador in Berlin handed the German Government a final note stating that, unless we heard from them by eleven o'clock that they were prepared at once to withdraw their troops from Poland, a state of war would exist between us. I have to tell you that no such undertaking has been received, and that consequently this country is at war with Germany.
Speech, London (September 3, 1939)

5 Hitler has missed the bus.
Speech to the British Parliament (April 4, 1940)

6 I have to inform the House that...in the event of any action which clearly threatened Polish independence...His Majesty's government would feel themselves bound at once to lend the Polish government all support in their power.
Speech to the British Parliament (March 31, 1939)

7 We should seek by all means in our power to avoid war...even if it does mean the establishment of personal contact with the dictators.
Speech to the British Parliament (October 6, 1938)

8 How horrible, fantastic, incredible, it is that we should be digging trenches and trying on gas-masks here because of a quarrel in a far-away country between people of whom we know nothing.
September 27, 1938. Referring to Germany's annexation of the Sudetenland. *Times,* London (September 28, 1938)

9 This is the second time in our history that there has come back from Germany to Downing Street peace with honour. I believe it is peace for our time.
September 30, 1938. Speech from 10 Downing Street, home of the British prime minister. *Times,* London (October 1, 1938)

10 This morning I had another talk with...Herr Hitler, and here is the paper which bears his name upon it as well as mine..."We regard the agreement signed last night...as symbolic of the

desire of our two peoples never to go to war with one another again."
1938. Said at Heston airport on returning from signing the Munich agreement.

Chamfort, Nicolas (Sébastien Roch Nicolas Chamfort; 1741–94) French writer

1 Man arrives as a novice at each age of his life.
Caractères et anecdotes (1795)

2 Someone said of a very great egotist: "He would burn your house down to cook himself a couple of eggs."
Caractères et anecdotes (1795)

3 However much a man might think ill of women, there is no woman who does not think greater ill of him.
Maximes et pensées (1795)

4 If one should love one's neighbor as one's self, it is at least as fair that one should love one's self as one's neighbor.
Maximes et pensées (1795)

5 Our gratitude to most benefactors is the same as our feeling for dentists who have pulled our teeth. We acknowledge the good they have done and the evil from which they have delivered us, but we remember the pain they occasioned and do not love them very much.
Maximes et pensées (1795)

6 Philosophy, like medicine, has plenty of drugs, few good remedies, and hardly any specific cures.
Maximes et pensées (1795)

7 The most wasted of all days is that on which one has not laughed.
Maximes et pensées (1795)

8 What I have learned I no longer know. The little that I do know, I guessed.
Maximes et pensées (1795)

9 The majority of those who put together collections of verses or epigrams resemble those who eat cherries or oysters: they begin by choosing the best and end by eating everything.
Maximes et pensées (1795), ch. 1

10 Living is an illness to which sleep provides relief every sixteen hours. It's a palliative. The remedy is death.
Maximes et pensées (1795), ch. 2

11 Love, in the form in which it exists in society, is nothing but the exchange of two fantasies and the superficial contact of two bodies.
Maximes et pensées (1795), ch. 6

12 I am tempted to say of metaphysicians what Scaliger used to say of the Basques: they are said to understand one another, but I don't believe a word of it.
Maximes et pensées (1795), ch. 7

13 The poor are Europe's blacks.
Maximes et pensées (1795), ch. 8

14 Be my brother or I kill you.
His interpretation of the revolutionary rallying cry: "Fraternité ou la mort!" ("Fraternity or death!") "Notice historique sur la vie et les écrits de Chamfort," *Oeuvres complètes* (P. R. Anguis, ed.; 1824)

15 The threat of a neglected cold is for doctors what the threat of purgatory is for priests—a gold mine.
Attrib.

Chandler, Raymond (1888–1959) U.S. novelist

1 When I split an infinitive, god damn it, I split it so it stays split.
Letter to Edward Weeks, his English publisher (January 18, 1947)

2 It was a blonde. A blonde to make a bishop kick a hole in a stained-glass window.
Farewell, My Lovely (1940), ch. 13

3 She gave me a smile I could feel in my hip pocket.
Farewell, My Lovely (1940), ch. 18

4 Alcohol is like love: the first kiss is magic, the second is intimate, the third is routine. After that you just take the girl's clothes off.
The Long Goodbye (1953)

5 California is poor drinking country in the summer. In New York you can handle four times as much with half the hangover.
The Long Goodbye (1953)

6 Mass production couldn't sell its goods next year unless it made what it sold this year look unfashionable a year from now.
The Long Goodbye (1953)

7 Pasadena, where the stuffy millionaires holed up after Beverly Hills was spoiled for them by the movie crowd.
The Long Goodbye (1953)

8 The law isn't justice. It's a very imperfect mechanism. If you press exactly the right buttons and are also lucky, justice may also turn up in the answer.
The Long Goodbye (1953)

9 There is no trap so deadly as the trap you set for yourself.
Said by Philip Marlowe. *The Long Goodbye* (1953)

10 Down these mean streets a man must go who is not himself mean; who is neither tarnished nor afraid.
The Simple Art of Murder (1950)

11 When in doubt have a man come through a door with a gun in his hand.
The Simple Art of Murder (1950)

12 If my books had been any worse I should not have been invited to Hollywood, and if they had been any better I should not have come.
December 12, 1945. Letter to Charles W. Morton, *Raymond Chandler Speaking* (Dorothy Gardner and Katherine S. Walker; 1962)

13 High prices and heavy taxation will destroy a society just as effectively as war.
Written to Carl Brandt. Quoted in *Selected Letters of Raymond Chandler* (Frank MacShane, ed.; 1981)

14 Hollywood is a world with all the personality of a paper cup.
Attrib.

Chandra, Vikram (b.1961) Indian-born U.S. writer

1 A kulfi-seller set up his cart near the bridge, and a crowd, mostly of young boys, formed around him; the boys shouted insults at him, and he replied to each in verse, never at a loss for an answer.
"The Book of Blood and Journeys," *Red Earth and Pouring Rain* (1995)

2 Those who cannot see the spirits are the dead. The gravity of the sometimes-glimpsed cold of the cities on the ocean's floor, the hiss of the guardian, impels us...what is sacred cannot be history, but memory...is divine.
"The Book of Learning and Desolation," *Red Earth and Pouring Rain* (1995)

3 If I must be reborn, I prefer not to be aware, to be always divided against myself, to be a monster; I have no doubt cursed myself through my actions, but have I done enough so that I will be reborn as an animal?
"The Book of Return," *Red Earth and Pouring Rain* (1995)

4 This world in which nothing is clear, where there is horror at every turn, I am sick of it. I know I will be reborn into it...Does it get any better?
The world is the world. It is you that makes the horror.
"The Book of Return," *Red Earth and Pouring Rain* (1995)

Chanel, Coco (Gabrielle Bonheur Chanel; 1883–1971) French fashion designer

1 Fashion is made to become unfashionable.
Life (1957)

2 Dressmaking is a technique, a craft, a trade...If a costume tries to match the beauty of a body or to accentuate the role of a sublime heroine, that's fine, but this does not mean the dressmaker should think, claim to be, act, or pose as an artist.
Quoted in *Chanel* (Jean Leymarie; 1987)

3 There is nothing more comfortable than a caterpillar and nothing more made for love than a butterfly. We need dresses that crawl and dresses that fly.
1920s. Quoted in *Chanel* (Jean Leymarie; 1987)

4 Women think of all colors except the absence of color. I have already said that black has it all. White too. Their beauty is absolute. It is the perfect harmony.
Quoted in *Chanel* (J. Leymarie; 1987)

5 Youth is something very new: twenty years ago no one mentioned it.
Coco Chanel, Her Life, Her Secrets (Marcel Haedrich; 1987)

6 Fashion is architecture: it is a matter of proportions.
Attrib. *Coco Chanel, Her Life, Her Secrets* (Marcel Haedrich; 1987)

7 Wherever one wants to be kissed.
When asked where one should wear perfume. Attrib. *Coco Chanel, Her Life, Her Secrets* (Marcel Haedrich; 1987)

8 Balenciaga? He dresses women to look like old Spaniards.
Referring to Cristóbal Balenciaga, a Spanish clothing designer. Quoted in *Dior* (Françoise Giroud, Stewart Spencer, tr.; 1987)

Chang, S. K. (b.1944) U.S. writer

1 You are living in American society now. You can't not fight. If you don't fight, how will you be able to persuade anyone of anything? If you don't fight, how will people know what your strong points are?
"The Amateur Cameraman" (Jeffery C. Bent, tr.; 1991)

Channing, William Ellery (1780–1842) U.S. clergyman

1 I call that mind free which jealously guards its intellectual rights and powers, which calls no man master, which does not content itself with a passive or hereditary faith, which opens itself to light whensoever it may come, which receives new truth as an angel from heaven.
Sermon. "Spiritual Freedom" (1830)

2 There are seasons...of inward and outward revolution, when new depths seem to be broken up in the soul, when new wants are unfolded in the multitudes, and a new and undefined good is thirsted for. These are periods when...to *dare* is the highest wisdom.
"The Union" (1829)

3 I see the marks of God in the heaven and the earth, but how much more in a liberal intellect, in magnanimity, in unconquerable rectitude...I thank God that my own lot is bound up with that of the human race.
Likeness to God (1828)

Channon, Henry (1897–1958) British politician and writer

1 A bore, a bounder and a prig. He was intoxicated with his own youth and loathed any milieu which he couldn't dominate. Certainly he had none of a gentleman's instincts, strutting about Peace Conferences in Arab dress.
Referring to T. E. Lawrence, who, having led Arab forces in the Middle East against Turkish rule, later tried but failed to secure Arab independence at the Paris Peace Conference (1919). *Diary*, May 23, 1935

Channon, Paul (b.1935) British politician

1 Contrary to popular mythology, it is not my Department's mission in life to tarmac over the whole of England.
Speech (September 1998)

Chaplin, Charlie, Sir (Charles Spencer Chaplin; 1889–1977) British actor and director

Quotations about Chaplin

1 I left the screen because I didn't want what happened to Chaplin to happen to me. When he discarded the little tramp, the little tramp turned around and killed him.
Mary Pickford (1893–1979) U.S. actor and film producer. Quoted in *New York Times* (Aljean Harmetz; March 28, 1971)

Quotations by Chaplin

2 The Zulus know Chaplin better than Arkansas knows Garbo.
Atlantic Monthly (August 1939)

3 Life is a tragedy when seen in close-up, but a comedy in long-shot.
Guardian, London (December 28, 1977), Obituary

4 PRIEST May the Lord have mercy on your soul.
VERDOUX Why not? After all, it belongs to Him.
Monsieur Verdoux (1947)

5 Wars, conflict, it's all business. One murder makes a villain. Millions a hero. Numbers sanctify.
Monsieur Verdoux (1947)

6 The saddest thing I can imagine is to get used to luxury.
My Autobiography (1964)

7 All I need to make a comedy is a park, a policeman and a pretty girl.
My Autobiography (1964), ch. 10

8 A tramp, a gentleman, a poet, a dreamer, a lonely fellow, always hopeful of romance and adventure.
Referring to the tramp character in his motion pictures. *My Autobiography* (1964), ch. 10

9 I am for people. I can't help it.
Observer, London (September 28, 1952), "Sayings of the Week"

10 I remain just one thing, and one thing only—and that is a clown. It places me on a far higher plane than any politician.
Observer, London (June 17, 1960), "Sayings of the Week"

11 I am known in parts of the world by people who have never heard of Jesus Christ.
Quoted in *My Life with Chaplin* (Lita Grey Chaplin; 1966)

12 I went into the business for the money, and the art grew out of it. If people are disillusioned by that remark, I can't help it. It's the truth.
Quoted in *The Reader's Digest* (January 1, 1982)

13 Timing! My mother gave me that. I was born with it. I don't think you can teach a person to act.
Attrib.

Chapman, George (1559?–1634) English poet and playwright

1 Young men think old men are fools; but old men know young men are fools.
All Fools (1605), Act 5, Scene 1

2 I know an Englishman,
Being flattered, is a lamb; threatened, a lion.
Alphonsus, Emperor of Germany (1654), Act 1, Scene 2

3 Danger, the spur of all great minds.
Co-written with Ben Jonson and John Marston. *The Revenge of Bussy D'Ambois* (1613), Act 5, Scene 1

Chapman, John Jay (1862–1933) U.S. writer

1 The New Testament, and to a very large extent the Old, *is* the soul of man. You cannot criticize it. It criticizes you.
Letter (March 26, 1898)

2 The present in New York is so powerful that the past is lost.
Letter (1909)

Char, René (1907–88) French poet

1 Poetry will steal death from me.
"La bibliothèque est en feu," *La Parole en archipel* (1961)

2 Wisdom, with tear-filled eyes.
"La paroi et la prairie, Lascaux," *La Parole en archipel* (1961)

3 Those who truly have a taste for nothingness burn their clothes before dying.
"Artine: La manne de Lola Abba," *Le Marteau sans maître* (1934)

Charcot, Jean Martin (1825–93) French pathologist and neurologist

1 Disease is very old, and nothing about it has changed. It is we who change, as we learn to recognize what was formerly imperceptible.
De l'expectation en médecine (1857)

2 If the clinician, as observer, wishes to see things as they really are, he must make a *tabula rasa* of his mind and proceed without any preconceived notions whatever.
Attrib.

Charlemagne, King of the Franks and Emperor of the West (Charles the Great; 742?–814) Frankish monarch

1 Our task is, with the aid of divine piety, to defend the Holy Church of Christ with arms...Your task, most holy father, is to lift up your hands to God, like Moses, so as to aid our troops.
Letter to Pope Leo III (796)

2 I should never have entered the church on that day, though it was an important feast, could I have known the Pope's intention in advance.
Referring to his coronation as emperor. Attrib. (December 25, 800)

Charles, Elizabeth (Elizabeth Rundle Charles; 1828–96) British writer

1 To know how to say what others only know how to think is what makes men poets or sages; and to dare to say what others only dare to think makes men martyrs or reformers—or both.
Chronicle of the Schönberg-Cotta Family (1863)

Charles, Prince, Prince of Wales (Philip Arthur George Charles; b.1948) British prince

1 Retirement, for a monarch, is not a good idea.
Speech (1974)

2 Well frankly, the problem as I see it at this moment in time is whether I should just lie down under all this hassle and let them walk all over me, or whether I should just say OK, I get the message, and do myself in.
At the presentation of the Thomas Cranmer Schools Prize (1989), suggesting a possible modern English version of Hamlet's soliloquy. The original version is:
To be, or not to be: that is the question:
Whether 'tis nobler in the mind to suffer
The slings and arrows of outrageous fortune,
Or to take arms against a sea of troubles,
And by opposing end them?
Speech (1989)

3 Do you seriously expect me to be the first Prince of Wales in history not to have a mistress?
Daily Mail, London (December 1994)

4 To get the best results you must talk to your vegetables.
Observer, London (September 28, 1986), "Sayings of the Week"

5 You have to give this much to the Luftwaffe—when it knocked down our buildings it did not replace them with anything more offensive than rubble. We did that.
Observer, London (December 6, 1987), "Sayings of the Week"

6 Like a carbuncle on the face of an old and valued friend.
May 10, 1984. Referring to a proposed modern extension to the National Gallery. *Times,* London (May 31, 1984)

7 I am afraid I believe we delude ourselves if we think that humanity is becoming ever more civilised, ever more sophisticated and ever more reasonable. It's simply not the case.
ITV television program, "Charles: The Private Man, the Public Role." (June 29, 1994)

8 I'm not very good at being a performing monkey.
ITV television program, "Charles: The Private Man, the Public Role." (June 29, 1994)

9 I personally would much rather see my title as Defender of Faith, not the Faith, because it means just one interpretation of the faith, which I think is sometimes something that causes a great deal of a problem.
ITV television program, "Charles: The Private Man, the Public Role." (June 29, 1994)

10 Yes...whatever that may mean.
On his engagement, when asked whether he was in love. (February 1981)

11 The monarchy is the oldest profession in the world.
Attrib.

12 The one advantage about marrying a princess—or someone from a royal family—is that they do know what happens.
Attrib.

Charles, Ray (Ray Charles Robinson; b.1932) U.S. pianist and singer

1 I'd like to think that when I sing a song, I can let you know all about the heartbreak, struggle, lies and kicks in the ass I've gotten over the years for being black and everything else, without actually saying a word about it.
Interview, *Playboy* (1970)

2 My version of "Georgia" became the state song of Georgia. That was a big thing for me, man. It really touched me. Here is a state that used to lynch people like me suddenly declaring my version of a song as its state song. That is touching.
Quoted in "Ray Charles," *Off the Record: An Oral History of Popular Music* (Joe Smith; 1988)

3 I don't know what would have happened to me if I hadn't been able to hear.
Ray Charles was born blind. Quoted in "Ray Charles," *Off the Record: An Oral History of Popular Music* (Joe Smith; 1988)

Charles I, King of England, Scotland, and Ireland (1600–49) Scottish-born monarch

Quotations about Charles I

1 He nothing common did or mean
Upon that memorable scene,
But with his keener eye
The axe's edge did try.
Andrew Marvell (1621–78) English poet and government official. Referring to the execution of Charles I. "An Horatian Ode upon Cromwell's Return from Ireland" (1650), st. 15

Quotations by Charles I

2 The nature of Presbyterian government is to steal or force the crown from the king's head.
Letter to his wife, Queen Henrietta Maria (March 3, 1646)

3 Never make a defence or apology before you be accused.
Letter to Lord Wentworth (September 3, 1636), quoted in *Letters to King Charles I* (Charles Petrie, ed.; 1935)

4 For the people; and truly I desire their liberty and freedom, as much as any body: but I must tell you, that their liberty and freedom consists in having the government of those laws by which their life and their goods may be most their own.
Speech on the scaffold (January 30, 1649), quoted in *Historical Collections* (J. Rushworth; 1701), pt. 4, vol. 2

5 I die a Christian, according to the Profession of the Church of England, as I found it left me by my Father.
Speech on the scaffold (January 30, 1649), quoted in *Historical Collections* (J. Rushworth; 1701), pt. 4, vol. 2

6 If I would have given way to an arbitrary way, for to have all laws changed according to the power of the sword, I needed not to have come here; therefore I tell you (and I pray God it be not laid to your charge) that I am the martyr of the people.
Speech on the scaffold (January 30, 1649), quoted in *Historical Collections* (J. Rushworth; 1701), pt. 4, vol. 2

7 Well, since I see all the birds are flown, I do expect from you that you shall send them unto me as soon as they return hither.
January 4, 1642. On entering the British Parliament to arrest five Members of Parliament. *Hansard Parliamentary History to the Year 1803* (1803), vol. 2, col. 1010

8 1. Urge no healths. 2. Profane no divine ordinances. 3. Touch no state matters. 4. Reveal no secrets. 5. Pick no quarrels. 6. Make no comparisons. 7. Maintain no ill opinions. 8. Keep no bad company. 9. Encourage no vice. 10. Make no long meals. 11. Repent no grievances. 12. Lay no wagers.
Attrib.

Charles I, Emperor of Austria (Charles Francis Joseph; also Charles IV, King of Hungary; 1887–1922) Austrian monarch

1 What should I do? I think the best thing is to order a new stamp to be made with my face on it.
On hearing of his accession as emperor to the Austro-Hungarian Empire, 1916. *Anekdotenschatz* (H. Hoffmeister; 1916)

Charles II, King of England, Scotland, and Ireland ("The Merry Monarch"; 1630–85) English monarch

Quotations about Charles II

1 He only treats with me to derive an advantage in his future negotiations with his subjects.
Louis XIV (1638–1715) French monarch. Attrib.

2 Whatever he may promise me he will break everything to get a regular income from his parliament.
1680
Louis XIV (1638–1715) French monarch. Attrib.

3 There were gentlemen and there were seamen in the navy of Charles the Second. But the seamen were not gentlemen; and the gentlemen were not seamen.
Thomas Babington Macaulay (1800–59) British politician, historian, and writer. *History of England from the Accession of James II* (1848–61), vol. 1, ch. 3

4 A merry monarch, scandalous and poor.
2nd Earl of Rochester (1647–80) English courtier and poet. *A Satire on King Charles II* (1697)

5 Here lies our sovereign lord the king,
Whose word no man relies on;
He never says a foolish thing,
Nor ever does a wise one.
2nd Earl of Rochester (1647–80) English courtier and poet. Written on the bedchamber door of Charles II. Attrib.

Quotations by Charles II

6 The thing which is nearest the heart of this nation is trade and all that belongs to it.
Letter to his sister, Henrietta (September 14, 1668)

7 You will have heard of our taking of New Amsterdam...It did belong to England heretofore, but the Dutch by degrees drove our people out and built a very good town, but we have got the better of it, and 'tis now called New York.
Remark (1664)

8 Brother, I am too old to go again to my travels.
Referring to his exile (1651–60). Remark to his brother, James (1650s), quoted in *History of England* (Hume; 1754–62), vol. 2, ch. 7

9 You had better have one King than five hundred.
After saying which he did not summon Parliament again. Speech (March 28, 1681)

10 He had been, he said, an unconscionable time dying; but he hoped that they would excuse it.
1685. Quoted in *History of England* (Lord Macaulay; 1849), vol. 1, ch. 4, p.437

11 Not a religion for gentlemen.
1724. Referring to Presbyterianism. *History of His Own Time* (Bishop Burnet; 1724–34), vol. 1, bk. 2. ch. 2

12 This is very true: for my words are my own, and my actions are my ministers'.
Replying to Lord Rochester's suggested epitaph: "God Bless our good and gracious King
Whose promise none relies on,
Who never said a foolish thing
Nor never did a wise one." *King Charles II* (A. Bryant; 1931)

13 I am sure no man in England will take away my life to make you King.
1678. Said to his brother James following revelation of the Popish Plot fabricated by Titus Oates. Attrib. *Political and Literary Anecdotes* (William King; 1818)

14 Of this you may be assured, that you shall none of you suffer for your opinions or religion, so long as you live peaceably, and you have the word of a king for it.
Said to a deputation of Quakers. *Single Works* (George Fox; 1661)

15 Then, my lord, be his blood on your own conscience. You might have saved him if you would. I cannot pardon him because I dare not.
Reply to the Earl of Essex, who had protested Saint Oliver Plunket's innocence of the treason for which he had been sentenced to death. *The Later Stuarts* (Sir George Clark; 1934)

16 It is upon the navy under the Providence of God that the safety, honour, and welfare of this realm do chiefly attend.
1652. "Articles of War," *The Naval Side of British History* (Sir Geoffrey Callender; 1952), pt. 1, ch. 8

17 Let not poor Nelly starve.
On his death bed, referring to his mistress, the actor Nell Gwynne. (1685)

18 Better than a play.
1670. Referring to the upper house of the British Parliament debate on the Divorce Bill. Attrib.

Charles V, Holy Roman Emperor (Charles I, King of Spain; 1500–58) Belgian-born Spanish monarch

1 Name me an emperor who was ever struck by a cannonball.
Responding to his military commanders' exhortations not to risk his life needlessly at the Battle of Mühlberg. Remark (April 23, 1547)

2 Depend on none but yourself.
Remark to his son, Philip II of Spain (1558)

3 My cousin Francis and I are in perfect accord—he wants Milan, and so do I.
Referring to his dispute with Francis I of France over Italian territory. *The Story of Civilization* (William Durant; 1950–67), vol. 5

4 I speak Spanish to God, Italian to women, French to men, and German to my horse.
Attrib.

5 I make war on the living, not on the dead.
1546. After the death of Martin Luther, when it was suggested that he hang the corpse on a gallows. Attrib.

Charles X (1757–1836) French monarch

1 There is no middle course between the throne and the scaffold.
Remark to Talleyrand, who is said to have replied, "You are forgetting the postchaise." Attrib.

Charles Albert, King of Sardinia-Piedmont (1798–1849) Piedmontese monarch

1 Italy will do it alone.
Referring to the movement to liberate and unify Italy. Remark (March 1848)

Charron, Pierre (1541–1603) French theologian and philosopher

1 The true science and the true study of man is man.
Traité de la sagesse (1601), bk. 1, ch. 1

Chase, Salmon P. (Salmon Portland Chase; 1808–73) U.S. politician and Supreme Court chief justice

1 The Constitution, in all its provisions, looks to an indestructible Union composed of indestructible States.
Decision on a law case (1868)

Chateaubriand, René, Vicomte (François Auguste René; 1768–1848) French writer and statesman

1 An original writer is not one who imitates nobody, but one whom nobody can imitate.
Génie du Christianisme (1802)

2 I wept and I believed.
Asserting his Christian faith. *Génie du Christianisme* (1802), preface

3 Let us not scorn glory too much: nothing, other than virtue, is more beautiful.
Itinéraire de Paris à Jérusalem (1811), pt. 1

4 Achilles exists only through Homer. Take away the art of writing from this world, and you will probably take away its glory.
Les Natchez (1826)

5 Memory is often the attribute of stupidity; it generally belongs

to heavy spirits whom it makes even heavier by the baggage it loads them down with.
Mémoires d'outre-tombe (1849–50)

6 One does not learn how to die by killing others.
Mémoires d'outre-tombe (1849–50)

7 I have within me an impossibility of obeying.
Mémoires d'outre-tombe (1849–50), bk. 2, ch. 8

8 The more serious the face, the more beautiful the smile.
Mémoires d'outre-tombe (1849–50), bk. 14, ch. 10

9 Life does not suit me; death might become me better.
Mémoires d'outre-tombe (1849–50), preface

10 One is not superior merely because one sees the world in an odious light.
Attrib.

Chaucer, Geoffrey (1343?–1400) English poet

Quotations about Chaucer

1 And Chaucer, with his infantine
Familiar clasp of things divine.
Elizabeth Barrett Browning (1806–61) British poet. "A Vision of Poets" (1844)

2 Chaucer, notwithstanding the praises bestowed on him, I think obscene and contemptible; he owes his celebrity merely to his antiquity.
Lord Byron (1788–1824) British poet. Attrib.

3 The worshipful father and first founder and embellisher of ornate eloquence in our English, I mean Master Geoffrey Chaucer.
William Caxton (1422?–91) English printer. *Caxton's edition of Chaucer's translation of Boethius, De Consolacione Philosophie* (1478), epilogue

4 Chaucer and Spenser are Normans, and their minds open most fairly southward.
James Russell Lowell (1819–91) U.S. poet, editor, essayist, and diplomat. Referring to Geoffrey Chaucer and Edmund Spenser. "Nationality in Literature" (1849), quoted in *The Great Critics* (James Harry Smith and Edd Winfield Parks, eds.; 1951)

5 I read Chaucer still with as much pleasure as any of our poets. He is a master of manners and of description and the first tale-teller in the true enlivened, natural way.
Alexander Pope (1688–1744) English poet. Attrib.

6 What was it Chaucer
Said once about the long toil
That goes like blood to the poem's making?
Leave it to nature and the verse sprawls,
Limp as bindweed, if it break at all
Life's iron crust.
R. S. Thomas (b.1913) Welsh poet and clergyman. "Poetry for Supper," *Poetry for Supper* (1958)

Quotations by Chaucer

7 Trouthe is the hyeste thyng that man may kepe.
"The Franklin's Tale," *The Canterbury Tales* (1390?), l. 1479, quoted in *The Works of Geoffrey Chaucer* (F. N. Robinson, ed.; 1957)

8 No berd hadde he, ne nevere sholde have;
As smothe it was as it were late shave.
I trow he were a geldyng or a mare.
Referring to the Pardoner. "The General Prologue," *The Canterbury Tales* (1390?), ll. 688–690, quoted in *The Works of Geoffrey Chaucer* (F. N. Robinson, ed.; 1957)

9 He was a verray, parfit gentil knyght.
Referring to the knight. "The General Prologue," *The Canterbury Tales* (1390?), l. 72, quoted in *The Works of Geoffrey Chaucer* (F. N. Robinson, ed.; 1957)

10 He was as fresh as is the month of May.
Referring to the squire. "The General Prologue," *The Canterbury Tales* (1390?), l. 92, quoted in *The Works of Geoffrey Chaucer* (F. N. Robinson, ed.; 1957)

11 He knew the tavernes wel in every toun.
Referring to the friar. "The General Prologue," *The Canterbury Tales* (1390?), l. 240, quoted in *The Works of Geoffrey Chaucer* (F. N. Robinson, ed.; 1957)

12 As leene was his hors as is a rake.
Referring to the clerk. "The General Prologue," *The Canterbury Tales* (1390?), l. 287, quoted in *The Works of Geoffrey Chaucer* (F. N. Robinson, ed.; 1957)

13 If gold ruste, what shall iren do?
"The General Prologue," *The Canterbury Tales* (1390?), l. 500, quoted in *The Works of Geoffrey Chaucer* (F. N. Robinson, ed.; 1957)

14 Whan that Aprill with his shoures soote
The droghte of March hath perced to the roote.
"The General Prologue," *The Canterbury Tales* (1390?), ll. 1–2, quoted in *The Works of Geoffrey Chaucer* (F. N. Robinson, ed.; 1957)

15 A Knyght ther was and that a worthy man,
That fro the tyme that he first bigan
To riden out, he loved chivalrie,
Trouthe and honour, fredom and curteisie.
Referring to the knight. "The General Prologue," *The Canterbury Tales* (1390?), ll. 43–46, quoted in *The Works of Geoffrey Chaucer* (F. N. Robinson, ed.; 1957)

16 Ful weel she soong the service dyvyne,
Entuned in hir nose ful semely.
Referring to the prioress. "The General Prologue," *The Canterbury Tales* (1390?), ll. 122–123, quoted in *The Works of Geoffrey Chaucer* (F. N. Robinson, ed.; 1957)

17 A Clerk ther was of Oxenford also,
That unto logyk hadde longe ygo.
"The General Prologue," *The Canterbury Tales* (1390?), ll. 285–286, quoted in *The Works of Geoffrey Chaucer* (F. N. Robinson, ed.; 1957)

18 Sownynge in moral vertu was his speche,
And gladly wolde he lerne and gladly teche.
Referring to the clerk. "The General Prologue," *The Canterbury Tales* (1390?), ll. 307–308, quoted in *The Works of Geoffrey Chaucer* (F. N. Robinson, ed.; 1957)

19 Nowher so bisy a man as he ther nas,
And yet he semed bisier than he was.
Referring to the man of law. "The General Prologue," *The Canterbury Tales* (1390?), ll. 321–322, quoted in *The Works of Geoffrey Chaucer* (F. N. Robinson, ed.; 1957)

20 For gold in phisik is a cordial,
Therfore he lovede gold in special.
Referring to the doctor. "The General Prologue," *The Canterbury Tales* (1390?), ll. 443–444, quoted in *The Works of Geoffrey Chaucer* (F. N. Robinson, ed.; 1957)

21 She was a worthy womman al hir lyve,
Housbondes at chirche dore she hadde fyve,
Withouten other compaignye in youthe.
Referring to the wife of Bath. "The General Prologue," *The Canterbury Tales* (1390?), ll. 459–461, quoted in *The Works of Geoffrey Chaucer* (F. N. Robinson, ed.; 1957)

22 For pitee renneth soone in gentil herte.
"The Knight's Tale," *The Canterbury Tales* (1390?), l. 1761, quoted in *The Works of Geoffrey Chaucer* (F. N. Robinson, ed.; 1957)

23 The smylere with the knyf under the cloke.
"The Knight's Tale," *The Canterbury Tales* (1390?), l. 1999, quoted in *The Works of Geoffrey Chaucer* (F. N. Robinson, ed.; 1957)

24 Myn be the travaille, and thyn be the glorie!
"The Knight's Tale," *The Canterbury Tales* (1390?), l. 2406, quoted in *The Works of Geoffrey Chaucer* (F. N. Robinson, ed.; 1957)

25 And whan a beest is deed he hath no peyne;
But man after his deeth moot wepe and pleyne.
"The Knight's Tale," *The Canterbury Tales* (1390?), ll. 1319–20, quoted in *The Works of Geoffrey Chaucer* (F.N. Robinson, ed.; 1957)

26 This world nys but a thurghfare ful of wo,
And we ben pilgrymes, passynge to and fro;
Deeth is an ende of every worldly sore.
"The Knight's Tale," *The Canterbury Tales* (1390?), ll. 2847–49, quoted in *The Works of Geoffrey Chaucer* (F. N. Robinson, ed.; 1957)

27 Thanne is it wysdom, as it thynketh me,
To maken vertue of necessitee.
"The Knight's Tale," *The Canterbury Tales* (1390?), ll. 3041–42, quoted in *The Works of Geoffrey Chaucer* (F. N. Robinson, ed.; 1957)

28 Tragedie is to seyn a certeyn storie,
As olde bokes maken us memorie,
Of him that stood in greet prosperitee
And is y-fallen out of heigh degree
Into miserie, and endeth wrecchedly.
"The Monk's Prologue," *The Canterbury Tales* (1390?), quoted in *The Works of Geoffrey Chaucer* (F. N. Robinson, ed.; 1957)

29 Mordre wol out, that see we day by day.
"The Nun's Priest's Tale," *The Canterbury Tales* (1390?), quoted in *The Works of Geoffrey Chaucer* (F. N. Robinson, ed.; 1957)

30 "Now, sires," quoth he, "if that you be so leef
To fynde Death, turne up this croked way,
For in that grove I lafte hym, by my fey,
Under a tree, and there he wole abyde."
The old man's advice to the three youths who have set out from a tavern to conquer death. "The Pardoner's Tale," *The Canterbury Tales* (1390?), ll. 760–764, quoted in *The Works of Geoffrey Chaucer* (F. N. Robinson, ed.; 1957)

31 This is to seyn, to syngen and to rede,
As smale children doon in hire childhede.
"The Prioress's Tale," *The Canterbury Tales* (1390?), l. 500, quoted in *The Works of Geoffrey Chaucer* (F. N. Robinson, ed.; 1957)

32 The gretteste clerkes been noght wisest men.
"The Reeves Tale," *The Canterbury Tales* (1390?), l. 4054, quoted in *The Works of Geoffrey Chaucer* (F. N. Robinson, ed.; 1957)

33 And what is better than wisedoom? Womman. And what is better than a good womman? Nothyng.
"The Tale of Melibee," *The Canterbury Tales* (1390?), l. 1107, quoted in *The Works of Geoffrey Chaucer* (F. N. Robinson, ed.; 1957)

34 In th'olde dayes of the King Arthour,
Of which that Britons speken greet honour,
Al was this land fulfild of fayerye.
"The Wife of Bath's Tale," *The Canterbury Tales* (1390?), quoted in *The Works of Geoffrey Chaucer* (F. N. Robinson, ed.; 1957)

35 Wommen desiren to have sovereynetee
As wel over hir housbond as hir love.
"The Wife of Bath's Tale," *The Canterbury Tales* (1390?), quoted in *The Works of Geoffrey Chaucer* (F. N. Robinson, ed.; 1957)

36 A thousand tymes have I herd men telle
That ther ys joy in hevene and peyne in helle,
And I acorde wel that it ys so;
But, natheless, yet wot I wel also
That ther nis noon dwellyng in this contree,
That eyther hath in hevene or helle ybe.
"The Prologue," *The Legend of Good Women* (1380–86), quoted in *The Works of Geoffrey Chaucer* (F. N. Robinson, ed.; 1957)

37 That lyf so short, the craft so long to lerne,
Th' assay so hard, so sharp the conquerynge.
The Parliament of Fowls (1380?), ll. 1–2, quoted in *The Works of Geoffery Chaucer* (F. N. Robinson, ed.; 1957)

38 It is nought good a slepyng hound to wake.
Troilus and Criseyde (1380–86), bk. 3, 1. 764, quoted in *The Works of Geoffrey Chaucer* (F. N. Robinson, ed.; 1957)

39 Oon ere it herde, at tother out it wente.
Troilus and Criseyde (1380–86), bk. 4, 1. 434, quoted in *The Works of Geoffrey Chaucer* (F. N. Robinson, ed.; 1957)

Chausen, Dave U.S. restaurateur

1 Bogart's a helluva nice guy till 11.30 p.m. After that he thinks he's Bogart.
Remark, quoted in *The Filmgoer's Book of Quotes* (L. Halliwell; 1973)

Cheever, John (1912–82) U.S. short-story writer and novelist

1 Homesickness is...absolutely nothing. Fifty percent of the people in the world are homesick all the time...You don't really long for another country. You long for something in yourself that you don't have, or haven't been able to find.
"The Bella Lingua," *The Stories of John Cheever* (1978)

2 Fear tastes like a rusty knife and do not let her into your home. Courage tastes of blood. Stand up straight. Admire the world. Relish the love of a gentle woman. Trust in the Lord.
The Wapshot Chronicle (1957), ch. 36

Chekhov, Anton (Anton Pavlovich Chekhov; 1860–1904) Russian playwright and short-story writer

Quotations about Chekhov

1 Politically speaking, he might as well have been living on the moon as in Imperial Russia.
Ronald Hingley (b.1920) British biographer and critic. *A New Life of Anton Chekhov* (1976)

2 We are certainly entitled to deduce that he was somewhat undersexed.
Ronald Hingley (b.1920) British biographer and critic. *A New Life of Anton Chekhov* (1976)

3 When I had read this story to the end, I was filled with awe. I could not remain in my room and went out of doors. I felt as if I were locked up in a ward too.
Vladimir Ilyich Lenin (1870–1924) Russian revolutionary leader. On reading "Ward Number Six" by Anton Chekhov (1892). Quoted in *Anton Chekhov* (W. H. Bruford; 1957)

Quotations by Chekhov

4 She was always alone, always wearing the same toque, followed by the white pomeranian. No one knew who she was, and she became known simply as the lady with the lapdog.
"Lady with Lapdog" (1899), sect. 1

5 They were like two migrating birds, male and female, who had been caught and forced to live in separate cages.
"Lady with Lapdog" (1899), sect. 4

6 When all is said and done, no literature can outdo the cynicism of real life; you won't intoxicate with one glass someone who has already drunk up a whole barrel.
Letter (1887)

7 Doctors are just the same as lawyers; the only difference is that lawyers merely rob you, whereas doctors rob you and kill you, too.
Ivanov (1887), Act 1

8 LIBOV ANDREEVNA Are you still a student?
TROFIMOV I expect I shall be a student to the end of my days.
The Cherry Orchard (1904), Act 1

9 When a lot of remedies are suggested for a disease, that means it can't be cured.
The Cherry Orchard (1904), Act 1

10 But if we're to start living in the present isn't it abundantly clear that we've first got to redeem our past and make a clean break with it? And we can only redeem it by suffering and getting down to some real work for a change.
The Cherry Orchard (1904), Act 2

11 Before the cherry orchard was sold everybody was worried and upset, but as soon as it was all settled finally and once for all, everybody calmed down, and felt quite cheerful.
The Cherry Orchard (1904), Act 4

12 MEDVEDENKO Why do you wear black all the time?
MASHA I'm in mourning for my life, I'm unhappy.
The Seagull (1896), Act 1

13 NINA Your play's hard to act, there are no living people in it.
TREPLEV Living people! We should show life neither as it is nor as it ought to be, but as we see it in our dreams.
The Seagull (1896), Act 1

14 Women can't forgive failure.
The Seagull (1896), Act 2

15 We'll be forgotten. Such is our fate and we can't do anything about it.
The Three Sisters (1901), Act 1

16 Do let's go to Moscow. We must go. Please! There's nowhere in the world like Moscow.
The Three Sisters (1901), Act 3

17 The time's come: there's a terrific thunder-cloud advancing upon us, a mighty storm is coming to freshen us up....It's going to blow away all this idleness and indifference, and prejudice against work....I'm going to work, and in twenty-five or thirty years' time every man and woman will be working.
Three Sisters (1901), Act 1

18 People who don't even notice whether it's summer or winter are lucky!
Three Sisters (1901), Act 2

19 Man has been endowed with reason, with the power to create, so that he can add to what he's been given. But up to now he hasn't been a creator, only a destroyer. Forests keep disappearing, rivers dry up, wild life's become extinct, the climate's ruined and the land grows poorer and uglier every day.
Uncle Vanya (1897), Act 1

20 SONYA I'm not beautiful.
HELEN You have lovely hair.
SONYA No, when a woman isn't beautiful, people always say, "You have lovely eyes, you have lovely hair."
Uncle Vanya (1897), Act 3

21 When an actor has money he doesn't send letters, he sends telegrams.
"Nanka," *Complete Works and Letters in Thirty Volumes* (1980), Works, Notebook 4, vol. 17, p. 181

22 There is no national science just as there is no national multiplication table; what is national is no longer science.
Quoted in *Mysli o nauke Kishinev* (V. P. Ponomarev; 1973)

23 If I had listened to the critics I'd have died drunk in the gutter.
Quoted in *Timebends* (Arthur Miller; 1987)

Chen Duxiu (also known as Ch'en Tu-hsiu; 1879–1942) Chinese reformer

1 We love a country that brings the people happiness, not a country that demands the people sacrifice themselves.
Remark (1915)

2 We really don't know which, if any, of our traditional institutions can be adapted for survival in the modern world. I would rather see the destruction of our "national essence" than the final extinction of our race because it is unable to adapt.
Quoted in *Origins of the Chinese Revolution, 1915–1949* (Lucien Bianco; 1967), "Intellectual Origins of the Revolution"

3 When Chinese want to praise someone, they say, "Even though he's young, he acts like a man of mature years." What do English and Americans say when they want to give one another moral support? "Stay young in your heart, no matter what your age is."
Quoted in *Origins of the Chinese Revolution, 1915–1949* (Lucien Bianco; 1967), "Intellectual Origins of the Revolution"

4 If we have committed all these crimes, it is solely because of our support for two gentlemen, Mr. Democracy, and Mr. Science. As supporters of Democracy, we are obliged to attack Confucianism, rituals, womanly chastity, traditional morality, and old-style politics.
January 1919. Said in defense of his criticism of traditional Confucian culture. Quoted in *Origins of the Chinese Revolution, 1915–1949* (Lucien Bianco; 1967), "Intellectual Origins of the Revolution"

Chen Muhua (b.1920) Chinese politician

1 Eugenics not only affects the success of the state and the

prosperity of the race, but also the well-being of the people and social stability.

1991. Quoted in *Imperfect Conceptions: Medical Knowledge, Birth Defects, and Eugenics in China* (Frank Dikotter; 1998)

Chen Yi, Marshal (1901–72) Chinese military leader and statesman

1 It's man who decides, not heaven.

To My Children (1961), quoted in *Literature of the People's Republic of China* (Kai-yu Hsu, ed.; 1980)

Cher (Cherilyn Sarkisian La Piere; b.1946) U.S. singer and actor

1 I don't know how many more times I can beat this face into submission.

Referring to cosmetic surgery. "The Many Faces of Cher," *Newsweek* (Charles Leerhsen, co-written with Jennifer Foote and Peter McKillop; November 30, 1987)

Chernow, Ron (b.1949) U.S. journalist and author

1 I fear the tyranny of a stock market that favors boring financial conglomerates over innovative, enterprising firms.

Wall Street Journal (September 30, 1997)

Chesneau, Ernest (1833–90) French art critic

1 To satisfy taste while we satisfy the demands of utility: the problem, stated in these apparently simple terms is...the whole mystery of decorative art.

The Education of the Artist (1886)

Chesnut, Mary (originally Mary Boykin Miller; 1823–86) U.S. diarist

1 Does anybody wonder so many women die. Grief and constant anxiety kill nearly as many women as men die on the battlefield.

June 9, 1862. *A Diary from Dixie* (1905)

Chesnutt, Charles W. (1858–1932) U.S. writer and educator

1 Impossibilities are merely things of which we have not learned, or which we do not wish to happen.

The Marrow of Tradition (1901)

2 Our boasted civilization is but a thin veneer, which cracks and scales off at the first impact of primal passions.

The Marrow of Tradition (1901)

Chesterfield, Lord, 4th Earl of Chesterfield (Philip Dormer Stanhope; 1694–1773) British statesman and writer

Quotations about Chesterfield

1 This man I thought had been a Lord among wits; but, I find, he is only a wit among Lords.

1754

Samuel Johnson (1709–84) British lexicographer and writer. *Life of Samuel Johnson* (James Boswell; 1791)

2 They teach the morals of a whore, and the manners of a dancing master.

1754

Samuel Johnson (1709–84) British lexicographer and writer. Referring to Lord Chesterfield's *Letters*. *Life of Samuel Johnson* (James Boswell; 1791)

3 He was a man of much wit, middling sense, and some learning; but as absolutely void of virtue as any Jew, Turk or Heathen that ever lived.

John Wesley (1703–91) English religious leader. *Journal* (October 11, 1775)

Quotations by Chesterfield

4 Religion is by no means a proper subject of conversation in a mixed company.

1766? *Letters to His Godson* (1890)

5 Advice is seldom welcome; and those who want it the most always like it the least.

January 29, 1748. *Letters to his Son* (1774)

6 An injury is much sooner forgotten than an insult.

October 9, 1746. *Letters to his Son* (1774)

7 Be wiser than other people if you can, but do not tell them so.

November 19, 1745. *Letters to his Son* (1774)

8 Do as you would be done by is the surest method that I know of pleasing.

October 16, 1747. *Letters to his Son* (1774)

9 Due attention to the inside of books, and due contempt for the outside, is the proper relation between a man of sense and his books.

January 10, 1749. *Letters to his Son* (1774)

10 Every woman is infallibly to be gained by every sort of flattery, and every man by one sort or other.

March 16, 1752. *Letters to his Son* (1774)

11 Idleness is only the refuge of weak minds.

July 20, 1749. *Letters to his Son* (1774)

12 I recommend you to take care of the minutes: for hours will take care of themselves.

November 6, 1747. *Letters to his Son* (1774)

13 It must be owned, that the Graces do not seem to be natives of Great Britain; and I doubt, the best of us here have more of rough than polished diamond.

November 18, 1748. *Letters to his Son* (1774)

14 Take the tone of the company you are in.

October 9, 1747. *Letters to his Son* (1774)

15 The knowledge of the world is only to be acquired in the world, and not in a closet.

October 4, 1746. *Letters to His Son* (1774)

16 There is a Spanish proverb, which says very justly, Tell me whom you live with, and I will tell you who you are.

October 9, 1747. *Letters to His Son* (1774)

17 Whatever is worth doing at all is worth doing well.

March 10, 1746. *Letters to his Son* (1774)

18 The chapter of knowledge is very short, but the chapter of accidents is a very long one.

February 16, 1753. Letter to Solomon Dayrolles, *Miscellaneous Works* (M. Maty, ed.; 1778), vol. 2, no. 79

19 The pleasure is momentary, the position ridiculous and the expense damnable.

On sex. Attrib.

20 Make him a bishop, and you will silence him at once.
When asked what steps might be taken to control the evangelical preacher George Whitefield. Attrib.

Chesterton, G. K. (Gilbert Keith Chesterton; 1874–1936) British writer and poet

Quotations about Chesterton

1 Remote and ineffectual Don
That dared attack my Chesterton.
Hilaire Belloc (1870–1953) French-born British writer. "Lines to a Don," *Verses* (1910), quoted in *Complete Verse* (1991)

2 Chesterton, who was a very witty and a very wise man, said of someone who had been accused of imitating Virgil that a debt to Virgil is like a debt to nature. It is not a case of plagiarism.
Jorge Luis Borges (1899–1986) Argentinian writer and poet. "Poetry," *Borges on Writing* (N. T. Giovanni, D. Halpern, and F. MacShane, eds.; 1973), pt. 2

3 Chesterton is like a vile scum on a pond....All his slop—it is really modern Catholicism to a great extent, the *never* taking a hedge straight, the mumbo-jumbo of superstition dodging behind clumsy fun and paradox...he creates a milieu in which art is impossible.
Ezra Pound (1885–1972) U.S. poet, translator, and critic. Letter to John Quinn (August 21, 1917)

Quotations by Chesterton

4 The strangest whim has seized me...After all
I think I will not hang myself today.
"A Ballade of Suicide" (1915)

5 For the great Gaels of Ireland
Are then men that God made mad,
For all their wars are merry,
And all their songs are sad.
"Ballad of the White Horse" (1911)

6 I tell you naught for your comfort,
Yea, naught for your desire,
Save that the sky grows darker yet
and the sea rises higher.
Trevor Huddleston took the title of his book, *Naught for Your Comfort* (1956), from the opening line. "The Ballad of the White Horse" (1911)

7 Before the Roman came to Rye or out to Severn strode,
The rolling English drunkard made the rolling English road.
"The Rolling English Road" (1914)

8 For there is good news yet to hear and fine things to be seen,
Before we go to Paradise by way of Kensal Green.
"The Rolling English Road" (1914)

9 The modern world...has no notion except that of simplifying something by destroying nearly everything.
"All I Survey," *A Book of Essays* (1933)

10 A great deal of contemporary criticism reads to me like a man saying: "Of course I do not like green cheese: I am very fond of brown sherry."
"On Jonathan Swift," *All I Survey* (1933)

11 We do not get good laws to restrain bad people. We get good people to restrain bad laws.
All Things Considered (1908)

12 Mankind is not a tribe of animals to which we owe compassion. Mankind is a club to which we owe our subscription.
Daily News (April 10, 1906)

13 A man's opinion on tramcars matters; his opinion on Botticelli matters; his opinion on all things does not matter.
Heretics (1905)

14 There is no such thing on earth as an uninteresting subject; the only thing that can exist is an uninterested person.
Heretics (1905), ch. 1

15 The word "orthodoxy" not only no longer means being right; it practically means being wrong.
Heretics (1905), ch. 1

16 As enunciated today, "progress" is simply a comparative of which we have not settled the superlative.
Heretics (1905), ch. 2

17 Happiness is a mystery like religion, and should never be rationalized.
Heretics (1905), ch. 7

18 Carlyle said that men were mostly fools. Christianity, with a surer and more reverend realism, says that they are all fools.
Heretics (1905), ch. 12

19 Charity is the power of defending that which we know to be indefensible. Hope is the power of being cheerful in circumstances which we know to be desperate.
Heretics (1905), ch. 12

20 A good novel tells us the truth about its hero; but a bad novel tells us the truth about its author.
Heretics (1905), ch. 15

21 The artistic temperament is a disease that afflicts amateurs.
Heretics (1905), ch. 17

22 Democracy means government by the uneducated, while aristocracy means government by the badly educated.
New York Times (February 1, 1931)

23 There is nothing the matter with Americans except their ideals. The real American is all right; it is the ideal American who is all wrong.
New York Times (February 1, 1931)

24 Education is simply the soul of a society as it passes from one generation to another.
Observer, London (July 6, 1924), "Sayings of the Week"

25 The cosmos is about the smallest hole that a man can hide his head in.
Orthodoxy (1909), ch. 1

26 The madman is not the man who has lost his reason. The madman is the man who has lost everything except his reason.
Orthodoxy (1909), ch. 1

27 Mathematicians go mad, and cashiers; but creative artists very seldom.
Orthodoxy (1909), ch. 2

28 Reason is itself a matter of faith. It is an act of faith to assert that our thoughts have any relation to reality at all.
Orthodoxy (1909), ch. 3

29 All conservatism is based upon the idea that if you leave things alone you leave them as they are. But you do not. If you leave a thing alone you leave it to a torrent of change.
Orthodoxy (1909), ch. 7

30 Angels can fly because they take themselves lightly.
Orthodoxy (1909), ch. 7

31 Talk about the pews and steeples
And the cash that goes therewith!
But the souls of Christian peoples...
Chuck it, Smith!
"Antichrist or the Reunion of Christendom," *Poems* (1915)

32 One sees great things from the valley; only small things from the peak.
"The Hammer of God," *Storyteller* (1924)

33 All slang is metaphor, and all metaphor is poetry.
The Defendant (1901)

34 "My country, right or wrong" is a thing that no patriot would think of saying, except in a desperate case. It is like saying "My mother, drunk or sober."
The Defendant (1901)

35 The one stream of poetry which is continually flowing is slang.
The Defendant (1901)

36 There is a road from the eye to the heart that does not go through the intellect.
The Defendant (1901)

37 The rich are the scum of the earth in every country.
The Flying Inn (1914), ch. 15

38 To be clever enough to get all that money, one must be stupid enough to want it.
The Innocence of Father Brown (1911)

39 Is ditchwater dull? Naturalists with microscopes have told me that it teems with quiet fun.
"The Spice of Life," *The Listener* (1936)

40 Evil comes at leisure like the disease; good comes in a hurry like the doctor.
The Man who was Orthodox (1963)

41 You can only find truth with logic if you have already found truth without it.
The Man who was Orthodox (1963)

42 Thieves respect property; they merely wish the property to become their property that they may more perfectly respect it.
The Man who was Thursday (1908), ch. 4

43 Hardy became a sort of village atheist brooding and blaspheming over the village idiot.
Referring to the writer Thomas Hardy. *The Victorian Age in Literature* (1912)

44 He could not think up to the height of his own towering style.
The Victorian Age in Literature (1912)

45 Compromise used to mean that half a loaf was better than no bread. Among modern statesmen it really seems to mean that half a loaf is better than a whole loaf.
What's Wrong with the World (1910)

46 If a thing is worth doing, it is worth doing badly.
"Folly and Female Education," *What's Wrong with the World* (1910), pt. 4

47 The Christian ideal has not been tried and found wanting; it has been found difficult and left untried.
"The Unfinished Temple," *What's Wrong with the World* (1910), pt. 1

48 Just the other day in the Underground I enjoyed the pleasure of offering my seat to three ladies.
Suggesting that fatness had its consolations. Quoted in *Das Buch des Lachens* (W. Scholz; 1938)

49 Am in Market Harborough. Where ought I to be?
Telegram to his wife during a lecture tour. Later versions of the story give Birmingham as the town. *Portrait of Barrie* (C. Asquith; 1954)

50 I want to reassure you I am not this size, really—dear me no, I'm being amplified by the mike.
At a lecture in Pittsburgh. Attrib. *The Outline of Sanity: A Life of G. K. Chesterton* (A. S. Dale; 1983)

51 A puritan's a person who pours righteous indignation into the wrong things.
Attrib.

52 Journalism largely consists of saying "Lord Jones is dead" to people who never knew Lord Jones was alive.
Attrib.

53 New roads: new ruts.
Attrib.

54 Psychoanalysis is confession without absolution.
Attrib.

55 The only way to be sure of catching a train is to miss the one before it.
Attrib.

56 How beautiful it would be for someone who could not read.
Referring to the lights on Broadway. Attrib.

Chevalier, Albert (1861–1923) British entertainer

1 There ain't a lady livin' in the land
As I'd swop for my dear old Dutch!
"My Old Dutch" (1901)

Chevalier, Maurice (1888–1972) French singer and actor

1 I prefer old age to the alternative.
1962. Attrib.

2 Many a man has fallen in love with a girl in a light so dim he would not have chosen a suit by it.
1955. Attrib.

Chevalier, Michel (1806–79) French economist

1 In America...a merger means: Increase our salaries, or we go West.
Lettres sur l'Amérique du nord (1827), vol. 1, no. 13

2 In everything the Frenchman needs lightly to feel his neighbor's elbow, as in a line of battle.
Lettres sur l'Amérique du nord (1827), vol. 2, no. 23

Chia, Thye Poh (b.1941) Singaporean dissident

1 Nobody knows you. Nobody remembers you. You are not a man of steel. Even if you are a man of steel, we can break you and there's no one to come to your rescue. We have limitless manpower and unlimited time.
Referring to the threats of his internal security interrogators. *Guardian*, London (February 7, 1992)

Chicago, Judy (Judith Cohen Gerowitz; b.1939) U.S. sculptor and installation artist

1 One thing I find myself very uncomfortable with is the present role of art—its powerlessness. In the Middle Ages art functioned educatively, spiritually. I really believe that art has an incredible capacity to illuminate reality, bring a new perspective and bridge gaps.
Through the Flower (1975)

Child, Julia (originally Julia McWilliams; b.1912) U.S. chef, writer, and television personality

1 Learn how to cook! That's the way to save money. You don't save it buying...prepared foods; you save it buying fresh foods in season...and you prepare them from scratch at home.
Julia Child's Kitchen (1975)

2 Too many cooks spoil the broth, but it only takes one to burn it.
Referring to the Woman Suffrage movement. *Julia Child's Kitchen* (1975), Introduction

3 Sometimes...it takes me an entire day to write a recipe, to communicate it correctly. It's really like writing a little short story.
Quoted in "The Making of a Masterpiece," *McCall's* (Patricia Simon; October 1970)

Child, Lydia Maria (originally Lydia Maria Francis; 1802–80) U.S. abolitionist, suffrage campaigner, and writer

1 None speaks of the bravery, the might, or the intellect of Jesus; but the devil is always imagined as being of acute intellect, political cunning, and the fiercest courage.
December 8, 1842. *Letters from New York* (1852), no. 33

2 Not in vain is Ireland pouring itself all over the earth...The Irish, with their glowing hearts and reverent credulity, are needed in this cold age of intellect and skepticism.
December 8, 1842. *Letters from New York* (1852), vol. I, no. 33

3 I sometimes think the gods have united human beings by some mysterious principle, like the according notes of music. Or is it as Plato has supposed, that souls originally one have been divided, and each seeks the half it lost.
Philothea: A Romance (1836), ch. 1

4 But men never violate the laws of God without suffering the consequences, sooner or later.
"Toussaint L'Ouverture," *The Freedmen's Book* (1865)

5 England may as well dam up the waters from the Nile with bulrushes as to fetter the step of Freedom, more proud and firm in this youthful land.
The Rebels (1825), ch. 4

6 Genius hath electric power
Which earth can never tame.
Attrib.

Childers, Erskine (Erskine Robert Childers; 1870–1922) British-born Irish nationalist and writer

1 Take a step forward, lads. It will be easier that way.
November 24, 1922. Last words before being executed by firing squad. *The Riddle of Erskine Childers* (A. Boyle; 1977)

Childers, Lee U.S. soldier

1 We got more trouble for killing a water-buffalo than we did for killing people. That was something I could never adjust to.
Referring to the Vietnam War (1959–75). Quoted in *Everything We Had: An Oral History of the Vietnam War by Thirty-Three American Soldiers Who Fought It* (Al Santoli; 1981)

Children's Verse

1 Tom, he was a piper's son,
He learnt to play when he was young,
And all the tune that he could play
Was "Over the hills and far away."
Nursery rhyme. "The Piper's Son" (1785)

2 Tom, Tom, the piper's son,
Stole a pig and away he run;
The pig was eat
And Tom was beat,
And Tom went howling down the street.
Nursery rhyme. "The Piper's Son" (1785)

3 Where are you going to, my pretty maid?
I'm going a-milking, sir, she said.
Nursery rhyme. *Archaeologia Cornu-Britannica* (William Pryce; 1790)

4 What is your fortune, my pretty maid?
My face is my fortune, sir, she said.
Then I can't marry you, my pretty maid.
Nobody asked you, sir, she said.
Nursery rhyme. *Archaeologia Cornu-Britannica* (William Pryce; 1790)

5 There was an old woman
Lived under a hill,
And if she's not gone
She lives there still.
Nursery rhyme. *Academy of Complements* (1714)

6 Little Boy Blue,
Come blow your horn,
The sheep's in the meadow,
The cow's in the corn.
Nursery rhyme. *Famous Tommy Thumb's Little Story Book* (1760)

7 Simple Simon met a pieman,
Going to the fair;
Says Simple Simon to the pieman,
Let me taste your ware.

Says the pieman to Simple Simon,
Show me first your penny;
Says Simple Simon to the pieman,
Indeed I have not any.
Nursery rhyme. *Simple Simon* Chapbook Advertisement (1764)

8 Hot cross buns!
Hot cross buns!
One a penny, two a penny,
Hot cross buns!
Nursery rhyme. From the street vendor's cry. *Christmas Box* (1797)

9 My mother said that I never should
Play with the gypsies in the wood;
If I did, she would say,
Naughty girl to disobey.
Nursery rhyme. *Come Hither* (Walter de la Mare; 1922)

10 Three blind mice, see how they run!
They all run after the farmer's wife,
Who cut off their tails with a carving knife,
Did you ever see such a thing in your life,
As three blind mice?
Nursery rhyme. *Deuteromelia* (Thomas Ravenscroft; 1609)

11 The Queen of Hearts
She made some tarts,
All on a summer's day;
The Knave of Hearts
He stole the tarts,
And took them clean away.
Nursery rhyme. *European Magazine* (1782)

12 Come, let's to bed
Says Sleepy-head;
Tarry a while, says Slow;
Put on the pan;
Says Greedy Nan,
Let's sup before we go.
Nursery rhyme. *Gammer Gurton's Garland* (1810)

13 Goosey, goosey gander,
Whither shall I wander?
Upstairs and downstairs
And in my lady's chamber.
Nursery rhyme. *Gammer Gurton's Garland* (1784)

14 Humpty Dumpty sat on a wall,
Humpty Dumpty had a great fall.
All the king's horses,
And all the king's men,
Couldn't put Humpty together again.
Nursery rhyme. *Gammer Gurton's Garland* (1810)

15 I love sixpence, jolly little sixpence,
I love sixpence better than my life;
I spent a penny of it, I lent a penny of it,
And I took fourpence home to my wife.
Nursery rhyme. *Gammer Gurton's Garland* (1810)

16 I see the moon,
And the moon sees me;
God bless the moon,
And God bless me.
Nursery rhyme. *Gammer Gurton's Garland* (1810)

17 Little Bo-peep has lost her sheep,
And can't tell where to find them;
Leave them alone, and they'll come home,
Bringing their tails behind them.
Nursery rhyme. *Gammer Gurton's Garland* (1810)

18 Ride a cock-horse to Banbury Cross,
To see a fine lady upon a white horse;
Rings on her fingers and bells on her toes,
And she shall have music wherever she goes.
Nursery rhyme. *Gammer Gurton's Garland* (1810)

19 There was an old woman who lived in a shoe,
She had so many children she didn't know what to do;
She gave them some broth without any bread;
She whipped them all soundly and put them to bed.
Nursery rhyme. *Gammer Gurton's Garland* (1810)

20 Curly locks, Curly locks,
Wilt thou be mine?
Thou shalt not wash dishes
Nor yet feed the swine,
But sit on a cushion
And sew a fine seam,
And feed upon strawberries,
Sugar and cream.
Nursery rhyme. *Infant Institutes* (1810)

21 A frog he would a-wooing go,
Heigh ho! says Rowley,
A frog he would a-wooing go,
Whether his mother would let him or no.
With a rowley, powley, gammon and spinach,
Heigh ho! says Anthony Rowley.
Nursery rhyme. *Melismata* (Thomas Ravenscroft; 1611)

22 The twelfth day of Christmas,
My true love sent to me
Twelve lords a-leaping,
Eleven ladies dancing,
Ten pipers piping,
Nine drummers drumming,
Eight maids a-milking,
Seven swans a-swimming,
Six geese a-laying,
Five gold rings,
Four colly birds,
Three French hens,
Two turtle doves,
And a partridge in a pear tree.
Nursery rhyme. *Mirth without Mischief* (1780)

23 Hush a bye, baby, on the tree top,
When the wind blows the cradle will rock;
When the bough breaks the cradle will fall,
Down will come baby, cradle, and all.
1765? Lullaby. *Mother Goose; or, the Old Nursery Rhymes* (Kate Greenway; 1881)

24 Ding dong, bell,
Pussy's in the well.
Who put her in?
Little Johnny Green.
Who pulled her out?
Little Tommy Stout.

1765. Nursery rhyme. *Mother Goose; or, the Old Nursery Rhymes* (Kate Greenway; 1881)

25 Hey diddle diddle,
The cat and the fiddle,
The cow jumped over the moon;
The little dog laughed
To see such sport,
And the dish ran away with the spoon.

1765? Nursery rhyme. *Mother Goose; or, the Old Nursery Rhymes* (Kate Greenway; 1881)

26 Jack and Jill went up the hill
To fetch a pail of water;
Jack fell down and broke his crown,
And Jill came tumbling after.

1765. Nursery rhyme. *Mother Goose; or, the Old Nursery Rhymes* (Kate Greenway; 1881)

27 Two little dicky birds,
Sitting on a wall;
One named Peter,
The other named Paul,
Fly away, Peter!
Fly away, Paul!
Come back, Peter!
Come back, Paul!

1765? Nursery rhyme. *Mother Goose; or, the Old Nursery Rhymes* (Kate Greenway; 1881)

28 Ring-a-ring o'roses,
A pocket full of posies,
A-tishoo! A-tishoo!
We all fall down.

1665? Nursery rhyme. Based on the symptoms of the Great Plague, which often began with a rash and ended with a prolonged sneezing fit. *Mother Goose; or, the Old Nursery Rhymes* (Kate Greenway; 1881)

29 See-saw, Margery Daw,
Jacky shall have a new master;
He shall have but a penny a day,
Because he can't work any faster.

Nursery rhyme. *Mother Goose's Melody* (1765)

30 As I was going to St. Ives,
I met a man with seven wives.
Each wife had seven sacks
Each sack had seven cats,
Each cat had seven kits,
How many were going to St. Ives?

Nursery rhyme. *Mother Goose's Quarto* (1825)

31 Little Jack Horner
Sat in the corner,
Eating a Christmas pie;
He put in his thumb,
And pulled out a plum,
And said, What a good boy am I!

Nursery rhyme. *Namby Pamby* (Henry Carey; 1725)

32 I had a little nut tree,
Nothing would it bear
But a silver nutmeg
And a golden pear;
The King of Spain's daughter
Came to visit me,
And all for the sake
Of my little nut tree.

Nursery rhyme. *Newest Christmas Box* (1797)

33 What are little boys made of?
Frogs and snails
And puppy-dogs' tails,
That's what little boys are made of.
What are little girls made of?
Sugar and spice
And all that's nice,
That's what little girls are made of.

Nursery rhyme. *Nursery Rhymes* (J. O. Halliwell; 1844)

34 This is the farmer sowing his corn,
That kept the cock that crowed in the morn,
That waked the priest all shaven and shorn,
That married the man all tattered and torn,
That kissed the maiden all forlorn,
That milked the cow with the crumpled horn.

Nursery rhyme. "The House that Jack Built," *Nurse Truelove's New-Year-Gift* (1755)

35 Jack Sprat could eat no fat,
His wife could eat no lean,
And so between them both you see,
They licked the platter clean.

Nursery rhyme. *Paroemiologia Anglo-Latina* (John Clark; 1639)

36 Peter Piper picked a peck of pickled pepper;
A peck of pickled pepper Peter Piper picked;
If Peter Piper picked a peck of pickled pepper,
Where's the peck of pickled pepper Peter Piper picked?

Nursery rhyme. *Peter Piper's Practical Principles of Plain and Perfect Pronunciation* (1819)

37 Tinker,
Tailor,
Soldier,
Sailor,
Rich man,
Poor man,
Beggarman,
Thief.

Nursery rhyme. *Popular Rhymes and Nursery Tales* (J. O. Halliwell; 1849)

38 Bobby Shafto's gone to sea,
Silver buckles on his knee;
He'll come back and marry me,
Bonny Bobby Shafto!

Nursery rhyme. *Songs for the Nursery* (1805)

39 How many miles to Babylon?
Three score miles and ten.
Can I get there by candle-light?

Yes, and back again.
If your heels are nimble and light,
You may get there by candle-light.
Nursery rhyme. *Songs for the Nursery* (1805)

40 Little Miss Muffet
Sat on a tuffet,
Eating her curds and whey;
There came a big spider,
Who sat down beside her
And frightened Miss Muffet away.
Nursery rhyme. *Songs for the Nursery* (1805)

41 One, two,
Buckle my shoe;
Three, four,
Knock at the door.
Nursery rhyme. *Songs for the Nursery* (1805)

42 Pussy cat, pussy cat, where have you been?
I've been to London to look at the queen.
Pussy cat, pussy cat, what did you there?
I frightened a little mouse under her chair.
Nursery rhyme. *Songs for the Nursery* (1805)

43 Old Mother Hubbard
Went to the cupboard,
To fetch her poor dog a bone;
But when she got there
The cupboard was bare,
And so the poor dog had none.
Nursery rhyme. *The Comic Adventures of Old Mother Hubbard and Her Dog* (Sarah Catherine Martin; 1805)

44 This little piggy went to market,
This little piggy stayed at home,
This little piggy had roast beef,
This little piggy had none,
And this little piggy cried, Wee-wee-wee-wee-wee,
All the way home.
Nursery rhyme. *The Famous Tommy Thumb's Little Story Book* (1760)

45 Doctor Foster went to Gloucester
In a shower of rain:
He stepped in a puddle,
Right up to his middle,
And never went there again.
Nursery rhyme. *The Nursery Rhymes of England* (J. O. Halliwell; 1842)

46 Georgie Porgie, pudding and pie,
Kissed the girls and made them cry;
When the boys came out to play,
Georgie Porgie ran away.
Nursery rhyme. *The Nursery Rhymes of England* (J. O. Halliwell; 1842)

47 Solomon Grundy,
Born on Monday,
Christened on Tuesday,
Married on Wednesday,
Took ill on Thursday,
Worse on Friday,
Died on Saturday,
Buried on Sunday.
This is the end
Of Solomon Grundy.
Nursery rhyme. *The Nursery Rhymes of England* (J. O. Halliwell; 1842)

48 There was a crooked man, and he walked a crooked mile,
He found a crooked sixpence against a crooked stile:
He bought a crooked cat, which caught a crooked mouse,
And they all lived together in a little crooked house.
Nursery rhyme. *The Nursery Rhymes of England* (J. O. Halliwell; 1842)

49 All the birds of the air
Fell a-sighing and a-sobbing,
When they heard the bell toll
For poor Cock Robin.
Nursery rhyme. *Tommy Thumb's Pretty Song Book* (1744)

50 Baa, baa, black sheep,
Have you any wool?
Yes, sir, yes, sir,
Three bags full;
One for the master,
And one for the dame,
And one for the little boy
Who lives down the lane.
Nursery rhyme. *Tommy Thumb's Pretty Song Book* (1744)

51 Hickory, dickory, dock,
The mouse ran up the clock.
The clock struck one,
The mouse ran down,
Hickory, dickory, dock.
Nursery rhyme. *Tommy Thumb's Pretty Song Book* (1744)

52 Ladybird, ladybird,
Fly away home,
Your house is on fire
And your children all gone.
Nursery rhyme. *Tommy Thumb's Pretty Song Book* (1744)

53 Little Tommy Tucker,
Sings for his supper:
What shall we give him?
White bread and butter
How shall he cut it
Without a knife?
How will he be married
Without a wife?
Nursery rhyme. *Tommy Thumb's Pretty Song Book* (1744)

54 Mary, Mary, quite contrary,
How does your garden grow?
With silver bells and cockle shells,
And pretty maids all in a row.
Nursery rhyme. *Tommy Thumb's Pretty Song Book* (1744)

55 Sing a song of sixpence,
A pocket full of rye;
Four and twenty blackbirds,
Baked in a pie.
When the pie was opened,
The birds began to sing;
Was not that a dainty dish,
To set before the king?
Nursery rhyme. *Tommy Thumb's Pretty Song Book* (1744)

56 Who killed Cock Robin?
I, said the Sparrow,
With my bow and arrow,
I killed Cock Robin.
Who saw him die?
I, said the Fly,
With my little eye,
I saw him die.
Nursery rhyme. *Tommy Thumb's Pretty Song Book* (1744)

57 Oranges and lemons,
Say the bell of St Clement's.
You owe me five farthings,
Say the bells of St Martin's.
When will you pay me?
Say the bells of Old Bailey.
When I grow rich,
Say the bells of Shoreditch.
When will that be?
Say the bells of Stepney.
I'm sure I don't know,
Says the great bell at Bow.
Nursery rhyme. Based on church peals in the City of London. *Tommy Thumb's Pretty Song Book* (1744)

58 Monday's child is fair of face,
Tuesday's child is full of grace,
Wednesday's child is full of woe,
Thursday's child has far to go,
Friday's child is loving and giving,
Saturday's child works hard for his living,
And the child that is born on the Sabbath day
Is bonny and blithe, and good and gay.
Nursery rhyme. *Traditions of Devonshire* (A. E. Bray; 1838)

59 Boys and girls come out to play,
The moon doth shine as bright as day.
Nursery rhyme. *Useful Transactions in Philosophy* (William King; 1708–09)

60 Old King Cole
Was a merry old soul,
And a merry old soul was he;
He called for his pipe,
And he called for his bowl,
And he called for his fiddlers three.
Nursery rhyme. *Useful Transactions in Philosophy* (William King; 1708–09)

61 Wee Willie Winkie runs through the town
Upstairs and downstairs and in his nightgown,
Rapping at the window, crying through the lock,
Are the children all in bed? It's past eight o'clock.
Nursery rhyme. *Whistle-Binkie* (John D. Carrick, ed.; 1832)

62 Rain, rain, go away, come again another day.

63 Here we come gathering nuts in May
Nuts in May...On a cold and frosty morning.
Nursery rhyme.

64 Pat-a-cake, pat-a-cake, baker's man,
Bake me a cake as fast as you can;
Pat it and prick it, and mark it with B,
And there will be plenty for baby and me.
Nursery rhyme.

65 Polly put the kettle on,
Polly put the kettle on,
Polly put the kettle on,
We'll all have tea.
Sukey take it off again,
Sukey take it off again,
Sukey take it off again,
They've all gone away.
Nursery rhyme.

66 Rub-a-dub-dub,
Three men in a tub,
And who do you think they be?
The butcher, the baker,
The candlestick-maker,
And they all sailed out to sea.
1890. Nursery rhyme.

Childress, Alice (1920–94) U.S. playwright, novelist, and editor

1 I continue to create because writing is a labor of love and also an act of defiance, a way to light a candle in a gale wind.
"A Candle in a Gale Wind," *Black Women Writers 1950–1980: A Critical Evaluation* (Mari Evans, ed.; 1984), p.111

2 I think women need kindness more than love. When one human being is kind to another, it's a very deep matter.
Quoted in *Interviews with Contemporary Women Playwrights* (Rachael Koenig and Karen Betsko; 1987)

Chisholm, Shirley (b.1924) U.S. state legislator, educator, and U.S. representative

1 I don't measure America by its achievement, but by its potential.
Unbought and Unbossed (1970)

2 Of my two "handicaps," being female put many more obstacles in my path than being black.
Unbought and Unbossed (1970)

3 There is little place in the political scheme of things for an independent, creative personality, for a fighter. Anyone who takes that role must pay a price.
Unbought and Unbossed (1970)

4 When morality comes up against profit, it is seldom that profit loses.
Unbought and Unbossed (1970)

5 Service is the rent that you pay for room on this earth.
I Dream a World: Portraits of Black Women Who Changed America (Brian Lanker; 1989), p.106

Chitty, Susan (Susan Epstein Chitty; b.1929) British author

1 But goodness, how we lose our heads at the mention of a wedding! Especially the older women, who should know better. At the sound of the word all basic standards of elegance fly to the wind.
The Intelligent Woman's Guide to Good Taste (1958)

Choate, Rufus (1799–1859) U.S. lawyer and senator

1 History shows you prospects by starlight, or, at best, by the waning moon.
The Romance of New England History (1902)

Chomsky, Noam (Avram Noam Chomsky; b.1928) U.S. linguist and political activist

1 Loss of the Royal Family's symbolism together with Britain's other problems may have serious outcomes. Those are pre-fascist conditions.
Independent, London (October 18, 1994)

2 As soon as questions of will or decision or reason or choice of action arise, human science is at a loss.
Television interview. *Listener*, London (March 30, 1978)

3 My own suggestion is that a central part of what we call "learning" is actually better understood as the growth of cognitive structures...We may usefully think of the language faculty, the number faculty, and others, as "mental organs."
Rules and Representations (1980)

4 Colorless green ideas sleep furiously.
Used by Chomsky to demonstrate that an utterance can be grammatical without having meaning. *Syntactic Structures* (1957), ch. 2

5 The empiricist view is so deep-seated in our way of looking at the human mind that it almost has the character of a superstition.
Quoted in *Listener* London (May 30, 1968)

Chopin, Kate (originally Katherine O'Flaherty; 1850–1904) U.S. novelist, short-story writer, and poet

1 The voice of the sea speaks to the soul.
The Awakening (1899), ch. 6

2 The past was nothing to her; offered no lesson which she was willing to heed. The future was a mystery which she never attempted to penetrate. The present alone was significant.
The Awakening (1899), ch. 15

3 There are some people who leave impressions not so lasting as the imprint of an oar upon the water.
The Awakening (1899), ch. 34

Chow, Selina Hong Kong politician

1 The worst fears of the Hong Kong people have been confirmed by the events in Peking.
Referring to the massacre in Tiananmen Square. *Times*, London (June 4, 1989)

Christie, Agatha, Dame (originally Agatha Mary Clarissa Miller; 1890–1976) English novelist and playwright

1 I don't think necessity is the mother of invention—invention, in my opinion, arises directly from idleness, possibly also from laziness. To save oneself trouble.
An Autobiography (1977)

2 One doesn't recognize in one's life the really important moments—not until it's too late.
Endless Night (1967), bk. 2, ch. 14

3 Where large sums of money are concerned, it is advisable to trust nobody.
Endless Night (1967), bk. 2, ch. 15

4 Hercule Poirot tapped his forehead. "These little grey cells, It is 'up to them' as you say over here."
The Mysterious Affair at Styles (1920), ch. 10

5 If one sticks too rigidly to one's principles one would hardly see anybody.
Towards Zero (1944)

6 TREVES In my experience, pride is a word often on women's lips—but they display little sign of it where love affairs are concerned.
Towards Zero (1944)

7 Curious things, habits. People themselves never knew they had them.
Witness for the Prosecution (1924)

8 An archaeologist is the best husband any woman can have: the older she gets, the more interested he is in her.
March 8, 1954. Attrib.

Christie, Linford (b.1960) Jamaican-born British athlete

1 I'm proving that if you're on drugs then you're in trouble because those drugs aren't working. I'm clean and I'm beating you.
Independent, London (June 10, 1994)

2 I'm old, but I'm not cold.
Referring to his victory in the 100 m. at the Weltklasse Grand Prix, Zurich. *Independent*, London (August 18, 1994)

3 Whoever said losing wasn't important was a loser himself; it's rubbish. Who cares about the people who took part? The only people who are remembered are the winners.
Independent on Sunday, London (August 21, 1994)

Christina, Queen of Sweden (1626–89) Swedish monarch

1 We grow old more through indolence, than through age.
"Maxims (1660–1680)," *The Works of Christina of Sweden* (1753)

Christine de Pisan (1364?–1431?) Italian-born French poet

1 If it were customary to send little girls to school and to teach them the same subjects as are taught to boys, they would learn just as fully and would understand the subtleties of all arts and sciences. Indeed, maybe they would understand them better.
The City of Women (1405), Prologue

2 You ask whether woman possesses any natural intelligence. Yes. It can be developed to become wisdom, and then it is most beautiful.
The City of Women (1405), Prologue

3 Honour to Womankind. It needs must be
That God loves Woman, since He fashioned Thee.
Referring to Joan of Arc. *Of Six Medieval Women* (Alice Kemp-Welch; 1913)

4 He loved me, and 'twas right that he should, for I had come to him as a girl-bride...our two hearts were moved in all things, whether of joy or of sorrow, by a common wish, more united in love than the hearts of brother and sister.
Referring to her husband, Etienne du Castel. *Women in All Ages and All Countries* (Pierce Butler; 1907–08), vol. 5

Christy, David (1802–68?) U.S. writer

1 His majesty, King Cotton, is forced to continue the employment of his slaves; and, by their toil, is riding on, conquering and to conquer.
Cotton is King: or Slavery in the Light of Political Economy (1860)

Chrysoloras, Emanuel (1355?–1415) Byzantine-born Italian classical scholar

1 Why is it that when we see a live horse or a dog or a lion...we are not roused to admiration, are not delighted by its beauty and attach little value to its appearance...but when we see the picture of a horse or a bull or a plant or a bird or a man, or even of a fly, a worm, a mosquito or some other foul animal, we are greatly moved by the sight of such pictures and make much of them?
1411. Quoted in *Patrologiae cursus completus, Series latina* (J. P. Migne; 1844)

Chrysostom, Saint John (345?–407) Syrian divine

1 Fasting is a medicine.
Homilies on the Statutes, 3

Chuo Wên-chün (179?–117 B.C.) Chinese poet

1 Why should marriage bring only tears?
All I wanted was a man
With a single heart,
And we would stay together
As our hair turned white,
Not somebody always after wriggling fish
With his big bamboo rod.
Quoted in *Orchid Boat, Women Poets of China* (Kenneth Rexroth and Ling Chung; 1972)

Churchill, Caryl (b.1938) British playwright

1 Women, children and lunatics can't be Pope.
Top Girls (1982), Act 1, Scene 1

2 Most theatres are still controlled by men and people do tend to be able to see promise in people who are like themselves.
Quoted in *Interviews with Contemporary Women Playwrights* (Rachael Koenig and Karen Betsko; 1987)

Churchill, Charles (1731–64) British poet

1 The danger chiefly lies in acting well,
No crime's so great as daring to excel.
"An Epistle to William Hogarth" (1763), l. 51

2 By different methods different men excel;
But where is he who can do all things well?
"An Epistle to William Hogarth" (1763), ll. 573–574

3 Old-age, a second child, by Nature cursed
With more and greater evils than the first,
Weak, sickly, full of pains; in ev'ry breath
Railing at life, and yet afraid of death.
Gotham (1764), I, l. 215

4 Keep up appearances; there lies the test
The world will give thee credit for the rest.
Night (1761), l. 311

5 Be England what she will,
With all her faults, she is my country still.
The Farewell (1764), l. 27

6 England—a happy land we know,
Where follies naturally grow.
The Ghost (1763), bk. 1, l. 111

7 Who wit with jealous eye surveys,
And sickens at another's praise.
The Ghost (1763), bk. 2, ll. 663–664

8 A joke's a very serious thing.
The Ghost (1763), bk. 4, l. 386

9 Genius is of no country.
The Rosciad (1761), l. 207

10 So much they talk'd, so very little said.
The Rosciad (1761), l. 550

11 The two extremes appear like man and wife,
Coupled together for the sake of strife.
The Rosciad (1761), l. 1005

12 Where he falls short, 'tis Nature's fault alone;
There he succeeds, the merit's all his own.
Referring to the actor Thomas Sheridan. *The Rosciad* (1761), l. 1025

13 Fashion a word which knaves and fools may use,
Their knavery and folly to excuse.
The Rosciad (1761), ll. 455–456

Churchill, Jennie (Jennie Jerome; 1854–1921) U.S.-born British hostess and writer

1 You seem to have no real purpose in life and won't realize at the age of twenty-two that for a man life means work, and hard work if you mean to succeed.
Letter to Winston Churchill (February 26, 1897), quoted in *Jennie* (Ralph G. Martin), vol. II

2 There is no such thing as a moral dress...It's people who are moral or immoral.
Daily Chronicle, London (February 16, 1921)

3 ALMA I rather suspect her of being in love with him.
MARTIN Her own husband? Monstrous! What a selfish woman!
His Borrowed Plumes (1909)

4 We owe something to extravagance, for thrift and adventure seldom go hand in hand.
"Extravagance," *Pearson's* (1915)

Churchill, Randolph, Lord (Randolph Henry Spencer Churchill; 1849–95) British statesman

1 The duty of an opposition is to oppose.
1880? *Lord Randolph Churchill* (W. S. Churchill; 1906)

2 Ulster will fight; Ulster will be right.
May 7, 1886. Public letter. *Lord Randolph Churchill* (R. F. Foster; 1981)

3 I never could make out what those damned dots meant.
1880? Referring to decimal points. *Lord Randolph Churchill* (W. S. Churchill; 1906)

Churchill, Randolph (Randolph Frederick Edmund Spencer Churchill; 1911–68) British journalist

Quotations about Churchill

1 Dear Randolph, utterly unspoiled by failure.
Noel Coward (1899–1973) British playwright, actor, and songwriter. Attrib.

2 At social gatherings he was liable to engage in heated and noisy arguments which could ruin a dinner party, and made him the dread of hostesses on both sides of the Atlantic. The tendency was exacerbated by an always generous, and occasionally excessive alcoholic intake.
Malcolm Muggeridge (1903–90) British journalist. In Randolph Churchill's obituary notice. *Times*, London (June 7, 1968)

Quotations by Churchill

3 I should never be allowed out in private.
Apologizing to a hostess whose dinner party he had ruined. *Randolph: A Study of Churchill's Son* (B. Roberts; 1984)

Churchill, Sarah, Duchess of Marlborough (originally Sarah Jennings; 1660–1744) English courtier

1 For painters, poets and builders have very high flights, but they must be kept down.
Letter to the Duchess of Bedford (June 21, 1734)

2 The Duke returned from the wars today and did pleasure me in his top-boots.
1704? Attributed to her in various forms; a more ambitious version goes "...pleasured me three times in his top-boots." Attrib.

Churchill, Winston, Sir (Winston Leonard Spencer Churchill; 1874–1965) British prime minister and writer

Quotations about Churchill

1 It hasn't taken Winston long to get used to American ways. He hadn't been an American citizen for three minutes before attacking an ex-secretary of state!
1963
Dean Acheson (1893–1971) U.S. lawyer and statesman. At a ceremony to make Winston Churchill an honorary American citizen, Churchill obliquely attacked Acheson's reference to Britain's losing an empire. Quoted in *Randolph Churchill, the Young Pretender* (Kay Halle; 1971)

2 I thought he was a young man of promise; but it appears he was a young man of promises.
1899
Arthur Balfour (1848–1930) British prime minister. Said of Winston Churchill on his entry into politics. *Winston Churchill* (Randolph Churchill; 1966), vol. 1

3 Churchill on top of the wave has in him the stuff of which tyrants are made.
Max Aitken, Lord Beaverbrook (1879–1964) Canadian-born British newspaper owner and politician. *Politicians and the War* (1928–32)

4 He is a man suffering from petrified adolescence.
Aneurin Bevan (1897–1960) Welsh-born British politician. *Aneurin Bevan* (Vincent Brome; 1953), ch. 11

5 In private conversation he tries on speeches like a man trying on ties in his bedroom to see how he would look in them.
Lionel Curtis (1872–1955) British writer and administrator. Letter to Nancy Astor (1912)

6 Mr. Churchill is proud of Britain's stand alone after France had fallen and before America entered the war. Could he not find in his heart the generosity to acknowledge that there is a small nation that stood alone, not for one year or two, but for several hundred years against aggression?
Eamon de Valera (1882–1975) U.S.-born Irish statesman. Replying to Winston Churchill's criticism of Irish neutrality in World War II. Radio broadcast (May 16, 1945), quoted in *Phrases Make History Here* (Conor O'Clery; 1986)

7 He mobilized the English language and sent it into battle.
John Fitzgerald Kennedy (1917–63) U.S. president. Speech at a ceremony to confer honorary U.S. citizenship on Winston Churchill (April 9, 1963)

Quotations by Churchill

8 An iron curtain has descended across the Continent.
Address to Westminster College, Fulton, United States (March 5, 1946)

9 Men will forgive a man anything except bad prose.
Election speech, Manchester (1906)

10 Perhaps it is better to be irresponsible and right than to be responsible and wrong.
Party political broadcast in London (August 26, 1950)

11 Give us the tools, and we will finish the job.
Referring to Lend-Lease, which was being legislated in the United States. Radio broadcast (February 9, 1941)

12 We are waiting for the long-promised invasion. So are the fishes.
Radio broadcast to the French people (October 21, 1940)

13 They say you can rat, but you can't re-rat.
Referring to changing political parties more than once. Remark (January 26, 1941), quoted in *The Fringes of Power* (John Colville; 1985), vol. 1

14 Would a special relationship between the United States and the British Commonwealth be inconsistent with our over-riding loyalty to the World Organization?
Speech (March 5, 1946)

15 I have not become the King's First Minister in order to preside over the liquidation of the British Empire.
Speech at Mansion House, London (November 10, 1942)

16 This is not the end. It is not even the beginning of the end. But it is, perhaps, the end of the beginning.
Referring to the increasingly successful Allied offensive in North Africa against German-led troops. Speech at Mansion House, London (November 10, 1942)

17 The maxim of the British people is "Business as usual".
Speech at the Guildhall, London (November 9, 1914)

18 India is a geographical term. It is no more a united nation than the Equator.
Speech at the Royal Albert Hall (March 18, 1931)

19 Of all tyrannies in history the Bolshevik tyranny is the worst, the most destructive, the most degrading.
Speech, London (April 11, 1919)

20 The loss of India would mark and consummate the downfall of the British Empire. That great organism would pass at a stroke out of life into history. From such a catastrophe there could be no recovery.
Speech, London (December 12, 1930)

21 This is *your* victory.
Speech, London (May 8, 1945)

22 The nation had the lion's heart. I had the luck to give the roar.
Speech to both houses of the British Parliament on his 80th birthday (1954)

23 He is one of those orators of whom it was well said, "Before they get up they do not know what they are going to say; when they are speaking, they do not know what they are saying; and when they sit down, they do not know what they have said."
Referring to Lord Charles Beresford. Speech to the British Parliament (December 20, 1912)

24 The day must come when the nation's whole scale of living must be reduced. If that day comes, Parliament must lay the burden equally on all classes.
Speech to the British Parliament (August 7, 1925)

25 A hopeful disposition is not the sole qualification to be a prophet.
Speech to the British Parliament (April 10, 1927)

26 We have sustained a defeat without a war.
Referring to the Munich Pact. Speech to the British Parliament (October 5, 1938)

27 Victory at all costs, victory in spite of all terror, victory however long and hard the road may be; for without victory there is no survival.
Speech to the British Parliament (May 13, 1940)

28 I have nothing to offer but blood, toil, tears and sweat.
Said on becoming prime minister. Speech to the British Parliament (May 13, 1940)

29 We shall fight in France, we shall fight on the seas and oceans, we shall fight...in the air, we shall defend our island, whatever the cost may be, we shall fight on the beaches, we shall fight on the landing grounds, we shall fight in the fields and in the streets, we shall fight in the hills; we shall never surrender.
Speech to the British Parliament (June 4, 1940)

30 If we can stand up to Hitler, all Europe may be free and the life of the world may move forward into broad, sunlit uplands.
Speech to the British Parliament (June 18, 1940)

31 The battle of Britain is about to begin.
Speech to the British Parliament (July 1, 1940)

32 This was their finest hour.
Referring to the Dunkirk evacuation. Speech to the British Parliament (July 1, 1940)

33 Like the Mississippi, it just keeps rolling along. Let it roll. Let it roll on full flood, inexorable, irresistible, benignant, to broader lands and better days.
Referring to cooperation with the United States. Speech to the British Parliament (August 20, 1940)

34 Never in the field of human conflict was so much owed by so many to so few.
Referring to the pilots who took part in the Battle of Britain. Speech to the British Parliament (August 20, 1940)

35 The Bomb brought peace but man alone can keep that peace.
Speech to the British Parliament (August 16, 1945)

36 To jaw-jaw is better than to war-war.
Speech, Washington (June 26, 1954)

37 We must build a kind of United States of Europe.
Speech, Zurich (September 19, 1946)

38 We must have a better word than "prefabricated". Why not "ready-made"?
Closing the Ring (1951), appendix C

39 Well, the principle seems the same. The water still keeps falling over.
When asked whether the Niagara Falls looked the same as when he first saw them. *Closing the Ring* (1951), ch. 5

40 Nothing recalls the past so potently as a smell.
My Early Life (1930)

41 Headmasters have powers at their disposal with which Prime Ministers have never yet been invested.
My Early Life (1930), ch. 2

42 Which brings me to my conclusion upon Free Will and Predestination, namely let the reader mark it that they are identical.
My Early Life (1930), ch. 3

43 It is a good thing for an uneducated man to read books of quotations.
My Early Life (1930), ch. 9

44 Those who can win a war well can rarely make a good peace and those who could make a good peace would never have won the war.
My Early Life (1930), ch. 26

45 I am always ready to learn although I do not always like being taught.
Observer, London (November 9, 1952)

46 Everybody has a right to pronounce foreign names as he chooses.
Observer, London (August 5, 1951), "Sayings of the Week"

47 Without measureless and perpetual uncertainty the drama of human life would be destroyed.
The Gathering Storm (1948)

48 The redress of the grievances of the vanquished should precede the disarmament of the victors.
The Gathering Storm (1948), ch. 3

49 I felt as if I were walking with destiny, and that all my past life had been but a preparation for this hour and this trial.
Referring to the outbreak of World War II. *The Gathering Storm* (1948), ch. 38

50 When you have to kill a man it costs nothing to be polite.
Justifying the fact that the declaration of war against Japan was made in the usual diplomatic language. *The Grand Alliance* (1950)

51 Before Alamein we never had a victory. After Alamein we never had a defeat.
The Hinge of Fate (1951), ch. 33

52 No one can guarantee success in war, but only deserve it.
Their Finest Hour (1949)

53 When I look back on all these worries I remember the story of the old man who said on his deathbed that he had had a lot of trouble in his life, most of which had never happened.
Their Finest Hour (1949)

54 Wars are not won by evacuations.
Referring to Dunkirk. *Their Finest Hour* (1949)

55 In Franklin Roosevelt there died the greatest American friend we have ever known and the greatest champion of freedom who has ever brought help and comfort from the New World to the Old.
The Second World War (1948–53)

56 In war, resolution; in defeat, defiance; in victory, magnanimity; in peace, goodwill.
Epigram used by Sir Edward Marsh after World War II; used as "a moral of the work" in Churchill's book. *The Second World War* (1948–53)

57 I must point out that my rule of life prescribed as an absolutely sacred rite smoking cigars and also the drinking of alcohol before, after, and if need be during all meals and in the intervals between them.
Said during a lunch with the Arab leader Ibn Saud, when he heard that the king's religion forbade smoking and alcohol. *The Second World War* (1948–53)

58 In wartime, truth is so precious that she should always be attended by a bodyguard of lies.
Said to Stalin. *The Second World War* (1948–53)

59 The Germans turned upon Russia the most grisly of all weapons. They transported Lenin in a sealed truck like a plague bacillus from Switzerland to Russia.
The World Crisis (1923–29)

60 Peace with Germany and Japan on our terms will not bring much rest....As I observed last time, when the war of the giants is over the wars of the pygmies will begin.
Triumph and Tragedy (1954), ch. 25

61 Dictators ride to and fro upon tigers which they dare not dismount. And the tigers are getting hungry.
While England Slept (1938)

62 In defeat unbeatable; in victory unbearable.
Referring to Sir Bernard Law Montgomery. Attrib. *Ambrosia and Small Beer* (Edward Marsh; 1964), ch. 5

63 I'm so bored with it all.
Said to be his last words. Attrib. *Clementine* (M. Soames; 1965)

64 Don't talk to me about naval tradition. It's nothing but rum, sodomy, and the lash.
Former Naval Person: Winston Churchill and the Royal Navy (Sir Peter Gretton; 1968), ch. 1

65 Call that a maiden speech? I call it a brazen hussy of a speech.
Said to A. P. Herbert. *Immortal Jester* (Leslie Frewin; 1973)

66 If it is a blessing, it is certainly very well disguised.
1945. Said to his wife after his defeat in the general election, when she said that it was a blessing in disguise. *Memoirs of Richard Nixon* (R. Nixon; 1978)

67 If you were my wife, I'd drink it.
Replying to Lady Astor who had said, "If you were my husband, I'd put poison in your coffee." Attrib. *Nancy Astor and Her Friends* (E. Langhorne; 1974)

68 This is the sort of English up with which I will not put.
Said to be a comment written in the margin of a report by a civil servant, referring to the person's use of a preposition at the end of a sentence. An alternative version of the remark substitutes "bloody nonsense" for "English." Attrib. *Plain Words* (E. Gowers; 1948), ch. 9

69 You may take the most gallant sailor, the most intrepid airman, or the most audacious soldier, put them at a table together—what do you get? *The sum of their fears*.
November 16, 1943. Talking about the Chiefs of Staffs system. *The Blast of War* (H. Macmillan; 1967), ch. 16

70 Labour is not fit to govern.
1920. Election speech.

71 I cannot forecast to you the action of Russia. It is a riddle wrapped in a mystery inside an enigma.
October 1, 1939. Radio broadcast.

72 There is no finer investment for any community than putting milk into babies.
March 21, 1943. Radio broadcast.

73 You do your worst, and we will do our best.
July 14, 1941. Speech addressed to Hitler.

74 I am ready to meet my Maker. Whether my Maker is ready for the ordeal of meeting me is another matter.
November 30, 1949. Speech on his 75th birthday.

75 They are the only people who like to be told how bad things are—who like to be told the worst.
1921. Speech referring to the British.

76 An appeaser is one who feeds a crocodile—hoping that it will eat him last.
1954. Attrib.

77 Do not criticize your government when out of the country. Never cease to do so when at home.
Attrib.

78 Golf is a game whose aim is to hit a very small ball into an even smaller hole, with weapons singularly ill-designed for the purpose.
Attrib.

79 I know of no case where a man added to his dignity by standing on it.
Attrib.

80 Nothing would induce me to vote for giving women the franchise. I am not going to be henpecked into a question of such importance.
Attrib.

81 The art of making deep sounds from the stomach sound like important messages from the brain.
Referring to the art of speechmaking. Attrib.

82 And you, madam, are ugly. But I shall be sober in the morning.
Replying to the Member of Parliament Bessie Braddock, who told him he was drunk. Attrib.

83 Haven't you learned yet that I put something more than whisky into my speeches.
Said to his son Randolph. Attrib.

84 Madam, all babies look like me.
When a woman said her baby looked like him. Attrib.

85 Dead birds don't fall out of their nests.
When someone told him that his trouser fly-buttons were undone. Attrib.

Ciano, Galeazzo, Conte di Cortellazzo (1903–44) Italian politician

1 As always, victory finds a hundred fathers, but defeat is an orphan.
Speech (September 9, 1942)

Ciardi, John (1916–86) U.S. poet and critic

1 Modern art is what happens when painters stop looking at girls and persuade themselves that they have a better idea.
Attrib.

Cibber, Colley (1671–1757) British actor and playwright

1 One had as good be out of the world, as out of the fashion.
Love's Last Shift (1696), Act 2

2 We shall find no fiend in hell can match the fury of a disappointed woman, scorned,—slighted, dismissed without a parting pang.
Love's Last Shift (1696), Act 4

3 Oh! how many torments lie in the small circle of a wedding-ring!
The Double Gallant (1707), Act 1, Scene 2

4 Old houses mended,
Cost little less than new before they 're ended.
The Double Gallant (1707), Prologue

5 Losers must have leave to speak.
The Rival Fools (1709), Act 1

6 Stolen sweets are best.
The Rival Fools (1709), Act 1

7 Possession is eleven points in the law.
Woman's Wit (1697), Act 1

8 Words are but empty thanks.
Woman's Wit (1697), Act 5

Cicero (Marcus Tullius Cicero; 106–43 B.C.) Roman orator and statesman

1 As a matter of fact, if there is any art which really pleases me it is painting.
Ad Familiares VII (61 B.C.)

2 There is nothing so absurd but some philosopher has said it.
De Divinatione (44? B.C.), bk. 2, sect. 58

3 If it is fated for you to recover from this illness, you will recover whether or not you call a doctor; similarly if it is fated for you not to recover from this illness, you will not recover whether or not you call a doctor...there is no point in calling a doctor.
An example of the "Idle Argument." *De Fato* (D. Charles, tr.; 43? B.C.), ll. 12, 28–29

4 Law is founded not on theory but upon nature.
De Legibus (1st century B.C.), bk. 1, ch. 10, sect. 28

5 A mental stain can neither be blotted out by the passage of time nor washed away by any waters.
De Legibus (52 B.C.), bk. 2

6 The good of the people is the chief law.
De Legibus (45 B.C.), bk. 3, ch. 3, sect. 8

7 Extreme justice is extreme injustice.
De Officiis (1st century B.C.)

8 The greatest good.
De Officiis (November 44 B.C.), bk. 1, ch. 5

9 A careful physician..., before he attempts to administer a remedy to his patient, must investigate not only the malady of the man he wishes to cure, but also his habits when in health, and his physical constitution.
De Oratore (55 B.C.)

10 If the truth were self-evident, eloquence would be unnecessary.
De Oratore (55 B.C.)

11 While the sick man has life, there is hope.
Epistolarum ad Atticum (68–43 B.C.), bk. 9

12 What times! What customs!
In Catilinam (63 B.C.), speech 1, ch. 1

13 Exercise and temperance can preserve something of our early strength even in old age.
On Old Age (45–44 B.C.), bk. 10

14 When you have no basis for an argument, abuse the plaintiff.
Pro Flacco (1st century B.C.), sect. 10

15 To whose profit?
Quoting L. Cassius Longinus Ravilla. *Pro Milone* (51 B.C.), ch. 12, sect. 32

16 Diseases of the soul are more dangerous and more numerous than those of the body.
Tusculanae Disputationes (45–44 B.C.), bk. 3

17 In a disordered mind, as in a disordered body, soundness of health is impossible.
Tusculanae Disputationes (45–44 B.C.), bk. 3

18 No sober man dances, unless he happens to be mad.
Quoted in *World History of Dance* (Curt Sachs; 1937)

19 Physicians, when the cause of disease is discovered, consider that the cure is discovered.
Attrib.

Cisneros, Sandra (b.1954) U.S. poet and writer

1 Mama can no longer climb up and down the stairs anymore in her condition since the baby they will name Reynaldo is asleep inside her Mama's belly, the child her Mama hopes will anchor her Papa home nights and mend the marriage.
"Divine Providence," *New Chicana/Chicano Writing* (Charles M. Tatum, ed.; 1992)

2 What they don't understand about birthdays and what they never tell you is that when you're eleven, you're also ten, and nine, and eight, and seven, and six, and five, and four, and three, and two, and one.
"Eleven," *Women Hollering Creek* (1991)

Cixi (also known as Tz'u-hsi; 1835–1908) Chinese monarch

1 Ever since the foundation of the dynasty, foreigners coming to China have been kindly treated...At first they were amenable to Chinese control, but for the past thirty years they...trample on Chinese people and...absorb the wealth of the Empire.
The Boxer Rising was a nationalistic insurrection aimed at purging China of foreigners and foreign influence. Declaration at the start of the Boxer Rising (June 21, 1900)

Clapton, Eric (Eric Patrick Clapton; b.1945) British rock guitarist, singer, and songwriter

1 You were at school and you were pimply and no one wanted to know you. You get into a group and you've got thousands of chicks there.
Quoted in *Rock 'n' Roll Babylon* (Gary Herman; 1994)

Clare, John (1793–1864) British poet

1 They took me from my wife, and to save trouble
I wed again, and made the error double.
"Child Harold" (1841), l. 152

2 I am! Yet what I am who cares, or knows?
My friends forsake me like a memory lost.
I am the self-consumer of my woes;
rise and vanish, an oblivious host,
Shadows of life, whose very soul is lost.
Written in Northampton County Asylum, where he spent the last 22 years of his life. "I am" (1848)

Clarendon, Edward Hyde, Lord (1609–74) English statesman and historian

1 He will be looked upon by posterity as a brave, bad man.
Referring to Oliver Cromwell. Remark (1704), quoted in *History of the Rebellion and Civil Wars in England* (W. D. Macray, ed.; 1888)

2 He had a head to contrive, a tongue to persuade, and a hand to execute any mischief.
Referring to the Parliamentarian John Hampden. Remark (1703), quoted in *History of the Rebellion and Civil Wars in England* (W. D. Macray, ed.; 1888)

Clark, Abraham (1726–94) U.S. politician

1 We set out to oppose Tyranny in all its Strides, and I hope we shall persevere.
Letter to John Hart (February 8, 1777)

Clark, Joe (Charles Joseph Clark; b.1939) Canadian prime minister

1 Political freedom is rare enough in the world, but the kind of social and cultural freedom which is the hallmark of Canada is even less common.
Speech to the Canadian Parliament (February 18, 1977)

Clark, John Bates (1847–1938) U.S. economist

1 A nearly ideal situation would be that in which, in every department or industry, there should be one great corporation working without friction and with enormous economy, and compelled to give to the public the full benefit of that economy.
The Control of Trusts (co-written with John Maurice Clark; 1912)

2 Free competition tends to give to labor what labor creates, to capitalists what capital creates, and to entrepreneurs what the coordinating function creates.
The Distribution of Wealth (1899)

Clark, Kenneth (1850–1921) U.S. politician

1 I hope to see the day when the American flag will gloat over every square foot of the British North American possessions clear to the North Pole.
Speech to the House of Representatives (June 1911)

Clark, Kenneth, Baron (Kenneth MacKenzie Clark; 1903–83) British art historian

1 All great civilisations, in their early stages, are based on success in war.
Civilisation (1969)

2 French Classical architecture...was the work not of craftsmen but of wonderfully gifted civil servants.
Civilisation (1969)

3 Machines from the Maxim gun to the computer, are for the most part means by which a minority can keep free men in subjection.
Civilisation (1969)

4 Marriage without love means love without marriage.
Civilisation (1969)

5 One of the reasons why medieval and Renaissance architecture is so much better than our own is that the architects were artists. Bernini, one of the great artists of seventeenth-century Rome, was a sculptor.
Civilisation (1969)

6 You have no idea what portrait painters suffer from the vanity of their sitters.
Observer, London (March 29, 1959)

Clark, Mark (Mark Wayne; 1896–1984) U.S. general

1 I was the first American commander to put his signature to a paper ending a war when we did not win it.
1953. Upon his retirement as supreme commander, UN Forces, Korea. Quoted in *Speaking Freely* (Stuart Berg Flexner and Anne H. Soukhanov; 1997)

Clark, Septima Poinsette (1898–1987) U.S. educator

1 I have great belief in the fact that whenever there is chaos, it creates wonderful thinking. I consider chaos a gift.
Ready From Within (1986)

Clarke, Arthur C. (Arthur Charles Clarke; b.1917) British writer and scientist

1 If we relate the life of a star to the life of a man...the Sun is but a week old...Life has existed on this planet for two or three days of the week that has passed; the whole of human history lies within the last second, and there are eighty years to come.
By Space Possessed (1993)

2 When the Sun shrinks to a dull red dwarf, it will not be dying. It will just be starting to live and *everything that has gone*

before will be merely a fleeting prelude to its real history.
By Space Possessed (1993)

3 When a distinguished but elderly scientist states that something is possible, he is almost certainly right. When he states that something is impossible, he is very probably wrong.
Profiles of the Future (1962)

4 Any sufficiently advanced technology is indistinguishable from magic.
The Lost Worlds of 2001 (1972)

5 The only way of finding the limits of the possible is by going beyond them into the impossible.
The Lost Worlds of 2001 (1972)

6 There is no reason to assume that the universe has the slightest interest in intelligence—or even in life. Both may be random accidental by-products of its operations like the beautiful patterns on a butterfly's wings. The insect would fly just as well without them.
The Lost Worlds of 2001 (1972)

Clarke, Austin (1896–1974) Irish writer

1 Burn Ovid with the rest. Lovers will find
A hedge-school for themselves and learn by heart
All that the clergy banish from the mind.
1938. "Penal Law," *Collected Poems* (1974), ll. 1–3

2 And O she was the Sunday
In every week.
1928. "The Planter's Daughter," *Collected Poems* (1974), ll. 16–17

Clarke, Gerald (b.1937) U.S. journalist

1 During World War II a man of middle age entertained a Marine..."Where would you like to go?" he asked. The Marine...had heard of only one fancy and expensive place in New York, and he said: "Let's have breakfast at Tiffany's."
Referring to Truman Capote's *Breakfast at Tiffany's* (1958). *Capote: A Biography* (1988)

Clarke, Gillian (b.1937) Welsh poet

1 This spring a lamb sips caesium on a Welsh hill.
A child, lifting her face to drink the rain,
Takes into her blood the poisoned arrow.
Written about the aftermath of the Chernobyl disaster. "Neighbours," *Letting in the Rumour* (1989)

Clarke, John (*fl.* 17th century) English scholar

1 Home is home, though it be never so homely.
Paraemiologia Anglo-Latina (1639)

Clarke, John Henrik (1915–98) U.S. historian and educator

1 You cannot subjugate a man and recognize his humanity, his history, and his personality; so systematically, you must take this away from him. You begin by telling lies about this man's role in history.
Address to Jewish Currents conference, New York (February 15, 1969)

2 The final interpretation of African history is the responsibility of scholars of African descent.
Address to the Regional Conference on Afro-American History, University of Detroit (May 11–13, 1967), "A New Approach to African History"

3 History is a clock that people use to tell their political and cultural time of day. It is also a compass that people use to find themselves on the map of human geography.
African People in World History (1993)

4 Powerful people never teach powerless people how to take their power away from them.
Essence (September 1989)

5 It is too often forgotten that when the Europeans gained enough maritime skill and gunpowder to conquer most of the world, they not only colonized the bulk of the world's people but they colonized the interpretation of history itself...The roots of modern racism can be traced to this conquest and colonization.
"Race: An Evolving Issue in Western Thought," *Journal of Human Relations* (1970)

Clarke, Kenneth (Kenneth Harry Clarke; b.1940) British politician

1 The public are usually more sensible than politicians or the press.
Speech at the Mansion House, London (June 15, 1994)

2 I have never read it. You should not waste your time.
Referring to the Maastricht Treaty (1995). *Independent*, London (March 17, 1995)

3 I have acquired a deep and abiding respect for all those engaged in the difficult business of commerce.
Observer, London (June 20, 1993), "Sayings of the Week"

Claudel, Paul (Paul Louis Charles Marie Claudel; 1868–1955) French writer and diplomat

1 The poem is not made up of these letters that I plant like nails, but of the white that remains on the paper.
"Les Muses," *Cinq Grandes Odes* (1910)

2 O God...I am free, deliver me from freedom!
"L'esprit et l'eau," *Cinq Grandes Odes* (1910)

3 When man tries to imagine Paradise on earth, the immediate result is a very respectable Hell.
Conversations dans le Loir-et-Cher (1929)

4 You explain nothing, O poet, but thanks to you all things become explicable.
La Ville (1890), Act 1

5 It is not that there isn't time, it is that we lose it.
Partage de midi (1906), Act 1

Claudius Caecus, Appius (*fl.* 300 B.C.) Roman statesman

1 Each man the architect of his own fate.
De Civitate (300? B.C.), bk. 1 (Sallust)

Clausen, A. W. (Aiden Winship Clausen; b.1923) U.S. banker

1 A cow is not an animal that produces milk and cheese. Rather, it's something to be eviscerated, hacked up and sold piecemeal. In short, you have to kill the cow.
Referring to the economics of the Chicago stockyards. Speech (May 19, 1988)

Clausewitz, Karl Marie von (Karl Philip Gottlieb von Clausewitz; 1780–1831) Prussian general

1 It is politics which begets war. Politics represents the intelligence, war merely its instrument, not the other way around. The only possible course in war is to subordinate the military viewpoint to the political.
On War (1833)

2 War belongs, not to the arts and sciences, but to the province of social life.
On War (1833)

3 War is nothing but a continuation of politics with the admixture of other means.
Often misquoted as "War is nothing but a continuation of politics by other means." *On War* (1833)

Clay, Henry ("The Great Pacificator"; 1777–1852) U.S. politician

1 I had rather be right than be President.
Speech in the Senate (1850)

2 It was in the provinces that were laid the seeds of the ambitious projects that overturned the liberties of Rome.
Referring to popular approval of President Andrew Jackson's foreign policy outside Washington, D.C. Speech to the Senate (May 1818)

Cleaver, Eldridge (b.1935) U.S. writer and civil rights activist

1 A general law of causes may be that their toxic content gains potency in proportion to their shrinkage in volume. Outworn organizations are not half as malignant as worn-out causes.
Soul on Fire (1978)

2 Black history began with Malcolm X.
Soul on Ice (1968)

3 In the culture that secretly subscribes to the piratical ethic of "every man for himself"...the logical culmination of this ethic, on a person-to-person level, is that the weak are seen as the natural and just prey of the strong.
Soul on Ice (1968)

4 Too much agreement kills a chat.
"A Day in Folsom Prison," *Soul on Ice* (1968)

5 All the gods are dead except the god of war.
"Four Vignettes," *Soul on Ice* (1968)

6 The price of hating other human beings is loving oneself less.
"On Becoming," *Soul on Ice* (1968)

7 Americans think of themselves collectively as a huge rescue squad on a twenty-four-hour call to any spot on the globe where dispute and conflict may erupt.
"Rallying Round the Flag," *Soul on Ice* (1968)

8 We don't need a War on Poverty. What we need is a war on the rich.
1967. *Eldridge Cleaver: Post-Prison Writings and Speeches* (Robert Scheer, ed.; 1968)

Cleese, John (John Marwood Cleese; b.1939) British comic actor and writer

1 Pretentious? *Moi?*
As Basil Fawlty. *Fawlty Towers*, BBC Television (co-written with Connie Booth; 1979)

2 Don't mention the war.
Instruction of hotel manager Basil Fawlty (played by John Cleese) to his staff before the arrival of German guests. *Fawlty Towers*, BBC Television (co-written with Connie Booth; 1975)

Clemenceau, Georges ("The Tiger"; 1841–1929) French prime minister and journalist

Quotations about Clemenceau

1 Foch, Clemenceau, de Gaulle—it is the same thing; and it is important the French people have no doubts on that score.
Charles De Gaulle (1890–1970) French president. Referring to Marshal Ferdinand Foch and Georges Clemenceau, France's military and political leaders at the end of World War I. Remark to his political staff (June 18, 1946)

Quotations by Clemenceau

2 The good Lord needed only Ten Commandments.
Said upon reading Woodrow Wilson's "Fourteen Points," which were aimed at establishing a just and lasting peace after World War I. Remark (1918)

3 I shall fight before Paris, I shall fight in Paris, I shall fight behind Paris.
June, 1918. Speech (June 1918)

4 It is far easier to make war than to make peace.
Speech at Verdun (July 20, 1919), quoted in *Discours de Paix* (1938)

5 My home policy? I wage war. My foreign policy? I wage war. Always, everywhere, I wage war...And I shall continue to wage war until the last quarter of an hour.
Speech to the French Chamber of Deputies (March 8, 1918)

6 It is thanks to the armies of the Republic that France, yesterday the soldier of God and today the soldier of Humanity, will be forever the soldier of the Ideal.
Referring to the signing of the armistice ending World War I. Speech to the French Chamber of Deputies (November 11, 1918)

7 We have won the war: now we have to win the peace, and it may be more difficult.
Clemenceau (D. R. Watson; 1974)

8 War is too important to be left to the generals.
Clemenceau and the Third Republic (Hampden Jackson; 1946)

9 The only time in his life he ever put up a fight was when we asked him for his resignation.
Referring to Marshal Joffre. *Here I Lie* (A.M. Thomson; 1937)

10 America is the only nation in history which miraculously has gone directly from barbarism to degeneration without the usual interval of civilization.
Attrib. *Saturday Review of Literature* New York (December 1, 1945)

Clement XIII, Pope (1693–1769) Italian pope

1 Let them be as they are or not be at all.
January 27, 1762. Reply to request for changes in the constitutions of the Society of Jesus. *Clément XIV et les Jésuites* (J. A. M. Crétineau-Joly; 1847)

Cleobulus (*fl.* 6th century B.C.) Greek sage

1 Safeguard the health both of body and soul.
Attrib.

Cleveland, Grover (Stephen Grover Cleveland; 1837–1908) U.S. president

1 And let us not trust to human effort alone, but humbly acknowledging the power and goodness of Almighty God, who presides over the destiny of nations, and who at all times has been revealed in our country's history, let us invoke His aid and His blessings upon our leaders.
Inaugural address (March 4, 1885)

2 Party honesty is party expediency.
New York Commercial Advertiser (September 19, 1889)

Cliff, Michelle (b.1946) U.S. novelist, essayist, and lecturer

1 Sin should not be effortless.
Free Enterprise (1993)

2 Tourism is whorism.
No Telephone to Heaven (1987)

Clifton, Lucille (b.1936) U.S. novelist and poet

1 She is a poet
she don't have no sense.
Admonitions (1969)

2 I got a long memory and I came from a line of black and goin on women.
"For De Lawd," *Good Times* (1969)

Clinton, Bill (William Jefferson Clinton; b.1946) U.S. president

Quotations about Clinton

1 My dog Millie knows more about foreign policy than these two bozos.
George Bush (b.1924) U.S. president. Referring to Bill Clinton and Al Gore, his Democratic opponents in the 1992 presidential election. Remark (October 1992)

2 We're not running against the comeback kids, we're running against the Karaoke Kids—they'd sing any tune to get elected.
George Bush (b.1924) U.S. president. Referring to Bill Clinton and Al Gore, his Democratic opponents in the 1992 presidential election. Bill Clinton called himself "the Comeback Kid." Speech (1992)

3 There is another thing that connects Bill Clinton, Boris Yeltsin and François Mitterrand; we all like to eat, I perhaps most of all.
Helmut Kohl (b.1930) German statesman. *Observer*, London (June 12, 1994), "Sayings of the Week"

4 We have never said to the press that Clinton is a philandering, pot-smoking draft dodger.
Mary Matalin (b.1953?) U.S. political adviser. Remark (1992)

Quotations by Clinton

5 The light may be fading on the twentieth century, but the sun is still rising on America.
December 31, 1999. Address to the nation

6 If you'll be my voice today, I'll be yours for the next four years.
Election day, while suffering from laryngitis. Speech (November 3, 1992)

7 We must not let the iron curtain be replaced with a veil of indifference.
Speech to NATO (January 10, 1994)

8 You do not need to glamorize addiction to sell clothes.
Criticizing the popularity, during the 1990s, of "heroin chic," a style in which fashion models looked emaciated and unwell. *Guardian*, London (May 23, 1997)

9 We know there have always been gays in the military. The issue is whether they can be in the military without lying about it.
Independent, London (November 17, 1992)

10 Sure enough at Oxford, I was another Yank half a step behind.
Bill Clinton was a Rhodes Scholar at Oxford. *Observer*, London (June 12, 1994), "Sayings of the Week"

11 There have been no scandals in this administration.
PBS's Washington Week in Review (February 25, 1994)

12 America can no longer afford to get the Nobel Prizes while our competitors get the profits.
Putting People First: How We Can All Change America (co-written with Al Gore; 1992)

13 America needs a new approach to economics that will give new hope to our people and breathe new life into the American Dream.
Putting People First: How We Can All Change America (co-written with Al Gore; 1992)

14 In the emerging global economy, everything is mobile: capital, factories, even entire industries. The only resource that's really rooted in a nation and the ultimate source of all its wealth is its people.
Putting People First: How We Can All Change America (co-written with Al Gore; 1992)

15 The only preparation for prospering in the global economy is investing in ourselves.
Putting People First: How We Can All Change America (co-written with Al Gore; 1992)

16 To build a twenty-first-century economy, America must revive a nineteenth-century habit—investing in the common, national economic resources that enable every person and every firm to create wealth and value.
Putting People First: How We Can All Change America (co-written with Al Gore; 1992)

17 We should not reward China with improved trade status when it has...failed to make sufficient progress on human rights since the Tiananmen Square massacre.
The Tiananmen Square Protest took place in 1989. *Putting People First: How We Can All Change America* (co-written with Al Gore; 1992)

18 Over time, the more we bring China into the world, the more the world will bring freedom to China.
Time (1998)

19 Throughout the Middle East, there is a great yearning for the quiet miracle of a normal life.
Referring to the Israeli-PLO peace accord. *Times*, London (September 14, 1993)

20 When I was in England, I experimented with marijuana a time or two and I didn't like it. I didn't inhale.
Remark made during the U.S. presidential election campaign replying to Republican accusations that he had taken drugs and had played a leading role in the movement against the Vietnam War. *Washington Post* (March 30, 1992)

21 There is nothing wrong with America that cannot be cured by what is right with America.
Attrib.

Clinton, Hillary (Hillary Rodham Clinton; b.1947) U.S. lawyer and first lady

1 In every era, society must strike the right balance between the freedom businesses need to compete for a market share and to make profits and the preservation of family and community values.
Speech at Sydney Opera House (November 21, 1996)

2 Issues affecting women are not soft or marginal, but are central to decisions involving all nations.
It Takes a Village (1996)

3 We desperately need...a national and global economy in which people act not only as consumers but as citizens, in which workers reassert their responsibility for themselves and the success of their companies.
It Takes a Village (1996)

4 I believe that I have created a lot of cognitive dissonance in the minds of people who are comfortable with stereotypes.
Observer, London (May 15, 1994), "Sayings of the Week"

Clive, Robert, Baron Clive of Plassey ("Clive of India"; 1725–74) British soldier and colonial administrator

Quotations about Clive

1 What I like about Clive
Is that he is no longer alive.
There is a great deal to be said
For being dead.
Edmund Clerihew Bentley (1875–1956) British writer and journalist. "Clive," *Biography for Beginners* (1905)

Quotations by Clive

2 By God, Mr. Chairman, at this moment I stand astonished at my own moderation!
1773. Exclamation uttered during a British parliamentary cross-examination. *The Life of Robert, First Lord Clive* (G. R. Gleig; 1848), ch. 29

Clough, Arthur Hugh (1819–61) British poet

1 'Tis better to have fought and lost,
Than never to have fought at all.
A parody of Tennyson's "'Tis better to have loved and lost." "Peschiera" (1854)

2 Say not the struggle nought availeth,
The labour and the wounds are vain,
The enemy faints not, nor faileth,
And as things have been, things remain.
"Say Not the Struggle Nought Availeth" (1855)

3 Do not adultery commit;
Advantage rarely comes of it.
"The Latest Decalogue" (1862)

4 Thou shalt not steal; an empty feat,
When it's so lucrative to cheat.
"The Latest Decalogue" (1862)

5 Thou shalt have one God only; who
Would be at the expense of two?
"The Latest Decalogue" (1862), ll. 1–2

6 Thou shalt not kill; but needst not strive
Officiously to keep alive.
"The Latest Decalogue" (1862), ll. 11–12

7 *Action will furnish belief*, but will that belief be the true one?
This is the point, you know.
Amours de voyage (1858)

8 Am I prepared to lay down my life for the British female?
Really, who knows?
Amours de Voyage (1858), Act 2, Scene 4

9 How pleasant it is to have money.
Dipsychus (1865), Scene 4, "In a gondola"

10 This world is very odd we see,
We do not comprehend it;
But in one fact can all agree,
God won't, and we can't mend it.
Dipsychus (1865), Scene 4, "In a gondola"

11 And almost every one when age,
Disease, or sorrows strike him,
Inclines to think there is a God,
Or something very like Him.
Said to Dipsychus by the Spirit. *Dipsychus* (1865), Scene 5, "The Lido"

12 Grace is given of God, but knowledge is bought in the market.
The Bothie of Tober-na-Vuolich (1848), pt. 4, l.159

13 A world where nothing is had for nothing.
The Bothie of Tober-na-Vuolich (1848), pt. 8, l. 5

Coate, John U.S. academic

1 Let us build into...networks a pervasive community spirit that invigorates our society at every level, from local to global, with a new democratic awareness.
Quoted in "Cyberspace Innkeeping," *Reinventing Technology* (Philip E. Agre and Douglas Schuler, eds.; 1997)

2 Online conversation is...talking by writing.
Quoted in "Cyberspace Innkeeping," *Reinventing Technology* (Philip E. Agre and Douglas Schuler, eds.; 1997)

Cobain, Kurt (1967–94) U.S. rock musician

1 Here's the one who likes all our pretty songs
And he likes to sing along
And he likes to shoot his gun
But he don't know what it means.
Song lyric. "Nevermind" (1991)

2 I'm worst at what I do best and for this gift I feel blest.
Song lyric. "Nevermind" (1991)

3 When I finally heard punk music...I found my calling. There were so many things going on at once because it expressed the way I felt socially, politically, emotionally. I cut my hair and started trying to play my own style of punk rock and guitar: fast, with a lot of distortion.
Observer, London (August 1993)

4 The worst crime is faking it.
Observer, London (April 17, 1994), "Sayings of the Week"

5 Holding my baby is the best drug in the world. I don't want my daughter to grow up with people telling her that her parents were junkies.
1993. Quoted in *Rock 'n' Roll Babylon* (Gary Herman; 1994)

Cobb, Irvin S. (Irvin Shrewsbury Cobb; 1876–1944) U.S. humorist and journalist

1 But after all, when all is said and done, the king of all topics is operations.
Speaking of Operations (1916)

2 A good storyteller is a person who has a good memory and hopes other people haven't.
Attrib.

3 I would rather that any white rabbit on earth should have the Asiatic cholera twice than that I should have it just once.
Attrib.

Cobb, Ty (Tyrus Raymond Cobb, "The Georgia Peach"; 1886–1961) U.S. baseball player

1 Learn the fundamentals.
Study and work at the game as if it were a science.
Keep in top physical condition.
Make yourself as effective as possible.
Get the desire to win.
Keeping in the best physical condition and having an intense spirit to succeed is the combination for winning games.
"Six Keys to Baseball Success," *The Sporting News* (February 20, 1957)

2 I had to fight all my life to survive. They were all against me...but I beat the bastards and left them in the ditch.
He was one of the greatest and fiercest players in the history of baseball. Quoted in *Baseball: The Early Years* (Harold Seymour; 1960)

3 Speed is a great asset; but it's greater when it's combined with quickness—and there's a big difference.
Quoted in *The Tumult and Shouting* (Grantland Rice; 1954)

Cobbett, William (1763–1835) British writer, journalist, and reformer

1 Machines are the produce of the mind of man; and their existence distinguishes the civilised man from the savage.
Letter to the Luddites of Nottingham (1816)

2 To be poor and independent is very nearly an impossibility.
Advice to Young Men (1829)

3 From a very early age, I had imbibed the opinion, that it was every man's duty to do all that lay in his power to leave his country as good as he had found it.
Cobbett's Weekly Political Register (December 22, 1832)

4 A couple of flitches of bacon are worth fifty thousand Methodist sermons and religious tracts. They are great softeners of temper and promoters of domestic harmony.
Cottage Economy (1821)

5 But what is to be the fate of the great wen of all? The monster, called..."the metropolis of the empire"?
January 5, 1822. Referring to London. *Rural Rides* (1830)

Cobden, Richard ("The Apostle of Free Trade"; 1804–65) British economist and politician

1 I believe it has been said that one copy of *The Times* contains more useful information than the whole of the historical works of Thucydides.
Referring to the *Times* (London). Speech, Manchester, England (December 27, 1850)

2 The progress of freedom depends more upon the maintenance of peace, the spread of commerce, and the diffusion of education, than upon the labours of cabinets and foreign offices.
Speech to the British Parliament (June 26, 1850)

3 Is it that war is a luxury? Is it that we are fighting—to use a cant phrase of Mr Pitt's time—to secure indemnity for the past and security for the future? Are we to be the Don Quixotes of Europe, to go about fighting for every cause where we find that someone has been wronged?
Referring to the Crimean War. Speech to the British Parliament (December 22, 1854)

Cockburn, Catherine (1679–1749) English poet, playwright, and essayist

1 When a Woman appears in the World under any distinguishing Character, she must expect to be the mark of ill Nature.
Fatal Friendship (1698)

Cockburn, Claud (1904–81) British journalist and writer

1 Small earthquake in Chile. Not many dead.
According to the author, the winning entry in a competition in the *Times* (London) for the most lacklustre newspaper headline. *Time of Trouble* (1956), ch. 10

Cocteau, Jean (1889–1963) French film director, novelist, and playwright

1 A film is a petrified fountain of thought.
Esquire (February 1961)

2 Celebrity: I picture myself as a marble bust with legs to run everywhere.
"Des beaux-arts considérés comme un assassinat," *Essai de critique indirecte* (1932)

3 To write is an act of love. If it isn't it's just writing.
"Des Moeurs," *La Difficulté d'être* (1947)

4 Being tactful in audacity is knowing how far one can go too far.
"Le Coq et l'arlequin," *Le Rappel à l'ordre* (1926)

5 A very simple way of saying complicated things.
A definition of style. *Le Secret professionel* (1924)

6 Life is a horizontal fall.
Opium (1930)

7 A true poet does not bother to be poetical. Nor does a nursery gardener scent his roses.
Professional Secrets (1922)

8 Mirrors should think longer before they reflect.
Sunday Times, London (October 20, 1963)

9 You don't make a poem with thoughts; you must make it with words.
Sunday Times, London (October 20, 1963)

10 He is one of those beasts who died in a cage. He lived as one dreams of living: on the road.
Referring to Django Reinhardt. Quoted in *Stephane Grappelli* (Geoffrey Smith; 1987), ch. 11

Coe, Sebastian (b.1956) British athlete and politician

1 It's altogether quieter, more reflective, less controversial and more physical.
On taking up a career in politics. Remark (1989)

Coggan, Donald, Baron Coggan of Canterbury and Sissinghurst (Frederick Donald Coggan; b.1909) British bishop

1 Abortion leads to an appalling trivialization of the act of procreation.
Remark during his time as Archbishop of York (October 2, 1973)

Cohan, George M. (George Michael Cohan; 1878–1942) U.S. actor, playwright, and producer

1 Give my regards to Broadway,
Remember me to Herald Square,
Tell all the gang at Forty-Second Street
That I will soon be there.
Song lyric. "Give My Regards to Broadway," *Little Johnny Jones* (1904)

2 I'm a Yankee Doodle Dandy,
A Yankee Doodle do or die;
A real live nephew of my Uncle Sam's
Born on the Fourth of July.
Song lyric. "Yankee Doodle Dandy," *Little Johnny Jones* (1904)

Cohen, Henry, Lord Cohen of Birkenhead (1900–77) British surgeon

1 The feasibility of an operation is not the *best* indication for its performance.
Annals of the Royal College of Surgeons of England (1950)

Cohen, Jack, Sir (1898–1979) British business executive

1 Pile it high, sell it cheap.
Business motto (1960s)

Cohen, Leonard (Leonard Norman Cohen; b.1934) Canadian poet, singer, and songwriter

1 History! they shouted. Give us back our History! The English have stolen our History!
Referring to French Canadians. *Beautiful Losers* (1966)

Cohn, Harry (1891–1958) U.S. film producer

Quotations about Cohn

1 It proves what they say, give the public what they want to see and they'll come out for it.
March 2, 1958
Red Skelton (1913–97) U.S. actor and comedian. Said while attending the funeral (1958) of Hollywood producer Harry Cohn. It has also been attributed to Samuel Goldwyn while attending Louis B. Mayer's funeral (1957). "Foreground," *King Cohn* (Bob Thomas; 1967)

Quotations by Cohn

2 I don't have ulcers; I give them.
Attrib.

Cohn, Nik U.S. journalist

1 Entertainment always turns soft when times turn tough.
AwopbopaloobopAlopbamboom (1969)

2 Simple songs, one-line lyrics, gimmicks, big smiles and a dash of good clean filth for flavoring. It's a format that's changed only fractionally with time.
Referring to successful pop music. *AwopbopaloobopAlopbamboom* (1969)

Cohn, Roy (Roy Marcus Cohn; 1927–86) U.S. lawyer

1 I don't want to know what the law is, I want to know who the judge is.
Attrib. *American Heritage: Dictionary of American Quotations* (Margaret Miner and Hugh Rawson, eds.; 1997)

Coke, Edward, Sir (1552–1634) English lawyer and politician

1 We have a maxim in the House of Commons...that old ways are the safest and surest ways.
Speech, London (May 8, 1628)

2 The law of the realm cannot be changed but by Parliament.
Articuli Cleri (1605)

3 The house of every one is to him as his castle and fortress.
"Semayne's Case," *Reports* (1600–15), vol. 5, no. 91

Coker, Cheo Hodari U.S. journalist

1 An excuse for white teenagers in the Midwest to...assume the posture without feeling the pain.
Referring to gangsta rap music's depiction of urban violence and sexuality, and its appeal to white American teenagers. "Tupac. Thug Life Vol. 1," *Vibe* (1994)

Cole, Johnetta Betsch (b.1936) U.S. educator and cultural anthropologist

1 To teach well is to be a lifelong student.
Conversations: Straight Talk with America's Sister President (1993)

2 While it is true that without a vision the people perish, it is doubly true that without action the people and their vision perish as well.
Conversations: Straight Talk with America's Sister President (1993)

Cole, Nat King (Nathaniel Adams Coles; 1919–65) U.S. singer and jazz pianist

1 A lot of notes lying around on that old piano. I just pick at the ones I like.
Describing his style of piano playing. *Saturday Evening Post* (1943)

Cole, Thomas (1801–48) English-born U.S. painter

1 It is generally thought that the liberal arts tend to soften our manners; but they do more—they carry with them the power to mend our hearts.
"Essay on American Scenery 2," *The American Monthly Magazine* (January 1836), New Series, 1

Coleridge, Hartley (David Hartley Coleridge; 1796–1849) British poet

1 But what is Freedom? Rightly understood,
A universal licence to be good.
"Liberty" (1833)

Coleridge, Mary (Mary Elizabeth Coleridge; 1861–1907) British poet

1 Some hang above the tombs,
Some weep in empty rooms,
I, when the iris blooms,
Remember.
Poems (1907), no. 146

Coleridge, Samuel Taylor (1772–1834) British poet

Quotations about Coleridge

1 Let simple Wordsworth chime his childish verse,
And brother Coleridge lull the babe at nurse.
Lord Byron (1788–1824) British poet. Referring to Samuel Taylor Coleridge and William Wordsworth. "English Bards and Scotch Reviewers" (1809), l. 917

2 I wish he would explain his explanation.
Lord Byron (1788–1824) British poet. *Don Juan* (1819–24), can. 1, Dedication, st. 2

3 How great a possibility; how small a realized result.
Thomas Carlyle (1795–1881) Scottish historian and essayist. Letter to Ralph Waldo Emerson (August 12, 1834)

4 This illustrious man, the largest and most spacious intellect, the subtlest and the most comprehensive, in my judgement, that has yet existed amongst men.
Thomas De Quincey (1785–1859) British essayist and critic. *Recollections of the Lake Poets* (1863)

5 He talked on for ever; and you wished him to talk on for ever.
William Hazlitt (1778–1830) British essayist and critic. "On the Living Poets," *Lectures on the English Poets* (1818), Lecture 8

6 His thoughts did not seem to come with labour and effort; but as if borne on the gusts of genius, and as if the wings of his imagination lifted him from off his feet.
William Hazlitt (1778–1830) British essayist and critic. "On the Living Poets," *Lectures on the English Poets* (1818), Lecture 8

7 To tell the story of Coleridge without the opium is to tell the story of Hamlet without mentioning the Ghost.
Leslie Stephen (1832–1904) British biographer, critic, and philosopher. "Coleridge," *Hours in a Library* (1874–79)

Quotations by Coleridge

8 A sight to dream of, not to tell!
"Christabel" (1816), pt.1, l. 252

9 Joy is the sweet voice, joy the luminous cloud
We in ourselves rejoice!
And thence flows all that charms or ear or sight,
All melodies the echoes of that voice,
All colours a suffusion from that light.
Written April 4, 1802, in despair at the difficulties presented by his extramarital love for Sara Hutchinson (younger sister of Wordsworth's wife, Mary), and first sent in a letter to the poet Robert Southey, July 19, 1802. "Dejection: An Ode" (1802), quoted in *The Portable Coleridge* (I. A. Richards, ed.; 1950)

10 I see them all so excellently fair,
I see, not feel, how beautiful they are!...
I may not hope from outward forms to win
The passion and the life, whose fountains are within.
Written April 4, 1802, in despair at the difficulties presented by his extramarital love for Sara Hutchinson (younger sister of Wordsworth's wife, Mary), and first sent in a letter to the poet Robert Southey, July 19, 1802. "Dejection: An Ode" (1802), quoted in *The Portable Coleridge* (I. A. Richards, ed.; 1950)

11 What is an Epigram? a dwarfish whole,
Its body brevity, and wit its soul.
"Epigram" (1809)

12 That he who many a year with toil of breath
Found death in life, may here find life in death.
Epitaph for himself. "Epitaph" (November 9, 1833), ll. 5–6, quoted in *The Portable Coleridge* (I. A. Richards, ed.; 1950)

13 Ere sin could blight or sorrow fade,
Death came with friendly care;
The opening bud to heaven conveyed,
And bade it blossom there.
"Epitaph on an Infant" (1794)

14 In Xanadu did Kubla Khan
A stately pleasure-dome decree:
Where Alph, the sacred river, ran
Through caverns measureless to man
Down to a sunless sea.
"Kubla Khan" (1797), ll. 1–5, quoted in *The Portable Coleridge* (I. A. Richards, ed.; 1950)

15 A savage place! as holy and enchanted
As e'er beneath a waning moon was haunted
By woman wailing for her demon-lover!
"Kubla Khan" (1797), ll. 14–16, quoted in *The Portable Coleridge* (I. A. Richards; 1950)

16 And 'mid this tumult Kubla heard from far
Ancestral voices prophesying war!
"Kubla Khan" (1797), ll. 29–30, quoted in *The Portable Coleridge* (I. A. Richards, ed.; 1950)

17 It was a miracle of rare device,
A sunny pleasure-dome with caves of ice!
"Kubla Khan" (1797), ll. 35–36, quoted in *The Portable Coleridge* (I. A. Richards, ed.; 1950)

18 To know, to esteem, to love, and then to part,
Makes up life's tale to many a feeling heart!
"On taking Leave of—, 1817" (1817)

19 I have heard of reasons manifold
Why Love must needs be blind,
But this the best of all I hold—
His eyes are in his mind.
"Reason for Love's Blindness" (1811?), ll. 1–4

20 Reviewers are usually people who would have been poets, historians, biographers, &c., if they could; they have tried their talents at one or the other, and have failed; therefore they turn critics.
1811–12. *Seven Lectures on Shakespeare and Milton* (1856)

21 Her very frowns are fairer far,
Than smiles of other maidens are.
"She is Not Fair" (1833)

22 A mother is a mother still,
The holiest thing alive.
"The Three Graves" (1798)

23 "Alas!" said she, "we ne'er can be
Made happy by compulsion!"
"The Three Graves" (1798), pt. 4, st. 12

24 To believe and to understand are not diverse things, but the same things in different periods of growth.
Aids to Reflection (1825)

25 He who begins by loving Christianity better than Truth will proceed by loving his own sect or church better than Christianity, and end by loving himself better than all.
"Moral and Religious Aphorisms," *Aids to Reflection* (1825), no. 25

26 If a man could pass through Paradise in a dream, and have a flower presented to him as a pledge that his soul had really been there, and if he found that flower in his hand when he awoke—Aye, and what then?
Anima Poetae (1816)

27 Until you understand a writer's ignorance, presume yourself ignorant of his understanding.
Biographia Literaria (1817), ch. 12

28 The Fancy is indeed no other than a mode of memory emancipated from the order of time and space.
Biographia Literaria (1817), ch. 13

29 The primary imagination I hold to be the living Power and prime Agent of all human Perception, and as a repetition in the finite mind of the eternal act of creation in the infinite I AM.
Biographia Literaria (1817), ch. 13

30 Nothing can permanently please, which does not contain in itself the reason why it is so, and not otherwise.
Biographia Literaria (1817), ch. 14

31 That willing suspension of disbelief for the moment, which constitutes poetic faith.
Biographia Literaria (1817), ch. 14

32 No man was ever yet a great poet, without being at the same time a profound philosopher.
Biographia Literaria (1817), ch. 15

33 Our myriad-minded Shakespeare.
Coleridge says he borrowed this phrase from a Greek monk who applied it to a patriarch of Constantinople. *Biographia Literaria* (1817), ch. 15

34 Poetry is not the proper antithesis to prose, but to science. Poetry is opposed to science, and prose to metre.
Lectures and Notes of 1818 (1818), Lecture 1

35 It is an ancient Mariner,
And he stoppeth one of three.
"By thy long grey beard and glittering eye,
Now wherefore stopp'st thou me?"
"The Rime of the Ancient Mariner," *Lyrical Ballads* (1798), pt. 1

36 He holds him with his glittering eye...
He cannot choose but hear;
And thus spake on that ancient man,
The bright-eyed Mariner.
"The Rime of the Ancient Mariner," *Lyrical Ballads* (1798), pt. 1

37 The Sun came up upon the left,
Out of the sea came he!
And he shone bright, and on the right
Went down into the sea.
"The Rime of the Ancient Mariner," *Lyrical Ballads* (1798), pt. 1

38 The ice was here, the ice was there,
The ice was all around:
It cracked and growled, and roared and howled,
Like noises in a swound!
"The Rime of the Ancient Mariner," *Lyrical Ballads* (1798), pt. 1

39 "God save thee, ancient Mariner!
From the fiends that plague thee thus!—
Why look'st thou so?"—"With my cross-bow
I shot the Albatross."
"The Rime of the Ancient Mariner," *Lyrical Ballads* (1798), pt. 1

40 The fair breeze blew, the white foam flew,
The furrow followed free;
We were the first that ever burst
Into that silent sea.
"The Rime of the Ancient Mariner," *Lyrical Ballads* (1798), pt. 2

41 As idle as a painted ship
Upon a painted ocean.
"The Rime of the Ancient Mariner," *Lyrical Ballads* (1798), pt. 2

42 Water, water, every where,
And all the boards did shrink;
Water, water, every where,
Nor any drop to drink.
"The Rime of the Ancient Mariner," *Lyrical Ballads* (1798), pt. 2

43 Alone, alone, all, all alone,
Alone on a wide wide sea!
And never a saint took pity on
My soul in agony.
"The Rime of the Ancient Mariner," *Lyrical Ballads* (1798), pt. 4

44 The many men, so beautiful!
And they all dead did lie:
And a thousand thousand slimy things
Lived on; and so did I.
"The Rime of the Ancient Mariner," *Lyrical Ballads* (1798), pt. 4

45 The moving Moon went up the sky,
And no where did abide:
Softly she was going up,
And a star or two beside.
"The Rime of the Ancient Mariner," *Lyrical Ballads* (1798), pt. 4

46 Oh Sleep! it is a gentle thing,
Beloved from pole to pole!
"The Rime of the Ancient Mariner," *Lyrical Ballads* (1798), pt. 5

47 Quoth he, "The man hath penance done,
And penance more will do."
"The Rime of the Ancient Mariner," *Lyrical Ballads* (1798), pt. 5

48 Like one, that on a lonesome road
Doth walk in fear and dread,

And having once turned round walks on,
And turns no more his head;
Because he knows, a frightful fiend
Doth close behind him tread.

"The Rime of the Ancient Mariner," *Lyrical Ballads* (1798), pt. 6

49 No voice; but oh! the silence sank
Like music on my heart.

"The Rime of the Ancient Mariner," *Lyrical Ballads* (1798), pt. 6

50 I pass, like night, from land to land;
I have strange power of speech.

"The Rime of the Ancient Marlner," *Lyrical Ballads* (1798), pt. 7

51 He prayeth best, who loveth best
All things both great and small;
For the dear God who loveth us,
He made and loveth all.

"The Rime of the Ancient Mariner," *Lyrical Ballads* (1798), pt. 7

52 A sadder and a wiser man,
He rose the morrow morn.

"The Rime of the Ancient Mariner," *Lyrical Ballads* (1798), pt. 7

53 The faults of great authors are generally excellences carried to an excess.

Miscellanies (1884), 149

54 If men could learn from history, what lessons it might teach us! But passion and party blind our eyes and the light which experience gives is a lantern on the stern, which shines only on the waves behind us!

December 18, 1831. *Table Talk* (1835)

55 I wish our clever young poets would remember my homely definitions of prose and poetry; that is, prose = words in their best order;—poetry = the *best* words in the best order.

July 12, 1827. *Table Talk* (1835)

56 No mind is thoroughly well organized that is deficient in a sense of humour.

1833. *Table Talk* (1835)

57 The most happy marriage I can picture or imagine to myself would be the union of a deaf man to a blind woman.

Table Talk (1835)

58 The principle of the Gothic architecture is infinity made imaginable.

Table Talk (1835)

59 What comes from the heart, goes to the heart.

1833. *Table Talk* (1835)

60 To see him act, is like reading Shakespeare by flashes of lightning.

April 27, 1823. Referring to Edmund Kean. *Table Talk* (1835)

61 Swans sing before they die—'twere no bad thing,
Did certain persons die before they sing.

"On a Volunteer Singer," *The Complete Poetical Works of Samuel Taylor Coleridge* (1912)

62 The dwarf sees farther than the giant, when he has the giant's shoulder to mount on.

"On the Principles of Political Knowledge," *The Friend* (1818), vol. 2

63 The history of man for the nine months preceding his birth would, probably, be far more interesting and contain events of greater moment than all the three-score and ten years that follow it.

Aesthetic and Literary Miscellanies (T. Ashe, ed.; 1885)

64 Readers may be divided into four classes: 1. Sponges, who absorb all they read and return it nearly in the same state, only a little dirtied. 2. Sand-glasses, who retain nothing, and are content to get through a book for the sake of getting through the time. 3. Strain-bags, who retain merely the dregs of what they read, and return it nearly in the same state, only a little dirtied. 4. Mogul diamonds, equally rare and valuable, who profit by what they read, and reflecting, refracting, and enlarging upon it enable others to profit by it also.

Quoted in *The Jingle Bell Principle* (Miloslav Holub; 1992)

65 Laudanum gave me repose, not sleep; but you, I believe, know how divine this repose is, what a spot of enchantment, a green spot of fountain and flowers and trees in the very heart of a waste of sands.

Attrib.

Coleridge-Taylor, Samuel (1875–1912) British composer, conductor, and teacher

1 Really great people always see the best in others; it is the little man who looks for the worst—and finds it.

1912. *Croydon Guardian and Surrey Country Gazette* (February 1912), quoted in *Staying Power: The History of Black People in Britain* (Peter Fryer; 1984)

Colette (Sidonie Gabrielle Colette; 1873–1954) French novelist

1 My virtue's still far too small, I don't trot it out and about yet.

Claudine at School (1900)

2 Smokers, male and female, inject and excuse idleness in their lives every time they light a cigarette.

"Freedom," *Earthly Paradise: An Autobiography* (1966)

3 Don't ever wear artistic jewelry; it wrecks a woman's reputation.

Gigi (1944)

4 It's nothing to be born ugly. Sensibly, the ugly woman comes to terms with her ugliness and exploits it as a grace of nature.

Journey for Myself (1971)

5 Nothing ages a woman like living in the country.

"On Tour," *Music Hall Sidelines* (1913)

6 It's pretty hard to retain the characteristics of one's sex after a certain age.

"My Mother and Illness," *My Mother's House* (1922)

7 One of those refined people who go out to sew for the rich because they cannot bear contact with the poor.

The Other One (1929)

Collier, Price (1860–1913) U.S. writer

1 Germany is the only country I have visited where the hands of the men are better cared for than the hands of women.

Germany and the Germans: From an American Point of View (1913)

Collingbourne, William (?–1484) English landowner

1 The Cat, the Rat, and Lovell our dog
Rule all England under a hog.
The cat was Sir William Catesby, the rat Sir Richard Ratcliffe, the dog Lord Lovell, who had a dog on his crest. The hog refers to the emblem of Richard III, a wild boar. Quoted in *Chronicles* (Raphael Holinshed; 1577), vol. 3

Collingwood, Cuthbert, Baron (1748–1810) British admiral

1 Now, gentlemen, let us do something today which the world may talk of hereafter.
October 21, 1805. Said before the Battle of Trafalgar. *A Selection from the Correspondence of Lord Collingwood* (G. L. Newnham Collingwood, ed.; 1828), vol. 1

Collingwood, R. G. (Robin George Collingwood; 1889–1943) British philosopher, historian, and archaeologist

1 So, perhaps, I may escape otherwise than by death the last humiliation of an aged scholar, when his juniors conspire to print a volume of essays and offer it to him as a sign that they now consider him senile.
Autobiography (1939)

Collins, Merle (b.1950) Grenadian poet, novelist, and lecturer

1 Discovered that art
in England
comes in Black and White
in rich and poor
that an art called Black
exists
for England
in some region called the Fringe.
"Visiting Yorkshire—Again," *Rotten Pomerack* (1992)

Collins, Michael (1890–1922) Irish politician

1 Think—what have I got for Ireland? Something which she has wanted these past seven hundred years...I tell you this—early this morning I signed my death warrant.
Referring to signing the agreement with Great Britain that established the Irish Free State. He was assassinated in an ambush some months later. Letter to John O'Kane (December 6, 1921), quoted in *Michael Collins and the Treaty* (T. R. Dwyer; 1981)

2 We've been waiting 700 years, you can have the seven minutes.
1922. Said on being told he was 7 minutes late for the hand-over of British military jurisdiction to Irish Free State. Attrib. *Michael Collins: A Biography* (Tim Pat Coogan; 1990)

3 I found that those fellows we put on the spot were going to put a lot of us on the spot, so I got in first.
November 21, 1920. Referring to the killing of unnamed protestors on "Bloody Sunday." Quoted in *Phrases Make History Here* (Conor O'Clery; 1986)

4 We only succeeded after we had begun to get back our Irish ways...after we had made a serious effort to speak our own language, after we had striven again to govern ourselves.
Quoted in *The Oxford Illustrated History of Ireland* (R. F. Foster, ed.; 1989)

Collins, Wilkie (William Wilkie Collins; 1824–89) British novelist

1 Cultivate a superiority to reason, and see how you pare the claws of all the sensible people when they try to scratch you for your own good!
The Moonstone (1868), ch. 21

2 There, in the middle of the broad, bright high-road...stood the figure of a solitary Woman, dressed from head to foot in white garments, her face bent in grave inquiry on mine, her hand pointing to the dark cloud over London, as I faced her.
The Woman in White (1860), ch. 1

Colman, George ("The Younger"; 1762–1836) British playwright and theater owner

1 Mum's the word.
The Battle of Hexham (1789), Act 2, Scene 1

2 Lord help you! Tell 'em Queen Anne's dead.
A phrase which came to be applied to news everyone already knows. *The Heir at Law* (1797), Act 1, Scene 1

3 Oh, London is a fine town,
A very famous city,
Where all the streets are paved with gold,
And all the maidens pretty.
The Heir at Law (1797), Act 1, Scene 2

4 Not to be sneezed at.
The Heir at Law (1797), Act 2, Scene 2

Colton, Charles (Charles Caleb Colton; 1780–1832) British cleric and writer

1 Examinations are formidable even to the best prepared, for the greatest fool may ask more than the wisest man can answer.
Lacon (1820), vol. 1

2 Imitation is the sincerest form of flattery.
Lacon (1820), vol. 1

3 Law and equity are two things which God hath joined, but which man hath put asunder.
Lacon (1820), vol. 1

4 Lawyers are the only civil delinquents whose judges must of necessity be chosen from themselves.
Lacon (1820), vol. 1

5 Men will wrangle for religion; write for it; fight for it; anything but—live for it.
Lacon (1820), vol. 1

6 Physicians must discover the weaknesses of the human mind, and even condescend to humour them, or they will never be called in to cure the infirmities of the body.
Lacon (1820), vol. 1

Coltrane, John (John William Coltrane; 1926–67) U.S. jazz musician, composer, and bandleader

Quotations about Coltrane

1 Coltrane sounds like nothing so much as a club bore who has been metamorphosed by a fellow-member of magical powers into a pair of bagpipes.
1965
Philip Larkin (1922–85) British poet. "The Tenor Player with Fifty Legs," *All What Jazz: A Record Diary* (1970)

Quotations by Coltrane

2 If the music doesn't say it, how can words say it *for* the music?
Jazz Is (Nat Hentoff; 1976)

Colum, Padraig (1881–1972) Irish poet, playwright, and folklorist

1 She stepped away from me and she moved through the fair,
And fondly I watched her go here and go there,
Then she went her way homeward with one star awake,
As the swan in the evening moves over the lake.
"She Moved Through the Fair," *The Poet's Circuits* (1960)

Columbus, Christopher (1451–1506) Italian explorer and colonialist

Quotations about Columbus

1 Columbus did not seek a new route to the Indies in response to a majority directive.
Milton Friedman (b.1912) U.S. economist. *The Reader's Digest* (June 1, 1978)

Quotations by Columbus

2 I should be judged as a captain who went from Spain to the Indies to conquer a people numerous and warlike, whose manners and religion are very different from ours, who live in sierras and mountains, without fixed settlements.
Letter to Dona Juana de Torres (October 1500)

3 I believe that the earthly Paradise lies here, which no one can enter except by God's leave. I believe that this land which your Highnesses have commanded me to discover is very great, and that there are many other lands in the south of which there have never been reports.
Account of his third voyage, on which he sighted South America from Trinidad, July 31, 1498. Narrative of his third voyage (1498)

4 Here the people could stand it no longer and complained of the long voyage; but the Admiral cheered them as best he could, holding out good hope of the advantages they would have. He added that it was useless to complain, he had come to go to the Indies, and so had to continue it until he found them, with the help of Our Lord.
Journal of the First Voyage to America, 1492–1493 (October 10, 1492)

5 Presently we saw several of the natives advancing towards our party, and one of them came up to us, to whom we gave some hawk's bells and glass beads, with which he was delighted.
Journal of the First Voyage to America, 1492–1493 (October 21, 1492)

6 These people have no religion, neither are they idolaters, but are a very gentle race, without the knowledge of any iniquity; they neither kill, nor steal, nor carry weapons...they have a knowledge that there is a God above, and are firmly persuaded that we have come from heaven.
Journal of the First Voyage to America, 1492–1493 (November 12, 1492)

7 They handed all sails and set the *treo*, which is the mainsail without bonnets, and lay-to waiting for daylight Friday, when they arrived at an island of the Bahamas that was called in the Indians' tongue Guanahaní (San Salvador).
Journal of the First Voyage to America, 1492–1493 (October 12, 1492)

8 When you have nothing to say, say nothing.
Attrib.

Comden, Betty (b.1915) U.S. librettist and lyricist

1 New York, New York—a helluva town,
The Bronx is up but the Battery's down.
"New York, New York," *New York, New York* (co-written with Adolph Green; 1945)

Commager, Henry Steele (1902–98) U.S. historian

1 With the United States, history was rather a creation of the nation, and it is suggestive that in the New World the self-made nation was as familiar as the self-made man.
"The Search for a Usable Past," *American Heritage* (February 1965)

2 History is a jangle of accidents, blunders, surprises and absurdities, and so is our knowledge of it, but if we are to report it at all we must impose some order upon it.
The Nature and the Study of History (1965)

3 History is as all-embracing as life itself and the mind of man.
The Nature and the Study of History (1965)

4 To yearn for a single, and usually simple, explanation of the chaotic materials of the past, to search for a single thread in that most tangled of all skeins, is a sign of immaturity.
The Nature and the Study of History (1965)

5 For a people to be without History, or to be ignorant of its history, is as for a man to be without memory—condemned forever to make the same discoveries that have been made in the past, invent the same techniques, wrestle with the same problems, commit the same errors; and condemned, too, to forfeit the rich pleasures of recollection.
The Study of History (1966)

6 History is organized memory, and the organization is all important!
The Study of History (1966)

7 The historian is not God but I think it's inevitable that historians use judgment.
Attrib. *The Meaning of History* (N. Gordon and Joyce Carper; 1991)

Committee on Science and Creationism, National Academy of Sciences U.S. academic body

1 The goal of science is to seek naturalistic explanations for phenomena...within the framework of natural laws and principles and the operational rule of testability.
Science and Creationism: A View from the National Academy of Sciences (1984), conclusion

Compton, Karl Taylor (1887–1954) U.S. physicist

1 In recent times, modern science has developed to give mankind, for the first time in the history of the human race, a way of securing a more abundant life which does not simply consist in taking away from someone else.
Speech to the American Philosophical Society (1938)

Compton-Burnett, Ivy, Dame (1884–1969) British novelist

1 People don't resent having nothing nearly as much as too little.
A Family and a Fortune (1939), ch. 4

2 Appearances are not held to be a clue to the truth. But we seem to have no other.
Manservant and Maidservant (1947)

3 There is more difference within the sexes than between them.
Mother and Son (1955)

4 "She still seems to me in her own way a person born to command," said Luce.
"I wonder if anyone is born to obey," said Isabel. "That may be why people command rather badly, that they have no suitable material to work on."
Parents and Children (1941), ch. 3

Comte, Auguste (1798–1857) French philosopher and sociologist

1 Positivism becomes, in the true sense of the word, a religion; the only religion which is real and complete; destined therefore to replace all imperfect and provisional systems resting on the primitive basis of theology.
A General View of Positivism (J. H. Bridges, tr.; 1852)

2 The ignorance of the true laws of social life under which Communists labor is evident in their dangerous tendency to suppress individuality.
A General View of Positivism (J. H. Bridges, tr.; 1852)

3 The human mind has created celestial and terrestrial physics, mechanics and chemistry, vegetable and animal physics, we might say, but we still have to complete the system of observational sciences with *social physics*.
Course in Positive Philosophy (M. Clarke, tr.; 1830–42)

4 Each of our principal conceptions, each branch of our knowledge passes successively through three different theoretical states: the theological, or fictitious; the metaphysical, or abstract; and the scientific, or positive.
Referring to the unifying principle of Positivism. Quoted in *The Essential Comte* (S. Andreski, ed., M. Clarke, tr.; 1974)

Conant, James Bryant (1893–1978) U.S. chemist and diplomat

1 There is only one proved method of assisting the advancement of pure science—that of picking men of genius, backing them heavily, and leaving them to direct themselves.
Letter to the editor, *New York Times* (August 13, 1945)

2 The stumbling way in which even the ablest of scientists in every generation have had to fight through thickets of erroneous observations, misleading generalizations, inadequate formulations, and unconscious prejudice is rarely appreciated by those who obtain their scientific knowledge from textbooks.
Science and Common Sense (1951)

Confucius (Kong Fuzi, or K'ung Fu-tzu; 551–479 B.C.) Chinese philosopher, administrator, and moralist

1 A man who has committed a mistake and doesn't correct it, is committing another mistake.
Analects (5th century B.C.)

2 Choose a job you love, and you will never have to work a day in your life.
Analects (5th century B.C.)

3 Desire to have things done quickly prevents their being done thoroughly.
Analects (5th century B.C.)

4 Everything has beauty, but not everyone sees it.
Analects (5th century B.C.)

5 Fine words and an insinuating appearance are seldom associated with true virtue.
Analects (5th century B.C.)

6 Have no friends not equal to yourself.
Analects (5th century B.C.)

7 He who requires much from himself and little from others, will keep himself from being the object of resentment.
Analects (5th century B.C.)

8 In a country well governed poverty is something to be ashamed of. In a country badly governed wealth is something to be ashamed of.
Analects (5th century B.C.)

9 It is man that makes truth great, not truth that makes man great.
Analects (5th century B.C.)

10 It is only the wisest and the stupidest that cannot change.
Analects (5th century B.C.)

11 Learning without thought is labor lost; thought without learning is perilous.
Analects (5th century B.C.)

12 Men's natures are alike; it is their habits that carry them far apart.
Analects (5th century B.C.)

13 Music produces a kind of pleasure which human nature cannot do without.
Analects (5th century B.C.)

14 Our greatest glory is not in never falling, but in rising every time we fall.
Analects (5th century B.C.)

15 Real knowledge is to know the extent of one's ignorance.
Analects (5th century B.C.)

16 Recompense injury with justice, and recompense kindness with kindness.
Analects (5th century B.C.)

17 Straightforwardness, without the rules of propriety, becomes rudeness.
Analects (5th century B.C.)

18 Study the past, if you would divine the future.
Analects (5th century B.C.)

19 The people may be made to follow a course of action, but they may not be made to understand it.
Analects (5th century B.C.)

20 The superior man is distressed by his want of ability.
Analects (5th century B.C.)

21 The superior man is satisfied and composed; the mean man is always full of distress.
Analects (5th century B.C.)

22 They must often change, who would be constant in happiness or wisdom.
Analects (5th century B.C.)

23 To be able to practice five things everywhere under heaven constitutes perfect virtue...gravity, generosity of soul, sincerity, earnestness, and kindness.
Analects (5th century B.C.)

24 To be wrong is nothing unless you continue to remember it.
Analects (5th century B.C.)

25 To love a thing means wanting it to live.
Analects (5th century B.C.)

26 To see what is right, and not do it, is want of courage, or of principle.
Analects (5th century B.C.)

27 What the superior man seeks is in himself. What the mean man seeks is in others.
Analects (5th century B.C.)

28 What you do not want done to yourself, do not do to others.
Analects (5th century B.C.)

29 When you have faults, do not fear to abandon them.
Analects (5th century B.C.)

30 When you meet someone better than yourself, turn your thoughts to becoming his equal. When you meet someone not as good as you are, look within and examine your own self.
Analects (5th century B.C.)

31 The Master said, "At fifteen I set my heart on learning; at thirty I took my stand; at forty I came to be free from doubts; at fifty I understood the Decree of Heaven; at sixty my ear was attuned; at seventy I followed my heart's desire without overstepping the line."
5th century B.C. Quoted in *The Analects* (D. C. Lau, tr.; 1979), bk. 2, no. 4

32 The Master said, "If one learns from others but does not think, one will be bewildered. If, on the other hand, one thinks but does not learn from others, one will be in peril."
5th century B.C. Quoted in *The Analects* (D. C. Lau, tr.; 1979), bk. 2, no. 15

33 The Master said, "It is only the benevolent man who is capable of liking or disliking other men."
5th century B.C. Quoted in *The Analects* (D. C. Lau, tr.; 1979), bk. 4, no. 3

34 The Master said, "The gentleman understands what is moral. The small man understands what is profitable."
5th century B.C. Quoted in *The Analects* (D. C. Lau, tr.; 1979), bk. 4, no. 16

35 The Master said, "In serving your father and mother you ought to dissuade them from doing wrong in the gentlest way. If you see your advice being ignored, you should not become disobedient but remain reverent. You should not complain even if in doing so you wear yourself out."
5th century B.C. Quoted in *The Analects* (D. C. Lau, tr.; 1979), bk. 4, no. 18

36 Ji Wen Zi always thought three times before taking action. When the Master was told of this, he commented, "Twice is quite enough."
5th century B.C. Quoted in *The Analects* (D. C. Lau, tr.; 1979), bk. 5, no. 20

37 When I have pointed out one corner of a square to anyone and he does not come back with the other three, I will not point it out to him a second time.
5th century B.C. Quoted in *The Analects* (D. C. Lau, tr.; 1979), bk. 7, no. 8

38 A woman's business is simply the preparation and supplying of food and wine. She may take no step of her own motion, and may come to no conclusion in her own mind. Beyond the threshold of her apartments she should not be known for good or evil. She may not cross the boundaries of a state to accompany a funeral.
Quoted in *The Sayings of Confucius* (Lionel Giles, ed.; 1993)

39 Shall I teach you what knowledge is? When you know a thing, to hold that you know it; and when you do not know a thing, to allow that you do not know it. This is knowledge.
Quoted in *The Sayings of Confucius* (Lionel Giles, ed.; 1993)

40 He who keeps danger in mind will rest safely in his seat; he who keeps ruin in mind will preserve his interests secure; he who sets the dangers of disorder before himself will maintain a state of order.
An idea frequently referred to by leaders in China and Singapore. Attrib.

Congreve, William (1670–1729) English playwright and poet

1 I confess freely to you I could never look long upon a Monkey, without very Mortifying Reflections.
Letter to John Dennis (July 10, 1695)

2 I am always of the opinion with the learned, if they speak first.
Incognita (1692)

3 I came upstairs into the world; for I was born in a cellar.
Love for Love (1695), Act 2, Scene 7

4 O fie miss, you must not kiss and tell.
Love for Love (1695), Act 2, Scene 10

5 I know that's a secret, for it's whispered every where.
Love for Love (1695), Act 3, Scene 3

6 He that first cries out stop thief, is often he that has stolen the treasure.
Love for Love (1695), Act 3, Scene 14

7 Women are like tricks by slight of hand,
Which, to admire, we should not understand.
Love for Love (1695), Act 4, Scene 21

8 There is nothing more unbecoming a man of quality than to laugh; Jesu, 'tis such a vulgar expression of the passion!
The Double Dealer (1694), Act 1, Scene 4

9 Tho' marriage makes man and wife one flesh, it leaves 'em still two fools
The Double Dealer (1694), Act 2, Scene 3

10 She lays it on with a trowel.
The Double Dealer (1694), Act 3, Scene 10

11 When people walk hand in hand there's neither overtaking nor meeting.
The Double Dealer (1694), Act 4, Scene 2

12 See how love and murder will out.
The Double Dealer (1694), Act 4, Scene 6

13 No mask like open truth to cover lies,
As to go naked is the best disguise.
The Double Dealer (1694), Act 5, Scene 7

14 Heaven has no rage like love to hatred turned,
Nor hell a fury like a woman scorned.
The Mourning Bride (1697), Act 3, Scene 8

15 We never are but by ourselves betrayed.
The Old Bachelor (1693), Act 3, Scene 1

16 Eternity was in that moment.
The Old Bachelor (1693), Act 4, Scene 7

17 SHARPER Thus grief still treads upon the heels of pleasure:
Marry'd in haste, we may repent at leisure.
SETTER Some by experience find those words mis-plac'd:
At leisure marry'd, they repent in haste.
The Old Bachelor (1693), Act 5, Scene 1

18 Courtship to marriage, as a very witty prologue to a very dull Play.
The Old Bachelor (1693), Act 5, Scene 10

19 Ay, ay, I have experience: I have a wife, and so forth.
The Way of the World (1700), Act 1, Scene 3

20 I always take blushing either for a sign of guilt, or of ill breeding.
The Way of the World (1700), Act 1, Scene 9

21 Say what you will, 'tis better to be left than never to have been loved.
The Way of the World (1700), Act 2, Scene 1

22 Beauty is the lover's gift.
The Way of the World (1700), Act 2, Scene 4

23 Love's but a frailty of the mind
When 'tis not with ambition join'd.
The Way of the World (1700), Act 3, Scene 12

24 I hope you do not think me prone to any iteration of nuptials.
The Way of the World (1700), Act 4, Scene 12

25 O, she is the antidote to desire.
The Way of the World (1700), Act 4, Scene 14

26 Defer not till to-morrow to be wise,
To-morrow's sun to thee may never rise.
Letter to Cobham. "Verses to the Right Honourable the Lord Viscount Cobham," *Mr Congreve's Last Will and Testament, with Characters of his Writings* (Dryden, Blackmore, Addison, Pack; 1729)

Connell, James (1852–1929) Irish socialist

1 Psychoanalysis is spending 40 dollars an hour to squeal on your mother.
Bartlett's Unfamiliar Quotations (Leonard Louis Levinson; 1972)

2 The people's flag is deepest red;
It shrouded oft our martyred dead,
And ere their limbs grew stiff and cold,
Their heart's blood dyed its every fold.
Then raise the scarlet standard high!
Within its shade we'll live or die.
Tho' cowards flinch and traitors sneer,
We'll keep the red flag flying here.
1889. Traditionally sung at the close of annual conferences of the British Labour Party. "The Red Flag," *Songs that made History* (H. E. Piggott; 1937), ch.6

Connery, Sean (Thomas Sean Connery; b.1930) Scottish actor

1 I don't think a single other role changes a man quite so much as Bond. It's a cross, a privilege, a joke, a challenge. And it's as bloody intrusive as a nightmare.
Sunday Mirror, London (May 2, 1971), quoted in *Chambers Film Quotes* (Tony Crawley, ed.; 1991)

Connolly, Billy (b.1942) Scottish comedian and actor

1 This town was made to make money in and it has no other function. It has no pretence to longevity because it was never designed like that in the first place.
Referring to Los Angeles. *Times*, London (December 15, 1990)

2 Marriage is a wonderful invention; but then again so is a bicycle repair kit.
Billy Connolly (Duncan Campbell; 1976)

Connolly, Cyril (Cyril Vernon Connolly; 1903–74) British writer and journalist

1 A great writer creates a world of his own and his readers are proud to live in it. A lesser writer may entice them in for a moment, but soon he will watch them filing out.
Enemies of Promise (1938), ch. 1

2 An author arrives at a good style when his language performs what is required of it without shyness.
Enemies of Promise (1938), ch. 3

3 As repressed sadists are supposed to become policemen or butchers so those with irrational fear of life become publishers.
Enemies of Promise (1938), ch. 3

4 Literature is the art of writing something that will be read twice; journalism what will be grasped at once.
Enemies of Promise (1938), ch. 3

5 Whom the gods wish to destroy they first call promising.
Enemies of Promise (1938), ch. 13

6 There is no more sombre enemy of good art than the pram in the hall.
"Pram" means baby carriage. *Enemies of Promise* (1938), ch. 14

7 All charming people have something to conceal, usually their total dependence on the appreciation of others.
Enemies of Promise (1938), ch. 16

8 Boys do not grow up gradually. They move forward in spurts like the hands of clocks in railway stations.
Enemies of Promise (1938), ch. 18

9 I have always disliked myself at any given moment; the total of such moments is my life.
Enemies of Promise (1938), ch. 18

10 English Law: where there are two alternatives: one intelligent, one stupid; one attractive, one vulgar; one noble, one ape-like; one serious and sincere, one undignified and false; one far-sighted, one short; EVERYBODY will INVARIABLY choose the latter.
Journal and Memoir (David Pryce-Jones, ed.; 1983)

11 Longevity is the revenge of talent upon genius.
Sunday Times, London (June 19, 1966)

12 It is closing time in the gardens of the West.
The Condemned Playground (1945)

13 A mistake which is commonly made about neurotics is to suppose that they are interesting. It is not interesting to be always unhappy, engrossed with oneself, malignant and ungrateful, and never quite in touch with reality.
The Unquiet Grave (1944)

14 If one is too lazy to think, too vain to do a thing badly, too cowardly to admit it, one will never attain wisdom.
The Unquiet Grave (1944)

15 In the sex-war thoughtlessness is the weapon of the male, vindictiveness of the female.
The Unquiet Grave (1944)

16 Life is a maze in which we take the wrong turning before we have learnt to walk.
The Unquiet Grave (1944)

17 The one way to get thin is to re-establish a purpose in life.
The Unquiet Grave (1944)

18 The only way for writers to meet is to share a quick pee over a common lamp-post.
The Unquiet Grave (1944)

19 There are many who dare not kill themselves for fear of what the neighbours might say.
The Unquiet Grave (1944)

20 There is no fury like an ex-wife searching for a new lover.
The Unquiet Grave (1944)

21 Better to write for yourself and have no public, than write for the public and have no self.
Turnstile One (V. S. Pritchett, ed.; 1948)

22 The man who is master of his passions is Reason's slave.
Turnstile One (V. S. Pritchett, ed.; 1948)

Connolly, James (1868–1916) Irish political leader

1 It is an axiom enforced by all the experience of the ages, that they who rule industrially will rule politically.
Socialism Made Easy (1905)

Connors, Jimmy (James "Jimbo" Scott Connors; b.1952) U.S. tennis player

1 I hate to lose more than I like to win. I hate to see the happiness on their faces when they beat me.
New York Times (January 24, 1977)

Conrad, Joseph (Jósef Teodor Konrad Korzeniowski; 1857–1924) Polish-born British novelist

Quotations about Conrad

1 He is pretty certain to come back into favour. One of the surest signs of his genius is that women dislike his books.
George Orwell (1903–50) British writer. *New English Weekly* (July 23, 1936)

Quotations by Conrad

2 I have known the sea too long to believe in its respect for decency.
"Falk: A Reminiscence" (1903)

3 Exterminate all the brutes.
Said by Kurtz. *Heart of Darkness* (1902), ch. 2

4 Mistah Kurtz—he dead.
Heart of Darkness (1902), ch. 3

5 The horror! The horror!
Heart of Darkness (1902), ch. 3

6 Vanity plays lurid tricks with our memory.
Lord Jim (1900)

7 You shall judge of a man by his foes as well as by his friends.
Lord Jim (1900)

8 A work that aspires, however humbly, to the condition of art should carry its justification in every line.
The Nigger of the Narcissus (1897), Preface

9 The terrorist and the policeman both come from the same basket.
The Secret Agent (1907), ch. 4

10 All a man can betray is his conscience.
Under Western Eyes (1911)

11 Words as is well known, are great foes of reality.
Under Western Eyes (1911), Prologue

12 A belief in a supernatural source of evil is not necessary; men alone are quite capable of every wickedness.
Under Western Eyes (1911), pt. 2

13 The scrupulous and the just, the noble, humane, and devoted natures; the unselfish and the intelligent may begin a movement but it passes away from them. They are not the leaders of a revolution. They are its victims.
Under Western Eyes (1911), pt. 2

14 The Archipelago has lasting fascination. It is not easy to shake off the spell of island life.
Referring to the Malay Archipelago, extending from Indonesia, through the Philippines, to New Guinea. *Victory* (1915), pt. 2, ch. 1

Conran, Shirley (Shirley Ida Conran; b.1932) British designer, novelist, and journalist

1 Our motto: Life is too short to stuff a mushroom.
Superwoman (1975), Epigraph

2 I make no secret of the fact that I would rather lie on a sofa than sweep beneath it. But you have to be efficient if you're going to be lazy.
"The Reason Why," *Superwoman* (1975)

Conran, Terence, Sir (Terence Orby Conran; b.1931) British designer and entrepreneur

1 It's a fallacy that women are attracted by power and money. No one has fallen in love with me for ages.
Daily Express, London (April 21, 1986)

2 Design occupies a unique space between art and science. Designers must be sensitive to what is technically possible and what is humanly desirable.
Terence Conran on Design (1996)

3 As creative retailers, our policy simply amounts to a belief that if reasonable and intelligent people are offered products for their home that are well made, work well and are of decent quality, at a price they can afford, then they will buy them.
Interview, *Times*, London (October 5, 1981)

Constable, John (1776–1837) English landscape painter

1 Imagination alone never did and never can produce works that are to stand by a comparison with *realities*.
Lecture to the Royal Institution (1836)

2 There is nothing ugly; I never saw an ugly thing in my life: for let the form of an object be what it may, light, shade, and perspective will always make it beautiful.
October 23, 1821. *Memoirs of the Life of John Constable* (C. R. Leslie; 1843), ch. 17

3 There has never been a boy painter, nor can there be. The art requires a long apprenticeship, being *mechanical* as well as intellectual.
Attrib.

Constantine, Learie, Baron (Learie Nicholas Constantine; 1901–71) Trinidadian cricketer, lawyer, and politician

1 I am black. My grandfather and grandmother were the children of slaves born into slavery. I am neither proud nor ashamed of these things. They are facts.
Colour Bar (1954)

2 Of course, if the nations which put their splendid signatures to the Universal Declaration of Human Rights...had had the slightest intention of honouring that Declaration, there would have been very little in the subject of Black and White for me or anyone else to write about.
Colour Bar (1954)

3 Slavery has been abandoned, with much beating of religious breasts, but it is mostly the name that has gone.
Colour Bar (1954)

Constitution of the United States U.S. system of fundamental laws

1 Congress shall make no law respecting an establishment of religion, or prohibiting the free exercise thereof.
Part of the first amendment of the Constitution of the United States. *Amendments to the Constitution* (1791), Article 1

2 A well-regulated militia being necessary to the security of a free state, the right of the people to keep and bear arms shall not be infringed.
The second amendment of the Constitution of the United States. *Amendments to the Constitution* (1791), Article 2

3 Nor shall be compelled in any criminal case to be a witness against himself.
From the fifth amendment of the Constitution of the United States. *Amendments to the Constitution* (1791), Article 5

4 Neither slavery nor involuntary servitude, except as a punishment for crime whereof the party shall have been duly convicted, shall exist within the United States, or any place subject to their jurisdiction.
Section 1 of the thirteenth amendment of the Constitution of the United States. *Amendments to the Constitution* (1865), Article 13

5 After one year from the ratification of this article the manufacture, sale, or transportation of intoxicating liquors within, the importation thereof into, or the exportation thereof from the United States and all territory subject to the jurisdiction thereof for beverage purposes is hereby prohibited.
Section 1 of the eighteenth amendment of the Constitution of the United States. This ban on alcohol was repealed in 1933. *Amendments to the Constitution* (1919), Article 18

6 The right of citizens of the United States to vote shall not be denied or abridged by the United States or by any State on account of sex.
From the nineteenth amendment of the Constitution of the United States. *Amendments to the Constitution* (1920), Article 19

7 The right of the citizens of the United States to vote shall not be denied or abridged by the United States or by any State on account of race, color, or previous condition of servitude.
Section 1 of the fifteenth amendment of the Constitution of the United States. *Amendments to the Constitution* (1870), Article 15

Cooder, Ry (Ryland Peter Cooder; b.1947) U.S. musician and composer

1 These "haircut" guys can't just play it. They need their cartridges and programs and tape to make their shit work.
Referring to manufactured pop music, as opposed to live performances. Quoted in "Ry Cooder," *Off the Record: An Oral History of Popular Music* (Joe Smith; 1988)

Cook, Daniel John (b.1926) U.S. journalist

1 The opera ain't over till the fat lady sings.
Washington Post (June 13, 1978)

Cook, Eliza (1818–89) British poet

1 Better build schoolrooms for "the boy",
Than cells and gibbets for "the man".
"A Song for the Ragged Schools" (1853)

Cook, James, Captain (1728–79) British explorer and cartographer

1 At daylight in the morning we discovered a bay which appeared to be tolerably well sheltered from all winds, into which I resolved to go with the ship.
April 20, 1770. Recording his arrival at Botany Bay. Attrib.

Cook, Peter (Peter Edward Cook; 1937–95) British writer, actor, and comedian

1 I am very interested in the Universe—I am specializing in the universe and all that surrounds it.
Beyond the Fringe (1959)

2 You know, I go to the theatre to be entertained...I don't want to see plays about rape, sodomy and drug addiction...I can get all that at home.
Caption to cartoon. *Observer,* London (July 8, 1962)

3 Neither am I.
On being told that the person sitting next to him at a dinner party was "writing a book." Attrib.

Cook, Samuel D. (b.1928) U.S. historian

1 In the final analysis, history, like nature...has no favorites. History has a tragic dimension...As the Negro realizes, then, the tragic element of history, he will see his own history in perspective.
"A Tragic Conception of Negro History," *Journal of Negro History* (October 1960)

2 Knowledge of the tragic dimension of history is no more a justification of tragedy than knowledge of the brevity of human life is a justification of death.
"A Tragic Conception of Negro History," *Journal of Negro History* (October 1960)

3 Of the many mysteries of Negro history, the greatest is the absence of a deep sense of tragedy. In spite of the degrading and harrowing character of his odyssey, the Negro has been in the main, consistently optimistic about his historic destiny.
"A Tragic Conception of Negro History," *Journal of Negro History* (October 1960)

4 The study of time and history is always different from the endless flow and drama of time and history.
"A Tragic Conception of Negro History," *Journal of Negro History* (October 1960)

Cooke, Alistair (Alfred Alistair Cooke; b.1908) British-born U.S. broadcaster and writer

1 The green damp England of Oregon.
Alistair Cooke's America (1973)

2 Canned music is like audible wallpaper.
Quoted in *Brewer's Twentieth Century Music* (David Pickering; 1994)

3 I find baseball fascinating. It strikes me as a native American ballet—a totally different dance form. Nearly every move in baseball—the windup, the pitch, the motion of the infielders—is different from other games. Next to a triple play, baseball's double play is the most exciting and graceful thing in sports.
Attrib.

Coolidge, Calvin (John Calvin Coolidge; 1872–1933) U.S. president

Quotations about Coolidge

1 Mr. Coolidge's genius for inactivity is developed to a very high point. It is far from being an indolent activity. It is a grim, determined, alert inactivity which keeps Mr. Coolidge occupied constantly.
Walter Lippmann (1889–1974) U.S. writer and editor. *Men of Destiny* (1927)

2 He looks as if he had been weaned on a pickle.
Alice Lee Longworth (1884–1980) U.S. society figure. *Crowded Hours* (1933)

3 Here, indeed, was his one really notable talent. He slept more than any other President, whether by day or by night....Nero fiddled, but Coolidge only snored...He had no ideas, and he was not a nuisance.
H. L. Mencken (1880–1956) U.S. journalist, critic, and editor. *American Mercury* (April 1933)

4 How do they know?
Dorothy Parker (1893–1967) U.S. writer and wit. Reaction to news of the death of U.S. president Calvin Coolidge. Also attributed to H. L. Mencken. Remark (1933), quoted in *Writers at Work* (Malcolm Cowley; 1958)

5 Coolidge is a better example of evolution than either Bryan or Darrow, for he knows when not to talk, which is the biggest asset the monkey possesses over the human.
Will Rogers (1879–1935) U.S. actor, writer, and humorist. Referring to the Scopes trial, with Darrow defending a teacher being prosecuted for teaching evolution in the state of Tennessee. "Rogers Thesaurus," *Saturday Review* (August 25, 1962)

6 Calvin Coolidge believed that the least government was the best government; he aspired to become the least President the country had ever had; he attained his desire.
Irving Stone (1903–89) U.S. novelist and playwright. "Calvin Coolidge: A Study in Inertia" (1949), quoted in *The Aspirin Age: 1919–1941* (Isabel Leighton, ed.; 1949)

Quotations by Coolidge

7 I do not choose to run for President in 1928.
Speech (August 2, 1927)

8 Prosperity is only an instrument to be used, not a deity to be worshipped.
Speech, Boston, Massachusetts (June 11, 1928)

9 Civilization and profits go hand in hand.
Speech, New York City (November 27, 1920)

10 The chief business of the American people is business.
Speech, Washington (January 17, 1925)

11 One with the law is a majority.
Vice-presidential nomination acceptance speech to the Republican National Convention (July 27, 1920)

12 When a great many people are unable to find work, unemployment results.
City Editor (1929)

13 We review the past, not in order to return to it, but that we may find in what direction it points to the future.
Quoted in *The Meaning of History* (N. Gordon and Joyce Carper; 1991)

14 Baseball is our national game.
Attrib.

15 Patriotism is easy to understand in America; it means looking out for yourself while looking out for your country.
Attrib.

16 There is no right to strike against the public safety by anybody, anywhere, any time.
September 14, 1919. Referring to the Boston police strike. Attrib.

17 They hired the money, didn't they?
1925. Referring to the war debts incurred by England and others. Attrib.

18 He said he was against it.
Reply when asked what a clergyman had said regarding sin in his sermon. Attrib.

19 You lose.
When a woman at a dinner told him that someone had bet her that she would not get more than two words out of him. Attrib.

Cooper, Astley, Sir (Astley Paston; 1768–1841) British surgeon

1 I have made many mistakes myself; in learning the anatomy of the eye I dare say, I have spoiled a hatful; the best surgeon,

like the best general, is he who makes the fewest mistakes.
The Lectures of Sir Astley Cooper on the Principles and Practice of Surgery (1824)

2 My lectures were highly esteemed, but I am of the opinion my operations rather kept down my practice.
Quoted in *Bulletin of the New York Academy of Medicine* (F. H. Garrison; 1929), 5:155

3 If you are too fond of new remedies, first you will not cure your patients; secondly, you will have no patients to cure.
Attrib.

Cooper, James Fenimore (1789–1851) U.S. novelist

1 The people of the United States...speak, as a body, incomparably better English than the people of the mother country.
Notions of the Americans (1828)

2 The loftiest interests of man are made up of a collection of those that are lowly; he who makes a faithful picture of only a single important scene in the events of a single life, is doing something towards painting the greatest historical piece of his day.
Satanstoe (1845)

3 Hurry was one of those theorists who believed in the inferiority of all the human race who were not white. His notions on the subject were not very clear, nor were his definitions at all well settled; but his opinions were none the less dogmatical or fierce.
The Deerslayer: Or the First War Path (1841), quoted in *The Leatherstocking Saga* (Allan Nevins, ed.; 1955)

4 Next to arms, eloquence offers the great avenue to popular favor, whether it be in civilized or savage life.
The Deerslayer: Or the First War Path (1841), quoted in *The Leatherstocking Saga* (Allan Nevins, ed.; 1955)

5 When a thing is to be told, why, tell it, and don't hang back like a Yankee lawyer pretending he can't understand a Dutchman's English, just to get a double fee out of him.
The Deerslayer: Or the First War Path (1841), quoted in *The Leatherstocking Saga* (Allan Nevins, ed.; 1955)

6 The Last of the Mohicans
Title of novel. (1826)

7 As for myself, I can brain a Huron as well as a better man; but when it comes to a race, the knaves would prove too much for me.
The Last of the Mohicans (1826), quoted in *The Leatherstocking Saga* (Allan Nevins, ed.; 1955)

8 "Book!" repeated Hawkeye, with singular and ill-concealed disdain..."Book! what have such as I, who am a warrior of the wilderness, though a man without a cross, to do with books?"
The Last of the Mohicans (1826), quoted in *The Leatherstocking Saga* (Allan Nevins, ed.; 1955)

9 History, like love, is apt to surround her heroes with an atmosphere of imaginary brightness.
The Last of the Mohicans (1826), quoted in *The Leatherstocking Saga* (Allan Nevins, ed.; 1955)

10 I have lived to see two things in my old age, that never did I expect to behold. An Englishman afraid to support a friend, and a Frenchman too honest to profit by his advantage.
The Last of the Mohicans (1826), quoted in *The Leatherstocking Saga* (Allan Nevins, ed.; 1955)

11 More than two thousand raving savages broke from the forest at the signal, and threw themselves across the fatal plain with instinctive alacrity.
The Last of the Mohicans (1826), quoted in *The Leatherstocking Saga* (Allan Nevins, ed.; 1955)

12 So a judgmatical rap over the head stiffened the lying impostor for a time...and stringing him up atween two saplings, I made free with his finery.
The Last of the Mohicans (1826), quoted in *The Leatherstocking Saga* (Allan Nevins, ed.; 1955)

13 The imbecility of her military leaders abroad, and the fatal want of energy in her councils at home, had lowered the character of Great Britain from the proud elevation on which it had been placed.
The Last of the Mohicans (1826), quoted in *The Leatherstocking Saga* (Allan Nevins, ed.; 1955)

14 Natur' is natur', and it is an Injun's natur' to be found where he is least expected.
The Pathfinder: Or the Inland Sea (1840), quoted in *The Leatherstocking Saga* (Allan Nevins, ed.; 1955)

15 Well, I want no delicate ladies or king's majesties (God bless 'em) in the canoe, in going over these falls; for a boat's breadth, either way, may make a drowning matter of it.
The Pathfinder: Or the Inland Sea (1840), quoted in *The Leatherstocking Saga* (Allan Nevins, ed.; 1955)

16 "It is time to be doing," he said, interrupting the controversy that was about to ensue between the naturalist and the bee hunter; "it is time to leave off books and moanings, and to be doing."
The Pioneers: Or the Sources of the Susquehanna (1823), quoted in *The Leatherstocking Saga* (Allan Nevins, ed.; 1955)

17 The ancient amusement of shooting the Christmas turkey is one of the few sports that the settlers of a new country seldom or never neglect to observe.
The Pioneers: Or the Sources of the Susquehanna (1823), quoted in *The Leatherstocking Saga* (Allan Nevins, ed.; 1955)

18 There's sloops on the river, boy, that would give a hard time on't to the stoutest vessel King George owns...I wish I was captain in one of them...and we'd soon see what good Yankee stuff is made on.
The Pioneers: Or the Sources of the Susquehanna (1823), ch. 23, quoted in *The Heath Anthology of American Literature* (Paul Lauter, ed.; 1998), vol. 1

Cooper, Lady Diana, Viscountess Norwich (1892–1986) British actor and writer

1 Servants should not be ill. We have quite enough illnesses of our own without them adding to the symptoms.
Diana Cooper (Philip Ziegler; 1981)

Cope, Wendy (b.1945) British poet

1 In Dundee and Penzance and Ealing
We're imbued with appropriate feeling:
We're British and loyal

And love every royal
And tonight we shall drink till we're reeling.
"All-Purpose Poem for State Occasions," *Making Cocoa for Kingsley Amis* (1986)

2 Decapitating the spring onions,
She made this mental note:
You can tell it's love, the real thing,
When you dream of slitting his throat.
"From June to December, 5: Some People," *Making Cocoa for Kingsley Amis* (1986)

3 Some people like sex more than others—
You seem to like it a lot.
There's nothing wrong with being innocent or high-minded
But I'm glad you're not.
"From June to December, 5: Some People," *Making Cocoa for Kingsley Amis* (1986)

4 For he is the kind of man who has been driving women round
the bend for generations.
For sad to say this thought does not bring you to your senses.
For he is charming.
For he is good with animals and children.
"My Lover," *Making Cocoa for Kingsley Amis* (1986)

5 Bloody men are like bloody buses
You wait for about a year
And as soon as one approaches your stop
two or three others appear.
"Bloody Men," *Serious Concerns* (1992)

Copland, Aaron (1900–90) U.S. composer

1 So long as the human spirit thrives on this planet, music in some living form will accompany and sustain it and give it expressive meaning.
From a radio broadcast. "Music as an Aspect of the Human Spirit" (1954)

2 The greatest moments of the human spirit may be deduced from the greatest moments in music.
From a radio broadcast. "Music as an Aspect of the Human Spirit" (1954)

3 Music is in a continual state of becoming.
Music and Imagination (1952)

4 First-rate orchestras, brilliant conductors...cannot by themselves constitute an important musical culture...the crux...the composer—for it is he who must create the music.
Our New Music (1941)

5 I can see three important ways in which music helps a picture. The first is by intensifying the emotional impact of any given scene, the second by creating an illusion of continuity, and the third by providing a kind of neutral background music.
Our New Music (1941)

6 I have no quarrel with masterpieces. I think I revere and enjoy them as well as the next fellow. But when they are used...to stifle contemporary effort, then I am almost tempted to take the most extreme view and say that we should be better off without them.
Our New Music (1941)

7 There was never a great composer who left music exactly as he found it.
Our New Music (1941)

8 The whole problem can be stated quite simply by asking, "Is there a meaning to music?" My answer would be, "Yes." And "Can you state in so many words what the meaning is?" My answer to that would be "No."
What to Listen for in Music (1939)

9 It was great to be 20 in the twenties.
Quoted in *Fascinating Rhythm* (Deena Rosenberg; 1991)

Coppola, Francis Ford (b.1939) U.S. film director, producer, and screenwriter

1 *Apocalypse Now* is not about Vietnam, it is Vietnam. We were in the jungle; there were too many of us; we had access to too much money, too much equipment; and, little by little, we went insane.
Attrib. *Films Illustrated* (October 1979)

2 It's like I'm at a poker table with five guys. And they're all betting two or three thousand dollars a hand, and I've got about eighty-seven cents in front of me. So I'm always having to take off my shirt and bet my pants. Because I want to be in the game. I want to play.
Quoted in *Francis Ford Coppola: A Film-Maker's Life* (Michael Schumacher; 1999)

3 The new technology is as important to modern man as the discovery of fire was to early man. We are going to turn in the distant future into a race of people who possess extraordinary communication with one another—and the language of communication will be art.
Quoted in *Francis Ford Coppola: A Film-Maker's Life* (Michael Schumacher; 1999)

4 When you start you want to make the greatest film in the world, but when you get into it, you just want to get it done, let it be passable and not embarrassing.
Quoted in *Francis Ford Coppola: A Film-Maker's Life* (Michael Schumacher; 1999)

Corbett, Richard (1582–1635) English bishop and poet

1 Farewell, rewards and Fairies,
Good housewives now may say,
For now foul sluts in dairies
Do fare as well as they.
"The Fairies' Farewell," *Certain Elegant Poems* (1647)

Core, Philip (1951–89?) U.S. painter and writer

1 Camp is a lie that tells the truth.
Adapting John Cocteau's phrase, "the lie that tells the truth." *Camp* (1984), quoted in *A Queer Reader* (Patrick Higgins, ed.; 1993)

Coren, Alan (b.1938) British writer and humorist

1 No visit to Dove Cottage, Grasmere, is complete without examining the outhouse where Hazlitt's father, a Unitarian minister of strong liberal views, attempted to put his hand up Dorothy Wordsworth's skirt.
"Bohemia," *All Except the Bastard* (1969)

2 The Act of God designation on all insurance policies; which means, roughly, that you cannot be insured for the accidents that are most likely to happen to you.
"A Short History of Insurance," *The Lady from Stalingrad Mansions* (1977)

3 They are short, blue-vested people who carry their own onions

when cycling abroad, and have a yard which is 3.37 inches longer than other people's.
"All You Need to Know about Europe," *The Sanity Inspector* (1974)

4 Apart from cheese and tulips, the main product of the country is advocaat, a drink made from lawyers.
Referring to Holland. "All You Need to Know about Europe," *The Sanity Inspector* (1974)

5 Since both its national products, snow and chocolate, melt, the cuckoo clock was invented solely in order to give tourists something solid to remember it by.
Referring to Switzerland. "And Though They Do Their Best," *The Sanity Inspector* (1974)

6 Democracy means choosing your dictators, after they've told you what it is you want to hear.
Attrib.

Cormac mac Airt, King (*fl.* 9th century) Irish legendary king

1 I was a listener in woods,
I was a gazer at stars...
I was silent in a wilderness,
I was talkative among many,
I was mild in the mead-hall.
9th century. Referring to his youth. Quoted in "The Instructions of King Cormac," *The Faber Book of Irish Verse* (John Montague, ed., Kuno Meyer, tr.; 1974)

Corneille, Pierre (1606–84) French playwright

1 What destroys one man preserves another.
Cinna (1641), Act 2, Scene 1

2 Who is all-powerful should fear all things.
Cinna (1641), Act 2, Scene 2

3 All evils are equal when they are extreme.
Horace (1640), Act 2, Scene 8

4 Do your duty and leave the rest to the Gods.
Horace (1640), Act 2, Scene 8

5 A first impulse was never a crime.
Horace (1640), Act 5, Scene 3

6 We triumph without glory when we conquer without danger.
Le Cid (1636–37), Act 2, Scene 2

7 And the combat ceased from lack of combatants.
Le Cid (1636–37), Act 4, Scene 3

8 The manner of giving is worth more than the gift.
Le Menteur (1644), Act 1, Scene 1

9 A liar is always lavish of oaths.
Le Menteur (1644), Act 3, Scene 5

10 A good memory is needed after one has lied.
Le Menteur (1644), Act 4, Scene 5

11 I owe my fame only to myself.
"Excuse à Ariste," *Poésies* (1660)

12 You often lighten your troubles by telling of them.
Polyeucte (1642), Act 1, Scene 3

Cornfeld, Bernard (b.1927) U.S. business executive

1 Do you sincerely want to be rich?
His stock question to salesmen. Quoted in *Do You Sincerely Want To Be Rich?* (Charles Raw; 1971)

Cornford, F. M. (Frances MacDonald Cornford; 1874–1943) British philosopher

1 Every public action which is not customary, either is wrong or, if it is right, is a dangerous precedent. It follows that nothing should ever be done for the first time.
Microcosmographia Academica (1908), ch. 7

2 Propaganda is that branch of the art of lying which consists in nearly deceiving your friends without quite deceiving your enemies.
Attrib. *New Statesman*, London (September 15, 1978)

Cornforth, John, Sir (John Warcup Cornforth; b.1917) Australian-born British chemist

1 Truth is so seldom the sudden light that shows new order and beauty; more often, truth is the uncharted rock that sinks his ship in the dark.
Referring to scientists. Remark (1975)

Cornish, Samuel Eli (1795?–1858) U.S. clergyman and newspaper editor

1 If the Press, a "FREE PRESS," be a foe to the tyrant—if its blessings be so great and innumerable, the Question naturally presents itself, why may we not have one of our own?
A Documentary History of the Negro People in the United States (Herbert Aptheker; 1951), vol. 1, p.164

Cornuel, Anne-Marie Bigot de (1605–94) French society hostess and courtier of Louis XIV

1 No man is a hero to his valet.
Letter 13, "De Paris" (August 13, 1728), quoted in *Lettres de Mlle Aïssé* (1787)

Cornwallis, Charles (1580?–1629) English diplomat

1 In general sorrow that so monstrous a wickedness should be found harboured within the breast of any of their religion.
Describing Spanish reaction to the Gunpowder Plot. Letter to Lord Salisbury (November 1605)

Corry, John U.S. writer

1 Loneliness seems to have become the great American disease.
New York Times (April 25, 1984)

Corso, Gregory (Nunzio Gregory Corso; b.1930) U.S. poet

1 Bomb you are as cruel as man makes you
and you're no crueller than cancer.
"Bomb," *Minefield* (1989)

2 The heavens are with you
hosannah incalescent glorious liaison
BOMB O havoc antiphony molten cleft BOOM
Bomb mark infinity a sudden furnace

spread thy multitudinous encompassed Sweep
set forth awful agenda.
"Bomb," *Minefield* (1989)

3 O God, and the wedding! All her family and her friends
and only a handful of mine all scroungy and bearded
just wait to get at the drinks and food.
"Marriage," *The Happy Birthday of Death* (1960), quoted in *The Penguin Book of American Verse* (Geoffrey Moore, ed.; 1977)

4 Should I get married? Should I be good?
Astound the girl next door with my velvet suit and faustus
hood?
"Marriage," *The Happy Birthday of Death* (1960), quoted in *The Penguin Book of American Verse* (Geoffrey Moore, ed.; 1977)

Cortez, Jayne (b.1936) U.S. musician and poet

1 Reactors breed plutonium
bloodcells pay their dues
radiation keeps leaking & seeping
and i've got the Chernobyl Three Mile Island Blues.
"Deadly Radiation Blues," *Poetic Magnetic* (1991)

Corvisart des Marets, Jean Nicolas, Baron (1755–1821) French physician

1 Medicine is a conjectural art.
Attrib.

Cosby, Bill (b.1937) U.S. actor, author, and comedian

1 The thing that best defines a child is the total inability to receive information from anything not plugged in.
Childhood (1991)

2 The truth is that parents are not really interested in justice. They just want quiet.
Fatherhood (1986)

3 God is trying to solve the race relations problem without making it look like a miracle.
NBC-TV (April 4, 1970)

4 It isn't a matter of black is beautiful as much as it is white is not *all* that's beautiful.
Interview, *Playboy* (May 1969)

5 It is a point of pride for the American male to keep the same size Jockey shorts for his entire life. He can lose his house in a crap game and his wife to the mailman, but his ego cannot tolerate an increase in his Jockey short size.
Time Flies (1987)

6 Like everyone else who makes the mistake of getting older, I begin each day with coffee and obituaries.
Time Flies (1987)

7 I got tired of seeing television shows that consist of a car crash, a gunman, and a hooker talking to a black pimp. It was cheaper to do a new series than to throw out my family's television sets.
The Cosby Wit (Bill Adler; 1988)

8 The national pastime in this country is not sex and it's not baseball. It's lying.
The Cosby Wit (Bill Adler; 1988)

Cosell, Howard (originally Howard William Cohen; 1918–95) U.S. sports commentator

1 Professional boxing is no longer worthy of civilized society. It's run by self-serving crooks, who are called promoters. Professional boxing is utterly immoral...You'll never clean it up. Mud can never be clean.
Attrib.

Costello, Elvis (Declan Patrick McManus; b.1955) British singer and songwriter

1 The only two things that matter to me, the only motivation points for me writing all these songs are revenge and guilt.
Interview, *New Musical Express*, London (August 27, 1977)

2 Sounds like a gameboy down a well.
Referring to techno music on a British television program. *The O Zone* (January 9, 1995)

3 The rock idiom...is immature and totally macho-orientated in its basic attitude. Only in country music can you find a guy singing about...deprivation honestly.
Reported in *The Dark Stuff* (Nick Kent; 1993)

Costello, Lou (Louis Francis Cristillo; 1908–59) U.S. comic actor

1 WOLFMAN You don't understand. Every night when the moon is full I turn into a wolf.
COSTELLO You and twenty million other guys!
Abbot and Costello Meet Frankenstein (Robert Lees, Frederick L. Rinaldo, John Grant; 1948)

Costello, Louisa (Louisa Stuart Costello; 1799–1870) Irish-born British travel writer and novelist

1 The Welsh peasants have the reputation...of being singularly false and never speaking their minds...If this be true, they are worthy descendants of their countrymen of old, who betrayed their chiefs, and those chiefs each other.
Falls, Lakes, and Mountains in North Wales (1845), ch. 8

Cotter, Joseph Seamon, Jr. (1895–1919) U.S. poet

1 I am so tired and weary
So tired of the endless fight
So weary of waiting the dawn
And finding endless night
That I ask but rest and quiet
Rest for days that are gone,
And quiet for the little space
That I must journey on.
"Supplication," *The Book of American Negro Poetry* (James Weldon Johnson, ed.; 1922)

Coubertin, Pierre de, Baron (1863–1937) French educator and thinker

1 The most important thing in the Olympic Games is not winning

but taking part....The essential thing in life is not conquering but fighting well.
Speech at a banquet for officials of the Olympic Games, London (July 24, 1908), quoted in *Fourth Olympiad* (T. A. Cook; 1909)

Coué, Émile (1857–1926) French psychotherapist and hypnotist

1 Every day, in every way, I am getting better and better.
Formula for a cure by autosuggestion. *De la suggestion et de ses applications* (1915)

Courbet, Gustave (Jean Désiré Gustave Courbet; 1819–77) French painter

1 To record the manners, ideas, and aspect of the age as I myself saw them—to be a man as well as a painter—in short to create a living art—that is my aim.
Preface to catalogue of exhibition in Avenue Montaigne, Paris. *Realism* (1855)

Courtauld, George (b.1938) British civil servant and author

1 Waiting for a bus is about as thrilling as fishing, with the similar tantalisation that something, sometime, somehow, will turn up.
The Travels of a Fat Bulldog (1996)

2 Only a toothbrush is really indispensable: starting from the top this will neaten the hair, remove scurf from the collar, clean the teeth, then the fingernails and then, if needs are dire, ream out between the toes and the welts of the shoes.
The lesson of traveling light, learned as a Queen's Messenger. *The Travels of a Fat Bulldog* (1996)

Cousin, Victor (1792–1867) French philosopher

1 Art for art's sake.
1818. Lecture at the Sorbonne, Paris. "Cours de Philosophie," *Du Vrai, du beau et du bien* (1853), pt. 2

Cousins, Norman (1915–90) U.S. newspaper editor

1 History is an accumulation of error.
Attrib. *Saturday Review* (April 15, 1978)

2 History is a vast early warning system.
Attrib. *Saturday Review* (April 15, 1978)

Cousteau, Jacques (Jacques-Yves Cousteau; 1910–97) French film director and underwater explorer

1 Population growth is the primary source of environmental damage.
Observer, London (January 15, 1989), "Sayings of the Week"

2 The sea is the universal sewer.
1971. Said to the U.S. House Committee on Science and Astronautics. Quoted in *Speaking Freely* (Stuart Berg Flexner and Anne H. Soukhanov; 1997)

Covey, Donna British labor leader

1 Black people are doing what they have been told and bettering themselves, but it is not getting them anywhere.
Independent, London (September 7, 1993)

Covey, Stephen R. (b.1932) U.S. educator, leadership consultant, author, and academic

1 Goal setting is obviously a powerful process...the manifestation of creative imagination and independent will. It's the practicality of...translating vision into achievable, actionable doing.
First Things First (co-written with A. Roger Merrill and Rebecca R. Merrill; 1994)

2 Management is efficiency in the ladder of success; leadership determines whether the ladder is leaning against the right wall.
The Seven Habits of Highly Effective People (1989)

3 The proactive approach to a mistake is to acknowledge it instantly, correct and learn from it. This literally turns a failure into a success.
The Seven Habits of Highly Effective People (1989)

Coward, Noel, Sir (Noel Pierce Coward; 1899–1973) British playwright, actor, and songwriter

Quotations about Coward

1 You can make a sordid thing sound like a brilliant drawing-room comedy. Probably a fear we have of facing up to the real issues. Could you say we were guilty of Noel Cowardice?
Peter De Vries (1910–93) U.S. novelist. *Comfort Me With Apples* (1956), ch. 15

Quotations by Coward

2 We then got into a long discussion of morals and sex taboos and homosexuality, which convinced me that he is one of the wisest and most thoroughly sensible men I have ever met. I shall go to him once a year.
Referring to the doctor he went to see about his health and nervous stomach. Diary (July 15, 1955), quoted in *The Noël Coward Diaries* (Graham Payn and Sheridan Morley, eds.; 1982)

3 I am all for audiences going mad with enthusiasm after a performance, but *not* incessantly *during* the performance, so that there ceases to be a performance.
Referring to seeing the Beatles play live. Diary entry (July 4, 1965)

4 Mad about the boy,
It's pretty funny but I'm mad about the boy
He has a gay appeal
that makes me feel
There may be something sad about the boy.
Song. "Mad about the Boy" (1932)

5 Mad dogs and Englishmen
Go out in the mid-day sun;
The Japanese don't care to, the Chinese wouldn't dare to;
Hindus and Argentines sleep firmly from twelve to one,
But Englishmen detest a siesta.
Song lyric. "Mad Dogs and Englishmen" (1931)

6 Just say your lines and don't trip over the furniture.
Advice for actors. Speech at the Gallery First-Nighters' Club (1962)

7 I believe that since my life began
The most I've had is just
A talent to amuse.
"If Love Were All," *Bitter Sweet* (1929)

8 We have no reliable guarantee that the afterlife will be any less exasperating than this one, have we?
Blithe Spirit (1941), Act 1

9 That one day this country of ours, which we love so much, will find dignity and greatness and peace again.
Cavalcade (1931), The toast

10 People are wrong when they say the opera isn't what it used to be. It is what it used to be. That's what's wrong with it.
Design for Living (1933)

11 Everybody was up to something, especially, of course, those who were up to nothing.
Future Indefinite (1954)

12 Mother love, particularly in America, is a highly respected and much publicised emotion and when exacerbated by gin and bourbon it can become extremely formidable.
Future Indefinite (1954)

13 I've over-educated myself in all the things I shouldn't have known at all.
1922. *Mild Oats* (1931)

14 I don't think pornography is very harmful, but it is terribly, terribly boring.
Observer, London (September 24, 1972), "Sayings of the Week"

15 Work is much more fun than fun.
Observer, London (June 21, 1963), "Sayings of the Week"

16 Poor Little Rich Girl
Song title. *On With the Dance* (1925)

17 The Stately Homes of England
How beautiful they stand,
To prove the upper classes
Have still the upper hand.
Song lyric. "The Stately Homes of England," *Operette* (1938)

18 It would take a far more concentrated woman than Amanda to be unfaithful every five minutes.
Private Lives (1930)

19 Strange how potent cheap music is.
Private Lives (1930)

20 She refused to begin the "Beguine"
Tho' they besought her to
And with language profane and obscene
She curs'd the man who taught her to
She curs'd Cole Porter too!
"Nina," *Sigh No More* (1945)

21 Never mind, dear, we're all made the same, though some more than others.
The Café de la Paix (1939)

22 Sunburn is very becoming—but only when it is even—one must be careful not to look like a mixed grill.
The Lido Beach (1928)

23 Nothing to be fixed except your performance.
Replying to a telegram from the actor Gertrude Lawrence—"Nothing wrong that can't be fixed"—referring to her part in Coward's play *Private Lives*. *Noël Coward and his Friends* (Cole Lesley, Graham Payn and Sheridan Morley; 1979)

24 Goodnight, my darlings. I'll see you tomorrow.
The Life of Noël Coward (Cole Lesley; 1976)

25 How strange, when I saw you acting in *The Glorious Adventure* I laughed all the time.
Said to Lady Diana Cooper who said she had not laughed once at his comedy *The Young Idea*. *The Noël Coward Diaries* (Graham Payn and Sheridan Morley, eds.; 1982)

26 The doggie in front has suddenly gone blind, and the other one has very kindly offered to push him all the way to St. Dunstan's.
Said to Lawrence Olivier's five-year-old daughter Tamsin, who asked what two dogs were doing together in the street. Saint Dunstan's is a British institution for the blind. *The Sound of Two Hands Clapping* (K. Tynan; 1975)

27 Two things should be cut: the second act and the child's throat.
Referring to a play featuring a child actor. *The Wit of Noël Coward* (Dick Richards; 1968)

28 I never realized before that Albert married beneath him.
After seeing a certain actor in the role of Queen Victoria. *Tynan on Theatre* (K. Tynan; 1964)

29 Don't Let's Be Beastly to the Germans
1943. Song title.

30 Don't Put Your Daughter on the Stage, Mrs Worthington
1935. Song title.

31 Dear 338171 (May I call you 338?).
1930. Starting a letter to T. E. Lawrence, who had retired from public life to become Aircraftsman Brown, 338171.

32 Dear Mrs A.—hooray hooray,
At last you are deflowered
On this as every other day
I love you. Noël Coward.
1940. Telegram to Gertrude Lawrence on her marriage to Richard S. Aldrich.

33 Television is for appearing on, not looking at.
Attrib.

34 It was very close to the real thing but it seemed to last twice as long and be just as noisy.
1962. Referring to the opening of Lionel Bart's musical *Blitz*. Attrib.

35 If you weren't the best light comedian in the country, all you'd be fit for would be the selling of cars in Great Portland Street.
Said to Rex Harrison. Attrib.

Cowley, Abraham (1618–67) English poet

1 Life is an incurable disease.
"To Dr Scarborough" (1656), st. 6

2 A mighty pain to love it is,
And 't is a pain that pain to miss;
But of all pains, the greatest pain
It is to love, but love in vain.
"Gold," *Anacreon* (1656), pt. 7

3 They mingled Fates, and both in each did share,
They both were *Servants*, they both *Princes* were...
And fortune's malice betwixt both was crost,
For striking one, it wounded th'other most.
"Davideis," *Poems* (1656), bk. 2, quoted in *Penguin Book of Homosexual Verse* (Stephen Coote, ed.; 1983)

4 God the first garden made, and the first city Cain.
The Garden (1664), essay 5

Cowley, Hannah (Hannah Parkhouse; 1743–1809) British poet and playwright

1 Vanity, like murder, will out.
The Belle's Stratagem (1780), Act 1, Scene 4

Cowper, William (1731–1800) British poet

Quotations about Cowper

1 That maniacal Calvinist and coddled poet.
Lord Byron (1788–1824) British poet. Attrib.

Quotations by Cowper

2 Rome shall perish—write that word
  In the blood that she has spilt.
"Boadicea: An Ode" (1782), ll. 13–14, quoted in *Cowper: Poetical Works* (H.S. Milford, ed.; 1934)

3 Regions Caesar never knew
  Thy posterity shall sway,
Where his eagles never flew,
  None invincible as they.
"Boadicea: An Ode" (1782), ll. 29–32, quoted in *Cowper: Poetical Works* (H.S. Milford, ed.; 1934)

4 He found it inconvenient to be poor.
Said of a burglar. "Charity" (1782), l. 189, quoted in *Cowper: Poetical Works* (H.S. Milford, ed.; 1934)

5 A noisy man is always in the right.
"Conversation" (1782), l. 114, quoted in *The Works of William Cowper* (Robert Southey, ed.; 1835–37)

6 A moral, sensible, and well-bred man
Will not affront me, and no other can.
"Conversation" (1782), ll. 193–194, quoted in *The Works of William Cowper* (Robert Southey, ed.; 1835–37)

7 A tale should be judicious, clear, succinct;
The language plain, and incidents well link'd;
Tell not as new what ev'ry body knows;
And, new or old, still hasten to a close.
"Conversation" (1782), ll. 235–238, quoted in *The Works of William Cowper* (Robert Southey, ed.; 1835–37)

8 War lays a burden on the reeling state,
And peace does nothing to relieve the weight.
"Expostulation" (1782), ll. 306–307, quoted in *The Works of William Cowper* (Robert Southey, ed.; 1835–37)

9 Absence from whom we love is worse than death.
"Hope" (1782), quoted in *Cowper: Poetical Works* (H. S. Milford, ed.; 1934)

10 Pleasure is labour too, and tires as much.
"Hope" (1782), l. 20, quoted in *The Works of William Cowper* (Robert Southey, ed.; 1835–37)

11 Men deal with life as children with their play,
Who first misuse, then cast their toys away.
"Hope" (1782), ll. 127–128

12 And diff'ring judgements serve but to declare
That truth lies somewhere, if we knew but where.
"Hope" (1782), ll. 423–424

13 The lie that flatters I abhor the most.
"Table Talk" (1782), l. 88, quoted in *The Works of William Cowper* (Robert Southey, ed.; 1835–37)

14 Stamps God's own name upon a lie just made,
To turn a penny in the way of trade.
"Table Talk" (1782), ll. 420–421

15 Manner is all in all, whate'er is writ,
The substitute for genius, sense, and wit.
"Table Talk" (1782), ll. 542–543

16 We perish'd, each alone:
But I beneath a rougher sea,
And whelm'd in deeper gulphs than he.
1799. "The Castaway" (1803), ll. 64–66, quoted in *Cowper: Poetical Works* (H. S. Milford, ed.; 1934)

17 The poplars are fell'd, farewell to the shade,
And the whispering sound of the cool colonnade.
"The Poplar Field" (1784), ll. 1–2

18 Remorse, the fatal egg by pleasure laid.
"The Progress of Error" (1782), l. 239

19 Mortals, whose pleasures are their only care,
First wish to be impos'd on, and then are.
"The Progress of Error" (1782), ll. 289–290

20 For 'tis a truth well known to most,
That whatsoever thing is lost—
We seek it, ere it come to light,
In ev'ry cranny but the right.
"The Retired Cat" (1791), ll. 95–98

21 Public schools 'tis public folly feeds.
"Tirocinium" (1785), l. 250, quoted in *The Works of William Cowper* (Robert Southey, ed.; 1835–37)

22 He has no hope who never had a fear
"Truth" (1782), l. 298, quoted in *The Works of William Cowper* (Robert Southey, ed.; 1835–37)

23 I am monarch of all I survey,
My right there is none to dispute;
From the centre all round to the sea
I am lord of the foul and the brute.
Oh, solitude! where are the charms
That sages have seen in thy face?
Better dwell in the midst of alarms,
Than reign in this horrible place.
"Verses supposed to be written by Alexander Selkirk" (1782), st. 1, quoted in *The Works of William Cowper* (Robert Southey, ed.; 1835–37)

24 God moves in a mysterious way
His wonders to perform;
He plants his footsteps in the sea,
And rides upon the storm.
"Light Shining out of Darkness," *Olney Hymns* (1779), no. 35, ll.1–4

25 The bud may have a bitter taste,
But sweet will be the flow'r.
"Light Shining out of Darkness," *Olney Hymns* (1779), no. 35, ll.19–20

26 God made the country, and man made the town.
The Task (1785), bk. 1, "The Sofa," l. 749

27 Mountains interposed
Make enemies of nations, who had else,
Like kindred drops, been mingled into one.
The Task (1785), bk. 2, "The Time-piece," ll. 17–19

28 England, with all thy faults, I love thee still,
My country!
The Task (1785), bk. 2, "The Time-piece," ll. 206–207

29 There is a pleasure in poetic pains
Which only poets know.
The Task (1785), bk. 2, "The Time-piece," ll. 285–286

30 Riches have wings, and grandeur is a dream.
The Task (1785), bk. 3, "The Garden," l. 263

31 Who loves a garden loves a greenhouse too.
The Task (1785), bk. 3, "The Garden," l. 566

32 Domestic happiness, thou only bliss
Of Paradise that has surviv'd the fall!
The Task (1785), bk. 3, "The Garden," ll. 41–42

33 Knowledge is proud that he has learn'd so much;
Wisdom is humble that he knows no more.
The Task (1785), bk. 6, "The Winter Walk at Noon," ll. 96–97

34 Nature is but a name for an effect
Whose cause is God.
The Task (1785), bk. 6, "The Winter Walk at Noon," ll. 223–224

35 Detested sport,
That owes its pleasures to another's pain.
On hunting. *The Task* (1785), bk. 3, "The Garden," ll. 326–327, quoted in *Cowper: Poetical Works* (H.S. Milford, ed.; 1934)

36 Variety's the very spice of life
That gives it all its flavour.
The Task (1785), bk. 2, "The Time-piece," ll. 606–607

Crabbe, George (1754–1832) British poet and clergyman

1 The ring so worn, as you behold,
So thin, so pale, is yet of gold.
"His Mother's Wedding-Ring" (1813), ll. 1–2, quoted in *George Crabbe: Poems* (Adolphus William Ward, ed.; 1905)

2 He tried the luxury of doing good.
Tales of the Hall (1819), bk. 3, "Boys at School," l. 139

3 Secrets with girls, like loaded guns with boys,
Are never valued till they make a noise.
Tales of the Hall (1819), bk. 11, "The Maid's Story," l. 84

4 Habit with him was all the test of truth,
"It must be right: I've done it from my youth."
Letter 3, "The Vicar," *The Borough* (1810), ll. 138–139

5 Books cannot always please, however good;
Minds are not ever craving for their food.
"Schools," *The Borough* (1810)

6 Our Farmers round, well pleased with constant gain,
Like other farmers, flourish and complain.
"Baptisms," *The Parish Register* (1807), pt. 1, l. 273

Craig, Edward Gordon, Sir (Edward Henry Gordon Craig; 1872–1966) British actor, director, and stage designer

1 Farce is the essential theatre. Farce refined becomes high comedy; farce brutalized becomes tragedy.
The Story of my Days (1957), Index

Craig, Gordon A. (Gordon Alexander Craig; b.1913) U.S. historian

1 The darkest pages in history are often the most instructive.
Germany, 1866–1945 (1978)

Crane, Hart (Harold Hart Crane; 1899–1932) U.S. poet

1 We have all seen
The moon in lonely alleys make
A grail of laughter of an empty ash can.
"Chaplinesque" (1926)

2 The swift red flesh, a winter king—
Who squired the glacier woman down the sky?
She ran the neighing canyons all the spring;
She spouted arms; she rose with maize to die.
"The Dance," *The Bridge* (1930)

3 Down Wall, from girder into street noon leaks,
A rip-tooth of the sky's acetylene;
All afternoon the cloud-flown derricks turn...
Thy cables breathe the North Atlantic still.
"To Brooklyn Bridge," *The Bridge* (1930), quoted in *The Penguin Book of American Verse* (Geoffrey Moore, ed.; 1977)

Crane, Stephen (1871–1900) U.S. writer and journalist

1 Every sin is the result of a collaboration.
"The Blue Hotel" (1898)

2 We picture the world as thick with conquering and elate humanity, but here, with the bugles of the tempest pealing, it was hard to imagine a peopled earth.
Referring to a storm. "The Blue Hotel" (1898)

3 "It is bitter—bitter," he answered;
"But I like it
Because it is bitter,
And Because it is my heart."
The reply of the creature in the desert, eating his own heart, to the poet's question: "Is it good, friend?" "The Heart," *The Black Riders* (1895), quoted in *The Penguin Book of American Verse* (Geoffrey Moore, ed.; 1977)

4 A singular disadvantage of the sea lies in the fact that after successfully surmounting one wave you discover that there is another behind it just as important and just as nervously anxious to do something effective in the way of swamping boats.
1897. "The Open Boat," *The Open Boat and Other Stories* (1898)

5 Shipwrecks are *apropos* of nothing. If men could only train for them and have them occur when the men had reached pink condition, there would be less drowning at sea.
1897. "The Open Boat," *The Open Boat and Other Stories* (1898)

6 When it occurs to a man that nature does not regard him as important, and that she feels she would not maim the universe by disposing of him, he at first wishes to throw books at the temple, and he hates deeply the fact that there are no bricks and no temples.
1897. "The Open Boat," *The Open Boat and Other Stories* (1898)

7 The Red Badge of Courage
Title of novel. (1895)

8 It would be impossible for him to escape from the regiment.

It inclosed him. And there were iron laws of tradition and law on four sides. He was in a moving box.
Referring to the American Civil War (1861–65). *The Red Badge of Courage* (1895), ch. 3

9 The corpse was dressed in a uniform that once had been blue...Over the gray skin of the face ran little ants. One was trundling some sort of a bundle along the upper lip.
Referring to the American Civil War (1861–65). *The Red Badge of Courage* (1895), ch. 6

10 Some of the men muttered and looked at the youth in awe-struck ways...It was revealed to him that he had been a barbarian, a beast. He had fought like a pagan who defends his religion.
The Red Badge of Courage (1895), ch. 12

11 There was the delirium that encounters despair and death, and is heedless and blind to the odds. It is a temporary but sublime absence of selfishness.
The Red Badge of Courage (1895), ch. 19

12 With serene regularity, as if controlled by a schedule, bullets buffed into men.
The Red Badge of Courage (1895), ch. 20

13 The guns on the slope roared out a message of warning...It became a din fitted to the universe. It was the whirring and thumping of gigantic machinery, complications among the minor stars.
The Red Badge of Courage (1895), ch. 22

14 He had been to touch the great death, and found that, after all, it was but the great death. He was a man.
The Red Badge of Courage (1895), ch. 24

15 A newspaper is a collection of half-injustices
...A newspaper is a court,
Where every one is unkindly and unfairly tried
By a Squalor of honest men.
"A Newspaper is a Collection of Half-Injustices," *War Is Kind* (1899), quoted in *The Penguin Book of American Verse* (Geoffrey Moore, ed.; 1977)

Cranmer, Thomas (1489–1556) English archbishop

Quotations about Cranmer

1 I perceive that that man hath the sow by the right ear.
Henry VIII (1491–1547) English monarch. Referring to Thomas Cranmer and his support for Henry's attempts to end his marriage to Catherine of Aragon, for which Cranmer was rewarded with the archbishopric of Canterbury. Letter (June 1529), quoted in *Henry VIII* (J. J. Scarisbrick; 1968)

Quotations by Cranmer

2 We should easily convert even the Turks to the obedience of our gospel, if only we would agree among ourselves and unite in some holy confederacy.
Letter to Joachim Vadian (1537)

3 This was the hand that wrote it, therefore it shall suffer first punishment.
March 21, 1556. Remark made at the stake, referring to the hand that signed his recantation. *Short History of the English People* (John Richard Green; 1874)

4 The roots of the weeds, is the popish doctrine of transubstantiation, of the real presence of Christ's flesh and blood in the sacrament of the altar (as they call it), and of the sacrifice and oblation of Christ by the priest, for the salvation of the quick and dead.
The beliefs for which Cranmer was executed. Quoted in *The Story of Anglican Ministry* (E. P. Echlin; 1974)

Crashaw, Richard (1613?–49) English poet

1 Love, thou art Absolute sole Lord
Of Life and Death.
"Hymn to the Name & Honour of the Admirable Saint Teresa" (1652), l. 1, quoted in *Steps to the Temple: Delights of the Muses and Other Poems* (A. R. Waller, ed.; 1904)

2 I would be married, but I'd have no wife,
I would be married to a single life.
"On Marriage" (1646), quoted in *Steps to the Temple: Delights of the Muses and Other Poems* (A. R. Waller, ed.; 1904)

Craven, Avery O. (1885–1980) U.S. historian

1 Behind the oft-repeated statement that each generation must write its own history lies a tragic situation...the historian is doomed to be forever writing in the sand.
"An Historical Adventure," *Journal of American History* (June 1964)

2 I am inclined to think that history pays its way largely in the personal satisfaction of sitting on the fence and enjoying vicariously the trials and tribulations of men and times now ended.
"An Historical Adventure," *Journal of American History* (June 1964)

Creeley, Robert (Robert White Creeley; b.1926) U.S. poet

1 There is nothing
but what thinking makes
it less tangible.
"I Keep to Myself Such Measures...," *Words* (1967), quoted in *The Penguin Book of American Verse* (Geoffrey Moore, ed.; 1977)

Creighton, Donald (Donald Grant Creighton; 1902–79) Canadian historian

1 History must be defended against attempts to abuse it in the cause of change; we should constantly be on our guard against theories which either dismiss the past or give it a drastically new interpretation.
Towards the Discovery of Canada (1972)

Creighton, Mandell (1843–1901) British churchman and historian

1 No people do so much harm as those who go about doing good.
The Life and Letters of Mandell Creighton (Louise Creighton; 1904)

2 Paradoxes are useful to attract attention to ideas.
The Life and Letters of Mandell Creighton (Louise Creighton; 1904)

Crescas, Hasdai ben Abraham (1340–1410) Spanish philosopher and Talmudist

1 Reason cannot be forced into belief.
Or Adonai (1412)

Crèvecoeur, Jean de (Michel-Guillaume Jean de Crèvecoeur, pen name J. Hector St. John; 1735–1813) French-born U.S. writer and farmer

1 Here individuals of all nations are melted into a new race of men, whose labors and posterity will one day cause great changes in the world.
Letters from an American Farmer (1782)

2 Men are like plants; the goodness and flavor of the fruit proceeds from the peculiar soil and exposition in which they grow.
Letters from an American Farmer (1782)

3 There is something in the proximity of the woods which is very singular. It is with men as it is with plants and animals that grow and live in the forests; they are different from those that live in the plains.
Letters from an American Farmer (1782)

4 These turtles are good to eat, and as long as we feed on what would feed on us, that seems to be founded on a just retaliation. Traps of various kinds are laid to catch the otters, and their furs are the only reward they yield.
Letters from an American Farmer (1782)

5 What then is the American, this new man?
Letters from an American Farmer (1782)

Crichton-Browne, James, Sir (1840–1938) British physician

1 We have institutes for mental hygiene in these days. I trust they have included in their syllabus "The Dog," for it is really a mental antiseptic and tonic of incalculable value. Many a man has been saved from madness by a Dandy Dinmont, or a fox terrier.
The Doctor's Second Thoughts (1931)

Crick, Francis (Francis Harry Compton Crick; b.1916) British biophysicist

Quotations about Crick

1 Already for thirty-five years he had not stopped talking and almost nothing of fundamental value had emerged.
James Dewey Watson (b.1928) U.S. biochemist. *The Double Helix* (1968), ch. 8

Quotations by Crick

2 I also suspect that many workers in this field and related fields have been strongly motivated by the desire, rarely actually expressed, to refute vitalism.
Referring to molecular biology. *British Medical Bulletin* (1965), vol. 21

3 We have discovered the secret of life!
1953. On entering a Cambridge pub with James Watson to celebrate the fact that they had unravelled the structure of DNA. *The Double Helix* (James D. Watson; 1968)

Cripps, Stafford, Sir (Richard Stafford Cripps; 1889–1952) British politician, lawyer, and economist

1 There is only a certain sized cake to be divided up, and if a lot of people want a larger slice they can only take it from others who would, in terms of real income, have a smaller one.
Speech at the British Trade Union Congress (September 7, 1945)

Crisp, Quentin (1908–99) British writer

1 If any reader of this book is in the grip of some habit of which he is deeply ashamed, I advise him not to give way to it in secret but to do it on television...People will cross the road at the risk of losing their own lives in order to say "We saw you on the telly".
How to Become a Virgin (1981)

2 The law is simply expediency wearing a long white dress.
Manners from Heaven (1984), ch. 8

3 The idea that He would take his attention away from the universe in order to give me a bicycle with three speeds is just so unlikely I can't go along with it.
Sunday Times, London (December 18, 1977)

4 An autobiography is an obituary in serial form with the last instalment missing.
The Naked Civil Servant (1968)

5 I became one of the stately homos of England.
The Naked Civil Servant (1968)

6 If one is not going to take the necessary precautions to avoid having parents one must undertake to bring them up.
The Naked Civil Servant (1968)

7 Keeping up with the Joneses was a full-time job with my mother and father. It was not until many years later when I lived alone that I realized how much cheaper it was to drag the Joneses down to my level.
The Naked Civil Servant (1968)

8 Life was a funny thing that happened to me on the way to the grave.
The Naked Civil Servant (1968)

9 Tears were to me what glass beads are to African traders.
The Naked Civil Servant (1968)

10 The...problem which confronts homosexuals is that they set out to win the love of a "real" man. If they succeed, they fail. A man who "goes with" other men is not what they would call a real man.
The Naked Civil Servant (1968)

11 There was no need to do any housework at all. After the first four years the dirt doesn't get any worse.
The Naked Civil Servant (1968)

12 The young always have the same problem—how to rebel and conform at the same time. They have now solved this by defying their parents and copying one another.
The Naked Civil Servant (1968)

13 Vice is its own reward.
The Naked Civil Servant (1968)

Critchley, Julian (Julian Michael Gordon Critchley; b.1930) British politician

1 Mrs. Thatcher is a woman of common views but uncommon abilities.
"Profile: Margaret Thatcher," *Times*, London (1980s)

Crittenden, John (John Jordan Crittenden; 1787–1863) U.S. politician

1 My country right or wrong.
1846. Responding to President James Polk's request for a declaration of war. Quoted in *Speaking Freely* (Stuart Berg Flexner and Anne H. Soukhanov; 1997)

Croce, Benedetto (1866–1952) Italian philosopher, historian, and politician

1 All history is the history of thought.
Referring to the role of imaginative re-creation in historical writing. Attrib.

Crockett, Davy (David Crockett; 1786–1836) U.S. frontiersman, pioneer, and politician

1 I leave this rule for others when I'm dead,
Be always sure you're right—then go ahead.
1812. His motto, originating in the War of 1812 (1812–15) beween the United States and Great Britain. *Narrative of the Life of David Crockett, of the State of Tennessee* (1834)

Croker, John Wilson (1780–1857) Irish-born British politician and essayist

1 A game which a sharper once played with a dupe, entitled "Heads I win, tails you lose."
A "sharper" is one who cheats or swindles. *Croker Papers* (1884)

2 We now are, as we always have been, decidedly and conscientiously attached to what is called the Tory, and which might with more propriety be called the Conservative, party.
The first use of the term "Conservative Party." *Quarterly Review* (January 1830)

Crompton, Richmal (Richmal Samuel Lamburn; 1890–1969) British author

1 Violet Elizabeth dried her tears. She saw that they were useless and she did not believe in wasting her effects. "All right," she said calmly, "I'll thcream then. I'll thcream, an' thcream, an' thcream till I'm thick".
Violet Elizabeth Bott, a character in the William books, had both a lisp and an exceptional ability to get her own way. *Just William* (1922)

Cromwell, Oliver (1599–1658) English soldier and statesman

Quotations about Cromwell

1 Cromwell was a man in whom ambition had not wholly suppressed, but only suspended, the sentiments of religion.
Edmund Burke (1729–97) Irish-born British statesman and political philosopher. Letter to a Member of Parliament (1791)

2 For he was great, ere fortune made him so.
John Dryden (1631–1700) English poet, playwright, and literary critic. Remark on the death of Oliver Cromwell. *Heroic Stanzas* (1659)

Quotations by Cromwell

3 I beseech you, in the bowels of Christ, think it possible you may be mistaken.
August 3, 1650. Letter to the General Assembly of the Church of Scotland, quoted in *Oliver Cromwell's Letters and Speeches* (Thomas Carlyle, ed.; 1845)

4 The people would be just as noisy if they were going to see me hanged.
Referring to a cheering crowd. Remark (1654)

5 Take away that fool's bauble, the mace.
Speech at the dismissal of the Rump Parliament (April 20, 1653), quoted in *Memorials of the English Affairs* (Bulstrode Whitelock; 1732)

6 Necessity hath no law.
Speech to the British Parliament (September 4, 1654), quoted in *Oliver Cromwell's Letters and Speeches* (Thomas Carlyle; 1845)

7 Mr. Lely, I desire you would use all your skill to paint my picture truly like me, and not flatter me at all; but remark all these roughnesses, pimples, warts, and everything as you see me, otherwise I will never pay a farthing for it.
The origin of the expression "warts and all." Attrib. *Anecdotes of Painting in England* (Horace Walpole; 1763), vol. 3, ch. 1

8 Nature can do more than physicians.
Attrib.

Cronenberg, David (b.1943) Canadian filmmaker

1 All films are subversive.
Interview, French television (1989), quoted in *Chambers Film Quotes* (Tony Crawley, ed.; 1991)

Cronin, Mary J. U.S. author

1 If global connectivity is the technological breakthrough of our decade, then the outburst of innovation is just beginning.
Doing More Business on the Internet (1995)

2 Just as "location, location, location" defines value in real estate, in business today it's connectivity that equals competitiveness.
Doing More Business on the Internet (1995)

3 The electronic highway is not merely open for business; it is relocating, restructuring, and literally redefining business in America.
Doing More Business on the Internet (1995)

4 For many businesses, the Internet is still a technology in search of a strategy.
Quoted in *Opening Digital Markets* (Walid Mougayar; 1997)

Cronkite, Walter (Walter Leland Cronkite, Jr.; b.1916) U.S. broadcast journalist

1 And that's the way it is.
Catchphrase, used as the closing words of the news. *Evening News*, CBS television (1962–81)

Crosby, David (b.1941) U.S. singer and songwriter

1 The show was like eating a banana nut Brillopad.
Reviewing a performance by The Velvet Underground, an avant-garde rock group known for its abrasive and often dissonant music. *Fire Island News* (1966)

Crosby, Philip B. (Philip Bayard Crosby; b.1926) U.S. business executive

1 If you don't delegate, then you are really just a supervisor working directly with the people and guiding their every movement.
The Art of Getting Your Own Sweet Way (1981)

2 Keeping neat records and overspending is not money management.
The Art of Getting Your Own Sweet Way (1981)

3 There are only two kinds of managers: the growing and the obsolete.
The Art of Getting Your Own Sweet Way (1981)

Cross, Douglas U.S. songwriter

1 I Left My Heart in San Francisco
1954. Song title. Popularized by Tony Bennett.

Crossman, Richard (Richard Howard Stafford Crossman; 1907–74) British politician

1 By yesterday morning British troops were patrolling the streets of Belfast. I fear that once Catholics and Protestants get used to our presence they will hate us more than they hate each other.
August 17, 1969. *Diaries of a Cabinet Minister 1964–1970* (1975), vol. 1

2 The Civil Service is profoundly deferential—"Yes, Minister! No, Minister! If you wish it, Minister!"
October 22, 1964. Comment on his first day as a cabinet minister. *Diaries of a Cabinet Minister 1964–1970* (1975), vol. 1

Crouse, Russell M. (1893–1966) U.S. writer

1 An optimist, in the atomic age, thinks the future is uncertain.
State of the Union (1946)

Crow, Tim J. (b.1938) British psychiatrist

1 Schizophrenia is the price that Homo sapiens pays for language.
British Journal of Psychiatry (1998), vol. 172

Crowley, Mart (Martino Crowley; b.1935) U.S. playwright

1 DONALD Are you calling me a screaming queen or a tired fairy?
MICHAEL Oh, I beg your pardon—six tired screaming fairy queens and one anxious queer.
The Boys in the Band (1968), Act 1

Crowther, Geoffrey, Baron (1907–72) British economist

1 Money, it has been said, has two properties. It is flat so that it can be piled up. But it is also round so that it can circulate.
An Outline of Money (1941), ch. 2

2 You do not haggle over the price when you are invited to climb onto a lifeboat. You scramble aboard while there is still a seat for you.
On the terms of entry into the European Common Market. *Observer*, London (August 1, 1971), "Sayings of the Week"

Crumb, R. (Robert Crumb; b.1943) U.S. cartoonist

1 Not everything's for children. Not everything's for everyone.
Commenting on the hostile response to the politically incorrect nature of his work. Quoted in *Crumb* (Terry Zwigoff; 1995)

Crummell, Alexander (1819–98) U.S. clergyman, teacher, and missionary

1 Any movement which passes by the female sex is an ephemeral thing.
August 15, 1883. Address to the Freedman's Aid Society, Ocean Grove, New Jersey, *Africa and America: Addresses and Discourses* (1891)

2 Nothing is more common in the world than man's eagerness for power, and his pride in the possession of it. It is a sad reflection, however, that a sense of the responsibility which comes with power is the rarest of things.
The Greatness of Christ and other Sermons (1882)

Crystal, Billy (b.1947) U.S. actor

1 No man can ever be friends with a woman that he finds attractive. He always wants to have sex with her.
As Harry Burns. *When Harry Met Sally* (Nora Ephron; 1989)

Cugoano, Ottobah (1757?–1803?) Ghanaian freed slave and abolitionist

1 If any man should buy another man without his consent, and compel him to his service and slavery without any agreement of that man to serve him, the enslaver is a robber, and a defrauder of that man every day. Wherefore it is as much the duty of a man who is robbed in that manner to get out of the hands of his enslaver, as it is for any honest community of men to get out of the hands of rogues and villains.
Thoughts and Sentiments on the Evil and Wicked Traffic of the Slavery and Commerce of the Human Species, Humbly Submitted to the Inhabitants of Great-Britain (1787)

2 I must own, to the shame of my own countrymen, that I was first kid-napped and betrayed by some of my own complexion, who were the first cause of my exile and slavery; but if there were no buyers there would be no sellers.
Thoughts and Sentiments on the Evil and Wicked Traffic of the Slavery and Commerce of the Human Species, Humbly Submitted to the Inhabitants of Great-Britain (1787)

Culbertson, Ely (1891–1955) U.S. bridge player

1 Power politics is the diplomatic name for the law of the jungle.
Must We Fight Russia? (1946)

Cullen, Countee (1903–46) U.S. poet, novelist, and playwright

1 One three centuries removed
From the scenes his fathers loved,
Spicy grove, cinammon tree,
What is Africa to me?
Color (1925)

2 Lord, forgive me if my need
Sometimes shapes a human creed.
"Heritage," *Color* (1925)

3 What is Africa to me: Copper sun or scarlet sea
Jungle star or jungle track
Strong bronzed men, or regal black
Women from whose loins I sprang
When the birds of Eden sang?
"Heritage," *Color* (1925)

4 "White folks is white," says uncle Jim;
"A platitude," I sneer;
And then I tell him so is milk,
And the froth upon his beer.
"Uncle Jim," *Color* (1925)

5 I doubt not God is good, well-meaning, kind ...
Yet do I marvel at this curious thing:
To make a poet black, and bid him sing!
"Yet Do I Marvel," *Color* (1925)

6 The loss of love is a terrible thing;
They lie who say that death is worse.
"Variations on a Theme (The Loss of Love) ," *Copper Sun* (1927)

7 Never love with all your heart,
It only ends in aching.
"Song in Spite of Myself," *The Black Christ and Other Poems* (1929)

cummings, e. e. (Edward Estlin Cummings; 1894–1962) U.S. poet and painter

1 I will not kiss your f.king flag.
"i sing of Olaf glad and big" (1931)

2 and nothing quite so least as truth
—i say though hate were why men breathe—
because my father lived his soul
love is the whole and more than all.
"my father moved through dooms of love" (1940)

3 And there're a
hun-dred-mil-lion-others, like
all of you successfully if
delicately gelded (or spaded)
gentlemen (and ladies).
"Poem, Or Beauty Hurts Mr. Vinal" (1926)

4 (i do not know what it is about you that closes
and opens; only something in me understands
the voice of your eyes is deeper than all roses)
nobody, not even the rain, has such small hands.
"somewhere i have never travelled" (1931)

5 a politician is an arse upon which everyone has sat except a man.
1 x 1 (1944), no. 10

6 listen: there's
a hell of a good universe next door; let's go.
1 x 1 (1944), no. 14

7 pity this busy monster, manunkind,
not. Progress is a comfortable disease.
1 x 1 (1944), no.14

8 anyone lived in a pretty how town
(with up so floating many bells down)
spring summer autumn winter
he sang his didn't he danced his did.
50 Poems (1940), no. 29

9 my father moved through dooms of love
through sames of am through haves of give,
singing each morning out of each night
my father moved through depths of height.
"my father moved through dooms of love," *50 Poems* (1940), quoted in *The Penguin Book of American Verse* (Geoffrey Moore, ed.; 1977)

10 a pretty girl who naked is
is worth a million statues.
Collected Poems (1938)

11 i remember we all cried like the Missouri
when my Uncle Sol's coffin lurched because
somebody pressed a button
(and down went
my Uncle
Sol
and started a worm farm).
"nobody loses all the time...," *Complete Poems 1913–1935* (1926), no. 29

12 who knows if the moon's
a balloon, coming out of a keen city
in the sky—filled with pretty people?
1925. Used as the title of David Niven's first volume of autobiography, *The Moon's a Balloon*, about his experiences in the film industry. "Seven Poems," *Complete Poems 1913–1935* (1968), no. 7, st. 1, ll. 1–3

13 A foolish world is more foolish than royalty can suppose. And what has been miscalled the Russian revolution is a more foolish than supposable world's attempt...to substitute for the royal incognito of humility the ignoble affectation of equality.
Eimi (1933)

14 The World with its smells hints its follies hatreds laughter mistakes whispers its sins...through doubtful certainties remembering each contradiction surely and beyond hideous victory all beautiful disasters.
Eimi (1933)

15 "I've seen all sorts of revolutions," he remarks, "and I've come to the conclusion that people are idiots. It doesn't make a darn bit of difference what the government is."
Referring to a man encountered on a train to Russia. *Eimi* (1933)

16 The churches are drowning with stars, everywhere stars blossom, frank and gold and keen...Now (touched by a resonance of sexually celestial forms) the little murdered adventure called Humanity becomes a selfless symbol.
Said after attending a Russian Orthodox Church service in Kiev. *Eimi* (1933)

17 my sweet old etcetera.
"my sweet old sweet etcetera," *is 5* (1926), quoted in *The Penguin Book of American Verse* (Geoffrey Moore, ed.; 1977)

18 Humanity i love you because
when you're hard up you pawn your
intelligence to buy a drink.
"La Guerre," *no. 2* (1925)

19 Buffalo Bill's
defunct
who used to
ride a watersmooth-silver
stallion
and break onetwothreefourfive pigeons—
justlikethat.
Portraits (1923), no. 8

20 Jesus
he was a handsome man
and what i want to know is
how do you like your blueeyed boy
Mister Death.
"Buffalo Bill's," *Tulips and Chimneys* (1922), quoted in *The Penguin Book of American Verse* (Geoffrey Moore, ed.; 1977)

21 i thank You God for most this amazing
day: for the leaping greenly spirits of the trees
and a blue dream of sky; and for everything
which is natural which is infinite which is yes.
"i thank You God for most this amazing," *XAIPE* (1950), quoted in *The Penguin Book of American Verse* (Geoffrey Moore, ed.; 1977)

22 now the ears of my ears awake and
now the eyes of my eyes are opened.
"i thank You God for most this amazing," *XAIPE* (1950), quoted in *The Penguin Book of American Verse* (Geoffrey Moore, ed.; 1977)

23 To like an individual because he's black is just as insulting as to dislike him because he isn't white.
Attrib.

Cunard, Lady "Emerald" (Maud Cunard; 1872–1948) U.S.-born British society figure

1 Why didn't you bring him with you? I should be delighted to meet him.
Said to Somerset Maugham, who said he was leaving a dinner party early "to keep his youth." Quoted in *Emerald and Nancy: Lady Cunard and her Daughter* (D. Fielding; 1968)

Cunningham, Allan (1784–1842) Scottish poet and writer

1 While the hollow oak our palace is,
Our heritage the sea.
"A Wet Sheet and a Flowing Sea," *The Songs of Scotland* (1825), st. 1

Cunningham, J. V. (James Vincent Cunningham; 1911–85) U.S. poet

1 *Arms and the man I sing*, and sing for joy,
Who was last year all elbows and a boy.
"Arms and the man I sing" quotes the opening to the *Aeneid* (19 B.C.) by Virgil. "A Century of Epigrams," *The Collected Poems and Epigrams of J. V. Cunningham* (1971), no. 68

Cunningham, Merce (b.1919) U.S. dancer and choreographer

1 I compare...dance...to water...Everyone knows what water is or what dance is, but...fluidity makes them intangible...Music at least has a literature, a notation.
Quoted in *The Dancer and the Dance* (in conversation with Jacqueline Lesschaeve; 1991)

2 Oh I think dancers have to be a little stupid to go through with what they do every day...wholly innocent or foolish.
Quoted in *The Dancer and the Dance* (in conversation with Jacqueline Lesschaeve; 1991)

3 I didn't *become* a dancer, I've always danced.
Response on being asked how he became a dancer. Quoted in *The Dancer and the Dance* (in conversation with Jacqueline Lesschaeve; 1991)

Cuomo, Mario (Mario Matthew Cuomo; b.1932) U.S. politician

1 You campaign in poetry. You govern in prose.
New Republic (April 8, 1985)

Cuppy, Will (William Jacob Cuppy; 1884–1949) U.S. humorist and critic

1 The Dodo never had a chance. He seems to have been invented for the sole purpose of becoming extinct and that was all he was good for.
"The Dodo," *How to Become Extinct* (1941)

Curie, Irène (Irène Joliot-Curie; 1897–1956) French nuclear physicist

1 That one must do some work seriously and must be independent and not merely amuse oneself in life—this our mother has told us always, but never that science was the only career worth following.
Recalling her mother's advice. *A Long Way from Missouri* (Mary Margaret McBride; 1959), ch. 10

Curie, Marie (originally Manya Sklodowska; 1867–1934) Polish-born French chemist and physicist

Quotations about Curie

1 Marie Curie is, of all celebrated beings, the only one whom fame has not corrupted.
Albert Einstein (1879–1955) German-born U.S. physicist. *Madame Curie* (Eve Curie; 1938)

Quotations by Curie

2 I have no dress except the one I wear every day. If you are going to be kind enough to give me one, please let it be practical and dark so that I can put it on afterwards to go to the laboratory.
Referring to a wedding dress. Letter to a friend (1894)

3 One never notices what has been done; one can only see what remains to be done.
Letter to her brother (March 18, 1894)

4 After all, science is essentially international, and it is only through lack of the historical sense that national qualities have been attributed to it.
"Intellectual Co-operation," *Memorandum* (1926)

5 The various reasons we have just enumerated lead us to believe that the new radioactive substance contains a new element to which we propose to give the name of RADIUM.
December 26, 1898. The first report of the new element, in pitchblende. Quoted in *Marie Curie* (Eve Curie; 1938)

6 When one studies strongly radioactive substances special precautions must be taken...Dust, the air of the room, and one's clothes all become radioactive.
Marie Curie coined the word "radioactivity." Quoted in "Notebooks," *Marie Curie* (Eve Curie; 1938)

7 All my life through, the new sights of Nature made me rejoice like a child.
1923. Attrib.

Curran, John Philpot (1750–1817) Irish judge and orator

1 The condition upon which God hath given liberty to man is eternal vigilance; which condition if he break, servitude is at once the consequence of his crime and the punishment of his guilt.
On the Right of Election of Lord Mayor. Speech, Dublin (July 10, 1790), quoted in *Speeches* (John Philpot Curran; 1808)

2 I have never yet heard of a murderer who was not afraid of a ghost.
Said to an Irish peer who hated the sight of the late Irish Parliament building, for whose abolition he had voted. Attrib. *A Book of Irish Quotations* (Sean McMahon, ed.; 1984)

Currie, Edwina (b.1946) British politician and novelist

1 One wants to mutter deeply that apart from having two good legs I also have two good degrees and it is just possible that I do know what I'm talking about.
Remark (November 1986)

2 If someone asks for a soft drink at a party, we no longer think he is a wimp.
Speech (December 1988)

3 Instead of drinking Coca Colas, turn on the tap and drink what the good Lord gave us.
Speech (November 1988)

4 My message to the businessmen of this country when they go abroad on business is that there is one thing above all they can take with them to stop them catching AIDS, and that is the wife.
Speech (February 12, 1987), quoted in *Observer,* London (February 15, 1987)

5 The strongest possible piece of advice I would give to any young woman is: Don't screw around and don't smoke.
Observer, London (April 3, 1988), "Sayings of the Week"

Curtiz, Michael (Mihaly Kertész; 1888–1962) Hungarian-born U.S. film director

1 Bring on the empty horses!
Said during the filming of *The Charge of the Light Brigade*, and referring to riderless horses. David Niven used the remark as the title for the second volume of his autobiography. *Bring on the Empty Horses* (David Niven; 1936)

Curzon, George Nathaniel, Marquess, Lord Curzon of Kedleston (1859–1925) British statesman

1 It is only when you get to see and realize what India is—that she is the strength and the greatness of England—it is only then that you feel that every nerve a man may strain, every energy he may put forward, cannot be devoted to a nobler purpose than keeping tight the cords that hold India to ourselves.
Speech, Southport, England (March 15, 1893)

2 I hesitate to say what the functions of the modern journalist may be; but I imagine that they do not exclude the intelligent anticipation of facts even before they occur.
Speech to the British Parliament (March 29, 1898)

3 Better send them a Papal Bull.
Written in the margin of a British Foreign Office document. The phrase "the monks of Mount Athos were violating their vows" had been misprinted as "...violating their cows." Quoted in *Life of Lord Curzon* (Lawrence Zetland; 1928)

4 I never knew the lower classes had such white skins.
Referring to seeing soldiers bathing. Attrib.

5 Ladies never move.
Said to his second wife, referring to love-making. Attrib.

Cushing, Harvey (Harvey Williams Cushing; 1869–1939) U.S. neurosurgeon

1 There is only one ultimate and effectual preventive for the maladies to which flesh is heir, and that is death.
"Medicine at the Crossroads," *The Medical Career and Other Papers* (1928)

2 A physician is obligated to consider more than a diseased organ, more even than the whole man—he must view the man in his world.
Attrib. *Man Adapting* (Rene Dubos; 1965)

Cuvier, Georges, Baron (Georges Léopold Chrétien Frédéric Dagobert Cuvier; 1769–1832) French zoologist and anatomist

1 Nurse, it was I who discovered that leeches have red blood.
1832. On his deathbed when the nurse came to apply leeches. Attrib.

Cyrano de Bergerac, Savinien (1619–55) French poet, playwright, and soldier

1 Perish the Universe, provided I have my revenge.
La Mort d'Agrippine (1654), Act 4

Dd

D, Chuck U.S. vocalist and writer

1 Rap music is information that has never been delivered to people so young or poor. A rap song has three times as many words as a singing song...Rap music is the invisible TV station that black people never had.
Speech, Black Expo Seminar on Rap, Indiana (July 22, 1989)

2 Don't be satisfied with just selling a song.
Advising fans and artists alike to become politically active. "Who's Gonna Take the Weight?," *Vibe* (February 1994)

d'Abo, Jennifer (Jennifer Mary Victoria d'Abo; b.1945) British business executive

1 I often get invited to boardroom lunches as the token woman; I think it tempting to say something outrageous.
Quoted in *Times*, London (May 3, 1985)

Daché, Lilly (1892?–1989) French-born U.S. fashion designer and writer

1 Glamor is what makes a man ask for your telephone number. But it also is what makes a woman ask for the name of your dressmaker.
1955. *Woman's Home Companion* (July 1955)

Dacier, Anne Lefevre (1654–1720) French writer and translator

1 History does not tempt only by flattery. It leads on to the strengthening of the heart and the fostering of wisdom.
Attrib. *The Meaning of History* (N. Gordon and Joyce Carper; 1991)

Dacre, Harry (1860–1922) British songwriter

1 Daisy, Daisy, give me your answer, do!
I'm half crazy, all for the love of you!
It won't be a stylish marriage,
I can't afford a carriage,
But you'll look sweet upon the seat
Of a bicycle made for two!
Song lyric. "Daisy Bell" (1892)

Dagerman, Stig (1923–54) Swedish writer

1 Creative imagination awakens early. As children we are all "makers." Later, as a rule, we're broken of the habit; so the art of being a creative writer consists, among other things, in not allowing life or people or money to turn us aside from it.
"A Child's Memories," *Our Need of Faith* (Naomi Walford, tr.; 1955)

Dahl, Roald (1916–90) British writer

1 Do you *know* what breakfast cereal is made of? It's made of all those little curly wooden shavings you find in pencil sharpeners!
Charlie and the Chocolate Factory (1964), ch. 27

Dai Wangshu (Dai Meng'ou; 1905–50) Chinese writer

1 My memory is loyal to me, more loyal than my best friends.
"My Memory," *Anthology of Modern Chinese Poetry* (Michelle Yeh, ed., tr.; 1992)

Daladier, Édouard (1884–1970) French prime minister

1 It is a phony war.
The early period of World War II before the evacuation of British troops at Dunkirk (1940) was known in Europe as "the phony war." Speech to Chamber of Deputies, Paris (December 22, 1939)

Dalai Lama (Tenzin Gyatso; b.1935) Tibetan spiritual leader

Quotations about Dalai Lama

1 The Dalai Lama has developed his philosophy of peace from a great reverence for all things living and upon the concept of universal responsibility embracing all mankind as well as nature.
Nobel Peace Prize Committee, Swedish prize-giving committee elected by parliament. *Citation of the Committee of the Nobel Peace Prize* (December 10, 1989)

Quotations by Dalai Lama

2 Any relationship between Tibet and China will have to be based on the principles of equality, respect, trust, and mutual benefit.
Speech on acceptance of a Nobel Prize in peace, Stockholm, Sweden (December 10, 1989)

3 No matter what part of the world we come from, we are all basically the same human beings. We all seek happiness and try to avoid suffering.
Speech on acceptance of a Nobel Prize in peace, Stockholm, Sweden (December 10, 1989)

4 We know our cause is just. Because violence can only breed more violence and suffering, our struggle must remain nonviolent and free of hatred. We are trying to end the suffering of our people, not to inflict suffering on others.
Speech on acceptance of a Nobel Prize in peace, Stockholm, Sweden (December 10, 1989)

5 It is my dream that the entire Tibetan plateau should become a free refuge where humanity and nature can live in peace and in harmonious balance. It would be a place where people from

all over the world could come to seek the true meaning of peace within themselves, away from the tensions and pressures of much of the rest of the world.
Speech, Oslo (December 11, 1989)

6 All six million Tibetans should be on the list of endangered peoples. This struggle is thus my first responsibility.
My Tibet (co-written with Galen Rowell; 1990)

7 Nobody can understand Tibet without some understanding of our religion.
My Tibet (co-written with Galen Rowell; 1990)

8 It is the enemy who can truly teach us to practice the virtues of compassion and tolerance.
Ocean of Wisdom: Guidelines for Living (1989)

9 There should be a balance between material and spiritual progress, a balance achieved by the principles based on love and compassion. Love and compassion are the essence of all religion.
Ocean of Wisdom: Guidelines for Living (1989)

10 Unless the cruel and inhuman treatment of my people is brought to an end, and until they are given their due right to self determination, there will always be obstacles in finding a solution to the Tibetan issue.
Ocean of Wisdom: Guidelines for Living (1989)

Daley, Janet (b.1944) U.S.-born British journalist

1 We are programmed (by biology or conditioning—who cares which?) to respond to social signals and pressures, and so find it almost impossible to be as single-mindedly ruthless as men.
Attrib.

Daley, Richard (Richard Joseph Daley; 1902–76) U.S. politician

1 Gentlemen, get the thing straight once and for all. The policeman isn't there to *create* disorder, the policeman is there to *preserve* disorder.
Said during anti-Vietnam War riots. Speech at the Democratic National Convention (1968)

Daley, William (b.1951) U.S. politician

1 Technology is reshaping this economy and transforming businesses and consumers. This is about more than e-commerce, or e-mail, or e-trades, or e-files. It is about the "e" in economic opportunity.
Quoted in *Business@the Speed of Thought: Using a Digital Nervous System* (Bill Gates, co-written with Collins Hemingway; 1999)

Dalí, Salvador (Salvador Felipe Jacinto Dalí; 1904–89) Spanish surrealist painter

1 Those who do not want to imitate anything, produce nothing.
Dalí by Dalí (1970)

2 I do not paint a portrait to look like the subject, rather does the person grow to look like his portrait.
Diary of a Genius (Richard Howard, tr.; 1966)

3 I'm going to live forever. Geniuses don't die.
1986. *Observer*, London (Jeffrey Care, ed.; 1989), "Sayings of the Eighties"

4 Beauty will be edible or will not exist.
Quoted in *Surrealist Art* (Sarane Alexandrian; 1970)

5 Every good painter who aspires to the creation of genuine masterpieces should first of all marry my wife.
1969. Quoted in *Surrealist Art* (Sarane Alexandrian; 1970)

6 It's either easy or impossible.
Reply when asked if he found it hard to paint a picture. Attrib.

Dalton, John (1766–1844) British scientist

1 This paper will no doubt be found interesting by those who take an interest in it.
Said on many occasions when chairing scientific meetings. Attrib. *Recollections and Reflections* (J. J. Thomson; 1890)

Daly, Daniel (1874–1937) U.S. Marine sergeant

1 Come on, you sons of bitches! Do you want to live forever?
Said during Allied resistance at Belleau Wood. Remark (June 14, 1918)

Daly, John (b.1966) U.S. golfer

1 I wasn't this nervous playing golf when I was drinking. It's the first tournament I've won on the PGA Tour in a sober manner, so it's a great feeling knowing I can do it sober. I don't think two years ago I could have pulled this off.
Independent, London (May 10, 1994)

Daly, Mary (b.1928) U.S. feminist and theologian

1 The liberation of language is rooted in the liberation of ourselves.
Beyond God the Father, Toward a Philosophy of Women's Liberation (1973)

2 I had explained that a woman's asking for equality in the church would be comparable to a black person's demanding equality in the Ku Klux Klan.
The Church and the Second Sex (1968)

Daly, T. A. (1871–1948) U.S. poet

1 Philadelphia—most colonial of our true Colonial Dames—
Curtseying, leads the ceremonial March of quaint and State-ly names:
Bethlehem, Emmaus, Kingsessing,
Libitz, Darby, Conoquenessing,...
Gold, Lycoming,
Wissinoming,
Mustard, Muse, Morganza, Muff—
Oh, but surely that's enough!
Replying to an assertion in the *Los Angeles Times* that no other state could match California for "place-names rich in rhyme and rhythm." "Pennsylvanian Places," *Late Lark Singing* (1946), st. 2

Damian, Peter, Saint (Pietro Damiani; 1007–72) Italian bishop

1 As these two, the kingdom and the priesthood, are brought together by divine mystery, so are their two heads, by the force of mutual loves; the King may be found in the Roman pontiff, and the Roman pontiff be found in the King.
Written following the enthronement of Pope Alexander II. *Disceptatio Synodalis* (1061)

Damien, Father (Joseph Damien de Veuster; 1840–89) Belgian missionary

1 What would you do with it? It is full of leprosy.
1889. When asked on his deathbed whether he would leave another priest his mantle, like Elijah. *Memoirs of an Aesthete* (Harold Acton; 1970)

Dana, Richard Henry (1815–82) U.S. sailor, writer, and lawyer

1 It is always observable that the physical and exact sciences are the last to suffer under despotisms.
To Cuba and Back (1859)

2 There is not so pitiable an object in the world as a landsman beginning a sailor's life.
Two Years Before the Mast (1840)

Dando, Malcolm British author

1 It would be quite extraordinary if a major new development in science was *not* applied in warfare, and there is probably little that we can do to prevent it.
Biological Warfare in the 21st Century (1994)

Dangerfield, Rodney (originally Jacob Cohen; b.1921) U.S. actor and comedian

1 I can't get no respect.
Comedy catchphrase. Attrib.

Daniel, Samuel (1562–1619) English poet and playwright

1 Unless above himself he can
Erect himself, how poor a thing is man!
"To the Ladie Margret, Countesse of Cumberland" (1600?), quoted in *The Complete Works in Verse and Prose of Samuel Daniel* (Rev. Alexander B. Grosart, ed.; 1885), bk. 2, st. 12

2 Love is a sickness full of woes,
All remedies refusing;
A plant that with most cutting grows,
Most barren with best using.
Why so?
More we enjoy it, more it dies;
If not enjoyed, it sighing cries,
Hey ho.
Hymen's Triumph (1615)

3 This many-headed monster, Multitude.
The Civil Wars (1595–1609), bk. 2, st. 13

Daniels, R. G. (Robert George Reginald Daniels; 1916–93) British magistrate

1 The most delightful advantage of being bald—one can hear snowflakes.
Observer, London (July 11, 1976), "Sayings of the Week"

Dante Alighieri (1265–1321) Italian poet

Quotations about Dante Alighieri

1 All right, then, I'll say it: Dante makes me sick.
Lope de Vega (1562–1635) Spanish playwright and poet. Said on being informed he was about to die. Attrib. (1635)

Quotations by Dante Alighieri

2 Midway along the path of our life.
"Inferno," *The Divine Comedy* (1307?–21?), can. 1, l. 1

3 The dear and kindly paternal image.
"Inferno," *The Divine Comedy* (1307?–21?), can. 15, l. 83

4 Consider your origins: you were not made to live as brutes, but to follow virtue and knowledge.
"Inferno," *The Divine Comedy* (1307?–21?), can. 26, l. 118

5 In His will is our peace.
"Paradiso," *The Divine Comedy* (1307?–21?), can. 3, l. 85

6 And ere it turned full circle, a new throng
Within a second circle closed it round,
And motion matched with motion, song with song.
Perhaps influenced by circle dances, such as one described in Florence, with monks alternating with choir boys on the inner circle, then the young clergy, and finally citizens on the outside circle. "Paradiso," *The Divine Comedy* (1307?–21?), can. 12, ll. 4–6, quoted in *World History of the Dance* (Curt Sachs; 1937)

7 And as a lady turns her when she dances,
With feet close to the ground and to each other,
And one before the other scarce advances.
Describing the woman's *aere* (or *aiere*), the Italian dance term for bearing or gesture. "Purgatorio," *The Divine Comedy* (1307?–21?), can. 28, ll. 52–54, quoted in *World History of the Dance* (Curt Sachs; 1937)

8 Pure and disposed to mount unto the stars.
"Purgatorio," *The Divine Comedy* (1307?–21?), can. 33, l. 145

Danton, Georges Jacques (1759–94) French revolutionary leader

1 Boldness, and again boldness, and always boldness!
September 2, 1792. Speech to the French Legislative Committee of General Defense, Paris, *Le Moniteur* (September 4, 1792)

2 Thou wilt show my head to the people: it is worth showing.
April 5, 1794. Said as he mounted the scaffold. *The French Revolution* (Thomas Carlyle; 1837), vol. 3, bk. 6, ch. 2

Darling, Charles John, Baron (1849–1936) British judge and writer

1 A timid question will always receive a confident answer.
Scintillae Juris (1877)

2 If a man stays away from his wife for seven years, the law presumes the separation to have killed him; yet according to our daily experience, it might well prolong his life.
Scintillae Juris (1877)

3 Much truth is spoken, that more may be concealed.
Scintillae Juris (1877)

4 Perjury is often bold and open. It is truth that is shamefaced—as, indeed, in many cases is no more than decent.
Scintillae Juris (1877)

5 The Law of England is a very strange one; it cannot compel anyone to tell the truth...But what the Law can do is to give you seven years for not telling the truth.
The Life of Lord Darling (Derek Walker Smith; 1938), ch. 27

6 The law-courts of England are open to all men, like the doors of the Ritz Hotel.
Attrib.

Darnton, Robert (Robert Choate Darnton; b.1939) U.S. historian

1 Historians like to nail things down, not pry them loose.
"The Symbolic Element in History," *Journal of Modern History* (March 1986)

Darrow, Clarence (Clarence Seward Darrow; 1857–1938) U.S. lawyer

1 We know life is futile. A man who considers that his life is of very wonderful importance is awfully close to a padded cell.
Lecture, University of Chicago (1929)

2 I do not consider it an insult but rather a compliment to be called an agnostic. I do not pretend to know where many ignorant men are sure.
Speech at the trial of John Scopes for teaching evolution in Tennessee (July 13, 1925)

3 To think is to differ.
Speech at the trial of John Scopes for teaching evolution in Tennessee (July 13, 1925)

4 Hanging men in our country jails does not prevent murder. It makes murderers.
Speech to prisoners, Cook County Jail (1902)

5 The world is made up for the most part of morons and natural tyrants, sure of themselves, strong in their own opinions, never doubting anything.
Personal Liberty (1928)

6 I go to a better tailor than any of you and pay more for my clothes. The only difference is that you probably don't sleep in yours.
Reply when teased by reporters about his appearance. *2500 Anecdotes* (Edmund Fuller; 1943)

7 When I was a boy I was told that anybody could become President of the United States. I am beginning to believe it.
Quoted in *Clarence Darrow for the Defense* (Irving Stone; 1941), ch. 6

8 The history of the past is a record of man's cruel inhumanity to man—of one imperfect vessel accusing and shattering another for the faults of both...There might be some excuse if man could turn from the frail, cracked vessels, and bring to trial the great potter for the imperfect work of his hand.
Quoted in *The Meaning of History* (N. Gordon and Joyce Carper; 1991)

Darwin, Charles (Charles Robert Darwin; 1809–82) British naturalist

Quotations about Darwin

1 It is no secret that...there are many to whom Mr. Darwin's death is a wholly irreparable loss. And this not merely because of his wonderfully genial, simple, and generous nature; his cheerful and animated conversation, and the infinite variety and accuracy of his information; but because the more one knew of him, the more he seemed the incorporated ideal of a man of science.
T. H. Huxley (1825–95) British biologist. *Nature* (1882)

Quotations by Darwin

2 Vivisection...is justifiable for real investigations on physiology; but not for mere damnable and detestable curiosity.
Letter (March 22, 1871)

3 I must begin with a good body of facts and not from a principle (in which I always suspect some fallacy) and then as much deduction as you please.
Letter to J. Fiske (December 8, 1874)

4 It may be said that natural selection is daily and hourly scrutinizing, throughout the world, every variation, even the slightest; rejecting that which is bad, preserving and adding up all that is good; silently and insensibly working, wherever and whenever opportunity offers, at the improvement of each organic being in relation to its organic and inorganic conditions of life.
On the Origin of Species by Means of Natural Selection (1859)

5 We will now discuss in a little more detail the Struggle for Existence.
On the Origin of Species by Means of Natural Selection (1859), ch. 3

6 It is generally admitted that with woman the powers of intuition, of rapid perception, and perhaps of imitation, are more strongly marked than in man; but some, at least, of these faculties are characteristic of the lower races, and therefore of a past and lower state of civilisation.
The Descent of Man (1871)

7 The chief distinction in the intellectual powers of the two sexes is shewn by man attaining to a higher eminence, in whatever he takes up, than woman can attain—whether requiring deep thought, reason, or imagination, or merely the use of the senses and hands.
The Descent of Man (1871)

8 The main conclusion arrived at in this work, namely, that man is descended from some lowly organized form, will, I regret to think, be highly distasteful to many. But there can hardly be a doubt that we are descended from barbarians.
The Descent of Man (1871)

9 Any animal whatever, endowed with well-marked social instincts, the parental and filial affections being here included, would inevitably acquire a moral sense or conscience, as soon as its intellectual powers had become as well, or nearly as well developed, as in man.
His reply to those who maintained that human conscience was implanted by God at the Creation. *The Descent of Man* (1871)

10 Man is developed from an ovule, about 125th of an inch in diameter, which differs in no respect from the ovules of other animals.
The Descent of Man (1871), ch. 1

11 The highest possible stage in moral culture is when we recognize that we ought to control our thoughts.
The Descent of Man (1871), ch. 4

12 We must, however, acknowledge, as it seems to me, that man with all his noble qualities...still bears in his bodily frame the indelible stamp of his lowly origin.
Closing words. *The Descent of Man* (1871), ch. 21

13 Every new body of discovery is mathematical in form, because there is no other guidance we can have.
Quoted in *Mathematical Maxims and Minims* (N. Rose, ed.; 1988)

Darwin, Charles Galton, Sir (1887–1962) British physicist

1 The evolution of the human race will not be accomplished in the ten thousand years of tame animals, but in the million years of wild animals, because man is and will always be a wild animal.
The Next Ten Million Years (1952), ch. 4

Darwin, Erasmus (1731–1802) British physician, biologist, and poet

1 No, Sir, because I have time to think before I speak, and don't ask impertinent questions.
Reply when asked whether he found his stammer inconvenient. "Reminiscences of My Father's Everyday Life," *Autobiography, Charles Darwin* (Sir Francis Darwin, ed.; 1877), Appendix 1

2 The mass starts into a million suns;
Earths round each sun with quick explosions burst,
And second planets issue from the first.
The first proposal of a "big bang" theory of the universe. *The Botanic Garden* (1789–91)

3 Soon shall thy arm, unconquer'd steam! afar
Drag the slow barge, or drive the rapid car;
Or on wide-waving wings expanded bear
The flying chariot through the field of air.
The Botanic Garden (1789–91), pt. 1, can. 1, l. 289

4 A fool...is a man who never tried an experiment in his life.
Quoted in Letter to Sophy Ruxton (Maria Edgeworth; March 9, 1792)

Darwin, Francis, Sir (1848–1925) British scientist

1 But in science the credit goes to the man who convinces the world, not to the man to whom the idea first occurs.
First Galton Lecture before the Eugenics Society, *Eugenics Review* (1914), April 1914, 6: 1

Darwish, Mahmoud (b.1942) Palestinian poet

1 This land absorbs the skins of martyrs.
This land promises wheat and stars.
Worship it!
We are its salt and its water.
We are its wound, but a wound that fights.
"Diary of a Palestinian Wound," *Modern Arabic Poetry* (Salma Khadra Jayyusi, ed.; 1987), no. 11

2 Where should we go after the last frontiers,
where should the birds fly after the last sky?
"Earth Scrapes Us," *Modern Arabic Poetry* (Salma Khadra Jayyusi, ed.; 1987), no. 1

3 We have a country full of words. Speak, speak so that I can rest my road against a rock.
We have a country full of words. Speak, speak, so that we may know what is the limit of this travelling.
"We Travel like Other People," *Modern Arabic Poetry* (Salma Khadra Jayyusi, ed.; 1987), ll. 9–10

4 Black tulips in my heart,
flames on my lips:
from which forest did you come to me,
all you crosses of anger?
"To the Reader," *When the Words Burn* (John Mikhail Asfour, ed., tr.; 1988), ll. 1–4

Das, Kamala (b.1934) Indian writer and poet

1 After the marriage when the young man asked her if she had loved anyone she said yes I have I have loved my english teacher miss laha and instead of being jealous he threw back his head and laughed revealing teeth all darkened by cigarette and iron tonics.
"Running Away from Home," *Panorama* (Mulk Raj Anand and S. Balu Rao, eds.; 1986)

2 When I die
do not throw the meat and bones away
but pile them up
and
let them tell
by their smell
what life was worth
on this earth
what love was worth
in the end.
"A Request," *Women Poets of India* (Pranab Bandyopadhyay, ed.; 1977)

Daudet, Alphonse (Louis Marie Alphonse Daudet; 1840–97) French writer

1 During the day beings live, at night things live.
"Les Étoiles," *Lettres de mon moulin* (1869)

2 Where would the merit be if heroes were never afraid?
Tartarin de Tarascon (1872), episode 3, ch. 5

Davenant, Charles (1656–1714) English political economist

1 Custom, that unwritten law,
By which the people keep even kings in awe.
Circe (1677), Act 2, Scene 3

Davenant, William, Sir (1606–68) English poet and playwright

1 For I must go where lazy Peace
Will hide her drowsy head;
And, for the sport of Kings, increase
The number of the Dead.
"The Soldier Going to the Field" (1673)

Davenport, Guy (Guy Mattison Davenport; b.1927) U.S. writer, translator, and educator

1 A dictionary is a vocabulary restricted by the concept of diction.
"Dictionary," *The Geography of the Imagination* (1984)

2 There are pioneer Bibles in the library of the University of Texas bound in Indian skin...A *neat idea!* Something to go look at on our vacation, Bibles bound in Indian skin. Genocide may well be an American invention.
"The Indian and His Image," *The Geography of the Imagination* (1984)

3 The Indian's subtlest enemy was, and probably still is,

humanitarianism bred of Enlightenment hope for reason in all things and universal *bon ton.*
Bon ton is French for sophisticated manners. "The Indian and His Image," *The Geography of the Imagination* (1984)

4 Metric derives from the dance; the music of poetry is therefore addressed to and originates in the muscles...Like music and painting, it arises from the total organism.
"Where Poems Come From," *The Geography of the Imagination* (1984)

5 Poetry is the voice of a poet at its birth, the voice of a people in its ultimate fulfilment as a successful and useful work of art.
"Where Poems Come From," *The Geography of the Imagination* (1984)

David, Jacques-Louis (Jacques-Louis Jules David; 1748–1825) French painter

1 To give a body and a perfect form to your thought, this alone is what it is to be an artist.
1796. Statement to his pupils, *Le peintre Louis David 1748–1825: Souvenirs et documents inédits* (1880)

David, Larry U.S. television producer, screenwriter, and actor

1 You're treating your body like an amusement park!
As George, recounting what his mother said on discovering him masturbating. "The Contest," *Seinfeld* (November 1992)

Davidson, Donald (b.1917) U.S. philosopher

1 Conceptual relativism is a heady and exotic doctrine, or would be if we could make good sense of it. The trouble is, as so often in philosophy, it is hard to improve intelligibility while retaining the excitement.
Inquiries into Truth and Interpretation (1984)

2 The most obvious semantic difference between simile and metaphor is all similes are true and most metaphors are false...We say Mr. S. is like a pig because we know he isn't one.
Inquiries into Truth and Interpretation (1984)

Davie, Donald (Donald Alfred Davie; 1922–95) British poet, critic, and translator

1 Hearing one saga, we enact the next.
We please our elders when we sit enthralled;
But then they're puzzled; and at last they're vexed
To have their youths so avidly recalled.
"Remembering the 'Thirties" (1955), quoted in *Oxford Book of Twentieth-Century Verse* (Philip Larkin, ed.; 1973)

Davies, John, Sir (1569–1626) English poet and jurist

1 Skill comes so slow, and life so fast doth fly,
We learn so little and forget so much.
"Nosce Teipsum" (1599), st. 19

2 This oppression did of force and necessity make the Irish a craftie people, for such as are oppressed and live in slavery are ever put to their shifts.
1612? Quoted in *The Oxford Illustrated History of Ireland* (R. F. Foster, ed.; 1989)

Davies, Norman (b.1939) British historian and writer

1 The Greeks do not appear either licentious or puritanical so much as practical and open-minded. Their world was full of explicit erotica, about which they were sublimely unembarrassed.
Europe: A History (1996), ch. 2

2 The "scramble for Africa" took place on the assumption that the land and the peoples were there for the taking.
Referring to the efforts by European nations to colonize all of Africa's land and people during the 19th and 20th centuries. As well as involving the genocide of African peoples, the struggle increased antagonisms between the European powers. *Europe: A History* (1996), ch. 10

3 All historians must tell their tale convincingly, or be ignored.
Europe: A History (1996), introduction

Davies, Paul (Paul Charles William Davies; b.1946) British-born Australian physicist

1 Chaos evidently provides us with a bridge between the laws of physics and the laws of chance.
New Scientist Guide to Chaos (1991)

2 Every atom is offered billions of trajectories by the quantum randomization, and in the many-worlds theory it accepts them all, so every conceivable atomic arrangement will come about somewhere.
Other Worlds: Space, Superspace and the Quantum Universe (1980)

Davies, Ray (Raymond Douglas Davies; b.1944) British pop musician

1 One week he's in polka dots, the next week he's in stripes.
'Cos he's a dedicated follower of fashion.
Song lyric. "Dedicated Follower of Fashion" (1966)

Davies, Rhys (1903–78) Welsh novelist and short-story writer

1 Sewn on, so to speak, like a patch of different material to England's robe of state, Wales nevertheless has succeeded in retaining its own texture and colour.
The Story of Wales (1943)

Davies, Robertson (William Robertson Davies; 1913–95) Canadian novelist and critic

1 There's more to marriage than four bare legs in a blanket.
A Jig for the Gypsy (1954)

2 All education is bad which is not self-education.
A Voice from the Attic (1960)

3 As a general rule, people marry most happily with their own kind. The trouble lies in the fact that people usually marry at an age where they do not really know what their own kind is.
A Voice from the Attic (1960)

4 Our age has robbed millions of the simplicity of ignorance, and has so far failed to lift them to simplicity of wisdom.
A Voice from the Attic (1960)

5 To pretend to be less intelligent than one is deceives nobody and begets dislike, for intelligence cannot be hidden; like a cough, it will out, stifle it how you may.
A Voice from the Attic (1960)

6 Children, having decided that a joke is funny, go on repeating it, laughing more loudly each time, until they collapse in hysteria. The mental age of a man might be gauged by observing how often he can laugh at the same joke.
Samuel Marchbanks' Almanack (1967)

Davies, Scrope (Scrope Berdmore Davies; 1783?–1852) British dandy

1 Babylon in all its desolation is a sight not so awful as that of the human mind in ruins.
Letter to Thomas Raikes (May 25, 1835), quoted in *Journal, 1831–1847* (T. Raikes, ed.; 1856), vol. 2

Davies, Sharron (Sharron Elizabeth Davies; b.1962) British swimmer and model

1 I've got a career that depends a lot on being tall and blonde, and if I ended up growing a beard I don't think it would do me much good.
Explaining why she did not take performance-enhancing drugs. Interview (1989)

Davies, W. H. (William Henry Davies; 1871–1940) British poet

1 A rainbow and a cuckoo's song
May never come together again;
May never come
This side the tomb.
"A Great Time" (1914)

2 The simple bird that thinks two notes a song.
Referring to the cuckoo. "April's Charms" (1916)

3 It was the Rainbow gave thee birth,
And left thee all her lovely hues.
"The Kingfisher" (1910)

4 I love thee for a heart that's kind—
Not for the knowledge in thy mind.
"Sweet Stay-at-Home," *Foliage* (1913)

5 Sweet Stay-at-Home, sweet Well-content.
"Sweet Stay-at-Home," *Foliage* (1913)

6 Teetotallers lack the sympathy and generosity of men that drink.
Introduction (1922)

7 What is this life if, full of care,
We have no time to stand and stare?
"Leisure," *Songs of Joy* (1911)

Davis, Adelle (Daisie Adelle Davis; 1904–74) U.S. nutritionist and writer

1 Nutritional research, like a modern star of Bethlehem, brings hope that sickness need not be a part of life.
"The Great Adelle Davis Controversy," *New York Times Magazine* (May 20, 1973)

Davis, Angela (b.1944) U.S. civil rights activist, educator, and writer

1 Jails and prisons are designed to break human beings, to convert the population into specimens in a zoo—obedient to our keepers, but dangerous to each other.
Angela Davis: An Autobiography (1974)

2 One small twist of fate and I might have drowned in the muck of poverty and disease and illiteracy. That is why I never felt I had the right to look upon myself as being any different from my sisters and brothers who did *all* the suffering, for *all* of us.
Angela Davis: An Autobiography (1974)

3 Racism, in the first place, is a weapon used by the wealthy to increase the profits they bring in—by paying Black workers less for their work.
Angela Davis: An Autobiography (1974)

4 The psychological impact of anti-communism on ordinary people in this country runs very deep. There is something about the word "communism" that, for the unenlightened, evokes not only the enemy, but also something immoral, something dirty.
Angela Davis: An Autobiography (1974)

5 When white people are indiscriminately viewed as the enemy, it is virtually impossible to develop a political solution.
Angela Davis: An Autobiography (1974)

6 The offense of the political prisoner is his political boldness.
If They Come in the Morning... (1971)

7 Black women have had the burden or the privilege of being spokespersons for all the oppressed in this society. And sometimes, of course, black women have just argued for the right to be tired.
I Dream a World: Portraits of Black Women Who Changed America (Brian Lanker; 1989)

Davis, Bette (Ruth Elizabeth Davis; 1908–89) U.S. actor

1 Don't let's ask for the moon! We have the stars!
Said by Bette Davis in the motion picture which was based on Oliver Higgins Prouty's 1941 book of the same name. *Now Voyager* (Oliver Higgins Prouty; 1942)

2 Fasten your seatbelts. It's going to be a bumpy night.
All About Eve (Joseph Mankiewicz; 1950)

3 But my biggest problem all my life was men. I never met one yet who could compete with the image the public made out of Bette Davis.
Quoted in *Conversations in the Raw* (Rex Reed; 1969)

4 I see—she's the original good time that was had by all.
Referring to a starlet of the time. *The Filmgoer's Book of Quotes* (Leslie Halliwell; 1973)

5 I am a woman meant for a man, but I never found a man who could compete.
Attrib.

6 The male ego with few exceptions is elephantine to start with.
Attrib.

7 When a man gives his opinion he's a man. When a woman gives her opinion she's a bitch.
Attrib. (1989)

8 Pray to God and say the lines.
Advice to the actor Celeste Holm. Attrib.

Davis, Bob (b.1943) U.S. business executive and educator

1 Praise progress—it's at least a moving target.
Quoted in *Management of Organizational Behavior* (Kenneth H. Blanchard and Paul Hersey; 1993)

Davis, Clive U.S. record company executive

1 Here I was...at a major record company on the New York Stock Exchange signing...artists whose appeal was almost inherently based on eschewing materialism.
Quoted in "Clive Davis," *Off the Record: An Oral History of Popular Music* (Joe Smith; 1988)

Davis, Elmer (Elmer Holmes Davis; 1890–1958) U.S. writer and broadcaster

1 The first and great commandment is, Don't let them scare you.
But We Were Born Free (1954), ch. 1

Davis, Jefferson (1808–89) U.S. Confederate president

1 All we ask is to be let alone.
Inaugural Address as President of the Confederate States of America (February 18, 1861)

Davis, Miles (1926–91) U.S. jazz musician, composer, and trumpeter

Quotations about Davis

1 He is so honest about music that he wants to catch the kernel of creativity as it's being created. If you rehearse too much, you're not going to get it.
Herbie Hancock (b.1940) U.S. jazz musician. Herbie Hancock worked with Miles Davis during the 1960s. Quoted in "Herbie Hancock," *Off the Record: An Oral History of Popular Music* (Joe Smith; 1988)

Quotations by Davis

2 I usually don't buy jazz records. They make me tired and depressed.
1982. *Jazz Review* (December 1958)

Davis, Philip J. (b.1923) U.S. mathematician

1 One began to hear it said that World War I was the chemists' war, World War II was the physicists' war, World War III (may it never come) will be the mathematicians' war.
The Mathematical Experience (co-written with Reuben Hersh; 1981)

Davis, Sammy, Jr. (1925–90) U.S. singer and entertainer

1 Being a star has made it possible for me to get insulted in places where the average Negro could never hope to go and get insulted.
Yes I Can (1965)

2 Fame creates its own standard. A guy who twitches his lip is just another guy with a lip twitch—unless he's Humphrey Bogart.
Yes I Can (1965)

3 I gotta be me.
Attrib.

4 I'm a colored, one-eyed Jew.
Said when asked what his handicap was during a game of golf. Attrib.

Davis, Steve (b.1957) British snooker player

1 Sport is cut and dried. You always know when you succeed...You are not an actor; you don't wonder "did my performance go down all right?" You've lost.
Attrib.

Davis, Thomas (1814–45) Irish writer and nationalist

Quotations about Davis

1 He shall not hear the bittern cry
In the wild sky, where he is lain,
Nor voices of the sweeter birds
Above the wailing of the rain.
Francis Ledwidge (1891–1917) Irish poet. Referring to Irish nationalist Thomas Davis, who called for Irish autonomy. "Lament for the Death of Thomas McDonagh" (1916–17), ll. 1–4

Quotations by Davis

2 And then I prayed I yet might see
Our fetters rent in twain,
And Ireland, long a province, be
A Nation once again.
"A Nation Once Again" (1846)

3 Be my epitaph writ on my country's mind,
"He served his country and loved his kind".
Quoted in "My Grave," *A Book of Irish Quotations* (Sean McMahon, ed.; 1984)

Davy, Humphry, Sir (1778–1829) British chemist

1 The wealth of our island may be diminished, but the strength of mind of the people cannot easily pass away...We cannot lose our liberty, because we cannot cease to think.
Letter to Thomas Poole (August 28, 1807)

2 The finest collection of frames I ever saw.
When asked what he thought of the Paris art galleries. Attrib.

Davys, Mary (1674–1732) English playwright

1 When Women write, the Criticks, now-a-days
Are ready, e'er they see, to damn their Plays;
Wit, as the Men's Prerogative, they claim,
And with one Voice, the bold Invader blame.
The Self-Rival: A Comedy (1725), prologue

Dawkins, Richard (Clinton Richard Dawkins; b.1941) British ethologist

1 We are survival machines—robot vehicles blindly programmed to preserve the selfish molecules known as genes. This is a truth which still fills me with astonishment.
The Selfish Gene (1976)

Dawson, Christopher, Professor (1889–1970) U.S. academic

1 The great curse of our modern society is not so much the lack of money as the fact that the lack of money condemns a man to a squalid and incomplete existence.
The Modern Dilemma (1932)

Day, Clarence Shepard (1874–1935) U.S. writer

1 Imagine the Lord talking French! Aside from a few odd words in Hebrew, I took it completely for granted that God had never spoken anything but the most dignified English.
"Father Interferes," *Life with Father* (1935)

2 "If you don't go to other men's funerals," he told Father stiffly, "they won't go to yours."
"Father Plans," *Life with Father* (1935)

3 Will and wisdom are both mighty leaders. Our times worship will.
"Humpty Dumpty and Adam," *The Crow's Nest* (1921)

4 It is fair to judge people by the rights they will sacrifice the most for.
This Simian World (1920)

5 The artistic impulse seems not to wish to produce finished work. It certainly deserts us halfway, after the idea is born; and if we go on, art is labor.
This Simian World (1920)

6 When eras die, their legacies
Are left to strange police.
Professors in New England guard
The glory that was Greece.
"Thoughts on Deaths," *Thoughts Without Words* (1928)

Day, Graham, Sir (Judson Graham Day; b.1933) British business executive

1 If you love your customer to death, you can't go wrong.
Daily Express, London (December 31, 1987)

2 For me the ideology is not the private sector, it is the avoidance of people eating at the public trough.
Interview, *Observer*, London (March 6, 1988)

3 I work on a "screw you" level. As long as I have enough resources to say "screw you" to anyone, that's fine.
Interview, *Sunday Times*, London (May 7, 1989)

4 When business is bad, always start weeding out at the top.
Interview, *Sunday Times*, London (May 7, 1989)

5 If I was given the choice of cleaning the floor and no job at all, I would say "pass me the goddam broom".
Sun, London (March 6, 1986)

Day, Robin, Sir (b.1923) British journalist and broadcaster

1 Abuse is in order, but it is best if it is supported by argument.
Election Call, BBC Radio (1987)

Dayan, Moshe (1915–81) Israeli general and archaeologist

1 Whenever you accept our views we shall be in full agreement with you.
Said to Cyrus Vance during Arab-Israeli negotiations. *Observer*, London (August 14, 1977), "Sayings of the Week"

2 If we lose this war, I'll start another in my wife's name.
Attrib.

Day-Lewis, Cecil (1904–72) Irish-born British writer

1 And when the Treaty emptied the British jails,
A haggard woman returned and Dublin went wild to greet her.
But it was still not enough: an iota
Of compromise, she cried, and the Cause fails.
Referring to Constance Markievicz, who, having fought in the Easter Uprising in Dublin (1916), was sentenced to death, and later reprieved in the general amnesty of 1917. In 1918 she became the first British woman member of parliament, but refused to take her seat. She was elected to the first Irish national assembly in 1919. "Remembering Con Markievicz" (1970)

2 A poet is not a public figure. A poet should be read and not seen.
Observer, London (January 7, 1968), "Sayings of the Week"

3 It is the logic of our times,
No subject for immortal verse—
That we who lived by honest dreams
Defend the bad against the worse.
Where are the War Poets? (1943)

4 Now the peak of summer's past, the sky is overcast
And the love we swore would last for an age seems deceit.
Hornpipe (1943)

Deakin, Ralph (1888–1952) British journalist

1 Nothing is news until it has appeared in *The Times*.
Attrib.

Dean, John (b.1938) U.S. presidential counsel

1 We have a cancer within, close to the Presidency, that is growing. It is growing daily.
1973. From a taped conversation with the president, Richard Nixon. Referring to the Watergate scandal. *The White House Transcripts* (1974)

Deane, Seamus (Seamus Francis Deane; b.1940) Irish writer and academic

1 If you ever met anyone with one green and one brown eye we were to cross ourselves, for that was a human child that had been taken over by the fairies. The brown eye was the sign it had been human.
Reading in the Dark (1996), ch. 1

2 My chief desire is to let you see that there is that which is rational, that which is irrational and that which is non-rational—and to leave you weltering in that morass thereafter.
Reading in the Dark (1996), ch. 5

de Benedetti, Carlo (b.1934) Italian business executive

1 Exports are becoming obsolete, because they are too slow. Marketers today must sell the latest product everywhere at once and that means producing locally.
Observer, London (February 14, 1988)

de Blank, Joost (1908–68) Dutch-born British churchman

1 Christ in this country would quite likely have been arrested under the Suppression of Communism Act.
Referring to South Africa. *Observer*, London (October 27, 1963), "Sayings of the Week"

2 I suffer from an incurable disease—colour blindness.
Attrib.

de Bono, Edward (Edward Francis Charles Publius de Bono; b.1933) Maltese-born British psychologist and writer

1 As computers come to provide wonderful tools for information processing the emphasis is shifting back to the importance of ideas...the ideas that make sense of the computer output.
Lateral Thinking for Management (1971)

2 Lateral thinking is a way of using information in order to bring about creativity.
Lateral Thinking for Management (1971)

3 Man owes his success to his creativity. No one doubts the need for it. It is most useful in good times and essential in bad.
Lateral Thinking for Management (1971)

4 Unhappiness is best defined as the difference between our talents and our expectations.
Observer, London (June 12, 1977), "Sayings of the Week"

5 Values are determined by systems, contexts and circumstances.
Parallel Thinking: From Socratic to de Bono Thinking (1994)

6 Most people...are put off science because maths is the gateway and they can't handle it. What we should be teaching is operational maths because, in general, the maths we need to carry out science is pretty straightforward.
Times, London (September 24, 1990)

7 Western traditions of education have emphasized knowledge analysis, description and debate. They all have a part to play, but today there is a whole vast aspect of doing that has just been left out. Operacy is what keeps society going.
Times, London (September 24, 1990)

de Botton, Alain (b.1969) British writer

1 There is always the option of being emotionally lazy, that is, of quoting.
Essays in Love (1994)

Debs, Eugene Victor (1855–1926) U.S. labor leader, socialist, and pacifist

1 The purpose of the Allies is exactly the purpose of the Central Powers, and that is the conquest and spoliation of the weaker nations that have always been the purpose of war.
Speech, Canton, Ohio (June 16, 1918)

2 When great changes occur in history, when great principles are involved, as a rule the majority are wrong. The minority are right.
1918. From a speech at his trial for sedition in Cleveland, Ohio. *Speeches* (1928)

3 It is the government that should ask me for a pardon.
When released from prison (1921) on the orders of President Harding after being jailed for sedition (1918). *The People's Almanac* (D. Wallechinsky; 1921)

Debussy, Claude (Claude Achille Debussy; 1862–1918) French composer

Quotations about Debussy

1 I have already heard it. I had better not go: I will start to get accustomed to it and finally like it.
Nikolay Rimsky-Korsakov (1844–1908) Russian composer. Referring to music by Claude Debussy. Quoted in *Conversations with Stravinsky* (Igor Stravinsky and Robert Craft; 1979)

Quotations by Debussy

2 I am more and more convinced that music, by its very nature, is something that cannot be poured into a tight and traditional form. It is made up of colors and rhythms.
Letter to J. Durand (September 3, 1907)

3 A century of airplanes deserves its own music. As there are no precedents I must create anew.
La Revue S. I. M. (1913)

4 Music is a sum total of scattered forces.
Monsieur Croche, antidilettante (1921)

5 The attraction of the virtuoso for the public is very like that of the circus for the crowd. There is always the hope that something dangerous may happen.
Monsieur Croche, antidilettante (1921)

6 You can't order the masses to love beauty any more than you can reasonably insist that they must walk on their hands.
Monsieur Croche, antidilettante (1921)

7 I love music passionately, and because I love it I try to free it from the barren conditions that stifle it.
Attrib.

8 Music is the arithmetic of sounds as optics is the geometry of light.
Attrib.

Decatur, Stephen (1779–1820) U.S. naval officer

1 Our country! In her intercourse with foreign nations, may she always be in the right; but our country, right or wrong.
Speech, Norfolk, Virginia (1816), quoted in *Life of Stephen Decatur* (A. S. Mackenzie; 1846)

De Chirico, Giorgio (1888–1978) Italian painter

1 Architecture completes nature.
The Sense of Architecture (1920)

Dee, John (1527–1608) English mathematician and alchemist

1 Most excellent Royall Majesty, of our Elizabeth sitting at the Helm of this Imperiall Monarchy: or rather, at the Helm of the Imperiall Ship.
General and Rare Memorials pertaining to the Perfect Arte of Navigation (1577)

Dee, Ruby (b.1923) U.S. actor, writer, and civil rights activist

1 Classism and greed are making insignificant all other kinds of isms.
I Dream a World: Portraits of Black Women Who Changed America (Brian Lanker; 1989)

Deffand, Marie du, Marquise du Deffand (Marie de Vichy-Chamrond; 1697–1780) French literary hostess

1 The distance doesn't matter; it is only the first step that is the most difficult.
Referring to the legend of Saint Denis, who is traditionally believed to have carried his severed head for six miles after his execution. Letter to d'Alembert (July 7, 1763)

Defoe, Daniel (1660–1731) English novelist and journalist

1 Self-destruction is the effect of cowardice in the highest extreme.
An Essay upon Projects (1697), "Of Projectors"

2 The best of men cannot suspend their fate:
The good die early, and the bad die late.
Character of the late Dr. S. Annesley (1697)

3 We lov'd the doctrine for the teacher's sake.
Character of the late Dr. S. Annesley (1697)

4 He bade me observe it, and I should always find, that the calamities of life were shared among the upper and lower part of mankind; but that the middle station had the fewest disasters.
Robinson Crusoe (1719), pt. 1

5 I takes my man Friday with me.
Robinson Crusoe (1719), pt. 1

6 I thought a woman was a free agent, as well as a man, and was born free, and could she manage herself suitably, might enjoy that liberty to as much purpose as the men do; that the laws of matrimony were indeed otherwise...and those such that a woman gave herself entirely away from herself, in marriage, and capitulated only to be, at best, but an upper servant.
Roxana (1724)

7 In trouble to be troubled
Is to have your trouble doubled.
1719. *The Farther Adventures of Robinson Crusoe* (G. Aitkin, ed.; 1895)

8 Nature has left this tincture in the blood,
That all men would be tyrants if they could.
The History of the Kentish Petition (1712–13), Addenda, l.11

9 Necessity makes an honest man a knave.
The Serious Reflections of Robinson Crusoe (1720), ch. 2

10 Wherever God erects a house of prayer,
The Devil always builds a chapel there;
And 'twill be found, upon examination,
The latter has the largest congregation.
The True-Born Englishman (1701), pt. 1, l. 1

11 From this amphibious ill-born mob began
That vain, ill-natured thing, an Englishman.
The True-Born Englishman (1701), pt. 1, l. 132

12 And of all plagues with which mankind are curst,
Ecclesiastic tyranny's the worst.
The True-Born Englishman (1701), pt. 2, l. 299

13 When kings the sword of justice first lay down,
They are no kings, though they possess the crown.
Titles are shadows, crowns are empty things,
The good of subjects is the end of kings.
The True-Born Englishman (1701), pt. 2, l. 313

14 Trade in general is built upon, and supported by two essential and principal foundations, viz., Money and Credit.
The Villainy of Stock-Jobbers Detected (1710)

15 Sometimes we see these mountains rising up at once, from the lowest valleys, to the highest summits which makes the height look horrid and frightful, even worse than those mountains abroad.
1725. Referring to the Welsh mountains. Quoted in *A Tour Through the Whole Island of Great Britain* (Pat Rogers, ed.; 1971), vol.2, letter 6

16 Middle age is youth without its levity,
And age without decay.
Attrib.

Degas, Edgar (Hilaire Germain Edgar Degas; 1834–1917) French artist

Quotations about Degas

1 Ah, they were lucky, who were drawn from life
By river banks in summer, in cafe scenes,
The way they were, for all their speechless pains,
That absinthe drinker and his sober wife.
Douglas Dunn (b.1942) British poet and critic. Referring to a painting by Edgar Degas. "The Gallery," *St Kilda's Parliament* (1981)

2 Edgar Degas purchased once
A fine El Greco, which he kept
Against the wall beside his bed
To hang his pants on while he slept.
Richard Wilbur (b.1921) U.S. poet. "Museum Piece," *Ceremony and Other Poems* (1950)

Quotations by Degas

3 I will not admit that a woman can draw so well.
Referring to the painter Mary Cassatt. Quoted in *An American Painter in Paris: A Life of Mary Cassatt* (Ellen Wilson; 1971)

4 Art is vice, you don't marry it legitimately, you rape it!
Degas (Paul Lafond; 1918)

5 I marry? Oh, I could never bring myself to do it. I would have been in mortal misery all my life for fear my wife might say, "That's a pretty little thing," after I had finished a picture.
Degas by Himself: Drawings, Prints, Paintings, Writings (Richard Kendall, ed.; 1987)

6 It is very good to copy what one sees; it is much better to draw what you can't see any more but is in your memory. It is a transformation in which imagination and memory work together. You only reproduce what struck you, that is to say the necessary.
Degas by Himself: Drawings, Prints, Paintings, Writings (Richard Kendall, ed.; 1987)

7 There are some women who should barely be spoken to; they should only be caressed.
Degas by Himself: Drawings, Prints, Paintings, Writings (Richard Kendall, ed.; 1987)

8 I feel as a horse must feel when the beautiful cup is given to the jockey.
On seeing one of his pictures sold at auction. Attrib.

de Gaulle, Charles, General (Charles André Joseph Marie de Gaulle; 1890–1970) French president

Quotations about de Gaulle

1 He is like a female llama surprised in her bath.
Winston Churchill (1874–1965) British prime minister and writer. Attrib.

2 Just look at him! He might be Stalin with 200 divisions.
Winston Churchill (1874–1965) British prime minister and writer. Attrib.

Quotations by de Gaulle

3 The French will only be united under the threat of danger. Nobody can simply bring together a country that has 265 kinds of cheese.
Election speech (1951)

4 At the present time there cannot be any other Europe than a Europe of states, apart of course from myths, stories, and parades.
Press conference, Paris (May 15, 1962)

5 I, General de Gaulle, now in London, call on all French officers and men who are at present on British soil, or who may be in the future...to get in touch with me. Whatever happens the flame of French resistance must not and shall not be extinguished.
Radio broadcast, London (June 18, 1940)

6 To all Frenchmen: France has lost a battle but France has not lost the war.
Radio broadcast, London (June 18, 1940) "Proclamation," *Discours, messages et déclarations du Général de Gaulle* (1941)

7 Treaties are like roses and young girls—they last while they last.
Speech at the Élysée Palace, Paris (July 2, 1963)

8 From her very beginning the vocation of France, the purpose of France, has been a calling to serve humanity.
Speech, Dakar, Senegal (December 13, 1959)

9 For all of us Frenchmen, the guiding rule of our epoch is to be faithful to France.
Speech, Lyon, France (September 28, 1963)

10 I always thought I was Jeanne d'Arc and Bonaparte—how little one knows oneself.
Referring to being compared with Robespierre. *Figaro Littéraire* (1958)

11 Deliberation is the work of many men. Action, of one alone.
Mémoires de guerre (1954–59), vol. 2

12 In the tumult of great events, solitude was what I hoped for. Now it is what I love. How is it possible to be contented with anything else when one has come face to face with History?
Mémoires de guerre (1954–59), vol. 3

13 What could I have done at Potsdam?
Referring to the Potsdam Conference (1945) held after the surrender of Germany and attended by Britain, the United States, and the Soviet Union, but not France. Among other things, it decided the administration of Germany pending the establishment of a new government. *Mémoires de guerre* (1954–59), vol. 3

14 I respect only those who resist me; but I cannot tolerate them.
New York Times Magazine (May 12, 1966)

15 I myself have become a Gaullist only little by little.
Observer, London (December 29, 1963), "Sayings of the Year"

16 I have come to the conclusion that politics is too serious a matter to be left to the politicians.
Replying to Clement Attlee's remark that "De Gaulle is a very good soldier and a very bad politician." *A Prime Minister Remembers* (Clement Attlee; 1961), ch. 4

17 One does not arrest Voltaire.
Explaining why he had not arrested Jean-Paul Sartre for urging French soldiers in Algeria to desert. *Encounter*, London (June 1975)

18 They really are bad shots.
Remark after narrowly escaping death in an assassination attempt. *Ten First Ladies of the World* (Pauline Frederick; 1962)

19 Old age is a shipwreck.
The Life of Arthur Ransome (Hugh Brogan; 1984)

20 In order to become the master, the politician poses as the servant.
Attrib. (1969)

21 Since a politician never believes what he says, he is surprised when others believe him.
Attrib. (1962)

22 I can see her in about ten years from now on the yacht of a Greek oil millionaire.
Referring to Jacqueline Kennedy after the assassination of President Kennedy. She later married the oil tycoon Aristotle Onassis. Attrib.

23 Change your friends.
Replying to Jacques Soustelle who complained that he was being attacked by his own friends. Attrib.

de Geus, Arie Dutch author

1 Companies die because their managers focus on the economic activity of producing goods and services, and they forget that their organization's true nature is that of a community of humans.
The Living Company (1997)

2 Concentrated power means no freedom. No freedom means little knowledge creation and, worse, little knowledge propagation. No propagation means little institutional learning and, thus, no effective action if the world changes.
The Living Company (1997)

3 If corporate health falters, the priority should be to mobilize human potential, to restore or maintain trust and civic behavior and to increase professionalism and good citizenship.
The Living Company (1997)

4 Like all organisms, the living company exists primarily for its own survival and improvement: to fulfil its own potential and to become as great as it can be.
The Living Company (1997)

5 The horizons of individual businesses are growing while political horizons shrink.
The Living Company (1997)

Degler, Carl N. (Carl Neumann Degler; b.1921) U.S. historian

1 All human beings seek to locate themselves in the stream of time.
"Remaking American History," *Journal of American History* (June 1980)

2 American history is perceived by most people as a luxury, an entertainment at best, and at worst, an escape from the present.
"Remaking American History," *Journal of American History* (June 1980)

3 Sex is to women's history as color is to black history: a prime basis of differentiation and therefore a source of conflict.
"Remaking American History," *Journal of American History* (June 1980)

4 The present, after all, is merely a nation's skin, its body is the past.
"Remaking American History," *Journal of American History* (June 1980)

5 When historians and social critics have exhausted their resources in a vain attempt to find a thread of consistency in a body of data, they invariably take refuge in the discovery of paradox.
"Understanding the South," *Journal of Southern History* (November 1964)

de Jars, Marie (1565–1645) French writer

1 The common man believes that in order to be chaste a woman must not be clever: in truth it is doing chastity too little honor to believe it can be found beautiful only by the blind.
Proumenoir (1594)

de Jesús, Carolina Maria (1913–77) Brazilian writer and lecturer

1 Actually we are slaves to the cost of living.
July 15, 1955. *Beyond All Pity: The Diary of Carolina Maria de Jesus* (1960)

2 I classify São Paolo this way: The Governor's Palace is the living room. The mayor's office is the dining room and the city is the garden. And the *favela* is the back yard where they throw the garbage.
May 15, 1958. *Beyond All Pity: The Diary of Carolina Maria de Jesus* (1960)

3 The poor don't rest nor are they permitted the pleasure of relaxation.
1955. *Beyond All Pity: The Diary of Carolina Maria de Jesus* (1960)

4 The voice of the poor has no poetry.
November 27, 1958. *Beyond All Pity: The Diary of Carolina Maria de Jesus* (1960)

de Jouvenel, Bertrand (Édouard Bertrand de Jouvenel des Ursins; 1903–87) French political scientist, economist, and journalist

1 Year by year we are becoming better equipped to accomplish the things we are striving for. But what are we actually striving for?
1970. Quoted in *The Jingle Bell Principle* (Miroslav Holub; 1992)

Dekker, Thomas (1572?–1632?) English playwright

1 A wise man poor
Is like a sacred book that's never read,
To himself he lives, and to all else seems dead.
This age thinks better of a gilded fool
Than of a threadbare saint in wisdom's school.
Old Fortunatus (1600), Act 1, Scene 1

2 Golden slumbers kiss your eyes,
Smiles awake you when you rise.
Patient Grissil (1603), Act 4, Scene 2

3 The Englishman's dress is like a traitor's body that hath been hanged, drawn, and quartered, and is set up in various places; his cod-piece is in Denmark, the collar of his doublet and the belly in France; the wing and narrow sleeve in Italy; the short waist hangs over a Dutch butcher's stall in Utrecht; his huge slops speak Spanishly...And thus we that mock every nation for keeping of one fashion, yet steal patches from every one of them to piece out our pride.
Seven Deadly Sins of London (1606)

4 Sleep is that golden chaine that ties health and our bodies together.
The Guls Horn-Booke (1609), ch. 2

5 We are ne'er like angels till our passion dies.
The Honest Whore (1630), pt.2, Act 1, Scene 2

6 Turn over a new leaf.
The Honest Whore (1630), pt. 2, Act 2, Scene 1

de Klerk, F. W. (Frederik Willem de Klerk; b.1936) South African president

1 Today we have closed the book on apartheid.
After a referendum of white South Africans had endorsed his government's reform program. *Independent*, London (March 19, 1992)

2 There is no such thing as a nonracial society in a multiracial country.
Time (1994)

de Klerk, Marike South African wife of F. W. de Klerk

1 We are unimportant. We are here to serve, to heal the wounds and give love.
Referring to the role of women. *Observer*, London (May 12, 1991)

de Kooning, Willem (1904–97) Dutch-born U.S. painter and sculptor

1 The trouble with being poor is that it takes up all your time.
Attrib.

Delacroix, Eugène (Ferdinand Victor Eugène Delacroix; 1798–1863) French painter

1 A book by a great man is a compromise between the reader and himself.
Letter to Honoré de Balzac, *Correspondances* (1832)

2 One has always slightly to spoil a painting to finish it.
April 13, 1853. *Journal* (1893–95)

3 Painting is only a bridge linking the painter's mind with that of the viewer.
October 8, 1822. *Journal* (1893–95)

4 The first virtue of a painting is to be a feast for the eyes.
Journal (1893–95)

5 The secret of not having worries, for me at least, is to have ideas.
July 14, 1850. *Journal* (1893–95)

6 Oh, young artist, you search for a subject—everything is a subject. Your subject is yourself, your impressions, your emotions in the presence of nature.
Oeuvres littéraires (1923)

de la Mare, Walter (Walter John de la Mare; 1873–1956) British poet and novelist

1 Until we learn the use of living words we shall continue to be waxworks inhabited by gramophones.
Observer, London (May 12, 1929), "Sayings of the Week"

2 Alas, Alack
Come! quick as you can!
There's a fish that *talks*
In the frying-pan.
"Alas, Alack," *Peacock Pie* (1913)

3 It's a very odd thing—
As odd as can be—
That whatever Miss T eats
Turns into Miss T.
"Miss T," *Peacock Pie* (1913)

4 Slowly, silently, now the moon
Walks the night in her silver shoon.
"Silver," *Peacock Pie* (1913)

5 Very old are we men;
Our dreams are tales
Told in dim Eden
By Eve's nightingales.
1912. "All That's Past," *The Complete Poems of Walter de la Mare* (1969)

6 Look thy last on all things lovely,
Every hour. Let no night
Seal thy sense in deathly slumber
Till to delight
Thou have paid thy utmost blessing.
1918. "Fare Well," *The Complete Poems of Walter de la Mare* (1969)

7 This Prince of Commerce spent his days
In crafty, calm, cold, cozening strife:
He thus amassed a million pounds,
And bought a pennyworth of life.
1953. "Hard Labour," *The Complete Poems of Walter de la Mare* (1969)

8 "Is there anybody there?" said the Traveller,
Knocking on the moonlit door.
1912. "The Listeners," *The Complete Poems of Walter de la Mare* (1969)

9 Alas, Alack
Oh, no man knows
Through what wild centuries
Roves back the rose.
"All That's Past," *The Listeners* (1912)

10 Too late for fruit, too soon for flowers.
On being asked, as he lay seriously ill, whether he would like some fruit or flowers. Attrib. *The Faber Book of Anecdotes* (Clifton Fadiman; 1985)

Delaney, Lucy A. (1830?–90) U.S. slave and writer

1 Oh! ye prosperous! prate of the uses of adversity as poetically as you please, we who are obliged to learn of them by bitter experience would greatly prefer a change of surroundings.
From The Darkness Cometh The Light or Struggles For Freedom (1891?)

2 Old people are like old trees, uproot them, and transplant to other scenes, they droop and die, no matter how bright the sunshine, or how balmy the breezes.
From The Darkness Cometh The Light or Struggles For Freedom (1891?)

Delaney, Shelagh (b.1939) British playwright

1 I'm not frightened of the darkness outside. It's the darkness inside houses I don't like.
A Taste of Honey (1958), Act 1, Scene 1

2 Women never have young minds. They are born three thousand years old.
A Taste of Honey (1958), Act 1, Scene 1

3 In this country there are only two seasons, winter and winter.
Referring to England. *A Taste of Honey* (1958), Act 1, Scene 2

Delany, Annie Elizabeth "Bessie" (1891–1995) U.S. doctor of dental surgery

1 Turning one hundred was the worst birthday of my life. I wouldn't wish it on my worst enemy. Turning 101 was not so bad. Once you're past that century mark, it's just not as shocking.
Having Our Say: The Delany Sisters' First 100 Years (1994)

Delany, Martin Robinson (1812–85) U.S. physician, abolitionist, and newspaper editor

1 Heathenism and Liberty, before Christianity and Slavery.
Letter (May 14, 1852), quoted in *The Mind of the Negro As Reflected In Letters Written During the Crisis, 1800–1860* (Carter G. Woodson, ed.; 1926)

2 A moral and mental, is as obnoxious as a physical servitude, and not to be tolerated; as the one may, eventually lead to the other.
The Condition, Elevation, Emigration and Destiny of the Colored People of the United States, Politically Considered (1852)

3 Every people should be the originators of their own designs, the projector of their own schemes, and creators of the events that lead to their destiny—the consummation of their desires.
The Condition, Elevation, Emigration and Destiny of the Colored People of the United States, Politically Considered (1852)

de la Renta, Oscar (b.1932) Dominican-born U.S. fashion designer

1 We have become world businessmen. In the old days fashion designers—seamstresses really—made and sold only dresses; today we sell a lifestyle to the whole world.
Quoted in *The Fashion Conspiracy* (Nicholas Coleridge; 1989), ch. 1

Delaunay, Sonia (Sonia Delaunay-Terk; 1885–1979) Ukrainian-born French painter and designer

1 Between me and painting there is nothing.
1970. Quoted in *Art Talk: Conversations with 15 Women Artists* (Cindy Nemser; 1975)

2 If you are an artist you are doing pictures like you do furniture. You must do what you want and be ready not to sell. You can't be too ambitious for money.
1970. Quoted in *Art Talk: Conversations with 15 Women Artists* (Cindy Nemser; 1975)

Delille, Jacques (1738–1813) French poet and abbot

1 Fate chooses your relations, you choose your friends.
Malheur et pitié (1803)

DeLillo, Don (b.1936) U.S. novelist

1 Men with secrets tend to be drawn to each other, not because they want to share what they know but because they need the company of the like-minded, the fellow-afflicted.
Said by Walter Everett, Jr. *Libra* (1988)

2 Tourism is the march of stupidity.
Said by James Axton. *The Names* (1982)

3 I've come to think of Europe as a hardcover book, America as the paperback version.
Said by Owen Brademas. *The Names* (1982)

4 Madness is a final distillation of self, a final editing down. It's the drowning out of false voices.
Said by Owen Brademas. *The Names* (1982)

5 It is not some peaceful use of atomic energy with some heating applications. It is a red bomb that spouts a great white cloud like some thunder god of ancient Eurasia.
Underworld (1998)

6 Longing on a large scale is what makes history.
Underworld (1998)

7 There is no space or time out here, or in here...There are only connections. Everything is connected. All human knowledge gathered and linked...this site leading to that, this fact referenced to that, a keystroke, a mouse-click, a password—world without end, amen.
Underworld (1998)

8 Men shout as they die, to be noticed, remembered for a second or two. To die in an apartment instead of a house can depress the soul, I would imagine, for several lives to come.
White Noise (1985)

9 The family is strongest where objective reality is most likely to be misinterpreted.
White Noise (1985)

Dell, Michael (b.1964) U.S. business executive

1 Ideas are a commodity. Execution of them is not.
Fortune (June 14, 1993)

2 The challenge in a start-up is that you always have to spread your wings pretty far to see what will work.
Quoted in *In the Company of Giants* (Rama Dev Jager; 1997)

3 When a business goes wrong, look only to the people who are running it.
Quoted in *In the Company of Giants* (Rama Dev Jager; 1997)

Deloria, Vine (Vine Victor Deloria, Jr.; b.1933) U.S. Native American leader, writer, educator, and lawyer

1 Tribalism is the strongest force at work in the world today.
Custer Died for Your Sins: An Indian Manifesto (1969), ch. 11

2 This country was a lot better off when the Indians were running it.
Quoted in *New York Times* (1970), magazine

Delors, Jacques (Jacques Lucien Jean Delors; b.1925) French statesman

1 You can't be a true idealist without being a true realist.
Speech to the European Union Summit, Corfu (June 21, 1994)

2 Europe is not just about material results, it is about spirit. Europe is a state of mind.
Independent, London (May 19, 1994)

3 My ideal is a society full of responsible men and women who show solidarity to those who can't keep up.
Independent, London (June 22, 1994)

4 Populism is on the increase—a populism that rejects anything different, anyone with a different-colored skin, or a different race or religion. This is the real danger and unspoken risk that threatens to pollute democracy.
Independent, London (May 19, 1994)

5 The construction of Europe is not a boxing match.
Independent, London (May 19, 1994)

6 The hardest thing is to convince European citizens that even the most powerful nation is no longer able to act alone.
As president of the European Union (1985–95), Jacques Delors was responsible for the Maastricht Treaty (1992) which reflected the intention of member states to broaden their political and economic cooperation. *Independent*, London (May 19, 1994)

Demarest, Ellen (1824–98) U.S. business executive

1 I do not claim that all women, or a large portion of them, should enter into independent business relations with the world, but I do claim that all women should cultivate and respect in themselves an ability to make money.
1872. Quoted in *Feminine Ingenuity* (Anne L. MacDonald; 1992)

de Mille, Agnes (Agnes George de Mille; 1905–93) U.S. dancer and choreographer

1 A kind of madness is involved. When pubescent girls have any inclination toward dancing at all, they are fairly driven by the frenzy.
1952. "Ballet and Sex," *Dance to the Piper* (1987), ch. 8

2 At the end of a thousand years of growing refinements and ceaseless efforts, dancing had completed its course from altar to gutter.
1952. Referring to the association between dance and prostitution. "Ballet and Sex," *Dance to the Piper* (1987), ch. 8

3 It is the one physical performance possible to women that does not carry with it either moral responsibility or physical hazard. It constitutes a true recapturing of pagan freedom and childish play. It can be even a complete although unconscious substitute for physical love, and in the lives of the greatest dancers it usually assumes this function.
1952. Referring to women ballet dancers. "Ballet and Sex," *Dance to the Piper* (1987), ch. 8

De Mille, Cecil B. (Cecil Blount De Mille; 1881–1959) U.S. film producer and director

1 Every time I make a picture the critics' estimate of American public taste goes down ten percent.
Halliwell's Filmgoer's and Video Viewer's Companion (Leslie Halliwell; 1984)

2 I didn't write the Bible and didn't invent sin.
Halliwell's Filmgoer's and Video Viewer's Companion (Leslie Halliwell; 1984)

3 I make my pictures for people, not for critics.
Halliwell's Filmgoer's and Video Viewer's Companion (Leslie Halliwell; 1984)

4 Remember you are a star. Never go across the alley even to dump garbage unless you are dressed to the teeth.
Halliwell's Filmgoer's and Video Viewer's Companion (Leslie Halliwell; 1984)

Deming, W. Edwards (William Edwards Deming; 1900–93) U.S. management expert

1 Anyone, when he has brought his work to a state of statistical control, whether he trained well or badly, is in a rut. He has completed his learning in a particular job.
Out of the Crisis (1982)

2 The aim of leadership should be to improve the performance of man and machine, to improve quality, to increase output, and simultaneously to bring pride of workmanship to people.
Out of the Crisis (1982)

3 The central problem in management and in leadership...is failure to understand the information in variation.
Out of the Crisis (1982)

4 The customer is the most important part of the production line.
Strategy and Business (1997), "Noteworthy Quotes"

Democritus (460?–370? B.C.) Greek philosopher

Quotations about Democritus

1 Children are to be won to follow liberal studies by exhortations and rational motives, and on no account to be forced thereto by whipping.
Plutarch (46?–120?) Greek biographer and philosopher. "Of the Training of Children" (1st–2nd century)

Quotations by Democritus

2 In reality we apprehend nothing for certain, but only as it changes according to the condition of our body, and of the things that impinge or offer resistance to it.
5th–4th century B.C. Attrib.

3 The atoms struggle and move in the void because of dissimilarities between them and other differences; and as they move they collide and become entangled in such a way as to cling in close contact to one another.
5th–4th century B.C. Attrib.

Dempsey, Jack (William Harrison Dempsey; 1895–1983) U.S. boxer

1 Kill the other guy before he kills you.
Quoted in his obituary. *Times*, London (June 2, 1983)

2 I just forgot to duck.
September 23, 1926. Said to his wife, when he lost the World Heavyweight boxing title. *Dempsey* (J. and B. P. Dempsey; 1977)

Deng To (1912–66) Chinese editor

1 Let us all honestly own our ignorance when confronted with what we do not know.
Evening Talks at Yenshan (1961–62), quoted in *Literature of the People's Republic of China* (Kai-yu Hsu, ed.; 1980)

2 Study more and criticize less. This is a correct attitude toward learning.
Evening Talks at Yenshan (1961–62), quoted in *Literature of the People's Republic of China* (Kai-yu Hsu, ed.; 1980)

Deng Xiaoping (1904–97) Chinese statesman

1 By Marxism we mean Marxism that is integrated with Chinese conditions, and by socialism we mean socialism that is tailored to Chinese conditions and has Chinese characteristics.
"Build Socialism with Chinese Characteristics" (June 30, 1984), quoted in *Deng Xiaoping: Speeches and Writings* (Robert Maxwell, ed.; 1987)

2 Democracy has to be institutionalized and written into law, so as to make sure that institutions and laws do not change whenever the leadership changes, or whenever the leaders change their views or shift the focus of their attention.
"Emancipate the Mind, Seek Truth from Facts and Unite as One in Looking to the Future" (December 13, 1978), quoted in *Deng Xiaoping: Speeches and Writings* (Robert Maxwell, ed.; 1987)

3 Revolution takes place on the basis of the needed material benefit. It would be idealism to emphasize the spirit of sacrifice to the neglect of material benefit.
"Emancipate the Mind, Seek Truth from Facts and Unite as One in Looking to the Future" (December 13, 1978), quoted in *Deng Xiaoping: Speeches and Writings* (Robert Maxwell, ed.; 1987)

4 No individual in the present Chinese leadership can determine any of our policies on his own. All important decisions are made through collective discussions.
Interview with Robert Maxwell (1984), quoted in *Deng Xiaoping: Speeches and Writings* (Robert Maxwell, ed.; 1987)

5 The socialist system is practiced by the one billion people on the mainland, but a capitalist system will be allowed to exist in certain regions, such as Hong Kong and Taiwan.
"One Country, Two Systems" (1984), quoted in *Deng Xiaoping: Speeches and Writings* (Robert Maxwell, ed.; 1987)

6 No foreign country can expect China to be its vassal nor can it expect China to accept anything harmful to China's interests.
Opening Speech to the 12th National Congress of the Communist Party of China (September 1, 1982), quoted in *Deng Xiaoping: Speeches and Writings* (Robert Maxwell, ed.; 1987)

7 For the same reason every party member must cultivate the style of work which stresses serving the people, holding himself responsible to them, never failing to consult them and being ever ready to share their joys and sorrow.
Report on the Revision of the Constitution of the Communist Party of China (September 16, 1956), quoted in *Deng Xiaoping: Speeches and Writings* (Robert Maxwell, ed.; 1987)

8 Yellow cat, black cat, as long as it catches mice, it is a good cat.
Speech (1962)

9 Backwardness must be recognized before it can be changed. One must learn from those who are more advanced before he can catch up with and surpass them.
Speech at the Opening Ceremony of the National Conference on Science (March 18, 1978), quoted in *Deng Xiaoping: Speeches and Writings* (Robert Maxwell, ed.; 1987)

10 The key to the four modernizations is the modernization of science and technology.
Speech at the Opening Ceremony of the National Conference on Science (March 18, 1978), quoted in *Deng Xiaoping: Speeches and Writings* (Robert Maxwell, ed.; 1987)

11 The more our agriculture, industry, national defense, and science and technology are modernized, the stronger we will be in the struggle against forces which sabotage socialism, and the more our people will support the socialist system.
Speech at the Opening Ceremony of the National Conference on Science (March 18, 1978), quoted in *Deng Xiaoping: Speeches and Writings* (Robert Maxwell, ed.; 1987)

12 Broadcasting offers an important means of developing education with greater, faster, better and more economical results, and we should take full advantage of it.
Speech to the National Conference on Education (April 22, 1978), quoted in *Deng Xiaoping: Speeches and Writings* (Robert Maxwell, ed.; 1987)

13 If we are to catch up with and surpass the advanced countries in science and technology, we must improve not only the quality of our higher education but, first of all, that of our primary and secondary education.
Speech to the National Conference on Education (April 22, 1978), quoted in *Deng Xiaoping: Speeches and Writings* (Robert Maxwell, ed.; 1987)

14 To train qualified personnel for socialist construction, we must try to find improved ways of combining education with productive labor, ways that are suited to our new conditions.
Speech to the National Conference on Education (April 22, 1978), quoted in *Deng Xiaoping: Speeches and Writings* (Robert Maxwell, ed.; 1987)

15 All Chinese have at the very least a sense of pride in the Chinese nation, no matter what clothes they wear or what political stand they take.
One Country, Two Systems (1984), quoted in *Deng Xiaoping: Speeches and Writings* (Robert Maxwell, ed.; 1987)

16 The modern image of China was not created by the government of the Qing Dynasty, nor by the northern warlords, nor by Chiang Kai-shek and his son. It is the People's Republic of China that has transformed China's image.
One Country, Two Systems (1984), quoted in *Deng Xiaoping: Speeches and Writings* (Robert Maxwell, ed.; 1987)

17 If you want China to beg, it can't be arranged. Even if it extended 100 years, the Chinese people will not beg for the lifting of sanctions.
Response to an American threat of economic sanctions in the aftermath of the Tiananmen massacre (1989). *Straits Times*, Singapore (November 5, 1993)

18 Even if they're functioning out of ignorance, they are still participating and must be suppressed. In China, even one million people can be considered a small sum.
Referring to the prodemocracy demonstrators in Tiananmen Square. *Times*, London (June 5, 1989)

19 It's impossible for a big country like China to live on borrowed money or achieve growth by imitating others.
Quoted in *Deng Xiaoping: Speeches and Writings* (Robert Maxwell, ed.; 1987)

20 In carrying out our modernization program we must...unite the universal truth of Marxism with the concrete realities of China, proceed along our own path, and build socialism with Chinese characteristics.
September 1982. Quoted in *Political and Social Change in China Since 1978* (Charles Burton; 1990)

Denham, John, Sir (1615–69) Irish poet

1 Such is our pride, our folly, or our fate,
That few, but such as cannot write, translate.
"To Richard Fanshaw" (1648)

De Niro, Robert (b.1943) U.S. actor

1 Someday a real rain will come and wash all this scum off the streets.
As Travis Bickle, referring to prostitutes and pimps on the streets of New York City. *Taxi Driver* (Paul Schrader; 1976)

Denisova, Galina Russian shopkeeper

1 The Democrats only come here when they want votes. They brought sweets to bribe us.
The Communists used to bring vodka. It was more successful.
August, 1993. Speaking to her neighbor. *Times*, London (August 11, 1993)

Denman, Thomas, 1st Baron Denman (1779–1854) British judge

1 Trial by jury itself, instead of being a security to persons who are accused, will be a delusion, a mockery, and a snare.
Speech to the House of Lords, the upper house of the British parliament (September 4, 1844)

Denning, Lord, Baron Denning of Whitchurch (Alfred Thompson Denning; 1899–1999) British judge

1 When a diplomat says yes, he means perhaps. When he says perhaps he means no. When he says no, he is not a diplomat. When a lady says no, she means perhaps. When she says perhaps, she means yes. But when she says yes, she is no lady.
Speech to the Magistrates Association (October 14, 1982)

2 There are many things in life more worthwhile than money. One is to be brought up in this our England which is still the envy of less happy lands.
August, 1968. *Observer*, London (August 4, 1968), "Sayings of the Week"

Dennis, John (1657–1734) English critic and playwright

1 A man who could make so vile a pun would not scruple to pick a pocket.
The Gentleman's Magazine (1781), vol. 51, pt. 1, l. 1

Dennis, Nigel (Nigel Forbes Dennis; 1912–89) British writer and playwright

1 But then one is always excited by descriptions of money changing hands. It's much more fundamental than sex.
Cards of Identity (1955)

2 This man, she reasons, as she looks at her husband, is a poor fish. But he is the nearest I can get to the big one that got away.
Cards of Identity (1955)

Depardieu, Gérard (b.1948) French actor

1 Acting in English...I'm like a blind man. When you can't see, you develop other senses. In one sense I am blind, but other faculties develop by way of compensation: the sense of hearing, of morbid curiosity, of tolerance. These are the ways you communicate if you don't speak the language.
Observer, London (April 10, 1994), Life Magazine

2 You don't have the same resistance to alcohol. You lose the arrogance you have when you are 20. Thank God.
Observer, London (April 10, 1994), Life Magazine

3 I appreciate teamwork. I don't like a one-man show. I'm an interpreter, a sort of tool—I don't mean an object. The right tool is quite essential. Try pounding a nail in with a screwdriver.
1990. Publicity release for *Cyrano de Bergerac* (1990). Attrib.

Depew, Chauncey (1834–1928) U.S. lawyer and public official

1 I get my exercise acting as a pallbearer to my friends who exercise.
Attrib.

de Pree, Max (Max Owen de Pree; b.1924) U.S. business executive and author

1 Leaders should leave behind them assets and a legacy.
Leadership is an Art (1994)

2 Managers who have no beliefs but only understand methodology and quantification are modern-day eunuchs. They can never engender competence or confidence. They can never be truly intimate.
Leadership is an Art (1994)

3 The best management process for today's environment is participative management based on covenantal relationships.
Leadership is an Art (1994)

4 The first responsibility of a leader is to define reality. The last is to say thank you.
Leadership is an Art (1994)

De Quincey, Thomas (1785–1859) British essayist and critic

1 Murder Considered as One of the Fine Arts
Essay title. *Blackwood's Magazine*, Edinburgh (1827)

2 Even imperfection itself may have its ideal or perfect state.
"Murder Considered as One of the Fine Arts," *Blackwood's Magazine*, Edinburgh (1827)

3 So much beauty, and so much native good-breeding and refinement, I do not remember to have seen before or since in any cottage.
Referring to the young Welsh people whose hospitality he enjoyed while wandering in North Wales. *Confessions of an English Opium Eater* (Alethea Hayter, ed.; 1821), pt. 1

4 It was a Sunday afternoon, wet and cheerless: and a duller spectacle this earth of ours has not to show than a rainy Sunday in London.
Confessions of an English Opium Eater (1821), pt. 2

5 Opium gives and takes away. It defeats the steady habit of exertion; but it creates spasms of irregular exertion! It ruins the natural power of life; but it develops preternatural paroxysms of intermitting power.
Confessions of an English Opium Eater (1821), pt. 2

6 Thou hast the keys of Paradise, oh, just, subtle, and mighty opium!
Confessions of an English Opium Eater (1821), pt. 2

7 Books, we are told, propose to instruct or to amuse. Indeed!...The true antithesis to knowledge, in this case, is not *pleasure*, but *power*. All that is literature seeks to communicate power; all that is not literature, to communicate knowledge.
"Letters to a Young Man Whose Education has been Neglected," *London Magazine* (1823), no. 3

Derrida, Jacques (b.1930) Algerian-born French philosopher

Quotations about Derrida

1 As usual with pithy little formulae, the Derridian claim that "There is nothing outside the text" is right about what it explicitly denies and wrong about what it explicitly asserts.
Richard Rorty (b.1931) U.S. philosopher. *Consequences of Pragmatism* (1982)

Quotations by Derrida

2 The writer writes *in* a language and *in* a logic whose proper system, laws, and life his discourse by definition cannot dominate absolutely.
Of Grammatology (1967)

3 An ineffaceable trace is not a trace.
Writing and Difference (1967)

4 The conscious text is...not a transcription, because there is no text *present elsewhere* as an unconscious one to be transposed or transported.
Writing and Difference (1967)

5 We have no language—no syntax and no lexicon—which is foreign to this history; we can pronounce not a single destructive proposition which has not already had to slip into the form, the logic, and the implicit postulations of that which it seeks to contest.
Writing and Difference (1967)

Dershowitz, Alan (Alan Morton Dershowitz; b.1938) U.S. lawyer

1 Judges are the weakest link in our system of justice and they are also the most protected.
Newsweek (February 20, 1978)

2 The courtroom oath—"to tell the truth, the whole truth and nothing but the truth"—is applicable only to witnesses...because the American justice system is built on a foundation of not telling the whole truth.
The Best Defense (1982)

3 I have great compassion for God now, because I think Bill is going to start filing lawsuits as soon as he gets to heaven.
Referring to William Kunstler, a well-known lawyer. *USA Today* (September 5, 1995)

Descartes, René (1596–1650) French philosopher and mathematician

Quotations about Descartes

1 It is often more convenient to possess the ashes of great men than to possess the men themselves during their lifetime.
Karl Gustav Jakob Jacobi (1804–51) German mathematician. Referring to the return of René Descartes' remains to France. Quoted in *Mathematical Circles Adieu* (H. Eves; 1977)

2 The *Cogito* depreciated the perception of others, teaching me as it did that the I is accessible only to itself, since it defined *me* as the thought which I have of myself, and which clearly I am alone in having.
Maurice Merleau-Ponty (1908–61) French existentialist philosopher. Referring to the *cogito ergo sum* of René Descartes. Quoted in *The Essential Writings of Merleau-Ponty* (A. L. Fisher, ed.; 1969)

3 The dogma of the Ghost in the Machine.
Gilbert Ryle (1900–76) British philosopher. Referring to Descartes' mental-conduct concepts. *The Concept of Mind* (1949), ch. 1

Quotations by Descartes

4 Good sense is the best distributed thing in the world: for everyone thinks himself so well endowed with it that even those who are the hardest to please in everything else do not usually desire more of it than they possess.
Discourse on Method (1637)

5 It is not enough to have a good mind. The main thing is to use it well.
Discourse on Method (1637)

6 Observing that this truth "I am thinking, therefore I exist" was so firm and sure...the sceptics were incapable of shaking it, I decided that I could accept it...as the first principle of the philosophy I was seeking.
Discourse on Method (1637)

7 The greatest minds are capable of the greatest vices as well as of the greatest virtues.
Discourse on Method (1637)

8 While I could pretend that I had no body and that there was no world and no place for me to be in, I could not for all that pretend that I did not exist...Accordingly this "I"...is entirely distinct from the body.
The original statement of "Cartesian Dualism." *Discourse on Method* (1637)

9 The reading of all good books is like a conversation with the finest men of past centuries.
Discourse on Method (1637), pt. 1

10 Traveling is almost like talking with men of other centuries.
Discourse on Method (1637), pt. 1

11 I think, therefore I am.
Discourse on Method (1637), pt. 4

12 But what then am I? A thing that thinks. What is that? A thing that doubts, understands, affirms, denies, is willing, is unwilling, and also imagines and has sensory perceptions.
Meditations on First Philosophy (1641), Second Meditation

13 There is a great difference between the mind and the body, inasmuch as the body is by its very nature always divisible, while the mind is utterly indivisible.
Meditations on First Philosophy (1641), Sixth Meditation

14 It is contrary to reason to say that there is a vacuum or space in which there is absolutely nothing.
Principia Philosophiae (1644), pt. 2, sect. 16

15 Neither, though we have mastered all the arguments of Plato and Aristotle, if yet we have not the capacity for passing a solid judgment on these matters, shall we become Philosophers; we should have acquired the knowledge not of a science, but of history.
Quoted in *Rules for the Direction of the Mind* (Elizabeth Haldane and G. R. T. Ross, trs.; 1952)

Deschamps, Eustache (1340?–1406?) French poet

1 Who will bell the cat?
"Ballade: Le Chat et les souris" (14th century)

des Rieux, Virginie French writer

1 Marriage is a lottery in which men stake their liberty and women their happiness.
La Satyre (1967)

Dessalines, Jean Jacques (1758–1806) West African-born Haitian revolutionary and monarch

1 Peace to our neighbors, but anathema to the name of France.
Dessalines was the self-proclaimed emperor of Haiti (1804–06). *From Dessalines to Duvalier* (David Nicholls; 1988)

Destouches, Philippe (Philippe Néricault; 1680–1754) French playwright

1 The absent are always in the wrong.
L'Obstacle imprévu (1717), Act 1, Scene 6

Deutsch, Babette (1895–1982) U.S. writer and poet

1 But the poet's job is, after all, to translate God's poem (or is it the Fiend's?) into words.
"Poetry at the Mid-Century," *The Writer's Book* (Helen Hull, ed.; 1950)

2 The poet...like the lover...is a person unable to reconcile what he knows with what he feels. His peculiarity is that he is under a certain compulsion to do so.
"Poetry at the Mid-Century," *The Writer's Book* (Helen Hull, ed.; 1950)

de Valera, Eamon (1882–1975) U.S.-born Irish statesman

Quotations about de Valera

1 You may assassinate us but you won't intimidate us.
1922
Arthur Griffith (1872–1922) Irish nationalist. Referring to Eamon de Valera's threats to kill Free State supporters. Attrib. *Michael Collins: a Biography* (Tim Pat Coogan; 1990)

2 If this nation had achieved its present political and economic structure a century or so ago, my great-grandfather might never have left New Ross, and I might, if fortunate, be sitting down here with you. Of course, if your own President had never left Brooklyn, he might be standing up here instead of me.
John Fitzgerald Kennedy (1917–63) U.S. president. Referring to Eamon de Valera's birth in America.

Speech to the Irish parliament (June 28, 1963), quoted in *Phrases Make History Here* (Conor O'Clery; 1986)

3 Negotiating with de Valera...is like trying to pick up mercury with a fork.
David Lloyd-George (1863–1945) British prime minister. A comment to which Eamon de Valera replied, "Why doesn't he use a spoon?" Quoted in *Eamon de Valera* (M. J. MacManus; 1944)

Quotations by de Valera

4 They are part of Ireland. They have always been part of Ireland, and their people, Catholic and Protestant, are our people.
Referring to the six counties of Northern Ireland. Letter to Winston Churchill (May 26, 1941)

5 A land whose countryside would be bright with cozy homesteads, whose fields and villages would be joyous with the sounds of industry, with the rompings of sturdy children, the contests of athletic youths, and the laughter of comely maidens.
His vision of Ireland. Radio broadcast, St. Patrick's Day (March 17, 1943), quoted in *Phrases Make History Here* (Conor O'Clery; 1986)

6 Future Volunteers would have to wade through Irish blood, through the blood of the soldiers of the Irish Government, perhaps, the blood of some of the members of Government in order to get Irish freedom.
Known as the "rivers of blood" speech, advocating civil war. Speech, Thurles (March 17, 1922), quoted in *Phrases Make History Here* (Conor O'Clery; 1986)

7 Whenever I wanted to know what the Irish people wanted, I had only to examine my own heart and it told me straight off what the Irish people wanted.
Speech to the Irish Parliament (January 6, 1922), quoted in *Phrases Make History Here* (Conor O'Clery; 1986)

Devereux, Robert, 2nd Earl of Essex (1566–1601) English soldier

1 Reasons are not like garments, the worse for wearing.
Letter to Lord Willoughby (January 4, 1599), quoted in *Notes & Queries, 10th series*, vol. 2

Devi, Mahasweta (b.1926) Indian writer

1 I can't see you. But I say to you in great humility, you can't do anything for us. We became unclean as soon as you entered our lives. No more roads, no more relief—what will you give to a people in exchange for the vanished land, home-field, burial ground?
Referring to economic development in rural parts of India. *Imaginary Maps* (Gayatri Chakravorty Spivak, tr.; 1989)

Devlin, Denis (1908–59) Irish poet

1 Her beauty was like silence in a cup of water.
"Little Elegy," *Collected Poems* (1964)

Devlin, Polly (b.1944) Irish writer

1 There is the squeeze of pain in every episode, and although people sometimes say that the Irish are great lickers of wounds, they have had many to lick.
All of Us There (1983)

DeVoto, Bernard (Bernard Augustine DeVoto; 1897–1955) U.S. writer and historian

1 Art is the terms of an armistice signed with fate.
Mark Twain at Work (1942)

2 The dawn of knowledge is usually the false dawn.
The Course of Empire (1952), ch. 2

De Vries, Peter (1910–93) U.S. novelist

1 We know the human brain is a device to keep the ears from grating on one another.
Comfort Me With Apples (1956), ch. 1

2 Gluttony is an emotional escape, a sign something is eating us.
Comfort Me With Apples (1956), ch. 7

3 I wanted to be bored to death, as good a way to go as any.
Comfort Me With Apples (1956), ch. 17

4 That dark day when a man decides he must wear his belt under instead of over his cascading paunch.
Consenting Adults, or The Duchess Will Be Furious (1980)

5 Or look at it this way. Psychoanalysis is a permanent fad.
Opening words. *Forever Panting* (1973)

6 Anyone informed that the universe is expanding and contracting in pulsations of eighty billion years has a right to ask, "What's in it for me?"
The Glory of the Hummingbird (1974), ch. 1

7 It is the final proof of God's omnipotence that he need not exist in order to save us.
The Mackerel Plaza (1958), ch. 1

8 Let us hope...that a kind of Providence will put a speedy end to the acts of God under which we have been laboring.
The Mackerel Plaza (1958), ch. 3

9 There are times when parenthood seems nothing but feeding the mouth that bites you.
The Tunnel of Love (1954)

10 The value of marriage is not that adults produce children but that children produce adults.
The Tunnel of Love (1954), ch. 8

11 Everybody hates me because I'm so universally liked.
The Vale of Laughter (1967), pt. 1

Dewey, George (1837–1917) U.S. admiral

1 You may fire when you are ready, Gridley.
May 1898. Said to the captain of his flagship during the Battle of Manila Bay (May 1, 1898). Attrib.

Dewey, John (1859–1952) U.S. philosopher and educator

1 Old ideas give way slowly; for they are more than abstract logical forms and categories. They are habits, predispositions, deeply engrained attitudes of aversion and preference.
"The Influence of Darwinism on Philosophy" (1909)

2 We do not solve them: we get over them.
Referring to dealing with philosophical, and other, questions. "The Influence of Darwinism on Philosophy" (1909)

3 Inner harmony is attained only when, by some means, terms are made with the environment.
Art as Experience (1934)

4 While man is other than a bird and beast, he shares basic vital functions with them and has to make the same basal adjustments if he is to continue the process of living.
Art as Experience (1934)

5 The educational process has no end beyond itself; it is its own end.
Democracy and Education (1916)

6 In the traditional method the child must say something that he has merely learned. There is all the difference in the world between having something to say, and having to say something.
Dewey on Education (Martin S. Dworkin, ed.; 1959)

7 All history is necessarily written from the standpoint of the present, and is, in an inescapable sense, the history not only of the present but of that which is contemporaneously judged to be important in the present.
Logic: The Theory of Inquiry (1938)

8 Consciousness can neither be described nor defined.
Psychology (1887)

9 Feeling is the subjective side of consciousness, knowledge its objective side. Will is the relation between the subjective and the objective.
Psychology (1887)

10 Hunger and satisfaction are the two most intense states of consciousness, and they are very intimately connected.
Psychology (1887)

11 In short, the activity of intelligence consists in identifying the apparently unlike, and in discriminating the apparently like.
Psychology (1887)

12 Intelligence begins with the external and least representative state, and advances to the *internal* and most *symbolic*.
Psychology (1887)

13 Judgment is the typical act of intelligence...Perception is a judgment of place; memory, a judgment of time; imagination, a judgment of ideal worth.
Psychology (1887)

14 Language is not an excrescence of mind or graft upon it, but...an essential mode of the expression of its activity...The abstract idea is projected into real existence through the medium of language.
Psychology (1887)

15 Nothing can be in consciousness which consciousness does not put there. Consciousness is an active process.
Psychology (1887)

16 Psychologically, the bond of union in society and the state is not law in a legal or judicial sense; much less force. It is love.
Psychology (1887)

17 Psychology is not concerned with the distinction between false and true judgments, as both are equally psychological processes.
Psychology (1887)

18 The various fine arts, architecture, sculpture, painting, music, and poetry, are the successive attempts of the mind adequately to express its own ideal nature.
Psychology (1887)

19 Truth, in short, from a psychological standpoint, is agreement of relations; falsity, disagreement of relations.
Psychology (1887)

20 Popular psychology is a mass of cant, of slush and of superstition worthy of the most flourishing days of the medicine man.
The Public and Its Problems (1927), ch. 5

21 Every great advance in science has issued from a new audacity of imagination.
The Quest for Certainty (1929), ch. 11

De Wolfe, Elsie (Ella Anderson De Wolfe; 1865–1950) U.S. interior designer

1 In my philosophy of food, the perfect meal is the short meal. Naturally, one presupposes in a short meal that the few dishes served will be perfection and served generously.
Recipes for Successful Dining (1934)

2 Just a few words to add as to the decoration of your table. Never have high flower vases, or other things that obstruct the view of the beautiful woman across the table, or prevent the witticism of the clever man, who is your opposite, reaching you.
Recipes for Successful Dining (1934)

3 It's beige! My color!
1933. On first sighting the Acropolis. *Elsie de Wolfe: A Life in High Style* (J. Smith; 1982)

de Wyzewa, Téodor (1862–1914) Polish-born French critic and theorist

1 The necessity of realism in art; not a realism which transcribes the vain appearances that we think real, with no other end, but an artistic realism, which tears these appearances from the false reality of interest where we perceive them, in order to transport them into the higher reality of a disinterested life.
1886. "L'Art wagnérien: la peinture," *Nos Maîtres* (1897)

Diana, Princess, Princess of Wales (Diana Frances Spencer; 1961–97) British princess

Quotations about Diana

1 I never heard a minute's silence like that.
Glenn Hoddle (b.1957) British soccer player and national team coach. Describing the Wembley tribute after the death of Princess Diana. *Observer*, London (December 28, 1997)

2 Goodbye Norma Jean
Though I never knew you at all
You had the grace to hold yourself
While those around you crawled.
Bernie Taupin (b.1950) British songwriter. Referring to Marilyn Monroe. In 1997, the song was reissued with different lyrics after the death of Princess Diana. "Candle in the Wind" (music by Elton John; 1973)

Quotations by Diana

3 The vicious circle of fear, prejudice and ignorance has increased the spread of Aids to an alarming level. Due to fear and

prejudice, many still do not want to listen. After all, Aids is a killer.
February 1993. *Independent*, London (February 17, 1993)

4 If men had to have babies they would only ever have one each.
July 29,1984. *Observer*, London (July 29, 1984), "Sayings of the Week"

5 There were three of us in this marriage, so it was a bit crowded.
Referring to the relationship between her husband and Camilla Parker-Bowles. *Panorama* (1995)

6 Eating disorders, whether it be anorexia or bulimia, show how individuals can turn the nourishment of the body into a painful attack on themselves and they have at the core a far deeper problem than mere vanity.
April, 1993. *Times*, London (April 28, 1993)

7 By focussing their energies on controlling their bodies, they had found a refuge from having to face the more painful issues at the centre of their lives.
April 1993. Referring to sufferers from eating disorders. *Times*, London (April 28, 1993)

8 I don't even know how to use a parking meter, let alone a phone box.
August 1994. Replying to allegations that she had been making nuisance telephone calls. *Times*, London (August 22, 1994)

Diane de Poitiers, Duchesse de Valentinois (1499–1566) French courtier and mistress of Henry II

1 The years that a woman subtracts from her age are not lost. They are added to the ages of other women.
Attrib.

Díaz, Porfirio (José de la Cruz Porfirio Díaz; 1830–1915) Mexican president

1 Poor Mexico, so far from God and so near to the United States.
Referring to the beginning of the Mexican War (1846–48). Attrib.

Díaz Ordaz, Gustavo (1911–79) Mexican president

1 My government will protect all liberties but one—the liberty to do away with other liberties.
Inaugural speech as president (1964)

Dibdin, Charles (1745–1814) British actor, composer, and playwright

1 Did you ever hear of Captain Wattle?
He was all for love and a little for the bottle.
"Captain Wattle and Miss Roe" (1797)

2 What argufies pride and ambition?
Soon or late death will take us in tow:
Each bullet has got its commission,
And when our time's come we must go.
"Each Bullet Has its Commission" (1803)

3 In every mess I finds a friend,
In every port a wife.
"Jack in his Element" (1790)

4 Then trust me, there's nothing like drinking
So pleasant on this side the grave;
It keeps the unhappy from thinking,
And makes e'en the valiant more brave.
"Nothing like Grog" (1803)

5 Oh! what a snug little Island,
A right little, tight little Island!
"The Snug Little Island," *The British Raft* (1797)

Dick, Philip K. (Philip Kindred Dick; 1928–82) U.S. science-fiction writer

1 Drug misuse is not a disease, it's a decision, like the decision to step out in front of a moving car. You would call that not a disease but an error of judgment.
"Author's Note," *A Scanner Darkly* (1977)

2 Reality is that which, when you stop believing in it, doesn't go away.
1972. "How to Build a Universe That Doesn't Fall Apart Two Days Later," *I Hope I Shall Arrive Soon* (1986), introduction

3 Science fiction writers, I am sorry to say, really do not know anything. We can't talk about science, because our knowledge of it is limited and unofficial, and usually our fiction is dreadful.
1972. "How to Build a Universe That Doesn't Fall Apart Two Days Later," *I Hope I Shall Arrive Soon* (1986), introduction

4 The basic tool for the manipulation of reality is the manipulation of words. If you can control the meaning of words, you can control the people who must use the words.
"How to Build a Universe That Doesn't Fall Apart Two Days Later," *I Hope I Shall Arrive Soon* (1986), introduction

5 Do Androids Dream of Electric Sheep?
1968. Novel title. It was later filmed as *Blade Runner* (1982).

Dickens, Charles (1812–70) British novelist

Quotations about Dickens

1 Of all the great Victorian writers, he was probably the most antagonistic to the Victorian age itself.
Edmund Wilson (1895–1972) U.S. critic and writer. "The Two Scrooges," *The Wound and the Bow* (1941)

Quotations by Dickens

2 "God bless us every one!" said Tiny Tim, the last of all.
A Christmas Carol (1843)

3 In came Mrs. Fezziwig, one vast substantial smile.
A Christmas Carol (1843)

4 It was a turkey! He could never have stood upon his legs, that bird. He would have snapped 'em off short in a minute, like sticks of sealing-wax.
A Christmas Carol (1843)

5 "Man of the worldly mind!" replied the Ghost, "do you believe in me or not?" "I do," said Scrooge. "I must."
A Christmas Carol (1843)

6 Pittsburgh is like Birmingham in England, at least its townspeople say so...It certainly has a great quantity of smoke hanging about.
American Notes (1842)

7 It is sometimes called the City of Magnificent Distances but it

might with greater propriety be termed the City of Magnificent Intentions.
Referring to Washington, D.C. *American Notes* (1842)

8 A wonderful fact to reflect upon, that every human creature is constituted to be that profound secret and mystery to every other.
A Tale of Two Cities (1859), bk. 1, ch. 1

9 It was the best of times, it was the worst of times, it was the age of wisdom, it was the age of foolishness, it was the epoch of belief, it was the epoch of incredulity, it was the season of Light, it was the season of Darkness, it was the spring of hope, it was the winter of despair, we had everything before us, we had nothing before us, we were all going direct to Heaven, we were all going direct the other way.
The opening words of the book. *A Tale of Two Cities* (1859), bk.1, ch.1

10 It is a far, far, better thing that I do, than I have ever done; it is a far, far, better rest that I go to, than I have ever known.
Sidney Carton's last words on the scaffold. *A Tale of Two Cities* (1859), bk. 2, ch. 15

11 Minds like bodies, will often fall into a pimpled, ill-conditioned state from mere excess of comfort.
Barnaby Rudge (1841), ch. 7

12 "There are strings", said Mr Tappertit, "in the human heart that had better not be wibrated."
Barnaby Rudge (1841), ch. 22

13 Oh gracious, why wasn't I born old and ugly?
Said by Miss Miggs. *Barnaby Rudge* (1841), ch. 70

14 "This is a London particular...A fog, miss."
Said by Kenge and Carboy's of Lincoln's Inn. *Bleak House* (1853), ch. 3

15 I expect a judgment. Shortly on the day of Judgment.
Said by Miss Flite. *Bleak House* (1853), ch. 3

16 I only ask to be free. The butterflies are free. Mankind will surely not deny to Harold Skimpole what it concedes to the butterflies!
Said by Harold Skimpole. *Bleak House* (1853), ch. 6

17 "Old girl," said Mr. Bagnet, "give him my opinion. You know it."
Referring to a marriage proposal. *Bleak House* (1853), ch. 27

18 It is a melancholy truth that even great men have their poor relations.
Bleak House (1853), ch. 28

19 I have known him come home to supper with a flood of tears, and a declaration that nothing was now left but a jail; and go to bed making a calculation of the expense of putting bow-windows to the house, "in case anything turned up," which was his favourite expression.
Referring to Mr. Micawber. *David Copperfield* (1850), ch. 11

20 Annual income twenty pounds, annual expenditure nineteen nineteen and six, result happiness. Annual income twenty pounds, annual expenditure twenty pounds ought and six, result misery.
Said by Mr. Micawber. *David Copperfield* (1850), ch. 12

21 I am well aware that I am the 'umblest person going....My mother is likewise a very 'umble person. We live in a numble abode.
Said by Uriah Heep. *David Copperfield* (1850), ch. 16

22 We are so very 'umble.
Said by Uriah Heep. *David Copperfield* (1850), ch. 17

23 I only ask for information.
Said by Miss Rosa Dartle. *David Copperfield* (1850), ch. 20

24 What a world of gammon and spinnage it is, though, ain't it!
Said by Miss Mowcher, using a euphemism for humbug and deception. *David Copperfield* (1850), ch. 22

25 Accidents will occur in the best-regulated families; and in families not regulated by that pervading influence which sanctifies while it enhances them I would say, in short, by the influence of Woman, in the lofty character of Wife, they may be expected with confidence, and must be borne with philosophy.
Said by Mr. Micawber. *David Copperfield* (1850), ch. 28

26 Mrs Crupp had indignantly assured him that there wasn't room to swing a cat there; but, as Mr Dick justly observed to me, sitting down on the foot of the bed, nursing his leg, "You know, Trotwood, I don't want to swing a cat. I never do swing a cat. Therefore, what does that signify to me!"
David Copperfield (1850), ch. 35

27 I'm Gormed—and I can't say no fairer than that.
Mr. Peggotty on the fact of Mrs. Gummidge's marriages. *David Copperfield* (1850), ch. 63

28 There was no light nonsense about Miss Blimber...she was dry and sandy with working in the graves of deceased languages. None of your live languages for Miss Blimber. They must be dead—stone dead—and then Miss Blimber dug them up like a Ghoul.
Dombey and Son (1848), ch. 11

29 Train up a fig-tree in the way it should go, and when you are old sit under the shade of it.
Said by Captain Cuttle. *Dombey and Son* (1848), ch. 19

30 Cows are my passion.
Said by Mrs. Skewton. *Dombey and Son* (1848), ch. 21

31 Stranger, pause and ask thyself the question, Canst thou do likewise? If not, with a blush retire.
Edwin Drood (1870), ch. 4

32 "He calls the knaves, Jacks, this boy," said Estella with disdain, before our first game was out.
Pip's first encounter with Estella. *Great Expectations* (1861), ch. 8

33 I had cherished a profound conviction that her bringing me up by hand, gave her no right to bring me up by jerks.
Said by Pip, referring to his sister, Mrs. Joe Gargery. *Great Expectations* (1861), ch. 8

34 On the Rampage, Pip, and off the Rampage, Pip; such is Life!
Said by Joe Gargery. *Great Expectations* (1861), ch. 15

35 Get hold of portable property.
Said by Wemmick. *Great Expectations* (1861), ch. 24

36 You don't object to an aged parent, I hope?
Said by Wemmick. *Great Expectations* (1861), ch. 25

37 "Halloa! Here's a church! ... Let's go in! ... Here's Miss Skiffins! Let's have a wedding."
Said by Wemmick. *Great Expectations* (1861), ch. 55

38 Now, what I want is Facts...Facts alone are wanted in life.
Said by Mrs. Gradgrind. *Hard Times* (1854), bk. 1, ch. 1

39 I have seen so little happiness come of money; it has brought within my knowledge so little peace to this house, or to any one belonging to it; that it is worth less to me than to another.
Little Dorrit (1857)

40 Whatever was required to be done, the Circumlocution Office was beforehand with all the public departments in the art of perceiving HOW NOT TO DO IT.
Little Dorrit (1857), bk. 1, ch. 10

41 Look here. Upon my soul you mustn't come into the place saying you want to know, you know.
Said by Barnacle Junior. *Little Dorrit* (1857), bk. 1, ch. 10

42 In company with several other old ladies of both sexes.
Said by Mr. Meagles. *Little Dorrit* (1857), bk. 1, ch. 17

43 It was not a bosom to repose upon, but it was a capital bosom to hang jewels upon.
Referring to Mrs. Merdle. *Little Dorrit* (1857), bk. 1, ch. 21

44 Father is rather vulgar, my dear. The word Papa, besides, gives a pretty form to the lips. Papa, potatoes, poultry, prunes, and prism, are all very good words for the lips: especially prunes and prism.
Said by Mrs. General. *Little Dorrit* (1857), bk. 2, ch. 5.

45 Any man may be in good spirits and good temper when he's well dressed. There ain't much credit in that.
Said by Mark Tapley. *Martin Chuzzlewit* (1844), ch. 5

46 With affection beaming in one eye, and calculation shining out of the other.
Description of Mrs. Todgers. *Martin Chuzzlewit* (1844), ch. 8

47 As she frequently remarked when she made any such mistake, it would be all the same a hundred years hence.
Referring to Mrs. Squeers. *Martin Chuzzlewit* (1844), ch. 9

48 Let us be moral. Let us contemplate existence.
Martin Chuzzlewit (1844), ch. 10

49 Here's the rule for bargains: "Do other men, for they would do you." That's the true business precept. All others are counterfeits.
Said by Jonas. *Martin Chuzzlewit* (1844), ch. 11

50 Buy an annuity cheap, and make your life interesting to yourself and everybody else that watches the speculation.
Said by Jonas. *Martin Chuzzlewit* (1844), ch. 18

51 "She's the sort of woman now," said Mould ..."one would almost feel disposed to bury for nothing: and do it neatly, too!"
Mr. Mould referring to Mrs. Gamp. *Martin Chuzzlewit* (1844), ch. 25

52 He'd make a lovely corpse.
Said by Mrs. Gamp. *Martin Chuzzlewit* (1844), ch. 25

53 All the wickedness of the world is print to him.
Said by Mrs. Gamp. *Martin Chuzzlewit* (1844), ch. 26

54 We never knows wot's hidden in each other's hearts; and if we had glass winders there, we'd need keep the shutters up, some on us, I do assure you!
Said by Mrs. Gamp. *Martin Chuzzlewit* (1844), ch. 29

55 The words she spoke of Mrs Harris, lambs could not forgive...nor worms forget.
Referring to Mrs. Gamp. *Martin Chuzzlewit* (1844), ch. 49

56 Youth are boarded, clothed, booked, furnished with pocket-money, provided with all necessaries, instructed in all languages living and dead, mathematics, orthography, geometry, astronomy, trigonometry, the use of the globes, algebra, single stick (if required), writing, arithmetic, fortification, and every other branch of classical literature. Terms, twenty guineas per annum. No extras, no vacations, and diet unparalleled.
Nicholas Nickleby (1839), ch. 3

57 He had but one eye, and the popular prejudice runs in favour of two.
Description of Mr. Squeers. *Nicholas Nickleby* (1839), ch. 4

58 Subdue your appetites my dears, and you've conquered human nature.
Said by Mr. Squeers. *Nicholas Nickleby* (1839), ch. 5

59 When he has learnt that bottinney means a knowledge of plants, he goes and knows 'em. That's our system, Nickleby; what do you think of it?
Mr Squeers' educational method. *Nicholas Nickleby* (1839), ch. 8

60 There are only two styles of portrait painting; the serious and the smirk.
Said by Miss La Creevy. *Nicholas Nickleby* (1839), ch. 10

61 Sir, My pa requests me to write to you, the doctors considering it doubtful whether he will ever recuvver the use of his legs which prevents his holding a pen.
Said by Fanny Squeers. *Nicholas Nickleby* (1839), ch. 15

62 We've got a private master comes to teach us at home, but we ain't proud, because ma says it's sinful.
Said by Mrs. Kenwigs. *Nicholas Nickleby* (1839), ch. 16

63 Language was not powerful enough to describe the infant phenomenon.
Referring to Nicholas Nickleby. *Nicholas Nickleby* (1839), ch. 23

64 Every baby born into the world is a finer one than the last.
Nicholas Nickleby (1839), ch. 36

65 All is gas and gaiters.
Nicholas Nickleby (1839), ch. 49

66 Bring in the bottled lightning, a clean tumbler, and a corkscrew.
Said by the Gentleman in the Small-clothes. *Nicholas Nickleby* (1839), ch. 49

67 Oliver Twist has asked for more.
Oliver Twist (1838), ch. 2

68 Known by the sobriquet of "The artful Dodger."
Oliver Twist (1838), ch. 8

69 There is a passion for hunting something deeply implanted in the human breast.
Referring to chasing pickpockets. *Oliver Twist* (1838), ch. 10

70 Oh, Mrs Corney, what a prospect this opens! What a opportunity for a jining of hearts and house-keepings!
Said by Bumble. *Oliver Twist* (1838), ch. 27

71 "If the law supposes that," said Mr Bumble..., "the law is a ass—a idiot."
Oliver Twist (1838), ch. 51

72 The question about everything was, would it bring a blush to the cheek of a young person?
Pondered by Mr. Podsnap. *Our Mutual Friend* (1865), bk. 1, ch. 11

73 I think...that it is the best club in London.
Mr. Tremlow describing the British Parliament. *Our Mutual Friend* (1865), bk. 2, ch. 3

74 He'd be sharper than a serpent's tooth, if he wasn't as dull as ditch water.
A reference to *King Lear* by William Shakespeare. *Our Mutual Friend* (1865), bk. 3, ch. 10

75 I want to be something so much worthier than the doll in the doll's house.
Said by Bella. *Our Mutual Friend* (1865), bk. 4, ch. 5

76 The dodgerest of the dodgers.
Referring to Mr. Fledgeby. *Our Mutual Friend* (1865), bk. 4, ch. 8

77 "It wasn't the wine," murmured Mr Snodgrass, in a broken voice, "It was the salmon."
Referring to his hangover. *Pickwick Papers* (1837), ch. 8

78 I wants to make your flesh creep.
Said by the Fat Boy. *Pickwick Papers* (1837), ch. 8

79 "Can I unmoved see thee dying
On a log,
Expiring frog!"
Mrs. Leo Hunter's poem. *Pickwick Papers* (1837), ch. 15

80 Battledore and shuttlecock's a wery good game, vhen you an't the shuttlecock and two lawyers the battledores, in which case it gets too excitin' to be pleasant.
Said by Mr. Weller. *Pickwick Papers* (1837), ch. 20

81 Dumb as a drum vith a hole in it, sir.
Said by Sam Weller. *Pickwick Papers* (1837), ch. 25

82 A double glass o' the inwariable.
Said by Mr. Weller. *Pickwick Papers* (1837), ch. 33

83 Never sign a walentine with your own name.
Said by Sam Weller. *Pickwick Papers* (1837), ch. 33

84 A Being, erect upon two legs, and bearing all the outward semblance of a man, and not of a monster.
Said by Buzfuz. *Pickwick Papers* (1837), ch. 34

85 They don't mind it; it's a regular holiday to them—all porter and skittles.
Said by Sam Weller. *Pickwick Papers* (1837), ch. 41

86 A smattering of everything, and a knowledge of nothing.
Sketches by Boz (1836), ch. 3; "Tales"

87 Grief never mended no broken bones, and as good people's wery scarce, what I says is, make the most on 'em.
Sketches by Boz (1836), ch. 22; "Gin-Shops"

88 O let us love our occupations,
Bless the squire and his relations,
Live upon our daily rations,
And always know our proper stations.
The Chimes (1844), "2nd Quarter"

89 If there were no bad people there would be no good lawyers.
Said by Mr. Brass. *The Old Curiosity Shop* (1841), ch. 56

90 "Did you ever taste beer?"
"I had a sip of it once," said the small servant.
"Here's a state of things!" cried Mr Swiveller..."She never tasted it—it can't be tasted in a sip!"
The Old Curiosity Shop (1841), ch. 57

91 Kent, sir—everybody knows Kent—apples, cherries, hops and women.
The Pickwick Papers (1837), ch. 2

92 "It's always best on these occasions to do what the mob do."
"But suppose there are two mobs?" suggested Mr Snodgrass.
"Shout with the largest," replied Mr Pickwick.
The Pickwick Papers (1837), ch. 13

93 Take example by your father, my boy, and be very careful o' vidders all your life.
Referring to widows. *The Pickwick Papers* (1837), ch. 13

94 "It's a wery remarkable circumstance, sir," said Sam, "that poverty and oysters always seem to go together."
The Pickwick Papers (1837), ch. 22

95 It's over, and can't be helped, and that's one consolation, as they always says in Turkey, ven they cuts the wrong man's head off.
Said by Sam Weller. *The Pickwick Papers* (1837), ch. 23

96 Wery glad to see you indeed, and hope our acquaintance may be a long 'un, as the gen'l'm'n said to the fi' pun' note.
The Pickwick Papers (1837), ch. 25

97 Our noble society for providing the infant negroes in the West Indies with flannel waistcoats and moral pocket handkerchiefs.
The Pickwick Papers (1837), ch. 27

98 It's my opinion, sir, that this meeting is drunk.
The Pickwick Papers (1837), ch. 33

99 Poetry's unnat'ral; no man ever talked poetry 'cept a beadle on boxin' day.
The Pickwick Papers (1837), ch. 33

100 "Do you spell it with a 'V' or a 'W'?" inquired the judge.
"That depends upon the taste and fancy of the speller, my Lord," replied Sam.
The Pickwick Papers (1837), ch. 34

101 "Yes I have a pair of eyes," replied Sam, "and that's just it. If they was a pair o' patent double million magnifyin' gas microscopes of hextra power, p'raps I might be able to see through a flight o' stairs and a deal door; but bein' only eyes, you see, my vision's limited."
The Pickwick Papers (1837), ch. 34

102 Miss Bolo rose from the table considerably agitated, and went straight home, in a flood of tears and a Sedan chair.
The Pickwick Papers (1837), ch. 35

103 "That 'ere young lady," replied Sam. "She knows wot's wot, she does."
The Pickwick Papers (1837), ch. 37

104 Anythin' for a quiet life, as the man said wen he took the sitivation at the lighthouse.
The Pickwick Papers (1837), ch. 43

Dickey, James (James Lafayette Dickey; 1923–97) U.S. poet and novelist

1 We have all been in rooms we cannot die in.
Adultery (1967)

Dickinson, Emily (Emily Elizabeth Dickinson; 1830–86) U.S. poet

Quotations about Dickinson

1 I saw her but twice, face to face, and brought away the impression of something as unique and remote as Undine or Mignon or Thekla.
Anonymous. *Bookman* (October 1924)

2 In a life so retired it was inevitable that the main events should be the death of friends, and Emily Dickinson became a prolific writer of notes of condolence.
Northrop Frye (1912–91) Canadian academic. Quoted in *Major Writers of America* (Perry Miller, ed.; 1962)

Quotations by Dickinson

3 Success is counted sweetest
By those who ne'er succeed.
No. 67 (1859?), st. 1, ll. 1–2, quoted in *The Complete Works of Emily Dickinson* (Thomas H. Johnson, ed.; 1970)

4 Surgeons must be very careful
When they take the knife!
Underneath their fine incisions
Stirs the culprit—*Life!*
No. 108 (1859), quoted in *The Complete Poems of Emily Dickinson* (Thomas H. Johnson, ed.; 1970)

5 "Hope" is the thing with feathers—
That perches in the soul—
And sings the tune without the words—
And never stops—at all.
No. 254 (1861), st. 1, quoted in *The Complete Poems of Emily Dickinson* (Thomas H. Johnson, ed.; 1970)

6 This is the Hour of Lead
Remembered, if outlived,
As Freezing persons, recollect the Snow
First—Chill—then Stupor—then the letting go.
No. 341 (1862?), st. 3, ll. 1–4, quoted in *The Complete Works of Emily Dickinson* (Thomas H. Johnson, ed.; 1970)

7 Much Madness is divinest Sense—
To a discerning Eye—
Much Sense—the starkest Madness.
No. 435 (1862?), st. 1, ll. 1–3, quoted in *The Complete Works of Emily Dickinson* (Thomas H. Johnson, ed.; 1970)

8 I heard a Fly buzz—when I died.
With Blue—uncertain stumbling Buzz
Between the light—and me
And then the Windows failed—and then
I could not see to see.
No. 465 (1862?), st. 1, ll. 1–5, quoted in *The Complete Works of Emily Dickinson* (Thomas H. Johnson, ed.; 1970)

9 Our journey had advanced;
Our feet were almost come
To that odd fork in Being's road,
Eternity by term.
No. 615 (1862?), st. 1, ll. 1–4, quoted in *The Complete Works of Emily Dickinson* (Thomas H. Johnson, ed.; 1970)

10 Pain—has an Element of Blank—
It cannot recollect
When it begun—or if there were
A time when it was not.
No. 650 (1862?), st. 1, ll. 1–4, quoted in *The Complete Works of Emily Dickinson* (Thomas H. Johnson, ed.; 1970)

11 Because I could not stop for Death,
He kindly stopped for me;
The carriage held but just ourselves
And Immortality.
No. 712 (1863?), st. 1, ll. 1–4, quoted in *The Complete Works of Emily Dickinson* (Thomas H. Johnson, ed.; 1970)

12 'Twas my one Glory—
Let it be
Remembered
I was owned of Thee.
No. 1028 (1865), quoted in *The Complete Works of Emily Dickinson* (Thomas H. Johnson, ed.; 1970)

13 My life closed twice before its close;
It yet remains to see
If Immortality unveil
A third event to me,
So huge, so hopeless to conceive
As these that twice befell.
Parting is all we know of heaven
And all we need of hell.
No. 1732, , st. 1–2, quoted in *The Complete Works of Emily Dickinson* (Thomas H. Johnson, ed.; 1970)

14 One need not be a Chamber—to be Haunted—
One need not be a House—
The Brain has Corridors-surpassing
Material Place—
Far safer, of a Midnight Meeting
External Ghost
Than its interior Confronting—
That Cooler Host.
"One Need Not Be a Chamber" (1830–86)

15 The first Day's Night had come—
And grateful that a thing
So terrible—had been endured—
I told my Soul to sing.
1862? "The First Day's Night Had Come" (1947), ll. 1–4, quoted in *Beyond Bedlam: Poems Written out of Mental Distress* (Ken Smith and Matthew Sweeney, eds.; 1997)

16 And Something's odd—within—
That person that I was—

And this One—do not feel the same—
Could it be Madness—this?
1862? "The First Day's Night Had Come" (1947), ll. 17–20, quoted in *Beyond Bedlam: Poems Written out of Mental Distress* (Ken Smith and Matthew Sweeney, eds.; 1997)

17 Of consciousness, her awful Mate
The Soul cannot be rid.
1864? "Of Consciousness Her Awful Mate," *Bolts of Melody* (1945), ll. 1–2, quoted in *A Choice of Emily Dickinson's Verse* (Ted Hughes, ed.; 1977)

18 After great pain, a formal feeling comes—
The Nerves sit ceremonious like tombs.
1862? "After Great Pain, a Formal Feeling Comes," *Further Poems* (1929), quoted in *The Penguin Book of American Verse* (Geoffrey Moore, ed.; 1977)

19 How slow the Wind—
how slow the sea—
how late their feathers be!
1883? "How Slow the Wind," *Letters of Emily Dickinson* (1894), st. 1, quoted in *A Choice of Emily Dickinson's Verse* (Ted Hughes, ed.; 1977)

20 Presentiment—is that long Shadow—on the Lawn—
Indicative that suns go down—

The Notice to the startled Grass
That Darkness—is about to pass.
1863? "Presentiment Is That Long Shadow on the Lawn," *Poems by Emily Dickinson* (1890), quoted in *A Choice of Emily Dickinson's Verse* (Ted Hughes, ed.; 1977)

21 The soul selects her own Society—
Then—shuts the Door.
1862? "The Soul Selects Her Own Society," *Poems by Emily Dickinson* (1890), quoted in *The Penguin Book of American Verse* (Geoffrey Moore, ed.; 1977)

Dickinson, John (1732–1808) U.S. politician and writer

1 Then join hand in hand, brave Americans all!
By uniting we stand, by dividing we fall.
"The Liberty Song" (1768)

Diddley, Bo (Ellas Bates McDaniel; b.1928) U.S. singer, guitarist, and songwriter

1 You don't have to be good with figures to know you've been had.
Referring to his first album, *Bo Diddley* (1955), not making him any money despite its popularity. Quoted in "Bo Diddley," *Off the Record: An Oral History of Popular Music* (Joe Smith; 1988)

2 We were the originators of all of this stuff, but nobody ever pays us any attention when one of us dies.
Referring to the fact that the riff to his debut album *Bo Diddley* (1955) is thought to have started rock and roll. Quoted in "Bo Diddley," *Off the Record: An Oral History of Popular Music* (Joe Smith; 1988)

Diderot, Denis (1713–84) French encyclopedist and philosopher

Quotations about Diderot

1 All your work is done on paper, which does not mind how you treat it...But I, poor Empress, must work upon human skin, which is much more ticklish and irritable.
Catherine the Great (1729–96) German-born Russian empress. Comparing her relationship with her political subjects with that of Denis Diderot to his writing. Letter to Denis Diderot (1770)

Quotations by Diderot

2 The word *freedom* has no meaning; there are and there can be no free beings.
Letter to Landois (1756)

3 Wandering in a vast forest at night, I have only a faint light to guide me. A stranger appears and says to me: "My friend, you should blow out your candle in order to find your way more clearly." This stranger is a theologian.
Addition aux pensées philosophiques (1762?)

4 But who shall be master? The writer or the reader?
Jacques le fataliste et son maître (1796)

5 It has been said that love robs those who have it of their wit, and gives it to those who have none.
Paradoxe sur le comédien (1830)

6 Staircase wit.
The witty retort one thinks of just too late, as one is leaving and on the way downstairs. *Paradoxe sur le comédien* (1830)

7 Examine the history of all nations and all centuries and you will always find men subject to three codes: the code of nature, the code of society, and the code of religion...these codes were never in harmony.
Supplément au Voyage de Bougainville (1935)

8 There is less harm to be suffered in being mad among madmen than in being sane all by oneself.
Supplément au Voyage de Bougainville (1935)

9 A sketch is generally more spirited than a picture. It is the artist's work when he is full of inspiration and ardor, when reflection has toned down nothing; it is the artist's soul expressing itself freely on canvas.
1765. Quoted in *Diderot on Art* (John Goodman, tr.; 1995)

10 The great landscapist has his own peculiar obsession; it is a kind of scared horror. His caverns are deep and gloomy; precipitous rocks threaten the sky...man passes through the domain of demons and gods.
1767. Quoted in *Diderot on Art* (John Goodman, tr.; 1995)

11 What a fine comedy this world would be if one did not play a part in it!
Quoted in *Diderot's Letters to Sophie Volland* (Peter France, tr.; 1974)

12 Religion is a support that in the end always ruins the edifice.
Quoted in *Encyclopedia of Philosophy* (P. Edwards, ed.; 1967)

13 Doctors are always working to preserve our health and cooks to destroy it, but the latter are the more often successful.
Attrib.

Didion, Joan (b.1934) U.S. journalist and writer

1 I learned early to keep death in my line of sight, keep it under surveillance, keep it on cleared ground and away from any brush where it might coil unnoticed.
A Book of Common Prayer (1977)

2 A good part of any day in Los Angeles is spent driving alone, through streets devoid of meaning to the driver, which is one

reason the place exhilarates some people, and floods others with an amorphous unease.
1991. "Pacific Distances," *Sentimental Journeys* (1992)

3 I was ten years old when "the atomic age"...came forcibly to the world's notice...I recall being told that the device which ended World War II was "the size of a lemon" (this was not true).
1991. "Pacific Distances," *Sentimental Journeys* (1992)

4 The intense blue in the pool water, the Cerenkov radiation around the fuel rods...the blue like light itself, the blue that is actually a shock wave in the water and is the exact blue of the glass at Chartres.
1991. Referring to a visit to a nuclear reactor. "Pacific Distances," *Sentimental Journeys* (1992)

5 Writers are always selling somebody out.
Slouching Towards Bethlehem (1968), preface

6 California is a place in which a boom mentality and a sense of Chekhovian loss meet in uneasy suspension; in which the mind is troubled by some buried but ineradicable suspicion that things had better work here, because here, beneath that immense bleached sky, is where we run out of continent.
"Notes from a Native Daughter," *Slouching Towards Bethlehem* (1968)

7 We tell ourselves stories in order to live...We look for the sermon in the suicide, for the social or moral lesson in the murder of five.
1978. *The White Album* (1979), pt. 1

8 The idea that truth lies on the far side of madness informs not only a considerable spread of Western literature but also, so commonly is it now held, an entire generation's experiment with hallucinogens.
1971. "Doris Lessing," *The White Album* (1979), pt. 3

9 Ask anyone committed to Marxist analysis how many angels on the head of a pin, and you will be asked in return to never mind the angels, tell me who controls the production of pins.
1972. "The Women's Movement," *The White Album* (1979), pt. 3

10 The astral discontent with actual lives, actual men, the denial of the real generative possibilities of adult sexual life, somehow touches beyond words...These are converts...who believe not in the oppression of women but in their own choices.
1972. "The Women's Movement," *The White Album* (1979), pt. 3

Diefenbaker, John (John George Diefenbaker; 1895–1979) Canadian statesman

1 Freedom is the right to be wrong, not the right to do wrong.
Quoted in *Reader's Digest* (September 1979)

Dietrich, Marlene (Maria Magdalene Dietrich von Losch; 1901–92) German-born U.S. actor and singer

1 Once a woman has forgiven her man, she must not reheat his sins for breakfast.
Marlene Dietrich's ABC (1962)

2 Latins are tenderly enthusiastic. In Brazil they throw flowers at you. In Argentina they throw themselves.
Newsweek (August 24, 1959)

3 Most women set out to try to change a man, and when they have changed him they do not like him.
Attrib.

4 The average man is more interested in a woman who is interested in him than he is in a woman—any woman—with beautiful legs.
Attrib.

Diggins, John P. (John Patrick Diggins; b.1935) U.S. historian

1 A history without moral dimension is a history without human causation and hence what is natural is what occurs and what occurs is natural.
"Consciousness and Ideology in American History," *American Historical Review* (February 1971)

2 If the problem of history is the problem of consciousness, the problem of consciousness is the problem of value.
"Consciousness and Ideology in American History," *American Historical Review* (February 1971)

DiLeonardo, Robert U.S. architect

1 My job is to create an environment that relaxes morality.
Referring to casinos in Atlantic City, New Jersey. *Wall Street Journal* (January 10, 1983)

Dillard, Annie (b.1945) U.S. writer

1 I cherish mental images I have of three perfectly happy people. One collects stones. Another—an Englishman, say—watches clouds. The third lives on a coast and collects drops of seawater which he examines microscopically and mounts.
Pilgrim at Tinker's Creek (1974), ch. 2

2 At this latitude I'm spinning 836 miles an hour round the earth's axis...I close my eyes and I see stars, deep stars giving way to deeper stars, deeper stars bowing to deepest stars at the crown of an infinite cone.
Pilgrim at Tinker's Creek (1974), ch. 3

3 Oh, it's mysterious lamplit evenings, here in the galaxy...Terror and a beauty insoluble are a ribband of blue woven into the fringes of garments of things both great and small.
Pilgrim at Tinker's Creek (1974), ch. 3

4 There are seven or eight categories of phenomena in the world that are worth talking about, and one of them is the weather.
Pilgrim at Tinker's Creek (1974), ch. 3

5 Shadows...inform my eyes of my location here, here O Israel, here in the world's flawed sculpture, here in the flickering shade of the nothingness between me and the light.
Pilgrim at Tinker's Creek (1974), ch. 4

6 The one thing that all religions recognize as separating us from our creator—our very self-consciousness—is also the one thing that divides us from our fellow creatures. It was a bitter birthday present from evolution, cutting us off at both ends.
Pilgrim at Tinker's Creek (1974), ch. 6

7 You don't run down the present, pursue it with baited hooks

and nets. You wait for it, empty-handed, and you are filled. You'll have fish left over.
Pilgrim at Tinker's Creek (1974), ch. 6

8 Look, in short, at practically anything—the coot's feet, the mantis's face, a banana, the human ear—and see that not only did the creator create everything, but that he is apt to create *anything*. He'll stop at nothing.
Pilgrim at Tinker's Creek (1974), ch. 8

9 Our planet alone has death. I have to acknowledge that the sea is a cup of death and the land is a stained altar stone.
Pilgrim at Tinker's Creek (1974), ch. 10

10 Divinity is not playful. The universe was not made in jest but in solemn incomprehensible earnest. By a power that is unfathomably secret, and holy, and fleet.
Pilgrim at Tinker's Creek (1974), ch. 15

Diller, Barry (b.1942) U.S. media executive

1 Like what?
Reply to his boss, Rupert Murdoch's comment that "we all share certain values." Quoted in *Rupert Murdoch, Ringmaster of the Information Circus* (William Shawcross; 1993)

Diller, Phyllis (b.1917) U.S. writer, comedian, and pianist

1 Cleaning your house while your kids are still growing
Is like shoveling the walk before it stops snowing.
Phyllis Diller's Housekeeping Hints (1966)

2 Never go to bed mad. Stay up and fight.
Phyllis Diller's Housekeeping Hints (1966)

3 I'm at an age when my back goes out more than I do.
The Joys of Aging and How to Avoid Them (1981)

Dillingham, Charles Bancroft (1868–1934) U.S. theatrical manager and producer

1 I bet you a hundred bucks he ain't in here.
Referring to the escapologist Harry Houdini; said at his funeral, while carrying his coffin. Attrib.

Dillon, Wentworth, 4th Earl of Roscommon (1633?–85) Irish-born British poet

1 But words once spoke can never be recall'd.
Art of Poetry (1680)

2 My God, my Father, and my Friend,
Do not forsake me at my end.
Translation of "Dies Irae"

3 Choose an author as you choose a friend.
"Essay on Translated Verse" (1684), l. 96

DiMaggio, Joe (Joseph Paul DiMaggio; 1914–99) U.S. baseball player

Quotations about DiMaggio

1 "I would like to take the great DiMaggio fishing," the old man said. "They say his father was a fisherman. Maybe he was poor as we are and would understand."
Ernest Hemingway (1899–1961) U.S. writer. *The Old Man and the Sea* (1952)

Quotations by DiMaggio

2 Now I've had everything except the thrill of watching Babe Ruth play.
Referring to being inducted into the Baseball Hall of Fame. Remark (1995)

3 A ball player's got to be kept hungry to become a big-leaguer. That's why no boy from a rich family ever made the big leagues.
Attrib.

Dimma, William U.S. business executive

1 Greed is essential to the proper functioning of our economic system...On the supply side we call it hustle or ambition or push and shove. On the demand side, we call it consumerism or, playfully, "shop till you drop."
Time (November 15, 1989)

Dinesen, Isak, Baroness (Karen Christence von Blixen-Finecke, born Dinesen; 1885–1962) Danish writer

1 What is man, when you come to think upon him, but a minutely set, ingenious machine for turning, with infinite artfulness, the red wine of Shiraz into urine?
"The Dreamers," *Seven Gothic Tales* (1934)

Ding Ling (pen name of Jiang Weizhi; 1904–86) Chinese novelist

1 She handed him lots of money, all in ten dollar notes. Some of it she had got from clients and some from gambling. Now she was handing it all over to him. The two of them would spend the rest of their lives together in peace.
"A House in Qingyun Lane" (1929)

Diogenes (Diogenes of Sinope, "The Cynic"; 412?–323 B.C.) Greek philosopher

1 If only it were as easy to banish hunger by rubbing the belly as it is to masturbate.
4th century B.C. "Diogenes," *Lives of the Philosophers* (Diogenes Läertius; 3rd century A.D.)

2 I am a citizen of the world.
Replying to a question concerning his nationality. Attrib. "Diogenes," *Lives of the Philosophers* (Diogenes Läertius; 3rd century A.D.)

3 The mountains too, at a distance, appear airy masses and smooth, but seen near at hand they are rough.
4th century B.C. Quoted in "Pyrrho," *Lives of the Philosophers* (Diogenes Läertius; 3rd century A.D.)

4 Stand a little less between me and the sun.
4th century B.C. When Alexander the Great asked if there was anything he wanted. "Alexander," *Parallel Lives* (Plutarch; 1st Century A.D.), ch. 14, sect. 4

5 I had rather be mad than delighted.
Attrib.

Diogenes Läertius (*fl.* 3rd century) Greek historian and biographer

1 It was a saying of his that education was an ornament in prosperity and a refuge in adversity.
"Aristotle," quoted in *Lives of Eminent Philosophers* (C. D. Yonge, tr.; 1853)

2 Nothing can be produced out of nothing.
"Diogenes of Apollonia," quoted in *Lives and Opinions of the Eminent Philosophers* (C. D. Yonge, tr.; 1853)

3 Diogenes lighted a candle in the daytime, and went round saying, "I am looking for an honest man."
Referring to Diogenes of Sinope, "the Cynic". "Diogenes," *Lives of the Philosophers* (3rd century?), 6

4 It was a common saying of Myson that men ought not to investigate things from words, but words from things; for that things are not made for the sake of words, but words for things.
"Myson," *Lives of the Philosophers* (3rd century?), 3

Dionysius of Halicarnassus (*fl.* 30 B.C.) Greek historian and critic

Quotations about Dionysius of Halicarnassus

1 I have read somewhere or other, in Dionysius of Halicarnassus, I think, that history is philosophy teaching by examples.
Henry St. John Bolingbroke (1678–1751) English statesman. *Letters on the Study and Use of History* (1752), Letter 2

Quotations by Dionysius of Halicarnassus

2 History is philosophy teaching by examples.
Ars Rhetorica (1st century B.C.), ch. 11, sect. 2

Dionysius the Areopagite (*fl.* 1st century) Greek church leader and martyr

1 One can take eternity and time to be predicates of God since, being the Ancient of Days, he is the cause of all time and eternity. Yet he is before time and beyond time and is the source of the variety of time and of seasons.
1st century A.D. Some modern scholars now identify the work attributed to Dionysius to a 6th-century Neoplatonist known as Pseudo-Dionysius. Quoted in "The Divine Names," *Pseudo-Dionysius, The Complete Works* (C. Luibheid, tr.; 1987)

2 We make assertions and denials of what is next to it, but never of it, for it is both beyond every assertion, being the perfect and unique cause of all things, and, by virtue of its preeminently simple and absolute nature, free of every limitation, beyond every limitation; it is also beyond every denial.
1st century A.D. Some modern scholars now identify the work attributed to Dionysius to a 6th-century Neoplatonist known as Pseudo-Dionysius. Quoted in "The Mystical Theology," *Pseudo-Dionysius, The Complete Works* (C. Luibheid, tr.; 1987), ch. 5

Dior, Christian (1905–57) French couturier

1 Women are most fascinating between the ages of thirty-five and forty, after they have won a few races and know how to pace themselves. Since few women ever pass forty, maximum fascination can continue indefinitely.
Colliers Magazine (June 10, 1955)

2 My models—they're the life of my dresses, and I want my dresses to be happy.
Quoted in *Dior* (Françoise Giroud; Stewart Spencer, tr.; 1987)

Diphilus (*fl.* 4th century B.C.) Greek poet

1 Time is a physician that heals every grief.
300 B.C. Attrib.

Dipoko, Mbella Sonne (b.1936) Cameroon novelist and poet

1 She didn't know that love was the fear that tenderness always has an end. She didn't know that love was passionate fear on the frontiers of sentimental departure.
Because of Women (1968)

2 We become like all mankind
Decent without Indecent within.
"Our Destiny," *Black & White in Love* (1972)

Dirac, Paul (Paul Adrien Maurice Dirac; 1902–84) British physicist and Nobel laureate

1 God is a mathematician of a very high order, and He used very advanced mathematics in constructing the universe.
Scientific American (May 1963)

2 In science one tries to tell people, in such a way as to be understood by everyone, something that no one ever knew before. But in poetry, it's the exact opposite.
Quoted in *Mathematical Circles Adieu* (H. Eves; 1977)

Disney, Walt (Walter Elias Disney; 1901–66) U.S. film producer and animator

Quotations about Disney

1 I do not know whether he draws a line himself. But I assume that his is the direction...It makes Disney the most significant figure in graphic art since Leonardo.
David Low (1891–1963) British cartoonist. Quoted in *The Disney Version* (Richard Schickel; 1985), ch. 20

Quotations by Disney

2 Sheer animated fantasy is still my first and deepest production impulse. The fable is the best storytelling device ever conceived, and the screen is its best medium.
Quoted in *The Disney Touch* (Ron Grover; 1996)

3 Of all the things I've done, the most vital is coordinating the talents of those who work for us and pointing them towards a certain goal.
Quoted in *The Disney Version* (Richard Schickel; 1968)

4 Girls bored me—they still do. I love Mickey Mouse more than any woman I've ever known.
You Must Remember This (W. Wagner; 1975)

5 If you can dream it you can do it.
Attrib.

6 Too many people grow up. That's the real trouble with the world, too many people grow up. They forget. They don't remember what it's like to be 12 years old. They patronize, they treat children as inferiors. Well I won't do that.
Attrib.

Disposable Heroes of Hiphoprisy U.S. rap group

1 Television—the drug of the nation
Breeding ignorance and feeding radiation.
"Television: The Drug of the Nation" (1992)

Disraeli, Benjamin, 1st Earl of Beaconsfield (1804–81) British prime minister and writer

Quotations about Disraeli

1 He was without any rival whatever, the first comic genius who ever installed himself in Downing Street.
Michael Foot (b.1913) British politician and writer. *Debts of Honour* (1980)

Quotations by Disraeli

2 Apologies only account for that which they do not alter.
Speech (July 28, 1871)

3 The health of the people is really the foundation upon which all their happiness and all their powers as a State depend.
Speech (June 24, 1877)

4 Protection is not a principle, but an expedient.
Speech in the British Parliament (March 17, 1845)

5 Upon the education of the people of this country the fate of this country depends.
Speech in the British Parliament (June 15, 1874)

6 No Government can be long secure without a formidable Opposition.
Coningsby (1844), bk. 2, ch. 1

7 "A sound Conservative government," said Taper, musingly. "I understand: Tory men and Whig measures."
Coningsby (1844), bk. 2, ch. 6

8 Almost everything that is great has been done by youth.
Coningsby (1844), bk. 3, ch. 1

9 Youth is a blunder; Manhood a struggle; Old Age a regret.
Coningsby (1844), bk. 3, ch. 1

10 Man is only truly great when he acts from the passions.
Coningsby (1844), bk. 4, ch. 13

11 Read no history: nothing but biography, for that is life without theory.
Contarini Fleming (1832), pt. 1, ch. 23

12 The practice of politics in the East may be defined by one word—dissimulation.
Contarini Fleming (1832), pt. 5, ch. 10

13 The world is a wheel, and it will all come round right.
Endymion (1880), ch. 70

14 "Sensible men are all of the same religion."
"And pray what is that?" inquired the prince.
"Sensible men never tell."
Endymion (1880), ch. 81

15 Though I sit down now, the time will come when you will hear me.
Maiden speech. Speech in the British Parliament, *Hansard* (December 7, 1837), col. 807

16 Thus you have a starving population, an absentee aristocracy, and an alien Church, and in addition the weakest executive in the world. That is the Irish Question.
Speech in the British Parliament, *Hansard* (February 16, 1844), col. 1016

17 A Conservative government is an organized hypocrisy.
Speech in the British Parliament, *Hansard* (March 17, 1845), col. 1028

18 Assassination has never changed the history of the world.
Speech in the British Parliament, *Hansard* (May 1, 1865), col. 1246

19 He has to learn that petulance is not sarcasm, and that insolence is not invective.
Referring to Sir Charles Wood. Speech in the British Parliament, *Hansard* (December 16, 1852), col. 1653

20 What we anticipate seldom occurs; what we least expected generally happens.
Henrietta Temple (1837), bk. 2, ch. 4

21 Time is the great physician.
Henrietta Temple (1837), bk. 6, ch. 9

22 A Protestant, if he wants aid or advice on any matter, can only go to his solicitor.
Lothair (1870), ch. 27

23 London: a nation, not a city.
Lothair (1870), ch. 27

24 When a man fell into his anecdotage it was a sign for him to retire from the world.
Lothair (1870), ch. 28

25 Every woman should marry—and no man.
Lothair (1870), ch. 30

26 "My idea of an agreeable person", said Hugo Bohun, "is a person who agrees with me".
Lothair (1870), ch. 35

27 You know who the critics are? The men who have failed in literature and art.
Lothair (1870), ch. 35

28 The Egremonts had never said anything that was remembered, or done anything that could be recalled.
Sybil (1845), bk. 1, ch. 3

29 To be conscious that you are ignorant is a great step to knowledge.
Sybil (1845), bk. 1, ch. 5

30 To do nothing and get something, formed a boy's ideal of a manly career.
Sybil (1845), bk. 1, ch. 5

31 "Two nations; between whom there is no intercourse and no sympathy; who are as ignorant of each other's habits, thoughts, and feelings, as if they were dwellers in different zones, or inhabitants of different planets; who are formed by a different breeding, are fed by a different food, are ordered by different manners, and are not governed by the same laws."
Referring to the rich and the poor. The inspiration for the "One Nation" Conservatism of Stanley Baldwin. *Sybil* (1845), bk. 2, ch. 5

32 Little things affect little minds.
Sybil (1845), bk. 3, ch. 2

33 Frank and explicit—that is the right line to take when you wish to conceal your own mind and confuse the minds of others.
Sybil (1845), bk. 6 ch. 1

34 That fatal drollery called a representative government.
Tancred (1847), bk. 2, ch. 13

35 All is race; there is no other truth.
Tancred (1847), bk. 2, ch. 14

36 A majority is always the best repartee.
Tancred (1847), bk. 2, ch. 14

37 London is a modern Babylon.
Tancred (1847), bk. 5, ch. 5

38 A good eater must be a good man; for a good eater must have a good digestion, and a good digestion depends upon a good conscience.
The Young Duke (1831)

39 It destroys one's nerves to be amiable every day to the same human being.
The Young Duke (1831)

40 Lord Salisbury and myself have brought you back peace—but a peace I hope with honour.
July 16, 1878. Remark on his return from the Congress of Berlin, where he succeeded in curbing Russian influence in southeastern Europe after the Russo-Turkish war. *Times*, London (July 17, 1878)

41 I hold that the characteristic of the present age is craving credulity.
November 25, 1864. Said to the Society for Increasing Endowments of Small Livings in the Diocese of Oxford, England. *Times*, London (November 26, 1864)

42 Party is organized opinion.
November 25, 1864. Said to the Society for Increasing Endowments of Small Livings in the Diocese of Oxford, England. *Times*, London (November 26, 1864)

43 An author who speaks about his own books is almost as bad as a mother who talks about her own children.
November 19, 1873. Speech at a banquet held in Glasgow for his installation as Lord Rector. *Times*, London (November 20, 1873)

44 The question is this: Is man an ape or an angel? I, my lord, am on the side of the angels.
November 25, 1864. Speech at the Diocesan Conference, *Times*, London (November 26, 1864)

45 I believe that without party Parliamentary government is impossible.
April 3, 1872. Speech, Manchester, England, *Times*, London (April 4, 1872)

46 Increased means and increased leisure are the two civilizers of man.
April 3, 1872. Speech, Manchester, England, *Times*, London (April 4, 1872)

47 There is moderation even in excess.
Vivian Grey (1826), bk. 6, ch. 1

48 I repeat...that all power is a trust—that we are accountable for its exercise—that, from the people, and for the people, all springs, and all must exist.
Vivian Grey (1826), bk. 6, ch. 7

49 Man is not the creature of circumstances. Circumstances are the creatures of men.
Vivian Grey (1826), bk. 6, ch. 7

50 Thank you for the manuscript; I shall lose no time in reading it.
His customary reply to those who sent him unsolicited manuscripts. Attrib. *An Irreverent Social History of the Bathroom* (Frank Muir; 1982)

51 There are three kinds of lies: lies, damned lies and statistics.
Attrib. *Autobiography* (Mark Twain; 1924), vol. 1

52 Everyone likes flattery; and when you come to Royalty you should lay it on with a trowel.
Said to Matthew Arnold. Attrib. *Collections and Recollections* (G. W. E. Russell; 1898), ch. 23

53 I will not go down to posterity talking bad grammar.
March 31, 1881. Remark made when correcting proofs of his last parliamentary speech. *Disraeli* (Robert Blake; 1966), ch. 32

54 No, it is better not. She will only ask me to take a message to Albert.
1881. On his deathbed, declining an offer of a visit from Queen Victoria. Attrib. *Disraeli* (Robert Blake; 1966), ch. 32

55 Pray remember, Mr Dean, no dogma, no Dean.
Attrib. *Life of Benjamin Disraeli* (W. Monypenny and G. Buckle; 1916), vol. 4, ch. 10

56 Yes, I have climbed to the top of the greasy pole.
1869. Said after being appointed prime minister. Attrib. *Life of Benjamin Disraeli* (W. Monypenny and G. Buckle; 1916), vol. 4, ch. 16

57 I am dead: dead, but in the Elysian fields.
Said on his elevation to the House of Lords. Attrib. *Life of Benjamin Disraeli* (W. Monypenny and G. Buckle; 1920), vol. 5, ch. 13

58 When I want to read a novel I write one.
Attrib. *Life of Benjamin Disraeli* (W. Monypenny and G. Buckle; 1920), vol. 6, ch. 17

59 I know he is, and he adores his maker.
Replying to a remark made in defense of the reformer John Bright (1818–89) that he was a self-made man. Attrib. *The Fine Art of Political Wit* (Leon A. Harris; 1965)

60 Nobody is forgotten when it is convenient to remember him.
Attrib.

61 When I meet a man whose name I can't remember, I give myself two minutes; then, if it is a hopeless case, I always say, And how is the old complaint?
Attrib.

62 She is an excellent creature, but she never can remember which came first, the Greeks or the Romans.
Referring to his wife. Attrib.

63 Her Majesty is not a subject.
Responding to Gladstone's taunt that Disraeli could make a joke out of any subject, including Queen Victoria. Attrib.

Dix, Dorothea (Dorothea Lynde Dix; 1802–87) U.S. reformer and nurse

1 I have myself seen more than nine thousand idiots, epileptics and insane in the United States...bound with galling chains, bowed beneath fetters, lacerated with ropes, scourged with rods.
1848? Dorothea Dix's lifelong crusade for improved treatment of people with mental illness led to the establishment of numerous state mental hospitals in the United States, Canada, and Europe. First Petition to Congress (1848)

2 In a world where there is so much to be done, I felt strongly

impressed that there must be something for me to do.
December 31, 1944. Letter (December 31, 1844), quoted in *Letters from New York* (Lydia Maria Child, ed.; 1852), vol. 2

Dix, Dorothy (Elizabeth Meriwether Gilmer; 1861–1951) U.S. journalist and writer

1 Now one of the great reasons why so many husbands and wives make shipwreck of their lives together is because a man is always seeking for happiness, while a woman is on a perpetual still hunt for trouble.
Dorothy Dix, Her Book (1926), ch. 1

2 I have learned to live each day as it comes, and not to borrow trouble by dreading tomorrow. It is the dark menace of the future that makes cowards of us.
Dorothy Dix, Her Book (1926), Introduction

3 It is only the women whose eyes have been washed clear with tears who get the broad vision that makes them little sisters to all the world.
Dorothy Dix, Her Book (1926), Introduction

4 The reason that husbands and wives do not understand each other is because they belong to different sexes.
Attrib.

Dix, Gregory, Dom (George Eglinton Alston Dix; 1901–52) British monk

1 It is no accident that the symbol of a bishop is a crook, and the sign of an archbishop is a double-cross.
Attrib. Letter to *Times*, London (December 3, 1977)

Dix, Otto (1891–1969) German painter

1 I have never made written confessions, since, as you will see if you inspect them, my pictures are confessions of the most candid sort such as you will rarely find in this age...He who has eyes to see, let him see!
Quoted in *Otto Dix: Life and Work* (Fritz Löffler; 1982)

Dixon, Willie (1915–92) U.S. blues musician, composer, and record producer

1 Don't get mad. Get smart.
I Am The Blues: The Willie Dixon Story (1989)

Djilas, Milovan (1911–95) Montenegrin-born Yugoslavian politician, writer, and dissident

1 Though man may endure his ordeal like Sisyphus, the time must come for him to revolt like Prometheus before his powers are exhausted by the ordeal.
The Unperfect Society (1969)

Dobie, J. Frank (James Frank Dobie; 1888–1964) U.S. folklorist and academic

1 Conform and be dull.
Voice of the Coyote (1949)

2 Putting on the spectacles of science in expectation of finding the answer to everything looked at signifies inner blindness.
Voice of the Coyote (1949), Introduction

Dobrée, Bonamy (1891–1974) British scholar and writer

1 It is difficult to be humble. Even if you aim at humility, there is no guarantee that when you have attained the state you will not be proud of the feat.
John Wesley (1974)

Dobson, Austin (Henry Austin Dobson; 1840–1921) British poet

1 Fame is a food that dead men eat,
I have no stomach for such meat.
1906. "Fame Is a Food that Dead Men Eat," *Collected Poems: By Austin Dobson: Ninth Edition* (1913), ll. 1–2

2 Time goes, you say? Ah no!
Alas, Time stays, *we* go.
1877. A variation on Ronsard: "Le temps s'en va, le temps s'en va, ma dame! Las! le temps non: mais *nous* nous en allons!" "The Paradox of Time," *Collected Poems: By Austin Dobson: Ninth Edition* (1913)

do Carmo, Isabel (b.1940) Portuguese politician

1 In our party, being a woman is no problem. After all, it is a revolutionary party.
Referring to the Portuguese Communist Party. *Time* (October 30, 1975)

Doctorow, E. L. (Edgar Lawrence Doctorow; b.1931) U.S. novelist

1 At moments when our attention is painfully acute, we notice peripheral things...as if to reaffirm to ourselves our basic irresponsibility.
The Waterworks (1994)

2 Death is no more than an obituary. Anyone's death, including our own, is yesterday's news.
The Waterworks (1994)

3 Like art and politics, gangsterism is a very important avenue into mainstream society.
Quoted in *International Herald Tribune* (October 1, 1990)

4 There is no longer any such thing as fiction or non-fiction; there's only narrative.
Quoted in *New York Times Book Review* (1988)

5 The writer isn't made in a vacuum. Writers are witnesses. The reason we need writers is because we need witnesses to this terrifying century.
Quoted in *Writers at Work* (George Plimpton, ed.; 1988)

6 It's like driving a car at night. You never see further than your headlights, but you can make the whole trip that way.
Referring to his own creative technique. Quoted in *Writers at Work* (George Plimpton, ed.; 1988)

Doddridge, Philip (1702–51) English clergyman and hymnwriter

1 Live while you live, the epicure would say,
And seize the pleasures of the present day;
Live while you live, the sacred preacher cries,
And give to God each moment as it flies.
Lord, in my views, let both united be:
I live in pleasure when I live to thee.
Epigram on his Family Arms (1745)

Dole, Bob (Robert Joseph Dole; b.1923) U.S. politician

1 History buffs probably noted the reunion at a Washington party a few weeks ago of three ex-presidents: Carter, Ford, and Nixon—See No Evil, Hear No Evil, and Evil.
Speech, Gridiron Club, Washington, D.C. (March 26, 1983)

Dolson, Hildegarde (Hildegarde Dolson Lockridge; 1908–81) U.S. fiction writer

1 Perhaps the surest way to tell when a female goes over the boundary from childhood into meaningful adolescence is to watch how long it takes her to get to bed at night.
"How Beautiful with Mud," *We Shook the Family Tree* (1946)

Domino, "Fats" (Antoine Domino, Jr.; b.1928) U.S. pianist and singer

1 A lot of fellows nowadays have a B.A., M.D., or Ph.D. Unfortunately, they don't have a J.O.B.
Attrib.

Donahue, Phil (Philip John Donahue; b.1935) U.S. television talk-show host

1 A little nonsense now and then is treasured by the best of men.
Quoted in *Speaking Freely—a Guided Tour of American English* (Stuart Berg Flexner and Anne H. Soukhanov; 1997)

Donatello (Donato di Niccolò di Betto Bardi; 1386?–1466) Italian sculptor

1 Tell the Patriarch I don't want to go to him, and that I am just as much the Patriarch in my art as he is in his.
Response to a patron's numerous summonses. Quoted in *Le facezie dei secoli d'oro* (G. Abrami, ed.; 1944)

Donatus, Aelius (*fl.* 4th century) Roman grammarian

1 To the devil with those who published before us.
4th century. Quoted by Saint Jerome, his pupil. Attrib.

Donleavy, J. P. (James Patrick Donleavy; b.1926) U.S. novelist

1 I got disappointed in human nature as well and gave it up because I found it too much like my own.
Fairy Tales of New York (1960)

2 To more than a few, Ireland remains a glowingly sweet emerald vision having the fifteenth beer over some bereft bar counter at three a.m., in some outskirt corner of San Francisco, Hawaii, Boston, or the Bronx.
J. P. Donleavy's Ireland (1986)

3 Occasionally the tranquillity would be broken by a hungover poet rustling his paper who would sit examining the day's racing form at the courses while nursing in his celibacy his agonizing impure thoughts.
Referring to the poets in Bewley's Café, Dublin. *J. P. Donleavy's Ireland* (1986)

4 To marry the Irish is to look for poverty.
The Ginger Man (1955)

5 When I die I want to decompose in a barrel of porter and have it served in all the pubs in Dublin.
The Ginger Man (1955)

6 But Jesus, when you don't have any money, the problem is food. When you have money, it's sex. When you have both it's health... If everything is simply jake then you're frightened of death.
"Simply jake" means "simply fine." *The Ginger Man* (1955), ch. 5

7 Writing is turning one's worst moments into money.
Quoted in *Playboy* (May 1979)

Donne, John (1572?–1631) English metaphysical poet and divine

Quotations about Donne

1 Here lies a King that ruled, as he thought fit,
The universal monarchy of wit.
Thomas Carew (1595?–1639?) English poet and diplomat. "An Elegy upon the Death of Dr John Donne" (1640), ll. 93–96

2 Few writers have shown a more extraordinary compass of powers than Donne; for he combined what no other man has ever done—the last sublimation of subtlety with the most impassioned majesty.
Thomas De Quincey (1785–1859) British essayist and critic. *Blackwood's Magazine*, Edinburgh (December 1828)

3 Reader! I am to let thee know,
Donne's Body only, lyes below:
For, could the grave his Soul comprize,
Earth would be richer than the skies.
Epitaphs. Written on the wall above John Donne's grave the day after his burial. (1631)

4 Dr Donne's verses are like the peace of God; they pass all understanding.
James I (1566–1625) English monarch
Recorded by Archdeacon Plume (1603–1704). Attrib.

Quotations by Donne

5 John Donne, Anne Donne, Un-done.
Referring to his dismissal from the service of his father-in-law after marrying Anne. Letter to his wife (1601), quoted in *The Life and Death of Dr Donne* (Izaak Walton; 1658)

6 On a huge hill,
Cragged, and steep, Truth stands, and he that will
Reach her, about must, and about must go.
"On Religion" (1594–95), ll. 79–81, Satyre 3

7 Come live with me, and be my love,
And we will some new pleasures prove
Of golden sands, and crystal brooks,
With silken lines, and silver hooks.
"The Bait" (1635), ll. 1–4

8 Sir, more than kisses, letters mingle souls.
"Verse Letter to Sir Henry Wotton" (1597–98), l. 1

9 She, she is dead; she's dead; when thou know'st this,
Thou know'st how dry a cinder this world is.
An Anatomy of the World: The First Anniversary (1611), l. 427

10 And new Philosophy calls all in doubt,
The Element of fire is quite put out;
The Sun is lost, and th'earth, and no man's wit
Can well direct him where to look for it.
An Anatomy of the World: The First Anniversary (1611), ll. 205–208

11 But I do nothing upon myself, and yet I am mine own Executioner.
"Meditation XII," *Devotions upon Emergent Occasions* (1624)

12 No man is an Island, entire of itself; every man is a piece of the Continent, a part of the main; if a clod be washed away by the sea, Europe is the less, as well as if a promontory were, as well as if a manor of thy friends or of thine own were; any man's death diminishes me, because I am involved in Mankind; And therefore never send to know for whom the bell tolls; It tolls for thee.
"Meditation XVII," *Devotions upon Emergent Occasions* (1624)

13 Death be not proud, though some have called thee
Mighty and dreadful, for, thou art not so,
For, those, whom thou think'st, thou dost overthrow,
Die not, poor death, nor yet canst thou kill me.
Holy Sonnets, *Divine Poems* (1633), no. 10, ll. 1–4

14 From rest and sleep, which but thy pictures be,
Much pleasure, then from thee, much more must flow,
And soonest our best men with thee do go,
Rest of their bones and souls delivery.
Holy Sonnets, *Divine Poems* (1633), no. 10, ll. 5–8

15 One short sleep past, we wake eternally,
And death shall be no more; Death, thou shalt die.
Holy Sonnets, *Divine Poems* (1633), no. 10, ll. 13–14

16 What if this present were the world's last night?
Holy Sonnets, *Divine Poems* (1633), no. 13, l. 1

17 Take me to you, imprison me, for I
Except you enthrall me, never shall be free,
Nor ever chaste, except you ravish me.
Holy Sonnets, *Divine Poems* (1633), no. 14, ll. 12–14

18 He was the Word, that spake it:
He took the bread and brake it;
And what that Word did make it,
I do believe and take it.
1607. "On the Sacrament," *Divine Poems* (1633)

19 Love built on beauty, soon as beauty, dies.
1595. "The Anagram," *Elegies* (1633), l. 27

20 She, and comparisons are odious.
"The Comparison," *Elegies* (1633), l. 54

21 Licence my roving hands, and let them go,
Before, behind, between, above, below
O my America! my new-found-land,
My kingdom, safeliest when with one man mann'd.
"To His Mistress Going to Bed," *Elegies* (1633), ll. 25–28

22 At the round earth's imagin'd corners, blow
Your trumpets, Angels, and arise, arise
From death you numberless infinities
Of souls, and to your scattered bodies go.
Holy Sonnets (1618), no. 7

23 Batter my heart, three person'd God; for, you
As yet but knock, breathe, shine, and seek to mend;
That I may rise, and stand, o'erthrow me, and bend
Your force, to break, blow, burn and make me new.
Holy Sonnets (1618), no. 14

24 A memory of yesterday's pleasures, a fear of tomorrow's dangers, a straw under my knee, a noise in mine ear, a light in mine eye, an anything, a nothing, a fancy, a Chimera in my brain, troubles me in my prayer.
December 12, 1626. Oration at the funeral of Sir William Cokayne. *LXXX Sermons* (1640)

25 I neglect God and his angels for the noise of a fly, for the rattling of a coach, for the whining of a door.
December 12, 1626. Oration at the funeral of Sir William Cokayne. *LXXX Sermons* (1640)

26 It comes equally to us all, and makes us all equal when it comes. The ashes of an Oak in the Chimney, are no epitaph of that Oak, to tell me how high or how large that was. It tells me not what flocks it sheltered while it stood, nor what men it hurt when it fell.
LXXX Sermons (1640), no. 15

27 Thou art the proclamation; and I am
The trumpet, at whose voice the people came.
Of the Progress of the Soul: The Second Anniversary (1612), ll. 527–528

28 In such white robes heav'n's angels used to be
Receiv'd by men, thou angel bringst with thee
A heaven like Mahomet's paradise; and though
Ill spirits walk in white, we easily know
By this these angels from an evil sprite:
Those set our hairs, but these our flesh upright.
"To His Mistress Going to Bed" (Elegy 19), *Poems* (1669)

29 I long to talk with some old lover's ghost,
Who died before the god of Love was born.
"Loves Deity," *Poems By J. D.: With Elegies on Author's Death* (1633), ll. 1–2

30 Love is a growing, or full constant light;
And his first minute, after noon, is night.
"A Lecture upon the Shadow," *Songs and Sonnets* (1635), ll. 25–26

31 'Tis the year's midnight, and it is the day's.
Saint Lucy's Day (December 13) is the day of the winter solstice. "A Nocturnal upon St. Lucy's Day, Being the Shortest Day," *Songs and Sonnets* (1635), l. 1

32 Thy firmness makes my circle just
And makes me end, where I begun.
"A Valediction Forbidding Mourning," *Songs and Sonnets* (1635), ll. 35–36

33 If yet I have not all thy love,
Dear, I shall never have it all.
It is possible the title was originally, *Love's Infiniteness.* "Lovers' Infiniteness," *Songs and Sonnets* (1635), ll. 1–2

34 Rebell and Atheist too, why murmure I,
As though I felt the worst that love could doe?
"Love's Deity," *Songs and Sonnets* (1635), ll. 22–23

35 Go, and catch a falling star,
Get with child a mandrake root,
Tell me, where all past years are,
Or who cleft the Devil's foot.
"Song" ("Go, and Catch a Falling Star"), *Songs and Sonnets* (1635), ll. 1–4

36 And swear
No where
Lives a woman true and fair...
Though she were true, when you met her,
And last, till you write your letter,
Yet she

will be
False, ere I come, to two, or three.
"Song" ("Go, and Catch a Falling Star"), *Songs and Sonnets* (1635), st. 2–3

37 Sweetest love, I do not go,
For weariness of thee,
Nor in hope the world can show
A fitter Love for me;
But since that I
Must die at last, 'tis best,
To use my self in jest
Thus by feigned deaths to die.
"Song" ("Sweetest Love, I Do Not Go"), *Songs and Sonnets* (1635), st. 1

38 All other things, to their destruction draw,
Only our love hath no decay;
This, no to-morrow hath, nor yesterday,
Running it never runs from us away,
But truly keeps his first, last, everlasting day.
"The Anniversary," *Songs and Sonnets* (1635), ll. 6–10

39 A naked thinking heart, that makes no show,
Is to a woman, but a kind of ghost.
"The Blossom," *Songs and Sonnets* (1635), ll. 27–28

40 For God's sake hold your tongue and let me love.
"The Canonization," *Songs and Sonnets* (1635), l. 1

41 Where, like a pillow on a bed,
A pregnant bank swelled up, to rest
The violet's reclining head,
Sat we two, one another's best.
"The Ecstasy," *Songs and Sonnets* (1635)

42 I wonder by my troth, what thou, and I
Did, till we lov'd? were we not wean'd till then?
But suck'd on country pleasures, childishly?
Or snorted we in the Seven Sleepers den?
"The Good-Morrow," *Songs and Sonnets* (1635), ll. 1–4

43 And now good morrow to our waking souls,
Which watch not one another out of fear.
"The Good-Morrow," *Songs and Sonnets* (1635), ll. 8–9

44 Busy old fool, unruly Sun,
Why dost thou thus,
Through windows, and through curtains call on us?
Must to thy motions lovers' seasons run?
"The Sun Rising," *Songs and Sonnets* (1635), ll. 1–4

45 Who are a little wise the best fools be.
"The Triple Fool," *Songs and Sonnets* (1635), l. 22

46 I am two fools, I know,
For loving, and for saying so
In whining Poetry.
"The Triple Fool," *Songs and Sonnets* (1635), ll. 1–3

47 That All, which alwayes is All everywhere,
Which could not sinne, and yet all sinnes did beare,
Which could not die, yet could not chuse but die.
The Progress of the Soul (1612), st. 8, ll. 4–6

48 She knew treachery,
Rapine, deceit, and lust, and ills enow
To be a woman.
The Progress of the Soul (1612), st. 51, ll. 507–509

49 As *sickness* is the greatest misery so the greatest misery of sickness is *solitude*. *Solitude* is a torment which is not threatened in *hell* itself.
Quoted in *Awakenings* (Oliver W. Sacks; 1973)

Donovan (Donovan Leitch) British folksinger

1 Pop is the perfect religious vehicle. It's as if God had come down to earth and seen all the ugliness that was being created and chosen pop to be the great force for love and beauty.
1968. Quoted in *Rock 'n' Roll Babylon* (Gary Herman; 1994)

Donovan, Carrie U.S. fashion journalist

1 Fashion's job is to combat the tedium of routine existence.
New York Times (May 4, 1986)

Dorati, Antal (1906–88) Hungarian-born U.S. conductor

1 When I was 25, Bartók needed me, a young man who would get up on the podium, play his music and be whistled at for it.
Referring to Béla Bartók. Remark (April 1986)

Dorrington, Sue British rugby player

1 I think women as a group are better team members than men. We communicate better and are more compatible. We're also more perfectionist and take instruction better.
Times, London (May 3, 1994)

Dors, Diana (Diana Fluck; 1931–84) British actor

1 I don't think men and women were meant to live together. They are totally different animals.
Attrib.

Dos Passos, John (John Roderigo Dos Passos; 1896–1970) U.S. novelist

1 A funny thing weather...When I was a boy once I saw it rain on one side of the street an' a house was struck by lightnin' an' on our side not a drop fell.
Manhattan Transfer (1925), pt. 2

2 A policeman's ballbearing eyes searched his face as he passed, a stout blue column waving a nightstick. Then suddenly he clenched his fists and walked off. "O God everything is hellish," he said aloud.
Manhattan Transfer (1925), pt. 2

3 Every sentence...that appears in the public press is perused and revised and deleted in the interests of advertisers and bondholders. The fountain of national life is poisoned at the source.
Manhattan Transfer (1925), pt. 2

4 Obsession of all the beds in all the pigeonhole bedrooms...Obsession of feet creaking on the stairs of

lodginghouses, hands fumbling at doorknobs. Obsession of pounding temples and solitary bodies rigid on their beds.
Manhattan Transfer (1925), pt. 2

5 The only thing an incomplete organism can do is drink...You complete organisms don't need to drink...I'm going to lie down and go byby.
Manhattan Transfer (1925), pt. 2

6 Those goddam French are so degenerate all they can do is fight duels and sleep with each other's wives. I bet the Germans are in Paris in two weeks.
Referring to World War I. *Manhattan Transfer* (1925), pt. 2

7 The trouble with the workers is we don't know nothin', we don't know how to eat, we don't know how to live, we don't know how to protect our rights.
Manhattan Transfer (1925), pt. 3

8 What the hell's an import and export firm got to do in politics? Our business is the price of beans...and it's goddam low.
Manhattan Transfer (1925), pt. 3

9 "Say will you give me a lift?" he asks the redhaired man at the wheel. How fur ye going? I dunno...Pretty far.
Closing words. *Manhattan Transfer* (1925), pt. 3

10 People don't choose their careers; they are engulfed by them.
New York Times (October 25, 1959)

11 Be a good boy one two three four five six get A's in some courses but don't be a grind be interested in literature but remain a gentleman don't be seen with Jews or Socialists.
The 42nd Parallel (1930)

12 He was terribly afraid of committing the sin against the Holy Ghost, which his mother hinted was inattention in church or in Sunday school or when she was reading him the Bible.
The 42nd Parallel (1930)

13 The needle went rasp rasp and far away a band played and out of a grindy noise in the little black horn came *God Save the King* and the little dogs howled.
The 42nd Parallel (1930)

14 They wrapped me in the stars and stripes I never remembered whether they brought me home or buried me at sea but anyway I was wrapped up in Old Glory.
The 42nd Parallel (1930)

15 Tim, I tellyer I feel like a whipped cur. It's the system, John, it's the goddam lousy system.
The 42nd Parallel (1930)

16 Up north they were dying in the mud and the trenches but business was good in Bordeaux and the winegrowers and the shipping agents and the munitionsmakers crowded into the Chapon Fin.
The 42nd Parallel (1930)

Dostoyevsky, Anna (originally Anna Snitkina; 1846–1918) Russian diarist and writer

1 From a timid, shy girl I had become a woman of resolute character, who could not longer be frightened by the struggle with troubles.
Dostoyevsky Portrayed by His Wife (1887)

2 It seems to me that he has never loved, that he has only imagined that he has loved, that there has been no real love on his part. I even think that he is incapable of love; he is too much occupied with other thoughts and ideas to become strongly attached to anyone earthly.
Referring to her husband, Fyodor Mikhailovich Dostoyevsky. *Dostoyevsky Portrayed by His Wife* (1887)

3 America our nation has been beaten by strangers who have brought the laws and fenced off the meadows and cut down the woods for pulp and turned our pleasant cities into slums and sweated the wealth out of our people and when they want to they hire the executioner to throw the switch.
"They Have Clubbed Us off the Streets," *The Big Money* (1936)

Dostoyevsky, Fyodor (Fyodor Mikhailovich Dostoyevsky; 1821–81) Russian novelist

1 It's a burden to us even to be human beings—men with our own real body and blood; we are ashamed of it, we think it a disgrace and try to contrive to be some sort of impossible generalized man.
Notes from the Underground (1864)

2 The formula "Two and two make five" is not without its attractions.
Notes from the Underground (1864)

3 To be conscious is an illness—a real thorough-going illness.
Notes from the Underground (1864)

4 If you were to destroy in mankind the belief in immortality, not only love but every living force maintaining the life of the world would at once be dried up. Moreover, nothing then would be immoral, everything would be permissible, even cannibalism.
The Brothers Karamazov (1879–80), bk. 2, ch. 6

5 I like Leo Tolstoy enormously, but in my opinion he won't write much of anything else. (I could be wrong.)
Referring to Leo Tolstoy's novel, *War and Peace* (1869). Tolstoy subsequently published *Anna Karenina* (1874). Attrib.

Douglas, Alfred, Lord (Alfred Bruce "Bosie" Douglas; 1870–1945) British writer and poet

1 What a funny little man you are.
Reply to his father's letter concerning his homosexual relationship with Oscar Wilde. Letter to his father, the Marquess of Queensbury (1894), quoted in *Homosexuality: A History* (Colin Spencer; 1995)

2 I am the Love that dare not speak its name.
Poem about homosexual love. "Two Loves" (1896)

Douglas, Archibald, 5th Earl of Angus (1449–1514) Scottish nobleman

1 I'll bell the cat.
Of his proposed capture of Robert Cochrane (executed 1482). The phrase "bell the cat" was earlier used by Eustache Deschamps in his "Ballade: le chat et le souris" (14th century). Remark (1482)

Douglas, Gawin (also spelled Gavin Douglas; 1474?–1522) Scottish poet and bishop

1 And all small fowlys singis on the spray:
Welcum the lord of lycht and lamp of day.
Eneados (1513?), bk. 12, prologue, l. 251

Douglas, Keith (Keith Castellain Douglas; 1920–44) British poet

1 Remember me when I am dead
and simplify me when I'm dead.
"Simplify me when I'm Dead" (May 1941)

2 But she would weep to see today
How on his skin the swart flies move;
The dust upon the paper eye
And the burst stomach like a cave.
For here the lover and killer are mingled
Who had one body and one heart
And death who had the soldier singled
Has done the lover mortal hurt.
On coming across the three-week dead body of a German soldier killed in a skirmish with his unit. "Vergissmeinnicht" (1944), ll. 17–24

Douglas, Michael (Michael Kirk Douglas; b.1944) U.S. film actor

1 Oh, I get it. It's simple. PG means the hero gets the girl, 15 means that the villain gets the girl and 18 means that everybody gets the girl.
Referring to British censor ratings. *Film Yearbook 1989* (1989), quoted in *Chambers Film Quotes* (Tony Crawley, ed.; 1991)

2 If you want to know I'm really tired of feminists, sick of them. They've really dug themselves into their own grave. Any man would be a fool who didn't agree with equal rights and pay, but some women, now, juggling with career, lover, children, wifehood, have spread themselves too thin, and are very unhappy.
You (March 6, 1988)

Douglas, Norman (George Norman Douglas; 1868–1952) British writer

1 It is the drawback of all sea-side places that half the landscape is unavailable for purposes of human locomotion, being covered by useless water.
"Mentone," *Alone* (1921)

2 Bouillabaisse is only good because cooked by the French, who, if they cared to try, could produce an excellent and nutritious substitute out of cigar stumps and empty matchboxes.
"Rain on the Hills," *Siren Land* (1911)

3 Many a man who thinks to found a home discovers that he has merely opened a tavern for his friends.
South Wind (1917), ch. 24

Douglas, Stephen A. (Stephen "Little Giant" Arnold Douglas; 1813–61) U.S. senator

1 Slavery cannot exist a day or an hour anywhere unless it is supported by local police regulations.
Speech (August 27, 1858)

Douglas, William (1672–1748) Scottish poet

1 And for bonnie Annie Laurie
I'll lay me doune and dee.
"Annie Laurie" (1700), ll. 3–8

2 What is there to make so much of in the Thames? I am quite tired of it. Flow, flow, flow, always the same.
Quoted in *Century of Anecdote* (J. Timbs; 1864)

Douglas, William Orville (1898–1980) U.S. jurist

1 The right to be let alone is indeed the beginning of all freedom.
An Almanac of Liberty (1954)

2 The right to revolt has sources deep in our history.
An Almanac of Liberty (1954)

Douglas-Home, Alec, Baron Home of the Hirsel (Alexander Frederick Douglas-Home; 1903–95) British prime minister

Quotations about Douglas-Home

1 A young man with so superior a voice that he might have been to Oxford twice.
Vernon Bartlett (b.1894) British journalist and writer. *Tomorrow Always Comes* (1943)

Quotations by Douglas-Home

2 There are two problems in my life. The political ones are insoluble and the economic ones are incomprehensible.
Speech (January 1964)

3 As far as the 14th Earl is concerned, I suppose Mr Wilson, when you come to think of it, is the 14th Mr Wilson.
October 21, 1963. When he renounced his peerage as 14th Earl of Home to become Prime Minister, opposition leader Harold Wilson commented that the democratic process had "ground to a halt with a fourteenth Earl." *Daily Telegraph*, London (October 22, 1963)

Douglas-Home, Caroline, Lady (b.1937) British aristocrat

1 He is used to dealing with estate workers. I cannot see how anyone can say he is out of touch.
October, 1963. Referring to her father's suitability for his new role as prime minister. *Daily Herald*, London (October 21, 1963)

Douglass, Frederick (1817–95) U.S. abolitionist, writer, and orator

1 This Fourth of July is *yours*, not *mine*. *You* may rejoice, *I* must mourn. To drag a man in fetters into the grand illuminated temple of liberty, and call upon him to join you in joyous anthems, were inhuman mockery and sacrilegious irony.
Address, Rochester, New York (July 1852), quoted in *The Life and Writings of Frederick Douglass* (Philip S. Foner, ed.; 1950), vol. 2

2 America is false to the past, false to the present, and solemnly binds herself to be false to the future.
Comment (July 1852)

3 He who will, intelligently, lay down his life for his country, is a man whom it is not in human nature to despise.
Speech (July 5, 1852)

4 If a slave has a bad master, his ambition is to get a better; when he gets a better, he aspires to have the best; and when

he gets the best, he aspires to be his own master.
Speech, Moorfields, England (May 12, 1846) "An Appeal to the British People," *The Life and Writings of Frederick Douglass* (Philip S. Foner, ed.; 1950), vol. 1

5 If there is no struggle there is no progress.
West India Emancipation speech, Canandaigua, New York (August 4, 1856)

6 Power concedes nothing without demand. It never did and it never will...The limits of tyrants are prescribed by the endurance of those whom they oppress.
West India Emancipation speech, Canandaigua, New York (August 4, 1856), quoted in *The Life and Writings of Frederick Douglass* (Philip S. Foner, ed.; 1950), vol. 2

7 Men who travel should leave their prejudices at home.
Douglass' Monthly (April 1859)

8 The fact is, white Americans find it hard to tell the truth about colored people. They see us with a dollar in their eyes.
Douglass' Monthly (May 1861)

9 The price of Liberty is eternal vigilance.
Douglass' Monthly (January 1863)

10 Fealty to party has no claims against fidelity to truth.
Frederick Douglass' Paper (September 10, 1852)

11 From my earliest recollection, I date the entertainment of a deep conviction that slavery would not always be able to hold me within its foul embrace; and in the darkest hours of my career in slavery, this living word of faith and spirit of hope departed not from me, but remained like ministering angels to cheer me through the gloom.
Narrative of the Life of Frederick Douglass, an American Slave (1845)

12 In coming to a fixed determination to run away, we did more than Patrick Henry, when he resolved upon liberty or death. With us it was a doubtful liberty at most, and almost certain death if we failed. For my part, I should prefer death to hopeless bondage.
Narrative of the Life of Frederick Douglass, an American Slave (1845)

13 It was considered as being bad enough to be a slave; but to be a poor man's slave was deemed a disgrace indeed!
Narrative of the Life of Frederick Douglass, an American Slave (1845)

14 The songs of the slave represent the sorrows of his heart; and he is relieved by them, only as an aching heart is relieved by its tears.
Narrative of the Life of Frederick Douglass, an American Slave (1845)

15 You have seen how a man was made a slave; you shall see how a slave was made a man.
Narrative of the Life of Frederick Douglass, an American Slave (1845)

16 Captain Anthony...would at times seem to take great pleasure in whipping a slave. I have often been awakened at the dawn of day by the most heartrending shrieks of an old aunt of mine, whom he used to tie up to a joist, and whip upon her naked back.
Narrative of the Life of Frederick Douglass, an American Slave (1845), ch. 1, quoted in *The Heath Anthology of American Literature* (Paul Lauter, ed.; 1998), vol. 1

17 I have often been utterly astonished, since I came to the north, to find persons who could speak of the singing, among slaves, as evidence of their contentment and happiness. It is impossible to conceive of a greater mistake. Slaves sing most when they are most unhappy.
Narrative of the Life of Frederick Douglass, an American Slave (1845), ch. 2, quoted in *The Heath Anthology of American Literature* (Paul Lauter, ed.; 1998), vol. 1

18 Slaves are like other people, and imbibe prejudices quite common to others. They think their own better than others.
Narrative of the Life of Frederick Douglass, an American Slave (1845), ch. 3, quoted in *The Heath Anthology of American Literature* (Paul Lauter, ed.; 1998), vol. 1

19 We were all ranked together at the valuation. Men and women, old and young, married and single, were ranked with horses, sheep and swine. There were horses and men, cattle and women, pigs, and children, all holding the same rank in the scale of being.
Narrative of the Life of Frederick Douglass, an American Slave (1845), ch. 4, quoted in *The Heath Anthology of American Literature* (Paul Lauter, ed.; 1998), vol. 1

20 This whole fiendish transaction was soon hushed up...It was a common saying, even among little white boys, that it was worth a half-cent to kill a "nigger," and a half-cent to bury one.
Referring to compensation paid to an owner following the murder of a slave. *Narrative of the Life of Frederick Douglass, an American Slave* (1845), ch. 4, quoted in *The Heath Anthology of American Literature* (Paul Lauter, ed.; 1998), vol. 1

21 A man who will not labor to gain his rights, is a man who would not, if he had them, prize and defend them.
The North Star (July 14, 1848)

22 Fellow-citizens!...The existence of slavery in this country brands your republicanism as a sham, your humanity as a base pretense, and your Christianity as a lie. It destroys your moral power abroad; it corrupts your politicians at home.
What to the Slave is the Fourth of July? (1852), appendix, quoted in *The Heath Anthology of American Literature* (Paul Lauter, ed.; 1998), vol. 1

23 Right is of no sex.
1847. Slogan on masthead of *The North Star*. *The Life and Writings of Frederick Douglass* (Philip S. Foner, ed.; 1950), vol. 1

24 The whole history of the progress of human liberty shows that all concessions yet made to her august claims have been born of earnest struggle.
Attrib. *The Meaning of History* (N. Gordon and Joyce Carper; 1991)

25 When the history of the emancipation movement shall have been fairly written, it will be found that the abolitionists of the nineteenth century were the only men who dared to defend the Bible from the blasphemous charge of sanctioning and sanctifying negro slavery.
Attrib.

Dove, Rita (b.1952) U.S. poet

1 There is a parrot imitating spring
in the palace, its feathers parsley green.
"Parsley" (1983), ll. 1–3

2 He used to sleep like a glass of water
held up in the hand of a very young girl.
"Straw Hat" (1986), ll. 8–9

3 To him,
work is a narrow grief
and the music afterwards
is like a woman

reaching into his chest
to spread it around.
"Straw Hat" (1986), ll. 19–23

4 There are ways to make of the moment a topiary so the pleasure's in walking through.
"Flirtation," *Museum* (1983)

Dow, Lorenzo (1777–1834) U.S. churchman

1 Observing the doctrine of Particular Election, and those who preached it up to make the Bible clash and contradict itself, by preaching somewhat like this: You can and you can't—You shall and you shan't—You will and you won't—And you will be damned if you do—And you will be damned if you don't.
Reflections on the Love of God (1836), ch. 6, "The Doctrine of Particular Election"

Dowler, Harold British churchman

1 When you go to church where two men stand behind the Communion table, and ten men serve Communion, and another man stands at the lectern and reads the scripture, and another man stands up and preaches, and three more men stand in the aisles handing out bulletins, you hear a fairly loud statement about the nature of the Church.
Ms (March 1982)

Downey, Robert, Jr. (b.1965) U.S. actor

1 Anything worth doing is worth doing poorly at first.
The Charlie Rose Show (December 21, 1995)

Dowson, Ernest (Ernest Christopher Dowson; 1867–1900) British lyric poet

1 I have forgot much, Cynara! gone with the wind,
Flung roses, roses, riotously, with the throng,
Dancing, to put thy pale, lost lilies out of mind;
But I was desolate and sick of an old passion,
Yea, all the time, because the dance was long:
I have been faithful to thee, Cynara! in my fashion.
"Non Sum Qualis Eram" (1896)

2 They are not long, the days of wine and roses.
"Vitae Summa Brevis Spem Nos Vetat Incohare Longam" (1896)

Doyle, Arthur Conan, Sir (1859–1930) Scottish-born British writer and physician

1 London, that great cesspool into which all the loungers of the Empire are irresistibly drained.
"A Study in Scarlet" (1887), ch. 1

2 "It is my duty to warn you that it will be used against you," cried the Inspector, with the magnificent fair play of the British criminal law.
"The Dancing Men" (1905)

3 Depend upon it, there is nothing so unnatural as the commonplace.
"A Case of Identity," *The Adventures of Sherlock Holmes* (1892)

4 It has long been an axiom of mine that the little things are infinitely the most important.
"A Case of Identity," *The Adventures of Sherlock Holmes* (1892)

5 The husband was a teetotaller, there was no other woman, and the conduct complained of was that he had drifted into the habit of winding up every meal by taking out his false teeth and hurling them at his wife.
"A Case of Identity," *The Adventures of Sherlock Holmes* (1892)

6 It is my belief, Watson, founded upon my experience, that the lowest and vilest alleys of London do not present a more dreadful record of sin than does the smiling and beautiful countryside.
"Copper Beeches," *The Adventures of Sherlock Holmes* (1892)

7 A man should keep his little brain attic stocked with all the furniture that he is likely to use, and the rest he can put away in the lumber room of his library, where he can get it if he wants it.
"Five Orange Pips," *The Adventures of Sherlock Holmes* (1892)

8 You know my method. It is founded upon the observance of trifles.
"The Boscombe Valley Mystery," *The Adventures of Sherlock Holmes* (1892)

9 It is quite a three-pipe problem.
"The Red-Headed League," *The Adventures of Sherlock Holmes* (1892)

10 When a doctor does go wrong he is the first of criminals. He has nerve and he has knowledge.
"The Speckled Band," *The Adventures of Sherlock Holmes* (1892)

11 They were the footprints of a gigantic hound!
The Hound of the Baskervilles (1902), ch. 2

12 "Excellent!" I cried.
"Elementary," said he.
Watson talking to Sherlock Holmes. Holmes's reply is often misquoted as "Elementary, my dear Watson." "The Crooked Man," *The Memoirs of Sherlock Holmes* (1894)

13 He is the Napoleon of crime.
Referring to Professor Moriarty. "The Final Problem," *The Memoirs of Sherlock Holmes* (1894)

14 "Is there any point to which you would wish to draw my attention?"
"To the curious incident of the dog in the night-time".
"The dog did nothing in the night-time".
"That was the curious incident", remarked Sherlock Holmes.
"The Silver Blaze," *The Memoirs of Sherlock Holmes* (1894)

15 An experience of women which extends over many nations and three continents.
The Sign of Four (1889)

16 It is an old maxim of mine that when you have excluded the impossible, whatever remains, however improbable, must be the truth.
The Sign of Four (1889), ch. 6

17 "For me," said Sherlock Holmes, "there still remains the cocaine bottle."
"The Strange Story of Jonathan Small," *The Sign of Four* (1889)

18 Mediocrity knows nothing higher than itself, but talent instantly recognizes genius.
The Valley of Fear (1915), ch. 1

19 You will, I am sure, agree with me that if page 534 finds us

only in the second chapter, the length of the first one must have been really intolerable.
In the words of Sherlock Holmes. Quoted in *The Jingle Bell Principle* (Miroslav Holub; 1992)

Doyle, Francis (Sir Francis Hastings Charles Doyle; 1810–88) British poet

1 His creed no parson ever knew,
For this was still his "simple plan",
To have with clergymen to do
As little as a Christian can.
The Unobtrusive Christian (1866)

Doyle, Roddy (b.1958) Irish novelist and playwright

1 There's a big trend in Hollywood of taking very good European films and turning them into very bad American films. I've been offered a few of those, but it's really a perverse activity. I'd rather go on the dole.
Independent, London (April 25, 1994)

2 From my experience and observation, if a family is held together in difficult circumstances, nine times out of ten it's the woman who's doing it...You'll find women in their late thirties who look 50, and their husbands of the same age who look 28 or 29—like the eldest sons. Because, in many ways, they are the eldest sons.
Observer, London (May 1, 1994)

3 I wasn't even aware of the Year of the Family. I couldn't give a toss. These things—the year of the family, the year of the three-legged dog. I think it's all trash.
Observer, London (May 1, 1994)

4 The only thing I don't like about the press is I can give as many answers as you want, and be totally honest, but finally it's you who shapes the final product...often what comes out isn't what I meant at all.
Observer, London (May 1, 1994)

5 A song belongs to no man, said Joey The Lips. The Lord holds copyright on all songs.
Me arse, said Outspan.
The Commitments (1987)

6 Soul is the rhythm o' sex. It's the rhythm o' the factory too. The workin' man's rhythm. Sex an' factory. Not the factory I'm in, said Natalie. There isn't much rhythm guttin' fish.
The Commitments (1987)

7 Hormonal changes are perfectly normal. Part an' parcel of the pregnancy, if yeh follows me. But sometimes there are side effects. Snottiness or depression or actin' a bit queer.
The Snapper (1990)

Drabble, Margaret (b.1939) British novelist and writer

Quotations about Drabble

1 She is becoming the chronicler of contemporary Britain, the novelist people will turn to a hundred years from now to find out how things were, the person who will have done for late 20th century London what Dickens did for Victorian London, what Balzac did for Paris.
Phyllis Rose (b.1942) U.S. writer. *New York Times Book Review* (September 1980)

Quotations by Drabble

2 And there isn't any way that one can get rid of the guilt of having a nice body by saying that one can serve society with it, because that would end up with oneself as what? There simply doesn't seem to be any moral place for flesh.
A Summer Bird-Cage (1963), ch. 10

3 Sex isn't the most important thing in life, she decided, wriggling her body slightly to see if her movement would affect Anthony. It did: he stiffened slightly, but slept on. But if sex isn't the most important thing, what is?
The Ice Age (1977), pt. 2

4 Civilized woman can't do the right thing without paying too high a price.
The Middle Ground (1980)

5 When nothing is sure, everything is possible.
The Middle Ground (1980)

6 Poverty, therefore, was comparative. One measured it by a sliding scale. One was always poor, in terms of those who were richer.
The Radiant Way (1987)

7 Thrift has nearly killed her on several occasions, through the agency of old sausages, slow-punctured tyres, rusty blades.
The Radiant Way (1987)

Dragnet U.S. television series

1 All we want is the facts, ma'am.
Catchphrase of Sergeant Joe Friday. *Dragnet* (1951–58)

Drake, Francis, Sir (1540?–96) English navigator and admiral

1 The advantage of time and place in all practical actions is half a victory; which being lost is irrecoverable.
While awaiting news of the coming of the Spanish Armada. Letter to Queen Elizabeth I (1588)

2 There must be a beginning of any great matter, but the continuing unto the end until it be thoroughly finished yields the true glory.
Dispatch to Sir Francis Walsingham. *Navy Records Society* (May 17, 1587), vol. 11

3 I have singed the Spanish king's beard.
1587. Referring to the raid on Cadiz harbor in 1587. Attrib. *Considerations Touching a War with Spain* (Francis Bacon; 1629)

4 There is plenty of time to win this game, and to thrash the Spaniards too.
July 20, 1588. Referring to the sighting of the Armada during a game of bowls. Attrib. *Dictionary of National Biography* (1917), vol. 5

5 I must have the gentleman to haul and draw with the mariner, and the mariner with the gentleman. I would know him, that would refuse to set his hand to a rope, but I know there is not any such here.
Drake and the Tudor Navy (J. S. Corbett; 1898), vol. 1, ch. 9

Drake, Joseph Rodman (1795–1820) U.S. poet

1 Flag of the free heart's hope and home!

By angel hands to valour given!
Thy stars have lit the welkin dome,
And all thy hues were born in heaven.
Forever float that standard sheet!
"The American Flag" (May 29, 1819), ll. 58–61

Draper, John (John William Draper; 1811–82) British-born U.S. chemist

1 The history of science is not a mere record of isolated discoveries; it is a narrative of the conflict of two contending powers, the expansive force of the human intellect on one side, and the compression arising from the traditional faith and human interest on the other.
History of the Conflict Between Religion and Science (1874), preface

2 How is it that the Church produced no geometers in her autocratic reign of twelve hundred years?
History of the Conflict Between Religion and Science (1874)

Drayton, Michael (1563–1631) English poet

1 Farewell sweet friend, with thee my joys are gone,
Farewell my Piers, my lovely Gaveston.
Referring to Piers Gaveston, Earl of Cornwall, favorite of King Edward II. "Piers Gaveston" (1593), quoted in *Gay Love Poetry* (Neil Powell, ed.; 1997)

2 I pray thee leave, love me no more,
Call home the heart you gave me
I but in vain the saint adore,
That can, but will not, save me.
"To His Coy Love" (1619)

3 Since there's no help, come let us kiss and part,
Nay, I have done: you get no more of me,
And I am glad, yea glad with all my heart,
That thus so cleanly, I myself can free,
Shake hands for ever, cancel all our vows,
And when we meet at any time again
Be it not seen in either of our brows,
That we one jot of former love retain.
"Idea," *Poems* (1619), Sonnet 61, ll. 1–8

4 Ill news hath wings, and with the wind doth go,
Comfort's a cripple and comes ever slow.
The Barons' Wars (1603), can. 2, st. 27

5 He of a temper was so absolute
As that it seem'd when Nature him began,
She meant to shew all, that might be in man.
The Barons' Wars (1603), can. 2, st. 40

6 Fair stood the wind for France
When we our sails advance.
"Agincourt," *To the Cambro-Britons* (1619)

7 O that Ocean did not bound our style
Within these strict and narrow limits so:
But that the melody of our sweet isle
Might now be heard to Tiber, Arne, and Po:
That they might know how far Thames doth outgo
The music of declined Italy.
Referring to the English language. *The Reign of Elizabeth, 1558–1603* (John Bennett Black; 1936), ch. 8

Dreiser, Theodore (Theodore Herman Albert Dreiser; 1871–1945) U.S. novelist

1 Life is a God-damned, stinking, treacherous game and nine hundred and ninety-nine men out of a thousand are bastards.
Quoting an unnamed newspaper editor. *A Book About Myself* (1922)

2 Art is the stored honey of the human soul, gathered on wings of misery and travail.
Life, Art and America (1917)

3 The true meaning of money yet remains to be popularly explained and comprehended. When each individual realizes for himself that this thing...should only be accepted as a moral due...many of our social, religious, and political troubles will have permanently passed.
Sister Carrie (1900)

4 Shakespeare, I come!
1945? His intended last words. *The Constant Circle: H. L. Mencken and his Friends* (Sara Mayfield; 1968)

Drennan, William (1754–1820) Irish poet

1 Hapless Nation! hapless Land
Heap of uncementing sand!
Crumbled by a foreign weight:
And by worse, domestic hate.
"The Wake of William Orr" (1797)

Driberg, Tom, Baron Bradwell (Thomas Edward Neil Driberg; 1905–76) British politician and journalist

1 Sincerity is all that counts. It's a wide-spread modern heresy. Think again. Bolsheviks are sincere. Fascists are sincere. Lunatics are sincere. People who believe the earth is flat are sincere. They can't all be right.
Daily Express, London (1937)

Droste-Hülshoff, Annette Elisabeth von, Baroness (1797–1848) German poet

1 Dreams release the soul's love urge.
"Sleepless Night," *An Anthology of German Poetry from Hölderlin to Rilke* (Angel Flores, ed., Herman Salinger, tr.; 1960)

2 So still the pond in morning's gray
A quiet conscience is not clearer.
"The Pond," *An Anthology of German Poetry from Hölderlin to Rilke* (Angel Flores, ed., Herman Salinger, tr.; 1960)

Drucker, Peter (Peter Ferdinand Drucker; b.1909) Austrian-born U.S. management consultant

1 Before an executive can think of tackling the future, he must be able therefore to dispose of the challenges of today in less time and with greater impact and permanence.
Managing for Results (1964), ch. 1

2 Management is the generic organ of all organizations.
"Introduction," *Mary Parker Follett: Prophet of Management* (Pauline Graham, ed.; 1995)

3 Modern organizations have to be built on making conflict constructive.
"Introduction," *Mary Parker Follett: Prophet of Management* (Pauline Graham, ed.; 1995)

4 A small country can now join an economic region and thus get the best of two worlds: cultural and political independence and economic integration.
Post-capitalist Society (1993)

5 Every organization of today has to build into its very structure the management of change.
Post-capitalist Society (1993)

6 No one before 1929...expected governments to be able to manage the economic weather. Since then every government in every country promises to be able to cure recessions.
Post-capitalist Society (1993)

7 Power must always be balanced by responsibility. Otherwise it is tyranny.
Post-capitalist Society (1993)

8 The non-productivity of its knowledge, more than anything else, is at the root of the slow and steady erosion of the British economy.
Post-capitalist Society (1993)

9 The right model for the information-based organization is not the military...it is the symphony orchestra.
Post-capitalist Society (1993)

10 The worker under capitalism was totally dependent on the machine. In the employee society the employee and the tools of production are interdependent.
Post-capitalist Society (1993)

11 To make knowledge productive...requires the systematic exploitation of opportunities for change.
Post-capitalist Society (1993)

12 Management and union may be likened to that serpent of the fables who on one body had two heads that, fighting each other with poisonous fangs, killed themselves.
The New Society (1951), ch. 14

13 Markets are not created by God, nature, or by economic forces, but by businessmen.
1954. Quoted in *Key Management Ideas* (Stuart Crainer; 1996)

14 Management is doing things right; leadership is doing the right things.
Quoted in *The Seven Habits of Highly Effective People* (Stephen R. Covey; 1989)

15 No institution can possibly survive if it needs geniuses or supermen to manage it. It must be organized in such a way as to be able to get along under a leadership composed of average human beings.
1995. Attrib.

16 The only things that evolve by themselves in an organization are disorder, friction, and malperformance.
Attrib.

17 Whenever you see a successful business, someone once made a courageous decision.
Attrib.

Drumgoold, Kate (*fl.* 19th-century) U.S. slave and teacher

1 No subject can surely be a more delightful study than the history of a slave girl, and the many things that are linked to this life that man may search and research in the ages to come.
A Slave Girl's Story, Being an Autobiography of Kate Drumgoold (1898)

Drummond, Thomas (1797–1840) British engineer and government official

1 Property has its duties as well as its rights.
May 22, 1838. Letter to the Earl of Donoughmore (1838), quoted in *Thomas Drummond: Life and Letters* (Richard Barry O'Brien; 1889)

Drummond, William (William Drummond of Hawthornden; 1585–1649) Scottish poet

1 Not to be born, or, being born, to die.
Poems (1656)

2 I long to kiss the *Image* of my *Death*.
1614. "Son," *The Poetical Works of William Drummond of Hawthornden* (L. E. Kastner, ed.; 1973), l. 14

3 Only the echoes which he made relent,
Ring from their marble caves repent, repent.
1623. "For the Baptiste," *The Poetical Works of William Drummond of Hawthornden* (L. E. Kastner, ed.; 1973), ll. 14–15

Dr. Who British television series

1 You will be exterminated.
Catchphrase of the Daleks, Dr. Who's most famous adversaries. *Dr. Who* (1963–89)

Dryden, John (1631–1700) English poet, playwright, and literary critic

Quotations about Dryden

1 Aside from the impossibility of equaling Dryden and Pope in their medium, Byron was really a comedian, not a satirist.
W. H. Auden (1907–73) British poet. Referring to John Dryden, Alexander Pope, and Lord Byron. *The Dyer's Hand* (1963)

2 The father of English criticism.
Samuel Johnson (1709–84) British lexicographer and writer. "Dryden," *Lives of the English Poets* (1779–81)

3 His imagination resembled the wings of an ostrich. It enabled him to run, though not to soar.
1828
Thomas Babington Macaulay (1800–59) British politician, historian, and writer. "On John Dryden," *Essays Contributed to the Edinburgh Review* (1843)

Quotations by Dryden

4 Errors, like Straws, upon the surface flow;
He who would search for Pearls must dive below.
"All for Love" (1678), prologue

5 By viewing Nature, Nature's handmaid, art,
Makes mighty things from small beginnings grow.
"Annus Mirabilis" (1667)

6 Ill fortune seldom comes alone.
"Cymon and Iphigenia" (1700), l. 392, quoted in *The Poems and Fables of John Dryden* (James Kinsley, ed.; 1962)

7 Bold knaves thrive without one grain of sense,
But good men starve for want of impudence.
"Epilogue to Constantine the Great" (1683), ll. 19–20, quoted in *The Poems and Fables of John Dryden* (James Kinsley, ed.; 1962)

8 Lord of yourself, uncumber'd with a wife.
"Epistle to John Driden of Chesterton" (1700), l. 18

9 A thing well said will be wit in all languages.
"Of Dramatick Poesy" (1688)

10 If by the people you understand the multitude, the *hoi polloi*, 'tis no matter what they think; they are sometimes in the right, sometimes in the wrong; their judgement is a mere lottery.
"Of Dramatick Poesy" (1688)

11 Beware the Fury of a Patient Man.
Absalom and Achitophel (1681), pt. 1

12 Did wisely from Expensive Sins refrain,
And never broke the Sabbath, but for Gain.
Absalom and Achitophel (1681), pt. 1

13 For Politicians neither love nor hate.
Absalom and Achitophel (1681), pt. 1

14 Great Wits are sure to Madness near alli'd
And thin Partitions do their Bounds divide.
Absalom and Achitophel (1681), pt. 1

15 Nor is the People's Judgment always true:
The Most may err as grossly as the Few.
Absalom and Achitophel (1681), pt. 1

16 What e'er he did was done with so much ease,
In him alone, 'twas Natural to please.
Absalom and Achitophel (1681), pt. 1

17 All empire is no more than power in trust.
Absalom and Achitophel (1681), pt. 1, l. 411

18 Never was patriot yet, but was a fool.
Absalom and Achitophel (1681), pt. 1, l. 968

19 A man so various, that he seemed to be
Not one, but all mankind's epitome.
Stiff in opinions, always in the wrong;
Was Everything by starts, and nothing long,
But, in the course of one revolving moon,
Was chemist, fiddler, statesman, and buffoon.
Referring to the character Zimri, who represents George Villiers, 2nd Duke of Buckingham. Villiers had himself parodied Dryden in his comedy *The Rehearsal* (1671). *Absalom and Achitophel* (1681), pt. 1, ll. 545–550

20 Arms, and the man I sing, who, forced by fate,
And haughty Juno's unrelenting hate,
Expelled and exiled, left the Trojan shore.
Translation of Virgil's *Aeneid*. *Aeneis* (1697), bk. 1, ll. 1–3

21 We must beat the iron while it is hot, but we may polish it at leisure.
Aeneis (1697), Dedication

22 Happy, happy, happy, pair!
None but the brave,
None but the brave,
None but the brave deserves the fair.
Alexander's Feast (1697), l. 4

23 Drinking is the soldier's pleasure;
Rich the treasure;
Sweet the pleasure;
Sweet is pleasure after pain.
Alexander's Feast (1697), l. 57

24 Whistling to keep myself from being afraid.
Amphitryon (1690), Act 3, Scene 1

25 For, Heaven be thanked, we live in such an age,
When no man dies for love, but on the stage.
Mithridates is a play by Nathaniel Lee. *A Prologue Spoken at Mithridates King of Pontus* (1681), epilogue

26 But here content with our own homely joys,
We had no relish of the fair fac'd boys.
Till you came in and with your Reformation,
Turn'd all things Arsy Versy in the nation.
Don Sebastian (1690), quoted in *Homosexuality: A History* (Colin Spencer; 1995)

27 And virtue, though in rags, will keep me warm.
Imitation of Horace (1685), bk. 3, ode 29, l. 87

28 All heiresses are beautiful.
King Arthur (1691), Act 2, Scene 2

29 War is the trade of kings.
King Arthur (1691), Act 2, Scene 2

30 Ovid, the soft philosopher of love.
Love Triumphant (1694), Act 2, Scene 1

31 All humane things are subject to decay,
And, when Fate summons, Monarchs must obey.
MacFlecknoe (1682)

32 I am to be married within these three days; married past redemption.
Marriage à la Mode (1672), Act 1, Scene 1

33 Whatever is, is in its causes just.
Oedipus (co-written with Nathaniel Lee; 1679), Act 3, Scene 1

34 Like pilgrims to th'appointed place we tend;
The world's an inn, and death the journey's end.
Palamon and Arcite (1700), bk. 3, ll. 883–884

35 A man is to be cheated into passion, but to be reasoned into truth.
Religio Laici (1682), preface

36 For secrets are edged tools,
And must be kept from children and from fools.
Sir Martin Mar-All (1667), Act 2, Scene 2

37 Forgiveness to the injured does belong;
But they ne'er pardon, who have done the wrong.
The Conquest of Granada (1680), pt. 2, Act 1, Scene 2

38 Thou strong seducer, opportunity!
The Conquest of Granada (1680), pt. 2, Act 4, Scene 3

39 And kind as kings upon their coronation day.
The Hind and the Panther (1687), pt. 1, l. 271

40 Reason to rule, but mercy to forgive:
The first is law, the last prerogative.
The Hind and the Panther (1687), pt. 1, ll. 261–262

41 For those whom God to ruin has designed,
He fits for fate, and first destroys their mind.
The Hind and the Panther (1687), pt. 3, l. 1093

42 For present joys are more to flesh and blood
Than a dull prospect of a distant good.
The Hind and the Panther (1687), pt. 3, ll. 364–365

43 And love's the noblest frailty of the mind.
The Indian Emperor (1665), Act 2, Scene 2

44 Repentance is the virtue of weak minds.
The Indian Emperor (1665), Act 3, Scene 1

45 I am resolved to grow fat and look young till forty, and then slip out of the world with the first wrinkle and the reputation of five-and-twenty.
The Maiden Queen (1668), Act 3, Scene 1

46 But treason is not own'd when 'tis descried;
Successful crimes alone are justified.
The Medal (1682), ll. 207–208

47 There is a pleasure sure
In being mad which none but madmen know.
The Spanish Friar (1681), Act 1, Scene 1

48 Self-preservation is the first of Laws:...
When Subjects are oppress'd by Kings,
They justify Rebellion by that Law.
The Spanish Friar (1681), Act 4, Scene 2

49 Happy the Man, and happy he alone,
He who can call today his own:
He who, secure within, can say,
Tomorrow do thy worst, for I have liv'd today.
Translation of Horace's Odes (1685), bk. 3, ode 29

50 Not Heav'n itself upon the past has pow'r;
But what has been, has been, and I have had my hour.
Translation of Horace's Odes (1685), bk. 3, ode 29

51 All delays are dangerous in war.
Tyrannic Love (1669), Act 1, Scene 1

du Bartas, Guillaume, Seigneur du Bartas (Guillaume de Salluste; 1544–90) French poet

1 I take the world to be but as a stage,
Where net-maskt men do play their personage.
"Dialogue Between Heraclitus and Democritus" (16th century)

2 For where's the state beneath the firmament
That doth excel the bees for government?
"First Week, Fifth Day," *Divine Weekes and Workes* (1578)

3 And swans seem whiter if swart crowes be by.
"First Week, First Day," *Divine Weekes and Workes* (1578)

4 The world's a stage where God's omnipotence,
His justice, knowledge, love, and providence
Do act the parts.
"First Week, First Day," *Divine Weekes and Workes* (1578)

5 What is well done is done soon enough.
"First Week, First Day," *Divine Weekes and Workes* (1578)

6 Much like the French (or like ourselves, their apes),
Who with strange habit do disguise their shapes;
Who loving novels, full of affectation,
Receive the manners of each other nation.
"First Week, Second Day," *Divine Weekes and Workes* (1578)

7 Even as a surgeon, minding off to cut
Some cureless limb,—before in ure he put
His violent engins on the vicious member,
Bringeth his patient in a senseless slumber,
And grief-less then (guided by use and art),
To save the whole, sawes off th'infested part.
"First Week, Sixth Day," *Divine Weekes and Workes* (1578)

8 Or almost like a spider, who, confined
In her web's centre, shakt with every wind,
Moves in an instant if the buzzing fly
Stir but a string of her lawn canapie.
"First Week, Sixth Day," *Divine Weekes and Workes* (1578)

9 Two souls in one, two hearts into one heart.
"First Week, Sixth Day," *Divine Weekes and Workes* (1578)

10 To man the earth seems altogether
No more a mother, but a step-dame rather.
"First Week, Third Day," *Divine Weekes and Workes* (1578)

11 In every hedge and ditch both day and night
We fear our death, of every leafe affright.
"Second Week, First Day," *Divine Weekes and Workes* (1578)

12 In the jaws of death.
"Second Week, First Day," *Divine Weekes and Workes* (1578)

13 Yielding more wholesome food than all the messes
That now taste-curious wanton plenty dresses.
"Second Week, First Day," *Divine Weekes and Workes* (1578)

14 My lovely living boy,
My hope, my hap, my love, my life, my joy.
"Second Week, Fourth Day," *Divine Weekes and Workes* (1578)

15 Who well lives, long lives; for this age of ours
Should not be numbered by years, days, and hours.
"Second Week, Fourth Day," *Divine Weekes and Workes* (1578)

16 Will change the pebbles of our puddly thought
To orient pearls.
"Second Week, Third Day," *Divine Weekes and Workes* (1578)

Dubček, Alexander (1921–92) Czech statesman

1 Socialism with a human face must function again for a new generation. We have lived in the darkness for long enough.
Speech, Wenceslas Square, Prague (November 4, 1989)

2 In the service of the people we followed such a policy that socialism would not lose its human face.
A resolution by the party group in the Ministry of Foreign Affairs, on March 14, 1968, referred to Czechoslovak foreign policy acquiring "its own defined face." Often misquoted as "Communism with a human face." *Rudé Právo* (July 19, 1968)

du Bellay, Joachim (1522?–60) French poet

1 France, mother of arts, of warfare, and of laws.
Sonnet 9, *Les Regrets* (1558)

2 Happy he who like Ulysses has made a glorious journey.
Sonnet 31, *Les Regrets* (1558)

Dubin, Al (1891–1945) U.S. songwriter

1 You may not be an angel
'Cause angels are so few,
But until the day that one comes along
I'll string along with you.
"Twenty Million Sweethearts" (1934)

2 Tiptoe through the tulips with me.
Song lyric. "Tiptoe Through the Tulips," *Gold Diggers of Broadway* (1935)

Du Bois, W. E. B. (William Edward Burghardt Du Bois; 1868–1963) U.S. sociologist, poet, and novelist

1 Any discrimination based simply on race or color is barbarous, we care not how hallowed it be by custom, expedience, or prejudice.
The Niagara Movement was founded in 1905 to protest against racial segregation in the United States. The Niagara Movement Declaration of Principles (1905)

2 Especially do I believe in the Negro Race: in the beauty of its genius, the sweetness of its soul, and its strength in that meekness which shall yet inherit this turbulent earth.
"Credo," *Darkwater: Voices from Within the Veil* (1920)

3 I believe that all men, black and brown and white, are brothers, varying through time and opportunity, in form and gift and feature, but differing in no essential particular, and alike in soul and the possibility of infinite development.
"Credo," *Darkwater: Voices from Within the Veil* (1920)

4 All womanhood is hampered today because the world on which it is emerging is a world that tries to worship both virgins and mothers and in the end despises motherhood and despoils virgins.
"The Damnation of Women," *Darkwater: Voices from Within the Veil* (1920)

5 Europe has never produced and never will in our day bring forth a single human soul who cannot be matched and over-matched in every line of human endeavor by Asia and Africa.
"The Souls of White Folk," *Darkwater: Voices from Within the Veil* (1920)

6 The Dark World is going to submit to its present treatment just as long as it must and not one moment longer.
"The Souls of White Folk," *Darkwater: Voices from Within the Veil* (1920)

7 A great silence has fallen on the real soul of this nation.
On McCarthyism (1951)

8 The blacker the mantle the mightier the man
My purpl'ing midnights no day may ban
I am carrying God in night,
I am painting hell in white.
I am the smoke king,
I am black.
"The Song of the Smoke," *Selected Poems of W. E. B. Du Bois* (1899)

9 The day is past when historians glory in war. Rather, with all thoughtful men, they deplore the barbarism of mankind which has made war so large a part of human history.
The Gift of Black Folk (1924)

10 Most men in this world are colored. A belief in humanity means a belief in colored men. The future world will, in all reasonable probability, be what colored men make it.
The Negro (1915)

11 Men of America, the problem is plain before you. Here is a race transplanted through the criminal foolishness of your fathers. Whether you like it or not the millions are here, and here they will remain. If you do not lift them up, they will pull you down.
The Negro Problem (1903)

12 The Negro race, like all races, is going to be saved by its exceptional men. The problem of education, then, among Negroes must first of all deal with the Talented Tenth; it is the problem of developing the Best of this race that they may guide the Mass away from the contamination and death of the Worst, in their own and other races.
"The Talented Tenth," *The Negro Problem* (1903)

13 One ever feels his twoness—an American, a Negro; two souls, two thoughts, two unreconciled strivings; two warring ideals in one dark body, whose dogged strength alone keeps it from being torn asunder.
The Souls of Black Folk (1903)

14 The chief problem in any community cursed with crime is not the punishment of the criminals, but the preventing of the young from being trained to crime.
The Souls of Black Folk (1903)

15 The history of the American Negro is the history of this strife,—this longing to attain self-conscious manhood, to merge his double self into a better and truer self...He simply wishes to make it possible for a man to be both a Negro and an American, without being cursed and spit upon by his fellows, without having the doors of Opportunity closed roughly in his face.
The Souls of Black Folk (1903)

16 The problem of the twentieth century is the problem of the color-line.
The Souls of Black Folk (1903)

17 This is the history of a human heart,—the tale of a black boy who many long years ago began to struggle with life that he might know the world and know himself.
The Souls of Black Folk (1903)

Dubos, René (René Jules Dubos; 1901–82) French-born U.S. bacteriologist

1 It can be said that each civilization has a pattern of disease peculiar to it. The pattern of disease is an expression of the response of man to his total environment (physical, biological, and social); this response is, therefore, determined by anything that affects man himself or his environment.
Industrial Medicine and Surgery (1961)

2 Epidemics have often been more influential than statesmen and

soldiers in shaping the course of political history, and diseases may also color the moods of civilizations.
The White Plague (1953), ch. 5

3 Many ancient, ancestral mechanisms persisting in modern man have to find some outlet, even if they no longer correspond to any real needs.
1965. Quoted in *The Jingle Bell Principle* (Miroslav Holub; 1992)

Ducas (also known as Doukas or Dukas; *fl.* 15th century) Byzantine historian

1 It would be better to see the royal turban of the Turks in the midst of the city than the Latin mitre.
Opposing the Emperor Constantine XI's attempted reunification of the Orthodox and Roman Churches (1452), in an attempt to save the Byzantine Empire from the Turks. Attrib.

Duchamp, Marcel (1887–1968) French-born U.S. artist

1 Art may be bad, good or indifferent, but, whatever adjective is used, we must call it art, and bad art is still art in the same way as a bad emotion is still an emotion.
"The Creative Act," *Art News* (Summer 1957), 56, no. 4

2 All in all the creative act is not performed by the artist alone; the spectator brings the work in contact with the external world by deciphering and interpreting its inner qualifications and thus adds his contribution to the creative act.
Quoted in "The Creative Act," *Marcel Duchamp* (Robert Lebel, ed., George Heard Hamilton, tr.; 1959)

3 I am still a victim of chess. It has all the beauty of art—and much more. It cannot be commercialized. Chess is much purer than art in its social position.
Attrib.

Dudar, Helen U.S. writer

1 Contrary to the folklore of abortion as life-long trauma, it is not necessarily a profoundly scarring one either.
April, 1973. "Abortion for the Asking," *Saturday Review of the Society* (April 1973)

Dudley Edwards, Ruth (b.1944) Irish historian and journalist

1 In these days of computer viruses, asking if you may put your disk into someone's computer is the technological equivalent of unsafe sex.
Independent, London (January 9, 1995)

Duffield, George (1794–1868) U.S. minister

1 Stand up!—stand up for Jesus!
Ye soldiers of the Cross.
Opening line of a hymn inspired by the dying words of American evangelist Dudley Atkins Tyng to Duffield. "Stand Up, Stand Up for Jesus" (1858)

Duffy, Carol Ann (b.1955) British poet

1 And we're all owed joy
sooner or later
The trick's to remember whenever
it was, or to see it coming.
"Crush," *Mean Time* (1993)

Du Fresnoy, Charles-Alphonse (also known as Charles-Alphonse Dufresnoy; 1611–68) French painter and theorist

1 Art must be subservient to the painter.
1655. Quoted in *The Art of Painting* (John Dryden, tr.; 1695)

2 'Tis labor in vain to paint a high noon or midday light in your picture, because we have no colors which can sufficiently express it.
1665. Quoted in *The Art of Painting* (John Dryden, tr.; 1695)

3 Let no day pass without a line.
1665. Referring to painting. Quoted in *The Art of Painting* (John Dryden, tr.; 1695)

Du Fu (also known as Tu Fu; 712–770) Chinese poet

1 Lone goose, not drinking or pecking for food,
it cries out in flight, voice yearns for the flock.
"Lone Wild Goose" (8th century), quoted in *An Anthology of Chinese Literature* (Stephen Owen, tr.; 1996)

2 Oh, where's my name
among the poets?
Official rank?
"Retired for ill-health."

Drifting, drifting,
what am I more than
A single gull
between earth and sky?
"Night Thoughts Afloat" (8th century), quoted in *Li Po and Tu Fu* (Arthur Cooper, tr.; 1973), st. 3 and 4

3 The capital is taken. The hills and streams are left,
And with spring in the city the grass and trees grow dense.
Mourning the times, the flowers trickle their tears;
Saddened with parting, the birds make my heart flutter.
"Spring Prospect" (8th century), quoted in *China's Imperial Past* (Charles O. Hucker; 1975)

4 The din of wagons! Whinnying horses!
Each marcher at his waist has bow and quiver;
Old people, children, wives, running alongside,
Who cannot see, for dust, bridge over river.
"The Ballad of the Army Wagons" (8th century), quoted in *Li Po and Tu Fu* (Arthur Cooper, tr.; 1973), st. 1

5 But have you not seen
On the Black Lake's shore
The white bones there of old no one has gathered,
Where new ghosts cry aloud, old ghosts are bitter,
Rain drenching from dark clouds their ghostly chatter?
"The Ballad of the Army Wagons" (8th century), quoted in *Li Po and Tu Fu* (Arthur Cooper, tr.; 1973), st. 8

Duhamel, Georges (1884–1966) French writer and physician

1 I hold that the novelist is the historian of the present, just as the historian is the novelist of the past.
Chronique: La Nuit de Saint-Jean (1937), preface

2 Civilization: if it is not in man's heart—well, then, it is nowhere.
Civilization (1918)

3 One half of the world will soon be playing the role of prison guard to the other half.
"Biographie de mes fantômes," *Light on My Days* (1948), ch. 5

4 Courtesy is not dead—it has merely taken refuge in Great Britain.
Observer, London (May 31, 1953), "Sayings of Our Times"

Dühem, Pierre (Pierre-Maurice-Marie Dühem; 1861–1916) French physicist and philosopher

1 A physical theory is not an explanation. It is a system of mathematical propositions, deduced from a small number of principles, which aim to represent as simply, as completely, and as exactly as possible a set of experimental laws.
Quoted in *The Aim and Structure of Physical Theory* (P. P. Wiener, tr.; 1906)

Dulles, John Foster (1888–1959) U.S. statesman and diplomat

Quotations about Dulles

1 The greatest mistake I ever made was not to die in office.
March 27, 1959
Dean Acheson (1893–1971) U.S. lawyer and statesman. Said on hearing the funeral eulogies for John Foster Dulles, U.S. secretary of state (1953–59). Dean Acheson had also been secretary of state (1947–53). Attrib.

Quotations by Dulles

2 Our capacity to retaliate must be, and is, massive in order to deter all forms of aggression.
Speech, Chicago, Illinois (December 8, 1955)

3 The ability to get to the verge without getting into the war is the necessary art. If you cannot master it, you inevitably get into war. If you try to run away from it, if you are scared to go to the brink, you are lost.
Dulles's use of the word "brink" in this context led to the invention of the word "brinkmanship." *Life* (January 16, 1956)

4 Natural science has outstripped moral and political science. That is too bad; but it is a fact, and the fact does not disappear because we close our eyes to it.
War or Peace (1950)

5 There is no nook or cranny into which Communist influence does not penetrate.
War or Peace (1950)

6 Yes, once—many, many years ago. I thought I had made a wrong decision. Of course, it turned out that I had been right all along. But I was wrong to have *thought* that I was wrong.
Said on being asked whether he had ever been wrong. Attrib. *Facing the Music* (H. Temianka; 1954)

Du Ma (Li Feng; b.1968) Chinese writer and academic

1 I was just like those patriotic Chinese years ago who had initially lost hope in the motherland and gone abroad, only to pack their bags and come scurrying home as soon as they heard that there'd been some sort of disaster.
"Into Parting Arms" (Helen Wang, tr.; 1994)

Dumas, Alexandre (Alexandre Davy de la Pailleterie Dumas, "Dumas père"; 1802–70) French novelist and playwright

Quotations about Dumas

1 You are one of the forces of nature.
Jules Michelet (1798–1874) French historian. From a letter received by Alexandre Dumas. Quoted in *My Memoirs* (E. M. Waller, tr.; 1907–09), vol. 6, ch. 138

Quotations by Dumas

2 Let us look for the woman.
Les Mohicans de Paris (1854)

3 All for one, and one for all.
The Three Musketeers (1844)

4 A good surgeon operates with his hand, not with his heart.
Attrib.

5 All generalizations are dangerous, even this one.
Attrib.

6 It is only rarely that one can see in a little boy the promise of a man, but one can almost always see in a little girl the threat of a woman.
1865. Attrib.

Dumas, Henry (1934–68) U.S. writer and poet

1 It is time to make the time.
"Emoyeni, Place of Winds," *Knees of A Natural Man: The Selected Poetry of Henry Dumas* (Eugene B. Redmond, ed.; 1989)

2 Hate is also creative: it creates more hate.
"Thought," *Knees of A Natural Man: The Selected Poetry of Henry Dumas* (Eugene B. Redmond, ed.; 1989)

Dumas, Roland (b.1922) French lawyer, journalist, and politician

1 I always believed that the arbitrary division of Germany was senseless. Since no one can permanently divide a nation, a people, a country, German unity will put an end to one of history's anomalies.
1990. "Towards a Confederal System," *New York Times* (March 13, 1990)

du Maurier, Daphne, Dame (1907–89) British writer

1 Last night I dreamt I went to Manderley again.
Rebecca (1938), ch. 1

du Maurier, George (George Louis Palmella Busson du Maurier; 1834–96) French-born British novelist and illustrator

1 "What sort of doctor is he?"
"Oh, well, I don't know much about his ability; but he's got a very good bedside manner!"
Punch, London (March 15, 1884)

Du Mu (also known as Tu Mu; 803–852) Chinese poet and essayist

1 By rivers and lakes at odds with life I journeyed, wine my freight:
Slim waists of Ch'u broke my heart, light bodies danced into my palm.
Ten years late I wake at last out of my Yangzhou dream
With nothing but the name of a drifter in the blue houses.
A "blue house" is a brothel. "Easing My Heart" (9th century), quoted in *Poems of the Late T'ang* (A. C. Graham, tr.; 1965)

2 Passion too deep seems like none.

While we drink, nothing shows but the smile which will not come.
The wax candles feel, suffer at partings:
Their tears drip for us till the sky brightens.
"Farewell Poem" (9th century), quoted in *Poems of the Late T'ang* (A. C. Graham, tr.; 1965)

Dunayevskaya, Raya (1910–87) Ukrainian-born U.S. author and philosopher

1 Ever since the myth of Eve giving Adam the apple was created, women have been presented as devils or angels, but definitely not as human beings.
Notes on Women's Liberation (1970)

Dunbar, Paul Laurence (1872–1906) U.S. poet, novelist, and playwright

1 The statement has been so strongly and so frequently urged that the Negro should work with his hands, that the opposite of the proposition has been implied. People are taking it for granted that he ought not to work with his head.
1898. *Independent,* (August 18, 1898)

2 But it's easy 'nough to titter w'en de stew is smokin' hot,
But hit's mighty ha'd to giggle w'en dey's nuffin' in de pot.
"Philosophy," *The Complete Poems* (1895)

3 I know why the caged bird sings,
ah me, When his wing is bruised and his bosom sore,—
When he beats his bars and he would be free;
It is not a carol of joy or glee,
But a prayer that he sends from his heart's deep core,
But a plea, that upward to Heaven he flings—
I know why the caged bird sings!
The first line of this poem was used as the title of Maya Angelou's autobiographical novel, published in 1970. "Sympathy," *The Complete Poems* (1895)

4 We wear the mask that grins and lies,
It hides our cheeks and shades our eyes,—
This debt we pay to human guile;
With torn and bleeding hearts we smile.
"We Wear the Mask," *The Complete Poems* (1895)

Dunbar, William (1460?–1520?) Scottish poet and priest

1 I that in heill wes and gladnes
Am trublit now with gret seiknes
And feblit with infirmitie:
Timor mortis conturbat me.
"Lament for the Makaris" (1507?), quoted in *The New Oxford Book of English Verse* (Helen Gardner, ed.; 1972)

2 Fair be their wives, right lovesom, white and small.
"London, Thou Art of Townes a Per Se" (1510?)

3 Strong be thy wallis that about thee standis;
Wise be the people that within thee dwellis.
The attribution to William Dunbar is now thought to be doubtful. "London, Thou Art of Townes a Per Se" (1510?), st. 6, ll. 1–8

Dunbar-Nelson, Alice (1875–1935) U.S. novelist, social worker, and teacher

1 The American public does not want to be uplifted, ennobled—it wants to be amused.
(December 4, 1921), quoted in *Give Us Each Day: The Diary of Alice Dunbar-Nelson* (Gloria T. Hull, ed.; 1984)

Duncan, Isadora (1877–1927) U.S. dancer

Quotations about Duncan

1 Unaccustomed to seeing an almost naked body on the stage, I could hardly notice and understand the art of the dancer...But after a few of the succeeding numbers...I could no longer remain indifferent to the protests of the general public and began to applaud demonstratively.
Constantin Stanislavsky (1863–1938) Russian actor and theater director. Quoted in *My Life* (Isadora Duncan; 1927)

Quotations by Duncan

2 America has all that Russia has not. Russia has things America has not. Why will America not reach out a hand to Russia, as I have given my hand?
Speaking at Symphony Hall, Boston, in support of Russia following the 1917 Revolution. Comment (1922)

3 I would rather live in Russia on black bread and vodka than in the United States at the best hotels. America knows nothing of food, love, or art.
Interview (1922)

4 Any intelligent woman who reads the marriage contract, and then goes into it, deserves all the consequences.
My Life (1927)

5 Before I go out on the stage, I must place a motor in my soul...if I do not get time to put that motor in my soul, I cannot dance.
My Life (1927)

6 I have discovered the dance. I have discovered the art which has been lost for two thousand years.
My Life (1927)

7 I have sometimes been asked whether I consider love higher than art, and I have replied that I cannot separate them, for the artist is the only lover, he alone has the pure vision of beauty, and love is the vision of the soul when it is permitted to gaze upon immortal beauty.
My Life (1927)

8 It seems to me that if the marriage ceremony is needed as a protection to ensure the enforced support of children, then you are marrying a man who, you suspect, would, under certain conditions, refuse to support his children, and it is a pretty low-down proposition.
My Life (1927)

9 When I was 16, I danced before an audience without music. At the end someone suddenly cried from the audience "It is Death and the Maiden"...The dance...should have been called "Life and the Maiden."
My Life (1927)

10 Before our very eyes she turned to many colored shining orchids, to a wavering, flowering sea-flower.
Referring to Loie Fuller, a modern dance pioneer famous for using scarves in her dances. *My Life* (1927)

11 So that ends my first experience with matrimony, which I always thought a highly overrated performance.
Said on her separation from Sergey Yesenin. *New York Times* (1923)

12 Farewell, my friends, I go to glory.
1927. Last words. She was strangled when her long scarf became entangled in the wheel of a sports car. *Isadora Duncan's End* (Mary Desti; 1929), ch. 25

Duncan, Robert (Robert Edward Duncan; born Edward Howard Duncan; 1919–88) U.S. poet

1 *The light foot hears you and the brightness begins*
god-step at the margins of thought,
quick adulterous tread at the heart.
Who is that goes there?
"A Poem Beginning with a Line by Pindar" (1960), quoted in *The Norton Anthology of American Literature* (Nina Baym, ed.; 1998), vol. 2

2 Long slumbering, often coming forward,
haunting the house I am the house I live in
resembles so, does he recall me or I
recall him?
"Interrupted Forms" (1984), quoted in *The Norton Anthology of American Literature* (Nina Baym, ed.; 1998), vol. 2

3 Often I am permitted to return to a meadow
as if it were a given property of the mind
that certain bounds hold against chaos,
that is a place of first permission,
everlasting omen of what is.
"Often I am Permitted to Return to a Meadow" (1960), quoted in *The Norton Anthology of American Literature* (Nina Baym, ed.; 1998), vol. 2

4 Salmon not in the well where the hazelnut falls
but at the falls battling, inarticulate,
blindly making it.
"Poetry, a Natural Thing," *The Opening of the Field* (1960), quoted in *The Penguin Book of American Verse* (Geoffrey Moore, ed.; 1977)

5 The poem
feeds upon thought, feeling, impulse,
to breed itself,
a spiritual urgency at the dark ladders leaping.
"Poetry, a Natural Thing," *The Opening of the Field* (1960), quoted in *The Penguin Book of American Verse* (Geoffrey Moore, ed.; 1977)

Dunham, Katherine (b.1912) U.S. choreographer, dancer, and scholar

1 To develop a technique that will be as important to the white man as to the Negro. To attain a status in the dance world that will give to the Negro dance student the courage really to study, and a reason to do so. And to take *our* dance out of the burlesque to make it a more dignified art.
Stating her intentions upon establishing a small school in Chicago in 1938. Quoted in *Black Dance* (Edward Thorpe; 1989)

Dunn, Douglas (Douglas Eaglesham Dunn; b.1942) British poet and critic

1 Death, the best of all mysteries.
"Supreme Death" (1972)

2 Planthouses force Italian heat
On melon, pepper, peach and vine
And horticultural conceit
Perfects a Scottish aubergine.
"Seventy-five Degrees: V," *Northlight* (1988)

Dunne, Finley Peter (1867–1936) U.S. humorist and journalist

1 There's always wan encouragin' thing about th' sad scientific facts that come out ivry week in th' papers. They're usually not thrue.
"On the Descent of Man," *Mr. Dooley on Making a Will* (1919)

2 A man's idea in a card game is war cool, devastating, and pitiless. A lady's idea of it is a combination of larceny, embezzlement, and burglary.
"On the Game of Cards," *Mr. Dooley on Making a Will* (1919)

3 Miracles are laughed at by a nation that reads thirty million newspapers a day and supports Wall Street.
Mr. Dooley's Opinions (1900)

4 A fanatic is a man who does what he thinks th' Lord wud do if He knew th' facts iv the case.
"Casual Observations," *Mr. Dooley's Opinions* (1900)

5 If th' Christyan Scientists had some science an' th' doctors more Christyanity, it wudden't make anny diff'rence which ye called in If ye had a good nurse.
"Christian Science," *Mr. Dooley's Opinions* (1900)

6 The further you get away from any period, the better you can write about it. You aren't subject to interruptions by people that were there.
Quoted in *Mr. Dooley Remembers: the Informal Memoirs of Finley Peter Dunne* (Philip Dunne, ed.; 1963)

7 History is a post-mortem examination. It tells ye what a counthry died iv. But I'd like to know what it lived iv.
Said by Mr. Dooley, an Irish saloonkeeper, whose opinions formed a well-known series of sketches written by Finley Peter Dunne. Quoted in *Mr. Dooley Remembers: the Informal Memoirs of Finley Peter Dunne* (Philip Dunne, ed.; 1963)

8 I know histhry isn't thrue, Hinnessy, because it ain't like what I see ivry day in Halsted Sthreet. If any wan comes along with a histhry iv Greece or Rome that'll show me the' people fightin', gettin' drunk, makin' love, gettin' married, owin' the grocery man an' bein' without hard-coal, I'll believe they was a Greece or Rome, but not befure.
Said by Mr. Dooley, an Irish saloonkeeper, whose opinions formed a well-known series of sketches written by Finley Peter Dunne. Quoted in *Mr. Dooley Remembers: the Informal Memoirs of Finley Peter Dunne* (Philip Dunne, ed.; 1963)

Dunning, John, 1st Baron Ashburton (1731–83) British lawyer and politician

1 The influence of the Crown has increased, is increasing, and ought to be diminished.
Defending the motion passed by the British parliament. (April 6, 1780)

Dunning, William A. (William Archibald; 1857–1922) U.S. historian

1 For very, very much history there is more importance in the ancient error than in the new-found truth.
Truth in History and Other Essays (1937)

Dunsany, Lord, 18th Baron Dunsany (Edward John Moreton Drax Plunkett; 1878–1957) British-born Irish poet, playwright, and novelist

1 Logic, like whiskey, loses its beneficial effect when taken in too large quantities.
Quoted in *The World of Mathematics* (J. R. Newman, ed.; 1956)

Duport, James (1606–79) English classicist

1 Whom God would destroy He first sends mad.
Homeri Gnomologia (1660)

Durand, Asher B. (Asher Brown Durand; 1796–1886) U.S. painter, engraver, and illustrator

1 Learn first to perceive with truthfulness, and then aim to embody your perceptions; take no thought on the question of genius or of future fame; with these you have nothing to do. Seek not to rival or surpass a brother artist, and above all, let not the love of money overlap the love of art.
"The Crayon," *Letters on Landscape Painting* (1855)

Durant, Will (William James Durant; 1885–1981) U.S. historian

1 Every science begins as philosophy and ends as art.
Story of Philosophy (1926)

2 History assures us that civilizations decay quite leisurely.
The Lessons of History (co-written with Ariel Durant; 1968)

3 History in the large is the conflict of minorities; the majority applauds the victor and supplies the human material of social experiment.
The Lessons of History (co-written with Ariel Durant; 1968)

4 History is a fragment of biology: the life of man is a portion of the vicissitudes of organisms on land and sea.
The Lessons of History (co-written with Ariel Durant; 1968)

5 History is color-blind, and can develop a civilization (in any favorable environment) under almost any skin.
The Lessons of History (co-written with Ariel Durant; 1968)

6 History is so indifferently rich that a case for almost any conclusion from it can be made by a selection of instances.
The Lessons of History (co-written with Ariel Durant; 1968)

7 History offers some consolation by reminding us that sin has flourished in every age.
The Lessons of History (co-written with Ariel Durant; 1968)

8 History repeats itself in the large because human nature changes with geological leisureliness.
The Lessons of History (co-written with Ariel Durant; 1968)

9 History smiles at all attempts to force its flow into theoretical patterns or logical grooves; it plays havoc with our generalizations, breaks all our rules; history is baroque.
The Lessons of History (co-written with Ariel Durant; 1968)

10 Human history is a brief spot in space, and its first lesson is modesty.
The Lessons of History (co-written with Ariel Durant; 1968)

11 Most history is guessing, and the rest is prejudice.
The Lessons of History (co-written with Ariel Durant; 1968)

12 One lesson of history is that religion has many lives, and a habit of resurrection.
The Lessons of History (co-written with Ariel Durant; 1968)

13 The present is the past rolled up for action, and the past is the present unrolled for understanding.
The Lessons of History (co-written with Ariel Durant; 1968)

14 There is no humorist like history.
The Lessons of History (co-written with Ariel Durant; 1968)

15 The South creates the civilizations, the North conquers them, ruins them, borrows from them, spreads them: this is one summary of history.
The Lessons of History (co-written with Ariel Durant; 1968)

16 War is one of the constants of history, and has not diminished with civilization or democracy.
The Lessons of History (co-written with Ariel Durant; 1968)

17 One of the lessons of history is that nothing is often a good thing to do and always a clever thing to say.
Attrib. *Reader's Digest* (November 1972)

18 There is nothing in Socialism that a little age or a little money will not cure.
Attrib.

Durante, Jimmy (James Francis Durante, "Schnozz"; 1893–1980) U.S. entertainer

1 Dese are de conditions dat prevail.
Catchphrase. Attrib.

Durbin, Karen U.S. music journalist

1 Criticism has lost touch with the pleasure principle. You wouldn't know it's music to move to. Rock criticism is more overwhelmingly male than rock itself.
1975. "Can the Stones Still Cut It?," *The Village Voice* (June 23, 1975)

Durcan, Paul (b.1944) Irish poet

1 Daddy and I were lovers
From the beginning, and when I was six
We got married...
My mother gave me away.
My sister was best man.
"Crinkle, Near Birr," *Daddy, Daddy* (1988)

2 At the funeral of the marriage
My wife and I paced
On either side of the hearse,
Our children racing behind it.
"At the Funeral of the Marriage," *The Berlin Wall Café* (1985)

3 "Follow me"—he said—"my name is Jesus:

Have no fear of me—I am a travelling actor.
We'll have a drink together in the nearby inn."
"The Haulier's Wife Meets Jesus on the Road near Moone," *The Berlin Wall Café* (1985)

Dürer, Albrecht (1471–1528) German painter and graphic artist

1 Love and delight are better teachers of the Art of Painting than compulsion is.
"On Painting" (1512), quoted in *The Literary Remains of Albrecht Dürer* (William Martin Conway; 1889)

2 Geometry, without which no one can either be or become an absolute artist.
The Art of Measurement (1525)

3 The Creator fashioned men once and for all as they must be, and I hold that the perfection of form and beauty is contained in the sum of all men.
1528. Quoted in "Four Books on Human Proportion," *The Painter's Manual* (Walter L. Strauss, tr.; 1977)

4 Whoever...proves his point and demonstrates the prime truth geometrically should be believed by all the world, for there we are captured.
Attrib.

Durocher, Leo (Leo Ernest "Leo the Lip" Durocher; 1905–91) U.S. baseball player

1 Show me a good loser and I'll show you an idiot.
Nice Guys Finish Last (1975)

2 I called off his players' names as they came marching up the steps behind him... All nice guys. They'll finish last. Nice guys. Finish last.
1946. Remark at a baseball field, July 1946. *Nice Guys Finish Last* (1975), pt. 1

Durrell, Gerald (Gerald Malcolm Durrell; 1925–95) British naturalist and writer

1 The only mornings that I was ever on time for my lessons were those which were given up to natural history.
My Family and Other Animals (1956)

2 The sneeze in English is the harbinger of misery, even death. I sometimes think the only pleasure an Englishman has is in passing on his cold germs.
My Family and Other Animals (1956)

Durrell, Lawrence (Lawrence George Durrell; 1912–90) British novelist and poet

1 No one can go on being a rebel too long without turning into an autocrat.
Balthazar (1958), pt. 2

2 Music was invented to confirm human loneliness.
Clea (1960)

3 There are only three things to be done with a woman. You can love her, you can suffer for her, or you can turn her into literature.
Justine (1957)

4 History is an endless repetition of the wrong way of living.
Listener, London (1978)

5 The weird mixture of smells which together compose the anthology of a Greek holiday under the pines—petrol, garlic, wine and goat.
Reflections on a Marine Venus (1953)

6 No more about sex, it's too boring. Everyone's got one. Nastiness is a real stimulant though—but poor honest sex, like dying, should be a private matter.
1945. *Tunc* (1968)

7 She has the smile of a woman who has just dined off her husband.
Referring to the Mona Lisa. Attrib.

Dürrenmatt, Friedrich (1921–90) Swiss writer

1 He who confronts the paradoxical exposes himself to reality.
The Physicists (1962)

2 The content of physics is the concern of physicists, its effect the concern of all men.
The Physicists (1962)

3 What concerns everyone can only be resolved by everyone.
The Physicists (1962)

4 What was once thought can never be unthought.
The Physicists (1962)

Dury, Ian (1942–2000) British songwriter and singer

1 Sex & Drugs & Rock & Roll
1977. Song title. The song was co-written with Chaz Jankel.

Duvalier, François ("Papa Doc"; 1907–71) Haitian president

1 Gratitude is cowardice.
Haiti: The Duvaliers and Their Legacy (Elizabeth Abbott; 1991)

2 My government has not been all that I had hoped for.
1971. *Papa Doc, Baby Doc* (James Ferguson; 1987)

Dworkin, Andrea (b.1946) U.S. writer and feminist

1 Coitus is punishment, I say. I am a feminist, not the fun kind. Coitus is the punishment for cowardice, for the fear of being alone.
Ice and Fire (1986)

2 When two individuals come together and leave their gender outside the bedroom door, then they make love. If they take it inside with them, they do something else, because society is in the room with them.
Intercourse (1987)

3 You think intercourse is a private act; it's not, it's a social act. Men are sexually predatory in life; and women are sexually manipulative.
Intercourse (1987)

4 She is the pin-up, the centerfold, the poster, the postcard, the dirty picture, naked, half-dressed, laid out, legs spread, breast or ass protruding. She is the thing she is supposed to be: the thing that makes him erect.
Pornography: Men Possessing Women (1981)

5 Women do not believe that men believe what pornography

says about women. But they do. From the worst to the best of them, they do.
Pornography: Men Possessing Women (1981)

Dyer, Edward, Sir (1543–1607) English courtier and poet

1 Some have too much, yet still do crave;
I little have, and seek no more:
They are but poor, though much they have,
And I am rich with little store.
They poor, I rich; they beg, I give;
They lack, I leave; they pine, I live.
"In Praise of a Contented Mind" (1588)

Dyer, John (1699–1757) Welsh poet

1 And he that will this health deny,
Down among the dead men let him lie.
Published in the early part of the reign of George I. "Toast: Here's a Health to the King" (1714?)

2 A little rule, a little sway,
A sunbeam in a winter's day,
Is all the proud and mighty have
Between the cradle and the grave.
Grongar Hill (1726)

3 Ever charming, ever new,
When will the landscape tire the view?
Grongar Hill (1726)

Dylan, Bob (Robert Allen Zimmerman; b.1941) U.S. singer and songwriter

Quotations about Dylan

1 If Dylan had just been a poet with no guitar saying those same things, it wouldn't have worked; but you can't ignore poetry when it shoots into the Top Ten.
Andy Warhol (1928?–87) U.S. artist and filmmaker. *Popism* (1980)

Quotations by Dylan

2 A Hard Rain's A-Gonna Fall
Song title. "A Hard Rain's Gonna Fall" (1963)

3 Because something is happening here
But you don't know what it is
Do you, Mister Jones?
Song lyric. "Ballad of a Thin Man" (1965)

4 How many roads must a man walk down
Before you call him a man?
Song lyric. "Blowin' in the Wind" (1962)

5 I've made shoes for everyone, even you, while I still go barefoot.
Song lyric. "I and I" (1983)

6 She takes just like a woman, yes, she does
She makes love just like a woman, yes, she does
And she aches just like a woman
But she breaks just like a little girl.
Song lyric. "Just Like a Woman" (1966)

7 Knock, knock, knockin' on Heaven's door.
Song lyric. "Knockin' on Heaven's Door" (1973)

8 How does it feel
To be without a home
Like a complete unknown
Like a rolling stone?
Song lyric. "Like a Rolling Stone" (1965)

9 She knows there's no success like failure
And that failure's no success at all.
Song lyric. "Love Minus Zero No Limit" (1965)

10 I ain't gonna work on Maggie's farm no more.
Song lyric. "Maggie's Farm" (1965)

11 Good intentions can be evil,
Both hands can be full of grease.
You know that sometimes Satan comes as a man of peace.
Song lyric. "Man of Peace" (1983)

12 Hey! Mr Tambourine Man, play a song for me.
I'm not sleepy and there is no place I'm going to.
Song lyric. A "Tambourine Man" is a drug dealer. "Mr Tambourine Man" (1965)

13 You don't need a weather man
To know which way the wind blows.
Song lyric. The U.S. revolutionary terrorist group, the Weathermen, took their name from these lines. "Subterranean Homesick Blues" (1965)

14 Come mothers and fathers
Throughout the land
And don't criticize
What you can't understand.
Song lyric. "The Times They Are A-Changin' " (1964)

15 The Times They Are A-Changin'
Song title. "The Times They Are A-Changin' " (1964)

16 I saw thousands who could have overcome the darkness,
For the love of a lousy buck, I've watched them die.
Song lyric. "When the Night Comes Falling from the Sky" (1985)

17 Ah, but I was so much older then
I'm younger than that now.
Song lyric. "My Back Pages," *Another Side of Bob Dylan* (1964)

18 To live outside the law, you must be honest.
Song lyric. "Absolutely Sweet Marie," *Blonde on Blonde* (1966)

19 Even the president of the United States
Sometimes must have to stand naked.
Song lyric. "It's Alright Ma (I'm Only Bleeding)," *Bringing It All Back Home* (1965)

20 He not busy being born is a-busy dying.
Song lyric. "It's Alright Ma (I'm Only Bleeding)," *Bringing It All Back Home* (1965)

21 Women rule the world...no man has ever done anything that a woman either hasn't allowed him to do or encouraged him to do.
Rolling Stone (June 21, 1984)

22 If I had a good quote, I'd be wearing it.
Said when a French journalist asked him for a good quote. *Times,* London (July 1981)

23 I've made my statement and I don't think I could make it any better than in some of those songs. Once I've said what I need to say in a song, that's it. I don't want to repeat myself.
1980. Quoted in *Bob Dylan Performing Artist, 1974–1986 The Middle Years* (Paul Williams; 1992)

24 There's no more rock 'n' roll, it's an imitation, we can forget

about that; rock 'n' roll has turned itself inside out. I never did do rock 'n' roll.

1977. Quoted in *Rock 'n' Roll Babylon* (Gary Herman; 1994)

25 I don't believe you. You're a liar.

1966. Said to a heckler who called him "Judas" for introducing electric guitars into his music. Quoted in *The Wheel's on Fire* (Levon Helm; 1993)

26 Decay turns me off, I'll die first before I decay.

Quoted in *The Wit and Wisdom of Rock and Roll* (Maxim Jabukowski, ed.; 1983)

27 Some of them are about ten minutes long, others five or six.

1965? Said during an interview, when asked what his songs were about. Attrib.

Dyson, Freeman (Freeman John Dyson; b.1923) British-born U.S. physicist

1 We cannot hope either to understand or to manage the carbon in the atmosphere unless we understand and manage the trees and the soil too.

From Eros to Gaia (1993)

2 It was hay that allowed populations to grow and civilizations to flourish among the forests of Northern Europe. Hay moved the greatness of Rome to Paris and London, and later to Berlin and Moscow and New York.

Hay was unknown in the Roman Empire, as grass grows all year round in Mediterranean countries. *Infinite in All Directions* (1988)

3 Science is a conspiracy of brains against ignorance...a revenge of victims against oppressors...a territory of freedom and friendship in the midst of tyranny and hatred.

The credo of the science club he founded to escape bullying at his preparatory school. Quoted in *The Faber Book of Science* (John Carey, ed.; 1995)

Eadmer (Eadner or Edmer; 1060?–1128?) English monk and historian

1 No one before Anselm became a bishop or abbot who did not first become the king's man and from his hand receive investiture by the gift of the pastoral staff.
Saint Anselm of Bec (1033–1109) became Archbishop of Canterbury in 1093 during the so-called Investiture Controversy, which concerned laymen's formerly uncontested rights to invest clerics with ecclesiastical offices. *Historia Novorum in Anglia* (1115?)

Eames, Emma (1865–1949) U.S. opera singer

1 I would rather be a brilliant memory than a curiosity.
1926. Referring to her retirement at the age of 47. Quoted in *The Elephant that Swallowed a Nightingale* (Charles Neilson Gattey; 1981)

Earhart, Amelia (Amelia Mary Earhart; 1897–1937) U.S. aviator

Quotations about Earhart

1 I have no hesitation in stating that they were exaggerated or slanted or untrue. We were united by one common bond of interest. We spoke each other's language—and that was the language of pioneer women of the air.
Ruth Rowland Nichols (1901–61) U.S. pioneer aviator. Referring to press reports about rivalry between herself and Amelia Earhart. *Wings for Life* (1957)

Quotations by Earhart

2 Of course I realized there was a measure of danger. Obviously I faced the possibility of not returning when first I considered going. Once faced and settled there really wasn't any good reason to refer to it.
Referring to her flight in the *Friendship*. *20 Hours: 40 Minutes—Our Flight in the Friendship* (1928), ch. 5

3 Courage is the price that Life exacts for granting peace.
Courage (1927)

Eastman, George (1854–1932) U.S. inventor, industrialist, and philanthropist

1 My work is done. Why wait?
Suicide note (1932)

Eastwood, Clint (Clinton Eastwood, Jr.; b.1930) U.S. film actor and director

1 Being as this is a .44 Magnum, the most powerful handgun in the world, and would blow your head clean off, you've got to ask yourself one question: "Do I feel lucky?" Well, do ya, punk?
As the police detective "Dirty Harry" Callahan. *Dirty Harry* (Harry Julian Fink; 1976)

2 Every actor should direct at least once. It gives you a tolerance, an understanding of the problems involved in making a film. In fact every director should act.
Playboy (February 1974), quoted in *Chambers Film Quotes* (Tony Crawley, ed.; 1991)

3 Go ahead, make my day.
As the police detective "Dirty Harry" Callahan. *Sudden Impact* (Joseph C. Stinson; 1983)

4 It's a hell of a thing killin' a man. You take away all he's got and all he's ever gonna have.
As William Munny. *Unforgiven* (Ben Maddow; 1992)

Eban, Abba (originally Aubrey Solomon; b.1915) South African-born Israeli statesman

1 History teaches us that men and nations behave wisely once they have exhausted all other alternatives.
December 16, 1970. Speech, *Times*, London (December 17, 1970)

Ebbinghaus, Hermann (1850–1909) German psychologist

1 Psychology has a long past, but only a short history.
Summary of Psychology (1885)

Eberhart, Richard (Richard Ghormley Eberhart; b.1904) U.S. poet

1 It is what man does not know of God
Composes the visible poem of the world.
"On a Squirrel Crossing the Road in Autumn in New England," *Collected Poems 1930–1976* (1976)

Ebner-Eschenbach, Marie von, Baroness (originally Countess Dubsky; 1830–1916) Austrian novelist and poet

1 We are so vain that we even care for the opinion of those we don't care for.
Aphorism (1905)

2 We don't believe in rheumatism and true love until after the first attack.
Aphorism (1905)

3 "Good heavens!" said he, "if it be our clothes alone which fit us for society, how highly we should esteem those who make them."
The Two Countesses (1893)

4 He says a learned woman is the greatest of all calamities.
Quoted in *The New Quotable Woman* (Elaine Partnow; 1993)

5 He who believes in freedom of the will has never loved and never hated.
Quoted in *The New Quotable Woman* (Elaine Partnow; 1993)

6 Only the thinking man lives his life, the thoughtless man's life passes him by.
Quoted in *The New Quotable Woman* (Elaine Partnow; 1993)

7 Privilege is the greatest enemy of right.
Quoted in *The New Quotable Woman* (Elaine Partnow; 1993)

8 To be content with little is hard, to be content with much, impossible.
Quoted in *The New Quotable Woman* (Elaine Partnow; 1993)

9 Whenever two people argue over principles, they are both right.
Quoted in *The New Quotable Woman* (Elaine Partnow; 1993)

10 You can stay young as long as you can learn, acquire new habits and suffer contradictions.
Quoted in *The New Quotable Woman* (Elaine Partnow; 1993)

Eccles, David McAdam, 1st Viscount Eccles (b.1904) British politician

1 A small acquaintance with history shows that all Governments are selfish and the French Governments more selfish than most.
December 1962. *Observer*, London (December 29, 1962), "Sayings of the Year"

2 The only censor is the audience, which will decide whether it wants it and how soon it gets fed up with it.
Attrib.

Eckhart, Meister (Johannes Eckhart; 1260?–1328?) German theologian and mystic

1 The greatest power available to man is not to use it.
Quoted in *The Jingle Bell Principle* (Miroslav Holub; 1992)

Eco, Umberto (b.1932) Italian writer and literary scholar

1 The world is divided between users of the Macintosh computer and users of MS-DOS compatible computers. I am firmly of the opinion that the Macintosh is Catholic and that DOS is Protestant.
"La bustina di Minerva," *Espresso* (September 30, 1994)

2 Whenever a poet or preacher, chief or wizard spouts gibberish, the human race spends centuries deciphering the message.
Foucault's Pendulum (William Weaver, tr.; 1988)

3 I do not want to use the word "true." There are only opinions, some of which are preferable to others. One cannot say: "Ah, if it is just a matter of preference to hell with it."...One can die for an opinion which is only preferable.
Index on Censorship (May/June 1994), vol. 23

4 In the United States there's a Puritan ethic and a mythology of success. He who is successful is good. In Latin countries, in Catholic countries, a successful person is a sinner.
International Herald Tribune (December 14, 1988)

5 I would define the poetic effect as the capacity that a text displays for continuing to generate different readings, without ever being completely consumed.
"Telling the Process," *Reflections on the Name of the Rose* (William Weaver, tr.; 1983)

6 But laughter is weakness, corruption, the foolishness of our flesh.
The Name of the Rose (William Weaver, tr.; 1980)

7 The girl is lost; she is burnt flesh.
Referring to a suspected witch. *The Name of the Rose* (William Weaver, tr.; 1980)

8 Nothing gives a fearful man more courage than another's fear.
The Name of the Rose (William Weaver, tr.; 1980), Third Day: After Compline

9 The good of a book lies in being read. A book is made up of signs that speak of other signs, which in their turn speak of things. Without an eye to read them, a book contains signs that produce no concepts; therefore it is dumb.
The Name of the Rose (William Weaver, tr.; 1980), Fifth Day: Vespers

10 A dream is a scripture, and many scriptures are nothing but dreams.
The Name of the Rose (William Weaver, tr.; 1980), Sixth Day: After Terce

11 Fear prophets...and those prepared to die for the truth, for as a rule they make many others die with them, often before them, at times instead of them.
The Name of the Rose (William Weaver, tr.; 1980), Seventh Day: Night (2)

12 Perhaps the mission of those that love mankind is to make people laugh at the truth, *to make truth laugh*, because the only truth lies in learning to free ourselves from insane passion for the truth.
The Name of the Rose (William Weaver, tr.; 1980), Seventh Day: Night (2)

13 The comic is the perception of the opposite; humor is the feeling of it.
Travels in Hyperreality (William Weaver, tr.; 1986)

14 The pleasure of imitation, as the ancients knew, is one of the most innate in the human spirit.
Travels in Hyperreality (William Weaver, tr.; 1986)

15 The ideology of this America wants to establish reassurance through Imitation. But profit defeats ideology, because the consumers want to be thrilled not only by the guarantee of the Good but also by the shudder of the Bad.
"Ecology 1984 and Coco-Cola Made Flesh," *Travels in Hyperreality* (William Weaver, tr.; 1986)

16 There is a constant in the average American imagination and taste, for which the past must be preserved and celebrated in full-scale authentic copy; a philosophy of immortality as duplication.
"The Fortresses of Solitude," *Travels in Hyperreality* (William Weaver, tr.; 1986)

Eddington, Arthur, Sir (Arthur Stanley Eddington; 1882–1944) British astronomer and physicist

1 Man is slightly nearer to the atom than the stars. From his central position he can survey the grandest works of Nature with the astronomer, or the minutest works with the physicist.
Stars and Atoms (1928)

2 Electrical force is defined as something which causes motion of electrical charge; an electrical charge is something which exerts electric force.
The Nature of the Physical World (1928)

3 I believe there are 15,747,724,136,275,002,577,605,653,961,181, 555,468,044,717,914,527,116,709,366,231,425,076,185,631,031,296

protons in the universe and the same number of electrons.
The Philosophy of Physical Science (1939)

4 We used to think that if we knew one, we knew two, because one and one are two. We are finding that we must learn a great deal more about "and".
Quoted in *Mathematical Maxims and Minims* (N. Rose; 1988)

Eddy, Mary Baker (1821–1910) U.S. religious leader

1 Christian Science explains all cause and effect as mental, not physical.
Science and Health with Key to the Scriptures (1875)

2 Disease is an image of thought externalized...We classify disease as error, which nothing but Truth or Mind can heal...Disease is an experience of so-called mortal mind. It is fear made manifest on the body.
Science and Health with Key to the Scriptures (1875)

3 Sickness, sin and death, being inharmonious, do not originate in God, nor belong to His government.
Science and Health with Key to the Scriptures (1875)

4 Sin brought death, and death will disappear with the disappearance of sin.
Science and Health with Key to the Scriptures (1875)

5 Then comes the question, how do drugs, hygiene, and animal magnetism heal? It may be affirmed that they do not heal, but only relieve suffering temporarily, exchanging one disease for another.
Science and Health with Key to the Scriptures (1875)

6 The prayer that reforms the sinner and heals the sick is an absolute faith that all things are possible to God—a spiritual understanding of Him, an unselfed love.
Science and Health with Key to the Scriptures (1875)

Edelman, Marian Wright (b.1939) U.S. lawyer

1 We are willing to spend the least amount of money to keep a kid at home, more to put him in a foster home, and the most to institutionalize him.
Psychology Today (June 1975)

Edelman, Robert U.S. business executive

1 Internet-driven electronic commerce is essential for organizations entering a virtual distribution marketplace and wishing to survive in it.
Quoted in *Opening Digital Markets* (Walid Mougayar; 1997)

Eden, Anthony, 1st Earl of Avon (Robert Anthony Eden; 1897–1977) British prime minister

Quotations about Eden

1 He is not only a bore but he bores for England.
Malcolm Muggeridge (1903–90) British journalist. Quoted in "Boring for England," *New Statesmanship* (Edward Hyams; 1963)

Quotations by Eden

2 We are not at war with Egypt. We are in an armed conflict.
Speech to the British Parliament, *Hansard* (November 4, 1956)

3 We must face the fact that the United Nations is not yet the international equivalent of our own legal system and the rule of law.
Speech to the British Parliament, *Hansard* (November 1, 1956)

4 Everybody is always in favour of general economy and particular expenditure.
Observer, London (June 17, 1956), "Sayings of the Week"

5 REPORTER If Mr Stalin dies, what will be the effect on international affairs?
EDEN That is a good question for you to ask, not a wise question for me to answer.
March 4, 1953. *Times*, London (March 5, 1953)

Eden, Clarissa, Countess of Avon (b.1920) British aristocrat

1 During the last few weeks I have felt that the Suez Canal was flowing through my drawing room.
Said during the Suez crisis. Speech, Gateshead (November 1956)

Eden, Emily (1797–1869) British writer and traveler

1 I have always thought complaints of ill-usage contemptible, whether from a seduced disappointed girl or a turned out Prime Minister.
Following Lord Melbourne's dismissal by William IV. Letter to Mrs. Lister (November 23, 1834), quoted in *Miss Eden's Letters* (V. Dickinson, ed.; 1919)

2 People may go on talking for ever of the jealousies of pretty women; but for real genuine, hard-working envy, there is nothing like an ugly woman with a taste for admiration.
The Semi-Attached Couple, pt. 1, ch. 1

Edgar, King of the English (Eadgar, "Edgar the Peaceful"; 943–975) English monarch

1 Nevertheless, this measure is to be common to all the nation, whether Englishmen, Danes or Britons...to the end that poor men and rich may possess what they rightly acquire and that a thief may not find a place to bring what he has stolen.
Attrib.

Edgeworth, Maria (1767–1849) British-born Irish novelist

1 Our Irish blunders are never blunders of the heart.
"Essay on Irish Bulls" (1827)

2 Obtain power, then, by all means; power is the law of man; make it yours.
"An Essay on the Noble Science of Self-Justification," *Letters for Literary Ladies* (1795)

3 Alarmed successively by every fashionable medical terror of the day, she dosed her children with every specific which was publicly advertised or privately recommended...The consequence was, that the dangers, which had at first been imaginary, became real: these little victims of domestic medicine never had a day's health: they looked, and were, more dead than alive.
Patronage (1893)

4 Some people talk of morality, and some of religion, but give me a little snug property.
The Absentee (1812), ch. 2

Edgeworth de Firmont, Abbé (Henry Essex Edgeworth de Firmont; 1745–1807) Irish-born confessor to Louis XVI

1 Son of Saint Louis, ascend to heaven.
1793. Said to Louis XVI as he climbed up to the guillotine. Attrib.

Edison, Thomas Alva (1847–1931) U.S. inventor

Quotations about Edison

1 Edison, whose inventions did as much as any to add to our material convenience, wasn't what we would call a scientist at all, but a supreme "do-it-yourself" man—the successor to Benjamin Franklin.
Kenneth Clark (1903–83) British art historian. *Civilisation* (1969)

Quotations by Edison

2 Baseball is the greatest of American games. Some say football, but it is my firm belief, and it shall always be, that baseball has no superior.
St. Petersburg Times (February 25, 1927)

3 Keep on the lookout for novel ideas that others have used successfully. Your idea has to be original only in its adaption to the problem you're working on.
Quoted in *A Kick in the Seat of the Pants* (Roger von Oech; 1986)

4 Genius is one per cent inspiration and ninety-nine per cent perspiration.
Quoted in *Harper's Magazine* (September 1932)

Edward III, King of England (1312–77) English monarch

1 The king of France, hardened in his malice, would assent to no peace or treaty, but called together his strong host to take into his hand the duchy of Aquitaine, declaring against all truth that it was forfeit to him.
Proclamation on the outbreak of the Hundred Years' War (1337). *Foedera* (T. Rymer, ed.; 1337), vol. 4

2 Also say to them, that they suffre hym this day to wynne his spurres, for if god be pleased, I woll this journey be his, and the honoure therof.
1346. "Let the boy win his spurs": replying to a suggestion that he should send reinforcements to his son, the Black Prince, during the Battle of Crécy (1346). *The Chronicle of Froissart* (Sir John Bourchier, Lord Berners, tr.; 1523–25), ch. 130

Edward VII, King of Great Britain and Ireland (1841–1910) British monarch

Quotations about Edward VII

1 We shall not pretend that there is nothing in his long career which those who respect and admire him would wish otherwise.
Newspapers. On the accession (1901) of King Edward VII, referring to his lifestyle. *Times*, London (January 1901)

Quotations by Edward VII

2 My good man, I'm not a strawberry.
Rebuking a footman who had spilled cream on him. *The Last Country Houses* (C. Aslat; 1982)

Edward VIII, King of Great Britain and Northern Ireland, Duke of Windsor (1894–1972) British monarch

Quotations about Edward VIII

1 Our cock won't fight.
1936
Max Aitken, Lord Beaverbrook (1879–1964) Canadian-born British newspaper owner and politician. Said to Winston Churchill during the abdication crisis. *Edward VIII* (F. Donaldson; 1974), ch. 22

2 For not wanting to consent to the divorce, which then afterwards will be recognized as unworthy, the King of the islands will be forced to flee, and one put in his place who has no sign of kingship.
Nostradamus (1503–66) French astrologer and physician. Thought to refer to the abdication of Edward VIII. *The Prophecies of Nostradamus* (16th century), Century 20, st. 22

Quotations by Edward VIII

3 Perhaps one of the only positive pieces of advice that I was ever given was that supplied by an old courtier who observed: "Only two rules really count. Never miss an opportunity to relieve yourself; never miss a chance to sit down and rest your feet."
A King's Story (1951)

4 The thing that impresses me most about America is the way parents obey their children.
Look Magazine (March 5, 1957)

5 I wanted to be an up-to-date king. But I didn't have much time.
Observer, London (January 18, 1970), "Sayings of the Week"

6 I have found it impossible to carry the heavy burden of responsibility and to discharge my duties as King as I would wish to do without the help and support of the woman I love.
December 11, 1936. Radio broadcast after his abdication. *Times*, London (December 12, 1936)

7 When you're bored with yourself, marry and be bored with someone else.
1960. Attrib.

8 Of course, I do have a slight advantage over the rest of you. It helps in a pinch to be able to remind your bride that you gave up a throne for her.
Discussing the maintenance of happy marital relations. Attrib.

9 Now what do I do with *this*?
On being handed the bill after a lengthy stay in a luxury hotel. Attrib.

Edwardes, Michael, Sir (Michael Owen Edwardes; b.1930) South African-born British company executive

1 People will not readily bear pain unless there is hope.
Speech (July 2, 1980)

Edwards, Jonathan (1703–58) U.S. theologian and clergyman

1 The soul of a natural man is the habitation of the devil.
1754. Referring to the condition of anyone who has not experienced a religious conversion. "Sermon on Acts 16:29," *The Works of President Edwards* (1847)

Edwin, John (1749–90) British comic actor

1 A man's ingress into the world is naked and bare,
His progress through the world is trouble and care;
And lastly, his egress out of the world, is nobody knows where.

If we do well here, we shall do well there:
I can tell you no more if I preach a whole year.
The Eccentricities of John Edwin (1791), vol. 1

Egbuna, Obi (b.1938) Nigerian novelist and playwright

1 Puberty is the cradle of love, senility its cremation.
Wind versus Polygamy (1974)

Eggleston, Edward (1837–1902) U.S. writer and Methodist minister

1 Every history has one quality in common with eternity. Begin where you will, there is always a beginning back of the beginning. And for that matter, there is always a shadowy ending beyond the ending.
The Circuit Rider (1874)

Ehrenreich, Barbara (b.1941) U.S. sociologist, feminist, and writer

1 The working-class became, for many middle-class liberals, a psychic dumping-ground for such unstylish sentiments as racism, male chauvinism, and crude materialism: a rearguard population that loved white bread and hated black people.
Fear of Falling (1990)

2 Thus will the fondest dream of Phallic science be realized: a pristine new planet populated entirely by little boy clones of great scientific entrepreneurs...free to smash atoms, accelerate particles, or, if they are so moved, build pyramids—without any social relevance or human responsibility at all.
1988. "Phallic Science," *The Worst Years of Our Lives* (1991)

Ehrlich, Gretel (b.1946) U.S. writer

1 Dryness is the common denominator in Wyoming. We're drenched more often in dust than in water; it is the scalpel and the suit of armor that makes westerners what they are.
"On Water," *The Solace of the Open Spaces* (1985)

Ehrlichman, John D. (John Daniel Ehrlichman; b.1925) U.S. presidential aide

1 I think we ought to let him hang there. Let him twist slowly, slowly in the wind.
Said during the Watergate investigations. Referring to Patrick Gray, acting director of the FBI, who did not know his commission had been withdrawn. Recorded telephone conversation with John Dean (March 7–8, 1973)

Einstein, Albert (1879–1955) German-born U.S. physicist

Quotations about Einstein

1 Einstein said that "the most beautiful experience we can have is the mysterious." Then why do so many of us try to explain the beauty of music, thus apparently depriving it of its mystery?
Leonard Bernstein (1918–90) U.S. composer, conductor, and pianist. *The Unanswered Question* (1976)

2 Einstein said that if quantum mechanics is right, then the world is crazy. Well, Einstein was right. The world is crazy.
Daniel Greenberger U.S. physicist. Quoted in "Quantum Philosophy," *Scientific American* (John Horgan; July 1992)

3 Einstein—the greatest Jew since Jesus. I have no doubt that Einstein's name will still be remembered and revered when Lloyd George, Foch and William Hohenzollern share with Charlie Chaplin that ineluctable oblivion which awaits the uncreative mind.
J. B. S. Haldane (1892–1964) British geneticist. *Daedalus, or, Science and the Future* (1924)

4 It's as important an event as would be the transfer of the Vatican from Rome to the New World. The pope of Physics has moved and the United States will now become the center of the natural sciences.
1933
Paul Langevin (1872–1946) French physicist. Referring to Albert Einstein's departure from Berlin to Princeton University, Princeton, New Jersey (1933). Quoted in *Brighter than a Thousand Suns* (Robert Jungk; 1958)

5 The genius of Einstein leads to Hiroshima.
Pablo Picasso (1881–1973) Spanish painter and sculptor. Remark to Françoise Gilot (1964), quoted in *Life with Picasso* (Françoise Gilot and Carlton Lake; 1964), pt. 2

6 It is pretty safe to say that, so long as physics lasts, no one will again hack out three major breakthroughs in one year.
C. P. Snow (1905–80) British novelist and scientist. Referring to Albert Einstein's papers of 1905. *Variety of Men* (1969)

Quotations by Einstein

7 Concern for man himself and his fate must always form the chief interest of all technical endeavors...in order that the creations of our mind shall be a blessing and not a curse to mankind.
Address, California Institute of Technology (1931)

8 If my theory of relativity is proven correct, Germany will claim me as a German and France will declare that I am a citizen of the world. Should my theory prove untrue, France will say that I am a German and Germany will declare that I am a Jew.
Address, Sorbonne, Paris (1929), quoted in *Einstein for Beginners* (J. Schwartz; 1979)

9 I do not believe in immortality of the individual, and I consider ethics to be an exclusively human concern with no superhuman authority behind it.
Draft response to Baptist pastor (1953), quoted in *Albert Einstein, The Human Side* (Helen Dukas and Banesh Hoffman; 1979)

10 By academic freedom I understand the right to search for truth and to publish and teach what one holds to be true. This right implies also a duty: one must not conceal any part of what one has recognized to be true.
Letter (March 13, 1954)

11 I do not believe in a personal God and I have never denied this but have expressed it clearly. If something is in me which can be called religious then it is the unbounded admiration for the structure of the world so far as our science can reveal it.
Letter (March 24, 1954), quoted in *Albert Einstein, The Human Side* (Helen Dukas and Banesh Hoffman; 1979)

12 It seems hard to sneak a look at God's cards. But that he plays dice and uses "telepathic" methods (as the present quantum theory requires of him) is something that I cannot believe for a single moment.
Letter to Cornelius Lanczos (February 14, 1938), quoted in *Albert Einstein, The Human Side* (Helen Dukas and Banesh Hoffman; 1979)

13 You imagine I look back on my life's work with calm satisfaction, but from nearby it looks quite different. There is not a single concept of which I am convinced it will stand firm, and I feel uncertain whether I am in general on the right track.
Letter to Maurice Solovine (March 28, 1949)

14 Some recent work by E. Fermi and L. Szilard...leads me to expect that the element uranium may be turned into a new and important source of energy in the immediate future. Certain aspects...call for watchfulness and, if necessary, quick action on the part of the Administration.
Referring to Enrico Fermi and Leo Szilard. Albert Einstein was expressing concern about possible Nazi development of an atomic bomb. His letter helped convince President Franklin D. Roosevelt to initiate the Manhattan Project to develop atomic weapons in the United States. Letter to President Franklin D. Roosevelt (August 2, 1939)

15 The minority, the ruling class at present, has the schools and press, usually the Church as well, under its thumb. This enables it to organize and sway the emotions of the masses, and make its tool of them.
Letter to Sigmund Freud (July 30, 1932)

16 It is the supreme art of the teacher to awaken joy in creative expression and knowledge.
Motto for the astronomy building of Junior College, Pasadena, California.Attrib.

17 Unless Americans come to realize that they are not stronger in the world because they have the bomb but weaker because of their vulnerability to atomic attack, they are not likely to conduct their policy at Lake Success or in their relations with Russia in a spirit that furthers the arrival at an understanding.
Following its establishment in 1945 the United Nations General Assembly met temporarily in Lake Success, New York State, pending the setting up of a permanent headquarters. Open letter (1947)

18 The discovery of nuclear chain reactions need not bring about the destruction of mankind...We only must do everything in our power to safeguard against its abuse. Only a supranational organization, equipped with a sufficiently strong executive power, can protect us.
Referring to the United Nations. Open letter (1953)

19 I think that only daring speculation can lead us further and not accumulation of facts.
Albert Einstein, Michele Besso: Correspondance 1903–1955 (1972)

20 I never think of the future. It comes soon enough.
Comment during an interview. *Belgenland* (December 1930)

21 The fairest thing we can experience is the mysterious. It is the fundamental emotion which stands at the cradle of true art and true science. He who knows it not and can no longer wonder, no longer feel amazement, is as good as dead, a snuffed-out candle.
Ideas and Opinions (1954)

22 To me the worst thing seems to be a school principally to work with methods of fear, force, and artificial authority. Such treatment destroys the sound sentiments, the sincerity and the self-confidence of pupils and produces a subservient subject.
Ideas and Opinions (1954)

23 Knowledge...resembles a statue of marble which stands in the desert and is continuously threatened with burial by the shifting sands. The hands of science must ever be at work in order that the marble column continue everlastingly to shine in the sun.
"On Education," address to the State University of New York, Albany, *Ideas and Opinions* (1954)

24 One should guard against preaching to young people success in the customary form as the main aim in life.The most important motive for work in school and in life is pleasure in work, pleasure in its result, and the knowledge of the value of the result to the community.
"On Education," address to the State University of New York, Albany, *Ideas and Opinions* (1954)

25 When you are courting a nice girl an hour seems like a second. When you sit on a red-hot cinder a second seems like an hour. That's relativity.
News Chronicle (March 14, 1949)

26 The school has always been the most important means of transferring the wealth of tradition from one generation to the next. This applies today in an even higher degree...for...the family as bearer of tradition and education has become weakened.
New York Times (October 16, 1936)

27 Every intellectual who is called before one of the committees ought to refuse to testify, i.e., he must be prepared...for the sacrifice of his personal welfare in the interest of the cultural welfare of the country...This kind of inquisition violates the spirit of the Constitution.
May 16, 1953. Referring to the Senate Internal Security Subcommittee. Letter to William Frauenglass, *New York Times* (June 12, 1953)

28 A man's ethical behavior should be based effectually on sympathy, education, and social ties and needs; no religious basis is necessary. Man would indeed be in a poor way if he had to be restrained by fear of punishment and hope of reward after death.
"Religion and Science," *New York Times* (November 9, 1930)

29 Education is that which remains, if one has forgotten everything one learned in school.
Out of My Later Years (1950)

30 Ethical axioms are found and tested not very differently from the axioms of science. Truth is what stands the test of experience.
Out of My Later Years (1950)

31 Science is the attempt to make the chaotic diversity of our sense-experience correspond to a logically uniform system of thought.
Out of My Later Years (1950)

32 The man of science is a poor philosopher.
Out of My Later Years (1950)

33 The point is to develop the childlike inclination for play and the childlike desire for recognition and to guide the child over to important fields for society. Such a school demands from the teacher that he be a kind of artist in his province.
Out of My Later Years (1950)

34 The whole of science is nothing more than a refinement of everyday thinking.
Out of My Later Years (1950)

35 We should take care not to make the intellect our god; it has, of course, powerful muscles, but no personality.
Out of My Later Years (1950)

36 If I were not a physicist, I would probably be a musician. I often think in music. I live my daydreams in music. I see my life in terms of music...I get most joy in life out of music.
"What Life Means to Einstein; An Interview by George Sylvester Viereck," *Saturday Evening Post* (October 26, 1929)

37 Science without religion is lame, religion without science is blind.
Science, Philosophy and Religion: a Symposium (1941), ch. 13

38 Most of the fundamental ideas of science are essentially simple, and may, as a rule, be expressed in a language comprehensible to anyone.
The Evolution of Physics (co-written with Leopold Infeld; 1938)

39 Physical concepts are free creations of the human mind, and are not, however it may seem, uniquely determined by the external world.
The Evolution of Physics (co-written with Leopold Infeld; 1938)

40 Equations are more important to me, because politics is for the present, but an equation is something for eternity.
1952? Quoted in *A Brief History of Time* (Stephen Hawking; 1988)

41 Never do anything against conscience, even if the state demands it.
Quoted in *Albert Einstein, Philosopher-Scientist* (Paul A. Schilpp, ed.; 1949)

42 Since the mathematicians have invaded the theory of relativity, I do not understand it myself anymore.
Quoted in *Albert Einstein, Philosopher-Scientist* (Paul A. Schilpp, ed.; 1949)

43 Nationalism is an infantile disease. It is the measles of mankind.
Albert Einstein, the Human Side (Helen Dukas and Banesh Hoffman; 1979)

44 If I had known that the Germans would not succeed in constructing the atom bomb, I would never have lifted a finger.
1947. Quoted in *Brighter Than a Thousand Suns* (Robert Jungk; 1958)

45 The real problem is in the hearts and minds of men. It is easier to denature plutonium than to denature the evil spirit of man.
Quoted in *Disturbing the Universe* (Freeman Dyson; 1979), ch. 5

46 God is subtle but he is not malicious.
1921. Inscribed over the fireplace in the Mathematical Institute, Princeton. It refers to Einstein's objection to quantum theory. *Einstein* (R. W. Clark; 1973), ch. 14

47 Concern for man himself and his fate must always form the chief interest of all technical endeavors...Never forget this in the midst of your diagrams and equations.
Quoted in *Knowledge for What?* (Robert S. Lynd; 1939)

48 Common sense is the collection of prejudices acquired by age eighteen.
Quoted in *Mathematics, Queen and Servant of the Sciences* (E. T. Bell; 1952)

49 If only I had known, I should have become a watchmaker.
Reflecting on his role in the development of the atom bomb. Attrib. *New Statesman*, London (April 16, 1965)

50 God does not care about our mathematical difficulties. He integrates empirically.
Quoted in *Quest* (L. Infield; 1942)

51 A theory can be proved by experiment; but no path leads from experiment to the birth of a theory.
Sunday Times, London (July 18, 1976)

52 I find the idea quite intolerable that an electron exposed to radiation should choose *of its own free will*, not only its moment to jump off, but also its direction. In that case I would rather be a cobbler, or even an employee in a gaming-house, than a physicist.
Referring to quantum theory. Quoted in *The Born-Einstein Letters* (I. Born, tr.; 1971)

53 Quantum mechanics is certainly imposing...but does not bring us any closer to the secret of the "old one." I, at any rate, am convinced that *He* is not playing dice.
The origin of "God does not play dice with the world." Quoted in *The Born-Einstein Letters* (I. Born, tr.; 1971)

54 As far as the laws of mathematics refer to reality, they are not certain, and as far as they are certain, they do not refer to reality.
The Tao of Physics (F. Capra; 1975), ch. 2

55 Well-being and happiness never appeared to me as an absolute aim. I am even inclined to compare such moral aims to the ambitions of a pig.
Quoted in *Variety of Men* (C. P. Snow; 1969)

56 Everything should be made as simple as possible, but not simpler.
Attrib.

57 No amount of experimentation can ever prove me right; a single experiment can prove me wrong.
Attrib.

58 The hardest thing in the world to understand is income tax.
Attrib.

59 My pacifism is not based on any intellectual theory but on a deep antipathy to every form of cruelty and hatred.
1914. Said on the outbreak of World War I. Attrib.

Eisenhower, Dwight D. (Dwight David Eisenhower, "Ike"; 1890–1969) U.S. general and president

Quotations about Eisenhower

1 Roosevelt proved a man could be president for life; Truman proved anybody could be president; and Eisenhower proved we don't need a president.
Anonymous

2 Eisenhower was President, and the entire country had been turned into a gigantic television commercial, an incessant harangue to buy more, make more, spend more, to dance around the dollar-tree until you dropped dead from the sheer frenzy of trying to keep up with everyone else.
Paul Auster (b.1947) U.S. writer. Dwight D. Eisenhower was U.S. president for two terms between 1953 and 1961. *Hand to Mouth* (1997)

3 It really looks as if Stevenson would get in, don't you think? At least it might be interesting to have someone nice & neurotic in the White House for a change.

Elizabeth Bishop (1911–79) U.S. poet. Referring to the 1952 presidential contest between Adlai Stevenson and Dwight D. Eisenhower, won by the latter. Letter to U. T. and Joseph Summers (September 17, 1952), quoted in *One Art: The Selected Letters of Elizabeth Bishop* (Robert Giroux, ed.; 1994)

4 As an intellectual he bestowed upon the games of golf and bridge all the enthusiasm and perseverance that he withheld from books and ideas.
Emmet John Hughes (1920–82) U.S. political scientist. *The Ordeal of Power* (1963)

5 He was the great tortoise upon whose back the world sat for eight years. We laughed at him; we talked wistfully about moving; and all the while we never knew the cunning beneath the shell.
Murray Kempton (1918–97) U.S. writer and commentator. "The Underestimation of Dwight D Eisenhower," *Esquire* (September 1967)

6 The best clerk I ever fired.
Douglas MacArthur (1880–1964) U.S. general. Attrib.

7 Perhaps his peculiar contribution to the art of politics was to make politics boring at a time when the people wanted any excuse to forget public affairs.
Arthur Schlesinger, Jr. (b.1917) U.S. historian. *Esquire* (January 1965)

8 He's a good man. The only trouble was, he had a lot of damn fool Republicans around him.
Harry S. Truman (1884–1972) U.S. president. Remark (December 1963), quoted in *Quotations in History* (Alan and Veronica Palmer; 1976)

Quotations by Eisenhower

9 The history of free men is never really written by chance but by choice—their choice.
Address at Pittsburgh (October 9, 1956)

10 The day will come when the people will make so insistent their demand that there be peace in the world that the Governments will get out of the way and let them have peace.
Broadcast discussion (August 1959)

11 In the councils of government, we must guard against the acquisition of unwarranted influence, whether sought or unsought, by the military-industrial complex. The potential for the disastrous rise of misplaced power exists and will persist.
Farewell address, Washington, D.C. (January 17, 1961)

12 A people that values its privileges above its principles soon loses both.
Inaugural address, Washington, D.C. (January 20, 1953)

13 History does not long entrust the care of freedom to the weak or the timid.
Inaugural address, Washington, D.C. (January 20, 1953)

14 We feel...moral strength because we know that we are not helpless prisoners of history. We are free men. We shall remain free, never to be proven guilty of the one capital offense against freedom, a lack of stanch faith.
Inaugural address, Washington, D.C. (January 20, 1953)

15 Whatever America hopes to bring to pass in this world must first come to pass in the heart of America.
Inaugural address, Washington, D.C. (January 20, 1953)

16 Politics is a profession; a serious, complicated and, in its true sense, a noble one.
Letter to Leonard V. Finder (January 22, 1948)

17 As men and women of character and of faith in the soundness of democratic methods, we must work like dogs to justify that faith.
Letter to Maime Eisenhower (September 15, 1942)

18 There are a number of things wrong with Washington. One of them is that everyone has been too long away from home.
Presidential press conference (May 11, 1955)

19 There can be no law if we were to invoke one code of international conduct for those who oppose us and another for our friends.
Said at the time of the Suez Crisis. Radio broadcast (October 31, 1956)

20 You have a row of dominoes set up; you knock over the first one, and what will happen to the last one is that it will go over very quickly.
The so-called "domino effect"; said during the Battle of Dien Bien Phu (1954), in which the French were defeated by the communist Vietminh. (The domino metaphor was first used by the French Minister-Resident, Jean de Tourneau, in April 1952.) Remark at press conference (April 7, 1954)

21 Every gun that is made, every warship launched, every rocket fired signifies, in the final sense, a theft from those who hunger and are not fed, those who are cold and are not clothed.
Speech, American Society of Newspaper Editors (April 16, 1953)

22 Don't join the book burners. Don't think you are going to conceal faults by concealing evidence that they ever existed.
Speech, Dartmouth College (June 14, 1953)

23 The opportunist thinks of me and today. The statesman thinks of us and tomorrow.
Speech, Lafayette College, Easton, Pennsylvania (November 1, 1946)

24 I have only one yardstick by which I test every major problem and that yardstick is: Is it good for America? Unlike presidential administrations, problems rarely have terminal dates.
State of the Union Address (January 12, 1961)

25 There is one thing about being President—nobody can tell you when to sit down.
Observer, London (August 9, 1953), "Sayings of the Week"

26 Without God, there could be no American form of government, nor American way of life.
1955. Quoted in *American Chronicle* (Lois and Alan Gordon; 1987)

27 Not making the baseball team at West Point was one of the greatest disappointments of my life, maybe the greatest.
Quoted in *Baseball: The People's Game* (Harold Seymour; 1990)

28 Your business is to put me out of business.
Addressing a graduating class at a university. Quoted in *Procession* (John Gunther; 1965)

29 Every GI in Europe—and that means all of us—has lost one of his best friends.
Quoted in *Speaking Freely* (Stuart Berg Flexner and Anne H. Soukhanov; 1997)

30 Neither a wise man nor a brave man lies down on the tracks of history to wait for the train of the future to run over him.
Quoted in *Time* (October 6, 1952)

31 The eyes of the world are upon you. The hopes and prayers of liberty-loving people everywhere march with you.
Address to troops on D-Day. (June 6, 1944)

Eisner, Michael (b.1942) U.S. entertainment executive

Quotations about Eisner

1 Stick Michael Eisner into a football game, and make him return a couple of punts. Let's just see if the guy is really worth big-league money.
Dave Barry (b.1947) U.S. humorist. Michael Eisner has been chief executive of Walt Disney productions. Interview, *Fortune* (July 7, 1997)

Quotations by Eisner

2 Failing is good as long as it doesn't become a habit.
Speech (April 19, 1996)

3 What I need is help, not succession.
Said after he had had a coronary bypass. *Business Week* (September 5, 1994)

4 Purpose is the central ingredient of power. Powerful people and organizations have a strong, sometimes even skewed, sense of purpose...A strong point of view is worth 80 IQ points.
Strategy and Business (1997), "Noteworthy Quotes"

5 I'm a child of the corporate struggle. I spent many years dealing with people trying to do me in. I determined that any operation I ran would be as nonpolitical as I could make it.
Time (April 25, 1988)

6 I've always been fearful that I'd end up in an industry like the railroads when they sneered at airplane travel.
Quoted in *New Yorker* (October 20, 1997)

Ekelöf, Gunnar (Bengt Gunnar Ekelöf; 1907–68) Swedish poet

1 Is there really any difference
Between Day and Night?
How blind we are when our eyes are open
How perceptive we are when we close them in sleep.
The Tale of Fatumeh (W. H. Auden and Leif Sjöberg, trs.; 1966)

2 To suffer is difficult
To suffer without loving is difficult
To love without suffering is impossible
To love is difficult.
The Tale of Fatumeh (W. H. Auden and Leif Sjöberg, trs.; 1966)

Ekland, Britt (Britt-Marie Eklund; b.1942) Swedish film actor

1 I say, I don't sleep with married men, but what I mean is that I don't sleep with happily married men.
Attrib.

Elaw, Zilpha (1790?–1846?) U.S. preacher, evangelist, and teacher

1 Pride and arrogancy are among the master sins of rational beings; an high look, a stately bearing, and a proud heart, are abominations in the sight of God, and insure a woeful reverse in a future life.
Memoirs of the Life, Religious Experience, Ministerial Travels and Labours of Mrs Zilpha Elaw, An American Female of Colour (1986)

Elgar, Edward, Sir (1857–1934) British composer, conductor, and violinist

1 Lovely day: sun—zephyr—view—window open—liver—pills—proofs—bills—weed-killer—yah!
Remark (May 20, 1900)

2 There is music in the air, music all round us: the world is full of it, and you simply take as much as you require.
Sir Edward Elgar (R. J. Buckley; 1905)

3 Teaching is like turning a grindstone with a dislocated shoulder.
Attrib.

Eliot, Charles William (1834–1926) U.S. educationist, mathematician, and chemist

1 Well, this year I'm told the team did well because one pitcher had a fine curve ball. I understand that a curve ball is thrown with a deliberate attempt to deceive. Surely that is not an ability we should want to foster at Harvard.
Reply when asked why he wished to drop baseball as a college sport. Attrib.

Eliot, George (pen name of Mary Ann Evans; 1819–80) British novelist

Quotations about Eliot

1 I found out in the first two pages that it was a woman's writing—she supposed that in making a door, you last of all put in the panels!
Thomas Carlyle (1795–1881) Scottish historian and essayist. Referring to *Adam Bede* by George Eliot. *George Eliot: a Biography* (Gordon Sherman Haight; 1968)

2 I never saw such a woman. There is nothing a bit masculine about her; she is thoroughly feminine and looks and acts as if she were made for nothing but to mother babies. But she has a power of *stating* an argument equal to any man.
John Fiske (1842–1901) U.S. historian and philosopher. Letter to his wife (1873)

Quotations by Eliot

3 By the time you receive this letter I shall have been married to Mr J. W. Ross, who now that I am alone sees his happiness in the dedication of his life to me.
Letter to Barbara Bodichon (May 5, 1880)

4 Few women, I fear, have had such reason as I have to think the long sad years of youth were worth living for the sake of middle age.
Letter to Mrs. Peter Taylor (December 31, 1857)

5 Oh may I join the choir invisible
Of those immortal dead who live again
In minds made better by their presence.
"Oh May I Join the Choir Invisible" (1867)

6 A patronizing disposition always has its meaner side.
Adam Bede (1854)

7 He was like a cock who thought the sun had risen to hear him crow.
Adam Bede (1854)

8 It's but little good you'll do a-watering the last year's crop.
Adam Bede (1854)

9 It's them that take advantage that get advantage i' this world.
Adam Bede (1854), ch. 32

10 We hand folks over to God's mercy, and show none ourselves.
Adam Bede (1854), ch. 42

11 I'm not denyin' the women are foolish: God Almighty made 'em to match the men.
Adam Bede (1854), ch. 53

12 A different taste in jokes is a great strain on the affections.
Daniel Deronda (1876), ch. 15

13 Friendships begin with liking or gratitude—roots that can be pulled up.
Daniel Deronda (1876), ch. 32

14 An election is coming. Universal peace is declared, and the foxes have a sincere interest in prolonging the lives of the poultry.
Felix Holt (1866), ch. 5

15 A woman dictates before marriage in order that she may have an appetite for submission afterwards.
Middlemarch (1871 72), ch. 9

16 Among all forms of mistake, prophecy is the most gratuitous.
Middlemarch (1871–72), ch. 10

17 Correct English is the slang of prigs who write history and essays. And the strongest slang of all is the slang of poets.
Middlemarch (1871–72), ch. 11

18 A woman, let her be as good as she may, has got to put up with the life her husband makes for her.
Middlemarch (1871–72), ch. 25

19 A man is seldom ashamed of feeling that he cannot love a woman so well when he sees a certain greatness in her: nature having intended greatness for men.
Middlemarch (1871–72), ch. 39

20 She was always attentive to the feelings of dogs, and very polite if she had to decline their advances.
Middlemarch (1871–72), ch. 39

21 Our deeds still travel with us from afar,
And what we have been makes us what we are.
Middlemarch (1871–72), ch. 70, heading

22 Errors look so very ugly in persons of small means—one feels they are taking quite a liberty in going astray; whereas people of fortune may naturally indulge in a few delinquencies.
"Janet's Repentance," *Scenes of Clerical Life* (1858), ch. 25

23 Animals are such agreeable friends—they ask no questions, they pass no criticisms.
"Mr Gilfil's Love Story," *Scenes of Clerical Life* (1858), ch. 7

24 "I never see'd a ghost myself, but then I says to myself, 'Very like I haven't got the smell for 'em'."
Landlord's comment. *Silas Marner* (1861)

25 Nothing is so good as it seems beforehand.
Silas Marner (1861), ch. 18

26 I should like to know what is the proper function of women, if it is not to make reasons for husbands to stay at home, and still stronger reasons for bachelors to go out.
The Mill on the Floss (1860), ch. 6

27 The happiest women, like the happiest nations, have no history.
The Mill on the Floss (1860), ch. 6

28 I am not an optimist but a meliorist.
Quoted in *A. E. H.* (Laurence Housman; 1937)

Eliot, T. S. (Thomas Stearns Eliot; 1888–1965) U.S.-born British poet and playwright

Quotations about Eliot

1 I seldom go to *films*. They are too exciting,
said the Honorable Possum.
John Berryman (1914–72) U.S. poet. "Possum" was a nickname for T. S. Eliot. *The Dream Songs* (1968)

2 He never hit a ball out of the infield in his life.
1950
Ernest Hemingway (1899–1961) U.S. writer. "The Pastime and the Literati," *New York Times* (April 8, 1981)

3 Who's left alive to understand my jokes?
My old brother in the arts...besides he was a smash of a poet.
Robert Lowell (1917–77) U.S. poet. According to Robert Lowell, Ezra Pound's assessment of T. S. Eliot. "Ezra Pound," *History* (1973), quoted in *The Penguin Book of American Verse* (Geoffrey Moore, ed.; 1977)

4 Here with a black suit and black briefcase; in the brief,
an abomination, Possum's hommage to Milton.
Robert Lowell (1917–77) U.S. poet. According to Robert Lowell, Ezra Pound's assessment of T. S. Eliot ("Possum"), while in St. Elizabeth's Hospital for the criminally insane (1946–58). "Ezra Pound," *History* (1973), quoted in *The Penguin Book of American Verse* (Geoffrey Moore, ed.; 1977)

5 It's balls to say he only
pretends to be Ezra...He's better though. This year,
he no longer wants to rebuild the Temple at Jerusalem.
Robert Lowell (1917–77) U.S. poet. According to Robert Lowell, T. S. Eliot's assessment of Ezra Pound. "Ezra Pound," *History* (1973), quoted in *The Penguin Book of American Verse* (Geoffrey Moore, ed.; 1977)

Quotations by Eliot

6 Because I do not hope to turn again
Because I do not hope
Because I do not hope to turn.
1930. "Ash Wednesday," pt. 1, ll. 1–3

7 Teach us to care and not to care
Teach us to sit still.
"Ash-Wednesday" (1930)

8 "And youth is cruel, and has no remorse
And smiles at situations which it cannot see."
I smile of course,
And go on drinking tea.
"Portrait of a Lady" (1917)

9 No poet, no artist of any sort, has his complete meaning alone. His significance, his appreciation is the appreciation of his relation to the dead poets and artists.
"Tradition and the Individual Talent" (1920)

10 Poetry is not a turning loose of emotion, but an escape from emotion; it is not the expression of personality, but an escape from personality.
"Tradition and the Individual Talent" (1920)

11 A cold coming we had of it,
Just the worst time of the year
For a journey, and such a long journey:
The ways deep and the weather sharp,
The very dead of winter.
1927. "Journey of the Magi," *Collected Poems 1909–1935* (1936)

12 Classicist in literature, royalist in politics, and anglo-catholic in religion.
Describing his "general point of view." "Preface," *For Lancelot Andrewes* (1928)

13 Footfalls echo in the memory
Down the passage which we did not take
Towards the door we never opened
Into the rose-garden. My words echo
Thus, in your mind.
"Burnt Norton," *Four Quartets* (1935)

14 Human kind
Cannot bear very much reality.
"Burnt Norton," *Four Quartets* (1935)

15 Time present and time past
Are both perhaps present in time future,
And time future contained in time past.
"Burnt Norton," *Four Quartets* (1935)

16 At the still point of the turning world. Neither flesh nor fleshless;
Neither from nor towards; at the still point, there the dance is,
But neither arrest nor movement.
"Burnt Norton," *Four Quartets* (1935), pt. 2

17 In my beginning is my end.
"East Coker," *Four Quartets* (1940)

18 The association of man and woman
In daunsinge, signifying matrimonie—
A dignified and commodious sacrament.
"East Coker," *Four Quartets* (1940)

19 The wounded surgeon plies the steel
That questions the distempered part;
Beneath the bleeding hands we feel
The sharp compassion of the healer's art
Resolving the enigma of the fever chart.
"East Coker," *Four Quartets* (1940)

20 We are only undeceived
Of that which, deceiving, could no longer harm.
"East Coker," *Four Quartets* (1940)

21 What we call the beginning is often the end
And to make an end is to make a beginning.
The end is where we start from.
"Little Gidding," *Four Quartets* (1942)

22 The last temptation is the greatest treason:
To do the right deed for the wrong reason.
Murder in the Cathedral (1935), Act 1

23 Macavity, Macavity, there's no one like Macavity,
There never was a Cat of such deceitfulness and suavity.
He always has an alibi, and one or two to spare:
At whatever time the deed took place—
MACAVITY WASN'T THERE!
"Macavity: The Mystery Cat," *Old Possum's Book of Practical Cats* (1939)

24 The Naming of Cats is a difficult matter
It isn't just one of your holiday games.
"The Naming of Cats," *Old Possum's Book of Practical Cats* (1939)

25 After such knowledge, what forgiveness? Think now
History has many cunning passages, contrived corridors
And issues, deceives with whispering ambitions.
"Gerontion," *Poems* (1920)

26 The host with someone indistinct
Converses at the door apart,
The nightingales are singing near
The Convent of the Sacred Heart.
"Sweeney Among the Nightingales," *Poems* (1919)

27 Webster was much possessed by death
And saw the skull beneath the skin.
"Whispers of Immortality," *Poems, 1920* (1920)

28 "Put your shoes at the door, sleep, prepare for life."
The last twist of the knife.
"Rhapsody on a Windy Night," *Prufrock and Other Observations* (1917)

29 I grow old...I grow old...
I shall wear the bottoms of my trousers rolled.
"The Love Song of J. Alfred Prufrock," *Prufrock and Other Observations* (1917)

30 I have measured out my life with coffee spoons.
"The Love Song of J. Alfred Prufrock," *Prufrock and Other Observations* (1917)

31 I have seen the moment of my greatness flicker,
And I have seen the eternal Footman hold my coat, and snicker,
And in short, I was afraid.
"The Love Song of J. Alfred Prufrock," *Prufrock and Other Observations* (1917)

32 In the room the women come and go
Talking of Michelangelo.
"The Love Song of J. Alfred Prufrock," *Prufrock and Other Observations* (1917)

33 Let us go then, you and I,
When the evening is spread out against the sky
Like a patient etherized upon a table.
"The Love Song of J. Alfred Prufrock," *Prufrock and Other Observations* (1917)

34 Shall I part my hair behind? Do I dare to eat a peach?
I shall wear white flannel trousers, and walk upon the beach.
I have heard the mermaids singing, each to each.
"The Love Song of J. Alfred Prufrock," *Prufrock and Other Observations* (1917)

35 The yellow fog that rubs its back upon the window panes.
Referring to a London fog. "The Love Song of J. Alfred Prufrock," *Prufrock and Other Observations* (1917)

36 In the seventeenth century a dissociation of sensibility set in from which we have never recovered.
"The Metaphysical Poets," *Selected Essays* (1932)

37 A dangerous person to disagree with.
Referring to Samuel Johnson. "The Metaphysical Poets," *Selected Essays* (1932)

38 Birth, and copulation, and death.

That's all the facts when you come to brass tacks:
Birth, and copulation and death.
I've been born, and once is enough.
Sweeney Agonistes (1932)

39 Well here again that don't apply
But I've gotta use words when I talk to you.
Sweeney Agonistes (1932)

40 Hell is oneself;
Hell is alone, the other figures in it
Merely projections. There is nothing to escape from
And nothing to escape to. One is always alone.
The Cocktail Party (1950), Act 1, Scene 3

41 We're all of us ill in one way or another:
We call it health when we find no symptom
Of illness. Health is a relative term.
The Family Reunion (1939), Act 1, Scene 3

42 Success is relative. It is what we can make of the mess we have made of things.
The Family Reunion (1939), Act 2, Scene 3

43 This is the way the world ends
Not with a bang but a whimper.
The Hollow Men (1925)

44 We are the hollow men
We are the stuffed men
Leaning together
Headpiece filled with straw. Alas!
The Hollow Men (1925)

45 The lot of man is ceaseless labour,
Or ceaseless idleness, which is still harder,
Or irregular labour, which is not pleasant.
The Rock (1934), chorus

46 The only way of expressing emotion in the form of art is by finding an "objective correlative"; in other words, a set of objects, a situation, a chain of events which shall be the formula of that *particular* emotion; such that when the external facts...are given, the emotion is immediately evoked.
1919. "Hamlet," *The Sacred Wood* (1920)

47 Immature poets imitate; mature poets steal.
"Philip Massinger," *The Sacred Wood* (1920)

48 And I will show you something different from either
Your shadow at morning striding behind you,
Or your shadow at evening rising to meet you
I will show you fear in a handful of dust.
"The Burial of the Dead," *The Waste Land* (1922)

49 April is the cruellest month, breeding
Lilacs out of the dead land, mixing
Memory and desire, stirring
Dull roots with spring rain.
"The Burial of the Dead," *The Waste Land* (1922)

50 I read, much of the night, and go south in the winter.
"The Burial of the Dead," *The Waste Land* (1922)

51 Unreal City,
Under the brown fog of a winter dawn,
A crowd flowed over London bridge, so many,
I had not thought death had undone so many.
"The Burial of the Dead," *The Waste Land* (1922)

52 What are the roots that clutch, what branches grow
Out of this stony rubbish? Son of man,
You cannot say, or guess, for you know only
A heap of broken images.
"The Burial of the Dead," *The Waste Land* (1922)

53 The time is now propitious, as he guesses,
The meal is ended, she is bored and tired,
Endeavours to engage her in caresses
Which still are unreproved, if undesired.
"The Fire Sermon," *The Waste Land* (1922)

54 These fragments I have shored against my ruin.
"What the Thunder Said," *The Waste Land* (1922)

55 The years between fifty and seventy are the hardest. You are always being asked to do things, and you are not yet decrepit enough to turn them down.
Time (October 23, 1950)

56 A book is not harmless merely because no one is consciously offended by it.
1935. "Religion and Literature," *T.S. Eliot Selected Essays* (1966)

Elizabeth, the Queen Mother (originally Lady Elizabeth Bowes-Lyon; b.1900) British queen consort

1 Now we can look the East End in the face.
Surveying the damage caused to Buckingham Palace by a bomb during the Blitz in World War II. Attrib. (1940)

Elizabeth I, Queen of England (1533–1603) English monarch

Quotations about Elizabeth I

1 The house is well, but it is you, Your Majesty, who have made me too great for my house.
Francis Bacon (1561–1626) English philosopher, statesman, and lawyer. Reply when Elizabeth I remarked on the smallness of his house. Attrib.

2 The queen did fish for men's souls, and had so sweet a bait that no one could escape her network.
Christopher Hatton (1540–91) English courtier. Attrib.

3 After all the stormy, tempestuous, and blustering windy weather of Queen Mary was overblown...it pleased God to send England calm and quiet season, a clear and lovely sunshine, a quitsest from former broils of a turbulent estate, and a world of blessings by good Queen Elizabeth.
Raphael Holinshed (1525?–80?) English chronicler. *The Chronicles of England, Scotland, and Ireland* (1577)

4 Upon a great adventure he was bond,
The greatest Gloriana to him gave,
(That greatest Glorious Queene of Faery lond)
To winne him worshippe, and her grace to have,
Which of all earthly thinges he most did crave.
Edmund Spenser (1552?–99) English poet. Dedicated to Elizabeth I. *The Faerie Queene* (1590), bk. 1, can. 1, st. 3

5 As just and merciful as Nero and as good a Christian as Mahomet.
John Wesley (1703–91) English religious leader. *Journal* (April 29, 1768)

Quotations by Elizabeth I

6 This judgment I have of you, that you will not be corrupted with any manner of gift and that you will be faithful to the state, and that, without respect of my private will, you will give me that counsel that you think best.
Remark (1558)

7 I muse how men of wit can so hardly use that gift they hold.
Speech to a delegation from the English Parliament (November 5, 1566)

8 As for me, I see no such great cause why I should either be fond to live or fear to die. I have had good experience of this world, and I know what it is to be a subject and what to be a sovereign. Good neighbours I have had, and I have met with bad: and in trust I have found treason.
Speech to a delegation from the English Parliament (November 12, 1586), quoted in *Elizabeth I and her Parliaments 1584–1601* (Sir John Neale; 1957)

9 Though God hath raised me high, yet this I count the glory of my crown: that I have reigned with your loves.
Known as the Golden Speech. Speech to a deputation from the English Parliament (November 30, 1601)

10 Of myself I must say this, I never was any greedy, scraping grasper, nor a strait fast-holding prince, nor yet a waster; my heart was never set on wordly goods, but only for my subjects' good.
Known as the Golden Speech. Speech to a deputation from the English Parliament (November 30, 1601), quoted in *The Journals of All The Parliaments* (Sir Simonds D'Ewes, ed.; 1682)

11 I am your anointed Queen. I will never be by violence constrained to do anything. I thank God that I am endued with such qualities that if I were turned out of the Realm in my petticoat I were able to live in any place in Christome.
Speech to the English Parliament (November 5, 1566), quoted in *Elizabeth I and her Parliaments, 1559–1581* (J. E. Neale; 1953), pt. 3, ch. 1

12 I know I have the body of a weak and feeble woman, but I have the heart and stomach of a King, and of a King of England too.
Speech to the troops at Tilbury on the approach of the Armada (1588), quoted in *A Third Collection of Scarce and Valuable Tracts* (Lord Somers; 1751)

13 The daughter of debate, that eke discord doth sow.
Referring to Mary Queen of Scots. "The Doubt of Future Woes" (1600), l. 11

14 Madam I may not call you; mistress I am ashamed to call you; and so I know not what to call you; but howsoever, I thank you.
Writing to the wife of the Archbishop of Canterbury, expressing her disapproval of married clergy. *A Brief View of the State of the Church of England* (Sir John Harington; 1653)

15 Anger makes dull men witty, but it keeps them poor.
Quoted in *Apophthegms* (Francis Bacon; 1625)

16 Must! Is *must* a word to be addressed to princes? Little man, little man! thy father, if he had been alive, durst not have used that word.
1603. Said to Robert Cecil, on her death bed. *A Short History of the English People* (J. R. Green; 1874), ch. 7

17 God may pardon you, but I never can.
Said to the dying Countess of Nottingham. Quoted in *History of England under the House of Tudor* (David Hume; 1759), vol. 2, ch. 7

18 The queen of Scots is this day leichter of a fair son, and I am but a barren stock.
Remark to her ladies in waiting (1567) *Memoirs of Sir James Melville* (Sir James Melville; 1827)

19 I will make you shorter by a head.
Said to the leaders of her council, who were opposing her course toward Mary Queen of Scots. *Sayings of Queen Elizabeth* (F. Chamberlin; 1923)

20 I have seen many a man turn his gold into smoke, but you are the first who has turned smoke into gold.
Speaking to Sir Walter Raleigh. *Sayings of Queen Elizabeth* (F. Chamberlin; 1923)

21 Good-morning, gentlemen both.
Addressing a group of eighteen tailors. *Sayings of Queen Elizabeth* (F. Chamberlin; 1923)

22 To me it shall be a full satisfaction both for the memorial of my name, and for the glory also, if when I shall let my last breath, it be engraven upon my marble tomb, "Here lieth Elizabeth, who reigned a virgin and died a virgin".
Said "to the Speaker, Knights and Burgesses of the Lower House who laid an address before her in the great gallery of Whitehall Palace urging her to marry." (February 6, 1559), quoted in *Sayings of Queen Elizabeth* (F. Chamberlin; 1923)

23 If thy heart fails thee, climb not at all.
Written on a window in reply to Sir Walter Raleigh's line "Fain would I climb, yet fear I to fall." *The History of the Worthies of England* (Thomas Fuller; 1662), vol. I

24 All my possessions for a moment of time.
Last words. Attrib. (1603)

Elizabeth II, Queen of the United Kingdom of Great Britain and Northern Ireland, and of Her other Realms and Territories Queen, Head of the Commonwealth (b.1926) British monarch

1 1992 is not a year I shall look back on with undiluted pleasure. In the words of one of my more sympathetic correspondents, it has turned out to be an "annus horribilis."
The Queen's televised address to the British nation, Christmas 1992, alluding to the separation of the Prince and Princess of Wales, and the fire at Windsor Castle. "Annus Mirabilis" is a poem by John Dryden. Speech (December 25, 1992)

2 I think that everyone will concede that—today of all days—I should begin by saying, "My husband and I".
On the celebration of her silver wedding anniversary. Speech at Guildhall, London (November 2, 1972)

3 These wretched babies don't come until they are ready.
Said of the expected birth of her fifth grandchild. Beatrice, the first daughter of the Duke and Duchess of York, was born five days later. *Today* London (August 1988)

4 I should like to be a horse.
When asked about her ambitions when a child. Attrib.

Elkin, Stanley (Stanley Lawrence Elkin; 1930–95) U.S. writer and educator

1 A beast in civilization does not even smell like a beast in the wild.
"The Making of Ashenden," *Searches and Seizures* (1973)

Elkington, John British author

1 It is at least conceivable that the 21st century business environment will be so fluid that it defies analysis, forcing executives to fall back upon hunch, or instinct.
Cannibals with Forks (1997)

2 It is often more effective to get a 20% solution into millions of homes than to get an 80% solution into tens of thousands.
Cannibals with Forks (1997)

Ellerton, John (1826–93) British churchman

1 The day Thou gavest, Lord, is ended
The darkness falls at Thy behest.
Hymn. *A Liturgy for Missionary Meetings* (1870)

Ellington, Duke (Edward Kennedy Ellington; 1899–1974) U.S. jazz bandleader, pianist, and composer

1 I read the Bible every night before retiring whether I'm "tight" or not. I got a lotta things to answer for.
Down Beat (July 1936)

2 Jazz is an international music...of such extraordinary variety that it is most consistently recognizable by its rhythmic vitality.
Music is My Mistress (1973)

3 Music is my mistress and she plays second fiddle to no one.
Music is My Mistress (1973)

4 Music to me is a sound sensation, assimilation, anticipation, adulation, and reputation.
Music is My Mistress (1973)

5 The City of Jazz is a place in which certain people live...The citizens...are more concerned with what they like than what they dislike.
Music is My Mistress (1973)

6 We run into some cats playing jazz at the Tokyo Hilton...They play really well. That is why Japan sometimes frightens me, because they have the ability here to do things better than the originals.
Music is My Mistress (1973)

7 When it sounds good, it *is* good.
Music is My Mistress (1973)

8 I maintain very happy relations...with my mistress. There are times when she herself provides the sound; at others, she waits for my echo.
Alluding to the title of his autobiography. *Music is My Mistress* (1973)

9 "Mr Ellington," he said, "we came here to hear Ellington. This is not Ellington!"...With that, of course, we had to tear up the programs and go back to before 1939.
Referring to an interruption during a concert in Paris in 1950. *Music is My Mistress* (1973)

10 If we had had Count Basie at the piano, and Freddie Green on guitar...Well, I don't know, maybe we might have scorched the moon.
Referring to his band's success at the Newport Jazz Festival (1956). *Music is My Mistress* (1973)

11 My band is my instrument.
New Yorker (July 1944)

12 The characteristic melancholy music of my race has been forged from the very white heat of our sorrows and from our gropings after something tangible in the primitiveness of our lives in the early days of our American occupation.
Rhythm (March 1931)

Elliot, Jane (or Jean; 1727–1805) Scottish poet

1 I've heard them lilting, at the ewe milking.
Lasses a' lilting, before dawn of day;
But now they are moaning, on ilka green loaning;
The flowers of the forest are a' wede away.
A version of an old lament for Flodden. "The Flowers of the Forest" (1769)

Elliott, Charlotte (1789–1871) British hymnwriter and poet

1 Just as I am, without one plea
But that Thy blood was shed for me,
And that Thou bidd'st me come to Thee,
O Lamb of God, I come!
1834. "Invalid's Hymn Book," *Hours of Sorrow Cheered and Comforted. Poems by Charlotte Elliot* (1869), st. 1, ll. 1–4

Ellis, Alice Thomas (pen name of Anna Margaret Haycraft, born Lindholm; b.1932) British writer

1 No wonder they were such a pasty lot. And so self-righteous about it, with their boundless contempt for garlic and messed-up foreign food with sauces. An exasperating people.
Referring to the English. *The 27th Kingdom* (1982)

2 Claudia...remembered that when she'd had her first baby she had realised with astonishment that the perfect couple consisted of a mother and child and not, as she had always supposed, a man and woman.
The Other Side of the Fire (1983)

Ellis, Bill British specialist in modern folklore

1 I've heard that myth quite seriously expressed in my church—that the beast in the Book of Revelation will be a monster computer.
Independent, London (December 13, 1994)

Ellis, George (1753–1815) British poet and journalist

1 Snowy, Flowy, Blowy,
Showery, Flowery, Bowery,
Hoppy, Croppy, Droppy,
Breezy, Sneezy, Freezy.
"The Twelve Months" (Undated)

Ellis, Havelock (Henry Havelock Ellis; 1859–1939) British psychologist

1 There is, however, a pathological condition which occurs so often, in such extreme forms, and in men of such pre-eminent intellectual ability, that it is impossible not to regard it as having a real association with such ability. I refer to gout.
A Study of British Genius (1904), ch. 8

2 The whole religious complexion of the modern world is due to the absence from Jerusalem of a lunatic asylum.
Impressions and Comments (1914)

3 What we call progress is the exchange of one nuisance for another nuisance.
Impressions and Comments (1914)

4 Pain and death are a part of life. To reject them is to reject life itself.
On Life and Sex: Essays of Love and Virtue (1922), vol. 2

5 The mathematician has reached the highest rung on the ladder of human thought.
The Dance of Life (1923)

6 The place where optimism most flourishes is the lunatic asylum.
The Dance of Life (1923)

7 The prevalence of suicide is a test of height in civilization; it means that the population is winding up its nervous and intellectual system to the utmost point of tension and that sometimes it snaps.
The Dance of Life (1923)

8 What we call morals is simply blind obedience to words of command.
The Dance of Life (1923)

9 When we reach the sphere of mathematics we are among processes which seem to some the most inhuman of all human activities and the most remote from poetry. Yet it is here that the artist has fullest scope for his imagination.
The Dance of Life (1923)

10 Every artist writes his own autobiography.
"Tolstoy," *The New Spirit* (1890)

11 There is nothing that war has ever achieved that we could not better achieve without it.
The Philosophy of Conflict (1919), Second series

12 Dancing is the loftiest, the most moving, the most beautiful of the arts, because it is no mere translation or abstraction from life; it is life itself.
Quoted in "The Dance of Life," *Dance to the Piper* (Agnes De Mille; 1987), foreword

Ellison, Ralph (Ralph Waldo Ellison; 1914–94) U.S. writer, jazz musician, and photographer

1 America is woven of many strands; I would recognize them and let it so remain...Our fate is to become one, and yet many—This is not prophecy, but description.
Invisible Man (1953)

2 Play the game, but don't believe in it.
Invisible Man (1953)

3 Power doesn't have to show off. Power is confident, self-assuring, self-starting and self-stopping, self-warming and self-justifying. When you have it, you know it.
Invisible Man (1953)

4 When I discover who I am, I'll be free.
Invisible Man (1953)

5 I am an invisible man, I am a man of substance, of flesh and bone, fiber and liquids—and I might even be said to possess a mind. I am invisible, understand, simply because people refuse to see me.
Invisible Man (1953), prologue

6 Good fiction is made of that which is real, and reality is difficult to come by.
Shadow and Act (1964), introduction

7 When American life is most American it is apt to be most theatrical.
"Change the Joke and Slip the Yoke," *Shadow and Act* (1964)

8 The blues is an art of ambiguity, an assertion of the irrepressibly human over all circumstance whether created by others or by one's own human failings. They...constantly remind us of our limitations while encouraging us to see how far we can actually go.
"Remembering Jimmy," *Shadow and Act* (1964)

9 Life is as the sea, art a ship in which man conquers life's crushing formlessness, reducing it to a course, a series of swells, tides and wind currents inscribed on a chart.
"Richard Wright's Blues," *Shadow and Act* (1964)

Ellmann, Richard (Richard David Ellmann; 1918–87) U.S. literary critic

1 Historians of literature like to regard a century as a series of ten faces, each grimacing in a different way.
Quoted in *New York Times* (February 5, 1967)

Elton, Ben (b.1959) British comedian and writer

1 Nothing kills passion faster than an exploding harpoon in the guts.
Stark (1992)

2 We're all wankers underneath...I'm a wanker, I have known the pleasures of the palm...why can't we be honest? Once we acknowledge everyone's a wanker it'll be easy—suddenly all authority figures disappear.
The Man from Auntie, BBC TV (1990)

Éluard, Paul (Eugène Grindel Éluard; 1895–1952) French surrealist poet

1 Farewell sadness
Good day sadness
You are written in the lines of the ceiling.
"À peine défigurée" (1932)

2 What has been understood no longer exists.
"Le Miroir d'un moment," *Capitale de la douleur* (1926)

3 The earth is blue like an orange.
L'Amour, la poésie (1929)

4 One day houses will be turned inside out like gloves.
Le Surréalisme au service de la Révolution (1933)

Elyot, Thomas, Sir (1490?–1546) English diplomat and writer

1 Wherein is nothing but beastly fury and extreme violence, whereof proceedeth hurt; and consequently rancour and malice do remain with them that be wounded.
Referring to soccer. *The Boke called the Governour* (1531)

Emecheta, Buchi (Florence Onye Buchi Emecheta; b.1944) Nigerian novelist and publisher

1 I am a woman and a woman of Africa. I am a daughter of Nigeria and if she is in shame, I shall stay and mourn with her in shame.
Destination Biafra (1982)

2 Why, oh why, do I always trust men, look up to them more than to people of my own sex, even though I was brought up by women?
Head Above Water (1986)

3 Sometimes it seemed that matrimony, apart from being a way of getting free sex when men felt like it, was also a legalized way of committing assault and getting away with it.
In The Ditch (1972)

4 Why was it that everybody would always judge one black person by the way another black person behaved. As long as you are black, any other black person is "your people."
In The Ditch (1972)

5 Nearly all the failures married white women. Maybe it was the only way of boosting their egos, or was it a way of getting even with their colonial masters?
Second-Class Citizen (1974)

6 That was life, she said to herself. Be as cunning as a serpent and as harmless as a dove.
Second-Class Citizen (1974)

7 In England you worship two goddesses; one is Christmas, the other one is holidays. As soon as they finish advertising for Christmas on television and in the papers, the next big thing is the annual holiday.
"Holidays" means vacations. *Second-Class Citizen* (1974)

8 God, when will you create a woman who will be fulfilled in herself, a full human being, not anybody's appendage?
The Joys of Motherhood (1979)

9 A writer is a writer, and writing is sexless.
1982. *In Their Own Voices: African Women Writers Talk* (Adeola James; 1990)

Emerson, Ralph Waldo (1803–82) U.S. poet and essayist

Quotations about Emerson

1 There comes Emerson first, whose rich words, every one,
Are like gold nails in temples to hang trophies on,
Whose prose is grand verse, while his verse, the Lord knows,
Is some of it pr—No, 'tis not even prose.
James Russell Lowell (1819–91) U.S. poet, editor, essayist, and diplomat. "Emerson," *A Fable for Critics* (1848), quoted in *The Penguin Book of American Verse* (Geoffrey Moore, ed.; 1977)

2 I could readily see in Emerson a gaping flaw. It was the insinuation that had he lived in those days when the world was made, he might have offered some valuable suggestions.
Herman Melville (1819–91) U.S. novelist. Attrib.

3 Waldo is one of those people who would be enormously improved by death.
Saki (1870–1916) British short-story writer. "The Feast of Nemesis," *Beasts and Super Beasts* (1914)

Quotations by Emerson

4 History is all party pamphlets.
Remark (February 18, 1855), quoted in *Journals* (Edward Waldo Emerson and Waldo Emerson Forbes, eds.; 1909–14)

5 The hearing ear is always found close to the speaking tongue.
"Race," *English Traits* (1856)

6 The wonder is always new that any sane man can be a sailor.
"Voyage to England," *English Traits* (1856)

7 Nothing great was ever achieved without enthusiasm.
"Circles," *Essays* (1841)

8 A Friend may well be reckoned the masterpiece of Nature.
"Friendship," *Essays* (1841)

9 An institution is the lengthened shadow of one man; as...the Reformation, of Luther; Quakerism, of Fox; Methodism, of Wesley; Abolition, of Clarkson...and all history resolves itself easily into the biography of a few stout and earnest persons.
"History," *Essays* (1841)

10 If the whole of history is in one man, it is all to be explained from individual experience.
"History," *Essays* (1841)

11 Man is explicable by nothing less than all his history.
"History," *Essays* (1841)

12 There is properly no history; only biography.
"History," *Essays* (1841)

13 I am ashamed to see what a shallow village tale our so-called history is.
Referring to the history of the United States. "History," *Essays* (1841)

14 All mankind love a lover.
"Love," *Essays* (1841)

15 In skating over thin ice, our safety is in our speed.
"Prudence," *Essays* (1841)

16 A foolish consistency is the hobgoblin of little minds, adored by little statesmen and philosophers and divines. With consistency a great soul has simply nothing to do.
"Self-Reliance," *Essays* (1841)

17 The centuries are conspirators against the sanity and authority of the soul. Time and space are but psychological colors which the eye makes, but the soul is light; where it is, is day; where it was, is night; and history is an impertinence and an injury if it be anything more than a cheerful apologue or parable of my being and becoming.
"Self-Reliance," *Essays* (1841)

18 To be great is to be misunderstood.
"Self-Reliance," *Essays* (1841)

19 Whoso would be a man must be a nonconformist.
"Self-Reliance," *Essays* (1841)

20 We are wiser than we know.
"The Over-Soul," *Essays* (1841)

21 The religions we call false were once true.
"Character," *Essays, Second Series* (1844)

22 The reward of a thing well done is to have done it.
"New England Reformers," *Essays, Second Series* (1844)

23 Every man is wanted, and no man is wanted much.
"Nominalist and Realist," *Essays, Second Series* (1844)

24 Homeopathy is insignificant as an act of healing, but of great value as criticism on the hygeia or medical practice of the time.
"Nominalist and Realist," *Essays, Second Series* (1844)

25 The reason of idleness and crime is the deferring of our hopes. Whilst we are waiting we beguile the time with jokes, with sleep, with eating, and with crimes.
"Nominalist and Realist," *Essays, Second Series* (1844)

26 Good men must not obey the laws too well.
"Politics," *Essays, Second Series* (1844)

27 What is a weed? A plant whose virtues have not been discovered.
Fortune of the Republic (1878)

28 Every man contemplates an angel in his future self.
1866. *Journals* (1860–66)

29 History is vanishing allegory.
Journals (1909–14)

30 In analyzing history do not be too profound, for often the causes are quite superficial.
Journals (1909–14)

31 I pay the schoolmaster, but 'tis the schoolboys that educate my son.
Journals (1860–66)

32 Old age brings along with its uglinesses the comfort that you will soon be out of it, which ought to be a substantial relief to such discontented pendulums as we are.
1864. *Journals* (1860–66)

33 Sanity is very rare: every man almost, and every woman, has a dash of madness.
1866. *Journals* (1860–66)

34 The book written against fame and learning has the author's name on the title page.
Journals (1860–66)

35 A record of the power of minorities, and of minorities of one.
Referring to history. "Progress of Culture," *Letters and Social Aims* (1876)

36 Wilt thou seal up the avenues of ill?
Pay every debt, as if God wrote the bill.
"Suum Cuique," *May-Day and Other Pieces* (1867)

37 It is a lesson which all history teaches wise men, to put trust in ideas, and not in circumstances.
"War," *Miscellanies* (1856)

38 Give me health and a day, and I will make the pomp of emperors ridiculous.
Nature (1836), ch. 3

39 Every hero becomes a bore at last.
"Uses of Great Men," *Representative Men* (1850)

40 Alcohol, hashish, prussic acid, strychnine are weak dilutions. The surest poison is time.
Society and Solitude (1870)

41 Hitch your wagon to a star.
"Civilization," *Society and Solitude* (1870)

42 One of our statesmen said, "The curse of this country is eloquent men."
"Eloquence," *Society and Solitude* (1870)

43 We boil at different degrees.
"Eloquence," *Society and Solitude* (1870)

44 America is a country of young men.
"Old Age," *Society and Solitude* (1870)

45 Men love to wonder, and that is the seed of our science, and such is the mechanical determination of our age, and so recent are our best contrivances, that use has not dulled our joy and pride in them...These arts open great gates of a future, promising to make the world plastic and to lift human life out of its beggary to a godlike ease and power.
"Works and Days," *Society and Solitude* (1870)

46 The use of history is to give value to the present hour and its duty.
"Works and Days," *Society and Solitude* (1870)

47 Whatever is old corrupts, and the past turns to snakes.
"Works and Days," *Society and Solitude* (1870)

48 There is less intention in history than we ascribe to it. We impute deep-laid, farsighted plans to Caesar and Napoleon; but the best of their power was in nature, not in them.
Spiritual Laws (1896)

49 Coal is a portable climate.
The Conduct of Life (1860)

50 The poisons are our principal medicines, which kill the disease and save the life.
The Conduct of Life (1860)

51 Man is physically as well as metaphysically a thing of shreds and patches, borrowed unequally from good and bad ancestors, and a misfit from the start.
"Beauty," *The Conduct of Life* (1860)

52 Nature tells every secret once.
"Behavior," *The Conduct of Life* (1860)

53 All sensible people are selfish, and nature is tugging at every contract to make the terms of it fair.
"Considerations by the Way," *The Conduct of Life* (1860)

54 A person seldom falls sick, but the bystanders are animated with a faint hope that he will die.
"Considerations by the Way," *The Conduct of Life* (1860)

55 History is the action and reaction of these two, nature and thought—two boys pushing each other on the curbstone of the pavement.
"Fate," *The Conduct of Life* (1860)

56 Art is a jealous mistress.
"Wealth," *The Conduct of Life* (1860)

57 We say the cows laid out Boston. Well there are worse surveyors.
"Wealth," *The Conduct of Life* (1860)

58 The louder he talked of his honor, the faster we counted our spoons.
"Worship," *The Conduct of Life* (1860)

59 The multitude of the sick shall not make us deny the existence of health.
"Worship," *The Conduct of Life* (1860)

60 'Tis a short sight to limit our faith in laws to those of gravity, of chemistry, of botany, and so forth.
"Worship," *The Conduct of Life* (1860)

61 In sculpture, did ever anybody call the Apollo a fancy piece? Or say of the Laocoön how it might be made different? A masterpiece of art has in the mind a fixed place in the chain of being, as much as a plant or a crystal.
"Thoughts on Art," *The Dial* (January 1841), vol. 1, no. 3

62 The conscious utterance of thought, by speech or action, to any end, is Art...Art is the spirit's voluntary use and combination of things to serve its end.
"Thoughts on Art," *The Dial* (January 1841), vol. 1, no. 3

63 Health is the first muse, and sleep is the condition to produce it.
"Resources," *Uncollected Lectures* (1932)

64 In the hands of the discoverer, medicine becomes a heroic art...wherever life is dear he is a demigod.
"Resources," *Uncollected Lectures* (1932)

65 To a physician, each man, each woman, is an amplification of one organ.
Bartlett's Unfamiliar Quotations (Leonard Louis Levinson, ed.; 1972)

66 If a man make a better mouse-trap than his neighbor, though he build his house in the woods, the world will make a beaten path to his door.
Often rendered as "The world will beat a path..." Attrib. *Borrowings* (Sarah S. B. Yule; 1889)

67 A good indignation makes an excellent speech.
Attrib.

68 Outside, among your fellows, among strangers, you must preserve appearances, a hundred things you cannot do, but inside, the terrible freedom!
Attrib.

Emmet, Robert (1778–1803) Irish nationalist

1 Let no man write my epitaph...When my country takes her place among the nations of the earth, then and not till then let my epitaph be written.
1803. Speech from the dock. Quoted in *This Most Distressful Country* (Robert Kee; 1972)

Emmett, Daniel Decatur (1815–1904) U.S. actor and songwriter

1 In Dixie Land, we'll take our stand,
To live and die in Dixie!
"Dixie" was adopted as the Confederate States' unofficial anthem during the Civil War. "Dixie" (1859), chorus

Empson, William, Sir (1906–84) British poet and literary critic

Quotations about Empson

1 What "literary people" did you see in England besides Empson? Why is English bohemianism more sordid than other kinds? I wonder. It's always seemed so to me that the English are so much dirtier than the Latins.
Elizabeth Bishop (1911–79) U.S. poet. Letter to Robert Lowell (August 26, 1963), quoted in *One Art: The Selected Letters of Elizabeth Bishop* (Robert Giroux, ed.; 1994)

Quotations by Empson

2 Waiting for the end, boys, waiting for the end.
1940. "Just a Smack at Auden," *Collected Poems* (1984)

3 No man is sure he does not need to climb.
It is not human to feel safely placed.
"Reflection from Anita Loos," *Collected Poems* (Robin Skelton, ed.; 1955)

4 I have mislaid the torment and the fear.
You should be praised for taking them away.
Those that doubt drugs, let them doubt which was here.
"Success," *Collected Poems* (Philip Larkin, ed.; 1955)

Engels, Friedrich (1820–95) German socialist

1 The British labor movement is today, and for many years has been, working in a narrow circle of strikes which are looked upon, not as an expedient, and not as a means of propaganda, but as an ultimate aim.
Letter to Eduard Bernstein (June 17, 1878)

2 Freedom does not consist in the dream of independence from natural laws, but in the knowledge of these laws, and in the possibility this gives of systematically making them work towards definite ends.
Anti-Dühring (1878)

3 Everything must justify its existence before the judgment seat of Reason, or give up existence.
Anti-Dühring (1878), pt. 3

4 The state is not "abolished," it withers away.
Anti-Dühring (1878), pt. 3, ch. 2

5 It was seen that all past history, with the exception of its primitive stages, was the history of class struggles.
Socialism: Utopian and Scientific (1892)

6 The political authority of the state dies out. Man, at last the master of his own form of social organization, becomes at the same time the lord over Nature, his own master—free.
Socialism: Utopian and Scientific (1892)

7 The proletariat seizes the public power, and by means of this transforms the socialized means of production, slipping from the hands of the bourgeoisie, into public property.
Socialism: Utopian and Scientific (1892)

English, Deirdre (Deirdre Elena English; b.1948) U.S. writer and editor

1 The fact remains that, no matter how disturbing violent fantasies are, as long as they stay within the world of pornography they are still only fantasies. The man masturbating in a theater showing a snuff film is still only watching a movie, not actually raping and murdering.
Mother Jones (April 1980)

English, Thomas Dunn (1819–1902) U.S. lawyer, physician, and writer

1 Oh! don't you remember sweet Alice, Ben Bolt,
Sweet Alice, whose hair was so brown,
Who wept with delight when you gave her a smile,
And trembled with fear at your frown?
"Ben Bolt" (1885)

Ennius, Quintus (239–169? B.C.) Roman poet

1 And the trumpet in terrible tones went taratantara.
3rd–2nd century B.C. *Annals of Q. Ennius* (O. Skutsch, ed.; 1985), l. 451

2 One man by delaying put the state to rights for us.
3rd–2nd century B.C. Referring to the Roman general Fabius Cunctator ("The Delayer"). *Annals of Q. Ennius* (O. Skutsch, ed.; 1985), bk. 12, l. 363

3 How like us is that ugly brute, the ape!
3rd–2nd century B.C. *De Divinatione* (Cicero; 1942 (tr. H. Rackham)), bk. 50

Enzensberger, Hans (Hans Magnus Enzensberger; b.1929) German poet

1 Those who live in the shadow
are difficult to kill.
"Shadow Realm," *Braille* (Michael Hamburger, tr.; 1964)

2 What else is Europe but a conglomeration of mistakes? Mistakes that are so diverse that they complement each other and balance one another. Taken separately, we're each unbearable in our own way.
1987. "Polish Incidents," *Europe, Europe* (Martin Chambers, tr.; 1989)

3 Hatred, too, is a precious habit.
1971. "The Force of Habit," *Poems 1955–1970* (Michael Hamburger, tr.; 1977)

4 That one gets used to everything—
one gets used to that.
The usual name for it is
a learning process.
1971. "The Force of Habit," *Poems 1955–1970* (Michael Hamburger, tr.; 1977)

5 The truth of the matter is that the Germans have a normality bordering on the tedious. They have become a nation of successful shopkeepers, incapable of a greatness that the world, in any case, is better off without.
"Rigmarole," *Time* (July 9, 1990)

Epictetus (55?–135?) Greek philosopher

1 If you hear that someone is speaking ill of you, instead of trying to defend yourself you should say: "He obviously does not know me very well, since there are so many other faults he could have mentioned."
Enchiridion (2nd century A.D.)

Epicurus (341–270 B.C.) Greek philosopher

1 For the end of all we do is to be free from pain and fear, and when once we have attained this, all turmoil of mind is dispersed and the living creature does not have to wonder as if in search of something missing, nor look for anything to complete the good of mind and body.
Letter to Menoeceus (3rd century B.C.)

2 So death, the most terrifying of ills, is nothing to us, since so long as we exist, death is not with us; but when death comes, then we do not exist.
Letter to Menoeceus (3rd century B.C.)

3 If you fight against all your sensations, you will have no standard to which to refer, and thus no means of judging even those judgments which you pronounce false.
The Principal Doctrines (4th century B.C.)

4 We begin every act of choice and avoidance from pleasure, and it is to pleasure that we return using our experience of pleasure as the criterion of every good thing.
Quoted in *Hellenistic Philosophy* (A. A. Long; 1986)

5 We must not make a pretense of doing philosophy, but really do it; for what we need is not the semblance of health but real health.
Quoted in *Hellenistic Philosophy* (A. A. Long; 1986)

6 When we say that pleasure is the goal we do not mean the pleasures of the dissipated and those which consist in the process of enjoyment...but freedom from pain in the body and from disturbance in the mind.
Quoted in *Hellenistic Philosophy* (A. A. Long; 1986)

7 It is not so much our friends' help that helps us as the confident knowledge that they will help us.
(3rd century B.C.)

Epitaphs

1 Here lies a poor woman who always was tired,
For she lived in a place where help wasn't hired
Her last words on earth
Dear friends I am going
Where washing ain't done nor sweeping nor sewing,
And everything there is exact to my wishes,
For there they don't eat and there's no washing of dishes.
Don't mourn for me now, don't mourn for me never,
For I'm going to do nothing for ever and ever.
1860? Bushey churchyard, England Letter, *Spectator,* London (September 23, 1922)

2 It is so soon that I am done for,
I wonder what I was begun for.
On a child who died at the age of three weeks. Cheltenham Churchyard, England

3 Here lie I by the chancel door;
They put me here because I was poor.
The further in, the more you pay,
But here lie I as snug as they.
Devon churchyard, England

4 Stranger! Approach this spot with gravity!
John Brown is filling his last cavity.
Epitaph of a dentist

5 Here lies my wife,
Here lies she;
Hallelujah!
Hallelujee!
Leeds churchyard, England

6 Here lies father and mother and sister and I,
We all died within the space of one short year;

They all be buried at Wimble, except I,
And I be buried here.
Staffordshire churchyard, England

7 All who come my grave to see
Avoid dampbeds and think of me.
St Michael's, Stoke, England

8 Here lies a man who was killed by lightning;
He died when his prospects seemed to be brightening.
He might have cut a flash in this world of trouble,
But the flash cut him, and he lies in the stubble.
Torrington, Devon, England

9 Here lies a valiant warrior
Who never drew a sword;
Here lies a noble courtier
Who never kept his word;
Here lies the Earl of Leicester
Who governed the estates
Whom the earth could never living love,
And the just heaven now hates.
Attrib. *Collection of Epitaphs* (Tissington; 1857)

10 Here lies Fred,
Who was alive and is dead:
Had it been his father,
I had much rather;
Had it been his brother,
Still better than another;
Had it been his sister,
No one would have missed her;
Had it been the whole generation,
Still better for the nation:
But since 'tis only Fred,
Who was alive and is dead,—
There's no more to be said.
Referring to Frederick, Prince of Wales, eldest son of George II and father of George III. *Memoirs of King George the Second* (Horace Walpole; 1846)

11 Here lies the body of Mary Ann Lowder,
She burst while drinking a Seidlitz powder.
Called from the world to her heavenly rest,
She should have waited till it effervesced.

12 Here lies the body of Richard Hind,
Who was neither ingenious, sober, nor kind.

13 Here lies Will Smith—and, what's something rarish,
He was born, bred, and hanged, all in the same parish.

14 This the grave of Mike O'Day
Who died maintaining his right of way.
His right was clear, his will was strong.
But he's just as dead as if he'd been wrong.

Epstein, Jacob, Sir (1880–1959) U.S.-born British sculptor

Quotations about Epstein

1 If people dug up the remains of this civilization a thousand years hence, and found Epstein's statues and that man Ellis, they would think we were just savages.
Doris Lessing (b.1919) British novelist and short-story writer. Referring to Jacob Epstein and the essayist and psychologist of sex Henry Havelock Ellis. *Martha Quest* (1952), pt. 1, ch. 1

Quotations by Epstein

2 Why don't they stick to murder and leave art to us?
Said on hearing that his statue of Lazarus in New College chapel, Oxford, England, kept Soviet statesman Nikita Khrushchev awake at night. Attrib.

Equiano, Olaudah (Gustavus Vassa; 1745?–97) African-born British former slave

1 Can any man be a Christian who asserts that one part of the human race were ordained to be in perpetual bondage to another?
Public Advertiser (February 5, 1788)

2 Well may I say my life has been
One scene of sorrow and of pain;
From early days I griefs have known,
And as I grew my griefs have grown.
The Interesting Narrative of the Life of Olaudah Equiano, or Gustavus Vassa (1789)

3 When you make men slaves you deprive them of half their virtue, you set them in your own conduct an example of fraud, rapine, and cruelty, and compel them to live with you in a state of war; and yet you complain that they are not honest or faithful!
The Interesting Narrative of the Life of Olaudah Equiano, or Gustavus Vassa (1789)

Erasmus, Desiderius (1466?–1536) Dutch humanist, scholar, and writer

1 I wished to be a citizen of the world, not of a single city.
Referring to his refusal of a suggestion that he be made a citizen of Zurich. Letter to Laurimus (February 1, 1523)

2 I believe firmly what I read in the holy Scriptures, and the Creed, called the Apostles', and I don't trouble my head any farther: I leave the rest to be disputed and defined by the clergy, if they please; and if any Thing is in common use with Christians that is not repugnant to the holy Scriptures, I observe it for this Reason, that I may not offend other people.
Commenting on the teachings of John Colet. *Colloquia* (1519)

3 If we must fight, why not go against the common enemy, the Turk? But wait. Is not the Turk also a man and a brother?
Querela Pacis (July 1517)

4 Let a king recall that to improve his realm is better than to increase his territory.
Querela Pacis (July 1517)

5 It is an unscrupulous intellect that does not pay to antiquity its due reverence...There are many kinds of genius; each age has its different gifts.
Works of Hilary (1523), preface

6 I have a Catholic soul, but a Lutheran stomach.
Replying to criticism of his failure to fast during Lent. Attrib.

Erdrich, Louise (Karen Louise Erdrich; b.1954) U.S. writer

1 The sky was so low that I felt the weight of it like a yoke. Clouds hung down, witch teats, a tornado's green-brown cones, and as I watched one flicked out and became a delicate probing thumb.
"Fleur," *Esquire* (August 1986)

2 I was in love with the whole world and all that lived in its rainy arms.
"The Good Tears," *Love Medicine* (1984)

Erhard, Ludwig (1897–1977) German economist and chancellor

1 The art of dividing a cake in such a way that everyone believes he has the biggest piece.
Referring to politics. Attrib.

Erikson, Erik (Erik Homburger Erikson; 1902–94) U.S. psychoanalyst

1 This sense of identity provides the ability to experience one's self as something that has continuity and sameness, and to act accordingly.
Childhood and Society (1950)

2 The identity crisis...occurs in that period of the life cycle when each youth must forge for himself some central perspective and direction, some working unity, out of the effective remnants of his childhood and the hopes of his anticipated adulthood.
Young Man Luther (1958)

Ernst, Max (1891–1976) German-born French artist

1 The virtue of pride, which was once the beauty of mankind, has given place to that fount of all ugliness, Christian humility.
Attrib.

Ertz, Susan (Mrs. Ronald McCrindle; 1894?–1985) U.S.-born British novelist and playwright

1 Millions long for immortality who do not know what to do with themselves on a rainy Sunday afternoon.
Anger in the Sky (1943)

Escrivá de Balaguer y Albas, José María Spanish priest

1 If you know that your body is your enemy, and the enemy of God's glory, why do you treat it so gently?
Quoted in *The Spaniards* (John Hooper; 1986)

Esslin, Martin (Martin Julius Esslin; b.1918) Austrian-born British critic

1 The Theatre of the Absurd strives to express its sense of the senselessness of the human condition and the inadequacy of the rational approach by the open abandonment of rational devices and discursive thought.
Theatre of the Absurd (1961)

Estienne, Henri (1528–98) French scholar and printer

1 If only youth knew, if only age could.
Les Prémices (1594), epigram 191

E. T. (The Extra-Terrestrial) U.S. film character

1 E. T. phone home.
Said by the alien E.T., who had been stranded on earth; and referring to his desire to contact his own planet. *E. T. The Extra-Terrestrial* (Melissa Mathison; 1982)

Etherege, George, Sir (1635?–91) English comic dramatist

1 Beyond Hyde Park all is a desert.
The Man of Mode; or, Sir Fopling Flutter (1676)

Etherington-Smith, Meredith British fashion journalist

1 The trouble with Yohji's clothes is that you can't get out of them in a hurry. Do you suppose those girls get any sex at all?
Referring to the clothes of Japanese fashion designer, Yohji Yamamoto. Quoted in *The Fashion Conspiracy* (Nicholas Coleridge; 1989), ch. 4

Euclid (*fl.* 300 B.C.) Greek mathematician

1 Which was to be proved.
The Latin version of this phrase is *Quod erat demonstrandum*, hence Q.E.D. *Elements* (300? B.C.), bk. 1, proposition 5

2 There is no "royal road" to geometry.
Reply to Ptolemy I when asked if there were an easier way to solve theorems. *Comment on Euclid* (Proclus; 300? B.C.), pt. 2, prologue

Euler, Leonhard (1707–83) Swiss mathematician

1 Now I will have less distraction.
1735. Referring to losing the sight of one eye. Quoted in *Mathematical Circles* (H. Eves; 1969)

Euripides (480?–406? B.C.) Greek playwright

Quotations about Euripides

1 I depict men as they ought to be, but Euripides portrays them as they are.
Sophocles (496?–406? B.C.) Greek playwright. Quoted in *Poetics* (Aristotle; 340? B.C.)

Quotations by Euripides

2 A bad beginning makes a bad ending.
Aeolus (5th century B.C.), fragment 32

3 Woman is woman's natural ally.
Alope (5th century B.C.), fragment 109

4 A worthy man is not mindful of past injuries.
Andromache (5th century B.C.), l. 1164

5 Man's best possession is a sympathetic wife.
Antigone (5th century B.C.), fragment 164

6 Bodies devoid of mind are as statues in the marketplace.
Electra (5th century B.C.), l. 386

7 A woman should always stand by a woman.
Helena (412 B.C.), l. 329

8 A weary thing is sickness and its pains!
Hippolytus (5th century B.C.), Scene 2, l. 176, quoted in *Greek Tragedies,* (Grene, David and Lattimore, Richard, eds.; 1968), vol.1

9 It's better to be sick than nurse the sick.
Sickness is single trouble for the sufferer:
but nursing means vexation of the mind,
and hard work for the hands besides.
Hippolytus (5th century B.C.), Scene 2, ll. 186–189, quoted in *Greek Tragedies,* (Grene, David and Lattimore, Richard, eds.; 1968), vol.1

10 What they say of us is that we have a peaceful time
Living at home, while they do the fighting in war.

How wrong they are! I would very much rather stand
Three times in the front of battle than bear one child.
Medea (431 B.C.)

11 It is said that gifts persuade even the gods.
Medea (431 B.C.), l. 964

12 Whoso neglects learning in his youth,
Loses the past and is dead for the future.
Phrixus (5th century B.C.), fragment 927

13 The gods
Visit the sins of the fathers upon the children.
Phrixus (5th century B.C.), fragment 970

14 Whom God wishes to destroy, he first makes mad.
Attrib.

Evangelista, Linda (b.1965) Canadian-born fashion model

1 I spend all my free time coloring my hair.
1990. Quoted in *Model: The Ugly Business of Beautiful Women* (Michael Gross; 1995)

Evans, Abel (1679–1737) English poet and divine

1 Under this stone, Reader, survey
Dead Sir John Vanbrugh's house of clay.
Lie heavy on him, Earth! for he
Laid many heavy loads on thee!
Epitaph on Sir John Vanbrugh, architect of Blenheim Palace (1726)

Evans, Edith, Dame (Edith Mary Evans; 1888–1976) British actor

1 Death is my neighbour now.
Said a week before her death. BBC Radio interview (October 14, 1976)

2 When a woman behaves like a man, why doesn't she behave like a nice man?
September 1956. *Observer,* London (September 30, 1956), "Sayings of the Week"

Evans, Harold (Harold Matthew Evans; b.1928) British-born U.S. publisher and newspaper editor

1 The camera cannot lie. But it can be an accessory to untruth.
Pictures on a Page (1978)

Evans, Mari (b.1923) U.S. poet, musician, and educator

1 I am a black woman
tall as a cypress
strong
beyond all definition still
defying place
and time
and circumstance
assailed
impervious
indestructible
Look
on me and
be renewed.
"I am a Black Woman," *I am a Black Woman* (1970)

2 I have never been contained except I made the prison, nor known a chain except those forged by me.
"The Silver Cell," *I am a Black Woman* (1970)

3 Hope I lives till I get home I'm tired of eatin'
What they eats in Rome.
"When in Rome," *I am a Black Woman* (1970)

4 Who can be born black and not exult!
"Who Can Be Born Black?," *Nightstar* (1981)

Evarts, William M. (William Maxwell Evarts; 1818–1901) U.S. lawyer and statesman

1 It was a brilliant affair; water flowed like champagne.
Describing a dinner given by President Rutherford B. Hayes, an advocate of temperance. Attrib.

Evelyn, John (1620–1706) English diarist

1 I went to the Society where were divers experiments in Mr Boyle's Pneumatic Engine. We put in a snake but could not kill it by exhausting the air, only making it extremely sick, but a chick died of convulsions in a short space.
Diary (April 22, 1661)

2 The Plague still increasing.
Diary (July 28, 1665)

3 She came into Whitehall laughing and jolly, as to a wedding, so as to seem quite transported.
Referring to Mary II's arrival in London. *Diary* (February 21, 1689)

4 This fatal night about ten, began that deplorable fire near Fish Street in London...all the sky were of a fiery aspect, like the top of a burning Oven, and the light seen above 40 miles round about for many nights.
The Fire of London (September 2–5, 1666) began in a bakehouse in Pudding Lane and spread to two thirds of the city. *Diary* (September 2–3, 1666)

5 His *Majestie* began first to Touch for the Evil according to costome: Thus, his Majestie sitting under his State in the *Banqueting*.
The King's touch was believed to cure scrofula ("The King's Evil"). *Diary* (July 6, 1660)

6 It was a fine silken thing which I spied walking th'other day through Westminster-Hall, that had as much Ribbon on him as would have plundered six shops, and set up Twenty Country Pedlars; all his body was dres't like a May-pole or a Tom-a Bedlam's Cap.
1661. "Tyrannus or the Mode in a Discourse of Sumptuary Lawes," *The Writings of John Evelyn* (Guy de la Bédoyère, ed.; 1995), ch. 6

Everett, David (1770–1813) U.S. lawyer and writer

1 You 'd scarce expect one of my age
To speak in public on the stage;
And if I chance to fall below
Demosthenes or Cicero,
Don't view me with a critic's eye,
But pass my imperfections by.
1776. Written at the age of seven. "Lines Written for a School Declamation" (1777)

Everett, Edward (1794–1865) U.S. clergyman and politician

1 When I am dead, no pageant train
Shall waste their sorrows at my bier,

Nor worthless pomp of homage vain
 Stain it with hypocritic tear.
"Dirge of Alaric the Visigoth," *Best Loved Story Poems* (Walter E. Thring, ed.; 1941)

Everett, Kenny (originally Maurice Cole; 1944–95) British disk jockey and television comedian

1 It's not affected my work—how healthy do you have to be to play "Da Do Ron Ron"?
Response to the confirmation that he was HIV positive. *Sun,* London (1992)

Everly, Phil (b.1939) U.S. pop singer

1 Everyone has the feeling that all you have to do is to achieve stardom and once you're there you can relax. It's just the opposite. Once you get there, then the war really starts. The pressures get larger because getting hit records is a miracle.
1981. Quoted in *Rock 'n' Roll Babylon* (Gary Herman; 1994)

Evers, Medgar (1925–63) U.S. civil rights leader

1 Freedom has never been free.
Speech (June 7, 1963)

Everyman

1 O Death, thou comest when I had thee least in mind!
Everyman (1509?–19?), l. 119

2 In prosperity men friends may find,
Which in adversity be full unkind.
Everyman (1509?–19?), ll. 309–310

3 Everyman, I will go with thee, and be thy guide,
In thy most need to go by thy side.
Spoken by Knowledge in the...morality play, *Everyman.* Used as the motto of the British publishing imprint, Everyman Library (founded 1906). *Everyman* (1509?–19?), pt. 1

Ewart, Gavin (Gavin Buchanan Ewart; 1916–95) British poet

1 We've given up the Georgian poets, teaching dance bands how
 to croon,
Bicycling in coloured goggles underneath a pallid moon.
"Audenesque for an Initiation" (1933), quoted in *Poetry of the Thirties* (Robin Skelton, ed.; 1964)

2 When a Beau goes in,
Into the drink,
It makes you think,
Because, you see, they always sink
But nobody says "Poor lad"
Or goes about looking sad
Because, you see, it's war,
It's the unalterable law.
"When a Beau Goes In" (1933), quoted in *The Oxford Book of Twentieth-Century English Verse* (Philip Larkin, ed.; 1965)

Ewer, William Norman (1885–1977) British writer, journalist, and humorist

1 I gave my life for freedom—This I know:
For those who bade me fight had told me so.
"Five Souls" (1917)

2 How odd
Of God
To choose
The Jews.
For a reply, see Cecil Browne. *Week-End Book* (1924)

Faber, Frederick William (1814–63) British priest, hymnwriter, and author

1 For right is right, since God is God,
And right the day must win;
To doubt would be disloyalty,
To falter would be sin.
"Right is Right," *The Treasury of Religious Verse* (Donald T. Kaufman; 1962)

Fabre, Jean Henri (1823–1915) French entomologist

1 What would one not do in the hope of an idea!
Souvenirs entomologiques (1879–1907)

2 It is in this triple blow that the infallibility, the infused science of instinct, appear in all their magnificence...We find what the Sphex knew long before the anatomist, three nerve centers far apart. Thence the fine logic of three stabs. Proud Science! humble thyself.
Referring to the method used by the Sphex wasp for paralyzing the host for its eggs. *Souvenirs entomologiques* (1879–1907)

3 Permanence of instinct must go with permanence of form...The history of the present must teach us the history of the past.
Referring to studying fossil remains of the weevil, largely unchanged to the present day. *The Life and Love of the Insect* (1911)

4 History...records the names of royal bastards, but cannot tell us the origin of wheat.
Attrib.

Fabyan, Robert (?–1513) English chronicler

1 This year, that is to mean ye 18 day of February, the Duke of Clarence and second brother to the king, then being prisoner in ye Tower, was secretly put to death and drowned in a barrel of malmesey within the said Tower.
This account is apocryphal and reflects popular rumor. "1478," *The New Chronicles of England and France* (1516), vol. 2

Fadiman, Clifton (b.1904) U.S. writer, editor, and broadcaster

1 We prefer to believe that the absence of inverted commas guarantees the originality of a thought, whereas it may be merely that the utterer has forgotten its source.
Any Number Can Play (1957)

2 Experience teaches you that the man who looks you straight in the eye, particularly if he adds a firm handshake, is hiding something.
Enter, Conversing (1962)

Fairchild, John B. (John Burr Fairchild; b.1927) U.S. publisher

1 Fashion is a sub-art and is not intellectual. Fashion is a business and operates best when it is born out of instincts. Fashion appeals to the senses and comes from gut feeling...True fashion comes straight out of the jungle.
Chic Savages (1989)

2 The truth is that many designers like to be copied. It's all part of the fashion sport.
Chic Savages (1989)

Fairfax, Lord, 3rd Baron Fairfax of Cameron (Thomas Fairfax; 1612–71) English general

1 Oh let that day from time be blotted quite,
And let belief of't in next age be waived.
In deepest silence th'act concealed might,
So that the Kingdom's credit might be saved.

But if the Power Divine permitted this,
His Will's the law and ours must acquiesce.
17th century. Referring to the execution of Charles I (1649). *The Faber Book of English History in Verse* (Kenneth Baker, ed.; 1988)

Fairfield, John (*fl.* 1400) Welsh receiver of Brecon

1 The whole of the Welsh nation in these parts are concerned in this rebellion.
Referring to the rebellion of Owen Glendower (1400–09). Letter to Henry IV (1400–09)

Faisal, King of Saudi Arabia (Malik Faisal ibn Abdul Aziz; 1905–75) Saudi Arabian monarch

1 We feel that the Arabs and the Jews are cousins in race, having suffered similar oppression at the hands of powers stronger than ourselves.
Quoted in *Dawn of the Promised Land* (Ben Wicks; 1997)

Faisal, Taujan (b.1949) Jordanian politician

1 Although we have some laws which are unfair to women, some women can live their whole lives and not know the law as it affects them.
On women and Islamic-based law. *Times*, London (June 15, 1994)

Falkenhayn, Erich von (Erich Georg Anton Sebastian von Falkenhayn; 1861–1922) German general

1 The forces of France will be bled to death, since there can be

no question of a voluntary withdrawal, whether or not we reach our goal.
Referring to plans for the conquest of Belfort and Verdun. Memorandum for Kaiser Wilhelm II (December 1915)

Falkland, Lucius Cary, 2nd Viscount Falkland (1610–43) English royalist

1 When it is not necessary to change, it is necessary not to change.
"A Speech concerning Episcopacy, 1641," *Discourses of Infallibility* (1660)

Fall, Aminata Sow (b.1941) Senegal novelist

1 You think that people give out of the goodness of their hearts? Not at all. They give out of an instinct for self-preservation.
The Beggar's Strike (1979)

Fallaci, Oriana (b.1930) Italian writer

1 Equality, Child, like freedom, exists only where you are now. Only as an egg in the womb are we all equal.
Letter to a Child Never Born (1975)

Fane, Violet, Lady (Mary Montgomerie Currie, born Violet Lamb; 1843–1905) British poet

1 Ah, "all things come to those who wait,"
(I say these words to make me glad),
But something answers soft and sad,
"They come, but often come too *late*".
"Tout vient à qui sait attendre," *Poems by Violet Fane* (1892), ll. 37–40

Fanon, Frantz (Frantz Omar Fanon; 1925–61) Martiniquan social scientist, physician, and psychiatrist

1 As a man, I undertake to face the possibility of annihilation in order that two or three truths may cast their eternal brilliance over the world.
Black Skin, White Masks (1952)

2 Fervor is the weapon of choice of the impotent.
Black Skin, White Masks (1952)

3 He who is reluctant to recognize me opposes me.
Black Skin, White Masks (1952)

4 I am my own foundation.
Black Skin, White Masks (1952)

5 I am not the slave of the Slavery that dehumanized my ancestors.
Black Skin, White Masks (1952)

6 It is the racist who creates his inferior.
Black Skin, White Masks (1952)

7 My final prayer: O my body make of me always a man who questions!
Black Skin, White Masks (1952)

8 To speak a language is to take on a world, a culture.
Black Skin, White Masks (1952)

9 Culture has never the translucidity of custom; it abhors all simplification.
"On National Culture," *The Wretched of the Earth* (1961)

10 The fact is that in guerilla warfare the struggle no longer concerns the place where you are, but the place where you are going. Each fighter carries his warring country between his bare toes.
"Spontaneity: Its Strength and Weakness," *The Wretched of the Earth* (1961)

11 If the building of a bridge does not enrich the awareness of those who work on it, then that bridge ought not to be built and the citizens can go on swimming across the river or going by boat.
"The Pitfalls of National Consciousness," *The Wretched of the Earth* (1961)

12 Public business ought to be the business of the public.
"The Pitfalls of National Consciousness," *The Wretched of the Earth* (1961)

Fanthorpe, U. A. (Ursula Askham Fanthorpe; b.1929) British poet

1 I wasn't good
At growing up. Never learned
The natives' art of life.
"Growing Up" (1984)

2 Kind Dr C., who is now dead, believed the best cure for depression was hope. "Remember," he said to me, in his most forceful way, "it is a self-limiting disease. It will go." And so it does, as if it's got bored with me and wants to toy with somebody else.
"Walking in Darkness," *Mind Readings* (1996)

Faraday, Michael (1791–1867) British scientist

1 I express a wish that you may, in your generation, be fit to compare to a candle; that you may, like it, shine as lights to those about you; that, in all your actions, you may justify the beauty of the taper by making your deeds honourable and effectual in the discharge of your duty to your fellow-men.
The first of his Christmas lectures for children at the Royal Institution. *A Course of Six Lectures on the Chemical History of a Candle* (1861)

2 Tyndall, I must remain plain Michael Faraday to the last; and let me now tell you, that if I accepted the honour which the Royal Society desires to confer upon me, I would not answer for the integrity of my intellect for a single year.
On being offered the Presidency of the Royal Society. "Illustrations of Character," *Faraday as a Discoverer* (J. Tyndall; 1868)

Farah, Nuruddin (b.1945) Somali novelist, playwright, and teacher

1 At the centre of every myth is another: that of the people who created it.
Gifts (1993)

2 To starve is to be of media interest these days.
Gifts (1993)

3 Unasked-for generosity has a way of making one feel obliged, trapped in a labyrinth of dependence.
Gifts (1993)

4 Good writing is like a bomb: it explodes in the face of the reader.
Sardines (1981)

5 Life is a kiln in which one bakes one's experiences: some are

taken out half done, some underdone and some undone.
Sardines (1981)

6 You must leave breathing-space in the architecture of your love.
Sardines (1981)

7 A writer depicting humdrum realities is comparable to a prophet incapable of performing miracles in which mountains are dislodged and rivers are turned into roads.
"In Praise of Exile," *Third World Affairs* (1988)

8 Truth never turns tail like a disinterested cat: it purrs, it winks its feline eyes, it sees, it envisions; truth is the breath in the air, the breath that someone somewhere in the world will inhale, and then speak, in the end.
"Why I Write," *Third World Quarterly* (July 1988), vol. 10, no. 4

Farb, Peter (1929–80) U.S. anthropologist and writer

1 Grasshoppers and other members of the locust family, for example, are exceptionally nutritious food. Merely a handful provides the daily allowance of vitamin A, as well as protein, carbohydrate, and fat.
Consuming Passions: the Anthropology of Eating (co-written with George Armelagos; 1980)

Farhi, Nicole (b.1946) French-born British fashion designer

1 I pay no attention to fashion at all. It is frivolous, not an important part of life. I really don't like clothes, though I like playing with shapes and colours and putting them together.
Daily Mail, London (October 2, 1992)

Farjeon, Herbert (1887–1945) British writer and playwright

1 I've danced with a man, who's danced with a girl, who's danced with the Prince of Wales.
Picnic (1927)

Farmer, Edward (1809–76) British writer

1 I have no pain, dear mother, now;
But oh! I am so dry:
Just moisten poor Jim's lips once more;
And, mother, do not cry!
A typical sentimental verse of the Victorian era. "The Collier's Dying Child" (19th century)

Farmer, Fannie (Fannie Merritt Farmer; 1857–1915) U.S. cookbook writer

1 Progress in civilization has been accompanied by progress in cookery.
The Boston Cooking-School Cookbook (1896), ch. 2

2 I certainly feel that the time is not far distant when a knowledge of the principles of diet will be an essential part of one's education. Then mankind will eat to live, be able to do better mental and physical work, and disease will be less frequent.
The Boston Cooking-School Cookbook (1896), preface to the first edition

Farmer, James (James Leonard Farmer; b.1920) U.S. civil rights leader

1 Evil societies always kill their consciences.
Lay Bare The Heart: An Autobiography of the Civil Rights Movement (1985)

2 We, who are the living, possess the past. Tomorrow is for our martyrs.
Lay Bare The Heart: An Autobiography of the Civil Rights Movement (1985)

Farouk I, King of Egypt (1920–65) Egyptian monarch

1 Soon there will be only five kings left the Kings of England, Diamonds, Hearts, Spades, and Clubs.
1948. Remark made to Lord Boyd-Orr at a conference in Cairo. *As I Recall* (Lord Boyd-Orr; 1966), ch. 21

Farquhar, George (1678–1707) Irish playwright

1 Money is the sinews of love, as of war.
Love and a Bottle (1698), Act 2, Scene 1

2 I'm privileged to be very impertinent, being an Oxonian.
Sir Harry Wildair (1701), Act 2, Scene 1

3 Says little, thinks less, and does nothing at all, faith.
The Beaux' Stratagem (1707)

4 I have fed purely upon ale; I have eat my ale, drank my ale, and I always sleep upon ale.
The Beaux' Stratagem (1707), Act 1, Scene 1

5 There is no scandal like rags, nor any crime so shameful as poverty.
The Beaux' Stratagem (1707), Act 1, Scene 1

6 We have heads to get money, and hearts to spend it.
The Beaux' Stratagem (1707), Act 1, Scene 1

7 No woman can be a beauty without a fortune.
The Beaux' Stratagem (1707), Act 2, Scene 2

8 It is a maxim that man and wife should never have it in their power to hang one another.
The Beaux' Stratagem (1707), Act 4, Scene 2

9 Spare all I have, and take my life.
The Beaux' Stratagem (1707), Act 5, Scene 2

10 I hate all that don't love me, and slight all that do.
The Constant Couple (1699), Act 1, Scene 2

11 Truth is only falsehood well disguised.
The Constant Couple (1699), Act 3, Scene 4

12 Grant me some wild expressions, Heavens, or I shall burst...Words, words, or I shall burst.
The Constant Couple (1699), Act 5, Scene 3

13 Hanging and marriage, you know, go by destiny.
The Recruiting Officer (1706), Act 3, Scene 2

Farrington, David (b.1944) British criminal psychologist

1 Problem children tend to grow up into problem adults and problem adults tend to produce more problem children.
Times, London (May 19, 1994)

Fassbinder, Rainer Werner (1946–82) German filmmaker, writer, and actor

1 I hope to build a house with my films. Some of them are the cellar, some are the walls, and some are the windows. But I hope in time there will be a house.
Quoted in *Halliwell's Filmgoer's Companion* (Leslie Halliwell; 1993)

Faulkner, William (1897–1962) U.S. novelist

Quotations about Faulkner

1 Faulkner's hallucinatory tendencies are not unworthy of Shakespeare.
Jorge Luis Borges (1899–1986) Argentinian writer and poet. *An Introduction to American Literature* (1967), ch. 8

Quotations by Faulkner

2 I believe that man will not merely endure; he will prevail. He is immortal, not because he alone among creatures has an inexhaustible voice, but because he has a soul, a spirit capable of compassion and sacrifice and endurance.
December 10, 1949. On receiving a Nobel Prize in Literature, Stockholm. Nobel Prize speech (1949), quoted in *Les Prix Nobel en 1950* (1951)

3 The last sound on the worthless earth will be two human beings trying to launch a homemade spaceship and already quarrelling about where they are going next.
Speech to UNESCO Commission, New York (1959)

4 The nihilists say it is the end; the fundamentalists, the beginning; when in reality it is no more than a single tenant or family moving out of a tenement or a town.
Referring to death. *As I Lay Dying* (1930)

5 No man can cause more grief than that one clinging blindly to the vices of his ancestors.
Intruder in the Dust (1948)

6 The Swiss who are not a people so much as a neat clean quite solvent business.
Intruder in the Dust (1948), ch. 7

7 Memory believes before knowing remembers. Believes longer than recollects, longer than knowing even wonders.
Light in August (1932)

8 He had surrendered all reality, all dread and fear, to the doctor beside him, as people do.
Light in August (1932), ch. 17

9 An artist is a creature driven by demons.
Interview, *Paris Review* (Spring 1956)

10 Since his capacity to do is forced into channels of evil through environment and pressures, man is strong before he is moral. The world's anguish is caused by people between twenty and forty.
Interview, *Paris Review* (Spring 1956)

11 The aim of every artist is to arrest motion, which is life, by artificial means and hold it fixed so that a hundred years later, when a stranger looks at it, it moves again since it is life.
Interview, *Paris Review* (Spring 1956)

12 The writer's only responsibility is to his art...If a writer has to rob his mother, he will not hesitate; the "Ode on a Grecian Urn" is worth any number of old ladies.
Interview, *Paris Review* (Spring 1956)

13 Maybe the only thing worse than having to give gratitude constantly all the time, is having to receive it.
Requiem For A Nun (1951), Act 2, Scene 1

14 Time is dead as long as it is being clicked off little wheels; only when the clock stops does time come to life.
"June Second 1910," *The Sound and the Fury* (1929)

15 *Yes*, he thought, *between grief and nothing I will take grief.*
Said by Wilborne. "Wild Palms," *The Wild Palms* (1939)

16 No man is himself, he is the sum of his past. There is no such thing as was because the past is. It is part of every man, every woman, and every moment. All of his and her ancestry, background, is all a part of himself and herself at any moment.
Quoted in *Faulkner in the University: Class Conferences at the University of Virginia 1957–1958* (Frederic L. Gwynn and Joseph L. Blotner, eds.; 1959)

17 The past is never dead, it is not even past.
Attrib. *Newsweek* (February 21, 1977)

18 Well, between Scotch and nothin', I suppose I'd take Scotch. It's the nearest thing to good moonshine I can find.
Quoted in *Speaking Freely* (Stuart Berg Flexner and Anne H. Soukhanov; 1997)

19 A man shouldn't fool with booze until he's fifty; then he's a damn fool if he doesn't.
Quoted in *William Faulkner of Oxford* (James M. Webb and A. Wigfall Green; 1965)

Fauset, Crystal Bird U.S. feminist activist

1 We should not want to think of America as a "melting pot," but as a great inter-racial laboratory where Americans can really begin to build the thing which the rest of the world feels that they stand for today, and that is real democracy.
Speech, Woman's Centennial Congress (November 26, 1940)

Fawconer, Samuel (*fl.* 1765) British sermonizer

1 Cloathing being merely artificial, runs into a thousand different forms and it often happens that those which are most fantastic and ridiculous are adopted in preference to such as are more useful, becoming and convenient, being qualified to answer the purposes of life, and preserve us in health.
An Essay on Modern Luxury (1765)

2 The proper design of cloathing is to be a covering for shame, a fence from the injuries of the weather, and a distinction of sexes and degrees.
An Essay on Modern Luxury (1765)

Fawkes, Guy (1570–1606) English conspirator

1 A desperate disease requires a dangerous remedy.
November 5, 1605. Justifying the Gunpowder Plot, on being questioned by the king and council immediately after his arrest. Quoted in *Dictionary of National Biography* (1917)

2 To blow the Scots back again into Scotland.
November 5, 1605. One of the professed objectives of the Gunpowder Plot, and referring to the Scottish-born Protestant King James I. Remark made on being questioned by the king and council immediately after his arrest. Quoted in *Dictionary of National Biography* (1917)

Fayol, Henri (1841–1925) French businessman

1 Dividing enemy forces to weaken them is clever, but dividing one's own team is a grave sin against the business.
General and Industrial Management (1949)

Fazil, Necip (1905–83) Turkish poet

1 I am the poet, prying locksmith of invisible things
I am the angel of inquisition, steering life's funerals.
"Poet," *Modern Turkish Poetry* (Feyyaz Kayacan Fergar, ed.; 1992), ll. 1–2

Feather, Leonard G. (Leonard Geoffrey Feather; 1914–94) British musical arranger, composer, and writer

1 "Asking for jazz in 3⁄4 time," he stated firmly, "is like asking for a red piece of green chalk.
Referring to the reply by the editor of the magazine *Melody Maker* (London) to a letter from Feather. "London," *The Jazz Years* (1986), pt. 1

Feather, Vic, Baron Feather of the City of Bradford (Victor Grayson Hardie Feather; 1908–76) British labor leader

1 Industrial relations are like sexual relations. It's better between two consenting parties.
Guardian Weekly (August 8, 1976)

Feiffer, Jules (b.1929) U.S. writer, cartoonist, and humorist

1 At sixteen I was stupid, confused, insecure, and indecisive. At twenty-five I was wise, self-confident, prepossessing, and assertive. At forty-five I am stupid, confused, insecure, and indecisive. Who would have supposed that maturity is only a short break in adolescence?
Observer, London (February 3, 1974)

Feinstein, Dianne (b.1933) U.S. politician

1 Ninety percent of leadership is the ability to communicate something people want.
Quoted in *Time* (June 18, 1990)

2 Toughness doesn't have to come in a pinstripe suit.
Quoted in *Time* (June 4, 1984)

Feinstein, Elaine (b.1930) British poet and novelist

1 When someone asked her if she had any money, she replied with a laugh that rumbled through her whole body, "Honey chile, what you talkin' about? I got a roll big enough to choke on."
Referring to Ma Rainey. *Bessie Smith: Empress of the Blues* (1985), ch. 2

Feldman, Marty (1933–82) British comedian

1 Comedy, like sodomy, is an unnatural act.
Times, London (1969)

Felker, Clay S. (Clay Schuette Felker; b.1925) U.S. editor

1 To beat his father...And to run the world.
Referring to the motives of Rupert Murdoch, who had acquired *New York* magazine in a hard-fought struggle with the editors and writers. Quoted in *Rupert Murdoch: Ringmaster of the Information Circus* (William Shawcross; 1993)

Fellini, Federico (1920–93) Italian film director

1 According to the doctors, I'm only suffering from a light form of premature baldness.
After spending four days in a clinic in Rome. *Variety* (1986)

2 I always direct the same film. I can't distinguish one from the other.
Quoted in *Halliwell's Filmgoer's Companion* (Leslie Halliwell; 1993)

3 Our dreams are our real life.
Quoted in *Halliwell's Filmgoer's Companion* (Leslie Halliwell; 1993)

4 Although my father wanted me to become an engineer and my mother a bishop, I myself am quite contented to have become an adjective.
Referring to the usage of the term "Felliniesque", meaning to blend fantasy and reality as Fellini does in his movies. Quoted in *Halliwell's Filmgoer's Companion* (Leslie Halliwell; 1993)

5 One should never think of a title first, only last, and it should be as encompassing as possible of its subject. If you limit yourself too early with a title, you will find what you look for instead of what is interesting; so you have to go into it with an open mind.
Quoted in *I, Fellini* (Charlotte Chandler; 1994)

6 She is abstract femininity...the prototype of a galactic New Woman.
Referring to the U.S. motion picture actor Kim Basinger. Attrib.

Femina, Jerry Della (b.1936) U.S. advertising executive

1 Advertising is the most fun you can have with your clothes on.
From those wonderful folks who gave you Pearl Harbor (Charles Sopkin, ed.; 1970)

Feng Zhi (also known as Feng Chih; 1905–93) Chinese poet

1 We often pass an intimate night
In a strange room. How it looks during
The day, we have no way of knowing,
Not to speak of its past or future.
"Sonnet 18" (1941)

2 From a pool of freely flowing, formless water,
The water carrier brings back a bottleful, ellipsoid in shape
Thus this much water has acquired a definite form.
"Sonnet 27" (1941)

Fenton, James (b.1949) British poet

1 There shouldn't be opposition between the classical Canon and the multicultural cause. Historically, things have always changed.
Independent, London (November 21, 1994)

2 His adult life resembled his childhood in the sense that he lorded it over admiring women.
Referring to Jean-Paul Sartre. *Times*, London (November 22, 1984)

Ferber, Edna (1885–1968) U.S. writer

1 I am not belittling the brave pioneer men, but the sunbonnet

as well as the sombrero has helped to settle this glorious land of ours.
Cimarron (1929), ch. 23

2 A woman can look both moral and exciting if she also looks as if it was quite a struggle.
Reader's Digest (December 1954)

3 Being an old maid is like death by drowning, a really delightful sensation after you cease to struggle.
"Completing the Circle," *Wit's End* (R. E. Drennan; 1973)

Ferdinand I, Holy Roman Emperor (1503–64) Spanish-born monarch

1 Let justice be done, though the world perish.
Motto. *Locorum Communium Collectanea* (Johannes Manlius; 1563), vol. 2

Ferdinand I, Emperor of Austria (1793–1875) Austrian monarch

1 I am the emperor, and I want dumplings.
The Fall of the House of Habsburg (Edward Crankshaw; 1963)

Ferguson, Samuel, Sir (1810–86) Irish antiquary and poet

1 The lions of the hill are gone,
And I am left alone—alone—
Dig the grave both wide and deep,
For I am sick, and fain would sleep.
"Deirdre's Lament for the Sons of Usnach" (1865), quoted in *The New Oxford Book of Irish Verse* (Thomas Kinsella, ed.; 1986)

Ferguson, Sarah, Duchess of York (Sarah Margaret Ferguson; b.1959) British ex-wife of Prince Andrew

1 I go to therapy, and I'm very proud of that.
August 26, 1993. *Times*, London

Fergusson, James (1808–86) British writer

1 With the aid of a few columns stuck here and there, or rich window dressings and rustications in another place, and aided by the fatal facility of stucco, they managed to get over an immense amount of space with a very slight expenditure of thought.
Referring to contemporary architects, such as John Nash (1752–1835). *History of Architecture* (1862), vol. 3

Ferlinghetti, Lawrence (Lawrence Ferling; b.1919) U.S. poet

1 Constantly risking absurdity
and death
whenever he performs
above the heads
of his audience
the poet like an acrobat
climbs on rime
to a high wire of his own making.
"A Coney Island of the Mind" (1958), quoted in *The Penguin Book of American Verse* (Geoffrey Moore, ed.; 1977)

2 exactly at the moment when
they first attained the title of
"suffering humanity."
"A Coney Island of the Mind" (1958), quoted in *The Penguin Book of American Verse* (Geoffrey Moore, ed.; 1977)

3 I have a feeling I'm falling
on rare occasions
but most of the time I have my feet on the ground
I can't help it if the ground itself is falling.
"Mock Confessional" (1973)

4 As I get older I perceive
Life has its tale in its mouth.
"Poet as Fisherman" (1988)

5 The world is a beautiful place
to be born into
if you don't mind some people dying
all the time
or maybe only starving
some of the time
which isn't half so bad
if it isn't you.
Pictures of the Gone World (1955)

Fermat, Pierre de (1601–65) French mathematician

1 To divide a cube into two other cubes, a fourth power or in general any power whatever into two powers of the same denomination above the second is impossible, and I have assuredly found an admirable proof of this, but the margin is too narrow to contain it.
1665. "Fermat's Last Theorem" was written in the margin of his copy of Diophantus' *Arithmetica*. A proof of the same was discovered in 1997. Attrib.

Fermi, Enrico (1901–54) Italian-born U.S. physicist

Quotations about Fermi

1 There is no democracy in physics. We can't say that some second-rate guy has as much right to an opinion as Fermi.
Luis Alvarez (b.1911) U.S. physicist. Quoted in *The Politics of Pure Science* (D. S. Greenberg; 1967)

2 The Italian navigator has reached the New World.
Arthur Holly Compton (1892–1962) U.S. physicist. Reporting the fact that Italian scientist Enrico Fermi had produced the first self-sustaining atomic chain reaction. Coded telephone message to James B. Conant (December 2, 1942)

Quotations by Fermi

3 Whatever Nature has in store for mankind, unpleasant as it may be, men must accept, for ignorance is never better than knowledge.
Atoms in the Family: My Life with Enrico Fermi (Laura Fermi; 1954)

Fern, Fanny (Sarah Payson Parton, born Willis; 1811–72) U.S. writer

1 The way to a man's heart is through his stomach.
Fern Leaves (1853)

Ferrier, James F. (James Frederick Ferrier; 1808–64) British philosopher

1 Every question in philosophy is the mask of another question;

and all these masking and masked questions require to be removed and laid aside, until the ultimate but *truly first* question has been reached.
"The Theory of Knowing and Being," *Institutes of Metaphysic* (1854)

Ferrier, Kathleen (1912–53) British contralto

1 Now I'll have *eine kleine* Pause.
Said shortly before her death. *Am I Too Loud?* (Gerald Moore; 1953)

Ferrier, Susan Edmonstone (1782–1854) Scottish novelist

1 But who can count the beatings of the lonely heart?
The Inheritance (1824), ch. 1.

Ferris, Richard J. U.S. airlines business executive

1 It is now possible for a flight attendant to get a pilot pregnant.
Attrib.

Feuerbach, Ludwig Andreas (1804–72) German philosopher

1 Religion is the dream of the human mind.
The Essence of Christianity (G. Eliot, tr.; 1841)

2 Food is the beginning of wisdom. The first condition of putting anything into your head and heart, is to put something into your stomach.
Quoted in *From Hegel to Marx* (Sidney Hook; 1936)

Feyerabend, Paul K. (Paul Karl Feyerabend; 1924–94) German philosopher

1 There is only *one* principle that can be defended under *all* stages of human development. It is the principle: *anything goes*.
Against Method (1975)

2 Unanimity of opinion may be fitting for a church, for the frightened or greedy victims of some (ancient or modern) myth, or for the weak and willing followers of some tyrant. Variety of opinion is necessary for objective knowledge.
Against Method (1975)

Feynman, Richard Phillips (1918–88) U.S. physicist

1 If I could explain it to the average person, I wouldn't have been worth the Nobel Prize.
He was awarded a Nobel Prize for his work on quantum electrodynamics. *People* (July 22, 1985)

2 For a successful technology, reality must take precedence over public relations.
Criticizing the response of the National Aeronautics and Space Administration (NASA) to the Challenger disaster. The space shuttle exploded on January 28, 1986, 73 seconds after take off, causing the death of the seven crew members. *Presidential Commission Report on the Challenger Explosion* (1986), appendix

3 Time comes, and this *tremendous* flash...white light changing into yellow and then into orange. Clouds form and disappear again...a big ball or orange...starts to rise and billow...The man standing next to me said, "What's that?" I said, "That was the Bomb."
Referring to the first successful testing of an atomic bomb in the Nevada desert, July 16, 1945. *Surely You're Joking, Mr. Feynman* (1985)

4 Science, indeed, makes an impact on many ideas associated with religion, but I do not believe it affects, in any strong way, moral conduct and ethical values.
Spring 1973. Lecture, University of Washington, *The Meaning of It All: Thoughts of a Citizen Scientist* (co-written with Michelle Feynman; 1998)

5 To every man is given the key to the gate of heaven; the same key opens the gates of hell.
What Do You Care What Other People Think? (1988)

6 Physicists like to think that all you have to do is say, these are the conditions, now what happens next?
Chaos: Making a New Science (James Gleick; 1988)

Fichte, Johann (1762–1814) German philosopher

1 Attend to yourself: turn your attention away from everything that surrounds you and towards your inner life; this is the first demand that philosophy makes of its disciple.
1794. *The Science of Knowledge* (P. Heath and J. Lachs, trs.; 1982)

2 Our doctrine here is therefore that all reality...is brought forth solely by the imagination.
1794. *The Science of Knowledge* (P. Heath and J. Lachs, trs.; 1982)

3 Our task is to *discover* the primordial, absolutely first principle of all human knowledge.
1794. *The Science of Knowledge* (P. Heath and J. Lachs, trs.; 1982)

4 *The self posits self*, and by virtue of this self-assertion it *exists*; and conversely, the self *exists* and *posits* its own existence by virtue of merely existing.
1794. *The Science of Knowledge* (P. Heath and J. Lachs, trs.; 1982)

5 In an uncorrupted woman the sexual impulse does not manifest itself at all, but only love; and this love is the natural impulse of a woman to satisfy a man.
The Science of Rights (1796)

Field, Eugene (1850–95) U.S. journalist and children's author

1 But I, when I undress me
Each night, upon my knees,
Will ask the Lord to bless me,
With apple pie and cheese.
"Apple Pie and Cheese" (1889)

2 Wynken, Blynken, and Nod one night
Sailed off in a wooden shoe
Sailed on a river of crystal light,
Into a sea of dew.
"Wynken, Blynken, and Nod" (1892), st. 1

3 A Chicago Papa is so Mean he Wont let his Little Baby have More than One Measle at a time.
"A Mean Man," *Nonsense for Old and Young* (1901)

4 What smells so? Has somebody been burning a Rag, or is there a Dead Mule in the Back yard? No, the Man is Smoking a Five-Cent Cigar.
"The Five-Cent Cigar," *The Denver Tribune Primer* (1882)

5 He played the King as though under momentary apprehension that someone else was about to play the ace.
Referring to Creston Clarke's performance in the role of King Lear in Denver (1880?). *The Denver Tribune* (1880)

Field, Marshall (1834–1906) U.S. entrepreneur

1 Give the lady what she wants!
Instruction to the manager of one of his large stores. Attrib.

Field, Sally (b.1946) U.S. actor

1 When I won my first one, I was so contained—numb. All I could think of was: Don't fall down.
Referring to winning an Oscar. Attrib. *Playboy* (March 1986)

Fielding, Henry (1707–54) British novelist and playwright

1 We must eat to live and live to eat.
The Miser (1733), Act 3, Scene 3

2 Penny saved is a penny got.
The Miser (1733), Act 3, Scene 12

3 It hath been often said, that it is not death, but dying, which is terrible.
Amelia (1751), bk. 3, ch. 4

4 When widows exclaim loudly against second marriages, I would always lay a wager, that the man, if not the wedding-day, is absolutely fixed on.
Amelia (1751), bk. 6, ch. 8

5 One fool at least in every married couple.
Amelia (1751), bk. 9, ch. 4

6 I am as sober as a Judge.
Don Quixote in England (1734), Act 3, Scene 14

7 Never trust the man who hath reason to suspect that you know he hath injured you.
Jonathan Wild (1743), bk. 3, ch. 4

8 He in a few minutes ravished this fair creature, or at least would have ravished her, if she had not, by a timely compliance, prevented him.
Jonathan Wild (1743), bk. 3, ch. 7

9 For clergy are men as well as other folks.
Joseph Andrews (1742), bk. 2, ch. 6

10 To whom nothing is given, of him can nothing be required.
Joseph Andrews (1742), bk. 2, ch. 8

11 Public schools are the nurseries of all vice and immorality.
Joseph Andrews (1742), bk. 3, ch. 5

12 Yes, I had two strings to my bow; both golden ones, egad! and both cracked.
Love in Several Masques (1728), Act 5, Scene 13

13 Enough is equal to a feast.
The Covent Garden Journal (1732), Act 5, Scene 1

14 Oh! The roast beef of England.
And old England's roast beef.
The Grub Street Opera (1731), Act 3, Scene 3

15 It is with jealousy as with the gout. When such distempers are in the blood, there is never any security against their breaking out; and that often on the slightest occasions, and when least suspected.
Tom Jones (1749), bk. 2, ch. 3

16 Every physician almost hath his favourite disease.
Tom Jones (1749), bk. 2, ch. 9

17 When I mention religion, I mean the Christian religion; and not only the Christian religion, but the Protestant religion; and not only the Protestant religion but the Church of England.
Tom Jones (1749), bk. 3, ch. 3

18 What is commonly called love, namely the desire of satisfying a voracious appetite with a certain quantity of delicate white human flesh.
Tom Jones (1749), bk. 6, ch. 1

19 His designs were strictly honourable, as the phrase is; that is, to rob a lady of her fortune by way of marriage.
Tom Jones (1749), bk. 11, ch. 4

20 Composed that monstrous animal a husband and wife.
Tom Jones (1749), bk. 15, ch. 9

21 All Nature wears one universal grin.
Tom Thumb the Great (1731), Act 1, Scene 1

Fielding, Sarah (1710–68) British author

1 I hope to be excused by those gentlemen who are quite sure they have found one woman who is a perfect angel, and that all the rest are perfect devils.
David Simple (1750)

Fields, W. C. (William Claude Dukenfield; 1879–1946) U.S. entertainer

1 It ain't a fit night out for man or beast.
W. C. Fields by Himself (1974), pt. 2

2 I exercise extreme self-control. I never drink anything stronger than gin before breakfast.
Quoted in *W. C. Fields, His Follies and Fortunes* (Robert Lewis Taylor; 1949)

3 Anybody who hates children and dogs can't be all bad.
Attrib.

4 Horse sense is a good judgment which keeps horses from betting on people.
Attrib.

5 I am free of all prejudice. I hate everyone equally.
Attrib.

6 If at first you don't succeed, try, try again. Then quit. No use being a damn fool about it.
Attrib.

7 Last week I went to Philadelphia, but it was closed.
Attrib.

8 Never give a sucker an even break.
1941. Attrib.

9 Fish fuck in it.
His reason for not drinking water. Attrib.

10 On the whole I'd rather be in Philadelphia.
Proposed inscription for his tombstone. Attrib.

11 I have spent a lot of time searching through the Bible for loopholes.
Said during his last illness. Attrib.

Fierstein, Harvey (b.1954) U.S. actor and playwright

1 I've lived my entire life with heterosexual hatred. All my life, I've been the queer down the hall.
Playboy (August 1988)

2 When you have AIDS, you're judged on how much sex you've had and what kind. There's nothing wrong with putting your arms around someone, holding them, feeling great.
Playboy (August 1988)

3 Gays grow up listening to heterosexual songs and watching heterosexual movies. It's good for them to see one of their own struggling to be himself, rather than watching *Now Voyager* and deciding whether they are Bette Davis or Paul Henreid.
Time (June 20, 1983)

Figes, Eva (b.1932) British writer

1 A woman's career, particularly if it is successful, is often blamed for the break-up of a marriage, but never a man's.
Patriarchal Attitudes (1970), ch. 8

2 When modern woman discovered the orgasm it was (combined with modern birth control) perhaps the biggest single nail in the coffin of male dominance.
Quoted in *The Descent of Woman* (Elaine Morgan; 1972)

Figes, Orlando (Orlando Guy Figes; b.1959) British historian

1 The revolution of 1917 has defined the shape of the contemporary world, and we are only now emerging from its shadow.
Referring to the Russian Revolution. *A People's Tragedy: The Russian Revolution 1891–1924* (1996), preface

Filarete (Antonio di Pietro Averlino; 1400?–69?) Italian sculptor and architect

1 We read of Giotto that as a beginner he painted flies, and his master Cimabue was so taken in that he believed they were alive and started to chase them off with a rag.
Treatise On Architecture (1460–64)

Filene, E. A. (Edward Albert Filene; 1860–1937) U.S. financier

1 When a man's education is finished, he is finished.
Attrib.

Finch, Anne, Countess of Winchilsea (originally Kingsmill; 1661–1720) English poet

1 Alas! a woman that attempts the pen,
Such an intruder on the rights of men,
Such a presumptuous creature, is esteemed,
The fault can by no virtue be redeemed.
"Written by a Lady," *Miscellany Poems on Several Occasions* (1713)

2 To write, or read, or think, or to inquire,
Would cloud our beauty, and exhaust our time,
And interrupt the conquests of our prime,
Whilst the dull manage of a servile house
Is held by some our utmost art and use.
The Spleen (1701)

Finch, Paul British architectural journalist

1 Design is the tribute art pays to industry.
Definitions of Design (1995)

Fionn MacCool (also known as Finn Mac Cumhail, Fionn mac Cumhaill; *fl.* 2nd century) mythical Irish chieftain

1 The music of what happens...that is the finest music in the world.
2nd century. Quoted in *Irish Fairy Tales* (James Stephens; 1920)

Firbank, Ronald (Arthur Annesley Ronald Firbank; 1886–1926) British novelist

1 There was a pause—just long enough for an angel to pass, flying slowly.
Vainglory (1915)

2 The world is disgracefully managed, one hardly knows to whom to complain.
Vainglory (1915)

3 To be sympathetic without discrimination is so very debilitating.
Vainglory (1915)

Fischer, Martin H. (1879–1962) German-born U.S. physician and author

1 A doctor must work eighteen hours a day and seven days a week. If you cannot console yourself to this, get out of the profession.
Fischerisms (Howard Fabing and Ray Marr, eds.; 1944)

2 All the world is a laboratory to the inquiring mind.
Fischerisms (Howard Fabing and Ray Marr, eds.; 1944)

3 A man who cannot work without his hypodermic needle is a poor doctor. The amount of narcotic you use is inversely proportional to your skill.
Fischerisms (Howard Fabing and Ray Marr, eds.; 1944)

4 Don't confuse *hypothesis* and *theory*. The former is a possible explanation; the latter, the correct one. The establishment of theory is the very purpose of science.
Fischerisms (Howard Fabing and Ray Marr, eds.; 1944)

5 Don't despise empiric truth. Lots of things work in practice for which the laboratory has never found proof.
Fischerisms (Howard Fabing and Ray Marr, eds.; 1944)

6 Facts are not science—as the dictionary is not literature.
Fischerisms (Howard Fabing and Ray Marr, eds.; 1944)

7 First need in the reform of hospital management? That's easy! The death of all dietitians, and the resurrection of a French chef.
Fischerisms (Howard Fabing and Ray Marr, eds.; 1944)

8 Half the modern drugs could well be thrown out the window except that the birds might eat them.
Fischerisms (Howard Fabing and Ray Marr, eds.; 1944)

9 Here's good advice for practice: go into partnership with

nature; she does more than half the work and asks none of the fee.
Fischerisms (Howard Fabing and Ray Marr, eds.; 1944)

10 I find that most men would rather have their bellies opened for five hundred dollars than have a tooth pulled for five.
Fischerisms (Howard Fabing and Ray Marr, eds.; 1944)

11 If you are physically sick, you can elicit the interest of a battery of physicians; but if you are mentally sick, you are lucky if the janitor comes around.
Fischerisms (Howard Fabing and Ray Marr, eds.; 1944)

12 In diagnosis think of the easy first.
Fischerisms (Howard Fabing and Ray Marr, eds.; 1944)

13 In the sick room, ten cents' worth of human understanding equals ten dollars' worth of medical science.
Fischerisms (Howard Fabing and Ray Marr, eds.; 1944)

14 Many a diabetic has stayed alive by stealing the bread denied him by his doctor.
Fischerisms (Howard Fabing and Ray Marr, eds.; 1944)

15 Medicine is the one place where all the show is stripped of the human drama. You, as doctors, will be in a position to see the human race stark naked—not only physically, but mentally and morally as well.
Fischerisms (Howard Fabing and Ray Marr, eds.; 1944)

16 None of the great discoveries was made by a "specialist" or a "researcher".
Fischerisms (Howard Fabing and Ray Marr, eds.; 1944)

17 Research has been called good business, a necessity, a gamble, a game. It is none of these—it's a state of mind.
Fischerisms (Howard Fabing and Ray Marr, eds.; 1944)

18 Some day when you have time, look into the business of prayer, amulets, baths, and poultices, and discover for yourself how much valuable therapy the profession has cast on the dump.
Fischerisms (Howard Fabing and Ray Marr, eds.; 1944)

19 The great doctors all got their education off dirt pavements and poverty—not marble floors and foundations.
Fischerisms (Howard Fabing and Ray Marr, eds.; 1944)

20 There is only one reason why men become addicted to drugs, they are weak men. Only strong men are cured, and they cure themselves.
Fischerisms (Howard Fabing and Ray Marr, eds.; 1944)

21 The specialist is a man who fears the other subjects.
Fischerisms (Howard Fabing and Ray Marr, eds.; 1944)

22 When a man lacks mental balance in pneumonia he is said to be delirious. When he lacks mental balance without the pneumonia, he is pronounced insane by all smart doctors.
Fischerisms (Howard Fabing and Ray Marr, eds.; 1944)

23 Whenever ideas fail, men invent words.
Fischerisms (Howard Fabing and Ray Marr, eds.; 1944)

24 When there is no explanation, they give it a name, which immediately explains everything.
Fischerisms (Howard Fabing and Ray Marr, eds.; 1944)

25 You must learn to talk clearly. The jargon of scientific terminology which rolls off your tongues is mental garbage.
Fischerisms (Howard Fabing and Ray Marr, eds.; 1944)

26 The practice of medicine is a thinker's art the practice of surgery a plumber's.
Fischerisms (Howard Fabing and Ray Marr, eds.; 1944)

Fischer-Mirkin, Toby U.S. fashion journalist

1 Although the ultratailored "menswear" look remains a strong component of a successful business wardrobe, it is no longer necessary for a woman to dress like her male colleagues to prove she is their equal.
Dress Code: Understanding the Hidden Meanings of Women's Clothing (1995), ch. 5

2 Of course, the more obvious dress code violations, such as charm bracelets, long dangling earrings, or four-inch heels, spell doom in conservative professions.
Dress Code: Understanding the Hidden Meanings of Women's Clothing (1995), ch. 5

Fischl, Eric (b.1948) U.S. painter

1 Art is like theater. If you want to whisper, you have to whisper loudly enough so that the audience hears you, and...has to know it's a whisper. So the artist has to be able to blow the subtleties up proportionately, and at the same time have them be recognized as subtle. It's what makes a good artist, even if he is painting badly.
Quoted in "Expressionism Today: An Artist's Symposium," *Art in America* (Carter Ratcliff; December 1982), 70, no. 2

Fish, Janet (b.1938) U.S. painter

1 Painting still lifes is like contemplation or meditation...You sit there with something very quiet. You are looking at it all day and you are constantly pushing through the thing you are looking at.
"Conversation with Janet Fish," *Feminist Art Journal* (Cindy Nemser; Fall 1976), no. 7

Fish, Michael (b.1944) British meteorologist

1 A woman rang to say she heard there was a hurricane on the way. Well don't worry, there isn't.
Television announcement just before a major hurricane. Weather Forecast, *BBC TV* (October 15, 1987)

Fisher, Carrie (b.1956) U.S. actor and writer

1 For *Star Wars*, they had me tape down my breasts because there are no breasts in space. I have some. I have two.
Playboy (July 1983)

2 I'm fond of kissing. It's part of my job. God sent me down to kiss a lot of people.
Playboy (July 1983)

3 Females get hired along procreative lines. After 40, we're kind of cooked.
Time (February 18, 1991)

4 I was born into big celebrity. It could only diminish.
Vanity Fair (August 1990)

5 You look at Harrison Ford and you *listen.* He looks like he's carrying a gun, even if he isn't.
Vanity Fair (August 1990)

Fisher, Geoffrey, Lord Fisher of Lambeth (Geoffrey Francis Fisher; 1887–1972) British archbishop

1 Consultant specialists are a degree more remote (like bishops!); and therefore (again like bishops) they need a double dose of grace to keep them sensitive to the personal and the pastoral.
Lancet (1949), 2:775

Fisher, Marve U.S. songwriter

1 I want an old-fashioned house
With an old-fashioned fence
And an old-fashioned millionaire.
Song lyric. The song is most closely associated with the singer Eartha Kitt. "An Old-Fashioned Girl" (1954)

Fisher, M. F. K. (originally Mary Frances Kennedy; 1908–92) U.S. writer

1 It must not simply be taken for granted that a given set of ill-assorted people, for no other reason than because it is Christmas, will be joyful to be reunited and to break bread together.
An Alphabet for Gourmets (1949)

Fisher, Ronald Aylmer, Sir (1890–1962) British biologist

1 To call in the statistician after the experiment is done may be no more than asking him to perform a postmortem examination: he may be able to say what the experiment died of.
Address to the Indian Statistical Congress, Sankhya (1938)

Fisher, Roy (b.1930) British poet

1 Because it could do it well
the poem wants to glorify suffering.
I mistrust it.
"It is Writing," *Poems, 1955–1987* (1988)

2 I saw
the mass graves dug
the size of workhouse wards
into the clay

ready for most of the people
the air-raids were going to kill.
Referring to preparations for air-raids on Birmingham, England, during World War II. "Wonders of Obligation," *Poems, 1955–1987* (1988)

Fitzgeffrey, Charles (1575?–1637) English poet

1 And bold and hard adventures t' undertake,
Leaving his country for his country's sake.
Sir Francis Drake (1596), st. 213

FitzGerald, Edward (1809–83) British poet and translator

1 Taste is the feminine of genius.
Letter to J. R. Lowell (October 1877), quoted in *Letters of Edward FitzGerald* (A. M. and A. B. Terhune, eds.; 1980)

2 Awake! for Morning in the Bowl of Night
Has flung the Stone that puts the Stars to Flight:
And Lo! the Hunter of the East has caught
The Sultán's Turret in a Noose of Light.
The Rubáiyát of Omar Khayyám (1859), st. 1

3 Come, fill the Cup, and in the Fire of Spring
The Winter Garment of Repentance fling:
The Bird of Time has but a little way
To fly—and Lo! the Bird is on the Wing.
The Rubáiyát of Omar Khayyám (1859), st. 7

4 The Wine of Life keeps oozing drop by drop,
The Leaves of Life keep falling one by one.
The Rubáiyát of Omar Khayyám (1859), st. 8

5 Here with a Loaf of Bread beneath the Bough,
A Flask of Wine, a Book of Verse—and Thou
Beside me singing in the Wilderness—
And Wilderness is Paradise enow.
The Rubáiyát of Omar Khayyám (1859), st. 11

6 Ah, take the Cash in hand and waive the Rest;
Oh, the brave Music of a *distant* Drum!
The Rubáiyát of Omar Khayyám (1859), st. 12

7 The Worldly Hope men set their Hearts upon
Turns Ashes—or it prospers; and anon,
Like Snow upon the Desert's dusty Face,
Lighting a little Hour or two is gone.
The Rubáiyát of Omar Khayyám (1859), st. 14

8 I sometimes think that never blows so red
The Rose as where some buried Caesar bled;
That every Hyacinth the Garden wears
Dropt in its Lap from some once lovely Head.
The Rubáiyát of Omar Khayyám (1859), st. 18

9 Ah, my Belovéd, fill the Cup that clears
TO-DAY of past Regrets and future Fears:
To-morrow!—Why, To-morrow I may be
Myself with Yesterday's Sev'n thousand Years.
The Rubáiyát of Omar Khayyám (1859), st. 20

10 One thing is certain, that Life flies;
One thing is certain, and the Rest is Lies;
The Flower that once has blown for ever dies.
The Rubáiyát of Omar Khayyám (1859), st. 26

11 Ah, fill the Cup:—what boots it to repeat
How Time is slipping underneath our Feet:
Unborn TO-MORROW, and dead YESTERDAY,
Why fret about them if TO-DAY be sweet!
The Rubáiyát of Omar Khayyám (1859), st. 37

12 The Moving Finger writes; and, having writ,
Moves on: nor all thy Piety nor Wit
Shall lure it back to cancel half a Line,
Nor all thy Tears wash out a Word of it.
The Rubáiyát of Omar Khayyám (1859), st. 51

13 And that inverted Bowl we call The Sky,
Whereunder crawling coop't we live and die,
Lift not thy hands to *It* for help—for It
Rolls impotently on as Thou or I.
The Rubáiyát of Omar Khayyám (1859), st. 52

14 "Who *is* the Potter, pray, and who the Pot?"
The Rubáiyát of Omar Khayyám (1859), st. 60

15 'Tis all a Chequer-board of Nights and Days
Where Destiny with Men for Pieces plays:
Hither and thither moves, and mates, and slays,
And one by one back in the Closet lays.
The Rubáiyát of Omar Khayyám (1868 edn.), st. 40

16 Strange, is it not? that of the myriads who
Before us pass'd the door of Darkness through,
Not one returns to tell us of the Road,
Which to discover we must travel too.
The Rubáiyát of Omar Khayyám (1868 edn.), st. 67

17 Drink! for you know not whence you came, nor why:
Drink! for you know not why you go, nor where.
The Rubáiyát of Omar Khayyám (1868 edn.), st. 80

18 Heav'n but the Vision of fulfill'd Desire,
And Hell the Shadow of a Soul on fire.
The Rubáiyát of Omar Khayyám (1868 edn.), st. 72

Fitzgerald, Ella (1918–96) U.S. jazz singer

1 I always thought my music was pretty much hollering.
Ella Fitzgerald (Bud Kliment; 1988), p.41

2 I found that all through the years you never appreciate anything if you get it in a hurry.
Ella: The Life and Times of Ella Fitzgerald (Sid Colin; 1986), p.36

Fitzgerald, F. Scott (Francis Scott Key Fitzgerald; 1896–1940) U.S. writer

Quotations about Fitzgerald

1 Fitzgerald was an alcoholic, a spendthrift and a superstar playboy possessed of a beauty and a glamour that only a Byron could support without artistic ruination.
Anthony Burgess (1917–93) British writer and critic. *Observer*, London (February 7, 1982)

2 The poor son-of-a-bitch!
Dorothy Parker (1893–1967) U.S. writer and wit. Quoting from *The Great Gatsby* (1925), on paying her last respects to F. Scott Fitzgerald. Remark (1940), quoted in *Thalberg: Life and Legend* (Bob Thomas; 1969)

3 The Fitzgeralds never got around to seeing the sights because, as Jazz Age celebrities, they were the sights. They wanted to have a good time and a good time was had by all for a short time.
1980
Gore Vidal (b.1925) U.S. novelist and essayist. Referring to F. Scott and Zelda Fitzgerald's stay in Europe. "F. Scott Fitzgerald's Case," *The Second American Revolution* (1982)

4 I am touched at your sending me a copy, for I feel that to your generation, which has taken such a flying leap into the future, I must represent the literary equivalent of tufted furniture and gas chandeliers.
Edith Wharton (1862–1937) U.S. novelist. Referring to F. Scott Fitzgerald's gift of a copy of *The Great Gatsby* (1925). Letter to F. Scott Fitzgerald (June 8, 1925), *The Letters of Edith Wharton* (R. W. B. Lewis and Nancy Lewis, eds.; 1988)

Quotations by Fitzgerald

5 Though the Jazz Age continued, it became less and less an affair of youth.
The sequel was like a children's party taken over by the elders.
1931. "Echoes of the Jazz Age", *The Crack-Up: with Other Uncollected Pieces, Note-Books and Unpublished Letters* (Edmund Wilson, ed.; 1945)

6 All good writing is *swimming under water* and holding your breath.
Letter to his daughter, Frances Scott Fitzgerald, *The Crack-Up: with Other Uncollected Pieces, Note-Books and Unpublished Letters* (Edmund Wilson, ed.; 1945)

7 Your life has been a disappointment, as mine has been too. But we haven't gone through this sweat for nothing.
Letter to his wife, Zelda (October 6, 1939), *The Letters of F. Scott Fitzgerald* (Andrew Turnbull; 1964)

8 FITZGERALD The rich are different from us.
HEMINGWAY Yes, they have more money.
1936. "Notebook E", *The Crack-Up: with Other Uncollected Pieces, Note-Books and Unpublished Letters* (Edmund Wilson, ed.; 1945)

9 Show me a hero and I will write you a tragedy.
1936. "Notebooks E", *The Crack-Up: with Other Uncollected Pieces, Note-Books and Unpublished Letters* (Edmund Wilson, ed.; 1945)

10 I entertained on a cruising trip that was so much fun that I had to sink my yacht to make my guests go home.
"Notebooks K", *The Crack-Up: with Other Uncollected Pieces, Note-Books and Unpublished Letters* (Edmund Wilson, ed.; 1945)

11 It appears that every man's insomnia is as different from his neighbor's as are their daytime hopes and aspirations.
"Sleeping and Waking", *The Crack-Up: with Other Uncollected Pieces, Note-Books and Unpublished Letters* (Edmund Wilson, ed.; 1945)

12 I remember riding in a taxi one afternoon between very tall buildings under a mauve and rosy sky; I began to bawl because I had everything I wanted and knew I would never be so happy again.
1932. "The Crack-Up", *The Crack-Up: with Other Uncollected Pieces, Note-Books and Unpublished Letters* (Edmund Wilson, ed.; 1945)

13 In the real dark night of the soul it is always three o'clock in the morning.
Referring to Saint John of the Cross's "The dark night of the soul." *Esquire* (March 1936)

14 A new generation grown to find all Gods dead, all wars fought, all faiths in man shaken.
Tales of the Jazz Age (1922)

15 So we beat on, boats against the current, borne back ceaselessly into the past.
Last line. *The Great Gatsby* (1925)

16 One of those men who reach such an acute limited excellence at twenty-one that everything afterward savours of anti-climax.
The Great Gatsby (1925), ch. 1

17 I was one of the few guests who had actually been invited. People were not invited—they went there.
The Great Gatsby (1925), ch. 3

18 One girl can be pretty—but a dozen are only a chorus.
The Last Tycoon (1941)

19 He differed from the healthy type that was essentially middle-class—he never seemed to perspire.
This Side of Paradise (1920), bk. 1, ch. 2

20 A big man has no time really to do anything but just sit and be big.
This Side of Paradise (1920), bk. 2, ch. 2

21 Beware of the artist who's an intellectual also. The artist who doesn't fit.
This Side of Paradise (1920), bk. 2, ch. 5

22 "I know myself," he cried, "but that is all."
This Side of Paradise (1920), bk. 2, ch. 5

23 First you take a drink, then the drink takes a drink, then the drink takes you.
1964. Attrib. "1964, May 7," *Ackroyd* (Jules Feiffer; 1977)

24 Sometimes I don't know whether Zelda and I are real or whether we are characters in one of my novels.
Said of himself and his wife. *A Second Flowering* (Malcolm Cowley; 1973)

25 Baseball is a game played by idiots for morons.
Quoted in *Confessions from Left Field* (Raymond Mungo; 1983)

26 Optimism is the content of small men in high places.
1936. *The Crack-Up: with Other Uncollected Pieces, Note-Books and Unpublished Letters* (Edmund Wilson, ed.; 1945)

27 The test of a first-rate intelligence is the ability to hold two opposed ideas in the mind at the same time, and still retain the ability to function.
1936. *The Crack-Up: with Other Uncollected Pieces, Note-Books and Unpublished Letters* (Edmund Wilson, ed.; 1945)

28 What we must decide is perhaps how we are valuable, rather than how valuable we are.
1936. *The Crack-Up: with Other Uncollected Pieces, Note-Books and Unpublished Letters* (Edmund Wilson, ed.; 1945)

29 You can stroke people with words.
1936. *The Crack-Up: with Other Uncollected Pieces, Note-Books and Unpublished Letters* (Edmund Wilson, ed.; 1945)

30 Nature's attempt to get rid of soft boys by sterilizing them.
Quoted in *The Notebooks of F. Scott Fitzgerald* (Matthew J. Bruccoli, ed.; 1978)

31 The Beautiful and the Damned
1922. Book title.

32 Tender Is the Night
1934. Book title taken from "Ode to a Nightingale," John Keats (l. 35): "Already with thee! tender is the night."

Fitzgerald, Zelda (1900–48) U.S. writer

1 I don't want to live—I want to love first, and live incidentally.
Letter to F. Scott Fitzgerald. (1919)

2 Don't you think I was made for you? I feel like you had me ordered—and I was delivered to you—to be worn—I want you to wear me, like a watch-charm or a button hole boquet—to the world.
Zelda actually wrote "boquet," not "bouquet." Letter to F. Scott Fitzgerald (1919)

3 A vacuum can only exist, I imagine, by the things which enclose it.
Journal (1932)

Fitz-Gibbon, Bernice (Bernice Bowles Fitz-Gibbon; 1895?–1982) U.S. advertising executive

1 Creativeness often consists in turning up what is already there. Did you know that left and right shoes were thought up only a little more than a century ago?
Attrib.

FitzNigel, Richard (1130?–98?) English cleric and official

1 The sanctuary and special delight of kings, where, laying aside their cares, they withdraw to refresh themselves with a little hunting; there, away from the turmoils inherent in a court, they breathe the pleasure of natural freedom.
Referring to the royal forests. *Dialogus de Scaccario: The course of the Exchequer* (1190?), bk. 1, ch. 11

Fitzsimmons, Bob (Robert Prometheus Fitzsimmons; 1862–1917) British-born New Zealand boxer

1 The bigger they come the harder they fall.
Brooklyn Daily Eagle (August 11, 1900)

Flack, Audrey (b.1931) U.S. painter and sculptor

1 For me art is a continuous discovery into reality, an exploration of visual data which has been going on for centuries, each artist contributing to the next generation's advancement. I wanted to go a step further and extend the boundaries.
1970. Quoted in *Art Talk: Conversations with 15 Women Artists* (Cindy Nemser; 1975)

Flammarion, Camille (1842–1925) French astronomer

1 There are men who would even be afraid to commit themselves to the doctrine that castor oil is a laxative.
Attrib.

Flanagan, Oliver J. (Oliver John Flanagan; 1920–87) Irish auctioneer and politician

1 It is popular in...Europe to talk of sex, divorce and drugs. These things are foreign in Ireland and to Ireland and we want them kept foreign.
Speech to the Irish Parliament (March 10, 1971), quoted in *Phrases Make History Here* (Conor O'Clery; 1986)

2 Let us hope and trust that there are sufficient proud and ignorant people left in this country to stand up to the intellectuals who are out to destroy faith and fatherland.
April 10, 1971. Attrib.

3 There was no sex in Ireland before television.
Attrib.

Flanders, Michael (1922–75) British comedian and songwriter

1 Eating people is wrong.
Song. "The Reluctant Cannibal" (1956)

Flaubert, Gustave (1821–80) French novelist

1 Books are made not like children but like pyramids...and they're just as useless! and they stay in the desert!...Jackals piss at their foot and the bourgeois climb up on them.
Letter to Ernest Feydeau (November/December 1857), quoted in *Correspondence, 1857–1864* (M. Nadeau, ed.; 1965)

2 All one's inventions are true, you can be sure of that. Poetry is as exact a science as geometry.
Letter to Louise Colet (August 14, 1853), quoted in *Correspondence, 1853–1856* (M. Nadeau, ed.; 1964)

3 Read in order to live.
Letter to Mme. de Chantepie (1857)

4 DOCTOR Always preceded by "the good." Among men, in familiar conversation, "Oh! balls, doctor!" Is a wizard when he enjoys your confidence, a jackass when you're no longer on terms. All are materialists: "You can't probe for faith with a scalpel."
Le Dictionnaire des idées reçues (1911)

5 HEALTHY Too much health, the cause of illness.
Le Dictionnaire des idées reçues (1911)

6 Erections—not mentioned unless speaking of monuments.
Le Dictionnaire des idées reçues (1911)

7 Fusillade—the only way to silence Parisians.
Le Dictionnaire des idées reçues (1911)

8 MONEY Cause of all evil...Politicians call it emoluments; lawyers, retainers; doctors, fees; employees, salary; workmen, pay; servants, wages.
Le Dictionnaire des idées reçues (1911)

9 Passions fade when one removes them from their usual surroundings.
L'Éducation sentimentale (1869), pt. 2, ch. 1

10 We shouldn't touch our idols: the gilt comes off on our hands.
Madame Bovary (1857), pt. 3, ch. 6

11 Anyone's death always releases something like an aura of stupefaction, so difficult is it to grasp this irruption of nothingness and to believe that it has actually taken place.
Madame Bovary (1857), pt. 3, ch. 9

Flecker, James Elroy (1884–1915) British poet

1 West of these out to seas colder than the Hebrides I must go
Where the fleet of stars is anchored and the young star-captains glow
The dragon-green, the luminous, the dark, the serpent-haunted sea.
"The Gates of Damascus" (1913)

2 It was so old a ship—who knows, who knows?
And yet so beautiful, I watched in vain
To see the mast burst open with a rose,
And the whole deck put on its leaves again.
"The Old Ships" (1915)

3 Sweet to ride forth at evening from the wells
When shadows pass gigantic on the sand,
And softly through the silence beat the bells
Along the Golden Road to Samarkand.
The Golden Journey to Samarkand (1913)

4 For lust of knowing what should not be known,
We make the Golden Journey to Samarkand.
The Golden Journey to Samarkand (1913), epilogue, quoted in *The Collected Poems of James Elroy Flecker* (Sir John Squire, ed.; 1946)

5 Last of all his shirt came flying. Ah, I tremble to disclose
How the shell came off the almond, how the lily showed its face,
How I saw a silver mirror taken flashing from its case.
"The Hammam Name," *The Penguin Book of Homosexual Verse* (Stephen Coote, ed.; 1983)

Fleming, Alexander, Sir (1881–1955) British microbiologist

Quotations about Fleming

1 He had in fact most of the qualities that make a great scientist: an innate curiosity and perceptiveness regarding natural phenomena, insight into the heart of a problem, technical ingenuity, persistence in seeing a job through and that physical and mental toughness that is essential to the top-class investigator.
Leonard Colebrook (1883–1967) British medical researcher. *Journal of Pathology and Bacteriology* (1956)

2 Had he not been an untidy man and apt to leave his cultures exposed on the laboratory table the spore of hyssop mould, the *penicillin notatum*, might never have floated in from Praed Street and settled on his dish of staphylococci.
André Maurois (1885–1967) French writer. *Life of Alexander Fleming* (1961)

3 Yet had Fleming not possessed immense knowledge and an unremitting gift of observation he might not have observed the effect of the hyssop mould. "Fortune," remarked Pasteur, "favors the prepared mind."
André Maurois (1885–1967) French writer. Referring to Alexander Fleming and Louis Pasteur. *Life of Alexander Fleming* (1961)

Quotations by Fleming

4 A good gulp of hot whisky at bedtime—it's not very scientific, but it helps.
Response when asked about a cure for colds. *News Report* (March 22, 1954)

5 It was astonishing that for some considerable distance around the mould growth the staphococcal colonies were undergoing lysis. What had formerly been a well-grown colony was now a faint shadow of its former self...I was sufficiently interested to pursue the subject.
September 1928. The first observation of penicillin. Quoted in *Portraits of Nobel Laureates in Medicine and Physiology* (Sarah R. Riedman and Elton T. Gustafson; 1963)

Fleming, Ian (Ian Lancaster Fleming; 1908–64) British writer

Quotations about Fleming

1 The trouble with Ian is that he gets off with women because he can't get on with them.
Rosamond Lehmann (1901–90) British novelist. *The Life of Ian Fleming* (John Pearson; 1966)

Quotations by Fleming

2 Most marriages don't add two people together. They subtract one from the other.
Diamonds Are Forever (1956)

3 Diamonds Are Forever
Book title originating from the advertising slogan for De Beers Consolidated Mines. *Diamonds Are Forever* (1956)

4 A medium vodka dry Martini—with a slice of lemon peel. Shaken and not stirred.
Dr. No (1958), ch. 14

5 A woman should be an illusion.
Life of Ian Fleming (John Pearson; 1966)

6 Older women are best because they always think they may be doing it for the last time.
Notebook entry. *Life of Ian Fleming* (John Pearson; 1966), ch. 8, sect. 1

Fleming, Marjory (1803–11) Scottish child writer

1 A direful death indeed they had
That would put any parent mad
But she was more than usual calm
She did not give a singel dam.
1810? *Journals, Letters and Verses* (A. Esdaille, ed.; 1934)

Fleming, Peter (Robert Peter Fleming; 1907–71) British travel writer

1 Long Island represents the American's idea of what God would have done with Nature if he'd had the money.
Letter (September 29, 1929)

2 With the possible exception of the equator, everything begins somewhere.
One's Company (1934)

Fletcher, John (1579–1625) English playwright

1 Our acts our angels are, or good or ill,
Our fatal shadows that walk by us still.
An Honest Man's Fortune (1647), Epilogue

2 And he that will go to bed sober,
Falls with the leaf still in October.
Also known as *Rollo, Duke of Normandy,* in collaboration with Jonson and others. *The Bloody Brother* (1616), Act 2, Scene 2

3 Best while you have it use your breath,
There is no drinking after death.
Also known as *Rollo, Duke of Normandy,* in collaboration with Jonson and others. *The Bloody Brother* (1616), Act 2, Scene 2

4 Drink to-day, and drown all sorrow;
You shall perhaps not do 't to-morrow.
Also known as *Rollo, Duke of Normandy,* in collaboration with Jonson and others. *The Bloody Brother* (1616), Act 2, Scene 2

5 Three merry boys, and three merry boys,
And three merry boys are we,
As ever did sing in a hempen string
Under the Gallows-Tree.
Song. Also known as *Rollo, Duke of Normandy,* in collaboration with Jonson and others. *The Bloody Brother* (1616), Act 3, Scene 2

6 Death hath so many doors to let out life.
The Custom of the Country (co-written with Philip Massinger; 1647), Act 2, Scene 2

7 He never is alone that is accompanied with noble thoughts.
"Love's Cure," *The Lover's Progress* (1623)

8 Hit the nail on the head.
"Love's Cure," *The Lover's Progress* (1623), Act 2, Scene 1

9 He went away with a flea in's ear.
"Love's Cure," *The Lover's Progress* (1623), Act 3, Scene 3

Fletcher, Phineas (1582–1650) English clergyman and poet

1 Love is like linen often chang'd, the sweeter.
Sicelides (1614), Act 3, Scene 4

2 The coward's weapon, poison.
Sicelides (1614), Act 5, Scene 3

Flintstones, The U.S. television cartoon series

1 Yabba Dabba Do!
1960–67. Catchphrase.

Florian, Jean-Pierre Claris de (1755–94) French playwright and novelist

1 Love's pleasure lasts but a moment; love's sorrow lasts all through life.
Celestine (1784)

Florio, John (1553?–1625) English lexicographer and translator

1 Patience is the best medicine.
First Frutes (1578)

2 England is the paradise of women, the purgatory of men, and the hell of horses.
Second Frutes (1591)

3 Of three things the devil makes his mess:
Of lawyers' tongues, of scriveners' fingers, you the third may guess.
Second Frutes (1591)

Flügel, J. C. (John Carl Flügel; 1884–1955) German-born British psychologist

1 There seems to be no escape from the view that the fundamental purpose of adopting a distinctive dress for the two sexes is to stimulate the sexual instinct.
The Psychology of Clothes (1930), ch. 13

Flusser, Alan U.S. menswear designer and author

1 In the 60s and 70s all the rules were ignored. The notion of doing your own thing was the main theme. I believe that people should do their own thing, but the 60s contributed to an incredible malaise of taste. Proper style was thrown to the wind.
New York Times (October 19, 1985)

Flynn, Errol (Leslie Thomson Flynn; 1909–59) Australian-born U.S. actor

Quotations about Flynn

1 I don't resent his popularity or anything else. Good Lord, I co-starred with Errol Flynn once.
December 1987
Ronald Reagan (b.1911) U.S. president and actor. Attrib.

Quotations by Flynn

2 If there's anyone listening to whom I owe money, I'm prepared to forget it if you are.
Attrib.

3 My problem lies in reconciling my gross habits with my net income.
Attrib.

Fo, Dario (b.1926) Italian playwright and actor

1 We Can't Pay! We Won't Pay!
1974. Play title.

Foch, Ferdinand (1851–1929) French soldier

1 This is not peace: it is an armistice for twenty years.
1919. Remark at the signing of the Treaty of Versailles. *Memoires* (Paul Reynaud; 1963), vol. 2

2 My center is giving way, my right is retreating; situation excellent. I shall attack.
Message sent during the second Battle of the Marne, 1918. Possibly apocryphal. "Ferdinand Foch," *Reputations Ten Years After* (B. H. Liddell Hart; 1928)

3 None but a coward dares to boast that he has never known fear.
Attrib.

4 What a marvellous place to drop one's mother-in-law!
Remark on being shown the Grand Canyon. Attrib.

Folk Verse

1 The sons of the prophet were brave men and bold,
And quite unaccustomed to fear,
But the bravest by far in the ranks of the Shah
Was Abdul the Bulbul Amir.
"Abdul the Bulbul Amir", quoted in *The American Songbook* (Carl Sandburg, ed.; 1927)

2 Matthew, Mark, Luke, and John,
The Bed be blest that I lie on
Four angels to my bed,
Four angels round my head,
One to watch, and one to pray,
And two to bear my soul away.
"A Candle in the Dark" (Thomas Ady; 1656)

3 From ghoulies and ghosties and long-leggety beasties
And things that go bump in the night,
Good Lord, deliver us!
Cornish prayer

4 Sumer is icumen in,
Lhude sing cuccu!
Groweth sed, and bloweth med,
And springth the wude nu.
"Cuckoo Song" (1250?)

5 Gold priests, wooden chalices
in Ireland in Patrick's time
Golden chalices, wooden priests
as the wretched world stands now.
"Epigram" (17th century), quoted in *The New Oxford Book of Irish Verse* (Thomas Kinsella, ed.; 1986)

6 Come landlord, fill the flowing bowl,
Until it doth run over...
For tonight we'll merry, merry be,
Tomorrow we'll be sober.
"Landlord, Fill the Flowing Bowl"

7 Ireland is a woman risen again
From the horrors of reproach...
She was owned for a while by foreigners
She belongs to Irishmen after that.
"Ode for the inauguration of Niall Mor O'Neill as King of Tir Eoghain" (1364), quoted in *The Oxford Illustrated History of Ireland* (R. F. Foster, ed.; 1989)

8 There is a lady sweet and kind,
Was never face so pleased my mind;
I did but see her passing by,
And yet I love her till I die.
Sometimes attributed to Thomas Forde. "Passing By" (1570)

9 I eat my peas with honey
I've done it all my life,
They do taste kind of funny,
But it keeps them on the knife.
Traditional nonsense rhyme. "Peas"

10 To this end, my fathers,
My mothers,
My children:
May you be blessed with light;
May your roads be fulfilled;
May you grow old;
May you be blessed in the chase.
Native American blessing. "Sayatasha's Night Chant", quoted in *The Heath Anthology of American Literature* (Paul Lauter, ed.; 1998), vol. 1

11 O, Shenandoah, I long to hear you
Away, you rolling river.
Song lyric. "Shenandoah"

12 The king sits in Dunfermline toon
Drinking the blude-red wine.
"I saw the new moon late yestreen
Wi' the auld moon in her arm;
And if we gang to sea master,
I fear we'll come to harm."
Scots ballad. "Sir Patrick Spens"

13 The bells of hell go ting-a-ling-a-ling
For you but not for me.
O Death, where is thy sting-a-ling-a-ling,
O Grave, thy victoree?
Sung by British troops, 1914–18 (See Bible: I Corinthians). Song, , st. 5

14 Farewell and adieu to you,
Fair Spanish Ladies,
Farewell and adieu to you, Ladies of Spain.
"Spanish Ladies"

15 Thirty days hath September,
April, June, and November;
All the rest have thirty-one,
Excepting February alone,
Which hath but twenty-eight, in fine,
Till leap year gives it twenty-nine.
Stevins MS (1555?)

16 Swing low sweet chariot,
Comin' for to carry me home,
I looked over Jordan an' what did I see?
A band of Angels coming after me,
Comin' for to carry me home.
Spiritual. Also sung by English Rugby Union supporters. "Sweet Chariot"

17 My father has no older son,
Mulan has no big brother.
I wish to go buy horse and gear
and march to the wars for father.
Referring to a girl who takes the place of her father in military service. "The Ballad of Mulan" (4th century–6th century), quoted in *An Anthology of Chinese Literature* (Stephen Owen, tr.; 1996)

18 O ye'll tak' the high road, and I'll tak' the low road,
And I'll be in Scotland afore ye,
But me and my true love will never meet again,
On the bonnie, bonnie banks o' Loch Lomond.
Folk song lyric attributed to a dying Scottish soldier. "The Bonnie Banks o' Loch Lomond"

19 I'll sing you twelve O.
Green grow the rushes O.
What is your twelve O?
Twelve for the twelve apostles,
Eleven for the eleven who went to heaven,
Ten for the ten commandments,
Nine for the nine bright shiners,
Eight for the eight bold rangers,
Seven for the seven stars in the sky,
Six for the six proud walkers,
Five for the symbol at your door,
Four for the Gospel makers,
Three for the rivals,
Two, two, the lily-white boys,
Clothed all in green O,
One is one and all alone
And ever more shall be so.
"The Dilly Song"

20 The holly and the ivy,
When they are both full grown,
Of all the trees that are in the wood,
The holly bears the crown.
O, the rising of the sun
And the running of the deer,
The playing of the merry organ,
Sweet singing in the choir.
"The Holly and the Ivy"

21 I know two things about the horse,
And one of them is rather coarse.
"The Horse" (20th century)

22 The rabbit has a charming face;
Its private life is a disgrace.
I really dare not name to you
The awful things that rabbits do.
"The Rabbit" (1925)

23 Adieu, adieu, kind friends, adieu, adieu, adieu,
I can no longer stay with you, stay with you.
I'll hang my harp on a weeping willow-tree.
And may the world go well with thee.
"There is a Tavern in the Town"

24 There is a tavern in the town,
And there my dear love sits him down,
And drinks his wine 'mid laughter free,
And never, never thinks of me.
Fare thee well, for I must leave thee,
Do not let this parting grieve thee,
And remember that the best of friends must part.
"There is a Tavern in the Town"

25 There were three ravens sat on a tree,
They were as black as they might be.
The one of them said to his mate,
"Where shall we our breakfast take?"
"The Three Ravens"

26 Now I am a bachelor, I live by myself and I work at the weaving trade,
And the only only thing that I ever did wrong
Was to woo a fair young maid.
She sighed, she cried, she damned near died: she said "What shall I do?"
So I took her into bed and covered up her head
Just to save her from the foggy, foggy dew.
"Weaver's Song"

27 What shall we do with the drunken sailor
Early in the morning?
Hoo-ray and up she rises
Early in the morning.
Traditional English song lyric. "What shall we do with the drunken sailor?"

28 Greensleeves was all my joy,
Greensleeves was my delight,
Greensleeves was my heart of gold,
And who but Lady Greensleeves.
The music has been attributed to Henry VIII. "A New Courtly Sonnet of the Lady Greensleeves, to the new tune of 'Greensleeves'," *A Handful of Pleasant Delights* (1584)

29 As I sat on a sunny bank,
On Christmas Day in the morning,
I spied three ships come sailing by.
"As I Sat on a Sunny Bank" (Traditional)

30 In Scarlet town, where I was born,
There was a fair maid dwellin',
Made every youth cry *Well-a-way!*
Her name was Barbara Allen.
All in the merry month of May,
When green buds they were swellin',
Young Jemmy Grove on his death-bed lay,
For love of Barbara Allen.
So slowly, slowly rase she up,

And slowly she came nigh him,
And when she drew the curtain by
"Young man, I think you're dyin'!"
Traditional English song lyric. *"Barbara Allen's Cruelty"*

31 Here lie I and my four daughters,
Killed by drinking Cheltenham waters.
Had we but stuck to Epsom salts,
We wouldn't have been in these here vaults.
"Cheltenham Waters"

32 Come lasses and lads, get leave of your dads,
And away to the Maypole hie,
For every he has got him a she,
And the fiddler's standing by.
Traditional English song lyric. *"Come Lasses and Lads"*

33 Early one morning, just as the sun was rising.
I heard a maid singing in the valley below:
"Oh, don't deceive me; Oh, never leave me!
How could you use a poor maiden so?"
Traditional English song lyric. *"Early One Morning"*

34 Frankie and Johnny were lovers, my gawd, how they could love,
Swore to be true to each other, true as the stars above;
He was her man, but he done her wrong.
U.S. song lyric. *"Frankie and Johnny"*

35 God rest you merry, gentlemen,
Let nothing you dismay.
"God Rest You Merry"

36 If all the world were paper,
And all the sea were ink,
And all the trees were bread and cheese,
What should we do for drink?
17th century. *"If All the World were Paper"*

37 Love me little, love me long,
Is the burden of my song.
"Love Me Little, Love Me Long" (1570)

38 My Love in her attire doth show her wit,
It doth so well become her:
For every season she hath dressings fit,
For winter, spring, and summer.
No beauty she doth miss,
When all her robes are on;
But beauty's self she is,
When all her robes are gone.
Madrigal (1602?)

39 He that fights and runs away
May live to fight another day.
Musarum Deliciae (17th century)

40 My Bonnie lies over the ocean,
My Bonnie lies over the sea,
My Bonnie lies over the ocean,
Oh, bring back my Bonnie to me.
"My Bonnie Lies Over the Ocean"

41 In Adam's fall
We sinnéd all.
New England Primer (1781)

42 My Book and Heart
Must never part.
New England Primer (1781)

43 Now I lay me down to sleep,
I pray the Lord my soul to keep.
If I should die before I wake,
I pray the Lord my soul to take.
New England Primer (1781)

44 The animals went in one by one,
There's one more river to cross.
"One More River"

45 God be in my head,
And in my understanding;
God be in my eyes,
And in my looking;
God be in my mouth,
And in my speaking;
God be in my heart,
And in my thinking;
God be at my end,
And at my departing.
Sarum Missal (11th century)

46 Thou art mine, I am thine,
Know thou this in joy and tine.
Thou art locked
Within my heart,
Lost the key that let thee in,
Needs must thou ever dwell therein.
12th century. One of the earliest known German love poems. Quoted in *A German Treasury* (Stanley Mason, tr.; 1993)

47 As the breath of the wind sweeps through the harp and the chords sing,
So the breath of the Lord's spirit sweeps through my members, and I sing in his love.
2nd century. The Odes of Solomon, inspired by the biblical *Song of Songs* but judged to be heretical, are thought possibly to be of Gnostic Christian authorship. Quoted in *Odes and Psalms of Solomon* (R. Harris and A. Mingana; 1920), 6

48 Mother makes brandy from cherries;
Pop distills whiskey and gin;
Sister sells wine from grapes on the vine—
Good grief, how the money rolls in!
Song lyric about Prohibition. Quoted in *Speaking Freely* (Stuart Berg Flexner and Anne H. Soukhanov; 1997)

49 Two ads a day keeps the sack away.
Saying among employees of the Saatchi & Saatchi advertising agency. Quoted in *The Book of Business Quotations* (Eugene Weber; 1991)

50 Get up at five, have lunch at nine,
Supper at five, retire at nine.
And you will live to ninety-nine.
Quoted in *The Complete Works of François Rabelais* (Sir Thomas Urquhart and Peter Motteux, tr.; 1927), bk. 4, ch. 64

51 My Lord Archbishop, what a scold you are
And when a man is down, how bold you are,

Of Christian charity how scant you are
You auld Lang Swine, how full of cant you are!
Archbishop Lang of Canterbury (Cantuar) was one of the chief opponents of Edward VIII's marriage to Mrs. Wallis Simpson (June, 3, 1937). *The Faber Book of English History in Verse* (Kenneth Baker; 1988)

52 Jack the Ripper's dead,
And lying in his bed.
He cut his throat
With Sunlight Soap.
Jack the Ripper's dead.
British schoolchildren's rhyme. *The Faber Book of English History in Verse* (Kenneth Baker; 1988)

53 I am of Ireland
And of the holy land of Ireland
Good sir, I pray you
Out of saintly charity
Come and dance with me
In Ireland.
14th century. Quoted in "Icham of Irlaunde," *The Faber Book of Irish Verse* (John Montague, ed.; 1974)

54 He that would be a stallion good
And can set straight his hood,
That monk shall have, without fear,
Twelve new wives each year.
14th century. Satirizing religious life. Quoted in "The Land of Cockaigne," *The Faber Book of Irish Verse* (John Montague, ed., Thomas Kinsella, tr.; 1974)

55 Three smiles that are worse than griefs: the smile of snow melting, the smile of your wife when another man has been with her, the smile of a mastiff about to spring.
9th century. Irish epigram. Quoted in "Triads," *The Faber Book of Irish Verse* (John Montague, ed., Thomas Kinsella, tr.; 1974)

56 I sometimes think I'd rather crow
And be a rooster than to roost
And be a crow. But I dunno.
Quoted in "I Sometimes Think I'd Rather Crow," *The Penguin Book of American Verse* (Geoffrey Moore, ed.; 1977)

57 Birth and death is a grave event;
How transient is life!
Every minute is to be judged,
Time waits for nobody.
Summons to communal meditation in a Zen monastery. Quoted in *The Spirit of Zen* (Alan Watts; 1991)

58 The law doth punish man or woman
That steals a goose from off the common,
But lets the greater felon loose
That steals the common from the goose.
1821. Referring to the General Enclosure Act (1801), in which common land was fenced and placed under private ownership. Quoted in *The Tickler Magazine* (February 1, 1821)

59 Lizzie Borden took an axe
And gave her mother forty whacks;
When she saw what she had done
She gave her father forty-one!
On August 4, 1892, in Fall River, Massachusetts, Lizzie Borden was acquitted of the murder of her stepmother and her father.

60 St. Swithin's Day, if thou dost rain, for forty days it will remain; St. Swithin's Day, if thou be fair, for forty days 'twill rain no more.
Proverb.

61 When Israel was in Egypt land,
Let my people go,
Oppressed so hard they could not stand,
Let my people go.
Go down, Moses,
Way-down in Egypt land,
Tell old Pharaoh
To let my people go.
Song lyric of African slaves in the United States.

62 We drove the Boche across the Rhine,
The Kaiser from his throne.
Oh, Lafayette, we've paid our debt,
For Christ's sake, send us home.
1918. U.S. World War I army song lyric. The Boche was the Allied soldiers' slang word for the German army during World War I. Kaiser Wilhelm (1859–1941) was the German emperor. The Marquis de Lafayette (1757–1834) fought on the side of the colonists during the American Revolution (1775–83) and later took a prominent part in the French Revolution (1789–99).

63 Hitler
Has only got one ball!
Goering
Has two, but very small!
Himmler
Has something similar,
But poor old Goebbels
Has no balls at all!
1939–45. World War II song, to the tune of "Colonel Bogey."

64 When I am dead, and laid in grave,
And all my bones are rotten,
By this may I remembered be
When I should be forgotten.
1736.

Follett, Mary Parker (1868–1933) U.S. social worker and management theorist

1 Germany's greatest power was her economic impotence.
Referring to Germany's international position after World War I. Lecture, Bureau of Business (January 1925)

2 Compromise is...on the same plane as fighting. War will continue—between capital and labor, between nation and nation—until we relinquish the ideas of concession and compromise.
The New State (1920)

3 The essence of democracy is creating. The technique of democracy is group organization.
The New State (1920)

Fonda, Jane (b.1937) U.S. actor and political activist

1 I am not a do-gooder. I am a revolutionary. A revolutionary woman.
Comment, *Los Angeles Weekly* (1971)

2 But the whole point of liberation is that you get out. Restructure your life. Act by yourself.
Quoted in "At Home with Tom and Jane", *Los Angeles Weekly* (Danae Brook; November 28, 1980)

Fontenelle, Bernard le Bovier, Sieur de (1657–1757) French philosopher

1 In vain we shall penetrate more and more deeply the secrets of the structure of the human body, we shall not dupe nature; we shall die as usual.
Dialogues des morts (1907?), Dialogue 5

2 I feel nothing, apart from a certain difficulty in continuing to exist.
1757. Remark made on his deathbed, at the age of 99. *Famous Last Words* (Barnaby Conrad; 1962)

3 We anatomists are like the porters in Paris, who are acquainted with the narrowest and most distant streets, but who know nothing of what takes place in the houses!
Attrib.

4 It is high time for me to depart, for at my age I now begin to see things as they really are.
1757. Remark on his deathbed, at the age of 99. Attrib.

Fonteyn, Margot, Dame (Margot Fonteyn de Arias, born Margaret Hookham; 1919–91) British ballet dancer

Quotations about Fonteyn

1 No one could be a more severe critic of Margot than Margot...She had done the performance, had received thunderous applause and ovations, yet when the curtain came down for good, she threw herself on the floor in tears because she felt she had danced it so badly.
Martha Graham (1893–1991) U.S. dancer and choreographer. *Blood Memory* (1991)

Quotations by Fonteyn

2 I'm sure if everyone knew how physically cruel dancing really is, nobody would watch—only those people who enjoy bullfights!
Quoted in *The Art of Margot Fonteyn* (Keith Money; 1965)

3 One cannot go prettily deranged; one needs to go out of one's mind with utter realism. The great jump in style to the second Act is an enormous stumbling block...Audiences...last century could accept such fanciful situations, just as they could accept crumbling ruins at the bottom of their gardens—ruins which had been built...only a year earlier.
Said about dancing *Giselle*. Quoted in *The Art of Margot Fonteyn* (Keith Money; 1965)

Foot, Lord, Baron Caradon (Hugh Mackintosh Foot; 1907–90) British administrator

1 Thirty years' imprisonment is...a declaration of society's intellectual bankruptcy in the field of penology.
Observer, London (March 9, 1969), "Sayings of the Week"

Foot, Michael (Michael Mackintosh Foot; b.1913) British politician and writer

1 A Royal Commission is a broody hen sitting on a china egg.
Speech to the British Parliament (1964)

2 Men of power have not time to read; yet men who do not read are unfit for power.
Debts Of Honour (1980)

3 Karl Marx wasn't a Marxist all the time. He got drunk in the Tottenham Court Road.
Behind The Image (Susan Barnes; 1974)

4 The members of our secret service have apparently spent so much time looking under the beds for Communists, they haven't had time to look in the bed.
1963. Referring to the Profumo affair. Attrib.

Foote, Samuel (1720–77) British actor and playwright

1 For as the old saying is,
When house and land are gone and spent
Then learning is most excellent.
Taste (1752), Act 1, Scene 1

2 Born in a cellar, and living in a garret.
The Author (1757), Act 2

3 So she went into the garden to cut a cabbage-leaf; to make an apple-pie; and at the same time a great she-bear, coming up the street, pops its head into the shop. What! no soap? So he died, and she very imprudently married the barber; and there were present the Picninnies, and the Joblillies, and the Garyalies, and the grand Panjandrum himself, with the little round button at top, and they all fell to playing the game of catch as catch can, till the gun powder ran out at the heels of their boots.
Nonsense composed to test the actor Charles Macklin's claim that he could memorize anything. *Harry and Lucy Concluded* (Maria Edgeworth; 1825), vol. 2

4 He is not only dull in himself, but the cause of dullness in others.
Referring to a dull law lord. Parody of Falstaff's famous line in *Henry IV, Part 2*: "I am not only witty in myself, but the cause that is wit in other men." *Life of Samuel Johnson* (James Boswell; 1791), Sunday, 30 March 1783, Aetat. 74

Forbes, Malcolm S. (1919–90) U.S. publisher

1 Risk-taking is an integral and intrinsic part of success or living a full life.
Quoted in *Tactics: The Art and Science of Success* (Edward de Bono; 1985)

Forbes, Miss C. F. (1817–1911) British writer

1 The sense of being well-dressed gives a feeling of inward tranquillity which religion is powerless to bestow.
Quoted in *Letters and Social Aims* (R. W. Emerson; 1876)

Forbes, Steve (Malcolm Stevenson Forbes, Jr.; b.1947) U.S. publisher

1 People who never get carried away, should be.
Town and Country (November 1976)

Forché, Carolyn U.S. poet

1 Every epoch bears its own ending within itself.
Fields of rape, canola fields, the white-eyed, walking dead.
The Angel of History (1991)

2 In every war someone puts the cigarette in the corpse's mouth.
The Angel of History (1991)

3 There is a cyclone fence between
ourselves and the slaughter and behind it
we hover in a calm protected world like
netted fish, exactly like netted fish.
It is either the beginning or the end
of the world, and the choice is ourselves
or nothing.
"Ourselves or Nothing," *The Country Between Us* (1981)

4 It was simple. She had come
to flesh out the memory of the poet
whose body was never found.
Referring to a refugee returning to her homeland in El Salvador after the civil war (1979–80). "The Island," *The Country Between Us* (1981)

Ford, Anna (b.1943) British broadcaster

1 Let's face it, there are no plain women on television.
Observer, London (September 23, 1979)

2 It is men who face the biggest problems in the future, adjusting to their new and complicated role.
Remark. (January 1981)

Ford, Ford Madox (Ford Hermann Hueffer; 1873–1939) British novelist

1 Only two classes of books are of universal appeal. The very best and the very worst.
Joseph Conrad (1924)

Ford, Gerald (Gerald Rudolph Ford; b.1913) U.S. president

Quotations about Ford

1 He looks like the guy in a science fiction movie who is the first to see the Creature.
David Frye (b.1934) U.S. comedian. Attrib.

2 Jerry Ford is so dumb that he can't fart and chew gum at the same time.
Lyndon Baines Johnson (1908–73) U.S. president. Quoted in *A Ford, Not a Lincoln: The Decline of American Political Leadership* (R. Reeves; 1976), ch. 1

Quotations by Ford

3 I am a Ford, not a Lincoln.
December 6, 1973. Said on taking the vice-presidential oath. *Washington Post* (December 7, 1973)

4 I guess it proves that in America anyone can be President.
Referring to his taking up the position of president after Nixon's resignation. *A Ford, Not a Lincoln* (Richard Reeves; 1975), ch. 4

5 Our long national nightmare is over. Our constitution works.
August 9, 1974. Remark on being sworn in as president following the resignation of Richard Nixon. *Gerald R. Ford* (J. G. Lankevich; 1977)

Ford, Harrison (b.1942) U.S. film actor

1 Los Angeles is where you've got to be an actor. You have no choice. You go there or New York. I flipped a coin...It came up New York. So I flipped it again.
Cinema (1981)

Ford, Henry (1863–1947) U.S. car manufacturer

Quotations about Ford

1 Henry Ford declared that history was bunk because it diminished the past he had come to venerate.
Oscar Handlin (b.1915) U.S. historian. *Truth in History* (1979)

Quotations by Ford

2 History is more or less bunk. It's tradition. We don't want tradition. We want to live in the present and the only history that is worth a tinker's damn is the history we make today.
Chicago Tribune (May 25, 1916)

3 The whole secret of a successful life is to find out what it is one's destiny to do, and then do it.
"Success," *Forum* (October 1928)

4 A dollar that stays 100 cents is as necessary as a pound that stays 16 ounces and a yard that stays 36 inches.
My Life and Work (1922)

5 It is not work that men object to, but drudgery. We must drive out drudgery wherever we find it. We shall never be wholly civilized until we remove the treadmill from the daily job.
My Life and Work (1922)

6 Money is like an arm or a leg—use it or lose it.
New York Times (1931)

7 Any color, so long as it's black.
Referring to the color options offered for the Model-T Ford car. *Ford* (Allan Nevins; 1957), vol. 2, ch. 15

8 I did not say it *was* bunk. It was bunk to *me*...I did not need it very bad.
Referring to history. Attrib. "Expansion and Challenge," *Ford* (Allan Nevins and Frank Hill; 1954)

9 Time waste differs from material waste in that there can be no salvage.
Quoted in *Key Management Ideas* (Stuart Crainer; 1996)

10 If you think you can or think you can't you're probably right.
Quoted in *Survival of the Smartest* (Haim Mendelson and Johannes Ziegler; 1999)

11 How come when I want a pair of hands I get a human being as well?
Quoted in *The Witch Doctors* (John Micklethwait and Adrian Wooldridge; 1996)

12 A business that makes nothing but money is a poor kind of business.
Attrib.

13 Accounting is a malicious extension of the banking conspiracy.
Attrib.

14 Exercise is bunk. If you are healthy, you don't need it: if you are sick, you shouldn't take it.
Attrib.

Ford, John (1586–1640?) English playwright

1 I am a mushroom
On whom the dew of heaven drops now and then.
The Broken Heart (1633), Act 1, Scene 3

2 Tempt not the stars, young man, thou canst not play
With the severity of fate.
The Broken Heart (1633), Act 1, Scene 3

3 He hath shook hands with time.
The Broken Heart (1633), Act 5, Scene 2

4 Tell us, pray, what devil
This melancholy is, which can transform
Men into monsters.
The Lady's Trial (1639), Act 3, Scene 1

5 'Tis Pity She's a Whore
1633. Play title.

Ford, John (Sean O'Feeney; 1895–1973) U.S. filmmaker

1 It is easier to get an actor to be a cowboy than to get a cowboy to be an actor.
Attrib.

Ford, Richard (b.1944) U.S. writer

1 Leaving reminds us what we can part with and what we can't, then offers us something new to look forward to, to dream about.
"An Urge for Going," *Harper's* (February 1992)

2 Reading is always a good way to define pleasure anew.
The Granta Book of the Long Story (Richard Ford, ed.; 1998), introduction

3 Married life requires shared mystery even when all the facts are known.
The Sportswriter (1986)

Foreman, George (b.1949) U.S. boxer

1 I have the body of a man half my age. Unfortunately, he's in terrible shape.
Guardian, London (December 28, 1996), Weekend

2 Muhammad Ali was so quick he would click off the light and be in bed before the room got dark.
Times, London (October 18, 1989)

Forgy, Howell Maurice (1908–83) U.S. naval chaplain

1 Praise the Lord and pass the ammunition!
December 7, 1941. Remark made during the Japanese attack on Pearl Harbor, December 1941. Later the title of a song by Frank Loesser, 1942. *New York Times* (November 1, 1942)

Formby, George (1904–61) British comedian and singer

1 I'm leaning on a lamp-post at the corner of the street,
In case a certain little lady walks by.
Song lyric. "Leaning on a Lamp-post" (1937)

Forrest, Nathan Bedford (1821–77) U.S. general

1 I got there fustest with the mostest.
1862. Popular misquotation of his remark after his successful capture of Murfreesboro (1862–63); his actual words were, "I just took the short cut and got there first with the most men." *A Civil War Treasury of Tales, Legends and Folklore* (Benjamin Albert Botkin, ed.; 1960)

2 Ah, colonel, all's fair in love and war, you know.
Remark to a captured enemy officer who had been tricked into surrendering. *A Civil War Treasury of Tales, Legends and Folklore* (Benjamin Albert Botkin, ed.; 1960)

Forster, E. M. (Edward Morgan Forster; 1879–1970) British novelist

1 I should have been a more famous writer if I had written or rather published more, but sex has prevented the latter.
Diary entry (December 31, 1964), quoted in *The Life to Come* (Oliver Stallybrass, ed.; 1972), introduction

2 My defence at the Last Judgement would be "I was trying to connect up and use all the fragments I was born with."
Letter to Forest Reid (1915), quoted in *A Queer Reader* (Patrick Higgins, ed.; 1993)

3 Nothing is more obdurate to artistic treatment than the carnal, but it has to be got in. I'm sure: everything has to be got in.
Letter to Siegfried Sassoon (1920), quoted in *A Queer Reader* (Patrick Higgins, ed.; 1993)

4 I want to love a strong young man of the lower classes and be loved by him and even hurt by him. That is my ticket.
Personal memorandum (1935), quoted in *The Life to Come* (Oliver Stallybrass, ed.; 1972), introduction

5 It is not that the Englishman can't feel—it is that he is afraid to feel. He has been taught at his public school that feeling is bad form. He must not express great joy or sorrow, or even open his mouth too wide when he talks—his pipe might fall out if he did.
"Notes on the English Character," *Abinger Harvest* (1936)

6 They go forth into it with well-developed bodies, fairly developed minds, and undeveloped hearts.
Referring to public schoolboys going into the world. "Notes on the English Character," *Abinger Harvest* (1936)

7 Everything must be like something, so what is this like?
"Our Diversions," *Abinger Harvest* (1936), "The Doll House"

8 The so-called white races are really pinko-gray.
A Passage to India (1924), ch. 7

9 God is Love. Is this the final message of India?
A Passage to India (1924), ch. 33

10 Yes—oh dear, yes—the novel tells a story.
Aspects of the Novel (1927), ch. 2

11 The very poor are unthinkable and only to be approached by the statistician and the poet.
Howards End (1910)

12 Beethoven's Fifth Symphony is the most sublime noise that has ever penetrated into the ear of man.
Howards End (1910), ch. 5

13 All men are equal—all men, that is to say, who possess umbrellas.
Howards End (1910), ch. 6

14 Personal relations are the important thing for ever and ever, and not this outer life of telegrams and anger.
Howards End (1910), ch. 19

15 Only connect! That was the whole of her sermon. Only connect the prose and the passion, and both will be exalted, and human love will be seen at its height.
"Only Connect!" is famous as the epigraph to *Howards End*. It also appears in the text of the novel. *Howards End* (1910), ch. 22

16 Death destroys a man, the idea of Death saves him.
Howards End (1910), ch. 27

17 Spoon feeding in the long run teaches us nothing but the shape of the spoon.
Observer, London (October 7, 1951), "Sayings of the Week"

18 Creative writers are always greater than the causes that they represent.
1943. "Gide and George," *Two Cheers for Democracy* (1951)

19 I hate the idea of causes, and if I had to choose between betraying my country and betraying my friend, I hope I should have the guts to betray my country.
"What I Believe," *Two Cheers for Democracy* (1951)

20 The memory of birth and the expectation of death always lurk within the human being, making him separate from his fellows and consequently capable of intercourse with them.
"What I Believe," *Two Cheers For Democracy* (1951)

Forte, Charles, Baron Forte of Ripley (b.1908) British hotelier

1 I may be wealthier than most but I still believe that real success is simply being able to put in a good day's work...and then go to sleep knowing that you have not—and will not—cause anything wrong to happen to anyone else.
Interview, *Daily Mail*, London (November 1, 1986)

2 When a taxi driver recognizes me, I feel I really belong.
Quoted in *Financial Times*, London (November 21, 1960)

Forten, James (1766–1842) U.S. abolitionist

1 Whilst so much is doing in the world, to ameliorate the condition of mankind, and the spirit of Freedom is marching with rapid strides, and causing tyrants to tremble, may America awake from the apathy in which she has long slumbered. She must, sooner or later, fall in with the irresistible current.
Letter to William Lloyd Garrison (December 31, 1830), quoted in *A Documentary History of the Negro People in the United States* (Herbert Aptheker; 1951), vol 1

Fortescue, John, Sir (1385?–1479?) English jurist

1 The greatest harm that cometh of a king's poverty is, that he shall by necessity be forced to find exquisite means of getting goods, as to put in default some of his subjects that be innocent, and upon the rich men more than the poor, because they may the better pay.
The Governance of England (1470?)

2 The king's council was wont to be chosen of the great princes, and of the greatest lords of the land, both spiritual and temporal....Wherethrough, when they came together they were so occupied with their own matters that they attended but little, and other whiles nothing, to the king's matters.
The Governance of England (1470?)

3 There is scarcely a man learned in the laws to be found in the realm who is not noble or sprung of noble lineage.
The Governance of England (1470?)

Fortunatus (Venantius Honorius Clementianus; 540?–600?) Italian poet and bishop

1 The banners of the king advance, the mystery of the cross shines bright; where his life went through with death, and from death brought forth life.
Hymn. "Vexilla Regis" (6th century)

Fortune, Timothy Thomas (1856–1928) U.S. journalist and orator

1 Let the history of the past be spread before the eyes of a candid and thoughtful people; let the bulky roll of misgovernment, incompetence, and blind folly be enrolled on the one hand, and then turn to the terrors of the midnight assassin and the lawless deeds which desecrate the sunlight of noontide.
Address to the Colored Press Association, Washington D.C. (June 27, 1882)

2 Necessity knows no law and discriminates in favor of no man or race.
Black and White: Land, Labor and Politics in the South (1884)

Fosdick, Henry Emerson (1878–1969) U.S. religious leader

1 An atheist is a man who has no invisible means of support.
Attrib.

Foss, Lukas (Lucas Fuchs; b.1922) German-born U.S. composer, conductor, and pianist

1 Composing is like making love to the future.
1975. Attrib.

Fosse, Bob (Robert Louis Fosse; 1927–87) U.S. choreographer and director

1 I've been accused of editing too much. But audiences get bored so quickly.
1980. *Cue* (February 1, 1980)

2 Directors are never in short supply of girlfriends.
Quoted in *Film Yearbook* (1985)

Foster, George E., Sir (George Eulas Foster; 1847–1931) Canadian classicist and statesman

1 In these somewhat troublesome days when the great Mother Empire stands splendidly isolated in Europe.
Speech to the Canadian Parliament (January 16, 1896)

Foster, Stephen (Stephen Collins Foster; 1826–64) U.S. composer of popular songs

1 Gwine to run all night!
Gwine to run all day!
I bet my money on the bob-tail nag.
Somebody bet on the bay.
Song. "Camptown Races" (1850)

2 Weep no more, my lady,
Oh! weep no more today!
We will sing one song for the old Kentucky Home,
For the old Kentucky Home far away.
Song. "My Old Kentucky Home" (1853)

3 O, Susanna! O, don't you cry for me,
I've come from Alabama, wid my banjo on my knee.
Song lyric. "O, Susanna" (1848)

4 I'm coming, I'm coming,
For my head is bending low
I hear their gentle voices calling, "Poor old Joe."
Also known as "Old Black Joe." "Poor Old Joe" (1860), st. 3

5 'Way down upon the Swanee River,
Far, far away,
There's where my heart is turning ever:
There's where the old folks stay.
All up and down the whole creation
Sadly I roam,
Still longing for the old plantation,
And for the old folks at home.
Song. "The Old Folks at Home" (1851), st. 1

Foucault, Michel (1926–84) French philosopher

1 A source of strong emotions and terrifying images which it arouses through fears of the Beyond, Catholicism frequently provokes madness; it generates delirious beliefs, entertains hallucinations, leads men to despair.
Madness and Civilization (1967)

2 For the nineteenth century, the initial model of madness would be to believe oneself to be God, while for the preceding centuries it had been to deny God.
Madness and Civilization (1967)

3 It is only by an artifice of language that the same meaning can be attributed to "illnesses of the body" and "illnesses of the mind".
Mental Illness and Psychology (1976)

4 Psychology can never tell the truth about madness because it is madness that holds the truth of psychology.
Mental Illness and Psychology (1976)

5 The world projected in the fantasy of delusion imprisons the consciousness that projects it.
Mental Illness and Psychology (1976)

6 Punishment has passed from being an art of unsupportable sensations to an economy of suspended rights.
Surveiller et punir (1975)

7 The coming into being of the notion of "author" constitutes the privileged moment of individualization in the history of ideas.
"What is an Author?," *The Foucault Reader* (1984)

Fourier, Charles (Charles François Marie Fourier; 1772–1837) French social scientist

1 The extension of women's rights is the basic principle of all social progress.
Theory of Four Movements (1808), vol. 2, ch. 4

Fowler, Gene (1890–1960) U.S. author

1 An editor should have a pimp for a brother, so he'd have somebody to look up to.
Attrib.

2 I always get the heaves in the presence of critics.
Attrib.

3 The best way to become a successful writer is to read good writing, remember it, and then forget where you remember it from.
Attrib.

Fowler, William Wyche (b.1940) U.S. politician

1 People have power when people think they have power.
Attrib.

Fowles, John (b.1926) British novelist

1 There are many reasons why novelists write, but they all have one thing in common—a need to create an alternative world.
Sunday Times Magazine, London (October 2, 1977)

2 The most odious of concealed narcissisms—prayer.
The Aristos (1980)

3 In essence the Renaissance was simply the green end of one of civilization's hardest winters.
The French Lieutenant's Woman (1969), ch. 10

4 We all write poems; it is simply that poets are the ones who write in words.
The French Lieutenant's Woman (1969), ch. 19

Fox, Charles James (1749–1806) British politician

1 How much the greatest event it is that ever happened in the world! and how much the best!
Referring to the fall of the Bastille, July 14, 1789. Letter to Richard Fitzpatrick (July 30, 1789), quoted in *Life and Times of C. J. Fox* (Lord John Russell; 1859), vol. 2

2 Kings govern by means of popular assemblies only when they cannot do without them.
Speech to the British Parliament (October 31, 1776)

3 He was uniformly of an opinion which, though not a popular one, he was ready to aver, that the right of governing was not property but a trust.
1785. Referring to William Pitt's plans for parliamentary reform. *C. J. Fox* (J. L. Hammond; 1903), ch. 4

4 I die happy.
1806. Last words. *Life and Times of C. J. Fox* (Lord John Russell; 1860), vol. 3

Fox, George (1624–91) English religious leader

1 When the Lord sent me forth into the world, He forbade me to put off my hat to any high or low.
Journal (1694)

2 I told them I lived in the virtue of that life and power that took away the occasion of all wars.
1651. Remark when offered a captaincy in Commonwealth army, against the King. *Journal* (1694)

Fox, Harrison W., Jr. U.S. author

1 A basic truism in Washington is that there is someone who knows everything about the thing you want to know.
Doing Business in Washington (co-written with Martin Schnitzer; 1981)

2 American corporations should abandon their old adversary role and adopt an advocacy strategy in their dealings with government.
Doing Business in Washington (co-written with Martin Schnitzer; 1981)

3 As long as we have a democratic system of government, there will be people seeking favors.
Doing Business in Washington (co-written with Martin Schnitzer; 1981)

4 Corporate leaders are increasingly seeing their jobs as quasi-public.
Doing Business in Washington (co-written with Martin Schnitzer; 1981)

5 Effective collaboration between government and business is a *sine qua non* for dealing with most of the major problems facing American society today.
Doing Business in Washington (co-written with Martin Schnitzer; 1981)

6 There is a general absence of political competence within most business organizations that results in an inability to attract public support for issues affecting the interest of business.
Doing Business in Washington (co-written with Martin Schnitzer; 1981)

7 Timing can be everything in selling an idea.
Doing Business in Washington (co-written with Martin Schnitzer; 1981)

8 Usually it is the accumulation of small gratuities rather than any direct bribe that gradually obligates the people in power.
Doing Business in Washington (co-written with Martin Schnitzer; 1981)

Fox, Henry Stephen (1791–1846) British diplomat

1 I am so changed that my oldest creditors would hardly know me.
Remark after an illness. Quoted in *Letter to John Murray* (Lord Byron; May 8, 1817)

Fox, Muriel (b.1928) U.S. business executive

1 Total commitment to family and total commitment to career is possible, but fatiguing.
New Woman (October 1971)

Frame, Janet (b.1924) New Zealand novelist and short-story writer

1 Many patients confined in other wards of Seacliff had no name, only a nickname, no past no future, only an imprisoned Now, an eternal Is-land without its accompanying horizons, foot or handhold, or even without its everchanging sky.
An Angel at my Table (1984)

France, Anatole (Jacques Anatole François Thibault; 1844–1924) French novelist, poet, and critic

1 It is only the poor who are forbidden to beg.
Crainquebille (1901)

2 To disarm the strong and arm the weak would be to change the social order which it's my job to preserve. Justice is the means by which established injustices are sanctioned.
Crainquebille (1901)

3 Without lies humanity would perish of despair and boredom.
The Bloom of Life (1922)

4 The Arab who builds himself a hut out of the marble fragments of a temple in Palmyra is more philosophical than all the curators of the museums in London, Munich, or Paris.
The Crime of Sylvestre Bonnard (1881)

5 Man is so made that he can only find relaxation from one kind of labor by taking up another.
The Crime of Sylvestre Bonnard (1881), pt. 2, ch. 4

6 Christianity has done a great deal for love by making a sin of it.
The Garden of Epicurus (1894)

7 The wonder is, not that the field of the stars is so vast, but that man has measured it.
The Garden of Epicurus (1894)

8 The majestic egalitarianism of the law, which forbids rich and poor alike to sleep under bridges, to beg in the streets, and to steal bread.
The Red Lily (1894), ch. 7

9 To die for an idea is to place a pretty high price upon conjectures.
The Revolt of the Angels (Mrs. Wilfrid Jackson, tr.; 1933)

10 It is only the poor who pay cash, and that not from virtue, but because they are refused credit.
Quoted in *A Cynic's Breviary* (J. R. Solly; 1925)

11 When a thing has been said and said well, have no scruple. Take it and copy it.
The Routledge Dictionary of Quotations (Robert Andrews, ed.; 1987)

12 It is his reasonable conversation which mostly frightens us in a madman.
Attrib.

13 One must never lose time in vainly regretting the past nor in complaining about the changes which cause us discomfort, for change is the very essence of life.
Attrib.

Francesca, Piero della (1420?–92) Italian painter

1 Although praise is given to many who are without perspective, it is given with false judgment by those who have no awareness of the potential of the art.
De Prospectiva Pingendi (G. N. Fasola, ed.; 1942)

Francis I, King of France (1494–1547) French monarch

1 Of all I had, only honor and life have been spared.
Referring to his defeat at the Battle of Pavia; usually misquoted as "All is lost save honor." Letter to his mother, Louise of Savoy (February 24, 1525)

Francis de Sales, Saint (1567–1622) French churchman and writer

1 Big fires flare up in a wind, but little ones are blown out unless they are carried in under cover.
Introduction to The Devout Life (1609), pt. 3, ch. 34

Francis Ferdinand, Archduke of Austria (also known as Franz Ferdinand; 1863–1914) Austrian heir to the Austro-Hungarian throne

1 Sophie dear, don't die! Stay alive for our children.
June 28, 1914. Said seconds after he and his wife were shot by the Serb nationalist Gavrilo Princip. Quoted in *Europe: A History* (Norman Davies; 1996), ch. 10

Francis Joseph I, Emperor of Austria (also known as Franz Josef; 1830–1916) Austrian monarch

1 Nothing has been spared in this world.
Said upon learning of the assassination of his wife, the Empress Elizabeth. Remark (September 10, 1898)

2 You see in me the last monarch of the old school.
Remark to Theodore Roosevelt (1910)

Franck, Sebastian (1499?–1542?) German theologian

1 The world wants to be deceived.
"Paradoxi ucenta Octoginta," *Paradoxa* (1534), no. 238

Franco, Francisco, General (1892–1975) Spanish general and dictator

Quotations about Franco

1 I picked Franco out when he was a nobody. He has double-crossed and deceived me at every turn.
Alfonso XIII (1886–1941) Spanish monarch. Quoted in *Franco* (Paul Preston; 1993)

Quotations by Franco

2 I must not conquer but liberate and liberating also means redeeming.
Remark (1937), quoted in *Franco* (Paul Preston; 1993)

3 In civil war, a systematic occupation of territory accompanied by the necessary purge is preferable to a rapid rout of the enemy armies which leaves the country still infested with enemies.
Remark (1937), quoted in *Franco* (Paul Preston; 1993)

4 If I didn't act with an iron hand, this would soon be chaos.
In reply to a protest by Vicente, his one-time contemporary at the Toledo military academy, at the execution of two soldiers who had committed a robbery and deserted service in Morocco. Remark (1921), quoted in *Franco* (Paul Preston; 1993)

5 Our war is not a civil war...but a Crusade...Yes, our war is a religious war. We who fight, whether Christians or Muslims, are soldiers of God and we are not fighting against men but against atheism and materialism.
Referring to the Nationalist campaign in the Spanish Civil War (from 1936). Remark (November 16, 1937), quoted in *Franco* (Paul Preston; 1993)

6 One Fatherland, One State, One Leader.
1936. Slogan. This deliberately echoed Hitler's *Ein Volk, ein Reich, ein Führer.* All newspapers in the Nationalist regions of Spain had to carry these words under the masthead. Quoted in *Franco* (Paul Preston; 1993)

Frank, Anne (1929–45) German diarist

1 I soothe my conscience now with the thought that it is better for hard words to be on paper than that Mummy should carry them in her heart.
January 2, 1944. *Anne Frank: The Diary of a Young Girl* (1947)

2 Laziness may *appear* attractive, but work *gives* satisfaction.
July 6, 1944. *Anne Frank: The Diary of a Young Girl* (1947)

3 Mummy herself has told us that she looked upon us more as her friends than her daughters. Now that is all very fine, but still, a friend can't take a mother's place. I need my mother as an example which I can follow, I want to be able to respect her.
January 15, 1944. *Anne Frank: The Diary of a Young Girl* (1947)

4 Parents can only give good advice or put them on the right paths, but the final forming of a person's character lies in their own hands.
July 15, 1944. *Anne Frank: The Diary of a Young Girl* (1947)

5 We all live with the objective of being happy; our lives are all different and yet the same.
July 6, 1944. *Anne Frank: The Diary of a Young Girl* (1947)

6 I must, indeed, try hard to control the talking habit, but I'm afraid that little can be done, as my case is hereditary. My mother, too, is fond of chatting, and has handed this weakness down to me.
August 12, 1943. "A Geometry Lesson," *Anne Frank: The Diary of a Young Girl* (1947)

7 I felt nothing, nothing but fear; I could neither eat nor sleep—fear clawed at my mind and body and shook me.
March 25, 1944. "Fear," *Anne Frank: The Diary of a Young Girl* (1947)

8 It was a terrible time through which I was living. The war raged about us, and nobody knew whether or not he would be alive the next hour.
March 25, 1944. "Fear," *Anne Frank: The Diary of a Young Girl* (1947)

Frankenthaler, Helen (b.1928) U.S. painter

1 I think when you're really painting, involved in a painting, what goes on in the art world doesn't matter. When you're making what you have to you're totally involved in the act.
Interview, *Artforum* (Henry Geldzahler; October 1965), 4, no. 2

2 I think relatively, there probably is chance and risk in all the history of painting. No matter how fine or meticulous or tortured a picture may be in execution, the risk or chance of its working or not is always there, no matter what the method.
Interview, *Arts magazine* (Cindy Nemser; November 1971)

3 Just as in relations with people, as in art, if you always stick to style, manners, and what will work, and you're never caught off guard, then some beautiful experiences never happen.
Interview, *Arts magazine* (Cindy Nemser; November 1971)

Frankfurter, Felix (1882–1965) U.S. jurist and teacher

1 There is no inevitability in history except as men make it.
Attrib. *Saturday Review* (October 30, 1954)

Franklin, Benjamin (1706–90) U.S. statesman and scientist

Quotations about Franklin

1 Franklin appeared at court in the dress of an American cultivator. His straight unpowdered hair, his round hat, his brown cloth coat, formed a contrast with the laced and

embroidered coats, and the powdered and perfumed heads of the courtiers of Versailles.
1777
Jeanne Louise Henriette Campan (1752–1822) French courtier. *Memoirs of the Private Life of Marie Antoinette* (1823), vol. I

2 I succeed him; no one can replace him.
Thomas Jefferson (1743–1826) U.S. president. Jefferson's reply to the question "Is it you sir, who replaces Dr. Benjamin Franklin?" Letter (1791)

3 A philosophical Quaker full of mean and thrifty maxims.
John Keats (1795–1821) British poet. Letter to George and Georgiana Keats (October 14–31, 1818), quoted in *Robert Gittings* (Letters of John Keats: A Selection; 1970)

4 He snatched the lightning shaft from heaven, and the scepter from tyrants.
Anne Robert Jacques Turgot (1727–81) French economist and administrator. An inscription for a bust of Benjamin Franklin, alluding to both his invention of the lightning conductor and his role in the American Revolution. Attrib.

Quotations by Franklin

5 Remember that credit is money.
"Advice to a Young Tradesman" (1748)

6 Remember that time is money.
"Advice to a Young Tradesman" (1748)

7 The body of
Benjamin Franklin, printer,
(Like the cover of an old book,
Its contents worn out,
And stript of its lettering and gilding)
Lies here, food for worms!
Yet the work itself shall not be lost,
For it will, as he believed, appear once more
In a new
And more beautiful edition,
Corrected and amended
By its Author!
Suggestion for his own epitaph. "Epitaph on Himself" (1728), quoted in *Complete Works* (John Bigelow, ed.; 1887), vol. 10

8 Here Skugg
Lies snug
As a bug
In a rug.
Epitaph for a squirrel, "skug" being another word for the animal. Letter to Georgiana Shipley (September 26, 1772), quoted in *Papers of Benjamin Franklin* (W.B. Willcox, ed.; 1975), vol. 19

9 In this world nothing can be said to be certain but death and taxes.
Letter to Jean-Baptiste Le Roy (November 13, 1789), quoted in *Works of Benjamin Franklin* (1817), ch. 6

10 There never was a good war or a bad peace.
Letter to Josiah Quincy (September 11, 1783), quoted in *Works of Benjamin Franklin* (1882), vol. 10, p. 11

11 Permit me, an American, to inform the gentleman...that Indian corn, taken for all and all, is one of the most agreeable grains in the world...and that johnny or hoecake, hot from the fire, is better than a Yorkshire muffin.
Letter to *The London Gazette* (January 2, 1776)

12 Blessed is he who expects nothing, for he shall not be disappointed.
Poor Richard's Almanack (1787)

13 Dost thou love life? Then do not squander time, for that's the stuff life is made of.
Poor Richard's Almanack (1746)

14 Happy that Nation, fortunate that age, whose history is not diverting.
Poor Richard's Almanack (1732)

15 He that falls in love with himself, will have no rivals.
Poor Richard's Almanack (1787)

16 He that goes a-borrowing goes a-sorrowing.
Poor Richard's Almanack (1754)

17 Historians relate, not so much what is done, as what they would have believed.
Poor Richard's Almanack (1732)

18 Many a long dispute among divines may be thus abridged: It is so. It is not so. It is so. It is not so.
Poor Richard's Almanack (1743)

19 Never leave that till to-morrow which you can do to-day.
Poor Richard's Almanack (1757)

20 Nothing is more fatal to *Health*, than an *over Care* of it.
Poor Richard's Almanack (1758)

21 You may give a man an office, but you cannot give him discretion.
Poor Richard's Almanack (1758)

22 Some are weather-wise, some are otherwise.
Poor Richard's Almanack (1735), February

23 Three may keep a secret, if two of them are dead.
Poor Richard's Almanack (1735), July

24 At twenty years of age, the will reigns; at thirty, the wit; and at forty, the judgment.
Poor Richard's Almanack (1741), June

25 Keep your eyes wide open before marriage, half shut afterwards.
Poor Richard's Almanack (1738), June

26 A little neglect may breed mischief,...for want of a nail, the shoe was lost; for want of a shoe the horse was lost; and for want of a horse the rider was lost.
Poor Richard's Almanack (1758), Preface

27 He that lives upon hope will die fasting.
Poor Richard's Almanack (1758), Preface

28 We must indeed all hang together, or most assuredly, we shall all hang separately.
On signing the Declaration of Independence. *Remark* (July 4, 1776)

29 Eat not to dullness; drink not to elevation.
1771–90. *The Autobiography* (1868), ch. 6

30 What is the use of a new-born child?
Response when asked the use of a new invention.
Quoted in *Life and Times of Benjamin Franklin* (J. Parton; 1864), pt. 4, ch. 17

31 Man is a tool-making animal.
Quoted in *Life of Samuel Johnson* (James Boswell; 1791), April 7, 1778

32 A lonesome man on a rainy day who does not know how to read.
On being asked what condition of man he considered the most pitiable. *Wit, Wisdom and Foibles of the Great* (C. A. Shriner; 1918)

33 God works wonders now and then;
Behold a lawyer, an honest man.
Attrib.

34 Quacks are the greatest liars in the world except their patients.
Attrib.

Franklin, John Hope (b.1915) U.S. historian

1 The new Negro history...will provide *all America* with a lesson in the wastefulness, nay, the wickedness of human exploitation and injustice that have characterized too much of this nation's past.
"The New Negro History," *Journal of Negro History* (April 1957)

Franks, Oliver, Baron (1905–92) British administrator

1 It is a secret in the Oxford sense: you may tell it to only one person at a time.
Sunday Telegraph, London (January 30, 1977)

Fraser, Antonia, Lady (originally Antonia Pakenham; b.1932) British historian

1 Women have done well in wartime when they have been able or compelled to act as substitutes for men, showing themselves resourceful, courageous and strong in every sense of the words...all those qualities generally described as masculine.
The Weaker Vessel (1984)

2 As with all forms of liberation, of which the liberation of women is only one example, it is easy to suppose in a time of freedom that the darker days of repression can never come again.
The Weaker Vessel (1984), epilogue

Fraser, Keath (b.1944) Canadian writer

1 Bad journeys, it seems, lead straight to the confession box. And as readers we take as much pleasure in listening to the blunders as writers do in confessing them.
Worst Journeys (Keath Fraser, ed.; 1991), introduction

2 Travel still suggests "travail" to those who know that by leaving home they risk wire-walking without a net.
Worst Journeys (Keath Fraser, ed.; 1991), introduction

3 Whoever claimed that travel is merely home in motion was traveling in an armchair.
Worst Journeys (Keath Fraser, ed.; 1991), introduction

Frayn, Michael (b.1933) British journalist, novelist, and playwright

1 No woman so naked as one you can see to be naked underneath her clothes.
Constructions (1974)

Frederick I, Holy Roman Emperor, King of Germany (called Frederick Barbarossa; 1123?–90) German-born emperor and monarch

1 Will you know where the ancient glory of your Rome, the gravity of your senate...the stainless and invincible courage in the conflict have gone?...All these things are with us Germans.
Referring to an antipapal revolt. Remark to envoys from the Senate of Rome (1155), quoted in *Quotations in History* (Alan and Veronica Palmer; 1976)

Frederick II, Holy Roman Emperor and King of Sicily (1194–1250) Italian-born emperor

1 We keep the students within view of their parents; we save them many toils and long foreign journeys; we protect them from robbers. They used to be pillaged while traveling abroad; now, they may study at small cost and short wayfaring, thanks to our liberality.
1224. *Foundation charter of Naples University*

Frederick II, King of Prussia ("Frederick the Great"; 1712–86) Prussian monarch

1 Every man has a wild beast within him.
Letter to Voltaire (1759)

2 Gentlemen, I have no allies save your valor and your good will...Our cause is just...farewell until we achieve the rendezvous with glory which awaits us.
Referring to the beginning of what was to become the War of Austrian Succession (1740–48). Speech to his generals (December 12, 1740)

3 It is a political error to practice deceit, if deceit is carried too far.
Antimachiavell (1740)

4 A crown is merely a hat that lets the rain in.
Attrib.

5 My people and I have come to an agreement which satisfies us both. They are to say what they please, and I am to do what I please.
Attrib.

6 Rascals, would you live for ever?
June 18, 1757. Addressed to reluctant soldiers at the Battle of Kolin. Attrib.

7 The King of England changes his ministers as often as he changes his shirts.
Referring to George III. Attrib.

Frederick William IV, King of Prussia (1795–1861) Prussian monarch

1 Henceforth Prussia merges into Germany.
Speech (March 21, 1848)

Freed, Arthur (1894–1973) U.S. film producer and songwriter

1 I'm singin' in the rain, just singin' in the rain;
What a wonderful feeling, I'm happy again.
Song. "Singin' in the Rain," *Hollywood Review* (1929)

Freeman, Richard Austin (1862–1943) British physician and writer

1 Simplicity is the soul of efficiency.
The Eye of Osiris (1911)

Freidank (*fl.* 1230) German poet

1 A dead man oft is showered with praise
Who earned not such in all his days.
13th century. Quoted in *A German Treasury* (Stanley Mason, tr.; 1993)

2 Hold no man's actions up to spite
If in the end he gets it right.
13th century. Quoted in *A German Treasury* (Stanley Mason, tr.; 1993)

3 The man who in himself can read,
That man, I say, is wise indeed.
13th century. Quoted in *A German Treasury* (Stanley Mason, tr.; 1993)

French, Marilyn (b.1929) U.S. novelist and feminist

1 The Bible demands suspension of belief, to have a story in which man produces woman at the very beginning is a reversal of nature from the very start.
Observer, London (April 24, 1994), "Sayings of the Week"

2 All men are rapists and that's all they are. They rape us with their eyes, their laws, and their codes.
The Women's Room (1977)

Freneau, Philip (1752–1832) U.S. poet

1 Far brighter scenes a future age,
The muse predicts, these states will hail,
Whose genius may the world engage,
Whose deeds may over death prevail,
And happier systems bring to view,
Than all the eastern sages knew.
"On the Emigration to America and Peopling the Western Country" (1785)

2 To western woods, and lonely plains,
Palemon from the crowd departs,
Where Nature's wildest genius reigns,
To tame the soil, and plant the arts
What wonders there shall freedom show,
What mighty states successive grow!
Traditionally any young man who sets out on a journey, "Palamon" appeared in Chaucer's *The Knight's Tale* (1390?). "On the Emigration to America and Peopling the Western Country" (1785), st. 1

3 Then rushed to meet the insulting foe;
They took the spear, but left the shield.
"To the Memory of the Americans who fell at Eutaw Springs," September 8, 1781 (1786), st. 5

4 Tobacco surely was designed
To poison, and destroy mankind.
"Tobacco," *Poems* (1795)

5 Hills sink to plains, and man returns to dust,
That dust supports a reptile or a flower;
Each changeful atom by some other nursed
Takes some new form, to perish in an hour.
The House of Night (1777–78), st. 134

6 No mystic wonders fired his mind;
He sought to gain no learned degree,
But only sense enough to find
The squirrel in the hollow tree.
1788. "The Indian Student or, Force of Nature," *The Penguin Book of American Verse* (Geoffrey Moore, ed.; 1977)

Frere, John Hookham (1769–1846) British diplomat, poet, and translator

1 And don't confound the language of the nation
With long-tailed words in *osity* and *ation*.
Prospectus and Specimen of an Intended National Work... by William and Robert Whistlecroft... relating to King Arthur and his Round Table (1817), ll. 47–48

Freud, Anna (1895–1982) Austrian-born British psychoanalyst

1 Freud...compared *psychotic* patients to crystals which, when broken up, reveal their structure by the manner in which they come apart.
Problems of Analytic Technique and Therapy (1972)

2 Neurotic nuclei are found in the minds of normal people as regularly as large areas of usual functioning are part of the makeup of every neurotic.
Problems of Analytic Technique and Therapy (1972)

3 Psychoanalysis came into being as a medical psychology, in answer to the lack of adequate therapeutic measures for the treatment of neurotic illness.
Problems of Analytic Technique and Therapy (1972)

4 The secret pathways between body and mind...remain invisible as such in adult patients unless they are brought to the surface by detailed analytic work.
Problems of Analytic Technique and Therapy (1972)

5 What the psychiatrist has learned so far are, as it were, the first single phrases of a foreign tongue which have to be linked up with each other, enlarged on, and built into the correct grammatical fabric of a language.
Problems of Analytic Technique and Therapy (1972)

Freud, Clement, Sir (Clement Raphael Freud; b.1924) British broadcaster and writer

1 Attila the Hen.
Referring to Margaret Thatcher. *News Quiz*, BBC Radio

2 If you resolve to give up smoking, drinking and loving, you don't actually live longer; it just seems longer.
Observer, London (December 27, 1964)

Freud, Lucien (b.1922) German-born British painter

1 A moment of complete happiness never occurs in the creation of a work of art. The promise of it is felt in the act of creation but disappears towards the completion of the work. For it is then that a painter realizes that it is only a picture he is painting.
"Some Thoughts on Painting," *Encounter* (July 1954), 3, no. 1

Freud, Sigmund (1856–1939) Austrian psychoanalyst

Quotations about Freud

1 To us he is no more a person
Now but a climate of opinion.
W. H. Auden (1907–73) British poet. "In Memory of Sigmund Freud" (1940), st. 17

2 Tranquillity comes with years, and that horrid thing which Freud calls sex is expunged.
E. F. Benson (1867–1940) British novelist. *Mapp and Lucia* (1931)

3 A few professional alienists understood his importance, but to most of the public he appeared as some kind of German sexologist...At least a decade would have to pass before Freud would have his revenge and see his ideas begin to destroy sex in America forever.
E. L. Doctorow (b.1931) U.S. novelist. *Ragtime* (1975)

4 Freud was one of the last representatives of Enlightenment philosophy. He genuinely believed in reason as the one strength man has and which alone could save him from confusion and decay.
1973
Erich Fromm (1900–80) German-born U.S. psychoanalyst and philosopher. *The Anatomy of Human Destructiveness* (1977)

5 In our talk together he rarely used any of the now overworked technical terms, invented by himself and elaborated on by...the International Psycho-Analytical Association.
1956
H. D. (1886–1961) U.S.-born British poet and writer. Referring to her psychoanalysis by Sigmund Freud (1933–34). *Tribute to Freud* (1971)

6 The old Professor...is Hercules struggling with death and he is the beloved, about to die. Moreover he himself, in his own character, has made the dead live, has summoned a host of dead and dying children from the living tomb.
1956
H. D. (1886–1961) U.S.-born British poet and writer. Referring to her psychoanalysis by Sigmund Freud, 1933–34. *Tribute to Freud* (1971)

7 Freud is midwife to the soul.
H. D. (1886–1961) U.S.-born British poet and writer. Referring to her psychoanalysis with Sigmund Freud (1933–34). Attrib.

8 I differ from Freud in that I think that most dreams are neither obscure nor bowdlerized, but rather that they are transparent and unedited...My position echoes Jung's notion of dreams as transparently meaningful and does away with any distinction between manifest and latent content.
J. Allan Hobson (b.1933) U.S. psychiatrist and educator. Referring to Sigmund Freud and Carl Gustav Jung. "The Dreaming Brain" (1988), quoted in *Evolutionary Psychiatry, a New Beginning* (Anthony Stevens and John Price; 1988)

9 Every reader of Freud, I imagine, remembers his first impressions: an incredible bias in favor of the least probable interpretations; a maniacal penchant for the sexual.
Maurice Merleau-Ponty (1908–61) French existentialist philosopher. Quoted in *The Essential Writings of Merleau-Ponty* (A. L. Fisher, ed.; 1969)

10 For Freud the ultimate psychological reality is the system of attractions and tensions which attaches the child to parental images, and then through these to all other persons.
Maurice Merleau-Ponty (1908–61) French existentialist philosopher. Quoted in *The Essential Writings of Merleau-Ponty* (A. L. Fisher, ed.; 1969)

11 There is no longer any risk that Freudian research will shock us by recalling what there is of the "barbarian" in us; the risk is rather that its findings will be too easily accepted in an "idealist" form.
Maurice Merleau-Ponty (1908–61) French existentialist philosopher. Quoted in *The Essential Writings of Merleau-Ponty* (A. L. Fisher, ed.; 1969)

12 But Malraux, like Sartre, has read Freud; and whatever they may think of him in the last analysis, it is with his help that they have learned to know themselves.
Maurice Merleau-Ponty (1908–61) French existentialist philosopher. Referring to André Malraux, Jean-Paul Sartre, and Sigmund Freud. Quoted in *The Essential Writings of Merleau-Ponty* (A. L. Fisher, ed.; 1969)

13 Freud is all nonsense; the secret of neurosis is to be found in the family battle of wills to see who can refuse longest to help with the dishes.
Julian Mitchell (b.1935) British writer and playwright. *As Far as You Can Go* (1963), pt. 1, ch. 1

14 Babies are, then, obviously narcissistic but not in the way adults are, not even Spinoza's God, and I am a little afraid that Freud sometimes forgets that the narcissistic baby has no sense of self.
Jean Piaget (1896–1980) Swiss psychologist. Referring to Baruch Spinoza and Sigmund Freud. "The First Year of Life of the Child" (1927), quoted in *The Essential Piaget* (H. E. Gruber and J. Jacques Vonèche, eds.; 1977)

15 Yes, you hate me. But didn't I try to atone? If I'd been a real Nazi I'd have chosen Jung, nicht wahr? But I chose Freud instead, the Jew. Freud's vision of the world had no Buchenwalds in it.
Thomas Pynchon (b.1937) U.S. novelist. Referring to Carl Gustav Jung and Sigmund Freud. Buchenwald, in Germany, was one of the main Nazi concentration camps. *The Crying of Lot 49* (1966), ch. 5

16 Freud...agreed in principle to the importance of sexual health. But he did not want what sexual health entailed, the attack on certain institutions which opposed it.
1952
Wilhelm Reich (1897–1957) Austrian psychoanalyst. Quoted in *Reich Speaks of Freud* (M. Higgins, ed.; 1967)

17 Freud was a peculiar mixture of a very progressive free thinker and a gentleman professor of 1860.
1952
Wilhelm Reich (1897–1957) Austrian psychoanalyst. Quoted in *Reich Speaks of Freud* (M. Higgins, ed.; 1967)

18 The two most original and creative figures in modern psychiatry, Freud and Jung were both proscribed by the Nazis...for both, though holding widely divergent views, upheld the value of the individual personality.
Anthony Storr (b.1920) British writer and psychiatrist. Referring to Sigmund Freud and Carl Gustav Jung. *The Integrated Personality* (1960)

19 Freud is constantly claiming to be scientific. But what he gives is *speculation*—something prior even to the formation of an hypothesis.
Ludwig Wittgenstein (1889–1951) Austrian philosopher. Quoted in *Lectures and Conversations* (Cyril Barnett, ed.; 1966)

20 Wisdom is something I would never expect from Freud. Cleverness, certainly; but not wisdom.
Ludwig Wittgenstein (1889–1951) Austrian philosopher. Quoted in *Lectures and Conversations* (Cyril Barnett, ed.; 1966)

21 Freud...has not given an explanation of the ancient myth. What he has done is to propound a new myth.

Ludwig Wittgenstein (1889–1951) Austrian philosopher. Referring to Sigmund Freud's work with myth in such areas as the Oedipus complex. Quoted in *Lectures and Conversations* (Cyril Barnett, ed.; 1966)

Quotations by Freud

22 What progress we are making. In the Middle Ages they would have burned me. Now they are content with burning my books.
Referring to the public burning of his books in Berlin. Letter to Ernest Jones (1933)

23 The great question...which I have not been able to answer, despite my thirty years of research into the feminine soul, is "What does a woman want?"
Letter to Maria Bonaparte, quoted in *Sigmund Freud: Life and Work* 3 vols. (Ernest Jones; 1953–55), vol. 3, ch. 16

24 A man like me cannot live without a hobby-horse, a consuming passion—in Schiller's words a tyrant. I have found my tyrant, and in his service I know no limits. My tyrant is psychology.
Letter to William Fliess (1895)

25 At bottom God is nothing more than an exalted father.
Totem and Taboo (1913), pt. 4, sect. 6

26 Anatomy is destiny.
Collected Writings (1924), vol. 5

27 A person who feels pleasure in producing pain in someone else in a sexual relationship is also capable of enjoying as pleasure any pain which he may himself derive from sexual relations. A sadist is always at the same time a masochist.
"Three Essays on Sexuality," *Complete Psychological Works* (1901–05), vol. 7

28 Psychoanalysis is in essence a cure through love.
Letter to Carl Jung, *Freud and Man's Soul* (Bruno Bettelheim; 1982)

29 The psychic development of the individual is a short repetition of the course of development of the race.
1910. *Leonardo da Vinci* (A. A. Brill, tr.; 1916)

30 It often seems that the poet's derisive comment is not unjustified when he says of the philosopher: "With his nightcaps and the tatters of his dressing-gown he patches up the gaps in the structure of the universe."
New Introductory Lectures on Psychoanalysis (James Strachey, tr.; 1933)

31 Religion is an illusion and it derives its strength from the fact that it falls in with our instinctual desires.
"A Philosophy of Life," *New Introductory Lectures on Psychoanalysis* (1933), Lecture 35

32 The only bodily organ which is really regarded as inferior is the atrophied penis, a girl's clitoris.
Freud was refuting claims that the "inferiority complex" can be traced back to self-perceived organic defects. "The Dissection of the Psychical Personality," *New Introductory Lectures on Psychoanalysis* (1933), Lecture 31

33 Among the examples of mistakes in speech...almost invariably I discover...a disturbing influence of something outside of the intended speech. The disturbing element is either a single unconscious thought...or it is a more general psychic motive.
Psychopathology of Everyday Life (1914)

34 It is easy to see that the ego is that part of the id which has been modified by the direct influence of the external world.
The Ego and the Id (1923)

35 The ego represents what we call reason and sanity, in contrast to the id which contains the passions.
The Ego and the Id (1923)

36 The sexual wishes in regard to the mother become more intense and the father is perceived as an obstacle to them; this gives rise to the Oedipus complex.
The Ego and the Id (1923)

37 We obtain our concept of the unconscious, therefore, from the theory of repression...We see, however, that we have two kinds of unconscious that which is latent but capable of becoming conscious, and that which is repressed and not capable of becoming conscious in the ordinary way.
The Ego and the Id (1923)

38 If the truth of religious doctrines is dependent on an inner experience that bears witness to the truth, what is one to make of the many people who do not have that experience?
The Future of an Illusion (1927)

39 The voice of the intellect is a soft one, but it does not rest till it has gained a hearing.
The Future of an Illusion (1927)

40 Religious ideas have sprung from the same need as all the other achievements of culture: from the necessity for defending itself against the crushing supremacy of nature.
The Future of an Illusion (1927), ch. 3

41 A poor girl may have an illusion that a prince will come and fetch her home. It is possible; some such cases have occurred. That the Messiah will come and found a golden age is much less probable.
The Future of an Illusion (1927), ch. 6

42 It would indeed be very nice if there were a God, who was both creator of the world and a benevolent providence, if there were a moral world order and a future life...It is very odd that this is all just as we should wish it ourselves.
The Future of an Illusion (1927), ch. 6

43 Religious doctrines...are all illusions, they do not admit of proof, and no one can be compelled to consider them as true or to believe in them.
The Future of an Illusion (1927), ch. 6

44 Where questions of religion are concerned people are guilty of every possible kind of insincerity and intellectual misdemeanor.
The Future of an Illusion (1927), ch. 6

45 Immorality, no less than morality, has at all times found support in religion.
The Future of an Illusion (1927), ch. 7

46 Our knowledge of the historical value of certain religious doctrines increases our respect for them, but it does not invalidate our proposal to exclude them from the motivation of cultural laws.
The Future of an Illusion (1927), ch. 8

47 The true believer is in a high degree protected against the danger of certain neurotic afflictions; by accepting the universal neurosis he is spared the task of forming a personal neurosis.
The Future of an Illusion (1927), ch. 8

48 They have been rash enough to withdraw the "opium" of religion from them and have been wise enough to give them a reasonable amount of sexual freedom.
1938. Referring to Soviet Russia. "Moses and Monotheism," *The Origins of Religion* (Albert Dickson, ed., Ken Jones, tr.; 1939)

49 With magnificent inflexibility he resisted every temptation to magical thought, and he rejected the illusion, so dear to Egyptians in particular, of a life after death.
Referring to the Pharaoh Akhenaton, "the heretic king" of the18th dynasty. "Moses and Monotheism," *The Origins of Religion* (Albert Dickson, ed., Ken Jones, tr.; 1939)

50 The sole criterion of frigidity is the absence of the vaginal orgasm.
Three Essays on the Theory of Sexuality (1905)

51 Conscience is the internal perception of the rejection of a particular wish operating within us.
Totem and Taboo (1913)

52 The conscious mind may be compared to a fountain playing in the sun and falling back into the great subterranean pool of subconscious from which it rises.
Bartlett's Unfamiliar Quotations (Leonard Louis Levinson, ed.; 1972)

53 The mind is an iceberg; it floats with only 17% of its bulk above water.
Bartlett's Unfamiliar Quotations (Leonard Louis Levinson, ed.; 1972)

54 The derivation of the religious attitude can be followed back in clear outline as far as the child's feeling of helplessness. There may be something else behind this, but for the present it is wrapped in obscurity.
1930. Quoted in *Civilization and Its Discontents* (Thomas Crofts, ed.; 1994), ch. 1

55 Religion circumscribes...choice and adaptation by...decrying the value of life and promulgating a view of the real world that is distorted like a delusion, and both of these imply a preliminary intimidating influence upon intelligence.
1930. Quoted in *Civilization and Its Discontents* (Thomas Crofts, ed.; 1994), ch. 2

56 My life and work has been aimed at one goal only: to infer or guess how the mental apparatus is constructed and what forces interplay and counteract in it.
Quoted in *Sigmund Freud: Life and Work* 3 vols. (Ernest Jones; 1953–55)

57 The poets and philosophers before me have discovered the unconscious; I have discovered the scientific method with which the unconscious can be studied.
1926. Remark on his 70th birthday. Quoted in *The Liberal Imagination* (Lionel Trilling; 1957)

58 Happiness is the deferred fulfilment of a prehistoric wish. That is why wealth brings so little happiness; money is not an infantile wish.
January 18, 1898. Said to Wilhelm Fliess. Quoted in *The Oxford Book of Money* (Kevin Jackson, ed.; 1995)

59 My discoveries are not primarily a heal-all. My discoveries are a basis for a very grave philosophy. There are very few who understand this, *there are very few who are capable of understanding this.*
1933–34. Said to Hilda Doolittle, who was psychoanalyzed by Sigmund Freud during 1933–34. Quoted in *Tribute to Freud* (Hilda Doolittle ("H. D."); 1971)

60 A man should not strive to eliminate his complexes, but to get into accord with them: they are legitimately what directs his conduct in the world.
Attrib.

61 The goal of psychoanalysis is a cultural achievement somewhat like the draining of the Zuyder Zee.
Attrib.

62 Sometimes a cigar is just a cigar.
When asked by one of his students whether there was any symbolism in the large cigars that Freud smoked. Attrib.

Friedan, Betty (Betty Naomi Friedan; b.1921) U.S. writer

1 If divorce has increased one thousand percent, don't blame the woman's movement. Blame our obsolete sex roles on which our marriages were based.
Remark (January 20, 1974)

Friedenberg, Edgar Z. (b.1921) U.S. sociologist

1 The examined life has always been pretty well confined to a privileged class.
"The Impact of the School," *The Vanishing Adolescent* (1959)

Friedman, Milton (b.1912) U.S. economist

1 There is no stable trade-off between inflation and unemployment.
Said on receiving the 1976 Nobel Prize in economics. "Inflation and Unemployment" (1976)

2 If freedom were not so economically efficient it certainly wouldn't stand a chance.
Remark (March 1987)

3 "Stagflation" emerged throughout the world as inflationary policies led in their turn to economic stagnation.
"The Invisible Hand in Economics and Politics" (1980)

4 History suggests that capitalism is a necessary condition for political freedom. Clearly it is not a sufficient condition.
Capitalism and Freedom (1962)

5 Freedom in economic arrangements is itself a component of freedom broadly understood, so economic freedom is an end in itself.
Capitalism and Freedom (1962), ch. 1

6 Factual evidence can never "prove" a hypothesis; it can only fail to disprove it, which is what we generally mean when we say, somewhat inexactly, that the hypothesis is "confirmed" by experience.
Essays in Positive Economics (1953)

7 Deflation is the easiest thing to avoid; you just print more money.
Interview, *Forbes* (December 29, 1997)

8 Inflation is the one form of taxation that can be imposed without legislation.
Interview, *Playboy* (February 1973)

9 There's only one place where inflation is made: that's in Washington.
1977. Attrib.

10 There's no such thing as a free lunch.
Used before Friedman but popularized by him. Attrib.

Friedman, Thomas L. U.S. journalist and author

1 No two countries that both have a McDonald's have ever fought a war against each other.
New York Times (December 8, 1996)

Friel, Brian (b.1929) Irish dramatist

1 It can happen that a civilisation can be imprisoned in a linguistic contour which no longer matches the landscape of...fact.
Translations (1980), Act 2

2 It is not the literal past, the "facts" of history, that shape us, but images of the past embodied in language.
Translations (1980), Act 3

Frisch, Max (1911–91) Swiss playwright and novelist

1 Technology is the knack of so arranging the world that we don't have to experience it.
Homo Faber (1957), pt. 2

2 He who fears change
More than disasters,
What can he do to forestall
The threatening disaster?
1958. *The Firebugs* (Michael Bullock, tr.; 1962), Scene 3

3 Joking is the third best method of hoodwinking people. The second best is sentimentality...But the best and safest method...is to tell the plain unvarnished truth.
1958. *The Firebugs* (Michael Bullock, tr.; 1962), Scene 4

Frisch, O.R. (Otto Robert Frisch; 1904–79) Austrian-born British physicist

1 I do not foresee meson guns or hyperon boilers, but if applications for these particles are ever found, it is unlikely that even the most imaginative of present science-fiction writers will have envisaged them correctly.
Quoted in *Science Survey 1* (A. W. Haslett and John St. John, eds.; 1960)

2 Physicists...just want to know what the world is made of, what are the smallest particles, and how they behave. Therefore they are always ahead of practical applications.
Quoted in *Science Survey 1* (A. W. Haslett and John St. John, eds.; 1960)

Frohman, Charles (1860–1915) U.S. theater producer

1 Why fear death? It is the most beautiful adventure in life.
May 7, 1915. Last words said before going down with the liner *Lusitania*, alluding to the line "To die will be an awfully big adventure," in J. M. Barrie's *Peter Pan* (1904), which Frohman had produced. Quoted in *Charles Frohman* (I. Marcosson and D. Frohman; 1916), ch. 19

Fromm, Erich (1900–80) German-born U.S. psychoanalyst and philosopher

1 Greed is a bottomless pit which exhausts the person in an endless effort to satisfy the need without ever reaching satisfaction.
Escape from Freedom (1941)

2 The paradoxical—and tragic—situation of a man is that his conscience is weakest when he needs it most.
Man for Himself (1947)

3 Man always dies before he is fully born.
Man for Himself (1947), ch. 3

4 Man's main task in life is to give *birth* to himself.
Man for Himself (1947), ch. 4

5 Chronic boredom—compensated or uncompensated—constitutes one of the major psychopathological phenomena in contemporary technotronic society.
The Anatomy of Human Destructiveness (1973)

6 Exploitation and manipulation produce boredom and triviality; they cripple man, and all factors that make man into a psychic cripple turn him also into a sadist or a destroyer.
The Anatomy of Human Destructiveness (1973)

7 It is the fully sane person who feels isolated in the insane society—and he may suffer so much from the incapacity to communicate that it is he who may become psychotic.
The Anatomy of Human Destructiveness (1973)

8 Neurosis can be understood best as the battle between two tendencies within an individual; deep character analysis leads, if successful, to the progressive solution.
The Anatomy of Human Destructiveness (1973)

9 Optimism is an alienated form of faith, pessimism an alienated form of despair.
The Anatomy of Human Destructiveness (1973)

10 People have committed suicide because of their failure to realize their passions for love, power, fame, revenge. Cases of suicide because of a lack of sexual satisfaction are virtually nonexistent.
The Anatomy of Human Destructiveness (1973)

11 Psychoanalysis is essentially a theory of unconscious strivings, of resistance, of falsification of reality according to one's subjective needs and expectations.
The Anatomy of Human Destructiveness (1973)

12 The existential split in man would be unbearable could he not establish a sense of unity within himself and with the natural and human world outside.
The Anatomy of Human Destructiveness (1973)

13 All forms of psychosis show the inability to be objective, to an extreme degree. For the insane person the only reality that exists is that within him, that of his fears and desires.
The Art of Loving (1956)

14 Narcissism is the earliest stage of human development, and the person who in later life has returned to this stage is incapable of love; in the extreme case he is insane.
The Art of Loving (1956)

15 Psychology as a science has its limitations, and, as the logical consequence of theology is mysticism, so the ultimate consequence of psychology is love.
The Art of Loving (1956)

16 The deepest need of man is the need to overcome his

separateness, to leave the prison of his aloneness.
The Art of Loving (1956)

17 The narcissistic orientation is one in which...the phenomena in the outside world have no reality in themselves, but are experienced only from the viewpoint of their being useful or dangerous to one.
The Art of Loving (1956)

18 Women are equal because they are not different any more.
The Art of Loving (1956)

19 Man does not only sell commodities, he sells himself and feels himself to be a commodity.
The Fear of Freedom (1942)

20 To feel completely alone and isolated leads to mental disintegration just as physical starvation leads to death.
The Fear of Freedom (1942)

21 The mother-child relationship is paradoxical and, in a sense, tragic. It requires the most intense love on the mother's side, yet this very love must help the child grow away from the mother and to become fully independent.
Attrib.

Frost, David, Sir (David Paradine Frost; b.1939) British television personality

1 Television is an invention that permits you to be entertained in your living room by people you wouldn't have in your home.
CBS Television (1971)

Frost, Robert (Robert Lee Frost; 1874–1963) U.S. poet

Quotations about Frost

1 His opinion of Housman is very low. Brainless, he calls him. A dry, classical scholar on the one hand, and a very limited poet on the other. Frost dislikes both the suicidal mood and the pretty technique.
Robert Francis (1901–87) U.S. poet. Referring to Robert Frost and A. E. Housman. "Robert Frost: a Time to Talk" (1933)

Quotations by Frost

2 Spades take up leaves
No better than spoons,
And bags full of leaves
Are light as balloons.
"Gathering Leaves" (1923), st.1, l.1–4, quoted in *The Poetry of Robert Frost* (Edward Connery Lathem, ed.; 1971)

3 No tears in the writer, no tears in the reader.
"The Figure a Poem Makes", quoted in Preface, *Collected Poems* (1939)

4 Mother : Folks think a witch who has familiar spirits
She could call up to pass a winter evening,
But won't, should be burned at the stake or something.
"The Witch of Coos" (1923)

5 They cannot scare me with their empty spaces
Between stars—on stars where no human race is
I have it in me so much nearer home
To scare myself with my own desert places.
"Desert Places," *A Further Range* (1936)

6 I never dared be radical when young, for fear it would make me conservative when old.
"Precaution," *A Further Range* (1936)

7 To err is human, not to, animal.
"The White-tailed Hornet," *A Further Range* (1936), l. 52, quoted in *The Poetry of Robert Frost* (Edward Connery Lathem, ed.; 1971)

8 The land was ours before we were the land's.
She was our land more than a hundred years
Before we were her people.
"The Gift Outright," *A Witness Tree* (1942), quoted in *The Poetry of Robert Frost* (Edward Connery Lathem, ed.; 1971)

9 Such as we were we gave ourselves outright
(The deed of gift was many deeds of war)
To the land vaguely realizing westward,
But still unstoried, artless, unenhanced,
Such as she was, such as she would become.
Frost read this poem at the inauguration of President John Fitzgerald Kennedy (1961), the first time a poem had been read at a presidential inauguration. "The Gift Outright," *A Witness Tree* (1941), ll. 12–16, quoted in *The Poetry of Robert Frost* (Edward Connery Lathem, ed.; 1971)

10 Some say the world will end in fire,
Some say in ice.
From what I've tasted of desire
I hold with those who favor fire.
1923. "Fire and Ice," *Collected Poems* (1930), quoted in *The Norton Anthology of American Literature* (Nina Baym, ed.; 1998), vol. 2

11 Forgive, O Lord, my little jokes on Thee
And I'll forgive Thy great big one on me.
"Cluster of Faith," *In the Clearing* (1962)

12 Two roads diverged in a wood, and I—
I took the one less traveled by,
And that has made all the difference.
"The Road Not Taken," *Mountain Interval* (1916), st. 4

13 I met a traveler from Arkansas
Who boasted of his state as beautiful
for diamonds and apples.
"New Hampshire," *New Hampshire* (1923), ll. 9–11, quoted in *The Poetry of Robert Frost* (Edward Connery Lathem, ed.; 1971)

14 I met a Californian who would
Talk California—a state so blessed.
He said, in climate, none had ever died there.
"New Hampshire," *New Hampshire* (1923), ll. 15–21, quoted in *The Poetry of Robert Frost* (Edward Connery Lathem, ed.; 1971)

15 The woods are lovely, dark, and deep,
But I have promises to keep,
And miles to go before I sleep,
And miles to go before I sleep.
"Stopping by Woods on a Snowy Evening," *New Hampshire* (1923), st. 4

16 My apple trees will never get across
And eat the cones under his pines, I tell him.
He only says, "Good fences make good neighbors."
"Mending Wall," *North of Boston* (1914)

17 Something there is that doesn't love a wall.
And wants it down.
"Mending Wall," *North of Boston* (1914)

18 Most of the change we think we see in life
Is due to truths being in and out of favor.
"The Black Cottage," *North of Boston* (1914)

19 Home is the place where, when you have to go there,
They have to take you in.
"The Death of the Hired Man," *North of Boston* (1914)

20 People are inexterminable—like flies and bed-bugs. There will always be some that survive in cracks and crevices—that's us.
Observer, London (March 29, 1959)

21 Writing free verse is like playing tennis with the net down.
Speech at the Milton Academy (May 17, 1935)

22 Poetry is what gets lost in translation. It is also what is lost in interpretation.
Quoted in *Robert Frost: A Backward Look* (Louis Untermeyer; 1964), ch. 1

23 A diplomat is a man who always remembers a woman's birthday but never remembers her age.
Attrib.

24 By working faithfully eight hours a day you may eventually get to be a boss and work twelve hours a day.
Attrib.

25 Poets are like baseball pitchers. Both have their moments. The intervals are the tough things.
Attrib.

26 The brain is a wonderful organ. It starts working the moment you get up in the morning, and does not stop until you get into the office.
Attrib.

27 The difference between a man and his valet; they both smoke the same cigars, but only one pays for them.
Attrib.

Froude, J. A. (James Anthony Froude; 1818–94) British historian

1 Men are made by nature unequal. It is vain, therefore, to treat them as if they were equal.
"Party Politics" (Short Studies on Great Subjects; 1877)

2 Wild animals never kill for sport. Man is the only one to whom the torture and death of his fellow-creatures is amusing in itself.
Oceana (1886), ch. 5

3 Experience teaches slowly, and at the cost of mistakes.
"Party Politics," *Short Studies on Great Subjects* (1877)

4 Fear is the parent of cruelty.
"Party Politics," *Short Studies on Great Subjects* (1877)

Fry, Christopher (Christopher Harris; b.1907) British playwright

1 Try thinking of love, or something.
Amor vincit insomnia.
Punning on the famous line from Virgil's 10th *Eclogue*: (*Amor vincit omnia*) "Love conquers all". *A Sleep of Prisoners* (1951)

2 He was caught
Red-handed with the silver and his Grace
Being short of staff at the time asked him to stay
And clean it.
Venus Observed (1950)

3 What is madness
To those who only observe, is often wisdom
To those to whom it happens.
A Phoenix Too Frequent (1946)

4 There may always be another reality
To make fiction of the truth we think we've arrived at.
A Yard of Sun (1970), Act 2

5 Religion
Has made an honest woman of the supernatural,
And we won't have it kicking over the traces again.
The Lady's Not for Burning (1949), Act 2

6 The moon is nothing
But a circumambulating aphrodisiac
Divinely subsidized to provoke the world
Into a rising birth-rate.
The Lady's Not for Burning (1949), Act 3

7 Where in this small-talking world can I find
A longitude with no platitude?
The Lady's Not for Burning (1949), Act 3

8 Poetry is the language in which man explores his own amazement.
Time (April 3, 1950)

9 A spade is never so merely a spade as the word
Spade would imply.
Venus Observed (1950), Act 2, Scene 1

10 Over all the world
Men move unhoming, and eternally
Concerned: a swarm of bees who have lost their queen.
Venus Observed (1950), Act 2, Scene 1

11 The Lady's Not for Burning
1949. Play title. Adapted in the 1980s by Margaret Thatcher as "the lady's not for turning."

Fry, Elizabeth (1780–1845) British prison reformer

1 Does capital punishment tend to the security of the people? By no means. It hardens the hearts of men, and makes the loss of life appear light to them; and it renders life insecure, inasmuch as the law holds out that property is of greater value than life.
Quoted in *Women's Record: Sketches of All Distinguished Women* (Sarah Josepha Hale; 1853)

2 Punishment is not for revenge, but to lessen crime and reform the criminal.
Quoted in *Women's Record: Sketches of All Distinguished Women* (Sarah Josepha Hale; 1853)

Frye, Northrop (Herman Northrop Frye; 1912–91) Canadian academic

1 Value judgments are founded on the study of literature; the study of literature can never be founded on value judgments.
Anatomy of Criticism (1957)

2 Criticism can talk, and all the arts are dumb.
Anatomy of Criticism (1957), ch. 4

3 Criticism is to art what history is to action and philosophy to wisdom.
Anatomy of Criticism (1957), ch. 12

4 Literature doesn't evolve or improve or progress.
The Educated Imagination (1964)

5 The Bible forms the lowest stratum in the teaching of literature. It should be taught so early and so thoroughly that it sinks straight to the bottom of the mind, where everything that comes along later can settle on it.
The Educated Imagination (1964)

6 Literature is a world that we try to build up and enter at the same time.
"The Motive for Metaphor," *The Educated Imagination* (1964)

7 The nation is rapidly ceasing to be the real defining unit of society.
The Modern Century (1967)

8 An aggregate of egos is a mob.
The Well-Tempered Critic (1963)

9 Historically, a Canadian is an American who rejects the revolution.
University of Toronto Quarterly (April 1953), vol. 22, no. 3

Fukuyama, Francis (b.1952) U.S. economist and historian

1 American democracy and the American economy were successful not because of individualism or communitarianism alone but because of the interaction of these two opposing tendencies.
Trust (1995)

2 If networks are to be more efficient...this will come about only on the basis of a high level of trust and the existence of shared norms of ethical behavior between network members.
Trust (1995)

3 In the future the optimal form of industrial organization will be neither small companies nor large ones but network structures that share the advantages of both.
Trust (1995)

4 It is very difficult to conceive of modern economic life in the absence of a minimum level of informal trust.
Trust (1995)

5 Modern liberal political and economic institutions not only coexist with religion and other traditional elements of culture, but many actually work better in conjunction with them.
Trust (1995)

6 Social capital is critical to prosperity and to what has come to be called competitiveness.
Trust (1995)

7 Social capital is like a ratchet that is more easily turned in one direction than another; it can be dissipated by the actions of government much more readily than those governments can build it up again.
Trust (1995)

8 The conventional wisdom that portrays America as the paradigm of individualism is wrong.
Trust (1995)

9 Trust is not the consequence of rational calculation; it arises from sources like religion or ethical habit that have nothing to do with modernity.
Trust (1995)

10 Virtually all economic activity in the contemporary world is carried out not by individuals but by organizations that require a high degree of social cooperation.
Trust (1995)

Fulbright, J. William (James William Fulbright; 1905–95) U.S. educator and politician

1 We must learn to explore all the options and possibilities that confront us in a complex and rapidly changing world...We must dare to think about "unthinkable things" because when things become unthinkable, thinking stops and action becomes mindless.
Speech to Senate (March 27, 1964)

2 Science has radically changed the condition of human life on earth. It has expanded our knowledge and our power but not our capacity to use them with wisdom.
Old Myths and New Realities (1964)

Fuller, Margaret (Sarah Margaret Fuller; 1810–50) U.S. writer and reformer

Quotations about Fuller

1 Hear me, ambitious souls,
Sex is the curse of life!
Edgar Lee Masters (1869–1950) U.S. poet and novelist. Margaret Fuller was regarded as the symbol of a liberated, intellectual woman. "Margaret Fuller Slack," *Spoon River Anthology* (1915), quoted in *The Norton Anthology of American Literature, 5th edn.* (Nina Baym, ed.; 1998), vol. 2

Quotations by Fuller

2 The critic is the historian who records the order of creation. In vain for the maker, who knows without learning it, but not in vain for the mind of his race.
A Short Essay on Critics in Art, Literature and the Drama (19th century)

3 There are three species: first, the servile American...Then there is the conceited American...3rd. The thinking American.
Referring to the types of "the American in Europe." "Things and Thoughts in Europe," *New York Daily Tribune* (November 27, 1847), quoted in *The Heath Anthology of American Literature* (Paul Lauter, ed.; 1998), vol. 1

4 The English character has the iron force of the Latins, but not the frankness and expansion. Like their fruits, they need a summer sky to give them more sweetness and a richer flavor.
"American Literature," *Papers on Literature and Art* (1846), quoted in *The Heath Anthology of American Literature* (Paul Lauter, ed.; 1998), vol. 1

5 The wives of the poorer settlers...very frequently become slatterns; but the ladies, accustomed to a refined neatness, feel that they cannot degrade themselves by its absence, and struggle under every disadvantage to keep up the necessary routine of small arrangements.
Referring to settlers on prairies of the Midwest. *Summer on the Lakes* (1843), ch. 3, quoted in *The Heath Anthology of American Literature* (Paul Lauter, ed.; 1998), vol. 1

6 The critic is...the younger brother of genius. Next to invention is the power of interpreting invention; next to beauty the power of appreciating beauty...The critic, then, should be not merely a poet, not merely a philosopher, not merely an observer, but tempered of all three.
"A Short Essay on Critics," *The Dial* (1840), quoted in *The Heath Anthology of American Literature* (Paul Lauter, ed.; 1998), vol. 1

7 Let Ulysses drive the beeves home, while Penelope there piles up the fragrant loaves; they are both employed well if these be done in thought and love, willingly. But Penelope is no more meant for a baker or weaver solely, than Ulysses for a cattle-herd.
Woman in the Nineteenth Century (1845), preface, quoted in *The Heath Anthology of American Literature* (Paul Lauter, ed.; 1998), vol. 1

8 The especial genius of Woman I believe to be electrical in movement, intuitive in function, spiritual in tendency. She excels not so easily in classification, or recreation, as in an instinctive seizure of causes.
Woman in the Nineteenth Century (1845), preface, quoted in *The Heath Anthology of American Literature* (Paul Lauter, ed.; 1998), vol. 1

9 The French Revolution, that strangely disguised angel, bore witness in favor of Woman, but interpreted her claims no less ignorantly than those of Man.
Woman in the Nineteenth Century (1845), preface, quoted in *The Heath Anthology of American Literature* (Paul Lauter, ed.; 1998), vol. 1

Fuller, R. Buckminster (Richard Buckminster Fuller; 1895–1983) U.S. architect, designer, and inventor

1 I look for what needs to be done...After all, that's how the universe designs itself.
Christian Science Monitor (November 3, 1964)

2 Here is God's purpose—
for God, to me, it seems,
is a verb,
not a noun,
proper or improper.
1940. "Untitled," *No More Secondhand God* (1963)

3 I am a passenger on the spaceship, Earth.
Operating Manual for Spaceship Earth (1969), ch. 1

4 The most important thing about Spaceship Earth—an instruction book didn't come with it.
Operating Manual for Spaceship Earth (1969), ch. 4

5 A ghost has made uneasy every bed.
You are not you without me and *The dead*
Only are pleased to be alone it said.
Royal Naval Air Station (1944)

6 I just invent, then wait until man comes round to needing what I've invented.
Time (June 10, 1964)

Fuller, Thomas (1608–61) English historian

1 There is a great difference between painting a face and not washing it.
The Church-History of Britain (1655), bk. 7

2 A proverb is much matter decocted into few words.
The History of the Worthies of England (1662), ch. 2

3 Anger is one of the sinews of the soul.
The Holy State and the Profane State (1642)

4 Fame is sometimes like unto a kind of mushroom, which Pliny recounts to be the greatest miracle in nature, because growing and having no root.
The Holy State and the Profane State (1642)

5 Learning hath gained most by those books by which the printers have lost.
The Holy State and the Profane State (1642)

6 Many have been the wise speeches of fools, though not so many as the foolish speeches of wise men.
The Holy State and the Profane State (1642)

7 Physicians, like beer, are best when they are old.
The Holy State and the Profane State (1642)

8 When he can keep life no longer in, he makes a fair and easie passage for it to go out.
The Holy State and the Profane State (1642)

9 Light (God's eldest daughter) is a principal beauty in building.
"Of Building," *The Holy State and the Profane State* (1642)

10 Know most of the rooms of thy native country before thou goest over the threshold thereof.
"Of Travelling," *The Holy State and the Profane State* (1642)

Fuller, Thomas (1654–1734) English physician and writer

1 A friend in the market is better than money in the chest.
Gnomologia (1732)

2 He that resolves to deal with none but honest men must leave off dealing.
Gnomologia (1732)

3 Study sickness while you are well.
Gnomologia (1732)

Furber, Douglas (1885–1961) British songwriter

1 Any time you're Lambeth way,
Any evening, any day,
You'll find us all doin' the Lambeth walk.
Song lyric. "Doin' the Lambeth Walk" (1937)

Fyleman, Rose (1877–1957) British writer of children's books

1 There are fairies at the bottom of our garden.
"The Fairies," *Fairies and Chimneys* (1918)

Gable, Clark (William Clark Gable; 1901–60) U.S. film actor

Quotations about Gable

1 Clark Gable has the best ears of our lives.
Milton Berle (b.1908) U.S. film and television entertainer. Attrib.

2 His ears make him look like a taxi-cab with both doors open.
Howard Hughes (1905–76) U.S. business executive, pilot, and film producer. Attrib.

Quotations by Gable

3 I'm just a lucky slob from Ohio who happened to be in the right place at the right time.
Attrib.

Gabor, Zsa Zsa (b.1918) Hungarian-born U.S. film actor

1 A man in love is incomplete until he has married. Then he's finished.
Newsweek (March 28, 1960)

2 Husbands are like fires. They go out when unattended.
Newsweek (March 28, 1960)

3 I never hated a man enough to give him diamonds back.
Observer, London (August 28, 1957), "Sayings of the Week"

4 Personally I know nothing about sex because I've always been married.
Observer, London (August 16, 1987), "Sayings of the Week"

Gadamer, Hans-Georg (b.1900) German philosopher

1 Those who have looked deeply into human nature have recognized that our capacity for play is an expression of the highest seriousness.
The Play of Art (1973)

Gainsborough, Thomas (1727–88) British portrait and landscape painter

Quotations about Gainsborough

1 His subjects are softened and sentimentalised too much. It is not simple unaffected nature that we see, but nature sitting for her picture.
William Hazlitt (1778–1830) British essayist and critic. Referring to Thomas Gainsborough's pictures. Attrib.

Quotations by Gainsborough

2 We are all going to Heaven, and Vandyke is of the company.
1788. Last words. *Thomas Gainsborough* (William B. Boulton; 1905), ch. 9

Gaitskell, Dora (1901–89) Russian-born British politician

1 All terrorists, at the invitation of the Government, end up with drinks at the Dorchester.
Letter, *Guardian*, London (August 23, 1977)

Gaitskell, Hugh (Hugh Todd Naylor Gaitskell; 1906–63) British politician

1 It means the end of a thousand years of history.
Referring to the prospect of Britain joining a European federation. Speech, Labour Party Conference (October 3, 1962)

2 Surely the right course is to test the Russians, not the bombs.
Observer, London (June 23, 1957), "Sayings of the Week"

Galbraith, J. K. (John Kenneth Galbraith; b.1908) Canadian-born U.S. economist

Quotations about Galbraith

1 Unless a reviewer has the courage to give you unqualified praise, I say ignore the bastard.
1958
John Steinbeck (1902–68) U.S. novelist. Remark made during a chance meeting with J. K. Galbraith; both men were reading a hostile review of Galbraith's book. Quoted in *The Affluent Society* (John Kenneth Galbraith; 1977), Introduction

Quotations by Galbraith

2 I have never understood why one's affections must be confined, as once with women, to a single country.
A Life in our Times (1981)

3 Politics is not the art of the possible. It consists in choosing between the disastrous and the unpalatable.
Ambassador's Journal (1969)

4 The salary of the chief executive of the large corporation is not a market award for achievement. It is frequently in the nature of a warm personal gesture by the individual to himself.
Annals of an Abiding Liberal (1980)

5 It's much easier to point out the problem than it is to say just how it should be solved.
Capitalism, Communism, and Coexistence (1988)

6 Had the Bible been in clear straightforward language, had the ambiguities and contradictions been edited out, and had the language been constantly modernised to accord with contemporary taste it would almost certainly have been, or become, a work of lesser influence.
Economics, Peace and Laughter (1971)

7 There are times in politics when you must be on the right side and lose.
Observer, London (February 11, 1968), "Sayings of the Week"

8 We all agree that pessimism is a mark of superior intellect.
Observer, London (April 3, 1977), "Sayings of the Week"

9 Nothing so weakens a government as persistent inflation.
The Affluent Society (1958)

10 One of the best ways of avoiding necessary and even urgent tasks is to seem to be busily employed on things that are already done.
The Affluent Society (1958), ch. 1

11 Wealth is not without its advantages, and the case to the contrary, although it has often been made, has never proved widely persuasive.
The Affluent Society (1958), ch. 1

12 These are the days when men of all social disciplines and all political faiths seek the comfortable and the accepted; when the man of controversy is looked upon as a disturbing influence; when originality is taken to be a mark of instability; and when, in minor modification of the scriptural parable, the bland lead the bland.
The Affluent Society (1958), ch. 1, sect. 3

13 Wealth has never been a sufficient source of honor in itself. It must be advertised, and the normal medium is obtrusively expensive goods.
The Affluent Society (1958), ch. 7

14 More die in the United States of too much food than of too little.
The Affluent Society (1958), ch. 9

15 Few things are as immutable as the addiction of political groups to the ideas by which they have once won office.
The Affluent Society (1958), ch. 13

16 In the affluent society no useful distinction can be made between luxuries and necessaries.
The Affluent Society (1958), ch. 21

17 All races have produced notable economists, with the exception of the Irish who doubtless can protest their devotion to higher arts.
The Age of Uncertainty (1977)

18 Only the man who finds everything wrong and expects it to get worse is thought to have a clear brain.
The Age of Uncertainty (1977)

19 Perhaps it is a sense of history that divides good economics from bad.
There is a book with the same title as the television series (1977). *The Age of Uncertainty*, television series (1977)

20 Men have been swindled by other men on many occasions. The autumn of 1929 was, perhaps, the first occasion when men succeeded on a large scale in swindling themselves.
The Great Crash, 1929 (1955)

21 The real accomplishment of modern science and technology consists in taking ordinary men, informing them narrowly and deeply and then, through appropriate organization, arranging to have their knowledge combined with that of other specialized but equally ordinary men. This dispenses with the need for genius.
The New Industrial State (1967), ch. 6

22 One of the greatest pieces of economic wisdom is to know what you do not know.
Time (1961)

23 Money differs from an automobile, a mistress, or cancer in being equally important to those who have it and those who do not.
Attrib.

Galen (Claudius Galenus; 129–199?) Greek physician and scholar

1 That physician will hardly be thought very careful of the health of others who neglects his own.
Of Protecting the Health (2nd century), bk. 5

2 Surgery is the ready motion of steady and experienced hands.
Quoted in *Definitiones Medicae* (Joannes Guinterius; 1539)

3 Confidence and hope do be more good than physic.
Attrib.

4 Employment is nature's physician, and is essential to human happiness.
Attrib.

Galileo (Galileo Galilei; 1564–1642) Italian scientist

Quotations about Galileo

1 Galileo was no idiot. Only an idiot could believe that science requires martyrdom—that may be necessary in religion, but in time a scientific result will establish itself.
David Hilbert (1862–1943) German mathematician and philosopher. Quoted in *Mathematical Circles Squared* (H. Eves; 1971)

2 What Galileo and Newton were to the seventeenth century, Darwin was to the nineteenth.
Bertrand Russell (1872–1970) British philosopher and mathematician. *A History of Western Philosophy* (1945)

Quotations by Galileo

3 In my studies of astronomy and philosophy I hold this opinion about the universe, that the Sun remains fixed in the centre of the circle of heavenly bodies, without changing its place; and the Earth, turning upon itself, moves round the Sun.
Letter to Cristina di Lorena, Grandduchess of Tuscany (1615)

4 It is not in the power of professors of demonstrative sciences to change their opinions at pleasure, and adopt first one side and then the other.
Letter to Cristina di Lorena, Grandduchess of Tuscany (1615)

5 It is the Holy Spirit's intention to teach us how to go to heaven, not how the heavens go.
Letter to Cristina di Lorena, Grandduchess of Tuscany (1615)

6 Yet it moves.
Referring to the earth, and supposedly said after his recantation before the Inquisition of belief in the Copernican system, which proposed that the earth revolved round the sun. Remark (1632). Attrib.

7 That sculpture is more admirable than painting for the reason that it contains relief and painting does not is completely false. For that very reason painting is more marvelous than sculpture, since the relief that is seen in sculpture does not look like sculpture but like painting.
Letter to Ludovico Cigoli, *Galileo as a Critic of the Arts* (Erwin Panofsky; 1954)

8 I feel sure that the surface of the Moon is not perfectly smooth, free from inequalities and exactly spherical...on the contrary, it is full of inequalities, uneven, full of hollows and protuberances, just like the surface of the Earth itself, which is varied everywhere by lofty mountains and deep valleys.
Referring to his observations with a telescope he had made. *The Starry Messenger* (March 1610)

9 I therefore concluded, and decided unhesitatingly, that there are three stars in the heavens moving about Jupiter, as Venus and Mercury round the Sun; which at length was established as clear as daylight by numerous other subsequent observations.
Referring to his observations with a telescope he had made. *The Starry Messenger* (March 1610)

10 Measure what is measurable, and make measurable what is not so.
Quoted in "Mathematics and the Laws of Nature," *The Armchair Science Reader* (I. Gordon and S. Sorkin, eds.; 1959)

Gallagher, Noel (b.1967) British rock musician

1 We'd always get in a van and go anywhere to play a gig, whereas your middle-class groups will say, "I'm not doing that, I've got college in the morning".
Guardian, London (March 17, 1995)

Gallup, George (George Horace Gallup; 1901–84) U.S. statistician and public opinion analyst

1 I could prove God statistically.
Attrib.

Galsworthy, John (1867–1933) British novelist and playwright

1 There is just one rule for politicians all over the world. Don't say in Power what you say in Opposition: if you do you only have to carry out what the other fellows have found impossible.
Maid in Waiting (1931)

2 Nobody ever tells me anything.
Repeatedly said by James Forsyte in *The Man of Property* (1906) and *In Chancery* (1920). *The Man of Property* (1906), pt. 1, ch. 1

3 Public opinion is always in advance of the law.
Windows (1922)

Galvin, Robert W. (Robert William Galvin; b.1922) U.S. business executive

1 No sanctuary.
Said when chief executive officer of Motorola, referring to his attitude toward Japanese competitors. *Fortune* (March 11, 1991)

Gambetta, Léon (Léon Michel Gambetta; 1838–82) French statesman

1 Clericalism—there is the enemy.
Speech, French Chamber of Deputies (May 5, 1877)

2 To remain a great nation or to become one, you must colonize.
Quoted in *Europe Since 1870* (James Joll; 1973), ch. 4

Games, Abram (b.1914) British graphic designer

1 Maximum meaning—minimum means.
Quoted in *Contemporary Designers* (Colin Naylor, ed.; 1990)

Gandhi, Indira (originally Indira Priyadarshini Nehru; 1917–84) Indian prime minister

Quotations about Gandhi

1 Her weapon is the snub, a regal, chilling silence. Her silences, as could be testified by ex-President Nixon, whom she disliked, can be disconcerting.
Trevor Fishlock (b.1941) British journalist. "Empress Indira," *Times*, London (March 22, 1982)

Quotations by Gandhi

2 There are moments in history when brooding tragedy and its dark shadows can be lightened by recalling great moments of the past.
Letter to U.S. president Richard Nixon (December 19, 1971)

3 You cannot shake hands with a clenched fist.
Remark, press conference, New Delhi (October 19, 1971)

4 Advanced countries of today have reached their present affluence through domination of other races and countries...Their sheer ruthlessness, undisturbed by feelings of compassion or by abstract theories of freedom, equality or justice, gave them a head start.
Speech, Stockholm, Sweden (June 14, 1973)

5 As for Western women, it seems to me that they have often had to struggle to obtain their own rights. That did not leave them much time to prove their abilities. The time will come.
Conversation with Vilallonga (1975)

6 I don't mind if my life goes in the service of the nation. If I die today every drop of my blood will invigorate the nation.
October 30, 1984. Said the night before she was assassinated. *Sunday Times*, London (December 3, 1989)

7 There exists no politician in India daring enough to attempt to explain to the masses that cows can be eaten.
Quoted in "Indira's Coup," *New York Review of Books* (Oriana Fallaci; 1975)

8 To bear many children is considered not only a religious blessing but also an investment. The greater their number, some Indians reason, the more alms they can beg.
Quoted in "Indira's Coup," *New York Review of Books* (Oriana Fallaci; 1975)

Gandhi, Mahatma (Mohandas Karamchand Gandhi; 1869–1948) Indian national leader

Quotations about Gandhi

1 A dear old man with his bald pate and spectacles, beaky nose and birdlike lips and benign but somewhat toothless smile.

Rodney Bennett, British journalist. *Teacher's World* (May 7, 1930)

2 I know of no other man in our time, or indeed in recent history, who so convincingly demonstrated the power of the spirit over things material.
Stafford Cripps (1889–1952) British politician, lawyer, and economist. Speech, Commonwealth Prime Ministers' Conference, London (October 1, 1948)

3 Friends and comrades, I do not quite know what to tell you and how to say it. Our beloved leader, Bapu as we called him, the father of our nation, is no more. The light has gone out...
Jawaharlal Nehru (1889–1964) Indian prime minister. Referring to the assassination of Mahatma Gandhi. Broadcast on All India Radio (January 30, 1948)

4 Gandhi was very keen on sex. He renounced it when he was 36, so thereafter it was never very far from his thoughts.
Woodrow Wyatt (1918–97) British journalist and writer. *Sunday Times*, London (November 27, 1977)

Quotations by Gandhi

5 Think of the poorest person you have ever seen and ask if your next act will be of any use to him.
Epitaph (1948)

6 As in law so in war, the longest purse finally wins.
Paper read to the Bombay Provincial Co-operative Conference (September 17, 1917)

7 It is a mark of wisdom not to kick away the very step from which we have risen higher. The removal of one step from a staircase brings down the whole of it.
Criticizing extremist political groups who spurned the heritage of former Congress moderates. Remark (1908)

8 Capital as such is not evil; it is its wrong use that is evil. Capital in some form or other will always be needed.
Harijan (1940)

9 Man becomes what he eats. The grosser the food the grosser the body.
Harijan (August 5, 1933)

10 Increase of material comforts, it may be generally laid down, does not in any way whatsoever conduce to moral growth.
Quoted in his obituary. *News Chronicle* (1948)

11 It is better to be violent, if there is violence in our hearts, than to put on the cloak of non-violence to cover impotence.
Non-Violence in Peace and War (1948)

12 Non-violence is not a garment to be put on and off at will. Its seat is in the heart and it must be an inseparable part of our very being.
Non-Violence in Peace and War (1948)

13 What is a man if he is not a thief who openly charges as much as he can for the goods he sells?
Non-Violence in Peace and War (1948)

14 Like opium production, the world manufacture of armaments needs to be restricted. The sword is probably responsible for more misery in the world than opium.
Young India (November 19, 1925)

15 Non-violence is the law of our species as violence is the law of the brute. The spirit lies dormant in the brute and he knows no law but that of physical might. The dignity of man requires obedience to another law—to the strength of the spirit.
Young India (August 11, 1920)

16 To a people famishing and idle, the only acceptable form in which God can dare to appear is work and promise of food and wages.
Young India (October 13, 1921)

17 A country that is governed by even its national army can never be morally free.
Quoted in *Questions in the Philosophy of Restraint* (Indira Rothermund; 1963)

18 Complete independence through truth and non-violence means the independence of every unit, be it the humblest of the nation, without distinction of race, colour or creed.
Quoted in *Questions in the Philosophy of Restraint* (Indira Rothermund; 1963)

19 If India won her freedom through truth and non-violence, India would not only point the way to all the exploited Asiatic nations, she would become a torch-bearer for the Negro races.
Quoted in *Questions in the Philosophy of Restraint* (Indira Rothermund; 1963)

20 If one man gains spiritually, the whole world gains with him, and if one man fails, the whole world fails to that extent.
Quoted in *Questions in the Philosophy of Restraint* (Indira Rothermund; 1963)

21 My service to my people is part of the discipline to which I subject myself in order to free my soul from the bonds of the flesh...For me the path of salvation leads through the unceasing tribulation in the service of my fellow countrymen and humanity.
Quoted in *Questions in the Philosophy of Restraint* (Indira Rothermund; 1963)

22 Willing submission to social restraint for the sake of the well-being of the whole of society, enriches both the individual and the society of which he is a member.
Quoted in *Questions in the Philosophy of Restraint* (Indira Rothermund; 1963)

23 You may, if you like, cut us to pieces. You may shatter us at the canon's mouth. If you act contrary to our will we shall not help you and without our help, we know that you cannot move one step forward. It is likely that you will laugh at all this in the intoxication of your power.
Addressing the British. Quoted in *Questions in the Philosophy of Restraint* (Indira Rothermund; 1963)

24 God has no religion.
Attrib.

25 I eat to live, to serve, and also, if it so happens, to enjoy, but I do not eat for the sake of enjoyment.
Attrib.

26 I think it would be a good idea.
On being asked for his view on Western civilization. Attrib.

Garbo, Greta (Greta Lovisa Gustafsson; 1905–90) Swedish-born U.S. film actor

Quotations about Garbo

1 The face of Garbo is an Idea, that of Hepburn, an Event.
Roland Barthes (1915–80) French philosopher and writer. Referring to Greta Garbo and Audrey Hepburn. *Mythologies* (1957)

2 She is every man's fantasy mistress. She gave you the impression

that, if your imagination had to sin, it could at least congratulate itself on its impeccable taste.
Alistair Cooke (b.1908) British-born U.S. broadcaster and writer. Quoted in *Words of Women* (Anne Stibbs; 1993)

3 What, when drunk, one sees in other women, one sees in Garbo sober.
Kenneth Tynan (1927–80) British theater critic. *Sunday Times*, London (August 25, 1963)

Quotations by Garbo

4 Gimme a viskey. Ginger ale on the side. And don't be stingy, baby.
Anna Christie (1930)

5 I want to be alone.
Words spoken by Garbo in the film *Grand Hotel*, and associated with her for the rest of her career. *Grand Hotel* (1932)

6 I never said, "I want to be alone." I only said, "I want to be *left* alone." There is all the difference.
Quoted in *Garbo* (John Bainbridge; 1955)

7 Ah, the sex thing. I'm glad that part of my life is over.
Attrib.

8 The story of my life is about back entrances and side doors and secret elevators and other ways of getting in and out of places so that people won't bother you.
Attrib.

Garcia, Jerry (Jerome John Garcia; b.1942) U.S. rock band leader, guitarist, and songwriter

1 Acid has changed consciousness entirely. The U.S. has changed in the last few years and it's because that whole first psychedelic thing meant: Here's this new consciousness, this new freedom, and it's here in yourself.
1970. Quoted in *Rock 'n' Roll Babylon* (Gary Herman; 1994)

García Lorca, Federico (1899–1936) Spanish poet and playwright

Quotations about García Lorca

1 Friends, carve a monument
out of dream stone
for the poet in the Alhambra,
over a fountain where the grieving water
shall say forever:
the crime was in Granada, his Granada.
1936
Antonio Machado (1875–1939) Spanish poet and playwright. Referring to Federico García Lorca, who was assassinated by nationalists near Granada in 1936. "The Crime Was in Granada," *Selected Poems* (Alan S. Trueblood, tr.; 1982), ll. 34–39

Quotations by García Lorca

2 To animate, in the precise sense of the word: to give life to.
1928. Inaugural lecture for the Granada Atheneum theater's season, *A Dream of Life* (Leslie Stainton; 1998)

3 I do not believe any artist works in a state of fever. Even the mystics begin working only after the ineffable dove of the Holy Spirit has already abandoned their cells.
1926. "The Poetic Imagination of Luis de Góngora," *Deep Song* (Christopher Maurer, tr.; 1980)

4 To see you naked is to recall the Earth.
"Casida of the Woman Prone," *Divan of the Tamarit* (1936)

5 And yet, hope pursues me, encircles me, bites me; like a dying wolf tightening its grip for the last time.
Doña Rosita the Spinster (1935), Act 3

6 The artist, and particularly the poet, is always an anarchist, and can only listen to the voices that rise up from within his own being, three imperious voices: the voice of Death, with all its presentiments; the voice of Love and the voice of Art.
1933. Newspaper interview, Léon, *Federico García Lorca* (Ian Gibson; 1989), pt. 2, ch. 6

7 At five o'clock in the afternoon. At exactly five o'clock in the afternoon.
Lament for Ignacio Sánchez Mejías (1935)

8 Success never satisfies me. Success is almost always a momentary stroke of luck that has nothing to do with a given work's intrinsic value.
Quoted in *A Dream of Life* (Leslie Stainton; 1998)

9 The poet is the medium
of Nature
who explains her grandeur
by means of words.
1918. From a poem on the poet written as an inscription in a copy of Antonio Machado Ruiz's *Campos de Castilla* (1912), belonging to his friend Antonio Gallego Búrin. Quoted in *Collected Poems* (Christopher Maurer, ed.; 1990)

10 I am and always will be on the side of the poor.
Quoted in *Federico García Lorca* (Ian Gibson; 1989), ch. 8

García Márquez, Gabriel (b.1928) Colombian novelist

1 "Homesickness starts with food," said Che Guevara, pining perhaps for the vast roasts of his native Argentina while they, men alone in the night in Sierra Maestra, spoke of war.
"Watching the Rain in Galicia," *Granta Book of Travel* (Bill Buford, ed.; 1991)

2 I don't know where the shame of being a tourist comes from...I like to join those lightning tours in which the guides explain everything you see out of the window.
"Watching the Rain in Galicia," *Granta Book of Travel* (Bill Buford, ed.; 1991)

3 Justice...limps along, but it gets there all the same.
Said by Guardiola to Judge Arcadio. *In Evil Hour* (1968)

4 An early-rising man...a good spouse but a bad husband.
Said by the widow Monteil. *In Evil Hour* (1968)

5 A man knows when he is growing old because he begins to look like his father.
Love in the Time of Cholera (1985)

6 He repeated until his dying day that there was no one with more common sense, no stonecutter more obstinate, no manager more lucid or dangerous, than a poet.
Love in the Time of Cholera (1985)

7 I don't believe in God, but I'm afraid of Him.
Love in the Time of Cholera (1985)

8 The problem with marriage is that it ends every night after making love, and it must be rebuilt every morning before breakfast.
Love in the Time of Cholera (1985)

9 She discovered with great delight that one doesn't love one's children just because they are one's children but because of the friendship formed when raising them.
Referring to Fermina Daza. *Love in the Time of Cholera* (1985)

10 A person doesn't die when he should but when he can.
One Hundred Years of Solitude (1967)

11 It had never occurred to him until then to think that literature was the best plaything that had ever been invented to make fun of people.
One Hundred Years of Solitude (1967)

12 The secret of good old age is simply an honorable pact with solitude.
Said by Aureliano Buendía. *One Hundred Years of Solitude* (1967)

13 The world must be all fucked up when men travel first class and literature goes as freight.
Said by the Catalan bookstore owner in Macondo. *One Hundred Years of Solitude* (1967)

14 If God hadn't rested on Sunday, He would have had time to finish the world.
The Funerals of Mama Grande (1974)

15 Ultimately, literature is nothing but carpentry. With both you are working with reality, a material just as hard as wood.
Quoted in *Writers at Work* (George Plimpton, ed.; 1985)

Gardner, Ed (1904–63) U.S. radio comedian

1 Opera is when a guy gets stabbed in the back and instead of bleeding he sings.
Duffy's Tavern, U.S. radio show (1940)

Gardner, John W. (1912–77) U.S. writer and public official

1 For every talent that poverty has stimulated, it has blighted a hundred.
Excellence: Can We be Equal and Excellent Too? (1961)

2 History never looks like history when you are living through it. It always looks confusing and messy, and it always feels uncomfortable.
No Easy Victories (1968)

3 The man who once cursed his fate, now, curses himself—and pays his psychoanalyst.
No Easy Victories (1968)

Gardner, Martin (b.1914) U.S. philosopher, mathematician, and writer

1 Scientists who falsify their results are regarded by their peers as committing an inexcusable crime. Yet the sad fact is that the history of science swarms with cases of outright fakery and instances of scientists who unconsciously distorted their work by seeing it through lenses of passionately held beliefs.
Science: Good, Bad and Bogus (1981)

2 In discussing extremes of unorthodoxy in science I consider it a waste of time to give rational arguments. Those who are in agreement do not need to be educated about such trivial matters, and trying to enlighten those who disagree is like trying to write on water.
Science: Good, Bad and Bogus (1981), introduction

Garfield, James A. (James Abram; 1831–81) U.S. statesman

Quotations about Garfield

1 Log Cabin to White House
William Roscoe Thayer (1859–1923) U.S. writer. The title of his biography of President James Garfield (1831–81). *Log Cabin to White House* (1910)

Quotations by Garfield

2 Suicide is not a remedy.
Inaugural address (March 4, 1881)

3 I am an advocate of paper money, but that paper money must represent what it professes on its face. I do not wish to hold in my hands the printed lies of government.
Speech to Congress (1866)

4 My fellow citizens, the President is dead, but the Government lives and God Omnipotent reigns.
April 14, 1865. Following the assassination of Abraham Lincoln. Speech, *New York Herald* (April 16, 1865), quoted in *Garfield: A Biography* (Allan Peskin; 1978), ch. 12

5 The lesson of history is rarely learned by the actors themselves.
Attrib. *Maxims of James Abram Garfield* (William Ralston Balch; 1880)

6 The world's history is a divine poem, of which the history of every nation is a canto, and every man a word.
Attrib. *The Meaning of History* (N. Gordon and Joyce Carper; 1991)

Garfield, Leon (1921–96) British writer

1 Lady Bullock, who had been at death's door for so long now that one might have been pardoned for mistaking her for its knocker.
The Prisoners of September (1975), ch. 29

Garibaldi, Giuseppe (1807–82) Italian nationalist leader

1 Anyone who wants to carry on the war against the outsiders, come with me. I can't offer you either honors or wages; I offer you hunger, thirst, forced marches, battles and death. Anyone who loves his country, follow me.
1882. *Garibaldi* (G. Guerzoni; 1929)

Garland, Hamlin (Hannibal Hamlin Garland; 1860–1940) U.S. novelist and critic

1 It is blind fetishism, timid provincialism, or commercial greed which puts the works of "the masters" above the living, breathing artist.
Crumbling Idols: Twelve Essays on Art and Literature (1894)

Garland, Judy (Frances Gumm; 1922–69) U.S. film actor and singer

1 I was born at the age of twelve on a Metro-Goldwyn-Mayer lot.
Observer, London (February 18, 1951), "Sayings of the Week"

2 We cast away priceless time in dreams, born of imagination, fed upon illusion, and put to death by reality.
Quoted in *Judy Garland* (Anne Edwards; 1974)

Garner, Alan (1934–96) British author

1 Possessive parents rarely live long enough to see the fruits of their selfishness.
The Owl Service (1967)

Garner, John Nance (1868–1967) U.S. vice president

1 A spare tire on the automobile of government.
Referring to the vice presidency. Speech (June 19, 1934)

Garnet, Henry Highland (1815–82) U.S. clergyman and abolitionist

1 However much you and all of us may desire it, there is not much hope of redemption without the shedding of blood. If you must bleed, let it all come at once—rather *die freemen, than live to be slaves.*
1843. "An address to the Slaves of the United States of America," *A Documentary History of the Negro People in the United States* (Herbert Aptheker; 1951), vol. 1

2 Millions have come from eternity into time, and have returned again to the world of spirits, cursed and ruined by American slavery.
1843. "An address to the Slaves of the United States of America," *A Documentary History of the Negro People in the United States* (Herbert Aptheker; 1951), vol. 1

3 The humblest peasant is as free in the sight of God as the proudest monarch that every swayed a sceptre. Liberty is a spirit sent out from God, and like its great Author, is no respecter of persons.
1843. "An address to the Slaves of the United States of America," *A Documentary History of the Negro People in the United States* (Herbert Aptheker; 1951), vol. 1

Garrick, David (1717–79) British actor-manager

Quotations about Garrick

1 I am disappointed by that stroke of death, which has eclipsed the gaiety of nations and impoverished the public stock of harmless pleasure.
Samuel Johnson (1709–84) British lexicographer and writer. Epitaph on David Garrick. "Edmund Smith," *Lives of the English Poets* (1779–81)

Quotations by Garrick

2 Prologues precede the piece—in mournful verse;
As undertakers—walk before the hearse.
Apprentice (Arthur Murphy; 1756), Prologue

Garrison, William Lloyd (1805–79) U.S. abolitionist

1 Our country is the world—our countrymen are all mankind.
"Prospectus," *The Liberator* (December 15, 1837)

2 I am in earnest—I will not equivocate—I will not excuse—I will not retreat a single inch; and I will be heard!
"Salutory Address," *The Liberator* (January 1, 1831), vol. 1, no. 1

3 The compact which exists between the North and the South is a covenant with death and an agreement with hell.
January 27, 1843. Resolution adopted by the Massachusetts Anti-Slavery Society. Quoted in *William Lloyd Garrison: The Abolitionist* (Archibald H Grimke; 1891), ch. 16

Garrod, Heathcote William (1878–1960) British classical scholar and literary critic

1 Madam, I am the civilization they are fighting to defend.
Replying to criticism during World War I (1914–18) that he was not fighting to defend civilization. Quoted in *Oxford Now and Then* (D. Balsdon; 1970)

Garth, Samuel, Sir (1661–1719) English physician and poet

1 The patient's ears remorseless he assails;
Murder with jargon where his medicine fails.
The Dispensary (1699)

2 See, one physician, like a sculler plies,
The patient lingers and by inches dies,
But two physicians, like a pair of oars
Waft him more swiftly to the Stygian shores.
Attrib.

Garvey, Marcus (Marcus Moziah Aurelius Garvey; 1887–1940) Jamaica-born black nationalist leader and publisher

1 Let no voice but your own speak to you from the depths.
"African Fundamentalism, A Racial Hierarchy and Empire for Negroes" (1923)

2 There is no humanity before that which starts with yourself.
"African Fundamentalism, A Racial Hierarchy and Empire for Negroes" (1923)

3 We believe in the freedom of Africa for the Negro people of the world, and by the principle of Europe for the Europeans, and Asia for the Asiatics, we also demand Africa for the Africans at home and abroad.
Bill of Rights adopted by the first International Convention of the Negro People of the World (August 1920)

4 There are more criminals out of jail than in jail, the only difference is that the majority of those who are out, are such skillful criminals that they know how to keep themselves out.
Speech, Carnegie Hall, New York (August 1, 1924)

5 We are not engaged in domestic politics, in church building, or in social uplift work, but we are engaged in nation building.
Speech to the Principles of the Universal Negro Improvement Society, New York (November 25, 1922)

6 I asked, "Where is the black man's Government?" "Where is his King and his kingdom?" "Where is his President, his country, and his ambassador, his army, his navy, his men of big affairs?" I could not find them, and then I declared, "I will help to make them."
"The Negro's Greatest Enemy" (1923)

7 All emancipation is from within. That is to say, real emancipation. As a man thinketh so is he.
1935. *The Black Man* (June–December 1935)

8 I know no national boundary where the Negro is concerned. The whole world is my province until Africa is free.
The Philosophy and Opinions of Marcus Garvey (Amy Jacques Garvey, ed.; 1923)

9 I would prefer to be honestly wealthy, than miserably poor.
The Philosophy and Opinions of Marcus Garvey (Amy Jacques Garvey, ed.; 1923)

10 No one knows when the hour of Africa's Redemption cometh. It is in the wind. It is coming. One day like a storm, it will be here. When that day comes all Africa will stand together.
The Philosophy and Opinions of Marcus Garvey (Amy Jacques Garvey, ed.; 1923)

11 Power is the only argument that satisfies man.
The Philosophy and Opinions of Marcus Garvey (Amy Jacques Garvey, ed.; 1923)

12 Climb ye the heights of liberty and cease not in well doing until you have planted the banner of the Red, the Black and the Green on the hilltops of Africa.
1923. The Red, Black, and Green were the colors of Marcus Garvey's Back to Africa movement. Attrib.

Garvey, Steve (b.1948) U.S. baseball player

1 We are not surgeons or even plumbers. Society cannot do without those skills; it can certainly do without ballplayers.
Attrib.

Gascoigne, George (1525?–77) English poet

1 Our bumbast hose, our treble double ruffes
Our sutes of silke, our comely guarded capes,
Our knit silk stockes, and spanish lether shoes...,
Are pricking spurres, provocking filthy pride,
And snares (unseen) which leade a man to hell.
The Steel Glas (1575), quoted in *The Complete Poems of George Gascoigne* (William Caven Hazlitt, ed.; 1870), vol. 2

Gaskell, Elizabeth (Elizabeth Cleghorn Stevenson; 1810–65) British novelist

1 Where evidence takes a supernatural character, there is no disproving it.
The story is set in Salem, Massachusetts, in 1692. "Lois the Witch" (1859)

2 A man...is *so* in the way in the house!
Cranford (1853), ch. 1

3 "It is very pleasant dining with a bachelor," said Miss Matty, softly, as we settled ourselves in the counting-house. "I only hope it is not improper; so many pleasant things are!"
Cranford (1853), ch. 4

4 That kind of patriotism which consists in hating all other nations.
Sylvia's Lovers (1863), ch. 1

Gassman, Vittorio (b.1922) Italian actor

1 Men don't understand anything about women and women understand nothing about men. And it's better that way.
Attrib.

Gates, Bill (William Henry Gates, III; b.1955) U.S. business executive

1 A fundamental new rule for business is that the Internet changes everything.
Business@the Speed of Thought: Using a Digital Nervous System (co-written with Collins Hemingway; 1999)

2 If the government, usually the largest "business" in any country, is a leader in the use of technology, it will automatically lift the country's technical skills and drive the move to an information market.
Business@the Speed of Thought: Using a Digital Nervous System (co-written with Collins Hemingway; 1999)

3 Information flow is the lifeblood of your company because it enables you to get the most out of your people and learn from your customers.
Business@the Speed of Thought: Using a Digital Nervous System (co-written with Collins Hemingway; 1999)

4 The CEO's role in raising a company's corporate IQ is to establish an atmosphere that promotes knowledge sharing and collaboration.
Business@the Speed of Thought: Using a Digital Nervous System (co-written with Collins Hemingway; 1999)

5 The Internet is becoming the town square for the global village of tomorrow.
Business@the Speed of Thought: Using a Digital Nervous System (co-written with Collins Hemingway; 1999)

6 You know you have built an excellent digital nervous system when information flows through your organization as quickly and naturally as thought in a human being...It's business at the speed of thought.
Business@the Speed of Thought: Using a Digital Nervous System (co-written with Collins Hemingway; 1999)

7 The growing technical prowess of nations such as India unnerves some people in developed countries who fear a loss of jobs and opportunities. I think these fears are misplaced. Economics is not a zero-sum game.
New York Times (April 8, 1997)

Gaule, John (*fl.* 1604–87) English cleric

1 Every old woman with a wrinkled face, a furr'd brow, a hairy lip, a gobber tooth, a squint eye, a squeaking voice, or a scolding tongue...a dog or cat by her side, is not only suspected but pronounced for a witch.
Referring to the activities of witch-finder General Matthew Hopkins. *Sermons on Witchcraft* (June 30, 1646)

Gaultier, Jean Paul (b.1952) French fashion designer

1 I never tried to be anti-establishment or to shock.
Quoted in "Jean Paul the First," *Elle* (Iain R. Webb; April 1998)

2 I want to make clothes that women want to have and want to wear and are not just sensational.
Quoted in "Jean Paul the First," *Elle* (Iain R. Webb; April 1998)

Gauss, Carl Friedrich (Johann Friedrich Carl Gauss; 1777–1855) German mathematician and astronomer

Quotations about Gauss

1 He is like the fox, who effaces his tracks in the sand with his tail.
Niels Henrik Abel (1802–29) Norwegian mathematician. Quoted in *Calculus Gems* (G. F. Simmons; 1992)

Quotations by Gauss

2 It is not knowledge, but the act of learning, not possession but the act of getting there, which grants the greatest enjoyment.
Letter to Farkas Bolyai (1808)

3 You know that I write slowly. This is chiefly because I am never satisfied until I have said as much as possible in a few words, and writing briefly takes far more time than writing at length.
Quoted in *Calculus Gems* (G. F. Simmons; 1992)

4 I have had my results for a long time: but I do not yet know how I am to arrive at them
Quoted in *The Mind and the Eye* (A. Arber; 1954)

5 God does arithmetic.
Attrib.

Gautier, Théophile (1811–72) French poet and critic

1 Yes, creation comes out more beautiful from a form rebellious to work, verse, marble, onyx, or enamel.
"L'Art," *Emaux et Camées* (1852)

2 I am a man for whom the outside world exists.
Journal des Goncourt (May 1, 1857)

Gay, John (1685–1732) English poet and playwright

1 Behold the bright original appear.
"A Letter to a Lady," l. 85, quoted in *The Poetical Works of John Gay* (G. C. Faber, ed.; 1926)

2 Variety's the source of joy below,
From whence still fresh revolving pleasures flow.
In books and love, the mind one end pursues,
And only change th'expiring flame renews.
"Lesser Epistles On a Miscellany To Bernard Linott," ll. 41–44, quoted in *The Poetical Works of John Gay* (G. C. Faber, ed.; 1926)

3 Life is a jest; and all things show it.
I thought so once; but now I know it.
"My Own Epitaph" (1720)

4 We only part to meet again.
Change, as ye list, ye winds; my heart shall be
The faithful compass that still points to thee.
"Sweet William's Farewell to Black-Eyed Susan" (1720)

5 Whence is thy learning? Hath thy toil
O'er books consum'd the midnight oil?
Fables (1727), Introduction, l. 15

6 'Tis a gross error, held in schools,
That Fortune always favours fools.
"Pan and Fortune," *Fables* (1727), st. 2, l. 12

7 And when a lady's in the case,
You know, all other things give place.
"The Hare and Many Friends," *Fables* (1727), l. 41

8 Fools may our scorn, not envy raise,
For envy is a kind of praise.
"The Hound and the Huntsman," *Fables* (1727), st. 1, l. 44

9 In every age and clime we see,
Two of a trade can ne'er agree.
"The Rat-Catcher and the Cats," *Fables* (1727), st. 1, l. 21

10 "While there is life, there's hope," he cried;
"Then why such haste?" so groaned and died.
"The Sick Man and the Angel," *Fables* (1727), st. 1, l. 27

11 "Is there no hope?" the sick Man said,
The silent doctor shook his head,
And took his leave with signs of sorrow,
Despairing of his fee to-morrow.
"The Sick Man and the Angel," *Fables* (1727), st. 1, ll. 1–4, quoted in *The Poetical Works of John Gay* (G. C. Faber, ed.; 1926)

12 No sir, tho' I was born and bred in England, I can dare to be poor, which is the only thing now-a-days men are asham'd of.
Polly (1729), Act 1, Scene 2

13 An inconstant woman, tho' she has no chance to be very happy, can never be very unhappy.
Polly (1729), Act 1, Scene 14

14 How, like a moth, the simple maid
Still plays about the flame!
The Beggar's Opera (1728), Act 1, Scene 4

15 Do you think your mother and I should have liv'd comfortably so long together, if ever we had been married?
The Beggar's Opera (1728), Act 1, Scene 8

16 If with me you'd fondly stray,
Over the hills and far away.
The Beggar's Opera (1728), Act 1, Scene 8

17 A moment of time may make us unhappy for ever.
The Beggar's Opera (1728), Act 2, Scene 5

18 I think you must ev'n do as other widows buy yourself weeds, and be cheerful.
The Beggar's Opera (1728), Act 2, Scene 11

19 She who has never loved has never lived.
The Captives (1724), Act 2, Scene 2

Gay, Peter (Peter Froehlich; b.1923) German-born U.S. cultural historian

1 Germany can be said to be the only country that could have taken seriously Shelley's famous dictum that "poets are the unacknowledged legislators of the world."
Weimar Culture: The Outsider as Insider (1968)

Gaye, Marvin (Marvin Pentz Gay, Jr.; 1939–84) U.S. singer and songwriter

1 Music, not sex, got me aroused.
Quoted in *Divided Soul: The Life of Marvin Gaye* (David Ritz; 1985)

2 I'm not going to be dictated to by fans, certainly. I'm dictated enough to by my record company to last me a million years.
Quoted in *Melody Maker* (Geoff Brown; October 9, 1976)

Geddes, Eric, Sir (Eric Campbell Geddes; 1875–1937) British politician

1 The Germans, if this Government is returned, are going to pay every penny; they are going to be squeezed, as a lemon is

squeezed—until the pips squeak. My only doubt is not whether we can squeeze hard enough, but whether there is enough juice.
Referring to German reparations after World War I (1914–18). Speech at Cambridge Guildhall, *Cambridge Daily News* (December 10, 1918)

Geldof, Bob (Robert Frederick Zenon Geldof; b.1954) Irish rock musician

1 Feed the World
Let them know it's Christmas.
Song lyric, written to raise money for the relief of famine in Ethiopia, and performed by Band Aid. "Do They Know It's Christmas" (1984)

2 I'm not interested in the bloody system! Why has he no food? Why is he starving to death?
Observer, London (October 27, 1985), "Sayings of the Week"

3 Irish Americans are about as Irish as Black Americans are African.
Observer, London (June 22, 1986), "Sayings of the Week"

Gellhorn, Martha (1908–98) U.S. journalist and author

1 The driver...said that Puerto Escondido was half an hour from Havana; my introduction to Cuban optimism. "No problem" might be the national motto.
"Cuba Revisited," *Granta Book of Travel* (Bill Buford, ed.; 1991)

2 The first morning in Havana, I stood by the sea-wall on the Malecon, feeling weepy with homesickness for this city.
"Cuba Revisited," *Granta Book of Travel* (Bill Buford, ed.; 1991)

3 The American war in Vietnam destroyed three ancient civilizations. They had survived through millennia everything history can do, which is always plenty, but they could not survive us, who understood nothing about them, nor valued them, and do not grieve for them.
"Last Words on Vietnam, 1987," *The Face of War* (1988)

4 The only aspect of our travels that is guaranteed to hold an audience is disaster.
Travels with Myself and Another (1978)

5 I offer that as a universal test of travel; boredom, called by any other name, is why you yearn for the first available transport out.
"What Bores Whom?," *Worst Journeys* (Keath Fraser, ed.; 1991)

Gell-Mann, Murray, Dr. (b.1929) U.S. particle physicist

1 Both biological and cultural diversity are now severely threatened and working for their preservation is a critical task.
The Quark and the Jaguar (1994)

2 I have always been astonished by the tendency of so many academic psychologists, economists, and even anthropologists to treat human beings as entirely rational. My own experience has always been that rationality is only one of many factors governing human behavior and by no means always the dominant factor.
The Quark and the Jaguar (1994)

Gellner, Ernest (Ernest Andre Gellner; 1925–95) British anthropologist and philosopher

1 Unlike Stoicism, psychoanalysis does not promise the good man that he will be happy even on the rack; but only that his unhappiness on the rack will be ordinary, and not neurotic.
The Psychoanalytic Movement (1985)

2 A cleric who loses his faith abandons his calling; a philosopher who loses his redefines his subject.
Words and Things (1968)

Geneen, Harold (Harold Sydney Geneen; 1910–97) U.S. business executive

1 Like mushrooms, they look enticing, but their nutritional value can be suspect. Some are even poisonous.
Referring to management consultancy concepts. *The Synergy Myth* (co-written with Brent Bowers, 1997)

2 If you keep working, you'll last longer, and I just want to keep vertical. I'd hate to spend the rest of my life trying to outwit an 18-inch fish.
Quoted in *New York Times* (November 23, 1997), obituary

3 My philosophy is to stay as close as possible to what's happening. If I can't solve something, how the hell can I expect my managers to?
Quoted in *New York Times* (November 23, 1997), obituary

Genet, Jean (1910–86) French writer

1 The eternal couple of the criminal and the saint.
The Maids (1947), Scene 2

2 Crimes of which a people is ashamed constitute its real history. The same is true of man.
The Screens (1973), preparatory notes

3 To achieve harmony in bad taste is the height of elegance.
The Thief's Journal (1949)

Genghis Khan (Temujin; 1167?–1227) Mongol ruler and conqueror

1 The words of the lad Kublai are well worth attention...One day he will sit in my seat and bring you good fortune such as you have had in my times.
Referring to his grandson, Kublai Khan. *Last words* (1227)

2 It is forbidden ever to make peace with a monarch, a prince or a people who have not submitted.
Genghis Khan's military abilities were reinforced by a ruthless approach. He habitually used massacre as a tool of conquest. *Laws* (1206?)

3 Man's greatest good fortune is to chase and defeat his enemy, seize his total possessions, leave his married women weeping and wailing, ride his gelding, use the bodies of his women as a nightshirt and support.
Quoted in "Flesh," *A History of Warfare* (John Keegan; 1993)

Genovese, Eugene D. (Eugene Dominick Genovese; b.1930) U.S. historian

1 Those who find America an especially violent and oppressive country have apparently never read the history of England or France, Germany or Russia, Indonesia or Burundi, Turkey or Uganda.
Quoted in *New York Times* (June 18, 1978)

Genscher, Hans-Dietrich (b.1927) German politician

1 The highlights and shadows of our history give us cause to reflect in these days, to reflect on that which was done in the name of Germany. That will not repeat itself.
Independent, London (October 5, 1990)

2 This is a day of jubilation, a day of remembrance and gratitude. Our common task now is to establish a new European order.
Referring to the conclusion of the agreement to reunite East and West Germany. *Independent*, London (September 10, 1990)

George, Dan, Chief (1899–1981) Canadian Native American leader and actor

1 When the white man came we had the land and they had the Bibles; now they have the land and we have the Bibles.
Attrib.

George, Daniel (Daniel George Bunting; 1890–1967) British writer

1 O Freedom, what liberties are taken in thy name!
A parody of the reputed last words of Madame Roland, a French revolutionary who was guillotined (1793). *The Perpetual Pessimist* (1963)

George, Henry (1839–97) U.S. economist

1 Capital is a result of labor, and is used by labor to assist it in further production. Labor is the active and initial force, and labor is therefore the employer of capital.
Progress and Poverty (1877–79)

2 It is but a truism that labor is most productive where its wages are largest. Poorly paid labor is inefficient labor, the world over.
Progress and Poverty (1877–79)

3 Society is an organism, not a machine.
Progress and Poverty (1877–79)

4 We cannot safely leave politics to politicians, or political economy to college professors. The people themselves must think, because the people alone can act.
Social Problems (1883)

5 The value of a thing is the amount of laboring or work that its possession will save the possessor.
The Science of Political Economy (1897)

George, Nelson U.S. journalist

1 A terrible school system, an addictive welfare system, and a government that lets drugs pour into the community have, along with twin turntables...conspired to make these young people come up with their own distinctive brand of entertainment.
Referring to the beginnings of rap music in the South Bronx and Harlem, New York City. *Musician* (1980)

2 It is Hollywood who originated the "hip hop de hippy hop the body rock" that lead to the rap-breaking graffiti scene labeled hip hop.
Referring to DJ Hollywood, a South Bronx rapping disc jockey credited by many as the originator of hip hop. *Village Voice* (1980)

George I, King of Great Britain and Ireland (1660–1727) German-born British monarch

Quotations about George I

1 The King, observing with judicious eyes
The state of both his universities,
To Oxford sent a troop of horse, and why?
That learned body wanted loyalty;
To Cambridge books, as very well discerning
How much that loyal body wanted learning.
Joseph Trapp (1679–1747) English scholar and churchman. Written after George I donated the Bishop of Ely's library to the University of Cambridge. Attrib.

Quotations by George I

2 I hate all Boets and Bainters.
The first of the Hanoverian line of British monarchs, George I never mastered English, which contributed to his unpopularity with his new subjects. Quoted in "Lord Mansfield," *Lives of the Chief Justices* (John Campbell; 1849)

George II, King of Great Britain and Ireland (1683–1760) German-born British monarch

1 There are kings enough in England. I am nothing there, I am old and want rest and should only go to be plagued and teased there about that D&-d House of Commons.
Reply when urged to leave Hanover and return to England. Quoted in Letter from Earl of Holderness to Duke of Newcastle (August 3, 1755)

2 No, I shall have mistresses.
Reply to Queen Caroline's suggestion, as she lay on her deathbed, that he should marry again after her death. *Memoirs of the Reign of George the Second* (John Hervey; 1848), vol. 2

3 Mad, is he? Then I hope he will *bite* some of my other generals.
1759? Replying to the Duke of Newcastle who told him that General James Wolfe was mad. Attrib. *The Life and Letters of James Wolfe* (Henry Beckles Willson; 1909), ch. 17

George III, King of the United Kingdom (1738–1820) British monarch

1 I can never suppose this country so far lost to all ideas of self-importance as to be willing to grant America independence; if that could ever be adopted I shall despair of this country being ever preserved from a state of inferiority and consequently falling into a very low class among the European States.
Letter to Lord North (March 7, 1780)

2 Take care of the woman—do not hurt her, for she is mad.
1786. Referring to Margaret Nicholson, who had attempted to kill him. Attrib.

George IV, King of the United Kingdom (1762–1830) British monarch

Quotations about George IV

1 So poor Prinney is really dead—on a Saturday too.
Thomas Creevey (1768–1838) British politician and diarist. Written on the day of George IV's death. As Prince of Wales he had been popularly known as "Prinney." Letter to Elizabeth Ord (June 26, 1830)

2 This is THE MAN—all shaven and shorn,
All cover'd with Orders—and all forlorn...
Who took to his counsels, in evil hour,
The Friends to the Reasons of lawless Power;
That back the Public Informer, who
Would put down the *Thing*, that, in spite of new Acts,
And attempts to restrain it, by Soldiers of Tax,
Will *poison* the Vermin,
That plunder the Wealth,
That lay in the House,
That Jack built.
William Hone (1780–1842) British writer and bookseller. *The Political House that Jack Built* (1819)

Quotations by George IV

3 Harris, I am not well; pray get me a glass of brandy.
On seeing his future wife, Caroline of Brunswick, for the first time. Quoted in *Diaries and Correspondence* (Earl of Malmesbury; 1795)

George V, King of the United Kingdom (1865–1936) British monarch

Quotations about George V

1 I'd punch him in the snoot.
William Thompson (1869–1944) U.S. politician. His reaction if ever King George V were to come to Chicago. Attrib.

Quotations by George V

2 How is the Empire?
Reputed last words. *Times*, London (January 21, 1936)

3 Bugger Bognor.
His alleged last words, when his doctor promised him he would soon be well enough to visit the coastal resort of Bognor Regis. Quoted in *King George V* (Kenneth Rose; 1983), ch. 9

George VI, King of the United Kingdom (1895–1952) British monarch

1 It is not the walls that make the city, but the people who live within them. The walls of London may be battered, but the spirit of the Londoner stands resolute and undismayed.
Announcement to the Empire near the start of the Blitz, the sustained German bombing of London and other British cities between September 1940 and mid-1941. Radio broadcast (September 23, 1940)

2 We're not a family; we're a firm.
Quoted in *Our Future King* (Peter Lane; 1978)

George-Brown, Lord, Baron George-Brown (George Alfred Brown; 1914–85) British politician

1 It is difficult to go on strike if there is no work in the first place.
Observer, London (February 24, 1980)

Gerald of Wales (Girald de Barri, "Giraldus Cambrensis"; 1146?–1223?) Welsh topographer, archdeacon, and writer

1 Kept a hearth-girl in his house who kindled his fire but extinguished his virtue.
Referring to the parish priest. *Gemma Ecclesiastica* (1210?), quoted in *Giraldus Cambrensis Opera*, 8 vols (J. S. Brewer, J. F. Dimmock, and G. F. Warner, eds.; 1861–91)

2 The English are striving for power, the Welsh for freedom; the English are fighting for national gain, the Welsh to avoid a disaster.
1194? "The Description of Wales," *The Journey Through Wales; and, the Description of Wales* (T. D. Lewis and W. Thorpe, trs.; 1978), book I, ch. 10

3 It is because of their sins, and more particularly the wicked and detestable vice of homosexuality, that the Welsh were punished by God and so lost first Troy and then Britain.
1194? Referring to the belief that the Welsh were orginally refugees from the civilization of Troy and subsequently dominant among the ancient Britons. "The Description of Wales," *The Journey Through Wales; and, the Description of Wales* (T. D. Lewis and W. Thorpe, trs.; 1978), book II, ch. 7

Gerasimov, Gennadi (b.1930) Russian journalist

1 There is a discussion in my country about a new name for the USSR...Philip Morris is sending us billions of cigarettes. So some people suggest our new name should be Marlboro Country.
Sunday Times, London (October 29, 1990)

Gere, Richard (b.1949) U.S. actor

1 I wonder if Deng Xiaoping is actually watching this right now with his children and grandchildren? And with the knowledge what a horrendous, horrendous human rights situation there is in China, and not only towards their own people but to Tibet as well.
Speech at Academy Awards ("Oscars") ceremony (May 1993)

Geronimo (Goyathlay; 1829–1909) Native American Chiricahua Apache leader

1 It is my land, my home, my father's land, to which I now ask to be allowed to return. I want to spend my last days there, and be buried among those mountains.
The land referred to is Arizona. He was writing from the reservations at Fort Sill, Oklahoma. Letter to President Ulysses S. Grant (1877)

2 Once I moved like the wind. Now I surrender to you, and that is all.
He escaped from military custody the next day. Remark to U.S. troops (March 27, 1886)

Gershwin, George (Jacob Gershvin; 1898–1937) U.S. composer

Quotations about Gershwin

1 I liked to do the songs just the way they were written, getting the words out clearly and putting in the meaning the songwriters intended—no less...you don't want to change a Gershwin song around. It's too good.
Fred Astaire (1899–1987) U.S. dancer and actor. Quoted in *Fascinating Rhythm* (Deena Rosenberg; 1991)

2 I've worked with quite a lot of composers and George's method of composing was the nearest thing to playfulness that I've ever known...George sat down as if he were going to have fun.
E. Y. Harburg (1896–1981) U.S. librettist and lyricist. Quoted in *Fascinating Rhythm* (Deena Rosenberg; 1991)

3 George Gershwin died last week. I don't have to believe it if I don't want to.
John O'Hara (1905–70) U.S. novelist and short-story writer. Remark (1937), quoted in *A Dictionary of Musical Quotations* (Ian Crofton and Donald Fraser, eds.; 1985)

Quotations by Gershwin

4 Not many composers have ideas. Far more of them know how to use strange instruments which do not require ideas.
The Composer in the Machine Age (1930)

5 I frequently hear music in the heart of noise.
Quoted in *George Gershwin* (Isaac Goldberg; 1931)

Gershwin, Ira (Israel Gershvin; 1896–1983) U.S. lyricist

1 Nice Work If You Can Get It
Song title. *A Damsel in Distress* (1937)

2 I got rhythm,
I got music,
I got my man—
Who could ask for anything more.
Song lyric. "I Got Rhythm," *Girl Crazy* (1930)

3 I got plenty o' nuttin'
And nuttin's plenty for me.
Song lyric. "I Got Plenty o' Nuttin'," *Porgy and Bess* (1935)

4 Summertime
And the livin' is easy.
Song lyric. "Summertime," *Porgy and Bess* (1935)

5 It ain't necessarily so—
The things that you're liable
To read in the Bible—
It ain't necessarily so.
Song lyric. "It ain't Necessarily So," *Porgy and Bess* (1935)

6 Let's Call the Whole Thing Off!
Song title. *Shall We Dance* (1937)

7 Love is Here to Stay
Song title. *The Goldwyn Follies* (1937)

8 I've Got a Crush on You
1920s. Song title.

Gersonides (Levi ben Gershom; 1288–1344) French rabbi, mathematician, and philosopher

1 By means of rational thought we have reached the opinion that God knows in advance the possibilities open to a man in his freedom, not the particular decisions he will make.
Milhamot ha-Shem (14th century)

Gerstner, Louis, Jr. (b.1942) U.S. business executive

1 Size is not a deterrent to success. I've never seen a small company that didn't want to be a big one. The challenge is being big without being slow.
Speech (October 9, 1996)

2 There is a misconception that small is always more beautiful than big. Just fragmenting an organization does not create conditions sufficient for success.
Fortune (May 31, 1993)

Geschke, Chuck (Charles M. Geschke; b.1939) U.S. business executive and computer scientist

1 Technology travels with people. You can't just throw it over the wall and, because it's such a good idea, expect another engineering group to simply pick it up and run with it.
Quoted in *In the Company of Giants* (Rama Dev Jager; 1997)

Getty, J. Paul (Jean Paul Getty; 1892–1976) U.S. oil magnate

1 Ability and achievement are *bona fides* no one dares question, no matter how unconventional the man who presents them.
How to be Rich (1966)

2 Be an individualist—and an individual. You'll be amazed at how much faster you'll get ahead.
How to be Rich (1966)

3 In business, the mystique of conformity is sapping the dynamic individualism that is the most priceless quality an executive or businessman can possess.
How to be Rich (1966)

4 The conformist is not born. He is made...Many teachers and professors seem hell-bent on imbuing their students with a desire to achieve "security" above all.
How to be Rich (1966)

5 The successful executive—the leader, the innovator—is the exceptional man.
How to be Rich (1966)

6 The truly successful businessman is essentially a dissenter, a rebel who is seldom if ever satisfied with the status quo.
How to be Rich (1966)

7 No one can possibly achieve any real or lasting success or "get rich" in business by being a conformist.
The International Herald Tribune (January 10, 1961)

8 You must never try to make all the money that's in a deal. Let the other fellow make some money too, because if you have a reputation for making all the money there is in a deal, you won't make many deals.
Quoted in *Getty on Getty* (Somerset de Chair; 1989)

9 If you can actually count your money you are not really a rich man.
"Gossip," *Observer*, London (Quoted by A. Barrow; November 3, 1957)

10 I buy when other people are selling.
Quoted in *The Great Getty* (Robert Lenzner; 1985)

11 The meek shall inherit the earth but not the mineral rights.
Attrib.

Giacometti, Alberto (1901–66) Swiss-born Italian sculptor and painter

1 It's impossible to reproduce what one sees...I've been wasting my life for over thirty years. The root of the nose is more than I can hope to manage.
1961. Quoted in "Giacometti: Reality at Cockcrow," *Art on the Edge: Creators and Situations* (Harold Rosenberg; 1975)

Giamatti, A. Bartlett (Angelo Bartlett Giamatti; 1938–89) U.S. scholar and baseball official

1 Merit will win, it was promised by baseball.
Take Time for Paradise (1989)

2 Baseball: it breaks your heart. It is designed to break your heart.
The Green Fields of the Mind (1977)

Gibbon, Edward (1737–94) British historian

Quotations about Gibbon

1 Gibbon is an ugly, affected, disgusting fellow, and poisons our literary club for me. I class him among infidel wasps and venomous insects.
James Boswell (1740–95) Scottish lawyer and biographer. *Diary entry* (1779)

Quotations by Gibbon

2 I was never less alone than when by myself.
Memoirs of My Life (1796)

3 The various modes of worship, which prevailed in the Roman world, were all considered by the people as equally true; by the philosopher, as equally false; and by the magistrate, as equally useful. And thus toleration produced not only mutual indulgence, but even religious concord.
The Decline and Fall of the Roman Empire (1776–88), ch. 2

4 The principles of a free constitution are irrecoverably lost, when the legislative power is nominated by the executive.
The Decline and Fall of the Roman Empire (1776–88), ch. 3

5 Twenty-two acknowledged concubines, and a library of sixty-two thousand volumes attested the variety of his inclinations; and from the productions which he left behind him, it appears that both the one and the other were designed for use rather than for ostentation.
On Emperor Gordian the Younger. *The Decline and Fall of the Roman Empire* (1776–88), ch. 7

6 Corruption, the most infallible symptom of constitutional liberty.
The Decline and Fall of the Roman Empire (1776–88), ch. 21

Gibbons, Orlando (1583–1625) English composer and organist

1 It is proportion that beautifies everything, this whole Universe consists of it, and Musicke is measured by it.
First Set of Madrigals (1612)

Gibbons, Stella (Stella Dorothea Gibbons; 1902–89) British poet and novelist

1 It was curious that persons who lived what the novelists called a rich emotional life always seemed to be a bit slow on the uptake.
Cold Comfort Farm (1933), ch. 6

2 Nature is all very well in her place, but she must not be allowed to make things untidy.
Cold Comfort Farm (1933), ch. 6

3 The dark flame of his male pride was a little suspicious of having its leg pulled.
Cold Comfort Farm (1933), ch. 7

4 Something nasty in the woodshed.
Cold Comfort Farm (1933), ch. 10

5 The life of the journalist is poor, nasty, brutish and short. So is his style.
Cold Comfort Farm (1933), foreword

6 There are some things (like first love and one's reviews) at which a woman in her middle years does not care to look too closely.
Cold Comfort Farm (1933), foreword

Gibbs, Wolcott (1902–58) U.S. writer

1 Backward ran sentences until reeled the mind.
Parodying the style of *Time* magazine. *More in Sorrow* (1958)

Gibran, Kahlil (Jubran Khalil Jubran; 1883–1931) Lebanese-born U.S. mystic, painter, and poet

1 Trees are poems that the earth writes upon the sky. We fell them down and turn them into paper that we may record our emptiness.
Sand and Foam (1926)

2 Love one another, but make not a bond of love:
Let it rather be a moving sea between the shores of your souls...
And stand together yet not too near together:
For the pillars of the temple stand apart,
And the oak tree and the cypress grow not in each other's shadow.
The Prophet (1923)

3 That which you love most in him (a friend) may be clearer in his absence.
The Prophet (1923)

4 You may give them your love but not your thoughts.
For they have their own thoughts.
You may house their bodies but not their souls,
For their souls dwell in the house of tomorrow, which you cannot visit, not even in your dreams.
"On Children," *The Prophet* (1923)

5 Much of your pain is self-chosen.
It is the bitter potion by which the physician within you heals your sick self.
"On Pain," *The Prophet* (1923)

6 Everyone has experienced that truth: that love, like a running brook, is disregarded, taken for granted; but when the brook freezes over, then people begin to remember how it was when it ran, and they want it to run again.
Quoted in *Beloved Prophet* (Virginia Hilu, ed.; 1972)

7 I now want to know all things under the sun, and the moon, too. For all things are beautiful in themselves, and become more beautiful when known to man. Knowledge is Life with wings.
Quoted in *Beloved Prophet* (Virginia Hilu, ed.; 1972)

8 No human relation gives one possession in another—every two souls are absolutely different. In friendship or in love, the two side by side raise hands together to find what one cannot reach alone.
Quoted in *Beloved Prophet* (Virginia Hilu, ed.; 1972)

Gibson, Althea (b.1927) U.S. tennis player, professional golfer, and singer

1 I am much richer in knowledge and experience. But I have no money.
Daily Mail, London (1956)

2 If I made it, it's half because I was game enough to take a wicked amount of punishment along the way and half because there were an awful lot of people who cared enough to help me.
I Always Wanted to Be Somebody (1958), p. 9

Gide, André (André Paul Guillaume Gide; 1869–1951) French novelist and critic

1 Drunkenness is never anything but a substitute for happiness. It amounts to buying the dream of a thing when you haven't money enough to buy the dreamed-of thing materially.
Journal (1939–51)

2 Fish die belly-upward and rise to the surface; it is their way of falling.
1930. *Journal* (1939–51)

3 Sadness is almost never anything but a form of fatigue.
1922. *Journal* (1939–51)

4 True kindness presupposes the faculty of imagining as one's own the suffering and joy of others.
"Pretexts," *Portraits and Aphorisms* (1903)

5 One does not discover new lands without consenting to lose sight of the shore for a very long time.
The Counterfeiters (1925)

6 The unmotivated action.
The Vatican Cellars (1914), bk. 4, ch. 7

Gielgud, John, Sir (Arthur John Gielgud; 1904–2000) British actor and producer

1 I never accept lengthy film roles nowadays, because I am always so afraid I will die in the middle of shooting and cause such awful problems.
Independent, London (March 26, 1994)

2 Film people find it difficult to *place* me. The number of films that deal with crowned heads of Europe is rather limited.
Radio Times, London (November 4, 1971)

3 When you're my age, you just never risk being ill—because then everyone says: Oh, he's done for.
Sunday Express, London (July 17, 1988)

Gigli, Beniamino (1890–1957) Italian tenor

1 Retirement from the concert world is like giving up smoking. You have got to finish completely.
Attrib.

Gilbert, Daniel J., Jr. U.S. author

1 Affirmative action is affirmative evidence that we need not apologize for thinking about business as an intellectual pursuit in a day and age when many people want...to turn business education into orientation for membership in the Chamber of Commerce.
Ethics Through Corporate Strategy (1996)

2 Game theory for managers is an anthem to bullying and to the heroism that the bully ascribes to himself.
Ethics Through Corporate Strategy (1996)

Gilbert, Fred (1850–1903) British songwriter

1 As I walk along the Bois Bou-long,
With an independent air,
You can hear the girls declare,
"He must be a millionaire",
You can hear them sigh and wish to die,
You can see them wink the other eye
At the man who broke the bank at Monte Carlo.
The Bois de Boulogne was a fashionable recreational area on the outskirts of Paris. "The Man who Broke the Bank at Monte Carlo" (1892)

Gilbert, Humphrey, Sir (1539?–83) English navigator

1 We are as near to heaven by sea as by land.
1583. Alleged remark made shortly before he went down with his ship, the *Squirrel*, in a storm off the Azores. Quoted in *Third and Last Voyages of the English Nation* (Richard Hakluyt; 1600)

Gilbert, W. S., Sir (William Schwenck Gilbert; 1836–1911) British librettist and playwright

Quotations about Gilbert

1 His foe was folly and his weapon wit.
Anthony Hope (1863–1933) British novelist and playwright. Written for the inscription on the memorial to W. S. Gilbert, Victoria Embankment, London. "Epitaph for W.S. Gilbert" (1915)

Quotations by Gilbert

2 And so do his sisters, and his cousins and his aunts!
His sisters and his cousins,
Whom he reckons up by dozens,
And his aunts!
HMS Pinafore (1878), Act 1

3 CAPTAIN I'm never, never sick at sea!
ALL What never?
CAPTAIN No, never!

ALL What, *never*?
CAPTAIN Hardly ever!
HMS Pinafore (1878), Act 1

4 I always voted at my party's call,
And I never thought of thinking for myself at all.
HMS Pinafore (1878), Act 1

5 I am the Captain of the *Pinafore*;
And a right good captain too!
HMS Pinafore (1878), Act 1

6 I'm called Little Buttercup—dear Little Buttercup,
Though I could never tell why.
HMS Pinafore (1878), Act 1

7 Stick close to your desks and never go to sea,
And you all may be Rulers of the Queen's Navee!
HMS Pinafore (1878), Act 1

8 When I was a lad I served a term
As office boy to an Attorney's firm.
I cleaned the windows and I swept the floor,
And I polished up the handle of the big front door.
I polished up that handle so carefullee
That now I am the Ruler of the Queen's Navee!
HMS Pinafore (1878), Act 1

9 For he might have been a Roosian,
A French, or Turk, or Proosian,
Or perhaps Ital-ian!
But in spite of all temptations
To belong to other nations,
He remains an Englishman!
HMS Pinafore (1878), Act 2

10 Things are seldom what they seem,
Skim milk masquerades as cream.
HMS Pinafore (1878), Act 2

11 I see no objection to stoutness, in moderation.
Iolanthe (1882), Act 1

12 When I went to the Bar as a very young man,
(Said I to myself—said I),
I'll work on a new and original plan,
(Said I to myself—said I).
Iolanthe (1882), Act 1

13 The Law is the true embodiment
Of everything that's excellent.
It has no kind of fault or flaw,
And I, my lords, embody the Law.
Iolanthe (1882), Act 1, "Lord Chancellor"

14 I often think it's comical
How Nature always does contrive
That every boy and every gal
That's born into the world alive
Is either a little Liberal
Or else a little Conservative!
Iolanthe (1882), Act 1, "Private Willis' Song"

15 The prospect of a lot
Of dull MPs in close proximity,
All thinking for themselves is what
No man can face with equanimity.
Iolanthe (1882), Act 2

16 To everybody's prejudice I know a thing or two;
I can tell a woman's age in half a minute—and I do!
Princess Ida (1884), Act 1, "Garna's Song"

17 Man is Nature's sole mistake.
Princess Ida (1884), Act 2

18 Bind up their wounds—but look the other way.
Princess Ida (1884), Act 3

19 He combines the manners of a Marquis with the morals of a Methodist.
Ruddigore (1887), Act 1

20 He uses language that would make your hair curl.
Ruddigore (1887), Act 1

21 This particularly rapid, unintelligible patter
Isn't generally heard, and if it is it doesn't matter.
Ruddigore (1887), Act 2, "Despard"

22 He led his regiment from behind
He found it less exciting.
The Gondoliers (1889), Act 1, "Duke's Song"

23 As some day it may happen that a victim must be found
I've got a little list—I've got a little list
Of society offenders who might well be underground,
And who never would be missed—who never would be missed!
The Mikado (1885), Act 1, "Ko-Ko's Song"

24 The idiot who praises, with enthusiastic tone,
All centuries but this, and every country but his own.
The Mikado (1885), Act 1, "Ko-Ko's Song"

25 A wandering minstrel I—
A thing of shreds and patches,
Of ballads, songs and snatches,
And dreamy lullaby!
The Mikado (1885), Act 1, "Nanky-Poo's Song"

26 I can trace my ancestry back to a protoplasmal primordial atomic globule. Consequently, my family pride is something in-conceivable. I can't help it. I was born sneering.
The Mikado (1885), Act 1, "Pooh-Bah"

27 Three little maids from school are we,
Pert as a school-girl well can be,
Filled to the brim with girlish glee.
The Mikado (1885), Act 1, "Trio for Yum-Yum, Peep-Bo and Pitti-Sing, with Chorus of Girls"

28 I have a left shoulder-blade that is a miracle of loveliness. People come miles to see it. My right elbow has a fascination that few can resist.
The Mikado (1885), Act 2

29 Something lingering, with boiling oil in it, I fancy.
The Mikado (1885), Act 2

30 The flowers that bloom in the spring,
Tra la,
Have nothing to do with the case.
I've got to take under my wing,

Tra la,
A most unattractive old thing,
Tra la,
With a caricature of a face.
The Mikado (1885), Act 2

31 On a tree by a river a little tom-tit
Sang "Willow, titwillow, titwillow!"
The Mikado (1885), Act 2, "Ko-Ko's Song"

32 My object all sublime
I shall achieve in time—
To let the punishment fit the crime—
The punishment fit the crime.
The Mikado (1885), Act 2, "The Mikado's Song"

33 Awaiting the sensation of a short, sharp shock,
From a cheap and chippy chopper on a big black block.
The Mikado (1885), Act 2, "Trio"

34 About binomial theorems I'm teeming with a lot of news,
With many cheerful facts about the square on the hypoteneuse.
The Pirates of Penzance (1879), Act 1

35 Poor wandering one!
Though thou hast surely strayed,
Take heart of grace,
Thy steps retrace,
Poor wandering one!
The Pirates of Penzance (1879), Act 1

36 It is, it is a glorious thing
To be a Pirate King.
The Pirates of Penzance (1879), Act 1, "Pirate King's Song"

37 I am the very model of a modern Major-General,
I've information vegetable, animal and mineral,
I know the kings of England, and I quote the fights historical,
From Marathon to Waterloo, in order categorical.
The Pirates of Penzance (1879), Act 1, "The Major General's Song"

38 When the foeman bares his steel,
Tarantara! tarantara!
We uncomfortable feel.
The Pirates of Penzance (1879), Act 2

39 When constabulary duty's to be done—
A policeman's lot is not a happy one.
The Pirates of Penzance (1879), Act 2, "Sergeant's Song"

40 Is life a boon
If so, it must befall
That Death, whene'er he call,
Must call too soon.
The lines are written on Arthur Sullivan's memorial in the Embankment gardens, London. *The Yeoman of the Guard* (1888), Act 1

41 I have a song to sing O!
Sing me your song, O!
The Yeoman of the Guard (1888), Act 1, "Jack Point's Song"

42 She may very well pass for forty-three
In the dusk, with a light behind her!
Trial by Jury (1875)

43 That whether you're an honest man or whether you're a thief
Depends on whose solicitor has given me my brief.
Utopia Limited (1893), Act I

44 Sir, I view the proposal to hold an international exhibition at San Francisco with an equanimity bordering on indifference.
Quoted in *Gilbert, His Life and Strife* (Hesketh Pearson; 1957)

45 Funny without being vulgar.
1893. Referring to Sir Henry Irving's Hamlet. Attrib.

46 My dear chap! Good isn't the word!
Speaking to an actor after a poor performance. Attrib.

Gill, Eric (Arthur Eric Rowton Gill; 1882–1940) British carver, engraver, and typographer

1 That state is a state of slavery in which a man does what he likes to do in his spare time and in his working time that which is required of him.
1918. "Slavery and Freedom," *Art-Nonsense and Other Essays* (1929)

Gillespie, Dizzy (John Birks Gillespie; 1917–93) U.S. jazz trumpeter and bandleader

1 It's taken me all my life to learn what not to play.
Jazz Is (Nat Hentoff; 1976), p.266

2 It was the most fun I've had since I've been black.
1956. Said in reply to Vice President Richard Nixon's question as to whether he had enjoyed a state department tour in 1956. Quoted in "Quincy Jones," *Off the Record: An Oral History of Popular Music* (Joe Smith; 1988)

Gilliatt, Penelope (originally Penelope Ann Douglass; 1932–93) English critic and screenwriter

1 It would be difficult for a woman to be, I should think, the production head of a studio or a manager without being called a bull-dyke.
Quoted in "Rebirth," *The Hollywood Screenwriters* (Richard Corliss, ed.; 1972)

Gilligan, Carol F. (b.1936) U.S. writer and psychologist

1 The psychology of women that has consistently been described as distinctive in its greater orientation toward relationships and interdependence implies a more contextual mode of judgment and a different moral understanding.
In a Different Voice (1982)

Gilman, Charlotte Perkins (originally Charlotte Anna Perkins; 1860–1935) U.S. feminist writer

1 However, one cannot put a quart in a pint cup.
The Living of Charlotte Perkins Gilman: An Autobiography (1935), ch. 4

2 New York...that unnatural city where every one is an exile, none more so than the American.
The Living of Charlotte Perkins Gilman: An Autobiography (1935), ch. 20

3 Where young boys plan for what they will achieve and attain, young girls plan for whom they will achieve and attain.
Women and Economics (1898), ch. 5

Gilot, Françoise (b.1921) French artist

1 You have to admit that most women who have done something

with their lives have been disliked by almost everyone.
Remnant (October 1987)

Gingold, Hermione (1897–1987) British actor

1 Fighting is essentially a masculine idea; a woman's weapon is her tongue.
Attrib.

Ginsberg, Allen (1926–97) U.S. poet

1 America I'm putting my queer shoulder to the
wheel.
"America" (1956)

2 America, I've given you all and now I'm nothing. America two dollars and twenty seven cents.
"America" (1956)

3 Hollywood will rot on the windmills of Eternity
Hollywood whose movies stick in the throat of God
Yes Hollywood will get what it deserves.
"America" (1956)

4 Maybe love will come
cause I am not so dumb
Tonight it fills my heart
heavy sad apart
from one or two I fancy
now I'm an old fairy.
"Maybe Love" (1979), quoted in *The Penguin Book of Homosexual Verse* (Stephen Coote, ed.; 1983)

5 The weight of the world
is love.
Under the burden
of solitude, under the
burden of dissatisfaction.
"Song" (1954)

6 Sheep speckle the mountainside, revolving their jaws with
empty eyes,
horses dance in the warm rain.
"Wales Visitation" (1967)

7 I saw the best minds of my generation destroyed by madness, starving hysterical naked.
Howl and Other Poems (1956)

8 Democracy! Bah! When I hear that word I reach for my feather Boa!
Journals: Early Fifties Early Sixties (October 1960)

9 Everything is holy! everybody's holy! everywhere is holy
everyday is an eternity, Everyman's an Angel.
"Kaddish," *Kaddish and Other Poems* (1961)

10 Seventh Avenue, the battlements of window office buildings
shouldering each other high, under a cloud, tall as the sky.
"Kaddish for Naomi Ginsberg 1894–1956," *Kaddish and Other Poems* (1961), pt. 1

Ginsburg, Ruth Bader (b.1933) U.S. jurist and educator

1 In commercial law, the person duped was too often a woman. In a section on land tenure, one 1968 textbook explains that "land, like women, was meant to be possessed."
1974. "Portia Faces Life–The Trials of Law School", *Ms.* (April 1974)

Giovanni, Nikki (b.1943) U.S. writer, activist, and educator

1 His headstone said
FREE AT LAST, FREE AT LAST
But death is a slave's freedom.
"The Funeral of Martin Luther King, Jr.," *Black Feeling, Black Talk, Black Judgement* (1968)

2 Black is a sacrament. It's an outward and visible sign of an inward and spiritual grace.
"A Spiritual View of Lena Horne," *Gemini* (1971)

3 The best anyone can do when dealing with weakness is to get as far away from it as possible.
"Convalescence—Compared to What?," *Gemini* (1971)

4 The minute you institutionalize a problem you don't intend to solve it.
"Gemini—A Prolonged Autobiographical Statement on Why," *Gemini* (1971)

5 Violence is like money in the bank; it's only helpful if you don't have to use it.
"About a Poem," *Sacred Cows... and Other Edibles* (1988)

Giraudoux, Jean (Hyppolyte Jean Giraudoux; 1882–1944) French playwright and writer

1 Human beings are like timid punctuation marks sprinkled among the incomprehensible sentences of life.
Siegfried (1922), ch. 2

2 I tell you, the only safeguard of order and discipline in the modern world is a standardized worker with interchangeable parts. That would solve the entire problem of management.
The Madwoman of Chaillot (1945), Act 1

3 Ask any soldier. To kill a man is to merit a woman.
Tiger at the Gates (1935), Act 1

4 It's odd how people waiting for you stand out far less clearly than people you are waiting for.
Tiger at the Gates (1935), Act 1

5 There's no better way of exercising the imagination than the study of law. No poet ever interpreted nature as freely as a lawyer interprets the truth.
Tiger at the Gates (1935), Act 1

6 Only the mediocre are always at their best.
Attrib.

Giroud, Françoise (originally Françoise Gourdji; b.1916) Swiss-born French politician, journalist, and editor

1 Are there still virgins? One is tempted to answer no. There are only girls who have not yet crossed the line, because they want to preserve their market value...Call them virgins if you wish, these travelers in transit.
Coronet (November 1960)

2 As though femininity is something you can lose the way you lose your pocketbook: hmm, where in the world did I put my femininity?
I Give You My Word (1974)

3 I don't for one moment believe that over the centuries some universal plot has been hatched by men to keep women in a state of servitude.
I Give You My Word (1974)

Gisborne, Thomas (Thomas Gisborne the Elder; 1758–1846) British clergyman

1 A physician ought to be extremely watchful against covetousness, for it is a vice imputed, justly or unjustly, to his Profession.
On the Duties of Physicians (1847)

Gish, Lillian (originally Lillian de Guiche; 1893–1993) U.S. actor

1 I don't care for modern films. Cars crashing over cliffs and close-ups of people's feet.
Attrib.

Gissing, George (George Robert Gissing; 1857–1903) English novelist

1 Time is money—says the vulgarest saw known to any age or people. Turn it round about, and you get a precious truth—money is time.
The Private Papers of Henry Ryecroft (1903)

Gladstone, William Ewart (1809–98) British statesman

Quotations about Gladstone

1 A sophistical rhetorician inebriated with the exuberance of his own verbosity.
July 28, 1878
Benjamin Disraeli (1804–81) British prime minister and writer. *Times*, London (July 29, 1878)

2 The G.O.M., when his life ebbs out,
Will ride in a fiery chariot,
And sit in state
On a red-hot plate
Between Pilate and Judas Iscariot.
Limericks. William Gladstone, British prime minister, known as the Grand Old Man, was blamed for the death of General Gordon at Khartoum (1885). *The Faber Book of English History in Verse* (Kenneth Baker; 1988)

3 He speaks to Me as if I was a public meeting.
Victoria (1819–1901) British monarch. *Collections and Recollections* (G. W. E. Russell; 1898), ch. 14

Quotations by Gladstone

4 We are part of the community of Europe, and we must do our duty as such.
Speech at Caernarfon, Wales (April 10, 1888)

5 All the world over, I will back the masses against the classes.
Speech at Liverpool (June 28, 1886)

6 The disease of an evil conscience is beyond the practice of all the physicians of all the countries in the world.
Speech at Plumstead, London (1887)

7 National injustice is the surest road to national downfall.
Speech at Plumstead, London (1878), quoted in *Gladstone's Speeches* (A. Tilney Bassett; 1916)

8 You cannot fight against the future. Time is on our side.
Speech on the second Reform Bill, which was intended to extend the franchise. It was defeated by an alliance between the Conservative opposition and Liberal dissidents, only to be passed the following year. *Hansard* (April 27, 1866), col. 152

9 Finance is, as it were, the stomach of the country, from which all the other organs take their tone.
1858. Quoted in *Gladstone 1809–1874* (H. C. G. Matthew; 1986), ch. 5

10 Swimming for his life, a man does not see much of the country through which the river winds.
December 31, 1868. Quoted in *The Gladstone Diaries* (M. R. D. Foot and H. C. G. Matthew, eds.; 1978)

Glaser, Milton (b.1929) U.S. graphic designer and illustrator

1 In fashion, you're always creating authority through provocation. The worst thing is to be overlooked because you're not provocative. You have to be on the edge of changing sensibilities.
Referring to the use of blatant sexuality in fashion advertising. *New York Times* (April 19, 1986)

Glasgow, Ellen (Ellen Anderson Gholson Glasgow; 1874–1945) U.S. novelist

1 You can't expect men not to judge by appearances.
The Sheltered Life (1932)

2 I ain't never seen a head so level that it could bear the lettin' in of politics. It makes a fool of a man and a worse fool of a fool. The government's like a mule; it's slow and sure; it's slow to turn, and it's sure to turn the way you don't want it.
The Voice of the People (1900), ch. 2

3 The war wasn't the worst thing...The worst thing is this sense of having lost our way in the universe. The worst thing is that the war has made peace seem so futile. It is just as if the bottom had dropped out of idealism.
They Stooped to Folly (1929), pt. 1, ch. 1

Glasse, Hannah (*fl.* 1708–70) British cookery writer

1 So in many other Things in Cookery, the great Cooks have such a high Way of expressing themselves that the poor Girls are at a Loss to know what they mean.
The Art of Cookery Made Plain and Easy (1747)

Gleick, James (b.1954) U.S. science writer

1 The irregular side of nature, the discontinuous and erratic side—these have been puzzles to science, or worse, monstrosities.
Chaos (1987)

2 To some physicists chaos is a science of process rather than state, of becoming rather than being.
Chaos (1987)

3 Simple systems give rise to complex behavior. Complex systems give rise to simple behavior. And most important, the laws of complexity hold universally, caring not at all for the details of a system's constituent atoms.
Attrib.

Gloucester, William, 1st Duke of (1743–1805) British nobleman

1 Another damned, thick, square book! Always scribble, scribble, scribble! Eh! Mr. Gibbon?
1781. Upon receiving from Edward Gibbon volume 2 of *The Decline and Fall of the Roman Empire.* Also attributed to George III and the Duke of Cumberland. Quoted in *Personal and Literary Memorials* (Henry Best; 1829)

Glover, Jane (b.1949) British conductor

1 This poor teacher was trying to keep control of this class of rowdy 13-year-olds, and after a while she just gave up and started playing the piano to us. She stopped and said "Does anybody know what key that is in?" Without thinking I said: "C sharp minor." And she looked at me and said: "See me afterwards."
On how she discovered she had perfect pitch. *Independent on Sunday*, London (June 5, 1994)

Glynn, Martin H. (1871–1924) U.S. politician

1 He kept us out of war!
Referring to President Woodrow Wilson. Speech, Democratic National Convention, St Louis (June 15, 1916)

Godard, Jean-Luc (b.1930) French film director

1 The dream of the Nouvelle Vague is to make *Spartacus* in Hollywood on a ten million dollar budget.
Cahiers du Cinéma (December 1962)

2 If World War I enabled American cinema to ruin French cinema, World War II, together with the advent of television, enabled it to finance, that is to say ruin, all the cinemas of Europe.
Histoires du Cinéma (1989)

3 The cinema is all about money but the money figures twice: first you spend all your time running to get the money to make the film but then in the film the money comes back again, in the image.
Quoted in *Godard: Images, Sounds, Politics* (Colin McCabe; 1980)

4 You don't make a movie, the movie makes you.
Quoted in *Halliwell's Filmgoer's Companion* (Leslie Halliwell; 1993)

5 I like a film to have a beginning, a middle, and an end, but not necessarily in that order.
Attrib. *Time* (September 14, 1981)

Goddard, Robert (Robert Hutchings Goddard; 1882–1945) U.S. physicist

1 God pity a one-dream man.
Quoted in *Broca's Brain* (Carl Sagan; 1980)

Godunov, Boris, Tsar (Boris Fyodorovich Godunov; 1551?–1605) Russian monarch

1 May God be my witness that there will not be a poor man in my Tsardom! And even to my last shirt I will share with all.
Coronation address, Moscow (September 1, 1598)

Goering, Hermann (Hermann Wilhelm Goering; 1893–1946) German Nazi leader

1 Guns will make us powerful; butter will only make us fat.
Referring to the summer Four Year Plan. Speech, Hamburg (Summer 1936), quoted in *Goering* (W. Frishauer; 1951), ch. 10

2 The Americans cannot build airplanes. They are very good at refrigerators and razor blades.
Assurance to Hitler. Quoted in *Alistair Cooke's America* (Alistair Cooke; 1978)

3 When I hear anyone talk of Culture, I reach for my revolver.
Probably derived from the Hanns Johst play, *Schlageter* (1933), Act 1, Scene 1. Attrib.

Goethe, Johann Wolfgang von (1749–1832) German poet, playwright, and scientist

Quotations about Goethe

1 Talent alone cannot make a writer. There must be a man behind the book.
Ralph Waldo Emerson (1803–82) U.S. poet and essayist. "Goethe; or, the writer," *Representative Men* (1850)

2 In extraversion and introversion it is clearly a matter of two antithetical, natural attitudes or trends, which Goethe once referred to as diastole and systole.
Carl Gustav Jung (1875–1961) Swiss psychoanalyst. *The Psychology of the Unconscious* (1912)

3 Official Germany celebrated Goethe, not as a poet and prophet, but above all as opium.
1932
Carl von Ossietzky (1889–1938) German pacifist and journalist. Quoted in *Weimar Culture* (Peter Gay; 1969)

Quotations by Goethe

4 More light!
Allegedly his last words. In fact he asked for a second shutter to be opened, to allow in more light. Remark (1832), quoted in *Oxford Dictionary of Quotations* (Angela Partington, ed.; 1992)

5 Nature proclaims her wisdom through Shakespeare...my characters are mere soap bubbles wafted about by fanciful whims.
"Shakespeare: a Tribute" (1771)

6 You must be master and win, or serve and lose, grieve or triumph, be the anvil or the hammer.
Der Gross-Cophta (1791), Act 2

7 Deny yourself! You must deny yourself! That is the never-ending song.
Faust (1808), pt. 1

8 I have often heard it said, That an actor can instruct a priest.
Faust (1808), pt. 1

9 Besides, civilization, which now licks
Us all so smooth, has taught even the Devil tricks;
The northern fiend's becoming a lost cause—
Where are his horns these days, his tail, his claws?
Said by Mephistopheles. *Faust* (1808), pt. 1

10 Omniscient am I not, but well-informed.
Said by Mephistopheles. *Faust* (1808), pt. 1

11 The fates of women mold her
With a nature kin to art.
Faust (1832), pt. 2

12 My peace is gone,
My heart is heavy.
"Gretchens Stube," *Faust* (1808), pt. 1

13 Eternal Woman draws us upward.
Last line. "Hochegebirg," *Faust* (1832), pt. 2

14 The deed is all, and not the glory.
"Hochgebirg," *Faust* (1832), pt. 2

15 Dear friend, theory is all gray,
And the golden tree of life is green.
"Studierzimmer," *Faust* (1808), pt. 1

16 I am the spirit that always denies.
"Studierzimmer," *Faust* (1808), pt. 1

17 Two souls dwell, alas! in my breast.
"Vor dem Thor," *Faust* (1808), pt. 1

18 But as for him, tell him he can kiss my arse!
Said by Götz to a messenger of an enemy captain asking him to surrender. *Götz von Berlichingen* (C. E. Passage, tr.; 1773), Act 3, Scene 17

19 A useless life is an early death.
Iphigenie auf Tauris (1787), Act 1, Scene 2

20 So far I have said nothing about the food—an important subject, after all. The vegetables are delicious, especially the lettuce, which is very tender and tastes like milk; one can understand why Americans call it *lactuca*.
Italian Journey (1816–17)

21 The Neopolitan not only enjoys his food, but insists that it be attractively displayed for sale.
Italian Journey (1816–17)

22 Verona. On market days the squares piled high with garlic and most every sort of vegetable and fruit. The people shout, throw things, scuffle, laugh and sing all day long. The mild climate and cheap food make life easy for them.
Italian Journey (1816–17)

23 Superstition is the poetry of life.
"Literatur und Sprache," *Maximen und Reflexionen* (1819), no. 908

24 If man thinks about his physical or moral state he usually discovers that he is ill.
Sprüche in Prosa (Rudolf Steiner, ed.; 1967), pt. 1, bk. 2

25 Painting...is able to reproduce on a panel a far more perfect visible world than the real world can ever be.
Theory of Colour (1810)

26 Talent develops in quiet places, character in the full current of human life.
Torquato Tasso (1790), Act 1

27 And if men in their torment must be mute. A god gave me the power to tell my pain.
Torquato Tasso (1790), Act 5

28 Art is long, life short; judgment difficult, opportunity transient.
Wilhelm Meisters Lehrjahre (1795–96), bk. 7, ch. 9

29 Never...have I moved so lightly. I was no longer a human being. To hold the most adorable creature in one's arms and fly around with her like the wind, so that everything around us fades away.
Describing the sensation of dancing. Quoted in *A Portrait of Mr. Balanchine* (Essay by Lincoln Kirstein; 1984)

30 I do not know myself, and God forbid that I should.
April 10, 1829. Quoted in *Conversations with Goethe* (Johann Peter Eckermann; 1836–48)

31 The world is so full of simpletons and madmen, that one need not seek them in a madhouse.
March 17, 1830. Quoted in *Conversations with Goethe* (Johann Peter Eckermann; 1836–48)

32 Thus I saw that most men only care for science so far as they get a living by it, and that they worship even error when it affords them a subsistence.
Quoted in *Conversations with Goethe* (Johann Peter Eckermann; 1836–48)

33 I must consider more closely this cycle of good and bad days which I find coursing within myself. Passion, attachment, the urge to action, inventiveness, performance, order all alternate and keep their orbit; cheerfulness, vigor, energy, flexibility and fatigue, serenity as well as desire.
Quoted in *The Encyclopedia of Alternative Medicine and Self-Help* (Malcolm Hulke, ed.; 1979)

34 From today and from this place there begins a new epoch in the history of the world.
1792. On witnessing the victory of the French revolutionary army over invading Prussian forces at the Battle of Valmy (September 1792). Quoted in *The Story of Civilization* (William Durant; 1950–67), vol. 2

35 I was not unaware that I had begotten a mortal.
1830. On learning of his son's death. Quoted in *The Story of Civilization* (William Durant; 1950–67), vol. 10

36 It was certainly a little rough to begin with, because so few knew how to dance it.
Referring to dancing the waltz. Quoted in *World History of the Dance* (Curt Sachs; 1937)

37 It is so hard that one cannot really have confidence in doctors and yet cannot do without them.
Attrib.

38 Medicine absorbs the physician's whole being because it is concerned with the entire human organism.
Attrib.

39 No skill or art is needed to grow old; the trick is to endure it.
Attrib.

Gogarty, Oliver St. John (1878–1957) Irish writer and physician

Quotations about Gogarty

1 I mistook Gogarty's white-robed maid for his wife—or his mistress. I expected every poet to have a spare wife.
Patrick Kavanagh (1904–67) Irish poet and novelist. *The Green Fool* (1938)

Quotations by Gogarty

2 Politics is the chloroform of the Irish people, or rather the hashish.
As I Was Going Down Sackville Street (1937)

3 If Hell is paved with good intentions, Dublin was paved with great affectations.
"The Most Magnificent of Snobs," *Intimations* (1950)

4 In England you will find people so desirous of titles that, if they cannot acquire them, they will stick two surnames together with an hyphen.
"The Most Magnificent of Snobs," *Intimations* (1950)

5 His Holiness, the Pope yesterday received The Most Reverend Dr Fogarty and the most irreverent Dr Gogarty.
1925. Referring to visiting Rome with Bishop Fogarty. Quoted in *Oliver St John Gogarty* (Ulick O'Connor; 1964), ch. 16

Gogh, Vincent van (1853–90) Dutch-born French painter

Quotations about van Gogh

1 Your passion strikes fire wherever you go.
You set a bouquet of yellow flowers ablaze in the sun,
And kindle the darkly somber yews.
Feng Zhi (1905–93) Chinese poet. "Sonnet 14: Van Gogh" (1941)

Quotations by van Gogh

2 Why do people see something decadent in Impressionism? It's completely the reverse.
Letter to his brother Théo (1888), quoted in *Complete Letters of Vincent van Gogh* (J. van Goch-Bonger and C. de Good, trs.; 1958)

Gogol, Nikolay (Nikolay Vasilyevich Gogol; 1809–52) Russian novelist and playwright

1 To be honest with you, if I'd known the sour look I was going to get from the head of our department I wouldn't have gone to the office at all.
Said by the "madman," a clerk hampered by his lowly social status. "Diary of a Madman" (1835), October 3rd, quoted in *Diary of a Madman and Other Stories* (Ronald Wilks, tr.; 1972)

2 Are you the gentleman who has lost his nose?
Yes, that's me.
It's been found...We caught it just as it was about to drive off in the Riga stagecoach.
"The Nose" (1836), quoted in *Diary of a Madman and Other Stories* (Ronald Wilks, tr.; 1972)

3 Ivan Yakovlevich, like any honest Russian working man, was a terrible drunkard.
"The Nose" (1836), quoted in *Diary of a Madman and Other Stories* (Ronald Wilks, tr.; 1972)

4 Russia is such an amazing country, that if you pass any remark about *one* collegiate assessor, every assessor from Riga to Kamchatka will take it personally.
"The Nose" (1836), quoted in *Diary of a Madman and Other Stories* (Ronald Wilks, tr.; 1972)

5 No one's more touchy than people in government departments.
"The Overcoat" (1842), quoted in *Diary of a Madman and Other Stories* (Ronald Wilks, tr.; 1972)

6 Only if a horse's muzzle appeared from out of nowhere, propped itself on his shoulder and fanned his cheek with a gust from its nostrils—only then did he realize he was not in the middle of a sentence but in the middle of the street.
Referring to an overworked clerk, the hero of the story. "The Overcoat" (1842), quoted in *Diary of a Madman and Other Stories* (Ronald Wilks, tr.; 1972)

7 As you pass from the tender years of youth into harsh and embittered manhood, make sure you take with you on your journey all the human emotions! Don't leave them on the road, for you will not pick them up afterwards!
Dead Souls (1842), pt. 1, ch. 6

Goizueta, Roberto (Roberto Crispulo Goizueta; b.1931) U.S. business executive

1 It is extremely important that you show some insensitivity to your past in order to show the proper respect for the future.
Fortune (December 11, 1995)

2 The moment you let avoiding failure becoming your motivator, you're down the path of inactivity. You can stumble only if you're moving.
Fortune (May 1, 1995)

3 The secret isn't counting the beans, it's growing more beans.
Fortune (November 13, 1995)

4 Energy is no. 1. Intellectual courage is extremely important too—intellectual courage to go out and do something.
Referring to the necessary qualities of a chief executive officer. *Fortune* (October 13, 1997)

5 You borrow money at a certain rate and invest it at a higher rate and pocket the difference. It's that simple.
The "Goizueta Rule of Investment." *Fortune* (October 13, 1997)

6 We don't know how to sell products based on performance. Everything we sell, we sell on image.
Wall Street Journal (February 3, 1997)

Goldberg, Whoopi (Caryn E. Johnson; b.1950) U.S. actor and comedian

1 You can see I'm black. It's not something I consciously think about. It's like having a dick. You don't think about having a dick. You just have one.
Attrib. *Playboy* (June 1987)

Goldblum, Jeff (b.1952) U.S. film actor

1 God creates man, man destroys God, man creates dinosaurs.
As Ian Malcolm. *Jurassic Park* (Michael Crichton and David Koepp; 1993)

Golden, Marita (b.1950) U.S. writer and teacher

1 I don't know much about love either, except that it gets all mixed up with things that don't have anything to do with it. And that it's awfully hard to find.
A Woman's Place (1986)

2 If you're ashamed of being human—weak, stupid, as well as God's greatest creation—you'll never be a good poet. Novelists have to love humanity to write anything worthwhile. Poets have to love themselves.
A Woman's Place (1986)

3 I grew up thinking men were some wonderful reward holding themselves back till women did something to deserve them.
A Woman's Place (1986)

4 In despair as in love, we are above all else, alone.
A Woman's Place (1986)

5 The only thing Africa has left is the future.
A Woman's Place (1986)

6 This world, whatever else it is, isn't safe and you might as well build up your defenses in the man's backyard, where he makes the rules. You'll have to deal with him sooner or later. Sooner just might give you an edge.
Referring to how a woman might get on best in what is perceived as a male-oriented society. *A Woman's Place* (1986)

7 I thank the Lord for friends. They can see you and your life so clear 'cause it's not their hearts all tangled up in it.
Long Distance Life (1989)

8 Never know what you made of if you ain't arguing with the world about something.
Long Distance Life (1989)

Golding, William, Sir (William Gerald Golding; 1911–93) British novelist

1 Ralph wept for the end of innocence, the darkness of man's heart, and the fall through the air of the true, wise friend called Piggy.
Lord of the Flies (1954), ch. 12

2 What is wrong with a revolution is that it is natural. It is as natural as natural selection, as devastating as natural selection, and as horrible.
Observer, London (1974), "Sayings of the Year"

3 How next to impossible is the exercise of virtue! It requires a constant watchfulness, constant guard.
"Colley's Letter," *Rites of Passage* (1980)

4 What a man does defiles him, not what is done by others.
"Next Day," *Rites of Passage* (1980)

5 Virginia, where charm is laid on so thick you could saw it off in chunks and export it.
The Hot Gates and Other Occasional Pieces (1965)

Goldman, Emma ("Red Emma"; 1869–1940) Lithuanian-born U.S. anarchist

Quotations about Goldman

1 Anyhow you did not tumble to Emma Goldman. She is beyond dispute the deviationingist old organiser of futility that ever dressed up in embellishing vanity as benevolence.
H. G. Wells (1866–1946) British writer. Letter to Bertrand Russell (March 7, 1929), quoted in *The Correspondence of H. G. Wells* (David C. Smith, ed.; 1998), vol. 3

Quotations by Goldman

2 If the production of any commodity necessitates the sacrifice of human life, society should do without that commodity, but it cannot do without that life.
Anarchism and Other Essays (1917)

3 Merely external emancipation has made of the modern woman an artificial being...Now, woman is confronted with the necessity of emancipating herself from emancipation, if she really desires to be free.
Anarchism and Other Essays (1917)

4 Politics is the reflex of the business and industrial world.
The Tragedy of Women's Emancipation (1911)

Goldman, William (William W. Goldman; b.1931) U.S. screenwriter

1 Studio executives are intelligent, brutally over-worked men and women who share one thing in common with baseball managers: they wake up every morning of the world with the knowledge that sooner or later they're going to get fired.
Referring to Hollywood. *Adventures in the Screen Trade* (1983)

2 Nobody knows anything.
Referring to the Hollywood motion picture studio system. *Adventures in the Screen Trade* (1983)

3 It's about a man who takes a woman to a booby hatch.
Said to an actor asking about Tennessee Williams's play *A Streetcar Named Desire* (1947). *Adventures in the Screen Trade* (1983)

Goldsmith, Edward (b.1928) British business executive and ecologist

1 The ethic of progress—in effect, the ethic of perpetual technospheric expansion—is in reality no more than an ethic of biospheric destruction...it is an anti-evolutionary ethic.
"Biospheric Ethics" (1992), quoted in *The Future of Progress* (Helena Norberg-Hodge, Peter Goering and Steven Gorelick, eds.; 1992)

Goldsmith, James, Sir (1933–97) French-born British businessman and politician

1 I can't tell you what a delight it is to be out of business. I've found a new virginity.
Referring to his retirement. *Sunday Times,* London (October 21, 1990)

2 Beauty is a social necessity.
Times, London (June 10, 1994)

3 Brussels is a madness. I will fight it from within.
Referring to the European Union, of which Brussels is the headquarters. He was elected a Member of the European Parliament (1994). *Times,* London (June 10, 1994)

4 The very best takeovers are thoroughly hostile. I've never seen a really good company taken over.
Quoted in *Financial Times,* London (March 21, 1989)

5 I'm not asset stripping...I prefer to think of it as unbundling.
Responding to accusations of asset-stripping. *Financial Times,* London (December 30, 1989), "Quotes of the Year"

6 I am a Jew to Catholics and a Catholic to Jews; an Englishman to the French and a Frenchman to the English.
Referring to his mixed ancestry as the son of a German-born Jewish father and a French Catholic mother. Quoted in *Times,* London (March 7, 1989)

7 If you pay peanuts, you get monkeys.
Attrib.

8 When you marry your mistress, you create a job vacancy.
Attrib.

Goldsmith, Oliver (1730–74) Irish-born British novelist, playwright, and poet

Quotations about Goldsmith

1 Here lies Nolly Goldsmith, for shortness called Noll,
Who wrote like an angel, and talk'd like poor Poll.

David Garrick (1717–79) British actor-manager. "Impromptu Epitaph" (1774)

2 No man was more foolish when he had not a pen in his hand, or more wise when he had.
Samuel Johnson (1709–84) British lexicographer and writer. Quoted in *Life of Samuel Johnson* (James Boswell; 1791)

3 To Oliver Goldsmith, A Poet, Naturalist, and Historian, who left scarcely any style of writing untouched, and touched none that he did not adorn.
June 22, 1776
Samuel Johnson (1709–84) British lexicographer and writer. Epitaph on Oliver Goldsmith. Quoted in *Life of Samuel Johnson* (James Boswell; 1791)

Quotations by Goldsmith

4 He writes indexes to perfection.
A Citizen of the World (1762), Letter 29

5 To a philosopher no circumstance, however trifling, is too minute.
A Citizen of the World (1762), Letter 29

6 The true use of speech is not so much to express our wants as to conceal them.
"The Use of Language," *Essays* (1765)

7 HARDCASTLE I love everything that's old: old friends, old times, old manners, old books, old wine.
She Stoops to Conquer (1773), Act 1

8 In my time, the follies of the town crept slowly among us, but now they travel faster than a stagecoach.
She Stoops to Conquer (1773), Act 1

9 The very pink of perfection.
She Stoops to Conquer (1773), Act 1

10 Let schoolmasters puzzle their brain,
With grammar, and nonsense, and learning,
Good liquor, I stoutly maintain,
Gives genius a better discerning.
Song lyric. *She Stoops to Conquer* (1773), Act 1

11 Ask me no questions, and I'll tell you no fibs.
She Stoops to Conquer (1773), Act 3

12 Women and music should never be dated.
She Stoops to Conquer (1773), Act 3

13 For he who fights and runs away
May live to fight another day;
But he who is in battle slain
Can never rise and fight again.
The Art of Poetry on a New Plan (1761), vol. 2

14 True genius walks along a line, and, perhaps, our greatest pleasure is in seeing it so often near falling, without being ever actually down.
"The Characteristics of Greatness," *The Bee* (1759), no. 4

15 Ill fares the land, to hast'ning ills a prey,
Where wealth accumulates, and men decay;
Princes and lords may flourish, or may fade;
A breath can make them, as a breath has made;
But a bold peasantry, their country's pride,
When once destroy'd, can never be supplied.
The Deserted Village (1770)

16 Ye friends to truth, ye statesmen who survey
The rich man's joys increase, the poor's decay,
'Tis yours to judge how wide the limits stand
Between a splendid and a happy land.
The Deserted Village (1770)

17 Thus to relieve the wretched was his pride,
And even his failings leaned to virtue's side.
Referring to the village preacher. *The Deserted Village* (1770)

18 And still they gazed, and still the wonder grew,
That one small head could carry all he knew.
The villagers' perception of the schoolmaster. *The Deserted Village* (1770)

19 Friendship is a disinterested commerce between equals; love, an abject intercourse between tyrants and slaves.
The Good-Natur'd Man (1768), Act 1

20 LEONTINE An only son, sir, might expect more indulgence.
CROAKER An only father, sir, might expect more obedience.
The Good-Natur'd Man (1768), Act 1

21 LEONTINE Don't let us make imaginary evils, when you know we have so many real ones to encounter.
The Good-Natur'd Man (1768), Act 1

22 We must touch his weaknesses with a delicate hand. There are some faults so nearly allied to excellence, that we can scarce weed out the fault without eradicating the virtue.
The Good-Natur'd Man (1768), Act 1

23 Silence is become his mother tongue.
The Good-Natur'd Man (1768), Act 2

24 Law grinds the poor, and rich men rule the law.
The Traveller (1764), l. 386

25 Where wealth and freedom reign, contentment fails,
and honour sinks where commerce long prevails.
The Traveller (1764), ll. 91–92

26 A book may be amusing with numerous errors, or it may be very dull without a single absurdity.
The Vicar of Wakefield (1766), Advertisement

27 Handsome is that handsome does.
The Vicar of Wakefield (1766), ch. 1

28 I...chose my wife, as she did her wedding gown, not for a fine glossy surface, but such qualities as would wear well.
The Vicar of Wakefield (1766), ch. 1

29 I was ever of opinion, that the honest man who married and brought up a large family, did more service than he who continued single and only talked of population.
The Vicar of Wakefield (1766), ch. 1

30 Conscience is a coward, and those faults it has not strength enough to prevent it seldom has justice enough to accuse.
The Vicar of Wakefield (1766), ch. 13

31 The man recovered of the bite,
The dog it was that died.
"Elegy on the Death of a Mad Dog," *The Vicar of Wakefield* (1766), ch. 17

32 The dog, to gain some private ends,
Went mad and bit the man.
"Elegy on the Death of a Mad Dog," *The Vicar of Wakefield* (1766), st. 5, ll. 12–14

33 When lovely woman stoops to folly,
And finds too late that men betray,
What charm can soothe her melancholy,
What art can wash her guilt away?
"Song," *The Vicar of Wakefield* (1766), st.1, ch. 24

34 As I take my shoes from the shoemaker, and my coat from the tailor, so I take my religion from the priest.
April 9, 1773. Quoted in *The Life of Samuel Johnson* (James Boswell; 1791)

Goldwater, Barry (Barry Morris Goldwater; 1909–98) U.S. politician

1 In your heart you know he's right.
His opponents retaliated with: "In your guts you know he's nuts!" Election slogan (1964)

2 You've got to forget about this civilian. Whenever you drop bombs, you're going to hit civilians.
Speech, New York (January 23, 1967)

3 I would remind you that extremism in the defense of liberty is no vice. And let me remind you also that moderation in the pursuit of justice is no virtue!
July 16, 1964. Acceptance speech for the Republican presidential nomination, San Francisco, *New York Times* (July 17, 1964)

4 The basic reason Russia has not attacked us is that we can outproduce her.
Phoenix Gazette (August 9, 1956)

5 A government that is big enough to give you all you want is big enough to take it all away.
Quoted in *Bachman's Book of Freedom Quotations* (M. Ivens and R. Dunstan; 1978)

Goldwyn, Samuel (Samuel Goldfish (Gelbfisz in Polish); 1882–1974) Polish-born U.S. film producer

Quotations about Goldwyn

1 You always knew where you were with Goldwyn—nowhere.
F. Scott Fitzgerald (1896–1940) U.S. writer. Quoted in *Some Sort of Epic Grandeur* (Matthew J. Bruccoli; 1981)

Quotations by Goldwyn

2 A wide screen just makes a bad film twice as bad.
Remark (1956)

3 For years I have been known for saying "Include me out"; but today I am giving it up forever.
Speech at Balliol College, Oxford, England (March 1, 1945)

4 Let's have some new clichés.
Observer, London (October 24, 1948), "Sayings of the Week"

5 Why should people go out and pay money to see bad movies when they can stay at home and see bad television for nothing?
Observer, London (September 9, 1956), "Sayings of the Week"

6 Tell me, how did you love my picture?
Quoted in *Colombo's Hollywood: Wit and Wisdom of the Moviemakers* (John Robert Colombo; 1979)

7 I'll give you a definite maybe.
Attrib. *Goldwyn* (A. Scott Berg; 1989)

8 I read part of it all the way through.
Attrib. *Goldwyn: the Man behind the Myth* (Arthur Marx; 1976), ch. 27

9 What we want is a story that starts with an earthquake and works its way up to a climax.
Quoted in *Leslie Halliwell's Filmgoer's and Video Viewer's Companion* (Leslie Halliwell; 1989)

10 Too caustic? To hell with cost; we'll make the picture anyway.
Attrib. *Moguls* (Norman Zierold; 1969)

11 You ought to take the bull between the teeth.
January 31, 1974. Recalled on his death bed. Attrib. *Moguls* (Norman Zierold; 1969)

12 I don't care if it doesn't make a nickel, I just want every man, woman, and child in America to see it!
Referring to his film *The Best Years of Our Lives* (1946). Attrib. *Moguls* (Norman Zierold; 1969)

13 Yes, I'm going to have a bust made of them.
Replying to an admiring comment about his wife's hands. Attrib. *Moguls* (Norman Zierold; 1969)

14 Any man who goes to a psychiatrist should have his head examined.
Quoted in *Moguls* (Norman Zierold; 1969), ch. 3

15 In two words: im-possible.
Attrib. "Samuel Goldwyn Presents," *Moguls* (Norman Zierold; 1969)

16 Chaplin is no business man. All he knows is that he can't take less.
Quoted in *My Autobiography* (Charlie Chaplin; 1964)

17 A verbal contract isn't worth the paper it's written on.
Quoted in *The Great Goldwyn* (Alva Johnston; 1937), ch. 1

18 That's the way with these directors, they're always biting the hand that lays the golden egg.
Quoted in *The Great Goldwyn* (Alva Johnston; 1937), ch. 1

19 I am willing to admit that I may not always be right, but I am never wrong.
Attrib.

20 I don't want any yes-men around me. I want everybody to tell me the truth even if it costs them their jobs.
Attrib.

21 If Roosevelt were alive he'd turn in his grave.
Attrib.

22 It's more than magnificent—it's mediocre.
Attrib.

23 The trouble with this business is the dearth of bad pictures.
Attrib.

24 This music won't do. There's not enough sarcasm in it.
Attrib.

25 We have all passed a lot of water since then.
Attrib.

26 We're overpaying him but he's worth it.
Attrib.

27 Please write music like Wagner, only louder.
January 31, 1974. Instructions to the composer of a movie score. Recalled on his death. Attrib.

28 "Why only twelve?" "That's the original number." "Well, go out and get thousands."
Referring to the number of disciples while filming a scene for *The Last Supper*. Attrib.

Goleman, Daniel U.S. author

1 A common core of personal and social abilities has proven to be the key ingredient in people's success: emotional intelligence.
Working with Emotional Intelligence (1998)

2 As work becomes more complex and collaborative, companies where people work together best have a competitive edge.
Working with Emotional Intelligence (1998)

3 Emotional intelligence carries much more weight than IQ in determining who emerges as a leader.
Working with Emotional Intelligence (1998)

4 If a company has the competencies that flow from self-awareness and self-regulation, motivation and empathy, leadership skills and open communication, it should prove more resilient no matter what the future brings.
Working with Emotional Intelligence (1998)

5 The people we get along with, trust, feel simpatico with, are the strongest links in our networks.
Working with Emotional Intelligence (1998)

Golzen, Godfrey (b.1930) British business writer

1 Young managers in the 1960s and 1970s, when pay was tied to seniority...used to argue, half-jokingly, that the pay pyramid was upside down. You ought to get paid more when you were young enough to enjoy it.
"The Colour of Money," *Smart Moves* (co-written with Andrew Garner; 1990)

2 Once one has got the money habit, it is extremely difficult to kick it.
"The Money Junkies," *Smart Moves* (co-written with Andrew Garner; 1990)

Gómez de la Serna, Ramón Spanish novelist

1 There is no more beautiful mission than to create the free novel, than to fabricate a world that we will never reach, regardless of how long we live!
Ismos (1931)

2 The wisest invention in the world is the flush mechanism for the toilet whose chain turns us all, when we pull it, into a miraculous Moses.
Quoted in "El Problema de la Greguería" (A. Hoyle; 1989)

3 Dogs show us their tongues as if they thought we were doctors.
Quoted in *The Spanish Avant Garde* (Derek Harris, ed.; 1995)

4 Laboratory guinea pigs say to themselves: I bet they would not do that to polar bears.
Quoted in *The Spanish Avant Garde* (Derek Harris, ed.; 1995)

5 Sculpture museums are places where parents hear their children say surprising things: Daddy my fig leaf hasn't grown yet!
Quoted in *The Spanish Avant Garde* (Derek Harris, ed.; 1995)

Gompers, Samuel (1850–1924) British-born U.S. labor leader

1 To protect workers in their inalienable rights to a higher and better life; to protect them, not only as equals before the law, but also in...their liberties as men, as workers, and as citizens; to overcome and conquer prejudices and antagonism...the glorious mission of the trade unions.
Speech (1898)

Goncharova, Natalia (1881–1962) Russian painter, printmaker, and stage designer

1 Sculpture cannot translate the emotion that comes from landscape, the moving fragility of a flower, the sweetness of a spring sky.
1937. "Natalia Goncharova," *Feminist Art Journal* (Gloria Fenman Orenstein; Summer 1974)

2 Untalented individuality is as useless as bad imitation.
1913. "Natalia Goncharova," *Feminist Art Journal* (Gloria Fenman Orenstein; Summer 1974)

Goncourt, Edmond de (Edmond Louis Antoine de Goncourt; 1822–96) French novelist and diarist

1 Never speak of yourself to others; make them talk about themselves instead: therein lies the whole art of pleasing. Everyone knows it and everyone forgets it.
Idées et sensations (co-written with Jules de Goncourt; 1866)

2 Antiquity was perhaps created to provide professors with their bread and butter.
January 6, 1866. *Le Journal des Goncourt* (co-written with Jules de Goncourt; 1887–96)

3 Commerce is the art of exploiting the need or desire someone has for something.
July 1864. *Le Journal des Goncourt* (co-written with Jules de Goncourt; 1887–96)

Gonne, Maud (became Maud MacBride; 1865–1953) Irish patriot and actor

1 Poets should never marry. The world should thank me for not marrying you.
Said to William Butler Yeats. Attrib.

Gooch, George Peabody (1873–1968) British historian and politician

1 We can now look forward with something like confidence to the time when war between civilized nations will be considered as antiquated as a duel.
History of Our Time 1855–1911 (1911)

Goodman, Benny (Benjamin David Goodman, "King of Swing"; 1909–86) U.S. jazz musician and bandleader

1 I'm absent-minded. I stare. I don't know what I'm staring at. Sometimes I'm in another city.
Referring to his "ray," a frightening stare that caused band-members to leave. Quoted in *The Penguin Encyclopedia of Popular Music* (Donald Clarke, ed.; 1989)

2 I dunno. How much does Toscanini get?
January 1938. Reply on being asked how long an intermission he wanted at his historic 1938 concert at Carnegie Hall. Referring to Arturo Toscanini. Quoted in *The Penguin Encyclopedia of Popular Music* (Donald Clarke, ed.; 1989)

Goodman, Paul (1911–72) U.S. writer, teacher, and psychotherapist

1 The philosophic aim of education must be to get each one out of his isolated class and into the one humanity.
Compulsory Mis-education (1964)

2 All men are creative but few are artists.
Growing Up Absurd (1960)

3 American society has tried so hard and so ably to defend the practice and theory of production for profit and not primarily for use that now it has succeeded in making its jobs and products profitable and useless.
Growing Up Absurd (1960)

4 Enjoyment is *not* a goal, it is a feeling that accompanies important ongoing activity.
Growing Up Absurd (1960)

5 In the modern world, we Americans are the old inhabitants. We first had political freedom, high industrial production, an economy of abundance.
Growing Up Absurd (1960)

6 Where there is official censorship it is a sign that speech is serious. Where there is none, it is pretty certain that the official spokesmen have all the loud-speakers.
Growing Up Absurd (1960)

7 It is by losing himself in the objective, in inquiry, creation, and craft, that a man becomes something.
The Community of Scholars (1962)

Gorbachev, Mikhail (Mikhail Sergeyevich Gorbachev; b.1931) Russian statesman

Quotations about Gorbachev

1 This man has a nice smile, but he has got iron teeth.
Andrey Gromyko (1909–89) Soviet statesman. Proposing Mikhail Gorbachev for the post of general secretary (leader) of the Soviet Communist Party. Speech, Moscow (1985)

2 Gorbachev is a president without a people—just an army, a party, and a KGB.
Vitaly Alekseyevich Korotych (b.1936) Russian editor and poet. Remark (March 1991)

3 You bring in your wake destruction, ruin, famine, cold, blood, and tears...Amid the applause of the West, Mikhail Sergeyevich has forgotten whose President he is.
December 1990
Sazhi Umalatova Soviet parliamentary deputy. Proposing a motion of no confidence in President Mikhail Gorbachev. Remark

4 I separate myself from the position and policies of Gorbachev, and I call for his immediate resignation. He has brought the country to dictatorship in the name of presidential rule.
Boris Yeltsin (b.1931) Russian president. Speech (February 1991)

Quotations by Gorbachev

5 No party has a monopoly over what is right.
Speech (March 1986)

6 The Soviet people want full-blooded and unconditional democracy.
Speech (July 1988)

7 Life is making us abandon established stereotypes and outdated views, it is making us discard illusions.
Speech to the United Nations (December 7, 1988)

8 We must look for ways to improve the international situation and build a new world—and we must do it together.
Speech to the United Nations (December 7, 1988)

9 Only socialism would put up with it for so long. Capitalism would have gone bankrupt years ago.
Talking of substandard manufacturing practices in the Soviet Union. TV documentary (March 23, 1987)

10 The market came with the dawn of civilization and it is not capitalism's invention.
Guardian, London (June 20, 1990)

11 Some comrades apparently find it hard to understand that democracy is just a slogan.
Observer, London (February 1, 1987), "Sayings of the Week"

12 And if the Russian word "perestroika" has easily entered the international lexicon, this is due to more than just interest in what is going on in the Soviet Union. Now the whole world needs restructuring, i.e. progressive development, a fundamental change.
Perestroika: New Thinking for Our Country and the World (1987)

13 Our rockets can find Halley's comet and fly to Venus with amazing accuracy, but side by side with these scientific and technical triumphs is an obvious lack of efficiency in using scientific achievements for economic needs, and many Soviet household appliances are of poor quality.
Perestroika: New Thinking for Our Country and the World (1987)

14 The essence of perestroika lies in the fact that *it unites socialism with democracy* and revives the feminist concept of socialist construction both in theory and in practice.
Perestroika: New Thinking for Our Country and the World (1987)

15 Democracy is the wholesome and pure air without which a socialist public organization cannot live a full-blooded life.
Report to the 27th Party Congress of the Communist Party of the USSR (February 25, 1986)

16 You cannot go to sleep with one form of economic system and wake up the next morning with another.
Quoted in *Guardian*, London (December 14, 1990)

Gordimer, Nadine (b.1923) South African novelist

1 Very often we support change, and then are swept away by the change. I think that...you just make your own response to your own generation. A response adequate to your time.
Times, London (June 1, 1990)

Gordon, Adam Lindsay (1833–70) Australian poet

1 Life is mostly froth and bubble;
Two things stand like stone,
Kindness in another's trouble,
Courage in your own.
Ye Wearie Wayfarer (1866), Fytte 8

Gore, Al (Albert Gore, Jr.; b.1948) U.S. politician

1 The presidency is not an academic exercise or seminar; it's a daily fight.
Time (January 17, 2000)

Gorky, Maksim (Alexey Maksimovich Peshkov; 1868–1936) Russian novelist, playwright, and short-story writer

1 A good man can be stupid and still be good. But a bad man must have brains.
The Lower Depths (1903)

2 When a woman gets married it is like jumping into a hole in the ice in the middle of winter; you do it once and you remember it the rest of your days.
The Lower Depths (1903)

3 When work is a pleasure, life is a joy! When work is a duty, life is slavery.
The Lower Depths (1903)

4 One has to be able to count, if only so that at fifty one doesn't marry a girl of twenty.
The Zykovs (1913)

5 When one loves somebody everything is clear—where to go, what to do—it all takes care of itself and one doesn't have to ask anybody about anything.
Attrib.

6 You must write for children in the same way as you do for adults, only better.
Attrib.

Gosaibi, Ghazi al- (b.1940) Saudi Arabian poet

1 Our words are dead
like the tyrant's conscience
They've never bathed in the fountain of life,
never known birth pangs or wounds,
the miracle of walking on spear points.
"Silence," *Modern Arabic Poetry* (Salma Khadra Jayyusi, ed.; 1987), ll. 1–5

2 When the brave poet is afraid to die
his best poem is silence!
"Silence," *Modern Arabic Poetry* (Salma Khadra Jayyusi, ed.; 1987), ll. 12–13

Gould, Stephen Jay (b.1941) U.S. geologist and writer

1 Science is all those things which are confirmed to such a degree that it would be unreasonable to withhold one's provisional consent.
Lecture, Cambridge University, England (1984)

2 I advocate a holistic recognition that biology and culture interpenetrate in an inextricable manner.
An Urchin in the Storm (1987)

3 Science is an integral part of culture. It's not this foreign thing, done by an arcane priesthood. It's one of the glories of human intellectual tradition.
Independent, London (January 24, 1990)

4 Evolution is an inference from thousands of independent sources, the only conceptual structure that can make unified sense of all this disparate information.
Leonardo's Mountain of Clams and the Diet of Worms: Essays on Natural History (1998)

5 Honorable errors do not count as failures in science, but as seeds for progress in the quintessential activity of correction.
Leonardo's Mountain of Clams and the Diet of Worms: Essays on Natural History (1998)

6 As to the supposed "conflict"...between science and religion, no such conflict should exist because each subject has a legitimate magisterium, or domain of teaching authority—and these magisteria do not overlap.
"Non-Overlapping Magisteria," *Leonardo's Mountain of Clams and the Diet of Worms: Essays on Natural History* (1998)

7 Nature is amoral, not immoral...It existed for eons before we arrived, didn't know we were coming, and doesn't give a damn about us.
Rocks of Ages: Science and Religion in the Fullness of Life (1999)

8 Humans arose, rather, as a fortuitous and contingent outcome of thousands of linked events, any one of which could have occurred differently and sent history on an alternative pathway that would not have led to consciousness.
"The Evolution of Life on Earth," *Scientific American* (October 1994)

9 Historical sciences...recognize the irreducible quirkiness that history entails, and acknowledge the limited power of present circumstances to impose or elicit optimal solutions.
The Flamingo's Smile (1985)

10 History employs evolution to structure biological events in time.
The Flamingo's Smile (1985)

11 History subverts the stereotype of science as a precise, heartless enterprise that strips the uniqueness from any complexity and reduces everything to timeless, repeatable, controlled experiments in a laboratory.
The Flamingo's Smile (1985)

12 Human equality is a contingent fact of history.
The Flamingo's Smile (1985)

Gourmont, Rémy de (1858–1915) French poet, novelist, and critic

1 Before undergoing a surgical operation arrange your temporal affairs—you may live.
Attrib.

Gournay, Jean-Claude-Marie-Vincent de, Seigneur (1712–59) French economist

1 Liberty of action, liberty of movement.
He reputedly first used the phrase in an economic context. Speech (September 1758)

Gove, Philip Babcock (1902–72) U.S. lexicographer

1 The responsibility of a dictionary is to record a language, not set its style.
Life (November 17, 1961)

Gower, John (1330?–1408) English poet

1 Who that well his warke beginneth,
The rather a good ende he winneth.
Confessio Amantis (1386–90)

2 It hath and schal ben evermor
That love is maister wher he wile.
Confessio Amantis (1386–90), prologue, l. 34

Goytisolo, Juan (b.1931) Spanish novelist and essayist

1 Soaring falcon, noble Poet, come to my aid: bear me aloft to the realm of more luminous truths: one's true homeland is not the country of one's birth: man is not a tree: help me to live without roots: ever on the move: my only sustenance your nourishing language.
Count Julian (1970)

2 The secret equation lying behind your twofold deviation: unproductive (onanastic) manipulation of the written word, self-sufficient (poetic) enjoyment of illicit pleasure.
Referring to Juan Sin Tierra (Juan the Landless), the novel's hero. *Juan the Landless* (1975)

3 The Babelization of great capitals and their cultural relativism are to me the unmistakeable sign of modernity.
1985. "Mudejarism Today," *Saracen Chronicles* (1992)

4 Today's hero, the urban animal...can no longer be exclusively national, or even European, but instead must be turned...inside out, scrambled, bastardized, fertilized by the contributions of any number of different civilizations and geographical regions.
1985. "Mudejarism Today," *Saracen Chronicles* (1992)

Grable, Betty (Elizabeth Ruth Grable; 1916–73) U.S. actor, dancer, and singer

1 There are two reasons why I am successful in show business and I am standing on both of them.
Attrib.

Grace, W. G. (William Gilbert Grace; 1848–1915) British cricketer

Quotations about Grace

1 It's not in support of cricket but as an earnest protest against golf.
Max Beerbohm (1872–1956) British essayist, critic, and caricaturist. Said when giving a shilling towards W. G. Grace's testimonial. *Carr's Dictionary of Extraordinary English Cricketers*

Quotations by Grace

2 They came to see me bat, not to see you bowl.
Refusing to leave the field after being bowled out on a first ball in front of a large crowd. Attrib.

Gracián, Baltasar (Baltasar Gracián y Morales; 1601–58) Spanish writer and Jesuit

1 Good things, when short, are twice as good.
The Art of Worldly Wisdom (1647)

2 Self-reflection is the school of wisdom.
The Art of Worldly Wisdom (1647)

Grade, Lew, Baron Grade of Elstree (Louis Winogradsky; b.1906) Ukrainian-born British film and television producer and impresario

1 All my shows are great. Some of them are bad. But they are all great.
Observer, London (September 14, 1975), "Sayings of the Week"

2 It would have been cheaper to lower the Atlantic.
Referring to the cost of his film, *Raise the Titanic* (1980). *The Sun*, London (December 22, 1987)

Graf, Steffi (b.1969) German tennis player

1 It doesn't hurt to lose my crown, it hurts to lose.
Independent, London (June 22, 1994)

Grafton, Richard (1513?–72?) English chronicler and printer

1 Thirty days hath November,
April, June and September,
February hath twenty-eight alone,
And all the rest have thirty-one.
Abridgement of the Chronicles of England (1562), Introduction

Graham, Billy (William Franklin Graham, Jr.; b.1918) U.S. evangelist

1 Decide for Christ.
Slogan (1950s)

2 Heaven is full of answers to prayers for which no one ever bothered to ask.
Encounter Weekly (1996)

Graham, Clementina Stirling (1782–1877) Scottish writer

1 The best way to get the better of temptation is just to yield to it.
"Soirée at Mrs Russel's," *Mystifications* (1859)

Graham, Harry (1874–1936) British writer, poet, and playwright

1 Aunt Jane observed, the second time
She tumbled off a bus,
"The step is short from the Sublime
To the Ridiculous."
"Equanimity," *Ruthless Rhymes for Heartless Homes* (1899)

2 "There's been an accident" they said,
"Your servant's cut in half; he's dead!"
"Indeed!" said Mr Jones, "and please
Send me the half that's got my keys."
"Mr. Jones," *Ruthless Rhymes for Heartless Homes* (1899)

3 Billy, in one of his nice new sashes,
Fell in the fire and was burnt to ashes;
Now, although the room grows chilly,
I haven't the heart to poke poor Billy.
"Tender-Heartedness," *Ruthless Rhymes for Heartless Homes* (1899)

Graham, Katharine (originally Katharine Meyer; b.1917) U.S. newspaper and magazine publisher

1 If one's rich and one's a woman, one can be quite misunderstood.
The Power That Didn't Corrupt (1974)

2 So few grown women like their lives.
The Power That Didn't Corrupt (1974)

Graham, Martha (1893–1991) U.S. dancer and choreographer

1 Modern dance dates so quickly. That is why I always use the term "contemporary" dance.
Blood Memory (1991)

2 For the contraction to the floor with the high arch: When arching back, think of Joan of Arc resisting a sword that is piercing her chest...For the use of the head and body: Think of Michelangelo's *Pietà*, or that extraordinary Bernini Ecstasy of St. Theresa.
Referring to the contraction, the basis of the Graham technique. *Blood Memory* (1991)

3 I wanted to spit. Respectable! Show me any artist who wants to be respectable.
1980. Reflecting on a fundraiser who complimented her on her respectability. *Blood Memory* (1991)

4 No artist is ahead of his time. He *is* his time; it is just that others are behind the times.
Observer Magazine (July 8, 1979)

Graham, Sheilah (1904–88) British-born U.S. writer

1 I think people still want to marry rich. Girls especially...It's simple. Don't date poor boys. Go where the rich are...You don't have to be rich to go where they go.
Los Angeles Times (October 13, 1974)

Grahame, Kenneth (1859–1932) British banker and children's writer

Quotations about Grahame

1 As a contribution to natural history, the work is negligible.
Anonymous. Referring to Kenneth Grahame's *The Wind in the Willows* (1908). Book review, *Times Literary Supplement*, London (1908), quoted in *The Life of Kenneth Grahame* (Peter Morris Green; 1959)

Quotations by Grahame

2 It is the restrictions placed on vice by our social code which makes its pursuit so peculiarly agreeable.
Pagan Papers (1893)

3 There is nothing—absolutely nothing—half so much worth doing as simply messing about in boats.
The Wind in the Willows (1908), ch. 1

4 The poetry of motion! The *real* way to travel! The *only* way to travel! Here today—in next week tomorrow! Villages skipped, towns and cities jumped—always somebody else's horizon!
Said by Mr. Toad about the motor car. *The Wind in the Willows* (1908), ch. 2

5 The clever men at Oxford
Know all that there is to be knowed.
But they none of them know one half as much
As intelligent Mr Toad.
The Wind in the Willows (1908), ch. 10

Grainger, James (1721?–66) British physician and poet

1 What is fame? an empty bubble;
Gold? a transient, shining trouble.
"Solitude" (1755), ll. 96–97

Grandma Moses (Anna Mary Robertson Moses; 1860–1961) U.S. artist

1 I don't advise any one to take it up as a business proposition, unless they really have talent, and are crippled so as to deprive them of physical labor.
Referring to painting. *New York Times* (May 11, 1947)

2 What a strange thing is memory, and hope; one looks backward, the other forward. The one is of today, the other is the Tomorrow. Memory is history recorded in our brain, memory is a painter, it paints pictures of the past and of the day.
Grandma Moses, My Life's History (Aotto Kallir, ed.; 1947), ch. 1

3 If I didn't start painting, I would have raised chickens.
Grandma Moses, My Life's History (Aotto Kallir, ed.; 1947), ch. 3

Grange, Red (Harold Edward Grange; 1903–91) U.S. football player

1 No one ever taught me and I can't teach anyone. If you can't explain it, how can you take credit for it?
Referring to his talent for eluding tackles. Attrib.

Grant, Cary (Alexander Archibald Leach; 1904–86) British-born U.S. film actor

1 In the spring a young man's fancy lightly turns to what he's been thinking about all winter.
As Jerry Warriner. *The Awful Truth* (Vina Delmar; 1937)

2 Old Cary Grant fine. How you?
Replying to a telegram sent to his agent inquiring: "How old Cary Grant?" *The Filmgoer's Book of Quotes* (Leslie Halliwell; 1973)

Grant, Ulysses S. (Ulysses Simpson Grant; 1822–85) U.S. general

Quotations about Grant

1 When Grant once gets possession of a place, he holds on to it as if he had inherited it.
Abraham Lincoln (1809–65) U.S. president. Letter (June 22, 1864)

2 Grant stood by me when I was crazy and I stood by him when he was drunk.
William Tecumseh Sherman (1820–91) U.S. general. Quoted in *Abraham Lincoln: The War Years* (Carl Sandburg; 1939)

Quotations by Grant

3 I purpose to fight it out on this line, if it takes all summer.
May 11, 1864. From his field headquarters. Despatch to George Washington (1869), quoted in *The Life and Campaigns of Lieut. Gen. U. S. Grant* (P. C. Headley; 1886), ch. 23

4 I know no method to secure the repeal of bad or obnoxious laws so effective as their stringent execution.
Inaugural address (March 4, 1869), quoted in *The Life and Campaigns of Lieut. Gen. U. S. Grant* (P. C. Headley; 1886), ch. 29

5 Let us have peace.
May 29, 1868. Accepting the Republican presidential nomination. Letter to General Joseph R. Hawkey (1869), quoted in *The Life and Campaigns of Lieut. Gen. U. S. Grant* (P. C. Headley; 1886), ch. 29

6 No terms except unconditional and immediate surrender can be accepted. I propose to move immediately upon your works.
Sent during siege of Fort Donelson, Tennessee. Message to Simon Bolivar Buckner, Confederate commander (February 16, 1862), quoted in *The Life and Campaigns of Lieut. Gen. U. S. Grant* (P. C. Headley; 1886), ch. 6

7 I feel we are on the eve of a new era, when there is to be great harmony between the Federal and the Confederate.
Personal Memoirs of Ulysses S. Grant (1885–86)

8 The much talked of surrendering of Lee's sword and my handing it back, this and much more that has been said about it is the purest romance.
Personal Memoirs of Ulysses S. Grant (1885–86)

9 Let no guilty man escape, if it can be avoided...No personal considerations should stand in the way of performing a public duty.
July 29, 1875. Referring to the Whiskey Ring, a tax-fraud scandal during his presidency that involved his secretary and a group of distillers. Quoted in *History of the United States Since the Civil War* (E. P. Oberholtzer; 1937), vol. 3, ch. 19

Granville, George, Baron Lansdowne (1666–1735) British poet and playwright

1 Cowards in scarlet pass for men of war.
The She Gallants (1696), Act 5

Grappelli, Stephane (1908–97) French jazz violinist

1 To serve people soup and make them believe it is chocolate.
Describing his "true gift" as a musician. Quoted in *Stephane Grappelli* (Geoffrey Smith; 1987), ch. 4

Grass, Günter (Günter Wilhelm Grass; b.1927) German writer

1 History offers no comfort. It hands out hard lessons. It makes absurd reading, mostly. Admittedly, it moves on, but progress is not the result of history. History is never-ending. We are always inside history, never outside it.
Documents on the Workings of Politics (1971)

2 A reunited Germany would be a colossus, bedevilled by complexes and blocking its own path and the path of European unity.
"Don't Reunify Germany," *New York Times* (January 27, 1990)

3 No one of sound mind and memory can ever again permit such a concentration of power in the heart of Europe.
Referring to plans to reunify Germany. Germany was divided after its defeat in World War II. The reunification of Germany took place on October 3, 1990. "Don't Reunify Germany," *New York Times* (January 27, 1990)

4 History is, to begin with at any rate, an absurd happening into which more or less gifted people attempt to introduce some perspectives.
The Citizen and His Vote (1974)

5 One of the mistakes the Germans made, in this century and also in the time before, was that they were not brave enough to be afraid.
Comment, *Voices*, Channel 4 television (June 27, 1985)

Grasso, Ella (originally Ella Rosa Giovanna Oliva Tambussi; 1919–89) U.S. politician

1 I'm opposed to abortion because I happen to believe that life deserves the protection of society.
Ms. (October 1974)

Graves, John Woodcock (1795–1886) British poet, hunter, and songwriter

1 D'ye ken John Peel with his coat so gay?
D'ye ken John Peel at the break of the day?
D'ye ken John Peel when he's far far away
With his hounds and his horn in the morning?
'Twas the sound of his horn called me from my bed,
And the cry of his hounds has me oft-times led;
For Peel's view-hollo would waken the dead,
Or a fox from his lair in the morning.
"John Peel" (1820)

Graves, Robert (Robert von Ranke Graves; 1895–1985) British poet and novelist

1 When the days of rejoicing are over,
When the flags are stowed safely away,
They will dream of another wild "War to End Wars"
And another wild Armistice day.

But the boys who were killed in the trenches,
Who fought with no rage and no rant,
We left them stretched out on their pallets of mud
Low down with the worm and the ant.
1918. "Armistice Day, 1918," *Beyond Giving* (1969), st. 7–8

2 Goodbye to All That
1929. Book title.

3 To be a poet is a condition rather than a profession.
1946. Reply to questionnaire. "The Cost of Letters," *Horizon* (September 1946)

4 Most poets are dead by their late twenties.
Observer, London (November 11, 1962)

5 In love as in sport, the amateur status must be strictly maintained.
Occupation: Writer (1950)

6 A well chosen anthology is a complete dispensary of medicine for the more common mental disorders, and may be used as much for prevention as cure.
On English Poetry (1922), ch. 29

7 Counting the beats,
Counting the slow heart beats,
The bleeding to death of time in slow heart beats,
Wakeful they lie.
"Counting the Beats," *Poems and Satires* (1951)

8 Why have such scores of lovely, gifted girls
Married impossible men?
Simple self-sacrifice may be ruled out,
And missionary endeavour, nine times out of ten.
"A Slice of Wedding Cake," *Robert Graves: Collected Poems* (1975)

Gray, Hanna (originally Hanna Holborn; b.1930) German-born U.S. educator

1 The university's characteristic state may be summarized by the words of the lady who said, "I have enough money to last me the rest of my life, unless I buy something."
Christian Science Monitor (November 26, 1986)

Gray, John (b.1948) British academic

1 Economic modernization...spawns indigenous types of capitalism that owe little to any western model.
False Dawn (1998)

2 Global democratic capitalism is as unrealizable a condition as worldwide communism.
False Dawn (1998)

3 The contemporary American faith that it is a universal nation implies that all humans are born American, and become anything else by accident—or error.
False Dawn (1998)

Gray, Lord Patrick (?–1612) Scottish nobleman

1 A dead woman bites not.
1587. Advocating the execution of Mary, Queen of Scots. Also attributed by oral tradition. Quoted in *Annals of the Reign of Queen Elizabeth* (William Camden; 1615 (1625 tr. by A. Darcy)), vol. 1

Gray, Simon (Simon James Holliday Gray; b.1936) British playwright

1 In my experience, the worst thing you can do to an important problem is to discuss it.
Otherwise Engaged (1975), Act 2

Gray, Thomas (1716–71) British poet

Quotations about Gray

1 He was dull in a new way, and that made many people think him *great.*
March 28, 1775
Samuel Johnson (1709–84) British lexicographer and writer. Quoted in *Life of Samuel Johnson* (James Boswell; 1791)

2 They are forced plants, raised in a hot-bed; and they are poor plants; they are but cucumbers after all.
1780
Samuel Johnson (1709–84) British lexicographer and writer. Referring to the poet Thomas Gray's *Odes.* Quoted in *Life of Samuel Johnson* (James Boswell; 1791)

3 I would rather have written those lines than take Quebec.
September 12, 1759
James Wolfe (1727–59) British general. On the eve of the Battle of Quebec, referring to Thomas Gray's "Elegy Written in a Country Churchyard". Attrib.

Quotations by Gray

4 The Curfew tolls the knell of parting day,
The lowing herd winds slowly o'er the lea,
The plowman homeward plods his weary way,
And leaves the world to darkness and to me.
"Elegy Written in a Country Churchyard" (1751), st. 1

5 Let not Ambition mock their useful toil,
Their homely joys, and destiny obscure;
Nor Grandeur hear with a disdainful smile
The short and simple annals of the poor.
"Elegy Written in a Country Churchyard" (1751), st. 8

6 The boast of heraldry, the pomp of pow'r,
And all that beauty, all that wealth e'er gave,
Awaits alike th' inevitable hour:
The paths of glory lead but to the grave.
"Elegy Written in a Country Churchyard" (1751), st. 9

7 Can storied urn or animated bust
Back to its mansion call the fleeting breath?
Can Honour's voice provoke the silent dust,
Or Flatt'ry soothe the dull cold ear of death?
"Elegy Written in a Country Churchyard" (1751), st. 11

8 Full many a gem of purest ray serene
The dark unfathom'd caves of ocean bear:
Full many a flower is born to blush unseen,
And waste its sweetness on the desert air.
"Elegy Written in a Country Churchyard" (1751), st. 14

9 Some village Hampden, that with dauntless breast
The little tyrant of his fields withstood,
Some mute inglorious Milton, here may rest,
Some Cromwell guiltless of his country's blood.
John Hampden (1594–1643) opposed taxation by Charles I without parliamentary sanction. He was imprisoned for his refusal to pay ship money (1637). "Elegy Written in a Country Churchyard" (1751), st. 15

10 Far from the madding crowd's ignoble strife
Their sober wishes never learn'd to stray;
Along the cool sequester'd vale of life
They kept the noiseless tenor of their way.
"Elegy Written in a Country Churchyard" (1751), st. 19

11 Their name, their years, spelt by th' unletter'd muse,
The place of fame and elegy supply:
And many a holy text around she strews,
That teach the rustic moralist to die.
"Elegy Written in a Country Churchyard" (1751), st. 21

12 Here rests his head upon the lap of Earth
A Youth to Fortune and to Fame unknown.
Fair Science frown'd not on his humble birth,
And Melancholy mark'd him for her own.
"Elegy Written in a Country Churchyard" (1751), The Epitaph, st. 1

13 He gave to Mis'ry all he had, a tear,
He gain'd from Heav'n ('twas all he wish'd) a friend.
"Elegy Written in a Country Churchyard" (1751), The Epitaph, st.2, ll. 3–4

14 What female heart can gold despise?
What cat's averse to fish?
"On a Favourite Cat, Drowned in a Tub of Gold Fishes" (1748), st. 4, ll. 5–6, quoted in *The Poems of Thomas Gray: William Collins: Oliver Goldsmith* (Roger Lonsdale, ed.; 1969)

15 A fav'rite has no friend.
"On a Favourite Cat, Drowned in a Tub of Gold Fishes" (1748), st. 6, l. 6, quoted in *The Poems of Thomas Gray: William Collins: Oliver Goldsmith* (Rogrt Lonsdale, ed.; 1969)

16 Not all that tempts your wand'ring eyes

And heedless hearts, is lawful prize;
Nor all that glisters, gold.
"On a Favourite Cat, Drowned in a Tub of Gold Fishes" (1748), st. 7, ll. 4–6, quoted in *The Poems of Thomas Gray: William Collins: Oliver Goldsmith* (Roger Lonsdale, ed.; 1969)

Grayson, Victor (1881–1920?) British politician

1 Never explain: your friends don't need it and your enemies won't believe it.
Attrib.

Greeley, Horace (1811–72) U.S. politician and journalist

1 Go West, young man, and grow up with the country.
Hints Toward Reforms (1850)

Green, Adolph (b.1915) U.S. librettist and lyricist

1 Why, o why, O why-o
Why did I ever leave Ohio,
Why did I wander
To see what lies yonder
When life was so happy at home?
Song lyric. "Wonderful Life" (co-written with Betty Comden; 1953)

Green, Al, Reverend (Albert Greene; b.1946) U.S. singer and songwriter

1 A buck is important, but you need to consider where you come from and what you are doing in order that you may possess your own soul.
Al Green became a "born again" Christian in 1973. Quoted in "Al Green," *Off the Record: An Oral History of Popular Music* (Joe Smith; 1988)

Green, Hannah (Joanne Greenberg; b.1932) U.S. novelist

1 I Never Promised You a Rose Garden
1964. Book and song title.

Green, Hetty (Henrietta Howland Green; 1834–1916) U.S. business executive

1 The thing I am proudest of in my whole business life is that I do not take, that I never took in all my life, and never, never! will take, one single penny more than 6% on any loan or any contract.
Quoted in *The Witch of Wall Street* (Boyden Sparkes and Samuel Taylor Moore; 1935)

Green, Matthew (1696–1737) British poet

1 Fling but a stone, the giant dies.
Laugh and be well.
The Spleen (Richard Glover, ed.; 1737), l. 92

Greene, Graham (Henry Graham Greene; 1904–91) British novelist

1 Those who marry God...can become domesticated too—it's just as humdrum a marriage as all the others.
A Burnt Out Case (1961), ch. 1

2 God forbid people should read our books to find the juicy passages.
Observer, London (October 14, 1979), "Sayings of the Week"

3 Fame is a powerful aphrodisiac.
Radio Times, London (September 10, 1964)

4 I have often noticed that a bribe...has that effect—it changes a relation. The man who offers a bribe gives away a little of his own importance; the bribe once accepted, he becomes the inferior, like a man who has paid for a woman.
The Comedians (1966), pt. 1, ch. 4

5 Catholics and Communists have committed great crimes, but at least they have not stood aside, like an established society, and been indifferent. I would rather have blood on my hands than water like Pilate.
The Comedians (1966), pt. 3, ch. 4

6 They had been corrupted by money, and he had been corrupted by sentiment. Sentiment was the more dangerous, because you couldn't name its price. A man open to bribes was to be relied upon below a certain figure, but sentiment might uncoil in the heart at a name, a photograph, even a smell remembered.
The Heart of the Matter (1948), bk. 1, pt. 1, ch. 2

7 That whisky priest, I wish we had never had him in the house.
The Power and the Glory (1940), pt. 1

8 Innocence is a kind of insanity.
The Quiet American (1955)

9 Perhaps if I wanted to be understood or to understand I would bamboozle myself into belief, but I am a reporter. God exists only for leader-writers.
The Quiet American (1955)

10 I am always ready to visit a new place.
Travels With My Aunt (1969)

11 The first sign of his approaching end was when my old aunts, while undressing him, removed a toe with one of his socks.
Travels With My Aunt (1969)

12 When a train pulls into a great city I am reminded of the closing moments of an overture.
Travels With My Aunt (1969)

13 I cannot bear being spoken to all the time by irrelevant loud-speakers...An airport always reminds me of a Butlin's Camp.
Butlin's Camps are places in the United Kingdom specifically built for short vacations, with all living and entertainment facilities provided on-site. *Travels With My Aunt* (1969), pt. 1, ch. 7

14 Writing is a form of therapy; sometimes I wonder how all those who do not write, compose or paint can manage to escape the madness, the melancholia, the panic fear which is inherent in the human situation.
Ways of Escape (1981)

15 Media is a word that has come to mean bad journalism.
Ways of Escape (1981)

Greene, Hunt U.S. venture capitalist

1 Everything is always impossible before it works. That is what

entrepreneurs are all about—doing what people have told them is impossible.
Fortune (May 27, 1996)

Greene, Robert (1560?–92) English poet and pamphleteer

1 Ah! were she pitiful as she is fair,
Or but as mild as she is seeming so.
Pandosto, The Triumph of Time (1588), ll. 12–13

2 Though men determine, the gods doo dispose; and oft times many things fall out betweene the cup and the lip.
Perimedes the Blacke-Smith (1588)

Greenspan, Alan (b.1926) U.S. economist

1 Inflation is never ultimately tamed. It only becomes subdued.
Financial Times, London (June 3, 1987)

2 I guess I should warn you. If I turn out to be particularly clear, you've probably misunderstood what I've said.
Financial Times, London (December 24, 1988), "Quotes of the Year"

3 Even a moderate rate of inflation can hamper economic performance. Moderate rates of deflation would most probably lead to similar problems.
New York Times (January 4, 1998)

4 Much of what we took for granted in our free-market system was not nature at all, but culture. The dismantling of the central planning function does not, as some had supposed, automatically establish market capitalism.
Quoted in "Genuflecting at the Altar of Market Economics," *International Herald Tribune* (William Pfaff; July 14, 1997)

Greer, Germaine (b.1939) Australian-born British writer and academic

Quotations about Greer

1 In London...I saw a lot of fashion-mad people, including the current Women's Lib idol, an absurd Australian giantess who made remarks like "We must make them understand that fucking is a political act."
Mary McCarthy (1912–89) U.S. writer. Letter to Hannah Arendt (December 11, 1970), quoted in *Between Friends: The Correspondence of Hannah Arendt and Mary McCarthy, 1949–1975* (Carol Brightman, ed.; 1995)

Quotations by Greer

2 Despite a lifetime of service to the cause of sexual liberation I have never caught a venereal disease, which makes me feel rather like an arctic explorer who has never had frostbite.
Observer, London (March 4, 1973), "Sayings of the Week"

3 Common morality now treats childbearing as an aberration. There are practically no good reasons left for exercising one's fertility.
Sex and Destiny (1984)

4 The management of fertility is one of the most important functions of adulthood.
Sex and Destiny (1984), ch. 2

5 If women are to cease producing cannon fodder for the final holocaust they must rescue men from the perversities of their own polarization.
The Female Eunuch (1970)

6 Mother is the dead heart of the family, spending father's earnings on consumer goods to enhance the environment in which he eats, sleeps, and watches the television.
The Female Eunuch (1970)

7 The most popular image of the female despite the exigencies of the clothing trade is all boobs and buttocks, a hallucinating sequence of parabolas and bulges.
The Female Eunuch (1970)

8 You can now see the Female Eunuch the world over...Wherever you see nail varnish, lipstick, brassieres, and high heels, the Eunuch has set up her camp.
The Female Eunuch (1991), Foreword (20th anniversary edition)

9 Women fail to understand how much men hate them.
"Loathing and Disgust," *The Female Eunuch* (1970)

10 Love, love, love—all the wretched cant of it, masking egotism, lust, masochism, fantasy under a mythology of sentimental postures, a welter of self-induced miseries and joys, blinding and masking the essential personalities in the frozen gestures of courtship.
"Obsession," *The Female Eunuch* (1970)

11 Probably the only place where a man can feel really secure is in a maximum security prison, except for the imminent threat of release.
"Security," *The Female Eunuch* (1970)

12 Freud is the father of psychoanalysis. It has no mother.
"The Psychological Sell," *The Female Eunuch* (1970)

13 For all the pseudo-sophistication of twentieth-century sex theory, it is still assumed that a man should make love as if his principal intention was to people the wilderness.
Attrib.

14 No sex is better than bad sex.
Attrib.

Gregoras, Nicephorus (1295–1360) Byzantine historian and scholar

1 The delineation of a sphere on a flat plane is similar to painting. For just as the painters seek to imitate objects exactly...geometricians and astronomers delineate on a flat plane solid objects, such as octahedrons and cubes and all spherical bodies, like the stars, the heavens, and the earth.
Astrolabica (14th century)

Gregory, Dick (Richard Claxton Gregory; b.1932) U.S. comedian and civil rights activist

1 In Chicago not only *your* vote counts, but all kinds of other votes—kids, dead folks, and so on.
Dick Gregory's Political Primer (1972)

2 And for those of you who don't know what the Ku Klux Klan is—that's people who get outta bed in the middle of the night—and take the sheet with 'em!...You always see pictures

of them wearing those pointed hoods? Those hoods are flat! It's the heads that are pointed...
From the Back of the Bus (1962)

3 I happen to know quite a bit about the South. Spent twenty years there one night.
From the Back of the Bus (1962)

4 I know a Southerner who owned an amusement park and almost went out of his mind over where to put us on the merry-go-round.
From the Back of the Bus (1962)

5 Just being a Negro doesn't qualify you to understand the race situation any more than being sick makes you an expert on medicine.
From the Back of the Bus (1962)

6 Let's see now. They've broken the four-minute mile; the sixteen-foot pole vault—how 'bout clearing the color bar next?
From the Back of the Bus (1962)

7 You gotta say this for the white race—its self confidence knows no bounds. Who else could go to a small island in the Pacific where there's no poverty, no crime, no unemployment, no war, and no worry—and call it a "primitive society"?
From the Back of the Bus (1962)

8 In America, with all of its evils and faults, you can still reach through the frost and see the sun. But we don't know yet whether that sun is rising or setting for our country.
"One Less Door," *Nigger* (1964)

Gregory, Richard Arman, Sir (1864–1952) British writer and editor

1 Science is not to be regarded merely as a storehouse of facts to be used for material purposes, but as one of the great human endeavours to be ranked with arts and religion as the guide and expression of man's fearless quest for truth.
Quoted in *The Harvest of a Quiet Eye: A Selection of Scientific Quotations* (Alan L. Mackay; 1977)

Gregory I, Saint ("Gregory the Great"; 540–604) Italian pope

1 Not Angles, but angels.
600? Traditionally Gregory's words when he beheld English slaves in a Roman market. Reported in *Ecclesiastical History of the English People* (Saint Bede the Venerable; 731), bk. 2, sect. 1

Gregory VII, Saint (originally Hildebrand; 1020?–85) Italian-born pope

1 It is the custom of the Roman Church which I unworthily serve with the help of God, to tolerate some things, to turn a blind eye to some, following the spirit of discretion rather than the rigid letter of the law.
Letter (March 9, 1078)

2 There for three days, before the castle gate, he laid aside all his royal gear; barefoot and wearing coarse wool, he stood pitifully, and did not stop begging for our apostolic help and compassion, until he had moved everyone there, or who heard tell of this, to great reverence and pity.
Referring to the Holy Roman Emperor Henry IV. Excommunicated by Gregory, Henry did penance at Canossa, northern Italy in order to regain admittance to the Church. Letter (January 28, 1077)

3 I have loved justice and hated iniquity; therefore I die in exile.
1085. Said to be his last words. Quoted in *The Life and Pontificate of Gregory VII* (J. W. Bowden; 1840), vol. 2, bk. 3, ch. 20

Grellet, Stephen (1773–1855) French-born U.S. cleric

1 I expect to pass through this world but once; any good thing therefore that I can do, or any kindness that I can show to any fellow-creature, let me do it now; let me not defer or neglect it, for I shall not pass this way again.
Quoted in *Treasure Trove* (John O'London; 1925)

Grenfell, Joyce (Joyce Irene Phipps Grenfell; 1910–79) British entertainer

1 I find I am not as closely in touch with modern life as I once was; I no longer seem to meet ladies in antique shops who are besotted about antlers.
1970. Said at the age of 60. Attrib.

Greville, Fulke, 1st Baron Brooke (1554–1628) English courtier and poet

1 The absence which you glory,
Is that which makes you sorry,
And burn in vain:
For thought is not the weapon,
Wherewith thought's ease men cheapen,
Absence is pain.
1590? "Caelica," *Caelica* (1633), quoted in *Selected Poems of Fulke Greville* (Neil Powell, ed.; 1990)

2 Oh wearisome condition of humanity!
Born under one law, to another bound.
Mustapha (1609), Act 5, Scene 4

Grey, Edward, 1st Viscount Grey of Fallodon (1862–1933) British statesman

1 In 1914 Europe had arrived at a point in which every country except Germany was afraid of the present, and Germany was afraid of the future.
Speech (July 24, 1924), quoted in *Quotations in History* (A. Palmer and V. Palmer; 1976)

2 The lamps are going out over all Europe; we shall not see them lit again in our lifetime.
August 3, 1914. From a speech made on the eve of Britain's declaration of war against Germany, at the beginning of World War I. *Twenty Five Years* (1925), vol. 2, ch. 18

Griffin, Susan (b.1943) U.S. poet, writer, and educator

1 Rape is a form of mass terrorism...The fear of rape keeps women off the streets at night. Keeps women at home. Keeps women passive and modest for fear that they be thought provocative.
Quoted in *Women: a Feminist Perspective* (Jo Freeman, ed.; 1979)

Griffith, Arthur (1872–1922) Irish nationalist

1 We have brought back the flag; we have brought back the evacuation of Ireland after 700 years by British troops and the formation of an Irish army. We have brought back to Ireland her full rights.
Supporting the Anglo-Irish Treaty. Speech, Dáil Éireann (Irish Parliament) (December 1921)

Griffith-Jones, Mervyn (John Mervyn Guthrie Griffith-Jones; 1909–79) British lawyer

1 You may think that one of the ways in which you can test this book, and test it from the most liberal outlook, is to ask yourselves the question when you have read it through: "Would you approve of your young sons and daughters—because girls can read as well as boys—reading this book?" Is it a book you would have lying around in your own house? Is it a book you would even wish your wife or your servants to read?
October 20, 1960. Remark during the *Lady Chatterley's Lover* obscenity trial, Central Criminal Court, London. *Times*, London (October 21, 1960)

Griffiths, Trevor (b.1935) British playwright

1 Comedy is medicine.
Comedians (1976), Act 1

Grimald, Nicholas (1519–62) English poet

1 Of all the heavenly gifts that mortal men commend,
What trusty treasure in the world can countervail a friend?
"Of Friendship" (1557)

Grimké, Angelina Emily (1805–79) U.S. abolitionist and social reformer

1 Our fathers waged a bloody conflict with England, because *they* were taxed without being represented...*They* were not willing to be governed by laws which *they* had no voice in making; but this is the way women are governed in this Republic.
Letter to Catherine Beecher (1836)

2 I know you do not make the laws but I also know that you are the wives and mothers, the sisters and daughters of those who do.
"Appeal to the Christian Women of the South," *The Anti-Slavery Examiner* (September 1836)

Grimké, Sarah Moore (1792–1873) U.S. abolitionist and social reformer

1 Brute force, the law of violence, rules to a great extent in the poor man's domicile; and woman is little more than his drudge.
Letter from Brookline (September 1837)

Grisham, John (b.1955) U.S. writer

1 I cannot write as well as some people; my talent is in coming up with good stories about lawyers. That is what I am good at.
Independent on Sunday, London (June 5, 1994)

Groening, Matt (b.1954) U.S. cartoonist

1 All life's answers are on TV.
Said by Homer, pater familias of "The Simpsons." "The Simpsons"

Gropius, Walter (Walter Adolph Gropius; 1883–1969) German-born U.S. architect

1 Architecture begins where engineering ends.
Speech, Harvard Department of Architecture, *Architects on Architecture* (Paul Heyer, ed.; 1978)

2 A modern, harmonic and lively architecture is the visible sign of an authentic democracy.
Observer, London (December 8, 1968), "Sayings of the Week"

Grossart, Angus, Sir (Angus McFarlane McLeod Grossart; b.1937) Scottish banker

1 I've got a great ambition to die of exhaustion rather than boredom.
Sunday Telegraph, London (September 16, 1984)

Grosseteste, Robert (1175?–1253) English scholar and cleric

1 They illuminate our whole country with the bright light of their preaching and teaching.
Referring to the Franciscan order. Letter to Pope Gregory IX (1238)

Grossman, Vasily (Vasily Semyonovich Grossman; 1905–64) Russian writer

1 The literature which called itself "realistic" was just as formalized and imaginary as the bucolic romances of the eighteenth century.
Referring to Socialist Realism. *Forever Flowing* (Thomas P. Whitney, tr.; 1970), ch. 11

2 Man's innate yearning for freedom can be suppressed but never destroyed.
1960. *Life and Fate* (Robert Chandler, tr.; 1980), pt. 1, ch. 50

3 Totalitarianism cannot renounce violence. If it does it perishes...Man does not renounce freedom voluntarily. This conclusion holds out hope for our time, hope for the future.
1960. *Life and Fate* (Robert Chandler, tr.; 1980), pt. 1, ch. 50

Grossmith, George (1847–1912) British entertainer, singer, and writer

1 If you were the only girl in the world,
And I were the only boy.
"If You were the Only Girl," *The Bing Boys* (co-written with Fred Thompson (1884–1949))

2 I left the room with silent dignity, but caught my foot in the mat.
The Diary of a Nobody (1892), ch. 1

3 What's the good of a home, if you are never in it?
The Diary of a Nobody (1892), ch. 1

Grove, Andrew S. (b.1936) Hungarian-born U.S. business executive

1 Consumers resent it when a company presumes to judge the quality of its products on their behalf.
Fortune (May 1, 1995)

2 Columbus didn't have a business plan when he discovered America.
New Yorker (April 11, 1994)

3 Is the Internet a typhoon force, a 10X force, or is it a bit of wind? Or is it a force that fundamentally alters our business?
Only the Paranoid Survive (1996)

4 Making the company into something of a self-sustaining institution, with its own methods and mores and organization—that's tough.
Quoted in *In the Company of Giants* (Rama Dev Jager; 1997)

5 The important things of tomorrow are probably going to be things that are overlooked today.
Quoted in *In the Company of Giants* (Rama Dev Jager; 1997)

6 You can't treat people like an expense item.
Quoted in *In the Company of Giants* (Rama Dev Jager; 1997)

Guan Hanqing (also known as Kuan Han-ch'ing; 1240?–1320?) Chinese playwright

1 DOU E I cry Injustice! Let Earth be moved, let Heaven quake! Soon my spirit will descend to the deep all-embracing Palace of Death.
Dou E, wrongly sentenced to death for the crime of murder, laments her fate. *The Injustice Done to Dou E* (13th–14th century), Act 2, quoted in *Six Yüan Plays* (Liu Jung-en, tr.; 1972)

Guare, John (b.1938) U.S. playwright

1 Show business offers more solid promises than Catholicism.
Independent, London (April 25, 1992)

2 We live in a world where amnesia is the most wished-for state. When did history become a bad word?
International Herald Tribune, Paris (June 13, 1990)

Guccione, Bob (Robert Charles Joseph Edward Sabatini Guccione; b.1930) U.S. publisher

1 Nobody can do this job unless he's a very sexy guy. And I don't know any guy more sexy than me.
Interview, *News of the World*, London (February 29, 1976)

Gu Cheng (1956–96) Chinese poet

1 For the sake of living on and on
People have invented souls
Have invented free and unhampered sails
That do not suffer the torture of ropes
And can sail on dry land.
"The Flag" (1980), quoted in *The Red Azalea* (Edward Morin, ed.; 1990)

Guedalla, Philip (1889–1944) British writer

1 Any stigma will do to beat a dogma.
"Ministers of State," *Masters and Men* (1923)

2 The work of Henry James always seemed divisible by a simple dynastic arrangement into three reigns: James I, James II, and the Old Pretender.
"Some Critics," *Supers and Supermen* (1920)

3 History repeats itself; historians repeat each other.
"Some Historians," *Supers and Supermen* (1920)

Guest, Edgar A. (Edgar Albert Guest; 1881–1959) British-born U.S. poet and journalist

1 It takes a heap o' livin' in a house t' make it home.
"Home," *The Collected Works of Edgar A. Guest* (1934)

2 He started to sing as he tackled the thing
That couldn't be done and he did it.
"It Couldn't Be Done," *The Collected Works of Edgar A. Guest* (1934)

Guevara, Che (Ernesto Guevara de la Serna; 1928–67) Argentinian-born revolutionary

1 I believe in the armed struggle as the only solution for those people who fight to free themselves, and I am consistent with my beliefs.
Written on leaving Cuba to resume an active role as a guerrilla leader, initially in the Congo and then Bolivia. Last letter to his parents (1965)

2 Many will call me an adventurer—and that I am, only one of a different sort: one of those who risks his skin to prove his platitudes.
Written on leaving Cuba to resume an active role as a guerrilla leader, initially in the Congo and then Bolivia. Last letter to his parents (1965)

Guinness, Alec, Sir (b.1914) British actor

1 It is now ten o'clock, Friday the 23rd of September, 1955. If you get in that car you will be found dead in it by this time next week.
1955. Said to James Dean, who died in the car on September 30, 1955. *Blessings in Disguise* (1985)

2 May the Force be with you.
As the Jedi knight, Obi-Wan Kenobi. His watchword to Luke Skywalker in the motion picture *Star Wars* (1977), as he prepares to attack the Death Star. *Star Wars* (George Lucas; 1977)

3 There is a great disturbance in the force.
As the Jedi knight, Obi-Wan Kenobi. This line has become a catchphrase. *Star Wars* (George Lucas; 1977)

Guitry, Sacha (Alexandre Georges Guitry; 1885–1957) Russian-born French actor and playwright

1 The others were only my wives. But you, my dear, will be my widow.
Allaying his fifth wife's jealousy of his previous wives. Attrib.

Guizot, François (François Pierre Guillaume Guizot; 1787–1874) French statesman and historian

1 The spirit of revolution, the spirit of insurrection is a spirit radically opposed to liberty.
Speech, Paris (December 29, 1830)

Gulbenkian, Nubar Sarkis (1896–1972) Turkish-born British philanthropist

1 The best number for a dinner party is two—myself and a dam' good head waiter.
Daily Telegraph, London (January 14, 1965)

2 I find it more satisfying to be a bad player at golf. The worse you play, the better you remember the occasional good shot.
Obituary, *Daily Telegraph,* London (January 12, 1972)

Gull, William Withey, Sir (1815–90) British physician

1 Never forget that it is not a pneumonia, but a pneumonic man who is your patient. Not a typhoid fever, but a typhoid man.
"Memoir II," *A Collection of the Published Writings of* W. W. Gull (T. D. Acland, ed.; 1894)

2 The foundation of the study of Medicine, as of all scientific inquiry, lies in the belief that every natural phenomenon, trifling as it may seem, has a fixed and invariable meaning.
"Study of Medicine," *A Collection of the Published Writings of* W. W. Gull (T. D. Acland, ed.; 1894)

Gummer, John Selwyn (b.1939) British politician

1 Eighty per cent of the people of Britain want more money spent on public transport—in order that other people will travel on the buses so that there is more room for them to drive their cars.
Independent, London (October 14, 1994)

Gunn, Neil (Neil Miller Gunn; 1891–1973) Scottish writer

1 No man gets away from his reckoning, but with luck he may learn how to face it.
Blood Hunt (1952)

Gunn, Thom (Thomson William Gunn; b.1929) British poet

1 He painted, elsewhere, that firm insolent
Young whore in Venus' clothes, those pudgy cheats,
Those sharpers; and was strangled, as things went,
For money, by one such picked off the streets.
Referring to Caravaggio. "In Santa Maria del Popolo," *My Sad Captains* (1961)

2 Now as I watch the progress of the plague,
The friends surrounding me fall sick, grow thin,
And drop away.
Referring to AIDS. "The Missing," *The Man with Night Sweats* (1992)

3 Fuzz is still on the peach,
Peach on the stem.
Your looks looked after you.
Look after them.
"San Francisco Streets," *The Passages of Joy* (1982)

4 He turns revolt into a style, prolongs
The impulse to a habit of the time.
"Elvis Presley," *The Sense of Movement* (1957)

5 At worst one is in motion; and at best,
Reaching no absolute in which to rest,
One is always nearer by not keeping still.
"On the Move," *The Sense of Movement* (1957)

6 On motorcycles up the road they come:
Small, black, as flies hanging in heat, the Boys,
Until the distance throws them forth, their hum
Bulges to thunder held by calf and thigh.
"On the Move," *The Sense of Movement* (1957)

Gunther, John (1901–70) U.S. author and journalist

1 I heard it said that the "architecture" of Atlanta is rococola.
Inside U.S.A. (1947)

Guo Moruo (also known as Kuo Mo-jo; 1892–1978) Chinese writer

1 Classical China did not really feel herself to be what one could call a nation. Rather, she thought of herself as a civilization with a message for all men and as a fatherland.
Quoted in *The Chinese* (Alain Peyrefitte (Graham Webb, tr.); 1977)

Gurdjieff, G. I. (George Ivanovich Gurdjieff, Georgi Ivanovich Gurdjieff; 1865?–1949) Armenian-born French philosopher and writer

1 Man is a machine. All his actions, words, thoughts, feelings, opinions, and habits are the results of external influences, external impressions...It is possible to stop being a machine, but for that it is necessary first of all to *know* the machine.
Quoted in *In Search of the Miraculous* (P. D. Ouspensky; 1950)

Guston, Philip (Philip Goldstein; 1913–80) Canadian-born U.S. painter

1 The visible world, I think, is abstract and mysterious enough, I don't think one needs to depart from it in order to make art.
1978. Quoted in "Philip Guston Talking," *Philip Guston* (Renee McKee, ed.; 1982)

Gutfreund, John (John Halle Gutfreund; b.1929) U.S. business executive

1 Ready to bite the ass of a bear.
Referring to the desired attitude of his employees. Quoted in *Liar's Poker* (Michael Lewis; 1989)

Guthrie, Woody (Woodrow Wilson Guthrie; 1912–67) U.S. folksinger and songwriter

1 This land is your land this land is my land,
From California to the New York Island,
From the redwood forest to the Gulfstream waters,
This land was made for you and me.
Song lyric. "This Land Is Your Land" (1956)

2 You can't write a good song about a whorehouse unless you've been in one.
Broadside (1964)

3 Looks like whatever you try to do, somebody jumps up and hollers and raises cain—then the feller next to him jumps up and hollers how much he likes it.
Quoted in *Music on My Beat: An Intimate Volume of Shop Talk* (Howard Taubman; 1943)

4 They called me everything from a rambling honky-tonk hitter to a waterlogged harmonica player. One paper down in

Kentucky said what us Okies needed next to three good square meals a day was some good music lessons.
Quoted in *Music on My Beat: An Intimate Volume of Shop Talk* (Howard Taubman; 1943)

Guy, Rosa (originally Rosa Cuthbert; b.1928) Trinidadian-born U.S. writer

1 Babies do more to women than make mothers of them.
A Measure of Time (1983), p. 38

2 Even forever comes to an end.
A Measure of Time (1983), p. 120

3 Them's that got, lose. Them what ain't got, got nothin' to lose.
A Measure of Time (1983), p. 210

4 If there were no poor, how do you think rich men would live?
My Love, My Love (1985), p. 8

5 Change is the one constant in life.
"The Human Spirit," *Caribbean Women Writers* (Selwyn R. Cudjoe, ed.; 1990), p.132

Gwenn, Edmund (1875–1959) British actor

1 It is. But not as hard as farce.
1959. Said on his deathbed, replying to the comment "It must be very hard." *Time* (January 30, 1984)

Gwyn, Nell (Eleanor Gwyn; 1650–87) English actor

1 Pray, good people, be civil. I am the Protestant whore.
1681. Said whilst surrounded in her coach by an angry mob in Oxford at the time of the so-called Popish Plot. In 1678, Titus Oates (1649–1703) gave details of a fictitious plot by Roman Catholics to murder Charles II. Quoted in *Nell Gwyn* (B. Bevan; 1969), ch. 13

2 Shall the dog lie where the deer once couched?
Said to a suitor after the death of Charles II. Attrib.

Gyllenhammar, Pehr G. (Pehr Gustaf Gyllenhammar; b.1935) Swedish business executive

1 Companies do not go bankrupt the way they used to, and countries are not declared in default. We talk about restructuring instead...We are prolonging the pains...I think this is detrimental.
Financial Times, London (November 15, 1983)

H. D. (pen name of Hilda Doolittle; 1886–1961) U.S.-born British poet and writer

1 All Greece hates
the still eyes in the white face,
the lustre as of olives
where she stands,
and the white hands.
"Helen" (1924), quoted in *Collected Poems 1912–1944* (Louis L. Martz, ed.; 1983)

2 The old-fashioned horsehair sofa...was the homely instrument of the original scheme of psychotherapy, of psychoanalysis, the science of the unravelling of the tangled skeins of the unconscious mind.
1956. Referring to Sigmund Freud's consulting couch. She was psychoanalyzed by Freud during 1933–34. *Tribute to Freud* (1971)

Haas, Robert (Robert Douglas Haas; b.1942) U.S. business executive

1 The idea of a person as a marionette whose arms and legs start moving whenever you pull the pay string is too simplistic a notion of what motivates people in organizations.
Harvard Business Review (September–October 1990)

2 The more you establish parameters and encourage people to take initiatives within those boundaries, the more you multiply your own effectiveness by the effectiveness of other people.
Harvard Business Review (September–October 1990)

3 Values are where the hard stuff and the soft stuff come together.
Harvard Business Review (September–October 1990)

4 You can't train anybody to do anything that he or she doesn't fundamentally believe in.
Harvard Business Review (September–October 1990)

5 The most visible differences between the corporation of the future and its present-day counterpart will not be the products they make or the equipment they use—but who will be working, how they will be working, why they will be working, and what work will mean to them.
Quoted in *Psychology for Leaders* (Dean Tjosvold and Mary M. Tjosvold; 1995)

Haber, Fritz (1868–1934) German chemist

1 For more than forty years I have selected my collaborators on the basis of their intelligence and their character and not on the basis of their grandmothers, and I am not willing for the rest of my life to change this method which I have found so good.
Remark (April 30, 1933)

Hadrian, Emperor of Rome (Publius Aelius Hadrianus; 76–138) Roman monarch

1 Ah! gentle, fleeting, wav'ring sprite,
Friend and associate of this clay!
To what unknown region borne,
Wilt thou now wing thy distant flight?
No more with wonted humor gay,
But pallid, cheerless, and forlorn.
"Adrian's Address to His Soul When Dying" (Lord Byron, tr.; 138?), quoted in *Minor Latin Poets* (J. W. Duff, ed.; 1934)

2 The crowd of physicians has killed me.
Quoted in *Essays* (Michel de Montaigne; 1580), bk. 2

Haeckel, Steve H. U.S. author

1 A firm's IQ is determined by the degree to which its IT infrastructure connects, shares and structures information. Isolated applications and data, no matter how impressive, can produce idiots savants but not a highly functional corporate behavior.
Quoted in "Managing by Wire: Using IT to Transform a Business," *Business@the Speed of Thought: Using a Digital Nervous System* (Bill Gates and Collins Hemingway; 1999)

Haggard, H. Rider, Sir (Henry Rider Haggard; 1856–1925) British novelist

1 She-who-must-be-obeyed.
She (1887), ch. 6

Hague, Frank (1876–1956) U.S. politician

1 We hear about constitutional rights, free speech, and the free press. Every time I hear those words I say to myself, "That man is a Red, that man is a Communist." You never heard a real American talk in that manner.
Speech, Jersey City Chamber of Commerce (January 12, 1938)

Hahnemann, Samuel (Christian Friedrich Samuel Hahnemann; 1755–1843) German physician

1 Like cures like.
Motto for homeopathy. Attrib.

Haig, Douglas, 1st Earl Haig of Bemersyde (1861–1928) British field marshal

1 Every position must be held to the last man: there must be no retirement. With our backs to the wall, and believing in the justice of our cause, each one of us must fight on to the end.
Order to the British troops (April 2, 1918), quoted in *Haig* (A. Duff Cooper; 1936), vol. 2, ch. 23

2 Please God—let there be victory, before the Americans arrive.
Diary (1917)

Haile Selassie I, Emperor of Ethiopia (originally Prince Ras Tafari Makonnen; 1891–1975) Ethiopian monarch

1 We have finished the job, what shall we do with the tools?
Mimicking Churchill's: "Give us the tools, and we will finish the job." Telegram to Winston Churchill (1941), quoted in *Ambrosia and Small Beer* (Edward Marsh; 1941), ch. 4

Hailey, Arthur (b.1920) British-born Canadian novelist

1 Who says auditors are human?
The Money Changers (1975)

Hailsham, Lord, Baron Hailsham of Saint Marylebone (Quintin McGarel Hogg; b.1907) British statesman

1 A great party is not to be brought down because of a scandal by a woman of easy virtue and a proved liar.
Referring to Christine Keeler, a leading protagonist in the Profumo Affair (1963), one of the greatest sex scandals in British political history. BBC interview (June 13, 1963), quoted in *The Pendulum Years* (Bernard Levin; 1970), ch. 3

2 A master of the English language does not need to exaggerate; an illiterate almost always does.
Observer, London (March 16, 1975)

3 Some of the worst men in the world are sincere and the more sincere they are the worse they are.
Observer, London (January 7, 1968), "Sayings of the Week"

4 You ought not to be ashamed of being bored. What you ought to be ashamed of is being boring.
Observer, London (October 12, 1975), "Sayings of the Week"

Halberstam, David (b.1934) U.S. journalist and author

1 By and large it is the sport that a foreigner is least likely to take to. You have to grow up playing it, you have to accept the lore of the bubblegum card, and believe that if the answer to the Mays-Snider-Mantle question is found, then the universe will be a simpler and more ordered place.
Referring to baseball. Quoted in *Confessions from Left Field* (Raymond Mungo; 1983)

Haldane, J. B. S. (John Burdon Sanderson Haldane; 1892–1964) British geneticist

1 Cancer's a Funny Thing:
I wish I had the voice of Homer
To sing of rectal carcinoma,
Which kills a lot more chaps, in fact,
Than were bumped off when Troy was sacked.
Written while mortally ill with cancer. "Cancer's a Funny Thing," *New Statesman*, London (February 21, 1964)

2 The layman finds such a law as dxdt = K(d^2xdy^2) much less simple than "it oozes", of which it is the mathematical statement.
Possible Worlds (1927)

3 My own suspicion is that the universe is not only queerer than we suppose, but queerer than we *can* suppose.
"On Being the Right Size," *Possible Worlds* (1927)

4 There are a few honest antivivisectionists...I have not met any of them, but I am quite prepared to believe that they exist.
"Some Enemies of Science," *Possible Worlds* (1927)

5 If human beings could be propagated by cutting, like apple trees, aristocracy would be biologically sound.
"The Inequality of Man," *The Inequality of Man* (1932)

6 An inordinate fondness for beetles.
Reply when asked what inferences could be drawn about the nature of God from a study of his works. Quoted in *Reader's Digest* (February 1979)

Hale, Edward Everett (1822–1909) U.S. author and cleric

1 "Do you pray for the senators, Dr. Hale?"
"No, I look at the senators and I pray for the country."
Quoted in *New England Indian Summer* (Van Wyck Brooks; 1940)

Hale, Matthew, Sir (1609–76) English judge

1 Christianity is part of the laws of England.
1676. Quoted in *Commentaries on the Laws of England* (Sir William Blackstone; 1769), vol. 4

Hale, Nathan (1755–76) American revolutionary

1 I only regret that I have but one life to lose for my country.
Prior to his execution by the British during the American Revolution. (September 22, 1776), quoted in *Nathan Hale* (Henry Phelps Johnston; 1914), ch. 7

Hale, Sarah Josepha (originally Sarah Josepha Buell; 1788–1879) U.S. editor

1 The whole process of home-making, house-keeping and cooking, which ever has been woman's special province, should be looked on as an art and a profession.
Godey's Lady's Book (1837–77)

2 Mary had a little lamb,
Its fleece was white as snow,
And everywhere that Mary went
The lamb was sure to go.
"Mary's Little Lamb," *Poems for Our Children* (1830), st.1

3 Of all kinds of knowledge, I consider antiquarian lore as the most unwomanly. It must be gained by so much research, and explained by such learned terms, and defended by so many arguments...heaven defend me from ever meeting with that anomaly in our species—an antiquarian without a beard.
Sketches of American Character (1838)

Haley, Alex (Alexander Murray Palmer Haley; 1921–92) U.S. writer

1 My fondest hope is that *Roots* may start black, white, brown, red, yellow people digging back for their own roots. Man, that would make me feel 90 feet tall.
Interview, *Playboy* (January 1977)

2 History is written by the winners.
Interview, *The David Frost Television Show* (April 20, 1972)

Haley, Bill (William John Clifton Haley; 1927–81) U.S. rock-and-roll singer and musician

1 *We* never sold no sex or sideburns. If we wanted to sell sex or sideburns, we'd have dressed differently.
Referring to the aims of his rock-and-roll group, The Comets. Quoted in *All You Need is Love* (Tony Palmer; 1977)

Haliburton, Thomas Chandler (1796–1865) Canadian writer and jurist

1 If you want to know how to value home, you should go abroad for a while among strangers.
"Sam Slick," *Nova Scotian* (1838)

2 Punctuality is the soul of business.
Sam Slick's Wise Saws (1853), ch. 3

Halifax, George Savile, 1st Marquis of Halifax ("The Trimmer"; 1633–95) English statesman

1 He had said he had known many kicked down stairs, but he never knew any kicked up stairs before.
April, 1684. Referring to Rochester's promotion to a post of higher rank, but carrying less advantage. Remark (April 1864), quoted in *History of My Own Time* (Gilbert Burnet; 1724), vol. 1

2 Popularity is a crime from the moment it is sought; it is only a virtue where men have it whether they will or no.
"Of Ambition," *Political, Moral and Miscellaneous Thoughts and Reflections* (1750)

3 It is flattering some men to endure them.
"Of Company," *Political, Moral and Miscellaneous Thoughts and Reflections* (1750)

4 Most men make little use of their speech than to give evidence against their own understanding.
"Of Folly and Fools," *Political, Moral and Miscellaneous Thoughts and Reflections* (1750)

5 Power is so apt to be insolent and Liberty to be saucy, that they are seldom upon good Terms.
"Of Prerogative, Power and Liberty," *Political, Moral and Miscellaneous Thoughts and Reflections* (1750)

6 When the People contend for their Liberty, they seldom get anything by their Victory but new masters.
"Of Prerogative, Power and Liberty," *Political, Moral and Miscellaneous Thoughts and Reflections* (1750)

7 Men are not hanged for stealing horses, but that horses may not be stolen.
"Of Punishment," *Political, Moral and Miscellaneous Thoughts and Reflections* (1750)

8 Our virtues and vices couple with one another, and get children that resemble both their parents.
"Of the World," *Political, Moral and Miscellaneous Thoughts and Reflections* (1750)

9 It is a general mistake to think the men we like are good for everything, and those we do not, good for nothing.
"Partiality," *Political, Moral and Miscellaneous Thoughts and Reflections* (1750)

Halifax, Lord, 1st Earl of Halifax (Edward Frederick Lindley Wood; 1881–1959) British statesman

1 I often think how much easier the world would have been to manage if Herr Hitler and Signor Mussolini had been at Oxford.
Speech, York (England) (November 4, 1937)

Hall, Charles Sprague (*fl.* 19th century) U.S. songwriter

1 John Brown's body lies a-mould'ring in the grave,
His soul is marching on!
Commemorates John Brown (1800–59), the militant U.S. abolitionist who died in the cause of ending slavery. "John Brown's Body" (1861) Attrib.

Hall, Jerry (b.1956) U.S. model

1 My mother said it was simple to keep a man, you must be a maid in the living room, a cook in the kitchen and a whore in the bedroom. I said I'd hire the other two and take care of the bedroom bit.
Observer, London (October 1985), quoted in *Sayings of the Eighties* (Jeffrey Care, ed.; 1989)

Hall, Joseph (1574–1656) British prelate and writer

1 Perfection is the child of Time.
Works (1625)

Hall, Peter, Sir (Peter Reginald Frederick Hall; b.1930) British theater director

1 We do not necessarily improve with age: for better or worse we become more like ourselves.
Observer, London (January 24, 1988), "Sayings of the Week"

Hallam, Arthur Henry (1811–33) British writer

Quotations about Hallam

1 For words, like Nature, half reveal
And half conceal the Soul within.
1833–49
Lord Tennyson (1809–92) British poet. Arthur Henry Hallam was the fiancé of Tennyson's sister Emily and died suddenly in September 1833. *In Memoriam A. H. H.* (1850), can. 5, st. 1

2 The last red leaf is whirl'd away,
The rooks are blown about the skies.
1833–49
Lord Tennyson (1809–92) British poet. Arthur Henry Hallam was the fiancé of Tennyson's sister Emily and died suddenly in September 1833. *In Memoriam A. H. H.* (1850), can. 15, st. 1

3 I envy not in any moods
The captive void of noble rage,
The linnet born within the cage,
That never knew the summer woods.
1833–49
Lord Tennyson (1809–92) British poet. Arthur Henry Hallam was the fiancé of Tennyson's sister Emily and died suddenly in September 1833. *In Memoriam A. H. H.* (1850), can. 27, st. 1

4 I hold it true, whate'er befall;
I feel it, when I sorrow most;
'Tis better to have loved and lost
Than never to have loved at all.
1833–49
Lord Tennyson (1809–92) British poet. Arthur Henry Hallam was the fiancé of Tennyson's sister Emily and died suddenly in September 1833. *In Memoriam A. H. H.* (1850), can. 27, st. 4

5 Short swallow-flights of song, that dip
Their wings in tears, and skim away.
1833–49
Lord Tennyson (1809–92) British poet. Arthur Henry Hallam was the fiancé of Tennyson's sister Emily and died suddenly in September 1833. *In Memoriam A. H. H.* (1850), can. 48, st. 4

6 Be near me when my light is low,
When the blood creeps, and the nerves prick
And tingle; and the heart is sick,
And all the wheels of Being slow.
1833–49
Lord Tennyson (1809–92) British poet. Arthur Henry Hallam was the fiancé of Tennyson's sister Emily and died suddenly in September 1833. *In Memoriam A. H. H.* (1850), can. 50, st. 1

7 How many a father have I seen,
A sober man, among his boys,
Whose youth was full of foolish noise,
Who wears his manhood hale and green.
1833–49
Lord Tennyson (1809–92) British poet. Arthur Henry Hallam was the fiancé of Tennyson's sister Emily and died suddenly in September 1833. *In Memoriam A. H. H.* (1850), can. 53, st. 1

8 Oh yet we trust that somehow good
Will be the final goal of ill.
1833–49
Lord Tennyson (1809–92) British poet. Arthur Henry Hallam was the fiancé of Tennyson's sister Emily and died suddenly in September 1833. *In Memoriam A. H. H.* (1850), can. 54, st. 1

9 But what am I?
An infant crying in the night:
An infant crying for the light:
And with no language but a cry.
1833–49
Lord Tennyson (1809–92) British poet. Arthur Henry Hallam was the fiancé of Tennyson's sister Emily and died suddenly in September 1833. *In Memoriam A. H. H.* (1850), can. 54, st. 5

10 Are God and Nature then at strife
That Nature lends such evil dreams?
So careful of the type she seems,
So careless of the single life.
1833–49
Lord Tennyson (1809–92) British poet. Arthur Henry Hallam was the fiancé of Tennyson's sister Emily and died suddenly in September 1833. *In Memoriam A. H. H.* (1850), can. 55, st. 2

11 O Sorrow, wilt thou live with me
No casual mistress, but a wife.
1833–49
Lord Tennyson (1809–92) British poet. Arthur Henry Hallam was the fiancé of Tennyson's sister Emily and died suddenly in September 1833. *In Memoriam A. H. H.* (1850), can. 59, st. 1

12 Sleep, Death's twin-brother, knows not Death,
Nor can I dream of thee as dead.
1833–49
Lord Tennyson (1809–92) British poet. Arthur Henry Hallam was the fiancé of Tennyson's sister Emily and died suddenly in September 1833. *In Memoriam A. H. H.* (1850), can. 68, st. 1

13 I dreamed there would be Spring no more,
That Nature's ancient power was lost.
1833–49
Lord Tennyson (1809–92) British poet. Arthur Henry Hallam was the fiancé of Tennyson's sister Emily and died suddenly in September 1833. *In Memoriam A. H. H.* (1850), can. 69, st. 1

14 So many worlds, so much to do,
So little done, such things to be.
1833–49
Lord Tennyson (1809–92) British poet. Arthur Henry Hallam was the fiancé of Tennyson's sister Emily and died suddenly in September 1833. *In Memoriam A. H. H.* (1850), can. 73, st. 1

15 Ring out, wild bells, to the wild sky,
The flying cloud, the frosty light:
The year is dying in the night;
Ring out, wild bells, and let him die.
1833–49
Lord Tennyson (1809–92) British poet. Arthur Henry Hallam was the fiancé of Tennyson's sister Emily and died suddenly in September 1833. *In Memoriam A. H. H.* (1850), can. 106, st. 1

16 Spring wakens too; and my regret
Becomes an April violet,
And buds and blossoms like the rest.
1833–49
Lord Tennyson (1809–92) British poet. Arthur Henry Hallam was the fiancé of Tennyson's sister Emily and died suddenly in September 1833. *In Memoriam A. H. H.* (1850), can. 115, st. 5

17 One God, one law, one element,
And one far-off divine event,
To which the whole creation moves.
1833–49
Lord Tennyson (1809–92) British poet. Arthur Henry Hallam was the fiancé of Tennyson's sister Emily and died suddenly in September 1833. *In Memoriam A. H. H.* (1850), Epilogue, st. 36, ll. 2–4

18 Our little systems have their day;
They have their day and cease to be.
1833–49
Lord Tennyson (1809–92) British poet. Arthur Henry Hallam was the fiancé of Tennyson's sister Emily and died suddenly in September 1833. *In Memoriam A. H. H.* (1850), Prologue, st. 5

Quotations by Hallam

19 Though...the basest passions have roused themselves in the deep caverns of my nature and swept like storm winds over me...I will struggle yet, and have faith in God, that when I ask for bread, I shall not receive a stone.
Letter to Richard Mockton Milnes (1829), quoted in *Homosexuality: A History* (Colin Spencer; 1995)

Halleck, Fitz-Greene (1790–1867) U.S. poet

1 Lord Stafford mines for coal and salt,
The Duke of Norfolk deals in malt,
The Douglas in red herrings.
"Alnwick Castle," *Alnwick Castle, with Other Poems* (1827)

Halliwell, Leslie (1929–89) British film critic

1 Cynics have claimed there are only six basic plots. *Frankenstein* and *My Fair Lady* are really the same story.
Filmgoer's Book of Quotes (1973)

Halm, Friedrich, pen name of Baron Eligius von Münch-Bellinghausen (1806–71) German playwright and poet

1 What love is, if thou wouldst be taught,
Thy heart must teach alone—
Two souls with but a single thought,
Two hearts that beat as one.
1842. Published in Germany in 1842. *Ingomar the Barbarian* (Maria Lovell, tr.; 1854), Act 2

Halsey, Margaret (Margaret Frances Halsey; 1910–97) U.S. writer

1 All of Stratford, in fact, suggests powdered history—add hot water and stir and you have a delicious, nourishing Shakespeare.
With Malice Toward Some (1938)

2 It takes a great deal to produce ennui in an Englishman and if you do, he only takes it as convincing proof that you are well-bred.
With Malice Toward Some (1938)

3 Living in England, provincial England, must be like being married to a stupid but exquisitely beautiful wife.
With Malice Toward Some (1938)

4 The attitude of the English...toward English history reminds one a good deal of the attitude of a Hollywood director toward love.
With Malice Toward Some (1938)

5 The English think of an opinion as something which a decent person, if he has the misfortune to have one, does all he can to hide.
With Malice Toward Some (1938)

Halsey, William (William Frederick Halsey, "Bull"; 1882–1959) U.S. admiral

1 Our ships have been salvaged and are retiring at high speed toward the Japanese fleet.
Response to Japanese claims that most of the American Third Fleet ships had been sunk or were retiring. Report (October 14, 1944), quoted in *Bull Halsey* (E. B. Potter; 1985), ch. 17

Hamel, Gary (b.1954) U.S. management writer

1 A company must be viewed not only as a portfolio of products and services, but a portfolio of competencies as well.
Competing for the Future (co-written with C. K. Prahalad; 1994)

2 All winning organizations are more akin to a pack of wolves than they are to a flock of sheep or wild ducks.
Competing for the Future (co-written with C. K. Prahalad; 1994)

3 Any company whose stake in the past or the present is bigger than its stake in the future runs the risk of becoming a laggard.
Competing for the Future (co-written with C. K. Prahalad; 1994)

4 It is essential for top management to set out an aspiration that creates, by design, a chasm between ambition and resources.
Competing for the Future (co-written with C. K. Prahalad; 1994)

5 Managers are spending too much time managing the present, and not enough creating the future.
Competing for the Future (co-written with C. K. Prahalad; 1994)

6 Most managers spend a disproportionate amount of time in the delivery room, waiting for the miracle of birth.
Competing for the Future (co-written with C. K. Prahalad; 1994)

7 Challenging the status quo has to be the starting point for anything that goes under the label of strategy.
Interview, *Strategy and Business* (1997)

8 In the airline business, you still have to put passengers in a metal tube to get them from A to B. We don't yet know how to overcome that particular orthodoxy.
Interview, *Strategy and Business* (1997)

9 I have talked in the past about the need for gene replacement therapy for top management.
Referring to lack of vision in business. Interview, *Strategy and Business* (1997)

Hamer, Fannie Lou (1917–77) U.S. civil rights activist

1 Ain't no such thing as I can hate anybody and hope to see God's face.
Sojourner (December 1982)

2 All my life I've been sick and tired. Now I'm sick and tired of being sick and tired.
The Nation (June 1, 1964)

Hamerow, Theodore S. (Theodore Stephen Hamerow; b.1920) U.S. historian

1 History appears at present to be a science in technique but an art in interpretation, objective in analysis, subjective in perception, logical or systematic in structure, but intuitive or imaginative in outlook.
Reflections on History and Historians (1987)

2 History...may teach moral lessons and illustrate spiritual truths, but it is too fragmented, too incoherent to guide civic conduct or public policy.
Reflections on History and Historians (1987)

Hamerton, Philip Gilbert (1834–94) British art critic

1 The art of reading is to skip judiciously.
The Intellectual Life (1873), pt. 4, letter 4

Hamilton, Alexander (1757–1804) U.S. president

Quotations about Hamilton

1 He smote the rock of the national resources, and abundant streams of revenue gushed forth. He touched the dead corpse of the public credit, and it sprang upon its feet.
Daniel Webster (1782–1852) U.S. lawyer, politician, and orator. Speech, New York City (1831)

Quotations by Hamilton

2 I believe it may be regarded as a position warranted by the history of mankind that, in the usual progress of things, the necessities of a nation, in every stage of its existence, will be found at least equal to its resources.
The Federalist (co-written with James Madison and John Jay; 1787–88)

3 Justice is the end of government. It is the end of civil society. It ever has been and ever will be pursued until it be obtained, or until liberty be lost in the pursuit.
The Federalist (co-written with James Madison and John Jay; 1787–88)

4 Let Americans disdain to be the instruments of European greatness. Let the Thirteen States, bound together in a strict and indissoluble union, concur in erecting one great American system.
The Federalist (co-written with James Madison and John Jay; 1787–88)

5 The history of Germany is a history of wars between the emperor and the princes and states...of the licentiousness of the strong, and the oppression of the weak; of foreign intrusions, and foreign intrigues...of general imbecility, confusion, and misery.
The Federalist (co-written with James Madison and John Jay; 1787–88)

6 To model our political systems upon speculations of lasting

tranquillity is to calculate on the weaker springs of the human character.
The Federalist (co-written with James Madison and John Jay; 1787–88)

Hamilton, William, Sir (1788–1856) Scottish philosopher

1 Truth, like a torch, the more it's shook it shines.
Discussions on Philosophy (1852), Title page

2 On earth there is nothing great but man; in man there is nothing great but mind.
Quoted in *Lectures on Metaphysics and Logic* (Mamsel and Veitch, eds.; 1859–69)

Hamilton, William (William Winter Hamilton; b.1917) Scottish politician

1 Britain is not a country that is easily rocked by revolution...In Britain our institutions evolve. We are a Fabian Society writ large.
My Queen and I (1975), ch. 9

2 The tourists who come to our island take in the Monarchy along with feeding the pigeons in Trafalgar Square.
My Queen and I (1975), ch. 9

Hamilton, William Rowan, Sir (1805–65) Irish mathematician

1 The hitherto strong-footed, but sore-eyed vixen, prejudice, is limping off, seeking the shade.
1834. *Minutes of the Fourth Annual Convention, for the improvement of the free people of colour* (June 2–13, 1834)

Hammarskjöld, Dag (Dag Hjalmar Agne Carl Hammarskjöld; 1905–61) Swedish statesman and diplomat

1 Do not seek death. Death will find you. But seek the road which makes death a fulfillment.
Markings (Leif Sjöberg and W. H. Auden, trs.; 1964)

2 Hunger is my native place in the land of the passions. Hunger for fellowship, hunger for righteousness—for a fellowship founded on righteousness, and a righteousness attained in fellowship.
Markings (Leif Sjöberg and W. H. Auden, trs.; 1964)

3 In a dream I walked with God through the deep places of creation...until, around me, was an infinity into which we all flowed together and lived anew, like the rings made by raindrops upon wide expanses of calm dark waters.
Markings (Leif Sjöberg and W. H. Auden, trs.; 1964)

4 Narcissus leant over the spring, enchanted by his own ugliness, which he prided himself upon having the courage to admit.
Markings (Leif Sjöberg and W. H. Auden, trs.; 1964)

5 Never let success hide its emptiness from you, achievement its nothingness, toil its desolation. And so...keep alive the incentive to push on further, that pain in the soul which drives us beyond ourselves.
Markings (Leif Sjöberg and W. H. Auden, trs.; 1964)

6 Never measure the height of a mountain, until you have reached the top. Then you will see how low it was.
Markings (Leif Sjöberg and W. H. Auden, trs.; 1964)

7 Pray that your loneliness may spur you into finding something to live for, great enough to die for.
Markings (Leif Sjöberg and W. H. Auden, trs.; 1964)

8 Time goes by: reputation increases, ability declines.
Markings (Leif Sjöberg and W. H. Auden, trs.; 1964)

9 You are your own god—and are surprised when you find that the wolf-pack is hunting you across the desolate ice-fields of winter.
Markings (Leif Sjöberg and W. H. Auden, trs.; 1964)

10 Your cravings as a human animal do not become a prayer just because it is God whom you must ask to attend to them.
Markings (Leif Sjöberg and W. H. Auden, trs.; 1964)

11 "The Army of Misfortune." Why should we always think of this as meaning "The Others"?
Referring to the idea of the enemy. *Markings* (Leif Sjöberg and W. H. Auden, trs.; 1964)

Hammer, Armand (1899–1990) U.S. business executive and philanthropist

1 When I work 14 hours a day, seven days a week, I get lucky.
Guardian, London (December 30, 1990)

2 The art world is a jungle echoing to the calls of vicious jealousies and ruthless combat...but I have been walking in the jungles of business all my life, and fighting tooth and nail for pictures comes as a form of relaxation for me.
Hammer, Witness to History (1987)

Hammer, Michael (b.1948) U.S. author and academic

1 No one, apart from investment managers, goes to work early because he or she is eager to make shareholders rich.
Beyond Re-engineering (1996)

2 Serving the customer is not a mechanical act but one that provides an opportunity for fulfillment and meaning.
Beyond Re-engineering (1996)

3 The feudal corporation—managers and workers in a lord-liege relationship—is gone forever.
Beyond Re-engineering (1996)

4 The heart of managing a business is managing its processes.
Beyond Re-engineering (1996)

Hammerstein, Oscar, II (1895–1960) U.S. lyricist and librettist

1 You'll Never Walk Alone
Song title. *Carousel* (music by Richard Rodgers; 1945)

2 The last time I saw Paris, her heart was warm and gay,
I heard the laughter of her heart in every street café.
Song lyric. "The Last Time I Saw Paris," *Lady Be Good!* (music by Jerome Kern; 1941)

3 People Will Say We're in Love
Song title. *Oklahoma!* (music by Richard Rodgers; 1943)

4 Oh, what a beautiful mornin'!
Oh, what a beautiful day!
Song lyric. "Oh, What a Beautiful Mornin'," *Oklahoma!* (music by Richard Rodgers; 1943)

5 The corn is as high as an elephant's eye.
Song lyric. "Oh, What a Beautiful Mornin'," *Oklahoma!* (music by Richard Rodgers; 1943)

6 Smoke Gets in Your Eyes
Song title. *Roberta* (music by Jerome Kern; 1933)

7 Ol' man river, dat ol' man river,
He must know sumpin', but don't say nothin',
He just keeps rollin', he keeps on rollin' along.
Song lyric. "Ol' Man River," *Show Boat* (music by Jerome Kern; 1927)

8 It's only make believe that I love you.
Song lyric. "Only Make Believe," *Show Boat* (music by Jerome Kern; 1927)

9 I'm Gonna Wash That Man Right Out of My Hair
Song title. *South Pacific* (music by Richard Rodgers; 1949)

10 There Is Nothin' Like a Dame
Song title. *South Pacific* (music by Richard Rodgers; 1949)

11 Fools give you reasons, wise men never try.
Song lyric. "Some Enchanted Evening," *South Pacific* (music by Richard Rodgers; 1949)

12 It Might as Well Be Spring
Song title. *State Fair* (music by Richard Rodgers; 1945)

13 I Whistle a Happy Tune
Song title. *The King and I* (music by Richard Rodgers; 1951)

14 Shall We Dance?
Song title. *The King and I* (music by Richard Rodgers; 1951)

15 Hello young lovers, wherever you are
Song lyric. "Hello Young Lovers," *The King and I* (music by Richard Rodgers; 1951)

16 Climb ev'ry mountain, ford ev'ry stream,
Follow ev'ry rainbow, till you find your dream.
Song lyric. "Climb Ev'ry Mountain," *The Sound of Music* (music by Richard Rodgers; 1959)

17 Girls in white dresses with blue satin sashes,
Snowflakes that stay on my nose and eyelashes,
Silver white winters that melt into springs,
These are a few of my favorite things.
Song lyric. "My Favorite Things," *The Sound of Music* (music by Richard Rodgers; 1959)

18 The hills are alive with the sound of music
With the songs they have sung
For a thousand years.
Song lyric. "The Sound of Music," *The Sound of Music* (music by Richard Rodgers; 1959)

Hammett, Dashiell (Samuel Dashiell Hammett; 1894–1961) U.S. detective-story writer

1 They brought their cult to California because everybody does, and picked San Francisco because it held less competition than Los Angeles.
1928. Said by the detective, referring to the origins of the Temple of the Holy Grail. *The Dain Curse* (1975)

2 Talking's something you can't do judiciously unless you keep in practice.
The Maltese Falcon (1930)

3 I keep these typewriters chiefly to remind myself I was once a writer.
Quoted in *Smithsonian* (May 1994)

4 It is the beginning of the end when you discover you have style.
Quoted in *Smithsonian* (May 1994)

5 Nobody ever created a more insufferably smug pair of characters!
Referring to Nick and Nora in his last novel, *The Thin Man* (1932). Quoted in *Smithsonian* (May 1994)

6 The Thin Man
1932. Book and movie title.

Hammon, Jupiter (1711–1800?) U.S. writer

1 Believe me now, my Christian friends, Believe your friend call'd Hammon: "You cannot to your God attend, And serve the God of Mammon."
A Dialogue Intitled the Kind Master and the Dutiful Servant (1783)

Hammond, Celia (b.1942) British fashion model

1 You had to carry about six or eight pairs of shoes, your rollers, different pairs of scarves, gloves, jewelry, accessories. You used to have to do a different hairstyle for every photograph. All your own makeup. You had to do everything yourself.
Referring to fashion modeling in the 1960s. Quoted in *Model: The Ugly Business of Beautiful Women* (Michael Gross; 1995)

Hammond, Percy (Percy Hunter Hammond; 1873–1936) U.S. drama critic

1 I have knocked everything but the knees of the chorus girls and Nature has anticipated me there.
Quoted in *The Frank Muir Book: An Irreverent Companion to Social History* (Frank Muir; 1976)

Hammurabi (or Hammurapi; *fl.* 1792?–1750? B.C.) Babylonian monarch

1 If a man destroy the eye of another man, they shall destroy his eye.
Quoted in *Right Thinking* (Edward Leigh; 1979)

Hampshire, Stuart (Stuart Newton Hampshire; b.1914) British philosopher

1 We should look in society not for consensus, but for ineliminable and acceptable conflicts, and for rationally controlled hostilities, as the normal condition of mankind...Harmony and inner consensus come with death.
Innocence and Experience (1989)

Hampton, Christopher (b.1946) British playwright

1 If I had to give a definition of capitalism I would say: the process whereby American girls turn into American women.
Savages (1973), Scene 16

2 Asking a working writer what he thinks about critics is like asking a lamp-post how it feels about dogs.
Sunday Times, Magazine London (October 16, 1977)

3 Masturbation is the thinking man's television.
The Philanthropist (1970)

4 You know very well that unless you're a scientist, it's much more important for a theory to be shapely, than for it to be true.
The Philanthropist (1970), Scene 1

5 You see, I always divide people into two groups. Those who live by what they know to be a lie, and those who live by what they believe, falsely, to be the truth.
The Philanthropist (1970), Scene 6

6 It's possible to disagree with someone about the ethics of non-violence without wanting to kick his face in.
Treats (1976), Scene 4

Hamsun, Knut (originally Knut Pedersen; 1859–1952) Norwegian novelist

1 When *The Cultural Life of America* is published, I'll send you a copy...I will surely never again be able to show myself in America...for it...asserts my biased view of that philistine land and is violently contra.
Letter to Victor Nilsson (March 4, 1889)

Hancock, John (1737–93) American patriot and statesman

1 There, I guess King George will be able to read that.
1776. Referring to his signature, written in a bold hand, on the Declaration of Independence. Quoted in *The American Treasury* (Clifton Fadiman; 1955)

Hand, Learned (Billings Learned Hand; 1872–1961) U.S. jurist

1 Liberty is so much latitude as the powerful choose to accord to the weak.
Address to University of Pennsylvania Law School (May 21, 1944)

2 There is no surer way to misread a document than to read it literally.
"Giuseppi v. Walling" (1944)

Handlin, Oscar (b.1915) U.S. historian

1 The historian must resist all pleas to solve the world's immediate problems. By the time this particular type of equipment is ready, the fire has moved elsewhere.
Truth in History (1979)

2 Where there is no evidence, there is no history.
Truth in History (1979)

Handy, Charles (Charles Brian Handy; b.1932) Irish-born British management educator and writer

1 Brains are becoming the core of organisations—other activities can be contracted out.
Strategy and Business (1998)

2 Most organisations are not designed, they grow.
Strategy and Business (1996)

3 I believe that corporations should be membership communities because I believe corporations are not things, they are the people who run them.
Interview, *Strategy and Business* (1995)

4 Not many people really do know how to design an organisation that is not a machine.
Interview, *Strategy and Business* (1995)

5 If you reward the good and ignore or forgive the bad, the good will occur more frequently and the bad will gradually disappear.
The Age of Unreason (1989)

6 Scrapbooks, I believe, are useful therapy—they are a way of putting the past to bed, decorously. Then we can move forward.
The Age of Unreason (1989)

7 We as individuals need to accept our past but then turn our backs on it. Organisations often do it by changing their name, individuals by moving house, or changing spouses. It does not have to be so dramatic.
The Age of Unreason (1989)

8 We need talents more than the intellect.
The Age of Unreason (1989)

9 Continuous change is comfortable change. The past is then the guide to the future.
Referring to the need for radical or "discontinuous" change in business. *The Age of Unreason* (1989)

10 If there is one general law of communication it is that we never communicate as effectively as we think we do.
Understanding Organisations (1976)

11 A consultant solves other people's problems. I could never do that. I want to help other people solve their own problems.
Quoted in *Key Management Ideas* (Stuart Crainer; 1996)

Handy, W. C. (William Christopher Handy; 1873–1958) U.S. composer, cornetist, and bandleader

1 Hits are like babies. To some they come every year or so and to others they never come.
Father of the Blues (1941)

2 Love, as everyone should know, is a strange disease.
Father of the Blues (1941)

3 The blues came from the man farthest down. The blues came from nothingness, from want, from desire. And when a man sang or played the blues, a small part of the want was satisfied from the music.
Quoted in *Hear Me Talkin' to Ya* (Nat Shapiro and Nat Hentoff, eds.; 1955)

Han Fei (also known as Han Fei Tzu; 280?–233? B.C.) Chinese philosopher

1 Water far away cannot put out a fire nearby.
The Book of Han Feizi (3rd century B.C.)

2 The ruler firmly bars his inner door, and from his room surveys the courtyard; he has provided the rules and yardsticks, so that all things know their place.
Quoted in *The Chinese Experience* (Raymond Dawson; 1978)

3 Those who talk about agriculture are many, but those who hold the plow are few.
Quoted in *The Chinese Experience* (Raymond Dawson; 1978)

Hanks, Tom (b.1956) U.S. film actor

1 My mama always said, life is like a box of chocolates. You never know what you're gonna get.
Said as Forrest Gump. *Forrest Gump* (Eric Roth; 1994)

Hansberry, Lorraine (Lorraine Vivian Hansberry; 1930–65) U.S. writer

1 There is always something left to love. And if you ain't learned that, you ain't learned nothing.
A Raisin in the Sun (1959)

2 Race—racism—is a device. No more, no less. It explains nothing at all.
Les Blancs (1963)

3 Take away the violence and who will hear the man of peace?
Les Blancs (1963)

4 I *care!* I care about it all. It takes too much energy *not* to care.
The Sign in Sidney Brustein's Window (1964)

5 Ball points belong to their age. They make everyone write alike.
To Be Young, Gifted and Black: An Informal Autobiography (Robert Nemiroff, ed.; 1970)

6 I think that the human race does command its own destiny and that that destiny can eventually embrace the stars.
To Be Young, Gifted and Black: An Informal Autobiography (Robert Nemiroff, ed.; 1970)

7 One cannot live with sighted eyes and feeling heart and not know and react to the miseries which afflict this world.
To Be Young, Gifted and Black: An Informal Autobiography (Robert Nemiroff, ed.; 1970)

Hansemann, David (1790–1864) German politician

1 Where it's the question of money, all good nature ends.
1847. Attrib.

Hansen, Karl-Heinz German politician

1 A people not prepared to face its own history cannot manage to face its own future.
1978. Attrib.

Hanson, Lord, Baron Hanson of Edgerton (James Edward Hanson; b.1922) British entrepreneur

1 I've always thought about the downside risk on a takeover rather than the upside potential—we don't gamble.
Financial Times, London (December 23, 1983)

2 It is perfectly reasonable to me that we should need to destroy large parts of the beautiful countryside, because there isn't a single thing in this country—not a hospital, not a school...you can build without destroying...countryside.
Spectator, London (October 7, 1989)

Hansson, Per Albin (1885–1946) Swedish statesman

1 Sweden should be *Folkhemmet*, the people's home, the good society which functions like a good home...where equality, consideration, cooperation, and helpfulness prevail.
Speech, Stockholm (1928)

Han Yu (768–824) Chinese writer and poet

1 The three grades of character are superior, medium and inferior: the superior is just good, the medium is capable of development either in an upward or a downward direction, and the inferior is just evil.
"The Truth About One's Underlying Character" (8th–9th century), quoted in *Essays by Han Yu* (A. C. Barnes, tr.; 1979)

2 The seven constituents of emotional make-up are: joy, anger, sorrow, fear, love, hatred, and desire. A man of superior emotional make-up will display these emotions in a balanced manner.
"The Truth About One's Underlying Character" (8th–9th century), quoted in *Essays by Han Yu* (A. C. Barnes, tr.; 1979)

Haraucourt, Edmond (1857–1941) French poet

1 To go away is to die a little, it is to die to that which one loves: everywhere and always, one leaves behind a part of oneself.
"Rondel de l'Adieu," *Seul* (1891)

Harbach, Otto (1873–1963) U.S. playwright and librettist

1 Tea for two, and two for tea
Song lyric. "Tea for Two, and Two for Tea," *No! No! Nanette* (1924)

2 She didn't say yes,
She didn't say no.
Song lyric. "She Didn't Say Yes," *The Cat and the Fiddle* (1931)

Harbord, James Guthrie (1866–1947) U.S. general and business executive

1 I met the great little man, the man who can be silent in several languages.
Referring to Colonel House. Quoted in *Mr. Wilson's War* (John Dos Passos; 1962), ch. 3

Harburg, E. Y. (Edgar Yipsel Harburg, "Yip"; 1896–1981) U.S. librettist and lyricist

1 Once I built a railroad,
Now it's done.
Brother, can you spare a dime?
Song lyric. Often misquoted as "Buddy, can you spare a dime?" "Brother, Can You Spare a Dime," *New Americana* (1932)

2 It's only a paper moon,
Sailing over a cardboard sea,
But it wouldn't be make-believe
If you believed in me.
Song lyric. "It's Only a Paper Moon," *The Great Magoo* (1933)

3 Follow the Yellow Brick Road
Song title. "Follow the Yellow Brick Road," *The Wizard of Oz* (1939)

4 Someday I'll wish upon a star.
Song lyric. "Over the Rainbow," *The Wizard of Oz* (1939)

5 Somewhere over the rainbow,
Way up high:

There's a land that I heard of
Once in a lullaby.
Song lyric. "Over the Rainbow," *The Wizard of Oz* (1939)

6 The World would be a safer place,
If someone had a plan,
Before exploring Outer Space,
To find the Inner Man.
Attrib.

Hardenberg, Friedrich Leopold von (pen name Novalis; 1772–1801) German poet

1 I often feel, and ever more deeply I realize, that fate and character are the same conception.
Often quoted as "Character is Destiny." *Heinrich von Ofterdingen* (1802), bk. 2

Harding, Gilbert (Gilbert Charles Harding; 1907–60) British broadcaster

1 If, sir, I possessed the power of conveying unlimited sexual attraction through the potency of my voice, I would not be reduced to accepting a miserable pittance from the BBC for interviewing a faded female in a damp basement.
Said to Mae West's manager, who suggested that he should be more "sexy" when interviewing her. Quoted in *Gilbert Harding by His Friends* (Stephen Grenfell, ed.; 1961)

Harding, Vincent (b.1931) U.S. historian

1 The struggle for black freedom has been tied to their history by cords of anguish and rivers of blood.
The Other American Revolution (1980)

Harding, Warren G. (Warren Gamaliel Harding; 1865–1923) U.S. president

Quotations about Harding

1 The only man woman or child who wrote a simple declarative sentence with seven grammatical errors "is dead."
e. e. cummings (1894–1962) U.S. poet and painter. *ViVa* (1931)

2 Harding, Wilson, Taft, Roosevelt,
idiots fumbling at the bride's door,
hear the cries of men in meaningless debt and war.
Where among these did the spirit reside
that restores the land to productive order?
Robert Duncan (1919–88) U.S. poet. Referring to U.S. presidents Warren G. Harding, Woodrow Wilson, William Howard Taft, and Franklin D. Roosevelt. "A Poem Beginning with a Line by Pindar" (1960), quoted in *The Norton Anthology of American Literature* (Nina Baym, ed.; 1998), vol. 2

Quotations by Harding

3 America's present need is not heroics but healing, not nostrums but normalcy.
Speech, Boston (May 14, 1920), quoted in *Rededicating America* (Frederick E. Schortemeier; 1920), ch. 17

4 I wish for an America no less alert in guarding against dangers from within than it is watchful against enemies from without.
New York Times (March 5, 1921)

5 It is everlastingly true that on the whole the best guide to the future is to be found in a proper understanding of the lessons of the past.
Quoted in *The Meaning of History* (N. Gordon and Joyce Carper; 1991)

Hardwick, Elizabeth (Elizabeth Bruce Hardwick; b.1916) U.S. writer

1 Women, wronged in one way or another, are given the overwhelming beauty of endurance, the capacity for high or low suffering, for violent feeling absorbed, finally tranquilized, for the radiance of humility, for silence, secrecy, impressive acceptance. Heroines are, then, heroic.
Seduction and Betrayal: Women in Literature (1974)

Hardy, Godfrey Harold (1877–1947) British mathematician

1 A science is said to be useful if its development tends to accentuate the existing inequalities of wealth, or more directly promotes the destruction of human life.
A Mathematician's Apology (1941)

2 Beauty is the first test: there is no permanent place in this world for ugly mathematics.
A Mathematician's Apology (1941)

3 I am interested in mathematics only as a creative art.
A Mathematician's Apology (1941)

4 Young men should prove theorems, old men should write books.
Quoted in *The College Mathematics Journal* (January 1994), vol. 25, no. 1

Hardy, Oliver (Norvell Hardy; 1892–1957) U.S. film comedian

1 Here's another fine mess you've gotten me into.
From 1926. Catchphrase said to Stan Laurel in various films. Sometimes quoted as "...another nice mess..."

Hardy, Thomas (1840–1928) British novelist and poet

Quotations about Hardy

1 He seems to me to have written as nearly for the sake of "self-expression" as a man well can; and the self which he had to express does not strike me as a particularly wholesome or edifying matter of communication.
T. S. Eliot (1888–1965) U.S.-born British poet and playwright. "After Strange Gods" (1934)

2 No one has written worse English than Mr Hardy in some of his novels...but at the same time so strangely expressive of something attractive...that we would not change it for the perfection of Sterne at his best.
Virginia Woolf (1882–1941) British novelist and critic. *The Moment* (1947)

Quotations by Hardy

3 I'm a labouring man, and know but little,
Or nothing at all;
But I can't help thinking that stone once echoed
The voice of Paul.
1930. "In the British Museum," st. 7, ll. 1–4

4 The land's sharp features seemed to be
The Century's corpse outleant,

His crypt the cloudy canopy,
The wind his death-lament.
"The Darkling Thrush" (1900), ll. 9–12

5 At once a voice arose among
The bleak twigs overhead
In a full-hearted evensong
Of joy unlimited;
An aged thrush, frail, gaunt, and small,
In blast-beruffled plume,
Had chosen thus to fling his soul
Upon the growing gloom.
Conceived as a farewell to the 19th century, the poem was first published under the title "By the Century's Deathbed" in *Graphic* (1900). "The Darkling Thrush" (1900), st. 3

6 Here's not a modest maiden elf
But dreads the final Trumpet,
Lest half of her should rise herself,
And half some sturdy strumpet!
"The Levelled Churchyard" (1882), st. 5, ll. 1–4

7 I shall be breakfasted before you are afield. In short, I shall astonish you all.
Bathsheba Everdene addressing the farm hands. *Far From the Madding Crowd* (1874)

8 A nice unparticular man.
Far From the Madding Crowd (1874), ch. 8

9 We ought to feel deep cheerfulness that a happy Providence kept it from being any worse.
Far From the Madding Crowd (1874), ch. 8

10 Ah! stirring times we live in—stirring times.
Far From the Madding Crowd (1874), ch. 15

11 Every branch big with it,
Bent every twig with it;
Every fork like a white web-foot;
Every street and pavement mute:
Some flakes have lost their way, and grope back upward, when
Meeting those meandering down they turn and descend again.
"Snow in the Suburbs," *Human Shows* (1925)

12 Done because we are too menny.
Suicide note of Jude's son. *Jude the Obscure* (1895), pt. 6, ch. 2

13 This is the weather the cuckoo likes,
And so do I;
When showers betumble the chestnut spikes,
And nestlings fly:
And the little brown nightingale bills his best,
And they sit outside at "The Travellers' Rest".
"Weathers," *Late Lyrics and Earlier* (1922), ll. 1–6

14 This is the weather the shepherd shuns,
And so do I.
"Weathers," *Late Lyrics and Earlier* (1922), ll. 10–11

15 Life's Little Ironies
Book title. *Life's Little Ironies* (1894)

16 If I pass during some nocturnal blackness, mothy and warm,
When the hedgehog travels furtively over the lawn,
One may say, "He strove that such innocent creatures should come to no harm,
But he could do little for them; and now he is gone."
"Afterwards," *Moments of Vision* (1917)

17 When the Present has latched its postern behind my tremulous stay,
And the May month flaps its glad green leaves like wings,
Delicate-filmed as new-spun silk, will the neighbours say,
"He was a man who used to notice such things"?
"Afterwards," *Moments of Vision* (1917), st. 1

18 I am the family face;
Flesh perishes, I live on.
"Heredity," *Moments of Vision* (1917)

19 "God's humbles, they!" I muse. Yet why?
They know Earth-secrets that know not I.
"An August Midnight," *Poems of the Past and Present* (1901)

20 Well: while was fashioning
This creature of cleaving wing,
The Immanent Will that stirs and urges everything

Prepared a sinister mate
For her—so gaily great—
A Shape of Ice, for the time far and dissociate.

And as the smart ship grew
In stature, grace, and hue,
In shadowy silent distance grew the Iceberg too.
Referring to the sinking of the *Titanic*, April 14, 1912. "The Convergence of the Twain," *Satires of Circumstance* (1914), sts. 6, 7, and 8

21 A little one-eyed, blinking sort o' place.
Tess of the D'Urbervilles (1891), ch. 1

22 Always washing, and never getting finished.
Tess of the D'Urbervilles (1891), ch. 4

23 "Justice" was done, and the President of the Immortals (in Aeschylean phrase) had ended his sport with Tess.
Tess of the D'Urbervilles (1891), ch. 59

24 That long drip of human tears.
"On an Invitation to the United States," *The Complete Poems* (James Gibson, ed.; 1979), st. 1, l. 6

25 A local thing called Christianity.
"Spirit of the Years," *The Dynasts* (1904), pt. 1, Act 1, Scene 6

26 My argument is that War makes rattling good history; but Peace is poor reading.
"Spirit Sinister," *The Dynasts* (1904), pt. 1, Act 2, Scene 5

27 A lover without indiscretion is no lover at all.
The Hand of Ethelberta (1876), ch. 20

28 Dialect words—those terrible marks of the beast to the truly genteel.
The Mayor of Casterbridge (1886), ch. 20

29 You was a good man, and did good things.
The Woodlanders (1887), ch. 48

30 Good, but not religious-good.
Under the Greenwood Tree (1872), ch. 2

31 That man's silence is wonderful to listen to.
Under the Greenwood Tree (1872), ch. 14

32 "Peace upon earth!" was said. We sing it,
And pay a million priests to bring it.
After two thousand years of mass
We've got as far as poison-gas.
"Christmas: 1924," *Winter Words* (1928), complete poem

33 If Galileo had said in verse that the world moved, the Inquisition might have let him alone.
Quoted in *The Later Years of Thomas Hardy, 1892–1928* (Florence Hardy; 1930)

Hare, David (b.1947) British playwright

1 And when it's gay priests, even the tabloids suddenly find they have a religious affairs correspondent.
Sunday Times, London (February 11, 1990)

2 I could always not deal with my problems by referring to God, my comfort...Religion was my protection against pain.
Sunday Times, London (February 11, 1990)

3 I wasn't born until I started to write.
Sunday Times, London (February 11, 1990)

Hare, Julius (Julius Charles Hare; 1795–1855) British writer and cleric

1 Half the failures in life arise from pulling in one's horse as he is leaping.
Series 1, *Guesses at Truth* (1827)

Hare, R. M. (b.1919) British philosopher

1 A moral judgment made about one situation commits us, on pain of logical inconsistency, to making the same judgment about any precisely similar situation.
"What Makes Choices Rational?" (1979)

2 I say that moral judgments are prescriptive because in their typical uses they are intended to guide our conduct; to accept one is to be committed to a certain line of action or to prescribing it to somebody else.
"What Makes Choices Rational?" (1979)

Hargreaves, W. F. (1846–1919) British songwriter

1 I'm Burlington Bertie:
I rise at ten-thirty.
Vaudeville song. "Burlington Bertie from Bow" (1915)

2 I walk down the Strand
With my gloves on my hand,
And I walk down again
With them off.
Vaudeville song. "Burlington Bertie from Bow" (1915)

Haring, Keith (1958–90) U.S. painter

1 Art lives through the imaginations of people who are seeing it. Without that contact there is no art.
Quoted in *Flash Art* (March 1984)

Harington, John, Sir (1561–1612) English writer and courtier

1 Treason doth never prosper: what's the reason?
For if it prosper, none dare call it treason.
"Of Treason," *Epigrams* (1618), bk. 4, no. 5

Harlan, John Marshall (1833–1911) U.S. jurist

1 The law regards man as man and takes no account of his surroundings or of his color when his civil rights as guaranteed by the supreme law of the land are involved.
Sole dissenting opinion in a legal case. *Plessy* v. *Ferguson* (1896), 163 U.S., 537

Harold II, King of England (1020?–66) Saxon monarch

Quotations about Harold II

1 I am...ready to risk my life against his in single combat to decide whether the kingdom of England should be his or mine.
William the Conqueror (1027–87) Norman-born English monarch. Referring to Harold II of England, shortly before the Battle of Hastings. Remark (October 14, 1066)

Quotations by Harold II

2 He will give him seven feet of English ground, or as much more as he may be taller than other men.
1066. Offer to Harald III (Hårdråde, The Hard Ruler), king of Norway (1047–66), whom he defeated at the Battle of Stamford Bridge, Yorkshire, 20 days before the Battle of Hastings. *King Harald's Saga* (Snorri Sturluson; 1260), sect. 91, Hemiskringla

Harper, Frances E. W. (originally Frances Ellen Watkins Harris; 1825–1911) U.S. writer and social reformer

1 Apparent failure may hold in its rough shell the germs of a success that will blossom in time, and bear fruit throughout eternity.
Speech (1875)

2 A towering intellect, grand in its achievements, and glorious in its possibilities, may, with the moral and spiritual faculties held in abeyance, be one of the most dangerous and mischievous forces in the world.
"A Factor in Human Progress," *African Methodist Episcopal Church Review* (1885)

3 The respect that is only bought by gold is not worth much.
"Our Greatest Want," *Anglo-African* (May 1859)

4 No golden weights can turn the scale
Of justice in His sight;
And what is wrong in woman's life
In man's cannot be right.
"A Double Standard," *Atlantic Offering* (1895)

5 I am not despondent of the future of my people; there is too much elasticity in their spirits, too much hope in their hearts, to be crushed out by unreasoning malice.
Iola Leroy, or Shadows Uplifted (1892)

6 Weep not, oh my well-sheltered sisters,
Weep not for the Negro alone,
But weep for your sons who must gather
The crops which their fathers have sown.
"An Appeal to My Country Women," *Poems* (1895)

7 Oh! how shall I speak of my proud country's shame?
Of the stains on her glory, how give them their name?
How say that her banner in mockery waves—

Her "star spangled banner"—o'er millions of slaves?
"Eliza Harris," *Poems on Miscellaneous Subjects* (1854)

Harragan, Betty Lehan (1921–98) U.S. management consultant, lecturer, and author

1 Never wear a man's tie. Never, never, never. A man's tie is a penis symbol. No woman with any self-respect wants to walk around advertising "I'm pretending I have a penis."
Games Mother Never Taught You (1977)

Harrington, James (1611–77) English political theorist

1 For the Colonies in the Indies, they are yet babes that cannot live without sucking the breasts of their mother-Cities, but such as I mistake, if when they come of age they do not wean themselves.
The Commonwealth of Oceana (1656)

2 No man can be a Politician, except he be first an Historian or a Traveller; (for except he can see what must be, or what may be, he is no Politician).
The Commonwealth of Oceana (1656)

Harrington, Michael (1928–89) U.S. socialist writer

1 America has the best-dressed poverty the world has ever known...It is much easier in the United States to be decently dressed than it is to be decently housed, fed, or doctored.
The Other America: Poverty in the United States (1962)

2 Our affluent society contains those of talent and insight who are driven to prefer poverty, to choose it, rather than to submit to the desolation of an empty abundance.
The Other America: Poverty in the United States (1962)

3 People who are much too sensitive to demand of cripples that they run races ask of the poor that they get up and act just like everyone else in society.
The Other America: Poverty in the United States (1962)

Harris, Corra May (originally Corra May White; 1869–1935) U.S. writer

1 A woman would rather visit her own grave than the place where she had been young and beautiful after she is aged and ugly.
Eve's Second Husband (1910), ch. 14

Harris, Frank (James Thomas Harris; 1854–1931) Irish-born editor and writer

Quotations about Harris

1 The great and terrible step was taken. What else could you expect from a girl so expectant? "Sex," said Frank Harris, "is the gateway to life." So I went through the gateway in an upper room in the Café Royal.
Enid Bagnold (1889–1981) British author and playwright. *Autobiography* (1969)

2 "Christianity, of course, but why journalism?"
1920
Arthur Balfour (1848–1930) British prime minister. In reply to Frank Harris's remark, "...all the faults of the age come from Christianity and journalism." *The Autobiography of Margot Asquith* (Margot Asquith; 1962), ch. 10

3 Dear Frank, we believe you; you have dined in every house in London once.
Oscar Wilde (1854–1900) Irish poet, playwright, and wit. Interrupting Frank Harris's interminable account of the houses at which he had dined. Attrib.

Quotations by Harris

4 A history of humanity to the present time in which Shakespeare is not mentioned and Jesus is dismissed in a page carelessly, as if not worth contempt, shocks me.
Referring to H. G. Wells's *The Outline of History* (1920). *My Life and Loves* (1925)

Harris, George (1844–1922) U.S. congressman

1 I intended to give you some advice but now I remember how much is left over from last year unused.
Said at the start of a new academic year. Address to students, quoted in *Braude's Second Encyclopedia* (J. Braude; 1957)

Harris, Janet (b.1915) U.S. writer and civil rights activist

1 I'm the ultimate in the throwaway society, the disposable woman.
The Prime of Ms. America (1975)

2 One searches the magazines in vain for women past their first youth. The middleaged face apparently sells neither perfume nor floor wax. The role of the mature woman in the media is almost entirely negative.
The Prime of Ms. America (1975)

3 Quite a few women told me, one way or another, that they thought it was sex, not youth, that's wasted on the young.
The Prime of Ms. America (1975)

4 We were born in an era in which it was a disgrace for a woman to be sexually responsible. We matured in an era in which it was an obligation.
The Prime of Ms. America (1975)

Harris, Joel Chandler (1848–1908) U.S. writer

1 Bred en bawn in a brier-patch!
"How Mr. Rabbit was too Sharp for Mr. Fox," *Uncle Remus and His Legends of the Old Plantation* (1881)

2 Tar-baby ain't sayin' nuthin', en Brer Fox, he lay low.
"The Wonderful Tar-Baby Story," *Uncle Remus and His Legends of the Old Plantation* (1881)

3 Hongry rooster don't cackle w'en he fine a wum.
"Plantation Proverbs," *Uncle Remus: His Songs and His Sayings* (1880)

4 Licker talks mighty loud w'en it git loose fum de jug.
"Plantation Proverbs," *Uncle Remus: His Songs and His Sayings* (1880)

5 You k'n hide de fier, but w'at you gwine do wid de smoke?
"Plantation Proverbs," *Uncle Remus: His Songs and His Sayings* (1880)

Harris, Wilson (Theodore Wilson Harris; b.1921) Guyanese-born writer

1 In an accident-prone, suicidal and conflict-ridden age, violence is a savage masquerade, is it not? It feeds on a void of sacrament and on the infliction of humiliation and shadow. It

not only feeds on these but remains blind to the pressures to which it is addicted.
Carnival (1985)

2 There are risks everywhere. Even heaven is a stage of risk.
Carnival (1985)

3 Man is frequently overwhelmed by the immense and alien power of the universe. But within that immense and alien power the frail heart-beat of man is the never-ending fact of creation. Man's survival is a continual tension and release of energy that approaches self-destruction, but is aware of self-discovery.
Tradition, The Writer and Society (1967)

Harrison, Jim (James Thomas Harrison; b.1937) U.S. novelist and screenwriter

1 I remember my grandfather telling me how each of us must live with a full measure of loneliness that is inescapable, and we must not destroy ourselves with our passion to escape this aloneness.
Dalva (1989)

Harrison, Tony (b.1937) British poet and filmmaker

1 *How you became a poet's a mystery!*
Wherever did you get your talent from?

I say, *I had two uncles, Joe and Harry—*
one was a stammerer, the other dumb.
"Heredity," *The School of Eloquence* (1978)

2 He shoves the frosted attic skylight, shouts:
Ah bloody can't ah've gorra Latin prose.
His bodiless head that's poking out's
like patriarchal Sissy-bleeding-ro's.
"Me Tarzan," *The School of Eloquence* (1978)

Harrison, William Henry (1773–1841) U.S. president

Quotations about Harrison

1 Sell a country! Why not sell the air, the great sea, as well as the earth? Did not the Great Spirit make them all for the use of his children?
1810
Tecumseh (1768?–1813) Native American Shawnee leader. Protesting to Governor William Henry Harrison over the breach of the Treaty of Greenville. Attrib.

Quotations by Harrison

2 We admit of no government by divine right...the only legitimate right to govern is an express grant of power from the governed.
Inaugural presidential address (March 4, 1841)

Harry, Deborah (b.1945) U.S. singer and actor

1 You don't have to be tough to survive, you have to be vulnerable...it's that sensitivity that makes you know how other people feel...to reach them.
Interview, *Mail on Sunday*, London (July 11, 1993), You magazine

2 An aggressive female front-person had never really been done in pop...It was very difficult to be in that position at the time—it's hard to be a ground breaker.
Referring to being lead singer in the band Blondie. Interview, *Mail on Sunday*, London (July 11, 1993), You magazine

3 I made my own image, then I was trapped in it.
Referring to being lead singer in the band Blondie. Interview, *Mail on Sunday*, London (July 11, 1993), You magazine

Hart, Lorenz (1895–1942) U.S. lyricist

1 My Funny Valentine
Song title. *Babes in Arms* (1937)

2 That's Why the Lady is a Tramp
Song title. *Babes in Arms* (1937)

3 Bewitched, Bothered, and Bewildered
Song title. *Pal Joey* (1940)

4 Falling in Love with Love
Song title. *The Boys from Syracuse* (1938)

Hart, Moss (1904–61) U.S. playwright and stage director

Quotations about Hart

1 Just what God would have done if he had the money.
Alexander Woollcott (1887–1943) U.S. writer and critic. Said after being shown round Moss Hart's country house and grounds. Attrib.

Quotations by Hart

2 The only credential the city asked was the boldness to dream. For those who did, it unlocked its gates and its treasures, not caring who they were or where they came from.
Act One (1959)

Harte, Bret (Francis Brett Harte; 1836–1902) U.S. writer

1 Behind the curtain's mystic fold
The glowing future lies unrolled.
Said at the opening of the California Theater. Speech, San Francisco (January 19, 1870)

2 Tell the boys I've got the Luck with me now.
"The Luck of Roaring Camp" (1868)

3 And he smiled a kind of sickly smile, and curled
up on the floor,
And the subsequent proceedings interested him
no more.
"The Society upon the Stanislaus" (1868), st. 7

4 The only sure thing about luck is that it will change.
The Outcasts of Poker Flat (1869)

Hartley, L. P. (Leslie Poles Hartley; 1895–1972) British novelist

1 Motorists (as they used to be called) were utterly irresponsible in their dealings with each other and with the pedestrian public; for their benefit homicide was legalised.
Facial Justice (1960), ch. 5

2 Uniformity isn't bad, as some people still think, because if the quality is good, it satisfies. People are never happy who want change.
Facial Justice (1960), ch. 13

3 The past is a foreign country: they do things differently there.
The Go-Between (1953), Prologue

Harvey, William (1578–1657) English physician

1 When I first gave my mind to vivisection, as a means of discovering the motions and uses of the heart...I found the task so truly arduous, so full of difficulties, that I was almost tempted to think with Fracastorius, that the motion of the heart was only to be comprehended by God.
Anatomical Essay on the Motion of the Heart and Blood in Animals (1628), ch. 1

2 Everything from an egg.
On the Generation of Animals (1651), Dedication

Harvey-Jones, John, Sir (John Henry Harvey-Jones; b.1924) British business executive and author

1 All in all, if one sought to design a life style which was destructive of the individual, the way that business has structured itself would seem to be almost ideal.
Making It Happen: Reflections on Leadership (1987)

2 I have worked with leaders whose style is so totally different to my own that I have found it incomprehensible that they achieve results, but nevertheless they do.
Making It Happen: Reflections on Leadership (1987)

3 Industry is a bit like the human body. The cells are continuously dying and unless new cells are created, sooner or later the whole thing will collapse and disappear.
Making It Happen: Reflections on Leadership (1987)

4 No amount of "tricks of the trade" will avoid the need to set some sort of priority when allocating one's time.
Making It Happen: Reflections on Leadership (1987)

5 Over the years I have only met one person who appeared totally impervious to jet lag. A life where you are never out of an aeroplane for more than a few days at a time is not a healthy one.
Making It Happen: Reflections on Leadership (1987)

6 The salesman that always gets the sale is selling too soft.
Making It Happen: Reflections on Leadership (1987)

7 Business is often about killing your favourite children to allow others to succeed.
Referring to the need to close part of a business to help the rest. *Troubleshooter* (1990)

8 Leadership is the priceless gift that you earn from the people who work for you. I have to earn the right to that gift and have to continuously re-earn that right.
Quoted in *International Management* (September 1985)

9 You've got to be approachable...I like being called by my first name. I loathe being called "Chairman".
Quoted in "Community of Interests," *The Roots of Excellence* (Ronnie Lessem; 1985), ch. 3

Haskins, Minnie Louise (1875–1957) U.S. writer and poet

1 And I said to the man who stood at the gate of the year: "Give me a light that I may tread safely into the unknown." And he replied: "Go out into the darkness and put your hand into the hand of God. That shall be to you better than light and safer than a known way."
Popularized in Britain by George VI, who quoted from it in his Christmas broadcast, 1939. Also known as "The Gate of the Year." "God Knows," *The Desert* (1908), Introduction

Hassall, Christopher (Christopher Vernon Hassall; 1912–63) British writer, poet, and librettist

1 She's genuinely bogus.
Attrib.

Hastings, Flora, Lady (Flora Elizabeth Hastings; 1806–39) British courtier and poet

1 Grieve not that I die young. Is it not well
To pass away ere life hath lost its brightness?
"Swan Song" (1839)

Hatshepsut (1520?–1483? B.C.) Egyptian queen

1 Now my heart turns to and fro,
In thinking what will the people say.
They who shall see my monument in after years,
And shall speak of what I have done.
Inscription from one of the obelisks she had erected in the temple of Amon at Karnak, near Luxor. Quoted in "The New Kingdom," *Ancient Egyptian Literature* (Miriam Lichtheim, ed.; 1976), vol. 2

Hatton, Christopher, Sir (1540–91) English courtier

1 England hath been accounted hitherto the most renowned kingdom for valour and manhood in all Christendom, and shall we now lose our old reputation? If we should, it would have been better for England we had never been born.
Calling for the voting of additional taxes after the defeat of the Spanish Armada. Speech to the House of Lords, the upper house of the British Parliament (February 4, 1589)

Hattori, Masaichi Japanese homeowner

1 In Japan, we live life with no guns. We hope that you too can live life without guns.
His 16-year-old son was shot dead by a trigger-happy homeowner, while on a student cultural exchange to the United States. *Independent*, London (November 19, 1993)

Haughey, Charles (Charles James Haughey; b.1925) Irish prime minister

1 I've been around so long now they know I don't eat babies.
Referring to the electorate's opinion of himself. In 1987 he was re-elected as Irish premier, after having been acquitted in a scandal trial. "Eating babies" was made synonymous with political scandal in Ireland by Jonathan Swift, whose satirical "A Modest Proposal" (1729) suggested that Ireland solve its hunger problems by consuming young children. Charles Haughey was later forced to resign as prime minister in February 1992, following allegations that he had known about the tapping of phones by his minister of justice in a previous administration. Quoted in *Irish Times*, Dublin (Maeve Binchy; February 14, 1987)

2 If you were to elect the head of the Orange Order as President of this Republic, the Unionists would still find we are doing something dishonest, deceitful and totally unacceptable to them.
The Orange Order is a group of Northern Irish Protestants who support Northern Ireland's continuing role in the United Kingdom, and are in opposition to a united Irish Republic. At the time of saying this Charles Haughey was an opposition leader in the Irish parliament. Quoted in *Irish Times*, Dublin (June 30, 1986)

Havel, Vaclav (b.1936) Czech statesman and playwright

1 The relationship of Germany to the family of European peoples and the relationship of that family to Germany is by tradition—simply because of its size, power and central position—the most important element in European stability.
Said on the occasion of the visit of the German president to Prague. Speech (February 15, 1990), quoted in *When the Wall Came Down* (Harold James and Marla Stone, eds.; 1992)

Hawes, Stephen (1475?–1525) English poet

1 For though the day be never so longe,
At last the belles ringeth to evensonge.
The Passetyme of Pleasure (1509), ch. 42

Hawken, Paul U.S. author

1 A mature economic system would appreciate an ancient forest or undisturbed grassland as the ideal for qualitative growth—fecund, abundant, and dynamic, mature but highly evolved.
The Ecology of Commerce (1993)

2 Companies must re-envision and re-imagine themselves as cyclical corporations, whose products either literally disappear into harmless components, or whose products are so specific and targeted to a specific function that there is no spillover effect.
The Ecology of Commerce (1993)

3 Markets are superb at setting prices, but incapable of recognizing costs.
The Ecology of Commerce (1993)

4 The restorative economy unites ecology and commerce into one sustainable act of production and distribution that mimics and enhances natural processes.
The Ecology of Commerce (1993)

5 Corporations, because they are the dominant institution on the planet, must squarely address the social and environmental problems that afflict mankind.
The Ecology of Commerce (1993), preface

Hawkes, Jacquetta (originally Jacquetta Hopkins; 1910–96) British archaeologist

1 The only inequalities that matter begin in the mind. It is not income levels but differences in mental equipment that keep people apart, breed feelings of inferiority.
New Statesman, London (January 1957)

Hawking, Stephen (Stephen William Hawking; b.1942) British physicist

1 Even if there is only one possible unified theory, it is just a set of rules and equations. What is it that breathes fire into the equations and makes a universe for them to describe?
A Brief History of Time (1988)

2 I was again fortunate in that I chose theoretical physics, because that is all in the mind. So my disability has not been a serious handicap.
Stephen Hawking has amyotrophic lateral sclerosis. *A Brief History of Time* (1988), Acknowledgment

3 Why does the universe go to all the bother of existing? Is the unified theory so compelling that it brings about its own existence? Or does it need a creator, and, if so, does he have any other effect on the universe? And who created him?
A Brief History of Time (1988), ch. 11

4 If we find the answer to that, it would be the ultimate triumph of human reason—for then we would know the mind of God.
The answer to the question: Why do we and the universe exist? *A Brief History of Time* (1988), ch. 11

5 God not only plays dice. He also sometimes throws the dice where they cannot be seen.
Referring to Albert Einstein's objection to quantum theory, "I shall never believe that God plays dice with the world." Quoted in *Nature* (1975), no. 257

Hawkins, Coleman (1904–69) U.S. jazz musician

1 I like most music unless it's wrong.
Quoted in *The World of Swing* (Stanley Dance; 1974)

Hawn, Goldie (b.1945) U.S. film actor

1 How long can you be cute?
Interview, *Playboy* (January 1985)

Hawthorne, Nathaniel (1804–64) U.S. novelist and short-story writer

1 If gentlemen love the pleasant titillation of the gout, it is all one to the Town Pump.
A Rill from the Town Pump (1857)

2 Houses of any antiquity in New England are so invariably possessed with spirits that the matter seems hardly worth alluding to. Our ghost used to heave deep sighs in a particular corner of the parlor, and sometimes rustled paper as if he were turning over a sermon in the long upper entry.
Mosses from an Old Manse (1846)

3 If cities were built by the sound of music, then some edifices would appear to be constructed by grave, solemn tones; others to have danced forth to light, fantastic airs.
Notebooks (1839)

4 We sometimes congratulate ourselves at the moment of waking from a troubled dream; it may be so the moment after death.
The American Notebooks (1836?), ch. 1

5 Is it fact, or have I dreamt it—that by means of electricity, the world of matter has become a great nerve, vibrating thousands of miles in a breathless point of time.
The House of Seven Gables (1851)

6 The past is but a coarse and sensual prophecy of the present and the future.
The House of Seven Gables (1851)

7 The Past lies upon the Present like a giant's dead body.
The House of Seven Gables (1851)

8 What other dungeon is so dark as one's own heart! What jailer so inexorable as one's self.
The House of Seven Gables (1851)

9 Life is made of marble and mud.
The House of Seven Gables (1851), ch. 2

10 Life, within doors, has few pleasanter prospects than a neatly arranged and well-provisioned breakfast-table.
The House of Seven Gables (1851), ch. 7

11 The world, that gray-bearded and wrinkled profligate, decrepit, without being venerable.
The House of Seven Gables (1851), ch. 12

12 The world owes all its onward impulse to men ill at ease. The happy man inevitably confines himself within ancient limits.
The House of Seven Gables (1851), ch. 20

13 Every crime destroys more Edens than our own.
The Marble Faun (1860), vol. 1, ch. 23

14 The founders of a new colony...have invariably recognized it among their earliest practical necessities to allot a portion of the virgin soil as a cemetery, and another as the site of a prison.
The Scarlet Letter (1850), ch. 1

15 That alchemy of quiet malice, by which women can concoct a subtile poison from ordinary trifles.
Referring to gossip. *The Scarlet Letter* (1850), ch. 5

16 A bodily disease, which we look upon as whole and entire within itself, may, after all, be but a symptom of some ailment in the spiritual part.
The Scarlet Letter (1850), ch. 10

17 Be true! Be true! Be true! Show freely to the world, if not your worst, yet some trait whereby the worst may be inferred.
The Scarlet Letter (1850), ch. 17

18 Human nature will not flourish, any more than a potato, if it be planted and replanted, for too long a series of generations, in the same worn-out soil.
"The Custom House," *The Scarlet Letter* (1850), introduction

19 My fortune somewhat resembled that of a person who should entertain an idea of committing suicide, and, altogether beyond his hopes, meet with the good hap to be murdered.
"The Custom House," *The Scarlet Letter* (1850), introduction

20 The moment when a man's head drops off is seldom or never, I am inclined to think, precisely the most agreeable of his life.
"The Custom House," *The Scarlet Letter* (1850), introduction

Hay, Charles, Lord (d.1760) British general

1 Gentlemen of the French Guard, fire first!
Said at the Battle of Fontenoy, during the War of the Austrian Succession. Remark (May 11, 1745)

Hay, Ian (pen name of John Hay Beith; 1876–1952) Scottish novelist and playwright

1 What do you mean, funny? Funny-peculiar or funny-ha-ha?
The Housemaster (1938), Act 3

Hay, John (John Milton Hay; 1838–1905) U.S. statesman and writer

1 There is a sanction like that of religion which binds us in partnership in the serious work of the world...We are joint ministers in the same sacred mission of freedom and progress.
Referring to Anglo-American relations. Speech, London (April 21, 1898)

Hay, William (1695–1755) English writer and politician

1 Another great Advantage of Deformity is, that it tends to the Improvement of the Mind. A man, that cannot shine in his Person, will have recourse to his Understanding: and attempt to adorn that Part of him, which alone is capable of ornament.
"Deformity: an Essay" (1754)

Hayden, Robert E. (Robert Earl Hayden; 1913–80) U.S. poet

1 This freedom, this liberty, this beautiful
and terrible thing, needful to man as air,
usable as earth.
1962. "Frederick Douglass, a Ballad of Remembrance," *Collected Poems* (1996)

Haydon, Benjamin Robert (1786–1846) British painter

1 I have loved Art always better than myself.
1841. Quoted in *The Autobiography and Journals of Benjamin Robert Haydon, 1786–1846* (Malcom Elwin, ed.; 1950)

Hayes, George, Sir (1805–69) British judge

1 Hard cases make bad law.
1854. Quoted in *History of English Law* (W. S. Holdsworth; 1926), ch. 9

Hayes, Helen (originally Helen Brown; 1900–93) U.S. actor

1 An actress's life is so transitory—suddenly you're a building!
Referring to the Broadway theater named in her honor. Remark on NBC television (July 7, 1987)

2 I decided long ago never to look at the right-hand side of the menu or the price tag of clothes—otherwise I would starve, naked.
Washington Post (May 7, 1990)

3 Charles...looked upon the poor little red thing and blurted "She's more beautiful than the Brooklyn Bridge!"
Her husband's response to their newborn daughter. Quoted in *Ever Since Eve: Personal Reflections on Childbirth* (Nancy C. Sorel, ed.; 1984)

Hayes, Rutherford B. (Rutherford Birchard Hayes; 1822–93) U.S. president

1 He serves his party best who serves his country best.
Inaugural address, Washington, D.C. (March 5, 1877)

2 Many, if not most, of our Indian wars have had their origin in broken promises and acts of injustice on our part.
Speech (December 4, 1877)

Hazlewood, Lee (b.1929) U.S. songwriter and singer

1 These boots are made for walking
And that's just what they'll do.
One of these days these boots
Are gonna walk all over you.
Song lyric. Popularized by Nancy Sinatra. "These Boots are Made for Walking" (1966)

Hazlitt, William (1778–1830) British essayist and critic

Quotations about Hazlitt

1 He is your only good damner, and if I am ever damned I should like to be damned by him.

John Keats (1795–1821) British poet. Attrib.

Quotations by Hazlitt

2 If you think you can win, you can win. Faith is necessary to victory.
"On Great and Little Things" (1836)

3 Man is an intellectual animal, and therefore an everlasting contradiction to himself. His senses centre in himself, his ideas reach to the ends of the universe; so that he is torn in pieces between the two, without a possibility of its ever being otherwise.
Characteristics (1823)

4 Death is the greatest evil, because it cuts off hope.
Characteristics (1823), no. 35

5 If the world were good for nothing else, it is a fine subject for speculation.
"In the Manner of Rochefoucauld's Maxims," *Characteristics* (1823), no. 302

6 The least pain in our little finger gives us more concern and uneasiness than the destruction of millions of our fellow-beings.
"American Literature—Dr. Channing," *Edinburgh Review* (October 1829)

7 Spleen can subsist on any kind of food.
"On Wit and Humour," *Essays on the English Comic Writers* (1819)

8 So have I loitered my life away, reading books, looking at pictures, going to plays, hearing, thinking, writing on what pleased me best. I have wanted only one thing to make me happy, but wanting that have wanted everything.
"My First Acquaintance with Poets," *Literary Remains of W. Hazlitt* (1836)

9 A person may be indebted for a nose or an eye, for a graceful carriage or a voluble discourse, to a great-aunt or uncle, whose existence he has scarcely heard of.
"On Personal Character," *London Magazine* (1821)

10 No young man believes he shall ever die.
"On the Feeling of Immortality in Youth," *Monthly Magazine* (1827)

11 But of all footmen the lowest class is *literary footmen*.
"Footmen," *Sketches and Essays* (William Carew Hazlitt, ed.; 1839)

12 A nickname is the heaviest stone that the devil can throw at a man.
"Nicknames," *Sketches and Essays* (William Carew Hazlitt, ed.; 1839)

13 The greatest offence against virtue is to speak ill of it.
"On Cant and Hypocrisy," *Sketches and Essays* (William Carew Hazlitt, ed.; 1839)

14 There is an unseemly exposure of the mind, as well as of the body.
"On Disagreeable People," *Sketches and Essays* (William Carew Hazlitt, ed.; 1839)

15 The most fluent talkers or most plausible reasoners are not always the justest thinkers.
"On Prejudice," *Sketches and Essays* (William Carew Hazlitt, ed.; 1839)

16 We never do anything well till we cease to think about the manner of doing it.
"On Prejudice," *Sketches and Essays* (William Carew Hazlitt, ed.; 1839)

17 Rules and models destroy genius and art.
"On Taste," *Sketches and Essays* (William Carew Hazlitt, ed.; 1839)

18 The English (it must be owned) are rather a foul-mouthed nation.
"On Criticism," *Table Talk* (1821–22)

19 We can scarcely hate any one that we know.
"On Criticism," *Table Talk* (1821–22)

20 One of the pleasantest things in the world is going on a journey; but I like to go by myself.
"On Going a Journey," *Table Talk* (1821–22)

21 When I am in the country I wish to vegetate like the country.
"On Going a Journey," *Table Talk* (1821–22)

22 There is not a more mean, stupid, dastardly, pitiful, selfish, spiteful, envious, ungrateful animal than the public. It is the greatest of cowards, for it is afraid of itself.
"On Living to One's-self," *Table Talk* (1821–22)

23 Those who make their dress a principal part of themselves, will, in general, become of no more value than their dress.
"On the Clerical Character," *Table Talk* (1821–22)

24 The most rational cure after all for the inordinate fear of death is to set a just value on life.
"On the Fear of Death," *Table Talk* (1821–22)

25 To great evils we submit, we resent little provocations.
"On the Great and the Little Things," *Table Talk* (1821–22)

26 How loathe were we to give up our pious belief in ghosts and witches, because we liked to persecute one and frighten ourselves to death with the other.
"On the Pleasure of Hating," *The Plain Speaker* (1826)

27 The dupe of friendship, and the fool of love; have I not reason to hate and to despise myself? Indeed I do; and chiefly for not having hated and despised the world enough.
"On the Pleasure of Hating," *The Plain Speaker* (1826)

28 There is nothing good to be had in the country, or, if there is, they will not let you have it.
"Observations on Mr. Wordsworth's Poem *The Excursion*," *The Round Table* (1817)

29 The art of pleasing consists in being pleased.
"On Manner," *The Round Table* (1817)

30 The love of liberty is the love of others; the love of power is the love of ourselves.
"Political Essays," *Times*, London (1819)

31 Well, I've had a happy life.
1830. Last words. Quoted in *Memoirs of William Hazlitt* (William Carew Hazlitt; 1867)

Head, Bessie (1937–86) South African writer

1 There's something wrong with God, expressed as masculine. You don't see the fire and thunder in him the way you do in his feminine counterpart.
God and the Underdog (1968)

2 It is preferable to change the world on the basis of love of mankind. But if that quality be too rare, then common sense seems the next best thing.
Maru (1971)

3 A ruler has to examine the dark side of human life and understand that men belong to that darkness.
Tales of Tenderness and Power (1989)

4 Poverty has a home in Africa—like a quiet second skin. It may be the only place on earth where it is worn with unconscious dignity.
Tales of Tenderness and Power (1989)

5 My motto is: live fast, die young, and have a good-looking corpse.
"Life," *The Collector of Treasures* (1977)

6 There are good women and good men but they seldom join their lives together.
"Life," *The Collector of Treasures* (1977)

7 The terrible thing is that those who fear are always in the majority.
The Woman from America (1966)

Healey, Denis, Baron Healey of Riddlesden (Denis Winston Healey; b.1917) British statesman

1 When you are in a hole, stop digging.
1983. Referring to U.S. politicians and the arms race. Remark (September 1983)

2 I warn you there are going to be howls of anguish from the 80,000 people who are rich enough to pay over 75% on the last slice of their income.
Referring to a proposed introduction of a supertax in the United Kingdom. Speech, Labour Party Conference (October 1, 1973)

3 Their Europeanism is nothing but imperialism with an inferiority complex.
October 1962. Referring to the policies of the Conservative Party. *Observer*, London (October 7, 1962), "Sayings of the Week"

4 You mustn't take out a man's appendix while he's moving a grand piano.
Quoted in *Mountbatten* (P. Ziegler; 1985)

Heaney, Seamus (b.1939) Irish poet

1 Between my finger and my thumb
The squat pen rests; snug as a gun...
I'll dig with it.
"Digging," *Death of a Naturalist* (1966), ll. 1–2, l. 31

2 Rained-on, flower-laden
Coffin after coffin
Seemed to float from the door
Of the packed cathedral
Like blossoms on slow water.
"Casualty," *Field Work* (1979), ll. 50–54

3 O charioteers, above your dormant guns,
It stands here still, stands vibrant as you pass,
The invisible, untoppled omphalos.
"The Toome Road," *Field Work* (1979), ll. 15–17

4 I have begun to pace
the Hadrian's Wall
of her shoulder, dreaming
of Maiden Castle.
"Bone Dreams," *North* (1975), st. 5

5 I am neither internee nor informer;
An inner émigré, grown long-haired
And thoughtful; a wood-kerne

Escaped from the massacre,
Taking protective colouring
From bole and bark.
"Exposure," *North* (1975), ll. 34–38

6 I shouldered a kind of manhood
stepping in to lift the coffins
of dead relations.
"Funeral Rites," *North* (1975), ll. 1–3

7 Of the "wee six" I sing
Where to be saved you only must save face
And whatever you say, you say nothing.
"Whatever You Say Say Nothing," *North* (1975), ll. 62–64

8 I think technique is different from craft. Craft is what you can learn from other verse...Technique...involves the discovery of ways to go out of...normal cognitive bounds and raid in the inarticulate.
October 1974. "Feeling into Words," *Preoccupations: Selected Prose 1968–1978* (1980)

9 Although they are an occupied nation
and their only border is an inland one
they yield to nobody in their belief
that the country is an island.
"Parable Island," *The Haw Lantern* (1987), ll. 1–4

Hearne, John (John Edgar Caulwell Hearne; b.1926) Canadian writer

1 That's why politics is such a sad thing. It's sad any way you play it. Sadder than war even. Because you get tied up in the procedure and think up reasons why you should have kindness and love.
Voices Under The Window (1955)

2 Funny how a man who can stay decent with everybody always find one other who turn him bad.
"At the Stelling," *West Indian Stories* (Andrew Salkey, ed.; 1960)

Hearst, William Randolph (1863–1951) U.S. newspaper publisher

Quotations about Hearst

1 Price of Herald three cents daily. Five cents Sunday. Bennett.
James Gordon Bennett, Jr. (1841–1918) U.S. newspaper owner and editor. Telegram to William Randolph Hearst, when he heard that Hearst was trying to buy his paper and had asked for a price. Quoted in *The Life and Death of the Press Barons* (Piers Brandon; 1982)

Quotations by Hearst

2 A politician will do anything to keep his job—even become a patriot.
Syndicated editorial (August 28, 1933)

3 Stop running those dogs on your page. I wouldn't have them peeing on my cheapest rug.
Referring to the publication of James Thurber's cartoons by one of his editors. Quoted in *The Years with Ross* (James Thurber; 1959)

Heath, Edward, Sir (Edward Richard George Heath; b.1916) British prime minister

1 We may be a small island, but we are not a small people.
Observer, London (June 21, 1970), "Sayings of the Week"

Heath, Neville George (Neville George Clevely Heath; 1917–46) British murderer

1 You might make that a double.
1946. Comment made when offered a drink before his execution. Attrib.

Heath, Roy A. K. (Roy Aubrey Kelvin Heath; b.1926) Guyanese novelist and teacher

1 There was a sky and an earth; there was the wind and the sun; and there was marriage.
From the Heat of the Day (1979)

2 He knew the value of money, because he had never had any.
Kwaku (1982)

3 Television was the ultimate evidence of cultural anemia.
Kwaku (1982)

4 Ugliness could only be cured with gold.
Kwaku (1982)

Heath-Stubbs, John (John Francis Alexander Heath-Stubbs; b.1918) British poet

1 Love, Love is a king uncrowned;
In their dumb motion
All the republican stars lament
His abdication.
"Carol for Advent," *Selected Poems* (1965)

Heat-Moon, William Least (originally William Lewis Trogdon; b.1939) U.S. writer

1 Some little towns get on the map only because some cartographer has a blank space to fill.
Blue Highways: A Journey into America (1982)

Heaviside, Oliver (1850–1925) British physicist

1 Should I refuse a good dinner simply because I do not understand the process of digestion?
Referring to being criticized for using formal mathematical manipulations without understanding how they worked. Attrib.

Heberden, William (1710–1801) British physician

1 This state I call the hypochondriac affection in men, and the hysteric in women...is a sort of waking dream, which, though a person be otherwise in sound health, makes him feel symptoms of every disease; and, though innocent, yet fills his mind with the blackest horrors of guilt.
Commentaries on the History and Cure of Diseases (W. Heberden the Younger, ed.; 1802), ch. 49

Hecht, Anthony (Anthony Evan Hecht; b.1923) U.S. poet

1 Human endeavor clumsily betrays
Humanity.
"Japan," *A Summoning of Stones* (1954), quoted in *The Penguin Book of American Verse* (Geoffrey Moore, ed.; 1977)

2 Now the quaint early image of Japan
That was so charming to me as a child
Seems like a bright design upon a fan.
"Japan," *A Summoning of Stones* (1954), quoted in *The Penguin Book of American Verse* (Geoffrey Moore, ed.; 1977)

Hecht, Ben (1894–1964) U.S. writer

1 There is hardly one in three of us who live in the cities who is not sick with unused self.
Child of the Century (1954)

2 There's nothing so nice as a new marriage.
Spellbound (1945)

Hefner, Hugh (Hugh Marston Hefner; b.1926) U.S. publisher, editor, and entrepreneur

1 The interesting thing is how one guy, through living out his own fantasies, is living out the fantasies of so many other people.
1979. Said on the 25th anniversary of *Playboy* magazine. *Newsweek* (January 1, 1979)

Hegel, G. W. F. (Georg Wilhelm Friedrich Hegel; 1770–1831) German philosopher

Quotations about Hegel

1 Hegel says somewhere that all great events and personalities in world history reappear in one fashion or another. He forgot to add: the first time as tragedy, the second as farce.
Karl Marx (1818–83) German philosopher. *The Eighteenth Brumaire of Louis Napoleon* (1852), sect. 1

Quotations by Hegel

2 Only one man ever understood me...And he didn't understand me.
Said on his deathbed. Remark (1831), quoted in *Famous Last Words* (Barnaby Conrad; 1962)

3 Political genius consists in identifying oneself with a principle.
Constitution of Germany (1802)

4 In England even the poorest of people believe they have rights: this is very different from what satisfies the poor in other lands.
Elements of the Philosophy of Right (1821)

5 Nothing, as thus immediate and equal to itself, is also conversely the same as Being is. The truth of Being and of Nothing is accordingly the unity of the two: and this unity is *Becoming.*
Encyclopaedia of the Philosophical Sciences (1817)

6 What experience and history teach is this—that people and governments have never learned anything from history, or acted upon any lessons they might have drawn from it.
1830. *Lectures on the Philosophy of History* (1837), Introduction

7 In everything that is supposed to be scientific, Reason must be awake and reflection applied. To him who looks at the world rationally the world looks rationally back. The relation is mutual.
Reason in History (Robert S. Hartman, tr.; 1953)

8 The nature of Spirit may be understood by a glance at its direct opposite—Matter. As the essence of Matter is Gravity, so...we may affirm that the substance, the essence of Spirit is Freedom.
Reason in History (Robert S. Hartman, tr.; 1953)

9 The question of how Reason is determined in itself and what its relation is to the world coincides with the question *What is the ultimate purpose of the world?*
Reason in History (Robert S. Hartman, tr.; 1953)

10 For consciousness is, on the one hand, consciousness of the object, on the other, consciousness of itself.
1807. *The Phenomenology of Mind* (J. B. Baillie, tr.; 1910)

11 In work consciousness becomes aware of itself as it in truth is, and its empty notion of itself disappears.
1807. *The Phenomenology of Mind* (J. B. Baillie, tr.; 1910)

12 Mind...becomes object, for it consists in the process of becoming an other to itself.
1807. *The Phenomenology of Mind* (J. B. Baillie, tr.; 1910)

13 Pure spirituality...is the soil of science, is thinking, and can be only in mind.
1807. *The Phenomenology of Mind* (J. B. Baillie, tr.; 1910)

14 The being of mind cannot be taken at any rate to be something completely rigid and immoveable. Man is free.
1807. *The Phenomenology of Mind* (J. B. Baillie, tr.; 1910)

15 The essential nature of individuality lies in the universal element of mind.
1807. *The Phenomenology of Mind* (J. B. Baillie, tr.; 1910)

16 The force of mind is only as great as its expression; its depth only as deep as its power to expand and lose itself.
1807. *The Phenomenology of Mind* (J. B. Baillie, tr.; 1910)

17 The life of the mind is not one that shuns death, and keeps clear of destruction; it endures its death and in death maintains its being.
1807. *The Phenomenology of Mind* (J. B. Baillie, tr.; 1910)

18 A state is then well constituted and internally powerful, when the private interest of its citizens is one with the common interest of the State; when the one finds its gratification and realization in the other.
The Philosophy of History (1832)

19 Reason has ruled, and is still ruling the world, and consequently the world's history.
The Philosophy of History (1832)

20 The final cause of the World at large, we allege to be the consciousness of its own freedom on the part of Spirit, and ipso facto, the reality of that freedom.
The Philosophy of History (1832)

21 The only Thought which Philosophy brings with it to the contemplation of History is the simple conception of Reason; that Reason is the Sovereign of the World; that the history of the world, therefore, presents us with a rational process.
The Philosophy of History (1832)

22 World-historical men—the heroes of an epoch—must be recognized as its clear-sighted ones; their deeds and their words are the best of their time.
The Philosophy of History (1832)

23 Money is not one particular type of wealth among others, but the universal form of all types so far as they are expressed in an external embodiment and so can be taken as "things."
1821. *The Philosophy of Right* (T. M. Knox, tr.; 1952)

24 The state is the march of God through the world.
1821. *The Philosophy of Right* (T. M. Knox, tr.; 1952)

25 What is rational is actual and what is actual is rational. On this conviction the plain man like the philosopher takes his stand, and from it philosophy starts in its study of the universe of mind as well as the universe of nature.
1821. *The Philosophy of Right* (T. M. Knox, tr.; 1952)

26 One word more about giving instruction as to what the world ought to be. Philosophy in any case always comes on the scene too late to give it...The owl of Minerva spreads its wings only with the falling of the dusk.
1821. The owl of Minerva represents wisdom. *The Philosophy of Right* (T. M. Knox, tr.; 1952)

Heide, Wilma Scott (b.1926) U.S. nurse and feminist

1 The only jobs for which no man is qualified are human incubators and wet nurse. Likewise, the only job for which no woman is or can be qualified is sperm donor.
NOW Official Biography (1971)

Heidegger, Martin (1889–1976) German philosopher

1 "Logic," "ethics," and "physics" begin to flourish only when original thinking has come to an end...the Greeks thought without such headings. They did not even call thinking "philosophy."
Letter on Humanism (1947)

2 Man is not the lord of beings. Man is the shepherd of Being.
Letter on Humanism (1947)

3 We are too late for the gods
and too early for Being. Being's poem,
just begun, is man.
Poetry, Language, Thought (1971)

4 All metaphysics, including its opponent, positivism, speaks the language of Plato.
The End of Philosophy (Joan Stambaugh, tr.; 1973)

Heifetz, Jascha (1901–87) Russian-born U.S. violinist

1 If the Almighty himself played the violin, the credits would still read "Rubinstein, God, and Piatigorsky," in that order.
Whenever he played with Artur Rubinstein (piano) and Gregor Piatigorsky (cello), Rubinstein always got top billing. *Los Angeles Times* (August 29, 1982)

Heilbroner, Robert (b.1919) U.S. economist and author

1 Less and less are we able to locate our lives meaningfully in the pageant of history. More and more do we find ourselves retreating to the sanctuary of an insulated individualism, sealed off in our private concerns from the larger events which surround us.
The Future as History (1960)

Heine, Heinrich (Christian Johann Heinrich Heine; 1797–1856) German poet

1 Sleep is good, death is better; but of course, the best thing would be never to have been born at all.
"Morphine"

2 Ordinarily he is insane, but he has lucid moments when he is only stupid.
A comment on Savoye, the French ambassador in Frankfurt. Remark (1848) Attrib.

3 I am breathing the air of home again!
My cheeks glow and understand.
And all this dirt on the road, it is
the filth of my fatherland.
1844. *Deutschland. A Winter's Tale* (T. J. Reed, tr.; 1986)

4 The French and the Russians have shared out the land,
Britannia rules the oceans;
we reign unchallenged in the realm
of dreamy abstract notions.
1844. *Deutschland. A Winter's Tale* (T. J. Reed, tr.; 1986), st. 7

5 There's no better place for sleep and dreams
than a German bed of feathers.
The German soul here feels itself free
of any earthly tethers.
1844. *Deutschland. A Winter's Tale* (T. J. Reed, tr.; 1986), st. 7

6 They served us pig's head, too. It says
a lot about German morals
that we stick to this quaint old custom. Our swine
still get decorated with laurels.
1844. *Deutschland. A Winter's Tale* (T. J. Reed, tr.; 1986), st. 9

7 The arrow belongs not to the archer when it has once left the bow; the word no longer belongs to the speaker when it has once passed his lips.
Religion and Philosophy (1840), preface

8 God will pardon me; it is His trade.
Last words. Quoted in *Heinrich Heine, Erinnerungen* (Alfred Meissner; 1856), ch. 5

9 We see here how small man is and how great is God! For gold is the God of our time and Rothschild is his prophet.
1854. Quoted in *Lutetia* (Charles Godfrey Leland, tr.; 1906)

10 No author is a man of genius to his publisher.
Attrib.

11 It is extremely difficult for a Jew to be converted, for how can he bring himself to believe in the divinity—of another Jew?
Born a Jew, Heine converted to Christianity in 1825 to secure his rights as a German citizen. Attrib.

Heinlein, Robert (Robert Anson Heinlein; 1907–88) U.S. writer

1 The Earth is just too small and fragile a basket for the human race to keep all its eggs in.
Speech (Undated)

2 Democracy can't work. Mathematicians, peasants, and animals, that's all there is—so democracy, a theory based on the assumption that mathematicians and peasants are equal, can never work.
Glory Road (1963), ch. 20

Heisenberg, Werner (Werner Karl Heisenberg; 1901–76) German physicist

1 An expert is someone who knows some of the worst mistakes that can be made in his subject, and how to avoid them.
Physics and Beyond (1971)

2 Natural science does not simply describe and explain nature, it is part of the interplay between nature and ourselves.
Physics and Philosophy (1958)

Hell, Richard (originally Richard Meyers; b.1949) U.S. singer and songwriter

1 Rock and roll is trying to convince girls to pay money to be near you.
Quoted in *Rock Talk* (Joe Kohut and John J. Kohut, eds.; 1994)

Heller, Joseph (1923–99) U.S. novelist

1 The Texan turned out to be good-natured, generous and likable. In three days no one could stand him.
Catch-22 (1961)

2 He had decided to live for ever or die in the attempt.
Catch-22 (1961), ch. 3

3 He was a self-made man who owed his lack of success to nobody.
Catch-22 (1961), ch. 3

4 Orr was crazy and could be grounded. All he had to do was ask; and as soon as he did, he would no longer be crazy and would have to fly more missions.
Catch-22 (1961), ch. 5

5 There was only one catch and that was Catch-22, which specified that a concern for one's own safety in the face of dangers that were real and immediate was the process of a rational mind.
Catch-22 (1961), ch. 5

6 He knew everything about literature except how to enjoy it.
Catch-22 (1961), ch. 8

7 Some men are born mediocre, some men achieve mediocrity, and some men have mediocrity thrust upon them. With Major Major it had been all three.
Paraphrase of William Shakespeare's: "Some are born great, some achieve greatness, and some have greatness thrust upon 'em." (*Twelfth Night*, Act 2, Scene 5). *Catch-22* (1961), ch. 9

8 Hungry Joe collected lists of fatal diseases and arranged them in alphabetical order so that he could put his finger without delay on any one he wanted to worry about.
Catch-22 (1961), ch. 17

9 How much reverence can you have for a Supreme Being who finds it necessary to include such phenomena as phlegm and tooth-decay in His divine system of Creation?
Catch-22 (1961), ch. 18

10 I'd like to see the government get out of war altogether and leave the whole feud to private industry.
Said by Milo Minderbinder. *Catch-22* (1961), ch. 24

11 Prostitution gives her an opportunity to meet people. It provides fresh air and wholesome exercise, and it keeps her out of trouble.
Catch-22 (1961), ch. 33

12 Abraham...circumcised himself. Now this is not an easy thing to do—try it sometime and see.
God Knows (1984), ch. 2

13 Almost one out of every four people in the world is Chinese, you know, even though many of them might not look it.
Good as Gold (1979)

14 In the long run, failure was the only thing that worked predictably.
Good as Gold (1979)

15 Mankind is resilient: the atrocities that horrified us a week ago become acceptable tomorrow.
Picture This (1988), ch. 37

Heller, Robert (Robert Gordon Barry Heller; b.1932) British management writer

1 Initiatives aimed at the radical improvement of performance are dangerous when they fail, but can also endanger a company's future when they work—either because success leads to complacency...or because success calcifies the new ways.
Signposts for Managers (1999)

2 Like the legal judge, the tycoon depends on the warders and hangman to obey his orders in utterly predictable conformity. So he needs predictable conformists, without imagination, independence, or pride.
The Decision Makers (1989)

3 The easiest way to extrapolate profitability into the future is to copy—for instance, from a geographical market which is leading the way. The United States has long served this function for European and Japanese entrepreneurs.
The Decision Makers (1989)

4 "Vision" is what, to put it crudely, the Japanese have and the West mostly hasn't.
The Decision Makers (1989)

5 Most of the truly great investors have belonged to the school that has come to be known as "contrarian". It isn't as simple as saying that, if everyone else is investing in gold, you sell, and vice versa. The true contrarian isn't interested in what others are doing at all.
The Decision Makers (1989), ch. 8

6 Roman generals during their triumphs were always reminded of their mortality, and business success, like human life, has its span.
The Decision Makers (1989), ch. 9

7 It's a sobering thought (or should be) that it took the ferocious competition of the Japanese to make Western managements set off in search of "competitive advantage".
The Decision Makers (1989), ch. 10

Heller, Walter W. (Walter Wolfgang Heller; 1915–87) U.S. economist and writer

1 One person's price is another person's income.
"What's Right with Economics?," *American Economic Review* (March 1975)

Hellman, Lillian (1905–84) U.S. playwright

1 It is a mark of many famous people that they cannot part with their brightest hour: what worked once must always work.
"Theater," *Pentimento* (1973)

2 Truth made you a traitor as it often does in a time of scoundrels.
Referring to the McCarthy era. *Scoundrel Time* (1976)

3 Cynicism is an unpleasant way of saying the truth.
The Little Foxes (1939), Act 1

4 Fashions in sin change.
The Watch on the Rhine (1941)

5 I cannot and will not cut my conscience to fit this year's fashions, even though I long ago came to the conclusion that I was not a political person and could have no comfortable place in any political group.
Hellman was called before the House Committee on Un-American Activities in 1952. She testified about her own activities, but refused to discuss those of anybody else. Letter to John S. Wood, House Committee on Un-American Activities, *U.S. Congress Committee Hearing on Un-American Activities* (May 19, 1952), pt. 8

6 It makes me feel masculine to tell you that I do not answer questions like this without being paid for answering them.
When asked by *Harper's Magazine* when she felt most masculine; this question had already been asked of several famous men. Quoted in *Reader's Digest* (July 1977)

Helmsley, Leona (originally Leona Rosenthal; b.1920) U.S. business executive

1 We don't pay taxes. The little people pay taxes.
Referring to her dispute with the U.S. Internal Revenue Service. *Time* (July 24, 1989)

Helpmann, Robert, Sir (Robert Murray Helpmann; 1909–86) Australian dancer and choreographer

1 The trouble with nude dancing is that not everything stops when the music stops.
After the opening night of *Oh, Calcutta!* (1969). Remark (1969), quoted in *The Frank Muir Book: An Irreverent Companion to Social History* (Frank Muir; 1976)

Helps, Arthur, Sir (1813–75) British historian

1 What a blessing this smoking is! perhaps the greatest that we owe to the discovery of America.
"Worry," *Friends in Council* (1859), vol. 1, ch. 1

Helvétius, Claude Adrien (1715–71) French philosopher

1 Education made us what we are.
"Discours 3," *De l'esprit* (1758), ch. 30

Hemans, Felicia (originally Felicia Dorothea Browne; 1793–1835) British poet

1 The boy stood on the burning deck
Whence all but he had fled;
The flame that lit the battle's wreck
Shone round him o'er the dead.

The boy was the 10-year-old son of naval officer Louis de Casabianca. He and his wounded father died when they refused to leave the *Orient*, flagship of Napoleon's fleet in the Battle of the Nile (1798). "Casabianca" (1829), ll. 1–4, *The Works of Mrs. Hemans* (Harriet Hughes, ed.; 1839)

2 What sought they thus afar?
Bright jewels of the mine?
The wealth of seas, the spoils of war?
They sought a faith's pure shrine!

"The Landing of the Pilgrim Fathers in New England," *The Works of Mrs. Hemans* (Harriet Hughes; 1839), ll. 33–36

Hemingway, Ernest (Ernest Miller Hemingway; 1899–1961) U.S. writer

Quotations about Hemingway

1 "Yes, a great writer," said Anna Andreevna. "I hate his fishing, though. Those hooks, those fish, those worms...No thank you!"

Anna Akhmatova (1888–1966) Russian poet. Referring to Ernest Hemingway and his book *Death in the Afternoon* (1932). (Milena Michalski and Sylva Rubashova, trs.; December 1939), quoted in *The Akhmatova Journals: 1938–1941* (Lydia Chukovskaya, ed.; 1989)

2 How clear, serene, and solid the best work still seems; it's as if there were a physical communion taking place among the fingers turning the page, the eyes taking in the words, the brain imaginatively recreating what the words stand for and, as Hemingway put it, "making it part of your experience."

November 17, 1985

Raymond Carver (1938–88) U.S. poet, short-story writer, and essayist. Review of *Along with Youth: Hemingway, the Early Years* (1985) by Peter Griffin and *Hemingway: A Biography* (1985) by Jeffrey Meyers in *New York Times Book Review*. "Coming of Age, Going to Pieces," *No Heroics, Please* (1991)

3 He has never been known to use a word that might send a reader to the dictionary.

William Faulkner (1897–1962) U.S. novelist. Attrib.

4 He has a capacity for enjoyment so vast that he gives away great chunks to those about him, and never even misses them... He can take you to a bicycle race and make it raise your hair.

Dorothy Parker (1893–1967) U.S. writer and wit. *New Yorker* (November 30, 1929)

Quotations by Hemingway

5 For a true writer each book should be a new beginning where he tries again for something that is beyond attainment.

Acceptance speech, Nobel Prize in literature (1954)

6 Don't you like writing letters? I do because it's such a swell way to keep from working and yet feel you've done something.

Letter to F. Scott Fitzgerald (July 1, 1925)

7 I don't buy a ticket. I just get on the train.

Referring to his go-getting approach to life. Letter to F. Scott Fitzgerald (1925)

8 The world breaks everyone and afterward many are strong at the broken places. But those that do not break it kills. It kills the very good and the very gentle and the very brave impartially. If you are none of these you can be sure it will kill you too but there will be no special hurry.

The first line was recalled on Ernest Hemingway's death, and also chosen as the frontispiece in Arthur M. Schlesinger, Jr.'s book on the John Fitzgerald Kennedy presidency, *A Thousand Days* (1965). *A Farewell to Arms* (1929), ch. 34

9 If you are lucky enough to have lived in Paris as a young man, then wherever you go for the rest of your life, it stays with you, for Paris is a moveable feast.

A Moveable Feast (1964), Epigraph

10 What is moral is what you feel good after, and what is immoral is what you feel bad after.

Death in the Afternoon (1932), ch. 1

11 Bullfighting is the only art in which the artist is in danger of death and in which the degree of brilliance in the performance is left to the fighter's honor.

Death in the Afternoon (1932), ch. 9

12 All good books are alike in that they are truer than if they had really happened and after you are finished reading one you will feel that all that happened to you and afterwards it all belongs to you: the good and the bad, the ecstasy, the remorse and sorrow, the people and the places and how the weather was.

"Old Newsman Writes," *Esquire* (December 1934)

13 But did thee feel the earth move?

For Whom the Bell Tolls (1940), ch. 13

14 If we win here we will win everywhere. The world is a fine place and worth the fighting for and I hate very much to leave it.

For Whom the Bell Tolls (1940), ch. 13

15 The most essential gift for any writer is a built-in, shock-proof, shit detector. This is the writer's radar and all great writers have had it.

Interview, *Paris Review* (Spring 1958)

16 A man can be destroyed but not defeated.

The Old Man and the Sea (1952)

17 Have faith in the Yankees, my son.

The Old Man and the Sea (1952)

18 This wine is too good for toast-drinking, my dear. You don't want to mix emotions up with a wine like that. You lose the taste.

The Sun Also Rises (1926), ch. 7

19 It makes one feel rather good deciding not to be a bitch...It's sort of what we have instead of God.

The Sun Also Rises (1926), ch. 19

20 Because I am a bastard.

1926. When asked why he had deserted his wife, Hadley, for Pauline Pfeiffer in 1926. Quoted in *Americans in Paris* (Brian Morton; 1984)

21 Grace under pressure.

Referring to being asked his definition of "guts" in an interview with Dorothy Parker. "The Artist's Reward," *New Yorker* (Dorothy Parker; November 30, 1929)

22 Does he really think big emotions come from big words? He thinks I don't know the ten-dollar words...there are older and

simpler and better words, and those are the ones I use.
In response to William Faulkner's jibe: "He has never been known to use a word that might send a reader to the dictionary." Quoted in *Papa Hemingway* (A. E. Hotchner; 1966), pt. 1, ch. 4

23 The Sun Also Rises
1926. Novel title.

Henderson, Leon (1895–1986) U.S. economist

1 Having a little inflation is like being a little pregnant.
Attrib.

Hendrick, Burton J. (Burton Jesse Hendrick; 1870–1949) U.S. journalist and biographer

1 The consultant's first obligation is to the patient, not to his brother physician.
Attrib.

2 The great glory of modern medicine is that it regards nothing as essential but the truth.
Attrib.

Hendrix, Jimi (James Marshall Hendrix; 1942–70) U.S. rock musician

1 'Scuse me while I kiss the sky.
Song lyric. "Purple Haze" (1967)

2 A musician, if he's a messenger, is like a child who hasn't been handled too many times by man, hasn't had too many fingerprints across his brain.
Life (1969)

3 Music is going to break the way. It's like the waves of the ocean. You can't just cut out the perfect wave and take it home with you. It's constantly moving all the time.
Quoted in *The Face of Black Music* (Valerie Wilmer; 1976)

4 It's funny the way most people love the dead. Once you are dead you are made for life. You have to die before they think you are worth anything.
1968? Quoted in *Those Who Died Young* (Marianne Sinclair; 1979)

Henley, William Ernest (1849–1903) British writer

1 It matters not how strait the gate,
How charged with punishments the scroll,
I am the master of my fate:
I am the captain of my soul.
"Invictus. In Memoriam R. T. H. B.," *Echoes* (1888), no. 4

2 In the fell clutch of circumstance,
I have not winced nor cried aloud;
Under the bludgeonings of chance
My head is bloody, but unbowed.
"Invictus. In Memoriam R. T. H. B.," *Echoes* (1888), no. 4, st. 2

3 Madam, Life's a piece in bloom
Death goes dogging everywhere;
She's the tenant of the room,
He's the ruffian on the stair.
"To W. R.," *Echoes* (1888), no. 9, ll. 1–4

4 What have I done for you,
England, my England?
What is there I would not do,
England, my own?
"Pro Rege Nostro," *For England's Sake* (1900), no. 3, ll. 1–4

Henri, Robert (1865–1929) U.S. painter and teacher

1 The object of painting is not to make a picture...The object, which is at the back of every true work of art is *the attainment of a state of being*, a state of high functioning, a more than ordinary moment of existence.
The Art Spirit (1923)

2 Art cannot be separated from life. It is the expression of the greatest need of which life is capable, and we value art not because of the skilled product, but because of its revelation of a life's experience.
"The New York Exhibition of Independent Artists," *The Craftsman* (1910)

3 It is not learning how to do something which people will call art, but rather inventing something that is absolutely necessary for the progress of our existence.
"The New York Exhibition of Independent Artists," *The Craftsman* (1910)

Henry I, King of England (called Henry Beauclerc; 1068–1135) English monarch

Quotations about Henry I

1 By intermarriage and by every means in his power he bound the two peoples into a firm union.
Walter Map (1140?–1210?) Welsh clergyman and writer. Referring to Henry I of England and his marriage (1182) to Matilda, a descendant of the Anglo-Saxon royal family. *De Nugis Curialum* (1182?), pt. 5, ch. 5

Quotations by Henry I

2 An illiterate king is a crowned ass.
Attrib. *Quotations in History* (Alan and Veronica Palmer; 1976)

Henry II, King of the English (1133–89) English monarch

Quotations about Henry II

1 Now in Ireland, now in England, now in Normandy, he must fly rather than travel by horse or ship.
Louis VII (1120?–80) French monarch. Quoted in *Imagines Historiarum* (Ralph de Diceto; 1202?)

Quotations by Henry II

2 Our kingdom and whatever anywhere is subject to our rule we place at your disposal and commit to your power...Let there be between us and our peoples an undivided unity of love and peace and safety of commerce, in such a way that to you, who are pre-eminent in dignity, be given the authority of command, and to us the will to obey shall not be lacking.
Henry made his promise to Frederick who was at the time in conflict with Pope Adrian who had claimed he only held lands as a fief from the pope. Letter to the Holy Roman Emperor Frederick Barbarossa (1157)

3 Will no one rid me of this turbulent priest?
Referring to Thomas à Becket, Archbishop of Canterbury, who opposed his attempts to remove the legal immunity of priests. Four of Henry's knights took his words literally and killed Becket in Canterbury Cathedral (December 1170). Remark (1170), quoted in *History of the Life of King Henry II* (G. Lyttleton; 1769), pt. 4

4 I order you to hold a free election, but forbid you to elect anyone but Richard my clerk.
Referring to the election of a new bishop. Richard d'Ilchester was one of the king's trusted servants. Writ to the electors of the See of Winchester, *Recueil des Historiens des Gaules et de la France* (J. J. Brial; 1806–22)

5 St. Thomas, guard for me my kingdom! To you I declare myself guilty of that for which others bear the blame.
Said at the outbreak of the Princes' Rebellion (1173–74), the first of the revolts by Henry's sons that marked his later years. One of Henry's first actions was to perform public penance for Thomas à Becket's murder. Quoted in *Chronique de la guerre entre les Anglois et les Écossais en 1173 et 1174* (Jordan Fantosme; 1173)

Henry III, King of England (1207–72) English monarch

Quotations about Henry III

1 There is very great honor for me in the peace which I am making with the King of England, since he is now my vassal, which before he was not.
Louis IX (1214–70) French monarch. Referring to the Treaty of Paris made with Henry III of England. Remark (1259)

Quotations by Henry III

2 All these things shall I keep faithfully and undiminished, as a man, as a Christian, as a soldier, and as a king, crowned and anointed.
Oath made to uphold the Provisions of Oxford, an agreement forced on Henry III by the barons, curbing the power of the monarchy and expanding the representative powers of Magna Carta. Oath (1258)

Henry IV, King of France (Henry of Navarre; 1553–1610) French monarch

1 Hang yourself, brave Crillon; we fought at Arques and you were not there.
Version, as given by Voltaire, of the king's more formally worded letter, to Crillon, a soldier noted for his bravery. Letter (September 20, 1597), quoted in *Lettres missives de Henri IV, Collection des documents inédits de l'histoire de France* (1847), vol. 4

2 Those who follow their conscience directly are of my religion; and, for my part, I am of the same religion as all those who are brave and true.
Henry had become a Roman Catholic, as a political move, in 1576. Letter to M. de Batz (1577)

3 I regret only two things I have had to leave behind in Paris, the mass and my wife. I can manage without the first, but not without the second.
Remark (1576)

4 Paris is worth a Mass.
Said on entering Paris, having secured its submission to his authority by becoming a Roman Catholic. Remark (March 1594) Attrib.

5 I want there to be no peasant in my kingdom so poor that he is unable to have a chicken in his pot every Sunday.
Quoted in *Histoire de Henri le Grand* (Hardouin de Péréfixe; 1681)

6 The wisest fool in Christendom.
Referring to James I of England (ruled 1603–25). Attrib.

Henry V, King of England (1387–1422) English monarch

1 Do you not believe that the Almighty, with this small force of men on his side, can conquer the hostile arrogance of the French, who pride themselves on their numbers and their own strength?
Said before the Battle of Agincourt. (October 25, 1415)

2 Everyone knows that I act in everything with kindness and mercy, for I am forcing Rouen into submission by starvation, not by fire, sword or bloodshed.
1418. Attrib.

3 I shall play such a ballgame with the French in their own courtyards, that they will lose their fun in the end and win grief instead of game.
Referring to a gift of tennis balls presented him by ambassadors returning from France. Attrib.

Henry VIII, King of England and Ireland (1491–1547) English monarch

Quotations about Henry VIII

1 In the midst stood Prince Henry, who showed already something of royalty in his demeanor, in which there was a certain dignity combined with singular courtesy.
Desiderius Erasmus (1466?–1536) Dutch humanist, scholar, and writer. Remark on first meeting the future Henry VIII. Attrib.

2 Junker Henry means to be God and do as he pleases.
Martin Luther (1483–1546) German theologian and religious reformer. Referring to Henry VIII's religious policy. Quoted in *The Earlier Tudors, 1485–1558* (J. D. Mackie; 1994)

3 The king of France is called the most Christian King, but this does him injustice, for he never did a Christian thing. I am called the most Invincible King, but I have been overcome. The Pope is called his Holiness, but he is the biggest scoundrel on earth. You are called the richest king, and this is true.
Maximilian I (1459–1519) Austrian-born monarch. Said to Henry VIII of England. Attrib.

4 The King has a way of making every man feel that he is enjoying his special favour, just as the London wives pray before the image of Our Lady by the Tower till each of them believes it is smiling upon her.
1518
Thomas More (1478–1535) English statesman and writer. Attrib.

5 Our king does not desire gold or gems or precious metals, but virtue, glory, immortality...The other day he wished he was more learned. I said, that is not what we expect of your Grace, but that you will foster and encourage learned men. Yea, surely, said he, for indeed without them we should scarcely exist at all.
Lord Mountjoy (*fl.* 16th century) English courtier and soldier. Letter to Erasmus (May 27, 1509)

6 He is a prince of royal courage and hath a princely heart; and rather than he will miss or want part of his appetite, he will hazard the loss of one-half of his kingdom.
Thomas Wolsey (1475–1530) English statesman and clergyman. Remark (November 1530)

Quotations by Henry VIII

7 Let him not suppose that either the king or his nobles will allow the fixed laws of his kingdom to be set aside.
Referring to Pope Clement VII. Remark (December 6, 1530)

8 The kings of England in times past never had any superior but God. Wherefore know you that we will maintain the rights of the Crown...as any of our progenitors.
Refusing to allow an ecclesiastical dispute to be referred to Rome. Remark (1515)

9 You have sent me a Flanders mare.
Said on meeting his fourth wife, Anne of Cleves, for the first time. Remark (January 1, 1540), quoted in *A Complete History of England* (Tobias Smollett; 1759, 3rd edition), vol. 6

10 We at no time stand so highly in our estate royal as in the time of Parliament, wherein we as head and you as members are conjoined and knit together into one body politic.
Speech to a deputation from the English Parliament (March 31, 1543)

11 I am very sorry to know and hear how unreverently that most precious jewel, the Word of God, is disputed, rhymed, sung and jangled in every ale-house and tavern, contrary to the true meaning and doctrine of the same.
Commenting on the translation of the Bible into English. Speech to the English Parliament (December 24, 1545)

Henry, Matthew (1662–1714) English clergyman

1 Many a dangerous temptation comes to us in fine gay colours that are but skin-deep.
An Exposition on the Old and New Testament (1710), Genesis ch. 3

2 The better day, the worse deed.
An Exposition on the Old and New Testament (1710), Genesis, ch. 3, v. 6, gloss 2

3 None so deaf as those that will not hear.
An Exposition on the Old and New Testament (1710), Psalm 58

4 They that die by famine die by inches.
An Exposition on the Old and New Testament (1710), Psalm 59, v. 15, gloss 5

5 All this and heaven too.
Life of Mr. Philip Henry (1698), ch. 5

Henry, O. (pen name of William Sydney Porter; 1862–1910) U.S. short-story writer

1 Turn up the lights, I don't want to go home in the dark.
His last words, quoting a popular song of the time, "I'm Afraid to Go Home in the Dark." Last words (1910), quoted in *O. Henry* (C. A. Smith; 1916), ch. 9

2 If men knew how women pass the time when they are alone, they'd never marry.
"Memoirs of a Yellow Dog," *The Four Million* (1906)

3 Life is made up of sobs, sniffles and smiles, with sniffles predominating.
"The Gift of the Magi," *The Four Million* (1906)

Henry, Patrick (1736–99) American statesman and orator

1 I am not a Virginian, but an American.
Speech to the First Continental Congress (September 5, 1774)

2 I know not what course others may take; but as for me, give me liberty or give me death!
Speech to the Virginia Convention (March 23, 1775)

3 I know of no way of judging the future but by the past.
Speech to the Virginia Convention (March 23, 1775)

4 Caesar had his Brutus—Charles the First, his Cromwell—and George the Third—"Treason," cried the Speaker...*may profit by their example*. If *this* be treason, make the most of it.
Referring to the Stamp Act. Speech to the Virginia Convention (May 1765)

Henry, Prince, Prince of Wales (1594–1612) English prince

1 Who but my father would keep such a bird in a cage?
Referring to Sir Walter Raleigh, who was imprisoned in the Tower of London for treason (1603–16). Remark (1603)

Henshaw, Joseph (1603–79) English prelate

1 Man's life is like unto a winter's day,
Some break their fast and so depart away;
Others stay dinner, then depart full fed;
The longest age but sups and goes to bed.
O reader, then behold and see!
As we are now, so must you be.
Horae Sucissivae (1631)

Henson, Josiah (1789–1883) U.S. preacher and social activist

1 Terror is the fiercest nurse of cruelty.
Truth Stranger Than Fiction: Father Henson's Story of His Own Life (1849)

Hentzner, Paul (*fl.* 1590) German tutor

1 Her face oblong, fair but wrinkled; her eyes small, yet black and pleasant; her nose a little hooked, her lips narrow and her teeth black, a defect the English seem subject to from their too great use of sugar...She wore false hair and that red.
1590? Referring to Elizabeth I. Quoted in *A Journey into England in the Year 1598* (R. Bentley, tr.; 1757)

Henze, Hans Werner (b.1926) German composer

1 There are limits to feats of skill, beyond which lie the realms of nonsense. Everything is quite difficult enough as it is, and what is simple actually comes hardest.
Music and Politics (1982)

Hepburn, Katharine (Katharine Houghton Hepburn; b.1907) U.S. actor

1 Nature, Mr. Allnut, is what we are put into this world to rise above.
As the missionary, Rosie Sayer. Charlie Allnut, captain of the river boat *The African Queen*, was played by Humphrey Bogart. *The African Queen* (James Agee and John Huston; 1951)

2 To be loved is very demoralizing.
The Dick Cavett Show, ABC television (April 4, 1975)

3 You never feel you have fame. It's always in back of you.
The Dick Cavett Show, ABC television (April 4, 1975)

4 First God made England, Ireland, and Scotland. That's when he corrected his mistakes and made Wales.
Time (August 7, 1978)

5 Acting is the most minor of gifts. After all, Shirley Temple could do it when she was four.
Attrib.

Hepworth, Barbara, Dame (Jocelyn Barbara Hepworth; 1903–75) British sculptor

1 You can't make a sculpture, in my opinion, without involving your body. You move and you feel and you breathe and you touch...One is physically involved and this is sculpture. It's not

architecture. It's rhythm and dance and everything.
1970. Quoted in *Art Talk: Conversations with 15 Women Artists* (Cindy Nemser; 1975)

2 I rarely draw what I see. I draw what I feel in my body.
Quoted in *Barbara Hepworth* (A. M. Hammacher; 1968)

He Qifang (1912–77) Chinese writer and editor

1 Nothing stays firm forever;
As the seasons turn, everything vanishes like morning dew.
"I'd Like to Talk to You About All Kinds of Pure Things" (1942), quoted in *Anthology of Modern Chinese Poetry* (Michelle Yeh (ed. and tr.); 1992)

Heraclitus (*fl.* 500 B.C.) Greek philosopher

1 Everything flows and nothing stays.
5th century? B.C. Quoted in *Cratylus* (Plato; 4th century? B.C.)

2 You can't step twice into the same river.
5th century? B.C. Quoted in *Cratylus* (Plato; 4th century? B.C.)

3 The foundation of the world is at rest, the world itself is in motion.
5th century? B.C. Quoted in *The Great Philosophers* (Karl Jaspers; 1966), vol. 2

4 A hidden connection is stronger than an obvious one.
480? B.C. Quoted in *The Presocratic Philosophers* (G. S. Kirk, J. E. Raven, and M. Schofield; 1983)

5 The way up and the way down are one and the same.
480? B.C. Quoted in *The Presocratic Philosophers* (G. S. Kirk, J. E. Raven, and M. Schofield; 1983)

6 We both step and do not step into the same rivers; we both are and are not.
480? B.C. Quoted in *The Presocratic Philosophers* (G. S. Kirk, J. E. Raven, and M. Schofield; 1983)

7 Listening not to me but to the Logos it is wise to agree that all things are one.
480? B.C. "Logos" refers to the divine wisdom of the word of God. Quoted in *The Presocratic Philosophers* (G. S. Kirk, J. E. Raven, and M. Schofield; 1983)

8 For in sleep, when the channels of perception are shut, our mind is sundered from its kinship with its surrounding...casts off its former power of memory. But in the waking state it again peeps out through the channels of perception as though through a kind of window, and...puts on its power of reason.
Attrib.

Herbert, A. P., Sir (Alan Patrick Herbert; 1890–1971) British writer and politician

1 Other people's babies—
That's my life!
Mother to dozens,
And nobody's wife.
"Other People's Babies," *A Book of Ballads* (1930)

2 Let's find out what everyone is doing,
And then stop everyone from doing it.
"Let's Stop Somebody," *Ballads for Broadbrows* (1930)

3 As my poor father used to say
In 1863,
Once people start on all this Art
Good-bye, moralitee!
And what my father used to say
Is good enough for me.
"Lines for a Worthy Person," *Ballads for Broadbrows* (1930)

4 Don't tell my mother I'm living in sin,
Don't let the old folks know:
Don't tell my twin that I breakfast on gin,
He'd never survive the blow.
Song lyric. "Don't Tell My Mother I'm Living in Sin," *Laughing Ann* (1925)

5 The concept of two people living together for 25 years without having a cross word suggests a lack of spirit only to be admired in sheep.
News Chronicle (1940)

6 It's hard to say why writing verse
Should terminate in drink or worse.
"Lines for a Worthy Person," *Punch*, London (1930)

7 He didn't ought to come to bed in boots.
"Riverside House, Hammersmith," *Riverside Nights* (1926)

8 For any ceremonial purposes the otherwise excellent liquid, water, is unsuitable in colour and other respects.
Uncommon Law (1935)

9 An Act of God was defined as "something which no reasonable man could have expected".
"Act of God," *Uncommon Law* (1935)

10 The Englishman never enjoys himself except for a noble purpose.
"Fox-Hunting Fun," *Uncommon Law* (1935)

11 People must not do things for fun. We are not here for fun. There is no reference to fun in any Act of Parliament.
"Is it a Free Country?," *Uncommon Law* (1935)

12 The critical period in matrimony is breakfast-time.
"Is Marriage Lawful?," *Uncommon Law* (1935)

13 The Common Law of England has been laboriously built about a mythical figure the figure of "The Reasonable Man".
"The Reasonable Man," *Uncommon Law* (1935)

Herbert, Edward, 1st Baron Herbert of Cherbury (1583–1648) English philosopher, historian, and diplomat

1 Now that the April of your youth adorns
The garden of your face.
"Ditty in Imitation of the Spanish: Entre tantoque L'Avril," *Occasional Verses* (1665), st. 1, ll. 1–2

Herbert, George (1593–1633) English poet and cleric

1 He that goes to bed thirsty rises healthy.
Jacula Prudentum (1640)

2 Would you know what money is, go borrow some.
Jacula Prudentum (1640)

3 He that makes a good war makes a good peace.
Outlandish Proverbs (1640), no. 420

4 I read, and sigh, and wish I were a tree;
For sure then I should grow

To fruit or shade; at least some bird would trust
Her household to me, and I should be just.
"Affliction," *The Temple: Sacred Poems and Private Ejaculations* (1633), ll. 57–60

5 Let all the world in every corner sing:
"My God and King!"
"Antiphon I," *The Temple: Sacred Poems and Private Ejaculations* (1633)

6 Oh that I were an orange-tree,
That busy plant!
Then I should ever laden be,
And never want
Some fruit for Him that dressed me.
"Employment: He That Is Weary, Let Him Sit," *The Temple: Sacred Poems and Private Ejaculations* (1633), st. 5

7 Death is still working like a mole,
And digs my grave at each remove.
"Grace," *The Temple: Sacred Poems and Private Ejaculations* (1633), st. 4, ll. 1–2

8 I made a posy while the day ran by:
Here will I smell my remnant out, and tie
My life within this band.
But Time did beckon to the flowers, and they
By noon most cunningly did steal away,
And withered in my hand.
"Life," *The Temple: Sacred Poems and Private Ejaculations* (1633), st. 1

9 Love bade me welcome; yet my soul drew back,
Guilty of dust and sin.
"Love: Love Bade Me Welcome," *The Temple: Sacred Poems and Private Ejaculations* (1633), ll. 1–2

10 "You must sit down," says Love, "and taste my meat."
So I did sit and eat.
"Love: Love Bade Me Welcome," *The Temple: Sacred Poems and Private Ejaculations* (1633), ll. 17–18

11 Oh mighty love! Man is one world, and hath
Another to attend him.
"Man," *The Temple: Sacred Poems and Private Ejaculations* (1633), ll. 47–48

12 To write a verse or two is all the praise
That I can raise.
"Praise," *The Temple: Sacred Poems and Private Ejaculations* (1633), st. 1, ll. 1–2

13 Exalted manna, gladness of the best,
Heaven in ordinarie, man well drest,
The milkie way, the bird of Paradise
Church-bels beyond the starres heard, the souls blood,
The land of spices; something understood.
"Prayer: Prayer the Church's Banquet," *The Temple: Sacred Poems and Private Ejaculations* (1633), ll. 10–14

14 The God of love my Shepherd is,
And He that doth me feed:
While He is mine, and I am His,
What can I want or need?
"The 23rd Psalm," *The Temple: Sacred Poems and Private Ejaculations* (1633), st. 1

15 Calmness is great advantage; he that lets another chafe may warm him at his fire, mark all his wand'rings and enjoy his frets, as cunning fencers suffer heat to tire.
"The Church Porch," *The Temple: Sacred Poems and Private Ejaculations* (1633), st. 53

16 Look not on pleasures as they come, but go.
"The Church Porch," *The Temple: Sacred Poems and Private Ejaculations* (1633), st. 77

17 I struck the board, and cried, "No more;
I will abroad."
What, shall I ever sigh and pine?
My lines and life are free; free as the road,
Loose as the wind, as large as store.
"The Collar," *The Temple: Sacred Poems and Private Ejaculations* (1633), ll. 1–5

18 But as I rav'd and grew more fierce and wild
At every word,
Methought I heard one calling, "Child";
And I replied, "My Lord".
"The Collar," *The Temple: Sacred Poems and Private Ejaculations* (1633), ll. 33–36

19 A man that looks on glass,
On it may stay his eye;
Or if he pleaseth, through it pass,
And then the heaven espy.
"The Elixir," *The Temple: Sacred Poems and Private Ejaculations* (1633), st. 3

20 Who would have thought my shrivelled heart
Could have recovered greenness?
"The Flower," *The Temple: Sacred Poems and Private Ejaculations* (1633), st. 2, ll. 8–9

21 And now in age I bud again,
After so many deaths I live and write;
I once more smell the dew and rain,
And relish versing; O, my only Light,
It cannot be
That I am he
On whom Thy tempests fell all night.
"The Flower," *The Temple: Sacred Poems and Private Ejaculations* (1633), st. 6

22 My friend may spit upon my curious floor;
Could he have gold? I lend it instantly;
But let the poor,
And Thou within them, starve at door:
I cannot use a friend, as I use Thee.
"Unkindness," *The Temple: Sacred Poems and Private Ejaculations* (1633), st. 3

23 Sweet day, so cool, so calm, so bright,
The bridal of the earth and sky.
"Virtue," *The Temple: Sacred Poems and Private Ejaculations* (1633), st. 1, ll. 1–2

24 Sweet spring, full of sweet days and roses,
A box where sweets compacted lie.
"Virtue," *The Temple: Sacred Poems and Private Ejaculations* (1633), st. 3, ll. 1–2

25 Only a sweet and virtuous soul,
Like season'd timber, never gives;
But though the whole world turn to coal,
Then chiefly lives.
"Virtue," *The Temple: Sacred Poems and Private Ejaculations* (1633), st. 4

Herford, Oliver (1863–1935) British-born U.S. poet, illustrator, and wit

1 Actresses will happen in the best regulated families.
Attrib.

2 A hair in the head is worth two in the brush.
Attrib.

3 I would like to throw an egg into an electric fan.
Said when asked if he had no ambition beyond making people laugh. Attrib.

Hermite, Charles (Oliver Brooke Herford; 1822–1901) French mathematician

1 There exists, if I am not mistaken, an entire world which is the totality of mathematical truths, to which we have access only with our mind, just as a world of physical reality exists, the one like the other independent of ourselves, both of divine creation.
Quoted in *The Mathematical Intelligencer*, vol. 5, no. 4

Herodotus (484?–425 B.C.) Greek historian

Quotations about Herodotus

1 Father of Lies.
Norman Davies (b.1939) British historian and writer. Name given to Herodotus by his more cynical contemporaries. He is more commonly called "The Father of History." *Europe: A History* (1996), ch. 2

Quotations by Herodotus

2 Death is a delightful hiding-place for weary men.
The Histories (450? B.C.), bk. 7, ch. 46

Herophilus (335?–280? B.C.) Greek anatomist

1 Medicines are nothing in themselves, if not properly used, but the very hands of the gods, if employed with reason and prudence.
Attrib.

Herr, Michael (b.1940) U.S. writer

1 Dozens of children broke from their hootches to run in toward the focus of our landing, the pilot laughing and saying, "Vietnam, man, bomb 'em and feed 'em, bomb 'em and feed 'em."
Dispatches (1977), ch. 1

2 In the coming hours he'd stand as faceless and quiet in the jungle as a fallen tree...he was a good killer, one of our best.
Referring to a U.S. soldier in the Vietnam War, affected by battle fatigue. *Dispatches* (1977), ch. 1

3 There wasn't anybody he wanted to thank for his food, but he was grateful that he was still alive to eat it...He hadn't been anything but tired and scared for six months.
Referring to a young soldier in the Vietnam War. *Dispatches* (1977), ch. 1

4 Going out at night the medics gave you pills, Dexedrine breath like dead snakes kept too long in a jar.
Referring to night patrols in the Vietnam War. *Dispatches* (1977), ch. 1

5 The saturating strangeness of the place...didn't lessen with exposure so often as it fattened and darkened in accumulating alienation.
Referring to the jungle environment of the Vietnam War. *Dispatches* (1977), ch. 1

Herrick, Robert (1591–1674) English poet

1 The Hag is astride,
The night for to ride;
The Devill and shee together;
Through thick, and through thin,
Now out, and then in,
Though ne'er so foule the weather.
"The Hag" (1648)

2 With thousand such enchanting dreams, that meet
To make sleep not so sound, as sweet.
"A Country Life: to His Brother, M. Tho. Herrick," *Hesperides* (1648), ll. 53–54

3 Thus times do shift, each thing his turn does hold;
New things succeed, as former things grow old.
"Ceremonies for Candlemas Eve," *Hesperides* (1648), ll. 21–22

4 Cherry ripe, ripe, ripe, I cry.
Full and fair ones; come and buy.
"Cherry Ripe," *Hesperides* (1648)

5 Get up, get up for shame, the blooming morn
Upon her wings presents the god unshorn.
"Corinna's Going a-Maying," *Hesperides* (1648), ll. 1–2

6 A sweet disorder in the dress
Kindles in clothes a wantonness.
"Delight in Disorder," *Hesperides* (1648), ll. 1–2

7 Roses at first were white,
Till they co'd not agree,
Whether my Sappho's breast,
Or they more white sho'd be.
"How Roses Came Red," *Hesperides* (1648), st. 1

8 'Twixt kings and tyrants there's this difference known;
Kings seek their subjects' good: tyrants their own.
"Kings and Tyrants," *Hesperides* (1648), ll. 1–2

9 You say to me-wards your affection's strong;
Pray love me little, so you love me long.
"Love Me Little, Love Me Long," *Hesperides* (1648), ll. 1–2

10 Here a little child I stand,
Leaving up my either hand;
Cold as paddocks though they be,
Here I lift them up to Thee,
For a benison to fall
On our meat, and on us all. Amen.
"Noble Numbers. Another Grace for a Child," *Hesperides* (1648), ll. 1–7

11 Attempt the end, and never stand to doubt;
Nothing's so hard but search will find it out.
"Seek and Find," *Hesperides* (1648), ll. 1–2

12 Fair daffodils, we weep to see
You haste away so soon:
As yet the early-rising sun
Has not attain'd his noon.
Stay, stay,
Until the hasting day
Has run
But to the even-song;
And, having pray'd together, we
Will go with you along.
We have short time to stay, as you,
We have as short a Spring;

As quick a growth to meet decay,
As you or any thing.
"To Daffodils," *Hesperides* (1648), ll. 1–14

13 If any thing delight me for to print
My book, 'tis this; that Thou, my God, art in't.
"To God," *Hesperides* (1648), ll. 1–2

14 He loves his bonds, who, when the first are broke,
Submits his neck unto a second yoke.
About a second marriage. "To Love," *Hesperides* (1648)

15 Her pretty feet, like snails, did creep
A little out, and then,
As if they played at bo-peep,
Did soon draw in again.
"To Mistress Susanna Southwell: Upon Her Feet," *Hesperides* (1648), ll. 1–5

16 Gather ye rosebuds while ye may,
Old time is still a-flying:
And this same flower that smiles today
Tomorrow will be dying.
"To the Virgins, To Make Much of Time," *Hesperides* (1648), st. 1

17 Then be not coy, but use your time;
And while ye may, go marry:
For having lost but once your prime,
You may for ever tarry.
"To the Virgins, To Make Much of Time," *Hesperides* (1648), st. 4

18 Whenas in silks my Julia goes
Then, then (methinks) how sweetly flows
That liquefaction of her clothes.
"Upon Julia's Clothes," *Hesperides* (1648), st. 1

Hershfield, Harry U.S. cartoonist

1 A city where everyone mutinies but no one deserts.
Referring to New York. *New York Post* (1974)

Hervey, James (1714–58) British devotional writer

1 E'en crosses from his sov'reign hand
Are blessings in disguise.
"Reflections on a Flower-Garden" (1746)

Hervey, John, Baron Hervey of Ickworth (1696–1743) English writer and pamphleteer

Quotations about Hervey

1 A cherub's face, a reptile all the rest.
Alexander Pope (1688–1744) English poet. *Epistle to Dr. Arbuthnot* (1735), l. 331

2 You know he is a lady himself; or at least such a nice composition of the two sexes that it is difficult to distinguish which is the most predominant.
William Pulteney (1684–1764) English statesman. Quoted in *Homosexuality: A History* (Colin Spencer; 1995)

Quotations by Hervey

3 Whoever would lie usefully should lie seldom.
Memoirs of the Reign of George II (J. W. Croker, ed.; 1848), vol. 1, ch. 19

Hervey, Thomas K. (Thomas Kibble Hervey; 1799–1859) British poet and editor

1 Like ships, that sailed for sunny isles,
But never came to shore.
The Devil's Progress (1830)

Herzberg, Frederick (b.1923) U.S. social psychologist

1 Ancient Egyptians, medieval people and contemporary man all have a kinship in sharing the feeling that the world is too complicated for them.
Work and the Nature of Man (1968)

Herzen, Aleksandr Ivanovich (1812–70) Russian writer and political thinker

1 Communism is Tsarist autocracy turned upside down.
My Past and Thoughts (1855)

Herzl, Theodor (1860–1904) Hungarian-born Zionist leader

1 Zionism...is a moral, lawful, humanitarian movement, directed towards the long yearned-for goal of our people.
Address to the First Zionist Congress, Basel, Switzerland (August 29, 1897)

2 This plan...is a reserve against more evil days.
Referring to the plan for a Jewish homeland. Letter to Rabbi Gudemann, Chief Rabbi of Vienna (1895)

3 England, the free and mighty England, whose vision embraces the seven seas, will understand our aspirations.
Referring to the aspirations of European Jews for a homeland in Palestine. Remark (August 13, 1900), *The Complete Diaries of Theodor Herzl* (Raphael Patai, ed.; 1960)

4 Zionism is our return to Judaism even before our return to the Jewish land!
Speech, First Zionist Congress, Basel (August 29, 1897)

5 At Basel I founded the Jewish State. If I said this out loud today, I would be answered by universal laughter. Perhaps in five years, and certainly in fifty, everyone will know it.
August 29, 1897. Speech, First Zionist Congress, Basel, *The Complete Diaries of Theodor Herzl* (Raphael Patai, ed.; 1960)

6 And if it should occur that men of other creeds and different nationalities come to live amongst us, we should accord them honorable protection and equality before the law.
The Jewish State (1896)

7 Anti-Semitism of today...is for the most part a movement among civilized nations by which they try to chase away the specters of their own past.
The Jewish State (1896)

8 The Promised Land, where we can have hooked noses, black or red beards, and bow legs, without being despised for it.
The Jewish State (1896)

9 We have learned toleration in Europe.
The Jewish State (1896)

10 We shall keep our priests within the confines of their temples in the same way as we shall keep our professional army within the confines of their barracks...they must not interfere in the administration of the state.
The Jewish State (1896)

11 We shall seek to bestow the moral salvation of work on men of every age and every class.
The Jewish State (1896)

12 When nations wandered in historic times, they let chance carry them, draw them, fling them hither and thither...but this modern Jewish migration must proceed in accordance with scientific principles.
The Jewish State (1896)

13 When we sink, we become a revolutionary proletariat, the subordinate officers of all revolutionary parties; and at the same time, when we rise, there rises also our terrible power of the purse.
The Jewish State (1896)

14 I must in the first place, guard my scheme from being treated as Utopian by superficial critics...this Utopia is far less attractive than any of those portrayed by Sir Thomas More.
Referring to his plan for a Jewish homeland. *The Jewish State* (1896)

15 We shall live at last as free men on our own soil, and die peacefully in our own homes. The world will be freed by our liberty, enriched by our wealth, magnified by our own greatness.
Referring to the plan for a Jewish homeland. *The Jewish State* (1896)

Heseltine, Michael (Michael Ray Dibdin Heseltine; b.1933) British politician

1 You can call an ecu a pound in Britain. A single currency does not need a single name, but it does need a single value.
Times, London (November 19, 1990)

Hesiod (*fl.* 8th century B.C.) Greek poet

1 Oft hath even a whole city reaped the evil fruit of a bad man.
Theogony (750? B.C.), l. 240

2 A bad neighbor is as great a misfortune as a good one is a great blessing.
Theogony (750? B.C.), l. 346

3 The dawn speeds a man on his journey, and speeds him too in his work.
Theogony (750? B.C.), l. 579

4 If a man avoids
Marriage and all the troubles women bring
And never takes a wife, at last he comes
To a miserable old age, and does not have
Anyone to care for the old man.
Theogony (750? B.C.), ll. 602–6

5 The half is greater than the whole.
Works and Days (750? B.C.), l. 40

Hesse, Eva (1936–70) German-born U.S. painter and sculptor

1 The best artists are those who *have* stood alone and who *can* be separated from whatever movements have been made about them.
1970. Quoted in *Art Talk: Conversations with 15 Women Artists* (Cindy Nemser; 1975)

Hesse, Hermann (1877–1962) German-born Swiss novelist and poet

1 If you hate a person, you hate something in him that is part of yourself. What isn't part of ourselves doesn't disturb us.
Demian (1919), ch. 6

2 Knowledge can be communicated but not wisdom.
Siddhartha (1922)

3 The bourgeois prefers comfort to pleasure, convenience to liberty, and a pleasant temperature to the deathly inner consuming fire.
"Treatise of the Steppenwolf," *Steppenwolf* (1927)

4 I believe that the struggle against death, the unconditional and self-willed determination to life, is the motive power behind the lives and activities of all outstanding men.
"Treatise of the Steppenwolf," *Steppenwolf* (1927)

5 You treat world history as a mathematician does mathematics, in which nothing but laws and formulae exist, no reality, no good and evil, no time, no yesterday, no tomorrow, nothing but an eternal, shallow, mathematical present.
The Glass Bead Game (1943)

Hewart, Gordon, 1st Viscount Hewart (1870–1943) British lawyer and politician

1 Justice should not only be done, but should manifestly and undoubtedly be seen to be done.
Quoted in *The Chief* (Robert Jackson; 1959)

2 If it's a boy I'll call him John. If it's a girl I'll call her Mary. But if, as I suspect, it's only wind, I'll call it F. E. Smith.
F. E. Smith had commented on the size of his stomach, saying "What's it to be—a boy or a girl?" Attrib.

Heym, Stefan (originally Helmut Flieg; b.1913) German writer

1 A socialist state in Germany is absolutely necessary for socialist development in the whole world.
Marxism Today, London (November 1989)

Heywood, John (1497?–1580?) English playwright and epigrammatist

1 All a green willow, willow,
All a green willow is my garland.
"A Ballad of the Green Willow" (1545?)

2 Wedding is destiny,
And hanging likewise.
Proverbs (1546), pt. 1, ch. 3.

3 Now for good lucke, cast an old shooe after me.
Proverbs (1546), pt. 1, ch. 9.

4 Much water goeth by the mill
That the miller knoweth not of.
Proverbs (1546), pt. 2, ch. 6

5 Enough is as good as a feast.
Proverbs (1546), pt. 2, ch. 11

Heywood, Thomas (1574–1641) English playwright and writer

1 Seven cities warr'd for Homer, being dead,
Who, living, had no roof to shroud his head.
"The Hierarchy of the Blessed Angels" (1635), ll. 4553–54

2 The world's a theatre, the earth a stage,
Which God and Nature do with actors fill.
Apology for Actors (1612)

3 A Woman Killed with Kindness
Play title. *A Woman Killed with Kindness* (1607)

4 What the dickens!
Edward IV (1600), Act 3, Scene 1

Hiatt, Arnold (b.1927) U.S. business executive

1 Ego is a treacherous and debilitating force. Nowhere is that more true than in marketing and product design.
Harvard Business Review (March–April 1992)

Hickman, Craig R. U.S. author

1 Complexity management can be used to build unity in the midst of diversity and to empower people to attain peak performance and individual fulfillment.
The Future 500 (co-written with Michael A. Silva; 1987)

2 Executives planning for the future must discover how to orchestrate corporate environments that nurture and harmonize subcultures and substrategies.
The Future 500 (co-written with Michael A. Silva; 1987)

3 Good architects nurture the psychological, mental, and spiritual needs of the people who will inhabit their structures.
The Future 500 (co-written with Michael A. Silva; 1987)

4 The accomplishment of individual and collective purposes in the most fulfilling ways possible will create winning organizations.
The Future 500 (co-written with Michael A. Silva; 1987)

5 The "dynamic network"...an organizational architecture that accommodates constant and accelerating change while at the same time stimulating components of the corporate environment to build deep and lasting relationships.
The Future 500 (co-written with Michael A. Silva; 1987)

6 The ethical leadership era requires an integration of corporate self-interest with the interests of all direct and indirect stakeholders in the corporate ecosystem.
The Future 500 (co-written with Michael A. Silva; 1987)

7 Whether a company is high tech or low tech, operating in an age-old industry or one of the newer service or knowledge ones...its success will depend, more than anything else, on the satisfaction of the needs and desires of each unique stakeholder.
The Future 500 (co-written with Michael A. Silva; 1987)

Hicks, Seymour, Sir (Edward Seymour Hicks; 1871–1949) British actor-manager

1 You will recognize, my boy, the first sign of old age: it is when you go out into the streets of London and realize for the first time how young the policemen look.
Quoted in *They Were Singing* (C. Pulling; 1952), ch. 7

Higgins, Andrew (b.1958) British journalist

1 The idea that if you inflict cruelty on the living animal immediately before slaughter the result will be greater flavour and tenderness in the carcass still exists today.
Independent on Sunday, London (August 25, 1991)

Higgins, Billy (b.1936) U.S. jazz musician

1 You're not supposed to *rape* the drums, you make love to them.
Quoted in "A Lesson in Lovemaking," *Jazz People* (Valerie Wilmer; 1970), ch. 5

Higley, Brewster (*fl.* 19th century) U.S. songwriter

1 Oh give me a home where the buffalo roam,
Where the deer and the antelope play,
Where seldom is heard a discouraging word
And the skies are not cloudy all day.
"Home on the Range" (1873?)

Hilbert, David (1862–1943) German mathematician and philosopher

1 Physics is much too hard for physicists.
Quoted in *Hilbert* (C. Reid; 1970)

2 One can measure the importance of a scientific work by the number of earlier publications rendered superfluous by it.
Quoted in *Mathematical Circles Revisited* (H. Eves; 1971)

Hildegarde of Bingen (1098–1179) German abbess, composer, and mystic

1 The body is truly the garment of the soul, which has a living voice; for that reason it is fitting that the body simultaneously with the soul repeatedly sing praises to God through the voice.
1178? Attrib.

Hilfiger, Tommy U.S. fashion designer

1 Absolutely I wear my own clothes! I wear my own jacket, my own pants, my own belts, my own eyewear.
Guardian, London (July 31, 1996)

Hill, Aaron (1685–1750) English poet and playwright

1 First, then, a woman will or won't, depend on 't;
If she will do 't, she will; and there 's an end on 't.
But if she won't, since safe and sound your trust is,
Fear is affront, and jealousy injustice.
The Tragedy of Zara (1736), epilogue

2 Tender-handed stroke a nettle,
And it stings you for your pains;
Grasp it like a man of mettle,
And it soft as silk remains.
"Tender Handed Stroke of a Nettle," *The Works of the Late Aaron Hill* (1753), st. 1

Hill, Benjamin H. (Benjamin Harvey Hill; 1823–82) U.S. politician

1 Tinkers may work, quacks may prescribe, and demagogues may deceive, but I declare to you that there is no remedy for us...but in adhering to the Constitution.
Quoted in *Senator Benjamin H. Hill: His Life, Speeches and Writings* (Benjamin Hill, Jr.; 1893)

Hill, Geoffrey (b.1932) British poet

1 I love my work and my children. God
Is distant, difficult. Things happen.
Too near the ancient troughs of blood
Innocence is no earthly weapon.
"Ovid in the Third Reich," *King Log* (1968), st. 1

2 King of the perennial holly-groves, the riven sandstone: overlord of the M5: architect of the historic rampart and ditch, the citadel at Tamworth...guardian of the Welsh Bridge and the Iron Bridge: contractor to the desirable new estates: saltmaster...the friend of Charlemagne. "I liked that," said Offa, "sing it again."
The M5 is a freeway crossing the area of the Anglo-Saxon kingdom of Mercia in the English Midlands. Offa was an 8th-century king of Mercia. "The Naming of Offa," *Mercian Hymns* (1971), no. 1

Hill, Joe (originally Joel Emmanuel Hägglund, also known as Joseph Hillstrom; 1879–1915) Swedish-born U.S. labor leader and songwriter

1 Work and pray, live on hay,
You'll get pie in the sky when you die.
"The Preacher and the Slave," *Songs of the Workers* (1911)

Hill, Rowland (1744–1833) British clergyman

1 I do not see any reason why the devil should have all the good tunes.
Quoted in *The Reverend Rowland Hill* (E. W. Broome; 1881), ch. 7

Hillary, Edmund, Sir (Edmund Percival Hillary; b.1919) New Zealand mountaineer

1 As far as I knew, he had never taken a photograph before, and the summit of Everest was hardly the place to show him how.
Referring to Tenzing Norgay. *High Adventure* (1955)

2 Well, we knocked the bastard off!
May 29, 1953. Referring to reaching the summit of Mount Everest with Tenzing Norgay. *Nothing Venture, Nothing Win* (1975), ch. 10

3 There is precious little in civilization to appeal to a Yeti.
June 1960. *Observer*, London (June 3, 1960), "Sayings of the Week"

Hillingdon, Alice, Lady (1857–1940) British diarist

1 I am happy now that Charles calls on my bedchamber less frequently than of old. As it is, I now endure but two calls a week and when I hear his steps outside my door I lie down on my bed, close my eyes, open my legs and think of England.
Often mistakenly attributed to Queen Victoria. *Journal* (1912)

Hillman, James (b.1926) U.S. author

1 Animal life is biologically aesthetic: each species presents itself in design, coats, tails, feathers, furs, curls, tusks, horns, hues, sheens, shells, scales, wings, songs, dances.
Paper for symposium, *Cosmos, Life, Religion: Beyond Humanism* (1988)

2 Each thing needs other things—once called "the sympathy of all things." Attachment is embedded in the soul of things, like an animal magnetism.
Paper for symposium, *Cosmos, Life, Religion: Beyond Humanism* (1988)

3 A cry went through late antiquity: "Great Pan is dead!"...Nature no longer spoke to us—or we could no longer hear...When Pan is alive, then nature is too, and it is filled with gods, so that the owl's hoot is Athena and the mollusk on the shore is Aphrodite.
Pan and the Nightmare (1972)

4 If God-given and man-made are an unnecessary, even false, opposition, then the city made by human hands is also natural in its own right...Cities belong to human nature; nature does not begin outside the city walls.
"Natural Beauty Without Nature," *Spring* (1985)

5 The first psychological difference between humans and animals resides in how we regard each other. Humans regard animals differently than animals regard animals (and humans), so a first step in restoring Eden would be to regain the animal eye.
Typologies (1986)

Himes, Chester (1909–84) U.S. novelist and short-story writer

1 American publishers are not interested in black writers unless they bleed from white torture.
The Quality of Hurt (1972)

2 My feelings are too intense. I hate too bitterly, I love too exaltingly, I pity too extravagantly, I hurt too painfully. We American blacks call that "soul."
The Quality of Hurt (1972)

3 The greatest failure for any man is to fail with a woman.
The Quality of Hurt (1972)

Himmelfarb, Gertrude (b.1922) U.S. historian

1 If historians have shown themselves, on occasion, to be strangely resistant to historical reality, they have also proved to be peculiarly vulnerable to boredom.
The New History and the Old (1987)

Himmler, Heinrich (1900–45) German Nazi chief of police

1 We Germans must finally learn not to regard the Jew and members of any organization who have been taught by the Jew as people of our kind or representatives of our manner of thinking.
Remark (March 5, 1936), quoted in *Germany, 1866–1945* (Gordon A. Craig; 1978), ch. 17

2 Most of you know what it means when a hundred corpses are lying together, when five hundred are lying there, or when a

thousand are lying there...This is an unwritten and never-to-be-written page of glory in our history.
Exhorting the S.S. to carry out mass murder in eastern Europe. Speech to the S.S. (Nazi security forces), Poznan, Poland (October 1943), quoted in *Germany, 1866–1945* (Gordon A. Craig; 1978)

Hinkle, Beatrice (originally Beatrice Moses; 1874–1953) U.S. psychiatrist

1 Fundamentally the male artist approximates more to the psychology of woman, who, biologically speaking, is a purely creative being and whose personality has been as mysterious and unfathomable to the man as the artist has been to the average person.
"The Psychology of the Artist," *Recreating the Individual* (1923)

Hippocleides (b.6th century? B.C.) Athenian aristocrat

1 Hippocleides doesn't care.
Comment after Cleisthenes told him he had ruined his chances of marrying Cleisthenes' daughter. Quoted in *The Histories* (Herodotus; 450? B.C.), bk. 6, ch. 129, l. 4

Hippocrates (460?–377? B.C.) Greek physician

1 Extreme remedies are most appropriate for extreme diseases.
Aphorisms (415? B.C.), sect. 1

2 The life so short, the craft so long to learn.
Describing medicine. It is often quoted in Latin as *Ars longa, vita brevis*, and interpreted as "Art lasts; life is short." *Aphorisms* (415? B.C.), sect. 1

3 In acute diseases it is not quite safe to prognosticate either death or recovery.
Aphorisms (415? B.C.), sect. 2

4 Sleep and watchfulness, both of them, when immoderate, constitute disease.
Aphorisms (415? B.C.), sect. 2

5 All men should know that the brain, and the brain only, is responsible for, and is the seat of, all our joys and happiness, our pain and sadness; here is seated wisdom, understanding, and the knowledge of the difference between good and evil.
Sacred Disease (5th century? B.C.)

6 As long as the brain is at rest the man enjoys his reason; depravement of the brain arises from phlegm and bile; those mad from phlegm are quiet, depressed, and oblivious; those from bile excited, noisy, and mischievous.
From his treatise on epilepsy. *Sacred Disease* (5th century? B.C.)

7 Foolish the doctor who despises the knowledge acquired by the ancients.
Quoted in *Entering the World: the Demedicalization of Childbirth* (Michel Odent and Christine Hauch, trs.; 1984)

8 Healing is a matter of time, but it is sometimes also a matter of opportunity.
Quoted in *Precepts* (W. H. S. Jones, tr.; 1923), ch. 1

Hippolytus of Rome, Saint (170?–235?) Roman theologian and antipope

1 Anyone taking part in baptismal instruction, or anyone already baptized who wants to become a soldier shall be sent away, for he has despised God.
218. Quoted in "The Apostolic Tradition," *The Early Christians* (E. Arnold; 1970)

Hirohito, Emperor (Showa Tenno Hirohito; 1901–89) Japanese monarch

1 The war situation has developed not necessarily to Japan's advantage.
Announcing Japan's unconditional surrender in World War II. Radio broadcast (August 15, 1945)

Hirschfeld, Al (Albert Hirschfeld; b.1903) U.S. caricaturist

1 I've always been interested in the insanities of people rather than nature; it would never occur to me to do the Grand Canyon.
Referring to his caricatures. Remark (November 9, 1991)

2 I was a sculptor. But that's really a drawing—a drawing you fall over in the dark, a three-dimensional drawing.
New York Times (June 21, 1988)

Hirst, Damien (b.1965) British artist

1 In terms of conceptual art, the sheep had already made its statement.
Referring to the vandalizing of one of his works, which featured a preserved dead sheep. *Observer*, London (August 21, 1994), "Sayings of the Week"

Hitchcock, Alfred, Sir (Alfred Joseph Hitchcock; 1899–1980) British-born U.S. film director

1 I made a remark a long time ago. I said I was very pleased that television was now showing murder stories, because it's bringing murder back into its rightful setting—in the home.
Observer, London (August 17, 1969), "Sayings of the Week"

2 Actors are cattle.
He afterwards insisted he had said, "Actors should be treated like cattle." *Saturday Evening Post*, London (May 22, 1943)

3 The cinema is not a slice of life but a piece of cake.
Sunday Times, London (March 6, 1977)

4 Never judge a country by its politics. After all, we English are quite honest by nature, aren't we?
A line from the film directed by Alfred Hitchcock. *The Lady Vanishes* (Screenplay by Sidney Gilliat and Frank Launder; 1938)

5 A filmmaker isn't supposed to say things, he's supposed to show them.
Quoted in *Filmgoer's Book of Quotes* (Leslie Halliwell; 1973)

6 Always make the audience suffer as much as possible.
Quoted in *Filmgoer's Book of Quotes* (Leslie Halliwell; 1973)

7 In a good movie the sound could go off and the audience would have a perfectly good idea of what was going on.
Quoted in *Filmgoer's Book of Quotes* (Leslie Halliwell; 1973)

8 A good film is when the price of the admission, the dinner, and the babysitter was well worth it.
Quoted in *Halliwell's Filmgoer's Companion* (Leslie Halliwell; 1993)

9 I'm not against the police; I'm just afraid of them.
Quoted in *New Society* (May 10, 1984)

10 You can't direct a Laughton picture. The best you can hope for is to referee.
Referring to the actor Charles Laughton. Attrib.

Hitler, Adolf (1889–1945) Austrian-born German political and military leader

Quotations about Hitler

1 I have only one purpose, the destruction of Hitler, and my life is much simplified thereby. If Hitler invaded Hell I would make at least a favourable reference to the Devil in the House of Commons.
Winston Churchill (1874–1965) British prime minister and writer. *The Grand Alliance* (1950)

2 Adolf Hitler was *sui generis*, a force without a real historical past, whose very Germanness was spurious because never truly felt and in the end, in the moment of defeat, repudiated...He stands alone.
Gordon A. Craig (b.1913) U.S. historian. *Germany, 1866–1945* (1978), ch. 15

3 Our leader said in Nuremberg, "We have made human beings once more of millions of people who were in misery." Anyone who will not deny himself a pound of butter for that is not worthy to be a German.
Hermann Goering (1893–1946) German Nazi leader. Speech, Sportpalast, Berlin (October 28, 1936)

4 In politics, as in grammar, one should be able to tell the substantives from the adjectives. Hitler was a substantive; Mussolini only an adjective. Hitler was a nuisance. Mussolini was bloody. Together a bloody nuisance.
Salvador de Madariaga y Rogo (1886–1978) Spanish diplomat and writer. Attrib.

5 I should be pleased, I suppose, that Hitler has carried out a revolution on our lines. But they are Germans. So they will end by ruining our idea.
1935
Benito Mussolini (1883–1945) Italian dictator. Referring to fascism, which he regarded as a uniquely Italian philosophy. Quoted in *Benito Mussolini* (C. Hibbert; 1975), pt. 2, ch. 1

6 The Italians will laugh at me; every time Hitler occupies a country he sends me a message.
Benito Mussolini (1883–1945) Italian dictator. Quoted in *Hitler* (Alan Bullock; 1952), ch. 8

7 Fascism is a religion; the twentieth century will be known in history as the century of Fascism.
1933
Benito Mussolini (1883–1945) Italian dictator. On Hitler's seizing power. Quoted in *Sawdust Caesar: the Untold History of Mussolini and Fascism* (George Seldes; 1935), ch. 24

8 That garrulous monk.
Benito Mussolini (1883–1945) Italian dictator. Quoted in *The Second World War* (Winston Churchill; 1948–53)

9 There is the racial policy of the Union of South Africa, which is in no sense different from the racial policy of Hitler, except that they have not gone to those extremes that Hitler went to.
Jawaharlal Nehru (1889–1964) Indian prime minister. Referring to South Africa's policy of Apartheid (1948–89) and to Adolf Hitler. Speech to the Lok-Sabha (the lower house of the Indian parliament) (September 30, 1956)

10 We have hired him...Within two months we will have pushed Hitler so far into the corner that he'll squeak.
February 1933
Franz von Papen (1879–1969) German soldier, diplomat, and politician. Said on Adolf Hitler's appointment as chancellor of Germany. Quoted in *Germany, 1866–1945* (Gordon A. Craig; 1978), ch. 16

11 Hitler's rule does not spell the end of the historical process. If ever the historical *raison d'être* of psychoanalysis and its sociological function was needed, the current phase of historical development must prove it.
1933
Wilhelm Reich (1897–1957) Austrian psychoanalyst. Quoted in *Reich Speaks of Freud* (M. Higgins, ed.; 1967)

12 Adolf is a swine. He will give us all away. He only associates with the reactionaries now.
Ernst Röhm (1887–1934) German Nazi leader. Remark (1934), quoted in *Germany, 1866–1945* (Gordon A. Craig; 1978), ch. 16

13 I wouldn't believe Hitler was dead, even if he told me so himself.
Hjalmar Schacht (1877–1970) Danish-born German economist and politician. Remark (May 8, 1945) Attrib.

14 It was Hitler's cognitive dissonance that enabled him to go on talking of victory as the Russians approached the suburbs of Berlin...Without this fatal schizotypal characteristic, the war may have ended somewhat earlier.
Anthony Stevens (b.1933) British psychiatrist. "Cognitive dissonance" is the disparity between facts and a perception of them. *Evolutionary Psychiatry* (1996), ch. 13

15 Germany was the cause of Hitler just as much as Chicago is responsible for the Chicago Tribune.
Alexander Woollcott (1887–1943) U.S. writer and critic. Radio interview (1943)

Quotations by Hitler

16 With us the Leader and the Idea are one, and every party member has to do what the Leader orders.
Conversation with Otto Strasser (as recounted by Strasser) (May 21, 1930), quoted in *Hitler and Stalin: Parallel Lives* (Alan Bullock; 1991), ch. 5

17 In the West it is important to leave the responsibility for opening hostilities unmistakably to England and France.
Germany attacked Poland on September 1, 1939. Britain and France declared war on Germany on September 3, 1939. Directive no. 1 for the Conduct of the War (September 3, 1939), quoted in *Hitler's War Directives 1939–1945* (H. R. Trevor-Roper; 1964)

18 For the last time our deadly enemies the Jewish Bolsheviks have launched their massive forces to the attack. Their aim is to reduce Germany to ruins and to exterminate our people.
Hitler's final formal Order claiming that Germany's enemies would "bleed to death" before Berlin and be defeated. He committed suicide 15 days later. The final capitulation was signed on May 7, 1945. Order of the day (April 15, 1945), quoted in *Hitler's War Directives 1939–1945* (H. R. Trevor-Roper; 1964)

19 Night and Fog.
Referring to the way in which people suspected of crimes against occupying forces would be dealt with: they would be spirited away into the night and fog. Remark (1941)

20 We are going to destroy the Jews. They are not going to get away with what they did on November 9, 1918. The day of reckoning has come.
Referring to the armistice ending World War I. Remark (January 21, 1939), quoted in *Germany, 1866–1945* (Gordon A. Craig; 1978), ch. 17

21 All our agreements with Poland have a purely temporary

significance. I have no intention of maintaining a serious relationship with Poland.
Referring to the German-Polish nonaggression treaty that was effective from 1924 and terminated in 1934. Poland tried to continue diplomatic relations, but German demands became increasingly aggressive and Germany eventually invaded Poland on September 1, 1939. Remark (October 18, 1934), quoted in *Germany, 1866–1945* (Gordon A. Craig; 1978), ch. 19

22 Now Poland is in the position in which I wanted her...I am only afraid that at the last moment some swine or other will submit to me a plan for mediation.
Said ten days before the German army invaded Poland. Remark (August 22, 1939), quoted in *Germany, 1866–1945* (Gordon A. Craig; 1978), ch. 19

23 The world belongs to the man with guts! God helps him!
Said after the successful German reoccupation of the Rhineland. Remark (March 1936), quoted in *Germany, 1866–1945* (Gordon A. Craig; 1978), ch. 19

24 It is not the neutrals or the lukewarm who make history.
Speech, Berlin (April 23, 1933)

25 A historical revision on a unique scale has been imposed on us by the Creator.
Announcing Germany's declaration of war on the United States. Speech, Berlin (December 11, 1941)

26 Before us stands the last problem that must be solved and will be solved. It is the last territorial claim which I have to make in Europe, but it is the claim from which I will not recede.
Referring to negotiations with Britain, France, and Italy which led to the Munich Agreement (September 29, 1938), allowing Germany to annex the Sudetenland, the German-speaking part of Czechoslovakia. Speech, Sportpalast, Berlin (September 26, 1938), quoted in *Hitler: Reden und Proklamationen 1932–1945* (Max Domarus, ed.; 1962)

27 I go the way that Providence dictates with the assurance of a sleepwalker.
Referring to his successful reoccupation of the Rhineland, in violation of the Versailles Treaty and despite being advised against the attempt. Speech, Munich (March 15, 1936), quoted in *Hitler: Reden und Proklamationen 1932–1945* (Max Domarus, ed.; 1962)

28 If today I stand here as a revolutionary, it is as a revolutionary against the revolution. There is no such thing as high treason against the traitors of 1918.
At his trial for treason following the unsuccessful Munich *putsch* (November 1923). Speech, Munich, Bavaria (February 26, 1924)

29 Success is the sole earthly judge of right and wrong.
Mein Kampf (1933)

30 With a suitcase full of clothes and underwear in my hand and an indomitable will in my heart, I set out for Vienna...I too hoped to become "something."
Mein Kampf (1933)

31 All those who are not racially pure are mere chaff.
Mein Kampf (1933), ch. 2

32 Only constant repetition will finally succeed in imprinting an idea on the memory of the crowd.
Mein Kampf (1933), ch. 6

33 The broad mass of a nation...will more easily fall victim to a big lie than to a small one.
Mein Kampf (1933), ch. 10

34 Germany will be either a world power or will not be at all.
Mein Kampf (1933), ch. 14

35 German misery must be broken by German steel! That time must come!
1919. Quoted in *Germany, 1866–1945* (Gordon A. Craig; 1978), ch. 19

36 Russia is our Africa, and the Russians are our Negroes.
Referring to the imperial and military ambition of Germany, compared with that of other European imperial powers in relation to Africa. Quoted in *Germany, 1866–1945* (Gordon A. Craig; 1978), ch. 20

37 Everything about the behavior of American society reveals that it is half judaised and half negrified. How can one expect a state like that to hold together?
Hitler's Table Talk (Norman Cameron and R. H. Stevens, trs.; 1953), pt. 2

38 Is Paris burning?
Referring to the liberation of Paris by the Allies. (August 25, 1944), quoted in *Is Paris Burning?* (Larry Collins and Dominique Lapierre; 1965), ch. 5

39 The final solution of the Jewish problem.
Referring to the proposed extermination of the Jews in the concentration camps. Quoted in *The Final Solution* (Gerald Reitlinger; 1968)

40 It was no secret that this time the revolution would have to be bloody...When we spoke of it, we called it "The Night of the Long Knives."
Referring to the murder of Hitler's opponents within the Nazi Party on June 29–30, 1934. "Night of the Long Knives" was taken by Hitler from an early Nazi marching song. Quoted in *The House Hitler Built* (S. H. Roberts; 1937), pt. 2, ch. 3

41 In starting and waging a war it is not right that matters, but victory.
Quoted in *The Rise and Fall of the Third Reich* (W. L. Shirer; 1960), ch. 16

42 When Barbarossa commences, the world will hold its breath and make no comment.
Referring to the invasion of the Soviet Union, Operation Barbarossa, which began on June 22, 1941. Attrib.

Hoagland, Edward (b.1932) U.S. novelist, naturalist, and essayist

1 Baseball has stood for loyalty to the verities, memories of innocence, patience with ritual; surely no one who cared about baseball could be an opportunist at heart.
"A Fan's Notes" (1977)

2 Man is different from animals in that he speculates, a high risk activity.
"Heaven and Nature," *Heart's Desire* (1988)

3 There are desperate suicides and crafty suicides, people who do it to cause others trouble and people who do it to save others trouble.
"Heaven and Nature," *Heart's Desire* (1988)

4 Texas is still a good place to be rich in.
1974. "Lament the Red Wolf," *Heart's Desire* (1988)

5 Whereas in the woods that fellow with the swamp shanty and two cabbagey acres owns everything the eye can see, on the prairie it takes a rich man to feel so proprietary.
1974. "Lament the Red Wolf," *Heart's Desire* (1988)

6 The great leveler nowadays is divorce; almost everybody thinks about it, whether because we expect to be happy all the time—daily, weekly—or because we want the smell of brimstone in lives made too affluent and easy.
1973. "Other Lives," *Heart's Desire* (1988)

7 The very root of my own hopefulness is a long stint I spent working in an army morgue—the odd smiles of most of the

dead as death had overtaken them and the nature of death had dawned on them.
1977. "The Ridge Slope and the Knife Thrower," *Heart's Desire* (1988)

8 Evolution has been a matter of days well-lived, chameleon strength, energy, zappy sex, sunshine stored up, inventiveness, competitiveness, and the whole fun of busy brain cells.
1972. "Thoughts on Returning to the City," *Heart's Desire* (1988)

9 One can risk one's life in the jungly districts of a city too, after all; that does not make it what we call a wilderness, there being no jubilation of *discovery*.
1973. "The New England Wilderness," *The Moose on the Wall* (1974)

10 Strength and a gift for physical feats are also unequally bestowed, and daring men look down just as condescendingly as some of the rich do on those passers-by who are unendowed.
1973. "The New England Wilderness," *The Moose on the Wall* (1974)

11 The contrast of absentee wealth and resident poverty, along with the fact that a kind of miniature frontier was preserved, have made for a special buccaneering spirit which is characteristic of Maine.
1973. "The New England Wilderness," *The Moose on the Wall* (1974)

Hoban, Russell (b.1925) U.S.-born British novelist, children's writer, and illustrator

1 When you suffer an attack of nerves you're being attacked by the nervous system. What chance has a man got against a system?
The Lion of Boaz-Jachin and Jachin-Boaz (1973), ch. 13

2 But when I don't smoke I scarcely feel as if I'm living. I don't feel as if I'm living unless I'm killing myself.
Turtle Diary (1975), ch. 7

Hobbes, Thomas (1588–1679) English philosopher and political thinker

1 Method, therefore, in the study of philosophy, is the shortest way of finding effects by their known causes, or of causes by their known effects.
Elements of Philosophy (1656)

2 Laughter is nothing else but sudden glory arising from some sudden conception of some eminency in ourselves, by comparison with the infirmity of others, or with our own formerly.
Human Nature (1650), ch. 9, sect. 13

3 A man that seeketh precise truth had need to remember what every name he uses stands for, and to place it accordingly, or else he will find himself entangled in words, as a bird in lime twigs, the more he struggles, the more belimed.
Leviathan (1651)

4 For it is most true that Cicero saith of them somewhere; that there can be nothing so absurd, but may be found in the books of the philosophers.
Leviathan (1651)

5 He that will do anything for his pleasure, must engage himself to suffer all the pains attached to it.
Leviathan (1651)

6 The opinions of the world, both in ancient and later ages, concerning the cause of madness, have been two. Some, deriving them from the passions; some from demons, or spirits, either good or bad, which they thought might enter into a man, possess him, and move his organs in such strange, and uncouth manner.
Leviathan (1651)

7 To this war of every man, against every man, this also is consequent; that nothing can be unjust. The notions of right and wrong, justice and injustice have there no place. Where there is no common power, there is no law; where no law, no injustice.
Leviathan (1651)

8 Geometry (which is the only science that it hath pleased God hitherto to bestow on mankind)—men begin at settling the significations of their words: which...they call Definitions.
Leviathan (1651), pt. 1, ch. 4

9 The condition of man...is a condition of war of everyone against everyone.
Leviathan (1651), pt. 1, ch. 4

10 True and False are attributes of speech, not of things. And where speech is not, there is neither Truth nor Falsehood.
Leviathan (1651), pt. 1, ch. 4

11 They that approve a private opinion, call it opinion; but they that mislike it, heresy: and yet heresy signifies no more than private opinion.
Leviathan (1651), pt. 1, ch. 11

12 Force and fraud are in war the two cardinal virtues.
Leviathan (1651), pt. 1, ch. 13

13 No arts; no letters; no society; and which is worst of all, continual fear and danger of violent death; and the life of man, solitary, poor, nasty, brutish, and short.
Leviathan (1651), pt. 1, ch. 13

14 Covenants without the sword are but words and of no strength to secure a man at all.
Leviathan (1651), pt. 2, ch. 17

15 The only way to erect such a common power, as may be able to defend them from the invasion of foreigners, and the injuries of one another...is, to confer all their power and strength upon one man, or upon one assembly of men, that may reduce all their wills, by plurality of voices, unto one will...This is the generation of that great Leviathan, or rather (to speak more reverently) of that Mortal God, to which we owe under the Immortal God, our peace and defence.
Leviathan (1651), pt. 2, ch. 17

16 They that are discontented under *monarchy*, call it *tyranny*; and they that are displeased with *aristocracy*, call it *oligarchy*; so also, they which find themselves grieved under a *democracy*, call it *anarchy*, which signifies the want of government; and yet I think no man believes, that want of government, is any new kind of government.
Leviathan (1651), pt. 2, ch. 19

17 The Papacy is no other than the ghost of the deceased Roman

empire, sitting crowned upon the grave thereof.
Leviathan (1651), pt. 4, ch. 47

18 In the mere state of nature, if you have a mind to kill, that state itself affords you a right.
Philosophical Rudiments: Concerning Government and Society (1642)

19 I am about to take my last voyage, a great leap in the dark.
1679. Last words. Quoted in *Anecdotes of Men of Learning* (John Watkins; 1808)

Hobson, John (John Atkinson Hobson; 1858–1940) British economist

1 Security is...the first essential in any shift of relative appeal to personal and social motives.
Economics and Ethics (1929)

Hoby, Edward, Sir (1560–1617) English politician, diplomat, and controversialist

1 On the 5th of November we began our Parliament, to which the King should have come in person, but refrained, through a practice but that morning discovered. The plot was to have blown up the King.
Referring to the Gunpowder Plot (November 5, 1605), the attempted assassination of James I by a group of Catholic conspirators, including most famously Guy Fawkes. Letter to Sir Thomas Edmondes (November 19, 1605)

Hochhuth, Rolf (b.1931) German playwright

1 The man who says what he thinks is finished, and the man who thinks what he says is an idiot.
The Representative (1963)

Hockney, David (b.1937) British artist

1 Art has to move you and design does not, unless it's a good design for a bus.
Guardian, London (October 26, 1988)

2 It is very good advice to believe only what an artist does, rather than what he says about his work.
Attrib.

Hodgins, Eric (1899–1971) U.S. writer and editor

1 A miracle drug is any drug that will do what the label says it will do.
Episode (1964)

Hodgkin, Dorothy (originally Dorothy Mary Crowfoot; 1910–94) Egyptian-born British crystallographer and chemist

1 I'm really an experimentalist. I used to say "I think with my hands." I just like manipulation.
Quoted in *A Passion for Science* (Lewis Wolpert and Alison Richards; 1988)

Hoff, Ted (Marcian Edward Hoff, Jr.; b.1937) U.S. electronics engineer

1 It's like a light bulb. When it's broken, unplug it, throw it away and plug in another.
Explaining how he would repair a computer. Attrib.

Hoffa, Jimmy (James Riddle Hoffa; 1913–75?) U.S. labor leader

1 You will only get what you are big enough to take.
Referring to labor unions and American businesses. Attrib.

Hoffer, Eric (1902–83) U.S. philosopher and longshoreman

1 To have a grievance is to have a purpose in life.
The Passionate State of Mind (1954)

2 When people are free to do as they please, they usually imitate each other.
The Passionate State of Mind (1954)

3 Man's chief goal in life is still to become and stay human, and defend his achievements against the encroachment of nature.
"The Return of Nature," *The Temper of Our Time* (1967)

4 We have rudiments of reverence for the human body, but we consider as nothing the rape of the human mind.
Quoted in *Bartlett's Unfamiliar Quotations* (Leonard Louis Levinson; 1972)

5 You can discover what your enemy fears most by observing the means he uses to frighten you.
Quoted in *The Faber Book of Aphorisms* (1964)

6 It is the malady of our age that the young are so busy teaching us that they have no time left to learn.
Attrib.

Hoffman, Abbie (Abbott Hoffman; 1936–89) U.S. political activist

1 In American society, the university is traditionally considered to be a psychosocial moratorium, an ivory tower where you withdraw from the problems of society and the world around you to work on important things like your career and your marriage.
Speech, University of South Carolina (September 16, 1987)

2 The Constitution was based on the old English law that a man's home is his castle. It was designed essentially to protect individuals from government intrusion. That is a good deal for men who own castles.
Speech, University of South Carolina (September 16, 1987)

3 The idea that the media is there to educate us, or to inform us, is ridiculous because that's about tenth or eleventh on their list. The first purpose of the media is to sell us shit.
Speech, University of South Carolina (September 16, 1987)

4 Sacred cows make the tastiest hamburger.
Attrib.

Hoffman, Charles Fenno (1806–84) U.S. poet

1 Sparkling and bright in liquid light
Does the wine our goblets gleam in;
With hue as red as the rosy bed
Which a bee would choose to dream in.
"Sparkling and Bright," *An American Anthology 1787–1900* (Edmund Clarence Steadman, ed.; 1900)

Hoffman, Dustin (b.1937) U.S. actor

1 Mrs. Robinson, if you don't mind me saying so, this conversation is getting a little strange.
As Benjamin, reacting to Mrs. Robinson's attempts to seduce him. *The Graduate* (Calder Willingham and Buck Henry; 1967)

Hoffman, Heinrich (1809–94) German physician and poet

1 At this, good Tray grew very red,
And growled, and bit him till he bled.
"Cruel Frederick," *Struwwelpeter* (1845)

2 Here is cruel Frederick, see!
A horrid wicked boy was he.
"Cruel Frederick," *Struwwelpeter* (1845)

3 Look at little Johnny there,
Little Johnny Head-in-Air.
"Johnny Head-in-Air," *Struwwelpeter* (1845)

4 Anything to me is sweeter
Than to see Shock-headed Peter.
"Shock-headed Peter," *Struwwelpeter* (1845)

5 The door flew open, in he ran,
The great, long, red-legged scissor-man
"Ah!" said Mamma, "I knew he'd come
To naughty little Suck-a-Thumb."
"The Little Suck-a-Thumb," *Struwwelpeter* (1845)

6 He finds it hard, without a pair
Of spectacles, to shoot the hare.
The hare sits snug in leaves and grass,
And laughs to see the green man pass.
"The Man Who Went Out Shooting," *Struwwelpeter* (1845)

Hoffmann, Amadeus (Ernst Theodor Wilhelm Hoffmann, "Amadeus"; 1776–1822) German writer and composer

1 He's a wicked man that comes after children when they won't go to bed and throws handfuls of sand in their eyes.
"The Sandman," *Fantastic Pieces in the Manner of Callot* (1815), vol. 2

Hoffmann, Max (1869–1927) German general

1 LUDENDORFF The English soldiers fight like lions.
HOFFMANN True. But don't we know that they are lions led by donkeys.
1915. Referring to the performance of the British army in World War I. Quoted in *The Donkeys* (Alan Clark; 1961), Epigraph

Hoffmann von Fallersleben, Heinrich (August Heinrich Hoffmann; 1798–1874) German poet, philologist, and composer

1 Germany, Germany before all else
Title of poem. "Deutschland, Deutschland über alles" (1841)

Hofmann, Hans (1880–1966) German-born U.S. painter and teacher

1 The ability to simplify means to eliminate the unnecessary so that the necessary may speak.
Search for the Real (1967)

Hofstadter, Douglas R. (b.1945) U.S. physicist and writer

1 Hofstadter's Law: It always takes longer than you expect, even when you take into account Hofstadter's Law.
Gödel, Escher, Bach: An Eternal Golden Braid (1979)

2 If I were meta-agnostic, I'd be confused over whether I'm agnostic or not—but I'm not quite sure if I feel that way; hence I must be meta-meta-agnostic, I guess.
Gödel, Escher, Bach: An Eternal Golden Braid (1979)

Hofstadter, Richard (1916–70) U.S. historian

1 It is ironic that the United States should have been founded by intellectuals; for throughout most of our political history the intellectual has been for the most part either an outsider, a servant, or a scapegoat.
Anti-Intellectualism in American Life (1963)

2 It is the nature of politics that conflict stands in the foreground, and historians usually abet the politicians in keeping it there.
The American Political Tradition and the Men Who Made It (1948)

3 Memory is the thread of personal identity, history of public identity.
The Progressive Historians (1968)

Hogarth, William (1697–1764) English painter and engraver

1 Serious dancing is a contradiction in terms.
Quoted in *Dance to the Piper* (Agnes De Mille; 1987)

2 Comedy in painting, as well as in writing, ought to be allotted the first place.
Quoted in *Hogarth Illustrated* (John Ireland; 1812)

Hogg, James ("The Ettrick Shepherd"; 1770–1835) Scottish writer and shepherd

1 Where the pools are bright and deep,
Where the grey trout lies asleep,
Up the river and o'er the lea,
That's the way for Billy and me.
"A Boy's Song," *A Poetic Mirror 1829–1831* (1831), st. 1

2 God bless our Lord the King!
God save our lord the king!
God save the king!
Make him victorious,
Happy, and glorious,
Long to reign over us:
God save the king!
"The King's Anthem," *Jacobite Relics of Scotland, Second Series* (1821)

Hogg, Michael, Sir (b.1925) British journalist

1 Good taste is, of course, an utterly dispensable part of any journalist's equipment.
Daily Telegraph, London (December 2, 1978)

Hokusai (Katsushika Hokusai; 1760–1849) Japanese painter and engraver

1 If heaven had granted me five more years, I could have become a real painter.
1849. Last words. Quoted in *Famous Last Words* (Barnaby Conrad; 1962)

Holanda, Francisco de (1517–84) Italian painter and writer

1 I declare that no nation or people (I except one or two Spaniards) can perfectly attain or imitate the Italian manner of painting (which is that of ancient Greece) in such a way that it will not immediately be seen to be foreign, however much they may strive and toil.
Quoted in *Four Dialogues on Painting* (Aubrey F. G. Bell, tr.; 1928)

Holberg, Ludvig, Baron Holberg (1684–1754) Danish poet, playwright, and philosopher

1 Do you call that thing under your hat a head?
Reply to the jibe: "Do you call that thing on your head a hat?" Attrib.

Hölderlin, Friedrich (Johann Christian Friedrich Hölderlin; 1770–1843) German poet

1 Things divine are believed in
But by those who themselves are so.
"Applause of Men" (1796–97), quoted in *Selected Poems* (J. B. Leishman, ed. and tr.; 1944)

2 I can conceive of no people more dismembered than the Germans. You see workmen but no human beings, thinkers but no human beings, priests but no human beings, masters and servants, youths and staid people, but no human beings.
Hyperion (1799), vol. 2, bk. 2

Holdsworth, Trevor, Sir (George Trevor Holdsworth; b.1927) British business executive

1 Most success comes from ignoring the obvious.
Quoted in *The New Elite* (Berry Ritchie and Walter Goldsmith; 1987)

Holiday, Billie (originally Eleanora Fagan, "Lady Day"; 1915–59) U.S. jazz singer

1 Them that's got shall get
Them that's not shall lose
So the Bible says
And it still is news
Mama may have
Papa may have,
But God bless the child that's got his own.
God Bless the Child (E. R. Marks; 1941)

2 I can't stand to sing the same song the same way two nights in succession, let alone two years or ten years. If you can, then it ain't music, it's close-order drill, or exercise or yodeling or something, not music.
Lady Sings the Blues (co-written with William Duffy; 1956)

3 Mom and Pop were just a couple of kids when they got married. He was eighteen, she was sixteen, and I was three.
Lady Sings the Blues (co-written with William Duffy; 1956)

4 People don't understand the sort of fight it takes to record what you want, to record the way you want to record it.
Lady Sings the Blues (co-written with William Duffy; 1956)

5 You can be up to your boobies in white satin, with gardenias in your hair and no sugar cane for miles, but you can still be working on a plantation.
Lady Sings the Blues (co-written with William Duffy; 1956)

Holland, Henry Fox, 1st Baron (1705–74) British statesman

1 If Mr. Selwyn calls again, shew him up: if I am alive I shall be delighted to see him; and if I am dead he would like to see me.
1774. Said during his last illness. George Selwyn was known for his morbid fascination with corpses. Quoted in *George Selwyn and his Contemporaries* (J. H. Jesse; 1843–44), vol. 3

Hollinghurst, Alan (b.1954) British novelist

1 It was the year of Trouble for Men, a talc and aftershave lotion of peculiar suggestiveness that, without any noticeable advertising, had permeated the gay world in a matter of weeks.
The Swimming-Pool Library (1988)

Holloway, David (b.1924) British literary editor

1 The business of being a child interests a child not at all. Children very rarely play at being other children.
Daily Telegraph, London (December 15, 1966)

Holloway, Joseph (1861–1944) Irish theater critic

1 Last year it was all Sean O'Casey: now it is all shun O'Casey.
"Impressions of a Dublin Playgoer" (August 30, 1926)

Holmes, John Haynes (1879–1964) U.S. clergyman

1 The universe is not hostile, nor yet is it friendly. It is simply indifferent.
A Sensible Man's View of Religion (1933), ch. 4

Holmes, Oliver Wendell (1809–94) U.S. physician and writer

1 Truth is the breath of life to human society. It is the food of the immortal spirit. Yet a single word of it may kill a man as suddenly as a drop of prussic acid.
Address at Harvard Commencement (March 10, 1858)

2 The mortmain of theorists extinct in science clings as close as that of ecclesiastics defunct in law.
Address, Massachusetts Medical Society, Boston, Massachusetts (May 30, 1860)

3 What I call a good patient is one who, having found a good physician, sticks to him till he dies.
Lecture, New York (March 2, 1871)

4 Wisdom has taught us to be calm and meek,
To take one blow, and turn the other cheek;
It is not written what a man shall do
If the rude caitiff smite the other too!
"Non-Resistance" (1861)

5 No families take so little medicine as those of doctors, except those of apothecaries.
"Apothecary" means "chemist," "pharmacist," or "druggist." "Currents and Counter-Currents in Medical Science," *Medical Essays* 1842–1882 (1891)

6 Science is the topography of ignorance.
Medical Essays 1842–1882 (1891)

7 It is so hard to get anything out of the dead hand of medical tradition!
"Currents and Counter-Currents in Medical Science," *Medical Essays* 1842–1882 (1891)

8 *Nature*, in medical language, as opposed to Art, means trust in the reactions of the living system against ordinary normal impressions.
Art, in the same language, as opposed to Nature, means an intentional resort to extraordinary abnormal impressions for the relief of disease.
"Currents and Counter-Currents in Medical Science," *Medical Essays* 1842–1882 (1891)

9 Opium...the Creator himself seems to prescribe, for we often see the scarlet poppy growing in the cornfields, as if it were foreseen that whatever hunger there is to be fed there must also be pain to be soothed.
"Currents and Counter-Currents in Medical Science," *Medical Essays* 1842–1882 (1891)

10 The truth is, that medicine, professedly founded on observation, is as sensitive to outside influences, political, religious, philosophical, imaginative, as is the barometer to the changes of atmospheric density.
"Currents and Counter-Currents in Medical Science," *Medical Essays* 1842–1882 (1891)

11 Homeopathy...a mingled mass of perverse ingenuity, of tinsel erudition, of imbecile credulity, and of artful misrepresentation, too often mingled in practice...with heartless and shameless imposition.
"Homeopathy and Its Kindred Delusions," *Medical Essays* 1842–1882 (1891)

12 So long as the body is affected through the mind, no audacious device, even of the most manifestly dishonest character, can fail of producing occasional good to those who yield it an implicit or even a partial faith.
"Homeopathy and Its Kindred Delusions," *Medical Essays* 1842–1882 (1891)

13 A good clinical teacher is himself a Medical School.
"Scholastic and Bedside Teaching," *Medical Essays* 1842–1882 (1891)

14 I would never use a long word, even, where a short one would answer the purpose. I know there are professors in this country who "ligate" arteries. Other surgeons only tie them, and it stops the bleeding just as well.
"Scholastic and Bedside Teaching," *Medical Essays* 1842–1882 (1891)

15 The bedside is always the true center of medical teaching.
"Scholastic and Bedside Teaching," *Medical Essays* 1842–1882 (1891)

16 The lancet was the magician's wand of the dark ages of medicine.
"Some of My Early Teachers," *Medical Essays* 1842–1882 (1891)

17 Three natural anesthetics...sleep, fainting, death.
"The Medical Profession in Massachusetts," *Medical Essays* 1842–1882 (1891)

18 Nature is a benevolent old hypocrite; she cheats the sick and the dying with illusions better than any anodynes.
"The Young Practitioner," *Medical Essays* 1842–1882 (1891)

19 Once in a while you will have a patient of sense, born with the gift of observation, from whom you may learn something.
"The Young Practitioner," *Medical Essays* 1842–1882 (1891)

20 Remember that even the learned ignorance of a nomenclature is something to have mastered, and may furnish pegs to hang facts upon which would otherwise have strewed the floor of memory in loose disorder.
"The Young Practitioner," *Medical Essays* 1842–1882 (1891)

21 A thought is often original, though you have uttered it a hundred times. It has come to you over a new route, by a new and express train of associations.
The Autocrat of the Breakfast-Table (1858), ch. 1

22 Insanity is often the logic of an accurate mind overtaxed.
The Autocrat of the Breakfast-Table (1858), ch. 2

23 Put not your trust in money, but put your money in trust.
The Autocrat of the Breakfast-Table (1858), ch. 2

24 The axis of the earth sticks out visibly through the center of each and every town or city.
The Autocrat of the Breakfast-Table (1858), ch. 6

25 The world's great men have not commonly been great scholars, nor great scholars great men.
The Autocrat of the Breakfast-Table (1858), ch. 6

26 Man has his will,—but woman has her way.
The Autocrat of the Breakfast-Table (1858), prologue

27 His home! the Western giant smiles,
And twirls the spotty globe to find it;
This little speck, the British Isles?
'T is but a freckle,—never mind it.
"A Good Time Going!," *The Complete Poetical Works of Oliver Wendell Holmes* (1912)

28 Go on, fair science, soon to thee
Shall nature yield her idle boast;
Her vulgar fingers formed a tree,
But thou hast trained it to a post.
The Meeting of the Dryads (1830)

29 Science is a first-rate piece of furniture for a man's upper chamber, if he has common sense on the ground floor.
The Poet at the Breakfast-Table (1872)

30 It is the province of knowledge to speak and it is the privilege of wisdom to listen.
The Poet at the Breakfast-Table (1872), ch. 10

31 Life is a fatal complaint, and an eminently contagious one.
The Poet at the Breakfast-Table (1872), ch. 12

32 A moment's insight is sometimes worth a life's experience.
The Professor at the Breakfast-Table (1860), ch. 10

33 The mind, once expanded to the dimensions of larger ideas, never returns to its original size.
Attrib.

34 Have a chronic disease and take care of it.
His formula for longevity. Attrib.

Holmes, Oliver Wendell, Jr. ("The Great Dissenter"; 1841–1935) U.S. judge

1 The law is the witness and external deposit of our moral life. Its history is the history of the moral development of the race.
Speech, Boston (January 8, 1897)

2 The most stringent protection of free speech would not protect a man in falsely shouting "Fire!" in a theater and causing a panic.
Supreme Court opinion, *Schenck vs. United States* (1919)

3 A page of history is worth a volume of logic.
New York Trust Co. vs. Eisner (1921)

4 The history of what the law has been is necessary to the knowledge of what the law is.
The Common Law (1881)

5 The life of the law has not been logic; it has been experience. The law embodies the story of a nation's development...it cannot be dealt with as if it contained the axioms and corollaries of a book of mathematics.
The Common Law (1881)

6 Oh, to be seventy again!
1928. Said in his 87th year, while watching a pretty girl. Quoted in *The American Treasury* (Clifton Fadiman; 1955)

7 Many ideas grow better when transplanted into another mind than in the one where they sprang up.
Quoted in *Yankee from Olympus* (C. Bowen; 1945)

8 War? War is an organized bore.
Quoted in *Yankee from Olympus* (C. Bowen; 1945)

Holmes à Court, Robert (Michael Robert Hamilton Holmes à Court; 1937–90) Australian entrepreneur

1 It's a well-known proposition that you know who's going to win a negotiation: it's he who pauses the longest.
Sydney Morning Herald (May 24, 1986)

2 Big business is only small business with an extra nought on the end.
Sydney Morning Herald (August 25, 1985), "Sayings of the Week"

Holst, Gustav (Gustave Theodore Holst; 1874–1934) British composer

1 Never compose anything unless the not composing of it becomes a positive nuisance to you.
Letter to W. G. Whittaker (1921)

Holub, Miroslav (1923–98) Czech poet and immunologist

1 Radioactivity created by people is a horror. Radioactivity in a piece of granite is fine, because it is natural.
"By Nature Alone," *Shedding Life* (1997)

2 The pastoral is an aesthetic category for aristocrats and city folk, not for stable hands.
"By Nature Alone," *Shedding Life* (1997)

3 To a human being who is allowed to go on living and pursuing questions about the meaning of life by means of a heart or kidney transplant and the discovery of cyclosporin A, the problem of interference with the wisdom of nature may appear to be rather an abstract question.
"From the Amoeba to the Philosopher," *Shedding Life* (1997)

4 By today's medical standards, Mozart would have written *La Clemenza di Tito* and the *Requiem* on dialysis, while awaiting a transplant.
"This Long Disease," *Shedding Life* (1997)

5 The angel of disease is kith and kin, identical with the historical phenomenon of people. There wouldn't be any people if there were no evolutionary pressures from disease and death.
"This Long Disease," *Shedding Life* (1997)

6 A scientific society is based on respect and dissent: it is by definition a democracy.
"Whatever the Circumstances," *Shedding Life* (1997)

7 Immunologists are the function of a culture in which jumping to conclusions means endangering the survival of men, women, and infants.
"Zen and the Thymus," *Shedding Life* (1997)

Homer (*fl.* 8th century B.C.) Greek poet

Quotations about Homer

1 I'm aggrieved when sometimes even excellent Homer nods.
Horace (*fl.* 65–8 B.C.) Roman poet. *Ars Poetica* (19–8 B.C.), l. 359

2 "It's like the question of the authorship of the *Iliad*," said Mr Cardan. "The author of that poem is either Homer or, if not Homer, somebody else of the same name."
Aldous Huxley (1894–1963) British novelist and essayist. *Those Barren Leaves* (1925), pt. 5, ch. 4

3 With the single exception of Homer, there is no eminent writer, not even Sir Walter Scott, whom I can despise so entirely as I despise Shakespeare when I measure my mind against his...It would positively be a relief to me to dig him up and throw stones at him.
George Bernard Shaw (1856–1950) Irish playwright. "Blaming the Bard," *Dramatic Opinions and Essays* (1907)

Quotations by Homer

4 The immortals will send you to the Elysian plain at the ends of the earth, where fair-haired Rhadamanthys is. There life is supremely easy for men. No snow is there, nor ever heavy winter storm, nor rain, and Ocean is ever sending gusts of the clear-blowing west wind to bring coolness to men.
The Elysian plains or fields (also known as Elysium), were the mythical land at the farthest corner of the earth where distinguished heroes were carried after they died and immortalized. They were considered to be a paradisal utopia. *Iliad* (8th century B.C.), bk. 4, ll. 563–569

5 Olympus, where they say there is an abode of the gods, ever unchanging: it is neither shaken by winds nor ever wet with rain, nor does snow come near it, but clear weather spreads cloudless about it, and a white radiance stretches above it.
Iliad (8th century B.C.), bk. 6, ll. 42–47

6 There were youths dancing, and maidens of costly wooing, their hands upon one another's wrists...And a great company stood round the lovely dance in joy; and among them a divine minstrel was making music on his lyre, and through the midst of them, leading the measure, two tumblers whirled.
Iliad (8th century B.C.), bk. 18, ll. 592–606

7 For who could see the passage of a goddess
unless she wished his mortal eyes aware?
Odyssey (Robert Fitzgerald, tr.; Late 8th century B.C.), bk. 10, ll. 575–576

8 Better, I say, to break sod as a farm hand
for some poor country man, on iron rations,
than lord it over all the exhausted dead.
Odyssey (Robert Fitzgerald, tr.; Late 8th century B.C.), bk. 11, ll. 495–497

9 Square in your ship's path are Seirênês, crying beauty
to bewitch men coasting by; woe to the innocent who hears
that sound!
Odyssey (Robert Fitzgerald, tr.; Late 8th century B.C.), bk. 12, ll. 41–42

10 The first prize was a woman skilled in graceful handicraft and a tripod with two handles holding twenty-two measures.
8th century B.C. First prize awarded by Achilles to the victor in a chariot race. Quoted in "Chariot Racing in the Ancient World," *History Today* (D. Bennett; December 1997)

Hone, William (1780–1842) British writer and bookseller

1 John Jones may be described as "one of the has beens".
Referring to the Welsh writer and poet, influenced by Thomas Paine and the French Revolution, who wrote satirical pamphlets under the pen name Jac Glan-y-Gors. *Every-Day Book* (1826–27), vol. 2, l. 820

Honegger, Arthur (1892–1955) French composer

1 The first requirement for a composer is to be dead.
Je suis compositeur (1951)

Hood, Samuel, 6th Viscount Hood (1910–81) British diplomat

1 Some people reach the age of 60 before others.
Observer, London (February 23, 1969), "Sayings of the Week"

Hood, Thomas (1799–1845) British poet and humorist

1 Straight down the Crooked Lane,
And all round the Square.
"A Plain Direction," , st. 1, ll. 7–8, quoted in *The Works of Thomas Hood* (1862–63)

2 When Eve upon the first of Men
The apple press'd with specious cant,
Oh! what a thousand pities then
That Adam was not Adamant!
"A Reflection" (1842)

3 When he's forsaken,
Wither'd and shaken,
What can an old man do but die?
"Ballad—Spring it is Cheery," , st. 1, ll. 4–6, quoted in *The Works of Thomas Hood* (1862–63)

4 His death, which happen'd in his berth,
At forty-odd befell:
They went and told the sexton, and
The sexton toll'd the bell.
"Faithless Sally Brown" (1826)

5 I remember, I remember,
The house where I was born,
The little window where the sun
Came peeping in at morn;
He never came a wink too soon,
Nor brought too long a day,
But now, I often wish the night
Had borne my breath away!
"I Remember" (1826)

6 For that old enemy the gout
Had taken him in toe!
"Lieutenant Luff," , ll. 35–36, quoted in *The Works of Thomas Hood* (1862–63)

7 For my part, getting up seems not so easy
By half as lying.
"Morning Meditations," , st. 1, ll. 3–4, quoted in *The Works of Thomas Hood* (1862–63)

8 No warmth, no cheerfulness, no healthful ease,
No comfortable feel in any member—
No shade, no shine, no butterflies, no bees,
No fruits, no flowers, no leaves, no birds,—
November!
"No!" (1844)

9 I saw old Autumn in the misty morn
Stand shadowless like Silence, listening
To silence.
"Ode: Autumn" (1827), st. 1

10 Alas for the rarity
Of Christian charity
Under the sun!
"The Bridge of Sighs" (1844), st. 9

11 He never spoils the child and spares the rod,
But spoils the rod and never spares the child.
"The Irish Schoolmaster," , ll. 106–107, quoted in *The Works of Thomas Hood* (1862–63)

12 But evil is wrought by want of thought,
As well as want of heart!
"The Lady's Dream" (1844)

13 O! men with sisters dear,
O! men with mothers and wives!
It is not linen you're wearing out,
But human creatures' lives!
"The Song of the Shirt" (1843), st. 4

14 Oh! God! that bread should be so dear,
And flesh and blood so cheap!
"The Song of the Shirt" (1843), st. 5

15 A wife who preaches in her gown,
And lectures in her night-dress!
"The Surplice Question," , ll. 11–12, quoted in *The Works of Thomas Hood* (1862–63)

16 There are three things which the public will always clamour for, sooner or later: namely, Novelty, novelty, novelty.
Comic Annual (1836)

17 For one of the pleasures of having a rout,
Is the pleasure of having it over.
"Her Dream," *Miss Kilmansegg and Her Precious Leg* (1841–43)

18 He lies like a hedgehog rolled up the wrong way,
Tormenting himself with his prickles.
"Her Dream," *Miss Kilmansegg and Her Precious Leg* (1841–43)

19 O bed! O bed! delicious bed!
That heaven upon earth to the weary head!
"Her Dream," *Miss Kilmansegg and Her Precious Leg* (1841–43)

20 Holland...lies so low they're only saved by being dammed.
"Letter from Martha Penny to Rebecca Page," *Up the Rhine* (1840)

21 Ben Battle was a soldier bold,
And used to war's alarms:
But a cannon-ball took off his legs,
So he laid down his arms!
"Faithless Nelly Gray," *Whims and Oddities* (1826)

22 What is a modern poet's fate?
To write his thoughts upon a slate;
The critic spits on what is done,
Gives it a wipe and all is gone.
Quoted in *Alfred Lord Tennyson: A Memoir* (Hallam Tennyson; 1895?), vol, 2, ch. 3

Hook, Sidney (1902–89) U.S. philosopher and educator

1 The history of societies, despite the succession of different political *forms*, is in substance nothing but the succession of different political elites.
The Hero in History: a Study in Limitation and Possibility (1943)

2 We must rule out as irrelevant the conception of the hero as a morally worthy man, not because ethical judgments are illegitimate in history, but because so much of it has been made by the wicked.
Attrib.

Hooker, Richard (1554?–1600) English theologian

1 He that goeth about to persuade a multitude, that they are not so well governed as they ought to be, shall never want attentive and favourable hearers.
Of the Laws of Ecclesiastical Polity (1594), bk. 1

2 To live by one man's will became the cause of all men's misery.
Of the Laws of Ecclesiastical Polity (1594), bk. 1

3 Change is not made without inconvenience, even from worse to better.
Quoted in *Johnson's English Dictionary* (Samuel Johnson; 1755), preface

hooks, bell (Gloria Watkins; b.1952) U.S. feminist writer, poet, and educator

1 Male domination has not destroyed the longing men and women have to love one another, even though it makes fulfilling that longing almost impossible to realize.
"feminist focus on men: a comment," *Talking Back* (1989)

2 Within patriarchal society, women who are victimized by male violence have had to pay a price for breaking the silence and naming the problem. They have had to be seen as fallen women, who have failed in their "feminine" role to sensitize and civilize the beast in the man.
"violence in intimate relationships: a feminist perspective," *Talking Back* (1989)

Hoover, Herbert (Herbert Clark Hoover; 1874–1964) U.S. president

Quotations about Hoover

1 He wouldn't commit himself to the time of day from a hatful of watches.
1929?
Westbrook Pegler (1894–1969) U.S. journalist. *Pegler: Angry Man of the Press* (1963)

2 Nothing doing on politics.
Babe Ruth (1895–1948) U.S. baseball player. Declining to have his photograph taken with presidential nominee Herbert Hoover. Remark (1928)

3 Such a little man could not have made such a big depression.
Norman Thomas (1884–1968) U.S. reformer and politician. Herbert Hoover was U.S. president during the Great Depression (1929–early 1940s). Letter to Murray B. Seidler (August 3, 1960)

Quotations by Hoover

4 In no nation are the fruits of accomplishment more secure...I have no fears for the future of our country. It is bright with hope.
Inaugural address, Washington, D.C. (March 4, 1929)

5 Our country has deliberately undertaken a great social and economic experiment, noble in motive and far-reaching in purpose.
Referring to Prohibition. Letter to Senator W. H. Borah (February 23, 1928)

6 We in America are nearer to the final triumph over poverty than ever before in the history of any land.
One year from this statement the stock market crashed, losing $40 billion. Speech (November 3, 1928), quoted in *Guide to Political Quotations* (Caroline Rathbone and Michael Stephenson; 1985)

7 We are challenged with a peace-time choice between the American system of rugged individualism and a European philosophy of diametrically opposed doctrines—doctrines of paternalism and state socialism.
Speech, New York City (October 22, 1928)

8 Older men declare war. But it is youth that must fight and die.
Speech to the Republican National Convention, Chicago (June 27, 1944)

9 The grass will grow in the streets of a hundred cities, a thousand towns; the weeds will overrun the fields of millions of farms if that protection is taken away.
October 31, 1932. Speech on proposals "to reduce the protective tariff to a competitive tariff for revenue." *State Papers of Herbert Hoover* (1934), vol. 2

10 The supreme purpose of history is a better world.
Quoted in *The Meaning of History* (N. Gordon and Joyce Carper; 1991)

11 Next to religion, baseball has furnished a greater impact on American life than any other institution.
Attrib.

Hoover, J. Edgar (John Edgar Hoover; 1895–1972) U.S. criminologist and government official

Quotations about Hoover

1 I'd much rather have that fellow inside my tent pissing out, than outside my tent pissing in.
Lyndon Baines Johnson (1908–73) U.S. president. Response when asked why he retained J. Edgar Hoover at the FBI. Quoted in *Guardian Weekly*, London (December 18, 1971)

Quotations by Hoover

2 You are honored by your friends...distinguished by your enemies. I have been very distinguished.
Quoted in *J. Edgar Hoover* (Curt Gentry; 1991)

Hope, Anthony (pen name of Sir Anthony Hope Hawkins; 1863–1933) British novelist and playwright

1 Economy is going without something you do want in case you should, some day, want something you probably won't want.
The Dolly Dialogues (1894), no. 12

2 "You oughtn't to yield to temptation."
"Well, somebody must, or the thing becomes absurd."
The Dolly Dialogues (1894), no. 14

3 Unless one is a genius, it is best to aim at being intelligible.
The Dolly Dialogues (1894), no. 15

4 "Boys will be boys—"
"And even that...wouldn't matter if we could only prevent girls from being girls."
The Dolly Dialogues (1894), no. 16

5 "*Bourgeois*," I observed, "is an epithet which the riff-raff apply to what is respectable, and the aristocracy to what is decent."
The Dolly Dialogues (1894), no. 17

6 He is very fond of making things which he does not want, and then giving them to people who have no use for them.
The Dolly Dialogues (1894), no. 17

7 I wish you would read a little poetry sometimes. Your ignorance cramps my conversation.
The Dolly Dialogues (1894), no. 22

8 Good families are generally worse than any others.
The Prisoner of Zenda (1894), ch. 1

Hope, Bob (Leslie Townes Hope; b.1903) British-born U.S. comedian and film actor

Quotations about Hope

1 There is nothing in the world I wouldn't do for Hope, and there is nothing he wouldn't do for me...We spend our lives doing nothing for each other.
Bing Crosby (1904–77) U.S. singer and actor. *Observer*, London (May 7, 1950), "Sayings of the Week"

Quotations by Hope

2 A bank is a place that will lend you money if you can prove that you don't need it.
Quoted in *Life in the Crystal Palace* (Alan Harrington; 1959)

3 I always enjoy appearing before a British audience. Even if they don't feel like laughing, they nod their heads to show they've understood.
Attrib.

4 Middle age is when your age starts to show around the middle.
Attrib.

Hope, Laurence (Adela Florence Cory Nicolson; 1865–1904) British poet

1 Pale hands I loved beside the Shalimar,
Where are you now? Who lies beneath your spell?
"Kashmiri Song," *The Garden of Kama and other Love Lyrics from India* (1901)

Hopkins, Anthony, Sir (b.1937) Welsh stage and film actor

1 All Stanislavsky ever said was: "Avoid generalities."
1980. Referring to Konstantin Stanislavsky. *Films Illustrated* (December 1980)

2 I'm more and more convinced that life is a dream. What has happened to me is surely a dream.
Independent, London (February 12, 1994)

3 Blank face is fine. The computer works faster than the brain, don't forget. The art of acting is not to act. Once you show them more, what you show them, in fact, is bad acting.
1980. *Knave* (November 1980)

4 A census taker once tried to test me. I ate his liver with some fava beans and a nice Chianti.
As the cannibalistic serial killer Hannibal Lecter in the motion picture, based on Thomas Harris's bestseller, *The Silence of the Lambs* (1988). *The Silence of the Lambs* (Ted Tally; 1990)

5 I do wish we could chat longer, but I'm having an old friend for dinner.
1991. Said as Hannibal Lecter, a cannibalistic psychopath, speaking by telephone to FBI agent Clarice Starling (Jodie Foster) in the final line from the motion picture, based on Thomas Harris's bestseller, *The Silence of the Lambs* (1988). *The Silence of the Lambs* (Ted Tally; 1990)

Hopkins, Gerard Manley (1844–89) British poet, priest, and classicist

1 That night, that year
Of now done darkness I wretch lay wrestling with
(my God!) my God.
"Carrion Comfort" (1885), quoted in *Poems* (Robert Bridges, ed.; 1918)

2 Cuckoo-echoing, bell-swarmèd, lark-charmèd,
rook-racked, river-rounded.
"Duns Scotus' Oxford" (1879), quoted in *Poems* (Robert Bridges, ed.; 1918)

3 The world is charged with the grandeur of God.
"God's Grandeur" (1877), quoted in *Poems* (Robert Bridges, ed.; 1918)

4 O the mind, mind has mountains; cliffs of fall
Frightful, sheer, no-man-fathomed. Hold them cheap
May who ne'er hung there...
Here! creep,
Wretch, under a comfort serves in a whirlwind: all
Life death does end and each day dies with sleep.
"No worst, there is none" (1885), quoted in *Poems* (Robert Bridges, ed.; 1918)

5 Glory be to God for dappled things—
For skies of couple-colour as a brindled cow;
For rose-moles all in stipple upon trout that swim.
"Pied Beauty" (1877), quoted in *Poems* (Robert Bridges, ed.; 1918)

6 Margaret, are you grieving
Over Goldengrove unleaving?
"Spring and Fall: To a Young Child" (1880), quoted in *Poems* (Robert Bridges, ed.; 1918)

7 Look at the stars! look, look up at the skies!

O look at all the fire-folk sitting in the air!
The bright boroughs, the circle-citadels there!
"The Starlight Night" (1877), quoted in *Poems* (Robert Bridges, ed.; 1918)

8 I caught this morning morning's minion, kingdom of daylight's dauphin, dapple-dawn-drawn Falcon.
"The Windhover" (1877), quoted in *Poems* (Robert Bridges, ed.; 1918)

Hopper, Edward (1882–1967) U.S. painter

1 A nation's art is greatest when it most reflects the character of its people.
Quoted in *Aroused by Books* (Anatole Broyard; 1974)

2 It's probably a reflection of my own, if I may say, loneliness...It could be the whole human condition.
Referring to his paintings, many of which depict stark, lonely scenes. Quoted in *Washington Post* (June 25, 1995)

Hopper, Grace Murray (1906–92) U.S. navy officer and mathematician

1 At any given moment, there is always a line representing what your boss will believe. If you step over it, you will not get your budget. Go as close to that line as you can.
Speech, Washington, D.C. (1987)

2 A ship in port is safe, but that's not what ships are built for.
Quoted in *Mothers of Invention* (E. A. Vare and G. Ptacek; 1987)

3 From then on, when anything went wrong with a computer, we said it had bugs in it.
1945. Referring to the extraction of a 2-inch-long moth from an experimental computer. Quoted in *Speaking Freely* (Stuart Berg Flexner and Anne H. Soukhanov; 1997)

4 You don't manage people, you manage things. You lead people.
Quoted in *Thick Face, Black Heart* (Chin-Ning Chu; 1992)

Horace (Quintus Horatius Flaccus; *fl.* 65–8 B.C.) Roman poet

1 "Painters and poets alike have always had license to dare anything." We know that, and we both claim and allow to others in their turn this indulgence.
The origin of "artistic license." *Ars Poetica* (19–8 B.C.), l. 9

2 I strive to be brief, and I become obscure.
Ars Poetica (19–8 B.C.), l. 25

3 Many terms which have now dropped out of favor, will be revived, and those that are at present respectable will drop out, if usage so choose, with whom resides the decision and the judgment and the code of speech.
Ars Poetica (19–8 B.C.), l. 70

4 Scholars dispute, and the case is still before the courts.
Ars Poetica (19–8 B.C.), l. 78

5 If you wish me to weep, you yourself must first feel grief.
Ars Poetica (19–8 B.C.), l. 102

6 It is hard to utter common notions in an individual way.
Ars Poetica (19–8 B.C.), l. 128

7 Mountains will heave in childbirth, and a silly little mouse will be born.
Ars Poetica (19–8 B.C.), l. 139

8 To the Greeks the Muse gave native wit, to the Greeks the gift of graceful eloquence.
Ars Poetica (19–8 B.C.), l. 323

9 Not gods, nor men, nor even booksellers have put up with poets being second-rate.
Ars Poetica (19–8 B.C.), l. 372

10 Let it be kept till the ninth year, the manuscript put away at home: you may destroy whatever you haven't published; once out, what you've said can't be stopped.
Ars Poetica (19–8 B.C.), l. 388

11 To save a man's life against his will is the same as killing him.
Ars Poetica (19–8 B.C.), l. 466

12 The happy state of getting the victor's palm without the dust of racing.
Epistles (20? B.C.), bk. 1, no. 1, l. 51

13 Let this be your wall of brass, to have nothing on your conscience, no guilt to make you turn pale.
Epistles (20? B.C.), bk. 1, no. 1, l. 60

14 If possible honestly, if not, somehow, make money.
Epistles (20? B.C.), bk. 1, no. 1, l. 66

15 Let me remind you what the wary fox said once upon a time to the sick lion: "Because those footprints scare me, all directed your way, none coming back."
Epistles (20? B.C.), bk. 1, no. 1, l. 73

16 We are just statistics, born to consume resources.
Epistles (20? B.C.), bk., 1, no. 2, l. 27

17 If there is anything the matter with your eyes, you hasten to get it put right; but if anything is the matter with your mind, you put off treatment for a year.
Epistles (20? B.C.), bk. 1, no. 2, l. 38

18 To have begun is half the job: be bold and be sensible.
Epistles (20? B.C.), bk. 1, no. 2, l. 40

19 Anger is a momentary madness, so control your passion or it will control you.
Epistles (20? B.C.), bk. 1, no. 2, l. 62

20 Believe each day that has dawned is your last. Some hour to which you have not been looking forward will prove lovely. As for me, if you want a good laugh, you will come and find me fat and sleek, in excellent condition, one of Epicurus' herd of pigs.
Epistles (20? B.C.), bk. 1, no. 4, l. 13

21 To marvel at nothing is just about the one and only thing, Numicius, that can make a man happy and keep him that way.
Epistles (20? B.C.), bk. 1, no. 6, l. 1

22 It is not the least praise to have pleased leading men. Not everyone is lucky enough to get to Corinth.
Epistles (20? B.C.), bk. 1, no. 7, l. 35

23 You may drive out nature with a pitchfork, yet she'll be constantly running back.
Epistles (20? B.C.), bk. 1, no. 10, l. 24

24 They change their clime, not their frame of mind, who rush across the sea. We work hard at doing nothing: we look for

happiness in boats and carriage rides. What you are looking for is here, is at Ulubrae, if only peace of mind doesn't desert you.
Epistles (20? B.C.), bk. 1, no. 11, l. 27

25 For it is your business, when the wall next door catches fire.
Epistles (20? B.C.), bk. 1, no. 18, l. 84

26 If you believe Cratinus from days of old, Maecenas, (as you must know) no verse can give pleasure for long, nor last, that is written by drinkers of water.
Epistles (20? B.C.), bk. 1, no. 19, l. 2

27 Greece, once overcome, overcame her wild conqueror, and brought the arts into rustic Latium.
Epistles (20? B.C.), bk. 2, no. 1, l. 156

28 And seek for truth in the groves of Academe.
Origin of the phrase "the groves of Academe." *Epistles* (20? B.C.), bk. 2, no. 2, l. 45

29 What pleasure does it give to be rid of one thorn out of many? If you don't know how to live right, give way to those who are expert at it. You have had enough fun, eaten and drunk enough: time you were off.
Epistles (20? B.C.), bk. 2, no. 2, l. 212

30 Hard to train to accept being poor.
Odes (23? B.C.), bk. 1, no. 1, l. 18

31 And if you include me among the lyric poets, I'll hold my head so high it'll strike the stars.
Odes (23? B.C.), bk. 1, no. 1, l. 35

32 Pale Death kicks his way equally into the cottages of the poor and the castles of kings.
Odes (23? B.C.), bk. 1, no. 4, l. 13

33 Life's short span forbids us to enter on far-reaching hopes.
Odes (23? B.C.), bk. 1, no. 4, l. 15

34 Drop the question what tomorrow may bring, and count as profit every day that Fate allows you.
Odes (23? B.C.), bk. 1, no. 9, l. 13

35 Do not try to find out—we're forbidden to know—what end the gods have in store for me, or for you.
Odes (23? B.C.), bk. 1, no. 11, l. 1

36 Seize the day, and put as little trust as you can in the morrow.
Odes (23? B.C.), bk. 1, no. 11, l. 7

37 When things are steep, remember to stay level-headed.
Odes (23? B.C.), bk. 2, no. 3, l. 1

38 Someone who loves the golden mean.
Odes (23? B.C.), bk. 2, no. 10, l. 5

39 Nothing is an unmixed blessing.
Odes (23? B.C.), bk. 2, no. 16. l. 27

40 Why should I exchange my Sabine valley for riches which just make more trouble?
Referrring to the poet's comfortable rural life. *Odes* (23? B.C.), bk. 3, no. 1, l. 47

41 It is a sweet and seemly thing to die for one's country.
Odes (23? B.C.), bk. 3, no. 2, l. 13

42 If the world should break and fall on him, its ruins would strike him unafraid.
Referring to the "just and tenacious man." *Odes* (23? B.C.), bk. 3, no. 3, l. 7

43 Force, if unassisted by judgment, collapses through its own mass.
Odes (23? B.C.), bk. 3, no. 4, l. 65

44 Undeservedly you will atone for the sins of your fathers.
Odes (23? B.C.), bk. 3, no. 6, l. 1

45 What do the ravages of time not injure? Our parents' age (worse than our grandparents') has produced us, more worthless still, who will soon give rise to a yet more vicious generation.
Odes (23? B.C.), bk. 3, no. 6, l. 45

46 With you I should love to live, with you be ready to die.
Odes (23? B.C.), bk. 3, no. 9, last line

47 My life with girls has ended, though till lately I was up to it and soldiered on not ingloriously; now on this wall will hang my weapons and my lyre, discharged from the war.
Odes (23? B.C.), bk. 3, no. 26, l. 1

48 I have executed a memorial longer lasting than bronze.
Odes (23? B.C.), bk. 3, no. 30, l. 1

49 I shall not altogether die.
Referring to the immortality he anticipates his poetry will confer on his name. *Odes* (23? B.C.), bk. 3, no. 30, l. 6

50 Not to hope for things to last for ever, is what the year teaches and even the hour which snatches a nice day away.
Odes (13? B.C.), bk. 4, no. 7, l. 7

51 The man worthy of praise the Muse forbids to die.
Odes (13? B.C.), bk. 4, no. 8, l. 28

52 Many brave men lived before Agamemnon's time; but they are all, unmourned and unknown, covered by the long night, because they lack their sacred poet.
Odes (13? B.C.), bk. 4, no. 9, l. 25

53 Not the owner of many possessions will you be right to call happy: he more rightly deserves the name of happy who knows how to use the gods' gifts wisely and to put up with rough poverty, and who fears dishonor more than death.
Odes (13? B.C.), bk. 4, no. 9, l. 45

54 Mix a little foolishness with your serious plans: it's lovely to be silly at the right moment.
Odes (13? B.C.), bk. 4, no. 12, l. 27

55 In Rome you long for the country; in the country—oh inconstant!—you praise the distant city to the stars.
Satires (35? B.C.), bk. 2, satire 7, l. 28

Horder, Thomas, Lord (1871–1955) British physician

1 It is the duty of a doctor to prolong life. It is not his duty to prolong the act of dying.
Speech to the House of Lords, the upper house of the British Parliament (December 1936)

Horne, Lena (Lena Calhoun Horne; b.1917) U.S. singer and actor

1 Don't grow old without money, honey.
Referring to her retirement, at 62. *People* (April 7, 1980)

Horne, Marilyn (Marilyn Bernice Horne; b.1934) U.S. opera singer

1 Ninety percent of what's wrong with singers today is that they don't breathe right.
Quoted in "Marilyn Horne," *Divas: Impressions of Six Opera Superstars* (Winthrop Sargeant; 1959)

2 The thing to do for insomnia is to get an opera score and read *that*. That will bore you to death.
Quoted in "Marilyn Horne," *Divas: Impressions of Six Opera Superstars* (Winthrop Sargeant; 1959)

Horne, Richard Henry (Richard Henry Hengist; 1803–84) British writer and colonialist

1 'Tis always morning somewhere in the world.
Orion (1843), bk. 3, can. 2

Horney, Karen (originally Karen Danielsen; 1885–1952) German-born U.S. psychoanalyst

1 All the pretenses to which a neurotic resorts in order to bridge the gap between his real self and his idealized image serve in the end only to widen it.
Our Inner Conflicts (1945)

2 As a result of innumerable outstanding contradictions in our civilization a general numbness of moral perception has developed.
Our Inner Conflicts (1945)

3 Compulsive drives are specifically neurotic; they are born of feelings of isolation, helplessness and fear, and represent ways of coping with the world despite these feelings...Their compulsive character is due to the anxiety lurking behind them.
Our Inner Conflicts (1945)

4 Every person, to the extent that he is neurotic, is like an airplane directed by remote control.
Our Inner Conflicts (1945)

5 For the sadist, exploitation becomes a kind of passion in its own right...The need to feed, vampirelike, on the emotional vitality of another person is as a rule completely unconscious.
Our Inner Conflicts (1945)

6 Fortunately, analysis is not the only way to resolve inner conflicts. Life itself remains a very effective therapist.
Our Inner Conflicts (1945)

7 Man has become to so great a degree merely a cog in an intricate social system that alienation from the self is almost universal, and human values themselves have declined.
Our Inner Conflicts (1945)

8 Neurotic conflicts cannot be resolved by rational decision.
Our Inner Conflicts (1945)

9 *Rationalization* may be defined as self-deception by reasoning.
Our Inner Conflicts (1945)

10 The analyst thinks it "unscientific" to have any moral values of his own or to take any interest in those of the patient.
Our Inner Conflicts (1945)

11 The most comprehensive formulation of therapeutic goals is the striving for *wholeheartedness*: to be without pretense, to be emotionally sincere, to be able to put the whole of oneself into one's feelings, one's work, one's beliefs.
Our Inner Conflicts (1945)

12 The most important therapeutic step is to bring the patient to see the reverse side of the medal: the incapacitating effects of his neurotic drives and conflicts.
Our Inner Conflicts (1945)

13 The neurotic person is not free to choose. He is driven by equally compelling forces in opposite directions, neither of which he wants to follow.
Our Inner Conflicts (1945)

14 The therapy effected by life itself is not, however, within one's control...Life as a therapist is ruthless.
Our Inner Conflicts (1945)

15 Whatever the starting point and however tortuous the road, we must finally arrive at a disturbance of the personality as the source of psychic illness.
Our Inner Conflicts (1945)

16 By simply radiating gloom he acts as a depressant.
Referring to the sadist's impulse to frustrate joy in others. *Our Inner Conflicts* (1945)

17 Neurotic girls cannot love a "weak" man because of their contempt for any weakness; but neither can they cope with a "strong" man because they expect their partner always to give in.
The Neurotic Personality of Our Time (1936)

18 Neurotic persons...feel and behave as if their existence, happiness, and security depended on being "liked."
The Neurotic Personality of Our Time (1936)

19 Neurotic suffering...is not what the person wants but what he pays, and the satisfaction he aims at is not suffering itself but a relinquishment of the self.
The Neurotic Personality of Our Time (1936)

20 The neurotic...feels caught in a cellar with many doors, and whichever door he opens leads only into new darkness. And all the time he knows that others are walking outside in sunshine.
The Neurotic Personality of Our Time (1936)

21 The neurotic striving for power...is born out of anxiety, hatred, and feelings of inferiority.
The Neurotic Personality of Our Time (1936)

22 When we realize the great import of cultural conditions on neuroses, the biological and physical conditions, which are considered by Freud to be their root, recede into the background.
The Neurotic Personality of Our Time (1936)

Horsley, Samuel (1733–1806) British bishop and writer

1 In *this* country, my Lords...the individual subject...has nothing to do with the laws but to obey them.
Speech to the House of Lords, the upper house of the British Parliament, *Hansard* (November 13, 1795), col. 268

Horton, George Moses (1797–1883?) U.S. poet

1 Alas! and am I born for this,
To wear this slavish chain?
Deprived of all created bliss,
Through hardship, toil and pain!
How long have I in bondage lain,
And anguished to be free!
Alas! and must I still complain—
Deprived of liberty.
On Liberty and Slavery (1829)

Horton, James Africanus Beale (1835–83) Sierra-Leonean political philosopher

1 I verily believe, my Lord, that in the government of a semi-barbarous race, where the aim is to bring up the governed rapidly to advancement in industrial pursuits, education, and general social condition, *a little despotism is absolutely necessary*.
Letter to Earl Granville (May 2, 1870), quoted in *African Aims and Attitudes* (Martin Minogue and Judith Molloy, eds.; 1979)

Hourani, Albert Egyptian historian and author

1 The rule of men of religion was a reaffirmation of tradition, but in another sense it went against tradition...it was dangerous to tie the eternal interests of Islam to the fate of a transient ruler of the world.
Referring to the rise of Islamic leaders in the Middle East. *A History of the Arab Peoples* (1991)

2 If more radical changes took place, it seemed more likely that in the 1980s they would take place in the name of an Islamic idea of the justice of God in the world. There was not one idea of Islam only, but a whole spectrum of them.
Referring to the role of Islam in Middle Eastern politics. *A History of the Arab Peoples* (1991)

Household, Geoffrey (Geoffrey Edward West Household; 1900–88) British novelist

1 I have noticed that what cats most appreciate in a human being is not the ability to produce food which they take for granted but his or her entertainment value.
Rogue Male (1939)

2 It's easy to make a man confess the lies he tells to himself; it's far harder to make him confess the truth.
Rogue Male (1939)

Housman, A. E. (Alfred Edward Housman; 1859–1936) British poet and classicist

1 Even when poetry has a meaning, as it usually has, it may be inadvisable to draw it out...Perfect understanding will sometimes almost extinguish pleasure.
Leslie Stephen Lecture, University of Cambridge (May 9, 1933)

2 If a line of poetry strays into my memory, my skin bristles so that the razor ceases to act.
Leslie Stephen Lecture, University of Cambridge (May 9, 1933)

3 The stars have not dealt me the worst they could do:
My pleasures are plenty, my troubles are two.
But oh, my two troubles they reave me of rest,
The brains in my head and the heart in my breast.
Additional Poems (1937), no. 17, quoted in *A. E. H.* (Lawrence Housman, ed.; 1937)

4 A Grecian lad, as I hear tell,
One that many loved in vain,
Looked into a forest well
And never looked away again.
Referring to Narcissus. *A Shropshire Lad* (1896), quoted in *The Collected Poems of A. E. Housman* (John Carter, ed.; 1967)

5 When I was one-and-twenty
I heard a wise man say,
"Give crowns and pounds and guineas
But not your heart away;
Give pearls away and rubies,
But keep your fancy free."
But I was one-and-twenty,
No use to talk to me.
A Shropshire Lad (1896), no. 13, quoted in *The Collected Poems of A. E. Housman* (John Carter, ed.; 1967)

6 Look not in my eyes, for fear
They mirror true the sight I see,
And there you find your face too clear
And love it and be lost like me.
A Shropshire Lad (1896), no. 15, quoted in *The Collected Poems of A. E. Housman* (John Carter, ed.; 1967)

7 Oh, when I was in love with you,
Then I was clean and brave,
And miles around the wonder grew
How well did I behave.
And now the fancy passes by,
And nothing will remain,
And miles around they'll say that I
Am quite myself again.
A Shropshire Lad (1896), no. 18, quoted in *The Collected Poems of A. E. Housman* (John Carter, ed.; 1967)

8 Shot? so quick, so clean an ending?
Oh that was right, lad, that was brave.
A Shropshire Lad (1896), no. 44, quoted in *The Collected Poems of A. E. Housman* (John Carter, ed.; 1967)

9 Loveliest of trees, the cherry now
Is hung with bloom along the bough,
And stands about the woodland ride
Wearing white for Eastertide.
"1887," *A Shropshire Lad* (1896), no. 2, quoted in *The Collected Poems of A. E. Housman* (John Carter, ed.; 1967)

10 Here of a Sunday morning
My love and I would lie,
And see the coloured counties,
And hear the larks so high
About us in the sky.
"Bredon Hill," *A Shropshire Lad* (1896), no. 21, quoted in *The Collected Poems of A. E. Housman* (John Carter, ed.; 1967)

11 Yes, lad, I lie easy,
I lie as lads would choose;

I cheer a dead man's sweetheart,
Never ask me whose.
"Is My Team Ploughing," *A Shropshire Lad* (1896), no. 27, quoted in *The Collected Poems of A. E. Housman* (John Carter, ed.; 1967)

12 Clay lies still, but blood's a rover;
Breath's a ware that will not keep
Up, lad: when the journey's over
There'll be time enough to sleep.
"Reveillé," *A Shropshire Lad* (1896), no. 4, quoted in *The Collected Poems of A. E. Housman* (John Carter, ed.; 1967)

13 And naked to the hangman's noose
The morning clocks will ring
A neck God made for other use
Than strangling in a string.
"Reveillé," *A Shropshire Lad* (1896), no. 9, quoted in *The Collected Poems of A. E. Housman* (John Carter, ed.; 1967)

14 They hang us now in Shrewsbury jail:
The whistles blow forlorn,
And trains all night groan on the rail
To men that die at morn.
"Reveillé," *A Shropshire Lad* (1896), no. 9, quoted in *The Collected Poems of A. E. Housman* (John Carter, ed.; 1967)

15 They put arsenic in his meat
And stared aghast to watch him eat;
They poured strychnine in his cup
And shook to see him drink it up.
"Terence, This is Stupid Stuff," *A Shropshire Lad* (1896), no. 62, quoted in *The Collected Poems of A. E. Housman* (John Carter, ed.; 1967)

16 East and west on fields forgotten
Bleach the bones of comrades slain,
Lovely lads and dead and rotten;
None that go return again.
"The Welsh Marches," *A Shropshire Lad* (1896), quoted in *The Collected Poems of A. E. Housman* (John Carter, ed.; 1967)

17 On Wenlock Edge the wood's in trouble;
His forest fleece the Wrekin heaves;
The wind, it plies the saplings double,
And thick on Severn snow the leaves.
"The Welsh Marches," *A Shropshire Lad* (1896), no. 31, quoted in *The Collected Poems of A. E. Housman* (John Carter, ed.; 1967)

18 Into my heart an air that kills
From yon far country blows:
What are those blue remembered hills,
What spires, what farms are those?
"The Welsh Marches," *A Shropshire Lad* (1896), no. 40, quoted in *The Collected Poems of A. E. Housman* (John Carter, ed.; 1967)

19 With rue my heart is laden
For golden friends I had,
For many a rose-lipt maiden
And many a lightfoot lad.
"The Welsh Marches," *A Shropshire Lad* (1896), no. 54, quoted in *The Collected Poems of A. E. Housman* (John Carter, ed.; 1967)

20 Eyes the shady night has shut
Cannot see the record cut,
And silence sounds no worse than cheers
After earth has stopped the ears.
"To an Athlete Dying Young," *A Shropshire Lad* (1896), no. 19, quoted in *The Collected Poems of A. E. Housman* (John Carter, ed.; 1967)

21 White in the moon the long road lies,
The moon stands blank above;
White in the moon the long road lies
That leads me from my love.
"White in the Moon the Long Road Lies," *A Shropshire Lad* (1896), no. 36, quoted in *The Collected Poems of A. E. Housman* (John Carter, ed.; 1967)

22 We'll to the woods no more,
The laurels all are cut,
The bowers are bare of bay
That once the Muses wore.
"Epigraph," *Last Poems* (1922), quoted in *The Collected Poems of A. E. Housman* (John Carter, ed.; 1967)

23 Tell me not here, it needs not saying,
What tune the enchantress plays
In aftermaths of soft September
Or under blanching mays,
For she and I were long acquainted
And I knew all her ways.
XL, *Last Poems* (1922), quoted in *The Collected Poems of A. E. Housman* (John Carter, ed.; 1967)

24 I sought them far and found them,
The sure, the straight, the brave,
The hearts I lost my own to,
The souls I could not save
They braced their belts about them,
They crossed in ships the sea,
They sought and found six feet of ground,
And there they died for me.
XXXII, *Last Poems* (1922), quoted in *The Collected Poems of A. E.Housman* (John Carter, ed.; 1967)

25 They say my verse is sad: no wonder;
Its narrow measure spans
Tears of eternity, and sorrow,
Not mine, but man's.
"Epigraph," *More Poems* (1936), quoted in *The Collected Poems of A. E. Housman* (John Carter, ed.; 1967)

26 This is for all ill-treated fellows
Unborn and unbegot,
For them to read when they're in trouble
And I am not.
"Epigraph," *More Poems* (1936), quoted in *The Collected Poems of A. E. Housman* (John Carter, ed.; 1967)

27 Because I liked you better
Than suits a man to say,
It irked you, and I promised
To throw the thought away.
XXXI, *More Poems* (1936), quoted in *The Collected Poems of A. E. Housman* (John Carter, ed.; 1967)

28 He would not stay for me; and who can wonder?
He would not stay for me to stand and gaze.

I shook his hand and tore my heart in sunder
And went with half my life about my ways.
"He Would Not Stay for Me; And Who Can Wonder?," *The Penguin Book of Homosexual Verse* (Stephen Coote, ed.; 1983)

29 Oh, who is that young sinner with the handcuffs on his wrists?
And what has he been after that they groan and shake their fists?
And wherefore is he wearing such a conscience-stricken air?
Oh they're taking him to prison for the colour of his hair.
"Oh Who is That Young Sinner...," *The Penguin Book of Homosexual Verse* (Stephen Coote, ed.; 1983)

30 That is indeed very good. I shall have to repeat that on the Golden Floor!
1936. Said to his doctor, who had told him a risqué story just before he died. Attrib.

Housman, Laurence (1865–1959) British writer and illustrator

1 If Nature had arranged that husbands and wives should have children alternately, there would never be more than *three* in a family.
Attrib.

Houston, Sam (Samuel Houston; 1793–1863) U.S. politician and military commander

1 Texas. Texas.
1863. His last words. He was leader in the fight for the independence of Texas from Mexico. Attrib.

Howard, Russell John (1875–1942) British surgeon

1 Diagnosis precedes treatment.
Quoted in *The Hip* (F. G. St. Clair Strange; 1965)

2 The first attribute of a surgeon is an insatiable curiosity.
Quoted in *The Hip* (F. G. St. Clair Strange; 1965), ch. 2

3 The most important person in the operating theatre is the patient.
Quoted in *The Hip* (F. G. St. Clair Strange; 1965), ch. 3

4 Speed in operating should be the achievement, not the aim, of every surgeon.
Quoted in *The Hip* (F. G. St. Clair Strange; 1965), ch. 9

Howard, Thomas, 2nd Duke of Norfolk (1443–1524) English soldier and courtier

1 He was my crowned King, and if the Parliamentary authority of England set the Crown upon a stock, I will fight for that stock: And as I fought then for him, I will fight for you, when you are established by the said authority.
Said to Henry VII, when asked why he had fought for Richard III at the Battle of Bosworth Field (August 22, 1485). Quoted in *Remains Concerning Britain* (William Camden; 1974)

Howatch, Susan (b.1940) British writer

1 Scientists are treated like gods handing down new commandments. People tend to assume that religion has been disproved by science. But the scientist may tell us how the world works, not why it works, not how we should live our lives, not how we face death or make moral decisions.
Observer, London (May 8, 1994)

Howe, Edgar Watson (1853–1937) U.S. novelist

1 A man should be taller, older, heavier, uglier, and hoarser than his wife.
Country Town Sayings (1911)

2 A whipping never hurts so much as the thought that you are being whipped.
Country Town Sayings (1911)

3 American freedom consists largely in talking nonsense.
Preaching from the Audience (1926)

4 Instead of loving your enemies, treat your friends a little better.
Attrib.

Howe, Geoffrey, Lord (Richard Edward Geoffrey Howe; b.1926) British politician

1 Megaphone diplomacy leads to a dialogue of the deaf.
Observer, London (September 29, 1985), "Sayings of the Week"

Howe, Joseph (1804–73) Canadian politician and journalist

1 We seek for nothing more than British subjects are entitled to; but we will be contented with nothing less.
Referring to the rights of Nova Scotians. Letter to Lord John Russell (1839)

2 Let the dog return to his vomit rather than Canada to division.
Referring to the possibility of Canadian confederation. He was prime minister of Nova Scotia (1860–63), and then a member of the federal parliament (1867–73). Speech, Halifax, Nova Scotia (August 13, 1864)

3 Poetry was the maiden I loved, but politics was the harridan I married.
Attrib.

Howe, Julia Ward (1819–1910) U.S. feminist and peace worker

1 Mine eyes have seen the glory of the coming of the Lord:
He is trampling out the vintage where the grapes of wrath are stored.
"Battle Hymn of the Republic" (1862), st. 1

Howe, Louis McHenry (1871–1936) U.S. presidential adviser

1 You can't adopt politics as a profession and remain honest.
Speech, Columbia University (January 17, 1933)

Howell, James (1594?–1666) English writer

1 Distance sometimes endears friendship, and absence sweeteneth it.
1645–55. *Familiar Letters of James Howell* (W. H. Bennett, ed.; 1890), bk. 1, pt. 1, no. 6

Howells, William Dean (1837–1920) U.S. writer and critic

1 Nothing is so hard to understand as that there are human beings in this world besides one's self and one's own set.
Their Wedding Journey (1872)

2 Some people can stay longer in an hour than others can in a week.
Attrib.

Howitt, Mary (1799–1888) British writer

1 "Will you walk into my parlour?" said a spider to a fly: "'Tis the prettiest little parlour that ever you did spy."
"The Spider and the Fly" (1834)

Hoyle, Edmond (1672–1769) English writer

1 When in doubt, win the trick.
"Whist, Twenty-Four Short Rules for Learners," *Hoyle's Games Improved* (Charles Jones, ed.; 1790)

Hoyle, Fred, Sir (Frederick Hoyle; b.1915) British astronomer, mathematician, and writer

1 It is the true nature of mankind to learn from mistakes, not from example.
Into Deepest Space (1975)

2 Space isn't remote at all. It's only an hour's drive away if your car could go straight upwards.
September 1979. *Observer*, London (September 9, 1979)

3 Once I had learnt my twelve times table (at the age of three) it was downhill all the way.
Attrib.

Hua Guofeng (also known as Hua Kuo-Feng; b.1920) Chinese premier

1 Don't be afraid of difficulties, don't be afraid of death, don't seek personal glory, don't seek profit...don't expect reward, don't consider your professional status.
Quoted in "The Great Leap," *Maoism: Slogans and Practice* (Vladimir Glebov; 1978)

Hubbard, Elbert (1856–1915) U.S. writer, printer, and editor

1 Little minds are interested in the extraordinary; great minds in the commonplace.
A Thousand and One Epigrams (1911)

2 One machine can do the work of fifty ordinary men. No machine can do the work of one extraordinary man.
A Thousand and One Epigrams (1911)

3 The probable fact is that we are descended not only from monkeys but from monks.
A Thousand and One Epigrams (1911)

4 An ounce of loyalty is worth a pound of cleverness.
The Note Book (1927)

5 If you want work well done, select a busy man: the other kind has no time.
The Note Book (1927)

6 The best preparation for good work tomorrow is to do good work today.
The Note Book (1927)

7 The love we give away is the only love we keep.
The Note Book (1927)

8 Life is just one damned thing after another.
The Philistine (1909)

9 Insomnia never comes to a man who has to get up exactly at six o'clock. Insomnia troubles only those who can sleep any time.
"In Re Muldoon," *The Philistine* (1909)

10 EDITOR: a person employed by a newspaper whose business it is to separate the wheat from the chaff and to see that chaff is printed.
The Roycroft Dictionary (1914)

11 HISTORY: a collection of epitaphs.
The Roycroft Dictionary (1914)

12 HISTORY: gossip well told.
The Roycroft Dictionary (1914)

13 OPTIMISM: A kind of heart stimulant—the digitalis of failure.
The Roycroft Dictionary (1914)

14 Cultivate only the habits that you are willing should master you.
Attrib.

15 The church saves sinners, but science seeks to stop their manufacture.
Attrib.

16 One who limits himself to his chosen mode of ignorance.
Definition of an expert. Attrib.

Hubbard, Frank McKinney ("Kin Hubbard"; 1868–1930) U.S. caricaturist

1 Some people are so sensitive they feel snubbed if an epidemic overlooks them.
Abe Martin's Broadcast (1930)

2 If there's one thing above all a vulture can't stand, it's a glass eye.
Attrib.

3 Why doesn't the fellow who says, "I'm no speechmaker," let it go at that instead of giving a demonstration.
Attrib.

Hubbard, L. Ron (Lafayette Ronald Hubbard; 1911–86) U.S. religious leader and science-fiction writer

1 A society in which women are taught anything at all but the management of a family, the care of men, and the creation of the future generation, is a society which is on the way out.
Questions for Our Time (1980)

Hubbard, Ruth (b.1924) U.S. biologist

1 To overturn orthodoxy is no easier in science than in philosophy, religion, economics, or any other disciplines through which we try to comprehend the world and the society in which we live.
"Have Only Men Evolved?," *Women Look at Biology Looking at Women* (co-written with Mary Sue Henfin and Barbara Fried, eds.; 1979)

Hu Feng (b.1903) Chinese writer and critic

1 The new literature, whose life blood is realism, has become a

national artery, a national nerve, and serves as a spiritual weapon of the people.
Realism Today (1943), quoted in *Literature of the People's Republic of China* (Kai-yu Hsu, ed.; 1980)

Huffington, Arianna (originally Arianna Stassinopoulos; b.1950) Greek-born U.S. socialite and writer

1 It would be futile to attempt to fit women into a masculine pattern of attitudes, skills, and abilities and disastrous to force them to suppress their specifically female characteristics...by keeping up the pretense that there are no differences between the sexes.
The Female Woman (1973)

2 Liberation is an evershifting horizon, a total ideology that can never fulfill its promises.
The Female Woman (1973)

Hügel, Friedrich, Baron von (1852–1925) Italian-born British theologian and philosopher

1 The golden rule is, to help those we love to escape from us; and never try to begin to help people, or influence them till they ask, but wait for them.
Advice to his niece. *Letters to a Niece* (1928), Introduction

Hughes, Charles (Charles Evans Hughes; 1862–1948) U.S. jurist and politician

1 How amazing it is that...one should expect unanimity of opinion upon difficult legal questions. In the highest ranges of thought...we find differences of view on the part of the most distinguished experts—theologians, philosophers, and scientists. The history of scholarship is a record of disagreements.
Speech, American Law Institute (May 7, 1936)

2 We are under a constitution, but the constitution is what the judges say it is, and the judiciary is the safeguard of our liberty and of our property under the constitution.
1907. Speech as Governor of New York State, *Addresses 1906–1916* (1916)

Hughes, Howard (Howard Robard Hughes; 1905–76) U.S. business executive, pilot, and film producer

1 Play off everyone against each other so you have more avenues of action open to you.
Quoted in *The Hughes Legacy: Scramble for the Billion* (1976)

Hughes, Langston (1902–67) U.S. novelist, playwright, and short-story writer

1 Negroes, like all other Americans, are being asked at the moment to prepare to defend democracy. But Negroes would very much like to have a little more democracy to defend.
Speech to Fourth American Writers' Congress (June 6–8, 1941), quoted in *Good Morning Revolution: Uncollected Writings of Langston Hughes* (Faith Berry, ed.; 1992)

2 We are considered exotic. When we cease to be exotic, we do not sell well.
Speech to Third American Writers' Congress (June 1939), quoted in *Good Morning Revolution: Uncollected Writings of Langston Hughes* (Faith Berry, ed.; 1992)

3 Life is a system of half-truths and lies,
Opportunistic, convenient evasion.
Elderly Leaders (1936)

4 Way down South in Dixie
(Break the heart of me)
They hung my black young lover
To a cross-roads tree.
"Song for a Dark Girl," *Fine Clothes to the Jew* (1927)

5 I swear to the Lord
I still can't see
Why Democracy means
Everybody but me.
"The Black Man Speaks," *Jim Crow's Last Stand* (1943)

6 Let America be America again.
Let it be the dream it used to be.
Let it be the pioneer on the plain
Seeking a home where he himself is free.
(America never was America to me.)
Let America Be America Again (1936)

7 What happens to a dream deferred?
Does it dry up
like a raisin in the sun?
Or fester like a sore—
and then run?
"Harlem," *Montage of a Dream Deferred* (1951)

8 But someday somebody'll
Stand up and talk about me
And write about me—
Black and beautiful.
Notes on Commercial Theater (1940)

9 When I get to be a composer
I'm gonna write me some music about
Daybreak in Alabama
...I'm gonna put some tall trees in it
And the scent of pine needles
And the smell of red clay after rain
And long red necks
And poppy colored faces
And big brown arms
And the field daisy eyes
Of black and white black white black people.
1940. "Daybreak in Alabama," *Selected Poems* (1959), ll. 1–3; 7–14

10 If you don't give a wife the last word, she will take it anyhow.
"Once in a Wife-Time," *The Best of Simple* (1961)

11 I am tired of working like a Negro all week in order to live like white folks on Saturday night.
"Present for Joyce," *The Best of Simple* (1961)

12 Two things, Miss Martin,
I cannot stand,
A bow-legged woman
And a cock-eyed man.

Two things, Miss Martin, I adore,

One is some loving—
and the other is some more!
1925. "Seven Rings," *The Best of Simple* (1961)

13 Sometimes, even if a woman no longer wants you in her arms, she wants you in her heart.
"Sometimes I Wonder," *The Best of Simple* (1961)

14 Humor is your own smile surprising you in the mirror.
The Book of Negro Folklore (1958)

15 Humor is laughing at what you haven't got when you ought to have it.
The Book of Negro Humor (1966)

16 It is the duty of the younger Negro Artist...to change through the force of his art that old whispering "I want to be white," hidden in the aspirations of his people to "Why should I want to be white? I am a Negro—and beautiful!"
"The Negro Artist and the Racial Mountain," *The Nation* (June 23, 1926)

17 My theory is, children should be born without parents—if born they must be.
The Life of Langston Hughes: Vol. 1, 1902–1941 (Arnold Rampersad; 1966)

Hughes, Richard (1900–76) British writer

1 A politician rises on the backs of his friends...but it is through his enemies he will have to govern afterwards.
The Fox in the Attic (1961)

2 Middle age snuffs out more talent than even wars or sudden deaths do.
The Fox in the Attic (1961)

3 Nature is as wasteful of promising young men as she is of fish spawn.
The Fox in the Attic (1961)

Hughes, Ted (Edward James Hughes; 1930–98) British writer and poet

1 Death invented the phone
It looks like the altar of death
Do not worship the telephone
It drags its worshippers into actual graves
With a variety of devices, through a variety of disguised voices.
"Do Not Pick Up the Telephone" (1979)

2 The war ended, the explosions stopped.
The men surrendered their weapons
And hung around limply.
Peace took them all prisoner.
"A Motorbike," *Earth-Numb* (1979), st. 2, ll. 1–4

3 Underwater eyes, an eel's
Oil of water body, neither fish nor beast is the otter:
Four-legged yet water-gifted, to outfish fish;
With webbed feet and long ruddering tail
And a round head like an old tomcat.
"An Otter," *Lupercal* (1960)

4 It took the whole of Creation
To produce my foot, my each feather:
Now I hold Creation in my foot.
"Hawk Roosting," *Lupercal* (1960)

5 You might not think that these two interests, capturing animals and writing poems, have much in common. But the more I think back the more sure I am that with me the two interests have been one interest.
Poetry in the Making (1967)

6 He spins from the bars, but there's no cage to him
More than to the visionary his cell:
His stride is wildernesses of freedom:
The world rolls under the long thrust of his heel.
Over the cage floor the horizons come.
"The Jaguar," *The Hawk in the Rain* (1957)

7 I imagine this midnight moment's forest:
Something else is alive
Beside the clock's loneliness
And this blank page where my fingers move.
"The Thought Fox," *The Hawk in the Rain* (1957)

Hughes, Thomas (1822–96) British writer

1 Life isn't all beer and skittles.
Tom Brown's Schooldays (1857), pt. 1, ch. 2

2 It's more than a game. It's an institution.
Referring to cricket. *Tom Brown's Schooldays* (1857), pt. 2, ch. 7

Hughes-Hallett, Lucy (Lucy Angela Hughes-Hallett; b.1951) British writer and critic

1 Each image of Cleopatra...provides clues to the nature of the culture which produced it, in particular to its sexual politics, its racial prejudices, its neuroses and its fantasies.
Cleopatra: Histories, Dreams and Distortions (1990)

Hugo, Victor (Victor Marie Hugo; 1802–85) French poet, novelist, and playwright

Quotations about Hugo

1 In Victor Hugo we have the average sensual man impassioned and grandiloquent; in Zola we have the average sensual man going near the ground.
Matthew Arnold (1822–88) British poet and critic. *Discourses in America* (1885)

2 Hugo—hélas!
André Gide (1869–1951) French novelist and critic. Reply when asked whom he considered the finest poet of the 19th century. Letter to Paul Valéry, quoted in *La Maturité d'André Gide* (Claude Martin; 1977)

3 !
Lacroix et Verboeckhoven. The entire contents of a telegram sent to Hugo by his publishers, in response to his "?", asking how *Les Misérables* was selling. Telegram (1862), quoted in *The Literary Life* (R. Hendrickson; 1981)

4 One day I read a novel by Victor Hugo which opened up a whole new world to me—that of literature, and gave me an interest in culture and the humanities.
1978
Yang Wenzhi (b.1954) Chinese writer. "Ah, Books!," *The Wounded* (Geremie Barmé, tr.; 1979)

Quotations by Hugo

5 If suffer we must, let's suffer on the heights.
"Les Malheureux," *Contemplations* (1856), bk. 5, no. 26

6 One can resist the invasion of an army; one cannot resist the invasion of ideas.
Histoire d'un crime (1852), vol. 5, ch. 10

7 It is nothing to die; it is frightful not to live.
Les Misérables (1862)

8 Indigestion is charged by God with enforcing morality on the stomach.
Les Misérables (1862), bk. 3, ch. 7

9 A man is not idle because he is absorbed in thought. There is visible labor and there is invisible labor.
"Cosette," *Les Misérables* (1862), bk. 7, ch. 8

10 The supreme happiness of life is the conviction that we are loved.
"Fantine," *Les Misérables* (1862), bk. 5, ch. 4

11 The misery of a child is interesting to a mother, the misery of a young man is interesting to a young woman, the misery of an old man is interesting to nobody.
"Saint Denis," *Les Misérables* (1862)

12 Thought is the labor of the intellect, reverie is its pleasure.
"Saint Denis," *Les Misérables* (1862), bk. 1, ch. 4

13 Popularity? It's glory's small change.
Ruy Blas (1838), Act 3, Scene 5

14 Rabelais is the wondrous mask of ancient comedy...henceforth a human living face, remaining enormous and coming among us to laugh at us and with us.
Attrib.

Hume, Basil, Cardinal (Basil George Hume; 1923–99) British Roman Catholic leader

1 If you become holy, it is because God has made you so. You will not know it anyway.
Observer, London (January 10, 1984), "Sayings of the Week"

2 There are times and occasions when it would be marvellous to have a wife.
Observer, London (February 6, 1981), "Sayings of the Week"

3 Such persons are often good, conscientious and faithful sons and daughters of the church.
Referring to Catholics who, against the tenets of their church, use contraceptives. *Observer*, London (March 30, 1980), "Sayings of the Week"

Hume, David (1711–76) Scottish philosopher and historian

1 Money is not, properly speaking, one of the subjects of commerce, but only the instrument which men have agreed upon to facilitate the exchange of one commodity for another.
"Of Money" (1752)

2 If we take in our hand any volume; of divinity or school metaphysics, for instance; let us ask, *Does it contain any abstract reasoning concerning quantity or number?* No. *Does it contain any experimental reasoning, concerning matter of fact and existence?* No. Commit it then to the flames: for it can contain nothing but sophistry and illusion.
An Enquiry Concerning Human Understanding (1748)

3 The Christian religion not only was at first attended with miracles, but even at this day cannot be believed by any reasonable person without one. Mere reason is insufficient to convince us of its veracity: and whoever is moved by faith to assent to it, is conscious of a continued miracle in his own person, which subverts all the principles of his understanding, and gives him a determination to believe what is most contrary to custom and experience.
"Of Miracles," *An Enquiry Concerning Human Understanding* (1748)

4 A gloomy, hare-brained enthusiast, after his death, may have a place in the calendar; but will scarcely ever be admitted, when alive, into intimacy and society, except by those who are as delirious and dismal as himself.
An Enquiry Concerning the Principles of Morals (1751)

5 It appears to be matter of fact, the circumstance of *utility*, in all subjects, is a source: of praise and approbation...and, in a word, that it is the foundation of the chief part of morals, which has a reference to mankind and our fellow-creatures.
An Enquiry Concerning the Principles of Morals (1751)

6 The hypothesis which we embrace is plain. It maintains that morality is determined by sentiment. It defines virtue to be *whatever mental action or quality gives to a spectator the pleasing sentiment of approbation*; and vice the contrary.
An Enquiry Concerning the Principles of Morals (1751)

7 All our simple ideas in their first impressions are derived from simple impressions, which are correspondent to them, and which they exactly represent.
A Treatise of Human Nature (1739–40)

8 All the perceptions of the human mind resolve themselves into two distinct kinds, which I shall call IMPRESSIONS and IDEAS.
A Treatise of Human Nature (1739–40)

9 *An object may exist and yet be nowhere*: and I assert, that this is not only possible, but that the greatest part of beings do and must exist after this manner.
A Treatise of Human Nature (1739–40)

10 Be a philosopher; but, amidst all your philosophy, be still a man.
A Treatise of Human Nature (1739–40)

11 Everyone has observed how much more dogs are animated when they hunt in a pack, than when they pursue their game apart. We might, perhaps, be at a loss to explain this phenomenon, if we had not experience of a similar in ourselves.
A Treatise of Human Nature (1739–40)

12 Generally speaking, the errors in religion are dangerous; those in philosophy only ridiculous.
A Treatise of Human Nature (1739–40)

13 Grief and disappointment give rise to anger, anger to envy, envy to malice, and malice to grief again, till the whole circle be completed.
A Treatise of Human Nature (1739–40)

14 I cannot compare the soul more properly to any thing than to a republic or commonwealth, in which the several members are united by the reciprocal ties of government and subordination.
A Treatise of Human Nature (1739–40)

15 If we believe, that fire warms, or water refreshes, 'tis only because it costs us too much pains to think otherwise.
A Treatise of Human Nature (1739–40)

16 I weigh the one miracle against the other...and always reject the greater miracle.
A Treatise of Human Nature (1739–40)

17 Morals excite passions, and produce or prevent actions. Reason of itself is utterly impotent in this particular. The rules of morality, therefore, are not conclusions for reason.
A Treatise of Human Nature (1739–40)

18 Our reason must be consider'd as a kind of cause, of which truth is the natural effect.
A Treatise of Human Nature (1739–40)

19 Philosophers never balance between profit and honesty, because their decisions are general, and neither their passions nor imaginations are interested in the objects.
A Treatise of Human Nature (1739–40)

20 Reason is nothing but a wonderful and unintelligible instinct in our souls, which carries us along a certain train of ideas, and endows them with particular qualities, according to their particular situations and relations.
A Treatise of Human Nature (1739–40)

21 The only connexion or relation of objects, which can lead us beyond the immediate impressions of our memory and senses, is that of cause and effect.
A Treatise of Human Nature (1739–40)

22 'Tis not contrary to reason to prefer the destruction of the whole world to the scratching of my finger...'Tis not the passion, properly speaking, which is unreasonable, but the judgment.
A Treatise of Human Nature (1739–40)

23 'Tis one thing to know virtue, and another to conform the will to it.
A Treatise of Human Nature (1739–40)

24 We have no other notion of cause and effect, but that of certain objects, which have *always conjoin'd* together, and which in all past instances have always been found inseparable.
A Treatise of Human Nature (1739–40)

25 We never remark any passion or principle in others, of which, in some degree or other, we may not find a parallel in ourselves.
A Treatise of Human Nature (1739–40)

26 How could things have been as they are, were there not an original, inherent principle or order somewhere?
Dialogues Concerning Natural Religion (1779)

27 Is he willing to prevent evil, but not able? then is he impotent. Is he able, but not willing? then is he malevolent. Is he both able and willing? whence then is evil?
Dialogues Concerning Natural Religion (1779)

28 Look round this universe...The whole presents nothing but the idea of blind nature, impregnated by a great vivifying principle, and pouring forth from her lap, without discernment or parental care, her maimed and abortive children.
Dialogues Concerning Natural Religion (1779)

29 Never literary attempt was more unfortunate than my Treatise of Human Nature. It fell *dead-born from the press*, without reaching such distinction, as even to excite a murmur among the zealots.
"My Own Life," *Essays, Moral and Political* (1741)

30 The life of man is of no greater importance to the universe than that of an oyster.
"Of Suicide," *Essays, Moral and Political* (1741)

31 Beauty in things exists in the mind which contemplates them.
"Of Tragedy," *Essays, Moral and Political* (1741)

32 Art may make a suit of clothes: but Nature must produce a man.
"The Epicurean," *Essays, Moral and Political* (1741)

33 Good and ill, both natural and moral, are entirely relative to human sentiment and affection.
"The Sceptic," *Essays, Moral and Political* (1741)

34 Even bear-baiting was esteemed heathenish and unchristian: the sport of it, not the inhumanity, gave offence.
History of England Under the House of Tudor (1754–62), vol. 1, ch. 62

Hume, John (b.1937) Northern Irish politician

1 Every party in Ireland was founded on the gun.
1995. Attrib.

Humphrey, Hubert H. (Hubert Horatio Humphrey, Jr.; 1911–78) U.S. vice president

Quotations about Humphrey

1 All that Hubert needs over there is a gal to answer the phone and a pencil with an eraser on it.
Lyndon Baines Johnson (1908–73) U.S. president. Attrib.

Quotations by Humphrey

2 There are those who say to you—we are rushing this issue of civil rights. I say we are 172 years late.
Speech, Democrat National Convention (July 14, 1948)

3 Much of our American progress has been the product of the individual who had an idea...tenaciously clung to it against all odds; and then produced it, sold it, and profited from it.
Speech, United States Junior Chamber of Commerce, Detroit (June 29, 1966)

4 The Politics of Joy.
April 26, 1968. Speech in Washington, D.C., *New York Times* (April 27, 1968)

5 In our nuclear age, the lack of a sense of history could have mortal consequences.
"What My Students Taught Me," *Today's Health* (August 1971)

Humphries, Rolfe (George Rolfe Humphries; 1894–1969) U.S. poet

1 Wales, which I have never seen,
Is gloomy, mountainous, and green,
And, as I judge from reading Borrow,
The people there rejoice in sorrow.
"For My Ancestors," *Collected Poems* (1965)

2 They practice magic out of season,

they hate the English with good reason,
Nor do they trust the Irish more,
And find the Scots an utter bore.
Referring to the Welsh. "For My Ancestors," *Collected Poems* (1965)

3 The weather veers from dull to foul,
The letter W's a vowel.
Referring to Wales. "For My Ancestors," *Collected Poems* (1965)

Huneker, James Gibbons (1860–1921) U.S. musician and critic

1 My corns ache, I get gouty, and my prejudices swell like varicose veins.
Old Fogy: His Musical Opinions and Grotesques (1913), ch. 1

2 Lawyers earn a living by the sweat of their browbeating.
Attrib.

Hungerford, Margaret Wolfe (1855?–97) Irish novelist

1 Beauty is altogether in the eye of the beholder.
Molly Bawn (1878)

Hunnicutt, Ellen U.S. writer

1 Even when it was easy, music's patterning shaped the emotions...Music proclaimed an orderly universe, promised a better place.
Suite for Calliope (1987)

Hunt, George William (1829?–1904) British writer

1 We don't want to fight, but, by jingo if we do,
We've got the ships, we've got the men, we've got the money too.
We've fought the Bear before, and while Britons shall be true,
The Russians shall not have Constantinople.
Song lyric, which gave rise to the use of the word "jingoism," meaning bombastic and xenophobic patriotism. "We Don't Want to Fight" (1878)

Hunt, Leigh (James Henry Leigh Hunt; 1784–1859) British poet and essayist

1 Abou Ben Adhem (may his tribe increase!)
Awoke one night from a deep dream of peace,
And saw, within the moonlight in his room,
Making it rich, and like a lily in bloom,
An angel writing in a book of gold.
"Abou Ben Adhem and the Angel" (1838)

2 And lo! Ben Adhem's name led all the rest.
"Abou Ben Adhem and the Angel" (1838)

3 "I pray thee then,
Write me as one that loves his fellow-men."
"Abou Ben Adhem and the Angel" (1838), ll. 13–14

4 Stolen sweets are always sweeter,
Stolen kisses much completer,
Stolen looks are nice in chapels,
Stolen, stolen, be your apples.
"Song of Fairies Robbing an Orchard" (1830)

5 The two divinest things this world has got,
A lovely woman in a rural spot!
"The Story of Rimini" (1816)

Hunt, Marsha (b.1946) U.S. singer, actor, and writer

1 Families ain't just born, you got to work at 'em, even when there ain't much to work with.
Joy (1990)

Hunter, Anne (originally Anne Home; 1742–1821) Scottish poet

1 My mother bids me bind my hair
With bands of rosy hue,
Tie up my sleeves with ribbons rare,
And lace my bodice blue.
"My Mother Bids Me Bind My Hair," *Poems, by Mrs John Hunter* (1807), ll. 1–4

Hupfeld, Herman (1894–1951) U.S. songwriter

1 You must remember this;
A kiss is still a kiss,
A sigh is just a sigh—
The fundamental things apply
As time goes by.
Song from the film *Casablanca* (1942). "As Time Goes By" (1931)

Hurd, Douglas, Baron (Douglas Richard Hurd; b.1930) British politician

1 The Communist Party, the KGB, and the army—the three ugly sisters—are the instruments of control in the Soviet Union.
Referring to an abortive coup in the Soviet Union. *Observer*, London (August 25, 1991)

Hurdis, James (1763–1801) British poet

1 Rise with the lark, and with the lark to bed.
"The Village Curate," *Poems: By The Rev. James Hurdis*, 3 vols. (1808), l. 275

Hurst, Fannie (originally Fannie Danielson; 1889–1968) U.S. writer

1 It's hard for a young girl to have patience for old age sitting and chewing all day over the past.
1917. Attrib.

Hurst, Gerald, Sir (1877–1957) British writer and judge

1 One of the mysteries of human conduct is why adult men and women all over England are ready to sign documents which they do not read, at the behest of canvassers whom they do not know, binding them to pay for articles which they do not want, with money which they have not got.
Closed Chapters (1942)

Hurston, Zora Neale (1891?–1960) U.S. writer and folklorist

Quotations about Hurston

1 That Zora Neale Hurston held her own, literally, against the flood of whiteness and maleness that diluted so much other black art of the period in which she worked is a testimony to her genius and her faith.
Alice Walker (b.1944) U.S. novelist and poet. *I Love Myself When I am Laughing...A Zora Neale Hurston Reader* (1979)

Quotations by Hurston

2 It seems to me that trying to live without friends is like milking a bear to get cream for your morning coffee. It is a whole lot of trouble, and then not worth much after you get it.
Dust Tracks on a Road (1942)

3 I want a busy life, a just mind and a timely death.
Dust Tracks on a Road (1942)

4 Love, I find, is like singing. Everybody can do enough to satisfy themselves, though it may not impress the neighbors as being very much.
Dust Tracks on a Road (1942)

5 Mama exhorted her children at every opportunity to "jump at de sun." We might not land on the sun, but at least we would get off the ground.
Dust Tracks on a Road (1942)

6 Nothing that God ever made is the same thing to more than one person.
Dust Tracks on a Road (1942)

7 People are prone to build a statue of the kind of person that it pleases them to be. And few people want to be forced to ask themselves, "What if there is no me like my statue?"
Dust Tracks on a Road (1942)

8 Research is formalized curiosity. It is poking and prying with a purpose.
Dust Tracks on a Road (1942)

9 There is no agony like bearing an untold story inside you.
Dust Tracks on a Road (1942)

10 There is nothing to make you like other human beings so much as doing things for them.
Dust Tracks on a Road (1942)

11 White man fret and worry and kill hisself. Colored folks fret uh lil' while and gwan tuh sleep.
Jonah's Gourd Vine (1934)

12 When one is too old for love, one finds great comfort in good dinners.
Moses: Man of the Mountain (1939)

13 An envious heart makes a treacherous ear.
Their Eyes Were Watching God (1937)

14 No hour is ever eternity, but it has its right to weep.
Their Eyes Were Watching God (1937)

15 So de white man throw down de load and tell de nigger tuh pick it up. He pick it up because he have to, but he don't tote it. He hand it to his womenfolks. De nigger woman is de mule uh de world so fur as Ah can see.
Their Eyes Were Watching God (1937)

16 When we sing the blues, we're singin' out our hearts, we're singin' out our feelings. Maybe we're hurt and just can't answer back, then we sing or maybe even hum the blues.
Quoted in *Hear Me Talkin' to Ya* (Nat Shapiro and Nat Hentoff eds.; 1955)

17 Sometimes, I feel discriminated against, but it does not make me angry. It merely astonishes me. How *can* any deny themselves the pleasure of my company? It's beyond me.
"How It Feels To Be Colored Me," *I Love Myself, a Zora Neale Hurston Reader* (Alice Walker, ed.; 1979)

Hurt, John (b.1940) British actor

1 There are two kinds of directors—allies and judges.
Radio Times, London (1971), quoted in *Chambers Film Quotes* (Tony Crawley, ed.; 1991)

Husain (Husayn ibn Ali ibn Abi Talib; 626–680) Islamic religious leader

1 When intention, ability, success, and correctness come together, there happiness is perfected.
Quoted in "The Lives of the Other Imams: Imam Ali ben al-Husayn," *The Book of Guidance Into the Lives of the Twelve Imams* (Abu al-Mufid; 10th century)

2 May you be exalted, O my God, above the pictures of You of those who try to describe You in human terms.
Referring to Allah. Quoted in "The Lives of the Other Imams: Imam Ali ben al-Husayn," *The Book of Guidance Into the Lives of the Twelve Imams* (Abu al-Mufid; 10th century)

3 I am the grandson of the one who brought the good news. I am the grandson of the warner. I am the grandson of the man who, with God's permission, summoned the people to God.
Husain was the grandson of Muhammad and younger son of Ali ibn Abi Talib. Quoted in "The Lives of the Other Imams: Imam al-Hasan ben Ali," *The Book of Guidance into the Lives of the Twelve Imams* (Abu al-Mufid; 10th century)

Husayn, Taha (1889–1973) Egyptian writer

1 Arabic language is not a foreign language among us, it is *our* language, and a thousand times closer to us than the language of the ancient Egyptians.
Quoted in *A History of the Arabic Peoples* (Albert Hourani; 1991)

Hu Shi (also known as Hu Shih; 1891–1962) Chinese reformer and philosopher

1 Only one who has loved knows the power of love.
Dreams and Poetry (1920), quoted in *Anthology of Modern Chinese Poetry* (Michelle Yeh, ed. and tr.; 1992)

2 I have the strongest desire to make my own people see that the methods of the West are not totally alien to the Chinese mind, and that...they are the instruments by which and in the light of which much of the lost treasures of Chinese philosophy can be recovered.
1917. Quoted in *Political and Social Change in China Since 1978* (Charles Burton; 1990)

Hüsnü Dag larca, Fazil (b.1914) Turkish poet

1 Hiroshima, the flower, petaled off into extinction.
How can it be? Where did I gather these multiples of death?
My mind becomes a fire-bird and erupts into dark, dark flights.
"Guilt Driven Madness," *Modern Turkish Poetry* (Feyyaz Kayacan Fergar, ed.; 1992)

Huss, John (Jan Hus; 1372?–1415) Bohemian religious reformer

1 O holy simplicity!
Said on noticing a peasant adding a piece of wood to the pile at his execution. *Apophthegmata* (Zincgreff-Weidner; 1653), pt. 3

Hussein, Saddam (b.1937) Iraqi president

1 They will drown in their own blood.
Referring to the coalition forces assembling in Saudi Arabia to expel the Iraqis from Kuwait. Iraqi News Agency (1990)

2 The mother of battles will be our battle of victory and martyrdom.
January 6, 1991. Referring to the imminent Persian Gulf War. Speech, Baghdad, *Times*, London (January 7, 1991)

Husserl, Edmund (Edmund Gustav Albrecht Husserl; 1859–1938) Czech-born German philosopher

1 Phenomenology proceeds by "seeing," clarifying, and determining meaning, and by distinguishing meanings.
The Idea of Phenomenology (1913)

Huston, John (John Marcellus Huston; 1906–87) U.S. film director and actor

1 It's not color, it's like pouring 40 tablespoons of sugar water over a roast.
Referring to the computer colorization of black-and-white films. Address, Directors' Guild of America (November 13, 1986)

2 Politicians, ugly buildings, and whores all get respectable if they last long enough.
Said as Noah Cross. *Chinatown* (Robert Towne; 1974)

3 The directing of a picture involves coming out of your individual loneliness and taking a controlling part in putting together a small world.
New York Journal (March 31, 1960)

4 Censorship hurts pictures, it damages them. The only form of censorship that's at all significant is what the French do—burn the theater down.
Rolling Stone (February 19, 1981), quoted in *Chambers Film Quotes* (Tony Crawley, ed.; 1991)

5 A work of art doesn't dare you to realize it. It germinates and gestates by itself.
Reply to a tribute from the Directors' Guild of America. *Variety* (April 26, 1982)

6 I don't try to guess what a million people will like. It's hard enough to know what I like.
Referring to making films. Attrib.

Hutcheson, Dan U.S. business executive

1 All new wealth comes from creative engineering types, who are difficult to manage and easy to offend. The mentality of a takeover is aggressive, a pirate mentality that upsets morale. The good people leave.
Forbes (July 7, 1997)

2 We are at risk of producing more technology than the world can adapt to.
New York Times (September 17, 1997)

Hutcheson, Francis (1694–1746) Irish-born English philosopher

1 Do we not find that we often desire the Happiness of others without any...selfish intention? How few have thought upon this part of our Constitution which we call a Publick Sense?
An Essay on the Nature and Conduct of the Passions and Affections (1728)

2 The Occasion of the imagined Difficulty in conceiving disinterested Desires, has probably been from the attempting to define this simple idea, Desire.
An Essay on the Nature and Conduct of the Passions and Affections (1728)

3 Wisdom denotes the pursuing of the best ends by the best means.
Inquiry into the Original of our Ideas of Beauty and Virtue (1725), pt. 1, sect. 5

4 That action is best, which procures the greatest happiness for the greatest numbers.
Inquiry into the Original of our Ideas of Beauty and Virtue (1725), pt. 2, sect. 3

Hutchins, Robert M. (Robert Maynard Hutchins; 1899–1977) U.S. educator

1 In the Middle West, the high school is the place where the band practices.
New York Herald Tribune (April 22, 1963)

2 We do not know what education can do for us, because we have never tried it.
The Atomic Bomb Versus Civilization (1945)

3 Whenever I feel like exercise, I lie down until the feeling passes.
Attrib.

Hutchinson, Anne (originally Anne Marbury; 1591–1643) English-born U.S. religious reformer

1 What from the Church at Boston? I know no such church, neither will I own it. Call it the whore and strumpet of Boston, no Church of Christ.
Remark (1638?)

Hutchison, Robert, Sir (1871–1960) British doctor

1 It is unnecessary—perhaps dangerous—in medicine to be too clever.
Lancet, London (1938), 2: 61

2 The scientific truth may be put quite briefly: eat moderately, having an ordinary mixed diet, and don't worry.
Newcastle Medical Journal (1932), vol. 12

3 Vegetarianism is harmless enough, though it is apt to fill a man with wind and self righteousness.
Attrib.

Hütter, Ralf (b.1946) German musician

1 After the war...German entertainment was destroyed. The German people were robbed of their culture, putting an American head on it.
Referring to World War II. Interview, *Creem* (September 1975), quoted in *The Faber Book of Pop* (Hanif Kureishi and Jon Savage, eds.; 1995)

Hutton, Maurice (1856–1940) British-born Canadian classicist

1 Canada's history is as dull as ditchwater and her politics is full of it.
Canadian Historical Review (1936)

Hutton, Will (William Nicholas Hutton; b.1950) British author and newspaper editor

1 We change the rules of football or cricket to improve the quality of the game; we can change the rules by which capitalism is played too. If we can't, what kind of democracy is it?
Stakeholding and its Critics (1997)

2 If the gentlemanly capitalists and international rentiers can operate offshore, with no democratic accountability, then democratisation of our national economy, polity and society will be permanently stymied.
The State We're In (1995)

3 The attempt to isolate economics from other disciplines—notably politics, history, philosophy, finance, constitutional theory and sociology—has fatally disabled its power to explain what is happening in the world.
The State We're In (1995)

Huxley, Aldous (Aldous Leonard Huxley; 1894–1963) British novelist and essayist

Quotations about Huxley

1 Mr. Huxley is perhaps one of those people who have to perpetrate thirty bad novels before producing a good one.
T. S. Eliot (1888–1965) U.S.-born British poet and playwright. Attrib.

2 Along with many scientists he considered the discovery of psychedelics one of the three major scientific break-throughs of the twentieth century, the other two being the splitting of the atom and the manipulation of genetic structures.
Laura Huxley (b.1911) Italian-born U.S. musician and writer. *This Timeless Moment* (1968)

3 Like a piece of litmus paper he has always been quick to take the colour of his times.
Anonymous. *Observer*, London (February 27, 1949), "Author Profile"

Quotations by Huxley

4 A majority of young people seem to develop mental arteriosclerosis forty years before they get the physical kind.
Interview, quoted in *Writers at Work: Second Series* (George Plimpton, ed.; 1977)

5 Thanks to words, we have been able to rise above the brutes; and thanks to words, we have often sunk to the level of the demons.
Adonis and the Alphabet (1956)

6 Why should human females become sterile in the forties, while female crocodiles continue to lay eggs into their third century?
After Many a Summer (1939), bk. 1, ch. 5

7 Science has "explained" nothing; the more we know the more fantastic the world becomes and the profounder the surrounding darkness.
"Places: Views of Holland," *Along the Road: Notes and Essays of a Tourist* (1925)

8 Since Mozart's day composers have learned the art of making music throatily and palpitatingly sexual.
"Popular Music," *Along the Road: Notes and Essays of a Tourist* (1925)

9 "Liberty Mr. Gumboil?" he said, "you don't suppose any serious minded person imagines a revolution is going to bring liberty do you?"
Antic Hay (1923)

10 "To make money", said Mr. Porteous, "one must be really interested in money."
Antic Hay (1923)

11 You sought the last resort of feeble minds with classical educations. You became a schoolmaster.
Antic Hay (1923)

12 There are few who would not rather be taken in adultery than in provincialism.
Antic Hay (1923), ch. 10

13 Mr. Mercaptan went on to preach a brilliant sermon on that melancholy sexual perversion known as continence.
Antic Hay (1923), ch. 18

14 Official dignity tends to increase in inverse ratio to the importance of the country in which the office is held.
Beyond the Mexique Bay (1934)

15 Before the time of our Ford.
In Huxley's futuristic anti-utopian satire, Henry Ford has become the presiding deity, with the president known as "his Fordship." *Brave New World* (1932), ch. 3

16 There can be no doubt that if tranquillizers could be bought as easily and cheaply as aspirin they would be consumed, not by the billions, as they are at present, but by the scores and hundreds of billions.
Brave New World Revisited (1958), ch. 8

17 Nobody can have the consolations of religion or philosophy unless he has first experienced their desolations.
Collected Essays (1958)

18 The proper study of mankind is books.
A reference to Alexander Pope's famous line: "The proper study of mankind is man," *An Essay on Man*, Epistle 2, ll. 1–2, *Crome Yellow* (1921), ch. 28

19 Thought must be divided against itself before it can come to any knowledge of itself.
Do What You Will (1929)

20 Consistency is contrary to nature, contrary to life. The only completely consistent people are the dead.
"Wordsworth in the Tropics," *Do What You Will* (1929)

21 Capitalism tends to produce a multiplicity of petty dictators each in command of his own little business kingdom. State Socialism tends to produce a single, centralised, totalitarian dictatorship, wielding absolute authority...through a hierarchy of bureaucratic agents.
Ends and Means (1937)

22 So long as men worship the Caesars and Napoleons, Caesars and Napoleons will arise to make them miserable.
Ends and Means (1937)

23 Science and art are only too often a superior kind of dope, possessing this advantage over booze and morphia: that they can be indulged in with a good conscience and with the conviction that, in the process of indulging, one is leading the "higher life".
"Beliefs," *Ends and Means* (1937)

24 One of the great attractions of patriotism—it fulfils our worst wishes. In the person of our nation we are able, vicariously, to bully and to cheat. Bully and cheat, what's more, with a feeling that we are profoundly virtuous.
Eyeless in Gaza (1936)

25 Revolution is delightful in the preliminary stages. So long as it's a question of getting rid of the people at the top.
Eyeless in Gaza (1936)

26 That was the chief difference between literature and life. In books, the proportion of exceptional to commonplace people is high; in reality, very low.
Eyeless in Gaza (1936)

27 People will insist...on treating the *mons Veneris* as though it were Mount Everest.
Eyeless in Gaza (1936), ch. 30

28 Death...It's the only thing we haven't succeeded in completely vulgarizing.
Eyeless in Gaza (1936), ch. 31

29 A million million spermatozoa,
All of them alive:
Out of their cataclysm but one poor Noah
Dare hope to survive.
Fifth Philosopher's Song (1920)

30 Christianity accepted as given a metaphysical system derived from several already existing and mutually incompatible systems.
Grey Eminence: A Study in Religion and Politics (1941), ch. 3

31 The quality of moral behaviour varies in inverse ratio to the number of human beings involved.
Grey Eminence: A Study in Religion and Politics (1941), ch. 10

32 "Bed," as the Italian proverb succinctly puts it, "is the poor man's opera."
Heaven and Hell (1956)

33 I can sympathize with people's pains, but not with their pleasures. There is something curiously boring about somebody else's happiness.
"Cynthia," *Limbo* (1920)

34 Most of one's life...is one prolonged effort to prevent oneself thinking.
"Green Tunnels," *Mortal Coils* (1922)

35 She was one of those indispensables of whom one makes the discovery, when they are gone, that one can get on quite as well without them.
"Nuns at Luncheon," *Mortal Coils* (1922)

36 What we think and feel and are is to a great extent determined by the state of our ductless glands and our viscera.
"Meditation on El Greco," *Music At Night And Other Essays* (1949)

37 Defined in psychological terms, a fanatic is a man who consciously over-compensates a secret doubt.
"Vulgarity in Literature," *Music At Night And Other Essays* (1949)

38 The aristocratic pleasure of displeasing is not the only delight that bad taste can yield. One can love a certain kind of vulgarity for its own sake.
"Vulgarity in Literature," *Music At Night And Other Essays* (1949)

39 A bad book is as much a labour to write as a good one; it comes as sincerely from the author's soul.
Point Counter Point (1928)

40 It takes two to make a murder. There are born victims, born to have their throats cut.
Point Counter Point (1928)

41 Silence is as full of potential wisdom and wit as the unhewn marble of great sculpture.
Point Counter Point (1928)

42 The instinct of acquisitiveness has more perverts, I believe, than the instinct of sex. At any rate people seem to be odder about money than about even their amours.
Point Counter Point (1928)

43 There is no substitute for talent. Industry and all the virtues are of no avail.
Point Counter Point (1928)

44 Happiness is like coke—something you get as a by-product in the process of making something else.
Coke is a by-product of coal that has been distilled to get rid of its volatile components. *Point Counter Point* (1928)

45 Facts do not cease to exist because they are ignored.
Proper Studies (1927)

46 That all men are equal is a proposition to which, at ordinary times, no sane individual has ever given his assent.
Proper Studies (1927)

47 Those who believe that they are exclusively in the right are generally those who achieve something.
Proper Studies (1927)

48 We participate in a tragedy; at a comedy we only look.
The Devils of Loudon (1952), ch. 11

49 A firm conviction of the material reality of Hell never prevented medieval Christians from doing what their ambition, lust or covetousness suggested.
The Doors of Perception (1954)

50 Most human beings have an almost infinite capacity for taking things for granted.
Themes and Variations (1950)

51 The ageing man of the middle twentieth century lives, not in the public world of atomic physics and conflicting ideologies, of welfare states and supersonic speed, but in his strictly private universe of physical weakness and mental decay.
"Variations on a Philosopher," *Themes and Variations* (1950)

52 The propagandist's purpose is to make one set of people forget that certain other sets of people are human.
The Olive Tree And Other Essays (1936)

53 I'm afraid of losing my obscurity. Genuineness only thrives in the dark. Like celery.
Those Barren Leaves (1925), pt. 1, ch. 1

54 Facts are ventriloquists' dummies. Sitting on a wise man's knee

they may be made to utter words of wisdom; elsewhere they say nothing or talk nonsense.
Time Must Have A Stop (1944)

55 How appallingly thorough these Germans always managed to be, how emphatic! In sex no less than in war—in scholarship, in science. Diving deeper than anyone else and coming up muddier.
Time Must Have A Stop (1944), ch. 6

56 You mean what everybody means nowadays... Ignore death up to the last moment; then, when it can't be ignored any longer, have yourself squirted full of morphia and shuffle off in a coma.
Time Must Have A Stop (1944), ch. 26

57 To see ourselves as others see us is a most salutary gift. Hardly less important is the capacity to see others as they see themselves.
Attrib.

Huxley, Julian, Sir (Julian Sorell Huxley; 1887–1975) British biologist

1 We all know how the size of sums of money appears to vary in a remarkable way according as they are being paid in or paid out.
Essays of a Biologist (1923)

2 Operationally, God is beginning to resemble not a ruler but the last fading smile of a cosmic Cheshire cat.
Referring to the Cheshire Cat in Lewis Carroll's children's classic, *Alice's Adventures in Wonderland* (1865). *Religion Without Revelation* (1957), ch. 3

3 The human race will be the cancer of the planet.
Attrib.

Huxley, T. H. (Thomas Henry Huxley; 1825–95) British biologist

1 I am too much of a sceptic to deny the possibility of anything.
Letter to Herbert Spencer (March 22, 1886), quoted in *Life and Letters of Thomas Henry Huxley* (Leonard Huxley, ed.; 1900)

2 A man has no reason to be ashamed of having an ape for his grandfather. If there were an ancestor whom I should feel shame in recalling it would rather be a *man*—a man of restless and versatile intellect—who...plunges into scientific questions with which he has no real acquaintance, only to obscure them by an aimless rhetoric, and distract the attention of his hearers from the real point at issue by eloquent digressions and skilled appeals to religious prejudice.
Replying to Bishop Samuel Wilberforce in the debate on Darwin's theory of evolution at the meeting of the British Association at Oxford, June 30, 1860. The version above is commonly quoted. After hearing Wilberforce's speech, and before rising himself, Huxley is said to have remarked, "The Lord has delivered him into my hands!" Speech (June 30, 1860), quoted in *Life and Letters of Thomas Henry Huxley* (Leonard Huxley, ed.; 1900)

3 The great tragedy of Science—the slaying of a beautiful hypothesis by an ugly fact.
"Biogenesis and Abiogenesis," *Collected Essays* (1893–94)

4 Science is nothing but trained and organized common sense, differing from the latter only as a veteran may differ from a raw recruit: and its methods differ from those of common sense only as far as the guardsman's cut and thrust differ from the manner in which a savage wields his club.
"The Method of Zadig," *Collected Essays* (1893–94)

5 Science...commits suicide when it adopts a creed.
"The Darwin Memorial," *Darwiniana* (1860)

6 I doubt if the philosopher lives, or ever has lived, who could know himself to be heartily despised by a street boy without some irritation.
Evolution and Ethics (1893)

7 One of the unpardonable sins, in the eyes of most people, is for a man to go about unlabelled. The world regards such a person as the police do an unmuzzled dog, not under proper control.
Evolution and Ethics (1893)

8 The chess-board is the world; the pieces are the phenomena of the universe; the rules of the game are what we call the laws of Nature. The player on the other side is hidden from us. We know that his play is always fair, just, and patient. But also we know, to our cost, that he never overlooks a mistake, or makes the smallest allowance for ignorance.
"A Liberal Education," *Lay Sermons* (1870)

9 Some experience of popular lecturing had convinced me that the necessity of making things plain to uninstructed people was one of the very best means of clearing up the obscure corners in one's own mind.
Man's Place in Nature (1894), Preface

10 If he my next-door neighbour is to be allowed to let his children go unvaccinated, he might as well be allowed to leave strychnine lozenges about in the way of mine.
"Administrative Nihilism," *Method and Results* (1870)

11 If some great Power would agree to make me always think what is true and do what is right, on condition of being turned into a sort of clock and wound up every morning before I got out of bed, I should instantly close with the offer.
"On Descartes' Discourse on Method," *Method and Results* (1870)

12 If a little knowledge is dangerous, where is the man who has so much as to be out of danger?
Referring to Alexander Pope's famous line: "A little learning is a dang'rous thing" (*An Essay on Criticism*, 1711). *On Elementary Instruction in Physiology* (1877)

13 Logical consequences are the scarecrows of fools and the beacons of wise men.
"On the Hypothesis that Animals are Automata," *Science and Culture and Other Essays* (1881)

14 Irrationally held truths may be more harmful than reasoned errors.
"The Coming of Age of the Origin of Species," *Science and Culture and Other Essays* (1881)

15 It is the customary fate of new truths to begin as heresies and to end as superstitions.
"The Coming of Age of the Origin of Species," *Science and Culture and Other Essays* (1881)

Huxtable, Ada Louise (originally Ada Louise Landman; b.1921?) U.S. architecture critic

1 This city has been an act of real estate rather than an act of God or man.
Referring to Texas City, Texas. *New York Times* (1977)

2 America the beautiful,
Let me sing of thee;
Burger King and Dairy Queen
From sea to shining sea.
"Goodbye History, Hello Hamburger," *New York Times* (March 21, 1971)

3 Water is the wine of architecture.
Quoted in *Of Rivers and the Sea* (Herbert E. French; 1970)

Hynde, Chrissie (b.1951) U.S. singer and musician

1 If you don't wear high heels and lipstick in this business, pal, you'd better get on to a model agency quick. If it was up to me, I'd get Yasmin Le Bon to go on the covers of all my albums and I'd just call it a day, just stay in the studio all the time.
Observer, London (October 1986)

Hypatia (370?–415) Greek philosopher, mathematician, and astronomer

1 He who influences the thought of his times, influences all the times that follow. He has made his impress on eternity.
Quoted in "Hypatia," *Little Journeys to the Homes of Great Teachers* (Elbert Hubbard; 1908)

2 Men will fight for superstition quite as quickly as for a living truth—often more so, since a superstition is so intangible you cannot get at it to refute it, but truth is a point of view, and so is interchangeable.
Quoted in "Hypatia," *Little Journeys to the Homes of Great Teachers* (Elbert Hubbard; 1908)

3 To rule by fettering the mind through fear of punishment in another world, is just as base as to use force.
Quoted in "Hypatia," *Little Journeys to the Homes of Great Teachers* (Elbert Hubbard; 1908)

I i

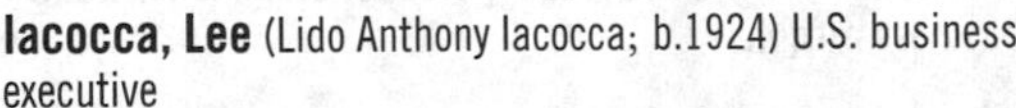

Iacocca, Lee (Lido Anthony Iacocca; b.1924) U.S. business executive

1 Hey boys, I've got a shotgun at your heads. I've got thousands of jobs at 17 bucks an hour. I've got none at 20. So you better come to your senses.
Negotiating with the workers at Chrysler. *Iacocca: An Autobiography* (co-written with William Novak; 1985)

2 In the end, all business operations can be reduced to three words: people, product, and profits.
Iacocca: An Autobiography (co-written with William Novak; 1985), ch. 15

3 The public has become pretty cynical about big business and for good reason. Sometimes our cars were so bad, they felt we built them that way on purpose.
Referring to the Chrysler Corporation. *Iacocca: An Autobiography* (co-written with William Novak; 1985), ch. 15

4 The cement in our whole democracy today is the worker who makes $15 an hour. He's the guy who will buy a house and a car and a refrigerator. He's the oil in the engine.
Iacocca: An Autobiography (co-written with William Novak; 1985), ch. 26

5 I have the feeling that when I die—and assuming that I go to heaven—St. Peter is going to meet me at the gate to talk to me about air bags.
Lee Iacocca was president of Ford (1970–78) and then Chief Executive Officer of the Chrysler Corporation (1978–92) for whom automobile safety features were a regular concern. *Iacocca: An Autobiography* (co-written with William Novak; 1985), ch. 27

6 The trick is to make sure you don't die waiting for prosperity to come.
Strategy and Business (1998)

7 Everybody in an organization has to believe their livelihood is based on the quality of the product they deliver.
Talking Straight (1988)

8 Perhaps the biggest responsibility of any corporation is to own up when it makes a mistake.
Talking Straight (1988)

9 Your legacy should be that you made it better than it was when you got it.
Talking Straight (1988)

Ibárruri, Dolores ("La Pasionaria"; 1895–1989) Spanish politician and journalist

1 Spain will either win as a free democratic country or will cease to exist altogether.
Address, People's Front meeting, Madrid (October 14, 1936)

2 You are the heroic example of democracy's solidarity and universality, in face of the shameful "accommodating" spirit of those who interpret democratic principles with their eyes on hoards of wealth or the industrial shares which they want to preserve from any risk.
Farewell speech to the International Brigades, after their defeat in the Spanish Civil War. "Goodbye, Brothers, Till Our Speedy Reunion," speech, Barcelona (September 1938)

3 It is better to die on your feet than to live on your knees.
Referring to the Spanish Civil War (1936–38). Speech in Paris, *L'Humanité* (September 4, 1936)

4 It is better to be the widow of a hero than the wife of a coward.
Speech, Valencia, *Radio Broadcast, Madrid* (1936)

5 They shall not pass!
July 19, 1936. A slogan originally used by French soldiers at the Battle of Verdun (1916), but taken up by Republican forces during the Spanish Civil War, following this famous radio broadcast from Madrid by Dolores Ibárruri. *Speeches and Articles 1936–1938* (1938)

6 We dip our colors in honor of you, dear women comrades, who march into battle together with the men.
1938. Referring to the women who fought in support of the Republic during the Spanish Civil War (1936–38).

Ibn Hanbal, Ahmad (780–855) Abbasid jurist and scholar

1 Command your children to perform ritual prayer when they are seven, and beat them for neglecting it when they are ten.
Musnad of Ibn Hanbal (9th century), quoted in *Salvation of the Soul and Islamic Devotions* (Muhammad Abdul Quasem; 1983)

Ibn Khaldun (Abu Zayd 'Abd-Ar-Rahman Ibn Khaldun; 1332–1406) Spanish-Arab historian

1 Geometry enlightens the intellect and sets one's mind right.
Muqaddimah (1376?)

Ibn Maja, Yazid al-Raba al-Qazwini (824–887) Arab compiler

1 Recite the Koran and weep. If you do not weep naturally, force yourselves to weep.
Sunan of Ibn Maja (9th century), quoted in *Salvation of the Soul and Islamic Devotions* (Muhammad Abdul Quasem; 1983)

Ibsen, Henrik (1828–1906) Norwegian playwright

1 I am not even quite sure what women's rights really are. To me it has been a question of human rights...Of course it is incidentally desirable to solve the problem of women; but that

has not been my whole object. My task has been the portrayal of human beings.
Speech, the Norwegian Society for Women's Rights (May 26, 1898)

2 No debts! Never borrow! Something of freedom's lost—and something of beauty too—from a home that's founded on borrowing and debt.
A Doll's House (1879), Act 1

3 DR STOCKMANN I've made a great discovery...The fact is, you see, that the strongest man in the world is he who stands most alone.
An Enemy of the People (1882)

4 Fools are in a terrible, overwhelming majority, all the wide world over.
An Enemy of the People (1882), Act 4

5 The majority has the might—more's the pity—but it hasn't right...The minority is always right.
An Enemy of the People (1882), Act 4

6 The worst enemy of truth and freedom in our society is the compact majority. Yes, the damned, compact, liberal majority.
An Enemy of the People (1882), Act 4

7 A man should never put on his best trousers when he goes out to battle for freedom and truth.
An Enemy of the People (1882), Act 5

8 But be consistent, do it all the time, not one thing one day and another the next. Be wholly what you are, not half and half. Everyone now is a little of everything.
Brand (1865), Act 1

9 It is not by spectacular achievements that man can be transformed, but by will.
Brand (1865), Act 2

10 It's not just what we inherit from our mothers and fathers that haunts us. It's all kinds of old defunct theories, all sorts of old defunct beliefs, and things like that. It's not that they actually live on in us; they are simply lodged there, and we cannot get rid of them. I've only to pick up a newspaper and I seem to see ghosts gliding between the lines.
Ghosts (1881), Act 2

11 Mother, give me the sun.
Ghosts (1881), Act 3

12 JUDGE BRACK But good God! People don't do such things!
Referring to Hedda Gabler's suicide by shooting herself in the temple. *Hedda Gabler* (1890)

13 Ten o'clock...and back he'll come. I can just see him. With vine leaves in his hair. Flushed and confident.
Hedda Gabler (1890), Act 2

14 You made my life a cause for singing. Bless you, for coming back at last!
Said by Solveig about Peer Gynt on the latter's return. *Peer Gynt* (1867)

15 What's a man's first duty? The answer's brief: To be himself.
Peer Gynt (1867), Act 4, Scene 1

16 There is no judge over us, and therefore we must do justice upon ourselves.
Rosmersholm (1886), Act 4

17 Youth will come here and beat on my door, and force its way in.
The Master Builder (1892), Act 1

18 Castles in the air—they're so easy to take refuge in. So easy to build, too.
The Master Builder (1892), Act 3

19 On the contrary!
Ibsen's last words, his nurse having just remarked that he was feeling a little better. Quoted in *True Remarkable Occurrences* (J. Train; 1906)

Icahn, Carl (Carl Celian Icahn; b.1936) U.S. financier and business executive

1 The chairman doesn't want someone under him who is a threat, so he picks someone a little less capable. It's like an anti-Darwinian theory—the survival of the unfittest.
Referring to American boardrooms. *Fortune* (December 9, 1985)

2 When nobody wants something, that creates an opportunity.
Referring to buying into Texaco and USX when both were troubled companies. *Fortune* (November 5, 1990)

Icke, David (b.1952) British television presenter and author

1 Green politics is not about being far left or far right, but being far-sighted.
Speech to the Green Party conference (September 1989)

Ickes, Harold L. (Harold LeClaire Ickes; 1874–1952) U.S. lawyer and government official

1 I am against government by crony.
Referring to his resignation as secretary of the interior after a dispute with President Harry S. Truman. Remark (February 1946)

Ignatieff, Michael (b.1947) Canadian-born British writer and broadcaster

1 The American model is a form of state capitalism in which the great corporations of the military-industrial complex fatten on the largess of the state, while the poor and disadvantaged get a firm dose of *laissez-faire*.
Observer, London (September 15, 1991)

2 This theory that memory images were stored in different parts of the brain was surely the origin of my belief that my mother's memories were still intact, like a butterfly collection left behind in the attic of an abandoned house.
Describing his mother's dementia. *Scar Tissue* (1993)

Ihara Saikaku (Togo Hirayama; 1642–93) Japanese poet and novelist

1 When you send a clerk on business to a distant province, a man of rigid morals is not your best choice.
Quoted in *The Japanese Family Storehouse* (G. W. Sargent, tr.; 1959), bk. 1, ch. 5

Illich, Ivan (b.1926) Austrian-born U.S. educator and researcher

1 Any attempt to reform the university without attending to the system of which it is an integral part is like trying to do urban renewal in New York City from the twelfth story up.
Deschooling Society (1971), ch. 3

2 Man must choose whether to be rich in things or in the freedom to use them.
Deschooling Society (1971), ch. 4

3 We must rediscover the distinction between hope and expectation.
Deschooling Society (1971), ch. 7

4 Effective health care depends on self care...The medicalization of early diagnosis not only hampers and discourages preventative health care but it also trains the patient-to-be to function...as an acolyte to his doctor. He learns to depend on the physician in sickness and in health. He turns into a life-long patient.
Medical Nemesis (1975)

5 Healthy people are those who live in healthy homes on a healthy diet; in an environment equally fit for birth, growth, work, healing, and dying...Healthy people need no bureaucratic interference to mate, give birth, share the human condition, and die.
Medical Nemesis (1975)

6 A just society would be one in which liberty for one person is constrained only by the demands created by equal liberty for another.
Tools for Conviviality (1973)

7 In a consumer society there are inevitably two kinds of slaves: the prisoners of addiction and the prisoners of envy.
Tools for Conviviality (1973), ch. 3

Imamura Shohei (b.1926) Japanese filmmaker

1 Above and beyond anything else, working as an artist means having a limitless curiosity about human beings. I have no interest in films made by directors who don't care about people.
Interview (Toichi Nakata; August 1994), quoted in *Projections 6* (John Boorman and Walter Donohue, eds.; 1996)

Imparato, Nicholas (b.1944) U.S. academic

1 Progress toward a global environment of vibrant democracies and free markets depends in great measure on our ability to accommodate the promise and the challenge of intellectual capital.
Capital for Our Time (1999)

2 Speaking about commercial enterprises means speaking about the creation, the management, the protection, and the application of intellectual capital.
Capital for Our Time (1999)

Inayama, Yoshihiro Japanese business executive

1 There is nothing Japan really wants to buy from foreign countries except, possibly, neckties with unusual designs.
Sydney Morning Herald (August 3, 1984), "Sayings of the Week"

Inge, William (William Motter Inge; 1913–73) U.S. playwright

1 Once we find the fruits of success, the taste is nothing like we had anticipated.
Attrib.

Inge, William Ralph ("The Gloomy Dean"; 1860–1954) British churchman

1 Democracy is only an experiment in government, and it has the obvious disadvantage of merely counting votes instead of weighing them.
"Possible Recovery?" (1922)

2 To become a popular religion, it is only necessary for a superstition to enslave a philosophy.
"The Idea of Progress," Romanes lecture, Oxford (May 27, 1920)

3 Literature flourishes best when it is half a trade and half an art.
"The Victorian Age" (1922)

4 Only those can care intelligently for the future of England to whom the past is dear.
Assessments and Anticipations (1929)

5 What we know of the past is mostly not worth knowing. What is worth knowing is mostly uncertain. Events in the past may roughly be divided into those which probably never happened and those which do not matter.
"Prognostications," *Assessments and Anticipations* (1929)

6 The command "Be fruitful and multiply" was promulgated according to our authorities, when the population of the world consisted of two people.
More Lay Thoughts of a Dean (1931)

7 Many people believe that they are attracted by God, or by Nature, when they are only repelled by man.
More Lay Thoughts of a Dean (1931), pt. 4, ch. 1

8 I think middle age is the best time, if we can escape the fatty degeneration of the conscience which often sets in at about fifty.
Observer, London (June 8, 1930)

9 The proper time to influence the character of a child is about a hundred years before he is born.
Observer, London (June 21, 1929)

10 The whole of nature is a conjugation of the verb to eat, in the active and the passive.
Outspoken Essays (1919), First Series

11 If...an outbreak of cholera might be caused either by an infected water supply or by the blasphemies of an infidel mayor, medical research would be in confusion.
"Confessio Fidei," *Outspoken Essays* (1922), Second series

12 Man as we know him is a poor creature; but he is halfway between an ape and a god and he is travelling in the right direction.
"Confessio Fidei," *Outspoken Essays* (1922), Second series

13 It takes in reality only one to make a quarrel. It is useless for the sheep to pass resolutions in favour of vegetarianism while the wolf remains of a different opinion.
"Patriotism," *Outspoken Essays* (1919), First series

14 The nations which have put mankind and posterity most in their debt have been small states—Israel, Athens, Florence, Elizabethan England.
"State, Visible and Invisible," *Outspoken Essays* (1922), Second series

15 A man may build himself a throne of bayonets, but he cannot sit on it.
Philosophy of Plotinus (1923), vol. 2, lecture 22

16 Hatred and the feeling of solidarity pay a high psychological dividend. The statistics of suicide show that, for noncombatants at least, life is more interesting in war than in peace.
The End of an Age (1948), ch. 3

17 The enemies of Freedom do not argue; they shout and they shoot.
The End of an Age (1948), ch. 4

18 The effect of boredom on a large scale in history is underestimated. It is a main cause of revolutions, and would soon bring to an end all the static Utopias and the farmyard civilization of the Fabians.
The End of an Age (1948), ch. 6

19 We tolerate shapes in human beings that would horrify us if we saw them in a horse.
Attrib.

Ingersoll, Robert G. (Robert Green Ingersoll, "The Great Agnostic"; 1833–99) U.S. lawyer

1 Few rich men own their property. The property owns them.
Address to the McKinley League, New York (October 29, 1896)

2 Every science has been an outcast.
"Liberty of Man, Woman, and Child," address, Troy, New York State (December 17, 1877)

3 Many people think they have religion when they are troubled with dyspepsia.
Liberty of Man, Woman, and Child (1903), pt. 3

4 In nature there are neither rewards nor punishments—there are consequences.
Some Reasons Why (1881), pt. 8, "The New Testament"

5 An honest God is the noblest work of man.
The Gods (1876)

6 Reason, Observation, and Experience—the Holy Trinity of Science.
The Gods (1876)

7 If I had my way I'd make health catching instead of disease.
Attrib.

Ingham, Bernard (b.1932) British journalist

1 Blood sport is brought to its ultimate refinement in the gossip columns.
Observer, London (December 28, 1986), "Sayings of the Week"

Ingrams, Richard (b.1937) British journalist

1 My own motto is publish and be sued.
Referring to his editorship of *Private Eye*, a satirical magazine. Remark on BBC Radio (May 4, 1977)

2 I have come to regard the law courts not as a cathedral but rather as a casino.
Guardian, London (July 30, 1977)

Ingres, Jean-Auguste Dominique (1780–1867) French artist

1 Drawing is the true test of art.
Pensées d'Ingres (1922)

2 The only way to be absolutely safe is never to try anything for the first time.
Attrib.

Innes, Hammond (Ralph Hammond Innes; b.1913) British novelist

1 I'm replacing some of the timber used up by my books. Books are just trees with squiggles on them.
Radio Times, London (August 18, 1984)

Innocent III, Pope (1160?–1216) Italian pope

1 It is a much more serious thing to offend the divine majesty than to offend the temporal power.
Letter (March 25, 1199)

2 Nothing which happens in the world should escape the notice of the supreme pontiff.
Letter (1199)

3 The King of kings and Lord of lords, Jesus Christ...has established in the Church His kingdom and His priesthood...He has set up one whom He has appointed as His Vicar on earth, so that, as every knee is bowed to Jesus...all men should obey His Vicar.
Letter to King John of England (April 21, 1214)

4 Just as the moon receives its light from the sun, which is greater by far, owing to the quantity and quality of its light, so the royal power takes all its reputation and prestige from the pontifical power.
Letter to rectors of Tuscany (1198)

5 This charter has been forced from the king. It constitutes an insult to the Holy See, a serious weakening of the royal power, a disgrace to the English nation, a danger to all Christendom, since this civil war obstructs the crusade.
Referring to Magna Carta. (August 24, 1215)

International Military Tribunal of the Nuremberg Trials international legal agreement

1 War is essentially an evil thing. Its consequences are not confined to the belligerent states alone, but affect the whole world.
1946. Part of the Judgment on the German war leaders by the International Military Tribunal of the Nuremberg Trials. Quoted in "Judgement: Law, Crime, and Punishment," *The Anatomy of the Nuremberg Trials* (T. Taylor; 1993), ch. 2

2 There is nothing to be said in mitigation.
1946. Concluding passage of the Judgment on Hermann Goering, the German Nazi leader. He was found guilty on all counts by the International Military Tribunal and was sentenced to death by hanging on October 15, 1946. "Judgement: Law, Crime, and Punishment," *The Anatomy of the Nuremberg Trials* (T. Taylor; 1993), ch. 21

Ionesco, Eugène (1909–94) Romanian-born French playwright

1 Explanation separates us from astonishment, which is the only gateway to the incomprehensible.
Découvertes (1969)

2 Everything that has been will be, everything that will be is, everything that will be has been.
Exit the King (1962)

3 Many people have delusions of grandeur but you're deluded by triviality.
Exit the King (1962)

4 We haven't the time to take our time.
Exit the King (1962)

5 Living is abnormal.
Rhinoceros (1959), Act 1

6 You can only predict things after they've happened.
Rhinoceros (1959), Act 3

7 Then, Madam, we must live in the same room and sleep in the same bed, dear Madam. Perhaps that is where we have met before.
The character is speaking to his own wife. *The Bald Prima Donna* (1950)

8 It's as we speak that we find our ideas, our words, ourselves too, in our words, and the city, the gardens, perhaps everything comes back and we're not orphans any more.
The Chairs (1951)

9 A civil servant doesn't make jokes.
The Killer (1958), Act 1

10 Nothing makes me more pessimistic than the obligation not to be pessimistic.
Attrib.

Iphicrates (410?–353 B.C.) Athenian general

1 The difference between us is that my family begins with me, whereas yours ends with you.
Reply to a descendant of Harmodius (an Athenian hero), who had derided Iphicrates for being the son of a cobbler. Attrib. *Apothegms* (Plutarch; 1st century? A.D.)

Irving, John (b.1942) U.S. author

1 It isn't what they put in that bothers me but what they left out. It's as if they took the family to the laundry. Still, I expected worse.
Referring to the film of his novel *The World According to Garp* (1982). *International Herald Tribune* (October 22, 1982)

Irving, Washington (1783–1859) U.S. writer

1 For what is history, but...huge libel on human nature, to which we industriously add page after page, volume after volume, as if we were holding up a monument to the honor, rather than the infamy of our species.
A History of New York (1809)

2 Whenever a man's friends begin to compliment him about looking young, he may be sure that they think he is growing old.
"Bachelors," *Bracebridge Hall* (1822)

3 There is nothing, however, that conquers John Bull's crustiness sooner than eating, whatever may be the cookery; and nothing brings him into good humor with his company sooner than eating together.
John Bull is a stereotype dating from about 1712, personifying the typical Englishman, the English people, or their government. *Tales of a Traveler* (1824)

4 There is a certain relief in change, even though it be from bad to worse; as I have found in traveling in a stagecoach, that it is often a comfort to shift one's position and be bruised in a new place.
"To the Reader," *Tales of a Traveler* (1824)

5 On the shore of this wondrous isle the kraken heaves its unwieldy bulk and wallows many a rood. Here the sea-serpent...lies coiled up during the intervals of its revelations to the eyes of true believers...the Flying Dutchman finds a port, and casts his anchor, and furls his shadowy sail, and takes a brief repose from his eternal cruisings.
The Phantom Island (1858)

6 A tart temper never mellows with age, and a sharp tongue is the only edged tool that grows keener with constant use.
"Rip Van Winkle," *The Sketch Book* (1819–20)

7 A woman's whole life is a history of the affections.
"The Broken Heart," *The Sketch Book* (1819–20)

8 History fades into fable; fact becomes clouded with doubt and controversy; the inscription molders from the tablet: the statue falls from the pedestal. Columns, arches, pyramids, what are they but heaps of sand; and their epitaphs, but characters written in the dust?
"Westminster Abbey," *The Sketch Book* (1819–20)

9 The almighty dollar, that great object of universal devotion throughout our land, seems to have no genuine devotees in these peculiar villages.
"The Creole Village," *Wolfert's Roost* (1855)

Isherwood, Christopher (1904–86) British-born U.S. writer

1 To Christopher, Berlin meant Boys.
Referring to himself. *Christopher and His Kind* (1976)

2 California is a tragic country—like Palestine, like every Promised Land. Its short history is a fever-chart of migrations—the land-rush, the gold-rush, the oil-rush, the movie-rush—followed, in each instance, by counter-migrations of the disappointed and unsuccessful.
1947. "Los Angeles," *Exhumations* (1966)

3 To live sanely in Los Angeles...you have to cultivate the art of staying awake.
1947. "Los Angeles," *Exhumations* (1966)

4 I am a camera with its shutter open, quite passive, recording, not thinking.
Autumn 1930. "Berlin Diary," *Goodbye to Berlin* (1939)

5 We live in stirring times—tea-stirring times.
Mr Norris Changes Trains (1935)

6 My novel is so terrific that I cannot put pen to paper.
1953. Quoted in *Diaries* (Stephen Spender; 1948–53)

Ivan IV, Tsar ("Ivan the Terrible"; 1530–84) Russian monarch

1 Did I ascend the throne by robbery or armed bloodshed? I was

born to rule by the grace of God; and I do not even remember my father bequeathing the kingdom to me and blessing me—I grew up upon the throne.
Letter to Prince Kurbsky (September 1577)

2 The autocracy of this Russian kingdom...has its beginning from the great Tsar Vladimir, who enlightened the whole Russian land with holy baptism...the great Tsar Vladimir Monomach...and the brave and great sovereign, Alexander Nevsky.
Letter to Prince Kurbsky (September 1577)

Iverson, Ken (Francis Kenneth Iverson; b.1925) U.S. industrialist

1 Don't study the idea to death with experts and committees. Get on with it and see if it works.
Speech (February 5, 1996)

2 We believe that there are two successful ways to manage in relationship to employees. That is: tell them everything or tell them nothing.
Speech (February 5, 1996)

3 We don't publicize our failures. When something doesn't work don't leave the corpse lying around.
Speech (February 5, 1996)

4 You do not get good people if you lay off half your workforce just because one year the economy isn't very good and then you hire them back.
Speech (February 5, 1996)

5 Entrepreneurs should be able to spend 80 percent of their time getting customers.
Inc. (April 1996)

6 When there's a deep-seated conflict between management and labor, it's because of autocratic management practices.
New Yorker (February 25, 1991)

Ives, Charles (Charles Edward Ives; 1874–1954) U.S. composer

1 Music is one of the ways God has of beating in on man.
"Epitaph for David Twitchell" (1924)

2 You goddam sissy!—When you hear strong masculine music like this, get up AND USE YOUR EARS LIKE A MAN!
Said to a noisy member of the audience during a performance of Carl Ruggles' *Men and Mountains.* Remark (1931)

3 Beauty in music is too often confused with something that lets the ears lie back in an easy chair.
Quoted in *Introduction to Contemporary Music* (Joseph Machlis; 1963)

Izetbegovic, Alija (b.1925) Bosnia and Herzogovinian president

1 Defend us, or let us defend ourselves.
Calling for an end to the arms embargo during the war in Bosnia. Speech (September 8, 1993)

Izzard, Eddie (b.1962) British comedian

1 At school I was quite sure I was a talentless bastard, but at 15 I got my first part in a school play and learnt the art of upstaging.
Independent, London (June 14, 1994)

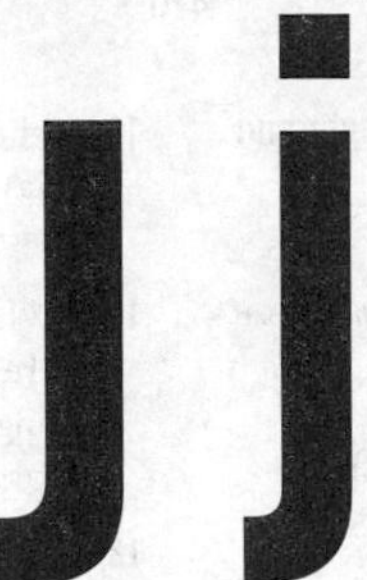

Jackson, Andrew (1767–1845) U.S. president

Quotations about Jackson

1 I—am—a man and you—are—another.
Black Hawk (1767–1838) Native American leader. Said to president Andrew Jackson. Quoted in *Abraham Lincoln, the Prairie Years* (Carl Sandburg; 1929)

2 He was too generous to be frugal, too kindhearted to be thrifty, too honest to live above his means.
Vernon Parrington (1871–1929) U.S. educator. *Main Currents in American Thought* (1927), vol. 1, bk. 2

3 I tread in the footsteps of illustrious men...In receiving from the people the sacred trust twice confined to my illustrious predecessor.
Martin Van Buren (1782–1862) U.S. president. Andrew Jackson was his presidential predecessor. Inaugural presidential address (March 4, 1837)

Quotations by Jackson

4 There are no necessary evils in government. Its evils exist only in its abuses.
Veto of the Bank Bill (July 10, 1832)

5 Elevate them guns a little lower.
Order given while watching the effect of the U.S. artillery on the British lines at the Battle of New Orleans (1815). Attrib.

Jackson, Bo (Vincent Edward Jackson; b.1962) U.S. football and baseball player

1 Baseball was fun when I was in college. It's my job now. But I like my 3–11 shift.
The Sporting News (July 3, 1989), quoted in *Baseball's Greatest Quotations* (Paul Dickson, ed.; 1991)

Jackson, Chevalier (1865–1958) U.S. laryngologist

1 In teaching the medical student the primary requisite is to keep him awake.
The Life of Chevalier Jackson: an Autobiography (1938), ch. 16

Jackson, George (1941–71) U.S. political activist and writer

1 The power of the people lies in its greater potential for violence.
Blood in My Eye (1972)

2 The ultimate expression of law is not order—it's prison.
Blood in My Eye (1972)

3 I'm part of a righteous people who anger slowly but rage undammed.
March 24, 1970. Letter, *Soledad Brother* (1970)

4 White people tend to grossly underestimate all blacks, out of habit. Blacks have been overestimating whites in a conditioned reflex.
June 10, 1970. Letter, *Soledad Brother* (1970)

5 He was out of place, out of season, too naive, too innocent, too cultured, too civil for these times. That is why his end was so predictable.
April 11, 1968. Referring to Martin Luther King, Jr, who was assassinated on April 4, 1968. Letter to his father, *Soledad Brother* (1970)

6 I don't care how long I live. Over this I have no control, but I do care about what kind of life I live, and I can control this. I may not live but another five minutes but it will be five minutes definitely on my terms.
January 23, 1967. Letter to his father, *Soledad Brother* (1970)

7 Love of self and kind is the first law of nature.
December 1964. Letter to his father, *Soledad Brother* (1970)

8 The payment for life is death.
April 18, 1965. Letter to his father, *Soledad Brother* (1970)

9 Men who read Lenin, Fanon, and Che don't riot, "they mass," "they rage," they dig graves.
April 1970. Letter to his lawyer, *Soledad Brother* (1970)

10 Love has never turned aside the boot, blade, or bullet. Neither has it ever satisfied my hunger of body or mind.
July 28, 1967. Letter to his mother, *Soledad Brother* (1970)

11 The real world calls for a predatory man's brand of thinking.
February 1965. Letter to his mother, *Soledad Brother* (1970)

Jackson, Glenda (b.1936) British actor and politician

1 My mother polishes them to an inch of their lives until the metal shows. That sums up the Academy Awards—all glitter on the outside and base metal coming through. Nice presents for a day. But they don't make you any better.
Referring to her two Oscars: *Women in Love* (1969) and *A Touch of Class* (1973). *People* (March 18, 1985), quoted in *Chambers Film Quotes* (Tony Crawley, ed.; 1991)

Jackson, Helen Hunt (originally Helen Maria Fiske; 1830–85) U.S. writer

1 My body, eh. Friend Death, how now?
Why all this tedious pomp of writ?
Thou hast reclaimed it sure and slow
For half a century, bit by bit.
"Habeas Corpus" (1885), st. 1

Jackson, Janet (Janet Damita Jackson; b.1966) U.S. singer and actress

1 Business...that's what I'm all about.
Quoted in *Out of the Madness: the Strictly Unauthorised Biography of Janet* (Bart Andrews and J. Randy Taraborrelli; 1994)

Jackson, Jesse (Jesse Louis Jackson; b.1941) U.S. clergyman, civil rights leader, and politician

1 Hands that picked cotton in 1864 will pick a president in 1984.
Address at the Lincoln Memorial (August 27, 1983), quoted in *Jesse Jackson* (Robert E. Jakoubek; 1991)

2 I am—Somebody. I may be poor, but I am—Somebody! I may be on welfare, but I am—Somebody! I may be uneducated, but I am—Somebody! I may be in jail, but I am—Somebody! I am—Somebody! I must be, I'm God's child. I must be respected and protected. I am black and I am beautiful! I am—Somebody! Soul Power!
Operation Breadbasket was launched with the aim of using economic pressure from the black community and its churches to compel U.S. companies to end discriminatory practices. Address to Operation Breadbasket rally (1966), quoted in *Jesse Jackson* (Robert E. Jakoubek; 1991)

3 His foreparents came to America in immigrant ships. My foreparents came to America in slave ships. But whatever the original ships, we are both in the same boat tonight.
Referring to Michael Dukakis who was of Greek origin. Dukakis was running against Jackson for the presidential nomination. Speech (July 1988)

4 I cast my bread upon the waters long ago. Now it's time for you to send it back to me—toasted and buttered on both sides.
Speech to black voters (January 30, 1984)

5 The great temptation in these difficult days of racial polarization and economic injustice is to make political arguments black and white and miss the moral imperative of wrong and right. Vanity asks, "Is it popular?" Politics asks "Will it win?" Morality and conscience ask, "Is it right?"
Speech to the Democratic National Convention (July 14, 1992)

6 America is not a blanket woven from one thread, one color, one cloth.
Speech to the Democratic National Convention, Atlanta (July 1988)

7 What makes New York so special? It's the invitation of the Statue of Liberty—give me your tired, your poor, your huddled masses who yearn to breathe free. Not restricted to English only.
Quoting a poem by Emma Lazarus. Speech to the Democratic National Convention, Atlanta (July 1988)

8 Our time has come! No lie can live forever. Our time has come. We must leave the racial battleground and come to the economic common ground and the moral high ground. America, our time has come!
Speech to the Democratic National Convention, San Francisco (July 17, 1984)

9 We must not measure greatness from the mansion down, but from the manger up.
Speech to the Democratic National Convention, San Francisco (July 17, 1984)

10 If I can conceive it and believe it, I can achieve it. It's not my *ap*titude but my *at*titude that will determine my *al*titude—*with a little intestinal fortitude!*
Ebony (August 1988)

11 I hear that melting pot stuff a lot, and all I can say is that we haven't melted.
Interview, *Playboy* (November 1969)

12 When we're unemployed, we're called lazy; when the whites are unemployed it's called a depression, which is the psycholinguistics of racism.
Interview by David Frost, *The Americans* (1970)

13 Drugs are the greatest threat to our national security.
The Koppel Report, ABC Television (September 13, 1988)

14 We have allowed death to change its name from Southern rope to Northern dope. Too many black youths have been victimized by pushing dope into their veins instead of hope into their brains.
Quoted in *Jesse Jackson* (Robert E. Jakoubek; 1991)

15 I am too controlled, I'm too clear. I'm too mature to be angry.
1988. On hearing that he had not been selected as Dukakis's running mate in the 1988 presidential election. Quoted in *Jesse Jackson* (Robert E. Jakoubek; 1991)

Jackson, Mahalia (1911–72) U.S. gospel singer

1 Blues are the songs of despair, but gospel songs are the songs of hope.
Movin' On Up (Mahalia Jackson and Evan McLeod Wylie; 1966)

2 The person who sings only the blues is like someone in a deep pit yelling for help.
Movin' On Up (Mahalia Jackson and Evan McLeod Wylie; 1966)

Jackson, Mattie J. (*fl.* 19th century) U.S. writer

1 Bondage and torture, scourges and chains
Placed on our backs indelible stains.
The Story of Mattie J. Jackson (1866), quoted in *Six Women's Slave Narratives* (William L. Andrews, ed.; 1988)

Jackson, Michael (b.1958) U.S. pop singer

1 It is in my family on my father's side. I use make-up to even out the blotches. When people make up stories that I don't want to be who I am it hurts me...what about all the millions of people who sit out in the sun to become darker, to become other than what they are? No one says anything about that.
Referring to vitiligo, a skin pigmentation disorder. Interview (1993)

2 I haven't scratched the surface yet of what my real purpose is for being here.
Interview, *Ebony* (May 1992), quoted in *Q Encyclopaedia of Rock Stars* (Dafydd Rees and Luke Crampton, eds.; 1996)

Jackson, Reggie (Reginald Martinez Jackson; b.1946) U.S. baseball player

1 A baseball swing is a very finely tuned instrument. It is repetition and more repetition, then a little more after that.
Remark (1984)

Jackson, Shirley (1916–65) U.S. novelist

1 I believe that all women, but especially housewives, tend to think in lists.
Life Among The Savages (1953)

Jackson, Shoeless Joe (Joseph Jefferson Jackson; 1887?–1951) U.S. baseball player

1 I ain't afraid to tell the world that it don't take school stuff to help a fella play ball.
Attrib.

Jackson, Stonewall (Thomas Jonathan Jackson; 1824–63) U.S. soldier

1 Always mystify, mislead, and surprise the enemy, if possible.
His strategic motto during the Civil War. Motto (1860s)

2 No, Captain, the men are right. Kill the brave ones, they lead the others on.
In response to an officer during the Civil War who told his men they should have captured a Union major instead of killing him. Remark (August 29, 1862)

Jacobi, Abraham (1830–1919) German-born U.S. physician

1 Treat the man who is sick and not a Greek name.
Bulletin of the New York Academy of Medicine (1928), no. 4

Jacobi, Karl Gustav Jakob (1804–51) German mathematician

1 One should always generalize.
Quoted in *The Mathematical Experience* (P. Davis and R. Hersh; 1981)

2 Mathematics is the science of what is clear by itself.
Quoted in *The World of Mathematics* (J. R. Newman, ed.; 1956)

Jacobs, Harriet Ann (pen name of Linda Brent; 1813–97) U.S. writer

1 Could you have seen that mother clinging to her child, when they fastened the irons upon his wrists; could you have heard her heart-rending groans, and seen her bloodshot eyes wander wildly from face to face, vainly pleading for mercy; could you have witnessed that scene as I saw it, you would exclaim, *Slavery is damnable!*
Incidents in the Life of a Slave Girl (1861)

2 Cruelty is contagious in uncivilized communities.
Incidents in the Life of a Slave Girl (1861)

Jacobs, Jane (originally Jane Butzner; b.1916) U.S. writer and urban theorist

1 Virtually all of urban Detroit is weak on vitality and diversity...It is ring superimposed upon ring of failed belts.
The Death and Life of Great American Cities: The Failure of Town Planning (1961)

2 In the big wild-animal reservations of Africa, tourists are warned to leave their car under no circumstances until they reach a lodge. This is also the technique practiced in...the vast, blind-eyed reservation of Los Angeles.
Referring to the response to Los Angeles' high crime rate. *The Death and Life of Great American Cities: The Failure of Town Planning* (1961)

Jacobs, Joe (1896–1940) U.S. boxing manager

1 We wuz robbed—We should have stood in bed.
Referring to Max Schmeling's defeat by Jack Sharkey in the heavyweight title fight, June 21, 1932. Quoted in *Strong Cigars and Lovely Women* (J. Lardner; 1932)

Jaeger, Gustav (1851–1927) German academic and clothing manufacturer

1 Animal Wool, which Nature has created to clothe the animal body, is the "survival of the fittest" clothing material. Vegetable fiber (linen and cotton) is not a natural clothing material, and is only used by Man.
Health Culture (1892), ch. 1

2 The modern trousers are largely responsible for the sparrow-like legs and protruding stomachs which are so common with men, and for the frequent inability or disinclination to walk, run or jump; further they are a cause of the hemorrhoids which set in when the first vigor of youth has passed away.
Health Culture (1892), ch. 5

Jagger, Mick (Michael Philip Jagger; b.1943) British rock musician and songwriter

Quotations about Jagger

1 He took my music. But he gave me my name.
Muddy Waters (1915–83) U.S. blues musician. Quoted in *All You Need Is Love* (Tony Palmer; 1976)

Quotations by Jagger

2 I can't get no satisfaction.
Song lyric. "Satisfaction" (co-written with Keith Richards; 1965)

3 Everywhere I hear the sound of marching, charging feet, boy. 'Cause summer's here and the time is right for fighting in the street.
Song lyric. "Street Fighting Man" (co-written with Keith Richards; 1968)

4 You can't always get what you want,
But, if you try sometimes, you just might find,
You get what you need.
Song lyric. "You Can't Always Get What You Want" (co-written with Keith Richards; 1969)

5 I don't understand the connection between music and violence. I just know that I get very aroused by music, but that it doesn't arouse me violently.
Quoted in *Rock 'n' Roll Babylon* (Gary Herman; 1994)

6 The only true performance is the one which attains madness.
Quoted in *The Wit and Wisdom of Rock and Roll* (Maxim Jabukowski, ed.; 1983)

7 I'd rather be dead than singing "Satisfaction" when I'm 45.
"(I Can't Get No) Satisfaction" was released in 1965. Quoted in *The Wit and Wisdom of Rock and Roll* (Maxim Jabukowski, ed.; 1983)

8 Let's Spend the Night Together
1967. Song title. The song was co-written with Keith Richards.

9 Street Fighting Man
1968. Song title. The song was co-written with Keith Richards.

10 Sympathy for the Devil
1968. Song title. The song was co-written with Keith Richards.

James I, King of England, Scotland, and Ireland (1566–1625) English monarch

Quotations about James I

1 I will that a king succeed me, and who but my kinsman the king of Scots.
1603
Elizabeth I (1533–1603) English monarch. Said shortly before she died, when pressed concerning the succession. Referring to James VI of Scotland, who became James I of England and Ireland in 1603. Quoted in *The Reign of Elizabeth, 1558–1603* (John Bennett Black; 1936), ch. 13

Quotations by James I

2 The state of monarchy is the supremest thing upon earth; for kings are not only God's Lieutenants upon earth, and sit upon God's throne, but even by God himself they are called Gods.
Speech to the English Parliament (March 21, 1609)

3 A branch of the sin of drunkenness, which is the root of all sins.
Referring to smoking. *A Counterblast to Tobacco* (1604)

4 A custom loathsome to the eye, hateful to the nose, harmful to the brain, dangerous to the lungs, and in the black, stinking fume thereof, nearest resembling the horrible Stygian smoke of the pit that is bottomless.
Referring to smoking. *A Counterblast to Tobacco* (1604)

5 After the end of divine service our good people be not disturbed...from any lawful recreation, such as...archery for men, leaping...account still as prohibited all unlawful games to be used upon Sundays only, as bear and bull-baiting...bowling.
The Book of Sports (1618)

6 I will govern according to the common weal, but not according to the common will.
1621. Quoted in *History of the English People* (J. R. Green; 1879), pt. 7, ch. 4

7 No Bishop, no King.
An expression, at a conference on doctrinal reform held at Hampton Court on January 14, 1604, of his belief that a nonepiscopal form of church government was incompatible with monarchy. Quoted in *Sum and Substance of the Conference* (William Barlow; January 14, 1604)

8 These are rare attainments for a damsel, but pray tell me, can she spin?
On being introduced to a young girl proficient in Latin, Greek, and Hebrew. Attrib.

James II, King of England, Scotland, and Ireland (1633–1701) English monarch

Quotations about James II

1 The best that I can wish you is that we shall never see each other again.
Louis XIV (1638–1715) French monarch. Said to James II, who was leaving for Ireland in an attempt to regain his throne. Attrib.

Quotations by James II

2 I have often heretofore ventured my life in defence of this nation; and I shall go as far as any man in preserving it in all its just rights and liberties.
Said on becoming king. Address to the Privy Council (1685)

3 This is a standard of rebellion.
Referring to a petition from seven bishops against his Declaration of Indulgence (1687; reissued May 7, 1688); the bishops were prosecuted for seditious libel, but acquitted. Remark (May 7, 1688)

James V, King of Scotland (1512–42) Scottish monarch

1 Adieu, farewell, it came with a lass, it will pass with a lass.
Said upon hearing of the birth of his daughter, Mary, as he lay dying after the Scottish defeat at the battle of Solway Moss, northern England. Remark (December 1542), quoted in *Quotations in History* (Alan and Veronica Palmer; 1976)

James, Alice (1848–92) U.S. diarist

1 I suppose one has a greater sense of intellectual degradation after an interview with a doctor than from any human experience.
September 27, 1890. *The Diary of Alice James* (Leon Edel, ed.; 1964)

2 Notwithstanding the poverty of my outside experience, I have always had a significance for myself, and every chance to stumble along my straight and narrow little path, and to worship at the feet of my Deity, and what more can a human soul ask for?
The Diary of Alice James (Leon Edel, ed.; 1964)

3 It is so comic to hear oneself called old, even at ninety I suppose!
June 14, 1889. Letter to William James, *The Diary of Alice James* (Leon Edel, ed.; 1964)

James, Clive (b.1939) Australian writer and broadcaster

1 Even today, when some oaf who has confused rudeness with blunt speech tells me exactly what he thinks, I tend to stand there wondering what I have done to deserve it, instead of telling him exactly what I think right back.
Falling Towards England (1985), ch. 4

2 The British hamburger thus symbolised, with savage neatness, the country's failure to provide its ordinary people with food which did anything more for them than sustain life.
Falling Towards England (1985), ch.17

James, C. L. R. (Cyril Lionel Robert James; 1901–89) Trinidadian writer, political theorist, and educator

1 A new type of woman arises. She is called a career woman. A man is never a career man. That is his right and privilege. But the woman is called career woman because her "career" in modern society demands she place herself in a subordinate position or even renounce normal life.
Letter to Constance Webb (1943), quoted in *The C.L.R. James Reader* (Anna Grimshaw, ed.; 1992)

2 Literary criticism today means nothing to anybody except literary critics.
Unpublished manuscript, quoted in *The C.L.R. James Reader* (Anna Grimshaw, ed.; 1992)

3 Time would pass, old empires would fall and new ones take their place...before I discovered that it is not quality of goods and utility which matter, but movement; not where you are or what you have, but where you have come from, where you are going and the rate at which you are getting there.
Beyond a Boundary (1963)

4 What do they know of cricket who only cricket know? West Indians crowding to Tests bring with them the whole past history and future hopes of the islands.
Beyond a Boundary (1963)

5 Body-line was not an incident, it was not an accident, it was not a temporary aberration. It was the violence and ferocity of our age expressing itself in cricket.
"Body-line" is the style of bowling first employed by English cricketer Harold Larwood in 1932, in which the bowler aims the ball hard and fast towards the body of the batsman. *Beyond a Boundary* (1963)

6 What is wrong with nuclear weapons?...there is nothing wrong with nuclear weapons as such, it is the persons who are in control of this society and use them.
C.L.R. James's 80th Birthday Lectures (1984)

7 Eminence engenders enemies.
The Black Jacobins (1938)

8 Great men make history, but only such history as it is possible for them to make. Their freedom of achievement is limited by the necessities of their environment.
The Black Jacobins (1938)

9 Men will say (and accept) anything in order to foster national pride or soothe a troubled conscience.
The Black Jacobins (1938)

10 The cruelties of property and privilege are always more ferocious than the revenges of poverty and oppression. For the one aims at perpetuating resented injustice, the other is merely a momentary passion soon appeased.
The Black Jacobins (1938)

11 The race question is subsidiary to the class question in politics, and to think of imperialism in terms of race is disastrous. But to neglect the racial factor as merely incidental is an error only less grave than to make it fundamental.
The Black Jacobins (1938)

12 A great work of art bears its meaning on its face.
Quoted in *The C.L.R. James Reader* (Anna Grimshaw, ed.; 1992)

James, Henry (1843–1916) U.S.-born British writer and critic

Quotations about James

1 Henry James has a mind so fine that no idea could violate it.
T. S. Eliot (1888–1965) U.S.-born British poet and playwright. Attrib.

2 Henry James was one of the nicest old ladies I ever met.
William Faulkner (1897–1962) U.S. novelist. Quoted in *The Battle and the Books: Some Aspects of Henry James* (Edward Stone; 1964)

3 Mr. James' cosmopolitanism is, after all, limited; to be really cosmopolitan, a man must be at home even in his own country.
Thomas Wentworth Higginson (1823–1911) U.S. writer and political reformer. *Short Studies of American Authors* (1879)

4 The sudden break-down of a solid equilibre character like Henry's is very different (& must be differently dealt with) from the chronic flares and twitches of the older brother—William o'the wisp James.
Edith Wharton (1862–1937) U.S. novelist. Letter to W. Morton Fullerton (March 24, 1910), quoted in *The Letters of Edith Wharton* (R. W. B. Lewis and Nancy Lewis, eds.; 1988)

5 I am embalmed in a book of Henry James; the American Scene: like a fly in amber. I don't expect to get out; but it is very quiet and luminous.
Virginia Woolf (1882–1941) British novelist and critic. Letter to Lady Robert Cecil (August 16, 1907), quoted in *The Letters of Virginia Woolf* (Nigel Nicolson, ed.; 1975), vol. 1

Quotations by James

6 I'm glad you like adverbs—I adore them; they are the only qualifications I really much respect.
Letter to Miss M. Bentham Edwards (January 5, 1912), quoted in *The Letters of Henry James* (Percy Lubbock, ed.; 1920)

7 It takes a great deal of history to produce a little literature.
Hawthorne (1879), ch. 1

8 Whatever question there may be of his talent, there can be none I think of his genius. It was a slim and crooked one, but it was eminently personal.
Hawthorne (1879), ch. 4

9 To kill a human being is, after all, the least injury you can do him.
My Friend Bingham (1867)

10 Experience is never limited, and it is never complete; it is an immense sensibility, a kind of huge spider-web of the finest silken threads suspended in the chamber of consciousness, and catching every air-borne particle in its tissue.
"The Art of Fiction," *Partial Portraits* (1888)

11 The only obligation to which in advance we may hold a novel, without incurring the accusation of being arbitrary, is that it be interesting.
"The Art of Fiction," *Partial Portraits* (1888)

12 Try to be one of the people on whom nothing is lost.
"The Art of Fiction," *Partial Portraits* (1888)

13 What is character but the determination of incident? What is incident but the illustration of character?
"The Art of Fiction," *Partial Portraits* (1888)

14 I am prepared with the confession that the "ghost story", as we for convenience call it, has ever been for me the most possible form of the fairy tale.
"The Altar of the Dead," *Prefaces* (1909)

15 In art economy is always beauty.
"The Altar of the Dead," *Prefaces* (1909)

16 The ever-importunate murmur, "Dramatize it, dramatize it!"
"The Altar of the Dead," *Prefaces* (1909)

17 The deep well of unconscious cerebration.
"The American," *Prefaces* (1909)

18 The historian, essentially, wants more documents than he can really use; the dramatist only wants more liberties than he can really take.
"The Aspern Papers," *Prefaces* (1909)

19 Live all you can; it's a mistake not to. It doesn't so much matter what you do in particular, so long as you have your life. If you haven't had that what *have* you had?
The Ambassadors (1903), bk. 5, ch. 2

20 The Story is just the spoiled child of art.
The Ambassadors (1903), preface

21 The terrible *fluidity of self-revelation.*
The Ambassadors (1903), preface

22 The biggest little place in America.
Referring to Concord, Massachusetts. *The American Scene* (1907), ch. 8

23 Experience was to be taken as showing that one might get a five-pound note as one got a light for a cigarette; but one had to check the friendly impulse to ask for it in the same way.
The Awkward Age (1899)

24 London doesn't love the latent or the lurking, has neither time, nor taste, nor sense for anything less discernable than the red flag in front of the steam-roller. It wants cash over the counter and letters ten feet high.
The Awkward Age (1899)

25 The standing quarrel between painters and *littérateurs* will probably never be healed. Writers will continue to criticize pictures from the literary point of view, and painters will continue to denounce their criticisms from the free-spoken atmosphere of the studio. Each party will, in a manner, to our sense, be in the right.
"On Some Pictures Lately Exhibited," *The Galaxy* (July 1875)

26 Cats and monkeys, monkeys and cats—all human life is there.
The Madonna of the Future (1879), vol. 1

27 There are few things in life more agreeable than the hour dedicated to the ceremony known as afternoon tea.
The Portrait of a Lady (1881), ch. 1

28 An Englishman is never so natural as when he is holding his tongue.
The Portrait of a Lady (1881), ch. 10

29 I think patriotism is like charity—it begins at home.
The Portrait of a Lady (1881), ch. 10

30 I don't care anything about reasons but I know what I like.
The Portrait of a Lady (1881), ch. 24

31 Money's a horrid thing to follow, but a charming thing to meet.
The Portrait of a Lady (1881), ch. 35

32 There were moments, for instance, when, as he bent over his papers, the light breath of his dead host was as distinctly in his hair as his own elbows were on the table before him.
"The Real Thing," *The Real Thing, and other tales* (1893)

33 The superiority of one man's opinion over another's is never so great as when the opinion is about a woman.
The Tragic Muse (1890), ch. 9

34 We were all alone with the quiet day, and his little heart, dispossessed, had stopped.
The Turn of the Screw (1898)

35 It was like fighting with a demon for a human soul.
Said by the governess, upon confronting the ghost of Peter Quint. *The Turn of the Screw* (1898)

36 What *is* he? He's a horror.
The governess-narrator describing the apparition she has seen to Mrs. Grose. *The Turn of the Screw* (1898)

37 It was an oddity of Mrs. Lowder's that her face in speech was like a lighted window at night, but that silence immediately drew the curtain.
The Wings of the Dove (1902), bk. 11 ch. 2

38 Summer afternoon—summer afternoon; to me those have always been the two most beautiful words in the English language.
Quoted in *A Backward Glance* (Edith Wharton; 1934)

39 So here it is at last, the distinguished thing!
1916. A "voice" heard in the room as he fell victim to his first stroke. Quoted in *A Backward Glance* (Edith Wharton; 1934), ch. 14

40 I can stand a great deal of gold.
Referring to seeing an ornate drawing room. Attrib. "Social Occasions," *The Legend of the Master* (Simon Nowell-Smith; 1947)

41 I hate American simplicity. I glory in the piling up of complications of every sort.
Quoted in *The Letters of Henry James* (Leon Edel, ed.; 1953–72), vol. 4, introduction

James, M. R. (Montague Rhodes James; 1862–1936) British writer and scholar

1 The Malice of Inanimate Objects
1933. Story title.

James, William (1842–1910) U.S. psychologist and philosopher

Quotations about James

1 Whenever I have time I now read James's "Varieties of Religious Experience." This book does me a *lot* of good...I think that it helps me get rid of the *Sorge*.
Ludwig Wittgenstein (1889–1951) Austrian philosopher. Referring to William James's work of 1902. *Sorge* approximates to melancholy. Letter to Bertrand Russell (June 22, 1912), quoted in *Ludwig Wittgenstein: Cambridge Letters* (B. McGuinness and G. H. von Wright, eds.; 1995)

Quotations by James

2 I wished by treating psychology *like* a natural science, to help her become one.
A Plea for Psychology as a Natural Science (1892)

3 The union of the mathematician with the poet, fervor and measure, passion with correctness, this surely is the ideal.
Clifford's Lectures and Essays (1879)

4 Everything real must be experienceable somewhere, and every kind of thing experienced must somewhere be real.
Essays in Radical Empiricism (1912)

5 History is a bath of blood.
Memories and Studies (1911)

6 Many persons nowadays seem to think that any conclusion must be very scientific if the arguments in favor of it are derived from twitching of frogs' legs—especially if the frogs are decapitated—and that—on the other hand—any doctrine chiefly vouched for by the feelings of human beings—with heads on their shoulders—must be benighted and supersititious.
Pragmatism: A New Name for Old Ways of Thinking (1907)

7 Test every concept by the question, "What sensible difference to anybody will its truth make?"
Pragmatism: A New Name for Old Ways of Thinking (1907)

8 The unrest which keeps the never stopping clock of metaphysics going is the thought that the non-existence of the world is just as possible as its existence.
Some Problems of Philosophy (1911)

9 A strictly voluntary act has to be guided by idea, perception, and volition, throughout its entire course.
The Principles of Psychology (1890), vol. 1

10 Consciousness, from our natal day, is of a teeming multiplicity of objects and relations, and what we call simple sensations are results of discriminative attention, pushed often to a very high degree.
The Principles of Psychology (1890), vol. 1

11 Consciousness, however small, is an illegitimate birth in any philosophy that starts without it, and yet professes to explain all the facts by continuous evolution.
The Principles of Psychology (1890), vol. 1

12 Consciousness...is nothing jointed; it flows. A "river" or a "stream" are the metaphors by which it is most naturally described.
The Principles of Psychology (1890), vol. 1

13 Consciousness...is only intense when nerve-processes are hesitant. In rapid, automatic, habitual action it sinks to a minimum.
The Principles of Psychology (1890), vol. 1

14 Everyone must know the tantalizing effect of the blank rhythm of some forgotten verse, restlessly dancing in one's mind, striving to be filled out with words.
The Principles of Psychology (1890), vol. 1

15 One great use of the Soul has always been to account for, and at the same time to guarantee, the closed individuality of each personal consciousness.
The Principles of Psychology (1890), vol. 1

16 Our psychological duty is to cling as closely as possible to the actual constitution of the thought we are studying. We may err as much by excess as by defect.
The Principles of Psychology (1890), vol. 1

17 Reason is only one out of a thousand possibilities in the thinking of each of us. Who can count all the silly fancies, the grotesque suppositions, the utterly irrelevant reflections he makes in the course of a day?
The Principles of Psychology (1890), vol. 1

18 Suppose we try to recall a forgotten name. The state of our consciousness is peculiar. There is a gap therein...A sort of wraith of the name is in it, beckoning us in a given direction.
The Principles of Psychology (1890), vol. 1

19 The *great* snare of the psychologist is the *confusion of his own standpoint with that of the mental fact* about which he is making his report. I shall hereafter call this the "psychologist's fallacy."
The Principles of Psychology (1890), vol. 1

20 The machinery of recall is thus the same as the machinery of association, and the machinery of association...is nothing but the elementary law of habit in the nerve centers.
The Principles of Psychology (1890), vol. 1

21 The only thing which psychology has the right to postulate at the outset is the fact of thinking itself, and that must first be taken up and analyzed.
The Principles of Psychology (1890), vol. 1

22 There are every year works published whose contents show them to be by real lunatics.
The Principles of Psychology (1890), vol. 1

23 The stream of our thought is like a river. On the whole easy simple flowing predominates...But at intervals an obstruction, a set-back, a log-jam occurs, stops the current, creates an eddy, and makes things move the other way.
The Principles of Psychology (1890), vol. 1

24 The transition between one thought and another is no more a break in the *thought* than a joint in a bamboo is a break in the wood. It is a part of the *consciousness* as much as the joint is a part of the *bamboo*.
The Principles of Psychology (1890), vol. 1

25 The truth is that large tracts of human speech are nothing but *signs of direction* in thought.
The Principles of Psychology (1890), vol. 1

26 When very fresh, our minds carry an immense horizon with them. The present image shoots its perspective far before it, irradiating in advance the regions in which lie the thoughts as yet unborn.
The Principles of Psychology (1890), vol. 1

27 If merely "feeling good" could decide, drunkenness would be the supremely valid human experience.
The Varieties of Religious Experience (1902)

28 Mohammed's revelations all came from the subconscious sphere.
The Varieties of Religious Experience (1902)

29 Our civilization is founded on the shambles, and every individual existence goes out in a lonely spasm of helpless agony.
The Varieties of Religious Experience (1902)

30 There is no worse lie than a truth misunderstood by those who hear it.
The Varieties of Religious Experience (1902)

31 The Sufis have existed in Persia from the earliest times, and as their pantheism is so at variance with the hot and rigid monotheism of the Arab mind, it has been suggested that Sufism must have been inoculated into Islam by Hindu influences.
The Varieties of Religious Experience (1902)

32 The sway of alcohol over mankind is unquestionably due to its power to stimulate the mystical faculties of human nature.
The Varieties of Religious Experience (1902)

33 We are thinking beings, and we cannot exclude the intellect from participating in any of our functions.
The Varieties of Religious Experience (1902)

34 Science, like life, feeds on its own decay. New facts burst old rules; then newly divined conceptions bind old and new together into a reconciling law.
The Will to Believe (1897)

35 Man lives for science as well as bread.
1875. "Vivisection," *The Works of William James* (1987), vol. 17, pt. 1

36 I take it that no man is educated who has never dallied with the thought of suicide.
Attrib.

Jami, Nur ad-Din Abd ar-Rahman ibn Ahmad (1414–92) Persian poet and mystic

1 The Prophet Muhammad is quoted as saying, "The believer is high-spirited and speaks pleasantly; the hypocrite is sullen and frowning."
The Beharistan; or The Abode of Spring (15th century), quoted in *Four Sufi Classics* (Idris Shah, ed.; 1980)

Jan III Sobieski, King of Poland (1624–96) Polish soldier and monarch

1 The immortal God...has blest us with so signal a victory as scarce the memory of man can equal. Thanks be to Heaven, now the half-moon triumphs no longer over the cross.
1683. Letter to his wife, referring to his victory over the Turks at Vienna (1683).

2 I came; I saw; God conquered.
1683. Announcing to the pope his victory over the Turks at Vienna (paraphrasing Caesar's famous phrase "veni, vidi, vici"). Attrib.

Janner, Greville Ewan, Baron Janner of Braunstone (b.1928) British writer and broadcaster

1 Executive style and commercial success are synonymous.
Janner on Presentation (1981), ch. 2

Janov, Arthur U.S. therapist and author

1 Primal therapy shuts off any transference and does not permit neurotic behavior of any kind because that means the patient isn't feeling; he is acting out.
"The Primal Scream" (1970), quoted in *A Complete Guide to Therapy* (Joel Kovel, ed.; 1976)

Janowitz, Tama (b.1957) U.S. writer

1 With publicity comes humiliation.
International Herald Tribune, Paris (September 8, 1992)

Jarrell, Randall (1914–65) U.S. author and poet

1 When I died they washed me out of the turret with a hose.
"The Death of the Ball Turret Gunner" (1945), quoted in *The Penguin Book of American Verse* (Geoffrey Moore, ed.; 1977)

2 President Robbins was so well adjusted to his environment that sometimes you could not tell which was the environment and which was President Robbins.
Pictures from an Institution (1954), pt. I, ch. 4

3 To Americans English manners are far more frightening than none at all.
Pictures from an Institution (1954), pt. I, ch. 5

4 One of the most obvious facts about grown-ups to a child is that they have forgotten what it is like to be a child.
Quoted in *The Man Who Loved Children* (Christina Stead; 1965), Introduction

Jarry, Alfred (1873–1907) French playwright and poet

1 Death is only for the mediocre.
Gestes et Opinions du Docteur Faustroll, Pataphysicien (1911)

2 Forgetfulness is an indispensable condition of the memory.
"Toomai et les Éléphants," *Le Périple de la Littérature et de l'Art* (1903)

3 Madame, I would have given you another!
Said on being reprimanded by a woman for firing his pistol in the vicinity of her child, who might have been killed. Quoted in *Recollections of a Picture Dealer* (Ambroise Vollard; 1936)

Jaspers, Karl (Karl Theodor Jaspers; 1883–1969) German philosopher

1 The history of the German nation-state is at an end. What we...can achieve as a great nation is insight into the world's situation: that today the idea of the nation-state is a calamity for Europe and all the continents.
Freedom and Reconciliation (1960)

2 Freedom is the most-used word of our time. What it is seems obvious to all...Yet there is nothing more obscure, more ambiguous, more abused.
Future of Mankind (1958)

3 I know I am free, and so I admit I am guilty.
Philosophy (1932), vol. 2

4 The will does not choose between good and evil; it is its choice, rather, that makes it good or evil.
Philosophy (1932), vol. 2

Jáuregui, Juan de (Juan Martinez de Jáuregui y Aguilar; 1583–1641) Spanish poet

1 Sculpture: Your humble genealogy should make you silent. Painting: Well, yours is not astonishing either. Sculpture: You began in shadow. Painting: And you, in idolatry.
"Diálogo entre la naturaleza y las dos artes pintura y escultura, de cuya preeminencia se disputa y juzga," *Rimas* (1618)

Jaurès, Jean (Jean Joseph Marie Auguste Jaurès; 1859–1914) French politician and philosopher

Quotations about Jaurès

1 I choose neither Wilson nor Lenin. I choose Jaurès.
Léon Blum (1872–1950) French statesman, lawyer, and critic. Referring to U.S. president Woodrow Wilson, Russian revolutionary Vladimir Ilyich Lenin, and Jean Jaurès, whose ideas and actions provided the foundation for the French socialist tradition. Quoted in *Europe Since 1870* (James Joll; 1973), ch. 9

Quotations by Jaurès

2 You have finally torn the people away from the protection of the church and its dogma...You have interrupted the old song which lulled human misery, and human misery has risen up and is crying out.
Referring to the anticlericalism of the French Chamber of Deputies. Speech to the Chamber of Deputies, Paris, quoted in *Europe Since 1870* (James Joll; 1973), ch. 2

3 It is the duty of every one of you not to miss any opportunity

to show that you belong to that international socialist party which, at this hour when the storm is breaking, represents the sole prospect of maintaining peace or of restoring peace.
Referring to his attempts to create an international socialist alliance, the possibility of which vanished when he was assassinated in July 1914. As a member of the French Chamber of Deputies he warned against the threat of world war. Speech, Vaise, France (July 24, 1914)

Jay, Douglas (b.1907) British writer and politician

1 For in the case of nutrition and health, just as in the case of education, the gentleman in Whitehall really does know better what is good for people than the people know themselves.
The Socialist Case (1939), ch. 30

Jean Baptist de la Salle, Saint (1651–1719) French cleric and educational reformer

1 It is necessary to clean the teeth frequently, more especially after meals, but not on any account with a pin, or the point of a penknife, and it must never be done at table.
"The Rules of Christian Decorum and Civility" (1684), quoted in *The Complete Works of Saint John Baptist de La Salle* (Richard Arnandez, tr.; Gregory Wright, ed.; 1988), vol. 2

Jeans, James, Sir (James Hopwood Jeans; 1877–1946) British mathematician, physicist, and astronomer

1 Life exists in the universe only because the carbon atom possesses certain exceptional properties.
The Mysterious Universe (1930), ch. 1

2 Science should leave off making pronouncements: the river of knowledge has too often turned back on itself.
The Mysterious Universe (1930), ch. 5

3 The universe begins to look more like a great thought than like a great machine.
The Mysterious Universe (1930), ch. 5

Jefferies, Richard (John Richard Jefferies; 1848–87) British naturalist and writer

1 From space to the sky, from the sky to the hills, and the sea; to every blade of grass, to every leaf, to the smallest insect, to the million waves of ocean...this earth itself appears but a mote in that sunbeam by which we are conscious of one narrow streak in the abyss.
The Story of My Heart (1883)

2 I verily believe that the earth in one year produces enough food to last for thirty. Why, then, have we not enough?
The Story of My Heart (1883)

3 I was inhaling the richness of the sea, all the strength and depth of meaning of the sea and earth came to me again...I held my hand so that I could see the sunlight gleam on the slightly moist surface of the skin. The earth and sun were to me like my flesh and blood, and the air of the sea life.
The Story of My Heart (1883)

4 I was utterly alone with the sun and the earth...I thought of the earth's firmness—I felt it bear me up; through the grassy couch there came an influence as if I could feel the great earth speaking to me.
The Story of My Heart (1883)

5 There is nothing human in nature. The earth, though loved so dearly, would let me perish on the ground...the great sun, of whose company I have been so fond, would merely burn on and make no motion to assist me.
The Story of My Heart (1883)

Jeffers, Robinson (John Robinson Jeffers; 1887–1962) U.S. poet and dramatist

1 But for my children, I would have them keep their distance
from the thickening center; corruption
Never has been compulsory, when the cities lie at the monster's
feet there are left the mountains.
"Shine, Perishing Republic," *Taman and Other Poems* (1924), quoted in *The Penguin Book of American Verse* (Geoffrey Moore, ed.; 1977)

Jefferson, Thomas (1743–1826) U.S. president

Quotations about Jefferson

1 His attachment to those of his friends whom he could make useful to himself was thoroughgoing and exemplary.
John Quincy Adams (1767–1848) U.S. president. *Diary* (July 29, 1836)

2 Thomas Jefferson...said, not less than two hours a day should be devoted to exercise...If the man who wrote the Declaration of Independence, was Secretary of State, and twice President, could give it two hours, our children can give it ten or fifteen minutes.
1961
John Fitzgerald Kennedy (1917–63) U.S. president. Attrib.

3 A gentleman of thirty-two who could calculate an eclipse, survey an estate, tie an artery, plan an edifice, try a cause, break a horse, dance a minuet, and play the violin.
James Parton (1822–91) U.S. writer. *Life of Thomas Jefferson: Third President of the United States* (1874), ch. 19

Quotations by Jefferson

4 Freedom of religion; freedom of the press, and freedom of person under the protection of the *habeas corpus*, and trial by juries impartially selected. These principles form the bright constellation which has gone before us, and guided our steps through an age of revolution and reformation.
Inaugural Address, Washington, D.C. (March 4, 1801)

5 Peace, commerce, and honest friendship with all nations, entangling alliances with none.
Inaugural address, Washington, D.C. (March 4, 1801)

6 Knowledge indeed is a desirable, a lovely possession, but I do not scruple to say that health is more so. It is of little consequence to store the mind with science if the body be permitted to become debilitated. If the body be feeble, the mind will not be strong.
Journal (August 27, 1786)

7 Blest is that nation whose silent course of happiness furnishes nothing for history to say.
Letter to Diodati (1807)

8 One of the most successful physicians I have ever known, has assured me, that he used more bread pills, drops of colored water, and powders of hickory ashes, than of all other

medicines put together. It was certainly a pious fraud.
Letter to Dr. Caspar Wistar (June 21, 1807)

9 The natural course of the human mind is certainly from credulity to skepticism.
Letter to Dr. Caspar Wistar (June 21, 1807)

10 The patient, treated on the fashionable theory, sometimes gets well in spite of the medicine. The medicine therefore restored him, and the young doctor receives new courage to proceed in his bold experiments on the lives of his fellow creatures.
Letter to Dr. Caspar Wistar (June 21, 1807)

11 His mind must be strong indeed, if, rising above juvenile credulity, it can maintain a wise infidelity against the authority of his instructors, and the bewitching delusions of their theories.
Letter to Dr. Casper Wistar (June 21, 1807)

12 The only sure foundations of medicine are, an intimate knowledge of the human body, and observation on the effects of medicinal substances on that.
Letter to Dr. Casper Wistar (June 21, 1807)

13 If nature has made any one thing less susceptible than all others of exclusive property, it is the action of the thinking power called an idea.
Letter to Isaac McPherson (August 13, 1813)

14 A bill of rights is what the people are entitled to against every government on earth, general or particular, and what no just government should refuse to rest on inference.
Letter to James Madison (December 20, 1787)

15 A little rebellion now and then is a good thing.
Letter to James Madison (January 30, 1787)

16 A morsel of genuine history is a thing so rare as to be always valuable.
Letter to John Adams (1817)

17 And even should the cloud of barbarism and despotism again obscure the science and libraries of Europe, this country remains to preserve and restore light and liberty to them.
Letter to John Adams (September 12, 1821)

18 Bodily decay is gloomy in prospect, but of all human contemplations the most abhorrent is body without mind.
Letter to John Adams (August 1, 1816)

19 He is happiest of whom the world says least, good or bad.
Letter to John Adams (1786)

20 If science produces no better fruits than tyranny, murder, rapine, and destitution of national morality, I would rather wish our country to be ignorant, honest, and estimable, as our neighboring savages are.
Letter to John Adams (January 21, 1812)

21 This momentous question, like a firebell in the night, awakened and filled me with terror. I considered it at once as the knell of the Union.
Referring to the Missouri Compromise. Letter to John Holmes (April 22, 1820)

22 Tranquillity is now restored to the capital: the shops are again opened; the people resuming their labors, and if the want of bread does not disturb our peace, we may hope a continuance of it. The demolition of the Bastille is going on.
Referring to Paris during the French Revolution. Letter to John Jay (July 19, 1789)

23 The new circumstances...call for new words...An American dialect will therefore be formed...And should the language of England continue stationary, we shall probably enlarge our employment of it, until its new character may separate it in name as well as in power, from the mother tongue.
Letter to John Wald (August 16, 1813)

24 The art of life is the art of avoiding pain.
Letter to Maria Cosway (October 12, 1786)

25 Idleness begets ennui, ennui the hypochondriac, and that a diseased body. No laborious person was ever yet hysterical.
Letter to Martha Jefferson (March 28, 1787)

26 It is New Orleans, through which the produce of three-eighths of our territory must pass to market, and from its fertility it will ere long yield more than half of our whole produce, and contain more than half of our inhabitants.
Underlining the importance of successfully negotiating the acquisition of at least part of the Louisiana colony, the territory in North America acquired by France from Spain in 1800. Letter to Robert Livingston, U.S. ambassador to France (1803)

27 Some men look at constitutions with sanctimonious reverence and deem them like the ark of the covenant, too sacred to be touched.
Letter to Samuel Kercheval (July 12, 1816)

28 Man is fed with fables through life, and leaves it in the belief he knows something of what has been passing, when in truth he has known nothing but what has passed under his own eye.
Letter to Thomas Cooper (1823)

29 A more virtuous man, I believe, does not exist, nor one who is more enthusiastically devoted to better the condition of mankind.
Referring to Tsar Alexander I. Letter to William Duane (July 20, 1807)

30 The tree of liberty must be refreshed from time to time with the blood of patriots and tyrants. It is its natural manure.
Letter to William Stevens Smith (November 13, 1787)

31 There is not a single crowned head in Europe whose talents or merits would entitle him to be elected a vestryman by the people of any parish in America.
Letter written from Paris (May 2, 1788)

32 When a man assumes a public trust, he should consider himself as public property.
Remark to Baron von Humboldt (1807), quoted in *Life of Jefferson* (B. L. Rayner; 1834)

33 We hold these truths to be self-evident: that all men are created equal; that they are endowed by their Creator with certain unalienable rights; that among these are life, liberty, and the pursuit of happiness.
Declaration of Independence (July 4, 1776)

34 We hold these truths to be sacred and undeniable; that all men are created equal and independent, that from that equal creation they derive rights inherent and inalienable, among which are the preservation of life, and liberty, and the pursuit of happiness.
Declaration of Independence (July 4, 1776), original draft

35 When in the course of human events, it becomes necessary for one people to dissolve the political bonds which have connected them with another, and to assume among the powers of the earth the separate and equal station to which the laws of nature and of Nature's God entitle them, a decent respect to the opinions of mankind requires that they should declare the causes which impel them to the separation.
Declaration of Independence (July 4, 1776), Preamble

36 No free man shall ever be debarred the use of arms. The strongest reason for the people to retain the right to keep and bear arms is, as a last resort, to protect themselves against tyranny in government
Proposed Virginia Constitution, *Jefferson Papers* (1776)

37 Every government degenerates when trusted to the rulers of the people alone. The people themselves therefore are its only safe depositories.
Notes on the State of Virginia (1785)

38 Ignorance is preferable to error; and he is less remote from the truth who believes nothing, than he who believes what is wrong.
Notes on the State of Virginia (1785)

39 The whole commerce between master and slave is a perpetual exercise of the most boisterous passions, the most unremitting despotism on the one part, and degrading submissions on the other.
Notes on the State of Virginia (1785)

40 I tremble for my country when I reflect that God is just; and that his justice cannot sleep forever...an exchange of situation is among possible events; that it may become probable by supernatural interference.
Referring to slavery in the United States. *Notes on the State of Virginia* (1785)

41 It is the trade of lawyers to question everything, yield nothing, and to talk by the hour.
Quoted in *The Writings of Thomas Jefferson* (H. A. Washington, ed.; 1853–54), vol. 1

42 History, in general, only informs us of what bad government is.
Quoted in *The Writings of Thomas Jefferson* (H. A. Washington, ed.; 1853–54), vol. 9

43 I like the dreams of the future better than the history of the past.
Quoted in *Time* (January 9, 1978)

44 That Indian swamp in the wilderness.
Referring to Washington, D.C. Attrib.

Jeffreys, George, 1st Baron Jeffreys of Wembley ("The Hanging Judge"; 1648–89) English judge

1 I was not half bloody enough for him who sent me thither.
Referring to his "Bloody Assizes" after the defeat of the Duke of Monmouth's rebellion at the Battle of Sedgemoor (1685), and to his imprisonment in the Tower of London following the Glorious Revolution (1688). Remark to the chaplain of the Tower of London (April 1689)

Jekyll, Lady (originally Agnes Graham; 1861–1937) British writer

1 Matters of taste must be felt, not dogmatized about. A large crayfish or lobster rearing itself menacingly on its tail seems quite at home on the sideboard of a Brighton hotel-de-luxe, but will intimidate a shy guest at a small dinner party.
Kitchen Essays (1922)

Jellicoe, Ann (Patricia Ann Jellicoe; b.1927) British playwright

1 That white horse you see in the park could be a zebra synchronized with the railings.
The Knack (1962), Act 3

Jenkins, David, Bishop of Durham (David Edward Jenkins; b.1925) British theologian and prelate

1 What sort of God are we portraying and believing in if we insist on what I will nickname "the divine laser beam" type of miracle as the heart and basis of the Incarnation and Resurrection?
Speech (July 1986)

Jenkins, Roy, Baron Jenkins of Hillhead (Roy Harris Jenkins; b.1920) British statesman

1 The permissive society has been allowed to become a dirty phrase. A better phrase is the civilized society.
Speech, Abingdon, Oxfordshire, England (July 19, 1969)

2 There are always great dangers in letting the best be the enemy of the good.
Speech to the British Parliament (1975)

Jenner, Edward (1749–1823) British physician

1 The deviation of man from the state in which he was originally placed by nature seems to have proved to him a prolific source of diseases.
Attrib.

Jenner, William, Sir (1815–98) British physician and pathologist

1 Never believe what a patient tells you his doctor has said.
Attrib.

Jennings, Elizabeth (b.1926) British poet and writer

1 Critics are more malicious about poetry than about other books—maybe because so many manqué poets write reviews.
Remark (December 1987)

2 Now deep in my bed I turn
and the world turns on the other side.
1955. "In the Night," *Collected Poems 1953–1985* (1986)

3 Do not suppose that I do not fear death
Because I trust it is no end. You say
It must be a great comfort to live with
Such a faith, but you don't know the way
I battle on this earth
With faults of character I try to change
But they bound back on me like living things.
"The Fear of Death," *The Oxford Book of Death* (D. J. Enright, ed.; 1987)

4 Who doesn't regret Lazarus was not
Questioned about after-lives? Of course
He only reached death's threshhold. I fear what
Dark exercises may with cunning power

Do when I am brought
To my conclusion.
"The Fear of Death," *The Oxford Book of Death* (D. J. Enright, ed.; 1987)

Jennings, Paul (1918–89) British writer

1 Of all musicians, flautists are most obviously the ones who know something we don't know.
"Flautists Flaunt Afflatus," *The Jenguin Pennings* (1963)

Jenrette, Richard U.S. business executive

1 It seems to me the worst thing many CEOs do is announce huge cuts before the fact, thereby upsetting the entire organization so that no one feels secure.
Fortune (July 22, 1996)

2 Tired people make bad decisions.
Fortune (July 22, 1996)

3 If you've been chairman and running things, you shouldn't sit there and second-guess successors. If you're going to get out, get out.
Wall Street Journal (February 14, 1996)

Jenyns, Soame (1704–87) English poet and politician

1 Hence, with her sister arts, shall dancing claim
An equal right to universal fame;
And Isaac's Rigadoon shall live as long
As Raphael's painting, or as Virgil's song.
"The Art of Dancing: a Poem" (1727), quoted in *World History of Dance* (Curt Sachs; 1937)

Jepson, Edgar (1863–1938) British novelist

1 I know nothing about platonic love except that it is not to be found in the works of Plato.
Quoted in *Ego 5* (James Agate, ed.; August 24, 1940)

Jerome, Jerome K. (Jerome Klapka Jerome; 1859–1927) British novelist and playwright

1 Conceit is the finest armour a man can wear.
Idle Thoughts of an Idle Fellow (1886)

2 If you are foolish enough to be contented, don't show it, but grumble with the rest.
Idle Thoughts of an Idle Fellow (1886)

3 It is easy enough to say that poverty is no crime. No; if it were men wouldn't be ashamed of it. It is a blunder, though, and is punished as such. A poor man is despised the whole world over.
Idle Thoughts of an Idle Fellow (1886)

4 It is impossible to enjoy idling thoroughly unless one has plenty of work to do.
"On Being Idle," *Idle Thoughts of an Idle Fellow* (1886)

5 Love is like the measles; we all have to go through with it.
"On Being in Love," *Idle Thoughts of an Idle Fellow* (1886)

6 We drink one another's health and spoil our own.
"On Eating and Drinking," *Idle Thoughts of an Idle Fellow* (1886)

7 Time is but the shadow of the world upon the background of Eternity.
Three Men in a Boat (1889)

8 I never read a patent medicine advertisement without being impelled to the conclusion that I am suffering from the particular disease therein dealt with in its most virulent form.
Three Men in a Boat (1889), ch. 1

9 But there, everything has its drawbacks, as the man said when his mother-in-law died, and they came down upon him for the funeral expenses.
Three Men in a Boat (1889), ch. 3

10 I like work; it fascinates me. I can sit and look at it for hours. I love to keep it by me; the idea of getting rid of it nearly breaks my heart.
Three Men in a Boat (1889), ch. 15

11 Mere bald fabrication is useless; the veriest tyro can manage that. It is in the circumstantial detail, the embellishing touches of probability, the general air of scrupulous veracity, that the experienced angler is seen.
Three Men in a Boat (1889), ch. 17

Jerome, Saint (Eusebius Hieronymus; 347?–419 or 420) Roman monk and scholar

1 Of gold she would not wear so much as a seal-ring, choosing to store her money in the stomachs of the poor rather than to keep it at her own disposal.
Letters, 127

2 I have revered always not crude verbosity, but holy simplicity.
"Ad Pammachium," *Patrologia Latina* (1864), vol. 22, col. 579

Jerrold, Douglas (Douglas William Jerrold; 1803–57) British playwright

1 Honest bread is very well—it's the butter that makes the temptation.
The Catspaw (1850), Act 3

2 Religion's in the heart, not in the knees.
The Devil's Ducat (1830), Act 1, Scene 2

3 The surest way to hit a woman's heart is to take aim kneeling.
The Wit and Opinions of Douglas Jerrold (1859)

4 Earth is here so kind, that just tickle her with a hoe and she laughs with a harvest.
Referring to Australia. "A Land of Plenty," *The Wit and Opinions of Douglas Jerrold* (1859)

5 Love's like the measles—all the worse when it comes late in life.
"A Philanthropist," *The Wit and Opinions of Douglas Jerrold* (1859)

6 The ugliest of trades have their moments of pleasure. Now, if I were a grave-digger, or even a hangman, there are some people I could work for with a great deal of enjoyment.
"Ugly Trades," *The Wit and Opinions of Douglas Jerrold* (1859)

7 The best thing I know between France and England is—the sea.
"The Anglo-French Alliance," *Wit and Opinions of Douglas Jerrold* (1859)

8 The only athletic sport I ever mastered was backgammon.
Quoted in *Douglas Jerrold* (Walter Jerrold; 1914), vol. 1, ch. 1

9 If an earthquake were to engulf England to-morrow, the English would manage to meet and dine somewhere among the rubbish, just to celebrate the event.
The Life and Remains of Douglas Jerrold (Blanchard Jerrold; 1859), ch. 14

10 Sir, you are like a pin, but without either its head or its point.
Speaking to a small thin man who was boring him. Attrib.

Jersild, P. C. (b.1935) Swedish writer

1 And another thing; he had learned at school that people really see the world upside down; that was how their eyes functioned. Reine...wanted to see the world as it really was.
1976. *Children's Island* (Joan Tate, tr.; 1986)

Jevons, William Stanley (1835–82) British economist and logician

1 It is clear that Economics, if it is to be a science at all, must be a mathematical science.
Theory of Political Economy (1871)

Jewett, Sarah Orne (Theodora Sarah Orne Jewett; 1849–1909) U.S. writer

1 In the life of each of us, I said to myself, there is a place remote and islanded, and given to endless regret or secret happiness.
The Country of the Pointed Firs (1896), ch. 15

Jhabvala, Ruth Prawer (b.1927) German-born writer

1 These diseases that people get in India, they're not physical, they're purely psychic. We only get them because we try to resist India—because we shut ourselves up in our little Western egos and don't want to give ourselves. But once we learn to yield, then they must fall away.
Travelers (1972)

Jia Dao (also known as Chia Tao; 779–845) Chinese poet

1 The master has gone to pick herbs.
He is somewhere out there in the hills,
but the clouds are so deep I know not where.
"Looking for the Recluse and Not Finding Him Home" (8th–9th century), quoted in *An Anthology of Chinese Literature* (Stephen Owen, tr.; 1996)

Jiang Zemin (b.1926) Chinese president

1 History shows that anything conducive to our national stability is good.
Referring to the massacre in Tiananmen Square (1989). *Times*, London (May 14, 1994)

Jiles, Paulette (b.1943) U.S.-born Canadian poet and writer

1 At a thousand feet we make quick decisions about our loyalties, the other engine might fail.
"Night Flight to Attiwapiskat," *Worst Journeys* (Keath Fraser, ed.; 1991)

Jiménez, Juan Ramón (1881–1958) Spanish poet

1 Daybreak
has that sadness of arriving
by train at a station that's not yours.
"Daybreak," *Roots and Wings: Poetry from Spain, 1900–1975* (Hardie St. Martin, ed.; 1976)

2 One would think
that the earth was the road
Of the body,
that the sea was the road
Of the soul.
"Dream Nocturne," *Roots and Wings: Poetry from Spain, 1900–1975* (Hardie St. Martin, ed.; 1976), ll. 6–10

3 How like
Is a journey by sea
To death,
To eternal life!
"Dream Nocturne," *Roots and Wings: Poetry from Spain, 1900–1975* (Hardie St. Martin, ed.; 1976), ll. 17–20

4 My feet, so deep in the earth!
My wings, so far into the heavens!
—And so much pain
in the heart torn between!
"My Feet So Deep in the Earth," *Roots and Wings: Poetry from Spain, 1900–1975* (Hardie St. Martin, ed.; 1976)

5 All the names that I gave
to the universe that I created again for you
are now turning into one name, into one
god.
"The Name Drawn From the Names," *Roots and Wings: Poetry from Spain, 1900–1975* (Hardie St. Martin, ed.; 1976)

6 You find in solitude only what you take to it.
Selected Writings (1957)

7 The urban man is an uprooted tree, he can put out leaves, flowers and grow fruit but what a nostalgia his leaf, flower, and fruit will always have for mother earth.
"Aristocracy and Democracy," *Selected Writings* (1957)

8 A permanent state of transition is man's most noble condition.
"Heroic Reason," *Selected Writings* (1957)

9 Every country should realize that its turn at world domination, domination because its rights coincided more or less with the character or progress of the epoch, must terminate with the change brought about by this progress.
"Heroic Reason," *Selected Writings* (1957)

10 I do not cut my life up into days but my days into lives, each day, each hour, an entire life.
"Heroic Reason," *Selected Writings* (1957)

11 The greatest assassin of life is haste, the desire to reach things before the right time which means overreaching them.
"Heroic Reason," *Selected Writings* (1957)

12 The world is like a map of antipathies, almost of hates, in which everyone picks the symbolic color of his difference.
"Heroic Reason," *Selected Writings* (1957)

13 The background reveals the true being and state of being of the man or thing. If I do not possess the background, I make the man transparent, the thing transparent.
"José Marti," *Selected Writings* (1957)

14 Literature is a state of culture, poetry is a state of grace, before and after culture.
"Poetry and Literature," *Selected Writings* (1957)

15 A fantasy can be equivalent to a paradise and if the fantasy passes, better yet, because eternal paradise would be very boring.
"To Burn Completely," *Selected Writings* (1957)

16 If you go slowly,
Time will walk behind you
Like a submissive ox.
"To Miss Rápida," *Selected Writings* (1957)

Jin Guantao (b.1947) Chinese writer

1 The Chinese feudal system is fragile in that its three subsystems—economic, political, and ideological—must be maintained at a specific point of equilibrium; deviation by any subsystem from this point will bring down the whole structure.
"The Shadow of History," *Behind the Phenomena of History* (1983)

Joad, C. E. M. (Cyril Edwin Mitchinson Joad; 1891–1953) British philosopher

1 It will be said of this generation that it found England a land of beauty and left it a land of beauty spots.
Observer, London (May 31, 1953), "Sayings of Our Times"

2 There was never an age in which useless knowledge was more important than in our own.
Observer, London (September 30, 1951), "Sayings of the Week"

Joan of Arc, Saint (Jeanne d'Arc, "The Maid of Orleans"; 1412?–31) French patriot and martyr

1 If I said that God did not send me, I should condemn myself; truly God did send me.
Remark at her trial (February–May 1431) Attrib.

2 I was in my thirteenth year when God sent a voice to guide me. At first, I was very much frightened. The voice came towards the hour of noon, in summer, in my father's garden.
Remark at her trial (February–May 1431) Attrib.

3 Deliver the keys of all the good towns you have taken and violated in France to the Maid who has been sent by God the King of Heaven! Go away, for God's sake, back to your own country; otherwise, await news of the Maid, who will soon visit you to your great detriment.
1429. "The Maid" refers to Joan of Arc herself. She was commonly called "the Maid of Orléans." Quoted in *Saint Joan of Arc* (Vita Sackville-West; 1936)

Jobs, Steve (Steven Paul Jobs; b.1955) U.S. computer executive

Quotations about Jobs

1 As the guru of personal computing...he'd become the leader of a technological youth cult that was out to change the world.
Frank Rose U.S. author. *West of Eden* (1989)

2 Apple has to be more pragmatic and less religious. And the only one who can do that is the person who created the religion in the first place.
John Sculley (b.1939) U.S. business executive. Steve Jobs was a co-founder of Apple Computer Inc. *Newsweek* (August 18, 1997)

Quotations by Jobs

3 Real artists ship.
Speech (1983), quoted in *West of Eden* (Frank Rose; 1989)

4 I'm just a guy who probably should have been a semi-talented poet on the Left Bank. I got sort of sidetracked here.
Fortune (October 1, 1984)

5 Do you want to spend the rest of your life selling sugared water or do you want the chance to change the world?
Said to John Sculley, then president of Pepsico, when inviting him to join Apple. *Fortune* (September 14, 1987)

Joel, Billy (William Martin Joel; b.1949) U.S. pop singer

1 Everybody is sleeping with everybody else in this business, but the artist is the only one that's getting screwed.
Independent, London (June 24, 1994)

Joffre, Joseph Jacques Césaire (1852–1931) French general

1 We are about to engage in a battle on which the fate of our country depends...all our efforts must be directed to attacking and driving back the enemy. Troops that can advance no farther must...die on the spot rather than give way.
Referring to the counterattack at the first Battle of the Marne (1914). *The Memoirs of Marshall Joffre* (T. Bentley Mott, tr.; 1932)

2 If the women working in the factories stopped for twenty minutes, France would lose the war.
Referring to World War I. Quoted in *La Grande Guerre 1914–1918* (Marc Ferro; 1969)

John, Elton, Sir (Reginald Kenneth Dwight; b.1947) British pop singer and songwriter

1 They can say I'm a fat old sod, they can say I'm an untalented bastard, they can call me a poof, but they musn't lie about me because I'm determined to fight.
Referring to his successful libel action against the *Sun* newspaper (London). Interview (1988), quoted in *Rock 'n' Roll Babylon* (Gary Herman; 1994)

2 Every artist who makes it big goes through a period where it seems like they're invincible.
Quoted in "Elton John," *Off the Record: An Oral History of Popular Music* (Joe Smith; 1988)

3 I became much happier as a person when I took on Elton John. It became my real name and I could do things I wanted.
Referring to his name change in 1970. Quoted in "Elton John," *Off the Record: An Oral History of Popular Music* (Joe Smith; 1988)

John XXII, Pope (Jacques Duèse; 1245?–1334) French pope

1 There are as many miracles as there are articles of the *Summa*.
Referring to the *Summa Theologiae* (1265–73) of Thomas Aquinas, who was in the process of being canonized. Attrib.

John XXIII, Pope (Angelo Giuseppe Roncalli; 1881–1963) Italian pope

1 I am able to follow my own death step by step. Now I move softly towards the end.
Remark made two days before he died. *Guardian*, London (June 3, 1963)

2 Anybody can be Pope; the proof of this is that I have become one.
Quoted in *Wit and Wisdom of Good Pope John* (Henri Fresquet; 1964)

3 It is easier for a father to have children than for children to have a real father.
Attrib.

4 It often happens that I wake at night and begin to think about a serious problem and decide I must tell the Pope about it. Then I wake up completely and remember I am the Pope.
Attrib.

John of Gaunt, Duke of Lancaster (1340–99) Belgian-born English soldier and prince

1 For, he said, albeit unworthy, he was a king's son and one of the greatest lords in the kingdom after the king: and what had been so evilly spoken of him could rightly be called plain treason...And if any man were so bold as to charge him with treason or other disloyalty or with anything prejudicial to the realm, he was ready to defend himself with his body as though he were the poorest bachelor in the land.
1377? Report of a speech to Richard II's first Parliament. *Rotuli Parliamentorum*, vol. 3

John of Lancaster, Duke of Bedford (1389–1435) English soldier and statesman

1 A disciple and limb of the fiend, called the Pucelle, that used false enchantments and sorcery.
Referring to Joan of Arc. *Proceedings and Ordinances of the Privy Council* (N. H. Nicolas, ed.), vol. 4

John of Salisbury (1115?–80) English philosopher and humanist

1 The common people say, that physicians are the class of people who kill other men in the most polite and courteous manner.
Policraticus (1159?), bk. 2, ch. 29

2 The brevity of our life, the dullness of our senses, the torpor of our indifference, the futility of our occupation, suffer us to know but little: and that little is soon shaken and then torn from the mind by that traitor to learning, that hostile and faithless stepmother to memory, oblivion.
Prologue to the Policraticus (C. C. J. Webb, ed.; 1909), vol. 1, ll. 13–16

3 The wanton and effeminate sound produced by caressing, chiming and intertwining melodies, a veritable harmony of sirens.
Referring to polyphony in music, contrasted with the unison of Gregorian chant. Quoted in *Richard the Lionheart* (John Gillingham; 1978), ch. 3

John of the Cross, Saint (Juan de Yepes y Álvarez; 1542–91) Spanish poet, mystic, and Doctor of the Church

1 I die because I do not die.
"Coplas del alma que pena por ver a dios" (1578)

2 The dark night of the soul.
"Noche obscura del alma" (1578?)

John Paul II, Pope (Karol Jozef Wojtyla; b.1920) Polish pope

1 War should belong to the tragic past, to history: it should find no place on humanity's agenda for the future.
Speech in Coventry, England (1982)

2 Christ called as his Apostles only men. He did this in a totally free and sovereign way.
Observer, London (September 25, 1988), "Sayings of the Week"

3 Only before the eyes of God can the human body remain nude and uncovered while fully conserving its splendor and beauty.
Observer, London (April 10, 1994), "Sayings of the Week"

4 We thus denounce the false and dangerous program of the arms race, of the secret rivalry between peoples for military superiority.
Observer, London (December 19, 1976), "Sayings of the Week"

5 The legitimate desire to have a child cannot be interpreted as the right to have a child at any cost.
Times, London (August 1, 1994)

6 Science can purify religion from error and superstition. Religion can purify science from idolatry and false absolutes.
Quoted in *Galileo, A Life* (James Reston; 1994)

7 The two thousand years which have passed since the Birth of Christ represent an extraordinary great Jubilee; not only for Christians but indirectly for the whole of humanity, given the prominent role played by Christianity during these two millennia.
Quoted in *Tertio Millennio Adveniente* (Catholic Truth Society; 1994)

8 It is unbecoming for a cardinal to ski badly.
Replying to the suggestion that it was inappropriate for him, a cardinal, to ski. Attrib.

Johns, Jasper (b.1930) U.S. painter

1 Meaning implies that something is happening; you can say meaning is determined by the use of the thing, the way an audience uses a painting once it is put in public.
Quoted in "What is Pop Art? Interviews with Eight Painters," *Art News* (G. R. Swenson; February 1964), issue 62, no. 10

2 Sometimes I see it and then paint it. Other times I paint it and then see it. Both are impure situations, and I prefer neither.
Quoted in *Sixteen Americans* (Dorothy C. Miller, ed.; 1959)

Johnson, Adam (1975–93) British poet

1 I stare at death in a mirror behind the bar
And wonder when I sacrificed my blood,
And how I could not recognise the face
That smiled with the mouth, the eyes, of death—
In Manchester, London or Amsterdam.
I do not hate that face, only the bell.
"The Playground Bell" (1992)

Johnson, Amy (1903–41) British aviator

1 Had I been a man I might have explored the Poles or climbed Mount Everest, but as it was my spirit found outlet in the air.
Quoted in *Myself When Young* (Margot Asquith, ed.; 1938)

Johnson, Andrew (1808–75) U.S. president

1 The only safety of the nation lies in a generous and expansive plan of conciliation.
Quoted in *The Critical Year: A Study of Andrew Johnson* (Howard K. Beale; 1930)

Johnson, Georgia Douglas (originally Georgia Douglas Camp; 1886–1966) U.S. writer, poet, and songwriter

1 The strong demand, contend, prevail; the beggar is a fool!
"The Suppliant", quoted in *Shadowed Dreams: Women's Poetry of the Harlem Renaissance* (Maureen Honey, ed.; 1989)

2 The heart of a woman falls back with the night,
And enters some alien cage in its plight,
And tries to forget it has dreamed of the stars
While it breaks, breaks, breaks on the sheltering bars.
"The Heart of a Woman," *The Heart of a Woman* (1918)

Johnson, Hiram W. (Hiram Warren Johnson; 1866–1945) U.S. politician and reformer

1 The first casualty when war comes is truth.
Speech, U.S. Senate (1917)

Johnson, Jack (John Arthur Jackson; 1878–1946) U.S. boxer

1 It was not the fights but the fights to get those fights that proved the hardest part of the struggle. It was my color.
Quoted in *World's Great Men of Color* (Joel Augustus Rogers; 1947), vol. 2

Johnson, James Weldon (1871–1938) U.S. writer, lawyer, and diplomat

1 London was a city not to be visited, but to be captured.
Along This Way (1933)

2 Rhetorical oratory is the foundation upon which all the humbug in our political system rests.
Along This Way (1933)

3 The time of the psychological passing over from boyhood to manhood is a movable feast. The legal date fixed on the twenty-first birthday has little or no connection with it. There are men in their teens, and there are boys in their forties.
Along This Way (1933)

4 Young man—Young man—Your arm's too short to box with God.
"The Prodigal Son," *God's Trombones* (1927)

5 Sing a song full of the faith that the dark past has taught us,
Sing a song full of hope that the present has brought us,
Facing the rising sun of our new day begun,
Let us march on till victory is won.
Lift Every Voice and Sing (1900)

6 O black and unknown bards of long ago,
How came your lips to touch the sacred fire?
How, in your darkness, did you come to know
The power and beauty of the minstrel's lyre?
"O Black and Unknown Bards," *Saint Peter Relates an Incident* (1930)

7 New York is the most fatally fascinating thing in America.
The Autobiography of an Ex-Colored Man (1912)

8 Paris practices its sins as lightly as it does its religion, while London practices both very seriously.
The Autobiography of an Ex-Colored Man (1912)

Johnson, Lady Bird (originally Claudia Alta Taylor; b.1912) U.S. first lady

1 A politician ought to be born a foundling and remain a bachelor.
Time (December 1, 1975)

2 The coach has turned into a pumpkin and the mice have all run away.
Said on leaving the White House, after the election of Republican Richard Nixon (1969). Quoted in *The Vantage Point* (Lyndon B. Johnson; 1971)

3 Lyndon acts like there was never going to be a tomorrow.
Referring to her husband. Attrib.

Johnson, Linton Kwesi (b.1952) Jamaican-born British poet, musician, and political activist

1 Inglan is a bitch dere's no escapin' it
Inglan is a bitch dere's no runnin' way fram it.
"Inglan Is a Bitch," *Inglan Is a Bitch* (1980)

Johnson, Luke British business executive

1 The medical profession is reaching near-paralysis in certain U.S. states thanks to malpractice lawsuits.
Sunday Telegraph, London (March 29, 1998)

Johnson, Lyndon Baines (1908–73) U.S. president

Quotations about Johnson

1 He wanted everyone with him all the time, and when they weren't, it broke his heart.
Max Frankel (b.1930) U.S. journalist. Quoted in *Lyndon* (Richard Harwood and Haynes Johnson; 1973)

2 An extraordinarily gifted president who was the wrong man from the wrong place at the wrong time under the wrong circumstances.
Eric F. Goldman (b.1915) U.S. biographer. *The Tragedy of Lyndon Johnson* (1969), ch. 18

3 Kennedy promised, Johnson delivered.
Arthur Schlesinger, Jr. (b.1917) U.S. historian. *Observer*, London (November 20, 1983)

4 Lyndon Johnson came into office seeking a Great Society in America and found instead an ugly little war that consumed him.
Tom Wicker (b.1926) U.S. writer. Referring to the Vietnam War. *JFK and LBJ* (1968)

Quotations by Johnson

5 All I have, I would have given gladly not to be standing here today.
First address to Congress as president. Address to Congress (November 27, 1963)

6 Yesterday is not ours to recover, but tomorrow is ours to win or lose.
Address to the nation (November 28, 1963)

7 When I was a boy growing up we never had these issues of our relations with other nations so much. We didn't wake up with Viet Nam and have Cyprus for lunch...folks...just kept

us debating whether we were "wet" or "dry"...prohibitionists or anti-prohibitionists.
Informal speech, White House, Washington, D.C. (March 1, 1965)

8 It is the genius of our constitution that under its shelter of enduring institutions and rooted principles there is ample room for the rich fertility of American political invention.
Message to Congress (January 12, 1966)

9 Public participation in the process of government is the essence of democracy.
Message to Congress (May 25, 1967)

10 We are not about to send American boys nine or ten thousand miles away from home to do what Asian boys ought to be doing for themselves.
Denying an escalation of U.S. involvement in Vietnam. Remark at Akron University, Akron, Ohio (October 21, 1964)

11 The great society is a place where men are more concerned with the quality of their goods than the quantity of their goods.
"The great society" was his campaign slogan. Speech (May 22, 1964)

12 I am going to build the kind of nation that President Roosevelt hoped for, President Truman worked for, and President Kennedy died for.
Speech (December 1964), quoted in *Sunday Times*, London (December 27, 1964)

13 Power is where power goes.
Referring to the vice presidency. Speech, Democratic Party Convention, Los Angeles (July 14, 1960)

14 It is a common failing of totalitarian regimes that they cannot really understand the nature of our democracy. They mistake dissent for disloyalty. They mistake restlessness for a rejection of policy...They mistake individual speeches for public policy.
Speech, San Antonio, Texas (September 29, 1967)

15 The vote is the most powerful instrument ever devised by man for breaking down injustice and destroying the terrible walls which imprison men because they are different from other men.
Speech, Washington, D.C. (August 6, 1965)

16 This Administration here and now declares unconditional war on poverty in America.
State of the Union message (January 8, 1964)

17 It is true that a house divided against itself is a house that cannot stand...I have concluded that I should not permit the Presidency to become involved in the partisan divisions that are developing in this political year. Accordingly, I shall not seek, and I will not accept, the nomination of my party for another term as your President.
Announcing his intention not to run again for election. Televised speech (March 31, 1968)

18 A nation, like a person, not conscious of its own past is adrift without purpose or protection against the contending forces of dissolution.
Thanksgiving Day proclamation (November 25, 1964)

19 In your time we have the opportunity to move not only toward the rich society and the powerful society but upward to the Great Society.
May 22, 1964. Speech, University of Michigan, *Public Papers of the Presidents of the United States: Lyndon B. Johnson* (1963–64), vol. 1

20 You let a bully come into your front yard, the next day he'll be on your porch.
Often-used formulation when referring to North Vietnam and justifying U.S. involvement (from 1965) in the Vietnam War (1959–75). *Time* (April 15, 1984)

21 Did y'ever think, Ken, that making a speech on economics is a lot like pissing down your leg? It seems hot to you, but it never does to anyone else.
Said to the economist J. K. Galbraith. Quoted in *A Life in Our Times* (J. K. Galbraith; 1981)

22 When things haven't gone well for you, call in a secretary or a staff man and chew him out. You will sleep better and they will appreciate the attention.
Quoted in "Love It or Loathe It, Here's the Wit and Wisdom of LBJ," *People* (February 2, 1987)

23 If you're in politics and you can't tell when you walk into a room who's for you and who's against you, then you're in the wrong line of work.
Quoted in *The Lyndon Johnson Story* (B. Mooney; 1956)

24 I don't believe I'll ever get credit for anything I do in foreign affairs, no matter how successful it is, because I didn't go to Harvard.
Quoted in *The Wise Men* (Walter Isaacson and Evan Thomas; 1986)

25 Son, they are all my helicopters.
Johnson was moving towards the wrong helicopter and an officer said to him, "Your helicopter is over there." Attrib.

26 Come now, let us reason together.
Often-used phrase Attrib.

Johnson, "Magic" (Earvin Johnson; b.1959) U.S. basketball player

1 I'm going to beat it and I'm going to have fun.
Referring to his HIV-positive status. *Guardian*, London (December 23, 1991)

Johnson, Paul (b.1928) British historian and journalist

1 For me this is a vital litmus test: no intellectual society can flourish where a Jew feels even slightly uneasy.
Sunday Times Magazine, London (February 6, 1977)

Johnson, Philander Chase (1866–1939) U.S. journalist

1 Cheer up, the worst is yet to come.
"Shooting Stars," *Everybody's Magazine* (1920)

Johnson, Philip (b.1906) U.S. architect

1 Architecture is the art of how to waste space.
New York Times (December 27, 1964)

2 Monuments last much longer than words. Civilizations are remembered by buildings. There's nothing more important than architecture.
1964. Quoted in *Modern Movements in Architecture* (Charles Jencks; 1973)

Johnson, Richard W. British writer and historian

1 Among the workers, the effects of recession are...that a large underclass of the unemployed and downwardly mobile is created.
The Politics of Recession (1985)

2 Recession and public spending cuts increase the social power of the rich.
The Politics of Recession (1985)

3 Recession creates diffuse social influences towards conservatism...Businessmen—previously viewed, mundanely, as mere managers—are now seen as leaders and possible saviours.
The Politics of Recession (1985)

4 The economic crisis of the 1930s saw a remarkably even progression of the social democratic left (with a few fascist exceptions).
The Politics of Recession (1985)

5 The post-1973 recession...far from producing new fascist states...laid them low wherever they existed (Greece, Portugal, Spain).
The Politics of Recession (1985)

6 In the 1930s it was possible for fascists and social democrats alike to see the solutions to their problems in the attainment of national economic autonomy and the application of...Keynesian policy at national level.
Referring to the policies of economist John Maynard Keynes. *The Politics of Recession* (1985)

Johnson, Samuel (1709–84) British lexicographer and writer

Quotations about Johnson

1 That great Cham of Literature, Samuel Johnson.
Tobias Smollett (1721–71) Scottish novelist. Letter to John Wilkes (March 16, 1759)

2 Johnson made the most brutal speeches to living persons; for though he was good-natured at bottom he was ill-natured at top.
Horace Walpole (1717–97) British writer. Attrib.

Quotations by Johnson

3 Illness makes a man a scoundrel.
Letter to Fanny Burney (January 1788)

4 Here falling houses thunder on your head,
And here a female atheist talks you dead.
"London" (1738)

5 Deign on the passing world to turn thine eyes,
And pause awhile from letters to be wise;
Mark there what ills the scholar's life assail,
Toil, envy, want, the patron, and the jail.
"The Vanity of Human Wishes" (1749)

6 Life protracted is protracted woe.
"The Vanity of Human Wishes" (1749)

7 See nations slowly wise and meanly just,
To buried merit raise the tardy bust.
If dreams yet flatter, once again attend,
Here Lydiat's life, and Galileo's end.
"The Vanity of Human Wishes" (1749)

8 When first the college rolls receive his name,
The young enthusiast quits his ease for fame;
Through all his veins the fever of renown
Burns from the strong contagion of the gown.
"The Vanity of Human Wishes" (1749)

9 *Cough*. A convulsion of the lungs, vellicated by some sharp serosity.
A Dictionary of the English Language (1755)

10 *Excise*. A hateful tax levied upon commodities.
A Dictionary of the English Language (1755)

11 *Lexicographer*. A writer of dictionaries, a harmless drudge.
A Dictionary of the English Language (1755)

12 *Network*. Anything reticulated or decussated at equal distances, with interstices between the intersections.
A Dictionary of the English Language (1755)

13 *Oats*. A grain, which in England is generally given to horses, but in Scotland supports the people.
A Dictionary of the English Language (1755)

14 *Patron*. Commonly a wretch who supports with insolence, and is paid with flattery.
A Dictionary of the English Language (1755)

15 *Dull*. To make dictionaries is dull work.
A Dictionary of the English Language (1755), "Dull" (8th definition)

16 But these were the dreams of a poet doomed at last to wake a lexicographer.
A Dictionary of the English Language (1755), Preface

17 I am not yet so lost in lexicography, as to forget that words are the daughters of earth, and that things are the sons of heaven. Language is only the instrument of science, and words are but the signs of ideas.
A Dictionary of the English Language (1755), Preface

18 I have protracted my work till most of those whom I wished to please have sunk into the grave; and success and miscarriage are empty sounds.
A Dictionary of the English Language (1755), Preface

19 The chief glory of every people arises from its authors.
A Dictionary of the English Language (1755), Preface

20 Every quotation contributes something to the stability or enlargement of the language.
On citations used in a dictionary. *A Dictionary of the English Language* (1755), Preface

21 A Scotchman must be a very sturdy moralist who does not love Scotland better than truth.
"Ostig in Sky," *Journey to the Western Islands of Scotland* (1775)

22 Small debts are like small shot; they are rattling on every side, and can scarcely be escaped without a wound: great debts are like cannon; of loud noise, but little danger.
1759. Letter to Joseph Simpson, *Life of Samuel Johnson* (James Boswell; 1791)

23 Dublin, though a place much worse than London, is not so bad as Iceland.
Letter to Mrs. Christopher Smart, *Life of Samuel Johnson* (James Boswell; 1791)

24 The reciprocal civility of authors is one of the most risible scenes in the farce of life.
Life of Sir Thomas Browne (1756)

25 A man, doubtful of his dinner, or trembling at a creditor, is not much disposed to abstracted meditation, or remote enquiries.
"Collins," *Lives of the English Poets* (1779–81)

26 The true genius is a mind of large general powers, accidentally determined to some particular direction.
"Cowley," *Lives of the English Poets* (1779–81)

27 We are perpetually moralists, but we are geometricians only by chance. Our intercourse with intellectual nature is necessary; our speculations upon matter are voluntary, and at leisure.
"Milton," *Lives of the English Poets* (1779–81)

28 Notes are often necessary, but they are necessary evils.
Plays of William Shakespeare, with Notes (1765), Preface

29 Human life is everywhere a state in which much is to be endured, and little to be enjoyed.
Rasselas (1759), ch. 11

30 Marriage has many pains, but celibacy has no pleasures.
Rasselas (1759), ch. 26

31 Integrity without knowledge is weak and useless, and knowledge without integrity is dangerous and dreadful.
Rasselas (1759), ch. 41

32 The power of punishment is to silence, not to confute.
Sermons (1788), no. 23

33 How is it that we hear the loudest yelps for liberty among the drivers of negroes?
Referring to white Americans. *Taxation No Tyranny* (1775)

34 Pleasure is very seldom found where it is sought; our brightest blazes of gladness are commonly kindled by unexpected sparks.
The Idler (1758)

35 We are inclined to believe those whom we do not know because they have never deceived us.
The Idler (1758)

36 When two Englishmen meet, their first talk is of the weather.
The Idler (June 24, 1758), no. 11

37 I know not, that by living dissections any discovery has been made by which a single malady is more easily cured.
The Idler (August 5, 1758), no. 17

38 Money and time are the heaviest burdens of life, and...the unhappiest of all mortals are those who have more of either than they know how to use.
The Idler (November 11, 1758), no. 30

39 Condemned to hope's delusive mine,
As on we toil from day to day,
By sudden blasts or slow decline
Our social comforts drop away.
"On the Death of Mr. Robert Levet, a Practiser in Physic," *The New Oxford Book of English Verse* (Helen Gardner, ed.; 1972)

40 The modest wants of every day
The toil of every day supplied.
"On the Death of Mr. Robert Levet, a Practiser in Physic," *The New Oxford Book of English Verse* (Helen Gardner, ed.; 1972)

41 Almost every man wastes part of his life in attempts to display qualities which he does not possess, and to gain applause which he cannot keep.
The Rambler (1750–52)

42 Hope is necessary in every condition. The miseries of poverty, sickness, of captivity, would, without this comfort, be insupportable.
The Rambler (1750–52)

43 I have laboured to refine our language to grammatical purity, and to clear it from colloquial barbarisms, licentious idioms, and irregular combinations.
The Rambler (1750–52)

44 The love of life is necessary to the vigorous prosecution of any undertaking.
The Rambler (1750–52)

45 There is a certain race of men that either imagine it their duty, or make it their amusement, to hinder the reception of every work of learning or genius, who stand as sentinels in the avenues of fame, and value themselves upon giving Ignorance and Envy the first notice of a prey.
The Rambler (1750–52)

46 A translator is to be like his author, it is not his business to excel him.
Quoted in *A History of Reading* (Alberto Manguel; 1996)

47 If the man who turnips cries,
Cry not when his father dies,
'Tis a proof that he had rather
Have a turnip than his father.
Quoted in *Anecdotes of the Late Samuel Johnson* (Hester Lynch Piozzi; 1786)

48 It is very strange, and very melancholy, that the paucity of human pleasures should persuade us ever to call hunting one of them.
Quoted in *Anecdotes of the Late Samuel Johnson* (Hester Lynch Piozzi; 1786)

49 GOLDSMITH Here's such a stir about a fellow that has written one book, and I have written many.
JOHNSON Ah, Doctor, there go two-and-forty sixpences you know to one guinea.
Referring to James Beattie's *Essay on the Nature and Immutability of Truth* (1770). Quoted in *Anecdotes of the Late Samuel Johnson* (Hester Lynch Piozzi; 1786)

50 What is written without effort is in general read without pleasure.
Quoted in *Biographia* (William Seward; 1799)

51 Madam, before you flatter a man so grossly to his face, you should consider whether or not your flattery is worth his having.
August 1778. Said to Hannah More. Quoted in *Diary and Letters of Madame d'Arblay* (Charlotte Barrett, ed.; 1842–46), vol. 1, ch. 2

52 Every man has, some time in his life, an ambition to be a wag.
Quoted in *Diary and Letters of Madame d'Arblay* (Charlotte Barrett, ed.; 1842–46), vol. 3, ch. 46

53 Fly fishing may be a very pleasant amusement; but angling or float fishing I can only compare to a stick and a string, with a worm at one end and a fool at the other.
Quoted in *Instructions to Young Sportsmen* (Hawker; 1859)

54 The only sensual pleasure without vice.
1784. Referring to music. Quoted in *Johnsoniana* (Sir John Hawkins; 1787)

55 Dear Doctor (said he one day to a common acquaintance, who lamented the tender state of his *inside*), do not be like the

spider, man, and spin conversation thus incessantly out of thy own bowels.
Quoted in *Johnsonian Miscellanies* (G. B. Hill, ed.; 1897), vol. 1

56 A man is in general better pleased when he has a good dinner upon his table, than when his wife talks Greek.
Quoted in *Johnsonian Miscellanies* (G. B. Hill, ed.; 1897), vol. 2

57 Love is the wisdom of the fool and the folly of the wise.
Quoted in *Johnsonian Miscellanies* (G. B. Hill, ed.; 1897), vol. 2

58 A tavern chair is the throne of human felicity.
1755. Quoted in "Extracts from Hawkin's *Life of Samuel Johnson*," *Johnsonian Miscellanies* (G. B. Hill, ed.; 1897), vol. 2

59 A cucumber should be well sliced, and dressed with pepper and vinegar, and then thrown out, as good for nothing.
October 5, 1773. Quoted in *Journal of a Tour to the Hebrides* (James Boswell; 1785)

60 A lawyer has no business with the justice or injustice of the cause which he undertakes, unless his client asks his opinion, and then he is bound to give it honestly. The justice or injustice of the cause is to be decided by the judge.
August 15, 1773. Quoted in *Journal of a Tour to the Hebrides* (James Boswell; 1785)

61 I am always sorry when any language is lost, because languages are the pedigree of nations.
September 18, 1773. Quoted in *Journal of a Tour to the Hebrides* (James Boswell; 1785)

62 I am sorry I have not learned to play at cards. It is very useful in life: it generates kindness and consolidates society.
November 21, 1773. Quoted in *Journal of a Tour to the Hebrides* (James Boswell; 1785)

63 I have, all my life long, been lying till noon; yet I tell all young men, and tell them with great sincerity, that nobody who does not rise early will ever do any good.
September 14, 1773. Quoted in *Journal of a Tour to the Hebrides* (James Boswell; 1785)

64 Smoking...is a shocking thing, blowing smoke out of our mouths into other people's mouths, eyes and noses, and having the same thing done to us.
1773. Quoted in *Journal of a Tour to the Hebrides* (James Boswell; 1785)

65 Come, let me know what it is that makes a Scotchman happy!
1773. Ordering for himself a glass of whisky. Quoted in *Journal of a Tour to the Hebrides* (James Boswell; 1785)

66 No, Sir; there were people who died of dropsies, which they contracted in trying to get drunk.
1773. Scornfully criticizing the strength of the wine in Scotland before the Act of Union (1707) in response to James Boswell's claim that there had been a lot of drunkenness. Quoted in *Journal of a Tour to the Hebrides* (James Boswell; 1785)

67 A country governed by a despot is an inverted cone.
April 14, 1778. Quoted in *Life of Samuel Johnson* (James Boswell; 1791)

68 A Frenchman must be always talking, whether he knows anything of the matter or not; an Englishman is content to say nothing, when he has nothing to say.
1780. Quoted in *Life of Samuel Johnson* (James Boswell; 1791)

69 All censure of a man's self is oblique praise. It is in order to shew how much he can spare.
April 25, 1778. Quoted in *Life of Samuel Johnson* (James Boswell; 1791)

70 All knowledge is of itself of some value. There is nothing so minute or inconsiderable, that I would not rather know it than not.
April 14, 1775. Quoted in *Life of Samuel Johnson* (James Boswell; 1791)

71 Always, Sir, set a high value on spontaneous kindness. He whose inclination prompts him to cultivate your friendship of his own accord, will love you more than one whom you have been at pains to attach to you.
May 1781. Quoted in *Life of Samuel Johnson* (James Boswell; 1791)

72 A man ought to read just as inclination leads him; for what he reads as a task will do him little good.
July 14, 1763. Quoted in *Life of Samuel Johnson* (James Boswell; 1791)

73 A man who exposes himself when he is intoxicated, has not the art of getting drunk.
April 24, 1779. Quoted in *Life of Samuel Johnson* (James Boswell; 1791)

74 A man who has not been in Italy, is always conscious of an inferiority, from his not having seen what it is expected a man should see. The grand object of travelling is to see the shores of the Mediterranean.
April 11, 1776. Quoted in *Life of Samuel Johnson* (James Boswell; 1791)

75 A man who is good enough to go to heaven, is good enough to be a clergyman.
April 5, 1772. Quoted in *Life of Samuel Johnson* (James Boswell; 1791)

76 A man will turn over half a library to make one book.
April 6, 1775. Quoted in *Life of Samuel Johnson* (James Boswell; 1791)

77 As I know more of mankind I expect less of them, and am ready now to call a man *a good man*, upon easier terms than I was formerly.
September 1783. Quoted in *Life of Samuel Johnson* (James Boswell; 1791)

78 A woman's preaching is like a dog's walking on his hinder legs. It is not done well; but you are surprised to find it done at all.
July 30, 1763. Quoted in *Life of Samuel Johnson* (James Boswell; 1791)

79 BOSWELL I do indeed come from Scotland, but I cannot help it...
JOHNSON That, Sir, I find, is what a very great many of your countrymen cannot help.
May 16, 1763. Quoted in *Life of Samuel Johnson* (James Boswell; 1791)

80 Claret is the liquor for boys; port for men; but he who aspires to be a hero must drink brandy.
April 7, 1779. Quoted in *Life of Samuel Johnson* (James Boswell; 1791)

81 Classical quotation is the *parole* of literary men all over the world.
May 8, 1781. Quoted in *Life of Samuel Johnson* (James Boswell; 1791)

82 Depend upon it that if a man talks of his misfortunes there is something in them that is not disagreeable to him; for where there is nothing but pure misery there never is any recourse to the mention of it.
1780. Quoted in *Life of Samuel Johnson* (James Boswell; 1791)

83 ELPHINSTON What, have you not read it through?...
JOHNSON No, Sir, do *you* read books *through*?
April 19, 1773. Quoted in *Life of Samuel Johnson* (James Boswell; 1791)

84 Fine clothes are good only as they supply the want of other means of procuring respect.
March 27, 1776. Quoted in *Life of Samuel Johnson* (James Boswell; 1791)

85 George the First knew nothing, and desired to know nothing; did nothing, and desired to do nothing: and the only good thing that is told of him is, that he wished to restore the crown to its hereditary successor.
April 6, 1775. Quoted in *Life of Samuel Johnson* (James Boswell; 1791)

86 Great abilities are not requisite for an Historian... Imagination is not required in any high degree.
July 6, 1763. Quoted in *Life of Samuel Johnson* (James Boswell; 1791)

87 He did not care to speak ill of any man behind his back, but he believed the gentleman was an *attorney*.
1770. Quoted in *Life of Samuel Johnson* (James Boswell; 1791)

88 He who praises everybody praises nobody.
1777. Quoted in *Life of Samuel Johnson* (James Boswell; 1791)

89 How few of his friends' houses would a man choose to be at when he is sick.
October 10, 1783. Quoted in *Life of Samuel Johnson* (James Boswell; 1791)

90 I am willing to love all mankind, *except an American*.
April 15, 1778. Quoted in *Life of Samuel Johnson* (James Boswell; 1791)

91 I deny the lawfulness of telling a lie to a sick man for fear of alarming him. You have no business with consequences; you are to tell the truth...It may bring his distemper to a crisis, and that may cure him. Of all lying, I have the greatest abhorrence of this, because I believe it has been frequently practised on myself.
Quoted in *Life of Samuel Johnson* (James Boswell; 1791)

92 If a madman were to come into this room with a stick in his hand, no doubt we should pity the state of his mind; but our primary consideration would be to take care of ourselves. We should knock him down first, and pity him afterwards.
April 3, 1776. Quoted in *Life of Samuel Johnson* (James Boswell; 1791)

93 If a man does not make new acquaintance as he advances through life, he will soon find himself left alone. A man, Sir, should keep his friendship in *constant repair*.
1755. Quoted in *Life of Samuel Johnson* (James Boswell; 1791)

94 If I had no duties, and no reference to futurity, I would spend my life in driving briskly in a post-chaise with a pretty woman.
September 19, 1777. Quoted in *Life of Samuel Johnson* (James Boswell; 1791)

95 I hate a fellow whom pride, or cowardice, or laziness drives into a corner, and who does nothing when he is there but sit and *growl*; let him come out as I do, and *bark*.
October 10, 1782. Quoted in *Life of Samuel Johnson* (James Boswell; 1791)

96 I have got no further than this: Every man has a right to utter what he thinks truth, and every other man has a right to knock him down for it. Martyrdom is the test.
1780. Quoted in *Life of Samuel Johnson* (James Boswell; 1791)

97 In lapidary inscriptions a man is not upon oath.
1775. Quoted in *Life of Samuel Johnson* (James Boswell; 1791)

98 In my early years I read very hard. It is a sad reflection, but a true one, that I knew almost as much at eighteen as I do now.
July 21, 1763. Quoted in *Life of Samuel Johnson* (James Boswell; 1791)

99 I think the full tide of human existence is at Charing-Cross.
April 2, 1775. Quoted in *Life of Samuel Johnson* (James Boswell; 1791)

100 It is better that some should be unhappy than that none should be happy, which would be the case in a general state of equality.
April 7, 1776. Quoted in *Life of Samuel Johnson* (James Boswell; 1791)

101 It matters not how a man dies, but how he lives. The act of dying is not of importance, it lasts so short a time.
October 26, 1769. Quoted in *Life of Samuel Johnson* (James Boswell; 1791)

102 I would not give half a guinea to live under one form of government rather than another. It is of no moment to the happiness of an individual.
March 31, 1772. Quoted in *Life of Samuel Johnson* (James Boswell; 1791)

103 Knowledge is of two kinds. We know a subject ourselves, or we know where we can find information upon it.
April 18, 1775. Quoted in *Life of Samuel Johnson* (James Boswell; 1791)

104 My dear friend, clear your *mind* of cant... You may *talk* in this manner; it is a mode of talking in Society: but don't *think* foolishly.
May 15, 1783. Quoted in *Life of Samuel Johnson* (James Boswell; 1791)

105 No man but a blockhead ever wrote, except for money.
April 5, 1776. Quoted in *Life of Samuel Johnson* (James Boswell; 1791)

106 No man will be a sailor who has contrivance enough to get himself into a jail; for being in a ship is being in a jail, with the chance of being drowned...A man in a jail has more room, better food, and commonly better company.
1759. Quoted in *Life of Samuel Johnson* (James Boswell; 1791)

107 Norway, too, has noble wild prospects; and Lapland is remarkable for prodigious noble wild prospects. But, Sir, let me tell you, the noblest prospect which a Scotchman ever sees, is the high road that leads him to England!
July 6, 1763. Quoted in *Life of Samuel Johnson* (James Boswell; 1791)

108 Our tastes greatly alter. The lad does not care for the child's rattle, and the old man does not care for the young man's whore.
Spring 1766. Quoted in *Life of Samuel Johnson* (James Boswell; 1791)

109 Patriotism is the last refuge of a scoundrel.
April 7, 1775. Quoted in *Life of Samuel Johnson* (James Boswell; 1791)

110 Politicks are now nothing more than a means of rising in the world.
April 18, 1775. Quoted in *Life of Samuel Johnson* (James Boswell; 1791)

111 Questioning is not the mode of conversation among gentlemen.
March 25, 1776. Quoted in *Life of Samuel Johnson* (James Boswell; 1791)

112 Round numbers are always false.
1778. Quoted in *Life of Samuel Johnson* (James Boswell; 1791)

113 Seeing Scotland, Madam, is only seeing a worse England. It is seeing the flower fade away to the naked stalk.
April 7, 1778. Quoted in *Life of Samuel Johnson* (James Boswell; 1791)

114 Sir, I look upon every day to be lost, in which I do not make a new acquaintance.
November 1784. Quoted in *Life of Samuel Johnson* (James Boswell; 1791)

115 Sir, it is not so much to be lamented that Old England is lost, as that the Scotch have found it.
May 15, 1776. Quoted in *Life of Samuel Johnson* (James Boswell; 1791)

116 Sir, the insolence of wealth will creep out.
April 18, 1778. Quoted in *Life of Samuel Johnson* (James Boswell; 1791)

117 Swallows certainly sleep all winter. A number of them conglobulate together, by flying round and round, and then all in a heap throw themselves under water, and lie in the bed of a river.
Quoted in *Life of Samuel Johnson* (James Boswell; 1791)

118 That all who are happy, are equally happy, is not true. A peasant and a philosopher may be equally *satisfied*, but not equally *happy*.
February, 1766. Quoted in *Life of Samuel Johnson* (James Boswell; 1791)

119 That is the happiest conversation where there is no competition, no vanity, but a calm quiet interchange of sentiments.
April 14, 1775. Quoted in *Life of Samuel Johnson* (James Boswell; 1791)

120 The booksellers are generous liberal-minded men.
1756. Quoted in *Life of Samuel Johnson* (James Boswell; 1791)

121 The Irish are a FAIR PEOPLE; they never speak well of one another.
February 18, 1775. Quoted in *Life of Samuel Johnson* (James Boswell; 1791)

122 There are few ways in which a man can be more innocently employed than in getting money.
March 27, 1775. Quoted in *Life of Samuel Johnson* (James Boswell; 1791)

123 There are innumerable questions to which the inquisitive mind can in this state receive no answer: Why do you and I exist? Why was this world created? Since it was to be created, why was it not created sooner?
1778. Quoted in *Life of Samuel Johnson* (James Boswell; 1791)

124 There is a wicked inclination in most people to suppose an old man decayed in his intellects. If a young or middle-aged man, when leaving a company, does not recollect where he laid his hat, it is nothing; but if the same inattention is discovered in an old man, people will shrug up their shoulders, and say, "His memory is going."
1783. Quoted in *Life of Samuel Johnson* (James Boswell; 1791)

125 There is no idolatry in the Mass. They believe God to be there, and they adore him.
October 26, 1769. Quoted in *Life of Samuel Johnson* (James Boswell; 1791)

126 There is nothing which has yet been contrived by man, by which so much happiness is produced as by a good tavern or inn.
March 21, 1776. Quoted in *Life of Samuel Johnson* (James Boswell; 1791)

127 There is now less flogging in our great schools than formerly, but then less is learned there; so that what the boys get at one end, they lose at the other.
1775. Quoted in *Life of Samuel Johnson* (James Boswell; 1791)

128 This was a good dinner enough, to be sure; but it was not a dinner to *ask* a man to.
August 5, 1763. Quoted in *Life of Samuel Johnson* (James Boswell; 1791)

129 Walpole was a minister given by the King to the people: Pitt was a minister given by the people to the King.
May 9, 1772. Quoted in *Life of Samuel Johnson* (James Boswell; 1791)

130 Were it not for imagination, Sir, a man would be as happy in the arms of a chambermaid as of a Duchess.
May 9, 1778. Quoted in *Life of Samuel Johnson* (James Boswell; 1791)

131 We would all be idle if we could.
April 3, 1776. Quoted in *Life of Samuel Johnson* (James Boswell; 1791)

132 When a man is tired of London, he is tired of life; for there is in London all that life can afford.
September 20, 1777. Quoted in *Life of Samuel Johnson* (James Boswell; 1791)

133 When men come to like a sea-life, they are not fit to live on land.
March 19, 1776. Quoted in *Life of Samuel Johnson* (James Boswell; 1791)

134 Why, Sir, most schemes of political improvement are very laughable things.
October 26, 1769. Quoted in *Life of Samuel Johnson* (James Boswell; 1791)

135 Your levellers wish to level *down* as far as themselves; but they cannot bear levelling *up* to themselves.
July 21, 1763. Quoted in *Life of Samuel Johnson* (James Boswell; 1791)

136 It is as bad as bad can be: it is ill-fed, ill-killed, ill-kept, and ill-drest.
June 3, 1784. About the roast mutton at an inn. Quoted in *Life of Samuel Johnson* (James Boswell; 1791)

137 When the messenger who carried the last sheet to Millar returned, Johnson asked him, "Well, what did he say?"—"Sir (answered the messenger), he said, thank God I have done with him."—"I am glad (replied Johnson, with a smile) that he thanks God for anything."
April 8, 1755. After the final page of his Dictionary had been delivered. Quoted in *Life of Samuel Johnson* (James Boswell; 1791)

138 Nay, Madam, when you are declaiming, declaim; and when you are calculating, calculate.
April 29, 1776. Commenting on Mrs. Thrale's discourse on the price of children's clothes. Quoted in *Life of Samuel Johnson* (James Boswell; 1791)

139 Ignorance, madam, pure ignorance.
1755. His reply on being questioned, by a female reader of his Dictionary, why he had defined "pastern" as the "knee" of a horse. Quoted in *Life of Samuel Johnson* (James Boswell; 1791)

140 Sir, your wife, under pretence of keeping a bawdy-house, is a receiver of stolen goods.
1780. Johnson's reply to a man while sailing, an example of the customary badinage between travelers on the River Thames. Quoted in *Life of Samuel Johnson* (James Boswell; 1791)

141 Read over your compositions, and where ever you meet with a passage which you think is particularly fine, strike it out.
April 30, 1773. Recalling the advice of a college teacher. Quoted in *Life of Samuel Johnson* (James Boswell; 1791)

142 That fellow seems to me to possess but one idea, and that is a wrong one.
1770. Referring to "a dull tiresome fellow, whom he chanced to meet." Quoted in *Life of Samuel Johnson* (James Boswell; 1791)

143 But if he does really think that there is no distinction between virtue and vice, why, Sir, when he leaves our houses let us count our spoons.
July 14, 1763. Referring to an "impudent fellow" from Scotland. Quoted in *Life of Samuel Johnson* (James Boswell; 1791)

144 A fly, Sir, may sting a stately horse and make him wince; but one is but an insect, and the other is a horse still.
1754. Referring to critics. Quoted in *Life of Samuel Johnson* (James Boswell; 1791)

145 He is the richest author that ever grazed the common of literature.
July 1, 1763. Referring to Dr. John Campbell. Quoted in *Life of Samuel Johnson* (James Boswell; 1791)

146 Their learning is like bread in a besieged town: every man gets a little, but no man gets a full meal.
April 18, 1775. Referring to education in Scotland. Quoted in *Life of Samuel Johnson* (James Boswell; 1791)

147 I will be conquered; I will not capitulate.
November 1784. Referring to his final illness. Quoted in *Life of Samuel Johnson* (James Boswell; 1791)

148 He was a vicious man, but very kind to me. If you call a dog *Hervey*, I shall love him.
1737. Referring to his late friend, the honorable Henry Hervey, third son of the first Earl of Bristol. Quoted in *Life of Samuel Johnson* (James Boswell; 1791)

149 The woman's a whore, and there's an end on't.
May 7, 1773. Referring to Lady Diana Beauclerk. Quoted in *Life of Samuel Johnson* (James Boswell; 1791)

150 Much may be made of a Scotchman, if he be *caught* young.
Spring 1772. Referring to Lord Mansfield. Quoted in *Life of Samuel Johnson* (James Boswell; 1791)

151 A very unclubbable man.
Spring 1764. Referring to Sir John Hawkins. Quoted in *Life of Samuel Johnson* (James Boswell; 1791)

152 Truth, Sir, is a cow, which will yield such people no more milk, and so they are gone to milk the bull.
July 21, 1763. Referring to skeptics. Quoted in *Life of Samuel Johnson* (James Boswell; 1791)

153 I have two very cogent reasons for not printing any list of subscribers;—one, that I have lost all the names,—the other, that I have spent all the money.
May 1781. Referring to subscribers to his *Dictionary of the English Language.* Quoted in *Life of Samuel Johnson* (James Boswell; 1791)

154 It is no matter what you teach them first, any more than what leg you shall put into your breeches first.
July 26, 1763. Referring to the education of children. Quoted in *Life of Samuel Johnson* (James Boswell; 1791)

155 Depend upon it, Sir, when a man knows he is to be hanged in a fortnight, it concentrates his mind wonderfully.
September 19, 1777. Referring to the forthcoming execution of Dr. William Dodd. Quoted in *Life of Samuel Johnson* (James Boswell; 1791)

156 Worth seeing? yes; but not worth going to see.
October 12, 1779. Referring to the Giant's Causeway, County Antrim, Northern Ireland. Quoted in *Life of Samuel Johnson* (James Boswell; 1791)

157 The triumph of hope over experience.
1770. Referring to the hasty remarriage of an acquaintance following the death of his first wife, with whom he had been most unhappy. Quoted in *Life of Samuel Johnson* (James Boswell; 1791)

158 You *may* abuse a tragedy, though you cannot write one. You may scold a carpenter who has made you a bad table, though you cannot make a table. It is not your trade to make tables.
June 25, 1763. Referring to the qualifications needed to indulge in literary criticism. Quoted in *Life of Samuel Johnson* (James Boswell; 1791)

159 I refute it *thus*.
August 6, 1763. Replying to James Boswell's contention that they were unable to refute Bishop Berkeley's theory that matter cannot be conceived to exist independent of the mind, by kicking a large stone with his foot. Quoted in *Life of Samuel Johnson* (James Boswell; 1791)

160 A cow is a very good animal in the field; but we turn her out of a garden.
April 15, 1772. Replying to James Boswell's objections to the expulsion of six Methodists from Oxford University. Quoted in *Life of Samuel Johnson* (James Boswell; 1791)

161 "Why yes, Sir, but I have had cats whom I liked better than this"; and then as if perceiving Hodge to be out of countenance, adding, "but he is a very fine cat, a very fine cat indeed."
1783. Replying to James Boswell's observation that Johnson's cat, Hodge, was a fine cat. Quoted in *Life of Samuel Johnson* (James Boswell; 1791)

162 Why Sir, it is much easier to say what it is not. We all *know* what light is; but it is not easy to *tell* what it is.
April 12, 1776. Reply when asked, "What is poetry?" Quoted in *Life of Samuel Johnson* (James Boswell; 1791)

163 It is incident to physicians, I am afraid, beyond all other men, to mistake subsequence for consequence.
Reviewing Dr. Charles Lucas's *Essay on Waters* (1756). Quoted in *Life of Samuel Johnson* (James Boswell; 1791)

164 All argument is against it; but all belief is for it.
March 31, 1778. Rreferring to the ghost of a dead person. Quoted in *Life of Samuel Johnson* (James Boswell; 1791)

165 Sir, I have found you an argument but I am not obliged to find you an understanding.
June, 1784. Said to an opponent in a drawn-out argument, who had said to Johnson, "I don't understand you, Sir." Quoted in *Life of Samuel Johnson* (James Boswell; 1791)

166 Sir, I perceive you are a vile Whig.
March 31, 1772. Said to Sir Adam Fergusson. Quoted in *Life of Samuel Johnson* (James Boswell; 1791)

167 I'll come no more behind your scenes, David; for the silk stockings and white bosoms of your actresses excite my amorous propensities.
1750. Said to the actor-manager David Garrick. What Johnson was actually reported as saying was: "I'll come no more behind your scenes, David, for the white bubbies and silk stockings of your actresses excite my genitals." Quoted in *Life of Samuel Johnson* (James Boswell; 1791)

168 Yes, Sir, many men, many women, and many children.
May 24, 1763. When asked by Dr. Blair whether any man of their own time could have written the poems of Ossian. Quoted in *Life of Samuel Johnson* (James Boswell; 1791)

169 Towering in the confidence of twenty-one.
January 9, 1758. Quoted in Letter to Bennet Langton, *Life of Samuel Johnson* (James Boswell; 1791)

170 Are you sick, or are you sullen?
November 3, 1784. Quoted in Letter to Boswell, *Life of Samuel Johnson* (James Boswell; 1791)

171 Resolve not to be poor: whatever you have, spend less. Poverty is a great enemy to human happiness; it certainly destroys liberty, and it makes some virtues impracticable and others extremely difficult.
December 7, 1782. Quoted in Letter to Boswell, *Life of Samuel Johnson* (James Boswell; 1791)

172 Is not a Patron, my Lord, one who looks with unconcern on a man struggling for life in the water, and, when he has reached ground, encumbers him with help? The notice which you have been pleased to take of my labours, had it been

early, had been kind; but it has been delayed till I am indifferent, and cannot enjoy it; till I am solitary, and cannot impart it; till I am known, and do not want it.
February 7, 1755. Quoted in Letter to Lord Chesterfield, *Life of Samuel Johnson* (James Boswell; 1791)

173 Every man has a lurking wish to appear considerable in his native place.
July 17, 1771. Quoted in Letter to Sir Joshua Reynolds, *Life of Samuel Johnson* (James Boswell; 1791)

174 Difficult do you call it, Sir? I wish it were impossible.
Said on hearing a famous violinist. Quoted in *Supplement to the Anecdotes of Distinguished Persons* (William Seward; 1797)

175 Abuse is often of service. There is nothing so dangerous to an author as silence.
Attrib.

Johnson, Sonia (b.1936) U.S. feminist and writer

1 I am a warrior in the time of women warriors; the longing for justice is the sword I carry, the love of womankind my shield.
From Housewife to Heretic (1981)

Johnston, Jill (b.1929) British-born U.S. writer and feminist

1 I never said I was a dyke even to a dyke because there wasn't a dyke in the land who thought she should be a dyke or even thought she was a dyke so how could we talk about it.
Lesbian Nation: The Feminist Solution (1973)

Johst, Hanns (1890–1978) German novelist and playwright

1 Whenever I hear the word "culture"...I reach for my gun.
Popularly attributed to Hermann Goering. The actual line Johst wrote was: "Whenever I hear the word culture...I release the safety-catch of my Browning." *Schlageter* (1933), Act 1, Scene 1

Jolson, Al (Asa Yoelson; 1886–1950) Russian-born U.S. actor and singer

Quotations about Jolson

1 Nobody ever dominated a theater like Jolson. And nobody was ever as quick to admit it as he was, either.
George Burns (1896–1996) U.S. comedian and actor. *All My Best Friends* (1989)

Quotations by Jolson

2 You ain't heard nothin' yet, folks.
July 1927. The first speech in a "talkie" film, *The Jazz Singer*; later adopted as a catch phrase by President Ronald Reagan. *The Jazz Singer* (1927)

Jones, Amanda Theodosia (1835–1914) U.S. inventor, poet, businesswoman, and psychic

1 This is a woman's industry. No man will vote our stock, transact our business, pronounce on woman's wages, supervise our factories. Give men whatever work is suitable, but keep the governing power.
From an address to employees of the Women's Canning and Preserving Company, a business that Amanda Theodosia Jones founded in Chicago after inventing a canning process. *A Psychic's Autobiography* (1910)

Jones, Chris U.S. business consultant

1 Companies have to devote five man-years to finding out whether the Internet is an opportunity or a rat hole.
Fortune (March 7, 1994)

Jones, David (David Michael Jones; 1895–1974) British poet and graphic artist

1 Rotary steel hail split and lashed in sharp spasms along the vibrating line; great solemn guns leisurely manipulated their expensive discharges at rare intervals, bringing weight and full recession to the rising orchestration.
Describing an artillery bombardment in World War I. "Starlight Order," *In Parenthesis* (1937), pt. 3

2 This all depriving darkness split now by crazy flashing; marking hugely clear the spilled bowels of trees, splinter-spike, leper-ashen, sprawling the receding, unknowable, wall of night.
Describing an artillery bombardment in World War I. "Starlight Order," *In Parenthesis* (1937), pt. 3

3 Are the scarred ridges
his dented greaves
do the trickling gullies
yet drain his hog-wounds?
Does the land wait the sleeping lord
or is the wasted land
that very lord who sleeps?
"The Sleeping Lord," *The Sleeping Lord and Other Fragments* (1974)

Jones, James Earl (b.1931) U.S. actor

1 There is not enough magic in a bloodline to forge an instant, irrevocable bond.
James Earl Jones: Voices and Silences (Jones & Niven; 1993)

Jones, John Paul (1747–92) Scottish-born U.S. naval officer

1 I have not yet begun to fight.
September 23, 1779. Supposed retort when informed his ship was sinking. He captured the British frigate *Serapis* in a hard-fought engagement off Flamborough Head, England, but his ship sank two days later. Quoted in *Life and Letters of J. P. Jones* (De Koven, ed.; 1779), vol. 1

Jones, Mablen U.S. rock journalist

1 Rock'n'roll stars look dangerous. These frenetic heroes and goddesses in costumes ranging from glamorous to grotesque assault high culture.
Getting it On: the Clothing of Rock 'n' Roll (1987)

Jones, Mother (Mary Harris Jones; 1830–1930) Irish-born U.S. labor leader

1 Pray for the dead and fight like hell for the living.
Autobiography (1925)

Jones, Owen (1809–74) British architect

1 Style in architecture is the peculiar form that expression takes under the influence of climate and materials at command.
The Grammar of Ornament (1856)

Jones, Quincy (b.1933) U.S. record producer and musician

1 The most deadly thing about cocaine is that it separates you from your soul.
Quoted in *Divided Soul* (David Ritz; 1985)

2 And then came *Thriller*, which was mind-boggling. It scared me. I thought, "Holy shit, what is going on?" I mean, everybody wants a big record, but this was outrageous.
Quoted in *Off the Record: An Oral History of Popular Music* (Joe Smith; 1988)

3 He's not the weirdo people think he is.
On Michael Jackson. Quoted in *Off the Record: An Oral History of Popular Music* (Joe Smith; 1988)

4 That was the band that turned everything around, where black musicians for the first time said, "We don't want to be just entertainers. We want to be artists."
Referring to Billy Eckstine's band that included Dizzy Gillespie, Donald Byrd, Sarah Vaughan, and Miles Davis. Quoted in "Quincy Jones," *Off the Record: An Oral History of Popular Music* (Joe Smith; 1988)

Jones, Reginald (Reginald Harold Jones; b.1917) U.S. business executive

1 The main problems of business these days are external to the company and are determined in the area of public policy.
Quoted in *Doing Business in Washington* (Harrison W. Fox, Jr., and Martin Schnitzer; 1981)

2 When business managers bring their experience in the formation of policy and law, they speak for millions of affected people and deserve a hearing.
Quoted in *Doing Business in Washington* (Harrison W. Fox, Jr., and Martin Schnitzer; 1981)

Jones, Spike (Lindley Armstrong Jones; 1911–65) U.S. bandleader

1 Thank-you, music-lovers.
Catch phrase. His act featured such things as a goat trained to bleat rhythmically and a lyre made from a lavatory seat. Attrib.

Jones, Stephen (b.1957) British milliner

1 A baseball cap is just as valid as a felt hat was 20 years ago.
Observer, London (April 17, 1994), "Sayings of the Week"

Jones, Steve (b.1944) British geneticist

1 A useless but amusing fact is that if all the DNA in all the cells in a single human being were stretched out it would reach the moon and back eight thousand times.
The Language of the Genes (1991)

2 There have been claims that we may soon find the gene that makes us human. The ancestral message will then at last allow us to understand what we really are. The idea seems to me ridiculous.
The Language of the Genes (1991)

Jones, Thomas K. U.S. public official

1 Dig a hole, cover it with a couple of doors and then throw three feet of dirt on top...It's the dirt that does it...You know, dirt is just great stuff...If there are enough shovels to go round, everybody's going to make it.
Referring to civil defense precautions in the event of a nuclear war. Quoted in *With Enough Shovels: Reagan, Bush and Nuclear War* (Robert Scheer; 1981)

Jones, William, Sir (1746–94) British jurist and orientalist

1 My opinion is, that power should always be distrusted, in whatever hands it is placed.
Letter to Lord Althrope (October 5, 1782), quoted in *Life of Sir William Jones* (Lord Teignmouth; 1835), vol. 1

Jong, Erica (originally Erica Mann; b.1942) U.S. writer

1 Men have always detested women's gossip because they suspect the truth: their measurements are being taken and compared.
Fear of Flying (1973)

2 Solitude is un-American.
Fear of Flying (1973)

3 The zipless fuck is the purest thing there is. And it is rarer than the unicorn. And I have never had one.
Fear of Flying (1973)

4 All the cosmetics' names seemed obscenely obvious to me in their promise of sexual bliss. They were all firming or uplifting or invigorating. They made you *tingle*. Or *glow*. Or feel *young*.
How to Save your Own Life (1977)

5 Jealousy is all the fun you *think* they had.
How to Save Your Own Life (1977)

6 Success, for women, is always partly failure.
1973. "The Artist as Housewife," *The First Ms. Reader* (Francine Klagsburn, ed.; 1982)

7 It was the ecstasy of striking matches in the dark.
Referring to writing poetry. *What Do Women Want?* (1998), preface

8 Without farts, there are no flowers. Without pricks, there are no poems.
"Deliberate Lewdness and the Creative Imagination: Should We Censor Pornography?," *What Do Women Want?* (1998), ch. 10

Jonson, Ben (Benjamin Jonson; 1572–1637) English playwright and poet

Quotations about Jonson

1 O Rare Ben Jonson.
John Young (*fl.* 17th century) English patron of arts. Sometimes read as "Orare Ben Jonson" (Latin for "pray for Ben Jonson"). Ben Jonson's Epitaph, Westminster Abbey, London (17th century)

Quotations by Jonson

2 Drink to me only with thine eyes,
And I will pledge with mine;
Or leave a kiss but in the cup,
And I'll not look for wine.
The thirst that from the soul doth rise
Doth ask a drink divine;
But might I of Jove's nectar sup,
I would not change for thine.
I sent thee late a rosy wreath,
Not so much honouring thee,
As giving it a hope that there
It could not wither'd be.
"To Celia" (1616), st. 1

3 Soul of the Age!
The applause, delight, the wonder of our stage!

My Shakespeare, rise; I will not lodge thee by
Chaucer, or Spenser, or bid Beaumont lie
A little further, to make thee a room.
"To the Memory of My Beloved, the Author, Mr William Shakespeare" (1623)

4 Neither do thou lust after that tawney weed tobacco.
Bartholomew Fair (1614), Act 2, Scene 6

5 The drunkards they are wading,
The punks and chapmen trading;
Who'd see the Fair without his lading?
Batholomew Fair (1614), Act 2, Scene 1

6 Youth, youth, thou had'st better been starv'd by thy nurse,
Than to live to be hanged for cutting a purse.
Batholomew Fair (1614), Act 3, Scene 1

7 Alas, all the castles I have, are built with air, thou know'st.
Eastward Ho (1604), Act 2, Scene 2

8 As he brews, so shall he drink.
Every Man in His Humour (1598), Act 2, Scene 1

9 Helter skelter, hang sorrow, care'll kill a cat, up-tails all, and a louse for the hangman.
Every Man in His Humour (1598), Act 2, Scene 3

10 I have it here in black and white
It must be done like lightning
Every Man in His Humour (1598), Act 4, Scene 5

11 Blind Fortune still
Bestows her gifts on such as cannot use them.
Every Man Out of His Humour (1599), Act 2, Scene 2

12 Ods me, I marvel what pleasure or felicity they have in taking their roguish tobacco. It is good for nothing but to choke a man, and fill him full of smoke and embers.
Every Man Out of His Humour (1599), Act 3, Scene 5

13 A prince's power makes all his actions virtue.
Sejanus, His Fall (1603), Act 3, Scene 3

14 Thither, too,
He hath his boys, and beauteous girls ta'en up,
Out of our noblest houses, the best formed,
Best nurtured, and most modest: what's their good
Serves to provoke his bad.
Sejanus, His Fall (1603), Act 4, Scene 4

15 If his dream lasts, he'll turn the age to gold.
The Alchemist (1610), Act 1, Scene 1

16 Fortune, that favours fools.
The Alchemist (1610), Prologue

17 When I mock poorness, then heaven make me poor.
The Case is Altered (1599), Act 3, Scene 1

18 That old bald cheater, Time.
The Poetaster (1601), Act 1, Scene 1

19 Ramp up my genius, be not retrograde;
But boldly nominate a spade a spade.
The Poetaster (1601), Act 5, Scene 1

20 She is Venus when she smiles;
But she's Juno when she walks,
And Minerva when she talks.
"Celebration of Charis. His Discourse with Cupid," *The Underwood* (1640)

21 Talking and eloquence are not the same: to speak, and to speak well, are two things.
Timber, or, Discoveries Made upon Men and Matter (1640)

22 They say princes learn no art truly, but the art of horsemanship. The reason is, the brave beast is no flatterer. He will throw a prince as soon as his groom.
Timber, or, Discoveries Made upon Men and Matter (1640)

23 Good morning to the day: and, next, my gold!—
Open the shrine, that I may see my saint.
Volpone (1606), Act 1, Scene 1

24 Calumnies are answered best with silence.
Volpone (1606), Act 2, Scene 2

25 O health! health! the blessing of the rich! the riches of the poor! who can buy thee at too deare a rate, since there is no enjoying this world, without thee?
Volpone (1606), Act 2, Scene 2

26 Come, my Celia, let us prove,
While we can, the sports of love,
Time will not be ours for ever,
He, at length, our good will sever.
Volpone (1606), Act 3, Scene 5

27 Honour! tut, a breath:
There's no such thing in nature: a mere term
Invented to awe fools.
Volpone (1606), Act 3, Scene 5

28 The seasoning of a play, is the applause.
Volpone (1606), Act 5, Scene 8

29 Many funerals discredit a physician.
Attrib.

Joplin, Janis (1943–70) U.S. rock singer

Quotations about Joplin

1 Janis Joplin...wanted brandy-and-Benedictine in a water tumbler. Music people never wanted ordinary drinks. They wanted sake, or champagne cocktails, or tequila neat. Spending time with music people was confusing.
1978
Joan Didion (b.1934) U.S. journalist and writer. "The White Album," *The White Album* (1979), pt. 1

Quotations by Joplin

2 Lord, won't you buy me a Mercedes-Benz,
My friends all drive Porsches,
I must make amends.
Song lyric. "Mercedes-Benz" (co-written with Michael McClure and Bob Neuwirth; 1970)

3 It's not what isn't, it's what you wish *was* that makes unhappiness. The hole, the vacuum...I think I think too much. That's why I drink.
Quoted in *Rock 'n' Roll Babylon* (Gary Herman; 1994)

4 On stage I have to make love to 25,000 different people, then I go home alone.
Quoted in *The Wit and Wisdom of Rock and Roll* (Maxim Jabukowski, ed.; 1983)

5 People like their blues singers dead.
She died from a heroin overdose on October 8, 1970. Quoted in *The Wit and Wisdom of Rock and Roll* (Maxim Jabukowski, ed.; 1983)

Jordan, Barbara (Barbara Charline Jordan; 1936–96) U.S. congresswoman, lawyer, and educator

1 What the people want is very simple. They want an America as good as its promise.
Harvard commencement speech (1977)

2 The American dream is not dead. True, it is gasping for breath but it is not dead.
Keynote address to the Democratic National Convention (July 13, 1992)

3 We, the people...a very eloquent beginning. But when the document was completed on the 17th of September in 1787 I was not included in that "We, the people."...But through...amendment, interpretation, and court decision I have finally been included in "We, the people."
Referring to the U.S. Constitution, and the Equal Rights Amendment of 1972 and other legal developments facilitating equality of the sexes. Speech to the House of Representatives (July 24, 1974)

Jordan, June (b.1936) U.S. journalist, writer, and activist

1 The only leadership I can respect is one that enables every man and woman to be his and her own leader.
Civil Wars (1980)

2 I am a feminist, and what that means to me is much the same as the meaning of the fact that I am Black: it means that I must undertake to love myself and to respect myself as though my very life depends upon self-love and self-respect.
1978. "Where Is the Love?," *Civil Wars* (1980)

3 It is a sad thing to consider that this country has given its least to those who have loved it the most.
For My American Family (1986)

4 What will we do
when there is nobody left
to kill?
"Poem for Nana," *Haruko/Love Poems* (1993)

5 Well, would I like to see Mike Tyson a free man again? He was never free!
Requiem For The Champ (1992)

6 Some people despise me because I have a Venus mound
and not a penis
Does that *sound*
right
to you?
"Some People," *Things that I Do in the Dark* (1981)

7 I am stranded in a hungerland
of great prosperity.
1968. "Who Look at Me," *Things that I Do in the Dark* (1981)

8 There is difference, and there is power. And who holds the power shall decide the meaning of difference.
Toward a Manifest New Destiny (1992)

9 A democratic nation of persons, of individuals, is an impossibility, and a fratricidal goal. Each American one of us must consciously choose to become a willing and outspoken part of the people who, together, will determine our individual chances for happiness, and justice.
Waking Up In The Middle Of Some American Dreams (1986)

10 Calling somebody a Communist is an entirely respectable, and popular, middle-class way to call somebody a low-down dirty dog.
Where Are We And Whose Country Is This Anyway? (1986)

Jordan, Michael (Michael Jeffrey Jordan; b.1963) U.S. basketball player

1 Talent wins games, but teamwork wins championships.
Attrib.

Jordan, Neil (b.1950) Irish film director and writer

1 The crew that shot the film contained many English technicians and when we filmed the sequence as the Union Jack is lowered in the forecourt of Dublin Castle and the tricolour of the Irish Free State run up, there was an almost tangible tenseness that felt as if it had been passed on from 75 years before.
Referring to the making of the movie *Michael Collins* (1996). Interview, *Evening Standard*, London (September 3, 1996)

2 I think I'd have failed if, in dealing with such a story, it didn't affront or even alienate some people.
Referring to the movie *Michael Collins* (1996). Interview, *Evening Standard*, London (September 3, 1996)

Jordan, Thomas (1612?–85) English poet

1 They pluck't communion tables down
And broke our painted glasses;
They threw our altars to the ground
And tumbled down the crosses.
They set up Cromwell and his heir
The Lord and Lady Claypole
Because they hated Common Prayer,
The organ and the maypole.
Referring to the (Protestant) "Roundheads" at the start of the English civil wars (1642–49). "How the War Began" (1664)

Joseph II, Holy Roman Emperor (1741–90) Austrian emperor

1 Convinced...of the...great benefits accruing to religion and the State from true Christian tolerance, we...grant the right of private worship to the Lutheran, Calvinist and non-Uniate Greek religions.
Edict of Toleration (October 13, 1781)

2 Here lies Joseph, who failed in everything he undertook.
18th century. Suggesting his own epitaph when reflecting upon the disappointment of his hopes for reform. Attrib.

Joseph, Chief (In-mut-too-yah-lat-lat, "thunder coming up from the water over the land"; 1840?–1904) Native American Nez Percé leader

1 Hear me, my chiefs, I am tired; my heart is sick and sad. From where the sun now stands, I will fight no more forever.
Said to his men at the end of the Nez Percé War. Speech (October 1877)

2 The earth is the mother of all people, and all people should have equal rights upon it. You might as well expect the rivers to run backward as that any man who was born a free man should be contented when penned up and denied liberty.
"An Indian's View of Indian Affairs," *North American Review* (1879)

3 Words do not pay for my dead people.
Attrib.

Joseph, Jenny (b.1932) British poet

1 When I am an old woman I shall wear purple
With a red hat that doesn't go, and doesn't suit me,
And I shall spend my pension on brandy and summer gloves
And satin sandals, and say we've no money for butter.
"Warning" (1973)

Joseph, Keith, Sir (Keith Sinjohn Joseph; 1918–94) British politician

1 Incomes policy alone as a way to abate inflation caused by excessive money supply is like trying to stop water coming out of a leaky hose without turning off the tap.
Speech, Preston, England (September 5, 1974)

2 Problems reproduce themselves from generation to generation...I refer to this as a "cycle of deprivation".
Speech to the Pre-School Playgroups Association (June 29, 1972)

3 This is a very fine country to be acutely ill or injured in, but take my advice and do not be old and frail or mentally ill here—at least not for a few years. This is definitely not a good country to be deaf or blind in either.
Observer, London (July 1, 1973), "Sayings of the Week"

Joseph, Michael (1897–1958) British publisher

1 Authors are easy to get on with—if you're fond of children.
Observer, London (1949)

Jouvet, Louis (1887–1951) French actor, director, and writer

1 There are performances where the public is quite without talent.
Quoted in *The Jingle Bell Principle* (Miroslav Holub; 1992)

Jowett, Benjamin (1817–93) British scholar

1 My dear child, you must believe in God in spite of what the clergy tell you.
1892. Quoted in *Autobiography* (Margot Asquith; 1920–22), ch. 8

2 Nowhere probably is there more true feeling, and nowhere worse taste, than in a churchyard—both as regards the monuments and the inscriptions. Scarcely a word of true poetry anywhere.
Quoted in *Letters of Benjamin Jowett* (E. Abbott and L. Campbell, eds.; 1897)

3 Young men make great mistakes in life; for one thing, they idealize love too much.
Quoted in *Letters of Benjamin Jowett* (E. Abbott and L. Campbell, eds.; 1897)

4 Logic is neither a science or an art, but a dodge.
Quoted in *The World of Mathematics* (J. R. Newman, ed.; 1956)

5 Research! A mere excuse for idleness; it has never achieved, and will never achieve any results of the slightest value.
Quoted in *Unforgotten Years* (Logan Pearsall Smith; 1938)

6 The way to get things done is not to mind who gets the credit of doing them.
Attrib.

7 If you don't find a God by five o'clock this afternoon you must leave the college.
Said to a student who had asserted that he could find no evidence for the existence of a God. Attrib.

Joyce, James (James Augustine Aloysius Joyce; 1882–1941) Irish writer

Quotations about Joyce

1 That bloody Joyce whom I kept in my youth has written a book you can read on all the lavatory walls of Dublin.
1922
Oliver St. John Gogarty (1878–1957) Irish writer and physician. Referring to James Joyce's *Ulysses* (1922). Quoted in *Oliver St John Gogarty* (Ulick O'Connor; 1964), ch. 6

2 To end up in a draughty lamplit station
After the trains have gone, the wet track
Bared and tense as I am, all attention
For your step following and damned if I look back.
Seamus Heaney (b.1939) Irish poet. The step following is that of James Joyce's ghost. "The Underground," *Station Island* (1984)

3 My God, what a clumsy *olla putrida* James Joyce is! Nothing but old fags and cabbage stumps of quotations from the Bible and the rest, stewed in the juice of deliberate, journalistic dirty-mindedness.
D. H. Lawrence (1885–1930) British writer. Letter to Aldous Huxley (August 15, 1928)

Quotations by Joyce

4 Once upon a time and a very good time it was there was a moocow coming down along the road and this moocow that was coming down along the road met a nicens little boy named baby tuckoo.
Opening sentence. *A Portrait of the Artist as a Young Man* (1916)

5 The language in which we are speaking is his before it is mine. How different are the words *home, Christ, ale, master*, on his lips and on mine.
Referring to the English language. *A Portrait of the Artist as a Young Man* (1916)

6 April 26 Welcome, O life! I go to encounter for the millionth time the reality of experience and to forge in the smithy of my soul the uncreated conscience of my race.
A Portrait of the Artist as a Young Man (1916), ch. 5

7 Ireland is the old sow that eats her farrow.
A Portrait of the Artist as a Young Man (1916), ch. 5

8 Pity is the feeling which arrests the mind in the presence of whatsoever is grave and constant in human sufferings and unites it with the human sufferer. Terror is the feeling which

arrests the mind in the presence of whatsoever is grave and constant in human sufferings and unites it with the secret cause.
A Portrait of the Artist as a Young Man (1916), ch. 5

9 The mystery of æsthetic like that of material creation is accomplished. The artist, like the God of the creation, remains within or behind or beyond or above his handiwork, invisible, refined out of existence, indifferent, paring his fingernails
A Portrait of the Artist as a Young Man (1916), ch. 5

10 Snow was general all over Ireland. It was falling on every part of the dark central plain, on the treeless hills, falling softly upon the Bog of Allen and, further westward, softly falling into the dark mutinous Shannon waves.
"The Dead," *Dubliners* (1914)

11 All moanday, tearsday, wailsday, thumpsday, frightday, shatterday.
Finnegans Wake (1939)

12 That ideal reader suffering from an ideal insomnia.
Finnegans Wake (1939)

13 The Gracehoper was always jigging ajog, hoppy on akkant of his joyicity.
Finnegans Wake (1939)

14 When is a man not a man? when he is a—yours till the rending of the rocks—Sham
Finnegans Wake (1939)

15 The flushpots of Euston and the hanging garments of Marylebone.
Euston and Marylebone are London railway stations. *Finnegans Wake* (1939)

16 riverrun, past Eve and Adam's, from swerve of shore to bend of bay, brings us by a commodius vicus of recirculation back to Howth Castle and Environs.
Opening words of novel. *Finnegans Wake* (1939)

17 Three quarks for Muster Mark!
The word quark has since been adopted by physicists for hypothetical elementary particles. *Finnegans Wake* (1939)

18 Always see a fellow's weak point in his wife.
Ulysses (1922)

19 A—sudden—at—the—moment—though—not—from—lingering—illness—often—previously—expectorated—demise, Lenehan said. And with a great future behind him.
Ulysses (1922)

20 Every life is many days, day after day. We walk through ourselves, meeting robbers, ghosts, giants, old men, young men, wives, widows, brothers-in-love. But always meeting ourselves.
Ulysses (1922)

21 Greater love than this, he said, no man hath that a man lay down his wife for a friend. Go thou and do likewise. Thus, or words to that effect, saith Zarathustra, sometime regius professor of French letters to the University of Oxtail.
Ulysses (1922)

22 He can't wear them, Buck Mulligan told his face in the mirror. Etiquette is etiquette. He kills his mother but he can't wear grey trousers.
Ulysses (1922)

23 "History", Stephen said, "is a nightmare from which I am trying to awake."
Ulysses (1922)

24 I'm the queerest young fellow that ever you heard.
My mother's a jew, my father's a bird.
With Joseph the joiner I cannot agree,
So here's to disciples and Calvary.
Ulysses (1922)

25 Ineluctable modality of the visible: at least that if no more thought through my eyes.
Signatures of all things I am here to read,
seaspawn and seawrack, the nearing tide, that rusty boot. Snot-green, bluesilver, rust: coloured signs.
Ulysses (1922)

26 It is a symbol of Irish art. The cracked looking glass of a servant.
Ulysses (1922)

27 Mr Leopold Bloom ate with relish the inner organs of beasts and fowls.
Ulysses (1922)

28 Silently, in a dream she had come to him after her death, her wasted body within its loose brown graveclothes giving off an odour of wax and rosewood.
Ulysses (1922)

29 The bard's snotrag. A new art colour for our Irish poets: snot-green. You can almost taste it, can't you?
Ulysses (1922)

30 The heaventree of stars hung with humid nightblue fruit.
Ulysses (1922)

31 The now, the here, through which all future plunges to the past.
Ulysses (1922)

32 The snotgreen sea. The scrotumtightening sea.
Ulysses (1922)

33 "When I makes tea I makes tea," as old mother Grogan said. "And when I makes water I makes water."
Ulysses (1922)

34 Will someone tell me where I am least likely to meet these necessary evils?
Ulysses (1922)

35 You behold in me, said Stephen with grim displeasure, a horrible example of free thought.
Ulysses (1922)

36 Stately, plump Buck Mulligan came from the stairhead, bearing a bowl of lather on which a mirror and a razor lay crossed.
Opening sentence. *Ulysses* (1922)

37 The statue of the onehandled adulterer Nelson.
Referring to the statue of Nelson in Dublin. *Ulysses* (1922)

38 And I thought well as well him as another and then I asked

him with my eyes to ask again yes and then he asked me would I yes to say yes my mountain flower and first I put my arms around him yes and drew him down to me so he could feel my breasts all perfume yes and his heart was going like mad and yes I said yes I will Yes.
The closing words of Molly Bloom's soliloquy, and the closing words of the novel. *Ulysses* (1922)

39 The desire of the moth for the star.
Commenting on the interruption of a music recital when a moth flew into the singer's mouth. Quoted in *James Joyce* (Richard Ellmann; 1959)

40 Never mind about my soul, just make sure you get my tie right.
Responding to the painter Patrick Tuohy's assertion that he wished to capture Joyce's soul in his portrait of him. Quoted in *James Joyce* (Richard Ellmann; 1959)

41 No, it did a lot of other things, too.
Response to a young man who asked, "May I kiss the hand that wrote *Ulysses*?" Quoted in *James Joyce* (Richard Ellmann; 1959)

42 When I die, Dublin will be written on my heart.
1939. Quoted in *Oliver St John Gogarty* (Ulick O'Connor; 1964), ch. 6

Joyce, William ("Lord Haw-Haw"; 1906–46) U.S.-born British traitor

1 Germany calling, Germany calling.
Often quoted as "Jairmany calling ...," emphasizing his upper-class British ("haw-haw") accent. Radio Hamburg broadcasts (1939–45)

Julia (39 B.C.–14 A.D.) Roman daughter of Emperor Augustus

1 Today I dressed to meet my father's eyes; yesterday it was for my husband's.
On being complimented by her father, the emperor Augustus, on her choice of a more modest dress than the one she had worn the previous day. Quoted in *Saturnalia* (Macrobius; 400? A.D.)

2 He sometimes forgets that he is Caesar, but I always remember that I am Caesar's daughter.
Replying to suggestions that she should live in the simple style of her father, which contrasted with her own extravagance. Quoted in *Saturnalia* (Macrobius; 400? A.D.)

Julian of Norwich (also known as Juliana; 1342?–1416?) English mystic

1 Wouldest thou wit thy Lord's meaning in this thing? Wit it well: Love was his meaning. Who shewed it thee? Love. What shewed He thee? Love. Wherefore shewed it He? for Love. Thus was I learned that Love is our Lord's meaning
"Wit" means "know." *Revelations of Divine Love* (1373?), ch. 86, Revelation 16

Jung, Carl Gustav (1875–1961) Swiss psychoanalyst

1 We need more understanding of human nature, because the only real danger that exists is man himself...We know nothing of man, far too little. His psyche should be studied because we are the origin of all coming evil.
BBC television interview (1959)

2 Wherever an inferiority complex exists, there is a good reason for it.
Interview (1943)

3 Judaism has a morally ambivalent God; Christianity a Trinity and Summum Bonum.
Letter to Pere Lachat (1958), quoted in *Psychology and Western Religion* (Albert Dickson, ed.; 1988), pt. 3

4 The action of the Holy Spirit does not meet us in the atmosphere of a normal, bourgeois (or proletarian!), sheltered, regular life, but only in the insecurity outside the human economy, in the infinite spaces where one is alone with the *providentia Dei.*
Letter to Pere Lachat (1958), quoted in *Psychology and Western Religion* (Albert Dickson, ed.; 1988), pt. 3

5 Even on the highest peak we shall never be "beyond good and evil", and the more we experience of their inextricable entanglement the more uncertain and confused will our moral judgment be.
1958. "A Psychological Approach to the Dogma of the Trinity," *Collected Works* (1969), vol. 2

6 Faith is a charisma not granted to all; instead man has the gift of thought, which can strive after the highest things.
1958. "A Psychological Approach to the Dogma of the Trinity," *Collected Works* (1969), vol. 2

7 Nobody can doubt the manifest superiority of the Christian revelation over its pagan precursors.
1958. "A Psychological Approach to the Dogma of the Trinity," *Collected Works* (1969), vol. 2

8 The central symbol of Christianity must have, above all else, a psychological meaning, for without this it...would have been relegated long ago to the dusty cabinet of spiritual monstrosities.
1958. "A Psychological Approach to the Dogma of the Trinity," *Collected Works* (1969), vol. 2

9 The Lucifer legend is in no sense an absurd fairytale; like the story of the serpent in the Garden of Eden, it is a "therapeutic" myth.
1958. "A Psychological Approach to the Dogma of the Trinity," *Collected Works* (1969), vol. 2

10 We should be careful not to pare down God's omnipotence to the level of our human opinions.
1958. "A Psychological Approach to the Dogma of the Trinity," *Collected Works* (1969), vol. 2

11 God does nothing to stop this nefarious activity and leaves it all to man (who is notoriously stupid, unconscious, and easily led astray).
1958. Referring to the problem of evil. "A Psychological Approach to the Dogma of the Trinity," *Collected Works* (1969), vol. 2

12 Out of the tension of duality life always produces a "third" that seems somehow incommensurable or paradoxical.
1958. Referring to the psychological provenance of "the idea of the Holy Ghost." "A Psychological Approach to the Dogma of the Trinity," *Collected Works* (1969), vol. 2

13 We say to the brother within us "Raca," and condemn and rage against ourselves.
1955. "Raca" is a Chaldee word, meaning "worthless." "Transformation Symbolism in the Mass," *Collected Works* (1969), vol. 2

14 The pendulum of the mind oscillates between sense and nonsense, not between right and wrong.
Memories, Dreams, Reflections (1962), ch. 5

15 A man who has not passed through the inferno of his passions has never overcome them.
Memories, Dreams, Reflections (1962), ch. 9

16 As far as we can discern, the sole purpose of human existence

is to kindle a light in the darkness of mere being.
Memories, Dreams, Reflections (1962), ch. 11

17 Every form of addiction is bad, no matter whether the narcotic be alcohol or morphine or idealism.
Memories, Dreams, Reflections (1962), ch. 12

18 Among all my patients in the second half of life...there has not been one whose problem in the last resort was not that of finding a religious outlook on life.
Modern Man in Search of a Soul (1933)

19 It is indeed high time for the clergyman and the psychotherapist to join forces.
Modern Man in Search of a Soul (1933)

20 The least of things with a meaning is worth more in life than the greatest of things without it.
Modern Man in Search of a Soul (1933)

21 Fortunately, in her kindness and patience, Nature has never put the fatal question as to the meaning of their lives into the mouths of most people. And where no one asks, no one needs to answer.
The Development of Personality (1934)

22 Show me a sane man and I will cure him for you.
Quoted in *Observer*, London (July 19, 1975)

23 Sentimentality is a superstructure covering brutality.
Quoted in *Psychological Reflections: an anthology of the writings of C. G. Jung* (Jolande Jacobi, ed.; 1953)

24 We cannot change anything unless we accept it. Condemnation does not liberate, it oppresses.
Quoted in *Psychological Reflections: an anthology of the writings of C. G. Jung* (Jolande Jacobi, ed.; 1953)

25 Neurosis is always a substitute for legitimate suffering.
Attrib.

26 One looks back with appreciation to the brilliant teachers, but with gratitude to those who touched our human feelings. The curriculum is so much necessary raw material, but warmth is the vital element for the growing plant and for the soul of the child.
Attrib.

27 Psychoanalysis cannot be considered a method of education if by education we mean the topiary art of clipping a tree into a beautiful artificial shape. But those who have a higher conception of education will prize most the method of cultivating a tree so that it fulfils to perfection its own natural conditions of growth.
Attrib.

28 The cinema, like the detective story, makes it possible to experience without danger all the excitement, passion and desirousness which must be suppressed in a humanitarian ordering of society.
Attrib.

29 The discussion of the sexual problem is the somewhat crude beginning of a far deeper question, namely, that of the psyche of human relationships between the sexes.
Attrib.

Jung Chang (b.1952) Chinese-born British writer and lecturer

1 A Japanese teacher passing by was like a whirlwind sweeping through a field of grass—you just saw the grass bending as the wind blew by.
Describing the Japanese in Manchuria (1931–45), to whom all Chinese had to bow. *Wild Swans* (1991)

2 Gentleness was considered "bourgeois"...Over the years of the Cultural Revolution, I was to witness people being attacked for saying "thank you" too often, which was branded as "bourgeois hypocrisy."
Wild Swans (1991), ch. 16

3 In spring 1989...I saw the build up of demonstrations from Chengdu to Tiananmen Square. It struck me that fear had been forgotten to such an extent that few of the millions of demonstrators perceived danger. Most seemed to be taken by surprise when the army opened fire.
Wild Swans (1991), Epilogue

Junius (*fl.* 1769–72) British unidentified polemicist

1 The injustice done to an individual is sometimes of service to the public.
Letter, *Public Advertiser* (November 14, 1770)

Junot, Andoche, Duc d'Abrantès ("La Tempête"; 1771–1813) French general

1 I am my own ancestor.
Said on being made a duke. Attrib.

Justinian I, Emperor of the East Roman Empire (Flavius Petrus Sabbatius Justinianus, "Justinian the Great"; 483–565) Byzantine emperor

1 Justice is the constant and perpetual wish to render to everyone his due.
Institutes (533?), bk. 1, ch. i, para. 1

Justin Martyr, Saint (100?–165?) Samarian philosopher and theologian

1 God has foreknowledge of what all men will do, and it is his principle to reward or punish every person in the future according to the merits of his actions.
155? From a defense of Christianity addressed to the Roman emperor Antoninus Pius. Quoted in "First Apology," *The Early Christians* (E. Arnold; 1970)

2 We know that the followers of the Stoic school were also hated and killed because, at least in their ethical teaching, they showed a love of order by virtue of the seed of the Logos implanted in all mankind.
161. From a defense of Christianity addressed to the Roman Senate. Quoted in "Second Apology," *The Early Christians* (E. Arnold; 1970)

Juvenal (Decimus Junius Juvenalis; 65?–128?) Roman poet

1 He who secretly meditates crime is as guilty as if he had committed the offense.
Satires (98?–128?), 13, l. 209

2 What man have you ever seen who was content with one crime only?
Satires (98?–128?), 13, l. 243

3 It's hard not to write satire.
Satires (98?–128?), no. 1, l. 30

4 Even if nature says no, indignation makes me write verse.
Satires (98?–128?), no. 1, l. 79

5 No one ever suddenly became depraved.
Satires (98?–128?), no. 2, l. 83

6 The misfortunes of poverty carry with them nothing harder to bear than that it makes men ridiculous.
Satires (98?–128?), no. 3, l. 152

7 It's not easy for people to rise out of obscurity when they have to face straitened circumstances at home.
Satires (98?–128?), no. 3, l. 164

8 Postumus, are you really
Taking a wife?...
Isn't it better to sleep with a pretty boy?
Boys don't quarrel all night, or nag you for little presents
While they're on the job, or complain that you don't come
Up to their expectations, or demand more gasping passion.
Satires (98?–128?), no. 6

9 When the first few wrinkles appear,
When her skin goes dry and slack, when her teeth begin
To blacken, when her eyes turn lustreless, then: "Pack
Your bags!" his steward will tell her. "Be off with you!"
Satires (98?–128?), no. 6

10 "Bolt her in, keep her indoors." But who is to guard the guards themselves? Your wife arranges accordingly and begins with them.
Satires (98?–128?), no. 6, l. 137

11 I will have this done, so I order it done; let my will replace reasoned judgment.
Satires (98?–128?), no. 6, l. 223

12 Many suffer from the incurable disease of writing, and it becomes chronic in their sick minds.
Satires (98?–128?), no. 7, l. 51

13 Count it the greatest sin to prefer mere existence to honor, and for the sake of life to lose the reasons for living.
Satires (98?–128?), no. 8, l. 83

14 But worse than any loss of limb is the failing mind, which forgets the names of slaves, and cannot recognize the face of the old friend who dined with him last night, not those of the children whom he has begotten and brought up.
Satires (98?–128?), no. 10

15 Travel light and you can sing in the robber's face.
Satires (98?–128?), no. 10, l. 22

16 The people long eagerly for just two things—bread and circuses.
Satires (98?–128?), no. 10, l. 80

17 You should pray to have a sound mind in a sound body.
Satires (98?–128?), no. 10, l. 356

18 Indeed, it's always a paltry, feeble, tiny mind that takes pleasure in revenge. You can deduce it without further evidence than this, that no one delights more in vengeance than a woman.
Satires (98?–128?), no. 13, l. 189

19 A child deserves the maximum respect; if you ever have something disgraceful in mind, don't ignore your son's tender years.
Satires (98?–128?), no. 14, l. 47

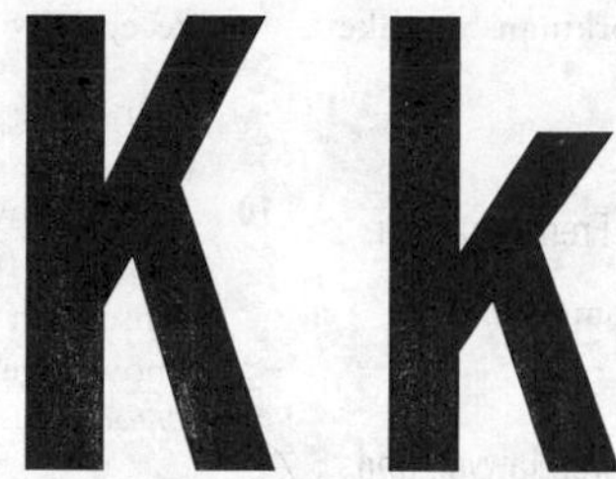

Kabbani, Rana (b.1958) Syrian cultural historian

1 Arabs today...see a travesty of modernism, neither genuinely Western nor properly Eastern, and certainly not satisfactory. The frenzy of Islamic revivalism must surely be a reaction to this state of affairs.
A Letter to Christendom (1989)

2 The Koran becomes prosaic in any tongue but its own...A Muslim reading the Koran in Arabic and a non-Muslim reading it in translation are simply not reading the same book.
A Letter to Christendom (1989)

3 Unlike Westerners, Muslims are for the most part too poor and insecure to afford the luxury of individual feelings.
A Letter to Christendom (1989)

4 Fundamentalism is a specter that is stalking the globe, but Islam is not its synonym.
Imperial Fictions: Europe's Myths of the Orient (1994)

5 Islam, at the end of the twentieth century, has been made into the religion the West loves to hate; a seething cauldron of sexism, and a dumping ground for all blame.
Imperial Fictions: Europe's Myths of the Orient (1994)

6 Just as Western feminists dress in "un-feminine" ways to reject the stereotype of femininity, so...Muslim women taking on Islamic dress are saying: No, we are not sex symbols, and this is our way of expressing it.
Women in Muslim Society (1992)

Kael, Pauline (b.1919) U.S. film critic

1 Good movies make you care, make you believe in possibilities again.
Going Steady (1970)

2 The lowest action trash is preferable to wholesome family entertainment. When you clean them up, when you make movies respectable, you kill them.
Going Steady (1970)

3 The words, "Kiss Kiss Bang Bang", which I saw on an Italian movie poster, are perhaps the briefest statement imaginable of the basic appeal of movies.
Kiss Kiss Bang Bang (1968)

4 The innocent vulgarity of the big numbers is charming and uproarious, and aesthetically preferable to the pretentious ballet finales of fifties musicals like *An American in Paris*. Even those of us who were children at the time did not mistake *Gold Diggers* for art—and certainly no one took it for life.
1968. Referring to Mervyn Le Roy and Busby Berkeley's *Gold Diggers of 1933*. Quoted in *Halliwell's Film Guide* (Leslie Halliwell; 1987)

Kafka, Franz (1883–1924) Czech writer

1 You've obviously never spoken to a ghost. You'll never get a straight answer out of one of them.
"Unhappiness" (J. A. Underwood, tr.; 1913)

2 Don't despair, not even over the fact that you don't despair.
Diary (1913)

3 No sooner is it a little calmer with me than it is almost too calm. As though I have a true feeling of myself only when I am unbearably unhappy. That is probably true, too.
The Diaries of Franz Kafka (Max Brod, ed.; 1948)

4 Utter despair, impossible to pull myself together; only when I have become satisfied with my sufferings can I stop.
The Diaries of Franz Kafka (Max Brod, ed.; 1948)

5 It's often safer to be in chains than to be free.
The Trial (Edwin and Willa Muir, trs.; 1953), ch. 8

6 Let me remind you of the old maxim: people under suspicion are better moving than at rest, since at rest they may be sitting in the balance without knowing it, being weighed together with their sins.
The Trial (Edwin and Willa Muir, trs.; 1953), ch. 8

Kahn, Gus (Gustav Gerson Kahn; 1886–1941) German-born U.S. lyricist

1 I'll See You in My Dreams
1920s. Song title. The music was by Isham Jones.

2 Makin' Whoopee
1928. Song title. The music was by Walter Donaldson.

Kalashnikov, Mikhail (Mikhail Timofeievich Kalashnikov; b.1917) Russian gun designer

1 Bad children would not have been adopted by other countries. The military knows what to choose. They need reliability and simplicity.
Referring to the AK-47 assault rifle. Interview, *Esquire* (September 1997)

Kalendarian, Tom U.S. merchandise manager

1 Men have a keener awareness of what's chic or elegant. Young men today make a sport out of shopping. They come in knowing exactly what they want. There's a new status

associated with knowing about fabrics and workmanship, like knowing about the best restaurants or wines.
New York Times (November 29, 1988)

Kandinsky, Wassily (1866–1944) Russian-born French painter

1 Modern art can only be born where signs become symbols.
1926. Quoted in *Point and Line to Plane* (H. Rebay, ed.; 1947)

Kane, Cheikh Hamidou (b.1928) Senegalese writer, lawyer, and politician

1 Civilization is an architecture of responses. Its perfection, like that of any dwelling house, is measured by the comfort man feels in it, by the added portion of liberty it procures for him.
Ambiguous Adventure (1961), p. 69

Kang Youwei (also known as K'ang Yu-Wei; 1858–1927) Chinese reformer and scholar

1 Down to the present day, subjects prostrate themselves in awe of the ruler's majesty and dare not speak out; wives are held down as inferiors and, being uneducated, are kept in ignorance.
Quoted in "Dynastic Reform and Reaction," *The Fall of Imperial China* (Frederic Wakeman, Jr.; 1975)

Kant, Immanuel (1724–1804) German philosopher

1 The knowledge of the other world can be obtained here only by losing some of that intelligence which is necessary for this present world.
"Dream of a Spirit-Seer" (E. F. Goerwicz, tr.; 1766)

2 Laughter is an affection arising from the sudden transformation of a strained expectation into nothing.
Critique of Judgement (1790)

3 Now I say: the beautiful is the symbol of the morally good.
Critique of Judgement (1790)

4 The *beautiful* is that which pleases universally without a concept.
Critique of Judgement (1790)

5 The *sublime* is what pleases immediately through its opposition to the interest of sense.
Critique of Judgement (1790)

6 Two things fill the mind with ever new and increasing wonder and awe, the more often and the more intensely reflection concentrates upon them: the starry heaven above me and the moral law within me.
Critique of Practical Reason (1788), Conclusion

7 I entitle *transcendental* all knowledge which is occupied not so much with objects as with the mode of our knowledge of objects.
Critique of Pure Reason (1781), A 11–12, B 25

8 Hitherto it has been assumed that all our knowledge must conform to objects...We must therefore make trial whether we may not have more success in the tasks of metaphysics, if we suppose that objects must conform to our knowledge.
Critique of Pure Reason (1781), A 13

9 What objects may be in themselves, and apart from all this receptivity of our sensibility, remains completely unknown to us.
Critique of Pure Reason (1781), A 42, B 59

10 Thoughts without content are empty, intuitions without concepts are blind...The understanding can intuit nothing, the senses can think nothing. Only through their union can knowledge arise.
Critique of Pure Reason (1781), A 51, B 75

11 Psychologists have hitherto failed to realize that imagination is a necessary ingredient of perception itself.
Critique of Pure Reason (1781), A 120

12 All our knowledge falls within the bounds of possible experience.
Critique of Pure Reason (1781), A 146, B 185

13 It is therefore correct to say that the senses do not err—not because they always judge rightly, but because they do not judge at all.
Critique of Pure Reason (1781), A 293, B 350

14 *Philosophical* knowledge is the *knowledge gained by reason from concepts*; mathematical knowledge is the knowledge gained by reason from the *construction* of concepts.
Critique of Pure Reason (1781), A 713, B 741

15 It is precisely in knowing its limits that philosophy consists.
Critique of Pure Reason (1781), A 727, B 755

16 I have therefore found it necessary to deny *knowledge* in order to make room for *faith*.
Critique of Pure Reason (1781), B 30

17 I have no *knowledge* of myself as I am, but merely as I appear to myself.
Critique of Pure Reason (1781), B 158

18 Finally, there is an imperative which commands a certain conduct immediately...This imperative is Categorical...This imperative may be called that of Morality.
Fundamental Principles of the Metaphysics of Ethics (1785)

19 Happiness is not an ideal of reason but of imagination.
Fundamental Principles of the Metaphysics of Ethics (1785)

20 We do not need science and philosophy to know what we should do to be honest and good, yea, even wise and virtuous.
Fundamental Principles of the Metaphysics of Ethics (1785)

21 Act only according to that maxim by which you can at the same time will that it should become a universal law.
Grounding for the Metaphysics of Morals (1785)

22 A good will is good not because of what it effects or accomplishes, nor because of its fitness to attain some proposed end; it is good only through its willing, i.e. it is good in itself.
Grounding for the Metaphysics of Morals (1785)

23 There is no possibility of thinking of anything at all in the world, or even out of it, which can be regarded as good without qualification, except a good will.
Grounding for the Metaphysics of Morals (1785)

24 Out of the crooked timber of humanity no straight thing can ever be made.
Idea for a General History with a Cosmopolitan Purpose (1784), Proposition 6

25 The Germans are praised in that, when constancy and sustained diligence are demanded, they can go further than other peoples.
Prolegomena to Any Future Metaphysics (1783)

26 Physicians think they do a lot for a patient when they give his disease a name.
Attrib.

Kanter, Rosabeth Moss (b.1943) U.S. management educator, consultant, and writer

1 Ambivalence about family responsibilities has a long history in the corporate world.
When Giants Learn to Dance (1989)

2 Competition is a performance stimulant.
When Giants Learn to Dance (1989)

3 It is dangerous to be playing a cooperative game if one's opponent is playing a competitive one.
When Giants Learn to Dance (1989)

4 Post-entrepreneurial organizations...want people to form close relationships—but not too close.
When Giants Learn to Dance (1989)

5 We must combine the power of corporate teamwork and cooperation with the creativity and agility of the entrepreneur, without slipping into the excesses of either corpocrat or cowboy.
When Giants Learn to Dance (1989)

6 One of the lessons America's mythologized cowboys supposedly learned in the rough-and-tumble days of the American frontier was that paranoia was smart psychology.
Referring to the roots of American business culture. *When Giants Learn to Dance* (1989)

Kao, John J. (b.1950) U.S. teacher of business creativity

1 Jazz musicians can be great teachers of business. Their creativity is not dependent on their mood, it does not have to be coaxed out of them, it has nothing to do with the phases of the moon or even how they feel that day.
Referring to using a jazz band to train executives. Interview, *Strategy and Business* (1996)

Karan, Donna (Donna Faske Karan; b.1948) U.S. fashion designer

Quotations about Karan

1 She feminized corporate attire and said it was OK for a woman to show off her body and still be considered respectable. Her designs were shapely and still corporate. She was the first one who did it and Wall Street women loved her.
Justine Cook, U.S. fashion journalist. Commenting on the appeal of Donna Karan. *Guardian*, London (August 14, 1997)

Quotations by Karan

2 I've never considered myself a fashion designer. I'm more a sort of doctor for women's problems. A garment has to work on me and not just some gorgeous model.
August 14, 1997. *Guardian*, London (August 18, 1997)

Karloff, Boris (William Henry Pratt; 1887–1969) British-born U.S. actor

1 The monster was indeed the best friend I could ever have.
Referring to his success in the movie role of Frankenstein's monster. Quoted in *Connoisseur* (January 1991)

Karr, Alphonse (Jean Baptiste Alphonse Karr; 1808–90) French writer

1 If we are to abolish the death penalty, I should like to see the first step taken by our friends the murderers.
The Wasps, 6th Series (1849), January 1849

Kassia (*fl.* 840?) Byzantine poet

1 Wealth covers sin—the poor
Are naked as a pin.
9th century. Quoted in *Women Poets of the World* (Joanna Bankier and Deirdre Lashgari, eds.; 1983)

Kauffman, Ewing M. (Ewing Marion Kauffman, "Mr. K."; 1916–93) U.S. pharmaceutical executive and philanthropist

1 Produce or get out.
His maxim for salesmen while working at Marion Laboratories. Attrib.

Kauffmann, Stanley (b.1916) U.S. author and critic

1 Film journals will feast for years on shots from this picture.
Referring to the movie *Cabaret* (1972). Quoted in *Halliwell's Film Guide* (Leslie Halliwell; 1989)

Kaufman, George S. (George Simon Kaufman; 1889–1961) U.S. playwright and director

1 Merrily We Roll Along
Song title. *The Band Wagon* (1931)

2 Over my dead body!
On being asked to suggest his own epitaph. Attrib. *The Algonquin Wits* (R. Drennan, ed.; 1968)

3 God finally caught his eye.
Referring to a dead waiter. *The Portable Curmudgeon* (Jon Winokur; 1987)

Kaunda, Kenneth David (b.1924) Zambian president

1 Let the West have its Technology and Asia its Mysticism! Africa's gift to world culture must be in the realm of Human relationships.
A Humanist in Africa (1966)

2 Revolution has become the intellectually acceptable form of modern war. To call any large-scale conflict revolution and identify one side as the revolutionaries is enough to win the sympathy and support of well-meaning people...And, of course, the combination of "left-wing" and "revolution" is a double pedigree.
Quoted in *Kaunda on Violence* (Colin M. Morris, ed.; 1980)

3 War is just like bush-clearing—the moment you stop, the jungle comes back even thicker, but for a little while you can plant and grow a crop in the ground you have won at such terrible cost.
Quoted in *Kaunda on Violence* (Colin M. Morris, ed.; 1980)

4 I pray the Good Lord to give us courage to recognize our weaknesses and to give us wisdom to recognize the truth and, having recognized that truth, moral power to get committed to it through thick and thin.
July 23, 1984. Quoted in *Kenneth Kaunda* (Philip Brownrigg; 1989)

5 The battle still remains the same. It is not anti-white, but anti-wrong.
1961. Quoted in *Kenneth Kaunda* (Philip Brownrigg; 1989)

6 The decoration on the front of the Mercedes has almost become our national emblem instead of the pick and hoe displayed on our coat of arms.
June 1975. Quoted in *Kenneth Kaunda* (Philip Brownrigg; 1989)

Kavanagh, Patrick (1904–67) Irish poet and novelist

1 To be a poet and not to know the trade
To be a lover and repel all women;
Twin ironies by which great saints are made,
The agonising pincer-jaws of Heaven.
"Sanctity" (1936), ll.1–4, quoted in *Selected Poems* (Antoinette Quinn, ed.; 1996)

2 I have lived in important places, times
When great events were decided, who owned
That half a rood of rock, a no-man's land
Surrounded by our pitchfork-armed claims.
"Epic," *Collected Poems* (1964), ll. 1–4

3 He Tarry Flynn loved virtuous girls, and that was one of the things he admired the Catholic religion for—because it kept girls virtuous until such time as he'd meet them.
Tarry Flynn (1948)

Kaye, Danny (David Daniel Kominski; 1913–87) U.S. stage, film, and television entertainer

1 The pellet with the poison's in the vessel with the pestle, and the chalice from the palace has the brew that is true.
The Court Jester (1956)

Kaye, Lenny U.S. guitarist and songwriter

1 The fact that you could learn to play three chords and get up onstage within a week...that's the kind of thing that makes rock and roll tick.
Quoted in "Blank Generation," *Dancing in the Street* (Robert Palmer; 1996)

Kazin, Alfred (b.1915) U.S. writer and critic

1 A classic book is a book that survives the circumstances that made it possible yet alone keeps those circumstances alive.
Quoted in *The New Republic* (August 29, 1988)

Keane, Molly (originally Mary Nesta Skrine, pen name M. J. Farrell; 1904–96) Irish writer

1 I was born in 1904, and by 1908 I had accepted the fact that nursery food was so disgusting that greed, even hunger, must be allayed elsewhere.
Nursery Cooking (1985)

Kearney, Denis (1847–1907) Irish-born U.S. labor leader

1 Horny-handed sons of toil.
Taken from the poem "A Glance behind the Curtain" by James Russell Lowell: "And blessèd are the horny hands of toil!" Speech, San Francisco (1887?)

Keating, Paul (Paul John Keating; b.1944) Australian statesman

1 Good economics is good politics.
Sydney Morning Herald (August 27, 1988), "Sayings of the Week"

Keats, John (1795–1821) British poet

Quotations about Keats

1 Who killed John Keats?
"I," says the Quarterly,
So savage and Tartarly;
"Twas one of my feats."
Lord Byron (1788–1824) British poet. Byron blamed a hostile review in *The Quarterly* for hastening the death of John Keats. "John Keats" (1821)

2 Here is Johnny Keats' piss-a-bed poetry. No more Keats, I entreat; flay him alive; if some of you don't I must skin him myself; there is no bearing the idiotism of the Mankin.
Lord Byron (1788–1824) British poet. "Mankin"—human race or mankind. Letter to John Murray (October 12, 1821)

3 That man goes to Rome—to death, despair;
And no one notes him now but you and I:
A hundred years, and the world will follow him there,
And bend with reverence where his ashes lie.
Thomas Hardy (1840–1928) British novelist and poet. "At Lulworth Cove a Century Back," *Selected Poems of Thomas Hardy* (David Wright, ed.; 1978)

4 In what other English poet (however superior to him in other respects) are you so *certain* of never opening a page without lighting upon the loveliest imagery and the most eloquent expressions? Name one.
Leigh Hunt (1784–1859) British poet and essayist. *Imagination and Fancy* (1844)

5 I weep for Adonais—he is dead!
O, weep for Adonais! though our tears
Thaw not the frost which binds so dear a head!
Percy Bysshe Shelley (1792–1822) English poet. An elegy on the death of John Keats. *Adonais* (1821), st. 1

6 He hath awakened from the dream of life—
'Tis we, who lost in stormy visions, keep
With phantoms an unprofitable strife,
And in mad trance, strike with our spirit's knife
Invulnerable nothings.
Percy Bysshe Shelley (1792–1822) English poet. An elegy on the death of John Keats. *Adonais* (1821), st. 23

7 Life, like a dome of many-coloured glass,
Stains the white radiance of eternity.
Percy Bysshe Shelley (1792–1822) English poet. An elegy on the death of John Keats. *Adonais* (1821), st. 52

8 The Poet of Immortal Youth.
Henry Van Dyke (1852–1933) U.S. clergyman, poet, and theologian. Attrib.

9 Mr Wordsworth is never interrupted.
Mary Wordsworth (1770–1850) British wife of William Wordsworth. Rebuking John Keats for interrupting a long monologue. Attrib.

Quotations by Keats

10 Bright star, would I were steadfast as thou art—
Not in lone splendour hung aloft the night
And watching, with eternal lids apart,
Like nature's patient, sleepless Eremite,
The moving waters at their priestlike task
Of pure ablution round earth's human shores.

Originally written on a blank page of Shakespeare's *Poems.* "Eremite" means "hermit." "Bright Star" (1819), quoted in *Life, Letters and Literary Remains of John Keats* (R. M. Milnes, ed.; 1848)

11 Ever let the fancy roam,
Pleasure never is at home.

"Fancy" (1820), ll. 1–2

12 Where's the cheek that doth not fade,
Too much gaz'd at? Where's the maid
Whose lip mature is ever new?

"Fancy" (1820), ll. 69–71

13 I see a lily on thy brow,
With anguish moist and fever dew;
And on thy cheek a fading rose
Fast withereth too.

"La Belle Dame Sans Merci" (May 10, 1820), st. 3

14 I met a lady in the meads
Full beautiful, a faery's child;
Her hair was long, her foot was light,
And her eyes were wild.
... I set her on my pacing steed,
And nothing else saw all day long;
For sideways would she lean, and sing
A faery's song.

"La Belle Dame Sans Merci" (May 10, 1820), st. 4 and st. 5

15 I saw pale kings, and princes too,
Pale warriors, death-pale were they all;
They cried—"La Belle Dame sans Merci
Hath Thee in thrall!"

"La Belle Dame Sans Merci" (May 10, 1820), st. 10

16 Love in a hut, with water and a crust,
Is—Love, forgive us!—cinders, ashes, dust;
Love in a palace is perhaps at last
More grievous torment than a hermit's fast.

"Lamia" (1820), pt. 2, l. 1

17 That purple-lined palace of sweet sin.

"Lamia" (1820), pt. 2, l. 31

18 Do not all charms fly
At the mere touch of cold philosophy?

"Lamia" (1820), pt. 2, l. 229

19 I shall soon be laid in the quiet grave—thank God for the quiet grave—O! I can feel the cold earth upon me —the daisies growing over me—O for this quiet—it will be my first.

Keats's words as reported by Joseph Severn. Letter from Joseph Severn to John Taylor (March 6, 1821), quoted in *Letters of John Keats* (H. E. Rollins, ed.; 1958), vol. 2

20 I am quite disgusted with literary men.

Letter to Benjamin Bailey (October 8, 1817)

21 Scenery is fine—but human nature is finer.

Letter to Benjamin Bailey (March 13, 1818)

22 A long poem is a test of invention which I take to be the Polar star of poetry, as fancy is the sails, and imagination the rudder.

Letter to Benjamin Bailey (October 8, 1817), quoted in *Letters of John Keats* (H. E. Rollins, ed.; 1958), vol. 1

23 I am certain of nothing but the holiness of the heart's affections and the truth of imagination—what the imagination seizes as beauty must be truth—whether it existed before or not.

Letter to Benjamin Bailey (November 22, 1817), quoted in *Letters of John Keats* (H. E. Rollins, ed.; 1958), vol. 1

24 I am in that temper that if I were under water I would scarcely kick to come to the top.

Letter to Benjamin Bailey (May 21, 1818), quoted in *Letters of John Keats* (H. E. Rollins, ed.; 1958), vol. 1

25 I do think better of womankind than to suppose they care whether Mister John Keats five feet high likes them or not.

Letter to Benjamin Bailey (July 18, 1818), quoted in *Letters of John Keats* (H. E. Rollins, ed.; 1958), vol. 1

26 My friends should drink a dozen of Claret on my Tomb.

Letter to Benjamin Bailey (August 14, 1819), quoted in *Letters of John Keats* (H. E. Rollins, ed.; 1958), vol. 1

27 O for a Life of Sensations rather than of Thoughts!

Letter to Benjamin Bailey (November 22, 1817), quoted in *Letters of John Keats* (H. E. Rollins, ed.; 1958), vol. 1

28 There is an old saying "well begun is half done"—'tis a bad one. I would use instead—Not begun at all 'til half done.

Letter to Benjamin Robert Haydon (May 10–11, 1817), quoted in *Letters of John Keats* (Robert Gittings, ed.; 1970)

29 Is there another life? Shall I awake and find all this a dream? There must be, we cannot be created for this sort of suffering.

Letter to Charles Brown (September 30, 1820), quoted in *Letters of John Keats* (Robert Gittings, ed.; 1970)

30 "If I should die," said I to myself, "I have left no immortal work behind me—nothing to make my friends proud of my memory—but I have loved the principle of beauty in all things, and if I had had time I would have made myself remembered."

Letter to Fanny Brawne (February (?) 1820), quoted in *Letters of John Keats* (H. E. Rollins, ed.; 1958), vol. 2

31 I have two luxuries to brood over in my walks, your loveliness and the hour of my death. O that I could have possession of them both in the same minute.

Letter to Fanny Brawne (July 25, 1819), quoted in *Letters of John Keats* (H. E. Rollins, ed.; 1958), vol.2

32 I wish to believe in immortality—I wish to live with you for ever.

Letter to Fanny Brawne (July 1820), quoted in *Letters of John Keats* (H. E. Rollins, ed.; 1958), vol. 2

33 Love is my religion—I could die for that.

Letter to Fanny Brawne (October 13, 1819), quoted in *Letters of John Keats* (H. E. Rollins, ed.; 1958), vol. 2

34 Give me books, fruit, French wine and fine weather and a little music out of doors, played by somebody I do not know.

Letter to Fanny Keats (August 28, 1819), quoted in *Letters of John Keats* (Robert Gittings, ed.; 1970)

35 I never can feel certain of any truth but from a clear perception of its Beauty.
Letter to George and Georgiana Keats (December 16, 1818 – January 4, 1819), quoted in *Letters of John Keats* (Robert Gittings, ed.; 1970)

36 I go among the fields and catch a glimpse of a stoat or a fieldmouse peeping out of the withered grass—The creature hath a purpose and its eyes are bright with it—I go amongst the buildings of a city and I see a man hurrying along—to what? The Creature has a purpose and his eyes are bright with it.
Journal letter written over several months. Letter to George and Georgiana Keats (October 14, 1818–April 19, 1819), quoted in *Letters of John Keats* (H. E. Rollins, ed.; 1958), vol. 1

37 A man's life of any worth is a continual allegory.
Letter to George and Georgiana Keats (February 18, 1819), quoted in *Letters of John Keats* (H. E. Rollins, ed.; 1958), vol. 2

38 I think I shall be among the English Poets after my death.
Letter to George and Georgiana Keats (October 14, 1818), quoted in *Letters of John Keats* (H. E. Rollins, ed.; 1958), vol. 2

39 Nothing ever becomes real till it is experienced—even a proverb is no proverb to you till your life has illustrated it.
Letter to George and Georgiana Keats (March 19, 1818), quoted in *Letters of John Keats* (H. E. Rollins, ed.; 1958), vol. 2

40 Though a quarrel in the streets is a thing to be hated, the energies displayed in it are fine; the commonest man shows a grace in his quarrel.
Letter to George and Georgiana Keats (March 19, 1819), quoted in *Letters of John Keats* (H. E. Rollins, ed.; 1958), vol. 2

41 I think we may class the lawyer in the natural history of monsters.
Discussing the relative merits of different professions. Letter to George and Georgiana Keats (March 13, 1819), quoted in *The Letters of John Keats* (Maurice Buxton Forman, ed.; 1931), letter 114

42 The roaring of the wind is my wife and the stars through the window pane are my children...The opinion I have of the generality of women—who appear to me as children to whom I would rather give a sugar plum than my time, forms a barrier against matrimony which I rejoice in.
Letter to George and Georgiana Keats (October 14, 1818), vol. 1, quoted in *Letters of John Keats* (H. E. Rollins, ed.; 1958), vol. 1

43 *Negative Capability*, that is, when a man is capable of being in uncertainties, mysteries, doubts, without any irritable reaching after fact and reason.
Letter to George and Thomas Keats (December 21, 1817), quoted in *Letters of John Keats* (H. E. Rollins, ed.; 1958), vol. 1

44 The excellence of every art is its intensity, capable of making all disagreeables evaporate, from their being in close relationship with beauty and truth.
Letter to George and Thomas Keats (December 21, 1817), quoted in *Letters of John Keats* (H. E. Rollins, ed.; 1958), vol. 1

45 There is nothing stable in the world; uproar's your only music.
Letter to Georgiana and Thomas Keats (January 13, 1818), quoted in *Letters of John Keats* (H. E. Rollins, ed.; 1958), vol. 1

46 Upon the whole I dislike mankind: whatever people on the other side of the question may advance, they cannot deny that they are always surprised at hearing of a good action and never of a bad one.
Letter to Georgiana Keats (January 13, 15, 17, and 28, 1820), quoted in *Letters of John Keats* (Robert Gittings, ed.; 1970)

47 I would sooner fail than not be among the greatest.
Letter to James Hessey (October 8, 1818), quoted in *Letters of John Keats* (H. E. Rollins, ed.; 1958), vol. 1

48 We hate poetry that has a palpable design upon us...Poetry should be great and unobtrusive, a thing which enters into one's soul, and does not startle or amaze it with itself, but with its subject.
Letter to John Hamilton Reynolds (February 3, 1818), quoted in *Letters of John Keats* (H. E. Rollins, ed.; 1958), vol.1

49 I never was in love—yet the voice and the shape of a woman has haunted me these two days.
Referring to Jane Cox, Reynolds's cousin, whom Keats had met the week before. Letter to John Hamilton Reynolds (September 22, 1818), quoted in *Letters of John Keats* (H. E. Rollins, ed.; 1958), vol. 1

50 I am convinced more and more day by day that fine writing is next to fine doing, the top thing in the world.
Letter to John Hamilton Reynolds (August 24, 1819), quoted in *Letters of John Keats* (H. E. Rollins, ed.; 1958), vol. 2

51 If Poetry comes not as naturally as Leaves to a tree it had better not come at all.
Countering his publisher's attempts to get him to amend *Endymion*. Letter to John Taylor (February 27, 1818), quoted in *Letters of John Keats* (H. E. Rollins, ed.; 1958), vol. 1

52 A poet is the most unpoetical of anything in existence, because he has no Identity—he is continually infor(ming?)—and filling some other body.
Letter to Richard Woodhouse (October 27, 1818), quoted in *Letters of John Keats* (H. E. Rollins, ed.; 1958), vol. 1

53 As to the poetical character itself (I mean that sort of which, if I am anything, I am a member; that sort distinguished from the Wordsworthian or egotistical sublime; which is a thing *per se* and stands alone) it is not itself—it has no self.
Letter to Richard Woodhouse (October 27, 1818), quoted in *Letters of John Keats* (H. E. Rollins, ed.; 1958), vol. 1

54 Heard melodies are sweet, but those unheard
Are sweeter; therefore, ye soft pipes, play on;
Not to the sensual ear, but, more endear'd,
Pipe to the spirit ditties of no tone.
"Ode on a Grecian Urn" (1820), st. 2

55 Who are these coming to the sacrifice?
To what green altar, O mysterious priest,
Lead'st thou that heifer lowing at the skies,
And all her silken flanks with garlands drest?
"Ode on a Grecian Urn" (1820), st. 4

56 "Beauty is truth, truth beauty,"—that is all
Ye know on earth, and all ye need to know.
"Ode on a Grecian Urn" (1820), st. 5, l. 9

57 Ay, in the very temple of delight
Veil'd Melancholy has her sovran shrine.
Though seen of none save him whose strenuous tongue
Can burst Joy's grape against his palate fine.
"Ode on Melancholy" (1820), st. 3

58 'Tis not through envy of thy happy lot,
But being too happy in thine happiness,—
That thou, light-winged Dryad of the trees,
In some melodious plot
Of beechen green, and shadows numberless,
Singest of summer in full-throated ease.
"Ode to a Nightingale" (1820), st. 1

59 My heart aches, and a drowsy numbness pains
My sense, as though of hemlock I had drunk.
The opening lines of the poem. "Ode to a Nightingale" (1820), st. 1

60 O, for a draught of vintage! that hath been
Cool'd a long age in the deep-delvéd earth.
"Ode to a Nightingale" (1820), st. 2

61 Away! away! for I will fly to thee,
Not charioted by Bacchus and his pards,
But on the viewless wings of Poesy,
Though the dull brain perplexes and retards:
Already with thee! tender is the night,
And haply the Queen-Moon is on her throne,
Clustered around by all her starry Fays.
"Pards" are leopards. "Ode to a Nightingale" (1820), st. 4

62 I cannot see what flowers are at my feet,
Nor what soft incense hangs upon the boughs.
"Ode to a Nightingale" (1820), st. 5

63 Now more than ever seems it rich to die,
To cease upon the midnight with no pain,
While thou art pouring forth thy soul abroad
In such an ecstasy!
"Ode to a Nightingale" (1820), st. 6

64 The voice I hear this passing night was heard
In ancient days by emperor and clown:
Perhaps the self-same song that found a path
Through the sad heart of Ruth, when sick for home,
She stood in tears amid the alien corn.
In the Bible, the loyal and modest Moabite Ruth won her Israelite husband Boaz while gleaning corn in his fields. "Ode to a Nightingale" (1820), st. 7

65 Forlorn! the very word is like a bell
To toll me back from thee to my sole self!
Adieu! the fancy cannot cheat so well
As she is fam'd to do, deceiving elf.
"Ode to a Nightingale" (1820), st. 8

66 Much have I travell'd in the realms of gold...
That deep-brow'd Homer ruled as his demesne,
Yet did I never breathe its pure serene
Till I heard Chapman speak out loud and bold:
Then felt I like some watcher of the skies
When a new planet swims into his ken;
Or like stout Cortez when with eagle eyes
He star'd at the Pacific—and all his men
Look'd at each other with a wild surmise—
Silent, upon a peak in Darien.
George Chapman, the translator of Homer's *Iliad*, was a contemporary of Shakespeare's. In fact, Balboa, not Cortez, was the first European to see the Pacific from Darien in Panama. "On First Looking into Chapman's Homer" (1817)

67 They sway'd about upon a rocking horse,
And thought it Pegasus.
1817. Referring to the Augustan poets, including Alexander Pope. "Sleep and Poetry" (1820), l. 186

68 Turn the key deftly in the oiled wards,
And seal the hushed Casket of my Soul.
"Sonnet to Sleep" (1819)

69 St Agnes' Eve—Ah, bitter chill it was!
The owl, for all his feathers, was a-cold;
The hare limp'd trembling through the frozen grass,
And silent was the flock in woolly fold.
The poem takes the old superstition that virgins who observe the ritual of Eve of Saint Agnes, January 20, the coldest winter night, will see a vision of their husband-to-be, and dramatizes it. "The Eve of Saint Agnes" (1820), st. 1, ll. 1–4

70 And soft adorings from their loves receive
Upon the honey'd middle of the night.
"The Eve of Saint Agnes" (1820), st. 6, l. 3

71 The music, yearning like a God in pain.
"The Eve of Saint Agnes" (1820), st. 7, l. 2

72 Sudden a thought came like a full-blown rose,
Flushing his brow, and in his pained heart
Made purple riot.
"The Eve of Saint Agnes" (1820), st. 16

73 As though a rose should shut, and be a bud again.
"The Eve of Saint Agnes" (1820), st. 27

74 And still she slept an azure-lidded sleep,
In blanched linen, smooth, and lavender'd,
While he from forth the closet brought a heap
Of candied apple, quince, and plum, and gourd...
Manna and dates, in argosy transferr'd
From Fez; and spiced dainties, every one,
From silken Samarcand to cedar'd Lebanon.
Fez is Morocco, and Samarcand (Samarqand) and Lebanon were places associated with luxury and wealth. "The Eve of Saint Agnes" (1820), st. 30

75 And they are gone: aye, ages long ago
These lovers fled away into the storm.
"The Eve of Saint Agnes" (1820), st. 42

76 Four seasons fill the measure of the year;
There are four seasons in the mind of man.
"The Human Seasons" (1819)

77 Season of mists and mellow fruitfulness,
Close bosom-friend of the maturing sun;
Conspiring with him how to load and bless
With fruit the vines that round the thatch-eaves run.
"To Autumn" (1820), st. 1, l. 1

78 Where are the songs of Spring? Ay, where are they?
"To Autumn" (1820), st. 3

79 When I have fears that I may cease to be
Before my pen has glean'd my teeming brain.
"When I Have Fears" (1818), quoted in *Life, Letters, and Literary Remains of John Keats* (R. M. Milnes, ed.; 1848)

80 When I behold, upon the night's starr'd face,
Huge cloudy symbols of a high romance,
...then on the shore

Of the wide world I stand alone, and think
Till love and fame to nothingness do sink.
"When I Have Fears" (1818), quoted in *Life, Letters, and Literary Remains of John Keats* (R. M. Milnes, ed.; 1848)

81 Woman! when I behold thee flippant, vain,
Inconstant, childish, proud, and full of fancies.
"Woman! When I Behold Thee" (1817)

82 The grandeur of the dooms
We have imagined for the mighty dead.
Endymion (1818), bk. 1, l. 20

83 A thing of beauty is a joy for ever:
Its loveliness increases; it will never
Pass into nothingness; but still will keep
A bower quiet for us, and a sleep
Full of sweet dreams, and health, and quiet breathing.
The opening lines of the poem. *Endymion* (1818), bk. 1, ll. 1–5

84 The imagination of a boy is healthy, and the mature imagination of a man is healthy; but there is a space of life between, in which the soul is in a ferment, the character undecided, the way of life uncertain, the ambition thick-sighted.
Endymion (1818), Preface

85 Deep in the shady sadness of a vale
Far sunken from the healthy breath of morn,
Far from the fiery noon, and eve's one star,
Sat gray-hair'd Saturn, quiet as a stone.
The opening lines of the poem. *Hyperion: A Fragment* (1820), bk. 1, ll. 1–4

86 The days of peace and slumberous calm are fled.
Hyperion: A Fragment (1820), bk. 2, l. 335

87 O aching time! O moments big as years!
Hyperion: A Fragment (1820), bk. 4, l. 64

88 The poet and the dreamer are distinct,
Diverse, sheer opposite, antipodes.
The one pours out a balm upon the world,
The other vexes it.
The Fall of Hyperion: A Dream (1819), can. 1, l. 199

89 Fanatics have their dreams, wherewith they weave
A paradise for a sect.
The Fall of Hyperion: A Dream (1819), can. 1, ll. 1–2

90 Dry your eyes—O dry your eyes,
For I was taught in Paradise
To ease my breast of melodies.
"A Faery Song," quoted in *Life, Letters, and Literary Remains of John Keats* (R. M. Milnes, ed.; 1848)

91 Axioms in philosophy are not axioms until they are proved upon our pulses; we read fine things but never feel them to the full until we have gone the same steps as the author.
May 3, 1818. Quoted in *Letters of John Keats* (Robert Gittings, ed.; 1970)

92 Here lies one whose name was writ in water.
1821. Suggesting his own epitaph, and recalling a line from *Philaster* (1609?) by Beaumont and Fletcher. Quoted in *Life, Letters, and Literary Remains of John Keats* (R. M. Milnes, ed.; 1848), ch. 2

Keats, John (b.1920) U.S. writer

1 Americans have plenty of everything and the best of nothing.
You Might As Well Live (1970)

Keble, John (1792–1866) British poet and cleric

1 A style of architecture which, to me at least, is, in comparison with all others, the most beautiful of all, and by far the most in harmony with the mysteries of religion.
Referring to Gothic architecture. *Lectures on Poetry, 1832–1841* (1844)

2 Abide with me from morn till eve,
For without Thee I cannot live;
Abide with me when night is nigh,
For without Thee I dare not die.
"Evening," *The Christian Year* (1827)

Keegan, William (William James Gregory Keegan; b.1938) British author and journalist

1 Communism has failed, but capitalism has not succeeded.
The Spectre of Capitalism (1992)

2 "Primitive capitalism" is capitalism in a state of nature, red in tooth and claw—a state where those employers whose ideal would be mastery over slaves, find they can rub along by...displaying scant regard for the labour force.
The Spectre of Capitalism (1992)

3 The failure of communism as an economic system is made all the more ironic by the arrogance of the original conception, which was no less than to export the "revolution" to the entire world.
The Spectre of Capitalism (1992)

4 The human tendency to search for panaceas and magic solutions is well represented among politicians and economists.
The Spectre of Capitalism (1992)

5 Totalitarianism is not so good at industrial innovation and adaptation to consumer demand.
The Spectre of Capitalism (1992)

Keeler, William (William Henry Keeler, "Wee Willie"; 1872–1923) U.S. baseball player

1 I keep my eyes clear and hit 'em where they ain't.
1897. Said to Abe Tyler of the Brooklyn *Eagle*, when asked to explain his success.

Keen, Peter U.S. business executive

1 Capital is built in the past, owned in the present, and deployed to create future value.
"Transforming Intellectual Property into Intellectual Capital: Competing in the Trust Economy," *Capital for Our Time* (Nicholas Imparato, ed.; 1999)

2 Complexity and trust go together...the more firms downsize and outsource, the more they need partnerships, alliances, and joint ventures.
"Transforming Intellectual Property into Intellectual Capital: Competing in the Trust Economy," *Capital for Our Time* (Nicholas Imparato, ed.; 1999)

3 Innovation, everyday entrepreneurship, and creativity are the aims of collaboration.
"Transforming Intellectual Property into Intellectual Capital: Competing in the Trust Economy," *Capital for Our Time* (Nicholas Imparato, ed.; 1999)

4 Trust...is the foundation for innovation and coordination of the supply chain, customer interaction, and market, product and service development.
"Transforming Intellectual Property into Intellectual Capital: Competing in the Trust Economy," *Capital for Our Time* (Nicholas Imparato, ed.; 1999)

5 Electronic commerce on the Internet will, before the end of the century, profoundly redefine many basics of business.
Quoted in *Opening Digital Markets* (Walid Mougayar; 1997)

Keenan, Brian (b.1950) Irish writer

1 I am trying to cope with the paradox of being a public figure while desperately wanting to be a man unseen, and at the same time trying to cope with a deeply felt moral and emotional responsibility about the remaining hostages.
Keenan was a hostage in Lebanon in the 1980s. *Times*, London (1990)

2 Sometimes it seems that the adulation, affection and warmth in which I am cocooned by friends and family is a kind of hothouse of obligations...This psychological, emotional and social temperature change...knocks the personality out of balance and makes difficult any meaningful response to the world.
Keenan was a hostage in Lebanon in the 1980s. *Times*, London (1990)

3 The strange paradox of the situation is that on being released, we who have spent so much time on our own still desperately need to be left alone. We need to lick and heal the wounds gradually and unmolested.
Keenan was a hostage in Lebanon in the 1980s. *Times*, London (1990)

Keillor, Garrison (Gary Edward Keillor; b.1942) U.S. writer and broadcaster

1 That's the news from Lake Wobegon, where all the women are strong, the men are good-looking, and all the children are above average.
The regular closing words to his weekly show on Minnesota Public Radio. *A Prairie Home Companion* (1974–87)

2 A good newspaper is never nearly good enough but a lousy newspaper is a joy forever.
"That Old Picayune-Moon," *Harper's* (September 1990)

3 The town of Lake Wobegon, Minnesota, lies on the shore against Adams Hill...the highway aims for the lake...bringing the traveler in on Main Street toward the town's one traffic light, which is almost always green.
"Home," *Lake Wobegon Days* (1985)

4 They say such nice things about people at their funerals that it makes me sad to realize I'm going to miss mine by just a few days.
December 13, 1984. "Lecture in San Francisco," *Lake Wobegon Days* (1985)

5 If God had not meant everyone to be in bed by ten-thirty, He would never have provided the ten o'clock newscast.
"News," *Lake Wobegon Days* (1985)

6 Some luck lies in not getting what you thought you wanted but getting what you have, which once you have it you may be smart enough to see is what you would have wanted had you known.
"Revival," *Lake Wobegon Days* (1985)

7 Ha! Easy for nuns to talk about giving up things. That's what they do for a living.
"Winter," *Lake Wobegon Days* (1985)

8 The gospel is meant to comfort the afflicted and afflict the comfortable.
"Winter," *Lake Wobegon Days* (1985)

9 People always are encouraging about a terrible loss, so that sometimes the loser would like to strangle them.
Lake Wobegone Days (1985), preface

10 Foreign places help your mind to float free
And reduce you to such simplicity
You only know the words for Good night and Good day
And Please.
You don't know how to say
"My life is torn between immutable existential uncertainties."
Leaving Home (1987)

11 Men peak at age nineteen and go downhill.
Leaving Home (1987)

12 Sweet corn was our family's weakness. We were prepared to resist atheistic Communism, immoral Hollywood, hard liquor, gambling and dancing, smoking, fornication, but if Satan had come around with sweet corn, we at least would have listened to what he had to say.
Leaving Home (1987), foreword to the 1988 edition

13 Book reading is a solitary and sedentary pursuit, and those who do are cautioned that a book should be used as an integral part of a well-rounded life...*A book should not be used as a substitute or an excuse.*
The Book of Guys (1993)

14 Humor, a good sense of it, is to Americans what manhood is to Spaniards and we will go to great lengths to prove it.
We Are Still Married (1989), introduction

Keith, Penelope (b.1940) British actor

1 Shyness is just egotism out of its depth.
Remark (July 1988)

Keith of Kinkel, Lord (b.1922) British judge

1 Marriage in modern times is regarded as a partnership of equals and no longer one in which the wife must be the subservient chattel of the husband.
Giving judgment in the House of Lords, the upper house of the British Parliament, that rape can occur within marriage. *Independent*, London (October 24, 1991)

Kelber, Michel (b.1908) Ukrainian-born French cinematographer

1 They wanted to create a revolution, invent a new kind of cinema and get rid of all the old "classical" directors. But all they invented were things which we had all known for years.
Referring to the *nouvelle vague* (New Wave) directors of the late 1950s and early 1960s. Quoted in *Projections 6* (John Boorman and Walter Donohue, eds.; 1996)

Keller, Helen (Helen Adams Keller; 1880–1968) U.S. writer and lecturer

Quotations about Keller

1 I wish all Americans were as blind as you.
George Bernard Shaw (1856–1950) Irish playwright. Said to Helen Keller, who, deaf and blind from the age of 19 months, overcame her physical disabilities, lecturing and writing about her experiences, and working for the cause of people with disabilities. George Bernard Shaw regarded her as an exemplary figure of learning and commitment. Quoted in *Bernard Shaw* (Hesketh Pearson; 1975)

2 She likes stories that make her cry—I think we all do, it's so nice to feel sad when you've nothing particular to be sad about.
Anne Sullivan (1866–1936) U.S. teacher. Letter (December 12, 1887)

Quotations by Keller

3 We could never learn to be brave and patient, if there were only joy in the world.
Atlantic Monthly (May 1890)

4 That the sky is brighter than the earth means little unless the earth itself is appreciated and enjoyed. Its beauty loved gives the right to aspire to the radiance of the sunrise and the stars.
My Religion (1927)

5 The heresy of one age becomes the orthodoxy of the next.
Optimism (1903)

6 How reconcile this world of fact with the bright world of my imagining? My darkness has been filled with the light of intelligence, and behold, the outer daylight world was stumbling and groping in social blindness.
The Cry for Justice (Upton Sinclair, ed.; 1915)

7 Militarism...is one of the chief bulwarks of capitalism, and the day that militarism is undermined, capitalism will fail.
The Story of My Life (1903)

8 Now I feel as if I should succeed in doing something in mathematics, although I cannot see why it is so very important...The knowledge doesn't make life any sweeter or happier, does it?
The Story of My Life (1903)

Keller, Maryann U.S. business analyst

1 Planting flags around the world, like the British Empire, is not a strategy for success.
Speech (April 2, 1997)

2 Almost anyone who has worked for GM could get every organ in his body replaced and it would not cost him a dime.
Referring to General Motors. *Economist*, London (December 5, 1992)

3 The car industry used to be a Western Hemisphere business and it's becoming an Eastern Hemisphere business and we don't understand that. It's not going to be answerable to our wonderful economic philosophy.
One World, Ready or Not (William Greider; 1997)

Kellogg, John Harvey (1852–1943) U.S. doctor and inventor

1 The tobacco business is a conspiracy against womanhood and manhood. It owes its origin to that scoundrel Sir Walter Raleigh, who was likewise the founder of American slavery.
Attrib.

Kelly, Ellsworth (b.1923) U.S. painter and sculptor

1 All art since the Renaissance seemed too men-oriented. I liked the object quality...The form of my painting is the content.
"Notes of 1969" (1969), quoted in *Ellsworth Kelly* (Stedelijk Museum catalog, Amsterdam; 1980)

Kelly, Gene (Eugene Curran Kelly; 1912–96) U.S. dancer, actor, choreographer, and director

1 The one-eye lens of the camera allows the audience to see only that portion of the scenery behind the dancer and he becomes a 2-dimensional figure. So you lose one of the most vital aspects of the dance—the sense of kinetic force and the feeling of that Third Dimension.
Quoted in *The Films of Gene Kelly* (Tony Thomas; 1991)

2 You learn to use the camera as part of the choreography. Film dancing will always be a problem because the eye of the camera is coldly realistic, demanding that everything looks natural, and dancing is unrealistic.
Quoted in *The Films of Gene Kelly* (Tony Thomas; 1991)

3 Stage dancers couldn't understand what concerned us. Ours was a kind of splendid isolation.
Referring to choreography. Quoted in *The Films of Gene Kelly* (Tony Thomas; 1991)

4 So many young men who have talent are put off by the belief that it is an effeminate business.
Referring to dancing. Quoted in *The Films of Gene Kelly* (Tony Thomas; 1991)

5 It's dated now, of course, because the techniques gradually became common and the theme of sailors on a spree has been done to death, but...it paved the way for musicals like *West Side Story*.
Referring to the film *On The Town* (1950). Quoted in *The Films of Gene Kelly* (Tony Thomas; 1991)

6 The real work for this one was done by the technicians who had to pipe two city blocks on the backlot with overhead sprays and the poor cameraman who had to shoot through all that water. All I had to do was dance.
1952. Referring to the title number of the film *Singin' in the Rain* (1952). Quoted in *The Films of Gene Kelly* (Tony Thomas; 1991)

7 The musical is the victim of changing times. To make good musicals you need a team of performers, musicians...choreographers, writers, etc., etc. The economics of the business have killed all that.
Said while directing the film, *Hello Dolly* (1969). Quoted in *The Films of Gene Kelly* (Tony Thomas; 1991)

Kelly, Kevin (b.1952) U.S. author and editor

1 A neo-biological technology is far more rewarding than a world of clocks, gears, and predictable simplicity.
Out of Control (1994)

Kelly, Patrick C. (Patrick Chastain Kelly; b.1947) U.S. sales executive

1 I've come to the belief that banks are not in the business of banking. They're in the business of collecting fees.
Inc. (October 1995)

2 My personal goal for the last 10 years has been to grow 100 CEOs like me.
Inc. (October 1995)

Kelman, James (b.1946) Scottish writer

1 One of the few remaining freedoms we have is the blank page. No one can prescribe how we should fill it.
Guardian, London (October 12, 1994)

Kelvin, William Thomson, 1st Baron Kelvin of Largs (1824–1907) British mathematician and physicist

1 At what time does the dissipation of energy begin?
Said on realizing that his wife was planning an afternoon excursion. Quoted in *Memories of a Scientific Life* (Sir John Ambrose Fleming; 1934)

Kemal, Yasar (b.1923) Turkish novelist

1 Look not for fire in Hell, each man brings his own fire...Yes, Mahmut murmured, from this earth each takes his own fire.
Mahmut, the hero of the novel, is reflecting on an inscription he has seen written on the side of a cart in Istanbul. *The Birds Have Also Gone* (1987)

2 Ankara might be able to drain the sea, but it will not be able to catch the fish.
Referring to the limits to freedom of expression in Turkey. Ankara is the capital of Turkey. Quoted in *Kurdistan* (Jonathan C. Randal; 1998)

Kemble, Charles (1775–1854) British actor

1 Sir, I now pay you this exorbitant charge, but I must ask you to explain to her Majesty that she must not in future look upon me as a source of income.
On being obliged to hand over his income tax to the tax collector. Attrib.

Kemble, Fanny (Frances Anne Kemble; 1809–93) British actor and writer

1 These New England States, I do believe, will be the noblest country in the world in a little while. They will be the salvation of that great body with a very little soul, the rest of the United States.
A Year of Consolation (1837)

2 Mr Stephenson having taken me on the bench of the engine with him, we started at about ten miles an hour. You cannot imagine how strange it seemed to be journeying on thus, without any visible cause of progressing other than that magical machine.
Referring to George Stephenson, inventor of the railroad locomotive the *Rocket* (1829). *Record of a Girlhood* (1879)

Kemble, John Philip (1757–1823) British actor

1 Ladies and gentlemen, unless the play is stopped, the child cannot possibly go on.
Said to the audience when the play he was in was interrupted by a child crying. Attrib.

Kempe, Margery (1373?–1440?) English mystic and writer

1 I have oftentimes told thee, daughter, that thinking, weeping, and high contemplation are the best life on earth, and thou shalt have more merit in Heaven for one year of thinking in thy mind than for a hundred years of praying with thy mouth.
The Booke of Margery Kempe (1435?)

Kempis, Thomas à (Thomas Hemerken; 1379?–1471) German monk and religious writer

1 If thou may not continually gather thyself together, do it some time at least once a day, morning or evening.
The Imitation of Christ (1415–24?), bk. 1

2 If you cannot mould yourself as you would wish, how can you expect other people to be entirely to your liking?
The Imitation of Christ (1415–24?), bk. 1

3 Oh how quickly the glory of the world passes away.
Generally misquoted as "*Sic transit gloria mundi.* (Thus passes the glory of the world)," a formula spoken during papal coronations from 1409. *The Imitation of Christ* (1415–24?), bk. 1, ch. 3

4 It is much safer to obey than to rule.
The Imitation of Christ (1415–24?), bk. 1, ch. 9, sect. 1

5 Man proposes but God disposes.
The Imitation of Christ (1415–24?), bk. 1, ch. 19, sect. 2

6 And when he is out of sight, quickly also is he out of mind.
Referring to death. *The Imitation of Christ* (1415–24?), bk. 1, ch. 23

7 Would to God that we might spend a single day really well!
The Imitation of Christ (1415–24?), bk. 1, ch. 23, sect. 2

8 Love feels no burden, thinks nothing of trouble, attempts what is above its strength, pleads no excuse of impossibility; for it thinks all things lawful for itself, and all things possible.
The Imitation of Christ (1415–24?), bk. 3, ch. 6

9 Of two evils, the lesser is always to be chosen.
The Imitation of Christ (1415–24?), bk. 3, ch. 12

Ken, Thomas (1637–1711) English bishop

1 Redeem thy mis-spent time that's past;
Live this day, as if 'twere thy last.
Song lyric. "A Morning Hymn" (1709), verse 2

2 Teach me to live, that I may dread
The grave as little as my bed.
Song lyric. "Glory to Thee My God This Night: An Evening Hymn" (1695), verse 3

Kennan, George F. (George Frost Kennan; b.1904) U.S. diplomat and scholar

1 If we are to regard ourselves as a grown-up nation...we must, as the Biblical phrase goes, put away childish things...self-idealization and the search for absolutes in world affairs: for absolute security, absolute amity, absolute harmony.
Russia and the West under Lenin and Stalin (1961), ch. 25

2 A war regarded as inevitable or even probable, and therefore much prepared for, has a very good chance of being fought.
The Cloud of Danger (1977), ch. 11

3 There is no political or ideological difference between the Soviet Union and the United States—nothing which either side would like, or would hope, to achieve at the expense of the other—that would be worth the risks and sacrifices of a military encounter.
The Cloud of Danger (1977), ch. 11

Kennedy, Edward M. (Edward Moore Kennedy; b.1932) U.S. politician

1 Frankly, I don't mind not being President. I just mind that someone else is.
Speech, Gridiron Club, Washington, D.C. (March 22, 1986)

2 I even opposed the death penalty for the man who killed my brother.
Referring to the assassination of his brother, Robert Kennedy (1968). *Washington Post* (April 29, 1990)

Kennedy, Florynce R. (Florynce Rae Kennedy; b.1916) U.S. lawyer and activist

1 If you want to know where the apathy is, you're probably sitting on it.
Color Me Flo: My Hard Life and Good Times (1976)

2 The biggest sin is sitting on your ass.
Ms. (March 1973)

3 There are very few jobs that actually require a penis or vagina. All other jobs should be open to everybody.
1974. "Freelancer with No Time to Write", *Writer's Digest* (February 1974)

4 It must be realized that racism is more serious than sexism. Black people are often killed for no reason other than they are Black. Racism is to sexism what cancer is to a toothache.
Quoted in *Contributions of Black Women to America* (Marianna W. Davis, ed.; 1982), vol. 1

5 Being a mother is a noble status, right? Right. So why does it change when you put "unwed" or "welfare" in front of it?
1973. Quoted in "The Verbal Karate of Florynce R. Kennedy, Esq.," *Ms.* (Gloria Steinem; March 1973)

6 If men could get pregnant, abortion would be a sacrament.
Quoted in "The Verbal Karate of Florynce R. Kennedy, Esq.," *Ms.* (Gloria Steinem; March 1973)

7 Unity in a movement situation is overrated. If you were the Establishment, which would you rather see coming in the door, five hundred mice or one lion?
Quoted in *Outrageous Acts & Everyday Rebellions* (Gloria Steinem; 1983)

8 Oppressed people are frequently very oppressive when first liberated. And why wouldn't they be? They know best two positions. Somebody's foot on their neck or their foot on somebody's neck.
Quoted in "Institutionalized Oppression vs. the Female," *Sisterhood is Powerful* (Robin Morgan, ed.; 1970)

9 Where a system of oppression has become institutionalized it is unnecessary for individuals to be oppressive.
Quoted in "Institutionalized Oppression vs. the Female," *Sisterhood is Powerful* (Robin Morgan, ed.; 1970)

10 Women are dirt searchers; their greatest worth is eradicating rings on collars and tables.
Quoted in "Institutionalized Oppression vs. the Female," *Sisterhood is Powerful* (Robin Morgan, ed.; 1970)

Kennedy, John Fitzgerald (1917–63) U.S. president

1 If we cannot now end our differences, at least we can help make the world safe for diversity.
Address, American University, Washington D.C. (June 10, 1963)

2 When power narrows the areas of man's concern, poetry reminds him of the richness and diversity of his existence.
Address at the Dedication of the Robert Frost Library (October 26, 1963)

3 In free society art is not a weapon...Artists are not engineers of the soul.
Taking issue with Stalin's 1932 pronouncement that artists should be the "engineers of human souls." Address at the Dedication of the Robert Frost Library (October 26, 1963)

4 No costs have increased more rapidly in the last decade than the cost of medical care. And no group of Americans has felt the impact of these sky-rocketing costs more than our older citizens.
Address on the 25th Anniversary of the Social Security Act (August 14, 1960)

5 I believe that this nation should commit itself to achieving the goal, before this decade is out, of landing a man on the Moon and returning him safely to earth.
Address to joint session of Congress (May 25, 1961)

6 The supreme reality of our time is...our common vulnerability on this planet.
Address to the Irish Parliament, Dublin (June 28, 1963)

7 And so, my fellow Americans: ask not what your country can do for you—ask what you can do for your country. My fellow citizens of the world: ask not what America will do for you, but what together we can do for the freedom of man.
Inaugural address as president of the United States (January 20, 1961)

8 Let both sides seek to invoke the wonders of science instead of its terrors. Together let us explore the stars, conquer the deserts, eradicate disease, tap the ocean depths, and encourage the arts and commerce.
Inaugural address as president of the United States (January 20, 1961)

9 Let us never negotiate out of fear, but let us never fear to negotiate.
Inaugural address as president of the United States (January 20, 1961)

10 The torch has been passed to a new generation of Americans...unwilling to witness or permit the slow undoing of those human rights to which...we are committed today at home and around the world.
Inaugural address as president of the United States (January 20, 1961)

11 There are no "white" or "colored" signs on the foxholes or graveyards of battle.
Referring to race relations. Message to Congress (June 19, 1963)

12 We are confronted primarily with a moral issue...whether all Americans are to be afforded equal rights and equal opportunities, whether we are going to treat our fellow Americans as we want to be treated.
Referring to race riots in Alabama. Radio broadcast (June 11, 1963)

13 I guess this is the week I earn my salary.
Referring to the Cuban missile crisis. Remark, quoted in *Nobody Said It Better* (M. Ringo; 1962)

14 I am sorry to say that there is too much point to the wisecrack that life is extinct on other planets because their scientists were more advanced than ours.
Speech (December 11, 1959)

15 If a free society cannot help the many who are poor, it cannot save the few who are rich.
Speech (January 20, 1961)

16 I think it's the most extraordinary collection of talent, of human knowledge, that has ever been gathered together at the White House—with the possible exception of when Thomas Jefferson dined alone.
Speech at a dinner for Nobel prizewinners (April 29, 1962)

17 A medical revolution has extended the life of our elder citizens without providing the dignity and security those later years deserve.
Speech at the Democratic National Convention, Los Angeles (July 15, 1960)

18 We stand today on the edge of a new frontier.
Said on his nomination as presidential candidate. Speech at the Democratic Party Convention (July 15, 1960)

19 The war against hunger is truly mankind's war of liberation.
Speech at the World Food Congress (June 4, 1963)

20 Freedom has many flaws and our democracy is imperfect, but we have never had to put up a wall to keep our people in.
Referring to the Berlin Wall, the fortified wall that was erected in 1961 by the communist GDR (German Democratic Republic) to divide East Berlin from West Berlin. Speech, City Hall, West Berlin, Germany (June 26, 1963)

21 Democracy is a difficult kind of government. It requires the highest qualities of self-discipline, restraint, a willingness to make commitments and sacrifices for the general interest, and it also requires knowledge.
Speech, Dublin Castle, Republic of Ireland (June 28, 1963)

22 The greater our knowledge increases the more our ignorance unfolds.
Speech, Rice University (September 12, 1962)

23 There can be no progress if people have no faith in tomorrow.
Speech to the Inter-American Press Association, Miami Beach (November 18, 1963)

24 Today...every man, woman and child lives under a nuclear sword of Damocles, hanging by the slenderest of threads, capable of being cut at any moment by accident or miscalculation or madness.
Speech to the United Nations General Assembly, New York City (September 1961)

25 The time to repair the roof is when the sun is shining.
State of the Union Address, Washington, D.C. (January 11, 1962)

26 The great battleground for the defense and expansion of freedom today is the whole southern half of the globe...Their revolution is the greatest in human history. They seek an end to injustice, tyranny, and exploitation. More than an end, they seek a beginning.
Supplementary State of the Union Address (May 25, 1961)

27 No man who witnessed the tragedies of the last war, no man who can imagine the unimaginable possibilities of the next war can advocate war out of irritability or frustration or impatience.
Veterans' Day Address, Arlington National Cemetery, Virginia (November 11, 1961)

28 All free men, wherever they may live, are citizens of Berlin. And therefore, as a free man, I take pride in the words *Ich bin ein Berliner.*
June 26, 1963. Speech at City Hall, West Berlin. Kennedy's speech writers had failed to discover that such citizens never call themselves "Berliners." That term refers to a certain kind of breakfast sweet. Therefore, Kennedy was saying, literally: "I am a jelly-filled doughnut." *New York Times* (June 27, 1963)

29 Arms alone are not enough to keep the peace—it must be kept by men.
Observer, London (1962), "Sayings of the Decade"

30 The United States has to move very fast to even stand still.
Observer, London (July 29, 1963), "Sayings of the Week"

31 We must use time as a tool, not as a couch.
Observer, London (December 10, 1961), "Sayings of the Week"

32 I can't see that it's wrong to give him a little legal experience before he goes out to practice law.
On being criticized for making his brother Robert attorney general. *Time* (February 3, 1961)

33 Democracy is the superior form of government, because it is based on a respect for man as a reasonable being.
Why England Slept (1940)

34 It was involuntary. They sank my boat.
Response made when asked how he became a hero. Quoted in *A Thousand Days* (Arthur M. Schlesinger, Jr.; 1965), ch. 4

35 I had plenty of problems when I came into office. But wait until the fellow who follows me sees what he will inherit.
Quoted in *John F. Kennedy, President: A Reporter's Inside Story* (Hugh Sidey; 1963)

36 Washington is a city of southern efficiency and northern charm.
1962. Quoted in *Portrait of a President* (William Manchester; 1967)

37 Last year, more Americans went to symphonies than went to baseball games. This may be viewed as an alarming statistic, but I think that both baseball and the country will endure.
Quoted in *The Kennedy Wit* (Bill Adler, ed.; 1964)

38 The worse I do, the more popular I get.
Referring to his popularity following the failure of the U.S. invasion of Cuba. *The People's Almanac* (D. Wallechinsky; 1962)

39 Mothers all want their sons to grow up to become president, but they don't want them to become politicians in the process.
Attrib.

40 Victory has a thousand fathers but defeat is an orphan.
Attrib.

Kennedy, Joseph (Joseph Patrick Kennedy; 1888–1969) U.S. business executive and government official

1 Don't get mad, get even.
Attrib. *Conversations with Kennedy* (B. Bradlee; 1976)

2 I think the primary notion back of most gambling is the excitement of it. While gamblers naturally want to win, the majority of them derive pleasure even if they lose. The desire to win, rather than the excitement involved, seems to me the compelling force behind speculation.
Quoted in *The Kennedys* (Peter Collier and David Horowitz; 1984), ch. 2

Kennedy, Robert (Robert Francis Kennedy; 1925–68) U.S. statesman

Quotations about Kennedy

1 Marilyn Monroe committed suicide because she had been having an affair with Bobby Kennedy and the White House

intervened...Our age begins to sound like some awful colossal movie about the late Roman Emperors and their Messalinas.
Mary McCarthy (1912–89) U.S. writer. Letter to Hannah Arendt (September 28, 1962), quoted in *Between Friends: the Correspondence of Hannah Arendt and Mary McCarthy, 1949–1975* (Carol Brightman, ed.; 1995)

Quotations by Kennedy

2 It is from numberless diverse acts of courage and belief that human history is shaped.
Speech, University of Cape Town, South Africa (June 6, 1966)

3 Some men see things as they are and say why? I dream things that never were and say "Why not?"
Esquire (1969)

4 One fifth of the people are against everything all the time.
Observer, London (May 10, 1964), "Sayings of the Week"

5 What is objectionable, what is dangerous about extremists is not that they are extreme but that they are intolerant.
The Pursuit of Justice (1964)

6 I was the seventh of nine children. When you come from that far down you have to struggle to survive.
The Kennedy Neurosis (Nancy G. Clinch; 1973)

7 Always forgive your enemies—but never forget their names.
Attrib.

8 Assassins have never changed history.
Referring to the assassination of his brother, President John Fitzgerald Kennedy (1963). Attrib.

Kennedy, Terry (Terrence Edward Kennedy; b.1956) U.S. baseball player and manager

1 We play like King Kong one day and like Fay Wray the next.
Sports Illustrated (May 9, 1983), quoted in *Baseball's Greatest Quotations* (Paul Dickson, ed.; 1991)

Kennedy, William (William Joseph Kennedy; b.1928) U.S. screenwriter and novelist

1 I don't hold no grudges more'n five years.
Said by the character Francis Phelan. *Ironweed* (1983)

Kenny, Elizabeth ("Sister Kenny"; 1886–1952) Australian nurse

1 Panic plays no part in the training of a nurse.
And They Shall Walk (co-written with Martha Ostenso; 1951)

2 Some minds remain open long enough for the truth not only to enter but to pass on through by way of a ready exit without pausing anywhere along the route.
And They Shall Walk (co-written with Martha Ostenso; 1951)

Kent, Bruce (b.1929) British peace campaigner and cleric

1 Preparing for suicide is not a very intelligent means of defence.
Referring to the nuclear deterrent. *Observer,* London (August 10, 1986), "Sayings of the Week"

Kent, Corita (1918–86) U.S. graphic artist

1 Women's Liberation is the liberation of the feminine in the man and the masculine in the woman.
Los Angeles Times (July 11, 1974)

Kenyatta, Jomo (1897?–1978) Kenyan president

1 God said this is our land, land in which we flourish as people...we want our cattle to get fat on our land so that our children grow up in prosperity; and we do not want the fat removed to feed others.
Speech, Nyeri, Kenya (July 26, 1952)

2 The African is conditioned, by the cultural and social institutions of centuries, to a freedom of which Europe has little conception, and it is not in his nature to accept serfdom for ever.
Facing Mount Kenya (1938), p. 318

3 We reject a blue-print of the Western model of a two-party system of government because we do not subscribe to the notion of the government and the governed in opposition to one another. One clamouring for duties and the other crying for rights.
Quoted in *Nationalism and New States in Africa* (Ali Mazrui & Ali Al'Amin Tidy; 1984), p. 285

Kepler, Johannes (1571–1630) German astronomer

1 Nature uses as little as possible of anything.
Harmonice mundi (1619)

2 Where there is matter, there is geometry.
Quoted in *Solid Shape* (J. Koenderink; 1990)

Kerbis, Gertrude Lempp (originally Gertrude Mary Lempp; b.1926) U.S. architect

1 It was hell for women architects then. They didn't want us in school or in the profession. One thing I've never understood about this prejudice is that it's so strange in view of the fact that the drive to build has always been in women.
Quoted in *Women at Work* (Betty Medsger; 1975)

Kerkonian, Kirk (b.1917) U.S. business executive

1 If economists were good at business, they would be rich men instead of advisers to rich men.
Attrib.

Kerner, Otto, Jr. (1908–76) U.S. politician

1 Our nation is moving towards two societies, one black, one white—separate and unequal.
Quoted in *Report of the National Advisory Commission on Civil Disorders* (1968)

Kerouac, Jack (Jean Louis Lebris de Kerouac; 1922–69) U.S. writer

Quotations about Kerouac

1 Jack Kerouac sat beside me on a busted rusty iron pole, companion,
we thought the same thoughts of the sun, bleak and blue and sad-eyed, surrounded
by the gnarled steel roots of trees of machinery.
Allen Ginsberg (1926–97) U.S. poet. "Sunflower Sutra," *Howl and Other Poems* (1956)

Quotations by Kerouac

2 A peaceful sorrow at home is the best I'll be able to offer the

world in the end, and so I told my desolation angels goodbye. A new life for me.
Desolation Angels (1965)

3 It is not my fault that certain so-called Bohemian elements have found in my writings something to hang their peculiar beatnik theories on.
New York Journal-American (December 8, 1960)

4 Holy flowers floating in the air, were all these tired faces in the dawn of Jazz America.
On the Road (1957), ch. 4

5 Boom, kick, that drummer was kicking his drums to the cellar and rolling the beat back upstairs with his murderous sticks, rattlety-boom!
Referring to jazz in San Francisco. *On the Road* (1957), ch. 4

6 George Shearing...He played innumerable choruses with amazing chords that mounted higher and higher till the sweat splashed all over the piano and everybody listened in fright and awe.
On the Road (1957), ch. 10

7 It came from angelical smiling lips upon the mouthpiece and it was a soft, sweet, fairy-tale solo on an alto. Lonely as America, a throatpierced sound in the night.
Referring to jazz in Chicago. *On the Road* (1957), ch. 10

8 Lester Young...that gloomy, saintly goof in whom the history of jazz was wrapped; for when he held his horn high and horizontal from his mouth he blew the greatest.
Referring to Lester "Prez" Young. *On the Road* (1957), ch. 10

9 Because the only people for me are the mad ones...the ones who never yawn or say a commonplace thing, but burn, burn, burn, like fabulous yellow roman candles exploding like spiders across the stars and in the middle you see the blue centerlight pop and everybody goes "Awww!"
On the Road (1957), pt. 1

10 We're really all of us bottomly broke. I haven't had time to work in weeks.
On the Road (1957), pt. 1

11 You can't teach the old maestro a new tune.
On the Road (1957), pt. 1

12 Now I could see Denver looming ahead of me like the Promised Land, way out there beneath the stars, across the prairies of Iowa and the plains of Nebraska.
On the Road (1957), pt. 1, ch. 3

13 The prettiest girls in the world live in Des Moines.
On the Road (1957), pt. 1, ch. 3

14 There is something brown and holy about the East; and California is white, like washlines, and emptyheaded.
On the Road (1957), pt. 1, ch. 11

15 I wandered out like a haggard ghost, and there she was, Frisco—long, bleak streets with trolley wires all shrouded in fog and whiteness.
Said by Sal Paradise (Jack Kerouac), on first arriving, by bus, in San Francisco. *On the Road* (1957), pt. 1, ch. 11

16 LA is the loneliest and most brutal of American cities; New York gets god-awful cold in the winter but there's a feeling of wacky comradeship...LA is a jungle.
On the Road (1957), pt. 1, ch. 13

17 All the cops in LA looked like handsome gigolos; obviously they'd come to LA to make the movies. Everybody had come to make the movies, even me.
Said by Sal Paradise (Jack Kerouac), on trying to find work in Los Angeles and Hollywood. *On the Road* (1957), pt. 1, ch. 13

18 New York with its millions and millions hustling forever for a buck among themselves, the mad dream—grabbing, taking, giving, sighing, dying, just so they could be buried in those awful cemetery cities beyond Long Island City.
Said by Sal Paradise (Jack Kerouac), on first returning to New York after his trip to the West Coast. *On the Road* (1957), pt. 1, ch. 14

19 I had nothing to offer anybody except my own confusion.
On the Road (1957), pt. 2

20 The air was so sweet in New Orleans it seemed to come in soft bandannas; and you could smell the river...and every kind of tropical exhalation with your nose suddenly removed from the dry ices of a Northern winter.
On the Road (1957), pt. 2, ch. 6

21 Tucson...was one great big construction job; the people transient, wild, ambitious, busy, gay; washlines, trailers; bustling downtown streets with banners; altogether very Californian.
On the Road (1957), pt. 2, ch. 8

22 At dusk we were in the Salt Lake flats with the lights of Salt Lake City infinitesimally glimmering almost a hundred miles across the mirage of the flats, twice showing, above and below the curve of the earth, one clear, one dim.
On the Road (1957), pt. 3, ch. 5

23 What a man most wishes to hide, revise, and unsay, is precisely what literature is waiting and bleeding for. Every doctor knows, every Prophet knows the convulsion of truth.
Letter to Malcolm Cowley, *Selected Letters 1940–1956* (Ann Cowley, ed.; 1996)

24 What does it mean that I am in this endless universe, thinking that I'm a man sitting under the stars on this terrace of earth, but actually empty and awake through the emptiness and awakedness of everything?
The Dharma Bums (1958)

25 Nothing in the world matters; not even success in America but just void and emptiness await the career of a soul of a man.
1951–52. *Visions of Cody* (1972)

26 We're a *beat* generation.
1948. Phrase used by John Clellon Holmes, and then by Kerouac. *Playboy* (June 1959)

27 We are beat, man. Beat means beatific, it means you get the beat.
Quoted in *Playboy* (1988)

28 All of life is a foreign country.
Quoted in *The Rolling Stone Book of the Beats* (Holly George-Warren, ed.; 1999)

Kerr, Clark (b.1911) U.S. educator and economist

1 I find the three major administrative problems on a campus

are sex for the students, athletics for the alumni, and parking for the faculty.
Time (November 17, 1958)

Kerr, Jean (b.1923) U.S. playwright and humorist

1 Man is the only animal that learns by being hypocritical. He pretends to be polite and then, eventually, he *becomes* polite.
Finishing Touches (1973)

2 One of the most difficult things to contend with in a hospital is the assumption on the part of the staff that because you have lost your gall bladder you have also lost your mind.
Please Don't Eat the Daisies (1960)

3 The average, healthy, well-adjusted adult gets up at seven-thirty in the morning feeling just plain terrible.
Please Don't Eat the Daisies (1960)

4 The real menace in dealing with a five-year-old is that in no time at all you begin to sound like a five-year-old.
Please Don't Eat the Daisies (1960)

5 Even though a number of people have tried, no one has yet found a way to drink for a living.
Poor Richard (1963)

6 You don't seem to realize that a poor person who is unhappy is in a better position than a rich person who is unhappy. Because the poor person has hope. He thinks money would help.
Poor Richard (1963)

7 I feel about airplanes the way I feel about diets. It seems to me that they are wonderful things for other people to go on.
"Mirror, Mirror, on the Wall," *The Snake Has All the Lines* (1958)

8 Marrying a man is like buying something you've been admiring in a shop window. You may love it when you get home, but it doesn't always go with everything else in the house.
Attrib.

Kesey, Ken (Ken Elton Kesey; b.1935) U.S. writer

1 You don't lead by pointing a finger and telling people some place to go. You lead by going to that place and making a case.
Interview, *Esquire* (June 1970)

2 But it's the truth even if it didn't happen.
One Flew Over The Cuckoo's Nest (1962), pt. 1

3 We are always acting on what just finished happening. It happened at least one thirtieth of a second ago. We think we're in the present but we aren't. The present we know is only a movie of what happened in the past.
Quoted in *The Electric Kool-aid Acid Test* (Tom Wolfe; 1968)

4 I'd rather be a lightning rod than a seismograph.
Referring to writing. Quoted in *The Electric Kool-aid Acid Test* (Tom Wolfe; 1968)

Kettering, Charles (Charles Franklin Kettering; 1876–1958) U.S. inventor and business executive

1 Problems are the price of progress. Don't bring me anything but trouble. Good news weakens me.
Strategy and Business (1997)

2 Teach a highly educated person that it is not a disgrace to fail and he must analyze every failure to find its cause. He must learn how to fail intelligently, for failing is one of the greatest arts in the world.
Strategy and Business (1997)

3 The difference between intelligence and education is this: intelligence will make you a good living.
Attrib.

Key, Ellen (Ellen Karolina Sofia Key; 1849–1926) Swedish reformer and educationalist

1 People work better, feel better, and are more amiable and happier if they experience beautiful shapes and colors in the objects with which they surround themselves at home, however humble it may be.
1899. *Beauty for Everyone* (Michael Snodin, tr.; 1997)

2 The emancipation of women is practically the greatest egoistic movement of the nineteenth century, and the most intense affirmation of the right of the self that history has yet seen.
The Century of the Child (1900), ch. 2

3 At every step the child should be allowed to meet the real experiences of life; the thorns should never be plucked from his roses.
The Century of the Child (1900), ch. 3

4 Nothing would more effectively further the development of education than for all flogging pedagogues to learn to educate with the head instead of with the hand.
The Century of the Child (1900), ch. 3

5 Love is moral even without legal marriage, but marriage is immoral without love.
"The Morality of Woman," *The Morality of Woman and Other Essays* (1911)

6 Woman, however, as the bearer and guardian of the new lives, has everywhere greater respect for life than man, who for centuries, as hunter and warrior, learned that the taking of lives may be not only allowed, but honorable.
The Renaissance of Motherhood (1914), ch. 2

7 Everything, everything in war is barbaric...But the worst barbarity of war is that it forces men collectively to commit acts against which individually they would revolt with their whole being.
War, Peace, and the Future (1916), ch. 6

Key, Francis Scott (1779–1843) U.S. lawyer and poet

1 O say can you see, by the dawn's early light,
What so proudly we hailed at the twilight's last gleaming—
Whose broad stripes and bright stars, through clouds of the fight,
O'er ramparts we watched were so gallantly streaming!
"The Star-Spangled Banner" (1857), quoted in *The Penguin Book of American Verse* (Geoffrey Moore, ed.; 1977)

2 O! say, does that star-spangled banner yet wave
O'er the land of the free, and the home of the brave?
"The Star-Spangled Banner" (1857), quoted in *The Penguin Book of American Verse* (Geoffrey Moore, ed.; 1977)

Keynes, Geoffrey, Sir (Geoffrey Langdon Keynes; 1887–1982) British surgeon and literary scholar

1 The affluent society has made everyone dislike work, and come to think of idleness as the happiest life.
Observer, London (October 25, 1981)

Keynes, John Maynard, 1st Baron Keynes of Tilton (1883–1946) British economist

1 *Long run* is a misleading guide to current affairs. *In the long run* we are all dead.
"A Tract on Monetary Reform" (1923), ch. 3

2 Does that mean that because Americans won't listen to sense, you intend to talk nonsense to them?
Said before a monetary conference. Remark (1945?)

3 There is...no surer means of overturning the existing basis of society than to debauch the currency.
Economic Consequences of the Peace (1919)

4 If irreligious capitalism is ultimately to defeat religious Communism, it is not enough that it should be economically more efficient—it must be many times as efficient.
Essays in Persuasion (1925)

5 Modern capitalism is absolutely irreligious, without internal union, without much public spirit, often, though not always, a mere congeries of possessors and pursuers.
Essays in Persuasion (1925)

6 The moral problem of our age is concerned with the love of money.
Essays in Persuasion (1925)

7 At the same time a persecuting and missionary religion and an experimental economic technique.
Referring to Leninism. *Essays in Persuasion* (1925)

8 We take it as a fundamental psychological rule of any modern community that, when its real income is increased, it will not increase its consumption by an equal *absolute* amount.
General Theory of Employment, Interest and Money (1936), ch. 8

9 Of the maxims of orthodox finance, none, surely, is more antisocial than the fetish of liquidity...It forgets that there is no such thing as liquidity of investment for the community as a whole.
General Theory of Employment, Interest and Money (1936), ch. 12

10 There are no intrinsic reasons for the scarcity of capital.
General Theory of Employment, Interest and Money (1936), ch. 12

11 Worldly wisdom teaches that it is better for the reputation to fail conventionally than to succeed unconventionally.
General Theory of Employment, Interest and Money (1936), ch. 12

12 It is better that a man should tyrannize over his bank balance than over his fellow citizens.
General Theory of Employment, Interest and Money (1936), ch. 24

13 Practical men, who believe themselves to be quite exempt from any intellectual influences, are usually the slaves of some defunct economist. Madmen in authority, who hear voices in the air, are distilling their frenzy from some academic scribbler of a few years back.
General Theory of Employment, Interest and Money (1936), ch. 24

14 There are the *Trade-Unionists*, once the oppressed, now the tyrants, whose selfish and sectional pretensions need to be bravely opposed.
Liberalism and Labour (1926)

15 I do not know which makes a man more conservative—to know nothing but the present, or nothing but the past.
The End of Laissez-Faire (1925), bk. 1

16 Marxian Socialism must always remain a portent to the historians of Opinion—how a doctrine so illogical and so dull can have exercised so powerful and enduring an influence over the minds of men, and, through them, the events of history.
The End of Laissez-Faire (1925), ch. 3

17 The important thing for Government is not to do things which individuals are doing already, and to do them a little better or a little worse; but to do those things which at present are not done at all.
The End of Laissez-Faire (1925), ch. 4

18 I think that Capitalism, wisely managed, can probably be made more efficient for attaining economic ends than any alternative system yet in sight, but that in itself it is in many ways extremely objectionable.
The End of Laissez-Faire (1925), ch. 5

19 If Enterprise is afoot, Wealth accumulates whatever may be happening to Thrift; and if Enterprise is asleep, Wealth decays, whatever Thrift may be doing.
Treatise on Money (1930)

20 I will not be a party to debasing the currency.
On refusing to pay more than a small tip on having his shoes polished, while on a visit to Africa. Quoted in *John Maynard Keynes* (Charles C. Hession; 1984)

21 The avoidance of taxes is the only pursuit that still carries any reward.
Attrib.

Kgositsile, Keorapetse (b.1938) South African poet, journalist, and teacher

1 The Present Is a Dangerous Place to Live
Poem title. *Contemporary African Literature* (Edris Makward & Leslie Lacy (eds); 1972), p.305

Khasoggi, Adnan (b.1935) Saudi Arabian entrepreneur

1 Making a billion dollars on a new deal is not difficult for me. Making it in a way that gives me satisfaction is the real challenge.
Daily Express, London (August 26, 1986)

2 You never know when you might need the Pope.
Referring to meeting Pope John Paul II. *Daily Mail*, London (February 19, 1987)

3 If a man does things for you which seem to be a miracle, you pay him. Why grumble?
Referring to bribery. *News of the World*, London (May 24, 1986)

Khomeini, Ruhollah, Ayatollah (1900–89) Iranian religious and political leader

1 A learned man who is not cleansed is more dangerous than an ignorant man.
Speech (July 6, 1980)

2 A Muslim will inherit from an infidel but an infidel will not inherit from a Muslim even though he is the deceased's father or son.
A Clarification of Questions (J. Borujerdi, tr.; 1984)

3 If an infidel pronounces the Twin Blessings, that is if he says "I witness that there is no God but God and I witness that Muhammad was God's prophet," he becomes a Muslim.
A Clarification of Questions (J. Borujerdi, tr.; 1984)

4 Radio and television have lawful intellectual benefits as well as unlawful benefits, from the point of view of Islam.
A Clarification of Questions (J. Borujerdi, tr.; 1984)

5 The alms of nine things are obligatory: First, wheat; second, barley; third, dates; fourth, currants; fifth, gold; sixth, silver; seventh, camels; eighth, cows; ninth, sheep.
A Clarification of Questions (J. Borujerdi, tr.; 1984)

6 The most generous Prophet (God's salutations be upon Him and His relatives) bade: A person who does not heed prayer and takes it lightly deserves the torture of the Day of Judgment.
A Clarification of Questions (J. Borujerdi, tr.; 1984)

7 Touching the writings of the Koran...is unlawful for a person who does not possess ablution. But if the Koran is translated into Persian or other languages touching it is of no concern.
A Clarification of Questions (J. Borujerdi, tr.; 1984)

8 Do you know what justice is? If you do not know, ask your reason, for reason acts like an eye for man.
1943. "A Warning to the Nation," *Islam and Revolution* (H. Algar, tr.; 1985)

9 The whole world is a name of God, for a name is a sign, and all the creatures that exist in the world are signs of the Sacred Essence of God.
1979. "Everything is a Name of God," *Islam and Revolution* (H. Algar, tr.; 1985)

10 In Islam the legislative power and competence to establish laws belongs exclusively to God Almighty. The Sacred Legislator of Islam is the sole legislative power.
1971. "Islamic Government," *Islam and Revolution* (H. Algar, tr.; 1985)

11 Islam is the religion of militant individuals who are committed to truth and justice. It is the religion of those who desire freedom and independence. It is the school of those who struggle against imperialism.
1971. "Islamic Government," *Islam and Revolution* (H. Algar, tr.; 1985)

12 Muslim peoples! Leaders of the Muslim peoples! Presidents and kings of the Muslim peoples! Come to our aid! Shah of Iran, save yourself.
1964. Calling on Iranians to overthrow the Shah. Khomeini led the Islamic revolution (1979) based on a fundamentalist interpretation of Islamic principles. "The Granting of Capitulatory Rights to the U.S.," *Islam and Revolution* (H. Algar, tr.; 1985)

13 Neither East nor West.
Referring to his political philosophy, and his opposition to the superpowers, the United States and the Soviet Union. Quoted in *Living Islam* (Akbar Ahmed; 1993)

Khrushchev, Nikita (Nikita Sergeyevich Khrushchev; 1894–1971) Soviet statesman

Quotations about Khrushchev

1 Khruschev reminds me of the tiger hunter who had picked a place on the wall to hang the tiger's skin long before he has caught the tiger. This tiger has other ideas.
John Fitzgerald Kennedy (1917–63) U.S. president. *New York Times* (December 24, 1961)

Quotations by Khrushchev

2 We will bury you.
November 18, 1956. Another possible translation of this sentence is: "We shall be present at your funeral" (meaning "We shall outlive you.") Remark at a Kremlin reception (1956), quoted in *Times*, London (November 19, 1956)

3 Politicians are the same all over. They promise to build a bridge even where there's no river.
Remark to journalists while on a visit to the United States (1960)

4 Every year humanity takes a step towards Communism. Maybe not you, but at all events your grandson will surely be a Communist.
Remark to Sir William Hayter (June 1956)

5 Revolutions are not made for export.
Speech to the 21st Congress of the Communist Party of the Soviet Union, Moscow (January 27, 1959)

6 We had no use for the policy of the Gospels: if someone slaps you, just turn the other cheek. We had shown that anyone who slapped us on our cheek would get his head kicked off.
Khrushchev Remembers (1971), vol. 2

7 If you start throwing hedgehogs under me, I shall throw two porcupines under you.
Observer, London (November 10, 1963), "Sayings of the Week"

8 When you are skinning your customers, you should leave some skin on to grow so that you can skin them again.
Addressed to British businessmen. *Observer*, London (May 28, 1961), "Sayings of the Week"

9 They talk about who won and who lost. Human reason won. Mankind won.
Referring to the Cuban missile crisis. *Observer*, London (November 11, 1962), "Sayings of the Week"

10 Economics is a subject that does not greatly respect one's wishes.
Attrib.

11 If you feed people just with revolutionary slogans they will listen today, they will listen tomorrow, they will listen the day after tomorrow, but on the fourth day they will say "To hell with you!"
Attrib.

12 Those who wait for that must wait until a shrimp learns to whistle.
Referring to the chances of the Soviet Union rejecting communism. Attrib.

Kickham, Charles Joseph (1826–82) Irish writer

1 I have time enough in fourteen years.
Referring to being asked to hurry up with his prison work. *Knocknagow* (1970), introduction

Kieko, Yamamuro (1874–1915) Japanese evangelist and philanthropist

1 I realize that if I were a man, I would be at the battlefront fighting amid bullets and explosives, instead of sitting serenely at my desk.
Untitled essay (1895)

Kierkegaard, Søren (Søren Aabye Kierkegaard; 1813–55) Danish philosopher

1 Each age has its own characteristic depravity. Ours is perhaps not pleasure or indulgence or sensuality, but rather a dissolute pantheistic contempt for the individual man.
Concluding Unscientific Postscript (1846)

2 It is subjectivity that Christianity is concerned with, and it is only in subjectivity that its truth exists, if it exists at all; objectively, Christianity has absolutely no existence.
Concluding Unscientific Postscript (1846)

3 There has been said much that is strange, much that is deplorable, much that is revolting about Christianity; but the most stupid thing ever said about it is that it is to a certain degree true.
Concluding Unscientific Postscript (1846)

4 The scribbling modern philosophy holds passion in contempt; and yet passion is the culmination of existence for an existing individual—and we are all of us existing individuals.
Concluding Unscientific Postscript (1846)

5 What is a poet? A poet is an unhappy being whose heart is torn by secret sufferings, but whose lips are so strangely formed that when the sighs and the cries escape them, they sound like beautiful music.
Either/Or (1843)

6 Job endured everything—until his friends came to comfort him, then he grew impatient.
Journal (1849)

7 The supreme paradox of all thought is the attempt to discover something that thought cannot think.
Philosophical Fragments (1844)

8 Psychology...delineates sin, while again and again it is alarmed by the sketch it produces.
1844. *The Concept of Dread* (W. Lowrie, tr.; 1957)

9 Sin, however, is not a theme for psychological interest, and it would only be to abandon oneself to the service of a misunderstood cleverness if one were to treat it thus.
1844. *The Concept of Dread* (W. Lowrie, tr.; 1957)

10 Spirit is dreaming in man.
1844. *The Concept of Dread* (W. Lowrie, tr.; 1957)

11 That which can concern psychology and with which it can concern itself is the question how sin came into existence, not the fact that it exists.
1844. *The Concept of Dread* (W. Lowrie, tr.; 1957)

12 The psychological observer ought to be more agile than the tightrope dancer in order to be able to insinuate himself under the skin of other people.
1844. *The Concept of Dread* (W. Lowrie, tr.; 1957)

13 The sophistry which insane remorse is every instant capable of producing, no dialectic is able to overcome.
1844. *The Concept of Dread* (W. Lowrie, tr.; 1957)

14 His silence in confidential moments ought to be seductive and voluptuous in order that the hidden thing may find pleasure in slipping out and chatting quietly with itself in this fictitious inattention.
1844. Referring to the observing psychologist. *The Concept of Dread* (W. Lowrie, tr.; 1957)

15 In relation to their systems most systematizers are like a man who builds an enormous castle and lives in a shack close by; they do not live in their own enormous systematic buildings.
The Journals of Søren Kierkegaard (Alexander Dru, tr.; 1938)

16 The method which begins by doubting in order to philosophize is just as suited to its purpose as making a soldier lie down in a heap in order to teach him to stand up straight.
The Journals of Søren Kierkegaard (Alexander Dru, tr.; 1938)

17 The greatest hazard of all, losing one's self, can occur very quietly in the world, as if it were nothing at all. No other loss can occur so quietly; any other loss—an arm, a leg, five dollars, a wife, etc.—is sure to be noticed.
The Sickness unto Death (1849)

18 That is the road we all have to take—over the Bridge of Sighs into eternity.
Quoted in *Kierkegaard* (W. H. Auden; 1955)

Kiesler, Frederick (1890–1965) Austrian-born U.S. architect and sculptor

1 Our Western World has been overrun by masses of art objects. What we really need are not more and more objects, but an objective.
March 1965. "Second Manifesto of Correalism," *Art International* (March 1965)

Kieslowski, Krzysztof (1941–96) Polish film director

1 We all steal but if we're smart we steal from great directors. Then, we can call it influence.
7 Days (May 6, 1990), quoted in *Chambers Film Quotes* (Tony Crawley, ed.; 1991)

2 I can understand Fellini and most of the others who build streets, houses and even artificial seas in the studio: in this way not so many people get to see the shameful and insignificant job of directing.
Referring to Federico Fellini. *Kieslowski on Kieslowski* (1993), epigraph

Killens, John Oliver (1916–87) U.S. novelist, film scriptwriter, and educator

1 A people needs legends, heroes, myths. Deny them these and you have won half the battle against them.
"The Black Writer Vis-à-Vis His Country," *Black Man's Burden* (1965)

2 Who will uninvent the Negro?
"The Black Writer Vis-à-Vis His Country," *Black Man's Burden* (1965)

3 My fight is not to be a white man in a black skin, but to inject some black blood, some black intelligence into the pallid

mainstream of American life, culturally, socially, psychologically, philosophically.
"Explanation of the Black Psyche," *New York Times* (June 7, 1964)

Kilmer, Joyce (Alfred Joyce Kilmer; 1886–1918) U.S. poet

1 I think that I shall never see
A poem lovely as a tree.
"Trees," *Trees and Other Poems* (1914)

2 Poems are made by fools like me,
But only God can make a tree.
"Trees," *Trees and Other Poems* (1914)

Kilvert, Francis (Robert Francis Kilvert; 1840–79) British diarist and cleric

1 Of all noxious animals, too, the most noxious is a tourist. And of all tourists the most vulgar, ill-bred, offensive and loathsome is the British tourist.
April 5, 1870. *Diary* (W. Plomer, ed.; 1938)

2 It is a fine thing to be out on the hills alone. A man can hardly be a beast or a fool alone on a great mountain.
May 29, 1871. On the Black Mountain in Wales. *Diary* (W. Plomer, ed.; 1938)

Kimball, Spencer W. (1895–1985) U.S. Mormon leader

1 We plead with you fathers to return to your little kingdoms and, with kindness, justice, proper discipline, and love, to inspire your family. We appeal to mothers to help create that happy family relationship.
The Teachings of Spencer W. Kimball (1976)

Kincaid, Jamaica (b.1949) Antiguan-born U.S. novelist, short-story writer, and journalist

1 We were afraid of the dead because we never could tell when they might show up again.
Annie John (1986), p. 4

2 A tourist is an ugly human being.
A Small Place (1988), p. 14

3 He did not draw your attention to how handsome he was; he didn't draw attention to anything about him. This was a nice trait in a man.
Lucy (1991), p. 48

4 Lying is the beginning of fiction.
New York Times (October 7, 1990)

King, B. B. (Riley B. King; b.1925) U.S. blues singer and guitarist

1 Being a blues singer is like being black two times.
Quoted in *The Wit and Wisdom of Rock and Roll* (Maxim Jabukowski, ed.; 1983)

2 Nobody loves me but my mother,
And she could be jiving, too.
Song lyric. Attrib.

King, Benjamin Franklin (1857–94) U.S. humorist

1 Nothing to do but work,
Nothing to eat but food,
Nothing to wear but clothes,
To keep one from going nude.
"The Pessimist" (19th century)

King, Billie Jean (originally Billie Jean Moffitt; b.1943) U.S. tennis player

1 I've always wanted to equalize things for us...Women can be great athletes. And I think we'll find in the next decade that women athletes will finally get the attention they deserve.
Interview (September 1973)

2 It's really impossible for athletes to grow up. As long as you're playing, no one will let you.
Billie Jean (1982)

King, Carole (b.1942) U.S. singer and songwriter

1 Winter, spring, summer or fall,
All you have to do is call
And I'll be there.
You've got a friend.
Song lyric. "You've Got a Friend" (1971)

King, Don (b.1931) U.S. boxing impresario

1 People just don't like me for the same reason they didn't like Muhammad Ali. We're the wrong kind of nigger.
Quoted in *The Black Lights: Inside the World of Professional Boxing* (Thomas Hauser; 1986)

King, Henry (1592–1669) English bishop and poet

1 Sleep on, my Love, in thy cold bed,
Never to be disquieted!
My last good night! Thou wilt not wake,
Till I thy fate shall overtake;
Till age, or grief, or sickness, must
Marry my body to that dust
It so much loves, and fill the room
My heart keeps empty in thy tomb.
Written for his wife Anne. "The Exequy," *Poems, Elegies, Paradoxes and Sonnets* (1657), ll. 81–88

King, Larry (Lawrence Harvey Zeiger; b.1933) U.S. talk-show host

1 Talk wrestling.
His term for aggressive talk shows. Quoted in "A Bumpy Ride for TV's High Flyer," *Manhattan, Inc.* (August 1989)

2 An absolute ungovernable curiosity.
1991. Referring to the secret of his success. Attrib.

King, Martin Luther, Jr. (1929–68) U.S. civil rights leader

1 Yes, if you want to say that I was a drum major, say that I was a drum major for justice; say that I was a drum major for righteousness. And all of the other shallow things will not matter.
Comment (February 4, 1968)

2 I just want to do God's will. And he's allowed me to go up to the mountain. And I've looked over. And I've seen the promised land. I may not get there with you. But I want you

to know...we as people will get to the promised land.
Final speech (April 3, 1968)

3 Nonviolent direct action seeks to create such a crisis and foster such a tension that a community which has constantly refused to negotiate is forced to confront the issue.
Letter from Birmingham Jail, Alabama (April 16, 1963)

4 Injustice anywhere is a threat to justice everywhere.
Letter from Birmingham Jail, Alabama (April 16, 1963), quoted in *Right Thinking* (Edward Leigh; 1979)

5 If a man hasn't discovered something that he will die for, he isn't fit to live.
Speech, Detroit, Michigan (June 23, 1963)

6 The security we profess to seek in foreign adventures we will lose in our decaying cities.
1967. Referring to U.S. Vietnam policy. Address, Riverside Church, New York, *History Today* (April 1998), vol. 48

7 Freedom is never voluntarily given up by the oppressor.
1963. He was briefly in prison on civil disorder charges in Birmingham, Alabama. Letter from Birmingham Jail, *History Today* (April 1998), vol. 48

8 I want to be the white man's brother, not his brother-in-law.
New York Journal-American (September 10, 1962)

9 I have a dream that one day on the red hills of Georgia the sons of former slaves and sons of former slaveowners will be able to sit down together at the table of brotherhood...I have a dream that my four little children will one day live in a nation where they will be not judged by the color of their skin but by the content of their character.
August 28, 1963. Speech at civil rights march in Washington, D.C., *New York Times* (August 29, 1963)

10 We can never be satisfied as long as a Negro in Mississippi cannot vote and a Negro in New York believes he has nothing for which to vote...we will not be satisfied until justice rolls down like waters and righteousness like a mighty stream.
August 28, 1963. Speech at civil rights march in Washington, D.C., *New York Times* (August 29, 1963)

11 I have a dream that one day this nation will rise up, live out the true meaning of its creed: we hold these truths to be self-evident, that all men are created equal.
August 28, 1963. Referring to the Declaration of Independence (1776). Speech at civil rights march in Washington, D.C., *New York Times* (August 29, 1963)

12 Human salvation lies in the hands of the creatively maladjusted.
Strength To Love (1963)

13 Moral principles have lost their distinctiveness. For modern man, absolute right and absolute wrong are a matter of what the majority is doing.
Strength To Love (1963)

14 Nothing in the world is more dangerous than sincere ignorance and conscientious stupidity.
Strength To Love (1963)

15 The means by which we live have outdistanced the ends for which we live. Our scientific power has outrun our spiritual power. We have guided missiles and misguided men.
Strength To Love (1963)

16 The ultimate measure of a man is not where he stands in moments of comfort and convenience, but where he stands at times of challenge and controversy.
Strength To Love (1963)

17 We have genuflected before the god of science only to find that it has given us the atomic bomb, producing fears and anxieties that science can never mitigate.
Strength To Love (1963)

18 A religion true to its natures must also be concerned about man's social conditions. Religion deals with both earth and heaven, both time and eternity. Religion operates not only on the vertical plane but also on the horizontal. It seeks not only to integrate men with God but to integrate men with men and each man with himself.
Stride Toward Freedom (1964)

19 He who passively accepts evil is as much involved in it as he who helps to perpetrate it.
Stride Toward Freedom (1964)

20 In order to be true to one's conscience and true to God, a righteous man has no alternative but to refuse to cooperate with an evil system.
Stride Toward Freedom (1964)

21 The best way to solve any problem is to remove its cause.
Stride Toward Freedom (1964)

22 Today the choice is no longer between violence and nonviolence. It is either nonviolence or nonexistence.
Stride Toward Freedom (1964)

23 We are out to defeat injustice and not white persons who may be unjust.
Stride Toward Freedom (1964)

24 Urban riots must now be recognized as a durable social phenomenon. They are a special form of violence...mainly intended to shock the white community.
The American Psychologist (1968)

25 It may be true that the law cannot make a man love me, but it can keep him from lynching me, and I think that's pretty important.
Wall Street Journal (November 13, 1962)

26 A good many observers have remarked that if equality could come at once the Negro would not be ready for it. I submit that the white American is even more unprepared.
Where Do We Go From Here: Chaos or Community? (1967)

27 A riot is at bottom the language of the unheard.
Where Do We Go From Here: Chaos or Community? (1967)

28 Being a Negro in America means trying to smile when you want to cry. It means trying to hold on to physical life amid psychological death. It means the pain of watching your children grow up with clouds of inferiority in their mental skies. It means having your legs cut off, and then being condemned for being a cripple.
Where Do We Go From Here: Chaos or Community? (1967)

29 What is needed is a realization that power without love is reckless and abusive and that love without power is sentimental and anemic. Power at its best is love implementing the demands

of justice. Justice at its best is love correcting everything that stands against love.
Where Do We Go From Here: Chaos or Community? (1967)

30 Nonviolence is a powerful and just weapon. It is a weapon unique in history, which cuts without wounding and ennobles the man who wields it. It is a sword that heals.
Why We Can't Wait (1964), p. 26

31 Communism will never be defeated by atomic bombs...Our greatest defense against Communism is to take offensive action on behalf of justice and righteousness...We must...seek to remove...conditions of poverty, injustice, and racial discrimination.
Quoted in *Rebels Against War* (Lawrence Wittner; 1969)

32 The old law of an eye for an eye leaves everybody blind.
1955. Attrib.

King, Rodney (b.1966) U.S. construction worker

1 Please, we can get along here. We can all get along. We've just got to. I mean we're all stuck here for a while. Let's try to work it out.
May 1, 1992. During the Los Angeles riots. *Facts on File* (May 7, 1992)

King, Stephen (Stephen Edwin King; b.1947) U.S. novelist

1 The night roared like a lion with a poisoned spear stuck in its throat.
Needful Things (1991)

2 I believe there is an unseen world all around us.
Nightmares and Dreamscapes (1993), introduction

3 You have to start knowing yourself so well that you begin to know other people. A piece of us is in every person we can ever meet.
Night Shift (1978)

King, W. L. Mackenzie (William Lyon Mackenzie King; 1874–1950) Canadian prime minister

1 U.S. foreign policy at bottom is to bring Canada into as many situations affecting themselves as possible with a view to leading ultimately to the annexation of our two countries.
Diary (June 30, 1950)

Kingsley, Charles (1819–75) British novelist and cleric

1 For men must work, and women must weep,
And there's little to earn, and many to keep,
Though the harbour bar be moaning.
"The Three Fishers" (1851), st. I

2 To be discontented with the divine discontent, and to be ashamed with the noble shame, is the very germ and first upgrowth of all virtue.
Health and Education (1874)

3 When all the world is young, lad,
And all the trees are green;
And every goose a swan, lad,
And every lass a queen;
Then hey for boot and horse, lad,
And round the world away:
Young blood must have its course, lad,
And every dog his day.
"Young and Old," *Songs from The Water Babies* (1863), Song 2, st. 1

4 He did not know that a keeper is only a poacher turned outside in, and a poacher a keeper turned inside out.
The Water Babies (1863), ch. 1

5 Mrs Bedonebyasyoudid is coming.
The Water Babies (1863), ch. 5

6 The loveliest fairy in the world; and her name is Mrs Doasyouwouldbedoneby.
The Water Babies (1863), ch. 5

7 More ways of killing a cat than choking her with cream.
Westward Ho! (1855), ch. 20

8 Some say that the age of chivalry is past, that the spirit of romance is dead. The age of chivalry is never past, so long as there is a wrong left unredressed on earth.
Quoted in *Charles Kingsley: His Letters and Memories of His Life* (Mrs C. Kingsley; 1879), vol. 2, ch. 28

Kingsley, Mary (Mary Henrietta Kingsley; 1862–1900) British explorer

1 To my taste there is nothing so fascinating as spending a night out in an African forest or plantation; but I beg you to note I do not advise anyone to follow the practice.
Travels in West Africa (1897)

Kingsmill, Hugh (Hugh Kingsmill Lunn; 1889–1949) British writer, critic, and anthologist

1 It is difficult to love mankind unless one has a reasonable private income and when one has a reasonable private income one has better things to do than loving mankind.
Quoted in *God's Apology* (R. Ingrams; 1977)

2 Friends are God's apology for relations.
Quoted in *The Best of Hugh Kingsmill* (Michael Holroyd; 1970), Introduction

Kingston, Maxine Hong (Maxine Ting Ting Hong Kingston; b.1940) U.S. writer

1 Ocean people are different from land people. The ocean never stops saying and asking into ears, which don't sleep like eyes.
China Men (1980)

2 San Francisco supplemented the anti-Chinese state laws with...a queue tax, a "cubic air ordinance" requiring that every residence have so many cubic feet of air per inhabitant, a pole law prohibiting the use of carrying baskets on poles, cigar taxes, shoe taxes, and laundry taxes.
China Men (1980)

3 The ocean and hunger and some other urge made the Cantonese people explorers and Americans.
China Men (1980)

4 The Navy continues to bomb Kaho'olawe and the Army blasts

the green skin off the red mountains of Oahu. But the land sings.
Oahu and Kaho'olawe are two islands in Hawaii. Pearl Harbor is on Oahu, where the U.S. Pacific fleet was attacked on December 7, 1941 by Japanese airplanes and submarines. *China Men* (1980)

Kington, Miles (Miles Beresford Kington; b.1941) British writer and broadcaster

1 I recently reported that a computer had been programmed to enjoy modern concert music (as very few people seemed to want to).
Attrib.

Kinnock, Neil (Neil Gordon Kinnock; b.1942) British politician

1 I warn you not to be ordinary, I warn you not to be young, I warn you not to fall ill, and I warn you not to grow old.
Referring to the prospects of a Conservative election victory. Election rally, Bridgend, Glamorgan (June 7, 1983)

2 It's a pity others had to leave theirs on the ground at Goose Green to prove it.
1983. Replying to a heckler who said Margaret Thatcher "showed guts" in the Falklands War. Goose Green was the location of the decisive battle in the Falklands War (1982), fought between the United Kingdom and Argentina over the sovereignty of the Falkland Islands, or Islas Malvinas. Live television interview (June 6, 1983)

3 You don't play politics with people's jobs.
Addressing the Labour Party's "Militant Tendency." Speech at the Labour Party Conference (October 1985)

4 I would die for my country, but I would not let my country die for me.
Speech on Nuclear Disarmament (1987)

5 When you see the way she was done down, you are bound to think that the people who organised the coup must have had a conscience bypass.
Referring to the removal of Margaret Thatcher as leader of the Conservative Party (1990). *Guardian*, London (August 19, 1991)

6 Proportional Representation, I think, is fundamentally counter-democratic.
Marxism Today (1983)

7 Switzerland only seems small because it's all folded up. If you opened it out it would be bigger than the U.S.
Time (April 7, 1997)

8 You cannot fashion a wit out of two half-wits.
Times, London (1983)

9 We cannot remove the evils of capitalism without taking its source of power: ownership.
Tribune (1975)

Kinsey, Alfred (Alfred Charles Kinsey; 1894–1956) U.S. biologist

1 The vagina walls are quite insensitive in the great majority of females...There is no evidence that the vagina is ever the sole source of arousal, or even the primary source of erotic arousal in any female.
Sexual Behaviour in the Human Female (1953)

Kinsley, Michael (b.1951) U.S. journalist and magazine editor

1 The scandal is not what's illegal. The scandal is what's legal.
Attrib.

Kipling, Rudyard (Joseph Rudyard Kipling; 1865–1936) Indian-born British writer and poet

Quotations about Kipling

1 Kipling tries so hard to celebrate and justify true authority, the work and habit and wisdom of the world, because he feels so bitterly the abyss of pain and insanity that they overlie.
1961
Randall Jarrell (1914–65) U.S. author and poet. "On Preparing to Read Kipling," *Kipling, Auden, & Co.: Essays and Reviews, 1935–1964* (1981)

2 Will there never come a season
Which shall rid us from the curse
Of a prose which knows no reason
And an unmelodious verse?
When there stands a muzzled stripling,
Mute, beside a muzzled bore:
When the Rudyards cease from Kipling
And the Haggards Ride no more.
James Kenneth Stephen (1859–92) British writer. Referring to Rudyard Kipling and H. Rider Haggard. "To R. K.," *Lapsus Calami* (1891)

Quotations by Kipling

3 There are only two classes of mankind in the world—doctors and patients.
Address to medical students at London's Middlesex Hospital (October 1, 1908)

4 For all we have and are,
For all our children's fate,
Stand up and take the war.
The Hun is at the gate!
"For All We Have and Are" (1914)

5 Words are, of course, the most powerful drug used by mankind.
Speech (1923)

6 England's on the anvil—hear the hammers ring
Clanging from the Severn to the Tyne!
Never was a blacksmith like our Norman King—
England's being hammered, hammered, hammered into line!
"The Anvil" (1927)

7 Oh, Adam was a gardener, and God who made him sees
That half a proper gardener's work is done upon his knees,
So when your work is finished, you can wash your hands and pray
For the Glory of the Garden, that it may not pass away!
"The Glory of the Garden," st. 8, quoted in *A History of England* (C.R.L. Fletcher; 1911)

8 In the Carboniferous Epoch we were promised abundance for all,
By robbing selected Peter to pay for collective Paul;
But though we had plenty of money, there was nothing our money could buy,
And the Gods of the Copybook Headings said: "If you don't work, you die."
"The Gods of the Copybook Headings" (1927)

9 Brothers and Sisters, I bid you beware
Of giving your heart to a dog to tear.
"The Power of the Dog" (1909)

10 But remember, please, the Law by which we live,
We are not built to comprehend a lie,
We can neither love nor pity nor forgive,
If you make a slip in handling us you die!
One of many songs Kipling wrote for C. R. L. Fletcher's book. "The Secret of Machines", quoted in *A History of England* (C. R. L. Fletcher; 1911)

11 Down to Gehenna or up to the Throne,
He travels the fastest who travels alone.
"The Story of the Gadsbys" (1890), l. 6

12 Take up the White Man's burden—
And reap his old reward:
The blame of those ye better,
The hate of those ye guard.
"The White Man's Burden" (1899)

13 When the Himalayan peasant meets the he-bear in his pride,
He shouts to scare the monster, who will often turn aside.
But the she-bear thus accosted rends the peasant tooth and nail
For the female of the species is more deadly than the male.
One of the many songs that Kipling wrote for C. R. L. Fletcher's book. "The Female of the Species," *A History of England* (C. R. L. Fletcher; 1911), st. 1

14 And that is called paying the Dane-geld;
But we've proved it again and again,
That if once you have paid him the Dane-geld
You never get rid of the Dane.
One of many songs Kipling wrote for C. R. L. Fletcher's book. "What Dane-Geld Means," *A History of England* (C. R. L. Fletcher; 1911)

15 And the talk slid north, and the talk slid south
With the sliding puffs from the hookah-mouth
Four things greater than all things are,
Women and Horses and Power and War.
1890. "Ballad of the King's Jest," *Barrack-Room Ballads and Other Verses* (1892)

16 I've a head like a concertina, I've a tongue like a button-stick,
I've a mouth like an old potato, and I'm more than a little sick,
But I've had my fun o' the Corp'ral's Guard; I've made the cinders fly,
And I'm here in the Clink for a thundering drink and blacking the Corporal's eye.
"Cells," *Barrack-Room Ballads and Other Verses* (1892)

17 So 'ere's to you, Fuzzy-Wuzzy, at your 'ome in the Soudan;
You're a pore benighted 'eathen but a first-class fightin' man.
1890. "Fuzzy-Wuzzy," *Barrack-Room Ballads and Other Verses* (1892)

18 An' for all 'is dirty 'ide
'E was white, clear white, inside
When 'e went to tend the wounded under fire!
"Gunga Din," *Barrack Room Ballads and Other Verses* (1892)

19 The uniform 'e wore
Was nothin' much before,
An' rather less than 'arf o' that be'ind.
"Gunga Din," *Barrack Room Ballads and Other Verses* (1892)

20 Though I've belted you an' flayed you,
By the livin' Gawd that made you,
You're a better man than I am, Gunga Din!
"Gunga Din," *Ballads and Barrack Room Ballads* (1892)

21 An' I seed her first a-smokin' of a whackin' white cheroot,
An' a-wastin' Christian kisses on an 'eathen idol's foot.
1890. "Mandalay," *Barrack-Room Ballads and Other Verses* (1892)

22 By the old Moulmein Pagoda, lookin' eastward to the sea,
There's a Burma girl a-settin', and I know she thinks o' me;
For the wind is in the palm-trees, an' the temple-bells they say:
"Come you back, you British soldier; come you back to Mandalay!"
1890. "Mandalay," *Barrack-Room Ballads and Other Verses* (1892)

23 Ship me somewheres east of Suez, where the best is like the worst,
Where there aren't no Ten Commandments, an' a man can raise a thirst:
For the temple-bells are callin', an' it's there that I would be—
By the old Moulmein Pagoda, looking lazy at the sea.
1890. "Mandalay," *Barrack-Room Ballads and Other Verses* (1892)

24 Oh, East is East, and West is West, and never the twain shall meet...
But there is neither East nor West, Border, nor Breed, nor Birth,
When two strong men stand face to face, though they come from the ends of the earth.
1889. "The Ballad of East and West," *Barrack-Room Ballads and Other Verses* (1892)

25 We know that the tail must wag the dog, for the horse is drawn by the cart;
But the Devil whoops, as he whooped of old: "It's clever, but is it Art?"
1890. "The Conundrum of the Workshops," *Barrack-Room Ballads and Other Verses* (1892)

26 But it's "Thin red line of 'eroes" when the drums begin to roll.
1890. "Tommy," *Barrack-Room Ballads and Other Verses* (1892)

27 It's Tommy this, an' Tommy that, an' "Chuck him out, the brute!"
But it's "Saviour of 'is country" when the guns begin to shoot
Then it's Tommy this, an' Tommy that, an' "Tommy 'ow's yer soul?"
1890. "Tommy," *Barrack-Room Ballads and Other Verses* (1892)

28 Oh, it's Tommy this, an' Tommy that, an' "Tommy, go away";
But it's "Thank you, Mister Atkins," when the band begins to play.
1890. "Tommy"*Barrack-Room Ballads and Other Verses* (1892)

29 Father, Mother, and Me,
Sister and Auntie say
All the people like us are We,
And every one else is They.
"We and They," *Debits and Credits* (1926)

30 We are very slightly changed

From the semi-apes who ranged
India's prehistoric clay.
"A General Summary," *Departmental Ditties and Other Verses* (1886)

31 The toad beneath the harrow knows
Exactly where each tooth-point goes;
The butterfly upon the road
Preaches contentment to that toad.
"Pagett M.P.," *Departmental Ditties and Other Verses* (1886)

32 A woman is only a woman, but a good cigar is a smoke.
"The Betrothed," *Departmental Ditties and Other Verses* (1886)

33 If any question why we died,
Tell them because our fathers lied.
"Common Form," *Epitaphs of The War* (1914–18)

34 No one as yet has approached the management of New York in a proper spirit; that is to say, regarding it as the shiftless outcome of squalid barbarism and reckless extravagance.
"Across a Continent," *From Tideway to Tideway* (1897)

35 "Humph yourself!"
And thc Camel humphed himself.
"How the Camel Got His Hump," *Just So Stories* (1902)

36 He walked by himself, and all places were alike to him.
"The Cat That Walked by Himself," *Just So Stories* (1902)

37 I keep six honest serving-men
They taught me all I knew;
Their names are What and Why and When
And How and Where and Who.
"The Elephant's Child," *Just So Stories* (1902)

38 Asia is not going to be civilized after the methods of the West. There is too much Asia and she is too old.
"The Man Who Was," *Life's Handicap* (1891)

39 Now it is not good for the Christian's health to hustle the Aryan brown,
Now the Christian riles, and the Aryan smiles, and it weareth the Christian down;
And the end of the fight is a tombstone white with the name of the late deceased,
And the epitaph drear: "A Fool lies here who tried to hustle the East."
Chapter heading. "The Naulahka," *Naulahka* (1892), ch. 5

40 Every one is more or less mad on one point.
"On the Strength of a Likeness," *Plain Tales from the Hills* (1888)

41 The silliest woman can manage a clever man; but it needs a very clever woman to manage a fool.
"Three and—an Extra," *Plain Tales from the Hills* (1888)

42 She was as immutable as the hills.
But not quite so green.
"Venus Annodomini," *Plain Tales from the Hills* (1888)

43 If you wake at midnight, and hear a horse's feet,
Don't go drawing back the blind, or looking in the street,
Them that asks no questions isn't told a lie.
Watch the wall, my darling, while the Gentlemen go by!
"A Smuggler's Song," *Puck of Pook's Hill* (1906)

44 Mithras, God of the Morning, our trumpets waken the Wall!
"Rome is above the Nations, but Thou art over all!"
Mithras was the ancient Persian god of light and wisdom, and in the 1st century B.C. began to be adopted by the Romans as the sun god. Mithraism rapidly became one of the major religious cults of the Roman Empire. "A Song to Mithras" in "On the Great Wall," *Puck of Pook's Hill* (1906)

45 Teach us delight in simple things,
And mirth that has no bitter springs;
Forgiveness free of evil done,
And love to all men 'neath the sun!
"The Children's Song," *Puck of Pook's Hill* (1906)

46 No one thinks of winter when the grass is green!
"A St Helena Lullaby," *Rewards and Fairies* (1910)

47 I tell this tale, which is strictly true,
Just by way of convincing you
How very little, since things were made,
Things have altered in the building trade.
"A Truthful Song" in "The Wrong Thing," *Rewards and Fairies* (1910)

48 Gold is for the mistress—silver for the maid—
Copper for the craftsman cunning at his trade.
"Good!" said the Baron, sitting in his hall,
"But Iron—Cold Iron—is master of them all."
"Cold Iron," *Rewards and Fairies* (1910)

49 If you can fill the unforgiving minute
With sixty seconds' worth of distance run,
Yours is the Earth and everything that's in it,
And—which is more—you'll be a Man my son!
"If," *Rewards and Fairies* (1910)

50 If you can keep your head when all about you
Are losing theirs and blaming it on you,
If you can trust yourself when all men doubt you,
But make allowance for their doubting too.
"If," *Rewards and Fairies* (1910)

51 If you can make one heap of all your winnings
And risk it on one turn of pitch-and-toss,
And lose, and start again at your beginnings
And never breathe a word about your loss.
"If," *Rewards and Fairies* (1910)

52 A Nation spoke to a Nation,
A Throne sent word to a Throne:
"Daughter am I in my mother's house,
But mistress in my own.
The gates are mine to open,
As the gates are mine to close,
And I abide by my Mother's House,"
Said our Lady of the Snows.
1897. Referring to Canada. "Our Lady of the Snows," *The Five Nations* (1903)

53 Take up the White Man's burden—
Send forth the best ye breed—
Go, bind your sons to exile
To serve your captives' need;
To wait in heavy harness
On fluttered folk and wild—
Your new-caught, sullen peoples,
Half devil and half child.
"The White Man's Burden," *The Five Nations* (1903)

54 Now Chil the Kite brings home the night
That Mang the Bat sets free—
The herds are shut in byre and hut
For loosed till dawn are we.
"Night-Song in the Jungle"—chapter-heading quotation. The song of the wolf pack. "Mowgli's Brothers," *The Jungle Book* (1894)

55 The dance—the elephant-dance! I have seen it, and—I die.
Said by Little Toomai. Petersen Sahib had told him that he might enter the Keddah, the elephant stockade, when he had seen the elephants dance. "Toomai of the Elephants," *The Jungle Book* (1894)

56 The Light that Failed
Novel title. (1890)

57 The Law of the Jungle—which is by far the oldest law in the world—has arranged for almost every kind of accident that may befall the Jungle People, till now its code is as perfect as time and custom can make it.
"How Fear Came," *The Second Jungle Book* (1895)

58 Now this is the Law of the Jungle—as old and as true as the sky;
And the Wolf that shall keep it may prosper, but the Wolf that shall break it must die.
"The Law of the Jungle," *The Second Jungle Book* (1895)

59 The 'eathen in 'is blindness must end where 'e began,
But the backbone of the Army is the Non-commissioned man!
"The 'Eathen," *The Seven Seas* (1896)

60 English they be and Japanese that hang on the Brown Bear's flank,
And some be Scot, but the worst of the lot, and the boldest thieves, be Yank!
1894. "The Rhyme of the Three Sealers," *The Seven Seas* (1896)

61 I'm the Prophet of the Utterly Absurd,
Of the Patently Impossible and Vain.
1895. "The Song of the Banjo," *The Seven Seas* (1896)

62 I could not look on Death, which being known,
Men led me to him, blindfold and alone.
"Epitaphs—The Coward," *The Years Between* (1919)

63 Ah! What avails the classic bent
And what the cultured word,
Against the undoctored incident
That actually occurred?
"The Benefactors," *The Years Between* (1919)

64 'Tisn't beauty, so to speak, nor good talk necessarily. It's just It.
"Mrs. Bathurst," *Traffics and Discoveries* (1904)

65 Anything green that grew out of the mould
Was an excellent herb to our fathers of old.
Quoted in *Grandmother's Secrets* (Jean Palaiseul; 1973)

66 Power without responsibility—the prerogative of the harlot throughout the ages.
Better known for its subsequent use by Kipling's cousin, Stanley Baldwin, in 1931. Quoted in *Kipling Journal* (December 1971), vol. 38, no. 180

67 I've just read that I am dead. Don't forget to delete me from your list of subscribers.
Writing to a magazine that had mistakenly published an announcement of his death. Attrib.

Kirkland, Lane (Joseph Lane Kirkland; b.1922) U.S. labor leader

1 If hard work were such a wonderful thing, surely the rich would have kept it all to themselves.
Quoted in *Fortune* (October 31, 1983)

2 You know, my pappy told me never to bet my bladder against a brewery or get into an argument with people who buy ink by the barrel.
Quoted in *Fortune* (December 23, 1985)

Kirkpatrick, Jeane Jordan (b.1926) U.S. political scientist and diplomat

1 Look, I don't even agree with *myself* at times.
Referring to leaving the Democratic Party to join the Republicans. Interview (NBC television) (April 3, 1985)

2 Words can destroy. What we call each other ultimately becomes what we think of each other, and it matters.
Speech, Anti-Defamation League (February 11, 1982), "Israel as Scapegoat"

Kirkup, James (b.1919) British poet

1 The old are always serious. They have to be.
It was for that I loved them.
"The Love of Older Men," *The Penguin Book of Homosexual Verse* (Stephen Coote, ed.; 1983)

2 This most unwelcoming outpost of the American way of life.
Referring to Anchorage, Alaska. *These Horned Islands* (1962)

Kirstein, Lincoln (Lincoln Edward Kirstein; 1907–96) U.S. ballet director and writer

Quotations about Kirstein

1 Lincoln...said, "I admire your dance." I replied, "Well, that isn't what you recently wrote. You call me the goddess who belched and I have never forgotten that." He said, "But that was before I knew you." I said, "You don't know me now."
Martha Graham (1893–1991) U.S. dancer and choreographer. *Blood Memory* (1991)

Quotations by Kirstein

2 As much as half the force and efficiency of a supporting corps is fueled as much by resentment as by ambition. Fury at failure to advance or achieve a desired status is not negligible as a source of negative energy.
Portrait of Mr. B (1984)

3 Promising aspirants who are marked for eventual soloist standing, often disappoint teachers, parents and, worst of all, themselves. Cute kittens turn into scraggly cats.
Portrait of Mr. B (1984)

4 The ballet dancer's mode of existence may seem to outsiders as circumscribed as that of a convent or cloister.
Portrait of Mr. B (1984)

Kissinger, Henry (Henry Alfred Kissinger; b.1923) German-born U.S. politician and diplomat

Quotations about Kissinger

1 Kissinger brought peace to Vietnam the same way Napoleon brought peace to Europe: by losing.

Joseph Heller (1923–99) U.S. novelist. Referring to Henry Kissinger and Napoleon I. *Good as Gold* (1979), ch. 7

2 Satire died the day they gave Henry Kissinger the Nobel Peace Prize. There were no jokes left after that.
Tom Lehrer (b.1928) U.S. mathematician and songwriter. *Daily Telegraph*, London (April 28, 1998)

Quotations by Kissinger

3 We have no intention of buying an illusory tranquillity at the expense of our friends. The United States will never knowingly sacrifice the interests of others. But the perception of common interests is not automatic; it requires constant redefinition.
Speech, New York City (April 23, 1971)

4 The pursuit of peace must...begin with the pragmatic concept of existence—especially in a period of ideological conflict.
Speech, Washington, D.C. (October 8, 1973)

5 History is the memory of states.
A World Restored: Castlereagh, Metternich and the Restoration of Peace, 1812–1822 (1957)

6 The lessons of historical experience, as of personal experience, are contingent. They teach the consequences of certain actions, but they cannot force a recognition of comparable situations.
A World Restored: Castlereagh, Metternich and the Restoration of Peace, 1812–1822 (1957)

7 The conventional army loses if it does not win. The guerrilla wins if he does not lose.
"The Vietnam Negotiations," *Foreign Affairs* (January 1969), ch. 13

8 The art of government is to deal with threats before they become overwhelming.
Meet the Press, NBC television (July 31, 1988)

9 China remains too important for America's national security to risk the relationship on the emotions of the moment...No government in the world would have tolerated having the main square of its capital occupied by tens of thousands of demonstrators.
Referring to the massacre in Tiananmen Square, Beijing, China (June 1989). *New York Times* (August 20, 1989)

10 Power is the ultimate aphrodisiac.
Sometimes quoted as "Power is the great aphrodisiac." *New York Times* (January 19, 1971)

11 Moderation is a virtue only in those who are thought to have an alternative.
Observer, London (January 24, 1982)

12 The nice thing about being a celebrity is that when you bore people, they think it's their fault.
Reader's Digest (April 1985)

13 We are all the President's men.
Said with reference to the invasion of Cambodia (1970). *Sunday Times Magazine*, London (May 4, 1975)

14 The capacity to admire others is not my most fully developed trait.
The White House Years (1979)

15 Even a paranoid can have enemies.
Time (January 24, 1977)

16 Baseball is the most intellectual game because most of the action goes on in your head.
Attrib.

17 I want to thank you for stopping the applause. It is impossible for me to look humble for any period of time.
Attrib.

Kitchin, Robert U.S. author and academic

1 Cyberspace does allow people to freely communicate with everybody else who is on-line...but it is largely owned and controlled by transnational corporations and regulated within current government policies.
Cyberspace (1998)

Klein, Allen U.S. music business manager and lawyer

1 It's a game, for Chrissakes, and winning is everything. It's a shame it has to get nasty sometimes.
1971. Referring to his business dealings with The Beatles. Quoted in "Don't Play Golf with Richard Branson," *Expensive Habits: the Dark Side of the Music Industry* (Simon Garfield; 1986)

Klein, Calvin (Calvin Richard Klein; b.1942) U.S. fashion designer

1 What should I do? Show the underwear on a clothesline? I'm going to put it on the most beautiful body I can find.
Referring to the controversy over his revealing underwear advertisements. *New York Times* (April 19, 1986)

2 I look upon advertising as my statement about my work. When Vogue comes in and borrows my clothes, and chooses the photographer and the model and the location, that's Vogue's statement about Calvin Klein, not Calvin Klein's statement.
Quoted in *The Fashion Conspiracy* (Nicholas Coleridge; 1989)

3 In America possibilities always exist. It's always out there if you really want it, and have the talent and are prepared for the hard work. Then any new designer can achieve something far greater than I've achieved or Ralph Lauren or anyone else.
Quoted in *The Fashion Conspiracy* (Nicholas Coleridge; 1989)

Klein, Melanie (1882–1960) Austrian psychoanalyst

1 In the analysis of the effects of early disturbances on the whole development lies, I believe, our greatest hope of helping our patients.
"A Study of Envy and Gratitude" (1956), quoted in *The Selected Melanie Klein* (Juliet Mitchell, ed.; 1986)

2 Smashing things, tearing them up, using the tongs as a sword—these represent the other weapons of the child's primary sadism, which employs his teeth, nails, muscles, and so on.
"Infantile Anxiety Situations" (1929), quoted in *The Selected Melanie Klein* (Juliet Mitchell, ed.; 1986)

3 In normal mourning early psychotic anxieties are reactivated; the mourner is in fact ill, but, because this state of mind is so common and seems so natural to us, we do not call mourning an illness.
"Mourning and Manic-Depressive States" (1940), quoted in *The Selected Melanie Klein* (Juliet Mitchell, ed.; 1986)

4 The greatest danger for the mourner comes from the turning of his hatred against the lost loved person himself. One of the

ways in which hatred expresses itself in the situation of mourning is in feelings of triumph over the dead person.
"Mourning and Manic-Depressive States" (1940), quoted in *The Selected Melanie Klein* (Juliet Mitchell, ed.; 1986)

5 The impulse to control other people is...an essential element in obsessional neurosis. The need to control others can to some extent be explained by a deflected drive to control parts of the self.
"Notes on Some Schizoid Mechanisms" (1946), quoted in *The Selected Melanie Klein* (Juliet Mitchell, ed.; 1986)

6 Reaction to psychoanalysis is different in early childhood from what it is later. We are often surprised at the facility with which *for the time being* our interpretations are accepted: sometimes children even express considerable pleasure in them.
"Psychological Principles of Infant Analysis" (1926), quoted in *The Selected Melanie Klein* (Juliet Mitchell, ed.; 1986)

7 In children schizophrenia is less obvious and striking than in adults. Traits which are characteristic of this disease are less noticeable in a child because, in a lesser degree, they are natural in the development of normal children.
"The Importance of Symbol Formation in the Development of the Ego" (1930), quoted in *The Selected Melanie Klein* (Juliet Mitchell, ed.; 1986)

8 In fantasy the excreta are transformed into dangerous weapons: wetting is regarded as cutting, stabbing, burning, drowning, while the fecal mass is equated with weapons and missiles.
"The Importance of Symbol Formation in the Development of the Ego" (1930), quoted in *The Selected Melanie Klein* (Juliet Mitchell, ed.; 1986)

9 He...threw them about the room saying: "We always smash our Christmas presents straight away; we don't want any." Smashing his toys thus stood in his unconscious for smashing his father's genitals. During this first hour he did in fact break several toys.
"The Psycho-Analytic Play Technique" (1955), quoted in *The Selected Melanie Klein* (Juliet Mitchell, ed.; 1986)

10 In paranoia the characteristic defenses are chiefly aimed at annihilating the "persecutors," while anxiety on the ego's account occupies a prominent place in the picture.
"The Psychogenesis of Manic-Depressive States" (1935), quoted in *The Selected Melanie Klein* (Juliet Mitchell, ed.; 1986)

Klein, Yves (1928–62) French painter

1 Color is sensibility turned into matter, matter in its primordial state.
"My Position in the Battle between Line and Color" (1958), quoted in *Yves Klein* (Sidra Dtich; 1995)

2 Through color I feel a total identification with space; I am truly free.
"My Position in the Battle between Line and Color" (1958), quoted in *Yves Klein* (Sidra Dtich; 1995)

Kleiner, Art U.S. editor and journalist

1 Modern heretics are not burned at the stake. They are relegated to backwaters or pressured to resign.
The Age of Heretics (1996)

Kleist, Heinrich von (Bernd Heinrich Wilhelm von Kleist; 1777–1811) German dramatist

1 Oh how infirm man is, you Gods.
1808. *Penthesilea* (M. Greenberg, tr.; 1988), Scene 24

Kline, Franz (Franz Josef Kline; 1910–62) U.S. painter

1 Immediacy can be accomplished in a picture that's been worked on for a long time just as well as if it's been done rapidly, you see. But I don't find that any of these things prove anything really.
Quoted in "An Interview with Franz Kline," *Living Arts* (David Sylvester; 1963)

2 I rather feel that painting is a form of drawing and the painting that I like has a form of drawing to it. I don't see how it could be disassociated from the nature of drawing.
Quoted in "An Interview with Franz Kline," *Living Arts* (David Sylvester; 1963)

Kline, Morris (1908–92) U.S. mathematician

1 Universities hire professors the way some men choose wives—they want the ones the others will admire.
Why the Professor Can't Teach (1977)

2 Logic is the art of going wrong with confidence.
Quoted in *Mathematical Maxims and Minims* (N. Rose; 1988)

3 Statistics: the mathematical theory of ignorance.
Quoted in *Mathematical Maxims and Minims* (N. Rose; 1988)

Kline, Nancy U.S. author

1 A manager's ability to turn meetings into a thinking environment is probably an organization's greatest asset.
Time to Think (1999)

2 Diversity raises the intelligence of groups.
Time to Think (1999)

3 Even in a hierarchy people can be equal as thinkers.
Time to Think (1999)

4 Homogeneity is a form of denial...because diversity, the differences between groups, is still the excuse for discrimination, disempowerment and even genocide. We have been taught to hate or deny our differences rather than to welcome them.
Time to Think (1999)

5 Synergy takes place best in structure.
Time to Think (1999)

6 Teams are now the primary force of organizations. They are worth cultivating at their core. Their core is the *mind* of each team member.
Time to Think (1999)

7 The quality of your attention determines the quality of other people's thinking.
Time to Think (1999)

8 To take time to think is to gain time to live.
Time to Think (1999)

9 Withholding information from someone is an act of intellectual

imperialism. Not bothering to seek accurate information is an act of intellectual recklessness.
Time to Think (1999)

Kline, Stephen U.S. economist

1 Each market need entering the innovation cycle leads in time to a new design, and every successful new design, in time, leads to new market conditions.
Quoted in *Evolutionary Innovations* (Maureen D. McKelvey; 1996)

Klinger, Friedrich Maximilian von (1752–1831) German playwright and novelist

1 Storm and Stress
Play title which was adopted as the name for a German literary movement of the late 18th century. (1777)

Knight, Frank Hyneman (1885–1972) U.S. economist

1 I have been...moved to wonder whether my job is a job or a racket, whether economists....may not be in the position that Cicero...ascribed to the augurs of Rome—that they should cover their faces or burst into laughter when they met on the street.
Essays on the History and Method of Economics (1956)

2 Costs merely register competing attractions.
Risk, Uncertainty and Profit (1971)

3 The businessman has the same fundamental psychology as the artist, inventor, or statesman. He has set himself at a certain work and the work absorbs and becomes himself. It is the expression of his personality; he lives in its growth and perfection according to his plans.
Risk, Uncertainty and Profit (1971)

4 The fact that so many opportunities for the profitable investment of resources in the development of human potentialities are neglected, and so many wasteful investments of the same kind made, is perhaps one of the most serious criticisms of existing society.
Risk, Uncertainty and Profit (1971)

5 To find men capable of managing business efficiently and secure to them the positions of responsible control is perhaps the most important single problem of economic organization on the efficiency scale.
Risk, Uncertainty and Profit (1971)

6 Sociology is the science of talk, and there is only one law in sociology. Bad talk drives out good.
Quoted in *The Samuelson Sampler* (Paul A. Samuelson; 1973)

Knopf, Alfred A. (1892–1984) U.S. publisher

1 Gone today, here tomorrow.
Referring to the publishing industry's readiness to allow stores to return unsold books. Attrib.

Knox, John (1513?–72) Scottish religious reformer

Quotations about Knox

1 Here lies he who neither feared nor flattered any flesh.
November 26, 1572

James Douglas (1516?–81) Scottish nobleman. Said of John Knox at his funeral. Quoted in *The Life of John Knox* (George R. Preedy; 1940), ch. 7

Quotations by Knox

2 A man with God is always in the majority.
Inscription on Reformation monument, Geneva, Switzerland (16th century)

3 To promote a Woman to bear rule, superiority, dominion or empire, above any Realm, Nation, or City, is repugnant to Nature; contumely to God, a thing most contrarious to his revealed will and approved ordinance, and finally it is the subversion of good Order, of all equity and justice.
The opening words of the pamphlet. *The First Blast of the Trumpet Against the Monstrous Regiment of Women* (1558)

Knox, Ronald, Right Reverend Monsignor (Ronald Arbuthnott Knox; 1888–1957) British priest and writer

1 It is so stupid of modern civilization to have given up believing in the devil when he is the only explanation of it.
Let Dons Delight (1939)

2 The baby doesn't understand English and the Devil knows Latin.
Said when asked to conduct a baptism service in English. Quoted in *The Life of Ronald Knox* (Evelyn Waugh; 1962), pt. I, ch. 5

3 A loud noise at one end and no sense of responsibility at the other.
Definition of a baby. Attrib.

4 There once was a man who said, "God
Must think it exceedingly odd,
If he find that this tree
Continues to be
When there's no one about in the Quad."
Referring to Bishop Berkeley's axiom: *Esse est Percipi* (To be is to be perceived). Attrib.

Knox, Vicesimus (1752–1821) British writer

1 Can anything be more absurd than keeping women in a state of ignorance, and yet so vehemently to insist on their resisting temptation?
"On the Literary Education of Women," *Liberal Education* (1792), vol. 1

Koch, Ed (Edward Irving Koch; b.1924) U.S. lawyer and politician

1 If you turn your back on these people, you yourself are an animal. You may be a well-dressed animal, but you are nevertheless an animal.
Referring to people with AIDS. State of the City Address, New York City (March 16, 1987)

Koehler, Ted (1894–1973) U.S. lyricist

1 Stormy weather,
Since my man and I ain't together.
Song lyric. "Stormy Weather" (music by Harold Arlen; 1933)

Koestler, Arthur (1905–83) Hungarian-born British writer and journalist

1 In my youth I regarded the universe as an open book, printed in the language of physical equations, whereas now it appears to me as a text written in invisible ink, of which in our rare

moments of grace we are able to decipher a small fragment.
Bricks to Babel (1980), epilogue

2 One may not regard the world as a sort of metaphysical brothel for emotions.
Darkness at Noon (Daphne Hardy, tr.; 1940)

3 If the creator had a purpose in equipping us with a neck, he surely meant us to stick it out.
Encounter (May 1970)

4 The most persistent sound which reverberates through men's history is the beating of war drums.
Janus: A Summing Up (1978), Prologue

5 Einstein's space is no closer to reality than Van Gogh's sky.
The Act of Creation (1964), pt. 2, ch. 10

6 God seems to have left the receiver off the hook, and time is running out.
The Ghost in the Machine (1967), ch. 18

7 Two half-truths do not make a truth, and two half-cultures do not make a culture.
The Ghost in the Machine (1967), Preface

8 Hitherto man had to live with the idea of death as an individual; from now onward mankind will have to live with the idea of its death as a species.
Referring to the development of the atomic bomb. Attrib.

Koffka, Kurt (1886–1941) German-born U.S. psychologist

1 Far from being compelled to banish concepts like meaning and value from psychology and science in general, we must use these concepts for a full understanding of the mind and the world.
Referring to the theory of Gestalt. Attrib.

Kohl, Helmut (b.1930) German statesman

1 Only through resolute commitment to the realization of European unification can we obviate a relapse into the destructive nationalism of the past.
Speech to the Bundestag, Bonn (June 17, 1992)

2 Only peace will emanate from German soil in future.
Following the unification of Germany and referring to Germany's role in two world wars. *Daily Telegraph*, London (December 29, 1990)

3 Germany is our fatherland, the united Europe our future.
On the unification of Germany. *Times*, London (October 1990)

4 The Germans, who are now coming together in the spirit of freedom, will never pose a threat. Rather will they, I am convinced, be an asset to a Europe which is growing more and more together.
1989. Quoted in *When the Wall Came Down* (Harold James and Marla Stone, eds.; 1992)

Kolb, Barbara (b.1939) U.S. composer

1 Composing a piece of music is very feminine. It is sensitive, emotional, contemplative. By comparison, doing housework is positively masculine.
Attrib.

Kollwitz, Käthe (originally Käthe Schmidt; 1867–1945) German artist

1 Although my leaning towards the male sex was dominant, I also felt frequently drawn towards my own sex. In fact I believe that bisexuality is almost a necessary factor in artistic production.
Diaries and Letters (1942)

2 I do not want to die...until I have faithfully made the most of my talent and cultivated the seed that was placed in me until the last small twig has grown.
Diaries and Letters (February 15, 1915)

3 Where do all the women who have watched so carefully over the lives of their beloved ones get the heroism to send them to face the cannon?
Diaries and Letters (August 27, 1914)

Komachi (834–880) Japanese poet

1 Alas! the colours of the flowers
Have faded in the long continued rain;
My beauty ageing, too, as in this world
I gazed, engrossed, on things that were but vain.
"The Colours of Flowers" (9th century)

2 So lonely am I
My body is a floating weed
Severed at the roots.
Were there water to entice me,
I would follow it, I think.
Kokinshu (10th century), quoted in *Anthology of Japanese Literature* (Donald Keene, ed.; 1968)

Komisar, Lucy (b.1942) U.S. writer

1 Advertising...legitimizes the idealized, stereotyped roles of women as temptress, wife, mother, and sex object.
Women in Sexist Society (1971)

Konchalovsky, Andrei (Andrei Sergeyevich Mikhalkov-Konchalovsky; b.1937) Russian-born film director

1 Hollywood is a corporate mentality—like Socialist mentality. All the people are paid to say no. Very few to say yes. Because if you say yes and you're wrong—you're fired.
Knave (October 1986), quoted in *Chambers Film Quotes* (Tony Crawley, ed.; 1991)

Koran

1 In the name of God, Most Gracious, Most Merciful.
Praise be to God, The Cherisher and Sustainer of the Worlds;
Most Gracious, Most Merciful;
Master of the Day of Judgment.
Thee do we worship, and Thine aid we seek.
Show us the straight way,
The way of those on whom Thou hast bestowed Thy Grace,
Those whose (portion) is not wrath, and who go not astray.
7th century. The Fatiha, or opening verses, of the Koran, the Holy Book of Islam. Recited as part of every prayer and on many other occasions, it is incumbent upon every Muslim to memorize the Fatiha in Arabic. The Koran records revelations made by Allah to Muhammad. A definitive version was set down during the reign of the Caliph Uthman (644–656). *Koran* (A. Yusuf Ali, tr.; 1934), Sura 1

2 But the Jews will not be pleased with thee, neither the Christians, until thou follow their religion; say, The Direction of God is the true direction. And verily if thou follow their desires, after the knowledge which hath been given thee, thou shalt find no patron or protector against God.
Koran (7th century), Sura 2

3 The Infidels...will ask thee concerning the sacred month, whether they may war therein: Answer, To war therein is grievous; but to obstruct the way of God, and infidelity towards him, and to keep men from the holy temple, and to drive out his people from thence, is more grievous in the sight of God.
Koran (7th century), Sura 2

4 The month of Ramadan shall ye fast, in which the Koran was sent down from heaven, a direction unto men, and declarations of direction, and the distinction between good and evil.
Koran (7th century), Sura 2

5 Say ye: "We believe in God and the revelation given to us and
To Abraham, Ismail, Isaac
Jacob, and the tribes, and that given to Moses
and Jesus, and that give to (all) Prophets from their Lord: We make no difference
Between one and another of them: and we bow to God."
7th century. Summing up the belief in one God and that the basis of Islam is the message taught by the prophets listed and their scriptures. *Koran* (A. Yusuf Ali, tr.; 1934), Sura 2, v. 136

6 It is not righteousness that ye turn your faces
Towards East or West;
But it is righteousness to believe in God
And the Last Day and the Angels and the Book,
And the Messengers;
To spend of your substance out of love for Him for your kin and the orphans, for the needy,
For the wayfarer, for those who ask, and for the ransom of slaves
To be steadfast in prayer and practice regular charity.
7th century. Warning against the practise of the external forms of religion without real virtue and belief. *Koran* (A. Yusuf Ali, tr.; 1934), Sura 2, v. 177

7 Fighting is obligatory for you, much as you dislike it. But you may hate a thing although it is good for you, and love a thing although it is bad for you. Allah knows, but you do not.
The Koran (7th century), Sura 2, v. 216

8 God! There is no god but he
— the Living, the Self-Subsisting, Eternal
No slumber can seize Him, nor sleep
His are all things in the heavens and on earth.
Who is there can intercede in his presence except as he permitteth?
He knoweth what appeareth to His creatures as before or
After or Behind them
Nor shall they compass aught of his knowledge except as He willeth.
His throne doth extend over the heavens and the earth,
And he feeleth no fatigue in guarding and preserving them.
7th century. One of the most famous verses of the Koran, the Ayat al-Kursi ("Verse of the throne"), it includes the most fundamental tenet of Islam, that there is no god but God. *Koran* (A. Yusuf Ali, tr.; 1934), Sura 2, v. 255

9 O ye who believe!
Cancel not your charity by reminders of your generosity.
7th century. *Koran* (A. Yusuf Ali, tr.; 1934), Sura 2, v. 264

10 On no soul doth God place a burden greater than it can bear.
...Our Lord,! Lay not on us a burden greater than we can bear.
Blot out our sins
and grant us forgiveness.
Have mercy on us.
Thou art our Protector
Help us against those who stand against Faith.
7th century. Closing lines of the longest chapter (sura) of the Koran. *Koran* (A. Yusuf Ali, tr.; 1934), Sura 2, v. 286

11 They plotted and Allah plotted. Allah is the supreme Plotter.
Referring to those people opposed to Jesus Christ, who is regarded as a prophet by Muslims. *The Koran* (7th century), Sura 3, l. 54

12 Men are the protectors and maintainers of women
because God has given the one more strength than the other
and because they support them from their means.
Koran (7th century), Sura 4, v. 34

13 Ye are forbidden to eat that which dieth of itself, and blood, and swine's flesh, and that on which the name of any besides God hath been invocated; and that which hath been strangled, or killed by a blow, or by a fall, or by the horns of another beast, and that which hath been eaten by a wild beast, except what ye shall kill yourselves; and that which hath been sacrificed unto idols.
Koran (7th century), Sura 5

14 Children of Allah, dress well when you attend your mosques. Eat and drink, but avoid excess. He does not love the intemperate.
The Koran (7th century), Sura 7, l. 31

15 Then We sent forth Moses and Aaron with our signs to Pharaoh and his nobles. But they rejected them with scorn, for they were wicked men. When Our truth was shown to them they said: "This is plain magic." Moses replied: "Do you call the truth magic? Magicians never prosper."
The Koran (7th century), Sura 10, ll. 76–78

16 God changes not what is in a people, until they change what is in themselves.
Koran (7th century), Sura 13, v. 11

17 Do you not see that Allah has created the heavens and the earth with truth? He can destroy you if He wills and bring into being a new creation: that is no difficult thing for Him.
The Koran (7th century), Sura 14, ll. 19–20

18 If we opened for the unbelievers a gate in heaven and they ascended through it higher and higher, still they would say: "Our eyes were dazzled: truly, we must have been bewitched."
The Koran (7th century), Sura 15, ll. 14–15

19 We created man from dry clay, from black moulded loam, and before him Satan from smokeless fire.
The Koran (7th century), Sura 15, ll. 26–27

20 Walk not on the earth exultantly, for thou canst not cleave the earth, neither shalt thou reach to the mountains in height.
Koran (7th century), Sura 17, v. 37

21 Wealth and children are the ornaments of this life. But deeds

of lasting merit are better rewarded by your Lord and hold for you a greater hope of salvation.
The Koran (7th century), Sura 18, l. 47

22 Man is exceedingly contentious.
The Koran (7th century), Sura 18, l. 55

23 Those who say: "The Lord of Mercy has begotten a son" preach a monstrous falsehood, at which the very heavens might crack, the earth break asunder, and the mountains crumble to dust. That they should ascribe a son to the Merciful, when it does not become Him to beget one!
Referring to the belief that Jesus Christ is the son of God. *The Koran* (7th century), Sura 19, ll. 88–92

24 On that day We shall roll up the heaven like a scroll of parchment. As we first created man, so will We bring him back to life.
Referring to the resurrection of human life after the world has been brought to an end. *The Koran* (7th century), Sura 21, l. 104

25 Yet men have divided themselves into different sects, each rejoicing in its own doctrines. Leave them in their error until death overtakes them.
The Koran (7th century), Sura 23

26 Blessed are the believers, who are humble in their prayers; who avoid profane talk, and give alms to the destitute; who restrain their carnal desires (except with their wives and slave-girls, for these are lawful to them).
The Koran (7th century), Sura 23, ll. 1–6

27 Marry those who are single among you, and such as are honest of your men-servants and your maid-servants: if they be poor, God will enrich them of his abundance; for God is bounteous and wise.
Koran (7th century), Sura 24

28 O ye who believe! Enter not houses
other than your own
until ye have asked permission and saluted those in them.
7th century. *Koran* (A. Yusuf Ali, tr.; 1934), Sura 24

29 The whore, and the whoremonger, shall ye scourge with a hundred stripes.
Koran (7th century), Sura 24

30 Poets are followed by none save erring men. Behold how aimlessly they rove in every valley, preaching what they never practise. Not so the true believers who do good works and remember Allah and defend themselves when attacked.
The Koran (7th century), Sura 26, ll. 224–227

31 We have taught Mohammed no poetry, nor does it become him to be a poet.
The Koran (7th century), Sura 36, l. 68

32 None but the unbelievers dispute the revelations of Allah. Do not be deceived by their prosperous dealings in the land.
The Koran (7th century), Sura 40, l. 4

33 Jesus was no more than a mortal whom We favoured and made an example to the Israelites...He is a portent of the Hour of Doom. Have no doubt about its coming and follow me.
The Koran (7th century), Sura 43, ll. 59–61

34 We gave the Scriptures to the Israelites and bestowed on them wisdom and prophethood...We gave them their plain commandments: yet it was not till knowledge had been vouchsafed them that they disagreed among themselves from evil motives.
The Koran (7th century), Sura 45, ll. 16–17

35 They say: "There is this life and no other. We live and die; nothing but time destroys us." Surely of this they have no knowledge. They are merely guessing.
The Koran (7th century), Sura 45, ll. 24

36 We created you
From a single (pair) of a male and a female
And made you into tribes
that ye may know each other (not that ye may despise each other)
Verily the most honoured of you
In the sight of God is (he who is) the most righteous of you.
7th century. *Koran* (A. Yusuf Ali, tr.; 1934), Sura 49, v. 13

37 They shall recline on jewelled couches face to face, and there shall wait on them immortal youths with...a cup of purest wine...with fruits of their own choice and flesh of fowls that they relish. And theirs shall be the dark-eyed houris, chaste as hidden pearls.
Referring to the afterlife of true believers of Islam. *The Koran* (7th century), Sura 55, ll. 15–24

38 Those to whom the burden of the Torah was entrusted and yet refused to bear it are like a donkey laden with books. Wretched is the example of those who deny Allah's revelations.
Referring to the afterlife of true believers of Islam. *The Koran* (7th century), Sura 62, l. 5

39 Suffer the women whom ye divorce to dwell in some part of the houses wherein ye dwell; according to the room and conveniences of the habitations which ye possess; and make them not uneasy, that ye may reduce them to straits.
Koran (7th century), Sura 65

40 Let man reflect on the food he eats: how We pour down the rain in torrents and cleave the earth asunder; how We bring forth the corn, the grapes, and the fresh vegetation; the olive and the palm, the thickets, the fruit-trees and the green pasture, for you and for your cattle to delight in.
The Koran (7th century), Sura 70, ll. 19–21

41 Indeed, man was created impatient. When evil befalls him he is despondent; but blessed with good fortune he grows niggardly.
The Koran (7th century), Sura 70, ll. 19–21

42 When the sky is rent asunder; when the stars scatter and the oceans roll together; when the graves are hurled about; each soul shall know what it has done and what it has failed to do.
The Koran (7th century), Sura 82, ll. 1–5

43 Verily the life to come shall be better for thee than this present life: and thy Lord shall give thee a reward wherewith thou shalt be well pleased. Did he not find thee an orphan, and hath he not taken care of thee? And did he not find thee wandering in error, and hath he not guided thee into the truth?
Koran (7th century), Sura 93

44 Read! In the name of thy Lord

Who created
Created man out of a clot of blood
Read! And thy Lord is Most Bountiful
He who taught the use of the Pen
Taught man that which he knew not.
7th century. The first revelation that came to the prophet Mohammed. In the cave of Hira, near Mecca, the Angel Gabriel appeared to him with these words, exhorting him to preach the word of God. *Koran* (A. Yusuf Ali, tr.; 1934), Sura 96, ll. 1–5

Korda, Alexander, Sir (Sándor Lászlo Kellner; 1893–1956) Hungarian-born British film director and producer

1 It's not enough to be Hungarian, you must have talent too.
Quoted in *Alexander Korda* (K. Kulik; 1975)

Kosinski, Jerzy (Jerzy Nikodem Kosinski; 1933–91) Polish-born U.S. novelist

1 I rent everything, other than the gift of life itself, which was given to me without any predictable lease, a gift that can be withdrawn at any time.
Interview, *Guardian*, London (May 25, 1991)

Kosuth, Joseph (b.1945) U.S. conceptual artist

1 Being an artist now means to question the nature of art. If one is questioning the nature of painting, one cannot be not questioning the nature of art. If an artist accepts painting (or sculpture) he is accepting the tradition that goes with it.
Quoted in *Arte Povera* (Germano Celant; 1968)

Kotler, Philip (b.1931) U.S. author and educator

1 Companies pay too much attention to the cost of doing something. They should worry more about the cost of not doing it.
Quoted in *Key Management Principles* (Stuart Crainer; 1996)

Kotter, John P. (John Paul Kotter; b.1947) U.S. academic

1 An industry with a low level of competitiveness can be a sanctuary from tough times for a while, but never long term.
The New Rules (1995)

2 Anyone in a large organization who thinks major change is impossible should probably get out.
The New Rules (1995)

3 Bureaucratic and risk-averse environments are career killers because of their impact on learning.
The New Rules (1995)

4 Ethical traps are more common now than a generation ago...In a volatile world, it is easy to step over moral boundaries.
The New Rules (1995)

5 The goal of a big business person should be to create a new organization that feels and operates like a smaller business, yet retains the resource advantages of big business.
The New Rules (1995)

6 The number one impediment to cultural change in large organizations is a lack of urgency fostered by too much historical success.
The New Rules (1995)

Kotzebue, August Friedrich Ferdinand von (1761–1819) German playwright

1 There is another and a better world.
1790. *The Stranger* (N. Schink, tr.; 1798), Act 1, Scene 1

Kounellis, Jannis (b.1936) Greek-born Italian multimedia artist

1 Conceptual art is another kind of artistic style. And style blocks any attempt at revolutionary thinking and activity.
Quoted in "Structure and Sensibility: An interview with Jannis Kounellis," *Avalanche* (Willoughby Sharp; Summer 1972), no. 5

Koussevitzky, Serge (Sergei Alexandrovitch Koussevitsky; 1874–1951) Russian-born U.S. conductor, composer, and musician

1 When my stick touches the air, you play.
Attrib.

Kovacs, Ernie (1919–62) U.S. entertainer

1 A medium, so called because it is neither rare nor well done.
Referring to television. Attrib.

Kovel, Joel (b.1936) U.S. psychiatrist

1 Is it not true that defining life's problems in psycho-therapeutic categories has ill served those who suffer from real loss of power? In particular, has not more harm than good been done to women, whose legitimate struggles were redefined and undercut by the male-dominated institution of therapy?
A Complete Guide to Therapy (1976)

Kozyrev, Andrey Vladimirovich (b.1951) Russian politician

1 It is one thing if a small poodle tries to walk through these gates but quite another matter when an elephant like Russia tries to do the same thing.
Referring to the NATO Partnership for Peace agreement. *Observer*, London (June 26, 1994), "Sayings of the Week"

Kramer, Larry (b.1935) U.S. playwright

1 We're all going to go crazy, living this epidemic every minute, while the rest of the world goes on out there, all around us, as if nothing is happening...We're living through war, but where they're living it's peacetime, and we're all in the same country.
The Normal Heart (1985)

Kraus, Karl (1874–1936) Austrian writer

1 Diplomacy is a game of chess in which the nations are checkmated.
1918. Quoted in *Karl Kraus* (Harry Zohn; 1971)

2 I master the language of others. Mine does what it wants with me.
1918. Quoted in *Karl Kraus* (Harry Zohn; 1971)

3 Psychoanalysts are father confessors who like to listen to the sins of the fathers as well.
1918. Quoted in *Karl Kraus* (Harry Zohn; 1971)

4 The development of technology will leave only one problem: the infirmity of human nature.
1918. Quoted in *Karl Kraus* (Harry Zohn; 1971)

5 Through my satire I make little people so big that afterwards they are worthy objects of my satire and no one can reproach me any longer.
1918. Quoted in *Karl Kraus* (Harry Zohn; 1971)

6 War is, at first, the hope that one will be better off; then, the expectation that the other fellow will be worse off; then, the satisfaction that he isn't any better off; and finally, the surprise at everyone's being worse off.
1918. Quoted in *Karl Kraus* (Harry Zohn; 1971)

7 A journalist is stimulated by a deadline. He writes worse when he has time.
1912. Quoted in "Pro domo et mundo," *Karl Kraus* (Harry Zohn; 1971)

8 A linguistic work translated into another language is like someone going across the border without his skin and putting on the local garb on the other side.
1912. Quoted in "Pro domo et mundo," *Karl Kraus* (Harry Zohn; 1971)

9 I am not for women but against men.
1912. Quoted in "Pro domo et mundo," *Karl Kraus* (Harry Zohn; 1971)

10 The making of a journalist: no ideas and the ability to express them.
1912. Quoted in "Pro domo et mundo," *Karl Kraus* (Harry Zohn; 1971)

11 A good stylist should have a narcissistic enjoyment as he works. He must be able to objectivize his work to such an extent that he catches himself feeling envious...In short, he must display that highest degree of objectivity which the world calls vanity.
1909. Quoted in "Sprüche und Widersprüche," *Karl Kraus* (Harry Zohn; 1971)

12 A woman whose sensuality never ceases and a man who constantly has ideas: two human ideals which mankind regards as sick.
1909. Quoted in "Sprüche und Widersprüche," *Karl Kraus* (Harry Zohn; 1971)

13 In the beginning was the review copy, and a man received it from the publisher. Then he wrote a review. Then he wrote a book which the publisher accepted and sent on to someone else as a review copy. The man who received it did likewise. This is how modern literature came into being.
1909. Quoted in "Sprüche und Widersprüche," *Karl Kraus* (Harry Zohn; 1971)

14 It is better not to express what one means than to express what one does not mean.
1909. Quoted in "Sprüche und Widersprüche," *Karl Kraus* (Harry Zohn; 1971)

15 It is not easy to get a truly and constantly productive spirit to read. He is to a reader as a locomotive is to a tourist. Also, one does not ask a tree how it likes the scenery.
1909. Quoted in "Sprüche und Widersprüche," *Karl Kraus* (Harry Zohn; 1971)

16 Moral responsibility is what is lacking in a man when he demands it of a woman.
1909. Quoted in "Sprüche und Widersprüche," *Karl Kraus* (Harry Zohn; 1971)

17 Nothing is more narrow-minded than chauvinism or race hatred. To me all men are equal: there are jackasses everywhere, and I have the same contempt for all. No petty prejudices.
1909. Quoted in "Sprüche und Widersprüche," *Karl Kraus* (Harry Zohn; 1971)

18 People don't understand German. But I can tell things to them in journalese.
1909. Quoted in "Sprüche und Widersprüche," *Karl Kraus* (Harry Zohn; 1971)

19 The most incomprehensible talk comes from people who have no other use for language than to make themselves understood.
1909. Quoted in "Sprüche und Widersprüche," *Karl Kraus* (Harry Zohn; 1971)

20 There are writers who can express in as little as twenty pages what I occasionally need as many as two for.
1909. Quoted in "Sprüche und Widersprüche," *Karl Kraus* (Harry Zohn; 1971)

21 The triumph of morality: A thief who has broken into a bedroom claims his sense of shame has been outraged, and by threatening the occupants with exposure of an immoral act he blackmails them into not bringing charges for burglary.
1909. Quoted in "Sprüche und Widersprüche," *Karl Kraus* (Harry Zohn; 1971)

22 The world is a prison in which solitary confinement is preferable.
1909. Quoted in "Sprüche und Widersprüche," *Karl Kraus* (Harry Zohn; 1971)

23 Truth is a clumsy servant that breaks the dishes while cleaning them.
1909. Quoted in "Sprüche und Widersprüche," *Karl Kraus* (Harry Zohn; 1971)

24 When there were no human rights, the exceptional individual had them. That was inhuman. Then equality was created by taking the human rights away from the exceptional individual.
1909. Quoted in "Sprüche und Widersprüche," *Karl Kraus* (Harry Zohn; 1971)

25 Lord, forgive them, for they know what they do!
1909. Ironic misquoting of Jesus Christ's words from the cross. Quoted in "Sprüche und Widersprüche," *Karl Kraus* (Harry Zohn; 1971)

26 He who lacks temperament must look for ornament.
Quoted in *The Jingle Bell Principle* (Miroslav Holub; 1992)

Krishnamurti, Jiddu (1895–1986) Indian theosophist

1 What canst thou know of happiness,
If in the vale of misery thou hast not walked?
What canst thou know of freedom,
If against bondage thou hast not cried aloud?
The Song of Life (1931), pt. 13, st. 2

2 Heaven and hell
Are words
To frighten thee to right action.
The Song of Life (1931), pt. 28, st. 3

3 Meditation is not a means to an end. It is both the means and the end.
Quoted in *The Penguin Krishnamurti Reader* (Mary Lutyens, ed.; 1970)

Kristofferson, Kris (b.1936) U.S. film actor and pop singer

1 Freedom's just another word for nothing left to lose,
And nothin' ain't worth nothin' but it's free.
Song, co-written with Fred Foster. "Me and Bobby McGee" (1969)

Kroc, Ray (Raymond Albert Kroc; 1902–84) U.S. restaurateur

1 It's ridiculous to call this an industry—it's not. This is rat eat rat, dog eat dog.
Referring to the fast food industry. Quoted in *Big Mac* (Maxwell Boas and Steve Chain; 1976)

2 In business for yourself, not by yourself.
Quoted in *McDonald's: Behind the Arches* (John F. Love; 1986)

3 I believe in God, family, and McDonald's and in the office, that order is reversed.
Ray Kroc was the founder and president of the McDonald's chain. Quoted in *McDonald's: Behind the Arches* (John F. Love; 1986)

4 Creativity is a highfalutin word for the work I have to do between now and Tuesday.
Attrib.

5 While formal schooling is an important advantage, it is not a guarantee of success nor is its absence a fatal handicap.
Attrib.

Kronecker, Leopold (1823–91) German mathematician

1 Number theorists are like lotus-eaters—having once tasted of this food they can never give it up
Quoted in *Mathematical Circles Squared* (H. Eves; 1972)

Kronenberger, Louis (1904–80) U.S. writer and critic

1 There seems to be a terrible misunderstanding on the part of a great many people to the effect that when you cease to believe you may cease to behave.
Company Manners (1954)

2 This is, I think, very much the Age of Anxiety, the age of the neurosis, because along with so much that weighs on our minds there is perhaps even more that grates on our nerves.
"The Spirit of the Age," *Company Manners* (1954)

3 The American Way is so restlessly creative as to be essentially destructive; the American Way is to carry common sense itself almost to the point of madness.
"Last Thoughts," *Company Matters* (1954)

4 It is disgusting to pick your teeth. What is vulgar is to use a gold toothpick.
The Cart and the Horse (1964)

Kruger, Barbara (b.1945) U.S. artist

1 I'm interested in *coupling* the ingratiation of wishful thinking with the criticality of knowing better. To use the device to get people to look at the picture, and then to displace the conventional meaning that the image usually carries.
Quoted in "Pictures and Words," *Arts* (June 1987)

Krugman, Paul (b.1953) U.S. economist

1 A world awash in information is one in which information has very little market value.
New York Times (September 29, 1996)

2 Downsizing suddenly became news because for the first time, white-collar, college-educated workers were being fired in large numbers, even while skilled machinists and other blue-collar workers were in demand.
New York Times (September 30, 1996), magazine

3 I don't think the pace of change has accelerated...We look at our changes and we say "Wow, aren't those spiffy?" and forget how incredible the changes were that went through the lives of our parents and our...great-grandparents.
Interview, *Strategy and Business* (1998)

4 We are a microelectronic-driven service economy, whereas our grandfathers lived in a diesel-driven manufacturing economy. Nonetheless...a depression looks pretty much the same.
Interview, *Strategy and Business* (1998)

5 Nothing disrupts global markets quite as well as submarines.
Referring to the effect of world wars on economics. Interview, *Strategy and Business* (1998)

6 I was 90% wrong...everybody else was 150% wrong.
Referring to predicting the 1990s Asian economic crisis. Interview, *Strategy and Business* (1998)

Krutch, Joseph Wood (1893–1970) U.S. essayist and naturalist

1 It is...sometimes easier to head an institute for the study of child guidance than it is to turn one brat into a decent human being.
"Whom Do We Picket Tonight?," *If You Don't Mind My Saying* (1964)

2 The impulse to mar and to destroy is as ancient and almost as nearly universal as the impulse to create. The one is an easier way than the other of demonstrating power.
The Best of Two Worlds (1950)

3 Being the inventor of sex would seem to be a sufficient distinction for a creature just barely large enough to be seen by the naked eye.
Referring to Volvox, a microscopic freshwater organism, indeterminately both plant and animal in its reproductive cycle. *The Great Chain of Life* (1957)

4 If only the fit survive and if the fitter they are the longer they survive, then Volvox must have demonstrated its superb fitness more conclusively than any higher animal ever has.
Volvox is a microscopic freshwater organism, indeterminately both plant and animal in its reproductive cycle. *The Great Chain of Life* (1957)

5 Surrendering its pretensions so far as any ability to establish truths of reference is concerned and proclaiming itself essentially an art rather than a science, Metaphysics, which promised so much, thus ends by confirming the very despair which it set out to combat.
The Modern Temper (1929)

6 The world of poetry, mythology, and religion represents the world as a man would like to have it, while science represents the world as he gradually comes to discover it.
The Modern Temper (1929)

7 The most serious charge which can be brought against New England is not Puritanism, but February.
"February," *The Twelve Seasons* (1949)

8 When a man wantonly destroys one of the works of man we call him a vandal. When he destroys one of the works of God we call him a sportsman.
Referring to hunting. Attrib.

Kübler-Ross, Elisabeth (b.1926) Swiss-born U.S. psychiatrist and author

1 There is no need to go to India or anywhere else to find peace. You will find that deep place of silence right in your room, your garden, or even your bathtub.
Speech (1976)

2 The more we are making advancements in science, the more we seem to fear and deny the reality of death.
On Death and Dying (1969), ch. 1

3 We have to ask ourselves whether medicine is to remain a humanitarian and respected profession or a new but depersonalized science in the service of prolonging life rather than diminishing human suffering.
On Death and Dying (1969), ch. 2

Kubrick, Stanley (1928–99) U.S. film director

1 The great nations have always acted like gangsters, and the small nations like prostitutes.
Guardian, London (June 5, 1963)

2 The very meaninglessness of life forces man to create his own meaning. If it can be written or thought, it can be filmed.
Halliwell's Filmgoer's and Video Viewer's Companion (1999)

Kuhn, Maggie (1905–95) U.S. social activist

1 The ultimate indignity is to be given a bedpan by a stranger who calls you by your first name.
Observer, London (August 20, 1978)

Kuhn, Thomas S. (Thomas Samuel Kuhn; 1922–96) U.S. philosopher and historian of science

1 There is no appropriate scale available with which to weigh the merits of alternative paradigms: they are incommensurable.
The Structure of Scientific Revolutions (1962)

Kulyk Keefer, Janice (b.1952) Canadian writer

1 Like Henry James, my mother has "the imagination of disaster"; in her eyes I could see the watery ghosts of the *Titanic*, *Lusitania*, *Andrea Doria* as she kissed me farewell.
"Aboard the *Alexander Pushkin*," *Worst Journeys* (1991)

Kumin, Maxine (originally Maxine Winokur; b.1925) U.S. poet and writer

1 In the county there are thirty-seven churches
and no butcher shop. This could be taken
as a matter of all form and no content.
"Living Alone with Jesus" (1975), ll. 10–12

Kundera, Milan (b.1929) Czech novelist

1 Culture is perishing in overproduction, in an avalanche of words, in the madness of quantity.
Immortality (1991)

2 Even stupidity is the product of highly organized matter.
Quoted in *Shedding Life* (Miroslav Holub; 1997)

Küng, Hans (b.1928) Swiss-born German priest and theologian

1 When a pope's theoretically infallible, doctrinal opinions are treated as infallible, authoritarian abuse of power begins.
Infallible? An Enquiry (1970)

Kunitz, Stanley (Stanley Jasspon Kunitz; b.1905) U.S. poet

1 In every house of marriage
there's room for an interpreter.
"Route Six" (1979)

2 That pack of scoundrels
tumbling through the gate
emerges
as the Order of the State.
"The System" (1971)

3 The thing that eats the heart is mostly heart.
Final line. "The Thing That Eats the Heart" (1958)

Kunze, Reiner (b.1933) German poet

1 In the center stands
mankind

Not
this man or that man.
"Ethics," *East German Poetry* (Michael Hamburger, ed.; 1972)

Kureishi, Hanif (b.1954) British writer and filmmaker

1 England has become a squalid, uncomfortable, ugly place...an intolerant, racist, homophobic, narrow-minded, authoritarian rat-hole run by vicious suburban-minded, materialistic philistines.
1988. Quoted in *A Queer Reader* (Patrick Higgins, ed.; 1993)

Kurosawa, Akira (1910–98) Japanese film director

1 In all my films, there's three or maybe four minutes of real cinema.
1987. Quoted in *Chambers Film Quotes* (Tony Crawley, ed.; 1991)

Kutuzov, Mikhail Ilarionovich, Prince of Smolansk (1745–1813) Russian field marshal

1 Napoleon is a torrent which as yet we are unable to stem. Moscow will be the sponge that will suck him dry.
Remark (September 13, 1812)

Kyd, Thomas (1558–94) English playwright

1 I am never better than when I am mad. Then methinks I am a brave fellow; then I do wonders. But reason abuseth me, and there's the torment, there's the hell.
The Spanish Tragedy (1592?), Act 3, Scene 7, l. 169

2 My son—and what's a son? A thing begot
Within a pair of minutes, thereabout,
A lump bred up in darkness
The Spanish Tragedy (1592?), Act 3, Scene 11; Additions, l. 5

3 For what's a play without a woman in it?
The Spanish Tragedy (1592?), Act 4, Scene 1, l. 96

Labé, Louise (originally Louise Charly, "La Belle Cordière"; 1524?–66) French poet

1 A woman's heart always has a burned mark.
Sonnet 2, *Oeuvres* (1555)

La Bruyère, Jean de (1645–96) French essayist and moralist

1 A long illness seems to be placed between life and death, in order to make death a comfort both to those who die and to those who remain.
Characters, or the Manners of the Age (1688)

2 A pious man is one who would be an atheist if the king were.
Characters, or the Manners of the Age (1688)

3 A slave has but one master; an ambitious man has as many masters as there are people who may be useful in bettering his position.
Characters, or the Manners of the Age (1688)

4 As long as men are liable to die and are desirous to live, a physician will be made fun of, but he will be well paid.
Characters, or the Manners of the Age (1688)

5 Everything has been said, and we are more than seven thousand years of human thought too late.
Characters, or the Manners of the Age (1688)

6 If poverty is the mother of crime, stupidity is its father.
Characters, or the Manners of the Age (1688)

7 If we heard it said of Orientals that they habitually drank a liquor which went to their heads, deprived them of reason, and made them vomit, we should say: "How very barbarous!"
Characters, or the Manners of the Age (1688)

8 Liberality lies less in giving liberally than in the timeliness of the gift.
Characters, or the Manners of the Age (1688)

9 One must laugh before one is happy, or one may die without ever laughing at all.
Characters, or the Manners of the Age (1688)

10 Party loyalty lowers the greatest of men to the petty level of the masses.
Characters, or the Manners of the Age (1688)

11 The doctors allow one to die, the charlatans kill.
Characters, or the Manners of the Age (1688)

12 The majority of men devote the greater part of their lives to making their remaining years unhappy.
Characters, or the Manners of the Age (1688)

13 The pleasure of criticizing robs us of the pleasure of being moved by some very fine things.
Characters, or the Manners of the Age (1688)

14 There are only three events in a man's life; birth, life, and death; he is not conscious of being born, he dies in pain, and he forgets to live.
Characters, or the Manners of the Age (1688)

15 There are some who speak one moment before they think.
Characters, or the Manners of the Age (1688)

16 There exist some evils so terrible and some misfortunes so horrible that we dare not think of them... but if they happen to fall on us, we find ourselves stronger than we imagined, we grapple with our ill luck, and behave better than we expected we should.
Characters, or the Manners of the Age (1688)

17 "There is a report that Piso is dead; it is a great loss; he was an honest man, who deserved to live longer; he was intelligent and agreeable, resolute and courageous, to be depended upon, generous and faithful." Add: "provided he is really dead".
Characters, or the Manners of the Age (1688)

18 The shortest and best way to make your fortune is to let people see clearly that it is in their interests to promote yours.
Characters, or the Manners of the Age (1688)

19 To endeavor to forget anyone is a certain way of thinking of nothing else.
Characters, or the Manners of the Age (1688)

20 Women run to extremes; they are either better or worse than men.
Characters, or the Manners of the Age (1688)

21 The duty of a judge is to administer justice, but his practice is to delay it.
Attrib.

Lacan, Jacques (1901–81) French philosopher and psychologist

1 How can we be sure that we are not impostors?
The Four Fundamental Concepts of Psycho-Analysis (Jacques-Alain Miller, ed., Alan Sheridan, tr.; 1977)

La Chaussée, Nivelle de (Pierre Claude Nivelle de la Chaussée; 1692–1754) French playwright

1 When everyone is wrong, everyone is right.
La Gouvernante (1747), Act 1, Scene 2

Laclos, Pierre Choderlos de (Pierre Ambroise François Choderlos de Laclos; 1741–1803) French novelist and politician

1 How lucky we are that women defend themselves so poorly! We should, otherwise, be no more to them than timid slaves.
Les Liaisons dangereuses (1782), Letter 4

2 Prudence is, it seems to me, the virtue which must be preferred above the rest when one is determining the fate of others; and especially when it is a case of sealing that fate with sacred and indissoluble promises, such as those of marriage.
Les Liaisons dangereuses (1782), Letter 104

3 Have you not as yet observed that pleasure, which is undeniably the sole motive force behind the union of the sexes, is nevertheless not enough to form a bond between them? And that, if it is preceded by desire which impels, it is succeeded by disgust which repels? That is a law of nature which love alone can alter.
Les Liaisons dangereuses (1782), Letter 131

4 Who would not shudder to think of the misery that may be caused by a single dangerous intimacy? And how much suffering could be avoided if it were more often thought of!
Les Liaisons dangereuses (1782), Letter 175

Lacroix, Christian (Christian Marie Marc Lacroix; b.1951) French fashion designer

1 Nowadays a woman can go skiing in pearls or nightclubbing in a ballgown if she feels like it.
Lacroix by Lacroix (1992), ch. 8

2 We're all in the lifestyle game now, because you have to create your own stage. So much contemporary art and design is a parody, a joke, and full of allusions to the past.
Sunday Times Magazine, London (October 1987), quoted in *Sultans of Style* (Georgina Howell; 1990), ch. 20

La Follette, Suzanne (1893–1983) U.S. writer and politician

1 Rights that depend on the sufferance of the state are of uncertain tenure.
Concerning Women (1926)

La Fontaine, Jean de (1621–95) French writer and poet

1 Help thyself, and God will help thee.
Fables (1668), bk. 6

2 Death never takes the wise man by surprise; he is always ready to go.
Fables (1668), bk. 8

3 A mountain in labor shouted so loud that everyone, summoned by the noise, ran up expecting that she would be delivered of a city bigger than Paris; she brought forth a mouse.
"La Montagne qui accouche," *Fables* (1668), bk. 5

4 Rather suffer than die is man's motto.
"La Mort et le Bûcheron," *Fables* (1668), bk. 1

5 People must help one another; it is nature's law.
"L'Âne et le Chien," *Fables* (1668), bk. 8

6 Be advised that all flatterers live at the expense of those who listen to them.
"Le Corbeau et le Renard," *Fables* (1668), bk. 1

7 What God does, He does well.
"Le Gland et la Citrouille," *Fables* (1668), bk. 9

8 One should oblige everyone to the extent of one's ability. One often needs someone smaller than oneself.
"Le Lion et le Rat," *Fables* (1668), bk. 2

9 Patience and passage of time do more than strength and fury.
"Le Lion et le Rat," *Fables* (1668), bk. 2

10 A hungry stomach has no ears.
"Le Milan et le Rossignol," *Fables* (1668), bk. 9

11 This fellow did not see farther than his own nose.
"Le Renard et la Boue," *Fables* (1668), bk. 3

12 But the shortest works are always the best.
"Les Lapins," *Fables* (1668), bk. 10

13 He told me never to sell the bear's skin before one has killed the beast.
"L'Ours et les deux Compagnons," *Fables* (1668), bk. 5

14 By the work one knows the workman.
"The Hornets and the Bees," *Fables* (1668)

Laforgue, Jules (1860–87) French poet

1 O what an everyday business life is!
"Complainte sur certains ennuis," *Les Complaintes* (1885)

Lagerfeld, Karl (Karl Otto Lagerfeld; b.1938) German-born French fashion designer

1 Fashion is the image of an age and can tell its story better than a speech.
Daily Telegraph, London (October 20, 1994)

Lagerlöf, Selma (Selma Ottiliana Lovisa Lagerlöf; 1858–1940) Swedish writer

1 If you have learned anything at all from us, Tummetott, you no longer think that the humans should have the whole earth to themselves.
1907. Said by Akka, leader of the wild geese, to the boy Nils Holgersson, who, changed into an elf-sized version of himself, has been able to journey with the birds. *The Further Adventures of Nils* (Velma Swanston Howard, tr.; 1911)

2 Women can do nothing that has permanence.
The Miracles of Anti-Christ (1899)

Lagrange, Joseph Louis, comte de (1736–1813) French mathematician and astronomer

1 It took the mob only a moment to remove his head; a century will not suffice to reproduce it.
Referring to the execution of the chemist Antoine-Laurent Lavoisier. Quoted in *An Introduction to the History of Mathematics* (Howard Whitley; 1964)

2 When we ask advice, we are usually looking for an accomplice.
Attrib.

La Guardia, Fiorello (Fiorello Henry La Guardia; 1882–1947) U.S. politician

1 Ticker tape ain't spaghetti.
Speech to the United Nations Relief and Rehabilitation Commission, New York City (March 29, 1946)

2 I've never belonged to any political party for more than fifteen minutes.
Quoted in *Inside USA* (John Gunther; 1947)

Lahr, Bert (Irving Lahrheim; 1895–1967) U.S. actor

1 If I'd made a hit as a *human being* then perhaps I'd be sailing in films now.
Referring to his Cowardly Lion performance in *The Wizard of Oz* (1939). Quoted in *Notes on a Cowardly Lion* (John Lahr; 1969)

2 Believe me, it was a tonic for my inferiority complex which is so readily developed in Hollywood.
Referring to his success in *The Wizard of Oz*. Quoted in *Notes on a Cowardly Lion* (John Lahr; 1969)

3 Metro's going to keep me for life after what I've done for this picture. I'm going to stay out here a long time.
Shortly afterwards MGM decided to stop making musicals for financial reasons, and Lahr returned to New York. Quoted in *Notes on a Cowardly Lion* (John Lahr; 1969)

Laing, B. Kojo (b.1946) Ghanaian novelist, poet, and educator

1 One of the joys of being a judge is to grin ruefully at your own secret faults while you deal with the faults of others.
Major Gentl and the Achimota Wars (1992)

Laing, Dilys (1906–60) Canadian poet and editor

1 Women receive
the insults of men
with tolerance,
having been bitten
in the nipple
by their toothless gums.
"Veterans," *Collected Poems* (1967)

Laing, R. D. (Ronald David Laing; 1927–89) Scottish psychiatrist

1 Philosophy does not exist. It is nothing but an hypostatized abstraction.
Reason and Violence (1964), ch. 1

2 The greatest psychopathologist has been Freud. Freud was a hero. He descended to the "Underworld" and met there stark terrors. He carried with him his theory as a Medusa's head which turned these terrors to stone.
The Divided Self (1965), ch. 1

3 No one *has* schizophrenia, like having a cold. The patient has not "got" schizophrenia. He is schizophrenic.
The Divided Self (1965), ch. 2

4 I am quite sure that a good number of "cures" of psychotics consist in the fact that the patient has decided, for one reason or other, once more to *play at being sane*.
The Divided Self (1965), ch. 7

5 A man who prefers to be dead rather than Red is normal. A man who says he has lost his soul is mad. A man who says that men are machines may be a great scientist. A man who says he *is* a machine is "depersonalized" in psychiatric jargon.
The Divided Self (1965), preface

6 In the best places, where straitjackets are abolished, doors are unlocked, leucotomies largely foregone, these can be replaced by more subtle lobotomies and tranquillizers that place the bars of Bedlam and the locked doors *inside* the patient.
The Divided Self (1965), preface

7 The statesmen of the world who boast and threaten that they have Doomsday weapons are far more dangerous, and far more estranged from "reality," than many of the people on whom the label "psychotic" is affixed.
The Divided Self (1965), preface

8 Children do not give up their innate imagination, curiosity, dreaminess easily. You have to love them to get them to do that.
The Politics of Experience (1967), ch. 3

9 Schizophrenic behaviour is a special strategy that a person invents in order to live in an unlivable situation.
The Politics of Experience (1967), ch. 5

10 We are effectively destroying ourselves by violence masquerading as love.
The Politics of Experience (1967), ch. 13

11 Madness need not be all breakdown. It may also be break-through. It is potential liberation and renewal as well as enslavement and existential death.
The Politics of Experience (1967), ch. 16

12 Few books today are forgivable.
The Politics of Experience (1967), introduction

13 A mental healer may be a psychiatrist. A psychiatrist may or may not be a mental healer.
Wisdom, Madness and Folly: The Making of a Psychiatrist, 1927–1957 (1985)

14 I remember remarks made in all seriousness by psychiatrists. "Hamlet was just a badly conditioned rat." "If Lear had been given electric shocks there would have been no need for all that nonsense."
Wisdom, Madness and Folly: The Making of a Psychiatrist, 1927–1957 (1985)

15 The human mind *has* to ask "Who, what, whence, whither, why am I?" And it is very doubtful if the human mind can answer any of these questions.
Wisdom, Madness and Folly: The Making of a Psychiatrist, 1927–1957 (1985)

16 Where can you scream? It's a serious question: where can you go in society and scream?
Quoted in *Mad to be Normal: Conversations with R. D. Laing* (Bob Mullan, ed.; 1995), introduction

Laker, Freddie, Sir (Frederick Alfred Laker; b.1922) British airline entrepreneur

1 The LA Skytrain can't possibly fail.
His Laker Airways "Skytrain" project briefly pioneered low-cost flights across the Atlantic before its collapse (1982). *Daily Express*, London (December 1, 1978)

2 Every businessman should have one day in his life to see what it's like coming down.
Said after the collapse of the Laker Airways Skytrain. *Observer,* London (September 11, 1983), "Sayings of the Week"

3 If they get you down, sue the bastards.
Referring to larger airlines that use unfair business practices. Quoted in *How to Get Ahead in Business* (Tom Cannon, ed.; 1993), foreword

Lamarr, Hedy (Hedwig Eva Maria Kiesler; 1913–2000) Austrian-born U.S. film actor

1 Any girl can be glamorous. All you have to do is stand still and look stupid.
Quoted in *The Stars* (Richard Schickel; 1962)

Lamartine, Alphonse de (Alphonse Marie Louis Prat de Lamartine; 1790–1869) French poet and politician

1 At its birth the Republic gave voice to...three words, "Liberty, Equality, Fraternity"...If Europe is wise and just, each of these words signifies peace.
Referring to the French Revolution. "A Manifesto to the Powers" (March 4, 1848)

2 France is revolutionary or she is nothing at all. The Revolution of 1789 is her political religion.
Histoire des Girondins (1847)

3 How cruel God would be, if he were not so great!
Les Oiseaux (1842)

4 O Time! arrest your flight, and you, propitious hours!
Stay your course.
"Le Lac," *Méditations poétiques* (1820), st. 6

5 Just one being is lacking, and the whole world is empty of people.
"L'Isolement," *Méditations poétiques* (1820)

6 God is but a word invented to explain the world.
"Le Tombeau d'une mère," *Nouvelles harmonies poétiques et religieuses* (1832)

Lamb, A. J. (1870–1928) British songwriter

1 She's only a Bird in a Gilded Cage
Song title. (1900)

Lamb, Caroline, Lady (originally Caroline Ponsonby; 1785–1828) British novelist

1 It is said there is no happiness, and no love to be compared to that which is felt for the first time...but love like other arts requires experience, and terror and ignorance, on its first approach, prevent our feeling it as strongly as at a later period.
Glenarvon (1816), vol. 1, ch. 11

Lamb, Charles (pen name Elia; 1775–1834) British essayist

Quotations about Lamb

1 At Godwin's they were disputing fiercely which was the best—Man as he was, or man as he is to be. "Give me," says Lamb, "man as he is not to be".
William Hazlitt (1778–1830) British essayist and critic. "My First Acquaintance with Poets," quoted in *Hazlitt on English Literature* (1913), ch. 17

2 His sayings are generally like women's letters; all the pith is in the postscript.
William Hazlitt (1778–1830) British essayist and critic. *Conversations of James Northcote* (1826–27)

Quotations by Lamb

3 Gone before
To that unknown and silent shore.
"Hester" (1803), st. 7, quoted in *The Oxford Book of English Verse, 1250–1918* (Sir Arthur Quiller-Couch, ed.; 1939)

4 Pain is life—the sharper, the more evidence of life.
Letter to Bernard Barton (January 9, 1824)

5 Damn the age; I'll write for Antiquity.
Describing his reaction to one of his sonnets being rejected. Letter to B. W. Proctor (1829)

6 This very night I am going to leave off tobacco! Surely there must be some other world in which this unconquerable purpose shall be realized. The soul hath not her generous aspirings implanted in her in vain.
Letter to Thomas Manning (December 26, 1815)

7 Separate from the pleasure of your company, I don't much care if I never see another mountain in my life.
Letter to William Wordsworth (January 30, 1801)

8 What have I gained by health? intolerable dullness. What by early hours and moderate meals?—a total blank.
Letter to William Wordsworth (January 22, 1830)

9 I have had playmates, I have had companions
In my days of childhood, in my joyful schooldays—
All, all are gone, the old familiar faces.
"The Old Familiar Faces" (1798)

10 May my last breath be drawn through a pipe and exhaled in a pun.
Diary (January 9, 1834)

11 Nothing is to me more distasteful than that entire complacency and satisfaction which beam in the countenances of a new-married couple.
"A Bachelor's Complaint of the Behaviour of Married People," *Essays of Elia* (1823)

12 We are nothing; less than nothing, and dreams. We are only what might have been, and must wait upon the tedious shores of Lethe millions of ages before we have existence, and a name.
In Greek mythology, Lethe was a river in the underworld whose waters were drunk by souls about to be reborn in order to forget their past lives. "Dream Children," *Essays of Elia* (1823)

13 I hate a man who swallows it, affecting not to know what he is eating. I suspect his taste in higher matters.
Referring to food. "Grace before Meat," *Essays of Elia* (1823)

14 Man is a gaming animal. He must always be trying to get the better in something or other.
"Mrs Battle's Opinions on Whist," *Essays of Elia* (1823)

15 Boys are capital fellows in their own way, among their mates; but they are unwholesome companions for grown people.
"The Old and the New Schoolmaster," *Essays of Elia* (1823)

16 In everything that relates to science, I am a whole Encyclopaedia behind the rest of the world.
"The Old and the New Schoolmaster," *Essays of Elia* (1823)

17 The human species, according to the best theory I can form of it, is composed of two distinct races, the men who *borrow*, and *the men who lend*.
"The Two Races of Men," *Essays of Elia* (1823)

18 Your *borrowers of books*—those mutilators of collections, spoilers of the symmetry of shelves, and creators of odd volumes.
"The Two Races of Men," *Essays of Elia* (1823)

19 Credulity is the man's weakness, but the child's strength.
"Witches and other Night Fears," *Essays of Elia* (1823)

20 I love to lose myself in other men's minds. When I am not walking, I am reading; I cannot sit and think. Books think for me.
"Detached Thoughts on Books and Reading," *Last Essays of Elia* (1833)

21 Newspapers always excite curiosity. No one ever lays one down without a feeling of disappointment.
"Detached Thoughts on Books and Reading," *Last Essays of Elia* (1833)

22 A poor relation—is the most irrelevant thing in nature.
"Poor Relations," *Last Essays of Elia* (1833)

23 A pun is a pistol let off at the ear; not a feather to tickle the intellect.
"Popular Fallacies," *Last Essays of Elia* (1833)

24 To be sick is to enjoy monarchal prerogatives.
"The Convalescent," *Last Essays of Elia* (1833)

25 The greatest pleasure I know, is to do a good action by stealth, and to have it found out by accident.
"Table Talk by the late Elia," *The Athenaeum* (January 4, 1834)

26 For thy sake, Tobacco, I
Would do any thing but die.
"A Farewell to Tobacco," *The Poetical Works of Charles Lamb* (1836), ll. 122–123

27 Riddle of destiny, who can show
What thy short visit meant, or know
What thy errand here below?
"On an Infant Dying as soon as Born," *The Poetical Works of Charles Lamb* (1836), ll. 13–15

Lamb, Mary Ann (1764–1847) British writer

1 A child's a plaything for an hour.
Sometimes attributed to Charles Lamb, with whom she sometimes collaborated. "Parental Recollections," *Poetry for Children* (1809)

Lambert, Jack (b.1952) U.S. football player

1 Who's Nureyev?
Response on being described as "the Nureyev of American Football." Remark (1976)

Lambert, Kit (Christopher Sebastian Lambert; 1935–81) British pop group manager

1 Once you've arranged the entire seating of Lancing College Chapel to sit next to the boy you fancy, anything is possible.
Quoted in *The Lamberts* (Andrew Motion; 1986)

La Mettrie, Julien Offroy de (1709–51) French philosopher and physician

1 The brain has muscles for thinking as the legs have muscles for walking.
The Man-Machine (1747)

2 The human body is a machine which winds its own springs: the living image of perpetual movement.
The Man-Machine (1747)

Lamming, George (b.1927) Barbadian writer

1 The architecture of our future is not only unfinished; the scaffolding has hardly gone up.
"The West Indian People" (1966), quoted in *Caribbean Essays* (Andrew Salkey, ed.; 1973)

2 The only England he had known was a kind of corpse in future argument with itself, a dead voice bearing witness to its own achievement, passionate in incest with its past.
Season of Adventure (1960), p. 36

3 Different man, different land, but de same outlook. Dat's de meanin' o' West Indies.
The Emigrants (1954), p. 62

4 A man is always resident in the castle of his skin. If the castle is deserted, then we know the Devil has been at work.
The Pleasures of Exile (1960), p. 75

Lamont, Norman (b.1942) British politician

1 Rising unemployment and the recession have been the price that we've had to pay to get inflation down: that is a price well worth paying.
Observer, London (May 19, 1991)

2 We give the impression of being in office but not in power.
Observer, London (June 13, 1993)

Lampton, William James (Andrew George Little; 1859–1917) British writer

1 Same old slippers,
Same old rice,
Same old glimpse of
Paradise.
"June Weddings" (Undated)

Lancaster, Burt (Burton Stephen Lancaster; 1913–94) U.S. actor

1 Tits and sand—that's what we used to call sex and violence in Hollywood.
Photoplay (April 1983), quoted in *Chambers Film Quotes* (Tony Crawley, ed.; 1991)

Lancaster, Osbert, Sir (1908–86) English cartoonist and writer

1 What I particularly admired about the debate was the way that every speaker managed to give the impression that he personally had never met a homosexual in his life.
July 1960. Caption to a cartoon of two women talking at a party. *A Queer Reader* (Patrick Higgins, ed.; 1993)

2 It's an odd thing, but now one knows it's profoundly moral

and packed with deep spiritual significance a lot of the old charm seems to have gone.
Caption to cartoon in the *Daily Express* (London) referring to D. H. Lawrence's novel *Lady Chatterley's Lover*, after the obscenity trial. *Daily Express*, London (1960)

3 No other form of transport in the rest of my life has ever come up to the bliss of my pram.
"Pram" means baby carriage. *Observer*, London (January 25, 1976), "Sayings of the Week"

Lance, Bert (b.1931) U.S. government official

1 If it ain't broke, don't fix it.
Nation's Business (1977)

Lanchester, Elsa (1902–86) British-born U.S. actor

1 She looked as though butter wouldn't melt in her mouth—or anywhere else.
Referring to Maureen O'Hara. Attrib.

Land, Edwin Herbert (1909–91) U.S. scientist and inventor

1 Anything worth doing is worth doing to excess.
Attrib.

2 The bottom line is in heaven.
1977. Referring to the worth of a product, dismissing the idea that the bottom line is on the balance sheet. Attrib.

Landers, Ann (Esther Pauline Friedman Lederer, "Eppie"; b.1918) U.S. journalist

1 Women complain about sex more often than men. Their gripes fall into two major categories: (1) Not enough; (2) Too much.
Ann Landers Says Truth Is Stranger... (1968)

2 I don't want anybody calling me Ms.
Time (August 21, 1989)

3 Opportunities are usually disguised as hard work, so most people don't recognize them.
Attrib.

Landon, Letitia Elizabeth (pen name L. E. L.; 1802–38) British poet and novelist

1 Were it not better to forget
Than but remember and regret?
"Despondency," ll. 5–6, quoted in *Life and Literary Remains of L. E. L.* (Laman Blanchard; 1841)

2 Few, save the poor, feel for the poor.
"The Poor," l. 1, quoted in *Life and Literary Remains of L. E. L.* (Laman Blanchard; 1841)

3 We might have been!—These are but common words,
And yet they make the sum of life's bewailing.
"We Might Have Been," ll. 1–2, quoted in *Life and Literary Remains of L. E. L.* (Laman Blanchard; 1841)

Landor, Walter Savage (1775–1864) British poet and writer

1 Prose on certain occasions can bear a great deal of poetry: on the other hand, poetry sinks and swoons under a moderate weight of prose.
"Archdeacon Hare and Walter Landor," *Imaginary Conversations* (1853)

2 Goodness does not more certainly make men happy than happiness makes them good.
"Lord Brooke and Sir Philip Sidney," *Imaginary Conversations of Literary Men and Statesmen* (1824)

3 Clear writers, like clear fountains, do not seem so deep as they are; the turbid look the most profound.
"Southey and Porson," *Imaginary Conversations of Literary Men and Statesmen* (1824)

4 George the First was always reckoned
Vile, but viler George the Second;
And what mortal ever heard
Any good of George the Third?
When from earth the Fourth descended
God be praised the Georges ended!
April 28, 1855. "Notes & Queries," *The Atlas* (May 3, 1902), Epigram

5 Good God, I forgot the violets!
Having thrown his cook out of an open window on to the flowerbed below. Quoted in *The Frank Muir Book: An Irreverent Companion to Social History* (Frank Muir; 1976)

Landowska, Wanda (1877–1959) Polish-born harpsichordist and teacher

1 Oh, well, you play Bach *your* way. I'll play him *his*.
Remark to fellow musician. Quoted in *The Faber Book of Anecdotes* (Clifton Fadiman; 1985)

Landseer, Edwin Henry, Sir (1802–73) British painter and sculptor

1 If people only knew as much about painting as I do, they would never buy my pictures.
Said to W. P. Frith. Quoted in *Landseer: the Victorian Paragon* (Campbell Lennie; 1976), ch. 12

Lane, Geoffrey Dawson, Baron Lane of Saint Ippollitts (b.1918) British judge

1 We take the view that the time has now arrived when the law should declare that a rapist remains a rapist and is subject to the criminal law, irrespective of his relationship with his victim.
Dismissing the appeal of a man who argued, on the 1736 principle of Chief Justice Hale, that he could not be guilty of raping his wife. *Times*, London (March 15, 1991)

Lang, Andrew (1844–1912) Scottish writer and scholar

1 Politicians use statistics in the same way that a drunken man uses lamp-posts—for support rather than illumination.
Speech (1910), quoted in *The Harvest of a Quiet Eye* (Alan L. Mackay; 1977)

lang, k.d. (Katherine Dawn Lang; b.1961) Canadian singer and songwriter

1 I see God in everything, whether it's a pair of running shoes or a whale.
Interview, *Rolling Stone* (Mim Udovitch; August 5, 1993)

Langbridge, Frederick (1849–1922) British writer and priest

1 Two men look out through the same bars:
One sees the mud, and one the stars.
"A Cluster of Quiet Thoughts" (1896)

Lange, Dorothea (originally Dorothea Nutzhorn; 1895–1965) U.S. photographer

1 The camera is an instrument that teaches people how to see without a camera.
Los Angeles Times (August 13, 1978)

Langer, Susanne K. (Susanne Knauth Langer; 1895–1985) U.S. philosopher

1 Art is the objectification of feeling, and the subjectification of nature.
Mind (1967), vol. 1, pt. 2, ch. 4

Langland, William (1330?–1400?) English poet

1 Bakers and brewers, bouchers and cokes
For thees men doth most harme to the mene peple.
The Vision of Piers Plowman (1365–86), Passus 4, l. 80

2 Dowel, Dobet and Dobest.
Do well, do better, and do best: three concepts central to the search for Truth in *The Vision of Piers Plowman*, in which they appear as allegorical characters. *The Vision of Piers Plowman* (1365–86), Passus 8, l. 109

3 Grammere, that grounde is of al.
The Vision of Piers Plowman (1365–86), Passus 18, l. 107

4 "After sharpest shoures," quath Pees, "most sheene is the sonne;
Is no weder warmer than after watery cloudes."
"Pees" means "Peace." *The Vision of Piers Plowman* (1365–86), Passus 18, l. 456

5 In a somer seson, whan softe was the sonne.
Opening line. *The Vision of Piers Plowman* (1365–86), Prologue, l. 1

6 A glotoun of wordes.
The Vision of Piers Plowman (1365–86), Prologue, l. 139

Langton, Stephen (1150?–1228) English clergyman

1 Any service rendered to the temporal king to the prejudice of the eternal king is, without doubt, an act of treachery.
Letter to the barons of England (1207)

Langton, Thomas (1440?–1501) Welsh clergyman

1 He contents the people where he goes best that ever did Prince, for many a poor man that hath suffered wrong many days has been relieved and helped by him.
Referring to Richard III. Remark (late 15th century)

Lanier, Sidney (1842–81) U.S. poet and critic

1 Oh, might I through these tears
But glimpse some hill my Georgia high uprears,
Where white the quartz and pink the pebble shine,
The hickory heavenward strives, the muscadine
Swings o'er the slope, the oak's far-falling shade
Darkens the dogwood in the bottom glade.
"From the Flats," *Sidney Lanier: Poems and Letters* (Charles R. Anderson, ed.; 1960), v. 3, ll. 1–7

Laozi (also spelled Lao-tse; 570?–490? B.C.) Chinese philosopher

1 A good calculator does not need artificial aids.
The *Daode Jing* is an early Chinese Taoist text. While attributed to Laozi, it probably dates from the 3rd century B.C. *Daode Jing* (Unknown)

2 He cannot be got and benefitted;
He cannot be got and harmed;
He cannot be got and honored;
He cannot be got and humbled;
Therefore arises the world's honor.
Referring to attributes of the Taoist holy man. *Daode Jing* (Unknown), quoted in *Sacred Texts of the World* (Ninian Smart and Richard D. Hecht, eds.; 1982)

3 He produces but does not own,
He acts and makes no claim.
He achieves merit and does not dwell in it.
In that he does not dwell in it
It does not depart.
Referring to attributes of the Taoist holy man. *Daode Jing* (Unknown), quoted in *Sacred Texts of the World* (Ninian Smart and Richard D. Hecht, eds.; 1982)

4 Great I call the elusive.
The elusive I call the far.
The far I call the returning.
The *Daode Jing* is an early Chinese Taoist text. While attributed to Laozi, it probably dates from the 3rd century B.C. *Daode Jing* (Unknown), quoted in *Sacred Texts of the World* (Ninian Smart and Richard D. Hecht, eds.; 1982)

5 He who is eternally without desire
Perceives the spiritual side of it;
He who is permanently with desire
Perceives the limit of it.
The *Daode Jing* is an early Chinese Taoist text. While attributed to Laozi, it probably dates from the 3rd century B.C. *Daode Jing* (Unknown), quoted in *Sacred Texts of the World* (Ninian Smart and Richard D. Hecht, eds.; 1982)

6 Not exalting the worthy means the people do not envy;
Not prizing hard-to-get valuables means the people do not steal.
Not looking at that which creates desire makes the heart undisturbed.
The *Daode Jing* is an early Chinese Taoist text. While attributed to Laozi, it probably dates from the 3rd century B.C. *Daode Jing* (Unknown), quoted in *Sacred Texts of the World* (Ninian Smart and Richard D. Hecht, eds.; 1982)

7 The great Way declines:
We have humanity and justice:
Prudence and wisdom appear;
There is cultivation of behavior.
The *Daode Jing* is an early Chinese Taoist text. While attributed to Laozi, it probably dates from the 3rd century B.C. *Daode Jing* (Unknown), quoted in *Sacred Texts of the World* (Ninian Smart and Richard D. Hecht, eds.; 1982)

8 Therefore hold to the things which are reliable.
Look to simplicity; embrace purity;
Lessen the self; diminish desire.
The *Daode Jing* is an early Chinese Taoist text. While attributed to Laozi, it probably dates from the 3rd century B.C. *Daode Jing* (Unknown), quoted in *Sacred Texts of the World* (Ninian Smart and Richard D. Hecht, eds.; 1982)

9 The valley spirit does not die:
It is called the mysterious woman.

The gate of the mysterious woman
Is called the root of the universe.
The *Daode Jing* is an early Chinese Taoist text. While attributed to Laozi, it probably dates from the 3rd century B.C. *Daode Jing* (Unknown), quoted in *Sacred Texts of the World* (Ninian Smart and Richard D. Hecht, eds.; 1982)

10 The way that can be spoken of
Is not the constant way;
The name that can be named
Is not the constant name.
The nameless was the beginning of heaven and earth;
The named was the mother of the myriad creatures.
Opening lines of the *Daode Jing*, an early Chinese Taoist text. While attributed to Laozi, the book probably dates from the 3rd century B.C. *Daode Jing* (Unknown), quoted in *Tao Te Ching* (D. C. Lau, tr.; 1963), bk. 1, pt. 1

11 The sage keeps to the deed that consists in taking no action and practices the teaching that uses no words.
The *Daode Jing* is an early Chinese Taoist text. While attributed to Laozi, it probably dates from the 3rd century B.C. *Daode Jing* (Unknown), quoted in *Tao Te Ching* (D. C. Lau, tr.; 1963), bk. 1, pt. 2

12 Thus Something and Nothing produce each other;
The difficult and the easy complement each other;
The long and the short off-set each other;
The high and the low incline toward each other.
The *Daode Jing* is an early Chinese Taoist text. While attributed to Laozi, it probably dates from the 3rd century B.C. *Daode Jing* (Unknown), quoted in *Tao Te Ching* (D. C. Lau, tr.; 1963), bk. 1, pt. 2

13 Heaven and earth are ruthless, and treat the myriad creatures as straw dogs; the sage is ruthless, and treats the people like dogs.
The *Daode Jing* is an early Chinese Taoist text. While attributed to Laozi, it probably dates from the 3rd century B.C. *Daode Jing* (Unknown), quoted in *Tao Te Ching* (D. C. Lau, tr.; 1963), bk. 1, pt. 5

14 Cut out doors and windows in order to make a room. Adapt the nothing therein to the purpose in hand, and you will have the use of the room.
The *Daode Jing* is an early Chinese Taoist text. While attributed to Laozi, it probably dates from the 3rd century B.C. *Daode Jing* (Unknown), quoted in *Tao Te Ching* (D. C. Lau, tr.; 1963), bk. 1, pt. 11

15 The five colors make a man's eyes blind;
The five notes make his ears deaf;
The five tastes injure his palate;
Riding and hunting make his mind go wild with excitement.
The *Daode Jing* is an early Chinese Taoist text. While attributed to Laozi, it probably dates from the 3rd century B.C. *Daode Jing* (Unknown), quoted in *Tao Te Ching* (D. C. Lau, tr.; 1963), bk. 1, pt. 12

16 When the great way falls into disuse
There are benevolence and rectitude;
When cleverness emerges
There is great hypocrisy;
When the six relations are at variance
There are filial children;
When the state is benighted
There are loyal ministers.
The six relations are: father and son, elder and younger brother, and husband and wife. *Daode Jing* (Unknown), quoted in *Tao Te Ching* (D. C. Lau, tr.; 1963), bk. 1, pt. 18

17 He who tiptoes cannot stand; he who strides cannot walk.
He who shows himself is not conspicuous;
He who considers himself right is not illustrious;
He who brags will have no merit;
He who boasts will not endure.
The *Daode Jing* is an early Chinese Taoist text. While attributed to Laozi, it probably dates from the 3rd century B.C. *Daode Jing* (Unknown), quoted in *Tao Te Ching* (D. C. Lau, tr.; 1963), bk. 1, pt. 24

18 A journey of a thousand miles must begin with a single step.
The *Daode Jing* is an early Chinese Taoist text. While attributed to Laozi, it probably dates from the 3rd century B.C. *Daode Jing* (Unknown), 1

19 One may know the world without going out of doors.
One may see the Way of Heaven without looking through the windows.
The further one goes, the less one knows.
The *Daode Jing* is an early Chinese Taoist text. While attributed to Laozi, it probably dates from the 3rd century B.C. *Daode Jing* (Unknown), 47

20 Learning builds daily accumulation, but the practice of Tao builds daily simplification. Simplify and simplify, until all contamination from relative, contradictory thinking is eliminated.
The *Daode Jing* is an early Chinese Taoist text. While attributed to Laozi, it probably dates from the 3rd century B.C. *Daode Jing* (Unknown), 48

Laplace, Pierre Simon, Marquis de (1749–1827) French mathematician and astronomer

1 Man follows only phantoms.
1827. Alleged last words. Quoted in *Budget of Paradoxes*, 8th ed. (Augustus De Morgan; 1872)

2 What we know is not much. What we do not know is immense.
1827. Alleged last words. Quoted in *Budget of Paradoxes*, 8th ed. (Augustus De Morgan; 1872)

3 Sire, I had no need of that hypothesis.
1827. Referring to his *Exposition du système du Monde* (1796), and responding to the words of Napoleon I, "You have written this huge book on the system of the world without once mentioning the author of the universe." Quoted in *Budget of Paradoxes*, 8th ed. (Augustus De Morgan; 1872)

Lappë, Frances Moore (b.1944) U.S. ecologist and author

1 The act of putting into your mouth what the earth has grown is perhaps the most direct interaction with the earth.
Diet for a Small Planet (1971), pt. 1

Lardner, Ring (Ringgold Wilmer Lardner; 1885–1933) U.S. humorist and writer

1 How do you look when I'm sober?
Speaking to a flamboyantly dressed stranger who walked into the club where he was drinking. Quoted in *Ring* (J. Yardley; 1977)

2 Frenchmen drink wine just like we used to drink water before Prohibition.
Quoted in *Wit's End* (R. E. Drennan, ed.; 1973)

3 The only exercise I get is when I take the studs out of one shirt and put them in another.
Attrib.

4 The only real happiness a ballplayer has is when he is playing a ball game and accomplishes something he didn't think he could do.
Attrib.

Larkin, Philip (1922–85) British poet

1 Get stewed:
Books are a load of crap.
"Stewed" means "drunk." "A Study of Reading Habits" (1960), st. 3, ll. 5–6, quoted in *Philip Larkin Collected Poems* (Anthony Thwaite, ed.; 1988)

2 Home is so sad. It stays as it was left,
Shaped to the comfort of the last to go
As if to win them back.
"Home is so Sad" (1958), quoted in *Philip Larkin Collected Poems* (Anthony Thwaite, ed.; 1988)

3 The difficult part of love
Is being selfish enough,
Is having the blind persistence
To upset an existence
Just for your own sake.
"Love" (1966), quoted in *Philip Larkin Collected Poems* (Anthony Thwaite, ed.; 1988)

4 Clearly money has something to do with life,
In fact, they've a lot in common, if you enquire:
You can't put off being young until you retire.
"Money" (1973), st. 2, l. 4 and st. 3, ll. 1–2, quoted in *Philip Larkin Collected Poems* (Anthony Thwaite, ed.; 1988)

5 He married a woman to stop her getting away,
Now she's there all day.
"Self's The Man" (1958), st. 1, ll. 3–4, quoted in *Philip Larkin Collected Poems* (Anthony Thwaite, ed.; 1988)

6 It becomes still more difficult to find
Words at once true and kind,
Or not untrue and not unkind.
"Talking in Bed" (1960), quoted in *Philip Larkin Collected Poems* (Anthony Thwaite, ed.; 1988)

7 Perhaps being old is having lighted rooms
Inside your head, and people in them, acting.
People you know, yet can't quite name.
"The Old Fools" (1973), st. 3, ll. 1–3, quoted in *Philip Larkin Collected Poems* (Anthony Thwaite, ed.; 1988)

8 At first, I didn't notice what a noise
The weddings made
Each station that we stopped at: sun destroys
The interest of what's happening in the shade.
"The Whitsun Weddings" (1958)

9 They fuck you up, your mum and dad.
They may not mean to, but they do.
They fill you with the faults they had
And add some extra, just for you.
"This be the Verse" (1971), st. 1, ll. 1–4, quoted in *Philip Larkin Collected Poems* (Anthony Thwaite, ed.; 1988)

10 Hooker has a curiously archaic manner: after singing a line, his guitar breaks into a series of rapid, aimless little runs proliferating through a whole back-country of melancholy.
1963. Referring to John Lee Hooker. "The Prospect Behind Us," *All What Jazz: A Record Diary* (1970)

11 Sexual intercourse began
In nineteen sixty-three
(Which was rather late for me)—
Between the end of the *Chatterley* ban
And the Beatles' first LP.
"Annus Mirabilis," *High Windows* (1974)

12 Man hands on misery to man.
It deepens like a coastal shelf.
Get out as early as you can,
And don't have any kids yourself.
"This Be the Verse," *High Windows* (1974)

13 Far too many relied on the classic formula of a beginning, a muddle, and an end.
Referring to modern novels. *New Fiction* (January 1978)

14 I wouldn't mind seeing China if I could come back the same day. I hate being abroad.
Interview, *Observer*, London (1979)

15 One reason for writing, of course, is that no-one's written what you want to read.
Interview, *Paris Review* (1982)

16 Poetry isn't a kind of paint-spray you use to cover selected objects with. A good poem about failure is a success.
Interview, *Paris Review* (1982)

17 I don't suppose I'm unhappier there than I should be anywhere else.
Reply on being asked if he liked living in Hull, England. Interview, *Paris Review* (1982)

18 What are days for?
Days are where we live
They come they wake us
Time and time over
They are to be happy in;
Where can we live but days?
1953. "Days," *Philip Larkin Collected Poems* (Anthony Thwaite, ed.; 1988), st. 1, ll. 1–6

19 Nothing, like something, happens anywhere.
1954. "I Remember, I Remember," *Philip Larkin Collected Poems* (Anthony Thwaite, ed.; 1988), st. 8

20 What will survive of us is love.
"An Arundel Tomb," *The Whitsun Weddings* (1964)

21 Give me your arm, old Toad;
Help me down Cemetery Road.
"Toads Revisited," *The Whitsun Weddings* (1964)

La Rochefoucauld, François (1613–80) French epigrammatist and moralist

1 There are very few people who are not ashamed of having been in love when they no longer love each other.
Reflections, or Sentence and Moral Maxims (1665), no. 71

2 Most usually our virtues are only vices in disguise.
Reflections, or Sentences and Moral Maxims (1665), Epigraph

3 Our repentance is not so much regret for the ill we have done as fear of the ill that may happen to us in consequence.
Reflections, or Sentences and Moral Maxims (1665), maxim 80

4 We are all strong enough to bear the misfortunes of others.
Reflections, or Sentences and Moral Maxims (1665), no. 19

5 Philosophy triumphs easily over past evils and future evils; but present evils triumph over it.
Reflections, or Sentences and Moral Maxims (1665), no. 22

6 We need greater virtues to sustain good fortune than bad.
Reflections, or Sentences and Moral Maxims (1665), no. 25

7 Neither the sun nor death can be looked at with a steady eye.
Reflections, or Sentences and Moral Maxims (1665), no. 26

8 If we had no faults of our own, we would not take so much pleasure in noticing those of others.
Reflections, or Sentences and Moral Maxims (1665), no. 31

9 Self-interest speaks all sorts of tongues, and plays all sorts of roles, even that of disinterestedness.
Reflections, or Sentences and Moral Maxims (1665), no. 39

10 We are never so happy nor so unhappy as we imagine.
Reflections, or Sentences and Moral Maxims (1665), no. 49

11 To succeed in the world, we do everything we can to appear successful.
Reflections, or Sentences and Moral Maxims (1665), no. 50

12 If one judges love by its visible effects, it looks more like hatred than like friendship.
Reflections, or Sentences and Moral Maxims (1665), no. 72

13 The love of justice in most men is simply the fear of suffering injustice.
Reflections, or Sentences and Moral Maxims (1665), no. 78

14 Silence is the best tactic for him who distrusts himself.
Reflections, or Sentences and Moral Maxims (1665), no. 79

15 It is more shameful to distrust one's friends than to be deceived by them.
Reflections, or Sentences and Moral Maxims (1665), no. 84

16 Everyone complains of his memory, but no one complains of his judgment.
Reflections, or Sentences and Moral Maxims (1665), no. 89

17 In the misfortune of our best friends, we always find something which is not displeasing to us.
Reflections, or Sentences and Moral Maxims (1665), no. 99

18 One gives nothing so freely as advice.
Reflections, or Sentences and Moral Maxims (1665), no. 110

19 One had rather malign oneself than not speak of oneself at all.
Reflections, or Sentences and Moral Maxims (1665), no. 138

20 To refuse praise reveals a desire to be praised twice over.
Reflections, or Sentences and Moral Maxims (1665), no. 149

21 To preserve one's health by too strict a regime is in itself a tedious malady.
Reflections, or Sentences and Moral Maxims (1665), no. 208

22 Hypocrisy is the homage paid by vice to virtue.
Reflections, or Sentences and Moral Maxims (1665), no. 218

23 The height of cleverness is to be able to conceal it.
Reflections, or Sentences and Moral Maxims (1665), no. 245

24 There is scarcely a single man sufficiently aware to know all the evil he does.
Reflections, or Sentences and Moral Maxims (1665), no. 269

25 In most of mankind gratitude is merely a secret hope for greater favors.
Reflections, or Sentences and Moral Maxims (1665), no. 298

26 We only confess our little faults to persuade people that we have no large ones.
Reflections, or Sentences and Moral Maxims (1665), no. 327

27 The accent of one's birthplace lingers in the mind and in the heart as it does in one's speech.
Reflections, or Sentences and Moral Maxims (1665), no. 342

28 We seldom attribute common sense except to those who agree with us.
Reflections, or Sentences and Moral Maxims (1665), no. 347

29 The greatest fault of a penetrating wit is to go beyond the mark.
Reflections, or Sentences and Moral Maxims (1665), no. 377

30 Our minds are lazier than our bodies.
Reflections, or Sentences and Moral Maxims (1665), no. 490

31 Quarrels would not last so long if the fault were on only one side.
Reflections, or Sentences and Moral Maxims (1665), no. 496

32 Temperance is the love of health, or the inability to overindulge.
Reflections, or Sentences and Moral Maxims (1665), no. 583

Larsen, Nella (1891–1964) U.S. novelist, nurse, and librarian

1 I'm really not such an idiot that I don't realize that if a man calls me a nigger, it's his fault the first time, but mine if he has the opportunity to do it again.
Passing (1929)

2 Religion had, after all, its uses. It blunted the perceptions. Robbed life of its crudest truths. Especially it had its uses for the poor—and the blacks.
Quicksand (1928)

3 Some day you'll learn that lies, injustice, and hypocrisy are a part of every ordinary community. Most people achieve a sort of protective immunity, a kind of callousness, toward them. If they didn't, they couldn't endure.
Quicksand (1928)

Lasch, Christopher (1932–94) U.S. historian and social critic

1 The advertising industry thus encourages the pseudo-emancipation of women, flattering them with its insinuating reminder, You've come a long way, baby, and disguising the freedom to consume as genuine autonomy.
The Culture of Narcissism (1979)

Laski, Harold (Harold Joseph Laski; 1893–1950) British political theorist and economist

1 The meek do not inherit the earth unless they are prepared to fight for their meekness.
Attrib.

Lasky, Jesse L. (Jesse Louis Lasky; 1880–1958) U.S. film producer

1 The producer must be a prophet and a general, a diplomat and a peacemaker, a miser and a spendthrift. He must have vision tempered by hindsight, daring governed by caution, the patience of a saint, and the iron of a Cromwell.
Attrib.

Latham, Peter Mere (1789–1875) U.S. poet and essayist

1 The practice of physic is jostled by quacks on the one side, and by science on the other.
"In Memoriam" (Undated), quoted in *Collected Works* (Sir Thomas Watson), vol. 1

2 Medicine is a strange mixture of speculation and action. We have to cultivate a science and to exercise an art. The calls of science are upon our leisure and our choice; the calls of practice are of daily emergence and necessity.
"Diseases of the Heart," *Lectures on Subjects connected with Clinical Medicine* (1836)

3 Truths without exception are not the truths most commonly met with in medicine.
"Diseases of the Heart," *Lectures on Subjects connected with Clinical Medicine* (1836)

Latimer, Hugh (1485?–1555) English clergyman and reformer

1 The drop of rain maketh a hole in the stone, not by violence, but by oft falling.
Sermon preached before Edward VI (April 19, 1549)

2 Therefore for the love of God appoint teachers and schoolmasters, you that have the charge of youth; and give the teachers stipends worthy of the pains.
Attrib.

Laud, William (1573–1645) English clergyman

1 Unity cannot long continue in the Church, when Uniformity is shut out at the Church door.
William Laud was impeached for treason, after his controversial attempts to impose Catholic conformity on Christian practices in England and Scotland. Although cleared of treason, he was beheaded for subverting the laws, attempting to overthrow the Protestant religion, and acting as an enemy of Parliament. Speech at his impeachment trial (March 12, 1640)

2 The poor Church of England...which all the Jesuits' machinations could not ruin, is fallen into danger by her own.
William Laud was impeached for treason, after his controversial attempts to impose Catholic conformity on Christian practices in England and Scotland. Although cleared of treason, he was beheaded for subverting the laws, attempting to overthrow the Protestant religion, and acting as an enemy of Parliament. Words spoken on the scaffold (January 10, 1645)

3 I laboured nothing more than that the external public worship of God, too much slighted in most parts of this kingdom, might be preserved.
(March 12, 1644)

Lauder, Estée (originally Estée Mentzer; b.1910?) U.S. cosmetics company executive

1 Even if your anger is justified, don't ever sever relationships, especially business relationships.
Estée, a Success Story (1985)

2 For most women...a half-boudoir, half-boardroom image is the image that works best, and neither is stronger than the other.
Estée, a Success Story (1985)

3 Observing your own and your competitors' successes and failures makes your inner business voice more sure and vivid.
Estée, a Success Story (1985)

Lauder, Harry, Sir (Harry MacLennan; 1870–1950) Scottish singer and comedian

1 Roamin' in the gloamin',
By the bonny banks of Clyde.
"Roamin' in the Gloamin" (1911)

2 I Love a Lassie
1905. Song title.

3 Keep Right on to the End of the Road
1905. Song title.

Lauren, Ralph (Ralph Lifshitz; b.1939) U.S. fashion designer

1 I don't design clothes, I design dreams.
New York Times (April 19, 1986)

2 I didn't create the designer mystique.There was always a mystique in the fashion business with names and people.
Quoted in *Ralph Lauren: The Man Behind the Mystique* (Jeffrey A. Trachtenberg; 1988)

3 When people go to a movie they come out wanting to wear what the movie star was wearing. "I want that hat, I want that dress." Why? Because they liked that person. They were romanced by the mood, not necessarily by what a person was wearing.
Quoted in *Ralph Lauren: The Man Behind the Mystique* (Jeffrey A. Trachtenberg; 1988)

4 We sell a way of life, we sell a lifestyle.
Quoted in *The Fashion Conspiracy* (Nicholas Coleridge; 1989)

Laurence, William L. (William Leonard Laurence; 1888–1977) U.S. journalist

1 At first it was a giant column that soon took the shape of a supramundane mushroom.
July 16, 1945. Referring to the explosion of the first atomic bomb in New Mexico. *New York Times* (September 26, 1945)

Laurier, Wilfrid, Sir (1841–1919) Canadian statesman

1 It has been my lot to run the whole gamut of prejudices in Canada. In 1896 I was excommunicated by the Roman priests, and in 1917 by Protestant parsons.
Letter (1917)

2 If you please, paint me as a ruler of men.
Remark to a portrait painter (1916)

3 I am a subject of the British Crown, but whenever I have to choose between the interests of England and Canada it is manifest to me that the interests of my country are identical with those of the United States of America.
Speech, Boston, Massachusetts (November 17, 1891)

4 As the nineteenth century was that of the United States, so I

think the twentieth century shall be filled by Canada.
Speech, Canadian Club, Ottawa (January 18, 1904)

5 For us, sons of France, political sentiment is a passion; while, for the Englishmen, politics are a question of business.
Speech, Montreal (May 19, 1884)

6 I have too much respect for the faith in which I was born to ever use it as the basis of a political organization.
Speech, Quebec City (June 26, 1877)

7 I have had before me as a pillar of fire by night and a pillar of cloud by day a policy of true Canadianism, of moderation, of conciliation.
Speech, St. John, Quebec (1911)

8 The French Canadian father who today does not have his son learn English does not do justice to his child, for he forces him to remain behind in the struggle for existence.
Speech to the Canadian Parliament (February 17, 1890)

9 When Britain is at war, Canada is at war; there is no distinction.
Speech to the Canadian Parliament (January 12, 1910)

10 We answer to a higher destiny.
Referring to the possibility of U.S. annexation of Canada. Quoted in *Willison's Monthly* (1928)

11 Quebec does not have opinions, but only sentiments.
Attrib.

Law, Bonar (Andrew Bonar Law; 1858–1923) Canadian-born British prime minister

1 If I am a great man, then a good many of the great men of history are frauds.
Attrib.

Law, John (1671–1729) Scottish financier

1 National Power and Wealth consists in numbers of People, and Magazines of Home and Foreign Goods. These depend on Trade, and Trade depends on Money.
Money and Trade Considered (1705)

2 The best Laws without Money cannot employ the People, improve the Product, or advance Manufacture and Trade.
Money and Trade Considered (1705)

3 To be Powerful and Wealthy in proportion to other Nations, we should have Money in proportion with them.
Money and Trade Considered (1705)

Lawrence, D. H. (David Herbert Lawrence; 1885–1930) British writer

Quotations about Lawrence

1 This pictorial account of the day-to-day life of an English gamekeeper is full of considerable interest to outdoor minded readers, as it contains many passages on pheasant-raising, the apprehending of poachers, ways to control vermin, and other chores and duties of the professional gamekeeper. Unfortunately, one is obliged to wade through many pages of extraneous material in order to discover and savour those sidelights on the management of a midland shooting estate, and in this reviewer's opinion the book cannot take the place of J. R. Miller's *Practical Gamekeeping*.
Anonymous. Review of D. H. Lawrence's novel *Lady Chatterley's Lover* (1928). Quoted in *Field and Stream* (1940s)

2 He said that, by God, D. H. Lawrence was right when he had said there must be a dumb, dark, dull, bitter belly-tension between a man and woman, and how else could this be achieved save in the long monotony of marriage?
Stella Gibbons (1902–89) British poet and novelist. *Cold Comfort Farm* (1933), ch. 20

3 Mr Lawrence has penned another novel, *Women in Love*, which justly merits the fate of its predecessor. I do not claim to be a literary critic, but I know dirt when I smell it and here it is in heaps—festering, putrid heaps.
W. Charles Pilley (1885–1937) British barrister, journalist, and critic. Review of *Women in Love* (1921) by D. H. Lawrence. *John Bull* (September 17, 1921)

4 Detestable person but needs watching. I think he learned the proper treatment of modern subjects before I did.
Ezra Pound (1885–1972) U.S. poet, translator, and critic. Remark (March 1913)

5 *Lady Chatterley's Lover* is a book that all Christians might read with profit.
John Robinson (1919–83) British clergyman and theologian. Giving evidence as a defense witness in the prosecution of Penguin Books for publishing *Lady Chatterley's Lover* by D. H. Lawrence. *Times*, London (October 28, 1960)

6 The Christian view of sex is that it is, indeed, a form of holy communion.
John Robinson (1919–83) British clergyman and theologian. Giving evidence as a defense witness in the prosecution of Penguin Books for publishing *Lady Chatterley's Lover* by D. H. Lawrence. *Times*, London (October 28, 1960)

7 His excessive emphasis on sex was due to the fact that in sex alone he was compelled to admit that he was not the only human being in the universe.
Bertrand Russell (1872–1970) British philosopher and mathematician. *The Autobiography of Bertrand Russell* (1967–69)

Quotations by Lawrence

8 I'm not sure if a mental relation with a woman doesn't make it impossible to love her. To know the *mind* of a woman is to end in hating her. Love means the pre-cognitive flow...it is the honest state before the apple.
Letter to Dr. Trigant Burrow (August 3, 1927)

9 I cannot get any sense of an enemy—only of a disaster.
Referring to World War I. Letter to Edward Marsh (October 1914)

10 The dead don't die. They look on and help.
On the death of Katherine Mansfield, who was married to Murry. Letter to J. Middleton Murry (February 2, 1923)

11 I like to write when I feel spiteful: it's like having a good sneeze.
Letter to Lady Cynthia Asquith (November 1913)

12 You mustn't think I advocate perpetual sex. Far from it. Nothing nauseates me more than promiscuous sex in and out of season.
Referring to *Lady Chatterley's Lover*. Letter to Lady Ottoline Morrell (December 20, 1928)

13 We know these new English Catholics. They are the last words in Protest. They are Protestants protesting against Protestantism.
"Review of Eric Gill," *Art Nonsense* (1936)

14 I had made a mistake, I didn't know him,
This grey, monotonous soul in the water,
This intense individual in shadow,
Fish-alive.

I didn't know his God,
I didn't know his God.
"Fish," *Birds, Beasts and Flowers* (1923)

15 A snake came to my water-trough
On a hot, hot day, and I in pyjamas for the heat,
To drink there.
"Snake," *Birds, Beasts and Flowers* (1923)

16 There are terrible spirits, ghosts, in the air of America.
Edgar Allan Poe (1924)

17 To the Puritan all things are impure, as somebody says.
"Cerveteri," *Etruscan Places* (1932)

18 The refined punishments of the spiritual mode are usually much more indecent and dangerous than a good smack.
Fantasia of the Unconscious (1922), ch. 4

19 The Romans and Greeks found everything human. Everything had a face, and a human voice. Men spoke, and their fountains piped an answer.
Fantasia of the Unconscious (1922), ch. 4

20 Morality which is based on ideas, or on an ideal, is an unmitigated evil.
Fantasia of the Unconscious (1922), ch. 7

21 When Eve ate this particular apple, she became aware of her own womanhood, mentally. And mentally she began to experiment with it. She has been experimenting ever since. So has man. To the rage and horror of both of them.
Fantasia of the Unconscious (1922), ch. 7

22 The highest function of *mind* is its function of messenger.
Kangaroo (1923)

23 There isn't much newness in *man*, whatever the country.
Kangaroo (1923)

24 The very best that is in the Jewish blood: a faculty for pure disinterestedness, and warm, physically warm love, that seems to make the corpuscles of the blood glow.
Kangaroo (1923)

25 But tha mun dress thysen, an' go back to thy stately homes of England, how beautiful they stand. Time's up! Time's up for Sir John, an' for little Lady Jane! Put thy shimmy on, Lady Chatterley!
Lady Chatterley's Lover (1928)

26 It's all this cold-hearted fucking that is death and idiocy.
Lady Chatterley's Lover (1928)

27 Some things can't be ravished. You can't ravish a tin of sardines.
Lady Chatterley's Lover (1928)

28 John Thomas says good-night to Lady Jane, a little droopingly, but with a hopeful heart.
The closing words of the book. *Lady Chatterley's Lover* (1928), ch. 19

29 Nobody can have the soul of me. My mother has had it, and nobody can have it again. Nobody can come into my very self again, and breathe me like an atmosphere.
Letters (1950)

30 How beastly the bourgeois is
especially the male of the species.
"How Beastly the Bourgeois Is," *Pansies* (1929)

31 I never saw a wild thing
Sorry for itself.
A small bird will drop frozen dead
From a bough
Without ever having felt sorry for itself.
"Self Pity," *Pansies* (1929)

32 Water is H_2O, hydrogen two parts, oxygen one,
but there is also a third thing, that makes it water
and nobody knows what that is.
"The Third Thing," *Pansies* (1929)

33 To every man who struggles with his own soul in mystery, a book that is a book flowers once, and seeds, and is gone.
"A Bibliography of D. H. L.," *Phoenix* (1929)

34 Pornography is the attempt to insult sex, to do dirt on it.
"Pornography and Obscenity," *Phoenix* (1929)

35 Away with all ideals. Let each individual act spontaneously from the for ever incalculable prompting of the creative wellhead within him. There is no universal law.
Preface to *All Things are Possible* by Leo Shostov, *Phoenix* (1929)

36 Russia will certainly inherit the future. What we already call the greatness of Russia is only her pre-natal struggling.
Preface to *All Things are Possible* by Leo Shostov, *Phoenix* (1929)

37 Neither can you expect a revolution, because there is no new baby in the womb of our society. Russia is a collapse, not a revolution.
"The Good Man," *Phoenix* (1929)

38 It is no good casting out devils. They belong to us, we must accept them and be at peace with them.
"The Reality of Peace," *Phoenix* (1929)

39 I am a man, and alive...For this reason I am a novelist. And being a novelist, I consider myself superior to the saint, the scientist, the philosopher, and the poet, who are all great masters of different bits of man alive, but never get the whole hog.
"Why the Novel Matters," *Phoenix* (1929)

40 One realizes with horror, that the race of men is almost extinct in Europe. Only Christ-like heroes and woman-worshipping Don Juans, and rabid equality-mongrels.
Sea and Sardinia (1921)

41 And suddenly she craved again for the more absolute silence of America. English stillness was so soft, like an inaudible murmur of voices, of presences.
St. Mawr (1925)

42 Ideal mankind would abolish death, multiply itself million upon million, rear up city upon city, save every parasite alive, until the accumulation of mere existence is swollen to a horror.
St. Mawr (1925)

43 It always seemed to me that men wore their beards, like they wear their neckties, for show. I shall always remember Lewis for saying his beard was part of him.
St. Mawr (1925)

44 The modern pantheist not only sees the god in everything, he takes photographs of it.
St. Mawr (1925)

45 There's nothing so artificial as sinning nowadays. I suppose it once was real.
St. Mawr (1925)

46 Why doesn't the past decently bury itself, instead of sitting and waiting to be admitted by the present?
St. Mawr (1925)

47 You may have my husband, but not my horse. My husband won't need emasculating, and my horse I won't have you meddle with. I'll preserve one last male thing in the museum of this world, if I can.
St. Mawr (1925)

48 Never trust the artist. Trust the tale. The proper function of a critic is to save the tale from the artist who created it.
Studies in Classic American Literature (1923), ch. 1

49 You must always be a-waggle with LOVE.
Referring to a dog. "Bibbles," *The Complete Poems of D. H. Lawrence* (Vivian de Sola Pinto and Warren Roberts, eds.; 1964)

50 We have all lost the war. All Europe.
"The Ladybird," *The Ladybird* (1923)

51 Be a good animal, true to your animal instincts.
The White Peacock (1911), pt. 2, ch. 2

52 No absolute is going to make the lion lie down with the lamb unless the lamb is inside.
Twilight in Italy (1916)

Lawrence, George (*fl.* 19th century) U.S. abolitionist

1 As the continual dropping of water has a tendency to wear away the hardest and most flinty substance, so likewise shall we, abounding in good works, and causing our examples to shine forth as the sun at noon day, melt their callous hearts, and render sinewless the arm of sore oppression.
"An Oration on the Abolition of the Slave Trade" (January 1, 1813)

2 There could be many reasons given, to prove that the mind of an African is not inferior to that of an European; yet to do so would be superfluous. It would be like adding hardness to the diamond, or luster to the sun.
"An Oration on the Abolition of the Slave Trade" (January 1, 1813)

Lawrence, James (1781–1813) U.S. naval officer

1 Don't give up the ship.
Last words as he lay dying in his ship, the U.S. frigate *Chesapeake*, during the battle with the British frigate *Shannon.* Attrib. (1813)

Lawrence, T. E. (Thomas Edward Lawrence, "Lawrence of Arabia"; 1888–1935) British adventurer, soldier and writer

Quotations about Lawrence

1 He had a genius for backing into the limelight.
Lord Berners (1883–1950) British composer and painter. Attrib.

2 There are those who have tried to dismiss his story with a flourish of the Union Jack, a psycho-analytical catchword, or a sneer. It should move our deepest admiration and pity. Like Shelley and like Baudelaire it may be said of him that he suffered, in his own person, the neurotic ills of an entire generation.
Christopher Isherwood (1904–86) British-born U.S. writer. "Lawrence of Arabia," *Exhumations* (1966)

Quotations by Lawrence

3 All men dream: but not equally. Those who dream by night... wake in the day to find that it was vanity: but the dreamers of the day are dangerous men, for they may act their dream with open eyes, to make it possible.
Seven Pillars of Wisdom (1926), ch. 1

Lazarus, Emma (1849–87) U.S. poet

1 Give me your tired, your poor,
Your huddled masses yearning to breathe free.
Used as an inscription on the Statue of Liberty, New York City (1886). "The New Colossus" (1883)

2 Night and beneath star-blazened summer skies
Behold the spirit of the musky South,
A creole with still-burning, languid eyes,
Voluptuous limbs and incense-breathing mouth.
"The South," *The Poems of Emma Lazarus* (Mary and Annie Lazarus, ed.; 1889), ll. 1–4

Leach, Bernard (Bernard Howell Leach; 1887–1979) British potter

1 There can be no fullness or complete realization of utility without beauty, refinement and charm, for the simple reason that their absence must...be intolerable to both maker and consumer.
The Potter's Book (1940)

Leach, Edmund, Sir (Edmund Ronald Leach; 1910–89) British social anthropologist

1 Far from being the basis of the good society, the family, with its narrow privacy and tawdry secrets, is the source of all our discontents.
BBC Reith Lecture, *Listener*, London (November 30, 1967)

Leach, Penelope (b.1937) British psychologist and writer

1 Kids haven't changed much, but parents seem increasingly unhappy with the child-raising phase of their lives.
Remark (October 1988)

Leacock, Stephen (Stephen Butler Leacock; 1869–1944) British-born Canadian writer and economist

1 Independent, we could not survive a decade.
Speech, Empire Club, Toronto (1907)

2 The classics are only primitive literature. They belong in the

same class as primitive machinery and primitive music and primitive medicine.
"Homer and Humbug," *Behind the Beyond* (1913)

3 If every day in the life of a school could be the last day but one, there would be little fault to find with it.
"Memories and Miseries of a Schoolmaster," *College Days* (1923)

4 Advertising may be described as the science of arresting human intelligence long enough to get money from it.
Garden of Folly (1924)

5 In Canada we have enough to do keeping up with two spoken languages without trying to invent slang, so we just go right ahead and use English for literature, Scotch for sermons, and American for conversations.
How to Write (1944)

6 It is the wishes and likings of the mass which largely dictate what the rest of us shall see and hear.
Humour: Its Theory and Technique (1935)

7 The Americans...admire us for the way we hang criminals. They...say, "You certainly do hang them, don't you!" My! they'd like to hang a few! The day may be coming when they will. Meantime we like to hang people to make the Americans sit up.
I'll Stay in Canada. Funny Pieces (1931)

8 I am a great believer in luck, and I find the harder I work the more I have of it.
Literary Lapses (1910)

9 Many a man in love with a dimple makes the mistake of marrying the whole girl.
Literary Lapses (1910)

10 Astronomy teaches the correct use of the sun and the planets.
"A Manual of Education," *Literary Lapses* (1910)

11 The landlady of a boarding-house is a parallelogram—that is, an oblong angular figure, which cannot be described, but which is equal to anything.
"Boarding-House Geometry," *Literary Lapses* (1910)

12 Get your room full of good air, then shut up the windows and keep it. It will keep for years. Anyway, don't keep using your lungs all the time. Let them rest.
"How to Live to be 200," *Literary Lapses* (1910)

13 I detest life-insurance agents; they always argue that I shall some day die, which is not so.
"Insurance: Up to Date," *Literary Lapses* (1910)

14 It takes a good deal of physical courage to ride a horse. This, however, I have. I get it at about forty cents a flask, and take it as required.
"Reflections on Riding," *Literary Lapses* (1910)

15 The great man...walks across his century and leaves the marks of his feet all over it, ripping out the dates on his galoshes as he passes.
"The Life of John Smith," *Literary Lapses* (1910)

16 Higher education in America flourished chiefly as a qualification for entrance into a moneymaking profession, and not as a thing in itself.
My Discovery of England (1922)

17 A "Grand Old Man". That means on our continent any one with snow-white hair who has kept out of jail till eighty.
"Three Score and Ten," *My Remarkable Uncle* (1942)

18 Golf may be played on Sunday, not being a game within the view of the law, but being a form of moral effort.
"Why I Refuse to Play Golf," *Over the Footlights* (1923)

19 He had broken the law. How he had come to do so, it passed his imagination to recall. Crime always seems impossible in retrospect.
"The Hostelry of Mr. Smith," *Sunshine Sketches of a Little Town* (1912)

20 I have always found that the only kind of statement worth making is an overstatement. A half-truth, like half a brick, is always more forcible as an argument than a whole one. It carries further.
"The Perfect Salesman," *The Garden of Folly* (1924)

21 I am a Liberal Conservative, or, if you will, a Conservative Liberal with a strong dash of sympathy with the Socialist idea, a friend of Labour, and a believer in Progressive Radicalism. I...would take a seat in the Canadian Senate at five minutes' notice.
The Hohenzollerns in America (1919)

22 Medieval education was supposed to fit people to die. Any schoolboy of today can still feel the effect of it.
Too Much College (1939)

23 The colonial status is a worn-out, by-gone thing. The sense and feeling of it has become harmful to us. It limits the ideas...impairs the mental vigor and narrows the outlook of those who are reared and educated in our midst.
University Magazine (1907)

24 The general idea, of course, in any first-class laundry is to see that no shirt or collar ever comes back twice.
Winnowed Wisdom (1926), ch. 6

Leadbelly (Huddie Ledbetter; 1888–1949) U.S. folk and blues musician

1 No white man ever had the blues.
Attrib.

Leahy, Frank (Frank William Leahy; 1908–73) U.S. football coach

1 Egotism is the anesthetic that dulls the pains of stupidity.
Look (January 10, 1955)

Lear, Amanda (b.1946) U.S. singer

1 Disco is the lowest form of music, but the quickest way to fame.
1978. Quoted in *Rock 'n' Roll Babylon* (Gary Herman; 1994)

Lear, Edward (1812–88) British writer and artist

1 There was an Old Man with a beard,
Who said, "It is just as I feared!—
Two Owls and a Hen,

Four Larks and a Wren,
Have all built their nests in my beard!"

"There was an old man with a beard," *A Book of Nonsense* (1846), quoted in *The Complete Nonsense of Edward Lear* (Holbrook Jackson, ed.; 1947)

2 And those who watch at that midnight hour
From Hall or Terrace, or lofty Tower,
Cry, as the wild light passes along,–
"The Dong!—the Dong!
The wandering Dong through the forest goes!
The Dong! the Dong!
The Dong with a luminous Nose!"

"The Dong with a Luminous Nose," *Laughable Lyrics* (1877), ll. 19–25, quoted in *The Complete Nonsense of Edward Lear* (Holbrook Jackson, ed.; 1947)

3 The Pobble who has no toes
Had once as many as we;
When they said, "Some day you may lose them all";
He replied,–"Fish fiddle de-dee!"

"The Pobble who has no Toes," *Laughable Lyrics* (1877), st. 1, quoted in *The Complete Nonsense of Edward Lear* (Holbrook Jackson, ed.; 1947)

4 And she made him a feast at his earnest wish
Of eggs and buttercups fried with fish;—
And she said,—"It's a fact the whole world knows,
That Pobbles are happier without their toes."

"The Pobble Who Has No Toes," *Laughable Lyrics* (1877), st. 6, quoted in *The Complete Nonsense of Edward Lear* (Holbrook Jackson, ed.; 1947)

5 "But the longer I live on this Crumpetty Tree
The plainer than ever it seems to me
That very few people come this way
And that life on the whole is far from gay!"
Said the Quangle-Wangle Quee.

"The Quangle-Wangle's Hat," *Laughable Lyrics* (1877), st. 2, quoted in *The Complete Nonsense of Edward Lear* (Holbrook Jackson, ed.; 1947)

6 "And what can we expect if we haven't any dinner,
But to lose our teeth and eyelashes and keep on growing
thinner?"

"The Two Old Bachelors," *Laughable Lyrics* (1877), ll. 7–8, quoted in *The Complete Nonsense of Edward Lear* (Holbrook Jackson, ed.; 1947)

7 There was an old man of Thermopylae,
Who never did anything properly;
But they said, "If you choose
To boil eggs in your shoes,
You shall never remain in Thermopylae."

"There was an old man of Thermopylae," *More Nonsense* (1872), quoted in *The Complete Nonsense of Edward Lear* (Holbrook Jackson, ed.; 1947)

8 There was an old person of Slough,
Who danced at the end of a bough;
But they said, "If you sneeze,
You might damage the trees,
You imprudent old person of Slough."

"There was an old person of Slough," *More Nonsense* (1872), quoted in *The Complete Nonsense of Edward Lear* (Holbrook Jackson, ed.; 1947)

9 There was an old person of Ware,
Who rode on the back of a bear:
When they asked,"Does it trot?"
He said, "Certainly not!
He's a Moppsikon Floppsikon bear."

"There was an old person of Ware," *More Nonsense* (1872), quoted in *The Complete Nonsense of Edward Lear* (Holbrook Jackson, ed.; 1947)

10 How pleasant to know Mr Lear!
Who has written such volumes of stuff!
Some think him ill-tempered and queer,
But a few think him pleasant enough.

Edward Lear's self-description and the preface to *Nonsense Songs.* "How pleasant to know Mr Lear," *Nonsense Songs* (1871), ll. 1–4, quoted in *The Complete Nonsense of Edward Lear* (Holbrook Jackson, ed.; 1947), Preface

11 He reads but he cannot speak Spanish,
He cannot abide ginger-beer:
Ere the days of his pilgrimage vanish,
How pleasant to know Mr Lear!

"How pleasant to know Mr Lear," *Nonsense Songs* (1871), ll. 29–32, quoted in *The Complete Nonsense of Edward Lear* (Holbrook Jackson, ed.; 1947), Preface

12 He has many friends, laymen and clerical;
Old Foss is the name of his cat;
His body is perfectly spherical,
He weareth a runcible hat.

Preface, *Nonsense Songs* (1871), ll. 17–20, quoted in *The Complete Nonsense of Edward Lear* (Holbrook Jackson, ed.; 1947)

13 Who, or why, or which, or *what*,
Is the Akond of SWAT?

"The Akond of Swat," *Nonsense Songs* (1871), quoted in *The Complete Nonsense of Edward Lear* (Holbrook Jackson, ed.; 1947)

14 They went to sea in a sieve, they did
In a sieve they went to sea.

"The Jumblies," *Nonsense Songs* (1871), ll. 1–2, quoted in *The Complete Nonsense of Edward Lear* (Holbrook Jackson, ed.; 1947)

15 Far and few, far and few,
Are the lands where the Jumblies live;
Their heads are green, and their hands are blue,
And they went to sea in a Sieve.

"The Jumblies," *Nonsense Songs* (1871), ll. 11–14, quoted in *The Complete Nonsense of Edward Lear* (Holbrook Jackson, ed.; 1947)

16 The Owl and the Pussy-Cat went to sea
In a beautiful pea-green boat,
They took some honey, and plenty of money,
Wrapped up in a five-pound note.

"The Owl and the Pussy-Cat," *Nonsense Songs* (1871), st. 1, quoted in *The Complete Nonsense of Edward Lear* (Holbrook Jackson, ed.; 1947)

17 The Owl looked up to the Stars above
And sang to a small guitar,
"Oh lovely Pussy! O Pussy, my love,
What a beautiful Pussy you are, You are,
You are!
What a beautiful pussy you are!"

"The Owl and the Pussy-Cat," *Nonsense Songs* (1871), st. 1, quoted in *The Complete Nonsense of Edward Lear* (Holbrook Jackson, ed.; 1947)

18 Pussy said to the Owl, "You elegant fowl!
How charmingly sweet you sing!
O let us be married! too long we have tarried:
But what shall we do for a ring?"

"The Owl and the Pussy-Cat," *Nonsense Songs* (1871), st. 2, quoted in *The Complete Nonsense of Edward Lear* (Holbrook Jackson, ed.; 1947)

19 They sailed away for a year and a day,
To the land where the Bong-tree grows,

And there in a wood a Piggy-wig stood
With a ring at the end of his nose.
"The Owl and the Pussy-Cat," *Nonsense Songs* (1871), st. 2, quoted in *The Complete Nonsense of Edward Lear* (Holbrook Jackson, ed.; 1947)

Leary, Timothy (1920–96) U.S. psychologist and guru

1 Science is all metaphor.
Remark (September 24, 1980)

2 Like Communism and Christianity, psychoanalysis was a revered orthodoxy that brought respectability and fortune to an elite.
Flashbacks: an Autobiography (1983)

3 In four hours by the swimming pool in Cuernavaca I learned more about the mind, the brain, and its structure than I did in the preceding fifteen as a diligent psychologist.
Referring to his first experience of psychedelic drugs. *Flashbacks: an Autobiography* (1983)

4 They had changed on the objective indices so dear to the heart of the psychologist. They showed less depression, hostility, anti-social tendencies; more energy, responsibility, cooperation.
Referring to results of drug therapy with convicts. *Flashbacks: an Autobiography* (1983)

5 It's better to die than become a victim of the whole dying industry—religion, morticians, politicians.
Guardian, London (December 2, 1995)

6 All that Freud said is that modern man and modern society are completely dishonest.
The Politics of Ecstasy (1968)

7 Emotions are the lowest form of consciousness. Emotional actions are the most contracted, narrowing, dangerous form of behavior.
The Politics of Ecstasy (1968)

8 Modern psychology, like modern man, does not like to see the sparse, wrinkled-skin facts about human transience. The personality chess game is blown up to compelling importance.
The Politics of Ecstasy (1968)

9 Pursuing the religious life today without using psychedelic drugs is like studying astronomy with the naked eye because that's how they did it in the first century A.D.
The Politics of Ecstasy (1968)

10 Turn on, tune in, drop out.
June 1966. Lecture, *The Politics of Ecstasy* (1968)

Lease, Mary Elizabeth (originally Mary Elizabeth Clyens; 1853–1933) U.S. reformer

1 The farmers of Kansas must raise less corn and more Hell.
Campaign speech (1890)

2 The people are at bay, let the bloodhounds of money beware.
Campaign speech, Wichita, Kansas (October 1894)

Lebed, Alexander (Alexander Ivanovich Lebed; b.1950) Russian general and politician

1 He who doesn't take risks, doesn't drink champagne.
New York Times (January 23, 1997)

2 The highest skyscraper in the world cannot be built next to the Kremlin. We cannot allow anyone spitting from the roof of the skyscraper on the Kremlin.
Said in response to Donald Trump's building ambitions in Moscow. *New York Times* (January 23, 1997)

Lebowitz, Fran (b.1951?) U.S. writer and columnist

1 Food is an important part of a balanced diet.
Metropolitan Life (1978)

2 Girls who put out are tramps. Girls who don't are ladies. This is, however, a rather archaic use of the word. Should one of you boys happen upon a girl who doesn't put out, do not jump to the conclusion that you have found a lady.
Metropolitan Life (1978)

3 Life is something to do when you can't get to sleep.
Metropolitan Life (1978)

4 Never judge a cover by its book.
A twist on the usual saying: "Never judge a book by its cover." *Metropolitan Life* (1978)

Leboyer, Frédérick (b.1918) French obstetrician

1 Birth may be a matter of a moment. But it is a unique one.
Birth Without Violence (1991)

2 Making love is the sovereign remedy for anguish.
Birth without Violence (1991)

Lebrecht, Norman (b.1948) British writer

1 A woman may be elected Prime Minister. She may administer justice in the High Courts, and the sacraments in the Church, but she cannot be trusted with a symphony orchestra for a couple of hours.
The Maestro Myth: Great Conductors in Pursuit of Power (1991)

Lec, Stanislaw (Stanislaw Jerzy Lec; 1909–66) Polish writer

1 I give you bitter pills in sugar coating. The pills are harmless, the poison is in the sugar.
Unkempt Thoughts (1962)

2 The dispensing of injustice is always in the right hands.
Unkempt Thoughts (1962)

3 All people are actors, but where do we find them a repertoire?
1964. Quoted in *The Jingle Bell Principle* (Miroslav Holub; 1992)

4 Everything has been said already. But not everyone has said it.
1964. Quoted in *The Jingle Bell Principle* (Miroslav Holub; 1992)

5 Illiterates have to dictate.
1964. Quoted in *The Jingle Bell Principle* (Miroslav Holub; 1992)

6 In order to be yourself you first have to be somebody.
1964. Quoted in *The Jingle Bell Principle* (Miroslav Holub; 1992)

Le Carré, John (pen name of David John Moore Cornwell; b.1931) British novelist

1 A committee is an animal with four back legs.
Tinker, Tailor, Soldier, Spy (1974)

Le Corbusier (professional name of Charles Édouard Jeanneret; 1887–1965) Swiss-born French architect

1 A house is a machine for living in.
1923. *Towards a New Architecture* (Frederick Etchells, tr.; 1927)

2 Architecture is the masterly, correct, and magnificent play of masses brought together in light.
1923. *Towards a New Architecture* (Frederick Etchells, tr.; 1927)

3 It is a question of building which is at the root of the social unrest of today: architecture or revolution.
1923. *Towards a New Architecture* (Frederick Etchells, tr.; 1927)

4 Profile and contour are the touchstone of the Architect. Here he reveals himself as artist or mere engineer.
1923. *Towards a New Architecture* (Frederick Etchells, tr.; 1927)

5 Absence of verbosity, good arrangement, a single idea, daring and unity in construction, the use of elementary shapes. A sane morality.
1923. Referring to the architecture of ancient Rome. *Towards a New Architecture* (Frederick Etchells, tr.; 1927)

6 Demand bare walls in your bedroom, your living room, and your dining room...Buy only practical furniture and never buy "decorative" pieces. If you want to see bad taste, go into the houses of the rich. Put only a few pictures on your walls and none but good ones.
Attrib.

7 The materials of city planning are: sky, space, trees, steel, and cement; in that order and that hierarchy.
Attrib.

Ledru-Rollin, Alexandre Auguste (1807–74) French lawyer and politician

1 Let me pass, I have to follow them, I am their leader.
1848. Trying to force his way through a mob during the Revolution of 1848, of which he was one of the chief instigators. The Fine Art of Political Wit, *Les contemporains,* (E. de Mirecourt; 1857), vol. 14, "Ledru-Rollin"

Lee, Gypsy Rose (Louise Rose Hovick; 1914–70) U.S. entertainer

1 God is love, but get it in writing.
Attrib.

Lee, Hannah Farnham (Hannah Farnham Sawyer Lee; 1780–1865) U.S. writer

1 Time had robbed her of her personal charms, and that scourge of the human race, the gout, was racking her bones and sinews.
Referring to Catherine de Medici. *The Huguenots in France and America* (1843)

2 A good nurse is of more importance than a physician.
The Log-Cabin (1844)

Lee, Harper (Nelle Harper Lee; b.1926) U.S. writer

1 Introductions inhibit pleasure, kill the joy of anticipation, frustrate curiosity.
Interview, *Times,* London (August 26, 1995)

2 Being Southerners, it was a source of shame to some members of the family that we had no recorded ancestors on either side of the Battle of Hastings.
To Kill a Mockingbird (1960), ch. 1

3 Shoot all the bluejays you want, if you can hit 'em, but remember it's a sin to kill a mockingbird.
To Kill a Mockingbird (1960), ch. 10

4 The one thing that doesn't abide by majority rule is a person's conscience.
To Kill a Mockingbird (1960), ch. 11

5 Folks don't like to have somebody around knowin' more than they do. It aggravates 'em. You're not gonna change any of them by talkin' right, they've got to want to learn themselves.
To Kill a Mockingbird (1960), ch. 12

Lee, Jennie, Baroness Lee of Ashridge (1904–88) Scottish politician

1 Better to enjoy and suffer than sit around with folded arms. You know the only true prayer? Please God, lead me into temptation.
My Life with Nye (1980)

Lee, Kuan Yew (b.1923) Singaporean statesman

1 We got one little island—600 square kilometres. You unwind this, you will not drop on soft paddy fields, it is hard, hard concrete, your bones are broken and it's kaput.
Referring to the consequences of Singapore's embracing Western values. Speech, National Day, *Independent,* London (November 24, 1995)

2 I'm not sure China can improve her performance by allowing populist politics. It has no tradition of democratic restraint. It's a tradition of winner takes all.
Referring to the Tiananmen Square massacre (1989). Interview, *Newsweek* (December 10, 1990)

3 They're not in prison with their fingernails pulled out.
Replying to an interviewer's suggestion that he was too tough on his political opponents in Singapore. Interview, *Newsweek* (December 10, 1990)

4 I had one simple guiding principle of survival from the very start, that Singapore had to be better organised than the countries of the region.
Explaining that to survive as a city state, Singapore had to leapfrog its neighbors economically. *Straits Times,* Singapore (June 8, 1996)

5 If you were to allow me to speak without inhibitions, I would say simply that you have carried the rights of individuals to the point where the individual now threatens the rest of society.
Referring to western individualism and the fight against crime. *Straits Times,* Singapore (June 6, 1996)

Lee, Laurie (1914–97) British novelist and poet

1 As the drought continued, prayer was abandoned and more devilish steps adopted. Finally soldiers with rifles marched to the tops of the hills and began shooting at passing clouds.
"First Names," *Cider With Rosie* (1959)

2 But the horse was king, and almost everything grew around him...This was what we were born to, and all we knew at first. Then, to the scream of the horse, the change began. The

brass-lamped motor-car came coughing up the road.
"Last Days," *Cider With Rosie* (1959)

3 Being so recently born, birth had no meaning; it was the other extreme that enthralled me. Death was absorbing, and I saw much of it; it was my childhood's continuous fare.
"Public Death, Private Murder," *Cider with Rosie* (1959)

4 "The Workhouse"—always a word of shame, grey shadow falling on the close of life, most feared by the old (even when called The Infirmary); abhorred more than debt, or prison, or beggary, or even the stain of madness.
"Public Death, Private Murder," *Cider with Rosie* (1959)

Lee, Richard Henry (1732–94) American revolutionary leader

1 That these United Colonies are, and of right ought to be, free and independent states.
This resolution, of the Continental Congress, Philadelphia (1776) gave rise to the Declaration of Independence. (June 7, 1776)

Lee, Robert E. (Robert Edward Lee; 1807–70) U.S. general

1 My experience through life has convinced me that, while moderation and temperance in all things are commendable and beneficial, abstinence from spirituous liquors is the best safeguard of morals and health.
Remark (December 9, 1869)

2 I should be trading on the blood of my men.
Refusing to write his memoirs. Quoted in *Nobody Said It Better!* (Miriam Ringo; 1980)

3 It is well that war is so terrible; else we would grow too fond of it.
Speaking to another general during the battle of Fredericksburg. *The Reader's Digest Treasury of American Humor* (Clifton Fadiman; 1862)

Lee, Spike (Shelton Jackson Lee; b.1957) U.S. film director

1 I agree that agents are necessary, but they're still one of the lowest forms of life.
Do The Right Thing (Spike Lee and Ralph Jones; 1989), p. 94

2 A lot of people are disappointed when they meet me.
Spike Lee's Gotta Have It (1987), p. 47

Lee-Potter, Linda British journalist

1 Powerful men often succeed through the help of their wives. Powerful women only succeed in spite of their husbands.
Daily Mail, London (May 16, 1984)

Leeuwenhoek, Antoni van (1632–1723) Dutch maker of microscopes

1 Examining this water...I found floating therein divers earthy particles, and some green streaks, spirally wound serpent-wise...and I judge that some of these little creatures were above a thousand times smaller than the smallest ones I have ever yet seen, upon the rind of cheese, in wheaten flour, mould, and the like.
September 7, 1674. The first recorded observation of protozoa. Quoted in *Antony van Leeuwenhoek and his 'Little Animals'* (Clifford Dobell, ed., tr.; 1958)

Lefèvre, Théo (1914–73) Belgian statesman and lawyer

1 In Western Europe there are now only small countries—those that know it and those that don't know it yet.
Observer, London (1963), "Sayings of the Week"

Le Guin, Ursula (originally Ursula Kroeber; b.1929) U.S. writer

1 He had grown up in a country run by politicians who sent the pilots to man the bombers to kill the babies to make the world safe for children to grow up in.
The Lathe of Heaven (1971)

Lehman, Ernest (b.1915) U.S. screenwriter

1 The Sweet Smell of Success
1957. Novel and film title.

Lehmann, Rosamond (Rosamond Nina Lehmann; 1901–90) British novelist

1 One can present people with opportunities. One cannot make them equal to them.
The Ballad and the Source (1945)

Lehrer, Keith (b.1936) U.S. philosopher

1 When I was young, I thought that any philosopher who abandoned minute analytical method to construct a philosophical system was done for. But I feel all right.
"Metamental Ascent," *Proceedings of the American Philosophical Association* (1990)

Lehrer, Tom (Thomas Andrew Lehrer; b.1928) U.S. mathematician and songwriter

1 He was into animal husbandry—until they caught him at it.
Record album. *An Evening Wasted with Tom Lehrer* (1953)

2 Life is like a sewer. What you get out of it depends on what you put into it.
Record album. *We Will All Go Together When We Go* (1953)

Leiber, Jerry (b.1933) U.S. lyricist and producer

1 You ain't nothin' but a hound dog,
Cryin' all the time.
"Hound Dog" (with Mike Stoller; 1956)

2 The Beatles are second to none in all departments. I don't think there has ever been a better song written than "Eleanor Rigby."
Quoted in "Jerry Leiber," *Off the Record: An Oral History of Popular Music* (Joe Smith; 1988)

Leibniz, Gottfried Wilhelm (Baron Gottfried Wilhelm von Leibniz; 1646–1716) German philosopher and mathematician

1 Since all possible things have a claim to existence in God's understanding in proportion to their perfections, the result of all these claims must be the most perfect actual world which is possible.
"The Principles of Nature and Grace, based on Reason" (1714), quoted in *G. W. Leibniz: Philosophical Essays and Letters* (L. E. Loemker, ed.; 1969)

2 Music charms us, although its beauty consists only in the agreement of numbers and in the counting.
"The Principles of Nature and Grace, based on Reason" (1714), quoted in *G. W. Leibniz: Philosophical Papers and Letters* (L. E. Loemker, ed.; 1969)

3 The supreme wisdom, united to a goodness that is no less infinite, cannot have chosen but the best...So it may be said that if this were not the best of all possible worlds, God would not have created any.
The origin of the notion "the best of all possible worlds" as espoused by Doctor Pangloss in Voltaire's *Candide* (1759). *Essays in Theodicy on the Goodness of God, the Liberty of Man, and the Origin of Evil* (1710), bk. 1, sect. 8

4 Pleasure is a knowledge or feeling of perfection, not only in ourselves, but also in others, for in this way some further perfection is aroused in us.
"Felicity," *Leibniz: Political Writings* (Patrick Riley, ed., tr.; 1988)

5 To love is to find pleasure in the perfection of another.
"Felicity," *Leibniz: Political Writings* (Patrick Riley, ed., tr.; 1988)

6 Virtue is the habit of acting according to wisdom. It is necessary that practice accompany knowledge.
"Felicity," *Leibniz: Political Writings* (Patrick Riley, ed., tr.; 1988)

7 As there is an infinite number of possible universes in the ideas of God, and as only one can exist, there must be a sufficient reason for God's choice, to determine him to one rather than to another.
Monadology (1714)

8 There are two kinds of truths: truths of *reasoning* and truths of *fact*. Truths of *reasoning* are necessary and their opposite is impossible; those of *fact* are contingent and their opposite is possible.
Monadology (1714)

9 There is nothing waste, nothing sterile, nothing dead in the universe; no chaos, no confusions, save in appearance.
Monadology (1714)

10 The soul follows its own laws, and the body its own likewise, and they accord by virtue of the *harmony pre-established* among all substances, since they are all representations of one and the same universe.
Monadology (1714)

11 It is one of my most important and best verified maxims that *nature makes no leaps*. This I have called the *law of continuity*.
New Essays Concerning Human Understanding (1703)

12 Music is the pleasure the human soul experiences from counting without being aware that it is counting.
Quoted in *Mathematical Maxims and Minims* (N. Rose; 1988)

Leigh, Dorothy (d.1616) English author

1 A woman fit to be a man's wife is too good to be his servant.
The Mother's Blessing (1616), ch. 13

Leigh, Vivien (1913–67) Indian-born British actor

1 In Britain, an attractive woman is somehow suspect. If there is talent as well it is overshadowed. Beauty and brains just can't be entertained; someone has been too extravagant.
Light of a Star (1967)

Lekachman, Robert U.S. author

1 Capitalists are a self-nominating group. To join them is a matter of seizing an opportunity, mobilizing one's savings, borrowing from relatives, friends, and banks, working hard and intelligently, and testing one's acumen and luck.
Capitalism for Beginners (1981)

LeMay, Curtis Emerson ("Old Iron Pants"; 1906–90) U.S. air force chief

1 My solution to the problem would be to tell them...they've got to draw in their horns or we're going to bomb them into the Stone Age.
Referring to the North Vietnamese. *Mission with LeMay* (1965)

Lemmon, Jack (John Uhler Lemmon III; b.1925) U.S. film actor

1 You know, I used to live like Robinson Crusoe, shipwrecked among eight million people. Then one day I saw a footprint in the sand and there you were.
As C. C. Baxter, owner of the apartment of the movie title, to Miss Kubelik (Shirley MacLaine). *The Apartment* (Billy Wilder and I. A. L. Diamond; 1960)

Lenclos, Ninon de (Anne de Lenclos; 1620–1705) French courtesan

1 Old age is woman's hell.
Attrib.

Lenin, Vladimir Ilyich (Vladimir Ilyich Ulyanov; 1870–1924) Russian revolutionary leader

Quotations about Lenin

1 Lenin was greatly influenced by the scholarship of Marx, in much the same way as many contemporary business leaders are influenced by the works of leading economists and management scholars.
Warren Bennis (b.1925) U.S. educationalist and writer. *Beyond Leadership: Balancing Economics, Ethics and Ecology* (co-written with Jagdish Parikh and Ronnie Lessem; 1994)

2 Their worst misfortune was his birth; their next worst—his death.
Winston Churchill (1874–1965) British prime minister and writer. *The World Crisis* (1923–29)

3 What hope is there for Russia if Lenin, who transformed her most, did not destroy but strengthened the tie between Russian progress and Russian slavery?
Vasily Grossman (1905–64) Russian writer. *Forever Flowing* (Thomas P. Whitney, tr.; 1970), ch. 22

4 Lenin was the first to discover that capitalism "inevitably" caused war; and he discovered this only when the First World War was already being fought... Capitalism obviously "caused" the First World War; but just as obviously it had "caused" the previous generation of Peace.
A. J. P. Taylor (1906–90) British historian. *The Origins of the Second World War* (1961), ch. 6

5 Lenin's method leads to this: the party organization at first substitutes itself for the party as a whole. Then the central committee substitutes itself for the party organization, and

finally a single dictator substitutes himself for the central committee.
Leon Trotsky (1879–1940) Russian revolutionary leader. Attrib.

Quotations by Lenin

6 Do everything so that the people will see, tremble, and groan for miles and miles around...P.S. Search out hard people.
Directive sent to Bolshevik forces at Penza (August 11, 1918), quoted in *Corriere della Sera* (February 13, 1992)

7 From today I shall cease being a socialist and shall become a communist.
Referring to the vote by the German Social Democrats in the Reichstag for war credits. Remark (August 1914), quoted in *Europe: A History* (Norman Davies; 1996), ch. 10

8 We shall now proceed to construct the socialist order.
Speech at the Congress of Soviets (October 26, 1917)

9 Dear comrades, soldiers, sailors and workers! I am happy to greet in you the victorious Russian Revolution!
Speech at the Finland Station, Petrograd (April 1917)

10 Any day, if not today or tomorrow, the crash of the whole of European imperialism may come...Hail the worldwide socialist revolution.
Speech to the crowd on his arrival at the Finland Station, Petrograd (April 3, 1917), quoted in *Europe Since 1870* (James Joll; 1973), ch. 8

11 Communism is Soviet power plus the electrification of the whole country.
Political slogan of 1920, promoting the program of electrification. Report to 8th Congress, *Collected Works* (1920), vol. 42

12 A mighty accelerator of events.
Referring to war. *Letters from Afar* (1917), quoted in *Collected Works of V. I. Lenin* (Alexander Trachtenberg, ed.; 1930)

13 One step forward, two steps back...It happens in the lives of individuals, and it happens in the history of nations and in the development of parties.
One Step Forward, Two Steps Back (1904)

14 When a liberal is abused, he says: Thank God they didn't beat me. When he is beaten, he thanks God they didn't kill him. When he is killed, he will thank God that his immortal soul has been delivered from its mortal clay.
December 1906. Lenin heard this characterization at a meeting, and repeated it with approval. "Proletary," *The Government's Falsification of the Duma and the Tasks of the Social-Democrats* (1906)

15 In a state worthy of the name there is no liberty. The people want to exercise power but what on earth would they do with it if it were given to them?
The State and Revolution (1919)

16 The substitution of the proletarian for the bourgeois state is impossible without a violent revolution.
The State and Revolution (1919), ch. 1

17 A democracy is a state which recognizes the subjecting of the minority to the majority.
The State and Revolution (1919), ch. 4

18 Under capitalism we have a state in the proper sense of the word, that is, a special machine for the suppression of one class by another.
The State and Revolution (1919), ch. 5

19 While the state exists there can be no freedom. When there is freedom there will be no state.
The State and Revolution (1919), ch. 5

20 Under socialism *all* will govern in turn and will soon become accustomed to no one governing.
The State and Revolution (1919), ch. 6

21 It is true that liberty is precious—so precious that it must be rationed.
Attrib. *Soviet Communism* (Sidney and Beatrice Webb; 1936)

22 Any cook should be able to run the country.
Quoted in *The First Circle* (Alexander Solzhenitsyn; 1968)

23 But I can't listen to music too often. It affects your nerves, makes you want to say stupid, nice things, and stroke the heads of people who could create such beauty while living in this vile hell.
Remark to Maksim Gorky, while listening to Beethoven. Quoted in *The History of the Russian Revolution* (Leon Trotsky; M. Easterman, tr.; 1933)

24 The most important thing in illness is never to lose heart.
Quoted in *The Secret of Soviet Strength* (Hewlett Johnson; 1943), bk. 2, ch. 3, sect. 2

Lennon, John (John Winston Lennon; 1940–80) British rock musician

Quotations about Lennon

1 Imagine six apartments
It isn't hard to do
One is full of fur coats
The other's full of shoes.
1980
Elton John (b.1947) British pop singer and songwriter. Message in the card sent to John Lennon on his 40th birthday. The words mimic the lyrics of Lennon's song "Imagine" (1971). Quoted in "Favourites," *Small Talk Big Names* (Myles Palmer; 1993)

2 In truth, they were never great collaborators in the sense of Rogers and Hart...It was a competitive collaboration. In fact, Paul misses it terribly now. He misses that spark of John being rude to him, saying, "You can't write that, Paul. It's awful".
George Martin (b.1926) British record producer. Referring to John Lennon and Paul McCartney. Quoted in "George Martin," *Off the Record: An Oral History of Popular Music* (Joe Smith; 1988)

3 I felt the weight of the break-up because he had been communicating and having an extremely intense and stimulating exchange with three very intelligent...guys and now he expected all that to be replaced by me.
Yoko Ono (b.1933) Japanese-born U.S. musician, writer, campaigner, and artist. Referring to John Lennon, and The Beatles' split. Quoted in "Yoko Ono," *Off the Record: An Oral History of Popular Music* (Joe Smith; 1988)

Quotations by Lennon

4 Life is what happens to you while you're busy making other plans.
"Beautiful Boy" (1979)

5 All we are saying is Give Peace a Chance.
Song lyric. "Give Peace A Chance" (1969)

6 Imagine there's no heaven
It's easy if you try
No hell below us

Above us only sky
Imagine all the people
Living for today.
"Imagine" (1971)

7 Would the people in the cheaper seats clap your hands? And the rest of you, if you'll just rattle your jewellery.
Remark, Royal Variety performance (November 4, 1963)

8 A working class hero is something to be.
Song lyric. "Working Class Hero" (1970)

9 We're more popular than Jesus Christ now. I don't know which will go first. Rock and roll or Christianity.
Evening Standard, London (March 4, 1966)

10 Rock 'n' roll was not fun anymore. I chose not to take the standard options in my business—going to Vegas and singing your great hits, if you're lucky, or going to hell, which is where Elvis went.
Interview, *Playboy* (1980)

11 I don't know how much money I've got...I did ask the accountant how much it came to. I wrote it down on a bit of paper. But I've lost the bit of paper.
Quoted in *The Beatles* (Hunter Davies; 1968)

12 My little rebellion was to have my tie loose, with the top button of my shirt undone, but Paul'd always come up to me and put it straight.
Quoted in *The Wit and Wisdom of Rock and Roll* (Maxim Jabukowski, ed.; 1983)

13 Women should be obscene and not heard.
Quoted in *The Wit and Wisdom of Rock and Roll* (Maxim Jabukowski, ed.; 1983)

Lennon & McCartney (John Winston Lennon, 1940–80, and Paul McCartney, b. 1942) British rock musicians

1 Waits at the window, wearing the face that she keeps in a jar by the door.
Who is it for? All the lonely people, where do they all come from?
All the lonely people, where do they all belong?
Song lyric. "Eleanor Rigby" (1966)

2 Well here's another clue for you all
The walrus was Paul.
Song lyric. "Glass Onion" (1968)

3 She Loves You, Yeh, Yeh, Yeh
Song title. "She Loves You" (1963)

4 I get by with a little help from my friends.
Song lyric. "With a Little Help from My Friends" (1967)

5 It's been a hard day's night.
Originally said by Ringo Starr, during filming of the then untitled Beatles film, *A Hard Day's Night.*
"A Hard Day's Night," *A Hard Day's Night* (1964)

6 For I don't care too much for money,
For money can't buy me love.
"Can't Buy Me Love," *A Hard Day's Night* (1964)

7 All You Need Is Love
Song title. *Magical Mystery Tour* (1968?)

8 If there's anything that you want,
If there's anything I can do,
Just call on me,
And I'll send it along with love from me to you.
"From Me to You," *Please Please Me* (1963)

9 He's a real Nowhere Man,
Sitting in his Nowhere Land,
Making all his nowhere plans for nobody.
Doesn't have a point of view,
Knows not where he's going to,
Isn't he a bit like you and me?
"Nowhere Man," *Rubber Soul* (1965)

10 Yesterday, all my troubles seemed so far away.
"Yesterday," *Rubber Soul* (1965)

11 Sergeant Pepper's Lonely Hearts Club Band
Album title.

12 I've got to admit it's getting better.
It's a little better all the time.
"Getting Better," *Sergeant Pepper's Lonely Hearts Club Band* (1967)

13 When I caught a glimpse of Rita
Filling in a ticket in her little white book
In a cap she looked much older
And the bag across her shoulder
Made her look a little like a military man
Lovely Rita Meter Maid.
"Lovely Rita," *Sergeant Pepper's Lonely Hearts Club Band* (1967)

14 Picture yourself in a boat on a river with tangerine trees and marmalade skies.
Somebody calls you, you answer quite slowly a girl with kaleidoscope eyes.
"Lucy in the Sky with Diamonds," *Sergeant Pepper's Lonely Hearts Club Band* (1967)

15 She's leaving home after living alone for so many years.
"She's Leaving Home," *Sergeant Pepper's Lonely Hearts Club Band* (1967)

16 Will you still need me, will you still feed me
When I'm sixty-four?
"When I'm Sixty-Four," *Sergeant Pepper's Lonely Hearts Club Band* (1967)

17 Happiness is a Warm Gun
1968. Song title.

18 I Want to Hold Your Hand
1963. Song title.

19 Let It Be
1970. Song title.

20 Why Don't We Do It in the Road?
1968. Song title.

Lenthall, William (1591–1662) English parliamentarian

1 I have neither eye to see, nor tongue to speak here, but as the House is pleased to direct me.
January 4, 1642. Reply in the English Parliament when asked by Charles I if he had seen five MPs whom the King wished to arrest. It was a succinct restatement of the Speaker's traditional role.
Historical Collections. The Third Part (John Rushworth; 1692), vol. 2

Leo X, Pope (Giovanni de' Medici; 1475–1521) Italian pope

1 Arise, O Lord, plead Thine own cause; remember how the foolish man reproacheth Thee daily; the foxes are wasting

Thy vineyard, which Thou hast given to Thy Vicar Peter, the boar out of the wood doth waste it, and the wild beast of the field doth devour it.
Exsurge Domine, *Papal Bull*, preface, quoted in *Oratio Constantii Moventini de virtute Clauiu, & Bulla Condemnationis Leonis Decimi* (Constantius Eubulus; 1521)

2 Since God has given us the papacy, let us enjoy it.
Quoted in *Men of Art* (Thomas Craven; 1933)

León, Luis Ponce de (1527–91) Spanish monk, poet, and scholar

1 As I was saying the other day.
Remark on resuming a lecture interrupted by five years imprisonment. Attrib.

Leonard, Graham, Sir (Graham Douglas Leonard; b.1921) British churchman

1 The purpose of population is not ultimately peopling earth. It is to fill heaven.
Contribution to a debate on the Church and the Bomb. Remark, General Synod of the Church of England (February 10, 1983)

Leonard, Sugar Ray (Ray Charles Leonard; b.1956) U.S. boxer

1 People in boxing is against me. People is jealous and envious. I'm like a diamond in the mud.
Sunday Times, London (September 20, 1981)

2 What helped me develop my quickness was fear. I think the rougher the opponent, the quicker I am.
Attrib.

Leonardo da Vinci (1452–1519) Italian artist, engineer, and inventor

Quotations about Leonardo da Vinci

1 He was the most relentlessly curious man in history. Everything he saw made him ask how and why. Why does one find sea-shells in the mountains? How do they build locks in Flanders?...Find out; write it down; if you can see it, draw it.
1970
Kenneth Clark (1903–83) British art historian. *Civilisation* (1969)

2 He bores me. He ought to have stuck to his flying machines.
Pierre Auguste Renoir (1841–1919) French painter. Attrib.

3 Leonardo undertook for Francesco Zanobi del Giocondo the portrait of his wife Mona Lisa...He engaged people to play and sing, and jesters to keep her merry, and remove that melancholy which painting usually gives to portraits. This figure of Leonardo's has such a pleasant smile that it seems rather divine than human.
Giorgio Vasari (1511–74) Italian biographer, writer, architect, and painter. "Leonardo da Vinci," *The Lives of the Most Eminent Italian Architects, Painters, and Sculptors* (1550)

4 Leonardo da Vinci used to convince his patrons that his thinking time was worth...even more than his painting time and that may have been true for him, but I know that my thinking time isn't worth anything. I only expect to get paid for my "doing" time.
Andy Warhol (1928?–87) U.S. artist and filmmaker. *The Philosophy of Andy Warhol: From A to B and Back Again* (1975)

Quotations by Leonardo da Vinci

5 Painting can be shown to be philosophy because it deals with the motion of bodies in the promptitude of their actions, and philosophy too deals with motion.
"The Paragone," *First Part of the Book on Painting* (1651)

6 Painting is poetry which is seen and not heard, and poetry is a painting which is heard but not seen.
"The Paragone," *First Part of the Book on Painting* (1651)

7 A man with wings large enough and duly attached might learn to overcome the resistance of the air, and conquering it succeed in subjugating it and raise himself upon it.
Notebooks (1508–18)

8 Mechanics is the paradise of the mathematical sciences, because by means of it one comes to the fruits of mathematics.
Notebooks (1508–18)

9 Those who are enamored of practice without science are like a pilot who goes into a ship without rudder or compass and never has any certainty where he is going.
Practice should always be based upon a sound knowledge of theory.
Notebooks (1508–18)

10 You know that medicines when well used restore health to the sick: they will be well used when the doctor together with his understanding of their nature shall understand also what man is, what life is, and what constitution and health are. Know these well and you will know their opposites; and when this is the case you will know well how to devise a remedy.
Notebooks (1508–18)

11 The poet ranks far below the painter in the representation of visible things, and far below the musician in that of invisible things.
Notebooks (1508–18), quoted in *Selections from the Notebooks of Leonardo da Vinci* (Irma A. Richter, ed.; 1952)

12 While I thought that I was learning how to live, I have been learning how to die.
Notebooks (1508–18), quoted in *Selections from the Notebooks of Leonardo da Vinci* (Irma A. Richter, ed.; 1952)

13 Whatever exists in the universe, whether in essence, in act, or in the imagination, the painter has first in his mind and then in his hands.
Notebooks (1508–18), quoted in *Treatise On Painting* (A. P. McMahon, tr.; 1956)

14 When I painted Our Lord as a boy, you put me in gaol; if I were now to paint him as a grown man, you would do worse to me.
Quoted in *Homosexuality: A History* (Colin Spencer; 1995)

15 A bird is an instrument working according to a mathematical law, which instrument it is within the capacity of man to reproduce, with all its movements.
Quoted in *The Notebooks of Leonardo da Vinci* (Edward McCurdy, tr.; 1928)

16 The peaks of the Apennines once stood up in a sea, in the form of islands surrounded by salt water, and above the plains of Italy where flocks of birds are flying today, fishes were once moving in large shoals.
Quoted in *The Notebooks of Leonardo da Vinci* (Edward McCurdy, tr.; 1928)

Leonidas, King of Sparta (d.480? B.C.) Spartan monarch

1 Go, stranger, and tell the Lacedaemonians that here we lie, obedient to their commands.
Inscription over the tomb in which he and his followers were buried after their defeat at Thermopylae. Epitaph (480 B.C.)

Leopold, Aldo (Rand Aldo Leopold; 1886–1948) U.S. naturalist, conservationist, and philosopher

1 Conservation is a state of harmony between men and land.
"The Land Ethic," *A Sand County Almanac* (1949), pt. 3

2 Wild things were taken for granted until progress began to do away with them...we face the question whether a still higher "standard of living" is worth its cost in things natural, wild, and free.
Quoted in *National Geographic Magazine* (November 1981)

3 We abuse land because we regard it as a commodity belonging to us. When we see land as a community to which we belong, we may begin to use it with love and respect.
Quoted in *The Quiet Crisis* (Stewart L. Udall; 1963)

Leopold II, King of Belgium (1835–1909) Belgian monarch

1 A constitutional king must learn to stoop.
Instructing Prince Albert, the heir apparent, to pick up some papers that had fallen onto the floor. Quoted in *The Mistress: the Domestic Scandals of Nineteenth Century Monarchs* (Betty Kelen; 1966)

Lermontov, Mikhail (Mikhail Yuryevich Lermontov; 1814–41) Russian poet and novelist

1 I was travelling post from Tiflis. The only luggage I had on my cart was one small portmanteau half-filled with travel notes on Georgia. Luckily for you most of them have been lost.
Opening words. *A Hero of Our Time* (Paul Foote, tr.; 1840)

Lerner, Alan Jay (1918–86) U.S. lyricist and librettist

1 Don't let it be forgot
That once there was a spot
For one brief shining moment that was known
As Camelot.
Song lyric. "Camelot," *Camelot* (1960)

2 Oh, yes I remember it well.
Song lyric. "I Remember It Well," *Gigi* (1958)

3 Thank heaven for little girls,
For little girls get bigger every day.
Song lyric. "Thank Heaven for Little Girls," *Gigi* (1958)

4 I Could Have Danced All Night
Song title. *My Fair Lady* (1956)

5 An Englishman's way of speaking absolutely classifies him
The moment he talks he makes some other Englishman despise him.
My Fair Lady (1956), Act 1, Scene 1

6 All I want is a room somewhere,
Far away from the cold night air;
With one enormous chair...
Oh, wouldn't it be loverly?
Song lyric. *My Fair Lady* (1956), Act 1, Scene 1

7 I'd be equally as willing
For a dentist to be drilling
Than to ever let a woman in my life.
Song lyric. *My Fair Lady* (1956), Act 1, Scene 2

8 Oozing charm from every pore,
He oiled his way around the floor.
Song lyric. *My Fair Lady* (1956), Act 2, Scene 1

9 I'm getting married in the morning?
Ding dong! the bells are gonna chime.
Pull out the stopper!
Let's have a whopper!
But get me to the church on time!
Song lyric. *My Fair Lady* (1956), Act 2, Scene 3

10 Why can't a woman be more like a man?
Men are so honest, so thoroughly square;
Eternally noble, historically fair.
Song lyric. *My Fair Lady* (1956), Act 2, Scene 4

11 I've grown accustomed to the trace
Of something in the air,
Accustomed to her face.
Song lyric. *My Fair Lady* (1956), Act 2, Scene 6

12 On a Clear Day You Can See Forever
1965. Song title.

13 You write a hit the same way you write a flop.
Attrib.

Lerner, Gerda (b.1920) Austrian-born U.S. educator and historian

1 Women's history is the primary tool for women's emancipation.
On the Future of Our Past (1981)

Lerner, Max (1902–92) Russian-born U.S. editor and social scientist

1 It is not science that has destroyed the world, despite all the gloomy forebodings of the earlier prophets. It is man who has destroyed man.
"The Human Heart and the Human Will," *Actions and Passions* (1949)

2 Sometimes I think that dancing, like youth, is wasted on the young.
The Unfinished Country (1959)

3 What is dangerous about the tranquilizers is that whatever peace of mind they bring is a packaged peace of mind. Where you buy a pill and buy peace with it, you get conditioned to cheap solutions instead of deep ones.
The Unfinished Country (1959)

Lesage, Alain René (1668–1747) French writer

1 Justice is such a fine thing that we cannot pay too dearly for it.
Crispin rival de son maître (1707), pt. 9

2 I wish you all sorts of prosperity with a little more taste.
Gil Blas (1715–35), bk. 7, ch. 4

3 Isocrates was in the right to insinuate, in his elegant Greek expression, that what is got over the Devil's back is spent under his belly.
Gil Blas (1715–35), bk. 8, ch. 9

4 They made peace between us; we embraced, and we have been mortal enemies ever since.
Le Diable boiteux (1707), ch. 3

Leslie, Eliza (1787–1858) U.S. writer

1 She had always found occupation to be one of the best medicines for an afflicted mind.
"Constance Allerton; or the Mourning Suits," *Pencil Sketches; or, Outlines of Character and Manners* (1833)

Lessing, Doris (b.1919) British novelist and short-story writer

1 In university they don't tell you that the greater part of the law is learning to tolerate fools.
Martha Quest (1952), pt. 3, ch. 2

2 If a fish is the movement of water embodied, given shape, then cat is a diagram and pattern of subtle air.
Particularly Cats (1967), ch. 2

3 That is what learning is. You suddenly understand something you've understood all your life, but in a new way.
The Four-Gated City (1969)

4 When old settlers say "One has to understand the country," what they mean is, "You have to get used to our ideas about the native." They are saying, in effect, "Learn our ideas, or otherwise get out; we don't want you."
Referring specifically to South Africa. *The Grass is Singing* (1950), ch. 1

5 When a white man in Africa by accident looks into the eyes of a native and sees the human being (which it is his chief preoccupation to avoid), his sense of guilt, which he denies, fumes up in resentment and he brings down the whip.
The Grass is Singing (1950), ch. 8

Lessing, Gotthold Ephraim (1729–81) German playwright and critic

1 A man who does not lose his reason over certain things has none to lose.
Emilia Galotti (1772), Act 4, Scene 7

2 What we find beautiful in a work of art is not found beautiful by the eye, but by our imagination through the eye.
Laokoon (1766), ch. 6, quoted in *Laocoon, Nathan the Wise & Minna von Barnhelm* (W. A. Steel, ed.; 1930)

3 It is not right to seem richer than one really is.
Minna von Barnhelm (1763), Act 3, Scene 7, quoted in *Laocoon, Nathan the Wise & Minna von Barnhelm* (W. A. Steel, ed.; 1930)

4 This is medicine, not poison that I bring.
Spoken by Nathan, referring to the healing power of the plain truth. *Nathan the Wise* (1779), Act 1, Scene 2, quoted in *Laocoon, Nathan the Wise & Minna von Barnhelm* (W. A. Steel, ed.; 1930)

5 The true beggar...is the true king.
Nathan the Wise (1779), Act 2, Scene 9, quoted in *Laocoon, Nathan the Wise & Minna von Barnhelm* (W. A. Steel, ed.; 1930)

6 We can only tolerate miracles in the physical world; in the moral everything must retain its neutral course, because the theater is to be the school of the moral.
1767. Quoted in *Hamburg Dramaturgy* (Victor Lange, ed.; 1962), no. 2

7 Nothing is great that is not true.
1767. Quoted in *Hamburg Dramaturgy* (Victor Lange, ed.; 1962), no. 30

Lester, Julius (b.1939) U.S. writer, educator, and political activist

1 It might help things a helluva lot if Justice would take off that blindfold. Seeing a few things might help her out, 'cause it's obvious her hearing ain't none too good.
Look Out Whitey! Black Power's Gon' Get Your Mama (1968), p. 8

2 If anyone wonders why the anger of blacks is so often turned upon the white liberal, it is because, while professing to be a friend, the white liberal has generally turned out to be more white than liberal whenever blacks assert themselves.
Look Out Whitey! Black Power's Gon' Get Your Mama (1968), p. 53

3 The human ego is like an insatiable tick. If it is not killed, it can burrow under the layers of the soul and feed upon the man within, gorging itself until there is no man left.
November 23, 1968. *Revolutionary Notes* (1970), p. 177

4 In Vietnam I learned that the revolutionary is he who cries for those he has killed.
Search for the New Land (1969), p. 129

L'Estrange, Roger, Sir (1616–1704) English journalist and pamphleteer

1 Though this may be play to you, 'tis death to us.
Aesop's Fables (1692), no. 398

Lethaby, W. R. (William Richard Lethaby; 1857–1931) British architect

1 Art is not a special sauce applied to ordinary cooking; it is the cooking itself if it is good.
"Art and Workmanship," *Form in Civilization: Collected Papers on Art and Labour* (1922)

Letterman, David (b.1947) U.S. entertainer

1 New York now leads the world's great cities in the number of people around whom you shouldn't make a sudden move.
Late Night with David Letterman (February 9, 1984)

2 For the love of God, folks, don't do this at home.
Demonstrating the Donut-o-pult. *Late Show*, CBS television (1995)

Lettsom, John Coakley (1744–1815) British physician

1 Medicine is not a lucrative profession. It is a divine one.
Letter to a friend (September 6, 1791)

Levant, Oscar (1906–72) U.S. pianist and actor

Quotations about Levant

1 There is absolutely nothing wrong with Oscar Levant that a miracle cannot fix.
Alexander Woollcott (1887–1943) U.S. writer and critic. Quoted in *The Vicious Circle* (M. C. Harriman; 1951)

Quotations by Levant

2 I'm a controversial figure. My friends either dislike me or hate me.
Artemus Ward, His Book (1964), introduction

3 Strip the phony tinsel off Hollywood and you'll find the real tinsel underneath.
Attrib.

4 Play us a medley of your hit.
Replying to George Gershwin's barb "If you had it all over again, would you fall in love with yourself?" Attrib.

Leverhulme, William Hesketh Lever, 1st Viscount (1851–1925) British industrialist and philanthropist

1 Half the money I spend on advertising is wasted, and the trouble is I don't know which half.
Quoted in *Confessions of an Advertising Man* (David Ogilvy; 1964)

Leverson, Ada (pen name Elaine; 1862–1933) British writer and journalist

1 It is an infallible sign of the second-rate in nature and intellect to make use of everything and everyone.
The Limit (1911)

2 I'm sure he had a fork in the other.
Reply when told by Oscar Wilde of a devoted apache (Parisian gangster) who used to follow him with a knife in one hand. Attrib.

Levertov, Denise (1923–97) British-born U.S. poet and writer

1 Your eyes were the brown gold of pebbles under water.
I never crossed the bridge over the Roding, dividing
the open field of the present from the mysteries,
the wraiths and shifts of time-sense Wanstead Park held
suspended,
without remembering your eyes.
An elegy for her sister, Olga Levertov. "Olga Poems" (1966), quoted in *The Norton Anthology of American Literature* (Nina Baym, ed.; 1998), vol. 2

2 This is the year the old ones,
the old great ones
leave us alone on the road.
In 1961 William Carlos Williams and Hilda Doolittle both had severe strokes, and Ezra Pound stopped writing. "September 1961" (1964), quoted in *The Norton Anthology of American Literature* (Nina Baym, ed.; 1998), vol. 2

3 It's not terror, it's pain we're talking about:
those places in us, like your dog's bruised head,
that are bruised forever, that time
never assuages, never.
"Zeroing In" (1987), quoted in *The Norton Anthology of American Literature* (Nina Baym, ed.; 1998), vol. 2

Levi, Primo (1919–87) Italian writer and chemist

1 The future of humanity is uncertain, even in the most prosperous of countries, and the quality of life deteriorates; and yet I believe what is being discovered about the infinitely large and infinitely small is sufficient to absolve the end of the century and millennium.
Other People's Trade (1985)

Levin, Bernard (b.1928) British journalist and author

1 Once, when a British Prime Minister sneezed, men half a world away would blow their noses. Now when a British Prime Minister sneezes nobody else will even say "Bless You."
Times, London (1976)

Levin, Kurt German social psychologist

1 Nothing is so practical as a good theory.
Quoted in *The Age of Heretics* (Art Kleiner; 1996)

Levinas, Emmanuel (1905–95) Lithuanian-born French philosopher

1 Humanism must be denounced because it is not sufficiently human.
1974. *Otherwise than Being, or Beyond Essence* (Alphonso Lingis, tr.; 1981)

2 Politics is opposed to morality, as philosophy to naïveté.
Totality and Infinity (1969)

3 What could an entirely rational being speak of with another entirely rational being?
Totality and Infinity (1969)

Levine, Sherrie (b.1947) U.S. photographer and conceptual artist

1 A painting's meaning lies not in its origin, but in its destination. The birth of the viewer must be at the cost of the painter.
"Five Comments" (1981), quoted in *Blasted Allegories: An Anthology of Writings by Contemporary artists* (Brian Wallis, ed.; 1987)

2 A picture is a tissue of quotations drawn from the innumerable centers of culture...We can only imitate a gesture that is always interior, never original.
"Five Comments" (1981), quoted in *Blasted Allegories:An Anthology of Writings by Contemporary Artists* (Brian Wallis, ed.; 1987)

Lévis, Pierre Marc Gaston de, Duc (1755–1830) French writer and soldier

1 Nobility has its own obligations.
"Morale: Maximes et Préceptes," *Maximes et Réflexions* (1812), no. 73

Lévi-Strauss, Claude (Claude Gustave Lévi-Strauss; b.1908) French anthropologist

1 Language is a form of human reason and has its reasons which are unknown to man.
The Savage Mind (1966)

2 The anthropologist respects history, but he does not accord it a special value. He conceives it as a study complementary to his own: one of them unfurls the range of human societies in time, the other in space.
The Savage Mind (1966)

3 For us European earth-dwellers, the adventure played out in the...New World signifies in the first place that it was not our

world and that we bear responsibility for the crime of its destruction.
Tristes Tropiques (1955), ch. 38

Levy, Paul (b.1941) British author and broadcaster

1 The southern Chinese...will eat almost anything...Southerners themselves tell the story about the Indian and the Cantonese confronted by a creature from outer space: the Indian falls to his knees and begins to worship it, while the Chinese searches his memory for a suitable recipe.
Out to Lunch (1986)

Lévy, Bernard Henri (b.1949) Algerian-born French philosopher

1 The totalitarian state is not unleashed force, it is truth in chains.
La Barbarie à visage humain (1977)

Lewes, George Henry (1817–78) British philosopher and writer

Quotations about Lewes

1 Women who are content with light and easily broken ties do *not* act as I have done. They obtain what they desire and are still invited to dinner.
George Eliot (1819–80) British novelist. Referring to her life with George Lewes. Attrib.

Quotations by Lewes

2 Murder, like talent, seems occasionally to run in families.
The Physiology of Common Life (1859), ch. 12

Lewis, Alun (1915–44) Welsh poet

1 Forgive this strange inconstancy of soul,
The face distorted in a jungle pool
That drowns its image in a mort of leaves.
"The Jungle," *The Oxford Book of Welsh Verse in English* (Gwyn Jones, ed.; 1977)

2 I have begun to die
And the guns' implacable silence
Is my black interim, my youth and age,
In the flower of fury, the folded poppy,
Night.
"The Sentry," *Twentieth Century Anglo-Welsh Poetry* (Dannie Abse, ed.; 1997)

Lewis, C. S. (Clive Staples Lewis; 1898–1963) Irish-born British novelist

1 Many things—such as loving, going to sleep or behaving unaffectedly—are done worst when we try hardest to do them.
Studies in Medieval and Renaissance Literature (1966)

2 Telling us to obey instinct is like telling us to obey "people." People say different things: so do instincts. Our instincts are at war...Each instinct, if you listen to it, will claim to be gratified at the expense of the rest.
The Abolition of Man (1943)

3 Compared with this revolution the Renaissance is a mere ripple on the surface of literature.
Referring to the appearance of the concept of courtly love in the 12th century. *The Allegory of Love* (1936)

4 Friendship is unnecessary, like philosophy, like art.... It has no survival value; rather it is one of those things that give value to survival.
"Friendship," *The Four Loves* (1960)

5 There must be several young women who would render the Christian life intensely difficult to him if only you could persuade him to marry one of them.
The Screwtape Letters (1942)

6 The Future is something which everyone reaches at the rate of sixty minutes an hour, whatever he does, whoever he is.
The Screwtape Letters (1942), no. 25

7 She's the sort of woman who lives for others—you can always tell the others by their hunted expression.
The Screwtape Letters (1942), no. 26

8 There is wishful thinking in Hell as well as on earth.
The Screwtape Letters (1942), preface

Lewis, D. B. Wyndham (Dominic Bevan Wyndham Lewis; 1891–1969) British journalist and writer

1 I am one of those unfortunates to whom death is less hideous than explanations.
Welcome to All This (1931)

Lewis, Drew U.S. presidential envoy

1 Saying sulfates do not cause acid rain is the same as saying that smoking does not cause lung cancer.
1985. Quoted in *Speaking Freely* (Stuart Berg Flexner and Anne H. Soukhanov; 1997)

Lewis, Flora U.S. journalist

1 Any realistic sense of the world today leaves it clear that there isn't going to be any German reunification this century, nor probably in the lifetime of anyone who can read this.
1984. Germany was reunified on October 3, 1990. *New York Times* (September 7, 1984)

Lewis, George Cornewall, Sir (1806–63) British statesman and writer

1 Life would be tolerable, were it not for its amusements.
Times, London (September 18, 1872)

Lewis, Jerry Lee (b.1935) U.S. rock-and-roll singer and pianist

1 I'm draggin' the audience to hell with me.
Referring to his stage performances. Quoted in *Hellfire: The Jerry Lee Lewis Story* (Nick Tosches; 1982)

2 Elvis was the greatest but I'm the best.
Quoted in *Man on Fire, The Face* (Nick Kent; 1989)

Lewis, Joe E. (Joe E. Klewan; 1902–71) U.S. comedian

1 Whenever someone asks me if I want water with my Scotch, I say I'm thirsty, not dirty.
Quoted in *Speaking Freely* (Stuart Berg Flexner and Anne H. Soukhanov; 1997)

Lewis, John L. (John Llewellyn Lewis; 1880–1969) U.S. labor leader

1 No tin-hat brigade of goose-stepping vigilantes or Bible-babbling mob of blackguarding and corporation-paid

scoundrels will prevent the onward march of labor.
Time (September 9, 1937)

2 I'm not interested in classes...Far be it from me to foster inferiority complexes among the workers by trying to make them think they belong to some special class. That has happened in Europe but it hasn't happened here yet.
Quoted in *The Coming of the New Deal* (A. M. Schlesinger, Jr.; 1958), pt. 7, ch. 25

Lewis, Roy U.S. writer

1 We know more about the motives, habits, and most intimate arcana of the primitive peoples of New Guinea or elsewhere, than we do of the denizens of the executive suites in Unilever House.
Referring to the international industrial company Unilever and its headquarters in London. *The Boss* (co-written with Rosemary Stewart; 1958)

Lewis, Sinclair (Harry Sinclair Lewis; 1885–1951) U.S. novelist

Quotations about Lewis

1 He was a writer who drank, not, as so many have believed, a drunk who wrote.
James Lundquist (b.1941) U.S. writer and critic. *The Mervill Guide to Sinclair Lewis* (1970)

Quotations by Lewis

2 A sensational event was changing from the brown suit to the gray the contents of his pockets. He was earnest about these objects. They were of eternal importance, like baseball or the Republican party.
Babbitt (1922)

3 In fact there was but one thing wrong with the Babbitt house; it was not a home.
Babbitt (1922), ch. 2

4 In other countries, art and literature are left to a lot of shabby bums living in attics and feeding on booze and spaghetti, but in America the successful writer or picture-painter is indistinguishable from any other decent business man.
Babbitt (1922), ch. 14

5 She did her work with the thoroughness of a mind that reveres details and never quite understands them.
Babbitt (1922), ch. 18

6 It Can't Happen Here
1935. Book title.

7 Our American professors like their literature clear and cold and pure and very dead.
On receiving a Nobel Prize in literature. (December 12, 1930)

8 A smile that snapped back after using, like a stretched rubber band.
Attrib.

Lewis, Wyndham (Percy Wyndham Lewis; 1882–1957) British novelist and painter

1 "Dying for an idea," again, sounds well enough, but why not let the idea die instead of you?
The Art of Being Ruled (1926), pt. 1, ch. 1

2 I believe that (in one form or another) castration may be the solution. And the feminization of the white European and American is already far advanced, coming in the wake of the war.
The Art of Being Ruled (1926), pt. 2, ch. 2

3 The "homo" is the legitimate child of the "suffragette."
The Art of Being Ruled (1926), pt. 8, ch. 4

LeWitt, Sol (b.1928) U.S. artist

1 In Conceptual art the idea or concept is the most important aspect of the work...all planning and decisions are made beforehand and the execution is a perfunctory affair. The idea becomes the machine that makes the art.
"Paragraphs on Conceptual Art," *Artforum* (Summer, 1967)

Leybourne, George (Joseph Saunders; 1842–84) British songwriter

1 O, he flies through the air with the greatest of ease,
This daring young man on the flying trapeze.
Song lyric. "The Man on the Flying Trapeze" (1868)

Liang Qichao (also known as Liang Ch'i-ch'ao; 1873–1929) Chinese scholar and political reformer

1 The countries of Europe compare their systems and are continually spurring one another on. In this way the talents of their peoples get richer by emulation. China proudly considers herself great and powerful and declares that no one is her equal.
Late 19th century. Quoted in *The Chinese* (Alain Peyrefitte, ed.; Graham Webb, tr.; 1977)

Li Bai (also known as Li Po; 701–762) Chinese poet

1 Seafarers tell of the Fairy Isles
Hid in sprays of great seas, not easily sought;
Yue people say the Queen of the Skies
Can for moments be seen in a rainbow's light.
"A Song of Adieu to the Queen of the Skies, after a Dream Voyage to Her" (8th century), quoted in *Li Po and Tu Fu* (Arthur Cooper, tr.; 1973), ll. 1–4

2 And never let a goblet of gold
face the bright moon empty.
Heaven bred in me talents,
and they must be put to use.
"Bring in the Wine" (8th century), quoted in *An Anthology of Chinese Literature* (Stephen Owen, tr.; 1996)

3 Here among flowers one glass of wine,
with no close friends, I pour it alone.
I lift cup to bright moon, beg its company,
then facing my shadow, we become three.
"Drinking Alone by Moonlight" (8th century), quoted in *An Anthology of Chinese Literature* (Stephen Owen, tr.; 1996)

4 You rode up on your bamboo steed,
Round garden beds we juggled green plums;
Living alike in Changgan village
We were both small, without doubts or guile.
"The Ballad of Changgan" (8th century), quoted in *Li Po and Tu Fu* (Arthur Cooper, tr.; 1973)

Liberace (Wladziu Valentino Liberace; 1919–87) U.S. pianist and entertainer

Quotations about Liberace

1 Liberace has always been my total hero, just for the way he can take the piss out of himself and yet stop the traffic at the same time.

Ian Dury (b.1942) British songwriter and singer. Referring to the U.S. pianist Liberace, who performed popular classics in a flamboyant style. Quoted in *The Wit and Wisdom of Rock and Roll* (Maxim Jabukowski, ed.; 1983)

Quotations by Liberace

2 When the reviews are bad I tell my staff that they can join me as I cry all the way to the bank.

Said when asked whether he minded being criticized. *Liberace: An Autobiography* (1973), ch. 2

Lichtenberg, Georg Christoph (1742–99) German physicist and writer

1 Great men too make mistakes, and many among them do it so often that one is almost tempted to call them little men.

Aphorisms (1764–99)

2 Man is a masterpiece of creation; if only because no amount of determinism can prevent him from believing that he acts as a free being.

Aphorisms (1764–99)

3 Nothing is more conducive to peace of mind than not having an opinion.

Aphorisms (1764–99)

4 Probably no invention came more easily to man than Heaven.

Aphorisms (1764–99)

5 That man is the noblest of all creatures may also be inferred from the fact that no other creature has yet denied him the title.

Aphorisms (1764–99)

6 The most accomplished monkey cannot draw a monkey, this too only man can do; just as it is also only man who regards this as his merit.

Aphorisms (1764–99)

7 There can hardly be a stranger commodity in the world than books. Printed by people who don't understand them; sold by people who don't understand them; bound, criticized and read by people who don't understand them; and now even written by people who don't understand them.

Aphorisms (1764–99)

8 After all, is our idea of God anything more than personified incomprehensibility?

Quoted in *The Reflections of Lichtenberg* (Norman Alliston, tr.; 1908)

Lichtenstein, Roy (1923–97) U.S. painter

1 Everybody has called Pop Art "American" painting, but it's actually industrial painting.

1963. Quoted in "What is Pop Art? Interviews with Eight Painters," *Art News* (G. R. Swenson; February 1964), 62, no. 10

2 Organized perception is what art is all about...It is a process. It has nothing to do with any external form the painting takes, it has to do with a way of building a unified pattern of seeing.

1963. Quoted in "What is Pop Art? Interviews with Eight Painters," *Art News* (G. R. Swenson; February 1964), 62, no. 10

Lie, Trygve (Trygve Halvdan Lie; 1896–1968) Norwegian statesman

1 Now we are in a period which I can characterize as a period of cold peace.

Observer, London (August 21, 1949), "Sayings of the Week"

2 A real diplomat is one who can cut his neighbor's throat without having his neighbor notice it.

Attrib.

Liebig, Justus, Baron von (1803–73) German chemist and educator

1 We are too much accustomed to attribute to a single cause that which is the product of several, and the majority of our controversies come from that.

Attrib.

Li He (also known as Li Ho; 791–817) Chinese poet

1 A Tartar horn tugs at the north wind,
Thistle Gate shines whiter than the stream.
The sky swallows the road to Kokonor.
On the Great Wall, a thousand miles of moonlight.

"On the Frontier" (early 9th century), st. 1, quoted in *Poems of the Late T'ang* (A. C. Graham, tr.; 1965)

Li Jinfa (also known as Li Shuliang; 1900–76) U.S. poet and diplomat

1 Spring is not on the willow tips nor in the grassy pond.

"Thou Mayest Come Naked" (1922), quoted in *Anthology of Modern Chinese Poetry* (Michelle Yeh, ed., tr.; 1992)

Lillie, Beatrice, Lady Peel (Constance Sylvia Muston; 1894–1989) Canadian-born British actor

1 I'll simply say here that I was born Beatrice Gladys Lillie at an extremely tender age because my mother needed a fourth at meals.

Every Other Inch a Lady (1972), ch. 1

2 At one early, glittering dinner party at Buckingham Palace, the trembling hand of a nervous waiter spilled a spoonful of decidedly hot soup down my neck. How could I manage to ease his mind...except to...say, without thinking: "Never darken my Dior again!"

Every Other Inch a Lady (1972), ch. 14

3 Heard there was a party. Came.

On arriving breathlessly at a friend's house seeking help after a car crash. Attrib.

Lillo, George (1693–1739) English playwright

1 As the name of the merchant never degrades the gentleman, so by no means does it exclude him.

The London Merchant (1731), Act 1, Scene 1

Limericks

1 There was a faith-healer of Deal,
Who said, "Although pain isn't real,
If I sit on a pin
And it punctures my skin,
I dislike what I fancy I feel."
Quoted in *The Week-End Book* (1925)

2 A maiden at college, named Breeze,
Weighed down by B.A.s and M.D.s
Collapsed from the strain.
Said her doctor, "It's plain
You are killing yourself by degrees!"

3 There was an old man from Darjeeling,
Who boarded a bus bound for Ealing,
He saw on the door:
"Please don't spit on the floor,"
So he stood up and spat on the ceiling.

4 There was an old man of Boulogne
Who sang a most topical song.
It wasn't the words
That frightened the birds,
But the horrible double-entendre.

5 There was a young lady of Riga,
Who went for a ride on a tiger;
They returned from the ride
With the lady inside,
And a smile on the face of the tiger.

6 There was a young man of Japan
Whose limericks never would scan;
When they said it was so,
He replied, "Yes, I know,
But I always try to get as many words into the last line as ever I possibly can."

7 There's a wonderful family called Stein,
There's Gert and there's Ep and there's Ein;
Gert's poems are bunk,
Ep's statues are junk,
And no one can understand Ein.
Current in the United States in the 1920s, the lines refer to Gertrude Stein, Jacob Epstein, and Albert Einstein.

Lin, Maya (b.1959) U.S. architect and sculptor

1 Sculpture to me is like poetry, and architecture like prose.
Observer, London (May 14, 1994), "Sayings of the Week"

Linacre, Thomas (1460?–1524) English physician and humanist

1 Either this is not the gospel or we are not Christians.
Referring to reading the Christian gospels for the first time, late in his life. Attrib.

Lin Biao (also known as Lin Piao or Lin Yu-yung; 1907–71) Chinese revolutionary and politician

Quotations about Lin Biao

1 A bourgeois careerist, intriguer, a man of two faces and a traitor to his country. Lin Biao...used Confucius's teaching as a reactionary ideological weapon in his dirty attempts to usurp leadership in the Party, seize power, and restore capitalism.
Anonymous. Written during the campaign to denigrate Mao Zedong's political opponent Lin Biao. *People's Daily,* Beijing (February 2, 1974), editorial, quoted in "People's War," *Maoism: Slogans and Practice* (Vladimir Glebov; 1978)

Quotations by Lin Biao

2 The whole cause of world revolution hinges on the revolutionary struggles of the Asian, African, and Latin American people who make up the overwhelming majority of the world's population.
"Long Live the Victory of People's War" (1965), quoted in *Occidentalism* (Liu Xiaomei; 1995)

Lincoln, Abraham (1809–65) U.S. president

Quotations about Lincoln

1 Mr. Lincoln is like a waiter in a large eating house where all the bells are ringing at once; he cannot serve them all at once and so some grumblers are to be expected.
John Bright (1811–89) British politician. *Cincinnati Gazette* (1864)

2 My heart burned within me with indignation and grief; we could think of nothing else. All night long we had but little sleep, waking up perpetually to the sense of a great shock and grief. Everyone is feeling the same. I never knew such a universal feeling.
Elizabeth Gaskell (1810–65) British novelist. Referring to the assassination of Abraham Lincoln. Letter to C. E. Norton (April 28, 1865)

3 Lincoln had faith in time, and time has justified his faith.
Benjamin Harrison (1833–1901) U.S. president. Lincoln Day Address (1898)

4 Lincoln was not a type. He stands alone—no ancestors, no fellows, no successors.
Robert G. Ingersoll (1833–99) U.S. lawyer. *Reminiscences of Abraham Lincoln* (Allen T. Rice; 1886)

5 The color of the ground was in him, the red earth,
The smack and tang of elemental things.
Edwin Markham (1852–1940) U.S. poet. "Lincoln, the Man of the People," *Lincoln and Other Poems* (1901), st. 1

6 Now he belongs to the ages.
Edwin Stanton (1814–69) U.S. lawyer and public official. Referring to the assassination of Abraham Lincoln. Remark (April 15, 1865)

7 He said that he was too old to cry, but it hurt too much to laugh.
Adlai Stevenson (1900–65) U.S. statesman. Quoting Abraham Lincoln. Speech, after losing the presidential election (November 5, 1952)

8 This dust was once the man,
Gentle, plain, just, and resolute, under whose cautious hand,
Against the foulest crime in history known in any land or age,
Was saved the Union of these States.
1871
Walt Whitman (1819–92) U.S. poet. The last of four poems published originally under the title "President Lincoln's Burial Hymn." "This Dust Was Once the Man," *Leaves of Grass* (1892), Memories of President Lincoln

9 Ever-returning spring, trinity sure to me you bring,
Lilac blooming perennial and drooping star in the west,
And thought of him I love.
1865

Walt Whitman (1819–92) U.S. poet. Composed after the assassination of Abraham Lincoln (April 14, 1865). "When Lilacs Last in the Dooryard Bloom'd," *Sequel to Drum-Taps* (1866)

10 When lilacs last in the dooryard bloom'd,
And the great star early dropp'd in the western sky in the night,
I mourn'd, and yet shall mourn with ever-returning spring.
1865
Walt Whitman (1819–92) U.S. poet. Composed after the assassination of Abraham Lincoln (April 14, 1865). "When Lilacs Last in the Dooryard Bloom'd," *Sequel to Drum-Taps* (1866)

Quotations by Lincoln

11 Let us have faith that right makes might; and in that faith let us to the end, dare to do our duty as we understand it.
Address at Cooper Union, New York (February 27, 1860)

12 The world will little note, nor long remember, what we say here, but it can never forget what they did here. It is for us, the living, rather to be dedicated here to the unfinished work which they who fought here have thus far so nobly advanced. It is rather for us...that government of the people, by the people, and for the people, shall not perish from the earth.
The dedication of the national cemetery on the site of the Battle of Gettysburg, known as the Gettysburg Address. Address, Gettysburg (November 19, 1863)

13 This country, with its institutions, belongs to the people who inhabit it. Whenever they shall grow weary of the existing government, they can exercise their constitutional right of amending it, or their revolutionary right to dismember or overthrow it.
First inaugural address, Washington, D.C. (March 4, 1861)

14 In your hands my dissatisfied fellow-countrymen, and not in mine, is the momentous issue of civil war. The government will not assail you.
Referring to the southern states. First inaugural address, Washington, D.C. (March 4, 1861)

15 I claim not to have controlled events, but confess plainly that events have controlled me.
Letter to A. G. Hodges (April 4, 1864)

16 I think the necessity of being *ready* increases—Look to it.
Message for the Governor of Pennsylvania. Letter to Andrew Curtin (April 8, 1861), quoted in *Collected Works of Abraham Lincoln* (R. P. Baster, ed.; 1953), vol. 4

17 If you don't want to use the army, I should like to borrow it for a while. Yours respectfully, A. Lincoln.
General George B. McClellan's lack of activity during the American Civil War irritated Lincoln. Letter to General George B. McClellan (1862)

18 Those who deny freedom to others, deserve it not for themselves.
Letter to H. L. Pierce and others (April 6, 1859)

19 If I could save the Union without freeing any slave, I would do it; and if I could save it by freeing all the slaves, I would do it...I intend no modification of my oft-expressed personal wish that all men everywhere could be free.
Letter to Horace Greeley (August 22, 1862)

20 Discourage litigation. Persuade your neighbors to compromise whenever you can...As a peacemaker the lawyer has a superior opportunity of being a good man. There will still be business enough.
Notes for a law lecture (1850), quoted in *The Collected Works of Abraham Lincoln* (Roy P. Basler, ed.; 1953)

21 So you're the little woman who wrote the book that made this great war!
Said on meeting Harriet Beecher Stowe, the author of *Uncle Tom's Cabin* (1852), which stimulated opposition to slavery before the Civil War. Remark (1860?), quoted in *Abraham Lincoln: The War Years* (Carl Sandburg; 1936), vol. 2, ch. 39

22 The Lord prefers common-looking people. That is why he makes so many of them.
Remark (December 23, 1863), quoted in *Our Presidents* (James Morgan; 1928), ch. 6

23 A farce or a comedy is best played; a tragedy is best read at home.
Said to John Hay after seeing *The Merchant of Venice*. Remark (1863), quoted in *The Guinness Dictionary of Theatrical Quotations* (Michele Brown; 1993)

24 In giving freedom to the slave, we assure freedom to the free—honorable alike in what we give and what we preserve.
Second annual message to Congress (December 1, 1862)

25 Let us strive on to finish the work we are in: to bind up the nation's wounds; to care for him who shall have borne the battle, and for his widow and his orphan, to do all which may achieve and cherish a just and lasting peace among ourselves, and with all nations.
Second inaugural address (March 4, 1865)

26 It is not our frowning battlements...or the strength of our gallant and disciplined army. These are not our reliance against a resumption of tyranny...Our defense is in the preservation of the spirit which prizes liberty as the heritage of all men, in all lands, everywhere.
Speech (September 11, 1858)

27 What is conservatism? Is it not adherence to the old and tried, against the new and untried?
Speech (February 27, 1860)

28 I am not, nor ever have been, in favor of bringing about in any way the social and political equality of the white and black races—I am not...in favor of making voters or jurors of Negroes, nor of qualifying them to hold office.
The first Lincoln-Douglas debate. Speech (August 21, 1858)

29 The ballot is stronger than the bullet.
Speech at Bloomington, Illinois (May 19, 1856)

30 No man is good enough to govern another man without that other's consent.
Speech at Peoria, Illinois (October 16, 1854)

31 I believe this government cannot endure permanently, half slave and half free.
Speech, Republican State Convention, Springfield, Illinois (June 16, 1858)

32 Enough lives have been sacrificed. We must extinguish our resentments if we expect harmony and union.
Said hours before he was assassinated. Speech to his cabinet (April 14, 1865)

33 It is best not to swap horses in mid-stream.
June 9, 1864. Reply to the National Union League. *Collected Works of Abraham Lincoln* (R. P. Baster, ed.; 1953), vol. 7

34 People who like this sort of thing will find this is the sort of thing they like.
A comment on a book. Attrib. *"Collections and Recollections"* (G. W. E. Russell; 1898), ch. 30

35 The man who murdered his parents, then pleaded for mercy on the grounds that he was an orphan.
Defining a hypocrite. Quoted in *Lincoln's Own Stories* (Anthony Gross, ed.; 1912)

36 Die when I may, I want it said of me by those who know me best, that I have always plucked a thistle and planted a flower where I thought a flower would grow.
Quoted in *Presidential Anecdotes* (Paul F. Boller, Jr.; 1981)

37 You can fool some of the people all the time and all the people some of the time; but you can't fool all the people all the time.
Attrib.

38 As President, I have no eyes but constitutional eyes, I cannot see you.
Reply to the South Carolina commissioners. Attrib. (1865)

39 I can't spare this man; he fights.
Resisting demands for the dismissal of Ulysses S. Grant. Attrib.

40 I don't know who my grandfather was; I am much more concerned to know what his grandson will be.
Taking part in a discussion on ancestry. Attrib.

Lindbergh, Anne Morrow (originally Anne Spencer Morrow; b.1906) U.S. writer

1 The punctuation of anniversaries is terrible, like the closing of doors, one after another between you and what you want to hold on to.
On the first anniversary of her son's kidnapping. Diary entry (1933)

2 Men seem to kick friendship around like a football, but it doesn't seem to crack. Women treat it as glass and it goes to pieces.
Attrib.

Lindgren, Astrid (originally Astrid Ericsson; b.1907) Swedish writer

1 "Have I behaved badly?" asked Pippi..."You understand, ma'am, that when your mother is an angel and your father a Cannibal King, and you've travelled all your life on the seas, you don't really know how you oughter behave in a school."
1945. Said by Pippi Longstocking. *Pippi Longstocking* is a children's book. *Pippi Longstocking* (Edna Hurup, tr.; 1950)

2 And then spring came like a shout of joy to the woods..."I have to scream a spring scream or I'll burst." Ronia explained.
Ronia, the Robber's Daughter (Patricia Crampton, tr.; 1981)

Lindner, Robert (1915–56) U.S. psychoanalyst

1 A calming influence on the nervous system, they say, can be obtained from travel on the Volga.
1954. Quoting a remark by a Russian psychiatrist. *The Fifty-Minute Hour* (1986), ch. 2

2 To treat a psychopath—at any time, in any place, or under any set of conditions—is the most onerous and unrewarding job a clinician can undertake.
1954. *The Fifty-Minute Hour* (1986), ch. 4

3 Psychoanalysis...has raised understanding to an art so fine that it can actually be practiced as a legitimate occupation...A psychoanalyst is, therefore, nothing but an artist at understanding.
1954. *The Fifty-Minute Hour* (1986), foreword

Lindsay, Vachel (Nicholas Vachel Lindsay; 1879–1931) U.S. poet

1 Booth died blind and still by faith he trod,
Eyes still dazzled by the ways of God.
"General William Booth Enters Heaven" (1913)

2 A nation of one hundred fine, mob-hearted, lynching, relenting, repenting millions.
Referring to the United States. "Bryan, Bryan, Bryan, Bryan," *Collected Poems* (1923)

3 Yes I have walked in California,
And the rivers there are blue and white.
Thunderclouds of grapes hang on the mountains.
Bears in the meadows pitch and fight.
"The Golden Whales of California, I: A Short Walk Along the Coast," *Collected Poems* (1923)

4 Not by the earthquake daunted
Nor by new fears made tame,
Painting her face and laughing
Plays she a new-found game.
Referring to San Francisco. "The Lily that will not Repent," *Collected Poems* (1923)

5 The flower-fed buffaloes of the spring
In the days of long ago,
Ranged where the locomotives sing
And the prairie flowers lie low.
"The Flower-fed Buffaloes," *New Oxford Book of American Verse* (Richard Ellmann, ed.; 1976)

6 And who will bring white peace
That he may sleep upon his hill again?
"Abraham Lincoln Walks at Midnight," *The Congo and Other Poems* (1914)

Linklater, Eric (Eric Robert Russell Linklater; 1899–1974) British writer

1 With a heavy step Sir Matthew left the room and spent the morning designing mausoleums for his enemies.
Juan in America (1931), Prologue

2 She looks like a million dollars, but she only knows a hundred and twenty words and she's only got two ideas in her head. The other one's hats.
Juan in America (1931), pt. 2, ch. 5

3 There won't be any revolution in America...The people are too clean. They spend all their time changing their shirts and washing themselves. You can't feel fierce and revolutionary in a bathroom.
Juan in America (1931), pt. 5, ch. 3

4 All I've got against it is that it takes you so far from the club house.
Referring to golf. *Poet's Pub* (1929), ch. 3

Linkletter, Art (b.1912) Canadian-born U.S. radio and television broadcaster

1 Skin is like wax paper that holds everything in without dripping.
From a collection of statements by unidentified children. *A Child's Garden of Misinformation* (1965), ch. 5

2 The four stages of man are infancy, childhood, adolescence, and obsolescence.
A Child's Garden of Misinformation (1965), ch. 8

Linnaeus, Carolus (Carl von Linné; 1707–78) Swedish naturalist

1 Before I was 23, I had conceived everything.
Autobiographical sketch (Neil Tomkinson, tr.; 1978)

2 He cared little about a man's appearance and therefore never answered those who wrote against him. He used to say, "If I am wrong, I shall never win; if I am right, I shall be right as long as nature lasts."
Referring to himself. Autobiographical sketch (Neil Tomkinson, tr.; 1978)

Lin Yutang (1895–1976) Chinese-born writer and philologist

1 The Chinese do not draw any distinction between food and medicine.
The Importance of Living (1937)

2 Few men who have liberated themselves from the fear of God and the fear of death are yet able to liberate themselves from the fear of man.
The Importance of Living (1937)

3 I believe world civilization can be built only upon the common basis of international living...The ideal life...to live in an English cottage, with American heating, and have a Japanese wife, a French mistress, and a Chinese cook.
Quoted in *Lin Yutang: The Best of An Old Friend* (A. J. Anderson, ed.; 1975)

Liotta, Ray (b.1955) U.S. actor

1 As far back as I can remember, I always wanted to be a gangster.
As Henry Hill. *GoodFellas* (Martin Scorsese and Nicholas Pileggi; 1990)

Li Peng (b.1928) Chinese premier

1 If some Western politician claims he is in a position to use the normal Western methods to feed and clothe 1.2 billion Chinese, we would be happily prepared to elect him president of China.
Independent, London (July 6, 1994)

2 If a new party is designed...to try to negate the leadership of the Communist party, then it will not be allowed to exist.
Quoted in "From Spring to Fall," *Time* (Nisid Najari; December 14, 1998)

3 The party has already drawn the correct conclusion, which will not be changed in any way.
Referring to the decision to send in troops on June 3–4, 1989, to suppress prodemocracy supporters in Tiananmen Square. The action led to the deaths of hundreds of demonstrators and injury to an estimated 10,000 more. Quoted in "From Spring to Fall," *Time* (Nisid Najari; December 14, 1998)

4 Since China has a population of 1.1 billion, it won't feel lonely even if it becomes the only socialist country.
On the world's dwindling number of socialist governments. Attrib.

Lipman, Maureen (Maureen Diane Lipman; b.1946) British actor and comedian

1 You know the worst thing about oral sex? The view.
(1990)

Lippmann, Walter (1889–1974) U.S. writer and editor

1 Even God has been defended with nonsense.
A Preface to Politics (1913)

2 Politicians tend to live *in character* and many a public figure has come to imitate the journalism which describes him.
A Preface to Politics (1913)

3 You cannot endow even the best machine with initiative. The jolliest steam-roller will not plant flowers.
A Preface to Politics (1913)

4 The tendency of the casual mind is to pick out or stumble upon a sample which supports or defines its prejudices, and then to make it representative of a whole class.
Public Opinion (1922)

5 In a free society the state does not administer the affairs of men. It administers justice among men who conduct their own affairs.
The Good Society (1937)

Li Qingzhao (also known as Li Ch'ing-chao; 1084–1151?) Chinese poet

1 Now the sun is high above the curtain's hook;
Arising from my bed, I sit
Before the dusty mirror,
Idly combing my hair.
"Feng Huang Tai Shang Yi Chui Xiao" (12th century), quoted in *Anthology of Song-Dynasty Ci-Poetry* (Huang Hongquan, tr.; 1988)

2 In piles chrysanthemums fill the ground,
looking all wasted, damaged—
who could pick them, as they are now?
I stay by the window,
how can I wait alone until blackness comes?
"Note after Note" (12th century), quoted in *An Anthology of Chinese Literature* (Stephen Owen, tr.; 1996)

3 "How about the haitang flowers," I ask
The maid who is rolling the curtains.
"Just the same," she lies to me.
"The Same Tune" (12th century), quoted in *Anthology of Song-Dynasty Ci-Poetry* (Huang Hongquan, tr.; 1988)

4 Now I hear spring is nice in the Twin Stream,
I even think to row my little boat.
Alas! I dread my Locust Boat should fail
To bear mine heavy woe.
"Wu Ling Chun" (12th century), quoted in *Anthology of Song-Dynasty Ci-Poetry* (Huang Hongquan, tr.; 1988)

5 The scene remains the same,
But my love is forever gone,
And forever gone my life's joy.
"Wu Ling Chun" (12th century), quoted in *Anthology of Song-Dynasty Ci-Poetry* (Huang Hongquan, tr.; 1988)

Li Shangyin (813–858) Chinese poet

1 Chang E must surely repent
the theft of that magic herb—
in the sapphire sea, the blue heavens,
her heart night after night.
Chang E is the moon goddess. "Chang E" (9th century), quoted in *An Anthology of Chinese Literature* (Stephen Owen, tr.; 1996)

2 When shall we, side by side, trim a candle at the west window,
And talk back to the time of the night rains on Mount Pa?
"Night Rains: to my Wife up North" (9th century), quoted in *Poems of the Late T'ang* (A. C. Graham, tr.; 1965)

Lister, Joseph, 1st Baron Lister of Lyme Regis (1827–1912) British surgeon

1 Since the antiseptic treatment has been brought into full operation, and wounds and abscesses no longer poison the atmosphere with putrid exhalations, my wards...have completely changed their character; so that during the last nine months not a single instance of pyaemia, hospital gangrene or erysipelas has occurred in them.
British Medical Journal (1867)

2 There are people who do not...object to shooting a pheasant with the considerable chance that it may be only wounded and may have to die after lingering in pain...and yet who consider it something monstrous to introduce under the skin of a guinea pig a little inoculation of some microbe to ascertain its action.
British Medical Journal (1897)

Little, A. G. (1863–1945) British historian

1 The pulpit was the cradle of English prose.
English Historical Review (1934), no. 49

Little, James (James Lawrence Little; 1836–85) U.S. physician

1 The first qualification for a physician is hopefulness.
Attrib.

Little Richard (Richard Wayne Penniman; b.1932) U.S. rock-and-roll singer and pianist

1 I decided to come back and teach goodness in this business. To teach love, because music is the universal language. We are God's bouquet, and through music we become one.
Quoted in *The Life and Times of Little Richard* (Charles White; 1984)

2 My music made your liver quiver, your bladder splatter, and your knees freeze. And your big toe shoot right up in your boot!
The Life and Times of Little Richard (Charles White; 1984), p.124

Littlewood, John (John Edensor Littlewood; 1885–1977) British mathematician

1 A good mathematical joke is better, and better mathematics, than a dozen mediocre papers.
A Mathematician's Miscellany (1953)

2 I recall once saying that when I had given the same lecture several times I couldn't help feeling that they really ought to know it by now.
A Mathematician's Miscellany (1953)

3 The surprising thing about this paper is that a man who could write it would.
A Mathematician's Miscellany (1953)

Littlewood, Sydney, Sir (Sidney Charles Thomas Littlewood; 1895–1967) British lawyer

1 The Irish don't know what they want and are prepared to fight to the death to get it.
Speech (April 13, 1961)

Litvinov, Maxim Maximovich (1876–1951) Soviet statesman

1 Peace is indivisible.
Speech to the League of Nations, Geneva (July 1, 1936)

Liu Binyan (b.1925) Chinese writer

1 Smashing a mirror is no way to make any ugly person beautiful, nor is it a way to make social problems evaporate.
1979. "Listen Carefully to the Voice of the People," *People or Monsters* (Perry Link, ed.; 1983)

2 Nothing causes self-delusion quite so readily as power.
1979. "People or Monsters," *People or Monsters* (Perry Link, ed.; 1983)

3 But old man history tells us that it's better to be a little more noisy. A silent era cannot be a little more noisy.
1979. "Sound is Better than Silence," *People or Monsters* (Perry Link, ed.; 1983)

Liu Shahe (Yu Xuntan; b.1931) Chinese writer and editor

1 Being misunderstood by someone is vexation. Being misunderstood by everyone is tragedy.
1957. Quoted in *The Red Azalea* (Edward Morin, ed.; 1990)

2 The saws are sawing wood, But wood is also sawing the saws...The wood sawn into boards is fashioned into furniture. Saws just break and are discarded.
1972. Quoted in *The Red Azalea* (Edward Morin, ed.; 1990)

Livermore, Mary Ashton (originally Mary Ashton Rice; 1820–1905) U.S. social reformer and writer

1 Other books have been written by men physicians...One would suppose in reading them that women possess but one class of physical organs, and that these are always diseased. Such teaching is pestiferous, and tends to cause and perpetuate the very evils it professes to remedy.
What Shall We Do with Our Daughters? (1883), ch. 2

2 Above the titles of wife and mother, which, although dear, are transitory and accidental, there is the title human being, which precedes and out-ranks every other.
What Shall We Do with Our Daughters? (1883), ch. 7

Liverpool, Lord, 2nd Earl of Liverpool and 2nd Baron Hawkesbury of Hawkesbury (Robert Banks Jenkinson; 1770–1828) British statesman

1 We must prevent these scandalous practices in such a way that

the public is kept ignorant of the disgrace of them.
1808. Referring to homosexuality. Quoted in *Homosexuality: A History* (Colin Spencer; 1995)

Livingstone, Ken (b.1945) British politician

1 The problem is that many MPs never see the London that exists beyond the wine bars and brothels of Westminster.
Times, London (February 19, 1987)

2 The working classes are never embarrassed by money—only the absence of it.
September 1987

Livingstone, William U.S. editor and critic

1 Whenever a dance fever has gripped the public, moralists have inveighed against it as the work of the devil...Hopping dances and ring dances were condemned...in 1209, and the waltz was violently opposed for its "immorality" at the end of the eighteenth century.
The Tango Project, recording (1982), sleeve notes

Livy (Titus Livius; 59? B.C.–17 A.D.) Roman historian

1 Down with the defeated.
Proverbial cry of Brennus, the Gallic king, on capturing Rome in 390 B.C. *History of Rome from its Foundation* (1st century B.C.), bk. 5, ch. 48, sect. 9

Liyong, Taban Lo (b.1939) Sudanese poet, novelist, and short-story writer

1 Progress has gone full circle to regress.
"Why Be Good if Goodness Can Be Misused?," *Ballads of Underdevelopment* (1976)

2 A genius is somebody a computer cannot programme.
Meditations of Taban Lo Liyong (1975)

3 Let each man make himself, Oh Lord, and let each woman herself find.
Meditations of Taban Lo Liyong (1975)

4 Everybody is an artist until he begins to learn: everybody becomes an artist after he has stopped learning.
The Uniformed Man (1971)

Llewellyn, Richard (pen name of Richard Dafydd Vivian Llewellyn Lloyd; 1906–83) Welsh novelist and playwright

1 None But the Lonely Heart
Adapted from the English title of Tchaikovsky's song "None But the Weary Heart" (original words by Goethe). *None But the Lonely Heart* (1943)

Lloyd, Cecil Francis (1884–1938) English-born Canadian poet

1 I like history because my reading of it is accompanied by the comforting certainty that all the people I meet in its pages are dead.
Sunlight and Shadow (1928)

Lloyd, Harold (Harold Clayton Lloyd; 1893–1971) U.S. film actor

1 I am just turning forty and taking my time about it.
Reply when, aged 77, he was asked his age. *Times,* London (September 23, 1970)

Lloyd, Henry Demarest (1847–1903) U.S. journalist and reformer

1 We must either regulate, or own, or destroy, perishing by the sword we take.
Quoted in *The Entrepreneurs* (David B. Sicilia; 1986)

Lloyd, Marie (Matilda Alice Victoria Wood; 1870–1922) British singer and entertainer

1 Oh, mister porter, what shall I do?
I wanted to go to Birmingham, but they've carried me on to Crewe.
Song lyric. "Oh Mister Porter" (1890?)

Lloyd-George, David, 1st Earl of Dwyfor (1863–1945) British prime minister

1 They do not even need a medical certificate. They need not be sound either in body or mind. They only require a certificate of birth—just to prove that they are first of the litter. You would not choose a spaniel on these principles.
1909. Referring to the House of Lords, the unelected upper house of the British Parliament. Budget speech

2 You cannot feed the hungry on statistics.
1904. Advocating tariff reform. Speech

3 Every man has a House of Lords in his own head. Fears, prejudices, misconceptions—those are the peers, and they are hereditary.
1927. The House of Lords is the unelected upper house of the British Parliament. Speech, Cambridge, England

4 A fully equipped Duke costs as much to keep up as two Dreadnoughts, and Dukes are just as great a terror, and they last longer.
Speech, Limehouse, London (July 30, 1909)

5 The world is becoming like a lunatic asylum run by lunatics.
1933. *Observer,* London (January 8, 1953), "Sayings of Our Times"

6 You get to know more of the character of a man in a round of golf than you can get to know in six months with only political experience.
Observer, London (January 27, 1924), "Sayings of the Week"

7 A politician is a person with whose politics you did not agree. When you did agree, he was a statesman.
Speech, Central Hall, Westminster, London, *Times,* London (July 2, 1935)

8 If a situation were to be forced upon us, in which peace could only be preserved by the surrender of the great and beneficent position Britain has won by centuries of heroism and achievement...I say emphatically that peace at that price would be a humiliation intolerable for a great country like ours to endure.
Quoted in *British Documents on the Origins of the War, 1898–1914* (G. P. Gooch and Harold Temperley, eds.; 1927), vol. 7

9 Like a cushion, he always bore the impress of the last man who sat on him.
Referring to Lord Derby. This remark is also credited to Earl Haig. Quoted in *Listener,* London (September 7, 1978)

10 What an extraordinary mixture of idealism and lunacy. Hasn't she the sense to see that the very worst method of campaigning for the franchise is to try and intimidate or blackmail a man

into giving her what he would gladly give her otherwise.
Quoted in *Lloyd George* (Richard Lloyd George; 1960)

11 The doctors are always changing their opinions. They always have some new fad.
After being told that a well-known surgeon recommended that people sleep on their stomachs. Quoted in *Lord Riddell's War Diary, 1914–1918* (Lord Riddell; 1933), ch. 36

12 I see some rats have got in; let them squeal, it doesn't matter.
Said when suffragettes interrupted a meeting. Quoted in *The Faber Book of English History in Verse* (Kenneth Baker, ed.; 1988)

13 Well, I find that a change of nuisances is as good as a vacation.
On being asked how he maintained his cheerfulness when beset by numerous political obstacles. Attrib.

14 The Right Hon. gentleman has sat so long on the fence that the iron has entered his soul.
Referring to Sir John Simon. Attrib.

15 This war, like the next war, is a war to end war.
Referring to the popular opinion that World War I would be the last major war. Attrib.

Lo, Kenneth H. (Hsiao Chien Lo; 1913–95) British cookbook writer

1 To write about Peking's food and cooking one has to write about Peking itself, for they are such an integral part of the city's life.
Peking Cooking (1970)

Lo, Vivienne (Luo Weiqian; b.1958) British historian and writer

1 Almost all Chinese, whatever their social status, live by and for their bellies.
150 Recipes from the Teahouse (1997)

2 Eating cannot be a solitary affair, but must be shared with the people you love or are doing business with; it increases the pleasure.
150 Recipes from the Teahouse (1997)

Lobachevsky, Nikolay (Nikolay Ivanovich Lobachevsky; 1793–1856) Russian mathematician

1 The shortest distance between two points is not always a straight line.
Quoted in *The Jingle Bell Principle* (Miroslav Holub; 1992)

Locke, Alain Le Roy (1886–1954) U.S. writer and editor

1 It is the "man farthest down" who is most active in getting up.
"Enter the New Negro," *Survey Graphic* (March 1925)

Locke, John (1632–1704) English philosopher

1 Let us then suppose the Mind to be, as we say, white Paper, void of all Characters, without any *Ideas*; How comes it to be furnished?...Whence has it all the materials of Reason and Knowledge? To this I answer, in one word, From *Experience*.
An Essay Concerning Human Understanding (1690), bk. 2

2 Madmen do not appear to me to have lost the faculty of reasoning, but having joined together some of the ideas very wrongly, they mistake them for truths...For, by the violence of their imaginations, having taken their fancies for realities, they make right deductions from them.
An Essay Concerning Human Understanding (1690), bk. 2

3 Whatsoever the Mind perceives in itself, or is the immediate object of Perception, Thought, or Understanding, that I call *Idea*.
An Essay Concerning Human Understanding (1690), bk. 2

4 The use...of words is to be sensible marks of ideas, and the ideas they stand for are their proper and immediate signification.
An Essay Concerning Human Understanding (1690)

5 It is one thing to show a man that he is in an error, and another to put him in possession of truth.
Essay Concerning Human Understanding (1690), bk. 4

6 New opinions are always suspected, and usually opposed, without any other reason but because they are not already common.
An Essay Concerning Human Understanding (1690), Dedicatory epistle

7 Freedom of men under government is to have a standing rule to live by, common to every one in that society...and not to be subject to the inconstant, uncertain, unknown, arbitrary will of another man.
Second Treatise on Civil Government (1690)

8 Government has no other end but the preservation of property.
Second Treatise on Civil Government (1690)

9 When a King has Dethron'd himself and put himself in a state of War with his People, what shall hinder them from prosecuting him who is no King?
Second Treatise on Civil Government (1690)

10 A sound mind in a sound body.
Alluding to Juvenal's original in Latin: "Mens sana in corpore sano." *Second Treatise on Civil Government* (1690)

11 When a nation is running to decay and ruin, the merchant and monied man, do what you can, will be sure to starve last.
Some Considerations of the Consequences of the Lowering of Interests and Raising the Value of Money (1692)

12 The Liberty of Man, in Society, is to be under no other Legislative Power, but that established by consent, in the Common-wealth, nor under the Domination of any Will, or Restraint of any Law, but what the Legislative shall enact, according to the trust put in it.
Two Treatises of Government (1690)

Lockier, Francis (1667–1740) British writer and priest

1 In all my travels I never met with any one Scotchman but what was a man of sense. I believe everybody of that country that has any, leaves it as fast as they can.
Quoted in *Anecdotes* (Joseph Spence; 1820), pt. 2, "1730–32"

Lodge, David (David John Lodge; b.1935) British novelist and critic

1 The British, he thought, must be gluttons for satire: even the weather forecast seemed to be some kind of spoof, predicting every possible combination of weather for the next twenty-

four hours without actually committing itself to anything specific.

A visiting U.S. academic's first experience of Britain and the British. *Changing Places* (1975), ch. 2

2 There was sex of course, but although both of them were extremely interested in sex, and enjoyed nothing better than discussing it, neither of them, if the truth be told, was quite so interested in actually having it, or at any rate in having it very frequently.

Nice Work (1988), ch. 1

3 Universities are the cathedrals of the modern age. They shouldn't have to justify their existence by utilitarian criteria.

Nice Work (1988), ch. 4

4 Literature is mostly about having sex and not much about having children; life is the other way round.

The British Museum is Falling Down (1965), ch. 4

5 There is a vanity and a paranoia about writers—which makes excellent dramatic material—but which also makes me question the nature of writing.

Times Educational Supplement, London (May 18, 1990)

Loesser, Frank (Frank Henry Loesser; 1910–69) U.S. composer and songwriter

1 I'd like to get you
On a slow boat to China.

Song lyric. "On a Slow Boat to China" (1948)

2 Yes, time heals all things,
So I needn't cling to this fear,
It's merely that Spring
Will be a little late this year.

Song lyric. "Spring Will Be a Little Late This Year," *Christmas Holiday* (1944)

3 See What the Boys in the Backroom Will Have

Song title. Sung by Marlene Dietrich in the film *Destry Rides Again* (music by Frank Skinner; 1939)

4 Luck be a Lady Tonight

Song title. *Guys and Dolls* (1950)

5 Sit Down, You're Rockin' the Boat

Song title. *Guys and Dolls* (1950)

6 The Guy's Only Doin' it for Some Doll

Song title. *Guys and Dolls* (1950)

7 How to Succeed in Business without Really Trying

1961. Musical title.

Loewy, Raymond (Raymond Fernand Loewy; 1893–1986) U.S. industrial designer

1 Between two products, equal in function, quality and price, the better looking will outsell the other.

1934. Quoted in *Royal Designers on Design: a Selection of Addresses by Royal Designers for Industry* (The Design Council, London; 1986)

2 If you design something too well, you don't get another job for 30 years.

1934. Quoted in *Royal Designers on Design: a Selection of Addresses by Royal Designers for Industry* (The Design Council, London; 1986)

Lofting, Hugh (Hugh John Lofting; 1886–1947) British-born U.S. children's writer and illustrator

1 "But animals don't always speak with their mouths," said the parrot in a high voice, raising her eyebrows. "They talk with their ears, with their feet, with their tails—with everything. Sometimes they don't want to make a noise."

The Story of Dr. Doolittle (1922)

2 Oh, sometimes people annoy me dreadfully—such airs they put on—talking about the "dumb animals". Dumb! Huh! Why, I knew a macaw once who could say "Good morning!" in seven different ways without once opening his mouth.

Said by Polynesia the parrot. *The Story of Dr. Doolittle* (1922)

Logau, Friedrich von, Baron (pen name Salomon von Golaw; 1604–55) German poet and writer

1 Joy and Temperance and Repose
Slam the door on the doctor's nose.

Deutscher Sinngedichte Drietausend (1654)

2 Man-like is it to fall into sin,
Fiend-like is it to dwell therein;
Christ-like is it for sin to grieve,
God-like is it all sin to leave.

Deutscher Sinngedichte Drietausend (1654)

3 Though the mills of God grind slowly, yet they grind exceeding small;
Though with patience He stands waiting, with exactness grinds He all.

The first line of the poem is a translation of anonymous verse in Sextus Empiricus, *Adversus Mathematicus*, bk. 1, sect. 287. *Deutscher Sinngedichte Drietausend* (1654)

4 Friendships made o'er wine are slight;
Like it, they only act one night.

1654? Quoted in *A German Treasury* (Stanley Mason, tr.; 1993)

5 What use is it that knowledge mounts?
It's knowing something good that counts.

1654? Quoted in *A German Treasury* (Stanley Mason, tr.; 1993)

Logue, Christopher (b.1926) British poet, playwright, and actor

1 Said Marx: "Don't be snobbish, we seek to abolish
The 3rd Class, not the 1st."

"M," *Abecedary* (1977)

Lombardi, Vince (Vincent Thomas Lombardi; 1913–70) U.S. football coach

1 Winning isn't everything, but wanting to win is.

Interview (1962)

Lombroso, Cesare (1836–1909) Italian physician and criminologist

1 The ignorant man always adores what he cannot understand.

The Man of Genius (1891), pt. 3, ch. 3

London, Jack (John Griffith London; 1876–1916) U.S. writer

Quotations about London

1 It is very consistent and well-assimilated Darwinism, adorned,

unfortunately, by a cheap and poorly comprehended Nietzscheanism. However, it poses as the wisdom of nature itself and as the permanent law of life.
Osip Mandelstam (1891–1938) Russian poet, writer, and translator. Referring to the anti-intellectual philosophy of Jack London's writing as a response to technological progress. "Jack London" (1912), quoted in *The Collected Critical Prose and Letters of Osip Mandelstam* (J. G. Harris, ed., tr., C. Link, tr.; 1991)

Quotations by London

2 Nature did not care. To life she set one task, gave one law. To perpetuate was the task of life, its law was death.
"The Law of Life" (1901)

3 The proper function of man is to live, not to exist. I shall not waste my days in trying to prolong them. I shall use my time.
Bulletin (December 2, 1916)

4 After God had finished the rattlesnake, the toad, the vampire, he had some awful substance left with which he made a scab.
A scab is a worker who continues to work or who does a striker's job during a labor union's strike. "A Scab," *C.I.O. News* (September 13, 1946)

5 A scab is a two-legged animal with a corkscrew soul, a waterlogged brain, a combination backbone of jelly and glue. Where others have hearts, he carries a tumor of rotten principles.
A scab is a worker who continues to work or who does a striker's job during a labor union's strike. "A Scab," *C.I.O. News* (September 13, 1946)

6 Hawaii is a paradise—and I can never cease proclaiming it; but I must append one word of qualification: *Hawaii is a paradise for the well to do.*
My Hawaiian Aloha (1916)

7 In what other land save this one is the commonest form of greeting not "Good day," nor "How d'ye do," but "Love"? That greeting is *Aloha*–love, I love you, my love to you...It is a positive affirmation of the warmth of one's own heart-giving.
Referring to Hawaii. *My Hawaiian Aloha* (1916)

8 And those who have undergone life in Alaska claim that in the making of the world God grew tired, and when He came to the last barrowload, "just dumped it anyhow," and that was how Alaska happened to be.
"Gold Hunters of the North," *Revolution and other Essays* (1910)

9 There is a patience of the wild...that holds motionless for endless hours the spider in its web, the snake in its coils, the panther in its ambuscade; this patience belongs primarily to life when it hunts its living food.
The Call of the Wild (1903)

10 He must master or be mastered; while to show mercy was a weakness. Mercy did not exist in the primordial life. It was misunderstood for fear, and such misunderstandings made for death.
Referring to Buck, the dog-hero. *The Call of the Wild* (1903)

11 He was older than the days he had seen and the breaths he had drawn. He linked the past with the present, and the eternity behind him throbbed through him in a mighty rhythm to which he swayed as the tides and seasons swayed.
Referring to Buck, the dog-hero. *The Call of the Wild* (1903)

12 When I have done some such thing, I am exalted. I glow all over...Every fiber of me is thrilling with it. It is very natural. It is a mere matter of satisfaction at adjustment to environment. It is success.
The Cruise of the Snark (1911)

13 With my own hands I had done my trick at the wheel and guided a hundred tons of wood and iron through a few million tons of wind and waves.
The Cruise of the Snark (1911)

14 In an English ship, they say, it is poor grub, poor pay, and easy work; in an American ship, good grub, good pay, and hard work. And this is applicable to the working populations of both countries.
The People of the Abyss (1903)

15 He preferred suffering in freedom to all the happiness of a comfortable servility. He did not care to serve God. He cared to serve nothing. He was no figure-head. He stood on his own legs. He was an individual.
Referring to Wolf Larsen. *The Sea-Wolf* (1904)

16 In our loins are the possibilities of millions of lives. Could we but find time and opportunity and utilize the last bit and every bit of the unborn life that is in us, we could become the fathers of nations and populate continents.
Said by Wolf Larsen. *The Sea-Wolf* (1904)

17 The earth is as full of brutality as the sea is full of motion. And some men are made sick by the one, and some by the other.
Said by Wolf Larsen. *The Sea-Wolf* (1904)

Long, Clarisa U.S. academic

1 Intellectual property must adapt to the globalization of technology and markets.
Quoted in *Capital for Our Time* (Nicholas Imparato, ed.; 1999)

2 Nations that cheat innovators fail to attract capital investment, are unsuitable partners for technology transfers, and have no savings to pass on to their citizens.
Quoted in *Capital for Our Time* (Nicholas Imparato, ed.; 1999)

3 The most successful economies in the decades to come will be those that can best harness their brain power to generate economic growth.
Quoted in *Capital for Our Time* (Nicholas Imparato, ed.; 1999)

Long, Huey (Huey Pierce Long, "Kingfish"; 1893–1935) U.S. politician

1 Evangeline wept bitter tears in her disappointment, but it lasted only through one lifetime. Your tears in this country, around this oak, have lasted for generations. Give me the chance to dry the tears of those who still weep here!
At the oak tree said to have inspired Henry Wadsworth Longfellow's narrative poem *Evangeline* (1847). Campaign speech, Louisiana (November 1928)

2 Every man a king but no man wears a crown.
Quoting William Jennings Bryan. Slogan (1928)

3 The man who pulls the plow gets the plunder in politics.
Speech, U.S. Senate (January 30, 1934)

4 I looked around at the little fishes present and said, "I'm the Kingfish."
On his nickname "Kingfish." Quoted in *The Politics of Upheaval* (A. Schlesinger, Jr.; 1961)

Long, Russell B. (Russell Billiu Long; b.1918) U.S. politician

Quotations about Long

1 The trouble with Senator Long is that he is suffering from halitosis of the intellect. That's presuming Emperor Long has an intellect.
Harold L. Ickes (1874–1952) U.S. lawyer and government official. Quoted in *The Politics of Upheaval* (A. M. Schlesinger, Jr.; 1988), pt. 2, ch. 14

Quotations by Long

2 The first rule of politics is not to lie to somebody unless it is absolutely necessary.
Attrib.

Longfellow, Henry Wadsworth (1807–82) U.S. poet

Quotations about Longfellow

1 The gentleman was a sweet beautiful soul, but I have entirely forgotten his name.
1882
Ralph Waldo Emerson (1803–82) U.S. poet and essayist. On attending Henry Wadsworth Longfellow's funeral. Attrib.

Quotations by Longfellow

2 Lives of great men all remind us
We can make our lives sublime,
And, departing, leave behind us
Footprints on the sands of time
Let us, then, be up and doing,
With a heart for any fate;
Still achieving, still pursuing,
Learn to labor and to wait.
"A Psalm of Life" (1838), st. 7

3 The shades of night were falling fast,
As through an Alpine village passed
A youth, who bore, 'mid snow and ice,
A banner with the strange device,
Excelsior!
Opening of a poem best known as a Victorian drawing-room ballad, and the butt of many music-hall jokes. Excelsior means "higher" (Latin). "Excelsior" (1841)

4 All houses wherein men have lived and died
Are haunted houses. Through the open doors
The harmless phantoms on their errands glide,
With feet that make no sound upon the floors.
"Haunted Houses" (1858)

5 You would attain to the divine perfection,
And yet not turn your back upon the world.
"Michael Angelo" (1883)

6 The men that women marry,
And why they marry them, will always be
A marvel and a mystery to the world.
"Michael Angelo" (1883), pt. 1, sect. 5

7 A hurry of hoofs in a village street,
A shape in the moonlight, a bulk in the dark,
And beneath, from the pebbles, in passing, a spark
Struck out from a steed flying fearless and fleet:
That was all! And yet, through the gloom and the light,
The fate of a nation was riding that night.
"Paul Revere's Ride" (1863)

8 I shot an arrow into the air,
It fell to earth, I knew not where.
"The Arrow and the Song" (1845)

9 I stood on the bridge at midnight,
As the clocks were striking the hour.
"The Bridge" (1904)

10 In the elder days of Art,
Builders wrought with greatest care
Each minute and unseen part;
For the gods see everywhere.
"The Builders" (1849)

11 Thou, too, sail on, O Ship of State!
Sail on, O Union, strong and great!
Humanity with all its fears,
With all the hopes of future years,
Is hanging breathless on thy fate!
"The Building of the Ship" (1849)

12 The heights by great men reached and kept
Were not attained by sudden flight,
But they, while their companions slept,
Were toiling upward in the night.
"The Ladder of Saint Augustine" (1850)

13 Know how sublime a thing it is
To suffer and be strong.
"The Light of Stars in Knickerbocker" (1839)

14 There is a Reaper whose name is Death,
And, with his sickle keen,
He reaps the bearded grain at a breath,
And the flowers that grow between.
"The Reaper and the Flowers" (1886)

15 "Wouldst thou"—so the helmsman answered—
"Learn the secret of the sea?
Only those who brave its dangers
Comprehend its mystery!"
"The Secret of the Sea" (1904)

16 Looks the whole world in the face,
For he owes not any man.
"The Village Blacksmith" (1839)

17 Under a spreading chestnut tree
The village smithy stands;
The smith, a mighty man is he,
With large and sinewy hands;
And the muscles of his brawny arms
Are strong as iron bands.
"The Village Blacksmith" (1839)

18 It was the schooner Hesperus,
That sailed the wintry sea;

And the skipper had taken his little daughter,
To bear him company.
"The Wreck of the Hesperus" (1839)

19 Art is long, and Time is fleeting,
And our hearts, though stout and brave,
Still, like muffled drums, are beating
Funeral marches to the grave.
A Psalm of Life (1838)

20 There is no flock, however watched and tended,
But one dead lamb is there!
There is no fireside, howsoe'er defended,
But has one vacant chair!
A Psalm of Life (1838)

21 Into each life some rain must fall.
"The Rainy Day," *Ballads and Other Poems* (1842), st. 3

22 Death is better than disease.
Christus: A Mystery (1872)

23 If you would hit the mark, you must aim a little above it;
Every arrow that flies feels the attraction of earth.
Elegiac Verse (1880)

24 The wondrous, beautiful prairies,
Billowy bays of grass ever rolling in shadow and in sunshine,
Bright with luxuriant clusters of roses and purple amorphae.
Evangeline (1847), pt. 2

25 Over them wander the buffalo herds, and the elk and the roebuck;
Over them wander the wolves, and herds of riderless horses;
Fires that blast and blight, and winds that are weary with travel.
Referring to the North American prairies. *Evangeline* (1847), pt. 2

26 Sorrow and silence are strong, and patient endurance is godlike.
Evangeline (1847), pt. 2, l. 60

27 We judge ourselves by what we feel capable of doing, while others judge us by what we have already done.
Kavanagh (1849), ch. 1

28 Our ingress into the world
Was naked and bare;
Our progress through the world
Is trouble and care.
"The Student's Tale," *Tales of a Wayside Inn* (1874)

29 Ships that pass in the night, and speak each other in passing...
Only a look and a voice; then darkness again and a silence.
"The Theologian's Tale: Elizabeth," *Tales of a Wayside Inn* (1874)

30 From the waterfall he named her,
Minnehaha, Laughing Water.
"Hiawatha and Mudjekeewis," *The Song of Hiawatha* (1855), pt. 4

31 By the shore of Gitche Gumee,
By the shining Big-Sea-Water,
Stood the wigwam of Nokomis,
Daughter of the Moon, Nokomis.
Dark behind it rose the forest...
Bright before it beat the water,
Beat the clear and sunny water,
Beat the shining Big-Sea-Water.
"Hiawatha's Childhood," *The Song of Hiawatha* (1855), pt. 3

32 Onaway! Awake, beloved!
Opening of the song sung by Chibiabos at Hiawatha's wedding feast; best known in the setting by Samuel Taylor Coleridge. "Hiawatha's Wedding-feast," *The Song of Hiawatha* (1855), pt. 11

33 As unto the bow the cord is,
So unto the man is woman;
Though she bends him, she obeys him,
Though she draws him, yet she follows;
Useless each without the other!
"Hiawatha's Wooing," *The Song of Hiawatha* (1855), pt. 10

34 There was a little girl
Who had a little curl
Right in the middle of her forehead;
When she was good
She was very very good,
But when she was bad she was horrid.
1850? Sung to his daughter as a baby in his arms. "There was a Little Girl," *The Home Life of Henry W. Longfellow* (B. R. Tucker-Macchetta; 1882)

Longford, Elizabeth, Countess of (Elizabeth Harman Pakenham; b.1906) British writer

1 Dr. Simpson's first patient, a doctor's wife in 1847, had been so carried away with enthusiasm that she christened her child, a girl, "Anaesthesia".
Queen Victoria (1964), ch. 17

Longford, Lord, 7th Earl of Longford (Francis Aungier Pakenham; b.1905) British politician

1 No sex without responsibility.
Observer, London (May 3, 1954), "Sayings of the Week"

2 On the whole I would not say that our Press is obscene. I would say that it trembles on the brink of obscenity.
Observer, London (1963), "Sayings of the Year"

Longley, Michael (b.1939) Northern Irish poet

1 He was preparing an Ulster fry for breakfast
When someone walked into the kitchen and shot him:
A bullet entered his mouth and pierced his skull,
The books he had read, the music he could play.
"Wreaths," *Collected Poems 1963–1983* (1991), ll. 1–4

Longworth, Alice Lee (originally Alice Lee Roosevelt; 1884–1980) U.S. society figure

1 If you haven't anything nice to say about anyone, come and sit by me.
Embroidered on a cushion at her home. *Time* (December 9, 1966)

2 I have a simple philosophy. Fill what's empty. Empty what's full. And scratch where it itches.
Quoted in *The Best* (Peter Passell and Leonard Ross; 1987)

Lonsdale, Kathleen, Dame (originally Kathleen Yardley; 1903–71) Irish-born British crystallographer

1 Any scientist who has ever been in love knows that he may understand everything about sex hormones but the actual experience is something quite different.
Universities Quarterly (1963), no. 17, 1963

Loos, Anita (Corinne Anita Loos; 1888–1981) U.S. writer

Quotations about Loos

1 You are the first American to make sex funny.
Anonymous. Said to Anita Loos by a friend on reading her book *Gentlemen Prefer Blondes* (1928).

Quotations by Loos

2 So I am beginning to wonder if maybe girls wouldn't be happier if we stopped demanding so much respeckt for ourselves and developped a little more respeckt for husbands.
A Mouse is Born (1951), ch. 19

3 Gentlemen always seem to remember blondes.
Gentlemen Prefer Blondes (1925), ch. 1

4 So this gentleman said a girl with brains ought to do something with them besides think.
Gentlemen Prefer Blondes (1925), ch. 1

5 Any girl who was a lady would not even think of having such a good time that she did not remember to hang on to her jewelry.
Gentlemen Prefer Blondes (1925), ch. 4

6 Kissing your hand may make you feel very very good but a diamond and sapphire bracelet lasts forever.
Gentlemen Prefer Blondes (1925), ch. 4

7 So then Dr Froyd said that all I needed was to cultivate a few inhibitions and get some sleep.
Gentlemen Prefer Blondes (1925), ch. 5

8 I'm furious about the Women's Liberationists. They keep getting up on soapboxes and proclaiming that women are brighter than men. That's true, but it should be kept very quiet or it ruins the whole racket.
Observer, London (December 30, 1973), "Sayings of the Year"

Lord, Betty Bao U.S. writer

1 I was an insider and an outsider. I was at home and I was exiled. I had never been happier, nor had I been so sad.
Referring to her years in China during the 1980s. *Legacy* (1989)

Lorde, Audre (1934–92) U.S. poet, novelist, and feminist

1 Every Black woman in America lives her life somewhere along a wide curve of ancient and unexpressed angers.
"Eye to Eye: Black Women, Hatred, and Anger," *Sister Outsider* (1984)

2 The Master's Tools Will Never Dismantle the Master's House
September 29, 1979. Title of a speech. Speech given at the Second Sex Conference, *Sister Outsider* (1984)

3 We have been raised to fear the *yes* within ourselves, our deepest cravings.
"Uses of the Erotic: The Erotic as Power," *Sister Outsider* (1984)

4 Once I accept the existence of dying, as a life process, who can ever have power over me again?
The Cancer Journals (1980)

5 Any world which did not have a place for me loving women was not a world in which I wanted to live, nor one which I could fight for.
Zami: A New Spelling of My Name (1982)

Lorenz, Edward (Edward Norton Lorenz; b.1917) U.S. meteorologist and educator

1 Predictability: Does the Flap of a Butterfly's Wings in Brazil Set Off a Tornado in Texas?
1979. Paper title. The best known illustration of "chaos theory," a term first used by mathematician James Yorke in 1972.

Lorenz, Konrad (Konrad Zacharias Lorenz; 1903–89) Austrian zoologist

1 I think I know of no other rodent that plays in such an intelligent way, quite like dogs and cats, as the golden hamster...I think the golden hamster was created expressly for the sake of the poor animal lover in the city.
King Solomon's Ring (Marjorie Kerr Wilson, tr.; 1949)

2 Just as the transmitting apparatus of animals is considerably more efficient than that of man, so also is their receiving apparatus.
King Solomon's Ring (Marjorie Kerr Wilson, tr.; 1949)

3 There is no faith which has never yet been broken, except that of a truly faithful dog.
King Solomon's Ring (Marjorie Kerr Wilson, tr.; 1949)

4 To me it is a strangely appealing and even elevating thought that the age-old covenant between man and dog was "signed" voluntarily and without obligation by each of the contracting parties.
King Solomon's Ring (Marjorie Kerr Wilson, tr.; 1949)

5 We do need the dog, but not as a watchdog...I have derived, from the mere fact of his existence, a great sense of inward security, such as one finds in a childhood memory or in the prospect of the scenery of one's own home country.
King Solomon's Ring (Marjorie Kerr Wilson, tr.; 1949)

6 Without supernatural assistance, our fellow creatures can tell us the most beautiful stories, and that means true stories, because the truth about nature is always far more beautiful even than what our great poets sing of it.
King Solomon's Ring (Marjorie Kerr Wilson, tr.; 1949)

7 It is a good morning exercise for a research scientist to discard a pet hypothesis every day before breakfast. It keeps him young.
On Aggression (1963), ch. 2

8 Man appears to be the missing link between anthropoid apes and human beings.
New York Times Magazine (John Pfeiffer; April 11, 1965)

Lorimer, James (1818–90) Scottish jurist and political philosopher

1 Jane Eyre strikes us as a personage much more likely to have sprung ready-armed from the head of a man and that head a pretty hard one, than to have experienced, in any shape, the softening influence of a female creation.
Referring to the authorship of Charlotte Brontë's *Jane Eyre*, published under the pseudonym Currer Bell (1847). *North British Review* (August 1849)

Lorre, Peter (Lászlo Loewenstein; 1904–64) Hungarian-born U.S. film actor

1 What is time? The Swiss manufacture it. Italians want it. The Americans say it is money. Hindus say it does not exist. I say time is a crook.
As O'Hara. *Beat the Devil* (Truman Capote and John Huston; 1953)

Lothian, Lord, 11th Marquis of Lothian (Philip Henry Kerr; 1882–1940) British journalist and statesman

1 The only lasting solution is that Europe itself should gradually find its way to an internal equilibrium and a limitation of armaments by political appeasement.
Times, London (May 4, 1934)

Loud, Pat (b.1926) U.S. writer and television personality

1 Housework isn't bad in itself—the trouble with it is that it's inhumanely lonely.
Pat Loud: a Woman's Story (with Nora Johnson; 1974)

Louis, Joe (Joseph Louis Barrow; 1914–81) U.S. boxer

1 He can run, but he can't hide.
Referring to the speed for which his coming opponent, Billy Conn, was renowned. Remark (June 19, 1941)

2 Once that bell rings you're on your own. It's just you and the other guy.
Quoted in *A Hard Road to Glory* (Arthur Ashe; 1988)

3 Yeah, I'm scared. I'm scared I might kill Schmeling.
June 1938. Referring to his rematch with Max Schmeling. Quoted in *A Hard Road to Glory* (Arthur Ashe; 1988)

4 We gonna do our part, and we will win, because God's on our side.
1942. On World War II. This became a popular slogan among American troops. *Joe Louis: 50 years an American Hero* (Joe Barrow Jr.; 1988), p.141

Louis VII, King of France ("Louis the Young"; 1120?–80) French monarch

1 Your lord the King of England, who lacks nothing, has men, horses, gold, silk, jewels, fruits, game, and everything else. We in France have nothing but bread and wine and gaiety.
By "France" Louis meant the comparatively small area around Paris that he ruled directly. Quoted in *Richard the Lionheart* (John Gillingham; 1978), ch. 4

Louis IX, King of France ("Saint Louis"; 1214–70) French monarch

1 Our clothing and our armor ought to be of such a kind that men of mature experience will not say we have spent too much on them, nor younger men say we have spent too little.
Attrib.

Louis XI, King of France ("The Spider"; 1423–83) French monarch

1 I have chased the English out of France...with venison pies and good wine.
Remark at a banquet after the Treaty of Pecquigny (August 29, 1475)

Louis XIV, King of France ("The Sun King"; 1638–1715) French monarch

Quotations about Louis XIV

1 I have often seen the King consume four plates of different soups, a whole pheasant, a partridge, a large plate of salad, two big slices of ham, a dish of mutton in garlic sauce, a plateful of pastries followed by fruit and hard-boiled eggs. The King and Monsieur greatly like hard-boiled eggs.
Duchess of Orléans (1652–1722) French sister-in-law to Louis XIV. Letter (1682?)

Quotations by Louis XIV

2 The function of kings consists primarily of using good sense, which always comes naturally and easily. Our work is sometimes less difficult than our amusements.
Memoir for the Instruction of the Dauphin (1661)

3 I almost had to wait.
Referring to an occasion when a coach he had ordered arrived just in time. Quoted in *L'Esprit dans Histoire* (E. Fournier; 1857), ch. 48

4 Why are you weeping? Did you imagine that I was immortal?
1715. Noticing as he lay on his deathbed that his attendants were crying. Attrib. *Louis XIV* (Vincent Cronin; 1964)

5 There are no more Pyrenees.
1700. On the accession of his grandson to the Spanish throne; attributed by Voltaire but attributed also to the Spanish ambassador to France in the *Mercure Gallant* (Paris), November 1700. Attrib. *Siècle de Louis XIV* (Voltaire; 1753), ch. 26

6 Every time I make an appointment, I make one ungrateful person and a hundred with a grievance.
1669? After the disgrace of the Duke of Lauzun. Quoted in *Siècle de Louis XIV* (Voltaire; 1751), ch. 26

7 Ah, if I were not king, I should lose my temper.
Attrib.

8 First feelings are always the most natural.
First impressions at the Battle of Malplaquet. Attrib. (Mme. de Sévigné; September 11, 1709)

9 Try to keep peace with your neighbors. I have loved war too much; do not copy me in that nor in my extravagance.
Advice given to the future Louis XV. Attrib.

10 Has God then forgotten what I have done for him?
Reportedly said after Marlborough's pyrrhic victory over the French at the Battle of Malplaquet. Attrib. (September 11, 1709)

Louis XVI, King of France (1754–93) French monarch

Quotations about Louis XVI

1 Citizens, we are talking of a republic, and yet Louis lives! We are talking of a republic, and the person of the King still stands between us and liberty.
Maximilien Robespierre (1758–94) French lawyer and revolutionary. Convention (December 3, 1792)

2 It imprints a grand character on the National Convention and makes it worthy of the confidence of the French.
Maximilien Robespierre (1758–94) French lawyer and revolutionary. Referring to the execution of Louis XVI earlier that day. Remark (January 21, 1793), quoted in "Impure Blood, August 1792-January 1793," *Citizens: A Chronicle of the French Revolution* (S. Schama; 1989)

Quotations by Louis XVI

3 Nothing.
Diary entry on the day the Bastille fell. Diary (July 14, 1789)

Louis XVIII, King of France (Louis Xavier; 1755–1824) French monarch

Quotations about Louis XVIII

1 The courtiers who surround him have forgotten nothing and learned nothing.
Charles-François Dumouriez (1739–1823) French general. Said of Louis XVIII at the time of the Declaration of Verona; also quoted by Napoleon on his return from Elba. *Examen impartial d'un Écrit intitulé Déclaration de Louis XVIII* (September 1795)

Quotations by Louis XVIII

2 Punctuality is the politeness of kings.
Attrib.

Louis-Philippe, King of France ("The Citizen King"; 1773–1850) French monarch

1 The friendly understanding that exists between my government and hers.
Referring to an informal understanding reached between Britain and France on December 27, 1843. The more familiar phrase, "entente cordiale," was first used in 1844. Remark (December 27, 1843)

Lovecraft, H. P. (Howard Phillips Lovecraft; 1890–1937) U.S. writer

1 The most merciful thing in the world, I think, is the inability of the human mind to correlate all its contents.
The Call of Cthulhu (1928), ch. 1

Lovelace, Richard (1618–57) English poet

1 When flowing cups run swiftly round
With no allaying Thames...
When thirsty grief in wine we steep,
When healths and draughts go free,
Fishes, that tipple in the deep,
Know no such liberty.
"To Althea, From Prison" (1649)

2 When Love with unconfinèd wings
Hovers within my gates;
And my divine Althea brings
To whisper at the grates:
When I lie tangled in her hair,
And fettered to her eye;
The Gods, that wanton in the air,
Know no such liberty.
"To Althea, From Prison" (1649)

3 Stone walls do not a prison make,
Nor iron bars a cage;
Minds innocent and quiet take
That for an hermitage;
If I have freedom in my love,
And in my soul am free,
Angels alone that soar above
Enjoy such liberty.
"To Althea, From Prison" (1649), st. 4

4 Tell me not, Sweet, I am unkind,
That from the nunnery
Of thy chaste breast and quiet mind
To war and arms I fly...
I could not love thee, Dear, so much,
Loved I not Honour more.
"To Lucasta, Going to the Wars" (1649)

Lovell, Bernard, Sir (Alfred Charles Bernard Lovell; b.1913) British astronomer

1 Out of all possible universes, the only one which can exist, in the sense that it can be known, is simply the one which satisfies the narrow conditions necessary for the development of intelligent life.
In the Centre of Immensities (1979)

2 A study of history shows that civilizations that abandon the quest for knowledge are doomed to disintegration.
Observer, London (May 14, 1972), "Sayings of the Week"

Lovell, James (James Arthur Lovell; b.1928) U.S. astronaut

1 OK, Houston, we have had a problem here...Houston, we have a problem.
April 11, 1970. His message to mission control after an explosion on Apollo 13.

Lovell, Maria (Maria Anne Lovell; 1803–77) British actor and dramatist

1 Two souls with but a single thought,
Two hearts that beat as one.
Translated from Friedrich Halm's *Der Sohn der Wildniss* (1843). *Ingomar the Barbarian* (1855), Act 2

Lovelock, James (James Ephraim Lovelock; b.1919) British scientist

1 In the current fashionable denigration of technology, it is easy to forget that nuclear fission is a natural process. If something as intricate as life can assemble by accident, we need not marvel at the fission reactor, a relatively simple contraption, doing likewise.
Gaia: A New Look at Life on Earth (1979)

2 Our planet...consists largely of lumps of fall-out from a star-sized hydrogen bomb...Within our bodies, no less than three million atoms rendered unstable in that event still erupt every minute, releasing a tiny fraction of the energy stored from that fierce fire of long ago.
Gaia: A New Look at Life on Earth (1979)

3 The climate and the chemical properties of the Earth now and throughout its history seem always to have been optimal for life. For this to have happened by chance is as unlikely as to

survive unscathed a drive blindfold through rush hour traffic.
Gaia: a New Look at Life on Earth (1979)

4 The hazards of nuclear and of ultra-violet radiation are much in mind these days and some fear that they may destroy all life on Earth. Yet the very womb of life was flooded by the light of these fierce energies.
Gaia: A New Look at Life on Earth (1979)

5 We have since defined Gaia as a complex entity involving the Earth's biosphere, atmosphere, oceans, and soil; the totality constituting a feedback or cybernetic system which seeks an optimal physical and chemical environment for life on this planet.
Gaia: a New Look at Life on Earth (1979)

Lover, Samuel (1797–1868) Irish novelist and songwriter

1 Andy Rooney was a fellow who had the most singularly ingenious knack of doing everything the wrong way; disappointment waited upon all affairs in which he bore a part, and destruction was at his fingers' end; so the nickname the neighbours stuck upon him was Handy Andy.
Handy Andy (1842)

2 When once the itch of literature comes over a man, nothing can cure it but the scratching of a pen.
Handy Andy (1842)

Low, David, Sir (David Alexander Cecil Low; 1891–1963) British cartoonist

1 Very well, alone.
The cartoon shows a single British soldier defiantly shaking his fist at a hostile sea and a sky full of war planes. After the fall of France in June 1940 Britain was Hitler's one remaining active enemy in Europe. *Evening Standard* (June 18, 1940)

Lowe, Robert, Viscount Sherbrooke (1811–92) British lawyer and politician

1 I believe it will be absolutely necessary that you should prevail on our future masters to learn their letters.
Popularized as "We must educate our masters," which became the slogan of the 1870 Education Act. Speech to the British Parliament (July 15, 1867)

Lowell, A. Lawrence (Abbott Lawrence Lowell; 1856–1943) U.S. political scientist and educator

1 Anyone who sees in his own occupation merely a means of earning money degrades it; but he that sees in it a service to mankind ennobles both his labor and himself.
1930s. Quoted in *Intellectual Capital* (Thomas A. Stewart; 1997)

Lowell, Amy (Amy Lawrence Lowell; 1874–1925) U.S. poet and critic

1 I must be mad, or very tired
When the curve of a blue bay beyond a railroad track
Is shrill and sweet to me like the sudden springing of a tune.
"Meeting-House Hill" (1925), quoted in *The Penguin Book of American Verse* (Geoffrey Moore, ed.; 1977)

Lowell, James Russell (1819–91) U.S. poet, editor, essayist, and diplomat

1 I first drew in New England's air, and from her hearty breast
Sucked in the tyrant-hating milk that will not let me rest.
"On the Capture of Fugitive Slaves near Washington" (1854), st. 2, ll. 1–2

2 Truly there is a tide in the affairs of men; but there is no gulf-stream setting forever in one direction.
"New England Two Centuries Ago," *Literary Essays* (1899), vol. 2

3 Democracy gives every man a right to be his own oppressor.
The Bigelow Papers (1867), vol. 2

Lowell, Robert (Robert Traill Spence Lowell, Jr.; 1917–77) U.S. poet

1 Yours the lawlessness
of something simple that has lost its law.
"Caligula" (1964)

2 I saw the spiders marching through the air,
Swimming from tree to tree that mildewed day...
Let there pass
A minute, ten, ten trillion; but the blaze
Is infinite, eternal, this is death,
To die and know it. This is the Black Widow, death.
"Mr. Edwards and the Spider" (1950)

3 The man is killing time—there's nothing else.
"The Drinker" (1964)

4 Is getting well ever an art
Or art a way to get well?
"Unwanted" (1977)

5 Those blessed structures, plot and rhyme—why are they no help to me now
I want to make
something imagined, not recalled?
"Epilogue," *Day by Day* (1977)

6 Pray for the grace of accuracy
Vermeer gave to the sun's illumination
stealing like the tide across a map
to his girl solid with yearning.
Referring to the Dutch painter Jan Vermeer. "Epilogue," *Day by Day* (1977)

7 If we see light at the end of the tunnel it is the light of an oncoming train.
"Since 1939," *Day by Day* (1977)

8 But I suppose even God was born
too late to trust the old religion—
all those settings out
that never left the ground,
beginning in wisdom, dying in doubt.
"For the Union Dead," *For the Union Dead* (1964)

9 Everywhere,
giant finned cars nose forward like fish; a savage servility slides by on grease.
"For the Union Dead," *For the Union Dead* (1964)

10 I often sigh still

for the dark downward and vegetating kingdom
of the fish and reptile.

"For the Union Dead," *For the Union Dead* (1964)

11 He is out of bounds now. He rejoices in man's lovely
peculiar power to choose life and die—
when he leads his black soldiers to death,
he cannot bend his back.

Referring to Colonel Shaw, the white commander of the black regiment commemorated by the monument in Boston. "For the Union Dead," *For the Union Dead* (1964)

12 The monument sticks like a fishbone
in the city's throat.

Referring to the monument in Boston commemorating Colonel Shaw and his mainly black infantry. "For the Union Dead," *For the Union Dead* (1964), st. 8, ll. 1–2

13 The elect, the elected...they come here bright as dimes,
and die dishevelled and soft.

"July in Washington," *For the Union Dead* (1964)

14 I was a fire-breathing Catholic C.O.,
and made my manic statement,
Telling off the state and president, and then
I sat waiting sentence in the bull pen
beside a Negro boy with curlicues
Of marijuana in his hair.

Refers to Lowell's stance as a conscientious objector, when he refused to be drafted to fight during World War II. "Memories of West Street and Lepke," *Life Studies* (1959), st. 2

15 I myself am hell,
nobody's here.

"Skunk Hour," *Life Studies* (1956), quoted in *The Penguin Book of American Verse* (Geoffrey Moore, ed.; 1977)

16 On a thousand small town New England greens,
the old white churches hold their air
of sparse, sincere rebellion; frayed flags
quilt the graveyards of the Grand Army of the Republic.

"Waking in the Blue," *Life Studies* (1956), quoted in *The Penguin Book of American Verse* (Geoffrey Moore, ed.; 1977)

17 O that the spirit could remain
tinged but untarnished by its strain!

"Waking Early Sunday Morning," *Near the Ocean* (1967), st. 6

18 Pity the planet, all joy gone
from this sweet volcanic cone.

"Waking Early Sunday Morning," *Near the Ocean* (1967), st. 14

19 Life is too short to silver over this tarnish.
The gods, employed to haunt and punish
husbands, have no hand for trigger-fine distinctions,
their myopia makes all error mortal.

1968. "New Year's Eve," *Notebook* (1970), ll. 6–9

20 My Darling, prickly hedgehog of the hearth,
chocolates, cherries, hairshirts, pinks and glass—
when we joined in the sublime blindness of
courtship
loving lost all its vice with half its virtue.

1968. "New Year's Eve," *Notebook* (1970), ll. 10–13

21 You could cut the brackish winds with a knife
Here in Nantucket, and cast up the time
When the Lord God formed man from the sea's slime
And breathed into his face the breath of life.

"The Quaker Graveyard in Nantucket," *Poems 1938–1949* (1950)

22 This is the end of the whaleroad and the whale
Who spewed Nantucket bones on the thrashed swell
And stirred the troubled waters to whirlpools
To send the Pequod packing off to hell.

Nantucket is an island in southeastern Massachusetts, in the Atlantic Ocean. *Pequod* was the name of the whaling ship led by Captain Ahab in Herman Melville's novel *Moby Dick* (1851). "The Quaker Graveyard in Nantucket," *Poems 1938–1949* (1950)

23 When the whale's viscera go and the roll
Of its corruption shall overrun this world,
Beyond tree-swept Nantucket and Wood's Hole
And Martha's Vineyard, Sailor, will your sword
Whistle and fall and sink into the fat?

"The Quaker Graveyard in Nantucket," *Poems 1938–1949* (1950), pt. 3, ll. 1–5

24 They died
When time was open-eyed,
Wooden and childish; only bones abide
There, in the nowhere, where their boats were tossed
Sky-high, where mariners had fabled news
Of IS, the whited monster.

"The Quaker Graveyard in Nantucket," *Poems 1938–1949* (1950), pt. 3, ll. 13–18

25 The Lord survives the rainbow of His will.

Closing line. "The Quaker Graveyard in Nantucket," *Poems 1938–1949* (1950), pt. 4, l. 6

26 I saw the sky descending, black and white,
Not blue, and Boston where the winters wore
The skulls to jack-o'-lanterns on the slates,
And Hunger's skin-and-bone retrievers tore
The chickens and the shrike.

"Where the Rainbow Ends," *Poems 1938–1949* (1950), ll. 1–5

27 Age is our reconciliation with dullness.

"Last Summer at Milgate," *The Dolphin* (1973)

Lower, A. R. M. (Arthur Reginald Marsden Lower; 1899–1988) Canadian writer

1 Canada is a secondary and second-rate country without much depth of experience: everyone admits that—too freely, sometimes.

Canadian Historical Review (1941)

2 In Canada, democracy has been even more of a condition and less of a theory than it has been in the United States.

Report of the Canadian Historical Association (1930)

3 The history of much of North America might be termed the history of the rivalry of New York and Montreal.

The North American Assault on the Canadian Forest (1938)

Lowry, L. S. (Laurence Stephen Lowry; 1887–1976) British painter

1 A bachelor lives like a king and dies like a beggar.

Attrib.

Lowry, Malcolm (Clarence Malcolm Lowry; 1909–57) British novelist

1 Malcolm Lowry

Late of the Bowery
His prose was flowery
And often glowery
Who worked nightly
And sometimes daily,
And died playing the ukulele.

"Epitaph," quoted in *The Collected Poetry of Malcolm Lowry* (Kathleen Scherf, ed.; 1992)

2 Where are the children I might have had? You may suppose I might have wanted them. Drowned to the accompaniment of the rattling of a thousand douche bags.
Under the Volcano (1947), ch. 10

3 How alike are the groans of love to those of the dying.
Under the Volcano (1947), ch. 12

Loyden, Eddie (b.1923) British politician

1 If there was a war tomorrow you wouldn't be discriminating against gays and lesbians. You'd be dragging them in, just as you did in 1939.
Referring to the ban on homosexuals in the military. *Guardian Weekend*, London (December 28, 1996)

Loyola, Ignatius of, Saint (Inigo de Oñez y Loyola; 1491–1556) Spanish theologian

1 A sound mind in a sound body is the most useful instrument wherewith to serve God.
Letter to Francis Borgia (1548–49)

2 To give and not to count the cost;
To fight and not to heed the wounds;
To toil and not to seek for rest;
To labor and not ask for any reward
Save that of knowing that we do Thy will.
"Prayer for Generosity" (1548)

3 I have never left the army: I have only been seconded for the service of God.
Remark to Pope Paul III, Rome (1539)

4 To arrive at the truth in all things, we ought always to be ready to believe that what seems to us white is black if the hierarchical Church so defines it.
Spiritual Exercises (1548)

5 Let me look at the foulness and ugliness of my body. Let me see myself as an ulcerous sore running with every horrible and disgusting poison.
Spiritual Exercises (1548), no. 58

Lucan (Marcus Annaeus Lucanus; 39–65) Roman poet

1 Pygmies placed on the shoulders of giants see more than the giants themselves.
Didacus Stella (65?), 10

2 I have a wife, I have sons: all of them hostages given to fate.
Pharsalia (62–63), bk. 6, l. 661

Lucas, E. V. (Edward Verrall Lucas; 1868–1938) British publisher and writer

1 Americans are people who prefer the Continent to their own country but refuse to learn its languages.
Wanderings and Diversions (1926)

Luce, Clare Boothe (1903–87) U.S. playwright, journalist, and public official

1 I don't have a warm personal enemy left. They've all died off. I miss them terribly because they helped define me.
Remark on *The Dick Cavett Show*, ABC television (July 21, 1981)

2 NORA But if God had wanted us to think with our womb, why did He give us a brain?
Slam the Door Softly (1970)

3 When a man can't explain a woman's actions, the first thing he thinks about is the condition of her uterus.
Slam the Door Softly (1970)

4 What generally passes for "thought" among the majority of mankind is the time one takes out to rearrange one's prejudices.
Today's Woman (April 1946)

Luce, Henry R. (Henry Robinson Luce; 1898–1967) U.S. editor and publisher

Quotations about Luce

1 Mr. Luce's unique contribution to American journalism is that he placed into the hands of the people yesterday's newspaper and today's garbage homogenized into one package.
Herbert Lawrence Block (b.1909) U.S. cartoonist. Referring to the publisher Henry Luce, founder of *Time* (1923), *Fortune* (1929), and *Life* (1936) magazines. Attrib.

Quotations by Luce

2 Service is not a kind of blackmail paid to representatives of social morality; it is the way money is made.
Quoted in *The American Idea of Success* (Richard M. Huber; 1971)

3 Service is what the typical American businessman would do his best to render even if there weren't a cop or preacher in sight.
Quoted in *The American Idea of Success* (Richard M. Huber; 1971)

4 The businessman makes money in America, typically by serving his fellow man in ways his fellow man wants to be served.
Quoted in *The American Idea of Success* (Richard M. Huber; 1971)

Lucian (120?–after 180) Greek satirist and rhetorician

1 The poor wretches have got it into their heads that they are altogether immortal.
Late 2nd century. Referring to a Christian who publicly committed suicide in 165. "Peregrinus," *The Early Christians* (E. Arnold; 1970)

Luciano, Lucky (Charles Luciano, born Salvatore Lucania; 1897–1962) Italian-born U.S. gangster

1 I never wanted to be a crumb. If I had to be a crumb, I'd rather be dead.
Quoted in *Thomas E. Dewey* (Richard Norton Smith; 1982)

Lucretius (Titus Lucretius Carus; 99?–55? B.C.) Roman philosopher and poet

1 Nothing can be created out of nothing.
De Rerum Natura (1st century B.C.), pt. 1, l. 101

2 So much wrong could religion induce.
De Rerum Natura (1st century B.C.), pt. 1, l. 101

3 Constant dripping hollows out a stone.
De Rerum Natura (1st century B.C.), pt. 1, l. 314

4 Lovely it is, when the winds are churning up the waves on the great sea, to gaze out from the land on the great tribulations of someone else.
Referring not to enjoying another's troubles, but knowing yourself spared from problems. *De Rerum Natura* (1st century B.C.), pt. 2, l. 1

5 The generations of living things pass in a short time, and like runners hand on the torch of life.
De Rerum Natura (1st century B.C.), pt. 2, l. 75

6 The mind like a sick body can be healed and changed by medicine.
De Rerum Natura (1st century B.C.), pt. 3

7 And life is given to none freehold, but it is leasehold for all.
De Rerum Natura (1st century B.C.), pt. 3, l. 971

8 What is food to one man is bitter poison to others.
De Rerum Natura (1st century B.C.), pt. 4, l. 637

9 In the midst of the fountain of bliss there arises something bitter, which stings him even amid the very flowers.
Referring to sexual lust poisoning a man's happiness. *De Rerum Natura* (1st century B.C.), pt. 4, l. 1133

Ludendorff, Erich von (1865–1937) German general

1 They shall now eat the soup they have brewed for us.
Referring to Germany's democratic parties, which he hoped would be blamed for signing the armistice with the Allies. Remark (September 28, 1918), quoted in *Europe Since 1870* (James Joll; 1973), ch. 8

Ludwig, Emil (originally Emil Cohn; 1881–1948) German writer

1 Nature puts upon no man an unbearable burden; if her limits be exceeded, man responds by suicide. I have always respected suicide as a regulator of nature.
Quoted in *I Believe* (Clifton Fadiman, ed.; 1940)

Lueger, Karl (1844–1910) Austrian politician

1 I decide who is a Jew.
Also attributed to Hermann Goering. Attrib. *Europe Since 1870* (James Joll; 1973), ch. 4

Lugosi, Bela (Bela Feranc Denzso Blasko; 1884–1956) Hungarian-born U.S. film actor

1 Mr. Liveright, I understand your concern but the performance is not until a week from tomorrow ev-e-nink...yes, we save the atmosphere for a week from tomorrow ev-e-nink.
Said to Horace Liveright, producer of the stage version *Dracula*, a week before the opening night, which turned out to be a resounding success. Remark (1927), quoted in *Lugosi: The Man Behind the Cape* (Robert Cremer; 1977)

2 No! Not at any price...When I am through with this picture I hope never to hear of Dracula again. I cannot stand it...I do not intend that it shall possess me. No one knows what I suffer from the role.
1931. In response to a request by his agent that he play the Dracula role for 16 weeks in the theater. *Lugosi: The Man Behind the Cape* (Robert Cremer; 1977)

Lumière, Louis (1862–1954) French inventor and photographic pioneer

1 I have always been a technician and a researcher. I have never been what is called a director.
June 26, 1948. Quoted in "Founding Father: Louis Lumiere in conversation with Georges Sadoul," *Projections 4* (Pierre Hodgson; 1995)

Lumumba, Patrice (Patrice Hemery Lumumba; 1925–61) Congolese prime minister

1 A minimum of comfort is necessary for the practice of virtue.
Congo, My Country (1962), p. 57

2 No one is perfect in this imperfect world.
Congo, My Country (1962), p. 136

3 Without dignity there is no liberty, without justice there is no dignity, and without independence there are no free men.
1960. Letter to his wife, *Congo, My Country* (1962), p. 23

Luo Guanzhong (also known as Lo Kuan-chung; *fl.* 14th century?) Chinese author and playwright

1 Golden Lotus gazed at the handsome figure of Wu Song. "He's so big," she thought, "you'd never know they were born of the same mother. If I could have a man like that I wouldn't have lived in vain!"
Wu Song is a member of a group of bandits sworn to brotherhood and chastity. Golden Lotus, a name associated with the erotic in Chinese literature, attempts to seduce him. Here she compares him with his brother. "Wu Song Kills a Tiger on Jingyang Ridge," *Outlaws of the Marsh* (co-written with Shi Nai'an; 14th century?), ch. 10 (Sidney Shapiro, tr.; 1985)

2 Anyone using fire depends on the wind. This is now winter and only west winds blow...I am on the northwest and the enemy is on the south bank. If they use fire they will destroy themselves. I have nothing to fear.
Said by Cao Cao. *Romance of the Three Kingdoms* (C. H. Brewitt Taylor, tr.; 14th century?), ch. 48

Luther, Martin (1483–1546) German theologian and religious reformer

Quotations about Luther

1 The Diet of Worms. Luther's appearing there on 17th April 1521 may be considered as the greatest scene in Modern European history, the point, indeed, from which the whole subsequent history of civilisation takes its rise.
Thomas Carlyle (1795–1881) Scottish historian and essayist. *On Heroes, Hero-Worship, and the Heroic in History* (1841)

2 A single friar who goes counter to all Christianity for a thousand years must be wrong.
Charles V (1500–58) Belgian-born Spanish monarch. Speech at the Diet of Worms (April 19, 1521)

Quotations by Luther

3 Anyone who can be proved to be a seditious person is an

outlaw before God and the emperor; and whoever is the first to put him to death does right and well.
Referring to the "Peasants' War," an uprising (1524–25) of peasants in Germany partly inspired by Luther's teachings. "Against the Robbing and Murdering Hordes of Peasants" (Broadsheet) (May 1525)

4 I shall never be a heretic, I may err in dispute; but I do not wish to decide anything finally; on the other hand, I am not bound by the opinions of men.
Letter (August 28, 1518)

5 In my opinion it is better that all of these peasants should be killed rather than that the sovereigns and magistrates should be destroyed, because the peasants take up the sword without God's authorization.
Letter to Nicholas von Ansdorf (May 30, 1525)

6 Here stand I. I can do no other. God help me. Amen.
Speech at the Diet of Worms (April 18, 1521)

7 If I had heard that as many devils would set on me in Worms as there are tiles on the roofs, I should none the less have ridden there.
Referring to the Diet of Worms (April 18, 1521). Speech to the princes of Saxony (August 21, 1524), quoted in *Sämmtliche Schriften* (1745), vol. 16, ch. 10, sect. 1, no. 763: 15

8 In cases of melancholy...it is merely the work of the devil. Men are possessed by the devil in two ways; corporally or spiritually. Those whom he possesses corporally...he has permission from God to vex and agitate, but he has no power over their souls.
Colloquia Mensalia (1652)

9 The world degenerates and grows worse every day...The calamities inflicted on Adam...were light in comparison with those inflicted on us.
Commentary on the Book of Genesis (1545)

10 Be a sinner and sin strongly, but more strongly have faith and rejoice in Christ.
1521. Letter to Melanchthon, *Epistolae* (1556), vol.1, folio 345

11 For where God built a church, there the Devil would also build a chapel.
1540? *Table Talk* (1566), no. 67

12 Heavy thoughts bring on physical maladies; when the soul is oppressed so is the body.
"Of Temptation and Tribulation," *Table Talk* (1531–46)

13 Many devils are in woods, in waters, in wildernesses, and in dark pooly places...some are also in the thick black clouds...the philosophers and physicians say, it is natural, ascribing it to the planets, and showing I know not what reasons for such misfortunes and plagues as ensue.
1566. Quoted in *Table Talk* (William Hazlitt, tr.; 1821–22)

14 Wealth has in it neither material, formal, efficient, nor final cause, not anything else that is good; therefore our Lord God commonly gives riches to those from whom he withholds spiritual good.
Quoted in *Table Talk* (William Hazlitt; 1821–22)

15 Wealth is the smallest thing on earth, the least gift that God has bestowed on mankind.
Quoted in *Table Talk* (William Hazlitt; 1821–22)

16 A good servant is a real godsend; but truly 'tis a rare bird in the land.
Attrib.

17 Medicine makes sick patients, for doctors imagine diseases, as mathematics makes hypochondriacs and theology sinners.
Attrib.

18 The reproduction of mankind is a great marvel and mystery. Had God consulted me in the matter, I should have advised him to continue the generation of the species by fashioning them of clay.
Attrib.

19 Who loves not wine, woman and song,
Remains a fool his whole life long.
Inscribed in the Luther room in Wartburg, but with no proof of authorship. Attrib.

Luthuli, Albert (Albert John Mvumbi Luthuli; 1898–1967) Rhodesian-born South African nationalist leader

1 The struggle must go on...to make the opportunity for the building to begin. The struggle will go on...God giving me strength and courage enough, I shall die, if need be, for this cause. But I do not want to die until I have seen the building begun.
Let My People Go (1963), p. 206

2 Let your courage rise with danger.
Long Walk to Freedom (Nelson Mandela; 1994), p.523

Lutyens, Edwin Landseer, Sir (1869–1944) British architect

1 The answer is in the plural and they bounce.
Attrib.

Lutz, Mark U.S. author

1 Economics can no longer be seen as the theory of maximum possible production with consequent effects on welfare, but rather, in the opposite manner, as the theory of maximum possible welfare with consequent effects on production.
Quoted in "Humanistic Economics: History and Basic Principles," *Real-Life Economics* (Paul Ekins and Manfred Max-Neef, eds.; 1992)

Luxemburg, Rosa (1871–1919) Russian-born German socialist leader and revolutionary

1 Freedom is always and exclusively the freedom for the one who thinks differently.
The Russian Revolution (1918), sect. 4

Lu Xun (originally Zhou Shuren, also known as Lu Hsun; 1881–1936) Chinese writer

1 It is always a good idea for young people to be on the polite and amiable side. Politeness and amiability breed wealth, as they say.
"Divorce" (1925)

2 "Hope isn't the kind of thing that you can say either exists or doesn't exist," I thought to myself. "It's like a path across the land—it's not there to begin with, but when lots of people go the same way, it comes into being."
"Hair" (1921)

3 I began to realize that...I had neglected every last essential of human life for the sake of love alone...I'd forgotten about the business of making a living. A man has to be able to make a living before he can provide a place for love to dwell.
"Mourning the Dead" (1925)

4 "Master!..." I felt a shiver run through me; for I knew then what a lamentably thick wall had grown up between us. Yet I could not say anything.
The narrator is from a landlord family. As an adult he meets again his childhood friend, a peasant. "My Old Home" (January 1921)

5 If one can call the Creator to account, then I think he ought to be faulted for being too prodigal in the creation of life and too prodigal in its destruction.
"Some Rabbits and a Cat" (1922)

6 A biography of this type should start off something like this: "So-and-so, whose other name was so-and-so, was a native of such-and-such a place"; but I don't really know what Ah Q's surname was.
"The True Story of Ah Q" (December 1921)

7 It has long been noted that some conquerors prefer enemies as fierce as tigers and brave as eagles, for only then can they savor the true joy of victory.
"The True Story of Ah Q" (December 1921)

8 Ever since Chen Duxiu had put out the radical magazine *New Youth* and advocated scrapping the Chinese characters altogether in favor of spelling with a foreign alphabet, our "national heritage" had sunk into utter oblivion.
Referring to the advocacy of literary reform led by Chen Duxiu as part of the May Fourth Movement of the 1920s. "The True Story of Ah Q" (December 1921)

9 The majority of Chinese men could become saints and sages, were it not for the unfortunate fact that they are ruined by women.
"The True Story of Ah Q" (December 1921), ch. 4

10 Most people were dissatisified, because a shooting was not such a fine spectacle as a decapitation; and what a ridiculous culprit he had been too, to pass through so many streets without singing a single line from an opera.
Referring to the execution of Ah Q, the illiterate peasant protagonist. His ineffectual life is seen as symbolic of the state of China. "The True Story of Ah Q" (December 1921), ch. 9

11 Stay too long in a room filled with orchids and you no longer notice their fragrance. I must have lived in Beijing too long, for I no longer notice its quiet. To me, it was a very lively place indeed.
1922. "A Comedy of Ducks," *Diary of a Madman and Other Stories* (William A. Lyell, tr.; 1990)

12 Recalling the diagnoses and prescriptions given by my father's doctors and comparing them with this new knowledge of modern medicine, it gradually dawned on me that Chinese doctors were nothing more than quacks, whether intentional or unwitting.
1923. "Cheering from the Sidelines," *Diary of a Madman and Other Stories* (William A. Lyell, tr.; 1990)

13 There were no dates in this history, but scrawled this way and that across every page were the words BENEVOLENCE, RIGHTEOUSNESS, and MORALITY...finally I began to make out what was written between the lines; the whole volume was filled with a single phrase: EAT PEOPLE!
1918. Satirizing traditional Chinese historiography. Lu Xun is suggesting that the Confucian virtues of benevolence, righteousness, and morality hid a more sinister reality. "Diary of a Madman," *Diary of a Madman and Other Stories* (William A. Lyell, tr.; 1990)

14 My motive is to expose the illness in order to induce people to pay attention to its cure.
"How I Came to Write Fiction," *Literature of the People's Republic of China* (Kai-yu Hsu, ed.; 1980)

15 I am party to a history that comprises four thousand years of cannibalism.
1918. Referring to social injustice in the history of China. Quoted in *Origins of the Chinese Revolution, 1915–1949* (Lucien Bianco; 1967), "Intellectual Origins of the Revolution"

16 The Great Wall of China: a wonder and a curse.
1935. Attrib.

17 There is something about Heaven that displeases me; I do not wish to go there. There is something about Hell that displeases me...something about your future Golden Age that displeases me too; I do not wish to go there either.
September 24, 1924. Attrib.

Lydgate, John (1370?–1451?) English poet

1 All is not golde that outward shewith bright.
"As a Mydsomer Rose," , no. 63, l. 12, quoted in *The Minor Poems of John Lydgate* (Henry Noble MacCrauken, ed.; 1910–34)

2 Woord is but wynd; leff woord and tak the dede.
"Secretes of Old Philisoffres" (1430?), l. 1224

3 Comparisouns doon offte gret greuaunce.
The Fall of Princes (1431–38), bk. 3, l. 2188

Lyell, Charles, Sir (1797–1875) British geologist

1 Amidst the vicissitudes of the earth's surface, species cannot be immortal, but must perish, one after another, like the individuals which compose them. There is no possibility of escaping from this conclusion.
Principles of Geology (1830–33)

2 Millions of our race are now supported by lands situated where deep seas once prevailed in earlier ages. In many districts not yet occupied by man, land animals and forests now abound where the anchor once sank into the oozy bottom.
Principles of Geology (1830–33)

3 Notwithstanding, therefore, that we have not witnessed within the last three thousand years the devastation by deluge of a large continent, yet, as we may predict the future occurrence of such catastrophes, we are authorized to regard them as part of the present order of Nature.
Principles of Geology (1830–33)

4 When the aggregate amount of solid matter transported by rivers in a given number of centuries from a large continent, shall be reduced to arithmetical computation, the result will appear most astonishing to those...not in the habit of reflecting how many of the mightiest of operations in nature are effected insensibly, without noise or disorder.
Principles of Geology (1830–33)

Lyly, John (1554?–1606) English writer

1 CAMPASPE Were women never so fair, men would be false
APELLES Were women never so false, men would be fond.
Campaspe (1584), Act 3, Scene 3

2 O Love! has she done this to thee?
What shall, alas! become of me?
What bird so sings, yet so does wail?
O 'tis the ravish'd nightingale
Jug, jug, jug, jug, tereu, she cries,
And still her woes at midnight rise.
Campaspe (1584), Act 5, Scene 1

3 I can darken the Sunne by my skil, and remove the Moone out of her course.
Spoken by Dipsas, the old Enchantress. "Dipsas, the Old Enchantress," *Endimion* (1591)

4 A Rose is sweeter in the budde than full blowne.
Euphues: An Anatomy of Wit (1578)

5 As lyke as one pease is to another.
Euphues: An Anatomy of Wit (1578)

6 I mean not to run with the Hare and holde with the Hounde.
Euphues: An Anatomy of Wit (1578)

7 It seems to me (said she) that you are in some brown study.
Euphues: An Anatomy of Wit (1578)

8 Long quaffing maketh a short lyfe.
Euphues: An Anatomy of Wit (1578)

9 Ther can no great smoke arise, but there must be some fire.
Euphues: An Anatomy of Wit (1578)

10 Night hath a thousand eyes.
Maides Metamorphose (1600), Act 3, Scene 1

11 Wines indeed and girls are good,
But brave victuals feast the blood;
For wenches, wine, and lusty cheer,
Jove would leap down to surfeit here.
"A Serving Men's Song," *The New Oxford Book of English Verse* (Helen Gardner, ed.; 1972)

12 If all the earth were paper white
And all the sea were ink
'Twere not enough for me to write
As my poor heart doth think.
Quoted in *The Complete Works of John Lyly* (Bond, ed.; 1902), vol. 3

Lynch, Jack (John Lynch; b.1917) Irish prime minister

1 I would not like to leave contraception on the long finger too long.
Referring to the difficulties and controversy in trying to legalize contraceptives in Ireland. *Irish Times*, Dublin (May 23, 1971)

2 I have never and never will accept the right of a minority who happen to be a majority in a small part of the country to opt out of a nation.
Referring to Loyalists in Northern Ireland. *Irish Times*, Dublin (November 14, 1970), "This Week They Said"

Lynch, Michael (b.1946) Scottish historian

1 Politics and government in Victorian Scotland were a unique blend of deference and native idiosyncrasies.
Scotland: a New History (1991)

2 The eighteenth century is rightly hailed as the age when Scotland became one of the most important centres of intellectual culture in the western world.
Scotland: a New History (1991)

3 Bannockburn has been called one of the few decisive battles in Scottish history. Edward lost his shield, privy seal, court poet (who was obliged to compose victory verses for the Scots), and much of his credibility.
Referring to the Battle of Bannockburn (June 24, 1314), which is considered the victory by which Scottish independence was won, and to Edward II of England. The English army lost an estimated 10,000 men. *Scotland: a New History* (1991)

4 Culloden has become the symbol of the death of an old order as well as the emblem of the calculated brutality of the army of the Duke of Cumberland.
Referring to the Battle of Culloden (April 16, 1746), at which 5,000 highlanders led by Prince Charles Edward Stewart, who wanted to depose George III of England, were routed and massacred by 9,000 British regulars under the command of the Duke of Cumberland, George II's son. *Scotland: a New History* (1991)

5 The history of the Picts can be likened to a mystery with few clues and no satisfactory ending.
The Picts were the ancient inhabitants of Scotland and Northern Ireland. They were believed to have arrived in Scotland from continental Europe about 1000 B.C. *Scotland: a New History* (1991)

Lynch, Peter U.S. business executive

1 Never invest in any idea you can't illustrate with a crayon.
Beating the Street (1993)

2 You can't see the future through a rearview mirror.
Beating the Street (1993)

3 I like to buy a company any fool can manage because eventually one will.
Fortune (December 14, 1992)

4 You know you're in trouble when you need a Cray supercomputer to arrange your free time.
Inc. (February 1994)

5 Our popular culture saves its adulation for people ranging from Michael Jordan to Hootie and the Blowfish. They may be terrific individuals, but how many jobs did they create?
Wall Street Journal (September 20, 1996)

6 The United States is blessed with four elements missing in Europe: entrepreneurs, commercial banks looking for loans, large pools of venture capital, and outstanding capital markets.
Wall Street Journal (September 20, 1996)

7 There's no sense owning oil companies unless you're convinced that oil has a profitable future.
Worth (October 1996)

Lynd, Robert (Robert Wilson Lynd; 1879–1949) Irish essayist and journalist

1 As a rule, there is nothing that offends us more than a new type of money.
Attrib.

2 It is almost impossible to remember how tragic a place the world is when one is playing golf.
Attrib.

Lyndhurst, John Singleton Copley, Baron (1772–1863) U.S.-born British politician

1 Campbell has added another terror to death.
Referring to Lord Campbell's controversial *Lives of the Lord Chancellors* (1845–47), from which Lyndhurst was excluded because he was still alive. *Seventy-Two Years at the Bar* (E. Bowen-Rowlands; 1924), ch. 10

Lynn, Loretta (b.1937) U.S. country music singer

1 A woman's two cents' worth is worth two cents in the music business.
Quoted in *Los Angeles Times* (May 26, 1974)

Lysander (d.395 B.C.) Spartan naval commander

1 Deceive boys with toys, but men with oaths.
Quoted in *Lives* (Plutarch; 1st century?), 8

Lyte, Henry Francis (1793–1847) British hymnwriter

1 Abide with me; fast falls the eventide;
The darkness deepens; Lord, with me abide;
When other helpers fail, and comforts flee,
Help of the helpless, O, abide with me...
Change and decay in all around I see;
Thou, who changest not, abide with me.
"Abide with Me" (1847?)

Lyttelton, George, 1st Baron Lyttelton of Frankley (1709–73) English politician and writer

1 Where none admire, 'tis useless to excel;
Where none are beaux, 'tis vain to be a belle.
"Soliloquy on a Beauty in the Country," *Poems by the Right Honourable the Late George Lyttleton* (1777)

Lyttelton, Humphrey (Humphrey Richard Adeane Lyttelton; b.1921) British jazz trumpeter

1 Like actors in the days of Henry VIII, dance-band musicians—and jazzmen are inextricably mixed in with them—are generally regarded by their fellow men today as rogues and vagabonds.
Take It From the Top (1975), pt. 2, ch. 2

2 My experience is that jazzmen, particularly those who have fought their way almost single-handedly to the top of their profession, are as cuddly as man-eating tigers.
Take It From the Top (1975), pt. 3, ch. 7

3 The great jazz giants whom I have heard...have all made the same striking impression that, were the instrument to be suddenly wrenched from their lips, the music would continue to flow out of sheer creative momentum.
The Best of Jazz (1978), ch. 5

4 Spokesmen for Western civilisation reach for the word "primitive" whenever they encounter a music with strong rhythmic foundations.
The Best of Jazz (1978), ch. 14

Lytton, Bulwer (pseudonym of Edward George Earle Lytton Bulwer-Lytton; 1803–73) British novelist and politician

1 The extremes of life differ but in this:—Above, Vice smiles and revels—below, Crime frowns and starves.
Money (1840), Act 3, Scene 1

2 Beneath the rule of men entirely great,
The pen is mightier than the sword.
Richelieu (1839), Act 2, Scene 2

3 In the lexicon of youth, which Fate reserves
For a bright manhood, there is no such word
As fail?
Richelieu (1839), Act 2, Scene 3

4 There is no man so friendless but what he can find a friend sincere enough to tell him disagreeable truths.
What Will He Do With It? (1858), vol. 1, bk. 3, ch. 15

5 Nothing is so contagious as enthusiasm. It is the real allegory of the tale of Orpheus; it moves stones and charms brutes. It is the genius of sincerity and truth accomplishes no victories without it.
Attrib.

Mabley, Jackie (Loretta Mary Aiken, "Moms"; 1894?–1975) U.S. comedian and actor

1 There ain't nothin' an ol' man can do but bring me a message from a young one.
Her best-known line. Attrib.

MacArthur, Douglas (1880–1964) U.S. general

Quotations about MacArthur

1 The son of a bitch isn't going to resign on me, I want him fired.
Harry S. Truman (1884–1972) U.S. president. On removing General Douglas MacArthur from his command of UN forces in Korea. Remark to Omar Bradley, army chief of staff (1951)

2 I didn't fire him because he was a dumb son of a bitch, although he was, but that's not against the law for generals. If it was, half to three-quarters of them would be in jail.
Harry S. Truman (1884–1972) U.S. president. Quoted in *Plain Speaking* (Merle Miller; 1974), ch. 24

Quotations by MacArthur

3 Like the old soldier of the ballad, I now close my military career and just fade away.
Address to Congress (April 19, 1951)

4 People of the Philippines, I have returned.
Referring to his return to lead the reconquest of the Philippines from Japan (1944–45). Under orders, he had left the Philippines for Australia before the Japanese invasion in 1942. Radio broadcast, Leyte, Philippines (October 20, 1944)

5 A great victory has been won. A new era is upon us. We have had our last chance. If we do not devise some greater and more equitable system, Armageddon will be at our door.
Radio broadcast on Japan's surrender (September 2, 1945)

6 In war, indeed there can be no substitute for victory.
Speech to the U.S. Congress (April 19, 1951)

7 There is no security on this earth; there is only opportunity.
Quoted in *MacArthur: His Rendezvous with History* (Courtney Weaver; 1955)

8 I shall return.
March 30, 1942. Referring to leaving Corrigedor Island having lost the Philippines to advancing Japanese forces in World War II.

Macaulay, Robert B. Canadian politician

1 Fission is like kissing your wife. Fusion is like kissing your mistress.
Globe and Mail, Toronto (June 8, 1983)

Macaulay, Rose, Dame (Emilie Rose Macaulay; 1881–1958) British poet, novelist, and essayist

1 Oh, we'll lie quite still, nor listen nor look,
While the earth's bounds reel and shake,
Lest, battered too long, our walls and we
Should break...should break.
Referring to hearing the distant sound of an artillery bombardment in France. "Picnic" (1917), quoted in *The War Poets* (R. Giddings; 1988)

2 Gentlemen know that fresh air should be kept in its proper place—out of doors—and that, God having given us indoors and out-of-doors, we should not attempt to do away with this distinction.
Crewe Train (1926), pt. 1, ch. 5

3 He felt about books as doctors feel about medicines, or managers about plays—cynical but hopeful.
Crewe Train (1926), pt. 2, ch. 8

4 Poem me no poems.
Poetry Review (1963), Autumn

5 A group of closely related persons living under one roof; it is a convenience, often a necessity, sometimes a pleasure, sometimes the reverse; but who first exalted it as admirable, an almost religious ideal?
On the family. *The World My Wilderness* (1950), ch. 20

6 Decades have a delusive edge to them. They are not, of course, really periods at all, except as any other ten years would be. But we, looking at them, are caught by the different name each bears, and give them different attributes, and tie labels on them, as if they were flowers in a border.
Told by an Idiot (1923), pt. 2, ch.1

7 The Israelis are now what we call the "enemy-friends".
Quoted in *Independent*, London (July 5, 1994)

8 It was a book to kill time for those who like it better dead.
Attrib.

9 The great and recurrent question about abroad is, is it worth getting there?
Attrib.

Macaulay, Thomas Babington, 1st Baron Macaulay of Rothley (1800–59) British politician, historian, and writer

1 Ye diners-out from whom we guard our spoons.
Letter to Hannah Macaulay (June 29, 1831)

2 I shall not be satisfied unless I produce something that shall

for a few days supersede the last fashionable novel on the tables of young ladies.
Letter to Macvey Napier (November 5, 1841)

3 Free trade, one of the greatest blessings which a government can confer on a people, is in almost every country unpopular.
"On Mitford's *History of Greece*" (1824)

4 The history of nations, in the sense in which I use the word, is often best studied in works not professedly historical.
"On Mitford's *History of Greece*" (1824)

5 Night sank upon the dusky beach, and on the purple sea,
Such night in England ne'er had been, nor e'er again shall be.
"The Armada" (1833)

6 The reluctant obedience of distant provinces generally costs more than it is worth.
"Lord Mahon's War of the Succession," *Essays Contributed to the Edinburgh Review* (1843)

7 We know no spectacle so ridiculous as the British public in one of its periodical fits of morality.
"Moore's *Life of Lord Byron*," *Essays Contributed to the Edinburgh Review* (1843)

8 The business of everybody is the business of nobody.
1824. "On Hallam's *Constitutional History*," *Essays Contributed to the Edinburgh Review* (1843)

9 The gallery in which the reporters sit has become a fourth estate of the realm.
1824. Referring to the press gallery in the British Parliament. "On Hallam's *Constitutional History*," *Essays Contributed to the Edinburgh Review* (1843)

10 Knowledge advances by steps, and not by leaps.
1828. "On History," *Essays Contributed to the Edinburgh Review* (1843)

11 The English Bible, a book which, if everything else in our language should perish, would alone suffice to show the whole extent of its beauty and power.
1828. Referring to the King James Bible (1611). "On John Dryden," *Essays Contributed to the Edinburgh Review* (1843)

12 Nothing is so useless as a general maxim
1827. "On Machiavelli," *Essays Contributed to the Edinburgh Review* (1843)

13 As civilization advances, poetry almost necessarily declines.
1825. "On Milton," *Essays Contributed to the Edinburgh Review* (1843)

14 Many politicians...are in the habit of laying it down...that no people ought to be free till they are fit to use their freedom. The maxim is worthy of the fool in the old story, who resolved not to go into the water till he had learnt to swim. If men are to wait for liberty till they become wise and good in slavery, they may indeed wait for ever.
1825. "On Milton," *Essays Contributed to the Edinburgh Review* (1843)

15 Perhaps no person can be a poet, or can even enjoy poetry, without a certain unsoundness of mind.
1825. "On Milton," *Essays Contributed to the Edinburgh Review* (1843)

16 A single breaker may recede; but the tide is eventually coming in.
1830. "On Southey's *Colloquies of Society*," *Essays Contributed to the Edinburgh Review* (1843)

17 The highest intellects, like the tops of mountains, are the first to catch and to reflect the dawn.
"Sir James Mackintosh," *Essays Contributed to the Edinburgh Review* (1843)

18 Persecution produced its natural effect on them. It found them a sect; it made them a faction.
1848. Referring to the early Puritans and Calvinists. *History of England from the Accession of James II* (1848–61), vol. 1, ch. 1

19 The Puritan hated bear-baiting, not because it gave pain to the bear, but because it gave pleasure to the spectators.
1848. *History of England from the Accession of James II* (1848–61), vol. 1, ch. 2

20 In every age the vilest specimens of human nature are to be found among demagogues.
1848. *History of England from the Accession of James II* (1848–61), vol. 1, ch. 5

21 By the nine gods he swore
That the great house of Tarquin
Should suffer wrong no more
By the Nine Gods he swore it,
And named a trysting day,
And bade his messengers ride forth,
East and west and south and north,
To summon his array.
"Horatius," *Lays of Ancient Rome* (1842), st. 1

22 Then out spake brave Horatius,
The Captain of the Gate:
"To every man upon this earth
Death cometh soon or late.
And how can man die better
Than facing fearful odds,
For the ashes of his fathers,
And the temples of his Gods?"
"Horatius," *Lays of Ancient Rome* (1842), st. 27

23 Then none was for a party;
Then all were for the state;
Then the great man helped the poor,
And the poor man loved the great:
Then lands were fairly portioned;
Then spoils were fairly sold:
The Romans were like brothers
In the brave days of old.
"Horatius," *Lays of Ancient Rome* (1842), st. 32

24 Was none who would be foremost
To lead such dire attack;
But those behind cried "Forward!"
And those before cried "Back!"
"Horatius," *Lays of Ancient Rome* (1842), st. 50

25 Let no man stop to plunder,
But slay, and slay, and slay;
The Gods who live for ever
Are on our side to-day.
"The Battle of Regillus," *Lays of Ancient Rome* (1842), st. 35

26 The object of oratory alone is not truth, but persuasion.
"Essay on Athenian Orators," *Works* (1898), vol. 11

27 Thank you, madam, the agony is abated.
1804. Replying, aged four, to a woman who asked if he was hurt when hot coffee was spilled over his legs. Quoted in *Life and Letters of Macaulay* (G. M. Trevelyan; 1876), ch. 1

MacCarthy, Desmond, Sir (1878–1952) British poet and writer

1 When I meet those remarkable people whose company is coveted, I often wish they would show off a little more.
"Good Talk," *Theatre* (1954)

2 The whole of art is an appeal to a reality which is not without us but in our minds.
"Modern Drama," *Theatre* (1954)

3 More attentive to the minute hand of history than to the hour hand.
Referring to journalism. Quoted in *Curtains* (K. Tynan; 1961)

MacDiarmid, Hugh (pen name of Christopher Murray Grieve; 1892–1978) Scottish poet and writer

1 Killing
Is the ultimate simplification of life.
"England's Double Knavery" (1969)

2 It is very rarely that a man loves
And when he does it is nearly always fatal.
"The International Brigade" (1957)

3 Our principal writers have nearly all been fortunate in escaping regular education.
Observer, London (March 29, 1953), "Sayings of the Week"

MacDonagh, Donagh (1912–68) Irish playwright and broadcaster

1 Tallchief commented succinctly that she didn't mind being listed alphabetically, she just didn't want to be treated alphabetically.
Said about the New York City Ballet Company's policy of star billing. Maria Tallchief was a ballerina with the company. *George Balanchine* (1983)

MacDonald, Betty (originally Anne Elizabeth Campbell Baird; 1908–58) U.S. writer

1 In high school and college my sister Mary was very popular with the boys, but I had braces on my teeth and got high marks.
The Egg and I (1945), ch. 2

MacDonald, George (1824–1905) Scottish novelist and poet

1 The bliss of animals lies in this, that, on their lower level, they shadow the bliss of those—few at any moment on the earth—who do not "look before and after, and pine for what is not" but live in the holy carelessness of the eternal now.
"Sir Gibbie," *George MacDonald, an Anthology* (C. S. Lewis, ed.; 1946)

2 The ways of God go into the depths yet unrevealed to us: He knows his horses and dogs as we cannot know them, because we are not yet pure sons of God.
"The Inheritance," *George MacDonald, an Anthology* (C. S. Lewis, ed.; 1946), second series

3 There is no water in oxygen, no water in hydrogen; it comes bubbling fresh from under the imagination of the living God, rushing from under the great white throne of the glacier.
"The Truth," *George MacDonald, an Anthology* (C. S. Lewis, ed.; 1946), third series

4 To know a primrose is a higher thing than to know all the botany of it...Nature exists primarily for her face, her look...and not for the secrets to be discovered in her and turned to man's farther use.
"The Voice of Job," *George MacDonald, an Anthology* (C. S. Lewis, ed.; 1946), second series

Macdonald, John A., Sir (John Alexander Macdonald; 1815–91) Scottish-born Canadian statesman

1 I have no accord with the desire expressed...that by any mode whatever there should be an attempt made to oppress the one language or to render it inferior to the other; I believe that would be impossible...and it would be foolish and wicked if it were possible.
Referring to the use of both English and French in the federation of the Dominion of Canada, created in 1867. Speech, Canadian House of Commons (February 17, 1890)

2 A British subject I was born, and a British subject I hope to die.
When the Dominion of Canada was created in 1867, it remained part of the British Empire subject to the authority of the Crown. Speech, Canadian House of Commons (1882)

3 Give me better wood and I will make you a better cabinet.
Referring to criticism of his choice of cabinet ministers. Attrib.

MacDonald, John D. (1916–86) U.S. writer

1 The early bird who catches the worm works for someone who comes in late and owns the worm farm.
McGee (1975)

MacDonald, Ramsay (James Ramsay MacDonald; 1866–1937) British prime minister

Quotations about MacDonald

1 He died as he lived—at sea.
Anonymous

2 I remember, when I was a child, being taken to the celebrated Barnum's circus, which contained an exhibition of freaks and monstrosities, but the exhibit...which I most desired to see was ..."The Boneless Wonder". My parents judged that that spectacle would be too revolting and demoralising for my youthful eyes, and I have waited 50 years to see the boneless wonder sitting on the Treasury Bench.
Winston Churchill (1874–1965) British prime minister and writer. Speech to the British Parliament (January 30, 1931)

3 Well, what are you socialists going to do about me?
George V (1865–1936) British monarch. Said to Ramsay MacDonald, at their first meeting after MacDonald became Britain's first Labour prime minister. Remark (1924)Attrib.

Quotations by MacDonald

4 Society goes on and on and on. It is the same with ideas.
Speech (1935)

MacDougall, Donald, Sir (George Donald Alastair MacDougall; b.1912) British economist

1 I would not, however, push the case for a sense of history quite so far as the History Fellow of an Oxford college who criticised the reasoning behind the Bursar's investment policy

on the ground that the last two hundred years had been exceptional.
"In Praise of Economics," *Economic Journal* (December 1974)

Maceo, Antonio (Antonio Maceo y Grajales; 1845–96) Cuban soldier and revolutionary leader

1 Liberty is won with the edge of the machete: it is not asked for. To beg for rights is the domain of cowards incapable of exercising these rights.
Journal of the Knights of Labor (November 5, 1896), quoted in *Antonio Maceo: The "Bronze Titan" of Cuba's Struggle for Independence* (Philip S. Foner; 1977)

Macgregor, Douglas (1906–64) U.S. industrial psychologist

1 Successful leadership is not dependent on the possession of a single universal pattern of inborn traits and abilities.
Quoted in *Key Management Ideas* (Stuart Crainer; 1996)

Mach, Ernst (1838–1916) Austrian physicist and philosopher

1 The aim of research is the discovery of the equations which subsist between the elements of phenomena.
Popular Scientific Lectures (Thomas J. McCormack, tr.; 1910, 4th ed.)

2 Science itself, therefore, may be regarded as a minimal problem, consisting of the completest possible presentment of facts with the *least expenditure of thought*.
Quoted in *The Science of Mechanics: A Critical and Historical Account of its Development* (T. J. McCormack, tr.; 1915)

3 I can accept the theory of relativity as little as I can accept the existence of atoms and other such dogma.
1913? Attrib.

Machado, Antonio (1875–1939) Spanish poet and playwright

1 What does one day matter! Yesterday stands poised
to face tomorrow, tomorrow faces the infinite:
men of Spain, the past has never died
nor is tomorrow—nor yesterday—yet written.
"The Iberian God" (1913), ll. 59–62

2 Who has seen the face of the God of Spain?
My heart is waiting
for that man of Iberia with rough hands
who will know how to carve from the ilex of Castile
the austere God of that brown earth.
"The Iberian God" (1913), ll. 63–67

3 I live in peace with men and at war with my innards.
"Proverbs and Songs," *Castilian Landscapes* (1907–17), no. 23

4 Beware of the community in which blasphemy does not exist: underneath, atheism runs rampant.
Juan de Mairena (1943)

5 No one can shed light on vices he does not have or afflictions he has never experienced.
Juan de Mairena (1943)

6 The great philosophers are poets who believe in the reality of their own poems.
Juan de Mairena (1943)

7 The only living language is the language in which we think and have our being.
Juan de Mairena (1943)

8 There is no one so bound to his own face that he does not cherish the hope of presenting another to the world.
Juan de Mairena (1943)

9 Under all that we think, lives all we believe, like the ultimate veil of our spirits.
Juan de Mairena (1943)

10 Oh Time, oh Still and Now,
pregnant with things impending.
You travel the cold path with me,
arousing restlessness and hope.
"Last Lamentations of Abel Martin," *Selected Poems* (Alan S. Trueblood, tr.; 1982), ll. 22–25

11 The God of distance and of absence,
of the anchor in the sea, the open sea...
He frees us from the world in its omnipresence,
and opens up a way where we can walk.
"Siesta, In Memory of Abel Martin," *Selected Poems* (Alan S. Trueblood, tr.; 1982), ll. 9–12

12 By this glass filled with darkness to the brim
and this heart that's never full,
let us praise the Lord, matter of Nothingness,
who carved our reason out of faith.
"Siesta, In Memory of Abel Martin," *Selected Poems* (Alan S. Trueblood, tr.; 1982), ll. 13–16

13 Oh, empty spirit and full soul
facing the smoky bonfire,
the crackle of flames through roots,
the watchfire on the border
lighting up deep scars!
"The Death of Abel Martin," *Selected Poems* (Alan S. Trueblood, tr.; 1982), ll. 8–12

Machado de Assis, Joaquim Maria (1839–1908) Brazilian novelist and short-story writer

1 Life is so beautiful that the idea of death must itself arise first before it can be fulfilled.
Dom Casmurro (1899)

2 Purgatory is not to be confused with hell, which is an eternal shipwreck. Purgatory is a pawnshop which lends out against all virtues on short terms and at high interest.
Dom Casmurro (1899)

3 There is nothing worse than giving the longest of legs to the smallest of ideas.
Dom Casmurro (1899)

4 Believe in yourself, but do not always refuse to believe in others.
Epitaph of a Small Winner (1880)

5 Do not feel badly if your kindness is rewarded with ingratitude; it is better to fall from your dream clouds than from a third-story window.
Epitaph of a Small Winner (1880)

6 God deliver you, dear reader, from a fixed idea...it is they that make both supermen and mad men.
Epitaph of a Small Winner (1880)

7 I am a deceased writer not in the sense of one who has written and is now deceased, but in the sense of one who has died and is now writing.
Epitaph of a Small Winner (1880)

8 In justice to my father, one should note that he resorted to elaborate invention only after first experimenting with simple falsehood.
Epitaph of a Small Winner (1880)

9 Let no one trust the happiness of the moment; there is in it a drop of gall. When time has gone by and the spasm has ended, then, if ever, one can truly enjoy the event.
Epitaph of a Small Winner (1880)

10 Let Pascal say that man is a thinking reed. He is wrong; man is a thinking erratum. Each period in life is a new edition that corrects the preceding one and that in turn will be corrected by the next, until publication of the definitive edition, which the publisher donates to the worms.
Epitaph of a Small Winner (1880)

11 Remorse is nothing but the wry face that a conscience makes when it sees itself hideous.
Epitaph of a Small Winner (1880)

12 Tight boots are one of the greatest goods in the world, for, by making feet hurt, they create an opportunity to enjoy the pleasure of taking off your boots.
Epitaph of a Small Winner (1880)

13 We kill time; time buries us.
Epitaph of a Small Winner (1880)

14 If you desire something more than their aroma, I am sorry to have to tell you that I have kept neither portraits, nor letters, nor memories; even the emotion has vanished.
Referring to past loves. *Epitaph of a Small Winner* (1880)

15 Sometimes virtual crimes lie dormant, and operas are stored away in a maestro's head, only to await the creative influence of genius to inspire their opening bars.
Philosopher or Dog? (Clotilde Wilson, tr.; 1892)

16 The first thing that one loses in politics is one's freedom.
Philosopher or Dog? (Clotilde Wilson, tr.; 1892)

17 The universe has not yet come to an end for lack of a few poems that have died aflower in a man's head, be the man illustrious or obscure, but...Humanity must eat.
Philosopher or Dog? (Clotilde Wilson, tr.; 1892)

18 When roses are fresh, they are concerned little or not at all with man's anger; but if they are dying they will vex the human soul at the slightest provocation.
Philosopher or Dog? (Clotilde Wilson, tr.; 1892)

19 Our buttons operate in synchronization with ourselves; they form a sort of cheap and comfortable senate, which always votes in favor of our motions.
Referring to buttons on clothing. *Philosopher or Dog?* (Clotilde Wilson, tr.; 1892)

Machel, Samora (Samora Moïses Machel; 1933–86) Mozambiquan nationalist leader

1 War is the best university.
Quoted in *Mugabe* (David Smith and Colin Simpson; 1981)

Machiavelli, Niccolò (1469–1527) Italian historian, statesman, and political philosopher

1 A prince who desires to maintain his position must learn to be not always good, but to be so or not as needs may require.
1513–17. *Discourses on the First Ten Books of Titus Livy* (1531)

2 It never or rarely happens that a republic or monarchy is well constituted, or its old institutions entirely reformed, unless it is done by only one individual.
1513–17. *Discourses on the First Ten Books of Titus Livy* (1531)

3 We Italians then owe to the Church of Rome and to her priests our having become irreligious and bad, but we owe her a still greater debt, and one that will be the cause of our ruin, namely that the Church has kept and still keeps our country divided.
Discourses on the First Ten Books of Titus Livy (1531)

4 As a prince must be able to act just like a beast, he should learn from the fox and the lion; because the lion does not defend himself against traps, and the fox does not defend himself against wolves. So one has to be a fox in order to recognize traps, and a lion to frighten off wolves.
The Prince (1513)

5 Cunning and deceit will every time serve a man better than force.
The Prince (1513)

6 If an injury has to be done to a man it should be so severe that his vengeance need not be feared.
The Prince (1513)

7 It is better to be feared than loved, more prudent to be cruel than compassionate.
The Prince (1513)

8 It is the nature of men to be bound by the benefits they confer as much as by those they receive.
The Prince (1513)

9 Men are apt to deceive themselves in big things, but they rarely do so in particulars.
The Prince (1513)

10 The principal foundations of all states are good laws and good arms; and there cannot be good laws where there are not good arms.
The Prince (1513)

11 War should be the only study of a prince.
The Prince (1513)

12 It should be borne in mind that there is nothing more difficult to arrange, more doubtful of success and more dangerous to carry through than initiating changes in a state's constitution.
Quoted in *Key Management Ideas* (Stuart Crainer; 1996)

MacInnes, Colin (1914–76) British novelist and journalist

1 A coloured man can tell, in five seconds dead, whether a white

man likes him or not. If the white man *says* he does, he is instantly—and usually quite rightly—mistrusted.
"A Short Guide for Jumbles," *England, Half English* (1961)

2 England is...a country infested with people who love to tell us what to do, but who very rarely seem to know what's going on.
"Pop Songs and Teenagers," *England, Half English* (1961)

3 In England, pop art and fine art stand resolutely back to back.
"Pop Songs and Teenagers," *England, Half English* (1961)

4 Never have I met anyone who, condemning it completely, has turned out, on close enquiry, to know anything about it.
Referring to critics of pop music. Quoted in *The Faber Book of Pop* (Hanif Kureishi and Jon Savage, eds.; 1995)

Mackenzie, Compton, Sir (Edward Montague Compton Mackenzie; 1883–1972) British writer

1 I do wish you wouldn't wash your dirty Lenin at Council meetings, Mr MacLachlan.
Ben Nevis Goes East (1954), ch. 2

2 Well, people will put anything in a book. I don't read much, Hugh. But I've read enough to know that.
Ben Nevis Goes East (1954), ch. 2

3 I've never gone in much for poetry. It always seems to me rather a roundabout way of saying anything.
Hunting the Fairies (1949), ch. 5

4 I got tired of every blessed dog we had being called Luath, and I thought Bonzo would make a good change.
Hunting the Fairies (1949), ch. 8

5 Why the Lord should deport him to Hell for not listening to two and sometimes even three hours of preaching and praying in an alien tongue, for digging himself a few potatoes for his Sabbath dinner...was outside Ailean's conception of his Heavenly Father.
The "alien tongue" referred to is Latin, the liturgical language of the Catholic church. *Hunting the Fairies* (1949), ch. 11

6 Women do not find it difficult nowadays to behave like men; but they often find it extremely difficult to behave like gentlemen.
Literature in My Time (1933), ch. 2

7 Fancy the Government running out of whisky just before Lent. What a Government!
Whisky Galore (1947), ch. 1

8 I belong to the All One Association which is trying to bring about the religious union of all people, and we make no distinction at all between one creed and another. Except Communism.
Attrib.

Mackenzie, Henry (1745–1831) Scottish writer

1 Denominations of value are to nations what weights and measures are to individual countries.
Anecdotes and Egotisms (1827)

Mackie, J. L. (John Leslie Mackie; 1917–81) British philosopher

1 The present suggestion, then, is that a statement of the form "X caused Y" means "X occurred and Y occurred and Y would not have occurred if X had not".
The Cement of the Universe: A Study of Causation (1974)

2 Although, on this account, God could not have known what Adam and Eve, or Satan, would do if he created them, he could surely know what they *might* do...If so, he was taking, literally, a hell of a risk.
The Miracle of Theism (1982)

Mackintosh, James, Sir (1765–1832) Scottish lawyer, philosopher, and historian

1 Men are never so good or so bad as their opinions.
"Jeremy Bentham," *Ethical Philosophy* (1830)

2 The Commons, faithful to their system, remained in a wise and masterly inactivity.
Vindiciae Gallicae (1791)

Mackintosh, Margaret Macdonald (1865–1933) Scottish designer

1 The design of a pepper pot is as important as the conception of a cathedral.
Quoted in *Terence Conran on Design* (Terence Conran; 1996)

Mack Smith, Denis (b.1932) British historian

1 The "March on Rome" was a comfortable train ride, followed by a petty demonstration, and all in response to an express invitation from the monarch.
Referring to the October 1922 demonstration of Fascist power that led to the resignation of the administration and King Victor Emmanuel's request for Benito Mussolini to form a new government. "The March on Rome," *Mussolini* (1981)

Maclachlan, Jim U.S. business consultant

1 Dialogue is the oxygen of change.
Fortune (June 10, 1996)

MacLaine, Shirley (Shirley MacLean Beatty; b.1934) U.S. actor, dancer, and author

1 I've made so many movies playing a hooker that they don't pay me in the regular way any more. They leave it on the dresser.
Out on a Limb (1983)

MacLeish, Archibald (1892–1982) U.S. poet and educator

1 A Poem should be palpable and mute
As a globed fruit,
Dumb
As old medallions to the thumb,
Silent as the sleeve-worn stone
Of casement ledges where the moss has grown
A poem should be wordless
As the flight of birds.
"Ars Poetica" (1926)

2 A poem should not mean
But be.
"Ars Poetica" (1926)

3 We have learned the answers, all the answers:
It is the question that we do not know.
"The Hamlet of A. MacLeish" (1928)

Macleod, Iain (Iain Norman Macleod; 1913–70) British politician

1 We now have the worst of both worlds—not just inflation on the one side or stagnation on the other side, but both of them together. We have a sort of "stagflation" situation.
Speech to the British Parliament (November 17, 1965)

2 History is too serious to be left to historians.
Observer, London (July 16, 1961), "Sayings of the Week"

3 The nanny state.
Referring to overprotective government. *Spectator,* London (1960s)

4 Equality of opportunity means equal opportunity to be unequal.
Quoted in *Way Of Life* (John Boyd-Carpenter; 1980)

MacLeod, Sheila (b.1939) Scottish writer

1 In observing the behaviour of the slimmer and the anorexic, we may read the same text, "I want to lose weight". But the subtexts differ.
"The Art of Starvation" (1981), quoted in *Mind Readings* (Sara Dunn, Blake Morrison, and Michele Roberts, eds.; 1996)

MacMechan, Archibald (1862–1935) Canadian writer and scholar

1 Historically, Canada is a by-product of the United States.
The Canadian Historical Review (1920)

Macmillan, Harold, 1st Earl of Stockton (Maurice Harold Macmillan, "Supermac"; 1894–1986) British prime minister

Quotations about Macmillan

1 There is no reason to attack the monkey when the organ-grinder is present.
Aneurin Bevan (1897–1960) Welsh politician. The "monkey" was Selwyn Lloyd; the "organ-grinder" was Harold Macmillan. Speech in the British Parliament (May 16, 1957)

Quotations by Macmillan

2 When you're abroad you're a statesman: when you're at home you're just a politician.
Speech (1958)

3 After a long life I have come to the conclusion that when all the establishment is united, it is always wrong.
Speech, Carlton Club, London (October 1982)

4 Marxism is like a classical building that followed the Renaissance; beautiful in its way, but incapable of growth.
Speech to the Primrose League (April 29, 1981)

5 I am MacWonder one moment and MacBlunder the next.
Daily Telegraph, London (November 15, 1973)

6 Forever poised between a cliché and an indiscretion.
Referring to a British foreign secretary's life. *Newsweek* (April 30, 1956)

7 Memorial services are the cocktail parties of the geriatric set.
Quoted in *Macmillan 1957–1986* (Alistair Horne; 1991), vol. 2

8 If people want a sense of purpose they should get it from their archbishop. They should certainly not get it from their politicians.
Quoted in *The Life of Politics* (H. Fairlie; 1968)

9 Power? It's like a dead sea fruit; when you achieve it, there's nothing there.
Quoted in *The New Anatomy of Britain* (Anthony Sampson; 1971), ch. 37

MacNally, Leonard (1752–1820) Irish playwright and poet

1 On Richmond Hill there lives a lass,
More sweet than May day morn,
Whose charms all other maids' surpass,
A rose without a thorn.
"The Lass of Richmond Hill" (1789)

MacNeice, Louis (Frederick Louis MacNeice; 1907–63) Irish-born British poet

Quotations about MacNeice

1 The time is Auden and the place London.
1939
Randall Jarrell (1914–65) U.S. author and poet. Remarking on the critical judgments in Louis MacNeice's *Modern Poetry: A Personal Essay* (1938). "From That Island," *Kipling, Auden, & Co.: Essays and Reviews, 1935–1964* (1981)

2 That occupational disease of Englishmen, a real ignorance of anything American.
1939
Randall Jarrell (1914–65) U.S. author and poet. Remarking on the unfamiliarity with American work in Louis MacNeice's *Modern Poetry: A Personal Essay* (1938). "From That Island," *Kipling, Auden, & Co.: Essays and Reviews, 1935–1964* (1981)

3 His book is full of truisms you consent to without much pleasure, and half-truths you dissent from without much heat.
1939
Randall Jarrell (1914–65) U.S. author and poet. Reviewing Louis MacNeice's *Modern Poetry: A Personal Essay* (1938). "From That Island," *Kipling, Auden, & Co.: Essays and Reviews, 1935–1964* (1981)

Quotations by MacNeice

4 It's no go the picture palace, it's no go the stadium,
It's no go the country cot with a pot of pink geraniums,
It's no go the Government grants, it's no go the elections,
Sit on your arse for fifty years and hang your hat on a pension.
Set in Scotland, during the Great Depression (1930s) and pre-World War II. "Bagpipe Music" (1938), st.9

5 The glass is falling hour by hour, the glass will fall for ever,
But if you break the bloody glass, you won't hold up the weather.
"Bagpipe Music" (1938), st.10

6 I am tired to death of polygamy. I should like to live somewhere monogamously & work eight hours a day.
Letter to E. R. Dodds (November 6, 1939), quoted in *Louis MacNeice* (Jon Stallsworthy; 1995)

7 A poet like a pale candle guttering
On a worn window-sill in the wind.
"A Classical Education," *Blind Fireworks* (1929)

8 Time was away and somewhere else,
There were two glasses and two chairs
And two people with one pulse.
"Meeting Point," *Holes in the Sky* (1948)

9 I am not yet born; O fill me
With strength against those who would freeze my
humanity, would dragoon me into a lethal automaton,
would make me a cog in a machine, a thing with
one face, a thing.
1944. "Prayer Before Birth," *Holes in the Sky* (1948)

10 In doggerel and stout let me honour this country
Though the air is so soft that it smudges the words.
"Western Landscape," *Holes in the Sky* (1948), ll. 1–2

11 In my childhood trees were green
And there were plenty to be seen.
Come back early or never come.
September 1940. "Autobiography," *Plant and Phantom* (1941), ll. 1–3

12 The room was suddenly rich and the great bay-window was
Spawning snow and pink roses against it
Soundlessly collateral and incompatible:
World is suddener than we fancy it.
"Snow," *Poems* (1935), ll. 1–3

13 A house can be haunted by those who were never there
If there was where they were missed.
1957–60. "Selva Oscura," *Selected Poems of Louis MacNeice* (1964), ll. 1–2

14 A watched clock never moves, they said:
Leave it alone and you'll grow up.
Nor will the sulking holiday train
Start sooner if you stamp your feet.
"The Slow Starter," *Solstices* (1961)

15 He turned and saw the accusing clock
Race like a torrent round a rock.
"The Slow Starter," *Solstices* (1961), ll. 23–24

16 Age became middle: the habits
Made themselves at home, they were dressed
In quilted dressing-gowns and carried
A decanter, a siphon, and a tranquilliser.
"The Habits," *The Burning Perch* (1963), ll. 16–19

17 Take away your slogans; give us something to swallow,
Give us beer or brandy or schnapps or gin;
This is the only road for the self-betrayed to follow—
The last way out that leads not out but in.
December 1942. "Alcohol," *The Collected Poems of Louis MacNeice* (E. R. Dodds, ed.; 1966)

18 For the last blossom is the first blossom
And the first blossom is the best blossom
And when from Eden we take our way
The morning after is the first day.
1957. "Apple Blossom," *The Collected Poems of Louis MacNeice* (E. R. Dodds, ed.; 1966), st. 6, ll. 1–4

19 Sleep, my body, sleep, my ghost,
Sleep, my parents and grand-parents,
And all those I have loved most:
One man's coffin is another's cradle.
1938. "Autumn Journal," *The Collected Poems of Louis MacNeice* (E. R. Dodds, ed.; 1966)

20 And here we are—just as before—safe in our skins;
Glory to God for Munich.
And stocks go up and wrecks
Are salved and politicians' reputations
Go up like Jack-on-the-Beanstalk; only the Czechs
Go down and without fighting.
1938. "Autumn Journal," *The Collected Poems of Louis MacNeice* (E. R. Dodds, ed.; 1966), pt. 8, ll. 102–107

21 Popcorn peanuts clams and gum:
We whose Kingdom has not come
Have mouths like men but still are dumb.
July 1940. "Bar-Room Matins," *The Collected Poems of Louis MacNeice* (E. R. Dodds, ed.; 1966)

22 That the world will never be quite—what a cliché—the same
again
Is what we only learn by the event
When a friend dies out on us and is not there
To share the periphery of a remembered scent.
1946. "Tam Cari Capitis," *The Collected Poems of Louis MacNeice* (E. R. Dodds, ed.; 1966), ll. 1–4

23 The sunlight on the garden
Hardens and grows cold,
We cannot cage the minute
Within its nets of gold,
When all is told
We cannot beg for pardon.
1938. "The Sunlight on the Garden," *The Collected Poems of Louis MacNeice* (E. R. Dodds, ed.; 1966), st. 1

24 World is crazier and more of it than we think,
Incorrigibly plural.
1961. "The Taxis," *The Collected Poems of Louis MacNeice* (E. R. Dodds, ed.; 1966)

25 Your health, Master Yew.
My bones are few
And I fully admit my rent is due,
But do not be vexed, I will postdate a cheque for you.
1962. "Tree Party," *The Collected Poems of Louis MacNeice* (E. R. Dodds, ed.; 1966)

26 The cook Annie, who was a buxom girl from a farm in County Tyrone, was the only Catholic I knew and therefore my only proof that Catholics were human.
The Strings are False (1965), ch. 5

Madan, Geoffrey (1895–1947) British bibliophile

1 The devil finds some mischief still for hands that have not learnt how to be idle.
Livre sans nom: Twelve Reflections (1934)

Madariaga y Rogo, Salvador de (1886–1978) Spanish diplomat and writer

1 State education in Spain is not lay in the French sense of the word: it is religious, orthodox, and Catholic...Hence the

persistence of a rift in the nation, a state of mutual intolerance born of the intolerance of the Church, since one cannot be tolerant towards intolerance.
Spain (1930)

2 First the sweetheart of the nation, then the aunt, woman governs America because America is a land where boys refuse to grow up.
Quoted in "Americans are Boys," *The Perpetual Pessimist* (Sagittarius and George; 1963)

Madden, Samuel (1686–1765) Irish writer

1 Words are men's daughters, but God's sons are things.
Boulter's Monument (1745), l. 377

Madhubuti, Haki R. (Don L. Lee; b.1942) U.S. writer, publisher, and lecturer

1 Suppose those
who made
wars
had to fight them?
Quoted in "Nigerian Unity, or, Little Niggers Killing Little Niggers," *You Better Believe It* (Paul Breman, ed.; 1973)

Madison, James (1751–1836) U.S. president

1 Democracies...have in general been as short in their lives as they have been violent in their deaths.
Independent Journal (November 23, 1787), quoted in *The Federalist* (Alexander Hamilton, ed.; 1788), no. 10

2 The diversity in the faculties of men, from which the rights of property originate, is not less an insuperable obstacle to an uniformity of interests. The protection of these faculties is the first object of government.
Independent Journal (November 1787), quoted in *The Federalist* (Alexander Hamilton, ed.; 1788), no. 10

3 The proposed Constitution...is, in strictness, neither a national nor a federal constitution; but a composition of both.
Independent Journal (January 1788), quoted in *The Federalist* (Alexander Hamilton, ed.; 1788), no. 39

4 What is government itself but the greatest of all reflections on human nature?
Independent Journal (January 1788), quoted in *The Federalist* (Alexander Hamilton, ed.; 1788), no. 47

5 Money is the instrument by which men's wants are supplied, and many who possess it will part with it for that purpose, who would not gratify themselves at the expense of their visible property.
The National Gazette (1791)

6 A certain degree of preparation for war...affords also the best security for the continuance of peace.
Quoted in *Smithsonian* (September 1987)

Madonna (Madonna Louise Veronica Ciccone; b.1958) U.S. pop singer and film actor

Quotations about Madonna

1 Well, flower-print tight pants, a gold crucifix, Merry Widow black lace bras, chiffon strips as hair bows, and jeweled belts. A tumble of disheveled curls tops it all off.
Anonymous. Madonna's "Material Girl" fashion style. *New York Times* (June 7, 1985)

Quotations by Madonna

2 For being a single female. For having power and being rich and...having sex. For enjoying it and for saying that I enjoy it.
Referring to the negative press and public response to her book, *Sex* (1992), and album, *Erotica* (1992). "Je ne regrette rien," *The Face* (October 1994)

3 I live for meeting with the Suits. I love them because I know they had a really boring week and I walk in there with my orange-velvet leggings and drop popcorn in my cleavage and then fish it out and eat it.
Quoted in *Madonna Revealed* (Douglas Thompson; 1991)

4 Part of the reason I'm successful is because I'm a good businesswoman, but I don't think it is necessary for people to know that.
Quoted in *Madonna Revealed* (Douglas Thompson; 1991)

5 The more money you have, the more problems you have. I went from having no money to making comparatively a lot and all I've had is problems. Life was simpler when I had no money, when I just barely survived.
Quoted in *Madonna Revealed* (Douglas Thompson; 1991)

6 There's a wink behind everything I do.
Quoted in "Madonna," *Small Talk Big Names* (Myles Palmer; 1993)

Maeterlinck, Maurice, Count (Maurice Polydore Marie Bernard Maeterlinck; 1862–1949) Belgian playwright and poet

1 The living are just the dead on vacation.
Attrib.

Magee, John Gillespie (1922–41) British-born U.S. wartime pilot

1 Oh, I have slipped the surly bonds of earth,
And danced the skies on laughter silvered wings;
Sunward I've climbed and joined the tumbling mirth
Of sun-split clouds and done a hundred things
You have not dreamed of.
Quoted by President Ronald Reagan after the "Challenger" space shuttle disaster, January 28, 1986. "High Flight" (1941)

Magee, William Connor, Archbishop of York (1821–91) British clergyman

1 It would be better that England should be free than that England should be compulsorily sober.
Speaking on the Intoxicating Liquor Bill in the House of Lords (British Parliament's Upper Chamber). *Hansard* (May 2, 1872)

Magidson, Herbert (1906–86) U.S. songwriter

1 Music, Maestro, Please
1938. Song title.

Magna Carta

1 No freeman shall be taken, or imprisoned, or outlawed, or

exiled, or in any way harmed...except by the legal judgment of his peers or by the law of the land.
1215. The Magna Carta was a charter granted by King John of England to the English barons, subsequently regarded as the basis of English constitutional liberties.

2 To none will we sell, to none deny or delay, right or justice.
1215. The Magna Carta was a charter granted by King John of England to the English barons, subsequently regarded as the basis of English constitutional liberties.

Magruder, Jeb (Jeb Stuart Magruder; b.1934) U.S. political aide

1 Somewhere between my ambition and my ideals, I lost my ethical compass.
He was giving evidence to the Congressional investigation into Watergate. Quoted in *Time* (June 3, 1974)

Mahbubani, Kishore (b.1948) Singaporean diplomat

1 To have good government, you often need less, not more, democracy.
Observer, London (April 17, 1994), "Sayings of the Week"

Mahfouz, Naguib (b.1911) Egyptian writer

1 It is an indication of truth's jealousy that it has not made for anyone a path to it.
Arabian Nights and Days (1982)

2 Three years he had spent between fear and hope, death and expectation; three years spent in the telling of stories...Yet like everything, the stories had come to an end, had ended yesterday.
Referring to the Arabian Nights, in which after one thousand and one nights of storytelling by Scheherazade in order to suspend her death sentence, the sultan Schahriar sets her free. The end to her storytelling is the premise of Mahfouz's novel. *Arabian Nights and Days* (1982)

3 Beware, for I have found no trade more profitable than the selling of dreams.
Said by Sheikh Abd-Rabbih al-Ta-ih. *Echoes of an Autobiography* (1994)

4 Evil has encircled man from all sides, so man has devised good in all courses of action.
Said by Sheikh Abd-Rabbih al-Ta-ih. *Echoes of an Autobiography* (1994)

5 The breeze of love blows for an hour and makes amends for the ill winds of the whole of a lifetime.
Said by Sheikh Abd-Rabbih al-Ta-ih. *Echoes of an Autobiography* (1994)

6 When disasters come at the same time, they compete with each other.
Palace of Desire (1957)

7 Hating England is a form of self-defense. That kind of nationalism is nothing more than a local manifestation of a concern for human rights.
Said by Kamal. *Palace of Desire* (1957)

8 How beautiful it would be to see man wrestle with his illusions and vanquish them.
Said by Kamal. *Palace of Desire* (1957)

9 There's nothing to prevent a sensible person from admiring Sa'd Zaghlul as much as Copernicus, the chemist Oswald, or the physicist Mach; for an effort to link Egypt with the advance of human progress is noble and humane.
Said by Kamal. *Palace of Desire* (1957)

10 What I want is to draw inspiration only from the truth...My qualifications for this important role include a large head, an enormous nose, disappointment in love, and expectations of ill health.
Said by Kamal. *Palace of Desire* (1957)

Mahon, Derek (b.1941) Irish poet

1 I lie and imagine a first light gleam in the bay
After one more night of erosion and nearer the grave
Then stand and gaze from a window at break of day
As a shearwater skims the ridge of an incoming wave.
"Achill," *Antartica* (1985), ll. 1–4

2 I lie and imagine the lights going on in the harbour
Of white-housed Náousa, your clear definition at night,
And wish you were here to upstage my disconsolate labour
As I glance through a few thin pages and switch off the light.
"Achill," *Antartica* (1985), ll. 21–24

3 "I am just going outside and may be some time."
The others nod, pretending not to know.
At the heart of the ridiculous, the sublime.
Quoting Captain Oates's famous words, said during the return leg of Scott's expedition to the South Pole (1912) as he left the camp to die in the Antarctic cold, convinced that his injuries would jeopardize his companions' safe return. "Antartica," *Antartica* (1985), ll. 1–3

4 They are begging us, you see, in their wordless way,
To do something, to speak on their behalf...
Save us, save us, they seem to say.
"They" are mushrooms. "A Disused Shed in Co. Wexford," *Poems 1962–1978* (1979), ll. 51–52, l. 55

5 Elsewhere they are burning
Witches and heretics
In the boiling squares,

Thousands have died since dawn
In the service
Of barbarous kings;

But there is silence
In the houses of Nagoya
And the hills of Ise.
"The Snow Party," *Poems 1962–1978* (1979), ll. 16–24

Mahoney, Richard J. U.S. business executive

1 If you cite an R&D project in the chairman's letter in the annual report, the project will enjoy perpetual funding whether or not it even sees the light of day in the marketplace.
Speech (May 26, 1993)

2 Studies have shown that many of us carry a burden of subjective baggage about women and minorities in the workplace. For women and minorities striving to move up the corporate ladder, this can pose an enormous barrier.
Speech (November 9, 1993)

3 We are all gratified by advancing the frontiers of scientific knowledge, but the only thing that ever gets invoiced is the product.
Speech (May 26, 1993)

Mailer, Norman (b.1923) U.S. novelist and journalist

Quotations about Mailer

1 Mailer's sexual journalism reads like the sporting news grafted on to a series of war dispatches.

Kate Millett (b.1934) U.S. feminist and writer. *Washington Post* (July 30, 1970)

Quotations by Mailer

2 A novelist sits over his work like a god, but he knows he's a particularly minor god. Whereas a director making a small movie is a bona fide general of a small army.

Tough Guys Don't Dance publicity release (1987), quoted in *Chambers Film Quotes* (Tony Crawley, ed.; 1991)

3 Growth is a greater mystery than death. All of us can understand failure, we all contain failure and death within us, but not even the successful man can begin to describe the impalpable elations and apprehensions of growth.

Advertisements for Myself (1959)

4 America is a hurricane, and the only people who do not hear the sound are those fortunate if incredibly stupid and smug White Protestants who live in the center, in the serene eye of the big wind.

"Advertisements for 'Games and Ends'," *Advertisements for Myself* (1959)

5 The White Protestant's ultimate sympathy must be with science, factology, and committee rather than with sex, birth, heat, flesh, creation, the sweet and the funky.

"Advertisements for 'Games and Ends'," *Advertisements for Myself* (1959)

6 Each day a few more lies eat into the seed with which we are born, little institutional lies from the print of newspapers, the shock waves of television, and the sentimental cheats of the movie screen.

"First Advertisement for Myself," *Advertisements for Myself* (1959)

7 What characterizes a member of a minority group is that he is forced to see himself as both exceptional and insignificant, marvelous and awful, good and evil.

"A Speech at Berkeley on Vietnam Day," *Cannibals and Christians* (1966)

8 Sentimentality is the emotional promiscuity of those who have no sentiment.

"My Hope for America," *Cannibals and Christians* (1966)

9 A politician in...trouble can give away the last of his soul in order not to be forced to witness how much he has given away already.

"The Siege of Chicago," *Miami and the Siege of Chicago* (1968)

10 Punches did not often hurt in a fight, but there came a point in following hours when you descended into your punishment. Pain would begin; a slow exploration of the damage done.

"The Siege of Chicago," *Miami and the Siege of Chicago* (1968)

11 Being married six times shows a degree of optimism over wisdom, but I am incorrigibly optimistic.

Observer, London (January 17, 1988), "Sayings of the Week"

12 The horror of the twentieth century was the size of each event, and the paucity of the reverberation.

Of a Fire on the Moon (1970), ch. 2

13 If the Devil was devoted to destroying all belief in conservative values among the intelligent and prosperous, he could not have picked a finer instrument to his purpose than the war in Vietnam.

St. George and the Godfather (1972)

14 It had taken him...three divorces and four wives to decide that some female phenomena could be explained by no hypothesis less thoroughgoing than the absolute existence of witches.

"History as Novel: The Steps of the Pentagon," *The Armies of the Night* (1968), bk. 1, pt. 3, ch. 5

15 Two of them leaped on him at once in the cold clammy murderous fury of all cops at the existential moment of making their bust—all cops who secretly expect to be struck at that instant for their sins.

Referring to his own arrest during the anti-Vietnam War march on the Pentagon (1968). "History as Novel: The Steps of the Pentagon," *The Armies of the Night* (1968), bk. 1, pt. 3, ch. 5

16 The American Nazis were all fanatics, yes, poor mad tormented fanatics...but this man's conviction stood in his eyes as if his soul had been focused to a single point of light.

"History as Novel: The Steps of the Pentagon," *The Armies of the Night* (1968), bk. 1, pt. 4, ch. 2

17 The average good Christian American secretly loved the war in Vietnam...America needed the war. It would need a war so long as technology expanded on every road of communication, and the cities and corporations spread like cancer.

"History as Novel: The Steps of the Pentagon," *The Armies of the Night* (1968), bk. 1, pt. 4, ch. 7

18 Once a newspaper touches a story, the facts are lost forever, even to the protagonists.

The Presidential Papers (1963)

19 Ultimately a hero is a man who would argue with Gods, and awakens devils to contest his vision.

The Presidential Papers (1963)

20 A modern democracy is a tyranny whose borders are undefined; one discovers how far one can go only by traveling in a straight line until one is stopped.

The Presidential Papers (1963), Preface

21 At bottom, the FBI has nothing to do with Communism, it has nothing to do with catching criminals...it has nothing to do with anything but serving as a church for the mediocre.

"Sixth Presidential Paper—A Kennedy Miscellany: An Impolite Interview," *The Presidential Papers* (1963)

22 I'm hostile to men, I'm hostile to women. I'm hostile to cats, to poor cockroaches, I'm afraid of horses.

"Sixth Presidential Paper—A Kennedy Miscellany: An Impolite Interview," *The Presidential Papers* (1963)

23 We kill the spirit here, we are the experts at that. We use psychic bullets and kill each other cell by cell.

Contrasting the United States with Cuba, where Norman Mailer claims hatred runs over into the love of blood. "The Fourth Presidential Paper—Foreign Affairs: Letter to Castro," *The Presidential Papers* (1963)

24 But then the country is our religion. The true religion of America has always been America.

Interview, *Time* (September 27, 1984)

25 Hip is the sophistication of the wise primitive in a giant jungle.

"The White Negro," *Voices of Dissent* (1959)

26 The final purpose of art is to intensify, even, if necessary, to exacerbate, the moral consciousness of people.
"Hip, Hell, and the Navigator," *Western Review* (Winter 1959)

27 The sickness of our times for me has been just this damn thing that everything has been getting smaller and smaller and less and less important, that the romantic spirit has dried up.
"Hip, Hell, and the Navigator," *Western Review* (Winter 1959)

28 Writing books is the closest men ever come to childbearing.
Quoted in *Conversations with Norman Mailer* (J. Michael Lennon; 1988)

Maimonides (also known as Moses ben Maimon; 1135–1204) Spanish-born Jewish philosopher and physician

1 Medical practice is not knitting and weaving and the labor of the hands, but it must be inspired with soul and be filled with understanding and equipped with the gift of keen observation; these together with accurate scientific knowledge are the indispensable requisites for proficient medical practice.
Bulletin of the Institute of the History of Medicine (1935), vol. 3

2 A great disparity subsists between the knowledge an artificer has of the thing he has made and the knowledge someone else has of the artefact in question.
Guide to the Perplexed (1190)

3 One who is ill has not only the right but also the duty to seek medical aid.
Attrib.

4 Teach thy tongue to say "I do not know."
Attrib.

Maistre, Joseph Marie de, Comte (1753–1821) French political philosopher and diplomat

1 Every country has the government it deserves.
Letter (August 15, 1811), quoted in *Lettres et opuscules inédits* (1851), vol. 1, no. 53

2 Scratch the Russian and you will find the Tartar.
Attributed also to Napoleon and Prince de Ligne. *Lettres et opuscules inédits* (1851)

Major, John (b.1943) British prime minister

1 We cannot go on spilling blood in the name of the past. There is no excuse, no justification and no future for the use of violence in Northern Ireland.
Referring to the Anglo-Irish peace initiative. Press conference (December 15, 1993)

2 It is time to get back to basics: to self-discipline and respect for the law, to consideration for others, to accepting responsibility for yourself and your family, and not shuffling it off on the state.
Speech, Conservative party conference (October 8, 1993)

3 The harsh truth is that *if the policy isn't hurting, it isn't working.*
Referring to his government's determination to counter inflation with high interest rates. Speech, Northampton, England (October 27, 1989)

4 Gentlemen, I think we had better start again, somewhere else.
Said after an IRA mortar-bomb attack on 10 Downing Street during a Cabinet meeting. *Independent*, London (February 9, 1991)

5 Society needs to condemn a little more and understand a little less.
Interview, *Mail on Sunday*, London (February 21, 1993)

6 I think I'll stay cool, calm and elected.
He was defeated at the next British general election by the Labour leader, Tony Blair. *Time* (January 20, 1997)

7 Irish history records the Easter Uprising. Let us hope that this Easter records the Irish Settlement.
Referring to the Good Friday Agreement of April 1998, which provided for a provincial assembly for Northern Ireland and new mechanisms for cooperation between Northern Ireland and the Irish Republic. The Easter Uprising, or Rising, of 1916 was an armed rebellion of Irish nationalists against British rule. *Times*, London (April 11, 1998)

Makarios III, Archbishop of Cyprus (Mikhail Christodolou Mouskos; 1913–77) Greek Cypriot president

1 You should have known that it was not easy for me to die. But, tell me, were my obituaries good?
After mistaken reports of his death. Attrib.

Makeba, Miriam (b.1932) South African singer and political activist

1 Age is other things too. It is wisdom, if one has lived one's life properly. It is experience and knowledge. And it is getting to know all the ways the world turns, so that if you cannot turn the world the way you want, you can at least get out of the way so you won't get run over.
My Story (1988)

Makihara, Minoru (b.1931) Japanese business executive

1 In the United States, the shareholders are the owners. Period. They have the final say. But here it is an accepted fact that if you were to list who owns the company, it is first the employees and then the shareholders.
Referring to business in Japan. Quoted in "An Interview with Minoru Makihara," *Strategy and Business* (Joel Kurtzman; 1996)

Malamud, Bernard (1914–86) U.S. writer

1 Levin wanted friendship and got friendliness; he wanted steak and they offered spam.
A New Life (1961), pt. 6

2 There is no life that can be recaptured wholly; as it was. Which is to say that all biography is ultimately fiction.
Dublin's Lives (1979)

3 If your train's on the wrong track, every station you come to is the wrong station.
Quoted in *Natural Born Winners* (Robin Sieger; 1999)

Malcolm X (originally Malcolm Little, later El-Hajj Malik El-Shabazz; 1925–65) U.S. Black activist

Quotations about Malcolm X

1 Malcolm was our manhood, our living, black manhood! This was his meaning to his people. And, in honoring him, we honor the best in ourselves.
Ossie Davis (b.1917) U.S. playwright, film director, and civil rights activist. *The Autobiography of Malcolm X* (1965)

2 He spoke like a poor man and walked like a king.
Dick Gregory (b.1932) U.S. comedian and civil rights activist. Attrib.

3 He rose renewed renamed, became
much more than there was time for him to be.
Robert E. Hayden (1913–80) U.S. poet. "El-Hajj Malik El-Shabazz," *Words in the Mourning Time* (1970)

4 The brotherhood of Muslim men—in all colors—may exist...but part of the glue that holds them together is the thorough suppression of women.
Alice Walker (b.1944) U.S. novelist and poet. "To the Editors of Ms. Magazine," *In Search of Our Mothers' Gardens* (1983)

Quotations by Malcolm X

5 I see America through the eyes of a victim. I don't see any American dream. I see an American nightmare.
Comment (April 3, 1964)

6 Sitting at the table doesn't make you a diner, unless you eat some of what's on that plate. Being here in America doesn't make you an American.
Comment (April 3, 1964)

7 The question tonight, as I understand it, is "The Negro Revolt, and Where Do We Go From Here?" or "What Next?" In my little humble way of understanding it, it points toward either the ballot or the bullet.
Comment (April 3, 1964)

8 We don't go for segregation. We go for separation. Separation is when you have your own. You control your own economy; you control your own politics; you control your own society; you control your own everything. You have yours and you control yours; we have ours and we control ours.
Comment (January 23, 1963)

9 I think that what you should realize is that in America there are 20 million black people, all of whom are in prison. You don't have to go to Sing Sing to be in prison. If you're born in America with a black skin, you're born in prison.
Interview with Kenneth B. Clarke (June 1963)

10 There is nothing in our book, The Koran, that teaches us to suffer peacefully. Our religion teaches us to be intelligent. Be peaceful, be courteous, obey the law, respect everyone, but, if someone puts his hand on you, send him to the cemetery. That's a good religion.
Speech (November 1963), quoted in *Malcolm X Speaks* (George Breitman, ed.; 1965), ch. 1

11 You show me a capitalist, I'll show you a bloodsucker.
Speech at the Audubon ballroom (December 20, 1964), quoted in *Malcolm X Speaks* (George Breitman, ed.; 1965)

12 It's just like when you've got some coffee that's too black, which means it's too strong. What do you do? You integrate it with cream, you make it weak. But if you pour too much cream in it, you won't know you ever had coffee...It used to wake you up, now it puts you to sleep.
Referring to the state of black culture in United States. "Message to the Grass Roots," (November 1963), ch. 1, quoted in *Malcolm X Speaks* (George Breitman, ed.; 1965), ch. 1

13 And if I can die having brought any light, having exposed any meaningful truth that will help to destroy the racist cancer that is malignant in the body of America—then, all of the credit is due to Allah. Only the mistakes have been mine.
The Autobiography of Malcolm X (1965)

14 It has always been my belief that I, too, will die by violence. I have done all that I can to be prepared.
The Autobiography of Malcolm X (1965)

15 My feeling about in-laws was that they were outlaws.
The Autobiography of Malcolm X (1965)

16 New York was Heaven to me. And Harlem was Seventh Heaven.
The Autobiography of Malcolm X (1965), ch. 5

17 If it's necessary to form a Black Nationalist army, we'll form a Black Nationalist army. It'll be the ballot or the bullet. It'll be liberty or it'll be death.
April 1964. Quoted in *Malcolm X Speaks* (George Breitman, ed.; 1965)

18 Power never takes a back step—only in the face of more power.
Quoted in *Malcolm X Speaks* (George Breitman, ed.; 1965)

19 No *sane* black man really wants integration! No *sane* white man really wants integration!
1965. Quoted in *The Faber Book of America* (Christopher Ricks and William L. Vance, eds.; 1992)

20 All Negroes are angry and I am the angriest of all.
1965. Attrib.

21 I'm nonviolent with those who are nonviolent with me.
1965. Attrib.

Malesherbes, Chrétien de (Chrétien Guillaume de Lamoignon de Malesherbes; 1721–94) French statesman

1 A new maxim is often a brilliant error.
Pensées et maximes (18th century)

Malherbe, François de (1555–1628) French poet

Quotations about Malherbe

1 At last came Malherbe, and, the first ever in France, made a proper flow felt in verse.
Nicolas Boileau (1636–1711) French poet and critic. *L'Art poétique* (1674), pt. 1, l. 131

Quotations by Malherbe

2 But she was of the world where the fairest things have the worst fate. Like a rose, she has lived as long as roses live, the space of one morning.
"Consolation à Monsieur du Périer," *Stances Spirituelles* (1599)

Ma Lihua (b.1955) Tibetan writer

1 The sun turns the heart's agitation into tranquility
and love becomes profound because of it, after sublimation.
Quoted in *The Red Azalea* (Edward Morin, ed.; 1990)

Mallaby, George, Sir (Howard George Mallaby; 1902–78) British diplomat and writer

1 Never descend to the ways of those above you.
From My Level: Unwritten Minutes (1965)

Mallarmé, Stéphane (1842–98) French poet

1 The flesh, alas, is wearied; and I have read all the books there are.
"Brise marine," *Poésies* (1887)

2 That virgin, vital, fine day: today.
"Plusieurs sonnets," *Poésies* (1887), no. 1

3 Fundamentally, you see...the world is made to end in a fine book.
Réponses à des enquêtes: Sur l'évolution littéraire (1891)

4 To *name* an object is to destroy three-quarters of the pleasure given by a poem, which is gained little by little: to *suggest* it, that is the ideal.
Réponses à des enquêtes: Sur l'évolution littéraire (1891)

Malle, Louis (1932–95) French film director

1 It takes a long time to learn simplicity.
Referring to the art of filmmaking. *Films Illustrated* (March 1981), quoted in *Chambers Film Quotes* (Tony Crawley, ed.; 1991)

2 People found out I came from this upper-class background, a wealthy industrial family, very traditional. I had this reputation of being a playboy, making films for the sake of something to do. That really got on my nerves, because I was working very hard at what I was doing. If I'd been gifted, it would have been easier.
Today (January 28, 1990), quoted in *Chambers Film Quotes* (Tony Crawley, ed.; 1991)

Mallet, David (originally David Malloch; 1705?–65) Scottish poet

1 O grant me, Heaven, a middle state,
Neither too humble nor too great;
More than enough, for nature's ends,
With something left to treat my friends.
"Imitation of Horace" (Undated)

2 Maternity is on the face of it an unsocial experience. The selfishness that a woman has learned to stifle or to dissemble where she alone is concerned, blooms freely and unashamed on behalf of her offspring.
Attrib.

Mallet, Robert (b.1915) French writer and academic

1 How many pessimists end up by desiring the things they fear, in order to prove that they are right.
Apostilles, ou L'utile et le futile (1972)

Mallory, George (George Leigh Mallory; 1886–1924) British mountaineer

1 Because it is there.
In reply to the question "Why do you want to climb Mount Everest?" *New York Times* (March 18, 1923)

Malone, Michael S. (Michael Shawn Malone; b.1954) U.S. journalist

1 Because intellectual capital measurement is not confined to business but is likely to be the first universal measurement tool for *all* human institutions—we will be able to construct a more valuable society.
Quoted in *Capital for Our Time* (Nicholas Imparato, ed.; 1999)

2 One of the best ways to win any game is to write the rules.
Quoted in *Capital for Our Time* (Nicholas Imparato, ed.; 1999)

Malory, Thomas, Sir (?–1471?) English writer

1 Whoso pulleth out this sword of this stone and anvil is rightwise King born of all England.
Le Morte d'Arthur (1470), bk. 1, ch. 4

2 For, as I suppose, no man in this world hath lived better than I have done, to achieve that I have done.
Le Morte d'Arthur (1470), bk. 17, ch. 16

3 The month of May was come, when every lusty heart beginneth to blossom, and to bring forth fruit; for like as herbs and trees bring forth fruit and flourish in May, in likewise every lusty heart that is in any manner a lover, springeth and flourisheth in lusty deeds.
Le Morte d'Arthur (1470), bk. 18, ch. 25

4 For love that time was not as love is nowadays.
Le Morte d'Arthur (1470), bk. 20, ch. 3

5 And much more am I sorrier for my good knights' loss than for the loss of my fair queen; for queens I might have enough, but such a fellowship of good knights shall never be together in no company.
Le Morte d'Arthur (1470), bk. 20, ch. 9

6 Then Sir Launcelot saw her visage, but he wept not greatly, but sighed!
Le Morte d'Arthur (1470), bk. 21, ch. 11

Malraux, André (André Georges Malraux; 1901–76) French writer and statesman

1 The human mind invents its Puss-in-Boots and its coaches that turn into pumpkins at midnight because neither the believer nor the atheist is completely satisfied with appearances.
Antimémoires (1967), Preface

2 The attempt to force human beings to despise themselves...is what I call hell.
"La Condition humaine," *Antimémoires* (1967), pt. 2

3 The extermination camps, in endeavoring to turn man into a beast, intimated that it is not life alone which makes him man.
"La Condition humaine," *Antimémoires* (1967), pt. 2

4 The only domain where the divine is visible is that of art, whatever name we choose to call it.
La Métamorphose des dieux (1957), pt. 2, ch. 1

5 Man is what he does!
Les Noyers de l'Altenburg (1945), pt. 2, ch. 1

6 Man knows that the world is not made on a human scale; and he wishes that it were.
Les Noyers de l'Altenburg (1945), pt. 2, ch. 3

7 One cannot create an art that speaks to men when one has nothing to say.
L'Espoir (1938)

8 There are not fifty ways of fighting, there's only one, and that's to win. Neither revolution nor war consists in doing what one pleases.
L'Espoir (1938)

9 Art is a revolt against fate.
Les voix du silence (1951), pt. 4, ch. 7

10 There is...no death...There is only...*me...me...who is going to die...*
The Royal Way (Stuart Gilbert, tr.; 1935)

Malthus, Thomas (Thomas Robert Malthus; 1766–1834) British clergyman and economist

1 Population, when unchecked, increases in a geometrical ratio. Subsistence only increases in an arithmetical ratio.
Essay on the Principle of Population (1798), ch.1

2 The perpetual struggle for room and food.
Essay on the Principle of Population (1798), ch.3

Mama Cass (Cassandra Elliot, born Ellen Naomi Cohen; 1941–74) U.S. singer

1 Pop music is just long hours, hard work, and lots of drugs.
1970? Quoted in *Rock 'n' Roll Babylon* (Gary Herman; 1994)

Mamet, David (David Alan Mamet; b.1947) U.S. writer and film director

1 All professions, achievements, impulses, are thrown up to compete, to strive, to an end which is *not* chance, but is the effect of some Universal Will.
Lecture, Harvard University (December 11, 1988)

2 The law of life is to do evil and good, to eat and be eaten, and the most supposedly innocuous good is, perhaps, also and occasionally violence in disguise.
Lecture, Harvard University (December 11, 1988)

3 When you walk around you *hear* a lot of things, and what you got to do is keep clear who your friends are, and who treated you like what. Or else the rest is garbage.
American Buffalo (1976), Act 1

4 Superman comics are a fable, not of strength, but of disintegration. They appeal to the preadolescent mind not because they reiterate grandiose delusions, but because they reiterate a very deep cry for help.
"Kryptonite," *A Whore's Profession: Notes and Essays* (1994)

5 It is the strength to resist the extraneous that renders acting powerful and beautiful.
"Some Lessons from Television," *A Whore's Profession: Notes and Essays* (1994)

6 ROMA What I'm saying, what is our life?...It's looking forward or it's looking back. And that's our life. That's *it*.
Glengarry Glen Ross (1983), Act 1, Scene 3

7 I was born for a salesman. And now I'm back, and got my *balls* back.
Glengarry Glen Ross (1983), Act 2

8 A good film script should be able to do completely without dialogue.
Independent, London (November 11, 1988)

9 LANG We are all made of chemicals. We are the world in this respect...Why must I distinguish between inorganic and organic? All things come from hydrogen. They all come from the earth.
The Water Engine (1977)

10 LOHR The mind of man is less perturbed by a mystery he cannot explain than by an explanation he cannot understand.
The Water Engine (1977)

11 Demons and the fear of sleep have been eradicated by the watchmen of the modern order. Now we are characters within a dream of industry.
Voice-over. *The Water Engine* (1977)

12 Drama never changed anybody's mind about anything.
Times, London (September 15, 1993)

13 We respond to a drama to that extent to which it corresponds to our dreamlife.
"A National Dream-Life," *Writing in Restaurants* (1986)

14 We Americans have always considered Hollywood, at best, a sinkhole of depraved venality. And, of course, it is. It is not a Protective Monastery of Aesthetic Truth. It is a place where everything is incredibly expensive.
"A Playwright in Hollywood," *Writing in Restaurants* (1986)

15 The product of the artist has become less important than the *fact* of the artist...In our society this person is much more important than anything he might create.
"Exuvial Magic," *Writing in Restaurants* (1986)

16 The proclamation and repetition of first principles is a constant feature of life in our democracy. Active adherence to these principles, however, has always been considered un-American.
"First Principles," *Writing in Restaurants* (1986)

17 In a world we find terrifying, we ratify that which doesn't threaten us.
"Notes for a Catalog for Raymond Saunders," *Writing in Restaurants* (1986)

18 We live in oppressive times. We have, as a nation, become our own thought police; but instead of calling the process by which we limit our expression of dissent and wonder "censorship," we call it "concern for commercial viability."
"Radio Drama," *Writing in Restaurants* (1986)

19 Policemen so cherish their status as keepers of the peace and protectors of the public that they have occasionally been known to beat to death those citizens or groups that question that status.
"Some Thoughts on Writing in Restaurants," *Writing in Restaurants* (1986)

Mamonova, Tatyana (b.1944) Russian painter, poet, and translator

1 I have been stripped of my Soviet citizenship and exiled from the Soviet Union, and now, as citizen of the world, I hope that all people of goodwill will support women's moral resistance to the forces of evil and violence.
Referring to being exiled because of her feminist views. *New Directions For Women* (November–December 1980)

Mancroft, Stormont Samuel, Baron Mancroft (1914–87) British business executive and writer

1 Happy is the man with a wife to tell him what to do and a secretary to do it.
Observer, London (December 18, 1966), "Sayings of the Week"

2 All men are born equal, but quite a few get over it.
Attrib.

3 A speech is like a love affair: any fool can start one but to end it requires considerable skill.
Attrib.

Mandela, Nelson (Nelson Rolihlahla Mandela; b.1918) South African president and lawyer

Quotations about Mandela

1 Mr Mandela has walked a long road and now stands at the top of the hill. A traveller would sit down and admire the view. But a man of destiny knows that beyond this hill lies another and another. The journey is never complete.
May 2, 1994
F. W. de Klerk (b.1936) South African president. *Observer*, London (May 8, 1994), "Sayings of the Week"

2 Life with him was a life without him.
Winnie Mandela (b.1934) South African social worker and political activist. *Part of My Soul Went With Him* (1985)

Quotations by Mandela

3 Years of imprisonment could not stamp out our determination to be free. Years of intimidation and violence could not stop us. And we will not be stopped now.
Press conference (April 26, 1994)

4 I have cherished the ideal of a democratic and free society in which all persons live together in harmony and with equal opportunites...if needs be, it is an ideal for which I am prepared to die.
After his release from prison. Mandela was reiterating his words at his trial in 1964. Remark (February 11, 1990)

5 We stand for majority rule, we don't stand for black majority rule.
Referring to the first meeting between the government and the African National Congress. Remark (April 24, 1994)

6 Only free men can negotiate; prisoners cannot enter into contracts.
Replying to an offer to release him if he renounced violence. Remark (February 10, 1985)

7 I am not less life-loving than you are. But I cannot sell my birthright, nor am I prepared to sell the birthright of the people to be free.
February 1985. Response to the offer of freedom from P. W. Botha. Remark, quoted in *Part of My Soul Went With Him* (Winnie Mandela; 1985)

8 The task at hand will not be easy, but you have mandated us to change South Africa from a land in which the majority lived with little hope, to one in which they can live and work with dignity, with a sense of self-esteem and confidence in the future.
At his inauguration as president. Speech (May 10, 1994)

9 My fellow South Africans, today we are entering a new era for our country and its people. Today we celebrate not the victory of a party, but a victory for all the people of South Africa.
Following his election to the presidency. Speech, Cape Town (May 9, 1994)

10 It indicates the deadly weight of the terrible tradition of a dialogue between master and servant which we have to overcome.
Referring to the first meeting between the government and the African National Congress. *Independent*, London (May 5, 1990), "Quote Unquote"

11 In South Africa, to be poor and black was normal, to be poor and white was a tragedy.
Long Walk to Freedom (1994)

12 Man's goodness is a flame that can be hidden but never extinguished.
Long Walk to Freedom (1994)

13 I have discovered the secret that after climbing a great hill, one only finds that there are many more hills to climb.
Long Walk to Freedom (1994)

14 The soil of our country is destined to be the scene of the fiercest fight and the sharpest struggles to rid our continent of the last vestiges of white minority rule.
Observer, London (June 15, 1980), "Sayings of the Eighties"

15 Let there be work, bread, water and salt for all.
From his inaugural address as president. *Observer*, London (May 15, 1994), "Sayings of the Week"

16 Between the anvil of united mass action and the hammer of the armed struggle we shall crush apartheid and white minority racist rule.
June 1980. *The Struggle is My Life* (1990 ed.)

17 Since my release, I have become more convinced than ever that the real makers of history are the ordinary men and women of our country; their participation in every decision about the future is the only guarantee of true democracy and freedom.
1990. *The Struggle is My Life* (1990 ed.)

18 The past is a rich resource on which we can draw in order to make decisions for the future, but it does not dictate our choices. We should look back at the past and select what is good, and leave behind what is bad.
February 25, 1990. *The Struggle is My Life* (1990 ed.)

19 The spectre of Belsen and Buchenwald is haunting South Africa. It can only be repelled by the united strength of the people of South Africa.
October 1955. *The Struggle is My Life* (1990 ed.)

20 To overthrow oppression has been sanctioned by humanity and is the highest aspiration of every free man.
1953. *The Struggle is My Life* (1990 ed.)

21 There is no easy walk to freedom anywhere and many of us will have to pass through the valley of the shadow of death again and again before we reach the mountain tops of our desires.
September 21, 1953. Adapted from a statement by Nehru. Presidential address to ANC Conference, *The Struggle is My Life* (1990 ed.)

22 The struggle is my life. I will continue fighting for freedom until the end of my days.
June 26, 1961. Press statement, *The Struggle is My Life* (1990 ed.)

23 I stand here before you not as a prophet but as a humble servant of you, the people. Your tireless and heroic sacrifices have made it possible for me to be here today. I therefore place the remaining years of my life in your hands.
February 11, 1990. Speech on his release from prison, *The Struggle is My Life* (1990 ed.)

24 The freedom flame can never be put down by anybody.
December 31, 1999. Said whilst passing a memorial candle to Thabo Mbeki, his successor as South Africa's president, in a New Year's Eve visit to the prison cell on Robben Island where he had been imprisoned for over 20 years. *Time* (January 1, 2000)

25 I cannot and will not give any undertaking at a time when I, and you, the people, are not free. Your freedom and mine cannot be separated.
Message from prison, read by his daughter to a rally in Soweto. (February 10, 1985)

Mandela, Winnie (Nkosikazi Nomzamo Madikizela; b.1934) South African social worker and political activist

1 I am a living symbol of the white man's fear.
Part of My Soul Went With Him (1985)

2 Together, hand in hand, with our matches and our necklaces, we shall liberate this country.
The "necklace" was a burning tire placed over a victim's neck. *Times,* London (April 13, 1986)

3 Part of My Soul Went With Him
1985. Book title. Referring to Nelson Mandela's imprisonment.

Mandelstam, Nadezhda (Nadezhda Yakovlevna Mandelstam; 1899–1980) Russian writer

1 If the first way of evading responsibility is not to recollect at all, the second and most widespread way of silencing the voice of memory is to embellish and streamline one's recollections...The operation can be performed on an individual life history, or on the past of a whole nation.
1970. *Hope Abandoned* (Max Hayward, tr.; 1972), ch. 18, "Memory"

2 The members of the exterminating profession had a little saying: "Give us the man, and we'll make a case."
Referring to the Russian secret police. *Hope Against Hope* (Max Hayward, tr.; 1970), ch. 3

Mandelstam, Osip (Osip Yemilyevich Mandelstam; 1891–1938) Russian poet, writer, and translator

Quotations about Mandelstam

1 But in the room of the poet in disgrace
Fear and the muse keep watch in turn.
The night presses on,
Which knows no dawn.
Anna Akhmatova (1888–1966) Russian poet. Dedicated to the poet Osip Mandelstam in exile. "Voronezh" (Peter Norman, tr.; March 4, 1936), quoted in *The Akhmatova Journals: 1938–1941* (Lydia Chukovskaya; 1989), no. 42

2 Receive from me this city not made by hand,
My strange, my beautiful brother.
Marina Tsvetaeva (1892–1941) Russian poet. "Receive from me this city not made by hand..." (March 31, 1916), quoted in *Tsvetaeva* (Peter Norman, tr.; 1992)

Quotations by Mandelstam

3 For the resounding glory of eras to come,
For the lofty tribe of people then,
I've relinquished the cup at the elder's feast
And my happiness and my honor.
"Wolf" (1931), ll. 1–4, quoted in *The Eyesight of Wasps* (James Greene, tr.; 1989)

4 A plant in the world is an event, a happening, an arrow, and not a boring, bearded development.
Journey to Armenia (Clarence Brown, tr.; 1931–32), ch. 3

5 Parting is the younger sister of death.
Journey to Armenia (Clarence Brown, tr.; 1931–32), ch. 3

6 Who has not felt envious of chess players? You sense in the room a peculiar field of alienation from which a chill inimical to nonparticipants flows.
Journey to Armenia (Clarence Brown, tr.; 1931–32), ch. 3

7 To live in Petersburg is to sleep in a grave.
"O Lord, Help Me to Live Through This Night...," *Osip Mandelstam: Selected Poems* (Clarence Brown and W. S. Merwin, tr.; 1973), l. 3

8 No, I am no one's contemporary—ever.
That would have been above my station...
How I loathe that other with my name.
He certainly never was me.
Poems (1928), no. 141

9 O life of earth! O dying age!
I'm afraid no one will understand you
but the man with the helpless smile
of one who has lost himself.
1924. "1 January 1924," *Poems* (1928), ll. 1–4, quoted in *Osip Mandelstam: Selected Poems* (Clarence Brown and W. S. Merwin, tr.; 1973)

10 Now I'm dead in the grave with my lips moving
And every schoolboy repeating my words by heart.
"Now I'm Dead in the Grave," *Poems* (1928), no. 306

11 My animal, my age, who will ever be able
to look into your eyes?
Who will ever glue back together the vertebrae
of two centuries with his blood?
1923. "The Age," *Poems* (1928), ll. 1–4, quoted in *Osip Mandelstam: Selected Poems* (Clarence Brown and W. S. Merwin, tr.; 1973)

12 Hagia Sophia—here the Lord ordained
That nations and emperors must halt!
1912. Referring to the church built in Istanbul (532–537) under the auspices of Justinian I, and which became a mosque following the Ottoman conquest (1453). "Hagia Sophia," *Stone* (Robert Tracy, tr.; 1915), ll. 1–2

13 This is a day that yawns like a caesura:
Quiet since dawn, and wearily drawn out.
1914. "Orioles in the Woods...," *Stone* (Robert Tracy, tr.; 1915), ll. 5–6

14 Sleeplessness. Homer. The sails tight.
I have the catalog of ships half read:
That file of cranes, long fledgling line that spread
And lifted once over Hellas, into flight.
Hellas means ancient Greece, its islands and colonies. "Sleeplessness. Homer...," *Stone* (Robert Tracy, tr.; 1915), ll. 1–4

15 My desire is not to speak about myself but to track down the age, the noise and germination of time.
The Noise of Time (Clarence Brown, tr.; 1923), ch. 13

16 A *raznochinetz* needs no memory—it is enough for him to tell the books he has read, and his biography is done.
Raznochinetz is a Russian word meaning a classless scholar. *The Noise of Time* (Clarence Brown, tr.; 1923), ch. 13

17 I have studied the science of saying goodbye.
1918. "Tristia," *Tristia* (Robert Tracy, tr.; 1922), l. 1, quoted in *Leopard II: Turning the Page* (Christopher MacLehose, ed.; 1993)

18 Who can know, when he hears the word "farewell"
What kind of separation is before us,
Or what it is the crowing cock foretells.
1918. "Tristia," *Tristia* (Robert Tracy, tr.; 1922), ll. 9–11, quoted in *Leopard II: Turning the Page* (Christopher MacLehose, ed.; 1993)

19 Fat fingers as oily as maggots,
Words sure as forty-pound weights,
With his leather-clad gleaming calves
And his large laughing cockroach eyes.
1934. The "Stalin Lampoon," as it was known, was the direct cause of Mandelstam's exile to Veronezh in 1934. This translation (by John Crowfoot) is based on the autographed copy found in Mandelstam's KGB file by Vitaly Shentalinsky. Quoted in *The KGB's Literary Archive* (Vitaly Shentalinsky; 1995)

Mandeville, Bernard (1670–1733) English physician and satirist

1 One of the greatest reasons why so few people understand themselves, is, that most writers are always teaching men what they should be, and hardly ever trouble their heads with telling them what they really are.
An Enquiry into the Origin of Moral Virtue (1725)

Mangan, James Clarence (1803–49) Irish poet

1 O! the Erne shall run red
With redundance of blood,
The earth shall rock beneath our tread,
And flames wrap hill and wood,
And gun-peal, and slogan cry,
Wake many a serene glen,
Ere you shall fade, ere you shall die,
My Dark Rosaleen!
My own Rosaleen!
Translation from a medieval poem by Owen Roe MacWard. "My Dark Rosaleen," *The Faber Book of Irish Verse* (John Montague, ed.; 1974), ll.73–8

Mangipan, Theodore French physician

1 The number of unexplained cures has dropped enormously in the last few years and...will continue to drop.
Referring to Lourdes, where he worked for 18 years. *Independent*, London (May 12, 1994)

Manguel, Alberto (b.1948) Argentinian writer

1 Translating is the ultimate act of comprehending.
A History of Reading (1996)

2 Reading—I discovered—comes before writing. A society can exist—many do exist—without writing, but no society can exist without reading.
"The Last Page," *A History of Reading* (1996)

Manikan, Ruby Indian religious leader

1 If you educate a man you educate a person, but if you educate a woman you educate a family.
Observer, London (March 30, 1947), "Sayings of the Week"

Mankiewicz, Herman J. (Herman Jacob Mankiewicz; 1897–1953) U.S. screenwriter and film producer

1 It's the only disease you don't look forward to being cured of.
Referring to death. *Citizen Kane* (1941)

2 You know it's hard to hear what a bearded man is saying. He can't speak above a whisker.
Quoted in *Wit's End, Days and Nights of the Algonquin Round Table* (James R. Gaines; 1977)

3 It's all right, Arthur, the white wine came up with the fish.
After vomiting at the table of a fastidious host. Attrib.

Manley, Michael (Michael Norman Manley; 1924–96) Jamaican prime minister

1 I think that so long as politics is seen as the rather undignified contest between groups that are struggling for nothing more dignified than power, so long as that is true, then so long is shame the proper attitude to apply to the process.
Speech (September 12, 1974), quoted in *Michael Manley: The Making of a Leader* (Darrell E. Levi; 1989)

2 We all become so immersed in the habits of American culture that if we are not careful we mistake them for life itself.
Jamaica: Struggle in the Periphery (1982)

3 Where poverty is shared it may be endured. Where poverty is mocked by extravagance it becomes the condition within which resentment smoulders.
Jamaica: Struggle in the Periphery (1982)

Mann, Golo (Gottfried Mann; 1909–94) German historian

1 At times the Germans seem a philosophical people, at others the most practical and most materialist; at times the most patient and peaceful, at others the most domineering and brutal.
The History of Germany Since 1789 (1958), pt. 1

2 Nations have always managed to find some rational necessity, some ideological reasons for murdering each other.
The History of Germany Since 1789 (1958), pt. 1

Mann, Heinrich (1871–1950) German novelist and essayist

1 Each one of us is as nothing, but massed in ranks as Neo-Teutons, soldiers, bureaucrats, priests and scientists...we taper up like a pyramid to the point at the top where Power itself stands, graven and dazzling.
Man of Straw (1918)

Mann, Horace (1796–1859) U.S. educator

1 Be ashamed to die until you have won some victory for humanity.
Commencement Address, Antioch College, Yellow Springs, Ohio (1859)

2 Lost, yesterday, somewhere between sunrise and sunset, two

golden hours, each set with sixty diamond minutes. No reward is offered, for they are gone forever.
Attrib.

Mann, Thomas (1875–1955) German writer

1 Freedom is a more complex and delicate thing than force. It is not as simple to live under as force is.
Letter (December 1938), quoted in *Letters of Thomas Mann 1889–1955* (Richard Winston and Clara Winston, trs.; 1975)

2 National Socialism was not imposed on the German people from outside but has century-old roots in German life itself.
Letter (March 30, 1945), quoted in *Letters of Thomas Mann 1889–1955* (Richard Winston and Clara Winston, trs.; 1975)

3 We are not free, separate, and independent entities, but like links in a chain, and we could not by any means be what we are without those who went before us and showed us the way.
1902. *Buddenbrooks: The Decline of a Family* (H. T. Lowe-Porter, tr.; 1924), pt.3, ch.10

4 Often, the outward and visible material signs and symbols of happiness and success only show themselves when the process of decline has already set in.
1901. *Buddenbrooks: The Decline of a Family* (H. T. Lowe-Porter, tr.; 1924), pt. 7, ch. 6

5 The German is the eternal student, the eternal searcher, among the peoples of the earth.
1947. *Doctor Faustus* (H. T. Lowe-Porter, tr.; 1949), ch. 14

6 The German's revolutions are the puppet shows of world history.
1947. *Doctor Faustus* (H. T. Lowe-Porter, tr.; 1949), ch. 14

7 Youth in the ultimate sense has nothing to do with political history, nothing to do with history at all. It is a metaphysical endowment, an essential factor, a structure, a conditioning.
1947. *Doctor Faustus* (H. T. Lowe-Porter, tr.; 1949), ch. 14

8 A great truth is a truth whose opposite is also a great truth.
Essay on Freud (1937)

9 I don't want politics. I want impartiality, order and propriety. If that is philistine, then I want to be a philistine.
Reflections of a Non-Political Man (1918)

10 I hate politics and the belief in politics, because it makes men arrogant, doctrinaire, obstinate, and inhuman.
Reflections of a Non-Political Man (1918)

11 I tell them that if they will occupy themselves with the study of mathematics they will find in it the best remedy against the lusts of the flesh.
The Magic Mountain (1924)

12 Man is a master of contradictions, they exist through him, and so he is grander than they. Grander than death, too grand for it—that is the freedom of his head. Grander than life, too grand for it—that is the piety in his heart.
The Magic Mountain (1924)

13 What we call mourning for our dead is perhaps not so much grief at not being able to call them back as it is grief at not being able to want to do so.
The Magic Mountain (1924)

14 Disease makes men more physical, it leaves them nothing but body.
The Magic Mountain (1924), ch. 4

15 All interest in disease and death is only another expression of interest in life.
The Magic Mountain (1924), ch. 6

16 A man's dying is more the survivors' affair than his own.
The Magic Mountain (1924), ch. 6

17 Speech is civilization itself. The word, even the most contradictory word, preserves contact—it is silence which isolates.
The Magic Mountain (1924), ch. 6

18 Every intellectual attitude is latently political.
Quoted in *Observer,* London (August 11, 1974)

Manners, Lord John, 7th Duke of Rutland (John James Robert Manners; 1818–1906) British politician

1 Let wealth and commerce, laws and learning die,
But leave us still our old nobility!
England's Trust and Other Poems (1841), pt. 3, ch. 1

Man Ray (Emmanuel Rudnitsky; 1890–1976) U.S. painter and photographer

1 Each one of us, in his timidity, has a limit beyond which he is outraged.
"The Age of Light," *Photographs by Man Ray* (1934), introduction

2 For, whether a painter...introduces bits of ready-made chromos alongside his handiwork, or whether another, working directly with light and chemistry, so deforms the subject as almost to hide the identity of the original...the ensuing violation of the medium employed is the most perfect assurance of the author's convictions.
"The Age of Light," *Photographs by Man Ray* (1934), introduction

3 No plastic expression can ever be more than a residue of an experience.
"The Age of Light," *Photographs by Man Ray* (1934), introduction

Mansfield, Katherine (originally Kathleen Mansfield Beauchamp; 1888–1923) New Zealand-born British short-story writer and poet

1 How idiotic civilization is! Why be given a body if you have to keep it shut up in a case like a rare, rare fiddle?
"Bliss," *Bliss and Other Stories* (1920)

2 Smiling encouragement like a clumsy dentist.
Referring to the character Professor Leonard. "Bank Holiday," *The Garden Party* (1922)

3 Whenever I prepare for a journey I prepare as though for death. Should I never return, all is in order. This is what life has taught me.
January 29, 1922. *The Journal of Katherine Mansfield* (1927)

4 If you wish to live, you must first attend your own funeral.
Quoted in *Katherine Mansfield* (Antony Alpers; 1954)

5 I must say I hate money but it's the lack of it I hate most.
1910s. Quoted in *Katherine Mansfield* (Anthony Alpers; 1954)

6 Make it a rule of life never to regret and never to look back.

Regret is an appalling waste of energy; you can't build on it; it's only good for wallowing in.
Attrib.

Mansfield, William Murray, 1st Earl Mansfield of Caen Wood (1705–93) Scottish-born British judge and politician

1 Every man who comes to England is entitled to the protection of the English law, whatever oppression he may hereto have suffered, and whatever may be the colour of his skin, whether it is black or whether it is white.
From the judgment in the case of James Somersett, a fugitive Negro slave. It established the principle that slaves enjoyed the benefits of freedom while in England. Remark (May 1772)

2 Consider what you think justice requires, and decide accordingly. But never give your reasons; for your judgement will probably be right, but your reasons will certainly be wrong.
18th century. Advice given to a new colonial governor ignorant in the law. *Lives of the Chief Justices of England* (Campbell; 1849), vol. 2, ch. 40

3 God help the patient.
Attrib.

Manson, Charles (b.1934) U.S. cult leader and murderer

Quotations about Manson

1 The sixties ended abruptly on August 9, 1969, ended at the exact moment when word of the killings on Cielo Drive traveled like bushfire through the community...The tension broke that day. The paranoia was fulfilled.
1978
Joan Didion (b.1934) U.S. journalist and writer. Referring to the murders of Sharon Tate and others committed by Charles Manson and his followers. "The White Album," *The White Album* (1979), pt. 1

Quotations by Manson

2 Death is psychosomatic.
Esquire (1971)

Manzoni, Piero (1933–63) Italian painter and multimedia artist

1 A common vice among artists—or rather bad artists—is a certain kind of mental cowardice because of which they refuse to take up any position whatsoever, invoking a misunderstood notion of the freedom of art, or other equally crass commonplaces.
"For the Discovery of Zone of Images" (1957), quoted in *Piero Manzoni* (Tate Gallery, London; 1974)

Mao Yushi Chinese economist

1 The idea that we should expect sudden freedom is simplistic.
Referring to China, in particular to economic reform and the possibility of political liberalization. "Hayek's Children," *Far Eastern Economic Review* (1998)

Mao Zedong (formerly anglicized as Mao Tse-Tung; 1893–1976) Chinese statesman

Quotations about Mao Zedong

1 He wasn't one of those people who, having gained power, settled down to enjoy it. He was restless. He loved upheavals. He loved people fighting each other. It was like a game.
Jung Chang (b.1952) Chinese-born British writer and lecturer. Interview, *Straits Times*, Singapore (May 17, 1997)

2 Half of his bed was piled a foot high with books, so he could just roll over and pick one up. Books were specially printed for him. Sometimes the print run was two copies—one for the record, one for Mao.
Jung Chang (b.1952) Chinese-born British writer and lecturer. Referring to Mao Zedong and banned books in China. Interview, *Straits Times*, Singapore (May 5, 1997)

Quotations by Mao Zedong

3 What then, from the point of view of the broad masses of the people, should be the criteria today for distinguishing fragrant flowers from poisonous weeds?
"On the Correct Handling of Contradictions among the People" (1957), quoted in *Selected Readings from Mao Zedong* (1967)

4 We are advocates of the abolition of war, we do not want war; but war can only be abolished through war, and in order to get rid of the gun it is necessary to take up the gun.
"Problems of War and Strategy" (November 6, 1938)

5 A revolution is not a dinner party...or doing embroidery; it cannot be so refined, so leisurely.
Remark (1927)

6 Reading books is learning, but application is also learning and the more important form of learning.
"The Important Problem is to be Good at Learning" (1935), quoted in *Mao Tsetung: An Anthology of His Writings* (Anne Fremantle, ed.; 1962)

7 China is a vast country—"When the east is still dark, the west is lit up; when night falls in the south, the day breaks in the north"; hence one need not worry about whether there is room enough to move round.
Characteristics of China's Revolutionary War (1935), quoted in *Mao Tsetung: An Anthology of His Writings* (Anne Fremantle, ed.; 1962)

8 Liberalism is a manifestation of opportunism and conflicts fundamentally with Marxism.
Combat Liberalism (1937), quoted in *Mao Tsetung: An Anthology of His Writings* (Anne Fremantle, ed.; 1962)

9 All counter-revolutionary wars are unjust, all revolutionary wars are just.
How to Study War (1935), quoted in *Mao Tsetung: An Anthology of His Writings* (Anne Fremantle, ed.; 1962)

10 War is the highest form of struggle, existing ever since the emergence of private property and social classes, for settling contradictions between classes, between nations, between states, or between political groups at five stages of their development.
How to Study War (1935), quoted in *Mao Tsetung: An Anthology of His Writings* (Anne Fremantle, ed.; 1962)

11 War, this monster of mutual slaughter among mankind, will be finally eliminated through the progress of human society, and in no distant future too.
How to Study War (1935), quoted in *Mao Tsetung: An Anthology of His Writings* (Anne Fremantle, ed.; 1962)

12 To read too many books is harmful.
New Yorker (March 7, 1977)

13 The law of contradiction in things, that is, the law of the unity

of opposites, is the most basic law in materialist dialectics.
On Contradiction (1937), quoted in *Mao Tsetung: An Anthology of His Writings* (Anne Fremantle, ed.; 1962)

14 Imperialist aggression shattered the fond dreams of the Chinese about learning from the West.
On People's Democratic Dictatorship (1949)

15 In a class society everyone lives within the status of a particular class and every mode of thought is invariably stamped with the brand of a class.
On Practice (1937)

16 The genuine knowledge originates in direct experience.
On Practice (1937)

17 When the whole of mankind consciously remoulds itself and changes the world, the era of world communism will dawn.
On Practice (1937)

18 Democracy sometimes seems to be an end, but it is in fact only a means.
On the Correct Handling of Contradiction (1957), quoted in *Mao Tsetung: An Anthology of His Writings* (Anne Fremantle, ed.; 1962)

19 Questions of right and wrong in the arts and sciences should be settled through free discussion in artistic and scientific circles and in the course of practical work in the arts and sciences.
On the Correct Handling of Contradiction (1957), quoted in *Mao Tsetung: An Anthology of His Writings* (Anne Fremantle, ed.; 1962)

20 "War is the continuation of politics." In this sense war is politics and war itself is a political action.
Quotations of Chairman Mao (1966)

21 Letting a hundred flowers blossom and a hundred schools of thought contend is the policy for promoting the progress of the arts and the sciences and a flourishing socialist culture in our land.
February 27, 1957. Speech, *Quotations of Chairman Mao* (1966)

22 The atom bomb is a paper tiger which the United States reactionaries use to scare people.
August 1946. Interview, *Selected Works* (1961), vol. 4

23 Every Communist must grasp the truth, "Political power grows out of the barrel of a gun."
November 6, 1938. Speech, *Selected Works* (1961), vol. 2

24 All reactionaries are paper tigers.
November 1957. Speech to Communist International Congress, Moscow, *Selected Works* (1961), vol. 4

25 As to the so-called "love of mankind," there has been no such all-embracing love since humanity was divided into classes.
Talks at the Yan'an Forum on Art and Literature (1942), quoted in *Mao Tsetung: An Anthology of His Writings* (Anne Fremantle, ed.; 1962)

26 One of the principal methods of struggle in the artistic and literary sphere is art and literary criticism.
Talks at the Yan'an Forum on Art and Literature (1942), quoted in *Mao Tsetung: An Anthology of His Writings* (Anne Fremantle, ed.; 1962)

27 The wind from the East prevails over the West.
September 5, 1958. Quoted in *Maoism: Slogans and Practice* (Vladimir Glebov; 1978)

28 Many dare not openly admit that contradictions still exist among the people of our country, although it is these very contradictions that are pushing our society forward.
Quoted in "Continuation of the Revolution under the Dictatorship of the Proletariat," *Maoism: Slogans and Practice* (Vladimir Glebov; 1978)

29 The enemy advances, we retreat; the enemy halts, we harass; the enemy retreats, we pursue.
August 24, 1964. Quoted in "People's War," *Maoism: Slogans and Practice* (Vladimir Glebov; 1978)

30 Everything in Yan'an has been created by having guns. All things grow out of the barrel of a gun.
August 1965. Yan'an is a town in the northern Shaanxi province where the Communist Party of China Central Committee and the Chinese Red Army Command were stationed (1936–37). Quoted in "Power Grows out of the Barrel of a Gun," *Maoism: Slogans and Practice* (Vladimir Glebov; 1978)

31 We cannot take the old road of developing technology, which all countries took; we cannot crawl in the tracks of others. We must break the fixed norms...This is the meaning of what we call the great leap.
Quoted in "The Great Leap," *Maoism: Slogans and Practice* (Vladimir Glebov; 1978)

32 China's 600 million people...are, first of all, poor, and secondly blank... Poor people want change...revolution. A clean sheet of paper has no blotches, and so the newest and most beautiful words can be written.
1958. Quoted in "Permanent Revolution: The Ideological Origins of the Great Leap," *Mao's China* (Maurice Meisner; 1977)

33 Contemporary China has grown out of the China of the past; we are Marxist in our historical approach and must not lop off our history. We should sum up our history from Confucius to Sun Yat-sen and take over this valuable legacy.
1938. Quoted in *The Chinese* (Alain Peyrefitte, Graham Webb, tr.; 1977)

34 Let the ancient serve the present, let the foreign serve the national; by developing that which has been accomplished, one creates something that is new.
1950s. Quoted in *The Chinese* (Alain Peyrefitte, Graham Webb, tr.; 1977)

35 We must tell the people and tell our comrades that there will be twists and turns in our road. There are still many obstacles and difficulties along the road of revolution. We must be prepared to follow the road which exists and turns.
1945. Quoted in *The Chinese* (Alain Peyrefitte, Graham Webb, tr.; 1977)

36 You must despise your enemy strategically, but respect him tactically.
Attrib.

37 The government burns down whole cities while the people are forbidden to light lamps.
On his Nationalist opponents during a period of civil war. Attrib.

Map, Walter (also spelled Mapes or Mahap; 1140?–1210?) Welsh clergyman and writer

1 If die I must, let me die drinking in an inn.
De Nugis Curialum (1182?)

2 Rich, noble, lovable, eloquent, handsome, gallant, every way attractive, a little lower than the angels—all these gifts he turned to the wrong side.
Referring to Henry, "The Young King," eldest son of Henry II of England. *De Nugis Curialum* (1182?), pt. I, ch. 1

3 The rustics vie with each other in bringing up their ignoble and degenerate offspring to the liberal arts.
Drawing a comparison with the aristocracy, who were "too proud or too lazy to put their children to learning." *De Nugis Curialum* (1182?), pt. I, ch. 10

Mapanje, Jack (b.1945) Malawian poet, theoretical linguist, and educator

1 Hope is our only hope.
"If Chiuta Were Man," *Of Chameleons and Gods* (1991), p. 7

Maradona, Diego (b.1960) Argentinian soccer player

1 I didn't take drugs and above all I did not let down those who love me.
Having been expelled from the soccer 1994 World Cup for taking drugs. *Independent,* London (July 1, 1994)

2 The goal was scored a little bit by the hand of God and a little bit by the head of Maradona.
Referring to a goal he scored against England in the 1986 soccer World Cup quarter-final; although it was scored illegally with his hand, the referee allowed it to stand. Interview, *Observer,* London (December 28, 1986), "Sayings of the Week"

Maragall, Joan (1860–1911) Catalan poet

1 I see the Pyrenees, the gilded peaks of snow,
and all of Catalonia, stretched out at their feet,
And I feel drawn.
Quoted in *Barcelona* (Felipe Fernández-Armesto; 1992), "Oda Nova a Barcelona"

Marat, Jean Paul (1743–93) French revolutionary politician and journalist

1 It is through violence that one must achieve liberty, and the moment has come for us to organize a temporary despotism of liberty to crush the despotism of kings.
Referring to the French Revolution (1789–99). Jean Paul Marat was one of the chief advocates of violence and dictatorial measures to defend the Revolution. He was assassinated by a young aristocrat, Charlotte Corday, on July 13, 1793. *L'Ami du peuple* (April 1793)

2 It seems to be the inevitable outcome for man never to be entirely free: everywhere princes head towards despotism, and the people towards servitude.
Les Chaînes de l'esclavage (1793)

Marceau, Marcel (b.1923) French mime artist

1 Words can be deceitful, but pantomime necessarily is simple, clear and direct.
Theater Arts (March 1958)

Marcos, Subcomandante (b.1958) Mexican revolutionary leader

1 All the government gives us is charity at election time. Afterwards, death returns to our homes.
Leader of the Zapatistas, a rebel movement in the Chiapas region of Mexico. *Independent,* London (January 12, 1994)

Marcus, Bernie (Bernard Marcus; b.1929) U.S. business executive

1 If you pay commissions, you imply that the small customer isn't worth anything.
Fortune (May 31, 1993)

2 People create problems by not trusting their own judgment. By creating a committee. By constantly needing validation.
Fortune (March 4, 1996)

Marcus, Greil U.S. writer

1 Four days after John Lennon was shot I woke up to find Beatles music off the radio and the story off the front page...Does this mean, I thought, that it's over? That he's not dead any more?
Quoted in *Rock 'n' Roll Babylon* (Gary Herman; 1994)

Marcus, Leah S. (b.1945) U.S. literary critic

1 Shakespeare becomes inseparable from the landscape—he incarnates "Merry England."
Referring to Shakespeare's *The Merry Wives of Windsor.* *Unediting the Renaissance* (1995)

Marcus Aurelius, Emperor (originally Marcus Annius Verus; reigned as Marcus Aurelius Antoninus Augustus.; 121–180) Roman emperor and philosopher

1 Whatever this is that I am, it is a little flesh and breath, and the ruling part.
Meditations (170–180), bk. 2, sect. 2

2 And thou wilt give thyself relief, if thou doest every act of thy life as if it were the last.
Meditations (170–180), bk. 2, sect. 5

3 All things from eternity are of like forms and come round in a circle.
Meditations (170–180), bk. 2, sect. 14

4 Remember that no man loses any other life than this which he now lives, nor lives any other than this which he now loses.
Meditations (170–180), bk. 2, sect. 14

5 Nowhere can man find a quieter or more untroubled retreat than in his own soul.
Meditations (170–180), bk. 4, sect. 3

6 Everything is only for a day, both that which remembers and that which is remembered.
Meditations (170–180), bk. 4, sect. 35

7 The universe is transformation; our life is what our thoughts make it.
Meditations (170–180), bk. 4, sect. 35

8 Time is like a river made up of the events which happen, and its current is strong; no sooner does anything appear than it is swept away, and another comes in its place, and will be swept away too.
Meditations (170–180), bk. 4, sect. 35

9 Nothing happens to any man that he is not formed by nature to bear.
Meditations (170–180), bk. 5, sect. 18

10 Live with the gods. And he does so who constantly shows them that his soul is satisfied with what is assigned to him.
Meditations (170–180), bk. 5, sect. 27

11 Remember that to change your mind and follow him who sets you right is to be none the less free than you were before.
Meditations (170–180), bk. 8, sect. 16

12 Whatever may happen to you was prepared for you from all eternity; and the implication of causes was from eternity spinning the thread of your being.
Meditations (170–180), bk. 10, sect. 5

13 Everything that happens happens as it should and if you observe carefully, you will find this to be so.
150?

Marcuse, Herbert (1898–1979) German-born U.S. philosopher

1 Not every problem someone has with his girlfriend is necessarily due to the capitalist mode of production.
Listener, London (1978)

2 The closed operational universe of advanced industrial civilization with its terrifying harmony of freedom and oppression, productivity and destruction, growth and regression is pre-designed in this idea of Reason as a specific historical project.
One-dimensional Man (1964)

Marcy, William Learned (1786–1857) U.S. politician

1 They see nothing wrong in the rule that to the victor belong the spoils of the enemy.
Referring to the practice known as the "spoils system," whereby appointments to public office are made on the basis of political connection or personal relationship. In defense of the nomination of Martin Van Buren (later president) as minister to Britain. Speech to the Senate (January 1832)

Marden, Brice (b.1938) U.S. painter

1 Painters are amongst the priests—worker priests of the cult of man—searching to understand but never to know. As a painter I believe in the indisputability of The Plane.
1974. Quoted in "Statements, Notes and Interviews: 1963–1981," *Brice Marden: Paintings, Drawings and Prints 1975–1980* (Whitechapel Gallery, London; 1981)

Marechera, Dambudzo (1952–87) Zimbabwean writer and poet

1 Nothing lasts long enough to make any sense.
"The House of Hunger," *The House of Hunger* (1978)

2 The lives of small men are like spiders' webs; they are studded with minute skeletons of greatness.
"The House of Hunger," *The House of Hunger* (1978)

Margaret of Valois, Queen of Navarre (1553–1615) French queen consort

1 Science conducts us, step by step, through the whole range of creation, until we arrive, at length, at God.
Mémoires (1594–1600), Letter 12

Mariana, Juan de, Father, Spanish historian

1 In a Republic in which some are overstuffed with riches and others lack the very necessities, neither peace nor happiness is possible.
De Rege et Regis Institutione (1599)

2 It is a duty of humanity for us to open to all men the riches which God gave in common to all, since to all he gave the earth as a patrimony, so that all without distinction might live by its fruits.
De Rege et Regis Institutione (1599)

Marias, Javier Spanish novelist

1 The tongue in the ear is always the most persuasive of kisses...the tongue that probes and disarms, whispers and kisses, that almost obliges.
A Heart So White (Margaret Jull Costa, tr.; 1995)

2 Using one's imagination avoids many misfortunes...the person who anticipates his own death rarely kills himself.
A Heart So White (Margaret Jull Costa, tr.; 1995)

Marie-Antoinette, Queen of France (Josèphe Jeanne Marie Antoinette; 1755–93) Austrian-born French queen consort

1 Courage! I have shown it for years; think you I shall lose it at the moment when my sufferings are to end?
October 16, 1793. Said on the way to the guillotine. Quoted in *Women of Beauty and Heroism* (Frank B. Goodrich; 1859)

2 Let them eat cake.
1780? On being told that the people had no bread to eat; in fact she was repeating a much older saying. Attrib.

Marinetti, Filippo Tommaso (Filippo Tommaso Emilio Marinetti; 1876–1944) Italian writer, poet, and political activist

1 The essential elements of our poetry will be courage, audacity, and revolt. We wish to exalt too aggressive movement, feverish insomnia, running the perilous leap, the cuff, the blow.
"Founding and First Manifesto of Futurism" (1909), quoted in *Cubism, Futurism and Constructivism* (J. M. Nash; 1974)

2 We will destroy museums and libraries, and fight against moralism, feminism, and all utilitarian cowardice.
"Founding and First Manifesto of Futurism" (1909), quoted in *Cubism, Futurism and Constructivism* (J. M. Nash; 1974)

3 We will glorify war—the world's only hygiene—militarism, patriotism, the destructive gesture of the Anarchist, the beautiful ideas that kill, contempt for women.
"Founding and First Manifesto of Futurism" (1909), quoted in *Cubism, Futurism and Constructivism* (J. M. Nash; 1974)

4 The splendor of the world has been enriched by a new form of beauty, the beauty of speed. A racing-car adorned with great pipes like serpents with explosive breath...is more beautiful than the *Victory of Samothrace*.
The *Victory of Samothrace*, or *Winged Victory*, which is housed in the Louvre, Paris, is a famous Greek sculpture of the Hellenistic period. "Founding and First Manifesto of Futurism" (1909), quoted in *Cubism, Futurism and Constructivism* (J. M. Nash; 1974)

5 Let's break away from rationality as out of a horrible husk...Let's give ourselves up to the unknown, not out of desperation but to plumb the depths of the absurd.
Quoted in *Cubism, Futurism and Constructivism* (J. M. Nash; 1974)

Mark, Robert, Sir (b.1917) British police officer

1 You cannot control a free society by force.
Observer, London (July 25, 1976), "Sayings of the Week"

Markham, Edwin (Charles Edward Anson; 1852–1940) U.S. poet

1 O masters, lords and rulers in all lands,
Is this the handiwork you give to God?
"The Man with the Hoe," *The Man with the Hoe and Other Poems* (1899), st. 1

Marks, Johnny (John D. Marks; 1909–85) U.S. songwriter

1 Rudolph the Red-Nosed Reindeer
Had a very shiny nose,
And if you ever saw it,
You would even say it glows.
Song lyric. "Rudolph, the Red-Nosed Reindeer" (1949)

Marlborough, John Churchill, 1st Duke of (1650–1722) English general

1 I have not time to say more, but to beg you will give my duty to the Queen, and let her know her army has had a glorious victory. Monsieur Tallard and two other generals are in my coach, and I am following the rest.
Referring to the Battle of Blenheim. Message written on a tavern bill (August 13, 1704)

Marley, Bob (Robert Nesta Marley; 1945–81) Jamaican musician, singer, and songwriter

1 Stolen from Africa,
brought to America,
Fighting on arrival,
fighting for survival.
Song lyric. "Buffalo Soldier" (1983)

2 Get up, stand up
Stand up for your rights
Get up stand up
Don't give up the fight.
Song lyric. "Get Up, Stand Up" (1980)

3 Open your eyes and look within.
Are you satisfied with the life you're living?
Song lyric. "Exodus," *Exodus* (1977)

4 They gave me star treatment because I was making a lot of money. But I was just as good when I was poor.
Radio Times, London (September 18, 1981)

5 Emancipate yourselves from mental slavery.
None but ourselves can free our minds.
"Redemption Song," *Uprising* (1980)

6 Well I know that, wey I figure seh, maybe things get worse for the better?
1980. Quoted in *Bob Marley: Conquering Lion of Reggae* (Stephen Davis; 1983)

7 Well, reggae music is a music created by Rasta people, and it carry earth force, people rhythm...it is a rhythm of working people, movement, a music of the masses, see?
1979. Quoted in *Bob Marley: Conquering Lion of Reggae* (Stephen Davis; 1983)

8 Name wailers from the Bible, some place in the Bible. There's plenty of places you meet up with weeping and wailing. Children always wail, yunno, cryin' out for justice and alla dat.
1974. The Wailers was the name of Bob Marley's reggae group. Quoted in *Bob Marley: Conquering Lion of Reggae* (Stephen Davis; 1983)

9 I handle fame by not being famous...I'm not famous to me.
December 1974. Quoted in *Bob Marley in His Own Words* (Ian McCann; 1993)

10 Reggae is a music that has plenty fight. But only the music should fight, not the people.
1977. Quoted in *Bob Marley in His Own Words* (Ian McCann; 1993)

11 Every day people come forward with new songs. Music goes on forever.
Attrib.

Marlowe, Christopher (1564–93) English playwright and poet

1 Come live with me, and be my love;
And we will all the pleasures prove
That valleys, groves, hills and fields,
Woods or steepy mountain yields.
"The Passionate Shepherd to his Love" (1599), st. 1

2 And I will make thee beds of roses
And a thousand fragrant posies.
"The Passionate Shepherd to his Love" (1599), st. 3, ll. 1–2

3 What doctrine call you this? Che sera, sera:
What will be, shall be?
Doctor Faustus (1592?), Act 1, Scene 1

4 FAUSTUS And what are you that live with Lucifer?
MEPHISTOPHELES Unhappy spirits that fell with Lucifer,
Conspired against our God with Lucifer,
And are for ever damned with Lucifer.
Doctor Faustus (1592?), Act 1, Scene 3

5 Why this is hell, nor am I out of it.
Doctor Faustus (1592?), Act 1, Scene 3

6 When all the world dissolves,
And every creature shall be purified,
All place shall be hell that is not heaven.
Doctor Faustus (1592?), Act 2, Scene 1

7 Oh, thou art fairer than the evening's air
Clad in the beauty of a thousand stars.
Doctor Faustus (1592?), Act 5, Scene 1

8 Was this the face that launch'd a thousand ships
And burnt the topless towers of Ilium?
Sweet Helen, make me immortal with a kiss.
Doctor Faustus (1592?), Act 5, Scene 1, ll. 97–99

9 Now hast thou but one bare hour to live,
And then thou must be damn'd perpetually!
Stand still, you ever-moving spheres of heaven,
That time may cease, and midnight never come.
Doctor Faustus (1592?), Act 5, Scene 2

10 *O lente, lente currite noctis equi.*
The stars move still, time runs, the clock will strike,
The devil will come, and Faustus must be damned.
Doctor Faustus (1592?), Act 5, Scene 2, ll. 152–154

11 Oh, I'll leap up to my God: who pulls me down?
See, see, where Christ's blood streams in the firmament.
One drop would save my soul, half a drop. Ah, my Christ!
Doctor Faustus (1592?), Act 5, Scene 2, ll. 155–157

12 O soul, be changed into little water drops

And fall into the ocean, ne'er be found.
My God, my God, look not so fierce on me!
Doctor Faustus (1592?), Act 5, Scene 2, ll. 195–197

13 Ugly hell, gape not! come not, Lucifer!
I'll burn my books!
Doctor Faustus (1592?), Act 5, Scene 2, ll. 199–200

14 Cut is the branch that might have grown full straight,
And burned is Apollo's laurel bough,
That sometime grew within this learned man.
Doctor Faustus (1592?), Epilogue, ll. 1–3

15 I must have wanton poets, pleasant wits,
Musicians, that with touching of a string
May draw the pliant king which way I please.
Edward II (1593), Act 1, Scene 1

16 My men, like satyrs grazing on the lawns,
Shall with their goat-feet dance an antic hay.
Edward II (1593), Act 1, Scene 1, ll. 59–60

17 Sometime a lovely boy in Dian's shape,
With hair that gilds the water as it glides,
Crownets of pearl about his naked arms,
And in his sportful hands an olive-tree,
To hide those parts which men delight to see,
Shall bathe him in a spring.
Edward II (1593), Act 1, Scene 1, ll. 61–66

18 It lies not in our power to love, or hate,
For will in us is over-rul'd by fate
When two are stripped, long ere the course begin,
We wish that one should lose, the other win;
And one especially do we affect
Of two gold ingots, like in each respect.
Hero and Leander (1593)

19 Treason was in her thought,
And cunningly to yield herself she sought.
Seeming not won, yet won she was at length;
In such wars women use but half their strength.
Hero and Leander (1593)

20 The reason no man knows; let it suffice,
What we behold is censured by our eyes
Where both deliberate, the love is slight;
Who ever loved that loved not at first sight?
Hero and Leander (1593)

21 Our swords shall play the orators for us.
Tamburlaine the Great (1587?), Act 1, Scene 2, l. 132

22 Is it not passing brave to be a king,
And ride in triumph through Persepolis?
Tamburlaine the Great (1587?), pt. 1, Act 2, Scene 5

23 Virtue is the fount whence honour springs.
Tamburlaine the Great (1587?), pt. 1, Act 4, Scene 4

24 Excess of wealth is cause of covetousness.
The Jew of Malta (1590?), Act 1, Scene 2

25 FRIAR BARNARDINE Thou hast committed—
BARABAS Fornication: but that was in another country;
And besides the wench is dead.
The Jew of Malta (1590?), Act 4, Scene 1

26 I count religion but a childish toy,
And hold there is no sin but ignorance.
The Jew of Malta (1590?), prologue

27 Shy as a leveret, swift as he,
Straight and slight as a young larch tree,
Sweet as the first wild violets, she,
To her wild self. But what to me?
"The Farmer's Bride," *The Oxford Book of Twentieth-Century English Verse* (Philip Larkin, ed.; 1973)

Marlowe, Derek (b.1938) British writer

1 Life to me is like boarding-house wallpaper. It takes a long time to get used to it, but when you finally do, you never notice that it's there. And then you hear the decorators are arriving.
A Dandy in Aspic (1966)

Marmion, Shackerley (also Shakerley Marmion; 1603–39) English playwright

1 Great joys, like griefs, are silent.
Holland's Leaguer (1632), Act 5, Scene 1

Marnoch, Alex British police officer

1 The police are the only 24-hour social service in the country.
Remark (February 1983)

Marquis, Don (Donald Robert Perry Marquis; 1878–1937) U.S. journalist and writer

1 if you make people think they're thinking, they'll love you:
but if you really make them think, they'll hate you.
"archy and mehitabel" (1927)

2 an optimist is a guy
that never had
much experience.
"certain maxims of archy," *archy and mehitabel* (1927)

3 procrastination is the art of keeping up with yesterday.
"certain maxims of archy," *archy and mehitabel* (1927)

4 here i am ben says bill nothing but a lousy playwright
and with anything like luck
in the breaks i might have been
a fairly decent sonnet writer
i might have been a poet.
Referring to William Shakespeare's supposed complaint to Ben Jonson. "pete the parrot and shakespeare," *archy and mehitabel* (1927)

5 well archy the world is full of ups and downs but toujours gai
is my motto.
mehitabel the cat to archy the cockroach. "the song of mehitabel," *archy and mehitabel* (1927)

6 dear boss it wont be long now it wont be long...
till the earth is barren as the moon...
i relay this information without any fear

that humanity will take warning and reform
signed archy.
A warning letter, typed by archy the cockroach, who is too small and light to use the shift key. "what the ants are saying," *archy does his part* (1935)

7 what man calls civilization
always results in deserts.
A warning letter, typed by archy the cockroach, who is too small and light to use the shift key. "what the ants are saying," *archy does his part* (1935)

8 now and then
there is a person born
who is so unlucky
that he runs into accidents
which started out to happen
to somebody else.
"archy says," *archy's life of mehitabel* (1933)

9 An idea isn't responsible for the people who believe in it.
New York Sun (1918?)

10 To stroke a platitude until it purrs like an epigram.
New York Sun (1918?)

11 Censors are necessary, increasingly necessary, if America is to avoid having a vital literature.
Prefaces: Foreword to a Literary Censor's Autobiography (1919)

12 Alas! The hours we waste in work
And similar inconsequence,
Friends, I beg you do not shirk
Your daily task of indolence.
The Almost Perfect State (1927)

Marryat, Frederick ("Captain Marryat"; 1792–1848) British naval officer and novelist

1 If you please, ma'am, it was a very little one.
Said by the nurse to excuse the fact that she had had an illegitimate baby. *Mr Midshipman Easy* (1836), ch. 3

2 I think it much better that...every man paddle his own canoe.
Settlers in Canada (1844), ch. 8

3 I never knows the children. It's just six of one and half-a-dozen of the other.
The Pirate (1836), ch. 4

Marsalis, Wynton (b.1961) U.S. trumpet player and jazz musician

1 Jazz is music that really deals with what it means to be American...Louis Armstrong, the grandson of a slave, is the one more than anybody else who could translate into music that feeling of what it is to be an American.
"We Must Preserve Our Jazz Heritage," *Ebony*, Chicago (February 1986)

Marsh, Richard (b.1928) British civil servant and politician

1 In so far as socialism means anything, it must be about the wider distribution of smoked salmon and caviar.
Remark (October 1976)

2 If we had a hundred Beatles we would not have any balance of payments problems.
Referring to The Beatles. *Daily Mail*, London (June 17, 1965)

3 There are some lines where it would be cheaper to give every one a Bentley and ask them to drive to work.
Referring to the British railway system. *Liverpool Daily Post*, England (April 7, 1971)

4 You can cut any public expenditure except the civil service, those lads spent a hundred years learning to look after themselves.
Observer, London (September 19, 1976), "Sayings of the Week"

Marsh, Rodney (b.1944) British soccer player

1 In England, soccer is a grey game played by grey people on grey days.
Describing soccer to an audience on Florida television. Remark (1979)

Marshall, Alfred (1842–1924) British economist

1 In the nineties it became clear that in the future Englishmen must take business as seriously as their grandfathers had done, and as their American and German rivals were doing...the time had passed at which they could afford merely to teach foreigners and not learn from them in return.
Referring to British manufacturers. "Memorandum," *White Paper* (1908)

Marshall, George (George Catlett Marshall; 1880–1959) U.S. military commander and politician

1 Our policy is directed not against any country or doctrine but against hunger, poverty, desperation, and chaos. Its purpose should be the revival of a working economy in the world so as to permit the emergence of political and social conditions in which free institutions can exist.
Announcing the European Recovery Plan (the Marshall Plan). Address, Harvard University (June 5, 1947)

2 If man does find the solution for world peace it will be the most revolutionary reversal of his record we have ever known.
1945. *Biennial Report of the Chief of Staff, United States Army* (September 1, 1945)

3 It is not enough to fight. It is the spirit which we bring to the fight that decides the issue. It is morale that wins the victory.
Military Review (October 1948)

4 It is logical that the USA should do whatever it is able to do to assist in the return of normal economic health in the world.
June 5, 1947. Advocating the European Recovery Program, the so-called Marshall Plan. Quoted in *The Spectre of Capitalism* (William Keegan; 1992)

Marshall, John (1755–1835) U.S. Supreme Court chief justice

1 The people made the Constitution, and the people can unmake it. It is the creature of their own will, and lives only by their will.
Decision in law case (1821)

2 The power to tax involves the power to destroy.
Decision in law case (1819)

Marshall, Paule (b.1929) U.S. novelist, teacher, and journalist

1 Mothers? Hell, they seldom die!
Brown Girl, Brownstones (1954)

2 There was no question that they were truly men; they could so easily prove it by flashing a knife or smashing out with their fists or tumbling one of the whores in the bar onto a bed. But

what of those...to whom these proofs of manhood were alien? Who must find other, more sanctioned ways?
Brown Girl, Brownstones (1954)

3 Some days called for the blues.
Praisesong for the Widow (1983)

4 A man can't help his feelings sometime. He don't even understand his damn self half the time and there the trouble starts.
The Chosen Place, The Timeless People (1969)

5 A person can run for years but sooner or later he has to take a stand in the place which, for better or worse, he calls home, do what he can to change things there.
The Chosen Place, The Timeless People (1969)

6 The church and the rumshop! ... They're one and the same, you know. Both a damn conspiracy to keep us pacified and in ignorance.
The Chosen Place, The Timeless People (1969)

Marshall, Thomas R. (Thomas Riley Marshall; 1854–1925) U.S. vice president

1 What this country needs is a really good 5-cent cigar.
New York Tribune (January 4, 1920)

2 I come from Indiana, the home of more first-rate second-class men than any State in the Union.
Recollections (1925)

Marshall, Thurgood (1908–93) U.S. civil rights lawyer and jurist

1 If the First Amendment means anything, it means that a state has no business telling a man, sitting in his own house, what books he may read or what films he may watch. Our whole constitutional heritage rebels at the thought of giving government the power to control men's minds.
Stanley v. Georgia (1969)

2 I'm the world's original gradualist. I just think ninety-odd years is gradual enough.
Referring to President Dwight D. Eisenhower's call for patience regarding the progress of civil rights. Quoted in *I. F. Stone's Weekly* (May 19, 1958)

3 The United States has been called the melting pot of the world. But it seems to me that the colored man either missed getting into the pot or he got melted down.
The Encyclopaedia of Black Folklore and Humor (Henry D. Spalding; 1972)

Martí, José (José Julian Martí; 1853–95) Cuban writer and patriot

1 Charm is a product of the unexpected.
Attrib.

2 The dagger plunged in the name of Freedom is plunged into the breast of Freedom.
Attrib.

Martial (Marcus Valerius Martialis; 40?–104?) Spanish-born Roman satirical poet

1 Believe me, wise men don't say "I shall live to do that," tomorrow's life's too late; live today.
Epigrams (1st century), bk. 1, no. 15

2 Life is not living, but living in health.
Epigrams (1st century), bk. 6, no. 70

3 Why, Hyllus, do you tease me so,
Who loved me a mere day ago?
If then a boy, how, without warning,
Have you become a man this morning?
Quoted in *Gay Love Poetry* (Neil Powell, ed.; 1997)

4 I am Scorpus, the glory of the roaring circus, the object of Rome's cheers, and her short-lived darling. The fates, counting not my years but the number of my victories, judged me to be an old man.
Late 1st century. Quoted in "Chariot Racing in the Ancient World," *History Today* (D. Bennett; December 1997), vol. 47

Martin, Agnes (b.1912) Canadian-born U.S. painter

1 Senility is looking back with nostalgia
senility is lack of inspiration in life
Art restimulates inspirations and awakens sensibilities
that's the function of art.
1972. "The Untroubled Mind," *Agnes Martin* (Barbara Haskell, ed.; 1973)

Martin, Chester Bailey (1882–1958) Canadian historian

1 Nobody knows better than the historian how much courage it still takes to tell the truth about American-Canadian relations, and how near the surface these antiquated but latent prejudices are still to be found.
The Canadian Historical Review (1937)

Martin, Graham Dunstan (b.1932) British writer and academic

1 Dogma thinks it knows. Belief knows it does not. Dogma is credulous. Belief is sceptical, but for ever open-minded.
Shadows in the Cave: Mapping the Conscious Universe (1990)

Martin, John U.S. critic and writer

1 A man of the hour who has appeared at a time when he is needed.
July 22, 1928. Referring to Busby Berkeley. Quoted in *New York Times* review, *Showstoppers: Busby Berkeley and the Tradition of Spectacle* (Martin Rubin; 1993)

Martin, Steve (b.1945) U.S. comedian, actor, and writer

1 Talking about music is like dancing about architecture.
Attrib.

Martin IV (Simon de Brie; 1210?–85) French-born pope

1 I wish I were a stork and the Germans were frogs in the marshes, so I could devour them all.
Attrib.

Martineau, Harriet (1802–76) British writer and economist

1 I am in truth very thankful for not having married at all.
Harriet Martineau's Autobiography (1877), vol. 1

2 I believe no one attempts to praise the climate of New England.
Retrospect of Western Travel (1838)

3 They told me I saw Albany; but I was no means sure of it.

This large city lay in the landscape like an anthill in a meadow.
Referring to Albany, New York. *Retrospect of Western Travel* (1838)

4 Any one must see at a glance that if men and women marry those whom they do not love, they must love those whom they do not marry.
"Marriage," *Society in America* (1837), vol.3

5 If there is any country on earth where the course of true love may be expected to run smooth, it is America.
"Marriage," *Society in America* (1837), vol.3

6 In no country, I believe, are the marriage laws so iniquitous as in England, and the conjugal relation, in consequence, so impaired.
"Marriage," *Society in America* (1837), vol.3

7 Is it to be understood that the principles of the Declaration of Independence bear no relation to half of the human race?
"Marriage," *Society in America* (1837), vol. 3

8 The early marriages of silly children...where...every woman is married before she well knows how serious a matter human life is.
"Marriage," *Society in America* (1837), vol.3

Martínez de la Mata, Don (*fl.* 17th century) Spanish economist

1 The most obvious defect which one finds in the body of this republic is that there does not exist in any one of its parts any love or regard for the conservation of the whole; for every man thinks solely of present utility and not at all of the future.
Discursos (1659)

Martínez-Sarrión, Antonio (b.1939) Spanish poet, critic, and translator

1 Time is a traitor, millimeter by millimeter it betrays
the hope of uniting discontinuity,
of securing the incomplete,
all time is treachery.
"Umma Gumma," *A Bilingual Anthology of Contemporary Spanish Poetry* (Luis A. Ramos-Garcia; 1997)

Marvell, Andrew (1621–78) English poet and government official

1 So restless Cromwell could not cease
In the inglorious arts of peace.
"An Horatian Ode upon Cromwell's Return from Ireland" (1650), st. 3, ll. 1–2

2 My love is of a birth as rare
As 'tis for object strange and high:
It was begotten by despair
Upon impossibility.
Magnanimous Despair alone
Could show me so divine a thing,
Where feeble Hope could ne'er have flown
But vainly flapt its tinsel wing.
"The Definition of Love" (1650–52), st. 1 and st. 2

3 Therefore the love which does us bind,
But Fate so enviously debars,
Is the conjunction of the mind,
And opposition of the stars.
"The Definition of Love" (1650–52), st. 8

4 How vainly men themselves amaze
To win the palm, the oak, or bays.
"Palm," "oak," and "bays" describe the wreaths awarded for athletic, civic, and poetic achievements.
"The Garden" (1650?), st. 1

5 Annihilating all that's made
To a green thought in a green shade.
"The Garden" (1650?), st. 6, ll. 7–8

6 Such was that happy garden-state,
While man there walk'd without a mate.
"The Garden" (1650?), st. 8, ll. 1–2

7 The world in all doth but two nations bear,
The good, the bad; and these mixed everywhere.
"The Loyal Scot" (1650–52)

8 Ye living lamps, by whose dear light
The nightingale does sit so late,
And studying all the summer night,
Her matchless songs does meditate. Ye country comets, that portend
No war, nor prince's funeral,
Shining unto no higher end
Then to presage the grasses fall.
"The Mower to the Glow-worms" (1650?), st. 1–2

9 I have a garden of my own,
But so with roses overgrown,
And lilies, that you would it guess
To be a little wilderness.
"The Nymph Complaining for the Death of her Fawn" (1681), ll. 71–74, quoted in *The Complete Poems* (Elizabeth Story Donno, ed.; 1972)

10 Who can foretell for what high cause
This darling of the Gods was born?
Probably referring to Theophila Cornewall, whose family was severely reduced by infant mortality.
"The Picture of Little T.C. in a Prospect of Flowers" (1650?), st. 2, ll. 1–2, quoted in *The Complete Poems* (Elizabeth Story Donno, ed.; 1972)

11 Gather the flowers, but spare the buds.
Probably referring to Theophila Cornewall, whose family was severely reduced by infant mortality.
"The Picture of Little T.C. in a Prospect of Flowers" (1650?), st. 5, l. 3, quoted in *The Complete Poems* (Elizabeth Story Donno, ed.; 1972)

12 Had we but world enough, and time,
This coyness, lady, were no crime.
"To His Coy Mistress" (1650?), ll. 1–2

13 But at my back I always hear
Time's wingèd chariot hurrying near
And yonder all before us lie
Deserts of vast eternity
Thy beauty shall no more be found;
Nor, in thy marble vault, shall sound
My echoing song: then worms shall try
That long preserved virginity:
And your quaint honour turn to dust;
And into ashes all my lust.
"To His Coy Mistress" (1650?), ll. 21–30

14 The grave's a fine and private place,
But none, I think, do there embrace.
"To His Coy Mistress" (1650?), ll. 31–32

15 Let us roll all our strength and all

Our sweetness up into one ball,
And tear our pleasures with rough strife
Through the iron gates of life:
Thus, though we cannot make our sun
Stand still, yet we will make him run.
"To His Coy Mistress" (1650?), ll. 41–46

Marx, Chico (Leonard Marx; 1891–1961) U.S. comedian and film actor

1 But I wasn't kissing her. I was whispering in her mouth.
Response when his wife caught him kissing a chorus girl. *The Marx Brothers Scrapbook* (G. Marx and R. Anobile; 1974), ch. 24

Marx, Groucho (Julius Henry Marx; 1895–1977) U.S. comedian and film actor

Quotations about Marx

1 The world would not be in such a snarl, had Marx been Groucho instead of Karl.
1966
Irving Berlin (1888–1989) Russian-born U.S. composer and lyricist. Telegram to Groucho Marx, on the comedian and actor's seventy-first birthday. Attrib.

Quotations by Marx

2 A man is only as old as the woman he feels.
Remark (1950?) Attrib.

3 No, Groucho is not my real name. I'm breaking it in for a friend.
Remark (1950?) Attrib.

4 Time wounds all heels.
Remark (1950?) Attrib.

5 Whoever named it necking was a poor judge of anatomy.
Remark (1950?) Attrib.

6 Either he's dead or my watch has stopped.
On taking a man's pulse. *A Day at the Races* (R. Pirosh, G. Seaton, and G. Oppenheimer; 1937)

7 Do they allow tipping on the boat?
—Yes, sir.
Have you got two fives?
—Oh, yes, sir.
Then you won't need the ten cents I was going to give you.
A Night at the Opera (George S. Kaufman and Morrie Ryskind; 1935)

8 I don't have a photograph, but you can have my footprints. They are upstairs in my socks.
A Night at the Opera (George S. Kaufman and Morrie Ryskind; 1935)

9 The strains of Verdi will come back to you tonight, and Mrs. Claypool's check will come back to you in the morning.
A Night at the Opera (George S. Kaufman and Morrie Ryskind; 1935)

10 Send two dozen roses to Room 424 and put "Emily, I love you" on the back of the bill.
A Night in Casablanca (Joseph Fields, Roland Kibbee, and Frank Tashlin; 1946)

11 One morning I shot an elephant in my pajamas.
How he got into my pajamas I'll never know.
From a musical written by Morrie Ryskind and George S. Kaufman. *Animal Crackers* (Morrie Ryskind; 1930)

12 You're the most beautiful woman I've ever seen, which doesn't say much for you.
From a musical written by Morrie Ryskind and George S. Kaufman. *Animal Crackers* (Morrie Ryskind; 1930)

13 A child of five would understand this.
Send somebody to fetch a child of five.
Duck Soup (Bert Kalmar, Harry Ruby, Arthur Sheekman, and Nat Perrin; 1933)

14 Go, and never darken my towels again!
Duck Soup (Bert Kalmar, Harry Ruby, Arthur Sheekman, and Nat Perrin; 1933)

15 I could dance with you till the cows come home. Better still, I'll dance with the cows till *you* come home.
Duck Soup (Bert Kalmar, Harry Ruby, Arthur Sheekman, and Nat Perrin; 1933)

16 My husband is dead.
—I'll bet he's just using that as an excuse.
I was with him to the end.
—No wonder he passed away.
I held him in my arms and kissed him.
—So it was murder!
Duck Soup (Bert Kalmar, Harry Ruby, Arthur Sheekman, and Nat Perrin; 1933)

17 Remember, men, we're fighting for this woman's honor; which is probably more than she ever did.
Duck Soup (Bert Kalmar, Harry Ruby, Arthur Sheekman, and Nat Perrin; 1933)

18 Please accept my resignation. I don't want to belong to any club that will accept me as a member.
1950? Resigning from the Friar's Club in Hollywood. *Groucho and Me* (1959), ch. 26

19 I never forget a face, but I'll make an exception in your case.
Guardian, London (June 18, 1965)

20 There's a man outside with a big black mustache.
—Tell him I've got one.
Horse Feathers (Bert Kalmar, Harry Ruby, S. J. Perelman, and Will B. Johnstone; 1932)

21 You've got the brain of a four-year-old boy, and I bet he was glad to get rid of it.
Horse Feathers (Bert Kalmar, Harry Ruby, S. J. Perelman, and Will B. Johnstone; 1932)

22 You're a disgrace to our family name of Wagstaff, if such a thing is possible.
Said to his brother Zeppo. *Horse Feathers* (Bert Kalmar, Harry Ruby, S. J. Perelman, and Will B. Johnstone; 1932)

23 Do you suppose I could buy back my introduction to you?
Monkey Business (S. J. Perelman, Will B. Johnstone, and Arthur Sheekman; 1931)

24 I want to register a complaint. Do you know who sneaked into my room at three o'clock this morning?...
—Who?...
Nobody, and that's my complaint.
Monkey Business (S. J. Perelman, Will B. Johnstone, and Arthur Sheekman; 1931)

25 Look at me: I worked my way up from nothing to a state of extreme poverty.
Monkey Business (S. J. Perelman, Will B. Johnstone, and Arthur Sheekman; 1931)

26 Sir, you have the advantage of me.
—Not yet I haven't, but wait till I get you outside.
Monkey Business (S. J. Perelman, Will B. Johnstone, and Arthur Sheekman; 1931)

27 Since my daughter is only half-Jewish, could she go in the water up to her knees?
When excluded from a beach club on ethnic grounds. *Observer,* London (August 21, 1977)

28 What's a thousand dollars? Mere chicken feed. A poultry matter.
The Cocoanuts (George S. Kaufman and Morrie Ryskind; 1929)

29 Your eyes shine like the pants of my blue serge suit.
The Cocoanuts (George S. Kaufman and Morrie Ryskind; 1929)

30 From the moment I picked up your book until I laid it down, I was convulsed with laughter. Some day I intend reading it.
Quoted in *The Last Laugh* (S. J. Perelman; 1981)

31 I eat like a vulture. Unfortunately the resemblance doesn't end there.
Attrib.

32 I was so long writing my review that I never got around to reading the book.
1950? Attrib.

33 Only one man in a thousand is a leader of men—the other 999 follow women.
Attrib.

34 We in this industry know that behind every successful screenwriter stands a woman. And behind her stands his wife.
Attrib.

35 Marriage is a wonderful institution, but who wants to live in an institution?
Also attributed to Mae West. Attrib.

Marx, Karl (Karl Heinrich Marx; 1818–83) German philosopher

Quotations about Marx

1 The intellectual rigour of Marxism proved to be far inferior to its emotive power...Marx had unwittingly provided...yet another substitute religion.
Norman Davies (b.1939) British historian and writer. *Europe: A History* (1996), ch. 10

2 According to the materialist conception of history, the ultimate determining element in history is the production and reproduction of real life. More than this neither Marx nor I have ever asserted. Hence if somebody twists this into saying that the economic element is the only determining one, he transforms that proposition into a meaningless, abstract, senseless phrase.
Friedrich Engels (1820–95) German socialist. Letter to J. Bloch (1895)

3 Just as Darwin discovered the law of evolution of organic matter, so Marx discovered the law of evolution of human history.
Friedrich Engels (1820–95) German socialist. Said at the funeral of Karl Marx. Remark (1883), quoted in *Europe Since 1870* (James Joll; 1976), ch. 3

4 Real socialism is inside man. It wasn't born with Marx. It was in the communes of Italy in the Middle Ages. You can't say it's over.
Dario Fo (b.1926) Italian playwright and actor. *Times,* London (April 6, 1992)

5 Much of the world's work, it has been said, is done by men who do not feel quite well. Marx is a case in point.
J. K. Galbraith (b.1908) Canadian-born U.S. economist. *The Age of Uncertainty* (1977), ch. 3

6 He is the apostle of class-hatred, the founder of a Satanic anti-religion, which resembles some religions in its cruelty, fanaticism and irrationality.
William Ralph Inge (1860–1954) British churchman. *Assessments and Anticipations* (1929)

7 But not even Marx is more precious to us than the truth.
1933
Simone Weil (1909–43) French philosopher, mystic, and political activist. "Revolution proletarienne," *Oppression and Liberty* (1958)

Quotations by Marx

8 What I did that was new was to prove ... that class struggle necessarily leads to the dictatorship of the proletariat.
Letter to Georg Weydemeyer (March 5, 1852)

9 The first requisite for the happiness of the people is the abolition of religion.
A Criticism of the Hegelian Philosophy of Right (1844)

10 From each according to his abilities, to each according to his needs.
Criticism of the Gotha Programme (1875)

11 The sum total of these relations of production constitutes the economic structure of society—the real foundation, on which rise legal and political superstructures and to which correspond definite forms of social consciousness.
Critique of Political Economy (1859)

12 Religion is the soul of soulless conditions, the heart of a heartless world, the opium of the people.
Critique of the Hegelian Philosophy of Right (1844), Introduction

13 The centralization of the means of production and the socialization of labor reach a point where they prove incompatible with their capitalist husk. This bursts asunder. The knell of private property sounds. The expropriators are expropriated.
Das Kapital (1867)

14 Capitalist production begets, with the inexorability of a law of nature, its own negation.
Das Kapital (1867), ch. 15

15 The devaluation of the world of men is in direct proportion to the increasing value of the world of things.
Economic and Philosophic Manuscripts (1844)

16 The worker becomes an ever cheaper commodity the more commodities he creates.
Economic and Philosophic Manuscripts (1844)

17 It is the common whore, the common procurer of people and nations.
Referring to the nature and power of money. *Economic and Philosophic Manuscripts* (1844)

18 The history of all hitherto existing society is the history of class struggles.
The Communist Manifesto (co-written with Friedrich Engels; 1848)

19 The workers have nothing to lose but their chains. They have a world to gain. WORKERS OF THE WORLD, UNITE.
Closing words. *The Communist Manifesto* (co-written with Friedrich Engels; 1848)

20 A specter is haunting Europe—the specter of communism.
Opening words. *The Communist Manifesto* (co-written with Friedrich Engels; 1848)

21 As soon as labor is distributed, each man has a particular, exclusive sphere of activity which is forced upon him and from which he cannot escape. He is a hunter, a fisherman, a shepherd, or a critic, and must remain so if he does not want to lose his means of livelihood.
The German Ideology (1846)

22 In communist society...society regulates the general production and thus makes it possible for me to do one thing today and another tomorrow, to hunt in the morning, fish in the afternoon, rear cattle in the evening, criticize after dinner, just as I have a mind.
The German Ideology (1846)

23 We set out from real, active men, and on the basis of their real life process we demonstrate the development of the ideological reflexes and echoes of this life process.
Referring to the methodology of historical materialism. *The German Ideology* (1846)

24 The materialist doctrine that men are products of circumstances and upbringing, and that, therefore, changed men are products of other circumstances and changed upbringing, forgets that it is men that change circumstances, and that the educator himself needs educating.
Theses on Feuerbach (1845)

25 The philosophers have only interpreted the world in various ways; the point is to change it.
Theses on Feuerbach (1845)

26 Money is the external, universal means and power (not derived from man as man nor from human society as society) to change representation into reality and reality into mere representation.
1844. Quoted in *Economical and Philosophical Manuscripts* (T. B. Bottomore, tr.; 1963)

27 Money saves me the trouble of being dishonest; therefore, I am presumed honest.
1844. Quoted in *Economical and Philosophical Manuscripts* (T. B. Bottomore, tr.; 1963)

28 All I know is that I am not a Marxist.
Attrib.

Mary I, Queen of England and Ireland (Mary Tudor, "Bloody Mary"; 1516–58) English monarch

1 My father made the most part of you almost out of nothing.
Reply when threatened, during the reign of Edward VI, because of her Catholicism. Remark (1550?), quoted in *The Earlier Tudors, 1485–1558* (J. D. Mackie; 1994)

2 When I am dead and opened, you shall find "Calais" lying in my heart.
1550? Quoted in *Holinshed's Chronicles of England, Scotland, and Ireland*, 6 vols. (J. Johnson et al., eds.; 1808), vol. 4

Mary of Teck, Queen (Victoria Mary Augusta Louise Olga Pauline Claudine Agnes; 1867–1953) British queen consort

1 Well, Mr Baldwin! *this* is a pretty kettle of fish!
1937. Referring to the abdication of Edward VIII. Quoted in *Life of Mary of Teck* (James Pope-Hennessy; 1959)

2 So *that's* what hay looks like.
Quoted in *Life of Queen Mary* (James Pope-Hennessy; 1959), ch. 7

Mary, Queen of Scots (Mary Stuart; 1542–87) Scottish monarch

1 In my end is my beginning.
Motto embroidered on her canopy of state

2 No more tears now; I will think upon revenge.
Said after the murder of her secretary, David Rizzio, by an opposing faction led by her husband, Lord Darnley, on March 9, 1566. Lord Darnley was murdered the following year. Remark (1566)Attrib.

Maschwitz, Eric (1901–69) British songwriter and theater producer

1 The sigh of midnight trains in empty stations...
The smile of Garbo and the scent of roses
These foolish things
Remind me of you.
Song lyric. "These Foolish Things Remind Me of You" (1935)

Masefield, John (1878–1967) British poet and playwright

1 Quinquireme of Nineveh from distant Ophir
Rowing home to haven in sunny Palestine,
With a cargo of ivory,
And apes and peacocks,
Sandalwood, cedarwood, and sweet white wine.
"Cargoes" (1903), st. 1

2 Dirty British coaster with a salt-caked smoke stack,
Butting through the Channel in the mad March days,
With a cargo of Tyne coal,
Road-rail, pig-lead,
Firewood, iron-ware, and cheap tin trays.
Referring to coastal trading vessels. "Cargoes" (1903), st. 3

3 The stars grew bright in the winter sky,
The wind came keen with a tang of frost,
The brook was troubled for new things lost,
The copse was happy for old things found,
The fox came home and he went to ground.
"Reynard the Fox" (1919)

4 I must down to the seas again, to the lonely sea and the sky,
And all I ask is a tall ship and a star to steer her by,
And the wheel's kick and the wind's song and the white sail's shaking,
And a grey mist on the sea's face and a grey dawn breaking.
Often quoted using "sea" rather than "seas." "Sea Fever" (1902)

5 I look on martyrs as mistakes
But still they burned for it at stakes.
"The Everlasting Mercy" (1911)

6 In the dark womb where I began
My mother's life made me a man.
Through all the months of human birth
Her beauty fed my common earth.
I cannot see, nor breathe, nor stir,
But through the death of some of her.
1910. "C. L. M.," *The Collected Poems of John Masefield* (1923), st. 1, ll. 1–6

7 Only stay quiet while my mind remembers
The beauty of fire from the beauty of embers.
"On Growing Old," *The Collected Poems of John Masefield* (1923), st. 1, ll. 13–14

Maslow, Abraham (1908–70) U.S. psychologist

1 A musician must make music, an artist must paint, a poet must write, if he is to be ultimately at peace with himself. What one can be, one must be.
Motivation and Personality (1954)

2 Duty cannot be contrasted with pleasure, nor work with play when duty *is* pleasure, when work *is* play, and the person doing his duty and being virtuous is simultaneously seeking his pleasure and being happy.
Motivation and Personality (1954)

3 If the only tool you have is a hammer, all problems begin to look like nails.
Motivation and Personality (1954)

4 The most stable and therefore most healthy self-esteem is based on *deserved* respect from others rather than on external forms or celebrity and unwarranted adulation.
Motivation and Personality (1954)

Mason, Donald (b.1913) U.S. naval officer

1 Sighted sub, sank same.
January 28, 1942. Referring to sinking a Japanese submarine in the Atlantic, the first U.S. naval success of World War II. *New York Times* (February 27, 1942)

Mason, George (1725–92) U.S. statesman

1 Government is, or ought to be, instituted for the common benefit, protection and security of the people, nation, or community; of all the various modes and forms of government, that is best which is capable of producing the greatest degree of happiness and safety, and is most effectively secured against the danger of maladministration.
Virginia Bill of Rights (June 12, 1776), Article 1

2 That all men are by nature equally free and independent, and have certain inherent rights, of which, when they enter into a state of society, they cannot by any compact deprive or divest their posterity; namely, the enjoyment of life and liberty, with the means of acquiring and possessing property, and pursuing and obtaining happiness and safety.
Virginia Bill of Rights (June 12, 1776), Article 1

3 The freedom of the press is one of the greatest bulwarks of liberty, and can never be restrained but by despotic governments.
Virginia Bill of Rights (June 12, 1776), Article 1

Mason, John, Sir (b.1940) British politician and solicitor

1 The weather forecast has no effect on the weather but the economics forecast may well affect the economy.
Presidential Address to the British Association (1983)

Massinger, Philip (1583–1640) English playwright

1 Ambition, in a private man a vice,
Is in a prince the virtue.
The Bashful Lover (1636), Act 1, Scene 2

2 He that would govern others, first should be
The master of himself.
The Bondman (1623), Act 1, Scene 3

3 Soar not too high to fall; but stoop to rise.
The Duke of Milan (1623), Act 1, Scene 2

4 I am driven
Into a desperate strait and cannot steer
A middle course
The Great Duke of Florence (1627), Act 3, Scene 1

5 All words,
And no performance!
The Parliament of Love (1624), Act 4, Scene 2

Masson, Jeffrey (Jeffrey Moussaieff Masson; b.1940) U.S. psychoanalyst and author

1 My experiences with the dogs in my life convince me that...the dog truly loves us...beyond measure, beyond what we deserve, more indeed than we love ourselves.
Dogs Never Lie About Love (1997)

2 There is some profound essence, something about being a dog, which corresponds to our notion of an inner soul, the core of our being that makes us most human.
Dogs Never Lie About Love (1997)

3 No one who has ever had a dog or cat can doubt the animal capacity for happiness...Like uninhibited human happiness, the pleasure is contagious, and pets serve as a conduit to joyful feelings.
When Elephants Weep: The Emotional Lives of Animals (co-written with Susan McCarthy; 1995)

Masters, Edgar Lee (1869–1950) U.S. poet and novelist

1 What is this I hear of sorrow and weariness,
Anger, discontent and drooping hopes?
Degenerate sons and daughters,
Life is too strong for you—
It takes life to love life.
"Lucinda Matlock," *Spoon River Anthology* (1915), quoted in *The Norton Anthology of American Literature* (Nina Baym, ed.; 1998), vol. 2

2 Where are Elmer, Herman, Bert, Tom and Charley,
The weak of will, the strong of arm, the clown, the boozer, the fighter?
All, all, are sleeping on the hill.
"The Hill," *Spoon River Anthology* (1915), quoted in *The Penguin Book of American Verse* (Geoffrey Moore, ed.; 1977)

Masters, John (1914–83) British writer

1 Join a Highland regiment, me boy. The kilt is an unrivalled garment for fornication and diarrhoea.
Bugles and a Tiger (1956)

2 In the West, the past is very close. In many places, it still believes it's the present.
Pilgrim Son (1971)

Mastroianni, Marcello (1924–96) Italian film actor

1 The less you do, the better you do it.
Advice on being a successful actor. Interview, *Il Corriere della Sera* (August 3, 1985), quoted in *Chambers Film Quotes* (Tony Crawley, ed.; 1991)

Mata Hari (Gertrud Margarete Zelle; 1876–1917) Dutch spy and dancer

1 I am a woman who enjoys herself very much; sometimes I lose, sometimes I win.
Quoted in *Mata Hari, the True Story* (Russell Howe; 1986)

Mather, Cotton (1663–1728) U.S. cleric and writer

1 I write the wonders of the Christian religion, flying from the depravations of Europe, to the American strand: and, assisted by the Holy Author of that religion...I report the wonderful displays of His infinite power, wisdom, goodness, and faithfulness, wherewith his Divine Providence hath irradiated an Indian wilderness.
Magnalia Christi Americana (1702), Introduction

Mathew, James, Sir (1830–1908) British judge

1 In England, Justice is open to all, like the Ritz hotel.
1870? Quoted in *Miscellany-at-Law* (R. E. Megarry; 1955)

Matisse, Henri (Henri Émile-Benoît; 1869–1954) French painter and sculptor

Quotations about Matisse

1 It is comparatively easy to achieve a certain unity in a picture by allowing one colour to dominate, or by muting all the colours. Matisse did neither. He clashed his colours together like cymbals and the effect was like a lullaby.
John Berger (b.1926) British novelist, essayist, and art critic. *Toward Reality: Essays in Seeing* (1962)

Quotations by Matisse

2 What I dream of is an art of balance, of purity and serenity...a soothing, calming influence on the mind, rather like a good armchair which provides relaxation from physical fatigue.
Notes d'un peintre (1908), quoted in *Écrits et propos sur l'art* (Dominique Fourcade; 1972)

3 There is nothing more difficult for a truly creative painter than to paint a rose, because before he can do so he has first to forget all the roses that were ever painted.
Quoted in Obituary (November 5, 1954)

4 Exactitude is not truth.
Quoted in *Matisse on Art* (Jack D. Flam; 1973)

Matlovich, Leonard (?–1991) U.S. soldier in the Air Force

1 When I was in the military, they gave me a medal for killing two men, and a discharge for loving one.
Quoted in *Homosexuality: A History* (Colin Spencer; 1995)

Matos Guerra, Gregório de (1636?–96) Brazilian poet

1 Of two fs,
as I see it,
is this city composed: one fraud, the other fornication.
Referring to Salvador, Brazil. "He Defines His City," *Crônica do Viver Bahiano* (1882)

Matthews, Brander (James Brander Matthews; 1852–1929) U.S. writer and academic

1 A gentleman need not know Latin, but he should at least have forgotten it.
1900? Attrib.

Matthiessen, Peter (b.1927) U.S. novelist and travel writer

1 Last night I dreamin dat de sun rose up out of de west, and dat we livin on de wrong side of de night. I dreamed dat we was dead and did not know it.
Far Tortuga (1975)

2 Customs at Belem is a famous joke, for the town depends on contraband for its economy, and the customs officials themselves expect neither more nor less than their fair share.
The Cloud Forest: A Chronicle of the South American Wilderness (1961), ch. 1

3 The waters of Amazona harbor...a sliver-like little fish of wretched bent called the *candiru*, which seeks out even the smallest orifices of the body and lodges itself with its spines; once implanted, it has to be cut out.
The Cloud Forest: A Chronicle of the South American Wilderness (1961), ch. 2

4 I have come to regard myself...as a connoisseur of bad moments in the air, and it is my heartfelt opinion that the take-off was worse than the landing.
The Cloud Forest: A Chronicle of the South American Wilderness (1961), ch. 4

5 Two young women...vomited dolefully where they lay. The Spanish are rarely sentimental about suffering, and, the occasion being a festive one, the girls' misery provoked friends and family alike to shouts and seizures of uncontrollable mirth.
Referring to a truck journey to a soccer match in Argentina. *The Cloud Forest: A Chronicle of the South American Wilderness* (1961), ch. 4

6 Of all things in nature, the one that most abhors a vacuum is a cartographer, and the most dreaded vacuums in all of mapdom...are the interiors of Australia, Siberia, and the Estados Unidos do Brasil.
The Cloud Forest: A Chronicle of the South American Wilderness (1961), ch. 5

7 On the trail we talked to a handsome booted Brazilian who is a wanted killer—though it must be remembered that the term "killer" in these parts describes a fair percentage of the male population and lacks our perjorative connotation.
The Cloud Forest: A Chronicle of the South American Wilderness (1961), ch. 5

8 I slept happily last night on top of a bin of cacao beans, having first searched the shed with a flashlight for snakes, tarantulas, and scorpions.
The Cloud Forest: A Chronicle of the South American Wilderness (1961), ch. 6

9 Confronted with the pain of Asia, one cannot look and cannot turn away. In India, human misery seems so pervasive that one takes in only stray details: a warped leg or a dead eye...an ancient woman lifting her sari to move her shrunken bowels by the road.
The Snow Leopard (1978), pt. 1

10 In Zen thought, even attachment to the Buddha's "golden words" may get in the way of ultimate perception; hence the Zen expression "Kill the Buddha!".
The Snow Leopard (1978), pt. 1

11 To the beat of tom-toms, a buffalo is slowly killed for Durga Puja and its fresh blood drunk...one of the blood-drinkers has the loveliest face of any child I have ever seen.
The Snow Leopard (1978), pt. 1

Maudling, Reginald (1917–79) British politician

1 I don't think one can speak of defeating the IRA, of eliminating them completely, but it is the design of the security forces to reduce their level of violence to something like an acceptable level.
1971. The phrase "an acceptable level of violence" was bitterly resented by Ulster Unionists. Comment at press conference, Northern Ireland (December 15, 1971)

2 There comes a time in every man's life when he must make way for an older man.
November 1976. Remark made on being replaced in the British shadow cabinet by John Davies, his elder by four years. *Guardian*, London (November 20, 1976)

Maudsley, Henry (1835–1918) British psychiatrist

1 Insanity is in fact disorder of brain producing disorder of mind...it is a disorder of the supreme nerve-centres of the brain...producing derangement of thought, feeling and action, together or separately, of such degree or kind as to incapacitate the individual for the relations of life.
Responsibility in Mental Disease (1906)

2 A possible apprehension now is that the surgeon be sometimes tempted to supplant instead of aiding Nature.
Attrib.

Maugham, Somerset (William Somerset Maugham; 1874–1965) British writer

1 American women expect to find in their husbands a perfection that English women only hope to find in their butlers.
A Writer's Notebook (1949)

2 At a dinner party one should eat wisely but not too well, and talk well but not too wisely.
A Writer's Notebook (1949)

3 Few misfortunes can befall a boy which bring worse consequences than to have a really affectionate mother.
A Writer's Notebook (1949)

4 I learned that love was only the dirty trick played on us to achieve continuation of the species.
A Writer's Notebook (1949)

5 Most people are such fools that it is really no great compliment to say that a man is above the average.
A Writer's Notebook (1949)

6 Music-hall songs provide the dull with wit, just as proverbs provide them with wisdom.
A Writer's Notebook (1949)

7 No action is in itself good or bad, but only such according to convention.
A Writer's Notebook (1949)

8 Sentimentality is only sentiment that rubs you up the wrong way.
A Writer's Notebook (1949)

9 Hypocrisy is the most difficult and nerve-racking vice that any man can pursue; it needs an unceasing vigilance and a rare detachment of spirit. It cannot, like adultery or gluttony, be practised at spare moments; it is a whole-time job.
Cakes and Ale (1930), ch. 1

10 From the earliest times the old have rubbed it into the young that they are wiser than they, and before the young had discovered what nonsense this was they were old too, and it profited them to carry on the imposture.
Cakes and Ale (1930), ch. 11

11 I've always been interested in people, but I've never liked them.
Observer, London (August 28, 1949), "Sayings of the Week"

12 The trouble with our younger authors is that they are all in their sixties.
Observer, London (October 17, 1951), "Sayings of the Week"

13 Of Human Bondage
1915. Book title, after one of the books in Baruch Spinoza's *Ethics Demonstrated with Geometrical Order* (1674).

14 The new-born child does not realize that his body is more a part of himself than surrounding objects,...and it is only by degrees, through pain, that he understands the fact of the body.
Of Human Bondage (1915), ch. 13

15 Mrs. Carey thought there were only four professions for a gentleman, the Army, the Navy, the Law, and the Church. She had added medicine...but did not forget that in her young days no one ever considered the doctor a gentleman.
Of Human Bondage (1915), ch. 33

16 Like all weak men he laid an exaggerated stress on not changing one's mind.
Of Human Bondage (1915), ch. 39

17 People ask you for criticism, but they only want praise.
Of Human Bondage (1915), ch. 50

18 Money is like a sixth sense without which you cannot make a complete use of the other five.
Of Human Bondage (1915), ch. 51

19 You will have to learn many tedious things,...which you will forget the moment you have passed your final examination, but in anatomy it is better to have learned and lost than never to have learned at all.
Given as advice to first-year medical students. A pun on the phrase, "better to have loved and lost..." *Of Human Bondage* (1915), ch. 54

20 The degree of a nation's civilization is marked by its disregard for the necessities of existence.
Our Betters (1917), Act 1

21 The right people are rude. They can afford to be.
Our Betters (1917), Act 2

22 What makes old age hard to bear is not the failing of one's faculties, mental and physical, but the burden of one's memories.
Points of View (1958), ch. 1

23 You know, of course, that the Tasmanians, who never committed adultery, are now extinct.
The Bread-Winner (1930)

24 It is very unfair to expect a politician to live in private up to the statements he makes in public.
The Circle (1921)

25 When you have loved as she has loved you grow old beautifully.
The Circle (1921)

26 You can do anything in this world if you are prepared to take the consequences.
The Circle (1921)

27 A woman will always sacrifice herself if you give her the opportunity. It is her favourite form of self-indulgence.
The Circle (1921), Act 3

28 When married people don't get on they can separate, but if they're not married it's impossible. It's a tie that only death can sever.
The Circle (1921), Act 3

29 You can't learn too soon that the most useful thing about a principle is that it can always be sacrificed to expediency.
The Circle (1921), Act 3

30 She's too crafty a woman to invent a new lie when an old one will serve.
The Constant Wife (1926), Act 2

31 The mystic sees the ineffable, and the psychopathologist the unspeakable.
The Moon and Sixpence (1919), ch. 1

32 Impropriety is the soul of wit.
The Moon and Sixpence (1919), ch. 4

33 Because women can do nothing except love, they've given it a ridiculous importance.
The Moon and Sixpence (1919), ch. 41

34 For to write good prose is an affair of good manners. It is, unlike verse, a civil art. Poetry is baroque.
The Summing Up (1938)

35 I knew that suffering did not ennoble; it degraded. It made men selfish, mean, petty and suspicious. It absorbed them in small things...it made them less than men.
The Summing Up (1938)

36 I'll give you my opinion of the human race...Their heart's in the right place, but their head is a thoroughly inefficient organ.
The Summing Up (1938)

37 It has been said that good prose should resemble the conversation of a well-bred man.
The Summing Up (1938)

38 I would sooner read a time-table or a catalogue than nothing at all. They are much more entertaining than half the novels that are written.
The Summing Up (1938)

39 Life is too short to do anything for oneself that one can pay others to do for one.
The Summing Up (1938)

40 Perfection has one grave defect; it is apt to be dull.
The Summing Up (1938)

41 The future will one day be the present and will seem as unimportant as the present does now.
The Summing Up (1938)

42 There is an impression abroad that everyone has it in him to write one book; but if by this is implied a good book the impression is false.
The Summing Up (1938)

43 Dying is a very dull, dreary affair. And my advice to you is to have nothing whatever to do with it.
Quoted in *Escape from the Shadows* (Robin Maugham; 1972)

44 To eat well in England you should have breakfast three times a day.
Attrib.

Mauldin, Bill (William Henry Mauldin; b.1921) U.S. cartoonist

1 I feel like a fugitive from th' law of averages.
Cartoon caption. *Up Front* (1944)

2 Look at an infantryman's eyes and you can tell how much war he has seen.
Cartoon caption. *Up Front* (1944)

Maunick, Edouard J. (b.1931) Mauritian poet and radio producer

1 If I could find a kingdom between midday and midnight I would go forth and proclaim my mixed blood to the core.
Quoted in "Seven Sides and Seven Syllables," *Poems of Black Africa* (Wole Soyinka, ed.; 1975)

Maupassant, Guy de (Henri René Albert Guy de Maupassant; 1850–93) French writer

1 A man who looks a part has the soul of that part.
Mont-Oriol (1887)

2 The least thing contains something unknown. Let us find it.
Pierre et Jean (1887), preface

3 Conversation...is the art of never appearing a bore, of knowing how to say everything interestingly, to entertain with no matter what, to be charming with nothing at all.
Sur l'eau (1888)

4 History, that excitable and lying old lady.
Sur l'eau (1888)

Maupin, Armistead (b.1944) U.S. novelist

1 Outing is a nasty word for telling the truth.
Outing is the practice of making public the fact that somebody is homosexual when that person wants the information kept private. Remark (June 1991), quoted in *A Queer Reader* (Patrick Higgins, ed.; 1993)

2 I think a lot of gay people who are not dealing with their homosexuality get into right-wing politics.
Guardian, London (April 22, 1988)

3 If *Tales of the City* is radical, it's because...the gay characters are on exactly the same footing as the straight characters.
Sunday Times, London (February 4, 1990)

4 People either think I'm famous or they've never heard of me.
Sunday Times, London (February 4, 1990)

5 Terry and I are both from the South and were subjected to the most heterosexual propaganda of all. If propaganda worked we'd be straight.
Sunday Times, London (February 4, 1990)

6 There's nothing I'd like better than to live in a world where my sexuality was utterly irrelevant.
Sunday Times, London (February 4, 1990)

7 Cruising, he had long ago decided, was a lot like hitchhiking. It was best to dress like the person you wanted to pick up.
Tales of the City (1978), quoted in *A Queer Reader* (Patrick Higgins, ed.; 1993)

8 PBS are engaging in a very serious game of self-censorship. Because they are publicly funded, they're desperately afraid their life's blood will be taken from them for making homosexuals look like regular human beings...I'm making personal pleas to everyone I know who can write a check.
Referring to the banning of the television adaptation of *Tales of the City* by the U.S. television network Public Broadcasting Service (PBS). *Times*, London (June 15, 1994)

Maura, Antonio Spanish politician

1 A swarm of high and low agents of the Government falls on villages and towns and unfolds the whole repertory of its overbearing acts, puts in practice all the arts of abuse, and realizes the most outrageous falsifications and manipulations and tries on the most ingenious tricks and deceits.
Referring to election activities. Speech made to Congress, Madrid (April 8, 1891)

2 It is a tradition in our country that the public authorities should not attempt to act so as to enforce the law, to secure justice, to further culture, to increase prosperity, or to direct the life of the people toward the destinies that its peculiar genius and vocation point to.
Quoted in *The Spanish Labyrinth* (Gerald Brenan; 1943)

3 Let those govern who prevent anyone else from doing so.
1917. Referring to the rise of regionalism, labor protests, and action by anarcho-syndicalists which was creating crisis conditions for the government. Quoted in *The Spanish Labyrinth* (Gerald Brenan; 1943)

Maurois, André (Émile Salomon Wilhelm Herzog; 1885–1967) French writer

1 If men could regard the events of their own lives with more open minds they would frequently discover that they did not really desire the things they failed to obtain.
The Art of Living (1940)

2 Growing old is no more than a bad habit which a busy man has no time to form.
"The Art of Growing Old," *The Art of Living* (1940)

3 In England there is only silence or scandal.
Attrib.

4 When you become used to never being alone you may consider yourself Americanized.
Attrib.

Maurras, Charles (Charles Marie-Photius Maurras; 1868–1952) French poet, journalist, and political thinker

1 It is the revenge of Dreyfus.
Referring to his life sentence for his support of the Vichy regime in France, which collaborated with the Germans during World War II. The French Jew Alfred Dreyfus was accused of treason (1893) for allegedly intending to pass French military documents on to the German embassy in Paris, for which he was sentenced to life imprisonment. In 1899 Dreyfus was pardoned. Remark (1945)

Mauthner, Fritz (1849–1923) German writer

1 If Aristotle had spoken Chinese or Dakota, he would have had to adopt an entirely different Logic, or at any rate an entirely different theory of categories.
Beiträge zu einer Kritik der Spracher (1902), vol. 3

Maximilian I, King of Germany and Holy Roman Emperor (1459–1519) Austrian-born monarch

1 Since Christendom comprehends only a small part of the globe, should not everyone who believes in a God be saved by his own religion?
Addressed to Abbot Tritemius. Comment (1508)

Maxwell, Elsa (1883–1963) U.S. society figure and columnist

1 The secret of my success is that no woman has ever been jealous of me.
Quoted in *The Natives Were Friendly* (Noël Barber; 1977)

Maxwell, James Clerk (1831–79) British physicist

1 A molecule of hydrogen...whether in Sirius or in Arcturus, executes its vibrations in precisely the same time. Each molecule therefore throughout the universe bears impressed upon it the stamp of a metric system as distinctly as does the metre of the Archives at Paris, or the double royal cubit of the temple of Karnac.
Discourse on Molecules (1873)

Maxwell, Robert (Robert Ian Maxwell, born Jan Ludvik Hoch; 1923–91) Czech-born British politician, business executive, and publisher

1 I came from a farm-labouring family and I don't go in for owning yachts or going to big parties.
Eleven years later, he died after falling overboard from his yacht, the *Lady Ghislaine*. *Bookseller*, London (August 1980), quoted in *Maxwell: The Outsider* (Tom Bower; 1988)

2 If I had been a woman, I would be constantly pregnant because I simply cannot say no.
Observer, London (August 7, 1988), "Sayings of the Week"

3 I defy anyone who's ever done a deal with Bob Maxwell to say he didn't get a full 12 annas for his rupee.
There are 16 annas to a rupee. Quoted in *The Risk Takers* (Jeffrey Robinson; 1985)

May, Brian (b.1947) British rock guitarist and songwriter

1 I know it's like a Nuremberg Rally, but our fans are sensible people.
Referring to a concert by Queen. Quoted in *The Wit and Wisdom of Rock and Roll* (Maxim Jabukowski, ed.; 1983)

Mayakovsky, Vladimir (Vladimir Vladimirovich Mayakovsky; 1893–1930) Russian poet and playwright

Quotations about Mayakovsky

1 Mayakovsky is deafeningly novel, but at the same time he is unfruitful, barren: he brought Russian poetry to the edge of an abyss, one step further—and it would have disintegrated.
Anna Akhmatova (1888–1966) Russian poet. (Milena Michalski and Sylva Rubashova, trs.; June 8, 1940), quoted in *The Akhmatova Journals: 1938–1941* (Lydia Chukovskaya; 1989)

Quotations by Mayakovsky

2 All poetry
is a journey
into the unknown.
"A Conversation with the Inspector of Taxes about Poetry" (1926), quoted in *Mayakovsky* (Herbert Marshall, ed., tr.; 1965)

3 A rhyme's
a bill of exchange
in your mode of speech.
Discount after a line!—
that's the regulation.
The subtleties of suffixes and inflections,
we seek
in the emptying cash-box of declensions
and conjugations.
"A Conversation with the Inspector of Taxes about Poetry" (1926), quoted in *Mayakovsky* (Herbert Marshall, ed., tr.; 1965)

4 I'm fed up to the teeth with agit-prop, too,
I'd like to scribble love ballads for you—
they're profitable, charming and halcyon.
But I mastered myself, and crushed under foot
the throat of my very own songs.
"At the Top of My Voice" (1930), quoted in *Mayakovsky* (Herbert Marshall, ed., tr.; 1965)

5 As a beauty-drunk artist
thrusts his eyes
into a museum-madonna
love-gazing sharp-edged,
so I,
enveloped
in star-studded skies,
look
at New York
through Brooklyn Bridge.
"Brooklyn Bridge" (1925), quoted in *Mayakovsky* (Herbert Marshall, ed., tr.; 1965)

6 Today's poetry—is the poetry of strife.
Each word must, like a soldier in the army, be made of meat
that is healthy, meat that is red!
Those who have it—join us!
"We Also Want Meat!" (Helen Segall, tr.; 1914), quoted in *The Ardis Anthology of Russian Futurism* (Ellendea Proffer and Carl R. Proffer, eds.; 1980)

7 "I'll see you at four," said Maria.
Eight.
Nine
Ten.
A Cloud in Trousers (1914–15), sect. 1, quoted in *Mayakovsky* (Herbert Marshall, ed., tr.; 1965)

8 I saw one thing only:
You were—a Giaconda
that had to be stolen!
A Cloud in Trousers (1914–15), sect. 1, quoted in *Mayakovsky* (Herbert Marshall, ed., tr.; 1965)

9 In the sky, red as the Marseillaise,
shuddering in its death throes, the sunset died.
A Cloud in Trousers (1914–15), sect. 3, quoted in *Mayakovsky* (Herbert Marshall, ed., tr.; 1965)

10 Art is not a mirror to reflect the world, but a hammer with which to shape it.
1925? Quoted in *Guardian*, London (December 11, 1974)

Maynard, John, Sir (1602–90) English judge and politician

1 I have forgotten more law than you ever knew, but allow me to say, I have not forgotten much.
1680? Replying to Judge Jeffreys' suggestion that he was so old he had forgotten the law. Attrib.

Mayo, Charles Horace (1865–1939) U.S. physician

1 While there are several chronic diseases more destructive to life than cancer, none is more feared.
Annals of Surgery (1926)

2 The prevention of disease today is one of the most important factors in the line of human endeavor.
Collected Papers of the Mayo Clinic and Mayo Foundation (1913)

3 There are two objects of medical education: To heal the sick, and to advance the science.
Collected Papers of the Mayo Clinic and Mayo Foundation (1913)

4 The trained nurse has given nursing the human, or shall we say, the divine touch, and made the hospital desirable for patients with serious ailments regardless of their home advantages.
Collected Papers of the Mayo Clinic and Mayo Foundation (1913)

5 Good health is an essential to happiness, and happiness is an essential to good citizenship.
Journal of the American Dental Association (1919)

6 The sooner patients can be removed from the depressing influence of general hospital life the more rapid their convalescence.
Lancet, London (1916)

7 The safest thing for a patient is to be in the hands of a man engaged in teaching medicine. In order to be a teacher of medicine the doctor must always be a student.
Proceedings of the Staff Meetings of the Mayo Clinic (1927)

8 Worry affects circulation, the heart, and the glands, the whole nervous system, and profoundly affects the heart. I have never known a man who died from overwork, but many who died from doubt.
Quoted in *Bartlett's Unfamiliar Quotations* (Leonard Louis Levinson; 1972)

Mayo, William James (1861–1939) U.S. physician

Quotations about Mayo

1 As he approached the place where a meeting of doctors was being held, he saw some elegant limousines and remarked, "The surgeons have arrived." Then he saw some cheaper cars and said, "The physicians are here, too."...And when he saw a row of overshoes inside, under the hat rack, he is reported to have remarked, "Ah, I see there are laboratory men here."
Walter Bradford Cannon (1871–1945) U.S. physiologist. *The Way of an Investigator* (1945), ch. 19

Quotations by Mayo

2 Unfortunately, only a small number of patients with peptic ulcer are financially able to make a pet of an ulcer.
Journal of the American Medical Association (1922)

3 The examining physician often hesitates to make the necessary examination because it involves soiling the finger.
Lancet, London (1915)

4 Specialist—A man who knows more and more about less and less.
Also attributed to Nicholas Butler. *Modern Hospital* (September 1939)

5 The aim of medicine is to prevent disease and prolong life, the ideal of medicine is to eliminate the need of a physician.
National Education Association: Proceedings and Addresses (1928)

6 Given one well-trained physician of the highest type he will do better work for a thousand people than ten specialists.
Attrib.

Mays, Benjamin E. (1894–1984) U.S. baptist minister and educator

1 I have never sought "acceptance" as such, but I have wanted respect from all mankind. Love is wonderful; but if I could not have both, I would prefer respect.
Born to Rebel—An Autobiography (1971)

2 Make no mistake. We will abolish war or war will abolish mankind.
1968. *Born to Rebel—An Autobiography* (1971)

Mays, Willie (Willie Howard Mays, Jr., "Say Hey Kid"; b.1931) U.S. baseball player

1 I remember the last season I played. I went home after a ballgame one day, lay down on my bed, and tears came to my eyes...It's like crying for your mother after she's gone. You cry because you love her. I cried I guess, because I knew I had to leave it.
Attrib.

Mazarin, Jules (Giulio Raimondo Mazarini; 1602–61) Italian-born French statesman and cardinal

1 The French are nice people. I allow them to sing and to write, and they allow me to do whatever I like.
Attrib.

2 A woman will not go to sleep until she has talked over affairs of state with her lover or her husband.
Referring to French women. Attrib.

Mazzini, Giuseppe (1805–72) Italian revolutionary and political theorist

1 A nation is the universality of citizens speaking the same tongue.
La Giovine Italia (1831)

Mboya, Tom (1930–69) Kenyan nationalist leader

1 White people have often confused the symbol of our poverty with our culture.
From an article written shortly before his death. *New York Times* (1969), quoted in *The Challenge of Nationhood* (Tom Mboya; 1970)

2 We cannot, through ignorant prejudice, afford to under-use the talents and potential of half our citizens, merely because they are women.
The Challenge of Nationhood (1970)

McCaig, Norman (Norman Alexander McCaig; 1910–96) Scottish poet

1 Now I remember the name
but have forgotten the flower.
—The curse of literacy.
"1,800 Feet Up" (1977)

2 Can you say over and over again
"Love", till its incantation makes us
Forget how much we are alone?
"After" (1955)

3 Hear my words carefully.
Some are spoken
not by me, but
by a man in my position.
"A Man in My Position" (1969)

4 I took my mind a walk
or my mind took me a walk—
whichever was the truth of it.
"An Ordinary Day" (1966)

5 The sea rips in between two claws of stone
Or races out, as meaning does with words.
"Ardmore" (1960)

6 Built like a gorilla but less timid,
thick-fleshed, steak-coloured, with two
hieroglyphs in his face that mean
trouble.
"Brooklyn Cop" (1968)

7 I sit with my back to the future, watching
time pouring away into the past.
"Crossing the Border" (1968)

8 I learned words, I learned words: but half of them
died for lack of exercise. And the ones I use
often look at me
with a look that whispers, *Liar.*
"Ineducable Me" (1980)

9 Scotland, I rush towards you
into my future that,
every minute,
grows smaller and smaller.
"London to Edinburgh" (1988)

10 A hen stares at nothing with one eye,
Then picks it up.
"Summer Farm" (1955)

11 Self under self, a pile of selves I stand
Threaded on time, and with a metaphysic hand
Lift the farm like a lid and see
Farm within farm, and in the centre, me.
"Summer Farm" (1955)

12 I can no more describe you
than I can put a thing for the first time
where it already is.
"Sure Proof" (1969)

13 Petitions pour into the Big House.
Haven't the people learned yet that God
is an absentee landlord?
"The Kirk" (1980)

14 You burn yourself with anger at yourself
For being an empty house, in a waste ground.
"To a Poet, Grown Old" (1968)

15 How extraordinary ordinary
things are, like the nature of the mind
and the process of observing.
"An Ordinary Day," *An Ordinary Day* (1966)

McCarthy, Eugene J. (Eugene Joseph McCarthy; b.1916) U.S. politician and writer

1 Have you ever tried to split sawdust?
Answering the charge that he divided the Democrats in 1968. Interview, NBC television (October 23, 1969)

2 In every other great war of this century, we have had the support of what is generally accepted as the decent opinion of mankind. We do not have that today.
Referring to the Vietnam War (1959–75). *The Limits of Power* (1967)

McCarthy, John (b.1957) British journalist

Quotations about McCarthy

1 He has come out of a black hole into glaring light and he will be overwhelmed by it.
Jill Morrell, British campaigner. Referring to the release of hostage John McCarthy. *Times*, London (August 9, 1991)

Quotations by McCarthy

2 Well hello. It's very nice to be here after five years...I want to go home, to be with my family, to try to make up the time I have lost.
Returning home after five years as a hostage in Lebanon. Comment (August 1991)

McCarthy, Joseph (1885–1943) U.S. lyricist

1 In my sweet little Alice blue gown,
When I first wandered out in the town.
Song lyric. "Alice Blue Gown" (1919)

McCarthy, Joseph (Joseph Raymond McCarthy; 1909–57) U.S. politician

Quotations about McCarthy

1 No one can terrorize a whole nation, unless we are all his accomplices.
Ed Murrow (1908–65) U.S. journalist and broadcaster. Closing words of his investigation into Senator Joseph McCarthy's campaign against "Un-American Activities." *See It Now*, CBS television (March 7, 1954)

Quotations by McCarthy

2 McCarthyism is Americanism with its sleeves rolled.
McCarthy gave his name to the anticommunist movement in the 1940s and 1950s, which was institutionalized as the House Un-American Activities Committee. Speech, Wisconsin (1952), quoted in *Senator Joe McCarthy* (Richard Rovere; 1973), ch. 1

3 It looks like a duck, walks like a duck, and quacks like a duck.
Suggested method of identifying a communist. McCarthy gave his name to the anticommunist movement in the 1940s and 1950s, which was institutionalized as the House Un-American Activities Committee. Attrib.

McCarthy, Mary (Mary Therese McCarthy; 1912–89) U.S. writer

1 Stupidity is caused, not by brain failure, but by a wicked heart. Insensitiveness, opacity, inability to make connection, often accompanied by low animal cunning...this mental oblivion is *chosen*, by the heart or the moral will.
Letter to Hannah Arendt (June 9, 1971), quoted in *Between Friends: The Correspondence of Hannah Arendt and Mary McCarthy, 1949–1975* (Carol Brightman, ed.; 1995)

2 And yet I *am* tempted, perhaps partly by the money...and partly by a kind of glamor, a purple-gold glamor, that the name Jerusalem has for me.
Referring to a publisher's proposal that she write a book on Jerusalem. Letter to Hannah Arendt (August 17, 1959), quoted in *Between Friends: The Correspondence of Hannah Arendt and Mary McCarthy, 1949–1975* (Carol Brightman, ed.; 1995)

3 Despite your warning that nobody ever changes for a woman, I think we shall both change a little. What's the use of falling in love if you both remain inertly as-you-were?
Referring to her relationship with James West, who became her fourth husband in 1961. Letter to Hannah Arendt (May 25, 1960), quoted in *Between Friends: The Correspondence of Hannah Arendt and Mary McCarthy, 1949–1975* (Carol Brightman, ed.; 1995)

4 Nothing happens to the very rich; that seems to be the definition of their state of being, which is close to burial alive.
Written during her six-week stay in Tripoli as the guest of Countess Anna Maria Cicogna. Letter to Hannah Arendt (November 11, 1959), quoted in *Between Friends: The Correspondence of Hannah Arendt and Mary McCarthy, 1949–1975* (Carol Brightman, ed.; 1995)

5 Catholics had a great appetite for reading about gruesome diseases, especially those involving the rotting or falling off of parts of the body.
How I Grew (1986), ch. 1

6 In those days modern literature (like "creative writing") was not taught in school *or* in college...As with Prohibition liquor,

you had to know somebody to get hold of the good stuff. Professional librarians were no help.
How I Grew (1986), ch. 2

7 In my first year at Annie Wright Seminary, I lost my virginity. I am not sure whether this was an "educational experience" or not.
How I Grew (1986), ch. 3

8 Although a rebel, I did not care to picture authority as weak...For self-realization, a rebel demands a strong authority, a worthy opponent, God to his Lucifer.
How I Grew (1986), ch. 5

9 I was not interested in being a lesbian myself, having been groped more than once by hairy girls who had had me to stay the night. My heart was set on men...even though the male organs were far from beauteous in my eyes.
How I Grew (1986), ch. 6

10 And I don't feel the attraction of the Kennedys at all...I don't think they are Christians; they may be Catholics but they are not Christians, in my belief anyway.
Observer, London (October 14, 1979)

11 An interviewer asked me what book I thought best represented the modern American woman. All I could think of to answer was: *Madame Bovary*.
"America the Beautiful," *On the Contrary* (1961)

12 If someone tells you he is going to make "a realistic decision," you immediately understand that he has resolved to do something bad.
"America the Beautiful," *On the Contrary* (1961)

13 The immense popularity of American movies abroad demonstrates that Europe is the unfinished negative of which America is the proof.
"America the Beautiful," *On the Contrary* (1961)

14 When an American heiress wants to buy a man, she at once crosses the Atlantic. The only really materialistic people I have ever met have been Europeans.
"America the Beautiful," *On the Contrary* (1961)

15 Modern neurosis began with the discoveries of Copernicus. Science made man feel small by showing him that the earth was not the center of the universe.
"Tyranny of the Orgasm," *On the Contrary* (1961)

16 There are no new truths, but only truths that have not been recognized by those who have perceived them without noticing.
"Vita Activa," *On the Contrary* (1961)

McCartney, Paul, Sir (James Paul McCartney; b.1942) British rock musician and composer

1 The issues are the same. We wanted peace on earth, love, and understanding between everyone around the world. We have learned that change comes slowly.
Observer, London (June 7, 1987), "Sayings of the Week"

McClellan, George (George Brinton McClellan; 1826–85) U.S. soldier

1 All quiet along the Potomac.
A frequent report from his Union headquarters. Attrib.

McCloud, Beverley Thomas U.S. academic

1 Islam...allowed blacks the ultimate protest—the discarding of Christianity.
"African-American Muslim Women" (1991), quoted in *The Muslims of America* (Yvonne Y. Haddad, ed.; 1991)

McCormack, Mark (Mark Hume McCormack; b.1930) U.S. sports agent, promoter, and lawyer

1 Form a team, not a committee.
McCormack on Managing (1985)

2 If new ideas are the lifeblood of any thriving organization...managers must learn to revere, not merely tolerate, the people who come up with the ideas.
McCormack on Managing (1985)

3 In our business, the windows of opportunity open and close with dazzling rapidity...I constantly have to remind people to seize the moment.
McCormack on Managing (1985)

4 We seriously undervalue the passion...a person brings to an enterprise. You can rent a brain, but you can't rent a heart.
McCormack on Managing (1985)

5 When in doubt, don't call a meeting.
McCormack on Managing (1985)

6 If you have to boil down your negotiating attitude to two things, you can do a lot worse than *question everything* and *think big*.
McCormack on Negotiating (1995)

7 When was the last time someone praised you for "taking advice well"? In the advice game, we all would rather be perceived as the one dispensing wisdom rather than seeking it.
The 110% Solution (1991)

8 Anger can be an effective negotiating tool.
What They Don't Teach You at Harvard Business School (1984)

9 A "powerful" office is either a very big one or one that is neat, clean and efficient, a place where one can tell that business gets done.
What They Don't Teach You at Harvard Business School (1984)

10 Discretion is the better part of reading people...If you let them know what you know, you will blow any chance of using your own insight effectively.
What They Don't Teach You at Harvard Business School (1984)

11 Do something for his kids. It always means far more to a customer than doing anything for him.
What They Don't Teach You at Harvard Business School (1984)

12 If Thomas Edison had gone to business school, we would all be reading by larger candles.
What They Don't Teach You at Harvard Business School (1984)

13 If you aren't afraid to fail, then you probably don't care enough about success.
What They Don't Teach You at Harvard Business School (1984)

14 Observation is an aggressive act. People are constantly revealing themselves in ways that will go unnoticed unless you are aggressively involved in noticing them.
What They Don't Teach You at Harvard Business School (1984)

15 Organize for the next day at the end of the previous day. This is what gives me peace of mind at night, a feeling that I am on top of things.
What They Don't Teach You at Harvard Business School (1984)

16 People aren't inconsistent, but their behavior is.
What They Don't Teach You at Harvard Business School (1984)

17 Simply by arranging the next day—defining on paper what I want to accomplish—I feel that I have a head start.
What They Don't Teach You at Harvard Business School (1984)

18 The Inner Game of Business...is understanding the Business Paradox: the better you think you are doing, the greater should be your cause for concern.
What They Don't Teach You at Harvard Business School (1984)

19 To manage time well you have to *believe in your own knowledge*.
What They Don't Teach You at Harvard Business School (1984)

McCormick, Robert Rutherford (1880–1955) U.S. editor and publisher

1 The dangers of atomic war are underrated. It would be hard on little, concentrated countries like England. In the United States we have lots of space.
Chicago Tribune (February 23, 1950)

McCourt, Frank (b.1930) Irish-born U.S. writer

1 Men have been dying for Ireland since the beginning of time and look at the state of the country.
Angela's Ashes (1996)

McCoy, Horace (1897–1955) U.S. novelist and screenwriter

1 They Shoot Horses Don't They?
1935. Book and movie title.

McCrae, John (1872–1918) Canadian poet and physician

1 In Flanders fields the poppies blow
Between the crosses, row on row,
That mark our place.
"In Flanders Fields" (May 3, 1915)

McCullers, Carson (originally Lula Carson Smith; 1917–67) U.S. writer

1 The Heart Is a Lonely Hunter
1940. Book title, taken from the poem "The Lonely Hunter" by William Sharp: "My heart is a lonely hunter that hunts on a lonely hill."

2 I suppose my central theme is the theme of spiritual isolation. Certainly I have always felt alone.
Quoted in *The World We Imagine* (Mark Schorer; 1968)

McDaniel, Hattie (1898–1952) U.S. actor

1 Much better to play a maid than to be one.
Black Hollywood: The Black Performer in Motion Pictures (Gary Null; 1990)

McDonnell, Evelyn U.S. music journalist

1 Female artists are no longer accepting tokenization: militant, angry, diverse, they understand the fight for power. You become part of an emerging dialog that changes not just conception of gender, but changes music itself.
"The Feminine Critique: The Secret History of Women and Rock Journalism," *The Village Voice Rock and Roll Quarterly* (Autumn 1992)

McEnroe, John (John Patrick McEnroe, Jr.; b.1959) U.S. tennis player and broadcaster

1 This taught me a lesson, but I'm not sure what it is.
Referring to losing the Ebel U.S. Pro Indoor Championships to Tim Mayotte. *New York Times* (February 9, 1987)

2 I've never tolerated phoniness in anyone and there's a lot of it at Wimbledon.
Observer, London (August 16, 1981), "Sayings of the Eighties"

3 You are the pits.
Said to an umpire at the Wimbledon grand slam tournament. *Sunday Times*, London (June 24, 1981)

McEwan, Ian (Ian Russell McEwan; b.1948) British writer

1 Dreams culminating in emission may reveal the object of the dreamer's desire as well as his inner conflicts. An orgasm cannot lie.
In Between the Sheets and Other Stories (1978)

2 Film throws up an enormous amount of dust and heat and noise, urgent meetings and so on, which have nothing to do with making a film, but to do with people who are not creatively involved guarding their investments. I suppose it's what you should expect when people are spending the GNP of small countries to make other people less bored for 100 minutes.
Independent, London (August 19, 1993)

McGahern, John (b.1934) Irish writer

1 It is heartless and it is mindless and it is a lie.
Referring to pornography. *The Pornographer* (1979)

McGee, Thomas D'Arcy (1825–68) Irish-born Canadian politician and writer

1 I do not believe it is our destiny to be engulfed into a Republican union, renovated and inflamed with the wine of victory, of which she now drinks so deeply.
Speech, Quebec, Canada (May 10, 1862)

2 We Irishmen, Protestant and Catholic, born and bred in a land of religious controversy, should never forget that we now live and act in a land of the fullest religious and civil liberty.
Referring to Canada. *Home-sick Stanzas* (1858)

McGhee, Howard (1918–87) U.S. jazz trumpeter and composer

1 I got up one morning and I looked like a bowl of kraut...So I

said I'm gonna quit because I didn't have a razor, a clock or a window. I said if this is the way the process goes, this I don't need.
Referring to the end of his eight years of heroin addiction. "Maggie's Back in Town," *Jazz People* (Valerie Wilmer; 1970), ch. 12

McGinley, Phyllis (1905–78) U.S. poet

1 Nothing fails like success; nothing is so defeated as yesterday's triumphant Cause.
"How to Get Along with Men," *The Province of the Heart* (1959)

2 Sin...has been made out not only ugly but passé. People are no longer sinful, they are only immature or underprivileged or frightened or, more particularly, sick.
"In Defense of Sin," *The Province of the Heart* (1959)

McGinley, Robert U.S. musician

1 Sex is on the up. All this hooplah about Aids is rubbish. People I know rarely wear condoms. If it was true that Aids was a threat, swingers would be dropping like flies.
Sunday Times, London (June 14, 1992)

McGonagall, William (1830–1902) Scottish poet and novelist

1 The New Yorkers boast about their Brooklyn Bridge,
But in comparison to thee it seems like a midge,
Because thou spannest the silvery Tay
A mile and more longer I venture to say;
Besides the railway carriages are pulled across by a rope,
Therefore Brooklyn Bridge cannot with thee cope.
"An Address to the New Tay Bridge" (1890)

2 Welcome! thrice welcome! to the year 1893,
For it is the year I intend to leave Dundee,
Owing to the treatment I receive,
Which does my heart sadly grieve.
"A New Year's Resolution to Leave Dundee" (1893)

3 Arabi's army was about seventy thousand in all,
And, virtually speaking, it wasn't very small;
But if they had been as numerous again,
The Irish and Highland brigades would have beaten them, it is plain.
Referring to the battle of Tel-El-Kebir in Lebanon (September 13, 1882). "The Battle of Tel-El-Kebir" (1890)

4 How beautiful thou look'st on a summer morn,
When thou sheddest thy effulgence among the yellow corn.
"The Beautiful Sun" (1890)

5 'Twas in the year of 1887 he married the Lady Ada Louisa Bennett,
And by marrying that noble lady he ne'er did regret;
And he was ever ready to give his service in any way,
Most willingly and cheerfully by night or by day.
"The Death of Lord and Lady Dalhousie" (1890)

6 Alas! Lord and Lady Dalhousie are dead, and buried at last,
Which causes many people to feel a little downcast.
"The Death of Lord and Lady Dalhousie" (1890)

7 Beautiful Moon, with thy silvery light,
Thou cheerest the farmer in the night,
And makest his heart beat high with delight,
As he views his crops by thy light in the night.
"The Moon" (1890)

8 Beautiful Railway Bridge of the Silv'ry Tay!
Alas, I am very sorry to say
That ninety lives have been taken away
On the last Sabbath day of 1879,
Which will be remember'd for a very long time.
"The Tay Bridge Disaster" (1890)

9 Oh! ill-fated bridge of the Silv'ry Tay,
I must now conclude my lay
By telling the world fearlessly without the least dismay,
That your central girders would not have given way,
At least many sensible men do say,
Had they been supported on each side with buttresses.
"The Tay Bridge Disaster" (1890)

McGough, Roger (b.1937) British poet, playwright, and performer

1 You will put on a dress of guilt
and shoes with broken high ideals.
"Comeclose and Sleepnow" (1967)

2 If the heart bleeds love, bare it,
If the martyr's crown fits, wear it.
"Russian Bear," *Watchwords* (1969), st. 6, ll. 8–9

McGovern, George (George Stanley McGovern; b.1922) U.S. politician

1 The whole campaign was a tragic case of mistaken identity.
Referring to his defeat in the 1972 U.S. presidential election. *New York Times* (May 6, 1973)

2 I must admit, it would be nice if I had a few more exciting personal qualities than I do.
Interview, *Playboy Magazine* (August 1971)

McGrath, Charles U.S. newspaper editor

1 Fashion, the semioticians keep telling us, is a language.
"Fashions of the Times," *New York Times* (Spring 1996)

McGregor, Douglas M. (1906–64) U.S. management theorist

1 For many wage earners work is perceived as a form of punishment which is the price to be paid for various kinds of satisfactions away from the job.
The Human Side of Enterprise (1960), ch. 3

2 Paternalism has become a nasty word, but it is by no means a defunct managerial philosophy.
The Human Side of Enterprise (1960), ch. 3

McGregor, Ian, Sir (Ian Kinloch McGregor; 1912–98) British-born business executive

1 People are now discovering the price of insubordination and insurrection. And boy, are we going to make it stick!
Referring to the miners' strike (1984–85), which was called to oppose British Coal's plan to close most deep-mine pits in 1992. *Sunday Telegraph*, London (March 10, 1985)

McGregor, Peter (1871–1916) British soldier

1 Some of the places we passed were liquid mud up to our knees. The town we passed through was an absolute ruin, not a house that is not blown to bits...what devastation—a day of judgement more like.
Letter to his wife (June 21, 1916)

McInerney, Jay U.S. writer

1 Models are the apex of consumer society. Pure image...Modeling is the purest kind of performance, uncomplicated by content.
Model Behavior (1998)

McKay, Claude (1890–1948) Jamaican-born U.S. writer

1 And I must walk the way of life a ghost
Among the sons of earth, a thing apart.
For I was born, far from my native clime,
Under the white man's menace, out of time.
"Outcast," *Harlem Shadows* (1922)

2 Although she feeds me bread of bitterness,
And sinks into my throat her tiger's tooth,
Stealing my breath of life, I will confess
I love this cultured hell that tests my youth!
"America," *Liberator* (December 1921)

3 If we must die, let it not be like hogs
Hunted and penned in an inglorious spot,
While round us bark the mad and hungry dogs
Making their mock at our accursed lot.
...
Like men we'll face the murderous, cowardly pack,
Pressed to the wall, dying, but fighting back!
"If We Must Die," *Liberator* (July 1919)

McKay, David O. (David Oman McKay; 1873–1970) U.S. Mormon leader

1 Be true to your families, loyal to them. Protect your children. Guide them, not arbitrarily, but through the kind example of a father.
Speech, Conference Report (1969)

McKellen, Ian, Sir (Ian Murray McKellen; b.1939) British actor

1 I also wanted to be an actor because I thought I could meet queers.
Remark (March 1991), quoted in *A Queer Reader* (Patrick Higgins, ed.; 1993)

2 Constant conditioning in my youth and social pressure in every department of my life all failed to convert me to heterosexuality.
Times, London (December 5, 1991)

3 The way to stop the spread of HIV is not to make sex illegal, but to make it safe.
Times, London (December 5, 1991)

4 Those lesbians and gay men who do have difficulties with their sexuality suffer them because of the prejudice and discrimination they face.
Times, London (December 5, 1991)

McKinley, William (1843–1901) U.S. president

Quotations about McKinley

1 This face of McKinley's, this placid, kindly, unchipped mask of a kindly, dull gentleman, is a cast...to represent American politics; on the whole decent...and rarely reaching above the least common multiple of the popular intelligence.
William Allen White (1868–1944) U.S. writer. *Masks in a Pageant* (1928)

Quotations by McKinley

2 There was nothing left for us to do but to take them all, and to educate the Filipinos, and uplift and civilize and Christianize them, and by God's grace do the very best we could for them, as our fellowmen for whom Christ also died.
1899. Referring to his decision to claim the Philippine Islands for the United States. Attrib.

McKinney, Joyce (b.1950) U.S. beauty queen

1 I loved Kirk so much, I would have skied down Mount Everest in the nude with a carnation up my nose.
Ms. McKinney was accused of kidnapping an ex-lover who had rejected her. Evidence to British court (1977)

McLaren, Anne, Dame (Anne Laura McLaren; b.1927) British geneticist

1 You don't destroy the mystery of a rainbow by understanding the light processes that form it.
Independent, London (September 5, 1994)

McLaren, Malcolm British musician and manager

1 We live in a Christian society concerned with order: rock 'n' roll was always concerned with disorder. Punk rock promoted blatantly the word chaos.
Time Out, London (May 27–June 2, 1983)

McLaurin, A. J. U.S. politician

1 There is always some basic principle that will ultimately get the Republican party together. If my observations are worth anything, that basic principle is the cohesive power of public plunder.
Speech, U.S. Senate (May 1906)

McLean, Don (b.1945) U.S. singer and songwriter

1 The day the music died.
Song lyric, referring to the death of Buddy Holly, Ritchie Valens, and the Big Bopper in a plane crash in 1959. "American Pie" (1972)

McLuhan, Marshall (Herbert Marshall McLuhan; 1911–80) Canadian sociologist

1 Baseball is doomed. It is the inclusive mesh of the TV image, in particular, that spells...the doom of baseball now, but it'll come back. Games go in a cycle.
Remark (1969) Attrib.

2 It's misleading to suppose there's any basic difference between education and entertainment.
Explorations (1957), ch. 6

3 Television brought the brutality of war into the comfort of

the living room. Vietnam was lost in the living rooms of America—not on the battlefields of Vietnam.
Montreal Gazette (May 16, 1975)

4 Projecting current trends, the love machine would appear a natural development in the near future—not just the computerized datefinder, but a machine whereby ultimate orgasm is achieved by direct mechanical stimulation of the pleasure circuits of the brain.
Playboy (March 1969)

5 The business of the advertiser is to see that we go about our business with some magic spell or tune or slogan throbbing quietly in the background of our minds.
The Age of Advertising (1953)

6 A point of view can be a dangerous luxury when substituted for insight and understanding.
The Gutenberg Galaxy (1962)

7 The new electronic interdependence recreates the world in the image of a global village.
The Gutenberg Galaxy (1962)

8 You've heard money talking? Did you understand the message?
The Mechanical Bridge (1951)

9 For tribal man space was the uncontrollable mystery. For technological man it is time that occupies the same role.
"Magic that Changes Mood," *The Mechanical Bridge* (1951)

10 An expensive ad represents the toil, attention, testing, wit, art, and skill of many people. Far more thought and care go into the composition of any prominent ad in a newspaper or magazine than go into the writing of their features and editorials.
Understanding Media (1964)

11 The medium is the message. This is merely to say that the personal and social consequences of any medium...result from the new scale that is introduced into our affairs by each extension of ourselves or by any new technology.
Understanding Media (1964), ch. 1

12 The car has become the carapace, the protective and aggressive shell, of urban and suburban man.
Understanding Media (1964), ch. 22

13 If the nineteenth century was the age of the editorial chair, ours is the century of the psychiatrist's couch.
Understanding Media (1964), Introduction

14 Explore the situation. Statements are expendable. Don't keep on looking in the rearview mirror and defending the status quo which is outmoded the moment it happened.
Weekend Magazine (March 18, 1967), no. 11

15 The dinosaur didn't know it was extinct either. Dinosaurs never had it so good, as just before they vanished.
Weekend Magazine (March 18, 1967), no. 11

16 Money is a poor man's credit card.
Quoted in *Maclean's Magazine,* Toronto (Peter C. Newman, ed.; June 1971)

17 Advertising is an environmental striptease for a world of abundance.
Quoted in *Subliminal Seduction* (Wilson Key; 1973)

McMillan, Terry (b.1951) U.S. novelist and teacher

1 A BMW can't hug and kiss you at night.
Essence (May 1993)

2 Our hearts are surviving at the poverty level. We're scared to death that getting "too close" will cost us too much.
Essence (May 1993)

3 Hell, any woman can have a baby, Mildred thought, but can't every woman get the man.
Mama (1987)

4 Marrying a man is a way of letting him know you want to be with him forever. It don't make no different if it don't last but two weeks.
Mama (1987)

5 These white folks didn't actually hate colored people, they just didn't like being too close to them.
Mama (1987)

6 What good is roots if you can't go back to 'em?
Mama (1987)

7 I think life is one long introductory course in tolerance, but in order for a woman to get her Ph.D. she's gotta pass Men 101.
Waiting to Exhale (1992)

8 It's not that marriage itself is bad; it's the people we marry who give it a bad name.
Waiting to Exhale (1992)

9 I worry about if and when I'll ever find the *right* man, if I'll ever be able to exhale. The more I try not to think about it, the more I think about it.
Waiting to Exhale (1992)

10 Unfortunately, most men are deaf.
Waiting to Exhale (1992)

McMurry, Robert N. (b.1901) U.S. business executive

1 Chief executives repeatedly fail to recognize that for communication to be effective, it must be two-way.
"Clear Communications for Chief Executives," *Harvard Business Review* (1965)

McMurtry, Larry (Larry Jeff McMurtry; b.1936) U.S. writer

1 "We'll be the Indians, if we last another twenty years," Augustus said. "The way this place is settling up it'll be nothing but churches and dry-goods stores before you know it. Next thing you know they'll...stick us on a reservation to keep us from scaring the ladies."
Lonesome Dove (1985), ch. 42

2 Self-parody is the first portent of age.
Some Can Whistle (1989), pt. 1, ch. 14

3 But the sorrowing are nomads, on a plain with few landmarks and no boundaries; sorrow's horizons are vague and its demands are few.
Some Can Whistle (1989), pt. 4, ch. 9

McNamara, Robert (Robert Strange McNamara; b.1916) U.S. politician and business executive

1 Although we sought to do the right thing—and believed we

were doing the right thing—in my judgment, hindsight proves us wrong.
In Retrospect: The Tragedy and Lessons of Vietnam (co-written with Brian Van de Mark; 1995)

2 I don't object to it being called "McNamara's war"...It is a very important war and I am pleased to be identified with it and do whatever I can to win it.
Referring to the Vietnam War (1959–75). *New York Times* (April 25, 1964)

3 One cannot fashion a credible deterrent out of an incredible action.
Referring to nuclear weapons. *The Essence of Security: Reflections in Office* (1968)

McNealy, Scott (b.1954) U.S. business executive

1 In some situations the right answer is the best answer, the wrong answer is the second best answer, and no answer is the worst answer.
Quoted in *Steve Jobs and the NeXT Big Thing* (Randall Stross; 1993)

McPherson, Aimee Semple (originally Aimee Elizabeth Kennedy; 1890–1944) Canadian-born U.S. evangelist and writer

1 O Hope! dazzling radiant Hope!—What a change thou bringest to the hopeless; brightening the darkened paths, and cheering the lonely way.
This is That (1923)

2 We are all making a crown for Jesus out of these daily lives of ours, either a crown of golden, divine love, studded with gems of sacrifice and adoration, or a thorny crown, filled with the cruel briars of unbelief, or selfishness, and sin, and placing it upon His brow.
This is That (1923)

McTaggart, John (John Ellis McTaggart; 1866–1925) British philosopher

1 I believe that nothing that exists can be temporal, and that therefore time is unreal.
The Nature of Existence (1921)

McWilliams, Carey (b.1905) U.S. lawyer, historian, and journalist

1 Tolerance is not acceptance, and indifference is not assimilation.
Brothers Under the Skin (1945)

McWilliams, Monica Irish sociologist

1 The mainstream male politics of Northern Ireland have been not only macho in style but macho in agenda.
Irish Times, Dublin (October 25, 1997), "This Week They Said"

Mead, Margaret (1901–78) U.S. anthropologist

Quotations about Mead

1 She was a patron saint of the peripheral.
Jane Howard (1935–96) U.S. author and biographer. *Margaret Mead: A Life* (1984)

Quotations by Mead

2 I had no reason to doubt that brains were suitable for a woman. And as I had my father's kind of mind—which was also his mother's—I learned that the mind is not sex-typed.
Blackberry Winter (1972)

3 A society which is clamoring for choice...will give each new generation no peace until all have chosen or gone under, unable to bear the conditions of choice.
Coming of Age in Samoa (1928)

4 Chief among our gains must be reckoned this possibility of choice, the recognition of many possible ways of life, where other civilizations have recognized only one.
Coming of Age in Samoa (1928)

5 The negative cautions of science are never popular. If the experimentalist would not commit himself, the social philosopher, the preacher, and the pedagogue tried the harder to give a short-cut answer.
Coming of Age in Samoa (1928)

6 The prophet who fails to present a bearable alternative and yet preaches doom is part of the trap that he postulates.
Culture and Commitment (1970), Introduction

7 It is of very doubtful value to enlist the gifts of women if bringing women into fields that have been defined as male frightens the men, unsexes the women, muffles and distorts the contribution women could make.
Male and Female (1949)

8 Our humanity rests upon a series of learned behaviors, woven together into patterns that are infinitely fragile and never directly inherited.
Male and Female (1949), ch. 9

9 I think certain government officials, industrialists and celebrated persons should make it clear they are prepared to be sacrificed if taken hostage. If that were done, what gain would there be for terrorists in taking hostages?
Parade (May 20, 1979)

10 Women want mediocre men, and men are working to be as mediocre as possible.
Quote Magazine (May 15, 1958)

11 A city must be a place where groups of women and men are seeking and developing the highest things they know.
Redbook (August 1978)

12 We are living beyond our means. As a people we have developed a life-style that is draining the earth of its priceless and irreplaceable resources without regard for the future of our children and people all around the world.
"The Energy Crisis—Why Our World Will Never Again Be the Same," *Redbook* (1974)

13 A city is a place where there is no need to wait for next week to get the answer to a question, to taste the food of any country, to find new voices to listen to and familiar ones to listen to again.
World Enough (1975)

14 Nobody has ever before asked the nuclear family to live all by itself in a box the way we do. With no relatives, no support, we've put it in an impossible situation.
Quoted in *New Realities* (June 1978)

15 No matter how many communes anybody invents, the family always creeps back.
Attrib.

16 The only way a woman can marry now is to agree to become a charwoman, regardless of her education and skills.
Attrib.

17 We won't have a society if we destroy the environment.
Attrib.

Mead, Walter Russell U.S. economist

1 The politics of the East and the economics of the future pull in the opposite directions.
Explaining why he believes eastern European economies will not achieve the affluence of those of western Europe. *Worth* (September 1994)

Meany, George (1894–1980) U.S. labor leader

1 The one profession where you can gain great eminence without ever being right.
Referring to economists. Attrib.

Mearns, Hughes (1875–1965) U.S. writer and educator

1 As I was walking up the stair
I met a man who wasn't there.
He wasn't there again to-day.
I wish, I wish he'd stay away.
Set to music in 1939 as "The Little Man Who Wasn't There." *The Psycho-ed* (1910)

Medawar, Peter, Sir (Peter Brian Medawar; 1915–87) Brazilian-born British biologist

1 One of the great revolutions brought about by scientific research has been the democratization of learning. Anyone who combines strong common sense with an ordinary degree of imaginativeness can become a creative scientist.
Pluto's Republic (1982)

2 What are we to make of luck in our methodology of science? In the inductive view, luck strikes me as completely inexplicable; it can arise only from the gratuitous obtrusion of something utterly unexpected upon the senses.
Pluto's Republic (1982)

3 Considered in its entirety, psychoanalysis won't do. It's an end product, moreover, like a dinosaur or a zeppelin; no better theory can ever be erected on its ruins, which will remain for ever one of the saddest and strangest of all landmarks in the history of twentieth century thought.
"Further Comments on Psychoanalysis," *The Hope of Progress* (1972)

4 The human mind treats a new idea in the same way the body treats a strange protein; it rejects it.
Attrib.

Medici, Catherine de' (Queen of France; 1519–89) Italian-born French monarch

1 Ah, sentiments of mercy are in unison with a woman's heart.
Quoted in *The Huguenots in France and America* (Hannah Farnham Lee; 1843), vol. 1, ch. 3

Medici, Lorenzo de' ("Lorenzo the Magnificent"; 1449–92) Italian banker and statesman

1 How beautiful is youth, that is always slipping away! Whoever wants to be happy, let him be so: about tomorrow there's no knowing.
"The Triumph of Bacchus and Ariadne" (15th century)

2 Three things in my judgment are called for for a perfect work of painting, namely, a good support, a wall or wood or cloth or whatever it may be, on which the paint is applied; a master who is very good both in drawing and in color; and, besides this, that the matters painted be, in their own nature, attractive and pleasant to the eyes.
Opera (1939), vol. 1

Meier-Graefe, Julius (Alfred Julius Meier-Graefe; 1867–1935) German writer and critic

1 Loftiness of character, or of intelligence, are not essential to the comprehension of art. The greatest men of our age have notoriously known nothing about it, and what is remarkable, artists themselves often understand it least of all.
1904. *Modern Art: Being a Contribution to a New System of Aesthetics* (F. Simmonds and G. Chrystal, trs.; 1908)

Meir, Golda (originally Goldie Mabovich; 1898–1978) Russian-born Israeli prime minister

1 There are not enough prisons and concentration camps in Palestine to hold all the Jews who are ready to defend their lives and property.
Speech (May 2, 1940)

2 Women's Liberation is just a lot of foolishness. It's the men who are discriminated against. They can't bear children. And no one's likely to do anything about that.
Newsweek (October 23, 1972)

3 Pessimism is a luxury that a Jew never can allow himself.
Observer, London (December 29, 1974), "Sayings of the Year"

4 Being seventy is not a sin.
"The Indestructible Golda Meir," *Reader's Digest* (July 1971)

5 We intend to remain alive. Our neighbors want to see us dead. This is not a question that leaves much room for compromise.
"The Indestructible Golda Meir," *Reader's Digest* (July 1971)

6 A leader who doesn't hesitate before he sends his nation into battle is not fit to be a leader.
Quoted in *As Good as Golda* (Israel and Mary Shenker, ed.; 1967)

7 I can honestly say that I was never affected by the question of the success of an undertaking. If I felt it was the right thing to do, I was for it regardless of the possible outcome.
Quoted in *Golda Meir: Woman with a Cause* (Marie Syrkin; 1964)

8 There's no difference between one's killing and making decisions that will send others to kill. It's exactly the same thing, or even worse.
Quoted in *L'Europeo* (Oriana Fallaci; 1973)

Melba, Nellie, Dame (originally Helen Porter Mitchell; 1861–1931) Australian operatic soprano

1 Music is not written in red, white and blue. It is written in the heart's blood of the composer.
Melodies and Memories (1925)

2 One of the drawbacks of Fame is that one can never escape from it.
Melodies and Memories (1925)

3 The first rule in opera is the first rule in life: see to everything yourself.
Melodies and Memories (1925)

4 So you're going to Australia! Well, I made twenty thousand pounds on my tour there, but of course *that* will never be done again. Still, it's a wonderful country, and you'll have a good time. What are you going to sing? All I can say is—sing 'em muck! It's all they can understand!
Speaking to Dame Clara Butt. Quoted in *Clara Butt: Her Life Story* (W. H. Ponder; 1928), ch. 12

Melbourne, Lord, 2nd Viscount Melbourne (Henry William Lamb; 1779–1848) British prime minister

1 Things have come to a pretty pass when religion is allowed to invade the sphere of private life.
On hearing an evangelical sermon. Quoted in *Collections and Recollections* (G. W. E. Russell; 1898), ch. 6

2 What I want is men who will support me when I am in the wrong.
Replying to a politician who said he would support Melbourne as long as he was in the right. Quoted in *Lord M* (Lord David Cecil; 1954), ch. 4

3 I like the Garter; there is no damned merit in it.
Referring to the "Order of the Garter," an honor awarded by the Crown. Quoted in "On the Order of the Garter," *Lord Melbourne* (H. Dunckley; 1890)

4 I wish I was as cocksure of anything as Tom Macaulay is of everything.
Quoted in *Lord Melbourne's Papers* (Earl Cowper; 1889), Preface

5 Nobody ever did anything very foolish except from some strong principle.
Quoted in *The Young Melbourne* (Lord David Cecil; 1939)

6 The worst of the present day is that men hate one another so damnably. For my part I love them all.
Attrib.

7 I don't know, Ma'am, why they make all this fuss about education; none of the Pagets can read or write, and they get on well enough.
Said to Queen Victoria, referring to the Pagets, an aristocratic family. Attrib.

Mellon, Andrew (Andrew William Mellon; 1855–1937) U.S. financier, public official, and philanthropist

1 A nation is not in danger of financial disaster merely because it owes itself money.
1933. Attrib.

Melly, George (Alan George Heywood Melly; b.1926) British jazz singer and author

1 I went home in a state of hysterical happiness. I was a singer in a jazz band.
Said after being asked to join a jazz band after his first extemporary public performance. *Owning Up* (1965), ch. 2

2 "You hear that!" he announced as he swayed about, "that's the death of jazz. We've had it. In six months we'll all be in the bread line!"
Quoting jazz trombonist and professional cricketer Frank "Normal" Parr on the advent of rock and roll in London. *Owning Up* (1965), ch. 11

3 Modern jazz was like the Roman Catholic Church at the time of the Reformation. It had developed historically from the origins of jazz but had, in the eyes of the early revivalists, become decadent.
Referring to the revival of New Orleans jazz in the 1950s. *Owning Up* (1965), ch. 11

4 Jazz is an impure art. There's a great deal of romantic nostalgia involved.
Owning Up (1965), ch. 12

5 Mr Peg-Leg Bates...danced in a surprisingly agile manner on his single artificial limb...but was not exactly full of high jazz content.
Referring to vaudeville performers who accompanied a Louis Armstrong tour in the 1950s. *Owning Up* (1965), ch. 12

6 The basis of that sound, the instrument which provided the heartbeat of the trad Frankenstein monster, was...a banjo played chung, chung, chung, chung, smack on the beat.
Referring to the British traditional jazz revival of the 1950s. *Owning Up* (1965), ch. 15

Meltzer, Jay (b.1944) U.S. business executive and lawyer

1 Fashion is a high-risk investment. If it works, it's wonderful...But there is a substantial downside risk just because it is the fashion business.
New York Times (May 4, 1986)

Meltzer, Samuel J. (1851–1920) Russian-born U.S. physician and physiologist

1 The fact that your patient gets well does not prove that your diagnosis was correct.
Attrib.

Melville, Herman (1819–91) U.S. novelist

Quotations about Melville

1 If it is true that talent recreates life while genius has the additional gift of crowning it with myths, Melville is first and foremost a creator of myths.
Albert Camus (1913–60) Algerian-born French novelist, essayist, and playwright. "Herman Melville" (1952), quoted in *Albert Camus: Selected Essays and Notebooks* (P. Thody, ed., tr.; 1970)

2 Melville's...books...are at one and the same time both obvious and obscure, as dark as the noonday sun and yet as clear as deep water.
Albert Camus (1913–60) Algerian-born French novelist, essayist, and playwright. "Herman Melville" (1952), quoted in *Albert Camus: Selected Essays and Notebooks* (P. Thody, ed., tr.; 1970)

Quotations by Melville

3 Our Handsome Sailor had as much of masculine beauty as one can expect anywhere to see.
Billy Budd, Foretopman (1924), quoted in *A History of Gay Literature* (Gregory Woods; 1998)

4 A whale ship was my Yale College and my Harvard.
Moby Dick (1851)

5 I always go to sea a sailor, because they make a point of paying me for my trouble, whereas they never pay passengers a single penny.
Moby Dick (1851)

6 The urbane activity with which a man receives money is really marvelous, considering that we so earnestly believe money to be the root of all earthly ills.
Moby Dick (1851)

7 You've been beating this steak too much, cook; it's too tender. Don't I always say that to be good, a whale-steak must be tough?
Moby Dick (1851)

8 Better sleep with a sober cannibal than a drunken Christian.
Ishmael, the narrator of Melville's novel, on his first meeting with Queequeg, the harpooner, with whom he is obliged to share a bed. *Moby Dick* (1851)

9 The human body...indeed is like a ship; its bones being the stiff standing-rigging, and the sinews the small running ropes, that manage all the motions.
Redburn (1849), ch. 13

10 There is no counting the names, that surgeons and anatomists give to the various parts of the human body...which keep increasing every day, and hour...But people seem to have a great love for names; for to know a great many names seems to look like knowing a good many things.
Redburn (1849), ch. 13

11 I am a man who, from his youth upwards, has been filled with a profound conviction that the easiest way of life is the best.
1853. "Bartleby the Scrivener," *The Piazza Tales* (1856), quoted in *The Penguin Book of American Short Stories* (James Cochrane, ed.; 1966)

12 John Jacob Astor; a name which, I admit, I love to repeat; for it hath rounded and orbicular sound to it, and rings like unto bullion.
1853. "Bartleby the Scrivener," *The Piazza Tales* (1856), quoted in *The Penguin Book of American Short Stories* (James Cochrane, ed.; 1966)

13 The heart of the eternal pyramids, it seemed, wherein, by some strange magic, through the clefts, grass-seed, dropped by birds, had sprung.
1853. "Bartleby the Scrivener," *The Piazza Tales* (1856), quoted in *The Penguin Book of American Short Stories* (James Cochrane, ed.; 1966)

14 What shall I do? I now said to myself, buttoning up my coat to the last button. What shall I do? what ought I to do? what does conscience say I *should* do with this man?
1853. "Bartleby the Scrivener," *The Piazza Tales* (1856), quoted in *The Penguin Book of American Short Stories* (James Cochrane, ed.; 1966)

15 Ah, Bartleby! Ah, humanity!
1853. Closing words. "Bartleby the Scrivener," *The Piazza Tales* (1856), quoted in *The Penguin Book of American Short Stories* (James Cochrane, ed.; 1966)

16 The sins for which the cities of the plain were overthrown still lingers in some of these wooden-walled Gomorrahs of the deep.
Referring to homosexuality on board ships. According to the Bible, the cities of Sodom and Gomorrah were associated with homosexuality. They were destroyed by a rain of brimstone. *White-Jacket; or the World in a Man-of-War* (1850)

17 A man of true science...uses but few hard words, and those only when none other will answer his purpose; whereas the smatterer in science...thinks, that by mouthing hard words, he proves that he understands hard things.
White-Jacket; or the World in a Man-of-War (1850), ch. 63

18 No country will more quickly dissipate romantic expectations than Palestine—particularly Jerusalem...Is the desolation of the land the result of the fatal embrace of the Deity? Hapless are the favorites of heaven.
January 25, 1857. Quoted in *Journal of a Visit to Europe and the Levant* (H. C. Horsford, ed.; 1955)

19 Priests at Jerusalem sell...tickets for heaven. Printed paper with Dove in middle & Father & Son each side. Divided into seats like plan of theater on benefit night.
February 5, 1857. Quoted in *Journal of a Visit to Europe and the Levant* (H. C. Horsford, ed.; 1955)

20 *Talk of the Guides* "Here is the stone Christ leaned against, & here is the English Hotel." Yonder is the arch where Christ was shown to the people, & just by that open window is sold the best coffee in Jerusalem.
January 25, 1857. Quoted in *Journal of a Visit to Europe and the Levant* (H. C. Horsford, ed.; 1955)

21 Then to the Cistern of 1001 columns...Terrible place to be robbed or murdered in. At whatever point you look, you see lines of pillars, like trees in an orchard arranged in the quincus style.
December 13, 1856. Referring to the Cistern of Philoxenus in Istanbul. Quoted in *Journal of a Visit to Europe and the Levant* (H. C. Horsford, ed.; 1955)

22 The horrible grimy tragic air of these streets. The rotten & wicked looking houses. So gloomy and grimy seems as if a suicide hung from every rafter within.
December 13, 1856. Referring to the Galata district of Istanbul. Quoted in *Journal of a Visit to Europe and the Levant* (H. C. Horsford, ed.; 1955)

23 It is not the sense of height, or breadth or length or depth that is stirred, but the sense of immensity...After seeing the pyramid, all other architecture seems but pastry.
January 3, 1857. Referring to visiting the pyramids at Giza. Quoted in *Journal of a Visit to Europe and the Levant* (H. C. Horsford, ed.; 1955)

24 Duckworth, the English resident, came off early. Talked with him. Said he had been *a day's shooting in the Vale of Tempe*—Ye Gods! whortleberrying on Olympus, &c.
December 7, 1856. Written in Salonica. Quoted in *Journal of a Visit to Europe and the Levant* (H. C. Horsford, ed.; 1955)

Menander (342? –291? B.C.) Greek playwright and poet

1 Whom the gods love dies young.
Dis Exapaton (327?–320? B.C.)

2 The man who does no wrong needs no law.
Fragments, no. 845

Mencius (Mengzi, or Mengtse; 371? –288? B.C.) Chinese philosopher

1 A territory of a hundred *li* square...is sufficient to enable its ruler to become a true king. If Your Majesty practices benevolent government towards the people, reduces punishment and taxation, gets the people to plow deeply and weed promptly...then they can be made to inflict defeat on the strong armor and sharp weapons of Qin and Chu, armed with nothing but staves.
4th century B.C. Quoted in *Mencius* (D. C. Lau, tr.; 1970), bk. 1

2 If you say...“I am unable to do it,” when the task is one of striding over the North Sea...a genuine case of inability to act. But if you say, “I am unable to do it,” when it is one of massaging an elder’s joints for him...a case of refusal to act, not of inability.
4th century B.C. Quoted in *Mencius* (D. C. Lau, tr.; 1970), bk. 1

3 The King blushed and said, “It is not the music of the Former Kings that I am capable of appreciating. I am merely fond of popular music.“
4th century B.C. Quoted in *Mencius* (D. C. Lau, tr.; 1970), bk. 1

4 When people die, you simply say, “It is none of my doing. It is the fault of the harvest.” In what way is that different from killing a man by running him through, while saying all the time, “It is none of my doing. It is the fault of the weapon.”
4th century B.C. Quoted in *Mencius* (D. C. Lau, tr.; 1970), bk. 1

5 When the people have more grain, more fish and turtles than they can eat, and more timber than they can use, then in the support of their parents when alive and in the mourning of them when they are dead, they will be able to have no regrets over anything left undone. This is the first step along the Kingly way.
4th century B.C. Quoted in *Mencius* (D. C. Lau, tr.; 1970), bk. 1

Mencken, H. L. (Henry Louis Mencken; 1880–1956) U.S. journalist, critic, and editor

1 Verse libre; a device for making poetry easier to read and harder to write.
A Book of Burlesques (1916)

2 Conscience is the inner voice that warns us somebody may be looking.
A Little Book in C Major (1916)

3 Democracy is the theory that the common people know what they want, and deserve to get it good and hard.
A Little Book in C Major (1916)

4 Puritanism—the haunting fear that someone, somewhere, may be happy.
A Mencken Chrestomathy (1949), ch. 30

5 When women kiss, it always reminds me of prize-fighters shaking hands.
A Mencken Chrestomathy (1949), ch. 30

6 Self-respect—the secure feeling that no one, as yet, is suspicious.
“Sententiae: The Mind of Men,” *A Mencken Chrestomathy* (1949)

7 Nineteen suburbs in search of a metropolis.
Referring to Los Angeles. *Americana* (1925)

8 The average schoolmaster is and always must be essentially an ass, for how can one imagine an intelligent man engaging in so puerile an avocation?
“The Educational Process,” *New York Evening Mail* (January 23, 1918)

9 I’ve made it a rule never to drink by daylight and never to refuse a drink after dark.
New York Post (September 18, 1945)

10 A society made up of individuals who were all capable of original thought would probably be unendurable. The pressure of ideas would simply drive it frantic.
“Minority Report,” *Notebooks* (1956)

11 God is the immemorial refuge of the incompetent, the helpless, the miserable. They find not only sanctuary in His arms, but also a kind of superiority, soothing to their macerated egos; He will set them above their betters.
“Minority Report,” *Notebooks* (1956)

12 It is now quite lawful for a Catholic woman to avoid pregnancy by a resort to mathematics, though she is still forbidden to resort to physics and chemistry.
“Minority Report,” *Notebooks* (1956)

13 It takes a long while for a naturally trustful person to reconcile himself to the idea that after all God will not help him.
“Minority Report,” *Notebooks* (1956)

14 Man is a beautiful machine that works very badly. He is like a watch of which the most that can be said is that its cosmetic effect is good.
“Minority Report,” *Notebooks* (1956)

15 Metaphysics is almost always an attempt to prove the incredible by an appeal to the unintelligible.
“Minority Report,” *Notebooks* (1956)

16 One of the things that makes a Negro unpleasant to white folk is the fact that he suffers from their injustice. He is thus a standing rebuke to them.
“Minority Report,” *Notebooks* (1956)

17 The chief contribution of Protestantism to human thought is its massive proof that God is a bore.
“Minority Report,” *Notebooks* (1956)

18 The Christian church, in its attitude toward science, shows the mind of a more or less enlightened man of the Thirteenth Century. It no longer believes that the earth is flat, but it is still convinced that prayer can cure after medicine fails.
“Minority Report,” *Notebooks* (1956)

19 The effort to reconcile science and religion is almost always made, not by theologians, but by scientists...the theologians...are smart enough to see that the two things are implacably and eternally antagonistic.
“Minority Report,” *Notebooks* (1956)

20 The scientist who yields anything to theology, however slight, is yielding to ignorance and false pretenses, and as certainly as if he granted that a horse-hair put into a bottle of water will turn into a snake.
“Minority Report,” *Notebooks* (1956)

21 The worst government is the most moral. One composed of cynics is often very tolerant and human. But when fanatics are on top there is no limit to oppression.
"Minority Report," *Notebooks* (1956)

22 War will never cease until babies begin to come into the world with larger cerebrums and smaller adrenal glands.
"Minority Report," *Notebooks* (1956)

23 We must respect the other fellow's religion, but only in the sense and to the extent that we respect his theory that his wife is beautiful and his children smart.
"Minority Report," *Notebooks* (1956)

24 What men value in this world is not rights but privileges.
"Minority Report," *Notebooks* (1956)

25 A sense of humor always withers in the presence of the messianic delusion, like justice and truth in front of patriotic passion.
Prejudices (1919–27)

26 Injustice is relatively easy to bear; what stings is justice.
Prejudices (1919–27)

27 It is hard to believe that a man is telling the truth when you know that you would lie if you were in his place.
Prejudices (1919–27)

28 The chief business of the nation, as a nation, is the setting up of heroes, mainly bogus.
Prejudices (1923)

29 Thousands of American women know far more about the subconscious than they do about sewing.
Prejudices (1919–27)

30 Urbanity, *politesse*, chivalry? Go to! It was in Virginia that they invented the device for searching for contraband whiskey in women's underwear.
Prejudices (1920)

31 When one hears of a poet past thirty-five he seems somehow unnatural and obscene.
Prejudices (1919–27)

32 No man is genuinely happy, married, who has to drink worse gin than he used to drink when he was single.
"Reflections on Monogamy," *Prejudices* (1922)

33 Hygiene is the corruption of medicine by morality.
"The Physician," *Prejudices* (1922)

34 The aim of medicine is surely not to make men virtuous; it is to safeguard and rescue them from the consequences of their vices.
"The Physician," *Prejudices* (1922)

35 Poetry is a comforting piece of fiction set to more or less lascivious music.
"The Poet and his Art," *Prejudices* (1922)

36 The New England shopkeepers and theologians never really developed a civilization, all they ever developed was a government.
"The Sahara of the Bozart," *Prejudices* (1921)

37 The older I grow, the more I distrust the familiar doctrine that age brings wisdom.
"Third Series," *Prejudices* (1922), ch. 3

38 Faith may be defined briefly as an illogical belief in the occurrence of the improbable.
"Types of Men," *Prejudices* (1922)

39 If, after I depart this vale, you ever remember me and have thought to please my ghost, forgive some sinner and wink your eye at some homely girl.
Epitaph. *The Smart Set* (December 1921)

40 Adultery is the application of democracy to love.
1920. Sententiæ, *The Vintage Mencken* (Alistair Cooke, ed.; 1955)

41 Democracy is...a form of religion; it is the worship of jackals by jackasses.
1920. Sententiæ, *The Vintage Mencken* (Alistair Cooke, ed.; 1955)

42 If I were building a house tomorrow it would certainly not follow the lines of a dynamo or steam shovel.
Referring to Le Corbusier's remark that "a house is a machine for living in." Quoted in *American Art Since 1900* (Barbara Rose; 1967)

43 Opera in English is, in the main, just about as sensible as baseball in Italian.
1950? Quoted in *The Frank Muir Book: An Irreverent Companion to Social History* (Frank Muir; 1976)

44 An idealist is one who, on noticing that a rose smells better than a cabbage, concludes that it will also make better soup.
1916. *The Vintage Mencken* (Alistair Cooke, ed.; 1955)

45 A cynic is a man who, when he smells flowers, looks around for a coffin.
Attrib.

46 A judge is a law student who marks his own examination papers.
Attrib.

47 A teacher is one who, in his youth, admired teachers.
Attrib.

48 Love is based on a view of women that is impossible to those who have had any experience with them.
Attrib.

49 No one ever went broke underestimating the intelligence of the American people.
Attrib.

50 The only really happy people are married women and single men.
Attrib.

Mendelson, Stuart U.S. journalist

1 What they wanted was Monte Carlo. They didn't want Las Vegas. What they got was Las Vegas.
Referring to the introduction of legalized gambling in Atlantic City, New Jersey. *Times*, London (May 29, 1978)

Mendelssohn, Felix (Jakob Ludwig Felix Mendelssohn-Bartholdy; 1809–47) German composer

1 Anything but national music! May ten thousand devils take all

folklore. Here I am in Wales...a harpist sits in the lobby of every inn of repute playing so-called folk melodies at you—i.e. dreadful, vulgar, fake stuff, and *simultaneously* a hurdy-gurdy is tootling out melodies...it's even given me a toothache.
August 8, 1829. Written during a visit to Llangollen. Quoted in *A Life in Letters* (Rudolf Elvers, ed., Craig Tomlinson, tr.; 1986)

Mendelssohn, Moses (Moses Dessau; 1729–86) German author and philosopher

1 I hate religious disputes and especially those which are conducted in the eye of the public. Experience teaches that they are useless, they lead more to hatred than to enlightenment.
Collected Writings (1929), vol. 7, ch. 10

Mendes, Chico (Francisco Alves Mendes Filho; 1944–88) Brazilian rubber tapper and ecological campaigner

1 I became an ecologist long before I heard the word.
Attrib.

Menninger, Karl (Karl Augustus Menninger; 1893–1990) U.S. psychiatrist

1 The Encyclopedia Britannica devotes many columns to the topic of love, and many more to faith. But hope, poor little hope! She is not even listed!
American Journal of Psychiatry (December 1959)

2 Illness is in part what the world has done to a victim, but in a larger part it is what the victim has done with his world, and with himself.
Illness as Metaphor (Susan Sontag; 1978), ch. 6

3 Neurotic means he is not as sensible as I am, and psychotic means he's even worse than my brother-in-law.
Attrib.

Menon, V. K. Krishna (Vengalil Krishnan Krishna Menon; 1896–1974) Indian politician and diplomat

1 The expression "positive neutrality" is a contradiction in terms. There can be no more positive neutrality than there can be a vegetarian tiger.
New York Times (October 18, 1960)

Menuhin, Yehudi, Sir (1916–99) U.S.-born British violinist

1 Music creates order out of chaos; for rhythm imposes unanimity upon the divergent, melody imposes continuity upon the disjointed, and harmony imposes compatibility upon the incongruous.
Sunday Times, London (October 10, 1976)

Menzies, Robert, Sir (Robert Gordon Menzies; 1894–1978) Australian prime minister

1 Considering the company I keep in this place, that is hardly surprising.
When accused of having a superiority complex in the British Parliament. *Time* (May 29, 1978)

2 If I were the Archangel Gabriel, madam, I'm afraid you would not be in my constituency.
Replying to a heckler who shouted, "I wouldn't vote for you if you were the Archangel Gabriel." Quoted in *The Wit of Sir Robert Menzies* (R. Robinson; 1966)

Mercer, Johnny (John H. Mercer; 1909–76) U.S. lyricist and composer

1 Jeepers Creepers—where'd you get them peepers?
Song lyric. "Jeepers Creepers" (1938)

2 That old black magic has me in its spell.
Song lyric. "That Old Black Magic" (1942)

Mercier, Louis-Sébastien (1740–1814) French writer

1 These deaths suit everybody, since black clothes go very nicely with mud, bad weather, thrift, and a reluctance to devote hours to one's toilet.
Referring to the convenience of wearing mourning clothes. *Tableaux de Paris* (1782), vol. 1, quoted in *The Culture of Clothing* (Daniel Roche; 1996)

2 I know a man who maintains that the pleasures of the table are the greatest of pleasures. Mankind, he says, begins by feeding at the breast and never loses his appetite till he dies.
The Picture of Paris (1781–89)

Merck, George (George Wilhelm Emanuel; 1894–1957) U.S. business executive

1 Medicine is for the patient. Medicine is for the people. It is not for the profits.
Attrib.

Mercouri, Melina (Anna Amalia Mercouri; 1923–94) Greek actor and politician

1 When you are born they tell you "what a pity that you are so clever, so intelligent, so beautiful but you are not a man."
Comment (1973)

Meredith, George (1828–1909) British novelist and poet

1 A kiss is but a kiss now! and no wave
Of a great flood that whirls me to the sea
But, as you will! we'll sit contentedly,
And eat our pot of honey on the grave.
"Modern Love" (1862)

2 And if I drink oblivion of a day,
So shorten I the stature of my soul.
"Modern Love" (1862)

3 God, what a dancing spectre seems the moon.
"Modern Love" (1862)

4 He fainted on his vengefulness, and strove
To ape the magnanimity of love.
"Modern Love" (1862)

5 Not till the fire is dying in the grate,
Look we for any kinship with the stars.
"Modern Love " (1862)

6 Enter these enchanted woods,
You who dare.
"The Woods of Westermain" (1883), st. 1

7 The well of true wit is truth itself.
Diana of the Crossways (1885), ch. 1

8 She whom I love is hard to catch and conquer,
Hard, but O the glory of the winning were she won!
Love in the Valley (1883), ch. 2

9 Confirmed dispepsia is the apparatus of illusions.
The Ordeal of Richard Feverel (1859)

10 I expect that Woman will be the last thing civilized by Man.
The Ordeal of Richard Feverel (1859), ch. 1

11 Who rises from prayer a better man, his prayer is answered.
The Ordeal of Richard Feverel (1859), ch. 12

12 Golden lie the meadows; golden run the streams; red gold is on the vine-stems. The sun is coming down to earth, and walks the fields and the waters. The sun is coming down to earth, and the fields and the waters shout to him golden shouts.
The Ordeal of Richard Feverel (1859), ch. 19

13 Kissing don't last: cookery do!
The Ordeal of Richard Feverel (1859), ch. 28

14 Speech is the small change of Silence.
The Ordeal of Richard Feverel (1859), ch. 34

15 Much benevolence of the passive order may be traced to a disinclination to inflict pain upon oneself.
Vittoria (1866), ch. 42

Meredith, James (James Howard Meredith; b.1933) U.S. civil rights advocate

1 There are a million Negroes in Mississippi. I think they'll take care of me.
June 7, 1966. Said after he had been shot by white supremacists at the start of a civil rights march. He rejoined the march on June 25. Attrib.

2 The day for the Negro man being a coward is over.
1966. Said while recovering from injuries, having been shot by white supremacists at the start of a civil rights march (June 7, 1966). He rejoined the march on June 25. Attrib.

Mérimée, Prosper (1803–70) French writer and historian

1 Remember to be on your guard.
Words engraved on the ring that he always wore. *Lettre à une inconnue* (1873)

Merleau-Ponty, Maurice (1908–61) French existentialist philosopher

1 Every object is the mirror of all other objects.
Phenomenology of Perception (1945)

2 Phenomenology...is a transcendental philosophy...for which the world is always "already there" before reflection begins.
Phenomenology of Perception (1945)

3 The world is not what I think, but what I live through.
Phenomenology of Perception (1945)

4 Time presupposes a view of time. It is, therefore, not like a river, not a flowing substance.
Phenomenology of Perception (1945)

5 We should not ask ourselves if we perceive the world truly; on the contrary: the world is that which we perceive.
Phenomenology of Perception (1945)

6 The "sane" man is not the one who has eliminated all contradictions from himself so much as the one who uses these contradictions and involves them in his work.
Signes (1960)

7 If the suggestions of the analyst can never be proven, neither can they be eliminated.
Quoted in *The Essential Writings of Merleau-Ponty* (A. L. Fisher, ed.; 1969)

8 It is psychoanalysis that has returned our myths to us. What will become of all this if the tamed sphinx soberly takes its place in a new philosophy of enlightenment?
Quoted in *The Essential Writings of Merleau-Ponty* (A. L. Fisher, ed.; 1969)

9 Phenomenology permits psychoanalysis to recognize...a world on the margin of, and counter to, the true world, a lived history beneath the effective history—a world called illness.
Quoted in *The Essential Writings of Merleau-Ponty* (A. L. Fisher, ed.; 1969)

10 Psychoanalysis does not make freedom impossible; it teaches us to think of this freedom concretely, as a creative repetition of ourselves, always, in retrospect, faithful to ourselves.
Quoted in *The Essential Writings of Merleau-Ponty* (A. L. Fisher, ed.; 1969)

11 Psychoanalytic concepts, weakened and banalized, have lost their enigmas and furnish the themes of a new dogmatism.
Quoted in *The Essential Writings of Merleau-Ponty* (A. L. Fisher, ed.; 1969)

12 The certainty of ideas is not the foundation of the certainty of perception but is, rather, based on it—in that it is perceptual experience which gives us the passage from one moment to the next and thus realizes the unity of time.
Quoted in *The Essential Writings of Merleau-Ponty* (A. L. Fisher, ed.; 1969)

13 There are two senses, and two only, of the word "exist": one exists as a thing or else one exists as a consciousness.
Quoted in *The Essential Writings of Merleau-Ponty* (A. L. Fisher, ed.; 1969)

14 Today we no longer seek...Our thinking is a thought in retreat or in reply.
Quoted in *The Essential Writings of Merleau-Ponty* (A. L. Fisher, ed.; 1969)

15 We must ask ourselves whether it is not essential to psychoanalysis...to remain, not exactly a disreputable enterprise or a secret science, but at least a paradox and an interrogation.
Quoted in *The Essential Writings of Merleau-Ponty* (A. L. Fisher, ed.; 1969)

Mernissi, Fatima (b.1941) Moroccan writer

1 Can the West realize its ideal of one world where all can flourish together while continuing to base much of its economy on the military?
Islam and Democracy (1992)

2 The Gulf War is over...life goes on. You are surprised to find yourself singing in the springtime, putting a flower in your hair, trying a new lipstick.
Islam and Democracy (1992)

3 The Gulf War...plunged the peoples terrorized by the power of destruction into a search for guideposts in the area that

eludes understanding: myth and its language of ambiguity.
Islam and Democracy (1992)

4 Western democracy, although it seems to carry within it the seeds of life, is too linked in our history with the seeds of death.
Islam and Democracy (1992)

5 Women are no longer cooped up in harems, nor are they veiled and silent. They have massively infiltrated forbidden territory.
Islam and Democracy (1992)

Merrill, Bob (Robert Merrill; 1921–98) U.S. lyricist and composer

1 People who need people are the luckiest people in the world.
Song lyric. "People Who Need People" (1964)

Merrill, James (James Ingram Merrill; 1926–95) U.S. poet

1 Goodby to childhood, that unhappy haven.
1966. "Family Week at Oracle Ranch," *A Scattering of Salts* (1995)

2 As usual in New York, everything is torn down
Before you have had time to care for it.
1960. "An Urban Convalescence," *Water Street* (1962), st. 2, ll. 1–2

Merriman, Brian (1747–1805) Irish poet

1 The Court considered the country's crisis,
And what do you think its main advice is—
That unless there's a spurt in procreation
We can bid goodbye to the Irish nation.
The Midnight Court (1786?), quoted in *The Faber Book of Irish Verse* (John Montague, ed., David Marcus, tr.; 1974)

Merritt, Dixon Lanier (1879–1972) U.S. writer and editor

1 A wonderful bird is the pelican,
His bill will hold more than his belican.
He can take in his beak
Food enough for a week,
But I'm damned if I see how the helican.
1910. "The Pelican," *Nashville Banner* (1913)

Merton, Robert K. (Robert King Merton; b.1910) U.S. sociologist

1 It would be a curious reading of the history of thought to suggest that the absence of disagreement testifies to a developing discipline.
1961. Defending internal differences within the field of sociology. "Now the Case *for* Sociology," *New York Times* (July 16, 1961)

Merton, Thomas (1915–68) U.S. monk, religious writer, and poet

1 The keen, thin scent of decay that pervades everything and accuses with a terrible accusation the superficial youthfulness, the abounding undergraduate noise, that fills those ancient buildings.
He studied at Cambridge University for a while. *The Seven Story Mountain* (1948), pt. 1, ch. 3

Merwin, W. S. (William Stanley Merwin; b.1927) U.S. poet and writer

1 Every year without knowing it I have passed the day.
"For the Anniversary of My Death" (1967)

2 The dead will think the living are worth it we will know
Who we are
And we will all enlist again.
"When the War is Over" (1967)

3 The thing that makes poetry different from all of the other arts...is you're using language, which is what you use for everything else—telling lies and selling socks, advertising, and conducting law. Whereas we don't write little concerts or paint little pictures.
Said on receiving the $100,000 Tanning Prize for poetry. Quoted in *Washington Post* (September 30, 1994)

Metternich (Prince Klemens Wenzel Nepomuk Lothar von Metternich; 1773–1859) Austrian diplomat and statesman

Quotations about Metternich

1 Every time I come near him, I pray God to preserve me from the Devil.
Nicholas I (1796–1855) Russian monarch. Remark (1833)

Quotations by Metternich

2 When Paris sneezes, Europe catches cold.
Reflecting his anxiety preceding the July Revolution in France (1830), which caused the abdication of King Charles X. Letter, *Liberalism* (January 26, 1830)

3 Italy is a geographical expression.
August 6, 1847. Discussing the Italian question with the British foreign secretary Lord Palmerston. Letter, *Mémoires, documents, etc. de Metternich publiés par son fils* (1883), vol. 7

4 The disease which must be cured, the volcano which must be extinguished, the gangrene which must be burned out with a hot iron, the hydra with jaws open to swallow up the social order.
Referring to French-style democracy. Quoted in *Europe: A History* (Norman Davies; 1996), ch. 10

Meyer, Lawrence H. U.S. banker

1 Giving the speech is fun. Dealing with the aftermath of the speech is the only thing where there's stress.
Wall Street Journal (April 25, 1997)

Meyer, Melissa (b.1923) U.S. painter

1 Published information about the origins of collage is misleading. Picasso and Braque are credited with inventing it. Many artists made collage before they did, Picasso's father for one and Sonia Delaunay for another.
"Waste Not Want Not: An Inquiry into What Women Saved and Assembled—FEMMAGE" (1977), quoted in *Heresies* (Winter 1977–78), vol. I, no. 4

Meyers, John (b.1929) U.S. business executive and magazine publisher

1 We've replaced the concept of having a job with having a mission.
U.S. News & World Report (September 2, 1985)

Meynell, Alice (originally Alice Christiana Gertrude Thompson; 1847–1922) British poet and literary critic

1 I must not think of thee; and, tired yet strong,
I shun the thought that lurks in all delight—
The thought of thee—and in the blue heaven's height,
And in the sweetest passage of a song.
"Renouncement" (1875)

2 My heart shall be thy garden.
"The Garden" (1875)

Mezzrow, Mezz (Milton Mesirow; 1899–1972) U.S. jazz musician

Quotations about Mezzrow

1 He plays the blues better than any other white musician...Mezzrow is by far the greatest jazz clarinettist that the white race has produced.
Hugues Panassie (1912–74) French jazz writer and impresario. *The Real Jazz* (1942), ch. 7

Quotations by Mezzrow

2 Music school? Are you kidding? I learned to play the sax in Pontiac Reformatory.
Opening words. *Really the Blues* (1946), ch. 1

3 Get this straight, we pure-and-simple jazzmen didn't scoff at the serious composers exactly, but...symphony means slavery in any jazzman's dictionary. Jazz and freedom are synonymous.
Really the Blues (1946), ch. 8

4 Bix played a cornet...that looked like it came from the junkpile...The whiskey fumes that he blew out of that beat-up old cornet almost gassed me.
Referring to Bix Beiderbecke. *Really the Blues* (1946), ch. 8

5 Out of the belly-spasms of this frenzy-jammed country a brand-new voice sang out...It was the voice of jazz making itself heard above the rattle of machine guns and the clink of whiskey bottles.
Referring to the growing popularity of jazz during the Prohibition era in the United States (1920–33). *Really the Blues* (1946), ch. 8

6 The colored chef came running out of the kitchen...and yelled "Boy, you is the saxophonest blowinest man I ever heard in all my born days. Where'd you come from poppa?"
Really the Blues (1946), ch. 9

7 Nothing could hold us back now. King Jazz was moving in, heading up his whole army of horn-tooters and skin-beaters, and I was right in there with them, ready to cover all spots.
Referring to the exodus of musicians to New York in 1928 after the suppression of Chicago's speakeasies. *Really the Blues* (1946), ch. 9

8 Our music hit Legs' girl friend so hard, she jumped out on the dance floor and began rolling her hips like she was fresh in from Waikiki, with ball-bearings where her pelvis should've been.
Referring to the gangster Legs Diamond and his companion. *Really the Blues* (1946), ch. 10

9 I could tickle the clarinet keys and squeeze out the only language in the whole world that would let me say my piece. And you know what my piece was? A very simple story: *Life is good, it's great to be alive.*
Really the Blues (1946), ch. 17

Michael, George (originally Yorgos Kyriatou Panayiotou; b.1963) British pop singer and songwriter

1 There is no such thing as resignation for an artiste in the music industry. Effectively, you sign a piece of paper at the beginning of your career and you are expected to live with that decision, good or bad, for the rest of your professional life.
Referring to his court action against Sony, who refused to release him from a recording contract he signed in his youth. *Times*, London (May 22, 1994)

Michaels, Anne (b.1958) Canadian poet and novelist

1 Do you realize Beethoven composed all his music without ever having looked upon the sea?
Fugitive Pieces (1997)

Michelangelo (Michelangelo di Lodovico Buonarroti Simoni; 1475–1564) Italian sculptor, painter, architect, and poet

1 There is no clime or country outside the kingdom of Italy where one can paint well...We call good painting Italian, and if good painting be produced in Flanders or in Spain...it will still be Italian painting.
Quoted in *On Ancient Painting* (Francisco de Hollanda; 1548)

Michelet, Jules (1798–1874) French historian

1 England is an empire, Germany is a nation, a race, France is a person.
1867. "Tableau de la France," *History of France* (1833–67)

2 The sea is English by inclination; she doesn't like France; she breaks up our boats; she silts up our ports.
1867. "Tableau de la France," *History of France* (1833–67)

3 With the world a war began, which will end with the world, and not before: that of man against nature, of the spiritual against the material, of freedom against fate. History is nothing more than the account of this unending struggle.
L'histoire universelle (1831), Introduction

4 There is no such thing as an old woman. Any woman, of any age, if she loves, if she is good, gives a man a sense of the infinite.
Love (1859), bk. 5, ch. 4

5 What is the first part of politics? Education. The second? Education. And the third? Education.
The People (1846)

Michelson, Albert A. (Albert Abraham Michelson; 1852–1931) German-born U.S. physicist

1 The most important fundamental laws of physical science have all been discovered, and these are now so firmly established that the possibility of their ever being supplemented in consequence of new discoveries is exceedingly remote.
1903. Quoted in *The Arrow of Time* (Peter Coveney and Roger Highfield; 1991)

Michitsuna no Haha (935?–995) Japanese diarist

1 Have you any idea
How long a night can last, spent
Lying alone and sobbing?
974? Quoted in *Hundred Poets, A Poem Apiece* (13th century)

Micklethwait, John U.S. author

1 The arrival of multicultural companies means that people can no longer rely on shared backgrounds and tacit understanding to bind them together.
The Witch Doctors (co-written with Adrian Wooldridge; 1996)

Middleton, Peter, Sir (b.1934) British banker

1 It would be a dreadful mistake to equate economics with real life.
Times, London (February 26, 1983)

Middleton, Thomas (1580?–1627) English playwright

1 Anything for a Quiet Life
1620? Title of play (possibly written with John Webster).

2 Hold their noses to the grindstone.
Blurt, Master-Constable (1602), Act 3, Scene 3

3 Sometimes he jets it like a Gentleman
Otherwhiles much like a wanton Courtesan
But truth to tell a man or woman whether,
I cannot say she's excellent in either.
But if Report may certifie a truth,
She's neither or either, but a Cheating youth.
Ingling Pyander (1599), quoted in *Homosexuality: A History* (Colin Spencer; 1995)

4 Our eyes are sentinels unto our judgments,
And should give certain judgment what they see;
But they are rash sometimes, and tell us wonders
Of common things, which when our judgments find,
They can then check the eyes, and call them blind.
The Changeling (co-written with William Rowley; 1622), Act 1, Scene 1

5 Why, are you not as guilty, in (I'm sure)
As deep as I? And we should stick together.
The Changeling (co-written with William Rowley; 1622), Act 3, Scene 4

6 Ground not upon dreams; you know they are ever contrary.
The Family of Love (1602), Act 4, Scene 3

7 Have you summoned your wits from wool-gathering?
The Family of Love (1602), Act 5, Scene 3

8 On his last legs.
The Old Law (1656), Act 5, Scene 1

9 Though I be poor, I'm honest.
The Witch (1609–16), Act 3, Scene 2

Midgley, Mary (b.1919) British philosopher

1 Human moral capacities are just what could be expected to evolve when a highly social creature becomes intelligent enough to become aware of profound conflicts among his motives.
The Ethical Primate (1994)

2 The core reductive mistake is...the idea of a single fundamental explanation.
The Ethical Primate (1994)

Midler, Bette (b.1945) U.S. singer and actor

1 A woman who pulled herself up by her bra straps.
Introducing the singer Madonna at a concert in New York City. Comment (1985)

2 If sex is such a natural phenomenon, how come there are so many books on how to?
Attrib.

Mies van der Rohe, Ludwig (originally Ludwig Mies; 1886–1969) German-born U.S. architect

1 Less is more.
Also said by Robert Browning in "Andrea del Sarto," l. 78. *New York Herald Tribune* (1959)

2 God is in the details.
New York Times (August 19, 1969)

Mikes, George (1912–87) Hungarian-born British writer and humorist

1 Britain is the society where the ruling class does not rule, the working class does not work, and the middle class is not in the middle.
English Humour for Beginners (1980)

2 An Englishman, even if he is alone, forms an orderly queue of one.
How to be an Alien (1946)

3 Continental people have a sex life; the English have hot-water bottles.
How to be an Alien (1946)

4 In England only uneducated people show off their knowledge; nobody quotes Latin or Greek authors in the course of conversation, unless he has never read them.
How to be an Alien (1946)

5 Many continentals think life is a game, the English think cricket is a game.
How to be an Alien (1946)

6 On the Continent people have good food; in England people have good table manners.
How to be an Alien (1946)

7 When people say England, they sometimes mean Great Britain, sometimes the United Kingdom, sometimes the British Isles—but never England.
How to be an Alien (1946)

8 It was twenty-one years ago that England and I first set foot on each other. I came for a fortnight; I have stayed ever since.
How to be Inimitable (1961)

Miles, Sarah (b.1941) British actor

1 Isn't it amazing that there's no copyright on your own life.
Observer, London (February 2, 1994), "Sayings of the Week"

Mill, John Stuart (1806–73) British philosopher and social reformer

Quotations about Mill

1 John Stuart Mill

By a mighty effort of will
Overcame his natural bonhomie
And wrote "Principles of Political Economy".
Edmund Clerihew Bentley (1875–1956) British writer and journalist. "John Stuart Mill," *Biography for Beginners* (1905)

Quotations by Mill

2 The most important thing women have to do is to stir up the zeal of women themselves.
Letter to Alexander Bain (July 14, 1869), quoted in *Letters of John Stuart Mill* (Hugh S. R. Elliot, ed.; 1910), vol. 2

3 As often as a study is cultivated by narrow minds, they will draw from it narrow conclusions.
Auguste Comte and Positivism (1865), pt. 1

4 The notion that truths external to the human mind may be known by intuition or consciousness, independently of observation and experience, is, I am persuaded, in these times, the great intellectual support of false doctrines and bad institutions.
Autobiography (1873)

5 Ask yourself whether you are happy, and you cease to be so.
Autobiography (1873), ch. 5

6 The only part of the conduct of any one, for which he is amenable to society, is that which concerns others. In the part which merely concerns himself, his independence is, of right, absolute. Over himself, over his own body and mind, the individual is absolute.
On Liberty (1859)

7 A party of order or stability, and a party of progress or reform, are both necessary elements of a healthy state of political life.
On Liberty (1859), ch. 2

8 He who knows only his own side of the case knows little of that.
On Liberty (1859), ch. 2

9 If all mankind minus one were of one opinion, and only one person were of the contrary opinion, mankind would be no more justified in silencing that one person, than he, if he had the power, would be justified in silencing mankind.
On Liberty (1859), ch. 2

10 All good things which exist are the fruits of originality.
On Liberty (1859), ch. 3

11 The liberty of the individual must be thus far limited; he must not make himself a nuisance to other people.
On Liberty (1859), ch. 3

12 The worth of a State in the long run is the worth of the individuals composing it.
On Liberty (1859), ch. 5

13 Instead of governing, for which it is radically unfit, the proper office of a representative assembly is to watch and control the government.
Representative Government (1861)

14 The opinion in favour of the present system which entirely subordinates the weaker sex to the stronger, rests upon theory only; for there was never trial made of any other.
The Subjection of Women (1869)

15 The principle which regulates the existing social relations between the two sexes—the legal subordination of one sex to the other—is wrong in itself, and now one of the chief hindrances to human improvement.
The Subjection of Women (1869)

16 The reason why the old painters were so greatly superior to the modern is that a greatly superior class of men applied themselves to the art.
The Subjection of Women (1869)

17 Whether the institution to be defended is slavery, political absolutism, or the absolutism of the head of a family, we are always supposed to judge of it from its best instances...Meanwhile, laws and institutions require to be adapted not to good men, but to bad.
The Subjection of Women (1869)

18 It is better to be a human being dissatisfied than a pig satisfied; better to be Socrates dissatisfied than a fool satisfied.
Utilitarianism (1863)

19 The only proof capable of being given that an object is visible is that people actually see it...In like manner, I apprehend, the sole evidence it is possible to produce that anything is desirable is that people do actually desire it.
Utilitarianism (1863)

20 To desire anything, except in proportion as the idea of it is pleasant, a physical and metaphysical impossibility.
Utilitarianism (1863)

Millay, Edna St. Vincent (1892–1950) U.S. poet

1 Childhood is the kingdom where nobody dies.
Nobody that matters, that is.
"Childhood is the Kingdom Where Nobody Dies" (1934)

2 Man has never been the same since God died.
He has taken it very hard.
"Conversation at Midnight" (1937)

3 It is not true that life is one damn thing after another—it's one damn thing over and over.
Letter to Arthur Davison Ficke (October 24, 1930), quoted in *Letters of Edna St. Vincent Millay* (Allan Ross Macdougall, ed.; 1952)

4 My candle burns at both ends;
It will not last the night;
But ah, my foes, and oh, my friends—
It gives a lovely light!
"First Fig," *A Few Figs from Thistles* (1920)

5 What lips my lips have kissed, and where, and why,
I have forgotten, and what arms have lain
Under my head till morning; but the rain
Is full of ghosts tonight.
"What Lips My Lips Have Kissed, and where, and why," *Collected Poems* (1923), sonnet 42, quoted in *The Penguin Book of American Verse* (Geoffrey Moore, ed.; 1977)

Miller, Arthur (b.1915) U.S. playwright

Quotations about Miller

1 EGGHEAD WEDS HOURGLASS.
Anonymous. On the marriage of the playwright Arthur Miller to the film star Marilyn Monroe. *Variety* (1956), headline

Quotations by Miller

2 ALFIERE But this is Red Hook, not Sicily. This is the slum that faces the bay on the seaward side of Brooklyn Bridge. This is the gullet of New York swallowing the tonnage of the world.
A View from the Bridge (1955), Act 1

3 I am inclined to notice the ruin in things, perhaps because I was born in Italy.
A View from the Bridge (1955), Act 1

4 My first thought was that he had committed a crime, but soon I saw it was only a passion that had moved into his body like a stranger.
A View from the Bridge (1955), Act 1

5 Everyone likes a kidder, but no one lends him money.
Death of a Salesman (1949)

6 He's liked, but he's not well liked.
Death of a Salesman (1949), Act 1

7 I don't say he's a great man. Willy Loman never made a lot of money. His name was never in the paper. He's not the finest character that ever lived. But he's a human being, and a terrible thing is happening to him. So attention must be paid.
Death of a Salesman (1949), Act 1

8 Never fight fair with a stranger, boy. You'll never get out of the jungle that way.
Death of a Salesman (1949), Act 1

9 A salesman has got to dream, boy. It comes with the territory.
Death of a Salesman (1949), Act 2

10 For a salesman, there is no rock bottom to the life. He don't put a bolt to a nut, he don't tell you the law or give you medicine. He's a man way out there in the blue, riding on a smile and a shoeshine.
"Requiem," *Death of a Salesman* (1949)

11 The structure of a play is always the story of how the birds came home to roost.
"Shadows of the Gods," *Harper's Magazine* (August 1958)

12 A good newspaper, I suppose, is a nation talking to itself.
Observer, London (November 26, 1961), "Sayings of the Week"

13 No one wants the truth if it is inconvenient.
Observer, London (January 8, 1989), "Sayings of the Week"

14 All organization is and must be grounded in the idea of exclusion and prohibition just as two objects cannot occupy the same space.
The Crucible (1953), Act 1

15 There are many who stay away from church these days because you hardly ever mention God any more.
The Crucible (1953), Act 1

16 PROCTOR Oh, Elizabeth, your justice would freeze beer!
Said to his wife. *The Crucible* (1953), Act 1

17 The witch-hunt was a perverse manifestation of the panic which set in among all classes when the balance began to turn toward greater individual freedom.
Referring to the Salem witchcraft trials (1692). *The Crucible* (1953), Act 1, overture

18 PROCTOR How may I live without my name?
Considering whether ignominiously to confess to witchcraft and thus escape execution. *The Crucible* (1953), Act 4

19 Years ago a person, he was unhappy, didn't know what to do with himself—he'd go to church, start a revolution—something. Today you're unhappy? Can't figure it out? What is the salvation? Go shopping.
The Price (1968), Act 1

20 To a very important degree the theater we have is the theater the critics have permitted us to have, since they filter out what they consider we ought not see, enforcing laws that have never been written, laws, among others, of taste and even ideological content.
Timebends (1987), pt. 2

21 It must be said, nevertheless, whatever its shortcomings, in a different theatrical time this play might well have stuck to the wall instead of oozing down.
Referring to the opening of his play *The Man Who Had All the Luck* (1944). *Timebends* (1987), pt. 2

Miller, Henry (Henry Valentine Miller; 1891–1980) U.S. novelist

Quotations about Miller

1 Miller is not really a writer but a non-stop talker to whom someone has given a typewriter.
Gerald Brenan (1894–1987) Maltese-born British writer and novelist. "Literature," *Thoughts in a Dry Season* (1978)

2 At last, an unprintable book that is readable.
Ezra Pound (1885–1972) U.S. poet, translator, and critic. Referring to *Tropic of Cancer* by Henry Miller; also quoted as "A dirty book worth reading." Remark (1934)

Quotations by Miller

3 The great artist is one who conquers the romantic in himself.
Black Spring (1936)

4 You can travel fifty thousand miles in America without once tasting a piece of good bread.
"The Staff of Life," *Remember to Remember* (1947)

5 Freedom includes everything. Freedom converts everything to its basic nature, which is perfection.
Sexus (1949)

6 Sex is one of the nine reasons for reincarnation...The other eight are unimportant.
Sexus (1949)

7 The neurotic is the flounder that lies on the bed of the river, securely settled in the mud, waiting to be speared. For him

death is the only certainty, and the dread of that grim certainty immobilizes him.
Sexus (1949)

8 When our very lives are threatened we begin to live. Even the psychic invalid throws away his crutches in such moments.
Sexus (1949)

9 I have never been able to look upon America as young and vital, but rather as prematurely old, as a fruit which rotted before it had a chance to ripen.
The Air-Conditioned Nightmare (1945)

10 It isn't the oceans which cut us off from the rest of the world—it's the American way of looking at things.
"Letter to Lafayette," *The Air-Conditioned Nightmare* (1945)

11 The study of crime begins with the knowledge of oneself.
"The Soul of Anæsthesia," *The Air-Conditioned Nightmare* (1945)

12 Music is a beautiful opiate, if you don't take it too seriously.
"With Edgar Varèse in the Gobi Desert," *The Air-Conditioned Nightmare* (1945)

13 In recommending a book to a friend the less said the better. The moment you praise a book too highly you awaken resistance in your listener.
The Books In My Life (1957)

14 Everyman has his own destiny: The only imperative is to follow it, to accept it, no matter where it leads him.
The Wisdom of the Heart (1941)

15 The aim of life is to live, and to live means to be aware, joyously, drunkenly, serenely, divinely aware.
"Creative Death," *The Wisdom of the Heart* (1941)

16 Art teaches nothing, except the significance of life.
"Reflections on Writing," *The Wisdom of the Heart* (1941)

17 All my life I had been looking forward to something happening, some extrinsic event that would alter my life, and now suddenly, inspired by the abusive hopelessness of everything, I felt relieved.
Tropic of Cancer (1934)

18 Do anything, but let it produce joy.
Tropic of Cancer (1934)

19 I have found God, but he is insufficient. I am only spiritually dead. Physically I am alive. Morally I am free.
Tropic of Cancer (1934)

20 I have no money, no resources, no hopes. I am the happiest man alive.
Tropic of Cancer (1934)

21 I love everything that flows: rivers, sewers, lava, semen, blood, bile, words, everything that has time in it and becoming, that brings us back to the beginning where there is never end.
Tropic of Cancer (1934)

22 The wallpaper with which the men of science have covered the world of reality is falling to tatters.
Tropic of Cancer (1934)

23 We are living a million lives in the space of a generation.
Tropic of Cancer (1934)

24 Every man with a belly full of the classics is an enemy to the human race.
"Dijon," *Tropic of Cancer* (1934)

25 Even if everything I say is wrong, is prejudiced, spiteful, malevolent, even if I am a liar and a poisoner, it is nevertheless the truth and it will have to be swallowed.
Tropic of Capricorn (1939)

26 My home is not in this world, nor in the next. I am a man without a home, without a friend, without a wife. I am a monster who belongs to a reality that does not exist yet.
Tropic of Capricorn (1939)

27 Nothing is determined in advance. The future is absolutely uncertain, the past is non-existent.
Tropic of Capricorn (1939)

28 Confusion is a word we have invented for an order which is not understood.
"On the Ovarian Trolley: An Interlude," *Tropic of Capricorn* (1939)

29 One has to be a lowbrow, a bit of a murderer, to be a politician, ready and willing to see people sacrificed, slaughtered for the sake of an idea, whether a good one or a bad one.
Quoted in *Writers at Work* (Malcolm Crowley, ed.; 1958)

Miller, Joaquin (Cincinnatus Hiner Miller; 1839–1913) U.S. poet

1 A mighty nation moving west,
With all its steely sinews set
Against the living forest.
Hear the shouts, the shots of pioneers,
The rended forests, rolling wheels.
"Westward Ho!," *Songs of the Sierra* (1871), ll. 3–7

Miller, Jonathan (Jonathan Wolfe Miller; b.1934) British psychologist, director, and writer

1 They do those little personal things people sometimes do when they think they are alone in railway carriages; things like smelling their own armpits.
Beyond the Fringe (1960)

2 I'm not really a Jew; just Jew-ish, not the whole hog.
"Real Class," *Beyond the Fringe* (1960)

3 I wasn't driven into medicine by a social conscience but by rampant curiosity.
Observer, London (February 5, 1983)

4 The human body is private property. We have to have a search warrant to look inside, and even then an investigator is confined to a few experimental tappings here and there, some gropings on the party wall, a torch flashed rather hesitantly into some of the dark corners.
"Perishable Goods," *The Body in Question* (February 15, 1979)

Miller, Kelly (1863–1939) U.S. sociologist, educator, and civil rights activist

1 There may be some argument for suffrage for unfortunate females, such as widows and hopeless spinsters, but such

status is not contemplated as a normal social relation.
"The Risk of Woman Suffrage," *The Crisis* (November 1915)

Miller, Max (Thomas Henry Sargent, "The Cheeky Chappie"; 1895–1963) British music-hall comedian

1 There was a little girl
Who had a little curl
Right in the middle of her forehead,
When she was good she was very very good
And when she was bad she was very very popular.
Quoted in *The Max Miller Blue Book* (Barry Took, ed.; 1975)

Miller, Roger (Roger Dean Miller; 1936–92) U.S. singer and songwriter

1 King of the Road
1964. Song title, referring to a hobo.

Miller, Steven E. U.S. author

1 Markets can be adaptive and flexible, agents of..."creative destruction" that is sometimes necessary for various kinds of progress.
Civilizing Cyberspace (1996)

2 Markets require deliberate guidance from nonmarket institutions to achieve stability or even to avoid self-destruction.
Civilizing Cyberspace (1996)

3 The real force behind the debasement of our culture is the freedom of our business to pursue profit without constraint from the non-market institutions that are the repository of community values.
Civilizing Cyberspace (1996)

4 Unregulated markets create and reinforce hierarchy by allowing the strong to get stronger and the rich to get richer.
Civilizing Cyberspace (1996)

5 We have exchanged our communities for jobs, our stable social connections for the ability to purchase products.
Civilizing Cyberspace (1996)

Milligan, Spike (Terence Alan Milligan; b.1918) Indian-born British humorist, writer, and actor

1 I am not going to thank anybody—because I did it all myself.
On receiving the British Comedy Award for Lifetime Achievement. Speech (1994)

2 Only on the third class tourist class passengers' deck was it a sultry overcast morning, but then if you do things on the cheap you must expect these things.
A Dustbin of Milligan (1963)

3 I have for instance among my purchases...several original Mona Lisas and all painted (according to the Signature) by the great artist Kodak.
"Letters to Harry Secombe," *A Dustbin of Milligan* (1963)

4 His thoughts, few that they were, lay silent in the privacy of his head.
Puckoon (1963)

5 I'm a hero with coward's legs. I'm a hero from the waist up.
Puckoon (1963)

6 Money can't buy friends, but you can get a better class of enemy.
Puckoon (1963)

7 When she saw the sign "Members Only" she thought of him.
Puckoon (1963)

8 "Do you come here often?"
"Only in the mating season."
BBC radio series. *The Goon Show* (1951–59)

9 I'm walking backwards till Christmas.
BBC radio series. *The Goon Show* (1951–59)

10 MORIARTY How are you at Mathematics?
HARRY SECOMBE I speak it like a native.
BBC radio series. *The Goon Show* (1951–59)

11 SEAGOON I want you to accompany me on the safari.
BLOODNOCK Gad sir, I'm sorry, I've never played one.
BBC radio series. *The Goon Show* (1951–59)

12 One day the don't-knows will get in, and then where will we be?
Remark made about a pre-election poll. Attrib.

Mills, Hugh (1913–71) British screenwriter

1 Nothing unites the English like war. Nothing divides them like Picasso.
Prudence and the Pill (1968)

Milman, Henry Hart (1791–1868) British historian, clergyman, and poet

1 Ride on! ride on in majesty!
In lowly pomp ride on to die.
Hymn. "Ride on! Ride on in Majesty" (1827)

2 Too fair to worship, too divine to love.
Newdigate Prize Poem, Oxford. *The Belvedere Apollo* (1812)

Milne, A. A. (Alan Alexander Milne; 1882–1956) British writer

1 I am old enough to be—in fact am—your mother.
Belinda (1922)

2 For one person who dreams of making fifty thousand pounds, a hundred people dream of being left fifty thousand pounds.
"The Future," *If I May* (1920)

3 What I say is that, if a fellow really likes potatoes, he must be a pretty decent sort of fellow.
Not That It Matters (1919)

4 I think I am an Elephant,
Behind another Elephant
Behind *another* Elephant who isn't really there.
"Busy," *Now We are Six* (1927)

5 King John was not a good man—
He had his little ways.
And sometimes no-one spoke to him
For days and days and days.
"King John's Christmas," *Now We are Six* (1927)

6 If the English language had been properly organized...then there would be a word which meant both "he" and "she", and I could write, "If John or Mary comes heesh will want to play tennis," which would save a lot of trouble.
The Christopher Robin Birthday Book (1930)

7 Pooh began to feel a little more comfortable, because when you are a Bear of Very Little Brain, and you Think of Things, you find sometimes that a Thing which seemed very Thingish inside you is quite different when it gets out into the open and has other people looking at it.
The House at Pooh Corner (1928)

8 Supposing Pooh, said Piglet, we were walking in the forest and a tree fell on us. Supposing it didn't, said Pooh after careful consideration.
The House at Pooh Corner (1928)

9 Well, it's when people call out at you just as you're going off to do it, "What are you going to do, Christopher Robin?" and you say "Oh, nothing", and then you go and do it.
In reply to Piglet's question, "How do you do Nothing?" "An Enchanted Place," *The House at Pooh Corner* (1928)

10 Tiggers always eat thistles, so that was why we came to see you, Eeyore.
"Tigger Has Breakfast," *The House at Pooh Corner* (1928)

11 They're changing guard at Buckingham Palace—
Christopher Robin went down with Alice.
Alice is marrying one of the guard.
"A soldier's life is terrible hard,"
Says Alice.
"Buckingham Palace," *When We Were Very Young* (1924)

12 James James
Morrison Morrison
Weatherby George Dupree
Took great
Care of his Mother,
Though he was only three.
"Disobedience," *When We Were Very Young* (1924)

13 You must never go down to the end of the town if you don't go down with me.
"Disobedience," *When We Were Very Young* (1924)

14 Halfway down the stairs
Is a stair
Where I sit.
There isn't any
Other stair
Quite like
It.
"Halfway Down," *When We Were Very Young* (1924)

15 And some of the bigger bears try to pretend
That they came round the corner to look for a friend;
And they'll try to pretend that nobody cares
Whether you walk on the lines or squares.
"Lines and Squares," *When We Were Very Young* (1924)

16 *What* is the matter with Mary Jane?
She's perfectly well and she hasn't a pain,
And it's lovely rice pudding for dinner again!—
What *is* the matter with Mary Jane?
"Rice Pudding," *When We Were Very Young* (1924)

17 The King asked
The Queen, and
The Queen asked
The Dairymaid:
"Could we have some butter for
The Royal slice of bread?"
"The King's Breakfast," *When We Were Very Young* (1924)

18 Little Boy kneels at the foot of the bed,
Droops on the little hands little gold head.
Hush! Hush! Whisper who dares!
Christopher Robin is saying his prayers.
"Vespers," *When We Were Very Young* (1924)

19 Isn't it funny
How a bear likes honey?
Buzz! Buzz! Buzz!
I wonder why he does?
Winnie the Pooh (1926), ch. 1

20 I am a Bear of Very Little Brain, and long words Bother me.
Winnie the Pooh (1926), ch. 4

21 Time for a little something.
Winnie the Pooh (1926), ch. 6

22 "Good morning, Little Piglet," said Eeyore. "If it *is* a good morning," he said. "Which I doubt," said he. "Not that it matters," he said.
Typical of Eeyore's gloomy outlook. "Eeyore Has a Birthday," *Winnie the Pooh* (1926)

23 "It is hard to be brave," said Piglet, sniffing slightly, "when you're only a Very Small Animal."
"Kanga and Baby Roo," *Winnie the Pooh* (1926)

24 I have my friends. Somebody spoke to me only yesterday.
Said by Eeyore. Typical of his gloomy outlook. "We Say Good-bye," *Winnie the Pooh* (1926)

Milner, Alfred, 1st Viscount Milner (1854–1925) German-born British politician and colonial administrator

1 If we believe a thing to be bad, and if we have a right to prevent it, it is our duty to try to prevent it and to damn the consequences.
Speech, Glasgow, quoted in *Times*, London (November 27, 1909)

Milton, John (1608–74) English writer

Quotations about Milton

1 He was so fair that they called him the *lady of* Christ's College.
Late 17th century
John Aubrey (1626–97) English antiquary. *Brief Lives* (1813)

2 The whole of Milton's poem, *Paradise Lost*, is such barbarous trash, so outrageously offensive to reason and to common sense that one is naturally led to wonder how it can have been tolerated by a people amongst whom astronomy, navigation and chemistry are understood.
William Cobbett (1763–1835) British writer, journalist, and reformer. *Journal of a Year's Residence in The United States* (1817–19)

3 Oh many a peer of England brews

Livelier liquor than the Muse
And malt does more than Milton can
To justify God's ways to man.
A. E. Housman (1859–1936) British poet and classicist. Referring to beer, of which malt is one of the ingredients. "The Welsh Marches," *A Shropshire Lad* (1896), no. 62, st. 2, quoted in *The Collected Poems of A. E. Housman* (John Carter, ed.; 1967)

4 Milton, Madam, was a genius that could cut a Colossus from a rock; but could not carve heads upon cherry-stones.
June 13, 1784
Samuel Johnson (1709–84) British lexicographer and writer. When Miss Hannah More had wondered why Milton could write the epic *Paradise Lost* (1667) but only very poor sonnets. Quoted in *Life of Samuel Johnson* (James Boswell; 1791)

5 Milton almost requires a solemn service of music to be played before you enter upon him.
Charles Lamb (1775–1834) British essayist. "Detached Thoughts on Books and Reading," *Last Essays of Elia* (1833)

6 Milton's Devil as a moral being is far superior to his God...Milton has so far violated the popular creed...as to have alleged no superiority of moral virtue to his God over his Devil. And this bold neglect of direct moral purpose is the most decisive proof of Milton's genius.
Percy Bysshe Shelley (1792–1822) English poet. *A Defence of Poetry* (1821), quoted in *Essays, Letters from Abroad, Translations and Fragments* (Mrs. Shelley, ed.; 1840)

7 Milton! thou shouldst be living at this hour:
England hath need of thee: she is a fen
Of stagnant waters: altar, sword, and pen,
Fireside, the heroic wealth of hall and bower,
Have forfeited their ancient English dower
Of inward happiness.
September 1802
William Wordsworth (1770–1850) British poet. "London, 1802," *Poems in Two Volumes* (1807), vol. 1, ll. 1–6

Quotations by Milton

8 His words ... like so many nimble and airy servitors trip about him at command.
"An Apology for Smectymnuus" (1642), sect. 12

9 For what can war, but endless war still breed.
"On the Lord General Fairfax at the siege of Colchester" (1648), Sonnet XV, l. 10

10 Fly, envious Time, till thou run out thy race,
Call on the lazy leaden-stepping hours.
"On Time" (1645), l. 1

11 A good book is the precious life-blood of a master spirit, embalmed and treasured up on purpose to a life beyond life.
Areopagitica (1644)

12 Let her and Falsehood grapple; who ever knew Truth put to the worse, in a free and open encounter?
Areopagitica (1644)

13 Who kills a man kills a reasonable creature, God's image; but he who destroys a good book, kills reason itself, kills the image of God, as it were in the eye.
Areopagitica (1644)

14 What hath night to do with sleep?
Comus (1637), l. 122

15 Virtue may be assailed, but never hurt,
Surprised by unjust force, but not enthralled.
Comus (1637), l. 589

16 Bacchus, that first from out the purple grape
Crushed the sweet poison of misused wine.
Comus (1637), ll. 46–47

17 O thievish Night
Why shouldst thou, but for some felonious end,
In thy dark lantern thus close up the stars,
That Nature hung in heaven, and filled their lamps
With everlasting oil, to give due light
To the misled and lonely traveller?
Comus (1637), ll. 195–200

18 A thousand fantasies
Begin to throng into my memory
Of calling shapes, and beckoning shadows dire,
And airy tongues, that syllable men's names
On sands, and shores, and desert wildernesses.
Comus (1637), ll. 205–209

19 How charming is divine philosophy!
Not harsh, and crabbed as dull fools suppose,
But musical as is Apollo's lute,
And a perpetual feast of nectared sweets,
Where no crude surfeit reigns.
Comus (1637), ll. 475–479

20 Beauty is Nature's brag, and must be shown
In courts, at feasts, and high solemnities
Where most may wonder at the workmanship;
It is for homely features to keep home,
They had their name thence; coarse complexions
And cheeks of sorry grain will serve to ply
The sampler, and to tease the housewife's wool.
Comus (1637), ll. 744–750

21 Mortals that would follow me,
Love virtue, she alone is free.
The Attendant Spirit. *Comus* (1637), ll. 1017–18

22 Peace hath her victories
No less renowned than war.
1652. "To Oliver Cromwell," *Letters of State...Together with Several of his Poems* (1694), ll. 9–10

23 Of man's first disobedience, and the fruit
Of that forbidden tree, whose mortal taste
Brought death into the world, and all our woe,
With loss of Eden.
The opening lines. *Paradise Lost* (1667), bk. 1, ll. 1–4

24 What in me is dark
Illumine, what is low raise and support;
That to the highth of this great argument
I may assert eternal providence,
And justify the ways of God to men.
The poet's invocation to God. *Paradise Lost* (1667), bk. 1, ll. 22–26

25 Him the almighty power
Hurled headlong flaming from the ethereal sky
With hideous ruin and combustion down
To bottomless perdition, there to dwell

In adamantine chains and penal fire,
Who durst defy the omnipotent to arms.
Satan's descent to hell. *Paradise Lost* (1667), bk. 1, ll. 44–49

26 A dungeon horrible, on all sides round
As one great furnace flamed, yet from those flames
No light, but rather darkness visible
Served only to discover sights of woe,
Regions of sorrow, doleful shades, where peace
And rest can never dwell, hope never comes
That comes to all.
Describing Hell. *Paradise Lost* (1667), bk. 1, ll. 61–67

27 What though the field be lost?
All is not lost; the unconquerable will,
And study of revenge, immortal hate,
And courage never to submit or yield:
And what is else not to be overcome?
Said by Satan. *Paradise Lost* (1667), bk. 1, ll. 105–109

28 Fallen cherub, to be weak is miserable,
Doing or suffering: but of this be sure,
To do aught good never will be our task,
But ever to do ill our sole delight.
Satan addressing the cherubim. *Paradise Lost* (1667), bk. 1, ll. 157–160

29 The will
And high permission of all-ruling heaven
Left him at large to his own dark designs,
That with reiterated crimes he might
Heap on himself damnation.
Referring to Satan. *Paradise Lost* (1667), bk. 1, ll. 211–215

30 A mind not to be changed by place or time.
The mind is its own place, and in itself
Can make a heaven of hell, a hell of heaven.
Said by Satan. *Paradise Lost* (1667), bk. 1, ll. 253–255

31 Here we may reign secure, and in my choice
To reign is worth ambition though in hell:
Better to reign in hell, than serve in heaven.
Paradise Lost (1667), bk. 1, ll. 261–263

32 His spear, to equal which the tallest pine
Hewn on Norwegian hills, to be the mast
Of some great ammiral, were but a wand,
He walked with to support uneasy steps
Over the burning marl.
Referring to Satan's spear. *Paradise Lost* (1667), bk. 1, ll. 292–296

33 Awake, arise, or be forever fallen.
Satan's exhortation to the fallen angels. *Paradise Lost* (1667), bk. 1, l. 330

34 For Spirits when they please
Can either sex assume, or both, so soft
And uncompounded is their essence pure,
Not tied or manacled with joint or limb,
Nor founded on the brittle strength of bones,
Like cumbrous flesh, but in what shape they choose.
Referring to the nature of angels. *Paradise Lost* (1667), bk. 1, ll. 423–428

35 Care
Sat on his faded cheek, but under brows
Of dauntless courage.
Referring to Satan. *Paradise Lost* (1667), bk. 1, ll. 601–603

36 Thrice he essayed, and thrice in spite of scorn,
Tears such as angels weep, burst forth.
Satan weeps before addressing the fallen angels. *Paradise Lost* (1667), bk. 1, ll. 620–621

37 Who overcomes
By force hath overcome but half his foe.
Said by Satan. *Paradise Lost* (1667), bk. 1, ll. 648–649

38 From morn
To noon he fell, from noon to dewy eve,
A summer's day; and with the setting sun
Dropped from the zenith like a falling star.
Mulciber's fall from heaven. *Paradise Lost* (1667), bk. 1, ll. 742–745

39 Long is the way
And hard, that out of hell leads up to light.
Satan to the fallen angels. *Paradise Lost* (1667), bk. 2, ll. 432–433

40 Vain wisdom all, and false philosophy.
Paradise Lost (1667), bk. 2, l. 565

41 Whence and what art thou, execrable shape?
Satan addresses Death at the gates of Hell. *Paradise Lost* (1667), bk. 2, l. 681

42 Incensed with indignatio Satan stood
Unterrified, and like a comet burned,
That fires the length of Ophiucus huge
In the Arctic sky, and from his horrid hair
Shakes pestilence and war.
Paradise Lost (1667), bk. 2, ll. 707–711

43 Grim Death my son and foe.
Said by Sin, the daughter of Satan and mother of Death. *Paradise Lost* (1667), bk. 2, l. 804

44 Where eldest Night
And Chaos, ancestors of Nature, hold
Eternal anarchy, amidst the noise
Of endless wars, and by confusion stand.
For Hot, Cold, Moist, and Dry, four champions fierce
Strive here for mastery.
Paradise Lost (1667), bk. 2, ll. 894–899

45 Chaos umpire sits,
And by decision more embroils the fray
By which he reigns: next him high arbiter
Chance governs all.
Paradise Lost (1667), bk. 2, ll. 907–1000

46 High on a throne of royal state, which far
Outshone the wealth of Ormuz and of Ind,
Or where the gorgeous East with richest hand
Showers on her kings barbaric pearl and gold,
Satan exalted sat, by merit raised
To that bad eminence.
Paradise Lost (1667), bk. 2, ll. 1–10

47 Our torments also may in length of time
Become our elements.
Said by Mammon. *Paradise Lost* (1667), bk. 2, ll. 274–275

48 To sit in darkness here
Hatching vain empires.
Said by Beelzebub. *Paradise Lost* (1667), bk. 2, ll. 377–378

49 Others apart stand on a hill retired,
In thoughts more elevate, and reasoned high

Of providence, foreknowledge, will, and fate,
Fixed fate, free will, foreknowledge absolute,
And found no end, in wand'ring mazes lost.
Referring to the fallen angels. *Paradise Lost* (1667), bk. 2, ll. 557–561

50 For neither man nor angel can discern
Hypocrisy, the only evil that walks
Invisible, except to God alone.
Paradise Lost (1667), bk. 3, ll. 682–684

51 Me miserable! which way shall I fly
Infinite wrath, and infinite despair?
Which way I fly is hell; myself am hell;
And in the lowest deep a lower deep
Still threatening to devour me opens wide,
To which the hell I suffer seems a heaven.
Said by Satan. *Paradise Lost* (1667), bk. 4, ll. 73–78

52 So farewell hope, and with hope farewell fear,
Farewell remorse: all good to me is lost;
Evil be thou my good.
Said by Satan. *Paradise Lost* (1667), bk. 4, ll. 108–110

53 A heaven on earth.
Referring to the garden of Eden. *Paradise Lost* (1667), bk. 4, l. 208

54 And by her yielded, by him best received,
Yielded with coy submission, modest pride,
And sweet reluctant amorous delay.
Referring to Eve. *Paradise Lost* (1667), bk. 4, l. 309

55 And with necessity,
The tyrant's plea, excus'd his devilish deeds.
Satan plots humankind's downfall. *Paradise Lost* (1667), bk. 4, l. 393

56 Imparadised in one another's arms.
Referring to Adam and Eve. *Paradise Lost* (1667), bk. 4, l. 506

57 Now came still evening on, and twilight grey
Had in her sober livery all things clad.
Paradise Lost (1667), bk. 4, l. 598

58 God is thy law, thou mine: to know no more
Is woman's happiest knowledge and her praise.
With thee conversing I forget all time.
Eve to Adam. *Paradise Lost* (1667), bk. 4, l. 637

59 Hail wedded love, mysterious law, true source
Of human offspring, sole propriety
In Paradise of all things common else.
Paradise Lost (1667), bk. 4, l. 750

60 Sleep on
Blest pair; and O yet happiest if ye seek
No happier state, and know to know no more.
Referring to Adam and Eve. *Paradise Lost* (1667), bk. 4, l. 773

61 Squat like a toad, close at the ear of Eve.
Referring to Satan. *Paradise Lost* (1667), bk. 4, l. 800

62 Abashed the devil stood,
And felt how awful goodness is, and saw
Virtue in her shape how lovely, saw, and pined.
Paradise Lost (1667), bk. 4, l. 846

63 Wherefore with thee
Came not all hell broke loose.
Gabriel questions Satan who has been discovered in Eden. *Paradise Lost* (1667), bk. 4, ll. 918–919

64 The lower still I fall, only supreme
in misery; such joy ambition finds.
Said by Satan. *Paradise Lost* (1667), bk. 4, ll. 91–92

65 On the tree of life
The middle tree and highest there that grew,
Sat like a cormorant.
Referring to Adam and Eve. *Paradise Lost* (1667), bk. 4, ll. 194–196

66 For contemplation he and valour formed,
For softness she and sweet attractive grace,
He for God only, she for God in him: His fair large front and
eye sublime declared
Absolute rule; and hyacinthine locks
Round from his parted forelock manly hung
Clustering, but not beneath his shoulders broad.
Paradise Lost (1667), bk. 4, ll. 297–303

67 What if earth
Be but the shadow of heaven, and things therein
Each to other like, more than on earth is thought?
Raphael to Adam. *Paradise Lost* (1667), bk. 5, ll. 574–576

68 Midnight brought on the dusky hour
Friendliest to sleep and silence.
Paradise Lost (1667), bk. 5, ll. 667–668

69 My fairest, my espoused, my latest found,
Heaven's last best gift, my ever new delight.
Paradise Lost (1667), bk. 5, ll. 18–19

70 Arms on armour clashing brayed
Horrible discord, and the madding wheels
Of brazen chariots raged; dire was the noise
Of conflict.
The war in Heaven. *Paradise Lost* (1667), bk. 6, ll. 209–212

71 But pain is perfect misery, the worst
Of evils, and excessive, overturns
All patience.
Paradise Lost (1667), bk. 6, ll. 462–465

72 Far off his coming shone.
Paradise Lost (1667), bk. 6, l. 768

73 Headlong themselves they threw
Down from the verge of heaven, eternal wrath
Burnt after them to the bottomless pit.
Christ drives the fallen angels out of Heaven. *Paradise Lost* (1667), bk. 6, ll. 864–866

74 The planets in their station listening stood,
While the bright pomp ascended jubilant.
Open, ye everlasting gates, they sung,
Open, ye heavens, your living doors; let in
The great creator from his work returned
Magnificent, his six days' work, a world.
The Creation. *Paradise Lost* (1667), bk. 7, ll. 563 –568

75 Be lowly wise:
Think only what concerns thee and thy being.
Raphael to Adam. *Paradise Lost* (1667), bk. 8, ll. 173–174

76 Accuse not nature, she hath done her part;
Do thou but thine.
Raphael to Adam. *Paradise Lost* (1667), bk. 8, ll. 561–562

77 Oft times nothing profits more
Than self-esteem, grounded on just and right
Well managed.
Raphael to Adam. *Paradise Lost* (1667), bk. 8, ll. 571–573

78 In solitude
What happiness, who can enjoy alone,
Or all enjoying, what contentment find?
Adam to God. *Paradise Lost* (1667), bk. 8, ll. 364–366

79 Yet when I approach
her loveliness, so absolute she seems
And in her self complete, so well to know
Her own, that what she wills to do or say,
Seems wisest, virtuousest, discreetest, best.
Adam of Eve to Raphael. *Paradise Lost* (1667), bk. 8, ll. 546–550

80 A broad and ample road, whose dust is gold
And pavement stars, as stars to thee appear,
Seen in the galaxy, that Milky Way
Which nightly as a circling zone thou seest
Powdered with stars.
Paradise Lost (1667), bk. 8, ll. 577–581

81 The serpent subtlest beast of all the field.
Paradise Lost (1667), bk. 9, l. 86

82 Revenge, at first though sweet,
Bitter ere long back on itself recoils.
Paradise Lost (1667), bk. 9, ll. 171–172

83 For solitude sometimes is best society,
And short retirement urges sweet return.
Paradise Lost (1667), bk. 9, ll. 249–250

84 She fair, divinely fair, fit love for gods.
Satan to Eve. *Paradise Lost* (1667), bk. 9, l. 489

85 Hope elevates, and joy
Brightens his crest.
Satan of Adam. *Paradise Lost* (1667), bk. 9, ll. 633–634

86 Earth felt the wound, and Nature from her seat
Sighing through all her works gave signs of woe,
That all was lost.
Referring to the Fall. *Paradise Lost* (1667), bk. 9, ll. 782–784

87 O fairest of creation, last and best
Of all God's works, creature in whom excelled
Whatever can to sight or thought be formed,
Holy, divine, good, amiable, or sweet!
Adam to Eve. *Paradise Lost* (1667), bk. 9, ll. 896–899

88 What thou art is mine;
Our state cannot be severed, we are one,
One flesh; to lose thee were to lose my self.
Adam to Eve. *Paradise Lost* (1667), bk. 9, ll. 957–959

89 The evening star,
Love's harbinger.
Paradise Lost (1667), bk. 11, ll. 588–589

90 Yet know withal,
Since thy original lapse, true liberty
Is lost, which always with right reason dwells
Twinned, and from her hath no dividual being.
Paradise Lost (1667), bk. 12, ll. 82–85

91 The world was all before them, where to choose
Their place of rest, and Providence their guide:
They hand in hand with wandering steps and slow,
Through Eden took their solitary way.
The expulsion of Adam and Eve from the Garden of Eden; the last lines of Milton's epic. *Paradise Lost* (1667), bk. 12, ll. 646–649

92 Rhyme being no necessary adjunct or true ornament of poem or good verse, in longer works especially, but the invention of a barbarous age, to set off wretched matter and lame metre.
Milton's note on "the Verse," meaning his use of blank verse, was added as a preface to the 2nd edition (1674). "The Verse," *Paradise Lost* (1674)

93 The troublesome and modern bondage of rhyming.
Milton's note on "the Verse," meaning his use of blank verse, was added as a preface to the 2nd edition (1674). "The Verse," *Paradise Lost* (1674)

94 Ask for this great deliverer now, and find him
Eyeless in Gaza at the mill with slaves.
"Samson Agonistes," *Paradise Regain'd...To Which is added Samson Agonistes* (1671), l. 40

95 O dark, dark, dark, amid the blaze of noon,
Irrecoverably dark, total eclipse
Without all hope of day!
"Samson Agonistes," *Paradise Regain'd...To Which is added Samson Agonistes* (1671), l. 80

96 To live a life half dead, a living death.
"Samson Agonistes," *Paradise Regain'd...To Which is added Samson Agonistes* (1671), l. 100

97 Love-quarrels oft in pleasing concord end.
"Samson Agonistes," *Paradise Regain'd...To Which is added Samson Agonistes* (1671), l. 1008

98 For evil news rides post, while good news baits.
"Samson Agonistes," *Paradise Regain'd...To Which is added Samson Agonistes* (1671), l. 1538

99 A little onward lend thy guiding hand
To these dark steps, a little further on.
"Samson Agonistes," *Paradise Regain'd...To Which is added Samson Agonistes* (1671), ll. 1–2

100 Yet beauty, though injurious, hath strange power,
After offence returning, to regain
Love once possessed.
"Samson Agonistes," *Paradise Regain'd...To Which is added Samson Agonistes* (1671), ll. 1003–04

101 He's gone, and who knows how he may report
Thy words by adding fuel to the flame?
The chorus to Samson. "Samson Agonistes," *Paradise Regain'd...To Which is added Samson Agonistes* (1671), ll. 1350–51

102 Most men admire
Virtue, who follow not her lore.
Satan to Christ. *Paradise Regained* (1671), bk. 1, l. 482

103 Beauty stands

In the admiration only of weak minds
Led captive.

Satan rebukes Belial who has suggested tempting Christ with woman. *Paradise Regained* (1671), bk. 2, l. 220

104 For where no hope is left, is left no fear.

Paradise Regained (1671), bk. 3, l. 206

105 He who seeking asses found a kingdom.

Referring to Saul, who, looking for his father's asses, found Samuel who anointed him as the Lord's "captain." *Paradise Regained* (1671), bk. 3, l. 242

106 The childhood shows the man,
As morning shows the day. Be famous then
By wisdom; as thy empire must extend,
So let extend thy mind o'er all the world.

Satan to Christ. *Paradise Regained* (1671), bk. 4, l. 220

107 New *Presbyter* is but old *Priest* writ large.

1646? "On the New Forcers of Conscience under the Long Parliament," *Poems &c. Upon Several Occasions* (1673), l. 20

108 When I consider how my light is spent,
Ere half my days, in this dark world and wide,
And that one talent which is death to hide,
Lodged with me useless.

Sonnet 16, "On Blindness," *Poems &c. Upon Several Occasions* (1673), complete poem

109 Blest pair of sirens, pledges of heaven's joy,
Sphere-borne harmonious sisters, Voice, and Verse.

"At a Solemn Music," *Poems of Mr. John Milton* (1645), ll. 1–2

110 Where more is meant than meets the ear.

"Il Penseroso," *Poems of Mr. John Milton* (1645), l. 120

111 And looks commercing with the skies,
Thy rapt soul sitting in thine eyes.

"Il Penseroso," *Poems of Mr. John Milton* (1645), ll. 39–40

112 Sweet bird, that shunn'st the noise of folly,
Most musical, most melancholy!

Referring to the nightingale. "Il Penseroso," *Poems of Mr. John Milton* (1645), ll. 61–62

113 Where glowing embers through the room
Teach light to counterfeit a gloom,
Far from all resort of mirth,
Save the cricket on the hearth.

"Il Penseroso," *Poems of Mr. John Milton* (1645), ll. 79–82

114 Then to the spicy nut-brown ale.

"L'Allegro," *Poems of Mr. John Milton* (1645), l. 100

115 Come, and trip it as you go
On the light fantastic toe.

"L'Allegro," *Poems of Mr. John Milton* (1645), ll. 33–34

116 Mirth, admit me of thy crew
To live with her, and live with thee,
In unreproved pleasures free.

"L'Allegro," *Poems of Mr. John Milton* (1645), ll. 38–40

117 The melting voice through mazes running;
Untwisting all the chains that tie
The hidden soul of harmony.

"L'Allegro," *Poems of Mr. John Milton* (1645), ll. 142–144

118 As killing as the canker to the rose.

1638. "Lycidas," *Poems of Mr. John Milton* (1645), l. 45

119 Yet once more, O ye laurels, and once more
Ye myrtles brown, with ivy never sere,
I come to pluck your berries harsh and crude,
And with forced fingers rude,
Shatter your leaves before the mellowing year.

1638. "Lycidas," *Poems of Mr. John Milton* (1645), ll. 1–5

120 But O the heavy change, now thou art gone,
Now thou art gone, and never must return!

1638. "Lycidas," *Poems of Mr. John Milton* (1645), ll. 37–38

121 Thee Shepherd, thee the woods, and desert caves,
With wild thyme and the gadding vine o'ergrown,
And all their echoes mourn.

1638. "Lycidas," *Poems of Mr. John Milton* (1645), ll. 39–40

122 Were it not better done as others use,
To sport with Amaryllis in the shade,
Or with the tangles of Neaera's hair?

1638. Better than to "meditate the thankless muse." "Lycidas," *Poems of Mr. John Milton* (1645), ll. 68–69

123 Fame is the spur that the clear spirit doth raise
(That last infirmity of noble mind)
To scorn delights, and live laborious days.

1638. "Lycidas," *Poems of Mr. John Milton* (1645), ll. 70–72

124 At last he rose, and twitched his mantle blue:
Tomorrow to fresh woods, and pastures new.

1638. "Lycidas," *Poems of Mr. John Milton* (1645), ll. 192–193

125 How soon hath time the subtle thief of youth,
Stol'n on his wing my three and twentieth year!

Sonnet 7, *Poems of Mr. John Milton* (1645), ll. 1–2

126 It is not miserable to be blind; it is miserable to be incapable of enduring blindness.

Second Defence (1654)

127 Truth...never comes into the world but like a bastard, to the ignominy of him that brought her forth.

Introduction, *The Doctrine and Discipline of Divorce* (1643)

128 No man who knows aught, can be so stupid to deny that all men naturally were born free.

The Tenure of Kings and Magistrates (1649)

129 None can love freedom heartily, but good men; the rest love not freedom, but licence.

The Tenure of Kings and Magistrates (1649)

130 The power of kings and magistrates is nothing else, but what only is derivative, transformed and committed to them in trust from the people to the common good of them all, in whom the power yet remains fundamentally, and cannot be taken from them, without a violation of their natural birthright.

The Tenure of Kings and Magistrates (1649)

131 Why, in truth, should I not bear gently the deprivation of sight, when I may hope that it is not so much lost as revoked and retracted inwards, for the sharpening rather than the blunting of my mental edge?

Attrib.

132 One tongue is sufficient for a woman.

On being asked whether he would allow his daughters to learn foreign languages. Attrib.

Mingus, Charles (1922–79) U.S. jazz musician

1 Now, Mingus, here's how to save yourself from depending on what rich punks think and critics say about jazz, true jazz, your work...A good jazz musician has got to turn to pimpdom to be free and keep his soul straight.
Quoting Billy Bones, a wealthy black pimp. *Beneath the Underdog* (1971), ch. 29

2 I could always hypnotize people. Even when I lost sight of God, I could hypnotize with music.
Beneath the Underdog (1971), ch. 30

3 On the third day at Belle Vue I was sitting in the gymnasium writing a song called "All The Things You Could Be If Sigmund Freud's Wife Was Your Mother," which I later recorded.
Referring to his period of psychiatric treatment in New York's Bellevue Hospital. *Beneath the Underdog* (1971), ch. 36

4 You had your Shakespeare and Marx and Freud and Einstein and Jesus Christ and Guy Lombardo but we came up with *jazz*...and all the pop music in the world today is from that primary cause.
Beneath the Underdog (1971), ch. 38

5 Anger is an emotion that has some hope in it.
Beneath the Underdog (1971)

Minnelli, Liza (b.1946) U.S. singer, dancer, and actor

1 Reality is something you rise above.
Attrib.

Minogue, Kylie (b.1968) Australian actor and pop singer

1 I prefer it this way, instead of people leaning out of car windows and shouting obscenities at you.
Referring to her move out of the public eye. *The Face* (1994)

Mintzberg, Henry (b.1939) Canadian management writer

1 "Professional management" is the great invention of this century, an invention that produced gains in organizational *efficiency* so great that it eventually destroyed organizational *effectiveness*.
Mintzberg on Management (1989)

2 There is no science in managerial work. Managers work essentially as they always have—with verbal information and intuitive (nonexplicit) processes.
The Nature of Managerial Work (1973), ch. 1

3 Someone once defined the manager, only half in jest, as that person who sees the visitors so that everyone else can get the work done.
The Structure of Organizations (1979), ch. 2

Minucius Felix, Marcus (?–250?) Roman writer

1 To venerate an executed criminal and the gallows, the wooden cross on which he was executed, is to erect altars which befit lost and depraved wretches.
3rd century. Said by a pagan character, referring to Jesus Christ. This quotation comes from a dialogue written by Minucius, known as *Octavius*, in which a Christian defends his religion against the charges made by the pagan. Quoted in *The Early Christians* (Eberhard Arnold; 1970)

Mirabeau, Comte de (Honoré Gabriel Riqueti; 1749–91) French revolutionary statesman

1 No National Assembly ever threatened to be so stormy as that which will decide the fate of the monarchy, and which is gathering in such haste, and with so much distrust on both sides.
Remark (December 6, 1788)

Mirman, Sophie (b.1956) British business executive

1 I don't think women are embarrassed to talk about money. I just don't think they measure achievement and success in personal financial terms. The pleasure is in the success of the business rather than the financial reward.
Times, London (March 9, 1987)

Miró, Joan (1893–1983) Spanish painter

1 After the contemporary liberation of the arts we will see artists under no flag emerge with the strings of their spirits vibrating to different kinds of music.
Letter to J. F. Ràfols (September 13, 1917)

2 We cannot use Impressionism when we paint a huge street in New York, nor can we use Futurism when we paint a beautiful woman who is before us. May our brush keep time with our vibrations.
Letter to J. F. Ràfols (September 13, 1917)

3 There is always an aristocracy in art.
Letter to Michel Leiris (August 10, 1924)

4 To look nature in the face and *dominate it* is enormously attractive and exciting. It's as though by the strength of your eyes you bring down a panther at your feet in the middle of the jungle.
Letter to Pierre Matisse (February 12, 1937)

5 Courage consists of staying at home, close to nature, which could not care less about our disasters.
Interview, *Cahiers D'Art*, Paris (1936)

6 Poetry and painting are done in the same way you make love; it's an exchange of blood, a total embrace—without caution, without any thought of protecting yourself.
Interview, *Cahiers D'Art*, Paris (1936)

7 You don't gain even a centimeter of freedom from art that's governed by cold formulas. You only get your freedom by sweating for it, by an inner struggle.
Interview, *Correo Literario*, Barcelona (March 15, 1951)

8 The simpler the alphabet, the easier it is to read.
Interview, *El País*, Madrid (June 18, 1978)

9 As far as the passionate spirit is concerned, it will always be easier for me to understand the man who kills three people because somebody's touched a hair of his wife's head than it will be to understand a French ménage à trois.
Interview, *La Publicitat*, Barcelona (July 14, 1928)

10 A form is never something abstract; it is always a sign of something. It is always a man, a bird, or something else...painting is never form for form's sake.
Interview, *Partisan Review*, New York (February 1948)

11 We Catalans believe you must always plant your feet firmly on the ground if you want to be able to jump up in the air. The fact that I come down to earth from time to time makes it possible for me to jump all the higher.
Interview, *Partisan Review*, New York (February 1948)

12 I work like a gardener or a wine grower. Everything takes time. My vocabulary of forms, for example, did not come to me all at once. It formulated itself almost in spite of me.
Interview, *XXe Siècle*, Paris (February 15, 1959)

Mirren, Helen (Helen Lydia Mironoff; b.1945) British actor

1 You come into the world alone, you go out alone. In between it's nice to know a few people, but being alone is a fundamental quality of human life, depressing as that is.
Remark (January 1989)

2 The part never calls for it. And I've never ever used that excuse. The box office calls for it.
Referring to nudity. *Observer*, London (March 27, 1994), "Sayings of the Week"

Mistral, Gabriela (Lucila Godoy de Alcayaga; 1889–1957) Spanish poet, diplomat, and educator

1 He kissed me and now I am someone else.
"He Kissed Me," *Desolación* (1922)

2 My grief and my smile begin in your face, my son.
"Poem of the Son," *Desolación* (1922)

3 I have all that I lost
and I go carrying my childhood
like a favorite flower
that perfumes my hand.
"We Were All to be Queens," *Tala* (1938)

4 Of the enemies of the soul—
the world, the devil, the flesh—
the *world* is the most serious and most dangerous.
"We Were All to be Queens," *Tala* (1938)

5 All these are yours, baby born of woman,
if you'll only go to sleep.
"If You'll Only Go to Sleep," *Tenura* (1924)

6 I will leave behind me the dark ravine, and climb up gentler slopes toward that spiritual mesa where at last a wide light will fall upon my days.
Quoted in *Selected Poems of Gabriela Mistral* (Doris Dana, ed., tr.; 1971)

Mitchell, Adrian (b.1932) British poet and playwright

1 I want to be a movement
But there's no one on my side.
"Loose Leaf Poem" (1971)

2 England, unlike junior nations,
Wears officers' long combinations.
So no embarrassment was felt
By the Church, the Government or the Crown.
But I saw the Thames like a dirty old belt
And England's trousers falling down.
1964. Referring to the Suez Crisis (1956). "Remember Suez?," *Adrian Mitchell's Greatest Hits* (1991)

3 Some say corn liquor done it
Or ruttin' a bad whore
But I guess he blew so much out
He couldn't think no more.
Referring to the collapse into insanity of jazz trumpeter Buddy Bolden. "Buddy Bolden," *Poems* (1964)

Mitchell, Alexander British psychiatrist

1 Putting a label on a patient can invalidate the patient—"You are an invalid, and what you say is therefore invalid. You are sick because your label says so."
"What's on Your Label?," *Mind and Mental Health Magazine* (1973)

Mitchell, George (b.1933) U.S. politician and peace negotiator

1 Peace, political stability, and reconciliation are not too much to ask for. They are the minimum that a decent society provides.
Referring to Northern Ireland. *Irish Post*, Dublin (April 18, 1998)

Mitchell, Joan (1926–92) U.S. painter

1 Abstract is not a style...This is just a use of space and form: it's an ambivalence of forms and space.
Quoted in "Conversations with Joan Mitchell," *Joan Mitchell: New Paintings* (Yves Michaud; 1986)

Mitchell, John (1815–75) Irish writer and nationalist

1 An exile in my circumstances is a branch cut from its tree; it is dead but it has an affectation of life.
Jail Journal (1854)

Mitchell, Joni (b.1943) Canadian singer and songwriter

1 Abstract Expressionism was invented by New York drunks.
BBC television program (1985)

2 They paved Paradise,
Put up a parking lot.
Song lyric. "Big Yellow Taxi" (1970)

3 I've looked at life from both sides now
From win and lose and still somehow
It's life's illusions I recall
I really don't know life at all.
Song. "Both Sides Now" (1967)

4 It's a mystery, the creative process, inspiration is a mystery, but I think that as long as you still have questions the muse has got to be there. You throw a question out to the muses and maybe they drop something back on you.
Maclean's (June 1974)

5 To see teenagers sitting around trying to solve the problems of the world, I figured, all things considered, I'd rather be dancing.
Quoted in "Joni Mitchell," *Off the Record: An Oral History of Popular Music* (Joe Smith; 1988)

6 A good piece of art should be androgynous.
Attrib.

7 I'm not a feminist. That's too divisional for me.
Attrib.

Mitchell, Julian (b.1935) British writer and playwright

1 It has been said that a careful reading of *Anna Karenina*, if it teaches you nothing else, will teach you how to make strawberry jam.
Radio Times, London (October 30, 1976)

Mitchell, Liz U.S. wife of the baseball player Paul Mitchell

1 You've got to time your babies for the off-season and get married in the off-season and get divorced in the off-season. Baseball always comes first.
Quoted in *High and Inside: Memoirs of a Baseball Wife* (Danielle Gagnon Torrez; 1983)

Mitchell, Margaret (1900–49) U.S. novelist

1 Gone with the Wind
1936. Book title from the poem "Non Sum Qualis Eram" by Ernest Dowson (1896): "I have forgotten much, Cynara! gone with the wind..."

2 Here in north Georgia, a lack of the niceties of classical education carried no shame, provided a man was smart in the things that mattered. And raising good cotton, riding well, shooting straight, dancing lightly, squiring the ladies with elegance and carrying one's liquor like a gentleman were the things that mattered.
Gone with the Wind (1936), ch. 1

3 Until you've lost your reputation, you never realize what a burden it was or what freedom really is.
Said by Rhett Butler. *Gone with the Wind* (1936), ch. 9

4 Any fool can be brave on a battle field when it's be brave or else be killed.
Gone with the Wind (1936), ch. 31

5 Fighting is like champagne. It goes to the heads of cowards as quickly as of heroes.
Said by Ashley Wilkes. *Gone with the Wind* (1936), ch. 31

6 The town was roaring—wide open like a frontier village, making no effort to cover its vices and sins. Saloons blossomed overnight...Gambling houses ran full blast...Respectable citizens were scandalized to find Atlanta had a large and thriving red-light district.
Referring to Atlanta in the immediate post-Civil War, Reconstruction era. *Gone with the Wind* (1936), ch. 37

7 Death and taxes and childbirth! There's never any convenient time for any of them!
Gone with the Wind (1936), ch. 38

8 After all, tomorrow is another day.
The closing words of the book. *Gone with the Wind* (1936), ch. 63

9 The people who settled in the town called successively Terminus, Marthasville, and Atlanta were a pushy people. Restless, energetic people...drawn to this town that sprawled around the junction of the railroads at its center.
Referring to Atlanta in the immediate post-Civil War, Reconstruction era. *Gone with the Wind* (1936), pt. 2, ch. 8

10 Savannah and Charleston had the dignity of their years...they had always seemed like aged grandmothers fanning themselves placidly in the sun. But Atlanta was of her own generation, crude with the crudities of youth and as headstrong and impetuous as herself.
Referring to Scarlett O'Hara. *Gone with the Wind* (1936), pt. 2, ch. 8

11 The usual masculine disillusionment is discovering that a woman has a brain.
Gone with the Wind (1936), pt. 4, ch. 36

12 Frankly, my dear, I don't give a damn.
Rhett Butler to Scarlett O'Hara. *Gone with the Wind*, screen version (Sidney Howard; 1939)

Mitchell, S. Weir (Silas Weir Mitchell; 1829–1914) U.S. physician and writer

1 The moral world of the sick-bed explains in a measure some of the things that are strange in daily life, and the man who does not know sick women does not know women.
Introduction, *Doctor and Patient* (1887)

Mitchum, Robert (1917–97) U.S. film actor

1 What's history going to say about the movies? All those rows of seats facing a blank screen? Crazy!
Attrib.

Mitford, Jessica (Jessica Lucy Mitford; 1917–96) British writer

1 I have nothing against undertakers personally. It's just that I wouldn't want one to bury my sister.
Saturday Review (February 1, 1964)

Mitford, Mary Russell (1787–1855) British writer

1 A sick man is as wayward as a child.
Julian (1823, 2nd ed.), Act 1, Scene 1

Mitford, Nancy (Nancy Freeman Mitford; 1904–73) British writer

1 "Twenty-three and a quarter minutes past," Uncle Matthew was saying furiously, "in precisely six and three-quarter minutes the damned fella will be late."
Love in a Cold Climate (1949), pt. 1, ch.13

2 An aristocracy in a republic is like a chicken whose head has been cut off: it may run about in a lively way, but in fact it is dead.
Noblesse Oblige (1956)

3 I have only read one book in my life and that is *White Fang*.
The Pursuit Of Love (1945)

4 Like all the very young we took it for granted that making love is child's play.
The Pursuit Of Love (1945), ch. 3

5 Abroad is unutterably bloody and foreigners are fiends.
The Pursuit Of Love (1945), ch. 15

6 English women are elegant until they are ten years old, and perfect on grand occasions.
Quoted in *The Wit of Women* (Lore and Maurice Cowan; 1969)

7 I love children—especially when they cry, for then someone takes them away.
Attrib.

Mitford, William (1744–1827) British historian

1 Men fear death as if unquestionably the greatest evil, and yet no man knows that it may not be the greatest good.
Attrib.

Mitterrand, François (François Maurice Marie Mitterrand; 1916–96) French president

1 Government obliges it: absolute power has its reasons that the Republic does not know of.
Le Coup d'état permanent (1964), pt. 3

2 Nothing is won forever in human affairs, but everything is always possible.
Observer, London (June 12, 1994), "Sayings of the Week"

Miyake, Issey (b.1938) Japanese fashion designer

1 I want women to be able to wear my clothes in the kitchen, when they're pregnant. My clothes are for the young, the old, the short, the tall. They're ageless.
Guardian, London (July 19, 1997)

2 Design is not a philosophy—it's for life.
Attrib.

Mizner, Addison (1872–1933) U.S. architect

1 Where there's a will, there's a lawsuit.
Pun on the saying, "Where there's a will, there's a way." Attrib.

Mizner, Wilson (1876–1933) U.S. playwright

1 A trip through a sewer in a glass-bottomed boat.
Referring to Hollywood. Quoted in *The Incredible Mizners* (Rupert Hart-Davis; 1953)

2 When you steal from one author, it's plagiarism; if you steal from many, it's research.
Quoted in *The Legendary Mizners* (Alva Johnston; 1953)

3 Be nice to people on your way up because you'll meet 'em on your way down.
1920? Also attributed to Jimmy Durante. Quoted in *The Legendary Mizners* (Alva Johnston; 1953)

4 A drama critic is a person who surprises the playwright by informing him what he meant.
Attrib.

5 A good listener is not only popular everywhere, but, after a while, knows something.
Attrib.

6 Life's a tough proposition, and the first 100 years are the hardest.
Attrib.

7 Popularity is exhausting. The life of the party almost always winds up in a corner with an overcoat over him.
Attrib.

8 Some of the greatest love affairs I've known involved one actor—unassisted.
Attrib.

9 The only sure thing about luck is that it will change.
Attrib.

Mo, Timothy (Timothy Peter Mo; b.1950) Hong Kong-born British novelist

1 Their major commodity was...people. They exported people—domestic servants to Kuwait, prostitutes to Japan and Lagos, nurses to Dubai, tailors to Jeddah, construction workers to Iraq.
Referring to the economy of the Philippines. *Brownout on Breadfruit Boulevard* (1995), ch. 1

2 The country was on the slide, in the mire, had teetered on the brink of the crater so long no one suffered from vertigo any more. They were a nation as blasé as steeplejacks and as irresponsible as crows.
Referring to the Philippines. *Brownout on Breadfruit Boulevard* (1995), ch. 1

Modayil, Anna Sujartha (b.1934) Indian poet

1 The sun has only memory of flame
and for centuries has watched
the earth dance like a clown
upon one foot,
someday it will drop and die,
laughing laughing madly.
"On the Beach at Baga," *The Voice of the Indian Poets* (Pranab Bandyopadhyay, ed.; 1975)

2 Life is a kind doctor who gives us death
in small daily doses
so that when at last, we drink
death's dark wine,
we have already tasted its bitterness.
"Stones," *The Voice of the Indian Poets* (Pranab Bandyopadhyay, ed.; 1975)

Modersohn-Becker, Paula (originally Paula Becker; 1876–1907) German painter

1 There is no need to be too much concerned with nature in painting. The color sketch should exactly reflect something you have felt in nature. But personal feeling is the main thing.
1902. Quoted in "Paula Modersohn-Becker: Struggle between Life and Art," *Feminist Art Journal* (Martha Davidson; Winter 1973–74)

Modigliani, Franco (b.1918) Italian-born U.S. economist

1 On money: Save it when you need it least. Spend it when you need it most.
Attrib.

Mohamad, Mahathir bin (Datuk Seri Mahathir bin Mohamad; b.1925) Malaysian prime minister

1 It is only natural that old people would have to go, but the problem is that there is a young man who is too impatient to wait for me.
Complaining about his chief political rival, "young" Tengku Razaleigh. *Straits Times*, Singapore (October 6, 1990)

2 All meritocracies are limited.
Referring to advancement in Malaysia being based on race rather than ability. *Straits Times*, Singapore (June 9, 1996)

3 It's no use if we win the applause but lose the fight.
Referring to concentrating on economic growth over other political concerns. *Straits Times*, Singapore (September 1, 1990)

4 We no longer choose people who are qualified and capable in terms of party leadership calibre. We choose people who offer us money or gifts or other things.
He cut off public sector trade with Britain, accusing the press of spreading lies about political corruption in Malaysia. *Times*, London (June 20, 1994)

Mola, Emilio (Emilio Mola Vidal; 1887–1937) Spanish general

1 We shall raze Bilbao to the ground and its bare desolate site will remove the British desire to support Basque Bolsheviks against our will.
Referring to the Nationalist-supported German bombing of the Basque town Guernica. Remark (1937), quoted in *Franco* (Paul Preston; 1993)

2 The Fifth Column.
Reply when asked which of four Nationalist armies would capture Madrid; Mola was referring to Nationalist elements within the city. Speech (October 1936), quoted in *The Spanish Civil War* (Hugh Thomas; 1961), ch. 4

Molière (Jean-Baptiste Poquelin; 1622–73) French playwright

Quotations about Molière

1 He pleases all the world, but cannot please himself.
Nicolas Boileau (1636–1711) French poet and critic. *Satires* (1666)

Quotations by Molière

2 Birth counts for nothing where virtue is absent.
Don Juan (1665), Act 4, Scene 6

3 I shouldn't be surprised if the greatest rule of all weren't to give pleasure.
La Critique de L'école des femmes (1663), Scene 7

4 All the disasters of mankind, all the fatal misfortunes that histories are so full of, the blunders of politicians, the miscarriages of great commanders, all this comes from want of skill in dancing.
Le Bourgeois gentilhomme (1670), Act 1, Scene 2

5 All that is not prose is verse; and all that is not verse is prose.
Le Bourgeois gentilhomme (1670), Act 2, Scene 4

6 Good heavens! I have been talking prose for over forty years without realizing it.
Le Bourgeois gentilhomme (1670), Act 2, Scene 4

7 One dies only once, and it's for such a long time.
Le Dépit amoureux (1656), Act 5, Scene 3

8 He must have killed a lot of men to have made so much money.
Le Malade imaginaire (1673), Act 1, Scene 5

9 Most men die of their remedies, and not of their illnesses.
Le Malade imaginaire (1673), Act 3, Scene 3

10 GERONTE There was just one thing which surprised me—that was the positions of the liver and the heart. It seemed to me that you got them the wrong way about, that the heart should be on the left side, and the liver on the right.
SGANARELLE Yes, it used to be so but we have changed all that. Everything's quite different in medicine nowadays.
Le Médecin malgré lui (1667), Act 2, Scene 4

11 The mind has great influence over the body, and maladies often have their origin there.
Le Médecin malgré lui (1667), Act 3

12 He who is the friend of all humanity is not my friend.
Le Misanthrope (1666), Act 1, Scene 1

13 It is a stupidity second to none, to busy oneself with the correction of the world.
Le Misanthrope (1666), Act 1, Scene 1

14 Age will bring all things, and everyone knows, Madame, that twenty is no age to be a prude.
Le Misanthrope (1666), Act 3, Scene 4

15 One should examine oneself for a very long time before thinking of condemning others.
Le Misanthrope (1666), Act 3, Scene 4

16 Grammar, which can govern even kings.
Les Femmes savantes (1672), Act 2, Scene 6

17 I live on good soup, not fine words.
Les Femmes savantes (1672), Act 2, Scene 7

18 Rags they may be, but I love my rags.
Les Femmes savantes (1672), Act 2, Scene 7

19 A knowledgeable fool is a greater fool than an ignorant fool.
Les Femmes savantes (1672), Act 4, Scene 3

20 An encomium in Greek has a marvelous effect on the title page of a book.
Les Précieuses ridicules (1659), preface

21 Improvisation is the touchstone of wit.
Les Précieuses ridicules (1659), Scene 10

22 Things only have the value that we give them.
Les Précieuses ridicules (1659), Scene 10

23 Here they hang a man first and then they try him.
Monsieur de Pourceaugnac (1670), Act 3, Scene 2

24 It is a public scandal that gives offense, and it is no sin to sin in secret.
Tartuffe (1664), Act 4, Scene 5

25 One should eat to live, and not live to eat.
The Miser (1668), Act 3, Scene 1

26 Our minds need relaxation, and give way,
Unless we mix with work, a little play.
Attrib.

27 The only good thing about him is his cook. The world visits his dinners, not him.
Attrib.

Molotov, Vyacheslav Mikhailovich (originally Vyacheslav Mikhailovich Skriabin; 1890–1986) Soviet statesman

1 That bastard of the Versailles treaty.
Referring to Poland. Attrib.

Moltke, Helmuth Johannes von, Graf von Moltke (Helmuth Johannes Ludwig; 1848–1916) German military commander

1 A European war must come sooner or later in which ultimately

the struggle will be one between Germany and Slavism...but the aggression must come from the Slavs.
Letter to Conrad von Hoetzendorff, chief of staff of the Austrian army (February 1913), quoted in *Europe Since 1870* (James Joll; 1973), ch. 7

2 Perpetual peace is a dream, and not even a beautiful dream. War is part of God's order...In it, man's most noble virtues are displayed.
Letter to Dr. J. K. Bluntschi (December 11, 1880), quoted in *Europe: A History* (Norman Davies; 1996)

3 Germany, when it mobilizes against Russia, must also reckon on a war with France.
Memorandum to Conrad von Hoetzendorff, chief of staff of the Austrian army (January 1909), quoted in *Germany, 1866–1945* (Gordon A. Craig; 1978)

4 If this war were to break out, no one could foresee how long it would last nor how it would end...woe to the man who...first throws the match into the powder keg.
Speech, Reichstag, Berlin (May 1890), quoted in *Europe: A History* (Norman Davies; 1996)

5 The moment Russia mobilizes, Germany will also mobilize.
1908. Said to Conrad von Hoetzendorff, chief of staff of the Austrian army, following the Austrian annexation of Bosnia and Herzegovina. Quoted in *Europe Since 1870* (James Joll; 1973), ch. 7

Molyneux, William (1656–98) Irish philosopher and politician

1 The rights of parliament should be preserved sacred and inviolable, wherever they are found. This kind of government, once so universal all over Europe, is now almost vanished from amongst the nations thereof. Our king's dominions are the only supporters of this noble Gothic constitution.
Pamphlet. *The Case of Ireland's being Bound by Acts of Parliament in England Stated* (1698)

Momaday, N. Scott (Navarre Scott Momaday; b.1934) Native American writer

1 Houses are like sentinels in the plain, old keepers of the weather watch...All colors wear soon away in the wind and rain, and then the wood is burned gray and the grain appears and the nails turn red with rust.
The Way to Rainy Mountain (1969), Introduction, quoted in *The Heath Anthology of American Literature* (Paul Lauter, ed.; 1998), vol. 2

2 Kiowas...abide the cold and keep to themselves, but when the season turns and the land becomes warm and vital they cannot hold still; an old love of going returns upon them.
The Way to Rainy Mountain (1969), Introduction, quoted in *The Heath Anthology of American Literature* (Paul Lauter, ed.; 1998), vol. 2

3 That most brilliant shower of Leonid meteors has a special place in the memory of the Kiowa people...The falling stars seemed to image the sudden and violent disintegration of an old order.
Referring to the meteor showers of 1833 as an omen of the Kiowa's 1837 treaty with the U.S. government. *The Way to Rainy Mountain* (1969), Introduction, quoted in *The Heath Anthology of American Literature* (Paul Lauter, ed.; 1998), vol. 2

4 The way to Rainy Mountain is preeminently the history of an idea, man's idea of himself...What remains is fragmentary: mythology, legend, lore, and hearsay—and of course the idea itself.
The Way to Rainy Mountain (1969), Prologue, quoted in *The Heath Anthology of American Literature* (Paul Lauter, ed.; 1998), vol. 2

5 The journey began one day long ago on the edge of the northern Plains. It was carried on over a course of many generations...In the end there were many things to remember, to dwell upon and talk about.
Referring to the origins of Kiowa culture. *The Way to Rainy Mountain* (1969), Prologue, quoted in *The Heath Anthology of American Literature* (Paul Lauter, ed.; 1998), vol. 2

Mondale, Walter (Walter Frederick Mondale; b.1928) U.S. vice president and lawyer

1 I don't want to spend the next two years in Holiday Inns.
Referring to his withdrawal from the 1976 presidential campaign. Press conference (November 21, 1974)

2 If you are sure you understand everything that is going on, you are hopelessly confused.
Attrib.

Mondeville, Henri de (1260?–1320?) French surgeon

1 Keep up the spirits of your patient with the music of the viol and the psaltery, or by forging letters telling of the death of his enemies or (if he be a cleric) by informing him that he has been made a bishop.
Quoted in *Bartlett's Unfamiliar Quotations* (Leonard Louis Levinson; 1972)

Mondlane, Eduardo Chivambo (1920–69) Mozambiquan politician and activist

1 War is an extreme of political action, which tends to bring about social change more rapidly than any other instrument.
The Struggle for Mozambique (1969)

Mondrian, Piet (Pieter Cornelis Mondriaan; 1872–1944) Dutch painter

1 Great masters of painting have emphasized the tension characterizing the contour...What I have in mind is the most extreme transformation of the tension of the line, until it finally becomes the absolutely straight line.
1937. "Plastic Art and Pure Plastic," *Modern Artists on Art: 10 Unabridged Essays* (L. Herbert, ed.; 1964)

Monet, Claude (Claude Oscar Monet; 1840–1926) French painter

1 Could they have a title for the catalog, it really couldn't pass for a view of Le Havre; I answered: "Put: 'Impression'." From this came Impressionism, and the jokes abounded.
The painting is probably *Impression: Sunrise* (1872)—now in the Musée Marmottan, Paris—which gave rise to the press's intended derisory term "Impressionism." Attrib.

Monk, Thelonious (Thelonious Sphere Monk; 1920–82) U.S. jazz composer and pianist

Quotations about Monk

1 With a name like that he was made from an early age—all he needed was a hustle.
Anonymous. Quoted in "Round About Monk," *Jazz People* (Valerie Wilmer; 1970), ch. 4

2 I acquired a strong affection for that prodding, unseductive piano style...Monk always seemed to me to play the piano like

a man who had only that day discovered the instrument.
Humphrey Lyttelton (b.1921) British jazz trumpeter. *Take It From the Top* (1975), pt. 3

3 "Bird believes in God, Mingus?" You know he does. Someday one of us put-down, outcast makers of jazz music should show those church-going clock-punchers that people like Monk and Bird are dying for what they believe.
Charles Mingus (1922–79) U.S. jazz musician. In conversation with jazz trumpeter Fats Navarro. Referring to Charlie "Bird" Parker and Thelonious Monk. *Beneath the Underdog* (1971), ch. 39

4 When asked to bring a new Monk tune to a particular recording session, he turned up with the hymn "Abide With Me," which, he blandly informed the assembled company, was written by one William H. Monk. It was recorded.
Valerie Wilmer (b.1941) British writer and photographer. "Round About Monk," *Jazz People* (1970), ch. 4

Quotations by Monk

5 I hit the piano with my elbow sometimes because of a certain sound I want to hear. You can't hit that many notes with your hands.
Quoted in "Round About Monk," *Jazz People* (Valerie Wilmer; 1970), ch. 4

Monmouth, James Scott, Duke of (1649–85) Dutch-born English pretender

1 Do not hack me as you did my Lord Russell.
Said to the headsman before his execution. Quoted in *History of England* (Macaulay; 1685), vol. 1, ch. 5

Monod, Jacques Lucien (1910–76) French biochemist

1 But the Universe exists, things must happen in it, all equally improbable, and man is one of these things.
Inaugural lecture on taking the chair of molecular biology, Collège de France (November 3, 1967)

2 There are living systems; there is no living "matter."
Inaugural lecture on taking the chair of molecular biology, Collège de France (November 3, 1967)

3 Man knows in the end that he is alone in the indifferent immensity of the Universe from which he has emerged by chance. Neither his destiny nor his duty is written down anywhere.
Le Hasard et la nécessité (1970)

Monroe, Harriet (1860–1936) U.S. poet and editor

1 Poetry, "The Cinderella of the Arts."
Quoted in "Harriet Monroe," *Famous American Women* (Hope Stoddard; 1970)

Monroe, James (1758–1831) U.S. president

1 The mention of Greece fills the mind with the most exalted sentiments and arouses in our bosoms the best feelings of which our nature is susceptible.
Message to Congress (December 1822)

2 The American continents, by the free and independent condition which they have assumed and maintain, are henceforth not to be considered as subjects for future colonization by any European powers...In the wars of the European powers in matters relating to themselves we have never taken any part, nor does it comport with our policy to do so.
A statement of principle that became a cornerstone of U.S. foreign policy. "The Monroe Doctrine" (December 2, 1823)

3 A little flattery will support a man through great fatigue.
Attrib.

Monroe, Marilyn (originally Norma Jean Mortenson, known as Norma Jean Baker; 1926–62) U.S. film actor

Quotations about Monroe

1 If she was a victim of any kind, she was a victim of her friends.
George Cukor (1899–1983) U.S. film director. Quoted in *On Cukor* (Gavin Lambert; 1972)

2 So we think of Marilyn who was every man's love affair with America, Marilyn Monroe who was blonde and beautiful and had a sweet little rinky-dink of a voice and all the cleanliness of all the clean American backyards.
Norman Mailer (b.1923) U.S. novelist and journalist. *Marilyn* (1973)

3 Why should I go? She won't be there.
1962
Arthur Miller (b.1915) U.S. playwright. Said when asked if he would attend Marilyn Monroe's funeral. Attrib.

4 Directing her was like directing Lassie. You needed fourteen takes to get each one of them right.
Otto Preminger (1906–86) Austrian-born U.S. film director and producer. Attrib.

5 It was like going to the dentist making a picture with her. It was hell at the time, but after it was all over, it was wonderful.
Billy Wilder (b.1906) Austrian-born U.S. film director and screenwriter. Quoted in *The Show Business Nobody Knows* (Earl Wilson; 1972)

Quotations by Monroe

6 Hollywood is a place where they'll pay you a thousand dollars for a kiss and fifty cents for your soul.
Quoted in "Acting," *Marilyn Monroe* (Guus Luijters; 1990)

7 A career is born in public—talent in privacy.
Attrib.

8 I don't want to make money. I just want to be wonderful.
Attrib.

9 I've been on a calendar, but never on time.
Attrib.

10 JOURNALIST Didn't you have anything on?
M. M. I had the radio on.
Attrib.

11 The trouble with censors is that they worry if a girl has cleavage. They ought to worry if she hasn't any.
Attrib.

Monsell, John (John Samuel Bewley Monsell; 1811–75) British hymnwriter

1 Fight the good fight with all thy might,
Christ is thy strength and Christ thy right,
Lay hold on life, and it shall be
Thy joy and crown eternally.
Hymn. "Fight the Good Fight with all thy Might" (1834)

Montagu, Ashley (Montague Francis Ashley Montagu; b.1905) British-born U.S. anthropologist

1 Science has proof without any certainty. Creationists have certainty without any proof.
Attrib.

Montagu, Elizabeth (originally Elizabeth Robinson; 1720–1800) English writer and literary hostess

Quotations about Montagu

1 Mrs Montagu has dropt me. Now, Sir, there are people whom one should like very well to drop, but would not wish to be dropped by.
Samuel Johnson (1709–84) British lexicographer and writer. Elizabeth Montagu, an essayist on Shakespeare, took issue with Johnson over his work, *Lives of the Poets*. Remark (March 1781), quoted in *Life of Samuel Johnson* (James Boswell; 1791)

Quotations by Montagu

2 If she (Catherine the Great) is not a good woman, she is a great Prince.
Letter to Lord Lyttleton (1739)

3 Wit in women is apt to have bad consequences; like a sword without a scabbard, it wounds the weaker and provokes assailants. I am sorry to say the generality of women who have excelled in wit have failed in chastity.
1750. Quoted in *Reconstructing Aphra* (Angeline Goreau; 1980)

Montagu, Mary Wortley, Lady (originally Mary Pierrepont; 1689–1762) British writer

1 A woman, till five-and-thirty, is only looked upon as a raw girl, and can possibly make no noise in the world till about forty.
Letter to Lady Rich (September 20, 1716)

2 The Small Pox so fatal and so general amongst us is here entirely harmless by the invention of engrafting...Every year thousands undergo this Operation, and the French Ambassador says pleasantly that they take the Small Pox here by way of diversion as they take the Waters in other Countrys.
Letter to Sarah Chiswell (1717)

3 Civility costs nothing and buys everything.
Letter to the Countess of Bute (May 30, 1756)

4 Satire should, like a polished razor keen,
Wound with a touch that's scarcely felt or seen.
Verses Addressed to the Imitator of the First Satire of the Second Book of Horace (1733), bk. 2

5 It was formerly a terrifying view to me that I should one day be an old woman. I now find that Nature has provided pleasures for every state.
Attrib.

Montague, C. E. (Charles Edward Montague; 1867–1928) British novelist and essayist

1 To be amused at what you read—that is the great spring of happy quotation.
A Writer's Notes on his Trade (1930)

2 War hath no fury like a non-combatant.
Disenchantment (1922), ch. 16

Montague, John (b.1929) U.S.-born Irish poet

1 The whole landscape a manuscript
We had lost the skill to read.
1972. "A Lost Tradition," *Collected Poems* (1995), ll. 16–17

2 Hinge of silence
creak for us
Rose of darkness
unfold for us
Wood anemone
sway for us.
1975. "For the Hillmother," *Collected Poems* (1995), ll. 1–6

3 Like dolmens round my childhood, the old people.
1972. "Like Dolmens Round My Childhood," *Collected Poems* (1995), l. 1

Montaigne, Michel de (Michel Eyquem de Montaigne; 1533–92) French essayist

1 If it be a short and violent death, we have no leisure to fear it; if otherwise, I perceive that according as I engage myself in sickness, I do naturally fall into some disdain and contempt of life.
Essays (1580–88)

2 It is good to rub and polish our brain against that of others.
Essays (1580–88), bk. 1

3 The daughter-in-law of Pythagoras said that a woman who goes to bed with a man ought to lay aside her modesty with her skirt, and put it on again with her petticoat.
Essays (1580–88), bk. 1

4 The greatest thing in the world is to know how to be self-sufficient.
Essays (1580–88), bk. 1

5 Unless a man feels he has a good enough memory, he should never venture to lie.
Essays (1580–88), bk. 1

6 He who would teach men to die would at the same time teach them to live.
Essays (1580–88), bk. 1, ch. 20

7 I want death to find me planting my cabbages, but caring little for it, and much more for my imperfect garden.
Essays (1580–88), bk. 1, ch. 20

8 A man should keep for himself a little back shop, all his own, quite unadulterated, in which he establishes his true freedom and chief place of seclusion and solitude.
Essays (1580–88), bk. 1, ch. 39

9 Fame and tranquility can never be bedfellows.
Essays (1580–88), bk. 1, ch. 39

10 Health is a precious thing, and the only one, in truth, which deserves that we employ in its pursuit not only time, sweat, trouble, and worldly goods, but even life...As far as I am concerned, no road that would lead us to health is either arduous or expensive.
Essays (1580–88), bk. 2

11 When I play with my cat, who knows whether she is not amusing herself with me more than I with her?
Essays (1580–88), bk. 2

12 Living is my job and my art.
Essays (1580–88), bk.2, ch. 6

13 Arts and sciences are not cast in a mold, but are formed and perfected by degrees, by often handling and polishing, as bears leisurely lick their cubs into form.
Essays (1580–88), bk. 2, ch. 12

14 Man is quite insane. He wouldn't know how to create a maggot and he creates Gods by the dozen.
Essays (1580–88), bk. 2, ch. 12

15 Those who have likened our life to a dream were more right, by chance, than they realized. We are awake while sleeping, and waking sleep.
Essays (1580–88), bk. 2, ch. 12

16 What do I know?
Essays (1580–88), bk. 2, ch. 12

17 One may be humble out of pride.
Essays (1580–88), bk. 2, ch. 17

18 Nature forms us for ourselves, not for others; to be, not to seem.
Essays (1580–88), bk.2, ch. 37

19 A man who fears suffering is already suffering from what he fears.
Essays (1580–88), bk. 3

20 Marriage is like a cage; one sees the birds outside desperate to get in, and those inside equally desperate to get out.
Essays (1580–88), bk. 3

21 Poverty of goods is easily cured; poverty of soul, impossible.
Essays (1580–88), bk. 3

22 The world is but a school of inquiry.
Essays (1580–88), bk. 3

23 Many a man has been a wonder to the world, whose wife and valet have seen nothing in him that was even remarkable. Few men have been admired by their servants.
Essays (1580–88), bk. 3, ch. 2

24 It could be said of me that in this book I have only made up a bunch of other men's flowers, providing of my own only the string that ties them together.
Essays (1580–88), bk. 3, ch. 7

25 The oldest and best known evil was ever more supportable than one that was new and untried.
Essays (1580–88), bk. 3, ch. 9

26 There is no man so good, who, were he to submit all his thoughts and actions to the laws, would not deserve hanging ten times in his life.
Essays (1580–88), bk. 3, ch. 9

27 Every man carries the entire form of human condition.
"Of Repentance," *Essays* (1580–88), bk. 3, ch. 2

28 Old age puts more wrinkles in our minds than on our faces.
"Of Repentance," *Essays* (1580–88), bk. 3, ch. 2

29 For myself, I have not been able without distress to see pursued and killed an innocent animal which is defenseless and which does us no harm.
"On Cruelty," *Essays* (1580–88)

30 For a desperate disease a desperate cure.
"The Custom of the Isle of Cea," *Essays* (1580–88), bk. 2, ch. 3

31 It is quite unnecessary for me to bend and bow my reason, for that my knees will suffice.
Quoted in *The Jingle Bell Principle* (Miroslav Holub; 1992)

32 We are more sensible of one little touch of a surgeon's lancet than of twenty wounds with a sword in the heat of fight.
Attrib.

Montale, Eugenio (1896–1981) Italian poet

1 Too many lives are needed just to make one.
Le Occasioni (1939)

2 Man cannot produce a single work without the assistance of the slow, assiduous, corrosive worm of thought.
Poet in Our Time (1972)

3 The most dangerous aspect of present-day life is the dissolution of the feeling of individual responsibility. Mass solitude has done away with any difference between the internal and external, between the intellectual and the physical.
Poet in Our Time (1972)

4 The new man is born too old to tolerate the new world...He looks but he does not contemplate, he sees but he does not think. He runs away from time, which is made of thought, and yet all he can feel is his own time, the present.
Poet in Our Time (1972)

5 Holidays
Have no pity.
"Eastbourne," *Selected Poems* (G. S. Fraser, tr.; 1965)

Montalvo, Juan (1832–89) Ecuadorian writer

1 Old age is an island surrounded by death.
Attrib.

Montand, Yves (Ivo Livi; 1921–91) Italian-born French actor and singer

1 God, why didn't you make women first—when you were fresh?
Attrib.

Montanus (*fl.* 2nd century) Phrygian prophet and religious leader

1 When we call this a case of Melancholia, we understand that it is an affection of the brain; it is the brain then that is at fault, but to what is it due?
Consultationes medicae (200?)

Montefiore, Hugh (Hugh William Montefiore; b.1920) British bishop and author

1 Why did He not marry? Could the answer be that Jesus was not by nature the marrying sort?
Remark at a conference, Oxford (July 26, 1967)

Montejo, Esteban (1860–1968?) Cuban African slave

1 If you want my opinion, it's best not to die, because a few days later no one remembers you, not even your closest friends.
The Autobiography of a Runaway Slave (1968)

Monterroso, Augusto (b.1921) Guatemalan-born Mexican writer

1 History never stops. It progresses ceaselessly day and night. Trying to stop it is like trying to stop Geography.
"Aforismos, dichos, etc.," *The Rest is Silence* (1978)

Montesquieu, Baron de la Brède et de (Charles Louis de Secondat Montesquieu; 1689–1755) French writer and jurist

Quotations about Montesquieu

1 I am but a crow strutting about in peacock feathers. If I were Pope I would certainly canonize Montesquieu, and that without listening to a devil's advocate.
Catherine the Great (1729–96) German-born Russian empress. Referring to her admiration for Montesquieu's Enlightenment philosophy, which demanded that a ruler favor reason over passion. She felt that this embodied her governing style, contrary to her public image. It is said that Montesquieu's *The Spirit of Laws* (1748) became her prayer book. Letter to King Frederick II of Prussia (1767)

Quotations by Montesquieu

2 An empire founded by war has to maintain itself by war.
Considérations sur les causes de la grandeur des Romains et de leur décadence (1734), ch. 8

3 A really intelligent man feels what other men only know.
Essai sur les causes qui peuvent affecter les esprits et les caractères (1736)

4 Liberty is the right to do everything which the laws allow.
L'Esprit des lois (1748)

5 There is a very good saying that if triangles invented a god, they would make him three-sided.
Lettres persanes (1721)

6 No kingdom has ever had as many civil wars as the kingdom of Christ.
Lettres persanes (1721), no. 29

7 I suffer from the disease of writing and being ashamed of them when they are finished.
Pensées et fragments inédits (1899)

8 Great lords have their pleasures, but the people have fun.
Pensées et fragments inédits (1899), vol. 2, no. 992

9 The English are busy; they don't have time to be polite.
Pensées et fragments inédits (1899), vol. 2, no. 1428

10 The English kill themselves without any apparent reason for doing so; they kill themselves in the very lap of happiness.
Quoted in *Madness and Civilization* (Michel Foucault; 1960)

11 If one only wished to be happy, this could be easily accomplished; but we wish to be happier than other people, and this is always difficult, for we believe others to be happier than they are.
Attrib.

12 Lunch kills half of Paris, supper the other half.
Attrib.

13 What orators lack in depth they make up to you in length.
Attrib.

Montessori, Maria (1870–1952) Italian doctor and educator

1 And if education is always to be conceived along the same antiquated lines of a mere transmission of knowledge, there is little to be hoped from it in the bettering of man's future. For what is the use of transmitting knowledge if the individual's total development lags behind?
The Absorbent Mind (1949)

2 We teachers can only help the work going on, as servants wait upon a master.
The Absorbent Mind (1949)

3 The task of the educator of young children lies in seeing that the child does not confound good with immobility, and evil with activity.
Attrib.

Montgomery, James (1771–1854) Scottish poet and hymnwriter

1 Friend after friend departs;
Who hath not lost a friend?
There is no union here of hearts
That finds not here an end.
"Friends" (1824)

2 Hope against hope, and ask till ye receive.
"The World Before the Flood," *The Poetical Works of James Montgomery* (1840–41), can. 5

Montgomery, L. M. (Lucy Maud Montgomery; 1874–1942) Canadian writer

1 The point of good writing is knowing when to stop.
Anne's House of Dreams (1917), ch. 24

Montgomery, Robert (1807–55) British clergyman and poet

1 Home, the spot of earth supremely blest,
A dearer, sweeter spot than all the rest.
Attrib.

Montgomery of Alamein, Sir Bernard Law, 1st Viscount Montgomery of Alamein (1887–1976) British field marshal

1 The U.S. has broken the second rule of war. That is, don't go fighting with your land army on the mainland of Asia. Rule One is don't march on Moscow. I developed these two rules myself.
Referring to American policy in Vietnam. Speech to the House of Lords (the upper house of the British Parliament), quoted in *Hansard* (May 30, 1962)

2 This sort of thing may be tolerated by the French, but we are British—thank God.
Comment on a bill to relax the laws against homosexuals. Speech, *Daily Mail*, London (May 27, 1965)

Montherlant, Henri de (Henri Marie Joseph Millon de

Montherlant; 1896–1972) French novelist and playwright

1 To publish a book is to talk at the dinner table in front of the servants.
Carnets 1930–1944 (1957)

2 A lot of people, on the verge of death, utter famous last words or stiffen into attitudes...they still want to arouse admiration and adopt a pose and tell a lie with their last gasp.
Explicit Mysterium (1931)

3 It's when the thing itself is missing that you have to supply the word.
La Reine morte (1942), Act 2, Scene 1

4 Most affections are habits or duties we lack the courage to end.
La Reine morte (1942), Act 2, Scene 3

5 Noble values, in the end, are always overcome; history tells the story of their defeat over and over again.
Le Maître de Santiago (1947)

6 Colonies are made to be lost.
Le Maître de Santiago (1947), Act 1, Scene 4

7 Great ideas are not charitable.
Le Maître de Santiago (1947), Act 1, Scene 4

8 There is only one way to be prepared for death: to be sated. In the soul, in the heart, in the spirit, in the flesh. To the brim.
Mors et vita (1932)

9 Stupidity does not consist in being without ideas. Such stupidity would be the sweet, blissful stupidity of animals, mollusks, and the gods. Human Stupidity consists in having lots of ideas, but stupid ones.
Notebooks (1930–44)

Montpensier, Duchesse de (Anne Marie Louise d'Orléans, "la Grande Mademoiselle"; 1627–93) French aristocrat

1 I paid a visit of condolence to the Queen of England. Her husband had been beheaded by order of the British parliament. The court did not go into general mourning on this occasion, for want of funds. I found her not so deeply affected as she should have been.
Referring to the French court. *Mémoires* (February 1649)

Montrose, James Graham, 5th Earl and 1st Marquess of Montrose (1612–50) Scottish royalist general and poet

1 Let them bestow on every airth a limb;
Then open all my veins, that I may swim
To thee, my Maker! in that crimson lake;
Then place my parboiled head upon a stake—
Scatter my ashes—strew them in the air;—
Lord! since thou know'st where all these atoms are,
I'm hopeful thou'lt recover once my dust,
And confident thou'lt raise me with the just.
"Lines Written on the Window of His Jail the Night Before His Execution" (1650)

2 He either fears his fate too much,
Or his deserts are small,
That puts it not unto the touch
To win or lose it all.
"My Dear and Only Love" (1642)

3 I'll make thee glorious by my pen,
And famous by my sword.
"My Dear and Only Love" (1642)

Montrose, Percy (*fl.* 19th century) U.S. songwriter

1 But I kissed her little sister,
And forgot my Clementine.
Song lyric. "Clementine" (1884)

2 In a cavern, in a canyon,
Excavating for a mine
Dwelt a miner, Forty-niner,
And his daughter, Clementine.
Oh, my darling, Oh, my darling, Oh, my darling Clementine!
Thou art lost and gone for ever, dreadful sorry, Clementine.
Song lyric. "Clementine" (1884)

Monty Python's Flying Circus British television series

1 Of course, we had it tough. We used to have to get out of our shoebox at 12 o'clock at night, and lick road clean with tongue.
Monty Python's Flying Circus (co-written by John Cleese, Michael Palin, Eric Idle, Graham Chapman, Terry Jones and Terry Gilliam; 1969–74)

2 And now for something completely different.
Catchphrase. *Monty Python's Flying Circus* (co-written by John Cleese, Michael Palin, Eric Idle, Graham Chapman, Terry Jones and Terry Gilliam; 1969–74)

3 Nudge, nudge, wink, wink. Know what I mean? Say no more!
Catchphrase. *Monty Python's Flying Circus* (co-written by John Cleese, Michael Palin, Eric Idle, Graham Chapman, Terry Jones and Terry Gilliam; 1969–74)

4 Spam, spam, lovely spam, wonderful spam.
Song lyric. Spam was a canned meat product made mainly from ham, ubiquitous in the 1950s. *Monty Python's Flying Circus* (co-written by John Cleese, Michael Palin, Eric Idle, Graham Chapman, Terry Jones and Terry Gilliam; 1969–74)

5 It's not pining, it's passed on. This parrot is no more. It's ceased to be. It's expired. It's gone to meet its maker. This is a late parrot. It's a stiff. Bereft of life it rests in peace. It would be pushing up the daisies if you hadn't nailed it to the perch. It's rung down the curtain and joined the choir invisible. It's an ex-parrot.
"Dead Parrot" sketch, *Monty Python's Flying Circus* (December 14, 1969), Episode 8

6 I'm a lumberjack and I'm OK,
I sleep all night and I work all day,
I cut down trees, I skip and jump,
I like to press wild flowers.
I put on women's clothing,
And hang around in bars.
Song lyric. "The Lumberjack Song," *Monty Python's Flying Circus* (co-written by John Cleese, Michael Palin, Eric Idle, Graham Chapman, Terry Jones and Terry Gilliam; 1969–74)

Moodie, Susanna (originally Susanna Strickland; 1803–85) British-born Canadian writer

1 There are no ghosts in Canada. The country is too new for ghosts. No Canadian is afearded of ghosts.
Roughing it in the Bush, or Life in Canada (1852), ch. 12

Moore, Clement (Clement Clarke Moore; 1779–1863) U.S. educator and poet

1 Happy Christmas to all, and to all a good night!
"A Visit from St. Nicholas" (December 1823)

2 'Twas the night before Christmas, when all through the house
Not a creature was stirring—not even a mouse;
The stockings were hung by the chimney with care,
In hopes that St. Nicholas soon would be there.
"A Visit from St. Nicholas" (December 1823)

Moore, Edward (1712–57) English playwright

1 This is adding insult to injuries.
The Foundling (1747–48), Act 5

2 I am rich beyond the dreams of avarice.
The Gamester (1753), Act 2

3 'Tis now the summer of your youth. Time has not cropt the roses from your cheek, though sorrow long has washed them.
The Gamester (1753), Act 3, Scene 4

Moore, G. E. (George Edward Moore; 1873–1958) British philosopher

1 The assertion "I am morally bound to perform this action" is identical with the assertion, "This action will produce the greatest possible amount of good in the Universe".
Principia Ethica (1903)

2 The value of a whole must not be assumed to be the same as the sum of the values of its parts.
Principia Ethica (1903)

3 Remorse: beholding heaven and feeling hell.
Attrib.

Moore, George (George Augustus Moore; 1852–1933) Irish writer

1 If you were Jane Austens, George Eliots, and Rosa Bonheurs, it would be of no use if you weren't married. A husband is better than talent.
A Drama in Muslin (1886), bk. 1, ch. 8

2 Ireland is a little Russia in which the longest way round is the shortest way home.
Hail and Farewell (1911–14)

3 One of Ireland's many tricks is to fade away to a little speck down on the horizon of our lives, and then to return suddenly in tremendous bulk, frightening us.
Hail and Farewell (1911–14)

4 Acting is therefore the lowest of the arts, if it is an art at all.
"Mummer-Worship," *Impressions and Opinions* (1891)

5 A man travels the world in search of what he needs and returns home to find it.
The Brook Kerith (1916), ch. 11

6 "But you'll sit here drinking all night," and the priest's eyes went toward the corner where the women had gathered, and Bryden felt that the priest looked on the women as more dangerous than the porter.
"Home Sickness," *The Untilled Field* (1903)

7 To be aristocratic in Art one must avoid polite society.
Quoted in *Enemies of Promise* (Cyril Connolly; 1938), ch. 15

Moore, Grace U.S. writer

1 I think that to get under the surface and really appreciate the beauty of any country, one has to go there poor.
You're Only Human Once (1944)

Moore, Henry (Henry Spencer Moore; 1898–1986) British sculptor

Quotations about Moore

1 Sculptor Henry Moore has been asked not to leave any holes in which boys could trap their heads when he carves *Family Group* for Harlow New Town.
Anonymous. Henry Moore's work is noted for its abstraction of the human form to simple shapes, often with holes. *News Chronicle*, London (1960s)

Quotations by Moore

2 Purely abstract sculpture seems to me to be an activity that would be better fulfilled in another art, such as architecture...Abstract sculptures are too often but models for monuments that are never carried out.
Observer, London (1960)

3 The observation of nature is part of an artist's life, it enlarges his form and knowledge, keeps him fresh and from working only by formula, and feeds inspiration.
Attrib.

4 There is a right physical size for every idea.
Attrib.

Moore, J. Earle (1892–1957) U.S. physician

1 Two minutes with Venus, two years with mercury.
Alluding to the former use of mercury compounds in the treatment of syphilis. Attrib.

Moore, Marianne (Marianne Craig Moore; 1887–1972) U.S. poet

1 Psychology which explains everything
explains nothing,
and we are still in doubt.
"Marriage," *Collected Poems* (1951)

2 The Mind is an Enchanting Thing
is an enchanted thing
like the glaze on a
katydid-wing.
"The Mind is an Enchanting Thing," *Nevertheless* (1944), ll. 1–3

3 Fanaticism? No. Writing is exciting and baseball is like writing.
"Baseball and Writing," *New Yorker* (December 9, 1961)

4 I, too, dislike it: there are things that are important beyond all

this fiddle.
Reading it, however, with perfect contempt for it, one discovers
in it after all, a place for the genuine.
"Poetry," *Poems* (1921), quoted in *The Penguin Book of American Verse* (Geoffrey Moore, ed.; 1977)

5 A place as kind as it is green,
the greenest place I've never seen.
Referring to Ireland. "Poetry," *Poems* (1921), quoted in *The Penguin Book of American Verse* (Geoffrey Moore, ed.; 1977)

6 When I buy pictures
or what is closer to the truth,
when I look at that of which I may regard myself as the
imaginary possessor.
"When I Buy Pictures," *Poems* (1921), quoted in *The Penguin Book of American Verse* (Geoffrey Moore, ed.; 1977)

7 It comes to this: of whatever sort it is,
it must be "lit with piercing glances into the life of things";
it must acknowledge the spiritual forces which have made it.
Referring to works of art. "When I Buy Pictures," *Poems* (1921), quoted in *The Penguin Book of American Verse* (Geoffrey Moore, ed.; 1977)

8 The mind
feeling its way as though blind,
walks along with its eyes on the ground.
"The Mind is an Enchanting Thing," *Nevertheless* (1944), ll. 10–12

9 It has memory's ear
that can hear without
having to hear.
"The Mind is an Enchanting Thing," *Nevertheless* (1944), ll. 13–15

Moore, Roger (Roger George Moore; b.1927) British film actor

1 You're not a star until they can spell your name in Karachi.
Film Yearbook (1987), quoted in *Chambers Film Quotes* (Tony Crawley, ed.; 1991)

2 I enjoy being a highly overpaid actor.
Attrib.

Moore, Thomas (1779–1852) Irish poet

1 I never nurs'd a dear gazelle,
To glad me with its soft black eye
But when it came to know me well,
And love me, it was sure to die!
"Lalla Rookh" (1817)

2 But Faith, fanatic Faith, once wedded fast
To some dear falsehood, hugs it to the last.
"Lalla Rookh" (1817), can. 3, l. 356

3 Yet, who can help loving the land that has taught us
Six hundred and eighty-five ways to dress eggs?
"The Fudge Family in Paris" (1818)

4 No, the heart that has truly lov'd never forgets,
But as truly loves on to the close,
As the sun-flower turns on her god, when he sets,
The same look which she turn'd when he rose.
"Believe Me, If All Those Endearing Young Charms," *Irish Melodies* (1807)

5 She is far from the land where her young hero sleeps,
And lovers are round her, sighing:
But coldly she turns from their gaze, and weeps,
For her heart in his grave is lying.
"She is Far," *Irish Melodies* (1807)

6 The harp that once through Tara's halls
The soul of music shed,
Now hangs as mute on Tara's walls
As if that soul were fled.—
So sleeps the pride of former days,
So glory's thrill is o'er;
And hearts, that once beat high for praise,
Now feel that pulse no more.
"The Harp that Once," *Irish Melodies* (1807)

7 The Minstrel Boy to the war is gone,
In the ranks of death you'll find him;
His father's sword he has girded on,
And his wild harp slung behind him.
"The Minstrel Boy," *Irish Melodies* (1807)

8 'Tis the last rose of summer
Left blooming alone;
All her lovely companions
Are faded and gone.
"'Tis the Last Rose," *Irish Melodies* (1807)

9 'Twere more than woman to be wise;
'Twere more than man to wish thee so!
"The Ring," *Juvenile Poems* (1812)

10 To love you was pleasant enough,
And, oh! 'tis delicious to hate you!
"When I Lov'd You," *Juvenile Poems* (1812)

11 Oft in the stilly night,
Ere Slumber's chain has bound me,
Fond Memory brings the light
Of other days around me;
The smiles, the tears,
Of boyhood's years,
The words of love then spoken;
The eyes that shone,
Now dimmed and gone,
The cheerful hearts now broken!
"Oft in the Stilly Night," *National Airs* (1815)

12 This embryo capital, where Fancy sees
Squares in morasses, obelisks in trees;
Which second-sighted seers, ev'n now, adorn
With shrines unbuilt and heroes yet unborn.
Referring to Washington, D.C. "To Thomas Hume, Esq., M.D., from the City of Washington," *Poems Relating to America* (1806)

13 All that 's bright must fade,—
The brightest still the fleetest;
All that 's sweet was made
But to be lost when sweetest.
"All That 's Bright Must Fade," *The Poetical Works of Thomas Moore* (1840–41)

14 Shall I ask the brave soldier who fights by my side
In the cause of mankind, if our creeds agree?
"Come, Send Round the Wine," *The Poetical Works of Thomas Moore* (1840–41)

15 If I speak to thee in friendship's name
Thou think'st I speak too coldly;
If I mention love's devoted flame,
Thou say'st I speak too boldly.
"How Shall I Woo?," *The Poetical Works of Thomas Moore* (1840–41)

16 Earth hath no sorrow that heaven cannot heal.
Attrib.

Moore, Thomas Sturge (1870–1944) British poet, wood-engraver, and illustrator

1 Two buttocks of one bum.
Referring to Hilaire Belloc and G. K. Chesterton. Attrib.

Morand, Paul (1888–1976) French writer and diplomat

1 The world is a vale of tears, but, that said, well irrigated.
"La nuit de Babylone," *Fermé la nuit* (1923)

2 All that I do, I do quickly and badly, for fear of stopping too soon to want to do it.
"La nuit des six-jours," *Ouvert la nuit* (1922)

3 The apéritif is the evensong of the French.
"La nuit des six-jours," *Ouvert la nuit* (1922)

4 Mirrors are ices which do not melt: what melts are those who admire themselves in them.
"La nuit écossaise...," *Ouvert la nuit* (1922)

Moravia, Alberto (Alberto Pincherle; 1907–90) Italian novelist

1 Every method is used to prove to men that in given political, economic, and social situations they are bound to be happy, and those who are unhappy are mad or criminals or monsters.
Man as an End (Bernard Wall, tr.; 1964)

2 Modern man...can never for one moment forget that he is living in a world in which he is a means and whose end is not his business.
Man as an End (Bernard Wall, tr.; 1964)

3 The ratio of literacy to illiteracy is constant, but nowadays the illiterates can read and write.
Observer, London (October 14, 1979)

More, Hannah (1745–1833) British writer and philanthropist

1 For you'll ne'er mend your fortunes, nor help the just cause,
By breaking of windows, or breaking of laws.
"Address to the Meeting in Spa Field" (1817), quoted in *Life* (H. Thompson; 1838)

2 Going to the opera, like getting drunk, is a sin that carries its own punishment with it.
Letter to her sister (1775), quoted in *The Letters of Hannah More* (R. Brimley Johnson, ed.; 1925)

3 I used to wonder why people should be so fond of the company of their physician, till I recollected that he is the only person with whom one dares to talk continually of oneself, without interruption, contradiction or censure; I suppose that delightful immunity doubles their fees.
1789. Attrib.

4 Life is a short day; but it is a working day. Activity may lead to evil, but inactivity cannot lead to good.
Attrib.

5 Perish discretion when it interferes with duty.
Attrib.

More, Henry (1614–87) English philosopher and poet

1 Virtue is to herself the best reward.
Cupid's Conflict (1646)

More, Thomas, Sir (1478–1535) English statesman and writer

1 To morowe longe I to goe to God...I neuer liked your maner towarde me better then when you kissed me laste for I loue when doughterly loue and deere charitie hathe no laisor to looke to worldely curtesye. Fare well my deere childe and praye for me, and I shall for you and all your friendes that we maie merily meete in heaven.
Addressed to his daughter on the eve of his execution. Letter (July 6, 1535)

2 This hath not offended the king.
Said as he drew his beard aside before putting his head on the block. Remark (July 7, 1535)

3 I pray you, Master Lieutenant, see me safe up, and for coming down let me shift for myself.
Referring to climbing onto the scaffold prior to his execution. Remark (July 7, 1535), quoted in *Life of Sir Thomas More* (William Roper; 1626)

4 Of hearte couragious, politique in counsaile, in adversitie nothynge abashed, in peace juste and mercifull, in warre sharpe and fyerce, in the fielde bolde and hardye...Whose warres whoso will consyder, hee shall no lesse commende hys wysedome where he voyded than hys mannehode where he vanquished.
Referring to Edward IV. "The Historie of Kyng Rycharde the Thirde", quoted in *Miscellaneous Works* (Paul Kendall, ed.; 1965)

5 Yea, marry, now it is somewhat, for now it is rhyme; before, it was neither rhyme nor reason.
On reading an unremarkable book recently rendered into verse by a friend of his. Quoted in *Apophthegms New and Old* (Francis Bacon; 1625)

6 Is not this house as nigh heaven as my own?
Referring to the Tower of London; More was imprisoned there for treason arising from his defiance of Henry VIII's religious policies. Quoted in *Life of Sir Thomas More* (William Roper; 1626)

7 Pluck up thy spirits, man, and be not afraid to do thine office; my neck is very short; take heed therefore thou strike not awry, for saving of thine honesty.
July 7, 1535. Said to the headsman at his execution. Quoted in *Life of Sir Thomas More* (William Roper; 1626)

8 The state of things and the dispositions of men were then such, that a man could not well tell whom he might trust or whom he might fear.
Referring to England. Quoted in *The English Works of Sir Thomas More* (W. E. Campbell, ed.; 1931), vol. 1

Moreau, Jeanne (b.1928) French actor

1 I don't think success is harmful, as so many people say. Rather, I believe it indispensable to talent, if for nothing else than to increase the talent.
The Egotists (Oriana Fallaci; 1963)

2 Age doesn't protect you from love. But love, to some extent, protects you from age.
Attrib.

3 Feed yourself and feed others. Then, if you have to say goodbye, it won't matter. You will have shared love.
Attrib.

Morell, Thomas (1703–84) British classicist

1 See, the conquering hero comes!
Sound the trumpets, beat the drums!
1747. The libretto for Handel's oratorio. "A Chorus of Youths," *Judas Maccabeus* (1746), pt. 3

2 The first great gift we can bestow on others is a good example.
Attrib.

Morelli, Giovanni (1816–91) Italian art critic

1 Avoid falsehoods like the plague except in matters of taxation, which do not count, since here you are not lying to take someone else's goods, but to prevent your own from being unjustly seized.
Attrib.

Morgan, Edwin (Edwin George Morgan; b.1920) Scottish poet

1 And history? What use is history? Is history not the opium of the imagination?
1972. "The Resources of Scotland," *Crossing the Border* (1990)

2 An old pot seething with dissatisfactions which fortunately can be relied on never to come to the boil—might be the English politician's view of Scotland.
1972. "The Resources of Scotland," *Crossing the Border* (1990)

3 Anything that earnestly concerns the cultural health of a nation is political.
1972. "The Resources of Scotland," *Crossing the Border* (1990)

Morgan, Elaine (b.1920) British writer and educator

1 The trouble with specialists is that they tend to think in grooves.
The Descent of Woman (1972), ch. 1

2 The rumblings of women's liberation are only one pointer to the fact that you already have a discontented work force. And if conditions continue to lag so far behind the industrial norm and the discomfort increases, you will find...that you will end up with an inferior product.
The Descent of Woman (1972), ch. 11

3 Housewives and mothers seldom find it practicable to come out on strike.They have no union, anyway.
Attrib.

Morgan, John Pierpont (1837–1913) U.S. financier, art collector, and philanthropist

Quotations about Morgan

1 Mr. Morgan buys his partners; I grow my own.
Andrew Carnegie (1835–1919) Scottish-born U.S. industrialist and philanthropist. Quoted in *Life of Andrew Carnegie* (Burton J. Hendrick; 1932)

Quotations by Morgan

2 A man always has two reasons for what he does—a good one and the real one.
Quoted in *Roosevelt: The Story of a Friendship* (Owen Wister; 1930)

3 Any man who has to ask about the annual upkeep of a yacht can't afford one.
Attrib.

4 I don't know as I want a lawyer to tell me what I cannot do. I hire him to tell me how to do what I want to do.
Attrib.

5 Never be on the bear side but on the bull side when the United States is in question.
Attrib.

6 You can't pick cherries with your back to the tree.
Attrib.

Morgan, Robin (b.1941) U.S. writer

1 It isn't until you begin to fight in your own cause that you (a) become really committed to winning, and (b) become a genuine ally of other people struggling for their freedom.
Sisterhood Is Powerful: an Anthology of Writings from the Women's Liberation Movement (1970), Introduction

2 Sisterhood is Powerful
1970. Book title.

Morgenstern, Christian (1871–1914) German poet

1 There is a ghost
That eats handkerchiefs;
It keeps you company
On all your travels.
"Gespenst," quoted in *Der Gingganz* (Margareta Morgenstern, ed.; 1923)

2 Home is not where you live, but where they understand you.
Attrib.

Morison, Samuel Eliot (1887–1976) U.S. historian

1 America was discovered accidentally by a great seaman who was looking for something else; when discovered it was not wanted; and most of the exploration for the next fifty years was done in the hope of getting through or around it.
The Oxford History of the American People (1965), ch. 2

2 America was named after a man who discovered no part of the New World. History is like that, very chancy.
The Oxford History of the American People (1965), ch. 2

3 If the American Revolution had produced nothing but the Declaration of Independence, it would have been worthwhile.
The Oxford History of the American People (1965), ch. 14

Morisot, Berthe (Berthe Marie Pauline Morisot; 1841–95) French painter

1 The truth is that our value lies in feeling, in intention, in our vision that is subtler than that of men, and we can accomplish a great deal provided that affectation, pedantry, and sentimentalism do not come to spoil everything.
Quoted in *Correspondence of Berthe Morisot* (Denis Rouart, ed.; 1957)

Morissette, Alanis (b.1974) Canadian singer

1 What I have to say is far more important than how long my eyelashes are.
1995. Attrib.

Morita Akio (b.1921) Japanese business executive

1 Recession isn't the fault of the workers. If management take the risk of hiring them, we have to take the responsibility for them.
Daily Telegraph, London (February 24, 1982)

2 The glory and the nemesis of Japanese business, the life's blood of our industrial engine, is good old-fashioned competition.
Made in Japan (1987)

3 Communication is the most important form of marketing.
Times, London (March 26, 1982)

4 We believe if you have a family you can't just eliminate certain members of that family because profits are down.
One of the perceived differences between Western and Japanese approaches to business noted by Sony's chairman and cofounder. Quoted in *International Management* (September 1988)

5 No matter how successful you are or how clever or crafty, your business and its future are in the hands of the people you hire. To put it a bit more dramatically, the fate of your business is actually in the hands of the youngest recruit.
Quoted in *Strategy and Business* (1998)

Moritz, Karl Philipp (1757–93) German writer

1 When you see how in this happy country the lowest and poorest member of society takes an interest in all public affairs; when you see how high and low, rich and poor, are all willing to declare their feelings and convictions; when you see how a carter, a common sailor, a beggar is still a man, nay, even more, an Englishman...you find yourself very differently affected from the experience you feel when staring at our soldiers drilling in Berlin.
1782. Reaction to a by-election at Westminster. Attrib.

Morley, Christopher Darlington (1890–1957) U.S. writer and journalist

1 A human being, he wrote, is a whispering in the steam pipes on a cold night; dust sifted through a locked window; one or the other half of an unsolved equation; a pun made by God; an ingenious assembly of portable plumbing.
Human Being (1932), ch. 11

2 The courage of the poet is to keep ajar the door that leads to madness.
Inward Ho (1923)

3 There are three ingredients in the good life: learning, learning, and yearning.
Parnassus on Wheels (1917), ch. 10

4 Life is a foreign language: all men mispronounce it.
Thunder on the Left (1925), ch. 14

5 Why do they put the Gideon Bibles only in the bedrooms where it's usually too late?
1940? Quoted in *Quotations for Speakers and Writers* (Allen Andrews, ed.; 1969)

6 A man who has never made a woman angry is a failure in life.
Attrib.

7 My theology, briefly, is that the universe was dictated but not signed.
Attrib.

8 There is only one rule for being a good talker—learn to listen.
Attrib.

9 Timid roach, why be so shy? We are brothers, thou and I. In the midnight, like thyself, I explore the pantry shelf.
Attrib.

Morley, John, Viscount Morley of Blackburn (1838–1923) British statesman and writer

1 You have not converted a man because you have silenced him.
On Compromise (1874), ch. 5

2 The proper memory for a politician is one that knows when to remember and when to forget.
Recollections (1917)

3 Where it is a duty to worship the sun it is pretty sure to be a crime to examine the laws of heat.
Voltaire (1872)

Morley, Lord, 3rd Earl of Morley (1843–1905) British aristocrat

1 I am always very glad when Lord Salisbury makes a great speech. It is sure to contain at least one blazing indiscretion which it is a delight to remember.
Speech, Hull, England (November 25, 1887)

Morley, Robert (1908–92) British actor and playwright

1 Beware of the conversationalist who adds "in other words". He is merely starting afresh.
Observer, London (December 6, 1964), "Sayings of the Week"

2 No man is lonely while eating spaghetti.
Attrib.

3 Show me a man who has enjoyed his school days and I'll show you a bully and a bore.
Attrib.

Morpurgo, J. E. (Jack Eric Morpurgo; b.1918) British writer and academic

1 Austria is Switzerland speaking pure German and with history added.
The Road to Athens (1963)

Morris, Charles (1745–1838) British songwriter

1 His taxes now prove
His great love for the people,
So wisely they're managed
To starve the poor souls.
Referring to William Pitt the Younger. Quoted in *The Faber Book of English History in Verse* (Kenneth Baker, ed.; 1988)

Morris, Desmond (Desmond John Morris; b.1928) British ethnologist and writer

1 The very act of smoking a cigarette is, for many, a major source of Displacement Activities...smoking can play a valuable role in a society full of minute-by-minute tensions and pressures. It is so much more than a question of inhaling smoke.
"Displacement Activities," *Manwatching* (1977)

2 Observe diners arriving at any restaurant and you will see them make a bee-line for the wall-seats. No one ever voluntarily selects a centre table in an open space. Open seating positions are only taken when all the wall-seats are already occupied. This dates back to a primeval feeding practice of avoiding sudden attack during the deep concentration involved in consuming food.
"Feeding Behaviour," *Manwatching* (1977)

3 A true bond of friendship is usually only possible between people of roughly equal status. This equality is demonstrated in many indirect ways, but it is reinforced in face-to-face encounters by a matching of the posture of relaxation or alertness.
"Postural Echo," *Manwatching* (1977)

4 Clearly, then, the city is not a concrete jungle, it is a human zoo.
The Human Zoo (1969), Introduction

5 He is proud that he has the biggest brain of all the primates, but attempts to conceal the fact that he also has the biggest penis.
The Naked Ape (1967), Introduction

6 There are one hundred and ninety-three living species of monkeys and apes. One hundred and ninety-two of them are covered with hair. The exception is a naked ape self-named *Homo sapiens*.
The Naked Ape (1967), Introduction

Morris, George Pope (1802–64) U.S. journalist and poet

1 Woodman, spare that tree!
Touch not a single bough!
In youth it sheltered me,
And I'll protect it now.
"Spare That Tree" (1830)

2 A song for our banner! The watchword recall
Which gave the Republic her station:
"United we stand, divided we fall!"
It made and preserves us a nation!
The union of lakes, the union of lands,
The union of States none can sever,
The union of hearts, the union of hands,
And the flag of our Union forever!
"The Flag of Our Union" (1851)

Morris, Jan (originally James Morris; b.1926) British travel writer

1 The devotion of the Welsh to their land is proverbial, and homesickness is much the best-publicized of their national emotions—*hiraeth*, that sense of longing which has been sentimentalized in so many treacly songs.
The Matter of Wales (1984), ch. 1

2 After a distinctly uncomfortable introduction to the practice of travel, if I could possibly help it, I would never travel disagreeably again.
"My Worst Journey," *Worst Journeys* (Keath Fraser, ed.; 1991)

3 For forty years I have made a professional speciality of the happy journey. When things have gone wrong, I have resolutely forgotten them.
"My Worst Journey," *Worst Journeys* (Keath Fraser, ed.; 1991)

4 Principles of travel, like any other rules, can only be proved by exception.
"My Worst Journey," *Worst Journeys* (Keath Fraser, ed.; 1991)

Morris, Mary (b.1947) U.S. writer

1 Gender often forms a bond between women travellers. Women confide in other women.
Virago Book of Women Travellers (1993), Introduction

Morris, Robert Tuttle (1857–1945) U.S. surgeon and writer

1 It is the patient rather than the case which requires treatment.
Doctors Versus Folks (1915), ch. 2

2 One must not count upon all of his patients being willing to steal in order to pay doctor's bills.
Doctors Versus Folks (1915), ch. 3

3 The greatest triumph of surgery today...lies in finding ways for avoiding surgery.
Doctors Versus Folks (1915), ch. 3

4 There is no royal road to diagnosis.
Doctors Versus Folks (1915), ch. 4

5 A vain surgeon is like a milking stool, of no use except when sat upon.
Attrib.

Morris, William (1834–96) British designer, socialist reformer, and poet

Quotations about Morris

1 Of course he was a wonderful all-round man, but the act of walking round him has always tired me.
Max Beerbohm (1872–1956) British essayist, critic, and caricaturist. Quoted in *Conversations with Max* (Samuel Nathaniel Behrman; 1960), ch. 2

Quotations by Morris

2 Between complete Socialism and Communism there is no difference whatever in my mind. Communism is in fact the completion of Socialism; when that ceases to be militant and becomes triumphant, it will be Communism.
Speech to Hammersmith Socialist Society, London (1893)

3 Had she come all the way for this,
To part at last without a kiss?
Yea, had she borne the dirt and rain

That her own eyes might see him slain
Beside the haystack in the floods?
"The Haystack in the Floods" (1858)

4 If you want a golden rule that will fit everybody, this is it: Have nothing in your houses that you do not know to be useful, or believe to be beautiful.
Hopes and Fears for Art? The Beauty of Life? (1882)

5 Art will make our streets as beautiful as the woods, as elevating as the mountain-side: it will be a pleasure and a rest, and not a weight upon the spirits to come from the open country into a town. Every man's house will be fair and decent, soothing to his mind and helpful to his work.
Quoted in *The Arts and Crafts Movement* (Thomas Sanderson; 1905)

6 I don't want art for a few, any more than education for a few, or freedom for a few.
Quoted in *The Arts and Crafts Movement* (Thomas Sanderson; 1905)

7 It is not this or that tangible steel or brass machine which we want to get rid of, but the great intangible machine of commercial tyranny which oppresses the lives of us all.
Quoted in *The Arts and Crafts Movement* (Thomas Sanderson; 1905)

8 Nothing should be made by man's labour which is not worth making or which must be made by labour degrading to the makers.
Quoted in *The Arts and Crafts Movement* (Thomas Sanderson; 1905)

Morrison, Danny Irish nationalist

1 Who here really believes we can win the war through the ballot box? But will anyone here object if, with a ballot paper in this hand, and an armalite rifle in this hand, we take power in Ireland.
Known as the "gun-and-ballot-box" strategy. Speech, Sinn Féin Árd Fheis (November 2, 1981), quoted in *Phrases Make History Here* (Conor O'Clery; 1986)

Morrison, Jim (1943–71) U.S. rock singer and songwriter

1 I am interested in anything about revolt, disorder, chaos—especially activity that seems to have no meaning. It seems to me to be the road toward freedom.
Elektra Records press release (1967)

2 Come on baby, light my fire.
Song lyric. "Light My Fire" (1967)

3 What have they done to the earth?...
Ravaged and plundered and ripped her and did her,
Struck her with knives in the side of the dawn
And tied her with fences and dragged her down.
Song lyric. "When the Music's Over" (1967)

4 Fear is very exciting. People like to get scared. It's exactly like the moment before you have an orgasm.
Quoted in *No One Here Gets out Alive* (Jerry Hopkins and Danny Sugerman; 1980)

5 The only time I really open up is onstage. The mask of performing gives it to me, a place where I hide myself then I can reveal myself.
Quoted in *No One Here Gets out Alive* (Jerry Hopkins and Danny Sugerman; 1980)

6 Let's just say I was testing the bounds of reality. I was curious to see what would happen. That's all it was: just curiosity.
1969. Referring to his exposing of himself on stage, which led to obscenity charges. They were later dropped. Quoted in *No One Here Gets out Alive* (Jerry Hopkins and Danny Sugerman; 1980)

7 The body exists for the sake of the eyes; it becomes a dry stalk to support these two insatiable jewels.
Attrib.

8 Those first songs I wrote, I was just taking notes at a fantastic rock concert that was going on inside my head.
Attrib.

Morrison, Rutherford (1853–1939) British doctor

1 In men nine out of ten abdominal tumors are malignant; in women nine out of ten abdominal swellings are the pregnant uterus.
The Practitioner (October 1965)

2 Never neglect the history of a missed menstrual period.
The Practitioner (October 1965)

Morrison, Toni (originally Chloe Anthony Wofford; b.1931) U.S. novelist

Quotations about Morrison

1 I read recently Toni Morrison doesn't watch TV, which astounds me. Why should I read her novels when she is totally divorced from American culture?
Camille Paglia (b.1947) U.S. academic and author. "My Cultural Life," *Guardian*, London (January 30, 1998), Friday Review

Quotations by Morrison

2 In Ohio seasons are theatrical. Each one enters like a prima donna, convinced its performance is the reason the world has people in it.
Beloved (1987)

3 It's good, you know, when you got a woman who is a friend of your mind.
Beloved (1987)

4 Not a house in the country ain't packed to its rafters with some dead Negro's grief.
Beloved (1987)

5 Once upon a time she had known more and wanted to.
Beloved (1987)

6 The sadness was at her center, the desolated center where the self that was no self made its home.
Beloved (1987)

7 Winter in Ohio was especially rough if you had an appetite for color. Sky provided the only drama, and counting on a Cincinnati horizon for life's principal joy was reckless indeed.
Beloved (1987)

8 "This is a city of water," said Mr. Garner. "Everything travels by water and what the rivers can't carry the canals take. A queen of a city...If you have to live in a city—this is it."
Referring to Cincinnati, Ohio. *Beloved* (1987)

9 A critic should be a conduit, a bridge, but not a law.
Interview, *Black Creation Annual* (1974–75)

10 I don't believe any real artists have ever been nonpolitical. They may have been insensitive to this particular plight or insensitive to that, but they were political because that's what an artist is—a politician.
Interview, *Black Creation Annual* (1974–75)

11 Our history as Black women is the history of women who could build a house *and* have some children, and there was no problem.
Interview, *Essence* (July 1981)

12 It's a marvelous beginning. It's a real renaissance. You know, we have spoken of renaissances before. But this one is ours, not somebody else's.
Referring to African American culture in the United States. Interview, *Essence* (July 1981)

13 How soon country people forget. When they fall in love with a city it is forever, and it is like forever...There, in a city, they are not so much new as themselves: their stronger, riskier selves.
Jazz (1991)

14 We have to acknowledge that the thing we call "literature" is more pluralistic now, just as society ought to be. The melting pot never worked. We ought to be able to accept on equal terms everybody from the Hasidim to Walter Lippmann, from the Rastafarians to Ralph Bunche.
Walter Lippmann was a political journalist and writer, and Ralph Bunche a scholar and diplomat. *Newsweek* (March 30, 1981)

15 All of us, readers and writers, are bereft when criticism remains too polite or too fearful to notice a disrupting darkness before its eyes.
Playing in the Dark: Whiteness and the Literary Imagination (1992)

16 Grab this land! Take it, hold it, my brothers, make it, my brothers, shake it, squeeze it, turn it, twist it, beat it, kick it, kiss it, whip it, stomp it, dig it, plow it, seed it, reap it, rent it, buy it, sell it, own it, build it, multiply it, and pass it on.
Song of Solomon (1977)

17 What difference do it make if the thing you scared of is real or not?
Song of Solomon (1977)

18 Except for World War II, nothing ever interfered with the celebration of National Suicide Day.
Sula (1973)

19 I don't know everything, I just do everything.
Sula (1973)

20 Like any artist with no art form she became dangerous.
Sula (1973)

21 The purpose of evil was to survive it.
Sula (1973)

22 At some point in life the world's beauty becomes enough. You don't need to photograph, paint or even remember it. It is enough.
Tar Baby (1981)

23 Was there anything so loathsome as a wilfully innocent man? Hardly. An innocent man is a sin before God. Inhuman and therefore unworthy. No man should live without absorbing the sins of his kind.
Tar Baby (1981)

24 A little black girl yearns for the blue eyes of a little white girl, and the horror at the heart of her yearning is exceeded only by the evil of fulfillment.
The Bluest Eye (1970)

25 There is a sense of being in anger. A reality and presence. An awareness of worth. It is a lovely surging.
The Bluest Eye (1970)

26 To be required to sleep with the same woman forever was a curious and unnatural idea to him; to be expected to dredge up enthusiasms for old acts, and routine ploys; he wondered at the arrogance of the female.
The Bluest Eye (1970)

27 If anything I do, in the way of writing novels (or whatever I write) isn't about the village or the community or about you, then it is not about anything.
1980. Quoted in "Rootedness: The Ancestor as Foundation," *Black Women Writers* (Mari Evans, ed.; 1984)

28 I wrote my first novel because I wanted to read it.
Quoted in *Conversations with American Writers* (Charles Ruas; 1985)

29 In this country American means white. Everybody else has to hyphenate.
Referring to the United States. Quoted in *Guardian*, London (January 29, 1992)

Morrison, Van (George Ivan Morrison; b.1945) Irish singer and songwriter

1 I've never been comfortable working live and I'm still not...When I played clubs...you walk through the audience, have a drink with some people from the audience. Nothing about you're up here, and they're down there.
Quoted in "Van Morrison," *Off the Record: An Oral History of Popular Music* (Joe Smith; 1988)

2 Music is spiritual. The music business is not.
Attrib.

Morrissey (Steven Patrick Morrissey; b.1959) British singer and songwriter

1 Punk was...a musical movement without music.
Interview, *The Face* (1985)

2 Rock 'n' roll, or the traditional incurable rock and roller never interested me remotely. He was simply a rather foolish, empty-headed figure who was peddling his brand of self-projection and very arch machismo that I could never relate to.
Interview, *The Face* (1985)

3 If you must write prose poems
the words you use should be your own
don't plagiarise or take "on loan".
There's always someone, somewhere
with a big nose who knows.
"Cemetery Gates," *The Queen is Dead* (1986)

4 MORRISSEY But I really do want to be remembered. I want some grain of immortality. I think it's been deserved...

INTERVIEWER Really. In two years?
MORRISSEY Oh yes...In two days!
Interview, *Time Out* (March 1985)

5 The industry is just rife with jealousy and hatred. Everybody in it is a failed bassist.
Interview, *Time Out* (March 1985)

Morrow, Dwight Whitney (1873–1931) U.S. diplomat and politician

1 The world is divided into people who do things and people who get the credit. Try, if you can, to belong to the first class. There's far less competition.
Letter to his son, quoted in *Dwight Morrow* (Harold Nicolson; 1935), ch. 3

2 Any party which takes credit for the rain must not be surprised if its opponents blame it for the drought.
Speech (October 1930)

Morrow, Lance U.S. journalist

1 The real 1960s began on the afternoon of November 22, 1963...It came to seem that Kennedy's murder opened some malign trap door in American culture, and the wild bats flapped out.
Time (November 14, 1983)

Morse, Samuel (Samuel Finley Breese Morse; 1791–1872) U.S. artist and inventor

1 Alas! My dear sir, the very name of *pictures* produces a sadness of heart I cannot describe. Painting has been a smiling mistress to many, but she has been a cruel jilt to me.
Letter to James Fenimore Cooper (November 20, 1849)

Mortimer, John (John Clifford Mortimer; b.1923) British lawyer, novelist, and playwright

1 No brilliance is needed in the law. Nothing but common sense, and relatively clean finger nails.
A Voyage Round My Father (1970)

2 The shelf life of the modern hardback writer is somewhere between the milk and the yoghurt.
Observer, London (June 28, 1987)

3 The worst fault of the working classes is telling their children they're not going to succeed, saying: "There is a life, but it's not for you."
Observer, London (June 5, 1988), "Sayings of the Week"

4 Great works of literature, perhaps the greatest—the Oresteia, Hamlet, even the Bible—have been stories of mystery and crime.
Sunday Times, London (April 1, 1990)

5 Life itself is a mystery which defies solution.
Sunday Times, London (April 1, 1990)

Morton, H. V. (Henry Vollam Morton; 1892–1979) British travel writer

1 The Welsh people possess that surest of all retreats from the outsider, their own language.
In Search of Wales (1932), ch. 1

Morton, J. C. (John Cameron Andrieu Bingham Michael Morton, "Beachcomber"; 1893–1979) British journalist and writer

1 Dr Strabismus (Whom God Preserve) of Utrecht is carrying out research work with a view to crossing salmon with mosquitoes. He says it will mean a bite every time for fishermen.
Daily Express, London (January 1931), "By the Way"

2 Vegetarians have wicked, shifty eyes, and laugh in a cold and calculating manner. They pinch little children, steal stamps, drink water, favour beards...wheeze, squeak, drawl and maunder.
Daily Express, London (June 4, 1931), "By the Way"

3 *Rush hour*: that hour when traffic is almost at a standstill.
Morton's Folly (1933)

4 Hush, hush
Nobody cares!
Christopher Robin
Has
Fallen
Down-
Stairs.
"By the Way," *Now We Are Sick* (1931)

5 Erratum. In my article on the Price of Milk, "Horses" should have read "Cows" throughout.
The Best of Beachcomber (1963)

6 SIXTY HORSES WEDGED IN A CHIMNEY
The story to fit this sensational headline has not turned up yet.
1936. "Mr Justice Cocklecarrot: Home Life," *The Best of Beachcomber* (1963)

7 Justice must not only be seen to be done but has to be seen to be believed.
Attrib.

8 Wagner is the Puccini of music.
Attrib.

Morton, Jelly Roll (Ferdinand Joseph La Menthe; 1885–1941) U.S. jazz pianist, composer, and bandleader

1 It is evidently known, beyond contradiction, that New Orleans is the cradle of *jazz*, and I, myself, happened to be the creator in the year 1902...*Jazz* music is a style, not compositions; any kind of music may be played in *jazz*, if one has the knowledge.
Downbeat (August 1938)

Morton, Rogers (1914–79) U.S. businessman and politician

1 I'm not going to re-arrange the furniture on the deck of the Titanic.
Refusing attempts to rescue President Gerald Ford's re-election campaign, 1976. *The Washington Post* (May 16, 1976)

Morton, Thomas (1764–1838) English playwright

1 I eat well, and I drink well, and I sleep well—but that's all.
A Roland for an Oliver (1819), Act 1, Scene 2

Moschino, Franco (1950–95) Italian fashion designer

1 If you can't be elegant, at least be extravagant.
Quoted in *Elle* (April 1998)

2 Stop the fashion system!
1980s. T-shirt slogan. Quoted in *Elle* (April 1998)

Mosley, Oswald, Sir (Oswald Ernald Mosley; 1896–1980) British politician

1 "Can't" will be the epitaph of the British Empire—unless we wake up in time.
Speech, Manchester (December 9, 1937)

2 I am not and never have been, a man of the right. My position was on the left and is now in the centre of politics.
Letter, *Times*, London (April 26, 1968)

3 A gun is the ideal weapon of the detached, the reticent, the almost autistic. It is the opposite of a relationship.
Attrib.

Mosley, Walter (b.1952) U.S. novelist

1 All I know about the future is that it is what you make of it.
Lecture, Purcell Room, Royal Festival Hall, London (January 28, 1998)

2 Mofass didn't trust his own mother; that's what made him such a good real estate agent.
A Red Death (1991)

3 Police and government officials have contempt for innocence; they are, in some way, offended by an innocent man.
A Red Death (1991), ch. 5

4 Whatever it is I read about Europe is war. Them white men is always fightin'. War'a the Roses, the Crew-sades, the Revolution, the Kaiser, Hitler, the com'unists. Shit! All they care 'bout, war an' money, money an' land.
A Red Death (1991), ch. 30

5 I didn't even believe in history, really. Real was what was happening to me right then. Real was a toothache and a man you trusted who did you the dirt.
A Red Death (1991), ch. 35

6 Before we launched the attack on D-Day I was frightened but I fought...The first time I fought a German hand-to-hand I screamed for help the whole time I was killing him.
Devil in a Blue Dress (1990), ch. 7

7 I was in a black division but all the superior officers were white. I was trained how to kill men but white men weren't anxious to see a gun in my hands. They didn't want to see me spill white blood.
Devil in a Blue Dress (1990), ch. 14

8 I thought that there might be some justice for a black man if he had the money to grease it. Money isn't a sure bet but it's the closest to God that I've seen in this world.
Devil in a Blue Dress (1990), ch. 18

9 My lapels were crimson, my shoes yellow suede. I had a light buzz on and my new Chrysler floated down the side streets like a yacht down some inland canals.
White Butterfly (1992), ch. 8

10 The jazzmen had found new arenas. Many had gone to Paris and New York. The blues was still with us. The blues would always be with us.
White Butterfly (1992), ch. 9

11 My wife had left me, had taken my child, had gone off with my friend. There was no song on the radio too stupid for my heart.
White Butterfly (1992), ch. 31

Moss, Kate (b.1974) British fashion model

1 But I know I'm going to be called a waif forever. And I hate it.
Kate Moss is distinguished by her slight physique. *Guardian*, London (April 21, 1995)

Moss, Stirling (Stirling Cranford Moss; b.1929) British racing car driver

1 It's necessary to relax your muscles when you can. Relaxing your brain is fatal.
Attrib.

2 One cannot really enjoy speed to the absolute limit if there's a destination involved.
Attrib.

Mossell, Mrs. N. F. (originally Gertrude E. H. Bustill; 1855–1948) U.S. journalist

1 The men who used when single to kiss the babies, pet the cat, and fail to kick the dog where they visited are the men who remain at home most when married.
The Work of the Afro-American Woman (1894)

2 She can gain more readily as an interviewer access to both sexes. Women know best how to deal with women and the inborn chivalry of a gentleman leads him to grant her request when a man might have been repulsed without compunction.
Referring to the advantages of a female reporter over her male counterpart. *The Work of the Afro-American Woman* (1894)

Motherwell, Robert (Robert Burns Motherwell; 1915–91) U.S. painter

1 I love painting...it can be a vehicle for human intercourse...True painting is a lot more than "picture-making." A man is neither a decoration nor an anecdote.
Quoted in *The New Decade* (Whitney Museum of American Art, New York; 1955)

Motherwell, William (1797–1835) Scottish poet and journalist

1 I've wandered east, I've wandered west,
Through many a weary way;
But never, never can forget
The love of life's young day.
"Jeanie Morrison", quoted in *The Poetical Works of William Motherwell* (James M'Conechy; 1849)

Motley, Arthur (Arthur Harrison Motley, "Red"; 1900–84) U.S. business executive

1 A well adjusted executive is one whose intake of pep pills overbalances his consumption of tranquillizers just enough to leave him sufficient energy for the weekly visit to the psychiatrist.
Quoted in *The Pyramid Builders* (Vance Packard; 1962)

Motley, John Lothrop (1814–77) U.S. historian and diplomat

1 Give us the luxuries of life, and we will dispense with its necessities.
Quoted in *The Autocrat of the Breakfast Table* (O. W. Holmes; 1905), ch. 6

Mott, Lucretia (originally Lucretia Coffin; 1793–1880) U.S. abolitionist and women's rights' leader

1 In the marriage union, the independence of the husband and the wife will be equal, their dependence mutual, and their obligations reciprocal.
"Discourse on Woman" (December 17, 1849)

2 Let woman then go on—not asking favors, but claiming as a right the removal of all hindrances to her elevation in the scale of being—let her receive encouragement for the proper cultivation of all her powers, so that she may enter profitably into the active business of life.
"Discourse on Woman" (December 17, 1849)

Mottos and Slogans

1 Labour isn't working.
1979. British Conservative Party general election slogan.

2 Who dares, wins.
Motto of the British Special Air Service (SAS) Regiment

3 You Never Had It So Good.
Subsequently used by Harold Macmillan in the run-up to the 1959 British general election. U.S. Democratic party election slogan (1952)

4 Burn your bra!
U.S. feminist slogan (1970s)

5 Careless talk costs lives.
British Ministry of Information (1940)

6 *Guandao, guandao* profiteering, profiteering! Strike hard against it; it will not disappear by itself.
Chinese pro-democracy slogan. Quoted in *June Four: A Chronicle of the Chinese Democratic Uprising* (Zi Jin and Qin Zhou, trs.; 1989)

7 People's police have the love of the people.
April 1989. Said by student pro-democracy demonstrators in Beijing as they broke police lines. Quoted in *June Four: A Chronicle of the Chinese Democratic Uprising* (Zi Jin and Qin Zhou, trs.; 1989)

8 Coffee for all.
The phrase gained political currency during the regime of Felipe González (1982–96), and referred to the policy of degrees of regional autonomy throughout Spain, with more regional power for Catalonia and the Basque country in particular. Quoted in *The Spaniards* (John Hooper; 1986)

9 K = (P+I)S
Slogan for Arthur Andersen, a London-based accountancy firm. K stands for Knowledge; P stands for People; I stands for Information; S stands for Power of Sharing. Quoted in *The Witch Doctors* (John Micklethwait and Adrian Wooldridge; 1996)

10 Make love not war.
1960s. Anti-Vietnam War slogan.

11 Hey, hey, LBJ, How many kids did you kill today?
1960s. Anti-Vietnam War slogan. "LBJ" refers to President Lyndon Baines Johnson.

12 In his heart, he knows your wife.
1976. Automobile bumper sticker. Following President Jimmy Carter's admission in a *Playboy* interview that he had "committed adultery in his heart many times." Adapted from Barry Goldwater's 1964 presidential election slogan: "In your heart you know he's right."

13 Every time you sleep with a boy you sleep with all his old girlfriends.
1987. British AIDS education slogan.

14 Someone, somewhere, wants a letter from you.
1960s. British Post Office slogan.

15 Your King and Country Need You.
1914. British World War I recruitment poster.

16 I am a human being: Do not fold, spindle or mutilate.
Hippie slogan, referring to instructions on computer-processed forms.

17 Freedom! Equality! Brotherhood!
Motto of the French Revolutionaries, but known to be of earlier origin. (18th century)

18 To the greater glory of God.
Motto of the Jesuits.

19 Through endeavor to the stars.
Motto of the Royal Air Force.

20 I want you for the U.S. Army.
1917. Often misquoted as "Uncle Sam wants you," these are the actual words that appeared on the recruiting poster beneath the famous image of Uncle Sam with his finger pointing toward the viewer.

21 Be realistic, demand the impossible.
May 1968. Paris Students' Revolt slogan.

22 Revolution is the ecstasy of history.
May 1968. Paris Students' Revolt slogan.

23 We can soar to heaven, and pierce the earth, because our Great Leader Chairman Mao is our supreme commander.
1960s. Red Guard slogan.

24 Save water—shower with a friend.
1976. Semi-official slogan during the California drought of the mid 1970s.

25 Never work with animals or children.
Show business maxim.

26 Work Makes One Free.
1940s. Slogan at the entrance to Auschwitz concentration camp.

27 Out of the closets and into the streets.
Slogan for U.S. Gay Liberation Front.

28 Say It Loud, "I'm Black and I'm Proud."
1970s. Slogan in the United States.

29 Ban the bomb.
1953? Slogan of nuclear disarmament campaigners worldwide.

30 Black is beautiful.
1962? Slogan of the Black Panther Movement, used especially by Stokely Carmichael.

31 Better red than dead.
1958? Slogan of the British nuclear disarmament movement.

32 One Realm, One People, One Leader.
1934. Slogan of the German National Socialist (Nazi) Party, referring to Adolf Hitler.

33 Our day will come.
Slogan of the Irish Republican Army (IRA).

34 Algeria is French.
1958. Slogan of the opponents of Algerian independence.

35 Votes for Women.
1906–14. Slogan of the Woman Suffrage Movement.

36 Peace, Bread and Land.
1917. Slogan of workers in Petrograd (St. Petersburg) during the February Revolution.

37 All Power to the Soviets!
1917. Slogan of workers in Petrograd (St. Petersburg) during the October Revolution.

38 Hell no, we won't go!
1965? U.S. antiwar chant during the time of the Vietnam War.

39 Your politicians will always be there when they need you.
U.S. T-shirt slogan.

Mougayar, Walid (b.1959) U.S. author

1 Millions of consumers and businesses are waiting in line to participate in the expansion of intergalactic and gigantic virtual marketplaces.
Opening Digital Markets (1997)

2 Most organizations now must compete in two marketplaces: a physical (traditional) one and the emerging electronic one, mediated by the Internet.
Opening Digital Markets (1997)

3 The Internet and electronic commerce have captured our imagination by giving us new dreams of success and power.
Opening Digital Markets (1997)

4 The Internet as a market can be compared to the Mediterranean Sea. Only if you navigate it with the right ships are you able to reach your new trading partners.
Opening Digital Markets (1997)

Mountbatten, Lord, 1st Earl Mountbatten of Burma (Louis Mountbatten, born Prince Louis Francis Albert Victor Nicholas of Battenberg; 1900–79) British naval commander and statesman

1 As a military man who has given half a century of active service, I say in all sincerity that the nuclear arms race has no military purpose. Wars cannot be fought with nuclear weapons; their existence only adds to our perils because of the illusions which they have generated.
Speech, Strasbourg (May 11, 1979)

2 You can divide my life into two. During the first part of my life I was an ordinary conventional naval officer, trying not to be different in the sense of being royal, trying not to show myself off as being rich and ostentatious—like always using a small car to drive to the dockyard instead of my Rolls-Royce.
Quoted in *Mountbatten, Hero of Our Time* (Richard Hough; 1980), ch. 9

3 Do you really think the IRA would think me a worthwhile target?
Declining special protection while on holiday in Ireland. Also quoted as: "What would they want with an old man like me?" Quoted in *Mountbatten, Hero of Our Time* (Richard Hough; 1980), ch. 11

4 Actually I vote Labour, but my butler's a Tory.
1945. Said to a Conservative Party campaign worker during the 1945 election.

Mou Sen Chinese theater director

1 I do not act in the play; I am action.
1995. Quoted in "File O," *China Review* (Fiona McConnon; Summer 1995)

2 I want to know what is in my file. It is my file, yet I don't know where it is, and what is inside. My file is the basis for all levels of institutions and officials to judge, assess, and control me. If my file is lost, it means my disappearance in this society.
Quoted in "File O," *China Review* (Fiona McConnon; Summer 1995)

Moyers, Bill (William Don Moyers; b.1934) U.S. broadcast journalist

1 That our political system is failing to solve the bedrock problems we face is beyond dispute. One reason is that our public discourse has become the verbal equivalent of mud wrestling.
New York Times (March 22, 1992)

2 Ideas are great arrows, but there has to be a bow. And politics is the bow of idealism.
Time (October 29, 1965)

Moynihan, Daniel Patrick (b.1927) U.S. academic and politician

1 Somehow liberals have been unable to acquire from life what conservatives seem to be endowed with at birth: namely, a healthy skepticism of the powers of government agencies to do good.
New York Post (May 14, 1969)

2 The national security state controls the President. It controls most of the executive departments.
New York Times Magazine (September 16, 1990)

3 If the newspapers of a country are filled with good news, the jails will be filled with good people.
Attrib.

Moynihan, Noël (1916–94) British doctor and writer

1 Statistics will prove anything, even the truth.
Attrib.

Mozart, Wolfgang Amadeus (1756–91) Austrian composer

Quotations about Mozart

1 Whether the angels play only Bach in praising God I am not quite sure; I am sure, however, that *en famille* they play Mozart.
1930
Vicki Baum (1888–1960) Austrian-born U.S. writer. Referring to Wolfgang Amadeus Mozart and Johann Sebastian Bach. *Results of an Accident* (M. Goldsmith, tr.; 1931)

2 Ah Mozart! he was happily married—but his wife wasn't.

Victor Borge (b.1909) Danish-born U.S. entertainer and pianist. Quoted in *The Guinness Dictionary of Poisonous Quotations* (Colin Jarman, ed.; 1991)

3 Mozart in his music was probably the most reasonable of the world's greatest composers...expressing himself with a spontaneity and refinement and breath-taking rightness that has never since been duplicated.
Aaron Copland (1900–90) U.S. composer. *Copland on Music* (1960)

4 I like to get the most effect out of the fewest notes. This is getting back to the Mozart idea—simplicity in composition.
George Gershwin (1898–1937) U.S. composer. Quoted in *Fascinating Rhythm* (Deena Rosenberg; 1991)

5 It is sobering to consider that when Mozart was my age he had already been dead for a year.
Tom Lehrer (b.1928) U.S. mathematician and songwriter. Quoted in *An Encyclopedia of Quotations about Music* (Nat Shapiro; 1978)

6 The sonatas of Mozart are unique; they are too easy for children, and too difficult for artists.
Artur Schnabel (1882–1951) Austrian pianist and composer. Attrib.

7 From Mozart I learned to say important things in a conversational way.
George Bernard Shaw (1856–1950) Irish playwright. *Conversation with Busoni* (1922–24?)

Quotations by Mozart

8 Music must never offend the ear; it must please the hearer. In other words, it must never cease to be music.
Attrib.

Mozi (470? –391? B.C.) Chinese philosopher

1 The physician who is attending a patient...has to know the cause of the ailment before he can cure it.
Ethical and Political Works (400? B.C.), bk. 4, ch. 14

Mphahlele, Es'kia (b.1919) South African novelist, teacher, and political activist

1 Every man fashions and stays with the gods he thinks support him in his need.
The African Image (1974)

2 "Moderate," "liberal." Bad words in a situation of conflict. In any situation that requires nothing less than militancy to redress wrongs done to any section of a people. To be a liberal you have to be white.
The African Image (1974)

3 Petty intrigues and dramatic scenes among the relatives as they prepare for the funeral are innumerable. Without them, a funeral doesn't look like one.
"In Corner B," *Stories from Central and Southern Africa* (Paul A. Scanlon, ed.; 1983)

Msham, Mwana Kupona Binti (1810–60) Kenyan poet

1 Let your husband be content with you, All the days that you dwell together. On the Day on which ye are chosen, May he be happy and hold it due to you.
Utendi of Mwana Kupona: The Advice of Mwana Kupona upon The Wifely Duty (1934)

2 Live with him befittingly. Do not provoke him to anger. If he rebukes you, do not answer back; Endeavour to control your tongue. Keep faith with him. That which he desires do not withhold. You and he, dispute not together. A quarreller always is hurt.
Utendi of Mwana Kupona: The Advice of Mwana Kupona upon The Wifely Duty (1934)

3 When he awakes, delay you not To prepare for him a meal. And to take care of his body, Perfuming him and bathing him. Shave him, that his skin be smooth, Let his beard be trimmed. Let him enjoy ablution and incense, Morning and evening.
Utendi of Mwana Kupona: The Advice of Mwana Kupona upon The Wifely Duty (1934)

Mu Dan (1918–77) Chinese poet and translator

1 Some were boisterous friendships,
Fullblown blossoms, innocent of coming fall.
Society damned the pulsing blood,
Life cast molten passion in reality's shell.
"Song of Wisdom" (1976), st. 3

Mugabe, Robert (Robert Gabriel Mugabe; b.1924) Zimbabwean president

1 It could never be a correct justification that, because the whites oppressed us yesterday when they had power, that the blacks must oppress them today because they have power.
Speech (March 1980)

2 Genuine independence can only come out of the barrel of a gun.
Quoted in *The Africans: Encounters from the Sudan to the Cape* (David Lamb; 1983)

Muggeridge, Malcolm (Thomas Malcolm Muggeridge; 1903–90) British journalist

1 Few men of action have been able to make a graceful exit at the appropriate time.
Chronicles of Wasted Time (1972)

2 I will lift up mine eyes unto the pills. Almost everyone takes them, from the humble aspirin to the multi-coloured, king-sized three deckers, which put you to sleep, wake you up, stimulate and soothe you all in one. It is an age of pills.
New Statesman, London (August 3, 1962)

3 It has to be admitted that we English have sex on the brain, which is a very unsatisfactory place to have it.
Observer, London (1964), "Sayings of the Week"

4 An orgy looks particularly alluring seen through the mists of righteous indignation.
"Dolce Vita in a Cold Climate," *The Most of Malcolm Muggeridge* (1966)

5 The orgasm has replaced the Cross as the focus of longing and the image of fulfillment.
"Down With Sex," *The Most of Malcolm Muggeridge* (1966)

6 It is not for nothing that, in the English language alone, to accuse someone of trying to be funny is highly abusive.
Tread Softly For You Tread on My Jokes (1966)

7 Its avowed purpose is to excite sexual desire, which, I should have thought, is unnecessary in the case of the young,

inconvenient in the case of the middle aged, and unseemly in the old.
Referring to pornography. *Tread Softly For You Tread on My Jokes* (1966)

8 History will see advertising as one of the real evil things of our time. It is stimulating people constantly to want things, want this, want that.
Attrib.

9 Old politicians, like old actors, revive in the limelight.
Attrib.

Muhammad (570?–632?) Arab religious leader and prophet

1 The change in the breath of the mouth of him who fasts is better in Allah's estimation than the smell of musk.
610?–632? Reported as spoken by Muhammad by Abu Hurairah, one of his companions. Quoted in *Forty Hadith Qudsi* (E. Ibrahim and D. Johnson-Davies, eds., trs.; 1988), 10th Hadith

2 Let him who finds good praise Allah and let him who finds other than that blame no one but himself.
610?–632? Reported as spoken by Muhammad by Abu Dharr al-Ghifari. Quoted in *Forty Hadith Qudsi* (E. Ibrahim and D. Johnson-Davies, eds., trs.; 1988), 17th Hadith

3 Pride is My cloak and greatness My robe, and he who competes with Me in respect of either of them I shall cast into Hell-fire.
610?–632? Reported as revealed through Muhammad by Abu Hurairah, one of his companions. Quoted in *Forty Hadith Qudsi* (E. Ibrahim and D. Johnson-Davies, eds., trs.; 1988), 19th Hadith

4 When Allah decreed the Creation He pledged Himself by writing in His book which is laid down with Him: My mercy prevails over My wrath.
610?–632? Reported as saying of Muhammad by Abu Harairah, one of his companions. Quoted in *Forty Hadith Qudsi* (E. Ibrahim and D. Johnson-Davies, eds., trs.; 1988), 1st Hadith

5 There shall come out of Hell-fire he who has said: There is no god but Allah and who has in his heart goodness weighing an atom.
610?–632? Reported as spoken by Muhammad by al-Bukhari, the great Islamic scholar. Quoted in *Forty Hadith Qudsi* (E. Ibrahim and D. Johnson-Davies, eds., trs.; 1988), 36th Hadith

6 Paradise and Hell-fire disputed together, and Hell-fire said: In me are the mighty and the haughty. Paradise said: In me are the weak and the poor.
610?–632? Reported as spoken by Muhammad by Abu Sa'id al-Khudri. Quoted in *Forty Hadith Qudsi* (E. Ibrahim and D. Johnson-Davies, eds., trs.; 1988), 39th Hadith

7 Sons of Adam inveigh against the vicissitudes of Time, and I am Time, in My hand is the night and the day.
610?–632? Reported as revealed through Muhammad by Abu Harairah, one of his companions. Quoted in *Forty Hadith Qudsi* (E. Ibrahim and D. Johnson-Davies, eds., trs.; 1988), 4th Hadith

8 Your Lord delights at a shepherd who, on the peak of a mountain crag, gives the call to prayer and prays.
610?–632? Reported as spoken by Muhammad by 'Uqbah ibn 'Amir. Quoted in *Forty Hadith Qudsi* (E. Ibrahim and D. Johnson-Davies, eds., trs.; 1988), 7th Hadith

9 A part of the excellence of a man's Islam is his leaving alone what does not concern him.
Originally reported as a saying of Muhammad by Abu Hurairah, one of his companions. Reported as spoken by Muhammad by Abu Dharr al-Ghifari. Quoted in *The Complete Forty Hadith* (Muhyid-Din al-Nawawi; 13th century), 12th Hadith

10 You must wage jihad for it is the monasticism of believers.
Reported as spoken by Muhammad by Abu Dharr al-Ghifari. Quoted in *The Complete Forty Hadith* (Muhyid-Din al-Nawawi; 13th century), 12th Hadith

11 Beware of newly introduced matters, for every newly introduced matter is an innovation, and every innovation is a going astray, and every straying is in the Fire.
Reported as a saying of Muhammad by Abu Sariyah, an early disciple. Reported as spoken by Muhammad by Abu Dharr al-Ghifari. Quoted in *The Complete Forty Hadith* (Muhyid-Din al-Nawawi; 13th century), 28th Hadith

12 The most intelligent people are the people of doing without, because they love what Allah loves and dislike the world which Allah dislikes.
Reported as spoken by Muhammad by Abu Dharr al-Ghifari. Quoted in *The Complete Forty Hadith* (Muhyid-Din al-Nawawi; 13th century), 31st Hadith

13 It is sufficient evil for a man that he should despise his brother.
Reported as spoken by Muhammad by Abu Dharr al-Ghifari. Quoted in *The Complete Forty Hadith* (Muhyid-Din al-Nawawi; 13th century), 36th Hadith

14 Certainly, every king has his forbidden pasturage. Certainly, Allah's forbidden pasturage is the things he has forbidden.
Originally reported as a saying of Muhammad by Ibn Bashir, an early disciple. Reported as spoken by Muhammad by Abu Dharr al-Ghifari. Quoted in *The Complete Forty Hadith* (Muhyid-Din al-Nawawi; 13th century), 6th Hadith

15 The five senses are as spies. Each one of them has been entrusted with making one of the arts, so the eye has been entrusted with the world of colors, hearing with the world of voices, and so on.
Reported as spoken by Muhammad by Abu Dharr al-Ghifari. Quoted in *The Complete Forty Hadith* (Muhyid-Din al-Nawawi; 13th century), 6th Hadith

16 The ink of the scholar is more sacred than the blood of the martyr.
Attrib.

Muhammad, Elijah (Elijah Poole; 1897–1975) U.S. Black Muslim leader

1 The Negro wants to be everything but himself...He wants to integrate with the white man, but he cannot integrate with himself or with his own kind. The Negro wants to lose his identity because he does not know his own identity.
Quoted in *Black Nationalism* (E. U. Essien-Udom; 1962)

Muir, Edwin (1887–1959) Scottish poet, translator, and critic

1 Time, teach us the art
That breaks and heals the heart.
"The Heart Could Never Speak" (1960)

2 I had read a good deal about psychoanalysis, the experiment itself attracted me, and I accepted. I have been glad ever since that I did, and will always feel grateful for the kindness of the analyst.
Referring to the offer of free psychoanalysis in 1919. *An Autobiography* (1954)

3 Those lumbering horses in the steady plough,
On the bare field—I wonder why, just now,
They seemed terrible, so wild and strange,
Like magic power on the stony grange.
"Horses," *First Poems* (1925)

Muir, Frank (1920–98) British writer and broadcaster

1 I've examined your son's head, Mr Glum, and there's nothing there.
Take It from Here (with Dennis Norden; 1957)

2 It has been said that a bride's attitude towards her betrothed can be summed up in three words: Aisle. Altar. Hymn.
Upon My Word! (1974)

3 Some breakfast food manufacturer hit upon the simple notion of emptying out the leavings of carthorse nosebags, adding a few other things like unconsumed portions of chicken layer's mash, and the sweepings of racing stables, packing the mixture in little bags and selling them in health food shops.
Upon My Word! (1974)

4 Another fact of life that will not have escaped you is that, in this country, the twenty-four-hour strike is like the twenty-four-hour flu. You have to reckon on it lasting at least five days.
"Great Expectations," *You Can't Have Your Kayak and Heat It* (co-written with Dennis Norden; 1973)

5 Dogs, like horses, are quadrupeds. That is to say, they have four rupeds, one at each corner, on which they walk.
"Ta-ra-ra-boom-de-ay!," *You Can't Have Your Kayak and Heat It* (co-written with Dennis Norden; 1973)

6 Strategy is buying a bottle of fine wine when you take a lady out for dinner. Tactics is getting her to drink it.
Attrib.

Muir, John (1838–1914) U.S. naturalist and explorer

1 I have precious little sympathy for the selfish propriety of civilized man, and if a war of races should occur between the beasts and Lord Man, I would be tempted to sympathize with the bears.
A Thousand Mile Walk to the Gulf (1916), quoted in *John Muir: The Eight Wilderness Discovery Books* (1992)

2 Music is one of the attributes of matter...Infinitesimal portions of air plash and sing about the angles and hollows of sand-grains, as perfectly composed and predestined as the rejoicing anthems of worlds.
A Thousand Mile Walk to the Gulf (1916), quoted in *John Muir: The Eight Wilderness Discovery Books* (1992)

3 I wandered away on a glorious botanical and geological excursion, which has lasted nearly fifty years and is not yet completed, always happy and free, poor and rich, without thought of a diploma or of making a name, urged on and on through endless, inspiring Godful beauty.
Referring to leaving the University of Wisconsin in 1867. *A Thousand Mile Walk to the Gulf* (1916), quoted in *John Muir: The Eight Wilderness Discovery Books* (1992)

4 Found the fragrant Washington lily, the finest of all the Sierra lilies...A lovely flower, worth going hungry and footsore endless miles to see. The whole world seems richer now that I have found this plant in so noble a landscape.
My First Summer in the Sierra (1911), quoted in *John Muir: The Eight Wilderness Discovery Books* (1992)

5 Climb Electric Peak when a big bossy, well-charged thunder-cloud is on it, to breathe the ozone set free, and get yourself kindly shaken and shocked...Every hair of your head will stand up and hum and sing like an enthusiastic congregation.
Our National Parks (1901), quoted in *John Muir: The Eight Wilderness Discovery Books* (1992)

6 Even the scenery habit in its most artificial forms, mixed with spectacles, silliness, and kodaks: its devotees arrayed more gorgeously than scarlet tanagers, frightening the wild game with red umbrellas—even this is encouraging, and may well be regarded as a hopeful sign of the times.
Our National Parks (1901), quoted in *John Muir: The Eight Wilderness Discovery Books* (1992)

7 God has cared for these trees, saved them from drought, disease, avalanches and a thousand straining, levelling tempests and floods; but he cannot save them from fools—only Uncle Sam can do that.
Our National Parks (1901), quoted in *John Muir: The Eight Wilderness Discovery Books* (1992)

8 Surely all God's people, however serious or savage, great or small, like to play; whales and elephants, dancing, humming gnats, and invisibly small mischievous microbes—all are warm with divine radium and must have lots of fun in them.
The Story of my Boyhood and Youth (1913), quoted in *John Muir: The Eight Wilderness Discovery Books* (1992)

9 Most people are on the world, not in it—having no conscious sympathy or relationship to anything about them—undiffused, separate, and rigidly alone like marbles of polished stone, touching but separate.
Quoted in *John of the Mountains* (Linnie Marsh Wolfe, ed.; 1938)

10 Climb the mountains and get their good tidings. Nature's peace will flow into you as sunshine flows into trees. The winds will blow their own freshness into you, and the storms their energy, while cares will drop off like autumn leaves.
Attrib.

Muldoon, Paul (Paul Benedict Muldoon; b.1951) Irish poet

1 To tell the range of the English longbows
At Agincourt, or Crécy,
We need look no further than the yews
That, even in Irish graveyards,
Are bent on Fitzwilliams, and de Courcys.
"Palm Sunday" (1982), ll. 1–6, quoted in *The Penguin Book of Contemporary British Poetry* (Blake Morrison and Andrew Motion, eds.; 1982)

2 They gave us six fishhooks
and two blankets embroidered with smallpox.
Narrated in the voice of a Native American, defeated by the British. "Meeting the British," *Meeting the British* (1987), ll. 17–18

Mulgan, Geoff (b.1961) British author and political analyst

1 Capitalism was born out of an ethos, an ethos of work and sacrifice, but today it lacks even the means to think about what it is for.
Connexity (1997)

2 Organizations are becoming like insects: their ethos, which is equivalent perhaps to a kind of cultural DNA, is held internally,

but their structure is like the insect's exoskeleton, carried on the outside not the inside.
Connexity (1997)

3 Organizations can be less heavily structured through internal architectures and more through interfaces. To grow it may be more efficient to spread like amoeba, or fungi, than like a building.
Connexity (1997)

4 Remoteness and isolation were once the condition of the poor. Today it is only the extremely rich who can easily escape other people.
Connexity (1997)

5 Systems governed by only one set of rules are more vulnerable than those with variety.
Connexity (1997)

6 Within a virtual market the real world truly is irrelevant, and the invisible hand becomes a blind hand, with no reason to take account of how it affects other people, or future generations.
Connexity (1997)

Müller, Max (Friedrich Max Müller; 1823–1900) German-born British philologist

1 Language is the autobiography of the human mind.
Quoted in *Scholar Extraordinary* (Nirad Chaudhuri; 1974)

Mumford, James Gregory (1863–1914) U.S. surgeon

1 We'll be over, we're coming over,
And we won't come back till it's over, over there.
Song lyric. "Over There" (1917)

2 I don't care what you say about me, as long as you say *something*.
Quoted in *George M. Cohan* (John McCabe; 1973)

3 The history of medicine does not depart from the history of the people.
Attrib.

Mumford, Lewis (1895–1990) U.S. social philosopher and urban planner

1 Every generation revolts against its fathers and makes friends with its grandfathers.
The Brown Decades (1931)

2 By his very success in inventing labor-saving devices modern man has manufactured an abyss of boredom that only the privileged classes in earlier civilizations have ever fathomed.
The Conduct of Life (1951)

3 Life is the only art that we are required to practice without preparation, and without being allowed the preliminary trials, the failures and botches, that are essential for training.
Attrib.

4 Traditionalists are pessimists about the future and optimists about the past.
Attrib.

Munch, Edvard (1863–1944) Norwegian artist

1 The sky was suddenly blood-red—I stopped and leaned against the fence, dead tired. I saw the flaming clouds like blood and a sword—the bluish-black fjord and town—my friends walked on—I stood there, trembling with anxiety—and I felt as though Nature were convulsed by a great unending scream.
Letter (1892)

2 Nothing is small, nothing is great. Inside us are worlds. What is small divides itself into what is great, the great into the small.
Notebook (1913–15)

3 I do not believe in the kind of art which has not forced its way out through man's need to open his heart—all art, literature as well as music, must be created with one's heart's blood.
Attrib.

Munro, Neil (1864–1930) Scottish novelist and journalist

1 Oh man! she wass the beauty! She was chust sublime!
Referring to the steam engine, *Vital Spark*. "The *Vital Spark*," *Para Handy, Master Mariner* (1906)

2 He once crept out of the fo'c'sle rubbing his eyes after a twelve-hours' sleep, saying, "Tell me this and tell me no more, am I going to my bed or comin' from it?"
Referring to the Tar's tiredness. "The *Vital Spark*," *The Malingerer* (1906)

Münster, Ernst Friedrich Herbert (1766–1839) Hanoverian statesman

1 Absolutism tempered by assassination.
Referring to the Russian Constitution. Letter, *Political Sketches of the State of Europe 1814–1867* (1868)

Münter, Gabriele (1887–1962) German painter

1 My main difficulty was that I could not paint fast enough. My pictures are all moments of my life, I mean instantaneous visual experiences, generally noted very rapidly and spontaneously.
"Interview with Gabriele Münter," *Arts* (Edouard Roditi; January 1960)

Murchison, Clint (Clinton Williams Murchison; 1895–1969) U.S. industrialist

1 Money is like manure. If you spread it around it does a lot of good. But if you pile it up in one place it stinks like hell.
Time (June 16, 1961)

Murdoch, Iris, Dame (Jean Iris Murdoch; 1919–99) Irish-born British novelist and philosopher

1 One doesn't have to get anywhere in a marriage. It's not a public conveyance.
A Severed Head (1961)

2 Only lies and evil come from letting people off.
A Severed Head (1961)

3 Love is the difficult realization that something other than oneself is real.
"The Sublime and the Good," *Chicago Review* (1959)

4 Falling out of love is very enlightening. For a short while you see the world with new eyes.
Observer, London (February 4, 1968), "Sayings of the Week"

5 The cry of equality pulls everyone down.
Observer, London (September 1987), "Sayings of the Week"

6 All art deals with the absurd and aims at the simple. Good art speaks truth, indeed *is* truth, perhaps the only truth.
"Bradley Pearson's Foreword," *The Black Prince* (1974)

7 Writing is like getting married. One should never commit oneself until one is amazed at one's luck.
"Bradley Pearson's Foreword," *The Black Prince* (1974)

8 "What are you famous *for*"
"For nothing. I am just famous."
The Flight from the Enchanter (1955)

9 I think being a woman is like being Irish...Everyone says you're important and nice but you take second place all the same.
The Red and the Green (1965)

10 He led a double life. Did that make him a liar? He did not feel a liar. He was a man of two truths.
The Sacred and Profane Love Machine (1974)

11 Freedom...is not an inconsequential chucking of one's weight about, it is the disciplined overcoming of self.
The Sovereignty of Good (1970)

12 Humility is not a peculiar habit of self-effacement, rather like having an inaudible voice, it is a selfless respect for reality and one of the most difficult and central of all the virtues.
The Sovereignty of Good (1970)

13 We live in a fantasy world, a world of illusion. The great task in life is to find reality.
Times, London (April 15, 1983)

14 All artists dream of a silence which they must enter, as some creatures return to the sea to spawn.
Attrib.

Murdoch, Rupert (Keith Rupert Murdoch; b.1931) Australian-born U.S. media entrepreneur

Quotations about Murdoch

1 Rupert is the only man I know who makes me feel like Liberace.
James Goldsmith (1933–97) French-born British businessman and politician. Referring to Rupert Murdoch's sang-froid, and to the flamboyant 20th-century Las Vegas performer, Liberace. Quoted in *The Risk Takers* (Jeffrey Robinson; 1985)

Quotations by Murdoch

2 In the 18th century, Voltaire said that every man had two countries: his own and France. In the 20th century, that has come to be true of the United States.
Speech, New York City (November 9, 1989)

3 There is no such thing as a global village. Most media are rooted in their national and local cultures.
Business Review Weekly (November 17, 1989)

4 British journalism will not suffer from a little less alcohol.
Referring to the lack of pubs near the *Times*'s new presses at Wapping in East London. *Sydney Morning Herald* (February 8, 1986), "Sayings of the Week"

5 I want to be at the table and a player when they move the pieces around in America.
1989. Referring to his desire to buy *Time* magazine. Quoted in *Rupert Murdoch, Ringmaster of the Information Circus* (William Shawcross; 1993)

6 I'm either part of your problem or part of your solution.
Said to the deputy chairman of the British publishing company William Collins, pointing out that he owned 31 percent of the company's stock. Quoted in *Rupert Murdoch, Ringmaster of the Information Circus* (William Shawcross; 1993)

Murphy, Arthur (1727–1805) Irish playwright, writer, and actor

1 Above the vulgar flight of common souls.
Zenobia (1768), Act 5

Murphy, C. W. (b.1909) British songwriter

1 Has anybody here seen Kelly?
Kelly from the Isle of Man?
Song lyric. "Has Anybody Here Seen Kelly?" (1909)

Murphy, Dervla (b.1931) Irish travel writer

1 We Irish are always being accused of looking backwards too much. Sometimes, however, we don't look back far enough—or carefully enough, or honestly enough.
A Place Apart (1978)

2 These roads have no corners, only curves; thus we went around in circles for another half-hour.
Muddling Through in Madagascar (1985)

3 Anthropologists and ethnologists get extraordinarily steamed up about the origins of Madagascar's pervasive taboos (a Polynesian word) or *fady* (an Indonesian word).
Muddling Through in Madagascar (1985), ch. 3

4 Rotten fish is a Malagasy delicacy, reserved for Festive Occasions or Honoured Guests, and this pungent compliment could not be discreetly smuggled away.
Muddling Through in Madagascar (1985), ch. 4

5 My most precious souvenir of Madagascar is a small packet of red earth such as the Malagasy take with them when they go abroad...to ensure their eventual return.
Muddling Through in Madagascar (1985), ch. 10

Murphy, Eddy (Edward Reagan Murphy; b.1961) U.S. comedian, actor, and director

1 What would be the first thing I'd do if I were president? Buy a bullet proof vest!
Ebony (July 1988)

Murphy, Richard (b.1927) Irish poet

1 But tonight we stay, drinking with people
Happy in the monotony of boats.
1963. "Sailing to an Island," *New Selected Poems* (1985), ll. 67–68

2 In bowler hats and Sunday suits
Orange sashes, polished boots,

Atavistic trainbands come
To blow the fife and beat the drum.
Referring to the Orange Order, who support the continuation of British rule in Northern Ireland. William III (William of Orange) defeated the Irish at Aughrim in 1691. "Orange March," *The Battle of Aughrim* (1968)

3 Slate I picked from a nettlebed
Had history, my neighbour said.

To quarry it, men had to row
Five miles, twelve centuries ago.
"Slate," *The Battle of Aughrim* (1968), ll. 1–4

Murray, Bill (b.1950) U.S. comedian and actor

1 I don't have to take this abuse from you. I've got hundreds of people waiting to abuse me.
As Dr. Peter Venkman. *Ghostbusters* (Dan Ackroyd and Harold Ramis; 1984)

Murray, David (1888–1962) British journalist and writer

1 A reporter is a man who has renounced everything in life but the world, the flesh, and the devil.
Observer, London (July 5, 1931), "Sayings of the Week"

Murray, Jenni (Jennifer Susan Murray; b.1950) British broadcaster

1 Marriage is an insult and women shouldn't touch it.
Independent, London (June 20, 1992)

Murray, John Fisher (1811–65) British writer

1 "She says, if you please, sir, she only wants to be let die in peace."
"What!...impossible! Tell her she can't be allowed to die in peace; it is against the rules of the hospital!"
The World of London (1843)

Murrow, Ed (Edward, born Egbert, Roscoe Murrow; 1908–65) U.S. journalist and broadcaster

1 We cannot defend freedom abroad by deserting it at home.
Attrib.

Musset, Alfred de (Louis Charles Alfred de Musset; 1810–57) French poet and playwright

1 The glass I drink from is not large, but at least it is my own.
"La Coupe et les lèvres" (1832), quoted in *Poésies complètes* (Maurice Allem, ed.; 1933)

2 I cannot help it;—in spite of myself, infinity torments me.
"L'Espoir en Dieu" (1834)

3 That which comes from the heart can be written, but that which is the heart itself cannot.
Emmeline (1841), ch. 7

4 Great artists have no country.
Lorenzaccio (1834), Act 1, Scene 5

5 The only good thing left to me is that I have sometimes wept.
"Tristesse," *Poèmes* (1841)

6 I have come too late into a world too old.
"Rolla," *Poésies nouvelles* (1833)

Mussolini, Benito (Benito Amilcare Andrea Mussolini, "Il Duce"; 1883–1945) Italian dictator

Quotations about Mussolini

1 The Duce is always right.
Mottos and Slogans. Italian Fascist slogan

Quotations by Mussolini

2 Fascism is not an article for export.
Reported in the German press. Remark (1932)

3 We have buried the putrid corpse of liberty.
Speech (1934), quoted in *Bolshevism, Fascism and the Liberal-Democratic State* (Maurice Farr Parmelee; 1935)

4 I could have transformed this gray assembly hall into an armed camp of Blackshirts, a bivouac for corpses. I could have nailed up the doors of Parliament.
Referring to the Fascist march on Rome, which had resulted in Mussolini's becoming prime minister (October 31, 1922). Speech, Chamber of Deputies, Rome (November 16, 1922)

5 This Berlin-Rome connection is not so much a diaphragm as an axis, around which can revolve all those states of Europe with a will towards collaboration and peace.
Speech, Milan (November 1, 1936)

6 I declare...that I, and I alone, assume the political, moral and historical responsibility for all that has happened...If Fascism has been a criminal association...the responsibility has been mine.
Speech, Rome (January 3, 1925), quoted in *Fascist Italy* (John Whittam; 1995)

7 The keystone of the Fascist doctrine is its conception of the State, of its essence, its functions, and its aims. For Fascism the State is absolute, individuals and groups relative.
Fascism: Doctrine and Institutions (1935)

8 To understand Nietzsche we must envisage a new race of "free spirits," strengthened in war, in solitude, in great danger.
Il Pensiero Romagnolo (November–December 1908)

9 The right to the political succession belongs to us because it was we who forced the country into the war and led it to victory.
Il Popolo d'Italia (March 24, 1919)

10 Italian in its particular institutions, universal in spirit.
Referring to Fascism. *Scritti e discorsi* (October 27, 1930)

11 Our fierce totalitarian will.
Quoted in *Europe Since 1870* (James Joll; 1973), ch. 9

12 For me Fascism is not an end in itself. It was a means to re-establish national equilibrium.
August 1921. Quoted in *Fascist Italy* (John Whittam; 1995), ch., 3

13 We cannot change our policy now. After all, we are not political whores.
Quoted in *Hitler* (Alan Bullock; 1952), ch. 8

14 War alone brings up to their highest tension all human energies and imposes the stamp of nobility upon the peoples who have the courage to make it.
1930? Quoted in *Mussolini's Roman Empire* (Dennis Mark-Smith; 1976)

15 Blood alone moves the wheels of history.
Attrib.

16 Youth is a malady of which one becomes cured a little every day.
1933. Said on his 50th birthday. Attrib.

Mussorgsky, Modest (Modest Petrovich Mussorgsky; 1839–81) Russian composer

Quotations about Mussorgsky

1 What bothered Stalin in *Boris*? That the blood of the innocent will sooner or later rise from the soil. That's the ethical center of the opera.
1971–75
Dmitri Shostakovich (1906–75) Russian composer. Referring to Modest Mussorgsky's opera *Boris Godunov* (1874). *Testimony: The Memoirs of Shostakovich* (Solomon Volkov, ed., Antonina W. Bouis, tr.; 1979), ch. 7

Quotations by Mussorgsky

2 Art is not an end in itself, but a means of addressing humanity.
Attrib.

Muste, A. J. (Abraham John Muste; 1885–1967) U.S. author and pacifist

1 There is no way to peace. Peace is the way.
New York Times (November 16, 1967)

Myhrvold, Nathan U.S. business executive

1 Anyone who says you should stick to your knitting is wrong. And anyone who says do or die, create something for the sake of being different, is wrong too.
Business Week (March 21, 1994)

2 Going to Europe gives us a way to hire people who bring new talents and new perspectives to our work that we couldn't get any other way.
Referring to Microsoft Corporation's decision to build an $80 million research center in Cambridge, England. *New York Times* (June 18, 1997)

3 Most decisions are seat-of-the-pants judgments. You can create a rationale for anything. In the end, most decisions are based on intuition and faith.
Quoted in *The Highwaymen: Warriors of the Information Superhighway* (Ken Auletta; 1997)

Nabokov, Vladimir (Vladimir Vladimirovich Nabokov; 1899–1977) Russian-born U.S. novelist, poet, and critic

1 Lolita, light of my life, fire of my loins. My sin, my Soul.
Opening words. *Lolita* (1955), ch. 1

2 Solitude is the playfield of Satan.
Pale Fire (1962)

3 Life is a great surprise. I do not see why death should not be an even greater one.
"Commentary," *Pale Fire* (1962)

4 Like so many aging college people, Pnin had long ceased to notice the existence of students on the campus.
Pnin (1957), ch. 3

5 Discussion in class, which means letting twenty young blockheads and two cocky neurotics discuss something that neither their teacher nor they know.
Pnin (1957), ch. 6

6 Literature and butterflies are the two sweetest passions known to man.
Radio Times, London (October 1962)

7 My fear of losing or corrupting, through alien influence, the only thing I had salvaged from Russia—her language—became positively morbid.
Speak, Memory (1967)

8 The cradle rocks above an abyss, and common sense tells us that our existence is but a brief crack of light between two eternities of darkness.
Speak, Memory (1967)

9 The nostalgia I have been cherishing all these years is a hypertrophied sense of lost childhood, not sorrow for lost banknotes.
Speak, Memory (1967), ch. 3, sect. 5

10 They are passing, posthaste, posthaste, the gliding years—to use a soul-rending Horatian term. The years are passing, my dear, and presently nobody will know what you and I know.
Speak, Memory (1967), ch. 3, sect. 5

11 What the Tsars had never been able to achieve, namely the complete curbing of minds to the government's will, was achieved by the Bolsheviks after the main contingent of the intellectuals had escaped abroad or been destroyed.
Speak, Memory (1967), ch. 14, sect. 2

12 A novelist is, like all mortals, more fully at home on the surface of the present than in the ooze of the past.
Strong Opinions (1951), ch. 20

13 Poor Knight! he really had two periods, the first—a dull man writing broken English, the second—a broken man writing dull English.
The Real Life of Sebastian Knight (1941), ch. 1

14 A good reader has imagination, memory, a dictionary, and some artistic sense.
Attrib.

15 My loathings are simple: stupidity, oppression, crime, cruelty, soft music.
Attrib.

Nader, Ralph (b.1934) U.S. author, lawyer, and consumer activist

1 I don't agree with workers' control of industry. I don't think workers should meld with management. That creates an impregnable coalition against the consumer.
Quoted in *International Management* (August 1986)

Naess, Arne (b.1912) Norwegian philosopher and author

1 We need the immense variety of sources of joy opened through increased sensitivity toward the richness and diversity of life, through the profound cherishing of free natural landscapes.
"Self Realization," lecture, quoted in *Thinking Like a Mountain* (John Seed, ed.; 1988)

2 In the Deep Ecology Movement we are biocentric or ecocentric. For us it is the ecosphere, the whole planet, Gaia, that is the basic unit, and every living being has an intrinsic value.
"The Basics of Deep Ecology," a Schumacher lecture, quoted in *The Green Fuse* (John Button, ed.; 1990)

3 The essence of Deep Ecology is to ask deeper questions...We ask which society, which education, which form of religion is beneficial for all life on the planet as a whole.
Quoted in Zen Center of Los Angeles newsletter, *Ten Directions* (Summer–Fall 1982)

Nagel, Thomas (b.1937) Yugoslavian-born U.S. philosopher and educator

1 In seeing ourselves from outside we find it difficult to take our lives seriously. This loss of conviction, and the attempt to regain it, is the problem of the meaning of life.
The View from Nowhere (1986)

2 Philosophy is the childhood of the intellect, and a culture that tries to skip it will never grow up.
The View from Nowhere (1986)

3 We are finite beings, and even if each of us possesses a large dormant capacity for objective self-transcendence, our knowledge of the world will always be fragmentary, however much we extend it.
The View from Nowhere (1986)

Nahmanides (originally Moses ben Nahman; 1194?–1270) Spanish scholar and Jewish religious leader

1 From the days of Jesus until now, the whole world has been full of violence and plundering.
Quoted in *Judaism on Trial* (Hyam Maccoby; 1982)

Naidu, Sarojini (1879–1949) Indian poet and politician

1 The Indian woman of today is once more awake and profoundly alive to her splendid destiny as the guardian and interpreter of the Triune Vision of national life—the Vision of Love, the Vision of Faith, the Vision of Patriotism.
The Broken Wing (1916)

Naimbanna, John Henry (1767–93) Sierra Leonean son of King Naimbanna

1 If a man should rob me of my money, I can forgive him; if a man should shoot at me, I can forgive him; if a man should sell me and all my family to a slave ship, so that we should pass all the rest of our lives in slavery in the West Indies, I can forgive him; but if a man takes away the character of the people of my country, I never can forgive him.
Quoted in *Black Writers in Britain 1760–1890* (Paul Edwards and David Dabydeen; 1991)

Naipaul, V. S., Sir (Vidiadhar Surajprasad Naipaul; b.1932) Trinidadian-born British novelist

1 Worse, to have lived without even attempting to lay claim to one's portion of the earth; to have lived and died as one had been born, unnecessary and unaccommodated.
A House for Mr. Biswas (1961), Prologue

2 One always writes comedy at the moment of deepest hysteria.
Observer, London (May 1, 1994), "Sayings of the Week"

Nairn, Tom (b.1932) Scottish sociologist and author

1 Modern patriotism has no natural persona in Scotland. Our old clothes are romantic rags, yet—embarrassingly, inexplicably—none of the new uniforms seems to fit either.
Faces of Nationalism (1997)

2 There are no longer fixed absolutes in the societal universe, any more than in the physical one. But in the latter case this did not entail the serious rehabilitation of astrology or palmistry.
Faces of Nationalism (1997)

3 Every single barrel of North Sea oil will go on being used to get the Crown Jewels back from the pawn-shop.
Referring to the use of North Sea oil revenues to redeem the British economy. *The Break-Up of Britain* (1977)

Nairne, Carolina, Baroness (originally Carolina Oliphant; 1766–1845) Scottish songwriter

1 Better lo'ed ye canna be,
Will ye no come back again?
Referring to Prince Charles Edward Stuart. "Bonnie Charlie's Now Away!" (1846)

2 Charlie is my darling, my darling, my darling,
Charlie is my darling, the young Chevalier.
Referring to Prince Charles Edward Stuart. "Charlie is my Darling" (1846)

3 Wi' a hundred pipers an' a', an' a'.
A glorification of the Jacobite Rebellion (1745). "The Hundred Pipers" (1846)

Nakhla, Fayed U.S. psychoanalyst

1 The doctor says, you have to keep cutting yourself. Go on cutting yourself: you have to stay in touch with your body, with yourself, in whatever way you can.
Referring to self-laceration as a symptom of depression. *Picking Up the Pieces* (1993), ch. 4

Namath, Joe (Joseph William Namath; b.1943) U.S. football quarterback

1 When you win, nothing hurts.
Attrib.

Nannakaiyar, Kaccipettu (*fl.* 3rd century) Indian poet

1 I grow lean
in loneliness,
like a water lily
gnawed by a beetle.
Interior Landscape: Love Poems from a Tamil Anthology (A. K. Ramanujan, ed.; 1967)

Napier, Charles James, Sir (1782–1853) British general and colonial administrator

1 I have sinned!
Reporting his subjugation of Sind, N. India. Remark (February 1843)Attrib.

2 Lads, war is declared with a numerous and bold enemy. Should they meet and offer battle, you know how to dispose of them. Should they remain in port, we must try and get at them. Success depends upon the quickness and precision of your firing.
Referring to the declaration of war against Russia. Signal to his command (1854)

Napoleon I, Emperor of the French (Napoleon Bonaparte; 1769–1821) French emperor

Quotations about Napoleon I

1 That infernal creature who is the curse of all the human race becomes every day more and more abominable.
Alexander I (1777–1825) Russian monarch. Letter to his sister Catherine (January 5, 1812)

2 I shall never forget the tokens of friendship afforded me by the Emperor Napoleon. The more I think of them, the more happy I am to have known him. What an extraordinary man!
Alexander I (1777–1825) Russian monarch. Remark to the French ambassador (July 1807)

3 He is an ordinary human being after all!...now he will put himself above everyone else and become a tyrant.

Ludwig van Beethoven (1770–1827) German composer. Referring to Napoleon, on hearing that he had declared himself emperor. Attributed to him by a pupil (1804)

4 Napoleon is a dangerous man in a free country. He seems to me to have the makings of a tyrant, and I believe that were he to be king he would be fully capable of playing such a part, and his name would become an object of detestation to posterity and every right-minded patriot.
Lucien Bonaparte (1775–1840) French ambassador. Letter to his brother Joseph (1790)

5 Napoleon never wished to be justified. He killed his enemy according to the Corsican tradition, and if he sometimes regretted his error, he never understood that it had been a crime.
Guillaume-Prosper (1782–1866) French diplomat. *Souvenirs* (1865?), vol. 7

6 Napoleon—mighty somnambulist of a vanished dream.
Victor Hugo (1802–85) French poet, novelist, and playwright. *Les Misérables* (1862)

7 Napoleon has not been conquered by men. He was greater than any of us. God punished him because he relied solely on his own intelligence until that incredible instrument was so strained that it broke.
Karl XIV Johan (1763–1844) French-born Swedish general and monarch. Referring to the death of Napoleon I. Public announcement (May 1821)

8 One could forgive the fiend for becoming a torrent, but to become an earthquake was really too much.
Charles Joseph de Ligne (1735–1814) Belgian-born soldier, statesman, and writer. Attrib.

9 Napoleon had the best method. He dissolved all representative institutions and decided himself who should run the state together with him.
September 1973
Mao Zedong (1893–1976) Chinese statesman. Quoted in "Line of the Masses," *Maoism: Slogans and Practice* (Vladimir Glebov; 1978)

10 We will not leave the monster to prowl the world unopposed.
William Pitt the Younger (1759–1806) British prime minister. Speech to the British Parliament (June 7, 1799)

11 Bonaparte's whole life, civil, political and military, was a fraud. There was not a transaction, great or small, in which lying and fraud were not introduced.
Duke of Wellington (1769–1852) Irish-born British general and prime minister. Letter (December 29, 1835)

12 I used to say of him that his presence on the field made the difference of forty thousand men.
November 2, 1831
Duke of Wellington (1769–1852) Irish-born British general and prime minister. *Notes of Conversations with the Duke of Wellington* (Philip Henry Stanhope; 1888)

Quotations by Napoleon I

13 My principle is: France before everything.
Letter to Eugène de Beauharnais (August 23, 1810)

14 The bullet that is to kill me has not yet been molded.
Replying to his brother Joseph, King of Spain, who had asked whether he had ever been hit by a cannonball. Remark (February 2, 1814)

15 It's the most beautiful battlefield I've ever seen.
Referring to carnage on the field of Borodino, near Moscow, after the battle. Remark (September 7, 1812)Attrib.

16 It is only one step from the sublime to the ridiculous.
Following the retreat from Moscow. Remark to the Abbé de Pradt, the Polish ambassador (1812), quoted in *Histoire de l'Ambassade dans le grand-duché de Varsovie en 1812* (D. G. de Pradt; 1815)

17 France has more need of me than I have need of France.
Speech (December 31, 1813)

18 Think of it, soldiers; from the summit of these pyramids, forty centuries look down upon you.
Speech before the Battle of the Pyramids (July 21, 1798), quoted in "Egypte, Bataille des Pyramides," *Mémoires* (Gaspard Gourgaud; 1823), vol. 2

19 In war, three-quarters turns on personal character and relations; the balance of manpower and materials counts only for the remaining quarter.
1808. Referring to the Spanish campaign. Letter to Saint-Cloud, *Correspondance de Napoléon I* (1854–69), xvii, no. 14276

20 As to moral courage, I have very rarely met with two o'clock in the morning courage: I mean instantaneous courage.
Les Cases, Mémorial de Ste-Hélène (1815)

21 The scientists had another idea...they adapted to themselves the decimal system, on the basis of the meter as a unit; they suppressed all complicated numbers. Nothing is more contrary to the organization of the mind, of the memory, and of the imagination.
On the introduction of the metric system. *Mémoires écrits à Ste-Hélène* (1823–25), vol. 4, ch. 16

22 Power is my mistress. I have worked too hard in conquering her to allow anyone to take her from me, or even to covet her.
The Journal of Roederer (1804)

23 I cannot receive you, gentlemen, since you and your Senate reek with French blood.
1797. Reply to two envoys from Venice immediately after the Venetians had fired on three small French boats off the Lido port. Quoted in "The Fall," *A History of Venice* (J. J. Norwich; 1982)

24 The great proof of madness is the disproportion of one's designs to one's means.
Quoted in *Maximes de Napoléon* (A. G. de Liancourt, ed.; 1842)

25 It is not everyone who has the right to be plainly dressed.
1802. Quoted in *Memoirs of Madame de Rémusat* (Mrs. Cashel Howey and John Lillie, trs.; 1880), vol. 1, ch. 2

26 England is a nation of shopkeepers.
Quoted in *Napoleon in Exile* (Barry O'Meara; 1822), vol. 2

27 Oh well, no matter what happens, there's always death.
1817. Attrib.

28 The worse the man the better the soldier. If soldiers be not corrupt they ought to be made so.
Attrib.

29 An army marches on its stomach.
Attributed by Charles Sainte-Beuve. Attrib.

30 Chief of the Army.
1821. Last words. Attrib.

31 I still love you, but in politics there is no heart, only head.
1809. Referring to his divorce, for reasons of state, from the Empress Josephine. Attrib.

32 There rises the sun of Austerlitz.
September 7, 1812. Said at the Battle of Borodino, near Moscow. The Battle of Austerlitz (December 2, 1805) was Napoleon's great victory over the Russians and Austrians. Attrib.

Napoleon III, Emperor of the French (Charles Louis Napoleon Bonaparte; 1808–73) French emperor

1 For too long Society has resembled a pyramid which has been turned upside down and made to rest on its summit. I have replaced it on its base.
Remark (March 29, 1852)

2 The army is the true nobility of our country.
Remark (March 20, 1855)

3 In a mood of defiance certain people are saying, "The Empire means War." Personally I say, "The Empire means Peace."
The Second Empire was established at Bordeaux in 1852. Remark (October 15, 1852)

4 I don't care for war, there's far too much luck in it for my liking.
Said after the narrow but bloody French victory at the Battle of Solferino (June 24, 1859). Quoted in *The Fall of the House of Habsburg* (Edward Crankshaw; 1963)

5 The cause of which my name is the symbol—that is to say, France regenerated by the Revolution and organized by the Emperor.
December 2, 1851. Issued during his coup d'état. Attrib.

6 This vice brings in one hundred million francs in taxes every year. I will certainly forbid it at once—as soon as you can name a virtue that brings in as much revenue.
Reply when asked to ban smoking. Attrib.

Narayan, R. K. (Rasipuram Krishnaswamy Narayan; b.1906) Indian writer

1 The astrologer transacted his business by the light of a flare which crackled and smoked up above the groundnut heap nearby. Half the enchantment of the place was due to the fact that it did not have the benefit of municipal lighting.
"An Astrologer's Day," *An Astrologer's Day and Other Stories* (1947)

2 When he told the person before him, gazing at his palm, "In many ways you are not getting the fullest results for your efforts," nine out of ten were disposed to agree with him.
"An Astrologer's Day," *An Astrologer's Day and Other Stories* (1947)

Narváez, Ramón María, Duque de Valencia (1800–68) Spanish general and politician

1 The time has come for Spaniards to be governed in accordance with the spirit of their history and the feelings which make up their better character.
Inaugurating a severe repression that led to the revolution of 1868. Speech, Madrid (1867)

2 I do not have to forgive my enemies, I have had them all shot.
1868. Said on his deathbed, when asked by a priest if he forgave his enemies. Attrib.

Nash, Ogden (Frederic Ogden Nash; 1902–71) U.S. humorist

1 Senescence begins
And middle age ends,
The day your descendants,
Outnumber your friends.
Complete poem. "Crossing the Border" (1957)

2 Women would rather be right than reasonable.
"Frailty, Thy Name is A Misnomer" (1942)

3 This creature fills its mouth with venom
And walks upon its duodenum.
He who attempts to tease the cobra
Is soon a sadder he, and sobra.
"Free Wheeling" (1931), quoted in *Selected Poems of Ogden Nash* (Anthony Burgess, ed.; 1983)

4 The only people who should really sin
Are the people who can sin with a grin.
"I'm a Stranger Here Myself" (1938)

5 When I consider how my life is spent,
I hardly ever repent.
"Reminiscent Reflection" (1931)

6 I think that I shall never see
A billboard lovely as a tree.
Perhaps unless the billboards fall,
I'll never see a tree at all.
"Song of the Open Road" (1933)

7 The cow is of the bovine ilk;
One end is moo, the other, milk.
"The Cow" (1931)

8 Some people's money is merited
And other people's is inherited.
"The Terrible People" (1933)

9 To be an Englishman is to belong to the most exclusive club there is.
England Expects (1950)

10 The only way I can distinguish proper from improper fractions
Is by their actions.
"Ask Daddy, He Won't Know," *Family Reunion* (1950)

11 Beneath this slab
John Brown is stowed.
He watched the ads,
And not the road.
"Lather as You Go," *Good Intentions* (1942)

12 I have a bone to pick with Fate,
Come here and tell me, girlie,
Do you think my mind is maturing late,
Or simply rotted early?
1937. "Lines on Facing Forty," *Good Intentions* (1942)

13 Children aren't happy with nothing to ignore,
And that's what parents were created for.
"The Parent," *Happy Days* (1933)

14 One would be in less danger
From the wiles of a stranger
If one's own kin and kith
Were more fun to be with.
"Family Court," *Hard Lines* (1931)

15 Candy

Is dandy
But liquor
Is quicker.
"Reflection on Ice-Breaking," *Hard Lines* (1931)

16 The Bronx
No thonx.
Referring to the Bronx, a borough of New York City. *New Yorker* (1931)

17 It's better to be dead, or even perfectly well, than to suffer from the wrong affliction. The man who owns up to arthritis in a beriberi year is as lonely as a woman in a last month's dress.
Saturday Evening Post (October 14, 1933)

18 There once was an umpire whose vision
Was cause for abuse and derision.
He remarked in surprise,
"Why pick on my eyes?
It's my heart that dictates my decision."
"An Ump's Heart," *Saturday Evening Post* (1966)

19 They all observe one rule which woe betide the banker who fails to heed it,
Which is you must never lend any money to anybody unless they don't need it.
1954. *The Face is Familiar* (1954, revised edition)

20 The trouble with a kitten is THAT
When it grows up, it's always a CAT.
"The Kitten," *The Face Is Familiar* (1942)

21 Sure, deck your lower limbs in pants;
Yours are the limbs, my sweeting.
You look divine as you advance—
Have you seen yourself retreating?
"What's the Use?," *The Face is Familiar* (1942)

22 Home is heaven and orgies are vile
But you *need* an orgy, once in a while.
"Home 99.44/100% Sweet Home," *The Primrose Path* (1935)

23 A door is what a dog is perpetually on the wrong side of.
"A Dog's Best Friend Is His Illiteracy," *The Private Dining Room* (1953)

24 Sweet talk is scant by Lake Cayuga,
But in Tennessee, they chatta nougat.
Referring to Lake Cayuga, New York, and Chattanooga, Tennessee. "Is it True What They Say About Dixie, or is it Just the Way They Say It?," *The Private Dining Room and Other New Verses* (1952)

25 I prefer to forget both pairs of glasses and pass my declining years saluting strange women and grandfather clocks.
"Peekaboo, I Almost See You," *The Private Dining Room and Other New Verses* (1952)

26 Middle age is when you've met so many people that every new person you meet reminds you of someone else.
Versus (1949)

27 A cough is something that you yourself can't help, but everybody else does on purpose just to torment you.
"Can I Get You a Glass of Water? Or Please Close the Glottis After You," *You Can't Get There from Here* (1957)

Nashe, Thomas (1567–1601) English playwright, satirist, novelist, and pamphleteer

1 O, tis a precious apothegmaticall Pedant, who will finde matter inough to dilate a whole day of the first invention of Fy, fa, fum, I smell the bloud of an English-man.
"Have with You to Saffron-walden" (1596), Folio 3

2 Lord have mercy on us
In Time of Pestilence
From winter, plague and pestilence, good lord, deliver us!
1592. *Songs from Summer's Last Will and Testament* (1600)

Nasreen, Taslima (b.1958) Bangladeshi writer

1 I hold the Koran, the Vedas, the Bible, and all such religious texts determining the lives of their followers, as out of place and out of time...We have to move beyond these ancient texts if we want progress.
Remark (1994)

2 In both fiction and non-fiction, women are making their voices heard. My interpretation of women's rights in Islam, like that of countless other Muslim-born feminists, clashes strongly with the conservative, official interpretation.
Times, London (June 18, 1994)

3 Our religion doesn't give women any human dignity. Women are considered slaves...I write against the religion because if women want to live like human beings, they will have to live outside the religion and Islamic law.
Times, London (June 22, 1994)

Nasser, Gamal Abdel (1918–70) Egyptian statesman

1 Egyptian politicians in the past...aimed their words at the instincts of people leaving their minds wandering in the desert.
The Philosophy of the Revolution (1952)

2 If time imposes on us its evolution, place also imposes upon us its reality.
The Philosophy of the Revolution (1952)

3 I thought of assassinating many whom I regarded as obstacles between our country and its future. I began to expose their crimes and set myself as a judge of their actions and of the harm that these brought upon the country.
The Philosophy of the Revolution (1952)

4 Power is not merely shouting aloud. Power is to act positively with all the components of power.
The Philosophy of the Revolution (1952)

5 The struggle of any nation in its successive generations is a structure that rises one stone upon another.
The Philosophy of the Revolution (1952)

6 We now live in two revolutions: one demanding that we should unite together, love one another and strain every nerve to reach our goal; the other forces us...to disperse and give way to hatred, everyone thinking of himself.
The Philosophy of the Revolution (1952)

Nathan, G. J. (George Jean Nathan; 1882–1958) U.S. drama critic

1 To speak of morals in art is to speak of legislature in sex. Art is the sex of the imagination.
American Mercury (July 1926)

2 Patriotism is often an arbitrary veneration of real estate above principles.
Testament of a Critic (1930)

Nation, Carry (originally Carrie Amelia Moore; 1846–1911) U.S. temperance campaigner

1 A woman is stripped of everything by them saloons. Her husband is torn from her; she is robbed of her sons, her home, her food, and her virtue.
1893? Quoted in *Cyclone Carry* (Carleton Beals; 1962)

2 You have put me in here a cub, but I will come out roaring like a lion, and I will make all hell howl!
1901? Referring to one of her many spells of imprisonment. Quoted in *Cyclone Carry* (Carleton Beals; 1962)

National Academy of Sciences U.S. organization

1 If there is a component of faith to science, it is the assumption that the universe operates according to regularities...Even the assumption of that regularity is tested...This "faith" is very different from religious faith.
Teaching About Evolution and the Nature of Science (1997)

Navarre, Margaret of, Queen of Navarre (also known as Marguerite d'Angoulême; 1492–1549) French writer and patron of literature

1 A father will have compassion on his son. A mother will never forget her child. A brother will cover the sin of his sister. But what husband ever forgave the faithlessness of his wife?
Mirror of the Sinful Soul (1531)

2 Spite will make a woman do more than love.
"The First Day," *The Heptameron, or Novels of the Queen of Navarre* (1548)

3 To me it seems much better to love a woman as a woman, than to make her one's idol, as many do. For my part I am convinced that it is better to use than to abuse.
"The Second Day," *The Heptameron, or Novels of the Queen of Navarre* (1548)

Navratilova, Martina (b.1956) Czech-born U.S. tennis player

1 I'm playing as well as I ever have in my career. It's just hard to get out of bed in the morning.
Guardian, London (June 30, 1993)

2 The moment of victory is much too short to live for that and nothing else.
Guardian, London (June 21, 1989)

3 I wanted one more chance and I'm there. This is what I dreamed about. This is what I wanted—to go out in style. Win or lose, I'll be going out in style. I'm going to enjoy the moment.
Referring to the Wimbledon women's singles championship, which she won 9 times (1978–79, 1982–87, 1990). In 1994 she was defeated in the finals. *Independent,* London (July 1, 1994)

4 I would have drunk a lot of Pinot Grigio if I'd lost after leading 5–2 in the third.
Times, London (May 7, 1994)

5 I just try to concentrate on concentrating.
U.S. (October 20, 1986)

6 Whoever said, "It's not whether you win or lose that counts," probably lost.
Attrib.

Naylor, Gloria (b.1950) U.S. novelist, producer, and playwright

1 Contempt mates well with pity.
Linden Hills (1985)

2 The world said you spelled black with a capital nothing.
Linden Hills (1985)

3 Hell was right now. Daddy always said that folks misread the Bible. Couldn't be no punishment worse than having to live here on earth, he said.
Mama Day (1988)

4 Home. You can move away from it, but you never leave it. Not as long as it holds something to be missed.
Mama Day (1988)

5 There are some times in your life when you have to call upon the best of all God gave you—and the best of what He didn't.
Mama Day (1988)

6 Sometimes being a friend means mastering the art of timing. There is a time for silence. A time to let go and allow people to hurl themselves into their own destiny. And a time to prepare to pick up the pieces when it's all over.
The Women of Brewster Place (1982)

7 When I want ready-made trouble, I dig up a handsome man.
The Women of Brewster Place (1982)

Neale, John Mason (1818–66) English clergyman and hymnwriter

1 Art thou weary, art thou languid,
Art thou sore distressed?
"Art Thou Weary?" (1912?)

2 Good King Wenceslas looked out,
On the Feast of Stephen;
When the snow lay round about,
Deep and crisp and even.
"Good King Wenceslas" (1912?)

3 Jerusalem the golden,
With milk and honey blest,
Beneath thy contemplation
Sink heart and voice opprest.
Translated from the Latin of Saint Bernard of Cluny (1100?). "Jerusalem the Golden" (1858)

Needham, Joseph (Joseph Terence Montgomery Needham; 1900–95) British biochemist and Sinologist

1 European scholars have of course long been dimly aware of that vast and complex civilisation, at least as intricate and rich as their own, away at the other extreme end of the "heartland" continent.
Referring to China. *Science and Civilisation in China* (1954)

2 How...did the Chinese succeed in...maintaining, between the 3rd and the 13th centuries, a level of scientific knowledge unapproached in the west?
Science and Civilisation in China (1954), vol. 1, Preface

3 The very term "Far East"...exemplifies that fundamental insularity of outlook which is so difficult for Europeans, even those who have the best intentions, to discard.
Science and Civilisation in China (1954), vol. 1, Preface

4 Laboratorium est oratorium. The place where we do our scientific work is a place of prayer.
Quoted in *The Harvest of a Quiet Eye* (A. L. Mackay; 1977)

Neel, Alice (Alice Hartley Neel; 1900–84) U.S. painter

1 But we are all creatures in a way, aren't we?
And both men and women are wretched.
Portraits of Four Decades (October 1973)

2 When portraits are good art they reflect the culture, the time, and many other things.
1977. Quoted in "Some Women Realists: Painters of the Figure," *Arts* (Linda Nochlin; December 1977), no. 31

Neff, Pat (Patrick Neff; 1871–1952) U.S. politician

1 Texas could wear Rhode Island as a watch fob.
Quoted in *Inside U.S.A.* (John Gunther; 1947)

Negroponte, Nicholas U.S. business executive and writer

1 Computers and art can bring out the worst in each other when they first meet...Technology can be a jalapeno pepper in a French sauce.
Being Digital (1995)

2 Computing corduroy, memory muslin, and solar silk might be the literal fabric of tomorrow's digital dress. Instead of carrying your laptop, wear it.
Being Digital (1995)

3 Like a force of nature, the digital age cannot be denied or stopped. It has four very powerful qualities that will result in its ultimate triumph: decentralizing, globalizing, harmonizing, and empowering.
Being Digital (1995)

4 Machines need to talk easily to one another in order to better serve people.
Being Digital (1995)

5 One way to look at the future being digital is to ask if the quality of one medium can be transposed to another.
Being Digital (1995)

6 The cost of the electronics in a modern car now exceeds the cost of its steel.
Being Digital (1995)

7 If you were to hire household staff to cook, clean, drive, stoke the fire, and answer the door, can you imagine suggesting that they *not* talk to each other, not see what each other is doing, not coordinate their functions?
Referring to communication in a modern office. *Being Digital* (1995)

8 It is almost genetic in its nature, in that each generation will become more digital than the preceding one.
Referring to the impact of computer technologies on society. *Being Digital* (1995)

9 Cyberspace is a topology, not a topography. There are no physical constructs like "beside," "above," "to the north of."
Quoted in *Opening Digital Markets* (Walid Mougayar; 1997)

Nehru, Jawaharlal (1889–1964) Indian prime minister

1 That great lover of peace, a man of giant stature who moulded, as few other men have done, the destinies of his age.
On the death of Joseph Stalin. Speech to the Indian Parliament (March 9, 1953)

2 At the stroke of the midnight hour, India will awake to life and freedom. A moment comes, which comes but rarely in history, when we step out from the old to the new, when an age ends, and when the sound of a nation, long suppressed, finds utterance.
Referring to Indian independence. Speech to the Lok Sabha, the lower house of the Indian parliament (August 14, 1947)

3 Communism has definitely allied itself to the approach of violence...It's language is of violence, its thought is violent, and it does not seek to change by persuasion but by coercion and, indeed, by destruction and determination.
"The Tragic Paradox of Our Age," *New York Times* (September 7, 1958), magazine

Nelson, David R. U.S. crystallographer

1 The main satisfaction we're getting...is the intellectual excitement. For me, that's plenty. Isn't that really the driving force of science?
Referring to research on crystals. *New York Times* (July 30, 1985)

Nelson, Horatio, Viscount (1758–1805) English naval commander

1 I believe my arrival was most welcome, not only to the Commander of the Fleet but almost to every individual in it; and when I came to explain to them the "Nelson touch", it was like an electric shock. Some shed tears...Some may be Judas's; but the majority are much pleased with my commanding them.
Letter to Lady Hamilton (October 1, 1805), quoted in *Life of Nelson* (Robert Southey; 1813), ch. 9

2 In case signals can neither be seen nor perfectly understood, no captain can do very wrong if he places his ship alongside that of an enemy.
Memorandum to the British fleet, off Cadiz (October 9, 1805)

3 You must consider every man your enemy who speaks ill of your king; and you must hate a Frenchman as you hate the devil.
1800. Quoted in *Life of Nelson* (Robert Southey; 1813), ch. 3

4 I have only one eye: I have a right to be blind sometimes: I really do not see the signal.
Said during the Battle of Copenhagen. Nelson ignored Admiral Parker's order to disengage by placing his telescope to his blind eye; an hour later, he was victorious. (April 2, 1801), quoted in *Life of Nelson* (Robert Southey; 1813), ch. 7

5 Thank God, I have done my duty. Kiss me, Hardy.
October 21, 1805. Dying words at Battle of Trafalgar, to Captain Hardy of *The Victory.* Quoted in *Life of Nelson* (Robert Southey; 1813), ch. 9

6 England expects every man will do his duty.
October 21, 1805. Signal hoisted prior to the Battle of Trafalgar. Quoted in *Life of Nelson* (Robert Southey; 1813), ch. 9

Nelson, Willie (b.1933) U.S. country music singer, guitarist, and songwriter

1 I'm a country songwriter and we write cry-in-your-beer songs. That's what we do. Something that you can slow dance to.
Independent, London (May 11, 1996)

Nemerov, Howard (1920–91) U.S. poet, novelist, and critic

1 I've never read a political poem that's accomplished anything. Poetry makes things happen, but rarely what the poet wants.
International Herald Tribune, Paris (October 14, 1988)

2 For a Jewish Puritan of the middle class, the novel is serious, the novel is work, the novel is conscientious application—why, the novel is practically the retail business all over again.
"Reflexions of the Novelist Felix Ledger," *Journal of the Fictive Life* (1965)

3 Till I, high in the tower of my time
Among familiar ruins, began to cry
For accident, sickness, justice, war and crime,
Because all died, because I had to die.
The snow fell, the trees stood, the promise kept,
And a child I slept.
"The View from an Attic Window," *New Poems* (1960)

Neruda, Pablo (Neftalí Ricardo Reyes y Basoalto; 1904–73) Chilean poet and diplomat

1 Peace goes into the making of a poem as flour goes into the making of bread.
Memoirs (1974)

2 Latin America is very fond of the word "hope." We like to be called the "continent of hope"...This hope is really something like a promise of heaven, an IOU whose payment is always being put off.
Memoirs (1974), ch. 11

Nerval, Gérard de (Gérard Labrunie; 1808–55) French symbolist writer

1 Despair and suicide are the result of certain fatal situations for those who have no faith in immortality, its joys and its sorrows.
Aurélia ou Le Rêve et la vie (1855)

2 Nothing is indifferent, nothing is powerless in the universe; an atom might destroy everything, an atom might save everything!
Aurélia ou Le Rêve et la vie (1855)

3 I am the darkly shaded, the bereaved, the unconsoled,
The Prince of Aquitaine, with the blasted tower:
My only star is dead, and my star-studded lute
Wears the black sun of melancholy.
"El Desdichado," *Les Chimères* (1854)

4 God is dead! Heaven is empty
Weep, children, you no longer have a father.
"Le Christ aux Oliviers," *Les Chimères* (1854), epigraph

5 Why should a lobster be any more ridiculous than a dog...or any other animal one chooses to take for a walk? I have a liking for lobsters. They are peaceful, serious creatures.
Gérard de Nerval used to take a lobster for walks on a leash in the gardens of the Palais-Royal. Quoted in *Portraits et souvenirs littéraires* (Théophile Gautier; 1875)

Neuberger, Julia, Rabbi (Julia Barbara Sarah Neuberger; b.1950) British rabbi, author, and broadcaster

1 On the whole, in the Jewish tradition we don't die very well.
On Being Jewish (1995)

2 A man thanks God for not making him a woman and the woman simply thanks God for making her as she is.
Referring to part of the liturgy of Orthodox Judaism. *On Being Jewish* (1995)

Neurath, Otto (1882–1945) Austrian philosopher and social theorist

1 We are like sailors who must rebuild their ship on the open sea, never able to dismantle it in dry-dock and to reconstruct it there out of the best materials.
"Protocol Sentences," *Logical Positivism* (A. J. Ayer, ed.; 1959)

Nevins, Allan (1890–1971) U.S. historian

1 The former allies had blundered in the past by offering Germany too little, and offering even that too late, until finally Nazi Germany had become a menace to all mankind.
Current History (May 1935)

Newbolt, Henry, Sir (Henry John Newbolt; 1862–1938) English poet, novelist, and historian

1 He clapped the glass to his sightless eye,
And "I'm damned if I see it," he said.
Referring to Lord Nelson at the Battle of Copenhagen. "Admirals All" (1897)

2 Drake he's in his hammock till the great Armadas come.
(Capten, art tha sleepin' there below?)
Slung atween the round shot, listenin' for the drum,
An dreamin' arl the time o' Plymouth Hoe.
"Drake's Drum" (1897)

3 There's a breathless hush in the Close tonight—
Ten to make and the match to win—
A bumping pitch and a blinding light,
An hour to play and the last man in.
"Vitai Lampada" (1897)

4 The sand of the desert is sodden red,—
Red with the wreck of a square that broke;—
The gatling's jammed and the colonel dead,
And the regiment blind with the dust and smoke.
The river of death has brimmed its banks
And England's far and honour a name.
But the voice of a schoolboy rallies the ranks:
"Play up! play up! and play the game!"
"Vitai Lampada" (1897)

Newley, Anthony (1931–99) British actor, composer, and comedian

1 Stop the World, I Want to Get Off
Musical title, co-written with Leslie Bricusse. (1961)

Newman, Ernest (William Roberts; 1868–1959) English music critic

1 I sometimes wonder which would be nicer—an opera without an interval, or an interval without an opera.
Quoted in *Berlioz, Romantic and Classic* (Peter Heyworth, ed.; 1972)

2 You may help a lame dog over a stile but he is still a lame dog on the other side.
Quoted in *Berlioz, Romantic and Classic* (Peter Heyworth, ed.; 1972)

3 The higher the voice the smaller the intellect.
Attrib.

Newman, John Henry, Cardinal (1801–90) English clergyman and theologian

1 We can believe what we choose. We are answerable for what we choose to believe.
Letter to Mrs. William Froude (June 27, 1848), quoted in *Letters and Diaries of John Henry Newman* (C. S. Dessain, ed.; 1962), vol. 12

2 It would be a gain to the country were it vastly more superstitious, more bigoted, more gloomy, more fierce in its religion than at present it shows itself to be.
"History of My Religious Opinions from 1833 to 1839," *Apologia pro Vita Sua* (1864)

3 It is very difficult to get up resentment towards persons whom one has never seen.
"Mr Kingsley's Method of Disputation," *Apologia pro Vita Sua* (1864)

4 She holds that it were better for sun and moon to drop from heaven, for the earth to fail, and for all the many millions who are upon it to die of starvation in extremest agony, as far as temporal affliction goes, than that one soul...should commit one single venial sin.
Referring to the Roman Catholic Church. *Lectures on Anglican Difficulties* (1852)

5 When men understand what each other means, they see, for the most part, that controversy is either superfluous or hopeless.
1839. "Faith and Reason, Contrasted as Habits of the Mind," *Oxford University Sermons* (1843), no. 10

6 It is almost a definition of a gentleman to say that he is one who never inflicts pain.
"Knowledge and Religious Duty," *The Idea of a University* (1852)

7 Lead, kindly Light, amid the encircling gloom,
Lead thou me on;
The night is dark, and I am far from home,
Lead thou me on
Keep Thou my feet; I do not ask to see
The distant scene; one step enough for me.
"Lead Kindly Light," *The Pillar of Cloud* (1833), st. 1

Newman, Paul (b.1925) U.S. film actor

1 Why have hamburger out when you've got steak at home? That doesn't mean it's always tender.
Observer, London (March 11, 1984), "Sayings of the Week"

2 The second you step out of the confines of the personality the public has set up for you, they get incensed. Public reaction tends to keep actors as personalities instead of allowing them to act. It's a very corrupting influence.
Photoplay (1977), quoted in *Chambers Film Quotes* (Tony Crawley, ed.; 1991)

Newman, Randy (b.1944) U.S. singer and songwriter

1 I'd be interested to know how many people who say they're going to write a hit song actually do. I've never done it...I just write what comes out.
Quoted in "Randy Newman," *Off the Record: An Oral History of Popular Music* (Joe Smith; 1988)

Newspapers

1 Advice to persons about to marry. "Don't."
Punch (1845), vol. 8

2 I'm afraid you've got a bad egg, Mr. Jones.
Oh no, my Lord, I assure you! Parts of it are excellent!
The origin of the expression, "a curate's egg." Punch (1895), vol. 109

3 The *Daily Mirror* does not believe that patriotism had to be proved in blood. Especially someone else's blood.
Referring to the Falklands War (1982). *Daily Mirror*, London (April 1982)

4 The Net still resembles a congested street: because users pay only for their car and fuel, rather than for the inconvenience their presence on the road imposes on others, they have no incentive to limit the use of their car to avoid traffic jams.
Economist, London (October 19, 1996)

5 An Englishman's home is his tax haven.
Alluding to the tendency of high earners to avoid taxation. *Economist*, London (November 17, 1979)

6 A derivative is like a razor. You can use it to shave yourself and make yourself attractive for your girlfriend. You can slit her throat with it. Or you can use it to commit suicide.
Financial Times (March 4, 1995)

7 Much of corporate America is still trying to find out what is really meant by "dress-down day." Is a blue shirt without a tie congenial enough?
Fortune (November 19, 1995)

8 What do we want? Radio 4! Where do we want it? Long wave! And what do we say? Please!
1993. Chanted by protesters in Britain who successfully opposed the BBC's plans to broadcast Radio 4 on FM only. Devoted listeners consider Radio 4 the station of "polite society." *Guardian*, London (April 5, 1993)

9 The most participatory form of mass speech yet developed...a never-ending worldwide conversation.
Referring to the Internet. *Guardian*, London (December 5, 1996)

10 Some time last month arrived in this town Mr. Andrew Ellicot...He was employed by the President of the United States of America to lay off a tract of land, ten miles square on the Potomac, for the use of Congress.
Report from Georgetown, then a separate community, on the beginning of the surveying of the land set aside for the new federal capital, Washington, D.C. *Maryland Gazette* (March 18, 1791), quoted in *A History of the United States* (R. B. Nye and J. E. Morpugo; 1965), vol. 1

11 Six million young men lie in premature graves, and four old men sit in Paris partitioning the earth.
New York Nation (1919)

12 NEGROES ALLOWED IN.
St. Louis, May 4 (AP)—The St. Louis major league baseball teams, the Cardinals and Browns, have discontinued their old policy of restricting Negroes to the bleachers and pavilion at Sportsman's Park. Negroes now may purchase seats in the grandstand.
New York Times Book of Baseball History (1944)

13 It became necessary to destroy the town of Ben Tre to save it.
Said by a U.S. major in Vietnam. *Observer*, London (February 11, 1968), "Sayings of the Week"

14 Take a Clear-Cut Stand against Unrest.
In response to pro-democracy demonstrations. *People's Daily*, China (April 26, 1989), editorial, quoted in *June Four: A Chronicle of the Chinese Democratic Uprising* (photographers and reporters of the Ming Pao News; Zi Jin and Qin Zhou, trs.; 1989)

15 The Chinese people are capable of doing what other people are incapable of doing...While others make one step, we make ten.
People's Daily, China (April 18, 1977), editorial, quoted in "The Party Rules All," *Maoism: Slogans and Practice* (Vladimir Glebov; 1978)

16 Carry Forward the May Fourth Spirit, Promote the Causes of Reform and Modernization.
"May Fourth" is an allusion to the Chinese May Fourth Movement of 1919, when intellectuals demanded modernization. Headline, *People's Daily*, China (1989), quoted in *June Four: A Chronicle of the Chinese Democratic Uprising* (photographers and reporters of the Ming Pao News; Zi Jin and Qin Zhou, trs.; 1989)

17 The almighty dollar is the only object of worship.
Philadelphia Public Ledger (December 2, 1836)

18 *Punch*—the official journal of dentists' waiting rooms.
Punch, London (October 7, 1981)

19 The daughters of England are too numerous, and if the Mother cannot otherwise get them off her hands, she must send them abroad into the world.
Punch, London (January 1850), quoted in *Britannia's Daughters* (Joanna Trollope; 1983), ch. 3

20 The early exhaustion of our fossil fuels will require the use of such other sources of power as water, wind, and sun.
Scientific American (May 14, 1921)

21 THE SKIBBEREEN EAGLE HAS ITS EYE ON THE TSAR.
Headline in one of Ireland's tiniest local newspapers on the eve of World War I. *Skibbereen Eagle* (1914), quoted in "Skibbereen Eagle," *Irish Days* (Terry Wogan; 1988)

22 The good time is approaching.
The season is at hand.
When the merry click of the two-base lick
Will be heard throughout the land.
From the first issue. *Sporting News* (1886)

23 The quality of Mersey is not strained.
Referring to the polluted condition of the River Mersey, England, and parodying Shakespeare's "The quality of mercy..." in the *Merchant of Venice*.. *Sunday Graphic* (August 14, 1932)

24 One way a peer can make a bit of extra money is by letting the public into his house. Another way is by letting the public into his head. Either way, the dottier the contents the better.
Referring to the Earl of Avon's column in the *Evening News* (London). *Sunday Times*, London (January 15, 1967)

25 Gotcha!
Headline. The newspaper's response to the sinking of the *General Belgrano*, an Argentinian warship, during the Falklands conflict. *Sun*, London (May 4, 1982)

26 World War II began last week at 5:20 a.m. (Polish time) Friday, September 1, when a German bombing plane dropped a projectile on Puck, fishing village and air base in the armpit of the Hel Peninsula.
Time (September 11, 1939)

27 The region is undergoing ethnic cleansing.
Referring to Bosnia and Herzegovina, and reporting a statement by the Serb (Yugoslav) government. *Times*, London (May 21, 1992)

28 We are all Home Rulers today.
Referring to the Irish Home Rule Campaign. *Times*, London (March 26, 1919)

29 It strikes us as rather a pity that a civilized language should have been allowed to mar the complete Cambrianism of the proceedings.
Referring to the use of spoken English as well as Welsh in the proceedings of the 1866 Eisteddfod. *Times*, London (September 8, 1866)

30 Reforms mean you can have a big car if you're in the mafia. Reforms mean hard-currency shops for a handful of people who have it. I'm a factory worker. I'll never have a big car or dollars, so reform for me will be when the milk isn't sour, that's all.
November 1992. Remark by a Russian woman while lining up for food. *Times*, London (November 25, 1992)

31 The nursing mother of half a continent.
Referring to Canada. *Toronto Globe* (December 10, 1861)

32 It will be gone by June.
Referring to rock and roll. *Variety* (1953), quoted in *Rock Talk* (Joe Kohut and John J. Kohut, eds.; 1994)

33 Choose your specialist and you choose your disease.
Westminster Review (May 18, 1906)

34 If you can remember the sixties, you weren't really there.
Quoted in *Guardian*, London (June 2, 1987)

35 Inflation must be called prosperity with high blood pressure.
Quoted in *Reader's Digest* (September 1966)

Newton, Huey P. (Huey Percy Newton; 1942–89) U.S. political activist

1 Twelve years of formal education is twelve years of formal ignorance.
1973. Attrib.

Newton, Isaac, Sir (1642–1727) English mathematician and physicist

Quotations about Newton

1 I believe the souls of five hundred Sir Isaac Newtons would go to the making up of a Shakespeare or a Milton.
Samuel Taylor Coleridge (1772–1834) British poet. Letter to Thomas Poole (March 23, 1801)

2 He lived the life of a solitary, and like all men who are occupied with profound meditation, he acted strangely. Sometimes, in getting out of bed, an idea would come to him, and he would sit on the edge of the bed, half dressed, for hours at a time.

1879
Louis Figuier (1819–94) French writer. *Vies de Savants* (B. H. Clark, tr.; 1897)

3 As a man he was a failure; as a monster he was superb.
Aldous Huxley (1894–1963) British novelist and essayist. Quoted in *Contemporary Mind* (John William Navin Sullivan; 1934)

4 On 15 April 1726 I paid a visit to Sir Isaac...he told me he was just in the same situation as when, formerly, the notion of gravitation came into his mind. It was occasioned by the fall of an apple, as he sat in a contemplative mood.
William Stukeley (1687–1765) English physician and antiquary. *Memoirs of Sir Isaac Newton's Life* (1752)

Quotations by Newton

5 If I have seen further it is by standing on the shoulders of giants.
Letter to Robert Hooke (February 5, 1676), quoted in *Correspondence of Isaac Newton* (H. W. Turnbull, ed.; 1959), vol. 1

6 Nature is very consonant and conformable with herself.
Opticks (1704), bk. 3

7 I feign no hypotheses.
Philosophiæ Naturalis Principia Mathematica (1687)

8 I do not know what I may appear to the world, but to myself I seem to have been only like a boy playing on the sea-shore, and diverting myself in now and then finding a smoother pebble or a prettier shell than ordinary, whilst the great ocean of truth lay all undiscovered before me.
1727. Quoted in *Isaac Newton* (Louis Trenchard More; 1934)

9 O Diamond! Diamond! thou little knowest the mischief done!
Said to a dog that set fire to some papers, representing several years' work, by knocking over a candle. Attrib.

Newton, John (1725–1807) British hymnwriter and clergyman

1 How sweet the name of Jesus sounds.
In a believer's ear!
"The Name of Jesus" (1779)

Ngugi wa Thiongo (b.1938) Kenyan writer

1 The arts then act like a reflecting mirror. The artist is like the hand that holds and moves the mirror, this way and that way, to explore all corners of the universe. But what is reflected in the mirror depends on where the holder stands in relation to the object.
"Freedom of the Artist: People's Artists Versus People's Rulers," *Barrel of a Pen* (1983)

2 Intellectual slavery masquerading as sophistication is the worst form of slavery.
Detained, A Writer's Prison Diary (1981)

3 Despair is the one sin that cannot be forgiven.
Devil on The Cross (1982)

4 Literature is the honey of a nation's soul, preserved for her children to taste forever, a little at a time!
Devil on The Cross (1982)

5 Write and risk damnation. Avoid damnation and cease to be a writer. That is the lot of the writer in a neocolonial state.
Writing Against Neocolonialism (1986)

Nicely, Thomas R. U.S. mathematician

1 Usually mathematicians have to shoot somebody to get this much publicity.
December 17, 1994. Referring to the attention he received after finding a flaw in the Intel Pentium microchip. *The Cincinnati Enquirer* (December 18, 1994)

Nicholas I, Tsar (Nikolay Pavlovich; 1796–1855) Russian monarch

1 We have on our hands a sick man—a very sick man.
Referring to Turkey, the "sick man of Europe," said to Sir G. H. Seymour, British envoy to St. Petersburg. Quoted in *Memoirs of Baron Stockmar* (F. Max Müller, ed.; 1853)

2 Russia has two generals in whom she can confide—Generals Janvier and Février.
March 10, 1855. Referring to the Russian winter. Nicholas himself succumbed to a February cold in 1855, the subject of the famous Punch Cartoon, "General Février turned traitor." Attrib.

Nicholas II, Tsar (Nikolay Aleksandrovich; 1868–1918) Russian monarch

Quotations about Nicholas II

1 The tzar is not treacherous but he is weak. Weakness is not treachery, but it fulfils all its functions.
William II (1859–1941) German monarch. Comment written on a despatch from the German ambassador to Russia (March 16, 1907)

Quotations by Nicholas II

2 I shall maintain the principle of autocracy just as firmly and unflinchingly as it was upheld by my own ever to be remembered dead father.
Declaration to representatives of Tver (January 17, 1896)

Nichols, Beverley Australian journalist

1 It looked as if it was something that had crawled out of the sea and was up to no good. It reminds me of one of those films where giant ants and things take over.
Referring to the Sydney Opera House, five years before its completion. *The Sydney Sun News Pictorial* (1968)

Nichols, Grace (b.1950) Guyanese journalist, poet, and novelist

1 Cradle a soft black woman and burn fingers as you trace revolution beneath her woolly hair.
"Of Course When They Ask for Poems About the 'Realities' of Black Women," *Lazy Thoughts of a Lazy Woman and Other Poems* (1989)

Nichols, Mike (Michael Igor Peschkowsky; b.1931) German-born U.S. stage and film director

1 Style is beginning something in the manner which will make it necessary for things that happen later to happen.
Film Comment (May 1991)

Nicholson, Jack (b.1937) U.S. film actor

1 Men are boring to women because there's only about 12 types of us, and they know all the keys. And they're bored by the fact we never escape our types.
Observer, London (August 21, 1994), "Sayings of the Week"

Nicklaus, Jack (Jack William Nicklaus, "The Golden Bear"; b.1940) U.S. golfer

1 I don't remember too much about the tournaments I lose.
New York Times (April 12, 1987)

2 Last week I made a double bogey and didn't even get mad. Now that's bad.
A bogey is a score of one over par for a hole in a game of golf. *New York Times* (July 24, 1977)

3 That's what you play for, to separate yourself from the crowd.
Sports Illustrated (March 8, 1971)

4 I will stop only when I think I can no longer win.
Sunday Telegraph, London (January 21, 1990)

5 Television controls the game of golf. It's a matter of the tail wagging the dog.
Sunday Times, London (June 3, 1984)

6 Golf is not and has never been a fair game.
Attrib.

7 I think I fail a bit less than everyone else.
Attrib.

Nicole d'Oresme, Bishop of Lisieux (1325?–82?) French prelate

1 Whenever kingship approaches tyranny it is near its end, for by this it becomes ripe for division, change of dynasty, or total destruction, especially in a temperate climate...where men are habitually, morally, and naturally free.
De Moneta (Charles Johnson, tr.; 1956)

Nicolson, Harold, Sir (Harold George Nicolson; 1886–1968) British diplomat, writer, and critic

1 The gift of broadcasting is, without question, the lowest human capacity to which any man could attain.
Observer, London (January 5, 1947), "Sayings of the Week"

Niebuhr, Reinhold (1892–1971) U.S. theologian

1 Man's capacity for justice makes democracy possible, but man's inclination to injustice makes democracy necessary.
Children of Light and Children of Darkness (1944), Foreword

Niederman, Andrew U.S. novelist

1 The weak, yellow light peeled away the darkness slowly and revealed the corpselike face, its teeth as white as bone.
Perfect Little Angels (1990)

Nietzsche, Friedrich Wilhelm (1844–1900) German philosopher and poet

1 Gradually it has become clear to me what every great philosophy so far has been: namely, the personal confession of its author and a kind of involuntary and unconscious memoir.
Beyond Good and Evil (1886)

2 "I have done that," says my memory. "I cannot have done that," says my pride, and remains inexorable. Eventually—memory yields.
Beyond Good and Evil (1886)

3 Insanity in individuals is something rare—but in groups, parties, nations, and epochs it is the rule.
Beyond Good and Evil (1886)

4 Is not life a hundred times too short for us to bore ourselves?
Beyond Good and Evil (1886)

5 Morality in Europe today is herd-morality.
Beyond Good and Evil (1886)

6 The abdomen is the reason why man does not easily take himself for a god.
Beyond Good and Evil (1886)

7 The degree and kind of a man's sexuality reach up into the ultimate pinnacle of his spirit.
Beyond Good and Evil (1886)

8 There is *master morality and slave morality*...Slave morality is essentially the morality of utility.
Beyond Good and Evil (1886)

9 The thought of suicide is a great source of comfort: with it a calm passage is to be made across many a bad night.
Beyond Good and Evil (1886)

10 What separates two people most profoundly is a different sense and degree of cleanliness.
Beyond Good and Evil (1886)

11 Whoever despises himself still respects himself as one who despises.
Beyond Good and Evil (1886)

12 If only those actions are moral...which are performed out of freedom of will, then there are no moral actions.
Daybreak (1881)

13 As an artist, a man has no home in Europe save in Paris.
Ecce Homo (1888)

14 My time has not yet come either; some are born posthumously.
Ecce Homo (1888)

15 The scholar—a decadent. This I have seen with my own eyes: natures gifted, rich and free already in their thirties "read to ruins," mere matches that have to be struck if they are to ignite—emit "thoughts."
Ecce Homo (1888)

16 Philosophy, as I have so far understood and lived it, means living voluntarily among ice and high mountains—seeking out everything strange and questionable in existence, everything so far placed under a ban by morality.
Ecce Homo (1888), Preface

17 The sick are the greatest danger for the healthy; it is not from the strongest that harm comes to the strong, but from the weakest.
Genealogy of Morals (1887), Essay 3, aphorism 14

18 All philosophers have the common failing of starting out from man as he is now and thinking they can reach their goal through an analysis of him...Lack of historical sense is the family failing of all philosophers.
Human, All Too Human (1878–80)

19 Art raises its head when religions relax their hold.
Human, All Too Human (1878–80)

20 One often contradicts an opinion when what is uncongenial is really the tone in which it was conveyed.
Human, All Too Human (1878–80)

21 The most dangerous physicians are those who can act in perfect mimicry of the born physician.
Human, All Too Human (1878–80), pt. 2

22 There is more wisdom in your body than in your deepest philosophy.
Human, All Too Human (1878–80), pt. 2

23 Insects sting, not from malice, but because they want to live. It is the same with critics—they desire our blood, not our pain.
Miscellaneous Maxims and Reflections (1880)

24 He who does not need to lie is proud of not being a liar.
Nachgelassene Fragmente (1882–89)

25 When a man is in love he endures more than at other times; he submits to everything.
The Antichrist (1888)

26 God created Woman. And boredom did indeed cease from that moment—but many other things ceased as well! Woman was God's second blunder.
The Antichrist (1888), Aphorism 48

27 I call Christianity the one great curse, the one enormous and innermost perversion, the one great instinct of revenge, for which no means are too venomous, too underhand, too underground and too petty—I call it the one immortal blemish of mankind.
The Antichrist (1888), Aphorism 62

28 Do you really believe that the sciences would ever have originated and grown if the way had not been prepared by magicians, alchemists, astrologers, and witches whose promises and pretensions first had to create a thirst, a hunger, a taste for hidden and forbidden.
The Gay Science (1882)

29 God is dead: but considering the state the species Man is in, there will perhaps be caves, for ages yet, in which his shadow will be shown.
The Gay Science (1882), bk. 3

30 The Christian resolution to find the world ugly and bad has made the world ugly and bad.
The Gay Science (1882), bk. 3

31 Believe me! The secret of reaping the greatest fruitfulness and the greatest enjoyment from life is to live dangerously!
The Gay Science (1882), bk. 4

32 Truths are illusions about which one has forgotten that this is what they are; metaphors which are worn out and without sensuous power; coins which have lost their pictures and now matter only as metal, no longer as coins.
"On Truth and Lie in an Extra-Moral Sense," *The Portable Nietzsche* (Walter Kaufmann, ed., tr.; 1954)

33 Species do not evolve toward perfection, but quite the contrary. The weak, in fact, always prevail over the strong, not only because they are in the majority, but also because they are the more crafty.
The Twilight of the Idols (1888)

34 Idleness is the parent of all psychology.
"Maxims and Missiles," *The Twilight of the Idols* (1888)

35 The sick man is a parasite of society. In certain cases it is indecent to go on living. To continue to vegetate in a state of cowardly dependence upon doctors and special treatments, once the meaning of life, the right to life has been lost, ought to be regarded with the greatest contempt by society.
"Skirmishes in a War with the Age," *The Twilight of the Idols* (1888)

36 Two great European narcotics, alcohol and Christianity.
"Things the Germans Lack," *The Twilight of the Idols* (1888)

37 To show pity is felt as a sign of contempt because one has clearly ceased to be an object of fear as soon as one is pitied.
The Wanderer and His Shadow (1880)

38 I teach you the Superman. Man is something that is to be surpassed.
Thus Spake Zarathustra (1883–92)

39 Man is a rope, tied between beast and Superman—a rope over an abyss.
Thus Spake Zarathustra (1883–92)

40 Unto thee did I spring: then fledst thou back from my bound;
And towards me waved thy fleeing, flying tresses round!
Away from thee did I spring, and from thy snaky tresses;
Then stoodst thou there half-turned, and in thine eye caresses.
"The Second Dance Song," *Thus Spake Zarathustra* (1883–92)

41 What I am doing is to recount the history of the next two centuries. I am describing what is coming, what can no longer come in any other form: the rise of nihilism.
Quoted in *Europe Since 1870* (James Joll; 1973)

Nightingale, Florence (1820–1910) British nurse, hospital reformer, and humanitarian

Quotations about Nightingale

1 What a comfort it was to see her pass. She would speak to one, and nod and smile to as many more; but she could not do it to all you know. We lay there by the hundreds; but we could kiss her shadow as it fell and lay our heads on the pillow again content.
Anonymous. *Florence Nightingale 1820–1910* (Cecil Woodham-Smith; 1950)

2 A Lady with a Lamp shall stand
In the great history of the land,
A noble type of good,
Heroic womanhood.
Henry Wadsworth Longfellow (1807–82) U.S. poet. "Santa Filomena" (1857)

Quotations by Nightingale

3 The first possibility of rural cleanliness lies in water supply.
Letter to the Medical Officer of Health (November 1891)

4 It may seem a strange principle to enunciate as the very first

requirement in a Hospital that it should do the sick no harm.
Notes on Hospitals (1859), Preface

5 No man, not even a doctor, ever gives any other definition of what a nurse should be than this—"devoted and obedient." This definition would do just as well for a porter. It might even do for a horse. It would not do for a policeman.
Notes on Nursing (1860)

6 To understand God's thoughts we must study statistics, for these are the measure of his purpose.
Quoted in *Life...of Francis Galton* (K. Pearson), vol. 2, ch. 13, sect. 1

Nilsen, Dennis (b.1948) British convicted mass murderer

1 A house is not a home and sex is not a relationship. We would only lend each other our bodies in a vain search for inner peace.
Quoted in *Killing for Company* (Brian Masters; 1985)

Nimier, Roger (Roger Nimier de la Perrière; 1925–62) French writer

1 War becomes an awful bore when everyone and everything dies, is extinguished, is buried. Limitations must be found for it...One should have war fields for those who like dying in the open air. Elsewhere everyone will be dancing and laughing.
Le Hussard bleu (1950), pt. 1

2 Philosophy is not bad, either. Unfortunately it's like Russia: full of bogs and often invaded by Germans.
Le Hussard bleu (1950), pt. 3

Nimitz, Chester (Chester William Nimitz; 1885–1966) U.S. naval commander

1 Uncommon valor was a common virtue.
Referring to U.S. Marines at the bloody battle of Iwo Jima (February-May 1945). Remark (1945)

Nin, Anaïs (1903–77) French writer

1 What I consider my weaknesses are feminine traits: incapacity to destroy, ineffectualness in battle.
January 1943. *The Diary of Anaïs Nin* (1969)

2 It's all right for a woman to be, above all, human. I am a woman first of all.
June 1933. *The Diary of Anaïs Nin* (1966), vol. 1

3 Each friend represents a world in us, a world possibly not born until they arrive, and it is only by this meeting that a new world is born.
March 1937. *The Diary of Anaïs Nin* (1967), vol. 2

4 Dreams are necessary to life.
June 1936. Letter to her mother, *The Diary of Anaïs Nin* (1967), vol. 2

Niven, David (James David Graham Nevins; 1909–83) British film actor

1 Volunteers usually fall into two groups. There are the genuinely courageous who are itching to get at the throat of the enemy, and the restless who will volunteer for anything in order to escape from the boredom of what they are presently doing.
The Moon's a Balloon (1972), ch. 12

2 War is a great accelerator of events so ten days later, we were married in the tiny Norman church of Huish village at the foot of the Wiltshire Downs.
The Moon's a Balloon (1972), ch. 12

Niven, Larry (b.1938) U.S. science-fiction writer

1 On my twenty-first birthday my father said, "Son, here's a million dollars. Don't lose it."
When asked "What is the best advice you have ever been given?" Attrib.

Nixon, Patricia (originally Thelma Catherine Patricia Ryan; 1912–93) U.S. first lady

1 I have sacrificed everything in my life that I consider precious in order to advance the political career of my husband.
Quoted in *Women at Work* (Betty Medsger; 1975)

Nixon, Richard (Richard Milhous Nixon; 1913–94) U.S. president

Quotations about Nixon

1 He has a deeper concern for his place in history than for the people he governs. And history will not fail to note that fact.
Shirley Chisholm (b.1924) U.S. state legislator, educator, and U.S. representative. *The Good Fight* (1973)

2 President Nixon's motto was, if two wrongs don't make a right, try three.
Norman Cousins (1915–90) U.S. newspaper editor. *Daily Telegraph,* London (July 17, 1969)

3 If Richard Nixon was second-rate, what in the world *is* third-rate?
Joseph Heller (1923–99) U.S. novelist. *Good as Gold* (1979), ch. 6

4 Do you realize the responsibility I carry? I'm the only person standing between Nixon and the White House.
1960
John Fitzgerald Kennedy (1917–63) U.S. president. Said to Arthur Schlesinger the year Richard Nixon was the Republican candidate in the presidential election. Quoted in *A Thousand Days* (Arthur M. Schlesinger, Jr.; 1965)

5 Yes, Nixon was still the spirit of television. Mass communication was still his disease—he thought he could use it to communicate with the masses.
Norman Mailer (b.1923) U.S. novelist and journalist. "Nixon and Miami," *Miami and the Siege of Chicago* (1968)

6 He was like a kamikaze pilot who keeps apologizing for the attack.
Mary McGrory (b.1918) U.S. journalist. Remark (November 8, 1962)

7 Would you buy a used car from this man?
1952
Mottos and Slogans. Referring to Richard Nixon when he was Eisenhower's running mate (1952), and subsequently.

8 Nixon is the kind of politician who would cut down a redwood tree and then mount the stump for a conservation speech.
1956
Adlai Stevenson (1900–65) U.S. statesman. Quoted in *The Fine Art of Political Wit*

9 You don't set a fox to watching the chickens just because he has a lot of experience in the hen house.
Harry S. Truman (1884–1972) U.S. president. Referring to Vice President Richard Nixon's presidential nomination. Remark (October 30, 1960)

10 Nixon is a shifty-eyed goddam liar...He's one of the few in the

history of this country to run for high office talking out of both sides of his mouth at the same time and lying out of both sides.
Harry S. Truman (1884–1972) U.S. president. Quoted in *Infinite Riches* (Leo Rosten; 1978)

11 Here is a man in a presidential debate who referred to army uniforms as costumes.
Robin Williams (b.1951) U.S. actor and comedian. Attrib.

Quotations by Nixon

12 People have got to know whether or not their President is a crook. Well, I am not a crook. I've earned everything that I've got.
Defending himself against charges of tax evasion. Press conference (November 17, 1973)

13 You won't have Nixon to kick around any more, gentlemen. This is my last Press Conference.
After losing the election for the Governorship of California. Press conference (November 2, 1962)

14 The only alternative to a balance of power is an imbalance of power—and history shows us that nothing so drastically escalates the danger of war as such an imbalance.
Press conference, Washington, D.C. (June 25, 1972)

15 The only way we're going to get our prisoners of war back is by...hitting military targets in North Vietnam, retaining a force in South Vietnam, and continuing the mining of North Vietnam.
Press conference, Washington, D.C. (June 29, 1972)

16 I don't give a shit what happens. I want you all to stonewall it, let them plead the Fifth Amendment, cover-up or anything else, if it'll save it, save the plan.
In a taped conversation referring to the Watergate cover-up. Remark (March 22, 1973)

17 It is time for the great silent majority of Americans to stand up and be counted.
Remark (October 1970)

18 And so, tonight—to you, the great silent majority of my fellow Americans—I ask for your support.
Referring to a plan for peace in Vietnam. Speech (November 3, 1969)

19 For the first time in history we showed independence of Anglo-French policies towards Asia and Africa which seemed to us to reflect the colonial tradition. That declaration has had an electrifying effect throughout the world.
Said after the Suez Crisis. Speech (November 2, 1956)

20 For in a time when the national focus is concentrated upon the unemployed, the impoverished and the dispossessed, the working Americans have become the forgotten Americans...they have become the silent Americans.
The origin of the slogan, "The Silent Majority." Speech (1968)

21 And this certainly has to be the most historic phone call ever made.
Telephone call to astronauts on the moon (July 20, 1969)

22 I'm not a quitter and incidentally Pat's not a quitter. After all, her name was Patricia Ryan and she was born on St. Patrick's Day.
Following allegations that he had misappropriated an $18,000 campaign fund. His wife was, in fact, born the day before St. Patrick's Day. Television broadcast (September 14, 1952)

23 There can be no whitewash at the White House.
Referring to the Watergate scandal. Television broadcast (April 30, 1973)

24 When the President does it, that means it is not illegal.
Television interview (May 19, 1977), quoted in *I Gave Them a Sword* (David Frost; 1978), ch.8

25 I brought myself down. I gave them a sword and they stuck it in and they twisted it with relish. And I guess if I'd been in their position I'd have done the same thing.
Television interview (May 19, 1977), quoted in *I Gave Them a Sword* (David Frost; 1978), ch. 10

26 Regardless of what they say about it, we are going to keep it.
Referring to "Checkers," a dog given to his daughters. He was defending himself against corruption charges. TV and radio speech (September 23, 1952)

27 We must never forget that if the war in Vietnam is lost...the right of free speech will be extinguished throughout the world.
New York Times (October 27, 1965)

28 This country needs good farmers, good businessmen, good plumbers.
August 9, 1974. The team that broke into the Democrat offices in the Watergate building was called "The Plumbers." Farewell address at White House, *New York Times* (August 10, 1974)

29 I let down my friends, I let down my country. I let down our system of government.
Observer, London (May 8, 1977), "Sayings of the Week"

30 This isn't going to be a good country for any of us to live in until it's a good country for all of us to live in.
Observer, London (September 29, 1968), "Sayings of the Week"

31 The American leader class has really had it in terms of their ability to lead...I enjoy very much more receiving labor leaders and people from middle America who still have a bit of character and guts and a bit of patriotism.
September 1971. Diary, *The Memoirs of Richard Nixon* (1978)

32 Let us begin by committing ourselves to the truth—to see it as it is, and tell it like it is—to find the truth, to speak the truth, and to live the truth.
1968. Said on accepting the Republican nomination for U.S. president. Speech to the Republican Party Convention, Miami, *The Memoirs of Richard Nixon* (1978)

33 You fellows, in your business, you have a way of handling problems like this. Somebody leaves a pistol in the drawer. I don't have a pistol.
August 7, 1974. Said to General Alexander Haig. Nixon resigned two days later. Quoted in *Final Days* (Bob Woodward and Carl Bernstein; 1976)

34 I have as my ideal the life of Jesus.
Attrib. *Nixon, A Life* (Jonathan Aitken; 1993)

35 A man is not finished when he is defeated. He is finished when he quits.
Attrib.

36 For years politicians have promised the moon, I'm the first one to be able to deliver it.
July 20, 1969. About the first moon landing. Attrib.

37 This is the greatest week in the history of the world since the creation.
July 24, 1969. Welcoming the Apollo 11 astronauts on board the USS *Hornet* after their moon landing. Attrib.

38 I'll speak for the man, or against him, whichever will do him most good.
When agreeing to support a politician. Attrib.

Nizer, Louis (1902–94) British-born U.S. lawyer and writer

1 I know of no higher fortitude than stubbornness in the face of overwhelming odds.
My Life in Court (1961)

Nkomo, Joshua (b.1917) Zimbabwean nationalist leader

1 The hardest lesson of my life has come to me late. It is that a nation can win freedom without its people becoming free.
The Story of My Life (1984)

2 The price of freedom can never be too high.
The Story of My Life (1984)

3 The real difference between Western interests in Africa and those of the Soviet Union is that, when asked to leave, the Soviet Union has always left.
The Story of My Life (1984)

Nkrumah, Kwame (1909–72) Ghanaian president

1 Circumstances can be changed by revolution and revolutions are brought about by men, by men who think as men of action and act as men of thought.
Consciencism: Philosophy and Ideology for Decolonisation and Development (1964)

2 The two party system has shown itself to be unsuitable in any African state. It has grown up in Britain to serve specific class interests.
Dark Days in Ghana (1968)

3 The gains of violence are transient, the fruits of patience are imperishable.
1955. *I Speak of Freedom* (1961)

4 We prefer self-government with danger to servitude in tranquility.
1948. *I Speak of Freedom* (1961)

5 As long as we are ruled by others we shall lay our mistakes at their door, and our sense of responsibility will remain dulled. Freedom brings responsibilities, and our experience can be enriched only by the acceptance of these responsibilities.
The Autobiography of Kwame Nkrumah (1959)

6 Never in the history of the world has an alien ruler granted self-rule to a people on a silver platter.
The Autobiography of Kwame Nkrumah (1959)

7 Seek ye first the political kingdom and all things shall be added unto you.
The Autobiography of Kwame Nkrumah (1959)

8 Without discipline true freedom cannot survive.
The Autobiography of Kwame Nkrumah (1959)

9 Imperialism knows no law beyond its own interests.
Towards Colonial Freedom (1947)

Noel, Caroline M. (1817–77) British poet

1 At the name of Jesus
Every knee shall bow,
Every tongue confess him
King of glory now.
"The Name of Jesus" (1861)

Nogarola, Isotta (1418–66) Italian scholar and author

1 There are already so many women in the world! Why then...was I born a woman, to be scorned by men in words and deeds?
Letter to Guarino Veronese (15th century)

Norberg-Hodge, Helena British ecologist and author

1 The average pound of food in America travels 1,200 miles before it reaches the kitchen table, and the total transport distances of the ingredients in a pot of German yoghurt totals over 6,000 miles.
"Globalisation Versus Community," *The Future of Progress* (co-edited with Peter Goering and Steven Gorelick; 1992)

2 The mobility of capital today means that the comparative advantage once enjoyed by states or regions has been usurped by transnational corporations.
"Globalisation Versus Community," *The Future of Progress* (co-edited with Peter Goering and Steven Gorelick; 1992)

3 Free trade policies work against the interests of the vast majority of producers and consumers—in both the North and South—by systematically dismantling locally-based economies.
Co-written with Peter Goering. "The Future of Progress," *The Future of Progress* (co-edited with Peter Goering and Steven Gorelick; 1992)

Norgaard, Richard (b.1943) U.S. author

1 As we push our technologies to exploit more and more resources, we now recognize that both the direct devastation and the unforeseen consequences are becoming increasingly global in nature.
Quoted in "Coevolution of Economy, Society and Environment," *Real-Life Economics* (Paul Ekins and Manfred Max-Neef, eds.; 1992)

2 The policy challenge of sustainable development consists of finding a path towards a positive social and ecological coevolution.
Quoted in "Coevolution of Economy, Society and Environment," *Real-Life Economics* (Paul Ekins and Manfred Max-Neef, eds.; 1992)

Norman, Barry (Barry Leslie Norman; b.1933) British film critic and broadcaster

1 Perhaps at fourteen every boy should be in love with some ideal woman to put on a pedestal and worship. As he grows up, of course, he will put her on a pedestal the better to view her legs.
Listener, London (1978)

Norman, Frank (Benjamin Franklin Morris; 1931–80) British playwright and novelist

1 Fings Ain't Wot They Used T'Be
1959. Musical title.

Norman, Greg (Gregory John Norman; b.1955) Australian golfer

1 It doesn't bother me what ball I use, what colour trousers I

wear or what I ate the night before. How can that sort of stuff have any effect on my game?
Sunday Times, London (September 23, 1984)

Norman, Marsha (originally Marsha Williams; b.1947) U.S. playwright

1 As women, our historical role has been to clean up the mess. Whether it's the mess left by war or death or children or sickness...we know that life is messy.
Quoted in "Marsha Norman," *Interviews with Contemporary Women Playwrights* (Kathleen Betsko and Rachel Koenig; 1987)

2 Success is always something that you have to recover from.
Quoted in "Marsha Norman," *Interviews with Contemporary Women Playwrights* (Kathleen Betsko and Rachel Koenig; 1987)

3 There are things that music can do that language could never do, that painting can never do, or sculpture. Music is capable of going directly to the source of the mystery. It doesn't have to explain it. It can simply celebrate it.
Quoted in "Marsha Norman," *Interviews with Contemporary Women Playwrights* (Kathleen Betsko and Rachel Koenig; 1987)

Norris, Frank (1870–1902) U.S. novelist

1 "Her husband!" *That*, was her husband in there—she could yet hear his snores—for life, for life.
McTeague: A Story of San Francisco (1899), ch. 10

2 She had even...slept all night upon the money, taking a strange and ecstatic pleasure in the touch of the smooth flat pieces the length of her entire body.
McTeague: A Story of San Francisco (1899), ch. 19

3 He was drunk; not with that drunkenness which is stupid, maudlin, wavering on its feet, but with that which is alert, unnaturally intelligent, vicious, perfectly steady, deadly wicked.
Describing McTeague before he beats his wife to death. *McTeague: A Story of San Francisco* (1899), ch. 19

4 Here, of all her cities, throbbed the true life—the true power and spirit of America...brutal in its ambition, arrogant in the new-found knowledge of its giant strength, prodigal of its wealth, infinite in its desires.
Referring to Chicago. *The Pit* (1903), ch. 2

5 Death and grief are little things. They are transient. Life must be before death, and joy before grief. Else there are no such things as death or grief. These are only negatives. Life is positive. Death is only the absence of life.
Vanamee from The Octopus (1901)

Norris, George W. (George William Norris; 1861–1944) U.S. politician

1 We are going into war on the command of gold. We are going to run the risk of sacrificing millions of our countrymen's lives in order that other countrymen may coin their lifeblood into money. We are about to do the bidding of wealth's terrible mandate.
Referring to U.S. entry into World War I. Speech to U.S. Congress (April 4, 1917)

Norris, John (1657–1711) English philosopher

1 How fading are the joys we dote upon!
Like apparitions seen and gone.
But those which soonest take their flight
Are the most exquisite and strong,
Like angels' visits, short and bright;
Mortality's too weak to bear them long.
"The Parting," *The Miscellanies* (1687)

Norris, Steven (b.1945) British politician

1 You have your own company, your own temperature control, your own music—and don't have to put up with dreadful human beings sitting alongside you.
Explaining why he preferred using his private car to public transport. *Independent*, London (February 9, 1995)

Norse, Harold U.S. writer

1 My experiences ranged from quickies in hot showers or behind park bushes to one-night stands. Straight boys, facing the threat of extinction, quickly yielded to the gods of nature, Priapus and Bacchus (who never die).
Memoirs of a Bastard Angel (1989), quoted in *A Queer Reader* (Patrick Higgins, ed.; 1993)

North, Christopher (John Wilson; 1785–1854) Scottish poet, essayist, and critic

1 Minds like ours, my dear James, must always be above national prejudices, and in all companies it gives me true pleasure to declare, that, as a people, the English are very little indeed inferior to the Scotch.
"Noctes Ambrosianae," *Blackwood's Magazine* (October 1826), no. 28

2 His Majesty's dominions, on which the sun never sets.
"Noctes Ambrosianae," *Blackwood's Magazine* (April 20, 1829), no. 42

3 Laws were made to be broken.
"Noctes Ambrosianae," *Blackwood's Magazine* (May 24, 1830), no. 49

Northbrooke, John (*fl.* 1570) British preacher

1 One swallowe prouveth not that summer is neare.
Treatise against Dancing (1577)

Northcliffe, Lord, 1st Viscount Northcliffe (Alfred Charles William Harmsworth; 1865–1922) Irish-born British publisher

1 When I want a peerage, I shall buy one like an honest man.
Quoted in *Swaff* (Tom Driberg; 1974), ch. 2

2 They are only ten.
Said to have been a notice to remind his staff of his opinion of the mental age of the general public. Attrib.

Northup, Solomon (1809–after 1853) U.S. slave

1 O! how heavily the weight of slavery pressed upon me then. I must toil day after day, endure abuse and taunts and scoffs, sleep on the hard ground, live on the coarsest fare, and not only this, but live the slave of a blood-seeking wretch, of whom I must stand henceforth in continued fear and dread.

Why had I not died in my young years—before God had given me children to love and live for?
Twelve Years A Slave: Narrative of Solomon Northup (1853)

2 There may be humane masters, as there certainly are inhuman ones—there may be slaves well-clothed, well-fed, and happy, as there surely are those half-clad, half-starved and miserable; nevertheless, the institution that tolerates such wrong and inhumanity as I have witnessed, is a cruel, unjust, and barbarous one.
Twelve Years A Slave: Narrative of Solomon Northup (1853)

Norton, Caroline (originally Caroline Elizabeth Sarah Sheridan; 1808–77) British writer and reformer

1 I do not love thee!—no! I do not love thee!
And yet when thou art absent I am sad.
"I Do Not Love Thee" (1829)

2 I do not ask for my rights. I have no rights; I have only wrongs.
Said when a court upheld her husband's refusal to maintain her. Remark (August 1853)

Norton, Charles Eliot (1827–1908) U.S. writer, editor, and educator

1 A knowledge of Greek thought and life...is essential to high culture. A man may know everything else, but without this knowledge he remains ignorant of the best intellectual and moral achievements of his own race.
Letter to F. A. Tupper (1885)

2 The voice of protest, of warning, of appeal is never more needed than when the clamor of fife and drum, echoed by the press and too often by the pulpit, is bidding all men fall in and keep step and obey in silence the tyrannous word of command.
True Patriotism (1898)

Norton, Eleanor Holmes (b.1937) U.S. politician

1 But feminist change is both irresistible and irreversible. American women are part of an international movement that affects virtually every country in the world.
Speech, National Women's Political Caucus Conference, Alberquerque, New Mexico (July 1981)

2 Racial oppression of black people in America has done what neither class oppression nor sexual oppression, with all their perniciousness, has ever done: destroyed an entire people and their culture.
"For Sadie and Maude," *Sisterhood is Powerful* (Robin Morgan, ed.; 1970)

3 There are not many males, black or white, who wish to get involved with a woman who's committed to her own development.
Quoted in "The Black Family and Feminism," *The First MS Reader* (Francine Klagsbrun, ed.; 1972)

Norworth, Jack (1879–1959) U.S. vaudeville comedian and songwriter

1 Oh! shine on, shine on, harvest moon
Up in the sky.
I ain't had no lovin'
Since April, January, June, or July.
Song lyric. "Shine On, Harvest Moon" (1908)

Nostradamus (Michel de Notredame; 1503–66) French astrologer and physician

1 At night they will think they have seen the sun, when they see the half pig man: Noise, screams, battle seen fought in the skies. The brute beasts will be heard to speak.
Thought to foretell a 20th-century air-battle. *The Prophecies of Nostradamus* (16th century), Century 1, st. 64

2 The blood of the just will be demanded of London burnt by fire in three times twenty plus six. The ancient lady will fall from her high position, and many of the same denomination will be killed.
Believed to refer to the Great Fire of London, 1666. The "ancient lady" is interpreted as the Cathedral of St Paul's, which was destroyed in the fire. *The Prophecies of Nostradamus* (16th century), Century 2, st. 51

Novalis (Friedrich Leopold, Freiherr von Hardenberg; 1772–1801) German poet and novelist

1 Activity is the only reality.
The Disciples at Sais (1801)

2 A Realist is an Idealist who knows nothing of himself.
The Disciples at Sais (1801)

3 Precisely because we are philosophers we need not bother ourselves about issues. We have the principle, that is enough; the rest can be left for commoner brains.
The Disciples at Sais (1801)

4 Not only England, but also every Englishman is an island.
1799. Quoted in *Fragments* (R. Martin, ed.; 1988)

Novello, Ivor (David Ivor Davies; 1893–1951) British actor, playwright, and composer

1 Keep the Home Fires Burning
Song title. It was a favorite of British troops in World War I. (co-written with Lena Guilbert Ford; 1914)

2 There's something Vichy about the French.
Quoted by Edward Marsh in a letter, March 1941. After the fall of France during World War II, the seat of the collaborationist French government (1940–45) moved to Vichy in the unoccupied zone. *Ambrosia and Small Beer* (Christopher Hassall, ed.; 1964), ch. 4

Noverre, Jean Georges (1727–1810) French dancer, choreographer, and ballet master

1 A beautiful painting is only a copy of nature; a beautiful ballet is nature herself, enhanced by all the charms of art...we must not merely practice steps; we must study the passions!
Quoted in *World History of the Dance* (Curt Sachs; 1937)

Noyes, Alfred (1880–1958) British poet

1 Look for me by moonlight;
Watch for me by moonlight;
I'll come to thee by moonlight, though hell should bar the way!
"The Highwayman" (1907)

2 The wind was a torrent of darkness among the gusty trees,
The moon was a ghostly galleon tossed upon cloudy seas,
The road was a ribbon of moonlight over the purple moor,
And the highwayman came riding—
Riding—riding—
The highwayman came riding, up to the old inn-door.
"The Highwayman" (1907)

Nozick, Robert (b.1938) U.S. philosopher and political theorist

1 Why does mixing one's labor with something make one the owner of it...If I own a can of tomato juice and spill it in the sea...do I thereby own the sea, or have I foolishly dissipated my tomato juice?
Anarchy, State and Utopia (1975)

2 Why are philosophers intent on forcing others to believe things? Is that a nice way to behave towards someone?
Philosophical Explanations (1981)

Nwapa, Flora (1931–93) Nigerian novelist and educator

1 We don't ask people how many children they have. It is not done. Children are not goats or sheep or yams to be counted.
Efuru (1966)

2 What is money? Can a bag of money go for an errand for you? Can a bag of money look after you in your old age? Can a bag of money mourn you when you are dead? A child is more valuable than money.
Efuru (1966)

3 What woman was not susceptible to flattery, especially if it comes from a man she loves.
Efuru (1966)

4 When God gives you a rash, he also gives you nails to scratch it with.
Idu (1970)

Nye, Bill (Edgar Wilson Nye; 1850–96) U.S. humorist

1 There are just two people entitled to refer to themselves as "we"; one is a newspaper editor and the other is a fellow with a tapeworm.
Attrib.

Nyerere, Julius Kambarage (1922–99) Tanzanian president

1 Increasingly it is possible for governments to choose only *between* evils.
Lecture at the Africa Education Trust, London, quoted in *Guardian*, London (June 10, 1997)

2 The survival of our wildlife is a matter of grave concern to all of us in Africa. These wild creatures...are an integral part of our natural resources and of our future livelihood and well-being.
The Arusha Declaration, Tanganyika (September 1961)

3 Africa must refuse to be humiliated, exploited, and pushed around. And with the same determination we must refuse to humiliate, exploit or push others around.
February 29, 1968. *Freedom and Development* (1973)

4 The right of a man to stand upright as a human being in his own country comes before questions of the kind of society he will create once he has that right.
October 2, 1969. *Freedom and Development* (1973)

5 If we are to live our lives in peace and harmony, and if we are to achieve our ambitions of improving the conditions under which we live, we must have both freedom and discipline. For freedom without discipline is anarchy; discipline without freedom is tyranny.
TANU policy paper, October 16, 1968. *Freedom and Development* (1973)

6 From no quarter shall we accept direction, or neo-colonialism, and at no time shall we lower our guard against the subversion of our Government or our people. Neither our principles, our country, nor our freedom to determine our own future are for sale.
June 4, 1965. Said in a speech at a state banquet for Chou en Lai, the first leader of the People's Republic of China. *Freedom and Socialism* (1968)

7 The man who creeps forward inch by inch may well arrive at his destination, when the man who jumps without being able to see the other side may well fall and cripple himself.
September 1967. Policy paper. "Socialism and Rural Development," *Freedom and Socialism* (1968)

8 If Kuwait and Saudi Arabia sold bananas or oranges, the Americans would not go there. They are there because Kuwait is an oil monarchy.
September 27, 1990. Referring to the international response to the Iraqi invasion of Kuwait (August 1990). *Independent*, London (September 28, 1990)

9 Those who receive this privilege of education have a duty to return the sacrifice which others have made. They are like the man who has been given all the food available...in order that he might have the strength to bring supplies back...If he takes this food and does not bring help...he is a traitor.
Quoted in *Nyerere of Tanzania* (William Edgett Smith; 1981)

Oakeley, Frederick (1802–80) British churchman

1 O come all ye faithful,
Joyful and triumphant,
O come ye, O come ye to Bethlehem.
Translated from the Latin hymn "Adeste Fideles." "O Come All Ye Faithful" (1841)

Oates, Joyce Carol (b.1938) U.S. writer

1 The worst cynicism: a belief in luck.
Do What You Will (1970), pt. 2, ch. 15

2 I used to think getting old was about vanity—but actually it's about losing people you love.
Guardian, London (August 18, 1989)

3 For what *is* passes so swiftly and irrevocably into what *was*, no human claim can be of the least significance.
What I Lived For (1994), prologue

Oates, Lawrence, Captain (Lawrence Edward Grace Oates; 1880–1912) British explorer

1 I am just going outside and may be some time.
Last words before leaving the tent and vanishing into the blizzard on the British expedition to the South Pole (1912). Journal (March 17, 1912)

O'Brien, Conor Cruise (Donal Conor Dermod David Donat Cruise O'Brien; b.1917) Irish historian, critic, and politician

1 My doctor has advised me to cut back on predictions.
Newspaper column (November 11, 1994)

2 It is a city where you can see a sparrow fall to the ground, and God watching it.
Referring to Dublin. Attrib.

O'Brien, Edna (b.1932) Irish novelist

1 Do you know what I hate about myself, I have never done a brave thing, I have never risked death.
"Over," *A Scandalous Woman* (1974)

2 I thought of the day I too had gone a bit mad, slipped from behind this girl with all these hopes to the woman who would count in morsels from that final moment onward the pleasures and excitements of her life.
The High Road (1988)

3 I did not sleep. I never do when I am over-happy, over-unhappy, or in bed with a strange man.
The Love Object (1968)

4 The vote, I thought, means nothing to women. We should be armed.
Quoted in *Fear of Flying* (Erica Jong; 1973), epigraph to ch. 16

O'Brien, Flann (Brian O'Nolan, also known as Myles na Gopaleen; 1911–66) Irish novelist and journalist

1 The conclusion of your syllogism, I said lightly, is fallacious, being based upon licensed premises.
At Swim-Two-Birds (1939)

2 When money's tight and it's hard to get
And your horse has also ran,
When all you have is a heap of debt—
A PINT OF PLAIN IS YOUR ONLY MAN.
At Swim-Two-Birds (1939)

3 A woman doesn't care if she hasn't a stomach, provided she looks as if she hasn't.
"Criticism," *Further Cuttings from Cruiskeen Lawn* (1989)

4 I know of only four languages, viz: Latin, Irish, Greek and Chinese. These are languages because they are the instruments of integral civilisations. English and French are not languages: they are mercantile codes.
"Criticism," *Further Cuttings from Cruiskeen Lawn* (1989)

5 Mr O'Connor and I are old friends, though heaven knows of whom, and I yield to nuns in my admiration for his work—if not for his literary work.
Referring to Frank O'Connor. "Criticism," *Further Cuttings from Cruiskeen Lawn* (1989)

6 Now for a change I am going to be serious—though only temporarily.
"Politics," *Further Cuttings from Cruiskeen Lawn* (1989)

7 The task of reviving Irish, we are told, would be hard "unless conversations could be limited to requests for food and drink." And who wants conversations on any other subject?
"The First Article," *Further Cuttings from Cruiskeen Lawn* (1989)

8 A thing of duty is a boy for ever.
Referring to the fact that policemen always seem to be young-looking, and punning on the first line of John Keats's long poem *Endymion*: "A thing of beauty is a joy forever." *Listener*, London (February 24, 1977)

9 People who spend most of their natural lives riding iron bicycles...get their personalities mixed up with the personalities of their bicycles as a result of the interchanging of the mollycules of each of them.
The Dalkey Archive (1964)

10 I dedicate these pages to my Guardian Angel, impressing upon

him that I'm only fooling and warning him to see to it that there is no misunderstanding when I go home.
The Dalkey Archive (1964), dedication

11 Our ancestors believed in magic, prayers, trickery, browbeating and bullying: I think it would be fair to sum that list up as "Irish politics".
The Hair of the Dogma (Kevin O'Nolan, ed.; 1977)

12 The majority of the members of the Irish parliament are professional politicians, in the sense that otherwise they would not be given jobs minding mice at crossroads.
The Hair of the Dogma (Kevin O'Nolan, ed.; 1977)

13 It is not that I half knew my mother. I knew half of her: the lower half—her lap, legs, feet, her hands and wrists as she bent forward.
The Hard Life (1961)

O'Brien, Tim (William Timothy O'Brien; b.1946) U.S. novelist

1 Any battle or bombing raid or artillery barrage has the aesthetic purity of absolute moral indifference—a powerful, implacable beauty.
The Things They Carried (1990)

2 If you don't care for obscenity, you don't care for the truth; if you don't care for the truth, watch how you vote. Send guys to war, they come home talking dirty.
The Things They Carried (1990)

3 The great American war chest—the fruits of science, the smokestacks, the canneries, the arsenals at Hartford, the Minnesota forests, the machine shops, the vast fields of corn and wheat.
The Things They Carried (1990)

4 They carried all they could bear, and then some, including a silent awe for the terrible power of the things they carried.
The Things They Carried (1990)

5 They carried the soldier's greatest fear, which was the fear of blushing. Men killed and died because they were embarrassed not to.
The Things They Carried (1990)

6 The war was over and there was no place in particular to go.
Referring to the Vietnam War (1959–75). *The Things They Carried* (1990)

Ocampo, Victoria (1891–1979) Argentinian writer and publisher

1 Moral, like physical, cleanliness is not acquired once and for all: it can only be kept and renewed by a habit of constant watchfulness and discipline.
"Scruples and Ambitions" (1947)

O'Casey, Sean (John Casey; 1880–1964) Irish playwright

1 I'd love to blow my own trumpet, but the work's too hard. And even if others supply the trumpet, they expect you to provide the wind.
Letter to R. M. Fox (October 27, 1924), quoted in *Sean O'Casey: a Life* (Garry O'Connor; 1988)

2 He's an oul' butty o' mine—oh, he's a darlin' man, a daarlin' man.
Juno and the Paycock (1924)

3 I ofen looked up at the sky an' assed meself the question—what is the stars, what is the stars?
Juno and the Paycock (1924)

4 The whole country's in a state o' chassis.
Referring to Ireland. *Juno and the Paycock* (1924)

5 There's no reason to bring religion into it. I think we ought to have as great a regard for religion as we can, so as to keep it out of as many things as possible.
The Plough and the Stars (1926)

6 I believe in the freedom of Ireland and that England has no right to be here. But I draw the line when I hear the gunmen blowin' about dyin' for the people, when it's the people that are dyin' for the gunmen.
The Shadow of a Gunman (1923)

7 I wouldn't go to heaven on a free ticket.
1920? Referring to being offered help with a train fare. Attrib. *Guardian*, London (May 5, 1995)

8 We should remember that God made us from the waist down as well as from the waist up.
Encouraging Christians, whom he felt were too puritanical, to have more tolerant views towards sexual behavior. Quoted in *Sean O'Casey and His World* (David Krause; 1928)

Ochs, Adolph Simon (1858–1935) U.S. newspaper proprietor

1 All the news that's fit to print.
The motto of *New York Times* from 1896. *New York Times* (1896)

Ockham, William of (also spelled Occam, "Doctor Invincibilis," "Venerabilis Inceptor"; 1285?–1349?) English philosopher and theologian

1 Entities should not be multiplied unnecessarily.
No more things should be presumed to exist than are absolutely necessary.
"Ockham's Razor": despite its attribution to William of Ockham, it was in fact a repetition of an ancient philosophical maxim. *Quodlibeta Septem* (1320?)

O'Connell, Daniel ("The Liberator"; 1775–1847) Irish politician

1 I am the hired servant of Ireland, and I glory in my servitude.
Letter (February 1848), quoted in *A Book of Irish Quotations* (Sean McMahon, ed.; 1984)

2 Thank God, I'll have the privilege of knocking down any man that now calls me, "My Lord."
Referring to giving up the Lord Mayorship of Dublin. Remark (1842), quoted in *A Book of Irish Quotations* (Sean McMahon, ed.; 1984)

3 The Union...was a crime, and it must still be criminal unless it shall be ludicrously pretended that crime, like wine, improves by old age.
Referring to the Act of Union of 1800, which joined Great Britain and Ireland. Repeal speech (1809)

4 Not for all the universe contains would I, in the struggle for what I conceive my country's cause, consent to the effusion of a single drop of human blood, except my own.
Speech (February 28, 1843)

O'Connell, Eibhlin Dubh (1743?–?) Irish poet

1 I knew nothing of your murder
Till your horse came to the stable
With the reins beneath her trailing,
And your heart's blood on her shoulders
Staining the tooled saddle.
Elegy on the death of her husband. "Lament for Art O'Leary," *The Faber Book of Irish Verse* (John Montague, ed.; 1974)

2 So stop your weeping now
Women of the soft, wet eyes
And drink to Art O'Leary
Before he enters the grave school
Not to study wisdom and song
But to carry earth and stone.
Elegy on the death of her husband. "Lament for Art O'Leary," *The Faber Book of Irish Verse* (John Montague, ed.; 1974)

O'Connell, William Henry (1859–1944) U.S. cardinal

1 If this tango-dancing female is the new woman, then God spare us from any further development of the abnormal creature.
Attrib.

O'Connor, Edwin (1918–68) U.S. writer

1 The Last Hurrah
1956. Title of novel based on the political career of James M. Curley.

O'Connor, Flannery (Mary Flannery O'Connor; 1925–64) U.S. novelist and short-story writer

1 I doubt if the texture of Southern life is any more grotesque than that of the rest of the nation, but it does seem evident that the Southern writer is particularly adept at recognizing the grotesque.
Lecture, Notre Dame University (Spring 1957)

2 There was a time when the average reader read a novel simply for the moral he could get out of it, and however naïve that may have been, it was a good deal less naïve than some of the limited objectives he has now.
Lecture, Wesleyan College, Macon, Georgia (1960), "Some Aspects of the Grotesque in Southern Fiction"

3 While the South is hardly Christ-centered, it is most certainly Christ-haunted.
Lecture, Wesleyan College, Macon, Georgia (1960), "Some Aspects of the Grotesque in Southern Fiction"

4 The novel is an art form and when you use it for anything other than art, you pervert it...If you manage to use it successfully for social, religious, or other purposes, it is because you make it art first.
Letter to Father John McCown (May 9, 1956)

5 Knowing who you are is good for one generation only.
"Everything That Rises Must Converge," *Everything That Rises Must Converge* (1965)

6 I preach there are all kinds of truth, your truth and somebody else's. But behind all of them there is only one truth and that is that there's no truth.
Said by Hazel Motes. *Wise Blood* (1952), ch. 10

O'Connor, Frank (Michael O'Donovan; 1903–66) Irish writer

1 "Father," I said, feeling I might as well get it over while I had him in good humour, "I had it all arranged to kill my grandmother."
"First Confession," *My Oedipus Complex and Other Stories* (1953)

2 Some kids are cissies by nature, but I was a cissy by conviction.
"The Genius," *My Oedipus Complex and Other Stories* (1953)

3 Shut up, Donovan! You don't understand me, but these lads do. They're not the sort to make a pal and kill a pal. They're not the tools of any capitalist.
Said by one of two English soldiers in the story, who have been captured by the IRA and are being held pending execution. "Guests of the Nation," *Stories by Frank O'Connor* (1956)

4 "By the hokies, there was a man in this place one time by the name of Ned Sullivan, and a queer thing happened to him late one night..." That is how, even in my own lifetime, stories began.
The Lonely Voice: A Study of the Short Story (1962), introduction

5 In its earlier phases storytelling, like poetry and drama, was a public art...But the short story, like the novel, is a modern art form; that is to say, it represents, better than poetry or drama, our own attitude to life.
The Lonely Voice: A Study of the Short Story (1962), introduction

O'Connor, Johnson (1891–1973) U.S. scientist

1 Three characteristics of top executives are slow speech, impressive appearance, and a complete lack of a sense of humor.
Quoted in *The Pyramid Builders* (Vance Packard; 1962)

O'Connor, Joseph (b.1963) Irish writer

1 This struggle for Irish national freedom often expresses itself in profoundly Oedipal terms. For if motherhood in our history is associated with revolution, fatherhood is often linked with authority.
"Playboys on Crutches," *The Secret World of the Irish Male* (1994)

2 Fighting the Tans was all very well, but sometimes you can't help feeling that if the Eamon de Valera generation had stayed at home and changed the occasional nappy Ireland might have been oddly better off.
The Tans were the "Black and Tans," a British armed auxiliary force sent to Ireland to quell the republicans between 1920 and 1921. A "nappy" is a diaper. "Playboys on Crutches," *The Secret World of the Irish Male* (1994)

3 Part of the problem with Ireland is that everything is named after someone. In Dublin, there is a railway station called Sydney Parade, and for many years, I thought Sydney Parade was one of the leaders in the 1916 Rising.
Referring to the nationalist Easter Rising (Easter Rebellion) of 1916. "The Write Stuff: Irish Writers and Writing," *The Secret World of the Irish Male* (1994)

O'Connor, Sandra Day (b.1930) U.S. Supreme Court justice

1 Despite the encouraging and wonderful gains and the changes for women which have occurred in my lifetime, there is still room to advance and to promote correction of the remaining deficiencies and imbalances.
Speech, Atlanta, *New York Times* (February 12, 1989)

2 The more education a woman has, the wider the gap between men's and women's earnings for the same work.
Phoenix Magazine (1971)

Odets, Clifford (1906–63) U.S. playwright and screenwriter

1 Go out and fight so life shouldn't be printed on dollar bills.
Awake and Sing! (1935), Act 1

Odom, Jim (John "Blue Moon" Odom) U.S. baseball player and umpire

1 No manager ever thinks he got a break. I call them like I see them, and I don't care what team it is. If I'm right only half the time, I'm batting .500—and I never saw a ball player bat .500.
1991. Attrib.

O'Donoghue, Bernard (b.1945) Irish poet and academic

1 The mid-point being passed, the pattern is clear.
This road I had taken for a good byway
Is the main thoroughfare.
"Nell Mezzo del Cammin," *Gunpowder* (1995)

Ó'Faoláin, Sean (John Francis Whelan; 1900–91) Irish writer

1 Our sins are tawdry, our virtues childlike, our revolts desultory and brief, our submissions formal and frequent. In Ireland a policeman's lot is a supremely happy one. God smiles, the priest beams, and the novelist groans.
"The Dilemma of Irish Letters" (1949)

Officer, Charles B. U.S. geologist

1 "Continental drift"—or "plate tectonics"...has permitted us a far greater understanding of the nature of such things as volcanoes. Understanding them does nothing to tame them...but it does serve to make the Earth appear a bit less whimsical in its outbursts.
Tales of the Earth: Paroxysms and Perturbations of the Blue Planet (co-written with Jake Page; 1993)

O'Flaherty, Liam (1896–1984) Irish writer

1 Then the sniper turned over the dead body and looked into his brother's face.
"The Sniper" (1937)

Ogilvy, David (David Mackenzie Ogilvy; b.1911) U.S. advertising executive

1 In the best institutions, promises are kept no matter what the costs in agony and overtime.
Confessions of an Advertising Man (1987)

2 Like a midwife, I make my living bringing new babies into the world, except that mine are new advertising campaigns.
Confessions of an Advertising Man (1987)

3 The consumer isn't a moron; she is your wife. You insult her intelligence if you assume that a mere slogan and a few vapid adjectives will persuade her to buy anything.
Confessions of an Advertising Man (1987)

4 Avoid clients whose ethos is incompatible with yours.
Ogilvy on Advertising (1983)

5 The American brand of democratic leadership doesn't work so well in Europe, where executives have a psychological need for more autocratic leadership.
Ogilvy on Advertising (1983)

6 The best leaders are apt to be found among those executives who have a strong component of unorthodoxy in their characters. Instead of resisting innovation, they symbolize it.
Ogilvy on Advertising (1983)

7 The most effective leader is the one who satisfies the psychological needs of his followers.
Ogilvy on Advertising (1983)

8 When you have nothing to say, sing it.
Ogilvy on Advertising (1983)

9 First, make yourself a reputation for being a creative genius. Second, surround yourself with partners who are better than you. Third, leave them to get on with it.
Referring to success in advertising. *Sunday Times*, London (April 23, 1978)

O'Hara, Frank (Francis Russell O'Hara; 1926–66) U.S. poet and writer

1 No expressive or faulty quiver in a battement...no squiggle in a painting and no adverb, seems ever to escape his attention as to its relevance in the work as a whole.
Referring to dance critic and writer Edwin Denby. Quoted in *Dancers, Buildings and People in the Streets* (Edwin Denby; 1965), introduction

O'Hara, Geoffrey (1882–1967) Canadian-born U.S. songwriter and composer

1 K-K-K-Katy, beautiful Katy,
You're the only g-g-g-girl that I adore,
When the m-m-m-moon shines over the cow-shed,
I'll be waiting at the k-k-k-kitchen door.
Song lyric. "K-K-K-Katy" (1918)

O'Hara, Theodore (1820–67) U.S. poet and soldier

1 On Fame's eternal camping-ground
Their silent tents are spread,
And Glory guards with solemn round
The bivouac of the dead.
"The Bivouac of the Dead" (1847), st. 1

2 A lawyer with his briefcase can steal more than a thousand men with guns.
Attrib.

3 He's a businessman. I'll make him an offer he can't refuse.
Attrib.

O'Hare, Dean (Dean Raymond O'Hare; b.1942) U.S. insurance broker

1 A culture that values integrity, combined with management that tries to address potential causes of unethical behavior, is perhaps the best means of ensuring integrity in business.
Speech (October 1995)

2 When the monetary damages are smaller, lawyers will find themselves less zealous in their pursuit of what they call justice.
Speech (October 1995)

3 Yesterday's lifesaving, fireproof building material is today's carcinogen.
Speech (October 1995)

Ohmae, Kenichi Japanese business strategist

1 Region states'...primary linkage is with the global economy.
"Putting Global Logic First," *Harvard Business Review* (January–February 1995)

2 Before national identity, before local affiliation, before German ego or Italian ego or Japanese ego—before any of this comes the commitment to a single, unified global mission.
Referring to the globalization of business. *The Borderless World: Power and Strategy in the Interlinked Economy* (1990)

3 More strategies fail because they are overripe than because they are premature.
The Mind of the Strategist (1982)

4 Most large U.S. corporations are run like the Soviet economy.
The Mind of the Strategist (1982)

5 The final technique for coming up with new business ideas is to maximize one's strategic degrees of freedom.
The Mind of the Strategist (1982)

6 To break out of a market-share stalemate, the strategic thinker must sometimes have the courage to burst these shackles.
The Mind of the Strategist (1982)

7 What we need today...is not a new theory, concept, or framework, but people who can think strategically.
The Mind of the Strategist (1982)

8 In a borderless world, traditional national interest—which has become little more than a cloak for subsidy and protection—has no meaningful place.
Quoted in "Economic Prophet of the Information Age," *Independent*, London (Bryan Appleyard; December 11, 1995)

9 The strategist's method...challenge the prevailing assumptions with a single question: Why? and to put the same question relentlessly to those responsible for the current way of doing things until they are sick of it.
Quoted in *Key Management Ideas* (Stuart Crainer; 1996)

O'Keefe, Patrick (1872–1934) U.S. advertising agent

1 Say it with flowers.
Slogan for the Society of American Florists. *Florist's Exchange* (December 15, 1917)

O'Keeffe, Georgia (1887–1986) U.S. artist

1 You paint *from* your subject, not what you see, so you can't be bothered with changes in light. I rarely paint anything I don't know very well.
The Artist's Voice: Talks with 17 Artists (Katherine Kuh; 1962)

O'Keeffe, John (1747–1833) Irish playwright and librettist

1 Fat, fair and forty were all the toasts of the young men.
Irish Mimic (1795), Scene 2

Okri, Ben (b.1959) Nigerian novelist, short-story writer, and poet

1 A man's greatest battles are the ones he fights within himself.
Flowers and Shadows (1980)

2 A dream can be the highest point of a life.
The Famished Road (1991)

3 The only power poor people have is their hunger.
The Famished Road (1991)

4 A novel is a river, but a short story is a glass of water. A novel is a forest, but the short story is a seed. It is more atomic. The atom may contain the secret structures of the universe.
Talking With African Writers (Jane Wilkinson; 1992)

5 One shouldn't offer hope cheaply.
Talking With African Writers (Jane Wilkinson; 1992)

Oldenburg, Claes (Claes Thure Oldenburg; b.1929) Swedish-born U.S. sculptor

1 I am for an art that tells you the time of day, or where such and such a street is. I am for an art that helps old ladies across the street.
Statement for exhibition catalogue (1961)

2 I am for Kool-art, 7-Up art, Pepsi-art, Sunshine art.
Statement for exhibition catalogue (1961)

Oldys, William (1696–1761) English poet, antiquarian, and bibliographer

1 Busy, curious, thirsty fly,
Drink with me, and drink as I.
"The Fly" (1732), st. 1

Olitski, Jules (b.1922) Russian-born U.S. painter and sculptor

1 What is of importance in painting is paint. Paint can be color. Paint becomes painting when color establishes surface.
1966. "Painting in Color," *Artforum* (January 1967)

Olivier, Laurence, Baron Olivier of Brighton (Laurence Kerr Olivier; 1907–89) British actor and director

1 You must have—besides intuition and sensitivity—a cutting edge that allows you to reach what you need. Also, you have to know life—bastards included—and it takes a bit of one to know one, don't you think?
Advice on being a successful actor. Interview, *Daily Mail*, London (March 28, 1986), quoted in *Chambers Film Quotes* (Tony Crawley, ed.; 1991)

2 The role of Othello is the biggest strain of all.
Attrib.

Olmedo, José Juaquín (1780–1847) Ecuadorian poet and statesman

1 He who does not hope to win has already lost.
Attrib.

Olmsted, Frederick Law (1822–1903) U.S. landscape architect

1 It is one of the great purposes of the Park to supply to the hundreds of thousands of tired workers...a specimen of God's handiwork that shall be to them, inexpensively, what a month

or two in the White Mountains or the Adirondacks is, at great cost, to those in easier circumstances.
Referring to Central Park, New York City. Report (co-written with Calvert Vaux; April 28, 1858)

2 The Park throughout is a single work of art, and as such subject to the primary law of every work of art, namely, that it shall be framed upon a single, noble motive, to which the design of all its parts, in some more or less subtle way, shall be confluent and helpful.
Referring to Central Park, New York City. Report (co-written with Calvert Vaux; April 28, 1858)

3 Washington *en petit*, seen through a reversed glass.
Referring to Austin, Texas. *A Journey through Texas* (1857)

Olsen, Tillie (b.1913) U.S. writer

1 Better mankind born without mouths and stomachs than always to worry about money to buy, to shop, to fix, to cook, to wash, to clean.
Tell me a Riddle (1961)

Olson, Charles (Charles John Olson; 1910–70) U.S. poet

1 Hear all, the newmoon new in all
the ancient sky.
Closing lines. "Celestial Evening, October 1967" (1975)

2 Get on with it, keep moving, keep in
speed, the nerves, their speed, the perceptions,
theirs, the acts, the split second acts, the
whole business, keep it moving as fast as you
can, citizen...fast, there's the dogma.
"Projective Verse" (1950)

3 The chain of memory is resurrection.
"A Newly Discovered 'Homeric' Hymn," *Charles Olson: Selected Poems* (Robert Creeley, ed.; 1993)

4 The lilac moon of the earth's backyard
which gives silence to the whole house
falls down
out of the sky
over the fence.
"May 31, 1961," *Charles Olson: Selected Poems* (Robert Creeley, ed.; 1993)

5 But that which matters, that which insists, that
which will last,
that! o my people, where shall you find it, how, where, where
shall you listen
when all is become billboards, when, all, even silence, is spray-
gunned?
"I, Maximus of Gloucester, to You," *The Maximus Poems 1–10* (1953)

6 Facts to be dealt with, as the sea is, the demand
that they be played by...the ear!
"I, Maximus of Gloucester, to You," *The Maximus Poems 1–10* (1953)

7 Off-shore, by islands hidden in the blood
jewels & miracles, I, Maximus
a metal hot from boiling water, tell you
what is a lance, who obeys the figures of
the present dance.
"I, Maximus of Gloucester, to You," *The Maximus Poems 1–10* (1953)

8 one loves form only
and form only comes
into existence when
the thing is born.
"I, Maximus of Gloucester, to You," *The Maximus Poems 1–10* (1953)

9 I have had to learn the simplest things
last.
"I, Maximus to Himself," *The Maximus Poems 1–10* (1953)

10 A poem is energy transferred from where the poet got it...by way of the poem itself to, all the way over to, the reader.
Quoted in *Norton Anthology of American Literature* (Nina Baym, ed.; 1998)

11 An archaeologist of morning.
Referring to his own preoccupation with the origin of things. Quoted in *Norton Anthology of American Literature* (Nina Baym, ed.; 1998)

O'Malley, Austin (1858–1932) U.S. writer

1 God shows his contempt for wealth by the kind of person he selects to receive it.
Attrib.

2 The worst misfortune that can happen to an ordinary man is to have an extraordinary father.
Attrib.

3 Ugliness is a point of view: an ulcer is wonderful to a pathologist.
Attrib.

Onassis, Aristotle (Aristotle Socrates Onassis; 1900?–75) Turkish-born Greek shipping magnate

1 In business we cut each other's throats, but now and then we sit around the same table and behave—for the sake of the ladies.
Referring to his rivalry with shipping tycoon Stavros Niarchos. Quoted in *Sunday Times*, London (March 16, 1969)

2 Keep looking tanned, live in an elegant building (even if you're in the cellar), be seen in smart restaurants (even if you nurse one drink), and if you borrow, borrow big.
Referring to the secret of success. Quoted in *Times*, London (August 15, 1986)

3 If women didn't exist, all the money in the world would have no meaning.
Attrib.

Onassis, Jacqueline Kennedy (originally Jacqueline Lee Bouvier; 1929–94) U.S. first lady

1 The one thing I do not want to be called is First Lady. It sounds like a saddle horse.
Quoted in *The Kennedys* (Peter Collier and David Horowitz; 1984)

Ondaatje, Michael (b.1943) Sri Lankan-born Canadian novelist and poet

1 She had always wanted words, she loved them, grew up on them. Words gave her clarity, brought reason, shape. Whereas I thought words bent emotions like sticks in water.
The English Patient (1992)

O'Neill, Eugene, Eugene Gladstone O'Neill (1888–1953) U.S. playwright

1 Life is for each man a solitary cell whose walls are mirrors.
Lazarus Laughed (1928)

2 None of us can help the things life has done to us. They're done before you realize it, and once they're done they make you do other things until at last everything comes between you and what you'd like to be, and you've lost your true self forever.
Long Day's Journey into Night (1956)

3 Life is perhaps most wisely regarded as a bad dream between two awakenings and every day is a life in miniature.
Marco Millions (1928)

4 Our lives are merely strange dark interludes in the electric display of God the Father.
Strange Interlude (1928)

5 For de little stealin' dey gits you in jail soon or late. For de big stealin' dey makes you emperor and put you in de Hall o' Fame when you croaks.
The Emperor Jones (1920)

6 Christ, can you imagine what a guilty skunk she made me feel. If she'd only admitted once she didn't believe any more in her pipe dream that some day I'd behave!
The Iceman Cometh (1946)

7 The Iceman Cometh
1946. Play title that has become a catchphrase.

O'Neill, Hugh, 3rd Baron Dungannon and 2nd Earl of Tyrone (1540?–1616) Irish patriot

1 Wherever man would not be on our side and would not spend his efforts for the right, we take it that that man is a man against us.
Letter to Sir John McCoughleyn (February 6, 1600), quoted in *A Celtic Miscellany* (Kenneth Hurlstone Jackson; 1951)

O'Neill, Terence, Baron O'Neill of the Maine (Terence Marne O'Neill; 1914–90) Irish politician

1 It is frightfully hard to explain to Protestants that if you give Roman Catholics a good job and a good house, they will live like Protestants...They will refuse to have eighteen children.
May 10, 1969. Quoted in *Phrases Make History Here* (Conor O'Clery; 1986)

Ono, Yoko (b.1933) Japanese-born U.S. musician, writer, campaigner, and artist

1 Remove your pants before resorting to violence.
Attrib.

Opie, John ("The Cornish Wonder"; 1761–1807) British painter

1 I mix them with my brains, sir.
When asked what he mixed his colors with. Quoted in *Self-Help* (Samuel Smiles; 1859), ch. 4

Oppen, George (1908–84) U.S. poet

1 Obsessed, bewildered

By the shipwreck
Of the singular

We have chosen the meaning
Of being numerous.
"Of Being Numerous," *Of Being Numerous* (1968), quoted in *The Norton Anthology of American Literature* (Nina Baym, ed.; 1998), vol. 2

2 I have not and never did have any motive of poetry
But to achieve clarity.
"Route," *Of Being Numerous* (1968), quoted in *The Norton Anthology of American Literature* (Nina Baym, ed.; 1998), vol. 2

3 We have begun to say good bye
To each other
And cannot say it.
"Anniversary," *Seascape: Needle's Eye* (1972), quoted in *The Norton Anthology of American Literature* (Nina Baym, ed.; 1998), vol. 2

4 In the small beauty of the forest
The wild deer bedded down—
That they are there!
"Psalm," *This is Which* (1965), quoted in *The Norton Anthology of American Literature* (Nina Baym, ed.; 1998), vol. 2

Oppenheimer, Harry (Harry Frederick Oppenheimer; b.1908) South African industrialist

1 We were consistently on the side of the angels.
Referring to his company's attitude toward apartheid. *Financial Times*, London (October 17, 1988)

Oppenheimer, J. Robert (Julius Robert Oppenheimer; 1904–67) U.S. nuclear physicist

1 The physicists have known sin; and this is a knowledge which they cannot lose.
Referring to the development of the nuclear bomb. Lecture at Massachusetts Institute of Technology (November 25, 1947)

2 Today, it is not only that our kings do not know mathematics, but our philosophers do not know mathematics and—to go a step further—our mathematicians do not know mathematics.
"The Tree of Knowledge," *Harper's Magazine* (1958)

3 The open society, the unrestricted access to knowledge, the unplanned and uninhibited association of men for its furtherance—these are what may make a vast, complex, ever growing, ever changing, ever more specialized and expert technological world, nevertheless a world of human community.
Science and the Common Understanding (1953)

4 Both the man of science and the man of art live always at the edge of mystery, surrounded by it. Both, as the measure of their creation, have always had to do with the harmonization of what is new with what is familiar.
1954? Quoted in *Brighter than a Thousand Suns* (Robert Jungk; 1956)

5 I am become death, the destroyer of worlds.
July 16, 1945. Quoting Vishnu from the Indian religious text the Bhagavad-Gita, at the first atomic test in New Mexico. Quoted in *The Decision to Drop the Bomb* (Len Giovanitti and Fred Freed; 1965)

6 We knew the world would not be the same. A few people

laughed, a few people cried. Most people were silent.
Referring to the first atomic bomb test at Alamagordo, New Mexico. Quoted in *The Decision to Drop the Bomb* (Len Giovanitti and Fred Freed; 1965)

7 In the most primitive societies...the principal function of ritual, religion, of culture as it is practiced is, in fact, almost to stop change...The principal function of the most vital and living traditions today is precisely to provide the instruments of rapid change.
1959. Quoted in *The Jingle Bell Principle* (Miroslav Holub; 1992)

8 The atomic bomb...made the prospect of future war unendurable. It has led us up those last few steps to the mountain pass; and beyond there is a different country.
Quoted in *The Making of the Atomic Bomb* (Richard Rhodes; 1987)

Orben, Robert (b.1927) U.S. writer and editor

1 Every morning, I get up and look through the "Forbes" list of the richest people in America. If I'm not there, I go to work.
Attrib.

Orczy, Baroness (Emmuska Magdalena Rosalia Marie Josepha Barbara Orczy, also known as Mrs Montague Barstow; 1865–1947) Hungarian-born British novelist and playwright

1 We seek him here, we seek him there,
Those Frenchies seek him everywhere.
Is he in heaven?—Is he in hell?
That demmed elusive Pimpernel?
The Scarlet Pimpernel (1905), ch. 12

2 The weariest nights, the longest days, sooner or later must perforce come to an end.
The Scarlet Pimpernel (1905), ch. 22

Orléans, Duchess of (1652–1722) French sister-in-law to Louis XIV

1 Our dear King James is good and honest, but the most incompetent man I have ever seen in my life. A child of seven years would not make such silly mistakes as he does.
Referring to James II, who was in exile in France. Letter to the Electress Sophia (June 6, 1692)

O'Rourke, P. J. (b.1947) U.S. writer and humorist

1 We spend all day broadcasting on the radio and TV telling people back home what's happening here. And we learn about what's happening here by spending all day monitoring the radio and TV broadcasts from back home.
Referring to the media during the Gulf War (1991). Remark (January 31, 1991)

2 Automobiles are free of egotism, passion, prejudice and stupid ideas about where to have dinner. They are, literally, selfless. A world designed for automobiles instead of people would have wider streets, larger dining rooms, fewer stairs to climb, and no smelly dangerous subway stations.
"An Argument in Favor of Automobiles vs Pedestrians," *Give War a Chance* (1992)

3 No drug, not even alcohol, causes the fundamental ills of society. If we're looking for sources of our troubles, we shouldn't test people for drugs, we should test them for stupidity, ignorance, greed, and love of power.
"Studying For Our Drug Test," *Give War a Chance* (1992)

4 Marijuana is...self-punishing. It makes you acutely sensitive and in this world, what worse punishment could there be?
Rolling Stone (November 1989)

5 Nothing bad's going to happen to us. If we get fired, it's not a failure; it's midlife vocational reassessment.
Rolling Stone (November 1989)

6 Except for the fact that they all speak English pretty well, they're indistinguishable from Americans.
Referring to Germans. "The Death of Communism," *Rolling Stone* (November 1989)

7 The Americans don't really understand what's going on in Bosnia. To them it's the unspellables killing the unpronounceables.
Sun, London (1993)

Ortega y Gasset, José (1883–1955) Spanish writer and philosopher

1 Hatred is a feeling which leads to the extinction of values.
Meditations on Quixote (1914)

2 He who wishes to teach us a truth should not tell it to us, but simply suggest it with a brief gesture, a gesture which starts an ideal trajectory in the air along which we glide until we find ourselves at the feet of the new truth.
Meditations on Quixote (1914)

3 I am myself plus my circumstance and if I do not save it, I cannot save myself.
Meditations on Quixote (1914)

4 In order to master the unruly torrent of life the learned man meditates, the poet quivers, and the political hero erects the fortress of his will.
Meditations on Quixote (1914)

5 Life is the eternal text, the burning bush by the edge of the path from which God speaks.
Meditations on Quixote (1914)

6 Sexual pleasure seems to consist in a sudden discharge of nervous energy. Aesthetic enjoyment is a sudden discharge of allusive emotions. Similarly, philosophy is like a sudden discharge of intellectual activity.
Meditations on Quixote (1914)

7 The good is, like nature, an immense landscape in which man advances through centuries of exploration.
Meditations on Quixote (1914)

8 Triumph cannot help being cruel.
Notes on the Novel (1925)

9 Every life is, more or less, a ruin among whose debris we have to discover what the person ought to have been.
"In Search of Goethe from Within," *Partisan Review* (December 1949)

10 Life is our reaction to the basic insecurity which constitutes its substance.
"In Search of Goethe from Within," *Partisan Review* (December 1949)

11 Nothing so saps the profound resources of life as finding life too easy.
"In Search of Goethe from Within," *Partisan Review* (December 1949)

12 The soul...remains as much *outside* the *I* which you are, as the landscape remains outside the body.
"In Search of Goethe from Within," *Partisan Review* (December 1949)

13 Thought is not a gift to man but a laborious, precarious, and volatile acquisition.
"In Search of Goethe from Within," *Partisan Review* (December 1949)

14 To excel the past we must not allow ourselves to lose contact with it; on the contrary, we must feel it under our feet because we raised ourselves upon it.
"In Search of Goethe from Within," *Partisan Review* (December 1949)

15 We do not live to think, but, on the contrary, we think in order that we may succeed in surviving.
"In Search of Goethe from Within," *Partisan Review* (December 1949)

16 We must get over the error which makes us think that a man's life takes place inside himself.
"In Search of Goethe from Within," *Partisan Review* (December 1949)

17 Being an artist means ceasing to take seriously that very serious person we are when we are not an artist.
The Dehumanization of Art (1925)

18 Life is a petty thing unless there is pounding within it an enormous desire to extend its boundaries. We live in proportion to the extent to which we yearn to live more.
The Dehumanization of Art (1925)

19 The metaphor is probably the most fertile power possessed by man.
The Dehumanization of Art (1925)

20 The poet begins where the man ends. The man's lot is to live his human life, the poet's to invent what is nonexistent.
The Dehumanization of Art (1925)

21 Thinking is the desire to gain reality by means of ideas.
The Dehumanization of Art (1925)

22 Barbarism is the absence of standards to which appeal can be made.
The Revolt of the Masses (1930)

23 Men play at tragedy because they do not believe in the reality of the tragedy which is actually being staged in the civilized world.
The Revolt of the Masses (1930)

24 Revolution is not the uprising against pre-existing order, but the setting-up of a new order contradictory to the traditional one.
The Revolt of the Masses (1930)

25 The form most contradictory to human life that can appear among the human species is the "self-satisfied man."
The Revolt of the Masses (1930)

26 The struggle with the past is not a hand-to-hand fight. The future overcomes it by swallowing it. If it leaves anything outside it is lost.
The Revolt of the Masses (1930)

27 Today violence is the rhetoric of the period.
The Revolt of the Masses (1930)

28 We are in the presence of the contradiction of a style of living which cultivates sincerity and is at the same time a fraud. There is truth only in an existence which feels its acts as irrevocably necessary.
The Revolt of the Masses (1930)

29 We have need of history in its entirety, not to fall back into it, but to see if we can escape it.
The Revolt of the Masses (1930)

30 We live at a time when man believes himself fabulously capable of creation, but he does not know what to create.
The Revolt of the Masses (1930)

31 Who is it that exercises social power today? Who imposes the forms of his own mind on the period? Without a doubt, the man of the middle class.
The Revolt of the Masses (1930)

Orton, Joe (John Kingsley Orton; 1933–67) British playwright

1 I'd the upbringing a nun would envy and that's the truth. Until I was fifteen I was more familiar with Africa than my own body.
Entertaining Mr Sloane (1964)

2 It's all any reasonable child can expect if the dad is present at the conception.
Entertaining Mr Sloane (1964)

3 Women are like banks, boy, breaking and entering is a serious business.
Entertaining Mr Sloane (1964)

4 The humble and meek are thirsting for blood.
Funeral Games (1970)

5 Every luxury was lavished on you—atheism, breast-feeding, circumcision. I had to make my own way.
Loot (1966)

6 God is a gentleman. He prefers blondes.
Loot (1966)

7 Policemen, like red squirrels, must be protected.
Loot (1966)

8 Reading isn't an occupation we encourage among police officers. We try to keep the paper work down to a minimum.
Loot (1966)

9 Your explanation had the ring of truth. Naturally I disbelieved it.
Loot (1966)

10 You were born with your legs apart. They'll send you to the grave in a Y-shaped coffin.
What the Butler Saw (1969)

11 Try a boy for a change. You're a rich man. You can afford the luxuries of life.
Advice to Dr. Prentice to employ a male secretary. *What the Butler Saw* (1969)

12 The kind of people who always go on about whether a thing is in good taste invariably have very bad taste.
Attrib.

Orwell, George (Eric Arthur Blair; 1903–50) British writer

Quotations about Orwell

1 He could not blow his nose without moralising on the state of the handkerchief industry.
Cyril Connolly (1903–74) British writer and journalist. *The Evening Colonnade* (1973)

Quotations by Orwell

2 At 50, everyone has the face he deserves.
Manuscript notebook (April 17, 1949)

3 I loathed the game...it was very difficult for me to show courage at it. Football, it seemed to me, is not really played for the pleasure of kicking a ball about, but is a species of fighting.
"Such, Such Were the Joys" (1946)

4 Part of the reason for the ugliness of adults, in a child's eyes, is that the child is usually looking upwards, and few faces are at their best when seen from below.
"Such, Such Were the Joys" (1946)

5 Comrade Napoleon is always right.
Animal Farm (1945)

6 Man is the only creature that consumes without producing.
Animal Farm (1945), ch. 1

7 Four legs good, two legs bad.
Animal Farm (1945), ch. 3

8 War is war. The only good human being is a dead one.
Animal Farm (1945), ch. 4

9 He intended, he said, to devote the rest of his life to learning the remaining twenty-two letters of the alphabet.
Referring to Boxer, the farm horse. *Animal Farm* (1945), ch. 9

10 All animals are equal, but some animals are more equal than others.
Animal Farm (1945), ch. 10

11 One cannot really be a Catholic and grown-up.
Collected Essays (1961)

12 I'm fat, but I'm thin inside. Has it ever struck you that there's a thin man inside every fat man, just as they say there's a statue inside every block of stone?
Coming Up for Air (1939), pt. 1, ch. 3

13 He was an embittered atheist, the sort of atheist who does not so much disbelieve in God as personally dislike Him.
Down and Out in Paris and London (1933), ch. 30

14 I have the most evil memories of Spain, but I have very few bad memories of Spaniards.
Homage to Catalonia (1938)

15 In trench warfare five things are important: firewood, food, tobacco, candles, and the enemy.
Homage to Catalonia (1938)

16 The high sentiments always win in the end, the leaders who offer blood, toil, tears and sweat always get more out of their followers than those who offer safety and a good time. When it comes to the pinch, human beings are heroic.
"The Art of Donald McGill," *Horizon* (September 1941)

17 Big Brother is watching you.
Nineteen Eighty-Four (1949)

18 Thoughtcrime was not a thing that could be concealed forever. You might dodge successfully for a while, even for years, but sooner or later they were bound to get you.
Nineteen Eighty-Four (1949)

19 It was a bright cold day in April and the clocks were striking thirteen.
Opening sentence. *Nineteen Eighty-Four* (1949), pt. 1, ch. 1

20 War is Peace. Freedom is Slavery. Ignorance is Strength.
The three tenets of "Ingsoc." *Nineteen Eighty-Four* (1949), pt. 1, ch. 1

21 Who controls the past controls...the future: who controls the present controls the past.
Nineteen Eighty-Four (1949), pt. 1, ch. 3

22 *Doublethink* means the power of holding two contradictory beliefs in one's mind simultaneously, and accepting both of them.
Nineteen Eighty-Four (1949), pt. 2, ch. 9

23 If you want a picture of the future, imagine a boot stamping on a human face—for ever...And remember that it is for ever.
Nineteen Eighty-Four (1949), pt. 3, ch. 3

24 The quickest way of ending a war is to lose it.
"Second thoughts on James Burnham," *Polemic* (1946)

25 Most people get a fair amount of fun out of their lives, but on balance life is suffering and only the very young or the very foolish imagine otherwise.
"Lear, Tolstoy and the Fool," *Shooting an Elephant* (1950)

26 In our time, political speech and writing are largely the defence of the indefensible.
"Politics and the English Language," *Shooting an Elephant* (1950)

27 One ought to recognize that the present political chaos is connected with the decay of language, and that one can probably bring about some improvement by starting at the verbal end.
"Politics and the English Language," *Shooting an Elephant* (1950)

28 The great enemy of clear language is insincerity. When there is a gap between one's real and one's declared aims, one turns as it were instinctively to long words and exhausted idioms, like a cuttlefish squirting out ink.
"Politics and the English Language," *Shooting an Elephant* (1950)

29 The essence of being human is that one does not seek perfection.
"Reflections on Gandhi," *Shooting an Elephant* (1950)

30 Serious sport has nothing to do with fair play. It is bound up with hatred, jealousy, boastfulness, disregard of all rules and sadistic pleasure in witnessing violence; in other words it is war minus the shooting.
"The Sporting Spirit," *Shooting an Elephant* (1950)

31 A family with the wrong members in control—that, perhaps, is as near as one can come to describing England in a phrase.
"England Your England," *The Lion and the Unicorn* (1941)

32 Freedom is the right to tell people what they do not want to hear.
The Road to Wigan Pier (1937)

33 The more you are in the right the more natural that everyone else should be bullied into thinking likewise.
The Road to Wigan Pier (1937)

34 It is brought home to you...that it is only because miners sweat their guts out that superior persons can remain superior.
The Road to Wigan Pier (1937), ch. 2

35 I sometimes think that the price of liberty is not so much eternal vigilance as eternal dirt.
The Road to Wigan Pier (1937), ch. 4

36 There can hardly be a town in the South of England where you could throw a brick without hitting the niece of a bishop.
The Road to Wigan Pier (1937), ch. 7

37 As with the Christian religion, the worst advertisement for Socialism is its adherents.
The Road to Wigan Pier (1937), ch. 11

38 To the ordinary working man, the sort you would meet in any pub on Saturday night, Socialism does not mean much more than better wages and shorter hours and nobody bossing you about.
The Road to Wigan Pier (1937), ch. 11

39 We have nothing to lose but our aitches.
Referring to the middle classes; a parody of Karl Marx. *The Road to Wigan Pier* (1937), ch. 13

40 To a surprising extent the war-lords in shining armour, the apostles of the martial virtues, tend not to die fighting when the time comes. History is full of ignominious getaways by the great and famous.
"Who Are the War Criminals?," *Tribune* (1941)

41 After his long fast, the toad has a very spiritual look, like a strict Anglo-Catholic towards the end of Lent.
"As I Please," *Tribune*, London (April 1946), quoted in *The Collected Essays, Journalism and Letters of George Orwell* (Sonia Orwell and Ian Angus, eds.; 1968), vol. 4

42 Each generation imagines itself to be more intelligent than the one that went before it, and wiser than the one that comes after it.
Attrib. Book review (1945)

Osborne, Charles (b.1927) British author and critic

1 I think that if a third of all the novelists and maybe two-thirds of all the poets now writing dropped dead suddenly, the loss to literature would not be great.
Remark (November 1985)

Osborne, John (John James Osborne; 1929–94) British playwright and screenwriter

1 Damn you, England. You're rotting now, and quite soon you'll disappear.
Letter to *Tribune* (August 1961)

2 He really deserves some sort of decoration...a medal inscribed "For Vaguery in the Field".
Look Back in Anger (1956), Act 1

3 They spend their time mostly looking forward to the past.
Look Back in Anger (1956), Act 2, Scene 1

4 Poor old Daddy—just one of those sturdy old plants left over from the Edwardian Wilderness, that can't understand why the sun isn't shining any more.
Look Back in Anger (1956), Act 2, Scene 2

5 In the teeth of life we seem to die, but God says no—in the teeth of death we live.
Luther (1961), Act 3, Scene 2

6 There's no such thing as an orderly revolution.
Luther (1961), Act 3, Scene 2

7 I never deliberately set out to shock, but when people don't walk out of my plays I think there is something wrong.
Observer, London (January 19, 1975), "Sayings of the Week"

8 The schoolteacher is certainly underpaid as a childminder, but ludicrously overpaid as an educator.
Observer, London (July 21, 1985), "Sayings of the Week"

9 You're a long time dead.
The Entertainer (1957), Scene 2

10 Don't clap too hard—it's a very old building.
The Entertainer (1957), Scene 7

11 Never believe in mirrors or newspapers.
The Hotel in Amsterdam (1968)

12 She's not going to walk in here...and turn it into a Golden Sanitary Towel Award Presentation.
The Hotel in Amsterdam (1968)

13 She's like the old line about justice—not only must be done, but must be seen to be done.
Time Present (1968), Act 1

O'Shaughnessy, Arthur William Edgar (1844–81) English poet and natural historian

1 We are the music makers,
We are the dreamers of dreams,
Wandering by lone sea-breakers,
And sitting by desolate streams;
World-losers and world-forsakers,
On whom the pale moon gleams:
We are the movers and shakers
Of the world for ever, it seems
For each age is a dream that is dying,
Or one that is coming to birth.
"Ode" (1874), ll. 1–10, quoted in *The Oxford Book of English Verse, 1250–1918* (Sir Arthur Quiller Couch, ed.; 1939)

Oshima Nagisa (b.1932) Japanese film director

1 I cast actors from rock because they're sensitive to what people want. They're performers. Their antennas are screwed on right. They don't mind getting right in there and having a go at the truth.
Photoplay (September 1983), quoted in *Chambers Film Quotes* (Tony Crawley, ed.; 1991)

Osler, William, Sir (1849–1919) Canadian physician

1 The extraordinary development of modern science may be her undoing. Specialism, now a necessity, has fragmented the

specialties themselves in a way that makes the outlook hazardous. The workers lose all sense of proportion in a maze of minutiae.
Address, Classical Association, Oxford University, England (May 16, 1919)

2 I have learned since to be a better student, and to be ready to say to my fellow students "I do not know."
"After Twenty-Five Years," *Aequanimitas, with Other Addresses* (1889)

3 Imperative drugging—the ordering of medicine in any and every malady—is no longer regarded as the chief function of the doctor.
"Medicine in the Nineteenth Century," *Aequanimitas, with Other Addresses* (1889)

4 The trained nurse has become one of the great blessings of humanity, taking a place beside the physician and the priest, and not inferior to either in her mission.
"Nurse and Patient," *Aequanimitas, with Other Addresses* (1889)

5 I desire no other epitaph—no hurry about it, I may say—than the statement that I taught medical students in the wards, as I regard this as by far the most useful and important work I have been called upon to do.
"The Fixed Period," *Aequanimitas, with Other Addresses* (1889)

6 Fed on the dry husks of facts, the human heart has a hidden want which science cannot supply.
Science and Immortality (1904)

7 The successful teacher is no longer on a height, pumping knowledge at high pressure into passive receptacles...He is a senior student anxious to help his juniors.
The Student Life (1905)

8 A physician who treats himself has a fool for a patient.
Quoted in *Sir William Osler: Aphorisms* (William B. Bean, ed.; 1950)

9 One of the first duties of the physician is to educate the masses not to take medicine.
Quoted in *Sir William Osler: Aphorisms* (William B. Bean, ed.; 1950)

10 Patients should have rest, food, fresh air, and exercise—the quadrangle of health.
Quoted in *Sir William Osler: Aphorisms* (William B. Bean, ed.; 1950)

11 Soap and water and common sense are the best disinfectants.
Quoted in *Sir William Osler: Aphorisms* (William B. Bean, ed.; 1950)

12 The surgical cycle in woman: Appendix removed, right kidney hooked up, gall-bladder taken out, gastro-enterostomy, clean sweep of uterus and adnexa.
Quoted in *Sir William Osler: Aphorisms* (William B. Bean, ed.; 1950)

13 Nothing in life is more wonderful than faith—the one great moving force which we can neither weigh in the balance nor test in the crucible.
1910. Quoted in *The Life of Sir William Osler* (Harvey Cushing; 1925), vol. 2, ch. 30

14 We doctors have always been a simple trusting folk. Did we not believe Galen implicitly for 1500 years and Hippocrates for more than 2000?
Attrib.

Ossietzky, Carl von (1889–1938) German pacifist and journalist

1 We cannot appeal to the conscience of the world when our own conscience is asleep.
"Defeated Germany" (1920), quoted in *The Stolen Republic. Selected Writings of Carl von Ossietzky* (Bruno Frei, ed.; 1971)

2 If there is a really difficult task for a nation, it is to bear a defeat with dignity.
Written after Germany's defeat in World War I. "Defeated Germany" (1920), quoted in *The Stolen Republic. Selected Writings of Carl von Ossietzky* (Bruno Frei, ed.; 1971)

3 Germany has been wrecked by the exaggerations of the idea of power, by the blind confidence that force and naked steel are the sole measure of all things, and that justice and truth are just phrases, possibly useful as a way of swindling the stupid.
"The Coming Germany" (1918), quoted in *The Stolen Republic. Selected Writings of Carl von Ossietzky* (Bruno Frei, ed.; 1971)

4 No reasonable person today can doubt that Germany can only be linked with the democratic world in the sign of pacifism.
"The Pacifists" (1924), quoted in *The Stolen Republic. Selected Writings of Carl von Ossietzky* (Bruno Frei, ed.; 1971)

5 Germany...has no tradition of liberty; it lacks real civil consciousness, it lacks civilian pride when confronted with a uniform.
Published on the day Ossietzky began a prison sentence. "Account Rendered," *Die Weltbühne* (May 10, 1932), quoted in *The Stolen Republic. Selected Writings of Carl von Ossietzky* (Bruno Frei, ed.; 1971)

O'Sullivan, John L. (1813–95) U.S. writer

1 Understood as a central consolidated power, managing and directing the various general interests of the society, all government is evil, and the parent of evil. The best government is that which governs least.
The United States Magazine and Democratic Review (1837), Introduction

2 A spirit of hostile interference against us...checking the fulfilment of our manifest destiny to overspread the continent allotted by Providence for the free development of our yearly multiplying millions.
Referring to opposition to the annexation of Texas by the United States. *United States Magazine and Democratic Review* (1845), vol. 17

3 A torchlight procession marching down your throat.
Referring to whiskey. Attrib. *Collections and Recollections* (G. W. E. Russell; 1898), ch. 19

Otis, James (1725–83) U.S. politician

1 Taxation without representation is tyranny.
As "No taxation without representation" this became the principal slogan of the American Revolution. Slogan (1761?) Attrib.

Otto III, King of Germany and Holy Roman Emperor (980–1002) German monarch

1 Are you not my own Romans? For you I have abandoned my own father and denied the Saxons and all the Germans.
Said to the Romans, as they rebelled. Speech, Rome (1000)

Otto of Freising (1111?–58?) German bishop and historian

1 How, not many years before, one John, King and Priest, who

dwells in the extreme Orient beyond Persia and Armenia...is said to be of the ancient race of those Magi who are mentioned in the Gospel.

1145. The first mention of Prester John. The legend of a great Christian Priest-King in Asia persisted throughout the Middle Ages. Attrib.

Otway, Thomas (1652–85) English playwright and poet

1 These are rogues that pretend to be of a religion now!
Well, all I say is, honest atheism for my money.

The Atheist (1683), Act 3, Scene 1

2 Destructive, damnable, deceitful woman!

The Orphan (1680), Act 3, l. 586

3 Oh woman! lovely woman! Nature made thee
To temper man: we had been brutes without you;
Angels are painted fair, to look like you;
There's in you all that we believe of heav'n,
Amazing brightness, purity, and truth,
Eternal joy, and everlasting love.

Venice Preserved (1682), Act 1, Scene 1

4 Bear my weakness,
If throwing thus my arms about thy neck,
I play the boy, and blubber in thy bosom.

Venice Preserved (1682), ll. 274–276

Ouida (Marie Louise de la Ramée; 1839–1908) British novelist

1 With peaches and women, it's only the side next the sun that's tempting.

Strathmore (1865)

2 Christianity has made even of death a terror which was unknown to the gay calmness of the Pagan.

"The Failure of Christianity," *Views and Opinions* (1895)

3 The song that we hear with our ears is only the song that is sung in our hearts.

"Ariadne," *Wisdom, Wit and Pathos* (1877)

4 A cruel story runs on wheels, and every hand oils the wheels as they run.

"Moths," *Wisdom, Wit and Pathos* (1877)

Ouspensky, Peter (1878–1947) Russian philosopher

1 Body and mind, like man and wife, do not always agree to die together.

Lacon (1920?), vol. 1

2 Death...a friend that alone can bring the peace his treasures cannot purchase, and remove the pain his physicians cannot cure.

Lacon (1920?), vol. 2

3 Hypochondriacs squander large sums of time in search of nostrums by which they vainly hope they may get more time to squander.

Lacon (1920?), vol. 2

4 Man, as he is, is not a genuine article. He is an imitation of something, and a very bad imitation.

The Psychology of Man's Possible Evolution (1950), ch. 2

Overbury, Thomas, Sir (1581–1613) English poet and courtier

1 He disdains all things above his reach, and preferreth all countries before his own.

"An Affected Traveller," *Miscellaneous Works* (1632)

Ovett, Steve (Steven Michael James Ovett; b.1955) British athlete

1 There is no way sport is so important that it can be allowed to damage the rest of your life.

Remark, Los Angeles Olympic Games (1984)

Ovid (Publius Ovidius Naso; 43 B.C.–A.D. 17?) Roman poet

Quotations about Ovid

1 The sweet witty soul of Ovid lives in mellifluous honey-tongued Shakespeare.

1594–1616?

Francis Meres (1565–1647) English clergyman and writer. Attrib.

Quotations by Ovid

2 What they love to yield
They would often rather have stolen. Rough seduction
Delights them, the boldness of near rape
Is a compliment.

Ars Amatoria (after 1 B.C.)

3 Whether a pretty woman grants or withholds her favors, she always likes to be asked for them.

Ars Amatoria (after 1 B.C.)

4 A sick mind cannot endure any harshness.

Epistulae Ex Ponto (13 A.D.), bk. 1

5 Drops of water hollow out a stone, a ring is worn away by use.

Epistulae Ex Ponto (13 A.D.), bk. 4, no. 10

6 Now there are fields where Troy once was.

Heroides (1? A.D.), bk. 1

7 The art of medicine is my discovery. I am called Help-Bringer throughout the world, and all the potency of herbs is known to me.

Said by Apollo. *Metamorphoses* (8? A.D.)

8 It is the mind that makes the man, and our vigor is in our immortal soul.

Metamorphoses (8? A.D.), bk. 13

9 Time the devourer of everything.

Metamorphoses (8? A.D.), bk. 15

10 Ill habits gather by unseen degrees,
As brooks make rivers, rivers run to seas.

"The Worship of Aesculapius," *Metamorphoses* (8? A.D.), bk. 15

11 The art of medicine is generally a question of time.

Remedia Amoris (1 A.D.), bk. 1

12 All things can corrupt perverted minds.

Tristia (9 A.D.)

13 Medicine sometimes snatches away health, sometimes gives it.

Tristia (9 A.D.)

14 The mind grows sicker than the body in contemplation of its suffering.
Tristia (9 A.D.), bk. 4

Owen, David, Baron Owen of the City of Plymouth (David Anthony Llewellyn Owen; b.1938) British politician

1 No general in the midst of battle has a great discussion about what he is going to do if defeated.
Referring to his dual leadership, with David Steel, of the SDLP. *Observer*, London (June 6, 1987), "Sayings of the Week"

Owen, Meredith, 1st Earl of Lytton (Edward Robert Bulwer-Lytton; 1831–91) British statesman and poet

1 Genius does what it must, and Talent does what it can.
"Last Words of a Sensitive Second-rate Poet" (1868)

2 He may live without books,—what is knowledge but grieving?
He may live without hope,—what is hope but deceiving?
He may live without love—what is passion but pining?
But where is the man that can live without dining?
"Lucile" (1860), pt. 1, can. 2, sect. 24

3 We may live without friends; we may live without books;
But civilized man cannot live without cooks.
"Lucile" (1860), pt. 1, can. 2, sect. 24

Owen, Wilfred (1893–1918) British poet

1 The shrill, demented choirs of wailing shells;
And bugles calling for them from sad shires.
"Anthem for Doomed Youth" (1917), quoted in *The Collected Poems of Wilfred Owen* (C. Day Lewis, ed.; 1963)

2 What passing-bells for these who die as cattle?
Only the monstrous anger of the guns.
Only the stuttering rifles' rapid rattle
Can patter out their hasty orisons.
"Anthem for Doomed Youth" (1917), quoted in *The Collected Poems of Wilfred Owen* (C. Day Lewis, ed.; 1963)

3 And in the happy no-time of his sleeping,
Death took him by the heart.
"Asleep" (1914?), quoted in *The Collected Poems of Wilfred Owen* (C. Day Lewis, ed.; 1963)

4 While it is true that the guns will effect a little useful weeding, I am furious with chagrin to think that the Minds, which were to have excelled the civilization of two thousand years, are being annihilated—and bodies, the product of aeons of Natural Selection, melted down to pay for political statues.
Comment (August 28, 1914)

5 The old Lie: Dulce et decorum est
Pro patria mori.
"Dulce et decorum est" (1914?), quoted in *The Collected Poems of Wilfred Owen* (C. Day Lewis, ed.; 1963)

6 Move him into the sun—
If anything might rouse him now
The kind old sun will know.
"Futility" (1918), quoted in *The Collected Poems of Wilfred Owen* (C. Day Lewis, ed.; 1963)

7 Was it for this the clay grew tall?
—O what made fatuous sunbeams toil
To break earth's sleep at all?
"Futility" (1918), quoted in *The Collected Poems of Wilfred Owen* (C. Day Lewis, ed.; 1963)

8 Red lips are not so red
As the stained stones kissed by the English dead.
"Greater Love" (1917), quoted in *The Collected Poems of Wilfred Owen* (C. Day Lewis, ed.; 1963)

9 I am the enemy you killed, my friend.
I knew you in this dark: for so you frowned
Yesterday through me as you jabbed and killed.
I parried; but my hands were loath and cold.
Let us sleep now.
"Strange Meeting" (1918), quoted in *The Collected Poems of Wilfred Owen* (C. Day Lewis, ed.; 1963)

10 Above all I am not concerned with Poetry. My subject is War, and the pity of War. The Poetry is in the pity.
1918. "Preface," *Poems* (1920)

11 All the poet can do today is to warn. That is why the true Poets must be truthful.
1918. "Preface," *Poems* (1920)

Owens, Jesse (James Cleveland Owens; 1913–80) U.S. athlete

1 I let my feet spend as little time on the ground as possible. From the air, fast down, and from the ground, fast up.
Attrib.

Oxenstierna, Axel, Count (Axel Gustafsson Oxenstierna; 1583–1654) Swedish statesman

1 Do you not know, my son, with how little wisdom the world is governed?
Letter to his son (1648), quoted in *Svensk Plutark* (J. F. af Lundblad; 1826), pt. 2

2 It is essential that Your Majesty should above all things labor to create a powerful fleet at sea...so that you may be master of every nook and cranny of the Baltic.
Letter to King Gustavus Adolphus (January 8, 1631)

Oz, Amos (Amos Klausner; b.1939) Israeli writer

1 City of my birth. City of my dreams...And here I was, stalking its streets clutching a submachine gun, like a figure in one of my childhood nightmares: an alien man in an alien city.
1968. "An Alien City," *Under This Blazing Light* (1979)

2 I was not born to blow rams' horns and liberate lands from the "foreign yoke." I can hear the groaning of oppressed people; I cannot hear the groaning of oppressed lands.
1968. "An Alien City," *Under This Blazing Light* (1979)

3 A Jew...is someone who *chooses* to share the fate of other Jews, or who is *condemned* to do so.
1967. "The Meaning of Homeland," *Under This Blazing Light* (1979)

4 The new Israel is not a reconstruction of the kingdom of David and Solomon...or the *shtetl* borne to the hills of Canaan on the wings of Chagall.
1967. "The Meaning of Homeland," *Under This Blazing Light* (1979)

5 The Zionist enterprise has no other objective justification than

the right of a drowning man to grasp the only plank that can save him.
1967. "The Meaning of Homeland," *Under This Blazing Light* (1979)

6 I believe in...a Zionism that recognizes both the spiritual implications and the political consequences of the fact that this small tract of land is the homeland of two peoples fated to live facing each other.
1967. Referring to the Israelis and the Palestinians. "The Meaning of Homeland," *Under This Blazing Light* (1979)

7 The murder of the European Jews was no *shoah*. It was the ultimate logical outcome of the ancient status of the Jews in Western Civilization.
1967. *Shoah* is a Hebrew word meaning "catastrophe." "The Meaning of Homeland," *Under This Blazing Light* (1979)

Ozick, Cynthia (b.1928) U.S. novelist and short-story writer

1 I wanted to use what I was, to be what I was born to be—not to have a "career," but to be that straightforward obvious unmistakable animal, a writer.
Metaphor and Memory (1989)

2 Yiddish is a household tongue, and God, like other members of the family, is sweetly informal in it.
Metaphor and Memory (1989)

3 The whole peninsula of Florida was weighted down with regret. Everyone had left behind a real life.
Rosa (1984)

4 Stella, an ordinary American, indistinguishable! No one could guess what hell she had crawled out of until she opened her mouth and up coiled the smoke of accent.
The thoughts of Rosa. Stella is a Jew who has migrated from Europe. *The Shawl* (1980)

5 In saying what is obvious, never choose cunning. Yelling works better.
Quoted in "We Are the Crazy Lady and Other Feisty Feminist Fables," *The First Ms. Reader* (Francine Klagsbrun, ed.; 1972)

6 People who mistake facts for ideas are incomplete thinkers; they are gossips.
Quoted in "We Are the Crazy Lady and Other Feisty Feminist Fables," *The First Ms. Reader* (Francine Klagsbrun, ed.; 1972)

Pacheco, Francisco (1564–1654) Spanish painter

1 It would be hard to overstate the good that holy images do: they perfect our understanding, move our will, refresh our memory of divine things....they instantly cause us to seek virtue and to shun vice, and thus put us on the roads that lead to blessedness.
El arte de la pintura (1649)

Packard, David (1912–96) U.S. business executive

1 Flextime is the essence of respect for and trust in people.
The HP Way (1995)

2 Straightforward as it sounds, there are some subtleties and requirements that go with MBWA...if it's done reluctantly or infrequently, it just won't work. It needs to be frequent, friendly, unfocused, and unscheduled—but far from pointless.
Referring to "Management By Walking Around." *The HP Way* (1995)

Packer, Kerry (Kerry Francis Bullmore Packer; b.1937) Australian media executive

1 If a British guy saw someone at the wheel of a Rolls-Royce, he'd say "come the revolution and we'll take that away from you, mate", where the American would say "one day I'll have one of those, when I have worked hard enough". It's unfortunate we Australians inherited the British mentality.
Guardian, London (September 1, 1977)

Padmore, George (1902–59) Trinidadian campaigner

1 England's detached position from the Continent gives certain politicians like those of the Beaverbrook school the illusion that Britain can pursue a policy of "splendid isolation." But the fact remains that, thanks to the aeroplane, England has become as much a part of Europe as any continental State.
Africa and World Peace (1937)

2 War is an essential part of capitalism and can only be abolished by changing the present social system. This is the task which history has assigned to all those who hate and suffer most by war.
Africa and World Peace (1937)

3 With the capitalists, class interests take precedence over all other factors. Would to Heaven the workers would do likewise! Then the future of humanity would be assured.
Africa and World Peace (1937)

4 Imperialism divides: Socialism unites.
How Russia Transformed Her Colonial Empire (1946)

5 Africans have lived so long on promises. What they want to see are a few concrete deeds. They are tired of listening to pious sermons about "democracy" and "freedom" while the chains of servitude still hang around their necks.
Pan-Africanism (1956)

6 However painful the birth-pangs of progress may be, once a colony has taken the plunge along the road to self-government and self-determination, there can be no turning back.
Pan-Africanism (1956)

7 The word "Communist" is just a term of abuse, used loosely by Europeans and reactionary black politicians to smear militant nationalists whose views they dislike.
Pan-Africanism (1956)

Paget, Stephen (1855–1926) British surgeon

1 Talk of the patience of Job, said a Hospital nurse, Job was never on night duty.
Confessio Medici (1908), ch. 6

2 The natural dignity of our work, its unembarrassed kindness, its insight into life, its hold on science—for these privileges, and for all that they bring with them, up and up, high over the top of the tree, the very heavens open, preaching thankfulness.
Confessio Medici (1908), Epilogue

Paglia, Camille (Camille Anna Paglia; b.1947) U.S. academic and author

1 Teenage boys, goaded by their surging hormones...run in packs like the primal horde. They have only a brief season of exhilarating liberty between control by their mothers and control by their wives.
"Homosexuality at the Fin de Siècle," *Esquire* (October 1991)

2 Nothing important in high art is happening now but I worshipped the high art of the past.
"My Cultural Life," *Guardian*, London (January 30, 1998), Friday Review

3 There is no true expertise in the humanities without knowing *all* of the humanities. Art is a vast, ancient interconnected web-work, a fabricated tradition. Over-concentration on any one point is a distortion.
Book review, *New York Times* (May 5, 1991)

4 American universities are organized on the principle of the nuclear rather than the extended family. Graduate students are grimly trained to be technicians rather than connoisseurs.

The old German style of universal scholarship has gone.
Sex, Art, and American Culture (1992)

5 I believe that history has shape, order, and meaning; that exceptional men, as much as economic forces, produce change; and that passé abstractions like beauty, nobility, and greatness have a shifting but continuing validity.
Sex, Art, and American Culture (1992)

6 Man is not merely the sum of his masks. Behind the shifting face of personality is a hard nugget of self, a genetic gift.
Sex, Art, and American Culture (1992)

7 There is no masculine power or privilege I did not covet. But slowly, step by step, decade by decade, I was forced to acknowledge that even a woman of abnormal will cannot escape her hormonal identity.
Sex, Art, and American Culture (1992)

8 I oppose intrusions of the state into the private realm—as in abortion, sodomy, prostitution, pornography, drug use, or suicide, all of which I would strongly defend as matters of free choice in a representative democracy.
Sex, Art, and American Culture (1992), introduction

9 The feminist of the *fin de siècle* will be bawdy, streetwise, and on-the-spot confrontational, in the prankish Sixties way.
Sex, Art, and American Culture (1992), introduction

10 A fetus is a benign tumor, a vampire who steals in order to live. The so-called miracle of birth is nature getting her own way.
Sexual Personae (1990)

11 Beauty is our weapon against nature; by it we make objects, giving them limit, symmetry, proportion. Beauty halts and freezes the melting flux of nature.
Sexual Personae (1990)

12 Capitalism is an art form, an Apollonian fabrication to rival nature. It is hypocritical for feminists and intellectuals to enjoy the pleasures and conveniences of capitalism while sneering at it.
Sexual Personae (1990)

13 Cats are autocrats of naked self-interest. They are both amoral and immoral, consciously breaking rules...the cat may be the only animal who savors the perverse or reflects upon it.
Sexual Personae (1990)

14 French rhetorical models are too narrow for the English tradition...The Parisian is a provincial when he pretends to speak for the universe.
Sexual Personae (1990)

15 Men know they are sexual exiles. They wander the earth seeking satisfaction, craving and despising, never content. There is nothing in that anguished motion for women to envy.
Sexual Personae (1990)

16 Profanation and violation are part of the perversity of sex, which never will conform to liberal theories of benevolence. Every model of morally or politically correct sexual behavior *will be subverted*, by nature's daemonic law.
Sexual Personae (1990)

17 There are no accidents, only nature throwing her weight around...After the bomb, nature will pick up the cards we have spilled, shuffle them, and begin her game again.
Sexual Personae (1990)

Pagnol, Marcel (Marcel Paul Pagnol; 1895–1974) French dramatist, filmmaker, and scriptwriter

1 The most difficult secret for a man to keep is his own opinion of himself.
Remark (March 15, 1954)

2 Once wine has been drawn it should be drunk, even if it's good.
César (1936)

3 One has to be wary of engineers—they begin with sewing machines and end up with the atomic bomb.
Critique des critiques (1949)

4 Honor is like a match: you can only use it once.
Marius (1929), Act 4, Scene 5

5 It's better to choose the culprits than to seek them out.
Topaze (1928), Act 1

Paine, Albert Bigelow (1861–1937) U.S. writer

1 The Great White Way
1901. Book title, later used as a name for Broadway.

Paine, Thomas (1737–1809) English writer and political philosopher

1 Government, even in its best state, is but a necessary evil; in its worst state, an intolerable one.
Common Sense (1776), ch. 1

2 As to religion, I hold it to be the indispensable duty of government to protect all conscientious professors thereof, and I know of no other business which government hath to do therewith.
Common Sense (1776), ch. 4

3 It is necessary to the happiness of man that he be mentally faithful to himself. Infidelity does not consist in believing, or in disbelieving, it consists in professing to believe what one does not believe.
The Age of Reason (1794), pt. 1

4 The sublime and the ridiculous are often so nearly related that it is difficult to class them separately. One step above the sublime makes the ridiculous; and one step above the ridiculous makes the sublime again.
The Age of Reason (1795), pt. 2

5 These are the times that try men's souls. The summer soldier and the sunshine patriot will, in this crisis, shrink from the service of their country; but he that stands it now, deserves the love and thanks of man and woman.
Referring to the American Revolution (1775–83). *The American Crisis* (December 23, 1776), no. 1

6 A bad cause will ever be supported by bad means and bad men.
The American Crisis (January 13, 1777), no. 2

7 Those who expect to reap the blessings of freedom must, like men, undergo the fatigue of supporting it.
The American Crisis (September 12, 1777), no. 4

8 We fight not to enslave, but to set a country free, and to make room upon the earth for honest men to live in.
The American Crisis (September 12, 1777), no. 4

9 Arms discourage and keep the invader and plunderer in awe, and preserve order in the world as well as property...Horrid mischief would ensue were the law-abiding deprived the use of them.
Thoughts on Defensive War (1775)

Paintin, David British chairman of the Birth Control Trust

1 More people die from pregnancy than from the effect of the Pill.
Times, London (February 18, 1993)

2 The Pill has so much bad press because we collectively feel guilty about sexual enjoyment.
Times, London (February 18, 1993)

Paisiello, Giovanni (1740–1816) Italian composer

1 Hope told a flattering tale,
That Joy would soon return;
Ah! naught my sighs avail,
For Love is doomed to mourn.
Quoted in *Universal Songster* (George Cruikshank and Robert Cruikshank; 1825–26)

Paisley, Ian, Reverend (Ian Richard Kyle Paisley; b.1926) Northern Irish politician

1 Trusting in the God of our fathers and confident that our cause is just, we will never surrender our heritage.
Guardian, London (August 21, 1968)

2 We are reasonable. We have always been reasonable. We are noted for our sweet reasonableness.
Observer, London (May 11, 1975), "Sayings of the Week"

3 I would rather be British than just.
Sunday Times, London (December 12, 1971)

Palafox, José (1780–1847) Spanish general

1 War to the knife.
Replying to the demand that he surrender at the siege of Saragossa. Remark (1808)

Paleotti, Gabriele, Cardinal (1524–97) Italian bishop of Bologna

1 One of the main praises that we give to a writer or a practitioner of any liberal art is that he knows how to explain his ideas clearly, and that even if his subject is lofty and difficult, he knows how to make it plain and intelligible to all by his easy discourse.
"Discourse on Sacred and Profane Images" (1582), quoted in *Trattati d'arte del Cinquecento* (Paola Barocchi, ed.; 1960)

Paley, William (1743–1805) British theologian and philosopher

1 Who can refute a sneer?
Principles of Moral and Political Philosophy (1785), bk. 5, ch. 9

Palin, Michael (Michael Edward Palin; b.1943) British actor and writer

1 My parents just didn't have that sense of innate superiority that the successful parents had.
Times, London (February 24, 1990)

2 You get to shout at people. It was very useful material for later.
Referring to his time in the army as a color sergeant. *Times,* London (February 24, 1990)

Palme, Olof (Sven Olof Joachim Palme; 1927–86) Swedish statesman

Quotations about Palme

1 After Palme's murder suddenly anything seemed possible in Sweden.
Björn Ranelid (b.1949) Swedish journalist. Referring to Palme's assassination. Remark (February 1997)

Quotations by Palme

2 It is an illusion to believe that you can meet demands for social justice with violence and military might. It is extremely difficult to gain people's loyalty with promises to defend a freedom which, in actuality, they have never been able to experience.
Speech, Social Democrat conference, Gävle, Sweden (1965)

Palmer, Samuel (1805–81) British painter and etcher

1 A picture has been said to be something between a thing and a thought.
Quoted in *William Blake* (Arthur Symons; 1907)

Palmerston, Lord, 3rd Viscount (Henry John Temple, "Firebrand"; 1784–1865) British prime minister

1 Die, my dear Doctor, that's the last thing I shall do!
Last words (1865), quoted in *Famous Sayings and their Authors* (E. Latham; 1904)

2 A barren island with hardly a house upon it.
Referring to Hong Kong, which was to grow into the major center of Asian finance. Remark (1842)

3 We have no eternal allies and we have no perpetual enemies. Our interests are eternal and perpetual, and those interests it is our duty to follow.
Speech to the British Parliament (March 1, 1848)

4 As the Roman, in days of old, held himself free from indignity when he could say *Civis Romanus sum*, so also a British subject in whatever land he may be, shall feel confident that the watchful eye and the strong arm of England will protect him against injustice and wrong.
Don Pacifico debate. Speech to the British Parliament (June 25, 1850)

5 There are only three men who have ever understood it: one was Prince Albert, who is dead; the second was a German professor, who became mad. I am the third—and I have forgotten all about it.
Referring to the Schleswig-Holstein question. Quoted in *Britain in Europe 1789–1914* (R. W. Seton-Watson; 1937), ch. 14

6 The function of a government is to calm, rather than to excite agitation.
Quoted in *Gladstone and Palmerston* (P. Guedela; 1928)

7 What is merit? The opinion one man entertains of another.
Quoted in *Shooting Niagara* (T. Carlyle; 1837), ch. 8

8 Yes we have. Humbug.
In response to being told there was no English word for the French *sensibilité*. Attrib.

Pamuk, Orhan (b.1952) Turkish novelist

1 If this realm of dreams that we call the world is a house into which we enter disorientated as a somnambulist, then the various literatures are like clocks hung up on the walls of the rooms.
The Black Book (Guneli Gun, tr.; 1990)

2 The apprehension that one is someone else is all that one needs to believe that the world has changed from top to bottom.
The Black Book (Guneli Gun, tr.; 1990)

3 To be confronted with the trace instead of the memory itself is like looking through tears at the indentations on the armchair left there by your lover who has abandoned you and will never return.
The Black Book (Guneli Gun, tr.; 1990)

4 You can give the hope of victory and happiness to your unfortunate brethren only by waging war against the enemy inside.
The Black Book (Guneli Gun, tr.; 1990)

5 Don't make observations on cats and dogs, concern yourself with the problems of your homeland.
Advice to columnists. *The Black Book* (Guneli Gun, tr.; 1990)

6 A good book is a piece of writing that implies that things don't exist, a kind of absence, or death...it is futile to look outside the book for a realm that is located beyond the words.
The New Life (Guneli Gun, tr.; 1994)

7 This newfangled plaything called the novel, which is the greatest invention of Western culture, is none of our culture's business.
The New Life (Guneli Gun, tr.; 1994)

Panassie, Hugues (Hugues Louis Marie Henri Panassie; 1912–74) French jazz writer and impresario

1 Jazz did not issue from the individual efforts of one composer, but from the spontaneous urge of a whole people.
The Real Jazz (1942), ch. 1

2 Jazz is a music which is perpetually in motion, a *living* music which will never fall...into the funereal sleep of many *chefs d'oeuvre* which often give the impression of having been imprisoned in a pickle jar.
The Real Jazz (1942), ch. 2

3 I wish long life to that beautiful cry of jazz music, a cry of joy, sorrow, and love. May it be taken as it is, heard where it comes from—for there is no way to distort it without destroying it.
The Real Jazz (1942), ch. 17

4 No one with the slightest knowledge of jazz music can pretend that the real, honest "rock 'n' roll" does not belong to jazz. It was jazz *before* getting this name.
The Real Jazz (1942), ch. 17

Pankhurst, Christabel, Dame (Christabel Harriette Pankhurst; 1880–1958) British campaigner for woman suffrage

1 We are not ashamed of what we have done, because, when you have a great cause to fight for, the moment of greatest humiliation is the moment when the spirit is proudest.
Speech, Albert Hall, London (March 19, 1908)

2 What we suffragettes aspire to be when we are enfranchised is ambassadors of freedom to women in other parts of the world, who are not so free as we are.
Speech, Carnegie Hall, New York (October 25, 1915)

3 We are here to claim our rights as women, not only to be free, but to fight for freedom. It is our privilege, as well as our pride and our joy, to take some part in this militant movement, which, as we believe, means the regeneration of all humanity.
Speech, "Votes for Women" (March 31, 1911)

4 So greatly did she care for freedom that she died for it. So dearly did she love women that she offered her life as their ransom. That is the verdict given at the great Inquest of the Nation on the death of Emily Wilding Davison.
Emily Davison threw herself under the King's racehorse during a race in protest at the imprisoning of campaigners for woman suffrage. *The Suffragette* (June 13, 1913)

5 Never lose your temper with the Press or the public is a major rule of political life.
Unshackled (1959), ch. 5

Pankhurst, Emmeline (originally Emmeline Goulden; 1858–1928) British campaigner for woman suffrage

Quotations about Pankhurst

1 She was as she instinctively knew, cast for a great role. She had a temperament akin to genius. She could have been a queen on the Stage or in the Salon.
Emmeline Pethwick-Lawrence (1867–1954) British campaigner for woman suffrage. *My Part in a Changing World* (1938)

Quotations by Pankhurst

2 We have taken this action, because as women...we realize that the condition of our sex is so deplorable that it is our duty even to break the law in order to call attention to the reasons why we do so.
Speech in court (October 21, 1908), quoted in *Shoulder to Shoulder* (Midge Mackenzie, ed.; 1975)

3 I have no sense of guilt. I look upon myself as a prisoner of war. I am under no moral obligation to conform to, or in any way accept, the sentence imposed upon me.
Speech in court (April 1913), quoted in *The Fighting Pankhursts* (David Mitchell; 1913)

4 If civilization is to advance at all in the future, it must be through the help of women, women freed of their political shackles, women with full power to work their will in society.
My Own Story (1914)

5 Women have always fought for men, and for their children. Now they were ready to fight for their own human rights. Our militant movement was established.
Referring to the woman suffrage movement in the United Kingdom. *My Own Story* (1914)

6 The argument of the broken window pane is the most valuable argument in modern politics.
Quoted in *The Strange Death of Liberal England* (George Dangerfield; 1936), pt. 2, ch. 3, sec. 4

Pankhurst, Sylvia (Estelle Sylvia Pankhurst; 1882–1960) British campaigner for woman suffrage

1 There is a reaction from the ideal of an intellectual and emancipated womanhood, for which the pioneers toiled and suffered, to be seen in painted lips and nails, and the return of trailing skirts...which betoken the slave-woman's intelligent companionship.
News of the World, London (April 1928)

2 I could not give my name to aid the slaughter in this war, fought on both sides for grossly material ends, which did not justify the sacrifice of a single mother's son. Clearly I must continue to oppose it, and expose it, to all whom I could reach with voice or pen.
Referring to World War I. *The Home Front* (1932), ch. 25

3 I have gone to war too...I am going to fight capitalism even if it kills me. It is wrong that people like you should be comfortable and well fed while all around you people are starving.
Quoted in *The Fighting Pankhursts* (David Mitchell; 1967)

Pankin, Boris (Boris Dimitrievich Pankin; b.1931) Russian diplomat

1 Recession is when you have to tighten the belt. Depression is when there is no belt to tighten. We are probably in the next degree of collapse when there are no trousers as such.
Referring to the Russian economy. *Independent*, London (July 25, 1992)

Papanek, Victor (b.1925) Austrian-born U.S. designer, teacher, and writer

1 Design is the conscious effort to impose meaningful order.
Design for the Real World: Human Ecology and Social Change (1984)

2 Today industrial design has put murder on a mass-production basis.
Design for the Real World: Human Ecology and Social Change (1984)

Papineau, Louis Joseph (1786–1871) French-Canadian politician

1 The most efficacious and the most immediate means which the Canadians have to protect themselves against the fury of their enemies, is to attack them in their dearest parts—their pockets—in their strongest entrenchments, the banks.
Montreal Gazette (December 11, 1834)

Paracelsus (Philippus Aureolus Theophrastus Bombastus von Hohenheim; 1493–1541) German alchemist and physician

1 Medicine is not only a science; it is also an art. It does not consist of compounding pills and plasters; it deals with the very processes of life, which must be understood before they may be guided.
Die grosse Wundartzney (1536)

2 The book of Nature is that which the physician must read; and to do so he must walk over the leaves.
Encyclopædia Britannica, vol. 28

Paré, Ambroise (1510?–90?) French surgeon

1 Always give the patient hope, even when death seems at hand.
Attrib.

Pareto, Vilfredo (1848–1923) French-born Italian economist and sociologist

1 This phenomenon of new elites, which...rise up from the lower strata of society, mount up to the higher strata, flourish there, and then fall into decadence, are annihilated or disappear—this is one of the motive forces of history.
Les Systèmes socialistes (1902)

Paris, Matthew (1200?–59?) English chronicler and monk

1 A certain versifier, a false one, said, "Just as England has been filthy with the defiler John, so now the filth of Hell is fouled by his foul presence"; but it is dangerous to write against a man who can easily do you wrong.
Referring to King John of England (reigned 1199–1216). This quotation is better known in the form used by J. R. Green in his *Short History of the English People* (1875): "Foul as it is, Hell itself is defiled by the fouler presence of King John." *Chronica Majora* (1216)

Park, Mungo (1771–1806) Scottish explorer

1 The sight of it gave me infinite pleasure, as it proved that I was in a civilized society.
Remark on finding a gibbet in an unexplored part of Africa. Attrib.

Parker, Alan (b.1944) British film producer and director

1 Just because a film is made under the commercial umbrella does not mean it is not valid as art.
Interview, *Sight and Sound* (November 1997)

Parker, Charlie (Charles Christopher Parker, Jr., "Yardbird" or "Bird"; 1920–55) U.S. jazz saxophonist and composer

Quotations about Parker

1 Parker was a modern jazz player just as Picasso was a modern painter and Pound a modern poet...Jazz had gone from Lascaux to Jackson Pollock in fifty years.
Philip Larkin (1922–85) British poet. Referring to the radical innovations achieved by Charlie Parker. *All What Jazz: a Record Diary* (1970), introduction

2 There go the critics, blinkin' eyes, clappin' hands, tryin' to act like they was listening. And get Bird playing as he walks off! Shuffle off to Buffalo! Ha ha! Ho ho!
Charles Mingus (1922–79) U.S. jazz musician. *Beneath the Underdog* (1971), ch. 31

3 He breathed in air, he breathed out light.
Charlie Parker was my delight.
Adrian Mitchell (b.1932) British poet and playwright. "Goodbye," *Poems* (1964)

4 I would not for one minute dispute that Charlie Parker had great creative gifts, but this is a book on real jazz.
Hugues Panassie (1912–74) French jazz writer and impresario. Panassie had an exclusive preference for traditional jazz idioms. *The Real Jazz* (1942), ch. 8

5 Bird was the supreme hipster. He made his own laws. His

arrogance was enormous, his humility profound.
Robert Reisner (1921–74) U.S. writer and humorist. *Bird: the Legend of Charlie Parker* (1962), ch. 1

6 As for religion, Parker described himself as a "devout musician." As for society, he said, "Civilization is a damned good thing if somebody would try it." He lived for pleasure intensely; luckily, one of his pleasures was music.
Robert Reisner (1921–74) U.S. writer and humorist. *Bird: the Legend of Charlie Parker* (1962), ch. 1

Quotations by Parker

7 Music is your own experience, your thoughts, your wisdom. If you don't live it, it won't come out of your horn.
Quoted in *Hear Me Talkin' to Ya* (Nat Shapiro and Nat Hentoff; 1955)

Parker, Dorothy (Dorothy Rothschild; 1893–1967) U.S. writer and wit

Quotations about Parker

1 One cubic foot less of space and it would have constituted adultery.
Robert Benchley (1889–1945) U.S. humorist, writer, editor, and critic. Describing an office shared with the writer Dorothy Parker. Attrib.

2 She has put into what she has written a voice, a state of mind, an era, a few moments of human experience that nobody else has conveyed.
Edmund Wilson (1895–1972) U.S. critic and writer. Attrib.

3 She is a combination of Little Nell and Lady Macbeth.
Alexander Woollcott (1887–1943) U.S. writer and critic. "Our Mrs Parker," *While Rome Burns* (1934)

Quotations by Parker

4 Men seldom make passes
At girls who wear glasses.
"News Item" (1937)

5 You can lead a whore to culture but you can't make her think.
Her response when challenged to use the word "horticulture" in a sentence. Speech to the American Horticultural Society, quoted in *You Might As Well Live* (John Keats; 1970)

6 Dear Mary, We all knew you had it in you.
Referring to the successful outcome of a much-publicized pregnancy. Telegram sent to a friend, quoted in "Our Mrs. Parker," *While Rome Burns* (Alexander Woollcott; 1934)

7 He's really awfully fond of colored people. Well, he says himself, he wouldn't have white servants.
"Arrangements in Black and White," *Collected Stories* (1939)

8 Every love is the love before
In a duller dress.
Death and Taxes (1931)

9 I never see that prettiest thing—
A cherry bough gone white with Spring—
But what I think, How gay 'twould be
To hang me from a flowering tree.
"Cherry White," *Death and Taxes* (1931)

10 Oh, life is a glorious cycle of song,
A medley of extemporanea;
And love is a thing that can never go wrong
And I am Marie of Roumania.
"Comment," *Enough Rope* (1926)

11 Four be the things I am wiser to know:
Idleness, sorrow, a friend, and a foe.
"Inventory," *Enough Rope* (1926), st. 1

12 Four be the things I'd been better without:
Love, curiosity, freckles, and doubt.
"Inventory," *Enough Rope* (1926), st. 2

13 Why is it no one ever sent me yet
One perfect limousine, do you suppose?
Ah no, it's always just my luck to get
One perfect rose.
"One Perfect Rose," *Enough Rope* (1926)

14 Lady, lady, should you meet,
One whose ways are all discreet,
One who murmurs that his wife
Is the lodestar of his life,
One who keeps assuring you
That he never was untrue,
Never loved another one...
Lady, lady, better run!
"Social Note," *Enough Rope* (1926)

15 Sorrow is tranquillity remembered in emotion.
Alluding to Wordsworth's phrase in the preface to *Lyrical Ballads* (1798) that poetry "takes its origin from emotion recollected in tranquillity." "Sentiment," *Here Lies* (1939)

16 How do people go to sleep? I'm afraid I've lost the knack. I might try busting myself smartly over the temple with the nightlight. I might repeat to myself, slowly and soothingly, a list of quotations beautiful from minds profound; if I can remember any of the damn things.
"The Little Hours," *Here Lies* (1939)

17 I'm never going to be famous...I don't do anything. Not one single thing. I used to bite my nails, but I don't even do that any more.
"The Little Hours," *Here Lies* (1939)

18 The thought of death came and stayed with her and lent her a sort of drowsy cheer. It would be nice, nice and restful, to be dead.
Laments for the Living (1930)

19 I wouldn't touch a superlative again with an umbrella.
"Excuse It, Please," *New Yorker* (February 18, 1928)

20 Most good women are hidden treasures who are only safe because nobody looks for them.
New York Times (June 8, 1967)

21 Razors pain you
Rivers are damp;
Acids stain you;
And drugs cause cramp.
Guns aren't lawful;
Nooses give;
Gas smells awful;
You might as well live.
"Résumé," *Not So Deep As A Well* (1936)

22 He lies below, correct in cypress wood,
And entertains the most exclusive worms.
"Tombstones in the Starlight," *Not So Deep As A Well* (1936)

23 It costs me never a stab nor squirm
To tread by chance upon a worm.
"Aha, my little dear," I say,
"Your clan will pay me back one day."
"Thought for a Sunshiny Morning," *Sunset Gun* (1928)

24 By the time you say you're his,
Shivering and sighing,
And he vows his passion is
Infinite, undying—
Lady, make a note of this:
One of you is lying.
Unfortunate Coincidence (1937)

25 The doctors were very brave about it.
Said after she had been seriously ill. Quoted in *Journal of the American Medical Association* (1965)

26 That should assure us of at least forty-five minutes of undisturbed privacy.
Pressing a button marked NURSE during a stay in hospital. Quoted in *The Algonquin Wits* (R. E. Drennan; 1968)

27 Where does she find them?
Replying to the remark, "Anyway, she's always very nice to her inferiors." Quoted in *The Lyttelton Hart-Davis Letters* (Rupert Hart-Davis, ed.; 1978)

28 If all the young ladies who attended the Yale promenade dance were laid end to end, no one would be the least surprised.
Quoted in "Our Mrs. Parker," *While Rome Burns* (Alexander Woollcott; 1934)

29 Excuse my dust.
1925. One of two suggestions Parker made for an epitaph. Quoted in "Our Mrs Parker," *While Rome Burns* (Alexander Woollcott; 1934)

30 You know, she speaks eighteen languages. And she can't say "No" in any of them.
Referring to an acquaintance. Quoted in "Our Mrs. Parker," *While Rome Burns* (Alexander Woollcott; 1934)

31 A list of authors who have made themselves most beloved and, therefore, most comfortable financially, shows that it is our national joy to mistake for the first-rate, the fecund rate.
Quoted in *Wit's End: Days and Nights of the Algonquin Round Table* (James R. Gaines; 1973)

32 You can't teach an old dogma new tricks.
Quoted in *Wit's End: Days and Nights of the Algonquin Round Table* (James R. Gaines; 1977)

33 This is not a novel to be tossed aside lightly. It should be thrown with great force.
Book review. Quoted in *Wit's End: Days and Nights of the Algonquin Round Table.* (James R. Gaines; 1977)

34 I was fired from there, finally, for a lot of things, among them my insistence that the Immaculate Conception was spontaneous combustion.
Quoted in *Writers at Work* (Malcolm Cowley; 1958)

35 Brevity is the soul of lingerie.
1916. Caption written for *Vogue. You Might As Well Live* (John Keats; 1970)

36 One more drink and I'd be under the host.
Quoted in *You Might As Well Live* (John Keats; 1970)

37 There, but for a typographical error, is the story of my life.
At a Halloween party, when someone remarked, "They're ducking for apples." Quoted in *You Might As Well Live* (John Keats; 1970)

38 Pearls before swine.
Clare Booth Luce, going through a door with her, said, "Age before beauty." Quoted in *You Might As Well Live* (John Keats; 1970)

39 Because he spills his seed on the ground.
Referring to naming her canary "Onan"; referring to Genesis 38:9, "And Onan knew that the seed should not be his; and it came to pass, when he went in unto his brother's wife, that he spilled it on the ground." Quoted in *You Might As Well Live* (John Keats; 1970)

40 He really needs to telephone, but he's too embarrassed to say so.
When a man asked to go to the men's room. Quoted in *You Might As Well Live* (John Keats; 1970)

41 Tell him I've been too fucking busy—or vice versa.
When asked why she had not delivered her copy on time. Quoted in *You Might As Well Live* (John Keats; 1970)

42 This is on me.
One of two suggestions Parker made for an epitaph. Quoted in *You Might As Well Live* (John Keats; 1970), pt. 1, ch. 5

43 It serves me right for putting all my eggs in one bastard.
Said on going into hospital for an abortion. Quoted in *You Might As Well Live* (John Keats; 1970), pt. 2, ch. 3

44 Oh, don't worry about Alan...Alan will always land on somebody's feet.
Said of her husband on the day their divorce became final. Quoted in *You Might As Well Live* (John Keats; 1970), pt. 4, ch. 1

45 Love is like quicksilver in the hand. Leave the fingers open and it stays. Clutch it, and it darts away.
Attrib.

46 Check enclosed.
Giving her version of the two most beautiful words in the English language. Attrib. (1953)

47 She ran the whole gamut of the emotions from A to B.
Referring to a first-night performance by Katherine Hepburn on Broadway. Attrib.

48 Outspoken by whom?
When told that she was "very outspoken." Attrib.

Parker, Henry Taylor (1867–1934) U.S. music critic

1 Those people on the stage are making such a noise I can't hear a word you're saying.
Rebuking some talkative members of an audience, near whom he was sitting. Quoted in *The Humor of Music* (L. Humphrey; 1971)

Parker, Hubert Lister (1900–72) British judge

1 A judge is not supposed to know anything about the facts of life until they have been presented in evidence and explained to him at least three times.
Observer, London (March 12, 1961), "Sayings of the Week"

Parker, John (1729–75) U.S. general

1 Stand your ground. Don't fire unless fired upon, but if they mean to have a war, let it begin here!
April 19, 1775. Command given at the start of the Battle of Lexington, Massachussetts. Attrib.

Parker, Sir Peter (b.1924) British business executive

1 It is nonsense to refer to business as "the private sector"—does anything have as much public impact as businesses?
"Most Quoted, Least Heeded: the 5 Senses of Follett," *Mary Parker Follett: Prophet of Management* (Pauline Graham, ed.; 1995)

2 To talk about a socialist manager is about as sensible as talking about a Christian mathematician or a Hindu plumber. What you want is a good mathematician or a good plumber.
Observer, London (March 28, 1976)

3 You must deodorise profits and make people understand that profit is not something offensive, but as important to a company as breathing.
Sunday Telegraph, London (September 5, 1976)

Parker, Theodore (1810–60) U.S. clergyman

1 A democracy—that is a government of all the people, by all the people, for all the people; of course, a government of the principles of eternal justice, the unchanging law of God; for shortness' sake I will call it the idea of Freedom.
Speech, "The American Idea," at the New England Anti-Slavery Convention, Boston (May 29, 1850)

Parkes, Francis Ernest Kobina (b.1932) Ghanaian poet, journalist, and editor

1 I nurse a beard, as rebel young men do
And I love to sit and watch its bohemian growth
Each hair a sonorous protest.
"A Call to Youth for Sanity," *An African Treasury* (Langston Hughes, ed.; 1961)

Parkinson, Cyril Northcote (1909–93) British political scientist, historian, and writer

1 The Law of Triviality. Briefly stated, it means that the time spent on any item of the agenda will be in inverse proportion to the sum involved.
Parkinson's Law (1958)

2 The number of people in any working group tends to increase regardless of the amount of work to be done.
Parkinson's Law (1958), ch. 1

3 The rise in the total of those employed is governed by Parkinson's Law and would be much the same whether the volume of work were to increase, diminish or even disappear.
Parkinson's Law (1958), ch. 1

4 Work expands so as to fill the time available for its completion.
Parkinson's Law (1958), ch. 1

5 It is now known...that men enter local politics solely as a result of being unhappily married.
Parkinson's Law (1958), ch. 10

6 Delay is the deadliest form of denial.
Parkinson's Law of Delay (1958)

7 Expenditure rises to meet income.
The Law and the Profits (1960), ch. 1

Parkman, Francis (1823–93) U.S. historian

1 A happier calamity never befell a people than the conquest of Canada by the British arms.
Attrib.

Parks, Rosa (Rosa Louise Parks; b.1913) U.S. civil rights activist

1 My only concern was to get home after a hard day's work.
Commenting on her refusal to leave a "whites only" seat in a bus. *Time* (December 15, 1975)

Parmenter, Ross (b.1912) Canadian-born U.S. music critic and writer

1 In remaking the world in the likeness of a steam-heated, air-conditioned metropolis of apartment buildings we have violated...our kinship with nature.
"Inward Sign," *The Plant in My Window* (1949)

Parnell, Charles Stewart (1846–91) Irish politician

Quotations about Parnell

1 Poor Parnell! he cried loudly. My dead King!
James Joyce (1882–1941) Irish writer. *A Portrait of the Artist as a Young Man* (1916), ch. 1

2 Parnell may be the Uncrowned King of Ireland; he is not the infallible Pope of Rome.
John O'Leary (1830–1907) Irish rebel. Charles Stewart Parnell's nickname was the "Uncrowned King of Ireland." Speech, Mullinahone, Ireland (August 1885), quoted in *A Book of Irish Quotations* (Sean McMahon, ed.; 1984)

3 Parnell came down the road, he said to a cheering man:
"Ireland shall get her freedom and you still break stone".
W. B. Yeats (1865–1939) Irish poet and playwright. Charles Parnell led the fight for Home Rule in the 1880s. "Parnell," *London Mercury* (1938)

Quotations by Parnell

4 No man has a right to fix the boundary of the march of a nation; no man has a right to say to his country—thus far shalt thou go and no further.
Speech, Cork (January 21, 1885)

5 Ireland has been knocking at the English door long enough with kid gloves, and now she will knock with a mailed hand.
Speech, Liverpool, England (1885), quoted in "Tuam Herald," *A Book of Irish Quotations* (Sean McMahon, ed.; 1984)

6 When a man takes a farm from which another has been evicted, you must show him...by leaving him severely alone, by putting him into a moral Coventry, by isolating him from his kind as if he were a leper of old—you must show him your detestation of the crimes he has committed.
The first person to be treated this way was a Captain Boycott—hence the verb "to boycott." *Ennis* (September 19, 1880)

Parnell, Thomas (1679–1718) Irish poet

1 Remote from man, with God he passed the days;
Prayer all his business, all his pleasure praise.
"The Hermit," *The Collected Poems of Thomas Parnell* (1989), l. 5

2 Still Angel appear to each lover beside,
But still be a woman to you.
"When thy Beauty Appears," *The Collected Poems of Thomas Parnell* (1989)

Parra, Nicanor (b.1914) Chilean poet

1 Our Father who art in Heaven
Full of all kinds of problems
Ceaselessly frowning
As if you were a simple man:
Stop thinking about us.
"Our Father," *Obra Guesa* (1969)

Parra, Violeta (1917–67) Chilean songwriter and political activist

1 I do not play the guitar for applause. I sing the difference between what is true and what is false; otherwise I do not sing.
Attrib.

Parris, Matthew (b.1949) British journalist

1 Wilde's captors were the police. But his persecutors were to be found on the letters page of the *Daily Telegraph*.
Times, London (April 7, 1993)

Parton, Dolly (b.1946) U.S. singer, songwriter, and actor

1 If people think I'm a dumb blonde because of the way I look, then they're dumber than they think I am. If people think I'm not very deep because of my wigs and outfits, then they're not very deep.
Ms (June 1979)

Pascal, Blaise (1623–62) French philosopher, mathematician, and physicist

1 I have made this letter longer than usual, only because I have not had the time to make it shorter.
Lettres Provinciales (1657), no. 16

2 If you want people to think well of you, do not speak well of yourself.
Pensées (1669), no. 1

3 I maintain that, if everyone knew what others said about him, there would not be four friends in the world.
Pensées (1669), no. 101

4 Man is only a reed, the weakest in nature, but he is a thinking reed...Let us then strive to think well; that is the basic principle of morality.
Pensées (1669), no. 200

5 Justice without force is impotent, force without justice is tyranny.
Pensées (1669), no. 298

6 Men are so necessarily mad, that not to be mad would amount to another form of madness.
Pensées (1669), no. 414

7 Let us say,"'Either God is or he is not"...Let us weigh up the gain and loss involved in calling heads that God exists...Let us assess the two cases: if you win you win everything, if you lose you lose nothing. Do not hesitate then: wager that he does exist.
Pensées (1669), no. 418

8 Men never do evil so completely and cheerfully as when they do it from religious conviction.
Pensées (1669), no. 894

9 The more intelligence one has the more people one finds original. Commonplace people see no difference between men.
Pensées (1669), sect. 1, no. 7

10 The last thing one knows in constructing a work is what to put first.
Pensées (1669), sect. 1, no. 976

11 I cannot forgive Descartes; in all his philosophy he did his best to dispense with God. But he could not avoid making Him set the world in motion with a flip of His thumb; after that he had no more use for God.
Pensées (1669), sect. 2, no. 77

12 Had Cleopatra's nose been shorter, the whole face of the world would have changed.
Pensées (1669), sect. 2, no. 162

13 The heart has its reasons which reason knows nothing of.
Pensées (1669), sect. 4, no. 277

14 Not to care for philosophy is to be a true philosopher.
Pensées (1669), sect. 6, no. 430

15 We know the truth, not only by the reason, but also by the heart.
Pensées (1669), sect. 10, no. 1

Pascal, Jacqueline (1625–61) French writer

1 To pass from impoverishment to poverty as one moves from humiliation to humility.
Letter to her brother, Blaise Pascal (January 19, 1655)

Pasolini, Pier Paolo (1922–75) Italian filmmaker

1 Sex, consolation for misery!
The whore is queen, her throne a ruin,
her land a piece of shitty field,
her scepter a purse of red patent leather:
she barks in the night.
"Sex, Consolation for Misery" (1961)

2 They came out of their mothers' bellies
to find themselves on sidewalks or in prehistoric fields,
inscribed in birth registers
which want all history to forget them.
"The Desire for Wealth of the Roman Lumpenproletariat" (1961)

3 The cinema must be naturalistic. If I wish to express a garbage man through the medium of cinema, I take a real garbage man and reproduce him: body and voice.
"Why that of Oedipus is a Story," *Oedipus Rex* (1967)

Pasternak, Boris (Boris Leonidovich Pasternak; 1890–1960) Russian poet and novelist

Quotations about Pasternak

1 To read the poems of Pasternak is to get one's throat clear, to fortify one's breathing, to renovate one's lungs; such poems must be a cure for tuberculosis. At present we have no poetry

healthier than this. This is *kumys* after tinned milk.
Osip Mandelstam (1891–1938) Russian poet, writer, and translator. *Kumys* is a drink made from fermented mare's milk. "Notes on Poetry" (Angela Livingstone, tr.; 1923), quoted in *Pasternak* (Donald Davie and Angela Livingstone, eds.; 1969)

Quotations by Pasternak

2 The artist's hand is more powerful still.
It washes all the dust and dirt away
so life, reality, the simple truth
come freshly coloured from his dye works.
"After the Storm" (1956), quoted in *Boris Pasternak: The Tragic Years 1930–1960* (Ann Pasternak Slater and Craig Raine, eds., trs.; 1990)

3 The buzz subsides. I have come on stage.
Leaning in an open door
I'll try to detect from the echo
What the future has in store.
"Hamlet" (1946), ll. 1–4, quoted in *Pasternak: Selected Poems* (Jon Stallworthy and Peter France, trs.; 1983)

4 But the order of the acts is planned,
The end of the road already revealed.
Alone among the Pharisees I stand.
Life is not a stroll across a field.
"Hamlet" (1946), ll. 13–16, quoted in *Pasternak: Selected Poems* (Jon Stallworthy and Peter France, trs.; 1983)

5 From the way the nurse was shaking
her head and the questions she asked,
he suddenly understood
he might not get through this alive.
"In the Hospital" (May 5, 1956), quoted in *Boris Pasternak: The Tragic Years 1930–1960* (Ann Pasternak Slater and Craig Raine, eds., trs.; 1990)

6 It's vulgar to be famous,
That isn't what makes you great...
You must work at your work
not dream of your destiny.
"It's vulgar to be famous..." (May 5, 1956), quoted in *Boris Pasternak: The Tragic Years 1930–1960* (Ann Pasternak Slater and Craig Raine, eds., trs.; 1990)

7 My sister, Life, is today overflowing
And smashing herself in spring rain on our coats.
"My Sister, Life" (Jon Stallworthy and Peter France, trs.; 1917)

8 Like a pilot, like a planet,
don't give way to drowsiness, poet.
You are the pledge we give to eternity
and so the slave of every second.
Written while Boris Pasternak was recovering from a stroke. "Night" (Craig Raine and Ann Pasternak Slater, trs.; 1956), ll. 37–40, quoted in *Leopard II: Turning the Page* (Christopher MacLehose, ed.; 1993)

9 Which way? I'm like an animal trapped.
Somewhere: people, freedom, light
Behind me, the howls of the hunt,
but the exit eludes me.
Pasternak was awarded the Nobel Prize in literature in 1958, which he initially accepted. However, he was later forced by the Soviet authorities to rescind his acceptance. "The Nobel Prize" (1959), quoted in *Boris Pasternak: The Tragic Years 1930–1960* (Ann Pasternak Slater and Craig Raine, eds., trs.; 1990)

10 Who should remain alive and praised,
Who should stay dead without renown—
Depends upon criteria
That powerful sycophants lay down.
"The Wind" (Henry Kamen, tr.; 1955–56), pt. 1, quoted in *In the Interlude. Poems 1945–1960* (Henry Kamen, tr.; 1962)

11 At the moment of childbirth, every woman has the same aura of isolation, as though she were abandoned, alone.
Doctor Zhivago (Max Hayward and Manya Harari, trs.; 1958), ch. 9, sec. 3

Pasteur, Louis (1822–95) French scientist

1 When meditating over a disease, I never think of finding a remedy for it, but, instead, a means of preventing it.
Address to the Fraternal Association of Former Students of the École Centrale des Arts et Manufactures, Paris (May 15, 1884)

2 Where observation is concerned, chance favors only the prepared mind.
Inauguration lecture, Faculty of Science, University of Lille (December 7, 1854), quoted in *La Vie de Pasteur* (R. Vallery-Radot; 1900), ch. 4

3 There are no such things as applied sciences, only applications of science.
Lecture (September 11, 1872), quoted in *Comptes rendus des travaux du Congrès viticole et séricicole de Lyon, 9–14 septembre 1872*

4 Physicians are inclined to engage in hasty generalizations...the more eminent they are...the less leisure they have for investigative work...Eager for knowledge...they are apt to accept too readily attractive but inadequately proven theories.
Études sur la bière (1876), ch. 3

5 Wine is the most healthful and most hygienic of beverages.
Études sur le vin (1873), pt. 1, ch. 2

6 I have just made a great discovery. I have separated the sodium ammonium protartrate with two salts of opposite action on the plane of polarization of light. The dextro-salt is in all respects identical with the dextroprotartrate. I am so happy and so overcome by such nervous excitement that I am unable again to place my eye to the polarization instrument.
Attrib. *Chemistry in the Service of Man* (Alexander Findlay; 1916)

Pater, Walter (Walter Horatio Pater; 1839–94) British critic

1 She is older than the rocks among which she sits.
Referring to "*The Mona Lisa*." "Leonardo da Vinci," *Studies on the History of the Renaissance* (1873)

2 All art constantly aspires towards the condition of music.
"The School of Giorgione," *Studies on the History of the Renaissance* (1873)

3 Yes! The beauty of these most beautiful of all people was a male beauty, far remote from female tenderness.
Quoted in *A History of Gay Literature* (Gregory Woods; 1998)

Paterson, A. B. (Andrew Barton, "Banjo" Paterson; 1864–1941) Australian journalist and poet

1 Once a jolly swagman camped by a billy-bong,
Under the shade of a coolibah tree,
And he sang as he sat and waited for his billy-boil,
"You'll come a-waltzing, Matilda, with me."
"Waltzing Matilda," *Bulletin* (1885)

Patil, Chandrashekhara (b.1939) Indian poet

1 I entered the old castles of the heart.
Pulled out wishes and longings that lay dead,
or wriggled half-dead, or danced
wild on the stage,
and threw them all out
for dogs, foxes, crows and vultures
to peck at and live on.

"Freak," *The Oxford Anthology of Modern Indian Poetry* (Viany Dharwadker and A. K. Ramanujan, eds.; 1994)

Patmore, Coventry (Coventry Kersey Dighton Patmore; 1823–96) British poet

1 Some dish more sharply spiced than this
Milk-soup men call domestic bliss.

"Olympus," , ll. 15–16, quoted in *Poems by Coventry Patmore* (Basil Champneys; 1906)

2 Love's perfect blossom only blows
Where noble manners veil defect.
Angels may be familiar; those
Who err each other must respect.

The Angel in the House (1862), bk. 1, prelude 2

3 Kind souls, you wonder why, I love you,
When you, you wonder why, love none
We love, Fool, for the good we do,
Not that which unto us is done!

"A Riddle Solved," *The Angel in the House* (1854–62), bk. 1, prelude 4, ll. 61–64

4 I drew my bride, beneath the moon,
Across my threshold; happy hour!
But, ah, the walk that afternoon
We saw the water-flags in flower!

"The Spirit's Epochs," *The Angel in the House* (1862), bk. 1, ch. 8, prelude 3, l. 9

5 With all my will, but much against my heart,
We two now part
My Very Dear,
Our solace is, the sad road lies so clear
It needs no art,
With faint, averted feet
And many a tear,
In our opposed paths to persevere.

"A Farewell," *The Unknown Eros* (1877), ll. 775–782

6 It was not like your great and gracious ways!
Do you, that have nought other to lament,
Never, my Love, repent
Of how, that July afternoon,
You went,
With sudden, unintelligible phrase,—And frightened eye,
Upon your journey of so many days,
Without a single kiss or a good-bye?

"Departure," *The Unknown Eros* (1877), bk. 1, ll. 345–353

7 So, till to-morrow eve, my Own, adieu!
Parting's well-paid with soon again to meet,
Soon in your arms to feel so small and sweet,
Sweet to myself that am so sweet to you!

"The Azalea," *The Unknown Eros* (1877), ll. 341–344

Paton, Alan Stewart (1903–88) South African novelist and political activist

1 Wise men write many books, in words too hard to understand.
But this, the purpose of our lives, the end of all our struggle,
is beyond all human wisdom.

Cry, The Beloved Country (1948)

Patrick, Saint (Succat; 389?–461?) Welsh?-born Irish bishop

1 Christ with me, Christ before me, Christ behind me, Christ on my right, Christ on my left, Christ when I lie down, Christ when I arise...Christ in every eye that sees me, Christ in every ear that hears me.

5th century. Also called "The Breastplate." "The Deer's Cry" (Kuno Meyer, tr.), quoted in *A Book of Irish Quotations* (Sean McMahon, ed.; 1984)

Patten, Brian (b.1946) British poet and playwright

1 It is the monster hiding in a child's dark room, it is the scar on a beautiful person's face. It is the last blade of grass being picked from the city park.

Referring to poetry. "Prose poem towards a definition of itself," *Grinning Jack* (1990)

2 We pass
And lit briefly by one another's light
Think the way we go is right.

Love Poems (1982)

Pattison, Mark (1813–84) British rector and author

1 In research the horizon recedes as we advance, and is no nearer at sixty than it was at twenty. As the power of endurance weakens with age, the urgency of the pursuit grows more intense.

Isaac Casaubon (1875), ch. 10

Patton, George S. (George Smith Patton, Jr.; 1885–1945) U.S. general

1 We are having one hell of a war.

Letter to A. D. Surles (December 15, 1944)

2 The quickest way to get it over with is to get the bastards.

Speech to troops (1944), quoted in *Speaking Freely* (Stuart Berg Flexner and Anne H. Soukhanov; 1997)

3 Twenty years from now when you are sitting by the fireplace with your grandson on your knee and he asks you what you did in the great World War Two, you can...say, "Son, your Granddaddy rode with the great Third Army and a son-of-a-bitch named George Patton."

Speech to troops, U.S. Sixth Armored Division (May 31, 1944)

4 Dear Ike, Today I spat in the Seine.

1944. Message sent to Eisenhower reporting his crossing of the Seine in World War II. Quoted in *The American Treasury, 1455–1955* (Clifton Fadiman; 1955)

Paul, Leslie (Leslie Allen Paul; 1905–85) British writer

1 Angry Young Man

1951. Book title. The phrase subsequently became associated with John Osborne's play *Look Back In Anger* (1956).

Paul, Nathaniel (1775–1839) U.S. cleric and abolitionist

1 I have not failed to give Uncle Sam due credit for his 2,000,000 slaves; nor to expose the cruel prejudices of the Americans to our colored race...And is this, they say, republican liberty? God deliver us from it.
Letter to William Lloyd Garrison (April 10, 1833), quoted in *A Documentary History of the Negro People in the United States* (Herbert Aptheker; 1951), vol. 1

Paul VI, Pope (originally Giovanni Battista Montini; 1897–1978) Italian pope

1 Excluded is every action that, either in anticipation of the conjugal act, or in its accomplishment, or in the development of its natural consequences, purposes, whether as an end or as a means, to render procreation impossible.
Humanae Vitae (1968)

2 Nationalism isolates people from their true good.
Referring to his concern about the international debts of poorer countries, part of a wider plea for social justice. *Populorum Progressio* (1967), no. 62

3 From the moment of conception, the life of every human being is to be respected in an absolute way...no one can, in any circumstance, claim for himself the right to destroy directly an innocent human being.
Quoted in *Instruction on Respect for Human Life in its Origin* (Catholic Truth Society; 1987)

Pauli, Wolfgang (1900–58) Austrian-born U.S. physicist

1 I don't mind your thinking slowly: I mind your publishing faster than you think.
Attrib.

Pauling, Linus (Linus Carl Pauling; 1901–94) U.S. scientist

1 I like people. I like animals, too—whales and quail, dinosaurs and dodos. But I like human beings especially, and I am unhappy that the pool of human germ plasm, which determines the nature of the human race, is deteriorating.
Said on winning the Nobel Prize for peace. Referring to radioactive fallout. *New York Times* (October 13, 1962)

2 Science is the search for truth.
No More War! (1958)

Pausanias (*fl.* 5th century B.C.) Greek general

1 When the physician said to him, "You have lived to be an old man," he said, "That is because I never employed you as my physician."
479 B.C. Quoted in "Sayings of Spartans," *Moralia* (Plutarch; 1st or 2nd century A.D.)

Pavese, Cesare (1908–50) Italian novelist and poet

1 Living is like working out one long addition sum, and if you make a mistake in the first two totals you will never find the right answer. It means involving oneself in a complicated chain of circumstances.
May 5, 1936. *The Burning Brand: Diaries 1935–1950* (1952)

2 One does not kill oneself for the love of *a* woman, but because love—any love—reveals us in our nakedness, our misery, our vulnerability, our nothingness.
March 25, 1950. *The Burning Brand: Diaries 1935–1950* (1952)

3 Perfect behavior is born of complete indifference.
February 21, 1940. *The Burning Brand: Diaries 1935–1950* (1952)

4 The richness of life lies in the memories we have forgotten.
February 13, 1940. *This Business of Living: A Diary 1935–1950* (1952)

5 One stops being a child when one realizes that telling one's trouble does not make it better.
This Business of Living: A Diary 1935–1950 (1952)

6 No one ever lacks a good reason for suicide.
Quoted in *The Savage God* (A. Alvarez; 1971)

7 Every luxury must be paid for, and everything is a luxury, starting with the world.
Attrib.

8 Many men on the point of an edifying death would be furious if they were suddenly restored to life.
Attrib.

Pavlov, Ivan Petrovich (1849–1936) Russian physiologist

1 School yourself to demureness and patience. Learn to inure yourself to drudgery in science. Learn, compare, collect the facts.
Bequest to the Academic Youth of Soviet Russia (February 27, 1936)

2 Experiment alone crowns the efforts of medicine, experiment limited only by the natural range of the powers of the human mind. Observation discloses in the animal organism numerous phenomena existing side by side, and interconnected now profoundly, now indirectly, or accidentally. Confronted with a multitude of different assumptions the mind must *guess* the real nature of this connection.
Experimental Psychology and Other Essays (1958), pt. 10

Pavlova, Anna (Anna Pavlovna Pavlova; 1882–1931) Russian ballet dancer

Quotations about Pavlova

1 Mindful of the feminine contradiction, the great Pavlova insisted that for photographs her feet be pared down to ethereal points by a skilled retoucher.
Susan Brownmiller (b.1935) U.S. journalist and writer. Referring to the contrast between the illusion created by dance and the reality of the dancer's feet. *Femininity* (1986)

2 She seemed to be made of steel and elastic...Her beautiful face took on the stern lines of a martyr...The mind...can only suffer in aloofness from this rigorous muscular discipline. This is just the opposite from all the theories on which I founded my school, by which the body becomes transparent and is a medium for the mind and spirit.
Isadora Duncan (1877–1927) U.S. dancer. *My Life* (1927)

Quotations by Pavlova

3 Although one may fail to find happiness in theatrical life, one never wishes to give it up after having once tasted its fruits. To enter the School of the Imperial Ballet is to enter a convent

whence frivolity is banned, and where merciless discipline reigns.
Quoted in "Pages of My Life," *Pavlova: A Biography* (A. H. Franks, ed.; 1956)

4 As is the case in all branches of art, success depends in a very large measure upon individual initiative and exertion, and cannot be achieved except by dint of hard work.
Quoted in "Pages of My Life," *Pavlova: A Biography* (A. H. Franks, ed.; 1956)

5 When a small child...I thought that success spelled happiness. I was wrong. Happiness is like a butterfly which appears and delights us for one brief moment, but soon flits away.
Quoted in "Pages of My Life," *Pavlova: A Biography* (A. H. Franks, ed.; 1956)

Payn, James (1830–98) British writer and editor

1 I had never had a piece of toast
Particularly long and wide,
But fell upon the sanded floor,
And always on the buttered side.
Chambers's Journal (February 2, 1884)

Payne, Cynthia (b.1934) British hostess

1 I know it does make people happy but to me it is just like having a cup of tea.
After her acquittal on a charge of controlling prostitutes in a famous "sex-for-luncheon-vouchers" case. Remark (November 8, 1987)

Payne, Daniel Alexander (1811–93) U.S. educator, clergyman, and poet

1 A useful life by sacred wisdom crowned
Is all I ask, let weal or woe abound.
"The Mournful Lute or the Preceptor's Farewell" (1835)

Payne, Frank (1840–1910) British physician

1 This basis of medicine is sympathy and the desire to help others, and whatever is done with this end must be called medicine.
English Medicine in the Anglo-Saxon Times (1904)

Payne, John Howard (1791–1852) U.S. actor and playwright

1 An exile from home splendor dazzles in vain,
Oh give me my lowly thatched cottage again;
The birds singing gaily, that came at my call,
Give me them, and that peace of mind dearer than all.
"Home, Sweet Home," *Clari, the Maid of Milan* (1823)

2 Mid pleasures and palaces though we may roam,
Be it ever so humble, there's no place like home;
...
Home, home, sweet, sweet home!
There's no place like home! there's no place like home!
"Home, Sweet Home," *Clari, the Maid of Milan* (1823)

Paz, Octavio (1914–98) Mexican author and poet

1 Given the natural differences between human beings, equality is an ethical aspiration that cannot be realized without recourse either to despotism or to an act of fraternity.
New York Times (December 8, 1991)

2 Our democratic capitalist society has converted Eros into an employee of Mammon.
Observer, London (June 19, 1994), "Sayings of the Week"

3 Modernity desacralized the human body, and advertising has used it as a marketing tool.
The Double Flame (1993)

4 Contemporary man has rationalized the myths, but he has not been able to destroy them.
Quoted in *The Labyrinth of Solitude* (Lysander Kemp, tr.; 1985)

p'Bitek, Okot (1931–82) Ugandan poet, novelist, and social anthropologist

1 Woman of Africa. What are you not?
Song of Ocol (1970), p. 41

Peabody, Elizabeth (Elizabeth Palmer Peabody; 1804–94) U.S. educator

1 I saw it, but I did not realize it.
Giving a transcendentalist explanation for her accidentally walking into a tree. Quoted in *The Peabody Sisters of Salem* (Louise Tharp; 1950)

Peacock, Thomas Love (1785–1866) British novelist and poet

Quotations about Peacock

1 Have you not heard
When a man marries, dies, or turns Hindoo,
His best friends hear no more of him?
July 21, 1820
Percy Bysshe Shelley (1792–1822) English poet. Referring to Thomas Love Peacock, who worked for the East India Company and who had recently married. "Letter to Maria Gisborne" (1820), l. 235, quoted in *Posthumous Poems* (Mrs. Shelley, ed.; 1824)

Quotations by Peacock

2 Respectable means rich, and decent means poor. I should die if I heard my family called decent.
Crotchet Castle (1831), ch. 3

3 Ancient sculpture is the true school of modesty. But where the Greeks had modesty, we have cant; where they had poetry, we have cant; where they had patriotism, we have cant; where they had anything that exalts, delights, or adorns humanity, we have nothing but cant, cant, cant.
Crotchet Castle (1831), ch. 7

4 A book that furnishes no quotations is, *me judice*, no book—it is a plaything.
Crotchet Castle (1831), ch. 9

5 I distinguish the picturesque and the beautiful, and I add to them, in the laying out of grounds, a third and distinct character, which I call unexpectedness.
Headlong Hall (1816), ch. 2

6 Indeed, the loaves and fishes are typical of a mixed diet; and the practice of the Church in all ages shows
That it never loses sight of the loaves and the fishes.
Headlong Hall (1816), ch. 2

7 Nothing can be more obvious than that all animals were created solely and exclusively for the use of man.
Headlong Hall (1816), ch. 2

8 There are two reasons for drinking; one is, when you are thirsty, to cure it; the other, when you are not thirsty, to prevent it...Prevention is better than cure.
Melincourt (1817)

9 Marriage may often be a stormy lake, but celibacy is almost always a muddy horse-pond.
Melincourt (1817), ch. 7

10 He was sent, as usual, to a public school, where a little learning was painfully beaten into him, and from thence to the university where it was carefully taken out of him.
Nightmare Abbey (1818), ch. 1

11 Laughter is pleasant, but the exertion is too much for me.
Said by the Hon. Mr. Listless. *Nightmare Abbey* (1818), ch. 5

12 Sir, I have quarrelled with my wife; and a man who has quarrelled with his wife is absolved from all duty to his country.
Nightmare Abbey (1818), ch. 11

13 The mountain sheep are sweeter,
But the valley sheep are fatter;
We therefore deemed it meeter
To carry off the latter.
"The War-Song of Dinas Vawr," *The Misfortunes of Elphin* (1823), ch. 11

Peake, Mervyn (Mervyn Laurence Peake; 1911–68) British novelist, poet, and artist

1 "What a long time life takes!" said Clarice at last. "Sometimes I think it's hardly worth encroaching on."
Gormenghast (1950), ch. 8

2 Home is where I was safe. Home is what I fled from.
Titus Alone (1959), ch. 50

3 All I want is to lie down quietly forever, on linen. Oh God, white linen, before I die.
Titus Alone (1959), ch. 64

4 Buy up the sunset! Buy it up! Buy it up! Buy...buy...buy. A copper for a seat, sirs. A copper for the view.
Titus Alone (1959), ch. 66

5 EQUALITY...is the thing. It is the only true and central premise from which constructive ideas can radiate freely and be operated without prejudice.
"The Sun Goes Down Again," *Titus Groan* (1946)

6 "Now, Clarice," says Cora at last, "you turn your lovely head to the right, so that I can see what I look like from the *side*".
"The Twins Again," *Titus Groan* (1946)

Peale, Norman Vincent (1899–1993) U.S. clergyman and writer

1 The Power of Positive Thinking
1952. Book title.

Pearce, Lord (1901–85) British judge

1 Artists, as a rule, do not live in the purple; they live mainly in the red.
Attrib.

Pearse, Patrick (Patrick Henry Pearse; 1879–1916) Irish poet and nationalist

1 People will say hard things of us now, but we shall be remembered by posterity and blessed by unborn generations.
Patrick Pearse was executed on May 3, 1916. Letter to his mother (May 1, 1916)

2 I think the Orangeman with a rifle a much less ridiculous figure than a Nationalist without a rifle.
"Orangeman" means a member of the Protestant Orange Order in Northern Ireland. Newspaper article (November 1913), quoted in *Phrases Make History Here* (Conor O'Clery; 1986)

3 The fools, the fools, the fools!—they have left us our Fenian dead, and while Ireland holds these graves, Ireland unfree shall never be at peace.
The Fenians were promoters of ending British rule in Ireland. Oration at funeral of the Irish nationalist Jeremiah O'Donovan Rossa (August 1, 1915), quoted in *Rebels: The Irish Rising of 1916* (Peter de Rosa; 1990)

4 There are in every generation those who shrink from the ultimate sacrifice, but there are in every generation those who make it with joy and laughter and these are the salt of the generations.
Robert Emmet Commemoration Address, New York (March 2, 1914), quoted in *A Book of Irish Quotations* (Sean McMahon, ed.; 1984)

5 In the name of God and of the dead generations from which she receives her old tradition of nationhood, Ireland...summons her children to her flag and strikes for her freedom...We hereby proclaim the Irish Republic as a Sovereign Independent State.
1916. Declaration signed and approved by Pearse and other republicans, and read on the steps of the General Post Office in Dublin. Quoted in *Rebels: The Irish Rising of 1916* (Peter de Rosa; 1990)

Pearson, Hesketh (1887–1964) British biographer

1 A widely-read man never quotes accurately...Misquotation is the pride and privilege of the learned.
Common Misquotations (1934), Introduction

2 Misquotations are the only quotations that are never misquoted.
Common Misquotations (1934), Introduction

3 I am inclined to think that one's education has been in vain if one fails to learn that most schoolmasters are idiots.
Attrib.

Pearson, Lester (Lester Bowles Pearson; 1897–1972) Canadian prime minister

1 We prepare for war like ferocious giants, and for peace like retarded pygmies.
Nobel Prize, acceptance speech (December 11, 1957)

Peary, Robert Edwin (1856–1920) U.S. explorer

1 The Eskimo, Ootah, had his own explanation. Said he: *The devil is asleep or having trouble with his wife, or we should never have come back so easily.*
Referring to a safe return after one of his many Arctic expeditions. *The North Pole* (1910)

2 Altogether, they are a people unique upon the face of the

earth. A friend of mine well calls them the philosophic anarchists of the North.
Referring to the Inuit. *The North Pole* (1910), ch. 5

3 Behind the cliffs is the great Greenland ice cap, silent, eternal, immeasurable—the abode, say the Eskimos, of evil spirits and the souls of the unhappy dead.
The North Pole (1910), ch. 6

4 Many times...during my twenty-three years of Arctic exploration, I have thanked God for even a bite of raw dog.
The North Pole (1910), ch. 9

5 It was so cold much of the time on this last journey that the brandy was frozen solid, the petroleum was white and viscid, and the dogs could hardly be seen for the steam of their breath.
The North Pole (1910), ch. 21

6 A silk American flag which Mrs. Peary gave me fifteen years ago...has done more traveling in high latitudes than any other ever made. I carried it wrapped about my body on every one of my expeditions northward.
The North Pole (1910), ch. 32

7 Nothing easier. One step beyond the pole, you see, and the north wind becomes a south one.
Explaining how he knew he had reached the North Pole. Attrib.

Peattie, Donald Culross (1898–1964) U.S. naturalist

1 I say that it touches a man that his blood is sea water and his tears are salt, that the seed of his loins is scarcely different from the same cells in a seaweed, and that of stuff like his bones are coral made.
"April First"', *An Almanac for Moderns* (1935)

Peck, Gregory (b.1916) U.S. film actor

1 If you have to tell them who you are, you aren't anybody.
Remarking upon the failure of anyone in a crowded restaurant to recognize him. Quoted in *Pieces of Eight* (Sydney J. Harris; 1982)

Peel, Arthur Wellesley, 1st Viscount (1829–1912) British politician

1 My father didn't create you to arrest me.
Protesting against his arrest by the police, recently established by his father. Remark (1850?)

Peele, George (1558?–97) English playwright

1 Live or die, sink or swim.
Edward I (1593)

2 When as the rye reach to the chin,
And chopcherry, chopcherry ripe within,
Strawberries swimming in the cream,
And schoolboys playing in the stream,
Then O, then O, then O, my true love said,
Till that time come again,
She could not live a maid.
The Old Wives' Tale (1595), l. 81

3 What thing is love for (well I wot) love is a thing
It is a prick, it is a sting,
It is a pretty, pretty thing;
It is a fire, it is a coal
Whose flame creeps in at every hole.
1591? "The Hunting of Cupid," *Works* (A. H. Bullen, ed.), ll. 1–5

Pegler, Westbrook (James Westbrook Pegler; 1894–1969) U.S. journalist

1 He will go from resort to resort getting more tanned and more tired.
Referring to the abdication of Edward VIII (1936). Quoted in *Six Men* (Alistair Cooke; 1977), pt. 2

Péguy, Charles Pierre (1873–1914) French writer and poet

1 He who does not bellow the truth when he knows the truth makes himself the accomplice of liars and forgers.
"Provincial Letter" (December 21, 1899), quoted in *Basic Verities* (A. and J. Green, trs.; 1943)

2 It is innocence that is full and experience that is empty. It is innocence that wins and experience that loses.
"Innocence and Experience," *Basic Verities* (A. and J. Green, trs.; 1943)

3 Short of genius, a rich man cannot imagine poverty.
"Socialism and the Modern World," *Basic Verities* (A. and J. Green, trs.; 1943)

4 A word is not the same with one writer as with another. One tears it from his guts. The other pulls it out of his overcoat pocket.
"The Honest People," *Basic Verities* (A. and J. Green, trs.; 1943)

5 One must always tell what one sees. Above all, which is more difficult, one must always see what one sees.
"The Honest People," *Basic Verities* (A. and J. Green, trs.; 1943)

6 It is better to have a war for justice than peace in injustice.
"The Rights of Man," *Basic Verities* (A. and J. Green, trs.; 1943)

7 Love is rarer than genius itself. And friendship is rarer than love.
"The Search for Truth," *Basic Verities* (A. and J. Green, trs.; 1943)

8 The life of an honest man must be a perpetual infidelity.
"The Search for Truth," *Basic Verities* (A. and J. Green, trs.; 1943)

9 Tyranny is always better organized than freedom.
"War and Peace," *Basic Verities* (A. and J. Green, trs.; 1943)

10 It is impossible to write ancient history because we do not have enough sources, and impossible to write modern history because we have far too many.
1909–12. *Clio* (1931)

11 Any father whose son raises a hand against him is guilty: of having produced a son who raised his hand against him.
Les Cahiers de la quinzaine (December 2, 1906)

12 A great philosophy is not a flawless philosophy, but a fearless one.
"Note sur M. Bergson et la philosophie bergsonienne," *Les Cahiers de la quinzaine* (April 8–26, 1914)

13 Homer is new this morning, and perhaps nothing is as old as today's newspaper.
"Note sur M. Bergson et la philosophie bergsonienne," *Les Cahiers de la quinzaine* (April 8–26, 1914)

14 When a man lies dying, he does not die from the disease alone. He dies from his whole life.
Quoted in "The Search for Truth," *Basic Verities* (Ann and Julian Green, trs.; 1943)

15 The classical artist can be recognized by his sincerity, the romantic by his laborious insincerity.
Quoted in *La Grève* (Jean Hugues; 1901), Preface

Peirce, Benjamin (1809–80) U.S. mathematician and astronomer

1 Mathematics is the science which draws necessary conclusions.
Speech to the National Academy of Sciences, Washington, D.C. (1870)

Peirce, C. S. (Charles Sanders Peirce; 1839–1914) U.S. physicist and philosopher

1 The pragmatist knows that doubt is an art which has to be acquired with difficulty.
Collected Papers (Undated)

2 The universe ought to be presumed too vast to have any character.
Collected Papers (1934), vol. 6

3 It is easy to be certain. One has only to be sufficiently vague.
Quoted in *Collected Papers* (Charles Hartshore and Paul Weiss, eds.; 1931–58), vol. 2

4 There are Real things, whose characters are entirely independent of our opinions of them.
Quoted in *Collected Papers* (Charles Hartshore and Paul Weiss, eds.; 1931–58), vol. 5

Pelagius (360?–420?) Romano-British monk

1 No one knows the extent of our powers better than He who gave us those powers...And He who is righteous has not will to command anything impossible; neither would He who is holy condemn a man for what he cannot help.
"Epistle to Demetriades," *Patrologia Latina* (400?)

2 If it is a necessity, then it is not a sin;
if it is optional, then it can be avoided.
Quoted in *The Jingle Bell Principle* (Miroslav Holub; 1992)

Pelevin, Viktor (b.1962) Russian novelist

1 The Marlboro Man has nothing to do with Russia. Why should we respond to it?
Business Week (January 27, 1997)

Pelli, Cesar (b.1926) Argentine-born U.S. architect

1 Architecture is not in the empty building, but in the vital interchange between building and participant.
Quoted in *Contemporary Architects* (Muriel Emmanuel, ed.; 1994)

Pembroke, Earl of, 2nd Earl of Pembroke (Henry Herbert; 1534?–1601) English aristocrat

1 A parliament can do any thing but make a man a woman, and a woman a man.
Quoted in a speech at Oxford by his son, the 4th Earl, on April 11, 1648. Quoted in *Harleian Miscellany* (1745), vol. 5

Penhaligon, David (David Charles Penhaligon; 1944–86) British politician

1 To adopt nuclear disarmament would be akin to behaving like a virgin in a brothel.
Guardian, London (1980)

Penn, William (1644–1718) English preacher and colonialist

1 No pain, no palm; no thorns, no throne; no gall, no glory; no cross, no crown.
1668. Referring to Quaker practice. Written when imprisoned in the Tower of London. *No Cross, No Crown* (1669)

2 I have led the greatest colony into America that ever any man did upon a private credit.
Report on Foundation of Pennsylvania (1684)

3 They have a right to censure, that have a heart to help.
Some Fruits of Solitude (1693)

4 They that love beyond the world cannot be separated by it. Death is but crossing the world, as friends do the seas; they live in one another still.
Some Fruits of Solitude (1693)

5 Truth often suffers more by the heat of its defenders than from the arguments of its opposers.
Some Fruits of Solitude (1693)

6 Drunkenness...spoils health, dismounts the mind, and unmans men.
Some Fruits of Solitude (1693), no. 72

7 Let the people think they govern and they will be governed.
Some Fruits of Solitude (1693), no. 337

8 It is a reproach to religion and government to suffer so much poverty and excess.
Some Fruits of Solitude (1693), pt. 1, no. 52

9 Men are generally more careful of the breed of their horses and dogs than of their children.
Some Fruits of Solitude (1693), pt. 1, no. 85

10 The taking of a Bribe or Gratuity, should be punished with as severe penalties as the defrauding of the State.
Some Fruits of Solitude (1693), pt. 1, no. 384

Pepys, Samuel (1633–1703) English diarist and civil servant

1 But Lord! to see the absurd nature of Englishmen, that cannot forbear laughing and jeering at everything that looks strange.
Diary (November 27, 1662)

2 But methought it lessened my esteem of a king, that he should not be able to command the rain.
Diary (July 19, 1662)

3 I see it is impossible for the King to have things done as cheap as other men.
Diary (July 21, 1662)

4 I went out to Charing Cross, to see Major-general Harrison hanged, drawn, and quartered; which was done there, he looking as cheerful as any man could do in that condition.
Diary (October 13, 1660)

5 Most of their discourse was about hunting, in a dialect I understand very little.
Diary (November 22, 1663)

6 Music and women I cannot but give way to, whatever my business is.
Diary (March 9, 1666)

7 My wife hath something in her gizzard, that only waits an opportunity of being provoked to bring up.
Diary (June 17, 1668)

8 Strange to say what delight we married people have to see these poor fools decoyed into our condition.
Diary (December 25, 1665)

9 Strange to see how a good dinner and feasting reconciles everybody.
Diary (November 9, 1665)

10 To church; and with my mourning, very handsome, and new periwig, make a great show.
Diary (March 31, 1667)

11 Went to hear Mrs Turner's daughter...play on the harpsichon; but, Lord! it was enough to make any man sick to hear her; yet was I forced to commend her highly.
Diary (May 1, 1663)

12 Pretty witty Nell.
Referring to Nell Gwyn. *Diary* (April 3, 1665)

13 Here out of the window it was a most pleasant sight to see the City from one end to the other with a glory about it, so high was the light of the bonfires, and so thick round the City, and the bells rang everywhere.
Referring to the celebrations in London at the end of the Commonwealth. *Diary* (February 21, 1660)

14 And so I betake myself to that course, which is almost as much as to see myself go into my grave—for which, and all the discomforts that will accompany my being blind, the good God prepare me!
The closing words of Pepys's Diary; he lived another 34 years and did not go blind. *Diary* (May 31, 1669)

15 And so to bed.
This famous phrase, ending a diary entry, occurs regularly throughout the diaries. *Diary* (April 20, 1660)

16 Thence I walked to the Tower; but Lord! how empty the streets are and how melancholy, so many poor sick people in the streets full of sores...in Westminster, there is never a physician and but one apothecary left, all being dead.
Written during the Great Plague, the last major outbreak of bubonic plague in England, and the worst since the Black Death of 1348. *Diary* (September 16, 1665)

Perelman, S. J. (Sidney Joseph Perelman; 1904–79) U.S. humorist

1 Philadelphia, a metropolis sometimes known as the City of Brotherly Love, but more accurately as the City of Bleak November Afternoons.
"Westward Ho!" (1948)

2 For years I have let dentists ride roughshod over my teeth: I have been sawed, hacked, chopped, whittled, bewitched, bewildered, tattooed, and signed on again; but this is cuspid's last stand.
"Nothing but the Tooth," *Crazy Like a Fox* (1944)

3 I'll dispose of my teeth as I see fit, and after they've gone, I'll get along. I started off living on gruel, and by God, I can always go back to it again.
"Nothing but the Tooth," *Crazy Like a Fox* (1944)

4 He bit his lip in a manner which immediately awakened my maternal sympathy, and I helped him bite it.
"The Love Decoy," *Crazy Like a Fox* (1944)

5 I tried to resist his overtures, but he plied me with symphonies, quartettes, chamber music, and cantatas.
"The Love Decoy," *Crazy Like a Fox* (1944)

6 I have Bright's disease and he has mine.
Caption for cartoon, *Judge* (November 16, 1926)

7 I loathe writing. On the other hand, I'm a great believer in money.
Interview, *Life* (1962)

8 A case of the tail dogging the wag.
Having escaped with some difficulty from the persistent attentions of some prostitutes in the street. Quoted in *Another Almanac of Words at Play* (Willard R. Epsy; 1980)

9 Love is not the dying moan of a distant violin—it's the triumphant twang of a bedspring.
Quoted in *Quotations for Speakers and Writers* (Allen Andrews; 1969)

10 Button-cute, rapier-keen, wafer-thin and pauper-poor.
Self-description. Attrib.

Peres, Shimon (Shimon Persky; b.1923) Israeli prime minister

1 Peace is made with yesterday's enemies. What is the alternative?
Observer, London (October 16, 1994), "Sayings of the Week"

Pérez de Cuéllar, Javier (b.1920) Peruvian diplomat

1 I am like a doctor...If the patient doesn't want all the pills I've recommended that's up to him. But I must warn that next time I will have to come as a surgeon with a knife.
Referring to his decision, as secretary-general of the United Nations, to introduce cost-cutting measures. *Guardian*, London (May 10, 1986)

2 I am a free man. I am as light as a feather.
Said on concluding his nine-year tenure as secretary-general of the United Nations. *Times*, London (January 2, 1992)

Pérez Galdós, Benito (1843–1920) Spanish novelist and playwright

1 Fine pictures, fine statues, beautiful music; pleasure for the senses, and let the devil take the soul!
Doña Perfecta (1876)

2 It is better to be an artist, and delight in the contemplation of beauty, though this be only represented by nude nymphs, than to be indifferent and incredulous in everything.
Doña Perfecta (1876)

3 I acquired a certain pedantic presumption and the slightest touch of ostentation, which subsequently, thank goodness, I've completely cured myself of.
El Amigo Manso (1882), ch. 2

4 The man of reflection discovers Truth; but the one who enjoys it and makes use of its heavenly gifts is the man of action.
El Amigo Manso (1882), ch. 39

5 Perversity is not very inventive, my son, and if we had the entry book of hell to hand, we'd be bored reading it, so monotonous is it.
Said by the priest to Polo. *Inferno* (1884)

6 I myself would be hard pressed if I had to decide who had written what I write. I accept no responsibility for the writing process; but I can vouch for the accuracy of what is depicted.
Nazarín (Jo Labanyi, tr.; 1895)

7 Moor and Spaniard are more brothers than it appears. Take away a bit of religion, and another bit of language, and the relationship and family resemblance are obvious...how many Spaniards do we see who are Moors disguised as Christians?
Quoted in *Saracen Chronicles* (Juan Goytisolo; 1992)

8 Nothing is so like a rising of Spanish revolutionaries, as a rising of Spanish reactionaries.
Quoted in *The Spanish Labyrinth* (Gerald Brenan; 1943)

Pericles (495?–429? B.C.) Greek statesman

1 Our love of what is beautiful does not lead to extravagance; our love of the things of the mind does not make us soft.
Part of the funeral oration, 430 B.C., for the dead of the first year of the Peloponnesian War. *Histories* (Rex Warner, tr.; 1961), bk. 2, ch. 40, sect. 1

2 For famous men have the whole earth as their memorial.
430 B.C. *Histories* (Rex Warner, tr.; 1961), bk. 2, ch. 43, sect. 3

3 Your great glory is not to be inferior to what God has made you, and the greatest glory of a woman is to be least talked about by men, whether they are praising you or criticizing you.
430 B.C. *Histories* (Rex Warner, tr.; 1961), bk. 2, ch. 45, sect. 2

Perkins, Carl (Carl Lee Perkins; b.1932) U.S. rock singer and songwriter

1 Well it's one for the money,
Two for the show,
Three to get ready,
now go, cat, go.
But don't you
Step on my blue suede shoes.
Song lyric. "Blue Suede Shoes" (1956)

Perkins, Frances (1882–1965) U.S. social reformer and politician

1 Call me madame.
Deciding the term of address she would prefer when made the first woman to hold a cabinet office in the United States. Quoted in *Familiar Quotations* (John Bartlett; 1863)

Perle, Richard (Richard Norman Perle; b.1941) U.S. politician

1 Arms control so easily becomes an incantation rather than policy.
Remark (March 1987)

Perlman, Itzhak (b.1945) Israeli-born U.S. violinist

1 You see, our fingers are circumcised, which gives it a very good dexterity, you know, particularly in the pinky.
Responding to an observation that many great violinists are Jewish. Remark (1980), quoted in *Close Encounters* (Mike Wallace and Gary Gates; 1984)

Perlman, Lawrence (b.1938) U.S. business executive

1 "Career commitment" is a euphemism for "what if she has a baby?"...If companies want stronger career commitment from women, they should hasten to correct pay inequities and create equal opportunities for promotion.
Speech (April 28, 1992)

2 When you ask children what they want to be when they grow up, they don't say, "I want a boring job where the only thing I look forward to is Friday."
Christian Science Monitor (December 20, 1994)

3 Business is the most important engine for social change in this country.
Twin Cities Business Monthly (November 1994)

4 You're not going to transform society until you transform business. But you're not going to transform business by pretending it's not a business.
Twin Cities Business Monthly (November 1994)

Perls, Fritz (Frederick Salomon Perls; 1893–1970) German-born U.S. psychiatrist

1 In the Freudian system, the guilt is very complicated. In Gestalt therapy, the guilt thing is much simpler. We see guilt as projected *resentment*...find out what you resent, and the guilt will vanish and you will try to make the other person feel guilty.
"Gestalt Therapy Verbatim" (1972), quoted in *A Complete Guide to Therapy* (Joel Kovel, ed.; 1976)

Perón, Eva (originally María Eva Duarte, "Evita"; 1919–52) Argentinian political figure

Quotations about Perón

1 Quite so. But I have not been on a ship for fifteen years and they still call me "Admiral."
Anonymous. Italian admiral to whom Eva Perón had complained that she had been called a "whore" on an Italian visit.

Quotations by Perón

2 Our president has declared that the only privileged persons in our country are the children.
Remark (December 5, 1949)

3 Almsgiving tends to perpetuate poverty; aid does away with it once and for all. Almsgiving leaves a man just where he was before. Aid restores him to society as an individual worthy of all respect and not as a man with a grievance. Almsgiving is the generosity of the rich; social aid levels up social inequalities.
Speech to the American Congress of Industrial Medicine (December 5, 1949)

Perón, Juan Domingo (1895–1974) Argentinian president

1 If I had not been born Perón, I would have liked to be Perón.
Observer, London (February 21, 1960), "Sayings of the Week"

2 Today a pacifist revolutionary is something akin to a vegetarian lion.
Quoted in *We Say No* (Eduardo Galeano; 1992)

Perot, H. Ross (Henry Ross Perot; b.1930) U.S. business executive, politician, and philanthropist

1 Revitalizing General Motors is like teaching an elephant to tap dance. You find the sensitive spots and start poking.
Referring to being a director of General Motors. Quoted in *International Management* (1987)

2 I come from an environment where, if you see a snake, you kill it. At General Motors, if you see a snake, the first thing you do is hire a consultant on snakes. Then, you spend a year talking about snakes.
Attrib.

Perry, Eleanor (Eleanor Rosenfeld Bayer Perry; 1915?–81) U.S. screenwriter

1 So long as a woman is dependent on a man for her self-image or her self-esteem she will remain without any sense of her own worth—can never be a fully realized human being.
1972. Attrib.

Perry, Oliver Hazard (1785–1819) U.S. naval commander

1 We have met the enemy, and they are ours.
Reporting his victory in a naval battle on Lake Erie. Remark (1813), quoted in *Familiar Quotations* (John Bartlett; 1863)

Pershing, John J. (John Joseph Pershing; 1860–1948) U.S. general

1 I hope that here on the soil of France and in the school of French heroes, our American soldiers may learn to battle and vanquish for the liberty of the world.
Said shortly after taking command of the American Expeditionary Force on the western front. Speech, at Lafayette's tomb, Paris (July 4, 1917)

Persius (Aules Persius Flaccus; 34–62) Roman satirist

1 Ask no one's view but your own.
1st century. *Satires* (Niall Rudd, tr.; 1973), no.1, l. 7

2 Nip disease in the bud.
1st century. *Satires* (Niall Rudd, tr.; 1973), no. 3, l. 64

3 Let them recognize virtue and rot for having lost it.
1st century. *Satires* (Niall Rudd, tr.; 1973), no. 3, l. 138

4 He who is given to drink, and whom the dice are despoiling, is the one who rots away in sexual vice.
1st century. *Satires* (Niall Rudd, tr.; 1973), no. 5

Perugino (Pietro di Cristoforo Vannucci; 1445?–1523) Italian painter

1 I am curious to see what happens in the next world to one who dies unshriven.
Giving his reasons for refusing to see a priest as he lay dying. Remark (1523)

Pestalozzi, Johann Heinrich (1746–1827) Swiss educational reformer

1 Good humor is the seasoning of truth.
Quoted in *The Education of Man: Aphorisms* (Heinz and Ruth Norden, trs.; 1951)

2 He who bears the interests of humanity in his breast, that man is blessed.
Quoted in *The Education of Man: Aphorisms* (Heinz and Ruth Norden, trs.; 1951)

3 Learning is not worth a penny when courage and joy are lost along the way.
Quoted in *The Education of Man: Aphorisms*. (Heinz and Ruth Norden, trs.; 1951)

4 Love is the sole and everlasting foundation on which our nature can be trained to humaneness.
Quoted in *The Education of Man: Aphorisms* (Heinz and Ruth Norden, trs.; 1951)

5 Not art, not books, but life itself is the true basis of teaching and education.
Quoted in *The Education of Man: Aphorisms* (Heinz and Ruth Norden, trs.; 1951)

6 Perhaps the most fateful gift an evil genius could bestow upon our times is knowledge without skill.
Quoted in *The Education of Man: Aphorisms* (Heinz and Ruth Norden, trs.; 1951)

7 Revolutions are like a water wheel, for in the end they always bring the worst mistakes of human nature to the top.
Quoted in *The Education of Man: Aphorisms*. (Heinz and Ruth Norden, trs.; 1951)

8 The greatest victory a man can win is victory over himself.
Quoted in *The Education of Man: Aphorisms* (Heinz and Ruth Norden, trs.; 1951)

9 What else is education but the reverent joining of the past to the gloom of the future by making wise use of the present?
Quoted in *The Education of Man: Aphorisms* (Heinz and Ruth Norden, trs.; 1951)

10 Whoever is unwilling to help himself can be helped by no one.
Quoted in *The Education of Man: Aphorisms* (Heinz and Ruth Norden, trs.; 1951)

Pétain, Henri Philippe (1856–1951) French political and military leader

1 They shall not pass.
"Vous ne les laisserez pas passer," *General R. G. Nirelle's Order of the Day* (June 1916)

2 To write one's memoirs is to speak ill of everybody except oneself.
Observer, London (May 26, 1946)

3 To make a union with Great Britain would be fusion with a corpse.
1940. Referring to Winston Churchill's suggestion for an Anglo-French union. Quoted in *Their Finest Hour* (Winston S. Churchill; 1949), ch. 10

Peter, Laurence J. (1919–90) Canadian writer

1 A pessimist is a man who looks both ways before crossing a one-way street.
Peter's Quotations (1977)

2 Speak when you are angry—and you'll make the best speech you'll ever regret.
Peter's Quotations (1977)

3 In a hierarchy every employee tends to rise to his level of incompetence.
The Peter Principle (1969), ch. 1

4 Work is accomplished by those employees who have not yet reached their level of incompetence.
The Peter Principle (1969), ch. 1

5 *Papyromania*—compulsive accumulation of papers... *Papyrophobia*—abnormal desire for "a clean desk."
The Peter Principle (1969), Glossary

6 An economist is an expert who will know tomorrow why the things he predicted yesterday didn't happen today.
Quoted in *The Financial Times Guide to Using the Financial Pages* (Romesh Vaitilingam; 1996)

7 Prison will not work until we start sending a better class of people there.
Attrib.

Peterborough, 3rd Earl of (Charles Mordaunt; 1658–1735) English military and naval commander, and diplomat

1 In the first place, I have only five guineas in my pocket; and in the second, they are very much at your service.
1710. Persuading an angry mob that he was not the Duke of Marlborough, notorious for his meanness. Quoted in *Dictionary of National Biography* (Sir Leslie K. C. B. Stephen; 1930)

Peters, Hugh (also known as Hugh Peter; 1598–1660) English preacher

1 I have lived in a country where in seven years I never saw a beggar, nor heard an oath, nor looked upon a drunkard: why should there be beggars in your Israel where there is so much work to do?
Comparing New England, where he lived from 1635 to 1641, with England. Sermon to Parliament and Assembly of Divines (April 2, 1646)

Peters, Tom (Thomas J. Peters; b.1942) U.S. management consultant and author

1 All business, from potato chips to washing machines to jet engines, is about people selling to people.
A Passion for Excellence (co-written with Nancy Austin; 1985)

2 Even if the company is not an exciting one, we observe *pockets of excellence*. Excellence is what you, the supervisor (or vice president), create on *your* turf.
A Passion for Excellence (co-written with Nancy Austin; 1985)

3 If we were allowed to be "business czars" for thirty seconds, our first act would be to remove the word "commodity" from the language of commerce.
A Passion for Excellence (co-written with Nancy Austin; 1985)

4 The brand of leadership we propose has a simple base of MBWA (Managing by Wandering Around). To "wander" with customers and vendors and our own people, is to be in touch with the first vibrations of the new.
A Passion for Excellence (co-written with Nancy Austin; 1985)

5 Ask dumb questions. "How come computer commands all come from keyboards?" Somebody asked that one first; hence, the mouse.
Liberation Management (1992)

6 Get fired. If you're not pushing hard enough to get fired, you're not pushing hard enough.
Liberation Management (1992)

7 Innovation is a low-odds business—and luck sure helps.
Liberation Management (1992)

8 Pursue failure. Failure is success's only launching pad. (The bigger the goof, the better!)
Liberation Management (1992)

9 Spend 50 percent of your time with "outsiders." Distributors and vendors will give you more ideas in five minutes than another five-hour committee meeting...Spend 50 percent of your "outsider time" with wacko outsiders.
Liberation Management (1992)

10 Spread confusion in your wake. Keep people off balance, don't let the ruts get deeper than they already are.
Liberation Management (1992)

11 Smile if it kills you. The physiology of smiling diffuses a lot of anger and angst. It makes your body and soul feel better.
The Pursuit of WOW! (1994)

12 "Experts" are those who don't need to bother with elementary questions anymore—thus, they fail to "bother" with the true sources of bottlenecks, buried deep in the habitual routines of the firm, labelled "we've always done it that way."
Thriving on Chaos (1987)

13 He says, "When I see a frown on a customer's face, I see $50,000 about to walk out the door." His good customers buy about $100 worth of groceries a week. Over ten years, that adds up to roughly $50,000. We all agree that repeat trade is the key to business success.
Thriving on Chaos (1987)

14 People are people...not personnel.
Thriving on Chaos (1987)

15 The best way to really train people is with an experienced mentor...and on the job.
Thriving on Chaos (1987)

16 Unreasonable conviction based on inadequate evidence.
Defining entrepreneurship. Quoted in *The Witch Doctors* (John Micklethwait and Adrian Wooldridge; 1996)

Peter the Great, Tsar (Peter I; 1672–1725) Russian emperor

1 Now indeed with God's help the final stone has been laid in the foundation of St. Petersburg.
Referring to his victory over Charles XII of Sweden at the Battle of Poltava (1709). Letter to Admiral Apraksin (June 27, 1709)

2 I have not spared and I do not spare my life for my fatherland and my people.
Letter to his son, Alexis (October 11, 1715)

3 It is your military genius that has inspired my sword.
Remark to King William III of England (September 11, 1697)

Petrarch (Francesco Petrarca; 1304–74) Italian poet and scholar

1 Who overrefines his argument brings himself to grief.
"To Laura in Life" (14th century), Canzoniere 11

2 Life in itself is short enough, but the physicians with their art, know to their amusement, how to make it still shorter.
Letter to Pope Clement VI, *Invectives* (14th century), Preface

3 It may be only glory that we seek here, but I persuade myself that, as long as we remain here, that is right. Another glory

awaits us in heaven...among mortals the care of things mortal should come first; to the transitory will then succeed the eternal...the natural progression.
Secretum (14th century)

4 It may be only glory that we seek here, but I persuade myself that, as long as we remain here, that is right. Another glory awaits us in heaven and he who reaches there will not wish even to think of earthly fame.
Secretum (14th century)

5 A well-painted picture gives us a pleasure that raises us to the realm of celestial love by leading us to its divine origin. For is there anyone who delights in the small brook and hates the spring where it is born?
Quoted in *El arte de la pintura* (Francisco Pacheco; 1649)

6 She closed her eyes; and in sweet slumber lying,
her spirit tiptoed from its lodging-place.
It's folly to shrink in fear, if this is dying;
for death looked lovely in her lovely face.
Quoted in *Triumphs* (Ernest Hatch Wilkins, tr.; 1962)

Petronius Arbiter (Gaius, or Titus, Petronius Niger; d.66) Roman writer

1 A huge dog, tied by a chain, was painted on the wall and over it was written in capital letters "Beware of the dog."
Satyricon (1st century)

2 A physician is nothing but a consoler of the mind.
Satyricon (1st century)

3 We trained hard, but it seemed every time we were beginning to form up into teams, we would be reorganized. I was to learn later in life that we tend to meet any new situation by reorganizing.
Satyricon (1st century)

4 I saw the Sibyl at Cumae
(One said) with mine own eye.
She hung in a cage, and read her rune.
To all the passers-by
Said the boys, "What wouldst thou, Sibyl?"
She answered, "I would die."
"Trimalchio's Feast," *Satyricon* (1st century)

5 He's gone to join the majority.
Referring to a dead man. "Trimalchio's Feast," *Satyricon* (1st century)

6 Delight of lust is gross and brief
And weariness treads on desire.
1st century. Quoted in *Poetae Latinae Minores* (A. Baehrens, ed.; 1882), vol. 4, no. 101

Pettifor, Ann British activist

1 My fervent hope is for a Copernican shift: from a money-centred world to a human-centred world. For the subordination of money values to human and environmental values.
Referring to her hopes for the new millennium. She is the director of the organisation Jubilee 2000, which campaigns for the elimination of debt of poorer nations to wealthy ones. *Observer* , London (January 2, 2000)

Petty, Sir William (1623–87) English economist

1 For Money is but the Fat of the Body-politick, whereof too much doth as often hinder its Agility, as too little makes it sick.
Verbum sapienti (1691)

Petzinger, Thomas, Jr. U.S. writer

1 The issue is not how much revenue companies are extracting from the Internet but how much efficiency they are gaining from it.
Wall Street Journal (May 9, 1997)

Pevsner, Nikolaus, Sir (Nikolaus Bernhard Leon Pevsner; 1902–83) German-born British architectural and art historian

1 No part of the walls is left undecorated. From everywhere the praise of the Lord is drummed into you.
1952. Referring to All Saints' church, London, designed by the British architect William Butterfield. *London, Except the Cities of London and Westminster* (1951–74)

Pfeffer, Jeffrey (b.1946) U.S. management writer

1 In today's world, knowledge and capability have become keys to success because everything else—product offerings, marketing strategy, sourcing schemes—is easily acquired or imitated.
"The Real Keys to High Performance" (1998)

2 Subordinates obey not because the supervisor has the power to compel them to; rather, they follow reasonable instructions related to the control of their work behavior because they expect that such directions will be given and followed.
Power in Organizations (1981), ch. 1

3 A company's...ability to generate those exceptional returns in a knowledge-based economy is dependent, in large measure, upon its ability to attract, retain, and develop the right work force—and whether it succeeds in unleashing their mental capabilities.
Interview, *Strategy and Business* (Joel Kurtzman; 1998)

4 There's this tendency to say to people: "I want you to get good results. But I also want to review you along the way, I want you to tell me how you're getting those results and I want to review all these processes"...it turns experts into novices.
Interview, *Strategy and Business* (Joel Kurtzman; 1998)

Phaer, Thomas (1510?–60) English lawyer, physician, and translator

1 Slepe is the nouryshment and food of a sucking child.
The Boke of Chyldren (1553)

Phelps, Edward John (1822–1900) U.S. lawyer and diplomat

1 The man who makes no mistakes does not usually make anything.
Speech, Mansion House, London (January 24, 1899)

Philby, Kim (Harold Adrian Russell Philby; 1912–88) British intelligence officer and spy

1 To betray, you must first belong. I never belonged.
Sunday Times, London (December 17, 1967)

Philemon (368?–264? B.C.) Greek playwright

1 There is not a doctor who desires the health of his friends; not a soldier who desires the peace of his country.
Fabulae Incertae (3rd century B.C.?), fragment 46

Philip, John Woodward (1840–1900) U.S. naval officer

1 Don't cheer, men; those poor devils are dying.
July 4, 1898. Restraining his victorious crew during the naval battle off Santiago in the Spanish-American War. Quoted in "John Woodward Philip," *Dictionary of American Biography* (1934), vol. 14

Philip, Prince, Duke of Edinburgh (Philip Mountbatten; b.1921) British consort of Queen Elizabeth II

1 The biggest waste of water in the country by far. You spend half a pint and flush two gallons.
Referring to toilets. Remark (1965)

2 I include "pidgin-English"...even though I am referred to in that splendid language as "Fella belong Mrs. Queen".
Speech to the English-Speaking Union Conference, Ottawa (October 29, 1958)

3 I don't think a prostitute is more moral than a wife, but they are doing the same thing.
Observer (December 1988), quoted in *Sayings of the Eighties* (Jeffrey Care, ed.; 1989)

4 Simply having a convention which says you must not make species extinct does not make a blind bit of difference.
Referring to the UN treaty on world conservation, March 1989. *Sunday Correspondent,* London (December 31, 1989)

5 Dentopedology is the science of opening your mouth and putting your foot in it. I've been practising it for years.
Attrib.

6 I am interested in leisure in the way that a poor man is interested in money. I can't get enough of it.
Attrib.

7 The monarchy is part of the fabric of the country. And, as the fabric alters, so the monarchy and its people's relations to it alters.
March 20, 1968. Attrib.

8 When a man opens the car door for his wife, it's either a new car or a new wife.
March 1988. Attrib.

9 I'm self-employed.
Answering a query as to what nature of work he did. Attrib.

10 I declare this thing open—whatever it is.
Opening a new annex at Vancouver City Hall. Attrib.

Philip II, King of France (1165–1223) French monarch

1 I have two huge lions tearing at my flanks, the so-called Emperor Otto and John, King of England. Both try with all their might to upset the Kingdom of France. I cannot leave the country myself or do without my son here.
Explaining his refusal to crusade against the Albigensian heretics. Remark to Pope Innocent III (13th century) Attrib.

Philip II, King of Spain and (as Philip I) Portugal (1527–98) Spanish monarch

1 England's chief defense depends upon the navy being always ready to defend the realm against invasion.
As husband of Mary I, he was King-Consort of England (1554–58). Submission to the Privy Council (1555?)

Philippe, Charles-Louis (1874–1909) French novelist

1 One always has the air of someone who is lying when one speaks to a policeman.
Les Chroniques du canard sauvage (1923)

Philips, Ambrose (1674?–1749) English poet, playwright, and politician

1 The flowers anew, returning seasons bring!
But beauty faded has no second spring.
"Lobbin," *The First Pastoral* (1708), l. 47

Phillips, Mark, Captain (Mark Anthony Peter Phillips; b.1948) British three-day event rider and former husband of Princess Anne

1 A person seeking a quiet life is greatly helped by not having a title.
Attrib.

Phillips, Wendell (1811–84) U.S. reformer

1 Every man meets his Waterloo at last.
Lecture, Brooklyn (November 1, 1859)

2 One on God's side is a majority.
Lecture, Brooklyn (November 1, 1859)

3 Revolutions are not made; they come.
Speech (January 28, 1852)

4 Revolutions never go backward.
Speech (February 12, 1861)

5 We live under a government of men and morning newspapers.
Speech (January 28, 1852)

Philostratus (Flavius Philostratus, "The Athenian"; 170?–245) Greek writer

1 Drink to me with your eyes alone.... And if you will, take the cup to your lips and fill it with kisses, and give it so to me.
Letter 24 (3rd century?)

Piaget, Jean (1896–1980) Swiss psychologist

1 Logical activity is not the whole of intelligence. One can be intelligent without being particularly logical.
"Egocentrism of Thought in the Child" (1924), quoted in *The Essential Piaget* (H. E. Gruber and J. Jacques Vonèche, eds.; 1977)

2 We are constantly hatching an enormous number of false ideas, conceits, Utopias, mystical explanations, suspicions, and

megalomaniacal fantasies, which disappear when brought into contact with other people.
"Egocentrism of Thought in the Child" (1924), quoted in *The Essential Piaget* (H. E. Gruber and J. Jacques Vonèche, eds.; 1977)

3 Psychoanalysis is a sort of individual history, an embryology of the personality.
"Psychoanalysis and its Relations with Child Psychology" (1920), quoted in *The Essential Piaget* (H. E. Gruber and J. Jacques Vonèche, eds.; 1977)

4 The aim of psychoanalysis is very daring. It consists in rediscovering, in the individual's unconscious, the hidden tendencies which guide the person without his knowledge and which influence the actual contents of consciousness.
"Psychoanalysis and its Relations with Child Psychology" (1920), quoted in *The Essential Piaget* (H. E. Gruber and J. Jacques Vonèche, eds.; 1977)

5 Is childhood a necessary evil, or have characteristics of the childish mentality a functional significance that defines a genuine activity?
"Science of Education and the Psychology of the Child" (1935), quoted in *The Essential Piaget* (H. E. Gruber and J. Jacques Vonèche, eds.; 1977)

6 As regards the idea of succession, it is surprising to find that children not only fail to affirm that they were born after their parents, but that many of them claim anteriority.
"The Child's Conception of Time" (1946), quoted in *The Essential Piaget* (H. E. Gruber and J. Jacques Vonèche, eds.; 1977)

7 The child's first year of life is unfortunately still an abyss of mysteries for the psychologist.
"The First Year of Life of the Child" (1927), quoted in *The Essential Piaget* (H. E. Gruber and J. Jacques Vonèche, eds.; 1977)

8 Even though the appearance of formal thought is not a direct consequence of puberty, could we not say that it is a manifestation of cerebral transformations due to the maturation of the nervous system?
"The Growth of Logical Thinking from Childhood to Adolescence" (1927), quoted in *The Essential Piaget* (H. E. Gruber and J. Jacques Vonèche, eds.; 1977)

Piatt, John James (1835–1917) U.S. journalist and poet

1 But look behind thee, where in sunshine lie
Thy boundless fields of harvest in the West.
Where savage garments from thy shoulders fly,
Where eagle clings in sunshine to thy crest!
"To the Statue on the Capitol: Looking Eastward at Dawn," *Landmarks and other Poems* (1872), v. 3

Picasso, Pablo (Pablo Ruiz y Picasso; 1881–1973) Spanish painter and sculptor

Quotations about Picasso

1 God created the world—so they say—
and on the seventh day,
when he was quietly resting,
He jumped up suddenly and said:
I've forgotten something:
The eyes and the hand of Picasso.
Rafael Alberti (b.1902) Spanish poet. Untitled, *The Eight Names of Picasso* (1992)

2 A Catalan wizard who fools with shapes.
Bernard Berenson (1865–1959) Lithuanian-born U.S. art historian. Quoted in *Berenson: A Biography* (Sylvia Sprigge; 1960)

3 His sickness has created atrocities that are repellent. Every one of his paintings deforms man, his body and his face.
Vladimir Semyonovich Kemenov, Russian art critic. Attrib.

Quotations by Picasso

4 The earth doesn't have a cleaning woman to dust it off.
Interview (October 20, 1943)

5 One starts to get young at the age of sixty and then it is too late.
Sunday Times, London (October 20, 1963)

6 If I like it, I say it's mine. If I don't I say it's a fake.
When asked how he knew which paintings were his. *Sunday Times*, London (October 10, 1965)

7 There's no such thing as a bad Picasso, but some are less good than others.
Quoted in *Come to Judgment* (Alden Whitman; 1980)

8 I paint objects as I think them, not as I see them.
Quoted in *Cubism: a History and Analysis, 1907–1914* (John Golding; 1959)

9 I hate that aesthetic game of the eye and the mind, played by these connoisseurs, these mandarins who "appreciate" beauty. What *is* beauty anyway? There's no such thing. I never "appreciate," any more than I "like." I love or hate.
Quoted in *Life with Picasso* (Françoise Gilot and Carlton Lake; 1964), ch. 2

10 God is really only another artist. He invented the giraffe, the elephant, and the cat. He has no real style, He just goes on trying other things.
Quoted in *Life with Picasso* (Françoise Gilot and Carlton Lake; 1964), pt. 1

11 My joining the Communist Party is the logical outcome of my whole life and of the whole body of my work.
Attrib. *New Masses: an Anthology of the Rebel Thirties* (Joseph North, ed.; 1969)

12 It's better like that, if you want to kill a picture all you have to do is to hang it beautifully on a nail and soon you will see nothing of it but the frame. When it's out of place you see it better.
Explaining why a Renoir in his apartment was hung crooked. Quoted in *Picasso: His Life and Work* (Sir Roland Penrose; 1958)

13 When I was their age, I could draw like Raphael, but it took me a lifetime to learn to draw like them.
Visiting an exhibition of drawings by children. Quoted in *Picasso: His Life and Work* (Sir Roland Penrose; 1958)

14 It would be very interesting to preserve photographically not the stages, but the metamorphoses of a picture. Possibly one might then discover the path followed by the brain in materializing a dream.
Quoted in *Success and Failure of Picasso* (John Berger; 1965)

15 Painting is a blind man's profession. He paints not what he sees, but what he feels, what he tells himself about what he has seen.
Quoted in "Childhood," *The Journals of Jean Cocteau* (Wallace Fowlie, tr.; 1957)

16 An artist must know how to convince others of the truth of his lies.
Attrib.

17 There are painters who transform the sun into a yellow spot,

but there are others who, thanks to their art and intelligence, transform a yellow spot into the sun.
Attrib.

18 There are two kinds of women—goddesses and doormats.
Attrib.

19 Work is necessary for man. Man invented the alarm clock.
Attrib.

Pickens, William (1881–1954) U.S. educator

1 An insignificant right becomes important when it is assailed.
"The Ultimate Effects of Segregation," *The New Negro: His Political, Civil and Mental Status and Related Essays* (1916)

2 It is not simply that the white storyteller will not do full justice to the humanity of the black race; he cannot.
The Black Aesthetic (Addison Gayle, ed.; 1972)

Pickens, T. Boone, Jr. (Thomas Boone Pickens, Jr; b.1928) U.S. business executive

1 It has become cheaper to look for oil on the floor of the New York Stock Exchange than in the ground.
Time (March 4, 1985)

Pickering, George White, Sir (1904–80) British medical scientist

1 Medicine is not yet liberated from the medieval idea that disease is the result of sin and must be expiated by mortification of the flesh.
Resident Physician (1965), vol. 2, no. 9

Piggott, Lester (b.1935) British jockey

1 Eating's going to be a whole new ball game. I may even have to buy a new pair of trousers.
1995. Referring to his retirement. Attrib.

Pindar (518–438 B.C.) Greek poet

1 The best of healers is good cheer.
"Nemean Ode" (5th century B.C.)

2 Weapons speak to the wise; but in general they need interpreters.
Olympian Odes (5th century B.C.), bk. 2, l. 83

Pinero, Arthur, Sir (Arthur Wing Pinero; 1855–1934) British playwright

Quotations about Pinero

1 Like the skins of some small mammal just not large enough to be used as mats.
Max Beerbohm (1872–1956) British essayist, critic, and caricaturist. Referring to Pinero's eyebrows. *Edward Marsh* (C. Hassall; 1959)

Quotations by Pinero

2 From forty to fifty a man is at heart either a stoic or a satyr.
The Second Mrs Tanqueray (1893)

Pinker, Steven (Steven Arthur Pinker; b.1954) U.S. cognitive scientist and author

1 At all ages children are driven to figure out what it takes to succeed among their peers and to give these strategies precedence over anything their parents foist on them.
"How the Mind Works," *Guardian*, London (January 17, 1998)

2 Blood really is thicker than water, and no aspect of human existence is untouched by that part of our psychology.
How the Mind Works (1997)

3 Geniuses are wonks. The typical genius pays dues for at least ten years before contributing anything of lasting value. (Mozart composed symphonies at eight, but they weren't very good.)
How the Mind Works (1997)

4 The biggest influence that parents have on their children is at the moment of conception.
How the Mind Works (1997)

5 The discovery by cognitive science...of the technical challenges overcome by our mundane mental activity is...an awakening of the imagination comparable to learning that the universe is made up of billions of galaxies.
How the Mind Works (1997)

6 The problems of science are close enough in structure to the problems of our foraging ancestors that we have made the progress that we have...we can glimpse *why* certain problems are beyond our ken.
How the Mind Works (1997)

7 We may have trouble defining intelligence but we recognize it when we see it.
How the Mind Works (1997)

Pinochet, Augusto (Augusto Pinochet Ugarte; b.1915) Chilean military dictator

1 I wasn't looking for this job. Destiny gave it to me.
Quoted in *A Nation of Enemies* (Pamela Constable and Arturo Valenzuela; 1991)

2 Neither my moral nor spiritual formation permits me to be a dictator...If I were a dictator, you can be certain many things would have happened.
Quoted in *A Nation of Enemies* (Pamela Constable and Arturo Valenzuela; 1991)

Pinter, Harold (b.1930) British playwright, theater director, and screenwriter

1 I'm not a theorist. I'm not an authoritative or reliable commentator on the dramatic scene, the social scene, any scene. I write plays, when I can manage it, and that's all.
Speech addressed to the National Student Drama Festival, Bristol (1962)

2 There are two silences. One where no word is spoken. The other where perhaps a torrent of language is being employed.
Speech addressed to the National Student Drama Festival, Bristol (1962)

3 I believe the U.S. is a truly monstrous force in the world, now off the leash for obvious reasons.
Independent, London (September 20, 1993)

4 I tend to believe that cricket is the greatest thing that God ever

created on earth...certainly greater than sex, although sex isn't too bad either.
Observer, London (October 5, 1980)

5 There are things I remember which may never have happened but as I recall them so they take place.
Old Times (1971)

6 The earth's about five thousand million years old. Who can afford to live in the past?
The Homecoming (1965)

7 In other words, apart from the known and the unknown, what else is there?
The Homecoming (1965), Act 2

8 The weasel under the cocktail cabinet.
Reply when asked what his plays were about. Quoted in *Anger and After* (J. Russell Taylor; 1962)

Piozzi, Hester Lynch (Harriet Lynch Thrale, born Salusbury; 1741–1821) Welsh writer

1 A physician can sometimes parry the scythe of death, but has no power over the sand in the hourglass.
Letter to Fanny Burney (November 22, 1781)

Pirandello, Luigi (1867–1936) Italian dramatist, novelist, and short-story writer

1 Don't you see that that blessed conscience of yours is nothing but other people inside you?
Each in His Own Way (Arthur Livingstone, tr.; 1924)

2 When you are in love with humanity, you are satisfied with yourself!
Each in His Own Way (Arthur Livingstone, tr.; 1924)

3 None of us can estimate what we do when we do it from instinct.
Henry IV (Edward Storer, tr.; 1922)

4 Phantoms in general are nothing more than trifling disorders of the spirit: images we cannot contain within the bounds of sleep.
Henry IV (Edward Storer, tr.; 1922)

5 Woe to him who doesn't know how to wear his mask, be he king or pope!
Henry IV (Edward Storer, tr.; 1922)

6 A fact is like a sack which won't stand up when it is empty. In order that it may stand up, one has to put into it the reason and sentiment which have caused it to exist.
Six Characters in Search of an Author (Edward Storer, tr.; 1921)

7 Each of us when he appears before his fellows is clothed in a certain dignity. But every man knows what unconfessable things pass within the secrecy of his own heart.
Six Characters in Search of an Author (Edward Storer, tr.; 1921)

8 If we could see all the evil that may spring from good, what should we do?
Six Characters in Search of an Author (Edward Storer, tr.; 1921)

9 Isn't everyone consoled when faced with a trouble or fact he does not understand, by a word, some simple word, which tells us nothing and yet calms us?
Six Characters in Search of an Author (Edward Storer, tr.; 1921)

10 Life is full of infinite absurdities, which, strangely enough, do not even need to appear plausible, since they are true.
Six Characters in Search of an Author (Edward Storer, tr.; 1921)

11 When the characters are really alive before their author, the latter does nothing but follow them in their action, in their words, in the situations which they suggest to him.
Six Characters in Search of an Author (Edward Storer, tr.; 1921)

12 What do you expect me to do if nobody writes good plays any more and we're reduced to putting on plays by Pirandello?
Six Characters in Search of an Author (1921), Act 1

13 Whoever has the luck to be born a character can laugh even at death. Because a character will never die! A man will die, a writer, the instrument of creation: but what he has created will never die!
Six Characters in Search of an Author (1921), Act 1

14 Whatever you touch and believe in and that seems real for you today, is going to be—like the reality of yesterday—an illusion tomorrow.
Six Characters in Search of an Author (1921), Act 3

15 Anyone can be heroic from time to time, but a gentleman is something which you have to be all the time. Which isn't easy.
The Pleasure of Honesty (William Murray, tr.; 1917)

16 Life is little more than a loan shark: it exacts a very high rate of interest for the few pleasures it concedes.
The Pleasure of Honesty (William Murray, tr.; 1917)

17 Our whole knowledge of the world hangs on this very slender thread: the re-gu-la-ri-ty of our experiences.
The Pleasure of Honesty (William Murray, tr.; 1917)

18 In bed my real love has always been the sleep that rescued me by allowing me to dream.
The Rules of the Game (William Murray, tr.; 1918)

19 The facts are to blame, my friend. We are all imprisoned by facts: I was born, I exist.
The Rules of the Game (William Murray, tr.; 1918)

Pirenne, Henri (1862–1935) Belgian historian

1 There happened in the Middle Ages what has happened so often since then. Those who were the beneficiaries of the established order were bent on defending it.
Medieval Cities, Their Origins and the Revival of Trade (1925)

Piron, Alexis (1689–1773) French poet and playwright

1 I think you would have been very glad if I had written it.
Discussing Voltaire's *Sémiramis* with him after its poor reception on the first night. Quoted in *Cyclopaedia of Anecdotes of Literature and the Fine Arts* (Kazlitt Arvine; 1856)

Pirsig, Robert T. (b.1928) U.S. writer

1 If you want to get out of an insane asylum the way to do it...is to persuade them that you fully understand that they know

more than you do and that you are fully ready to accept their intellectual authority.
Lila: an Inquiry into Morals (1991)

2 Sanity is not truth. Sanity is conformity to what is socially expected. Truth is sometimes in conformity, sometimes not.
Lila: an Inquiry into Morals (1991)

3 The insane person is running a private unapproved film which he happens to *like* better than the current cultural one.
Lila: an Inquiry into Morals (1991)

4 What anthropologists see over and over again is that insanity is culturally defined. It occurs in all cultures but each culture has different criteria for what constitutes it.
Lila: an Inquiry into Morals (1991)

5 Whenever you kill a human being you are killing a source of thought too. A human being is a collection of ideas, and these ideas take moral precedence over a society. Ideas are patterns of value.
Lila: an Inquiry into Morals (1991)

6 A motorcycle functions entirely in accordance with the laws of reason, and a study of the art of motorcycle maintenance is really a miniature study of the art of rationality itself.
Zen and the Art of Motorcycle Maintenance (1974)

7 Mental reflection is so much more interesting than T.V., it's a shame more people don't switch over to it. They probably think that what they hear is unimportant but it never is.
Zen and the Art of Motorcycle Maintenance (1974)

8 When people are fanatically dedicated to political or religious faiths or any other kind of dogmas or goals, it's always because these dogmas or goals are in doubt.
Zen and the Art of Motorcycle Maintenance (1974), pt. 2, ch. 13

9 One geometry cannot be more true than another; it can only be more.
Zen and the Art of Motorcycle Maintenance (1974), pt. 3, ch. 22

10 Traditional scientific method has always been at the very *best*, 20–20 hindsight. It's good for seeing where you've been.
Zen and the Art of Motorcycle Maintenance (1974), pt. 3, ch. 24

11 We keep passing unseen through little moments of other people's lives.
Zen and the Art of Motorcycle Maintenance (1974), pt. 3, ch. 24

12 That's the classical mind at work, runs fine inside but looks dingy on the surface.
Zen and the Art of Motorcycle Maintenance (1974), pt. 3, ch. 25

13 Zen and the Art of Motorcycle Maintenance
1974. Book title.

Pisar, Samuel (b.1929) Polish-born U.S. writer and lawyer

1 Building up arms is not a substitute for diplomacy.
Of Blood and Hope (1980)

Pitkin, Walter B. (Walter Boughton Pitkin; 1878–1953) U.S. writer

1 A country doctor needs more brains to do his work passably than the fifty greatest industrialists in the world require.
The Twilight of the American Mind (1928), ch. 10

Pitter, Ruth (1897–1992) British poet

1 The seldom female in a world of males!
"The Kitten's Eclogue," *On Cats* (1947)

Pitts, William Ewart (b.1900) British policeman

1 It is the overtakers who keep the undertakers busy.
Observer, London (December 22, 1963), "Sayings of the Week"

Pitt the Elder, William, 1st Earl of Chatham ("The Great Commoner"; 1708–78) British prime minister

1 The parks are the lungs of London.
Quoted by William Windham in the British Parliament (June 30, 1808)

2 I know that I can save this country and that no one else can.
During the political crisis at the start of the Seven Years War (1756–63) Pitt became Secretary of State for the Southern Division, and effective head of government. Remark to one of his private secretaries (November 1756)

3 The poorest man may in his cottage bid defiance to all the forces of the Crown. It may be frail—its roof may shake—the wind may blow through it—the storm may enter—the rain may enter—but the King of England cannot enter!—all his force dares not cross the threshold of the ruined tenement!
Speech (1763?), quoted in First Series, *Statesmen in the Time of George III* (Lord Brougham; 1845), vol. 1

4 Confidence is a plant of slow growth in an aged bosom.
Speech to the British Parliament (January 14, 1766)

5 I rejoice that America has resisted. Three millions of people, so dead to all the feelings of liberty, as voluntarily to submit to be slaves, would have been fit instruments to make slaves of the rest.
Speech to the British Parliament (January 14, 1766)

6 The atrocious crime of being a young man...I shall neither attempt to palliate nor deny.
Speech to the British Parliament (March 2, 1741)

7 Youth is the season of credulity.
Speech to the British Parliament (January 14, 1766)

8 If I were an American, as I am an Englishman, while a foreign troop was landed in my country, I never would lay down my arms,—never—never—never!
Speech to the House of Lords, the upper house of the British Parliament (November 18, 1777)

9 There is something behind the throne greater than the King himself.
Speech to the House of Lords, the upper house of the British Parliament (March 2, 1770)

10 Unlimited power is apt to corrupt the minds of those who possess it.
Speech to the House of Lords, the upper house of the British Parliament (January 9, 1770)

11 We have a Calvinistic creed, a Popish liturgy, and an Arminian clergy.
Speech to the House of Lords, the upper house of the British Parliament (May 19, 1772)

12 You cannot conquer America.
Referring to the American Revolution. Speech to the House of Lords, the upper house of the British Parliament (November 18, 1777)

Pitt the Younger, William (1759–1806) British prime minister

Quotations about Pitt the Younger

1 Not merely a chip off the old "block", but the old block itself.
February 1781
Edmund Burke (1729–97) Irish-born British statesman and political philosopher. Referring to the maiden parliamentary speech of William Pitt the Younger, February 26, 1781. Quoted in *Historical Memories of my Own Time* (N. W. Wraxhall; 1904), pt. 2

Quotations by Pitt the Younger

2 Necessity is the plea for every infringement of human freedom. It is the argument of tyrants; it is the creed of slaves.
Speech to the British Parliament (November 18, 1783)

3 We must recollect what it is we have at stake, what it is we have to contend for. It is for our property, it is for our liberty, it is for our independence, ay, for our existence as a nation; it is for our character, it is for our very name as Englishmen, it is for everything dear and valuable to man on this side of the grave.
Speech to the British Parliament (July 22, 1803)

4 What is the will of the people? It is the power of the French.
Referring to the French Revolution (from 1789), popularly considered to have been effected by the will of the people, which temporarily transformed the country from an absolute monarchy into a republic of theoretically free and equal citizens. Under William Pitt, Britain declared war on France in 1793. Speech to the British Parliament (February 1, 1793)

5 Roll up that map: it will not be wanted these ten years.
December 1805. Said of a map of Europe on learning that Napoleon had won the Battle of Austerlitz. Quoted in *Life of the Rt. Hon. William Pitt* (Earl Stanhope; 1862), vol. 4, ch. 43

6 Oh, my country! How I leave my country!
Last words. Attrib. (1806)

Pius II, Pope (Enea Silvio Piccolomini, "Aeneas Silvius"; 1405–64) Italian pope

1 We look upon pope and emperor only as names in a story or as heads in a picture. Every city has its own sovereign; there are as many princes as there are houses; how then will you persuade this multitude of rulers to take up arms?
Responding to a proposal to organize a crusade to recapture Constantinople from the Turks. Speech to the Congress of Regensburg, Germany (1454)

2 Of the two lights of Christendom, one has been extinguished.
Referring to the fall of Constantinople to the Turks (May 29, 1453). Attrib.

Pi y Margall, Francisco (1824–1901) Spanish politician and author

1 Every man who has power over another is a tyrant.
La Reacción y La Revolución (1854)

2 Revolution...is the idea of justice...It divides power quantitatively, not qualitatively as our constitutionalists do...It is atheist in religion and anarchist in politics: anarchist in the sense that it considers power as a very passing necessity: atheist in that it recognizes no religion, because it recognizes them all.
La Reacción y La Revolución (1854)

3 Since I cannot do without the system of votes, I shall universalize suffrage. Since I cannot do without supreme magistrates I shall make them as far as possible changeable. I shall divide and subdivide power, I shall make it changeable and will go on destroying it.
La Reacción y La Revolución (1854)

Plà, Josep Catalan writer

1 Everybody watching the television with open mouths, such is today's culture.
Remark (1972), quoted in *Spain: Dictatorship to Democracy* (Raymond Carr and Juan Pablo Fusi Aizpurna; 1979)

Planck, Max (Max Karl Ernst Ludwig Planck; 1858–1947) German physicist

1 A new scientific truth does not triumph by convincing its opponents and making them see the light, but rather because its opponents eventually die, and a new generation grows up that is familiar with it.
Scientific Autobiography and Other Papers (1949)

2 We have no right to assume that any physical laws exist, or if they have existed up to now, that they will continue to exist in a similar manner in the future.
Quoted in *The Universe in the Light of Modern Physics* (W. H. Johnston, tr.; 1931)

Plaschkina, Nelly (1903–88) Russian

1 Give women scope and opportunity, and they will be no worse than men.
Diary (October 1, 1918)

Plath, Sylvia (1932–63) U.S. poet and novelist

1 They always knew it was you.
Daddy, daddy, you bastard, I'm through.
"Daddy," *Ariel* (1965), quoted in *The Penguin Book of American Verse* (Geoffrey Moore, ed.; 1977)

2 You do not do, you do not do
Anymore, black shoe
In which I have lived like a foot
For thirty years.
"Daddy," *Ariel* (1965), quoted in *The Penguin Book of American Verse* (Geoffrey Moore, ed.; 1977)

3 Dying
is an art, like everything else.
I do it exceptionally well.
October 1962. "Lady Lazarus," *Ariel* (1965)

4 The hills step off into whiteness.
People or stars
Regard me sadly, I disappoint them.
1962–63. "Sheep in Fog," *Ariel* (1965)

5 A living doll, everywhere you look,
It can sew, it can cook,
It can talk, talk, talk.
"The Applicant," *Ariel* (1965)

6 Stars open among the lilies.
Are you not blinded by such expressionless sirens?
This is the silence of astounded souls.
April 1962. "Crossing the Water," *Crossing the Water* (1971)

7 They all wanted to adopt me in some way and, for the price

of their care and influence, have me resemble them.
The Bell Jar (1963)

8 It was a queer, sultry summer, the summer they executed the Rosenbergs, and I didn't know what I was doing in New York. I'm stupid about executions.
Opening words. *The Bell Jar* (1963), ch. 1

9 His mother said, "What a man wants is a mate and what a woman wants is infinite security," and, "What a man is is an arrow into the future and what a woman is is the place he shoots off from," until it made me tired.
The Bell Jar (1963), ch. 6

10 Then something bent down and took hold of me and shook me like the end of the world. Whee-ee-ee-ee-ee, it shrilled, through an air crackling with blue light, and with each flash a great jolt drubbed me.
Referring to electro-convulsive therapy. *The Bell Jar* (1963), ch. 12

11 Then I remembered that I had never cried for my father's death...I laid my face to the smooth face of the marble and howled my loss into the cold salt rain.
The Bell Jar (1963), ch. 13

12 All the heat and fear had purged itself. I felt surprisingly at peace. The bell jar hung, suspended, a few feet above my head. I was open to the circulating air.
The Bell Jar (1963), ch. 18,

13 The fountains are dry and the roses over.
Incense of death. Your day approaches.
The pears fatten like little buddhas.
A blue mist is dragging the lake.
1959. "The Manor Garden," *The Colossus* (1960)

14 The surgeon is quiet, he does not speak.
He has seen too much death, his hands are full of it.
October 1962. "The Courage of Shutting-Up," *Winter Trees* (1971)

15 I am no shadow
Though there is a shadow starting from my feet. I am a wife.
The city waits and aches. The little grasses
Crack through stone, and they are green with life.
March 1962. "Three Women," *Winter Trees* (1971)

16 It is only time that weighs upon our hands.
It is only time, and that is not material.
March 1962. "Three Women," *Winter Trees* (1971)

Plato (428?–347? B.C.) Greek philosopher

Quotations about Plato

1 The safest general characterization of the European philosophical tradition is that it consists of a series of footnotes to Plato.
A. N. Whitehead (1861–1947) British philosopher and mathematician. *Process and Reality* (1929)

Quotations by Plato

2 The cure of many diseases is unknown to the physicians of Hellas, because they are ignorant of the whole, which ought to be studied also; for the part can never be well unless the whole is well.... This is the great error of our day in the treatment of the human body, that the physicians separate the soul from the body.
Charmides (4th century? B.C.)

3 Cookery...a form of pandering which corresponds to medicine, and in the same way physical training has its counterfeit in beauty-culture.
Gorgias (4th century B.C.)

4 Medicine is an art, and attends to the nature and constitution of the patient, and has principles of action and reason in each case.
Gorgias (4th century B.C.)

5 I refuse to give the title of art to anything irrational, and if you want to raise objection on this point I am ready to justify my position.
Referring to cooking. *Gorgias* (4th century B.C.)

6 But at three, four, five, and even six years the childish nature will require sports; now is the time to get rid of self-will in him, punishing him, but not so as to disgrace him.
Laws (4th century? B.C.), bk. 7

7 The good is the beautiful.
Lysias (370? B.C.)

8 Mind is ever the ruler of the universe.
Philebus (4th century? B.C.)

9 A man who criticizes the length of an argument must be required to support his grumble with a proof that a briefer statement would have left him more able to demonstrate real truth by reasoned argument.
Sophist (370? B.C.)

10 And this is what the physician has to do, and in this the art of medicine consists: for medicine may be regarded generally as the knowledge of the loves and desires of the body, and how to satisfy them or not; and the best physician is he who is able to separate fair love from foul, or to convert one into the other; and he who knows how to eradicate and how to implant love, whichever is required, and can reconcile the most hostile elements in the constitution and make them loving friends, is a skillful practitioner.
Symposium (4th century? B.C.)

11 Education in music is most sovereign, because more than anything else rhythm and harmony find their way to the inmost soul and take strongest hold upon it, bringing with them and imparting grace, if one is rightly trained.
The Republic (370? B.C.)

12 If you admit the Muse of sweet pleasure, whether in lyrics or epic, pleasure and pain will rule as monarchs in your city, instead of the law and that rational principle which is always and by all thought to be the best.
The Republic (370? B.C.)

13 So too with sex, anger, and all the desires, pleasures and pains which we say follow us in every activity. Poetic imitation fosters these in us. It nurtures and waters them when they ought to wither.
The Republic (370? B.C.)

14 The music-lovers and theater-lovers are delighted by the beauty

of sound and color and form, and the works of art which make use of them, but their minds are incapable of seeing and delighting in the essential nature of beauty itself.
The Republic (370? B.C.)

15 The people always have some champion whom they set over them and nurse into greatness...This and no other is the root from which tyranny springs.
The Republic (370? B.C.)

16 The poetry of dramatic representation...seems to be injurious to minds which do not possess the antidote in a knowledge of its real nature...It is...easy to produce with no knowledge of the truth.
The Republic (370? B.C.)

17 The rulers of the State are the only ones who should have the privilege of lying, whether at home or abroad; they may be allowed to lie for the good of the State.
The Republic (370? B.C.)

18 The true creator is necessity, which is the mother of invention.
The Republic (370? B.C.)

19 The true lover of knowledge naturally strives for truth, and is not content with common opinion, but soars with undimmed and unwearied passion till he grasps the essential nature of things.
The Republic (370? B.C.)

20 They will cheerfully speak of a bad man as happy and load him with honors and social esteem, provided he be rich and otherwise powerful.
The Republic (370? B.C.), bk. 2

21 Our object in the construction of the State is the greatest happiness of the whole, and not that of any one class.
The Republic (370? B.C.), bk. 4

22 Riches and poverty. The one produces luxury and idleness, and the other low standards of conduct and workmanship.
The Republic (370? B.C.), bk. 4

23 I wonder if we could contrive...some magnificent myth that would in itself carry conviction to our whole community.
The Republic (370? B.C.), bk. 5

24 There will be no end to the troubles of states, or indeed, my dear Glaucon, of humanity itself, till philosophers become kings in this world, or till those we now call kings and rulers really and truly become philosophers.
The Republic (370? B.C.), bk. 5

25 Democracy is a charming form of government, full of variety and disorder, and dispensing a sort of equality to equals and unequals alike.
The Republic (370? B.C.), bk. 8

26 Democracy passes into despotism.
The Republic (370? B.C.), bk. 8

27 Oligarchy was established by men with a certain aim in life: the good they sought was wealth, and it was the insatiable appetite for money-making to the neglect of everything else that proved its undoing.
The Republic (370? B.C.), bk. 8

28 And as to the painter, is he the creator or maker of something of this sort? Not at all..... "This," he said, "seems to me to be the most accurate thing to call him the imitator of that which others create." "Well then," I said, "would you call him one who produces an imitation which is three stages away from the real existence?" "Yes, I would indeed," he said.
The Republic (370? B.C.), bk. 10

29 There are two kinds of folly, the one madness and the other ignorance.
Timaeus (4th century B.C.)

30 Let no one ignorant of mathematics enter here.
387 B.C. Inscription written over the entrance to the Academy. Quoted in *Biographical Encyclopedia* (I. Asimov)

31 Hence it is from the representation of things spoken by means of posture and gesture that the whole of the art of dance has been elaborated.
Quoted in *Dancing on my Grave* (Gelsey Kirkland with Greg Lawrence; 1986), Preliminaries

32 Attention to health is the greatest hindrance to life.
4th century? B.C. Attrib.

Platonov, Andrei (Andrei Platonovich Platonov; 1899–1951) Russian writer

1 All right then, make the whole republic into a collective farm—but it'll still end up the property of one man!
A peasant's prophetic response to collectivization. *The Foundation Pit* (Robert Chandler and Geoffrey Smith, trs.; December 1929–April 1930)

Platt, Lewis (Lewis Emmett Platt; b.1941) U.S. business executive

1 One of our managers...had a meeting with his staff to discuss work-life balance. The meeting started at 5 p.m. and ended at 9.
Speech (October 18, 1995)

2 It's counter to human nature, but you have to kill your business while it's still working.
Fortune (May 2, 1994)

Plautus (Titus Maccius Plautus; 254?–184 B.C.) Roman comic playwright

1 He whom the gods love dies young, while he has his strength and senses and wits.
Bacchides (3rd–2nd century B.C.), Act 4, Scene 8

2 There are occasions when it is undoubtedly better to incur loss than to make gain.
Captivi (3rd–2nd century B.C.), Act 2, Scene 2

3 Well in body
But sick in mind.
Epidicus (3rd–2nd century B.C.), Act 1, Scene 2

4 Nothing is there more friendly to a man than a friend in need.
Epidicus (3rd–2nd century B.C.), Act 3, Scene 3

5 Things which you do not hope happen more frequently than things which you do hope.
Mostellaria (3rd–2nd century B.C.), Act 1, Scene 3

6 Patience is the best remedy for every trouble.
Rudens (3rd–2nd century B.C.), Act 2, Scene 5

7 If you are wise, be wise; keep what goods the gods provide you.
Rudens (3rd–2nd century B.C.), Act 4, Scene 7

8 Not by years but by disposition is wisdom acquired.
Trinummus (3rd–2nd century B.C.), Act 2, Scene 2

9 Consider the little mouse, how sagacious an animal it is which never entrusts its life to one hole only.
Truculentus (3rd–2nd century B.C.), Act 4, Scene 4

Player, Gary (Gary Jim Player; b.1936) South African golfer

1 The harder you work, the luckier you get.
Attrib.

Plessis, Armand-Emmanuel du, Duc de Richelieu (1766–1822) French soldier and statesman

1 Madame, you must really be more careful. Suppose it had been someone else who found you like this.
Discovering his wife with her lover. Quoted in *The Book of Lists* (David Wallechinsky, Irving Wallace, Amy Wallace, eds.; 1977)

Pliny the Elder (Gaius Plinius Secundus; 23?–79) Roman scholar

1 There is nothing encourageth a woman sooner to be barren than hard travail in child bearing.
Natural History (77)

2 Amid the miseries of our life on earth, suicide is God's best gift to man.
Natural History (77), bk. 2

3 Attic wit.
Natural History (77), bk. 2

4 It is far from easy to determine whether she has proved a kind parent to man or a merciless step-mother.
Referring to nature. *Natural History* (77), bk. 7

5 To laugh, if but for an instant only, has never been granted to man before the fortieth day from his birth, and then it is looked upon as a miracle of precocity.
Natural History (77), bk. 7, sect. 2

6 Man alone at the very moment of his birth, cast naked upon the naked earth, does she abandon to cries and lamentations.
Referring to nature. *Natural History* (77), bk. 7, sect. 2

7 Man is the only one that knows nothing, that can learn nothing without being taught. He can neither speak nor walk nor eat, and in short he can do nothing at the prompting of nature only, but weep.
Natural History (77), bk. 7, sect. 4

8 It has been observed that the height of a man from the crown of the head to the sole of the foot is equal to the distance between the tips of the middle fingers of the two hands when extended in a straight line.
Natural History (77), bk. 7, sect. 77

9 There is always something new out of Africa.
Natural History (77), bk. 8

10 Truth comes out in wine.
Natural History (77), bk. 14

11 A stage built for public spectacles arranged by Claudius Pulcher won great praise for its painted decoration, because some crows, deceived by a painted representation of roof tiles, tried to alight on them.
Natural History (77), bk. 15

12 There exists...a magnificent oration by Agrippa, worthy of the greatest of citizens, on the subject of making all statues and paintings public property, which would have been a more satisfactory solution than banishing them as exiles to country villas.
Natural History (77), bk. 15

13 This then is the way things are: idleness has sent the arts to perdition, and because there are no portraits of our spirits, our bodies are neglected.
Natural History (77), bk. 15

14 Always act in such a way as to secure the love of your neighbor.
Natural History (77), bk. 18, sect. 44

15 The best plan is, as the common proverb has it, to profit by the folly of others.
Natural History (77), bk. 28, sect. 31

Pliny the Younger (Gaius Plinius Caecilius Secundus; 62–113) Roman politician and writer

1 But our dinner must have a limit, in time as well as in preparations and expense; for we are not the sort of people whom even our enemies cannot blame without a word of praise.
Letters (1st–2nd century)

2 Who are you, to accept my invitation to dinner and never come?
Letters (1st–2nd century)

3 Never do a thing concerning the rectitude of which you are in doubt.
Quoted in *The Letters of Pliny the Consul* (W. Melmoth, tr.; 1747), bk. 1, letter 18

4 The living voice is that which sways the soul.
Quoted in *The Letters of Pliny the Consul* (W. Melmoth, tr.; 1747), bk. 2, letter 3

5 An object in possession seldom retains the same charm that it had in pursuit.
Quoted in *The Letters of Pliny the Consul* (W. Melmoth, tr.; 1747), bk. 2, letter 15

6 That indolent but agreeable condition of doing nothing.
Quoted in *The Letters of Pliny the Consul* (W. Melmoth, tr.; 1747), bk. 8, letter 9

7 His only fault is that he has no fault.
Quoted in *The Letters of Pliny the Consul* (W. Melmoth, tr.; 1747), bk. 9, letter 16

8 Objects which are usually the motives of our travels by land and by sea are often overlooked and neglected if they lie under our eye...We put off from time to time going and seeing what we know we have an opportunity of seeing when we please.
Quoted in *The Letters of Pliny the Consul* (W. Melmoth, tr.; 1747), bk. 8, letter 10

Plomer, William (William Charles Franklyn Plomer; 1903–73) South African writer

1 The next day's headlines were the talk of Troy;
BIG BIRD SENSATION, MISSING LOCAL BOY.
In Greek mythology, the Trojan prince Ganymede was snatched away to Mt. Olympus by Zeus in the guise of an eagle. "Ganymede," *Collected Poems* (1973)

2 A pleasant old buffer, nephew to a lord,
Who believed that the bank was mightier than the sword,
And that an umbrella might pacify barbarians abroad:
Just like an old liberal
Between the wars.
Father and Son: 1939 (1945)

3 With first-rate sherry flowing into second-rate whores,
And third-rate conversation without one single pause:
Just like a young couple
Between the wars.
Father and Son: 1939 (1945)

4 On a sofa upholstered in panther skin
Mona did researches in original sin.
Mews Flat Mona (1960)

5 Patriotism is the last refuge of the sculptor.
Attrib.

Plotinus (205–270) Egyptian-born Roman philosopher

1 If the art, then, makes an object in conformity with what it is and what it has...it itself is more, and more truly, beautiful in that it possesses the beauty of art, a thing greater and fairer than whatever may exist in the external object.
Quoted in *Enneads* (Stephen MacKenna, tr.; 1930), vol. 5

2 It is bad enough to be condemned to drag around this image in which nature has imprisoned me. Why should I consent to the perpetuation of the image of this image?
Refusing to have his portrait painted. Attrib.

Plunkett, James (James Plunkett Kelly; b.1920) Irish novelist

1 "Name?" the sergeant barked.
"Christian name?"
"Rashers."
The sergeant put down his pen.
"They never poured holy water on the likes of that," he said.
Strumpet City (1970), bk. 1, ch. 1

2 "So far as you and me is concerned," he said to the dog, "God never shut one door but He closed another."
Strumpet City (1970), bk. 3, ch. 3

Plunkitt, George Washington (1842–1924) U.S. politician

1 The politician who steals is worse than a thief. He is a fool. With the grand opportunities all around for a man with political pull, there's no excuse for stealin' a cent.
Quoted in *Plunkitt of Tammany Hall* (William L. Riordan; 1905)

Plutarch (46?–120?) Greek biographer and philosopher

1 A prating barber asked Archelaus how he would be trimmed. He answered, "In silence."
"Archelaus" (1st–2nd century)

2 As Athenodorus was taking his leave of Caesar, "Remember," said he, "Caesar, whenever you are angry, to say or do nothing before you have repeated the four-and-twenty letters to yourself."
"Caesar Augustus" (1st–2nd century)

3 There are two sentences inscribed upon the Delphic oracle, hugely accommodated to the usages of man's life: "Know thyself," and "Nothing too much"; and upon these all other precepts depend.
"Consolation to Apollonius" (1st–2nd century)

4 He who cheats with an oath acknowledges that he is afraid of his enemy, but that he thinks little of God.
"Lysander" (1st–2nd century), 8

5 We are more sensible of what is done against custom than against Nature.
"Of Eating of Flesh" (1st–2nd century), Tract 1

6 He is a fool who lets slip a bird in the hand for a bird in the bush.
"Of Garrulity" (1st–2nd century)

7 That proverbial saying, "Ill news goes quick and far."
"Of Inquisitiveness" (1st–2nd century)

8 According to the proverb, the best things are the most difficult.
"Of the Training of Children" (1st–2nd century)

9 An old doting fool, with one foot already in the grave.
"Of the Training of Children" (1st–2nd century)

10 Democritus said, words are but the shadows of actions.
"Of the Training of Children" (1st–2nd century)

11 For water continually dropping will wear hard rocks hollow.
"Of the Training of Children" (1st–2nd century)

12 It is a point of wisdom to be silent when occasion requires, and better than to speak, though never so well.
"Of the Training of Children" (1st–2nd century)

13 Simonides said "that he never repented that he held his tongue, but often that he had spoken."
"Rules for the Preservation of Health" (1st–2nd century)

14 Custom is almost a second nature.
"Rules for the Preservation of Health" (1st–2nd century), 18

15 Anacharsis said a man's felicity consists not in the outward and visible favours and blessings of Fortune, but in the inward and unseen perfections and riches of the mind.
"The Banquet of the Seven Wise Men" (1st–2nd century), 11

16 As geographers, Sosius, crowd into the edges of their maps parts of the world which they do not know about, adding notes in the margin to the effect that beyond this lies nothing but sandy deserts full of wild beasts, and unapproachable bogs.
"Aemilius Paulus," *Lives* (1st century), sect. 5

17 For to err in opinion, though it be not the part of wise men, is at least human.
"Against Colotes," *Moralia* (1st–2nd century)

18 Gout is not relieved by a fine shoe nor a hangnail by a costly ring nor migraine by a tiara.
"Contentment," *Moralia* (1st–2nd century)

19 As those persons who despair of ever being rich make little account of small expenses, thinking that little added to a little will never make any great sum.
"Of Man's Progress in Virtue," *Moralia* (1st–2nd century)

20 The whole life of man is but a point of time; let us enjoy it, therefore, while it lasts, and not spend it to no purpose.
"Of the Training of Children," *Moralia* (1st–2nd century)

21 Medicine, to produce health, has to examine disease.
"Demetrius," *Parallel Lives* (1st–2nd century), 1

22 A Roman divorced from his wife, being highly blamed by his friends, who demanded, "Was she not chaste? Was she not fair? Was she not fruitful?" holding out his shoe, asked them whether it was not new and well made. "Yet," added he, "none of you can tell where it pinches me."
"Life of Aemilius Paulus," *Parallel Lives* (1st–2nd century)

23 Caesar said to the soothsayer, "The ides of March are come"; who answered him calmly, "Yes, they are come, but they are not past."
"Life of Caesar," *Parallel Lives* (1st–2nd century)

24 He who first called money the sinews of the state seems to have said this with special reference to war.
" Life of Cleomenes," *Parallel Lives* (1st–2nd century), 27

25 To conduct great matters and never commit a fault is above the force of human nature.
"Life of Fabius," *Parallel Lives* (1st–2nd century)

26 Be ruled by time, the wisest counsellor of all.
"Life of Pericles," *Parallel Lives* (1st–2nd century)

27 Even a nod from a person who is esteemed is of more force than a thousand arguments or studied sentences from others.
"Life of Phocion," *Parallel Lives* (1st–2nd century)

28 Anacharsis coming to Athens, knocked at Solon's door, and told him that he, being a stranger, was come to be his guest, and contract a friendship with him; and Solon replying, "It is better to make friends at home," Anacharsis replied, "Then you that are at home make friendship with me."
"Life of Solon," *Parallel Lives* (1st–2nd century)

29 I had rather be the first in this town than second in Rome.
"Caesar," *Roman Apophthegms*. (1st–2nd century)

30 Once Antigonis was told his son, Demetrius, was ill, and went to see him. At the door he met some young beauty. Going in, he sat down by the bed and took his pulse. "The fever," said Demetrius, "has just left me." "Oh, yes," replied the father, "I met it going out at the door."
Quoted in *Bartlett's Unfamiliar Quotations* (Leonard Louis Levinson; 1971)

Pobedonostsev, Konstantin (Konstantin Petrovich Pobedonostsev; 1827–1907) Russian administrator

1 Parliaments are the great lie of our time.
Moskovskii Sbornik (1896)

Poe, Edgar Allan (1809–49) U.S. poet and writer

Quotations about Poe

1 The United States was nothing but a vast prison house for Poe, within which he moved in a state of feverish imagination, like someone born to breathe a sweeter air.
Charles Baudelaire (1821–67) French poet. *Edgar Allan Poe, his Life and Works* (1856)

2 There comes Poe, with his raven, like Barnaby Rudge,
Three fifths of him genius and two fifths sheer fudge.
James Russell Lowell (1819–91) U.S. poet, editor, essayist, and diplomat. Referring to Edgar Allen Poe's poem "The Raven" (1845). "Poe," *A Fable for Critics* (1848), quoted in *The Penguin Book of American Verse* (Geoffrey Moore, ed.; 1977)

3 Poe gave the sense for the first time in America that literature is *serious*, not a matter of courtesy but of truth.
William Carlos Williams (1883–1963) U.S. poet, novelist, and physician. "Edgar Allan Poe," *In the American Grain* (1925)

Quotations by Poe

4 *I* was a child and *she* was a child,
In this kingdom by the sea,
But we loved with a love that was more than love—
I and my Annabel Lee—
With a love that the winged seraphs of Heaven
Coveted her and me.
First version published in *New York Tribune* on October 9, 1849. This final text, which appeared in *Union Magazine* in January 1850, is generally assumed to be referring to Poe's 13-year-old wife, Virginia Clemm. "Annabel Lee" (1849), st. 2

5 Keeping time, time, time,
In a sort of Runic rhyme,
To the tintinnabulation that so musically wells
From the bells, bells, bells, bells,
Bells, bells, bells.
"The Bells" (1849), st.1

6 When I first beheld this apparition—for I could scarcely regard it as less—my wonder and my terror were extreme. But at length reflection came to my aid. The cat, I remembered, had been hung in a garden adjacent to the house.
The apparition is the image of a hung cat on a plastered internal wall of a house destroyed by fire. "The Black Cat" (1897)

7 Once upon a midnight dreary, while I pondered, weak and weary,
Over many a quaint and curious volume of forgotten lore,
While I nodded, nearly napping, suddenly there came a tapping,
As of some one gently rapping, rapping at my chamber door.
"The Raven" (1845), st.1

8 Helen, thy beauty is to me
Like those Nicean barks of yore,
That gently, o'er a perfumed sea,
The weary, wayworn wanderer bore
To his own native shore.
On desperate seas long wont to roam,
Thy hyacinth hair, thy classic face,

Thy Naiad airs have brought me home
To the glory that was Greece
And the grandeur that was Rome.
"To Helen" (1831)

9 All that we see or seem
Is but a dream within a dream.
A Dream within a Dream (1827), l. 10

10 And this maiden she lived with no other thought
Than to love and be loved by me.
Annabel Lee (1849), st.1

11 Thank Heaven! the crisis,
The danger, is past,
And the lingering illness
Is over at last—
And the fever called "living"
Is conquered at last.
1849. "For Annie," *Collected Poems* (1850), st. 1, quoted in *The Penguin Book of American Verse* (Geoffrey Moore, ed.; 1977)

12 In an instant I seemed to rise from the ground. But I had no bodily, no visible, audible, or palpable presence.
"Tale of the Ragged Mountains," *Tales of Mystery and Imagination* (1839)

13 Thou wast that all to me, love,
For which my soul did pine—
A green isle in the sea, love,
A fountain and a shrine.
"To One in Paradise," *The Penguin Book of American Verse* (Geoffrey Moore, ed.; 1977)

14 I would define, in brief, the poetry of words as the rhythmical creation of Beauty.
The Poetic Principle (1850)

15 Take thy beak from out my heart, and take thy form from off my door!
Quoth the Raven, "Nevermore."
"The Raven," *The Raven and Other Poems* (1845), st. 1

16 To speak algebraically, Mr. M. is execrable, but Mr. C. is (x + 1)-ecrable.
Referring to the writers Cornelius Mathews and William Ellery Channing. Quoted in *Mathematical Maxims and Minims* (N. Rose; 1988)

Pöhl, Karl Otto (b.1929) German economist

1 We all know 1992 is coming. The question is when.
Referring to the removal of European trade barriers in 1992. Speech at the London School of Economics (November 10, 1990)

Poincaré, Jules Henri (1854–1912) French mathematician and scientist

1 Liberty is to Science what air is to the animal.
Dernières Pensées (1913), appendix

2 There can be no scientific morality; but then neither can science be immoral.
Dernières Pensées (1913), ch. 8

3 Science is built up of facts, as a house is built of stones; but an accumulation of facts is no more a science than a heap of stones is a house.
La Science et l'Hypothèse (1903), ch. 9

4 To doubt everything or to believe everything are two equally convenient solutions; both dispense with the necessity of reflection.
La Science et l'Hypothèse (1903), Introduction

5 Sociology is the science with the greatest number of methods and the least results.
Science et Méthode (1908), ch.1

6 Mathematics is the art of giving the same name to different things.
Quoted in *The Mathematical Intelligencer* (1991), vol 13, no. 1

7 Thought is only a flash between two long nights, but this flash is everything.
Quoted in *The World of Mathematics* (J. R. Newman; 1956)

Poincaré, Raymond (Raymond Nicolas Landry Poincaré; 1860–1934) French statesman

1 The sacred union materialized throughout the country as if by magic.
1933. Referring to the national unity he called for at the start of World War I. *Au Service de la France* (1926–33), bk. 5, ch. 1

Poiret, Paul (1879–1944) French fashion designer

1 Am I mad when I try to put art into my dresses, or when I say that couture is an art?
1918. Quoted in *Poiret* (Yvonne Deslandres; 1987)

2 You will not learn how to be beautiful from fashion magazines. What have you to do with fashion? Take no notice of it; just wear what suits you.
1927. Quoted in *Poiret* (Yvonne Deslandres; 1987)

Poisson, Siméon-Denis (1781–1840) French mathematician and physicist

1 Life is good for only two things, discovering mathematics and teaching mathematics.
Quoted in *Mathematics Magazine* (February 1991), vol. 64, no. 1

Polanski, Roman (b.1933) French-born Polish filmmaker

1 I had a patent on masturbation when I was 12. I thought I invented it.
Interview, *Playboy* (December 1971)

2 The best films are the best because of no one but the director.
Quoted in *Halliwell's Filmgoer's Book of Quotes* (Leslie Halliwell; 1973)

Polk, James Knox (1795–1849) U.S. president

1 The people of this continent alone have the right to decide their own destiny.
Speech to Congress (December 2, 1845)

Pollock, Jackson (Paul Jackson Pollock; 1912–56) U.S. artist

1 The idea of an isolated American painting, so popular in this country during the thirties, seems absurd to me, just as the idea of creating a purely American mathematics or physics would seem absurd.
Response to a questionnaire (February 1944)

2 When I am *in* my painting, I'm not aware of what I am doing. It's only after a sort of "get acquainted" period that I see what I have been about.
"Winter Possibilities I," *My Painting* (1947–48)

3 On the floor I am more at ease, I feel nearer, more a part of the painting, since this way I can walk around it, work from the four sides and literally be "in" the painting.
Famed for using the floor as his easel, dripping and flicking paint on the canvas. Quoted in *Pollock* (Italo Tomassoni; 1968)

4 The thing that interests me today is that painters do not have to go to a subject matter outside of themselves. Most modern painters work from a different source. They work from within.
1951. Quoted in *Pollock: A Catalogue Raisonné* (Francis V. O'Connor and Eugene Victor Thaw, eds.; 1978)

5 A critic is a legless man who teaches running.
Attrib.

Polo, Marco (1254–1324) Venetian merchant and traveler

1 I have not told half of what I saw.
Remark (1324), quoted in *The Story of Civilization* (William Durant; 1935), vol. 1

2 Emperors and kings, dukes and marquises, counts, knights, and townsfolk, and all people who wish to know the various races of men and the peculiarities of the various regions of the world, take this book and have it read to you.
Referring to his own book. *The Travels of Marco Polo* (1298–99)

3 He is the most potent man, as regards forces and lands and treasure that exists in the world.
Referring to Kublai Khan, Emperor of China. *The Travels of Marco Polo* (1298–99)

4 The whole city is arrayed in squares just like a chessboard, and disposed in a manner so perfect and masterly that it is impossible to give a description that should do it justice.
Referring to Kublai Khan's capital, Cambaluc (later Beijing). *The Travels of Marco Polo* (1298–99)

5 The walls of the halls and chambers are all covered with gold and silver and decorated with pictures of dragons and birds and horsemen and various breeds of beasts and scenes of battle. The ceiling is similarly adorned...nothing to be seen anywhere but gold and pictures.
Referring to Kublai Khan's palace, the inspiration for Samuel Taylor Coleridge's description of Kubla Khan's "stately pleasure-dome." "Kubilai Khan," *The Travels of Marco Polo* (1298–99)

Pomfret, John (1667–1702) English poet

1 From the time we first begin to know,
We live and learn, but not the wiser grow.
Reason (1700), l. 112

Pompadour, Madame de, Marquise de Pompadour (Jeanne Antoinette Poisson; 1721–64) French courtesan

1 After us the deluge.
1757. Reputed reply to Louis XV after the French defeat at the hands of Frederick the Great. Quoted in *Mémoires* (Mme du Hausset; 1824)

Pompidou, Georges (Georges Jean Raymond Pompidou; 1911–74) French president

1 A statesman is a politician who places himself at the service of the nation. A politician is a statesman who places the nation at his service.
Observer, London (December 30, 1973), "Sayings of the Year"

Pop, Iggy (James Newell Osterberg; b.1947) U.S. rock singer and songwriter

1 If all else fails, do "Louie Louie," right? That's what you learn playing in a fraternity band for five years.
Referring to the simple three-chord song, "Louie Louie," originally by The Kingsmen. Quoted in "The Piss Factory 1974–1975," *Please Kill Me. The Uncensored Oral History of Punk* (Legs McNeil and Gillian McCain, eds.; 1996)

Popcorn, Faith (Faith Beryl Popcorn; b.1947) U.S. management consultant, business executive, and author

1 Just before consumers stop doing something, they do it with a vengeance.
Attrib.

Pope, Alexander (1688–1744) English poet

Quotations about Pope

1 I hold it as certain, that no man was ever written out of reputation but by himself.
Richard Bentley (1662–1742) English classical scholar. Quoted in *The Works of Alexander Pope* (W. Warburton; 1751), vol. 4

2 It is a pretty poem, Mr Pope, but you must not call it Homer.
Richard Bentley (1662–1742) English classical scholar. Referring to Alexander Pope's translation of the *Iliad.* Quoted in "The Life of Pope," *The Works of Samuel Johnson* (Samuel Johnson; 1787), vol. 4

3 In Pope I cannot read a line,
But with a sigh I wish it mine;
When he can in one couplet fix
More sense than I can do in six:
It gives me such a jealous fit,
I cry, "Pox take him and his wit!"
Jonathan Swift (1667–1745) Irish writer and clergyman. "Verses on the Death of Dr. Swift" (1731)

Quotations by Pope

4 He best can paint them who can feel them Most.
"Eloisa to Abelard" (1717)

5 I am His Highness' dog at Kew;
Pray tell me sir, whose dog are you?
Referring to the Prince of Wales. "Epigram. Engraved on the Collar of a Dog Which I Gave to His Royal Highness" (1738)

6 How often are we to die before we go quite off this stage? In the death of every friend we lose a part of ourselves, and the best part.
Letter to Jonathan Swift (December 5, 1732), quoted in *Correspondence of Alexander Pope* (G. Sherburn, ed.; 1956), vol. 3

7 Teach me to feel another's woe,
To hide the fault I see;
That mercy I to others show,
That mercy show to me.
"The Universal Prayer," st. 10, quoted in *Alexander Pope: Minor Poems* (Norman Ault, ed.; 1954)

8 Who dare to love their country, and be poor.
"Verses on a Grotto by the River Thames at Twickenham, Composed of Marbles, Spars, and Minerals" (1740)

9 Of all the causes which conspire to blind
Man's erring judgment, and misguide the mind,
What the weak head with strongest bias rules,
Is Pride, the never-failing vice of fools.
An Essay on Criticism (1711)

10 'Tis hard to say, if greater want of skill,
Appear in writing or in judging ill.
An Essay on Criticism (1711)

11 'Tis with our judgments as our watches, none
Go just alike, yet each believes his own.
An Essay on Criticism (1711)

12 Whoever thinks a faultless piece to see,
Thinks what ne'er was, nor is, nor e'er shall be.
An Essay on Criticism (1711)

13 Nor in the critic let the man be lost.
An Essay on Criticism (1711), l. 523

14 To err is human; to forgive, divine.
An Essay on Criticism (1711), l. 525

15 And make each day a critic on the last.
An Essay on Criticism (1711), l. 571

16 For fools rush in where angels fear to tread.
An Essay on Criticism (1711), l. 625

17 One science only will one genius fit:
So vast is art, so narrow human wit.
An Essay on Criticism (1711), ll. 60–61

18 Words are like leaves; and where they most abound,
Much fruit of sense beneath is rarely found.
An Essay on Criticism (1711), ll. 109–110

19 A little learning is a dangerous thing;
Drink deep, or taste not the Pierian spring:
There shallow draughts intoxicate the brain,
And drinking largely sobers us again.
An Essay on Criticism (1711), ll. 215–218

20 True wit is nature to advantage dress'd;
What oft was thought, but ne'er so well express'd.
An Essay on Criticism (1711), ll. 297–298

21 True ease in writing comes from art, not chance,
As those move easiest who have learn'd to dance.
'Tis not enough no harshness gives offence,
The sound must seem an echo to the sense.
An Essay on Criticism (1711), ll. 362–365

22 Fondly we think we honour merit then,
When we but praise ourselves in other men.
An Essay on Criticism (1711), ll. 454–455

23 All seems infected that th' infected spy,
As all looks yellow to the jaundiced eye.
An Essay on Criticism (1711), ll. 558–559

24 The bookful blockhead, ignorantly read,
With loads of learned lumber in his head.
An Essay on Criticism (1711), ll. 612–613

25 Hope springs eternal in the human breast;
Man never Is, but always To be blest.
The soul, uneasy, and confin'd from home,
Rests and expatiates in a life to come.
An Essay on Man (1733), Epistle 1, ll. 95–96

26 All nature is but art, unknown to thee;
All chance, direction, which thou canst not see;
All discord, harmony, not understood;
All partial evil, universal good;
And spite of Pride, in erring Reason's spite,
One truth is clear, "Whatever IS, is RIGHT."
An Essay on Man (1733), Epistle 1, ll. 289–294

27 Know then thyself, presume not God to scan,
The proper study of Mankind is Man.
An Essay on Man (1733), Epistle 2, ll. 1–2

28 The learn'd is happy nature to explore,
The fool is happy that he knows no more.
An Essay on Man (1733), Epistle 2, ll. 263–264

29 Order is heaven's first law.
An Essay on Man (1733), Epistle 4, l. 49

30 Reason's whole pleasure, all the joys of sense,
Lie in three words, health, peace, and competence.
An Essay on Man (1733), Epistle 4, ll. 79–80

31 A wit 's a feather, and a chief a rod;
An honest man 's the noblest work of God.
An Essay on Man (1733), Epistle 4, ll. 247–248

32 That virtue only makes our bliss below,
And all our knowledge is ourselves to know.
An Essay on Man (1733), Epistle 4, ll. 397–398

33 A heap of dust alone remains of thee;
'Tis all thou art, and all the proud shall be!
Elegy to the Memory of an Unfortunate Lady (1717), ll. 71–72

34 How shall I lose the sin, yet keep the sense,
And love th'offender, yet detest the offence?
"Eloisa to Abelard," *Eloisa to Abelard* (1717), ll. 191–192

35 You beat your pate, and fancy wit will come;
Knock as you please, there's nobody at home.
Epigram (1732)

36 Do good by stealth, and blush to find it fame.
Epilogue to the Satires (1738), Dialogue 1

37 Ask you what provocation I have had?
The strong antipathy of good to bad.
Epilogue to the Satires (1738), Dialogue 2

38 Yes; I am proud, I must be proud to see
Men not afraid of God, afraid of me.
Epilogue to the Satires (1738), Dialogue 2, ll. 208–209

39 In men, we various ruling passions find;
In women, two almost divide the kind;
Those, only fix'd, they first or last obey,
The love of pleasure, and the love of sway.
Addressed to Mrs. M. Blount. "To a Lady," *Epistles to Several Persons* (1734), ll. 207–210

40 The ruling passion, be it what it will
The ruling passion conquers reason still.
"To Lord Bathurst," *Epistles to Several Persons* (1734), ll. 155–156

41 'Tis Education forms the common mind,
Just as the twig is bent, the tree's inclined.
"To Lord Cobham," *Epistles to Several Persons* (1734), l.101

42 Alas! in truth the man but chang'd his mind,
Perhaps was sick, in love, or had not din'd.
"To Lord Cobham," *Epistles to Several Persons* (1734), ll. 127–128

43 The Muse but serv'd to ease some friend, not wife,
To help me through this long disease, my life.
Epistle to Dr. Arbuthnot (1735), ll. 131–132

44 But still the great have kindness in reserve,
He helped to bury whom he helped to starve.
Referring to a noble patron. *Epistle to Dr. Arbuthnot* (1735), ll. 247–248

45 Curst be the verse, how well so'er it flow,
That tends to make one worthy man my foe.
Epistle to Dr. Arbuthnot (1735), ll. 283–284

46 In wit a man; simplicity a child.
Epitaph on Mr. Gay (1732), l. 2

47 Nature, and Nature's laws lay hid in night:
God said, *Let Newton be!* and all was light.
"Intended for Sir Isaac Newton," *Epitaphs* (1730)

48 For he lives twice who can at once employ
The present well, and e'en the past enjoy.
Imitation of Martial, bk. 10, Epigram 23, quoted in *Alexander Pope: Minor Poems* (Norman Ault, ed.; 1954)

49 Not to go back, is somewhat to advance,
And men must walk at least before they dance.
Imitations of Horace (1738), bk. 1, Epistle 1, l. 53

50 What will a child learn sooner than a song?
Imitations of Horace (1738), Epistle 2

51 Not to admire, is all the art I know
To make men happy, and to keep them so.
"To Mr. Murray," *Imitations of Horace* (1738), bk. 1, Epistle 6, ll. 1–2

52 A man should never be ashamed to own he has been in the wrong which is but saying, in other words, that he is wiser to-day than he was yesterday.
"Thoughts on Various Subjects," *Miscellanies* (1727)

53 I never knew any man in my life who could not bear another's misfortunes perfectly like a Christian.
"Thoughts on Various Subjects," *Miscellanies* (1727)

54 It is with narrow-souled people as with narrow-necked bottles; the less they have in them, the more noise they make in pouring it out.
"Thoughts on Various Subjects," *Miscellanies* (1727)

55 The most positive men are the most credulous.
"Thoughts on Various Subjects," *Miscellanies* (1727)

56 The vanity of human life is like a river, constantly passing away, and yet constantly coming on.
"Thoughts on Various Subjects," *Miscellanies* (1727)

57 Woman's at best a contradiction still.
Addressed to Mrs. M. Blount. "To a Lady," *Moral Essays* (1735), Epistle 2, l. 270

58 Men, some to business, some to pleasure take;
But every woman is at heart a rake.
"To a Lady," *Moral Essays* (1735), Epistle 2, ll. 215–216

59 To observations which ourselves we make.
We grow more partial for th' observer's sake.
"To Richard Temple, Viscount Cobham," *Moral Essays* (1735), ll. 11–12

60 He 's arm'd without that's innocent within.
Satires, Epistles, and Odes of Horace (1737), bk. 1, Epistle 1, l. 94

61 Authors, like coins, grow dear as they grow old.
Satires, Epistles, and Odes of Horace (1737), bk. 2, Epistle 1, l. 35

62 Years following years steal something every day;
At last they steal us from ourselves away.
Satires, Epistles, and Odes of Horace (1737), bk. 2, Epistle 2, l. 72

63 Ye gods! annihilate but space and time.
And make two lovers happy.
The Art of Sinking in Poetry (1727), l. 11

64 A wit with dunces, and a dunce with wits.
The Dunciad (1742), bk. 4, l. 90

65 The Right Divine of Kings to govern wrong.
The Dunciad (1742), bk. 4, l. 187

66 I mount! I fly!
O grave! where is thy victory?
O death! where is thy sting?
The Dying Christian to his Soul (1730)

67 But when at last distracted in his mind,
Forsook by Heaven, forsaking human kind,
Wide o'er the Aleian fields he chose to stray
A long forlorn uncomfortable way,
Woes heaped on woes consumed his wasted heart.
Description of the melancholia of Bellerophon. *The Iliad of Homer* (1715–20)

68 Words sweet as honey from his lips distill'd.
The Iliad of Homer (1715–20), bk. 1, l. 332

69 She moves a goddess, and she looks a queen.
The Iliad of Homer (1715–20), bk. 3, l. 208

70 'Tis man's to fight, but Heaven's to give success.
The Iliad of Homer (1715–20), bk. 6, l. 427

71 A decent boldness ever meets with friends.
The Iliad of Homer (1715–20), bk. 7, l. 67

72 A generous friendship no cold medium knows,
Burns with one love, with one resentment glows.
The Iliad of Homer (1715–20), bk. 9, l. 725

73 Injustice, swift, erect, and unconfin'd,
Sweeps the wide earth, and tramples o'er mankind,
While prayers, to heal her wrongs, move slow behind.
The Iliad of Homer (1715–20), bk. 9, ll. 628–630

74 He serves me most who serves his country best.
The Iliad of Homer (1715–20), bk. 10, l. 201

75 Praise from a friend, or censure from a foe,
Are lost on hearers that our merits know.
The Iliad of Homer (1715–20), bk. 10, l. 293

76 Without a sign his sword the brave man draws,
And asks no omen but his country's cause.
The Iliad of Homer (1715–20), bk. 12, ll. 283–284

77 And seem to walk on wings, and tread in air.
The Iliad of Homer (1715–20), bk. 13, l. 106

78 And for our country 't is a bliss to die.
The Iliad of Homer (1715–20), bk. 15, l. 583

79 Our business in the field of fight
Is not to question, but to prove our might.
The Iliad of Homer (1715–20), bk. 20, l. 304

80 When lo! appear'd along the dusky coasts,
Thin, airy shoals of visionary ghosts;
Fair, pensive youths, and soft-enamour'd maids,
And wither'd Elders, pale and wrinkled shades.
Ulysses consults the ghost of the prophet Tiresias. *The Odyssey of Homer* (1725)

81 Rosy-fingered dawn.
This phrase first appears in book 2, and is used throughout to describe Eos, the goddess of dawn. *The Odyssey of Homer* (1725), bk. 2, l. 1 and elsewhere

82 In youth and beauty wisdom is but rare!
The Odyssey of Homer (1725), bk. 7, l. 379

83 A gen'rous heart repairs a sland'rous tongue.
The Odyssey of Homer (1725), bk. 8, l. 432

84 And pines with thirst amidst a sea of waves.
The Odyssey of Homer (1725), bk. 11, l. 722

85 And what so tedious as a twice-told tale.
The Odyssey of Homer (1725), bk. 12, l. 538

86 He ceas'd; but left so pleasing on their ear
His voice, that list'ning still they seem'd to hear.
The Odyssey of Homer (1725), bk. 13, l. 1

87 How prone to doubt, how cautious are the wise!
The Odyssey of Homer (1725), bk. 13, l. 375

88 And wine can of their wits the wise beguile,
Make the sage frolic, and the serious smile.
The Odyssey of Homer (1725), bk. 14, l. 520

89 And taste
The melancholy joy of evils past:
For he who much has suffer'd, much will know.
The Odyssey of Homer (1725), bk. 15, l. 434

90 For love deceives the best of womankind.
The Odyssey of Homer (1725), bk. 15, l. 463

91 Yet taught by time, my heart has learn'd to glow
For others' good, and melt at others' woe.
The Odyssey of Homer (1725), bk. 17, l. 269

92 Whatever day
Makes man a slave, takes half his worth away.
The Odyssey of Homer (1725), bk. 17, l. 392

93 What dire offence from am'rous causes springs,
What mighty contests rise from trivial things.
The Rape of the Lock (1712), can. 1, ll. 1–2

94 Fair tresses man's imperial race insnare,
And beauty draws us with a single hair.
The Rape of the Lock (1712), can. 2, ll. 27–28

95 The hungry judges soon the sentence sign,
And wretches hang that jury-men may dine.
The Rape of the Lock (1712), can. 3, ll. 21–22

96 Not louder shrieks to pitying heav'n are cast,
When husbands, or when lap-dogs breathe their last.
The Rape of the Lock (1712), can. 3, ll. 157–158

97 Beauties in vain their pretty eyes may roll;
Charms strike the sight, but merit wins the soul.
The Rape of the Lock (1712), can. 5, ll. 33–34

98 Love seldom haunts the breast where learning lies,
And Venus sets ere Mercury can rise.
Written in imitation of Chaucer's *Canterbury Tales*. *The Wife of Bath. Her Prologue*, ll. 369–370, quoted in *The Works of Alexander Pope* (1736)

99 We may see the small value God has for riches, by the people he gives them to.
Thoughts on Various Subjects (1727)

100 The mouse that always trusts to one poor hole
Can never be a mouse of any soul.
1714. Paraphrase of *The Wife of Bath's Prologue* (1387?) by Geoffrey Chaucer. Quoted in *The Works of Alexander Pope* (1736)

Pope, Walter (1630–1714) English astronomer

1 May I govern my passion with absolute sway,
And grow wiser and better as my strength wears away.
The Old Man's Wish (1685?)

Popov, Gavril (Gavril Kharitonovich Popov; b.1936) Russian economist and politician

1 This is a historic moment. Russia has entered the family of civilized nations.
Remark on his election as the first elected mayor of Moscow. *Observer*, London (June 16, 1991)

Popper, Karl, Sir (Karl Raimund Popper; 1902–94) Austrian-born British philosopher

1 Our belief in any particular natural law cannot have a safer basis than our unsuccessful critical attempts to refute it.
Conjectures and Refutations (1963)

2 Our knowledge can only be finite, while our ignorance must necessarily be infinite.
Conjectures and Refutations (1963)

3 Science may be described as the art of systematic over-simplification.
Remark, *Observer*, London (August 1982), quoted in *Sayings of the Eighties* (Jeffrey Care, ed.; 1989)

4 Our civilization...has not yet fully recovered from the shock of its birth—the transition from the tribal or "closed society," with its submission to magical forces, to the "open society" which sets free the critical powers of man.
The Open Society and Its Enemies (1945)

5 There is no history of mankind, there are only many histories of all kinds of aspects of human life. And one of these is the history of political power. This is elevated into the history of the world.
The Open Society and Its Enemies (1945)

6 We may become the makers of our fate when we have ceased to pose as its prophets.
The Open Society and Its Enemies (1945)

7 We must plan for freedom, and not only for security, if for no other reason than that only freedom can make security secure.
The Open Society and Its Enemies (1945)

8 Piecemeal social engineering resembles physical engineering in regarding the *ends* as beyond the province of technology.
The Poverty of Historicism (1957), pt. 3, sect. 21

9 Science must begin with myths, and with the criticism of myths.
Quoted in *British Philosophy in the Mid-Century* (C. A. Mace, ed.; 1957)

Porchia, Antonio Italian-born Argentinian writer

1 Almost always it is the fear of being ourselves that brings us to the mirror.
Voces (W. S. Merwin, tr.; 1968)

2 He who does not fill his world with phantoms remains alone.
Voces (W. S. Merwin, tr.; 1968)

3 If you do not raise your eyes you will think that you are at the highest point.
Voces (W. S. Merwin, tr.; 1968)

4 I know what I have given you. I do not know what you have received.
Voces (W. S. Merwin, tr.; 1968)

5 In a full heart there is room for everything, and in an empty heart there is room for nothing.
Voces (W. S. Merwin, tr.; 1968)

6 No one is a light unto himself, not even the sun.
Voces (W. S. Merwin, tr.; 1968)

7 Now humanity does not know where to go because no one is waiting for it: not even God.
Voces (W. S. Merwin, tr.; 1968)

8 One lives in the hope of becoming a memory.
Voces (W. S. Merwin, tr.; 1968)

9 They will say that you are on the wrong road, if it is your own.
Voces (W. S. Merwin, tr.; 1968)

10 Yes, that is what good is: to forgive evil. There is no other good.
Voces (W. S. Merwin, tr.; 1968)

Porson, Richard (1759–1808) British classical scholar

1 When Dido found Aeneas would not come,
She mourn'd in silence, and was Di-do-dum.
"Epigram: On Latin Gerunds", quoted in *Life of Porson* (J. S. Watson; 1861)

Porter, Cole (Cole Albert Porter; 1893–1964) U.S. songwriter and composer

Quotations about Porter

1 Listen kid, take my advice, never hate a song that has sold half a million copies.
Irving Berlin (1888–1989) Russian-born U.S. composer and lyricist. Giving advice to Cole Porter. Attrib.

Quotations by Porter

2 In olden days, a glimpse of stocking
Was looked on as something shocking,
But now, Heaven knows,
Anything goes.
Song lyric. "Anything Goes," *Anything Goes* (1934)

3 I get no kick from champagne.
Mere alcohol doesn't thrill me at all,
So tell me why should it be true
That I get a kick out of you?
Song lyric. "I Get a Kick Out of You," *Anything Goes* (1934)

4 You're the Nile,
You're the Tower of Pisa,
You're the smile
On the Mona Lisa...
But if, Baby, I'm the bottom you're the top!
Song lyric. "You're the Top," *Anything Goes* (1936)

5 I've Got You Under My Skin
Song title. *Born to Dance* (1936)

6 I love Paris in the springtime.
Song lyric. "I Love Paris," *Can-Can* (1953)

7 Miss Otis regrets she's unable to lunch today.
"Miss Otis Regrets," *Hi Diddle Diddle* (1934)

8 HE Have you heard it's in the stars
Next July we collide with Mars?
SHE Well, did you evah! What a swell party this is.
"Well, Did You Evah!," *High Society* (1956)

9 And we suddenly know, what heaven we're in,
When they begin the beguine.
Song lyric. "Begin the Beguine," *Jubilee* (1935)

10 A trip to the moon on gossamer wings.
"Just One of Those Things," *Jubilee* (1935)

11 It was great fun,
But it was just one of those things.
"Just One of Those Things," *Jubilee* (1935)

12 So goodbye, dear, and amen.
"Just One of Those Things," *Jubilee* (1935)

13 But I'm always true to you, darlin', in my fashion,
Yes, I'm always true to you, darlin', in my way.
Song lyric. "Always True to You in My Fashion," *Kiss Me Kate* (1948)

14 He may have hair upon his chest
But, sister, so has Lassie.
"I Hate Men," *Kiss Me Kate* (1948)

15 My Heart Belongs to Daddy
Song title. *Leave It to Me* (1938)

16 Paris loves lovers.
Song lyric, from the film version of the play *Ninotchka* by Melchior Lengyel. "Silk Stockings," *Ninotchka* (1955)

17 Let's do it; let's fall in love.
Song lyric. "Let's Do It," *Paris* (1928)

18 It's delightful, it's delicious, it's de-lovely.
"It's De-Lovely," *Red, Hot and Blue* (1936)

19 Night and day, you are the one,
Only you beneath the moon and under the sun.
Song lyric. "Night and Day," *The Gay Divorce* (1932)

20 Who Wants to Be a Millionaire?
1956. Song title.

Porter, George, Sir, Baron Porter of Luddenham (b.1920) British chemist

1 Should we force science down the throats of those that have no taste for it? Is it our duty to drag them kicking and screaming into the twenty-first century? I am afraid that it is.
Speech (September 1986)

2 If sunbeams were weapons of war, we would have had solar energy long ago.
Observer, London (August 26, 1973), "Sayings of the Week"

Porter, Katherine Anne (1890–1980) U.S. writer

1 Miracles are instantaneous, they cannot be summoned, but come of themselves, usually at unlikely moments and to those who least expect them.
Ship of Fools (1962), pt. 3

Porter, Mark British physician and broadcaster

1 The first and most important point to remember is that eating should be a pleasure—do not eat purely for health, you won't live much longer, but it will feel like an eternity.
Radio Times, London (July 15, 1994)

Porter, Michael E. (b.1947) U.S. author

1 No nation can be competitive in (and can be a net exporter of) everything.
The Competitive Advantage of Nations (1990)

Porter, Peter (Peter Neville Frederick Porter; b.1929) Australian-born British poet and critic

1 Why hast thou
held talent above my head
and let me see it, O my God?
1981. "Good Ghost, Gaunt Ghost," *English Subtitles* (1992)

2 The copulation
of cats is harrowing; they
are unbearably fond of the moon.
"Two Poems with French Titles," *Preaching to the Converted* (1972)

3 I heard a voice which told me not to grieve,
I heard myself. "Tell them," I said to all,
"I've had a wonderful life. I'm dead."
Ludwig Wittgenstein's last words were "I've had a wonderful life." "Wittgenstein's Dream," *The Chair of Babel* (1992)

4 Language of the liberal dead speaks
From the soil of Highgate, tears
Show a great water table is intact.
You cannot leave England, it turns
A planet majestically in the mind.
"The Last of England," *The Last of England* (1970)

5 Much have I travelled in the realms of gold
for which I thank the Paddington and Westminster
Public Libraries: and I have never said sir
to anyone since I was seventeen years old.
The first line alludes to John Keats's sonnet, "On First Looking into Chapman's Homer" (1816). "The Sanitized Sonnets: 4," *The Last of England* (1970)

Porteus, Beilby (1731–1808) British cleric

1 War its thousands slays, Peace its ten thousands.
"Death" (1759), l. 179

Portland, Duke of, 6th Duke of Portland (William John Arthur Charles James Cavendish-Bentinck; 1857–1943) British peer

1 What! Can't a fellow even enjoy a biscuit any more?
On being informed that as one of several measures to reduce his own expenses he would have to dispense with one of his two Italian pastry cooks. Attrib. *Their Noble Lordships* (Simon Winchester; 1981)

Post, Emily (originally Emily Price; 1872–1960) U.S. writer and columnist

1 Ideal conversation must be an exchange of thought, and not, as many of those who worry most about their shortcomings believe, an eloquent exhibition of wit or oratory.
Etiquette (1922), ch. 6

2 The woman who is chic is always a little different. Not different in being behind fashion, but always slightly apart from it.
Etiquette (1922), ch. 33

3 Lapels are moderately small. Padded shoulders are an abomination. Peg-topped trousers equally bad. If you must be eccentric, save your efforts for the next fancy dress ball, where you may wear what you please, but in your business clothing be reasonable.
Etiquette (1922), ch. 34

4 To the old saying that man built the house but woman made of it a "home" might be added the modern supplement that woman accepted cooking as a chore but man has made of it a recreation.
Etiquette (1922), ch. 34

Poste, George (George Henry Poste; b.1944) British-born U.S. business executive

1 Any economy in which more individuals escape entrapment in sterile, bureaucratic corporate slots or menial roles and expand their potential can be argued to be morally superior.
Speech (June 14, 1997)

Potter, Beatrix (Helen Beatrix Potter; 1866–1943) British children's writer and illustrator

1 Don't go into Mr McGregor's garden: your Father had an accident there; he was put in a pie by Mrs McGregor.
The Tale of Peter Rabbit (1900 edition)

2 I shall tell you a tale of four little rabbits whose names were Flopsy, Mopsy, Cottontail and Peter.
The Tale of Peter Rabbit (1900 edition)

Potter, Dennis (Dennis Christopher George Potter; 1935–94) British playwright

1 Religion has always been the wound, not the bandage.
Observer, London (April 10, 1994), "Sayings of the Week"

Potter, Henry Codman (1835–1908) U.S. bishop

1 We have exchanged the Washingtonian dignity for the Jeffersonian simplicity, which in due time came to be only another name for the Jacksonian vulgarity.
Speech, Washington, D.C. (April 30, 1889)

Potter, Stephen (Stephen Meredith Potter; 1900–69) British writer

1 It is an important general rule always to refer to your friend's country establishment as a "cottage".
Lifemanship (1950), ch. 2

2 Donsmanship..."the art of criticizing without actually listening."
Lifemanship (1950), ch. 6

3 *How to be one up*—how to make the other man feel that something has gone wrong, however slightly.
Lifemanship (1950), Introduction

4 A good general rule is to state that the bouquet is better than the taste, and vice versa.
One-Upmanship (1952), ch. 14

5 It is WRONG to do what everyone else does—namely, to hold the wine list just out of sight, look for the second cheapest claret on the list, and say, "Number 22, please."
One-Upmanship (1952), ch. 14

6 Gamesmanship or The Art of Winning Games Without Actually Cheating
1947. Book title.

Pound, Ezra (Ezra Loomis Pound; 1885–1972) U.S. poet, translator, and critic

Quotations about Pound

1 Pound's crazy. All poets are...They have to be. You don't put a poet like Pound in the loony bin. For history's sake we shouldn't keep him there.
Ernest Hemingway (1899–1961) U.S. writer. Referring to Ezra Pound, who was arrested for treason in 1945, and then confined to a mental hospital until 1958. Quoted in *New York Post* (Leonard Lyons; January 24, 1957)

Quotations by Pound

2 Bah! I have sung women in three cities,
But it is all the same;
And I will sing of the sun.
"Cino" (1908)

3 Any general statement is like a check drawn on a bank. Its value depends on what is there to meet it.
ABC of Reading (1934), ch. 1

4 Literature is news that STAYS news.
ABC of Reading (1934), ch. 1

5 One of the pleasures of middle age is to *find out* that one WAS right, and that one was much righter than one knew at say 17 or 23.
ABC of Reading (1934), ch. 1

6 Real education must ultimately be limited to one who INSISTS on knowing, the rest is mere sheep-herding.
ABC of Reading (1934), ch. 8

7 Music begins to atrophy when it departs too far from the dance;...poetry begins to atrophy when it gets too far from music.
"Warning," *ABC of Reading* (1934)

8 And even I can remember
A day when the historians left blanks in their writings,
I mean for things they didn't know.
Cantos (1954), 13

9 The difference between a gun and a tree is a difference of tempo. The tree explodes every spring.
Criterion (July 1937)

10 As cool as the pale wet leaves
of lily-of-the-valley
She lay beside me in the dawn.
"A Pact," *Dramatis Personae* (1926), quoted in *The Penguin Book of American Verse* (Geoffrey Moore, ed.; 1977)

11 The apparition of these faces in the crowd;
Petals on a wet black bough.
"In a Station of the Metro," *Dramatis Personae* (1926), quoted in *The Penguin Book of American Verse* (Geoffrey Moore, ed.; 1977)

12 Great Literature is simply language charged with meaning to the utmost possible degree.
How to Read (1931), pt. 2

13 For three years, out of key with his time,
He strove to resuscitate the dead art
Of poetry to maintain "the sublime"
In the old sense. Wrong from the start.
"E. P. Ode pour l'élection de son sépulcre," *Hugh Selwyn Mauberley* (1920), pt. 1

14 Died some, pro patria,
non "dulce" non "et decor."
"E. P. Ode pour l'élection de son sépulcre," *Hugh Selwyn Mauberley* (1920), pt. 4

15 There died a myriad,
And of the best, among them,
For an old bitch gone in the teeth,
For a botched civilization.
"E. P. Ode pour l'élection de son sépulcre," *Hugh Selwyn Mauberley* (1920), pt. 5

16 The age demanded an image
Of its accelerated grimace,
Something for the modern stage,
Not, at any rate, an Attic grace.
"Life and Contacts," *Hugh Selwyn Mauberley* (1920), quoted in *The Penguin Book of American Verse* (Geoffrey Moore, ed.; 1977)

17 Winter is icummen in,
Lhude sing Goddamm,
Raineth drop and staineth slop

And how the wind doth ramm!
Sing: Goddamm.
A parody of the Middle English lyric "Sumer is icumen in" (1250?). "Ancient Music," *Lustra* (1917)

18 I make a pact with you, Walt Whitman
I have detested you long enough
It was you that broke the new wood,
Now is a time for carving
We have one sap and one root
Let there be commerce between us.
"A Pact," *Lustra* (1916)

19 What thou lovest well remains,
the rest is dross
What thou lov'st well shall not be reft from thee
What thou lov'st well is thy true heritage.
Pisan Cantos (1948)

20 Usura rusteth the chisel
It rusteth the craft and the craftsman.
1937. "Usura" means usury in Latin. *The Cantos* (1976), can. 45

21 And then went down to the ship,
Set keel to the breakers, forth on the godly sea.
1925. *The Cantos* (1976), can. 1

22 Every popular song has at least one line or sentence that is perfectly clear—the line that fits the music.
Attrib.

Poussin, Nicolas (1594–1665) French painter

1 Colors in painting are like allurements for persuading the eyes, as the sweetness of meter functions in poetry.
Quoted in *Lives of the Modern Painters, Sculptors and Architects* (Giovanni Pietro Bellori; 1672)

2 Painting is nothing but the image of incorporeal things, despite the fact that it depicts bodies, for it represents only the arrangements, proportions and shapes of things and is more concerned with the idea of beauty than any other.
Quoted in *Lives of the Modern Painters, Sculptors and Architects* (Giovanni Pietro Bellori; 1672)

3 The idea of beauty does not descend into matter unless this is prepared as carefully as possible.
Reported in *Lives of the Modern Painters, Sculptors and Architects* (Giovanni Pietro Bellori; 1672)

Powell, Adam Clayton, Jr. (1908–72) U.S. clergyman and civil rights leader

1 Black power does not mean violence, but it does not mean total nonviolence. It does not mean that you walk with a chip on your shoulder, but you walk letting the chips fly where they may.
Adam By Adam (1971)

2 A man's respect for law and order exists in precise relationship to the size of his paycheck.
"Black Power: A Form of Godly Power," *Keep the Faith, Baby* (1967)

3 Faith is a risk and a gamble. Absolute certainty can never be faith.
"Palm Sunday," *Keep the Faith, Baby* (1967)

4 We have produced a world of contented bodies and discontented minds.
"The Temptations of Modernity," *Keep the Faith, Baby* (1967)

5 It was not a riot. It was an open, unorganized protest against empty stomachs, overcrowded tenements, filthy sanitation, rotten foodstuffs, and chiseling landlords. It was not caused by Communists.
Referring to protests in Harlem, New York City. Letter to the editor, *New York Post* (1935)

Powell, Anthony (Anthony Dymoke Powell; 1905–2000) British novelist

1 Parents are sometimes a bit of a disappointment to their children. They don't fulfil the promise of their early years.
A Buyer's Market (1952), ch. 2

2 A Dance to the Music of Time
1951–75. The title of a series of novels, taken from the title of a painting by Nicolas Poussin.

Powell, Colin (Colin Luther Powell; b.1937) U.S. military commander

Quotations about Powell

1 Richard Wright wrote famously that the Negro is America's metaphor. Now we have Colin Powell as a metaphor for consolidation and O. J. as a metaphor for division.
Henry Louis Gates (b.1950) U.S. author and educator. At this time General Colin Powell, former chairman of the Joint Chiefs of Staff (1989–93), was being suggested as a possible Republican presidential candidate; O. J. Simpson, football player and actor, was being tried for the murder of his ex-wife. *New York Times* (October 5, 1995)

Quotations by Powell

2 But trust me.
During Operation Desert Storm. Remark to journalists (1991)

3 Leadership is the art of accomplishing more than the science of management says is possible.
A Soldier's Way (1995)

4 Avoid having your ego so close to your position that when your position falls, your ego goes with it.
"Colin Powell's Rules," *Parade* (August 1989)

5 Get mad, then get over it.
"Colin Powell's Rules," *Parade* (August 1989)

6 Our strategy in going after this army is very simple. First we are going to cut it off, and then we are going to *kill* it.
Referring to the Iraqi military during Operation Desert Storm (1991). Remark, *U.S. News and World Report* (February 4, 1991)

Powell, Enoch (John Enoch Powell; 1912–98) British politician

1 As I look ahead, I am filled with foreboding. Like the Roman, I seem to see "the River Tiber foaming with much blood".
Talking about immigration at the annual meeting of the West Midlands Area Conservative Political Association. Speech, Birmingham (April 20, 1968)

2 History is littered with all the wars which everybody knew would never happen.
Speech to the Conservative Party Conference (October 19, 1967)

3 All political lives, unless they are cut off in mid-stream at a

happy juncture, end in failure, because that is the nature of politics and of human affairs.
Joseph Chamberlain (1977)

Powell, John, Sir (1645–1713) English judge

1 Let us consider the reason of the case. For nothing is law that is not reason.
Coggs v. Bernard, *Reports* (Lord Raymond; 1765), vol. 2

Powell, John Wesley (1834–1902) U.S. ethnologist, geologist, and explorer

1 Fetiches may be fragments of bone or shell, the tips of the tails of animals, the claws of birds or beasts, perhaps dried hearts of little warblers, shards of beetles, leaves powdered and held in bags, or crystals from the rocks—anything curious may become a fetich.
"Sketch of the Mythology of the North American Indians," *First Annual Report of the Bureau of Ethnology* (1881)

2 In the production of a philosophy, phenomena must be *discerned*, *discriminated*, *classified*...A philosophy will be higher in the scale, nearer the truth, as the discernment is wider, the discrimination nicer, and the classification better.
"Sketch of the Mythology of the North American Indians," *First Annual Report of the Bureau of Ethnology* (1881)

3 In *Ute*, falling stars are the excrements of dirty little star-gods. In science—well, I do not know what falling stars are in science. I think they are cinders from the furnace where the worlds are forged. You may call this mythologic or scientific, as you please.
"Sketch of the Mythology of the North American Indians," *First Annual Report of the Bureau of Ethnology* (1881)

4 The savage is a positive man; the scientist is a doubting man.
"Sketch of the Mythology of the North American Indians," *First Annual Report of the Bureau of Ethnology* (1881)

5 The scalping scene is no more the true picture of savagery than the bayonet charge of civilization.
"Sketch of the Mythology of the North American Indians," *First Annual Report of the Bureau of Ethnology* (1881)

Powell, Michael (1905–90) British filmmaker

1 A dancer is rather like a nun. Not a nun like we had in *Black Narcissus*, but a devotee.
A Life in Movies (1986)

2 Of course all films are surrealist. They are making something that looks like the real world but isn't.
Quoted in *Halliwell's Filmgoer's Companion* (Leslie Halliwell; 1993)

Powys, John Cowper (1872–1963) British novelist, essayist, and poet

1 Ambition is the grand enemy of all peace.
The Meaning of Culture (1929)

2 Who has not watched a mother stroke her child's cheek or kiss her child *in a certain way* and felt a nervous shudder at the possessive outrage done to a free solitary human soul?
The Meaning of Culture (1929)

Praed, Winthrop (Winthrop Mackworth Praed; 1802–39) British poet

1 I remember, I remember
How my childhood fleeted by,—
The mirth of its December
And the warmth of its July.
"I remember, I remember" (1840?)

Prahalad, C. K. (Coimbatore Krishna Prahalad; b.1941) U.S. management writer

1 Mentoring requires special skills, but it does not require hierarchical position.
Interview, *Strategy and Business* (1996)

2 If you think about strategy as revolution...then you must acknowledge that no monarchy has ever fomented its own revolution. In other words, senior management does not have a great propensity for change.
1996. Attrib.

Pratt, Sir Charles, 1st Earl Camden (1714–94) British jurist and politician

1 The British parliament has no right to tax the Americans...Taxation and representation are inseparably united.
Speech in the upper chamber of the British Parliament (December 1765)

Prescott, William (1726–95) U.S. soldier

1 Don't fire until you see the whites of their eyes.
Command given at the Battle of Bunker Hill (1775)

Presley, Elvis (Elvis Aaron Presley; 1935–77) U.S. pop singer

1 I learned very early in life that: "Without a song, the day would never end; without a song, a man ain't got a friend; without a song, the road would never bend—without a song." So I keep singing a song. Goodnight. Thank you.
Acceptance speech, Ten Outstanding Young Men of the Year Awards (January 16, 1971)

2 When I was a child...I was a dreamer. I read comic books, and I was the hero of the comic book. I saw movies, and I was the hero in the movie. So every dream I ever dreamed has come true a hundred times.
Acceptance speech, Ten Outstanding Young Men of the Year Awards (January 16, 1971)

3 Some people tap their feet, some people snap their fingers, and some people sway back and forth. I just sorta do 'em all together, I guess.
Quoted in *Down at the End of Lonely Street: the Life and Death of Elvis Presley* (Pat S. Broeske and Peter Harry Brown; 1998)

4 I have no use for bodyguards, but I have very specific use for two highly trained certified public accountants.
Quoted in "Don't Play Golf with Richard Branson," *Expensive Habits: the Dark Side of the Music Industry* (Simon Garfield; 1986)

5 The image is one thing and a human being is another...It's very hard to live up to an image, put it that way.
1972. Attrib.

Press, Frank (b.1924) U.S. geophysicist

1 In a nation whose people depend on scientific progress for their health, economic gains, and national security, it is of the utmost importance that our students understand science.
Science and Creationism: A View from the National Academy of Sciences, Committee on Science and Creationism (1984), preface

Prévert, Jacques (1900–77) French poet and screenwriter

1 I am the way I am
That is the way I'm made.
"Je suis comme je suis," *Paroles* (1946)

2 Our Father which art in heaven
Stay there
And we shall stay on earth.
"Pater Noster," *Paroles* (1946)

3 Those who die of boredom on Sunday afternoon
because they see ahead of them Monday
and Tuesday, and Wednesday, and Thursday, and Friday
and Saturday
and Sunday afternoon.
"Tentative de description d'un dîner de têtes à Paris-France," *Paroles* (1946)

Previn, André (André George Previn; b.1929) German-born U.S. conductor and composer

1 The basic difference between classical music and jazz is that in the former the music is always greater than its performance—whereas the way jazz is performed is always more important than what is being played.
1967. Quoted in "A Performer's Art," *Serious Music and All That Jazz* (Henry Pleasants; 1969)

Price, Don K. (1915–?) U.S. scientist

1 Science...cannot exist on the basis of a treaty of strict nonaggression with the rest of society; from either side, there is no defensible frontier.
Science and Government (1954)

Price, Leontyne (Mary Leontyne Price; b.1927) U.S. opera singer

1 Accomplishments have no color.
I Dream a World: Portraits of Black Women Who Changed America (Brian Lanker; 1989)

2 Once you get on stage, everything is right. I feel the most beautiful, complete, fulfilled. I think that's why, in the case of noncompromising career women, parts of our personal lives don't work out. One person can't give you the feeling that thousands of people give you.
Quoted in *I Dream a World: Portraits of Black Women Who Changed America* (Brian Lanker; 1989)

Priestland, Gerald British broadcaster and writer

1 Journalists belong in the gutter because that is where ruling classes throw their guilty secrets.
Times, London (May 22, 1988)

Priestley, J. B. (John Boynton Priestley; 1894–1984) British writer

Quotations about Priestley

1 Playing a fuddled fiddle, somewhere in the muddled middle.
Aneurin Bevan (1897–1960) Welsh politician. Attrib.

Quotations by Priestley

2 Those no-sooner-have-I-touched-the-pillow people are past my comprehension. There is something bovine about them.
All About Ourselves (1956)

3 The first fall of snow is not only an event, it is a magical event. You go to bed in one kind of world and wake up in another quite different, and if this is not enchantment then where is it to be found?
Apes and Angels (1928)

4 Comedy, we may say, is society protecting itself—with a smile.
George Meredith (1926)

5 I have always been a grumbler. I am designed for the part—sagging face, weighty underlip, rumbling, resonant voice. Money couldn't buy a better grumbling outfit.
Guardian, London (August 15, 1984)

6 A novelist who writes nothing for 10 years finds his reputation rising. Because I keep on producing books they say there must be something wrong with this fellow.
Observer, London (September 21, 1969), "Sayings of the Week"

7 There are plenty of clever young writers. But there is too much genius, not enough talent.
Observer, London (September 29, 1968), "Sayings of the Week"

8 The greater part of critics are parasites, who, if nothing had been written, would find nothing to write.
Outcries and Asides (1974)

9 A loving wife will do anything for her husband except stop criticising and trying to improve him.
Rain on Godshill (1939)

10 History that ignores the god and the altar is as false as history that could forget the sword and the wheel.
The Linden Tree (1948), Act 2, Scene 2

11 The point is to be good—to be sensitive and sincere.
Time and the Conways (1937), Act 3

12 I know only two words of American slang, "swell" and "lousy." I think "swell" is lousy, but "lousy" is swell.
U.S. radio broadcast. Attrib.

Priestley, Joseph (1733–1804) British theologian and scientist

1 More is owing to what we call *chance*, that is, philosophically speaking, to the observation of events arising from *unknown causes*, than to any proper *design*, or pre-conceived theory of the business.
Experiments and Observations of Different Types of Air (1775)

Primo de Rivera, José Antonio (1903–36) Spanish politician

1 Fire—without hatred.
1936. Giving the order to open fire at the siege of the Alcázar, the fortress above Toledo, occupied by Nationalists during the Spanish Civil War. Quoted in *The Siege of the Alcázar* (C. Eby; 1965)

Primus, Pearl (1919–94) Trinidadian-born U.S. dancer, choreographer, and anthropologist

1 I dance not to entertain but to help people better understand each other...Because through dance I have experienced the wordless joy of freedom, I seek it more fully now for my people and for all people everywhere.
Referring to being black and a dancer. Quoted in *Black Dance* (Edward Thorpe; 1989)

Prince (Prince Rogers Nelson, the artist formerly known as Prince; b.1958) U.S. rock singer and songwriter

1 When I'm recording I could have orgasm on my mind and my bass player could have pickles on his. It makes it a little rough when you listen back to a track and it's not played with the same intensity.
Quoted in *The Wit and Wisdom of Rock and Roll* (Maxim Jabukowski, ed.; 1983)

Prince, Mary (1788?–1833?) Bermudan slave, editor, and writer

1 I dearly loved to go to the church, it was so solemn. I never knew rightly that I had much sin till I went there. When I found out that I was a great sinner, I was very sorely grieved, and very much frightened.
The History of Mary Prince, A West Indian Slave, Related by Herself (1831), quoted in *Six Women's Slave Narratives* (William L. Andrews, ed.; 1988)

Prior, Matthew (1664–1721) English diplomat and poet

1 Be to her virtues very kind;
Be to her faults a little blind;
Let all her ways be unconfined;
And clap your padlock—on her mind.
"An English Padlock" (1705), ll. 79–82

2 No, no; for my virginity,
When I lose that, says Rose, I'll die:
Behind the elms last night, cried Dick,
Rose, were you not extremely sick?
"A True Maid" (1718)

3 That if weak women went astray,
Their stars were more in fault than they.
"Hans Carvel" (1701)

4 The end must justify the means.
"Hans Carvel" (1701)

5 That air and harmony of shape express,
Fine by degrees, and beautifully less.
"Henry and Emma" (1708)

6 For the idiom of words very little she heeded,
Provided the matter she drove at succeeded,
She took and gave languages just as she needed.
"Jinny the Just" (1700?)

7 Who breathes must suffer, and who thinks must mourn;
And he alone is bless'd who ne'er was born.
"Solomon on the Vanity of the World" (1718), bk. 2, l. 240

8 Venus, take my votive glass;
Since I am not what I was,
What from this day I shall be,
Venus, let me never see.
"The Lady who Offers her Looking-Glass to Venus" (1718)

9 Cur'd yesterday of my disease,
I died last night of my physician.
"The Remedy Worse than the Disease" (1727)

10 Our hopes, like towering falcons, aim
At objects in an airy height;
The little pleasure of the game
Is from afar to view the flight.
"To the Hon. Charles Montague" (1692)

11 From ignorance our comfort flows,
The only wretched are the wise.
"To the Hon. Charles Montague" (1692), st. 9

12 They never taste who always drink;
They always talk who never think.
"Upon a Passage in the Scaligerana" (1740)

13 Of two evils I have chose the least.
Ode in Imitation of Horace (1692)

14 Virtue is its own reward.
Ode in Imitation of Horace (1692)

15 For hope is but the dream of those that wake.
Solomon (1718), bk. 2

16 What is a King?—a man condemned to bear
The public burden of the nation's care.
Solomon (1718), bk. 3, ll. 275–276

Pritchett, V. S., Sir (Victor Sawden Pritchett; 1900–97) British writer

1 The detective novel is the art-for-art's-sake of yawning Philistinism.
"Books in General," *New Statesman*, London (June 16, 1951)

Prochnow, Herbert V. (Herbert Victor Prochnow; b.1897) U.S. writer

1 Inexperience is what makes a young man do what an older man says is impossible.
Saturday Evening Post (December 4, 1948)

2 The best salesman we ever heard of was the one who sold two milking machines to a farmer who had only one cow. Then this salesman helped finance the deal by taking the cow as a down payment on the two milking machines.
Attrib. (Rolf White; 1987)

Proclus (410?–485) Greek philosopher

1 I am the things that are, and those that are to be, and those that have been. No one ever lifted my skirts; the fruit which I bore was the sun.
Inscription in the temple of Neith at Sais, Egypt. "On Plato's Timaeus" (5th century)

Procter, Adelaide Ann (pseudonym of Mary Berwick; 1825–64) British poet and writer

1 Seated one day at the organ,
I was weary and ill at ease,
And my fingers wandered idly
Over the noisy keys.
...
But I struck one chord of music,
Like the sound of a great Amen.

Best known in the song setting by Sir Arthur Sullivan. "A Lost Chord," *Legends and Lyrics* (1858)

Procter, Bryan Waller (pen name Barry Cornwall; 1787–1874) British poet

1 I'm on the sea! I 'm on the sea!
I am where I would ever be,
With the blue above and the blue below,
And silence wheresoe'er I go.

"The Sea" (1851)

2 I never was on the dull, tame shore,
But I loved the great sea more and more.

"The Sea" (1851)

Profumo, John (John Dennis Profumo; b.1915) British politician

1 There was no impropriety whatsoever in my acquaintanceship with Miss Keeler.

Referring to accusations of an affair with Christine Keeler, who had simultaneously been involved with a Russian naval attaché. Speech to the British Parliament (March 22, 1963)

2 I shall not hesitate to issue writs for libel and slander if scandalous allegations are made or repeated outside the House.

Referring to Parliamentary Privilege, which grants British members of Parliament immunity from prosecution for libel and slander for allegations made inside the House of Commons. Speech to the British parliament (March 22, 1963)

Propertius, Sextus (50? –15? B.C.) Roman poet

1 The seaman tells stories of winds, the plowman of bulls; the soldier details his wounds, the shepherd his sheep.

Elegies (1st century B.C.), bk. 2, no. 1, l. 43

2 Even if strength fail, boldness at least will deserve praise: in great endeavors even to have had the will is enough.

Elegies (1st century B.C.), bk. 2, no. 10, l. 5

3 Make way, you Roman writers, make way, Greeks! Something greater than the *Iliad* is born.

Referring to Virgil's *Aeneid*. *Elegies* (1st century B.C.), bk. 2, no. 34

Prost, Alain (b.1955) French racing car driver

1 When you start off as a driver, it is a sport; but when you get into Formula One, it suddenly becomes a job.

Sunday Telegraph, London (June 18, 1989)

2 There's nothing natural about Formula One—I can't stand the artificiality.

Sunday Times, London (July 22, 1984)

Protagoras (480? –411? B.C.) Greek philosopher

1 Concerning the gods I have no means of knowing either that they exist or that they do not exist nor what sort of form they have.

"On the Gods" (5th century B.C.)

2 Man is the measure of all things: of those which are, that they are; of those which are not, that they are not.

Quoted in *Theaetetus* (Plato; 450? B.C.), 160

Proudhon, Pierre Joseph (1809–65) French writer and political theorist

1 It is a proof of philosophical mediocrity, today, to look for a philosophy.

La Révolution sociale (1852)

2 Property is theft.

Qu'est-ce que la propriété (1840), ch.1

Proulx, E. Annie (b.1935) U.S. writer

1 The part of Quoyle that was wonderful was, unfortunately, attached to the rest of him.

Referring to his penis. "Love Knot," *The Shipping News* (1993), ch. 2

2 The Bay crawled with whitecaps like maggots seething in a broad wound.

"Oil," *The Shipping News* (1993), ch. 25

3 The father saw other failures multiply like an explosion of virulent cells—failure to speak clearly; failure to sit up straight; failure to get up in the morning; failure in attitude; failure in ambition and ability; indeed in everything.

"Quoyle," *The Shipping News* (1993), ch. 1

4 If you get the landscape right, the characters will step out of it, and they'll be in the right place.

Time (November 29, 1993)

Proust, Marcel (1871–1922) French novelist

Quotations about Proust

1 Creating is harrowing business. I work in a state of anguish all year. I shut myself up, don't go out. It's a hard life, which is why I understand Proust so well; I have such an admiration for what he has written about the agony of creation.

Yves Saint Laurent (b.1936) Algerian-born French couturier. Quoted in *The Fashion Conspiracy* (Nicholas Coleridge; 1989)

2 Reading Proust is like bathing in someone else's dirty water.

Alexander Woollcott (1887–1943) U.S. writer and critic. Attrib.

Quotations by Proust

3 A smile that floated without support in the air.

À la recherche du temps perdu (1913–27)

4 As soon as one is unhappy one becomes moral.

1918. À l'ombre des jeunes filles en fleurs, *À la recherche du temps perdu* (1913–27)

5 In theory one is aware that the earth revolves but in practice one does not perceive it, the ground on which one treads seems not to move, and one can live undisturbed. So it is with Time in one's life.

1918. À l'ombre des jeunes filles en fleurs, *À la recherche du temps perdu* (1913–27)

6 The human face is indeed, like the face of the God of some

Oriental theogony, a whole cluster of faces, crowded together but on different surfaces so that one does not see them all at once.
1918. À l'ombre des jeunes filles en fleurs, *À la recherche du temps perdu* (1913–27)

7 There can be no peace of mind in love, since the advantage one has secured is never anything but a fresh starting point for further desires.
1918. À l'ombre des jeunes filles en fleurs, *À la recherche du temps perdu* (1913–27)

8 People often say that, by pointing out to a man the faults of his mistress, you succeed only in strengthening his attachment to her, because he does not believe you; yet how much more so if he does!
1913. Du côté de chez Swann, *À la recherche du temps perdu* (1913–27)

9 The taste was that of the little crumb of madeleine which on Sunday mornings at Combray...when I used to say good-day to her in her bedroom, my aunt Léonie used to give me, dipping it first in her own cup of real or of lime-flower tea.
1913. Du côté de chez Swann, *À la recherche du temps perdu* (1913–27)

10 It is seldom indeed that one parts on good terms, because if one were on good terms one would not part.
1923. La Prisonnière, *À la recherche du temps perdu* (1913–27)

11 A doctor who doesn't say too many foolish things is a patient half-cured, just as a critic is a poet who has stopped writing verse and a policeman a burglar who has retired from practice.
1921. Le Côté de Guermantes, *À la recherche du temps perdu* (1913–27)

12 A PUSHING LADY What are your views on love?
MME. LEROI Love? I make it constantly but I never talk about it.
1921. Le Côté de Guermantes, *À la recherche du temps perdu* (1913–27)

13 As soon as he ceased to be mad he became merely stupid. There are maladies we must not seek to cure because they alone protect us from others that are more serious.
1921. Le Côté de Guermantes, *À la recherche du temps perdu* (1913–27)

14 Everything great in the world is done by neurotics; they alone founded our religions and created our masterpieces.
1921. Le Côté de Guermantes, *À la recherche du temps perdu* (1913–27)

15 His hatred of snobs was a derivative of his snobbishness, but made the simpletons (in other words, everyone) believe that he was immune from snobbishness.
1921. Le Côté de Guermantes, *À la recherche du temps perdu* (1913–27)

16 It has been said that the highest praise of God consists in the denial of Him by the atheist, who finds creation so perfect that he can dispense with a creator.
1921. Le Côté de Guermantes, *À la recherche du temps perdu* (1913–27)

17 It is in moments of illness that we are compelled to recognize that we live not alone but chained to a creature of a different kingdom, whole worlds apart, who has no knowledge of us and by whom it is impossible to make ourselves understood: our body.
1921. Le Côté de Guermantes, *À la recherche du temps perdu* (1913–27)

18 Neurosis has an absolute genius for malingering. There is no illness which it cannot counterfeit perfectly...If it is capable of deceiving the doctor, how should it fail to deceive the patient?
1921. Le Côté de Guermantes, *À la recherche du temps perdu* (1913–27)

19 Happiness is beneficial for the body, but it is grief that develops the powers of the mind.
1927. Le Temps Retrouvé, *À la recherche du temps perdu* (1913–27)

20 The true paradises are the paradises that we have lost.
1927. Le Temps Retrouvé, *À la recherche du temps perdu* (1913–27)

21 Distances are only the relation of space to time and vary with that relation.
1921. Sodome et Gomorrhe, *À la recherche du temps perdu* (1913–27)

22 Good-bye, I've barely said a word to you, it is always like that at parties, we never see the people, we never say the things we should like to say, but it is the same everywhere in this life. Let us hope that when we are dead things will be better arranged.
1921. Sodome et Gomorrhe, *À la recherche du temps perdu* (1913–27)

23 I have a horror of sunsets, they're so romantic, so operatic.
1921. Sodome et Gomorrhe, *À la recherche du temps perdu* (1913–27)

24 I have sometimes regretted living so close to Marie...because I may be very fond of her, but I am not quite so fond of her company.
1921. Sodome et Gomorrhe, *À la recherche du temps perdu* (1913–27)

Proverbs

1 A good case is not difficult to state.
African (Ashanti) proverb.

2 One falsehood spoils a thousand truths.
African (Ashanti) proverb.

3 Choose your neighbor before you buy your house.
African (Hausa) proverb.

4 Silence is talk too.
African (Hausa) proverb.

5 An axe is sharp on soft wood.
African (Ovambo) proverb.

6 Hate has no medicine.
African (Ovambo) proverb.

7 The death of many is not wailed.
African (Ovambo) proverb.

8 The tongue is harder than the stick.
African (Ovambo) proverb.

9 If you chase two hares one will escape.
African (Shona) proverb.

10 A fault confessed is half redressed.
African (Swahili) proverb.

11 Better to stumble with the toe than with the tongue.
African (Swahili) proverb.

12 If a snake bites your neighbor, you too are in danger.
African (Swahili) proverb.

13 If you destroy a bridge be sure you can swim.
African (Swahili) proverb.

14 Smooth seas do not make skillful sailors.
African (Swahili) proverb.

15 When poverty crosses the threshold love flies out the window.
African (Swahili) proverb.

16 Ashes fly back in the face of him that throws them.
African (Yoruba) proverb.

17 Benefits make a man a slave.
Arabic proverb.

18 Better a thousand enemies outside the house than one inside.
Arabic proverb.

19 Do not stand in a place of danger trusting in miracles.
Arabic proverb.

20 If you have much, give of your wealth; if you have little, give of your heart.
Arabic proverb.

21 A bit of fragrance always clings to the hand that gives you roses.
Chinese proverb.

22 A truly great man never puts away the simplicity of a child.
Chinese proverb.

23 A wise man makes his own decisions, an ignorant man follows the public opinion.
Chinese proverb.

24 Be not afraid of growing slowly, be afraid only of standing still.
Chinese proverb.

25 Better a live beggar than a dead king.
Chinese proverb.

26 Do not remove a fly from your friend's forehead with a hatchet.
Chinese proverb.

27 Don't climb a tree to look for fish.
Chinese proverb.

28 Don't curse the darkness—light a candle.
Chinese proverb.

29 Every book must be chewed to get out its juice.
Chinese proverb.

30 Get the coffin ready and the man won't die.
Chinese proverb.

31 He who has seen little marvels much.
Chinese proverb.

32 If you want your dinner, don't offend the cook.
Chinese proverb.

33 It is easier to visit your friends than to live with them.
Chinese proverb.

34 Learning is a treasure which accompanies its owner everywhere.
Chinese proverb.

35 Man fools himself. He prays for a long life, and he fears an old age.
Chinese proverb.

36 One does not insult the river god while crossing the river.
Chinese proverb.

37 One joy scatters a hundred griefs.
Chinese proverb.

38 Only the rich have distant relatives.
Chinese proverb.

39 Talk doesn't cook rice.
Chinese proverb.

40 The conquerors are kings; the defeated are bandits.
Chinese proverb.

41 The dog in the kennel barks at his fleas; the dog that hunts does not feel them.
Chinese proverb.

42 The rich add riches to riches; the poor add years to years.
Chinese proverb.

43 The tongue is like a sharp knife; it kills without drawing blood.
Chinese proverb.

44 When you want to test the depths of a stream, don't use both feet.
Chinese proverb.

45 Win your lawsuit and lose your money.
Chinese proverb.

46 You can't clap with one hand.
Chinese proverb.

47 A tyrannical sultan is better than constant anarchy.
Egyptian proverb.

48 Even a crust is bread.
Finnish proverb.

49 Even a small star shines in the darkness.
Finnish proverb.

50 Everything passes, everything perishes, everthing palls.
French proverb.

51 Who has never tasted what is bitter does not know what is sweet.
German proverb.

52 Old men are twice children.
Greek proverb.

53 Hunger will make a monkey eat pepper.
Haitian proverb.

54 Buttered bread always falls dry side up.
Hebrew proverb.

55 In the hour of distress, a vow; in the hour of release, forgetfulness.
Hebrew proverb.

56 Once a man repents, stop reminding him of what he did.
Hebrew proverb.

57 Stains are not seen at night.
Hebrew proverb.

58 The absent are always to blame.
Hebrew proverb.

59 There is no such thing as boneless meat.
Hebrew proverb.

60 To be a critic is easier than to be an author.
Hebrew proverb.

61 Wine in, secret out.
Hebrew proverb.

62 Anger has no eyes.
Hindustani proverb.

63 The world befriends the elephant and tramples on the ant.
Hindustani proverb.

64 Two are an army against one.
Icelandic proverb.

65 A meal without flesh is like feeding on grass.
Indian proverb.

66 In illness the physician is a father; in convalescence a friend; when health is restored, he is a guardian.
Indian proverb.

67 If fortune turns against you, even jelly breaks your tooth.
Iranian proverb.

68 The mud that you throw will fall on your own head.
Iranian proverb.

69 When its time has arrived, the prey goes to the hunter.
Iranian proverb.

70 Death never comes too late.
Irish proverb.

71 One look before is better than two behind.
Irish proverb.

72 The friend that can be bought is not worth having.
Irish proverb.

73 A cask of wine works more miracles than a church full of saints.
Italian proverb.

74 Break the legs of an evil custom.
Italian proverb.

75 Curses like chickens come home to roost.
Jamaican proverb.

76 It's the willing horse they saddle the most.
Jamaican proverb.

77 Too many cousins ruin the shopkeeper.
Jamaican proverb.

78 Heroes cannot stand side by side.
Japanese proverb.

79 Money grows on the tree of patience.
Japanese proverb.

80 Numerous words show scanty wares.
Japanese proverb.

81 One kind word can warm three winter months.
Japanese proverb.

82 When the time comes, even a rat becomes a tiger.
Japanese proverb.

83 An unlettered king is a crowned ass.
Latin proverb.

84 Beware of the man of one book.
Latin proverb.

85 Better one word less than one too many.
Maltese proverb.

86 The land is a mother that never dies.
Maori proverb.

87 Show not your teeth when you are unable to bite.
Mexican proverb.

88 You are sure to find another cross if you flee the one you bear.
Mexican proverb.

89 None sigh deeper than those who have no troubles.
Norwegian proverb.

90 The sleep of kings is on an anthill.
Pashto proverb.

91 Kissin' wears out. Cookin' don't.
Pennsylvania Dutch proverb.

92 He who has been bitten by a snake fears a piece of string.
Persian proverb.

93 A guilty conscience needs no accuser.
Philippine proverb.

94 Suspicion always haunts the guilty mind.
Philippine proverb.

95 A bad penny always turns up.
Proverb.

96 A bad workman always blames his tools.
Proverb.

97 A bird in the hand is worth two in the bush.
Proverb.

98 Absence makes the heart grow fonder.
Proverb.

99 A cat has nine lives.
Proverb.

100 A cat may look at a king.
Proverb.

101 A chain is no stronger than its weakest link.
Proverb.

102 A constant guest is never welcome.
Proverb.

103 Actions speak louder than words.
Proverb.

104 A dimple in the chin, a devil within.
Proverb.

105 A drowning man will clutch at a straw.
Proverb.

106 A fool and his money are soon parted.
Proverb.

107 A fool at forty is a fool indeed.
Proverb.

108 A fool believes everything.
Proverb.

109 A friend in need is a friend indeed.
Proverb.

110 A good drink makes the old young.
Proverb.

111 A good face is a letter of recommendation.
Proverb.

112 A good friend is my nearest relation.
Proverb.

113 A good offense is the best defense.
Proverb.

114 A good scare is worth more than good advice.
Proverb.

115 A judge knows nothing unless it has been explained to him three times.
Proverb.

116 A lawyer's opinion is worth nothing unless paid for.
Proverb.

117 A liar is worse than a thief.
Proverb.

118 All are not saints that go to church.
Proverb.

119 All cats are gray in the dark.
Proverb.

120 All good things must come to an end.
Proverb.

121 All is fair in love and war.
Proverb.

122 All roads lead to Rome.
Proverb.

123 All's grist that comes to the mill.
Proverb.

124 All's well that ends well.
Proverb.

125 All that glitters is not gold.
Proverb.

126 All the world loves a lover.
Proverb.

127 All work and no play makes Jack a dull boy.
Proverb.

128 A man can die but once.
Proverb.

129 A man is as old as he feels, and a woman as old as she looks.
Proverb.

130 A miss is as good as a mile.
Proverb.

131 An apple a day keeps the doctor away.
Proverb.

132 An apple-pie without some cheese is like a kiss without a squeeze.
Proverb.

133 An Englishman's home is his castle.
Proverb.

134 An honest man's word is as good as his bond.
Proverb.

135 An hour in the morning is worth two in the evening.
Proverb.

136 A nod is as good as a wink to a blind horse.
Proverb.

137 Any port in a storm.
Proverb.

138 Any publicity is good publicity.
Proverb.

139 A penny saved is a penny earned.
Proverb.

140 Appearances are deceptive.
Proverb.

141 A priest sees people at their best, a lawyer at their worst, but a doctor sees them as they really are.
Proverb.

142 Ask a silly question and you'll get a silly answer.
Proverb.

143 Ask no questions and hear no lies.
Proverb.

144 As soon as man is born he begins to die.
Proverb.

145 A still tongue makes a wise head.
Proverb.

146 A stitch in time saves nine.
Proverb.

147 A tale never loses in the telling.
Proverb.

148 A trouble shared is a trouble halved.
Proverb.

149 A watched pot never boils.
Proverb.

150 A woman's place is in the home.
Proverb.

151 A woman's work is never done.
Proverb.

152 A young physician fattens the churchyard.
Proverb.

153 Bad news travels fast.
Proverb.

154 Barking dogs seldom bite.
Proverb.

155 Beauty is in the eye of the beholder.
Proverb.

156 Beauty is only skin-deep.
Proverb.

157 Beauty is potent but money is omnipotent.
Proverb.

158 Beggars can't be choosers.
Proverb.

159 Believe nothing of what you hear, and only half of what you see.
Proverb.

160 Better a lie that heals than a truth that wounds.
Proverb.

161 Better be a fool than a knave.
Proverb.

162 Better be an old man's darling than a young man's slave.
Proverb.

163 Better be envied than pitied.
Proverb.

164 Better be safe than sorry.
Proverb.

165 Better late than never.
Proverb.

166 Birds of a feather flock together.
Proverb.

167 Blood is thicker than water.
Proverb.

168 Books and friends should be few but good.
Proverb.

169 Bread is the staff of life.
Proverb.

170 Charity begins at home.
Proverb.

171 Civility costs nothing.
Proverb.

172 Cold hands, warm heart.
Proverb.

173 Constant dripping wears away the stone.
Proverb.

174 Curiosity killed the cat.
Proverb.

175 Dead men tell no tales.
Proverb.

176 Death is the great leveler.
Proverb.

177 Desperate situations call for desperate measures.
Proverb.

178 Divide and conquer.
Proverb.

179 Do as I say, not as I do.
Proverb.

180 Do as you would be done by.
Proverb.

181 Doing is better than saying.
Proverb.

182 Don't cross the bridge till you come to it.
Proverb.

183 Don't cut off your nose to spite your face.
Proverb.

184 Don't drown the man who taught you to swim.
Proverb.

185 Don't kill the goose that lays the golden egg.
Proverb.

186 Don't meet troubles half-way.
Proverb.

187 Don't put all your eggs in one basket.
Proverb.

188 Don't throw the baby out with the bathwater.
Proverb.

189 Don't wash your dirty linen in public.
Proverb.

190 Early to bed and early to rise, makes a man healthy, wealthy, and wise.
Proverb.

191 Easier said than done.
Proverb.

192 East, west, home's best.
Proverb.

193 Easy come, easy go.
Proverb.

194 Eat to live and not live to eat.
Proverb.

195 Empty vessels make the greatest sound.
Proverb.

196 Even a worm will turn.
Proverb.

197 Every cloud has a silver lining.
Proverb.

198 Every dog has his day.
Proverb.

199 Every dog is allowed one bite.
Proverb.

200 Every family has a skeleton in the closet.
Proverb.

201 Every little bit helps.
Proverb.

202 Every man after his fashion.
Proverb.

203 Every man for himself, and the devil take the hindmost.
Proverb.

204 Every man is his own worst enemy.
Proverb.

205 Everyone is innocent until proven guilty.
Proverb.

206 Every picture tells a story.
Proverb.

207 Everything comes to him who waits.
Proverb.

208 Experience is the best teacher.
Proverb.

209 Experience is the mother of science.
Proverb.

210 Experience is the mother of wisdom.
Proverb.

211 Faith will move mountains.
Proverb.

212 Familiarity breeds contempt.
Proverb.

213 Fear of death is worse than death itself.
Proverb.

214 Fight fire with fire.
Proverb.

215 Finders keepers, losers weepers.
Proverb.

216 Fine feathers make fine birds.
Proverb.

217 Fingers were made before forks, and hands before knives.
Proverb.

218 First come, first served.
Proverb.

219 First impressions are the most lasting.
Proverb.

220 First things first.
Proverb.

221 Fish and guests smell in three days.
Proverb.

222 Fools live poor to die rich.
Proverb.

223 Footprints on the sands of time are not made by sitting down.
Proverb.

224 Forbidden fruit tastes the sweetest.
Proverb.

225 Forewarned is forearmed.
Proverb.

226 Forgive and forget.
Proverb.

227 For want of a nail the shoe was lost; for want of a shoe the horse was lost; for want of a horse the rider was lost.
Proverb.

228 From small beginnings come great things.
Proverb.

229 Genius is an infinite capacity for taking pains.
Proverb.

230 Give a dog a bad name and hang him.
Proverb.

231 Give a thief enough rope and he'll hang himself.
Proverb.

232 Give him an inch and he'll take a mile.
Proverb.

233 Give me a child for the first seven years, and you may do what you like with him afterward.
Proverb.

234 God defend me from my friends; from my enemies I can defend myself.
Proverb.

235 God heals, and the doctor takes the fee.
Proverb.

236 God helps those that help themselves.
Proverb.

237 God is always on the side of the big battalions.
Proverb.

238 Good fences make good neighbors.
Proverb.

239 Gray hairs are death's blossoms.
Proverb.

240 Great minds think alike.
Proverb.

241 Great oaks from little acorns grow.
Proverb.

242 Half a loaf is better than none.
Proverb.

243 Handsome is as handsome does.
Proverb.

244 Haste makes waste.
Proverb.

245 He that has no children brings them up well.
Proverb.

246 He that is his own lawyer has a fool for a client.
Proverb.

247 He that knows little, often repeats it.
Proverb.

248 He that knows nothing, doubts nothing.
Proverb.

249 He that lives long suffers much.
Proverb.

250 He travels fastest who travels alone.
Proverb.

251 He was a bold man that first ate an oyster.
Proverb.

252 He who drinks a little too much drinks much too much.
Proverb.

253 He who hesitates is lost.
Proverb.

254 He who lives by the sword dies by the sword.
Proverb.

255 He who pays the piper calls the tune.
Proverb.

256 He who rides a tiger is afraid to dismount.
Proverb.

257 He who sups with the devil should have a long spoon.
Proverb.

258 History repeats itself.
Proverb.

259 Honesty is the best policy.
Proverb.

260 Hope for the best.
Proverb.

261 Hunger is the best sauce.
Proverb.

262 If a job's worth doing, it's worth doing well.
Proverb.

263 If anything can go wrong, it will.
Proverb.

264 If at first you don't succeed, try, try, try again.
Proverb.

265 If ifs and ands were pots and pans, there'd be no trade for tinkers.
Proverb.

266 If silence be good for the wise, how much better for fools.
Proverb.

267 If wishes were horses, beggars would ride.
Proverb.

268 If you can't be good, be careful.
Proverb.

269 If you can't take the heat, get out of the kitchen.
Proverb.

270 If you play with fire you get burned.
Proverb.

271 If you want a thing well done, do it yourself.
Proverb.

272 If you want to clear the stream get the hog out of the spring.
Proverb.

273 In for a penny, in for a pound.
Proverb.

274 In the country of the blind, the one-eyed man is king.
Proverb.

275 In union there is strength.
Proverb.

276 It is easy to bear the misfortunes of others.
Proverb.

277 It is easy to be wise after the event.
Proverb.

278 It is no use crying over spilled milk.
Proverb.

279 It never rains but it pours.
Proverb.

280 It's an ill wind that blows nobody any good.
Proverb.

281 It's a small world.
Proverb.

282 It's never too late to learn.
Proverb.

283 It's too late to shut the barn door after the horse has been stolen.
Proverb.

284 It takes all sorts to make a world.
Proverb.

285 It takes two to make a quarrel.
Proverb.

286 It takes two to tango.
Proverb.

287 It will all come out in the wash.
Proverb.

288 It will be all the same in a hundred years.
Proverb.

289 Jack of all trades, master of none.
Proverb.

290 Keep a weather-eye open.
Proverb.

291 Keep your mouth shut and your eyes open.
Proverb.

292 Knowledge is power.
Proverb.

293 Knowledge is the mother of all virtue; all vice proceeds from ignorance.
Proverb.

294 Know thyself.
Proverb.

295 Laugh before breakfast, you'll cry before supper.
Proverb.

296 Laughter is the best medicine.
Proverb.

297 Least said soonest mended.
Proverb.

298 Leave well enough alone.
Proverb.

299 Lend only that which you can afford to lose.
Proverb.

300 Let bygones be bygones.
Proverb.

301 Let sleeping dogs lie.
Proverb.

302 Let the cobbler stick to his last.
Proverb.

303 Life begins at forty.
Proverb.

304 Life is just a bowl of cherries.
Proverb.

305 Life is not all peaches and cream.
Proverb.

306 Like breeds like.
Proverb.

307 Like father, like son.
Proverb.

308 Listeners never hear good of themselves.
Proverb.

309 Live and learn.
Proverb.

310 Look after number one.
Proverb.

311 Look before you leap.
Proverb.

312 Look on the bright side.
Proverb.

313 Long absent, soon forgotten.
Proverb.

314 Love conquers all.
Proverb.

315 Love is blind; friendship closes its eyes.
Proverb.

316 Love makes the world go round.
Proverb.

317 Love me, love my dog.
Proverb.

318 Lucky at cards, unlucky in love.
Proverb.

319 Make hay while the sun shines.
Proverb.

320 Make not the sauce till you have caught the fish.
Proverb.

321 Manners maketh man.
Proverb.

322 Man proposes, God disposes.
Proverb.

323 Many a true word is spoken in jest.
Proverb.

324 Many hands make light work.
Proverb.

325 Many irons in the fire, some must cool.
Proverb.

326 March comes in like a lion and goes out like a lamb.
Proverb.

327 March winds and April showers bring forth May flowers.
Proverb.

328 Marriages are made in heaven.
Proverb.

329 Marry in haste, and repent at leisure.
Proverb.

330 Meet on the stairs and you won't meet in heaven.
Proverb.

331 Mind your own business.
Proverb.

332 Moderation in all things.
Proverb.

333 More haste, less speed.
Proverb.

334 Music is the language of love.
Proverb.

335 Nature, time and patience are the three great physicians.
Proverb.

336 Necessity is the mother of invention.
Proverb.

337 Never do things by halves.
Proverb.

338 Never judge from appearances.
Proverb.

339 Never look a gift horse in the mouth.
Proverb.

340 Never put off till tomorrow what you can do today.
Proverb.

341 Never say die.
Proverb.

342 Never speak ill of the dead.
Proverb.

343 Ninety percent of inspiration is perspiration.
Proverb.

344 No love like the first love.
Proverb.

345 No man is infallible.
Proverb.

346 No news is good news.
Proverb.

347 Nothing is certain but death and taxes.
Proverb.

348 Nothing so bad but it might have been worse.
Proverb.

349 Nothing succeeds like success.
Proverb.

350 Nothing ventured, nothing gained.
Proverb.

351 Not to know is bad; not to wish to know is worse.
Proverb.

352 Old habits die hard.
Proverb.

353 Old soldiers never die, they simply fade away.
Proverb.

354 One good turn deserves another.
Proverb.

355 One hour's sleep before midnight, is worth two after.
Proverb.

356 One man's meat is another man's poison.
Proverb.

357 One swallow does not make a summer.
Proverb.

358 Only the good die young.
Proverb.

359 Opportunity seldom knocks twice.
Proverb.

360 Out of sight, out of mind.
Proverb.

361 Patience is a virtue.
Proverb.

362 Penny wise, pound foolish.
Proverb.

363 Pigs might fly, if they had wings.
Proverb.

364 Possession is nine tenths of the law.
Proverb.

365 Poverty is not a crime.
Proverb.

366 Practice makes perfect.
Proverb.

367 Practice what you preach.
Proverb.

368 Promises are like pie-crust, made to be broken.
Proverb.

369 Punctuality is the politeness of princes.
Proverb.

370 Red sky at night, shepherd's delight; red sky in the morning, shepherd's warning.
Proverb.

371 Revenge is a dish that tastes better cold.
Proverb.

372 Revenge is sweet.
Proverb.

373 Rome was not built in a day.
Proverb.

374 Save something for a rainy day.
Proverb.

375 Save your breath to cool your porridge.
Proverb.

376 Saying is one thing, and doing another.
Proverb.

377 Scratch my back and I'll scratch yours.
Proverb.

378 See a pin and pick it up, all the day you'll have good luck; see a pin and let it lie, you'll want a pin before you die.
Proverb.

379 Seeing is believing.
Proverb.

380 See Naples and die.
Proverb.

381 Self-praise is no recommendation.
Proverb.

382 Silence is golden.
Proverb.

383 Slow but sure wins the race.
Proverb.

384 Soon learned, soon forgotten.
Proverb.

385 Spare the rod and spoil the child.
Proverb.

386 Speak when you are spoken to.
Proverb.

387 Sticks and stones may break my bones, but words will never hurt me.
Proverb.

388 Still waters run deep.
Proverb.

389 Strike while the iron is hot.
Proverb.

390 Take a hair of the dog that bit you.
Proverb.

391 Take care of the pennies, and the dollars will take care of themselves.
Proverb.

392 Talk of the devil, and he is bound to appear.
Proverb.

393 Tell the truth and shame the devil.
Proverb.

394 The best of friends must part.
Proverb.

395 The best things come in small packages.
Proverb.

396 The best things in life are free.
Proverb.

397 The darkest hour is just before the dawn.
Proverb.

398 The devil finds work for idle hands to do.
Proverb.

399 The early bird catches the worm.
Proverb.

400 The end justifies the means.
Proverb.

401 The exception proves the rule.
Proverb.

402 The eyes are the windows of the soul.
Proverb.

403 The family that prays together stays together.
Proverb.

404 The first step is always the hardest.
Proverb.

405 The hand that rocks the cradle rules the world.
Proverb.

406 The last straw breaks the camel's back.
Proverb.

407 The law does not concern itself about trifles.
Proverb.

408 The nearer the bone, the sweeter the meat.
Proverb.

409 There are only twenty-four hours in the day.
Proverb.

410 There is a time and place for everything.
Proverb.

411 There is more than one way to skin a cat.
Proverb.

412 There is no accounting for tastes.
Proverb.

413 There is no honor among thieves.
Proverb.

414 There is no time like the present.
Proverb.

415 There is safety in numbers.
Proverb.

416 There's always room at the top.
Proverb.

417 There's many a good tune played on an old fiddle.
Proverb.

418 There's many a slip 'twixt the cup and the lip.
Proverb.

419 There's no fool like an old fool.
Proverb.

420 There's no place like home.
Proverb.

421 There's no smoke without fire.
Proverb.

422 There's nought so queer as folk.
Proverb.

423 There's one law for the rich, and another for the poor.
Proverb.

424 There's only one pretty child in the world, and every mother has it.
Proverb.

425 There will be sleeping enough in the grave.
Proverb.

426 The road to hell is paved with good intentions.
Proverb.

427 The shoemaker's son always goes barefoot.
Proverb.

428 Things are not always what they seem.
Proverb.

429 Third time lucky.
Proverb.

430 Throw enough dirt, and some will stick.
Proverb.

431 Time and tide wait for no man.
Proverb.

432 Time is a great healer.
Proverb.

433 Time will tell.
Proverb.

434 To deceive oneself is very easy.
Proverb.

435 Tomorrow is another day.
Proverb.

436 Tomorrow never comes.
Proverb.

437 Too many cooks spoil the broth.
Proverb.

438 Travel broadens the mind.
Proverb.

439 Truth fears no trial.
Proverb.

440 Truth is stranger than fiction.
Proverb.

441 Truth will out.
Proverb.

442 Two heads are better than one.
Proverb.

443 Two wrongs do not make a right.
Proverb.

444 United we stand, divided we fall.
Proverb.

445 Vice is often clothed in virtue's habit.
Proverb.

446 Visitors' footfalls are like medicine; they heal the sick.
Proverb.

447 Walls have ears.
Proverb.

448 Waste not, want not.
Proverb.

449 We must learn to walk before we can run.
Proverb.

450 What can't be cured, must be endured.
Proverb.

451 What must be, must be.
Proverb.

452 What's done cannot be undone.
Proverb.

453 What you don't know can't hurt you.
Proverb.

454 What you lose on the swings you gain on the roundabouts.
Proverb.

455 When one door shuts, another opens.
Proverb.

456 When the cat's away, the mice will play.
Proverb.

457 When the wine is in, the wit is out.
Proverb.

458 Where there's a will there's a way.
Proverb.

459 While there's life there's hope.
Proverb.

460 Who spits against the wind, it falls in his face.
Proverb.

461 Why buy a cow when milk is so cheap?
Proverb.

462 You can have too much of a good thing.
Proverb.

463 You can lead a horse to the water, but you can't make him drink.
Proverb.

464 You cannot run with the hare and hunt with the hounds.
Proverb.

465 You can't get blood out of a stone.
Proverb.

466 You can't make an omelette without breaking eggs.
Proverb.

467 You can't make bricks without straw.
Proverb.

468 You can't please everyone.
Proverb.

469 You can't take it with you when you go.
Proverb.

470 You can't teach an old dog new tricks.
Proverb.

471 You can't tell a book by its cover.
Proverb.

472 He lies like an eyewitness.
Russian proverb.

473 Better unborn than untaught.
Scottish proverb.

474 If marriages be made in heaven, some had few friends there.
Scottish proverb.

475 A man too busy to take care of his health is like a mechanic too busy to take care of his tools.
Spanish proverb.

476 Don't throw away the old bucket until you know whether the new one holds water.
Swedish proverb.

477 He who approves evil is guilty of it.
Tamil proverb.

478 It is no use trying to tug the glacier backwards.
Tibetan proverb.

479 Different strokes for different folks.
U.S. proverb.

480 Don't kick a fellow when he's down.
U.S. proverb.

481 Everything has its price.
U.S. proverb.

482 Great occasions make great men.
U.S. proverb.

483 Hear before you blame.
U.S. proverb.

484 Home is where the heart is.
U.S. proverb.

485 Laugh and the world laughs with you; weep and you weep alone.
U.S. proverb.

486 One cannot live on prospects.
U.S. proverb.

487 Paddle your own canoe.
U.S. proverb.

488 The bigger they are, the harder they fall.
U.S. proverb.

489 There is always a first time.
U.S. proverb.

490 The shortest way is the best way.
U.S. proverb.

491 Good wood is better than good paint.
Vietnamese proverb.

492 Be honorable with yourself if you wish to associate with honorable people.
Welsh proverb.

493 There is no prison like a guilty conscience.
Welsh proverb.

494 A friend you have to buy; enemies you get for nothing.
Yiddish proverb.

495 All brides are beautiful; all the dead are pious.
Yiddish proverb.

496 An example is no proof.
Yiddish proverb.

497 A trick is clever only once.
Yiddish proverb.

498 Even for bad luck you need luck.
Yiddish proverb.

499 Everyone is kneaded out of the same dough but not baked in the same oven.
Yiddish proverb.

500 He who is aware of his folly is wise.
Yiddish proverb.

501 If you want your dreams to come true, don't sleep.
Yiddish proverb.

502 It costs nothing to look.
Yiddish proverb.

503 Let it be worse, so long as it's a change.
Yiddish proverb.

504 Lost years are worse than lost dollars.
Yiddish proverb.

505 Money goes to money.
Yiddish proverb.

506 No choice is also a choice.
Yiddish proverb.

507 Not all troubles come from heaven.
Yiddish proverb.

508 The Rabbi's daughter is forbidden what the bathhouse keeper's daughter is allowed.
Yiddish proverb.

509 The worst libel is the truth.
Yiddish proverb.

510 Truth is the safest lie.
Yiddish proverb.

511 When distress doesn't show on the face, it lies in the heart.
Yiddish proverb.

512 When one comes to comfort a young widow, he does not mean to perform a good deed.
Yiddish proverb.

513 You may deal in rags and dress in velvet.
Yiddish proverb.

Proverbs, Modern

1 A budget is a method of worrying before you spend instead of afterwards.

2 A drug is that substance which, when injected into a rat, will produce a scientific report.

3 Advice would be more acceptable if it didn't always conflict with our plans.

4 An adult is one who has ceased to grow vertically but not horizontally.

5 An animal psychologist is a man who pulls habits out of rats.

6 A psychoanalyst is one who pretends he doesn't know everything.

7 Asthma is a disease that has practically the same symptoms as passion except that with asthma it lasts longer.

8 Capitalism is the exploitation of man by man. Communism is the complete opposite.

9 Doctors bury their mistakes. Lawyers hang them. But journalists put theirs on the front page.

10 Ever since dying came into fashion, life hasn't been safe.

11 Exploratory operation: a remunerative reconnaissance.

12 Forty is the old age of youth; fifty is the youth of old age.

13 Half of the secret of resistance to disease is cleanliness; the other half is dirtiness.

14 If you're not part of the solution, you're part of the problem.

15 It's a sign of age if you feel like the morning after the night before and you haven't been anywhere.

16 Just because you're paranoid doesn't mean they're not out to get you.

17 Man endures pain as an undeserved punishment; woman accepts it as a natural heritage.

18 Men are blind in their own cause.

19 Nothing is harder on your laurels than resting on them.

20 Removing the teeth will cure something, including the foolish belief that removing the teeth will cure everything.

21 Social tact is making your company feel at home, even though you wish they were.

22 The amount of sleep required by the average person is just five minutes more.

23 The best contraceptive is a glass of cold water: not before or after, but instead.

24 The best way to kill an idea is to take it to a meeting.

25 The law of heredity is that all undesirable traits come from the other parent.

26 The new definition of psychiatry is the care of the id by the odd.

27 The operation was successful—but the patient died.

28 The psychiatrist is the obstetrician of the mind.

29 There is a dignity in dying that doctors should not dare to deny.

30 Today's sales should be better than yesterday's—and worse than tomorrow's.

31 We've made great medical progress in the last generation. What used to be merely an itch is now an allergy.

32 You are getting old when the gleam in your eyes is from the sun hitting your bifocals.

33 You've reached middle age when all you exercise is caution.

Provisional Government of the Irish Republic Irish government body

1 Ireland, through us, summons her children to her flag and strikes for her freedom.
"Proclamation of the Irish Republic" (April 24, 1916)

Proxmire, William (Edward William Proxmire; b.1915) U.S. senator

1 I doubt there is any occupation that is more consistently and unfairly demeaned, degraded, denounced, and deplored than banking.
Fortune (1983)

Prynne, William (1600–69) English pamphleteer

1 A woman with cut hair is a filthy spectacle, and much like a monster...it being natural and comely to women to nourish their hair, which even God and nature have given them for a covering, a token of subjection, and a natural badge to distinguish them from men.
Histrio-Mastix (1633)

2 It hath evermore been the notorious badge of prostituted strumpets...to ramble abroad to plays and playhouses; whither no honest, chaste or sober girls or women, but only branded whores and infamous adulteresses, did usually resort in ancient times.
Histrio-Mastix (1633)

3 Stage plays are sinfull, heathenish, lewde, ungodly Spectacles, and most pernicious Corruptions, condemned in all ages, as intolerable Mischiefs to Churches, to Republickes, to the manners, mindes and soules of men.
Histrio-Mastix (1633)

Pryor, Richard (b.1940) U.S. comedian and actor

1 Kiss my happy, rich black ass.
Typical of his controversial style of addressing social problems like prejudice, racism, and street life in America. Remark at Save Our Human Rights benefit (September 1977), quoted in *Richard Pryor: A Man and His Madness* (Jim Haskins; 1984)

2 Family is a mixed blessing. You're glad to have one, but it's also like receiving a life sentence for a crime you didn't commit.
Pryor Convictions and other Life Sentences (1995)

3 If I ain't horny, I check to see if my heart's beatin'.
Quoted in *Richard Pryor: This Cat's Got 9 Lives* (Fred Robbins and David Ragan; 1982)

Publilius Syrus (*fl.* 1st century B.C.) Roman writer

1 A good reputation is more valuable than money.
Maxims (Darius Lyman, tr.; 1st century B.C.), 108

2 You should hammer your iron when it is glowing hot.
Maxims (Darius Lyman, tr.; 1st century B.C.), 262

3 When Fortune flatters, she does it to betray.
Maxims (Darius Lyman, tr.; 1st century B.C.), 277

4 Powerful indeed is the empire of habit.
Maxims (Darius Lyman, tr.; 1st century B.C.), 305

5 A cock has great influence on his own dunghill.
Maxims (Darius Lyman, tr.; 1st century B.C.), 357

6 A rolling stone gathers no moss.
Maxims (Darius Lyman, tr.; 1st century B.C.), 524

7 Never promise more than you can perform.
Maxims (Darius Lyman, tr.; 1st century B.C.), 528

8 No man is happy who does not think himself so.
Maxims (Darius Lyman, tr.; 1st century B.C.), 584

9 It matters not how long you live, but how well.
Maxims (Darius Lyman, tr.; 1st century B.C.), 829

10 It is vain to look for a defense against lightning.
Maxims (Darius Lyman, tr.; 1st century B.C.), 835

11 The madman thinks the rest of the world crazy.
Moral Sayings (1st century B.C.), 386

12 They live ill who expect to live always.
Moral Sayings (1st century B.C.), 457

13 Whom Fortune wishes to destroy she first makes mad.
Moral Sayings (1st century B.C.), 911

14 An unruly patient makes a harsh physician.
Sententiae (1st century B.C.)

15 If you share your friend's crime, you make it your own.
Sententiae (1st century B.C.)

16 Pain of mind is worse than pain of body.
Sententiae (1st century B.C.)

17 He gives twice who gives promptly.
1st century B.C. Attrib.

18 Necessity knows no law.
1st century B.C. Attrib.

Pugin, Augustus (Augustus Welby Northmore Pugin; 1812–52) British architect and writer

1 The two great rules for design are these: first, that there should be no features about a building which are not necessary for convenience, construction or propriety; second, that all ornament should consist of enrichment of the essential construction of the building.
The True Principles of Pointed or Christian Architecture (1841)

Pulteney, William, 1st Earl of Bath (1684–1764) English politician

1 Since twelve honest men have decided the cause,
Who are judges alike of the facts and the laws.
Referring to Sir Philip Yorke's unsuccessful prosecution of the journal the *Craftsman.* "The Honest Jury" (1729), st. 3

Puri, Rakshat Indian journalist and writer

1 History is thicker than
blood, and we who rock-faced
wash with our tears
the red river with corpses
might consider that men
have died for less than love
and more than marble arches.
"Bangladesh," *The Voice of the Indian Poets* (Pranab Bandyopadhyay, ed.; 1975)

Purim, Flora (b.1942) Brazilian jazz singer and songwriter

1 Clear days, feel so good and free,
So light as a feather can be.
Song lyric. "Light as a Feather" (1973)

Pushkin, Alexander (Alexander Sergeyvich Pushkin; 1799–1837) Russian poet and writer

1 A man who's active and incisive
can yet keep nail-care much in mind:
why fight what's known to be decisive?
custom is the despot of mankind.
1831. *Eugene Onegin* (Charles Johnstone, tr.; 1977), ch. 1, st. 25

2 With womankind, the less we love them,
the easier they become to charm.
1831. *Eugene Onegin* (Charles Johnstone, tr.; 1977), ch. 4, st. 7

3 With a sharp epigram it's pleasant
to infuriate a clumsy foe.
1831. *Eugene Onegin* (Charles Johnstone, tr.; 1977), ch. 6, st. 33

Pu Songling (also known as P'u Sung-ling; 1640–1715) Chinese writer of ghost stories

1 He heard a rustling by a crack in the window. A quick look showed him a small creature slipping in armed with a spear, who grew to man's size as soon as its feet touched the ground.
"Black Magic" (17th–18th century), quoted in *Selected Tales of Liaozhai* (Yang Xianyi and Gladys Yang, trs.; 1981)

2 "I'll tell you the truth," Hongyu replied. "I was lying when I told you I was your neighbor's daughter. I'm in fact a fox."
"Hongyu, a Fox-fairy" (17th–18th century), quoted in *Selected Tales of Liaozhai* (Yang Xianyi and Gladys Yang, trs.; 1981)

3 He opened his basket and took out a coil of rope, hundreds of feet in length. He grasped one end of this and threw it up, whereupon the rope stood straight up in the air as if suspended to something. It went higher and higher till it was lost in the clouds.
"The Rope Trick" (17th–18th century), quoted in *Selected Tales of Liaozhai* (Yang Xianyi and Gladys Yang, trs.; 1981)

Putnam, Hilary (b.1926) U.S. philosopher

1 The only criterion for what is a fact is what it is rational to accept.
Reason, Truth and History (1981)

Puttnam, David (David Terence Puttnam; b.1941) British film producer

1 The medium is too powerful and important an influence on the way we live—the way we see ourselves—to be left solely to the tyranny of the box-office or reduced to the sum of the lowest common denominator of public taste.
1989. Attrib.

Puzo, Mario (b.1920) U.S. novelist

1 A lawyer with his briefcase can steal more than a hundred men with guns.
The Godfather (1969)

2 I'll make him an offer he can't refuse.
The Godfather (1969)

Pynchon, Thomas (Thomas Ruggles Pynchon, Jr.; b.1937) U.S. novelist

1 A bad-cinema spring, full of paper leaves and cotton-wool blossoms and phony lighting.
Gravity's Rainbow (1973)

2 Now there grows among all the rooms, replacing the night's old smoke, alcohol and sweat, the fragile, musaceous odor of Breakfast...Is there any reason not to open every window, and let the kind scent blanket all Chelsea?
Gravity's Rainbow (1973)

3 The phone call, when it comes, rips easily across the room...like a rude metal double-fart.
Gravity's Rainbow (1973)

4 San Narciso lay further south, near L.A. Like many named places in California it was less an identifiable city than a group of concepts.
The Crying of Lot 49 (1966), ch. 2

5 God protect me...from these lib, overeducated broads with the soft heads and bleeding hearts.
The Crying of Lot 49 (1966), ch. 3

6 "I didn't think people invented anymore," said Oedipa..."I mean, who's there been, really, since Thomas Edison? Isn't it all teamwork now?"
The Crying of Lot 49 (1966), ch. 4

7 Despair came over her, as it will when nobody around has any sexual relevance to you.
The Crying of Lot 49 (1966), ch. 5

8 My big mistake was love. From this day I swear to stay off of love: hetero, homo, bi, dog or cat, car, every kind there is. I will found a society of isolates, dedicated to this purpose.
The Crying of Lot 49 (1966), ch. 5

9 She remembered drifters she had listened to, Americans speaking their own language carefully, scholarly, as if they were in exile from somewhere else invisible yet congruent with the cheered land she lived in.
The Crying of Lot 49 (1966), ch. 6

10 Squatters who...spent the night up some pole in a lineman's tent like caterpillars, swung among a web of telephone wires, living in the very copper rigging and secular miracle of communication.
The Crying of Lot 49 (1966), ch. 6

11 His had always been a vigorous, Italian sort of pessimism: like Machiavelli, he allowed the forces of *virtù* and *fortuna* to be about 5050.
1960. "Entropy," *The Slow Learner: Early Stories* (1984)

12 Back at the truck Picnic said, "Jesus Christ I hate rain." "You and Hemingway," Rizzo said. "Funny, ain't it. T. S. Eliot likes rain."
1959. "Slow Rain," *The Slow Learner: Early Stories* (1984)

Pyrrhus, King of Epirus (318?–272 B.C.) Epirian monarch

1 Such another victory and we are ruined.
279 B.C. Referring to the costliness of his victory at the Battle of Asculum, which gave rise to the phrase, a Pyrrhic victory. Quoted in "Pyrrhus," *Parallel Lives* (Plutarch), ch. 21, sect. 9

Qabbani, Nizar (b.1923) Syrian poet

1 My poor country,
you have changed me in a moment
from a poet who writes of love and longing
to a poet who writes with a knife.
"Marginal Notes on the Book of Defeat" (1967), pt. 3, quoted in *When the Words Burn* (John Mikhail Asfour, ed., tr.; 1988)

2 The secret of our tragedy is
that our screams are louder than our voices
and our swords taller than ourselves.
"Marginal Notes on the Book of Defeat" (1967), pt. 6, quoted in *When the Words Burn* (John Mikhail Asfour, ed., tr.; 1988)

3 When a man is in love
how can he use old words?
Should a woman
desiring her lover
lie down with grammarians and linguists?
"Language," *Modern Arabic Poetry* (Salma Khadra Jayyusi, ed.; 1987), ll. 1–6

4 The day I met you I tore up
all my maps
all my prophecies
like an Arab stallion I smelled the rain.
"Poems," *Modern Arabic Poetry* (Salma Khadra Jayyusi, ed.; 1987), no. 2, ll. 1–4

5 When God gave you to me
I felt that he had loaded
everything my way
and unsaid all his sacred books.
"Poems," *Modern Arabic Poetry* (Salma Khadra Jayyusi, ed.; 1987), no. 8, ll. 2–4

Qasim, Samih (b.1939) Palestinian poet

1 O virgin desert!
Here we are, sent by the heart and mind
on an official mission
to build the world anew.
To prepare it once again
for another Apocalypse!
"After the Apocalypse," *Modern Arabic Poetry* (Salma Khadra Jayyusi, ed.; 1987), ll. 79–84

Quant, Mary (b.1934) British fashion designer

1 A "look" can so easily become weak and diluted and disintegrated when garments have to be made in all sizes for all types. I have seen it slaughtered in mass production.
Quant by Quant (1966)

2 What a great many people still don't realize is that the Look isn't just the garments you wear. It's the way you put your make-up on, the way you do your hair, the sort of stockings you choose, the way you walk and stand; even the way you smoke your fag.
Quant by Quant (1966)

Quarles, Francis (1592–1644) English poet

1 Our God and soldiers we alike adore
Ev'n at the brink of danger; not before:
After deliverance, both alike requited,
Our God's forgotten, and our soldiers slighted.
"Of Common Devotion," *Divine Fancies* (1632)

2 Man is Heaven's masterpiece.
Emblems (1635), bk. 2, no. 6, epigram 6

3 It is the lot of man but once to die.
Emblems (1635), bk. 5, no. 7

4 My soul; sit thou a patient looker-on;
Judge not the play before the play is done:
Her plot hath many changes, every day
Speaks a new scene; the last act crowns the play.
"Respice Finem," *Emblems* (1635), bk. 1, no. 15

5 I wish thee as much pleasure in the reading, as I had in the writing.
"To the Reader," *Emblems* (1635)

6 No man is born unto himself alone;
Who lives unto himself, he lives to none.
Esther (1621), Sect. 1, Meditation 1

7 Physicians of all men are most happy; what success soever they have, the world proclaimeth, and what fault they commit, the earth covereth.
Hierogylphics of the Life of Man (1646), no. 4

Quasimodo, Salvatore (1901–68) Italian poet and critic

1 Poetry is the revelation of a feeling that the poet believes to be interior and personal but which the reader recognizes as his own.
New York Times (May 14, 1960)

Quayle, Dan (James Danforth Quayle; b.1947) U.S. politician

Quotations about Quayle

1 I served with Jack Kennedy. I knew Jack Kennedy. Jack

Kennedy was a friend of mine. Senator, you're no Jack Kennedy.
Lloyd Bentsen (b.1921) U.S. politician. Replying to Dan Quayle's claim, in a television debate, that he had as much experience of Congress as Kennedy did on accession to the presidency. Remark (1988)

Quotations by Quayle

2 What a waste it is to lose one's mind or not to have a mind is very wasteful.
In 1972 the Fund used an advertising slogan, "A mind is a terrible thing to waste." Address to United Negro College Fund (May 1989)

3 We're going to have the best-educated American people in the world.
Remark (September 21, 1988), quoted in *Esquire* (August 1992)

4 If you give a person a fish, they'll fish for a day. But if you train a person to fish, they'll fish for a lifetime.
October 13, 1992. This is a misappropriation of the saying, "If you give a man a fish, he'll eat for a day, but if you teach him how to fish, he'll eat for a lifetime." Speech, job training center, Atlanta, Georgia, quoted in *New York Times* (October 14, 1992)

5 Republicans understand the importance of bondage between a mother and child.
U.S. News and World Report (October 10, 1988)

6 I stand by all the misstatements that I've made.
August 17, 1989. Quoted in *Esquire* (August 1992)

7 A stirring victory for the forces of aggression against lawlessness.
Referring to the Persian Gulf War. Attrib.

Queenan, Joe U.S. journalist and writer

1 Movies are an inherently stupid art form that often relies on scams, tricks, stunts, gambits, ploys, ruses, or gags that are logically or physically impossible, and often both.
"Don't Try This At Home," *If You're Talking to Me Your Career Must Be In Trouble* (1994)

2 Between 1956 and 1969, Elvis Presley, in his spare time from being the biggest rock 'n' roll star of all time, managed to make thirty-one of the worst movies in motion picture history.
"The King And His Court," *If You're Talking to Me Your Career Must Be In Trouble* (1994)

Queneau, Raymond (1903–76) French writer

1 The monkey, without effort, the monkey became man who not much later split the atom.
Petite cosmogonie portative (1950), song 6

Quételet, Lambert Adolphe Jacques (1796–1874) Belgian astronomer and statistician

1 Society...prepares crimes; criminals are only the instruments necessary for executing them.
On Man (1835)

Quevedo y Villegas, Francisco Gómez de (1580–1645) Spanish poet and writer

1 So blind am I to my mortal entanglement
that I dare not call upon thee, Lord, for fear
that thou wouldst take me away from my sin.
"Psalm 6," *Heráclito Cristiano* (1613)

Quincy, Josiah (1772–1864) U.S. politician

1 As it will be the right of all, so it will be the duty of some, definitely to prepare for a separation, amicably if they can, violently if they must.
Part of a speech given on a state's constitutional rights of self-determination. *Abridgement of Debates of Congress* (January 14, 1811), vol. 4

Quine, Willard V. (Willard Van Orman Quine; b.1908) U.S. philosopher

1 A curious thing about the ontological problem is its simplicity. It can be put in three Anglo-Saxon monosyllables: "What is there?" It can be answered, moreover, in a word—"Everything."
From a Logical Point of View (1953)

2 We know what it is like to be conscious, but not how to put it into satisfactory scientific terms. Whatever it may precisely be, consciousness is a state of the body, a state of nerves.
Quiddities: An Intermittently Philosophical Dictionary (1987)

3 It is the tension between the scientist's laws and his own attempted breaches of them that powers the engines of science and makes it forge ahead.
"Anomaly," *Quiddities: An Intermittently Philosophical Dictionary* (1987)

4 Physics investigates the essential nature of the world, and biology describes a local bump. Psychology, human psychology, describes a bump on the bump.
Theories and Things (1981)

5 "Ouch" is a one-word sentence which a man may volunteer from time to time by way of laconic comment on the passing show...One has only to prick a foreigner to appreciate that it is an English word.
Word and Object (1960)

Quintilian (Marcus Fabius Quintilianus; 35?–95?) Roman rhetorician

1 A liar should have a good memory.
Institutio Oratoria (90?)

2 Divine Providence has granted this gift to man, that those things which are honest are also the most advantageous.
Institutio Oratoria (90?)

3 Medicine for the dead is too late.
Attrib.

Quinton, Anthony (b.1925) British philosopher and broadcaster

1 Nowadays there are no serious philosophers who are not looking forward to the pension to which their involvement with the subject entitles them.
Thoughts and Thinkers (1982)

2 Architecture is the most inescapable of the higher arts.
Times, London (1982)

Quinton, Sir John (John Grand Quinton; b.1929) British banker

1 Politicians are people who, when they see light at the end of the tunnel, order more tunnel.
Quoted in *Money* (June 1989)

Qurtubiyya, 'Aisha bint Ahmad al- (*fl.* 10th century) Spanish poet

1 I am a lioness
and will never allow my body
to be anyone's resting place.
10th century. Untitled, *Women Poets of the World* (Joanna Bankier and Deirdre Lashgari, eds.; 1983)

Qutb, Sayyid (1903?–66) Egyptian philosopher and political leader

1 The leadership of western man in the human world is coming to an end, not because western civilization is materially bankrupt or has lost its economic or military strength, but because the Western order has played its part and no longer possesses that "stock" of "values" which give it its predominance.
Ma'alim fi'l-tariq (1964)

2 The scientific revolution has finished its role, as have "nationalism" and the territorially limited communities which grew up in its age...the turn of Islam has come.
Ma'alim fi'l-tariq (1964)

Qu Yuan (also known as Ch'ü Yüan; 343?–289 B.C.) Chinese poet

1 I bade my phoenixes mount up in flight,
to continue their going both by day and by night.
Then the whirlwinds massed, drawing together,
they marshaled cloud-rainbows, came to withstand me.
"The Li Sao" (4th–3rd century B.C.), quoted in *An Anthology of Chinese Literature* (Stephen Owen, tr.; 1996)

2 I once thought that orchid could be steadfast:
it bore me no fruit, it was all show.
Forsaking its beauty, it followed the common;
it wrongly is ranked in the hosts of sweet scent.
"The Li Sao" (4th–3rd century B.C.), quoted in *An Anthology of Chinese Literature* (Stephen Owen, tr.; 1996)

3 Those men of faction had ill-gotten pleasures,
their paths went in shadow, narrow, unsafe.
"The Li Sao" (4th–3rd century B.C.), quoted in *An Anthology of Chinese Literature* (Stephen Owen, tr.; 1996)

Rr

Raban, Jonathan (b.1942) British author

1 It would be stretching the point to claim the Odyssey and the Book of Exodus as early travel books; but they help to underline the fact that as long as narrative literature has existed, it has taken the form of a journey, real or imagined, or...partly reported and partly invented.
1991. Quoted in *Writers Abroad* (The British Council; 1992)

2 There are no formal constituents to define the travel book...The writer is *abroad*—away from home, in that state of enhanced alertness that comes from being uprooted from one's natural habitat.
1991. Quoted in *Writers Abroad* (The British Council; 1992)

Rabelais, François (pseudonym of Alcofribas Nasier; 1494?–1553?) French humanist and satirist

1 Appetite comes with eating.
Gargantua (1534), bk. 1, ch. 5

2 I drink for the thirst to come.
Gargantua (1534), bk. 1, ch. 5

3 I drink no more than a sponge.
Gargantua (1534), bk. 1, ch. 5

4 Nature abhors a vacuum.
Quoting an article of classical wisdom. *Gargantua* (1534), bk. 1, ch. 5

5 How shall I be able to rule over others, that have not full power and command of myself?
Gargantua (1534), bk. 1, ch. 52

6 In their rules there was only one clause: Do what you will.
Referring to the fictional Abbey of Thélème. *Gargantua* (1534), bk. 1, ch. 57

7 He that has patience may compass anything.
Gargantua (1534), bk. 4, ch. 48

8 Science without conscience is the death of the soul.
Gargantua and Pantagruel (1546), bk. 2

9 Believe me, your creditors, with a more fervent devotion, will beseech Almighty God to prolong your life, they being of nothing more afraid than that you should die.
Gargantua and Pantagruel (1546), bk. 3

10 Be still indebted to somebody or other, that there may be somebody always to pray for you.
Gargantua and Pantagruel (1546), bk. 3

11 The Lord forbid that I should be out of debt, as if, indeed, I could not be trusted. Who leaves not some leaven overnight, will hardly have paste the next morning.
Gargantua and Pantagruel (1546), bk. 3

12 Who lendeth nothing is an ugly and wicked creature.
Gargantua and Pantagruel (1546), bk. 3

13 Man never found the deities so kindly
As to assure him that he'd live tomorrow.
Gargantua and Pantagruel (1546), bk. 3

14 Without health life is not life; it is unlivable.... Without health, life spells but languor and an image of death.
Gargantua and Pantagruel (1546), bk. 4, Prologue

15 Speak the truth and shame the Devil.
Gargantua and Pantagruel (1546), Prologue

16 One inch of joy surmounts of grief a span,
Because to laugh is proper to the man.
"Rabelais to the Reader," *Gargantua and Pantagruel* (1546), bk. 1

17 Not everyone is a debtor who wishes to be; not everyone who wishes makes creditors.
Pantagruel (1532), ch. 3

18 I am going in search of a great perhaps.
1553? Last words. A number of different quotations are attributed to Rabelais as his last words. Quoted in *Rabelais et ses Oeuvres* (Jean Fleury; 1877), vol. 1, ch. 3, pt. 15

19 Bring down the curtain, the farce is over.
1553? Last words. A number of different quotations are attributed to Rabelais as his last words. Attrib.

20 I owe much; I have nothing; the rest I leave to the poor.
1553? Last words. A number of different quotations are attributed to Rabelais as his last words. Attrib.

Rabin, Yitzhak (1922–95) Israeli statesman

Quotations about Rabin

1 A brilliant soldier who hated war, he was a man of battle who longed for peace.
Jonathan Sacks (b.1948) British rabbi. *Times Magazine,* London (December 30, 1995)

Quotations by Rabin

2 In the last decade of the 20th century...Walls of enmity have fallen, borders have disappeared, powers have crumbled and ideologies collapsed, states have been born, states have died and the gates of emigration have been flung open.
Speech to the Israeli parliament, Tel Aviv (July 13, 1992), quoted in *Murder in the Name of God* (Michael Karpin and Ina Friedman; 1999)

3 No longer are we necessarily "a people that dwells alone," and no longer is it true that "the whole world's against us." We must overcome the sense of isolation that has held us in its thrall for almost half a century.
Speech to the Israeli parliament, Tel Aviv (July 13, 1992), quoted in *Murder in the Name of God* (Michael Karpin and Ina Friedman; 1999)

4 We have been fated to live together on the same patch of land, in the same country...One hundred years of your bloodshed and terror against us have brought you only suffering, humiliation, bereavement, and pain.
Addressed to Palestinians. Speech to the Israeli parliament, Tel Aviv (July 13, 1992), quoted in *Murder in the Name of God* (Michael Karpin and Ina Friedman; 1999)

5 You who have never known a single day of joy and freedom in your lives...We offer you the fairest and most viable proposal from our standpoint today—autonomy, self-government—with all its advantages and limitations.
Addressed to Palestinians. Speech to the Israeli parliament, Tel Aviv (July 13, 1992), quoted in *Murder in the Name of God* (Michael Karpin and Ina Friedman; 1999)

Rachmaninov, Sergei Vasilyevich (1873–1943) Russian composer, pianist, and conductor

Quotations about Rachmaninov

1 Rachmaninov's immortalizing totality was his scowl. He was a six-and-a-half-foot-tall scowl.
Igor Stravinsky (1882–1971) Russian-born U.S. composer. *Conversations with Igor Stravinsky* (co-written with Robert Craft; 1958), ch.2

2 He was the only pianist I have ever seen who did not grimace. That is a great deal.
Igor Stravinsky (1882–1971) Russian-born U.S. composer. *Conversations with Igor Stravinsky* (co-written with Robert Craft, 1958), ch. 2

Quotations by Rachmaninov

3 My dear hands. Farewell, my poor hands.
On being informed that he was dying from cancer. Attrib. (1940?)

Racine, Jean (Jean Baptiste Racine; 1639–99) French playwright

1 Oh, I have loved him too much to feel no hate for him.
Andromaque (1667), Act 2, Scene 1

2 Now my innocence begins to weigh me down.
Andromaque (1667), Act 3, Scene 1

3 I loved you when you were inconstant. What should I have done if you had been faithful?
Andromaque (1667), Act 4, Scene 5

4 I fear God, dear Abner, and I have no other fear.
Athalie (1691), Act 1, Scene 1

5 To repair the irreparable ravages of time.
Athalie (1691), Act 2, Scene 5

6 The happiness of the wicked runs away like a raging stream.
Athalie (1691), Act 2, Scene 7

7 She floats, she hesitates; in a word, she's a woman.
Athalie (1691), Act 3, Scene 3

8 My only hope lies in my despair.
Bajazet (1672), Act 1, Scene 4

9 You are emperor, my lord, and yet you weep?
Bérénice (1670), Act 4, Scene 5

10 Tired of making himself loved, he wants to make himself feared.
Brittanicus (1669), Act 1, Scene 1

11 Pain is unjust, and all the arguments that do not soothe it only worsen suspicions.
Brittanicus (1669), Act 1, Scene 2

12 On the vault of the heavens our history is written.
La Religion (1785), chant 5

13 Extreme justice is often injustice.
La Thébaïde ou les Frères Ennemis (1664), Act 4, Scene 3

14 He who laughs on Friday will cry on Sunday.
Les Plaideurs (1668), Act 1, Scene 1

15 Honor, without money, is just a disease.
Les Plaideurs (1668), Act 1, Scene 1

16 Nothing for nothing, and my door stayed shut.
Les Plaideurs (1668), Act 1, Scene 1

17 It's no longer a burning within my veins: it's Venus entire latched onto her prey.
Phèdre (1677), Act 1, Scene 3

18 The wicked always have recourse to perjury.
Phèdre (1677), Act 2, Scene 4

19 I know not where I am going, I know not where I am.
Phèdre (1677), Act 4, Scene 1

20 Crime, like virtue, has its degrees.
Phèdre (1677), Act 4, Scene 2

Radcliffe, Ann (originally Ann Ward; 1764–1823) British novelist

1 The sea, trembling with a long line of radiance, and showing in the clear distance the sails of vessels stealing in every direction along its surface.
The Italian (1797)

2 Fate sits on these dark battlements, and frowns;
And as the portals open to receive me,
Her voice, in sullen echoes, through the courts,
Tells of a nameless deed.
Motto, *The Mysteries of Udolpho* (1794)

3 At first a small line of inconceivable splendour emerged on the horizon, which, quickly expanding, the sun appeared in all of his glory, unveiling the whole face of nature, vivifying every colour of the landscape, and sprinkling the dewy earth with glittering light.
The Romance of the Forest (1791)

Radhakrishnan, Sarvepalli, Sir (1888–1975) Indian philosopher and statesman

1 Hindu and Buddhist thinkers with a singular unanimity make out that *avidya* or ignorance is the source of our anguish, and *vidya* or wisdom, *bodhi* or enlightenment is our salvation.
Eastern Religions and Western Thought (1939), ch. 2

2 Let us prefer to be human.
Eastern Religions and Western Thought (1939), ch. 2

3 The deepest secret of spiritual life is hidden from the common view and can be attained only with an effort...As a matter of fact it is an escape from individualism.
Eastern Religions and Western Thought (1939), ch. 2

4 The Hindu ideal thus affirms that...the Kingdom of God is within us and we need not wait for its attainment till some undated future or look for an apocalyptic display in the sky.
Eastern Religions and Western Thought (1939), ch. 2

5 God is not a word or a concept but a consciousness we can realize here and now in the flesh. Religion is more than worship of a personal god.
Eastern Religions and Western Thought (1939), ch. 4

6 For a religion like Hinduism, which emphasizes Divine Immanence, the chosen people embraces all mankind. If we have something to teach our neighbours we also have something to learn from them.
Eastern Religions and Western Thought (1939), ch. 5

Radiguet, Raymond (1903–23) French writer

1 In the long run, order imposes itself on things.
The Devil in the Flesh (1923)

2 It is not in novelty but in habit that we find the greatest pleasure.
The Devil in the Flesh (1923)

3 The war for so many young boys was this: four years of long vacation.
The Devil in the Flesh (1923)

Rado, James (originally James Radomski; b.1939) U.S. composer and librettist

1 This is the dawning of the age of Aquarius.
Song lyric. "Aquarius," *Hair* (music by Galt MacDermot; 1968)

Raglan, Lord, Baron Raglan of Raglan (Fitzroy James Henry Somerset; 1788–1855) British military commander

1 Lord Raglan wishes the cavalry to advance rapidly to the front and try to prevent enemy carrying away the guns. Troop of Horse Artillery may accompany. French cavalry is on your left. Immediate.
The result of the order was the Charge of the Light Brigade. *Military Order* (October 25, 1854)

2 Don't carry away that arm till I have taken off my ring.
1815. Request immediately after his arm had been amputated following the battle of Waterloo. The ring had been given him by his new wife. Quoted in *Dictionary of National Biography* (1898), vol. 53

Rahman, Fazlur (1919–88) Pakistani educator and Islamic scholar

1 A divine response, through the prophet's mind, to the moral-social situation of the prophet's Arabia.
Referring to the Koran. Quoted in *A History of the Arab Peoples* (Albert Hourani; 1991)

Rainborowe, Thomas, Vice-Admiral (also Rainsborough, or Rainborow; d.1648) British soldier and Parliamentarian

1 The poorest he that is in England hath a life to live as the greatest he.
October 29, 1647. During the Army debates at Putney, after the execution of Charles I. Quoted in *Life of Rainborowe* (Edward Peacock; 1881)

Raleigh, Walter, Sir (1554–1618) British explorer, courtier, and writer

1 As you came from the holy land
Of Walsinghame,
Met you not with my true Love
By the way as you came?
"As You Came from the Holy Land" (1599), st. 1

2 Our passions are most like to floods and streams:
The shallow murmur, but the deep are dumb.
"Sir Walter Ralegh to the Queen" (1599?), st. 1

3 Even such is Time, that takes in trust
Our youth, our joys, and all we have,
And pays us but with age and dust;
Who in the dark and silent grave,
When we have wandered all our ways,
Shuts up the story of our days;
And from which earth, and grave, and dust,
The Lord shall raise me up, I trust.
Supposedly written on the night before his execution. Found in his Bible in the Gate-house at Westminster, London. "The Author's Epitaph, Made by Himself" (1618)

4 Go, Soul, the body's guest,
Upon a thankless warrant:
Fear not to touch the best;
The truth shall be thy errand:
Go, since I needs must die,
And give the world the lie.
Printed in *Poetical Rhapsody* (Francis Davison, 1608); manuscript copy traced to 1595. "The Lie" (1595), st. 1

5 If all the world and love were young,
And truth in every shepherd's tongue,
These pretty pleasures might me move
To live with thee, and be thy love.
Written in response to Christopher Marlowe's poem, "The Passionate Shepherd to His Love." "The Nymph's Reply to the Shepherd" (1600), st. 1

6 Give me my scallop-shell of quiet,
My staff of faith to walk upon,
My scrip of joy, immortal diet,
My bottle of salvation,
My gown of glory, hope's true gage,
And thus I'll take my pilgrimage.
A scallop shell is the sign of a pilgrim. A scrip is a pilgrim's bag. "The Passionate Man's Pilgrimage" (1603), st. 1

7 Now what is love? I pray thee, tell.
It is that fountain and that well,
Where pleasure and repentance dwell.
It is perhaps that sauncing bell,
That tolls all in to heaven or hell:
And this is love, as I hear tell.
Late 16th century. "The Shepherd's Description of Love," *The Poems of Sir Walter Raleigh* (J. Hannah, ed.; 1892)

8 'Tis a sharp remedy, but a sure one for all ills.
1618. Referring to the executioner's axe just before he was beheaded. Attributed in *History of Great Britain* (David Hume; 1754), vol. 1, ch. 4

9 I have a long journey to take, and must bid the company farewell.
1618. Last words. Quoted in *Sir Walter Raleigh* (William Stebbing; 1891), ch. 30

10 So the heart be right, it is no matter which way the head lies.
1618. On being asked which way he preferred to lay his head on the executioner's block. Quoted in *Sir Walter Raleigh* (William Stebbing; 1891), ch. 30

11 Fain would I climb, yet fear I to fall.
Scratched using a diamond on a window pane, resulting in Elizabeth I's retort, "If thy heart fails thee, climb not at all." Quoted in *Worthies of England* (Thomas Fuller; 1662), vol. 1

12 The world itself is but a large prison, out of which some are daily led to execution.
1603. Said when returning to prison after his trial for treason. Attrib.

Raleigh, Walter Alexander, Sir (1861–1922) British critic and essayist

1 An anthology is like all the plums and orange peel picked out of a cake.
Letter to Mrs. Robert Bridges (January 15, 1915)

2 We could not lead a pleasant life,
And 'twould be finished soon,
If peas were eaten with the knife,
And gravy with the spoon.
Eat slowly: only men in rags
And gluttons old in sin
Mistake themselves for carpet bags
And tumble victuals in.
"Stans puer ad mensam," *Laughter from a Cloud* (1923)

3 I wish I loved the Human Race;
I wish I loved its silly face;
I wish I liked the way it walks;
I wish I liked the way it talks;
And when I'm introduced to one
I wish I thought *What Jolly Fun!*
"Wishes of an Elderly Man," *Laughter from a Cloud* (1923)

Ramanujan, Srinivasa (Srinivasa Aaiyangar Ramanujan; 1887–1920) Indian mathematician

1 No, it is a very interesting number, it is the smallest number expressible as a sum of two cubes in two different ways.
The mathematician G. H. Hardy had referred to the number—1729—on the back of a taxi cab, as "dull." The two ways are $1^3 + 12^3$ or $9^3 + 10^3$. *Proceedings of the London Mathematical Society* (May 26, 1921)

Rambert, Dame Marie (originally Cyvia Rambam; 1888–1982) Polish-born British ballet dancer, teacher, and author

1 That scene began with the Chosen Virgin...her folded hands under her right cheek, her feet turned in, in a truly prehistoric and beautiful pose. But to the audience of the time it appeared ugly and comical...and yet now there is no doubt that a masterpiece had been created that night.
Referring to the Paris premiere of *Sacre du Printemps* with the Russian ballet dancer Vaslav Nijinsky. *Quicksilver* (1913)

2 Absurd theories were put forward about his anatomy. People said that the bones in his feet were like a bird's...in fact he *did* have an exceptionally long Achilles...As to his famous posing in the air, he...created the illusion of it by the ecstasy of his expression at the apex of the leap.
Referring to Vaslav Nijinsky. *Quicksilver* (1960)

3 One is often asked whether his jump was really as high as it is always described. To that I answer: "I don't know how far from the ground it was, but I know it was near the stars." Who would watch the floor when he danced?
Referring to Vaslav Nijinsky. *Quicksilver* (1972)

Ramey, Estelle (b.1917) U.S. endocrinologist

1 Women's chains have been forged by men, not by anatomy.
Men's Monthly Cycles (1972)

Ramón y Cajal, Santiago (1852–1934) Spanish scientist

1 As long as our brain is a mystery, the universe, the reflection of the structure of the brain, will also be a mystery.
Charlas de Café (1920)

Ramsay, Allan (1686–1758) Scottish poet

1 Farewell to Lochaber, farewell my Jean,
Where heartsome wi' thee I hae mony day been;
For Lochaber no more, Lochaber no more,
We'll maybe return to Lochaber no more.
"Lochaber No More" (1724), st. 1

Ramsey, Frank (Frank Plumpton Ramsey; 1903–30) British mathematical logician

1 The chief danger to our philosophy, apart from laziness and woolliness, is *scholasticism*, the essence of which is treating what is vague as if it were precise and trying to fit it into an exact logical category.
"The Foundations of Mathematics," *Philosophical Papers* (D. H. Mellor, ed.; 1990)

2 Theology and Absolute Ethics are two famous subjects which we have realized to have no real objects.
"The Foundations of Mathematics," *Philosophical Papers* (D. H. Mellor, ed.; 1990)

Rand, Ayn (1905–82) Russian-born U.S. writer and philosopher

1 Money demands that you sell, not your weakness to men's stupidity, but your talent to their reason.
Atlas Shrugged (1957)

2 Anarchism is founded on the observation that since few men are wise enough to rule themselves, even fewer are wise enough to rule others.
The Fountainhead (1943)

3 Civilization is the progress toward a society of privacy. The savage's whole existence is public, ruled by the laws of his tribe. Civilization is the process of setting man free from men.
The Fountainhead (1943)

4 Creation comes before distribution—or there will be nothing to distribute.
The Fountainhead (1943)

5 Great men can't be ruled.
The Fountainhead (1943)

6 Kill reverence and you've killed the hero in man.
The Fountainhead (1943)

Randolph, A. Philip (Asa Philip Randolph; 1889–1979) U.S. labor leader and civil rights activist

1 The regnant law of the life of political parties, like all other organisms, is self-preservation. They behave in obedience to the principle of the *greatest gain for the least effort.*
The Messenger (October 1924)

2 It's easy to get people's attention, what counts is getting their *interest.*
Contemporary Black Leaders (Elton Fax; 1970)

Randolph, John (1773–1833) U.S. politician

1 This bill is an attempt to reduce the country south of Mason and Dixon's line to a state of worse than colonial bondage.
The Mason-Dixon line is the popular name for the boundary line between Maryland and Pennsylvania. Its name derives from when it was surveyed (1763–67) by two British astronomers, Charles Mason and Jeremiah Dixon. Speech, Congress (April 15, 1820)

Ranke, Leopold von (1795–1886) German historian

1 As it actually was.
Referring to the way that history should be written. Attrib.

Rankin, Jeannette (1880–1973) U.S. legislator

1 You no more win a war than you can win an earthquake.
Quoted in *Jeannette Rankin: First Lady in Congress* (Hannah Josephson; 1974)

2 As a woman I can't go to war, and I refuse to send anyone else.
Quoted in *Jeannette Rankin: First Lady in Congress* (Hannah Josephson; 1974), Prologue

Ransome, Arthur (Arthur Michell Ransome; 1884–1967) British journalist and novelist

1 Grab a chance and you won't be sorry for a might have been.
We Didn't Mean to Go to Sea (1937)

Raphael (Raffaello Sanzio, or Santi; 1483–1520) Italian painter

1 In order to paint a fair one, I should need to see several fair ones, with the proviso that Your Lordship will be with me to select the best. But as there is a shortage both of good judges and of beautiful women, I am making use of some sort of idea which comes into my mind.
Letter to Count Baldassare Castiglione (1514), quoted in *Artists on Art* (Robert Goldwater and Marco Treves, eds.; 1945)

Raphael, Frederic (b.1931) British writer

1 Your idea of fidelity is not having more than one man in the bed at the same time.
Said by Dirk Bogarde to Julie Christie in the film *Darling*. *Darling* (1965)

2 Great restaurants are, of course, nothing but mouth-brothels. There is no point in going to them if one intends to keep one's belt buckled.
Sunday Times Magazine, London (September 25, 1977)

3 We thought philosophy ought to be patient and unravel people's mental blocks. Trouble with doing that is, once you've unravelled them, their heads fall off.
"A Double Life," *The Glittering Prizes* (1976), pt. 3, sect. 2

4 This is the city of perspiring dreams.
Referring to Cambridge, playing on the expression "dreaming spires," used to describe Oxford. "An Early Life," *The Glittering Prizes* (1976), pt. 3

5 I come from suburbia ... I don't ever want to go back. It's the one place in the world that's further away than anywhere else.
"A Sex Life," *The Glittering Prizes* (1976), pt. 1, sect. 3

Rathenau, Walther (also known as Walter Rathenau; 1867–1922) German industrialist, political economist, and statesman

1 There comes a painful moment in the life of every young German Jew...when he fully realizes for the first time that he has come into the world as a second-class citizen, and that no virtue and no merit can free him from this situation.
Quoted in *Europe Since 1870* (James Joll; 1973), ch. 4

Rattigan, Terence, Sir (Terence Mervyn Rattigan; 1911–77) British playwright

1 A nice respectable, middle-class, middle-aged maiden lady, with time on her hands and the money to help her pass it...Let us call her Aunt Edna...Aunt Edna is universal, and to those who feel that all the problems of the modern theatre might be solved by her liquidation, let me add that...she is also immortal.
Collected Plays (1953), Preface, vol. 2

2 When you're between any sort of devil and the deep blue sea, the deep blue sea sometimes looks very inviting.
The Deep Blue Sea (1952)

Rauschenberg, Robert (b.1925) U.S. painter

1 It is extremely important that art be unjustifiable.
1963. Quoted in "Note on Painting," *Pop Art Redefined* (John Russell and Suzi Gablik; 1969)

2 Painting is always strongest when in spite of composition, color, etc., it appears as a fact, or an inevitability, as opposed to a souvenir or arrangement.
Quoted in *Sixteen Americans* (Dorothy C. Miller, ed.; 1959)

3 Painting relates to both art and life. Neither can be made.
Quoted in *Sixteen Americans* (Dorothy C. Miller, ed.; 1959)

Raven, Simon (Simon Arthur Noel Raven; b.1927) British writer

1 As you get older you become more boring and better behaved.
Observer, London (August 22, 1976)

Ravenscroft, Thomas (1583?–1633?) English composer

1 Nose, nose, nose, nose!
And who gave thee that jolly red nose?

Sinament and Ginger, Nutmegs and Cloves,
And that gave me my jolly red nose.
Song lyric. *Deuteromelia* (1609), Song no. 7

Ravetch, Irving (b.1920) U.S. screenwriter

1 The Long Hot Summer
1958. Motion-picture title. Co-written with Harriet Frank, it was based on stories by William Faulkner. "The Long Summer" is the title of book three of *The Hamlet*.

Rawlings, Majorie (originally Majorie Kinnan; 1896–1953) U.S. novelist

1 Bear meat is good according to the condition of the bear and the manner in which it is cooked...But under proper conditions, a Florida bear may be fat and sweet at the end of the winter.
Cross Creek (1942)

2 A woman has got to love a bad man once or twice in her life, to be thankful for a good one.
The Yearling (1938), ch. 8

Rawls, John (b.1921) U.S. philosopher

1 All social primary goods are to be distributed equally unless an unequal distribution is to the advantage of everyone.
A Theory of Justice (1971)

2 Each person possesses an inviolability founded on justice that even the welfare of society as a whole cannot override.
A Theory of Justice (1971)

Ray, John (also spelled Wray; 1627–1705) English naturalist

1 Diseases are the tax on pleasures.
English Proverbs (1670)

Ray, Satyajit (1921–92) Indian film director

1 GHASIRAM It is our sacred duty to marry and procreate. You have no son by your first wife, do you? Then it is your duty to marry again and keep alive your lineage.
Deliverance (1981)

2 GHASIRAM So why be sad?...Take another wife. Nowhere does it say in the Scriptures that you cannot marry again. Look at me. My present wife is my third...You may suffer bereavement but life does not stop. It goes on.
Deliverance (1981)

3 The highly technical polish which is the hallmark of the standard Hollywood product would be impossible to achieve under existing Indian conditions...what our cinema needs above everything else is a style, an idiom...uniquely and recognizably Indian.
My Years with Apu (1994)

4 KALYANI But they won't be the same anymore—the nursery rhymes. Uncle Moon! How could Uncle Moon ever be the same with those Americans trampling all over him.
The Alien (1967)

5 MOHAN One-two-three-four-five-six-seven-eight-nine—zero! You put a zero after one and it becomes more than nine. Every zero added multiplies it ten times. Isn't that wonderful? Well *we* discovered that zero—an unknown Indian.
The Alien (1967)

Raymond, Lee R. (b.1938) U.S. business executive

1 We need economically and environmentally attractive alternative fuels, and those that meet these criteria will succeed in a free marketplace.
Speech (May 6, 1996)

2 Many people, politicians and the public alike, believe that global warming is a rock-solid certainty.
New York Times (December 12, 1997)

Reade, Charles (1814–84) British novelist and playwright

1 Make 'em laugh; make 'em cry; make 'em wait.
Advice to an aspiring writer. Attrib.

Reagan, Ronald (Ronald Wilson Reagan; b.1911) U.S. president and actor

Quotations about Reagan

1 Reaganomics consists of rearming the United States and (for all but those at the top) reducing U.S. standards of living.
Frank Ackerman, U.S. author and economist. Referring to the policies of Ronald Reagan. Quoted in *The Spectre of Capitalism* (William Keegan; 1992)

2 Voodoo economics.
George Bush (b.1924) U.S. president. Referring to Ronald Reagan's economic policies, during the 1980 presidential election campaign. Remark (1980)

3 That youthful sparkle in his eyes is caused by his contact lenses, which he keeps highly polished.
Sheilah Graham (1904–88) British-born U.S. writer. *Times*, London (August 22, 1981)

4 The president wants to take from farms and give to arms.
Charles E. Grassley (b.1933) U.S. politician. *Wall Street Journal* (February 1, 1985)

5 In a disastrous fire in President Reagan's library both books were destroyed. And the real tragedy is that he hadn't finished colouring one.
Jonathan Hunt (b.1938) New Zealand politician. *Observer*, London (August 30, 1981)

6 When you meet the president, you ask yourself, "How did it ever occur to anyone that he should be governor, much less president?"
Henry Kissinger (b.1923) German-born U.S. politician and diplomat. *U.S.* (June 2, 1986)

7 The idea behind Reaganomics is this: a rising tide lifts all yachts.
Walter Mondale (b.1928) U.S. vice president and lawyer. *Time* (September 3, 1984)

8 Reagan is the most popular figure in the history of the U.S. No candidate we put up would have been able to beat Reagan this year.
Tip O'Neill (1912–94) U.S. politician. Remark (1984)

9 This president is going to lead us out of this recovery. It will happen.
Dan Quayle (b.1947) U.S. politician. Speech, California State University, Fresno (January 17, 1992)

10 I was cooking breakfast this morning for my kids, and I thought, "He's just like a Teflon frying pan: nothing sticks to him."

Patricia Schroeder (b.1940) U.S. politician. *The Boston Globe* (Michael Kennedy; October 24, 1984)

11 The carefully packaged persona of the old-time movie star resembles nothing so much as the carefully packaged persona of today's politician. Was it not inevitable that the two would at last coincide in one person?
Gore Vidal (b.1925) U.S. novelist and essayist. "Ronnie and Nancy: A Life in Pictures," *Armageddon* (1987)

12 As the age of television progresses the Reagans will be the rule, not the exception. To be perfect for television is all a President has to be these days.
Gore Vidal (b.1925) U.S. novelist and essayist. Quoted in Interview, *Observer*, London (Martin Amis; February 7, 1982)

13 A triumph of the embalmer's art.
Gore Vidal (b.1925) U.S. novelist and essayist. Quoted in Interview, *Observer*, London (John Heilpern; April 26, 1981)

14 Satire is alive and well and living in the White House.
Robin Williams (b.1951) U.S. actor and comedian. Referring to Ronald Reagan's administration. *Rolling Stone* (February 25, 1985)

15 Ask him the time, and he'll tell you how the watch was made.
Jane Wyman (b.1914) U.S. actor. Referring to her former husband, Ronald Reagan. Quoted in *Times*, London (Sheilah Graham; August 22, 1981)

Quotations by Reagan

16 You on the cutting edge of technology have already made yesterday's impossibilities the commonplace realities of today.
Address to Nobel Prize winners and others, White House, Washington, D.C. (February 12, 1985)

17 I have long believed there was a divine plan that placed this land here to be found by people of a special kind, that we have a rendezvous with destiny.
Campaign letter (1976), quoted in *Sincerely, Ronald Reagan* (Helene von Damm; 1976)

18 Government exists to protect us from each other. We can't afford the government it would take to protect us from ourselves.
Comment (1983), quoted in *Gambling with History—Reagan in the White House* (Laurence I. Barrett)

19 We meant to change a nation, and instead, we changed a world.
Communication to the publisher of the *Presidential Biblical Scorecard* (January 11, 1989)

20 I will not make age an issue of this campaign. I am not going to exploit for political purposes my opponent's youth and inexperience.
Referring to presidential opponent, Walter Mondale. Live television debate (October 22, 1984)

21 There were so many candidates on the platform there were not enough promises to go round.
Referring to the Democrat presidential primary debate in New Hampshire. Press conference (February 6, 1984)

22 I will resist the efforts of some to obtain government endorsement of homosexuality.
Remark (August 18, 1984)

23 The focus of evil in the modern world...an evil empire.
Referring to the Soviet Union. Ronald Reagan borrowed the term "evil empire" from George Lucas's film, *Star Wars* (1977). Speech (March 1983), quoted in "The Decade in Review," *New York Times* (December 24, 1989)

24 I have only one thing to say to the tax increasers: Go ahead, make my day.
The final phrase was said by Clint Eastwood in the motion picture, *Sudden Impact* (1983). Speech at American Business Conference, Washington, D. C. (March 13, 1985)

25 Since I came to the White House I got two hearing aids, a colon operation, skin cancer, a prostate operation and I was shot. The damn thing is, I never felt better in my life.
Speech, Gridiron Club, Washington, D.C. (March 28, 1987)

26 Free enterprise is a rough and competitive game. It is a hell of a lot better than a government monopoly.
Speech to the National Association of Manufacturers, New York (1972)

27 A tree is a tree—how many more do you need to look at?
Speech, Western Wood Products Association (September 12, 1965)

28 All the waste in a year from a nuclear power plant can be stored under a desk.
Burlington Free Press (February 15, 1980)

29 Learn your lines, don't bump into the furniture—and in kissing scenes, keep your mouth closed.
Acting tips. *Films Illustrated* (1988), quoted in *Chambers Film Quotes* (Tony Crawley, ed.; 1991)

30 Surround yourself with the best people you can find, delegate authority, and don't interfere.
Fortune (September 1986)

31 It's silly talking about how many years we will have to spend in Vietnam when we could pave the whole country and put parking stripes on it and still be home for Christmas.
Interview, *Fresno Bee* (October 10, 1965)

32 Inflation is as violent as a mugger, as frightening as an armed robber, and as deadly as a hit man.
Los Angeles Times (October 20, 1978)

33 The deficit is big enough to take care of itself.
Newsweek (November 21, 1988)

34 You can tell a lot about a fellow's character by the way he eats jelly beans.
Ronald Reagan was very fond of jelly beans. *New York Times* (January 15, 1981)

35 Approximately 80% of our air pollution stems from hydrocarbons released by vegetation. So let's not go overboard in setting and enforcing tough emissions standards for man-made sources.
Sierra (September 10, 1980)

36 Honey, I forgot to duck.
March 30, 1981. Said to his wife, Nancy, after an assassination attempt by John Hinckley III. *Sunday Times*, London (December 3, 1989)

37 People don't start wars, governments do.
Time (March 18, 1985)

38 Sadly I have come to realize that a great many so-called liberals aren't liberal—they will defend to the death your right to agree with them.
Where's the Rest of Me? (1965)

39 The Communist plan for Hollywood was remarkably simple. It was merely to take over the motion picture business. Not

only for its profits, as the hoodlums had tried—but also for a grand worldwide propaganda base.
Where's the Rest of Me? (1965)

40 My fellow Americans, I am pleased to tell you I have signed legislation which outlaws Russia for ever. We begin bombing in five minutes.
August 11, 1984. Testing a radio microphone while on air, August 11, 1984. Reported in *New York Times* (August 13, 1984)

41 Please assure me that you are all Republicans!
March 30, 1981. Addressing the surgeons on being wheeled into the operating room for emergency treatment after an assassination attempt by John Hinckley III, March 30, 1981. Quoted in *Presidential Anecdotes* (P. Boller; 1981)

42 A recession is when your neighbor loses his job. A depression is when you lose yours. And a recovery is when Jimmy Carter loses his.
1982. Quoted in *President Reagan: The Role of a Lifetime* (Lou Cannon; 1991)

43 Politics is supposed to be the second oldest profession. I have come to realize that it bears a very close resemblance to the first.
March 2, 1977. At a conference in Los Angeles. Quoted in *Reagan Wit* (Bill Adler; 1981), ch. 5

44 Football. It's a game in which you can feel a clean hatred for your opponent.
Quoted in *Speaking Freely—a Guided Tour of American English* (Stuart Berg Flexner and Anne H. Soukhanov; 1997)

45 Politics is just like show business. You have a hell of an opening, coast for a while, and then have a hell of a close.
Remark to Stuart Spencer. Quoted in *There He Goes Again: Ronald Reagan's Reign of Error* (Mark Green and Gail MacColl; 1966)

46 A government agency is the nearest thing to eternal life we'll ever see on this earth.
Attrib.

47 Government is a referee; it shouldn't try to be a player in the game.
Attrib.

48 Government is not the solution to the problem—government is the problem.
Attrib.

49 The taxpayer is someone who works for the federal government but doesn't have to take a civil service examination.
Attrib.

50 They say hard work never hurt anybody, but I figure why take the chance?
Attrib.

Redding, Otis (1941–67) U.S. soul singer and songwriter

1 We all love each other, right? Let me hear you say "Yeah!"
1967. Said at the Monterey Pop Festival. Quoted in *Rock 'n' Roll Babylon* (Gary Herman; 1994)

Redford, Robert (Charles Robert Redford; b.1937) U.S. film actor and director

1 All critics are fueled by their own failed ambitions. I can't tell you the number of critics who slip me a script on the side. Then, they rip you apart as an actor because you haven't responded to their screenplay.
Premiere (March 1988), quoted in *Chambers Film Quotes* (Tony Crawley, ed.; 1991)

Reed, Henry (1914–86) British poet and radio playwright

1 Today we have naming of parts. Yesterday,
We had daily cleaning. And tomorrow morning
We shall have what to do after firing. But today,
Today we have naming of parts.
"Naming of Parts," *Lessons of the War* (1970)

2 In a civil war, a general must know—and I'm afraid it's a thing rather of instinct than of practice—he must know exactly when to move over to the other side.
Unpublished radio play. *Not a Drum was Heard: The War Memoirs of General Gland* (1959)

Reed, Ishmael (Ishmael Scott Reed; b.1938) U.S. writer

1 If violence is as American as apple pie, then Europe provided the oven, because on the public buildings, in the churches, and in the painting there are scenes of violence.
Reckless Eyeballing (1986)

2 Americans love being conned if you can do it in a style that is both grand and entertaining.
Yellow Back Radio Broke-Down (1969)

3 No one says a novel has to be one thing. It can be anything it wants to be, a vaudeville show, the six o'clock news, the mumblings of wild men saddled by demons.
Yellow Back Radio Broke-Down (1969)

4 One should always believe the other side is capable of doing anything it says.
Yellow Back Radio Broke-Down (1969)

5 Most Americans aren't educated to American culture; that's why they don't know themselves and are confused.
Interviews with Black Writers (John O'Brien, ed.; 1973)

Reed, John (1887–1920) U.S. journalist

1 Ten Days that Shook the World
1919. Book title, referring to the Bolshevik revolution in Russia.

Reed, Lou (Louis Firbank; b.1942) U.S. rock singer and songwriter

1 I'm going to try for the kingdom if I can,
'Cause it makes me feel like I'm a man,
When I put a spike into my vein,
And I tell you things aren't quite the same,
When I'm rushing on my run,
And I feel just like Jesus' son.
Song lyric. "Heroin" (1967)

2 How do you think it feels
when all you can say is if only.
Song lyric. "How Do You Think It Feels" (1973)

3 People were offended because we did a song called "Heroin" but there's plenty of stuff about that in literature and no one gives a shit but it's rock 'n' roll so we must be pushing drugs or something.
Interview, *Q* (1989)

4 Everyone should have a divorce once, I can recommend it.
Quoted in *Lou Reed: Between the Lines* (Michael Wrenn; 1993)

5 I don't think that people who listen to rock 'n' roll for a minute think that the guy who's making the music, or singing, is as hip as they are.
Quoted in *Lou Reed: Between the Lines* (Michael Wrenn; 1993)

6 Of course I'm Jewish, aren't all the best people?
Quoted in *Lou Reed: Between the Lines* (Michael Wrenn; 1993)

7 The music is all. People should die for it. People are dying for everything else, so why not the music?
Quoted in *Lou Reed: Between the Lines* (Michael Wrenn; 1993)

8 Someone told us that Jim Morrison had just died in a bathtub in Paris. And the immediate reaction was, "How fabulous, in a bathtub, in Paris, how *faaaantastic*."
Jim Morrison was the lead singer and songwriter for The Doors, the 1960s rock group. Quoted in *Lou Reed: Between the Lines* (Michael Wrenn; 1993)

9 Walk on the Wild Side
1972. Song title, taken from Nelson Algren's novel *A Walk on the Wild Side*, (1956, film 1962)

10 I'll Be Your Mirror
1967. Song title. Sung by Nico.

Reed, Rex (b.1938) U.S. columnist and actor

1 In Hollywood, if you don't have happiness you send out for it.
Quoted in *Colombo's Hollywood* (J. R. Colombo; 1979)

2 Cannes is where you lie on the beach and stare at the stars—or vice versa.
Referring to the Cannes Film Festival. Attrib.

Reeves, Keanu (b.1965) U.S. film actor

1 You killed Ted, you medieval dickweed!
As Bill, addressing Death. *Bill and Ted's Excellent Adventure* (Chris Matheson and Ed Solomon; 1988)

Reeves, Martha (b.1941) U.S. soul singer

1 On the whole, no one who sings is ever treated fairly.
Referring to the fact that Berry Gordy moved his Motown record company away from Reeves' native Detroit without informing her. Quoted in "Martha Reeves," *Off the Record: An Oral History of Popular Music* (Joe Smith; 1988)

Reich, Robert B. (b.1946) U.S. economist

1 We are living through a transformation that will rearrange the politics and economics of the coming century. There will be no *national* products or technologies, no national corporations, no national industries. There will no longer be national economies.
The Work of Nations (1991)

Reich, Wilhelm (1897–1957) Austrian psychoanalyst

1 The few bad poems which occasionally are created during abstinence are of no great interest.
The Sexual Revolution (1936–45)

2 A bad conscience creates malignant behavior. You make somebody else bad in order to free yourself from responsibility. We call that the Emotional Plague.
1952. Quoted in *Reich Speaks of Freud* (M. Higgins, ed.; 1967)

3 Cancer is due to the stagnation of the flow of the life energy in the organism.
1952. Quoted in *Reich Speaks of Freud* (M. Higgins, ed.; 1967)

4 It happened once or twice that I fell in love with a patient. Then I was frank about it. I stopped the treatment and I let the thing cool off. Then we decided either yes or no to go to bed.
1952. Quoted in *Reich Speaks of Freud* (M. Higgins, ed.; 1967)

5 It is not the task of psychoanalysis to save the world.
1952. Quoted in *Reich Speaks of Freud* (M. Higgins, ed.; 1967)

6 Slander will go on for a long time—the slander of love, the slander of genitality, the slander of life...To protect against that is part of the job. It is beyond psychoanalysis.
1952. Quoted in *Reich Speaks of Freud* (M. Higgins, ed.; 1967)

7 The intensity of an idea depends upon the somatic excitation with which it is connected.
1920. Quoted in *Reich Speaks of Freud* (M. Higgins, ed.; 1967)

8 There is a deadly orgone energy. It is in the atmosphere. You can demonstrate it on such devices as the Geiger counter. It's a swampy quality.
1952. Referring to what Sigmund Freud termed "the death instinct." Quoted in *Reich Speaks of Freud* (M. Higgins, ed.; 1967)

Reid, Jimmy Scottish labor leader

1 When you think of some of the high flats around us, it can hardly be an accident that they are as near as one can get to an architectural representation of a filing cabinet.
"Flats" means "apartments." Address as new Rector of Glasgow University, quoted in *Observer*, London (April 30, 1972), "Sayings of the Week"

Reid, Thomas (1710–96) Scottish philosopher

1 It is genius, and not the want of it, that adulterates philosophy, and fills it with error and false theory.
Inquiry into the Human Mind on the Principles of Common Sense (1764)

2 Men are often led into error by *the love of simplicity, which disposes us to reduce things to few principles, and to conceive a greater simplicity in nature than there really is.*
Inquiry into the Human Mind on the Principles of Common Sense (1764)

3 The weakness of human reason makes men prone, when they leave one extreme, to rush into the opposite...from ascribing active power to all things to conclude all things to be carried on by necessity.
Inquiry into the Human Mind on the Principles of Common Sense (1764)

Reik, Theodor (1888–1969) Austrian-born U.S. psychoanalyst

1 Work and love—these are the basics. Without them there is neurosis.
Attrib.

Reinhardt, Ad (Adolph Dietrich Friedrich Reinhardt; 1913–67) U.S. painter, multimedia artist, and photographer

1 The one thing to say about art is that it is one thing. Art is art-as-art and everything else is everything else. Art-as-art is nothing but art. Art is not what art is not.
1962. "Art-as-Art," *Art International* (1962)

2 Fine art can only be defined as exclusive, negative, absolute and timeless. It is not practical, useful, related, applicable, or subservient to anything else.
Twelve Rules for a New Academy (1953), quoted in *Art-As-Art: The Selected Writings of Ad Reinhardt* (Barbara Rose, ed.; 1975)

3 Fine art has its own thought, its own history and tradition, its own reason, its own discipline. It has its own "integrity" and not someone else's "integration" with something else.
Twelve Rules for a New Academy (1953), quoted in *Art-As-Art: The Selected Writings of Ad Reinhardt* (Barbara Rose, ed.; 1975)

Reinhardt, Gottfried (1913–94) German-born U.S. film producer

1 Money is good for bribing yourself through the inconveniences of life.
Quoted in "Looks Like We're Still in Business," *Picture* (Lillian Ross; 1997)

Reisner, Robert (Robert George Reisner; 1921–74) U.S. writer and humorist

1 Death is the greatest kick of all, that's why they save it for last.
"Death," *Graffiti: Two Thousand Years of Wall Writing* (1974)

Reith, Lord, Baron Reith of Stonehaven (John Charles Walsham Reith; 1889–1971) British engineer, administrator, and politician

1 You can't think rationally on an empty stomach, and a whole lot of people can't do it on a full one either.
Attrib.

2 Educate, Inform, Entertain.
Personal motto for the British Broadcasting Corporation (BBC). Attrib.

Remarque, Erich Maria (1898–1970) German-born U.S. novelist

1 All Quiet on the Western Front
1929. Title of a novel about World War I.

Remond, Charles Lenox (1810–73) U.S. abolitionist

1 Slavery is trembling, prejudice is falling, and I hope will soon be buried—buried beyond resurrection; and we will write over its grave as over Babylon—"Prejudice, the mother of abominations, the liar, the coward, the tyrant, the waster of the poor, the brand of the white man, the bane of the black man, is fallen! is fallen!"
Letter to Thomas Cole (July 3, 1838), quoted in *The Mind of the Negro As Reflected in Letter Written During the Crisis, 1800–1860* (Carter G. Woodson, ed.; 1926)

2 It is said we all look alike. If this is true it is not true that we all behave alike.
Supporting petitions against segregation in traveling. Speech to Legislative Committee of the Massachusetts House of Representatives (February 25, 1842), quoted in *A Documentary History of the Negro People in the United States* (Herbert Aptheker; 1951), vol. 1

Renan, Ernest (Joseph Ernest Renan; 1823–92) French philosopher, philologist, and historian

1 "Knowledge is power" is the finest idea ever put into words.
Dialogues et fragments philosophiques (1876)

2 The epic disappeared along with the age of personal heroism; there can be no epic with artillery.
Dialogues et fragments philosophiques (1876)

3 The alleged god of armies is always on the side of the nation that has the better artillery, the better generals.
"Certitudes," *Dialogues et fragments philosophiques* (1876)

4 The man who obeys is nearly always better than the man who commands.
"Certitudes," *Dialogues et fragments philosophiques* (1876)

5 Man makes holy what he believes as he makes beautiful what he loves.
"La Tentation du Christ," *Études d'histoire religieuse* (1857)

6 Good humor is a philosophic state of mind; it seems to say to Nature that we take her no more seriously than she takes us.
Feuilles détachées (1880)

7 What is human life? Is it not a maimed happiness—care and weariness, weariness and care, with the baseless expectation...of a brighter tomorrow?
Feuilles détachées (1880)

8 The way not to vary is not to think.
L'Avenir de la science: Pensées de 1848 (1890), Preface

9 The simplest schoolboy is now familiar with truths for which Archimedes would have sacrificed his life.
Souvenirs d'enfance et de jeunesse (1883)

10 Woman puts us back into communication with the eternal spring in which God looks at his reflection.
Souvenirs d'enfance et de jeunesse (1883)

11 The whole of history is incomprehensible without him.
Referring to Jesus Christ. *The Life of Jesus* (1863), introduction

Renard, Jules (1864–1910) French writer

1 Be modest! It is the kind of pride least likely to offend.
1895. *Journal* (1877–1910)

2 Certainly there are good times and bad times, but our mood changes more often than our fortune.
January 1905. *Journal* (1877–1910)

3 Clarity is the politeness of the man of letters.
October 7, 1892. *Journal* (1877–1910)

4 Do not ask me to be kind; just ask me to act as though I were.
April 1898. *Journal* (1877–1910)

5 Failure is not our only punishment for laziness: there is also the success of others.
January 1898. *Journal* (1877–1910)

6 How many people have wanted to kill themselves, and have been contented with tearing up their photograph!
December 29, 1888. *Journal* (1877–1910)

7 I am not sincere even when I am saying that I am not sincere.
1910. *Journal* (1877–1910)

8 I don't understand life at all, but don't say it is impossible that God may understand it a little.
March 1910. *Journal* (1877–1910)

9 Irony is humanity's sense of propriety.
April 30, 1892. *Journal* (1877–1910)

10 Look for the ridiculous in everything and you will find it.
February 1890. *Journal* (1877–1910)

11 Poor style reflects imperfect thought.
1898. *Journal* (1877–1910)

12 The bourgeois are other people
January 28, 1890. *Journal* (1877–1910)

13 There are moments when everything goes well; don't be frightened, it won't last.
1910. *Journal* (1877–1910)

14 There is a justice, but we do not always see it. Discreet, smiling, it is there, to one side, a little behind injustice, which makes a big noise.
December 1906. *Journal* (1877–1910)

15 There is false modesty, but there is no false pride.
1909. *Journal* (1877–1910)

16 We are in the world to laugh. In purgatory or in hell we shall no longer be able to do so. And in heaven it would not be proper.
June 1907. *Journal* (1877–1910)

17 We are so happy to advise others that occasionally we even do it in their interest.
1910. *Journal* (1877–1910)

18 We don't understand life any better at forty than at twenty, but we know this and admit it.
1910. *Journal* (1877–1910)

19 We spend our lives talking about this mystery: our life.
April 1894. *Journal* (1877–1910)

20 When the defects of others are perceived with so much clarity, it is because one possesses them oneself.
1908. *Journal* (1877–1910)

21 Words are the small change of thought.
November 15, 1888. *Journal* (1877–1910)

22 Writing is a way of talking without being interrupted.
April 10, 1895. *Journal* (1877–1910)

23 Writing is the only profession where no one considers you ridiculous if you earn no money.
1906 *Journal* (1877–1910)

Rendall, Montague John (1862–1950) British head teacher

1 Nation shall speak peace unto nation.
1927. Motto of the British Broadcasting Corporation (BBC).

Renoir, Jean (1894–1979) French film director

1 Is it possible to succeed without any betrayal?
"Nana," *My Life and My Films* (1974)

2 A director makes only one film in his life. Then he breaks it into pieces and makes it again.
Quoted in *Halliwell's Filmgoer's Companion* (Leslie Halliwell; 1993)

3 The saving grace of the cinema is that with time and patience, and a little love, we may arrive at that wonderfully complex creature which is called man.
Quoted in *Halliwell's Filmgoer's Companion* (Leslie Halliwell; 1993)

4 If I were the son of a nursery gardener, I would probably know a great deal about trees, and I would have an extraordinary taste for gardens. But I'm the son of a painter, so I'm more or less influenced by the painters who surrounded me...when I was young.
Quoted in *Jean Renoir: Projections of Paradise* (Ronald Bergan; 1992)

Renoir, Pierre Auguste (1841–1919) French painter

1 In a few generations you can breed a racehorse. The recipe for making a man like Delacroix is less well known.
Attrib.

2 One morning, one of us, lacking black, used blue: Impressionism was born.
Attrib.

3 I just keep painting till I feel like pinching. Then I know it's right.
Explaining how he achieved such life-like flesh tones in his nudes. Attrib.

4 The pain passes, but the beauty remains.
Explaining why he still painted when his hands were twisted with arthritis. Attrib.

Repington, Charles à Court, Lieutenant-Colonel (1858–1925) British soldier and journalist

1 We mutually agreed to call it *The First World War* in order to prevent the millennium folk from forgetting that the history of the world was the history of war.
September 10, 1918. Attrib.

Retz, Cardinal de (Jean-François-Paul de Gondi; 1613–79) French ecclesiastic and politician

1 A man who doesn't trust himself can never really trust anyone else.
Mémoires (1717)

2 Even that which is despicable is not always to be despised.
Mémoires (1717)

3 Nothing indicates the soundness of a man's judgment so much as knowing how to choose between two disadvantages.
Mémoires (1717)

4 Of all the passions fear weakens judgment most.
Mémoires (1717)

5 One of man's greatest failings is that he looks almost always for an excuse in the misfortune that befalls him through his

own fault, before looking for a remedy—which means he often finds the remedy too late.
Mémoires (1717)

6 Richelieu leaned to the good whenever his interests did not draw him towards evil.
Mémoires (1717)

7 Such is irresolution that nothing is more uncertain than its conclusion.
Mémoires (1717)

8 The least things are often more telling than the greatest.
Mémoires (1717)

9 The man who can own up to his error is greater than he who merely knows how to avoid making it.
Mémoires (1717)

10 The most distrustful are often the greatest dupes.
Mémoires (1717)

11 There is nothing more praiseworthy than generosity, but nothing less to be carried to excess.
Mémoires (1717)

12 There is nothing so annoying as being the minister of a prince of whom one is not the favorite.
Mémoires (1717)

13 What is necessary is never a risk.
Mémoires (1717)

Reuben, David (b.1933) U.S. doctor and author

1 Everything You Always Wanted to Know About Sex But Were Afraid to Ask
1969. Book title.

Reuther, Walter (Walter Philip Reuther; 1907–70) U.S. labor leader

1 If you're not big enough to lose, you're not big enough to win.
Attrib.

Revson, Charles (Charles Haskell Revson; 1906–75) U.S. business executive

1 In the factory we make cosmetics. In the store we sell hope.
Quoted in *Fire and Ice* (A. Tobias; 1976), ch. 8

Rexford, Eben (1848–1916) British songwriter

1 Darling, I am growing old,
Silver threads among the gold.
"Silver Threads Among the Gold" (1873)

Reynolds, Malvina (1900–78) U.S. folksinger and songwriter

1 Little boxes on the hillside...
And they're all made out of ticky-tacky
And they all look just the same.
From a song describing a housing scheme built in the hills south of San Francisco. "Little Boxes" (1962)

Reynolds, Sir Joshua (1723–92) British painter and writer

1 Could we teach taste or genius by rules, they would be no longer taste and genius.
Discourse to the students of the Royal Academy (December 14, 1770), quoted in *Discourses on Art* (R. Wark, ed.; 1975)

2 If you have great talents, industry will improve them: if you have but moderate abilities, industry will supply their deficiency.
Discourse to the students of the Royal Academy (December 11, 1769), quoted in *Discourses on Art* (R. Wark, ed.; 1975)

3 A mere copier of nature can never produce anything great.
Discourse to the students of the Royal Academy (December 14, 1770), quoted in *Discourses on Art* (R. Wark, ed.; 1975), no. 3

4 He who resolves never to ransack any mind but his own, will be soon reduced, from mere barrenness, to the poorest of all imitations; he will be obliged to imitate himself, and to repeat what he has before often repeated.
Discourse to the students of the Royal Academy (December 10, 1774), quoted in *Discourses on Art* (R. Wark, ed.; 1975), no. 15

5 Taste does not come by chance: it is a long and laborious task to acquire it.
Memoirs of Sir Joshua Reynolds (1813–15), vol. 1

6 He who would have you believe that he is waiting for the inspiration of genius, is in reality at a loss how to begin, and is at last delivered of his monsters, with difficulty and pain.
1769. Quoted in *Discourses* (Pat Rogers, ed.; 1992)

Rhodes, Cecil (Cecil John Rhodes; 1853–1902) British colonial statesman and financier

1 Remember that you are an Englishman, and have consequently won first prize in the lottery of life.
Quoted in *Dear Me* (Peter Ustinov; 1977), ch. 4

2 So little done, so much to do.
1902. Last words. Quoted in *Life of Rhodes* (Lewis Michell; 1910), vol. 2, ch. 39

3 How can I possibly dislike a sex to which Your Majesty belongs?
Replying to Queen Victoria's suggestion that he disliked women. Attrib.

Rhodes, William Barnes (1772–1826) British playwright

1 Another lion gave a grievous roar;
And the first lion thought the last a bore.
Bombastes Furioso (1810), Act 1, Scene 4

Rhys, Jean (Ellen Gwendolyn Rees Williams; 1894–1979) Dominican-born British novelist

1 I often want to cry. That is the only advantage women have over men—at least they can cry.
Good Morning, Midnight (1939), pt. 2

2 Next week, or next month, or next year I'll kill myself. But I might as well last out my month's rent, which has been paid up, and my credit for breakfast in the morning.
Good Morning, Midnight (1939), pt. 2

3 Age seldom arrives smoothly or quickly. It's more often a succession of jerks.
Observer, London (May 25, 1975), "Sayings of the Week"

4 The feeling of Sunday is the same everywhere, heavy, melancholy, standing still. Like when they say, "As it was in the beginning, is now, and ever shall be, world without end."
Voyage in the Dark (1934), ch. 4

Ribbentrop, Joachim von (1893–1946) German diplomat

1 We want war!
August 1939. Said to the Italian Foreign Minister, Count Galeazzo Ciano. Quoted in *Germany, 1866–1945* (Gordon A. Craig; 1978), ch. 19

Ricardo, David (1772–1823) British political economist

1 The interest of the landlord is always opposed to the interests of every other class in the community.
Principles of Political Economy and Taxation (1817)

2 The natural price of labour is that price which is necessary to enable the labourers, one with another, to subsist and perpetuate their race, without either increase or diminution.
Principles of Political Economy and Taxation (1817)

Rice, Grantland (Henry Grantland Rice, "Granny"; 1880–1954) U.S. sportswriter

1 For when the One Great Scorer comes to write against your name,
He marks—not that you won or lost—but how you played the Game.
"Alumnus Football" (1941)

2 All wars are planned by old men
In council rooms apart.
"Two Sides of War" (1955)

Rice, Stephen, Sir (1637–1715) Irish lawyer

1 I will drive a coach and six horses through the Act of Settlement.
Also given as "I will drive a coach and six through the Act of Parliament." Quoted in *State of the Protestants of Ireland* (W. King; 1672), ch. 3, sect. 8

Rice, Tim (Timothy Miles Bindon Rice; b.1944) British songwriter

1 Don't Cry for Me Argentina
Song title. *Evita* (music by Andrew Lloyd Webber; 1976)

Rice-Davies, Mandy (Marilyn Rice-Davies; b.1944) Welsh model and showgirl

1 He would, wouldn't he?
June 29, 1963. Said on being told, during the trial of Stephen Ward, that Lord Astor had denied her account of his involvement in orgies at Cliveden House.

Rich, Adrienne (Adrienne Cecile Rich; b.1929) U.S. poet and educator

1 Re-vision—the act of looking back, of seeing with fresh eyes, of entering an old text from a new critical direction—is for women more than a chapter in cultural history: it is an act of survival.
"When We Dead Awaken," *On Lies, Secrets, and Silence* (1979)

Richard I, King of England ("Coeur de Lion", "The Lionheart"; 1157–99) English monarch

Quotations about Richard I

1 As the earth darkens when the sun departs, so the face of this kingdom was changed by the absence of the king. All the barons were restless, castles were strengthened, towns fortified, moats dug.
Richard of Devizes (*fl.* 1190) English monk and chronicler. Referring to the absence of Richard I at the Crusades. *Chronicon de rebus gestis Ricardo Prim* (1192)

2 I have long since been aware that your king is a man of the greatest honor and bravery, but he is imprudent.
1192
Saladin (1138–93) Mesopotamian sultan. Attrib.

Quotations by Richard I

3 Thus we have defeated the king of France at Gisors but it is not we who have done it, but God and our right through us.
Letter to the Bishop of Durham (1198)

4 Dear Lord, I pray thee to suffer me not to see thy holy city, since I cannot deliver it from the hands of thy enemies.
Referring to Jerusalem. Prayer (1192)

5 Think no more of it, John; you are only a child who has had evil counsellors.
Said at his reconciliation, at Lisieux in May 1194, with his brother John, who had attempted to overthrow him while he was held prisoner in Germany (1193–94). Quoted in *Histoire de Guillaume le Maréchal* (Paul Meyer, ed.; 1891–1901)

6 I would sell London, if I could find a suitable purchaser.
1189? Comment while raising money for the third Crusade. Quoted in *Historia Rerum Anglicarum* (William of Newburgh; 1196–98?), bk. 4, ch. 5

7 Dieu et mon droit.
1198. Motto, meaning "God and my right," on the royal arms of Great Britain; originally used as a war cry, September 1198.

Richard II, King of England (1367–1400) English monarch

1 My God! this is a wonderful land and a faithless one; for she has exiled, slain, destroyed and ruined so many kings, so many rulers, so many great men, and she is always diseased and suffering from differences, quarrels and hatred between her people.
September 21, 1399. Remark made in the Tower of London, where he was forced to abdicate 10 days later. Attrib.

Richard, Duke of York, 3rd Duke of York (Richard Plantagenet; 1411–60) English nobleman

1 I know of no one in the realm who would not more fitly to come to me than I to him.
Reply when asked, in Parliament, whether he wished to go and see the king. York formally claimed the throne six days later. (October 10, 1460)

Richard, Cliff, Sir (originally Harry Roger Webb; b.1940) Indian-born British pop singer

1 The nice thing about having relatives' kids around is that they go home.
Remark (November 1988)

Richards, Gordon, Sir (1904–86) British jockey and trainer

1 Mother always told me my day was coming, but I never realized that I'd end up being the shortest knight of the year.
1953. Referring to his diminutive size, on learning of his knighthood. Attrib.

Richards, Keith (b.1943) British rock musician

1 If you're gonna get wasted, get wasted elegantly.
Quoted in *The Wit and Wisdom of Rock and Roll* (Maxim Jabukowski, ed.; 1983)

Richardson, Dorothy M. (Dorothy Miller Richardson; 1873–1957) British writer

1 They invent a legend to put the blame for the existence of humanity on women and, if she wants to stop it, they talk about the wonders of civilizations and the sacred responsibilities of motherhood. They can't have it both ways.
"The Tunnel Interim," *Pilgrimage* (1919), vol. 2, ch. 24

Richardson, Ralph, Sir (Ralph David Richardson; 1902–83) British actor

1 The art of acting consists in keeping people from coughing.
Observer, London (1947)

2 The most precious things in speech are pauses.
Attrib.

Richelieu, Cardinal, Duc de Richelieu (Armand Jean du Plessis; 1585–1642) French churchman and statesman

1 Nothing is as dangerous for the state as those who would govern kingdoms with maxims found in books.
Testament politique (1688)

2 Authority compels people to obedience, but reason persuades them to it.
Testament politique (1688), ch. 2

3 Great conflagrations are born of tiny sparks.
Testament politique (1688), ch. 8

4 It is essential to banish pity in judging crimes against the State.
1641. *Testament politique* (1688), maxims

5 It is unnecessary for a man to attend to public affairs without any interruption: such concentration is, indeed, more likely to render him useless than any other behavior.
1641. *Testament politique* (1688), maxims

6 Not least among the qualities in a great king is a capacity to permit his ministers to serve him.
Testament politique (1688), maxims

7 Secrecy is the first essential in affairs of the State.
Testament politique (1688), maxims

8 To know how to dissimulate is the knowledge of kings.
Testament politique (1688), maxims

9 To make a law, yet not see that it is enforced, is to authorize what you have yourself forbidden.
1641. *Testament politique* (1688), maxims

10 When the people are too comfortable it is not possible to restrain them within the bounds of their duty...They may be compared to mules who, being accustomed to burdens, are spoiled rather by rest than by labor.
1641. *Testament politique* (1688), maxims

11 Wounds inflicted by the sword heal more easily than those inflicted by the tongue.
1641. *Testament politique* (1688), maxims

12 If you give me six lines written by the most honest man, I will find something in them to hang him.
Attrib.

Richler, Mordecai (b.1931) Canadian novelist

1 Remember this, Griffin. The revolution eats its own. Capitalism re-creates itself.
Cocksure (1968), ch. 22

2 Everybody writes a book too many.
Observer, London (January 9, 1985), "Sayings of the Week"

Richter, Gerhard (b.1932) German painter

1 Since there are no longer any priests and philosophers in this world, artists have become the most important people.
1970. Quoted in *Gerhard Richter* (Rolf Günter Dienst; 1972)

Richter, Jean Paul (Johann Paul Friedrich Richter; 1763–1825) German novelist and humorist

1 Providence has given to the French the empire of the land, to the English that of the sea, and to the Germans that of the air.
Quoted in "Richter," *Critical and Miscellaneous Essays* (Thomas Carlyle; 1827)

Riddell, William Renwick (1852–1945) Canadian lawyer and historian

1 As it was in Canada that the death blow to the old British Empire was struck, so it was in Canada that the new British Empire had its birth.
Speech, Empire Club, Toronto, Canada (April 25, 1929)

Ridge, William Pett (1857–1930) British writer

1 When you take the bull by the horns...what happens is a toss up.
Love at Paddington Green, ch. 4

Ridolfi, Carlo (1594–1658) Italian art historian, painter, and etcher

1 There is no profession...in which you may expect less felicity and contentment than in painting.
Marvels of the Painter's Art (1648)

Rifkind, Malcolm, Sir (Malcolm Leslie Rifkind; b.1946) British politician

1 Everything that is most beautiful in Britain has always been in private hands.
Observer, London (January 17, 1988), "Sayings of the Week"

Riley, James Whitcomb ("The Hoosier Poet"; 1849–1916) U.S. poet

1 The ripest peach is highest on the tree.
"The Ripest Peach," st. 1

Riley, Janet Mary (b.1915) U.S. lawyer

1 The role of a mother is probably the most important career a woman can have.
Times, London (November 2, 1986)

Riley, Pat (Patrick James Riley; b.1945) U.S. basketball coach

1 Teamwork isn't simple. In fact, it can be a frustrating, elusive commodity...Teamwork doesn't appear magically just because someone mouths the words.
The Winner Within (1994)

Rilke, Rainer Maria (1875–1926) Austrian poet and novelist

Quotations about Rilke

1 Rilke wouldn't discuss the war. He felt betrayed by his friends when they insisted on talking about it. Not just because the present was too brutal and too formless to be talked about, but because you could only talk about it in newspaper expressions.
Saul Bellow (b.1915) Canadian-born U.S. writer. *The Dean's December* (1982)

Quotations by Rilke

2 We live our lives, for ever taking leave.
1923. "The Eighth Elegy," *Duino Elegies* (J. B. Leishman and Stephen Spender, trs.; 1939)

3 I never read anything concerning my work. I feel that criticism is a letter to the public which the author, since it is not directed to him, does not have to open and read.
Letters of Rainer Maria Rilke (Jane Bannard Greene and M. D. Norton, trs.; 1945)

4 Once the realization is accepted that even between the *closest* human beings infinite distances continue to exist, a wonderful living side by side can grow up, if they succeed in loving the distance between them.
Letters of Rainer Maria Rilke (Jane Bannard Greene and M. D. Norton, trs.; 1945)

5 Spring has returned. The earth is like a child that knows poems.
Sonnets to Orpheus (1923), sonnet 1, l. 21

Rimbaud, Arthur (Jean Nicolas Arthur Rimbaud; 1854–91) French poet

Quotations about Rimbaud

1 And I'll stay off Verlaine too; he was always chasing Rimbauds.
Dorothy Parker (1893–1967) U.S. writer and wit. "The Little Hours," *Here Lies* (1939)

Quotations by Rimbaud

2 I is somebody else.
Letters to Georges Izambard and Paul Demeny (May 1871), quoted in *Lettres du voyant: 13 et 15 mai 1871* (Gérald Schaeffer, ed.; 1975)

3 I say one must be a *seer*, make oneself *seer*.The poet makes himself a *seer* by an immense, long, deliberate *disordering* of the senses.
Letter to Paul Demeny (May 15, 1871), quoted in *Lettres du voyant: 13 et 15 mai 1871* (Gérald Schaeffer, ed.; 1975)

4 Black A, white E, red I, green U, blue O: vowels,
Some day I shall recount your latent births.
"Voyelles" (1871)

5 I have embraced the summer dawn.
"Aube," *Illuminations* (1886)

6 I have bathed in the Poem
Of the Sea, immersed in stars, and milky,
Devouring the green azures.
Le Bateau ivre (1871)

7 I long for Europe of the ancient parapets.
Le Bateau ivre (1871)

8 Lighter than a cork I danced on the waves.
Le Bateau ivre (1871)

9 One must be absolutely modern.
"Adieu," *Une Saison en enfer* (1873)

10 O seasons, O castles!
What soul is without fault?
"Faim: ô saisons, ô châteaux," *Une Saison en enfer* (1873)

11 I believe I am in hell, therefore I am.
"Nuit de l'enfer," *Une Saison en enfer* (1873)

Riney, Hal (b.1932) U.S. advertising executive

1 It's morning again in America.
Slogan for Ronald Reagan's campaign for a second presidential term. *Newsweek* (August 6, 1984)

Ripley, R. L. (Robert, born LeRoy Ripley; 1893–1949) U.S. writer and cartoonist

1 Believe It or Not
Title of newspaper column (1918)

Ritt, Martin (1914–90) U.S. director and actor

1 Most of the so-called new techniques were tried out 30 or 40 years ago and abandoned because they distracted from the essential. The best direction is that which is least visible.
Films Illustrated (February 1980), quoted in *Chambers Film Quotes* (Tony Crawley, ed.; 1991)

Rivarol, Antoine de (Antoine Rivaroli; 1753–1801) French journalist

1 Accurate, social, reasonable, it is no longer just the French language, it is the language of humanity.
Discours sur l'universalité de la langue française (1784)

2 The whole world needs France when England needs the whole world.
Discours sur l'universalité de la langue française (1784)

3 What is not clear is not French; what is not clear is, moreover, English, Italian, Greek, or Latin.
Discours sur l'universalité de la langue française (1784)

4 There are two truths in this world that should never be separated: 1. that sovereignty rests with the people; 2. that the people should never exercise it.
Journal politique national (1790), vol. 1, no. 13

5 It is no doubt a terrible advantage not to have done anything, but it shouldn't be abused.
Le Petit Almanach de nos grands hommes (1788), preface

6 There are men who gain from their wealth only the fear of losing it.
L'Esprit de Rivarol (1802)

7 Very good, but it has its *longueurs*.
Referring to a couplet by a mediocre poet. "Longueur," referring to poetry, is a derogatory term meaning overlong or labored. Quoted in *Das Buch des Lachens* (Wilhelm von Scholz; 1958)

Rivera, José Eustasio (1888–1928) Colombian poet and novelist

1 Before I felt passion for any woman, I gambled my heart and lost it to violence.
The Vortex (1924)

Rivers, Joan (Joan Alexandra Molinsky; b.1933) U.S. television comedian and actor

1 There is not one female comic who was beautiful as a little girl.
Los Angeles Times (May 10, 1974)

2 Omaha is a little like Newark—without Newark's glamor.
Referring to Newark, New Jersey. Attrib.

Rizzuto, Phil (Fiero Francis Rizzuto; b.1917) U.S. baseball player and broadcaster

1 Well, that kind of puts the damper on even a Yankee win.
August 6, 1978. Remark, while commentating on a baseball game involving the New York Yankees, on hearing that Pope Paul VI had died. Attrib.

Roach, Stephen S. U.S. economist

1 Tactics of open-ended downsizing and real wage compression are ultimately recipes for industrial extinction.
Financial Times, London (May 14, 1996)

2 It doesn't take much to derail a market that has gone to the moon.
Time (November 10, 1997)

3 Extreme trends are breeding grounds for equally powerful countertrends.
Referring to the workings of the free-market system. "A New Competitive Dilemma," *Wall Street Journal* (June 20, 1996)

Robbe-Grillet, Alain (b.1922) French novelist and screenwriter

1 The true writer has nothing to say, just a way of saying it.
Pour un nouveau roman (1963)

2 The function of art is not to illustrate a truth—or even a question—that is known in advance—but to put to the world questions (and perhaps also, eventually, answers) that themselves cannot yet be conceived.
"À quoi servent les théories," *Pour un nouveau roman* (1963)

Robbins, Tom (b.1936) U.S. writer

1 Human beings were invented by water as a device for transporting itself from one place to another.
Another Roadside Attraction (1971)

2 To emphasize the afterlife is to deny life. To concentrate on Heaven is to create hell.
Skinny Legs and All (1990)

Robens, Alfred, Baron Robens of Woldingham (b.1910) British labor leader and industrialist

1 Leadership, above all, consists of telling the truth, unpalatable though it may be. It is better to go down with the truth on one's lips than to rise high by innuendo and doubletalk.
Speech, Institute of Directors Annual Convention (November 7, 1974)

2 We should never be allowed to forget that it is the customer who, in the end, determines how many people are employed and what sort of wage companies can afford to pay.
Observer, London (May 1, 1977)

Robert, Yves (b.1920) French film director

1 Such is the life of man: brief moments of joy, soon obliterated by unforgettable sorrows.
Le Chateau de ma mère (1990)

Robeson, Paul (Paul Bustill Robeson; 1898–1976) U.S. singer, actor, and civil rights activist

1 My father was a slave, and my people died to build this country, and I am going to stay here and have a piece of it, just like you.
Statement to the House Committee on Un-American Activities (June 12, 1956)

2 "Gradualism" is a mighty long road. It stretches back 100 long and weary years, and looking forward it has no end.
Here I Stand (1958)

3 In Britain there was at hand the riches of English, Welsh and Gaelic folksongs. And as I sang these lovely melodies I felt that they, too, were close to my heart and expressed the same soulful quality that I knew in Negro music.
Here I Stand (1958)

4 No barriers can stand against the mightiest river of all the people's will for peace and freedom now surging in floodtide throughout the world!
Here I Stand (1958)

5 The American Negro has changed his temper. Now he wants

his freedom. Whether he is smiling at you or not, he wants his freedom.
April 12, 1944. *Here I Stand* (1958)

6 To be free—to walk the good American earth as equal citizens, to live without fear, to enjoy the fruits of our toil, to give our children every opportunity in life—that dream which we have held so long in our hearts is today the destiny that we hold in our hands.
Here I Stand (1958)

Robespierre, Maximilien (Maximilien François Marie Isidore de Robespierre; 1758–94) French lawyer and revolutionary

1 Any institution which does not suppose the people good, and the magistrate corruptible, is evil.
Declaration of the Rights of Man (April 24, 1793)

2 Any law which violates the indefeasible rights of man is essentially unjust and tyrannical; it is not a law at all.
Part of a declaration, this figured in Robespierre's "Projet" of April 21, 1793. *Declaration of the Rights of Man* (April 24, 1793), Article 6

3 The general will rules in society as the private will governs each separate individual.
Lettres à ses commettants (January 5, 1793), series 2

Robin, Leo (1895–1984) U.S. songwriter

1 Thanks for the Memory
Song title. Co-written with Ralph Rainger. (1938)

2 Diamonds Are A Girl's Best Friend
1949. Title of song sung by Marilyn Monroe in the film *Gentlemen Prefer Blondes* (1953).

Robinson, Edwin Arlington (1869–1935) U.S. poet

1 Life is the game that must be played.
"Ballade by the Fire," Envoy

2 I shall have more to say when I am dead.
"John Brown" (1920)

3 Love that's wise
Will not say all it means.
"Tristram" (1927), pt. 8

4 Joy shivers in the corner where she knits
And Conscience always has the rocking chair,
Cheerful as when she tortured into fits
The first cat that was ever killed by care.
Referring to Puritanism, which is satirized as destroying happiness. "New England," *Collected Poems* (1925), st. 2, ll. 1–6

5 And he was always quietly arrayed,
And he was always human when he talked;
But still he fluttered pulses when he said,
"Good-Morning," and he glittered when he walked.
"Richard Cory," *The Children of the Night* (1897), quoted in *The Penguin Book of American Verse* (Geoffrey Moore, ed.; 1977)

6 And Richard Cory, one calm summer night,
Went home and put a bullet through his head.
"Richard Cory," *The Children of the Night* (1897), quoted in *The Penguin Book of American Verse* (Geoffrey Moore, ed.; 1977)

7 Miniver Cheevy, child of scorn,
Grew lean while he assailed the seasons;
He wept that he was ever born,
And he had reasons.
"Miniver Cheevy," *The Town Down the River* (1907), quoted in *The Penguin Book of American Verse* (Geoffrey Moore, ed.; 1977)

Robinson, Frank (b.1935) U.S. baseball player and manager

1 It's nice to come to a town and be referred to as the manager of the Cleveland Indians instead of as the first black manager.
Sporting News (October 25, 1975)

2 Close don't count in baseball. Close only counts in horseshoes and grenades.
"Close only counts in horseshoes and hand grenades" is a commonly used phrase. *Time* (July 31, 1973)

Robinson, Jackie (Jack Roosevelt Robinson; 1919–72) U.S. baseball player

1 Above anything else, I hate to lose.
Quoted in *Giants of Baseball* (Bill Gutman; 1975)

2 Baseball is a poker game. Nobody wants to quit when he's losing; nobody wants you to quit when you're ahead.
Quoted in *Giants of Baseball* (Bill Gutman; 1975)

3 Baseball, like some other sports, poses as a sacred institution dedicated to the public good, but it is actually a big, selfish business with a ruthlessness that many big businesses would never think of displaying.
Quoted in *I Never Had It Made* (Jackie Robinson with Alfred Duckett; 1972)

4 A life is not important except in the impact it has on other lives.
Attrib.

Robinson, James Harvey (1863–1936) U.S. historian and educator

1 Partisanship is our great curse. We too readily assume that everything has two sides and that it is our duty to be on one or the other.
The Mind in the Making (1921)

Robinson, Joan (Joan Violet Robinson; 1903–83) British economist

1 The purpose of studying economics is not to acquire a set of ready-made answers to economic questions, but to learn how to avoid being deceived by economists.
Marx, Marshall and Keynes (1955)

Robinson, Mary (b.1944) Irish stateswoman

1 Instead of rocking the cradle, they rocked the system.
Paying tribute to Irish women who voted for her, helping her to become Ireland's first female president (1990–97). Victory speech following her election as president of the Republic of Ireland (November 10, 1990)

Robinson, Sugar Ray (Walker Smith; 1921–89) U.S. boxer

1 Every so often a boxer dies. Whenever that happens, some people like to shout that boxing should be outlawed...But an occasional death doesn't mean a sport should be abolished. If

that were the case, auto racing should be abolished. So should football.
Said after his fight with Jimmy Doyle, who died after being knocked out by Robinson. *Sugar Ray: The Sugar Ray Robinson Story* (1992)

2 I can hurt anybody. The question is, can I hurt him enough?
The Black Lights: Inside the World of Professional Boxing (Thomas Hauser; 1987)

3 Getting hit.
When asked what he liked least about boxing. *The Black Lights: Inside the World of Professional Boxing* (Thomas Hauser; 1987)

Roche, Boyle, Sir (1743–1807) Irish politician

1 What has posterity done for us?
Speech to the Irish Parliament (1780)

Rochefort, Henri, Marquis de Rochefort-Luçay (Victor-Henri; 1830–1913) French journalist

1 My scribbling pays me zero francs per line—not including the white spaces.
Referring to his salary as a writer. Attrib.

Rochester, 2nd Earl of (John Wilmot; 1647–80) English courtier and poet

1 Here lies our sovereign lord the King
Whose promise none relies on;
He never said a foolish thing,
Nor ever did a wise one.
Written on the bedchamber door of Charles II. A variant first line reads, "Here lies a great and mighty king." "The King's Epitaph," quoted in *Thomas Hearne: Remarks and Collections* (C. E. Doble et al; 1885–1921)

2 Huddled in dirt the reasoning engine lies,
Who was so proud, so witty, and so wise.
"Homo Sapiens," *The New Oxford Book of English Verse* (Helen Gardner, ed.; 1972)

3 Then talk not of inconstancy,
False hearts and broken vows;
If I, by miracle, can be
This livelong minute true to thee,
'Tis all that heaven allows.
"Love and Life," *The New Oxford Book of English Verse* (Helen Gardner, ed.; 1972)

Rockefeller, John D. (John Davison Rockefeller; 1839–1937) U.S. industrialist and philanthropist

1 I believe it is my duty to make money and still more money and to use the money I make for the good of my fellow man according to the dictates of my conscience.
Interview (1905)

2 I believe the power to make money is a gift of God.
Interview (1905)

3 A friendship founded on business is better than a business founded on friendship.
Attrib. *A Dictionary of Business Quotations* (Simon James and Robert Parker; 1990)

4 The growth of a large business is merely the survival of the fittest...The American beauty rose can be produced in the splendor and fragrance which brings cheer to the beholder only by sacrificing the early buds which grow up around it.
Quoted in *Our Benevolent Feudalism* (W. J. Ghent; 1902)

5 Good management consists in showing average people how to do the work of superior people.
Attrib.

6 If you want to succeed you should strike out on new paths rather than travel the worn paths of accepted success.
Attrib.

Rockefeller, Nelson A. (Nelson Aldrich Rockefeller; 1908–79) U.S. statesman

1 The brotherhood of man under the fatherhood of God.
Attrib.

Rockne, Knute (Knute Kenneth Rockne; 1888–1931) Norwegian-born U.S. football coach

1 Show me a good and gracious loser and I'll show you a failure.
Remark to Wisconsin basketball coach Walter Meanwell (1920s)

2 Drink the first. Sip the second slowly. Skip the third.
Advice to his players. Quoted in *Rockne* (Jerry Brondfield; 1976)

Roddick, Anita (originally Anita Lucia Perilli; b.1942) British business executive

1 To succeed you have to believe in something with such a passion that it becomes a reality.
Body and Soul (1991)

2 Being good is good business.
Sunday Express, London (November 2, 1986), magazine

3 Work is more fun than fun.
Quoted in *When a Woman Means Business* (Debbie Moore; 1989)

Roden, Claudia (b.1937) Egyptian-born British cookbook writer

1 Every cuisine tells a story. Jewish food tells the story of an uprooted, migrating people and their vanished worlds.
The Book of Jewish Food (1997)

Rodenberg, Julius (originally Julius Levy; 1831–1914) German poet and writer

1 It was so dismal and gloomy on these mountains, and so were my spirits. I felt as though we were wandering under the sea, and ought to climb over these basalt blocks and porphyry rocks to the surface and light of day.
1856. Referring to his only experience of mountain-walking in North Wales, which took place in dense mist. "Caernarvon and Llanberis," *An Autumn in Wales* (William Linnard, tr.; 1985)

2 This *Caru-ar-y-gwely*, called courting on the bed, is customary throughout Wales—the girl sits on the bed chatting with her beloved until morning.
1856. "The Schoolmaster of Llanfairfechan," *An Autumn in Wales* (William Linnard, tr.; 1985)

Rodgers, T. J. U.S. business executive

1 There are no safe harbors—the only safe harbor is competency.
Quoted in *In the Company of Giants* (Rama Dev Jager; 1997)

Rodin, Auguste (François Auguste René Rodin; 1840–1917) French sculptor

1 Really, there is no beautiful style, no beautiful design, and no beautiful color: there is just one beauty, that of the truth that is revealed.
Attrib.

2 What is ugly in Art is only that which is without character, that is, that which offers no truth at all, either exterior or interior.
Attrib.

Rodin, Robert U.S. business executive

1 You have to decisively say: Goodbye industrial age.
Referring to the coming of the information revolution in business. Quoted in *Opening Digital Markets* (Walid Mougayar; 1997)

Roentgen, Wilhelm Conrad (1845–1923) German physicist

1 All bodies are transparent to this agent...For brevity's sake I shall use the expression "rays"; and to distinguish them from others of this name I shall call them "X-rays".
December 28, 1895. His "Preliminary Communication" to the Würzburg Physical and Medical Society. Quoted in *William Conrad Roentgen and the Early History of the Roentgen Rays* (Otto Glasser; 1933)

Roepke Bahamonde, Gabriela (b.1920) Chilean playwright

1 OLD LADY The best thing others can do for us is to tell us lies.
A White Butterfly (1960)

2 SMITH The reflection in my shaving mirror tells me things nobody else would.
A White Butterfly (1960)

Roethke, Theodore (Theodore Huebner Roethke; 1908–63) U.S. poet

1 In a dark wood I saw
I saw my several selves
Come running from the leaves,
Lewd, tiny, careless lives
That scuttled under stones,
Or broke, but would not go.
"The Exorcism" (1958)

2 All finite things reveal infinitude.
The Far Field (1964)

3 In a dark time, the eye begins to see.
"In a Dark Time," *The Far Field* (1964), l. 1

4 What's madness but nobility of soul
At odds with circumstance?
"In a Dark Time," *The Far Field* (1964), ll. 7–8

5 A man goes far to find out what he is—
Death of the self in a long, tearless night,
All natural shapes blazing unnatural light.
"In a Dark Time," *The Far Field* (1964), ll. 16–18

6 I learned not to fear infinity,
The far field, the windy cliffs of forever,
The dying of time in the white light of tomorrow.
"The Far Field," *The Far Field* (1964)

7 May the eyes in your face
Survive the green ice
Of envy's mean gaze.
"To a Young Wife," *The Far Field* (1964)

8 Over the gulfs of dream
Flew a tremendous bird
Further and further away
Into a moonless black,
Deep in the brain, far back.
"Night Crow," *The Lost Son and Other Poems* (1948)

9 At Woodlawn I heard the dead cry;
I was lulled by the slamming of iron,
A slow drip over stones,
Toads brooding in wells.
"The Flight," *The Lost Son and Other Poems* (1948)

10 I wake to sleep, and take my waking slow.
I feel my fate in what I cannot fear.
I learn by going where I have to go.
The Waking (1953)

11 She was the sickle; I, poor I, the rake,
Coming behind her for her pretty sake
(But what prodigious mowing we did make).
"I Knew a Woman," *Words for the Wind: The Collected Verse of Theodore Roethke* (1957)

Rogers, Everett (Everett Mitchell Rogers; b.1931) U.S. sociologist

1 Invention is the process by which a new idea is discovered or created. In contrast, innovation occurs when that new idea is adopted.
Attrib.

Rogers, Jim U.S. investor

1 The 19th Century was the century of the U.K. The 20th Century was the century of the U.S. The 21st Century will be the century of China. Not Japan—China.
The Charlie Rose Show, U.S. Public Broadcasting Service (December 18, 1995)

Rogers, Roy (originally Leonard Slye; 1912–98) U.S. singer and film actor

1 Until we meet again, may the good Lord take a liking to you.
Catchphrase. *The Roy Rogers Show* (1951–57)

Rogers, Samuel (1763–1855) British poet and art collector

1 She was good as she was fair,
None—none on earth above her!
As pure in thought as angels are:
To know her was to love her.
"Jacqueline" (1814), st. 1

2 The good are better made by ill,
As odours crushed are sweeter still.
"Jacqueline" (1814), st. 3

3 A guardian angel o'er his life presiding,
Doubling his pleasures, and his cares dividing.
Human Life (1819)

4 The soul of music slumbers in the shell
Till waked and kindled by the master's spell;
And feeling hearts, touch them but rightly, pour
A thousand melodies unheard before!
Human Life (1819)

5 Think nothing done while aught remains to do.
Human Life (1819), l. 49

6 Never less alone than when alone.
Human Life (1819), l. 756

7 Those that he loved so long and sees no more,
Loved and still loves,—not dead, but gone before,—
He gathers round him.
Human Life (1819), l. 757

8 Sweet Memory! wafted by thy gentle gale,
Oft up the stream of Time I turn my sail.
The Pleasures of Memory (1792), pt. 2

9 That very law which moulds a tear
And bids it trickle from its source—
That law preserves the earth a sphere,
And guides the planets in their course.
"On a Tear," *The Poetical Works of Samuel Rogers* (1875)

10 It doesn't much signify whom one marries, for one is sure to find next morning that it was someone else.
Quoted in *Table Talk of Samuel Rogers* (Alexander Dyce, ed.; 1860)

11 When a new book is published, read an old one.
Attrib.

Rogers, Will (William Penn Adair Rogers; 1879–1935) U.S. actor, writer, and humorist

1 A comedian can only last till he either takes himself serious or his audience takes him serious.
Newspaper article (1931)

2 You can't say civilization don't advance, however, for in every war they kill you a new way.
New York Times (December 23, 1929)

3 Being a hero is about the shortest-lived profession on earth.
"A Rogers Thesaurus," *Saturday Review* (August 25, 1962)

4 I don't make jokes—I just watch the government and report the facts.
"A Rogers Thesaurus," *Saturday Review* (August 25, 1962)

5 The more you read and observe about this politics thing, you got to admit that each party is worse than the other.
"A Rogers Thesaurus," *Saturday Review* (August 25, 1962)

6 It has made more liars out of the American people than golf.
Referring to income tax. "A Rogers Thesaurus," *Saturday Review* (August 25, 1962)

7 The English should give Ireland home rule—and reserve the motion picture rights.
The Autobiography of Will Rogers (1949)

8 The best doctor in the world is the Veterinarian. He can't ask his patients what is the matter—he's got to just know.
The Autobiography of Will Rogers (1949)

9 England elects a Labour Government. When a man goes in for politics over here, he has no time to labor, and any man that labors has no time to fool with politics. Over there politics is an obligation; over here it's a business.
The Autobiography of Will Rogers (1949)

10 Everything is funny, as long as it's happening to somebody else.
The Illiterate Digest (1924)

11 Communism is like prohibition, it's a good idea but it won't work.
1927. *Weekly Articles* (1981), vol. 3

12 If we ever pass out as a great nation, we ought to put on our tombstone, "America died of the delusion she had moral leadership."
The Autobiography of Will Rogers (1949)

13 You can't spring a new plot on an audience the first time and expect it to go. It takes a movie audience years to get on to a new plot.
The Autobiography of Will Rogers (1949)

14 See what will happen to you if you don't stop biting your fingernails.
Message written on a postcard of the Venus de Milo that he sent to his young niece. Also attributed to others. Quoted in *The Faber Book of Anecdotes* (Clifton Fadiman, ed.; 1985)

15 So live that you wouldn't be ashamed to sell the family parrot to the town gossip.
Attrib.

Roland, Madame (Jeanne Manon Philipon Roland de La Platière; 1754–93) French revolutionary

1 Oh liberty! Oh liberty! What crimes are committed in thy name!
1793. Said as she mounted the steps of the guillotine at her execution. Attrib. *Histoire des Girondins* (A. de Lamartine; 1847), bk. 51, ch. 8

Rolland, Romain (1866–1944) French writer

1 A hero is the one who does what he can. The others do not.
1912. "L'adoléscent," *Jean-Christophe* (1903–12), vol. 3

2 France, the eternal resort of Germany in disorder.
"La révolte," *Jean-Christophe* (1903–12), vol. 4

3 Passion is like genius: a miracle.
1912. "Le Buisson ardent," *Jean-Christophe* (1903–12), vol. 9

4 Where the character is not great, there is no great man...Never mind success. It is a question of being great, not seeming it.
The Life of Beethoven (1903), Preface

Rolleston, Humphrey, Sir (1862–1944) British physician and writer

1 First they get *on*, then they get *honour*, then they get *honest*.
Referring to physicians. Quoted in *Confessions of an Advertising Man* (David Ogilvy; 1963)

2 Medicine is a noble profession but a damn bad business.
Quoted in *The Wit of Medicine* (Lore and Maurice Cowan; 1972)

Romains, Jules (Louis Farigoule; 1885–1972) French writer

1 Every man who feels well is a sick man neglecting himself.
Doctor Knock, ou le Triomphe de la médecine (1923)

2 For my part, I only know people more or less overcome by more or less numerous diseases of more or less rapid progression.
Doctor Knock, ou le Triomphe de la médecine (1923)

Romer, Paul M. (b.1955) U.S. academic

1 Every generation has underestimated the potential for finding new ideas...Possibilities do not add up. They multiply.
Fortune (October 18, 1993)

Romero, Oscar (Oscar Arnulfo Romero; 1917–80) Salvadoran archbishop

1 Liberation will only arrive when the poor are the controllers of, and protagonists in, their own struggle and liberation.
Sermon, San Salvador (February 2, 1980), quoted in *The War of Gods* (Michael Löwy; 1996)

2 I would like to make a special appeal to the members of the Army...In the name of God, in the name of your tormented people whose cries rise up...I beseech you, I beg you, I command you: STOP THE REPRESSION!
Said on the day before his murder by paramilitary death squads. Sermon, San Salvador (March 23, 1980), quoted in *The War of Gods* (Michael Löwy; 1996)

3 Martyrdom is a grace of God which I do not think that I deserve. But if God accepts the sacrifice of my life, let my blood be a seed of freedom and the sign that hope will soon become reality.
Oscar Romero was murdered by paramilitary death squads (March 24, 1980). Quoted in *The War of Gods* (Michael Löwy; 1996)

Ronsard, Pierre de (1524–85) French poet

1 When you are very old, and sit in the candle-light at evening spinning by the fire, you will say, as you murmur my verses, a wonder in your eyes, "Ronsard sang of me in the days when I was fair."
Sonnets for Hélène (1578), bk. 2, no 42

Rooke, Sir Denis (Denis Eric Rooke; b.1924) British business executive

1 The only things that create wealth in the world are things like fishing and farming and mining and taking resources and creating something.
Financial Times, London (July 1, 1984)

Rooney, Mickey (originally Joe Yule, Jr.; b.1920) U.S. film actor

1 Had I been brighter, the ladies been gentler, the Scotch been weaker, had the gods been kinder, had the dice been hotter, this could have been a one-sentence story: Once upon a time I lived happily ever after.
Attrib.

Roosevelt, Edith Carow (originally Edith Kermit Carow; 1861–1948) U.S. first lady

1 Women who marry pass their best and happiest years in giving life and fostering it.
Quoted in "American Backlogs," *First Ladies* (Betty Boyd Caroli; 1967)

Roosevelt, Eleanor (Anna Eleanor Roosevelt; 1884–1962) U.S. diplomat, author, and human rights campaigner

Quotations about Eleanor Roosevelt

1 She would rather light candles than curse the darkness, and her glow has warmed the world.
1962
Adlai Stevenson (1900–65) U.S. statesman. On learning of the death of Eleanor Roosevelt. *New York Times* (November 8, 1962)

Quotations by Eleanor Roosevelt

2 I have spent many years of my life in opposition and I rather like the role.
Letter to Bernard Baruch (November 18, 1952)

3 So—against odds, the women inch forward, but I'm rather old to be carrying on this fight!
Remark (February 13, 1946)

4 No one can make you feel inferior without your consent.
1937. *Catholic Digest* (August 1960)

5 I think if the people of this country can be reached with the truth, their judgment will be in favor of the many, as against the privileged few.
Ladies' Home Journal (1942)

6 Life has got to be lived—that's all there is to it. At 70, I would say the advantage is that you take life more calmly. You know that "this, too, shall pass!"
New York Times (October 8, 1954)

Roosevelt, Franklin D. (Franklin Delano Roosevelt, "FDR"; 1882–1945) U.S. president

Quotations about Franklin Roosevelt

1 A chameleon on plaid.
Herbert Hoover (1874–1964) U.S. president. Quoted in *The Lion and the Fox* (James McGregor Burns; 1956)

2 He would rather follow public opinion than lead it.
Harry L. Hopkins (1890–1946) U.S. politician. Attrib.

3 The man who started more creations since Genesis—and finished none.
Hugh Johnson (1882–1942) U.S. general and government official. Referring to Franklin D. Roosevelt's social and economic recovery projects during the Depression. Quoted in *All But the People: F. D. Roosevelt and His Critics* (George Wolfskill and John Hudson; 1969)

4 If he became convinced tomorrow that coming out for

cannibalism would get him the votes he so sorely needs, he would begin fattening a missionary on the White House backyard come Wednesday.
H. L. Mencken (1880–1956) U.S. journalist, critic, and editor. Quoted in *Franklin D. Roosevelt: A Profile* (W. E. Leuchtenburg, ed.; 1967)

5 I used to tell my husband that, if he could make *me* understand something, it would be clear to all the other people in the country.
Eleanor Roosevelt (1884–1962) U.S. diplomat, author, and human rights campaigner. Newspaper column. "My Day" (February 12, 1947)

6 Happy Days Are Here Again
1929
Jack Yellen (1892–1958) U.S. lyricist and music publisher. Song title. Used by Franklin D. Roosevelt as a campaign song in the 1932 election.

Quotations by Franklin Roosevelt

7 We must be the great arsenal of democracy.
Broadcast address to Forum on Current Problems (December 29, 1940)

8 The nation that destroys its soil destroys itself.
Urging soil conservation laws throughout the United States. Letter to the governors (February 26, 1937)

9 If factories close in Ireland and there is a great deal more suffering there, there will be less general sympathy in the United States than if it happened six months ago.
Expressing anger at Ireland's neutrality in World War II. Letter to the U.S. Ambassador to Ireland (August 21, 1941), quoted in *Phrases Make History Here* (Conor O'Clery; 1986)

10 We all know that books burn—yet we have the greater knowledge that books cannot be killed by fire. People die, but books never die. No man and no force can abolish memory...In this war, we know, books are weapons.
Message to the American Booksellers Association (May 6, 1942)

11 Never before have we had so little time in which to do so much.
Radio address (February 23, 1942)

12 The forgotten man at the bottom of the economic pyramid.
The man the New Deal was designed to help. Radio address (April 7, 1932)

13 I am reminded of four definitions. A radical is a man with both feet firmly planted—in the air; a conservative is a man with two perfectly good legs who, however, has never learned to walk; a reactionary is a somnambulist walking backwards; a liberal is a man who uses his legs and his hands at the behest of his head.
Radio broadcast (October 26, 1939)

14 There is a mysterious cycle in human events. To some generations much is given. Of other generations much is expected. This generation has a rendezvous with destiny.
Speech accepting the Democratic Party presidential nomination (June 26, 1936)

15 The hand that held the dagger has struck it into the back of its neighbor...Neither those who sprang from that ancient stock nor those who have come hither in later years can be indifferent to the destruction of freedom in their ancestral lands across the seas.
Said on the day that Italy declared war on France and Britain. Speech, Charlottesville, Virginia (June 10, 1940)

16 The country needs and, unless I mistake its temper, the country demands bold, persistent experimentation. It is common sense to take a method and try it; if it fails, admit it frankly and try another. But above all, try something.
Speech, Oglethorpe University, Atlanta, Georgia (May 22, 1932)

17 The arts cannot thrive except where men are free to be themselves and to be in charge of the discipline of their own energies and ardors. The conditions for democracy and art are one.
Speech on the occasion of the dedication of the Museum of Modern Art, New York City (May 10, 1939)

18 Better the occasional faults of a government that lives in a spirit of charity than the consistent omissions of a government frozen in the ice of its own indifference.
Speech, Philadelphia, Pennsylvania (June 27, 1936)

19 Nothing less than the unconditional surrender of Germany, Italy, and Japan.
Referring to the objectives of the U.S. and British governments. Statement to the press, Casablanca, Morocco (January 24, 1943)

20 Yesterday, December 7, 1941—a day that will live in infamy—the United States of America was suddenly and deliberately attacked by naval and air forces of the Empire of Japan.
Referring to the Japanese attack on Pearl Harbor, which brought the United States into World War II. War message to Congress (December 8, 1941)

21 When peace has been broken anywhere, the peace of all countries everywhere is in danger.
September 3, 1939. Radio broadcast. "Fireside Chat," *Public Papers* (1941), vol. 8

22 In the field of world policy, I would dedicate this nation to the policy of the good neighbor.
March 4, 1933. First inaugural address, *Public Papers* (1938), vol. 2

23 Let me assert my firm belief that the only thing we have to fear is fear itself.
March 4, 1933. First inaugural address, *Public Papers* (1938), vol. 2

24 I see one-third of a nation ill-housed, ill-clad, ill-nourished.
January 20, 1937. Second inaugural address, *Public Papers* (1941), vol. 6

25 I pledge you, I pledge myself, to a new deal for the American people.
July 2, 1932. Accepting the nomination for presidency. Speech, Chicago, *Public Papers* (1938), vol. 1

26 We look forward to a world founded upon four essential human freedoms. The first is freedom of speech and expression—everywhere in the world. The second is freedom of every person to worship God in his own way—everywhere in the world. The third is freedom from want—everywhere in the world. The fourth is freedom from fear—anywhere in the world.
Speech to Congress, *Public Papers* (January 6, 1941), vol. 10

27 I murdered my grandmother this morning.
His habitual remark to any guest at the White House he suspected of paying no attention to what he said. Quoted in *Ear on Washington* (Diana McClellan; 1982)

28 Big business collectivism in industry compels an ultimate collectivism in government.
Quoted in *The American Dream* (Esmond Wright; 1996)

29 Hello, Joe? It's Frank. Giants three, Dodgers nothing.
Telephone call to Joseph Stalin, said to be "almost surely apocryphal." Refers to two baseball teams. Attrib. *The Faber Book of Anecdotes* (Clifton Fadiman, ed.; 1995)

30 It is fun to be in the same decade with you.
1942. After Churchill had congratulated him on his 60th birthday. Quoted in *The Hinge of Fate* (Winston S. Churchill; 1950), ch. 4

31 Defeat of Germany means the defeat of Japan, probably without firing a shot or losing a life.
1942. Quoted in *The Hinge of Fate* (Winston S. Churchill; 1950), ch. 25

32 The best immediate defense of the United States is the success of Great Britain defending itself.
Said at a press conference. Quoted in *Their Finest Hour* (Winston S. Churchill; December 17, 1940), ch. 28

33 You know how I really feel? I feel like a baseball team going into the ninth inning with only eight men left to play.
(April 4, 1945. Said to Clark Griffith. Roosevelt died eight days later. Quoted in *This Week* (April 10, 1955)

34 The problem of economic loss due to sickness...a very serious matter for many families with and without incomes, and therefore, an unfair burden upon the medical profession.
Address on the problems of economic and social security. (November 14, 1934)

35 More than an end of this war, we want an end to the beginnings of all wars.
Address written for Jefferson Day, broadcast on the day after his death. (April 13, 1945)

36 A man who has never gone to school may steal from a freight car, but if he has a university education he may steal the whole railroad.
Attrib.

37 Be sincere, be brief, be seated.
Attrib.

38 Government cannot close its eyes to the pollution of waters, to the erosion of soil, to the slashing of forests any more than it can close its eyes to the need for slum clearance and schools.
Attrib.

39 When you get to the end of your rope, tie a knot and hang on.
Attrib.

Roosevelt, Theodore ("Teddy" Roosevelt; 1858–1919) U.S. president

Quotations about Theodore Roosevelt

1 Now look, that damned cowboy is President of the United States.
Mark Hanna (1837–1904) U.S. businessman and politician. Remark (September 1901)

2 I've always voted for Roosevelt as President. My father always voted for Roosevelt as President.
1944
Bob Hope (b.1903) British-born U.S. comedian and film actor. Quoted in *American Chronicle* (Lois and Alan Gordon; 1987)

3 Oh, Mr. President, do not let so great an achievement suffer from any taint of legality.
Philander Chase Knox (1853–1921) U.S. lawyer and politician. Responding to Theodore Roosevelt's request for a legal justification of his acquisition of the Panama Canal Zone. Quoted in *Violent Neighbours* (T. Buckley; 1903)

4 Father always wanted to be the bride at every wedding and the corpse at every funeral.
Nicholas Roosevelt (1893–1982) U.S. journalist. *A Front Row Seat* (1953)

5 I always enjoy his society, he is so hearty, so straightforward, outspoken and, for the moment, so absolutely sincere.
Mark Twain (1835–1910) U.S. writer and humorist. *Autobiography* (1913)

Quotations by Theodore Roosevelt

6 In the Western hemisphere the adherence of the United States to the Monroe Doctrine may force the United States, however reluctantly, in flagrant cases of wrongdoing or impotence, to the exercise of an international police power.
Annual Message to Congress: Corollary to the Monroe Doctrine (December 6, 1904)

7 The things that will destroy America are prosperity-at-any-price, peace-at-any-price, safety-first instead of duty-first, the love of soft living, and the get-rich-quick theory of life.
Letter to S. Stanwood Mencken (January 10, 1917)

8 A just war is in the long run far better for a nation's soul than the most prosperous peace obtained by acquiescence in wrong or injustice.
Message to Congress (December 4, 1906)

9 We have room in this country for but one flag, the Stars and Stripes...We have room for but one loyalty, loyalty to the United States...We have room for but one language, the English language.
Said two days before his death. Message to the American Defense Society (January 3, 1919)

10 The only tyrannies from which men, women and children are suffering in real life are the tyrannies of minorities.
Speech (March 22, 1912)

11 There is a homely adage which runs "Speak softly and carry a big stick, you will go far."
Speech at Minnesota State Fair (September 2, 1901)

12 A man who is good enough to shed his blood for the country is good enough to be given a square deal afterwards. More than that no man is entitled to, and less than that no man shall have.
Speech at Springfield, Illinois (July 4, 1903)

13 I wish to preach, not the doctrine of ignoble ease, but the doctrine of the strenuous life.
Speech before the Hamilton Club, Chicago (April 10, 1899)

14 No people is wholly civilized where a distinction is drawn between stealing an office and stealing a purse.
Speech, Chicago, Illinois (June 22, 1912)

15 The first requisite of a good citizen in this Republic of ours is that he shall be able and willing to pull his weight.
Speech, New York (November 11, 1902)

16 I stand for the square deal...I mean not merely that I stand for fair play under the present rules of the game, but that I stand for having those rules changed so as to work for a more substantial equality of opportunity and of reward for equally good service.
The Square Deal was Theodore Roosevelt's program of domestic reform. It aimed to break up concentrations of economic and political power that undermined equality of opportunity. Speech, Osawatomie, Kansas (August 31, 1910)

17 We are fighting in the quarrel of civilization against barbarism, of liberty against tyranny. Germany has become a menace to

the whole world. She is the most dangerous enemy of liberty now existing.
Speech, Oyster Bay, Long Island, New York City (April 1917)

18 The men with the muckrakes are often indispensable to the well-being of society; but only if they know when to stop raking the muck.
Referring to the exposing of political scandal. Muckrakes are rakes used to spread manure or compost. Speech, Washington, D.C. (April 14, 1906)

19 Do not hit at all if it can be avoided, but never hit softly.
Autobiography (1913)

20 Every reform movement has a lunatic fringe.
Autobiography (1913)

21 Practical efficiency is common, and lofty idealism not uncommon; it is the combination which is necessary, and the combination is rare.
Autobiography (1913)

22 Every immigrant who comes here should be required within five years to learn English or leave the country.
Kansas City Star (April 27, 1918)

23 The Cubists are entitled to the serious attention of all who find enjoyment in the colored puzzle pictures of the Sunday newspapers.
1913. Referring to the International Exhibition of Modern Art (the Armory Show) of new French work that toured New York, Chicago, and Boston in 1913. "A Layman's View of an Art Exhibition," *Outlook* (March 9, 1913)

24 There can be no fifty-fifty Americanism in this country. There is room here for only one hundred per cent Americanism.
July 19, 1918. Speech in Saratoga, New York, *Roosevelt Policy* (1919), vol. 3

25 No man is justified in doing evil on the ground of expediency.
The Strenuous Life: Essays and Addresses (1900)

26 There is no room in this country for hyphenated Americanism.
October 12, 1915. Speech before the Knights of Columbus, New York, *Works* (Memorial edition, 1923–26), vol. 20

27 Kings and such like are just as funny as politicians.
Quoted in *Mr. Wilson's War* (John Dos Passos; 1962), ch. 1

28 A man who will steal *for* me will steal *from* me.
Firing a cowboy who had applied Roosevelt's brand to a steer belonging to a neighboring ranch. Quoted in *Roosevelt in the Bad Lands* (Herman Hagedorn; 1921)

29 There is apt to be a lunatic fringe among the votaries of any forward movement.
Quoted in *Speaking Freely* (Stuart Berg Flexner and Anne H. Soukhanov; 1997)

Rorem, Ned (b.1923) U.S. composer and writer

1 It isn't evil that is ruining the earth, but mediocrity. The crime is not that Nero played while Rome burned, but that he played badly.
The Final Diary (1974)

2 Famous last words of Ned Rorem, crushed by a truck, gnawed by pox, stung by wasps, in dire pain: "How do I look?"
The Paris Diary of Ned Rorem (1966), quoted *A Queer Reader* (Patrick Higgins, ed.; 1993)

3 The phone: "How will I recognize you?" "I'm beautiful."
The Paris Diary of Ned Rorem (1966), quoted in *A Queer Reader* (Patrick Higgins, ed.; 1993)

Rorty, Richard (Richard McKay Rorty; b.1931) U.S. philosopher

1 There is nothing deep down inside us except what we have put there ourselves.
Referring to the notion that there is some kind of metaphysical "truth" within us that might answer the problems presented to us by the world. "Pragmatism and Philosophy," *Consequences of Pragmatism* (1982)

2 Openmindedness should not be fostered because, as Scripture teaches, Truth is great and will prevail, nor because, as Milton suggests, Truth will always win in a free and open encounter. It should be fostered for its own sake.
"The Contingency of Community," *Contingency, Irony and Solidarity* (1989), ch. 3

3 Always strive to excel, but only on weekends.
New York Times Magazine (February 12, 1990)

4 It is pictures rather than propositions, metaphors rather than statements, which determine most of our philosophical convictions.
Philosophy and the Mirror of Human Nature (1979)

Rosa, Salvator (1615–73) Spanish-born Italian painter

1 For twenty-two days I have known no rest in body or mind. As soon as I eat enough to keep alive I howl, I weep, and cannot stand the sight of a paintbrush. Now I really know that the errors of the wise are always greater than those of ordinary men.
Letter to Riccardi (1656), quoted in *Poesie e lettere inedite di Salvator Rosa* (Uberto Limentani, ed.; 1950)

Rose, Billy (William Samuel Rosenberg; 1899–1966) U.S. theatrical impresario and composer

1 Never invest your money in anything that eats or needs repainting.
New York Post (October 26, 1957)

2 Does the Spearmint Lose Its Flavor on the Bedpost Overnight?
Early 1920s. Song title.

3 Me and My Shadow
1927–28. Song title.

Rose, Frank U.S. author

1 The democratization of computer power would alter the balance between the individual and the institution.
West of Eden (1989)

2 Macintosh was an artificial arrangement of silicon and metal designed to manipulate electrons according to the strict rules of logic; but its appeal transcended logic...this was no mere "productivity tool" but a machine to free the human spirit.
Referring to a computer made by Apple Computer Inc. *West of Eden* (1989)

3 Computers seemed destined to be nodes on the network, not bastions of individual creativity.
Referring to the rise of the Internet. *West of Eden* (1989)

Rosenberg, Harold (1906–78) U.S. art historian

1 An artist is a person who has invented an artist.
Discovering the Present: Three Decades in Art, Culture and Politics (1973)

Rosenberg, Isaac (1890–1918) British poet and painter

1 A man's brains splattered on
A stretcher-bearer's face;
His shook shoulders slipped their load.
1916–18. "Dead Man's Dump," *Collected Works of Isaac Rosenberg* (1937)

2 We heard his weak scream,
We heard his very last sound,
And our wheels grazed his dead face.
1916–18. "Dead Man's Dump," *Collected Works of Isaac Rosenberg* (1937)

Rosewarne, V. A. (1916–40) British pilot

1 The universe is so vast and so ageless that the life of one man can only be justified by the measure of his sacrifice.
1940. Inscribed on the portrait of the "Young Airman" in the RAF Museum. Last letter to his mother, quoted in *Times*, London (June 18, 1940)

Ross, Alan Strode Campbell (1907–80) British linguist

1 U and Non-U, An Essay in Sociological Linguistics.
Essay title. *Neuphilologische Mitteilungen* (1954), quoted in *Noblesse Oblige* (Nancy Mitford, ed.; 1965)

Ross, Diana (Diana Ernestine Ross; b.1944) U.S. singer and actor

Quotations about Ross

1 It's hard for me to deal with other prima donnas.
Marvin Gaye (1939–84) U.S. singer and songwriter. Quoted in *Divided Soul: The Life of Marvin Gaye* (David Ritz; 1985)

Quotations by Ross

2 I've always said if one person believes in me, I will try to move mountains.
Secrets of a Sparrow (1993)

Ross, Harold W. (Harold Wallace Ross; 1892–1951) U.S. journalist

Quotations about Ross

1 His ignorance was an Empire State Building of ignorance. You had to admire it for its size.
Dorothy Parker (1893–1967) U.S. writer and wit. Attrib.

Quotations by Ross

2 I've never been in there...but there are only three things to see, and I've seen color reproductions of all of them.
Referring to the Louvre. Quoted in *A Farewell to Arms* (Ernest Hemingway; 1929)

3 I don't want you to think I'm not incoherent.
Quoted in *The Years with Ross* (James Thurber; 1957)

4 The *New Yorker* will not be edited for the old lady from Dubuque.
1925. Said upon founding the *New Yorker*. Attrib.

Ross, Nick (b.1947) British broadcaster

1 We're barking mad about crime in this country. We have an obsession with believing the worst, conning ourselves that there was a golden age—typically 40 years before the one we're living in.
Radio Times, London (June 26, 1993)

Ross, Pamela British mother

1 But do you value life less than sport?
Referring to the British government's decision not to ban all handguns. *Independent*, London (August 1, 1996)

Ross, Ronald, Sir (1857–1932) British physician and entomologist

Quotations about Ross

1 Once on this August day, an exiled man
Striving to read the hieroglyphics spelled
By changing speckles upon glass, beheld
A secret hidden since the world began.
August 20, 1957
John Masefield (1878–1967) British poet and playwright. Referring to the 60th anniversary of the discovery by Ronald Ross of the transmission of malaria by the mosquito *Anopheles stephensi*. *Times*, London (August 20, 1957)

Quotations by Ross

2 That evening I wrote to my wife: "I have seen something very promising indeed in my new mosquitoes".
Referring to his discovery of the transmission of malaria by the mosquito *Anopheles stephensi*. *Memoirs* (1923)

3 This day relenting God
Hath placed within my hand
A wondrous thing; and God
Be praised. At His command,
Seeking His secret deeds
With tears and toiling breath,
I find thy cunning seeds,
O million-murdering Death.
I know this little thing
A myriad men may save.
O Death, where is thy sting?
Thy victory, O Grave?
On his part in the discovery of the life-cycle of the malaria parasite. "In Exile," *Philosophies* (1910), pt. 6, reply 1

4 Science is the Differential Calculus of the mind. Art the Integral Calculus; they may be beautiful when apart, but are greatest only when combined.
Quoted in *The Complete Poems of Hugh MacDiarmid, 1920–1976* (Michael Grieve and W. R. Aitken, eds.; 1978)

Rossetti, Christina (Christina Georgina Rossetti; 1830–94) British poet

1 My heart is like a singing bird
Whose nest is in a watered shoot;
My heart is like an apple-tree
Whose boughs are bent with thickset fruit;
My heart is like a rainbow shell
That paddles in a halcyon sea;
My heart is gladder than all these
Because my love is come to me.
"A Birthday" (1861)

2 Come to me in the silence of the night;
Come in the speaking silence of a dream;
Come with soft rounded cheeks and eyes as bright
As sunlight on a stream;

Come back in tears,
O memory, hope, love of finished years.
"Echo" (1862)

3 For there is no friend like a sister
In calm or stormy weather;
To cheer one on the tedious way,
To fetch one if one goes astray,
To lift one if one totters down,
To strengthen whilst one stands.
"Goblin Market" (1862)

4 Cheek to cheek and breast to breast
Locked together in one nest.
"Goblin Market" (1862), ll. 196–197, quoted in *Penguin Book of Homosexual Verse* (Stephen Coote, ed.; 1983)

5 In the bleak mid-winter
Frosty wind made moan,
Earth stood hard as iron,
Water like a stone;
Snow had fallen, snow on snow,
Snow on snow,
In the bleak mid-winter,
Long ago.
"Mid-Winter" (1875)

6 The hope I dreamed of was a dream,
Was but a dream; and now I wake,
Exceeding comfortless, and worn, and old,
For a dream's sake.
"Mirage" (1862)

7 Better by far you should forget and smile
Than that you should remember and be sad.
"Remember" (1862)

8 Remember me when I am gone away,
Gone far away into the silent land.
"Remember" (1862)

9 Does the road wind up-hill all the way?
Yes, to the very end.
Will the day's journey take the whole long day?
From morn to night, my friend.
"Up-Hill" (1862)

10 Will there be beds for me and all who seek?
Yea, beds for all who come.
"Up-Hill" (1862)

11 When I am dead, my dearest,
Sing no sad songs for me;
Plant thou no roses at my head,
Nor shady cypress tree:
Be the green grass above me
With showers and dewdrops wet;
And if thou wilt, remember,
And if thou wilt, forget.
"When I am Dead" (1862)

12 Who has seen the wind?
Neither you nor I:
But when the trees bow down their heads,
The wind is passing by.
"Who Has Seen the Wind?" (1872)

Rossetti, Dante Gabriel (1828–82) British painter and poet

1 Was it a friend or foe that spread these lies?
Nay, who but infants question in such wise?
'Twas one of my most intimate enemies.
"Fragment"

2 I have been here before.
But when or how I cannot tell:
I know the grass beyond the door,
The sweet keen smell,
The sighing sound, the lights around the shore.
"Sudden Light" (1881), st. 1

3 The blessed damozel leaned out
From the gold bar of Heaven;
Her eyes were deeper than the depth
Of waters stilled at even;
She had three lilies in her hand,
And the stars in her hair were seven.
"The Blessed Damozel" (1870), st. 1

4 Her hair that lay along her back
Was yellow like ripe corn.
"The Blessed Damozel" (1870), st. 2

5 From perfect grief there need not be
Wisdom or even memory:
One thing then learnt remains to me,
The woodspurge has a cup of three.
"The Woodspurge" (1870), st. 4

6 Look in my face; my name is Might-have-been.
I am also called No-more, Too-late, Farewell.
"A Superscription," *The House of Life* (1881)

7 A sonnet is a moment's monument,—
Memorial from the Soul's eternity
To one dead deathless hour.
"Introduction," *The House of Life* (1881)

8 When vain desire at last and vain regret
Go hand in hand to death, and all is vain,
What shall assuage the unforgotten pain
And teach the unforgetful to forget?
"The One Hope," *The House of Life* (1881), pt. 2

Rossi, Hugo U.S. mathematician

1 In the fall of 1972 President Nixon announced that the rate of increase of inflation was decreasing. This was the first time a sitting president used the third derivative to advance his case for reelection.
Quoted in "Mathematics is an Edifice, Not a Toolbox," *Notices of the American Mathematical Society* (October 1996), vol. 43, no. 10

Rossini, Gioacchino (Gioacchino Antonio Rossini; 1792–1868) Italian composer

1 Give me a laundry-list and I'll set it to music.
Attrib.

Rostand, Edmond (1868–1918) French playwright

1 My nose is huge! Vile snub-nose, flat-nosed ass, flat-head, let me inform you that I am proud of such an appendage, since a big nose is the proper sign of a friendly, good, courteous, witty, liberal, and brave man, such as I am.
Cyrano de Bergerac (1898), Act 1, Scene 1

2 Only dreaming is of interest,
What is life without dreams?
La Princesse lointaine (1895)

Rostand, Jean (1894–1977) French biologist and writer

1 A married couple are well suited when both partners usually feel the need for a quarrel at the same time.
Marriage (1927)

2 Never feel remorse for what you have thought about your wife; she has thought much worse things about you.
Marriage (1927)

3 Kill a man, and you are a murderer. Kill millions of men, and you are a conqueror. Kill everyone, and you are a god.
Thoughts of a Biologist (1955)

Rosten, Norman (b.1914) U.S. poet and playwright

1 And there's the outhouse poet, anonymous:
Soldiers who wish to be a hero
Are practically zero
...But those who wish to be civilians
Jesus they run into millions.
The Big Road (1946), pt. 5

Roszak, Theodore (b.1933) U.S. writer and editor

1 High tech is embedded in the texture of industrial history; it needs to be planned into existence. Otherwise...it will become the same sort of jolting, humanly wasteful leap from one economic stage to another that produced the worst hardships of the first industrial revolution.
The Cult of Information (1986)

2 If computerized information services have any natural place in a democratic society, it is in the public library.
The Cult of Information (1986)

3 In the long run, no ideas, no information.
The Cult of Information (1986)

4 The hard-pressed weavers of Northern England who rallied around the mythical General Ludd appear to have had no grudge against technology in and of itself; their grievance was with those who used machines to lower wages or eliminate jobs.
The Cult of Information (1986)

5 The mind thinks, not with data, but with ideas whose creation and elaboration cannot be reduced to a set of predictable values.
The Cult of Information (1986)

6 The ongoing military-industrial drive toward rationalizing, disciplining, and ultimately dehumanizing the workplace is among the foundation stones of information technology.
The Cult of Information (1986)

7 The rise of the information economy in America is a matter of manifest industrial destiny, a change so vast and inevitable that it might almost be a natural process beyond human control.
The Cult of Information (1986)

8 Economics is as much a study in fantasy and aspiration as in hard numbers—maybe more so.
The Making of a Counter Culture (1995), Introduction

9 Revolutionary spirits of my father's generation waited for Lefty. Existentialist heroes of my youth waited for Godot. Neither showed up.
Unfinished Animal (1975)

10 People may still nostalgically honor prescientific faiths, but no one—no priest or prophet—any longer speaks with authority to us about the nature of things except the scientists.
Where the Wasteland Ends (1972), ch. 2

11 What science can measure is only a portion of what man can know. Our knowing reaches out to embrace the sacred; what bars its way, though it promises us dominion, condemns us to be prisoners of the empirical lie.
Where the Wasteland Ends (1972), ch. 2

12 Objective knowing is alienated knowing; and alienated knowing is sooner or later, ecologically disastrous knowing. Before the earth could become an industrial garbage can it had first to become a research laboratory.
Where the Wasteland Ends (1972), ch. 7

13 A nobler economics...is not afraid to discuss spirit and conscience, moral purpose and the meaning of life, an economics that aims to educate and elevate people, not merely to measure their low-grade behavior.
Defining a humanistic economics. Quoted in *Small is Beautiful: Economics as if People Mattered* (Ernst F. Schumacher; 1973)

Roth, David Lee (b.1954) U.S. musician

1 Most bands don't think about the future. Most musicians can't even spell future. Lunch is how far we think ahead.
Quoted in "David Lee Roth," *Off the Record: An Oral History of Popular Music* (Joe Smith; 1988)

2 Some people paint Picassos and some people fingerpaint. Rock and roll is a unique combination. Not one or the other.
Quoted in *Rock Talk* (Joe Kohut and John J. Kohut, eds.; 1994)

3 I didn't get into this business to become a responsible citizen.
Quoted in *The Wit and Wisdom of Rock and Roll* (Maxim Jabukowski, ed.; 1983)

Roth, Philip (Philip Milton Roth; b.1933) U.S. novelist

1 An infantryman 's heart...like his feet, at first aches and swells, but finally grows horny enough for him to travel the weirdest paths without feeling a thing.
"Defender of the Faith," *Goodbye, Columbus* (1959)

2 Long ago, someone had told Grossbart the sad law that only lies can get the truth.
"Defender of the Faith," *Goodbye, Columbus* (1959)

3 Sir, Marx here tells me Jews have a tendency to be pushy.
Said by Colonel Barrett, referring to Jewish parents whom narrator Marx has described as "protective." "Defender of the Faith," *Goodbye, Columbus* (1959)

4 Baseball—with its lore and legends, its cultural power, its seasonal associations...its mythic transformation of the immediate—was the literature of my boyhood.
"My Baseball Years," *New York Times* (April 2, 1973)

5 The road to hell is paved with works-in-progress.
New York Times Book Review (July 15, 1979)

6 Judaism makes my third great religion and I'm still not even thirty-five. I got a ways to go yet with God. I ought to sashay over tomorrow to the Muhammadans and sign on with them. They sound like they got it all together. Great on women.
Operation Shylock: A Confession (1993)

7 A Jewish man with parents alive is a fifteen-year-old boy, and will remain a fifteen-year-old boy until they die.
Portnoy's Complaint (1969)

8 Doctor, my doctor, what do you say—let's put the id back in yid!
Portnoy's Complaint (1969)

9 Is an intelligent human being likely to be much more than a large-scale manufacturer of misunderstanding?
The Counterlife (1986)

10 Just like those who are incurably ill, the aged know everything about their dying except exactly when.
"Opening letter to Zuckerman," *The Facts* (1988)

Rothko, Mark (originally Marcus Rothkovitch; 1903–70) Russian-born U.S. painter

1 I realize that historically the function of painting very large pictures has been grandiose and pompous. The reason I paint them...I want to be very intimate and human. To paint a small picture is to...look upon an experience as a stereopticon view with a reducing glass.
"A Symposium on How to Combine Architecture, Painting and Sculpture," *Interiors* (May 1951), 110, no. 10

2 It is a widely accepted notion among painters that it does not matter what one paints as long as it is well painted. This is the essence of academism. There is no such thing as good painting about nothing.
Letter to Edwin A. Jewell, *New York Times* (co-written with Adolph Gottlieb; June 13, 1943)

Rouget de Lisle, Claude-Joseph (1760–1836) French army officer and composer

1 Come, children of our native land,
The day of glory has arrived.
French national anthem. "La Marseillaise" (1792)

2 To arms! to arms! ye brave!
The avenging sword unsheathe!
March on! march on! all hearts resolved
On victory or death!
French national anthem. "La Marseillaise" (1792)

Rougier, Richard, Sir (Richard George Rougier; b.1932) British judge

1 Women are entitled to dress attractively, even provocatively if you like, be friendly with casual acquaintances and still say no at the end of the evening without being brutally assaulted...This sort of brutal violence, particularly to women, has got to be dealt with severely. You broke her jaw just because she wasn't prepared to go to bed with you.
March 3, 1988. Sentencing an attacker at the Old Bailey, London. *Daily Telegraph*, London (March 4, 1988)

Rousseau, Jean-Jacques (1712–78) French philosopher and writer

Quotations about Rousseau

1 Rousseau says that man is born free, but is everywhere in chains. That is like saying that sheep are born carnivores, but are everywhere herbivorous.
Joseph Marie de Maistre (1753–1821) French political philosopher and diplomat. Attrib.

2 Maybe it would have been better if neither of us had been born.
Napoleon I (1769–1821) French emperor. Said while looking at the tomb of the philosopher Jean-Jacques Rousseau, whose theories had influenced the French Revolution. Quoted in *The Story of Civilization* (William Durant; 1935), vol. 2

3 One of the most remarkable intuitions in Western thought was Rousseau's noble Savage: the idea that perhaps civilization has something to learn from the primitive.
1967
Gary Snyder (b.1930) U.S. poet, essayist, and translator. "Poetry and the Primitive," *Earth House Hold* (1969)

Quotations by Rousseau

4 It is not the criminal things which are hardest to confess, but the ridiculous and shameful.
1765–70. *Confessions* (1782)

5 The Catholic must adopt the decision handed down to him; the Protestant must learn to decide for himself.
1765–70. *Confessions* (1782)

6 Remorse sleeps during a prosperous period, but wakes up in adversity.
1765–70. *Confessions* (1782), bk. 2

7 At length I recalled the thoughtless words of a great princess, who, on being informed that the country people had no bread, replied, "Let them eat cake."
1765–70. This volume of the *Confessions* was written before Marie-Antoinette allegedly uttered those words. *Confessions* (1782), bk. 6

8 Money is the seed of money, and the first franc is sometimes more difficult to acquire than the second million.
Discourse on the Origin and Foundation of Inequality Among Men (1754)

9 As long as there are rich people in the world, they will be desirous of distinguishing themselves from the poor.
Discours sur l'économie politique (1758)

10 Everything is good when it leaves the Creator's hands; everything degenerates in the hands of man.
Émile (1762), bk. 1

11 Temperance and labor are the two real physicians of man:

labor sharpens his appetite and temperance prevents his abusing it.
Émile (1762), bk. 1

12 Do not judge, and you will never be mistaken.
Émile (1762), bk. 3

13 When woman complains...about unjust man-made inequality, she is wrong. This inequality...is the work not of prejudice but of reason. It is up to the sex that nature has charged with the bearing of children to be responsible for them to the other sex.
Émile (1762)

14 He who pretends to look on death without fear lies. All men are afraid of dying, this is the great law of sentient beings, without which the entire human species would soon be destroyed.
Julie ou la nouvelle Héloïse (1760)

15 In the strict sense of the term, there has never been a true democracy, and there never will be. It is contrary to the natural order that the greater number should govern and the smaller number be governed.
The Social Contract (1762)

16 Man's first law is to watch over his own preservation; his first care he owes to himself; and as soon as he reaches the age of reason, he becomes the only judge of the best means to preserve himself; he becomes his own master.
The Social Contract (1762)

17 Man was born free and everywhere he is in chains.
The Social Contract (1762)

18 The body politic, like the human body, begins to die from the moment of its birth, and bears in itself the causes of its destruction.
The Social Contract (1762)

19 The passing from the state of nature to the civil society produces a remarkable change in man; it puts justice as a rule of conduct in place of instinct, and gives his actions the moral quality they previously lacked.
The Social Contract (1762)

20 There is only one law which by its nature requires unanimous assent. This is the social pact: for the civil association is the most voluntary act in the world; every man having been born free and master of himself, no one else may on any pretext whatsoever subject him without his consent.
The Social Contract (1762)

21 Truth is no road to fortune.
The Social Contract (1762)

22 Happiness: a good bank account, a good cook, a good digestion.
Attrib.

Routh, Martin Joseph (1755–1854) British scholar

1 You will find it a very good practice always to verify your references.
Quoted in *Lives of Twelve Good Men* (John William Burgeon; 1888), vol. 1

Routsong, Alma (b.1924) U.S. writer and feminist

1 I wonder if what makes men walk lordlike and speak so masterfully is having the love of women.
A Place For Us (1969)

Rover, Constance (b.1910) British sociologist and feminist

1 Women have been emancipated on condition that they don't upset men, or interfere too much with men's way of life.
Quoted in *There's Always Been a Women's Movement this Century* (Dale Spender; 1983), ch. 5, "Constance Rover"

Rowan and Martin's Laugh-In U.S. television comedy series

1 This is beautiful downtown Burbank.
Catchphrase in the 1960s television comedy series.

Rowe, Arthur (1906–93) British soccer coach

1 You play nineteen-twentieths of the game without the ball and that's when you do your thinking. That's when you do your real playing. Any clown can play with the ball when he's got it. It's the good fellows who get into position to receive.
Quoted in *The Encyclopedia of Association Football* (1960)

Rowe, Nicholas (1674–1718) English playwright and poet

1 At length the morn and cold indifference came.
The Fair Penitent (1703), Act 1, Scene 1, Prologue

2 Is she not more than painting can express,
Or youthful poets fancy when they love?
The Fair Penitent (1703), Act 3, Scene 1

3 Death is the privilege of human nature,
And life without it were not worth our taking.
The Fair Penitent (1703), Act 5, Scene 1

Rowland, Edward ("Red Rowley"; b.1915) British songwriter

1 A mademoiselle from Armenteers,
She hasn't been kissed for forty years,
Hinky, dinky, par-lee-voo.
Armentières was completely destroyed (1918) in World War I. "Mademoiselle from Armenteers" (1914–18)

Rowland, Helen (1876–1950) U.S. writer, journalist, and humorist

1 A husband is what is left of the lover after the nerve has been extracted.
A Guide to Men (1922)

2 One man's folly is another man's wife.
A Guide to Men (1922)

3 The follies which a man regrets most in his life are those which he didn't commit when he had the opportunity.
A Guide to Men (1922)

4 It takes a woman twenty years to make a man of her son, and another woman twenty minutes to make a fool of him.
Reflections of a Bachelor Girl (1909)

5 When you see what some girls marry, you realize how they must hate to work for a living.
Reflections of a Bachelor Girl (1909)

6 Never trust a husband too far, nor a bachelor too near.
The Rubaiyat of a Bachelor (1915)

Rowland, Henry Augustus (1848–1901) U.S. physicist

1 American science is a thing of the future, and not of the present or past; and the proper course...is to consider what must be done to create a science of physics in this country, rather than to call telegrams, electric lights, and such conveniences by the name of science.
Address, American Association for the Advancement of Science (1883)

Rowland, Sherwood (Frank Sherwood Rowland; b.1927) U.S. chemist

1 The work is going well, but it looks like the end of the world.
Referring to his research into the destruction of the ozone layer. Attrib.

Rowley, William (1585?–1642?) British actor and playwright

1 Art thou gone in haste?
...I'll not forsake thee;
Run'st thou ne'er so fast,
...I'll o'ertake thee:
O'er the dales, o'er the downs,
Through the green meadows,
From the fields through the towns,
To the dim shadows.
The Thracian Wonder (1661), Act 1, Scene 1

Rowse, A. L. (Alfred Leslie Rowse; b.1903) British historian and critic

1 I regard everything that has happened since the last war as a decline in civilization.
Observer, London (June 15, 1975), "Sayings of the Week"

Roy, Arundhati (b.1960) Indian writer

1 In an unconscious gesture of television-enforced democracy, mistress and servant both scrabbled unseeingly in the same bowl of nuts.
The God of Small Things (1997), "Big Man the Laltain, Small Man the Mombatti"

2 The whole of contemporary history, the World Wars, the War of Dreams, the Man on the Moon, science, literature, philosophy, the pursuit of knowledge—was no more than a blink of the Earth Woman's eye.
The God of Small Things (1997), "Pappachi's Mouth"

3 The twins were too young to know that these were only history's henchmen...civilization's fear of nature, men's fear of women, power's fear of powerlessness. Man's subliminal urge to destroy what he could neither subdue or deify.
The God of Small Things (1997), "The History House"

Royden, Maud (Agnes Maud Royden; 1876–1956) British woman suffrage campaigner and writer

1 The Church should be no longer satisfied to represent only the Conservative Party at prayer.
Address at Queen's Hall, London (July 16, 1917)

2 If you want to be a dear old lady at seventy, you should start early, say about seventeen.
Attrib.

Roydon, Matthew (1564?–1622?) British poet

1 A sweet attractive kind of grace,
A full assurance given by looks,
Continual comfort in a face,
The lineaments of Gospel books;
I trow that countenance cannot lie,
Whose thoughts are legible in the eye.
Referring to Sir Philip Sidney. "An Elegy, or Friend's Passion, for his Astrophil," *Phoenix Nest* (1593), st. 18

Rubin, Jerry (1938–94) U.S. activist and author

1 To steal from the rich is a sacred and religious act.
Do It (1969)

2 Don't trust anyone over thirty.
Quoted in *Listening to America* (S. B. Flexner; 1982)

Rubin, Robert E. (b.1938) U.S. business executive and government official

1 I'm working on the supposition that good economics can also be good politics. I'll admit that not everyone believes that.
New York Times (September 22, 1996)

2 Doing nothing is the wrong thing to do if there is something to do that is clearly the right thing to do. But doing something that is not sensible...is a very bad idea.
Attrib.

Rubinstein, Helena (1870–1965) Polish-born U.S. business executive

1 I have always felt that a woman has the right to treat the subject of her age with ambiguity until, perhaps, she passes into the realm of over ninety. Then it is better she be candid with herself and with the world.
My Life for Beauty (1965), pt. I, ch. 1

Rudikoff, Sonya U.S. writer

1 The idea has gained currency that women have often been handicapped not only by a fear of failure—not unknown to men either—but by a fear of success as well.
"Women and Success," *Commentary* (October 1974)

Rudolf I (1218–91) German monarch and Holy Roman Emperor

1 By God, let any man who will come to me! I have not become King to live hidden in a wardrobe.
Remark after his coronation at Aachen (1273), quoted in *Quotations in History* (Alan and Veronica Palmer, eds.; 1976)

Rue, Danny La (Daniel Patrick Carroll; b.1928) British entertainer

1 The essence of any blue material is timing. If you sit on it, it becomes vulgar.
"Blue" means risqué. Attrib.

Ruhlen, Merritt (b.1944) U.S. linguist

1 If...Africans had...founded America and raided Europe and brought white slaves over, and this country ended up with a 10 percent white minority that...spoke white English, you'd find the same problems in reverse.
Referring to Ebonics. *Washington Post* (January 6, 1997)

Rule, Jane (Jane Vincent Rule; b.1931) U.S.-born Canadian writer

1 Morality, like language, is an invented structure for conserving and communicating order. And morality is learned, like language, by mimicking and remembering.
"Myth and Morality, Sources of Law and Prejudice," *Lesbian Images* (1975)

Rumbold, Richard (1622?–85) British revolutionary republican

1 I never could believe that Providence had sent a few men into the world, ready booted and spurred to ride, and millions ready saddled and bridled to be ridden.
1685. His words, as paraphrased by the historian Lord Macaulay, have passed into common usage. Richard Rumbold's actual words were: "I am sure there was no man born marked of God above another; for none comes into the world with a saddle upon his back, neither any booted and spurred to ride him" (State Trials, XL). Speech on the scaffold, quoted in *History of England,* (T. B. Macaulay; 1849), vol. 1, ch. 1

Rumi, Jalal al-Din Muhammad (1207–73) Persian mystic and poet

1 Whosoever knoweth the power of the dance, dwelleth in God.
Quoted in *Portrait of Mr. Balanchine* (Lincoln Kirstein; 1984)

Runcie, Robert, Baron Runcie of Cuddesdon (Robert Alexander Kennedy Runcie; b.1921) British archbishop

1 My advice was delicately poised between the cliché and the indiscretion.
July 13, 1981. To the press, referring to his advice to the Prince of Wales and Lady Diana Spencer on their approaching wedding.

2 In the middle ages people were tourists because of their religion, whereas now they are tourists because tourism is their religion.
Observer, London (December 11, 1988), "Sayings of the Week"

Runciman, Steven, Sir (James Cochran Stevenson Runciman; b.1903) British academic and diplomat

1 Unlike Christianity, which preached a peace that it never achieved, Islam unashamedly came with a sword.
1951. "The First Crusade," *A History of the Crusades* (1951–54)

Runciman of Doxford, Lady, Viscountess Runciman of Doxford (Ruth Runciman, born Hellmann; b.1936) British social reformer

1 There is a statistical terrorism inflicted on society by crime figures.
Times, London (January 20, 1995)

Runyon, Damon (Alfred Damon Runyon; 1880–1946) U.S. writer

1 You can keep the things of bronze and stone and give me one man to remember me just once a year.
Remark (1946)

2 It is against the law to commit suicide in this man's town...although what the law can do to a guy who commits suicide I am never able to figure out.
Guys and Dolls (1931)

3 My boy...always try to rub up against money, for if you rub up against money long enough, some of it may rub off on you.
"A Very Honorable Guy," *Guys and Dolls* (1931)

4 All she has to do is to walk around and about Georgie White's stage with only a few light bandages on, and everybody considers her very beautiful, especially from the neck down.
George White was a producer of musical revues featuring glamorous dancers. "A Very Honorable Guy," *Guys and Dolls* (1931)

5 And you cannot tell by the way a party looks or how he lives in this town, if he has any scratch, because many a party who is around in automobiles, and wearing good clothes, and chucking quite a swell is nothing but a phonus bolonus and does not have any real scratch whatever.
"The Snatching of Bookie Bob," *More than Somewhat* (1937)

6 She is a smart old broad. It is a pity she is so nefarious.
"Broadway Incident," *Runyon à la carte* (1944)

7 At such an hour the sinners are still in bed resting up from their sinning of the night before, so they will be in good shape for more sinning a little later on.
"The Idyll of Miss Sarah Brown," *Runyon à la carte* (1944)

8 I once knew a chap who had a system of just hanging the baby on the clothes line to dry and he was greatly admired by his fellow citizens for having discovered a wonderful innovation on changing a diaper.
"Diaper Dexterity," *Short Takes* (1946)

9 A freeloader is a confirmed guest. He is the man who is always willing to come to dinner.
"Freeloading Ethics," *Short Takes* (1946)

10 These citizens are always willing to bet that what Nicely-Nicely dies of will be over-feeding and never anything small like pneumonia, for Nicely-Nicely is known far and wide as a character who dearly loves to commit eating.
"Lonely Heart," *Take it Easy* (1938)

11 Guys and Dolls
1932. Book title.

12 More than Somewhat
Title of a collection of stories and a favorite phrase of Runyon's. (1937)

Rush, Benjamin (1745–1813) U.S. physician and statesman

1 Medicine is an occupation for slaves.
The Autobiography of Benjamin Rush (George Washington Corner, ed.; 1948)

Rushdie, Salman (Ahmad Salman Rushdie; b.1947) Indian-born British novelist

Quotations about Rushdie

1 The author of the Satanic Verses book, which is against Islam, the Prophet and the Koran, and all those involved in its publication who were aware of its content, are sentenced to

death. I ask all Muslims to execute them wherever they find them.
Ruhollah Khomeini (1900–89) Iranian religious and political leader. Statement announcing a death sentence against Salman Rushdie, following the publication of his novel *The Satanic Verses* (1988). Fatwa (February 14, 1989)

Quotations by Rushdie

2 I call upon the intellectual community in this country and abroad to stand up for freedom of the imagination, an issue much larger than my book or indeed my life.
Referring to the Fatwa issued against his life by Iranian Orthodox Muslims because of the purported blasphemy against Islam contained in his book *The Satanic Verses*. Public statement (February 14, 1989)

3 God, Satan, Paradise and Hell all vanished one day in my fifteenth year, when I quite abruptly lost my faith.
Imaginary Homelands (1991), pt. 12, ch. 2

4 My relationship with formal religious belief has been somewhat chequered.
Imaginary Homelands (1991), pt. 12, ch. 2

5 The idea of the sacred is quite simply one of the most conservative notions in any culture, because it seeks to turn other ideas—Uncertainty, Progress, Change—into crimes.
Imaginary Homelands (1991), pt. 12, ch. 4

6 I have been finding my own way towards an intellectual understanding of religion, and religion for me has always meant Islam.
Imaginary Homelands (1991), pt. 12, ch. 5

7 What I know of Islam is that tolerance, compassion and love are at its very heart.
Imaginary Homelands (1991), pt. 12, ch. 5

8 We who have grown up on a diet of honour and shame can still grasp what must seem unthinkable to people living in the aftermath of the death of God and of tragedy: that men will sacrifice their dearest love on the implacable altars of their pride.
Shame (1983), pt. 3, ch. 7

9 Mahound shakes his head, "Your blasphemy, Salman, can't be forgiven. Did you think I wouldn't work it out? To set your words against the Words of God."
The Satanic Verses (1988), pt. 6

10 I hate admitting that my enemies have a point.
Said by Hamza in the "Mahound" section of the novel. "Mahound," *The Satanic Verses* (1988)

Rusk, Dean (David Dean Rusk; 1909–94) U.S. educator and politician

1 We're eyeball to eyeball and I think the other fellow just blinked.
Referring to the Cuban Missile Crisis. Interview, quoted in *Political Dictionary* (W. Safire; October 24, 1962)

Ruskin, John (1819–1900) British art critic, writer, and reformer

1 You may either win your peace or buy it; win it by resistance to evil; buy it by compromise with evil.
"The Two Paths" (1859), lecture 5

2 No person who is not a great sculptor or painter can be an architect. If he is not a sculptor or painter, he can only be a *builder*.
Lectures on Architecture and Painting (1854), lectures 1 and 2 (addenda)

3 Life without industry is guilt, and industry without art is brutality.
"The Relation of Art to Morals," *Lectures on Art* (1870), lecture 3, sect. 95

4 One of the worst diseases to which the human creature is liable is its disease of thinking.
"A Joy For Ever," *Lectures on the Political Economy of Art* (1858)

5 All violent feelings...produce in us a falseness in all our impressions of external things, which I would generally characterize as the "Pathetic Fallacy".
"Pathetic fallacy" became a common 20th-century literary critical term. *Modern Painters* (1856), vol. 3, pt. 4, ch. 12

6 Mountains are the beginning and the end of all natural scenery.
Modern Painters (1856), vol. 4, pt. 5, ch. 20

7 But whether thus submissively or not, at least be sure that you go to the author to get at his meaning, not to find yours.
"Of Kings' Treasuries," *Sesame and Lilies* (1865)

8 How long most people would look at the best book before they would give the price of a large turbot for it!
"Of Kings' Treasuries," *Sesame and Lilies* (1865)

9 If a book is worth reading, it is worth buying.
"Of Kings' Treasuries," *Sesame and Lilies* (1865)

10 Which of us...is to do the hard and dirty work for the rest—and for what pay? Who is to do the pleasant and clean work, and for what pay?
"Of Kings' Treasuries," *Sesame and Lilies* (1865)

11 All books are divisible into two classes, the books of the hour, and the books of all time.
"Of Kings' Treasuries," *Sesame and Lilies* (1865)

12 In one point of view, Gothic is not only the best, but the only rational architecture, as being that which can fit itself most easily to all services, vulgar or noble.
Stones of Venice (1851–53)

13 No architecture is so haughty as that which is simple.
Stones of Venice (1851–53)

14 We may, without offending any laws of good taste, require of an architect, as we do of a novelist, that he should be not only correct, but entertaining.
Stones of Venice (1851–53)

15 Remember that the most beautiful things in the world are the most useless; peacocks and lilies for instance.
Stones of Venice (1851)

16 The only absolutely and unapproachably heroic element in the soldier's work seems to be—that he is paid little for it—and regularly.
The Crown of Wild Olive (1866)

17 They, on the whole, desire to cure the sick; and—if they are good doctors, and the choice were fairly put to them—would rather cure their patient and lose their fee, than kill him, and get it.
The Crown of Wild Olive (1866)

18 An architect should live as little in cities as a painter. Send him to our hills, and let him study there what nature understands by a buttress, and what by a dome.
The Seven Lamps of Architecture (1849)

19 Architecture concerns itself only with those characters of an edifice which are above and beyond its common use.
The Seven Lamps of Architecture (1849)

20 I believe the right question to ask, respecting all ornament, is simply this: Was it done with enjoyment—was the carver happy while he was about it?
"The Lamp of Life," *The Seven Lamps of Architecture* (1849), sect. 24

21 When we build let us think that we build for ever.
"The Lamp of Memory," *The Seven Lamps of Architecture* (1849), sect. 10

22 Fine art is that in which the hand, the head, and the heart of man go together.
The Two Paths (1859), lecture 2

23 No human being, however great, or powerful, was ever so free as a fish.
The Two Paths (1859), lecture 5

24 Labour without joy is base. Labour without sorrow is base. Sorrow without labour is base. Joy without labour is base.
Time and Tide (1867), letter 5

25 To make your children *capable of honesty* is the beginning of education.
Time and Tide (1867), letter 8

26 Whereas it has long been known and declared that the poor have no right to the property of the rich, I wish it also to be known and declared that the rich have no right to the property of the poor.
Unto this Last (1862), essay 3

27 There is no wealth but life.
Unto this Last (1862), essay 4

Russell, Anna (Claudia Anna Russell-Brown; b.1911) British-born Canadian singer and musical satirist

1 The reason there are so few female comics is that so few women can bear being laughed at.
Sunday Times, London (August 25, 1957)

Russell, Bertrand, 3rd Earl Russell (Bertrand Arthur William Russell; 1872–1970) British philosopher and mathematician

Quotations about Russell

1 Your discovery of the contradiction caused me the greatest surprise...not only the foundations of my arithmetic, but also the sole possible foundations of arithmetic, seem to vanish.
Gottlob Frege (1848–1925) German philosopher. Bertrand Russell had discovered a paradox in Frege's attempt to derive the principles of arithmetic from those of logic. Letter to Bertrand Russell (1902)

2 The beauty of Bertrand Russell's beautiful mathematical mind is absolute, like the third movement of Beethoven's A Minor Quartet.
Ethel Mannin (1900–84) British writer. *Confessions and Impressions* (1930)

Quotations by Russell

3 I have a certain hesitation in starting my biography too soon for fear of something important having not yet happened. Suppose I should end my days as President of Mexico; the biography would seem incomplete if it did not mention this fact.
Letter to Stanley Unwin (November 1930)

4 Since power over human beings is shown in making them do what they would rather not do, the man who is activated by love of power is more apt to inflict pain than to permit pleasure.
Nobel Prize acceptance speech, "Human Society in Ethics and Politics" (1950)

5 Almost everything that distinguishes the modern world from earlier centuries is attributable to science, which achieved its most spectacular triumphs in the seventeenth century.
A History of Western Philosophy (1945)

6 To teach how to live without certainty and yet without being paralysed by hesitation is perhaps the chief thing that philosophy, in our age, can do for those who study it.
A History of Western Philosophy (1945)

7 Matter...a convenient formula for describing what happens where it isn't.
An Outline of Philosophy (1927)

8 The more you are talked about, the more you will wish to be talked about. The condemned murderer who is allowed to see the account of his trial in the Press is indignant if he finds a newspaper which has reported it inadequately...Politicians and literary men are in the same case.
Human Society in Ethics and Politics (1954)

9 The point of philosophy is to start with something so simple as to seem not worth stating, and to end with something so paradoxical that no one will believe it.
Logic and Knowledge (1955)

10 In a logically perfect language, there will be one word and no more for every simple object, and everything that is not simple will be expressed by a combination of words.
"The Philosophy of Logical Atomism," *Logic and Knowledge* (1955)

11 America...where law and customs alike are based on the dreams of spinsters.
Marriage and Morals (1929)

12 Love as a relation between men and women was ruined by the desire to make sure of the legitimacy of the children.
Marriage and Morals (1929)

13 Marriage is for women the commonest mode of livelihood, and the total amount of undesired sex endured by women is probably greater in marriage than in prostitution.
Marriage and Morals (1929)

14 The fact that an opinion has been widely held is no evidence whatever that it is not utterly absurd.
Marriage and Morals (1929)

15 To fear love is to fear life, and those who fear life are already three parts dead.
Marriage and Morals (1929)

16 Civilized people cannot fully satisfy their sexual instinct without love.
Marriage and Morals (1929)

17 To a mind of sufficient intellectual power, the whole of mathematics would appear trivial, as trivial as the statement that a four-footed animal is an animal.
My Philosophical Development (1959)

18 Happiness is not best achieved by those who seek it directly.
Mysticism and Logic (1918)

19 Organic life, we are told, has developed gradually from the protozoon to the philosopher, and this development, we are assured, is indubitably an advance. Unfortunately it is the philosopher, not the protozoon, who gives us this assurance.
Mysticism and Logic (1918)

20 Our great democracies still tend to think that a stupid man is more likely to be honest than a clever man, and our politicians take advantage of this prejudice by pretending to be even more stupid than nature has made them.
New Hopes for a Changing World (1951)

21 The more we realise our minuteness and our impotence in the face of cosmic forces, the more amazing becomes what human beings have achieved.
New Hopes for a Changing World (1951)

22 Religions, which condemn the pleasures of sense, drive men to seek the pleasures of power. Throughout history power has been the vice of the ascetic.
New York Herald-Tribune Magazine (May 6, 1938)

23 The collection of prejudices which is called political philosophy is useful provided that it is not called philosophy.
Observer, London (1962), "Sayings of the Year"

24 No one gossips about other people's secret virtues.
On Education (1926)

25 Mathematics, rightly viewed, possesses not only truth, but supreme beauty—a beauty cold and austere, like that of sculpture.
1902. *Philosophical Essays* (1910), no. 4

26 I cannot see how to refute the arguments for the subjectivity of ethical values, but I find myself incapable of believing that all that is wrong with wanton cruelty is that I don't like it.
"Notes on Philosophy," *Philosophy* (1960), vol. 35

27 The human race may well become extinct before the end of the century.
Interview, *Playboy* (March 1963)

28 The fact that all Mathematics is Symbolic Logic is one of the greatest discoveries of our age; and when this fact has been established, the remainder of the principles of mathematics consists in the analysis of Symbolic Logic itself.
Principia Mathematica (co-written with A. N. Whitehead; 1913)

29 The most widely accepted philosophy of life at present is that what matters most to a man's happiness is his income. This philosophy, apart from other demerits, is harmful because it leads men to aim at a result rather than an activity.
Principles of Social Reconstruction (1916)

30 Mathematics may be defined as the subject in which we never know what we are talking about, nor whether what we are saying is true.
Recent Works on the Principles of Mathematics (1901), quoted in *International Monthly* (1901), vol. 4

31 The people who are regarded as moral luminaries are those who forego ordinary pleasures themselves and find compensation in interfering with the pleasures of others.
Sceptical Essays (1928)

32 Every man, wherever he goes, is encompassed by a cloud of comforting convictions, which move with him like flies on a summer day.
"Dreams and Facts," *Sceptical Essays* (1928)

33 We have, in fact, two kinds of morality side by side; one which we preach but do not practise, and another which we practise but seldom preach.
"Eastern and Western Ideals of Happiness," *Sceptical Essays* (1928)

34 The infliction of cruelty with a good conscience is a delight to moralists. That is why they invented Hell.
"On the Value of Scepticism," *Sceptical Essays* (1928)

35 It is obvious that "obscenity" is not a term capable of exact legal definition; in the practice of the Courts, it means "anything that shocks the magistrate".
"The Recrudescence of Puritanism," *Sceptical Essays* (1928)

36 Understanding words does not consist in knowing their dictionary definitions...Understanding language is more like understanding cricket: it is a matter of habits, acquired in oneself and rightly presumed in others.
The Analysis of Mind (1921)

37 I discovered to my amazement that average men and women were delighted at the prospect of war. I had fondly imagined what most pacifists contended, that wars were forced upon a reluctant population by despotic and Machiavellian governments.
The Autobiography of Bertrand Russell (1967–69)

38 The average man's opinions are much less foolish than they would be if he thought for himself.
The Autobiography of Bertrand Russell (1967–69)

39 The trouble with the world is that the stupid are cocksure and the intelligent full of doubt.
The Autobiography of Bertrand Russell (1967–69)

40 Three passions, simple but overwhelmingly strong, have governed my life: the longing for love, the search for knowledge, and unbearable pity for the suffering of mankind.
The Autobiography of Bertrand Russell (1967–69), Prologue

41 I was told that the Chinese said they would bury me by the Western Lake and build a shrine to my memory. I have some slight regret that this did not happen, as I might have become a god, which would have been very *chic* for an atheist.
The Autobiography of Bertrand Russell (1967–69), vol. 2, ch. 3

42 The nuns who never take a bath without wearing a bathrobe all the time. When asked why, since no man can see them, they reply "Oh, but you forget the good God."
The Basic Writings of Bertrand Russell (1961), pt. 2, ch. 7

43 Drunkenness is temporary suicide; the happiness that it brings is merely negative, a momentary cessation of unhappiness.
The Conquest of Happiness (1930)

44 Suspicion of one's own motives is especially necessary for the philanthropist.
The Conquest of Happiness (1930)

45 The megalomaniac differs from the narcissist by the fact that he wishes to be powerful rather than charming, and seeks to be feared rather than loved. To this type belong many lunatics and most of the great men of history.
The Conquest of Happiness (1930)

46 There are two motives for reading a book: one, that you enjoy it, the other that you can boast about it.
The Conquest of Happiness (1930)

47 Boredom is...a vital problem for the moralist, since half the sins of mankind are caused by the fear of it.
The Conquest of Happiness (1930), ch. 4

48 One should as a rule respect public opinion insofar as is necessary to avoid starvation and keep out of prison, but anything that goes beyond this is voluntary submission to an unnecessary tyranny.
The Conquest of Happiness (1930), ch. 9

49 Of all forms of caution, caution in love is perhaps the most fatal to true happiness.
The Conquest of Happiness (1930), ch. 12

50 Every proposition which we can understand must be composed wholly of constituents with which we are acquainted.
The Problems of Philosophy (1912)

51 Only mathematics and mathematical logic can say as little as the physicist means to say.
The Scientific Outlook (1931)

52 In America everybody is of the opinion that he has no social superiors, since all men are equal, but he does not admit that he has no social inferiors.
Unpopular Essays (1950)

53 The most savage controversies are those about matters as to which there is no good evidence either way.
Unpopular Essays (1950)

54 I say quite deliberately that the Christian religion, as organized in its Churches, has been and still is the principal enemy of moral progress in the world.
Why I Am Not a Christian (1927)

55 The peculiar importance attached, at present, to adultery is quite irrational. It is obvious that many forms of misconduct are more fatal to married happiness than an occasional infidelity.
Why I Am Not a Christian (1927)

56 I am as drunk as a lord, but then, I am one, so what does it matter?
Quoted in *Bertrand Russell, Philosopher of the Century* (Ralph Schoenman; 1967)

57 People don't seem to realize that it takes time and effort and preparation to think. Statesmen are far too busy making speeches to think.
Quoted in *Kenneth Harris Talking to Bertrand Russell* (Kenneth Harris; 1971)

58 You may reasonably expect a man to walk a tightrope safely for ten minutes; it would be unreasonable to do so without accident for two hundred years.
On the subject of nuclear war between the United States and the Soviets. Quoted as an epigraph in *The Tightrope Men* (D. Bagley; 1973)

59 Many people would sooner die than think. In fact they do.
Quoted as an epigraph in *Thinking About Thinking* (Anthony Flew; 1975)

60 Every time I talk to a savant I feel quite sure that happiness is no longer a possibility. Yet when I talk with my gardener, I'm convinced of the opposite.
Attrib.

61 Few people can be happy unless they hate some other person, nation or creed.
Attrib.

62 Nothing is so exhausting as indecision, and nothing is so futile.
Attrib.

63 Patriots always talk of dying for their country, and never of killing for their country.
1967. Attrib.

64 Science is what you know, philosophy is what you don't know.
Attrib.

65 To be without some of the things you want is an indispensable part of happiness.
Attrib.

66 Of course not. After all, I may be wrong.
On being asked whether he would be prepared to die for his beliefs. Attrib.

Russell, Dora, Countess Russell (originally Dora Winifred Black; 1894–1986) British feminist

1 We want better reasons for having children than not knowing how to prevent them.
Hypatia, or Women and Knowledge (1925), ch. 4

Russell, Lord, 1st Earl Russell of Kingston Russell (John Russell; 1792–1878) British prime minister

Quotations about Russell

1 If a traveller were informed that such a man was leader of the House of Commons, he may well begin to comprehend how the Egyptians worshipped an insect.
1852
Benjamin Disraeli (1804–81) British prime minister and writer. Attrib.

Quotations by Russell

2 If peace cannot be maintained with honour, it is no longer peace.
September 19, 1853. Speech at Greenock, *Times*, London (September 21, 1853)

3 A proverb is one man's wit and all men's wisdom.
Quoted in *Sir James Mackintosh* (R. J. Macintosh; 1835), vol. 2, ch. 7

4 Two mothers-in-law.
His answer when asked what he would consider a proper punishment for bigamy. Attrib.

5 There is no class of men whose rewards are so disproportionate to their usefulness to the community.
Referring to the low pay of British schoolteachers. Attrib.

Russell, William Howard, Sir (1821–1907) British journalist

1 They dashed on towards that *thin red line tipped with steel.*
November 14, 1854. Description of the Russian charge against the British at the battle of Balaclava, 1854, originally reported in slightly different words in a dispatch to *Times* (London). *The British Expedition to the Crimea* (1877)

Rustin, Bayard (1910–87) U.S. civil rights leader

1 Society, by waiting for riots to occur before responding to needs, deprives the more responsible Negro leaders of any possibility of leadership.
1967. "The Mind of the Black Militant," *Down The Line* (1971), p. 210

2 The resort to stereotype is the first refuge and chief strategy of the bigot.
1967. "The Premise of the Stereotype," *Down The Line* (1971), p. 171

Ruth, Babe (George Herman Ruth; 1895–1948) U.S. baseball player

1 All I can tell them is pick a good one and sock it. I get back to the dugout and they ask me what it was I hit and I tell them I don't know except it looked good.
Quoted in *The American Treasury, 1455–1955* (Clifton Fadiman; 1955)

2 That last one sounded kinda high to me.
Questioning the umpire about three fast pitches that he had not seen. Attrib.

3 I know, but I had a better year.
Reply when a club official objected that the salary he was demanding was greater than the U.S. president's. Attrib.

Rutherford, Ernest, 1st Baron Rutherford of Nelson and Cambridge (1871–1937) New Zealand-born British physicist

1 We haven't got the money, so we've got to think!
Quoted in *Bulletin of the Institute of Physics* (R. V. Jones; 1962), vol. 13

2 All science is either physics or stamp collecting.
Quoted in *Rutherford at Manchester* (J. B. Birks; 1962)

3 If your experiment needs statistics, you ought to have done a better experiment.
Quoted in *The Mathematical Approach to Biology and Medicine* (N. T. J. Bailey; 1967)

Ryan, Cornelius (1920–74) Irish writer

1 A Bridge Too Far
1974. Book title. Lieut. General Sir Frederick Browning said to Field Marshal Montgomery, "But, sir, we may be going a bridge too far;" referring to the airborne attack to capture 11 bridges over the Rhine, including the bridge at Arnhem, prior to the invasion of Germany in 1944.

Ryan, Desmond (1893–1964) British-born Irish socialist and historian

1 The triumph of failure.
Referring to the Easter Rising (April 24, 1916). *The Rising* (1949)

Ryder, Albert Pinkham (1847–1917) U.S. painter

1 Imitation is not inspiration, and inspiration only can give birth to a work of art. The least of man's original emanation is better than the best of a borrowed thought.
Quoted in *Albert Pinkham Ryder* (John Sherman; 1920)

Ryle, Gilbert (1900–76) British philosopher

1 A myth is, of course, not a fairy story. It is the presentation of facts belonging to one category in the idioms appropriate to another. To explode a myth is accordingly not to deny the facts but to re-allocate them.
The Concept of Mind (1949), Introduction

Ss

Saadawi, Nawal el- (b.1931) Egyptian novelist

1 The Arab feminist movement will...rise from the soil of Arab lands, rather than become another copy of feminist movements in the West.
"Arab Women and Politics," *The Nawal el-Saadawi Reader* (1997)

2 The major capitalist countries resist Islam where it is an instrument of progress and unity, and encourage it whenever it serves to divide and weaken...one of the sources of severe contradiction in the lives and struggles of Arab women.
"Arab Women and Politics," *The Nawal el-Saadawi Reader* (1997)

3 Arab unity is a goal and Arab women's unity and solidarity are important weapons in fighting for the liberation of women and of our land and economy.
1990. "Women in Resistance: the Arab World," *The Nawal el-Saadawi Reader* (1997)

Sachs, Jeffrey (Jeffrey David Sachs; b.1954) U.S. economist

1 Our living standard isn't being maintained by higher productivity or wages. It's maintained by foreign capital.
Time (January 30, 1989)

Sachs, Nelly (Nelly Leonie Sachs; 1891–1970) German-Swedish poet

1 And the snail
with the ticking luggage of God's time.
"White Serpent" (1959), quoted in *German Poetry 1910–1975* (Michael Hamburger, ed., tr.; 1977)

Sacks, Jonathan (b.1948) British chief rabbi

1 After the destruction of the Second Temple Jews lived by an ancient and fundamental insight, that God does not live in buildings but in the human heart.
Community of Faith (1995)

2 Israel is a people at whose centre is the space we make for God.
Community of Faith (1995)

3 Moses tells the Israelites to "Choose life". In the laws of purity, contact with death defiles, for God's presence is in life. Most of the vast code of Jewish law is an infinitely detailed discipline in not taking life for granted, but making a blessing of it and sanctifying it.
Community of Faith (1995)

4 Solitude, for the Torah, is not humanity's highest state, nor is it the condition in which we come most fully into the presence of God. The individual must share his life with others.
Community of Faith (1995)

5 The Torah is not meant for angels...Judaism is the sustained attempt to bring the Divine presence from the soul to the body, from poetry to prose, from the innermost mind to the public domain, from exalted moments into the texture of everyday life.
Community of Faith (1995)

6 Where once nine Jews in ten lived, today there are fewer than one in five. Jewish life has moved from Europe to Israel and the United States.
Community of Faith (1995)

7 A Jewish community that has lost its *edah* is on its way to ceasing to be an *am*.
Edah denotes the Jews as a religious group. *Am* denotes the historical and ethnic aspects of Judaism. *Community of Faith* (1995)

8 Hasidic communities gathered under...Rabbi Hayim Vidrowitz from Moscow, outside whose headquarters hung a sign, "Chief Rabbi of America". When asked who had conferred this title on him, he is reported to have replied, "The sign painter".
Referring to a period of rivalry and division among U.S. Jewry in the late 19th century. *Community of Faith* (1995)

9 Religious law is like the grammar of a language. Any language is governed by such rules; otherwise it ceases to be a language. But within them, you can say many different sentences and write many different books.
Independent, London (June 30, 1994)

10 We had a certain image of the Jewish woman as a mother. And now we have a generation of Jewish women with huge educational attainments. We had to learn that there is a huge tension between the roles these women are allotted in the outside world and the roles that have been open to them in, for example, synagogue management.
Independent, London (June 30, 1994)

Sacks, Oliver (Oliver Wolf Sacks; b.1933) British neurologist and writer

1 Sign language is the equal of speech, lending itself equally to the rigorous and the poetic, to philosophical analysis or to making love.
Times, London (June 16, 1994)

Sackville-West, Vita (Victoria Mary Sackville-West; 1892–1962) British poet and novelist

1 Men do kill women. Most women enjoy being killed; so I am told.
All Passion Spent (1931)

2 For observe, that to hope for Paradise is to live in Paradise, a very different thing from actually getting there.
Passenger to Tehran (1926), ch. 1

3 Travel is the most private of pleasures. There is no greater bore than the travel bore. We do not in the least want to hear what he has seen in Hong-Kong.
Passenger to Tehran (1926), ch. 1

4 Among the many problems which beset the novelist, not the least weighty is the choice of the moment at which to begin his novel.
The Edwardians (1930), ch. 1

5 The country habit has me by the heart,
For he's bewitched for ever who has seen,
Not with his eyes but with his vision, Spring
Flow down the woods and stipple leaves with sun.
"Winter," *The Land* (1926)

6 Those who have never dwelt in tents have no idea either of the charm or of the discomfort of a nomadic existence. The charm is purely romantic, and consequently very soon proves to be fallacious.
Twelve Days (1928), ch. 6

Sadat, Anwar al- (1918–81) Egyptian statesman

1 Most people seek after what they do not possess and they are enslaved by the very things they want to acquire.
In Search of Identity (1978)

2 Only when he has ceased to need things can a man truly be his own master and so really exist.
In Search of Identity (1978)

3 Peace is much more precious than a piece of land.
In Search of Identity (1978)

4 There can be hope only for a society which acts as one big family, and not as many separate ones.
In Search of Identity (1978)

Sade, Marquis de, Comte de Sade (Donatien Alphonse François; 1740–1814) French philosopher and novelist

1 All universal moral principles are idle fancies.
The 120 Days of Sodom (1785)

2 It is as unjust to possess a woman exclusively as to possess slaves.
The Bedroom Philosophers (1795)

Sagan, Carl (Carl Edward Sagan; 1934–96) U.S. astronomer and writer

1 A universe in which everything is known would be static and dull, as boring as the heaven of some weak-minded theologians...The ideal universe for us is one very much like the universe we inhabit...not really much of a coincidence.
Broca's Brain: The Romance of Science (1979)

2 Can we know, ultimately and in detail, a grain of salt?...In that grain of salt there are about...10 million billion atoms...Now, is this number more or less than the number of things which the brain can know?
Broca's Brain: The Romance of Science (1979)

3 Chlorine is a deadly poison gas employed on European battlefields in World War I. Sodium is a corrosive metal which burns upon contact with water. Together they make a placid and unpoisonous material, table salt. Why each of these substances has the properties it does is...chemistry.
Broca's Brain: The Romance of Science (1979)

4 It is an astonishing fact that there *are* laws of nature, rules that summarize conveniently—not just qualitatively but quantitatively—how the world works.
Broca's Brain: The Romance of Science (1979)

5 We are not in the habit of traveling close to the speed of light. The testimony of our common sense is suspect at high velocities.
Broca's Brain: The Romance of Science (1979)

6 Occasionally someone remarks on what a lucky coincidence it is that the Earth is perfectly suitable for life...But this is, at least in part, a confusion of cause and effect.
Cosmos (1980)

7 Our loyalties are to the species and the planet. We speak for Earth. Our obligation to survive is owed not just to ourselves but also to that cosmos, ancient and vast, from which we spring.
Cosmos (1980)

8 The secrets of evolution are death and time—the deaths of enormous numbers of life forms that were imperfectly adapted to the environment; and time for a long succession of small mutations.
Cosmos (1980)

9 To make an apple pie from scratch, you must first invent the universe.
Cosmos (1980)

10 A galaxy is composed of gas and dust and stars—billions upon billions of stars.
Carl Sagan became associated with the word "billions," often misquoted as "billions and billions," through the televison series he made from his book. *Cosmos* (1980)

11 Advances in medicine and agriculture have saved vastly more lives than have been lost in all wars in history.
The Demon-Haunted World: Science as a Candle in the Dark (1995)

12 Pseudoscience is easier to contrive than science...The standards of argument, what passes for evidence, are much more relaxed. In part for these reasons, it is much easier to present pseudoscience to the general public than science.
The Demon-Haunted World: Science as a Candle in the Dark (1995)

13 Pseudoscience is embraced, it might be argued, in exact proportion as real science is misunderstood.
The Demon-Haunted World: Science as a Candle in the Dark (1995)

14 Science is far from a perfect instrument of knowledge. It's just the best we have.
The Demon-Haunted World: Science as a Candle in the Dark (1995)

15 The reason science works so well is partly that built-in error-correcting machinery. There are no forbidden questions in

science, no matters too sensitive or delicate to be probed, no sacred truths.
The Demon-Haunted World: Science as a Candle in the Dark (1995)

16 We can pray over the cholera victim, or we can give her 500 milligrams of tetracycline every 12 hours.
The Demon-Haunted World: Science as a Candle in the Dark (1995)

17 Instead of acknowledging that in many areas we are ignorant, we have tended to say things like the Universe is permeated with the ineffable. A God of the Gaps is assigned responsibility for what we do not understand.
Contrasting science and theology. *The Demon-Haunted World: Science as a Candle in the Dark* (1995)

18 The consequences of scientific illiteracy are far more dangerous in our time than in any that has come before.
Written after noting Plato's words on the importance of science and mathematics to Athenian freemen. *The Demon-Haunted World: Science as a Candle in the Dark* (1995)

19 While our behavior is still significantly controlled by our genetic inheritance, we have, through our brains, a much richer opportunity to blaze new behavioral and cultural pathways on short timescales.
The Dragons of Eden (1977), introduction

Sagan, Françoise (Françoise Quoirez; b.1935) French writer

1 Every little girl knows about love. It is only her capacity to suffer because of it that increases.
Daily Express, London (1957)

2 To jealousy, nothing is more frightful than laughter.
La Chamade (1965), ch. 9

3 Art must take reality by surprise.
Interview, *Writers at Work* (1958)

Sagasta, Práxedes (d.1903) Spanish politician

1 When in a town they close the doors of justice, they open the doors of the Revolution.
Quoted in *The Spanish Labyrinth* (Gerald Brenan; 1943)

Said, Edward W. (Edward Wadi Said; b.1935) Palestinian-born U.S. writer and educator

1 Americans tend to identify with foreign societies or cultures projecting a pioneering spirit...On the other hand Americans often mistrust or do not have much interest in traditional cultures, even those in the throes of revolutionary renewal.
"The Formation of American Public Opinion on the Question of Palestine" (1980)

2 Until knowledge is understood in human and political terms as something to be won to the service of coexistence and community, not of particular races, nations, or religions, the future augurs badly.
Covering Islam (1981)

3 The orient...vacillates between the West's contempt for what is familiar and its shivers of delight in—or fear of—novelty.
Orientalism (1978)

4 Maps are always instruments of conquest; once projected, they are then implemented. Geography is therefore the art of war.
The Politics of Dispossession (1994), epilogue

5 There is no such thing as partial independence or limited autonomy. Without political independence there is neither sovereignty nor real freedom, and certainly not equality.
Referring to the desire for an independent Palestinian state. *The Politics of Dispossession* (1994), epilogue

Sainte-Beuve, Charles Augustin (1804–69) French critic

1 It is with medicine as with mathematics: we should occupy our minds only with what we continue to know; what we once knew is of little consequence.
Attrib.

Saint-Exupéry, Antoine de (Antoine Marie Roger de Saint-Exupéry; 1900–44) French writer and aviator

1 The soldier's body becomes a stock of accessories that are not his property.
Flight to Arras (1942)

2 To live is to be slowly born.
Flight to Arras (1942)

3 War is not an adventure. It is a disease. It is like typhus.
Flight to Arras (1942)

4 It is such a secret place, the land of tears.
The Little Prince (1943), ch. 7

5 You become responsible, forever, for what you have tamed. You are responsible for your rose.
The Little Prince (1943), ch. 21

6 Man's "progress" is but a gradual discovery that his questions have no meaning.
Posthumously published as *Citadelle*. *The Wisdom of the Sands* (Stuart Gilbert, tr.; 1948)

7 In the night reason disappears, only the lives of things remaining.
Vol de Nuit (1931)

8 Love does not consist in gazing at each other but in looking together in the same direction.
Wind, Sand and Stars (1939), ch. 8

Saint-Lambert, Jean François (Marquis de Saint-Lambert; 1716–1803) French poet and philosopher

1 Often I am still listening when the song is over.
"Le Printemps," *Les Saisons* (1769)

Saint Laurent, Yves (Yves Henri Donat Mathieu; b.1936) Algerian-born French couturier

Quotations about Saint Laurent

1 He is such a giant that I wonder if we are not asking too much of him. I wonder if he is bored. He's not working, he's not caring, something is broken there. He is just making the pretense.
Hebe Dorsey (1925–87) Tunisian-born French fashion journalist. Quoted in *The Fashion Conspiracy* (Nicholas Coleridge; 1986)

Quotations by Saint Laurent

2 We must never confuse elegance with snobbery.
Ritz (1984)

3 I have often said that I wish I had invented blue jeans, the most spectacular, the most practical, the most relaxed and nonchalant. They have expression, modesty, sex appeal, simplicity— all I hope for in my clothes.
Quoted in *Yves Saint Laurent* (Costume Institute Exhibition catalog, Metropolitan Museum, New York City; 1984), ch. 2

Sakharov, Andrei (Andrei Dmitriyevich Sakharov; 1921–89) Soviet nuclear physicist and human rights activist

1 There'll be a hard fight tomorrow.
Said to a friend shortly before his death. Remark (1989)

Saki (Hector Hugh Monro; 1870–1916) British short-story writer

1 "I believe I take precedence," he said coldly; "you are merely the club Bore: I am the club Liar."
"A Defensive Diamond," *Beasts and Super-Beasts* (1914)

2 A little inaccuracy sometimes saves tons of explanation.
"The Square Egg," *Clovis and the Alleged Business of Romance* (1924)

3 In baiting a mouse-trap with cheese, always leave room for the mouse.
"The Square Egg," *Clovis and the Alleged Business of Romance* (1924)

4 There may have been disillusionments in the lives of the medieval saints, but they would scarcely have been better pleased if they could have foreseen that their names would be associated nowadays chiefly with racehorses and the cheaper clarets.
"Reginald at the Carlton," *Reginald* (1904)

5 The young have aspirations that never come to pass, the old have reminiscences of what never happened. It's only the middle-aged who are really conscious of their limitations.
"Reginald at the Carlton," *Reginald* (1904)

6 The cook was a good cook, as cooks go; and as cooks go she went.
"Reginald on Besetting Sins," *Reginald* (1904)

7 People may say what they like about the decay of Christianity; the religious system that produced green Chartreuse can never really die.
"Reginald on Christmas Presents," *Reginald* (1904)

8 Even the Hooligan was probably invented in China centuries before we thought of him.
"Reginald on House-Parties," *Reginald* (1904)

9 Every reformation must have its victims. You can't expect the fatted calf to share the enthusiasm of the angels over the prodigal's return.
"Reginald on the Academy," *Reginald* (1904)

10 Her frocks are built in Paris but she wears them with a strong English accent.
"Reginald on Women," *Reginald* (1904)

11 The doctors said at the time that she couldn't live more than a fortnight, and she's been trying ever since to see if she could. Women are so opinionated.
"Reginald on Women," *Reginald* (1904)

12 I think she must have been very strictly brought up, she's so desperately anxious to do the wrong thing correctly.
"Reginald on Worries," *Reginald* (1904)

13 I always say beauty is only sin deep.
"Reginald's Choir Treat," *Reginald* (1904)

14 Addresses are given to us to conceal our whereabouts.
Reginald in Russia (1910)

15 But, good gracious, you've got to educate him first. You can't expect a boy to be vicious till he's been to a good school.
Reginald in Russia (1910)

16 By insisting on having your bottle pointing to the north when the cork is being drawn, and calling the waiter Max, you may induce an impression on your guests which hours of laboured boasting might be powerless to achieve. For this purpose, however, the guests must be chosen as carefully as the wine.
"The Chaplet," *The Chronicles of Clovis* (1911)

17 The people of Crete unfortunately make more history than they can consume locally.
"The Jesting of Arlington Stringham," *The Chronicles of Clovis* (1911)

18 To say that anything was a quotation was an excellent method, in Eleanor's eyes, for withdrawing it from discussion.
"The Jesting of Arlington Stringham," *The Chronicles of Clovis* (1911)

19 All decent people live beyond their incomes; those who aren't respectable live beyond other people's; a few gifted individuals manage to do both.
"The Match-Maker," *The Chronicles of Clovis* (1911)

20 He's simply got the instinct for being unhappy highly developed.
"The Match-Maker," *The Chronicles of Clovis* (1911)

21 Oysters are more beautiful than any religion...There's nothing in Christianity or Buddhism that quite matches the sympathetic unselfishness of an oyster.
"The Match-Maker," *The Chronicles of Clovis* (1911)

22 There are so many things to complain of in this household that it would never have occurred to me to complain of rheumatism.
"The Quest," *The Chronicles of Clovis* (1911)

23 Children with Hyacinth's temperament don't know better as they grow older; they merely know more.
"Hyacinth," *Toys of Peace and Other Papers* (1919)

24 Monogamy is the Western custom of one wife and hardly any mistresses.
Attrib.

Salinger, J. D. (Jerome David Salinger; b.1919) U.S. novelist

Quotations about Salinger

1 I HATED the Salinger story. It took me days to go through it, gingerly, a page at a time, and blushing with embarrassment for him every ridiculous sentence of the way. How can they let him do it?
Elizabeth Bishop (1911–79) U.S. poet. Referring to J. D. Salinger's novel, *The Catcher in the Rye* (1951). Letter to Pearl Kazin (September 9, 1959), quoted in *One Art: The Selected Letters of Elizabeth Bishop* (Robert Giroux, ed.; 1994)

2 Salinger was the perfect *New Yorker* writer, whose promise and celebrity delivered less and less.
Leo Brandy, U.S. academic. Quoted in "Naturalists, and Novelists of Manners," *Harvard Guide to Contemporary American Writing* (Daniel Hoffman, ed.; 1979)

3 That quality of sensitive innocence which Holden Caulfield retained beneath his rebellious mannerisms has developed into a note of religious mysticism.
Ian Ousby, British critic. Holden Caulfield is the hero of J. D. Salinger's novel, *The Catcher in the Rye* (1951). *50 American Novels* (1979)

Quotations by Salinger

4 I'm trying to hold on to some old, useful feelings of obscurity. If I had to do it over again, I'm pretty sure I'd use a pseudonym during publication years. It's a great pity that noms de plume have gone out of fashion.
Declining to appear in one of critic Kenneth Tynan's British television programs. Letter to Kenneth Tynan (1959)

5 Lane...sat back and briefly looked around the room with an almost palpable sense of well-being at finding himself...in the right place with an unimpeachably right-looking girl.
"Franny," *Franny and Zooey* (1961)

6 I'm sick of just liking people. I wish to God I could meet somebody I could respect.
Said by Franny. "Franny," *Franny and Zooey* (1961)

7 I mean they're not *real* poets. They're just people that write poems and get published and anthologized all over the place, but they're not *poets*.
Said by Franny, referring to the staff of her English department. "Franny," *Franny and Zooey* (1961)

8 Anyway I just got your beautiful letter and I love you to pieces, distraction, etc.
Written by Franny in a letter to Lane. "Franny," *Franny and Zooey* (1961)

9 To get straight to the worst, what I'm about to offer isn't really a short story at all but a sort of prose home movie.
"Zooey," *Franny and Zooey* (1961)

10 The facts at hand presumably speak for themselves, but a trifle more vulgarly, I suspect, than facts even usually do.
Opening line of "Zooey." "Zooey," *Franny and Zooey* (1961)

11 Both Testaments are full of pundits, prophets, disciples, favorite *sons*, Solomons, Isaiahs, Davids, Pauls—but, my God, who besides Jesus really knew which end was up? *Nobody*.
Said by Zooey. "Zooey," *Franny and Zooey* (1961)

12 A child is a guest in the house, to be loved and respected—never possessed, since he belongs to God.
Raise High the Roofbeams, Carpenters (1963)

13 What really knocks me out is a book that, when you're all done reading it, you wish the author that wrote it was a terrific friend of yours and you could call him up on the phone whenever you felt like it.
The Catcher in the Rye (1951)

14 If you really want to hear about it, the first thing you'll probably want to know is where I was born and what my lousy childhood was like, and how my parents were occupied and all before they had me, and all that David Copperfield kind of crap.
The opening words of the novel. *The Catcher in the Rye* (1951), ch. 1

15 Sex is something I really don't understand too hot. You never know *where* the hell you are. I keep making up these sex rules for myself, and then I break them right away.
The Catcher in the Rye (1951), ch. 9

16 They didn't act like people and they didn't act like actors. It's hard to explain. They acted more like they knew they were celebrities and all. I mean they were good, but they were *too* good.
Holden Caulfield's response to the Lunts' acting style. Alfred Lunt (1893–1977) and Lynn Fontanne (1887?–1983) were a husband and wife acting team and frequently worked together. *The Catcher in the Rye* (1951), ch. 17

Salisbury, Lord, 1st Earl of Salisbury and 1st Viscount Cranbourne (Robert Cecil; 1563–1612) English statesman

1 I have been, though unworthy, a member of this House in six or seven Parliaments, yet never did I see the House in so great confusion. This is more fit for a grammar school than a Court of Parliament.
Speech to the English Parliament (November 24, 1601)

Salk, Jonas E. (Jonas Edward Salk; 1914–95) U.S. physician and virologist

1 The people—could you patent the sun?
On being asked who owned the patent on his antipolio vaccine. Attrib.

Sallust (Gaius Sallustius Crispus; 86?–35? B.C.) Roman historian and politician

1 To like and dislike the same things, that is indeed true friendship.
Bellum Catilinae (43 B.C.)

Salvandy, Comte de (1795–1856) French nobleman

1 We are dancing on a volcano.
Remark made before the July Revolution (Paris, July 1830).

Sampras, Pete (b.1971) U.S. tennis player

1 I've been training for about 2 weeks...For once, I've had a normal life.
Independent, London (May 10, 1994)

Sampson, Anthony (b.1926) British writer and journalist

1 Members rise from CMG (known sometimes in Whitehall as "Call me God") to the KCMG ("Kindly Call me God") to...The GCMG ("God Calls me God").
Referring to names of the British Civil Service orders. CMG: Companion of St. Michael and St. George. KCMG: Knight Commander of St. Michael and St. George. GCMG: Grand Cross of St. Michael and St. George. *Anatomy of Britain* (1962), ch. 18

Samuel, Herbert, 1st Viscount Samuel (Herbert Louis Samuel; 1870–1963) British statesman and philosopher

1 Without doubt the greatest injury...was done by basing morals on myth, for sooner or later myth is recognized for what it

is, and disappears. Then morality loses the foundation on which it has been built.
Romanes lecture (1947)

2 A library is thought in cold storage.
A Book of Quotations (1947)

3 It takes two to make a marriage a success and only one a failure.
A Book of Quotations (1947)

4 The House of Lords must be the only institution in the world which is kept efficient by the persistent absenteeism of most of its members.
The House of Lords, the upper house of the British Parliament, is made up of unelected members. *News Review* (February 5, 1948)

Samuelson, P. A. (Paul Anthony Samuelson; b.1915) U.S. economist

1 The consumer, so it is said, is the king...each is a voter who uses his money as votes to get the things done that he wants done.
1948. *Economics: an Introductory Analysis* (1964)

2 Man does not live by GNP alone.
1948. GNP means gross national product. *Economics: an Introductory Analysis* (1964)

Sanchez, Sonia (b.1934) U.S. poet and writer

1 WE A badddDDD PEOPLE
Poem title. "WE A badddDDD PEOPLE," *A Blues Book For Blue Black Magical Women* (1974)

2 So much of growing up is an unbearable waiting. A constant longing for another time. Another season.
"Graduation Notes," *Under a Soprano Sky* (1987)

3 this country might have
been a pio
neer land
once.
but. there ain't
no mo
indians blowing
custer's mind
with a different
image of america.
"Right on: White America," *WE A badddDDD PEOPLE* (1973), quoted in *The Penguin Book of American Verse* (Geoffrey Moore, ed.; 1977)

Sancho, Ignatius (1729–80) British slave

1 One ounce of practical religion is worth all that ever the Stoics wrote.
October 16, 1775. Letter to Miss L., *The Letters of the Late Ignatius Sancho, An African* (1782), vol. 1

2 A man should know a little of Geography—History, nothing more useful, or pleasant.
1778. Letter to Mr J. W., *The Letters of the Late Ignatius Sancho, An African* (1782), vol. 2

3 In some one of your letters which I do not recollect—you speak (with honest indignation) of the treachery and chicanery of the Natives. My good friend, you should remember from whom they learnt those vices.
1778. Letter to Mr J. W., *The Letters of the Late Ignatius Sancho, An African* (1782), vol. 2

Sand, George (Amandine Aurore Lucile, Baronne Dudevant; 1804–76) French novelist

1 There is only one happiness in life, to love and be loved.
Letter to Lina Calamatta (March 31, 1862)

2 One is happy as a result of one's own efforts, once one knows...ingredients of happiness—simple tastes, a certain degree of courage, self denial to a point, love of work, and...a clear conscience. Happiness is no vague dream, of that I now feel certain.
Correspondence 1812–1876 (1882–84), vol. 5

3 Liszt said to me today that God alone deserves to be loved. It may be true, but when one has loved a man it is very different to love God.
Intimate Journal (1834)

4 Where love is absent there can be no woman.
Lelia (1833), vol. 1

5 Nothing is more horrible than the terror, the sufferings, and the revulsion of a poor girl, ignorant of the facts of life, who finds herself raped by a brute. As far as possible we bring them up as saints, and then we hand them over as if they were fillies.
1843. Attrib.

Sandburg, Carl (1878–1967) U.S. poet and biographer

1 The fog comes on little cat feet.
"Fog" (1916)

2 Poetry is the achievement of the synthesis of hyacinths and biscuits.
"Poetry Considered," *Atlantic Monthly* (1923)

3 Come and show me another city with lifted head singing so proud to be alive and coarse and strong and cunning.
1914. "Chicago," *Chicago Poems* (1916)

4 Hog Butcher for the World,
Tool Maker, Stacker of Wheat,
Player with Railroads and the Nation's Freight Handler;
Stormy, husky, brawling,
City of the Big Shoulders.
1914. "Chicago," *Chicago Poems* (1916), quoted in *The Norton Anthology of American Literature* (Nina Baym, ed.; 1998), vol. 2

5 They tell me you are wicked and I believe them, for I have seen your painted
women under the gas lamps luring the farm boys.
1914. "Chicago," *Chicago Poems* (1916), quoted in *The Norton Anthology of American Literature* (Nina Baym, ed.; 1998), vol. 2

6 Omaha, the roughneck feeds armies,
Eats and sweats from a dirty face.
Omaha works to get the world a breakfast.
Referring to Omaha, Nebraska. "Omaha," *Steel and Smoke* (1920)

7 Red barns and red heifers spot the green

grass circles around Omaha—the farmers
haul tanks of cream and wagon loads of cheese.
Referring to Omaha, Nebraska. "Omaha," *Steel and Smoke* (1920)

8 Money is power: so said one.
Money is a cushion: so said another.
Money is the root of evil: so said still another.
Money means freedom: so runs an old saying.
The People, Yes (1936)

9 Sometime they'll give a war and nobody will come.
The People, Yes (1936)

10 To the Chinese we have given
kerosene, bullets, Bibles
and they have given us radishes, soy beans, silk,
poems, paintings, proverbs,
porcelain, egg foo yong,
gunpowder, Fourth of July firecrackers, fireworks
and labor gangs for the first Pacific railways.
"The Copperfaces, the Red Men," *The People, Yes* (1936)

11 Here is the difference between Dante, Milton, and me. They wrote about hell and never saw the place. I wrote about Chicago after looking the town over for years and years.
Quoted in *Carl Sandburg* (Harry Golden; 1961)

Sanders, George (1906–72) British film actor

1 Dear World, I am leaving you because I am bored. I am leaving you with your worries. Good luck.
Suicide note. (1972)

Sanford, Charles, Jr. (Charles Steadman Sanford, Jr.; b.1936) U.S. business executive

1 I have yet to meet the famous Rational Economic Man theorists describe. Real people have always done inexplicable things from time to time, and they show no sign of stopping.
Speech (October 1994)

2 Intellectual honesty is more than what's legislated; it is inherent in the best people, those who take a broader view of their action than simply "What's in it for me?"
Speech (1995)

3 People wonder why they should adopt new processes...when they think the old ones work just fine...if I were going to have surgery tomorrow, I'd much rather have a shot of Demerol than a shot of Jack Daniels.
Speech (October 1994)

4 Getting someone to do something for you.
Defining politics. *Economist*, London (July 11, 1987)

Sanger, Margaret (originally Margaret Louise Higgins; 1879–1966) U.S. social reformer and leader of birth control movement

1 No woman can call herself free who cannot choose the time to be a mother or not as she sees fit.
The Case for Birth Control (1917)

Sankara, Thomas (1950–87) Burkina Fasoan soldier and president

1 The revolution and women's liberation go together. We do not talk of women's emancipation as an act of charity or because of a surge of human compassion. It is a basic necessity for the triumph of the revolution. Women hold up the other half of the sky.
October 2, 1983. *Thomas Sankara Speaks* (1988)

2 We should see in every prostitute an accusing finger pointing firmly at society as a whole. Every pimp, every partner in prostitution, turns the knife in this festering and gaping wound that disfigures the world.
March 8, 1987. Speech at International Women's Day celebration, Ouagadougou, *Thomas Sankara Speaks* (1988)

Santayana, George (Jorge Augustín Nicolás Ruiz de Santayana; 1863–1952) Spanish-born U.S. philosopher, poet, and novelist

Quotations about Santayana

1 He stood on the flat road to heaven and buttered slides to hell for all the rest.
Oliver Wendell Holmes (1841–1935) U.S. judge. Letter (December 5, 1913)

Quotations by Santayana

2 Philosophers are as jealous as women. Each wants a monopoly of praise.
Dialogues in Limbo (1926)

3 The diseases which destroy a man are no less natural than the instincts which preserve him.
Dialogues in Limbo (1926)

4 The young man who has not wept is a savage, and the old man who will not laugh is a fool.
Dialogues in Limbo (1926)

5 The tide of evolution carries everything before it, thoughts no less than bodies, and persons no less than nations.
Little Essays (1920), 44

6 If all the arts aspire to the condition of music, all the sciences aspire to the condition of mathematics.
Observer, London (March 4, 1928), "Sayings of the Week"

7 England is the paradise of individuality, eccentricity, heresy, anomalies, hobbies, and humors.
"The British Character," *Soliloquies in England* (1922)

8 Trust the man who hesitates in his speech and is quick and steady in action, but beware of long arguments and long beards.
"The British Character," *Soliloquies in England* (1922)

9 There is no cure for birth and death save to enjoy the interval.
"War Shrines," *Soliloquies in England* (1922)

10 The working of great institutions is mainly the result of a vast mass of routine, petty malice, self interest, carelessness, and sheer mistake. Only a residual fraction is thought.
The Crime of Galileo (1955)

11 There is nothing impossible in the existence of the supernatural: its existence seems to me to be decidedly probable.
The Genteel Tradition at Bay (1931)

12 America is the greatest of opportunities and the worst of influences.
The Last Puritan (1935)

13 Happiness is the only sanction of life; where happiness fails, existence remains a mad and lamentable experiment.
The Life of Reason (1905–06)

14 Progress, far from consisting in change, depends on retentiveness. Those who cannot remember the past are condemned to repeat it.
The Life of Reason (1905–06)

15 Popular poets are the parish priests of the Muse, retailing her ancient divinations to a long since converted public.
"Reason in Art," *The Life of Reason* (1905–06)

16 A body seriously out of equilibrium, either with itself or with its environment, perishes outright. Not so a mind. Madness and suffering can set themselves no limit.
"Reason in Common Sense," *The Life of Reason* (1905–06)

17 A life of pleasure requires an aristocratic setting to make it interesting.
"Reason in Society," *The Life of Reason* (1905–06)

18 A grateful environment is a substitute for happiness. It can quicken us from without as a fixed hope and affection, or the consciousness of a right life, can quicken us from within.
The Sense of Beauty (1896)

19 It is a great advantage for a system of philosophy to be substantially true.
The Unknowable (1923)

20 For an idea ever to be fashionable is ominous, since it must afterwards be always old-fashioned.
"Modernism and Christianity," *Winds of Doctrine* (1913)

21 Our occasional madness is less wonderful than our occasional sanity.
Quoted in *Interpretations of Poetry and Religion* (William G. Holzberger and Herman J. Saatkaup, Jr.; 1989)

22 Because there's no fourth class.
Referring to being asked why he always traveled third class. Quoted in *Living Biographies of Great Philosophers* (H. Thomas; 1946)

23 It is always pleasant to be urged to do something on the ground that one can do it well.
Quoted in *The Letters of George Santayana* (Daniel Cory, ed.; 1956)

24 Life is not a spectacle or a feast; it is a predicament.
Quoted in *The Perpetual Pessimist* (Sagittarius and George; 1963)

25 Sanity is madness put to good uses; waking life is a dream controlled.
Attrib.

Sappho (610?–580? B.C.) Greek poet

Quotations about Sappho

1 Sappho survives, because we sing her songs;
And Aeschylus, because we read his plays!
Robert Browning (1812–89) British poet. "Cleon," *Men and Women* (1855)

Quotations by Sappho

2 Gentle ladies, you will remember till old age what we did together in our brilliant youth.
Quoted in *Distinguished Women Writers* (Virginia Moore; 1934)

Sarasate, Pablo de (Pablo Martín Melitón Sarasate y Navascuez; 1844–1908) Spanish violinist and composer

1 A genius! For thirty-seven years I've practiced fourteen hours a day, and now they call me a genius!
On being hailed as a genius by a critic. Attrib.

Sargent, Epes (1813–80) U.S. writer and playwright

1 A life on the ocean wave,
A home on the rolling deep.
Song lyric. "A Life on the Ocean Wave" (1838)

Sargent, John Singer (1856–1925) U.S. portrait painter

1 Every time I paint a portrait I lose a friend.
Treasury of Humorous Quotations (N. Bentley and E. Esar; 1951)

Sargent, Malcolm, Sir (Harold Malcolm Watts Sargent; 1895–1967) British conductor

1 Just a little more reverence, please, and not so much astonishment.
Rehearsing the female chorus in "For Unto Us a Child Is Born" from Handel's *Messiah*. Attrib.

Sariegos, Quentin de Spanish Capuchin friar

1 Whenever you kiss a man, remember your last communion and think to yourself "Could the Sacred Host and the lips of this man come together on my lips without sacrilege?"
Advice on premarital contact between the sexes. Quoted in *The Spaniards* (John Hooper; 1986)

Sarnoff, David (1891–1971) Russian-born U.S. broadcasting executive

1 Freedom is the oxygen without which science cannot breathe.
"Electronics—Today and Tomorrow" (1954), quoted in *Profile of America* (Emily Davie, ed.; 1954)

2 I have learned to have more faith in the scientist than he does in himself.
Quoted in *Newsweek* (December 27, 1971), obituary

3 Atoms for peace. Man is still the greatest miracle and the greatest problem on this earth.
January 27, 1954. First message sent with atomic power.

Sarnoff, Robert W. U.S. business executive

1 Finance is the art of passing currency from hand to hand until it finally disappears.
Attrib.

Saro-Wiwa, Ken (1941–95) Nigerian writer and political and human rights activist

1 The most important thing for me is that I've used my talents as a writer to enable the Ogoni people to confront their tormentors. I was not able to do it as a politician or a

businessman. My writing did it. And it sure makes me feel good! I'm mentally prepared for the worst, but hopeful for the best. I think I have the moral victory.
Letter to William Boyd, *A Month and a Day: A Detention Diary* (1995)

2 The environment is man's first right. Without a safe environment, man cannot exist to claim other rights, be they political, social, or economic.
1995. Message sent from prison upon winning the 1995 Goldman Environmental prize for campaigning against oil companies' environmental destruction in his native Ogoniland. He was hanged in November 1995 on politically motivated charges of incitement to murder. Quoted in *National Geographic Magazine* (April 1996)

Saroyan, William (1908–81) U.S. novelist

1 Baseball can be trusted, as great art can, and bad art can't.
Sports Illustrated (June 8, 1959)

2 If you give to a thief he cannot steal from you, and he is then no longer a thief.
The Human Comedy (1943), ch. 4

3 Everybody has got to die, but I have always believed an exception would be made in my case. Now what?
1981. Last words. Quoted in *Time* (January 16, 1984)

Sarsfield, Patrick, Earl of Lucan (d.1693) Irish soldier

1 Would to God this was shed for Ireland.
1693. Last words, after being wounded fighting for France at Landen. Quoted in *A Book of Irish Quotations* (Sean McMahon, ed.; 1984)

2 Change kings, and we will fight it over again with you.
1691. Said after the Treaty of Limerick. Quoted in *A Book of Irish Quotations* (Sean McMahon, ed.; 1984)

Sarton, George (George Alfred Leon Sarton; 1884–1956) U.S. science historian

1 Scientific activity is the only one which is obviously and undoubtedly cumulative and progressive.
The History of Science and the History of Civilization (1930)

Sartre, Jean-Paul (1905–80) French philosopher, playwright, and novelist

Quotations about Sartre

1 He is a philosopher remarkable for the force, one might almost say the animal vigour, of his thought; a novelist of great fecundity...a playwright able to sustain themes apparently void of dramatic interest; and a political journalist with a word to say on all contemporary problems.
Anonymous. *Observer*, London (March 7, 1947)

2 The ineptitude of M. Sartre's political performance has tempted some British critics to dismiss him as a phoney, particularly as he rarely hesitates to adapt the facts to fit the cause for which he currently cares.
Anonymous. *Observer*, London (December 4, 1960)

Quotations by Sartre

3 If a Jew is fascinated by Christians it is not because of their virtues, which he values little, but because they represent anonymity, humanity without race.
Anti-Semite and Jew (George J. Becker, tr.; 1976)

4 Fear is of being in the world whereas anguish is anguish before myself.
Being and Nothingness (1943)

5 It is certain that we cannot overcome anguish, for we are anguish.
Being and Nothingness (1943)

6 The environment can act on the subject only to the exact extent that he comprehends it; that is, transforms it into a situation. Hence no objective description of this environment could be of any use to us.
Being and Nothingness (1943)

7 There is not a taste, a mannerism, or a human act which is not revealing.
Being and Nothingness (1943)

8 Man is condemned to be free.
Existentialism is a Humanism (1947)

9 So that's what Hell is. I'd never have believed it...Do you remember, brimstone, the stake, the gridiron? What a joke! No need of a gridiron—Hell is other people.
Huis clos (1944), Scene 5

10 I don't think the profession of historian fits a man for psychological analysis. In our work we have to deal only with simple feelings to which we give generic names such as Ambition and Interest.
Nausea (1938)

11 I know perfectly well that I don't want to do anything; to do something is to create existence—and there's quite enough existence as it is.
Nausea (1938)

12 My thought is *me*: that is why I can't stop. I exist by what I think...and I can't prevent myself from thinking.
Nausea (1938)

13 Things are entirely what they appear to be and *behind them*...there is nothing.
Nausea (1938)

14 Three o'clock is always too late or too early for anything you want to do.
Nausea (1938)

15 You get the impression that their normal condition is silence and that speech is a slight fever which attacks them now and then.
Nausea (1938)

16 Doctors, priests, magistrates, and officers know men as thoroughly as if they had made them.
"Shrove Tuesday," *Nausea* (1938)

17 I distrust an immediate morality, it involves too much bad faith, all the tepidness of ignorance.
Notebooks for an Ethics (1983)

18 If you seek authenticity for authenticity's sake, you are no longer authentic.
Notebooks for an Ethics (1983)

19 The one and only basis of the moral life must be spontaneity, that is, the immediate, the unreflective.
Notebooks for an Ethics (1983)

20 An American is either a Jew, or an anti-Semite, unless he is both at the same time.
The Condemned of Altona (1960)

21 I hate victims who respect their executioners.
The Condemned of Altona (1960), Act 1, Scene 1

22 When the rich wage war it is the poor who die.
The Devil and the Good Lord (1951), Act 1, Tableau 1

23 A desire is in fact never satisfied to the letter precisely because of the abyss that separates the real from the imaginary.
The Psychology of Imagination (1948)

24 All consciousness is consciousness *of* something.
The Psychology of Imagination (1948)

25 Any attempt to directly conceive death or the nothingness of existence is by nature bound to fail.
The Psychology of Imagination (1948)

26 If the schizophrenic imagines so many amorous scenes it is not only because his real love has been disappointed, but, above all, because he is no longer capable of loving.
The Psychology of Imagination (1948)

27 Imagination is not an empirical or superadded power of consciousness, it is the whole of consciousness as it realizes its freedom.
The Psychology of Imagination (1948)

28 A man evaporates without an eye-witness.
The Reprieve (1945)

29 A kiss without a mustache, they said then, is like an egg without salt; I will add to it: and it is like Good without Evil.
Words (1964)

30 She believed in nothing; only her skepticism kept her from being an atheist.
Words (1964)

31 The poor don't know that their function in life is to exercise our generosity.
Words (1964)

32 When we love animals and children too much we love them at the expense of men.
Words (1964)

33 There is no such thing as psychological. Let us say that one can improve the biography of the person.
Quoted in *The Divided Self* (R. D. Laing; 1960), ch. 8

34 In the first days of the revolt you must kill: to shoot down a European is to kill two birds with one stone, to destroy an oppressor and the man he oppresses at the same time: there remain a dead man, and a free man.
1961. Referring to the liberation of colonized people from European imperial powers. Quoted in *The Wretched of the Earth* (F. Fanon; 1965), preface

Sassoon, Siegfried (1886–1967) British poet and writer

1 And when the war is done and youth stone dead
I'd toddle safely home and die—in bed.
"Base Details" (1918)

2 Soldiers are citizens of death's grey land,
Drawing no dividend from time's tomorrows.
"Dreamers" (1918)

3 Who will remember, passing through this gate
The unheroic dead who fed the guns?
Who shall absolve the foulness of their fate—
Those doomed, conscripted, unvictorious ones?
"On Passing the New Menin Gate" (1928)

4 To these I turn, in these I trust;
Brother Lead and Sister Steel.
To his blind power I make appeal;
I guard her beauty clean from rust.
"The Kiss" (1917), st. 1, quoted in *The War Poets* (R. Giddings; 1988)

5 "Stick him between the eyes, in the throat, in the chest." "Don't waste good steel. Six inches are enough. What's the use of a foot of steel sticking out at the back of a man's neck?...when he coughs, go and look for another."
The army school instructor's lecture on the use of the bayonet. *Memoirs of an Infantry Officer* (1930), pt. 1, ch. 1

6 I am making this statement as a wilful defiance of military authority because I believe that the War is being deliberately prolonged by those who have the power to end it.
Memoirs of an Infantry Officer (1930), pt. 10, ch. 3

Satie, Erik (Erik Alfred Leslie Satie; 1866–1925) French composer

1 When I was young, I was told: "You'll see, when you're fifty." I am fifty and I haven't seen a thing.
Letter to his brother, quoted in *Erik Satie* (Pierre-Daniel Templier; 1932), ch. 1

2 My doctor has always told me to smoke. He even explains himself: "Smoke, my friend. Otherwise someone else will smoke in your place."
Mémoires d'un amnésique (1924)

3 To be played with both hands in the pocket.
Direction on one of his piano pieces. Attrib.

Saunders, Jennifer (b.1958) British comedian

1 Instant coffee is just old beans that have been cremated.
Said as Edina. *Absolutely Fabulous*, BBC television (1990s)

2 She was once cool but Mr. Gravity's been very unkind to that woman.
Said as Edina. *Absolutely Fabulous*, BBC television (1990s)

3 The only label she wears is "drip dry".
Said as Edina. *Absolutely Fabulous*, BBC television (1990s)

Savalas, Telly (originally Aristotle Savalas; 1926–94) Greek-born U.S. actor

1 Who loves ya, baby?
Catchphrase from the television detective series. *Kojak* (Abby Mann; 1974–78)

Savile, Sir George, 1st Marquess of Halifax (1633–95) English politician and pamphleteer

1 This innocent word "Trimmer" signifies no more than this, that if men are together in a boat, and one part of the company would weigh it down on one side, another would make it lean as much to the contrary.
Character of a Trimmer (1688), Preface

2 Anger is never without an argument, but seldom with a good one.
"Of Anger," *Political, Moral, and Miscellaneous Thoughts and Reflections* (1750)

3 Malice is of a low stature, but it hath very long arms.
"Of Malice and Envy," *Political, Moral, and Miscellaneous Thoughts and Reflections* (1750)

Savonarola, Girolamo (1452–98) Italian preacher and reformer

1 Art cannot imitate nature entirely, even if the artist is perfect, because, even if a painter makes something similar to man in everything, yet it will not have life.
Sermon on the Psalm *Quam Bonus* (1493), quoted in *Savonarola* (M. Ferrara, ed.; 1952)

2 Would you see true beauty? Look at the pious man or woman in whom spirit dominates matter; watch him when he prays, when a ray of the divine beauty glows upon him when his prayer is ended; you will see the beauty of God shining in his face.
28th sermon on Ezekiel (1489?)

Sayers, Dorothy L. (Dorothy Leigh Sayers; 1893–1957) British writer

1 I can't see that she could have found anything nastier to say if she'd thought it out with both hands for a fortnight.
"Prothalamion," *Busman's Holiday* (1937)

2 Time and trouble will tame an advanced young woman, but an advanced old woman is uncontrollable by any earthly force.
Clouds of Witness (1956), ch. 16

3 A facility for quotation covers the absence of original thought.
Said by Lord Peter Wimsey. *Gaudy Night* (1935)

4 Astronomers and mathematicians are much the most cheerful people of the lot...perpetually contemplating things on so vast a scale makes them feel either that it doesn't matter a hoot anyway, or that anything so large and elaborate must have some sense in it.
The Documents in the Case (co-written with R. Eustace; 1930)

Scanderbeg (George Kastrioti, also known as Georgios Kastriotes; 1405–68) Albanian patriot

1 Come what may, I am the friend of virtue and not of fortune.
Letter to Ferdinand I, King of Naples (1460)

Scannelli, Francesco (1616–63) Italian priest, physician, and writer

1 One can say that painting is purifying, and that it does not corrupt the emotions. Thus it shares common ground not only with poetry, rhetoric and history, but also as well with philosophy and with moral theology.
Il Microcosmo della Pittura (1657)

Scargill, Arthur (b.1938) British labor leader

1 My father still reads the dictionary every day. He says your life depends on your power to master words.
Sunday Times, London (January 10, 1982)

Scarron, Paul (1610–60) French writer

1 At last I am going to be well!
1660. As he lay dying. Attrib.

Schaffer, Bob (b.1962) U.S. politician

1 No taxation without respiration.
Advocating the abolition of inheritance tax. *Time* (August 4, 1997)

Schama, Simon (Simon Michael Schama; b.1945) British-born U.S. historian

1 If one had to look for one indisputable story of transformation in the French Revolution, it would be the creation of the juridical entity of the citizen.
Citizens: A Chronicle of the French Revolution (1989), epilogue

Scharlieb, Dame Mary Ann Dacomb (1845–1930) British gynecological surgeon

1 Pregnancy is not a disease, and the pregnant woman should not consider herself a patient, but she should be more careful than ever to lead a really physiological life.
A Woman's Words to Women on the Care of Their Health in England and in India (1895)

2 Girls are taught...that any exhibition of sexual feeling is unwomanly and intolerable; they also learn from an early age that if a woman makes a mistake it is upon her...alone that social punishment will descend.
The Seven Ages of Woman (1915)

Scharping, Rudolf (b.1947) German politician

1 Remembrance is the secret of reconciliation.
Observer, London (April 17, 1994), "Sayings of the Week"

Scheidemann, Philipp (1865–1939) German statesman

1 The Hohenzollerns have abdicated. Long live the great German Republic!
Address before the Reichstag, Berlin, announcing the formation of the Weimar Republic (November 9, 1918)

Schein, Edgar H. (Edgar Henry Schein; b.1928) U.S. educator and author

1 Dialogue cannot create the need to change, but it certainly facilitates the process of change.
Process Consultation Revisited: Building the Helping Relationship (1999)

2 Real help can only be delivered when both consultant and

client are using a common set of assumptions and have developed some common language.
Process Consultation Revisited: Building the Helping Relationship (1999)

Schell, Jonathan (b.1943) U.S. author

1 If it is "utopian" to want to survive, then it is "realistic" to want to be dead.
The Fate of the Earth (1982)

2 Reason must sit at the knee of instinct and learn reverence for the miraculous instinctual capacity for creation.
The Fate of the Earth (1982)

3 The lie that we have all come to live—the pretense that life lived on top of a nuclear stockpile can last.
The Fate of the Earth (1982)

4 If our economy were to produce a wonderful abundance of silverware, glasses, and table napkins but no food, people would quickly rebel and insist on a different system.
Alluding to the nuclear arms industry. *The Fate of the Earth* (1982)

5 It may not be until the human future has been restored to us that desire can again find a natural place.
Referring to the threat posed by nuclear weapons. *The Fate of the Earth* (1982)

6 The West in the wake of the Soviet collapse is like a person who has won fifty million dollars in the lottery and then declares, "Wonderful—now I can redecorate my living room."
The Gift of Time (1998), ch. 1

7 Vertical disarmament makes a catastrophe, should it ever occur, smaller. Horizontal disarmament makes a catastrophe of any size less likely to occur. The verticalist looks at the size of the arsenals. The horizontalist looks at its operation.
Referring to alternative types of nuclear disarmament. *The Gift of Time* (1998), ch. 3

Schelling, Friedrich Wilhelm Joseph von (1775–1854) German philosopher

1 Architecture in general is frozen music.
Philosophie der Kunst (1809)

Schiaparelli, Elsa (1890–1973) Italian fashion designer

1 A dress has no life of its own unless it is worn, and as soon as this happens another personality takes over from you and animates it, or tries to, glorifies or destroys it, or makes it into a song of beauty.
A Shocking Life (1954)

2 A good cook is like a sorceress who dispenses happiness.
A Shocking Life (1954)

3 Dress designing, incidentally, is to me not a profession but an art. I found that it was a most difficult and unsatisfying art, because as soon as a dress is born it has already become a thing of the past.
A Shocking Life (1954)

4 So fashion is born by small facts, trends, or even politics, never by trying to make little pleats and furbelows, by trinkets, by clothes easy to copy, or by the shortening or lengthening of a skirt.
A Shocking Life (1954)

Schick, Béla (1877–1967) Hungarian-born U.S. physician

1 First, the patient, second the patient, third the patient, fourth the patient, fifth the patient, and then maybe comes science. We first do everything for the patient; science can wait, research can wait.
Quoted in *Aphorisms and Facetiae of Béla Schick* (Israel J. Wolf; 1965)

2 In making theories always keep a window open so that you can throw one out if necessary.
Quoted in *Aphorisms and Facetiae of Béla Schick* (Israel J. Wolf; 1965)

3 The physician's best remedy is *Tincture of Time*.
Quoted in *Aphorisms and Facetiae of Béla Schick* (Israel J. Wolf; 1965)

4 After twenty years one is no longer quoted in the medical literature. Every twenty years one sees a republication of the same ideas.
Quoted in "Early Years," *Aphorisms and Facetiae of Béla Schick* (Israel J. Wolf; 1965)

5 It is too bad that we cannot cut the patient in half in order to compare two regimens of treatment.
Quoted in "Early Years," *Aphorisms and Facetiae of Béla Schick* (Israel J. Wolf; 1965)

6 The human body is like a bakery with a thousand windows. We are looking into only one window of the bakery when we are investigating one particular aspect of a disease.
Quoted in "Early Years," *Aphorisms and Facetiae of Béla Schick* (Israel J. Wolf; 1965)

Schiffer, Claudia (b.1970) German fashion model

Quotations about Schiffer

1 That's how she made her fortune. She's got an amazing body and big tits. She sold her body like I sold mine.
Kate Moss (b.1974) British fashion model. Remark (1992), quoted in *Model: The Ugly Business of Beautiful Women* (Michael Gross; 1995)

Quotations by Schiffer

2 I ate a whole chocolate bar.
Referring to her retirement from the catwalk. *Guardian*, London (September 27, 1996)

Schiller, Friedrich von (Johann Christoph Friedrich von Schiller; 1759–1805) German poet, playwright, and historian

1 Joy, beautiful radiance of the gods, daughter of Elysium, we set foot in your heavenly shrine dazzled by your brilliance. Your charms reunite what common use has harshly divided: all men become brothers under your tender wing.
"Ode to Joy" (1785), st. 1

2 The May of life blooms once, and not again.
"Resignation" (1788)

3 Art is a daughter of Freedom, and takes her orders from the necessity inherent in minds, not from the exigencies of matter.
Tenth letter (1793), quoted in *On the Aesthetic Education of Man* (E. M. Wilkinson and C. A. Willoughby, eds., trs.; 1967)

4 He who never ventures beyond actuality will never win the prize of truth.
Tenth letter (1793), quoted in *On the Aesthetic Education of Man* (E. M. Wilkinson and C. A. Willoughby, eds., trs.; 1967)

5 Ah! How happy are the dead.
Das Siegesfest (1804)

6 Freedom lives only in the realm of dreams,
And in song only blooms the beautiful.
Der Antritt des neuen Jahrhunderts (1801)

7 Life is not the highest blessing, but of evils sin's the worst.
Die Braut von Messina (1803)

8 Man is created free, all free,
E'en were he born in chains.
Die Worte des Glaubens (1798)

9 I am called
The richest monarch in the Christian world;
The sun in my dominion never sets.
Originally said by Philip II. *Don Carlos* (1787), Act 1, Scene 6

10 Love is only known by him who hopelessly persists in love.
Don Carlos (1787), Act 3, Scene 8

11 The history of the World is the World's court of justice.
Jena (May 26, 1789)

12 Kings are only slaves of their own position who may not follow their own heart.
Maria Stuart (1800), Act 2, Scene 2

13 All other forms of perception divide a man, because they are exclusively based either on the sensuous or on the intellectual part of his being; only the perception of the Beautiful makes something whole of him, because both his natures must accord with it.
On the Aesthetic Education of Man (1795)

14 Art, like Science, is absolved from all positive constraint and from all conventions introduced by man; both rejoice in absolute immunity from human arbitrariness.
On the Aesthetic Education of Man (1795)

15 Beauty alone makes all the world happy, and every being forgets its limitations as long as it experiences her enchantment.
On the Aesthetic Education of Man (1795)

16 What's the short meaning of this long harangue?
Piccolomini (1800), Act 1, Scene 2

17 Our life was but a battle and a march, and like the wind's blast, never resting, homeless, we stormed across the war-convulséd heath.
The Death of Wallenstein (1799), Act 3, Scene 15

18 Obedience is woman's duty on earth. Harsh suffering is her heavy fate.
The Maid of Orleans (1801), Act 1, Scene 10

19 Against stupidity the gods themselves struggle in vain.
The Maid of Orleans (1801), Act 3, Scene 6

20 I have a mission only, no opinions.
The Robbers and Wallenstein (1799), Act 1, Scene 5

21 Time is man's angel.
The Robbers and Wallenstein (1799), Act 5, Scene 11

22 The future winds no garlands for the actor.
The Robbers and Wallenstein (1799), prologue

23 The brave man thinks of himself the last of all.
Wilhelm Tell (Patrick Maxwell, tr.; 1804), Act 1, Scene 1

24 And cleave to your beloved fatherland;
Hold it firm with all your heart and soul;
Here are the hardy roots of all your power.
Wilhelm Tell (Patrick Maxwell, tr.; 1804), Act 2, Scene 1

Schirmacher, Käthe (1865–1930) German author and feminist

1 In the greater part of the world woman is a slave and a beast of burden.
The Modern Woman's Rights Movement (1905)

Schlegel, Friedrich von (1772–1829) German critic and philosopher

1 A historian is a prophet in reverse.
Das Athenäum (1798–1800)

Schlesinger, Arthur, Jr. (Arthur Meier Schlesinger, Jr.; b.1917) U.S. historian

1 All wars are popular for the first thirty days.
Attrib.

Schliemann, Heinrich (1822–90) German archaeologist

1 I have looked upon the face of Agamemnon.
1871. On discovering a gold death mask at an excavation in Mycenae. Quoted in *The Story of Civilization* (William Durant), vol. 2

Schnabel, Artur (1882–1951) Austrian pianist and composer

1 The notes I handle no better than many pianists. But the pauses between the notes—ah, that is where the art resides.
Quoted in *Chicago Daily News* (June 11, 1958)

2 I don't think there was ever a piece of music that changed a man's decision on how to work.
My Life and Music (1961), pt. 2, ch. 8

3 I know two kinds of audience only—one coughing and one not coughing.
My Life and Music (1961), pt. 2, ch. 10

4 Applause is a receipt, not a note of demand.
Saturday Review of Literature (September 29, 1951)

5 When a piece gets difficult make faces.
Advice given to the pianist Vladimir Horowitz. Quoted in *The Unimportance of Being Oscar* (Oscar Levant; 1968)

Schnabel, Julian (b.1951) U.S. painter and conceptual artist

1 Where artists can give to others...is in their discovery of a point of convergence where a physical fact denotes a state of consciousness. This is how art is generative.
1983. Quoted in *Julian Schnabel: Paintings 1975–1987* (Whitechapel Gallery, London; 1986)

Schneckenburger, Max (1819–49) German poet

1 The Watch on the Rhine
Song title. (1840)

Schneider, Florian (b.1947) German musician

1 We don't need a choir...We just turn this key, and there's the choir.
Referring to the ease with which synthesizers can create a wide variety of sounds. Interview, *Creem* (September 1975)

Schoenberg, Arnold (Arnold Franz Walter Schoenberg; 1874–1951) Austrian-born U.S. composer

1 If it is art, it is not for the masses.
Letter to W. S. Schlamm (July 1, 1945), quoted in *Arnold Schoenberg Letters* (Erwin Stein, ed.; 1964)

2 Very well, I can wait.
Replying to a complaint that his violin concerto would need a musician with six fingers. Attrib.

Schonfield, Hugh Joseph (1901–88) British writer and editor

1 Wars come because not enough people are sufficiently afraid.
News Review, London (February 26, 1948)

Schopenhauer, Arthur (1788–1860) German philosopher

1 A man has less conscience when in love than in any other condition.
"The World as Will and Ideas" (1819), quoted in *The Metaphysics of Love and the Sexes* (R. B. Haldane and J. Kemp, eds.; 1886)

2 Intellect is invisible to the man who has none.
Aphorismen zur Lebensweisheit (1919)

3 To be alone is the fate of all great minds—a fate deplored at times, but still always chosen as the less grievous of two evils.
Aphorismen zur Lebensweisheit (1919)

4 Every parting gives a foretaste of death; every coming together again a foretaste of the resurrection.
Gedanken über vielerlei Gegenstände (1851), no. 26

5 The fundamental fault of the female character is that it has no sense of justice.
Gedanken über vielerlei Gegenstände (1851), no. 27

6 After your death you will be what you were before your birth.
Parerga and Paralipomena (1851)

7 But what do I get from existence? If it is full I have only distress, if empty only boredom. How can you offer me so poor a reward for so much labor and so much suffering?
Parerga and Paralipomena (1851)

8 Hypochondria torments us not only with causeless irritation with the things of the present; not only with groundless anxiety on the score of future misfortunes entirely of our own manufacture; but also with unmerited self-reproach for our own past actions.
Parerga and Paralipomena (1851)

9 If the immediate and direct purpose of our life is not suffering then our existence is the most ill-adapted to its purpose in the world.
Parerga and Paralipomena (1851)

10 If you want to know how you really feel about someone take note of the impression an unexpected letter from him makes on you when you first see it on the doormat.
Parerga and Paralipomena (1851)

11 It is only in the microscope that our life looks so big. It is an indivisible point, drawn out and magnified by the powerful lenses of Time and Space.
Parerga and Paralipomena (1851)

12 Most men discover when they look back on their life that they have been living ad interim, and are surprised to see that which they let go by so unregarded and unenjoyed was precisely their life.
Parerga and Paralipomena (1851)

13 Our existence has no foundation on which to rest except the transient present. Thus its form is essentially unceasing motion, without any possibility of that repose which we continually strive after.
Parerga and Paralipomena (1851)

14 There are very many thoughts which have value for him who thinks them, but only a few of them possess the power of engaging the interest of a reader after they have been written down.
Parerga and Paralipomena (1851)

15 The thing-in-itself, the will-to-live, exists whole and undivided in every being, even in the tiniest; it is present as completely as in all that ever were, are, and will be, taken together.
Parerga and Paralipomena (1851)

16 The two main requirements for philosophizing are: firstly, to have the courage not to keep any question back; and secondly, to attain a clear consciousness of anything that goes without saying so as to comprehend it as a problem.
Parerga and Paralipomena (1851)

17 To expect a man to retain everything that he has ever read is like expecting him to carry about in his body everything that he has ever eaten.
Parerga and Paralipomena (1851)

18 Wealth is like seawater; the more we drink, the thirstier we become; and the same is true of fame.
Parerga and Paralipomena (1851)

19 We begin in the madness of carnal desire and the transport of voluptuousness, we end in the dissolution of all our parts and the musty stench of corpses.
Parerga and Paralipomena (1851)

20 Every man takes the limits of his own field of vision for the limits of the world.
"Psychological Observations," *Studies in Pessimism* (1851)

21 Women exist in the main solely for the propagation of the species.
Attrib.

Schrader, Paul (Paul Joseph Schrader; b.1946) U.S. film director, screenwriter, and actor

1 You can think up a shot in five seconds—five minutes to explain it—three hours to execute it.
Los Angeles Times (February 18, 1990), quoted in *Chambers Film Quotes* (Tony Crawley, ed.; 1991)

2 Screenplays are not works of art. They are invitations to others to collaborate on a work of art.
Quoted in *Writers in Hollywood 1915–1951* (Ian Hamilton; 1990), preface

Schreiber, Stuart L. (b.1956) U.S. organic chemist and educator

1 It was a flash of eureka.
Referring to his discovery of an aphrodisiac that controlled cockroaches. *New York Times* (September 26, 1984)

Schreiner, Olive (Olive Emily Albertina Schreiner, pen name Ralph Iron; 1855–1920) South African novelist and feminist

1 We have always borne part of the weight of war, and the major part...Men have made boomerangs, bows, swords, or guns with which to destroy one another; we have made the men who destroyed and were destroyed!...*We pay the first cost on all human life.*
Woman and Labour (1911), ch. 4

Schroeder, Patricia (b.1940) U.S. politician

1 Everyone is always talking about our defense effort in terms of defending women and children, but no one ever asks the women and children what they think.
American Political Women (1978)

Schulberg, Budd (b.1914) U.S. novelist, screenwriter, and journalist

1 I compare the great film with a horse race in which every one of the horses finishes at the wire in a dead heat...writer, director, cinematographer, and all the crew...Too often the victory is accorded to the director.
Interview, *Cineaste* (1981)

2 They take from other movies rather than from life. If they are middle class to begin with, without roots in other kinds of experiences, movies become the tool of their experience.
Referring to film-school students and the trend of "homage" to other movies. Interview, *Cineaste* (1981)

Schuler, Douglas U.S. author

1 Computer technology...could play a role in rebuilding community by improving communication, economic opportunity, civic participation, and education.
Reinventing Technology (Co-edited with Philip E. Agre; 1997)

2 "Electronic democracy" can open new doors for participation but it is no panacea...democracy without democratic processes is just a word.
Reinventing Technology (Co-edited with Philip E. Agre; 1997)

Schultze, Howard U.S. business executive

1 Hire people smarter than you and get out of the way.
Business Week (October 24, 1994)

Schumacher, E. F. (Ernst Friedrich Schumacher; 1911–77) German-born British economist

1 Call a thing immoral or ugly, soul destroying or a degradation of man, a peril to the peace of our world or to the well-being of future generations; as long as you have not shown it to be "uneconomic" you have not really questioned its right to exist, grow and prosper.
Lecture, Blackpool, England, "Clean Air and Future Energy" (October 19, 1967)

2 Ecology...ought to be a compulsory subject for all economists.
Lecture, Blackpool, England, "Clean Air and Future Energy" (October 19, 1967)

3 Modern economic thinking...is peculiarly unable to consider the long term and to appreciate man's dependence on the natural world.
Lecture, Blackpool, England, "Clean Air and Future Energy" (October 19, 1967)

4 Even with renewable primary products, man is not wholly in control of the productive process as he is in a factory but first must fit his actions into the rhythm of the seasons and the often mysterious requirements of organic life.
Referring to agriculture in contrast to industry. Seminar, University of Birmingham, England, "Some Problems of Coal Economics" (January 18, 1962)

5 It might be said that it is the ideal of the employer to have production without employees and the ideal of the employee is to have income without work.
Observer, London (May 4, 1975), "Sayings of the Week"

6 The heart of the matter, as I see it, is the stark fact that world poverty is primarily a problem of two million villages, and thus a problem of two thousand million villagers.
Small is Beautiful (1973), ch. 13

7 After all, for mankind as a whole there are no exports. We did not start developing by obtaining foreign exchange from Mars or the moon. Mankind is a closed society.
Small is Beautiful (1973), ch. 14

Schumpeter, Joseph Alois (1883–1950) Austrian-born U.S. economist

1 Bureaucracy is not an obstacle to democracy but an inevitable complement to it.
Capitalism, Socialism, and Democracy (1942)

2 Electric lighting is no great boon to anyone who has enough money to buy a sufficient number of candles and to pay servants to attend them.
Capitalism, Socialism, and Democracy (1942)

3 The capitalist achievement does not typically consist in providing more silk stockings for queens but in bringing them within the reach of factory girls in return for steadily decreasing amounts of effort.
Capitalism, Socialism, and Democracy (1942)

4 The cold metal of economic theory is in Marx's pages immersed in such a wealth of steaming phrases as to acquire a temperature not naturally its own.
Capitalism, Socialism, and Democracy (1942)

Schwarzenberg, Felix zu (1800–52) Austrian statesman

1 Austria will astound the world with the magnitude of her ingratitude.
1849. On being asked whether Austria was under any obligation to Russia for help received previously. Quoted in *The Fall of the House of Habsburg* (E. Crankshaw; 1963)

Schwarzenegger, Arnold (b.1947) Austrian-born U.S. bodybuilder and film actor

1 I'll be back.
As the android star of the movie. *Terminator* (James Cameron and Gale Anne Hurd; 1984)

2 Hasta La Vista, baby!
Spoken by the android star of the movie, while committing homicide. *Terminator 2: Judgement Day* (James Cameron and William Wisher; 1991)

3 Money doesn't make you happy. I now have $50 million but I was just as happy when I had $48 million.
Attrib.

Schwarzkopf, Norman (H. Norman Schwarzkopf, "Stormin' Norman"; b.1934) U.S. general

1 We're going around, over, through, on top, underneath.
Describing his tactics for attacking the Iraqi army during the "Desert Storm" offensive in the Persian Gulf War (1991). Press conference (February 24, 1991)

2 A very great man once said you should love your enemies and that's not a bad piece of advice. We can love them but, by God, that doesn't mean we're not going to fight them.
Referring to the Persian Gulf War (1991). *Observer*, London (July 14, 1991)

Schweitzer, Albert (1875–1965) German theologian, philosopher, physician, and musicologist

1 Here, at whatever hour you come, you will find light and help and human kindness.
Inscription on the lamp outside his hospital at Lambaréné (1913–65)

2 We must all die. But that I can save him from days of torture, that is what I feel as my great and ever new privilege. Pain is a more terrible lord of mankind than even death himself.
On the Edge of the Primeval Forest (1922), ch. 5

3 Truth has no special time of its own. Its hour is now—always.
Out of My Life and Thought (1949)

4 The purpose of human life is to serve and to show compassion and the will to help others.
Quoted in *The Schweitzer Album* (Erica Anderson; 1965)

5 Man has lost the capacity to foresee and to forestall. He will end by destroying the earth.
Attrib.

6 I too had thoughts once of being an intellectual, but I found it too difficult.
Remark made to an African who refused to perform a menial task on the grounds that he was an intellectual. Attrib.

Schwerin, David A. (b.1942) U.S. business executive and author

1 Business, with its global influence and its ability to adapt rapidly to changing conditions, has become one of the most effective vehicles for accelerating our self-conscious awareness.
Conscious Capitalism (1998)

Scooby Doo U.S. cartoon character

1 Scooby Dooby Doo!
Catchphrase. *Scooby Doo* (Hanna-Barbera; 1970–72)

Scorsese, Martin (b.1942) U.S. filmmaker

1 I don't think there is any difference between fantasy and reality in the way these should be approached in a film. Of course if you live that way you are clinically insane.
"Mean Streets—Alice Doesn't Live Here Anymore—Taxi Driver," *Scorsese on Scorsese* (Ian Christie and David Thompson, eds.; 1989), ch. 3

2 I always tell the younger film-makers and students: Do it like the painters used to...Study the old masters. Enrich your palette. Expand the canvas. There's always so much more to learn.
Scorsese: A Personal Journey Through American Movies (1997)

3 I don't really see a conflict between the church and the movies, the sacred and the profane...there are major differences, but I could also see great similarities...Both are places for people to come together and share.
Scorsese: A Personal Journey Through American Movies (1997)

4 *Mean Streets* dealt with the American Dream, according to which everybody thinks they can get rich quick, and if they can't do it by legal means then they'll do it by illegal ones.
"Mean Streets—Alice Doesn't Live Here Anymore—Taxi Driver," *Scorsese on Scorsese* (Ian Christie and David Thompson, eds.; 1989), ch. 3

5 When I made it, I didn't intend to have the audience react with that feeling, "Yes, let's do it! Let's go out and kill."
Referring to his film, *Taxi Driver* (1976). "Mean Streets—Alice Doesn't Live Here Anymore—Taxi Driver," *Scorsese on Scorsese* (Ian Christie and David Thompson, eds.; 1989), ch. 3

6 Cinema's a matter of what's in the frame and what's out.
Attrib.

Scot, Reginald (1538–99) English author

1 For as a looking glass sheweth the image or figure thereunto opposite, so in dreams the phantasy and imagination informs the understanding of such things as haunt the outward sense.
The Discoverie of Witchcraft (16th century)

2 Now if the fancy of a melancholic person may be occupied in causes which are both false and impossible, why should an old witch be thought free from such fantasies?
Suggesting that witches suffered from mental disorder. *The Discoverie of Witchcraft* (16th century)

Scott, Captain (Robert Falcon Scott; 1868–1912) British explorer

1 Had we lived, I should have had a tale to tell of the hardihood, endurance, and courage of my companions which would have stirred the heart of every Englishman. These rough notes and our dead bodies must tell the tale.
Message to the public (1912)

2 Great God! this is an awful place.
Referring to the South Pole. *Journal* (January 17, 1912)

Scott, C. P. (Charles Prestwich Scott; 1846–1932) British journalist

1 Its primary office is the gathering of news. At the peril of its soul it must see that the supply is not tainted...Comment is free but facts are sacred.
1921. Referring to journalism. *The Manchester Guardian* (May 5, 1922)

2 Television? No good will come of this device. The word is half Greek and half Latin.
Attrib.

Scott, Dennis (Dennis Courtney Scott; 1939–91) Jamaican editor, actor, and poet

1 To travel
is to return
to strangers.
Quoted in *Breaklight: an Anthology of Caribbean Poetry* (Andrew Salkey, ed.; 1971)

Scott, George C. (George Campbell Scott; b.1927) U.S. actor

1 I don't say we wouldn't get our hair mussed, but I do say no more than ten to twenty million people killed.
As General, referring to nuclear war with the USSR. *Dr. Strangelove, or How I Learned to Stop Worrying and Love the Bomb* (Stanley Kubrick, Terry Southern, and Peter George; 1963)

Scott, Hazel (1920–81) U.S. jazz musician, actor, and feminist

1 Any woman who has a great deal to offer the world is in trouble.
Ms (1974)

2 There's a time when you have to explain to your children why they're born, and it's a marvelous thing if you know the reason by then.
Ms (1974)

3 Who ever walked behind anyone to freedom? If we can't go hand in hand, I don't want to go.
Ms (1974)

Scott, Paul (Paul Mark Scott; 1920–78) British novelist

1 There were people in Mayapore who said I only kept up with Lady Manners for snob reasons, *Indian* snob reasons, like calling an English person by his Christian name.
The Jewel in the Crown (1965)

Scott, Sir Walter (1771–1832) Scottish novelist

Quotations about Scott

1 He writes as fast as they can read, and he does not write himself down.
William Hazlitt (1778–1830) British essayist and critic. "Sir Walter Scott," *Spirit of the Age* (1825)

2 His worst is better than any other person's best.
William Hazlitt (1778–1830) British essayist and critic. "Sir Walter Scott," *Spirit of the Age* (1825)

Quotations by Scott

3 All health is better than wealth.
Letter to C. Carpenter, *Familiar Letters* (August 4, 1812)

4 Women are but the toys which amuse our lighter hours; ambition is the serious business of life.
Ivanhoe (1820)

5 The rose is fairest when 'tis budding new,
And hope is brightest when it dawns from fears.
The rose is sweetest wash'd with morning dew,
And love is loveliest when embalm'd in tears.
Lady of the Lake (1810), can. 3, st. 1

6 Although too much of a soldier among sovereigns, no one could claim with better right to be a sovereign among soldiers.
Life of Napoleon (1827)

7 But search the land of living men,
Where wilt thou find their like agen?
Marmion (1808), can. 1, st. 11

8 And come he slow, or come he fast,
It is but Death who comes at last.
Marmion (1808), can. 2, st. 30

9 O, young Lochinvar is come out of the west,
Through all the wide Border his steed was the best.
Marmion (1808), can. 5, st. 12

10 So faithful in love, and so dauntless in war,
There never was knight like the young Lochinvar.
Marmion (1808), can. 5, st. 12

11 O what a tangled web we weave,
When first we practise to deceive!
Marmion (1808), can. 6, st. 17

12 O Woman! in our hours of ease
Uncertain, coy, and hard to please,
And variable as the shade
By the light quivering aspen made;
When pain and anguish wring the brow,
A ministering angel thou!
Marmion (1808), can. 6, st. 30

13 Just at the age 'twixt boy and youth,
When thought is speech, and speech is truth.
Marmion (1808), Introduction, can. 2

14 Ridicule often checks what is absurd, and fully as often smothers that which is noble.
Quentin Durward (1823)

15 But with the morning cool repentance came.
Rob Roy (1817), ch. 12

16 See yon pale stripling! when a boy,
A mother's pride, a father's joy!
Rokeby (1813), can. 3

17 O, Brignal banks are wild and fair,
And Gretna woods are green,
And you may gather garlands there
Would grace a summer queen.
Rokeby (1813), can. 3, st. 16

18 Thus aged men, full loth and slow,
The vanities of life forego,
And count their youthful follies o'er,
Till Memory lends her light no more.
Rokeby (1813), can. 5, st. 1

19 Fat, fair, and forty.
St. Ronan's Well (1823), ch. 7

20 Widowed wife, and married maid,
Betrothed, betrayer, and betrayed!
The Betrothed (1825), ch. 15

21 Woman's faith, and woman's trust
Write the characters in dust.
The Betrothed (1825), ch. 20

22 Look back, and smile at perils past.
The Bridal of Triermain (1813), Introduction

23 The hour is come, but not the man.
The Heart of Midlothian (1818), ch. 4

24 True love's the gift which God has given
To man alone beneath the heaven.
The Lay of the Last Minstrel (1805), can. 5

25 Breathes there the man, with soul so dead,
Who never to himself hath said,
This is my own, my native land!
Whose heart hath ne'er within him burn'd,
As home his footsteps he hath turn'd
From wandering on a foreign strand!
The Lay of the Last Minstrel (1805), can. 6, st. 1

26 O Caledonia! stern and wild,
Meet nurse for a poetic child!
Land of brown heath and shaggy wood,
Land of the mountain and the flood,
Land of my sires! what mortal hand
Can e'er untie the filial band
That knits me to thy rugged strand!
The Lay of the Last Minstrel (1805), can. 6, st. 1

27 His morning walk was beneath the elms in the churchyard; "for death," he said, "had been his next-door neighbour for so many years, that he had no apology for dropping the acquaintance."
The Legend of Montrose (1819), Introduction

28 I'll make thee famous by my pen,
And glorious by my sword.
The Legend of Montrose (1819), ch. 15

29 To that dark inn, the grave!
The Lord of the Isles (1813), can. 6

30 The ae half of the warld thinks the tither daft.
The Monastery (1820), ch. 7

31 And better had they ne'er been born,
Who read to doubt, or read to scorn.
The Monastery (1820), ch. 12

32 No, this right hand shall work it all off.
1826. Refusing offers of help following his bankruptcy (1826), and referring to his intention to write his way out of debt. Quoted in *Century of Anecdote* (J. Timbs; 1864)

Scott, William, Baron Stowell (1745–1836) British jurist

1 A dinner lubricates business.
Life of Samuel Johnson (James Boswell; 1791)

Scott, Winfield (1786–1866) U.S. army officer

1 Say to the seceded states: "Wayward sisters, depart in peace!"
Referring to the confederate Southern states, that had seceded from the federal Union. Letter to William Henry Seward (March 3, 1861)

Scott-Heron, Gil (b.1949) U.S. musician, writer, and poet

1 It's a mass of irony for all the world to see
It's the nation's capital, it's Washington, D.C.
Song lyric. "Washington D.C." (1982)

Scott-Maxwell, Florida (1883–?) U.S.-born British writer

1 No matter how old a mother is she watches her middle-aged children for signs of improvement.
The Measure of My Days (1968)

Sculley, John (b.1939) U.S. business executive

1 Anybody who runs a successful high-technology company has to be an eternal optimist, has to be able to take big risks.
Fortune (July 26, 1993)

2 We try to picture what the products will be and then say, what technology should we be working on today to help us get there?
Inc. (January 1988)

3 Coke was a little like the Wizard of Oz—so powerful was its image that few foresaw that the company was vulnerable to attack by new ideas.
Odyssey: from Pepsi to Apple (1987)

4 In America, projects have a beginning, a middle, and an end. In Japan, projects have direction, so that what you're pushing for is heading further and further out.
Odyssey: from Pepsi to Apple (1987)

5 If we hadn't put a man on the moon, there wouldn't be a Silicon Valley today.
U.S. News and World Report (1992)

6 The new leaders face new tests such as how to lead in this idea-intensive, interdependent network environment.
Quoted in "Leaders on Leadership" (Warren Bennis; 1991)

7 No great marketing decisions have ever been made on quantitative data.
Quoted in *The Intuitive Manager* (Roy Rowan; 1986)

8 Implementers aren't considered bozos anymore.
Quoted in *Thriving on Chaos* (Tom Peters; 1987)

Seaborg, Glenn (Glenn Theodore Seaborg; b.1912) U.S. chemist

1 People must understand that science is inherently neither a potential for good nor for evil. It is a potential to be harnessed by man to do his bidding.
Interview, Associated Press (September 29, 1964)

Seacole, Mary (1805?–84) Jamaican nurse, businesswoman, and adventurer

1 I wonder if the people of other countries are as fond of carrying with them everywhere their home habits as the English. I think not.
Wonderful Adventures of Mrs Seacole in many lands (1857)

2 Some people, indeed, have called me quite a female Ulysses. I believe that they intended it as a compliment; but from my experience of the Greeks, I do not consider it a very flattering one.
Wonderful Adventures of Mrs Seacole in many lands (1857)

Seale, Bobby (Robert George Seale; b.1936) U.S. civil rights activist

1 Power to the People.
Attrib.

2 You can jail a revolutionary, but you cannot jail the revolution.
1969. Attrib.

Sears, E. H. (Edmund Hamilton Sears; 1810–76) U.S. clergyman and hymnwriter

1 It came upon the midnight clear,
That glorious song of old,
From Angels bending near the earth
To touch their harps of gold;
"Peace on the earth; good will to man
From Heaven's all gracious King."
The world in solemn stillness lay
To hear the angels sing.
Song lyric. "The Angel's Song" (1850), st. 1

Sedgwick, Catharine Maria (1789–1867) U.S. writer

1 I expect no very violent transition.
Her reply, when told she spoke of her home town of Stockbridge, Massachussetts, as heaven. *Edie* (Jean Stein; 1982)

Sedgwick, John (1813–64) U.S. general

1 Nonsense, they couldn't hit an elephant at this dist—
His last words, in response to a suggestion that he should not show himself over the parapet during the Battle of the Wilderness. Attrib. (1864)

Sedley, Charles, Sir (1639–1701) English playwright and poet

1 Phyllis is my only joy,
Faithless as the winds or seas;
Sometimes coming, sometimes coy,
Yet she never fails to please
She deceiving,
I believing;
What need lovers wish for more?
"Song" (1702), st. 1

Seeckt, Hans von (Hans Friedrich Leopold von Seeckt; 1866–1936) German general and politician

1 Gentlemen, none but I in Germany can make a putsch and I assure you I shall not make one.
Referring to the army's support for the government in the face of the attempted Nazi coup (November 8–9, 1923). Quoted in *Europe Since 1870* (James Joll; 1973), ch. 9

Seeger, Alan (1888–1916) U.S. poet

1 I have a rendezvous with Death
At some disputed barricade.
"I Have a Rendezvous with Death" (1916)

Seeger, Pete (Peter R. Seeger; b.1919) U.S. folksinger and songwriter

1 Where have all the flowers gone?
Young girls picked them every one.
His rendering of the song "Where Have All the Flowers Gone?" made it famous. "Where Have All the Flowers Gone?" (Derek Collyer and David Cumming; 1961)

2 We Shall Overcome
1962. Song title.

3 If I Had a Hammer
1949. Song title. Popularized by Peter, Paul, and Mary.

Seferis, George (Georgios Stylianou Seferiadis; 1900–71) Greek poet and diplomat

1 As pine trees
hold the wind's imprint
after the wind has gone, is no longer there,
so words
retain a man's imprint
after the man has gone, is no longer there.
1966. "On Stage," *Complete Poems* (Edmund Keeley and Philip Sherrard, trs.; 1995)

Segal, Erich (b.1937) U.S. writer

1 Love means never having to say you're sorry.
Love Story (1970)

2 What can you say about a 25-year-old girl who died? That she was beautiful? And brilliant. That she loved Mozart and Bach. And the Beatles. And me.
Love Story (1970)

Seifert, Richard (b.1910) British architect

1 Many of my buildings are condemned now in advance.
Observer, London (August 6, 1972), "Sayings of the Week"

Sei Shonagon (966?–1013) Japanese diarist

1 If someone with whom one is having an affair keeps on mentioning some woman whom he knew in the past, however long ago it is since they separated, one is always irritated.
The Pillow Book (1002?), quoted in *Anthology of Japanese Literature* (Donald Keene, ed.; 1968)

Seitz, Frederick (b.1911) U.S. physicist

1 A good scientist is a person in whom the childlike quality of perennial curiosity lingers on. Once he gets an answer, he has other questions.
Fortune (April 1976)

Selden, John (1584–1654) English historian, jurist, and politician

1 Every law is a contract between the king and the people and therefore to be kept.
Table Talk (1689)

2 For a priest to turn to a man when he lies a-dying, is just like one that has a long time solicited a woman, and cannot obtain his end; at length makes her drunk, and so lies with her.
Table Talk (1689)

3 Pleasures are all alike simply considered in themselves...He that takes pleasure to hear sermons enjoys himself as much as he that hears plays.
Table Talk (1689)

4 *Scrutamini scripturas* (Let us look at the scriptures). These two words have undone the world.
"Bible Scripture," *Table Talk* (1689)

5 Old friends are best. King James used to call for his old shoes; they were easiest for his feet.
"Friends," *Table Talk* (1689)

6 Humility is a virtue all preach, none practise, and yet everybody is content to hear. The master thinks it good doctrine for his servant, the laity for the clergy, and the clergy for the laity.
"Humility," *Table Talk* (1689)

7 'Tis not the drinking that is to be blamed, but the excess.
"Humility," *Table Talk* (1689)

8 Ignorance of the law excuses no man; not that all men know the law, but because 'tis an excuse every man will plead, and no man can tell how to confute him.
"Law," *Table Talk* (1689)

9 Marriage is nothing but a civil contract.
"Marriage," *Table Talk* (1689)

10 A king is a thing men have made for their own sakes, for quietness' sake. Just as if in a family one man is appointed to buy the meat.
"Of a King," *Table Talk* (1689)

11 Pleasure is nothing else but the intermission of pain.
"Pleasure," *Table Talk* (1689)

12 Thou little thinkest what a little foolery governs the world.
"Pope," *Table Talk* (1689)

13 Preachers say, Do as I say, not as I do. But if the physician had the same disease upon him that I have, and he should bid me do one thing, and himself do quite another, could I believe him?
"Preaching," *Table Talk* (1689)

Seldes, Gilbert (Gilbert Vivian Seldes; 1893–1970) U.S. theater, film, and radio critic

1 As if excited by the dance to the point where they did not care whether they were graceful or not, the chorus assumed the most awkward postures...these seemingly grotesque elements were actually woven...into a pattern...gay and orgiastic and wild.
Referring to the *Charleston*. Quoted in *Black Dance from 1619 to Today* (Lynne Fauley Emery, ed.; 1972)

Selfridge, H. Gordon (Harry Gordon Selfridge; 1858–1947) U.S.-born British business executive

1 The customer is always right.
1909. Slogan followed by staff at his shops. Quoted in *No Name on the Door: A Memoir of Gordon Selfridge* (A. H. Williams; 1956)

2 This famous store needs no name on the door.
1930s? Quoted in *No Name on the Door: A Memoir of Gordon Selfridge* (A. H. Williams; 1956)

Sellar, W. C. (Walter Carruthers; 1898–1951) British humorous writer

1 The Roman Conquest was, however, a *Good Thing*, since the Britons were only natives at the time.
1066 And All That (co-written with R. J. Yeatman; 1930), ch. 1

2 Honi soie qui mal y pense ("Honey, your silk stocking's hanging down").
1066 And All That (co-written with R. J. Yeatman; 1930), ch. 24

3 The Cavaliers (Wrong but Wromantic) and the Roundheads (Right but Repulsive).
Referring to the Royalists and the Parliamentarians in the English Civil War. *1066 And All That* (co-written with R. J. Yeatman; 1930), ch. 35

4 The National Debt is a very Good Thing and it would be dangerous to pay it off for fear of Political Economy.
1066 And All That (co-written with R. J. Yeatman; 1930), ch. 38

5 Napoleon's armies used to march on their stomachs, shouting: "Vive l'intérieur!"
1066 And All That (co-written with R. J. Yeatman; 1930), ch. 48

6 Gladstone spent his declining years trying to guess the answer to the Irish Question; unfortunately, whenever he was getting warm, the Irish secretly changed the question.
Referring to William Ewart Gladstone. *1066 And All That* (co-written with R. J. Yeatman; 1930), ch. 57

7 Do not on any account attempt to write on both sides of the paper at once.
1066 And All That (co-written with R. J. Yeatman; 1930), Test Paper 5

8 For every person wishing to teach there are approximately thirty who don't want to learn much.
And Now All This (1932), Introduction

9 1066 And All That
1930. Book title. Co-written with R. J. Yeatman.

Sellers, Peter (1925–80) British comic actor

1 People will swim through shit if you put a few bob in it.
Quoted in *Halliwell's Filmgoer's Companion* (John Walker, ed.; 1999)

2 If you ask me to play myself, I will not know what to do. I do not know who or what I am.
Attrib.

3 There used to be a me behind the mask, but I had it surgically removed.
Attrib.

Selye, Hans (Hans Hugo Bruno Selye; 1907–82) Austrian-born Canadian physician and endocrinologist

1 The true scientist never loses the faculty of amazement. It is the essence of his being.
Newsweek (March 31, 1958)

Selznick, David O. (David Oliver Selznick; 1902–65) U.S. film producer

Quotations about Selznick

1 The son-in-law also rises.
Anonymous. Referring to the filmmaker Louis B. Mayer's promoting David Selznick, his daughter's

husband; also to the appointment by British prime minister James Callaghan of his son-in-law, Peter Jay, as British ambassador to the United States.

Quotations by Selznick

2 I have no middle name...I had an uncle...named David Selznick, so in order to avoid the growing confusion between the two of us, I decided to take a middle initial and went through the alphabet to find one that seemed to me to give the best punctuation, and decided on "O."
Quoted in *Memo from David O. Selznick* (Rudy Behlmer; 1973)

Sembène, Ousmane (b.1923) Senegalese writer, film director, and labor leader

1 Prison kills everything. It is something vile and loathsome with its unhealthiness, its venom which withers everything, its bitter gall. It is a leech preying on the soul, it neither contains nor combats offenses, it exacerbates and expands them, and you are condemned for the rest of your life.
Black Docker (1956)

2 What kills love is words.
Black Docker (1956)

3 If you really love Africa, she will still give herself to you—she is so generous that she never ceases to give; and so greedy that she will never stop devouring you.
God's Bits of Wood (1960)

4 It isn't those who are taken by force, put in chains and sold as slaves who are the real slaves: it is those who will accept it, morally and physically.
God's Bits of Wood (1960)

Semiramis (Sammuramat; *fl.* 9th century B.C.) semi-legendary Assyrian queen

1 Nature gave me the form of a woman; my actions have raised me to the level of the most valiant of men.
9th century B.C. Part of the myth attaching to Semiramis was her extraordinary bravery in war. Attrib. *Women of Beauty and Heroism* (Frank B. Goodrich; 1859)

Semler, Ricardo Brazilian business executive

1 A touch of civil disobedience is necessary to alert the organization that all is not right.
Maverick! (1993)

2 Few ideas are as capitalist as profit-sharing, which rewards with part of a company's earnings the people who help generate this blessed surplus.
Maverick! (1993)

3 I try to create an environment in which others make decisions. Success means not making them myself.
Maverick! (1993)

4 Large, centralized organizations foster alienation like stagnant ponds breed algae.
Maverick! (1993)

5 No one can expect the spirit of involvement and partnership to flourish without an abundance of information available even to the most humble employee.
Maverick! (1993)

6 People will perform at their potential only when they know almost everyone around them.
Maverick! (1993)

7 Rules freeze companies inside a glacier; innovation lets them ride sleighs over it.
Maverick! (1993)

8 The pyramid, the chief organizational principle of the modern organization, turns a business into a traffic jam.
Maverick! (1993)

9 We want people to advance because of competence, not longevity or conformity.
Maverick! (1993)

Semmelweis, Ignaz (Ignaz Philipp Semmelweis; 1818–65) Hungarian physician

1 When I look back upon the past, I can only dispel the sadness which falls upon me by gazing into that happy future when the infection will be banished...The conviction that such a time must inevitably sooner or later arrive will cheer my dying hour.
Semmelweis had discovered that it was the physicians who spread puerperal ("childbed") fever among women patients in hospitals, but he was not believed until after his death. *Etiology* (1861), Foreword

Sendak, Maurice (b.1928) U.S. writer and illustrator

1 A little like a quiet explosion in your head.
Referring to writing. Radio interview, Station WAMU, Washington (December 24, 1991)

Seneca, "the Elder" (Marcus Annaeus Seneca; 55? B.C.–40? A.D.) Roman rhetorician

1 A small debt makes a man your debtor, a large one makes him your enemy.
Epistulae Ad Lucilium (63?)

2 All art is but imitation of nature.
Quoted by his son, Lucius Annaeus Seneca, in *Epistulae Morales*. *Epistulae Morales* (63?), quoted in *Seneca. Epistulae Morales* (Richard M. Gummere; 1925)

Seneca, "the Younger" (Lucius Annaeus Seneca; 4? B.C.–65 A.D.) Roman writer, philosopher, and statesman

1 Time heals what reason cannot.
Agamemnon (45?), l. 130

2 There is no great genius without a tincture of madness.
De Tranquillitate Animi (63?), no. 17, sect. 10

3 Conversation has a kind of charm about it, an insinuating and insidious something that elicits secrets from us just like love or liquor.
Epistulae Morales (63?)

4 Nothing hinders a cure so much as frequent change of medicine.
Epistulae Morales (63?)

5 People pay the doctor for his trouble; for his kindness they still remain in his debt.
Epistulae Morales (63?)

6 Live among men as if God beheld you; speak to God as if men were listening.
Epistulae Morales (63?), no. 10, sect. 5

7 The physician cannot prescribe by letter the proper time for eating or bathing; he must feel the pulse.
Epistulae Morales (63?), no. 12

8 Everything may happen.
Epistulae Morales (63?), no. 70

9 Drunkenness is simply voluntary insanity.
Epistulae Morales (63?), no. 83

10 Remember that pain has this most excellent quality: if prolonged it cannot be severe, and if severe it cannot be prolonged.
Epistulae Morales (63?), no. 94

11 Old age is a disease which we cannot cure.
Epistulae Morales (63?), no. 108

12 The body is not a permanent dwelling, but a sort of inn (with a brief sojourn at that) which is to be left behind when one perceives that one is a burden to the host.
Epistulae Morales (63?), no. 120

13 Crime which is prosperous and lucky is called virtue.
Hercules Furens (1st century), l. 251

14 Death is a punishment to some, to some a gift, and to many a favor.
Hercules Oetaeus (63?)

15 It is part of the cure to wish to be cured.
Phaedra (63?), l. 249

Senge, Peter M. (b.1947) U.S. business executive and author

1 A shared vision is not an idea. It is not even an important idea such as freedom. It is, rather, a force in people's hearts, a force of impressive power...Shared vision is vital for the learning organization because it provides the focus and energy for learning.
The Fifth Discipline (1990)

2 Learning organizations are possible because not only is it our nature to learn but we love to learn.
The Fifth Discipline (1990)

3 Learning organizations may be a tool not just for the evolution of organizations, but for the evolution of intelligence.
The Fifth Discipline (1990)

4 The entire global business community is learning to learn together, becoming a learning community.
The Fifth Discipline (1990)

5 Vision paints the picture of what we want to create. Systems thinking reveals how we have created what we currently have.
The Fifth Discipline (1990)

6 We learn best from experience but we never directly experience the consequences of many of our most important decisions.
The Fifth Discipline (1990)

Senghor, Léopold (Léopold Sédar Senghor; b.1906) Senegalese president, poet, and intellectual

1 Negritude is the sum total of the values of the civilization of the African world. It is not racialism, it is culture.
1962. "Pierre Teilhard de Chardin et la Politique Africaine," *Léopold Sédar Senghor: Prose and Poetry* (John Reed and Clive Wake, eds.; 1965)

2 Lord God, forgive white Europe.
January 1945. "Prière de paix (pour grandes orgues)," *Selected Poems of Léopold Sédar Senghor* (Abiola Ire, ed.; 1977)

3 New York! I say to you: New York let black blood flow into your blood that it may rub the rust from your steel joints, like an oil of life.
"New York," *Seven African Writers* (Gerald Moore; 1962)

Senior, Nassau William (1790–1864) British economist

1 It is as difficult to elevate the poor as it is easy to depress the rich. In human affairs...it is much easier to do harm than good.
Quoted in *Nassau Senior and Classical Economics* (M. Bowley; 1937)

Senna, Ayrton (Ayrton Senna da Silva; 1960–94) Brazilian racecar driver

1 There are no small accidents on this circuit.
Remark made before the 1994 San Marino Grand Prix, during which he was killed. *Independent*, London (December 22, 1994)

2 The most important thing for me is to win. The few seconds of pleasure I get when I overtake, or gain a pole position, or win a race are my motivation.
Sunday Correspondent, London (November 5, 1989)

3 To survive in grand prix racing, you need to be afraid. Fear is an important feeling. It helps you to race longer and live longer.
Times, London (May 3, 1994)

4 The cars are very fast and difficult to drive. It's going to be a season with lots of accidents and I'll risk saying we'll be lucky if something really serious doesn't happen.
Referring to his fears for the 1994 season. *Times*, London (May 3, 1994)

Serlio, Sebastiano (1475–1554) Italian architect and theorist

1 It is necessary that the Architect or Workman should first or at the least...understand the principles of Geometry, that he may not be accounted amongst the number of stone spoilers, who bear the name of workmen.
1545. *The First Booke of Architecture* (1611)

2 The learning of Architecture comprehendeth in it many notable Arts.
1545. *The First Booke of Architecture* (1611)

Serrano, Andres (b.1950) U.S. artist

1 Artists often depend on the manipulation of symbols to present ideas and associations not always apparent in such symbols. If all ideas and associations were evident there would be little need for artists to give expression to them...no need to make art.
The letter was written in defense of a photograph by Andres Serrano that was criticized by Jesse

Helms in Congress. The addressee, Hugh Southern, was acting chairman of the National Endowment for the Arts. Letter to Hugh Southern (May 18, 1989), quoted in *Theories and Documents of Contemporary Art: A Sourcebook of Artists' Writings* (Kristine Stiles and Peter Selz, eds.; 1996)

Servetus, Michael (also known as Miguel Serveto; 1511–53) Spanish physician and theologian

1 I will burn, but this is a mere incident. We shall continue our discussion in eternity.
Said to the judges of the Inquisition after he was condemned to be burned at the stake as a heretic. Quoted in *Borges: A Reader* (E. Monegal; 1977)

Service, Robert W. (Robert William Service; 1874–1958) Canadian poet

1 Ah! the clock is always slow;
It is later than you think.
"It Is Later than You Think," *Ballads of a Bohemian* (1921)

2 When we, the Workers, all demand: "What are we fighting for?"...
Then, then we'll end that stupid crime, that devil's madness—War.
"Michael," *Ballads of a Bohemian* (1921)

3 A promise made is a debt unpaid.
McGee, a "fictitious" person, was the name of an accountholder at the bank where he worked. "The Cremation of Sam McGee," *Songs of a Sourdough* (1907)

4 This is the Law of the Yukon, that only the strong shall thrive;
That surely the weak shall perish, and only the Fit survive.
"The Law of the Yukon," *Songs of a Sourdough* (1907), st. 1

5 Back of the bar, in a solo game, sat Dangerous Dan McGrew,
And watching his luck was his light-o'-love, the lady that's known as Lou.
"The Shooting of Dan McGrew," *Songs of a Sourdough* (1907), st. 1

Seth, Vikram (b.1952) Indian novelist and poet

1 Irish dolphin, swift and single,
Dwelling off the coast of Dingle
Choosing now and then to mingle
With the flipperless and glum.
Prefatory poem to the libretto, dedicated to Funghie, the Irish dolphin. *Arion and the Dolphin* (1994)

2 Boredom provides a stronger inclination to write than anything.
Observer, London (May 1, 1994), "Sayings of the Week"

3 John looks about him with enjoyment.
What a man needs, he thinks, is health;
Well-paid, congenial employment;
A house; a modicum of wealth;
Some sunlight; coffee and the papers.
The Golden Gate (1986), ch. 6, st. 13

4 Catholic and Episcopalian,
Lutheran, Baptist, Methodist,
Jew, Muslim, Buddhist, atheist,
We are all here; no one is alien
Now radiation's common laws
Impel us into common cause.
The Golden Gate (1986), ch. 7, st. 20

5 Ten hostages is terrorism;
A million and it's strategy.
The Golden Gate (1986), ch. 7, st. 31

Seuss, Dr. (Theodor Seuss Geisel; 1904–91) U.S. writer and illustrator

1 I meant what I said
And I said what I meant...
An elephant's faithful
One hundred per cent!
Horton Hatches the Egg (1940)

2 Why for fifty-three years I've put up with it now.
I must stop Christmas from coming, but how?
Said by the Grinch. *How the Grinch Stole Christmas* (1957)

3 You will see something new.
Two things. And I call them
Thing One and Thing Two.
The Cat in the Hat (1957)

4 Green Eggs and Ham
1960. Book title.

5 The Cat in the Hat
1957. Book title.

6 You're Only Old Once!
1986. Book title.

7 Adults are obsolete children.
Attrib.

Sévigné, Madame de, Marquise de Sévigné (originally Marie de Rabutin-Chantal; 1626–96) French writer

1 I have been dragged against my will to the fatal period when *old age* must be endured; I see it, I have attained it; and I would, at least, contrive not to go beyond it, not to advance in the road of infirmities, pain, loss of memory, *disfigurements*, which are ready to lay hold of me.
Letter to her daughter (November 30, 1689)

2 It is sometimes best to slip over thoughts and not go to the bottom of them.
Letter to her daughter (17th century)

3 Youth is in itself so amiable, that were the soul as perfect as the body, we could not forbear adoring it.
Letter to her daughter (17th century)

4 The more I see of men, the more I admire dogs.
Attrib.

5 There is nothing so lovely as to be beautiful. Beauty is a gift of God and we should cherish it as such.
Attrib.

Sewall, Samuel (1652–1730) English-born American judge

1 The Numerousness of Slaves at this day in the Province, and the Uneasiness of them under their Slavery, hath put many upon thinking whether the Foundation of it be firmly and well laid...all Men...have equal Right unto Liberty, and all other outward Comforts of Life.
Referring to slavery in America. *The Selling of Joseph* (1700), quoted in *The Heath*

Anthology of American Literature (Paul Lauter, ed.; 1998), vol. 1

Seward, William Henry (1801–72) U.S. politician

1 It is an irrepressible conflict between opposing and enduring forces, and it means that the United States must and will, sooner or later, become either entirely a slave-holding nation, or entirely a free-labor nation.
Speech, Rochester, New York (October 25, 1858)

2 There is a higher law than the Constitution.
Arguing against the Fugitive Slave Law of 1850, which revised the Fugitive Slave Law of 1793 to appease slave owners and included additional penalties against those who aided runaway slaves. Speech to Senate (March 11, 1850)

Sewell, Sarah Ann (*fl.* 1870s) British writer and social critic

1 It is a man's place to rule, and a woman's to yield. He must be held up as the head of the house, and it is her duty to bend so unmurmuringly to his wishes, that the rest of the household will follow her example, and treat him with the due respect his sex demands.
Women and Times We Live In (1869)

Sexton, Anne (1928–74) U.S. poet

1 In a dream you are never eighty.
"Old," *All My Pretty Ones* (1962)

2 I'm no more a woman
than Christ was a man.
Consorting with Angels (February 1963)

3 A woman is her mother.
That's the main thing.
Housewife (1962)

Seymour, Edward, 1st Duke of Somerset (1506?–52) English soldier and statesman

1 This is to make an end of all wars, to conclude an eternal and perpetual peace.
Referring to the invasion of September 1547 and the English victory at the Battle of Pinkie. Open letter to the people of Scotland (January 1548)

Sforza, Caterina (1463–1509) Italian aristocrat

1 War is not for ladies and children like mine.
Letter to her uncle (August 27, 1498)

Shackleton, Lord (1911–94) British politician

1 A life peer is like a mule—no pride of ancestry, no hope of posterity.
Attrib.

Shadwell, Thomas (1642?–92) English playwright and poet

Quotations about Shadwell

1 The rest to some faint meaning make pretence,
But Shadwell never deviates into sense.
John Dryden (1631–1700) English poet, playwright, and literary critic. Each poet wrote satires attacking the other. *MacFlecknoe* (1682), ll. 19–20

Quotations by Shadwell

2 The haste of a fool is the slowest thing in the world.
A True Widow (1679), Act 3, Scene 1

3 Every man loves what he is good at.
A True Widow (1679), Act 5, Scene 1

4 Words may be false and full of art,
Sighs are the natural language of the heart.
Psyche (1675), Act 3

5 'Tis the way of all flesh.
The Sullen Lovers (1668), Act 5, Scene 2

Shaffer, Peter (b.1926) British playwright

1 Rehearsing a play is making the word flesh. Publishing a play is reversing the process.
Note (1973)

2 All my wife has ever taken from the Mediterranean—from that whole vast intuitive culture—are four bottles of Chianti to make into lamps, and two china condiment donkeys labelled Sally and Peppy.
Equus (1973), Act 1, Scene 18

Shahn, Ben (1898–1969) Lithuanian-born U.S. artist

1 An amateur is an artist who supports himself with outside jobs which enable him to paint. A professional is someone whose wife works to enable him to paint.
Outlining the difference between professional and amateur painters. Attrib.

Shakespeare, William (1564–1616) English poet and playwright

Quotations about Shakespeare

1 When he killed a calf he would do it in a high style, and make a speech.
John Aubrey (1626–97) English antiquary. *Brief Lives* (1898), "William Shakespeare"

2 Shakespeare himself was an actor and he must have known better than we do that playing him could never entirely do him justice.
John Barton (b.1928) British theater director. *Playing Shakespeare* (1995)

3 Renowned Spenser, lie a thought more nigh
To learned Chaucer; and rare Beaumont, lie,
A little nearer Spenser; to make more room
For Shakespeare, in your threefold, fourfold tomb.
William Basse (1583–1653?) English poet. "On Mr. Wm. Shakespeare" (1633)

4 I acknowledge Shakespeare to be the world's greatest dramatic poet, but regret that no parent could place the uncorrected book in the hands of his daughter, and therefore I have prepared *The Family Shakespeare*.
Thomas Bowdler (1754–1825) British editor. Referring to his censored edition of the works of William Shakespeare, which gave rise to the term "bowdlerize." *The Family Shakespeare* (1818), preface

5 Shakespeare was something of an Establishment creep...a man who could be trusted to have a safe pair of hands when it came to politics dramatised on the stage.
Howard Brenton (b.1942) British playwright. "Soundbites," *Guardian*, London (June 3, 1993)

6 Shakespeare's thought was quickened by the idea of actors and a stage but, more than this, his consciousness was fully involved with actors in performance. No element of an actor's experience was unknown to him or without his fascination.
John Russell Brown (b.1923) British academic and theater director. *Discovering Shakespeare* (1981)

7 Rome's just a city like anywhere else. A vastly overrated city, I'd say. It trades on belief just as Stratford trades on Shakespeare.
Anthony Burgess (1917–93) British writer and critic. *Mr. Enderby* (1963), pt. 2, ch. 2

8 Our great poet-teacher, has given us 126 clearly-drawn and thoroughly individual female characters, who has depicted women with full appreciation of their highest qualities, yet with accurate perception of their defects and foibles.
Mary Cowden Clarke (1809–98) British writer and critic. *Shakespeare as the Girl's Friend* (1887), vol. 4

9 I have tried lately to read Shakespeare, and found it so intolerably dull that it nauseated me.
1877
Charles Darwin (1809–82) British naturalist. *Autobiography* (G. de Beer, ed.; 1974)

10 Yet it must be allowed to the present age that the tongue in general is so much refined since Shakespeare's time that many of his words, and more of his phrases, are scarce intelligible.
John Dryden (1631–1700) English poet, playwright, and literary critic. *Troilus and Cressida* (1679), Preface

11 Shakespeare was not great literature lying conveniently to hand, which the literary institution then happily discovered: he is great literature because the institution constitutes him as such.
Terry Eagleton (b.1943) British academic. "Essay on Political Criticism," *Literary Theory* (1982)

12 We can say of Shakespeare, that never has a man turned so little knowledge to such great account.
April 15, 1942
T. S. Eliot (1888–1965) U.S.-born British poet and playwright. A presidential address given to the Classical Association. "The Classics and the Man of Letters" (1942)

13 Shakespeare is the only biographer of Shakespeare; and even he can tell nothing, except to the Shakespeare in us; that is, to our most apprehensive and sympathetic hour.
Ralph Waldo Emerson (1803–82) U.S. poet and essayist. "Shakespeare; or the Poet," *Representative Men* (1850)

14 Good friend, for Jesus' sake forbear
To dig the dust enclosed here!
Bless'd be the man that spares these stones,
And curs'd be he that moves my bones.
Epitaphs. On Shakespeare's grave, composed for the sexton, and sometimes attributed to Shakespeare. Epitaph (1616)

15 In the end, perhaps the reason why Shakespeare's language is "the best" is that it can express the most ordinary as well as the most exalted moments, and that his use of the arts of language has room for the most casual speech as well as the most elaborate rhetoric.
Inga-Stina Ewbank (b.1932) British academic and critic. "Shakespeare and the Arts of Language," *Companion to Shakespeare Studies* (1986)

16 Shakespeare's verbal imagination was also his dramatic imagination.
Inga-Stina Ewbank (b.1932) British academic and critic. "Shakespeare and the Arts of Language," *Companion to Shakespeare Studies* (1986)

17 Shakespeare enjoyed the advantage of living in a creative age in a vigorous Protestant country where the madness of bigotry was silent for a while.
Johann Wolfgang von Goethe (1749–1832) German poet, playwright, and scientist. "Shakespeare: a Tribute" (1771)

18 Shakespeare's works are one great bubbling fair, and he owes the richness of his wares to his native land...His Romans are Englishmen through and through.
Johann Wolfgang von Goethe (1749–1832) German poet, playwright, and scientist. "Shakespeare: a Tribute" (1771)

19 It is Fate that draws the plan; as the story issues from a deed of terror, and the hero is continually driven forward to a deed of terror, the work is tragic in the highest sense, and admits of no other than a tragic end.
1795
Johann Wolfgang von Goethe (1749–1832) German poet, playwright, and scientist. Referring to William Shakespeare's *Hamlet.* Quoted in *The Great Critics* (James Harry Smith and Edd Winfield Parks, eds.; 1951)

20 The remarkable thing about Shakespeare is that he is really very good—in spite of all the people who say he is very good.
Robert Graves (1895–1985) British poet and novelist. *Observer,* London (December 6, 1964), "Sayings of the Week"

21 Shakespeare's so bloody difficult, and I don't like failure. You can fail on film, but there's nobody actually there in the flesh to watch you failing.
Anthony Hopkins (b.1937) Welsh stage and film actor. *Independent,* London (February 12, 1994)

22 This is a play which all men admire, and which most women dislike. Many revolting expressions in the comic parts, much boisterous courage in some of the graver scenes, together with Falstaff's unwieldy person, offend every female auditor.
Elizabeth Inchbald (1753–1821) British actor, playwright, and novelist. On *Henry IV, Part 1* (1597). *The British Theatre* (1806–09)

23 It must be at last confessed that, as we owe everything to him, he owes something to us; that, if much of our praise is paid by perception and judgement, much is likewise given by custom and veneration. We fix our eyes upon his graces and turn them from his deformities, and endure in him what we should in another loathe or despise.
Samuel Johnson (1709–84) British lexicographer and writer. *Plays of William Shakespeare, with Notes* (1765), Preface

24 Shakespeare never had six lines together without a fault. Perhaps you may find seven, but this does not refute my general assertion.
October 29, 1769
Samuel Johnson (1709–84) British lexicographer and writer. Quoted in *Life of Samuel Johnson* (James Boswell; 1791)

25 Shakespeare has no heroes.
Samuel Johnson (1709–84) British lexicographer and writer. Attrib.

26 For a good poet's made, as well as born.
Ben Jonson (1572–1637) English playwright and poet. "To the Memory of My Beloved, the Author, Mr William Shakespeare" (1623)

27 He was not of an age, but for all time!
Ben Jonson (1572–1637) English playwright and poet. "To the Memory of My Beloved, the Author, Mr William Shakespeare" (1623)

28 Sweet Swan of Avon! what a sight it were
To see thee in our waters yet appear,
And make those flights upon the banks of Thames,
That so did take Eliza, and our James!
Ben Jonson (1572–1637) English playwright and poet. "To the Memory of My Beloved, the Author, Mr William Shakespeare" (1623)

29 Thou hadst small Latin, and less Greek.
Ben Jonson (1572–1637) English playwright and poet. "To the Memory of My Beloved, the Author, Mr William Shakespeare" (1623)

30 The players have often mentioned it as an honour to Shakespeare that in his writing (whatsoever he penned) he never blotted out a line. My answer hath been "Would he had blotted a thousand"...I had not told posterity this, but for their ignorance, who chose that circumstance to commend their friend by wherein he most faulted; and to justify mine own candour: for I loved the man, and do honour his memory, on this side idolatry, as much as any.
Ben Jonson (1572–1637) English playwright and poet. "De Shakespeare Nostrati," *Timber, or, Discoveries Made upon Men and Matter* (1641)

31 I have good reason to be content, for thank God I can read and perhaps understand Shakespeare to his depths.
John Keats (1795–1821) British poet. Letter to John Taylor (February 27, 1818), quoted in *Letters of John Keats* (H. E. Rollins, ed.; 1958), vol. 1

32 I would trust a Shakespeare but not a committee of Shakespeares.
Tadeusz Kotarbinski (1886–1981) Polish satirist. Quoted in "From the Amoeba to the Philosopher," *Shedding Life* (Miroslav Holub; 1997)

33 But the Lear of Shakespeare cannot be acted...the play is beyond all art, as the tamperings with it show: it is too hard and stony; it must have love scenes and a happy ending.
Charles Lamb (1775–1834) British essayist. Referring to Shakespeare's tragedy *King Lear*, and the late 17th-century and 18th-century trend to revise Shakespeare's tragedies by giving them happy endings. The most distinguished proponent of this was poet laureate Nahum Tate, whose widely performed *Tate's Lear* (a revision of *King Lear*), ended with Cordelia marrying Edgar. Attrib.

34 When I read Shakespeare I am struck with wonder
That such trivial people should muse and thunder
In such lovely language.
D. H. Lawrence (1885–1930) British writer. "When I Read Shakespeare," *Pansies* (1929)

35 What is it old Shakespeare says? In the Spring a young man's fancy does something or other about love. He's a wonderful fellow is old Shakespeare.
Compton Mackenzie (1883–1972) British writer. *Hunting the Fairies* (1949), ch. 1

36 Shakespeare alone had paved a road for himself to the pantheon of the arts. People are engrossed in Shakespeare, enraptured by Shakespeare.
Osip Mandelstam (1891–1938) Russian poet, writer, and translator. "Goethe's Youth: Radiodrama" (1935), quoted in *The Collected Critical Prose and Letters of Osip Mandelstam* (J. G. Harris, ed., tr., C. Link, tr.; 1991)

37 The reason I couldn't do the music is that I don't really like words by Shakespeare.
Paul McCartney (b.1942) British rock musician and composer. Referring to a proposition to do a musical version of Shakespeare's *As You Like It*. Letter to Kenneth Tynan (1968)

38 Immortal! William Shakespeare, there's none can you excel,
You have drawn out your characters remarkably well.
William McGonagall (1830–1902) Scottish poet and novelist. "An Address to Shakespeare" (1878)

39 William Shakespeare wrote for the masses. If he were alive today, he'd probably be the chief scriptwriter on *All in the Family* or *Dallas*.
Rupert Murdoch (b.1931) Australian-born U.S. media entrepreneur. *Sunday Express*, London (December 20, 1984), "Quotes of the Year"

40 In Greek tragedy the structure of the scenes and the concrete images convey a deeper wisdom than the poet was able to put into words and concepts. The same may be claimed of Shakespeare.
Friedrich Wilhelm Nietzsche (1844–1900) German philosopher and poet. *The Birth of Tragedy* (1872)

41 Shakespeare—the nearest thing in incarnation to the eye of God.
Laurence Olivier (1907–89) British actor and director. Quoted in "Sir Lawrence Olivier," *Kenneth Harris Talking To...* (Kenneth Harris; 1971)

42 Shakespeare absolutely belongs to everyone: the Japanese student struggling with the hieroglyphics, the muttering commuter, the professional, the club bore, everybody who quotes him without realising it every day.
Michael Pennington (b.1943) British actor and theater director. *The English Shakespeare Company* (1990)

43 A man can be forgiven a lot if he can quote Shakespeare in an economic crisis.
Prince Philip (b.1921) British consort of Queen Elizabeth II. Attrib.

44 Brush Up Your Shakespeare
Cole Porter (1893–1964) U.S. songwriter and composer. Song title from the musical *Kiss Me Kate*. Music composed by Jerome Kern (1885–1945). "Brush Up Your Shakespeare," *Kiss Me Kate* (1948)

45 The title of a "Tale of the Crusades" would resemble...the play-bill, which is said to have announced the tragedy of Hamlet, the character of the Prince of Denmark being left out.
Sir Walter Scott (1771–1832) Scottish novelist. Known since as "Hamlet Without the Prince." *The Talisman* (1825), Introduction

46 It does not follow...that the right to criticize Shakespeare involves the power of writing better plays. And in fact...I do not profess to write better plays.
George Bernard Shaw (1856–1950) Irish playwright. *Three Plays for Puritans* (1901), Preface

47 Besides Shakespeare and me, who do you think there is?
Gertrude Stein (1874–1946) U.S. writer. Speaking to a friend she considered ignorant about literature. Quoted in *Charmed Circle* (J. Mellow; 1974)

48 Wonderful women! Have you ever thought how much we all, and women especially, owe to Shakespeare for his vindication of women in these fearless, high-spirited, resolute, and intelligent heroines?
Ellen Terry (1847–1928) British actor. "Four Lectures on Shakespeare," *The Triumphant Women* (1911)

49 A strange, horrible business, but I suppose good enough for Shakespeare's day.
Victoria (1819–1901) British monarch. Giving her opinion of *King Lear*. Attrib.

Quotations by Shakespeare

50 HELENA Our remedies oft in ourselves do lie,
Which we ascribe to heaven.
All's Well That Ends Well (1603), Act 1, Scene 1

51 CLOWN It is like a barber's chair, that fits all buttocks.
All's Well That Ends Well (1603), Act 2, Scene 2

52 PAROLLES A young man married

is a man that's
marred.
All's Well That Ends Well (1603), Act 2, Scene 3

53 FIRST LORD The web of our life is of a mingled yarn, good and ill together.
All's Well That Ends Well (1603), Act 4, Scene 3

54 KING Praising what is lost
Makes the remembrance dear.
All's Well That Ends Well (1603), Act 5, Scene 3

55 KING Th' inaudible and noiseless foot of Time.
All's Well That Ends Well (1603), Act 5, Scene 3

56 HELENA Love looks not with the eyes, but with the mind;
And therefore is wing'd Cupid painted blind.
A Midsummer Night's Dream (1595–96), Act 1, Scene 1

57 PUCK I'll put a girdle round about the earth
In forty minutes.
A Midsummer Night's Dream (1595–96), Act 2, Scene 1

58 HELENA So we grew together,
Like to a double cherry, seeming parted,
But yet an union in partition,
Two lovely berries moulded on one stem;
So, with two seeming bodies, but one heart.
A Midsummer Night's Dream (1595–96), Act 3, Scene 2

59 PUCK Jack shall have Jill;
Nought shall go ill;
The man shall have his mare again,
And all shall be well.
A Midsummer Night's Dream (1595–96), Act 3, Scene 2

60 PUCK Lord, what fools these mortals be!
A Midsummer Night's Dream (1595–96), Act 3, Scene 2

61 BOTTOM I have had a dream, past the wit of man to say what dream it was.
A Midsummer Night's Dream (1595–96), Act 4, Scene 1

62 BOTTOM The eye of man hath not heard, the ear of man hath not seen, man's hand is not able to taste, his tongue to conceive, nor his heart to report, what my dream was.
A Midsummer Night's Dream (1595–96), Act 4, Scene 1

63 TITANIA My Oberon! what visions have I seen!
Methought I was enamour'd of an ass.
A Midsummer Night's Dream (1595–96), Act 4, Scene 1

64 PUCK If we shadows have offended,
Think but this, and all is mended,
That you have but slumber'd here
While these visions did appear.
A Midsummer Night's Dream (1595–96), Act 5, Scene 1

65 PUCK Not a mouse
Shall disturb this hallowed house,
I am sent with broom before,
To sweep the dust behind the door.
A Midsummer Night's Dream (1595–96), Act 5, Scene 1

66 QUINCE All for your delight
We are not here.
A Midsummer Night's Dream (1595–96), Act 5, Scene 1

67 THESEUS The lunatic, the lover, and the poet,
Are of imagination all compact.
A Midsummer Night's Dream (1595–96), Act 5, Scene 1

68 THESEUS The poet's eye, in a fine frenzy rolling,
Doth glance from heaven to earth, from earth to heaven;
And as imagination bodies forth
The forms of things unknown, the poet's pen
Turns them to shapes, and gives to airy nothing
A local habitation and a name.
A Midsummer Night's Dream (1595–96), Act 5, Scene 1

69 ANTONY I will to Egypt
And though I make this marriage for my peace,
I' the East my pleasure lies.
Antony and Cleopatra (1606–07)

70 ANTONY There's beggary in the love that can be reckon'd.
Antony and Cleopatra (1606–07), Act 1, Scene 1

71 CHARMIAN In time we hate that which we often fear.
Antony and Cleopatra (1606–07), Act 1, Scene 3

72 CLEOPATRA My salad days,
When I was green in judgment, cold in blood,
To say as I said then!
Antony and Cleopatra (1606–07), Act 1, Scene 5

73 CLEOPATRA Where's my serpent of old Nile?
Antony and Cleopatra (1606–07), Act 1, Scene 5

74 ENOBARBUS Age cannot wither her, nor custom stale
Her infinite variety. Other women cloy
The appetites they feed, but she makes hungry
Where most she satisfies.
Antony and Cleopatra (1606–07), Act 2, Scene 2

75 ENOBARBUS The barge she sat in, like a burnish'd throne,
Burn'd on the water. The poop was beaten gold;
Purple the sails, and so perfumed that
The winds were love-sick with them; the oars were silver,
Which to the tune of flutes kept stroke and made
The water which they beat to follow faster,
As amorous of their strokes. For her own person,
It beggar'd all description.
Antony and Cleopatra (1606–07), Act 2, Scene 2

76 ENOBARBUS I will praise any man that will praise me.
Antony and Cleopatra (1606–07), Act 2, Scene 6

77 CLEOPATRA Celerity is never more admir'd
Than by the negligent.
Antony and Cleopatra (1606–07), Act 3, Scene 7

78 ANTONY To business that we love we rise betime,
And go to't with delight.
Antony and Cleopatra (1606–07), Act 4, Scene 4

79 CLEOPATRA Lord of lords!
O infinite virtue! com'st thou smiling from
The world's great snare uncaught?
ANTONY My nightingale,
We have beat them to their beds.
Antony and Cleopatra (1606–07), Act 4, Scene 8

80 ANTONY I will be

A bridegroom in my death, and run into 't
As to a lover's bed.
Antony and Cleopatra (1606–07), Act 4, Scene 14

81 ANTONY Unarm, Eros; the long day's task is done,
And we must sleep.
Antony and Cleopatra (1606–07), Act 4, Scene 14

82 ANTONY I am dying, Egypt, dying; only
I here importune death awhile, until
Of many thousand kisses the poor last
I lay upon thy lips.
Antony and Cleopatra (1606–07), Act 4, Scene 15

83 ANTONY Not Caesar's valour hath o'erthrown Antony
But Antony's hath triumphed on itself.
CLEOPATRA So it should be, that none but Antony
Should conquer Antony.
Antony and Cleopatra (1606–07), Act 4, Scene 15

84 ANTONY The miserable change now at my end
Lament nor sorrow at; but please your thoughts
In feeding them with those my former fortunes
Wherein I liv'd the greatest prince o' the world,
The noblest; and do now not basely die,
Not cowardly put off my helmet to
My countryman; a Roman by a Roman
Valiantly vanquished.
Antony and Cleopatra (1606–07), Act 4, Scene 15

85 CLEOPATRA Hast thou no care of me? shall I abide
In this dull world, which in thy absence is
No better than a sty? O! see my women,
The crown o' the earth doth melt. My lord!
Antony and Cleopatra (1606–07), Act 4, Scene 15

86 CLEOPATRA O, wither'd is the garland of the war,
The soldier's pole is fall'n! Young boys and girls
Are level now with men. The odds is gone,
And there is nothing left remarkable
Beneath the visiting moon.
Antony and Cleopatra (1606–07), Act 4, Scene 15

87 AGRIPPA A rarer spirit never
Did steer humanity; but you, gods, will give us
Some faults to make us men.
Antony and Cleopatra (1606–07), Act 5, Scene 1

88 CAESAR She hath pursu'd conclusions infinite
Of easy ways to die.
Antony and Cleopatra (1606–07), Act 5, Scene 2

89 CAESAR She shall be buried by her Antony!
No grave upon the earth shall clip in it
A pair so famous.
Antony and Cleopatra (1606–07), Act 5, Scene 2

90 CLEOPATRA His legs bestrid the ocean; his rear'd arm
Crested the world. His voice was propertied
As all the tuned spheres, and that to friends;
But when he meant to quall and shake the orb,
He was as rattling thunder. For his bounty,
There was no winter in't; an autumn 'twas
That grew the more by reaping. His delights
Were dolphin-like: they show'd his back above
The element they liv'd in. In his livery
Walk'd crowns and crownets; realms and islands were
As plates dropp'd from his pocket.
Antony and Cleopatra (1606–07), Act 5, Scene 2

91 CLEOPATRA If thou and nature can so gently part,
The stroke of death is as a lover's pinch,
Which hurts, and is desir'd.
Antony and Cleopatra (1606–07), Act 5, Scene 2

92 CLEOPATRA My resolution's plac'd, and I have nothing
Of woman in me; now from head to foot
I am marble-constant, now the fleeting moon
No planet is of mine.
Antony and Cleopatra (1606–07), Act 5, Scene 2

93 IRAS The bright day is done,
And we are for the dark.
Antony and Cleopatra (1606–07), Act 5, Scene 2

94 CLEOPATRA Dost thou not see my baby at my breast
That sucks the nurse asleep?
Referring to the asp which (according to the stage direction) "she applies to her breast." *Antony and Cleopatra* (1606–07), Act 5, Scene 2

95 CLEOPATRA If she first meet the curled Antony,
He'll make demand of her, and spend that kiss
Which is my heaven to have. Come, thou mortal wretch,
With thy sharp teeth this knot intrinsicate
Of life at once untie. Poor venomous fool,
Be angry, and dispatch. O couldst thou speak,
That I might hear thee call great Caesar ass
Unpolicied.
Referring to the asp which (according to the stage direction) "she applies to her breast." *Antony and Cleopatra* (1606–07), Act 5, Scene 2

96 CELIA Well said; that was laid on with a trowel.
As You Like It (1599), Act 1, Scene 2

97 ROSALIND O, how full of briers is this working-day world!
As You Like It (1599), Act 1, Scene 3

98 DUKE SENIOR Sweet are the uses of adversity,
Which like the toad, ugly and venomous,
Wears yet a precious jewel in his head;
And this our life, exempt from public haunt,
Finds tongues in trees, books in the running brooks,
Sermons in stones, and good in everything.
As You Like It (1599), Act 2, Scene 1

99 ROSALIND Thou speakest wiser than thou art ware of.
As You Like It (1599), Act 2, Scene 4

100 TOUCHSTONE I had rather bear with you than bear you.
As You Like It (1599), Act 2, Scene 4

101 TOUCHSTONE We that are true lovers run into strange capers.
As You Like It (1599), Act 2, Scene 4

102 SILVIUS If thou remember'st not the slightest folly
That ever love did make thee run into,
Thou hast not lov'd.
Song lyric. *As You Like It* (1599), Act 2, Scene 4

103 JAQUES I can suck melancholy out of a song,
as a weasel sucks eggs.
As You Like It (1599), Act 2, Scene 5

104 AMIENS Under the greenwood tree
Who loves to lie with me,
And turn his merry note
Unto the sweet bird's throat,
Come hither, come hither, come hither.
Here shall he see
No enemy
But winter and rough weather.
Song lyric. *As You Like It* (1599), Act 2, Scene 5

105 JAQUES All the world's a stage,
And all the men and women merely players;
They have their exits and their entrances;
And one man in his time plays many parts,
His acts being seven ages.
As You Like It (1599), Act 2, Scene 7

106 JAQUES And so, from hour to hour, we ripe and ripe,
And then, from hour to hour, we rot and rot;
And thereby hangs a tale.
As You Like It (1599), Act 2, Scene 7

107 JAQUES Last scene of all,
That ends this strange eventful history,
Is second childishness and mere oblivion;
Sans teeth, sans eyes, sans taste, sans everything.
As You Like It (1599), Act 2, Scene 7

108 Blow, blow, thou winter wind,
Thou art not so unkind
As man's ingratitude.
Song lyric. *As You Like It* (1599), Act 2, Scene 7

109 Most friendship is feigning, most loving mere folly.
Song lyric. *As You Like It* (1599), Act 2, Scene 7

110 CELIA It is as easy to count atomies as to resolve the propositions of a lover.
As You Like It (1599), Act 3, Scene 2

111 CORIN He that wants money, means, and content, is without three good friends.
As You Like It (1599), Act 3, Scene 2

112 CORIN I earn that I eat, get that I wear, owe no man hate, envy no man's happiness, glad of other men's good, content with my harm.
As You Like It (1599), Act 3, Scene 2

113 JAQUES I do not like her name.
ORLANDO There was no thought of pleasing you when she was christened.
As You Like It (1599), Act 3, Scene 2

114 ORLANDO I do desire we may be better strangers.
As You Like It (1599), Act 3, Scene 2

115 ROSALIND Do you not know I am a woman? When I think, I must speak.
As You Like It (1599), Act 3, Scene 2

116 TOUCHSTONE The truest poetry is the most feigning.
As You Like It (1599), Act 3, Scene 3

117 ROSALIND Men are April when they woo,
December when they wed; maids are May when they are maids, but the sky changes when they are wives.
As You Like It (1599), Act 4, Scene 1

118 ROSALIND Men have died from time to time, and worms have eaten them, but not for love.
As You Like It (1599), Act 4, Scene 1

119 ORLANDO Oh! how bitter a thing it is to look into happiness through another man's eyes.
As You Like It (1599), Act 5, Scene 2

120 SECOND PAGE It was a lover and his lass,
With a hey and a ho, and a hey nonino,
That o'er the green corn-field did pass
In the spring time, the only pretty ring time,
When birds do sing, hey ding a ding, ding;
Sweet lovers love the spring.
As You Like It (1599), Act 5, Scene 3

121 TOUCHSTONE Your "If" is the only peace-maker; much virtue in "If".
As You Like It (1599), Act 5, Scene 4

122 ROSALIND If it be true that "good wine needs no bush," 'tis true that a good play needs no epilogue.
As You Like It (1599), Act 5, Scene 4, Epilogue

123 SICINIUS What is the city but the people?
Coriolanus (1608), Act 3, Scene 1

124 CORIOLANUS The beast with many heads butts me away.
Referring to the tribunes, who are running him out of Rome. *Coriolanus* (1608), Act 4, Scene 1

125 FIRST SERVANT Let me have war, say I; it exceeds peace as far as day does night; it's spritely, waking, audible, and full of vent. Peace is a very apoplexy, lethargy: mulled, deaf, sleepy, insensible; a getter of more bastard children than war's a destroyer of men.
Coriolanus (1608), Act 4, Scene 5

126 CORIOLANUS Chaste as the icicle
That's curdled by the frost from purest snow,
And hangs on Dian's temple.
Coriolanus (1608), Act 5, Scene 3

127 Hark, hark! the lark at heaven's gate sings
And Phoebus 'gins arise,
His steeds to water at those springs
On chalic'd flow'rs that lies;
And winking Mary-buds begin
To ope their golden eyes.
Cymbeline (1609–10), Act 2, Scene 3

128 POSTUMUS Is there no way for men to be, but women must be half-workers?
Cymbeline (1609–10), Act 2, Scene 5

129 IMOGEN O, for a horse with wings!
Cymbeline (1609–10), Act 3, Scene 2

130 BELARIUS O, this life
Is nobler than attending for a check,

Richer than doing nothing for a bribe,
Prouder than rustling in unpaid-for silk.
Cymbeline (1609–10), Act 3, Scene 3

131 IMOGEN Hath Britain all the sun that shines?
Cymbeline (1609–10), Act 3, Scene 4

132 GUIDERIUS Thersites' body is as good as Ajax'
When neither are alive.
Cymbeline (1609–10), Act 4, Scene 2

133 IMOGEN Society is no comfort
To one not sociable.
Cymbeline (1609–10), Act 4, Scene 2

134 GUIDERIUS Fear no more the heat o' the sun,
Nor the furious winter's rages;
Thou thy worldly task hast done,
Home art gone and ta'en thy wages.
Song, sung by Guiderius and Arviragus. *Cymbeline* (1609–10), Act 4, Scene 2

135 POSTHUMUS Every good servant does not all commands.
Cymbeline (1609–10), Act 5, Scene 1

136 GAOLER He that sleeps feels not the toothache.
Cymbeline (1609–10), Act 5, Scene 4

137 CYMBELINE By medicine life may be prolonged, yet death
Will seize the doctor too.
Cymbeline (1609–10), Act 5, Scene 5

138 POSTHUMUS Hang there like fruit, my soul,
Till the tree die!
Said on recognizing his wife Imogen, whom he thought lost. *Cymbeline* (1609–10), Act 5, Scene 5

139 FRANCISCO For this relief much thanks. 'Tis bitter cold,
And I am sick at heart.
Hamlet (1601), Act 1, Scene 1

140 HAMLET A little more than kin, and less than kind.
Hamlet (1601), Act 1, Scene 2

141 HAMLET But I have that within which passes show—
these but the trappings and the suits of woe.
Hamlet (1601), Act 1, Scene 2

142 HAMLET Frailty, thy name is woman!
Hamlet (1601), Act 1, Scene 2

143 HAMLET It is not, nor it cannot come to good.
Hamlet (1601), Act 1, Scene 2

144 HAMLET O! that this too too solid flesh would melt,
Thaw, and resolve itself into a dew.
Or that the Everlasting had not fix'd
His canon 'gainst self-slaughter! O God! O God!
How weary, stale, flat, and unprofitable,
Seem to me all the uses of this world!
Hamlet (1601), Act 1, Scene 2

145 HAMLET So excellent a king, that was to this
Hyperion to a satyr.
Hamlet (1601), Act 1, Scene 2

146 HAMLET Thrift, thrift, Horatio! The funeral bak'd-meats
Did coldly furnish forth the marriage tables.
Hamlet (1601), Act 1, Scene 2

147 HAMLET 'A was a man, take him for all in all,
I shall not look upon his like again.
Referring to his dead father. *Hamlet* (1601), Act 1, Scene 2

148 LAERTES The canker galls the infants of the spring
Too oft before her buttons be disclosed.
Hamlet (1601), Act 1, Scene 3

149 OPHELIA Do not, as some ungracious pastors do,
Show me the steep and thorny way to heaven,
Whiles, like a puff'd and reckless libertine,
Himself the primrose path of dalliance treads
And recks not his own rede.
Hamlet (1601), Act 1, Scene 3

150 POLONIUS Costly thy habit as thy purse can buy,
But not express'd in fancy; rich, not gaudy;
For the apparel oft proclaims the man.
Hamlet (1601), Act 1, Scene 3

151 POLONIUS Give every man thy ear, but few thy voice;
Take each man's censure, but reserve thy judgement.
Hamlet (1601), Act 1, Scene 3

152 POLONIUS Neither a borrower nor a lender be;
For loan oft loses both itself and friend,
And borrowing dulls the edge of husbandry.
This above all: to thine own self be true,
And it must follow, as the night the day,
Thou canst not then be false to any man.
Hamlet (1601), Act 1, Scene 3

153 MARCELLUS Something is rotten in the state of Denmark.
Hamlet (1601), Act 1, Scene 4

154 HAMLET But to my mind, though I am native here
And to the manner born, it is a custom
More honour'd in the breach than the observance.
The custom referred to is that of "wassail," which involved ritual toasts and heavy drinking. *Hamlet* (1601), Act 1, Scene 4

155 GHOST Murder most foul, as in the best it is;
But this most foul, strange, and unnatural.
Hamlet (1601), Act 1, Scene 5

156 GHOST O wicked wit and gifts, that have the power
So to seduce!—won to his shameful lust
The will of my most seeming-virtuous Queen.
Hamlet (1601), Act 1, Scene 5

157 GHOST Taint not thy mind, nor let thy soul contrive
Against thy mother aught. Leave her to heaven
And to those thorns that in her bosom lodge
To prick and sting her.
Hamlet (1601), Act 1, Scene 5

158 HAMLET O villain, villain, smiling, damned villain!
My tables,—meet it is I set it down,
That one may smile, and smile, and be a villain;
At least I'm sure it may be so in Denmark.
Hamlet (1601), Act 1, Scene 5

159 HAMLET There are more things in heaven and earth, Horatio,
Than are dreamt of in your philosophy.
Hamlet (1601), Act 1, Scene 5

160 HAMLET The time is out of joint; O cursed spite,
That ever I was born to set it right!
Hamlet (1601), Act 1, Scene 5

161 GUILDENSTERN Dreams indeed are ambition.
For the very substance of the ambitious is merely the shadow of a dream.
Hamlet (1601), Act 2, Scene 2

162 HAMLET But I am pigeon-liver'd, and lack gall
To make oppression bitter, or ere this
I should have fatted all the region kites
With this slave's offal. Bloody, bawdy villain!
Remorseless, treacherous, lecherous, kindless villain!
Hamlet (1601), Act 2, Scene 2

163 HAMLET I am but mad north-north-west; when the
wind is southerly, I know a hawk from a handsaw.
Hamlet (1601), Act 2, Scene 2

164 HAMLET I have heard,
That guilty creatures sitting at a play
Have by the very cunning of the scene
Been struck so to the soul that presently
They have proclaim'd their malefactions;
For murder, though it have no tongue, will speak
With most miraculous organ.
Hamlet (1601), Act 2, Scene 2

165 HAMLET O what a rogue and peasant slave am I!
Is it not monstrous that this player here,
But in a fiction, in a dream of passion,
Could force his soul so to his own conceit
Tears in his eyes, distraction in his aspect,
A broken voice, and his whole function suiting
With forms to his conceit? And all for nothing.
Hamlet (1601), Act 2, Scene 2

166 HAMLET The play, I remember, pleas'd not the million; 'twas caviare to the general.
Hamlet (1601), Act 2, Scene 2

167 HAMLET The play's the thing
Wherein I'll catch the conscience of the King.
Hamlet (1601), Act 2, Scene 2

168 HAMLET There is nothing either good or bad, but thinking makes it so.
Hamlet (1601), Act 2, Scene 2

169 HAMLET To be honest, as this world goes, is to be one man pick'd out of ten thousand.
Hamlet (1601), Act 2, Scene 2

170 HAMLET Use every man after his desert, and who should 'scape whipping?
Hamlet (1601), Act 2, Scene 2

171 HAMLET What a piece of work is a man! How noble in reason! how infinite in faculties! in form and moving, how express and admirable! in action, how like an angel! in apprehension, how like a god! the beauty of the world! the paragon of animals! And yet, to me, what is this quintessence of dust? Man delights not me—no, nor woman neither.
Hamlet (1601), Act 2, Scene 2

172 POLONIUS Brevity is the soul of wit.
Hamlet (1601), Act 2, Scene 2

173 POLONIUS Though this be madness, yet there is method in't.
Hamlet (1601), Act 2, Scene 2

174 ROSENCRANTZ For they say an old man is twice a child.
Hamlet (1601), Act 2, Scene 2

175 HAMLET For the power of beauty will sooner transform honesty from what it is to a bawd than the force of honesty can translate beauty into his likeness.
Hamlet (1601), Act 3, Scene 1

176 HAMLET Get thee to a nunnery: why wouldst thou be a breeder of sinners?
Hamlet (1601), Act 3, Scene 1

177 HAMLET The dread of something after death—
The undiscover'd country, from whose bourn
No traveller returns.
Hamlet (1601), Act 3, Scene 1

178 HAMLET Thus conscience does make cowards of us all;
And thus the native hue of resolution
Is sicklied o'er with the pale cast of thought.
Hamlet (1601), Act 3, Scene 1

179 HAMLET To be, or not to be—that is the question;
Whether 'tis nobler in the mind to suffer
The slings and arrows of outrageous fortune,
Or to take arms against a sea of troubles,
And by opposing end them? To die, to sleep—
No more; and by a sleep to say we end
The heart-ache and the thousand natural shocks
That flesh is heir to, 'tis a consummation
Devoutly to be wish'd. To die, to sleep;
To sleep, perchance to dream. Ay, there's the rub;
For in that sleep of death what dreams may come,
When we have shuffled off this mortal coil,
Must give us pause.
Hamlet (1601), Act 3, Scene 1

180 KING Madness in great ones must not unwatch'd go.
Hamlet (1601), Act 3, Scene 1

181 KING There's something in his soul
O'er which his melancholy sits on brood.
Hamlet (1601), Act 3, Scene 1

182 OPHELIA For to the noble mind
Rich gifts wax poor when givers prove unkind.
Hamlet (1601), Act 3, Scene 1

183 OPHELIA O, what a noble mind is here o'erthrown!
The courtier's, soldier's, scholar's, eye, tongue, sword,
Th'expectancy and rose of the fair state,
The glass of fashion and the mould of form,
Th'observed of all observers, quite, quite down!
Hamlet (1601), Act 3, Scene 1

184 POLONIUS 'Tis too much proved, that with devotion's visage
And pious action we do sugar o'er
The devil himself.
Hamlet (1601), Act 3, Scene 1

185 HAMLET Give me that man
That is not passion's slave, and I will wear him
In my heart's core, ay, in my heart of heart,
As I do thee.
Hamlet (1601), Act 3, Scene 2

186 HAMLET Let me be cruel, not unnatural;
I will speak daggers to her, but use none.
Hamlet (1601), Act 3, Scene 2

187 HAMLET O wonderful son, that can so 'stonish a mother!
Hamlet (1601), Act 3, Scene 2

188 HAMLET Speak the speech, I pray you, as I pronounced it to you, trippingly on the tongue; but if you mouth it, as many of your players do, I had as lief the town-crier spoke my lines. Nor do not saw the air too much with your hand, thus; but use all gently: for in the very torrent, tempest, and—as I may say—whirlwind of passion, you must acquire and beget a temperance, that may give it smoothness. O! it offends me to the soul to hear a robustious periwig-pated fellow tear a passion to tatters, to very rags, to split the ears of the groundlings, who for the most part are capable of nothing but inexplicable dumb-shows and noise: I would have such a fellow whipped for o'erdoing Termagant; it out-herods Herod: pray you, avoid it.
Hamlet (1601), Act 3, Scene 2

189 HAMLET Suit the action to the word, the word to the action; with this special observance, that you o'erstep not the modesty of nature.
Hamlet (1601), Act 3, Scene 2

190 HAMLET You would play upon me; you would seem to know my stops; you would pluck out the heart of my mystery; you would sound me from my lowest note to the top of my compass.
Hamlet (1601), Act 3, Scene 2

191 OPHELIA 'Tis brief, my lord.
HAMLET As woman's love.
Hamlet (1601), Act 3, Scene 2

192 QUEEN The lady doth protest too much, methinks.
Hamlet (1601), Act 3, Scene 2

193 POLONIUS Very like a whale.
Hamlet, feigning madness, leads Polonius on to make a fool of himself, persuading him that he can see contradictory shapes in the clouds—a camel, a weasel, a whale. *Hamlet* (1601), Act 3, Scene 2

194 KING My words fly up, my thoughts remain below:
Words without thoughts never to heaven go.
Hamlet (1601), Act 3, Scene 3

195 KING O! my offence is rank, it smells to heaven.
Hamlet (1601), Act 3, Scene 3

196 KING Whereto serves mercy
But to confront the visage of offence?
Hamlet (1601), Act 3, Scene 3

197 ROSENCRANTZ Never alone
did the king sigh, but with a general groan.
Hamlet (1601), Act 3, Scene 3

198 GERTRUDE Speak no more;
Thou turn'st mine eyes into my very soul.
Hamlet (1601), Act 3, Scene 4

199 HAMLET A king of shreds and patches.
Hamlet (1601), Act 3, Scene 4

200 HAMLET A station like the herald Mercury
New lighted on a heaven-kissing hill.
Hamlet (1601), Act 3, Scene 4

201 HAMLET Goodnight—but go not to my uncle's bed; Assume a virtue, if you have it not.
Hamlet (1601), Act 3, Scene 4

202 HAMLET I must be cruel only to be kind.
Hamlet (1601), Act 3, Scene 4

203 HAMLET That I essentially am not in madness,
But mad in craft.
Hamlet (1601), Act 3, Scene 4

204 HAMLET Thou wretched, rash, intruding fool, farewell!
I took thee for thy better.
On discovering that he has killed Polonius, who had been hiding in his mother's bedroom behind a tapestried wall hanging. *Hamlet* (1601), Act 3, Scene 4

205 HAMLET Indeed this counsellor
Is now most still, most secret, and most grave,
Who was in life a foolish prating knave.
Referring to Polonius. *Hamlet* (1601), Act 3, Scene 4

206 QUEEN Mad as the sea and wind when both contend
Which is the mightier.
Hamlet (1601), Act 4, Scene 1

207 HAMLET A knavish speech sleeps in a foolish ear.
Hamlet (1601), Act 4, Scene 2

208 HAMLET Nothing but to show you how a king may go progress through the guts of a beggar.
Hamlet (1601), Act 4, Scene 3

209 KING Diseases desperate grown
By desperate appliance are relieved,
Or not at all.
Hamlet (1601), Act 4, Scene 3

210 HAMLET How all occasions do inform against me,
And spur my dull revenge! What is a man,
If his chief good and market of his time
Be but to sleep and feed? a beast, no more.
Hamlet (1601), Act 4, Scene 4

211 HAMLET Rightly to be great
Is not to stir without great argument,
But greatly to find quarrel in a straw
When honour's at the stake.
Hamlet (1601), Act 4, Scene 4

212 HAMLET Some craven scruple
Of thinking too precisely on th' event.
Hamlet (1601), Act 4, Scene 4

213 KING There's such divinity doth hedge a king
That treason can but peep to what it would.
Hamlet (1601), Act 4, Scene 5

214 KING When sorrows come, they come not single spies,
But in battalions!
Hamlet (1601), Act 4, Scene 5

215 OPHELIA There's rosemary, that's for remembrance; pray, love, remember: and there is pansies, that's for thoughts.
Hamlet (1601), Act 4, Scene 5

216 KING She is so conjunctive to my life and soul
That, as the star moves not but in his sphere,
I could not but by her.
Hamlet (1601), Act 4, Scene 7

217 LAERTES Too much of water hast thou, poor Ophelia,
And therefore I forbid my tears.
Referring to Ophelia's death by drowning. *Hamlet* (1601), Act 4, Scene 7

218 FIRST CLOWN What is he that builds stronger than either the mason, the shipwright, or the carpenter?
SECOND CLOWN The gallows-maker; for that frame outlives a thousand tenants.
Hamlet (1601), Act 5, Scene 1

219 GERTRUDE I thought thy bride-bed to have decked,
And not have strewed thy grave.
Hamlet (1601), Act 5, Scene 1

220 HAMLET Alas, poor Yorick! I knew him, Horatio: a fellow of infinite jest, of most excellent fancy.
Hamlet (1601), Act 5, Scene 1

221 HAMLET Imperious Caesar, dead and turn'd to clay,
Might stop a hole to keep the wind away.
Hamlet (1601), Act 5, Scene 1

222 HAMLET Let Hercules himself do what he may,
The cat will mew, and dog will have his day.
Hamlet (1601), Act 5, Scene 1

223 HAMLET Why may not that be the skull of a lawyer?
Where be his quiddities now, his quillets, his cases, his tenures, and his tricks?
Hamlet (1601), Act 5, Scene 1

224 LAERTES Now pile your dust upon the quick and dead
Till of this flat a mountain you have made
T'o'ertop old Pelion or the skyish head of blue Olympus.
Hamlet (1601), Act 5, Scene 1

225 AMBASSADOR The ears are senseless that should give us hearing.
To tell him his commandment is fulfilled,
That Rosencrantz and Guildenstern are dead.
Hamlet (1601), Act 5, Scene 2

226 FORTINBRAS For he was likely, had he been put on,
To have prov'd most royal.
Hamlet (1601), Act 5, Scene 2

227 HAMLET He that hath killed my King and whor'd my mother,
Popped in between th'election and my hopes.
Hamlet (1601), Act 5, Scene 2

228 HAMLET If thou didst ever hold me in thy heart,
Absent thee from felicity awhile,
And in this harsh world draw thy breath in pain,
To tell my story.
Hamlet (1601), Act 5, Scene 2

229 HAMLET I have shot my arrow o'er the house
And hurt my brother.
Hamlet (1601), Act 5, Scene 2

230 HAMLET There's a divinity that shapes our ends,
Rough-hew them how we will.
Hamlet (1601), Act 5, Scene 2

231 HAMLET The rest is silence.
Hamlet (1601), Act 5, Scene 2

232 HORATIO I am more antique Roman than a Dane.
Hamlet (1601), Act 5, Scene 2

233 HORATIO Now cracks a noble heart. Good night, sweet Prince,
And flights of angels sing thee to thy rest!
Hamlet (1601), Act 5, Scene 2

234 PRINCE HENRY If all the year were playing holidays,
To sport would be as tedious as to work.
Henry IV, Part 1 (1597), Act 1, Scene 2

235 PRINCE HENRY Falstaff sweats to death
And lards the lean earth as he walks along.
Henry IV, Part 1 (1597), Act 2, Scene 2

236 HOTSPUR Out of this nettle, danger, we pluck this flower, safety.
Henry IV, Part 1 (1597), Act 2, Scene 3

237 FALSTAFF Company, villainous company, hath been the spoil of me.
Henry IV, Part 1 (1597), Act 3, Scene 3

238 FALSTAFF I have more flesh than another man, and therefore more frailty.
Henry IV, Part 1 (1597), Act 3, Scene 3

239 HOTSPUR Greatness knows itself.
Henry IV, Part 1 (1597), Act 4, Scene 3

240 FALSTAFF Honour pricks me on. Yea, but how if honour prick me off when I come on? How then? Can honour set to a leg? No. Or an arm? No. Or take away the grief of a wound? No. Honour hath no skill in surgery, then? No. What is honour? A word. What is in that word? Honour. What is that honour? Air.
Henry IV, Part 1 (1597), Act 5, Scene 1

241 WORCESTER For mine own part, I could be well content
To entertain the lag-end of my life
With quiet hours.
Henry IV, Part 1 (1597), Act 5, Scene 1

242 HOTSPUR Now, Esperance! Percy! and set on.
Henry IV, Part 1 (1597), Act 5, Scene 2

243 HOTSPUR The time of life is short;
To spend that shortness basely were too long.
Henry IV, Part 1 (1597), Act 5, Scene 2

244 FALSTAFF Lord, Lord, how this world is given to lying! I grant you I was down and out of breath; and so was he; but we rose both at an instant, and fought a long hour by Shrewsbury clock.
Henry IV, Part 1 (1597), Act 5, Scene 4

245 FALSTAFF The better part of valour is discretion; in the which better part I have saved my life.
Henry IV, Part 1 (1597), Act 5, Scene 4

246 HOTSPUR But thoughts, the slaves of life, and life, time's fool,
And time, that takes survey of all the world,
Must have a stop.
Henry IV, Part 1 (1597), Act 5, Scene 4

247 PRINCE HENRY Fare thee well, great heart!
Ill-weav'd ambition, how much art thou shrunk!
When that this body did contain a spirit,
A kingdom for it was too small a bound;
But now two paces of the vilest earth
Is room enough: this earth, that bears thee dead,
Bears not alive so stout a gentleman.
Henry IV, Part 1 (1597), Act 5, Scene 4

248 PRINCE HENRY For my part, if a lie may do thee grace,
I'll gild it with the happiest terms I have.
Referring to Falstaff, whom he mistakenly believes has been killed in the battle. *Henry IV, Part 1* (1597), Act 5, Scene 4

249 CHIEF JUSTICE God send the prince a better companion!
FALSTAFF God send the companion a better prince! I cannot rid my hands of him.
Henry IV, Part 2 (1597), Act 1, Scene 2

250 FALSTAFF I am not only witty in myself, but the cause that wit is in other men. I do here walk before thee like a sow that hath overwhelm'd all her litter but one.
Henry IV, Part 2 (1597), Act 1, Scene 2

251 FALSTAFF I can get no remedy against this consumption of the purse; borrowing only lingers and lingers it out, but the disease is incurable.
Henry IV, Part 2 (1597), Act 1, Scene 2

252 LORD BARDOLPH When we mean to build,
We first survey the plot, then draw the model;
And when we see the figure of the house,
Then we must rate the cost of the erection;
Which if we find outweighs ability,
What do we then but draw anew the model
In fewer offices, or at last desist
To build at all?
Henry IV, Part 2 (1597), Act 1, Scene 3

253 HOSTESS He hath eaten me out of house and home.
Henry IV, Part 2 (1597), Act 2, Scene 1

254 POINS Is it not strange that desire should so many years outlive performance?
Henry IV, Part 2 (1597), Act 2, Scene 4

255 KING HENRY IV Uneasy lies the head that wears a crown.
Henry IV, Part 2 (1597), Act 3, Scene 1

256 KING HENRY IV O sleep, O gentle sleep,
Nature's soft nurse, how have I frighted thee,
That thou no more wilt weigh my eyelids down,
And steep my senses in forgetfulness?
Henry IV, Part 2 (1597), Act 3, Scene 1

257 FALSTAFF Care I for the limb, the thews, the stature, bulk, and big assemblance of a man! Give me the spirit.
Henry IV, Part 2 (1597), Act 3, Scene 2

258 FALSTAFF Lord, Lord! how subject we old men are to this vice of lying.
Henry IV, Part 2 (1597), Act 3, Scene 2

259 FEEBLE I care not; a man can die but once; we owe God a death.
Henry IV, Part 2 (1597), Act 3, Scene 2

260 KING HENRY IV Commit
The oldest sins the newest kind of ways.
Henry IV, Part 2 (1597), Act 4, Scene 5

261 KING HENRY IV Thy wish was father, Harry, to that thought.
Henry IV, Part 2 (1597), Act 4, Scene 5

262 NYM Though patience be a tired mare, yet she will plod.
Henry V (1599), Act 2, Scene 1

263 KING HENRY V If little faults, proceeding on distemper,
Shall not be wink'd at, how shall we stretch our eye
When capital crimes, chew'd, swallow'd, and digested,
Appear before us?
Henry V (1599), Act 2, Scene 2

264 PISTOL Trust none;
For oaths are straws, men's faiths are wafer-cakes,
And hold-fast is the only dog, my duck.
Henry V (1599), Act 2, Scene 3

265 HOSTESS His nose was as sharp as a pen, and 'a babbl'd of green fields.
Referring to Falstaff on his deathbed. *Henry V* (1599), Act 2, Scene 3

266 KING HENRY V But when the blast of war blows in our ears,
Then imitate the action of the tiger;
Stiffen the sinews, summon up the blood,
Disguise fair nature with hard-favoured rage;
Then lend the eye a terrible aspect.
Henry V (1599), Act 3, Scene 1

267 KING HENRY V Once more unto the breach, dear friends, once more;
Or close the wall up with our English dead.
Henry V (1599), Act 3, Scene 1

268 KING HENRY V The game's afoot:
Follow your spirit; and, upon this charge
Cry "God for Harry! England and Saint George!"
Henry V (1599), Act 3, Scene 1

269 BOY Men of few words are the best men.
Henry V (1599), Act 3, Scene 2

270 KING HENRY V Every subject's duty is the King's; but every subject's soul is his own.
Henry V (1599), Act 4, Scene 1

271 KING HENRY V I think the King is but a man as I am: the violet smells to him as it doth to me.
Henry V (1599), Act 4, Scene 1

272 KING HENRY V 'Tis not the balm, the sceptre and the ball,
The sword, the mace, the crown imperial,
The intertissued robe of gold and pearl,

The farced title running 'fore the king,
The throne he sits on, nor the tide of pomp
That beats upon the high shore of this world,
No, not all these, thrice-gorgeous ceremony,
Can sleep so soundly as the wretched slave,
Who with a body fill'd and vacant mind
Gets him to rest, cramm'd with distressful bread;
Never sees horrid night, the child of hell,
But, like a lackey, from the rise to set
Sweats in the eye of Phoebus, and all night
Sleeps in Elysium.
Henry V (1599), Act 4, Scene 1

273 KING HENRY V What infinite heart's ease
Must kings neglect, that private men enjoy!
And what have kings that privates have not too,
Save ceremony, save general ceremony?
Henry V (1599), Act 4, Scene 1

274 KING HENRY V Old men forget; yet all shall be forgot,
But he'll remember, with advantages,
What feats he did that day.
Henry V (1599), Act 4, Scene 3

275 KING HENRY V We few, we happy few, we band of brothers;
For he to-day that sheds his blood with me
Shall be my brother; be he ne'er so vile
This day shall gentle his condition:
And gentlemen in England, now a-bed
Shall think themselves accurs'd they were not here,
And hold their manhoods cheap whiles any speaks
That fought with us upon Saint Crispin's day.
Henry V (1599), Act 4, Scene 3

276 FLUELLEN There is occasions and causes why and wherefore in all things.
Henry V (1599), Act 5, Scene 1

277 CHORUS O for a Muse of fire, that would ascend
The brightest heaven of invention,
A kingdom for a stage, princes to act,
And monarchs to behold the swelling scene!
Henry V (1599), Prologue

278 CHORUS Can this cockpit hold
The vasty fields of France? or may we cram
Within this wooden O the very casques
That did affright the air at Agincourt?
Probably referring to the Globe Theatre. *Henry V* (1599), Prologue

279 NORFOLK Heat not a furnace for your foe so hot
That it do singe yourself. We may outrun
By violent swiftness that which we run at,
And lose by over-running.
Henry VIII (1613), Act 1, Scene 1

280 ANN BULLEN I would not be a queen
For all the world.
Henry VIII (1613), Act 2, Scene 3

281 WOLSEY A peace above all earthly dignities,
A still and quiet conscience.
Henry VIII (1613), Act 3, Scene 2

282 WOLSEY Cromwell, I charge thee, fling away ambition:
By that sin fell the angels; how can man then,
The image of his Maker, hope to win by't?
Love thyself last: cherish those hearts that hate thee;
Corruption wins not more than honesty.
Still in thy right hand carry gentle peace,
To silence envious tongues: be just, and fear not.
Let all the ends thou aim'st at be thy country's,
Thy God's, and truth's: then if thou fall'st O Cromwell!
Thou fall'st a blessed martyr.
Henry VIII (1613), Act 3, Scene 2

283 WOLSEY Farewell, a long farewell, to all my greatness! This is the state of man: to-day he puts forth
The tender leaves of hopes: to-morrow blossoms
And bears his blushing honours thick upon him;
The third day comes a frost, a killing frost,
And when he thinks, good easy man, full surely
His greatness is a-ripening, nips his root,
And then he falls, as I do.
Henry VIII (1613), Act 3, Scene 2

284 WOLSEY Had I but serv'd my God with half the zeal
I serv'd my King, he would not in mine age
Have left me naked to mine enemies.
Henry VIII (1613), Act 3, Scene 2

285 GRIFFITH Men's evil manners live in brass: their virtues
We write in water.
Henry VIII (1613), Act 4, Scene 2

286 SUFFOLK She's beautiful and therefore to be woo'd;
She is a woman therefore to be won.
Referring to his prisoner, Margaret of Anjou, who later married Henry VI. *Henry VI, Part 1* (1592), Act 5, Scene 3

287 BOLINGBROKE Deep night, dark night, the silent of the night,
The time of night when Troy was set on fire,
The time when screech-owls cry, and ban-dogs howl,
And spirits walk, and ghosts break up their graves;
That time best fits the work we have in hand.
Henry VI, Part 2 (1592), Act 1, Scene 4

288 DICK The first thing we do, let's kill all the lawyers.
Henry VI, Part 2 (1592), Act 4, Scene 2, l. 73

289 YORK O tiger's heart wrapp'd in a woman's hide!
Said to Margaret, Queen of England, who taunts him with the death of his sons. *Henry VI, Part 3* (1592), Act 1, Scene 4

290 KING HENRY VI Gives not the hawthorn bush a sweeter shade
To shepherds, looking on their silly sheep,
Than doth a rich embroider'd canopy
To kings that fear their subjects' treachery?
About to lose the battle and his crown. *Henry VI, Part 3* (1592), Act 2, Scene 5

291 KING HENRY VI O God! methinks it were a happy life,
To be no better than a homely swain;
To sit upon a hill, as I do now,
To carve out dials, quaintly, point by point,
Thereby to see the minutes how they run,
How many make the hour full complete;
How many hours bring about the day;
How many days will finish up the year;
How many years a mortal man may live.
About to lose the battle and his crown. *Henry VI, Part 3* (1592), Act 2, Scene 5

292 QUEEN MARGARET Peace! impudent and shameless Warwick, peace;
Proud setter up and puller down of kings.
He has persuaded the king of France to transfer his support from Henry to Edward IV. *Henry VI, Part 3* (1592), Act 3, Scene 3

293 GLOUCESTER Down, down to hell; and say I sent thee thither.
Gloucester, the future Richard III, after he has stabbed Henry VI to death. *Henry VI, Part 3* (1592), Act 5, Scene 6

294 GLOUCESTER Suspicion always haunts the guilty mind;
The thief doth fear each bush an officer.
To Henry VI, who senses his impending murder. *Henry VI, Part 3* (1592), Act 5, Scene 6

295 CAESAR Let me have men about me that are fat;
Sleek-headed men, and such as sleep o' nights.
Yond Cassius has a lean and hungry look;
He thinks too much. Such men are dangerous.
Julius Caesar (1599), Act 1, Scene 2

296 CASCA For mine own part, it was Greek to me.
Julius Caesar (1599), Act 1, Scene 2

297 CASSIUS Well, honour is the subject of my story.
I cannot tell what you and other men
Think of this life: but, for my single self,
I had as lief not be as live to be
In awe of such a thing as I myself.
Persuading Brutus of Caesar's overbearing power. *Julius Caesar* (1599), Act 1, Scene 2

298 CASSIUS Why, man, he doth bestride the narrow world
Like a Colossus; and we petty men
Walk under his huge legs, and peep about
To find ourselves dishonourable graves.
Men at some time are masters of their fates:
The fault, dear Brutus, is not in our stars,
But in ourselves that we are underlings.
Referring to Julius Caesar. *Julius Caesar* (1599), Act 1, Scene 2

299 SOOTHSAYER Beware the ides of March.
Said as a warning to Caesar, foreshadowing his murder. *Julius Caesar* (1599), Act 1, Scene 2

300 CASSIUS Cassius from bondage will deliver Cassius.
Referring to Caesar's power. *Julius Caesar* (1599), Act 1, Scene 3

301 BRUTUS 'Tis a common proof,
That lowliness is young ambition's ladder,
Whereto the climber-upward turns his face;
But when he once attains the upmost round,
He then unto the ladder turns his back,
Looks in the clouds, scorning the base degrees
By which he did ascend.
Persuading himself of Caesar's ambition. *Julius Caesar* (1599), Act 2, Scene 1

302 CAESAR Cowards die many times before their deaths:
The valiant never taste of death but once.
Dismissing his wife's fears for his life. *Julius Caesar* (1599), Act 2, Scene 2

303 CASSIUS Why, he that cuts off twenty years of life
Cuts off so many years of fearing death.
Commenting on the murder of Caesar. *Julius Caesar* (1599), Act 3, Scene 1

304 ANTONY O mighty Caesar! dost thou lie so low?
Are all thy conquests, glories, triumphs, spoils,
Shrunk to this little measure?
Looking on Caesar's corpse. *Julius Caesar* (1599), Act 3, Scene 1

305 CAESAR Et tu, Brute?
On seeing that Brutus, too, is one of his murderers. *Julius Caesar* (1599), Act 3, Scene 1

306 ANTONY Cry "Havoc!" and let slip the dogs of war.
Prophesying that the spirit of Caesar will return, with the goddess Ate at his side, to take revenge. *Julius Caesar* (1599), Act 3, Scene 1

307 ANTONY O, pardon me, thou bleeding piece of earth,
That I am meek and gentle with these butchers!
Thou art the ruins of the noblest man
That ever lived in the tide of times.
Referring to the murdered Caesar. *Julius Caesar* (1599), Act 3, Scene 1

308 ANTONY For I have neither wit, nor words, nor worth,
Action, nor utterance, nor the power of speech,
To stir men's blood; I only speak right on.
Julius Caesar (1599), Act 3, Scene 2

309 ANTONY Friends, Romans, countrymen, lend me your ears
I come to bury Caesar, not to praise him.
Julius Caesar (1599), Act 3, Scene 2

310 ANTONY If you have tears, prepare to shed them now.
Julius Caesar (1599), Act 3, Scene 2

311 ANTONY The evil that men do lives after them;
The good is oft interred with their bones.
Julius Caesar (1599), Act 3, Scene 2

312 ANTONY For Brutus is an honourable man;
So are they all, all honourable men.
Ironic explanation to the citizens of Rome for the assassination of Caesar. *Julius Caesar* (1599), Act 3, Scene 2

313 BRUTUS Not that I lov'd Caesar less, but that I lov'd Rome more.
Justifying to the citizens of Rome why he slew Caesar. *Julius Caesar* (1599), Act 3, Scene 2

314 ANTONY Ambition should be made of sterner stuff.
Referring to Caesar, who wept for the poor. *Julius Caesar* (1599), Act 3, Scene 2

315 CASSIUS A friend should bear his friend's infirmities,
But Brutus makes mine greater than they are.
Answering Brutus' accusation of corruption. *Julius Caesar* (1599), Act 4, Scene 3

316 BRUTUS There is a tide in the affairs of men
Which, taken at the flood, leads on to fortune;
Omitted, all the voyage of their life
Is bound in shallows and in miseries.
On such a full sea are we now afloat,
And we must take the current when it serves,
Or lose our ventures.
As Mark Antony gathers forces against him at Philippi. *Julius Caesar* (1599), Act 4, Scene 3

317 BRUTUS Speak to me what thou art.
GHOST Thy evil spirit, Brutus.
BRUTUS Why com'st thou?
GHOST To tell thee thou shalt see me at Philippi.
Caesar's ghost appears to Brutus. Brutus later commits suicide at Philippi, having been defeated in battle by Mark Antony and Gaius Octavius, who became Emperor Augustus. *Julius Caesar* (1599), Act 4, Scene 3

318 ANTONY His life was gentle; and the elements
So mix'd in him that Nature might stand up
And say to all the world "This was a man"!
On hearing that Brutus has killed himself. *Julius Caesar* (1599), Act 5, Scene 5

319 ANTONY This was the noblest Roman of them all.

All the conspirators save only he
Did that they did in envy of great Caesar.
On hearing that Brutus has killed himself. *Julius Caesar* (1599), Act 5, Scene 5

320 PHILIP THE BASTARD Sweet, sweet, sweet poison for the age's tooth.
King John (1591–98), Act 1, Scene 1

321 AUSTRIA Courage mounteth with occasion.
King John (1591–98), Act 2, Scene 1

322 PHILIP THE BASTARD Mad world! mad kings! mad composition.
King John (1591–98), Act 2, Scene 1

323 PHILIP THE BASTARD That smooth-fac'd gentleman, tickling Commodity,
Commodity, the bias of the world.
King John (1591–98), Act 2, Scene 1

324 PHILIP THE BASTARD Well, whiles I am a beggar, I will rail
And say there is no sin but to be rich;
And being rich, my virtue then shall be
To say there is no vice but beggary.
King John (1591–98), Act 2, Scene 1

325 PHILIP THE BASTARD Bell, book, and candle, shall not drive me back,
When gold and silver becks me to come on.
King John (1591–98), Act 3, Scene 3

326 LEWIS Life is as tedious as a twice-told tale
Vexing the dull ear of a drowsy man.
King John (1591–98), Act 3, Scene 4

327 KING JOHN How oft the sight of means to do ill deeds
Makes ill deeds done!
King John (1591–98), Act 4, Scene 2

328 SALISBURY To gild refined gold, to paint the lily,
To throw a perfume on the violet,
To smooth the ice, or add another hue
Unto the rainbow, or with taper-light
To seek the beauteous eye of heaven to garnish,
Is wasteful and ridiculous excess.
King John (1591–98), Act 4, Scene 2

329 ARTHUR Heaven take my soul, and England my bones.
King John (1591–98), Act 4, Scene 3

330 KING JOHN I beg cold comfort.
King John (1591–98), Act 5, Scene 7

331 CORDELIA I want that glib and oily art
To speak and purpose not; since what I well intend,
I'll do't before I speak.
King Lear (1605–06), Act 1, Scene 1

332 FRANCE Fairest Cordelia, that art most rich, being poor;
Most choice, forsaken; and most lov'd, despis'd!
King Lear (1605–06), Act 1, Scene 1

333 LEAR Nothing will come of nothing. Speak again.
King Lear (1605–06), Act 1, Scene 1

334 EDMUND This is the excellent foppery of the world, that, when we are sick in fortune, often the surfeit of our own behaviour, we make guilty of our disasters the sun, the moon, and stars.
King Lear (1605–06), Act 1, Scene 2

335 LEAR Dost thou call me fool, boy?
FOOL All thy other titles thou hast given away; that thou was born with.
King Lear (1605–06), Act 1, Scene 4

336 LEAR How sharper than a serpent's tooth it is
To have a thankless child!
King Lear (1605–06), Act 1, Scene 4

337 LEAR Ingratitude, thou marble-hearted fiend,
More hideous when thou show'st thee in a child
Than the sea-monster!
King Lear (1605–06), Act 1, Scene 4

338 KENT Thou whoreson zed! thou unnecessary letter!
King Lear (1605–06), Act 2, Scene 2

339 LEAR Down, thou climbing sorrow,
Thy element's below.
King Lear (1605–06), Act 2, Scene 4

340 LEAR O, reason not the need! Our basest beggars
Are in the poorest thing superfluous.
Allow not nature more than nature needs,
Man's life is cheap as beast's.
King Lear (1605–06), Act 2, Scene 4

341 LEAR Touch me with noble anger,
And let not women's weapons, water-drops,
Stain my man's cheeks! No, you unnatural hags,
I will have such revenges on you both
That all the world shall—I will do such things,—
What they are yet I know not,—but they shall be
The terrors of the earth. You think I'll weep;
No, I'll not weep:
I have full cause of weeping, but this heart
Shall break into a hundred thousand flaws
Or ere I'll weep. O fool! I shall go mad.
King Lear (1605–06), Act 2, Scene 4

342 LEAR Blow, winds, and crack your cheeks; rage, blow.
You cataracts and hurricanoes, spout
Till you have drench'd our steeples, drown'd the cocks.
King Lear (1605–06), Act 3, Scene 2

343 LEAR I am a man
More sinn'd against than sinning.
King Lear (1605–06), Act 3, Scene 2

344 LEAR Rumble thy bellyful! Spit, fire! Spout rain!
Nor rain, wind, thunder, fire, are my daughters:
I tax not you, you elements, with unkindness.
King Lear (1605–06), Act 3, Scene 2

345 LEAR The art of our necessities is strange,
That can make vile things precious.
King Lear (1605–06), Act 3, Scene 2

346 LEAR O! that way madness lies; let me shun that.
King Lear (1605–06), Act 3, Scene 4

347 LEAR Poor naked wretches, wheresoe'er you are,
That bide the pelting of this pitiless storm,
How shall your houseless heads and unfed sides,

Your loop'd and window'd raggedness, defend you
From seasons such as these?
King Lear (1605–06), Act 3, Scene 4

348 LEAR Take physic, pomp;
Expose thyself to feel what wretches feel.
King Lear (1605–06), Act 3, Scene 4

349 LEAR Thou art the thing itself; unaccommodated man is no more but such a poor, bare, forked animal as thou art. Off, off, you lendings! Come; unbutton here.
King Lear (1605–06), Act 3, Scene 4

350 FOOL He's mad that trusts in the tameness of a wolf, a horse's health, a boy's love, or a whore's oath.
King Lear (1605–06), Act 3, Scene 6

351 GLOUCESTER I am tied to the stake, and I must stand the course.
King Lear (1605–06), Act 3, Scene 7

352 CORNWALL Out vile jelly!
Where is thy lustre now?
Spoken before putting out Gloucester's remaining eye. *King Lear* (1605–06), Act 3, Scene 7

353 EDGAR The worst is not
So long as we can say "This is the worst".
King Lear (1605–06), Act 4, Scene 1

354 GLOUCESTER As flies to wanton boys are we to th' gods—
They kill us for their sport.
King Lear (1605–06), Act 4, Scene 1

355 ALBANY Wisdom and goodness to the vile seem vile;
Filths savour but themselves.
King Lear (1605–06), Act 4, Scene 2

356 ALBANY You are not worth the dust which the rude wind
Blows in your face.
King Lear (1605–06), Act 4, Scene 2

357 LEAR A man may see how this world goes with no eyes. Look with thine ears: see how yond justice rails upon yond simple thief. Hark, in thine ear: change places; and, handy-dandy, which is the justice, which is the thief?
King Lear (1605–06), Act 4, Scene 6

358 LEAR Ay, every inch a king.
King Lear (1605–06), Act 4, Scene 6

359 LEAR Get thee glass eyes,
And, like a scurvy politician, seem
To see the things thou dost not.
King Lear (1605–06), Act 4, Scene 6

360 LEAR The wren goes to't, and the small gilded fly
Does lecher in my sight.
King Lear (1605–06), Act 4, Scene 6

361 LEAR Thou rascal beadle, hold thy bloody hand!
Why dost thou lash that whore? Strip thine own back;
Thou hotly lust'st to use her in that kind
For which thou whipp'st her.
King Lear (1605–06), Act 4, Scene 6

362 LEAR Through tatter'd clothes small vices do appear;
Robes and furr'd gowns hide all.
King Lear (1605–06), Act 4, Scene 6

363 LEAR When we are born, we cry that we are come
To this great stage of fools.
King Lear (1605–06), Act 4, Scene 6

364 LEAR I am a very foolish, fond old man,
Fourscore and upward, not an hour more or less;
And, to deal plainly,
I fear I am not in my perfect mind.
King Lear (1605–06), Act 4, Scene 7

365 LEAR Thou art a soul in bliss; but I am bound
Upon a wheel of fire, that mine own tears
Do scald like molten lead.
On waking to find Cordelia at his bedside. *King Lear* (1605–06), Act 4, Scene 7

366 EDGAR Men must endure
Their going hence, even as their coming hither:
Ripeness is all.
King Lear (1605–06), Act 5, Scene 2

367 EDGAR The gods are just, and of our pleasant vices
Make instruments to plague us.
King Lear (1605–06), Act 5, Scene 3

368 EDGAR We that are young
Shall never see so much or live so long.
King Lear (1605–06), Act 5, Scene 3

369 EDMUND The wheel is come full circle.
King Lear (1605–06), Act 5, Scene 3

370 KENT Vex not his ghost: O! let him pass; he hates him
That would upon the rack of this tough world
Stretch him out longer.
King Lear (1605–06), Act 5, Scene 3

371 LEAR And my poor fool is hang'd! No, no, no life!
Why should a dog, a horse, a rat have life,
And thou no breath at all? Thou'lt come no more,
Never, never, never, never.
King Lear (1605–06), Act 5, Scene 3

372 LEAR Come, let's away to prison;
We two alone will sing like birds i' the cage:
When thou dost ask me blessing, I'll kneel down,
And ask of thee forgiveness: and we'll live,
And pray, and sing, and tell old tales, and laugh
At gilded butterflies, and hear poor rogues
Talk of court news; and we'll talk with them too,
Who loses, and who wins; who's in, who's out;
And take upon 's the mystery of things,
As if we were God's spies; and we'll wear out,
In a wall'd prison, packs and sets of great ones
That ebb and flow by the moon.
King Lear (1605–06), Act 5, Scene 3

373 LEAR Her voice was ever soft,
Gentle and low, an excellent thing in woman.
King Lear (1605–06), Act 5, Scene 3

374 BEROWNE At Christmas I no more desire a rose
Than wish a snow in May's newfangled shows.
Love's Labour's Lost (1595), Act 1, Scene 1

375 NATHANIEL He hath never fed of the dainties that are bred in

a book; he hath not eat paper, as it were; he hath not drunk ink; his intellect is not replenished.
Love's Labour's Lost (1595), Act 4, Scene 2

376 BEROWNE For where is any author in the world
Teaches such beauty as a woman's eye?
Learning is but an adjunct to oneself.
Love's Labour's Lost (1595), Act 4, Scene 3

377 ROSALINE A jest's prosperity lies in the ear
Of him that hears it, never in the tongue
Of him that makes it.
Love's Labour's Lost (1595), Act 5, Scene 2

378 WINTER When icicles hang by the wall,
And Dick the shepherd blows his nail,
And Tom bears logs into the hall,
And milk comes frozen home in pail,
When blood is nipp'd, and ways be foul,
Then nightly sings the staring owl:
"Tu-who;
Tu-whit, Tu-who"—A merry note.
While greasy Joan doth keel the pot.
Love's Labour's Lost (1595), Act 5, Scene 2

379 FIRST WITCH When shall we three meet again
In thunder, lightning, or in rain?
Macbeth (1606), Act 1, Scene 1

380 WITCHES Fair is foul, and foul is fair;
Hover through the fog and filthy air.
Macbeth (1606), Act 1, Scene 1

381 BANQUO Oftentimes, to win us to our harm,
The instruments of darkness tell us truths;
Win us with honest trifles, to betray's
In deepest consequence.
Macbeth (1606), Act 1, Scene 3

382 MACBETH Come what come may,
Time and the hour runs through the roughest day.
Macbeth (1606), Act 1, Scene 3

383 MACBETH So foul and fair a day I have not seen.
Macbeth (1606), Act 1, Scene 3

384 MACBETH The Thane of Cawdor lives; why do you dress me
In borrow'd robes?
Macbeth (1606), Act 1, Scene 3

385 MACBETH This supernatural soliciting
Cannot be ill; cannot be good. If ill,
Why hath it given me earnest of success,
Commencing in a truth? I am Thane of Cawdor:
If good, why do I yield to that suggestion
Whose horrid image doth unfix my hair
And make my seated heart knock at my ribs,
Against the use of nature? Present fears
Are less than horrible imaginings;
My thought, whose murder yet is but fantastical,
Shakes so my single state of man that function
Is smother'd in surmise, and nothing is
But what is not.
Macbeth (1606), Act 1, Scene 3

386 MALCOLM Nothing in his life
Became him like the leaving it: he died
As one that had been studied in his death
To throw away the dearest thing he ow'd
As 'twere a careless trifle.
Macbeth (1606), Act 1, Scene 4

387 LADY MACBETH The raven himself is hoarse
That croaks the fatal entrance of Duncan
Under my battlements.
Macbeth (1606), Act 1, Scene 5

388 LADY MACBETH Yet do I fear thy nature;
It is too full o' th' milk of human kindness
To catch the nearest way.
Macbeth (1606), Act 1, Scene 5

389 LADY MACBETH Your face, my thane, is as a book where men
May read strange matters. To beguile the time,
Look like the time; bear welcome in your eye,
Your hand, your tongue: look like the innocent flower,
But be the serpent under't.
Macbeth (1606), Act 1, Scene 5

390 LADY MACBETH I have given suck, and know
How tender 'tis to love the babe that milks me:
I would, while it was smiling in my face,
Have plucked my nipple from his boneless gums,
And dash'd the brains out, had I so sworn as you
Have done to this.
MACBETH If we should fail—
LADY MACBETH We fail!
But screw your courage to the sticking-place,
And we'll not fail.
Macbeth (1606), Act 1, Scene 7

391 MACBETH False face must hide what the false heart doth know.
Macbeth (1606), Act 1, Scene 7

392 MACBETH I dare do all that may become a man;
Who dares do more is none.
Macbeth (1606), Act 1, Scene 7

393 MACBETH If it were done when 'tis done, then 'twere well
It were done quickly.
Macbeth (1606), Act 1, Scene 7

394 MACBETH I have no spur
To prick the sides of my intent, but only
Vaulting ambition, which o'er-leaps itself,
And falls on th' other.
Macbeth (1606), Act 1, Scene 7

395 MACBETH That but this blow
Might be the be-all and the end-all here—
But here upon this bank and shoal of time—
We'd jump the life to come.
Macbeth (1606), Act 1, Scene 7

396 MACBETH Is this a dagger which I see before me,
The handle toward my hand? Come, let me clutch thee:
I have thee not, and yet I see thee still.
Macbeth (1606), Act 2, Scene 1

397 LADY MACBETH The attempt and not the deed,
Confounds us.
Macbeth (1606), Act 2, Scene 2

398 MACBETH I am afraid to think what I have done;
Look on't again I dare not.
LADY MACBETH Infirm of purpose!
Give me the daggers. The sleeping and the dead
Are but as pictures; 'tis the eye of childhood
That fears a painted devil. If he do bleed
I'll gild the faces of the grooms withal;
For it must seem their guilt.
Macbeth (1606), Act 2, Scene 2

399 MACBETH Methought I heard a voice cry, "Sleep no more!
Macbeth doth murder sleep," the innocent sleep,
Sleep that knits up the ravell'd sleave of care,
The death of each day's life, sore labour's bath,
Balm of hurt minds, great nature's second course,
Chief nourisher in life's feast.
Macbeth (1606), Act 2, Scene 2

400 LADY MACBETH Had he not resembled
My father as he slept I had done't.
Referring to Macbeth's killing of Duncan. *Macbeth* (1606), Act 2, Scene 2

401 PORTER It provokes the desire, but it takes away the performance. Therefore much drink may be said to be an equivocator with lecher.
Macbeth (1606), Act 2, Scene 3

402 LADY MACBETH Nought's had, all's spent,
Where our desire is got without content.
'Tis safer to be that which we destroy,
Than by destruction dwell in doubtful joy.
Macbeth (1606), Act 3, Scene 2

403 FIRST MURDERER The west yet glimmers with some streaks of day:
Now spurs the lated traveller apace
To gain the timely inn.
Macbeth (1606), Act 3, Scene 3

404 LADY MACBETH Stand not upon the order of your going,
But go at once.
Macbeth (1606), Act 3, Scene 4

405 MACBETH I am in blood
Stepp'd in so far that, should I wade no more,
Returning were as tedious as go o'er.
Macbeth (1606), Act 3, Scene 4

406 MACBETH I had else been perfect,
Whole as the marble, founded as the rock,
As broad and general as the casing air,
But now I am cabin'd, cribb'd, confin'd, bound in
To saucy doubts and fears.
Macbeth (1606), Act 3, Scene 4

407 SECOND APPARITION Be bloody bold, and resolute, laugh to scorn
The power of man, for none of woman born
Shall harm Macbeth.
Macbeth (1606), Act 4, Scene 1

408 SECOND WITCH Eye of newt, and toe of frog,
Wool of bat, and tongue of dog,
Adder's fork, and blind-worm's sting,
Lizard's leg, and howlet's wing,
For a charm of powerful trouble,
Like a hell-broth boil and bubble.
Macbeth (1606), Act 4, Scene 1

409 THIRD APPARITION Macbeth shall never vanquish'd be until
Great Birnam wood to high Dunsinane hill
Shall come against him.
Macbeth (1606), Act 4, Scene 1

410 LADY MACBETH Here's the smell of the blood still. All the perfumes of Arabia will not sweeten this little hand.
Macbeth (1606), Act 5, Scene 1

411 LADY MACBETH What's done cannot be undone. To bed, to bed, to bed.
Macbeth (1606), Act 5, Scene 1

412 LADY MACBETH Yet who would have thought the old man to have had so much blood in him?
Macbeth (1606), Act 5, Scene 1

413 LADY MACBETH Out, damned spot! out, I say!
Referring to the blood on her hands. *Macbeth* (1606), Act 5, Scene 1

414 ANGUS Those he commands move only in command,
Nothing in love; now does he feel his title
Hang loose about him, like a giant's robe
Upon a dwarfish thief.
Macbeth (1606), Act 5, Scene 2

415 MACBETH Bring me no more reports; let them fly all:
Till Birnam wood remove to Dunsinane
I cannot taint with fear.
Macbeth (1606), Act 5, Scene 3

416 MACBETH Canst thou not minister to a mind diseas'd,
Pluck from the memory a rooted sorrow,
Raze out the written troubles of the brain,
And with some sweet oblivious antidote
Cleanse the stuff'd bosom of that perilous stuff
Which weighs upon the heart?
DOCTOR Therein the patient
Must minister to himself.
MACBETH Throw physic to the dogs; I'll none of it.
Macbeth (1606), Act 5, Scene 3

417 MACBETH I have liv'd long enough.
My way of life
Is fall'n into the sear, the yellow leaf;
And that which should accompany old age,
As honour, love, obedience, troops of friends,
I must not look to have.
Macbeth (1606), Act 5, Scene 3

418 MACBETH Hang out our banners on the outward walls;
The cry is still, "They come"; our castle's strength
Will laugh a siege to scorn.
Macbeth (1606), Act 5, Scene 5

419 MACBETH I gin to be aweary of the sun,

And wish th' estate o' th' world were now undone.
Macbeth (1606), Act 5, Scene 5

420 MACBETH I have supp'd full with horrors.
Macbeth (1606), Act 5, Scene 5

421 MACBETH Tomorrow, and tomorrow, and tomorrow,
Creeps in this petty pace from day to day
To the last syllable of recorded time,
And all our yesterdays have lighted fools
The way to dusty death. Out, out, brief candle!
Life's but a walking shadow, a poor player,
That struts and frets his hour upon the stage,
And then is heard no more; it is a tale
Told by an idiot, full of sound and fury,
Signifying nothing.
Macbeth (1606), Act 5, Scene 5

422 MACBETH She should have died hereafter;
There would have been a time for such a word.
On hearing the news of his wife's death on the eve of battle. *Macbeth* (1606), Act 5, Scene 5

423 MACBETH I bear a charmed life, which must not yield
To one of woman born.
MACDUFF Despair thy charm;
And let the angel whom thou still hast serv'd
Tell thee Macduff was from his mother's womb
Untimely ripp'd.
Macbeth (1606), Act 5, Scene 8

424 MACBETH Lay on, Macduff;
And damn'd be him that first cries, "Hold, enough!"
Macbeth (1606), Act 5, Scene 8

425 DUKE VINCENTIO Liberty plucks justice by the nose.
Measure for Measure (1604), Act 1, Scene 3

426 ANGELO We must not make a scarecrow of the law,
Setting it up to fear the birds of prey,
And let it keep one shape, till custom make it
Their perch and not their terror.
Measure for Measure (1604), Act 2, Scene 1

427 ANGELO Condemn the fault and not the actor of it?
Measure for Measure (1604), Act 2, Scene 2

428 ANGELO Is this her fault or mine?
The tempter or the tempted, who sins most?
Measure for Measure (1604), Act 2, Scene 2

429 ANGELO O, it is excellent
To have a giant's strength! But it is tyrannous
To use it like a giant.
Measure for Measure (1604), Act 2, Scene 2

430 ISABELLA But man, proud man
Dress'd in a little brief authority,
Most ignorant of what he's most assur'd,
His glassy essence, like an angry ape,
Plays such fantastic tricks before high heaven
As makes the angels weep.
Measure for Measure (1604), Act 2, Scene 2

431 ISABELLA That in the captain's but a choleric word
Which in the soldier is flat blasphemy.
Measure for Measure (1604), Act 2, Scene 2

432 CLAUDIO Ay, but to die, and go we know not where;
To lie in cold obstruction, and to rot;
This sensible warm motion to become
A kneaded clod; and the delighted spirit
To bathe in fiery floods or to reside
In thrilling region of thick-ribbed ice.
Measure for Measure (1604), Act 3, Scene 1

433 CLAUDIO If I must die,
I will encounter darkness as a bride,
And hug it in mine arms.
Measure for Measure (1604), Act 3, Scene 1

434 CLAUDIO The miserable have no other medicine
But only hope.
Measure for Measure (1604), Act 3, Scene 1

435 ISABELLA Dar'st thou die?
The sense of death is most in apprehension,
And the poor beetle, that we tread upon,
In corporal sufferance finds a pang as great
As when a giant dies.
Measure for Measure (1604), Act 3, Scene 1

436 LUCIO I am a kind of burr; I shall stick.
Measure for Measure (1604), Act 4, Scene 3

437 DUKE VINCENTIO Haste still pays haste, and leisure answers leisure;
Like doth quit like, and Measure still for Measure.
Measure for Measure (1604), Act 5, Scene 1

438 MARIANA They say best men are moulded out of faults
And, for the most, become much more the better
For being a little bad.
Measure for Measure (1604), Act 5, Scene 1

439 BEATRICE He is a very valiant trencher-man.
Much Ado About Nothing (1598–99), Act 1, Scene 1

440 BEATRICE I wonder that you will still be talking, Signior Benedick: nobody marks you.
BENEDICK
What! my dear Lady Disdain, are you yet living?
Much Ado About Nothing (1598–99), Act 1, Scene 1

441 BENEDICK Would you have me speak after my custom, as being a professed tyrant to their sex?
Much Ado About Nothing (1598–99), Act 1, Scene 1

442 LEONATO A victory is twice itself when the achiever brings home full numbers.
Much Ado About Nothing (1598–99), Act 1, Scene 1

443 MESSENGER I see, lady, the gentleman is not in your books.
Much Ado About Nothing (1598–99), Act 1, Scene 1

444 BEATRICE Speak, cousin, or, if you cannot, stop his mouth with a kiss.
Much Ado About Nothing (1598–99), Act 2, Scene 1

445 BEATRICE Would it not grieve a woman to be over-mastered with a piece of valiant dust? to make an account of her life to a clod of wayward marl?
Much Ado About Nothing (1598–99), Act 2, Scene 1

446 BENEDICK She speaks poniards, and every word stabs: if her

breath were as terrible as her terminations, there were no living near her; she would infect to the north star.
Much Ado About Nothing (1598–99), Act 2, Scene 1

447 CLAUDIO Friendship is constant in all other things
Save in the office and affairs of love.
Much Ado About Nothing (1598–99), Act 2, Scene 1

448 CLAUDIO Silence is the perfectest herald of joy: I were but little happy if I could say how much.
Much Ado About Nothing (1598–99), Act 2, Scene 1

449 BALTHASAR Sigh no more, ladies, sigh no more,
Men were deceivers ever;
One foot in sea, and one on shore,
To one thing constant never.
Then sigh not so,
But let them go,
And be you blithe and bonny,
Converting all your sounds of woe
Into Hey nonny, nonny.
Much Ado About Nothing (1598–99), Act 2, Scene 3

450 BENEDICK Doth not the appetite alter? A man loves the meat in his youth that he cannot endure in his age.
Much Ado About Nothing (1598–99), Act 2, Scene 3

451 BENEDICK The world must be peopled. When I said I would die a bachelor, I did not think I should live till I were married.
Much Ado About Nothing (1598–99), Act 2, Scene 3

452 BEATRICE Contempt, farewell! and maiden pride, adieu!
No glory lives behind the back of such.
And, Benedick, love on; I will requite thee,
Taming my wild heart to thy loving hand.
Much Ado About Nothing (1598–99), Act 3, Scene 1

453 HERO Disdain and scorn ride sparkling in her eyes.
Much Ado About Nothing (1598–99), Act 3, Scene 1

454 DOGBERRY To be a well-favoured man is the gift of fortune; but to write and read comes by nature.
Much Ado About Nothing (1598–99), Act 3, Scene 3

455 DOGBERRY Comparisons are odorous.
Much Ado About Nothing (1598–99), Act 3, Scene 5

456 DOGBERRY Our watch, sir, have, indeed comprehended two aspicious persons.
Much Ado About Nothing (1598–99), Act 3, Scene 5

457 VERGES I thank God I am as honest as any man living that is an old man and no honester than I.
Much Ado About Nothing (1598–99), Act 3, Scene 5

458 BENEDICK I do love nothing in the world so well as you; is not that strange?
Much Ado About Nothing (1598–99), Act 4, Scene 1

459 DOGBERRY Write down that they hope they serve God; and write God first; for God defend but God should go before such villains!
Much Ado About Nothing (1598–99), Act 4, Scene 2

460 BENEDICK In a false quarrel there is no true valour.
Much Ado About Nothing (1598–99), Act 5, Scene 1

461 LEONATO For there was never yet philosopher
That could endure the toothache patiently.
Much Ado About Nothing (1598–99), Act 5, Scene 1

462 LEONATO Patch grief with proverbs.
Much Ado About Nothing (1598–99), Act 5, Scene 1

463 BENEDICK No, I was not born under a rhyming planet.
Much Ado About Nothing (1598–99), Act 5, Scene 2

464 IAGO But I will wear my heart upon my sleeve
For daws to peck at: I am not what I am.
Othello (1602–04), Act 1, Scene 1

465 IAGO Even now, now, very now, an old black ram
Is tupping your white ewe.
Othello (1602–04), Act 1, Scene 1

466 IAGO In the following him, I follow but myself.
Othello (1602–04), Act 1, Scene 1

467 IAGO Your daughter and the Moor are now making the beast with two backs.
Othello (1602–04), Act 1, Scene 1

468 OTHELLO Keep up your bright swords, for the dew will rust them.
Othello (1602–04), Act 1, Scene 2

469 BRABANTIO But words are words; I never yet did hear
That the bruis'd heart was pierced through the ear.
Othello (1602–04), Act 1, Scene 3

470 DUKE OF VENICE The robb'd that smiles steals something from the thief.
Othello (1602–04), Act 1, Scene 3

471 DUKE OF VENICE To mourn a mischief that is past and gone
Is the next way to draw new mischief on.
Othello (1602–04), Act 1, Scene 3

472 IAGO Put money in thy purse.
Othello (1602–04), Act 1, Scene 3

473 IAGO There are many events in the womb of time which will be delivered.
Othello (1602–04), Act 1, Scene 3

474 IAGO Virtue! a fig! 'tis in ourselves that we are thus, or thus. Our bodies are our gardens, to the which our wills are gardeners.
Othello (1602–04), Act 1, Scene 3

475 OTHELLO She lov'd me for the dangers I had pass'd,
And I lov'd her that she did pity them.
This only is the witchcraft I have us'd.
Othello (1602–04), Act 1, Scene 3

476 DESDEMONA I am not merry, but I do beguile
The thing I am by seeming otherwise.
Othello (1602–04), Act 2, Scene 1

477 IAGO For I am nothing if not critical.
Othello (1602–04), Act 2, Scene 1

478 IAGO To suckle fools and chronicle small beer.
Othello (1602–04), Act 2, Scene 1

479 OTHELLO If it were now to die,

'Twere now to be most happy, for I fear
My soul hath her content so absolute
That not another comfort like to this
Succeeds in unknown fate.
DESDEMONA The heavens forbid
But that our loves and comforts should increase
Even as our days do grow!
Othello (1602–04), Act 2, Scene 1

480 CASSIO Out great Captain's Captain.
Referring to Othello's wife, Desdemona. *Othello* (1602–04), Act 2, Scene 1

481 CASSIO Reputation, reputation, reputation!
O, I have lost my reputation! I have lost the immortal part of myself, and what remains is bestial.
Othello (1602–04), Act 2, Scene 3

482 IAGO Come, come; good wine is a good familiar creature if it be well used; exclaim no more against it.
Othello (1602–04), Act 2, Scene 3

483 IAGO Good name in man and woman, dear my lord,
Is the immediate jewel of their souls:
Who steals my purse steals trash; 'tis something, nothing;
'Twas mine, 'tis his, and has been slave to thousands;
But he that filches from me my good name
Robs me of that which not enriches him
And makes me poor indeed.
Othello (1602–04), Act 3, Scene 3

484 IAGO O, beware, my lord, of jealousy;
It is the green-ey'd monster which doth mock
The meat it feeds on.
Othello (1602–04), Act 3, Scene 3

485 IAGO O wretched fool!
That liv'st to make thine honesty a vice.
O monstrous world! Take note, take note, O world!
To be direct and honest is not safe.
Othello (1602–04), Act 3, Scene 3

486 OTHELLO By heaven, he echoes me,
As if there were some monster in his thought
Too hideous to be shown.
Othello (1602–04), Act 3, Scene 3

487 OTHELLO Farewell the neighing steed and the shrill trump,
The spirit-stirring drum, th'ear piercing fife,
The royal banner, and all quality,
Pride, pomp, and circumstance, of glorious war!
Othello (1602–04), Act 3, Scene 3

488 OTHELLO He that is robb'd, not wanting what is stol'n,
Let him not know't, and he's not robb'd at all.
Othello (1602–04), Act 3, Scene 3

489 OTHELLO If she be false, O! then heaven mocks itself.
I'll not believe it.
Othello (1602–04), Act 3, Scene 3

490 OTHELLO I swear 'tis better to be much abused
Than but to know 't a little.
Othello (1602–04), Act 3, Scene 3

491 OTHELLO O curse of marriage,
That we can call these delicate creatures ours,
And not their appetites! I had rather be a toad,
And live upon the vapour of a dungeon,
Than keep a corner in the thing I love
For others' uses.
Othello (1602–04), Act 3, Scene 3

492 OTHELLO Excellent wretch! Perdition catch my soul
But I do love thee! and when I love thee not,
Chaos is come again.
Referring to Desdemona. *Othello* (1602–04), Act 3, Scene 3

493 EMILIA Jealous souls will not be answer'd so;
They are not ever jealous for the cause,
But jealous for they are jealous.
Othello (1602–04), Act 3, Scene 4

494 EMILIA Who would not make her husband a cuckold to make him a monarch?
Othello (1602–04), Act 4, Scene 3

495 IAGO This is the night
That either makes me or fordoes me quite.
Othello (1602–04), Act 5, Scene 1

496 IAGO He hath a daily beauty in his life.
That makes me ugly.
Referring to Cassio, Othello's lieutenant, of whose preferment Iago is jealous. *Othello* (1602–04), Act 5, Scene 1

497 EMILIA O! the more angel she,
And you the blacker devil.
Othello (1602–04), Act 5, Scene 2

498 OTHELLO Be not afraid, though you do see me weapon'd;
Here is my journey's end, here is my butt,
And very sea-mark of my utmost sail.
Othello (1602–04), Act 5, Scene 2

499 OTHELLO I kiss'd thee ere I kill'd thee, no way but this,
Killing myself to die upon a kiss.
Othello (1602–04), Act 5, Scene 2

500 OTHELLO Put out the light, and then put out the light.
If I quench thee, thou flaming minister,
I can again thy former light restore,
Should I repent me; but once put out thy light,
Thou cunning'st pattern of excelling nature,
I know not where is that Promethean heat
That can thy light relume.
Othello (1602–04), Act 5, Scene 2

501 OTHELLO Set you down this;
And say besides, that in Aleppo once,
Where a malignant and a turban'd Turk
Beat a Venetian and traduc'd the state,
I took by the throat the circumcised dog,
And smote him thus.
Othello (1602–04), Act 5, Scene 2

502 OTHELLO Then must you speak
Of one that lov'd not wisely, but too well;
Of one not easily jealous, but, being wrought,
Perplexed in the extreme; of one whose hand,
Like the base Indian, threw a pearl away
Richer than all his tribe.
Othello (1602–04), Act 5, Scene 2

503 OTHELLO This sorrow's heavenly,
It strikes where it doth love.
Othello (1602–04), Act 5, Scene 2

504 PERICLES Few love to hear the sins they love to act.
Pericles (1606–08), Act 1, Scene 1

505 3RD FISHERMAN Master, I marvel how the fishes live in the sea.
1ST FISHERMAN Why, as men do a-land—the great ones eat up the little ones.
Pericles (1606–08), Act 2, Scene 1

506 PERICLES O you gods!
Why do you make us love your goodly gifts
And snatch them straight away?
Pericles (1606–08), Act 3, Scene 1

507 KING RICHARD II We were not born to sue, but to command.
Richard II (1595), Act 1, Scene 1

508 MOWBRAY The purest treasure mortal times afford
Is spotless reputation; that away,
Men are but gilded loam or painted clay.
Richard II (1595), Act 1, Scene 1

509 BOLINGBROKE How long a time lies in one little word!
Four lagging winters and four wanton springs
End in a word; such is the breath of kings.
Richard II (1595), Act 1, Scene 3

510 GAUNT Teach thy necessity to reason thus:
There is no virtue like necessity.
Richard II (1595), Act 1, Scene 3

511 GAUNT Things sweet to taste prove in digestion sour.
Richard II (1595), Act 1, Scene 3

512 GAUNT This royal throne of kings, this sceptred isle,
This earth of majesty, this seat of Mars,
This other Eden, demi-paradise,
This fortress built by Nature for herself
Against infection and the hand of war,
This happy breed of men, this little world,
This precious stone set in the silver sea,
Which serves it in the office of a wall,
Or as a moat defensive to a house,
Against the envy of less happier lands;
This blessed plot, this earth, this realm, this England,
This nurse, this teeming womb of royal kings,
Fear'd by their breed, and famous by their birth,
Renowned for their deeds as far from home,
For Christian service and true chivalry,
As is the sepulchre in stubborn Jewry
Of the world's ransom, blessed Mary's Son.
Richard II (1595), Act 2, Scene 1

513 BOLINGBROKE I count myself in nothing else so happy
As in a soul remembering my good friends.
Richard II (1595), Act 2, Scene 3

514 BOLINGBROKE Eating the bitter bread of banishment.
Richard II (1595), Act 3, Scene 1

515 KING RICHARD II For God's sake let us sit upon the ground
And tell sad stories of the death of kings:
How some have been depos'd, some slain in war,
Some haunted by the ghosts they have depos'd,
Some poison'd by their wives, some sleeping kill'd,
All murder'd—for within the hollow crown
That rounds the mortal temples of a king
Keeps Death his court.
Richard II (1595), Act 3, Scene 2

516 KING RICHARD II Not all the water in the rough rude sea
Can wash the balm from an anointed king;
The breath of worldly men cannot depose
The deputy elected by the Lord.
Richard II (1595), Act 3, Scene 2

517 KING RICHARD II O villains, vipers, damn'd without redemption!
Dogs, easily won to fawn on any man!
Snakes, in my heart-blood warm'd, that sting my heart!
Three Judases, each one thrice worse than Judas!
Would they make peace? terrible hell make war
Upon their spotted souls for this offence!
Richard II (1595), Act 3, Scene 2

518 KING RICHARD II The worst is death, and death will have his day.
Richard II (1595), Act 3, Scene 2

519 SALISBURY O, call back yesterday, bid time return.
Richard II (1595), Act 3, Scene 2

520 KING RICHARD II Mine eyes are full of tears, I cannot see:
And yet salt water blinds them not so much
But they can see a sort of traitors here.
Nay, if I turn my eyes upon myself,
I find myself a traitor with the rest.
Richard II (1595), Act 4, Scene 1

521 KING RICHARD II You may my glories and my state depose,
But not my griefs; still am I king of those.
Richard II (1595), Act 4, Scene 1

522 KING RICHARD II I am sworn brother, sweet,
To grim Necessity, and he and I
Will keep a league till death.
Richard II (1595), Act 5, Scene 1

523 KING RICHARD II How sour sweet music is
When time is broke and no proportion kept!
So is it in the music of men's lives.
Richard II (1595), Act 5, Scene 5

524 KING RICHARD II I wasted time, and now doth time waste me.
Richard II (1595), Act 5, Scene 5

525 GLOUCESTER And therefore, since I cannot prove a lover,
To entertain these fair well-spoken days,
I am determined to prove a villain,
And hate the idle pleasures of these days.
Richard III (1591), Act 1, Scene 1

526 GLOUCESTER Grim-visag'd war hath smooth'd his wrinkl'd front;
And now, instead of mounting barbed steeds,
To fright the souls of fearful adversaries,—
He capers nimbly in a lady's chamber
To the lascivious pleasing of a lute.
But I, that am not shap'd for sportive tricks,

Nor made to court an amorous looking-glass;
I, that am rudely stamp'd, and want love's majesty
To strut before a wanton ambling nymph;
I, that am curtail'd of this fair proportion,
Cheated of feature by dissembling nature,
Deform'd, unfinish'd, sent before my time
Into this breathing world, scarce half made up,
And that so lamely and unfashionable
That dogs bark at me, as I halt by them;
Why, I, in this weak piping time of peace,
Have no delight to pass away the time.
Richard III (1591), Act 1, Scene 1

527 GLOUCESTER Now is the winter of our discontent
Made glorious summer by this sun of York.
Richard III (1591), Act 1, Scene 1

528 GLOUCESTER Teach not thy lip such scorn, for it was made
For kissing, lady, not for such contempt.
Richard III (1591), Act 1, Scene 2

529 GLOUCESTER Was ever woman in this humour woo'd?
Was ever woman in this humour won?
Referring to his wooing of Lady Anne, widow of Edward IV, as she mourns King Henry VI, her father-in-law. *Richard III* (1591), Act 1, Scene 2

530 GLOUCESTER And thus I clothe my naked villany
With odd old ends stol'n forth of holy writ,
And seem a saint when most I play the devil.
Richard III (1591), Act 1, Scene 3

531 QUEEN ELIZABETH An honest tale speeds best being plainly told.
Richard III (1591), Act 4, Scene 4

532 KING RICHARD III By the apostle Paul, shadows to-night
Have struck more terror to the soul of Richard
Than can the substance of ten thousand soldiers.
Richard III (1591), Act 5, Scene 3

533 KING RICHARD III I shall despair. There is no creature loves me;
And if I die, no soul will pity me:
Nay, wherefore should they, since that I myself
Find in myself no pity to myself?
Richard III (1591), Act 5, Scene 3

534 KING RICHARD III My conscience hath a thousand several tongues,
And every tongue brings in several tale,
And every tale condemns me for a villain.
Richard III (1591), Act 5, Scene 3

535 KING RICHARD III A horse! a horse ! my kingdom for a horse.
Richard III (1591), Act 5, Scene 4

536 KING RICHARD III I have set my life upon a cast,
And I will stand the hazard of the die.
Richard III (1591), Act 5, Scene 4

537 MERCUTIO O! then, I see Queen Mab hath been with you.
She is the fairies' midwife...
And in this state she gallops night by night
Through lovers' brains, and then they dream of love.
Romeo and Juliet (1595), Act 1, Scene 4

538 ROMEO O! she doth teach the torches to burn bright
It seems she hangs upon the cheek of night
Like a rich jewel in an Ethiop's ear;
Beauty too rich for use, for earth too dear.
Romeo and Juliet (1595), Act 1, Scene 5

539 JULIET My only love sprung from my only hate!
Too early seen unknown, and known too late!
Referring to Romeo, a Montague, and the enmity between the house of Montague and the house of Capulet, to which Juliet belongs. *Romeo and Juliet* (1595), Act 1, Scene 5

540 JULIET Good night, good night! Parting is such sweet sorrow
That I shall say good night till it be morrow.
Romeo and Juliet (1595), Act 2, Scene 2

541 JULIET My bounty is as boundless as the sea,
My love as deep; the more I give to thee,
The more I have, for both are infinite.
Romeo and Juliet (1595), Act 2, Scene 2

542 JULIET O Romeo, Romeo! wherefore art thou Romeo?
Romeo and Juliet (1595), Act 2, Scene 2

543 JULIET O, swear not by the moon, th' inconstant moon,
That monthly changes in her circled orb,
Lest that thy love prove likewise variable.
Romeo and Juliet (1595), Act 2, Scene 2

544 ROMEO He jests at scars, that never felt a wound.
But, soft! what light through yonder window breaks?
It is the east, and Juliet is the sun.
Romeo and Juliet (1595), Act 2, Scene 2

545 ROMEO It is my lady; O! it is my love;
O! that she knew she were.
Romeo and Juliet (1595), Act 2, Scene 2

546 ROMEO Love goes toward love, as schoolboys from their books;
But love from love, toward school with heavy looks.
Romeo and Juliet (1595), Act 2, Scene 2

547 ROMEO See! how she leans her cheek upon her hand:
O! that I were a glove upon that hand,
That I might touch that cheek.
Romeo and Juliet (1595), Act 2, Scene 2

548 ROMEO What's in a name? That which we call a rose
By any other name would smell as sweet.
Romeo and Juliet (1595), Act 2, Scene 2

549 FRIAR LAWRENCE Wisely and slow; they stumble that run fast.
Romeo and Juliet (1595), Act 2, Scene 3

550 FRIAR LAWRENCE Therefore love moderately: long love doth so;
Too swift arrives as tardy as too slow.
Romeo and Juliet (1595), Act 2, Scene 6

551 ROMEO O! I am Fortune's fool.
Romeo and Juliet (1595), Act 3, Scene 1

552 MERCUTIO A plague o' both your houses!
They have made worms' meat of me.
Fatally wounded in a street brawl, Mercutio curses the two noble families—the Montagues (Romeo's family) and the Capulets (Juliet's family)—whose enmity lies at the root of the dramatic action and is the direct cause of his death. *Romeo and Juliet* (1595), Act 3, Scene 1

553 JULIET Gallop apace, you fiery-footed steeds,
Towards Phoebus' lodging; such a waggoner
As Phaethon would whip you to the west,
And bring in cloudy night immediately.

Spread thy close curtain, love-performing night!
That runaway's eyes may wink, and Romeo
Leap to these arms, untalk'd of and unseen!
Lovers can see to do their amorous rites
By their own beauties; or, if love be blind,
It best agrees with night. Come, civil night,
Thou sober-suited matron, all in black.
Romeo and Juliet (1595), Act 3, Scene 2

554 JULIET Give me my Romeo: and, when he shall die,
Take him and cut him out in little stars,
And he will make the face of heaven so fine
That all the world will be in love with night,
And pay no worship to the garish sun.
Romeo and Juliet (1595), Act 3, Scene 2

555 CAPULET Thank me no thankings, nor proud me no prouds.
Romeo and Juliet (1595), Act 3, Scene 5

556 ROMEO Night's candles are burnt out, and jocund day
Stands tiptoe on the misty mountain tops.
Romeo and Juliet (1595), Act 3, Scene 5

557 SECOND SERVANT 'Tis an ill cook that cannot lick his own fingers.
Romeo and Juliet (1595), Act 4, Scene 2

558 PRINCE For never was a story of more woe
Than this of Juliet and her Romeo.
Romeo and Juliet (1595), Act 5, Scene 3

559 PROLOGUE From forth the fatal loins of these two foes
A pair of star-cross'd lovers take their life.
Romeo and Juliet (1595), Prologue

560 From fairest creatures we desire increase,
That thereby beauty's rose might never die.
Sonnet 1 (1609)

561 When forty winters shall besiege thy brow,
And dig deep trenches in thy beauty's field.
Sonnet 2 (1609)

562 Thou art thy mother's glass, and she in thee
Calls back the lovely April of her prime.
Sonnet 3 (1609)

563 Music to hear, why hear'st thou music sadly?
Sweets with sweets war not, joy delights in joy.
Sonnet 8 (1609)

564 If I could write the beauty of your eyes
And in fresh numbers number all your graces,
The age to come would say, "This poet lies;
Such heavenly touches ne'er touched earthly faces."
Sonnet 17 (1609)

565 Shall I compare thee to a summer's day?
Thou art more lovely and more temperate.
Rough winds do shake the darling buds of May,
And summer's lease hath all too short a date.
Sonnet 18 (1609)

566 But thy eternal summer shall not fade,
Nor lose possession of that fair thou ow'st,
Nor shall death brag thou wander'st in his shade,
When in eternal lines to time thou grow'st;
So long as men can breathe, or eyes can see,
So long lives this, and this gives life to thee.
Referring to poetry. Sonnet 18 (1609)

567 O, learn to read what silent love hath writ!
To hear with eyes belongs to love's fine wit.
Sonnet 23 (1609)

568 For thy sweet love remembered such wealth brings
That then I scorn to change my state with kings'.
Sonnet 29 (1609)

569 When in disgrace with fortune and men's eyes
I all alone beweep my outcast state,
And trouble deaf heaven with my bootless cries,
And look upon myself, and curse my fate,
Wishing me like to one more rich in hope
Featur'd like him, like him with friends possess'd,
Desiring this man's art, and that man's scope,
With what I most enjoy contented least.
Sonnet 29 (1609)

570 When to the sessions of sweet silent thought
I summon up remembrance of things past,
I sigh the lack of many a thing I sought,
And with old woes new wail my dear time's waste.
Sonnet 30 (1609)

571 Full many a glorious morning have I seen
Flatter the mountain-tops with sovereign eye.
Sonnet 33 (1609)

572 Roses have thorns, and silver fountains mud;
Clouds and eclipses stain both moon and sun,
And loathsome canker lives in sweetest bud.
All men make faults.
Sonnet 35 (1609)

573 Not marble, nor the gilded monuments
Of princes, shall outlive this powerful rhyme.
Sonnet 55 (1609)

574 So true a fool is love that in your will, Though you do anything, he thinks no ill.
Sonnet 57 (1609)

575 Like as the waves make towards the pebbled shore,
So do our minutes hasten to their end.
Sonnet 60 (1609)

576 That time of year thou mayst in me behold
When yellow leaves, or none, or few, do hang
Upon those boughs which shake against the cold,
Bare ruin'd choirs, where late the sweet birds sang.
"Choirs" refers to the choir stalls in an abbey stripped of its precious lead roof after the dissolution of the monasteries (1533). Sonnet 73 (1609)

577 Time's thievish progress to eternity.
Sonnet 77 (1609)

578 Farewell! thou art too dear for my possessing,
And like enough thou know'st thy estimate:
The charter of thy worth gives thee releasing;
My bonds in thee are all determinate.
Sonnet 87 (1609)

579 For sweetest things turn sourest by their deeds:
Lilies that fester smell far worse than weeds.
Sonnet 94 (1609)

580 That is my home of love: if I have rang'd,
Like him that travels, I return again.
Sonnet 109 (1609)

581 Let me not to the marriage of true minds
Admit impediments. Love is not love
Which alters when it alteration finds,
Or bends with the remover to remove.
O, no! it is an ever-fixed mark,
That looks on tempests and is never shaken.
Sonnet 116 (1609)

582 Love alters not with his brief hours and weeks,
But bears it out even to the edge of doom.
If this be error, and upon me prov'd,
I never writ, nor no man ever lov'd.
Sonnet 116 (1609)

583 Th' expense of spirit in a waste of shame
Is lust in action; and till action, lust
Is perjur'd, murd'rous, bloody, full of blame,
Savage, extreme, rude, cruel, not to trust;
Enjoy'd no sooner but despised straight.
Sonnet 129 (1609)

584 A bliss in proof and proved, a very woe;
Before, a joy proposed; behind a dream.
All this the world well knows, yet none knows well
To shun the heaven that leads men to this hell.
Referring to love. Sonnet 129 (1609)

585 My mistress' eyes are nothing like the sun;
Coral is far more red than her lips' red.
Sonnet 130 (1609)

586 When my love swears that she is made of truth,
I do believe her, though I know she lies.
Sonnet 138 (1609)

587 Two loves I have, of comfort and despair,
Which like two spirits do suggest me still;
The better angel is a man right fair,
The worser spirit a woman colour'd ill.
Sonnet 144 (1609)

588 Poor soul, the centre of my sinful earth,
Fool'd by these rebel powers that thee array,
Why dost thou pine within and suffer dearth,
Painting thy outward walls so costly gay!
Why so large cost, having so short a lease,
Dost thou upon thy fading mansion spend?
Sonnet 146 (1609)

589 For I have sworn thee fair, and thought thee bright,
Who art as black as hell, as dark as night.
Sonnet 147 (1609)

590 DROMIO Returned so soon! rather approach'd too late.
The capon burns, the pig falls from the spit;
The clock hath strucken twelve upon the bell
My mistress made it one upon my cheek;
She is so hot because the meat is cold,
The meat is cold because you have not come home,
You come not home because you have no stomach,
You have no stomach, having broke your fast;
But we, that know what 'tis to fast and pray,
Are penitent for your default to-day.
The Comedy of Errors (1594), Act 1, Scene 2

591 LUCIANA A man is master of his liberty
Time is their master, and when they see time,
They'll go or come.
The Comedy of Errors (1594), Act 2, Scene 1

592 LUCIANA How many fond fools serve mad jealousy!
The Comedy of Errors (1594), Act 2, Scene 1

593 DROMIO Marry, he must have a long spoon that must eat with the devil.
The Comedy of Errors (1594), Act 4, Scene 3

594 ABBESS The venom clamours of a jealous woman
Poison more deadly than a mad dog's tooth.
The Comedy of Errors (1594), Act 5, Scene 1

595 ANTIPHOLUS They brought one Pinch, a hungry lean-fac'd villain,
A mere anatomy, a mountebank,
A threadbare juggler, and a fortune-teller,
A needy, hollow-ey'd, sharp-looking wretch,
A living-dead man.
The Comedy of Errors (1594), Act 5, Scene 1

596 GRATIANO As who should say "I am Sir Oracle,
And when I ope my lips let no dog bark."
The Merchant of Venice (1596–98), Act 1, Scene 1

597 PORTIA If to do were as easy as to know what were good to do, chapels had been churches, and poor men's cottages princes' palaces.
The Merchant of Venice (1596–98), Act 1, Scene 2

598 ANTONIO The devil can cite Scripture for his purpose.
The Merchant of Venice (1596–98), Act 1, Scene 3

599 SHYLOCK Still have I borne it with a patient shrug,
For sufferance is the badge of all our tribe.
The Merchant of Venice (1596–98), Act 1, Scene 3

600 SHYLOCK You call me misbeliever, cut-throat dog,
And spit upon my Jewish gaberdine,
And all for use of that which is mine own.
The Merchant of Venice (1596–98), Act 1, Scene 3

601 PRINCE OF MOROCCO Mislike me not for my complexion,
The shadow'd livery of the burnish'd sun,
To whom I am a neighbour and near bred.
The Merchant of Venice (1596–98), Act 2, Scene 1

602 LAUNCELOT It is a wise father that knows his own child.
The Merchant of Venice (1596–98), Act 2, Scene 2

603 LAUNCELOT Truth will come to light; murder cannot be hid long.
The Merchant of Venice (1596–98), Act 2, Scene 2

604 JESSICA But love is blind, and lovers cannot see
The pretty follies that themselves commit.
The Merchant of Venice (1596–98), Act 2, Scene 6

605 JESSICA What! Must I hold a candle to my shames?
The Merchant of Venice (1596–98), Act 2, Scene 6

606 SHYLOCK My daughter! O my ducats! O my daughter!
Fled with a Christian! O my Christian ducats!
Justice! the law! my ducats, and my daughter!
The Merchant of Venice (1596–98), Act 2, Scene 8

607 NERISSA The ancient saying is no heresy:
Hanging and wiving goes by destiny.
The Merchant of Venice (1596–98), Act 2, Scene 9

608 PORTIA Thus hath the candle singed the moth.
O, these deliberate fools!
The Merchant of Venice (1596–98), Act 2, Scene 9

609 PRINCE OF ARAGON What many men desire!—that "many" may be meant
By the fool multitude, that choose by show,
Not learning more than the fond eye doth teach;
Which pries not to th' interior; but, like the martlet,
Builds in the weather on the outward wall,
Even in the force and road of casualty.
I will not choose what many men desire,
Because I will not jump with common spirits
And rank me with the barbarous multitudes.
The Merchant of Venice (1596–98), Act 2, Scene 9

610 SHYLOCK Hath not a Jew eyes? Hath not a Jew hands, organs, dimensions, senses, affections, passions, fed with the same food, hurt with the same weapons, subject to the same diseases, healed by the same means, warmed and cooled by the same winter and summer, as a Christian is? If you prick us, do we not bleed? If you tickle us, do we not laugh? If you poison us, do we not die? And if you wrong us, shall we not revenge?
The Merchant of Venice (1596–98), Act 3, Scene 1

611 SHYLOCK Let him look to his bond.
The Merchant of Venice (1596–98), Act 3, Scene 1

612 BASSANIO Ornament is but the guiled shore
To a most dangerous sea; the beauteous scarf
Veiling an Indian beauty; in a word,
The seeming truth which cunning times put on
To entrap the wisest.
The Merchant of Venice (1596–98), Act 3, Scene 2

613 BASSANIO So may the outward shows be least themselves:
The world is still deceived with ornament.
In law, what plea so tainted and corrupt
But, being season'd with a gracious voice,
Obscures the show of evil? In religion,
What damned error, but some sober brow
Will bless it and approve it with a text,
Hiding the grossness with fair ornament?
There is no vice so simple but assumes
Some mark of virtue on his outward parts.
The Merchant of Venice (1596–98), Act 3, Scene 2

614 LORENZO How every fool can play upon the word!
The Merchant of Venice (1596–98), Act 3, Scene 5

615 BASSANIO Wrest once the law to your authority:
To do a great right, do a little wrong.
The Merchant of Venice (1596–98), Act 4, Scene 1

616 CLERK I never knew so young a body with so old a head.
The Merchant of Venice (1596–98), Act 4, Scene 1

617 PORTIA The quality of mercy is not strain'd;
It droppeth as the gentle rain from heaven
Upon the place beneath. It is twice blest;
It blesseth him that gives and him that takes.
The Merchant of Venice (1596–98), Act 4, Scene 1

618 SHYLOCK A Daniel come to judgment! yea, a Daniel!
The Merchant of Venice (1596–98), Act 4, Scene 1

619 SHYLOCK What judgment shall I dread, doing no wrong?
The Merchant of Venice (1596–98), Act 4, Scene 1

620 JESSICA I am never merry when I hear sweet music.
The Merchant of Venice (1596–98), Act 5, Scene 1

621 LORENZO How sweet the moonlight sleeps upon this bank!
Here will we sit, and let the sounds of music
Creep in our ears; soft stillness and the night
Become the touches of sweet harmony.
The Merchant of Venice (1596–98), Act 5, Scene 1

622 LORENZO The man that hath no music in himself,
Nor is not mov'd with concord of sweet sounds,
Is fit for treasons, stratagems, and spoils.
The Merchant of Venice (1596–98), Act 5, Scene 1

623 LORENZO The moon shines bright: in such a night as this,
...in such a night
Troilus methinks mounted the Troyan walls,
And sigh'd his soul toward the Grecian tents,
Where Cressid lay that night.
The Merchant of Venice (1596–98), Act 5, Scene 1

624 PORTIA For a light wife doth make a heavy husband.
The Merchant of Venice (1596–98), Act 5, Scene 1

625 PORTIA How far that little candle throws his beams!
So shines a good deed in a naughty world.
The Merchant of Venice (1596–98), Act 5, Scene 1

626 SHALLOW I will make a Star-Chamber matter of it.
The Merry Wives of Windsor (1597), Act 1, Scene 1

627 MRS FORD We burn daylight.
The Merry Wives of Windsor (1597), Act 2, Scene 1

628 FALSTAFF Of what quality was your love, then?
FORD Like a fair house built upon another man's ground; so that I have lost my edifice by mistaking the place where I erected it.
The Merry Wives of Windsor (1597), Act 2, Scene 2

629 PISTOL Why, then the world's mine oyster,
Which I with sword will open.
The Merry Wives of Windsor (1597), Act 2, Scene 2

630 ANNE O, what a world of vile ill-favour'd faults
Looks handsome in three hundred pounds a year!
The Merry Wives of Windsor (1597), Act 3, Scene 4

631 FALSTAFF They say there is divinity in odd numbers, either in nativity, chance, or death.
The Merry Wives of Windsor (1597), Act 5, Scene 1

632 Crabbed age and youth cannot live together:
Youth is full of pleasure, age is full of care;
Youth like summer morn, age like winter weather;
Youth like summer brave, age like winter bare.
The Passionate Pilgrim (1599), st. 12

633 Beauty itself doth of itself persuade
The eyes of men without an orator.
The Rape of Lucrece (1594)

634 Time's glory is to calm contending kings,
To unmask falsehood, and bring truth to light.
The Rape of Lucrece (1594)

635 TRANIO No profit grows where is no pleasure ta'en;
In brief, sir, study what you most affect.
The Taming of the Shrew (1592), Act 1, Scene 1

636 KATHERINA She is your treasure, she must have a husband;
I must dance bare-foot on her wedding day,
And, for your love to her, lead apes in hell.
The Taming of the Shrew (1592), Act 2, Scene 1

637 PETRUCHIO Kiss me Kate, we will be married o' Sunday.
The Taming of the Shrew (1592), Act 2, Scene 1

638 PETRUCHIO This is a way to kill a wife with kindness.
The Taming of the Shrew (1592), Act 4, Scene 1

639 PETRUCHIO Our purses shall be proud, our garments poor;
For 'tis the mind that makes the body rich;
And as the sun breaks through the darkest clouds,
So honour peereth in the meanest habit.
The Taming of the Shrew (1592), Act 4, Scene 3

640 KATHERINA Fie, fie! unknit that threatening unkind brow,
And dart not scornful glances from those eyes,
To wound thy lord, thy king, thy governor.
The Taming of the Shrew (1592), Act 5, Scene 2

641 KATHERINA Such duty as the subject owes the prince,
Even such a woman oweth to her husband.
The Taming of the Shrew (1592), Act 5, Scene 2

642 ARIEL Full fathom five thy father lies;
Of his bones are coral made;
Those are pearls that were his eyes;
Nothing of him that doth fade
But doth suffer a sea-change
Into something rich and strange.
The Tempest (1611), Act 1, Scene 2

643 CALIBAN You taught me language; and my profit on't
Is, I know how to curse: the red plague rid you
For learning me your language!
The Tempest (1611), Act 1, Scene 2

644 ANTONIO They'll take suggestion as a cat laps milk.
The Tempest (1611), Act 2, Scene 1

645 TRINCULO Misery acquaints a man with strange bedfellows.
The Tempest (1611), Act 2, Scene 2

646 TRINCULO When they will not give a doit to relieve a lame beggar, they will lay out ten to see a dead Indian.
The Tempest (1611), Act 2, Scene 2

647 MIRANDA I am your wife, if you will marry me;
If not, I'll die your maid: to be your fellow
You may deny me; but I'll be your servant
Whether you will or no.
FERDINAND My mistress, dearest;
And thus I humble ever.
MIRANDA My husband then?
FERDINAND Ay, with a heart as willing
As bondage e'er of freedom; here's my hand.
MIRANDA And mine, with my heart in't.
The Tempest (1611), Act 3, Scene 1

648 CALIBAN Be not afeard. The isle is full of noises,
Sounds, and sweet airs, that give delight, and hurt not.
The Tempest (1611), Act 3, Scene 2

649 STEPHANO He that dies pays all debts.
The Tempest (1611), Act 3, Scene 2

650 PROSPERO Our revels now are ended. These our actors,
As I foretold you, were all spirits, and
Are melted into air, into thin air;
And, like the baseless fabric of this vision,
The cloud-capp'd towers, the gorgeous palaces,
The solemn temples, the great globe itself,
Yea, all which it inherit, shall dissolve,
And, like this insubstantial pageant faded,
Leave not a rack behind. We are such stuff
As dreams are made on; and our little life
Is rounded with a sleep.
The Tempest (1611), Act 4, Scene 1

651 ARIEL Where the bee sucks, There suck I;
In a cowslip's bell I lie;
There I couch when owls do cry,
On the bat's back I do fly
After summer merrily,
Merrily, merrily, shall I live now
Under the blossom that hangs on the bough.
The Tempest (1611), Act 5, Scene 1

652 MIRANDA How beauteous mankind is! O brave new world
That has such people in't!
The Tempest (1611), Act 5, Scene 1

653 PROSPERO I'll break my staff,
Bury it certain fathoms in the earth,
And deeper than did ever plummet sound
I'll drown my book.
The Tempest (1611), Act 5, Scene 1

654 VALENTINE Home-keeping youth have ever homely wits.
The Two Gentlemen of Verona (1592–93), Act 1, Scene 1

655 LUCETTA I have no other but a woman's reason:
I think him so, because I think him so.
The Two Gentlemen of Verona (1592–93), Act 1, Scene 2

656 Who is Silvia? What is she,
That all our swains commend her?
The Two Gentlemen of Verona (1592–93), Act 4, Scene 2

657 PROTEUS O heaven, were man
But constant, he were perfect!
The Two Gentlemen of Verona (1592–93), Act 5, Scene 4

658 MAMILLIUS A sad tale's best for winter. I have one
Of sprites and goblins.
The Winter's Tale (1610–11), Act 2, Scene 1

659 LEONTES I am a feather for each wind that blows.
The Winter's Tale (1610–11), Act 2, Scene 3

660 PAULINA It is an heretic that makes the fire,
Not she which burns in 't.
The Winter's Tale (1610–11), Act 2, Scene 3

661 PAULINA What's gone and what's past help
Should be past grief.
The Winter's Tale (1610–11), Act 3, Scene 2

662 SHEPHERD I would there were no age between ten and three and twenty, or that youth would sleep out the rest; for there is nothing in the between but getting wenches with child, wronging the ancientry, stealing, fighting.
The Winter's Tale (1610–11), Act 3, Scene 3

663 *Exit, pursued by a bear.*
Stage direction. *The Winter's Tale* (1610–11), Act 3, Scene 3

664 A snapper-up of unconsidered trifles.
Autolycus's description of himself. *The Winter's Tale* (1610–11), Act 4, Scene 3

665 AUTOLYCUS Ha, ha! what a fool Honesty is! and Trust, his sworn brother, a very simple gentleman!
The Winter's Tale (1610–11), Act 4, Scene 4

666 AUTOLYCUS Lawn as white as driven snow.
The Winter's Tale (1610–11), Act 4, Scene 4

667 AUTOLYCUS Though I am not naturally honest, I am so sometimes by chance.
The Winter's Tale (1610–11), Act 4, Scene 4

668 CAMILLO Good sooth, she is
The queen of curds and cream.
The Winter's Tale (1610–11), Act 4, Scene 4

669 CLOWN Though authority be a stubborn bear, yet he is oft led by the nose with gold.
The Winter's Tale (1610–11), Act 4, Scene 4

670 PERDITA The self-same sun that shines upon his court
Hides not his visage from our cottage, but
Looks on alike.
The Winter's Tale (1610–11), Act 4, Scene 4

671 PERDITA This dream of mine—
Being now awake, I'll queen it no inch farther,
But milk my ewes and weep.
The Winter's Tale (1610–11), Act 4, Scene 4

672 LEONTES O, she's warm!
If this be magic, let it be an art
Lawful as eating.
Referring to his Hermione, his wife, who until this moment he believes to have died 16 years before.
The Winter's Tale (1610–11), Act 5, Scene 3

673 APEMANTUS He that loves to be flattered is worthy o' the flatterer.
Timon of Athens (1607?), Act 1, Scene 1

674 APEMANTUS Like madness is the glory of this life.
Timon of Athens (1607?), Act 1, Scene 2

675 APEMANTUS Men shut their doors against a setting sun.
Timon of Athens (1607?), Act 1, Scene 2

676 TIMON You fools of fortune, trencher-friends, time's flies.
Timon of Athens (1607?), Act 3, Scene 6

677 FLAVIUS We have seen better days.
Timon of Athens (1607?), Act 4, Scene 2

678 DEMETRIUS She is a woman, therefore may be woo'd;
She is a woman therefore may be won;
She is Lavinia, therefore must be lov'd.
What, man! more water glideth by the mill
Than wots the miller of; and easy it is
of a cut loaf to steal a shive, we know.
Titus Andronicus (1590), Act 2, Scene 1

679 AARON If one good deed in all my life I did,
I repent it from my very soul.
Titus Andronicus (1590), Act 5, Scene 3

680 TAMORA Why hast thou slain thine only daughter thus?
TITUS Not I; 'twas Chiron and Demetrius.
They ravish'd her, and cut away her tongue;
And they, 'twas they, that did her all this wrong.
SATURNINUS Go, fetch them hither to us presently.
TITUS Why, there they are, both baked in this pie,
Whereof their mother daintily hath fed,
Eating the flesh that she herself hath bred.
Titus Andronicus (1590), Act 5, Scene 3

681 CRESSIDA That she belov'd knows nought that knows not this:
Men prize the thing ungain'd more than it is.
Troilus and Cressida (1602), Act 1, Scene 2

682 ULYSSES O, when degree is shak'd,
Which is the ladder of all high designs,
The enterprise is sick!
Troilus and Cressida (1602), Act 1, Scene 3

683 ULYSSES Take but degree away, untune that string,
And hark what discord follows! Each thing meets
In mere oppugnancy.
Troilus and Cressida (1602), Act 1, Scene 3

684 ULYSSES The heavens themselves, the planets, and this centre,
Observe degree, priority, and place,
Insisture, course, proportion, season, form,
Office, and custom, in all line of order.
Troilus and Cressida (1602), Act 1, Scene 3

685 CRESSIDA To be wise and love
Exceeds man's might.
Troilus and Cressida (1602), Act 3, Scene 2

686 TROILUS I am as true as truth's simplicity,
And simpler than the infancy of truth.
Troilus and Cressida (1602), Act 3, Scene 2

687 TROILUS This is the monstruosity in love, lady, that the will is infinite, and the execution confin'd; that the desire is boundless, and the act a slave to limit.
Troilus and Cressida (1602), Act 3, Scene 2

688 ULYSSES Time hath, my lord, a wallet at his back,
Wherein he puts alms for oblivion,
A great-siz'd monster of ingratitudes.
Troilus and Cressida (1602), Act 3, Scene 3

689 AGAMEMNON What's past, and what's to come is strew'd with husks
And formless ruin of oblivion.
Troilus and Cressida (1602), Act 4, Scene 5

690 HECTOR The end crowns all,
And that old common arbitrator, Time,
Will one day end it.
Troilus and Cressida (1602), Act 4, Scene 5

691 THERSITES Lechery, lechery! Still wars and lechery! Nothing else holds fashion.
Troilus and Cressida (1602), Act 5, Scene 2

692 TROILUS Words, words, mere words, no matter from the heart.
Troilus and Cressida (1602), Act 5, Scene 3

693 ORSINO If music be the food of love, play on,
Give me excess of it, that, surfeiting,
The appetite may sicken and so die.
Twelfth Night (1601), Act 1, Scene 1

694 SIR TOBY BELCH Is it a world to hide virtues in?
Twelfth Night (1601), Act 1, Scene 3

695 CLOWN Many a good hanging prevents a bad marriage.
Twelfth Night (1601), Act 1, Scene 5

696 MARIA My purpose is, indeed, a horse of that colour.
Twelfth Night (1601), Act 2, Scene 3

697 SIR TOBY BELCH Dost thou think, because thou art virtuous, there shall be no more cakes and ale?
Twelfth Night (1601), Act 2, Scene 3

698 SIR TOBY BELCH Not to be abed after midnight is to be up betimes.
Twelfth Night (1601), Act 2, Scene 3

699 CLOWN What is love? 'Tis not hereafter;
Present mirth hath present laughter;
What's to come is still unsure.
In delay there lies no plenty,
Then come kiss me, sweet and twenty;
Youth's a stuff will not endure.
Song lyric. *Twelfth Night* (1601), Act 2, Scene 3

700 DUKE ORSINO Let still the woman take
An elder than herself; so wears she to him,
So sways she level in her husband's heart.
Twelfth Night (1601), Act 2, Scene 4

701 VIOLA She never told her love,
But let concealment, like a worm i' th' bud,
Feed on her damask cheek. She pin'd in thought;
And with a green and yellow melancholy
She sat like Patience on a monument,
Smiling at grief.
Twelfth Night (1601), Act 2, Scene 4

702 MALVOLIO *reads* "Some are born great, some achieve greatness, and some have greatness thrust upon 'em."
Twelfth Night (1601), Act 2, Scene 5

703 MARIA Here comes the trout that must be caught with tickling.
Twelfth Night (1601), Act 2, Scene 5

704 OLIVIA Love sought is good, but given unsought is better.
Twelfth Night (1601), Act 3, Scene 1

705 VIOLA This fellow is wise enough to play the fool;
And to do that well craves a kind of wit.
Twelfth Night (1601), Act 3, Scene 1

706 FABIAN If this were play'd upon a stage now, I could condemn it as an improbable fiction.
Twelfth Night (1601), Act 3, Scene 4

707 FABIAN More matter for a May morning.
Twelfth Night (1601), Act 3, Scene 4

708 FABIAN Still you keep o' th' windy side of the law.
Twelfth Night (1601), Act 3, Scene 4

709 OLIVIA Why, this is very midsummer madness.
Twelfth Night (1601), Act 3, Scene 4

710 VIOLA I hate ingratitude more in a man
Than lying, vainness, babbling drunkenness,
Or any taint of vice whose strong corruption
Inhabits our frail blood.
Twelfth Night (1601), Act 3, Scene 4

711 CLOWN And thus the whirligig of time brings in his revenges.
Twelfth Night (1601), Act 5, Scene 1

712 MALVOLIO I'll be reveng'd on the whole pack of you.
Twelfth Night (1601), Act 5, Scene 1

713 Bid me discourse, I will enchant thine ear;
Or like a fairy, trip upon the green;
Or like a nymph, with long, dishevelled hair,
Dance on the sands, and yet no footing seen.
Love is a spirit all compact of fire
Not gross to sink, but light, and will aspire.
Venus and Adonis (1593)

Shange, Ntozake (originally Paulette Williams; b.1948) U.S. poet, novelist, essayist, and playwright

1 i found god in myself
& i loved her
i loved her fiercely.
"a laying on of hands," *for colored girls who have considered suicide when the rainbow is enuf* (1975)

2 i cdnt stand it
i cdnt stand being sorry & colored at the same time
it's so redundant in the modern world.
"no more love poems," *for colored girls who have considered suicide when the rainbow is enuf* (1975)

3 quite simply a poem shd fill you up with something
cd make you swoon, stop in yr tracks, change yr mind, or
make it up. a poem shd happen to you like cold water or a
kiss.
"i talk to myself," *nappy edges* (1978)

4 Give gifts to those who should know love. Give hell to those who take us lightly.
Sassafrass, Cypress & Indigo (1977)

5 Where there is a woman there is magic.
Sassafrass, Cypress & Indigo (1977)

6 Reading, to me, is simply the expansion of one's mind to include some people whom you just didn't get to meet before.
Black Women Writers at Work (Claudia Tate, ed.; 1983)

7 for colored girls who have considered suicide when the rainbow is enuf
1975. Play title.

Shankly, Bill (William Shankly; 1913–81) Scottish soccer manager

1 Some people think football is a matter of life and death—I can assure them it is much more important than that.
Referring to soccer. *Sunday Times*, London (October 4, 1981)

Shapiro, Karl (Karl Jay Shapiro; b.1913) U.S. poet, critic, and editor

1 Self-knowledge is a dangerous thing, tending to make man shallow or insane.
The Bourgeois Poet (1964)

2 America is the child society par excellence...a society of all rights and no obligations...the only society that ever raised gangsterism to the status of myth, and murder to the status of tragedy or politics.
"To Abolish Children," *To Abolish Children, and Other Essays* (1968)

Shapiro, Robert B. (b.1938) U.S. business executive

1 How do you react to the prospects of the world population doubling over the next few decades? First you may say, Great, 5 billion more customers.
Harvard Business Review (January–February 1997)

2 If an institution wants to be adaptive, it has to let go of some control and trust that people will work on the right things in the right way.
Harvard Business Review (January–February 1997)

3 If emerging economies have to relive the entire industrial revolution with all its waste, its energy use, and its pollution, I think it's all over.
Harvard Business Review (January–February 1997)

4 Today in most fields I know, the struggle is about creativity and innovation. There is no script.
Harvard Business Review (January–February 1997)

5 We're willing to place some bets because the world cannot avoid needing sustainability in the long run.
Harvard Business Review (January–February 1997)

6 We can't expect the rest of the world to abandon their aspirations just so we can continue to enjoy clean air and water.
Referring to the threat of global pollution and global warming. *Harvard Business Review* (January–February 1997)

Sharp, William (pen name Fiona MacLeod; 1856–1905) Scottish poet and writer

1 My heart is a lonely hunter that hunts on a lonely hill.
1896. "The Lonely Hunter," *Poems and Dramas by "Fiona MacLeod"* (1910), st. 6

Sharpe, Tom (Thomas Ridley Sharpe; b.1928) British novelist

1 Skullion had little use for contraceptives at the best of times. Unnatural, he called them, and placed them in the lower social category of things along with elastic-sided boots and made-up bow ties. Not the sort of attire for a gentleman.
Porterhouse Blue (1974), ch. 9

2 His had been an intellectual decision founded on his conviction that if a little knowledge was a dangerous thing, a lot was lethal.
Porterhouse Blue (1974), ch. 18

Shaw, George Bernard (1856–1950) Irish playwright

Quotations about Shaw

1 Shaw's judgements are often scatterbrained, but at least he has brains to scatter.
Max Beerbohm (1872–1956) British essayist, critic, and caricaturist. Quoted in *Conversation With Max* (S. N. Behrman; 1960)

2 When you were quite a little boy somebody ought to have said "hush" just once.
Mrs. Patrick Campbell (1865–1940) British actor. Letter to George Bernard Shaw (November 1, 1912)

3 A budding young anthologist sought to include a Shaw piece in a new collection. "I hope you understand," he wrote to Shaw, "that I cannot afford to pay your usual fee as I am a very young man." Shaw replied, "I'll wait for you to grow up."
Bennett Cerf (1898–1971) U.S. publisher and editor. *Shake Well Before Using* (1950)

4 Mr Shaw is (I suspect) the only man on earth who has never written any poetry.
G. K. Chesterton (1874–1936) British writer and poet. *Orthodoxy* (1909), ch. 3

5 Cannot make first night. Will come to second. If you have one.
Winston Churchill (1874–1965) British prime minister and writer. Replying to George Bernard Shaw's telegram: "Two tickets reserved for you, first night Pygmalion. Bring a friend. If you have one." Telegram to George Bernard Shaw (1916)

6 Shaw relished every opportunity to have himself painted, sketched, photographed or carved, because each likeness provided him with a new extension of himself.
Peter Conrad British writer and critic. "Multitude of Shaws," *Observer*, London (October 7, 1979)

7 I must say Bernard Shaw is greatly improved by music.
T. S. Eliot (1888–1965) U.S.-born British poet and playwright. Referring to *My Fair Lady* (1964), a musical based on George Bernard Shaw's play, *Pygmalion* (1914). Attrib.

8 He identified genius with immunity from the cravings and turpitudes which make us human. Hence his regime of sexual continence which so confused and dismayed the women he persisted in loving, and hence too his abstinent diet of grated vegetables.
Michael Holroyd (b.1935) British biographer. *The Genius of Shaw* (1979)

9 A good man fallen among Fabians.
Vladimir Ilyich Lenin (1870–1924) Russian revolutionary leader. Quoted in *Six Weeks in Russia in 1919* (Arthur Ransome; 1919), "Notes of Conversations With Lenin"

10 I remember coming across him at the Grand Canyon and finding him peevish, refusing to admire it or even look at it properly. He was jealous of it.
J. B. Priestley (1894–1984) British writer. *Thoughts In the Wilderness* (1957)

11 Sherard Blaw, the dramatist who had discovered himself, and who had given so ungrudgingly of his discovery to the world.
Saki (1870–1916) British short-story writer. *The Unbearable Bassington* (1912), ch. 13

12 It is disappointing to report that George Bernard Shaw appearing as George Bernard Shaw is sadly miscast in the part. Satirists should be heard and not seen.
Robert E. Sherwood (1896–1955) U.S. playwright. Reviewing a George Bernard Shaw play. Attrib.

13 Mr Bernard Shaw has no enemies but is intensely disliked by all his friends.
Oscar Wilde (1854–1900) Irish poet, playwright, and wit. Quoted in *Sixteen Self Sketches* (George Bernard Shaw; 1949), ch. 17

14 At 83 Shaw's mind was perhaps not quite as good as it used to be, but it was still better than anyone else's.
Alexander Woollcott (1887–1943) U.S. writer and critic. *While Rome Burns* (1934)

Quotations by Shaw

15 Whether you think Jesus was God or not, you must admit that he was a first-rate political economist.
"Jesus as Economist," *Androcles and the Lion* (1912), Preface

16 All great truths begin as blasphemies.
Annajanska (1919)

17 RAINA You are a very poor soldier: a chocolate cream soldier!
After feeding a fleeing soldier chocolate creams, who then shrinks from escaping down a drainpipe.
Arms and the Man (1894), Act 1

18 When a prisoner sees the door of his dungeon open he dashes for it without stopping to think where he shall get his dinner.
Back to Methuselah (1921), Preface

19 I enjoy convalescence. It is the part that makes the illness worth while.
Back to Methuselah (1921), pt. 2

20 Silence is the most perfect expression of scorn.
Back to Methuselah (1921), pt. 2

21 Life is a disease; and the only difference between one man and another is the stage of the disease at which he lives.
"Gospel of the Brothers Barnabas," *Back to Methuselah* (1921)

22 When a stupid man is doing something he is ashamed of, he always declares that it is his duty.
Caesar and Cleopatra (1901), pt. 3

23 I am only a beer teetotaller, not a champagne teetotaller.
Candida (1904), Act 3

24 Parentage is a very important profession; but no test of fitness for it is ever imposed in the interest of children.
Everybody's Political What's What (1944)

25 All that the young can do for the old is to shock them and keep them up to date.
Fanny's First Play (1912)

26 The pianoforte is the most important of all musical instruments: its invention was to music what the invention of printing was to poetry.
"The Religion of the Pianoforte," *Fortnightly Review* (1894)

27 Physically there is nothing to distinguish human society from the farm-yard except that children are more troublesome and costly than chickens and women are not so completely enslaved as farm stock.
Getting Married (1911), Preface

28 It isn't mere convention. Everyone can see that the people who hunt are the right people and the people who don't are the wrong ones.
Heartbreak House (1919)

29 Old men are dangerous; it doesn't matter to them what is going to happen to the world.
Heartbreak House (1919)

30 The surest way to ruin a man who doesn't know how to handle money is to give him some.
Heartbreak House (1919)

31 Truth telling is not compatible with the defence of the realm.
Heartbreak House (1919)

32 Peace is not only better than war, but infinitely more arduous.
Heartbreak House (1919), Preface

33 My way of joking is to tell the truth. It's the funniest joke in the world.
John Bull's Other Island (1907)

34 We must be thoroughly democratic and patronise everybody without distinction of class.
John Bull's Other Island (1907)

35 I am a millionaire. That is my religion.
Major Barbara (1907), Act 2

36 I am a sort of collector of religions: and the curious thing is that I find I can believe in them all.
Major Barbara (1907), Act 2

37 He knows nothing; and he thinks he knows everything. That points clearly to a political career.
Major Barbara (1907), Act 3

38 He never does a proper thing without giving an improper reason for it.
Major Barbara (1907), Act 3

39 Nothing is ever done in this world until men are prepared to kill each other if it is not done.
Major Barbara (1907), Act 3

40 CUSINS Do you call poverty a crime?
UNDERSHAFT The worst of all crimes. All the other crimes are virtues beside it.
Major Barbara (1907), Act 4

41 Property is organised robbery.
Major Barbara (1907), Preface

42 The universal regard for money is the one hopeful fact in our civilization. Money is the most important thing in the world.

It represents health, strength, honour, generosity and beauty.
Major Barbara (1907), Preface

43 A learned man is an idler who kills time by study.
Man and Superman (1903)

44 It is dangerous to be sincere unless you are also stupid.
Man and Superman (1903)

45 Kings are not born, they are made by artificial hallucination.
Man and Superman (1903)

46 The man with toothache thinks everyone happy whose teeth are sound.
Man and Superman (1903)

47 A lifetime of happiness: no man alive could bear it: it would be hell on earth.
Man and Superman (1903), Act 1

48 It is a woman's business to get married as soon as possible, and a man's to keep unmarried as long as he can.
Man and Superman (1903), Act 2

49 There is only one person an English girl hates more than she hates her eldest sister; and that is her mother.
Man and Superman (1903), Act 2

50 You can be as romantic as you please about love, Hector; but you mustn't be romantic about money.
Man and Superman (1903), Act 2

51 An Englishman thinks he is moral when he is only uncomfortable.
Man and Superman (1903), Act 3

52 I am a gentleman. I live by robbing the poor.
Man and Superman (1903), Act 3

53 Every man over forty is a scoundrel.
Man and Superman (1903), Act 4

54 There are two tragedies in life. One is to lose your heart's desire. The other is to gain it.
Man and Superman (1903), Act 4

55 Beware of the man who does not return your blow: he neither forgives you nor allows you to forgive yourself.
"Maxims for Revolutionists," *Man and Superman* (1903)

56 Democracy substitutes election by the incompetent many for appointment by the corrupt few.
"Maxims for Revolutionists," *Man and Superman* (1903)

57 Do not do unto others as you would they should do unto you. Their tastes may not be the same.
"Maxims for Revolutionists," *Man and Superman* (1903)

58 Do not love your neighbour as yourself. If you are on good terms with yourself it is an impertinence; if on bad, an injury.
"Maxims for Revolutionists," *Man and Superman* (1903)

59 He who can, does. He who cannot, teaches.
"Maxims for Revolutionists," *Man and Superman* (1903)

60 In heaven an angel is nobody in particular.
"Maxims for Revolutionists," *Man and Superman* (1903)

61 Lack of money is the root of all evil.
"Maxims for Revolutionists," *Man and Superman* (1903)

62 Life levels all men: death reveals the eminent.
"Maxims for Revolutionists," *Man and Superman* (1903)

63 Marriage is popular because it combines the maximum of temptation with the maximum of opportunity.
"Maxims for Revolutionists," *Man and Superman* (1903)

64 Self-denial is not a virtue; it is only the effect of prudence on rascality.
"Maxims for Revolutionists," *Man and Superman* (1903)

65 Self-sacrifice enables us to sacrifice
Other people without blushing.
"Maxims for Revolutionists," *Man and Superman* (1903)

66 The golden rule is that there are no golden rules.
"Maxims for Revolutionists," *Man and Superman* (1903)

67 Titles distinguish the mediocre, embarrass the superior, and are disgraced by the inferior.
"Maxims for Revolutionists," *Man and Superman* (1903)

68 Give women the vote, and in five years there will be a crushing tax on bachelors.
"Preface," *Man and Superman* (1903)

69 Common people do not pray; they only beg.
Misalliance (1914)

70 Heaven, as conventionally conceived, is a place so inane, so dull, so useless, so miserable, that nobody has ever ventured to describe a whole day in heaven, though plenty of people have described a day at the seaside.
Misalliance (1914), Preface

71 Optimistic lies have such immense therapeutic value that a doctor who cannot tell them convincingly has mistaken his profession.
Misalliance (1914), Preface

72 The secret of being miserable is to have leisure to bother about whether you are happy or not.
Misalliance (1914), Preface

73 There is nothing on earth intended for innocent people so horrible as a school. It is in some respects more cruel than a prison. In a prison, for example, you are not forced to read books written by the warders and the governor.
"Parents and Children," *Misalliance* (1914)

74 The fact is there are no rules, and there never were any rules, and there never will be any rules of musical composition except rules of thumb, and thumbs vary in length, like ears.
Music in London (1890–94)

75 You'll never have a quiet world till you knock the patriotism out of the human race.
O'Flaherty V.C. (1919)

76 Gin was mother's milk to her.
Pygmalion (1914)

77 He's a gentleman: look at his boots.
Pygmalion (1914)

78 I don't want to talk grammar, I want to talk like a lady.
Pygmalion (1914)

79 I have to live for others and not for myself; that's middle class morality.
Pygmalion (1914)

80 The English have no respect for their language, and will not teach their children to speak it...It is impossible for an Englishman to open his mouth, without making some other Englishman despise him.
Pygmalion (1914), Preface

81 A miracle is an event which creates faith. Frauds deceive. An event which creates faith does not deceive; therefore it is not a fraud, but a miracle.
Saint Joan (1924)

82 Don't think you can frighten me by telling me I am alone. France is alone; and God is alone; and what is my loneliness before the loneliness of my country and my God?
Saint Joan (1924)

83 We want a few mad people now. See where the sane ones have landed us!
Saint Joan (1924)

84 It is the sexless novel that should be distinguished: the sex novel is now normal.
Table-Talk of G. B. S. (1925), ch. 4

85 I never resist temptation because I have found that things that are bad for me never tempt me.
The Apple Cart (1930)

86 I never expect a soldier to think.
The Devil's Disciple (1901), Act 3

87 The most tragic thing in the world is a sick doctor.
The Doctor's Dilemma (1911), Act 1

88 DUBEDAT Morality consists in suspecting other people of not being legally married.
Said by the artist to the doctors diagnosing him, who jump to the conclusion that he's not married to his wife. *The Doctor's Dilemma* (1911), Act 2

89 Fashions, after all, are only induced epidemics.
The Doctor's Dilemma (1911), Preface

90 Make it compulsory for a doctor using a brass plate to have inscribed on it, in addition to the letters indicating his qualifications, the words "Remember that I too am mortal".
"Preface on Doctors," *The Doctor's Dilemma* (1911)

91 Use your health even to the point of wearing it out. That is what it is for. Spend all you have before you die, and do not outlive yourself.
"Preface on Doctors," *The Doctor's Dilemma* (1911)

92 Assassination is the extreme form of censorship.
"Limits to Toleration," *The Shewing-Up of Blanco Posnet* (1911)

93 We're from Madeira, but perfectly respectable, so far.
You Never Can Tell (1898), Act 1

94 Well, sir, you never can tell. That's a principle in life with me, sir, if you'll excuse my having such a thing, sir.
You Never Can Tell (1898), Act 2

95 Far too good to waste on children.
Reflecting upon youth. Quoted in *10,000 Jokes, Toasts, and Stories* (Lewis Copeland; 1940)

96 My reputation grew with every failure.
Referring to his unsuccessful early novels. Quoted in *Bernard Shaw* (Hesketh Pearson; 1975)

97 I've been offered titles, but I think they get one into disreputable company.
1946. Quoted in *Gossip: A History of High Society from 1920–1970* (A. Barrow; 1978)

98 It's a funny thing about that bust. As time goes on it seems to get younger and younger.
Referring to a portrait bust sculpted for him by Auguste Rodin. Quoted in *More Things I Wish I'd Said* (K. Edwards; 1978)

99 I quite agree with you, sir, but what can two do against so many?
Responding to a solitary hiss heard amid the applause at the first performance of *Arms and the Man* in 1894. *Oxford Book of Literary Anecdotes* (James Sutherland, ed.; 1975)

100 Certainly, there is nothing else here to enjoy.
Said at a party when his hostess asked him whether he was enjoying himself. Quoted in *Pass the Port Again* (Oxfam; 1980)

101 A perpendicular expression of a horizontal desire.
Referring to dancing. Quoted in *Revolt into Style* (George Melly; 1970)

102 The thought of two thousand people crunching celery at the same time horrified me.
Explaining why he had turned down an invitation to a vegetarian gala dinner. Quoted in *The Greatest Laughs of All Time* (Gerald Lieberman; 1961)

103 The trouble, Mr. Goldwyn, is that you are only interested in art and I am only interested in money.
Turning down Samuel Goldwyn's offer to buy the screen rights of his plays. Quoted in *The Great Goldwyn* (Alva Johnson; 1937), ch. 3

104 Better never than late.
Responding to an offer by a producer to present one of his plays after an earlier rejection of it. Quoted in *The Unimportance of Being Oscar* (Oscar Levant; 1968)

105 A character actor is one who cannot act and therefore makes an elaborate study of disguise and stage tricks by which acting can be grotesquely simulated.
Attrib.

106 A man never tells you anything until you contradict him.
Attrib.

107 A man of my spiritual intensity does not eat corpses.
Attrib.

108 An asylum for the sane would be empty in America.
Attrib.

109 Baseball has the great advantage over cricket of being sooner ended.
Attrib.

110 Changeable women are more endurable than monotonous ones. They are sometimes murdered but seldom deserted.
Attrib.

111 If all economists were laid end to end, they would not reach a conclusion.
Attrib.

112 Liberty means responsibility. That is why most men dread it.
Attrib.

113 LORD NORTHCLIFFE The trouble with you, Shaw, is that you

look as if there were famine in the land.
G.B.S. The trouble with you, Northcliffe, is that you look as if you were the cause of it.
Attrib.

114 No man can be a pure specialist without being in the strict sense an idiot.
Attrib.

115 Science is always wrong. It never solves a problem without creating ten more.
Attrib.

116 The British churchgoer prefers a severe preacher because he thinks a few home truths will do his neighbours no harm.
Attrib.

117 The national anthem belongs to the eighteenth century. In it you find us ordering God about to do our political work.
Attrib.

118 When a man wants to murder a tiger he calls it sport; when a tiger wants to murder him he calls it ferocity.
Attrib.

119 When the military man approaches, the world locks up its spoons and packs off its womankind.
Attrib.

120 England and America are two countries separated by the same language.
Attributed in this and other forms, but not found in Shaw's published writings. Attrib.

121 To correct an Englishman's pronunciation is to imply that he is not quite a gentleman.
When chairman of the BBC's committee on standard pronunciation. Attrib.

Shaw, Henry Wheeler ("Josh Billings", "Uncle Esek"; 1818–85) U.S. humorist

1 I have finally kum to the konklusion, that a good reliable sett ov bowels iz wurth more tu a man, than enny quantity ov brains.
Josh Billings: Hiz Sayings (1866), ch. 29

Shawcross, Lord, Baron Shawcross of Friston (Hartley William Shawcross; b.1902) German-born British politician and lawyer

1 The so-called new morality is too often the old immorality condoned.
Observer, London (November 17, 1963)

Shawqi, Ahmad (1868–1932) Egyptian poet

1 You have seen Caesar in his tyranny over us, making us slaves, his men driving us before them as one drives donkeys, and then defeated by a small band of noble conquerors.
Quoted in *A History of the Arab Peoples* (Albert Hourani; 1991)

Shaykh, Hanan al- (b.1945) Palestinian writer

1 The Arabs have the reputation of being uneducated, the people of camels, petrol, terrorism, etc. So how can a Westerner believe that Arabs have culture, literature, and woman writers?
Interview, *Michigan Quarterly Review* (Fall 1992)

Shea, Michael (Michael Sinclair MacAuslan Shea; b.1938) Scottish author and broadcaster

1 Facts influence. They are revered by people who cannot contradict them. Like statistics they are extremely dangerous. They must be controlled and only revealed where essential.
"Quote, Unquote," *Independent*, London (September 24, 1988)

2 Persuade the decision makers that the decision you want is their idea.
Influence (1988)

Sheen, Charlie (Carlos Irwin Esteves; b.1965) U.S. film actor

1 As I look back at the war, we did not fight the enemy. We fought ourselves, and the enemy was in us.
Said as Chris. *Platoon* (1986)

Sheen, Fulton J. (Fulton John Sheen; 1895–1979) U.S. Roman Catholic clergyman and broadcaster

1 The big print giveth and the fine print taketh away.
Referring to his contract for a television appearance. Attrib.

Sheffield, John, 3rd Earl of Mulgrave, afterward 1st Duke of Buckingham and Normanby (1648–1721) English poet and statesman

1 Learn to write well, or not to write at all.
Essay on Satire (1680?)

Shelley, Mary Wollstonecraft (Mary Wollstonecraft Godwin Shelley; 1797–1851) British novelist

1 My dreams were all my own; I accounted for them to nobody; they were my refuge when annoyed—my dearest pleasure when free.
Frankenstein (1818), preface

Shelley, Percy Bysshe (1792–1822) English poet

Quotations about Shelley

1 In his poetry as well as in his life Shelley was indeed "a beautiful and ineffectual angel", beating in the void his luminous wings in vain.
Matthew Arnold (1822–88) British poet and critic. "Shelley," *Literature and Dogma* (1873)

2 Shelley and Keats were the last English poets who were at all up to date in their chemical knowledge.
J. B. S. Haldane (1892–1964) British geneticist. *Daedalus, or, Science and the Future* (1924)

3 He had a fire in his eye, a fever in his blood, a maggot in his brain, a hectic flutter in his speech, which mark out the philosophic fanatic.
William Hazlitt (1778–1830) British essayist and critic. "On Criticism," *Table Talk* (1821–22)

4 You understand *Epipsychidion* best when you are in love; *Don Juan* when anger is subsiding into indifference. Why not Strindberg when you have a temperature?
Desmond MacCarthy (1878 1952) British poet and writer. Referring to the works of Percy Bysshe Shelley, Lord Byron, and August Strindberg. "Miss Julie and the Pariah," *Theatre* (1954)

Quotations by Shelley

5 I pursued a maiden and clasped a reed

Gods and men, we are all deluded thus!
It breaks in our bosom and then we bleed.
"Hymn of Pan" (1820), st. 3, quoted in *Posthumous Poems* (Mrs. Shelley, ed.; 1824)

6 The fountains mingle with the river,
And the rivers with the Ocean;
The winds of Heaven mix for ever
With a sweet emotion;
Nothing in the world is single;
All things, by a law divine,
In one another's being mingle.
Why not I with thine?
First published in *The Indicator.* "Love's Philosophy" (December 22, 1819), st. 1, quoted in *Posthumous Poems* (Mrs. Shelley, ed.; 1824)

7 Oh, lift me as a wave, a leaf, a cloud!
I fall upon the thorns of life! I bleed!
"Ode to the West Wind" (1819), ll. 53–54

8 If Winter comes, can Spring be far behind?
"Ode to the West Wind" (1819), l. 70

9 O wild West Wind, thou breath of Autumn's being,
Thou, from whose unseen presence the leaves dead
Are driven, like ghosts from an enchanter fleeing,

Yellow, and black, and pale, and hectic red,
Pestilence-stricken multitudes.
"Ode to the West Wind" (1819), ll. 1–5

10 "My name is Ozymandias, king of kings:
Look on my works, ye Mighty, and despair!"
"Ozymandias" (January 1818), quoted in *The Poetical Works* (Mrs. Shelley, ed.; 1839)

11 I met a traveller from an antique land
Who said: Two vast and trunkless legs of stone
Stand in the desert.
Referring to the legs of a broken statue of the Pharaoh Rameses II (1301–1234 B.C.; Greek name, Ozymandias). "Ozymandias" (January 1818), quoted in *The Poetical Works* (Mrs. Shelley, ed.; 1839)

12 Teas,
Where small talk dies in agonies.
A humorous follow-up to two earlier works on the Peter Bell theme, *A Tale* by William Wordsworth and *A Lyrical Ballad* by John Hamilton Reynolds. "Peter Bell the Third" (1819), quoted in *The Poetical Works* (Mrs. Shelley, ed.; 1839)

13 Hell is a city much like London—
A populous and smoky city.
A humorous follow-up to two earlier works on the Peter Bell theme, *A Tale* by William Wordsworth and *A Lyrical Ballad* by John Hamilton Reynolds. "Peter Bell the Third" (1819), pt. 3, st. 1, quoted in *The Poetical Works* (Mrs. Shelley, ed.; 1839)

14 Lift not the painted veil which those who live
Call life.
Sonnet (1818), quoted in *Posthumous Poems* (Mrs. Shelley, ed.; 1824)

15 I could lie down like a tired child,
And weep away the life of care
Which I have borne and yet must bear,
Till death like sleep might steal on me.
"Stanzas Written in Dejection, Near Naples" (1818), st. 4, quoted in *Posthumous Poems* (Mrs. Shelley, ed.; 1824)

16 I am the daughter of Earth and Water,
And the nursling of the Sky;
I pass through the pores of the ocean and shores;
I change, but I cannot die.
"The Cloud" (1819)

17 I wield the flail of the lashing hail,
And whiten the green plains under,
And then again I dissolve it in rain,
And laugh as I pass in thunder.
"The Cloud" (1819), ll. 9–12

18 I arise from dreams of thee
In the first sweet sleep of night.
When the winds are breathing low,
And the stars are shining bright.
First published in *The Liberal* as "Song Written for an Indian Air" (1822). Now known as "The Indian Serenade." "The Indian Serenade" (1822), quoted in *Posthumous Poems* (Mrs. Shelley, ed.; 1824)

19 Oh lift me from the grass!
I die! I faint! I fail!
First published in *The Liberal* as "Song Written for an Indian Air" (1822). Now known as "The Indian Serenade." "The Indian Serenade" (1822), quoted in *Posthumous Poems* (Mrs. Shelley, ed.; 1824)

20 His big tears, for he wept full well,
Turned to mill-stones as they fell.
And the little children, who
Round his feet played to and fro,
Thinking every tear a gem,
Had their brains knocked out by them.
"The Masque of Anarchy" (1819), st. 4 (Leigh Hunt, ed.; 1832)

21 It is a modest creed, and yet
Pleasant if one considers it,
To own that death itself must be,
Like all the rest, a mockery.
"The Sensitive Plant" (1820), Conclusion, st. 4

22 Music, when soft voices die,
Vibrates in the memory—
Odours, when sweet violets sicken,
Live within the sense they quicken.

Rose leaves, when the rose is dead,
Are heaped for the beloved's bed;
And so thy thoughts, when thou art gone,
Love itself shall slumber on.
"To —" (1821), quoted in *Posthumous Poems* (Mrs. Shelley, ed.; 1824)

23 Our sweetest songs are those that tell of saddest thought.
"To a Skylark" (1819), l. 90

24 Hail to thee, blithe Spirit!
Bird thou never wert,
That from Heaven, or near it,
Pourest thy full heart
In profuse strains of unpremeditated art.
"To a Skylark" (1819), ll. 1–5

25 When the lamp is shattered
The light in the dust lies dead
When the cloud is scattered—
The rainbow's glory is shed.
When the lute is broken,
Sweet tones are remembered not;

When the lips have spoken,
Loved accents are soon forgot.
"When the Lamp" (1822), st. 1, quoted in *Posthumous Poems* (Mrs. Shelley, ed.; 1824)

26 Poetry is the record of the best and happiest moments of the happiest and best minds.
A Defence of Poetry (1821), quoted in *Essays, Letters from Abroad, Translations and Fragments* (Mrs. Shelley, ed.; 1840)

27 The rich have become richer, and the poor have become poorer; and the vessel of the state is driven between the Scylla and Charybdis of anarchy and despotism.
A Defence of Poetry (1821), quoted in *Essays, Letters from Abroad, Translations and Fragments* (Mrs. Shelley, ed.; 1840)

28 Poets are...the trumpets which sing to battle and feel not what they inspire...Poets are the unacknowledged legislators of the world.
A Defence of Poetry (1821), quoted in *Essays, Letters from Abroad, Translations and Fragments* (Mrs. Shelley, ed.; 1840)

29 I never was attached to that great sect,
Whose doctrine is that each one should select
Out of the crowd a mistress or a friend,
And all the rest, though fair and wise, commend
To cold oblivion.
Epipsychidion (1821), ll. 149–153

30 I pant, I sink, I tremble, I expire!
Epipsychidion (1821), pt. 1, l. 591

31 True Love in this differs from gold and clay,
That to divide is not to take away.
Epipsychidion (1821), pt. 1, ll. 160–161

32 Life may change, but it may fly not;
Hope may vanish, but can die not;
Truth be veiled, but still it burneth;
Love repulsed,—but it returneth!
Inspired by the Greeks' revolt against Ottoman rule in 1821. *Hellas* (1822), ll. 34–37

33 Let there be light! said Liberty,
And like sunrise from the sea,
Athens arose!
Inspired by the Greeks' revolt against Ottoman rule in 1821. *Hellas* (1822), ll. 682–684

34 I love all waste
And solitary places; where we taste
The pleasure of believing what we see
Is boundless, as we wish our souls to be.
Julian and Maddalo (1818), ll. 14–17, quoted in *Posthumous Poems* (Mrs. Shelley, ed.; 1824)

35 Thou Paradise of exiles, Italy!
Julian and Maddalo (1818), l. 57, quoted in *Posthumous Poems* (Mrs. Shelley, ed.; 1824)

36 Most wretched men
Are cradled into poetry by wrong:
They learn in suffering what they teach in song.
Julian and Maddalo (1818), ll. 544–546, quoted in *Posthumous Poems* (Mrs. Shelley, ed.; 1824)

37 All spirits are enslaved which serve things evil.
Prometheus Unbound (1820), Act 2, Scene 4, l. 110

38 Death is the veil which those who live call life:
They sleep, and it is lifted.
Prometheus Unbound (1820), Act 3, Scene. 3, ll. 113–114

39 For she was beautiful—her beauty made
The bright world dim, and everything beside
Seemed like the fleeting image of a shade.
1820. *The Witch of Atlas*, st. 12, quoted in *Posthumous Poems* (Mrs. Shelley, ed.; 1824)

40 Reviewers, with some rare exceptions, are a most stupid and malignant race. As a bankrupt thief turns thief-taker in despair, so an unsuccessful author turns critic.
Passage cut by Shelley from an early version of his Preface to *Adonais* (1821). "Fragments of Adonais," *Relics of Shelley* (Richard Garnett, ed.; 1862)

Shenstone, William (1714–63) British poet

1 A Fool and his words are soon parted.
"On Reserve" (1764)

2 Health is beauty, and the most perfect health is the most perfect beauty.
"On Taste," *Essays on Men and Manners* (1794)

Shepard, Sam (Samuel Shepard Rogers, Jr.; b.1943) U.S. playwright and film actor

1 Collaboration—that's the word producers use. That means, don't forget to kiss ass from beginning to end.
Newsweek (November 11, 1985), quoted in *Chambers Film Quotes* (Tony Crawley, ed.; 1991)

2 Idaho decals. Now who in the hell want to eat offa' plate with the State of Idaho starin' ya' in the face. Every times ya' take a bite ya' get to see a little bit more.
True West (1980), Act 1, Scene 2

3 Nothin' like a shot a' orange juice after a round a' golf. Hot shower. Snappin' towels at each others' privates. Real sense a' fraternity.
True West (1980), Act 1, Scene 3

4 In this business we make movies, American movies. Leave the films to the French.
True West (1980), Act 2, Scene 5

Shepp, Archie (b.1937) U.S. jazz composer and saxophonist

1 "Funk"...means smelly and dirty, but it's the smell of a living people that makes jazz the most vital sound of the century...The jazz people did not achieve respectability, they had it thrust upon them.
Quoted in "The Fire This Time," *Jazz People* (Valerie Wilmer; 1970), ch. 14

Sheppard, Dick (Hugh Richard Lawrie Sheppard; 1880–1937) British clergyman and pacifist

1 If you see anybody fallen by the wayside and lying in the ditch, it isn't much good climbing into the ditch and lying by his side.
Quoted in *Dick Sheppard* (Carolyn Scott; 1977)

Sheridan, Philip Henry (1831–88) U.S. general

1 The only good Indians I ever saw were dead.
January 1869. Remark made at Fort Cobb. Quoted in *The People's Almanac* 2 (D. Wallechinsky; 1869)

2 If I owned Texas and Hell, I would rent out Texas and live in Hell.
Remark made as a junior officer stationed in Texas. Attrib.

Sheridan, Richard Brinsley (1751–1816) Irish-born British playwright and politician

Quotations about Sheridan

1 Good at a fight, but better at a play
God-like in giving, but the devil to pay.
Folk verse. Lines written on a cast of Richard Brinsley Sheridan's hand. Quoted in *Memoirs of the Life of Richard Brinsley Sheridan* (Thomas Moore; 1825), ch. 21

2 He could not make enemies. If anyone came to request the repayment of a loan from him he borrowed more. A cordial shake of his hand was a receipt in full for all demands.
William Hazlitt (1778–1830) British essayist and critic. *Monthly Magazine* (January 1824)

3 It is burning a farthing candle at Dover, to shew light at Calais.
Samuel Johnson (1709–84) British lexicographer and writer. Referring to the impact of Richard Brinsley Sheridan's works upon the English language. Quoted in *Life of Samuel Johnson* (James Boswell; 1791)

4 I'm sorry to hear that, sir, you don't happen to have the shilling about you now, do you?
Tom Sheridan (1775–1817) British administrator. To his father, on learning that he was to be cut off in his will with a shilling. *The Fine Art of Political Wit* (L. Harris; 1965)

Quotations by Sheridan

5 SURFACE It was an amiable weakness.
Claiming excessive generosity toward his extravagant brother. *School for Scandal* (1777), Act 5, Scene 1

6 The newspapers! Sir, they are the most villainous—licentious—abominable—infernal—Not that I ever read them—No—I make it a rule never to look into a newspaper.
The Critic (1779), Act 1, Scene 1

7 Certainly nothing is unnatural that is not physically impossible.
The Critic (1779), Act 2, Scene 1

8 I was struck all of a heap.
The Duenna (1775), Act 2, Scene 2

9 'Tis safest in matrimony to begin with a little aversion.
The Rivals (1775), Act 1, Scene 2

10 MRS. MALAPROP As headstrong as an allegory on the banks of the Nile.
Referring to Lydia Languish. *The Rivals* (1775), Act 3

11 MRS. MALAPROP If I reprehend any thing in this world, it is the use of my oracular tongue, and a nice derangement of epitaphs!
The Rivals (1775), Act 3, Scene 3

12 Our ancestors are very good kind of folks; but they are the last people I should choose to have a visiting acquaintance with.
The Rivals (1775), Act 4, Scene 1

13 The quarrel is a very pretty quarrel as it stands; we should only spoil it by trying to explain it.
The Rivals (1775), Act 4, Scene 3

14 You had no taste when you married me.
The School for Scandal (1777), Act 2, Scene 1

15 Be just before you are generous.
The School for Scandal (1777), Act 4, Scene 2

16 A man may surely be allowed to take a glass of wine by his own fireside.
February 24, 1809. As he sat in a coffeehouse watching his Drury Lane Theatre burn down. Quoted in *Memoirs of the Life of the Rt. Hon. Richard Brinsley Sheridan* (T. Moore; 1825), vol. 2

17 The Right Honourable gentleman is indebted to his memory for his jests, and to his imagination for his facts.
Replying to a speech in the British Parliament. Quoted in *Memoirs of the Life of the Rt. Hon. Richard Brinsley Sheridan* (T. Moore; 1825), vol. 2

18 Thank God, that's settled.
Handing one of his creditors an IOU. Quoted in *Wit, Wisdom, and Foibles of the Great* (C. Shriner; 1918)

19 My dear fellow, be reasonable; the sum you ask me for is a very considerable one, whereas I only ask you for twenty-five pounds.
Referring to being refused a further loan of £25 from a friend who wanted him to repay the £500 he had already borrowed. Attrib.

20 Won't you come into the garden? I would like my roses to see you.
Said to a young lady. Attrib.

21 It is not my interest to pay the principal, nor my principle to pay the interest.
Said to his tailor who had requested he pay a debt, or at least the interest on it. Attrib.

Sherman, William Tecumseh (1820–91) U.S. general

1 I am tired and sick of war. Its glory is all moonshine...War is hell.
Graduation address to the Michigan Military Academy (June 19, 1879)

2 I will not accept if nominated, and will not serve if elected.
It refers to his putative candidacy for presidential nomination. Message to the Republican National Convention (June 5, 1884)

3 There is many a boy here today who looks on war as all glory, but boys, it is all hell. You can bear this warning voice to generations yet to come. I look upon war with horror.
Speech, Columbus, Ohio (August 11, 1880)

Sherriff, R. C. (Robert Cedric Sherriff; 1896–1975) British author

1 When a man retires and time is no longer a matter of urgent importance, his colleagues generally present him with a clock.
Attrib.

Sherrill, Billy (b.1936) U.S. songwriter

1 Stand by Your Man
1975. Song title.

Sherrington, Charles Scott, Sir (1857–1952) British physiologist

1 As followers of natural science we know nothing of any relation between thoughts and the brain, except as a gross correlation in time and space.
Man on his Nature (1940)

Sherwood, Robert E. (Robert Emmet Sherwood; 1896–1955) U.S. playwright

1 The trouble with me is, I belong to a vanishing race. I'm one of the intellectuals.
The Petrified Forest (1935)

Shields, Brooke (Christa Brooke Camille Shields; b.1965) U.S. actor and model

1 Smoking kills, and if you're killed, you've lost a very important part of your life.
Attrib.

Shirley, James (1596–1666) English playwright

1 Death calls ye to the crowd of common men.
Cupid and Death (1653)

2 Only the actions of the just
Smell sweet, and blossom in their dust.
The Contention of Ajax and Ulysses (1659), Act 1, Scene 3

Shorter, Clement King (1857–1926) British journalist and literary critic

1 The latest definition of an optimist is one who fills up his crossword puzzle in ink.
Observer, London (February 22, 1925), "Sayings of the Week"

Shostakovich, Dmitri (Dmitri Dmitriyevich Shostakovich; 1906–75) Russian composer

1 There are few heroes or villains. Most people are average, neither black nor white, but gray...And it's in that gray middle ground that the fundamental conflicts of our age take place.
1971–75. *Testimony: The Memoirs of Shostakovich* (Solomon Volkov, ed., Antonina W. Bouis, tr.; 1979), ch. 1

2 These are not memoirs about myself. These are memoirs about other people. Others will write about us. And naturally they'll lie through their teeth—but that's their business.
1971–75. The opening paragraph of the composer's posthumously published memoirs. *Testimony: The Memoirs of Shostakovich* (Solomon Volkov, ed., Antonina W. Bouis, tr.; 1979), ch. 1

3 You have to treat everything with irony, especially the things you hold dear. There's more of a chance then that they'll survive. That is perhaps one of the greatest secrets of our life.
1971–75. *Testimony: The Memoirs of Shostakovich* (Solomon Volkov, ed., Antonina W. Bouis, tr.; 1979), ch. 3

Shuter, Edward (1728–76) British actor

1 A hole is the accident of a day, while a darn is premeditated poverty.
Explaining why he did not mend the holes in his stocking. Attrib. *Dictionary of National Biography* (1897)

Sibelius, Jean (Johan Julius Christian Sibelius; 1865–1957) Finnish composer

1 My heart sings, full of sadness—the shadows lengthen.
Written when trying to compose his Fifth Symphony against a background of troubling war news. Diary entry (October 1914)

2 When our conversation touched on the symphony, I said that I admired its style and severity of form, and the profound logic that created an inner connection between all the motifs ...Mahler's opinion was just the opposite. "No!" he said, "The symphony must be like the world. It must be all-embracing."
Said to Karl Ekman after Gustav Mahler's visit to Helsinki in 1907. Quoted in *Sibelius* (Robert Layton; 1965)

3 Pay no attention to what the critics say. No statue has ever been put up to a critic.
Attrib.

Sickert, Walter (Walter Richard Sickert; 1860–1942) German-born British painter

1 Nothing knits man to man, the Manchester School wisely taught, like the frequent passage from hand to hand of cash.
"The Language of Art," *New Age* (July 28, 1910)

Sidney, Algernon (1622–83) English politician

1 God helps those who help themselves.
Discourses Concerning Government (1698), ch. 2, pt. 23

2 'Tis not necessary to light a candle to the sun.
Discourses Concerning Government (1698), ch. 2, pt. 23

Sidney, Philip, Sir (1554–86) English poet, courtier, and soldier

1 Thy need is yet greater than mine.
Giving his own water bottle to a dying soldier after he had himself been wounded at the Battle of Zutphen (September 22, 1586). Quoted in *Life of the Renowned Sir Philip Sidney* (Sir Fulke Greville; 1652)

2 Biting my truant pen, beating myself for spite:
"Fool!" said my Muse to me; "look in thy heart and write."
Astrophel and Stella (1591), Sonnet 1

3 Come, Sleep! O Sleep, the certain knot of peace,
The bathing-place of wit, the balm of woe,
The poor man's wealth, the prisoner's release,
The indifferent judge between the high and low.
Astrophel and Stella (1591), Sonnet 39

4 There have been many most excellent poets that have never versified, and now swarm many versifiers that need never answer to the name of poets.
The Defence of Poesy (1595)

5 Love of honour and honour of love.
Referring to the ideal of chivalry. Quoted in *English Literature: Mediaeval* (W. P. Ker; 1912)

Sieff, Marcus, Baron Sieff of Brimpton (Marcus Joseph Sieff; b.1913) British business executive

1 Leaders must be seen to be up front, up to date, up to their job and up early in the morning.
Marcus Sieff on Management (1990)

2 Just as an employer should believe it is his duty to promote good human relations, so too should he see it as a duty to pursue the best possible relationship with the community.
Marcus Sieff was the chairman of the British retail chain, Marks & Spencer (1982–84). *Marcus Sieff on Management* (1990)

3 Top management must know how good or bad employees' working conditions are. They must eat in the employees' restaurants...visit the...lavatories. If they are not good enough for those in charge they are not good enough for anyone.
Quoted in Interview, *Sunday Telegraph*, London (July 1, 1984), magazine

Siegel, Jerry (1914–96) U.S. comic-strip writer

1 Faster than a speeding bullet, more powerful than a locomotive, able to leap tall buildings at a single bound—look, up there in the sky, it's a bird, it's a plane, it's Superman!
Comic strip. *Superman* (co-written with Joe Shuster; June 1938)

Sieger, Robin British business executive

1 Planning is as natural to the process of success as its absence is to the process of failure.
Natural Born Winners (1999)

2 When enthusiasm and commitment take root within a project, that project comes to life.
Natural Born Winners (1999)

Sieyès, Abbé (Emmanuel Joseph, Comte de Sieyès; 1748–1836) French clergyman and political theorist

1 Who will dare deny that the Third Estate contains within itself all that is needed to constitute a nation?
The "Third Estate" comprised all the French people except the nobility (the First Estate) and the clergy (the Second Estate). *Qu'est-ce que le Tiers État?* (January 1789)

2 I survived.
When asked what he had done during the French Revolution (1787–99). Quoted in *Notice historique sur la vie et les travaux de M. le Comte de Sieyès* (F. A. M. Mignet; 1836)

Sigerist, Henry E. (Henry Ernest Sigerist; 1891–1957) Swiss medical historian

1 The very popular hunting for "Fathers" of every branch of medicine and every treatment is, therefore, rather foolish; it is unfair not only to the mothers and ancestors but also to the obstetricians and midwives.
A History of Medicine (1951), Introduction, vol. 1

2 We must also keep in mind that discoveries are usually not made by one man alone, but that many brains and many hands are needed before a discovery is made for which one man receives the credit.
A History of Medicine (1951), Introduction, vol. 1

3 A determining point in the history of gynecology is to be found in the fact that sex plays a more important part in the life of woman than in that of man, and that she is more burdened by her sex.
American Journal of Obstetrics and Gynecology (1941)

4 Nicotinic acid cures pellagra, but a beefsteak prevents it.
Pellagra is niacin (vitamin B3) deficiency, caused by malnourishment. *Atlantic Monthly* (June 1939)

5 The development of industry has created many new sources of danger. Occupational diseases are socially different from other diseases, but not biologically.
Journal of the History of Medicine and Allied Sciences (1958)

6 Disease creates poverty and poverty disease. The vicious circle is closed.
Medicine and Human Welfare (1941), ch. 1

7 *Prevention* of disease must become the goal of every physician.
Medicine and Human Welfare (1941), ch. 3

8 The technology of medicine has outrun its sociology.
Medicine and Human Welfare (1941), ch. 3

9 Disease has social as well as physical, chemical, and biological causes.
Attrib.

Sigismund, Holy Roman Emperor (1368–1437) German-born emperor

1 Only do always in health what you have often promised to do when you are sick.
His advice on achieving happiness. *Biographiana* (14th–15th century), vol. 1

2 I am the Roman Emperor, and am above grammar.
Responding to criticism of his Latin. Attrib.

Siles, Jaime Spanish writer and critic

1 Can music be something more than shadows
made to the measure of an idea,
engraved on glass by one who forgets
that he causes a god to come forth from among his notes?
"Interiors," *A Bilingual Anthology of Contemporary Spanish Poetry* (Luis A. Ramos-García, ed.; 1997), pt. 2

Silius Italicus (Titus Catius Asconius Silius Italicus; 25/26?–101) Roman poet and politician

1 Virtue herself is her own fairest reward.
Punica (1st century?), bk. 13, l. 663

Silverman, Sime (1873–1933) U.S. newspaper publisher

1 Wall Street Lays An Egg
Headline following the Wall Street crash. *Variety* (October 1929)

Sima Guang (also known as Ssu-ma Kuang; 1019–86) Chinese writer

1 Even though a ruler may be wise as a sage, he must humble himself and yield to others. Then the intelligent will offer him their counsel and the brave will exert themselves to the fullest for him.
Zizhi tongjian (11th century), quoted in *China's Imperial Past* (Charles O. Hucker; 1975)

Simak, Clifford D. (Clifford Donald Simak; 1904–88) U.S. writer

1 The emergence of intelligence, I am convinced, tends to unbalance the ecology. In other words, intelligence is the great polluter. It is not until a creature begins to manage its environment that nature is thrown into disorder.
Shakespeare's Planet (1976)

2 What is the future of my kind of writing?...Perhaps in retirement...a quieter, narrower kind of life can be...adopted. Bounded by English literature and the Anglican Church and small pleasures like sewing and choosing dress material.
Attrib.

Sima Qian (also known as Ssu-ma Ch'ien; 145?–90? B.C.) Chinese historian

1 A multitude of evilly disposed people stir up strife, just as a crowd of mosquitoes can make a noise like thunder.
Biography of the King of Zhongsha (1st–2nd century B.C.), bk. 53, leaf 5

2 "I have heard that Han has offered a reward of a thousand catties of gold and a fief of ten thousand households for my head," said Xiang Yu. "I will do you the favor!" And with this he cut his own throat and died.
"The Basic Annals of Xiang Yu," *Records of the Historian* (Burton Watson, tr.; 1969)

Simenon, Georges (Georges Joseph Christian Simenon; 1903–89) Belgian-born French writer

1 Writing is not a profession but a vocation of unhappiness.
Interview, *Paris Review* (Summer 1955)

2 I have made love to ten thousand women since I was thirteen and a half.
His wife later said: "The true figure is no more than twelve hundred." Quoted in Interview, *L'Express* (Federico Fellini; February 21, 1977)

Simic, Charles (b.1938) Yugoslav-born U.S. poet and educator

1 Poetry proves again and again that any single overall theory of anything doesn't work. Poetry is always the cat concert under the window of the room in which the official version of reality is being written.
Quoted in *The Best of the Best American Poetry 1988–1997* (Harold Bloom, ed.; 1997)

Simon, Neil (Marvin Neil Simon; b.1927) U.S. playwright

1 PAUL Corie, there is one thing I learned in court. Be careful when you're tired and angry. You might say something you will soon regret.
Barefoot in the Park (1963)

2 CORIE A woman puts on rouge and powder to make her face more attractive. Maybe we can put some make-up on her personality.
Referring to her mother. *Barefoot in the Park* (1963)

3 I found a long gray hair on Kevin's jacket last night—If it's another woman's I'll kill him. If it's mine I'll kill myself.
Screenplay. *Only When I Laugh* (1981)

4 I've already had medical attention—a dog licked me when I was on the ground.
Screenplay. *Only When I Laugh* (1981)

5 There are two million interesting people in New York and only seventy-eight in Los Angeles.
Interview, *Playboy* (February 1979)

6 OSCAR Felix, leave everything alone. I'm not through dirtying-up for the night.
The Odd Couple (1965)

7 OSCAR *Poland* could live for a year on what my kids leave over from lunch.
The Odd Couple (1965)

8 OSCAR With my expenses and my alimony, a prisoner takes home more pay than I do!
The Odd Couple (1965)

9 OSCAR I'm eight hundred dollars behind in alimony, so let's up the stakes.
Referring to a poker game. *The Odd Couple* (1965)

10 ROY His refrigerator's been broken for two weeks—I saw milk standing in there that wasn't even in the bottle.
Referring to bachelor Oscar. *The Odd Couple* (1965)

11 OSCAR A world full of room-mates and I have to pick myself the Tin Man.
Referring to Felix. *The Odd Couple* (1965)

12 OSCAR Everything you do irritates me. And when you're not here, the things I know you're gonna do when you come back in irritate me.
Said to Felix. *The Odd Couple* (1965)

13 Everyone in Hollywood is looking for the blockbuster. They tell you their last movie "only grossed $70 million," as if that were some kind of crime.
Times, London (August 4, 1990)

14 The truth is that American audiences are still not altogether happy with Woody Allen or me when we stop doing the jokes.
Times, London (August 4, 1990)

15 You just can't have a leisurely farce, and the jokes have to come out of the *plot*, not the people.
Times, London (August 4, 1990)

Simon, Paul (b.1942) U.S. singer and songwriter

1 "Kathy," I said, as we boarded a Greyhound in Pittsburgh,
"Michigan seems like a dream to me now.
It took me four days to hitch-hike from Saginaw.
I've come to look for America."
Song lyric. "America" (1968)

2 Like a bridge over troubled water,
I will ease your mind.
Song lyric. "Bridge Over Troubled Water" (1970)

3 Here's to you, Mrs. Robinson,
Jesus loves you more than you will know.
Song lyric. "Mrs. Robinson" (1967)

4 People talking without speaking,
People listening without hearing,
People writing songs that voices never shared.
Song lyric. "The Sound of Silence" (1964)

5 Every time the industry gets powerful, and corporate thinking dominates what the music is, then the music really pales.
Quoted in "Paul Simon," *Off the Record: An Oral History of Popular Music* (Joe Smith; 1988)

6 If I liked the music, if it sounded good to me, it was popular for me, there was really no distinction between one culture and another.
Referring to "El Condor Pasa" by Los Incas, which he later recorded with Art Garfunkel. Quoted in "Paul Simon," *Off the Record: An Oral History of Popular Music* (Joe Smith; 1988)

Simone, Nina (originally Eunice Kathleen Waymon; b.1933) U.S. jazz singer, pianist, and songwriter

1 All record companies prefer third-rate talents to true genius because they can push them around more easily, make them change their clothes or politics just to sell more records.
I Put a Spell On You: The Autobiography (1991)

2 Getting stardom and, once you've got it, keeping it, is like fighting a war. You plan your campaign, recruit your troops, equip them properly, and then fight until you've stormed the cities you want. Then you dig in and defend your position.
I Put a Spell On You: The Autobiography (1991)

3 If an audience disrespects me it is insulting the music I play and I will not continue, because if they don't want to listen then I don't want to play. An audience chooses to come and see me perform; I don't choose the audience.
I Put a Spell On You: The Autobiography (1991)

4 Often you don't know how truly happy you were then until you look back and realize how much worse things could have been.
I Put a Spell On You: The Autobiography (1991)

Simpson, David (David Rae Fisher Simpson; b.1936) Scottish economist

1 To try to understand the workings of the economy by means of macroeconomics is rather like trying to understand how a clock works by observing the movements of the hands on its face.
"What Economists Need to Know," *Royal Bank of Scotland Review* (December 1988)

Simpson, N. F. (Norman Frederick Simpson; b.1919) British playwright

1 Knocked down a doctor? With an ambulance? How could she? It's a contradiction in terms.
One-Way Pendulum (1960), Act 1

Simpson, O. J. (Orenthal James Simpson; b.1947) U.S. football player, broadcaster, and actor

1 I am one hundred percent not guilty.
Read on television and often repeated. Open letter (June 17, 1994)

2 The only thing that endures is character. Fame and wealth—all that is illusion.
Said on his acquittal on murder charges. *Guardian*, London (December 30, 1995)

3 Right now I have to get twelve people to listen to all the facts, to listen to me, and for the first time in my life that's not going to be easy.
I Want to Tell You (1995)

Simpson, Wallis, Duchess of Windsor (originally Bessie Wallis Warfield; 1896–1986) U.S.-born British aristocrat

1 I don't remember any love affairs. One must keep love affairs quiet.
Los Angeles Times (April 11, 1974)

2 I married the Duke for better or worse but not for lunch.
Quoted in *The Windsor Story* (J. Bryan, III, and J. V. Murphy; 1979)

3 One can never be too thin or too rich.
Attrib.

Simpsons, The U.S. cartoon series

1 Funny noises are not funny.
Lines written as punishment on a chalkboard during the opening credits of *The Simpsons*. The content of the lines changes with each episode. *The Simpsons* (Matt Groening; 1990–)

2 I am not deliciously saucy.
Lines written as punishment on a chalkboard during the opening credits of *The Simpsons*. The content of the lines changes with each episode. *The Simpsons* (Matt Groening; 1990–)

3 I will not sell land in Florida.
Lines written as punishment on a chalkboard during the opening credits of *The Simpsons*. The content of the lines changes with each episode. *The Simpsons* (Matt Groening; 1990–)

4 The Pledge of Allegiance does not end with "Hail Satan."
Lines written as punishment on a chalkboard during the opening credits of *The Simpsons*. The content of the lines changes with each episode. *The Simpsons* (Matt Groening; 1990–)

Sinatra, Frank (Francis Albert Sinatra; 1915–98) U.S. singer and film actor

Quotations about Sinatra

1 He's the kind of guy that when he dies, he gives God a bad time for making him bald.
Marlon Brando (b.1924) U.S. actor. *Daily Mail*, London (March 30, 1977), quoted in *Chambers Film Quotes* (Tony Crawley, ed.; 1991)

Quotations by Sinatra

2 Rock and roll is phony and false, and it's sung, written, and played for the most part by cretinous goons.
Remark (1957)

3 People would often remark that I'm pretty lucky. Luck is only important insofar as getting the chance to sell yourself at the right moment. After that, you've got to have talent and know how to use it.
Quoted in *Bogie: the Biography of Humphrey Bogart* (Joe Hyams; 1971)

Sinclair, Clive, Sir (b.1940) British inventor and entrepreneur

1 An inventor is not just someone who comes up with ideas. Most people have ideas. The difference between the average person and the inventor is that the inventor for some reason has the urge to see his ideas through to fruition.
Quoted in "Creativity and Inventiveness," *The Roots of Excellence* (Ronnie Lessem; 1985), ch. 5

2 Computers today are superhuman in their ability to handle numbers, but still infantile in their ability to handle ideas and concepts.
Quoted in "Creativity and Inventiveness," *The Roots of Excellence* (Ronnie Lessem; 1985), ch. 5

3 It has suddenly become cheaper to have a machine to do a

mental task than for a man to do it...Just as men's muscles were replaced in the first industrial revolution, men's minds will be replaced in this second one.
Quoted in "Creativity and Inventiveness," *The Roots of Excellence* (Ronnie Lessem; 1985), ch. 5

4 Not too far in the future we will be able to put a machine into the home that is, in a real sense, intelligent, that can be a general factotum, an adviser, or a mentor.
Quoted in "Creativity and Inventiveness," *The Roots of Excellence* (Ronnie Lessem; 1985), ch. 5

5 Programming used to be thought of as a sort of arcane matter. Now it's become the province of children who are superb at it.
Quoted in "Creativity and Inventiveness," *The Roots of Excellence* (Ronnie Lessem; 1985), ch. 5

6 We're not going to enjoy the sort of society we're creating, unless we educate people to have a taste for living.
Quoted in "Creativity and Inventiveness," *The Roots of Excellence* (Ronnie Lessem; 1985), ch. 5

7 What I'd like to see, in due course, is a computer which has some sort of personality so that you can go round to it in the morning and talk to it.
Quoted in "Creativity and Inventiveness," *The Roots of Excellence* (Ronnie Lessem; 1985), ch. 5

Singer, Isaac Bashevis (Yitskhek Bashyevis Zinger; 1904–91) Polish-born U.S. writer

1 Children...have no use for psychology. They detest sociology. They still believe in God, the family, angels, devils, witches, goblins, logic, clarity, punctuation, and other such obsolete stuff...When a book is boring, they yawn openly. They don't expect their writer to redeem humanity, but leave to adults such childish illusions.
Nobel Prize address, Stockholm (December 10, 1978)

2 When I was a little boy they called me a liar but now that I am a grown up they call me a writer.
Remark (July 1983)

3 If Moses had been paid newspaper rates for the Ten Commandments, he might have written the Ten Thousand Commandments.
New York Times (June 30, 1985)

4 The greatness of art is not to find what is common but what is unique.
Interview, *New York Times Magazine* (November 28, 1978)

5 We know what a person thinks not when he tells us what he thinks, but by his actions.
Interview, *New York Times Magazine* (November 28, 1978)

6 Death is the Messiah. That's the real truth.
Closing lines. *The Family Moskat* (H. R. Gross, tr.; 1950)

7 We have to believe in free will. We've got no choice.
Times, London (June 21, 1982)

Siple, Paul Allman (1908–68) U.S. geographer and explorer

1 Even heavy automobile traffic out of New York City on a summer weekend minutely unbalances the earth as it rotates.
90 Degrees South (1959)

Sitting Bull (Tatanka Yotaka; 1834?–90) U.S. Sioux leader

Quotations about Sitting Bull

1 The contents of his pockets were often emptied into the hands of small, ragged little boys, nor could he understand how so much wealth should go brushing by, unmindful of the poor.
Annie Oakley (1860–1926) U.S. markswoman and performer. Quoted in *Annie Oakley: Woman at Arms* (Courtney Ryley Cooper; 1927), ch. 7

Quotations by Sitting Bull

2 The white man knows how to make everything, but he does not know how to distribute it.
Attrib.

Sitwell, Edith, Dame (1887–1964) British poet, critic, and writer

1 Still falls the Rain—
Dark as the world of man, black as our loss—
Blind as the nineteen hundred and forty nails
Upon the cross.
"Still Falls the Rain" (1942), ll. 1–4

2 My poems are hymns of praise to the glory of life.
"Some Notes on My Poetry," *Collected Poems* (1954)

3 Another little drink wouldn't do us any harm.
1922. "Scotch Rhapsody," *Façade* (1923)

4 When
Sir
Beelzebub called for his syllabub in the hotel in Hell
Where Proserpine first fell,
Blue as the gendarmerie were the waves of the sea,
(Rocking and shocking the bar-maid).
1922. "Sir Beelzebub," *Façade* (1923)

5 I have often wished I had time to cultivate modesty...But I am too busy thinking about myself.
Observer, London (April 30, 1950), "Sayings of the Week"

6 I wish the Government would put a tax on pianos for the incompetent.
Selected Letters, 1916–1964 (1971)

7 Why not be oneself? That is the whole secret of a successful appearance. If one is a greyhound why try to look like a Pekinese?
"Why I Look As I Do," *Sunday Graphic*, London (1955)

8 A lady asked me why, on most occasions, I wore black. "Are you in mourning?"
"Yes."
"For whom are you in mourning?"
"For the world."
Taken Care Of (1965), ch. 1

9 A pompous woman of his acquaintance, complaining that the head-waiter of a restaurant had not shown her and her husband immediately to a table, said, "We had to tell him who we were." Gerald, interested, enquired, "And who were you?"
Taken Care Of (1965), ch. 15

10 It is as unseeing to ask what is the *use* of poetry as it would be to ask what is the use of religion.
The Outcasts (1962), Preface

11 Who dreamed that Christ has died in vain?
He walks again on the Seas of Blood,
He comes in the terrible Rain.
The Shadow of Cain (1947)

12 Recreations: listening to music, silence.
In her *Who's Who* entry for many years. Quoted in *Who Was Who* (1972), vol. 6, 1961–70

Sitwell, Osbert, Sir, 5th Baronet Sitwell (Francis Osbert Sacheverell Sitwell; 1892–1969) British writer

1 In reality, *killing time*
Is only the name for another of the multifarious ways
By which Time kills us.
Milordo Inglese (1958)

Skelton, John (1460?–1529) English poet and satirist

1 There is nothynge that more dyspleaseth God,
Than from theyr children to spare the rod.
"Magnyfycence," ll. 1954–55

2 All to have promotion—
That is their whole devotion!
"The Prelates," *Collyn Clout* (1550?), quoted in *The Albatross Book of Verse* (Louis Untermeyer, ed.; 1933)

3 For, though my rhyme be ragged,
Tattered and jagged,
Rudely rain-beaten,
Rusty and moth-eaten,
If ye take well therewith
It hath in it some pith.
"The Prelates," *Collyn Clout* (1550?), quoted in *The Albatross Book of Verse* (Louis Untermeyer, ed.; 1933)

4 By Saint Mary, my lady,
Your mammy and your daddy
Brought forth a goodly baby!
"To Mistress Isabel Pennell," *The New Oxford Book of English Verse* (Helen Gardner, ed.; 1972)

5 On being desired to ask three things, which he would have granted, hee askt, 1st, as much ale as would serve him all his life; then what hee would have in the second place, as much tobacco as would serve his life; then, what in the third place, he stood awhile: the king prest him to speak quickly: he then said, more ale!
1525? A Welshman responding to the king's offer to grant three requests. Quoted in "Merie Tales of Skelton," *Shakespeare Jest-Books, vol. 2 of Old English Jest-Books* (William Carew Hazlitt, ed.; 1864), note to "Howe the Welshman dyd desyre Skelton to ayde hym in hys sute to the kynge..."

6 Old proverbe says,
That byrd ys not honest
That fyleth hys owne nest.
Quoted in *The Poetical Works of John Skelton* (Rev. Alexander Dyce; 1856), Poems against Garnesche

Skinner, B. F. (Burrhus Frederic Skinner; 1904–90) U.S. psychologist

1 All organisms, including humans, are greatly influenced by the consequences produced by their own behavior.
"The Behavior of Organisms" (1938)

2 When a given act is followed closely by a reinforcer, the organism tends to increase the frequency of that act under the same or similar conditions.
"The Behavior of Organisms" (1938)

3 The real problem is not whether machines think but whether men do.
Contingencies of Reinforcement (1969), ch. 9

4 Education is what survives when what has been learned has been forgotten.
"Education in 1984," *New Scientist* (May 21, 1964)

5 Indeed one of the ultimate advantages of an education is simply coming to the end of it.
The Technology of Teaching (1968)

Skinner, Cornelia Otis (1901–79) U.S. stage actor and writer

1 Woman's virtue is man's greatest invention.
Attrib.

Slezak, Leo (1873–1946) Czech-born tenor

1 What time's the next swan?
When the mechanical swan left the stage without him during a performance of *Lohengrin*. *What Time's the Next Swan?* (Walter Slezak; 1962)

Sloan, John (John French Sloan; 1871–1951) U.S. painter and etcher

1 Painting without drawing is just "coloriness", color excitement. To think of color for color's sake is like thinking of sound for sound's sake. Who ever heard of a musician who was passionately fond of B flat?
The Gist of Art: Principles and Practice Expounded in the Classroom and Studio (1939)

Sloan, Alfred P., Jr. (Alfred Pritchard Sloan, Jr.; 1875–1966) U.S. business executive and philanthropist

1 Bedside manners are no substitute for the right diagnosis.
Quoted in *Business@the Speed of Thought: Using a Digital Nervous System* (Bill Gates, co-written with Collins Hemingway; 1999)

2 Take my assets—but leave me my organization and in five years I'll have it all back.
Quoted in *Strategy and Business* (1998)

3 There are times when you have to spend money just to stay in business.
Quoted in *Strategy and Business* (1996)

4 There's no resting place for an enterprise in a competitive economy.
Quoted in *Strategy and Business* (1998)

5 Hard work. There is no short cut.
Attrib.

6 A car for every purse and purpose.
Sloan was president and chief executive of General Motors Corporation. Attrib.

Smart, Christopher (1722–71) British poet

Quotations about Smart

1 Sir, there is no settling the point of precedency between a louse and a flea.
1783
Samuel Johnson (1709–84) British lexicographer and writer. Said when Maurice Morgann asked him who he considered to be the better poet—Christopher Smart or Samuel Derrick. Quoted in *Life of Samuel Johnson* (James Boswell; 1791)

Quotations by Smart

2 For ADORATION seasons change,
And order, truth, and beauty range,
Adjust, attract, and fill:
The grass the polyanthus cheques;
And polished porphyry reflects,
By the descending rill.
"A Song to David" (1763), quoted in *The New Oxford Book of English Verse* (Helen Gardner, ed.; 1972)

3 God all-bounteous, all creative,
Whom no ills from good dissuade,
Is incarnate and a native
Of the very world he made.
"The Nativity of Our Lord and Saviour" (1765), quoted in *The New Oxford Book of English Verse* (Helen Gardner, ed.; 1972)

4 For I will consider my Cat Jeoffry.
For he is the servant of the Living God, duly and daily serving him.
Jubilate Agno (1758–63), Fragment B

5 For he counteracts the powers of darkness by his electrical skin and glaring eyes.
"For I Will Consider My Cat Jeoffry," *Jubilate Agno* (1758–63)

6 For he purrs in thankfulness, when God tells him he's a good Cat.
For he is an instrument for the children to learn benevolence upon.
"For I Will Consider My Cat Jeoffry," *Jubilate Agno* (1758–63)

7 For echo is the soul of the voice
exciting itself in hollow places.
Quoted in *The English Patient* (Michael Ondaatje; 1991)

Smart, Elizabeth (1913–86) U.S. poet and novelist

1 By Grand Central Station I Sat Down and Wept
1945. Book title. Paraphrasing Psalm 137:1.

Smiles, Samuel (1812–1904) Scottish writer

1 We often discover what *will* do, by finding out what will not do; and probably he who never made a mistake never made a discovery.
Self-Help (1859), ch. 11

2 A place for everything, and everything in its place.
Thrift (1875), ch. 5

Smith, Adam (1723–90) Scottish economist and philosopher

1 How selfish soever man may be supposed, there are evidently some principles in his nature, which interest him in the fortune of others, and render their happiness necessary to him, though he derives nothing from it except the pleasure of seeing it.
The Theory of Moral Sentiments (1759)

2 A man may sympathize with a woman in childbed, though it is impossible that he should conceive himself as suffering her pains in his own proper person and character.
The Theory of Moral Sentiments (1759), pt. 7

3 Consumption is the sole end and purpose of production; and the interest of the producer ought to be attended to only so far as it may be necessary for promoting that of the consumer.
The Wealth of Nations (1776), bk. 4, ch. 8

4 It is not from the benevolence of the butcher, the brewer, or the baker, that we expect our dinner, but from their regard to their own self-interest. We address ourselves, not to their humanity but their self-love.
Wealth of Nations (1776), bk. 1, ch. 2

5 People of the same trade seldom meet together but the conversation ends in a conspiracy against the public, or in some contrivance to raise prices.
Wealth of Nations (1776), bk. 1, ch. 10, pt. 2

6 With the great part of rich people, the chief employment of riches consists in the parade of riches.
Wealth of Nations (1776), bk. 1, ch. 11

7 Science is the great antidote to the poison of enthusiasm and superstition.
Wealth of Nations (1776), bk. 5, ch. 1

8 There is no art which one government sooner learns of another than that of draining money from the pockets of the people.
Wealth of Nations (1776), bk. 5, ch. 2

9 To found a great empire for the sole purpose of raising up a people of customers, may at first sight appear a project fit only for a nation of shopkeepers. It is, however, a project altogether unfit for a nation of shopkeepers; but extremely fit for a nation whose government is influenced by shopkeepers.
Wealth of Nations (1776), vol. 2, bk. 4, ch. 8

Smith, Al (Alfred Emanuel Smith; 1873–1944) U.S. politician

1 All the ills of democracy can be cured by more democracy.
Speech, Albany, New York (June 27, 1933), quoted in *New York Times* (July 28, 1933)

2 No matter how thin you slice it, it's still baloney.
Speech, *Campaign Speeches* (1936)

Smith, Anthony (Anthony John Francis Smith; b.1926) British zoologist and author

1 Someone once asked A. C. Aitken, professor at Edinburgh University, to make 4 divided by 47 into a decimal. After four seconds he started and gave another digit every three-quarters of a second...To many of us such a man is from another planet.
The Mind (1984)

2 We now have a brain more suited to our needs. Perhaps it will teach us one day how to tap its real potential.
The Mind (1984)

Smith, Bessie (Elizabeth Smith, "Empress of the Blues"; 1894?–1937) U.S. blues singer

Quotations about Smith

1 Blues comes from that sense of not being at the centre, "from nothingness, from want, from desire", as W. C. Handy put it. Bessie became the incarnation of that "absence, darkness, death."
Elaine Feinstein (b.1930) British poet and novelist. *Bessie Smith: Empress of the Blues* (1985), ch. 12

Quotations by Smith

2 No time to marry, no time to settle down,
I'm a young woman, and I ain't done runnin' aroun'.
Song lyric. "Young Woman's Blues" (1927)

3 It's mighty strange, without a doubt, Nobody knows you when you're down and out.
"Nobody Knows You When You're Down and Out," *Harlem: The Great Black Way* (Jervis Anderson; 1982)

Smith, Delia (b.1941) British cookery writer and broadcaster

1 Food is for eating, and good food is to be enjoyed...I think food is, actually, very beautiful in itself.
Times, London (October 17, 1990)

Smith, Dodie (C. L. Anthony; 1896–1990) British playwright, novelist, and theatrical producer

1 The family, that dear octopus from whose tentacles we never quite escape, nor in our innermost hearts never quite wish to.
Dear Octopus (1938)

2 Noble deeds and hot baths are the best cures for depression.
I Capture the Castle (1948), pt. 1, ch. 3

3 Truthfulness so often goes with ruthlessness.
One Hundred and One Dalmatians (1956)

Smith, F. E., 1st Earl of Birkenhead (Frederick Edwin Smith; 1872–1930) British politician

Quotations about Smith

1 He's very clever, but sometimes his brains go to his head.
Margot Asquith (1865–1945) British political hostess and writer. *As I Remember* (1922)

Quotations by Smith

2 The world continues to offer glittering prizes to those who have stout hearts and sharp swords.
Rectorial Address, Glasgow University, Scotland, quoted in *Times*, London (November 8, 1923)

3 JUDGE WILLIS You are extremely offensive, young man.
F. E. SMITH As a matter of fact, we both are, and the only difference between us is that I am trying to be, and you can't help it.
Frederick Edwin, Earl of Birkenhead (written by his son, the 2nd Earl of Birkenhead; 1933), vol. 1, ch. 9

4 Nature has no cure for this sort of madness, though I have known a legacy from a rich relative work wonders.
Referring to Bolshevism. *Law, Life and Letters* (1927), vol. 2, ch. 19

5 Possibly not, My Lord, but far better informed.
To a judge who complained that he had listened to Smith's argument but was still none the wiser. Quoted in *F. E.: the Life of F. E. Smith, First Earl of Birkenhead* (2nd Earl of Birkenhead; 1959 ed.)

Smith, Goldwin (1823–1910) British-born Canadian historian and journalist

1 History, without moral philosophy, is a mere string of facts; and moral philosophy, without history, is apt to become a dream.
Rational Religion (1861)

2 French Canada is a relic of the historical past preserved by isolation, as Siberian mammoths are preserved by ice.
The Political Destiny of Canada (1878)

Smith, Henry John Stephen (1826–83) Irish-born British mathematician

1 Pure mathematics, may it never be of any use to anyone.
A toast he often gave. Quoted in *Mathematical Circles Squared* (H. Eves; 1972)

Smith, Ian (Ian Douglas Smith; b.1919) Zimbabwean prime minister

1 I don't believe in black majority rule in Rhodesia...not in a thousand years.
Speech (March 1976)

Smith, Joan (b.1953) British writer and journalist

1 Most women decide to have abortions reluctantly, and with trepidation, as the lesser of two evils. No woman has an abortion for *fun*.
Misogynies (1989)

Smith, John (1579?–1631) English colonist

1 How was it possible such wise men could so torment themselves...making Religion their colour, when all their aime was nothing but present profit...by sending us so many Refiners, Goldsmiths, Jewellers...with all their appurtenances.
Referring to the Virginia Company. *Advertisements for the Unexperienced Planters of New England* (1631), quoted in *The Complete Works of Captain John Smith* (P. L. Barbour, ed.; 1986)

2 Two great stones were brought before *Powhatan*: then as many as could layd hands on him...to beate out his braines, *Pocahontas* the Kings dearest daughter...got his head in her armes, and laid her owne upon his to save him.
Referring to Smith's alleged rescue (1608) by Pocahontas, daughter of Powhatan, who was leader of the Powhatan confederacy of Algonquian peoples in what is now Virginia. *The Generall History of Virginia, New-England, and the Summer Isles* (1624), bk. 3, ch. 2, quoted in *The Complete Works of Captain John Smith* (P. L. Barbour, ed.; 1986)

3 *Powhatan*...came unto him and told him now they were friends, and presently he should go to *James* towne, to send him two great guns...for which he would give him the Country of

Capahowosick, and for ever esteeme him as his sonne *Nantaquoud*.
Referring to Smith's dealings (1608) with Powhatan, leader of the Powhatan confederacy of Algonquian peoples in what is now Virginia. *The Generall History of Virginia, New-England, and the Summer Isles* (1624), bk. 3, ch. 2, quoted in *The Complete Works of Captain John Smith* (P. L. Barbour, ed.; 1986)

4 Such things as shee delighted in, he would have given her; but with teares running down her cheekes, shee said shee durst not be seene to have any: for if Powhatan should know it, she were but dead.
Pocahontas had warned Smith of an intended raid by her father, Powhatan. *The Generall History of Virginia, New-England, and the Summer Isles* (1624), bk. 3, ch. 8, quoted in *The Complete Works of Captain John Smith* (P. L. Barbour, ed.; 1986)

Smith, Joseph (1805–44) U.S. founder of Mormon church

1 I told the brethren that the Book of Mormon was the most correct of any book on earth, and the keystone of our religion, and a man would get nearer to God by abiding by its precepts, than by any other book.
History of the Church of Jesus Christ of Latter-day Saints (co-written with B. H. Roberts; 1932–51)

2 He called me by name, and said unto me that he was a messenger sent from the presence of God to me, and that...God had a work for me to do.
In His Own Words (1844)

3 I have always declared God to be a distinct personage, Jesus Christ a separate and distinct personage from God the Father, and the Holy Ghost was a distinct personage and a Spirit.
Teachings of the Prophet Joseph Smith (Joseph Fielding Smith, ed.; 1938)

4 We are told, and very plainly too, that hot drinks—tea, coffee, chocolate, cocoa and all drinks of this kind are not good for man.
The Word of Wisdom (February 27, 1823)

Smith, Logan Pearsall (1865–1946) U.S.-born British writer

1 Don't tell your friends their social faults, they will cure the fault and never forgive you.
Afterthoughts (1931)

2 The denunciation of the young is a necessary part of the hygiene of older people, and greatly assists the circulation of their blood.
"Age and Death," *Afterthoughts* (1931)

3 There is more felicity on the far side of baldness than young men can possibly imagine.
"Age and Death," *Afterthoughts* (1931)

4 A best-seller is the gilded tomb of a mediocre talent.
"Arts and Letters," *Afterthoughts* (1931)

5 The test of a vocation is the love of the drudgery it involves.
"Arts and Letters," *Afterthoughts* (1931)

6 Eat with the rich, but go to the play with the poor, who are capable of joy.
"In the World," *Afterthoughts* (1931)

7 It is the wretchedness of being rich that you have to live with rich people.
"In the World," *Afterthoughts* (1931)

8 How awful to reflect that what people say of us is true.
"Life and Human Nature," *Afterthoughts* (1931)

9 There are few sorrows, however poignant, in which a good income is of no avail.
"Life and Human Nature," *Afterthoughts* (1931)

10 There are two things to aim at in life: first, to get what you want; and after that, to enjoy it. Only the wisest of mankind achieve the second.
"Life and Human Nature," *Afterthoughts* (1931)

11 People say that life is the thing, but I prefer reading.
"Myself," *Afterthoughts* (1931)

12 Thank heavens the sun has gone in and I don't have to go out and enjoy it.
"Myself," *Afterthoughts* (1931)

13 Married women are kept women, and they are beginning to find it out.
"Other People," *Afterthoughts* (1931)

14 Most people sell their souls, and live with a good conscience on the proceeds.
"Other People," *Afterthoughts* (1931)

15 When people come and talk to you of their aspirations, before they leave you had better count your spoons.
"Other People," *Afterthoughts* (1931)

16 I am one of the unpraised, unrewarded millions without whom Statistics would be a bankrupt science. It is we who are born, who marry, who die, in constant ratios.
Trivia (1902)

17 I cannot forgive my friends for dying: I do not find these vanishing acts of theirs at all amusing.
Trivia (1902)

18 I might give my life for my friend, but he had better not ask me to do up a parcel.
Trivia (1902)

19 Yes there is a meaning; at least for me, there is one thing that matters—to set a chime of words tinkling in the minds of a few fastidious people.
Contemplating whether life has any meaning, shortly before his death. Quoted in Obituary, *New Statesman*, London (Cyril Connolly; March 9, 1946)

Smith, Patti (Patti Lee Smith; b.1946) U.S. rock singer and songwriter

1 Most of my poems are written to women because women are most inspiring. Who are most artists? Men. Who do they get inspired by? Women. The masculinity in me gets inspired by the female...I can use her as my muse.
Quoted in *Please Kill Me* (Legs McNeil and Gillian McCain; 1996)

Smith, Paul (b.1946) British fashion designer

1 I can't think how many times I've wanted to leave a dinner table after spending too long in a designer chair.
Observer, London (December 12, 1995)

2 Fashion is about profit and expansion, and trends reduced to the level of soundbites—Long is the new short! Brown is the

new black!...Whatever happened to character and honesty and individuality?
Vogue, London (May 1998)

Smith, Raymond W. (b.1937) U.S. business executive

1 Administrators are cheap and easy to find and cheap to keep. Leaders—risk takers: they are in very short supply. And ones with vision are pure gold.
Speech (August 1, 1988)

2 The assumptions on which my whole generation of management built our careers—have been blown to bits by global competition.
Speech (November 1, 1995)

3 Today's information technology makes controlled information flow unproductive—it also makes it impossible.
Speech (October 17, 1995)

4 Traditional management structures were devised when information was a scarce commodity, so that knowledge about how to run the business could be communicated layer by layer.
Speech (October 17, 1995)

5 We're good at sending people to diversity training, using politically correct language, and making sure we have people of color in our Annual Report photos. But...the deep-seated issues of intolerance and exclusivity go unexamined.
Speech (November 1, 1995)

Smith, Roland, Sir (b.1928) British business executive

1 I'll answer some of your questions, the more difficult ones will be answered by my colleagues.
Speech, Annual General Meeting, British Aerospace, *Observer,* London (May 15, 1988), "Quotes of the Week"

Smith, Samuel Francis (1808–95) U.S. poet and clergyman

1 My country, 'tis of thee,
Sweet land of liberty,
Of thee I sing:
Land where my fathers died,
Land of the pilgrims' pride,
From every mountainside
Let freedom ring.
"America" (1831), st. 1

Smith, Stevie (Florence Margaret Smith; 1902–71) British poet and novelist

1 Nobody heard him, the dead man,
But still he lay moaning:
I was much further out than you thought
And not waving but drowning.
"Not Waving But Drowning" (1957)

2 This Englishwoman is so refined
She has no bosom and no behind.
"This Englishwoman" (1937)

3 Dearest Evelyn, I think of you
Out with the guns in the jungle stew
Yesterday I hittapotamus
I put the measurements down for you but they got lost in the fuss.
"The Jungle Husband," *Collected Poems* (1975)

4 The nearly right
And yet not quite
In love is wholly evil
And every heart
That loves in part
Is mortgaged to the devil.
"To the Tune of the Coventry Carol," *Collected Poems* (1975)

5 I do really think that death will be marvellous...If there wasn't death, I think you couldn't go on.
Observer, London (November 9, 1969)

6 A Good Time Was Had by All
Book title. (1937)

Smith, Sydney (1771–1845) British clergyman, essayist, and wit

1 I am convinced digestion is the great secret of life.
Letter to Arthur Kinglake (1837)

2 You must not think me necessarily foolish because I am facetious, nor will I consider you necessarily wise because you are grave.
Letter to Bishop Blomfield (1840)

3 He who drinks a tumbler of London water has literally in his stomach more animated beings than there are men, women and children on the face of the globe.
Letter to Countess Grey (1834)

4 I have no relish for the country; it is a kind of healthy grave.
Letter to Miss G. Harcourt (1838), quoted in *Letters of Sydney Smith* (N. C. Smith, ed.; 1953)

5 People of wealth and rank never use ugly names for ugly things. Apoplexy is an affection of the head; paralysis is nervousness; gangrene is pain and inconvenience in the extremities.
Remark (January 1844)

6 Mankind are always happy for having been happy, so that if you make them happy now, you make them happy twenty years hence by the memory of it.
1804–06. *Sketches of Moral Philosophy* (1849)

7 If you choose to represent the various parts in life by holes upon a table, of different shapes,—some circular, some triangular, some square, some oblong,—and the persons acting these parts by bits of wood of similar shapes, we shall generally find that the triangular person has got into the square hole, the oblong into the triangular, and a square person has squeezed himself into the round hole.
Sketches of Moral Philosophy (1849), Lecture 9

8 Have the courage to be ignorant of a great number of things, in order to avoid the calamity of being ignorant of everything.
The Letters of Peter Plymley (1807)

9 Oh! When I have the gout, I feel as if I was walking on my eyeballs.
Quoted in *A Memoir of the Rev. Sydney Smith* (Lady Holland; 1855), ch. 11

10 Take short views, hope for the best, and trust in God.
Quoted in *A Memoir of the Rev. Sydney Smith* (Lady Holland; 1855), vol. 1, ch. 6

11 Ah, you flavour everything; you are the vanilla of society.
Quoted in *A Memoir of the Rev. Sydney Smith* (Lady Holland; 1855), vol. 1, ch. 9

12 As the French say, there are three sexes—men, women, and clergymen.
Quoted in *A Memoir of the Rev. Sydney Smith* (Lady Holland; 1855), vol. 1, ch. 9

13 How can a bishop marry? How can he flirt? The most he can say is, "I will see you in the vestry after service."
Quoted in *A Memoir of the Rev. Sydney Smith* (Lady Holland; 1855), vol. 1, ch. 9

14 My living in Yorkshire was so far out of the way, that it was actually twelve miles from a lemon.
Quoted in *A Memoir of the Rev. Sydney Smith* (Lady Holland; 1855), vol. 1, ch. 9

15 No furniture so charming as books.
Quoted in *A Memoir of the Rev. Sydney Smith* (Lady Holland; 1855), vol. 1, ch. 9

16 "Heat, ma'am!" I said; "it was so dreadful here that I found there was nothing left for it but to take off my flesh and sit in my bones."
Discussing the hot weather with a lady acquaintance. Quoted in *A Memoir of the Rev. Sydney Smith* (Lady Holland; 1855), vol. 1, ch. 9

17 My definition of marriage:...it resembles a pair of shears, so joined that they cannot be separated; often moving in opposite directions, yet always punishing anyone who comes between them.
Quoted in *A Memoir of the Rev. Sydney Smith* (Lady Holland; 1855), vol. 1, ch. 11

18 He has occasional flashes of silence, that make his conversation perfectly delightful.
Referring to Lord Macaulay. Quoted in *A Memoir of the Rev. Sydney Smith* (Lady Holland; 1855), vol. 1, ch. 11

19 Serenely full, the epicure would say,
Fate cannot harm me, I have dined to-day.
Quoted in "Recipe for Salad," *A Memoir of the Rev. Sydney Smith* (Lady Holland; 1855), vol. 1, ch. 11

20 What you don't know would make a great book.
Quoted in "Recipe for Salad," *A Memoir of the Rev. Sydney Smith* (Lady Holland; 1855), vol. 1, ch. 11

21 They are written as if sin were to be taken out of man like Eve out of Adam—by putting him to sleep.
Referring to boring sermons. Quoted in *Anecdotes of the Clergy* (Jacob Larwood; 1890)

22 Poverty is no disgrace to a man, but it is confoundedly inconvenient.
Quoted in *Sydney Smith: His Wit and Wisdom* (J. Potter Briscoe, ed.; 1900)

23 I never read a book before reviewing it; it prejudices a man so.
Quoted in *The Smith of Smiths* (H. Pearson; 1934), ch. 3

24 Minorities...are almost always in the right.
Quoted in *The Smith of Smiths* (H. Pearson; 1934), ch. 9

25 What a pity it is that we have no amusements in England but vice and religion!
Quoted in *The Smith of Smiths* (H. Pearson; 1934), ch. 10

26 Death must be distinguished from dying, with which it is often confused.
Quoted in *The Smith of Smiths* (H. Pearson; 1934), ch. 11

27 I am just going to pray for you at St Paul's, but with no very lively hope of success.
Referring to meeting an acquaintance. Quoted in *The Smith of Smiths* (H. Pearson; 1934), ch. 13

28 I am not fond of expecting catastrophes, but there are cracks in the universe.
Attrib.

29 The birds seem to consider the muzzle of my gun as their safest position.
Attrib.

Smith, Theobald (1859–1934) U.S. pathologist

1 Research is fundamentally a state of mind involving continual reexamination of the doctrines and axioms upon which current thought and action are based. It is, therefore, critical of existing practices.
American Journal of Medical Science (1929), no. 178

Smith, Thorne (1892–1934) U.S. humorist and writer

1 Steven's mind was so tolerant that he could have attended a lynching every day without becoming critical.
The Jovial Ghosts (1933), ch. 11

Smith, Will (Willard Smith; b.1968) U.S. singer and actor

1 I know your feet must be tired 'cuz you been running through my mind *all* day!
As Will, the Fresh Prince of Bel-Air. "That's No Lady, That's My Cousin," *The Fresh Prince of Bel-Air* (1995)

Smithson, Robert (Robert Irving Smithson; 1938–73) U.S. artist and art theorist

1 Size determines an object, but scale determines art.
"The Spiral Jetty," *Arts of the Environment* (Gyorgy Kepes, ed.; 1972)

Smollett, Tobias (Tobias George Smollett; 1721–71) Scottish novelist

1 Some folk are wise, and some are otherwise.
The Adventures of Roderick Random (1748), ch. 6

2 True patriotism is of no party.
The Adventures of Sir Launcelot Greaves (1762)

Smoot, George (George Fitzgerald Smoot, III; b.1945) U.S. astrophysicist

1 We now have direct evidence of the birth of the Universe and its evolution...ripples in space-time laid down earlier than the first billionth of a second. If you're religious, it's like seeing God.
Wrinkles in Time (co-written with Keay Davidson; 1993)

Smythe, Tony (b.1938) British civil rights activist

1 Censorship is more depraving and corrupting than anything pornography can produce.
Observer, London (September 18, 1972), "Sayings of the Week"

Snow, C. P., Baron Snow of Leicester (Charles Percy Snow; 1905–80) British novelist and scientist

1 The official world, the corridors of power, the dilemmas of conscience and egotism—she disliked them all.
Homecomings (1956), ch. 22

2 "I grant you that he's not two-faced," I said. "But what's the use of that when the one face he has got is so peculiarly unpleasant?"
The Affair (1959), ch. 4

Snyder, Gary (Gary Sherman Snyder; b.1930) U.S. poet, essayist, and translator

1 If we are lucky we may eventually arrive at a totally integrated world culture with matrilineal descent, free-form marriage, natural credit communist economy, less industry, far less population, and lots more national parks.
"Buddhism and the Coming Revolution," *Earth House Hold* (1969)

2 Three-fourths of philosophy and literature is the talk of people trying to convince themselves that they really like the cage they were tricked into entering.
October 24, 1956. "Japan First Time Around," *Earth House Hold* (1969)

3 Forest equals crop Scenery equals recreation Public equals money: The shopkeeper's view of nature.
June 27, 1953. "Lookout's Journal: Sourdough," *Earth House Hold* (1969)

4 In a culture where the aesthetic experience is denied and atrophied, genuine religious ecstasy rare, intellectual pleasure scorned—it is only natural that sex should become the only personal epiphany of most people.
August 9, 1953. "Lookout's Journal: Sourdough," *Earth House Hold* (1969)

5 The foamy wake behind the boat *does* look like the water of Hokusai. Water in motion is precise and sharp, clearly formed, holding specific postures for infinitely small frozen moments.
June 30, 1953. Hokusai (1760–1849) was a Japanese painter and wood engraver. "Lookout's Journal: Sourdough," *Earth House Hold* (1969)

6 Americans are splendid while working—attentive, cooperative, with dignity and sureness—but the same ones seen later at home or bar are sloppy, bored, and silly.
March 30, 1957. "Tanker Notes," *Earth House Hold* (1969)

7 A clear attentive mind
Has no meaning but that which sees is truly seen.
"Piute Creek," *Riprap* (1959)

8 In the spiritual and political loneliness of America of the fifties you'd hitch a thousand miles to meet a friend.
1971. "North Beach," *The Old Ways* (1977)

9 Sometime in the last ten years the best brains of the Occident discovered to their amazement that we live in an Environment. This discovery has been forced on us by the realization that we are approaching the limits of something.
1976. Referring to the increasing prominence of ecological matters in Western thought. 'Re-Inhabitation," *The Old Ways* (1977)

10 Wrap in cold weather in a blanket and just read.
"Things to Do Around a Lookout," *The Penguin Book of American Verse* (Geoffrey Moore, ed.; 1977)

11 Americans would rather live by a Chamber-of-Commerce Creationism...satisfied with a divinely presented Shopping Mall. The integrity and character of our own ancestors is dismissed with "I couldn't live like that" by people who barely know how to live *at all*.
"Ancient Forests of the Far West," *The Practice of the Wild* (1990)

12 Taste all, and hand the knowledge down.
"Ethnobotany," *Turtle Island* (1975)

Sobukwe, Robert Mangaliso (1924–78) South African nationalist leader

1 Africa never forgets.
Speech at Fort Hare University (October 21, 1949), quoted in *How Can Man Die Better...Sobukwe and Apartheid* (Benjamin Pogrund; 1990)

2 On the liberation of the African depends the liberation of the whole world. The future of the world lies with the oppressed and the Africans are the most oppressed people on earth.
Speech at Fort Hare University (October 21, 1949), quoted in *How Can Man Die Better...Sobukwe and Apartheid* (Benjamin Pogrund; 1990)

3 There are no Communists in South Africa: only Communist quacks. Like Christianity, Communism has been unfortunate in its choice of representatives here.
Profiles of Africa (1983)

Socrates (470?–399? B.C.) Greek philosopher

Quotations about Socrates

1 Socrates was the first to call philosophy down from the heavens and to place it in cities, and even to introduce it into homes and compel it to enquire about life and standards and good and ill.
Cicero (106–43 B.C.) Roman orator and statesman. *Tusculanae Disputationes* (45–44 B.C.)

2 He was so orderly in his way of life that on several occasions when pestilence broke out in Athens he was the only man who escaped infection.
3rd century
Diogenes Läertius (*fl.* 3rd century) Greek historian and biographer. *Lives of the Philosophers* (3rd century?)

3 He declared that he knew nothing, except the fact of his ignorance.
Diogenes Läertius (*fl.* 3rd century) Greek historian and biographer. "Socrates," *Lives of the Philosophers* (3rd century?)

4 Socrates said, "Bad men live that they may eat and drink, whereas good men eat and drink that they may live."
Plutarch (46?–120?) Greek biographer and philosopher. "How a Young Man Ought To Hear Poems" (1st–2nd century), sect. 4

5 Socrates said he was not an Athenian or a Greek, but a citizen of the world.
Plutarch (46?–120?) Greek biographer and philosopher. "Of Banishment" (1st–2nd century)

Quotations by Socrates

6 Nothing can harm a good man, either in life or after death.
399? B.C. Quoted in *Apology* (Plato)

7 Socrates is a doer of evil, who corrupts the youth; and who does not believe in the gods of the state, but has other new divinities of his own. Such is the charge.
399? B.C. Summarizing the main charges against him at his trial. Quoted in *Apology* (Plato)

8 The unexamined life is not worth living.
399? B.C. Quoted in *Apology* (Plato), 38a

9 But already it is time to depart, for me to die, for you to go on living; which of us takes the better course, is concealed from anyone except God.
399? B.C. Quoted in closing words, *Apology* (Plato), 42a

10 Living well and beautifully and justly are all one thing.
399? B.C. Quoted in *Crito* (Plato)

11 How many things I can do without!
5th century B.C. Examining the range of goods on sale at a market. Quoted in *Lives of the Philosophers* (Diogenes Läertius; 3rd century), bk. 2, ch. 25

12 Crito, we owe a cock to Aesculapius; please pay it and don't let it pass.
399 B.C. Last words before his execution by drinking hemlock. Quoted in *Phaedo* (Plato)

Sokolov, Raymond (b.1941) U.S. writer

1 A narrow island off the coast of New Jersey devoted to the pursuit of lunch.
Referring to Manhattan, New York City. *Wall Street Journal* (1984)

Solanas, Valerie (b.1940) U.S. writer

1 The male is a biological accident: the y (male) gene is an incomplete x (female) gene, that is, has an incomplete set of chromosomes. In other words, the male is an incomplete female, a walking abortion, aborted at the gene stage.
1968. From the manifesto for "SCUM" (the "Society for Cutting Up Men"). Quoted in *Feminist Experiences: The Woman's Movement in Four Cultures* (Susan Bassnett; 1986)

Solomon, Robert C. (Robert Charles Solomon; b.1942) U.S. author

1 Economics without ethics is a discipline without substance.
The New World of Business (1994)

2 Either the business community recognizes values other than its own bottom line and supports interests other than its own or it will be...like the feudal lords of the eleventh century.
The New World of Business (1994)

3 If business is successful in America, it is because business gives America what it wants.
The New World of Business (1994)

4 Imperialism is imposing unwanted values on other people, even if not by physical force, even in the guise of free-market choices.
The New World of Business (1994)

5 Morality transcends not only markets but cultural boundaries too.
The New World of Business (1994)

6 The notion of businessman as a "pillar of the community" was as plausible as the idea of a peasant-king in that aristocratic society.
Referring to Classical Greece. *The New World of Business* (1994)

Solon (638?–559? B.C.) Greek statesman

Quotations about Solon

1 As some say, Solon was the author of the apophthegm, "Nothing in excess."
Diogenes Läertius (*fl.* 3rd century) Greek historian and biographer. "Solon," *Lives of the Philosophers* (3rd century?)

Quotations by Solon

2 Wrongdoing can only be avoided if those who are not wronged feel the same indignation at it as those who are.
Quoted in *Greek Wit* (Frederick Paley; 1880–81)

3 Laws are like spiders' webs: if some poor weak creature come up against them, it is caught; but a bigger one can break through and get away.
Quoted in *Lives of the Philosophers* (Diogenes Läertius; 3rd century), bk. 1, ch. 58

Solzhenitsyn, Alexander (Alexander Isayevich; b.1918) Russian novelist

Quotations about Solzhenitsyn

1 What is there about the *Gulag Archipelago* that made it a kind of last straw and that drove the politburo to arbitrary arrest and expulsion of its author?
Robert Conquest (b.1917) British literary editor. Referring to the book that caused the arrest and expulsion of Alexander Solzhenitsyn from the USSR (1974). Attrib.

Quotations by Solzhenitsyn

2 This universal, obligatory force-feeding with lies is now the most agonizing aspect of existence in our country—worse than all our material miseries, worse than any lack of civil liberties.
Letter to the Soviet leaders (1974), ch. 6

3 The salvation of mankind lies only in making everything the concern of all.
Nobel lecture (1972)

4 A man is happy so long as he chooses to be happy and nothing can stop him.
Cancer Ward (1968)

5 The whole of his life had prepared Podduyev for living, not for dying.
Cancer Ward (1968), pt. 1, ch. 8

6 Nowadays we don't think much of a man's love for an animal; we laugh at people who are attached to cats. But if we stop loving animals, aren't we bound to stop loving humans too?
Cancer Ward (1968), pt. 1, ch. 20

7 The camps had taught him that people who say nothing carry something within themselves.
Cancer Ward (1968), pt. 2, ch. 10

8 When truth is discovered by someone else, it loses something of its attractiveness.
Candle in the Wind (1972), Act 3

9 The people are not masters in their own house and therefore there is no democracy in Russia.
Independent, London (July 22, 1994)

10 For us in Russia communism is a dead dog, while, for many people in the West, it is still a living lion.
Listener, London (February 15, 1979)

11 In our country the lie has become not just a moral category but a pillar of the State.
Observer, London (December 29, 1974), "Sayings of the Year"

12 You only have power over people so long as you don't take *everything* away from them. But when you've robbed a man of everything, he's no longer in your power—he's free again.
The First Circle (1968), ch. 17

13 You took my freedom away a long time ago and you can't give it back because you haven't got it yourself.
The First Circle (1968), ch. 17

14 Their teacher had advised them not to read Tolstoy novels, because they were very long and would easily confuse the clear ideas which they had learned from reading critical studies of him.
The First Circle (1968), ch. 40

15 No regime has ever loved great writers, only minor ones.
The First Circle (1968), ch. 57

16 Forget the outside world. Life has different laws in here. This is Campland, an invisible country. It's not in the geography books, or the psychology books or the history books. This is the famous country where ninety-nine men weep while one laughs.
Referring to the world of Soviet labor camps known as the Gulag Archipelago. *The Love-Girl and the Innocent* (1969), Act 1, Scene 3

Somerville, Edith (Edith Anna Oenone Somerville; 1858–1949) Irish writer

1 Neither principalities nor powers should force me into the drawing-room, where sat the three unhappy women of my party, being entertained within an inch of their lives by Mrs McRory.
"Sharper Than a Ferret's Tooth," *Further Experiences of an Irish R.M.* (1899)

2 I have endured the Sandhurst riding-school, I have galloped for an impetuous general, I have been steward at regimental races, but none of these feats have altered my opinion that the horse, as a means of locomotion, is obsolete.
"Great-Uncle McCarthy," *Some Experiences of an Irish R.M.* (1899)

3 It is an ancient contention of my wife that I, in common with all other men, in any dispute between a female relative and a tradesman, side with the tradesman, partly from fear, partly from masculine clannishness, and most of all from a desire to stand well with the tradesman.
"The Pug-nosed Fox," *Some Experiences of an Irish R.M.* (1899)

Somoza Debayle, Anastasio (1925–80) Nicaraguan dictator

1 You won the elections, but I won the count.
Replying to allegations of ballot-rigging. *Guardian*, London (June 17, 1977)

Sondheim, Stephen (Stephen Joshua Sondheim; b.1930) U.S. composer and lyricist

1 Send in the Clowns
Song title. "A Little Night Music" (1973)

2 Everything's Coming up Roses
Song title. "Gypsy" (1959)

Song Lin (b.1959) Chinese writer

1 For poets, language is a maze, not a way forward.
"Prison Letter" (1991)

2 Language can be created only by talking to oneself, groaning, raving, crying, and even keeping silence.
"Prison Letter" (1991)

Sontag, Susan (b.1933) U.S. writer

1 Interpretation is the revenge of the intellect upon art.
Against Interpretation (1966)

2 Real art has the capacity to make us nervous. By reducing the work of art to its content and then interpreting *that*, one tames the work of art.
"Against Interpretation," *Against Interpretation* (1966)

3 Perversity is the muse of modern literature.
"Camus," *Against Interpretation* (1966)

4 Camp is a vision of the world in terms of style—but a particular style. It is the love of the exaggerated.
"Notes on Camp," *Against Interpretation* (1966)

5 If tragedy is an experience of hyperinvolvement, comedy is an experience of underinvolvement, of detachment.
"Notes on Camp," *Against Interpretation* (1966)

6 Sanity is a cozy lie.
"Notes on Camp," *Against Interpretation* (1966)

7 Taste has no systems and no proofs.
"Notes on Camp," *Against Interpretation* (1966)

8 The two pioneering forces of modern sensibility are Jewish seriousness and homosexual aestheticism and irony.
"Notes on Camp," *Against Interpretation* (1966)

9 What is most beautiful in virile men is something feminine; what is most beautiful in feminine women is something masculine.
"Notes on Camp," *Against Interpretation* (1966)

10 The felt unreliability of human experience brought about by the inhuman acceleration of historical change has led every sensitive modern mind to the recording of some kind of nausea, of intellectual vertigo.
"The Anthropologist as Hero," *Against Interpretation* (1966)

11 AIDS obliges people to think of sex as having, possibly the direst of consequences: suicide. Or murder.
AIDS and its Metaphors (1989), ch. 7

12 Although none of the rules for becoming more alive is valid it is healthy to keep formulating them.
"Debriefing," *American Review* (September 1973)

13 A large part of the popularity and persuasiveness of psychology comes from its being a sublimated spiritualism: a secular, ostensibly scientific way of affirming the primacy of "spirit" over matter.
Illness as Metaphor (1978), ch. 7

14 Everyone who is born holds dual citizenship, in the kingdom of the well and in the kingdom of the sick. Although we all prefer to use only the good passport, sooner or later each of us is obliged, at least for a spell, to identify ourselves as citizens of that other place.
New York Review of Books (January 26, 1978)

15 A photograph is not only an image (as a painting is an image), an interpretation of the real; it is also a trace, something directly stencilled off the real, like a footprint or a death mask.
On Photography (1977)

16 The freakish is no longer a private zone, difficult of access. People who are bizarre, in sexual disgrace, emotionally violent are seen daily on the newsstands, on TV, in the subways. Hobbesian man roams the streets, quite visible, with glitter in his hair.
"America, Seen Through Photographs, Darkly," *On Photography* (1977)

17 What pornography is really about, ultimately, isn't sex but death.
"The Pornographic Imagination," *Styles of Radical Will* (1969)

18 The truth is always something that is told, not something that is known. If there were no speaking or writing there would be no truth about anything. There would only be what is.
The Benefactor (1963), ch. 1

19 The pure examples of Camp are unintentional...Genuine camp—for instance, the numbers devised for the Warner Brothers' musicals of the early thirties (*42nd Street*; *The Gold Diggers*...) by Busby Berkeley—does not *mean* to be funny.
1964. Quoted in *A Susan Sontag Reader* (Elizabeth Hardwick; 1987)

Sophocles (496?–406? B.C.) Greek playwright

1 Nobody loves life like an old man.
Acrisius (5th century B.C.), fragment 64

2 Wonders are many, and none is more wonderful than man.
Antigone (after 441 B.C.), l. 332

3 Death is not the greatest of ills; it is worse to want to die, and not be able to.
Electra (418–410? B.C.), l. 1007

4 It is hope that maintains most of mankind.
Fragments (406? B.C.)

5 In a just cause the weak o'ercome the strong.
Oedipus at Colonus (5th century B.C.), l. 880

6 Everything is dear to its parent.
Oedipus at Colonus (5th century B.C.), l. 1108

7 A man should live only for the present day.
Oedipus Tyrannus (430–415? B.C.), l. 1013

8 It is better not to live at all than to live disgraced.
Peleus (5th century B.C.), fragment 445

9 Fortune is not on the side of the faint-hearted.
Phaedra (5th century B.C.), fragment 842

10 No oath too binding for a lover.
Phaedra (5th century B.C.), fragment 848

11 Sleep's the only medicine that gives ease.
Philoctetes (409? B.C.), l. 766

12 Old age and the wear of time teach many things.
Tyro (406? B.C.), fragment

13 Someone asked Sophocles, "How is your sex-life now? Are you still able to have a woman?" He replied, "Hush, man; most gladly indeed am I rid of it all, as though I had escaped from a mad and savage master."
5th century B.C. Quoted in *Republic* (Plato), bk. 1, 329b

Soros, George (b.1930) Hungarian-born U.S. investor and philanthropist

1 As an anonymous participant in financial markets, I never had to weigh the social consequences of my actions...I felt justified in ignoring them on the grounds that I was playing by the rules.
The Crisis of Global Capitalism (1998)

2 Financial markets...resent any kind of government interference but they hold a belief deep down that if conditions get really rough the authorities will step in. This belief has now been shaken.
The Crisis of Global Capitalism (1998)

3 I have been endowed with the reputation of a magician, particularly in Asian countries.
The Crisis of Global Capitalism (1998)

4 In the case of expectations, the outcome serves as a reality check; in the case of values it does not.
The Crisis of Global Capitalism (1998)

5 Market fundamentalism undermines the democratic political process and the inefficiency of the political process is a powerful argument in favor of market fundamentalism.
The Crisis of Global Capitalism (1998)

6 Politics does work better when citizens are guided by a sense of right or wrong rather than sheer expediency.
The Crisis of Global Capitalism (1998)

7 Studying economics is not a good preparation for dealing with it.
The Crisis of Global Capitalism (1998)

8 The Chinese Communist Party lost the "mandate to heaven" in the Tiananmen Square massacre, so it must provide prosperity on earth in order to be tolerated.
The Crisis of Global Capitalism (1998)

9 The stock market adopts a thesis and tests it; when it fails, as it usually does, it tries out another...that is what produces market fluctuations.
The Crisis of Global Capitalism (1998)

10 It is difficult to escape the conclusion that the international financial system itself constituted the main ingredient in the meltdown process.
Referring to the Asian economic crisis of 1997. *The Crisis of Global Capitalism* (1998)

Soule, John Lane Babsone (1815–91) U.S. writer and editor

1 Go West, young man, go West!
Also said by Horace Greeley. *Terre Haute Express*, Indiana (1851), Editorial

Sousa, John Philip (1854–1932) U.S. composer and conductor

1 Jazz will endure just as long as people hear it through their feet instead of their brains.
Attrib.

Southern, Terry (1924–95) U.S. novelist and screenwriter

1 They advertise they want tourists...they tell you that you'll be welcome in their country—then we come over here, pour plenty of good dollars into the economy, and what happens? We get the cold shoulder from a bum like that.
Said by an American tourist in India whose six-year-old daughter's request for an autograph from a holy man had been ignored. *Candy* (1958)

Southerne, Thomas (1660–1746) Irish playwright

1 Pity's akin to love.
Oroonoko (1696), Act 2, Scene 1

Southey, Robert (1774–1843) English poet and writer

Quotations about Southey

1 Your works will be read after Shakespeare and Milton are forgotten—and not till then.
Richard Porson (1759–1808) British classical scholar. Giving his opinion of the poems of Robert Southey. Attrib.

Quotations by Southey

2 Now tell us all about the war,
And what they fought each other for.
"The Battle of Blenheim" (1800)

3 He passed a cottage with a double coach-house—
A cottage of gentility;
And he owned with a grin,
That his favourite sin
Is pride that apes humility.
"The Devil's Walk" (1830), st. 8

4 In the days of my youth I remembered my God!
And He hath not forgotten my age.
"The Old Man's Comforts, and How he Gained Them" (1799)

5 You are old, Father William, the young man cried,
The few locks which are left you are grey;
You are hale, Father William, a hearty old man,
Now tell me the reason, I pray.
"The Old Man's Comforts, and How he Gained Them" (1799)

6 My name is death; the last best friend am I.
"The Dream," *Carmen Nuptiale: The Lay of the Laureate* (1816)

7 The arts babblative and scribblative.
Colloquies on the Progress and Prospects of Society (1829), Collection 10, pt. 2

8 They sin who tell us love can die;
With life all other passions fly,
All others are but vanity.
The Curse of Kehama (1810), can. 10, st. 10

9 Curses are like young chickens, they always come home to roost.
The Curse of Kehama (1810), Motto

10 Your true lover of literature is never fastidious.
The Doctor (1812), ch. 17

11 Show me a man who cares no more for one place than another, and I will show you in that same person one who loves nothing but himself. Beware of those who are homeless by choice.
The Doctor (1812), ch. 34

12 Man is a dupable animal. Quacks in medicine, quacks in religion, and quacks in politics know this, and act upon that knowledge.
The Doctor (1812), ch. 87

13 Live as long as you may, the first twenty years are the longest half of your life.
The Doctor (1812), ch. 130

South Park U.S. cartoon series

1 Oh my God, they killed Kenny!
Catchphrase, said by Stan whenever Kenny is killed in *South Park*. *South Park* (1998–)

Southwell, Robert (1561–95) English poet and martyr

1 Hoist up saile while gale doth last,
Tide and wind stay no man's pleasure.
"St Peter's Complaint" (1595)

2 Times go by turns, and chances change by course,
From foul to fair, from better hap to worse.
"Times go by Turn" (1595?), st. 1

Soyinka, Wole (Akinwande Oluwole Soyinka; b.1934) Nigerian novelist, playwright, poet, and lecturer

1 There is only one home to the life of a tortoise; there is only one shell to the soul of man: there is only one world to the spirit of our race. If that world leaves its course and smashes on the boulder of the great void, whose world will give us shelter?
Death and the King's Horseman (1975), Act 1

2 Disgust is cheap. I asked for self-disgust.
Madmen and Specialists (1971)

3 Your bounty threatens me, Mandela,
that taut Drumskin of your heart on which our millions
Dance. I fear we latch, fat leeches
On your veins.
"Your Logic Frightens Me Mandela," *Mandela's Earth and Other Poems* (1988)

4 When the present is intolerable, the unknown harbours no risks.
The Bacchae of Euripides (1973)

5 Americans expect to be loved.
The Interpreters (1965)

6 Is it so impossible to seal off the past and let it alone? Let it stay in its harmless anachronistic unit so we can dip into it at will and leave it without commitment, without impositions! A man needs that especially when the present, equally futile, distinguishes itself only by a particularly abject lack of courage.
The Interpreters (1965)

7 Any event is welcome in prison, even the threat of cerebrospinal meningitis and unpleasant needle jabs.
The Man Died (1975)

8 A war, with its attendant human suffering, must, when that evil is unavoidable, be made to fragment more than buildings: it must shatter the foundations of thought and re-create. Only in this way does every individual share in the cataclysm and understand the purpose of sacrifice.
The Man Died (1975)

9 The cold reality of power is, of course, that it has to be endured. Even when it is culpable and seen to be so, its effective reality is that it cannot be escaped for a duration.
The Man Died (1975)

10 The man dies in all who keep silent in the face of tyranny.
The Man Died (1975)

11 A man gets tired of feeling too much.
The Road (1965)

12 Well, some people say I'm pessimistic because I recognize the eternal cycle of evil. All I say is, look at the history of mankind *right up to this moment* and what do you find?
Talking With African Writers (Jane Wilkinson; 1992)

13 Foreign Publishers hovered like benevolent vultures over the still-born foetus of the African Muse.
"The Writer in a Modern African State," *The Writer in Modern Africa* (Per Wästburg, ed.; 1968)

Spaak, Paul Henri (1899–1972) Belgian prime minister

1 Our agenda is now exhausted. The secretary general is exhausted. All of you are exhausted. I find it comforting that, beginning with our very first day, we find ourselves in such complete unanimity.
Concluding the first General Assembly meeting of the United Nations, in San Francisco. Speech (1946)

Spark, Muriel, Dame (Muriel Sarah Spark; b.1918) British novelist

Quotations about Spark

1 Her prose is like a bird darting from place to place, palpitating with nervous energy; but a bird with a bright beady eye and a sharp beak as well.
Francis Hope (1938–74) British journalist and poet. *Observer,* London (April 28, 1963)

Quotations by Spark

2 Being over seventy is like being engaged in a war. All our friends are going or gone and we survive amongst the dead and the dying as on a battlefield.
Memento Mori (1959), ch. 4

3 A short neck denotes a good mind...You see, the messages go quicker to the brain because they've shorter to go.
The Ballad of Peckham Rye (1960), ch. 7

4 Parents learn a lot from their children about coping with life.
The Comforters (1957), ch. 6

5 Every communist has a fascist frown, every fascist a communist smile.
The Girls of Slender Means (1963), ch. 4

6 "Sex," she says, "is a subject like any other subject. Every bit as interesting as agriculture."
The Hothouse by the East River (1973), ch. 4

7 All my pupils are the crème de la crème.
The Prime of Miss Jean Brodie (1961)

8 Give me a girl at an impressionable age, and she is mine for life.
The Prime of Miss Jean Brodie (1961), ch. 1

9 One's prime is elusive. You little girls, when you grow up, must be on the alert to recognize your prime at whatever time of your life it may occur. You must then live it to the full.
The Prime of Miss Jean Brodie (1961), ch. 1

10 Art and religion first; then philosophy; lastly science. That is the order of the great subjects of life, that's their order of importance.
The Prime of Miss Jean Brodie (1961), ch. 2

11 If you had been mine when you were seven you would have been the crème de la crème.
The Prime of Miss Jean Brodie (1961), ch. 2

12 To me education is a leading out of what is already there in the pupil's soul. To Miss Mackay it is a putting in of something that is not there, and that is not what I call education, I call it intrusion.
The Prime of Miss Jean Brodie (1961), ch. 2

13 Miss Brodie said: "Pavlova contemplates her swans in order to perfect her swan dance, she studies them. This is true dedication. You must all grow up to be dedicated women as I have dedicated myself to you."
The Prime of Miss Jean Brodie (1961), ch. 3

14 But I did not remove my glasses, for I had not asked for her company in the first place, and there is a limit to what one can listen to with the naked eye.
"The Dark Glasses," *Voices at Play* (1961)

Spaulding, Asa T. (1902–90) U.S. business executive

1 Any job will expand or shrink to the size of the man who holds it.
Quoted in "Asa T. Spaulding: Insurance Executive," *Getting It Together: Black Businessmen in America* (John Seder and Berkeley G. Burrell; 1971)

Spector, Phil (Harvey Philip Spector; b.1940) U.S. record producer and songwriter

1 Wall of Sound.
Phrase used to describe the dense orchestral effects in Phil Spector's productions. Quoted in *The Sound of The City* (Charlie Gillett; 1970)

2 You've Lost That Lovin' Feelin'
1964. Song title. Co-written with Barry Mann and Cynthia West, it was a hit for The Righteous Brothers.

Speght, Rachel (b.1597) English author and poet

1 Man was created of the dust of the earth, but woman was made of a part of man...yet was shee not produced from Adam's foote, to be his too low inferiour, nor from his head

to be his superiour, but from his side, neare his heart, to be his equall.
A Mouzell for Melastomus, the Cynicall Bayter of, and Foule Mouthed Barker Against Evahs Sex (1617)

Speicher, Eugene (Eugene Edward Speicher; 1883–1962) U.S. painter

1 A portrait is a picture in which there is something wrong with the mouth.
Attrib.

Spence, James Calvert, Sir (1892–1954) British pediatrician

1 The essential unit of medical practice is the occasion when, in the intimacy of the consulting room or sick room, a person who is ill, or believes himself to be ill, seeks the advice of a doctor whom he trusts.
The Purpose and Practice of Medicine (1960), ch. 18

Spencer, Herbert (1820–1903) British philosopher

Quotations about Spencer

1 I have called this principle...by the term Natural Selection... But the expression often used by Mr. Herbert Spencer of the Survival of the Fittest is more accurate, and is sometimes equally convenient.
Charles Darwin (1809–82) British naturalist. *On the Origin of Species* (1859), ch. 3

Quotations by Spencer

2 Science is organized knowledge.
Education (1861), ch. 2

3 The ultimate result of shielding men from the effects of folly, is to fill the world with fools.
"State Tamperings with Money and Banks," *Essays* (1891), vol. 3

4 The Republican form of Government is the highest form of government; but because of this it requires the highest type of human nature—a type nowhere at present existing.
"The Americans," *Essays* (1891)

5 Survival of the fittest.
A phrase often misattributed to Charles Darwin. *Principles of Biology* (1865), pt. 3, ch. 12

6 A clever theft was praiseworthy amongst the Spartans; and it is equally so amongst Christians, provided it be on a sufficiently large scale.
Social Statics (1850), pt. 2, ch. 16, sect. 3

7 Education has for its object the formation of character.
Social Statics (1850), pt. 2, ch. 17, sect. 4

8 The liberty the citizen enjoys is to be measured not by the governmental machinery he lives under, whether representative or other, but by the paucity of restraints it imposes on him.
The Man Versus the State (1884)

9 The preservation of health is a duty. Few seem conscious that there is such a thing as physical morality.
Attrib.

Spencer, Stanley, Sir (1891–1959) British artist

1 Beautifully done.
1959. Said to the nurse who had injected him, just before he died. *Stanley Spencer, a Biography* (Maurice Collis; 1962), ch. 19

Spender, Stephen, Sir (Stephen Harold Spender; 1909–95) British poet and critic

Quotations about Spender

1 When the muse first came to Mr. Spender he looked so sincere that her heart failed her, and she said: "Ask anything and I will give it to you," and he said: "Make me sincere."
1955
Randall Jarrell (1914–65) U.S. author and poet. Criticizing the poetry of Stephen Spender. "Recent Poetry," *Kipling, Auden, & Co.: Essays and Reviews, 1935–1964* (1981)

2 Stephen Spender is, I think, an open, awkward, emotional, conscientiously well-intentioned, and simple-minded poet.
1955
Randall Jarrell (1914–65) U.S. author and poet. "The Year in Poetry," *Kipling, Auden, & Co.: Essays and Reviews, 1935–1964* (1981)

Quotations by Spender

3 Born of the sun, they travelled a short while towards the sun
And left the vivid air signed with their honour.
"I Think Continually of Those Who Were Truly Great" (1933)

4 I think continually of those who were truly great—
The names of those who in their lives fought for life,
Who wore at their hearts the fire's centre.
"I Think Continually of Those Who Were Truly Great" (1933)

5 Marston, dropping it in the grate, broke his pipe.
Nothing hung on this act, it was no symbol
Ludicrous for calamity, but merely ludicrous.
"Marston, Dropping It in the Grate, Broke His Pipe" (1930–33)

6 Pylons, those pillars
Bare like nude giant girls that have no secret.
"The Pylons" (1933)

7 Who live under the shadow of a war,
What can I do that matters?
"Who Live Under the Shadow of a War" (1933)

8 These men who idle in the road,
I have the sense of falling light.
They lounge at corners of the street
And greet friends with a shrug of the shoulder
And turn their empty pockets out,
The cynical gestures of the poor.
"15," *Preludes* (1930–33)

9 Never Being, But Always at the Edge of Being
Title of poem. (1933)

Spenser, Edmund (1552?–99) English poet

1 Sweet Thames! run softly, till I end my Song.
"Prothalamion" (1596), refrain

2 So let us love, dear Love, like as we ought,
Love is the lesson which the Lord us taught.
Amoretti (1595), Sonnet 68

3 Go to my love, where she is careless laid,
Yet in her winter's bower not well awake:
Tell her the joyous Time will not be staid,
Unless she do him by the forelock take.
Apostrophizing the Spring to wake amorous feelings in his lover. *Amoretti* (1595), Sonnet 70

4 One day I wrote her name upon the strand,
But came the waves and washed it away:
Again I wrote it with a second hand,
But came the tide, and made my pains his prey.
Amoretti (1595), Sonnet 75

5 A gentle knight was pricking on the plain.
The opening line of the poem. *The Faerie Queene* (1596), bk. 1, can. 1, st. 1

6 The noblest mind the best contentment has.
The Faerie Queene (1596), bk. 1, can. 1, st. 35

7 A bold bad man, that dar'd to call by name
Great Gorgon, Prince of darkness and dead night.
The Faerie Queene (1596), bk. 1, can. 1, st. 37

8 And all for love, and nothing for reward.
The Faerie Queene (1596), bk. 1, can. 8, st. 2

9 Ill can he rule the great that cannot reach the small.
The Faerie Queene (1596), bk. 5, can. 2, st. 43

10 O sacred hunger of ambitious minds.
The Faerie Queene (1596), bk. 5, can. 12, st. 1

11 And he that strives to touch the stars,
Oft stumbles at a straw.
"July," *The Shepherd's Calendar* (1579)

12 So now they have made our English tongue a gallimaufry or hodgepodge of all other speeches.
"Letter to Gabriel Harvey," *The Shepherd's Calendar* (1579)

13 I was promised on a time
To have reason for my rhyme;
From that time unto this season,
I received nor rhyme nor reason.
"Lines on His Promised Pension," *Worthies of England* (Thomas Fuller; 1662)

Spice Girls, The British pop group

1 Colours of the world
Spice up your life.
Every boy and girl,
Spice up your life.
Song lyric. "Spice up Your Life" (co-written with Richard Stannard and Matt Rowe; 1997)

2 If you wanna be my lover, you gotta get with my friends.
Song lyric. "Wannabe" (co-written with Richard Stannard and Matt Rowe; 1996)

Spiel, Hilde (b.1911) Austrian writer

1 Malice is like a game of poker or tennis; you don't play it with anyone who is manifestly inferior to you.
The Darkened Room (1961)

Spielberg, Steven (b.1947) U.S. film director

1 I looked younger than 26. I looked 17, and I had acne, and that doesn't help instill confidence in seasoned film crews.
New Yorker (1994)

2 Failure is inevitable. Success is elusive.
OM (December 1984)

3 The most expensive habit in the world is celluloid not heroin and I need a fix every two years.
OM (December 1984)

4 I love *Rambo* but I think it's potentially a very dangerous movie. It changes history in a frightening way.
Rolling Stone (October 24, 1985)

5 When I grow up I still want to be a director.
Time (July 15, 1985)

6 I solve my problems with the movies I make. Where there's a character in conflict in a movie, some part of that character is part of me that needs to be straightened out.
1986. Quoted in *Film Yearbook 1987* (1987)

7 I always think of the audience when I'm directing—because I am the audience.
1987. Quoted in *Film Yearbook 1988* (1988)

8 Close Encounters of the Third Kind
1979. Film title.

9 Movies for me are a heightened reality. Making reality fun to live with, as opposed to something you run from and protect yourself from.
1978. Attrib.

Spinoza, Baruch (also known as Benedict de Spinoza; 1632–77) Dutch philosopher and theologian

Quotations about Spinoza

1 I like mathematics because it is *not* human and has nothing particular to do with this planet or with the whole accidental universe—because, like Spinoza's God, it won't love us in return.
Bertrand Russell (1872–1970) British philosopher and mathematician. Attrib.

Quotations by Spinoza

2 Desire is the very essence of man.
Ethics (1677), pt. 3, prop. 59, def. 1

3 None are more taken in with flattery than the proud, who wish to be the first and are not.
Ethics (1677), pt. 4, appendix, no. 21

4 We feel and know that we are eternal.
Ethics (1677), pt. 4, prop. 23, note

5 Man is a social animal.
Ethics (1677), pt. 4, prop. 45, note

6 I have striven not to laugh at human actions, not to weep at them, nor to hate them, but to understand them.
Tractatus Theologico-Politicus (1670), ch. 1, sect. 4

7 Everything, insofar as it is in itself, endeavors to persist in its own being.
Quoted in *The Jingle Bell Principle* (Miroslav Holub; 1992)

Spivak, Gayatri (Gayatri Chakravorty Spivak; b.1942) Indian-born U.S. educator and writer

1 If only enlightenment is granted, freedom is almost sure to follow; where enlightenment is little more than three or four years of the three Rs and freedom is freedom from poverty.
Reversing Immanuel Kant's concept that enlightenment follows freedom, to comment on the situation in rural Bangladesh. "Thinking Academic Freedom in Gendered Post-Coloniality" (August 11, 1992)

Spock, Benjamin, Dr. (Benjamin McLane Spock; 1903–98) U.S. pediatrician

1 To win in Vietnam, we will have to exterminate a nation.
Dr. Spock on Vietnam (1968), ch. 7

2 There are only two things a child will share willingly—communicable diseases and his mother's age.
Attrib.

Spooner, William Archibald (1844–1930) British clergyman and academic

1 You will find as you grow older that the weight of rages will press harder and harder on the employer.
1900? *Spooner* (Sir W. Hayter; 1977), ch. 6

2 Kinquering Congs their titles take.
Probably apocryphal. (1879)

3 I remember your name perfectly, but I just can't think of your face.
1900? Attrib.

4 Let us drink to the queer old Dean.
1900? Attrib.

5 Sir, you have tasted two whole worms; you have hissed all my mystery lectures and have been caught fighting a liar in the quad; you will leave Oxford by the town drain.
1900? Dismissing a student, attributed, possibly apocryphal. Attrib.

Springfield, Dusty (Mary Isobel Catherine Bernadette O'Brien; 1939–99) British singer

1 My sexuality has never been a problem to me but I think it has for some people.
Referring to her lesbianism. Quoted in *Dusty* (Lucy O'Brien; 1989)

Spring-Rice, Cecil Arthur, Sir (1859–1918) British diplomat

1 And her ways are ways of gentleness, and all her paths are peace.
Written on his departure from Washington. "I Vow to Thee, My Country" (January 12, 1918)

2 I vow to thee, my country—all earthly things above—
Entire and whole and perfect, the service of my love,
The love that asks no question: the love that stands the test,
That lays upon the altar the dearest and the best:
The love that never falters, the love that pays the price,
The love that makes undaunted the final sacrifice.
Written on his departure from Washington. "I Vow to Thee, My Country" (January 12, 1918)

Springsteen, Bruce (Bruce Frederick Joseph Springsteen; b.1949) U.S. rock singer and songwriter

1 Rock 'n' roll man, it changed my life. It was...the Voice of America, the real America coming to your home. It was the liberating thing, the way out of the pits. Once I found the guitar, I had the key to the highway!
Quoted in *Springsteen: Blinded by the Light* (Patrick Humphries and Chris Hunt; 1985)

2 Born in the USA
1984. Song title.

Spry, Constance (Constance Fletcher; 1886–1960) British cookbook writer

1 Cooking is a combination of science, art, invention...it calls for individual taste and latitude in adjustment of the formulae. There is another word to be underlined—taste—taste of course in both its meanings.
The Constance Spry Cookery Book (1956)

2 Friendliness and easy hospitality are more important than grandeur.
The Constance Spry Cookery Book (1956)

3 I cannot forbear to remind you how much respect ought to be paid to food, how carefully it should be treated, how shameful waste is...it is fortunately unlikely that your hearts will be wrung or your consciences nudged by the sight of starving people.
The Constance Spry Cookery Book (1956)

Spyri, Johanna (1827–1901) Swiss writer

1 Oh, I wish that God had not given me what I prayed for! It was not so good as I thought.
Heidi (1880–81), ch. 11

2 Anger has overpowered him, and driven him to a revenge which was rather a stupid one, I must acknowledge, but anger makes us all stupid.
Heidi (1880–81), ch. 23

Squire, J. C., Sir (John Collings Squire; 1884–1958) British writer

1 But I'm not so think as you drunk I am.
"Ballade of Soporific Absorption" (1931)

2 It did not last: the Devil howling "Ho!
Let Einstein be!" restored the status quo.
Answer to Pope's "Epitaph for Newton." "The Dilemma," *Epigrams* (1926)

3 God heard the embattled nations sing and shout:
"Gott strafe England!," "God save the King!"
"God this!," "God that!," and "God the other thing!"
"My God," said God, "I've got my work cut out."
"The Dilemma," *The Survival of the Fittest* (1916), Epigrams: no. 1

Stacpoole, Henry de Vere (1863–1951) Irish novelist and ship's doctor

1 In home-sickness you must keep moving—it is the only disease that does not require rest.
The Bourgeois (1901)

Staël, Madame de, Baroness of Staël-Holstein (Anne Louise Germaine Necker; 1766–1817) French writer and intellectual

1 Music revives the recollections it would appease.
Corinna, or Italy (1807)

2 To be totally understanding makes one very indulgent.
Corinna, or Italy (1807)

3 A nation has character only when it is free.
De la Littérature (1800)

4 A man can brave an opinion; a woman must submit to it.
Delphine (1802), epigraph

5 Love is above the laws, above the opinion of men; it is the truth, the flame, the pure element, the primary idea of the moral world.
Zulma and Other Tales (1813)

Stafford, William (1914–93) U.S. academic and poet

1 From that shore below the mountain the water
darkens; the whole surface of the lake livens,
and, upward, high miles of pine tops bend where a storm
walks the country. Deeper and deeper, autumn
floods in.
Referring to the Montana mountains as winter approaches. "Montana Eclogue," *Allegiances* (1970), ll. 16–20

Stalin, Joseph (Iosif Vissarionovich Dzhugashvili; 1879–1953) Soviet dictator

Quotations about Stalin

1 Stalin hates the guts of all your top people. He thinks he likes me better, and I hope he will continue to do so.
1942
Franklin D. Roosevelt (1882–1945) U.S. president. Quoted in *The Hinge of Fate* (Winston S. Churchill; 1950), ch. 11

2 The dialectics of history have already hooked him and will raise him up...Stalin will become dictator of the USSR.
1924
Leon Trotsky (1879–1940) Russian revolutionary leader. *Stalin: An Appraisal of the Man and His Influence* (1941)

3 I like old Joe Stalin. He's a good fellow but he's a prisoner of the Politburo. He would make certain agreements but they won't let him keep them.
Harry S. Truman (1884–1972) U.S. president. *News Review* (June 24, 1948)

Quotations by Stalin

4 To attempt to export revolution is nonsense.
Message sent to Roy Howard, U.S. newspaper owner (March 1, 1936)

5 National in form, socialist in content.
Referring to Soviet literature. Remark (1932)

6 Dialectics is the soul of Marxism.
Problems of Leninism (1940)

7 This war is not as in the past; whoever occupies a territory also imposes on it his own social system. Everyone imposes his own system as far as his army has power to do so. It cannot be otherwise.
1941–45. *Conversations with Stalin* (Milovan Djilas; 1962)

8 Who organized this standing ovation?
May 1944. Said on hearing that at a poetry reading in Moscow the whole audience had spontaneously risen at the appearance of the poet Anna Akhmatova. Quoted in *Hope Abandoned* (Nadezhda Mandelstam (tr. Max Hayward); 1972), ch. 31

9 Communism fits Germany as a saddle does a cow.
August 1944. Quoted in *Quotations in History* (A. Palmer and V. Palmer; 1976)

10 The Pope! How many divisions has *he* got?
May 13, 1935. When urged by Pierre Laval to tolerate Catholicism in the Soviet Union to appease the Pope. *The Second World War* (W. S. Churchill; 1948), vol. 1, ch. 8

11 Our hand will not tremble.
Reply to a telegraph from Lenin at the start of the Red Terror (1918), urging him to be merciless against the Bolsheviks' enemies. (1918)

12 A single death is a tragedy; a million is a statistic.
Attrib.

13 Personnel selection is decisive. People are our most valuable capital.
Attrib.

14 To slacken the tempo...would mean falling behind. And those who fall behind get beaten...
We are fifty or a hundred years behind the advanced countries. We must make good this distance in ten years. Either we do it, or they crush us.
Attrib.

15 I will shake my little finger—and there will be no more Tito. He will fall.
Said to Nikita Khrushchev. Attrib.

Standing Bear, Luther (1868?–1939?) U.S. Native American leader and writer

1 The white man does not understand the Indian for the reason that he does not understand America. He is too far removed from its formative process. The roots of the tree of his life have not yet grasped the rock and soil.
Land of the Spotted Eagle (1933)

2 Only to the white man was nature a "wilderness"...To us it was tame. Earth was bountiful and we were surrounded with the blessings of the Great Mystery.
The Great Mystery, Wakan Tanka, is the Sioux's one and omnipotent god. *Land of the Spotted Eagle* (1933)

Stanley, Edward Geoffrey Smith, 14th Earl of Derby (1799–1869) British prime minister

1 When I first came into Parliament, Mr Tierney, a great Whig authority, used always to say that the duty of an Opposition was very simple—it was, to oppose everything, and propose nothing.
Speech to the British Parliament, *Hansard* (June 4, 1841)

2 The foreign policy of the noble Earl...may be summed up in two truly expressive words: "meddle" and "muddle".
Referring to Lord Russell's policy towards the American Civil War. Speech to the British parliament, *Hansard* (February 1864), col. 28

Stanley, Henry Morton, Sir (1841–1904) British-born U.S. explorer and journalist

1 Dr. Livingstone, I presume?
October 28, 1871. Said on finding the missionary David Livingstone at Ujiji on Lake Tanganyika. *How I found Livingstone* (1872), ch. 11

Stanshall, Vivian (1943–95) British rock musician and humorist

1 If I had all the money I've spent on drink, I'd go out and spend it on drink.
Attrib.

Stanton, Charles E. (1859–1933) U.S. colonel

1 Lafayette, we are here!
July 4, 1917. Following the arrival of the first American troops to join the Allied forces in World War I. Lafayette (1757–1834) aided the colonists during the American Revolution. Address at the tomb of the Marquis de Lafayette, Paris (July 14, 1917), reported in *New York Tribune* (September 6, 1917)

Stanton, Elizabeth Cady (originally Elizabeth Cady; 1815–1902) U.S. campaigner for woman suffrage

Quotations about Stanton

1 As usual when she had fired her gun she went home and left me to finish the battle.
1860
Susan B. Anthony (1820–1906) U.S. social reformer. Remark after Elizabeth Cady Stanton had addressed a convention on the subject of divorce. Quoted in *Words of Women* (Anne Stibbs; 1993)

Quotations by Stanton

2 I have been into many of the ancient cathedrals—grand, wonderful, mysterious. But I always leave them with a feeling of indignation because of the generations of human beings who have struggled in poverty to build these altars to the unknown god.
Diary (1882)

3 Though motherhood is the most important of all the professions—requiring more knowledge than any other department in human affairs—there was no attention given to preparation for this office.
Eighty Years and More: 1815–1897 (1898)

4 The Bible and Church have been the greatest stumbling block in the way of woman's emancipation.
Free Thought Magazine (September 1896)

5 It is impossible for one class to appreciate the wrongs of another.
History of Woman Suffrage (co-written with Susan B. Anthony and Matilda Gage; 1881), vol. 1

6 The prolonged slavery of women is the darkest page in human history.
History of Woman Suffrage (co-written with Susan B. Anthony and Matilda Gage; 1881), vol. 1

7 We still wonder at the stolid incapacity of all men to understand that woman feels the invidious distinctions of sex exactly as the black man does those of color, or the white man the more transient distinctions of wealth, family, position, place, and power; that she feels as keenly as man the injustice of disfranchisement.
History of Woman Suffrage (co-written with Susan B. Anthony and Matilda Gage; 1881), vol. 1

8 Womanhood is the great fact in her life; wifehood and motherhood are but incidental relations.
History of Woman Suffrage (co-written with Susan B. Anthony and Matilda Gage; 1881), vol. 1

9 We hold these truths to be self-evident: that all men and women are created equal.
July 19–20, 1848. "Declaration of Sentiments" at the First Women's Rights Convention, Seneca Falls, New York. *History of Woman Suffrage* (co-written with Susan B. Anthony and Matilda Gage; 1881), vol. 1

Stanton, Frank L. (Frank Lebby Stanton; 1857–1927) U.S. journalist and poet

1 Sweetes' li'l' feller,
Everybody knows;
Dunno what to call 'im,
But he's mighty lak' a rose!
Song lyric. "Mighty Lak' a Rose" (1901)

Stanwyck, Barbara (originally Ruby Stevens; 1907–90) U.S. film actor

1 My only problem is finding a way to play my fortieth fallen female in a different way from my thirty-ninth.
Interview (Hedda Hopper; 1933)

Stapledon, Olaf (1886–1950) British philosopher and science-fiction writer

1 That strange blend of the commercial traveller, the missionary, and the barbarian conqueror, which was the American abroad.
Last and First Men (1930), ch. 3

2 For suddenly it was clear to me that virtue in the creator is not the same as virtue in the creature. For the creator, if he should love his creature, would be loving only a part of himself; but the creature, praising the creator, praises an infinity beyond himself.
Star Maker (1937), ch. 13

Star Trek U.S. television series

1 Beam us up, Mr. Scott.
Often quoted wrongly as "Beam me up, Scotty." *Star Trek* (1966)

2 Space—the final frontier...These are the voyages of the starship *Enterprise*. Its five-year mission...to boldly go where no man has gone before.
Star Trek (1966–69), opening titles

Star Wars U.S. film series

1 A long time ago in a galaxy far, far away.
Opening words. *Star Wars* (George Lucas; 1977)

Stead, Christina (1902–83) Australian writer

1 A self-made man is one who believes in luck and sends his son to Oxford.
The House of All Nations (1938), "Credo"

2 A mother! What are we worth really? They all grow up whether you look after them or not.
The Man Who Loved Children (1940), ch. 10

Stead, W. T. (William Thomas Stead; 1849–1912) British journalist

1 If all persons guilty of Oscar Wilde's offences were to be clapped into gaol, there would be a very surprising exodus from Eton and Harrow, Rugby and Winchester, to Pentonville and Holloway.
Eton, Harrow, Rugby, and Winchester are English private schools; Pentonville and Holloway are prisons. *The Pall Mall Gazette*, London (1895), quoted in *A Queer Reader* (Patrick Higgins, ed.; 1993)

Steele, Richard, Sir (1672–1729) Irish-born English essayist, playwright, and politician

1 A little in drink, but at all times yr faithful husband.
Letter to his wife (September 27, 1708)

2 The insupportable labour of doing nothing.
Spectator, London (May 2, 1711), no. 54

3 I have heard Will Honeycomb say, A Woman seldom Writes her Mind but in her Postscript.
Spectator, London (May 31, 1711), no. 79

4 There are so few who can grow old with a good grace.
Spectator, London (January 1, 1712), no. 263

5 Though her mien carries much more invitation than command, to behold her is an immediate check to loose behaviour; to love her is a liberal education.
Referring to Lady Elizabeth Hastings. *Tatler*, London (August 2, 1709), no. 49

6 Reading is to the mind what exercise is to the body.
The Tatler, London (March 18, 1710), no. 147

Steffens, Lincoln (Joseph Lincoln Steffens; 1866–1936) U.S. journalist

1 Liberty is the right of any person to stand up anywhere and say anything whatsoever that everybody thinks.
Autobiography (1931)

2 I have seen the future and it works.
Said originally to U.S. economist and financier Bernard Baruch, after visiting the Soviet Union in 1919. *Letters* (1938), vol. 1

3 The great struggle of a writer is to learn to write as he would talk.
1933. Attrib. *Lincoln Steffens: A Biography* (Justin Kaplan; 1974)

Steiger, Rod (b.1925) U.S. film actor

1 It sounds pompous, but it's the nearest thing I can do to being God. I'm trying to create human beings and so does He.
October 10, 1970. Attrib.

Stein, Gertrude (1874–1946) U.S. writer

Quotations about Stein

1 Gertrude Stein is the mama of dada.
Clifton Fadiman (b.1904) U.S. writer, editor, and broadcaster. *Party of One* (1955)

Quotations by Stein

2 She always says she dislikes the abnormal, it is so obvious. She says the normal is so much more simply complicated and interesting.
Autobiography of Alice B. Toklas (1933)

3 Remarks are not literature.
Autobiography of Alice B. Toklas (1933), ch. 7

4 There ain't no answer. There ain't going to be any answer. There never has been an answer. That's the answer.
Brewsie and Willie (1946), ch. 7

5 It takes a lot of time to be a genius, you have to sit around so much doing nothing, really doing nothing.
Everybody's Autobiography (1937)

6 Oklahoma City with its towers, that is its skyscrapers coming right up out of the oil country was as exciting as when...we first saw the Strasbourg Cathedral. They do come up wonderfully out of that flat country.
Everybody's Autobiography (1937), ch. 4

7 The trouble with Oakland is that when you get there, there isn't any there there.
Everybody's Autobiography (1937), ch. 4

8 Rose is a rose is a rose is a rose.
Sacred Emily (1913)

9 In the United States there is more space where nobody is than where anybody is. That is what makes America what it is.
The Geographical History of America (1936)

10 The thing that differentiates man from animals is money...the thing no animal can do is count, and the thing no animal can know is money.
The Saturday Evening Post (August 22, 1936)

11 The Jews have produced only three originative geniuses: Christ, Spinoza, and myself.
Quoted in *Charmed Circle* (J. Mellow; 1974)

12 I like familiarity. In me it does not breed contempt. Only more familiarity.
Quoted in *Dale Carnegie's Scrapbook* (Dorothy Carnegie, ed.; 1959)

13 That's what you are. That's what you all are. All of you young people who served in the war. You are all a lost generation.
Referring to World War I. Stein heard the phrase "lost generation" being used by a French mechanic abusing an apprentice. Epigraph in *The Sun Also Rises* (Ernest Hemingway; 1926)

14 What *is* the answer?...In that case, what is the question?
July 27, 1946. Last words. Quoted in *What Is Remembered* (Alice B. Toklas; 1963)

Steinbeck, John (John Ernst Steinbeck; 1902–68) U.S. novelist

1 Lee Chong is...an Asiatic planet held to its orbit by the pull of Lao Tze and held away from Lao Tze by the centrifugality of abacus and cash register.
"Lao Tze" is Laozi, the semi-mythical early Taoist sage. *Cannery Row* (1945), ch. 2

2 Doc is the owner and operator of the Western Biological Laboratory...He wears a beard and his face is half Christ and half satyr and his face tells the truth.
Cannery Row (1945), ch. 5

3 Two generations of Americans know more about the Ford coil than the clitoris, about the planetary system of gears than about the solar system of stars.
Cannery Row (1945), ch. 11

4 Monterey is a city with a long and brilliant literary tradition. It remembers with pleasure and some glory that Robert Louis Stevenson lived there. Treasure Island certainly has the topography and the coastal plan of Pt. Lobos.
Cannery Row (1945), ch. 12

5 Cannery Row in Monterey in California is a poem, a stink, a grating noise, a quality of light, a tone, a habit, a nostalgia, a dream.
Opening words. *Cannery Row* (1945), introduction

6 The American Standard translation *orders* men to triumph over sin...The King James translation makes a promise in "Thou shalt," meaning that men will surely triumph over sin. But the Hebrew word, the word *timshel*—"Thou mayest"—that gives a choice.
Referring to Genesis 4:7. *East of Eden* (1952), ch. 24

7 Where does discontent start? You are warm enough, but you shiver. You are fed, yet hunger gnaws you. You have been loved, but your yearning wanders in new fields. And to prod all these there's time, the Bastard Time.
Sweet Thursday (1954)

8 To the red country and part of the gray country of Oklahoma, the last rains came gently, and they did not cut the scarred earth.
Opening sentence. *The Grapes of Wrath* (1939), ch. 1

9 Man, unlike any other thing organic or inorganic in the universe, grows beyond his work, walks up the stairs of his concepts, emerges ahead of his accomplishments.
The Grapes of Wrath (1939), ch. 14

10 Okie use' ta mean you was from Oklahoma. Now it means you're a dirty son-of-a-bitch. Okie means you're scum. Don't mean nothing itself, it's the way they say it.
The Grapes of Wrath (1939), ch. 18

11 And where a number of men gathered together, the fear went from the faces, and anger took its place. And the women sighed with relief, for they knew it was all right—the break had not come; and the break would never come as long as fear could turn to wrath.
The Grapes of Wrath (1939), ch. 29

12 The comfortable people in tight houses felt pity at first, and then distaste, and finally hatred for the migrant people.
The Grapes of Wrath (1939), ch. 29

13 No one wants advice—only corroboration.
The Winter of Our Discontent (1961)

14 Montana seems to me to be what a small boy would think Texas is like from hearing Texans.
Travels with Charley: In Search of America (1962)

15 Once a journey is designed, equipped, and put in process a new factor enters and takes over...it has personality, temperament, individuality, uniqueness. A journey is a person in itself, no two are alike.
Travels with Charley: In Search of America (1962)

16 We find after years of struggle that we do not take a trip; a trip takes us.
Travels with Charley: In Search of America (1962)

17 A journey is like a marriage. The certain way to be wrong is to think you can control it.
Travels with Charley: In Search of America (1962), pt. 1

18 American cities are like badger holes, ringed with trash—all of them—surrounded by piles of wrecked and rusting automobiles, and almost smothered with rubbish.
Travels with Charley: In Search of America (1962), pt. 2

19 As I went along I found that more and more people lusted towards Florida and that thousands had moved there and more thousands wanted to and would...the very name Florida carried the message of warmth and ease and comfort. It was irresistible.
Travels with Charley: In Search of America (1962), pt. 2

20 It is the nature of a man as he grows older to protest against change, particularly changes for the better.
Travels with Charley: In Search of America (1962), pt. 2

21 The natural New England taciturnity reaches its glorious perfection at breakfast...An early morning waitress in New England leads a lonely life.
Travels with Charley: In Search of America (1962), pt. 2

22 For all our enormous geographic range, for all of our sectionalism...we are a nation, a new breed. Americans are much more American than they are Northerners, Southerners, Westerners, or Easterners.
Travels with Charley: In Search of America (1962), pt. 3

23 I am in love with Montana. For other states I have admiration, respect, recognition, even some affection, but with Montana it is love.
Travels with Charley: In Search of America (1962), pt. 3

24 I was not prepared for the Bad Lands. They deserve this name. They are like the work of an evil child. Such a place the Fallen Angels might have made as a spite to Heaven, dry and sharp, desolate and dangerous.
Travels with Charley: In Search of America (1962), pt. 3

25 The Missouri River at Bismarck, North Dakota...Here is the boundary between east and west. On the Bismarck side it is eastern landscape, eastern grass...Across the Missouri, on the Mandan side, it is pure west, with brown grass and water scorings and small outcrops.
Bismarck and Mandan are cities in North Dakota, either side of the Missouri River. *Travels with Charley: In Search of America* (1962), pt. 3

26 I remembered Seattle as a town sitting on hills beside a matchless harborage—a little city of space and trees and gardens...It is no longer so. The tops of hills are shaved off to make level warrens for the rabbits of the present.
His first impressions of the impact of the population explosion on the United States West Coast. *Travels with Charley: In Search of America* (1962), pt. 3

27 I faced the South with dread. Here I knew were pain and

confusion and all the manic results of bewilderment and fear. And the South being a limb of the nation, its pain spread out to all America.
Travels with Charley: In Search of America (1962), pt. 4

28 Once you are in Texas it seems to take forever to get out, and some people never make it.
Travels with Charley: In Search of America (1962), pt. 4

29 There is no physical or geographical unity in Texas. Its unity lies in the mind.
Travels with Charley: In Search of America (1962), pt. 4

30 Writers facing the problem of Texas find themselves floundering in generalities, and I am no exception. Texas is a state of mind. Texas is an obsession. Above all, Texas is a nation in every sense of the word.
Travels with Charley: In Search of America (1962), pt. 4

31 When it comes right down to it, nothing has changed. The English sentence is just as difficult to write as it ever was.
1962. In a letter to his editor a week after accepting a Nobel Prize in literature. Quoted in *John Steinbeck* (Jay Parini; 1995)

32 Time is the only critic without ambition.
Quoted in "On Critics," *Writers at Work* (George Plimpton, ed.; 1977)

33 A book is like a man—clever and dull, brave and cowardly, beautiful and ugly. For every flowering thought there will be a page like a wet and mangy mongrel, and for every looping flight a tap on the wing and a reminder that wax cannot hold the feathers firm too near the sun.
Quoted in "On Publishing," *Writers at Work* (George Plimpton, ed.; 1977), 4th series

34 It is a common experience that a problem difficult at night is resolved in the morning after the committee of sleep has worked on it.
Attrib.

Steinberg, Saul (b.1914) Romanian-born U.S. artist and cartoonist

1 Baseball is an allegorical play about America, a poetic, complex, and subtle play of courage, fear, good luck, mistakes, patience about fate, and sober self-esteem...It's impossible to understand America without a thorough knowledge of baseball.
Quoted in *Saul Steinberg* (Harold Rosenberg; 1978)

Steinem, Gloria (b.1934) U.S. writer and feminist

1 What would happen if...men could menstruate and women could not? Clearly, menstruation would become an enviable, boast-worthy, masculine event: Men would brag about how long and how much. Young boys would talk about it as the envied beginning of manhood.
"If Men Could Menstruate" (1978)

2 Some of us are becoming the men we wanted to marry.
Speech, Yale University (September 1981)

3 If the men in the room would only think how they would feel graduating with a "spinster of arts" degree they would see how important this is.
Referring to language reform. Speech, Yale University (September 1981)

4 I learned that falsifying this one fact about my life made me feel phoney, ridiculous, complicit, and, worst of all, undermined by my own hand.
Referring to a time when she lied about her age. "Doing Sixty," *Moving Beyond Words* (1994)

5 Erotica is about sexuality, but pornography is about power and sex-as-weapon—in the same way we have come to understand that rape is about violence, and not really about sex at all.
"Erotica and Pornography, A Clear and Present Difference," *Ms* (November 1978)

6 For me, there was always this part of the brain reliably devoted to sex. Now there is this whole part of your brain which is freed up.
Observer Life Magazine, London (May 15, 1994)

7 I feel angry that the righteous anger I did manage to express in the past was denigrated as unprofessional or self-defeating, or more subtly suppressed when others praised me as calm, reasonable, not one of those "angry feminists."
Observer Life Magazine, London (May 15, 1994)

8 The false division of human nature into "feminine" and "masculine" is the root of all other divisions into subject and object, active and passive; the beginning of hierarchy.
Observer Life Magazine, London (May 15, 1994)

9 The only difference is that the stress and the violence is worse at home, because it happens younger, it happens at the hands of someone you love, and there is no recognition that this is the enemy.
Referring to the similarities between the trauma suffered by soldiers in war and female victims of recurrent domestic violence. *Observer Life Magazine*, London (May 15, 1994)

10 Men *would* support us (the feminists) we are told, if only we learned how to ask for their support in the right way. It's a subtle and effective way of blaming the victim.
Outrageous Acts and Everyday Rebellions (1983)

11 One day, an army of gray-haired women may quietly take over the earth.
Outrageous Acts and Everyday Rebellions (1983)

12 If the shoe doesn't fit, must we change the foot?
Referring to the position of women in western society. *Outrageous Acts and Everyday Rebellions* (1983)

13 Finding language that will allow people to act together while cherishing each other's individuality is probably the most feminist and therefore truly revolutionary function of writers.
Outrageous Acts and Everyday Rebellions (1983), Introduction

14 I've finally figured out why soap operas are, and logically should be, so popular with generations of housebound women. *They are the only place in our culture where grown-up men take seriously all the things that grown-up women have to deal with all day long.*
"Night Thoughts of a Media Watcher," *Outrageous Acts and Everyday Rebellions* (1983)

15 Outrageous Acts and Everyday Rebellions
1983. Book title.

16 A woman without a man is like a fish without a bicycle.
Attrib.

Steiner, George (b.1929) U.S. scholar and critic

1 To many men...the miasma of peace seems more suffocating than the bracing air of war.
"Has Truth a Future?" (1978)

2 The age of the book is almost gone.
Daily Mail, London (June 27, 1988)

3 There is something terribly wrong with a culture inebriated by noise and gregariousness.
Daily Telegraph, London (May 23, 1989)

4 Nothing is more symptomatic of the enervation, of the decompression of the Western imagination, than our incapacity to respond to the landings on the Moon. Not a single great poem, picture, metaphor has come of this breathtaking act, of Prometheus' rescue of Icarus or of Phaeton in flight towards the stars.
"Modernity, Mythology, and Magic," lecture, Salzburg Festival. *Guardian*, London (August 6, 1994)

5 We know that a man can read Goethe or Rilke in the evening, that he can play Bach or Schubert, and go to his day's work at Auschwitz in the morning.
Referring to Johann Sebastian Bach, Johann Wolfgang von Goethe, Rainer Maria Rilke, and Franz Peter Schubert. Auschwitz was a Nazi-run concentration camp in Poland during World War II (1939–45). *Language and Silence* (1967), preface

6 Words that are saturated with lies or atrocity, do not easily resume life.
"K," *Language and Silence* (1967)

7 Pornographers subvert this last, vital privacy; they do our imagining for us. They take away the words that were of the night and shout them over the roof-tops, making them hollow.
"Nightworks," *Language and Silence* (1967)

8 Language can only deal meaningfully with a special, restricted segment of reality. The rest, and it is presumably the much larger part, is silence.
"The Retreat from the Word," *Language and Silence* (1967)

Steiner, Rudolf (1861–1925) Austrian philosopher and scientist

1 The man of the present day would far rather believe that disease is connected only with immediate causes for the fundamental tendency in the modern view of life is always to seek what is more convenient.
1910. *The Manifestations of Karma* (1925), lecture 3

Stekel, Wilhelm (1868–1940) Austrian psychiatrist

1 The mark of the immature man is that he wants to die nobly for a cause, while the mark of the mature man is that he wants to live humbly for one.
Quoted in *The Catcher in the Rye* (J. D. Salinger; 1951), ch. 24

Stella, Frank (Frank Philip Stella; b.1936) U.S. painter

1 My painting is based on the fact that only what can be seen there *is* there...Any painting is an object and anyone who gets involved enough in this finally has to face up to the objectness of whatever it is that he's doing.
"Questions to Stella and Judd," *Art News* (September 1966) (Bruce Glazer)

Stendhal (Marie-Henri Beyle; 1783–1842) French writer

1 Prudery is a kind of avarice, the worst of all.
"Fragments," *De l'Amour* (1822)

2 One can acquire everything in solitude—except character.
"Miscellaneous Fragments," *De l'Amour* (1822)

3 Mathematics...allows for no hypocrisy and no vagueness.
La Vie d'Henri Brulard (1890)

4 Romanticism is the art of presenting people with the literary works which are capable of affording them the greatest possible pleasure, in the present state of their customs and beliefs. Classicism, on the other hand, presents them with the literature that gave the greatest possible pleasure to their great-grandfathers.
Racine and Shakespeare (1825), ch. 3

5 A novel is a mirror which passes over a highway. Sometimes it reflects to your eyes the blue of the skies, at others the churned-up mud of the road.
The Red and the Black (1830), bk. 2, ch. 19

Stengel, Casey (Charles Dillon Stengel; 1890?–1975) U.S. baseball player and manager

1 Don't cut my throat. I may want to do that later myself.
1935. Said after his Brooklyn Dodgers lost a doubleheader. Quoted in *Casey* (Joseph Durso; 1967)

2 Managing is getting paid for home runs someone else hits.
Attrib.

Stephens, James (1882–1950) Irish novelist and poet

1 Men come of age at sixty, women at fifteen.
Observer, London (October 1, 1944), "Sayings of the Week"

2 Curiosity will conquer fear even more than bravery will.
The Crock of Gold (1912)

Sterling, Andrew B. (1874–1955) U.S. songwriter

1 Meet me in St. Louis, Louis
meet me at the fair,
Don't tell me the lights are shining
any place but there.
Referring to the 1904 World's Fair at St. Louis, Missouri. The chorus from Sterling's poem was notably used in the film, *Meet Me in St. Louis* (1944). "Meet Me in St. Louis, Louis" (1904), chorus

Stern, Edith Mendel (1901–75) U.S. writer and social critic

1 For a woman to get a rewarding sense of total creation by way of the multiple monotonous chores that are her daily lot...as irrational as for an assembly line worker to rejoice that he had created an automobile because he had tightened a bolt.
"Women Are Household Slaves," *American Mercury* (January 1949)

Stern, Richard G. (b.1928) U.S. writer

1 Anybody can shock a baby, or a television audience. But it's too easy, and the effect is disproportionate to the effort.
Golk (1960), ch. 4

Sterne, Laurence (1713–68) Irish-born British writer and clergyman

1 "They order," said I, "this matter better in France."
Opening words. *A Sentimental Journey Through France and Italy* (1768)

2 I pity the man who can travel from Dan to Beersheba and cry, "T'is all barren!"
"In the Street, Calais," *A Sentimental Journey Through France and Italy* (1768)

3 God tempers the wind, said Maria, to the shorn lamb.
"Maria," *A Sentimental Journey Through France and Italy* (1768)

4 I am positive I have a soul; nor can all the books with which materialists have pestered the world ever convince me of the contrary.
"Maria, Moulines," *A Sentimental Journey Through France and Italy* (1768)

5 Vive l'amour! et vive la bagatelle!
"The Letter," *A Sentimental Journey Through France and Italy* (1768)

6 There are worse occupations in this world than feeling a woman's pulse.
"The Pulse, Paris," *A Sentimental Journey Through France and Italy* (1768)

7 You need not tell me what the proposal was, said she, laying her hand upon both mine, as she interrupted me. A man, my good Sir, has seldom an offer of kindness to make to a woman, but she has a presentiment of it some moments before.
"The Remise, Calais," *A Sentimental Journey Through France and Italy* (1768)

8 An ounce of a man's own wit is worth a ton of other people's.
Tristram Shandy (1759–67)

9 Sciences may be learned by rote, but Wisdom not.
Tristram Shandy (1759–67)

10 I wish either my father or my mother, or indeed both of them, as they were in duty both equally bound to it, had minded what they were about when they begot me.
Tristram Shandy (1759–67), bk. 1, ch. 1

11 So long as a man rides his *Hobby-Horse* peaceably and quietly along the king's highway, and neither compels you or me to get up behind him,—pray, Sir, what have either you or I to do with it?
Tristram Shandy (1759–67), bk. 1, ch. 7

12 'Tis known by the name of perseverance in a good cause,—and of obstinacy in a bad one.
Tristram Shandy (1759–67), bk. 1, ch. 17

13 Digressions, incontestably, are the sunshine; they are the life, the soul of reading; take them out of this book for instance, you might as well take the book along with them.
Tristram Shandy (1759–67), bk. 1, ch. 22

14 Writing, when properly managed (as you may be sure I think mine is), is but a different name for conversation.
Tristram Shandy (1759–67), bk. 2, ch. 11

15 A man should know something of his own country, too, before he goes abroad.
Tristram Shandy (1759–67), bk. 7, ch. 2

16 People who are always taking care of their health are like misers, who are hoarding a treasure which they have never spirit enough to enjoy.
Attrib.

17 Of all the soft, delicious functions of nature this is the chiefest; what a happiness it is to man, when the anxieties and passions of the day are over.
Referring to sleep. Attrib.

Sternhold, Thomas (1500–49) English psalmist

1 The Lord descended from above
And bow'd the heavens high;
And underneath his feet he cast
The darkness of the sky.
Gammer Gurton's Needle (1566), Act 2

Stevas, Norman St. John, Lord (b.1929) British politician

1 I mustn't go on singling out names. One must not be a name-dropper, as Her Majesty remarked to me yesterday.
Speech, Museum of the Year luncheon (June 20, 1979)

Stevens, Anthony (Anthony George Stevens; b.1933) British psychiatrist

1 The perfectionism of obsessional neurotics represents a desire to put themselves beyond rebuke.
Evolutionary Psychiatry (1996), ch. 4

2 Affective disorders...are exaggerations of the universal human capacity to experience sadness and elation.
Evolutionary Psychiatry (1996), ch. 5

3 The taxonomy of fear has long been a subject of interest to psychiatrists, who have delighted in compiling lists of phobias and calling them by Greek names.
Evolutionary Psychiatry (1996), ch. 8

4 When dealing with an assortment of facts or observations, the natural tendency of the human mind is to dichotomise.
Evolutionary Psychiatry (1996), ch. 10

5 If sleeping and dreaming do not perform vital biological functions, then they must represent nature's most stupid blunder and most colossal waste of time.
Evolutionary Psychiatry (1996), ch. 17

Stevens, Brooks U.S. industrial designer

1 Our whole economy is based on planned obsolescence...we make good products, we induce people to buy them, and then the next year we deliberately introduce something that will make these products old-fashioned, out of date, obsolete.
Quoted in *The Waste Makers* (Vance Packard; 1960), ch. 6

Stevens, Wallace (1879–1955) U.S. poet

1 Oh! Blessed rage for order, pale Ramon
The maker's rage to order words of the sea.
"The Idea of Order at Key West" (1935), quoted in *The Penguin Book of American Verse* (Geoffrey Moore, ed.; 1977)

2 Poetry is the supreme fiction, madame.
"A High-Toned Old Christian Woman," *Harmonium* (1923)

3 After the leaves have fallen, we return
To a plain sense of things. It is as if
We had come to an end of the imagination.
"Peter Quince at the Clavier," *Harmonium* (1923)

4 Beauty is momentary in the mind—
The fitful tracing of a portal;
But in the flesh it is immortal.
The body dies; the body's beauty lives.
"Peter Quince at the Clavier," *Harmonium* (1923)

5 Just as my fingers on these keys
Make music, so the selfsame sounds
On my spirit make a music, too.
"Peter Quince at the Clavier," *Harmonium* (1923), st. 1

6 Complacencies of the peignoir, and late
Coffee and oranges in a sunny chair.
And the green freedom of a cockatoo
Upon a rug mingle to dissipate
The holy hush of ancient sacrifice.
"Sunday Morning," *Harmonium* (1923), st. 1

7 The only emperor is the emperor of ice-cream.
"The Emperor of Ice-Cream," *Harmonium* (1923), st. 1

8 One must have a mind of winter
To regard the frost and the boughs
Of the pine-trees crusted with snow.
"The Snow Man," *Harmonium* (1923)

9 I do not know which to prefer,
The beauty of inflections
Or the beauty of innuendoes,
The blackbird whistling
Or just after.
"Thirteen Ways of Looking at a Blackbird," *Harmonium* (1923), st. 5

10 The poet is the priest of the invisible.
"Adagia," *Opus Posthumous* (1957)

11 I am the necessary angel of earth,
Since, in my sight, you see the earth again.
"Angel Surrounded by Paysans," *Selected Poems* (1955)

12 The angel in his cloud
Serenely gazing at the violent abyss,
Plucks on his strings to pluck abysmal glory.
"It Must Give Pleasure," *Selected Poems* (1955)

13 The mules that angels ride come slowly down
The blazing passes, from beyond the sun.
"Le Monocle de Mon Oncle," *Selected Poems* (1955), st. 7

14 I pursued,
And still pursue, the origin and course
Of love, but until now I never knew
That fluttering things have so distinct a shade.
"Le Monocle de Mon Oncle," *Selected Poems* (1955), st. 12

15 The major abstraction is the idea of man
And major man is its exponent, abler
In the abstract than in his singular.
"Notes Toward a Supreme Fiction," *Selected Poems* (1955)

16 The bear, the ponderous cinnamon, snarls in his mountain
At summer thunder and sleeps through winter snow.
"Notes Toward a Supreme Fiction," *Selected Poems* (1955)

17 Death is the mother of beauty:
hence from her,
Alone, shall come fulfillment to our dreams
And our desires.
"Sunday Morning," *Selected Poems* (1955)

18 What is divinity if it can come
Only in silent shadows and dreams?
"Sunday Morning," *Selected Poems* (1955), st. 2

19 I am content when wakened birds,
Before they fly, test the reality
Of misty fields with their sweet questionings.
"Sunday Morning," *Selected Poems* (1955), st. 4

20 Is there no change of death in paradise?
Does ripe fruit never fall?
"Sunday Morning," *Selected Poems* (1955), st. 6

21 Poetry is the supreme fiction, madame.
Take the moral law and make a nave of it
And from the nave build haunted heaven.
1923. "A High-Toned Old Christian Woman," *The Collected Poems of Wallace Stevens* (1954), ll. 1–3

22 I placed a jar in Tennessee,
And round it was, upon a hill.
It made the slovenly wilderness
Surround that hill.
1923. "Anecdote of the Jar," *The Collected Poems of Wallace Stevens* (1954), st. 1

23 They said, "You have a blue guitar,
You do not play things as they are."

The man replied, "Things as they are
Are changed upon the blue guitar."
"The Man with the Blue Guitar," *The Man with the Blue Guitar* (1937), ll. 3–6

24 Imagination...is the irrepressible revolutionist.
"Imagination as Value," *The Necessary Angel: Essays on Reality and the Imagination* (1951)

25 Of what value is anything to the solitary and those that live in misery and terror, except the imagination.
"Imagination as Value," *The Necessary Angel: Essays on Reality and the Imagination* (1951)

26 The imagination is the only genius. It is intrepid and eager and the extreme of its achievement lies in its abstraction. The achievement of the romantic, however, lies in minor wish-fulfillments and it is incapable of abstraction.
"Imagination as Value," *The Necessary Angel: Essays on Reality and the Imagination* (1951)

27 Few people realize that they are looking at the world of their own thoughts and the world of their own feelings.
"The Figure of the Youth as Virile Poet," *The Necessary Angel: Essays on Reality and the Imagination* (1951)

28 The poet...will decide to do as the imagination bids, because he has no choice, if he is to remain a poet. Poetry is the imagination of life.
"The Figure of the Youth as Virile Poet," *The Necessary Angel: Essays on Reality and the Imagination* (1951)

29 The mind has added nothing to human nature. It is a violence from within that protects us from a violence without.
"The Noble Rider and the Sound of Words," *The Necessary Angel: Essays on Reality and the Imagination* (1951)

30 There is no element more conspicuously absent from contemporary poetry than nobility.
"The Noble Rider and the Sound of Words," *The Necessary Angel: Essays on Reality and the Imagination* (1951)

31 An object is the sum of its complications, seen
And unseen. This is everybody's world.
Here the total artifice reveals itself
As the total reality.
"Three Academic Pieces," *The Necessary Angel: Essays on Reality and the Imagination* (1951)

Stevenson, Adlai (Adlai Ewing Stevenson; 1900–65) U.S. statesman

1 Let's talk sense to the American people. Let's tell them the truth, that there are no gains without pains.
Speech accepting presidential nomination, Democratic National Convention, Chicago (July 26, 1952), quoted in *Adlai Stevenson and Illinois* (J. B. Martin; 1976), ch. 8

2 My definition of a free society is a society where it is safe to be unpopular.
Speech, Detroit (October 7, 1952), quoted in *Major Campaign Speeches...1952* (1953)

3 Man has wrested from nature the power to make the world a desert or to make the deserts bloom. There is no evil in the atom, only in men's souls.
Speech, Hartford, Connecticut (September 18, 1952), quoted in "The Atomic Future," *Speeches* (1952)

4 When political ammunition runs low inevitably the rusty artillery of abuse is always wheeled into action.
Referring to critical press opinion claiming he was a "leftist egghead." Speech, New York City (September 22, 1952)

5 A lie is an abomination unto the Lord and a very present help in trouble.
Speech, Springfield (January 1951)

6 Communism is the corruption of a dream of justice.
Speech, Urbana (1951)

7 I suppose flattery hurts no one, that is, if he doesn't inhale.
Television broadcast (March 30, 1952), quoted in *Adlai E. Stevenson* (N. F. Busch; 1952), ch. 5

8 No administration can conduct a sound foreign policy when the future sits in judgment on the past and officials are held accountable as dupes, fools, or traitors for anything that goes wrong.
Call to Greatness (1954)

9 Since the beginning of time, governments have been mainly engaged in kicking people around. The astonishing achievement in modern times in the Western world is the idea that the citizen should do the kicking.
What I Think (1956)

10 A politician is a statesman who approaches every question with an open mouth.
1964. Also attributed to Arthur Goldberg. Quoted in *The Fine Art of Political Wit* (Leon Harris; 1966), ch. 10

11 An editor is one who separates the wheat from the chaff and prints the chaff.
Also attributed to Elbert Hubbard. Quoted in *The Stevenson Wit* (Bill Adler, ed.; 1966)

12 Man does not live by words alone, despite the fact that sometimes he has to eat them.
Attrib.

Stevenson, Juliet (b.1956) British actor

1 If drama shows people dealing nobly with their misery, it disenfranchises those watching who cannot cope like that.
Observer, London (May 22, 1994), "Sayings of the Week"

Stevenson, Robert Louis (Robert Louis Balfour Stevenson; 1850–94) Scottish novelist, essayist, and poet

Quotations about Stevenson

1 Stevenson seemed to pick the right word up on the point of his pen, like a man playing spillikins.
G. K. Chesterton (1874–1936) British writer and poet
Spillikins was a Victorian parlor game played with thin pointed sticks. *The Victorian Age in Literature* (1913)

Quotations by Stevenson

2 A child should always say what's true,
And speak when he is spoken to,
And behave mannerly at table:
At least as far as he is able.
"Whole Duty of Children," *A Child's Garden of Verses* (1885)

3 If your morals make you dreary, depend upon it, they are wrong.
Across the Plains (1892)

4 Here lies one who meant well, tried a little, failed much: surely that may be his epitaph, of which he need not be ashamed.
"A Christmas Sermon," *Across the Plains* (1892), pt. 4

5 Every one lives by selling something.
"Beggars," *Across the Plains* (1892), pt. 3

6 So long as we are loved by others I should say that we are almost indispensable; and no man is useless while he has a friend.
"Lay Morals," *Across the Plains* (1892)

7 "The cost of a thing," says he, "is the amount of what I will call life which is required to be exchanged for it, immediately or in the long run."
"Henry David Thoreau," *Familiar Studies of Men and Books* (1882)

8 Politics is perhaps the only profession for which no preparation is thought necessary.
"Yoshida-Torajiro," *Familiar Studies of Men and Books* (1882)

9 I've a grand memory for forgetting, David.
Kidnapped (1886), ch. 18

10 Vanity dies hard; in some obstinate cases it outlives the man.
Prince Otto (1885)

11 Wealth I seek not; hope nor love,
Nor a friend to know me;
All I seek, the heaven above
And the road below me.
"The Vagabond," *Songs of Travel* (1895), st. 4

12 Is there anything in life so disenchanting as attainment?
"The Adventure of a Hansom Cab," *The New Arabian Nights* (1882)

13 I regard you with an indifference closely bordering on aversion.
"The Rajah's Diamond: Story of the Bandbox," *The New Arabian Nights* (1882)

14 Ours was a California summer, and an earthquake was a far likelier accident than a shower of rain.
1883. "Toils and Pleasures," *The Silverado Squatters* (1917)

15 It's deadly commonplace, but, after all, the commonplaces are the great poetic truths.
The Weir of Hermiston (1896), ch. 6

16 Between the possibility of being hanged in all innocence, and the certainty of a public and merited disgrace, no gentleman of spirit could long hesitate.
The Wrong Box (co-written with Lloyd Osbourne; 1889), ch. 10

17 For my part, I travel not to go anywhere, but to go. I travel for travel's sake. The great affair is to move.
"Cheylard and Luc," *Travels with a Donkey in the Cévennes* (1879)

18 Fifteen men on the dead man's chest
Yo-ho-ho, and a bottle of rum!
Drink and the devil had done for the rest—
Yo-ho-ho, and a bottle of rum!
Treasure Island (1883), ch. 1

19 Pieces of eight!
Treasure Island (1883), ch. 10

20 The physician...is the flower (such as it is) of our civilization.
Underwoods (1887), Dedication

21 Go, little book, and wish to all
Flowers in the garden, meat in the hall,
A bin of wine, a spice of wit,
A house with lawns enclosing it,
A living river by the door,
A nightingale in the sycamore!
"Envoy," *Underwoods* (1887)

22 Of all my verse, like not a single line;
But like my title, for it is not mine.
That title from a better man I stole;
Ah, how much better, had I stol'n the whole!
"Foreword," *Underwoods* (1887)

23 Under the wide and starry sky
Dig the grave and let me lie.
Glad did I live and gladly die,
—And I laid me down with a will.
This is the verse you grave for me:
"Here he lies where he longed to be;
Home is the sailor, home from sea,
And the hunter home from the hill."
"Requiem," *Underwoods* (1887)

24 Give me the young man who has brains enough to make a fool of himself!
Virginibus Puerisque (1881)

25 Marriage; a long conversation chequered by disputes.
Virginibus Puerisque (1881)

26 When the torrent sweeps a man against a boulder, you must expect him to scream, and you need not be surprised if the scream is sometimes a theory.
Virginibus Puerisque (1881)

27 Even if the doctor does not give you a year, even if he hesitates about a month, make one brave push and see what can be accomplished in a week.
"Aes Triplex," *Virginibus Puerisque* (1881)

28 Books are good enough in their own way, but they are a mighty bloodless substitute for life.
"An Apology for Idlers," *Virginibus Puerisque* (1881)

29 He sows hurry and reaps indigestion.
"An Apology for Idlers," *Virginibus Puerisque* (1881)

30 There is no duty we so much underrate as the duty of being happy.
"An Apology for Idlers," *Virginibus Puerisque* (1881)

31 Old and young, we are all on our last cruise.
"Crabbed Age and Youth," *Virginibus Puerisque* (1881)

32 To travel hopefully is a better thing than to arrive, and the true success is to labour.
"El Dorado," *Virginibus Puerisque* (1881)

33 Lastly and this is, perhaps, the golden rule, no woman should marry a teetotaller, or a man who does not smoke.
"Virginibus Puerisque," *Virginibus Puerisque* (1881)

34 Even if we take matrimony at its lowest, even if we regard it as no more than a sort of friendship recognized by the police.
"Virginibus Puerisque," *Virginibus Puerisque* (1881), pt. 1

35 In marriage, a man becomes slack and selfish and undergoes a fatty degeneration of his moral being.
"Virginibus Puerisque," *Virginibus Puerisque* (1881), pt. 1

36 Marriage is a step so grave and decisive that it attracts light-headed, variable men by its very awfulness.
"Virginibus Puerisque," *Virginibus Puerisque* (1881), pt. 1

37 Marriage is like life in this—that it is a field of battle, and not a bed of roses.
"Virginibus Puerisque," *Virginibus Puerisque* (1881), pt. 1

38 Man is a creature who lives not upon bread alone, but principally by catchwords; and the little rift between the sexes is astonishingly widened by simply teaching one set of catchwords to the girls and another to the boys.
"Virginibus Puerisque," *Virginibus Puerisque* (1881), pt. 2

39 To marry is to domesticate the Recording Angel. Once you are married, there is nothing left for you, not even suicide, but to be good.
"Virginibus Puerisque," *Virginibus Puerisque* (1881), pt. 2

40 The cruellest lies are often told in silence.
"Virginibus Puerisque," *Virginibus Puerisque* (1881), pt. 4

41 Every man has a sane spot somewhere.
Attrib.

42 I never know whether to be more surprised at Darwin himself for making so much of natural selection, or at his opponents for making so little of it.
Attrib.

Stewart, Jackie (John Young Stewart; b.1939) British racing car driver

1 In my sport the quick are too often listed among the dead.
Attrib.

Stewart, Jimmy (James Maitland Stewart; 1908–97) British-born U.S. film actor

1 All our Western lore is exaggerated and distorted. The gunmen weren't very good shots. Audiences think they were daring men. In fact, they were a pretty desperate bunch, not romantic but very cowardly, very dirty and usually very drunk.
January 1966. Attrib.

Stewart, Maria W. (1803–79) U.S. lecturer, teacher, and essayist

1 O, ye daughters of Africa, awake! awake! arise! no longer slumber, but distinguish yourselves. Show forth to the world that ye are endowed with noble and exalted faculties.
Religion And The Pure Principles of Morality, The Sure Foundation On Which We Must Build (1831)

Stewart, Thomas A. (b.1948) U.S. journalist

1 Companies...have a hard time distinguishing between the cost of paying people and the value of investing in them.
Intellectual Capital (1997)

2 In companies whose wealth is intellectual capital, networks, rather than hierarchies, are the right organizational design.
Intellectual Capital (1997)

3 Information and knowledge are the thermonuclear weapons of our time.
Intellectual Capital (1997)

4 Intellectual capital is the sum of everything everybody in a company knows that gives it a competitive edge.
Intellectual Capital (1997)

5 Intelligence becomes an asset when some useful order is created out of free-floating brainpower.
Intellectual Capital (1997)

6 In the networked organization...the manager's job is DNA: Define, Nurture, Allocate.
Intellectual Capital (1997)

7 Managing intellectual assets has become the single most important task of business.
Intellectual Capital (1997)

8 Networks irrevocably subvert managerial authority.
Intellectual Capital (1997)

9 The rise of computers...is forcing machinery to adapt to our idiosyncratic humanity.
Intellectual Capital (1997)

Stipe, Michael (b.1960) U.S. rock musician and songwriter

1 Pop culture is still the one way in which someone who is without power can attain it and bring about a change.
Observer, London (May 21, 1989)

2 We don't get groupies. We get teenagers who want to read us their poetry.
Q (September 1, 1994)

Stockdale, James B. (b.1923) U.S. vice admiral

1 Who am I? Why am I here?
Said during the 1992 presidential election, when Stockdale was running-mate of independent candidate Ross Perot. Televised debate for vice presidential candidates (October 1992)

Stockhausen, Karlheinz (b.1928) German composer

1 Music is mathematics, the mathematics of listening, mathematics for the ears.
1981. Quoted in "In the Service of Music: The Quest for Perfection," *Conversations with Stockhausen* (Mya Tannenbaum; 1987)

Stocks, Mary, Baroness (1891–1975) British politician, writer, and broadcaster

1 It is clearly absurd that it should be possible for a woman to qualify as a saint with direct access to the Almighty while she may not qualify as a curate.
Still More Commonplace (1974)

Stockwood, Mervyn (Mervyn Arthur Stockwood; b.1913) British Anglican cleric

1 A psychiatrist is a man who goes to the Folies-Bergères and looks at the audience.
Observer, London (October 15, 1961), "Sayings of the Week"

Stoddard, Elizabeth (Elizabeth Drew Barstow Stoddard; 1823–1902) U.S. novelist and poet

1 A woman despises a man for loving her, unless she returns his love.
Two Men (1865), ch. 32

Stoker, Bram (Abraham Stoker; 1845–1912) Irish-born British writer

1 The mouth...was fixed and rather cruel-looking, with peculiarly sharp white teeth; these protruded over the lips, whose remarkable ruddiness showed astonishing vitality in a man of his years.
Describing Count Dracula. *Dracula* (1897), ch. 2

2 His eyes flamed red with devilish passion; the great nostrils of the white aquiline nose opened wide and quivered at the edges; and the white sharp teeth, behind the full lips of the blood dripping mouth; champed together like those of a wild beast....Further and further back he cowered, as we, lifting our crucifixes, advanced.
Dracula (1897), ch. 21

Stokes, Donald Gresham, Baron Stokes of Leyland (b.1914) British business executive

1 The ideal committee is a committee of one.
Daily Mail, London (January 18, 1968)

Stoll, Clifford U.S. astronomer and author

1 Footprints across an artificial reality are as evanescent as data on the Ethernet.
Ethernet is a trademark for a system for exchanging messages between computers on a local area network. *Silicon Snake Oil* (1995)

2 You're entering a non-existent universe. Consider the consequences.
His warning to people using the Internet. *Silicon Snake Oil* (1995)

3 For all its egalitarian promise, whole groups of people hardly show up on the network. Women, blacks, elderly, and the poor are all underrepresented.
Referring to the Internet. *Silicon Snake Oil* (1995)

4 Our networks aren't simple connections of cables and computers; they're cooperative communities.
Referring to use of the Internet among groups of people. *Silicon Snake Oil* (1995)

Stone, I. F. (Isidor Feinstein Stone; 1907–89) U.S. journalist and publisher

1 If you live long enough, the venerability factor creeps in; you get accused of things you never did and praised for virtues you never had.
Attrib.

Stone, Lucy (1818–93) U.S. reformer and editor

1 We want rights. The flour-merchant, the house-builder, and the postman charge us no less on account of our sex; but when we endeavor to earn money to pay all these, then, indeed, we find the difference.
Speech, "Disappointment Is the Lot of Women" (October 17–18, 1855)

Stone, Oliver (b.1946) U.S. film director and screenwriter

1 Not a historical document, but a metaphorical truth that represents a decade of aggression, a culture that worships aggression and makes money from it.
Referring to his movie *Natural Born Killers* (1994). *Independent,* London (February 21, 1995)

Stopes, Marie (Marie Charlotte Carmichael Stopes; 1880–1958) British scientist and birth-control campaigner

Quotations about Stopes

1 Her frontal attacks on old taboos, her quasi-prophetic tone, her flowery fervour, aroused strong opposition from those who disagreed with her for religious reasons or felt that she had overstepped the bounds of good taste.
Anonymous. Obituary, *Daily Telegraph,* London (October 3, 1958)

2 Dr Marie Stopes made contraceptive devices respectable in a somewhat gushing book, *Married Love.* For this she deserves to be remembered among the great benefactors of the age.
A. J. P. Taylor (1906–90) British historian. *English History 1914–1945* (1965)

Quotations by Stopes

3 I consider in a Christian country it is an immoral and outrageous act to tax me because I am living in Holy matrimony instead of as my husband's mistress.
Letter to George Bernard Shaw (June 29, 1925)

4 I do not believe that the normal man's sex needs are stronger than the normal woman's. The *average* man's undoubtedly are, owing to the utterly false repression of the woman's and the utterly unnatural stimulation of the man's which have been current for so long.
Remark (December 17, 1918)

5 An impersonal and scientific knowledge of the structure of our bodies is the surest safeguard against prurient curiosity and lascivious gloating.
Married Love (1918), ch. 5

6 Each coming together of man and wife, even if they have been mated for many years, should be a fresh adventure; each winning should necessitate a fresh wooing.
Married Love (1918), ch. 10

7 We are not much in sympathy with the typical hustling American business man, but we have often felt compunction for him, seeing him nervous and harassed...all but overshadowed by his overdressed, extravagant and idle wife...such wives imagine that they are upholding women's emancipation.
Quoted in *The Fighting Pankhursts* (David Mitchell; 1967)

Stoppard, Tom, Sir (Thomas Straussler; b.1937) Czech-born British playwright and screenwriter

1 The ordinary-sized stuff which is our lives...as mysterious to us as the heavens were to the Greeks. We're better at predicting events at the edge of a galaxy or inside the nucleus of an atom than whether it'll rain on auntie's garden party three Sundays from now.
Arcadia (1993)

2 Skill without imagination is craftsmanship and gives us many useful objects such as wickerwork picnic baskets. Imagination without skill gives us modern art.
Artist Descending a Staircase (1972)

3 It's better to be quotable than to be honest.
Guardian, London (1973)

4 If an idea's worth having once, it's worth having twice.
Indian Ink (1995)

5 This is a British murder inquiry and some degree of justice must be seen to be more or less done.
Jumpers (1972), Act 2

6 The media. It sounds like a convention of spiritualists.
Night and Day (1978), Act 1

7 He's someone who flies around from hotel to hotel and thinks the most interesting thing about any story is the fact that he has arrived to cover it.
Referring to foreign correspondents. *Night and Day* (1978), Act 1

8 Fifty-five crystal spheres geared to God's crankshaft is my idea

of a satisfying universe. I can't think of anything more trivial than quarks, quasars, big bangs and black holes.
Observer, London (May 22, 1994), "Sayings of the Week"

9 GUILDENSTERN Maidens aspiring to godheads.
ROSENCRANTZ And vice versa.
Rosencrantz and Guildenstern Are Dead (1966), Act 1

10 Eternity's a terrible thought. I mean, where's it going to end?
Rosencrantz and Guildenstern Are Dead (1966), Act 2

11 The bad end unhappily, the good unluckily. That is what tragedy means.
Imitating Miss Prism in Oscar Wilde's *The Importance of Being Earnest* (1895). *Rosencrantz and Guildenstern Are Dead* (1966), Act 2

12 Life is a gamble, at terrible odds—if it was a bet, you wouldn't take it.
Rosencrantz and Guildenstern Are Dead (1966), Act 3

13 War is capitalism with the gloves off.
Travesties (1974), Act 1

14 Your book has much in common with your dress. As an arrangement of words it is graceless without being random...as an experience it is like sharing a cell with a fanatic in search of a mania.
Travesties (1974), Act 2

Storr, Anthony (Charles Anthony Storr; b.1920) British writer and psychiatrist

1 When I was in practice, I was only consulted by creative people when their creativity was blocked in some way. I think the organisation required by producing creative work is protective against mental illness...Many would be mentally ill if they didn't create.
The Dynamics of Creation (1972)

2 A tolerant scepticism, an ability to doubt one's own ideas as well as those of other people, is a good test of maturity: fanaticism, insanity, and an infantile attitude to others are closely related.
The Integrated Personality (1960)

3 Delusions may be the only things which render life tolerable, and, as such, are jealously defended against all the assaults of reason.
The Integrated Personality (1960)

4 Only a very moderate acquaintance with psychology is required to recognize that men constantly deplore in others that which they cannot accept in themselves.
The Integrated Personality (1960)

Story, Jack Trevor (1917–91) British novelist

1 Live Now, Pay Later
1963. Novel title.

Stout, Rex (Rex Todhunter Stout; 1886–1975) U.S. writer

1 There are two kinds of statistics, the kind you look up and the kind you make up.
Death of a Doxy (1966), ch. 9

2 I like to walk around Manhattan, catching glimpses of its wild life, the pigeons and cats and girls.
"When a Man Murders," *Three Witnesses* (1956)

Stowe, Harriet Beecher (originally Harriet Elizabeth Beecher; 1811–96) U.S. writer and abolitionist

Quotations about Stowe

1 Harriet Beecher Stowe, whose *Uncle Tom's Cabin* was the first evidence to America that no hurricane can be so disastrous to a country as a ruthlessly humanitarian woman.
Sinclair Lewis (1885–1951) U.S. novelist. Quoted in *Henry Ward Beecher: An American Portrait* (Paxton Hibben; 1927), introduction

Quotations by Stowe

2 Women are the real architects of society.
"Dress, or Who Makes the Fashions," *Atlantic Monthly* (19th century)

3 The bitterest tears shed over graves are for words left unsaid and deeds left undone.
Little Foxes (1865), ch. 3

4 "Do you know who made you?" "Nobody, as I knows on," said the child, with a short laugh... "I 'spect I grow'd."
Uncle Tom's Cabin (1852), ch. 20

5 Whipping and abuse are like laudanum: You have to double the dose as the sensibilities decline.
Uncle Tom's Cabin (1852), ch. 20

6 "Who was your mother?" "Never had none!" said the child, with another grin. "Never had any mother? What do you mean? Where were you born?" "Never was born!" persisted Topsy.
Uncle Tom's Cabin (1852), ch. 20

7 I did not write it. God wrote it. I merely did his dictation.
Referring to *Uncle Tom's Cabin* (1852). Quoted in *The Faber Book of Anecdotes* (Clifton Fadiman, ed.; 1985)

Strachey, Lytton (Giles Lytton Strachey; 1880–1932) British writer

1 If this is dying, I don't think much of it.
1932. Last words. Quoted in *Lytton Strachey* (Michael Holroyd; 1967–68), pt. 5, ch. 17

Strasberg, Susan (Susan Elizabeth Strasberg; b.1938) U.S. actor

1 There's no such thing as The Method. The term method-acting is so much nonsense. There are many methods...My father merely used a method of teaching based on the ideas of Stanislavsky—self-discipline, how to think out a role and use imagination.
1961. Referring to her father, Lee Strasberg, who was the leading teacher of so-called method-acting, in a publicity release for *Scream of Fear* (1961). Attrib.

Strauss, Bill (William Strauss; 1947–?) U.S. satirist and entertainer

1 Hark, when Gerald Ford was king—
We were bored with everything.
Unemployment 6 per cent,
What a boring president.

Nothing major needed fixin'
So he pardoned Richard Nixon.
1982. Attrib.

Stravinsky, Igor (Igor Fyodorovich Stravinsky; 1882–1971) Russian-born U.S. composer

1 I don't write modern music. I only write good music.
Remark to journalists on his first visit to the United States (1925)

2 I had another dream the other day about music critics. They were small and rodent-like with padlocked ears, as if they had stepped out of a painting by Goya.
Evening Standard, London (October 29, 1969)

3 My music is best understood by children and animals.
Observer, London (October 8, 1961), "Sayings of the Week"

4 What are the connections that unite and separate music and dance? In my opinion, the one does not serve the other. There must be a harmonious accord, a synthesis of ideas. Let us speak, on the contrary, of the struggle between music and choreography.
Quoted in *A Portrait of Mr. Balanchine* (Lincoln Kirstein; 1984)

5 The more constraints one imposes, the more one frees one's self of the chains that shackle the spirit...the arbitrariness of the constraint only serves to obtain precision of execution.
Quoted in *The Jingle Bell Principle* (Miroslav Holub; 1992)

6 A good composer does not imitate; he steals.
Quoted in *Twentieth Century Music* (Peter Yates; 1967), pt. 1, ch. 8

7 Too many pieces of music finish too long after the end.
Attrib.

8 Hurry! I never hurry. I have no time to hurry.
Responding to his publisher's request that he hurry his completion of a composition. Attrib.

Streatfield, Geoffrey, Sir (Geoffrey Hugh Benbow Streatfield; 1897–1978) British lawyer

1 Facts speak louder than statistics.
Observer, London (March 19, 1950), "Sayings of the Week"

Streep, Meryl (Mary Louise Streep; b.1949) U.S. actor

1 Having wrinkles is at once strange and exciting.
Said on being asked whether she would have plastic surgery. *Independent*, London (March 26, 1994)

Streisand, Barbra (Barbara Joan Streisand; b.1942) U.S. singer, film actor, director, and producer

1 Success to me is having ten honeydew melons and eating only the top half of each one.
Life (September 20, 1963)

2 Why am I so famous? What am I doing right? What are the others doing so wrong?
Playboy (October 1977), quoted in *Chambers Film Quotes* (Tony Crawley, ed.; 1991)

3 Whether an album sells or not is not of consequence. The reward for me is in the process. If it sells...then that's a bonus.
Quoted in "Barbra Streisand," *Off the Record: An Oral History of Popular Music* (Joe Smith; 1988)

Strindberg, August (Johan August Strindberg; 1849–1912) Swedish dramatist

1 I loathe people who keep dogs. They are cowards who haven't got the guts to bite people themselves.
A Madman's Diary (1895), pt. 3

2 Impossible to know where you are with women. Whatever you do is wrong. One day they call you a satyr, the next day a Joseph...Oh this eternal torment of mutual recriminations, as if the bedroom held the keys to paradise!
An Occult Diary (Mary Sandbach, tr.; 1965)

3 Woman does not love; it is man who loves and woman who is loved.
An Occult Diary (Mary Sandbach, tr.; 1965)

4 ELEANORA For me there is neither time nor space. I am everywhere and of all times. I am in my father's prison and in my brother's schoolroom, I am in my mother's kitchen, and in my sister's shop, far away in America.
1900. *Easter* (Elizabeth Sprigge, tr.; 1955)

5 You wouldn't see anybody in our class behaving like that. But that's what happens when the gentry try to act like the common people—they become common!
Miss Julie (1889)

6 CAPTAIN A man has no children. Only women have children. So the future is theirs, while we die childless.
1887. *The Father* (Elizabeth Sprigge, tr.; 1955)

7 CAPTAIN Rude strength has fallen before treacherous weakness. Shame on you, woman of Satan, and a curse on all your sex!
1887. *The Father* (Elizabeth Sprigge, tr.; 1955)

8 STUDENT (*speaking of the hyacinth*). The bulb is...an image of the Cosmos. This is why Buddha sits holding the earth-bulb, his eyes brooding as he watches it grow, outward and upward, transforming itself into a heaven.
1907. *The Ghost Sonata* (Elizabeth Sprigge, tr.; 1955)

Strong, Maurice F. (b.1929) Canadian environmentalist and business executive

1 A citizen of an advanced industrialized nation consumes in six months the energy and raw materials that have to last the citizen of a developing country his entire lifetime.
Attrib.

Strunsky, Simeon (1879–1948) Russian-born U.S. editor and essayist

1 Famous remarks are seldom quoted correctly.
No Mean City (1944), ch. 38

Stubbes, Philip (or Stubbs; 1555?–1610?) English puritan pamphleteer

1 A ship is sooner rigged than a gentlewoman made ready.
Anatomy of Abuses (1583)

2 Football...causeth fighting, brawling, contention, quarrel picking, murder, homicide and great effusion of bloode, as daily experience teacheth.
"Football" means soccer. *Anatomy of Abuses* (1583)

Sturges, Preston (originally Edmund Preston Biden; 1898–1959) U.S. scriptwriter and film director

1 Now I've laid me down to die
I pray my neighbors not to pry
Too deeply into sins that I
Not only cannot here deny
But much enjoyed as life flew by.
Epitaph (1959)

Styron, William (William Clark Styron, Jr.; b.1925) U.S. novelist

1 Mysteriously and in ways that are totally remote from normal experience, the gray drizzle of horror induced by depression takes on the quality of physical pain...it is entirely natural that the victim begins to think ceaselessly of oblivion.
Darkness Visible (1990), quoted in *Depression* (Constance Hammen; 1997), ch. 1

Suckling, John, Sir (1609–42) English poet

1 Her feet beneath her petticoat
Like little mice stole in and out,
As if they feared the light;
But oh, she dances such a way!
No sun upon an Easter-day
Is half so fine a sight.
"A Ballad upon a Wedding," *Fragmenta Aurea* (1646), st. 8

2 But love is such a mystery,
I cannot find it out:
For when I think I'm best resolv'd,
I then am in most doubt.
"Song. I Prithee Send Me Back," *Fragmenta Aurea* (1646)

3 The prince of darkness is a gentleman.
The Goblins (1638)

Su Dongpo (also known as Su Tung-p'o, pen name of Su Shih, also known as Su Shi; 1036–1101) Chinese poet and writer

1 Eastwards goes the great river,
its waves have swept away
a thousand years of gallant men.
"The Charms of Nian-nu: Meditation on the Past at Red Cliff" (1082?), quoted in *An Anthology of Chinese Literature* (Stephen Lawson, tr.; 1996)

Suetonius (Gaius Suetonius Tranquillus; 69?–140?) Roman historian and biographer

1 On the night before his assassination, Caligula dreamed that he was standing beside Jupiter's throne in the heavens. The God kicked him with the big toe of his right foot, and sent him plummeting down to earth.
"Caligula," *Lives of the Caesars* (121?)

2 Strike him so that he can feel that he is dying.
Quoting the Emperor Caligula (ruled 37–41). "Caligula," *Lives of the Caesars* (121?)

3 Once at supper, reflecting that he had done nothing for any that day, he broke out into that memorable and justly admired saying, "My friends, I have lost a day!"
Referring to the Emperor Titus (ruled 79–81). "Titus," *Lives of the Caesars* (121?)

Sugar, Alan (Alan Michael Sugar; b.1947) British entrepreneur

1 Pan Am takes good care of you. Marks & Spencer loves you. Securicor cares, IBM say the customer is king. At Amstrad we want your money.
Speech, City University Business School, London (April 1987)

2 My accountants have told me that I can have one foot in Jersey, my left earlobe in the Isle of Man and my right foot in Zurich and pay little or no tax.
Guardian, London (March 29, 1984)

3 If there was a market in mass-produced portable nuclear weapons, we'd market them too.
Observer, London (September 14, 1986), "Quotes of the Week"

4 It's having the right stuff in the right place at the right time—and neither too much nor too little of it.
Referring to his formula for success. *Sun*, London (February 13, 1986)

Suharto (b.1921) Indonesian statesman

1 We must no longer be afraid of the multifarious views and opinions expressed by the people.
Referring to the day his information minister insisted that press controls remain in place. *Straits Times*, Singapore (September 1, 1990)

Sullivan, Anne (Joanna Mansfield Sullivan Macy; 1866–1936) U.S. teacher

1 It's queer how ready people always are with advice in any real or imaginary emergency, and no matter how many times experience has shown them to be wrong, they continue to set forth their opinions, as if they had received them from the Almighty!
Letter (June 12, 1887)

2 *Language* and *knowledge* are indissolubly connected; they are interdependent.
Speech to the American Association to Promote the Teaching of Speech to the Deaf (July 1894)

3 Language grows out of life, out of its needs and experiences.
Speech to the American Association to Promote the Teaching of Speech to the Deaf (July 1894)

Sully, Maximilien de Béthune, Duc de (1560–1641) French statesman

1 The English take their pleasures sadly after the fashion of their country.
Memoirs (1630?)

Sulpicia (*fl.* 63 B.C.–14 A.D.) Roman poet

1 I delight in sinning and hate to compose a mask for gossip.
1st century B.C. Quoted in *A Book of Women Poets* (Aliki and Willis Barnstone, eds.; 1980)

Sulzberger, Arthur Hays (1891–1968) U.S. newspaper proprietor

1 We tell the public which way the cat is jumping. The public will take care of the cat.
Referring to journalism. *Time* (May 8, 1950)

Summers, Lawrence H. (b.1954) U.S. politician and economist

1 I've always thought that underpopulated countries in Africa are vastly underpolluted.
Quoted in *Faith and Credit: The World Bank's Secular Empire* (Fabrizio Sabelli; 1994)

2 The economic logic behind dumping a load of toxic waste in the lowest wage country is impeccable and we should face up to it.
Quoted in *Faith and Credit: The World Bank's Secular Empire* (Fabrizio Sabelli; 1994)

Sumner, W. G. (William Graham Sumner; 1840–1910) U.S. sociologist and teacher

1 I suppose that the first chemists seemed to be very hard-hearted and unpoetical persons when they scouted the glorious dream of the alchemists that there must be some process for turning base metals into gold.
The Forgotten Man (1883)

Sun, Madame (Song Qingling, also known as Soong Ch'ing-ling; 1890–1981) Chinese writer and revolutionary

1 Let us exert every ounce of man's energy and everything produced by him to ensure that everywhere the common people of the world get their due from life.
Address, *The Chinese Women's Fight for Freedom* (July–August 1956)

Sun Yat-sen (also Sun Yixian, Sun Zhongshan; 1866–1925) Chinese revolutionary and nationalist leader

1 The foundation of the government of a nation must be built upon the rights of the people, but the administration must be entrusted to experts.
The Three Principles of the People (Frank W. Price; 1953)

2 Europe made the revolution in order to conquer liberty, of which she was deprived. We, on the other hand, want to make it because we suffer from an excess of liberty.
Quoted in *The Chinese* (Alain Peyrefitte (Graham Webb, tr.); 1977)

3 The civilization of Europe and America is completely materialistic. There is nothing more vulgar, more brutal, more evil. We Chinese call that barbarism. Our inferiority as a power derives from the fact that we have always scorned and avoided it. The Chinese Way is the way of mankind and morals.
1925. Quoted in *The Chinese* (Alain Peyrefitte (Graham Webb, tr.); 1977)

Supreme Court of the United States U.S. highest court

1 We conclude that in the field of public education the doctrine of "separate but equal" has no place. Separate educational facilities are inherently unequal.
The decision that outlawed segregated schooling in the United States. Court ruling (May 17, 1954)

Surrey, Henry Howard, Earl of (1517?–47) English courtier and poet

1 Martial, the things that do attain
The happy life be these, I find:
The riches left, not got with pain;
The fruitful ground, the quiet mind;
The equal friend; no grudge nor strife;
No charge or rule nor governance;
Without disease the healthful life;
The household of continuance.
"The Happy Life," *The Poems of Henry Howard, Earl of Surrey* (Frederick Morgan Padelford; 1928)

Susruta (fl.4th century) Hindu physician

1 Strong emotions and passions are the causes not only of mental but also of physical illness.
Attrib.

Sutherland, Donald (b.1934) Canadian-born U.S. film actor

1 When you're working for a good director, you become subjective and submissive. You become his concubine. All that you seek is his pleasure.
Quoted in *Film Yearbook 1986* (1986)

Su Xiaokang (b.1949) Chinese social scientist

1 This yellow river, it so happens, bred a nation identified by its yellow skin pigment. Moreover, this nation also refers to its earliest ancestor as the Yellow Emperor.
River Elegy (1991), quoted in *The Construction of Tacila Identities in China and Japan* (Frank Dikotter, ed.; 1997)

Svevo, Italo (Ettore Schmitz; 1861–1928) Italian writer

1 There are three things I always forget. Names, faces and—the third I can't remember.
Attrib.

Swaffer, Hannen (1879–1962) British journalist

1 Freedom of the press in Britain is freedom to print such of the proprietor's prejudices as the advertisers don't object to.
1928? Quoted in *Swaff* (Tom Driberg; 1974), ch. 2

Swanson, Gloria (originally Gloria Josephine Mae Swenson or Svensson; 1899–1983) U.S. film actor

1 I am big. It's the pictures that got small.
As the forgotten silent movie star Norma Desmond. *Sunset Boulevard* (Charles Brackett, Billy Wilder, and D. M. Marshman, Jr.; 1950)

2 When I die, my epitaph should read: *She Paid the Bills*. That's the story of my life.
The Saturday Evening Post (July 22, 1950)

Swartley, Ariel U.S. music journalist

1 It doesn't have anything to do with my life. It doesn't talk about kids. It doesn't talk about long-term relationships. I don't think there's any pop music directed at the peculiar class of anger women my age that I know feel.
"This Prince is No Pretender," *Real Paper* (March 1, 1980)

Sweeney, Matthew (b.1952) Irish poet

1 My father is writing in Irish.
The English language, with all its facts
will not do. It is too modern.

It is good for plane-crashes, for unemployment,
but not for the unexpected return
of the eagle to Donegal.
"The Eagle," *Cacti* (1992)

Swift, Jonathan, Dean (1667–1745) Irish writer and clergyman

Quotations about Swift

1 He washed himself with oriental scrupulosity.
Samuel Johnson (1709–84) British lexicographer and writer. "Swift," *Lives of the English Poets* (1779–81)

2 He delivered Ireland from plunder and oppression; and showed that wit, confederated with truth, had such force as authority was unable to resist.
Samuel Johnson (1709–84) British lexicographer and writer. Attrib.

Quotations by Swift

3 Laws are like cobwebs, which may catch small flies, but let wasps and hornets break through.
"A Critical Essay upon the Faculties of the Mind" (1709)

4 Now Betty from her master's bed had flown,
And softly stole to discompose her own.
"A Description of the Morning" (1709), ll. 3–4

5 I have been assured by a very knowing American of my acquaintance in London, that a young healthy child well nursed is at a year old a most delicious, nourishing, and wholesome food, whether stewed, roasted, baked, or boiled, and I make no doubt that it will equally serve in a fricassee, or a ragout.
"A Modest Proposal for Preventing the Children of Ireland from being a Burden to their Parents or Country" (1729)

6 'Tis an old maxim in the schools,
That flattery's the food of fools;
Yet now and then your men of wit
Will condescend to take a bit.
"Cadenus and Vanessa" (1713)

7 Here lies the body of Jonathan Swift, D.D., dean of this cathedral, where burning indignation can no longer lacerate his heart. Go, traveller, and imitate if you can a man who was an undaunted champion of liberty.
Jonathan Swift's epitaph, written by himself, on his tomb in St. Patrick's Cathedral, Dublin. Epitaph (1745)

8 My female friends, who could bear me very well a dozen years ago, have now forsaken me, although I am not so old in proportion to them as I formerly was: which I can prove by arithmetic, for then I was double their age, which now I am not.
Letter to Alexander Pope (February 7, 1736)

9 Proper words in proper places, make the true definition of a style.
"Letter to a Young Gentleman lately entered into Holy Orders" (January 9, 1720)

10 You have but a very few years to be young and handsome in the eyes of the world; and as few months to be so in the eyes of a husband, who is not a fool.
"Letter to a Young Lady on her Marriage" (1723)

11 Hail fellow, well met,
All dirty and wet:
Find out, if you can,
Who's master, who's man.
"My Lady's Lamentation" (1728)

12 So, naturalist observe, a flea
Hath smaller fleas that on him prey,
And these have smaller fleas to bite 'em.
And so proceed *ad infinitum.*
"On Poetry: A Rhapsody" (1733), ll. 353–356

13 Nor do they trust their tongue alone,
But speak a language of their own;
Can read a nod, a shrug, a look,
Far better than a printed book;
Convey a libel in a frown,
And wink a reputation down.
"The Journal of a Modern Lady" (1729)

14 Vision is the art of seeing things invisible.
"Thoughts on Various Subjects" (1726)

15 A poet, starving in a garret,
Conning old topics like a parrot,
Invokes his mistress and his muse,
And stays at home for want of shoes.
"To Stella Who Collected and Transcribed His Poems" (1723?)

16 What poet would not grieve to see
His brethren write as well as he?
"Verses on the Death of Dr. Swift" (1731)

17 Yet malice never was his aim;
He lashed the vice, but spared the name.
Referring to himself. "Verses on the Death of Dr. Swift" (1731)

18 Last week I saw a woman flayed, and you will hardly believe, how much it altered her person for the worse.
A Tale of a Tub (1704), ch. 9

19 I cannot but conclude the bulk of your natives to be the most pernicious race of little odious vermin that nature ever suffered to crawl upon the surface of the earth.
The king of Brobdingnag's opinion of the English. "A Voyage to Brobdingnag," *Gulliver's Travels* (1726), ch. 6

20 Whoever could make two ears of corn or two blades of grass to grow upon a spot of ground where only one grew before would deserve better of mankind and do more essential service to his country than the whole race of politicians put together.
The king of Brobdingnag's opinion of politicians. "A Voyage to Brobdingnag," *Gulliver's Travels* (1726), ch. 7

21 He had been eight years upon a project for extracting sunbeams out of cucumbers, which were to be put into vials hermetically sealed, and let out to warm the air in raw inclement summers.
"A Voyage to Laputa," *Gulliver's Travels* (1726), ch. 5

22 He showed me his bill of fare to tempt me to dine with him; Poh, said I, I value not your bill of fare, give me your bill of company.
Journal to Stella (September 2, 1711)

23 We were to do more business after dinner; but after dinner is

after dinner—an old saying and a true, "much drinking, little thinking."
Journal to Stella (February 26, 1712)

24 We are so fond of one another because our ailments are the same.
Stella was Swift's private name for Esther Johnson; they may have been secretly married. *Journal to Stella* (February 1, 1711)

25 No wise man ever wished to be younger.
Moral and Diverting (1711)

26 Money, the life-blood of the nation,
Corrupts and stagnates in the veins,
Unless a proper circulation
Its motion and its heat maintains.
1720. "The Run upon the Bankers," *Poems* (1735)

27 Bachelor's fare; bread and cheese, and kisses.
Polite Conversation (1738), Dialogue 1

28 If it had been a bear it would have bit you.
Polite Conversation (1738), Dialogue 1

29 I won't quarrel with my bread and butter.
Polite Conversation (1738), Dialogue 1

30 Promises and pie-crust are made to be broken.
Polite Conversation (1738), Dialogue 1

31 She wears her clothes, as if they were thrown on her with a pitchfork.
Polite Conversation (1738), Dialogue 1

32 He was a bold man that first ate an oyster.
Polite Conversation (1738), Dialogue 2

33 I always love to begin a journey on Sundays, because I shall have the prayers of the church, to preserve all that travel by land, or by water.
Polite Conversation (1738), Dialogue 2

34 May you live all the days of your life.
Polite Conversation (1738), Dialogue 2

35 Sweet things are bad for the teeth.
Polite Conversation (1738), Dialogue 2

36 The best doctors in the world are Doctor Diet, Doctor Quiet and Doctor Merryman.
Polite Conversation (1738), Dialogue 2

37 You must take the will for the deed.
Polite Conversation (1738), Dialogue 2

38 A penny for your thoughts.
Also attributed to John Heywood. *Polite Conversation* (1738), Introduction

39 Instead of dirt and poison we have rather chosen to fill our hives with honey and wax; thus furnishing mankind with the two noblest of things, which are sweetness and light.
The Battle of the Books (1704)

40 Satire is a sort of glass, wherein beholders do generally discover everybody's face but their own.
The Battle of the Books (1704), Preface

41 It is folly of too many to mistake the echo of a London coffee-house for the voice of the kingdom.
The Conduct of the Allies (1711)

42 I have heard of a man who had a mind to sell his house, and therefore carried a piece of brick in his pocket, which he shewed as a pattern to encourage purchasers.
The Drapier's Letters (August 4, 1724), no. 2

43 I never saw, heard, nor read, that the clergy were beloved in any nation where Christianity was the religion of the country. Nothing can render them popular, but some degree of persecution.
Published posthumously. *Thoughts on Religion* (1765)

44 It is impossible that anything so natural, so necessary, and so universal as death, should ever have been designed by Providence as an evil to mankind.
Published posthumously. *Thoughts on Religion* (1765)

45 Censure is the tax a man pays to the public for being eminent.
Thoughts on Various Subjects (1711)

46 I never wonder to see men wicked, but I often wonder to see them not ashamed.
Thoughts on Various Subjects (1711)

47 Most sorts of diversion in men, children, and other animals, are an imitation of fighting.
Thoughts on Various Subjects (1711)

48 Old men and comets have been reverenced for the same reason; their long beards, and pretences to foretell events.
Thoughts on Various Subjects (1727 edition)

49 We have just enough religion to make us hate, but not enough to make us love one another.
Thoughts on Various Subjects (1711)

50 When a true genius appears in the world, you may know him by this sign, that the dunces are all in confederacy against him.
Thoughts on Various Subjects (1711)

51 What they do in heaven we are ignorant of; what they do *not* we are told expressly, that they neither marry, nor are given in marriage.
Alluding to St. Matthew 92:3. *Thoughts on Various Subjects* (1711)

52 I shall be like that tree; I shall die from the top.
On seeing a tree with a withered crown. Quoted in *Works of Swift* (Sir Walter Scott; 1814), vol. 1

53 Good God! what a genius I had when I wrote that book.
Referring to *A Tale of a Tub* (1704) . Quoted in *Works of Swift* (Sir Walter Scott; 1814), vol. 1

54 Ah, a German and a genius! a prodigy, admit him!
October 19, 1745. Learning of the arrival of George Frideric Handel. Swift's last words. Attrib.

Swinburne, Algernon Charles (1837–1909) British poet

1 Glory to Man in the highest! for Man is the master of things.
"Hymn of Man" (1871)

2 Till life forget and death remember,
Till thou remember and I forget.
"Itylus" (1864)

3 Before the beginning of years
There came to the making of man

Time with a gift of tears,
Grief with a glass that ran.
"Before the Beginning of Years," *Atlanta in Calydon* (1865), chorus, st. 1, ll. 1–4

4 When the hounds of spring are on winter's traces,
The mother of months in meadow or plain
Fills the shadows and windy places
With lisp of leaves and ripple of rain.
"When the Hounds of Spring," *Atlanta in Calydon* (1865), chorus, st. 1

5 I remember the way we parted,
The day and the way we met;
You hoped we were both broken-hearted,
And knew we should both forget.
"An Interlude," *Poems and Ballads: First Series* (1866), st. 11

6 And the best and the worst of this is
That neither is most to blame,
If you have forgotten my kisses
And I have forgotten your name.
"An Interlude," *Poems and Ballads: First Series* (1866), st. 14

7 Change in a trice
The lilies and languors of virtue
For the raptures and roses of vice.
"Dolores," *Poems and Ballads: First Series* (1866), st. 9

8 Here, where the world is quiet;
Here, where all trouble seems
Dead winds' and spent waves' riot
In doubtful dreams of dreams.
"The Garden of Proserpine," *Poems and Ballads: First Series* (1866), st. 1

9 Sweet red splendid kissing mouth.
"Complaint of the Fair Amouress," *The Poems of Algernon Swinburne* (1905)

10 Bright with names that men remember, loud with names that men forget.
"Eton: An Ode," *The Poems of Algernon Swinburne* (1905)

Sydenham, Thomas ("The English Hippocrates"; 1624–89) English physician

1 The old saw is that "if you drink wine you have the gout and if you do not drink wine the gout will have you."
A Treatise on Gout and Dropsy (1683)

2 I watched what method Nature might take, with intention of subduing the symptom by treading in her footsteps.
Observationes Medicae (1676), ch. 2

3 The art of medicine was to be properly learned only from its practice and its exercise.
Observationes Medicae (1676), Dedicatory epistle

4 A man is as old as his arteries.
Quoted in *Bulletin of the New York Academy of Medicine* (F. H. Garrison; 1928)

Sylvester, Robert (1907–75) U.S. writer

1 I asked a coughing friend of mine why he doesn't stop smoking. "In this town it wouldn't do any good," he explained. "I happen to be a chain breather."
Attrib.

2 My brother-in-law wrote an unusual murder story. The victim got killed by a man from another book.
Attrib.

Symonds, John Addington (1840–93) British poet, writer, and historian

1 These things shall be! A loftier race
Than e'er the world hath known shall rise,
With flame of freedom in their souls,
And light of knowledge in their eyes.
"Hymn: The Days That Are To Be" (1880)

2 I love beauty above virtue, and think that nowhere is beauty more eminent than in young men.
Written in a letter to his daughter. Quoted in *A Queer Reader* (Patrick Higgins, ed.; 1993)

Synge, J. M. (John Millington Synge; 1871–1909) Irish playwright

1 "A man who is not afraid of the sea will soon be drownded," he said, "for he will be going out on a day he shouldn't. But we do be afraid of the sea, and we do only be drownded now and again."
The Aran Islands (1907), pt. 2

2 I've lost the only playboy of the western world.
Closing words. *The Playboy of the Western World* (1907), Act 3

3 In a good play every speech should be as fully flavoured as a nut or apple, and such speeches cannot be written by any one who works among people who have shut their lips on poetry.
The Playboy of the Western World (1907), preface

4 In countries where the imagination of the people, and the language they use, is rich and living, it is possible for a writer to be rich and copious in his words, and at the same time to give the reality, which is the root of all poetry, in a comprehensive and natural form.
The Playboy of the Western World (1907), preface

5 When I was writing *The Shadow of the Glen*, some years ago, I got more said than any learning could have given me from a chink in the floor of the old Wicklow house where I was staying, that let me hear what was being said by the servant girls in the kitchen.
The Shadow of the Glen was published in 1904. *The Playboy of the Western World* (1907), preface

Szasz, Thomas (Thomas Stephen Szasz; b.1920) Hungarian-born U.S. psychiatrist

1 As the primitive had spiritualized nature, so the psychiatrist now animalizes man...Who will correct the psychiatrist's mistake, and ours for supporting it?
Insanity: The Idea and its Consequences (1987)

2 Let us not consider mental illness an excusing condition. By treating offenders as responsible human beings, we offer them the chance, as I see it, to remain human.
Law, Liberty, and Psychiatry (1974)

3 Any behavior—for example, masturbation, homosexuality, eating too much or too little, smoking tobacco or marijuana—

may be *declared* to be a disease. This...may be likened to declaring that a piece of paper is money.
Said to Alan Kerr. *Psychiatric Bulletin* (1974), vol. 21

4 In the past, men created witches: now they create mental patients.
The Manufacture of Madness (1970), Introduction

5 Men are rewarded and punished not for what they do, but rather for how their acts are defined. This is why men are more interested in better justifying themselves than in better behaving themselves.
The Second Sin (1973)

6 A child becomes an adult when he realizes that he has a right not only to be right but also to be wrong.
"Childhood," *The Second Sin* (1973)

7 The proverb warns that, "You should not bite the hand that feeds you." But maybe you should, if it prevents you from feeding yourself.
"Control and Self-control," *The Second Sin* (1973)

8 A teacher should have maximal authority and minimal power.
"Education," *The Second Sin* (1973)

9 Happiness is an imaginary condition, formerly often attributed by the living to the dead, now usually attributed by adults to children, and by children to adults.
"Emotions," *The Second Sin* (1973)

10 The stupid neither forgive nor forget; the naive forgive and forget; the wise forgive but do not forget.
"Personal Conduct," *The Second Sin* (1973)

11 There is no psychology; there is only biography and autobiography.
"Psychology," *The Second Sin* (1973)

12 If you talk to God, you are praying; if God talks to you, you have schizophrenia. If the dead talk to you, you are a spiritualist; if God talks to you, you are a schizophrenic.
"Schizophrenia," *The Second Sin* (1973)

13 Formerly, when religion was strong and science weak, men mistook magic for medicine, now, when science is strong and religion weak, men mistake medicine for magic.
"Science and Scientism," *The Second Sin* (1973)

14 Masturbation: the primary sexual activity of mankind. In the nineteenth century it was a disease; in the twentieth, it's a cure.
"Sex," *The Second Sin* (1973)

15 Traditionally, sex has been a very private, secretive activity. Herein perhaps lies its powerful force for uniting people in a strong bond. As we make sex less secretive, we may rob it of its power to hold men and women together.
"Sex," *The Second Sin* (1973)

16 Semantic inflation.
Referring to the increasing hyperbole in language, for example, describing the common cold as "flu," a bad day as a "traumatic" one. Quoted in "A Sickness Called Therapy," *Guardian*, London (Dylan Evans; August 28, 1999)

17 Civil commitment and the insanity defense are like Siamese twins. They cannot be separated. Both are grave moral wrongs. But, for modern Western society, both are irresistibly convenient.
1997. Attrib.

18 We must remember that every "mental" symptom is a veiled cry of anguish. Against what? Against oppression, or what the patient experiences as oppression. The oppressed speak a million tongues.
Attrib.

Szent-Györgyi, Albert (Albert von Nagyrapolt Szent-Györgyi; 1898–1986) Hungarian-born U.S. biochemist

1 A substance that makes you ill if you don't eat it.
His definition of a vitamin. Attrib.

Szilard, Leo (1898–1964) Hungarian-born U.S. nuclear physicist

1 A scientist's aim in a discussion with his colleagues is not to persuade but to clarify.
Attrib.

2 We turned the switch, saw the flashes, watched for ten minutes, then switched everything off and went home. That night I knew the world was headed for sorrow.
May 30, 1964. Referring to the first atomic fission (1939). Attrib.

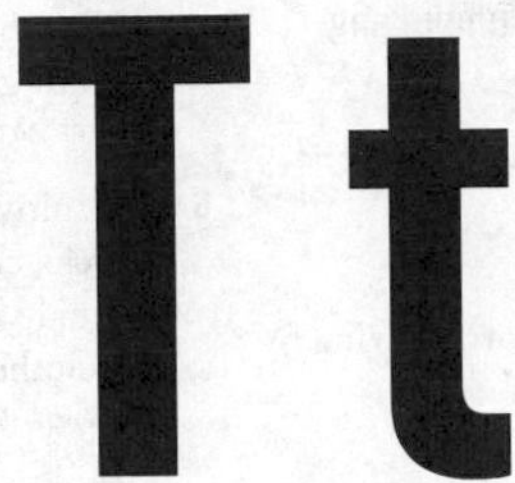

Taaffe, Eduard von, 11th Viscount Taaffe and Baron of Ballymote (Eduard Franz Joseph, Graf von Taaffe; 1833–95) Austrian statesman

1 It is my policy to keep all the nationalities in the monarchy in a balanced state of well-modulated dissatisfaction.
Letters (1881), quoted in *Europe: A History* (Norman Davies; 1996), ch. 10

Taber, Robert U.S. writer

1 The guerrilla fights the war of the flea, and his military enemy suffers the dog's disadvantages: too much to defend; too small, ubiquitous, and agile an enemy to come to grips with.
The War of the Flea (1965), ch. 2

Tacitus (Cornelius Tacitus; 55?–after 117?) Roman historian

1 They make a wilderness and call it peace.
De Vita Iulii Agricola (98?), ch. 30

2 It is part of human nature to hate the man you have hurt.
De Vita Iulii Agricola (98?), ch. 42

3 Whatever is unknown is taken for marvelous; but now the limits of Britain are laid bare.
De Vita Iulii Agricola (98?), ch. 30

4 Love of fame is the last thing even learned men can bear to be parted from.
Histories (104?–109?), bk. 4, ch. 6

Taleb, Ali ben Abi (d.660)

1 He who has a thousand friends has not a friend to spare,
And he who has one enemy will meet him everywhere.
Hundred Sayings (650?) (James Russell Lowell, tr.)

Talleyrand, Charles Maurice de (Charles Maurice de Talleyrand-Périgord; 1754–1838) French statesman and diplomat

1 I found there a country with thirty-two religions and only one sauce.
Referring to the United States. Quoted in *Autant en apportant les mots* (Mario Charlotte Pedrazzini; 1969)

2 They have learned nothing, and forgotten nothing.
January 1796. Quoted in *Mémoires et correspondance de Mallet du Pan* (A. Sayons; 1851), vol. 2

3 Accidentally.
Replying (during the reign of Louis Philippe) to the query, "How do you think this government will end?" Quoted in *The Wheat and the Chaff* (François Mitterrand; 1982)

4 Above all, gentlemen, not too much zeal.
Attrib.

5 Speech was given to man to disguise his thoughts.
Attrib.

6 Well, you might try getting crucified and rising again on the third day.
Giving his opinion upon what action might impress the French peasantry. Attrib.

7 War is much too serious a thing to be left to military men.
Quoted by French prime minister Aristide Briand to his British counterpart, David Lloyd George, during World War I. Also attributed to Georges Clemenceau. Attrib.

8 Mistrust first impulses; they are nearly always good.
Sometimes attributed to Count Montrond. Attrib.

Talmud body of Jewish law

1 A quotation at the right moment is like bread to the famished.
The Talmud (4th century? B.C.)

2 Examine the contents, not the bottle.
The Talmud (4th century? B.C.)

3 He who adds not to his learning diminishes it.
The Talmud (4th century? B.C.)

4 Power buries those who wield it.
The Talmud (4th century? B.C.)

5 The house which is not opened for charity will be opened to the physician.
The Talmud (4th century? B.C.)

6 The whole worth of a kind deed lies in the love that inspires it.
The Talmud (4th century? B.C.)

7 We presume none sins unless he stands to profit by it.
The Talmud (4th century? B.C.)

Tambo, Oliver (1917–93) South African nationalist leader

1 The history of the Christian church in South Africa is the history of a faith betrayed.
Address to World Consultation of the World Council of Churches (June 1980), quoted in *Oliver Tambo Speaks* (Adelaide Tambo, ed.; 1987)

2 The need for us to take up arms will never transform us into prisoners of the idea of violence.
1987. *Independent on Sunday*, London (April 25, 1993)

Tamerlane (Timur Lenk, "The Lame", also known as Timur Lang; 1336–1405) Turkic ruler and conqueror

1 It is better to be at the right place with 10 men than absent with 10,000.
Attrib.

2 The whole area of the inhabitable world is not worth having two monarchs.
Attrib.

Tang Min (b.1956) Chinese writer

1 Having children appears to be the fundamental duty of women. If a woman can't have a child herself, she must at least have one to adopt. Women and children, mother and child—these belong together as naturally as heaven and earth.
"I am not a cat" (Amy Dooling and Jeanne Tai, trs.; 1990), quoted in *Running Wild: New Chinese Writers* (1994)

Tang Xianzu (also known as T'ang Hsien-tsu; 1550–1617) Chinese playwright

1 DU LINIANG (*sings*) Back from dreams in orioles' warbling,
a tumult of bright spring weather
everywhere, and here I stand
in the heart of this small garden.
"Waking Suddenly from Dream," *Peony Pavilion* (1598), Scene 10, quoted in *An Anthology of Chinese Literature* (Stephen Owen, tr.; 1996)

Tao Qian (also known as Tao Yuanming or T'ao Ch'ien; 365–427) Chinese poet

1 They said that their ancestors had fled the upheavals during the Qin and had come to this region bringing their wives, children, and fellow townsmen. They had never left it since that time and thus had been cut off from people outside.
The Peach Blossom Spring, as depicted in Tao Qian's poem and its preface, a community secluded from human history and corruption, became a motif in Chinese literature. "An Account of Peach Blossom Spring" (4th–5th century), quoted in *An Anthology of Chinese Literature* (Stephen Owen, tr.; 1996)

2 Failure and success have no fixed abodes;
One man then another alternately share them.
For master Shao when he was in the melon field
How should it seem like his Dongling time?
Referring to Shao Ping, Marquis of Dongling, who fell from his high position into poverty and consequently grew melons, known as Dongling melons. "Drinking Wine" (4th–5th century), st. 1

3 In my household—no worldly infringements;
In my solitude—an abundance of leisure.
For too long cooped up in a cage,
I've now found my way back to nature.
"Returning to Live on the Farm" (4th–5th century), quoted in *China's Imperial Past* (Charles O. Hucker; 1975)

4 I plant my beans below the southern hill,
The grass grows thick, the beansprouts all too few.
At dawn I go to clear the choking weeds;
Beneath the moon I come home with my hoe.
"Returning to my Garden and Field" (4th–5th century), quoted in *The Chinese Experience* (Raymond Dawson; 1978)

5 Now I have realized that stopping is good;
This morning I have indeed truly stopped.
From this, once having stopped,
I shall go and stop upon the shores of Fusang.
Referring to giving up alcohol. "Stopping Wine" (4th–5th century), ll. 15–18

6 Uncultivated paths intersect into the distance;
Cocks crow and dogs bark to one another.
Ritual vessels are still of ancient pattern;
In clothes there are no new fashions.
"Poem," *Peach Blossom Spring* (4th–5th century), ll. 13–16

Tàpies, Antoni (b.1923) Spanish painter

1 An important element in modernism is the secularization of culture, our achievement of independence as artists from the Church and the monarchy.
Quoted in *Conversations with Antoni Tapies* (Barbara Catoir; 1991)

2 Artists go through periodic crises in which they feel an urge to destroy themselves. This is important, because if we succeed in mastering the crisis we rise again, as if reborn, from our own ashes.
Quoted in *Conversations with Antoni Tapies* (Barbara Catoir; 1991)

3 I regard mysticism as a state of mind which is necessary to scientific thinking, as well as to art: it enables one to discover things which cannot be found by any other means.
Quoted in *Conversations with Antoni Tapies* (Barbara Catoir; 1991)

Tarantino, Quentin (b.1963) U.S. film director, screenwriter, and actor

1 Violence in real life is terrible; violence in the movies can be cool. It's just another color to work with.
Observer, London (October 16, 1994), "Sayings of the Week"

2 To me, violence is a totally aesthetic subject. Saying you don't like violence in movies is like saying you don't like dance sequences in movies. I do like dance sequences in movies, but if I didn't, it doesn't mean I should stop dance sequences being made.
True Romance (1995), Introduction

Tarkington, Booth (Newton Booth Tarkington; 1869–1946) U.S. novelist

1 Mystics always hope that science will some day overtake them.
Looking Forward, and Others (1926)

2 There are two things that will be believed of any man whatsoever, and one of them is that he has taken to drink.
Penrod (1914), ch. 10

Tarkovsky, Andrey (Andrey Arsenyevich Tarkovsky; 1932–86) Russian filmmaker

1 The goal of all art is...to explain to people the reason for their appearance on this planet; or, if not to explain, at least to pose the question.
Sculpting in Time: Reflections on the Cinema (1989)

Tate, Allen (John Orley Allen Tate; 1899–1979) U.S. poet, critic, and biographer

1 Autumn is desolation in the plot
Of a thousand acres where these memories grow

From the inexhaustible bodies that are not
Dead, but feed the grass row after rich row.
"Ode to the Confederate Dead" (1926)

2 Row upon row with strict impunity
The headstones yield their names to the element.
"Ode to the Confederate Dead" (1926)

Tate, Nahum (1652–1715) Irish-born English poet and playwright

1 As pants the hart for cooling streams
When heated in the chase.
New Version of the Psalms (1696)

2 Through all the changing scenes of life.
New Version of the Psalms (1696)

3 While shepherds watch'd their flocks by night,
All seated on the ground,
The Angel of the Lord came down,
And Glory shone around.
Supplement to the New Version of the Psalms (1700)

Tatian (120?–173) Syrian writer and Christian thinker

1 Because we do not make any distinction in rank and outward appearance, or wealth and education, or age and sex, they devise an accusation against us that we practice cannibalism and sexual perversions.
160? Referring to the early Christian Church, which regarded as heretical his association with the ascetic religious community of Encratites, which combined Christianity and Stoicism. "Oratio ad Graecos," *The Early Christians* (E. Arnold; 1970)

Tattlewell, Mary (1640–?) English writer

1 If women be proud (or addicted to pride) it is ten to one to be laid, that it is the men that make them so; for like inchaunters, they do never leave or cease to bewitch & charme poore women with their flatteries.
Hearing the Abuse, Offeres to Women to Riseth out of her Grave and thus Saketh (17th century?)

Taubman, Alfred (b.1925) U.S. business executive and art collector

1 Selling art has much in common with selling root beer. People don't need root beer, and they don't need to buy a painting either.
Observer, London (July 2, 1989)

2 I guess you don't understand what buying this company seems like to an American. It's like coming over here and buying the throne.
Referring to buying the British auction house Sotheby's. *Times*, London (March 11, 1983)

Taupin, Bernie (b.1950) British songwriter

1 And it seems to me you lived your life
Like a candle in the wind.
Referring to Marilyn Monroe. In 1997, the song was reissued with different lyrics after the death of Princess Diana. "Candle in the Wind" (music by Elton John; 1973)

2 God it looks like Daniel
must be the clouds in my eyes.
Song lyric. "Daniel" (music by Elton John; 1973)

3 And all this science, I don't understand.
It's just my job, five days a week,
A rocket man.
Song lyric. "Rocket Man" (music by Elton John; 1972)

4 Goodbye Yellow Brick Road
1973. Song title. The music was by Elton John.

Taylor, A. J. P. (Alan John Percivale Taylor; 1906–90) British historian

1 Nothing is inevitable until it happens.
Daily Telegraph, London (January 7, 1980)

2 No historian achieves the highest excellence whose work cannot be read for pleasure as well as profit.
New Statesman and Nation, London (November 24, 1951)

3 The greatest problem about old age is the fear that it may go on too long.
Observer, London (November 1, 1981)

4 Human blunders usually do more to shape history than human wickedness.
The Origins of the Second World War (1961), ch. 10

5 It's no good asking "What factors caused the outbreak of war?" The question is rather "Why did the factors that had long preserved the peace of Europe fail to do so in 1914?"
Referring to secret diplomacy, the balance of power, and the standing armies. *The Struggle for Mastery in Europe* (1954), ch. 22

6 The modern delusion that if only we know enough facts we shall arrive at the answer.
Times Literary Supplement, London (April 27, 1951)

Taylor, Bayard (James Bayard Taylor; 1825–78) U.S. writer

1 Till the sun grows cold,
And the stars are old,
And the leaves of the Judgment Book unfold.
"Bedouin Song" (1855), Refrain

Taylor, Bert Leston (1866–1921) U.S. journalist

1 A bore is a man who, when you ask him how he is, tells you.
Attrib.

Taylor, Elizabeth (originally Elizabeth Coles; 1912–75) British novelist and short-story writer

1 She belongs to a Temperance Society and wears one of those badges in the shape of a bow of ribbon to show that she would never take a drink, not even brandy if she were dying. Of course by temperance they all mean the opposite—total abstinence.
"Angel," *A Dedicated Man* (1965)

2 It is very strange...that the years teach us patience; that the shorter our time, the greater our capacity for waiting.
A Wreath of Roses (1950)

3 She shrank from words, thinking of the scars they leave, which she would be left to tend when he had gone. If he spoke the

truth, she could not bear it; if he tried to muffle it with tenderness, she would look upon it as pity.
The Blush (1958)

4 Shyness is *common*...Self-consciousness it was always called when I was young, and that is what it is. To imagine that it shows a sense of modesty is absurd. *Modesty*. Why, I have never known a *truly* modest person to be the least bit shy.
"You'll Enjoy It When You Get There," *The Blush* (1958)

5 I don't pretend to be an ordinary housewife.
Attrib.

Taylor, James (Vernon James Taylor; b.1948) U.S. singer and songwriter

1 It's very strange making a living out of yourself.
Quoted in *The Wit and Wisdom of Rock and Roll* (Maxim Jabukowski, ed.; 1983)

Taylor, Jane (1783–1824) British poet

1 Twinkle, twinkle, little star,
How I wonder what you are!
Up above the world so high,
Like a diamond in the sky!
"The Star," *Rhymes for the Nursery* (1806)

2 Far from mortal cares retreating,
Sordid hopes and vain desires,
Here, our willing footsteps meeting,
Every heart to heaven aspires.
Hymn lyric. Attrib.

Taylor, Jeremy, Bishop (1613–67) English theologian

1 To preserve a man alive in the midst of so many chances and hostilities, is as great a miracle as to create him.
The Rule and Exercises of Holy Dying (1651)

2 As our life is very short, so it is very miserable, and therefore it is well it is short.
The Rule and Exercises of Holy Dying (1651)

3 Ignorance is the mother of devotion.
To a Person Newly Converted (1657)

4 He that loves not his wife and children, feeds a lioness at home and broods a nest of sorrows.
"Sermon 18," *Twenty-seven Sermons* (1651)

Taylor, Ron British teacher

1 Evil visited us yesterday.
Referring to the killing of schoolchildren and their teacher by Thomas Hamilton at Dunblane, Scotland. Remark (March 14, 1996)

Teagarden, Jack (Weldon John Leo Teagarden; 1905–64) U.S. jazz musician

1 Polyphony, flatted fifths, half-tones—they don't mean a thing. I just pick up my horn and play what I feel.
New York Times (January 16, 1964)

Teale, Edwin Way (Edwin Alfred Teale; 1899–1980) U.S. naturalist, writer, and photographer

1 Any fine morning a power saw can fell a tree that took a thousand years to grow.
Autumn Across America (1956)

2 The long fight to save wild beauty represents democracy at its best. It requires citizens to practice the hardest of virtues—self-restraint.
"February 2," *Circle of the Seasons* (1953)

Tebbit, Norman, Baron Tebbit (Norman Beresford Tebbitt; b.1931) British politician

1 The cricket test—which side do they cheer for?
Questioning the loyalties of immigrants to Britain. *Los Angeles Times* (April 1990)

Tecumseh (1768?–1813) Native American Shawnee leader

1 Where today are the Pequot? Where are the Narraganset, the Mohican, the Pocanet, and other powerful tribes of our people? They have vanished before the avarice and oppression of the white man, as snow before the summer sun.
1811. Quoted in *Bury My Heart at Wounded Knee* (Dee Brown; 1971), ch. 1

Teeter, Robert M. U.S. pollster and business executive

1 Diversity isn't a slogan—it's a reality when you're hiring people everywhere.
Fortune (November 13, 1995)

Teilhard de Chardin, Pierre (1881–1955) French priest, paleontologist, and theologian

1 From an evolutionary point of view, man has stopped moving, if he ever did move.
The Phenomenon of Man (1955), Postscript

Teller, Edward (b.1908) Hungarian-born U.S. physicist

1 The main purpose of science is simplicity and as we understand more things, everything is becoming simpler.
Conversations on the Dark Secrets of Physics (1991)

2 It took us eighteen months to build the first nuclear power generator; it now takes twelve years; that's progress.
Quoted in *Free to Choose* (Milton Friedman and Rose Friedman; 1979)

Temple, Sir William (1628–99) English statesman and essayist

1 When all is done, human life is, at the greatest and the best, but like a froward child, that must be played with and humoured a little to keep it quiet till it falls asleep, and then the care is over.
"Of Poetry," *Miscellanea, the Second Part* (1690)

Temple, William (1881–1944) British clergyman

1 In place of the conception of the Power-State we are led to that of the Welfare-State.
Citizen and Churchman (1941), ch. 2

2 Christianity is the most materialistic of all great religions.
Introduction, *Readings in St John's Gospel* (1939), vol. 1

3 I am greater than the stars for I know that they are up there and they do not know that I am down here.
Attrib.

4 I believe in the Church, One Holy, Catholic and Apostolic, and I regret that it nowhere exists.
Attrib.

Tennyson, Alfred, Lord, 1st Baron Tennyson of Freshwater and Aldworth (1809–92) British poet

Quotations about Tennyson

1 There was little about melancholia that he didn't know; there was little else that he did.
W. H. Auden (1907–73) British poet. *Tennyson: An Introduction and a Selection* (1946), Introduction

2 Every moment dies a man,
Every moment one and one sixteenth is born.
Charles Babbage (1792–1871) British mathematician and inventor. A parody of Tennyson's "Vision of Sin" in an unpublished letter from Babbage to the poet. *New Scientist*, London (December 4, 1958)

3 The misfortune is, that he has begun to write verses without very well understanding what metre is.
1833
Samuel Taylor Coleridge (1772–1834) British poet. *Table Talk* (1935)

4 Tennyson was not Tennysonian.
Henry James (1843–1916) U.S.-born British writer and critic. *The Middle Years* (1917)

Quotations by Tennyson

5 Sunset and evening star,
And one clear call for me!
And may there be no moaning of the bar
When I put out to sea.
"Crossing the Bar," *Demeter and Other Poems* (1889), st. 1

6 Twilight and evening bell,
And after that the dark!
And may there be no sadness of farewell,
When I embark;

For tho' from out our bourne of Time and Place
The flood may bear me far,
I hope to see my Pilot face to face
When I have crossed the bar.
"Crossing the Bar," *Demeter and Other Poems* (1889), sts. 4–5

7 That a lie which is all a lie may be met and fought with outright,
But a lie which is part a truth is a harder matter to fight.
July 16, 1859. "The Grandmother," *Enoch Arden* (1864), st. 8

8 The Gods themselves cannot recall their gifts.
February 1860. "Tithonus," *Enoch Arden* (1864), l. 49

9 The woods decay, the woods decay and fall,
The vapours weep their burthen to the ground,
Man comes and tills the field and lies beneath,
And after many a summer dies the swan.
February 1860. "Tithonus," *Enoch Arden* (1864), ll. 1–4

10 He makes no friend who never made a foe.
"Lancelot and Elaine," *Idylls of the King* (1859), l. 1081

11 He is all fault who hath no fault at all:
For who loves me must have a touch of earth.
"Lancelot and Elaine," *Idylls of the King* (1859), ll. 132–134

12 His honour rooted in dishonour stood,
And faith unfaithful kept him falsely true.
"Lancelot and Elaine," *Idylls of the King* (1859), ll. 871–872

13 It is the little rift within the lute,
That by and by will make the music mute,
And ever widening slowly silence all.
"Merlin and Vivien," *Idylls of the King* (1859), l. 388–391

14 Man dreams of fame while woman wakes to love.
"Merlin and Vivien," *Idylls of the King* (1859), l. 458

15 Man's word is God in man.
"The Coming of Arthur," *Idylls of the King* (1869), l. 132

16 For man is man and master of his fate.
"The Marriage of Geraint," *Idylls of the King* (1859), l. 355

17 An arm
Rose up from out the bosom of the lake,
Clothed in white samite, mystic, wonderful.
"The Passing of Arthur," *Idylls of the King* (1869), ll. 197–199

18 And slowly answer'd Arthur from the barge:
"The old order changeth, yielding place to new,
And God fulfils himself in many ways..."
"The Passing of Arthur," *Idylls of the King* (1869), ll. 407–409

19 For now I see the true old times are dead,
When every morning brought a noble chance,
And every chance brought out a noble knight.
"The Passing of Arthur," *Idylls of the King* (1869), ll. 397–399

20 If thou shouldst never see my face again,
Pray for my soul. More things are wrought by prayer
Than this world dreams of.
"The Passing of Arthur," *Idylls of the King* (1869), ll. 414–416

21 Authority forgets a dying king.
"The Passing of Arthur," *Idylls of the King* (1869), l. 289

22 The days darken round me, and the years,
Among new men, strange faces, other minds.
"The Passing of Arthur," *Idylls of the King* (1869), ll. 405–406

23 I am going a long way
With these thou seest—if indeed I go
(For all my mind is clouded with a doubt)—
To the island-valley of Avilion;
Where falls not hail, or rain, or any snow,
Nor ever wind blows loudly; but it lies
Deep-meadow'd, happy, fair with orchard lawns
And bowery hollows crown'd with summer sea,
Where I will heal me of my grievous wound.
"The Passing of Arthur," *Idylls of the King* (1869), ll. 424–432

24 Far off thou art, but ever nigh;
I have thee still, and I rejoice;
I prosper, circled with thy voice;
I shall not lose thee tho' I die.
In Memoriam A. H. H. (1850), can. 130, quoted in *Gay Love Poetry* (Neil Powell, ed.; 1997)

25 I hate that dreadful hollow behind the little wood,
Its lips in the field are dabbled with blood-red heath,
The red-ribb'd ledges drip with a silent horror of blood,
And echo there, whatever is ask'd her, answers "Death".
Maud: A Monodrama (1855), pt. 1, sect. 1, st. 1, ll. 1–4

26 She came to the village church,
And sat by a pillar alone;
An angel watching an urn
Wept over her, carved in stone.
Maud: A Monodrama (1855), pt. 1, sect. 8, ll. 301–304

27 A livelier emerald twinkles in the grass,
A purer sapphire melts into the sea.
Maud: A Monodrama (1855), pt. 1, sect. 8, st. 6, ll. 649–650

28 Come into the garden, Maud,
For the black bat, night, has flown,
Come into the garden, Maud,
I am here at the gate alone.
Maud: A Monodrama (1855), pt. 1, sect. 22, st. 1, ll. 850–853

29 But the churchmen fain would kill their church,
As the churches have kill'd their Christ.
Maud: A Monodrama (1855), pt. 2, sect. 5, st. 2, ll. 266–267

30 I embrace the purpose of God and the doom assigned.
Maud: A Monodrama (1855), pt. 3, sect. 6, st. 5, l. 59

31 Bury the Great Duke
With an empire's lamentation,
Let us bury the Great Duke
To the noise of the mourning of a mighty nation.
November 16, 1852. "Ode on the Death of the Duke of Wellington," *Maud and Other Poems* (1855), st. 1

32 The last great Englishman is low.
November 16, 1852. "Ode on the Death of the Duke of Wellington," *Maud and Other Poems* (1855), st. 3

33 For this is England's greatest son,
He that gain'd a hundred fights,
And never lost an English gun.
November 16, 1852. "Ode on the Death of the Duke of Wellington," *Maud and Other Poems* (1855), st. 6

34 I come from haunts of coot and hern,
I make a sudden sally
And sparkle out among the fern,
To bicker down a valley.
"The Brook," *Maud and Other Poems* (1855), ll. 23–26

35 For men may come and men may go
But I go on for ever.
"The Brook," *Maud and Other Poems* (1855), ll. 49–50

36 Half a league, half a league,
Half a league onward,
All in the valley of Death
Rode the six hundred.
December 9, 1854. "The Charge of the Light Brigade," *Maud and Other Poems* (1855), st. 1

37 "Forward the Light Brigade!"
Was there a man dismay'd?
Not tho' the soldier knew
Some one had blunder'd:
Their's not to make reply,
Their's not to reason why,
Their's but to do and die:
Into the valley of Death
Rode the six hundred.
December 9, 1854. "The Charge of the Light Brigade," *Maud and Other Poems* (1855), st. 2

38 Into the jaws of Death,
Into the mouth of Hell.
December 9, 1854. "The Charge of the Light Brigade," *Maud and Other Poems* (1855), st. 3

39 Break, break, break,
On thy cold gray stones, O Sea!
And I would that my tongue could utter
The thoughts that arise in me.
"Break, Break, Break," *Poems* (1842), st. 1

40 And the stately ships go on
To their haven under the hill;
But O for the touch of a vanish'd hand,
And the sound of a voice that is still!
"Break, Break, Break," *Poems* (1842), st. 3

41 Come not, when I am dead
To drop thy foolish tears upon my grave,
To trample round my fallen head,
And vex the unhappy dust thou wouldst not save.
1850. "Come Not When I Am Dead," *Poems* (1851), st. 1

42 The curate; he was fatter than his cure.
Subtitled "The Lake." "Edwin Morris," *Poems* (1842), l. 15

43 God made the woman for the man,
And for the good and increase of the world.
Subtitled "The Lake." "Edwin Morris," *Poems* (1842), ll. 43–44

44 Then she rode forth, clothed on with chastity.
"Godiva," *Poems* (1842), l. 53

45 A simple maiden in her flower
Is worth a hundred coats-of-arms.
"Lady Clara Vere de Vere," *Poems* (1842), st. 2

46 Kind hearts are more than coronets,
And simple faith than Norman blood.
"Lady Clara Vere de Vere," *Poems* (1842), st. 7

47 In the Spring a young man's fancy lightly turns to thoughts of love.
1837–38. "Locksley Hall," *Poems* (1842), l. 20

48 Science moves, but slowly slowly, creeping on from point to point.
1837–38. "Locksley Hall," *Poems* (1842), l. 134

49 I will take some savage woman, she shall rear my dusky race.
1837–38. "Locksley Hall," *Poems* (1842), l. 168

50 Comrades, leave me here a little, while as yet 'tis early morn:
Leave me here, and when you want me, sound upon the bugle-horn.
1837–38. "Locksley Hall," *Poems* (1842), ll. 1–2

51 Here about the beach I wander'd nourishing a youth sublime
With the fairy tales of science, and the long result of Time.
1837–38. "Locksley Hall," *Poems* (1842), ll. 11–12

52 Such a one do I remember, whom to look at was to love.
1837–38. "Locksley Hall," *Poems* (1842), ll. 72

53 Comfort? comfort scorn'd of devils! this is truth the poet sings,
That a sorrow's crown of sorrow is remembering happier things.
1837–38. "Locksley Hall," *Poems* (1842), ll. 75–76

54 O, I see thee old and formal, fitted to thy petty part,
With a little hoard of maxims preaching down a daughter's heart.
1837–38. "Locksley Hall," *Poems* (1842), ll. 93–94

55 So I triumph'd ere my passion, sweeping thro' me, left me dry,
Left me with the palsied heart, and left me with the jaundiced eye.
1837–38. "Locksley Hall," *Poems* (1842), ll. 131–132

56 Woman is the lesser man, and all thy passions match'd with mine,
Are as moonlight unto sunlight, and as water unto wine.
1837–38. "Locksley Hall," *Poems* (1842), ll. 151–152

57 Forward, forward let us range,
Let the great world spin forever down the ringing grooves of change.
1837–38. "Locksley Hall," *Poems* (1842), ll. 181–182

58 There lies a vale in Ida, lovelier
Than all the valleys of Ionian hills.
1830–32. "Oenone," *Poems* (1832), ll. 1–2

59 My strength is as the strength of ten,
Because my heart is pure.
"Sir Galahad," *Poems* (1842), st. 1

60 How sweet are looks that ladies bend
On whom their favours fall!
"Sir Galahad," *Poems* (1842), st. 2

61 A man had given all other bliss,
And all his worldly worth for this,
To waste his whole heart in one kiss
Upon her perfect lips.
Subtitled "A Fragment." "Sir Launcelot and Queen Guinevere," *Poems* (1842), st. 5

62 Battering the gates of heaven with storms of prayer.
1833. "St Simeon Stylites," *Poems* (1842), l. 7

63 And o'er the hills, and far away
Beyond their utmost purple rim,
Beyond the night, across the day,
Thro' all the world she follow'd him.
"The Day-Dream: The Departure," *Poems* (1842), st. 4

64 Half light, half shade,
She stood, a sight to make an old man young.
1833–34. Subtitled "The Pictures." "The Gardener's Daughter," *Poems* (1842), ll. 139–140

65 On either side the river lie
Long fields of barley and of rye,
That clothe the wold and meet the sky;
And thro' the field the road runs by
To many-tower'd Camelot.
"The Lady of Shalott," *Poems* (1832), pt. 1, st. 1

66 Willows whiten, aspens quiver,
Little breezes dusk and shiver.
"The Lady of Shalott," *Poems* (1832), pt. 1, st. 2

67 She has heard a whisper say,
A curse is on her if she stay
To look down to Camelot.
"The Lady of Shalott," *Poems* (1832), pt. 2, st. 1

68 Or when the moon was overhead,
Came two young lovers lately wed;
"I am half sick of shadows," said
The Lady of Shalott.
"The Lady of Shalott," *Poems* (1832), pt. 2, st. 4

69 "Tirra lirra," by the river
Sang Sir Lancelot.
"The Lady of Shalott," *Poems* (1832), pt. 3, st. 4

70 A bow-shot from her bower-eaves,
He rode between the barley-sheaves,
The sun came dazzling thro' the leaves
And flamed upon the brazen greaves
Of bold Sir Lancelot.
"The Lady of Shalott," *Poems* (1832), pt. 3, st. 5

71 The mirror crack'd from side to side;
"The curse is come upon me," cried
The Lady of Shalott.
"The Lady of Shalott," *Poems* (1832), pt. 3, st. 5

72 But Lancelot mused a little space;
He said, "She has a lovely face;
God in his mercy lend her grace,
The Lady of Shalott."
"The Lady of Shalott," *Poems* (1832), pt. 4, st. 6

73 Music that gentlier on the spirit lies,
Than tir'd eyelids upon tir'd eyes.
1830–32. "The Lotos-Eaters," *Poems* (1832), "Choric Song," st. 1

74 Death is the end of life; ah, why
Should life all labour be?
1830–32. "The Lotos-Eaters," *Poems* (1832), "Choric Song," st. 4

75 Time driveth onward fast,
And in a little while our lips are dumb.
Let us alone. What is it that will last?
All things are taken from us, and become
Portions and parcels of the dreadful Past.
1830–32. "The Lotos-Eaters," *Poems* (1832), "Choric Song," st. 4

76 "Courage!" he said, and pointed toward the land,
This mounting wave will roll us shoreward soon.
In the afternoon they came unto a land
In which it seemed always afternoon.
1830–32. "The Lotos-Eaters," *Poems* (1832), st. 1

77 You must wake and call me early, call me early, mother dear;
To-morrow 'ill be the happiest time of all the glad New-year,
Of all the glad New-year, mother, the maddest merriest day;
For I'm to be Queen o' the May, mother, I'm to be Queen o' the May.
"The May Queen," *Poems* (1832), st. 1

78 A still small voice spake unto me,

"Thou art so full of misery,
Were it not better not to be?"
"The Two Voices," *Poems* (1832), st. 1

79 No life that breathes with human breath
Has ever truly long'd for death.
"The Two Voices," *Poems* (1832), st. 132

80 Every moment dies a man,
Every moment one is born.
"The Vision of Sin," *Poems* (1842), pt. 4, st. 9

81 For now the Poet cannot die,
Nor leave his music as of old,
But round him ere he scarce be cold
Begins the scandal and the cry.
"To —, After Reading a Life and Letters," *Poems* (1842), st. 4

82 God gives us love. Something to love
He lends us; but, when love is grown
To ripeness, that on which it throve
Falls off, and love is left alone.
"To J.S.," *Poems* (1832), st. 4

83 The lights begin to twinkle from the rocks:
The long day wanes: the slow moon climbs: the deep
Moans round with many voices. Come, my friends,
'Tis not too late to seek a newer world.
1833. "Ulysses," *Poems* (1842), ll. 54–57

84 We are not now that strength which in old days
Moved earth and heaven; that which we are, we are;
One equal temper of heroic hearts,
Made weak by time and fate, but strong in will
To strive, to seek, to find, and not to yield.
1833. "Ulysses," *Poems* (1842), ll. 66–70

85 Dreams are true while they last, and do we not live in dreams?
"The Higher Pantheism," *The Holy Grail and Other Poems* (1869), st. 2

86 Man for the field and woman for the hearth:
Man for the sword and for the needle she:
Man with the head and woman with the heart:
Man to command and woman to obey;
All else confusion.
The Princess (1847), pt. 5

87 Man is the hunter; woman is his game:
The sleek and shining creatures of the chase,
We hunt them for the beauty of their skins.
The Princess (1847), pt. 5, l. 147–149

88 The moans of doves in immemorial elms,
And murmuring of innumerable bees.
"Come Down O Maid, from Yonder Mountain Height," *The Princess* (1847), pt. 7, song, ll. 30–31

89 Home they brought her warrior dead.
She nor swoon'd, nor utter'd cry:
All her maidens, watching said,
"She must weep or she will die."
"Home They Brought Her Warrior Dead," *The Princess* (1847), pt. 6, song, st. 1, ll. 1–4

90 O tell her, brief is life but love is long.
"O Swallow, Swallow, Flying, Flying South," *The Princess* (1847), pt. 4, song, st. 7, l. 1

91 So sad, so fresh, the days that are no more.
"Tears, Idle Tears, I Know Not What They Mean," *The Princess* (1847), pt. 4, song, l. 10

92 Dear as remember'd kisses after death,
And sweet as those by hopeless fancy feign'd
On lips that are for others: deep as love,
Deep as first love, and wild with all regret;
O Death in Life, the days that are no more.
"Tears, Idle Tears, I Know Not What They Mean," *The Princess* (1847), pt. 4, song, ll. 1–5

93 Tears, idle tears, I know not what they mean,
Tears from the depth of some divine despair.
"Tears, Idle Tears, I Know Not What They Mean," *The Princess* (1847), pt. 4, song, ll. 1–2

Terence (Publius Terentius Afer; 185–159 B.C.) Roman playwright and poet

1 The quarrels of lovers are the renewal of love.
Heauton Timoroumenos (2nd century B.C.)

2 Fortune favors the brave.
Phormio (2nd century B.C.)

3 So many men, so many opinions.
Phormio (2nd century B.C.)

4 There are vicissitudes in all things.
The Eunuch (161 B.C.), Act 2, Scene 2 (H. T. Riley, tr.)

5 I know the disposition of women: when you will, they won't; when you won't, they set their hearts upon you of their own inclination.
The Eunuch (161 B.C.), Act 4, Scene 7 (H. T. Riley, tr.)

6 Nothing has yet been said that's not been said before.
The Eunuch (161 B.C.), prologue, l. 41 (H. T. Riley, tr.)

7 I am a man, I count nothing human foreign to me.
The Self-Tormentor (2nd century B.C.)

8 Rigorous law is often rigorous injustice.
The Self-Tormentor (2nd century B.C.)

Teresa of Ávila, Saint (Teresa de Cepeda y Ahumada; 1515–82) Spanish mystic, author, and nun

1 Humility must always be doing its work like a bee making its honey in the hive: without humility all will be lost.
The Interior Castle (1577)

2 Accustom yourself continually to make many acts of love, for they enkindle and melt the soul.
"Maxims for Her Nuns" (1566?), quoted in *Selected Writings of St. Teresa of Avila* (William J. Doheny, ed.; 1950)

3 Be gentle to all and stern with yourself.
"Maxims for Her Nuns" (1566?), quoted in *Selected Writings of St. Teresa of Avila* (William J. Doheny, ed.; 1950)

4 Untilled soil, however fertile it may be, will bear thistles and thorns; and so it is with man's mind.
"Maxims for Her Nuns" (1566?), quoted in *Selected Writings of St. Teresa of Avila* (William J. Doheny, ed.; 1950)

5 Though rapture brings us delight, the weakness of our nature

at first makes us afraid of it, and we need to be resolute and courageous in life.
Life (1565)

6 Alas, O Lord, to what a state dost Thou bring those who love Thee!
The Interior Castle (1577), Mansion 6, ch. 11

7 The hour I have long wished for is now come.
1582. Last words. Quoted in *Distinguished Women Writers* (Virginia Moore; 1934)

8 About the injunction of the Apostle Paul that women should keep silent in church? Don't go by one text only.
Quoted in *Women of the Reformation* (Roland H. Bainton; 1977), vol. 3

9 It is true that we cannot be free from sin, but at least let our sins not be always the same.
Attrib.

Teresa of Calcutta, Mother (Agnes Gonxha Bojaxhiu; 1910–97) Albanian-born nun

Quotations about Teresa of Calcutta

1 Without her faith Mother Teresa would be remarkable only for her ordinariness, and she rejoices in this fact for it is evidence of the power for which she and many others with her are but channels.
Kathryn Spink (b.1953) British religious writer. *For the Brotherhood of Man Under the Fatherhood of God: Mother Teresa of Calcutta* (1981)

Quotations by Teresa of Calcutta

2 The greatest destroyer of peace is abortion because if a mother can kill her own child what is left but for me to kill you and you to kill me? There is nothing between.
Nobel Peace Prize lecture (1979)

3 This is not for me. The honour is for the poor.
November 24, 1983. Said on receiving the Order of Merit. *Sunday Times*, London (December 3, 1989)

4 The hunger for love is much more difficult to remove than the hunger for bread.
Time (December 4, 1989)

5 Loneliness and the feeling of being unwanted is the most terrible poverty.
"Saints Among Us," *Time* (December 29, 1975)

6 The poor are our brothers and sisters...people in the world who need love, who need care, who have to be wanted.
"Saints Among Us," *Time* (December 29, 1975)

7 To keep a lamp burning we have to keep putting oil in it.
"Saints Among Us," *Time* (December 29, 1975)

8 God is the friend of silence. Trees, flowers, grass grow in silence. See the stars, moon and sun, how they move in silence.
Quoted in *For the Brotherhood of Man Under the Fatherhood of God* (Kathryn Spink; 1981)

9 Facing the press is more difficult than bathing a leper.
Quoted in *Such a Vision of the Street* (Eileen Egan; 1985)

10 I would not give a baby from one of my homes for adoption to a couple who use contraception. People who use contraceptives do not understand love.
Said during a visit to London. Attrib.

Terrell, Mary Church (1863–1954) U.S. civil rights activist

1 Please stop using the word "Negro"...We are the only human beings in the world with fifty-seven varieties of complexions who are classed together as a single racial unit. Therefore, we are really colored people, and that is the only name in the English language which accurately describes us.
Letter, *Washington Post* (May 14, 1949)

Terry, Clark (b.1936) U.S. jazz musician

1 As for my jazz ability, it reminds me of that old saying, "Do you read music?" and the guy would say, "Not enough to hurt my playing."
Quoted in "The Sweet Smell of Success," *Jazz People* (Valerie Wilmer; 1970), ch. 9

2 Negroes used to brand any Caucasian jazz players as sad. But the way I see it a note doesn't care who plays it.
Quoted in "The Sweet Smell of Success," *Jazz People* (Valerie Wilmer; 1970), ch. 9

Terry, Ellen, Dame (1847–1928) British actor

1 Wonderful women! Have you ever thought how much we all, and women especially, owe to Shakespeare for his vindication of women in these fearless, high-spirited, resolute and intelligent heroines?
"The Triumphant Women," *Four Lectures on Shakespeare* (1911)

2 Imagination! imagination! I put it first years ago, when I was asked what qualities I thought necessary for success upon the stage.
The Story of My Life (1908), ch. 2

3 What is a diary as a rule? A document useful to the person who keeps it, dull to the contemporary who reads it, invaluable to the student, centuries afterwards, who treasures it!
The Story of My Life (1908), ch. 14

Terry, Jesse A. (b.1914) U.S. business executive

1 I am a businessman, not a crusader. I'm not making dresses for black women, I'm making dresses for women.
Quoted in "Jesse A. Terry: Clothing Manufacturer," *Getting It Together: Black Businessmen in America* (John Seder and Berkeley G. Burrell; 1971)

Terry, Quinlan (b.1937) British architect

1 Modern architecture is the absence of style.
Times, London (March 21, 1998)

Terry, Walter (1913–82) U.S. critic and writer

1 Modern dance in the 1930s had few followers outside New York and among college students.
The Dance in America (1971)

2 The principle was basic, its...application to dance was new. Between balance and unbalance, fall and recovery, lay the scope of all human movement. A simple step...threw the body off balance and certain compensatory movements...occurred to restore the balance.
Referring to the techniques developed by the dancers José Limón and Doris Humphreys. *The Dance in America* (1971)

Tertullian (Quintus Septimus Florens Tertullianus; 160?–220?) Carthaginian theological writer

1 To hinder a birth is merely speedier man-killing; nor does it matter whether you take away a life that is born, or destroy one that is coming to the birth. That is a man which is going to be one; you have the fruit already in its seed.
Apologeticus (197?)

2 See how these Christians love one another.
Apologeticus (197?), ch. 39

3 The blood of the martyrs is the seed of the Church.
Traditional misquotation: more accurately, "Our numbers increase as often as you cut us down: the blood of Christians is the seed." *Apologeticus* (197?), ch. 50, sect. 13

4 I believe because it is impossible.
The usual misquotation of "It is certain because it is impossible." *De Carne Christi* (2nd–3rd century), ch. 5

5 And do you know that you are an Eve? God's sentence hangs over all your sex and His punishment weighs down upon you. You are the devil's gateway; it was you who first violated the forbidden tree and broke God's law...You should always go in mourning and rags.
De Cultu Feminarum (2nd–3rd century)

6 He who flees will fight again.
De Fuga in Persecutione (2nd–3rd century), ch. 10

7 The nature of our meal and its purpose are explained by its very name. It is called *Agape*, as the Greeks call love in its purest sense.
Quoted in "Apology 39," *The Early Christians* (E. Arnold; 1970)

Tewodros II (Kassa Haylu; 1820?–68) Ethiopian emperor

1 I know their game. First, the traders and the missionaries, then the ambassadors; then the cannon. It's better to go straight to the cannon.
1860s. Quoted in *Africa in Modern History* (Basil Davidson; 1978), p.75

Thackeray, William Makepeace (1811–63) British novelist

1 There are some meannesses which are too mean even for man—woman, lovely woman alone, can venture to commit them.
A Shabby-Genteel Story (1840), ch. 3

2 He who meanly admires mean things is a Snob.
Book of Snobs (1846–47), ch. 2

3 We love being in love, that's the truth on't.
The History of Henry Esmond (1852), bk. 2, ch. 15

4 'Tis not the dying for a faith that's so hard, Master Harry—every man of every nation has done that—'tis the living up to it that is difficult.
The History of Henry Esmond (1852), ch. 6

5 'Tis strange what a man may do, and a woman yet think him an angel.
The History of Henry Esmond (1852), ch. 7

6 Remember, it is as easy to marry a rich woman as a poor woman.
The History of Pendennis (1848–50), ch. 28

7 The *Pall Mall Gazette* is written by gentlemen for gentlemen.
The History of Pendennis (1848–50), ch. 32

8 This I set down as a positive truth. A woman with fair opportunities and without a positive hump, may marry whom she likes.
Vanity Fair (1847–48), ch. 4

9 Whenever he met a great man he grovelled before him, and my-lorded him as only a free-born Briton can do.
Vanity Fair (1847–48), ch. 13

10 Nothing like blood, sir, in hosses, dawgs, and men.
Vanity Fair (1847–48), ch. 35

11 I think I could be a good woman if I had five thousand a year.
Vanity Fair (1847–48), ch. 36

Thales (625?–546? B.C.) Greek philosopher

Quotations about Thales

1 The apophthegm "Know thyself" is his.
Diogenes Lāertius (*fl.* 3rd century) Greek historian and biographer. "Thales," *Lives of the Philosophers* (3rd century?), 8

2 He said that men ought to remember those friends who were absent as well as those who were present.
Diogenes Lāertius (*fl.* 3rd century) Greek historian and biographer. "Thales," *Lives of the Philosophers* (3rd century?), 9

Quotations by Thales

3 I will be sufficiently rewarded if when telling it to others you will not claim the discovery as your own, but will say it was mine.
Quoted in *In Mathematical Circles* (H. Eves; 1969)

4 Because there is no difference.
Reply when asked why he chose to continue living after saying there was no difference between life and death. Quoted in *The Story of Civilization* (William Durant; 1935), vol. 2

Tharp, Twyla (b.1941) U.S. choreographer and dancer

1 The notion of doing something impossibly new usually turns out to be an illusion.
Independent, London (December 8, 1995)

Thatcher, Denis (b.1915) British businessman

1 I do, and I also wash and iron them.
Replying to the question "Who wears the pants in this house?" *Los Angeles Times* (April 21, 1981)

Thatcher, Margaret, Baroness Thatcher of Kesteven (Margaret Hilda Thatcher, born Roberts; b.1925) British prime minister

Quotations about Thatcher

1 The Iron Lady of British politics is seeking to revive the cold war.
Anonymous. Commenting on a speech by Margaret Thatcher. *Red Star*, Soviet defense ministry newspaper (Captain Y. Gavrilov; January 23, 1976)

2 The sort of woman who, if accidentally locked in alone in the National Gallery, would start rearranging the pictures.
Anonymous

3 I believe Mrs Thatcher's emphasis on enterprise was right.
Tony Blair (b.1953) British prime minister. *Sunday Times,* London (1995)

4 She is trying to wear the trousers of Winston Churchill.
Leonid Brezhnev (1906–82) Soviet president. Speech (1979)

5 She is clearly the best man among them.
Barbara Castle (b.1911) British politician. *The Castle Diaries* (1980)

6 I am not prepared to accept the economics of a housewife.
Jacques Chirac (b.1932) French president. *Sunday Times,* London (December 27, 1987)

7 She may be a woman but she isn't a sister; she may be a sister but she isn't a comrade.
Caryl Churchill (b.1938) British playwright. Quoted in *Interviews with Contemporary Women Playwrights* (Rachael Koenig and Karen Betsko; 1987)

8 She put back the chance of another woman becoming PM by 50 years—by going over the top, becoming a dictator, having illusions of infallibility, which of course brought her downfall.
Ann Clwyd (b.1937) British politician. *Independent,* London (April 28, 1992)

9 She cannot see an institution without hitting it with her handbag.
Julian Critchley (b.1930) British politician. *Times,* London (June 21, 1982)

10 She has no imagination and that means no compassion.
Michael Foot (b.1913) British politician and writer. Attrib.

11 Rather like the man who knows nothing about art but knows what he likes, she has groped her way from the fashion nadir of Bri-nylon, little scarves and plonking brooches to the perfectly good suit for all occasions.
Georgina Howell (b.1942) British fashion editor. Referring to the fashion sense of Margaret Thatcher. *Sultans of Style* (1990), ch. 21

12 Today, we were unlucky, but remember, we only have to be lucky once—you will have to be lucky always.
Provisional Irish Republican Army, Irish terrorist organization. Said after an assassination attempt on Margaret Thatcher. *Irish Times* Dublin (October 13, 1984), quoted in *Phrases Make History Here* (Conor O'Clery; 1986)

13 She sounded like the Book of Revelation read out over a railway address system by a headmistress of a certain age wearing calico knickers.
1979
Clive James (b.1939) Australian writer and broadcaster. Referring to Margaret Thatcher's television broadcasts. Attrib.

Quotations by Thatcher

14 Just as the Soviet Union was forced to recognize reality by dispersing power to its separate states and by limiting the powers of its central government, some people in Europe were...taking powers away from national states and concentrating them at the centre.
Remark (June 1991)

15 It will be years—and not in my time—before a woman will lead the party or become Prime Minister.
As minister for education and science. Remark (1974)

16 Children who need to be taught to respect traditional moral values are being taught that they have an inalienable right to be gay.
Remark (1987), quoted in *Homosexuality: A History* (Colin Spencer; 1995)

17 We must try to find ways to starve the terrorist and the hijacker of the oxygen of publicity on which they depend.
Speech to the American Bar Association, London (July 15, 1985)

18 It is exciting to have a real crisis on your hands, when you have spent half your political life dealing with humdrum issues like the environment.
Referring to the Falklands War (1982). Speech to the Scottish Conservative Party Conference (May 14, 1982)

19 Let our children grow tall, and some taller than others if they have it in them to do so.
Speech, U.S. tour (1975)

20 No one would have remembered the Good Samaritan if he'd only had good intentions. He had money as well.
Television interview (January 12, 1986)

21 I am sorry for all those who have lost. It's an experience I never had.
Referring to the 1997 general election. *Daily Telegraph,* London (May 3, 1997)

22 The battle for women's rights has been largely won.
Guardian, London (1982)

23 I can trust my husband not to fall asleep on a public platform and he usually claps in the right places.
Observer, London (August 20, 1978)

24 I owe nothing to Women's Lib.
Observer, London (December 1, 1974)

25 Any woman who understands the problems of running a home will be nearer to understanding the problems of running a country.
Following the Conservative general election victory, which made her Britain's first female prime minister. *Observer,* London (May 8, 1979)

26 I belong to a generation that don't spend until we have the money in hand.
Observer, London (February 13, 1977), "Sayings of the Week"

27 The charm of Britain has always been the ease with which one can move into the middle class.
Observer, London (October 27, 1974), "Sayings of the Week"

28 Pennies do not come from heaven. They have to be earned here on earth.
Sunday Telegraph, London (1982)

29 Had I faltered, we would have neither the success nor international reputation we have. Yet when a woman is strong, she is strident. If a man is strong, he's a good guy.
Times, London (November 19, 1990)

30 I don't mind how much my ministers talk—as long as they do what I say.
Times, London (1987)

31 I love argument, I love debate. I don't expect anyone just to sit there and agree with me, that's not their job.
Times, London (1980)

32 Young people ought not to be idle. It is very bad for them.
Times, London (1984)

33 I would not wish to be Prime Minister...I have not enough experience for that job.
Val Meets the VIPS, BBC television (1973)

34 Home is where you come to when you have nothing better to do.
What she claimed to have told her children. Interview, *Vanity Fair,* London (May 1991)

35 There is no such thing as Society. There are individual men and women, and there are families.
Woman's Own (October 31, 1987)

36 In politics, if you want anything said, ask a man; if you want anything done, ask a woman.
Quoted in *The Changing Anatomy of Britain* (Anthony Sampson; 1982)

Thayer, Ernest Lawrence (1863–1940) U.S. writer and poet

1 Oh! somewhere in this favored land the sun is shining bright;
The band is playing somewhere, and somewhere hearts are light,
And somewhere men are laughing, and somewhere children shout;
But there is no joy in Mudville—mighty Casey has struck out.
The last stanza of the most famous baseball poem ever published. "Casey at the Bat" (1888)

Theano (b.420? B.C.) Greek priestess

1 Put off your shame with your clothes when you go in to your husband, and put it on again when you come out.
Quoted in *Lives of the Philosophers* (Diogenes Läertius; 3rd century)

Themistocles (527?–460? B.C.) Athenian general and statesman

Quotations about Themistocles

1 He preferred an honest man that wooed his daughter, before a rich man. "I would rather," said Themistocles, "have a man that wants money than money that wants a man."
Plutarch (46?–120?) Greek biographer and philosopher. "Themistocles," *Parallel Lives* (1st–2nd century)

Quotations by Themistocles

2 Athens holds sway over all Greece; I dominate Athens; my wife dominates me; our newborn son dominates her.
Explaining an earlier remark to the effect that his baby son ruled all Greece. Attrib.

Theobald, Lewis (1688–1744) English playwright and critic

1 None but himself can be his parallel.
The Double Falsehood was claimed by Theobald to be a "lost" play by William Shakespeare. *The Double Falsehood* (1728)

Theodoric (also known as Theodoricus, "Theodoric the Great"; 454?–526) Ostrogoth monarch

1 If this man is not faithful to his God, how can he be faithful to me, a mere man?
Explaining why he had had a trusted minister beheaded, who had said he would adopt his master's religion. Quoted in *Dictionnaire encyclopédique* (Edmond Guérard; 1872)

Theognis of Megara (570?–490? B.C.) Greek elegiac poet

1 Wine is wont to show the mind of man.
Maxims (6th century B.C.), l. 500

Theophilus (*fl.* 2nd century) Syrian father of the church

1 We are forbidden so much as to look at gladiator fights lest we become privy to and participants in murder!
2nd century. Quoted in *The Early Christians* (E. Arnold; 1970)

Theroux, Paul (b.1941) U.S. writer

1 In every detail the subway is like a nightmare, complete with rats and mice and a tunnel and a low ceiling. It is manifest suffocation, straight out of Poe.
"Subterranean Gothic," *Granta Book of Travel* (Bill Buford, ed.; 1991)

2 The subway is New York City's best hope. The streets are impossible, the highways are a failure, there is nowhere to park.
"Subterranean Gothic," *Granta Book of Travel* (Bill Buford, ed.; 1991)

3 In the best comedy, there is clearly something wrong, but it is secret and understated—not even implied—comedy is the public version of a private darkness.
My Secret History (1996)

4 I should have worked just long enough to discover that I didn't like it.
Observer, London (April 1, 1979)

5 Travel is glamorous only in retrospect.
Observer, London (October 7, 1979), "Sayings of the Week"

6 A foreign swearword is practically inoffensive except to the person who has learned it early in life and knows its social limits.
Saint Jack (1973), ch. 12

7 Ever since childhood, when I lived within earshot of the Boston and Maine, I have seldom heard a train go by and not wished I was on it.
The Great Railway Bazaar (1975)

8 Extensive traveling includes a feeling of encapsulation, and travel, so broadening at first, contracts the mind.
The Great Railway Bazaar (1975), ch. 2

9 The Japanese have perfected good manners and made them indistinguishable from rudeness.
The Great Railway Bazaar (1975), ch. 2

10 They say that if the Swiss had designed these mountains they'd be rather flatter.
Referring to the Alps. *The Great Railway Bazaar* (1975), ch. 28

11 The ship follows Soviet custom: it is riddled with class distinctions so subtle, it takes a trained Marxist to appreciate them.
The Great Railway Bazaar (1975), ch. 30

12 It was an old society, with a long memory...1690 was considered just yesterday by people who were not sure whether they had their bus fare home tonight.
Referring to the Protestant community in Northern Ireland. *The Kingdom by the Sea* (1983)

13 It seemed to me that the real problem in Ulster—and the reason there were so many bloody killings—was that everyone believed in an after-life.
Referring to violence and religion in Northern Ireland. *The Kingdom by the Sea* (1983)

14 A travel book...is the simplest sort of narrative, an explanation which is its own excuse for the gathering up and the going.
The Old Patagonian Express: By Train Through the Americas (1979), ch. 1

15 For some, this was the train to Sullivan Square, or Milk Street, or at the very most Orient Heights; for me, it was the train to Patagonia.
The Old Patagonian Express: By Train Through the Americas (1979)

16 Travel is a vanishing act, a solitary trip down a pinched line of geography to oblivion.
The Old Patagonian Express: By Train Through the Americas (1979)

17 We have become used to life being a series of arrivals or departures, of triumphs and failures, with nothing noteworthy in between.
The Old Patagonian Express: By Train Through the Americas (1979)

Thiers, Adolphe (Louis Adolphe Thiers; 1797–1877) French statesman and historian

1 Everything must be taken seriously, nothing tragically.
Speech to the French National Assembly (May 24, 1873)

Thomas, Brandon (Walter Brandon Thomas; 1856–1914) British actor and playwright

1 I'm Charley's aunt from Brazil, where the nuts come from.
Charley's Aunt (1892), Act 1

Thomas, Clarence (b.1948) U.S. Supreme Court Judge

1 It is a hi-tech lynching for uppity blacks. Unless you kowtow, this is what will happen to you. You will be lynched by a committee rather than hanged from a tree.
On hearings into charges of sexual harassment. *Times*, London (October 12, 1991)

Thomas, Dylan (Dylan Marlais Thomas; 1914–53) Welsh poet, playwright, and short-story writer

Quotations about Thomas

1 Although there must have been things wrong, disastrously wrong, Dylan made most of our contemporaries seem small and disgustingly self-seeking and cautious and hypocritical and cold.
Elizabeth Bishop (1911–79) U.S. poet. Letter to Pearl Kazin (November 16, 1953), quoted in *One Art: The Selected Letters of Elizabeth Bishop* (Robert Giroux, ed.; 1994)

2 *Why* do some poets manage to get by and live to be malicious old bores like Frost or—probably—pompous old ones like Yeats, or crazy old ones like Pound—and some just don't!
Elizabeth Bishop (1911–79) U.S. poet. Referring to the premature death of Dylan Thomas in 1953. Letter to Pearl Kazin (November 16, 1953), quoted in *One Art: The Selected Letters of Elizabeth Bishop* (Robert Giroux, ed.; 1994)

3 At his worst he is a sort of *idiot savant* of language.
1940
Randall Jarrell (1914–65) U.S. author and poet. "Poetry in a Dry Season," *Kipling, Auden, & Co.: Essays and Reviews, 1935–1964* (1981)

4 Dylan Thomas is very Welsh (he reminds me a little of Owen Glendower) and very good.
1940
Randall Jarrell (1914–65) U.S. author and poet. "Poetry in a Dry Season," *Kipling, Auden, & Co.: Essays and Reviews, 1935–1964* (1981)

5 The first time I saw Dylan Thomas I felt as if Rubens had suddenly taken it into his head to paint a youthful Silenus.
Edith Sitwell (1887–1964) British poet, critic, and writer. *Taken Care Of: An Autobiography* (1965)

Quotations by Thomas

6 I, born of flesh and ghost, was neither
A ghost nor man, but mortal ghost.
And I was struck down by death's feather.
"Before I Knocked," *18 Poems* (1934)

7 Light breaks where no sun shines;
Where no sea runs, the waters of the heart
Push in their tides.
"Light Breaks Where No Sun Shines," *18 Poems* (1934), ll. 1–3

8 The force that through the green fuse drives the flower
Drives my green age.
"The Force That Through the Green Fuse Drives the Flower," *18 Poems* (1934), ll. 1–2

9 I can never remember whether it snowed for six days and six nights when I was twelve or whether it snowed for twelve days and twelve nights when I was six.
Originally written as a radio script. *A Child's Christmas in Wales* (1945)

10 The land of my fathers. My fathers can have it.
Referring to Wales. "Of Wales," *Adam* (1953)

11 These poems, with all their crudities, doubts, and confusions, are written for the love of Man and in praise of God, and I'd be a damn' fool if they weren't.
Collected Poems 1934–1952 (November 1952), Author's note

12 After the first death, there is no other.
"A Refusal to Mourn the Death, by Fire, of a Child in London," *Deaths and Entrances* (1946), l. 24

13 Now as I was young and easy under the apple boughs
About the lilting house and happy as the grass was green.
"Fern Hill," *Deaths and Entrances* (1946), ll. 1–2

14 Time held me green and dying
Though I sang in my chains like the sea.
"Fern Hill," *Deaths and Entrances* (1946), ll. 53–54

15 And the wild boys innocent as strawberries.
"The Hunchback in the Park," *Deaths and Entrances* (1946), l. 40

16 Do not go gentle into that good night,
Old age should burn and rave at close of day;
Rage, rage, against the dying of the light.
1951. Written when his father became seriously ill. "Do Not Go Gentle into that Good Night," *In Country Sleep* (1952), ll. 1–3

17 I missed the chance of a lifetime, too. Fifty lovelies in the rude and I'd left my Bunsen burner home.
"One Warm Saturday," *Portrait of the Artist as a Young Dog* (1940)

18 And Death Shall Have No Dominion
May 1933. Poem title. *Twenty-Five Poems* (1936)

19 Though they go mad they shall be sane,
Though they sink through the sea they shall rise again.
Though lovers be lost love shall not;
And death shall have no dominion.
"And Death Shall Have No Dominion," *Twenty-Five Poems* (1936), ll. 6–9

20 The hand that signed the treaty bred a fever,
And famine grew, and locusts came;
Great is the hand that holds dominion over
Man by a scribbled name.

"The Hand That Signed the Paper," *Twenty-Five Poems* (1936), ll. 9–12

21 Chasing the naughty couples down the grass-green gooseberried double bed of the wood.

Thomas's "play for voices," written for the BBC and first broadcast on January 25, 1954. *Under Milk Wood* (1954)

22 Every night of her married life she has been late for school.

Thomas's "play for voices," written for the BBC and first broadcast on January 25, 1954. *Under Milk Wood* (1954)

23 It is spring, moonless night in the small town, starless and bible-black, the cobblestreets silent and the hunched, courters'-and-rabbits' wood limping invisible down to the sloeblack, slow, black, crowblack, fishingboat-bobbing sea.

Thomas's "play for voices," written for the BBC and first broadcast on January 25, 1954. *Under Milk Wood* (1954)

24 MR PRITCHARD I must dust the blinds and then I must raise them.

MRS OGMORE-PRITCHARD And before you let the sun in, mind it wipes its shoes.

Thomas's "play for voices," written for the BBC and first broadcast on January 25, 1954. *Under Milk Wood* (1954)

25 Nothing grows in our garden, only washing. And babies.

Thomas's "play for voices," written for the BBC and first broadcast on January 25, 1954. *Under Milk Wood* (1954)

26 Oh, isn't life a terrible thing, thank God?

Thomas's "play for voices," written for the BBC and first broadcast on January 25, 1954. *Under Milk Wood* (1954)

27 Oh, what can I do? I'll never be refined if I twitch.

Thomas's "play for voices," written for the BBC and first broadcast on January 25, 1954. *Under Milk Wood* (1954)

28 Portraits of famous bards and preachers, all fur and wool from the squint to the kneecaps.

Thomas's "play for voices," written for the BBC and first broadcast on January 25, 1954. *Under Milk Wood* (1954)

29 It is very good, sometimes, to have nothing. I want society, not me, to have places to sit in and beds to lie in; and who wants a hatstand of his very own?

Quoted in *Dylan Thomas: Poet of His People* (Andrew Sinclair; 1975)

30 Somebody's boring me, I think it's me.

Remark made after he had been talking continuously for some time. Quoted in *Four Absentees* (Rayner Heppenstall; 1960)

31 An alcoholic is someone you don't like who drinks as much as you do.

Quoted in *Life of Dylan Thomas* (Constantine Fitzgibbon; 1965), ch. 6

32 Too many of the artists of Wales spend too much time going on about the position of the artist of Wales. There is only one position for an artist anywhere: and that is, upright.

Quoted in *New Statesman* London (December 18, 1964)

33 Whatever talents I possess may suddenly diminish or suddenly increase. I can with ease become an ordinary fool. I may be one now. But it doesn't do to upset one's own vanity.

Quoted in *Notebooks* (Robert Maud, ed.; 1968)

34 I've had eighteen straight whiskies. I think that's the record...After thirty-nine years, this is all I've done.

His early death was a result of alcoholic poisoning. Attrib.

Thomas, Edward (Phillip Edward Thomas; 1878–1917) British poet, biographer, and critic

1 Yes. I remember Adlestrop—
The name, because one afternoon
Of heat the express train drew up there
Unwontedly. It was late June.

Originally published under the pseudonym Edward Eastaway. "Adlestrop," *Poems* (1917)

2 The past is the only dead thing that smells sweet.

Originally published under the pseudonym Edward Eastaway. "Early One Morning," *Poems* (1917)

3 I have come to the borders of sleep,
The unfathomable deep
Forest where all must lose
Their way, however straight,
Or winding, soon or late;
They cannot choose.

Originally published under the pseudonym Edward Eastaway. "Lights Out," *Poems* (1917)

4 Now all roads lead to France
And heavy is the tread
Of the living; but the dead
Returning lightly dance.

Originally published under the pseudonym Edward Eastaway. "Roads," *Poems* (1917)

5 I wonder whether for a person like myself whose most intense moments were those of depression a cure that destroys the depression may not destroy the intensity—a desperate remedy.

Quoted in *Edward Thomas* (R. George Thomas; 1985)

Thomas, Gwyn (1913–81) Welsh writer and playwright

1 There are still parts of Wales where the only concession to gaiety is a striped shroud.

Punch, London (June 18, 1958)

Thomas, Irene (b.1920) British writer and broadcaster

1 Protestant women may take the Pill. Roman Catholic women must keep taking the Tablet.

The Tablet is a Roman Catholic periodical. *Guardian*, London (December 28, 1990)

2 It was the kind of show where the girls are not auditioned—just measured.

Attrib.

Thomas, Lewis (1913–93) U.S. physician and writer

1 Worrying is the most natural and spontaneous of all human functions. It is time to acknowledge this, perhaps even to learn to do it better.

"The Medusa and the Snail," *More Notes of a Biology Watcher* (1979)

2 It is from the progeny of this parent cell that we all take our looks; we still share genes around, and the resemblance of the enzymes of grasses to those of whales is in fact a family resemblance.

The Lives of a Cell (1974)

3 The uniformity of earth's life, more astonishing than its diversity, is accountable by the high probability that we derived, originally, from some single cell, fertilized in a bolt of lightning as the earth cooled.
The Lives of a Cell (1974)

4 We can take some gratification at having come a certain distance in just a few thousand years of our existence as language users, but it should be a deeper satisfaction, even an exhilaration, to recognize that we have such a distance still to go.
Epigraph. Quoted in *Shedding Life* (Miroslav Holub; 1997)

5 The mind of a cat is an inscrutable mystery, beyond human reach, the least human of all creatures and, at the same time, as any cat-owner will attest, the most intelligent.
Attrib.

Thomas, Lowell (Lowell Jackson Thomas; 1892–1981) U.S. traveler, writer, and broadcaster

1 They only got two things right, the camels and the sand.
Referring to the film *Lawrence of Arabia* (1962). *Times*, London (August 29, 1981)

Thomas, Norman (Norman Mattoon Thomas; 1884–1968) U.S. reformer and politician

1 While I'd rather be right than president, at any time I'm ready to be both.
Referring to his lack of success in presidential campaigns. Quoted in *Come to Judgment* (Alden Whitman; 1980)

Thomas, R. S. (Ronald Stuart Thomas; b.1913) Welsh poet and clergyman

1 Heaven affords
unlimited accommodation
to the simple-minded.
1986. "Revision," *Collected Poems* (1993)

2 We live in our own world,
A world that is too small
For you to stoop and enter
Even on hands and knees,
The adult subterfuge.
"Children's Song," *Song at the Year's Turning: Poems 1942–1954* (1955)

3 An impotent people,
Sick with inbreeding,
Worrying the carcase of an old song.
"Welsh Landscape," *Song at the Year's Turning: Poems 1942–1954* (1955)

Thompson, Bonar (1888–1963) British orator

1 Half the misery in the world is caused by ignorance. The other half is caused by knowledge.
Attrib.

Thompson, Clara (Clara Mabel Thompson; 1893–1958) U.S. psychoanalyst

1 People who have a low self-esteem...have a tendency to cling to their own sex because it is less frightening.
"A Study of Interpersonal Relations," *New Contributions to Psychiatry* (Patrick Mullahy, ed.; 1958)

Thompson, Daley (Francis Morgan Thompson; b.1958) British decathlete

1 In my sport you have to peak ten times.
Sunday Times, London (October 11, 1981)

Thompson, Emma (b.1959) British actor

1 I brought a lot of tranquillisers and my mother.
1992. Remark on receiving the Academy Award (Oscar) for Best Actress for her performance in *Howards End* (1991). Attrib.

2 This whole thing is like a cross between a very severe virus and getting married.
1992. Remark on receiving the Academy Award (Oscar) for Best Actress for her performance in *Howards End* (1991). Attrib.

Thompson, Francis (1859–1907) British poet and critic

1 I fled Him, down the nights and down the days;
I fled Him, down the arches of the years;
I fled Him, down the labyrinthine ways
Of my own mind; and in the mist of tears
I hid from Him, and under running laughter.
"The Hound of Heaven," *Poems* (1893)

2 There is no expeditious road
To pack and label men for God,
And save them by the barrel-load.
"A Judgment in Heaven," *Works* (Wilfred Meynell, ed.; 1913), Epilogue

3 The fairest things have fleetest end,
Their scent survives their close:
But the rose's scent is bitterness
To him that loved the rose.
"Daisy," *Works* (Wilfred Meynell, ed.; 1913), st. 10, ll. 1–4

4 Nothing begins and nothing ends
That is not paid with moan;
For we are born in others' pain,
And perish in our own.
"Daisy," *Works* (Wilfred Meynell, ed.; 1913), st. 15, ll. 1–4

5 O world invisible, we view thee,
O world intangible, we touch thee,
O world unknowable, we know thee,
Inapprehensible, we clutch thee!
Also known as "The Kingdom of God" from the epigraph to the poem, "The Kingdom of God is within you" (Luke ch. 17, v. 21). "In No Strange Land," *Works* (Wilfred Meynell, ed.; 1913), st. 1, ll. 1–4

6 Spring is come home with her world-wandering feet.
And all things are made young with young desires.
"Ode to Easter," *Works* (Wilfred Meynell, ed.; 1913)

Thompson, Hunter S. (Hunter Stockton Thompson; b.1939) U.S. writer and journalist

1 I felt like Othello. Here I'd been only in town for a few hours, and we'd already laid the groundwork for a classic tragedy. The hero was doomed; he had already sown the seed of his own downfall.
Fear and Loathing in Las Vegas (1972)

2 Ether is the perfect drug for Las Vegas. In this town they love a drunk. Fresh meat.
November 1971. *Fear and Loathing in Las Vegas* (1972), ch. 6

3 Mainline gambling is a very heavy business—and Las Vegas makes Reno seem like your friendly neighborhood grocery store. For a loser Vegas is the meanest town on earth.
November 1971. *Fear and Loathing in Las Vegas* (1972), ch. 6

4 A week in Vegas is like stumbling into a Time Warp, a regression to the late fifties. Which is wholly understandable when you see the people who come here, the Big Spenders from places like Denver and Dallas.
November 1971. *Fear and Loathing in Las Vegas* (1972), ch. 8

5 A career politician finally smelling the White House is not much different from a bull elk in the rut. He will stop at nothing, trashing anything that gets in his way; and anything he can't handle personally he will hire out—or, failing that, make a deal.
Fear and Loathing on the Campaign Trail, '72 (1972)

6 Defeat would be bad enough, but victory would be intolerable.
Referring to the dilemma facing Florida police as Vietnam veterans marched in protest on the 1972 Republican convention. *Fear and Loathing on the Campaign Trail, '72* (1972)

7 The Sixties were an era of extreme reality. I miss the smell of teargas. I miss the fear of getting beaten.
Independent on Sunday, London (October 12, 1997)

8 If I'd written all the truth I knew for the past ten years, about 600 people—including me—would be rotting in prison cells from Rio to Seattle today. Absolute truth is a very rare and dangerous commodity in the context of professional journalism.
"Fear and Loathing at the Superbowl," *Rolling Stone* (February 15, 1973), quoted in *The Great Shark Hunt* (Hunter S. Thompson; 1979), pt. 1

9 Going to trial with a lawyer who considers your life-style a Crime in Progress is not a happy prospect.
1990. "A Letter to *The Champion*: a production of the National Assoc. of Criminal Defence Lawyers," *Songs of the Doomed* (1991)

10 In a nation ruled by swine, all pigs are upwardly mobile—and the rest of us are fucked until we can put our acts together: not necessarily to win, but mainly to keep from losing completely.
"Jacket Copy for Fear and Loathing in Las Vegas," *The Great Shark Hunt* (1979)

11 Myths and legends die hard in America. We love them for the extra dimension they provide, the illusion of near-infinite possibility to erase the narrow confines of most men's reality.
1969. "Those Daring Young Men in their Flying Machines...Ain't What They Used to Be!" *The Great Shark Hunt* (1979), pt. 3, quoted in *Pageant* (September 1969)

12 Fear and Loathing in Las Vegas
1972. Book title. Subtitled: *A Savage Journey to the Heart of the American Dream.*

Thomson, James (1700–48) Scottish poet

1 When Britain first, at heaven's command,
Arose from out the azure main,
This was the charter of the land,
And guardian angels sung this strain:
"Rule, Britannia, rule the waves;
Britons never will be slaves."
This became the opening verse of "Rule, Britannia." *Alfred: a Masque* (1740), Act 2

Thomson, James (1834–82) British poet

1 The City is of Night; perchance of Death,
But certainly of Night.
"The City of Dreadful Night" (1874), can. 1

Thomson, Joseph (1858–95) Scottish geologist and explorer

1 Crossing Piccadilly Circus.
Replying to J. M. Barrie, who asked what was the most hazardous part of his expedition to Africa. Quoted in *J. M. Barrie* (Janet Dunbar; 1970)

Thoreau, Henry David (originally David Henry Thoreau; 1817–62) U.S. writer

Quotations about Thoreau

1 I love Henry, but I cannot like him; and as for taking his arm, I should as soon think of taking the arm of an elm tree.
Anonymous. Remark by an unknown friend

2 He was imperfect, unfinished, inartistic; he was worse than provincial—he was parochial.
Henry James (1843–1916) U.S.-born British writer and critic. *Hawthorne* (1879), ch. 4

3 A man may pay too dearly for his livelihood, by giving, in Thoreau's terms, his whole life for it...and becoming a slave till death.
Robert Louis Stevenson (1850–94) Scottish novelist, essayist, and poet. "Henry David Thoreau," *Familiar Studies of Men and Books* (1882)

Quotations by Thoreau

4 Not that the story need be long, but it will take a long while to make it short.
Letter to Harrison Blake (November 16, 1857)

5 Do not be too moral. You may cheat yourself out of much of life. So aim above morality. Be not simply good; be good for something.
Letter to Harrison Blake (March 27, 1848)

6 It takes two to speak the truth—one to speak, and another to hear.
"Wednesday," *A Week on the Concord and Merrimack Rivers* (1849)

7 He has something demoniacal about him who can discern a law or couple two facts.
Excursions (1863)

8 Life consists with wildness. The most alive is the wildest. Not yet subdued to man, its presence refreshes him.
"Walking," *Excursions* (1863)

9 In wildness is the preservation of the world.
Adopted as the motto of the Wilderness Society. "Walking," *Excursions* (1863)

10 I do not value any view of the universe into which man and the institutions of man enter very largely and absorb much of the attention. Man is but the place where I stand, and the prospect hence is infinite.
Journal (April 2, 1852)

11 Music is the crystallization of sound.
Journal (1841), quoted in *The Journal of Henry David Thoreau* (Bradford Torrey and Francis H. Allen, eds.; 1962)

12 When I hear music, I fear no danger. I am invulnerable. I see no foe. I am related to the earliest times and to the latest.
Journal (1857), quoted in *The Journal of Henry David Thoreau* (Bradford Torrey and Francis H. Allen, eds.; 1962)

13 Decay and disease are often beautiful, like the pearly tear of the shellfish and the hectic glow of consumption.
Journal (June 11, 1852), quoted in *The Writings of Henry David Thoreau* (1906)

14 Some circumstantial evidence is very strong, as when you find a trout in the milk.
Journal (1850), quoted in *The Writings of Henry David Thoreau* (1906)

15 Thank God men cannot as yet fly and lay waste the sky as well as the earth.
Journal (January 3, 1861), quoted in *The Writings of Henry David Thoreau* (1906)

16 The most attractive sentences are not perhaps the wisest, but the surest and soundest.
Journal (1842), quoted in *The Writings of Henry David Thoreau* (1906)

17 What does education often do? It makes a straight cut ditch of a free meandering brook.
Journal (October/November 1850), quoted in *The Writings of Henry David Thoreau* (1906)

18 What men call social virtues, good fellowship, is commonly but the virtue of pigs in a litter, which lie close together to keep each other warm. It brings men together in crowds and mobs in barrooms and elsewhere, but it does not deserve the name of virtue.
Journal (1852), quoted in *The Writings of Henry David Thoreau* (1906)

19 You do not get a man's most effective criticism until you provoke him. Severe truth is expressed with some bitterness.
Journal (March 15, 1854), quoted in *The Writings of Henry David Thoreau* (1906)

20 I heartily accept the motto, "That government is best which governs least"; and I should like to see it acted up to more rapidly and systematically. Carried out, it finally amounts to this, which I also believe, "That government is best which governs not at all."
On the Duty of Civil Disobedience (1849)

21 Under a government which imprisons any unjustly, the true place for a just man is also a prison.
On the Duty of Civil Disobedience (1849)

22 Every creature is better alive than dead, men and moose and pine trees, and he who understands it aright will rather preserve its life than destroy it.
"Chesuncook," *The Maine Woods* (1864)

23 Talk of mysteries! Think of our life in nature...rocks, trees, wind on our cheeks! the *solid* earth! the *actual* world! the *common sense! Contact! Contact! Who* are we? *where* are we?
"Ktaadn," *The Maine Woods* (1848)

24 Great God, I ask thee for no meaner pelf
Than that I may not disappoint myself.
"Pelf" is an archaic word for money, wealth. "Great God, I Ask Thee for No Meaner Pelf," *The Penguin Book of American Verse* (Geoffrey Moore, ed.; 1977)

25 I am a parcel of vain strivings tied
By a chance bond together.
"I Am a Parcel of Vain Strivings Tied," *The Penguin Book of American Verse* (Geoffrey Moore, ed.; 1977)

26 Whatever sentence will bear to be read twice, we may be sure was thought twice.
The Writings of Henry David Thoreau (1894)

27 Water is the only drink for a wise man.
Walden, or, Life in the Woods (1854)

28 What old people say you cannot do, you try and find that you can. Old deeds for old people, and new deeds for new.
Walden, or, Life in the Woods (1854)

29 If you give money, spend yourself with it.
Referring to giving aid to the poor. *Walden, or, Life in the Woods* (1854)

30 Explore thyself. Herein are demanded the eye and the nerve.
"Conclusion," *Walden, or, Life in the Woods* (1854)

31 If a man does not keep pace with his companions, perhaps it is because he hears a different drummer. Let him step to the music which he hears, however measured or far away.
"Conclusion," *Walden, or, Life in the Woods* (1854)

32 Superfluous wealth can buy superfluities only.
"Conclusion," *Walden, or, Life in the Woods* (1854)

33 The government of the world I live in was not framed, like that of Britain, in after-dinner conversations over the wine.
"Conclusion," *Walden, or, Life in the Woods* (1854)

34 As if you could kill time without injuring eternity.
"Economy," *Walden, or, Life in the Woods* (1854)

35 Beware of all enterprises that require new clothes.
"Economy," *Walden, or, Life in the Woods* (1854)

36 I have lived some thirty years on this planet, and I have yet to hear the first syllable of valuable or even earnest advice from my seniors.
"Economy," *Walden, or, Life in the Woods* (1854)

37 The mass of men lead lives of quiet desperation.
"Economy," *Walden, or, Life in the Woods* (1854)

38 There are nowadays professors of philosophy but not philosophers.
"Economy," *Walden, or, Life in the Woods* (1854)

39 I have a great deal of company in the house, especially in the morning when nobody calls.
"Solitude," *Walden, or, Life in the Woods* (1854)

40 I never found the companion that was so companionable as solitude.
"Solitude," *Walden, or, Life in the Woods* (1854)

41 By avarice and selfishness, and a groveling habit, from which none of us is free, of regarding the soil as property...the landscape is deformed.
"The Bean Field," *Walden, or, Life in the Woods* (1854)

42 I would rather sit on a pumpkin, and have it all to myself, than be crowded on a velvet cushion.
"Where I lived, and What I Lived For," *Walden, or, Life in the Woods* (1854)

43 Our life is frittered away by detail...Simplicity, simplicity.
"Where I Lived, and What I Lived For," *Walden, or, Life in the Woods* (1854)

44 Time is but the stream I go a-fishing in.
"Where I Lived, and What I Lived For," *Walden, or, Life in the Woods* (1854)

45 I once had a sparrow alight upon my shoulder for a moment while I was hoeing in a village garden, and I felt that I was more distinguished by that circumstance than I should have been by any epaulet I could have worn.
"Winter Animals," *Walden, or, Life in the Woods* (1854)

46 We are in great haste to construct a magnetic telegraph from Maine to Texas; but Maine and Texas, it may be, have nothing important to communicate.
Quoted in *Intellectual Capital* (Thomas A. Stewart; 1997)

47 'Tis healthy to be sick sometimes.
Attrib.

48 One world at a time.
Said on being asked his opinion of the hereafter a few days before his death. (May 1862) Attrib.

49 Yes—around Concord.
When asked whether he had traveled much, and referring to Concord, Massachusetts. Attrib.

50 I did not know that we had ever quarreled.
Said on being urged to make his peace with God. Attrib.

Thorndike, Sybil, Dame (Agnes Sybil Thorndike; 1882–1976) British actor

1 Divorce? Never. But murder often!
Replying to a query as to whether she had considered divorce from Sir Lewis Casson. Attrib.

Thornely, Nick British author

1 The first "managers" assumed that as the stick worked for animals it would also work for the managed.
Leadership: the Art of Motivation (co-written with Dan Lees; 1993)

Thornton, Charles ("Tex"; b.1915) U.S. business executive

1 When an executive has the authority and his subordinate has the responsibility...the subordinate in effect, then, is only a glorified clerk.
Quoted in *The Whiz Kids* (John A. Byrne; 1993)

Thorpe, Edward (b.1926) British writer

1 The continent from which the west first received Black dance contains a political system which separates Whites from Blacks both on and off stage. What, indeed, should the Black dancer dance about?
Black Dance (1989)

2 There still remained considerable prejudice about training for an art so associated with the white European cultural mainstream.
Referring to Arthur Mitchell and his role in a Balanchine ballet. *Black Dance* (1989)

Thorpe, Rose Hartwick (originally Rose Alnora Hartwick; 1850–1939) U.S. poet and novelist

1 And her face so sweet and pleading, yet with sorrow pale and worn,
Touched his heart with sudden pity—lit his eye with misty light;
"Go, your lover lives!" said Cromwell; "Curfew shall not ring tonight!"
"Curfew Shall Not Ring Tonight" (1866?)

Thorpe, Thomas Bangs (1815–78) U.S. writer and humorist

1 The Creation state, the finishin'-up country.
Referring to Arkansas. "The Big Bear of Arkansas," *Mysteries of the Backwoods* (1846)

Thucydides (460?–400? B.C.) Athenian historian and general

1 For we both alike know that into the discussion of human affairs the question of justice enters only where the pressure of necessity is equal, and that the powerful exact what they can, and the weak grant what they must.
History of the Peloponnesian War (431–400? B.C.)

2 What made war inevitable was the growth of Athenian power and the fear which this caused in Sparta.
History of the Peloponnesian War (431–400? B.C.)

3 The ability to understand a question from all sides meant one was totally unfit for action. Fanatical enthusiasm was the mark of the real man.
On the Athenian mood during Peloponnesian War 431–400? B.C. *History of the Peloponnesian War* (431–400? B.C.)

4 To famous men all the earth is a sepulcher.
History of the Peloponnesian War (431–400? B.C.), bk. 2, ch. 43

5 It is a great glory in a woman to show no more weakness than is natural to her sex, and not be talked of, either for good or evil by men.
History of the Peloponnesian War (431–400? B.C.), bk. 2, ch. 45

6 War, which robs people of the easy supply of their daily wants, is a violent schoolmaster matching most men's tempers to their condition.
History of the Peloponnesian War (431–400? B.C.), bk. 3, l. 83

Thurber, James (James Grover Thurber; 1894–1961) U.S. writer, cartoonist, and humorist

1 I was seized by the stern hand of Compulsion, that dark, unseasonable Urge that impels women to clean house in the middle of the night.
"There's a Time for Flags," *Alarms and Diversions* (1957)

2 It is better to have loafed and lost than never to have loafed at all.
"The Courtship of Arthur and Al," *Fables for Our Time* (1940)

3 You can fool too many of the people too much of the time.
"The Owl Who Was God," *Fables for Our Time* (1940)

4 Early to rise and early to bed makes a male healthy and wealthy and dead.
"The Shrike and the Chipmunks," *Fables for Our Time* (1940)

5 Old Nat Burge sat...He was...watching the moon come up lazily out of the old cemetery in which nine of his daughters were lying, and only two of them were dead.
"Bateman Comes Home," *Let Your Mind Alone* (1937)

6 No man...who has wrestled with a self-adjusting card table can ever quite be the man he once was.
"Sex ex Machina," *Let Your Mind Alone* (1937)

7 I suppose that the high-water mark of my youth in Columbus, Ohio, was the night the bed fell on my father.
My Life and Hard Times (1933), ch. 1

8 Her own mother lived the latter years of her life in the horrible suspicion that electricity was dripping invisibly all over the house.
My Life and Hard Times (1933), ch. 2

9 Then, with that faint fleeting smile playing about his lips, he faced the firing squad; erect and motionless, proud and disdainful, Walter Mitty, the undefeated, inscrutable to the last.
"The Secret Life of Walter Mitty," *My World—And Welcome to It* (1942)

10 The War between Men and Women
Title of a series of cartoons. *New Yorker* (January 20–April 28, 1934)

11 Well, if I called the wrong number, why did you answer the phone?
Cartoon caption, *New Yorker* (June 5, 1937)

12 Humor is emotional chaos remembered in tranquility.
New York Post (February 29, 1960)

13 The difference between our decadence and the Russians' is that while theirs is brutal, ours is apathetic.
Observer, London (February 5, 1961), "Sayings of the Week"

14 A man should not insult his wife publicly, at parties. He should insult her in the privacy of the home.
Thurber Country (1953)

15 It's a naive domestic Burgundy, without any breeding. But I think you'll be amused by its presumption.
Women and Dogs (1943)

16 All men should strive to learn before they die
What they are running from, and to, and why.
Attrib.

17 A woman's place is in the wrong.
Attrib.

18 I hate women because they always know where things are.
Attrib.

19 The majority of American males put themselves to sleep by striking out the batting order of the New York Yankees.
Attrib.

20 God bless...God damn.
1961. Last words. Attrib.

21 Surely you don't mean by unartificial insemination!
Responding to a woman at a party who said she wanted to have a baby by him. Attrib.

22 It had only one fault. It was kind of lousy.
Remark made about a play. Attrib.

Thurow, Lester (b.1938) U.S. management consultant

1 Every country that has caught up has done it by copying.
Harvard Business Review (September–October 1997)

Tichborne, Chidiock (1558?–86) English conspirator

1 My prime of youth is but a frost of cares;
My feast of joy is but a dish of pain;
My crop of corn is but a field of tares;
And all my good is but vain hope of gain.
The day is past, and yet I saw no sun;
And now I live, and now my life is done.
Written in the Tower of London before his execution. "Elegy" (1586)

Tichy, Noel M. U.S. management theorist and author

1 Everyone who holds a job is taking part in defining the new relationships between the individual and the corporation.
Control Your Destiny or Someone Else Will

2 Once all the surviving contendors in a market can offer value, the battle shifts to speed and innovation. To distinguish themselves, companies must offer something unique.
Control Your Destiny or Someone Else Will

3 Solve the problem yourself or accept a fate you may not like...from this perspective, the ethic of personal responsibility gains appeal.
Control Your Destiny or Someone Else Will

4 Success can deaden an organization's responses.
Control Your Destiny or Someone Else Will

Tickell, Thomas (1686–1740) English poet

1 Nor e'er was to the bowers of bliss conveyed
A fairer spirit or more welcome shade.
"To the Earl of Warwick. On the Death of Mr. Addison" (1721), ll. 45–46

Tiger, Lionel (b.1937) Canadian-born U.S. anthropologist

1 Eternal vigilance is the price of sexual confidence.
Referring to the uncertainty of male parentage. *Time* (November 25, 1985)

Tilberis, Liz (1947–?) U.S. editor

1 A love of fashion makes the economy go round.
Vogue (August 1987)

Tillich, Paul (Paul Johannes Tillich; 1886–1965) German-born U.S. theologian and philosopher

1 One can narrow the meaning of religion to the *cultus deorum* (the cult of the gods), thus excluding from the religious realm the pre-mythological as well as the post-mythological stages.
Christianity and the Encounter of the World Religions (1961), ch. 1

2 Religion is the state of being grasped by an ultimate concern...which itself contains the answer to the question of the meaning of our life.
Christianity and the Encounter of the World Religions (1961), ch. 1

3 The Christian missionaries there told me that they are much less worried about Buddhism and Shintoism than about the enormous amount of indifference to all religions.
Referring to the effect of modern technology on the Japanese. *Christianity and the Encounter of the World Religions* (1961), ch. 1

4 One of the radicalized and demoniacal quasi-religions—Nazism.
Christianity and the Encounter of the World Religions (1961), ch. 2

5 In the dialogue between Christianity and Buddhism two telos-formulas can be used: in Christianity the telos of every*one* and everything united in the Kingdom of God; in Buddhism the telos of every*thing* and everyone fulfilled in Nirvana.
Christianity and the Encounter of the World Religions (1961), ch. 3

6 The mystical and the ethical...There is no holiness and therefore no living religion without both elements.
Christianity and the Encounter of the World Religions (1961), ch. 3

7 Buddhism never conquered the principle of identity. Every Buddhist rock garden is a witness to its presence.
Christianity and the Encounter of the World Religions (1961), ch. 4

8 In Mahayana Buddhism the Buddha-Spirit appears in many manifestations of a personal character, making a nonmystical, often very primitive relation to a divine figure possible.
Christianity and the Encounter of the World Religions (1961), ch. 4

9 The question of the ultimate meaning of life cannot be silenced as long as men are men.
Christianity and the Encounter of the World Religions (1961), ch. 4

10 Neurosis is the way of avoiding non-being by avoiding being.
The Courage to Be (1952), pt. 2, ch. 3

11 Language has created the word loneliness to express the pain of being alone, and the word solitude to express the glory of being alone.
"Loneliness and Solitude," *The Eternal Now* (1963)

12 Islam...means surrender, devotion, subjection to the divine order, and all this without much sacramental thought even in doctrine. The commands of the Koran can be fulfilled, the commandment of love, however, can never be fulfilled.
1958. Quoted in *The Encounter of Religions and Quasi-Religions* (T. Thomas, ed.; 1991)

Timrod, Henry (1828–67) U.S. poet and editor

1 Thus girt without and garrisoned at home,
Day patient following day,
Old Charleston looks from roof, and spire, and dome,
Across her tranquil bay.
Referring to Charleston, South Carolina. "Charleston," *The Poems of Henry Timrod* (Paul H. Hayne, ed.; 1873), v. 7

Tintoretto (Jacopo Robusti; 1518?–94) Italian painter

1 Grant me paradise in this world; I'm not so sure I'll reach it in the next.
1581. Arguing that he be allowed to paint the *Paradiso* at the Doge's palace in Venice, despite his advanced age. Attrib.

Titian (Tiziano Vecellio; 1477?–1576) Italian painter

1 It is not bright colors but good drawing that makes figures beautiful.
Quoted in *Marvels of the Painter's Art* (Carlo Ridolfi; 1648)

Tito (Josip Broz; 1892–1980) Yugoslavian statesman

1 I am the only Yugoslav.
May 1980. Said shortly before his death. Attrib.

Tjosvold, Dean U.S. psychologist and author

1 Leaders are psychologists. They act upon their ideas about what drives and motivates people, what people want and how they plan to get it.
Psychology for Leaders (co-written with Mary M. Tjosvold; 1995)

2 Learning is a common journey that binds leaders and employers together...Learning unites leaders and followers in a common journey of self-discovery and team development.
Psychology for Leaders (co-written with Mary M. Tjosvold; 1995)

3 Managing conflict for mutual benefit moves people away from assuming that co-workers are arrogant and untrustworthy to seeing them as reliable colleagues.
Psychology for Leaders (co-written with Mary M. Tjosvold; 1995)

Tobias, Randall L. (Randall Lee Tobias; b.1942) U.S. business executive

1 Innovation is a necessary condition for business success—but not a sufficient condition for business success.
Speech (April 15, 1997)

Tocqueville, Alexis de (Alexis Charles Henri Maurice Clérel de Tocqueville; 1805–59) French writer and politician

1 A new world demands a new political science.
Democracy in America (1835–40)

2 I cannot believe that a republic could subsist if the influence of the lawyers in public business did not increase in proportion to the power of the people.
Democracy in America (1835–40), vol. 1, ch. 16

3 The profession of the law is the only aristocratic element which can be amalgamated without violence with the natural elements of democracy.
Democracy in America (1835–40), vol. 1, ch. 16

4 The French want no one to be their *superior*. The English want *inferiors*. The Frenchman constantly raises his eyes above him with anxiety. The Englishman lowers his beneath him with satisfaction. On either side it is pride, but understood in a different way.
May 8, 1835. *Voyage en Angleterre et en Irlande de 1835* (1835)

Toffler, Alvin (b.1928) U.S. writer

1 Man has a limited biological capacity for change. When this capacity is overwhelmed, it is in "future shock."
Future Shock (1970)

2 Technology feeds on itself. Technology makes more technology possible.
Future Shock (1970)

3 We are creating and using up ideas and images at a faster and faster pace. Knowledge, like people, places, things, and organizational forms, is becoming dispensable.
Future Shock (1970)

4 Even the seemingly "hardest" models and data are frequently based on "soft" assumptions, especially when these concern human affairs.
Powershift (1990)

5 A corporation without a strategy is like an airplane weaving

through stormy skies, hurled up and down, slammed by the wind, lost in the thunderheads. If lightning or crushing winds don't destroy it, it will simply run out of gas.
The Adaptive Corporation (1985)

6 Even the best strategies seldom take into account more than a few of the consequences that flow from them. In real life, the decision-maker must continually adjust to those consequences, and, in doing so, deviate from the clear course laid out in advance.
The Adaptive Corporation (1985)

7 It is always easier to talk about change than to make it. It is easier to consult than to manage.
The Adaptive Corporation (1985)

8 The adaptive manager today must be capable of radical action—willing to think beyond the thinkable: to reconceptualize products, procedures, programs, and purposes before crisis makes drastic change inescapable.
The Adaptive Corporation (1985)

9 Today's adaptive executives...must be experts not in bureaucracy, but in the co-ordination of ad-hocracy. They must adjust to immediate pressures—yet think in terms of long-term goals.
The Adaptive Corporation (1985)

Tolkien, J. R. R. (John Ronald Reuel Tolkein; 1892–1973) South African-born British scholar, philologist, and writer

1 Nearly all marriages, even happy ones, are mistakes: in the sense that almost certainly (in a more perfect world, or even with a little more care in this very imperfect one) both partners might be found more suitable mates. But the real soul-mate is the one you are actually married to.
Letter to Michael Tolkien (March 6–8, 1941)

2 In a hole in the ground there lived a hobbit.
The Hobbit (1937), ch. 1

3 Far over misty mountains cold,
To dungeons deep and caverns old,
We must away, ere break of day,
To seek the pale enchanted gold!
The dwarfs' song. *The Hobbit* (1937), ch. 1

4 One Ring to rule them all, One Ring to find them,
One Ring to bring them all and in the darkness bind them.
The Lord of the Rings, pt. 1: *The Fellowship of the Ring* (1954), ch. 2

5 Faithless is he that says farewell when the road darkens.
The Lord of the Rings, pt. 1: *The Fellowship of the Ring* (1954), ch. 3

6 Where iss it, where iss it: my Precious, my Precious? It's ours, it is, and we wants it.
Gollum, searching for the ring of power. *The Lord of the Rings*, pt. 2: *The Two Towers* (1955), ch. 1

7 He willed that the hearts of Men should seek beyond the world and should find no rest therein; but they should have a virtue to shape their life, amid the powers and chances of the world, beyond the Music of the Ainur, which is a fate to all things else.
Referring to Ilúvatar, the Creator. *The Silmarillion* (1977), ch. 1

Tolson, Melvin (Melvin Beaunorus; 1900–66) U.S. poet and teacher

1 A nagging woman is a bird beating her wings against the cage of matrimony. Henpecking is her revenge for her marital misery.
"Henpecked Husband: Comedy or Tragedy" (January 20, 1940)

2 It is hazardous to shake a family tree. One never knows what will fall out. Undesirable birds have an impish way of roosting among the finest genealogical branches.
"I am an Unprejudiced Negro" (August 26, 1939)

3 Youth has vision! Old age, dreams.
"Portrait of Jesus, the Young Radical" (June 4, 1938)

4 I may say here that no race is civilized until it produces a literature. A great work of literature is a race's ticket to immortality. Races do not live in history because they have produced Henry Fords.
"The Negro and Radicalism" (August 12, 1939)

5 When men are weak, they become moral. When men and nations are strong, they don't give a damn about morality.
"The Weapon of the Weak to Curb the Power of the Strong" (September 7, 1940)

6 It's easy to love God. It's easy to love Jesus. It's easy to pray for the heathen African ten thousand miles from the house where you live. It's hard to call a lousy tramp your brother and set him down at your table.
April 2, 1938. Quoted in "The Death of an Infidel," *Caviar and Cabbages: Selected Columns by Melvin B. Tolson* (Robert M. Farnsworth, ed.; 1982)

Tolstoy, Leo, Count (Lev Nikolayevich Tolstoy; 1828–1910) Russian writer

Quotations about Tolstoy

1 You must have noticed that the main idea of that great work is this: if a woman leaves her lawful husband to live with another man, this inevitably makes her a prostitute. Don't argue! That's exactly what it is.
Anna Akhmatora (1888–1966) Russian poet. Referring to Leo Tolstoy's novel *Anna Karenina* (1875–77). (Milena Michalski and Sylva Rubashova, trs.; May 18, 1939), quoted in *The Akhmatova Journals: 1938–1941* (Lydia Chukovskaya, ed.; 1989)

Quotations by Tolstoy

2 All happy families resemble one another, each unhappy family is unhappy in its own way.
Anna Karenina (1875–77), pt. 1, ch. 1

3 "There," she said to herself, looking in the shadow of the truck at the mixture of sand and coal dust which covered the sleepers. "There in the very middle, and I shall punish him and escape from them all and from myself."
Anna Karenina contemplating suicide. *Anna Karenina* (1875–77), pt. 1, sect. 18

4 In that brief glance Vronsky had time to notice the suppressed animation which played over her face and flitted between her sparkling eyes and the slight smile curving her red lips.
Describing Count Vronsky's first sight of Anna Karenina. *Anna Karenina* (1875–77), pt. 1, sect. 18

5 Just as her husband had done, her son produced on Anna a feeling akin to disappointment. In imagination she had pictured him nicer than he actually was. She had to descend to reality in order to enjoy him as he was.
Anna Karenina (1875–77), pt. 1, sect. 32

6 There are no conditions of life to which a man cannot get accustomed, especially if he sees them accepted by *everyone* about him.
Anna Karenina (1875–77), pt. 7, sect. 13

7 I have learned that every man lives not through care of himself, but by love.
Anna Karenina (1875–77), pt. 8, sect. 10

8 When Levin puzzled over what he was and what he was living for, he could find no answer and fell into despair; but when he left off worrying about the problem of his existence he seemed to know both what he was and for what he was living, for he acted and lived resolutely and unfalteringly.
Anna Karenina (1875–77), pt. 8, sect. 10

9 It is amazing how complete is the delusion that beauty is goodness.
The Kreutzer Sonata (1889)

10 The highest wisdom has but one science—the science of the whole—the science explaining the whole creation and man's place in it.
War and Peace (1865–69), bk. 5, ch. 2

11 The chief attraction of military service has consisted and will consist in this compulsory and irreproachable idleness.
War and Peace (1865–69), bk. 7, ch. 1

12 All, everything that I understand, I understand only because I love.
War and Peace (1865–69), bk. 7, ch. 16

13 Our body is a machine for living. It is organized for that, it is its nature. Let life go on in it unhindered and let it defend itself, it will do more than if you paralyze it by encumbering it with remedies.
War and Peace (1865–69), bk. 10, ch. 29

14 Pure and complete sorrow is as impossible as pure and complete joy.
War and Peace (1865–69), bk. 15, ch. 1

15 Art is not a handicraft, it is the transmission of feeling the artist has experienced.
What is Art? (1898), ch. 19

16 I sit on a man's back, choking him and making him carry me, and yet assure myself and others that I am very sorry for him and wish to ease his lot by all possible means—except by getting off his back.
What Then Must We Do? (1886), ch. 16

17 Historians are like deaf people who go on answering questions that no one has asked them.
Quoted in "Being an Historian," *A Discovery of Australia* (Manning Clark; 1976)

18 How do peasants die?
1910. Said on his deathbed. Quoted in "The Fallacies of Hope," *Civilization* (Kenneth Clark; 1969)

19 Even in the valley of the shadow of death, two and two do not make six.
November 1910. Refusing to reconcile himself with the Russian Orthodox Church as he lay dying. Attrib.

Tolstoy, Sofya (Sonia Andreyevna Bers; 1844–1919) Russian writer

1 He would like to destroy his old diaries and to appear before his children and the public only in his patriarchal robes. His vanity is immense!
1890. *A Diary of Tolstoy's Wife* (1860–91)

2 I am a source of satisfaction to him, a nurse, a piece of furniture, a *woman*—nothing more.
1863. *A Diary of Tolstoy's Wife* (1860–91)

3 One can't live on love alone; and I am so stupid that I can do nothing but think of him.
1862. *A Diary of Tolstoy's Wife* (1860–91)

Tomlinson, Rick U.S. campaigner for space exploration

1 This shows the moon is basically right there as a stepping stone, and calling us.
Referring to the discovery of large deposits of ice at the moon's poles by the NASA space probe *Lunar Prospector*. *Guardian*, London (March 6, 1998)

Tone, Wolfe (Theobald Wolfe Tone; 1763–98) Irish nationalist

1 Whatever I have said, written, or thought on the subject of Ireland I now reiterate: looking upon the connexion with England to have been her bane I have endeavoured by every means in my power to break that connexion.
Speech at his court martial (November 10, 1798), quoted in *Wolfe Tone: Prophet of Irish Independence* (Marianne Elliott; 1989)

Tooke, Horne (John Horne Tooke, born John Horne; 1736–1812) British lawyer, clergyman, and politician

1 With all my heart. Whose wife shall it be?
Replying to the suggestion that he take a wife. Attrib.

Toole, John Kennedy (1937–69) U.S. novelist

1 Mother doesn't cook...she burns.
A Confederacy of Dunces (1980)

2 You can always tell employees of the government by the total vacancy which occupies the space where most other people have faces.
A Confederacy of Dunces (1980)

Toomer, Jean (1894–1967) U.S. writer

1 Her skin is like the dusk on the eastern horizon
O can't you see it, O can't you see it,
Her skin is like the dusk on the eastern horizon
...when the sun goes down.
"Karintha," *Cane* (1923)

2 Life is water that is being drawn off.
"Rhobert," *Cane* (1923)

Toplady, Augustus Montague (1740–78) British hymnwriter and clergyman

1 Rock of ages, cleft for me,
Let me hide myself in Thee.
"Rock of Ages" (1775), st. 1, ll. 1–2

Toscanini, Arturo (1867–1957) Italian conductor

1 God tells me how he wants this music played—and you get in his way.
Said to players in his orchestra. Remark (1930)

2 After I die I am coming back to earth as the doorkeeper of a bordello. And I won't let any one of you in.
Said in a temper to an orchestra. Quoted in *Discord: Conflict and the Making of Music* (Norman Lebrecht; 1982)

3 When I was young, I kissed my first woman, and smoked my first cigarette on the same day. Believe me, never since have I wasted any more time on tobacco.
Attrib.

4 Can't you read? The score demands *con amore*, and what are you doing? You are playing it like married men!
Criticizing the playing of an Austrian orchestra during rehearsal. Attrib.

5 Madam, there you sit with that magnificent instrument between your legs, and all you can do is *scratch* it!
Rebuking a cellist. Attrib.

6 They are for prima donnas or corpses—I am neither.
Refusing a floral wreath at the end of a performance. Attrib.

7 It's too late to apologize.
Retort to the insult "Nuts to you!" shouted at him by a player he had just ordered from the stage during rehearsal. Attrib.

Touré, Kwame (originally Stokely Carmichael; b.1941) Trinidadian-born U.S. civil rights activist

1 Black power...is a call for a black people in this country to unite, to recognize their heritage, to build a sense of community...It is a call to reject the racist institutions and values of this society.
Kwame Touré is usually credited with creating the phrase "black power." *Black Power: The Politics of Liberation in America* (1967)

2 We cannot have the oppressors telling the oppressed how to rid themselves of the oppressor.
Speech, *Times*, London (September 15, 1966)

3 Violence is American as apple pie. The only position for women in SNCC is prone.
The SNCC was the Student Nonviolent Coordinating Committee. Remark (1966), Attrib.

Touré, Sékou (Ahmed Sékou Touré; 1922–84) Guinean president

1 We, for our part, have a first and indispensable need, that of our dignity. Now, there is no dignity without freedom.... We prefer freedom in poverty to riches in slavery.
1958. *Sekou Touré's Guinea: An Experiment in Nation Building* (Ladipo Adamolekun; 1976)

Tourneur, Cyril (1575?–1626) English playwright

1 A drunkard clasp his teeth and not undo 'em,
To suffer wet damnation to run through 'em.
The Revenger's Tragedy (1607), Act 3, Scene 1

Toussaint L'Ouverture (François Dominique Toussaint; 1743–1803) Haitian revolutionary leader and general

1 I am Toussaint L'Ouverture, my name is perhaps known to you. I have undertaken vengeance.
August 29, 1793. *The Black Jacobins* (C. L. R. James; 1938)

2 In overthrowing me, you have cut down in San Domingo only the trunk of the tree of liberty. It will spring up again by the roots for they are numerous and deep.
June 1802. *The Black Jacobins* (C. L. R. James; 1938)

3 My children, France comes to make us slaves. God gave us liberty; France has no right to take it away. Burn the cities, destroy the harvests, tear up the roads with cannon, poison the wells, show the white man the hell he comes to make!
This Gilded African (Wenda Parkinson; 1978)

Townley, Preston U.S. business executive

1 There are three forces driving restructuring: first, the need to react to excess capacity; second, the need to lift profitability in the teeth of recession; and third, the availability of more competitive wage rates in the global labor pool.
Speech (September 14, 1993)

Townsend, Robert (Robert Chase Townsend; b.1920) U.S. business executive

1 First get it through your head that computers are big, expensive, fast, dumb adding-machine-typewriters. Then realize that most of the computer technicians that you're likely to meet or hire are complicators, not simplifiers.
Further Up the Organization (1984)

2 True leadership must be for the benefit of the followers, not the enrichment of the leaders. In combat, officers eat last.
Further Up the Organization (1984)

3 When you give in, give in all the way. And when you win try to win all the way so that the responsibility to make it work rests squarely on you.
Further Up the Organization (1984)

4 20% of any group of salesmen will always produce 90% of the sales.
Up the Organization (1970)

5 Accountants *are* people.
Up the Organization (1970)

6 All decisions should be made as low as possible in the organization. The Charge of the Light Brigade was ordered by an officer who wasn't there looking at the territory.
Up the Organization (1970)

7 A personnel man with his arm around an employee is like a treasurer with his hand in the till.
Up the Organization (1970)

8 A premature announcement of what you are going to do unsettles potential supporters, gives opponents time to construct real and imaginary defenses and tends to ensure failure.
Up the Organization (1970)

9 A sure sign of frustration is putting on weight. Watch for it on the people who work for you. Remove the cause and the weight will come back off.
Up the Organization (1970)

10 Big companies are small companies that succeeded.
Up the Organization (1970)

11 Fire the whole purchasing department. They'd hire Einstein and then turn down his requisition for a blackboard.
Up the Organization (1970)

12 In a profit squeeze, management will come up with very creative reasons for changing the accounting system.
Up the Organization (1970)

13 Some meetings should be long and leisurely. Some should be mercifully brief. A good way to handle the latter is to hold the meeting with everybody standing up. The meetees won't believe you at first. Then they...can't wait to get the meeting over with.
Up the Organization (1970)

14 There are people who borrow your watch to tell you what time it is and then walk off with it.
Up the Organization (1970)

15 Titles are a form of psychic compensation.
Up the Organization (1970)

Townshend, Pete (Peter Dennis Blandford Townshend; b.1945) British rock musician

1 Hope I die before I get old.
Song lyric. "My Generation" (1965)

2 Plays by intuition, the digit counters fall.
That deaf, dumb and blind kid sure plays a mean pinball.
Song lyric. "Pinball Wizard," *Tommy* (1969)

Toynbee, Arnold (Arnold Joseph Toynbee; 1889–1975) British historian

1 At bottom, Nationalism and Communism are variations of the same perverse theme: man's self-centred worship of himself.
"What are the Criteria for Comparisons between Religions?," *Christianity Among the Religions of the World* (1958), pt. 1

2 Hinduism, if I have read it right, initially seeks to save the absoluteness of God at the cost of His goodness. The Judaic religions intuitively try to save His goodness at the cost of His absoluteness. And neither solution has been a true solution.
"What are the Criteria for Comparisons Between Religions?," *Christianity Among the Religions of the World* (1958), pt. 1

3 Plato means by "myth" a form of expression to which one turns when the resources of the intellect have been exhausted.
"What are the Criteria for Comparisons between Religions?," *Christianity Among the Religions of the World* (1958), pt. 1

4 Primitive religion is concerned, as I take it, not only with beliefs, but wholly with practice.
"What are the Criteria for Comparisons Between Religions?," *Christianity Among the Religions of the World* (1958), pt. 1

5 The equation of religion with belief is rather recent.
"What are the Criteria for Comparisons Between Religions?," *Christianity Among the Religions of the World* (1958), pt. 1

6 Death is the price paid by life for an enhancement of the complexity of a live organism's structure.
Life After Death (co-written with Arthur Koestler and others; 1975)

7 We have been God-like in our planned breeding of our domesticated plants and animals, but we have been rabbit-like in our unplanned breeding of ourselves.
National Observer (June 10, 1963)

8 Civilization is a movement, not a condition; it is a voyage, not a harbour.
Reader's Digest (October 1958)

9 The 20th century will be remembered chiefly, not as an age of political conflicts and technical inventions, but as an age in which human society dared to think of the health of the whole human race as a practical objective.
Attrib.

Tracy, Spencer (Spencer Bonaventure Tracy; 1900–67) U.S. film actor

1 There were times my pants were so thin I could sit on a dime and tell if it was heads or tails.
Attrib.

2 This is a movie, not a lifeboat.
Defending his demand for equal billing with Katharine Hepburn. Attrib.

3 Days off.
Explaining what he looked for in a script. Attrib.

Traherne, Thomas (1637–74) English poet and clergyman

1 You never enjoy the world aright, till the sea itself floweth in your veins, till you are clothed with the heavens, and crowned with the stars: and perceive yourself to be the sole heir of the whole world, and more than so, because men are in it who are every one sole heirs as well as you. Till you can sing and rejoice and delight in God, as misers do in gold, and kings in sceptres, you never enjoy the world.
Centuries of Meditations (1908), Cent. 1, pt. 29

Trajan (Marcus Ulpius Trajanus; 53?–117) Roman emperor

1 Anyone who denies that he is a Christian and actually proves this by worshipping our gods is pardoned on repentance, no matter how suspect his past may have been.
112. Quoted in Letters, Trajan with Pliny, *The Early Christians* (E. Arnold; 1970)

Tramp, The U.S. cartoon character

1 When you're footloose and collar-free, well, you take nothing but the best.
Lady and the Tramp (1955)

Travis, Dempsey J. (Dempsey Jerome Travis; b.1920) U.S. business executive and banker

1 I think every black entrepreneur has to have a whole lot of social worker in him.
Quoted in "Dempsey J. Travis: Mortgage Banker," *Getting It Together: Black Businessmen in America* (John Seder and Berkeley G. Burrell; 1971)

Travis, Merle (1917–83) U.S. country guitarist, singer, and composer

1 Sixteen tons, what do you get?
Another day older and deeper in debt.
Saint Peter, don't you call me 'cause I can't go.
I owe my soul to the company store.
Song lyric. Associated with singer Tennessee Ernie Ford. "Sixteen Tons" (1947)

Tree, Herbert Beerbohm, Sir (originally Herbert Draper Beerbohm; 1853–1917) British actor and theatrical impresario

1 Take that black box away. I can't act in front of it.
Referring to the presence of the camera while performing in a silent movie. Remark (1916), quoted in *Hollywood: The Pioneers* (Kevin Brownlow; 1979)

2 A committee should consist of three men, two of whom are absent.
Attrib. *Beerbohm Tree* (Hesketh Pearson; 1956)

3 I was born old and get younger every day. At present I am sixty years young.
Attrib. *Beerbohm Tree* (Hesketh Pearson; 1956)

4 The only man who wasn't spoilt by being lionized was Daniel.
Attrib. *Beerbohm Tree* (Hesketh Pearson; 1956)

5 My poor fellow, why not carry a watch?
Remark to a man carrying a grandfather clock. Attrib. *Beerbohm Tree* (Hesketh Pearson; 1956)

Tresckow, Henning von (1901–44) German general

1 The worth of a man is certain only if he is prepared to sacrifice his own life for his convictions.
1945. Henning von Tresckow plotted against Adolf Hitler. These words are from his suicide note. Attrib.

Trevelyan, G. M. (George Macaulay Trevelyan; 1876–1962) British historian

1 It is still too early to form a final judgement on the French Revolution.
Speech, National Book League (May 30, 1945)

2 Education...has produced a vast population able to read but unable to distinguish what is worth reading.
English Social History (1942), ch. 18

3 Disinterested intellectual curiosity is the life blood of real civilisation.
English Social History (1942), Preface

Trevor, William (William Trevor Cox; b.1928) Irish novelist, short-story writer, and playwright

1 He travelled in order to come home.
Matilda's England (1995)

2 The nice thing about having memories is that you can choose.
Matilda's England (1995)

Trilling, Lionel (1905–75) U.S. literary critic

1 The poet may be used as the barometer, but let us not forget he is also part of the weather.
"The Sense of the Past," *The Liberal Imagination* (1950)

Trinder, Tommy (Thomas Edward Trinder; 1909–89) British comedian and film actor

1 They're overpaid, overfed, oversexed and over here.
Expression associated with but not originated by Tommy Trinder, referring to U.S. troops in Britain during World War II. Attrib.

Tristan, Flora (1803–44) French feminist writer and revolutionary Socialist

1 Prostitution is a blight on the human race...for if you men did not impose chastity on women as a necessary virtue while refusing to practice it yourselves, they would not be rejected by society for yielding to the sentiments of their hearts, nor would seduced, deceived, and abandoned girls be forced into prostitution.
Promenades dans Londres (1840?)

Trollope, Anthony (1815–82) British novelist

Quotations about Trollope

1 He has a gross and repulsive face but appears *bon enfant* when you talk to him. But he is the dullest Briton of them all.
Henry James (1843–1916) U.S. born British writer and critic. Letter to his family (November 1, 1875)

Quotations by Trollope

2 The comic almanacs give us dreadful pictures of January and February; but, in truth, the months which should be made to look gloomy in England are March and April. Let no man boast himself that he has got through the perils of winter till at least the seventh of May.
Doctor Thorne (1858), ch. 47

3 With many women I doubt whether there be any more effectual way of touching their hearts than ill-using them and then confessing it. If you wish to get the sweetest fragrance from the herb at your feet, tread on it and bruise it.
Miss Mackenzie (1865), ch. 10

4 We cannot bring ourselves to believe it possible that a foreigner should in any respect be wiser than ourselves. If any such point out to us our follies, we at once claim those follies as the special evidences of our wisdom.
Orley Farm (1862), ch. 18

5 As for conceit, what man will do any good who is not conceited? Nobody holds a good opinion of a man who has a low opinion of himself.
Orley Farm (1862), ch. 22

6 No man thinks there is much ado about nothing when the ado is about himself.
The Bertrams (1859), ch. 27

7 Those who have courage to love should have courage to suffer.
The Bertrams (1859), ch. 27

8 I doubt whether any girl would be satisfied with her lover's mind if she knew the whole of it.
The Small House at Allington (1864), ch. 4

9 Contentment and fulfilment don't make for very good fiction.
Attrib. *Times,* London (June 25, 1994)

Trollope, Frances (originally Frances Milton; 1780–1863) British novelist and travel writer

1 I never saw any people who appeared to live so much without amusement as the Cincinnatians. Billiards are forbidden by law, so are cards...They have no public balls...They have no concerts. They have no dinner parties.
Domestic Manners of the Americans (1832), ch. 8

2 The religious severity of Philadelphian manners is in nothing more conspicuous than in the number of chains thrown across the streets on a Sunday to prevent horses and carriages passing.
Domestic Manners of the Americans (1832), ch. 26

3 Situated on an island...it rises, like Venice, from the sea, and like that fairest of cities in the days of her glory, receives into its lap tribute of all the riches of the earth.
Referring to New York City. *Domestic Manners of the Americans* (1832), ch. 30

Trollope, Joanna (b.1943) British writer

1 Jack's own Jill goes up the hill
To Murree or Chakrata,
Jack remains or dies in the plains
And Jill remarries soon after.
Murree or Chakrata were towns in northermost British India, now Pakistan. *Britannia's Daughters* (1983), ch. 6

2 Isabella Bird comes closest to admitting a passion for travel for travel's sake—her husband declared "I have only one formidable rival in Isabella's affections and that is the high tableland of Central Asia".
Isabella Bird (1831–1904), sent abroad for her health, became an inveterate traveler. *Britannia's Daughters* (1983), ch. 7

Trompenaars, Fons (b.1952) Dutch management consultant and author

1 When two values work with one another they are mutually facilitating and enhancing.
Riding the Waves of Culture (co-written with Charles Hampden-Turner; 1993)

Trotsky, Leon (Lev Davidovich Bronstein; 1879–1940) Russian revolutionary leader

1 Old age is the most unexpected of all the things that happen to a man.
Diary in Exile (May 8, 1935)

2 Revolution by its very nature is sometimes compelled to take in more territory than it is capable of holding. Retreats are possible—when there is territory to retreat from.
Diary in Exile (February 15, 1935)

3 The revolution does not choose its paths: it made its first steps toward victory under the belly of a Cossack's horse.
History of the Russian Revolution (1931), vol. 1, ch. 7

4 Revolutions are always verbose.
History of the Russian Revolution (1933), vol. 2, ch. 12

5 Insurrection is an art, and like all arts it has its laws.
History of the Russian Revolution (1933), vol. 3, ch. 6

6 If we had had more time for discussion we should probably have made a great many more mistakes.
My Life (1930)

7 For us, the tasks of education in socialism were closely integrated with those of fighting. Ideas that enter the mind under fire remain there securely and for ever.
My Life (1930), ch. 35

8 It was the supreme expression of the mediocrity of the apparatus that Stalin himself rose to his position.
My Life (1930), ch. 40

9 The dictatorship of the Communist Party is maintained by recourse to every form of violence.
Terrorism and Communism (1924)

10 An ally has to be watched just like an enemy.
Attrib. *Expansion and Coexistence* (A. Ulam; 1941)

11 Patriotism to the Soviet state is a revolutionary duty, whereas patriotism to a bourgeois state is treachery.
Attrib.

12 The end may justify the means as long as there is something that justifies the end.
Attrib.

Trotter, Reginald George (1888–1951) Canadian historian

1 Much Canadian history can only be read aright with one eye on the history of the United States.
Canadian Historical Review (1924)

Trotter, Wilfred (Wilfred Batten Lewis Trotter; 1872–1939) British surgeon and sociologist

1 Mr Anaesthetist, if the patient can keep awake, surely you can.
Attrib. *Lancet* (1965), 2:1340

Troubridge, Laura, Lady (Laura Gurney; d.1946) British writer

1 A bad woman always has something she regards as a curse—a real bit of goodness hidden away somewhere.
The Millionaire (1907)

Troubridge, T. St Vincent, Sir (1895–1963) British army officer

1 There is an iron curtain across Europe.
Also said by Winston Churchill and Joseph Goebbels. *Sunday Empire News* (October 21, 1945)

Troup, Bobby (1919–99) U.S. songwriter

1 If you ever plan to motor west,

Travel my way, take the highway, that's the best,
Get your kicks on Route 66.
"Route 66" (1946)

Trudeau, Garry (Garretson Beckman Trudeau; b.1948) U.S. cartoonist

1 Satire picks a one-sided fight, and the more its intended target reacts, the more the practitioner gains the advantage.
Wall Street Journal (January 20, 1993)

2 I've been trying for some time now to develop a lifestyle that doesn't require my presence.
Referring to avoiding parties in Washington, D.C. Quoted in *Ear on Washington* (Diana McLellan; 1982)

Trudeau, Pierre (Joseph Philippe Pierre Ives Elliott Trudeau; b.1919) Canadian statesman

1 The state has no business in the bedrooms of the nation.
New York Times (June 16, 1968)

2 Living next to you is in some ways like sleeping with an elephant. No matter how friendly and even-tempered is thc beast, one is affected by every twitch and grunt.
Referring to the United States. *New York Times* (March 26, 1969)

Truffaut, François (1932–84) French film director and screenwriter

1 Airing one's dirty linen never makes for a masterpiece.
Bed and Board (1972)

2 An actor is never so great as when he reminds you of an animal—falling like a cat, lying like a dog, moving like a fox.
Attrib.

Truman, Harry S. (1884–1972) U.S. president

Quotations about Truman

1 The captain with the mighty heart.
Dean Acheson (1893–1971) U.S. lawyer and statesman. *Present at the Creation* (1970)

Quotations by Truman

2 I want peace and I'm willing to fight for it.
Diary entry (May 22, 1945), quoted in *Off the Record* (Robert H. Ferrell; 1980)

3 I never think of anyone as the President but Mr. Roosevelt.
Written nearly six months after becoming president following Franklin D. Roosevelt's death on April 12, 1945. Letter to Eleanor Roosevelt (1945), quoted in *Off the Record* (Robert H. Ferrell; 1980)

4 And what I want to say to historians is that any Monday morning quarterback can win a ball game next Monday, but he can't do it on Saturday.
Press conference, Washington, D.C. (April 27, 1952)

5 Last night the moon, the stars and all the planets fell on me. If you fellows pray, pray for me.
Referring to President Franklin D. Roosevelt's death the previous day. Said to reporters (April 13, 1945)

6 Every segment of our population, and every individual, has a right to expect from his government a fair deal.
Speech to Congress (September 6, 1945)

7 Three things ruin a man—power, money, and women. I never wanted power, I never had any money, and the only woman in my life is up at the house right now.
Statement to reporters on his 75th birthday (May 8, 1959)

8 I never give them hell. I just tell the truth and they think it is hell.
Look (April 3, 1956)

9 If we see that Germany is winning the war we ought to help Russia, and if Russia is winning we ought to help Germany, and in that way let them kill as many as possible.
On the invasion of Russia by Germany during World War II. *New York Times* (July 24, 1941)

10 A politician is a man who understands government, and it takes a politician to run a government. A statesman is a politician who's been dead ten or fifteen years.
New York World Telegram and Sun (April 12, 1958)

11 It's a recession when your neighbor loses his job; it's a depression when you lose yours.
April 13, 1958. *Observer*, London (April 13, 958), "Sayings of the Week"

12 The President spends most of his time kissing people on the cheek in order to get them to do what they ought to do without getting kissed.
Observer, London (February 6, 1949), "Sayings of the Week"

13 It was said in the First World War that the French fought for their country, the British fought for freedom of the seas, and the Americans fought for souvenirs.
Quoted in *Harry S. Truman* (Margaret Truman; 1973)

14 A leader is a man who has the ability to get other people to do what they don't want to do, and like it.
Quoted in *Key Management Ideas* (Stuart Crainer; 1996)

15 Do your duty, and history will do you justice.
Attrib. *Memorial tribute to Truman, U.S. House of Representatives* (Edward T. Roybal; January 3, 1973)

16 It is ignorance that causes most mistakes. The man who sits here ought to know his American history, at least.
Referring to the office of President of the United States. Attrib. *Presidential Transitions* (Laurin L. Henry; 1960)

17 The buck stops here.
Motto kept on his desk during his term as president. Attrib. *The Man From Missouri* (Alfred Steinberg; 1962)

18 Give me a one-handed economist! All my economists say, "on the one hand...on the other."
Attrib.

Trumbull, John (1750–1831) U.S. lawyer and poet

1 No man e'er felt the halter draw,
With good opinion of the law.
M'Fingal (1775–82), can. 3, ll. 489–490

Trump, Donald (Donald John Trump; b.1946) U.S. real estate developer

1 I'm not running for president, but if I did I'd win.
October 1987. *Times*, London (October 29, 1987)

2 Deals are my art form. Other people paint beautifully on canvas or write wonderful poetry. I like making deals,

preferably big deals. That's how I get my kicks.
Trump: the Art of the Deal (co-written with Tony Schwartz; 1987)

3 In the end, you're measured not by how much you undertake but by what you finally accomplish.
Trump: the Art of the Deal (co-written with Tony Schwartz; 1987)

4 I wasn't satisfied just to earn a good living. I was looking to make a statement.
Trump: the Art of the Deal (co-written with Tony Schwartz; 1987)

5 You can create excitement, you can do wonderful promotion and get all kinds of press...But if you don't deliver the goods, people will eventually catch on.
Trump: the Art of the Deal (co-written with Tony Schwartz; 1987)

Truth, Sojourner (Isabella Truth; 1797?–1883) U.S. abolitionist, women's rights crusader, and preacher

1 Den dat little man in black dar, he say women can'y have as much rights as men, 'cause Christ wasn't a woman! Where did your Christ come from? From God and a woman! Man had notin' to do wid Him.
Speech to the Akron, Ohio convention (1851)

2 Ef women want any rights more'n dey's got, why don't dey jes' take 'em, an' not be talkin' about it?
1850. Speech at National Women's Rights Convention, *Narrative of Sojourner Truth* (1878)

3 If de fust woman God ever made was strong enough to turn the world upside down, all 'lone, dese togedder ought to be able to turn it back and get it right side up again, and now dey is asking to do it, de men better let em.
1851. Speech at Women's Rights Convention, Akron, Ohio, *Narrative of Sojourner Truth* (1878)

Tsvetaeva, Marina (Marina Ivanovna Tsvetaeva Efron; 1892–1941) Russian poet

Quotations about Tsvetaeva

1 Tsvetaeva was a woman with an actively male soul, decisive, militant, indomitable.
Boris Pasternak (1890–1960) Russian poet and novelist. *An Essay in Autobiography* (Manya Harari, tr.; 1957), ch. 5

Quotations by Tsvetaeva

2 What is life like with another,—
Simpler, no?—The stroke of an oar—
Did the memory of me soon
Fade away, a floating island.
"An Attempt at Jealousy" (Peter Norman, tr.; 1924), ll. 1–4, quoted in *Leopard II: Turning the Page* (Christopher MacLehose, ed.; 1993)

3 What is life like with one of a
Hundred thousand—you who have known Lilith!

Are you sated with new market
Goods? Now to witchery grown cold, and
Without a sixth sense, what is life
Like with a woman of this world?
"An Attempt at Jealousy" (Peter Norman, tr.; 1924), ll. 39–44, quoted in *Leopard II: Turning the Page* (Christopher MacLehose, ed.; 1993)

4 Homesickness! that
long exposed weariness!
"Homesickness" (1934), l. 1, quoted in *Marina Tsvetaeva: Selected Poems* (Elaine Feinstein, tr.; 1993)

5 I won't be seduced by the thought of
my native language, its milky call.
How can it matter in what tongue I
am misunderstood by whoever I meet?
"Homesickness" (1934), ll. 17–20, quoted in *Marina Tsvetaeva: Selected Poems* (Elaine Feinstein, tr.; 1993)

6 I didn't want this, not
this (but listen, quietly,
to want is what bodies do
and now we are ghosts only).
"Poem of the End" (1924), sect. 6, ll 1–4, quoted in *Marina Tsvetaeva: Selected Poems* (Elaine Feinstein, tr.; 1993)

7 What is this gypsy passion for separation, this
readiness to rush off when we've just met?
"What is this gypsy passion for separation" (1915), quoted in *Marina Tsvetaeva: Selected Poems* (Elaine Feinstein, tr.; 1993)

8 Where does this tenderness come from?
These are not the first curls I
have stroked slowly and lips I
have known are darker than yours.
"Where does this tenderness come from?" (1916), quoted in *Marina Tsvetaeva: Selected Poems* (Elaine Feinstein, tr.; 1993)

Tubman, Harriet (Araminta Ross; 1820?–1913) U.S. abolitionist

1 Dere's *two* things I've got a *right* to, and dese are, Death or Liberty—one or tother I mean to have.
Scenes in the Life of Harriet Tubman (Sarah Bradford; 1869)

Tuchman, Barbara (originally Barbara Wertheim; 1912–89) U.S. historian and writer

1 Dead battles, like dead generals, hold the military mind in their dead grip and Germans, no less than other peoples, prepare for the last war.
The Guns of August (1962), ch. 2

Tucholsky, Kurt (1890–1935) German philosopher

1 Human folly is international.
Quoted in "Selected Aphorisms," *Kurt Tucholsky. The Ironic Sentimentalist* (Bryan P. Grenville; 1981)

2 The condition of all human ethics can be summed up in two sentences: We ought to. But we don't.
Quoted in "Selected Aphorisms," *Kurt Tucholsky. The Ironic Sentimentalist* (Bryan P. Grenville; 1981)

3 The cruelty of most people is lack of imagination, their brutality is ignorance.
Quoted in "Selected Aphorisms," *Kurt Tucholsky. The Ironic Sentimentalist* (Bryan P. Grenville; 1981)

4 The intellect is part of life—not its counterpart.
Quoted in "Selected Aphorisms," *Kurt Tucholsky. The Ironic Sentimentalist* (Bryan P. Grenville; 1981)

5 To live is to choose and you should choose what is attainable and adequate. Ignore everything else.
Quoted in "Selected Aphorisms," *Kurt Tucholsky. The Ironic Sentimentalist* (Bryan P. Grenville; 1981)

6 In Europe people have thought a lot about the war. The English thought about it before, the French during the War, and the Germans after the War.
Referring to World War I (1914–18). Quoted in "Selected Aphorisms," *Kurt Tucholsky. The Ironic Sentimentalist* (Bryan P. Grenville; 1981)

7 Once in Spain a society for the protection of animals was founded which was hard up for money. They put on some large bullfights.
Quoted in *The Jingle Bell Principle* (Miroslav Holub; 1992)

Tucker, Laurie U.S. business executive

1 The glory of the Internet is that it provides global presence, and it's the great equalizer.
Quoted in *Opening Digital Markets* (Walid Mougayar; 1997)

Tucker, Sophie (Sophie Abuza; 1884–1966) Russian-born U.S. singer and entertainer

1 Keep breathing.
Her reply, at the age of 80, when asked the secret of her longevity. Remark (1964)

2 From birth to eighteen, a girl needs good parents. From eighteen to thirty-five, she needs good looks. From thirty-five to fifty-five, good personality. From fifty-five on, she needs good cash.
Remark (1953), quoted in *Sophie* (Michael Friedland; 1978)

3 The Last of the Red-Hot Mamas.
Description of herself used on the billing for her performances. Attrib.

Tuke, Samuel, Sir (1620?–74) English Royalist and playwright

1 He is a fool who thinks by force or skill
To turn the current of a woman's will.
The Adventures of Five Hours (1663), Act 5, Scene 3

Tupper, Martin Farquhar (1810–89) British writer

1 A good book is the best of friends, the same today and for ever.
"Of Reading," *Proverbial Philosophy: A Book of Thoughts and Arguments, Originally Treated* (1838)

Tuqan, Fadwa (b.1917) Palestinian poet

1 Why did my country become a gateway
to hell? Since when are apples bitter?
When did moonlight stop bathing orchards?
"Face Lost in the Wilderness," *Modern Arabic Poetry* (Salma Khadra Jayyusi, ed.; 1987), ll. 32–34

Turell, Jane (Jane Colman Turell; 1708–35) U.S. poet

1 Dauntless you undertake th' unequal strife,
And raise the dead virtue by your verse to life.
A woman's pen strikes the curs'd serpent's head,
And lays the monster gasping, if not dead.
"On reading 'The Warning' by Mrs Singer" (1735)

Turgenev, Ivan (Ivan Sergeyevich Turgenev; 1818–83) Russian novelist

1 Illness isn't the only thing that spoils the appetite.
A Month in the Country (1855)

2 I agree with no man's opinion. I have some of my own.
Fathers and Sons (1862), ch. 13

3 The temerity to believe in nothing.
Fathers and Sons (1862), ch. 14

4 Go and try to disprove death. Death will disprove you, and that's all!
Fathers and Sons (1862), ch. 27

5 Whatever a man prays for, he prays for a miracle. Every prayer reduces itself to this: "Great God, grant that twice two be not four."
"Prayer," *Poems in Prose* (1881)

Turing, Alan (Alan Mathison Turing; 1912–54) British mathematician

1 No, I'm not interested in developing a powerful brain. All I'm after is just a mediocre brain, something like the President of the American Telephone and Telegraph Company.
1943. Overheard in the cafeteria of the Bell Laboratories Corporation. Quoted in *Alan Turing: The Enigma of Intelligence* (Andrew Hodges; 1983)

Turlington, Christie (b.1969) U.S. fashion model

1 People don't want to like you. You're young and beautiful and successful.
Referring to being a model. Quoted in *Model: The Ugly Business of Beautiful Women* (Michael Gross; 1995)

Turnbull, Margaret (d.1942) Scottish-born U.S. writer and playwright

1 No man is responsible for his father. That is entirely his mother's affair.
Alabaster Lamps (1925)

2 When a man confronts catastrophe on the road, he looks in his purse—but a woman looks in her mirror.
The Left Lady (1926)

Turner, Henry M. (Henry McNeal Turner; 1834–1915) U.S. politician and cleric

1 The black man cannot protect a country, if the country doesn't protect him; and if, tomorrow, a war should arise, I would not raise a musket to defend a country where my manhood is denied.
Speech in the House of Representatives (September 3, 1868), quoted in *A Documentary History of the Negro People in the United States* (Herbert Aptheker; 1951), vol. 2

Turner, J. M. W. (Joseph Mallord William Turner; 1775–1851) British painter

1 I've lost one of my children this week.
His customary remark following the sale of one of his paintings. Attrib.

2 My business is to paint not what I know, but what I see.
Responding to a criticism of the fact that he had painted no portholes on the ships in a view of Plymouth, England. Attrib.

Turner, Nat (1800–31) U.S. popular religious leader

1 I had a vision—and I saw white spirits and black spirits engaged in battle, and the sun was darkened—the thunder rolled in the Heavens, and blood flowed in streams—and I heard a voice saying, "Such is your luck, such you are called to see; and let it come rough or smooth, you must surely bear it."
The Confessions of Nat Turner, the leader of the late insurrection in Southampton, Va. (1831)

Turner, Ted (Robert Edward Turner III; b.1938) U.S. media entrepreneur

1 Know what I want them to put on my tombstone? Do not disturb.
Evening Standard, London (December 14, 1988)

2 I have eight ranches and three plantations. If you have an olive, you want an olive tree.
New York Times (November 24, 1996)

3 I've been learning how to give. It's something you have to keep working on, because people like money the way they do their homes and their dogs.
New York Times (September 20, 1997)

4 We're gonna stay on until the end of the world. And when that day comes we'll cover it, play *Nearer My God to Thee* and sign off.
Referring to CNN television. Quoted in *The Corporate Warriors* (Douglas R. Ramsay; 1988)

Tusser, Thomas (1524–80) English farmer and writer

1 Sweet April showers
Do spring May flowers.
"April's Husbandry," *Hundredth Good Pointes of Husbandrie* (1557)

2 February, fill the dyke
With what thou dost like.
"February's Husbandry," *Hundredth Good Pointes of Husbandrie* (1557)

3 Seek home for rest,
For home is best.
"Instructions to Housewifery," *Hundredth Good Pointes of Husbandrie* (1557)

4 At Christmas play and make good cheer,
For Christmas comes but once a year.
"The Farmer's Daily Diet," *Hundredth Good Pointes of Husbandrie* (1557)

Tutu, Desmond, Archbishop (Desmond Mpilo Tutu; b.1931) South African clergyman and civil rights activist

1 Beware when you take on the Church of God. Others have tried and have bitten the dust.
Remark (April 1987)

2 It seems that the British Government sees black people as expendable.
Speech (June 1986)

3 If God be for us who can be against us?
Nobel Peace Prize speech of acceptance, *African Forum* (December 10, 1984), vol. 2, no 1

4 It is an incredible feeling, like falling in love.
Referring to voting in the first multiracial elections in South Africa. *Independent*, London (April 27, 1994)

5 We don't want apartheid liberalized. We want it dismantled. You can't improve something that is intrinsically evil.
Observer, London (March 10, 1985), "Sayings of the Week"

6 Improbable as it is, unlikely as it is, we are being set up as a beacon of hope for the world.
Times, London (October 11, 1994)

7 The paradox in South Africa is that after all these years of white racism, oppression and injustice there is hardly any anti-white feeling.
Quoted in *Black Sash: The Beginning of a Bridge in South Africa* (Kathryn Spink; 1991), Foreword

8 If we are to say that religion cannot be concerned with politics then we are really saying that there is a substantial part of human life in which God's writ does not run. If it is not God's, then whose is it? Who is in charge if not the God and Father of our Lord Jesus Christ?
The Words of Desmond Tutu (Naomi Tutu, ed.; 1989)

9 I want apartheid destroyed, not reformed.
The Words of Desmond Tutu (Naomi Tutu, ed.; 1989)

10 Nothing is too much trouble for love.
The Words of Desmond Tutu (Naomi Tutu, ed.; 1989)

11 White South Africans are not demons. White South Africans are ordinary human beings. Most of them are very scared human beings, and I ask the audience, "Wouldn't you be scared if you were outnumbered five to one?"
The Words of Desmond Tutu (Naomi Tutu, ed.; 1989)

12 Women, we need you to give us back our faith in humanity.
The Words of Desmond Tutu (Naomi Tutu, ed.; 1989)

Tutuola, Amos (1920–97) Nigerian novelist and short-story writer

1 One who wears only an apron is merely tying himself with a rope.
The Witch-Herbalist of the Remote Town (1981)

Tuwim, Julian (1894–1953) Polish poet

1 There are two kinds of blood, the blood that flows in the veins and the blood that flows out of them.
The Polish Jews (1984)

2 The brain is the means by which we think we think.
Quoted in *The Jingle Bell Principle* (Miroslav Holub; 1992)

Twain, Mark (Samuel Langhorne Clemens; 1835–1910) U.S. writer and humorist

Quotations about Twain

1 The most beautiful prose paragraph yet written by any American.

Harold Bloom (b.1930) U.S. literary critic and author. Referring to the opening of chapter 19 of Mark Twain's *The Adventures of Huckleberry Finn* (1884). *The Western Canon* (1991)

2 The average American loves his family. If he has any love left over for some other person, he generally selects Mark Twain.
Thomas Alva Edison (1847–1931) U.S. inventor. Attrib.

3 All modern American literature comes from one book by Mark Twain called *Huckleberry Finn*.
Ernest Hemingway (1899–1961) U.S. writer. *The Adventures of Huckleberry Finn* was published in 1884. *Green Hills of Africa* (1935), ch. 1

4 Mark Twain and I are in the same position. We have to put things in such a way as to make people, who would otherwise hang us, believe that we are joking.
George Bernard Shaw (1856–1950) Irish playwright. Attrib.

Quotations by Twain

5 Always do right. This will gratify some people, and astonish the rest.
Card to Greenpoint Presbyterian Church, Brooklyn (February 16, 1901)

6 Baseball is the very symbol, the outward and visible expression of the drive and push and rush and struggle of the raging, tearing, booming nineteenth century.
Said at a banquet in honor of baseball players returning from an around-the-world tour. Speech, New York (April 8, 1889)

7 And so I drink long life to the boys who plowed a new equator round the globe stealing bases on their bellies.
Toast proposed at a banquet in honor of baseball players returning from an around-the-world tour. Speech, New York (April 8, 1889)

8 Whenever the literary German dives into a sentence, that is the last you are going to see of him till he emerges on the other side of his Atlantic with his verb in his mouth.
A Connecticut Yankee at King Arthur's Court (1889)

9 Soap and education are not as sudden as a massacre, but they are more deadly in the long run.
"Facts Concerning the Recent Resignation," *A Curious Dream* (1872)

10 Surgeons and anatomists see no beautiful women in all their lives, but only a ghastly stack of bones with Latin names to them, and a network of nerves and muscles and tissues inflamed by disease.
Alta Californian (May 28, 1867)

11 The Germans are exceedingly fond of Rhine wines; they are put in small, slender bottles, and are considered pleasant beverage. One tells them from vinegar by the label.
A Tramp Abroad (1880)

12 I can understand German as well as the maniac that invented it, but I talk it best through an interpreter.
A Tramp Abroad (1880)

13 My philological studies have satisfied me that a gifted person should learn English (barring spelling and pronouncing) in thirty hours, French in thirty days, and German in thirty years.
"The Awful German Language," *A Tramp Abroad* (1880)

14 The noblest work of God? Man. Who found it out? Man.
Autobiography (1924)

15 That's the main charm of heaven—there's all kinds here—which wouldn't be the case if you let the preachers tell it.
Captain Stormfield's Visit to Heaven (1909)

16 Truth is the most valuable thing we have. Let us economize it.
Following the Equator (1897), ch. 7

17 It is by the goodness of God that in our country we have those three unspeakably precious things: freedom of speech, freedom of conscience, and the prudence never to practice either of them.
Following the Equator (1897), ch. 20

18 Man is the only animal that blushes. Or needs to.
Following the Equator (1897), ch. 27

19 There are several good protections against temptations, but the surest is cowardice.
Following the Equator (1897), ch. 36

20 It takes your enemy and your friend, working together, to hurt you to the heart; the one to slander you and the other to get the news to you.
Following the Equator (1897), ch. 45

21 When people do not respect us we are sharply offended; yet deep down in his heart no man much respects himself.
Following the Equator (1897), ch. 29

22 That astonishing Chicago—a city where they are always rubbing the lamps and fetching up the genii, and contriving and achieving new impossibilities.
Life on the Mississippi (1883)

23 Something that everybody wants to have read and nobody wants to read.
Definition of a literary classic. *New York Journal* (November 20, 1900)

24 The report of my death was an exaggeration.
Usually quoted as "Reports of my death have been greatly exaggerated." Note to the London office of the *New York Journal* on learning that his obituary had been published there. *New York Journal* (June 2, 1897)

25 Familiarity breeds contempt—and children.
Notebooks (1935)

26 Good breeding consists in concealing how much we think of ourselves and how little we think of the other person.
Notebooks (1935)

27 The radical invents the views. When he has worn them out, the conservative adopts them.
Notebooks (1935)

28 All say, "How hard it is that we have to die"—a strange complaint to come from the mouths of people who have had to live.
Pudd'nhead Wilson (1894)

29 Adam and Eve had many advantages, but the principal one was that they escaped teething.
Pudd'nhead Wilson (1894), ch. 4

30 When angry, count four; when very angry, swear.
Pudd'nhead Wilson (1894), ch. 10

31 Adam was but human—this explains it all. He did not want

the apple for the apple's sake, he wanted it only because it was forbidden.
"Pudd'nhead Wilson's Calendar," *Pudd'nhead Wilson* (1894), ch. 2

32 Cauliflower is nothing but cabbage with a college education.
"Pudd'nhead Wilson's Calendar," *Pudd'nhead Wilson* (1894), ch. 5

33 All scenery in California requires distance to give it its charm.
Roughing It (1872)

34 Morals are an acquirement—like music, like a foreign language, like piety, poker, paralysis—no man is born with them.
Seventieth Birthday (1907)

35 There was things which he stretched, but mainly he told the truth.
The Adventures of Huckleberry Finn (1884), ch. 1

36 You can't pray a lie—I found that out.
The Adventures of Huckleberry Finn (1884), ch. 3

37 Yes—en I's rich now, come to look at it. I owns mysef, en I's wuth eight hund'd dollars. I wisht I had de money, I wouldn' want no mo'.
Said by Jim. *The Adventures of Huckleberry Finn* (1884), ch. 8

38 It was fifteen minutes before I could work myself up to go and humble myself to a nigger—but I done it, and I warn't ever sorry for it afterwards, neither.
Describing Huckleberry Finn's befriending of Jim, his accomplice on many adventures. *The Adventures of Huckleberry Finn* (1884), ch. 15

39 It was enough to make a body ashamed of the human race.
Referring to the fraudulent display of grief put on by the "King" and the "Duke" on hearing the news of Peter Wilks' death. *The Adventures of Huckleberry Finn* (1884), ch. 24

40 That's always the way; it don't make no difference whether you do right or wrong, a person's conscience ain't got no sense, and it just goes for him *anyway*.
The Adventures of Huckleberry Finn (1884), ch. 33

41 But I reckon I got to light out for the Territory ahead of the rest, because Aunt Sally she's going to adopt me and sivilize me and I can't stand it. I been there before.
Huckleberry Finn's closing words. *The Adventures of Huckleberry Finn* (1884), ch. 43

42 I must have a prodigious quantity of mind; it takes me as much as a week, sometimes, to make it up.
The Innocents Abroad (1869), ch. 7

43 They spell it Vinci and pronounce it Vinchy; foreigners always spell better than they pronounce.
The Innocents Abroad (1869), ch. 19

44 There ain't no way to find out why a snorer can't hear himself snore.
Tom Sawyer Abroad (1894), ch. 10

45 In Boston they ask, How much does he know? In New York, How much is he worth? In Philadelphia, Who were his parents?
What Paul Bourger Thinks of Us (1897)

46 France has neither winter nor summer nor morals—apart from these drawbacks it is a fine country.
Quoted in *Notebooks* (1935)

47 There is a sumptuous variety about the New England weather that compels the stranger's admiration—and regret...In the Spring I have counted one hundred and twenty-six different kinds of weather inside of twenty-four hours.
1876. Quoted in *Speaking Freely* (Stuart Berg Flexner and Anne H. Soukhanov; 1997)

48 We Americans worship the almighty dollar! Well, it is a worthier god than Hereditary Privilege.
Quoted in *Speaking Freely* (Stuart Berg Flexner and Anne H. Soukhanov; 1997)

49 When I was a boy of 14 my father was so ignorant I could hardly stand to have the old man around. But when I got to be 21, I was astonished at how much he had learnt in 7 years.
Quoted in *The Jingle Bell Principle* (Miroslav Holub; 1992)

50 Golf is a good walk spoiled.
Attrib.

51 He has been a doctor a year now and has had two patients, no, three, I think—yes, it was three; I attended their funerals.
Attrib.

52 I have never let my schooling interfere with my education.
Attrib.

53 It usually takes more than three weeks to prepare a good impromptu speech.
Attrib.

54 Man is a museum of diseases, a home of impurities; he comes today and is gone tomorrow; he begins as dirt and departs as stench.
Attrib.

55 There are people who strictly deprive themselves of each and every eatable, drinkable, and smokable which has in any way acquired a shady reputation. They pay this price for health. And health is all they get for it.
Attrib.

56 The way it is now, the asylums can hold the sane people, but if we tried to shut up the insane we should run out of building materials.
Attrib.

57 When we remember that we are all mad, the mysteries disappear and life stands explained.
Attrib.

58 Woman is unrivaled as a wet nurse.
Attrib.

59 That's right. 'Tain't yours, and 'tain't mine.
Agreeing with a friend's comment that the money of a particular rich industrialist was "tainted." Attrib.

60 To cease smoking is the easiest thing I ever did. I ought to know because I've done it a thousand times.
Referring to giving up smoking. Attrib.

61 Scarce, sir. Mighty scarce.
Responding to the question "In a world without women what would men become?" Attrib.

Tweed, Boss (William Marcy Tweed; 1823–78) U.S. politician

1 As long as I count the votes, what are you going to do about it?
Referring to a ballot. Boss Tweed was notoriously corrupt. Remark, New York City (November 1871)

Tyler, Anne (originally Anne Modarressi; b.1941) U.S. novelist

1 There was something about the smell of a roasting Idaho that was so cozy, and also, well, *conservative.*
The Accidental Tourist (1985)

Tyler, Robin U.S. comedian

1 If Michelangelo had been straight, the Sistine Chapel would have been wallpapered.
Speech to a Gay Rights Rally, Washington (January 9, 1988)

Tyler, Wat (d.1381) English rebel leader

1 No man should be a serf, nor do homage or any manner of service to any lord, but should give fourpence rent for an acre of land, and that no one should work for any man but as his own will, and on terms of a regular covenant.
Attrib. *Anonimalle Chronicle* (14th century)

Tynan, Kenneth (1927–80) British theater critic

1 A novel is a static thing that one moves through; a play is a dynamic thing that moves past one.
Curtains (1961)

2 Even the youngest of us will know, in fifty years' time, exactly what we mean by "a very Noel Coward sort of person."
Curtains (1961)

3 A good many inconveniences attend play-going in any large city, but the greatest of them is usually the play itself.
New York Herald Tribune (1957)

4 A critic is a man who knows the way but can't drive the car.
New York Times Magazine (January 9, 1966)

5 A good drama critic is one who perceives what is happening in the theatre of his time. A great drama critic also perceives what is not happening.
Tynan Right and Left (1967), Foreword

6 Oh, Calcutta!
1969. Revue title. From the French: "Oh quel cul t'as" ("what a lovely ass you've got").

Tyndall, John (1820–93) Irish-born British physicist

1 Superstition may be defined as constructive religion which has grown incongruous with intelligence.
Science and Man (1863)

Tyson, Mike (b.1966) U.S. boxer

1 I'm "Mike Tyson," everyone likes me now.
1982. Remark at National Junior Olympics, quoted in *Mike Tyson: Money, Myth and Betrayal* (Monteith Illingworth; 1992)

2 Sometimes it's not easy being Mike Tyson.
Times, London (August 31, 1988)

3 After one of my fights I said something about trying to punch the other guy's bone into his brain. It was supposed to be a joke just for the people in the dressing room. A bad joke, but a joke...But I didn't mean anything by it. It just taught me to be more careful about what I said in future.
Mike Tyson: For Whom The Bell Tolls (Reg Gutteridge and Norman Giller; 1986)

4 I'm just a normal guy with heart.
Mike Tyson: Money, Myth and Betrayal (Monteith Illingworth; 1992)

U2 Irish rock group

1 I have climbed highest mountains,
I have run through the fields,
Only to be with you...
But I still haven't found what I'm looking for.
Song lyric. "I Still Haven't Found What I'm Looking For," *The Joshua Tree* (Larry Mullen, Adam Clayton, Paul Hewson, and David Evans; 1986)

2 I want to run, I want to hide,
I want to tear down the walls that hold me inside,
I want to reach out, and touch the flame,
Where the streets have no name.
Song lyric. "Where the Streets Have No Name," *The Joshua Tree* (Larry Mullen, Adam Clayton, Paul Hewson, and David Evans; 1986)

Uccello, Paolo (1397?–1475) Italian painter

1 What a delightful thing this perspective is.
Quoted in *Men of Art* (T. Craven; 1933)

Udall, Stewart L. (Stewart Lee Udall; b.1920) U.S. politician and conservationist

1 Over the long haul of life on the planet, it is the ecologists, and not the bookkeepers of business, who are the ultimate accountants.
Address, Congress of Optimum Population and Environment (June 9, 1970)

2 Mining is like a search-and-destroy mission.
1976—Agenda for Tomorrow (1968)

3 The most common trait of all primitive peoples is a reverence for lifegiving earth, and the native American shared this elemental ethic: the land was alive to his loving touch, and he, its son, was brother to all creatures.
The Quiet Crisis (1963), ch. 1

4 It is obvious that the best qualities in man must atrophy in a standing-room-only environment.
The Quiet Crisis (1963), ch. 13

5 A land ethic for tomorrow should...stress the oneness of our resources and the live-and-help-live logic of the great chain of life.
The Quiet Crisis (1963), ch. 14

Ude, Louis Eustache (*fl.* 1810s?) French chef

1 Broth is the foundation of Cookery.
The French Cook (1813)

2 Cookery cannot be done like pharmacy: the Pharmacist is obliged to weigh every ingredient that he employs, as he does not like to taste it; the Cook, on the contrary, must taste often, as the reduction increases the flavor.
The French Cook (1813)

Ullman, Ellen U.S. author

1 No crash-proof system can be built unless it is made for an idiot.
Referring to the design of computer software. "Out of Time: Reflections on the Programming Life," *Harper's* (June 1995)

Ulpian (Domitius Ulpianus; 170?–228?) Roman jurist

1 No injustice is done to someone who wants that thing done.
The Latin is "Nulla iniuria est, quae in volentem fiat." *Corpus Iuris Civilis* (212–217), Digests 47, X, i, 5

Unamuno y Jugo, Miguel de (1864–1936) Spanish writer and philosopher

1 Science robs men of wisdom and usually converts them into phantom beings loaded up with facts.
Essays and Soliloquies (1924)

2 Science says: "We must live," and seeks the means of prolonging, increasing, facilitating and amplifying life, of making it tolerable and acceptable; wisdom says: "We must die," and seeks how to make us die well.
"Arbitrary Reflections," *Essays and Soliloquies* (1924)

3 Cure yourself of the condition of bothering about how you look to other people. Be concerned only with how you appear to God, with the idea God has of you.
Life of Don Quixote and Sancho (1905), pt. 1

4 The reader of the novel will doubt, even for a brief moment, his own physical reality and will believe himself to be, like us, no more than a character from a novel.
Niebla (1914)

5 Life is doubt,
and faith without doubt is nothing but death.
"Salmo II," *Poesías* (1907)

6 An idea does not pass from one language to another without change.
The Tragic Sense of Life in Men and Peoples (1913)

7 May God deny you peace but give you glory!
Closing words of the book. *The Tragic Sense of Life in Men and Peoples* (1913)

8 Man, by the very fact of being man, by possessing

consciousness, is, in comparison with the ass or the crab, a diseased animal. Consciousness is a disease.
"The Man of Flesh and Blood," *The Tragic Sense of Life in Men and Peoples* (1913)

9 They will conquer, but they will not convince.
Referring to Franco rebels. Attrib.

Underhill, Frank H. (Frank Hawkins Underhill; 1889–1971) Canadian historian and social reformer

1 In Canada we have no revolutionary tradition; and our historians, political scientists, and philosophers have assiduously tried to educate us to be proud of this fact. How can such a people expect their democracy to be dynamic as the democracies of Britain and France and the United States have been?
Report of the Canadian Historical Association (1946)

United States Federal Emergency Management Agency

1 Following a nuclear attack on the United States, the U.S. Postal Service plans to distribute Emergency Change of Address Cards.
Executive Order 11490 (1969)

2 Every effort will be made to clear trans-nuclear attack checks, including those drawn on destroyed banks. You will be encouraged to buy U.S. Savings Bonds.
Referring to provision for nuclear attack. Executive Order 11490 (1969)

Universal Declaration of Human Rights

1 All human beings are born free and equal in dignity and rights.
Sometimes attributed to Eleanor Roosevelt. *Universal Declaration of Human Rights* (1948), Article 1

Updike, John (John Hoyer Updike; b.1932) U.S. writer

1 In general the churches, visited by me too often on weekdays...bore for me the same relation to God that billboards did to Coca-Cola: they promoted thirst without quenching it.
A Month of Sundays (1975), ch. 2

2 Americans have been conditioned to respect newness, whatever it costs them.
A Month of Sundays (1975), ch. 18

3 A healthy male adult bore consumes each year one and a half times his own weight in other people's patience.
"Confessions of a Wild Bore," *Assorted Prose* (1965)

4 Government is either organized benevolence or organized madness; its peculiar magnitude permits no shading.
Buchanan Dying (1974), Act 1

5 Every marriage tends to consist of an aristocrat and a peasant. Of a teacher and a learner.
Couples (1968), ch. 1

6 An affair wants to spill, to share its glory with the world. No act is so private it does not seek applause.
Couples (1968), ch. 2

7 Sex is like money; only too much is enough.
Couples (1968), ch. 5

8 The first breath of adultery is the freest; after it, constraints aping marriage develop.
Couples (1968), ch. 5

9 Writing criticism is to writing fiction and poetry as hugging the shore is to sailing the open sea.
Hugging the Shore (1983), foreword

10 Bankruptcy is a sacred state, a condition beyond conditions, as theologians might say, and attempts to investigate it are necessarily obscene, like spiritualism.
"The Bankrupt Man," *Hugging the Shore* (1983)

11 Customs and convictions change; respectable people are the last to know, or to admit, the change, and the ones most offended by fresh reflections of the facts in the mirror of art.
New Yorker (July 30, 1990)

12 Now that I am sixty, I see why the idea of elder wisdom has passed from currency.
New Yorker (1992)

13 It rots a writer's brain, it cretinizes you. You say the same thing again and again, and when you do that happily you're well on the way to being a cretin. Or a politician.
Referring to being interviewed. Interview, *Observer*, London (Martin Amis; August 30, 1987)

14 America is a vast conspiracy to make you happy.
"How to Love America and Leave It at the Same Time," *Problems* (1980)

15 That's one of my Goddamn precious American rights, not to think about politics.
Rabbit Redux (1971)

16 He is a man of brick. As if he was born as a baby literally of clay and decades of exposure have baked him to the color and hardness of brick.
Rabbit, Run (1960)

17 "I feel so guilty." "About what?" "About everything." "Relax. Not everything is your fault." "I can't accept that."
Rabbit, Run (1960)

18 Looking foolish does the spirit good. The need not to look foolish is one of youth's many burdens; as we get older we are exempted from more and more.
Self-Consciousness: Memoirs (1989)

19 Rain is grace; rain is the sky condescending to the earth; without rain there would be no life.
Self-Consciousness: Memoirs (1989), ch. 1

20 Among the repulsions of atheism for me has been its drastic uninterestingness as an intellectual position. Where was the ingenuity...of saying that the universe just happened to happen and that when we're dead we're dead?
Self-Consciousness: Memoirs (1989), ch. 4

21 Existence itself does not feel horrible; it feels like an ecstasy, rather, which we only have to be still to experience.
Self-Consciousness: Memoirs (1989), ch. 6

22 Truth should not be forced; it should simply manifest itself, like a woman who has in her privacy reflected and coolly decided to bestow herself upon a certain man.
Self-Consciousness: Memoirs (1989), ch. 6

23 Neutrinos, they are very small.
They have no charge and have no mass
And do not interact at all.
The earth is just a silly ball
To them, through which they simply pass,
Like dustmaids down a drafty hall
Or photons through a sheet of glass.
"Cosmic Gall," *Telephone Poles, and Other Poems* (1964)

24 Neutrinos, they are very small.
They have no charge and have no mass...
At night, they enter at Nepal
And pierce the lover and his lass
From underneath the bed—you call
It wonderful; I call it crass.
"Cosmic Gall," *Telephone Poles, and Other Poems* (1964)

25 The Founding Fathers in their wisdom decided that children were an unnatural strain on parents. So they provided jails called schools, equipped with tortures called an education.
The Centaur (1963), ch. 4

Urey, Harold C. (Harold Clayton Urey; 1893–1981) U.S. chemist

1 I thought it might have practical use in something like neon signs.
April 4, 1965. Referring to the discovery of heavy water (deuterium oxide), used in the construction of nuclear weapons. Attrib.

U.S. President's Science Advisory Committee U.S. committee

1 In science the excellent is not just better than the ordinary; it is almost all that matters.
Scientific Progress, the Universities and the Federal Government (1960)

Ussher, James (1581–1656) Irish prelate and scholar

1 Which beginning of time according to our Chronologie, fell upon the entrance of the night preceding the twenty third day of *Octob.*, in the year of the Julian Calendar, 710.
Referring to the Creation, as described in Genesis, which, he had calculated, took place on October 22, 4004 B.C.. *The Annals of the World* (1650–54)

Ustinov, Peter, Sir (Peter Alexander Ustinov; b.1921) British actor, director, and writer

1 Parents are the bones on which children sharpen their teeth.
Dear Me (1977)

2 Thanks to the movies, gunfire has always sounded unreal to me, even when being fired at.
Dear Me (1977), ch. 7

3 And here is the lesson I learned in the army. If you want to do a thing badly, you have to work at it as though you want to do it well.
Dear Me (1977), ch. 8

4 I told the officer I was interested in tanks...His eyes blazed with enthusiasm.
"Why tanks?" he asked keenly.
I replied that I preferred to go into battle sitting down.
Dear Me (1977), ch. 8

5 I am an optimist, unrepentant and militant. After all, in order not to be a fool an optimist must know how sad a place the world can be. It is only the pessimist who finds this out anew every day.
Dear Me (1977), ch. 9

6 There are no old men any more. *Playboy* and *Penthouse* have between them made an ideal of eternal adolescence, sunburnt and saunaed, with the grey drained out of it.
Dear Me (1977), ch. 18

7 Once we are destined to live out our lives in the prison of our mind, our one duty is to furnish it well.
Dear Me (1977), ch. 20

8 If Botticelli were alive today he'd be working for *Vogue*.
Observer, London (October 21, 1962), "Sayings of the Week"

9 Books, I don't know what you see in them...I can understand a person reading them, but I can't for the life of me see why people have to write them.
Photo-Finish (1962)

10 A diplomat these days is nothing but a head-waiter who's allowed to sit down occasionally.
Romanoff and Juliet (1956), Act 1

11 As for being a General, well, at the age of four with paper hats and wooden swords we're all Generals. Only some of us never grow out of it.
Romanoff and Juliet (1956), Act 1

12 This is a free country, madam. We have a right to share your privacy in a public place.
Romanoff and Juliet (1956), Act 1

13 People at the top of the tree are those without qualifications to detain them at the bottom.
Attrib.

Vachell, Horace Annesley (1861–1955) British writer

1 In nature there are no rewards or punishments; there are consequences.
The Face of Clay (1906), ch. 10

Vail, Amanda (Warren Miller; 1921–66) U.S. writer

1 Sometimes I think if there was a third sex men wouldn't get so much as a glance from me.
Love Me Little (1957), ch. 6

Valadon, Suzanne (Marie-Clémentine Valadon; 1865–1938) French painter

1 I don't understand the experts, neither their explanations nor their comparisons. When they speak of technique, balance, and values they simply make me dizzy. Only two things exist for me and all others who paint: good pictures and bad pictures, that's all.
Quoted in *L'Enfant Terrible: The Life and Work of Maurice Utrillo* (Peter de Polnay; 1969)

2 I paint with the stubbornness I need for living, and I've found that all painters who love their art do the same.
Quoted in *L'Enfant Terrible: The Life and Work of Maurice Utrillo* (Peter de Polnay; 1969)

Valentino (Valentino Garavani; b.1932) Italian fashion designer

1 A woman must cause heads to turn when she enters a room.
Quoted in *Valentino, Thirty Years of Magic* (Marie-Paule Pell; 1990)

Valenzuela, Luisa (b.1938) Argentinian writer

1 How good can freedom be if you're alone and broke, with just a few coins in the bottom of your purse, hidden in the lining, the forgotten coins nobody cares about.
"The Body" (1967)

2 In Victor's life, monotony and boredom had nothing to do with one another. He repeated his repertoire so often that even from miles away, Clara could follow his conversation with anyone who happened to be sitting next to him.
"The Body" (1967)

3 To wait, seated in a chair, is the deadest form of dead anticipation, and waiting the most uninspired form of death.
"Rituals of Rejection," *Other Weapons* (1982)

4 Cocaine—such a perfunctory, unintelligent drug. Ideal for those who seek euphoria and refuse to look inward.
The Lizard's Tail (Gregory Rabassa, tr.; 1983)

Valéry, Paul (Ambroise Paul Toussaint Jules Valéry; 1871–1945) French poet and philosopher

1 A poem is never finished; it's always an accident that puts a stop to it—that is to say, gives it to the public.
Littérature (1930)

2 A painter should not paint what he sees, but what will be seen.
Mauvaises pensées et autres (1942)

3 God made everything out of nothing. But the nothingness shows through.
Mauvaises pensées et autres (1942)

4 The only truths which are universal are those gross enough to be thought so.
Mauvaises pensées et autres (1942)

5 The term Science should not be given to anything but the aggregate of the recipes that are always successful. All the rest is literature.
Moralités (1932)

6 Liberty is the hardest test that one can inflict on a people. To know how to be free is not given equally to all men and all nations.
"On the Subject of Dictatorship," *Reflections on the World Today* (1933)

7 Politeness is organized indifference.
Tel quel (1943)

8 Politics is the art of preventing people from taking part in affairs which properly concern them.
Tel quel (1943)

9 The object of psychology is to give us a totally different idea of the things we know best.
Tel quel (1943)

10 Having verse set to music is like looking at a painting through a stained glass window.
Attrib.

Vallejo, César (César Abraham Vallejo; 1892–1938) Peruvian poet

1 Beware, Spain, of your own Spain!
Beware of the sickle without the hammer,
beware of the hammer without the sickle!
"Hymn to the Volunteers," *Spain, Take This Cup from Me* (1937–38), no. 14

2 I was born on a day
God was sick.
"Espergesia," *The Black Heralds* (1918)

Valois, Ninette de, Dame (Edris Stannus; b.1898) Irish-born British ballet dancer and choreographer

1 Ladies and gentleman, it takes more than one to make a ballet.
New Yorker (1950)

Vanbrugh, John, Sir (1664–1726) English architect and playwright

1 The want of a thing is perplexing enough, but the possession of it is intolerable.
The Confederacy (1705), Act 1, Scene 2

2 As if a woman of education bought things because she wanted 'em.
The Confederacy (1705), Act 2, Scene 1

3 Much of a muchness.
The Provok'd Husband (1728), Act 1, Scene 1

4 Once a woman has given you her heart you can never get rid of the rest of her.
The Relapse (1696), Act 2, Scene 1

5 Thinking is to me the greatest fatigue in the world.
The Relapse (1696), Act 2, Scene 1

6 No man worth having is true to his wife, or can be true to his wife, or ever was, or ever will be so.
The Relapse (1696), Act 3, Scene 2

Van Buren, Abigail (pen name of Pauline Esther Friedman Phillips; b.1918) U.S. advice columnist

1 Psychotherapy, unlike castor oil, which will work no matter how you get it down, is useless when forced on an uncooperative patient.
"Dear Abby" (July 11, 1974)

2 Religion, like water, may be free, but when they pipe it to you, you've got to help pay for the piping. And the piper!
"Dear Abby" (April 28, 1974)

3 Some people are more turned on by money than they are by love...In one respect they're alike. They're both wonderful as long as they last.
"Dear Abby" (April 26, 1974)

Vance, Jack (John Holbrook Vance; pen names Ellery Queen, Peter Held, Alan Wade; b.1916) U.S. writer

1 Somebody else's ignorance is bliss.
The Star King (1964)

Van de Geer, Richard (d.1975) U.S. soldier

1 I can envision a small cottage somewhere, with a lot of writing paper, a dog, and a fireplace and maybe enough money to give myself some Irish coffee now and then and entertain my two friends.
Richard Van de Geer was officially the last American to die in the Vietnam War (1959–75). Letter to a friend, *Time* (April 15, 1975)

Vanderbilt, Cornelius (known as "Commodore" Vanderbilt; 1794–1877) U.S. industrialist

1 You have undertaken to cheat me. I won't sue you, for the law is too slow. I'll ruin you.
Letter to former business associates (1853)

Vanderbilt, William Henry (1821–85) U.S. railroad magnate

1 I have had no real gratification or enjoyment of any sort more than my neighbor on the next block who is worth only half a million.
1885. Quoted in *Famous Last Words* (B. Conrad; 1961)

2 The public be damned. I am working for my stockholders.
Refusing to speak to a reporter, who was seeking to find out his views on whether the public should be consulted about luxury trains. Quoted in Letter from A. C. Cole, *New York Times* (August 25, 1918)

Van der Post, Laurens, Sir (Laurens Jan Van der Post; 1906–96) South African novelist and anthropologist

1 "The story is like the wind," the Bushman prisoner said. "It comes from a far off place, and we feel it."
A Story Like the Wind (1972)

2 Organized religion is making Christianity political rather than making politics Christian.
Observer, London (November 9, 1986), "Sayings of the Week"

3 They'd rather even govern themselves badly than have somebody else govern them.
Referring to Southeast Asians. *Straits Times*, Singapore (October 26, 1996)

4 Both in Indonesia and in Malaya, at around the age of forty, a male may suddenly seem to rebel against all this goodness and gentleness...he has displayed all his life, and run amok with his dagger, murdering anyone in his way.
Explaining the Malay origin of the English word "amok." *The Admiral's Baby* (1996)

5 One had the feeling that his vision, intense as it was, remained singularly a collective vision, and that he saw its realization as something uniquely to be established through THE PEOPLE, in capital letters, and through the power of his own voice.
Referring to Sukarno, Indonesia's first president (1945–67). *The Admiral's Baby* (1996)

6 They have not forgiven us Stamford Raffles yet, and they cannot forgive us that Malaya appears prosperous and peaceful to them, and their own islands so unsettled.
Referring to the Dutch who were facing rebellion in colonial Indonesia. In 1811 Sir Stamford Raffles had been involved in the capture of Java (Indonesia) from the Dutch, staying on as lieutenant-governor until 1816. *The Admiral's Baby* (1996)

7 Would you gentlemen please be so kind as to condescend to wait an honourable moment?
Said in Japanese to a startled patrol of Japanese soldiers who were about to bayonet him during a guerrilla skirmish in Java. Attrib.

Vanzetti, Bartolomeo (1888–1927) Italian-born U.S. anarchist

1 If it had not been for this thing, I might have lived out my life talking at street corners to scorning men. I might have died unmarked, unknown, a failure. Now we are not a failure. This is our career and our triumph.
Referring to his imminent execution, and that of Nicola Sacco, Vanzetti's fellow anarchist, and to the controversial trial at which they were condemned to death for murder and robbery. The charges were never conclusively proved. Letter to his son (April 1927)

2 Sacco's name will live in the hearts of the people when your name, your laws, institutions and your false god are but a dim remembering of a cursed past in which man was wolf to the man.
Referring to Nicola Sacco, Vanzetti's fellow anarchist, and to the controversial trial at which they were condemned to death for murder and robbery. The charges were never conclusively proved.
Speech (August 1927)

Vargas, Getúlio (Getúlio Dornelles Vargas; 1883–1954) Brazilian president

1 To the wrath of my enemies I leave the legacy of my death. I take the sorrow of not being able to give to the humble all that I wished.
August 24, 1954. Suicide note written after having been forced by 58 generals into resigning.

Vargas Llosa, Mario (Jorge Mario Pedro Vargas Llosa; b.1936) Peruvian writer

1 Sensuality is not, of necessity, a synonym of sexuality; it can, in certain cases—one of these cases is the artistic world of Botero—be an antonym.
Referring to the Colombian painter, Fernando Botero. "Botero: a Sumptuous Abundance" (1984)

2 Nationalism is a form of lack of culture that pervades all cultures and coexists with all ideologies, a chameleon resource at the service of politicians of every persuasion.
"Nations, Fictions" (1992)

3 Religious cultures produce poetry and theater but only rarely great novels. Fiction is an art of societies where faith is experiencing a certain crisis, *where one needs to believe something.*
"The Truth of Lies" (1989)

4 The lies of novels are never gratuitous: they compensate for the inadequacies of life.
"The Truth of Lies" (1989)

5 Prosperity or egalitarianism—you have to choose. I favor freedom—you never achieve real equality anyway: you simply sacrifice prosperity for an illusion.
Independent on Sunday, London (May 5, 1991)

6 Eroticism has its own moral justification because it says that pleasure is enough for me; it is a statement of the individual's sovereignty.
International Herald Tribune, Paris (October 23, 1990)

7 A liberal dreams of a better world, knowing the dream must ultimately be unattainable. Communism believed it was attainable and felt any means to reach it were justified. That was the corruption.
Observer, London (June 19, 1994), "Sayings of the Week"

8 It isn't true to say that convicts live like animals: animals have more room to move around.
The Real Life of Alejandro Mayta (1984)

9 Since it is impossible to know what's really happening, we Peruvians lie, invent, dream...Because of these strange circumstances, Peruvian life, a life in which so few actually do read, has become literary.
The Real Life of Alejandro Mayta (1984)

10 Real politics...has little to do with ideas, values, and imagination...and everything to do with maneuvers, intrigues, plots, paranoias, betrayals, a great deal of calculation, no little cynicism, and every kind of con game.
Quoted in *A Fish in the Water* (Helen Lane, tr.; 1994)

Varma, Monika (b.1916) Indian poet

1 The man in the slums...is a man,
he is not: poor man.
How dare we pity him, study him, write articles, treatises,
census reports;
gazeteers...and look him up in archives.
"Man," *Women Poets of India* (Pranab Bandyopadhyay, ed.; 1977)

Varro, Marcus Terentius (116–27 B.C.) Roman scholar

1 Divine nature gave the fields, human art built the cities.
De Re Rustica, bk. 3, sect. 1

2 The longest part of the journey is said to be the passing of the gate.
On Agriculture (37? B.C.), bk. 1, 2, 2

Vaucaire, Michel (b.1904) French songwriter

1 No, I have no regrets.
1961. Song title. It was one of Edith Piaf's greatest hits. Music by Charles Dumont.

Vaughan, Henry (1622–95) English poet and mystic

1 Man is the shuttle, to whose winding quest
And passage through these looms
God order'd motion, but ordain'd no rest.
"Man," *Silex Scintillans* (1650–55)

2 My soul, there is a country
Far beyond the stars,
Where stands a wingèd sentry
All skilful in the wars;
There, above noise and danger,
Sweet Peace is crown'd with smiles,
And One born in a manger
Commands the beauteous files.
"Peace," *Silex Scintillans* (1650–55)

3 Dear Night! this world's defeat;
The stop to busy fools; care's check and curb;
The day of spirits; my soul's calm retreat
Which none disturb!
"The Night," *Silex Scintillans* (1650–55), ll. 25–28

4 With what deep murmurs through time's silent stealth
Doth thy transparent, cool, and watery wealth
Here flowing fall
And chide and call.
"The Waterfall," *Silex Scintillans* (1650–55)

5 I saw Eternity the other night
Like a great Ring of pure and endless light.
"The World," *Silex Scintillans* (1650–55), quoted in *The Metaphysical Poets* (Helen Gardner, ed.; 1957)

6 They are all gone into the world of light,
And I alone sit lingering here;

Their very memory is fair and bright,
And my sad thoughts doth clear.
"They Are All Gone," *Silex Scintillans* (1650–55), ll. 1–4

7 Dear, beauteous death! the jewel of the just,
Shining nowhere but in the dark;
What mysteries do lie beyond thy dust,
Could man outlook that mark!
"They Are All Gone," *Silex Scintillans* (1650–55), ll. 17–20

8 And yet, as angels in some brighter dreams
Call to the soul when man doth sleep,
So some strange thoughts transcend our wonted themes,
And into glory peep.
"They Are All Gone," *Silex Scintillans* (1650–55), ll. 25–28

Vauvenargues, Marquis de (Luc de Clapiers de Vauvenargues; 1715–47) French soldier and moralist

1 Great thoughts come from the heart.
Réflexions et maximes (1746)

2 To achieve great things we must live as though we were never going to die.
Réflexions et maximes (1746)

3 We should expect the best and the worst from mankind, as from the weather.
Réflexions et maximes (1746)

Veblen, Thorstein Bunde (1857–1929) U.S. social scientist and economist

1 All business sagacity reduces itself in the last analysis to a judicious use of sabotage.
The Nature of Peace (1917)

2 The outcome of any serious research can only be to make two questions grow where only one grew before.
The Place of Science in Modern Civilization (1919)

3 Conspicuous consumption of valuable goods is a means of reputability to the gentleman of leisure.
The Theory of the Leisure Class (1899), ch. 4

4 Invention is the mother of necessity.
Quoted in *The Oxford Book of Aphorisms* (John Gross, ed.; 1983)

Vedova, Emilio (b.1919) Italian painter

1 Painting-acting means...going beyond the conventions that have lost their hope; it means constructing, in a primordial sense, a reason to believe.
"It's Not So Easy To Paint a Nose," *Il Matino del Popolo* (February 1948)

Vega, Lope de (Lope Félix de Vega Carpio; 1562–1635) Spanish playwright and poet

1 The most wise speech is not as holy as silence.
The Stupid Lady (1613), Act 3, Scene 4

Vegetius (Flavius Vegetius Renatus; *fl.* 4th century) Roman writer

1 Let him who desires peace, prepare for war.
Epitome Rei Militaris (373?), prologue pt. 3

Véliz, Claudio (b.1930) Chilean writer

1 English is the language of the fox; Castilian, the language of the hedgehog.
Referring to the saying of Archilochus, the early Greek lyric poet, "The fox knows many things but the hedgehog one big one." *The New World of the Gothic Fox* (1994)

Venner, Tobias (1577–1660) English medical writer

1 Tobacco drieth the brain, dimmeth the sight, vitiateth the smell, hurteth the stomach, destroyeth the concoction, disturbeth the humors and spirits, corrupteth the breath, induceth a trembling of the limbs, exsiccateth the windpipe, lungs, and liver, annoyeth the milt, scorcheth the heart, and causeth the blood to be adjusted.
1620. *Via Recta ad Vitam Longam* (1638 ed.)

Venning, Ralph (1621?–74) English writer

1 They spare the rod, and spoyle the child.
1647. *Mysteries and Revelations* (1649 ed.)

2 All the beauty of the world, 't is but skin deep.
1647. "The Triumph of Assurance," *Orthodoxe Paradoxes* (1650)

Venturi, Robert (Robert Charles Venturi; b.1925) U.S. architect and writer

1 Orthodox modern architecture is progressive, if not revolutionary, utopian, and puristic; it is dissatisfied with *existing* conditions...Architects have preferred to change the existing environment rather than enhance what is there.
"A Significance for A and P Parking Lots," *Learning from Las Vegas* (co-written with Denise Scott Brown and Stephen Izenour; 1972), pt. 1

2 In iconographic terms, the cathedral is a decorated shed.
"Historical and Other Precedents," *Learning from Las Vegas* (co-written with Denise Scott Brown and Stephen Izenour; 1972), pt. 2

3 The series of triumphal arches in Rome is a prototype of the billboard...The triumphal arches in the Roman Forum were spatial markers channeling processional paths within a complex urban landscape. On Route 66 the billboards...perform a similar formal-spatial function.
"Silent-White Majority Architecture," *Learning from Las Vegas* (co-written with Denise Scott Brown and Stephen Izenour; 1972), pt. 2

4 Less is a bore.
Criticizing the minimalist style of architecture, and a riposte to Ludwig Mies van der Rohe's maxim, "Less is more." Quoted in *Icons* (James Park, ed.; 1991)

Verdi, Giuseppe (Giuseppe Fortunino Francesco Verdi; 1813–1901) Italian composer

1 Our mistake, you see, was to write interminable large operas, which had to fill an entire evening...And now along comes someone with a one- or two-act opera without all that pompous nonsense...that was a happy reform.
Referring to Pietro Mascagni. Attrib.

Vergniaud, Pierre-Victurnien (1753–93) French revolutionary politician

1 There has been reason to fear that the Revolution may, like Saturn, devour each of her children one by one.
November 1793. Said at his trial. Attrib.

Verlaine, Paul (Paul Marie Verlaine; 1844–96) French poet

1 And all the rest is literature.
"Art poétique," *Jadis et naguère* (1884)

2 Laughter is as ridiculous as it is deceptive.
Poèmes Saturniens (1866), prologue

3 The drawn-out sobs of the violins of autumn wound my heart with a monotonous languor.
"Chanson d'Automne," *Poèmes Saturniens* (1866)

4 Hope flares like a bit of straw in the stable.
Sagesse (1881)

5 Tears fall in my heart
As rain falls on the city.
"Ariette oubliée," *Songs Without Words* (1874), no. 3

Verne, Jules (1828–1905) French writer

1 But from the final orders given him by his master when he left the *Mongolia* Passepartout realized that the same thing would happen in Bombay as had happened in Paris. And he began to wonder if that bet of Mr. Fogg's was not a serious business after all and if fate would not drag him around the world in eighty days in spite of his desire for a quiet life.
Around the World in Eighty Days (1873)

2 An Englishman does not joke about such an important matter as a bet.
Around the World in Eighty Days (1873)

3 My curiosity was aroused to fever-pitch, and my uncle tried in vain to restrain me. When he saw that my impatience was likely to do me more harm than the satisfaction of my curiosity, he gave way.
Journey to the Centre of the Earth (1864)

Verona, Virginia U.S. feminist

1 The American people will not stand up for their rights. They'll be violent, of course, but they will not stand up for their rights.
Los Angeles Times (January 5, 1975)

Verrall, Arthur Woollgar (1851–1912) British classicist

1 Oh, quite easy! The Septuagint minus the Apostles.
Reply to a person who found the number 58 difficult to remember. Attrib.

Versace, Donatella (b.1958) Italian fashion designer

1 To design clothes with an ideal woman in mind is *demodé*. Women today are so different, interesting, intelligent, with a lot of attitude. I think individuality is what inspires me.
Guardian, London (April 18, 1998)

Versace, Gianni (1946–97) Italian fashion designer

Quotations about Versace

1 Gianni always went for the grand entrance. He was uncompromisingly glitzy. He was glitz, glitz, glitz. But he was a modest man and a lot of fun.
Bruce Oldfield (b.1950) British fashion designer. Referring to Gianni Versace, after his death. *Independent*, London (July 16, 1997)

Quotations by Versace

2 At the beginning of each season there are fashion designers who discover all of a sudden that fashion is dead, perhaps confusing overall appreciation with a personal problem.
Guardian, London (September 12, 1996)

Vesey, Denmark (1767?–1822) U.S. abolitionist

1 We are free but the white people here won't let us be so, and the only way is to rise up and fight the whites.
1822. Testimony of Rolla, a slave at trial. *A Documentary History of the Negro People in the United States* (Herbert Aptheker; 1951), vol. 1

Vespasian (Titus Flavius Sabinus Vespasianus; 9–79) Roman emperor

1 Money has no smell.
Answering Titus's objection to tax on public lavatories. Quoted in "Vespasian, Afterwards Deified," *Lives of the Caesars* (Suetonius; 121?), ch. 23

2 Dear me, I believe I am becoming a god. An emperor ought at least to die on his feet.
79. Last words. Quoted in "Vespasian, Afterwards Deified," *Lives of the Caesars* (Suetonius; 121?), ch. 23

Vespucci, Amerigo (1454–1512) Italian navigator and explorer

1 These new regions of America which we found and explored with the fleet...we may rightly call a New World...a continent more densely peopled and abounding in animals than our Europe or Asia or Africa.
Letter to Lorenzo de' Medici (1503)

Vian, Boris (1920–59) French writer

1 What concerns me is not the happiness of all men, but that of each.
L'Écume des jours (1947)

Vicious, Sid (John Simon Ritchie; 1957–79) British rock musician

1 You can't arrest me. I'm a rock 'n' roll star.
1978. Quoted in *The Face*, London (1986)

Victoria, Queen of Great Britain and Empress of India (Alexandrina Victoria; 1819–1901) British monarch

Quotations about Victoria

1 Nowadays a parlourmaid as ignorant as Queen Victoria was when she came to the throne would be classed as mentally defective.
George Bernard Shaw (1856–1950) Irish playwright. Attrib.

2 Sparrowhawks, Ma'am.
1851
Duke of Wellington (1769–1852) Irish-born British general and prime minister. Advice when asked by Queen Victoria how to remove sparrows from the Crystal Palace. Attrib.

3 I would have liked to go to Ireland, but my grandmother would not let me. Perhaps she thought I wanted to take the little place.
William II (1859–1941) German monarch. His grandmother was Queen Victoria. Quoted in *Carson* (H. Montgomery Hyde; 1953), ch. 9

Quotations by Victoria

4 The Queen is most anxious to enlist every one who can speak or write to join in checking this mad, wicked folly of "Woman's Rights," with all its attendant horrors, on which her poor feeble sex is bent, forgetting every sense of womanly feeling and propriety.
Letter to Sir Theodore Martin (May 29, 1870)

5 Please understand that there is no one depressed in *this* house; we are not interested in the possibilities of defeat; they do not exist.
Remark to British prime minister Arthur Balfour, referring to the Boer War (1899–1902). *Life of Robert, Marquis of Salisbury* (1931)

6 I will be good.
1830. On learning that she would succeed to the throne. *The Prince Consort* (Sir Theodore Martin; 1875)

7 That old monkish place which I have a horror of.
Referring to Oxford. (October 31, 1859)

8 We are not amused!
Attrib.

Vidal, Gore (Gore Eugene Luther Vidal, Jr.; b.1925) U.S. novelist and essayist

1 Like so many blind people my grandfather was a passionate sightseer; not to mention a compulsive guide.
"At Home in Washington, DC," *Armageddon* (1987)

2 If nothing else, suicide really *validates*, to use lit-crit's ultimate verb, the life if not the poetry...Death and then—triumphant transfiguration as A Cautionary Tale.
"Tennessee Williams: Someone to Laugh at the Squares With," *Armageddon* (1987)

3 Since the individual's desire to dominate his environment is not a desirable trait in a society which every day grows more and more confining, the average man must take to daydreaming.
"Tarzan Revisited," *Esquire* (December 1963)

4 For certain people, after fifty, litigation takes the place of sex.
Evening Standard, London (1981)

5 The novel being dead, there is no point to writing made-up stories. Look at the French who will not and the Americans who cannot.
Myra Breckinridge (1968), ch. 2

6 Like all analysts Randolph is interested only in himself. In fact, I have often thought that the analyst should pay the patient for allowing himself to be used as a captive looking-glass.
Myra Breckinridge (1968), ch. 37

7 Certainly one knows more at forty than one did at twenty. And contrary to all American mythology, the novel is the rightful province not of the young but of the middle-aged.
"On Revising One's Own Work," *New York Times Book Review* (November 14, 1965)

8 Unless drastic reforms are made, we must accept the fact that every four years the United States will be up for sale, and the richest man or family will buy it.
Reflections upon a Sinking Ship (June 6, 1968), Postscript: The Holy Family

9 Whenever a friend succeeds, a little something in me dies.
Sunday Times Magazine (September 16, 1973)

10 For half a century photography has been the "art form" of the untalented...some pictures are better than others, but where is the credit due? To the designer of the camera? to the finger on the button? to the law of averages?
1978. "On Prettiness," *The Second American Revolution* (1982)

11 Since World War II, Italy has managed, with characteristic artistry, to create a society that combines a number of the least appealing aspects of socialism with practically all the vices of capitalism.
1979. "Sciasci's Italy," *The Second American Revolution* (1982)

12 American writers want to be not good but great; and so are neither.
Two Sisters (1970)

13 Never have children, only grandchildren.
Two Sisters (1970)

14 The astronauts!...Rotarians in outer space.
Two Sisters (1970)

15 It is not enough to succeed. Others must fail.
Antipanegyric for Tom Driberg (G. Irvine; 1976)

16 Teaching has ruined more American novelists than drink.
Quoted in "Conversations with Gore Vidal," *Oui* (Beverly Kempton; April 1975)

17 A narcissist is someone better looking than you are.
Quoted in *San Francisco Chronicle* (April 12, 1981)

18 To the right wing "law and order" is often just a code phrase, meaning "get the nigger." To the left wing it often means political oppression.
1975. Quoted in *The Cynic's Lexicon* (Jonathon Green, ed.; 1984)

19 I'm all for bringing back the birch, but only between consenting adults.
Said when asked by presenter David Frost in a British television interview for his views about corporal punishment. (1973)

20 Any American who is prepared to run for President should automatically, by definition, be disqualified from ever doing so.
Attrib.

21 Meretricious and a Happy New Year.
Said in reply to author Richard Adams who accused him of being meretricious. Attrib.

Vidor, King (King Wallis Vidor; 1894–1982) U.S. film director

1 Marriage isn't a word...it's a *sentence*!
Caption between scenes. *The Crowd* was a silent film. *The Crowd* (1928)

Vieira, António (1608–97) Portuguese Jesuit missionary, human rights activist, and writer

1 Never hesitate to say what ought to be said, even if the price of doing so is losing one's reputation. That is the true spirit of Christ. What if your hearers do not like it? That is their affair. Does the doctor worry about the particular taste of the patient when he wishes to cure him? What if the medicine be bitter, provided it cures?
World's Great Men of Color (Joel Augustus Rogers; 1947), vol. 2

Vigée-Lebrun, Élisabeth (Marie-Louise-Élisabeth Vigée-Lebrun; 1755–1842) French portraitist

1 Can you imagine that I, with my love of the picturesque, could ever tolerate a wig? I have always had a horror of them, to the point where I once refused a very advantageous offer of marriage because the gentleman wore a wig.
1835. *Memoirs of Elisabeth Vigée-Le Brun* (Siân Evans, ed., tr.; 1989), ch. 1

Vigny, Alfred de, Comte de Vigny (Alfred Victor de Vigny; 1797–1863) French poet, novelist, and playwright

1 The true God, the mighty God, is the God of ideas.
"La Bouteille à la mer" (1847)

2 Silence alone is great; all else is weakness.
"La Mort du loup" (1843)

3 Alas, Lord, I am powerful but alone. Let me sleep the sleep of the earth.
"Moïse" (1826)

4 I love the majesty of human suffering.
La Maison du Berger (1844)

5 An army is a nation within a nation; it is one of the vices of our age.
Servitude et grandeur militaire (1835), pt. 1, ch. 2

Village People U.S. pop group

1 It's fun to stay at the YMCA
They have everything there for young men to enjoy
You can hang out with all the boys.
Song lyric. "YMCA" (1979)

Villiers de L'Isle-Adam, Auguste (Philippe Auguste Mathias, Comte de Villiers de L'Isle Adam; 1840–89) French writer

1 Living? The servants will do that for us.
Axel (1890), Act 4, Scene 2

Villon, François (François de Montcorbier, or François des Loges; 1431?–63?) French poet

Quotations about Villon

1 Villon, our sad bad glad mad brother's name.
Algernon Charles Swinburne (1837–1909) British poet. "Ballad of François Villon," *Poems and Ballads: Second Series* (1878), refrain

Quotations by Villon

2 I know everything except myself.
"Ballade of Small Talk" (1460?), refrain

3 Brother men who after us live on,
Harden not your hearts against us,
For if you have some pity on us poor men,
The sooner God will show you mercy...
But pray to God that He absolve us all.
"Ballade of the Hanged" (1463?), ll. 1–5, quoted in *Complete Works of François Villon* (Anthony Bonner, tr.; 1960)

4 In this faith I wish to live and die.
"Ballade as a Prayer to Our Lady," *Le Grand Testament* (1461–62), refrain, quoted in *Complete Works of François Villon* (Anthony Bonner, tr.; 1960)

5 But where are the snows of yesteryear?
"Ballade des dames du temps jadis," *Le Grand Testament* (D. G. Rossetti, tr.; 1461), l. 16

Vincent de Paul, Saint (1581–1660) French priest

1 Mental disease is no different to bodily disease and Christianity demanded of the humane and powerful to protect, and the skilful to relieve, the one as well as the other.
Quoted in *The Life and Works of St. Vincent de Paul* (Père Coste; 1934)

Vionnet, Madeleine (1876–1975) French fashion designer

1 When a woman smiles her dress must smile too.
Quoted in *Madeleine Vionnet* (Jacqueline Demornex, Augusta Audubert, tr.; 1991)

Virchow, Rudolf (Rudolf Carl Virchow; 1821–1902) German politician, pathologist, archaeologist, and anthropologist

1 There can be no scientific dispute with respect to faith, for science and faith exclude one another.
"Disease, Life, and Man," *Cellular Pathology* (1858), "On Man"

2 As long as vitalism and spiritualism are open questions so long will the gateway of science be open to mysticism.
Bulletin of the New York Academy of Medicine (F. H. Garrison; 1928), 4:994

3 Marriages are not normally made to avoid having children.
Bulletin of the New York Academy of Medicine (F. H. Garrison; 1928), 4:995

Virgil (Publius Vergilius Maro; 70–19 B.C.) Roman poet

Quotations about Virgil

1 Thou art my master and my author, thou art he from whom alone I took the style whose beauty has done me honor.
Dante Alighieri (1265–1321) Italian poet. "Inferno," *Divine Comedy* (1307?–21?), pt. 1

2 Virgil's great judgement appears in putting things together, and in his picking gold out of the dunghills of old Roman writers.
Alexander Pope (1688–1744) English poet. Quoted in *Observations, Anecdotes and Characters of Books and Men* (Rev. Joseph Spence; 1820)

Quotations by Virgil

3 O you who have borne even heavier things, God will grant an end to these too.
Aeneid (29–19 B.C.), bk. 1

4 She spoke, and turned away; one saw the rosy glow of her cheek, and caught the ambrosial scent from her hair; her dress flowed down to her feet, and in her walk it showed, she was in truth a goddess.
Aeneid (29–19 B.C.), bk. 1

5 I sing of arms and the man who first from the shores
of Troy came destined an exile to Italy and the
Lavinian beaches, much buffeted he on land and on
the deep by force of the gods because of fierce
Juno's never-forgetting anger.
Referring to Aeneas. *Aeneid* (29–19 B.C.), bk. 1

6 Maybe one day we shall be glad to remember even these hardships.
Aeneid (29–19 B.C.), bk. 1, l. 203

7 I am learning to care for the unfortunate.
Motto on the seal of the New Jersey College of Medicine. *Aeneid* (29–19 B.C.), bk. 1, l. 630

8 Let us die even as we rush into the midst of the battle. The only safe course for the defeated is to expect no safety.
Aeneid (29–19 B.C.), bk. 2

9 A grief too much to be told, O queen, you bid me renew.
The opening words of Aeneas's account to Dido of the fall of Troy. *Aeneid* (29–19 B.C.), bk. 2, l. 3

10 Do not trust the horse, Trojans. Whatever it is, I fear the Greeks even when they bring gifts.
Aeneid (29–19 B.C.), bk. 2, l. 48

11 From the one crime recognize them all as culprits.
Aeneid (29–19 B.C.), bk. 2, l. 65

12 What do you not drive human hearts into, cursed craving for gold!
Aeneid (29–19 B.C.), bk. 3

13 Who could deceive a lover?
Aeneid (29–19 B.C.), bk. 4, l. 296

14 These success encourages: they can because they think they can.
Aeneid (29–19 B.C.), bk. 5, l. 231

15 That sweet, deep sleep, so close to tranquil death.
Aeneid (29–19 B.C.), bk. 6

16 I see wars, horrible wars, and the Tiber foaming with much blood.
Part of the Sibyl's prophecy to Aeneas, foretelling his difficulties in winning a home in Italy. *Aeneid* (29–19 B.C.), bk. 6, l. 86

17 The way down to Hell is easy.
Aeneid (29–19 B.C.), bk. 6, l. 126

18 These shall be your skills: to impose the way of peace, to spare the vanquished and to crush the proud.
Aeneid (29–19 B.C.), bk. 6, l. 852

19 If I am unable to make the gods above relent, I shall move Hell.
Aeneid (29–19 B.C.), bk. 7, l. 312

20 Fear lent wings to his feet.
Aeneid (29–19 B.C.), bk. 8

21 Oh if only Jupiter would give me back my past years.
Aeneid (29–19 B.C.), bk. 8, l. 560

22 Blessings on your young courage, boy; that's the way to the stars.
Aeneid (29–19 B.C.), bk. 9, l. 641

23 Fortune favors the bold.
Aeneid (29–19 B.C.), bk. 10, l. 284

24 Trust one who has gone through it.
Aeneid (29–19 B.C.), bk. 11, l. 283

25 He destroys his health by laboring to preserve it.
Aeneid (29–19 B.C.), bk. 12

26 Compare great things with small.
Eclogues (37 B.C.), no. 1, l. 23

27 Everyone is dragged on by their favorite pleasure.
Eclogues (37 B.C.), no. 2, l. 65

28 There's a snake hidden in the grass.
Eclogues (37 B.C.), no. 3, l. 93

29 Begin, baby boy: if you haven't had a smile for your parent, then neither will a god think you worth inviting to dinner, nor a goddess to bed.
Eclogues (37 B.C.), no. 4, l. 62

30 Restore, my charms,
My lovely Daphnis to my longing arms.
Eclogues (37 B.C.), no. 8

31 Now I know what Love is.
Eclogues (37 B.C.), no. 8, l. 43

32 We can't all do everything.
Eclogues (37 B.C.), no. 8, l. 63

33 Time carries all things, even our wits, away.
Eclogues (37 B.C.), no. 9, l. 51

34 Love conquers all things: let us too give in to Love.
Eclogues (37 B.C.), no. 10, l. 69

35 Lucky is he who could understand the causes of things.
Georgics (29 B.C.), no. 2, l. 490

36 All the best days of life slip away from us poor mortals first; illnesses and dreary old age and pain sneak up, and the fierceness of harsh death snatches away.
Georgics (29 B.C.), no. 3, l. 66

37 But meanwhile it is flying, irretrievable time is flying.
Georgics (29 B.C.), no. 3, l. 284

Vitruvius, Marcus (Marcus Vitruvius Pollio; 70?–25 B.C.) Roman architect and engineer

1 Pictures should not be given approbation which are not likenesses of reality; even if they are refined creations executed with artistic skill.
Vitruvius: The Ten Books on Architecture (M. H. Morgan, ed., tr.; 1960), bk. 7, pt. 5

Vittachi, Varindra Tarzie (b.1921) Sri-Lankan born writer

1 People who live on borrowed culture often go to extremes that their models and mentors had never intended.
The Brown Sahib (1962)

2 Very few people in the world can be relied upon to work without praise or recognition.
The Brown Sahib (1962)

3 The mother-tongue was relegated to the kitchen—it was a debased currency which was legal tender only for the exchanges one had with the servant, the *dhobi*, the rickshaw-wallah and the vegetable hawker.
Referring to how indigenous languages were regarded in the British colonies, where English was endorsed as the lingua franca. *The Brown Sahib* (1962)

Vizinczey, Stephen (b.1933) Hungarian-born British writer, editor, and broadcaster

1 I was told I am a true cosmopolitan. I am unhappy everywhere.
Guardian, London (March 7, 1968)

2 Don't let anybody tell you you're wasting your time when you're gazing into space. There is no other way to conceive an imaginary world...I daydream about my characters...take pen and paper and try to *report* what I've witnessed.
Truth and Lies in Literature (1986)

Vlaminck, Maurice de (1876–1958) French painter

1 Painting was an abscess which drained off the evil in me. Without a gift for painting I would have gone to the bad...What I could only have achieved in a social context by throwing a bomb...I have tried to express in art.
Quoted in *Fauvism* (Joseph Emile Muller; 1967)

Vogel, Eric Czechoslovakian jazz musician

1 We had to deliver all our musical instruments to the Gestapo...I soaked the valves in sulphuric acid to prevent anyone from playing military marches on the horn used to play jazz.
Down Beat Jazz (December 1961), quoted in *The Picador Book of Blues and Jazz* (James Campbell, ed.; 1995)

Voinovich, Vladimir (Vladimir Nikolayevich Voinovich; b.1932) Russian novelist

1 That night I slept badly. I dreamed of a white saucepan for milk...and I tried to answer the question: Could it be considered a writer? For some reason I decided that although it probably couldn't be considered a writer, it could be admitted into the Writers' Union.
The Life and Extraordinary Adventures of Private Ivan Chonkin (Richard Lourie, tr.; 1969), pt. 1

2 To study life you don't have to go on creative junkets and waste public funds. Study life where you live, it's more productive, and cheaper, too.
The Life and Extraordinary Adventures of Private Ivan Chonkin (Richard Lourie, tr.; 1969), pt. 1

3 From his close observation of life and his fathoming of life's laws, Chonkin had understood that it is usually warm in the summer and cold in winter.
The Life and Extraordinary Adventures of Private Ivan Chonkin (Richard Lourie, tr.; 1969), pt. 1, ch. 4

4 "I wonder what they teach them in the city."
"That's easy," announced Chonkin. "To live off the fat of the countryside."
The Life and Extraordinary Adventures of Private Ivan Chonkin (Richard Lourie, tr.; 1969), pt. 1, ch. 6

5 That's the story of our life—men tell lies and women believe them.
The Life and Extraordinary Adventures of Private Ivan Chonkin (Richard Lourie, tr.; 1969), pt. 1, ch. 7

6 A meeting is an arrangement whereby a large number of people gather together, some to say what they really do not think, some not to say what they really do.
The Life and Extraordinary Adventures of Private Ivan Chonkin (Richard Lourie, tr.; 1969), pt. 2, ch. 6

Volcker, Paul A. (b.1927) U.S. economist

1 Things continue in government unless you feel a crisis. In fact, we didn't have a crisis, so the deficit persisted.
Time (January 23, 1989)

2 You've got all the cards when you trade for the Fed.
Referring to the Federal Reserve Bank (central bank). *Time* (January 23, 1989)

3 At the rate we're borrowing from abroad, in the space of three years we will have wiped out all of the holdings we've built up overseas since the Second World War.
U.S. News & World Report (March 12, 1984)

Voltaire (François-Marie Arouet; 1694–1778) French writer and philosopher

Quotations about Voltaire

1 When he talked our language he was animated with the soul of a Briton. He had bold flights. He had humour. He had an extravagance.
James Boswell (1740–95) Scottish lawyer and biographer. Quoted in *Boswell on the Grand Tour* (F. A. Pottle, ed.; 1953)

2 He does not inflame his mind with grand hopes of the immortality of the soul. He says it may be, but he knows nothing of it. And his mind is in perfect tranquillity.
1764
James Boswell (1740–95) Scottish lawyer and biographer. Quoted in *Boswell on the Grand Tour* (F. A. Pottle, ed.; 1953), December 28, 1764

3 I have done but very little but read Voltaire since I saw you. He is an exquisite fellow. One thing in him is particularly striking—his clear knowledge of the limits of human understanding.
James Currie (1756–1805) Scottish physician and writer. Letter to Thomas Creevey (December 17, 1798)

4 I was born much too soon, but I do not regret it; I have seen Voltaire.
Frederick II (1712–86) Prussian monarch. Attrib.

5 There's a Bible on that shelf there. But I keep it next to Voltaire—poison and antidote.
Bertrand Russell (1872–1970) British philosopher and mathematician. Quoted in *Kenneth Harris Talking to Bertrand Russell* (Kenneth Harris; 1971)

Quotations by Voltaire

6 Men will always be mad and those who think they can cure them are the maddest of all.
Letter (1762)

7 The great consolation in life is to say what one thinks.
Letter (1765)

8 The man who leaves money to charity in his will is only giving away what no longer belongs to him.
Letter (1769)

9 There are two things for which animals are to be envied: they

know nothing of future evils, or of what people say about them.
Letter (1739)

10 I am not like a lady at the court of Versailles, who said: "What a dreadful pity that the bother at the tower of Babel should have got language all mixed up, but for that, everyone would always have spoken French."
French was the dominant language in the educated circles of 18th-century Europe. Letter to Catherine the Great, Empress of Russia (May 26, 1767)

11 Once the people begin to reason, all is lost.
Letter to Damilaville (April 1, 1766)

12 Whatever you do, stamp out abuses, and love those who love you.
Letter to M. d'Alembert (November 28, 1762)

13 It is said that God is always on the side of the heaviest battalions.
Letter to M. le Riche (February 6, 1770)

14 The ancient Romans built their greatest masterpieces of architecture, the amphitheaters, for wild beasts to fight in.
Letter to the Commissioner of the Paris Police (1733), quoted in *Dictionary of Art Quotations* (Ian Crofton; 1988)

15 All is for the best in the best of all possible worlds.
Candide (1759), ch. 1

16 If we do not find anything pleasant, at least we shall find something new.
Candide (1759), ch. 17

17 In this country it is good to kill an admiral from time to time, to encourage the others.
Referring to the execution of the British admiral Byng for failing to defeat the French at Minorca (1757). *Candide* (1759), ch. 23

18 Work banishes those three great evils, boredom, vice, and poverty.
Candide (1759), ch. 30

19 The best is the enemy of the good.
Originally from an Italian proverb quoted in Voltaire's *Dictionnaire philosophique*. "Art Dramatique": "Le meglio è l'inimico del bene." "La Bégueule," *Contes* (1772), l. 2

20 Men use thought only to justify their injustices, and speech only to conceal their thoughts.
"Le Chapon et la poularde," *Dialogue* (1763)

21 Let all the laws be clear, uniform, and precise; to interpret laws is almost always to corrupt them.
Dictionnaire philosophique (1764)

22 Man can have only a certain number of teeth, hair, and ideas; there comes a time when he necessarily loses his teeth, hair, and ideas.
"Fate," *Dictionnaire philosophique* (1764)

23 The wicked can have only accomplices, the voluptuous have companions in debauchery, self-seekers have associates, the politic assemble the factions, the typical idler has connections, princes have courtiers. Only the virtuous have friends.
"Friendship," *Dictionnaire philosophique* (1764)

24 What is madness? To have erroneous perceptions and to reason correctly from them.
"Madness," *Dictionnaire philosophique* (1764)

25 I never approved either the errors of his book, or the trivial truths he so vigorously laid down. I have, however, stoutly taken his side when absurd men have condemned him for these same truths.
Referring to Helvetius's *De L'Esprit*, which was publicly burned in 1758; usually misquoted as "I disapprove of what you say, but I will defend to the death your right to say it." "Man," *Dictionnaire philosophique* (1764)

26 Regimen is superior to medicine.
"Physicians," *Dictionnaire philosophique* (1764)

27 Superstition sets the whole world in flames; philosophy quenches them.
"Superstition," *Dictionnaire philosophique* (1764)

28 If God did not exist, it would be necessary to invent Him.
"À l'auteur du livre des trois Imposteurs," *Épîtres* (1769)

29 The secret of the arts is to correct nature.
"À M. de Verrière," *Épîtres* (1769)

30 This agglomeration which was called and which still calls itself the Holy Roman Empire was neither holy, nor Roman, nor an empire.
Essai sur l'histoire générale et sur les moeurs et l'esprit des nations (1756), ch. 70

31 Crime has its heroes, error has its martyrs:
Of true zeal and false, what vain judges we are.
Henriade (1728), chant 5

32 All our ancient history, as one of our wits remarked, is no more than accepted fiction.
Jeannot et Colin (1764)

33 All styles are good except the tiresome sort.
L'Enfant prodigue (1738), Preface

34 If God made us in His image, we have certainly returned the compliment.
Le Sottisier (1778?), ch. 32

35 Indeed, history is nothing more than a tableau of crimes and misfortunes.
L'Ingénu (1767), ch. 10

36 Extreme justice is extreme injury.
Oedipe (1718), Act 3, Scene 3

37 We owe respect to the living; to the dead we owe only truth.
"Première lettre sur Oedipe," *Oeuvres* (1785), vol. 1

38 Faith consists in believing when it is beyond the power of reason to believe. It is not enough that a thing be possible for it to be believed.
Questions sur l'encyclopédie (1770–72)

39 Love truth, but pardon error.
Sept discours en vers sur l'homme (1738), no. 3

40 Governments need to have both shepherds and butchers.
The Piccini Notebooks (1735–50?)

41 Nature has always had more power than education.
Vie de Molière (1733–34)

42 Never having been able to succeed in the world, he took his revenge by speaking ill of it.
Zadig (1747), ch. 4

43 Ah, the composition of a tragedy requires testicles.
When asked why no woman has ever written a tolerable tragedy. Quoted in Letter from Lord Byron to John Murray, *Byron's Letters and Journals* (L. A. Marchand, ed.; 1976), vol. 5, April 2, 1817

44 The human race is the only one that knows it must die, and it knows this only through its experience. A child brought up alone and transported to a desert island would have no more idea of death than a cat or a plant.
Quoted in *The Oxford Book of Death* (D. J. Enright; 1987)

45 There are no sects in geometry.
Quoted in *The Viking Book of Aphorisms* (W. H. Auden and L. Kronenberger, eds.; 1962)

46 It is one of the superstitions of the human mind to have imagined that virginity could be a virtue.
"The Leningrad Notebooks," *Voltaire's Notebooks* (T. Besterman, ed.; 1968), vol. 2

47 A physician is one who pours drugs of which he knows little into a body of which he knows less.
Attrib.

48 The art of medicine consists of amusing the patient while Nature cures the disease.
Attrib.

49 The fate of a nation has often depended upon the good or bad digestion of a prime minister.
Attrib.

50 Who are the greatest deceivers? The doctors? And the greatest fools? The patients?
Attrib.

51 Men of England! You wish to kill me because I am a Frenchman. Am I not punished enough in not being born an Englishman?
Addressing an angry London mob who desired to hang him because he was a Frenchman. Attrib.

52 He was a great patriot, a humanitarian, a loyal friend—provided, of course, that he really is dead.
Giving a funeral oration. Attrib.

53 I think it must be so, for I have been drinking it for sixty-five years and I am not dead yet.
On learning that coffee was considered a slow poison. Attrib.

54 I do not think this poem will reach its destination.
Reviewing Rousseau's poem "Ode to Posterity." Attrib.

55 Once: a philosopher; twice: a pervert!
Turning down an invitation to an orgy, having attended one the previous night for the first time. Attrib.

von Braun, Wernher (1912–77) German-born U.S. engineer

1 Everything in space obeys the laws of physics. If you know these laws and obey them, space will treat you kindly. And don't tell me that man doesn't belong out there. Man belongs wherever he wants to go; and he'll do plenty well when he gets there.
Time (February 17, 1958)

2 It was very successful, but it fell on the wrong planet.
Referring to the first V2 rocket to hit London during World War II. Attrib.

Vonnegut, Kurt (Kurt Vonnegut, Jr.; b.1922) U.S. novelist

1 Everybody in America was supposed to grab whatever he could and hold onto it. Some Americans were very good at grabbing and holding, were fabulously well-to-do. Others couldn't get their hands on doodley-squat.
Breakfast of Champions (1973), ch. 1

2 Fascism was a fairly popular political philosophy which made sacred whatever nation and race the philosopher happened to belong to.
Breakfast of Champions (1973), ch. 17

3 Beware of the man who works hard to learn something, learns it, and finds himself no wiser than before, Bokonon tells us. He is full of murderous resentment of people who are ignorant without having come by their ignorance the hard way.
Cat's Cradle (1963)

4 The American dream turned belly up, turned green, bobbed to the scummy surface of cupidity unlimited, filled with gas, went *bang* in the noonday sun.
God Bless You, Mr. Rosewater (1965), ch. 1

5 I think the main purpose of the Army, Navy, and Marine Corps is to get poor Americans into clean, pressed, unpatched clothes, so rich Americans can stand to look at them.
God Bless You, Mr. Rosewater (1965), ch. 3

6 Well, you get sick of it after a while. You think, honestly, you're so full of shit.
Referring to why he intended his novel, *Timequake* (1997), to be his last. Interview, *Independent on Sunday*, London (October 12, 1997)

7 People aren't supposed to look back...I've finished my war book now. The next one I write is going to be fun. This one is a failure...it was written by a pillar of salt.
Slaughterhouse-Five (1969), ch. 1

8 The British had no way of knowing it, but the candles and the soap were made from the fat of rendered Jews and Gypsies and fairies and communists, and other enemies of the state. So it goes.
Slaughterhouse-Five (1969), ch. 5

9 Their only English-speaking guard told them to memorize their simple address, in case they got lost in the city. Their address was this: "Schlachthof-fünf." *Schlachthof* meant *slaughterhouse*. *Fünf* was good old *five*.
Slaughterhouse-Five (1969), ch. 6

10 Billy had a tremendous cavalry pistol in his belt...That was one of the things about the war: Absolutely anybody who wanted a weapon could have one. They were lying all around.
Slaughterhouse-Five (1969), ch. 9

11 Robert Kennedy...died last night...Martin Luther King was shot a month ago...And every day my Government gives me a count of corpses created by military science in Vietnam. So it goes.
Slaughterhouse-Five (1969), ch. 10

Von Neumann, John (Johann von Neumann; 1903–57) Hungarian-born U.S. mathematician

1 In mathematics you don't understand things. You just get used to them.
Quoted in *The Dancing Wu Li Masters* (Gary Zukav; 1979)

Von Sternberg, Josef (Jonas Sternberg; 1894–1969) Austrian-born U.S. film director

1 The only way to succeed is to make people hate you. That way, they remember you.
Fun in a Chinese Laundry (1965)

2 You can seduce a man's wife there, attack his daughter and wipe your hands on his canary, but if you don't like his movie, you're dead.
Referring to Hollywood. Quoted in *20th Century Quotations* (Frank S. Pepper; 1984)

Vorster, John (Balthazar Johannes Vorster; 1915–83) South African prime minister and president

1 As far as criticism is concerned, we don't resent that unless it is absolutely biased, as it is in most cases.
Observer, London (November 9, 1969), "Sayings of the Week"

Voysey, Charles Francis Annesley (1857–1941) British designer and architect

1 Remember that cold vegetables are less harmful than ugly dishes. One affects the body, while the other affects the soul.
Quoted in *Terence Conran on Design* (Terence Conran; 1996)

Vukovich, Bill (1918–55) U.S. racing car driver

1 There's no secret. You just press the accelerator to the floor and steer left.
Explaining his success in the Indianapolis 500. Attrib.

Wacky Races U.S. television cartoon series

1 Drat and triple drat.
The villainous Dick Dastardly's catchphrase in the television cartoon series. *The Wacky Races* (1960s)

Wagner, Jane (b.1935) U.S. playwright and novelist

1 This morning I threw up at a board meeting. I was sure the cat was out of the bag, but no-one seemed to think anything about it; apparently it's quite common for people to throw up at board meetings.
Said by a character who has been trying to keep her pregnancy a secret for fear it may affect her employment. *The Search for Intelligent Signs in the Universe* (1986)

Wagner, Richard (Wilhelm Richard Wagner; 1813–83) German composer

Quotations about Wagner

1 A master is dead. Today we sing no more.
1883
Johannes Brahms (1833–97) German composer. Stopping a choral rehearsal on hearing of the death of Wagner. Quoted in *Brahms* (P. Latham; 1948)

2 Wagner has lovely moments but awful quarters of an hour.
April 1867
Gioacchino Rossini (1792–1868) Italian composer. Remark made to Émile Naumann. *Italienische Tondichter* (Émile Naumann; 1883)

3 I like Wagner's music better than anybody's. It is so loud that one can talk the whole time without other people hearing what one says.
Oscar Wilde (1854–1900) Irish poet, playwright, and wit. *The Picture of Dorian Gray* (1891)

Quotations by Wagner

4 It is a truth forever, that where the speech of man stops short there Music's reign begins.
"A Happy Evening" (1841), quoted in *Pilgrimage to Beethoven* (W. A. Ellis, tr.; 1994)

5 The only art that fully corresponds with the Christian belief is music.
1880. Quoted in *Religion and Art* (W. A. Ellis, tr.; 1994)

Wain, John (John Barrington Wain; 1925–94) British novelist and poet

1 Poetry is to prose as dancing is to walking.
BBC Radio broadcast (January 13, 1976)

2 Good news. It seems he loved them after all.
His orders were to fry their bones to ash.
He carried up the bomb and let it fall.
And then his orders were to take the cash,
A hero's pension.
Referring to Major Claude C. Eatherley, pilot of the aircraft that carried the atomic bomb to Nagasaki, who would not take up his military pension and was subsequently imprisoned for theft. "A Song About Major Eatherley," *The Oxford Book of Twentieth-Century English Verse* (Philip Larkin, ed.; 1973)

Waite, Terry (Terence Hardy Waite; b.1939) British religious adviser

Quotations about Waite

1 We apologize for having captured you. We recognize now that it was the wrong thing to do, that holding hostages achieves no useful, constructive purpose.
November 1991
Anonymous. Said by a Lebanese terrorist, on releasing Terry Waite. *Times*, London (November 19, 1991)

Quotations by Waite

2 Politics come from man. Mercy, compassion and justice come from God.
Observer, London (January 13, 1985), "Sayings of the Week"

3 All of us, all hostages, would plead with those who are holding the people of South Lebanon, innocent people being held as hostages, to release them soon; to put an end to this problem; to put an end to terrorism, and to find peaceful, humane and civilized ways of resolving the very complex problems that face the Middle East.
1991. *Times*, London (November 19, 1991)

Wakoski, Diane (b.1937) U.S. poet

1 All fathers in Western civilization must have
a military origin.
"The Father of My Country," *Inside the Blood Factory* (1967), quoted in *The Penguin Book of American Verse* (Geoffrey Moore, ed.; 1977)

Walcott, Derek (b.1930) St. Lucian poet and playwright

1 How can I turn from Africa and live?
1984. "In a Green Night," *Collected Poems: 1948–1984* (1986)

2 Because Rhyme remains the parentheses of palms
shielding a candle's tongue, it is the language's
desire to enclose the loved world in its arms.
Omeros (1990)

3 The worst crime is to leave a man's hands empty.
Men are born makers, with that primal simplicity

in every maker since Adam. This is pre-history.
Omeros (1990)

4 When one grief afflicts us we choose a sharper grief
in hope that enormity will ease affliction.
Omeros (1990)

5 I am tired of words,
and literature is an old couch stuffed with fleas,
of culture stuffed in the taxidermist's hides.
"North and South," *The Fortunate Traveller* (1982)

6 My race began as the sea began,
with no nouns, and with no horizon,
with pebbles under my tongue,
with a different fix on the stars.
"Names," *Caribbean Poetry Now* (Stewart Brown, ed.; 1984)

Walesa, Lech (b.1943) Polish labor leader and president

1 I've never worked for prizes...I'm as ready to receive prizes as I am to be thrown into prison, not that I'm ungrateful for this honor; it's just that neither the one nor the other could ever divert me from the course I've set myself.
1983. Said when awarded the Nobel Peace Prize. "Private Citizen," *A Path of Hope* (1987)

2 SOLIDARITY was born at that precise moment when the shipyard strike evolved from a local success in the shipyard, to a strike in support of other factories and business enterprises, large and small, in need of our protection.
"The Strike and the August Agreements," *A Path of Hope* (1987)

3 We have done all the things the West asked of us—now where is your investment?
1991. Said to a visiting European Community delegation. Attrib.

Walker, Alice (Alice Malsenior Walker; b.1944) U.S. novelist and poet

1 I don't like fond.
It sounds like something
you would tell a dog.
Give me love,
or nothing.
"I'm Really Very Fond," *Her Blue Body Everything We Know* (1991)

2 Tears left unshed
turn to poison
in the ducts.
"S M," *Her Blue Body Everything We Know* (1991)

3 Abortion, for many women, is more than an experience of suffering beyond anything most men will ever know, it is an act of mercy, and an act of self-defense.
April 8, 1989. Speech at Pro-Choice/Keep Abortion Legal Rally, Washington, D.C., *Her Blue Body Everything We Know* (1991)

4 My major advice to young black artists would be that they shut themselves up somewhere away from all debates about who they are and what color they are and just turn out paintings and poems and stories and novels.
In Search of Our Mothers' Gardens (1983)

5 Only Justice Can Stop a Curse
1982. Essay title. *In Search of Our Mothers' Gardens* (1983)

6 Ignorance, arrogance, and racism have bloomed as Superior Knowledge in all too many universities.
"A Talk: Convocation 1972," *In Search of Our Mothers' Gardens* (1983)

7 To me, the black, black woman is our essential mother—the blacker she is the more us she is—and to see the hatred that is turned on her is enough to make me despair, almost entirely, of the future of our people.
"If the Present Looks Like the Past, What Does the Future Look Like?" *In Search of Our Mothers' Gardens* (1983)

8 I've found, in my own writing, that a little hatred, keenly directed, is a useful thing.
"The Unglamorous But Worthwhile Duties of the Black Revolutionary Artist, or of the Black Writer Who Simply Works and Writes," *In Search of Our Mothers' Gardens* (1983)

9 The animals of the planet are in desperate peril...Without free animal life I believe we will lose the spiritual equivalent of oxygen.
"The Universe Responds: Or, How I Learned We Can Have Peace on Earth," *Living By the Word* (1988)

10 It is healthier, in any case, to write for the adults one's children will become than for the children one's "mature" critics often are.
"A Writer, Because of, Not in Spite of, Her Children," *Ms* (January 1976)

11 It no longer bothers me that I may be constantly searching for father figures; by this time, I have found several and dearly enjoyed knowing them all.
"In Search of Zora Neale Hurston," *Ms* (March 1975)

12 Writing saved me from the sin and inconvenience of violence.
"One Child of One's Own," *Ms* (August 1979)

13 I will concentrate on the beauty of one blue hill in the distance, and for me, that moment will be eternity.
Possessing the Secret of Joy (1992)

14 There are those who believe black people possess the secret of joy and that it is this that will sustain them through any spiritual or moral or physical devastation.
Possessing the Secret of Joy (1992)

15 World wars have been fought and lost; for every war is against the world and every war against the world is lost.
Possessing the Secret of Joy (1992)

16 This Book is Dedicated with Tenderness and Respect To the Blameless Vulva.
Possessing the Secret of Joy (1992), Dedication

17 To acknowledge our ancestors means we are aware that we did not make ourselves, that the line stretches all the way back, perhaps, to God; or to Gods.
"Fundamental Difference," *Revolutionary Petunias and Other Poems* (1973)

18 The quietly pacifist peaceful
always die
to make room for men
who shout.
"The QPP," *Revolutionary Petunias and Other Poems* (1973)

19 Africans are very much like white people back home, in that

they think they are the center of the universe and that everything that is done is done for them.
The Color Purple (1982)

20 Any God I ever felt in church I brought in with me.
The Color Purple (1982)

21 Anyhow, I say, the God I been praying and writing to is a man. And act just like all the other mens I know. Trifling, forgitful, and lowdown.
The Color Purple (1982)

22 But I don't know how to fight. All I know how to do is stay alive.
The Color Purple (1982)

23 Close up I see all this yellow powder caked up on her face. Red rouge. She look like she ain't long for this world but dressed well for the next.
The Color Purple (1982)

24 He laugh. Who you think you is? he say. You can't curse nobody. Look at you. You black, you pore, you ugly, you a woman. Goddam, he say, you nothing at all.
The Color Purple (1982)

25 I never truly notice nothing God make. Not a blade of corn (how it do that?) not the color purple (where it come from?). Not the little wildflowers. Nothing.
The Color Purple (1982)

26 I think it pisses God off if you walk by the color purple in a field somewhere and don't notice it.
The Color Purple (1982)

27 People think pleasing God is all God cares about. But any fool living in the world can see it always trying to please us back.
The Color Purple (1982)

28 Take off they pants, I say, and men look like frogs to me. No matter how you kiss 'em, as far as I'm concern, frogs is what they stay.
The Color Purple (1982)

29 The trouble with our people is that as soon as they got out of slavery they didn't want to give the white man nothing else. But the fact is, you got to give 'em something.
The Color Purple (1982)

30 When I found out I thought that God was white, and a man, I lost interest.
The Color Purple (1982)

31 If it is true that it is what we run from that chases us, then *The Color Purple*...is the book that ran me down while I sat with my back to it in a field.
1992. *The Color Purple* (1992, 10th anniversary edition), Preface

32 The animals of the world exist for their own reasons. They were not made for humans any more than black people were made for whites or women for men.
The Dreaded Comparison: Human and Animal Slavery (Marjorie Speigel; 1988), Introduction

33 Imagine thinking that black people write only about being black and not about being people.
"Fame," *You Can't Keep a Good Woman Down* (1981)

34 Not everyone's life is what they make it. Some people's life is what other people make it.
"Source," *You Can't Keep a Good Woman Down* (1981)

35 I'm always amazed that people will actually choose to sit in front of the television and just be savaged by stuff that belittles their intelligence.
I Dream a World: Portraits of Black Women Who Changed America (Brian Lanker; 1989)

Walker, David (1785–1830) U.S. abolitionist and writer

1 They think because they hold us in their infernal chains of slavery, that we wish to be white, or of their color—but they are dreadfully deceived—we wish to be just as it pleased our Creator to have made us.
Walker's Appeal, in Four Articles (September 1829), quoted in *A Documentary History of the Negro People in the United States* (Herbert Aptheker; 1951)

Walker, Jimmy (James John Walker; 1881–1946) U.S. politician

1 A reformer is a guy who rides through a sewer in a glass-bottomed boat.
Speech, New York (1928)

Walker, Margaret (Margaret Walker Alexander; b.1915) U.S. poet, novelist, and journalist

1 Friends and good manners will carry you where money won't go.
Jubilee (1966)

2 Only ways you can keep folks hating is to keep them apart and separated from each other.
Jubilee (1966)

3 Talk had feet and could walk and gossip had wings and could fly.
Jubilee (1966)

4 What I have here is a complete indictment of our present-day society, our whole world. What's wrong with it is money, honey, money.
Quoted in *Black Women Writers at Work* (Claudia Tate, ed.; 1983)

Wallace, Alfred Russel (1823–1913) British naturalist

Quotations about Wallace

1 An oyster has hardly any more reasoning power than a scientist has...this one jumped to the conclusion that the nineteen-million years was a preparation for *him*.
Mark Twain (1835–1910) U.S. writer and humorist. Mark Twain's riposte to Alfred Russel Wallace's "anthropocentric" theory, that the universe was created specifically for the evolution of mankind. "What Is Man?" (1903)

2 If the Eiffel Tower were now representing the world's age, the skin of paint on the pinnacle-knob at its summit would represent man's share of that age; and anybody would perceive that that skin was what the tower was built for.
Mark Twain (1835–1910) U.S. writer and humorist. Mark Twain's riposte to Alfred Russel Wallace's "anthropocentric" theory, that the universe was created specifically for the evolution of mankind. "What Is Man?" (1903)

Quotations by Wallace

3 Why do some die and some live?...The answer was clearly,

that on the whole the best fitted live...This self-acting process would necessarily *improve the race...the fittest would survive.*
The origin of the phrase "survival of the fittest," suggested by the writing of Thomas Robert Malthus.
My Life: A Record of Events and Opinions (1905)

Wallace, Edgar (Richard Horatio Edgar Wallace; 1875–1932) British thriller and detective-story writer

1 What is a highbrow? It is a man who has found something more interesting than women.
Interview, *New York Times* (January 24, 1932)

Wallace, George (George Corley Wallace; b.1919) U.S. politician

1 I draw the line in the dust and toss the gauntlet before the feet of tyranny, and I say segregation now, segregation tomorrow, segregation forever.
Inaugural address as governor of Alabama (1963)

Wallace, Henry A. (Henry Agard Wallace; 1888–1965) U.S. statesman, agriculturist, and editor

1 The century on which we are entering—the century which will come out of this war—can be and must be the century of the common man.
Address, "The Price of Free World Victory" (May 8, 1942)

2 I doubt if even China can equal our record for soil destruction.
Supporting soil-conservation movements in the United States. Attrib.

Wallace, Lew (Lewis Wallace; 1827–1905) U.S. soldier and writer

1 A man is never so on trial as in the moment of excessive good fortune.
Ben Hur: A Tale of the Christ (1880), bk. 5, ch. 7

2 Would you hurt a man keenest, strike at his self-love.
Ben Hur: A Tale of the Christ (1880), bk. 6, ch. 2

Wallace, Michele (b.1952) U.S. writer, critic, and educator

1 I am saying, among other things, that for perhaps the last fifty years there has been a growing distrust, even hatred, between black men and black women. It has been nursed along not only by racism on the part of whites but also by an almost deliberate ignorance on the part of blacks about the sexual politics of their experience in this country.
Black Macho and the Myth of the Superwoman (1978)

Wallace, Naomi (Naomi French Wallace; b.1960) U.S. writer

1 There is no essential sexuality. Maleness and femaleness are something we are dressed in.
Times, London (August 2, 1994)

Wallace, William Ross (1819–81) U.S. poet and songwriter

1 The hand that rocks the cradle
Is the hand that rules the world.
"What Rules the World" (1865), st. 1

Wallach, Eli (b.1915) U.S. film and stage actor

1 There's something about a crowd like that brings a lump to my wallet.
1964. Remarking upon the long line of people at the box office before one of his performances. Attrib.

Wallas, Graham (1858–1932) British political scientist

1 The little girl had the making of a poet in her who, being told to be sure of her meaning before she spoke, said: "How can I know what I think till I see what I say?"
The Art of Thought (1926), ch. 4

Waller, Edmund (1606–87) English poet

1 Go, lovely rose!
Tell her, that wastes her time and me,
That now she knows,
When I resemble her to thee,
How sweet and fair she seems to be.
"Go Lovely Rose!" (1645)

2 Give me but what this ribband bound,
Take all the rest the sun goes round.
"On a Girdle" (1645), quoted in *The Albatross Book of Verse* (Louis Untermeyer, ed.; 1933)

3 Could we forbear dispute and practise love,
We should agree as angels do above.
"Divine Love," *The Poems of Edmund Waller* (G. Thorn Drury; 1893), can. 3

4 Poets lose half the praise they should have got,
Could it be known what they discreetly blot.
"Upon Roscommon's Translation of Horace, De Arte Poetica," *The Poems of Edmund Waller* (G. Thorn Drury; 1893)

5 We might as well make up our minds that chastity is no more a virtue than malnutrition.
Attrib.

Waller, Fats (Thomas Wright Waller; 1904–43) U.S. jazz pianist, singer, and bandleader

1 Jazz isn't *what* you do, it's *how* you do it.
The Jazz Book (Joachim E. Berendt; 1983)

Wallingford, John of (d.1258) English historian

1 The Danes were effeminately gay in their dress, combed their hair once a day, bathed once a week, and often changed their attire, by these means they...frequently seduced the wives and daughters of the nobility.
13th century. Referring to the Danes during the invasions of Britain (1016–41). Quoted in *History of British Costume* (J. R. Planché; 1874)

Walpole, Horace, 4th Earl of Orford (1717–97) British writer

1 This world is a comedy to those who think, a tragedy to those who feel.
Letter to Anne, Countess of Upper Ossory (August 16, 1776), quoted in *Correspondence* (Yale ed.), vol. 32

2 The next Augustan age will dawn on the other side of the Atlantic. There will, perhaps, be a Thucydides at Boston, a

Xenophon at New York, and, in time, a Virgil in Mexico, and a Newton at Peru.
Letter to Sir Horace Mann (November 24, 1774), quoted in *Correspondence* (Yale ed.), vol. 24

3 Our supreme governors, the mob.
Letter to Sir Horace Mann (September 7, 1743), quoted in *Correspondence* (Yale ed.), vol. 18

4 It was easier to conquer it than to know what to do with it.
Referring to the East. Letter to Sir Horace Mann (March 27, 1772), quoted in *Correspondence* (Yale ed.), vol. 23

5 When will the world know that peace and propagation are the two most delightful things in it?
Letter to Sir Horace Mann (July 7, 1778), quoted in *Correspondence* (Yale ed.), vol. 24

Walpole, Hugh, Sir (Hugh Seymour Walpole; 1884–1941) New Zealand-born British novelist

1 'Tisn't life that matters! 'Tis the courage you bring to it.
Opening words of the book. *Fortitude* (1913), bk. 1, ch. 1

Walpole, Sir Robert, 1st Earl of Orford (1676–1745) English statesman

1 The balance of power.
Speech to the British Parliament (February 13, 1741)

2 Anything but history, for history must be false.
Walpoliana (1781), no. 141

3 All those men have their price.
1739. Said of fellow parliamentarians. *Memoirs of Sir Robert Walpole* (W. Coxe; 1798), vol. 1

Walsh, William (1663–1708) English poet

1 I can endure my own despair,
But not another's hope.
"Song: Of All the Torments," *The Poetical Works of William Walsh* (C. Cooke, ed.; 1797)

Walton, Izaak (1593–1683) English writer

1 Of this blest man, let his just praise be given,
Heaven was in him, before he was in heaven.
17th century. Inscription, referring to Dr. Richard Sibbes, in a copy of *The Returning Backslider* (in Salisbury Cathedral Library). *The Compleat Angler* (1653)

2 Angling is somewhat like poetry, men are to be born so.
The Compleat Angler (1653), ch. 1

3 I remember that a wise friend of mine did usually say, "that which is everybody's business is nobody's business."
The Compleat Angler (1653), ch. 2

4 I love such mirth as does not make friends ashamed to look upon one another next morning.
The Compleat Angler (1653), ch. 5

5 We may say of angling as Dr. Boteler said of strawberries, "Doubtless God could have made a better berry, but doubtless God never did."
The Compleat Angler (1653), ch. 5

6 Let the blessing of St. Peter's Master be...upon all that are lovers of virtue; and dare trust in His providence; and be quiet; and go a-Angling.
The Compleat Angler (1653), ch. 21

7 No man can lose what he never had.
The Compleat Angler (1653), pt. 1, ch. 5

8 Look to your health: and if you have it, praise God, and value it next to a good conscience; for health is the second blessing that we mortals are capable of; a blessing that money cannot buy.
The Compleat Angler (1653), pt. 1, ch. 21

Walton, Sam (Samuel Moore Walton; 1918–92) U.S. retail executive

1 It turned out that the first big lesson we learned was that there was much, much more business out there in small-town America than anybody, including me, had ever dreamed of.
Referring to the Wal-Mart department store chain which he founded in 1962. Quoted in *Sam Walton* (Keith Greenberg; 1993)

2 On the one hand, in the community, I really am an establishment kind of guy; on the other hand, in the marketplace, I have always been a maverick who enjoys shaking things up and creating a little anarchy.
Quoted in *Sam Walton* (Keith Greenberg; 1993)

3 If you can't make your books balance, you take however much they're off by and enter it under the heading ESP, which stands for Error Some Place.
Referring to Wal-Mart's early accounting methods. Quoted in *Sam Walton* (Keith Greenberg; 1993)

Wang Meng (b.1934) Chinese writer and politician

1 The more recent flood of pop culture and the secularization of literature have raised the alarm that serious culture is being engulfed.
"Literary Debates in China Today" (Taotao Liu, tr.; 1997)

Wang Shiduo (1802–98) Chinese government official

1 Because there are too many people, they are poor and there is not enough available land to support them...Heaven has its material for slaughter.
Written during the turbulent years of the Taiping Rebellion (1850–64). *Diary* (1850–64), quoted in *Imperfect Conceptions: Medical Knowledge, Birth Defects, and Eugenics in China* (Frank Dikotter; 1998)

Wang Tao (1828–97) Chinese journalist

1 The Chinese Way is the way of man. The Chinese Way will last as long as mankind.
1870. Quoted in *The Chinese* (Alain Peyrefitte; Graham Webb, tr.; 1977)

Wantling, William (1933–74) U.S. poet and novelist

1 Once, you know
I was quite religious
but now
there is nothing, nothing
yet I still pray.
The Awakening (1969)

2 Dreams
are cages
within which we
observe the cages
without.
"Dreams Are Cages," *The Awakening* (1969)

3 The world soon kills
what it cannot suffer.
"For Lenny Bruce, For Us," *The Awakening* (1969)

4 Let a man listen to his dream
so he may hear the story of all
men and let him say as he did
when he was a child: this is
true; it does not matter what
they tell me.
"For the Peyote Goddess," *The Awakening* (1969)

Warburton, William (1698–1779) English theologian

1 Orthodoxy is my doxy; heterodoxy is another man's doxy.
Letter to Lord Sandwich. Quoted in *Memoirs* (Joseph Priestley; 1807), vol. 1

Ward, Artemus (Charles Farrar Browne; 1834–67) U.S. humorist

1 They shoot folks here somewhat, and the law is rather partial than otherwise to first class murderers.
Referring to Carson City, Nevada. *Artemus Ward, His Travels* (1865)

2 Why care for grammar as long as we are good?
Artemus Ward in London (1867)

3 Let us all be happy, and live within our means, even if we have to borrer the money to do it with.
Artemus Ward in London (1867), ch. 7

4 I am happiest when I am idle. I could live for months without performing any kind of labor, and at the expiration of that time I should feel fresh and vigorous enough to go right on in the same way for numerous more months.
Artemus Ward in London (1867), ch. 9

5 Mr. C. had talent, but he couldn't spel. No man has a right to be a lit'rary man onless he knows how to spel. It is a pity that Chawcer, who had geneyus, was so unedicated. He's the wus speller I know of.
"Chaucer's Poems," *Artemus Ward in London* (1867), ch. 4

6 Why is this thus? What is the reason of this thusness?
"Heber C. Kimball's Harem," *Artemus Ward's Lecture* (1869)

Warhol, Andy (Andrew Warhola; 1928?–87) U.S. artist and filmmaker

Quotations about Warhol

1 I love Andy Warhol. He adores advertising, as I do. It's a great art form.
Camille Paglia (b.1947) U.S. academic and author. Interview, *Guardian*, London (Caroline Egan; 1998)

2 A genius with the IQ of a moron.
Gore Vidal (b.1925) U.S. novelist and essayist. Interview, *Observer*, London (June 18, 1989)

Quotations by Warhol

3 In the future, everyone will be famous for 15 minutes.
Catalogue of his photo exhibition in Stockholm (1968)

4 It's the place where my prediction from the sixties finally came true: "In the future everyone will be famous for fifteen minutes." I'm bored with that line. I never use it anymore. My new line is, "In fifteen minutes everybody will be famous."
Andy Warhol's Exposures (1979)

5 There should always be a lot of new girls in town, and there always are.
Angels, Angels, Angels (1975)

6 I'd asked around 10 or 15 people for suggestions...Finally one lady friend asked the right question, "Well, what do you love most?" That's how I started painting money.
"Andy Warhol Inc., Portrait of the Artist as a Middle-Aged Businessman," *Manhattan Inc.* (October 1984)

7 My instinct about painting says, "If you don't think about it, it's right."
The Philosophy of Andy Warhol: From A to B and Back Again (1975)

8 Being good in business is the most fascinating kind of art.
The Philosophy of Andy Warhol: From A to B and Back Again (1975), quoted in *Observer*, London (March 1, 1987)

9 An artist is someone who produces things that people don't need to have but that he—for *some reason*—thinks it would be a good idea to give them.
"Atmosphere," *The Philosophy of Andy Warhol: From A to B and Back Again* (1975)

10 Sports figures are to the '70s what movie stars were to the '60s.
Time (November 21, 1977)

11 Sex is the biggest nothing of all time.
Quoted in *Halliwell's Filmgoer's Companion* (John Walker, ed.; 1997)

12 If they can take it for ten minutes, then play it for fifteen. That's our policy. Always leave them wanting less.
Quoted in *Lou Reed: Between the Lines* (Michael Wrenn; 1993)

13 How can you say one style is better than another? You ought to be able to be an Abstract-Expressionist next week, or a Pop artist, or a realist, without feeling you've given up something.
Modern Arts Criticism (G. R. Swenson; 1963)

14 Suddenly we all felt like insiders because even though Pop was everywhere...to us, it was the new Art. Once you "got" Pop, you could never see a sign the same way again. And once you thought Pop, you could never see America the same way again.
The moment described occurred while Warhol and others drove to California in 1963. Quoted in *POPism: The Warhol '60s* (Andy Warhol and Pat Hackett; 1980)

15 As soon as you stop wanting something you get it. I've found that to be absolutely axiomatic.
Attrib.

Warner, Charles Dudley (1829–1900) U.S. writer

1 The thing generally raised on city land is taxes.
My Summer in a Garden (1870), sixteenth week

2 No man but feels more of a man in the world if he have a bit of ground that he can call his own. However small it is on the surface, it is four thousand miles deep; and that is a very handsome property.
My Summer in a Garden (1870), preliminary

Warren, Earl (1891–1974) U.S. jurist

1 Many people consider the things which government does for them to be social progress, but they consider the things government does for others as socialism.
Attrib.

Warren, Leonard (originally Leonard Varenov; 1911–60) U.S. baritone

1 Tenors are noble, pure, and heroic and get the soprano. But baritones are born villains in opera. Always the heavy and never the hero.
New York World Telegram (February 13, 1957)

Warren, Mercy (originally Mercy Otis; 1728–1814) U.S. writer

1 MARIA Men rail at weakness themselves create,
And boldly stigmatize the female mind,
As though kind nature's just impartial hand
Had form'd its features in a baser mold.
Poems Dramatic and Miscellaneous, *The Ladies of Castile* (1790), Act 1, Scene 5

Warren, Robert Penn (1905–89) U.S. novelist, poet, and critic

1 Long ago, in Kentucky, I, a boy, stood
By a dirt road, in first dark, and heard
The great geese hoot northward.
"Tell Me a Story," *Audubon* (1969)

2 Storytelling and copulation are the two chief forms of amusement in the South. They're inexpensive and easy to procure.
Newsweek (August 25, 1980)

3 I am not dead yet, though in years,
And the world's way is yet long to go,
And I love the world even in my anger,
And that's a hard thing to outgrow.
"America Portrait: Old Style," *Now and Then: Poems 1976–1978* (1978)

4 Who once would have thought that the heart,
Still ravening on the world's provocation and beauty, might,
After long time lost
In the tangled briars of youth,
Have picked today as payday, the payment

In life's dime-thin, thumb-worn, two-sided, two-faced coin.
"America Portrait: Old Style," *Now and Then: Poems 1976–1978* (1978)

Washington, Booker T. (Booker Taliaferro Washington; 1856–1915) U.S. educator and political activist

1 No race can wrong another race simply because it has the power to do so without being permanently in moral chaos. The Negro can endure the temporary inconvenience, but the injury to the white man is permanent. It is for the white man to save himself from his degradation that I plead.
Speech to the Institute of Arts and Sciences, New York (September 30, 1896), quoted in *Selected Speeches of Booker T. Washington* (E. Davidson Washington, ed.; 1932)

2 Do a common thing in an uncommon way.
Daily Resolves (1896)

3 After the coming of freedom there were two points upon which practically all the people on our place were agreed...that they must change their names, and that they must leave the old plantation for at least a few days or weeks in order that they might really feel sure that they were free.
Up From Slavery (1901)

4 From any point of view, I had rather be what I am, a member of the Negro race, than be able to claim membership with the most favored of any other race.
Up From Slavery (1901)

5 I have learned that success is to be measured not so much by the position that one has reached in life as by the obstacles which he has had to overcome while trying to succeed.
Up From Slavery (1901)

6 My experience is that there is something in human nature which always makes an individual recognize and reward merit, no matter under what color of skin merit is found.
Up From Slavery (1901)

7 My motto...is "Do not do that which others can do as well."
Up From Slavery (1901)

8 The world should not pass judgment upon the Negro, and especially the Negro youth, too quickly or too harshly. The Negro boy has obstacles, discouragements, and temptations to battle with that are little known to those not situated as he is. When a white boy undertakes a task, it is taken for granted that he will succeed. On the other hand, people are usually surprised if the Negro boy does not fail.
Up From Slavery (1901)

9 When freedom came, the slaves were almost as well fitted to begin life anew as the master, except in the matter of book learning and ownership of property. The slave owner and his sons had mastered no special industry.
Up From Slavery (1901)

10 No race can prosper till it learns there is as much dignity in tilling a field as in writing a poem. It is at the bottom of life we must begin, and not at the top. Nor should we permit our grievances to overshadow our opportunities.
September 18, 1895. Address, Atlanta Exposition, *Up From Slavery* (1901)

Washington, George (1732–99) U.S. president

Quotations about Washington

1 First in war, first in peace, first in the hearts of his countrymen.
Robert E. Lee (1807–70) U.S. general. Funeral address (December 1799)

2 The crude commercialism of America, its materializing spirit are entirely due to the country having adopted for its natural hero a man who could not tell a lie.
Oscar Wilde (1854–1900) Irish poet, playwright, and wit. "The Decay of Lying," *Intentions* (1889)

Quotations by Washington

3 It is our true policy to steer clear of permanent alliance with any portion of the foreign world.
Farewell Address, Washington, D.C. (September 17, 1796)

4 From some traits of his character which have lately come to my knowledge, he seems to have been so hackneyed in villainy, and so lost to all sense of honor and shame that while his facilities will enable him to continue his sordid pursuits there will be no time for remorse.
Referring to Benedict Arnold, who served in the Revolutionary Army during the American Revolution but later betrayed the American cause. Letter to John Laurens (October 13, 1780)

5 Associate yourself with men of good quality if you esteem your own reputation; for 'tis better to be alone than in bad company.
Washington's copybook when a schoolboy. "Rules of Civility and Decent Behavior" (1740?), quoted in *The Writings of George Washington* (Jared Sparks; 1834–37)

6 Labor to keep alive in your breast that little spark of celestial fire, called conscience.
Washington's copybook when a schoolboy. "Rules of Civility and Decent Behavior" (1740?), quoted in *The Writings of George Washington* (Jared Sparks; 1834–37), vol. 2

7 The merit of this gentleman is certainly great, and I heartily wish that fortune may distinguish him as one of her favourites. I am convinced that he will do everything that his prudence and valor shall suggest to add success to our arms.
Referring to Benedict Arnold, who served in the Revolutionary Army during the American Revolution but later betrayed the American cause. Quoted in *Benedict Arnold: The Proud Warrior* (Charles Coleman Sellers; 1930)

8 Father, I cannot tell a lie. I did it with my little hatchet.
Referring to cutting a cherry tree. Attrib. *Life of George Washington* (M. L. Weems; 1810, 10th edition), ch. 2

9 I heard the bullets whistle, and believe me, there is something charming in the sound.
Referring to a recent skirmish in the French and Indian War (1754–63). Quoted in *Presidential Anecdotes* (P. Boller; 1981)

10 I can answer but for three things: a firm belief in the justice of our cause, close attention in the prosecution of it, and the strictest integrity.
June 19, 1775. Said on being elected to command the army. Quoted in *Quotations in History* (Alan and Veronica Palmer; 1976)

Waters, Ethel (1896–1977) U.S. blues singer, actor, and songwriter

1 Poverty works like a steam roller, crushing a lot of people. But, like the steam roller, it's also a great leveller.
His Eye Is On The Sparrow (1951)

2 Find out how they like it, when they want it, and how they want it—then give it to them and you'll have no trouble.
On the secret of musical success. *Music on My Mind: The Memoirs of an American Pianist* (Willie the Lion Smith; 1978)

Waters, John (b.1946) U.S. film director

1 I like the audience to feel just a bit guilty about laughing.
Times, London (June 11, 1994), magazine section

2 People no longer need the jokes explained; everyone gets irony nowadays.
Times, London (June 11, 1994), magazine section

3 I base everything on the idea that all men are basically just seven years old.
Attrib.

Waters, Muddy (McKinley Morganfield; 1915–83) U.S. blues musician

1 All my life I was having trouble with women...Then after I quit having trouble with them, I could feel in my heart that somebody would always have trouble with them, so I kept writing those blues.
Quoted in *All You Need is Love* (Tony Palmer; 1977)

2 When you get in the music business, someone's gonna rip you anyway so that don't bother me.
Attrib.

Watson, James Dewey (b.1928) U.S. biochemist

1 Biology has at least 50 more interesting years.
Remark (December 31, 1984)

2 The thought could not be avoided that the best home for a feminist was in another person's lab.
The Double Helix (1968), ch. 2

3 It is necessary to be slightly underemployed if you want to do something significant.
Attrib.

Watson, John B. (John Broadus Watson; 1878–1958) U.S. psychologist and advertising executive

1 Psychology as the behaviorist views it is a purely objective experimental branch of natural science. Its theoretical goal is the prediction and control of behavior.
"Psychology as the Behaviorist Views It," *Psychological Review* (1913), vol. 20

2 When an emotionally exciting object stimulates the subject simultaneously with one not emotionally exciting, the latter may in time (often after one such joint stimulation) arouse the same emotional reaction as the former.
Psychology from the Standpoint of a Behaviorist (1919)

Watson, Thomas J. (Thomas John Watson; 1874–1956) U.S. industrialist

1 I think there is a world market for about five computers.
1943. Attrib.

2 You can do a lot of talking to your employees, and you can buy turkeys at Christmas if that's your hobby, but it isn't going to help you one bit to keep the employee happy.
Attrib.

Watson, Thomas, Jr. (Thomas John Watson, Jr.; 1914–93) U.S. business executive

1 The beliefs that mold great organizations frequently grow out of the character, the experience, and the convictions of a single person.
Quoted in *Key Management Ideas* (Stuart Crainer; 1996)

2 The secret I learned early on from my father was to run scared and never think I had made it.
Quoted in *Key Management Ideas* (Stuart Crainer; 1996)

Watson, William, Sir (John William Watson; 1858–1935) British poet

1 April, April,
Laugh thy girlish laughter;
Then, the moment after,
Weep thy girlish tears.
Song lyric. "April," *Collected Poems* (1898)

2 Pain with the thousand teeth.
"The Dream of Man," *The Poems of Sir William Watson* (1936)

Watt, James G. (James Gaius Watt; b.1938) U.S. lawyer and public official

1 I have a black, a woman, two Jews, and a cripple. And we have talent!
Referring to his staff. The remark precipitated his dismissal. Speech, U.S. Chamber of Commerce (September 21, 1983)

Watts, Alan (Alan Wetson Watts; 1915–73) British-born U.S. mystic and writer

1 Trying to define yourself is like trying to bite your own teeth.
Life (April 21, 1961)

2 For man's Karma travels with him, like his shadow. Indeed it is his shadow, for it has been said, "Man stands in his own shadow and wonders why it is dark."
The Spirit of Zen (1936)

3 The freedom and poverty of Zen is to leave everything and "Walk on," for this is what life itself does, and Zen is the religion of life.
The Spirit of Zen (1936)

4 There is the Zen saying, "Do not linger where the Buddha is, and as to where he is not, pass swiftly on."
The Spirit of Zen (1936)

5 Zen does not attempt to be intelligible, that is to say, capable of being understood by the intellect.
The Spirit of Zen (1936)

6 I have no castle; I make unmovable mind my castle. I have no sword; I make the sleep of the mind my sword.
Extract from the Samurai creed, referring to the condition of detachment known as "Muga." *The Spirit of Zen* (1936)

7 Whatever doubts and indecisions I had before were completely dissolved like a piece of thawing ice. I called out loudly "How wondrous! How wondrous!"
Referring to an account of the experience of enlightenment, or, in the Zen tradition, satori. *The Spirit of Zen* (1936)

8 Zen dispenses with all forms of theorization, doctrinal instruction and lifeless formality; these are treated as the mere symbols of wisdom.
The Spirit of Zen (1936), Foreword

9 To Taoism that which is absolutely still or absolutely perfect is absolutely dead, for without the possibility of growth and change there can be no Tao.
"The Origins of Zen," *The Spirit of Zen* (1936)

10 Zen...does not confuse spirituality with thinking about God while one is peeling the potatoes. Zen spirituality is just to peel the potatoes.
The Way of Zen (1957), pt. 2, ch. 2

Watts, Isaac (1674–1748) English theologian and hymnwriter

1 For Satan finds some mischief still
For idle hands to do.
"Against Idleness and Mischief," *Divine Songs for Children* (1715)

2 How doth the little busy bee
Improve each shining hour,
And gather honey all the day
From every opening flower!
"Against Idleness and Mischief," *Divine Songs for Children* (1715)

3 Let dogs delight to bark and bite,
For God hath made them so;
Let bears and lions growl and fight,
For 'tis their nature too.
"Against Quarrelling," *Divine Songs for Children* (1715)

4 Birds in their little nests agree
And 'tis a shameful sight,
When children of one family
Fall out, and chide, and fight.
"Love Between Brothers and Sisters," *Divine Songs for Children* (1715)

5 Lord, I ascribe it to Thy grace,
And not to chance, as others do,
That I was born of Christian race,
And not a Heathen, or a Jew.
"Praise for the Gospel," *Divine Songs for Children* (1715)

6 There's no repentance in the grave.
"Solemn Thoughts of God and Death," *Divine Songs for Children* (1715)

7 'Tis the voice of the sluggard, I heard him complain:
"You have waked me too soon, I must slumber again."
"The Sluggard," *Divine Songs for Children* (1715)

8 There is a land of pure delight,
Where saints immortal reign;
Infinite day excludes the night,
And pleasures banish pain.
Hymns and Spiritual Songs (1707)

9 When I survey the wondrous Cross,
On which the Prince of Glory died,
My richest gain I count but loss
And pour contempt on all my pride.
"Crucifixion to the World by the Cross of Christ," *Hymns and Spiritual Songs* (1707)

10 Our God, our help in ages past,
Our hope for years to come,
Our shelter from the stormy blast,
And our eternal home.
"Our Help in Ages Past," *The Psalms of David Imitated* (1719), Psalm 90

Waugh, Auberon (Alexander Auberon Waugh; b.1939) British novelist, journalist, and critic

1 It is a sad feature of modern life that only women for the most part have time to write novels, and they seldom have much to write about.
Remark (June 1981)

2 Politicians can forgive almost anything in the way of abuse; they can forgive subversion, revolution, being contradicted, exposed as liars, even ridiculed, but they can never forgive being ignored.
Observer, London (October 11, 1981)

Waugh, Evelyn (Evelyn Arthur St. John Waugh; 1903–66) British novelist

Quotations about Waugh

1 In our way we were both snobs, and no snob welcomes another who has risen with him.
Cecil Beaton (1904–80) British photographer and theatrical designer. Attrib.

2 I expect you know my friend Evelyn Waugh, who, like you, your Holiness, is a Roman Catholic.
Randolph Churchill (1911–68) British journalist. Remark made during an audience with the Pope. Attrib.

3 Mr. Waugh, I always feel, is an antique in search of a period, a snob in search of a class, perhaps even a mystic in search of a beatific vision.
Malcolm Muggeridge (1903–90) British journalist. *The Most of Malcolm Muggeridge* (1966)

Quotations by Waugh

4 Assistant masters came and went...Some liked little boys too little and some too much.
A Little Learning (1964), ch.4

5 We possess nothing certainly except the past.
Brideshead Revisited (1945)

6 I have lived carefully, sheltered myself from the cold winds, eaten moderately of what was in season, drunk fine claret, slept in my own sheets; I shall live long.
Said by Lord Marchmain, just before his death. *Brideshead Revisited* (1945)

7 O God, if there is a God, forgive him his sins, if there is such a thing as sin.
Brideshead Revisited (1945)

8 I expect you'll be becoming a schoolmaster sir. That's what most of the gentlemen does sir, that gets sent down for indecent behaviour.
Decline and Fall (1928), "Prelude"

9 We schoolmasters must temper discretion with deceit.
Decline and Fall (1928), pt. 1, ch. 1

10 That's the public-school system all over. They may kick you out, but they never let you down.
Decline and Fall (1928), pt. 1, ch. 3

11 I can't quite explain it, but I don't believe one can ever be unhappy for long provided one does just exactly what one wants to and when one wants to.
Decline and Fall (1928), pt. 1, ch. 5

12 Meanwhile you will write an essay on "self-indulgence." There will be a prize of half a crown for the longest essay, irrespective of any possible merit.
Decline and Fall (1928), pt. 1, ch. 5

13 Nonconformity and lust stalking hand in hand through the country, wasting and ravaging.
Decline and Fall (1928), pt. 1, ch. 5

14 There aren't many left like him nowadays, what with education and whisky the price it is.
Decline and Fall (1928), pt. 1, ch. 7

15 I have noticed again and again since I have been in the Church that lay interest in ecclesiastical matters is often a prelude to insanity.
Decline and Fall (1928), pt. 1, ch. 8

16 I haven't been to sleep for over a year. That's why I go to bed early. One needs more rest if one doesn't sleep.
Decline and Fall (1928), pt. 2, ch. 3

17 There is a species of person called a "Modern Churchman" who draws the full salary of a beneficed clergyman and need not commit himself to any religious belief.
Decline and Fall (1928), pt. 2, ch. 4

18 I came to the conclusion many years ago that almost all crime is due to the repressed desire for aesthetic expression.
Decline and Fall (1928), pt. 3. ch. 1

19 He was greatly pained at how little he was pained by the events of the afternoon.
Decline and Fall (1928), pt. 3, ch. 4

20 Instead of this absurd division into sexes they ought to class people as static and dynamic.
Decline and Fall (1928), pt. 3, ch. 7

21 Manners are especially the need of the plain. The pretty can get away with anything.
Observer, London (1962), "Sayings of the Year"

22 Enclosing every thin man, there's a fat man demanding elbow-room.
Officers and Gentlemen (1955), Interlude

23 No writer before the middle of the 19th century wrote about the working classes other than as grotesque or as pastoral decoration. Then when they were given the vote certain writers started to suck up to them.
Interview, *Paris Review* (1963)

24 He was gifted with the sly, sharp instinct for self-preservation that passes for wisdom among the rich.
Scoop (1938)

25 "I will not stand for being called a woman in my own house," she said.
Scoop (1938), bk. 1, ch. 5

26 News is what a chap who doesn't care much about anything wants to read. And it's only news until he's read it. After that it's dead.
Scoop (1938), bk. 1, ch. 5

27 Pappenhacker says that every time you are polite to a

proletarian you are helping to bolster up the capitalist system.
Scoop (1938), bk. 1, ch. 5

28 In the dying world I come from quotation is a national vice. It used to be the classics, now it's lyric verse.
The Loved One (1948)

29 Don't hold your parents up to contempt. After all, you are their son, and it is just possible that you may take after them.
The Tablet (May 9, 1951)

30 Mrs. Ape, as was her invariable rule, took round the hat and collected nearly two pounds. "Salvation doesn't do them the same good if they think it's free" was her favourite axiom.
Vile Bodies (1930)

31 Particularly against books the Home Secretary is. If we can't stamp out literature in the country, we can at least stop it being brought in from outside.
Vile Bodies (1930), ch. 2

32 When the war broke out she took down the signed photograph of the Kaiser and, with some solemnity, hung it in the menservants' lavatory; it was her one combative action.
Vile Bodies (1930), ch. 3

33 All this fuss about sleeping together. For physical pleasure I'd sooner go to my dentist any day.
Vile Bodies (1930), ch. 6

34 One forgets words as one forgets names. One's vocabulary needs constant fertilisation or it will die.
Diaries of Evelyn Waugh (Michael Davie, ed.; 1976)

35 Punctuality is the virtue of the bored.
March 26, 1962. "Irregular Notes," *Diaries of Evelyn Waugh* (Michael Davie, ed.; 1976)

36 We are all American at puberty; we die French.
July 18, 1961. "Irregular Notes," *Diaries of Evelyn Waugh* (Michael Davie, ed.; 1976)

37 I put the words down and push them a bit.
Referring to writing. Quoted in Obituary, *New York Times* (April 11, 1966)

38 Nurse unupblown.
Cable sent while a journalist serving in Ethiopia, referring to his inability to substantiate a rumor that an English nurse had been blown up in an Italian air raid. Quoted in *Our Marvellous Native Tongue* (R. Claiborne; 1935)

39 We cherish our friends not for their ability to amuse us, but for ours to amuse them.
Attrib.

40 Like German opera, too long and too loud.
1941. Giving his opinions on warfare after the Battle of Crete (1941). Attrib.

Wavell, Archibald Percival, 1st Earl Wavell (1883–1950) British soldier

1 It is like a cigar. If it goes out, you can light it again but it never tastes quite the same.
Referring to love. Attrib.

Wax, Ruby (b.1953) U.S. comedian and entertainer

1 The guys with that humble pouch, just big enough for some small change and maybe a buffalo.
Referring to the male strippers, *The Chippendales.* Attrib.

Wayne, John (Marion Michael Morrison, "The Duke"; 1907–79) U.S. film actor

1 Put a man aboard a horse, and right off you've got the makings of something magnificent. Physical strength, speed where you can feel it, plus heroism...You pit another strong man against him...and right off there's a simplicity of conflict you just can't beat.
Referring to cowboy films. Quoted in *Duke: The Life and Image of John Wayne* (Ronald L. Davis; 1998)

2 I play John Wayne in every picture regardless of the character, and I've been doing all right, haven't I? I never had a goddam artistic problem in my life, never, and I've worked with the best of them.
Quoted in *Halliwell's Filmgoer's Companion* (John Walker, ed.; 1997)

3 Westerns are closer to art than anything else in the motion picture business.
Quoted in *Halliwell's Filmgoer's Companion* (John Walker, ed.; 1997)

Weatherly, Frederic Edward (1848–1929) British lawyer and songwriter

1 Roses are flowering in Picardy,
But there's never a rose like you.
Song lyric. "Roses of Picardy" (1916)

2 Where are the boys of the Old Brigade?
Song lyric. "The Old Brigade" (1886)

Weaver, Sigourney (Susan Weaver; b.1949) U.S. actor

1 I'm an actor. An actress is someone who wears feather boas.
American Film (October 1983), quoted in *Chambers Film Quotes* (Tony Crawley, ed.; 1991)

Webb, Beatrice (originally Martha Beatrice Potter; 1858–1943) British economist and social reformer

1 Religion is love; in no case is it logic.
My Apprenticeship (1926), ch. 2

2 If I ever felt inclined to be timid as I was going into a room full of people, I would say to myself, "You're the cleverest member of one of the cleverest families in the cleverest class of the cleverest nation in the world, why should you be frightened?"
Quoted in *Portraits from Memory* (Bertrand Russell; 1956)

Webb, Sidney, Baron Passfield (Sidney James Webb; 1859–1947) British economist, social reformer, and politician

1 The inevitability of gradualness.
1923. Referring to social research and its effects. Presidential address to the Annual Conference of the British Labour Party (June 26, 1923)

2 Marriage is the waste-paper basket of the emotions.
Quoted in *Autobiography* (Bertrand Russell; 1967), vol. 1, ch. 4

Weber, Joseph (Joseph Morris Weber; 1867–1942) U.S. vaudeville comedian and theatrical producer

1 Who was that lady I saw you with last night?
She ain't no lady; she's my wife.
Vaudeville routine (co-written with Lew Fields; 1887)

Weber, Max (1864–1920) German economist and social historian

1 The concept of the "official secret" is bureaucracy's specific invention.
Politik als Beruf (1919)

2 If we thus ask, "*Why* should money be made out of men?" Benjamin Franklin himself, although he was a colorless deist, answers in his autobiography with a quotation from the Bible.
1904–05. *The Protestant Ethic and the Spirit of Capitalism* (Talcott Parsons, tr.; 1930)

3 The earning of money within the modern economic order is, so long as it is done legally, the result and the expression of virtue and proficiency in a calling.
1904–05. *The Protestant Ethic and the Spirit of Capitalism* (Talcott Parsons, tr.; 1930)

4 The impulse to acquisition, pursuit of gain, of money...has in itself nothing to do with capitalism...One may say that it has been common to all sorts and conditions of men at all times and in all cultures of the earth.
1904–05. *The Protestant Ethic and the Spirit of Capitalism* (Talcott Parsons, tr.; 1930)

5 Capital accounting in its formally most rational shape... presupposes *the battle of man with man.*
Quoted in *Economy and Society* (Guenther Roth and Claus Wittich, eds.; 1978), ch. 1

6 However many people complain about the "red tape," it would be sheer illusion to think...continuous administrative work can be carried out in any field except by means of officials working in offices...The choice is only that between bureaucracy and dilettantism.
1922. Quoted in *Economy and Society* (Guenther Roth and Claus Wittich, eds.; 1978), ch. 3

Webster, Daniel (1782–1852) U.S. lawyer, politician, and orator

1 Let our object be our country, our whole country, and nothing but our country.
1825. Address on laying the cornerstone of the Bunker Hill Monument, quoted in *The Writings and Speeches of Daniel Webster* (J. W. McIntyre, ed.; 1903), vol. 1

2 Mind is the great lever of all things; human thought is the process by which human ends are ultimately answered.
1825. Address on laying the cornerstone of the Bunker Hill Monument, quoted in *The Writings and Speeches of Daniel Webster* (J. W. McIntyre, ed.; 1903), vol. 1

3 The past, at least, is secure.
January 26, 1830. Speech to the U.S. Senate, quoted in *The Writings and Speeches of Daniel Webster* (J. W. McIntyre, ed.; 1903)

4 The people's government, made for the people, made by the people, and answerable to the people.
January 26, 1830. Referring to Foote's resolution. Speech to the U.S. Senate, quoted in *The Writings and Speeches of Daniel Webster* (J. W. McIntyre, ed.; 1903), vol. 6

5 I was born an American; I will live an American; I shall die an American.
July 17, 1850. Referring to the Compromise Bill. Speech to the U.S. Senate, quoted in *The Writings and Speeches of Daniel Webster* (J. W. McIntyre, ed.; 1903), vol. 10

6 On this question of principle...they raised their flag against a power...which has dotted over the surface of the whole globe with her possessions and military posts, whose morning drumbeat, following the sun, and keeping company with the hours, circles the earth with one continuous and unbroken strain of the martial airs of England.
Referring to the American colonies' fight for independence from British rule. Speech, U.S. Senate (May 7, 1834)

7 Age cannot wither her, nor custom stale her infinite virginity.
Paraphrasing words from William Shakespeare's *Antony and Cleopatra*, on hearing of Andrew Jackson's defense of Peggy Eaton's reputation. Quoted in *Presidential Anecdotes* (P. Boller; 1981)

8 There is no refuge from confession but suicide; and suicide is confession.
April 6, 1830. Said at the trial of John Francis Knapp for the murder of Captain Joseph White. Quoted in *The Writings and Speeches of Daniel Webster* (J. W. McIntyre, ed.; 1903), vol. 11

9 There is always room at the top.
When advised not to become a lawyer because the profession was overcrowded. John Braine (1922–86) borrowed the phrase for his novel *Room at the Top* (1957). Attrib.

Webster, John (1578?–1632?) English playwright

1 Ambition, madam, is a great man's madness.
The Duchess of Malfi (1623), Act 1, Scene 1

2 Indeed he rails at those things which he wants,
Would be as lecherous, covetous, or proud,
Bloody, or envious, as any man,
If he had means to be so.
The Duchess of Malfi (1623), Act 1, Scene 1

3 A politician is the devil's quilted anvil—
He fashions all sins on him, and the blows
Are never heard.
The Duchess of Malfi (1623), Act 3, Scene 2

4 I know death hath ten thousand several doors
For men to take their exits.
The Duchess of Malfi (1623), Act 4, Scene 2

5 Other sins only speak; murder shrieks out.
The Duchess of Malfi (1623), Act 4, Scene 2

6 Physicians are like kings,—they brook no contradiction.
The Duchess of Malfi (1623), Act 5, Scene 2

7 We are merely the stars' tennis-balls, struck and bandied
Which way please them.
The Duchess of Malfi (1623), Act 5, Scene 4

8 A mere tale of a tub, my words are idle.
The White Devil (1612), Act 2, Scene 1

9 There's nothing sooner dry than women's tears.
The White Devil (1612), Act 5, Scene 3

10 Call for the robin-redbreast and the wren,
Since o'er shady groves they hover,
And with leaves and flowers to cover
The friendless bodies of unburied men...
But keep the wolf far thence, that's foe to men,
For with his nails he'll dig them up again.
The White Devil (1612), Act 5, Scene 4

11 We think caged birds sing, when indeed they cry.
The White Devil (1612), Act 5, Scene 4

12 Let guilty men remember their black deeds
Do lean on crutches, made of slender reeds.
The White Devil (1612), Act 5, Scene 6

13 O happy they that never saw the court,
Nor ever knew great man but by report.
The White Devil (1612), Act 5, Scene 6

14 I saw him even now going the way of all flesh, that is to say towards the kitchen.
Westward Ho! (co-written with Thomas Dekker; 1604?), Act 2, Scene 2

15 Gold that buys health can never be ill spent.
Westward Ho! (co-written with Thomas Dekker; 1604?), Act 5

Webster, Noah (1758–1843) U.S. lexicographer and writer

1 No, my dear, it is *I* who am surprised; you are merely astonished.
Responding to his wife's comment that she had been surprised to find him embracing their maid. Attrib.

Wedderburn, Robert (1762?–1835?) Jamaican-born British preacher

1 Hath not a slave feelings? If you starve them, will they not die? If you wrong them will they not take revenge?
The Horrors of Slavery (1824)

Weidman, Jerome (1913–98) U.S. writer

1 "When I was your age," my mother said, "I ate herring and black bread for thirty-six days in the bottom of a ship to get from Antwerp to New York. Outside of New York there's nothing. Only a great big garbage pail they call Europe."
Praying for Rain (1986), ch. 1

2 Arrogance functions on the oxygen of its own modesty. The self-confidence that is part of being young is sensibly flexible.
Praying for Rain (1986), ch. 2

3 My father was an immigrant from Austria who...was considered by his peers to be one of the best pocket makers who ever carried an Amalgamated Clothing Workers of America union card.
Praying for Rain (1986), ch. 2

4 I learned to distinguish between the sounds made by a distant torpedo finding its target and the explosion of a depth charge; and I discovered...that it is possible...to survive sixteen consecutive days of being scared stiff.
Referring to crossing the Atlantic in convoy in 1941. *Praying for Rain* (1986), ch. 15

Weil, André (b.1906) French-born U.S. mathematician

1 God exists since mathematics is consistent, and the Devil exists since we cannot prove it.
Quoted in *Mathematical Circles Adieu* (H. Eves; 1977)

Weil, Simone (1909–43) French philosopher, mystic, and political activist

1 A work of art has an author and yet, when it is perfect, it has something which is anonymous about it.
"Gravity and Grace" (1947)

2 Imagination and fiction make up more than three quarters of our real life.
"Gravity and Grace" (1947)

3 Learn to reject friendship, or rather the dream of friendship. To want friendship is a great fault. Friendship ought to be a gratuitous joy, like the joys afforded by art, or life (like aesthetic joys).
"The Pre-War Notebook," *First and Last Notebooks* (Richard Rees, ed.; 1970)

4 The future is made of the same stuff as the present.
1940–42. "Some Thoughts on the Love of God," *On Science, Necessity and the Love of God* (Richard Rees, ed.; 1968)

5 The word "revolution" is a word for which you kill, for which you die, for which you send the laboring masses to their death, but which does not possess any content.
"Reflections Concerning the Causes of Liberty and Social Oppression," *Oppression and Liberty* (1958)

6 Culture is an instrument wielded by professors to manufacture professors, who when their turn comes will manufacture professors.
The Need for Roots (A. F. Wills, tr.; 1952)

7 The world only gives itself to Man in the form of food and warmth if Man gives himself to the world in the form of labor.
The Need for Roots (A. F. Wills, tr.; 1952)

8 Algebra and money are essentially levelers; the first intellectually, the second effectively.
Quoted in *The Viking Book of Aphorisms* (W. H. Auden and L. Kronenberger, eds.; 1966)

9 Love is not consolation, it is light.
Attrib.

Weill, Kurt (1900–50) German-born U.S. composer

1 I write for today. I don't care about posterity.
Quoted in *American Composers* (David Ewen; 1982)

2 Musical theater is the highest, the most expressive and the most imaginative form of theater...a composer who has a talent and a passion for the theater can express himself completely in this branch of musical creativeness.
Quoted in *American Composers* (David Ewen; 1982)

3 I am not struggling for new forms or new theories. I am struggling for a new public.
Quoted in *The World of Musical Comedy* (Stanley Green; 1962)

Weinberg, John Livingston (b.1925) U.S. investment banker

1 When the whale comes to the surface and spouts, that's when he gets harpooned.
Referring to investment company Goldman Sachs' dislike of publicity. *Independent on Sunday*, London (September 9, 1990)

Weinberg, Steven (b.1933) U.S. physicist

1 As we understand more and more about nature, the scientist's sense of wonder has not diminished but has rather become sharper, more narrowly focused on the mysteries that still remain.
Scientific American (October 1994)

2 The effort to understand the universe is one of the very few things that lifts human life a little above the level of farce and gives it some of the grace of tragedy.
The First Three Minutes (1977), ch. 8

3 The more the universe seems comprehensible, the more it also seems pointless.
The First Three Minutes (1977), Epilogue

Weinberger, Caspar (Caspar Willard Weinberger; b.1917) U.S. lawyer and public official

1 I have read the Book of Revelation and, yes, I believe the world is going to end—by an act of God, I hope—but every day I think that time is running out.
Interview, *New York Times* (August 23, 1982)

Weiner, Herb U.S. songwriter

1 It's my party and I'll cry if I want to.
Song lyric. First popularized by Leslie Gore in the United States (1963). Attrib.

Weiner, Norbert U.S. business executive

1 I have seriously considered the possibility of giving up my scientific productive effort because I know of no way to publish without letting my inventions go to the wrong hands.
Quoted in *The Cult of Information* (Theodore Roszak; 1986)

Weiss, Peter (Peter Ulrich Weiss; 1916–82) German-born Swedish novelist and playwright

1 Man has given a false importance to death
Any animal plant or man who dies
adds to Nature's compost heap
becomes the manure without which
nothing could grow nothing could be created
Death is simply part of the process.
The Persecution and Assassination of Marat as Performed by the Inmates of the Asylum of Charenton Under the Direction of the Marquis de Sade (1964), Act 1, Scene 12

2 We invented the Revolution
but we don't know how to run it.
The Persecution and Assassination of Marat as Performed by the Inmates of the Asylum of Charenton Under the Direction of the Marquis de Sade (1964), Act 1, Scene 15

Weisstein, Naomi (b.1939) U.S. experimental psychologist

1 Why have they been telling us women lately that we have no sense of humor—when we are always laughing?...And when we're not laughing, we're smiling.
Quoted in *All She Needs* (Ellen Levine; 1973)

Weizsäcker, Carl Friedrich von, Freiherr von Weizsäcker (b.1912) German physicist and philosopher

1 Classical physics has been superseded by quantum theory: quantum theory is verified by experiments. Experiments must be described in terms of classical physics.
Attrib.

Welch, Jack (originally John Francis Welch; b.1935) U.S. electronics executive

1 The leader's unending responsibility must be to remove every detour, every barrier to ensure that vision is first clear, then real.
Speech to the Bay Area Council, San Francisco (July 6, 1989)

2 If you're not in Germany, you're not in Europe. And if you're not in Asia, you're nowhere.
Speech to the Economic Club of Detroit (May 16, 1994)

3 The job for big companies, the challenge that we all face as bureaucrats, is to create an environment where people can reach their dreams—and they don't have to do it in a garage.
Fortune (May 29, 1996)

4 One of the things about leadership is that you cannot be a moderate, balanced, thoughtful, careful articulator of policy. You've got to be on the lunatic fringe.
Washington Post (March 23, 1997)

5 Companies can't promise lifetime employment, but by constant training and education we may be able to guarantee lifetime employability.
Quoted in *Control Your Destiny or Someone Else Will* (Noel M. Tichy and Stratford Sherman; 1993)

6 An overburdened, stretched executive is the best executive, because he or she doesn't have time to meddle, to deal in trivia, to bother people.
Quoted in *Financial Times*, London (December 30, 1989), "Quotes of the Year"

7 I want a revolution, and I want it to start in Crotonville.
The headquarters of General Electric Company are in Crotonville, New York. Quoted in *Jack Welch Speaks* (Janet C. Lowe; 1998)

8 Boundaryless behavior is what integrates us and turns this opportunity into reality, creating the real value of a multibusiness company—the big competitive advantage we call Integrated Diversity.
Quoted in *Survival of the Smartest* (Haim Mendelson and Johannes Ziegler; 1999)

9 Collocation is the ultimate boundaryless behavior and is as unsophisticated as can be...One room, one coffeepot, one team, one shared mission.
Quoted in *Survival of the Smartest* (Haim Mendelson and Johannes Ziegler; 1999)

10 What we are trying relentlessly to do is get that small-company soul—and small-company speed—inside our big company.
Quoted in *USA Today* (February 2, 1993)

Welch, Lew (Lewis Barrett Welch, Jr.; 1926–71) U.S. poet

1 Those who can't find anything to live for,
always invent something to die for.
Then they want the rest of us to die
for it too.
"The Basic Con," *Ring of Bone: Collected Poems 1950–1971* (Donald M. Allen, ed.; 1973)

Welch, Raquel (originally Raquel Tejada; b.1940) U.S. film actor

1 The mind can also be an erogenous zone.
Quoted in *Colombo's Hollywood* (J. R. Colombo; 1979)

2 What they say about footballers being ignorant is rubbish. I

spoke to a couple yesterday and they were quite intelligent.
1973. After a visit to see the British soccer club Chelsea play. Attrib.

Welch, William H. (William Henry Welch; 1850–1934) U.S. pathologist

1 Medical education is not completed at the medical school: it is only begun.
Bulletin of the Harvard Medical School Association (1892), no. 3

Weldon, Fay (b.1933) British writer

1 I think we owe our friends more, especially our female friends.
Praxis (1978)

2 Women who live by the goodwill of men have no control over their lives, and that's the truth of it.
The Heart of the Country (1989)

Welles, Orson (George Orson Welles; 1915–85) U.S. actor, director, producer, and writer

Quotations about Welles

1 "I want to do the history of jazz as a picture...While you're thinking about this," he continued, "you're on salary at a thousand dollars a week, and if you don't take it you're a sucker." "I accept," I said.
Duke Ellington (1899–1974) U.S. jazz bandleader, pianist, and composer. Referring to a meeting with Orson Welles in 1934. *Music is My Mistress* (1973)

2 There, but for the Grace of God, goes God.
1941
Herman J. Mankiewicz (1897–1953) U.S. screenwriter and film producer. Said of Orson Welles during the making of *Citizen Kane* (1941). Also attributed to others. Quoted in *The Citizen Kane Book* (Pauline Kael; 1971)

Quotations by Welles

3 My own start in movies was a lucky one, thanks to a contract that for almost 30 years remained unique in Hollywood history. That contract...challenged for a brief moment the basic premise of the whole studio system. Quite simply, I was left alone.
Referring to *Citizen Kane* (1941). *Look* (March 11, 1970), quoted in *Chambers Film Quotes* (Tony Crawley, ed.; 1991)

4 I hate television. I hate it as much as peanuts. But I can't stop eating peanuts.
New York Herald Tribune (October 12, 1956)

5 When you are down and out, something always turns up—and it is usually the noses of your friends.
New York Times (April 1, 1962)

6 There are only two emotions in a plane: boredom and terror.
Observer, London (May 12, 1985), "Sayings of the Week"

7 In Italy for thirty years under the Borgias they had warfare, terror, murder, bloodshed—they produced Michelangelo, Leonardo da Vinci and the Renaissance. In Switzerland they had brotherly love, five hundred years of democracy and peace, and what did they produce...? The cuckoo clock.
As Harry Lime in Carol Reed's celebrated film. *The Third Man* (co-written with Graham Greene and Carol Reed; 1949)

8 I would just like to mention Robert Houdini who in the eighteenth century invented the vanishing bird-cage trick and the theater matinée—may he rot and perish. Good afternoon.
Addressing the audience at the end of a matinée performance. Quoted in *Great Theatrical Disasters* (Gyles Brandreth; 1982)

9 It's the biggest electric train set a boy ever had.
Referring to the Radio-Keith-Orpheum (RKO) studios. Quoted in *The Fabulous Orson Welles* (Peter Noble; 1956), ch. 7

10 Every actor in his heart believes everything bad that's printed about him.
Attrib.

11 Everyone denies I am a genius—but nobody ever called me one!
Attrib.

12 I started at the top and worked my way down.
Attrib.

Wellington, Duke of, 1st Duke of Wellington (Arthur Wellesley, "The Iron Duke"; 1769–1852) Irish-born British general and prime minister

Quotations about Wellington

1 He accepted peace as if he had been defeated.
Napoleon I (1769–1821) French emperor. Attrib.

Quotations by Wellington

2 I have got an infamous army, very weak and ill-equipped, and a very inexperienced staff.
Written at the beginning of the Waterloo campaign. Letter to Lord Stewart (May 8, 1815)

3 Beginning reform is beginning revolution.
Remark (November 7, 1830)

4 I see no reason to suppose that these machines will ever force themselves into general use.
Referring to steam locomotives. Quoted in *Geoffrey Madan's Notebooks* (J. Gere, ed.; 1827)

5 I always say that, next to a battle lost, the greatest misery is a battle gained.
Recollections (Samuel Rogers; 1859)

6 Yes, and they went down very well too.
Replying to the observation that the French cavalry had come up very well during the Battle of Waterloo. Quoted in *The Age of Elegance, 1812–1822* (Arthur Bryant; 1950)

7 The battle of Waterloo was won on the playing fields of Eton.
Quoted in *Words on Wellington* (Sir William Fraser; 1889)

8 I don't know what effect these men will have on the enemy, but, by God, they frighten me.
1810. A paraphrase of words written in a dispatch of August 29, 1810, referring to his officers. Attrib.

9 It is not the business of generals to shoot one another.
1815. Refusing an artillery officer permission to fire upon Napoleon at the Battle of Waterloo, 1815. Attrib.

10 Very well, then I shall not take off my boots.
Responding, as he was going to bed, to news that the ship in which he was traveling seemed about to sink. Attrib.

11 Yes, about ten minutes.
Responding to a vicar who had asked whether there was anything he would like his forthcoming sermon to be about. Attrib.

Wells, H. G. (Herbert George Wells; 1866–1946) British writer

Quotations about Wells

1 Whatever Wells writes is not only alive, but kicking.
Henry James (1843–1916) U.S.-born British writer and critic. Attrib.

2 I doubt whether in the whole course of our history, any one individual has explored as many avenues, turned over so many stones, ventured along so many culs-de-sac. Science, history, politics, all were within his compass.
Malcolm Muggeridge (1903–90) British journalist. *Observer,* London (September 11, 1966)

Quotations by Wells

3 The cat is the offspring of a cat and the dog of a dog, but butlers and lady's maids do not reproduce their kind. They have other duties.
Bealby (1915), pt. 1, ch. 1

4 Miss Madeleine Philips was making it very manifest to Captain Douglas that she herself was a career; that a lover with any other career in view need not—as the advertisements say—apply.
Bealby (1915), pt. 5, ch. 5

5 He had one peculiar weakness; he had faced death in many forms but he had never faced a dentist. The thought of dentists gave him just the same sick horror as the thought of Socialism.
Bealby (1915), pt. 8, ch. 1

6 "It's giving girls names like that," said Buggins, "that nine times out of ten makes 'em go wrong. It unsettles 'em. If ever I was to have a girl, if ever I was to have a dozen girls, I'd call 'em all Jane."
Referring to the name Euphemia. *Kipps* (1905), bk. 1, ch. 4

7 "*Language*, man!" roared Parsons; "why, it's LITERATURE!"
The History of Mr. Polly (1910), pt. 1, ch. 3

8 Arson, after all, is an artificial crime...A large number of houses deserve to be burnt.
The History of Mr. Polly (1910), pt. 10, ch. 1

9 The Shape of Things to Come
Book title. (1933)

10 The War That Will End War
Book title. (1914)

11 To find goodness in the sinner and justification in the outcast is to condemn the law.
The Wife of Sir Isaac Harman (1914)

12 In England we have come to rely upon a comfortable time lag of fifty years or a century intervening between the perception that something ought to be done and a serious attempt to do it.
The Work, Wealth, and Happiness of Mankind (1931)

Weltsch, Robert (1891–1982) Czech-born German publisher

1 Wear it with pride, the yellow badge.
1933. Said in response to the onset of the Nazi anti-Semitic campaign, when Jews were forced to wear yellow stars sewn to their outer garments so that they could be easily identified. *Jüdische Rundschau* (April 1, 1933)

Welty, Eudora (b.1909) U.S. writer

1 I rather a man be anything than a woman be mean.
Livvie (1943)

2 For sure, you couldn't *buy* mayonnaise, and if you could, you wouldn't. For the generation bringing my generation up, everything made in the kitchen started from scratch, too.
The Jackson Cookbook (1971)

3 Our mothers were sans mixes, sans foil, sans freezer, sans blender, sans monosodium glutamate, but their ingredients were as fresh as the day; and they knew how to make bread.
The Jackson Cookbook (1971)

Wenders, Wim (Wilhelm Wenders; b.1945) German filmmaker

1 Someone asked me after a screening of *Paris, Texas*: "Is that a true story?" I said: "It is now."
The Act of Seeing (1988)

2 There have always been...two kinds of cinema: the purely industrial kind, no different than say the car industry, and the other sort with the blank sheet of paper, or the blank screen in the morning.
The Act of Seeing (1988)

Wentworth, Peter (1530–96) English parliamentary leader

1 In this House, which is termed a place of free speech, there is nothing so necessary for the preservation of the prince and state as free speech.
Speech to the English Parliament (February 8, 1576)

Wentworth, Thomas, 1st Earl of Strafford (1593–1641) English statesman

1 For howbeit the Irish might do very good Service, being a People removed from the Scottish, as well in Affections as Religion; yet it is not safe to train them up more than needs must in the military Way.
Letter to Charles I from Ireland (July 28, 1638)

2 If words spoken to friends, in familiar discourse, spoken in one's chamber, spoken at one's table, spoken in one's sick-bed...if these things shall be brought against a man as treason...it will be a silent world...and no man shall dare to impart his solitary thoughts or opinions to his friend and neighbour.
Remark at his trial (April 5, 1641)

3 That every man would lay his hand on his heart, and consider seriously whether the beginnings of the people's happiness should be written in letters of blood.
Remark before his execution (1641)

4 Divide not between Protestant and Papist...divide not nationally, betwixt English and Irish. The King makes no distinction betwixt you.
Referring to Charles I, for whom Thomas Wentworth was principal adviser. Charles I married a French Catholic princess, Henrietta Maria. Speech, Irish Parliament (July 15, 1634)

Wen Yiduo (also known as Wen I-to; 1899–1946) Chinese poet

1 Perhaps you hear earthworms turning the soil,
The grass roots sucking water.

Perhaps the music you hear now
Is lovelier than men's cursing voices.
"Perhaps (A Dirge)" (1927?), st. 3

Wesker, Arnold (b.1932) British playwright

1 Your work and your life should be part of one existence, not something hacked about by a bus queue and office hours.
Chicken Soup with Barley (1958), Act 2

2 You breed babies and you eat chips with everything.
Chips with Everything (1962), Act 1, Scene 2

3 There's nothing more pathetic than the laughter of people who have lost their pet faith.
I'm Talking About Jerusalem (1960), Act 2, Scene 1

Wesley, Charles (1707–88) English religious leader and hymnwriter

1 Gentle Jesus, meek and mild,
Look upon a little child;
Pity my simplicity,
Suffer me to come to thee.
"Gentle Jesus," *Hymns and Sacred Poems* (1742)

2 Love divine, all loves excelling,
Joy of heav'n to earth come down,
Fix in us thy humble dwelling,
All thy faithful mercies crown.
Hymn based on Dryden's "Fairest isle, all isles excelling" in *King Arthur* (1691). "Love Divine," *Hymns for Those that Seek...Redemption* (1747)

Wesley, John (1703–91) English religious leader

1 Though I am always in haste, I am never in a hurry.
Letter to Miss March (December 10, 1777), quoted in *Letters* (J. Telford, ed.; 1931), vol. 6

2 I look upon all the world as my parish.
Journal (June 11, 1739)

3 Do all the good you can,
By all the means you can,
In all the ways you can,
In all the places you can,
At all the times you can,
To all the people you can,
As long as ever you can.
Rule of Conduct (1784)

4 I want to know one thing—the way to heaven; how to land safe on that happy shore. God himself has condescended to teach the way; for this very end he came from heaven. He hath written it down in a book. O give me that book!
Sermons (1747), Preface

5 Let it be observed, that slovenliness is no part of religion; that neither this, nor any text of Scripture, condemns neatness of apparel. Certainly this is a duty, not a sin. "Cleanliness is, indeed, next to godliness."
"On Dress," *Sermons on Several Occasions* (1788), sermon 93

6 Beware you be not swallowed up in books! An ounce of love is worth a pound of knowledge.
Quoted in *Life of Wesley* (R. Southey; 1820), ch. 16

7 We should constantly use the most common, little, easy words (so they are pure and proper) which our language affords.
Advice for preaching to "plain people." Attrib.

West, Jessamyn (Mary Jessamyn West; 1902–84) U.S. writer

1 She intended to forgive. Not to do so would be un-Christian; but did not intend to do so soon, nor forget how much she had to forgive.
"The Buried Leaf," *The Friendly Persuasion* (1991)

West, Mae (1892–1980) U.S. actor and comedian

Quotations about West

1 In a non-permissive age, she made remarkable inroads against the taboos of her day, and did so without even lowering her neckline.
Leslie Halliwell (1929–89) British film critic. *The Filmgoer's Book of Quotes* (1973)

2 She stole everything but the cameras.
George Raft (1895–1980) U.S. actor. Attrib.

Quotations by West

3 A man in the house is worth two in the street.
Belle of the Nineties (1934)

4 I always say, keep a diary and some day it'll keep you.
Every Day's A Holiday (1937)

5 I have a lot of respect for that dame. There's one lady barber that made good.
Referring to Delilah in the screenplay of the film. *Going to Town* (1934)

6 Beulah, peel me a grape.
I'm No Angel (1933)

7 It's not the men in my life that count; it's the life in my men.
I'm No Angel (1933)

8 When I'm good I'm very good, but when I'm bad I'm better.
I'm No Angel (1933)

9 A gold rush is what happens when a line of chorus girls spot a man with a bank roll.
Klondike Annie (1936)

10 Whenever I'm caught between two evils, I take the one I've never tried.
Klondike Annie (1936)

11 "Goodness, what beautiful diamonds!"
"Goodness had nothing to do with it, dearie."
Night After Night (1932)

12 When you get the personality, you don't need the nudity.
Observer, London (August 4, 1968), "Sayings of the Week"

13 You're a fine woman, Lou. One of the finest women that ever walked the streets.
She Done Him Wrong (1933)

14 I always did like a man in uniform. And that one fits you grand. Why don't you come up sometime and see me?
Often misquoted as "Come up and see me some time." *She Done Him Wrong* (1933)

15 I knew what I wanted and determined at an early age that no

man would ever tell me what to do. I would make my own rules and down with the double standards.
Working Woman (1979)

16 Men have structured society to make a woman feel guilty if she looks after herself...I don't look down on men, but I don't look up to them either. I never found a man I could love—or trust—as much as myself.
"My Side, February," *Working Woman* (1979)

17 I never meant "Come up and see me some time" to be sexy.
Quoted in *Film Comment* (October 1984)

18 You can say what you like about long dresses, but they cover a multitude of shins.
Quoted in *Peel Me a Grape* (J. Weintraub; 1975)

19 It is better to be looked over than overlooked.
Quoted in *The Wit and Wisdom of Mae West* (J. Weintraub, ed.; 1967)

20 It's hard to be funny when you have to be clean.
Quoted in *The Wit and Wisdom of Mae West* (J. Weintraub, ed.; 1967)

21 I used to be Snow White...but I drifted.
Quoted in *The Wit and Wisdom of Mae West* (J. Weintraub, ed.; 1967)

22 When women go wrong, men go right after them.
Quoted in *The Wit and Wisdom of Mae West* (J. Weintraub, ed.; 1967)

23 Every man I meet wants to protect me. I can't figure out what from.
Attrib.

24 Love conquers all things except poverty and toothache.
Attrib.

25 Speak up for yourself, or you'll end up a rug.
Attrib.

26 Marriage is a great institution, but I'm not ready for an institution, yet.
Also attributed to Groucho Marx. Attrib.

27 I've been in *Who's Who*, and I know what's what, but this is the first time I ever made the dictionary.
Said after having a life jacket named after her. Attrib.

28 Everything.
When asked what she wanted to be remembered for. Attrib.

West, Nathanael (Nathan Wallenstein Weinstein; 1903–40) U.S. novelist and screenwriter

1 Are you in trouble? Do you need advice? Write to Miss Lonelyhearts and she will help.
Miss Lonelyhearts (1933)

2 He smiled bunching his fat cheeks like twin rolls of smooth pink toilet paper.
Miss Lonelyhearts (1933)

3 He thought of children dancing. Square replacing oblong and being replaced by circle. Every child, everywhere; in the whole world there was not one child who was not gravely, sweetly dancing.
Miss Lonelyhearts (1933)

4 Numbers constitute the only universal language.
Miss Lonelyhearts (1933)

5 You're morbid, my friend, morbid. Forget the crucifixion, remember the renaissance. There were no brooders then.
Miss Lonelyhearts (1933)

6 He knew now what this thing was—hysteria, a snake whose scales are tiny mirrors in which the dead world takes on a semblance of life.
"Miss Lonelyhearts and the Lamb," *Miss Lonelyhearts* (1933)

7 Miss Lonelyhearts, he of the singing heart—a still more swollen Mussolini of the soul.
Shrike's ironical description of Miss Lonelyhearts, the pen name of the male columnist whose life is the subject of the novel. "Miss Lonelyhearts Attends a Party," *Miss Lonelyhearts* (1933)

8 In the evening, on the blue lagoon, under the silvery moon, to your love you croon in the soft sylabelew and vocabelew of her langorour tongorour.
Shrike describes an ideal life in the South Seas to Miss Lonelyhearts. "Miss Lonelyhearts in the Dismal Swamp," *Miss Lonelyhearts* (1933)

West, Rebecca, Dame (Cicily Isabel Fairfield Andrews; 1892–1983) Irish-born British novelist, critic, and journalist

Quotations about West

1 She regarded me as a piece of fiction—like one of her novels—that she could edit and improve.
Anthony West (1914–87) British journalist and writer. *Heritage* (1984)

Quotations by West

2 But there are other things than dissipation that thicken the features. Tears, for example.
"Serbia," *Black Lamb and Grey Falcon* (1941)

3 Journalism—an ability to meet the challenge of filling the space.
New York Herald Tribune (April 22, 1956)

4 Any authentic work of art must start an argument between the artist and his audience.
The Court and the Castle (1957), pt. 1, ch. 1

5 There is no such thing as conversation. It is an illusion. There are intersecting monologues, that is all.
There is No Conversation (1935), ch. 1

6 The point is that nobody likes having salt rubbed into their wounds, even if it is the salt of the earth.
The Salt of the Earth (1935), ch. 2

7 God forbid that any book should be banned. The practice is as indefensible as infanticide.
"The Tosh Horse," *The Strange Necessity* (1928)

8 Just how difficult it is to write biography can be reckoned by anybody who sits down and considers just how many people know the real truth about his or her love affairs.
Vogue (1952)

9 If we had left it to the men *toilets* would have been the greatest obstacle to human progress. *Toilets* was always the reason women couldn't become engineers, or pilots...They didn't have women's toilets.
Quoted in *There's Always been a Women's Movement this Century* (Dale Spender; 1983)

10 My dear—the people we should have been seen dead with.
1945. Cable sent to Noël Coward after learning they had both been on a Nazi death list. Quoted in *Times Literary Supplement*, London (October 1, 1982)

Westmoreland, William C., General (William Childs Westmoreland; b.1914) U.S. military commander

1 We have reached an important point when the end begins to come into view.
Speech, National Press Club (November 21, 1967)

2 Vietnam was the first war ever fought without any censorship. Without censorship, things can get terribly confused in the public mind.
Time (April 5, 1982)

3 The military don't start wars. The politicians start wars.
Attrib.

Westwood, Vivienne (b.1941) British fashion designer

1 I think any man is either mad or stupid who wouldn't prefer me to every other woman in the room wherever I go.
Said on arriving for dinner at Kensington Palace, London, in a clinging, transparent dress. *Evening Standard*, London (June 3, 1992)

2 It is all about technique. The great mistake of this century is to put inspiration and creativity first.
Observer, London (May 15, 1994), "Sayings of the Week"

3 What I do is restricted by the cloth and the human body. My job is to make that cloth give expression to the body.
Times, London (November 16, 1992)

4 If you want to find out how much freedom you have, make some kind of explicit sexual statement and wait for it all to crash down around you.
Quoted in *Rock 'n' Roll Babylon* (Gary Herman; 1994)

Wexler, Jerry (b.1917) U.S. record producer

1 Since we're all capitalist enterprises, we have to capture the lowest possible denominator. What's wrong is that we have to cater to the rancid, infantile, pubescent tastes of the public.
Quoted in *The Wit and Wisdom of Rock and Roll* (Maxim Jabukowski, ed.; 1983)

Weyer, Johann (1515–88) German-Dutch physician

1 These evil spirits accomplish some wondrous feats, and they predict certain things on the basis of their knowledge of Holy Scripture.
1563. *De Praestigiis Daemonum* (John Shea, tr.; 1991), bk. 1, ch. 18

2 A most just and good God does not permit all the things which Satan might wish, or of which he is capable because of the subtlety of his nature.
1563. *De Praestigiis Daemonum* (John Shea, tr.; 1991), bk. 3, ch. 12

3 It has been abundantly demonstrated that a just and most merciful God has not subjected the air or the elements to the will and power of a malicious woman.
1563. *De Praestigiis Daemonum* (John Shea, tr.; 1991), bk. 3, ch. 18

Weygand, Maxime (1867–1965) Belgian-born French general

1 In three weeks England will have her neck wrung like a chicken.
1940. Said at the fall of France. Quoted in *Their Finest Hour* (Winston S. Churchill; 1948)

Weyl, Hermann (1885–1955) German-born U.S. mathematician

1 My work has always tried to unite the true with the beautiful and when I had to choose one or the other, I usually chose the beautiful.
Quoted in his obituary notice. Quoted in *Nature* (Freeman Dyson; March 10, 1956)

Wharton, Edith (Edith Newbold Wharton; 1862–1937) U.S. novelist

1 What is writing a novel like? The beginning: A ride through a spring wood. The middle: The Gobi desert. The end: Going down the cresta run...I am now (p. 166 of "The Buccaneers") in the middle of the Gobi desert.
Quoting from her diary of 1934. Letter to Bernard Berenson (January 12, 1937), quoted in *The Letters of Edith Wharton* (R. W. B. Lewis and Nancy Lewis, eds.; 1988)

2 Drop 30 per cent of your Latinisms...mow down every old cliché, uproot all the dragging circumlocutions, compress, diversify, clarify, vivify, & you'll make a book that will be read and talked of.
Letter to W. Morton Fullerton (March 24, 1910), quoted in *The Letters of Edith Wharton* (R. W. B. Lewis and Nancy Lewis, eds.; 1988)

3 I read the other day in a book by a fashionable essayist that ghosts went out when the electric light came in. What nonsense!
All Souls (1937)

4 In France everything speaks of long familiar intercourse between the earth and its inhabitants; every field has a name, a history, a distinct place of its own in the village polity.
A Motor-Flight Through France (1908), pt. 1, ch. 1

5 We live in the day of little noses: that once stately feature, intrinsically feudal and aristocratic in character—the *maschio naso* of Dante—has shrunk to democratic insignificance.
A Motor-Flight Through France (1908), pt. 1, ch. 2

6 There are several ways of leaving Paris by motor without touching even the fringe of what, were it like other cities, would be called its slums.
A Motor-Flight Through France (1908), pt. 3, ch. 1

7 The worst of doing one's duty was that it apparently unfitted one for doing anything else.
The Age of Innocence (1920)

8 An unalterable and unquestioned law of the musical world required that the German text of French operas sung by Swedish artists should be translated into Italian for the clearer understanding of English-speaking audiences.
The Age of Innocence (1920), bk. 1, ch. 1

9 She keeps on being Queenly in her own room with the door shut.
The House of Mirth (1905), bk. 2, ch. 1

10 I remember once saying to Henry James, in reference to a

novel of the type that used euphemistically to be called "unpleasant": "You know, I was rather disappointed; that book wasn't nearly as bad as I expected:"...he replied, with his incomparable twinkle: "Ah, my dear, the abysses are all so shallow."
The House of Mirth (1905), Introduction

11 Another unsettling element in modern art is that common symptom of immaturity, the dread of doing what has been done before.
The Writing of Fiction (1925), ch. 1

12 The beauty of Moroccan palaces is made up of details of ornament and refinements of sensuous delight too numerous to record.
"The Bahia," *Virago Book of Women Travellers* (Mary Morris, ed.; 1996)

13 All these many threads of the native life, woven of greed and lust, of fetishism and fear and blind hate of the stranger, form, in the *souks*, a thick network.
"The Bazaars," *Virago Book of Women Travellers* (Mary Morris, ed.; 1996)

14 Mrs. Ballinger is one of the ladies who pursue Culture in bands, as though it were dangerous to meet it alone.
Xingu (1916), ch. 1

Whately, Richard (1787–1863) British theologian and logician

1 Happiness is no laughing matter.
Apophthegms (1854)

2 Honesty is the best policy; but he who is governed by that maxim is not an honest man.
Apophthegms (1854)

3 It is a folly to expect men to do all that they may reasonably be expected to do.
Apophthegms (1854)

4 When a man says he wants to work, what he means is that he wants wages.
Attrib.

Wheatley, Phillis (1753?–84) Senegalese-born U.S. poet

1 Some view our sable race with scornful eye;
Their color is a diabolic dye.
Remember, *Christians*, *Negroes*, black as *Cain*,
May be refined, and join th' angelic train.
"On Being Brought from Africa to America," *Poems on Various Subjects, Religious and Moral* (1773)

2 I, young in life, by seeming cruel fate
Was snatched from *Afric's* fancy'd happy seat:
What pangs excruciating must molest,
What sorrows labor in my parent's breast!
Steel'd was that soul and by no misery mov'd,
That from a father seiz'd his babe belov'd:
Such, such my case. And can I then but pray
Others may never feel tyrannic sway?
"To the Right Honourable William, Earl of Dartmouth," *Poems on Various Subjects, Religious and Moral* (1773)

Wheeler, Hugh (1912–87) British-born U.S. novelist and playwright

1 To lose a lover or even a husband or two during the course of one's life can be vexing. But to lose one's teeth is a catastrophe.
A Little Night Music (1974)

Wheeler, John Archibald (b.1911) U.S. theoretical physicist

1 A black hole has no hair.
Referring to the No-Hair Theorem, which states that black holes are characterized by only a limited number of quantities. *Gravitation* (co-written with Charles W. Misner and Kip S. Thorne; 1973)

2 There is nothing in the world except empty curved space. Matter, charge, electromagnetism, and other fields are only manifestations of the curvature of space.
1957. Quoted in *New Scientist* (September 26, 1974)

3 Time is what prevents everything from happening at once.
1978. Attrib.

Whelan, Eugene (Eugene Francis Whelan; b.1924) Canadian politician

1 Canada has two official languages and I don't speak none of them.
Whelan (1986)

Whewell, William (1794–1866) British philosopher and mathematician

1 Hence no force however great can stretch a cord however fine into an horizontal line which is accurately straight: there will always be a bending downwards.
An example of unintentional versification. *Elementary Treatise on Mechanics* (1819), ch. 4

Whichcote, Benjamin (also spelled Whitchcote; 1609–83) English educator and cleric

1 Right and truth are greater than any power, and all power is limited by right.
Moral and Religious Aphorisms (1703)

Whistler, James Abbott McNeill (1834–1903) U.S. painter and etcher

Quotations about Whistler

1 With our James vulgarity begins at home, and should be allowed to stay there.
Oscar Wilde (1854–1900) Irish poet, playwright, and wit. Letter to *World* (Undated)

Quotations by Whistler

2 As music is the poetry of sound so painting is the poetry of sight, and the subject matter has nothing to do with harmony of sound or color.
The Gentle Art of Making Enemies (1890)

3 I am not arguing with you—I am telling you.
The Gentle Art of Making Enemies (1890)

4 Nature contains the elements, in color and form, of all pictures, as the keyboard contains the notes of all music.
The Gentle Art of Making Enemies (1890)

5 Nature is usually wrong.
The Gentle Art of Making Enemies (1890)

6 No, I ask it for the knowledge of a lifetime.
1878. Replying to the taunt, during the John Ruskin trial, that he was asking an exorbitant fee of 200 guineas for two days' painting. Whistler had brought a libel action against Ruskin for damning one of his paintings as "flinging a pot of paint in the public's face." *The Gentle Art of Making Enemies* (1890)

7 I maintain that two and two would continue to make four, in spite of the whine of the amateur for three, or the cry of the critic for five.
Whistler v. Ruskin. Art and Art Critics (1878)

8 Had silicon been a gas I would have been a major-general.
Referring to his failure in the chemistry paper of an entrance exam to West Point Military Academy. Quoted in *The Life of James McNeill Whistler* (Joseph Pennell; 1908)

9 Isn't it? I know in my case I would grow intolerably conceited.
Replying to the pointed observation that it was as well that we do not see ourselves as others see us. Quoted in *The Man Whistler* (H. Pearson; 1978)

10 A LADY I only know of two painters in the world: yourself and Velasquez.
WHISTLER Why drag in Velasquez?
Quoted in *Whistler Stories* (D. C. Seitz; 1913)

11 A LADY This landscape reminds me of your work.
WHISTLER Yes madam, Nature is creeping up.
Quoted in *Whistler Stories* (D. C. Seitz; 1913)

12 You shouldn't say it is not good. You should say you do not like it; and then, you know, you're perfectly safe.
Quoted in *Whistler Stories* (D. C. Seitz; 1913)

13 It is very simple. The artists retired. The British remained.
1888. Explaining his resignation as president of the Royal Society of British Artists. Quoted in *Whistler Stories* (D. C. Seitz; 1913)

14 I cannot tell you that, madam. Heaven has granted me no offspring.
Replying to a lady who had inquired whether he thought genius was hereditary. Quoted in *Whistler Stories* (D. C. Seitz; 1913)

15 Perhaps not, but then you can't call yourself a great work of nature.
Responding to a sitter's complaint that his portrait was not a great work of art. Quoted in *Whistler Stories* (D. C. Seitz; 1913)

16 Listen! There never was an artistic period. There never was an art-loving nation.
1885. Attrib.

17 Well, not bad, but there are decidedly too many of them, and they are not very well arranged. I would have done it differently.
His reply when asked if he agreed that the stars were particularly beautiful one night. Attrib.

18 The explanation is quite simple. I wished to be near my mother.
In reply to a snobbish lady who asked why he had been born in such an unfashionable place as Lowell, Massachusetts. Attrib.

White, Andrew Dickson (1832–1918) U.S. educator and diplomat

1 I will not permit thirty men to travel four hundred miles to agitate a bag of wind.
Refusing to allow the Cornell football team to visit Michigan to play a game. Quoted in *The People's Almanac* (D. Wallechinsky; 1978)

White, E. B. (Elwyn Brooks White; 1899–1985) U.S. writer and humorist

1 I am beginning to feel a little more like an author now that I have had a book banned. The literary life in this country begins in jail.
Referring to the banning by the U.S. military of *One Man's Meat* (1942). Letter to Stanley Hart White (June 1944)

2 Commuter—one who spends his life
In riding to and from his wife;
A man who shaves and takes a train,
And then rides back to shave again.
"The Commuter" (1929)

3 Here we are, busily preparing ourselves for a war already described as "unthinkable"...spying on each other, rewarding people on quiz programs with $100,000 for knowing how to spell "cat," and Zwicky wants to make a hundred *new* worlds.
June 14, 1956. Referring to astrophysicist Fritz Zwicky's proposal that 100 new planets could be created. "Coon Tree," *Essays of E. B. White* (1977)

4 In the country, one excuse is as good as another for a bit of fun, and just because a fire has grown cold is no reason for a fireman's spirits to sag.
December 10, 1955. "Home-Coming," *Essays of E. B. White* (1977)

5 You can certainly learn to spell "moccasin" while driving into Maine, and there is often little else to do except steer and avoid death.
December 10, 1955. "Home-Coming," *Essays of E. B. White* (1977)

6 The imaginary complaints of indestructible old ladies.
Harper's Magazine (November 1941)

7 MOTHER It's broccoli, dear.
CHILD I say it's spinach, and I say the hell with it.
Cartoon caption. *New Yorker* (December 8, 1928)

8 A good farmer is nothing more nor less than a handy man with a sense of humus.
"The Practical Farmer," *One Man's Meat* (1942)

9 As in the sexual experience, there are never more than two persons present in the act of reading—the writer who is the impregnator, and the reader who is the respondent.
The Second Tree from the Corner (1954)

10 To perceive Christmas through its wrapping becomes more difficult with every year.
The Second Tree from the Corner (1954)

11 In a man's middle years there is scarcely a part of the body he would hesitate to turn over to the proper authorities.
"A Weekend with the Angels," *The Second Tree from the Corner* (1954)

12 Is Sex Necessary?
1929. Book title. (co-written with James Thurber)

13 The trouble with the profit system has always been that it was highly unprofitable to most people.
Attrib.

White, Edmund (Edmund Valentine White III; b.1940) U.S. writer

1 If art is to confront AIDS more honestly than the media have

done, it must begin in tact, avoid humor and end in anger.
1987. Quoted in *A Queer Reader* (Patrick Higgins, ed.; 1993)

White, Henry Kirke (1785–1806) British poet

1 Much in sorrow, oft in woe,
Onward, Christians, onward go.
The first line is also known in the form, "Oft in danger, oft in woe." (1812?)

White, Patrick (Patrick Victor Martindale White; 1912–90) British-born Australian novelist

1 But bombs *are* unbelievable until they actually fall.
Riders in the Chariot (1961), Act 1, Scene 4

2 All my novels are an accumulation of detail. I'm a bit of a bower-bird.
Southerly: The Magazine of the Australian English Association, Attrib.

3 "I dunno," Arthur said. "I forget what I was taught. I only remember what I've learnt."
The Solid Mandala (1966), ch. 2

4 Well, good luck to you, kid! I'm going to write the Great Australian Novel.
The Vivisector (1970)

5 Names should be charms...I used to hope that, by saying some of them often enough, I might evoke reality.
Voss (1957)

White, Theodore H. (Theodore Harold White; 1915–86) U.S. author and journalist

1 The enmity of the community is not a matter to invite lightly.
1974. Said to Ray Kroc, chairman of fast-food chain McDonald's, which was planning to open on Manhattan's East Side. Quoted in *Big Mac* (Maxwell Boas and Steve Chain; 1976)

White, William Allen ("The Sage of Emporia"; 1868–1944) U.S. writer

1 All dressed up, with nowhere to go.
Referring to members of the Progressive Party after Theodore Roosevelt's failed attempt to win the U.S. presidential election (1916). Attrib.

Whitehead, A. N. (Alfred North Whitehead; 1861–1947) British philosopher and mathematician

1 As society is now constituted, a literal adherence to the moral precepts scattered throughout the Gospels would mean sudden death.
Adventures in Ideas (1933)

2 Life is an offensive, directed against the repetitious mechanism of the Universe.
1928. *Adventures of Ideas* (1933)

3 So far as the mere imparting of information is concerned, no university has had any justification for existence since the popularization of printing in the fifteenth century.
Aims of Education (1928)

4 Civilization advances by extending the number of important operations which we can perform without thinking about them.
An Introduction to Mathematics (1948)

5 If a dog jumps onto your lap it is because he is fond of you; but if a cat does the same thing it is because your lap is warmer.
Dialogues (1954)

6 What is morality in any given time or place? It is what the majority then and there happen to like and immorality is what they dislike.
Dialogues (1954)

7 There are no whole truths; all truths are half-truths. It is trying to treat them as whole truths that plays the devil.
Dialogues (1954), ch. 16

8 Intelligence is quickness to apprehend as distinct from ability, which is capacity to act wisely on the thing apprehended.
Dialogues (1954), ch. 135

9 Art is the imposing of a pattern on experience, and our aesthetic enjoyment is recognition of the pattern.
Dialogues (1954), ch. 228

10 A philosopher of imposing stature doesn't think in a vacuum. Even his most abstract ideas are, to some extent, conditioned by what is or what is not known in the time when he lives.
Dialogues (1954), Prologue

11 Philosophy is the product of wonder.
Nature and Life (1934), ch. 1

12 It requires a very unusual mind to undertake the analysis of the obvious.
Science and the Modern World (1925)

13 Mathematics is thought moving in the sphere of complete abstraction from any particular instance of what it is talking about.
Science and the Modern World (1925)

14 Everything of importance has been said before by somebody who did not discover it.
Quoted in *The World of Mathematics* (J. R. Newman; 1956)

15 A science which hesitates to forget its founders is lost.
Attrib.

16 It is more important that a proposition be interesting than that it be true.
Attrib.

17 "Necessity is the mother of invention" is a silly proverb. "Necessity is the mother of futile dodges" is much nearer the truth.
Attrib.

18 Seek simplicity, and distrust it.
Attrib.

19 We think in generalities, but we live in details.
Attrib.

Whitehorn, Katharine (b.1926) British journalist and writer

1 A food is not necessarily essential just because your child hates it.
How to Survive Children (1975)

2 The easiest way for your children to learn about money is for you not to have any.
How to Survive Children (1975)

3 When the middle classes, feeling poor, wring their hands and wonder what it is the working classes don't spend money on...one of the answers is—insurance.
"Insurance," *How to Survive Your Money Problems* (1983)

4 Sales techniques, as taught to the man on the move, include getting irritated or overbearing—they hope you'll buy something just to placate them.
"It's Your Money They're After," *How to Survive Your Money Problems* (1983)

5 But they underestimate the cumulative effect of always hearing Stone-Age man, postman, chairman; of the different reactions you have to "landlord" and "landlady" or "a bit of a bitch" and "a bit of a dog."
Observer, London (August 17, 1991)

6 It is a pity, as my husband says, that more politicians are not bastards by birth instead of vocation.
Observer, London (1964)

7 The best careers advice to give to the young is "Find out what you like doing best and get someone to pay you for doing it."
Observer, London (1964)

8 When an academic decries business for being so boring, you know he's never seen the thrills and spills of a boardroom.
Observer, London (March 29, 1987)

9 Why do born-again people so often make you wish they'd never been born the first time?
Observer, London (May 20, 1979)

10 With creative accountancy, who needs cheating?
Observer, London (1987)

11 "Think the unthinkable but wear a dark suit" is a handy maxim for the City.
Referring to London's business district, the City. *Observer*, London (January 25, 1987)

12 Have you ever taken anything out of the clothes basket because it had become, relatively, the cleaner thing?
"On Shirts," *Observer*, London (1964)

13 Hats divide generally into three classes: offensive hats, defensive hats, and shrapnel.
"Hats," *Shouts and Murmurs* (1963)

14 And what would happen to my illusion that I am a force for order in the home if I wasn't married to the only man north of the Tiber who is even untidier than I am?
"Husband-Swapping," *Sunday Best* (1976)

15 The Life and Soul, the man who will never go home while there is one man, woman or glass of anything not yet drunk.
"Husband-Swapping," *Sunday Best* (1976)

16 A good listener is not someone who has nothing to say. A good listener is a good talker with a sore throat.
Attrib.

17 Outside every thin girl there is a fat man trying to get in.
Attrib.

Whitelaw, William, 1st Viscount Whitelaw (William Stephen Ian Whitelaw, "Willie"; 1918–99) British politician

1 It is never wise to try to appear to be more clever than you are. It is sometimes wise to appear slightly less so.
Observer, London (1975), "Sayings of the Year"

2 I do not intend to prejudge the past.
Said on arriving in Ulster as minister for Northern Ireland. *Times*, London (December 3, 1973)

Whitfield, James M. (1830–70) U.S. poet

1 America, it is to thee, Thou boasted land of liberty,
—It is to thee I raise my song,
Thou land of blood, and crime, and wrong.
"America," *The Negro Caravan* (Sterling Brown, Arthur P. Davis, and Ulysses Lee, eds.; 1941)

Whiting, William (1825–78) British schoolmaster, poet, and hymnwriter

1 O hear us when we cry to Thee
For those in peril on the sea.
Hymn lyric. "Eternal Father Strong to Save" (1869)

Whitman, Walt (1819–92) U.S. poet

Quotations about Whitman

1 I saw you, Walt Whitman, childless, lonely old grubber, poking among the meats in the refrigerator and eyeing the grocery boys.
1955
Allen Ginsberg (1926–97) U.S. poet. "A Supermarket in California," *Howl and Other Poems* (1956)

2 Where are we going, Walt Whitman? The doors close in an hour. Which way does your beard point tonight? I touch your book and dream of our odyssey in the supermarket and feel absurd.
Allen Ginsberg (1926–97) U.S. poet. "A Supermarket in California," *Howl and Other Poems* (1956)

3 Well, he looks like a man.
Abraham Lincoln (1809–65) U.S. president. Referring to catching sight of Walt Whitman for the first time. Attrib.

4 Walt Whitman who laid end to end words never seen in each other's company before outside of a dictionary.
David Lodge (b.1935) British novelist and critic. *Changing Places* (1975), ch. 5

5 America...initiated her own particular philology from which Whitman emerged; and he, like a new Adam, began giving things names, began behaving like Homer himself, offering a model for a primitive American poetry of nomenclature.
Osip Mandelstam (1891–1938) Russian poet, writer, and translator. "On the Nature of the Word" (1925), quoted in *The Collected Critical Prose and Letters of Osip Mandelstam* (J. G. Harris, ed., tr., C. Link, tr.; 1991)

Quotations by Whitman

6 No one will ever get at my verses who insists upon viewing them as a literary performance.
"A Backward Glance O'er Travel'd Roads" (1888)

7 I will...let appear these burning fires that were threatening to
consume me,

I will lift what has too long kept down these smoldering fires—
I will now expose them and use them.
"Premonition" (1856–60)

8 City of orgies, walks, and joys.
Referring to Manhattan. "City of Orgies," *Calamus* (1860), no. 18

9 The United States are destined either to surmount the gorgeous history of feudalism, or else prove the most tremendous failure of time.
Democratic Vistas (1871)

10 Think of the United States today—the facts of these...fifty or sixty nations of equals...Think, in comparison, of the petty environage and limited area of the poets of past and present Europe.
Democratic Vistas (1871)

11 I will not have in my writing any elegance, or effect...to hang in the way between me and the rest like curtains...What I tell I tell for precisely what it is.
Leaves of Grass (1855), Preface

12 Logic and sermons never convince,
The damp of the night drives deeper into my soul.
Leaves of Grass (1855), st. 30

13 Flaunt of the sunshine I need not your bask—lie over!
Leaves of Grass (1855), st. 40

14 And as to you Life I reckon you are the leavings of many deaths,
(No doubt I have died myself ten thousand times before).
Leaves of Grass (1855), st. 49

15 If you do not say anything how can I say anything?
Of the turbid pool that lies in the autumn forest
Of the moon that descends the steeps of the soughing twilight.
Leaves of Grass (1855), st. 49

16 The earth does not argue,
Is not pathetic, has no arrangements,
Does not scream, haste, persuade, threaten, promise,
Makes no discriminations, has no conceivable failures,
Closes nothing, refuses nothing, shuts none out.
"A Song of the Rolling Earth," *Leaves of Grass* (1881), pt. 1

17 I too lived, Brooklyn of ample hills was mine,
I too walked the streets of Manhattan island, and bathed in the waters around it.
"Crossing Brooklyn Ferry," *Leaves of Grass* (1856), can. 5, ll. 4–6

18 Stand up, tall masts of Manhattan! stand up, beautiful hills of Brooklyn!
"Crossing Brooklyn Ferry," *Leaves of Grass* (1856), can. 9, l. 5

19 I will make divine magnetic lands,
With the love of comrades,
With the life-long love of comrades.
1860. "For You O Democracy," *Leaves of Grass* (1892), Calamus, no. 5

20 Give me Broadway, with the soldiers marching—give me the sound of the trumpets and the drums!
"Give Me the Splendid Silent Sun," *Leaves of Grass* (1881), can. 2, l. 9

21 Gliding o'er all, through all.
Through Nature, Time, and Space,
As a ship on the waters advancing,
The voyage of the soul—not life alone,
Death, many deaths I'll sing.
1871. Originally appeared as the epigraph to "Passage to India". "Gliding o'er All," *Leaves of Grass* (1892)

22 I hear it was charged against me that I sought to destroy institutions,
But really I am neither for nor against institutions.
1860. "I Hear It was Charged Against Me," *Leaves of Grass* (1881)

23 I proceed for all who are or have been young men,
To tell the secret of my nights and days,
To celebrate the need of my comrades.
1860. "In Paths Untrodden," *Leaves of Grass* (1892), Calamus, no. 1

24 Of physiology from top to toe I sing.
1855. "I Sing the Body Electric," *Leaves of Grass* (1881)

25 If anything is sacred the human body is sacred.
1855. "I Sing the Body Electric," *Leaves of Grass* (1881), pt. 8

26 O Captain! my Captain! our fearful trip is done,
The ship has weathered every rack, the prize we sought is won,
The port is near, the bells I hear, the people all exulting.
November 4, 1865. "O Captain! My Captain!," *Leaves of Grass* (1881)

27 O Magnet-South! O glistening perfumed South! my South!
O quick mettle, rich blood, impulse and love! good and evil!
O all dear to me!
1881. From the 1881 version of the poem, first published in 1860. "O Magnet-South," *Leaves of Grass* (1892), ll. 1–2

28 You came, taciturn, with nothing to give—we but look'd on each other,
When lo! more than all the gifts of the world you gave me.
1865. "O Tan-Faced Prairie Boy," *Leaves of Grass* (1892)

29 Camerado, this is no book,
Who touches this touches a man,
(Is it night? are we together alone?)
It is I you hold and who holds you,
I spring from the pages into your arms—decease calls me forth.
1877. "So Long!," *Leaves of Grass* (1892), ll. 53–57

30 I dote on myself, there is that lot of me and all so luscious.
1855. "Song of Myself," *Leaves of Grass* (1881)

31 I celebrate myself, and sing myself,
And what I assume you shall assume.
1855. "Song of Myself," *Leaves of Grass* (1881), pt. 1

32 I also say it is good to fall, battles are lost in the same spirit in which they are won.
1855. "Song of Myself," *Leaves of Grass* (1881), pt. 18

33 I think I could turn and live with animals, they're so placid and self-contained,
I stand and look at them long and long.
1855. "Song of Myself," *Leaves of Grass* (1881), pt. 32

34 Behold, I do not give lectures or a little charity,
When I give I give myself.
1855. "Song of Myself," *Leaves of Grass* (1881), pt. 40

35 I have said that the soul is not more than the body,

And I have said that the body is not more than the soul,
And nothing, but God, is greater to one than one's self is.
1855. "Song of Myself," *Leaves of Grass* (1881), pt. 48

36 Do I contradict myself?
Very well then I contradict myself,
I am large, I contain multitudes.
1855. "Song of Myself," *Leaves of Grass* (1881), pt. 51

37 Twenty-eight young men bathe by the shore,
Twenty-eight young men and all so friendly;
Twenty-eight years of womanly life and all so lonesome.
1855. "Song of Myself," *Leaves of Grass* (1881), st. 11

38 The bride unrumples her white dress, the minute-hand of the clock moves slowly,
The opium-eater reclines with rigid head and just-open'd lips,
The prostitute draggles her shawl, her bonnet bobs on her tipsy and pimpled neck.
1855. "Song of Myself," *Leaves of Grass* (1881), st. 15

39 What is man anyhow? what am I? what are you?
All I mark as my own you shall offset with your own,
Else it were time lost listening to me.
1855. "Song of Myself," *Leaves of Grass* (1881), st. 20

40 Something I cannot see puts up libidinous prongs,
Seas of bright juice suffuse heaven.
1855. "Song of Myself," *Leaves of Grass* (1881), st. 24

41 The orchestra whirls me wider than Uranus flies,
It wrenches such ardors from me I did not know I possess'd them,
It sails me I dab with bare feet.
1855. "Song of Myself," *Leaves of Grass* (1881), st. 26

42 A great city is that which has the greatest men and women.
1856. "Song of the Broad Axe," *Leaves of Grass* (1881), pt. 5

43 Where the populace rise at once against the never-ending audacity of elected persons.
1856. "Song of the Broad Axe," *Leaves of Grass* (1881), pt. 5

44 Afoot and light-hearted I take to the open road,
Healthy, free, the world before me,
The long brown path before me leading wherever I choose.
1871. First published as "Poem of the Road." "Song of the Open Road," *Leaves of Grass* (1881), pt. 1, ll. 1–3

45 We two boys together clinging,
One the other never leaving,
Up and down the roads going, North and South excursions making,
Power enjoying, elbows stretching, fingers clutching,
Arm'd and fearless, eating, drinking, sleeping, loving.
1860. "We Two Boys Together Clinging," *Leaves of Grass* (1892), Calamus, no. 26

46 For the one I love most lay sleeping by me under the same cover in the cool night...
And his arm lay lightly around my breast—and that night I was happy.
1860. "When I Heard at the Close of Day," *Leaves of Grass* (1892), Calamus, no. 11

47 I saw battle-corpses, myriads of them,
And the white skeletons of young men, I saw them.
1865. Composed after the assassination of Abraham Lincoln (April 14, 1865). "When Lilacs Last in the Dooryard Bloom'd," *Sequel to Drum-Taps* (1866)

48 Not for you, for one alone,
Blossoms and branches green to coffins all I bring,
For fresh as the morning, thus I would chant a song for you,
O sane and sacred death.
1865. Composed after the assassination of Abraham Lincoln (April 14, 1865). "When Lilacs Last in the Dooryard Bloom'd," *Sequel to Drum-Taps* (1866)

49 After you have exhausted what there is in business, politics, conviviality, and so on—have found that none of these finally satisfy, or permanently wear—what remains? Nature remains.
"New Themes Entered Upon," *Specimen Days and Collect* (1882)

50 Go on, my dear Americans, whip your horses to the utmost—Excitement; money! politics!—open all your valves and let her go...you will soon get under such momentum you can't stop if you would.
Two Rivulets Including Democratic Vistas (1876)

51 It would be sacrilege to put a name there—it would be like putting a name on the universe...at most I am only a mouthpiece.
Referring to the 1855 edition of *Leaves of Grass*, which he initially published anonymously. Attrib.

Whittemore, Reed (Edward Reed Whittemore II; b.1919) U.S. poet

1 The self, what a brute it is. It wants, wants.
"Clamming," *Poems* (1967), quoted in *The Penguin Book of American Verse* (Geoffrey Moore, ed.; 1977)

2 Antiquity doesn't matter. In but a decade
An empty house can gain centuries.
"Our Ruins," *The Fascination of Abomination* (1939), quoted in *The Penguin Book of American Verse* (Geoffrey Moore, ed.; 1977)

Whittier, John Greenleaf (1807–92) U.S. poet

1 "Shoot, if you must, this old gray head,
But spare your country's flag," she said.
A shade of sadness, a blush of shame,
Over the face of the leader came.
"Barbara Frietchie" (1863)

2 Up from the meadows rich with corn,
Clear in the cool September morn,
The clustered spires of Frederick stand
Green-walled by the hills of Maryland.
"Barbara Frietchie" (1863)

3 For of all sad words of tongue or pen,
The saddest are these: "It might have been!"
"Maud Muller" (1856)

4 Then the wife of the skipper lost at sea
Said, "God has touch'd him! Why should we?"
After Skipper Ireson abandoned his ship and crew at sea he went mad with remorse. "Skipper Ireson's Ride," *Home Ballads and Poems* (1860), quoted in *The Penguin Book of American Verse* (Geoffrey Moore, ed.; 1977)

5 Here's Flud Oirson, fur his horrd horrt,
Torr'd an' futherr'd an' corr'd in a corrt
By the women o' Morblehead!
The fate of a captain who abandoned his sinking ship and crew, whose number included the women's husbands and lovers. "Skipper Ireson's Ride," *Home Ballads and Poems* (1860), quoted in *The Penguin Book of American Verse* (Geoffrey Moore, ed.; 1977)

6 And step by step, since time began,
I see the steady gain of man.
"The Chapel of the Hermits," *The Poetical Works of John Greenleaf Whittier* (1894)

Whittington, Robert (b.16th century) English writer

1 As time requireth, a man of marvellous mirth and pastimes, and sometimes of as sad gravity, as who say: a man for all seasons.
Referring to Sir Thomas More. After Erasmus. "De Constructione Nominum," *Vulgaria* (1521), pt. 2

Whitton, Charlotte (Charlotte Elizabeth Whitton; 1896–1975) Canadian politician and writer

1 Whatever women do they must do twice as well as men to be thought half as good. Luckily, this is not difficult.
Canada Month (June 1963)

Wicks, Malcolm (b.1947) British sociologist

1 The most dramatic thing is that, even when you look at women who are working full time outside the home—as full time as their men—when it comes to ironing and cleaning, 60 or 70 per cent of that work is still done by the women.
1990. Quoted in *Move Over Darling* (Kathy Barnby and Loretta Loach)

Wideman, John Edgar (b.1941) U.S. writer

1 Takes all kinds to make my people.
Hiding Place (1984)

2 History is a cage, a conundrum we must escape or resolve before our art can go freely about its business.
Breaking Ice: An Anthology of Contemporary African-American Fiction (Terry McMillan, ed.; 1992), p.vi

3 A story is a formula for extracting meaning from chaos, a handful of water we scoop up to recall an ocean.
Breaking Ice: An Anthology of Contemporary African-American Fiction (Terry McMillan, ed.; 1992), p.x

Wieland, Christoph Martin (1733–1813) German writer

1 A single moment can change all.
Oberon (1780)

Wiener, Norbert (1894–1964) U.S. mathematician

1 The degradation of the position of the scientist as independent worker and thinker to that of a morally irresponsible stooge in a science-factory has proceeded even more rapidly and devastatingly than I had expected.
Bulletin of the Atomic Scientists (November 4, 1948)

2 We have decided to call the entire field of control and communication theory, whether in the machine or in the animal, by the name of Cybernetics, which we form from the Greek for steersman.
Cybernetics (1948)

3 The world of the future will be an ever more demanding struggle against the limits of our intelligence, not a comfortable hammock in which we can lie down to be waited upon by our robot slaves.
God and Golem, Inc. (1964)

4 The best material model of a cat is another, or preferably the same, cat.
Philosophy of Science (co-written with A. Rosenblueth; 1945)

5 The independent scientist who is worth the slightest consideration as a scientist has a consecration which comes entirely from within himself: a vocation which demands the possibility of supreme self-sacrifice.
The Human Use of Human Beings (1950)

6 The more we get out of the world the less we leave, and in the long run we shall have to pay our debts at a time that may be very inconvenient for our own survival.
The Human Use of Human Beings (1950)

Wiesel, Elie (Eliezer Wiesel; b.1928) Romanian-born U.S. writer

1 You'll try to reveal what should remain hidden, you'll try to incite people to learn from the past and rebel, but they will refuse to believe you. They will not listen to you...You'll possess the truth, you already do; but it's the truth of a madman.
A Beggar in Jerusalem (Lily Edelman and Elie Wiesel, trs.; 1970)

2 I was the accuser, God the accused. My eyes were open and I was alone—terribly alone in a world without God and without man.
Referring to the Holocaust. *Night* (Stella Rodway, tr.; 1958)

3 Rejected by mankind, the condemned do not go so far as to reject it in turn. Their faith in history remains unshaken...They do not despair. The proof: they persist in surviving not only to survive, but to testify...The victims elect to become witnesses.
Referring to the Holocaust. *One Generation After* (B. M. Mooyart, tr.; 1970)

Wilberforce, Samuel (1805–73) British churchman

Quotations about Wilberforce

1 For once reality and his brain came into contact, and the result was fatal.
T. H. Huxley (1825–95) British biologist. Referring to Wilberforce's death after falling from his horse. Quoted in *The Faber Book of Science* (John Carey, ed.; 1995)

Quotations by Wilberforce

2 And, in conclusion, I would like to ask the gentleman...whether the ape from which he is descended was on his grandmother's or his grandfather's side of the family.
Speech (June 30, 1860)

3 If I were a cassowary
On the plains of Timbuctoo,
I would eat a missionary,
Cassock, band, and hymn-book too.
Also attributed to W. M. Thackeray. Attrib.

Wilberforce, William (1759–1833) British abolitionist and politician

1 They charge me with fanaticism. If to be feelingly alive to the

sufferings of my fellow-creatures is to be a fanatic, I am one of the most incurable fanatics ever permitted to be at large.
Speech in the British Parliament (June 19, 1816)

2 God Almighty has set me two great objects, the suppression of the Slave Trade and the reformation of manners.
1787. Attrib.

Wilbur, Richard (Richard Purdy Wilbur; b.1921) U.S. poet

1 The soul descends once more in bitter love
To accept the waking body.
1956. "Love Calls Us to the Things of This World," *New and Collected Poems* (1988)

Wilcox, Ella Wheeler (1850–1919) U.S. poet

1 We flatter those we scarcely know,
We please the fleeting guest,
And deal full many a thoughtless blow
To those who love us best.
"Life's Scars" (1917)

2 No question is ever settled
Until it is settled right.
"Settle the Question Right" (1917)

3 Laugh, and the world laughs with you;
Weep, and you weep alone,
For the sad old earth must borrow its mirth,
But has trouble enough of its own.
"Solitude" (1917)

4 So many gods, so many creeds,
So many paths that wind and wind,
While just the art of being kind
Is all the sad world needs.
"The World's Need" (1917)

5 Talk health. The dreary, never-ending tale
Our mortal maladies is worn and stale;
You cannot charm or interest or please
By harping on that minor chord, disease.
"Speech," *Poems of Power* (1901)

6 Distrust that man who tells you to distrust.
Attrib.

Wilde, Oscar (Oscar Fingal O'Flahertie Wills Wilde; 1854–1900) Irish poet, playwright, and wit

Quotations about Wilde

1 He was one of the high priests of a school which attacks all wholesome, manly, simple ideals of English life, and sets up false gods of decadent culture and intellectual debauchery.
Anonymous. Referring to Oscar Wilde on the day of his conviction. *Evening News*, London (1895), editorial, quoted in *Homosexuality: A History* (Colin Spencer; 1995)

2 That sovereign of insufferables.
Ambrose Bierce (1842–1914?) U.S. writer and journalist. *Wasp* (1882)

3 The last gentleman in Europe.
Ada Leverson (1862–1933) British writer and journalist. "Reminiscences," *Letters to the Sphinx* (1930)

4 But remember the dismal, ridiculous condemnation of Oscar Wilde. Intellectual Europe will never forgive you for it.
Filippo Tommaso Marinetti (1876–1944) Italian writer, poet, and political activist. Referring to the persecution of writer and wit Oscar Wilde, who in 1895 was convicted for sodomy, served two years hard labor, and was subsequently driven to exile in Paris. Speech to the Lyceum Club, London (1910), quoted in *Marinetti: Selected Writings* (R. W. Flint, ed., tr., A. Coppotelli, tr.; 1972)

5 A ready means of being cherished by the English is to adopt the simple expedient of living a long time. I have little doubt that if, say, Oscar Wilde had lived into his nineties, instead of dying in his forties, he would have been considered a benign, distinguished figure suitable to preside at a school prize-giving or to instruct and exhort scoutmasters at their jamborees. He might even have been knighted.
Malcolm Muggeridge (1903–90) British journalist. *Tread Softly For You Tread on My Jokes* (1966)

6 If with the literate I am
Impelled to try an epigram
I never seek to take the credit
We all assume that Oscar said it.
Dorothy Parker (1893–1967) U.S. writer and wit. "Oscar Wilde," *Sunset Gun* (1928)

7 No, no, Oscar, you forget. When you and I are together we never talk about anything except me.
James Abbott McNeill Whistler (1834–1903) U.S. painter and etcher. Cable replying to Oscar Wilde's message: "When you and I are together we never talk about anything except ourselves." *The Gentle Art of Making Enemies* (1890)

8 You will, Oscar, you will.
James Abbott McNeill Whistler (1834–1903) U.S. painter and etcher. Replying to Oscar Wilde's exclamation "I wish I had said that!" Quoted in *Oscar Wilde* (R. Ellman; 1987), pt. 2, ch. 5

Quotations by Wilde

9 One would have to have a heart of stone to read the death of Little Nell without laughing.
Lecture on Dickens, quoted in *Lives of the Wits* (Hesketh Pearson; 1962)

10 It was like feasting with panthers; the danger was half the excitement.
After his conviction for sodomy. Remark (1895), quoted in *A Queer Reader* (Patrick Higgins, ed.; 1993)

11 The "Love that dare not speak its name" in this century is such a great affection of an elder for a younger man as there was between David and Jonathan...and such as you find in the sonnets of Michelangelo and Shakespeare.
Referring to homosexuality. Quoting a poem by Lord Alfred Douglas. Speech at his first trial for sodomy (1895), quoted in *A Queer Reader* (Patrick Higgins, ed.; 1993)

12 Musical people are so very unreasonable. They always want one to be perfectly dumb at the very moment when one is longing to be absolutely deaf.
An Ideal Husband (1895)

13 Other people are quite dreadful. The only possible society is oneself.
An Ideal Husband (1895), Act 2

14 To love oneself is the beginning of a lifelong romance.
An Ideal Husband (1895), Act 3

15 Every woman is a rebel, and usually in wild revolt against herself.
A Woman of No Importance (1893)

16 LORD ILLINGWORTH The Book of Life begins with a man and a

woman in a garden.
MRS ALLONBY It ends with Revelations.
A Woman of No Importance (1893), Act 1

17 MRS ALLONBY They say, Lady Hunstanton, that when good Americans die they go to Paris.
LADY HUNSTANTON Indeed? And when bad Americans die, where do they go to?
LORD ILLINGWORTH Oh, they go to America.
A Woman of No Importance (1893), Act 1

18 One can survive everything nowadays, except death.
A Woman of No Importance (1893), Act 1

19 One should never trust a woman who tells one her real age. A woman who would tell one that, would tell one anything.
A Woman of No Importance (1893), Act 1

20 Moderation is a fatal thing, Lady Hunstanton. Nothing succeeds like excess.
A Woman of No Importance (1893), Act 3

21 Ah! don't say you agree with me. When people agree with me I always feel that I must be wrong.
"The Critic as Artist," *Intentions* (1891), pt. 2

22 A little sincerity is a dangerous thing, and a great deal of it is absolutely fatal.
"The Critic as Artist," *Intentions* (1891), pt. 2

23 As long as war is regarded as wicked, it will always have its fascination. When it is looked upon as vulgar, it will cease to be popular.
"The Critic as Artist," *Intentions* (1891), pt. 2

24 The man who sees both sides of a question is a man who sees absolutely nothing at all.
"The Critic as Artist," *Intentions* (1891), pt. 2

25 There is much to be said in favour of modern journalism. By giving us the opinions of the uneducated, it keeps us in touch with the ignorance of the community.
"The Critic as Artist," *Intentions* (1891), pt. 2

26 There is no sin except stupidity.
"The Critic as Artist," *Intentions* (1891), pt. 2

27 Thinking is the most unhealthy thing in the world, and people die of it just as they die of any other disease.
"The Decay of Lying," *Intentions* (1891)

28 I can resist everything except temptation.
Lady Windermere's Fan (1892), Act 1

29 It is absurd to divide people into good and bad. People are either charming or tedious.
Lady Windermere's Fan (1892), Act 1

30 I am the only person in the world I should like to know thoroughly.
Lady Windermere's Fan (1892), Act 2

31 We are all in the gutter, but some of us are looking at the stars.
Lady Windermere's Fan (1892), Act 3

32 A man who knows the price of everything and the value of nothing.
Referring to a cynic. *Lady Windermere's Fan* (1892), Act 3

33 Experience is the name everyone gives to their mistakes.
Lady Windermere's Fan (1892), Act 3

34 What is it to thee if she dance on blood? Thou hast waded deep enough in it.
Said by Herodias to Herod, referring to Salomé's *Dance of the Seven Veils*. Salomé's dancing so pleased Herod that he granted her whatever she wished; at Herodias' behest she asked for the head of John the Baptist. *Salomé* (1893)

35 I never saw a man who looked
With such a wistful eye
Upon that little tent of blue
Which prisoners call the sky.
The Ballad of Reading Gaol (1898), pt. 1, st. 3

36 Yet each man kills the thing he loves,
By each let this be heard,
Some do it with a bitter look,
Some with a flattering word.
The coward does it with a kiss,
The brave man with a sword!
The Ballad of Reading Gaol (1898), pt. 1, st. 7

37 The Governor was strong upon
The Regulations Act:
The Doctor said that Death was but
A scientific fact:
And twice a day the Chaplain called,
And left a little tract.
The Ballad of Reading Gaol (1898), pt. 3, st. 3

38 Something was dead in each of us,
And what was dead was Hope.
The Ballad of Reading Gaol (1898), pt. 3, st. 31

39 For he who lives more lives than one
More deaths than one must die.
The Ballad of Reading Gaol (1898), pt. 3, st. 37

40 I know not whether Laws be right,
Or whether Laws be wrong;
All that we know who lie in gaol
Is that the wall is strong;
And that each day is like a year,
A year whose days are long.
The Ballad of Reading Gaol (1898), pt. 5, st. 1

41 All women become like their mothers. That is their tragedy. No man does. That's his.
The Importance of Being Earnest (1895), Act 1

42 Ignorance is like a delicate exotic fruit; touch it, and the bloom is gone.
The Importance of Being Earnest (1895), Act 1

43 I have invented an invaluable permanent invalid called Bunbury, in order that I may be able to go down into the country whenever I choose.
The Importance of Being Earnest (1895), Act 1

44 Nor do I in any way approve of the modern sympathy with

invalids. I consider it morbid. Illness of any kind is hardly a thing to be encouraged in others.
The Importance of Being Earnest (1895), Act 1

45 Really, if the lower orders don't set us a good example, what on earth is the use of them?
The Importance of Being Earnest (1895), Act 1

46 The amount of women in London who flirt with their own husbands is perfectly scandalous. It looks so bad. It is simply washing one's clean linen in public.
The Importance of Being Earnest (1895), Act 1

47 The old-fashioned respect for the young is fast dying out.
The Importance of Being Earnest (1895), Act 1

48 CECILY When I see a spade I call it a spade.
GWENDOLEN I am glad to say I have never seen a spade. It is obvious that our social spheres have been widely different.
The Importance of Being Earnest (1895), Act 2

49 I hope you have not been leading a double life, pretending to be wicked and being really good all the time. That would be hypocrisy.
The Importance of Being Earnest (1895), Act 2

50 I never travel without my diary. One should always have something sensational to read in the train.
The Importance of Being Earnest (1895), Act 2

51 On an occasion of this kind it becomes more than a moral duty to speak one's mind. It becomes a pleasure.
The Importance of Being Earnest (1895), Act 2

52 To lose one parent, Mr. Worthing, may be regarded as a misfortune; to lose both looks like carelessness.
The Importance of Being Earnest (1895), Act 2

53 In matters of grave importance, style, not sincerity, is the vital thing.
The Importance of Being Earnest (1895), Act 3

54 It is a terrible thing for a man to find out suddenly that all his life he has been speaking nothing but the truth.
The Importance of Being Earnest (1895), Act 3

55 Never speak disrespectfully of Society, Algernon. Only people who can't get into it do that.
The Importance of Being Earnest (1895), Act 3

56 No woman should ever be quite accurate about her age. It looks so calculating.
The Importance of Being Earnest (1895), Act 3

57 This suspense is terrible. I hope it will last.
The Importance of Being Earnest (1895), Act 3

58 A woman will flirt with anyone in the world as long as other people are looking on.
The Picture of Dorian Gray (1891)

59 There is only one thing in the world worse than being talked about, and that is not being talked about.
The Picture of Dorian Gray (1891), ch. 1

60 It is only shallow people who do not judge by appearances.
The Picture of Dorian Gray (1891), ch. 2

61 The only way to get rid of a temptation is to yield to it.
The Picture of Dorian Gray (1891), ch. 2

62 I can sympathize with everything, except suffering.
The Picture of Dorian Gray (1891), ch. 3

63 Women represent the triumph of matter over mind, just as men represent the triumph of mind over morals.
The Picture of Dorian Gray (1891), ch. 4

64 A cigarette is the perfect type of a perfect pleasure. It is exquisite, and it leaves one unsatisfied. What more can one want?
The Picture of Dorian Gray (1891), ch. 6

65 It is better to be beautiful than to be good. But...it is better to be good than to be ugly.
The Picture of Dorian Gray (1891), ch. 17

66 Anybody can be good in the country.
The Picture of Dorian Gray (1891), ch. 19

67 There is no such thing as a moral or an immoral book. Books are well written, or badly written.
The Picture of Dorian Gray (1891), Preface

68 As for the virtuous poor, one can pity them, of course, but one cannot possibly admire them.
The Soul of Man Under Socialism (1891)

69 Democracy means simply the bludgeoning of the people by the people for the people.
The Soul of Man Under Socialism (1891)

70 André came to London to start a salon, and has only succeeded in opening a saloon.
Referring to André Raffalovich, a rich Russian whose book of verse, *Tuberose and Meadowsweet* (1885), Oscar Wilde had mocked in the *Pall Mall Gazette.* Quoted in *Homosexuality: A History* (Colin Spencer; 1995)

71 A thing is not necessarily true because a man dies for it.
Quoted in *Oscariana* (1910)

72 The man who can dominate a London dinner-table can dominate the world.
Attrib. *Oscar Wilde* (R. Aldington; 1946)

73 Please do not shoot the pianist. He is doing his best.
1883. "Leadville," *Personal Impressions of America* (1893)

74 Oh, do let me go on. I want to see how it ends.
Said on being told to stop translating from the Greek text of the New Testament in an Oxford examination. Quoted in *The Life of Oscar Wilde* (Hesketh Pearson; 1946)

75 Arguments are to be avoided: they are always vulgar and often unconvincing.
Attrib.

76 Education is an admirable thing, but it is well to remember from time to time that nothing that is worth knowing can be taught.
Attrib.

77 If one plays good music, people don't listen, and if one plays bad music, people don't talk.
Attrib.

78 Work is the curse of the drinking classes.
Attrib.

79 If this is the way Queen Victoria treats her prisoners, she doesn't deserve to have any.
Complaining at having to wait in the rain for transport to take him to prison. Attrib.

80 It requires one to assume such indecent postures.
Explaining why he did not play cricket. Attrib.

81 I should be like a lion in a cave of savage Daniels.
Explaining why he would not be attending a function at a club whose members were hostile to him. Attrib.

82 Either that wallpaper goes, or I do.
1900. Last words, as he lay dying in a drab Paris bedroom. Attrib.

83 The play was a great success, but the audience was a disaster.
Referring to a play that had recently failed. Attrib.

84 Grief has turned her fair.
Referring to the fact that a recently bereaved lady friend had dyed her hair blond. Attrib.

85 Who am I to tamper with a masterpiece?
Refusing to make alterations to one of his own plays. Attrib.

86 Nothing, except my genius.
1882. Replying to a U.S. customs official on being asked if he had anything to declare. Attrib.

Wilder, Billy (Samuel Wilder; b.1906) Austrian-born U.S. film director and screenwriter

1 I've met a lot of hardboiled eggs in my time, but you're twenty minutes.
Ace in the Hole (co-written with Lesser Samuels and Walter Newman; 1951)

2 An audience is never wrong. An individual member of it may be an imbecile, but a thousand imbeciles together in the dark—that's critical genius.
Arena, BBC Television (January 24, 1992)

3 France is a country where the money falls apart in your hands and you can't tear the toilet paper.
Attrib.

4 Hindsight is always twenty-twenty.
Attrib.

5 I have ten commandments. The first nine are, thou shalt not bore. The tenth is, thou shalt have right of final cut.
Attrib.

6 You have Van Gogh's ear for music.
Said to Cliff Osmond. Attrib.

Wilder, Laura Ingalls (1867–1957) U.S. novelist

1 Once upon a time, sixty years ago, a little girl lived in the Big Woods of Wisconsin, in a little house made of logs. The great dark trees...stood all around the house, and beyond them were other trees and beyond them were more trees.
Little House in the Big Woods (1932), ch. 1

2 "Did little girls have to be as good as that?" Laura asked, and Ma said: "It was harder for little girls. Because they had to behave like little ladies...Little girls could never slide downhill, like boys. Little girls had to sit in the house and stitch samplers."
Little House in the Big Woods (1932), ch. 5

3 There was only the enormous, empty prairie, with grasses blowing in waves of light and shadow across it...there was no sign that any other human being had ever been there.
Little House on the Prairie (1935), ch. 4

4 "Yes," Pa said. "When white settlers come into a country the Indians have to move on...White people are going to settle this country, and we get the best land because we get here first and take our pick."
1935. Responding to the young Laura's question as to why, when they were in Indian Territory, the local Native Americans were packing up their camps and moving away. *Little House on the Prairie* (1975), ch. 18

Wilder, Thornton (Thornton Niven Wilder; 1897–1975) U.S. novelist and playwright

1 For what human ill does not dawn seem to be an alternative?
The Bridge of San Luis Rey (1927)

2 A living is made, Mr Kemper, by selling something that everybody needs at least once a year. Yes, sir! And a million is made by producing something that everybody needs every day. You artists produce something that nobody needs at any time.
The Matchmaker (1954), Act 2

3 The best part of married life is the fights. The rest is merely so-so.
The Matchmaker (1954), Act 2

4 Never support two weaknesses at the same time. It's your combination sinners—your lecherous liars and your miserly drunkards—who dishonor the vices and bring them into bad repute.
The Matchmaker (1954), Act 3

5 But there comes a moment in everybody's life when he must decide whether he'll live among human beings or not—a fool among fools or a fool alone.
The Matchmaker (1954), Act 4

6 Marriage is a bribe to make the housekeeper think she's a householder.
The Merchant of Yonkers (1939), Act 1

7 My advice to you is not to inquire why or whither, but just enjoy your ice cream while it's on your plate,—that's my philosophy.
The Skin of Our Teeth (1942), Act 1

8 When you're at war you think about a better life; when you're at peace you think about a more comfortable one.
The Skin of Our Teeth (1942), Act 3

9 True influence over another comes not from a moment's eloquence nor from any happily chosen word, but from the accumulation of a lifetime's thoughts stored up in the eyes.
The Woman of Andros (1930)

10 Literature is the orchestration of platitudes.
Time (January 12, 1953)

Wilford, John Noble (b.1933) U.S. journalist and author

1 Alone among all creatures, the species that styles itself wise, *Homo sapiens*, has an abiding interest in its distant origins,

knows that its allotted time is short, worries about the future, and wonders about the past.
New York Times (October 30, 1984)

Wilhelmina, Queen of the Netherlands (Wilhelmina Helena Pauline Maria; 1880–1962) Dutch monarch

1 And when we open our dikes, the waters are ten feet deep.
Replying to a boast by Wilhelm II that his guardsmen were all seven feet tall. Attrib.

Wilkes, John (1725–97) British politician and reformer

Quotations about Wilkes

1 Where laws end, tyranny begins.
William Pitt the Elder (1708–78) British prime minister. Referring to the trial of John Wilkes, regarded by many as a champion of freedom of the press. He was imprisoned for seditious libel (1769), elected an alderman (1770), and became lord mayor of London (1771). Speech to the House of Lords, the upper house of the British Parliament (January 9, 1770)

Quotations by Wilkes

2 LORD SANDWICH You will die either on the gallows, or of the pox.
WILKES That must depend on whether I embrace your lordship's principles or your mistress.
Also attributed to Samuel Foote. Quoted in *Portrait of a Patriot* (Charles Chenevix-Trench; 1962), ch. 3

3 The chapter of accidents is the longest chapter in the book.
Attrib. *The Doctor* (Robert Southey; 1847), ch. 18

Wilkins, James U.S. pioneer

1 Find a great many companies continually in sight. In fact it is one continued stream. As far as we can see, both in front and near the horizon is dotted with white wagon covers of emigrants, like a string of beads.
1850. Referring to the stream of wagons on the Oregon Trail. In 1850, 52,500 people emigrated to the West. Quoted in *The Oregon Trail* (W. E. Hill; 1987), Introduction

Wilkins, Roy (1901–81) U.S. civil rights activist, newspaper editor, and writer

1 Just give us a little time and one of these days we'll emancipate *you*!
Address to white people, quoted in *Contemporary Black Leaders* (Elton Fax; 1970)

Willebrands, Cardinal (b.1909) Dutch clergyman

1 The question of the rights of women to hold secular office is a quite separate matter and should not in any way be connected to or paralleled with the question of women's ordination.
Remark (June 1986)

William I, Emperor of Germany and King of Prussia (Wilhelm Friedrich Ludwig; 1797–1888) German monarch

1 I haven't got time to be tired.
Said during his final illness. (1888?) Attrib.

William II, Emperor of Germany and King of Prussia (Friedrich Wilhelm Viktor Albert, "Kaiser Bill"; 1859–1941) German monarch

1 The General Staff tells me nothing and never asks my advice. If people in Germany think I am the Supreme Commander, they are grossly mistaken.
Remark (November 1914), quoted in *Germany, 1866–1945* (Gordon A. Craig; 1978), ch. 10

2 We draw the sword with a clear conscience and with clean hands.
Remark, Berlin (August 4, 1914)

3 You will be home before the leaves have fallen from the trees.
August 1914. Said to troops leaving for the Front. Quoted in *The Guns of August* (Barbara W. Tuchman; 1962), ch. 9

4 The Admiral of the Atlantic salutes the Admiral of the Pacific.
Telegram sent to Tsar Nicholas II during a naval exercise. Quoted in *The Shadow of the Winter Palace* (Edward Crankshaw; 1976)

William III, King of England, Scotland, and Ireland, and Stadholder of the Netherlands ("William of Orange"; 1650–1702) English monarch

Quotations about William III

1 To long for and desire the landing of that Prince, whom they looked on as their deliverer from Popish tyranny, praying incessantly for an Easterly wind.
John Evelyn (1620–1706) English diarist. *Diary* (October 6, 1688)

Quotations by William III

2 There is one certain means by which I can be sure never to see my country's ruin; I will die in the last ditch.
Quoted in *History of England* (David Hume; 1757)

3 It seems to me a most extraordinary thing that one may not feel regard and affection for a young man without it being criminal.
Quoted in *Homosexuality: A History* (Colin Spencer; 1995)

4 Every bullet has its billet.
Quoted in *Journal* (John Wesley; June 6, 1765)

William of Malmesbury (1090?–1143?) English cleric and historian

1 Belching from daily excess he came hiccupping to the war.
Referring to Philip I of France. *Gesta Regum* (1135–40), bk. 2

William of Newburgh (1136?–98?) English monk and historian

1 The laity found him more than a king, the clergy more than a pope, and both an intolerable tyrant.
Referring to William Longchamp, justiciary and chancellor of England during Richard I's absence on the Third Crusade. *History of English Affairs* (1198), bk. 4, ch. 14

Williams, Dick (Richard Williams) U.S. baseball player

1 I've always gone back to the belief that you don't win—that the other team usually beats itself.
Christian Science Monitor (July 17, 1974)

Williams, Eric (1911–81) Trinidadian prime minister

1 In the 1950s we went to learn, now we go to teach.
1962. Referring to an upcoming tour of England by West Indian cricketers. Quoted in *Viv Richards: The Authorised Biography* (Trevor McDonald; 1984)

Williams, Hank (Hiram King Williams; 1923–53) U.S. country singer and songwriter

1 You got to have smelt a lot of mule manure before you can sing like a hillbilly.
1940? Quoted in *Look* (July 13, 1971)

Williams, Heathcote (b.1941) British poet and dramatist

1 In the last decade
Six of ten of the elephants in Africa
Have been massacred:
And the entire population
May soon be shovelled contemptuously
Into the realm of mythology.
Sacred Elephant (1989)

2 The shape of an African elephant's ear
Is the shape of Africa.
The shape of an Indian elephant's ear
Is the shape of India.
Sacred Elephant (1989)

3 When whaling boats have been overturned
And men have found themselves floundering helplessly in the seas,
They have been pushed up to the surface like bunches of frogs:
Forgivingly nudged by fellow mammals, until they regained their breath.
Whale Nation (1988)

4 The sullen killing continues.
The killing of the largest creatures in the world.
It is unthinkingly supposed
That the rest of life will not be shrivelled in the process.
Large creatures disappear;
Life becomes smaller.
Referring to the hunting of whales. *Whale Nation* (1988)

Williams, John A. (John Alfred Williams; b.1925) U.S. writer

1 Most people know things. All they want is a lie plausible enough to believe.
The Man Who Cried I Am (1968)

2 The French, for all their slogans, are becoming modern. Liberty, yes; equality, yes, of a sort; fraternity—with their women—highly questionable.
The Man Who Cried I Am (1968)

Williams, Robin (b.1951) U.S. actor and comedian

1 Nanoo nanoo!
One of the alien Mork's catchphrases. *Mork and Mindy* (1978–82)

2 Shazbot!
The alien Mork's version of a swearword. *Mork and Mindy* (1978–82)

3 My comedy is like emotional hang-gliding.
Playboy (October 1982)

4 My first film will be a very simple one. I'll need only $10 million. The film will be about a boy, his dog and his budget.
Playboy (October 1982)

5 Success? Ah yes, the first three-piece suit, first lawsuit.
Playboy (1979)

6 You're best when you're not in charge. The ego locks the muse.
Premiere (January 1988)

7 Cocaine is God's way of saying you're making too much money.
Screen International (December 15, 1990)

8 Golf is one of the few sports where a white man can dress like a black pimp and not look bad.
Attrib.

9 We're Americans, we're a simple people, but if you piss us off we'll bomb your cities.
Attrib.

Williams, Sherley Anne (b.1944) U.S. poet, writer, and teacher

1 Oh, we have paid for our children's place in the world again, and again.
Dessa Rose (1986)

Williams, Shirley, Dame, Baroness Williams (originally Shirley Vivien Teresa Brittain Catlin; b.1930) British politician

Quotations about Williams

1 You'll never get on in politics, dear, with *that* hat.
Nancy Astor (1879–1964) U.S.-born British politician. Said to the young Shirley Williams, who was later minister for education (1976–79), and then became a founder member of the Social Democratic Party (1980). Attrib.

Quotations by Williams

2 The British civil service...is a beautifully designed and effective braking mechanism.
Speech, Royal Institute of Public Administration (February 11, 1980)

Williams, Tennessee (Thomas Lanier Williams; 1911–83) U.S. playwright

1 Poker shouldn't be played in a house with women.
A Streetcar Named Desire (1947)

2 I can't stand a naked light bulb, any more than I can a rude remark or a vulgar action.
A Streetcar Named Desire (1947), Act 2, Scene 3

3 I have always depended on the kindness of strangers.
A Streetcar Named Desire (1947), Act 2, Scene 3

4 My suit is pale yellow. My nationality is French, and my normality has been often subject to question.
Camino Real (1953), block 4

5 Caged birds accept each other but flight is what they long for.
Camino Real (1953), block 7

6 We're all of us guinea pigs in the laboratory of God. Humanity is just a work in progress.
Camino Real (1953), block 12

7 It is a terrible thing for an old woman to outlive her dogs.
Camino Real (1953), Prologue

8 A vacuum is a hell of a lot better than some of the stuff that nature replaces it with.
Cat on a Hot Tin Roof (1955)

9 That Europe's nothin' on earth but a great big auction, that's all it is.
Cat on a Hot Tin Roof (1955), Act 1

10 You can be young without money but you can't be old without it.
Cat on a Hot Tin Roof (1955), Act 1

11 I think it's good for a writer to think he's dying; he works harder.
Observer, London (October 31, 1976), "Sayings of the Week"

12 I am the opposite of a stage magician. He gives you illusion that has the appearance of truth. I give you truth in the pleasant disguise of illusion.
The Glass Menagerie (1945), Scene 1

13 The play is memory. Being a memory play, it is dimly lighted, it is sentimental, it is not realistic. In memory everything seems to happen to music. That explains the fiddle in the wings.
The Glass Menagerie (1945), Scene 1

14 Couples would come outside, to the relative privacy of the alley. You could see them kissing behind ash pits and telephone poles. This was the compensation for lives...without any change or adventure.
The Glass Menagerie (1945), Scene 5

15 I didn't go to the moon, I went much further—for time is the longest distance between two places.
The Glass Menagerie (1945), Scene 7

16 Hysteria is a natural phenomenon, the common denominator of the female nature. It's the big female weapon, and the test of a man is his ability to cope with it.
The Night of the Iguana (1961)

17 I don't want to be involved in some sort of scandal, but I've covered the waterfront.
1970. Quoted in *A Queer Reader* (Patrick Higgins, ed.; 1993)

18 If people behaved in the way nations do they would all be put in straitjackets.
Attrib.

19 He was meddling too much in my private life.
Explaining why he had given up visiting his psychoanalyst. Attrib.

Williams, Velina U.S. pioneer

1 The quaking of the earth and the rumble of the rushing torrent continued for a long time, many estimating the herd to be from four to eight miles long...Surely many, many thousands of those animals.
1853. Referring to a herd of buffalo. Quoted in "Diaries," *The Oregon Trail* (W. E. Hill; 1987)

Williams, William Carlos (1883–1963) U.S. poet, novelist, and physician

Quotations about Williams

1 At dawn you rose & wrote—the books poured forth—
you delivered infinite babies, in one great birth.
John Berryman (1914–72) U.S. poet. "An Elegy for W. C. W., the Lovely Man," *The Dream Songs* (1968)

2 Mourn O Ye Angels of the Left Wing! that the poet
of the streets is a skeleton under the pavement now.
Allen Ginsberg (1926–97) U.S. poet. Referring to the death of William Carlos Williams. "Death News," *Howl and Other Poems* (1956), quoted in *The Penguin Book of American Verse* (Geoffrey Moore, ed.; 1977)

Quotations by Williams

3 So much depends
upon
a red wheel
barrow glazed with rain
water
beside the white
chickens.
"The Red Wheelbarrow" (1923)

4 Remember, now, Lawrence dead.
Blue squills in bloom—to
the scorched aridity of
the Mexican plateau.
"An Elegy for D. H. Lawrence," *An Early Martyr and other Poems* (1935), quoted in *The Penguin Book of American Verse* (Geoffrey Moore, ed.; 1977)

5 Rigor of beauty is the quest. But how will you find beauty when it is locked in the mind past all remonstrance?
"Paterson," *Paterson* (1946–58), *The Selected Poems of William Carlos Williams* (Charles Tomlinson, ed.; 1976)

6 Sniffing the trees,
just another dog
among a lot of dogs.
"Paterson," *Paterson* (1946–58), *The Selected Poems of William Carlos Williams* (Charles Tomlinson, ed.; 1976)

7 A cool of books
will sometimes lead the mind to libraries
of a hot afternoon, if books can be found
cool to the sense to lead the mind away.
"The Library," *Paterson* (1946–58), bk. 3, *The Selected Poems of William Carlos Williams* (Charles Tomlinson, ed.; 1976)

8 Minds like beds always made up,
(more stony than a shore)
unwilling or unable.
Paterson (1946–58), bk. 1, Preface

9 Beauty is a shell
from the sea
where she rules triumphant
till love has had its way with her.
"Song," *Pictures from Brueghel and Other Poems* (1962), *The Selected Poems of William Carlos Williams* (Charles Tomlinson, ed.; 1976)

10 His coat resembles the snow
deep snow
the male snow
which attacks and kills.
"The Polar Bear," *Pictures from Brueghel and Other Poems* (1962), *The Selected Poems of William Carlos Williams* (Charles Tomlinson, ed.; 1976)

11 I have eaten
the plums
that were in
the icebox
and which
you were probably
saving
for breakfast.
"This is Just to Say," *Poems* (1934), *The Penguin Book of American Verse* (Geoffrey Moore, ed.; 1977)

12 The crowd at the ball game
is moved uniformly
by a spirit of uselessness
which delights them.
"At the Ball Game," *Spring and All* (1923), *The Selected Poems of William Carlos Williams* (Charles Tomlinson, ed.; 1976)

13 Oh, oh, oh! she cried
as the ambulance men lifted
her to the stretcher—
Is this what you call
making me comfortable?
"The Last Words of My English Grandmother," *Spring and All* (1923), *The Selected Poems of William Carlos Williams* (Charles Tomlinson, ed.; 1976)

14 What are all those
fuzzy-looking things out there?
Trees? Well I'm tired
of them and rolled her head away.
"The Last Words of My English Grandmother," *Spring and All* (1923), *The Selected Poems of William Carlos Williams* (Charles Tomlinson, ed.; 1976)

15 The most marvelous is not
the beauty, deep as that is,
but the classic attempt
at beauty, at the swamp's center.
"The Hard Core of Beauty," *The Collected Later Poems* (1950), *The Selected Poems of William Carlos Williams* (Charles Tomlinson, ed.; 1976)

16 Through metaphor to reconcile
the people and the stones.
Compose. (No ideas but in things.) Invent!
"A Sort of Song," *The Wedge* (1944)

17 Is it any better in Heaven, my friend Ford,
than you found it in Provence?
"To Ford Madox Ford in Heaven," *The Wedge* (1944)

William the Conqueror, King of England (William I; 1027–87) Norman-born English monarch

1 By the splendour of God I have taken possession of my realm; the earth of England is in my two hands.
1066. Said after falling over when coming ashore at Pevensey with his army of invasion. Attrib.

Willis, Bruce (b.1955) U.S. film actor

1 Frankly, reviews are mostly for people who still read. Like most of the written word, it is going the way of the dinosaur.
Referring to poor reviews by the critics. *Time* (May 19, 1997)

Willison, George F. (George Findlay Willison; 1896–1972) U.S. writer

1 One man, his mind unhinged by slow starvation, killed his wife, "powdered salted her, and had eaten part of her before it was knowne," for which he was hanged.
Referring to the first winter (1607) in Jamestown, where four out of five died of starvation. *The American Heritage Cookbook* (1964)

Willkie, Wendell Lewis (1892–1944) U.S. politician and lawyer

1 The constitution does not provide for first and second class citizens.
An American Program (1944), ch. 2

2 There exists in the world today a gigantic reservoir of good will toward us, the American people.
One World (1943), ch. 10

3 Freedom is an indivisible word. If we want to enjoy it, and fight for it, we must be prepared to extend it to everyone, whether they are rich or poor, whether they agree with us or not, no matter what their race or the color of their skin.
One World (1943), ch. 13

Wilmer, Valerie (b.1941) British writer and photographer

1 He used a tough plastic reed, a Fibrecane No 4—the hardest—and had a sound that scared the shit out of people.
Referring to jazz saxophonist Albert Ayler. *As Serious as Your Life* (1977), ch. 6

Wilson, Angus, Sir (Angus Frank Johnstone Wilson; 1913–91) British writer

1 She was more than ever proud of the position of the bungalow, so almost in the country.
"A Flat Country Christmas," *A Bit Off the Map* (1957)

2 I have no concern for the common man except that he should not be so common.
No Laughing Matter (1967)

3 "God knows how you Protestants can be expected to have any sense of direction," she said. "It's different with us. I haven't been to mass for years, I've got every mortal sin on my conscience, but I know when I'm doing wrong. I'm still a Catholic."
"Significant Experience," *The Wrong Set* (1949)

Wilson, August (b.1945) U.S. playwright

1 You all line up at the door with your hands out. I give you the lint from my pockets. I give you my sweat and my blood. I ain't got no tears. I done spent them.
Fences (1985), Act 1, Scene 3

Wilson, Charles E. (Charles "Engine Charlie" Erwin Wilson; 1890–1961) U.S. politician and businessman

1 What's good for the country is good for General Motors, and what's good for General Motors is good for the country.
Statement to the Senate Armed Forces Committee (1952)

2 A bigger bang for a buck.
1954. Referring to testing the hydrogen bomb at Bikini (1954). Quoted in *Safire's Political Dictionary* (William Safire; 1978)

Wilson, Edmund (1895–1972) U.S. critic and writer

1 The great scientists have been occupied with values—it is only their vulgar followers who think they are not...They have imaginations as powerful as any poet's.
Letter to Allen Tate (July 20, 1931)

2 My contention is that Sherlock Holmes *is* literature on a humble but not ignoble level, whereas the mystery writers most in vogue now are not. The old stories are literature...by virtue of imagination and style.
Referring to the work of British author Sir Arthur Conan Doyle. *Classics and Commercials: A Literary Chronicle of the Forties* (1951)

3 All Hollywood corrupts; absolute Hollywood corrupts absolutely.
May 1938. Alluding to Lord Acton's famous saying: "Power tends to corrupt, and absolute power corrupts absolutely." "Old Antichrist's Sayings," *Letters on Literature and Politics 1912–1972* (1977)

4 We tended to imagine Canada as a vast hunting preserve convenient to the United States.
O Canada (1965)

Wilson, Edward O. (Edward Osborne Wilson; b.1929) U.S. evolutionary biologist

1 If history and science have taught us anything, it is that passion and desire are not the same as truth. The human mind evolved to believe in the gods. It did not evolve to believe in biology
Consilience: The Unity of Knowledge (1998)

2 The central idea of the consilience world view is that all tangible phenomena...are based on material processes that are ultimately reducible...to the laws of physics.
"To What End?," *Consilience: The Unity of Knowledge* (1998)

3 No species...possesses a purpose beyond the imperatives created by genetic history...The human mind is a device for survival and reproduction, and reason is just one of its various techniques.
"Dilemma," *On Human Nature* (1978)

4 We are compelled to drive toward total knowledge, right down to the levels of the neuron and the gene. When we have progressed enough to explain ourselves in these mechanistic terms...the result might be hard to accept.
"Man: From Sociobiology to Sociology," *Sociobiology: The New Synthesis* (1975)

5 In the process of natural selection, then, any device that can insert a higher proportion of certain genes into subsequent generations will come to characterize the species.
"The Morality of the Gene," *Sociobiology: The New Synthesis* (1975)

6 When you have seen one ant, one bird, one tree, you have not seen them all.
Time (October 13, 1986)

7 It's like having astronomy without knowing where the stars are.
Referring to the extinction of undiscovered species. *Time* (October 13, 1986)

Wilson, Harold, Baron Wilson of Rievaulx (James Harold Wilson; 1916–95) British prime minister

Quotations about Wilson

1 Lord George Brown drunk is a better man than the prime minister sober.
Anonymous. *Times*, London (March 6, 1976)

Quotations by Wilson

2 One man's wage rise is another man's price increase.
Observer, London (January 11, 1970), "Sayings of the Week"

3 Everybody should have an equal chance—but they shouldn't have a flying start.
Observer, London (1963), "Sayings of the Year"

4 I'm an optimist, but I'm an optimist who carries a raincoat.
Attrib.

5 A week is a long time in politics.
1964. Repeated on several occasions but first thought to have been said during the 1964 sterling crisis. Attrib.

Wilson, Harriette (originally Harriette Dubochet; 1789–1855) British writer and courtesan

Quotations about Wilson

1 Publish and be damned!
Duke of Wellington (1769–1852) Irish-born British general and prime minister. Said on being offered the chance to avoid mention in the memoirs of Harriette Wilson by giving her money. Attrib. *Wellington: The Years of the Sword* (Elizabeth Longford; 1969), ch. 10

Quotations by Wilson

2 I shall not say why and how I became, at the age of fifteen, the mistress of the Earl of Craven.
Opening lines. *Memoirs* (1825)

Wilson, Woodrow (Thomas Woodrow Wilson; 1856–1924) U.S. president

Quotations about Wilson

1 Like Odysseus, he looked wiser when seated.
John Maynard Keynes (1883–1946) British economist. Quoted in *The Worldly Philosophers* (R. Heilbroner; 1955)

2 Wilson is a noble failure and a Biblical prophet. The people followed Wilson because he promised immediate peace, while Lenin called them to civil war.
Osip Mandelstam (1891–1938) Russian poet, writer, and translator. "Jean-Richard Bloch" (1930), quoted in *The Collected Critical Prose and Letters of Osip Mandelstam* (J. G. Harris, ed., tr., C. Link, tr.; 1991)

3 He was the Messiah of the new age, and his crucifixion was yet to come.
George Edward Slocombe (1894–1963) British journalist. Referring to Woodrow Wilson and his visit to the Versailles Conference (1918). *Mirror to Geneva* (1937)

4 Well, I have one consolation. No candidate was ever elected ex-president by such a large majority!
1912
William Howard Taft (1857–1930) U.S. president. Referring to his disastrous defeat by Woodrow Wilson in the 1912 presidential election. Attrib.

Quotations by Wilson

5 Every people should be left free to determine its own policy, its own way of development, unhindered, unthreatened,

unafraid, the little along with the great and powerful...These are American principles.
Address to Congress (January 22, 1917)

6 Self-determination is not a mere phrase. It is an imperative principle which statesmen will henceforth ignore at their peril.
Address to Congress (February 11, 1918)

7 America's neutrality is ineffectual...at best...The world must be made safe for democracy.
Calling for a declaration of war. Address to Congress (April 2, 1917)

8 The world must be safe for democracy. Its peace must be planted upon trusted foundations of political liberty.
Calling for a declaration of war. Address to Congress (April 2, 1917)

9 It is not an army that we must train for war: it is a nation.
Address, Washington, D.C. (May 12, 1917)

10 The nation has been deeply stirred...The feelings with which we face this new age of right and opportunity sweep across our heartstrings like some air out of God's own presence.
Inaugural Address, Washington, D.C. (March 4, 1913)

11 We have stood apart, studiously neutral.
Message to Congress (December 7, 1915)

12 My message today was a message of death for our young men. How strange it seems to applaud that.
Referring to his speech to Congress calling for a declaration of war. Remark (1917)

13 There is no indispensable man. The government will not collapse and go to pieces if any one of the gentlemen who are seeking to be entrusted with its guidance should be left at home.
Remark (1912), quoted in *New York Times Magazine* (July 10, 1956)

14 Logic! Logic! I don't give a damn for logic. I am going to include pensions.
Addressed to his advisers on reparations at the Paris Peace Conference. Remark (April 1919), quoted in *Quotations in History* (Alan and Veronica Palmer; 1976)

15 Every man who takes office in Washington either grows or swells, and when I give a man office I watch him carefully to see whether he is growing or swelling.
Speech (May 15, 1916)

16 Liberty does not consist in mere declarations of the rights of man. It consists in the translation of those declarations into definite action.
Speech (July 4, 1914)

17 The United States must be neutral in fact as well as in name during these days that are to try men's souls. We must be impartial in thought as well as in action.
Speech (August 19, 1914)

18 One cool judgment is worth a thousand hasty councils.
Speech at Pittsburgh (January 29, 1916), quoted in *The Public Papers* (Ray S. Stannard and William E. Dodd, eds.; 1925)

19 You cannot become thorough Americans if you think of yourselves in groups. America does not consist of groups. A man who thinks of himself as belonging to a particular national group in America has not yet become an American.
Speech, Convention Hall, Philadelphia, Pennsylvania (May 10, 1915)

20 America cannot be an ostrich with its head in the sand.
Speech, Des Moines, Iowa (February 1, 1916)

21 There is a price which is too great to pay for peace, and that price can be put into one word. One cannot pay the price of self-respect.
Speech, Des Moines, Iowa (February 1, 1916)

22 I want to take this occasion to say that the United States will never again seek one additional foot of territory by conquest.
Speech, Mobile (October 27, 1913)

23 A general association of nations must be formed under specific covenants for the purpose of affording mutual guarantees of political independence and territorial integrity to great and small states alike.
The "Fourteen Points," were his proposals for a lasting peace, which formed the basis of the Treaty of Versailles (1919) and the League of Nations (1920–46). Speech to Congress, "Fourteen Points" (January 8, 1918)

24 Open covenants of peace, openly arrived at, after which there shall be no private international understandings of any kind but diplomacy shall proceed always frankly and in the public view.
The "Fourteen Points" were his proposals for a lasting peace, which formed the basis of the Treaty of Versailles (1919) and the League of Nations (1920–46). Speech to Congress, "Fourteen Points" (January 8, 1918)

25 What we demand in this war is nothing peculiar to ourselves. It is that the world be made fit and safe to live in.
The "Fourteen Points" were his proposals for a lasting peace, which formed the basis of the Treaty of Versailles (1919) and the League of Nations (1920–46). Speech to Congress, "Fourteen Points" (January 8, 1918), Preamble

26 The Declaration of Independence...is an eminently practical document, meant for the use of practical men; not a thesis for philosophers, but a whip for tyrants; not a theory of government, but a program for action.
The New Freedom (1913)

27 The war we have just been through, though it was shot through with terror, is not to be compared with the war we would have to face next time.
Referring to World War I. Quoted in *Mr Wilson's War* (John Dos Passos; 1917)

28 If you want me to talk for ten minutes I'll come next week. If you want me to talk for an hour I'll come tonight.
Answering an invitation to make a speech. Attrib.

Winchell, Walter (originally Walter Winchel; 1879–1972) U.S. journalist and broadcaster

1 I saw it at a disadvantage—the curtain was up.
Referring to a show starring Earl Carroll. Quoted in *Come to Judgment* (Alden Whiteman; 1980)

Windebank, Francis (1582–1646) English politician

1 That pig of a Henry VIII committed such sacrilege by profaning so many ecclesiastical benefices in order to give their goods to those who being so rewarded might stand firmly for the King in the Lower House; and now the King's greatest enemies are those who are enriched by these benefices.
Referring to the dissolution of the monasteries, and also to the lower house of the English Parliament. Remark to the Papal envoy (April 1635)

Winfrey, Oprah (b.1954) U.S. talk show host, actor, and businesswoman

1 I am the product of every other black woman before me who has done or said anything worthwhile. Recognizing that I am a part of history is what allows me to soar.
I Dream a World: Portraits of Black Women Who Changed America (Brian Lanker; 1989)

2 I luuuuuuv food. You can tell by the span of my hips.
Oprah! (Robert Waldron; 1987)

3 I was a token, but I was a happy, paid token.
Oprah! (Robert Waldron; 1987)

4 There is a commodity in human experience. If it's happened to one person, it has happened to thousands of others.
Quoted in *Time* (August 8, 1988)

Winkler, Paul (also known as Paul Winckler; 1630–86) German lawyer and writer

1 Who does nothing, makes no mistakes; and who makes no mistakes, never makes any progress.
Drei Tausend gute Gedanken (1685)

Winkworth, Catherine (1827–78) British writer

1 Now thank we all our God,
With hearts and hands and voices,
Who wondrous things hath done,
In whom his world rejoices.
"Now Thank We All Our God" (1858)

Winn, Mary Day (1888–1965) U.S. writer

1 Sex is the tabasco sauce which an adolescent national palate sprinkles on every course in the menu.
Adam's Rib (1931)

Winner, Michael (Michael Robert Winner; b.1935) British filmmaker

1 The hardest part of directing is staying awake for nine weeks at a stretch.
Attrib.

Winnicott, Donald W. (Donald Woods Winnicott; 1896–1971) British psychoanalyst and child psychiatrist

1 It is only when alone, that is to say in the presence of someone, that the infant can discover his personal life.
Attrib.

Winstanley, Gerrard (1609?–60?) English reformer

1 None ought to be lords or landlords over another, but the earth is free for every son and daughter of mankind to live free upon.
Letter to Lord Fairfax (1649)

2 Seeing the common people of England by joint consent of person and purse have cast out Charles our Norman oppressor, we have by this victory recovered ourselves from under his Norman yoke.
Referring to the trial and execution of Charles I after his defeat in the English Civil War. Remark to Lord Fairfax (December 8, 1649)

3 You noble Diggers all, stand up now,
The waste land to maintain, seeing Cavaliers by name
Your digging do disdain and persons all defame.
The Diggers were a radical group that believed in land reform and practiced an agrarian communism. Important in 1649, they were dispersed by the Commonwealth government in 1650. "The Diggers' Song" (1649)

Winterson, Jeanette (b.1959) British novelist

1 Praise and blame are much the same for the writer. One is better for your vanity, but neither gets you much further with your work.
Guardian, London (June 18, 1994)

2 There's nothing worse than the writer who learns to do something and then goes on doing it because it's comfortable and safe. It is a gift of wings, and you learn to trust yourself, that you will not fall—or if you do, that you will just swoop up again.
Guardian, London (June 18, 1994)

3 Whatever you think of the church, it does provide a coherence. It is better to have a framework to fight against than no framework at all.
Guardian, London (June 18, 1994)

4 And even the most solid of things and the most real, the best-loved and the well-known, are only hand-shadows on the wall. Empty space and points of light.
Sexing the Cherry (1989)

5 The Hopi, an Indian tribe, have a language as sophisticated as ours, but no tenses for past, present and future. The division does not exist. What does this say about time?
Sexing the Cherry (1989)

Winthrop, John (1588–1649) English-born North American colonial administrator

1 For we must consider that we shall be as a city upon a hill. The eyes of all people are upon us, so that if we shall deal falsely with our God in this work...and so cause Him to withdraw His present help from us, we shall be made a story and a byword through the world.
Sermon delivered on board the ship *Arabella*, bound for the New World. "A Model of Christian Charity" (1630)

Winthrop, Robert Charles (1809–94) U.S. politician

1 A Star for every State and a State for every Star.
Speech, Boston Common (August 27, 1862)

Wither, George (1588–1667) English poet and pamphleteer

1 And I oft have heard defended,
Little said is soonest mended.
The Shepherd's Hunting (1622)

Wittgenstein, Ludwig (Ludwig Josef Johann Wittgenstein; 1889–1951) Austrian philosopher

Quotations about Wittgenstein

1 "What is conceivable can happen too,"
Said Wittgenstein, who had not dreamt of you.
William Empson (1906–84) British poet and literary critic. "This Last Pain," *Collected Poems* (Michael Roberts and Donald Hall, eds.; 1955)

Quotations by Wittgenstein

2 The human body is the best picture of the human soul.
Philosophical Investigations (1953)

3 The philosopher's treatment of a question is like the treatment of an illness.
Philosophical Investigations (1953)

4 Philosophy, as we use the word, is a fight against the fascination which forms of expression exert upon us.
The Blue Book (1958)

5 The riddle does not exist. If a question can be framed at all, it is also possible to answer it.
Tractatus Logico-Philosophicus (1921)

6 The world is everything that is the case.
Tractatus Logico-Philosophicus (1921), ch. 1

7 Philosophy is not a theory but an activity.
Tractatus Logico-Philosophicus (1921), ch. 4

8 Logic must take care of itself.
Tractatus Logico-Philosophicus (1921), ch. 5

9 Whereof one cannot speak, thereof one must remain silent.
Tractatus Logico-Philosophicus (1921), ch. 7

10 In order to draw a limit to thinking, we should have to be able to think both sides of this limit.
Tractatus Logico-Philosophicus (1921), Preface

11 If there were a verb meaning "to believe falsely", it would not have any significant first person, present indicative.
Quoted in *A Certain World* (W. H. Auden; 1970)

12 Aim at being loved without being admired.
1940. Quoted in *Culture and Value* (G. H. von Wright and Heikki Nyman, eds.; 1980)

13 Philosophers use a language that is already deformed as though by shoes that are too tight.
1941. Quoted in *Culture and Value* (G. H. von Wright and Heikki Nyman, eds.; 1980)

14 Reading the Socratic dialogues one has the feeling: what a frightful waste of time! What's the point of these arguments that prove nothing and clarify nothing?
1931. Quoted in *Culture and Value* (G. H. von Wright and Heikki Nyman, eds.; 1980)

15 Someone who knows too much finds it hard not to lie.
1947. Quoted in *Culture and Value* (G. H. von Wright and Heikki Nyman, eds.; 1980)

16 Thoughts that are at peace. That's what someone who philosophizes yearns for.
1944. Quoted in *Culture and Value* (G. H. von Wright and Heikki Nyman, eds.; 1980)

17 If you are led by psychoanalysis to say that really you thought so and so or that really your motive was so and so, this is not a matter of discovery, but of persuasion.
1938. Quoted in *Lectures and Conversations* (Cyril Barnett, ed.; 1966)

18 When we are studying psychology we may feel there is something unsatisfactory, some difficulty about the whole subject or study—because we are taking physics as our ideal science.
Quoted in *Lectures and Conversations* (Cyril Barnett, ed.; 1966)

19 I am in one sense making propaganda for one style of thinking as opposed to another. I am honestly disgusted with the other.
1938. Referring to thinking based on a naïve reliance on scientific certainty. Quoted in *Lectures and Conversations* (Cyril Barnett, ed.; 1966)

20 Any logic good enough for a primitive means of communication needs no apology from us. Language did not emerge from some kind of ratiocination.
1950. Quoted in *On Certainty* (G. E. E. Anscombe, ed.; 1969)

21 A philosopher...says again and again "I know that's a tree," pointing to a tree that is near us. Someone else arrives and hears this, and I tell him: "This fellow isn't insane. We are only doing philosophy."
1950. Quoted in *On Certainty* (G. E. E. Anscombe, ed.; 1969)

22 If you tried to doubt everything you would not get as far as doubting anything. The game of doubting itself presupposes certainty.
1950. Quoted in *On Certainty* (G. E. E. Anscombe, ed.; 1969)

23 My *life* consists in my being content to accept many things.
1950. Quoted in *On Certainty* (G. E. E. Anscombe, ed.; 1969)

24 Our knowledge forms an enormous system. And only within this system has a particular bit the value we give it.
1950. Quoted in *On Certainty* (G. E. E. Anscombe, ed.; 1969)

Wittig, Monique (b.1935) French writer

1 The women say that they perceive their bodies in their entirety.They say they do not favor any of its parts on the grounds that it was formerly a forbidden object.
Les Guérillères (1969)

Wodehouse, P. G., Sir (Pelham Grenville Wodehouse; 1881–1975) British-born U.S. humorous writer

Quotations about Wodehouse

1 P. G. Wodehouse, whose works I place a little below Shakespeare's and any distance you like above anybody else's.
James Agate (1877–1947) British theater critic. *P. G. Wodehouse* (David A. Jasen; 1974)

2 A young, earnest American brought up the subject of nuclear warfare which, he said might well destroy the entire human race. "I can't wait," P. G. Wodehouse murmured.
Malcolm Muggeridge (1903–90) British journalist. *Tread Softly For You Tread on My Jokes* (1966)

3 English literature's performing flea.
Sean O'Casey (1880–1964) Irish playwright. Attrib.

Quotations by Wodehouse

4 Marriage isn't a process of prolonging the life of love, but of mummifying the corpse.
Bring on the Girls (co-written with Guy Bolton; 1953)

5 Memories are like mulligatawny soup in a cheap restaurant. It is best not to stir them.
Bring on the Girls (co-written with Guy Bolton; 1953)

6 "What ho!" I said, "What ho!" said Motty. "What ho! What ho!" "What ho! What ho! What ho!" After that it seemed rather difficult to go on with the conversation.
Carry On, Jeeves! (1925)

7 Judges, as a class, display, in the matter of arranging alimony, that reckless generosity that is found only in men who are giving away somebody else's cash.
Louder and Funnier (1963)

8 If I had had to choose between him and a cockroach as a companion for a walking-tour, the cockroach would have had it by a short head.
My Man Jeeves (1919)

9 His ideas of first-aid stopped short at squirting soda-water.
"Doing Clarence a Bit of Good," *My Man Jeeves* (1919)

10 I don't owe a penny to a single soul—not counting tradesmen, of course.
"Jeeves and the Hard-Boiled Egg," *My Man Jeeves* (1919)

11 She fitted into my biggest armchair as if it had been built round her by someone who knew they were wearing armchairs tight about the hips that season.
"Jeeves and the Unbidden Guest," *My Man Jeeves* (1919)

12 I spent the afternoon musing on Life. If you come to think of it, what a queer thing Life is! So unlike anything else, don't you know, if you see what I mean.
"Rallying Round Old George," *My Man Jeeves* (1919)

13 New York is a small place when it comes to the part of it that wakes up just as the rest is going to bed.
"The Aunt and the Sluggard," *My Man Jeeves* (1919)

14 The tragedy of life is that your early heroes lose their glamour...Now, with Doyle I don't have this feeling. I still revere his work as much as ever. I used to think it swell, and I still think it swell.
Referring to Sir Arthur Conan Doyle. *Performing Flea* (1962)

15 "Ah, love, love," he said. "Is there anything like it? Were you ever in love, Beach?"
"Yes, sir, on one occasion, when I was a young under-footman. But it blew over."
Pigs Have Wings (1952)

16 I can honestly say that I always look on Pauline as one of the nicest girls I was ever engaged to.
Thank You Jeeves (1934), ch. 6

17 All the unhappy marriages come from the husbands having brains. What good are brains to a man? They only unsettle him.
The Adventures of Sally (1920), ch.10

18 He spoke with a certain what-is-it in his voice, and I could see that, if not actually disgruntled, he was far from being gruntled.
The Code of the Woosters (1938), ch. 1

19 Big chap with a small mustache and the sort of eye that can open an oyster at sixty paces.
The Code of the Woosters (1938), ch. 2

20 It is no use telling me that there are bad aunts and good aunts. At the core they are all alike. Sooner or later, out pops the cloven hoof.
The Code of the Woosters (1938), ch.2

21 He is always called a nerve specialist because it sounds better, but everyone knows he's a sort of janitor in a loony bin.
The Inimitable Jeeves (1923), ch. 7

22 Jeeves coughed one soft, low, gentle cough like a sheep with a blade of grass stuck in its throat.
The Inimitable Jeeves (1923), ch. 13

23 It was my Uncle George who discovered that alcohol was a food well in advance of modern medical thought.
The Inimitable Jeeves (1923), ch. 16

24 It is a good rule in life never to apologize. The right sort of people do not want apologies, and the wrong sort take a mean advantage of them.
The Man Upstairs (1914)

25 There is only one cure for grey hair. It was invented by a Frenchman. It is called the guillotine.
The Old Reliable (1951)

26 The Right Hon. was a tubby little chap who looked as if he had been poured into his clothes and had forgotten to say "When!"
"Jeeves and the Impending Doom," *Very Good Jeeves!* (1930)

27 Like so many substantial Americans, he had married young and kept on marrying, springing from blonde to blonde like the chamois of the Alps leaping from crag to crag.
Quoted in *Wodehouse at Work to the End* (Richard Usborne; 1961), ch. 2

28 Unlike the male codfish which, suddenly finding itself the parent of three million five hundred thousand little codfish, cheerfully resolves to love them all, the British aristocracy is apt to look with a somewhat jaundiced eye on its younger sons.
Quoted in *Wodehouse at Work to the End* (Richard Usborne; 1961), ch. 5

29 He was either a man of about a hundred and fifty who was rather young for his years or a man of about a hundred and ten who had been aged by trouble.
Quoted in *Wodehouse at Work to the End* (Richard Usborne; 1961), ch. 6

30 Has anybody ever seen a dramatic critic in the daytime? Of course not. They come out after dark, up to no good.
Attrib.

31 You know, the more I see of women, the more I think that there ought to be a law. Something has got to be done about this sex, or the whole fabric of society will collapse, and then what silly asses we shall all look.
Attrib.

Wolf, Christa (originally Christa Ihlenfeld; b.1929) German writer

1 Every revolutionary movement also liberates language.
Speech, Berlin (November 4, 1989), quoted in *When the Wall Came Down* (Harold James and Marla Stone, eds.; 1992)

2 What is past is not dead; it is not even past. We cut ourselves off from it; we pretend to be strangers.
A Model Childhood (U. Molinaro and H. Rappott, trs.; 1976), ch. 1

3 Awe is composed of reverence and dread. I often think that people today have nothing left but the dread.
1983. *Cassandra. A Novel and Four Essays* (Jan van Heurck, tr.; 1984)

4 You can tell when a war starts, but when does the prewar start?
1983. *Cassandra. A Novel and Four Essays* (Jan van Heurck, tr.; 1984)

5 For women, writing is a medium which they place between themselves and the world of men.
1983. "A Work Diary," *Cassandra. A Novel and Four Essays* (Jan van Heurck, tr.; 1984)

6 The atomic threat...must...have brought us to the brink of silence...to the brink of endurance, to the brink of reserve about our fear and anxiety, and our true opinions.
1983. "A Work Diary," *Cassandra. A Novel and Four Essays* (Jan van Heurck, tr.; 1984)

7 It was still a time for open trust, for innocence and illusions.
Referring to the first few months after German reunification. "Gifts," *Im Dialog* (1990)

8 When we stop hoping, that which we fear will certainly come.
No Place on Earth (1979)

Wolf, L. J. U.S. writer

1 We spared the rod and wound up with the beat generation.
Attrib.

Wolf, Naomi (b.1962) U.S. writer

1 Of dancers, 38 percent show anorexic behavior. The average...dancer...is thinner than 95 percent of the female population...a near skeleton and the texture of men's musculature where the shape and feel of a woman used to be.
The Beauty Myth: How Images of Beauty are Used Against Women (1990)

2 The beauty myth of the present is more insidious than any mystique of femininity yet: A century ago, Nora slammed the door of the doll's house...where women are trapped today, there is no door to slam.
The Beauty Myth: How Images of Beauty are Used Against Women (1990)

3 The more legal and material hindrances women have broken through, the more strictly and heavily and cruelly images of female beauty have come to weigh upon us.
The Beauty Myth: How Images of Beauty are Used Against Women (1990)

4 We are in the midst of a violent backlash against feminism that uses images of female beauty as a political weapon against women's advancement: the beauty myth.
The Beauty Myth: How Images of Beauty are Used Against Women (1990)

Wolfard, Mary British radio journalist

1 I think a lot of the women's lib movement came from the war. The women who were growing up then are the mothers of today, and I'm sure they've been affected by the fact that their mothers worked then.
Referring to World War II. Quoted in *Don't You Know There's a War On?* (Jonathan Croall, ed.; 1988)

Wolfe, Charles (1791–1823) Irish poet and clergyman

1 Not a drum was heard, not a funeral note,
As his corpse to the rampart we hurried.
"The Burial of Sir John Moore at Corunna" (1817), st. 1, ll. 1–2

2 We carved not a line, and we raised not a stone—
But we left him alone with his glory.
"The Burial of Sir John Moore at Corunna" (1817), st. 8, ll. 3–4

Wolfe, Humbert (originally Umberto Wolff; 1886–1940) Italian-born British poet

1 You cannot hope
to bribe or twist,
thank God! the
British journalist.

But, seeing what
that man will do
unbribed, there's
no occasion to.
"Over the Fire," *The Uncelestial City* (1930), bk. 1

Wolfe, Thomas (Thomas Clayton Wolfe; 1900–38) U.S. novelist

1 Look Homeward, Angel
Book title. *Look Homeward, Angel* (1929)

2 Which of us has known his brother? Which of us has looked into his father's heart? Which of us has not remained forever prison-pent? Which of us is not forever a stranger and alone?
Look Homeward, Angel (1929), Foreword

3 Most of the time we think we're sick, it's all in the mind.
Look Homeward, Angel (1929), pt. 1, ch. 1

4 One belongs to New York instantly. One belongs to it as much in five minutes as in five years.
The Web and the Rock (1939)

5 If a man has talent and cannot use it, he has failed. If he has a talent and uses only half of it, he has partly failed. If he has a talent and learns somehow to use the whole of it, he has...won a satisfaction and a triumph few men ever know.
The Web and the Rock (1939), ch. 13

Wolfe, Tom (Thomas Kennerley Wolfe; b.1930) U.S. journalist and novelist

1 Writing a novel about this astonishing metropolis...cramming as much of New York City between the covers as you could, was the most tempting, the most challenging, and the most obvious idea that an American writer could possibly have.
Harper's (November 1989)

2 The Sideburn Fairy...had been...visiting young groovies in their sleep and causing them to awake with sideburns running down their cheeks.
Mauve Gloves and Madmen, Clutter and Vine (1976)

3 We are now in the Me Decade—seeing the upward roll of...the third great religious wave in American history...and this one has the mightiest, holiest roll of all, the beat that goes...Me...Me...Me...Me.
"The Me Decade and the Third Awakening," *Mauve Gloves and Madmen, Clutter and Vine* (1976)

4 Radical Chic, after all, is only radical in style; in its heart it is part of Society and its traditions—Politics, like Rock, Pop, and Camp, has its uses.
"Radical Chic and Mau-Mauing the Flak Catchers," *New Yorker* (June 8, 1970)

5 For decades the bond business had been the bedridden giant of Wall Street...twice as much money had always changed hands on the bond market as on the stock market.
The Bonfire of the Vanities (1987)

6 He was learning for himself the truth of the saying, "A liberal is a conservative who has been arrested."
The Bonfire of the Vanities (1987)

7 On Wall Street he and a few others—how many?—three hundred, four hundred, five hundred?—had become precisely that...Masters of the Universe.
The Bonfire of the Vanities (1987)

8 That's an electric doughnut...all I do all day is talk to other electric doughnuts.
A stockbroker describing his telephone. *The Bonfire of the Vanities* (1987)

9 The Rome, the Paris, the London of the 20th century, the dense magnetic rock, the irresistible destination of all those who insist on being where things are happening.
Referring to Manhattan, New York City. *The Bonfire of the Vanities* (1987)

10 By age forty you were either making a million a year or you were timid and incompetent.
Referring to the narrator's assessment of career expectations on Wall Street in the 1980s. *The Bonfire of the Vanities* (1987)

11 Pale yellow ties became the insignia of the worker bees in the business world.
Referring to the Wall Street neckwear of the late 1980s. *The Bonfire of the Vanities* (1987)

12 To compensate for the concupiscence missing from their juiceless ribs and atrophied backsides, they turned to the dress designers. This season no puffs, flounces, ruffles...were too extreme.
The Bonfire of the Vanities (1987)

13 The feeling of no sleep starts turning the body and the skull into a dried-out husk inside with a sour grease smoke like a tenement fire curdling in the brain pan.
The Electric Kool-Aid Acid Test (1968)

14 The heat waves are solidifying in the air like waves in a child's marble and the perspectives are all beserk, walls rushing up then sinking away back like a Titian banquet hall.
The Electric Kool-Aid Acid Test (1968)

15 A glorious age, a glorious age I tell you! A very Neon renaissance. And the myths that actually touched you at that time—not Hercules, Orpheus, Ulysses, and Aeneas—but Superman, Captain Marvel, Batman.
Referring to the 1940s and 1950s. *The Electric Kool-Aid Acid Test* (1968)

16 Bangs manes bouffants beehives Beatle caps butter faces brush-on lashes decal eyes puffy sweaters French thrust bras flailing leather blue jeans stretch pants stretch jeans honeydew bottoms.
The Kandy-Kolored Tangerine-Flake Streamline Baby (1965)

17 Single men are not shut out of social life in New York. Just the opposite. They are *terribly* desirable. They are invited everywhere...A single man, if he has anything going for him, is not going to get *lonely* in New York.
The Kandy-Kolored Tangerine-Flake Streamline Baby (1965)

18 The great public bath, vat, spa, regional physiotherapy tank, White Sulphur Springs, Marienbad, Ganges, River Jordan for a million souls...the Sunday *New York Times*.
The Painted World (1975)

19 The farmers of journalism...who love the good rich soil...and like to plunge their hands into the dirt.
Referring to tabloid journalists. *The Painted World* (1975)

20 Status is an influence at every level...all part of what I call plutography: depicting the acts of the rich.
Referring to his novel *The Bonfire of the Vanities* (1987). *Time* (February 13, 1989)

21 Writers can't back off from realism, just as an ambitious engineer cannot back off from electricity.
U.S. News and World Report (November 23, 1987)

22 The Right Stuff
Book title. Referring to people involved in the early days of the U.S. space program. (1979)

23 The Bonfire of the Vanities
1987. Novel title, deriving from political preacher Girolamo Savonarola's "burning of the vanities" in Florence, 1497.

Wolff, Charlotte (b.1904) German-born British psychiatrist and writer

1 Women have always been the guardians of wisdom and humanity which makes them natural, but usually secret, rulers. The time has come for them to rule openly, but together with and not against men.
Bisexuality: A Study (1977), ch. 2

2 I have no doubt that lesbianism makes a woman virile and open to *any* sexual stimulation, and that she is more often than not a more adequate and lively partner in bed than a "normal" woman.
Love Between Women (1971)

Wollaston, William (1659–1724) English philosopher

1 The foundation of religion lies in that difference between the acts of men, which distinguishes them into good, evil, indifferent.
The Religion of Nature Delineated (1724)

Wollstonecraft, Mary (Mary Wollstonecraft Godwin; 1759–97) British writer and feminist

1 If women be educated to dependence; that is, to act according to the will of another fallible being, and submit, right or wrong, to power, where are we to stop?
A Vindication of the Rights of Women (1792), ch. 3

2 The *divine right* of husbands, like the divine right of kings,

may, it is hoped, in this enlightened age, be contested without danger.
A Vindication of the Rights of Women (1792), ch. 3

3 A king is always a king—and a woman always a woman: his authority and her sex ever stand between them and rational converse.
A Vindication of the Rights of Women (1792), ch. 4

4 I do not wish them to have power over men; but over themselves.
Referring to women. *A Vindication of the Rights of Women* (1792), ch. 4

5 Teach him to think for himself? Oh, my God, teach him rather to think like other people!
1797? Referring to Mrs. Shelley's search for a school for her son, Percy Bysshe Shelley, who later became the husband of Mary Wollstonecraft's daughter, Mary. Quoted in "Shelley," *Essays in Criticism, Second Series* (Matthew Arnold; 1889)

Wolpert, Lewis (b.1929) British biologist and writer

1 Anxiety can be described as unresolved fear.
Malignant Sadness (1999)

2 It was the worst experience of my life. More terrible even than watching my wife die of cancer. I am ashamed to admit that my depression felt worse than her death but it is true.
Malignant Sadness (1999)

Wolsey, Thomas, Cardinal (1475–1530) English statesman and clergyman

1 Had I but served God as diligently as I have served the king, he would not have given me over in my grey hairs.
Remark to Sir William Kingston. Quoted in *Negotiations of Thomas Wolsey* (George Cavendish; 1641)

Wolstenholme, Kenneth British sports commentator

1 The crowd are on the pitch. They think it's all over. It is now.
Said at the end of his soccer commentary on the World Cup final between England and Germany when Geoff Hurst of England scored a goal in the final seconds of the game. *1966 World Cup Final,* BBC Television (1966)

Wonder, Stevie (Steveland Judkins Morris; b.1950) U.S. singer, songwriter, and activist

1 Pride is like a perfume. When it is worn, it radiates a sense of self the world reacts to.
Essence (January 1975)

2 Sometimes being blind enables you to see better than those who have sight. People who can see, often don't.
Essence (January 1975)

3 They say things are better for Blacks in this country. Oh, yeah? Well, they are just not better enough!
Essence (January 1975)

4 Most people think that entertainers see the world. But after the twenty-sixth city...your hotel room is your world.
Quoted in *The Wit and Wisdom of Rock and Roll* (Maxim Jabukowski, ed.; 1983)

Wong Kar Wai Hong Kong-born Chinese film director

1 No matter if the film is banned, the most important thing is believing in it.
Quoted in "Taking Risks," *China in Focus* (Tam Ly; 1998)

Wood, Natalie (originally Natasha Gurdin; 1938–81) U.S. film actor

1 The only time a woman really succeeds in changing a man is when he is a baby.
Attrib.

Wood, Victoria (b.1953) British writer and comedian

1 A man is designed to walk three miles in the rain to phone for help when the car breaks down—and a woman is designed to say, "You took your time," when he comes back dripping wet.
Attrib.

Woodcock, George (1912–95) Canadian educator and writer

1 There is a special ambivalence to journeys in which one's own discomfort seems mitigated by an awareness of the much greater misery of the people around one.
"My Worst Journeys," *Worst Journeys* (Keith Fraser, ed.; 1991)

Woodhatch, Alex British student in Peking

1 Students were sitting down and tanks were running over them. Other students had tanks run over them as they ran. Flame throwers are said to have been used afterwards on some of those who were run over so that the bodies could not be identified.
Referring to the events at Tiananmen Square in Beijing, China. *Times,* London (June 5, 1989)

2 The tension here is very high, the Chinese are enormously brave and they keep telling me they are not afraid to die for democracy but the students know that they will be the Army's first target.
Referring to the events at Tiananmen Square in Beijing, China. *Times,* London (June 5, 1989)

Woodruff, Wilford (1807–98) U.S. Mormon leader

1 I say to Israel, the Lord will never permit me or any other man who stands as president of this Church to lead you astray. It is not in the program. It is not in the mind of God.
Discourses of Wilford Woodruff (Scott G. Kenny, ed.; 1983–84)

Woods, Tiger (Eldrick Woods; b.1975) U.S. golfer

1 Growing up, I came up with this name: I'm a Cablinasian.
Referring to his rejection of the description "African American" for his Caucasian, African American, Native American, Thai, and Chinese ancestry. Interview (Oprah Winfrey; April 21, 1997)

Woodson, Carter G. (Carter Godwin Woodson; 1875–1950) U.S. historian

1 For me, education means to inspire people to live more abundantly, to learn to begin with life as they find it and make it better.
The Crisis (August 1931), quoted in *A Documentary History of the Negro People in the United States* (Herbert Aptheker; 1951), vol. 3

2 When you control a man's thinking you do not have to worry

about his actions. You do not have to tell him not to stand here or go yonder. He will find his "proper place" and will stay in it. You do not need to send him to the back door. He will go without being told. In fact, if there is no back door, he will cut one for his special benefit.
The Mis-Education of the Negro (1933)

Woodsworth, James S. (James Shaver Woodsworth; 1874–1942) Canadian cleric, reformer, and politician

1 I do not believe in moral issues being settled by physical force.
Speech, Winnipeg (June 4, 1916)

Woolf, Virginia (Adeline Virginia Stephen; 1882–1941) British novelist and critic

Quotations about Woolf

1 I do not believe that she wrote one word of fiction which does not put out boundaries a little way; one book which does not break new ground and form part of the total experiment.
Susan Hill (b.1942) British novelist and playwright. *Daily Telegraph*, London (May 5, 1974)

2 I enjoyed talking to her, but thought *nothing* of her writing. I considered her "a beautiful little knitter."
Edith Sitwell (1887–1964) British poet, critic, and writer. Letter to Geoffrey Singleton (July 11, 1955), quoted in *Selected Letters* (John Lehmann and Derek Palmer, eds.; 1970)

Quotations by Woolf

3 The older one grows the more one likes indecency.
"Monday or Tuesday" (1921)

4 Dearest I feel certain that I am going mad again: I feel we can't go through another of those terrible times. And I shan't recover this time. I begin to hear voices, and can't concentrate. So I am doing what seems the best thing to do...If anybody could have saved me it would have been you.
She was subject to bouts of severe depression, which culminated in her suicide by drowning after completing *Between the Acts*. Suicide note addressed to her husband, Leonard Woolf (March 18, 1941)

5 I would venture to guess that Anon, who wrote so many poems without signing them, was often a woman.
A Room of One's Own (1929)

6 Literature is strewn with the wreckage of men who have minded beyond reason the opinions of others.
A Room of One's Own (1929)

7 Why are women...so much more interesting to men than men are to women?
A Room of One's Own (1929)

8 Women have served all these centuries as looking-glasses possessing the magic and delicious power of reflecting the figure of man at twice its natural size.
A Room of One's Own (1929)

9 If we didn't live venturously, plucking the wild goat by the beard, and trembling over precipices, we should never be depressed, I've no doubt; but already should be faded, fatalistic and aged.
May 26, 1924. *A Writer's Diary* (1953)

10 Each has his past shut in him like the leaves of a book known to him by heart and his friends can only read the title.
Jacob's Room (1922), ch. 5

11 There is in the British Museum an enormous mind. Consider that Plato is there cheek by jowl with Aristotle; and Shakespeare with Marlowe. This great mind is hoarded beyond the power of any single mind to possess it.
Jacob's Room (1922), ch. 9

12 Frazer...left his children unbaptized—his wife did it secretly in the washing basin.
Referring to the British anthropologist J. G. Frazer. *Jacob's Room* (1922), ch. 9

13 The poet gives us his essence, but prose takes the mould of the body and mind entire.
"Reading," *The Captain's Death Bed* (1950)

14 It is just when opinions universally prevail and we have added lip service to their authority that we become sometimes most keenly conscious that we do not believe a word that we are saying.
The Common Reader (1929–35)

15 Humour is the first of the gifts to perish in a foreign tongue.
The Common Reader: First Series (1925)

16 *Middlemarch*, the magnificent book which with all its imperfections is one of the few English novels for grown up people.
"George Eliot," *The Common Reader: First Series* (1925)

17 Those comfortably padded lunatic asylums which are known, euphemistically, as the stately homes of England.
"Lady Dorothy Nevill," *The Common Reader: First Series* (1925)

18 Let us not take it for granted that life exists more fully in what is commonly thought big than in what is commonly thought small.
"Modern Fiction," *The Common Reader: First Series* (1925)

19 Fate has not been kind to Mrs. Browning. Nobody reads her, nobody discusses her, nobody troubles to put her in her place.
Referring to Elizabeth Barrett Browning. *The Common Reader: Second Series* (1932)

20 Considering how common illness is...it becomes strange indeed that illness has not taken its place with love and battle and jealousy among the prime themes of literature.
The Moment (1947)

21 If you do not tell the truth about yourself you cannot tell it about other people.
The Moment (1947)

22 Some element of the supernatural is so constant in poetry that one has come to look upon it as part of the normal fabric of the art, but in poetry, being etherealized, it scarcely evokes any emotion as gross as fear.
Referring to Dorothy Scarborough's *The Supernatural in Modern English Fiction* (1917). Review, *The Supernatural in Fiction* (1918)

23 The fear which we get from reading ghost stories of the supernatural is a refined and spiritualized essence of fear.
Referring to Dorothy Scarborough's *The Supernatural in Modern English Fiction* (1917). Review, *The Supernatural in Fiction* (1918)

Woollcott, Alexander (Alexander Humphreys Woollcott; 1887–1943) U.S. writer and critic

1 Subjunctive to the last, he preferred to ask, "And that, sir, would be the Hippodrome?"
"Our Mrs. Parker," *While Rome Burns* (1934)

2 All the things I really like to do are either immoral, illegal, or fattening.
Attrib.

3 I must get out of these wet clothes and into a dry Martini.
Attrib.

Woolley, Hannah (1623?–75?) English educator and writer

1 A woman in this age is considered learned enough if she can distinguish her husband's bed from that of another.
Remark (1675?), quoted in *The Stuarts in Love* (Maurice Ashley; 1864)

2 Vain man is apt to think we were merely intended for the world's propagation and to keep its humane inhabitants sweet and clean; but, by their leaves, had we the same literature he would find our brains as fruitful as our bodies.
The Gentlewoman's Companion (17th century)

Woolworth, Frank W. (Frank Winfield Woolworth; 1852–1919) U.S. merchant

1 I am the world's worst salesman, therefore, I must make it easy for people to buy.
Quoted in *Strategy and Business* (1998), "Noteworthy Quotes"

Wordsworth, Dorothy (1771–1855) British diarist

1 But as we went along there were more and yet more and at last under the boughs of the trees, we saw that there was a long belt of them along the shore, about the breadth of a country turnpike road. I never saw daffodils so beautiful they grew among the mossy stones about and about them, some rested their heads upon these stones as on a pillow for weariness and the rest tossed and reeled and danced and seemed as if they verily laughed with the wind that blew upon them over the lake.
The Grasmere Journals (April 15, 1802)

Wordsworth, William (1770–1850) British poet

Quotations about Wordsworth

1 He spoke, and loos'd our heart in tears.
He laid us as we lay at birth
On the cool flowery lap of earth.
Matthew Arnold (1822–88) British poet and critic. "Memorial Verses" (1852)

2 The great Metaquizzical poet.
Lord Byron (1788–1824) British poet. Letter to John Murray (January 19, 1821)

3 A drowsy frowzy poem, call'd the "Excursion",
Writ in a manner which is my aversion.
Lord Byron (1788–1824) British poet. On Wordsworth's poem, *The Excursion* (1814). *Don Juan* (1819–24), can. 3, st. 94

4 We learn from Horace, "Homer sometimes sleeps";
We feel without him, Wordsworth sometimes wakes.
Lord Byron (1788–1824) British poet. *Don Juan* (1819–24), can. 3, st. 98

5 The most original poet now living, and the one whose writings could the least be spared; for they have no substitutes elsewhere.
William Hazlitt (1778–1830) British essayist and critic. "Mr. Wordsworth," *Spirit of the Age* (1825)

6 For the sake of a few fine imaginative or domestic passages, are we to be bullied into a certain Philosophy engendered in the whims of an Egotist.
John Keats (1795–1821) British poet. Criticizing poetry such as Wordsworth's "that has a palpable design on us." Letter to John Hamilton Reynolds (February 3, 1818), quoted in *Selected Letters of John Keats* (Robert Gittings, ed.; 1970)

7 Deprivation is for me what daffodils were for Wordsworth.
Philip Larkin (1922–85) British poet. *Required Writing* (1983)

8 Mr. Wordsworth, a stupid man, with a decided gift for portraying nature in vignettes, never yet ruined anyone's morals, unless, perhaps, he has driven some susceptible persons to crime in a very fury of boredom.
Ezra Pound (1885–1972) U.S. poet, translator, and critic. *Future* (November 1917)

9 Wordsworth went to the Lakes, but he never was a lake poet. He found in stones the sermons he had already put there.
Oscar Wilde (1854–1900) Irish poet, playwright, and wit. "The Decay of Lying," *Intentions* (1891)

Quotations by Wordsworth

10 Small service is true service, while it lasts.
1834. "To a Child. Written in Her Album" (1835), l. 1

11 Nor less I deem that there are Powers
Which of themselves our minds impress;
That we can feed this mind of ours
In a wise passiveness.
May 23, 1798. Companion piece to "The Tables Turned." "Expostulation and Reply," *Lyrical Ballads* (1798), ll. 21–24

12 On that best portion of a good man's life,
His little, nameless, unremembered, acts
Of kindness and of love.
July 13, 1798. Subtitled: "On Revisiting the Banks of the Wye During a Tour, July 13, 1798." "Lines Composed a Few Miles Above Tintern Abbey," *Lyrical Ballads* (1798), ll. 33–35

13 That blessed mood,
In which the burthen of the mystery,
In which the heavy and the weary weight
Of all this unintelligible world,
Is lightened.
July 13, 1798. Subtitled: "On Revisiting the Banks of the Wye During a Tour, July 13, 1798." "Lines Composed a Few Miles Above Tintern Abbey," *Lyrical Ballads* (1798), ll. 37–41

14 We are laid asleep
In body, and become a living soul:
While with an eye made quiet by the power
Of harmony, and the deep power of joy,
We see into the life of things.
July 13, 1798. Subtitled: "On Revisiting the Banks of the Wye During a Tour, July 13, 1798." "Lines Composed a Few Miles Above Tintern Abbey," *Lyrical Ballads* (1798), ll. 45–49

15 For I have learned
To look on nature, not as in the hour

Of thoughtless youth; but hearing often-times
The still, sad music of humanity.
July 13, 1798. Subtitled: "On Revisiting the Banks of the Wye During a Tour, July 13, 1798." "Lines Composed a Few Miles Above Tintern Abbey," *Lyrical Ballads* (1798), ll. 88–91

16 A sense sublime
Of something far more deeply interfused,
Whose dwelling is the light of setting suns,
And the round ocean and the living air,
And the blue sky, and in the mind of man:
A motion and a spirit, that impels
All thinking things, all objects of all thought,
And rolls through all things.
July 13, 1798. Subtitled: "On Revisiting the Banks of the Wye During a Tour, July 13, 1798." "Lines Composed a Few Miles Above Tintern Abbey," *Lyrical Ballads* (1798), ll. 95–102

17 Knowing that Nature never did betray
The heart that loved her.
July 13, 1798. Subtitled: "On Revisiting the Banks of the Wye During a Tour, July 13, 1798." "Lines Composed a Few Miles Above Tintern Abbey," *Lyrical Ballads* (1798), ll. 122–123

18 Nor greetings where no kindness is, nor all
The dreary intercourse of daily life,
Shall e'er prevail against us, or disturb
Our cheerful faith, that all which we behold
Is full of blessings.
July 13, 1798. Subtitled: "On Revisiting the Banks of the Wye During a Tour, July 13, 1798." "Lines Composed a Few Miles Above Tintern Abbey," *Lyrical Ballads* (1798), ll.130–134

19 If this belief from heaven be sent,
If such be Nature's holy plan,
Have I not reason to lament
What man has made of man?
"Lines Written in Early Spring," *Lyrical Ballads* (1798), ll. 21–24

20 Come forth into the light of things,
Let Nature be your Teacher.
May 23, 1798. Subtitled "An Evening Piece on the Same Subject," referring to "Expostulation and Reply," to which it is a companion piece. "The Tables Turned," *Lyrical Ballads* (1798), ll. 15–16

21 One impulse from a vernal wood
May teach you more of man,
Of moral evil and of good,
Than all the sages can.
May 23, 1798. Subtitled "An Evening Piece on the Same Subject," referring to "Expostulation and Reply," to which it is a companion piece. "The Tables Turned," *Lyrical Ballads* (1798), ll. 21–24

22 Our meddling intellect
Misshapes the beauteous forms of things:
We murder to dissect.
May 23, 1798. Subtitled "An Evening Piece on the Same Subject," referring to "Expostulation and Reply," to which it is a companion piece. "The Tables Turned," *Lyrical Ballads* (1798), ll. 26–28

23 Every great and original writer, in proportion as he is great and original, must himself create the taste by which he is to be relished.
Lyrical Ballads, 2nd ed. (1800), Preface

24 It may be safely affirmed, that there neither is, nor can be, any *essential* difference between the language of prose and metrical composition.
Lyrical Ballads, 2nd ed. (1800), Preface

25 Poetry is the spontaneous overflow of powerful feelings: it takes its origin from emotion recollected in tranquillity.
Lyrical Ballads, 2nd ed. (1800), Preface

26 A slumber did my spirit seal;
I had no human fears:
She seemed a thing that could not feel
The touch of earthly years.
1799. One of the "Lucy poems." The identity of Lucy is uncertain. "A Slumber Did My Spirit Seal," *Lyrical Ballads,* 2nd ed. (1800), ll.1–4

27 The sweetest thing that ever grew
Beside a human door!
1799. Subtitled "Solitude." The identity of Lucy is uncertain "Lucy Gray," *Lyrical Ballads,* 2nd ed. (1800), ll. 7–8

28 There is a comfort in the strength of love;
'Twill make a thing endurable, which else
Would overset the brain, or break the heart.
"Michael: A Pastoral Poem," *Lyrical Ballads,* 2nd ed. (1800), ll. 448–450

29 A youth to whom was given
So much of earth—so much of heaven,
And such impetuous blood.
1799. "Ruth," *Lyrical Ballads,* 2nd ed. (1800), ll. 124–126

30 She dwelt among the untrodden ways
Beside the springs of Dove,
A maid whom there were none to praise
And very few to love.
1799. One of the "Lucy poems." The identity of Lucy is uncertain. "She Dwelt Among the Untrodden Ways," *Lyrical Ballads,* 2nd ed. (1800), ll. 1–4

31 A violet by a mossy stone
Half hidden from the eye!
—Fair as a star, when only one
Is shining in the sky.
1799. One of the "Lucy poems." The identity of Lucy is uncertain. "She Dwelt Among the Untrodden Ways," *Lyrical Ballads,* 2nd ed. (1800), ll. 5–8

32 She lived unknown, and few could know
When Lucy ceased to be;
But she is in her grave, and oh
The difference to me!
1799. One of the "Lucy poems." The identity of Lucy is uncertain. "She Dwelt Among the Untrodden Ways," *Lyrical Ballads,* 2nd ed. (1800), ll. 9–12

33 Strange fits of passion have I known:
And I will dare to tell,
But in the lover's ear alone,
What once to me befell.
1799. One of the "Lucy poems." The identity of Lucy is uncertain. "Strange Fits of Passion," *Lyrical Ballads,* 2nd ed. (1800), ll. 1–4

34 And yet the wiser mind
Mourns less for what age takes away
Than what it leaves behind.
1798. Subtitled "A Conversation." "The Fountain," *Lyrical Ballads,* 2nd ed. (1800), ll. 34–36

35 Three years she grew in sun and shower,
Then Nature said, "A lovelier flower
On earth was never sown;
This child I to myself will take;

She shall be mine, and I will make
A Lady of my own."

1799. One of the "Lucy poems." The identity of Lucy, the subject of the poems, is a matter of speculation. "Three Years She Grew in Sun and Shower," *Lyrical Ballads*, 2nd ed. (1800), st. 1, ll. 1–5

36 'Tis said that some have died for love.

"'Tis Said That Some Have Died," *Lyrical Ballads*, 2nd ed. (1800), l. 1

37 A primrose by a river's brim
A yellow primrose was to him,
And it was nothing more.

1798. *Peter Bell* (1819), part 1, st. 12, ll. 248–250

38 The gods approve
The depth, and not the tumult, of the soul.

1814. "Laodamia," *Poems* (1815), ll. 74–75

39 Surprised by joy—impatient as the Wind,
I turned to share the transport—Oh! with whom
But Thee, deep buried in the silent tomb.
That spot which no vicissitude can find?

1812–14. Referring to his second daughter, Catherine, who died aged three years in June 1812. "Surprised by Joy," *Poems* (1815), ll. 1–4

40 Earth has not anything to show more fair:
Dull would he be of soul who could pass by
A sight so touching in its majesty:
The City now doth, like a garment, wear
The beauty of the morning; silent, bare,
Ships, towers, domes, theatres, and temples lie
Open unto the fields, and to the sky;
All bright and glittering in the smokeless air.

September 3, 1802. "Composed Upon Westminster Bridge," *Poems in Two Volumes* (1807), vol. 1, ll. 1–8

41 Dear God! the very houses seem asleep;
And all that mighty heart is lying still!

September 3, 1802. "Composed Upon Westminster Bridge," *Poems in Two Volumes* (1807), vol. 1, ll. 13–14

42 It is a beauteous evening, calm and free,
The holy time is quiet as a nun,
Breathless with adoration; the broad sun
Is sinking down in its tranquillity;
The gentleness of heaven broods o'er the Sea.

August, 1802. Also known as "Evening on Calais Beach" and "Calais Sands." "It Is a Beauteous Evening, Calm and Free," *Poems in Two Volumes* (1807), vol. 1, ll. 1–5

43 We must be free or die, who speak the tongue
That Shakespeare spake; the faith and morals hold
Which Milton held.

1802. "It Is Not To Be Thought Of," *Poems in Two Volumes* (1807), vol. 1, ll. 11–13

44 I travelled among unknown men
In lands beyond the sea;
Nor, England! did I know till then
What love I bore to thee.

1799. Referring to his travels in Germany (1798–99), during which the "Lucy poems" (of which this is one) were written. "I Travelled Among Unknown Men," *Poems in Two Volumes* (1807), vol. 1, ll. 1–4

45 I wandered lonely as a cloud
That floats on high o'er vales and hills,
When all at once I saw a crowd,
A host, of golden daffodils.

1804. "I Wandered Lonely as a Cloud," *Poems in Two Volumes* (1807), vol. 2, ll. 1–4

46 For oft, when on my couch I lie
In vacant or in pensive mood,
They flash upon that inward eye
Which is the bliss of solitude.

1804. "I Wandered Lonely as a Cloud," *Poems in Two Volumes* (1807), vol. 2, ll. 19–22

47 Thy soul was like a star, and dwelt apart.

September 1802. "London, 1802," *Poems in Two Volumes* (1807), vol. 1, l. 9

48 My heart leaps up when I behold
A rainbow in the sky:
So was it when my life began;
So is it now I am a man;
So be it when I shall grow old,
Or let me die!
The Child is Father of the Man;
And I could wish my days to be
Bound each to each by natural piety.

March 26, 1802. "My Heart Leaps Up When I Behold," *Poems in Two Volumes* (1807), vol. 2

49 There was a time when meadow, grove, and stream,
The earth, and every common sight,
To me did seem
Apparelled in celestial light,
The glory and the freshness of a dream.

1802?–06. "Ode: Intimations of Immortality from Recollections of Early Childhood," *Poems in Two Volumes* (1807), vol. 2, st.1, ll. 1–5

50 The rainbow comes and goes,
And lovely is the Rose,
The Moon doth with delight
Look round her when the heavens are bare,
Waters on a starry night
Are beautiful and fair;
The sunshine is a glorious birth;
But yet I know, where'er I go,
That there hath passed away a glory from the earth.

1802?–06. "Ode: Intimations of Immortality from Recollections of Early Childhood," *Poems in Two Volumes* (1807), vol. 2, st. 2, ll. 10–18

51 Whither is fled the visionary gleam?
Where is it now, the glory and the dream?

1802?–06. "Ode: Intimations of Immortality from Recollections of Early Childhood," *Poems in Two Volumes* (1807), vol. 2, st. 4, ll. 56–57

52 Our birth is but a sleep and a forgetting:
The Soul that rises with us, our life's Star,
Hath had elsewhere its setting,
And cometh from afar:
Not in entire forgetfulness,
And not in utter nakedness,
But trailing clouds of glory do we come
From God, who is our home.

1802?–06. "Ode: Intimations of Immortality from Recollections of Early Childhood," *Poems in Two Volumes* (1807), vol. 2, st. 5, ll. 58–65

53 Why with such earnest pains dost thou provoke
The years to bring the inevitable yoke.
1802?–06. "Ode: Intimations of Immortality from Recollections of Early Childhood," *Poems in Two Volumes* (1807), vol. 2, st. 8, ll. 127–128

54 But for those obstinate questionings
Of sense and outward things,
Fallings from us, vanishings;
Blank misgivings of a Creature
Moving about in worlds not realised,
High instincts before which our mortal nature
Did tremble like a guilty Thing surprised.
1802?–06. "Ode: Intimations of Immortality from Recollections of Early Childhood," *Poems in Two Volumes* (1807), vol. 2, st. 9, ll. 145–151

55 Hence in a season of calm weather
Though inland far we be,
Our souls have sight of that immortal sea
Which brought us hither.
1802?–06. "Ode: Intimations of Immortality from Recollections of Early Childhood," *Poems in Two Volumes* (1807), vol. 2, st. 9, ll. 165–168

56 Though nothing can bring back the hour
Of splendour in the grass, of glory in the flower;
We will grieve not, rather find
Strength in what remains behind.
1802?–06. "Ode: Intimations of Immortality from Recollections of Early Childhood," *Poems in Two Volumes* (1807), vol. 2, st. 10, ll. 181–184

57 Thanks to the human heart by which we live,
Thanks to its tenderness, its joys and fears,
To me the meanest flower that blows can give
Thoughts that do often lie too deep for tears.
1802?–06. "Ode: Intimations of Immortality from Recollections of Early Childhood," *Poems in Two Volumes* (1807), vol. 2, st. 11, ll. 204–207

58 Stern Daughter of the Voice of God!
O Duty! if that name thou love
Who art a light to guide, a rod
To check the erring and reprove.
1805. "Ode to Duty," *Poems in Two Volumes* (1807), vol. 1, st.1, ll. 1–4,

59 But in the quietness of thought:
Me this unchartered freedom tires;
I feel the weight of chance-desires:
My hopes no more must change their name,
I long for a repose that ever is the same.
1805. "Ode to Duty," *Poems in Two Volumes* (1807), vol. 1, st. 5, ll. 4–8

60 O Nightingale! thou surely art
A creature of a "fiery heart":
These notes of thine—they pierce and pierce;
Tumultuous harmony and fierce!
1806. "O Nightingale!" *Poems in Two Volumes* (1807), vol. 2, ll. 1–4

61 Once did she hold the gorgeous East in fee;
And was the safeguard of the West.
1802. Venice, a republic since the Middle Ages, was conquered by Napoleon in 1797. "On the Extinction of the Venetian Republic," *Poems in Two Volumes* (1807), vol. 1, ll. 1–2

62 Venice, the eldest Child of Liberty.
She was a maiden City, bright and free.
1802. Venice, a republic since the Middle Ages, was conquered by Napoleon in 1797. "On the Extinction of the Venetian Republic," *Poems in Two Volumes* (1807), vol. 1, ll. 4–5

63 Men are we, and must grieve when even the shade
Of that which once was great is pass'd away.
1802. Venice, a republic since the Middle Ages, was conquered by Napoleon in 1797. "On the Extinction of the Venetian Republic," *Poems in Two Volumes* (1807), vol. 1, ll. 13–14

64 There was a roaring in the wind all night;
The rain came heavily and fell in floods;
But now the sun is rising, calm and bright.
1802. "Resolution and Independence," *Poems in Two Volumes* (1807), vol. 1, st. 1, ll. 1–3

65 Behold her, single in the field,
Yon solitary Highland lass!
November 1805. "The Solitary Reaper," *Poems in Two Volumes* (1807), vol. 2, ll. 1–2

66 The world is too much with us; late and soon,
Getting and spending, we lay waste our powers:
Little we see in Nature that is ours.
1802–04. "The World Is Too Much with Us," *Poems in Two Volumes* (1807), vol. 1, ll. 1–3

67 Great God! I'd rather be
A Pagan suckled in a creed outworn;
So might I, standing on this pleasant lea,
Have glimpses that would make me less forlorn;
Have sight of Proteus rising from the sea;
Or hear Old Triton blow his wreathèd horn.
"The World Is Too Much with Us," *Poems in Two Volumes* (1807), vol. 1, ll. 9–14

68 Two voices are there; one is of the sea,
One of the mountains; each a mighty voice:
In both from age to age thou didst rejoice,
They were thy chosen music, Liberty!
"Thought of a Briton on the Subjugation of Switzerland," *Poems in Two Volumes* (1807), vol. 1, ll. 1–4

69 Sweet childish days, that were as long
As twenty days are now.
April 20, 1802. Also known as "I've Watched You Now a Full Half Hour" to distinguish it from "To a Butterfly": "Stay near me—do not take thy flight," composed in March 1802 and also included in *Poems in Two Volumes.* "To a Butterfly," *Poems in Two Volumes* (1807), vol. 2, st. 2, ll. 9–10

70 But an old age, serene and bright,
And lovely as a Lapland night,
Shall lead thee to thy grave.
1802. The poem is also known by its first line: "Dear Child of Nature, Let Them Rail." "To a Young Lady Who Had Been Reproached for Taking Long Walks in the Country," *Poems in Two Volumes* (1807), vol. 1, ll. 16–18

71 O blithe new-comer! I have heard,
I hear thee and rejoice.
O Cuckoo! Shall I call thee bird,
Or but a wandering voice?
1802. "To the Cuckoo," *Poems in Two Volumes* (1807), vol. 2, ll. 1–4

72 Thrice welcome, darling of the Spring!
Even yet thou art to me
No bird, but an invisible thing,
A voice, a mystery.
1802. "To the Cuckoo," *Poems in Two Volumes* (1807), vol. 2, ll. 13–16

73 Thou unassuming common-place
Of Nature.
1802. Companion piece to "To the Daisy" ("In Youth from Rock to Rock I Went"). "To the Daisy," *Poems in Two Volumes* (1807), vol. 2, ll. 5–6

74 We meet thee, like a pleasant thought,
When such are wanted.
1802. "To the Daisy," *Poems in Two Volumes* (1807), vol. 2, ll. 23–24

75 Pleasures newly found are sweet
When they lie about our feet.
May 1, 1802. Companion piece to "To the Small Celandine (Pansies, Lilies, Kingcups, Daisies)." "To the Small Celandine," *Poems in Two Volumes* (1807), vol. 2, ll. 1–2

76 Thou hast great allies:
Thy friends are exultations, agonies,
And love, and man's unconquerable mind.
August 1802. Toussaint L'Ouverture, the son of a slave, led the rebellion that ended slavery in Haiti in 1794 and drove out the French. He resisted Napoleon's efforts to reestablish French control, was captured, and died in prison in 1803. "To Toussaint L'Ouverture," *Poems in Two Volumes* (1807), vol. 1, ll. 12–14

77 Plain living and high thinking are no more.
September 1802. Also known as "Oh Friend! I Know Not." "Written in London, September 1802," *Poems in Two Volumes* (1807), vol. 1, l. 11

78 Like an army defeated
The snow hath retreated.
April 16, 1802. "Written in March, While Resting on the Bridge at the Foot of Brother's Water," *Poems in Two Volumes* (1807), ll. 11–12

79 Ethereal minstrel! pilgrim of the sky!
Dost thou despise the earth where cares abound?
1825. "To a Skylark," *Poetical Works* (1827), ll. 1–2

80 Strongest minds
Are often those of whom the noisy world
Hears least.
"The Wanderer," *The Excursion* (1814), bk. 1, ll. 91–93

81 Oh, Sir! the good die first,
And they whose hearts are dry as summer dust
Burn to the socket.
"The Wanderer," *The Excursion* (1814), bk. 1, ll. 500–503

82 A boy I loved the sun,...
Not for his bounty to so many worlds—
But for this cause, that I had seen him lay
His beauty on the morning hills, had seen
The western mountain touch his setting orb.
The Prelude (1850), bk. 2

83 Fair seed-time had my soul, and I grew up
Fostered alike by beauty and by fear.
1799. "Childhood and School-Time," *The Prelude* (1850), bk. 1, ll. 301–302

84 And when the deed was done
I heard among the solitary hills
Low breathings coming after me, and sounds
Of undistinguishable motion, steps
Almost as silent as the turf they trod.
1799. The "deed" was the setting of a rabbit trap. "Childhood and School-Time," *The Prelude* (1850), bk. 1, ll. 321–325

85 And growing still in stature the grim shape
Towered up between me and the stars, and still,
For so it seemed, with purpose of its own
And measured motion like a living thing,
Strode after me.
1799. Describing the theft of a boat. "Childhood and School-Time," *The Prelude* (1850), bk. 1, ll. 381–385

86 And I was taught to feel, perhaps too much,
The self-sufficing power of Solitude.
1799. "Childhood and School-Time," *The Prelude* (1850), bk. 2, ll. 76–77

87 Bliss was it in that dawn to be alive,
But to be young was very heaven!
1804–05. Referring to the French Revolution. "France (Concluded)," *The Prelude* (1850), bk. 11, ll. 108–109

88 That which sets
...The budding rose above the rose full blown.
1804–05. Referring to the French Revolution. "France (Concluded)," *The Prelude* (1850), bk. 11, ll. 118, 121

89 There is
One great society alone on earth:
The noble living and the noble dead.
1804–05. "France (Concluded)," *The Prelude* (1850), bk. 11, ll. 393–395

90 That we were brothers all
In honour, as in one community,
Scholars and gentlemen.
1804–05. "Residence in France," *The Prelude* (1850), bk. 9, ll. 227–229

91 Still glides the Stream, and shall for ever glide;
The form remains, the function never dies.
1818–20. "After-Thought," *The River Duddon: A Series of Sonnets* (1820), sonnet 34, ll. 5–6

92 Why art thou silent! Is thy love a plant
Of such weak fibre that the treacherous air
Of absence withers what was once so fair?
1832. "Why Art Thou Silent!," *Yarrow Revisited and Other Poems* (1835), ll.1–3

93 A day spent in a round of strenuous idleness.
Attrib.

Work, Henry Clay (1832–84) U.S. songwriter

1 Father, dear father, come home with me now,
The clock in the steeple strikes one.
A temperance song. "Come Home, Father" (1864)

2 But it stopped short—never to go again—
When the old man died.
"Grandfather's Clock" (1876)

3 My grandfather's clock was too large for the shelf.
So it stood ninety years on the floor.
"Grandfather's Clock" (1876)

4 "Hurrah! hurrah! we bring the Jubilee!
Hurrah! hurrah! the flag that makes you free!"
So we sang the chorus from Atlanta to the sea
As we were marching through Georgia.
Commemorating the march (November-December 1864) by a Union army under General William Sherman through Confederate Georgia. "Marching Through Georgia" (1865)

Wotton, Henry, Sir (1568–1639) English poet and diplomat

1 Lord of himself, though not of lands;
And having nothing, yet hath all.
"The Character of a Happy Life" (1614)

2 An ambassador is an honest man sent to lie abroad for the good of his country.
Written in Christopher Fleckmore's album (1604), quoted in *Reliquiae Wottonianae* (Izaak Walton; 1651)

3 The itch of disputing will prove the scab of churches.
A Panegyric to King Charles (1649)

4 I am but a gatherer and disposer of other men's stuff.
Elements of Architecture (1624), Preface

5 In *Architecture* as in all other *Operative* Arts, the *end* must direct the *Operation*. The *end* is to build well. Well building hath three Conditions. *Commodity*, *Firmness*, and *Delight*.
Elements of Architecture (1624), pt. 1

6 Take heed of thinking. *The farther you go from the church of Rome, the nearer you are to God.*
Quoted in *Reliquiae Wottonianae* (Izaak Walton; 1651)

Wren, Christopher, Sir (1632–1723) English architect, scientist, and mathematician

1 Architecture has its political use; public buildings being the ornament of a country; it establishes a nation, draws people and commerce; makes the people love their native country.
Parentalia (1750)

Wright, Frank Lloyd (1867–1959) U.S. architect

1 No house should ever be built *on* a hill or *on* anything. It should be *of* the hill. Belonging to it. Hill and house should live together each the happier for the other.
An Autobiography (1932)

2 Architecture is life, or at least it is life itself taking form and therefore it is the truest record of life as it was lived in the world yesterday, as it is lived today or ever will be lived.
An Organic Architecture (1907)

3 Abandon it.
Referring to Pittsburgh, Pennsylvania. *New York Times* (1955)

4 An architect's most useful tools are an eraser at the drafting board, and a wrecking bar at the site.
Attrib.

5 An expert is a man who has stopped thinking. Why should he think? He is an expert.
Attrib.

6 Give me the luxuries of life and I will willingly do without the necessities.
Attrib.

7 The tall modern office building is the machine pure and simple...the engine, the motor, and the battleship are the works of art of the century.
Attrib.

8 Chewing gum for the eyes.
Referring to television. Attrib.

Wright, Orville (1871–1948) U.S. aviator

1 After these years of experience, I look with amazement on our audacity in attempting flights with a new and untried machine under such circumstances.
Referring to the first successful flight at Kitty Hawk, North Carolina (December 4, 1902). *Flying* (December 1913)

2 The airplane stays up because it doesn't have the time to fall.
Explaining the principles of powered flight. Attrib.

Wright, Richard (Richard Nathaniel Wright; 1908–60) U.S. novelist

1 How can law contradict the lives of millions of people and hope to be administered successfully?
Native Son (1940)

2 Injustice which lasts for three long centuries and which exists among millions of people over thousands of square miles of territory, is injustice no longer; it is an accomplished fact of life.
Native Son (1940)

3 Nobody but poor folks get happy in church.
Native Son (1940)

4 Public peace is the act of public trust; it is the faith that all are secure and will *remain* secure.
Native Son (1940)

5 The Negro is America's metaphor.
White Man, Listen! (1957)

6 I am black and I have seen black hands
raised in fists of revolt, side by side with the white fists of
white workers,
And some day—and it is only this which sustains me—
Some day there shall be millions and millions of them,
On some red day in a burst of fists on a new horizon!
"I Have Seen Black Hands," *The Poetry of the Negro, 1746–1949* (Langston Hughes and Arna Bontemps eds.; 1951)

Wright, Wilbur (1867–1912) U.S. engineer and inventor

1 Success. Four flights Thursday morning. All against twenty-one-mile wind. Started from level with engine power alone. Average speed through air thirty-one miles. Longest fifty-nine seconds. Inform press. Home Christmas.
Sent from Kitty Hawk, North Carolina, after having successfully completed the world's first powered flights. Telegram to the Reverend Milton Wright (co-written with Orville Wright; December 17, 1903)

Wrigley, William, Jr. (1861–1932) U.S. business executive

1 When two men in business always agree, one of them is unnecessary.
Attrib.

Wriston, Walter B. (Walter Bigelow Wriston; b.1919) U.S. banker

1 As long as capital—both human and money—can move toward opportunity, trade will not balance.
Speech (January 25, 1993)

2 When a system of national currencies run by central banks is transformed into a global electronic marketplace driven by currency traders, power changes hands.
Speech (January 25, 1993)

3 Banking is now about cooperating in the morning so that you can compete in the afternoon.
Quoted in *Capital for Our Time* (Nicholas Imparato, ed.; 1999)

4 Revolutions aren't made by gadgets and technology. They're made by a shift in power, which is taking place all over the world. Today, intellectual capital is at least as important as money capital and probably more so.
Quoted in *Opening Digital Markets* (Walid Mougayar; 1997)

5 Information about money has become as important as money itself.
Attrib.

Wrong, George M. (George MacKinnon Wrong; 1860–1948) Canadian historian

1 Quebec remained British because it was French.
Canada and the American Revolution (1935)

2 History is capricious in its awards of fame. It fixes on dramatic incident and ignores the quiet service that may count for much more.
Canadian Historical Review (1932)

3 History is the vast and complex tale of the working of the spirit of man.
Canadian Historical Review (1936)

4 It is one of the paradoxes of history that, had Canada been more completely anglicized in 1776, it would probably today be a part of the United States.
Canadian Historical Review (1922)

5 The study of history is the playground of patriotism.
Canadian Historical Review (1927)

6 While other animals have memory, man alone builds up a formal story of his life in the past and is governed by its traditions.
Referring to the writing of history. *Canadian Historical Review* (1933)

Wu, Harry (b.1937) Chinese civil rights activist

1 A few people were killed in Tiananmen Square. But millions of people have been lost in the labor camps.
Trouble Maker (co-written with George Vecsey; 1996)

2 If the Chinese want to sell their goods in the world, they must respect their own people.
Trouble Maker (co-written with George Vecsey; 1996)

3 I thought I was one of Chairman Mao's children. Everything we did was for him.
Trouble Maker (co-written with George Vecsey; 1996)

Wu Yingtao (1916–71) Taiwanese poet

1 Each time a tragedy ends
People return to their homes one by one
And set up a gray memorial
In another new ruin.
"The Ruins," *Anthology of Modern Chinese Poetry* (Michelle Yeh, ed., tr.; 1992)

Wyatt, Thomas, Sir (1503–42) English poet

1 Now is this song both sung and past:
My lute, be still, for I have done.
"My Lute Awake!" (1542?), quoted in *Silver Poets of the Sixteenth Century* (Gerald Bullett, ed.; 1947)

2 Her wily looks my wits did blind;
Thus as she would I did agree.
But ha! ha! ha! full well is me,
For I am now at liberty.
"Tangled I Was in Love's Snare" (1542?), quoted in *Silver Poets of the Sixteenth Century* (Gerald Bullett, ed.; 1947)

3 When her loose gown from her shoulders did fall,
And she caught me in her arms long and small,
Therewith all sweetly did me kiss,
And softly said, "Dear heart, how like you this?"
"They Flee from Me That Sometime Did Me Seek", quoted in *Silver Poets of the Sixteenth Century* (Gerald Bullett, ed.; 1947)

4 They flee from me, that sometime did me seek
With naked foot, stalking in my chamber:
I have seen them gentle, tame, and meek,
That now are wild, and do not remember.
"They Flee from Me That Sometime Did Me Seek," quoted in *Silver Poets of the Sixteenth Century* (Gerald Bullet, ed.; 1947)

Wycherley, William (1640–1716) English playwright

1 Temperance is the nurse of chastity.
Love in a Wood (1671), Act 3, Scene 3

2 A mistress should be like a little country retreat near the town, not to dwell in constantly, but only for a night and away.
The Country Wife (1675), Act 1, Scene 1

3 Bluster, sputter, question, cavil; but be sure your argument be intricate enough to confound the court.
The Plain Dealer (1676), Act 3, Scene 1

4 What easy, tame, suffering, trampled things does that little god of talking cowards make of us!
The Plain Dealer (1676), Act 4, Scene 1

5 Well, a widow, I see, is a kind of sinecure.
The Plain Dealer (1676), Act 5, Scene 3

Wycliffe, John (also spelled Wyclif, Wickliffe, or Wicliff; 1330?–84) English religious reformer

1 I believe that in the end the truth will conquer.
1381. John of Gaunt had withdrawn his patronage in 1379 after Wycliffe's repudiation of the doctrine of transubstantiation. Remark addressed to John of Gaunt, quoted in *Short History of the English People* (J. R. Green; 1874)

Wylie, Elinor (Elinor Morton Hoyt Wylie; 1885–1928) U.S. poet and writer

1 I love the look, austere, immaculate,
Of landscapes drawn in pearly monotones.
"Wild Peaches" (1921)

Wyndham, John (John Wyndham Parkes Lucas Benyon Harris; 1903–69) British science-fiction writer

1 Twentieth-century woman appears to regard sunlight as a kind

of cosmetic effulgence with a light aphrodisiac content...Men, of course, just go on sweating in it from century to century.
The Kraken Awakes (1953)

2 Wondering why one's friends chose to marry the people they did is unprofitable, but recurrent. One could so often have done so much better for them.
The Kraken Awakes (1953)

Wynne-Tyson, Jon (Timothy John Lyden Wynne-Tyson; b.1924)
British writer

1 The wrong sort of people are always in power because they would not be in power if they were not the wrong sort of people.
Attrib.

Xenophanes (560?–478? B.C.) Greek poet and philosopher

1 The Ethiopians say that their gods are snub-nosed and black, the Thracians that theirs have light blue eyes and red hair.
Fragment 15 (5th century B.C.)

Xenophon (430?–355? B.C.) Greek historian and soldier

1 The sea! the sea!
Shouted by the Greeks when they reached the safety of the coast following their military retreat across Armenia. *Anabasis* (355? B.C.), bk. 4, ch. 7, l. 24

Xerxes I, King of Persia (519?–465 B.C.) Persian monarch

1 I am moved to pity, when I think of the brevity of human life, seeing that of all this host of men not one will still be alive in a hundred years' time.
On surveying his army. Remark (480? B.C.)

X Files, The U.S. television series

1 THE TRUTH IS OUT THERE.
The creed of Fox Mulder, an FBI agent in the television series. *The X Files* (1990s)

Ximénèz, Augustin, Marquis de Ximénèz (Augustin Louis de Ximénèz; 1726–1817) French poet

1 Let us attack in her own waters perfidious Albion!
October 1793. "L'ère des Français," *Poésies Révolutionnaires et contre-révolutionnaires* (1821)

Xunzi (also known as Hsün-tzu; 300?–235? B.C.) Chinese philosopher

1 When his horse is uneasy harnessed to a carriage, a gentleman is not comfortable in the carriage; just so, when the common people are uneasy under an administration, a gentleman is not comfortable in his post.
3rd century B.C. Quoted in *China's Imperial Past* (Charles O. Hucker; 1975)

2 Heaven has its seasons; Earth has its resources; Man has his government. This means that man is capable of forming a trinity with the other two.
3rd century B.C. Quoted in *The Chinese Experience* (Raymond Dawson; 1978)

3 If man's nature is evil, where do rites and justice spring from? They all derive from the fabrication of the sages.
3rd century B.C. Quoted in *The Chinese Experience* (Raymond Dawson; 1978)

Xu Wenli (b.1944) Chinese dissident

1 My bag is always packed and behind the door.
Quoted in "From Spring to Fall," *Time* (Nisid Najari; December 14, 1998)

2 The focal point of all reforms should be human liberation, and the respect for human value and human rights. The free development of each individual is the basis for all social progress.
1980. Attrib.

3 It is impossible to modernize the country unless you let the intelligence of a thousand million individuals unfold.
February 1980. Referring to China. Attrib.

Xu Yunuo (1893–1958) Chinese writer and editor

1 What is a dream?
What is reality? Just a demarcation in human memory.
Little Poems (1922), quoted in *Anthology of Modern Chinese Poetry* (Michelle Yeh, ed., tr.; 1992)

Xu Zhimo (also known as Hsü Chih-mo; 1895–1931) Chinese poet

1 Silently I am going
As silently I came;
I shake my sleeves,
Not to bring away a patch of cloud.
"Second Farewell to Cambridge" (1925)

2 Come with me,
My love!
The world of man has fallen behind us—
Look, isn't this an immense ocean with its unlimited gleaming white?
"This is a Coward's World" (1925?)

3 Walking is a joy, but an even greater joy is to ride a bicycle. Bicycling is a universal skill in Cambridge: women, small children, old men alike relish the pleasure of the two-wheeled dance.
"The Cambridge I Knew," *Anthology of Chinese Literature* (Cyril Birch, ed.; 1972), vol. 2

Yy

Yamamoto Isoroku (1884–1943) Japanese naval commander

1 I fear we have only awakened a sleeping giant, and his reaction will be terrible.
Said after the Japanese attack on Pearl Harbor (December 7, 1941). Quoted in *Listener*, London (A. J. P. Taylor; September 9, 1976)

Yamani, Sheikh (Sheikh Ahmed Yamani; b.1930) Saudi Arabian politician

1 Oil, despite its vital and far-reaching importance, is a transient phenomenon, whose finite life-span will end, sooner or later. Islam is the eternal truth for us.
Quoted in *Arabia: the Islamic World Review* (October 1981)

2 When money is at stake, never be the first to mention sums.
Referring to negotiating. Quoted in *Yamani* (Jeffrey Robinson; 1988)

3 The first law of economics is that when the price goes up, consumption comes down. This is a divine law. You cannot change it.
Referring to the consequences of raising oil prices. Quoted in *Yamani* (Jeffrey Robinson; 1988)

Yan Fu (also known as Yen Fu; 1853–1921) Chinese reformer and translator

1 Using forced language we speak of a cosmic-historical process of Change. When such a process is at work, even sages have no power over it...The sage's role is merely to know its origins and foresee its movements.
1895. "On the Speed of World Change" (Charlotte Furth, tr.; 1916)

Yang Ping (b.1908) Chinese writer, political activist, and journalist

1 Women and Revolution! What tragic, unsung epics of courage lie silent in the world's history!
Fragments from a Lost Diary (1973)

Yang Wenzhi (b.1954) Chinese writer

1 With this new interest I became painfully aware of my ignorance and even stupidity, and I feel enthused by the novelty and attraction of knowledge.
1978. Referring to reading. "Ah, Books!" *The Wounded* (Geremie Barmé, tr.; 1979)

Yankwich, Léon R. U.S. lawyer and judge

1 There are no illegitimate children—only illegitimate parents.
Quoting columnist O. O. McIntyre. Decision of the State District Court, Southern District of California (June 1978)

Yan Yi (b.1927) Chinese writer

1 The truest probably don't look the most beautiful, the most beautiful probably aren't the truest.
"Pearls" (1982)

Ybarra, Thomas Russell (b.1880) Venezuelan-born U.S. journalist and traveler

1 A Christian is a man who feels
Repentance on a Sunday
For what he did on Saturday
And is going to do on Monday.
"The Christian" (1909)

Yeats, W. B. (William Butler Yeats; 1865–1939) Irish poet and playwright

Quotations about Yeats

1 Earth, receive an honoured guest:
William Yeats is laid to rest.
Let the Irish vessel lie
Emptied of its poetry.
W. H. Auden (1907–73) British poet. "In Memory of W. B. Yeats" (1940)

2 In the deserts of the heart
Let the healing fountain start,
In the prison of his days
Teach the free man how to praise.
W. H. Auden (1907–73) British poet. "In Memory of W. B. Yeats" (1940)

3 We have met too late. You are too old for me to have any effect on you.
James Joyce (1882–1941) Irish writer. On meeting W. B. Yeats. Quoted in *James Joyce* (Richard Ellmann; 1959)

4 Neath Ben Bulben's buttocks lies
Bill Yeats, a poet twoice the soize
Of William Shakespear, as they say
Down Ballykillywuchlin way.
1958
Ezra Pound (1885–1972) U.S. poet, translator, and critic. Epitaph on W. B. Yeats. Quoted in "Ez and Old Billyum," *a long the riverrun* (Richard Ellmann; 1988)

Quotations by Yeats

5 The Light of Lights
Looks always on the motive, not the deed,
The Shadow of Shadows on the deed alone.
The Countess Cathleen (1892), Act 4

6 Begin the preparation for your death

And from the fortieth winter by that thought
Test every work of intellect or faith,
And everything that your own hands have wrought.
"Vacillation" (1933), sect. 3, ll. 10–13

7 We begin to live when we have conceived life as a tragedy.
Autobiographies (1926)

8 When I think of all the books I have read...and of the hopes that I have had, all life weighed in the scales of my own life seems to me preparation for something that never happens.
Autobiographies (1926)

9 Out of the quarrel with others we make rhetoric; out of the quarrel with ourselves we make poetry.
"Anima Hominus," *Essays* (1924), sect. 5

10 If we understand our own minds, and the things that are striving to utter themselves through our minds, we move others, not because we have understood or thought about those others, but because all life has the same root.
"Samhain: 1905," *Explorations* (1962)

11 A line will take us hours maybe;
Yet if it does not seem a moment's thought,
Our stitching and unstitching has been naught.
"Adam's Curse," *In The Seven Woods* (1904), st. 1, ll. 4–6

12 Like a long-legged fly upon the stream
His mind moves upon silence.
"Long-Legged Fly," *Last Poems* (1936–39), ll. 9–10

13 How can I, that girl standing there,
My attention fix
On Roman or on Russian
Or on Spanish politics?
"Politics," *Last Poems* (1936–39), ll. 1–4

14 Did that play of mine send out
Certain men the English shot?
"The Man and the Echo," *Last Poems* (1936–39), ll. 11–12

15 None other knows what pleasures man
At table or in bed.
What shall I do for pretty girls
Now my old bawd is dead?
1938. "John Kinsella's Lament for Mrs. Mary Moore," *Last Poems and Plays* (1940), st. 1

16 Now that my ladder's gone
I must lie down where all the ladders start,
In the foul rag-and-bone shop of the heart.
1939. "The Circus Animals' Desertion," *Last Poems and Plays* (1940), pt. 3

17 Irish poets, learn your trade,
Sing whatever is well made,
Scorn the sort now growing up
All out of shape from toe to top.
September 4, 1938. "Under Ben Bulben," *Last Poems and Plays* (1940), pt. 5

18 Under bare Ben Bulben's head
In Drumcliff churchyard Yeats is laid...
On limestone quarried near the spot
By his command these words are cut:
Cast a cold eye
On life, on death.
Horseman, pass by.
September 4, 1938. W. B. Yeats's epitaph. "Under Ben Bulben," *Last Poems and Plays* (1940), pt. 6

19 An intellectual hatred is the worst.
June 1919. "A Prayer for My Daughter," *Michael Robartes and the Dancer* (1921), st. 8

20 All changed, changed utterly:
A terrible beauty is born.
September 25, 1916. Referring to the Easter Uprising in Dublin (1916). "Easter 1916," *Michael Robartes and the Dancer* (1921), st. 1

21 Too long a sacrifice
Can make a stone of the heart.
September 25, 1916. "Easter 1916," *Michael Robartes and the Dancer* (1921), st. 4

22 Things fall apart; the centre cannot hold;
Mere anarchy is loosed upon the world,
The blood-dimmed tide is loosed, and everywhere
The ceremony of innocence is drowned;
The best lack all conviction, while the worst
Are full of passionate intensity.
1919. "The Second Coming," *Michael Robartes and the Dancer* (1921), st. 1

23 Think where man's glory most begins and ends,
And say my glory was I had such friends.
1937. "The Municipal Gallery Re-visited," *New Poems* (1938), pt. 7, ll. 7–8

24 Never to have lived is best, ancient writers say;
Never to have drawn the breath of life,
Never to have looked into the eye of day.
The second best's a gay goodnight and quickly turn away.
March 1927. *Oedipus at Colonus* (1928)

25 In dreams begins responsibility.
Responsibilities (1914), Epigraph

26 Wine comes in at the mouth
And love comes in at the eye;
That's all we shall know for truth
Before we grow old and die.
February 17, 1910. "A Drinking Song," *The Green Helmet and Other Poems* (1910), ll. 1–4

27 Though leaves are many, the root is one;
Through all the lying days of my youth
I swayed my leaves and flowers in the sun;
Now I may wither into the truth.
March 1909. "The Coming of Wisdom with Time," *The Green Helmet and Other Poems* (1910), complete poem

28 But was there ever dog that praised his fleas?
April 1909. "To a Poet Who Would Have me Praise Certain Bad Poets, Imitators of His and Mine," *The Green Helmet And Other Poems* (1910), l. 4

29 She was more beautiful than thy first love,
This lady by the trees.
In the final version the second line reads: "But now lies under boards." "A Dream of Death," *The Rose* (1893), early version, ll. 11–12

30 I will arise and go now, and go to Innisfree,
And a small cabin build there, of clay and wattles made;
Nine bean-rows will I have there, a hive for the honey-bee,
And live alone in the bee-loud glade.
1890. "The Lake Isle of Innisfree," *The Rose* (1893), st. 1

31 While I stand on the roadway, or on the pavements grey,
I hear it in the deep heart's core.
1890. "The Lake Isle of Innisfree," *The Rose* (1893), st. 3

32 A pity beyond all telling
Is hid in the heart of love.
"The Pity of Love," *The Rose* (1893), ll. 1–2

33 When you are old and grey and full of sleep,
And nodding by the fire, take down this book,
And slowly read, and dream of the soft look
Your eyes had once, and of their shadows deep.
October 21, 1891. Based on Pierre Ronsard's sonnet "Quand vous serez bien vieille." "When You are Old," *The Rose* (1893), st. 1

34 Murmur, a little sadly, how Love fled
And paced upon the mountains overhead
And hid his face amid a crowd of stars.
October 21, 1891. "When You are Old," *The Rose* (1893), st. 3

35 O chestnut tree, great rooted blossomer,
Are you the leaf, the blossom or the bole?
O body swayed to music; O brightening glance,
How can we know the dancer from the dance?
June 14, 1926. "Among School Children," *The Tower* (1928), pt. 8

36 We had fed the heart on fantasies,
The heart's grown brutal from the fare;
More substance in our enmities
Than in our love.
"Meditations In Time of Civil War," *The Tower* (1928), "The Stare's Nest by My Window," ll. 16–19

37 That is no country for old men. The young
In one another's arms, birds in the trees,
—Those dying generations—at their song,
The salmon-falls, the mackerel-crowded seas.
September 26, 1926. "Sailing to Byzantium," *The Tower* (1928), pt. 1

38 An aged man is but a paltry thing
A tattered coat upon a stick, unless
Soul clap its hands and sing.
September 26, 1926. "Sailing to Byzantium," *The Tower* (1928), pt. 2

39 Through winter-time we call on spring,
And through the spring on summer call,
And when abounding hedges ring
Declare that winter's best of all.
"The Wheel," *The Tower* (1928), ll. 1–4

40 I think it better that in times like these
A poet's mouth be silent, for in truth
We have no gift to set a statesman right.
"On Being Asked for a War Poem," *The Wild Swans at Coole* (1919), ll. 1–3

41 The trees are in their autumn beauty,
The woodland paths are dry,
Under the October twilight the water
Mirrors a still sky;
Upon the brimming water among the stones
Are nine-and-fifty swans.
"The Wild Swans at Coole," *The Wild Swans at Coole* (1919), ll. 1–6

42 I have drunk ale from the Country of the Young
And weep because I know all things now.
"He Thinks of his Past Greatness when a Part of the Constellations of Heaven," *The Wind Among the Reeds* (1899), ll. 1–2

43 But weigh this song with the great and their pride;
I made it out of a mouthful of air,
Their children's children shall say they have lied.
"He Thinks of Those Who have Spoken Evil of his Beloved," *The Wind Among the Reeds* (1899), ll. 4–6

44 But I, being poor, have only my dreams;
I have spread my dreams under your feet;
Tread softly because you tread on my dreams.
"He Wishes for the Cloths of Heaven," *The Wind Among the Reeds* (1899), ll. 6–8

45 Out-worn heart, in a time out-worn,
Come clear of the nets of wrong and right;
Laugh, heart, again in the grey twilight,
Sigh, heart, again in the dew of the morn.
1893? "Into the Twilight," *The Wind Among The Reeds* (1899), st. 1

46 For the good arc always the merry,
Save by an evil chance,
And the merry love the fiddle,
And the merry love to dance.
November 1892. "The Fiddler of Dooney," *The Wind Among the Reeds* (1899), st. 4

47 Time drops in decay,
Like a candle burnt out.
"The Moods," *The Wind Among the Reeds* (1899), ll. 1–2

48 A woman of so shining loveliness
That men threshed corn at midnight by a tress,
A little stolen tress.
"The Secret Rose," *The Wind Among the Reeds* (1899), ll. 25–27

49 And pluck till time and times are done
The silver apples of the moon
The golden apples of the sun.
1893? "The Song of Wandering Aengus," *The Wind Among the Reeds* (1899), st. 3

50 Flinging from his arms I laughed
To think his passion such
He fancied that I gave a soul
Did but our bodies touch,
And laughed upon his breast to think
Beast gave beast as much.
1926. "A Woman Young and Old," *The Winding Stair and Other Poems* (1933), pt. 9, "A Last Confession," st. 2

51 Is every modern nation like the tower,
Half-dead at the top?
"Blood and the Moon," *The Winding Stair and Other Poems* (1933), pt. 4, ll. 5–6

52 Before me floats an image, man or shade,
Shade more than man, more image than a shade.
September 1930. "Byzantium," *The Winding Stair and Other Poems* (1933), ll. 9–10

53 That dolphin-torn, that gong-tormented sea.
September 1930. "Byzantium," *The Winding Stair and Other Poems* (1933), st. 5

54 A woman can be proud and stiff
When on love intent;

But Love has pitched his mansion in
The place of excrement.
November 1931. "Crazy Jane Talks with the Bishop," *The Winding Stair and Other Poems* (1933), "Words for Music Perhaps," st. 3, ll. 1–4

55 Nor dread nor hope attend
A dying animal;
A man awaits his end
Dreading and hoping all.
"Death," *The Winding Stair and Other Poems* (1933), ll. 1–4

56 Only God, my dear,
Could love you for yourself alone
And not your yellow hair.
September 1930. "For Anne Gregory," *The Winding Stair and Other Poems* (1933), st. 3

57 Two girls in silk kimonos, both
Beautiful, one a gazelle.
Referring to the youthful beauty of two of his friends. "In Memory of Eva Gore-Booth and Con Markiewicz," *The Winding Stair and Other Poems* (1933), ll. 3–4

58 The innocent and the beautiful
Have no enemy but time.
October 1927. "In Memory of Eva Gore-Booth and Con Markiewicz," *The Winding Stair and Other Poems* (1933), st. 2

59 I shudder and I sigh to think
That even Cicero
And many-minded Homer were
Mad as the mist and snow.
February 12, 1929. "Mad as the Mist and Snow," *The Winding Stair and Other Poems* (1933), "Words for Music Perhaps," no. 18, st. 3

60 Out of Ireland have we come.
Great hatred, little room,
Maimed us at the start.
I carry from my mother's womb
A fanatic heart.
August 28, 1931. "Remorse for Intemperate Speech," *The Winding Stair and Other Poems* (1933), ll. 11–15

61 The intellect of man is forced to choose
Perfection of the life, or of the work.
1932. "The Choice," *The Winding Stair and Other Poems* (1933), ll. 1–2

62 While on the shop and street I gazed
My body of a sudden blazed;
And twenty minutes more or less
It seemed, so great my happiness,
That I was blessèd and could bless.
1931. "Vacillation," *The Winding Stair and Other Poems* (1933), pt. 4, st. 2

63 O'CONNOR How are you?
W. B. Y. Not very well, I can only write prose today.
Attrib.

Yehoshua, A. B. (b.1936) Israeli novelist

1 I am anxious not for the survival of the Diaspora...but for the survival of Israel.
Interview (March 7, 1985), quoted in *Voices of Israel* (Joseph Cohen; 1990)

2 Our region is not the Middle East so much as it is a region of the Mediterranean. It is Greece and Italy and Egypt and Malta and Turkey.
Interview (March 7, 1985), quoted in *Voices of Israel* (Joseph Cohen; 1990)

3 Those perfect German Orientalists who know all the mysteries of the Koran but are unable to go to an Arab village and ask for a coffee.
Interview (March 7, 1985), quoted in *Voices of Israel* (Joseph Cohen; 1990)

Yeltsin, Boris (Boris Nikolayevich Yeltsin; b.1931) Russian president

Quotations about Yeltsin

1 Yeltsin got where he is by slogans. He is an old party communist and has the old mentality. He is good at leading from the top of a tank.
Zianon Pozniak, Belarusian politician. *Times*, London (February 4, 1995)

Quotations by Yeltsin

2 The market is not a panacea for all problems.
Speech to the Russian parliament (September 24, 1997)

3 A historic document which will allow us to continue our course towards entering Europe without the discrimination which took place in the past. We move forward as equal partners towards our mutual interests.
Signing a partnership and cooperation agreement with the European Union. *Guardian*, London (June 24, 1994)

4 Europe has not yet freed itself from the heritage of the Cold War and is in danger of plunging into a Cold Peace.
Independent, London (December 6, 1994)

5 I ask you to forgive me for not fulfilling some hopes of those people who believed that we would be able to jump from the totalitarian past into a bright, rich and civilized future in one go.
Said on his retirement as Russian president. *Observer*, London (January 2, 2000)

6 People in our country don't like it when foreigners take too active a hand in our affairs.
The View from the Kremlin (Catherine A. Fitzpatrick, tr.; 1994)

7 We are still too dependent upon dachas, cars, special government telephone lines, and armored doors—the prerequisites of power.
The View from the Kremlin (Catherine A. Fitzpatrick, tr.; 1994)

8 There, I've signed it.
1991. Yeltsin signed the agreement to end the USSR in December 1991. In response to the question, "For a little light relief, how about halting the work of the Communist Party?" Quoted in *Times*, London (August 24, 1994)

Yeo, George Singaporean politician

1 If the English language restricts...our mental images and emotional references to those of Anglo-Saxon societies, its use elsewhere may be resented and resisted.
Welcoming the "indigenization" of the English language. Speech (November 4, 1993), quoted in *Straits Times*, Singapore (November 5, 1993)

2 You cannot cane someone and expect it to be painless. You might as well give him a book to read.
Observer, London (May 1, 1994), "Sayings of the Week"

3 There is every likelihood that the center of world economy will shift to the Asia-Pacific in the next century. This economic

growth will be accompanied by a cultural renaissance of historical importance.
Quoted in *Singapore: Global City for the Arts* (Singapore Economic Development Board; 1994)

Ye Si (b.1948) Hong Kong-born Chinese writer

1 Even if my memory were to fail me in the future, I would still be able to retrace with certainty the footsteps of my soul.
"Transcendence and the Fax Machine" (Jeanne Tai, tr.; 1990)

Yetnikoff, Walter U.S. record company executive

1 I think I can tell a hit record as good as the next guy. It's from listening to the radio, not because of some musical ability.
Quoted in "Walter Yetnikoff," *Off the Record: An Oral History of Popular Music* (Joe Smith; 1988)

Yevtushenko, Yevgeny (Yevgeny Aleksandrovich Yevtushenko; b.1933) Russian poet

Quotations about Yevtushenko

1 They tried to destroy the memory of Babi Yar, first the Germans and then the Ukrainian government. But after Yevtushenko's poem, it became clear that it would never be forgotten. That is the power of art.
Dmitri Shostakovich (1906–75) Russian composer. Referring to the mass execution by Nazi troops of 30,000 Jews in a ravine at Babi Yar, near Kiev, in 1941, and to the poet Yevgeny Yevtushenko, who wrote a memorable poem about the event. *Testimony: The Memoirs of Shostakovich* (Solomon Volkov, ed., Antonina W. Bouis, tr.; 1979), ch. 5

Quotations by Yevtushenko

2 Leaves—we cannot have,
sky—we cannot have,
But there is so much we can have—
to embrace tenderly in a darkened room.
Babi Yar (1961)

3 No Jewish blood runs among my blood,
but I am as bitterly and hardly hated
by every anti-Semite
as if I were a Jew. By this
I am a Russian.
Babi Yar (1961)

4 The hell with it. Who never knew the price of happiness will not be happy.
Babi Yar (1961)

Young, Allen (b.1941) U.S. journalist

1 The artificial categories "heterosexual" and "homosexual" have been laid on us by a sexist society.
1992. Quoted in *Out of the Closets: Voices of Gay Liberation* (Karla Jay and Allen Young, eds.; 1994)

Young, Andrew (Andrew John Young; 1885–1971) Scottish poet and cleric

1 Stars lay like yellow pollen
That from a flower has fallen;
And single stars I saw
Crossing themselves in awe;
Some stars in sudden fear
Fell like a falling tear.
"The Stars," *The Collected Poems of Andrew Young* (1960)

Young, Andrew (b.1932) U.S. politician and civil rights activist

1 It's a blessing to die for a cause, because you can so easily die for nothing.
Playboy (July 1977)

2 Political morality is a long way from church morality.
1977. Attrib.

Young, Brigham (1801–77) U.S. Mormon leader

Quotations about Young

1 He is dreadfully married. He's the most married man I ever saw in my life.
Artemus Ward (1834–67) U.S. humorist. "Brigham Young's Palace," *Artemus Ward's Lecture* (1869)

Quotations by Young

2 I am here to answer. I shall be on hand to answer when I am called upon, for all the counsel and for all the instruction that I have given to this people.
Quoted in *Journal of Discourses* (John A. Widtsoe, ed.; 1954)

3 I say now, when...my discourses are copied and approved by me they are as good Scripture as is couched in this Bible.
Quoted in *Journal of Discourses* (John A. Widtsoe, ed.; 1954)

4 You are commencing anew. The soil, the air, the water are all pure and healthy. Do not suffer them to become polluted with wickedness.
Quoted in *Journal of Discourses* (John A. Widtsoe, ed.; 1954)

5 God has shown me that this is the spot to locate His people, and here is where they will prosper.
1847. Brigham Young led the Latter-day Saints from Nauvoo, Illinois, to the valley of the Great Salt Lake, Utah, the place he saw in a vision as the promised land. Quoted in *Journal of Discourses* (John A. Widtsoe, ed.; 1954)

6 Now if any of you will deny the plurality of wives, and continue to do so, I promise that you will be damned.
Polygamy is an accepted part of Mormon theology. Quoted in *Journal of Discourses* (John A. Widtsoe, ed.; 1954)

7 The only men who become Gods, even the sons of Gods, are those who enter into polygamy.
Polygamy is an accepted part of Mormon theology. Quoted in *Journal of Discourses* (John A. Widtsoe, ed.; 1954)

8 It is enough. That is the right place.
July 24, 1847. Referring to first seeing the Great Salt Lake Valley, Utah. The Mormons settled there after a 15-week journey westward to escape persecution. Attrib.

Young, Coleman (Coleman Alexander Young; 1918–97) U.S. politician

1 They've been operating jointly on me for years.
Said when mayor of Detroit. Referring to the joint operating agreement between the *Detroit Free Press* and the *Detroit News*. *Newsweek* (October 28, 1991)

Young, David Ivor, Baron Young of Graffham (b.1932) British politician and business executive

1 You never learn from success. Success you take as the natural order of things.
Guardian, London (February 25, 1985)

2 God helps those who train themselves.
Sunday Times, London (February 27, 1983)

Young, Edward (1683–1765) English poet

1 Some for renown, on scraps of learning dote,
And think they grow immortal as they quote.
Satire 1, *Love of Fame* (1725–28), ll. 89–90

2 Be wise with speed,
A fool at forty is a fool indeed.
Satire 2, *Love of Fame* (1725–28), ll. 281–282

3 Time flies, death urges, knells call, heaven invites,
Hell threatens.
The Complaint, or Night Thoughts on Life, Death, and Immortality (1742–45)

4 Procrastination is the thief of time.
The Complaint, or Night Thoughts on Life, Death, and Immortality (1742–45), bk. 1, l. 393

5 All men think all men mortal, but themselves.
The Complaint, or Night Thoughts on Life, Death, and Immortality (1742–45), bk. 1, l. 424

6 The bell strikes one. We take no note of time
But from its loss.
The Complaint, or Night Thoughts on Life, Death, and Immortality (1742–45), bk. 1, ll. 55–56

7 Man wants but little, nor that little long.
The Complaint, or Night Thoughts on Life, Death, and Immortality (1742–45), bk. 4, l. 222

8 By night an atheist half believes a God.
The Complaint, or Night Thoughts on Life, Death, and Immortality (1742–45), bk. 5, l. 176

9 To know the world, not love her is thy point,
She gives but little, nor that little long.
The Complaint, or Night Thoughts on Life, Death, and Immortality (1742–45), bk. 8, ll. 1276–77

Young, George W. (1846–1919) British writer

1 Your lips, on my own, when they printed "Farewell",
Had never been soiled by the "beverage of hell";
But they come to me now with the bacchanal sign,
And the lips that touch liquor must never touch mine.
Also attributed to Harriet Glazebrook. "The Lips That Touch Liquor Must Never Touch Mine" (1870?)

Young, Jock British criminologist

1 The person by far the most likely to kill you is yourself.
Observer, London (May 8, 1994), "Sayings of the Week"

Young, Mary Evans British dietician

1 You have a situation where girls of eight want to lose weight and at 12 they can tell you the fat content of an avocado...but they don't know what constitutes a healthy meal.
Observer, London (May 1, 1994)

Young, Michael, Baron Young of Dartington (b.1915) British educationist and consumer rights advocate

1 The Rise of the Meritocracy
1958. Book title.

Young, Neil (Neil Percival Young; b.1945) Canadian rock singer and songwriter

1 By MTV trying to visualize the music they automatically stripped it of most of its natural mystery and depth.
Quoted in "Favourites," *Small Talk Big Names* (Myles Palmer; 1993)

Young, Whitney M., Jr. (Whitney Moore Young, Jr.; 1921–71) U.S. social worker and civil rights leader

1 Black is beautiful when it is a slum kid studying to enter college...or a slum mother battling to give her kids a chance for a better life. But white is beautiful, too, when it helps to change society to make our system work for black people.
Beyond Racism: Building an Open Society (1969)

2 White is ugly when it oppresses blacks—and so is black ugly when black people exploit other blacks. No race has a monopoly on vice or virtue.
Beyond Racism: Building an Open Society (1969)

Yourcenar, Marguerite (Marguerite de Crayencour; 1903–87) Belgian-born French writer

1 A man who reads, who thinks, or who calculates, belongs to the species and not to the sex; in his better moments, he even escapes being human.
Memoirs of Hadrian (1951)

Yoxen, Edward British author and academic

1 Biotechnology has an ancient lineage. It is as old as the first fermented drink, the first bowl of yoghurt or the first piece of cheese.
The Gene Business (1983)

2 The term "technology transfer" is losing its meaning, since there is no motion or transfer. Conception *is* capitalization.
The Gene Business (1983)

3 No Winter Palace has been seized, no Bastille stormed, no monarchy abolished...(but) a technological assault is being prepared that will transform the economies of the developed and developing nations.
Referring to advances in biotechnology. *The Gene Business* (1983)

Yücel, Can (b.1926) Turkish poet

1 For politicians, politics is the art of staying
out of jail,
for convicts it is the prospect of freedom.
"Poem 26," *Modern Turkish Poetry* (Feyyaz Kayacan Fergar, ed.; 1992), ll. 5–7

2 People got so used to staying indoors
that curfews were declared illegal.
"The Latest Situation in Chile," *Modern Turkish Poetry* (Feyyaz Kayacan Fergar, ed.; 1992)

Yu Jie (b.1973) Chinese writer

1 From time immemorial, China has had people who obey, and people who are thugs, but China has never had citizens.
1990s. Quoted in "Fire and Ice," *Far Eastern Economic Review* (Matty Forney; April 1998)

Yusuf, Sa'di (b.1943) Iraqi poet

1 Once
twenty years ago
in the air-conditioned train
I kissed her the whole night long.
"A Woman," *Modern Arabic Poetry* (Salma Khadra Jayyusi, ed.; 1987), ll. 13–16

2 To a girl who knows something other than sex
and something more than soft colors
I sent postcards that never arrived.
"Six Poems (I)," *When the Words Burn* (John Mikhail Asfour, ed., tr.; 1988), ll. 3–6

Zz

Zaharias, Babe (originally Mildred Ella Didrikson; 1913–56) U.S. athlete

1 All my life I've been competing—and competing to win. I came to realize that in its way, this cancer was the toughest competition I'd faced yet. I made up my mind that I was going to lick it all the way.
Quoted in "'Babe' Didrikson Zaharias," *Famous American Women* (Hope Stoddard; 1970)

Zamyatin, Yevgeny (Yevgeny Ivanovich Zamyatin; 1884–1937) Russian writer

1 I cannot continue my work, because no creative activity is possible in an atmosphere of systematic persecution that increases in intensity from year to year.
"Letter to Stalin" (June 1931), quoted in *The Dragon and Other Stories* (Mirra Ginsburg, ed., tr.; 1966)

2 I know that while I have been proclaimed a Right winger here because of my habit of writing to my conscience rather than according to command, I shall sooner or later probably be declared a Bolshevik for the same reason abroad.
"Letter to Stalin" (June 1931), quoted in *The Dragon and Other Stories* (Mirra Ginsburg, ed., tr.; 1966)

3 The most wonderful thing in life is to be delirious and the most wonderful kind of delirium is being in love.
"The Fisher of Men" (1918), quoted in *Islanders and The Fisher of Men* (Sophie Fuller and Julian Sacchi, eds., trs.; 1984)

4 It is hereby proclaimed to all the members of The One State: Everyone who feels able to do so is obligated to compose treatises, poems, odes and/or other pieces on the beauty and grandeur of The One State.
We (Bernard Guilbert Guerney, tr.; 1920)

Zanuck, Darryl F. (Darryl Francis Zanuck; 1902–79) U.S. film producer and studio executive

1 When you get a sex story in biblical garb, you can open your own mint.
Referring to making movies on biblical subjects. Quoted in *Movie Talk* (David Shipman; 1988)

Zappa, Frank (Francis Vincent; 1940–93) U.S. rock musician and composer

1 I don't care if I'm known or remembered, respected or get famous. The reason I write music is because I like to listen to it. And if there are other people who like to listen to it, then that's fine.
Quoted in *Mother! The Frank Zappa Story* (Michael Gray; 1993)

2 Let me sum it up for you. Information is not knowledge. Knowledge is not wisdom. Wisdom is not truth. Truth is not beauty. Beauty is not love. Love is not music. Music is the best.
Quoted in *Mother! The Frank Zappa Story* (Michael Gray; 1993)

3 People who can't talk interviewed by people who can't write for people who can't read.
Referring to music journalism. Quoted in *Mother! The Frank Zappa Story* (Michael Gray; 1993)

4 If we cannot be free, at least we can be cheap!
Said in the late 1960s, referring to the idea of freedom, which inspired many contemporary social and political movements. Quoted in *Mother! The Frank Zappa Story* (Michael Gray; 1993)

5 Sometimes you can't write a chord ugly enough to say what you want to say.
Quoted in *Rock 'n' Roll Babylon* (Gary Herman; 1994)

Zayyad, Tawfiq (b.1932) Palestinian poet

1 When they ran over her,
the mulberry tree said:
"Do what you wish,
but remember
my right to bear fruit
will never die."
"Passing Remark," *Modern Arabic Poetry* (Salma Khadra Jayyusi, ed.; 1987), ll. 1–6

2 But they know that my country
has known a thousand conquerors
and they know
that the thousand
have all melted away
like driven snow.
"They Know," *Modern Arabic Poetry* (Salma Khadra Jayyusi, ed.; 1987), ll. 1–6

Zec, Philip (1910?–83) Russian-born British political cartoonist and editor

1 "Here you are—don't lose it again."
Cartoon caption showing a wounded soldier handing over "Victory and Peace in Europe." *Daily Mirror*, London (May 8, 1945)

Zeeman, E. C., Sir (Erik Christopher Zeeman; b.1923) British mathematician

1 Technical skill is mastery of complexity while creativity is mastery of simplicity.
Catastrophe Theory (1977)

Zeldin, Theodore (b.1933) British historian

1 Americans were originally thrifty; big business persuaded them to become consumers instead, insatiable, richer but more vulnerable.
An Intimate History of Humanity (1994)

2 If you choose to be a negotiator, you eliminate worry about whether you deserve to be successful.
An Intimate History of Humanity (1994)

3 Not everybody can be a leader, but everybody can be an intermediary.
An Intimate History of Humanity (1994)

4 The manager's job is to thrive in a chaotic world he cannot control. He is at last reconciled to being, openly, an intermediary.
An Intimate History of Humanity (1994)

5 The origin of the leisure society is the dream of living like a master.
An Intimate History of Humanity (1994)

6 The present century, in proclaiming the advent of a new age of communication and information...forgot to deal with the great problem of talk, which is how to find someone to listen.
An Intimate History of Humanity (1994)

7 To be a catalyst is the ambition most appropriate for those who see the world as being in constant change, and who, without thinking that they can control it, wish to influence its direction.
An Intimate History of Humanity (1994)

8 When Napoleon called England a nation of shopkeepers it was like calling them a nation of pimps. It has taken about twenty-five centuries for intermediaries to be appreciated.
An Intimate History of Humanity (1994)

9 Food isolates the French almost as much as their language. That would not be serious if France were at least certain of remaining a refuge for good food.
The French (1983)

Zell, Katharina (1497–1562) German church worker and hymnwriter

1 You remind me that the Apostle Paul told women to be silent in church. I would remind you of the word of this same apostle that in Christ there is no longer male or female.
Entschuldigung Katherina Schultzinn (1524)

Zhang Jie (b.1937) Chinese writer

1 I am thirty, the same as our People's Republic. For a republic thirty is still young. But a girl of thirty is virtually on the shelf.
Love Must Not be Forgotten (1982)

Zhanguo Ce Chinese historical account

1 Your lordship's mansion has plenty of gems and treasures; dogs and horses fill up the outbuildings; and there are a lot of beauties in the women's quarters. The only thing your household is short of is righteousness. So I brought your lordship some righteousness.
The *Zhanguo Ce* ("Intrigues of the Warring States", 2nd century? B.C.) gives political advice to rulers by drawing on historical examples. *China's Imperial Past* (Charles O. Hucker; 1975)

Zhang Xianliang (b.1936) Chinese writer

1 Our county Secretary talked like that. The loudspeaker even talked like that. What a load of rubbish. Being dead is fine, anyway. But if you were to take me as a living person, I'd come alive for you.
Half of Man is Woman (Martha Avery, tr.; 1986?)

Zhang Yimou (b.1950) Chinese film director

1 We wanted to use our limited artistic tools to paint a vast canvas of life, to use our "inks" to paint a world of resounding power.
"The Debate," *Seeds of Fire* (Geremie Barmé and John Minford, eds.; 1986)

2 The more they trusted me, the less I could afford to make a mistake.
Referring to the Chinese authorities. Quoted in "Turandot in the Forbidden City," *China Review* (Yu Peng; Autumn/Winter 1998)

Zhao, Henry Y. H. (Zhao Yiheng; b.1943) Chinese critic, fiction writer, and poet

1 New Wave literature is nothing more than canned soft drink, fashionable but not yet affordable for the majority of the Chinese people.
Sensing the Shift—New Wave Literature and Chinese Culture (1991)

2 Since very early times, Chinese culture has predominantly been a culture that values literature highly. Oral and other non-literate texts (music, for instance) did not have sufficient meaning.
Sensing the Shift—New Wave Literature and Chinese Culture (1991)

Zhou Peiyuan (1902–93) Chinese physicist and diplomat

1 Political democracy and academic freedom are very important to the development of science.
"China's Science in the Past Six Decades," *Red Flag* (June 1, 1979), quoted in *Remapping China* (Mary Brown Bullock; 1996)

Zhou Yang (b.1908) Chinese politician

1 All art forms and techniques of foreign origin when transplanted to China must be remodeled and assimilated so they possess national features and become our own.
The Path of Socialist Literature and Art in China (1960), quoted in *Literature of the People's Republic of China* (Kai-yu Hsu, ed.; 1980)

Zhuangzi (also known as Chuang-tzu; 369?–286 B.C.) Chinese philosopher and teacher

1 Both small and great things must equally possess form. The

mind cannot picture to itself a thing without form, nor conceive a form of unlimited dimensions.
"Autumn Floods," quoted in *Chuang Tzu* (Herbert A. Giles, tr.; 1980), ch. 17

2 Of all the myriad created things, man is but one. And of all those who inhabit the land...an individual man is but one. Is not he, as compared with all creation, but as the tip of a hair upon a horse's skin?
"Autumn Floods," quoted in *Chuang Tzu* (Herbert A. Giles, tr.; 1980), ch. 17

3 The life of man passes like a galloping horse, changing at every turn, at every hour. What should he do, or what should he not do, other than let his decomposition go on?
"Autumn Floods," quoted in *Chuang Tzu* (Herbert A. Giles, tr.; 1980), ch. 17

4 The Spirit of the River laughed for joy that all the beauty of the earth was gathered to himself. Down with the stream he journeyed east, until he reached the ocean. There, looking eastward and seeing no limit to its waves, his countenance changed.
"Autumn Floods," quoted in *Chuang Tzu* (Herbert A. Giles, tr.; 1980), ch. 17

5 I have heard that in Chu there is a sacred tortoise which has been dead some three thousand years...Now would this tortoise rather be dead and have its remains venerated, or be alive and wagging its tail in the mud?
Said in response to an invitation to take up public office. "Autumn Floods," quoted in *Chuang Tzu* (Herbert A. Giles, tr.; 1980), ch. 17

6 Books are what the world values as representing Tao. But books are only words, and the valuable part of words is the thought therein contained.
"The Tao of God," quoted in *Chuang Tzu* (Herbert A. Giles, tr.; 1980), ch. 13

7 In making a wheel...There must be co-ordination of mind and hand. Words cannot explain what it is, but there is some mysterious art herein. I cannot teach it to my son; nor can he learn it from me.
"The Tao of God," quoted in *Chuang Tzu* (Herbert A. Giles, tr.; 1980), ch. 13

8 There is a fish, called the Leviathan, many thousand *li* in size. This leviathan changes into a bird, called the Rukh, whose back is many thousand *li* in breadth. With a mighty effort it rises, and its wings obscure the sky like clouds.
"Transcendental Bliss," quoted in *Chuang Tzu* (Herbert A. Giles, tr.; 1980), ch. 1

9 I do not know whether I was then a man dreaming I was a butterfly, or whether I am now a butterfly dreaming I am a man.
Quoted in *Chuang Tzu* (Herbert A. Giles, tr.; 1980), ch. 2

Zhu Xi (also known as Chu Hsi; 1130–1200) Chinese philosopher

1 Understanding the good is fundamental, and if we hold this firm we shall have begun. If we enlarge it, we can become great; but if we regard it lightly, we shall shrivel. The potentiality of its flourishing rests with man and no other.
Jinsi lu (1175–76), quoted in *China's Imperial Past* (Charles O. Hucker; 1975)

Zinsser, Hans (1878–1940) U.S. bacteriologist and immunologist

1 The scientist takes off from the manifold observations of predecessors, and shows his intelligence...by selecting here and there the significant stepping stones that will lead across the difficulties to new understanding.
As I Remember Him (1940), ch. 20

Zinsser, William (William Knowlton Zinsser; b.1922) U.S. editor, writer, and educator

1 And as for Miss Charisse's legs, they are practically a national shrine.
Referring to dancer Cyd Charisse in *Silk Stockings* (1957), the musical version of *Ninotchka*. Quoted in *Starring Fred Astaire* (Stanley Green and Burt Goldblatt; 1973)

Zoshchenko, Mikhail (Mikhail Mikhailovich Zoshchenko; 1895–1958) Russian satirist

1 Nobody writes Halloween stories these days. For the good reason that there's nothing particularly hallowed left in our lives.
"A Halloween Story," *A Man is Not a Flea* (Serge Shishkoff, tr.; 1989)

2 The problem of civilization is a bitch of a problem...Things that are good in the bourgeois countries have a way of turning sour in our land.
"The Charms of Civilization," *A Man is Not a Flea* (Serge Shishkoff, tr.; 1989)

3 Phew! How tough it is to write literature.
You sweat buckets while trying to hack your way through impenetrable jungle.
And for what?
"What the Nightingale Sang About," *A Man is Not a Flea* (Serge Shishkoff, tr.; 1989)

4 The author is not at all impressed with humans. It is time, citizens, to renounce our senseless self-glorification. The author believes that if a slug can learn to live among wet slime, why shouldn't a human being get used to living among damp laundry?
"What the Nightingale Sang About," *A Man is Not a Flea* (Serge Shishkoff, tr.; 1989)

Zuccaro, Federico (1542–1609) Italian painter and theorist

1 Rules serve no purpose; they can only do harm...Not only must the artist's mind be clear, it should not be hindered and weighed down by a mechanical servility to such rules.
The Idea of Painters, Sculptors and Architects (1607)

Zucker, David (b.1947) U.S. playwright and director

1 She had the kind of body that could melt a cheese sandwich from across the room.
The Naked Gun: From the Files of Police Squad (co-written with Jerry Zucker, Jim Abrahams, and Pat Profit; 1988)

Zurita, Raul (Raul Zurita Canessa; b.1951) Chilean poet

1 MY OWN MIND THE DESERT OF CHILE
you thought it was no big
deal to walk out that way and then
come back after your own
never turned back stretched
like a plain before us.
"Purgatory" (1987), quoted in *The Gathering of Voices* (Mike Gonzalez and David Treece; 1992)

KEYWORD INDEX

Keyword Index

accomplished see what can be a. in a week STEVENSON, ROBERT LOUIS, 27
accomplishment a. of individual and collective purposes HICKMAN, CRAIG R., 4
accomplishments A. have no color PRICE, LEONTYNE, 1
accord My cousin Francis and I are in perfect a. CHARLES V, 3
accountancy With creative a., who needs cheating WHITEHORN, KATHARINE, 10
accountants A. *are* people TOWNSEND, ROBERT, 5
My a. have told me SUGAR, ALAN, 2
accounting A....malicious extension...banking conspiracy FORD, HENRY, 13
Capital a....presupposes *the battle of man with man* WEBER, MAX, 5
accuracy no fineness or a. of suppression BELLOW, SAUL, 24
Pray for the grace of a. LOWELL, ROBERT, 6
accuse A. not nature, she hath done her part MILTON, JOHN, 76
to a. someone of trying to be funny MUGGERIDGE, MALCOLM, 6
accuser I was the a., God the accused WIESEL, ELIE, 2
accustom A. yourself continually to...acts of love TERESA OF ÁVILA, SAINT, 2
accustomed A. to her face LERNER, ALAN JAY, 11
I will start to get a. to it DEBUSSY, CLAUDE, 1
achieve To a. great things we must live VAUVENARGUES, MARQUIS DE, 2
achievement do not let so great an a. suffer from...legality ROOSEVELT, THEODORE, 3
Achilles A. exists only through Homer CHATEAUBRIAND, RENÉ, 4
acid A. has changed consciousness entirely GARCIA, JERRY, 1
acne I looked 17, and I had a. SPIELBERG, STEVEN, 1
acquaintance auld a. be forgot BURNS, ROBERT, 9
hope our a. may be a long 'un DICKENS, CHARLES, 96
acquisition As an end...a. of wealth is ignoble CARNEGIE, ANDREW, 2
impulse to a....has in itself nothing to do with capitalism WEBER, MAX, 4
acquisitiveness a. has more perverts HUXLEY, ALDOUS, 42
act A. only according to...universal law KANT, IMMANUEL, 21
Can't a.. Can't sing ASTAIRE, FRED, 1
human a....not revealing SARTRE, JEAN-PAUL, 7
I do not a....I am action MOU SEN, 1
More of an a. than an actress BANKHEAD, TALLULAH, 1
the second a. and the child's throat COWARD, NOEL, 28
They didn't a. like people SALINGER, J. D., 16
When a given a. is followed closely SKINNER, B. F., 2
acting A. is the expression of a neurotic impulse BRANDO, MARLON, 7
A. is...the lowest of the arts MOORE, GEORGE, 4
A. is the most minor of gifts HEPBURN, KATHARINE, 5
art of a. is not to act HOPKINS, ANTHONY, 3
kind of a. in the United States BERGMAN, INGRID, 1
screen a. is no job for a lazy person ASTAIRE, FRED, 6
subtlest a....is by ordinary people BRANDO, MARLON, 2
The art of a. consists in keeping people from coughing RICHARDSON, RALPH, 1
The danger chiefly lies in a. well CHURCHILL, CHARLES, 1
The secret of a. is sincerity BURNS, GEORGE, 6
action *A. will furnish belief* CLOUGH, ARTHUR HUGH, 7
Let a single completed a....keep the theater packed BOILEAU, NICOLAS, 5
No a. is in itself good or bad MAUGHAM, SOMERSET, 7
Suit the a. to the word SHAKESPEARE, WILLIAM, 189
The true men of a....are...the scientists AUDEN, W. H., 31
without a. the people and their vision perish COLE, JOHNETTA BETSCH, 2
actions A. speak louder PROVERBS, 103
the a. of the just /...blossom in their dust SHIRLEY, JAMES, 2
activity A. is the only reality NOVALIS, 1
done almost every human a. inside a taxi BRIEN, ALAN, 1
Act of God A....no reasonable man...expected HERBERT, A. P., 9
The A. designation COREN, ALAN, 2
Act of Settlement drive a coach and six horses through the A. RICE, STEPHEN, 1
actor a. is something less than a man BURTON, RICHARD, 1
an a. can instruct a priest GOETHE, JOHANN WOLFGANG VON, 8
a....reminds you of an animal TRUFFAUT, FRANÇOIS, 2
be an a....I could meet queers MCKELLEN, IAN, 1
easier to get an a. to be a cowboy FORD, JOHN (1895–1973), 1
Every a. in his heart WELLES, ORSON, 10
Every a. should direct at least once EASTWOOD, CLINT, 2
greatest love affairs...involved one a. MIZNER, WILSON, 8
One can almost trick an a. ANTONIONI, MICHELANGELO, 1
When an a. has money CHEKHOV, ANTON, 21
actors A. are cattle HITCHCOCK, ALFRED, 2
All people are a. LEC, STANISLAW, 3
Public reaction...keep a. as personalities NEWMAN, PAUL, 2
Shakespeare's thought was quickened by the idea of a. and a stage SHAKESPEARE, WILLIAM, 6
actress An a.'s life is so transitory HAYES, HELEN, 1
a....someone who wears feather boas WEAVER, SIGOURNEY, 1
For an a. ... must have the face of Venus BARRYMORE, ETHEL, 2
actresses A. will happen HERFORD, OLIVER, 1
silk stockings and white bosoms of your a. JOHNSON, SAMUEL, 167
acts Our a. our angels are FLETCHER, JOHN, 1
Outrageous A. STEINEM, GLORIA, 15
the a., the split second acts OLSON, CHARLES, 2
actually As it a. was RANKE, LEOPOLD VON, 1
ad An expensive a. represents the toil MCLUHAN, MARSHALL, 10
Adam A....is the divine handwriting AL-GHAZALI, 1
A. was not Adamant HOOD, THOMAS, 2
first time A. had a chance ASTOR, NANCY, 6
grant that the old A. in this Child BOOK OF COMMON PRAYER, 20
In A.'s fall /We sinnéd all FOLK VERSE, 41
Oh, A. was a gardener KIPLING, RUDYARD, 7
When A. delved and Eve span BALL, JOHN, 2
adaptive a. manager...capable of radical action TOFFLER, ALVIN, 8
addiction Every form of a. is bad JUNG, CARL GUSTAV, 17
addictive All sin tends to be a. AUDEN, W. H., 20
Addison give his days and nights to the volumes of A. ADDISON, JOSEPH, 1
address Their a. was this: "Schlachthof-fünf." VONNEGUT, KURT, 9
addresses A....conceal our whereabouts SAKI, 14
adieu a., kind friends, adieu FOLK VERSE, 23
Adlestrop I remember A. THOMAS, EDWARD, 1
administrators A. are cheap and easy SMITH, RAYMOND W., 1
admiral good to kill an a. VOLTAIRE, 17
The A. of the Atlantic salutes the...Pacific WILLIAM II, 4

admire Not to a. POPE, ALEXANDER, 51
admired I am a. because I do things well BILLSON, CHRISTINE, 1
admit a. that I am more than fifty-two ASTOR, NANCY, 7
adolescence a man suffering from petrified a. CHURCHILL, WINSTON, 4
Adolf A. is a swine HITLER, ADOLF, 12
Adonais I weep for A. KEATS, JOHN (1795–1821), 5
adopt all wanted to a. me in some way PLATH, SYLVIA, 7
adoration For A. seasons change SMART, CHRISTOPHER, 2
adores he a. his maker DISRAELI, BENJAMIN, 59
ads Nobody counts the number of a. BERNBACH, WILLIAM, 2
Two a....keeps the sack away FOLK VERSE, 49
watched the a....not the road NASH, OGDEN, 11
adult An a....has ceased to grow vertically PROVERBS, MODERN, 4
His a. life resembled his childhood FENTON, JAMES, 2
adultery A....the application of democracy to love MENCKEN, H. L., 40
commit a. at one end CARY, JOYCE, 1
Do not a. commit CLOUGH, ARTHUR HUGH, 3
first breath of a. is the freest UPDIKE, JOHN, 8
I've committed a. in my heart CARTER, JIMMY, 6
rather...taken in a. than...provincialism HUXLEY, ALDOUS, 12
adults A. are obsolete children SEUSS, DR., 7
advance a. because of competence, not longevity SEMLER, RICARDO, 9
Every great a. in science DEWEY, JOHN, 21
Not to go back, is somewhat to a. POPE, ALEXANDER, 49
advanced closed operational universe of a. industrial civilization MARCUSE, HERBERT, 2
advancement a. of pure science...picking men of genius CONANT, JAMES BRYANT, 1
advantage a. not to have done anything RIVAROL, ANTOINE DE, 5
a. of time...half a victory DRAKE, FRANCIS, 1
take a....get advantage ELIOT, GEORGE, 9
The a. of doing one's praising BUTLER, SAMUEL (1835–1902), 14
you have the a. of me MARX, GROUCHO, 26
advent a. of a new age of communication and information ZELDIN, THEODORE, 6
adventurer Many will call me an a. GUEVARA, CHE, 2
adventures a. t' undertake FITZGEFFREY, CHARLES, 1
adverbs I'm glad you like a.—I adore them JAMES, HENRY, 6
adversity In his a. I ever prayed BACON, FRANCIS (1561–1626), 1
advertise It pays to a. ANONYMOUS, 77
They a. they want tourists SOUTHERN, TERRY, 1
advertisement the worst a. for Socialism ORWELL, GEORGE, 37
advertiser The business of the a. MCLUHAN, MARSHALL, 5
advertising A....arresting human intelligence long enough LEACOCK, STEPHEN, 4
a. industry thus encourages the pseudo-emancipation of women LASCH, CHRISTOPHER, 1
A. is an environmental striptease MCLUHAN, MARSHALL, 17
A. isn't a science BERNBACH, WILLIAM, 5
A. is the most fun FEMINA, JERRY DELLA, 1
A....legitimizes the idealized, stereotyped roles of women KOMISAR, LUCY, 1
a....my statement about my work KLEIN, CALVIN, 2
History will see a. as...evil MUGGERIDGE, MALCOLM, 8
Today's smartest a. style is tomorrow's corn BERNBACH, WILLIAM, 4
advice a. from people who take the subway BUFFETT, WARREN, 2
A. is seldom welcome CHESTERFIELD, LORD, 5
a....poised between the cliché RUNCIE, ROBERT, 1
A. to persons about to marry NEWSPAPERS, 1
A. would be more acceptable PROVERBS, MODERN, 3
gives nothing so freely as a. LA ROCHEFOUCAULD, FRANÇOIS, 18
how ready people always are with a. SULLIVAN, ANNE, 1
I intended to give you some a. HARRIS, GEORGE, 1
My a. to this investor BOESKY, IVAN, 4
No one wants a. STEINBECK, JOHN, 13
Parents can only give good a. FRANK, ANNE, 4
When we ask a. LAGRANGE, JOSEPH LOUIS, 2
advocaat a., a drink made from lawyers COREN, ALAN, 4
advocate I am an a. of paper money GARFIELD, JAMES A., 3
aeroplane a....destroys men and women BARNES, ERNEST WILLIAM, 1
life...never out of an a. HARVEY-JONES, JOHN, 5
thanks to the a., England has become as much a part of Europe PADMORE, GEORGE, 1
aesthetic a. experience is denied and atrophied SNYDER, GARY, 4
a. purity of absolute moral indifference O'BRIEN, TIM, 1
affair An a. wants to spill UPDIKE, JOHN, 6
affection a....in one eye, and calculation...the other DICKENS, CHARLES, 46
affections a. are habits or duties MONTHERLANT, HENRI DE, 4
a. must be confined...to a single country GALBRAITH, J. K., 2
affective A. disorders...are exaggerations STEVENS, ANTHONY, 2
affirmative action A. is affirmative evidence GILBERT, DANIEL J., JR., 1
affirmed He often a. with frequent laments ASSER, 1
affluence a. through domination of other races GANDHI, INDIRA, 4
affluent the a. society GALBRAITH, J. K., 16
The a. society...made everyone dislike work KEYNES, GEOFFREY, 1
afoot A. and light-hearted I take to the open road WHITMAN, WALT, 44
afraid are not a. to die for democracy WOODHATCH, ALEX, 2
be not a. to do thine office MORE, THOMAS, 7
man...not a. of the sea...soon be drownded SYNGE, J. M., 1
not...a. to die...don't want to be there ALLEN, WOODY, 15
We must no longer be a. of...opinions SUHARTO, 1
We were a. of the dead KINCAID, JAMAICA, 1
Who's A. of Virginia Woolf ALBEE, EDWARD, 5
Africa A. must refuse to be humiliated, exploited, and pushed around NYERERE, JULIUS KAMBARAGE, 3
A. never forgets SOBUKWE, ROBERT MANGALISO, 1
A.'s gift to world culture...Human relationships KAUNDA, KENNETH DAVID, 1
A. to me: Copper sun or scarlet sea CULLEN, COUNTEE, 3
How can I turn from A. and live WALCOTT, DEREK, 1
If you really love A., she will still give herself to you SEMBÈNE, OUSMANE, 3
more familiar with A. than my own body ORTON, JOE, 1
Only the best is good enough for A. AGGREY, JAMES EMMAN KWEGYIR, 1
only thing A. has left...the future GOLDEN, MARITA, 5
O, ye daughters of A., awake! awake! arise! STEWART, MARIA W., 1
Poverty has a home in A. HEAD, BESSIE, 4
something new out of A. PLINY THE ELDER, 9
Stolen from A., /brought to America MARLEY, BOB, 1
the hour of A.'s Redemption cometh GARVEY, MARCUS, 10
The "scramble for A." DAVIES, NORMAN, 2
underpopulated countries in A. are vastly underpolluted SUMMERS, LAWRENCE H., 1

We believe in the freedom of A. GARVEY, MARCUS, 3
What is A. to me CULLEN, COUNTEE, 1
Woman of A.. What are you not? P'BITEK, OKOT, 1
African fascinating...a night out in an A. forest KINGSLEY, MARY, 1
mind of an A....not inferior to...European LAWRENCE, GEORGE, 2
On the liberation of the A. depends the liberation of the whole world SOBUKWE, ROBERT MANGALISO, 2
The A. is conditioned...freedom of which Europe has little conception KENYATTA, JOMO, 2
the A....the burden-bearer of the world CASELY-HAYFORD, JOSEPH EPHRAIM, 2
the still-born foetus of the A. Muse SOYINKA, WOLE, 13
The two party system...unsuitable...A. state NKRUMAH, KWAME, 2
African-American A. language...very threatening ANGELOU, MAYA, 17
African history final interpretation of A. CLARKE, JOHN HENRIK, 2
Africans A. are very much like white people WALKER, ALICE, 19
A. have lived so long on promises PADMORE, GEORGE, 5
after-dinner a. conversations over the wine THOREAU, HENRY DAVID, 33
afterlife the a. will be...less exasperating COWARD, NOEL, 9
To emphasize the a. is to deny life ROBBINS, TOM, 2
against A. whom? ADLER, ALFRED, 10
He said he was a. it COOLIDGE, CALVIN, 18
I'm not a. the police HITCHCOCK, ALFRED, 9
age a. appears...best in four things BACON, FRANCIS (1561–1626), 3
A. became middle MACNEICE, LOUIS, 16
A. cannot wither her SHAKESPEARE, WILLIAM, 74
A. cannot wither her...infinite virginity WEBSTER, DANIEL, 7
A. doesn't protect you from love MOREAU, JEANNE, 2
A. is deformed, youth unkind BASTARD, THOMAS, 1
A. is our reconciliation with dullness LOWELL, ROBERT, 27
an a. in which useless knowledge was...important JOAD, C. E. M., 2
And now in a. I bud again HERBERT, GEORGE, 21
A. seldom arrives smoothly or quickly RHYS, JEAN, 3
a sign of a. if you feel PROVERBS, MODERN, 15
a. thinks better of a gilded fool DEKKER, THOMAS, 1
At twenty years of a. FRANKLIN, BENJAMIN, 24
A. will bring all things MOLIÈRE, 14
A. will not be defied BACON, FRANCIS (1561–1626), 53
a woman...treat...her a. with ambiguity RUBINSTEIN, HELENA, 1
characteristic of the present a....credulity DISRAELI, BENJAMIN, 41
I summon a. /To grant youth's heritage BROWNING, ROBERT, 34
Just at the a. 'twixt boy and youth SCOTT, SIR WALTER, 13
not of an a., but for all time SHAKESPEARE, WILLIAM, 27
Our a....nationalization of intellect BENDA, JULIEN, 1
Some people reach the a. of 60 HOOD, SAMUEL, 1
tell a woman's a. in half a minute GILBERT, W. S., 16
The mental a. of a man might be gauged DAVIES, ROBERTSON, 6
time for me to depart, for at my a. FONTENELLE, BERNARD LE BOVIER, 4
We do not necessarily improve with a. HALL, PETER, 1
what a. takes away WORDSWORTH, WILLIAM, 34
When you're my a....never risk being ill GIELGUD, JOHN, 3
aged An a. man...but a paltry thing YEATS, W. B., 38
don't object to an a. parent DICKENS, CHARLES, 36
agenda Our a. is now exhausted SPAAK, PAUL HENRI, 1
agents a....one of the lowest forms of life LEE, SPIKE, 1
age of chivalry The a. is never past KINGSLEY, CHARLES, 8
ages Nothing a. a woman like...the country COLETTE, 5
aggression the forces of a. against lawlessness QUAYLE, DAN, 7
aggressive a. female...never...done in pop HARRY, DEBORAH, 2
aggressor whole world...against an a. ATTLEE, CLEMENT, 6
agile danced in a surprisingly a. manner MELLY, GEORGE, 5
agitate I will not permit thirty men...to a. WHITE, ANDREW DICKSON, 1
agitation the a. of the subject of slavery CALHOUN, JOHN C., 3
agit-prop fed up to the teeth with a. MAYAKOVSKY, VLADIMIR, 4
agnostic a compliment to be called an a. DARROW, CLARENCE, 2
I must be meta-meta-a. HOFSTADTER, DOUGLAS R., 2
agony no a. like bearing an untold story inside you HURSTON, ZORA NEALE, 9
agree All colours will a. in the dark BACON, FRANCIS (1561–1626), 75
a. to a thing in principle BISMARCK, PRINCE OTTO VON, 23
don't say you a. with me WILDE, OSCAR, 21
I don't even a. with *myself* KIRKPATRICK, JEANE JORDAN, 1
agreeable an a. person...person who agrees with me DISRAELI, BENJAMIN, 26
agreement My people and I have come to an a. FREDERICK II (1712–86), 5
Too much a. kills a chat CLEAVER, ELDRIDGE, 4
agreements our a. with Poland...purely temporary significance HITLER, ADOLF, 21
Aids All this hooplah about A. is rubbish MCGINLEY, ROBERT, 1
A. obliges people to think of sex SONTAG, SUSAN, 11
business...stop them catching A. CURRIE, EDWINA, 4
ignorance has increased the spread of A. DIANA, PRINCESS, 3
ailments our a. are the same SWIFT, JONATHAN, 24
aim So a. above morality THOREAU, HENRY DAVID, 5
The a. of life is to live MILLER, HENRY, 15
air a. of someone...lying...to a policeman PHILIPPE, CHARLES-LOUIS, 1
fresh a. should be kept in its proper place MACAULAY, ROSE, 2
Get your room full of good a. LEACOCK, STEPHEN, 12
That a. and harmony of shape express PRIOR, MATTHEW, 5
air-conditioned in the a. train /I kissed her YUSUF, SA'DI, 1
airline In the a. business HAMEL, GARY, 8
airplane The a. stays up...doesn't have the time to fall WRIGHT, ORVILLE, 2
airplanes century of a. deserves its own music DEBUSSY, CLAUDE, 3
I feel about a. the way I feel about diets KERR, JEAN, 7
airport a....reminds me of...Butlin's GREENE, GRAHAM, 13
air-raids people /...a. were going to kill FISHER, ROY, 2
aisle A.. Altar. Hymn MUIR, FRANK, 2
Akond of Swat the A. LEAR, EDWARD, 13
Alamein Before A. we never had a victory CHURCHILL, WINSTON, 51
Alaska those who have undergone life in A. LONDON, JACK, 8
Albany They told me I saw A. MARTINEAU, HARRIET, 3
Albert that A. married beneath him COWARD, NOEL, 29
Albion perfidious A. XIMÉNEZ, AUGUSTIN, 1
album Whether an a. sells STREISAND, BARBRA, 3
alcohol A. is like love CHANDLER, RAYMOND, 4
If a. is Queen...tobacco is her consort BUÑUEL, LUIS, 5
Uncle George...discovered that a. was a food WODEHOUSE, P. G., 23
The sway of a. over mankind JAMES, WILLIAM, 32
alcoholic An a....drinks as much as you THOMAS, DYLAN, 31

ale a. from the Country of the Young YEATS, W. B., 42
as much a. as would serve him all his life SKELTON, JOHN, 5
the spicy nut-brown a. MILTON, JOHN, 114
Alexander A. wept when he heard...infinite number of worlds ALEXANDER THE GREAT, 4
If I were not A. ALEXANDER THE GREAT, 5
algebra A. and money are essentially levelers WEIL, SIMONE, 8
a....those three-cornered things BARRIE, J. M., 12
algebraically To speak a., Mr. M. is execrable POE, EDGAR ALLAN, 16
Algeria A. is French MOTTOS AND SLOGANS, 34
Alice In my sweet little A. blue gown MCCARTHY, JOSEPH (1885–1943), 1
alien the a. corn KEATS, JOHN (1795–1821), 64
alienate it didn't affront or even a. some people JORDAN, NEIL, 2
alike among so many million of faces,...none a. BROWNE, THOMAS, 26
alimony eight hundred dollars behind in a. SIMON, NEIL, 9
Judges...display, in the matter of arranging a., that reckless generosity WODEHOUSE, P. G., 7
alive All I know...is stay a. WALKER, ALICE, 22
A., we are like...black water beetle BLY, ROBERT, 2
grateful...he was still a. to eat HERR, MICHAEL, 3
if I am a. HOLLAND, HENRY FOX, 1
nobody knew whether...he would be a. the next hour FRANK, ANNE, 8
Not while I'm a., he ain't BEVAN, ANEURIN, 1
We intend to remain a. MEIR, GOLDA, 5
what matters is to come out a. BRECHT, BERTOLT, 4
all A. for one, and one for all DUMAS, ALEXANDRE, 3
A. good things...come to an end PROVERBS, 120
A. my life I've been sick and tired HAMER, FANNIE LOU, 2
A.'s well PROVERBS, 124
a. you can say is if only REED, LOU, 2
I shall never have it a. DONNE, JOHN, 33
That A., which alwayes is DONNE, JOHN, 47
Allah A. and He alone is the Hearer, the Seer, the Speaker AL-GHAZALI, 2
A....created...the earth with truth KORAN, 17
A. is the supreme Plotter KORAN, 11
A. knows, but you do not KORAN, 7
all of the credit is due to A. MALCOLM X, 13
A.'s forbidden pasturage MUHAMMAD, 14
better in A.'s estimation...smell of musk MUHAMMAD, 1
Children of A., dress well KORAN, 14
Let him who finds good praise A. MUHAMMAD, 2
unbelievers dispute the revelations of A. KORAN, 32
When A. decreed the Creation MUHAMMAD, 4
Wretched...those who deny A.'s revelations KORAN, 38
Allen Woody A. or me when we stop doing the jokes SIMON, NEIL, 14
alliance A....the union of two thieves BIERCE, AMBROSE, 5
policy to steer clear of permanent a. WASHINGTON, GEORGE, 3
allies I have no a. save your valor FREDERICK II (1712–86), 2
Thou hast great a. WORDSWORTH, WILLIAM, 76
allowed I should never be a. out in private CHURCHILL, RANDOLPH (1911–68), 3
ally An a. has to be watched TROTSKY, LEON, 10
almighty The a. dollar NEWSPAPERS, 17
Almighty Do you not believe that the A. HENRY V, 1
If the A. himself played the violin HEIFETZ, JASCHA, 1
almonds Don't eat too many a. BENÉT, STEPHEN VINCENT, 3
alms The a. of nine things are obligatory KHOMEINI, RUHOLLAH, 5
almsgiving A. tends to perpetuate poverty PERÓN, EVA, 3
Aloha *A.*–love, I love you, my love to you LONDON, JACK, 7
alone A., alone, all, all alone COLERIDGE, SAMUEL TAYLOR, 43
all a. with the quiet day JAMES, HENRY, 34
All we ask is to be let a. DAVIS, JEFFERSON, 1
better to be a. than in bad company WASHINGTON, GEORGE, 5
feel completely a....leads to mental disintegration FROMM, ERICH, 20
He never is a....with noble thoughts FLETCHER, JOHN, 7
I want to be a. GARBO, GRETA, 5
I was utterly a. with the sun and the earth JEFFERIES, RICHARD, 4
Never less a. than when alone ROGERS, SAMUEL, 6
never less a. than when by myself GIBBON, EDWARD, 2
only when a....the infant can discover WINNICOTT, DONALD W., 1
powerful but a. VIGNY, ALFRED DE, 3
The right to be let a. BRANDEIS, LOUIS D., 2
To be a....fate of...great minds SCHOPENHAUER, ARTHUR, 3
Very well, a. LOW, DAVID, 1
We perish'd, each a. COWPER, WILLIAM, 16
We two a. will sing like birds i' the cage SHAKESPEARE, WILLIAM, 372
You come into the world a. MIRREN, HELEN, 1
You'll Never Walk A. HAMMERSTEIN, OSCAR, II, 1
alphabet learning the remaining twenty-two letters of the a. ORWELL, GEORGE, 9
The simpler the a. MIRÓ, JOAN, 8
alter I dare not a. these things AUSTIN, ALFRED, 1
alternative only a. to a balance of power NIXON, RICHARD, 14
alternative fuels economically and environmentally attractive a. RAYMOND, LEE R., 1
alway lo, I am with you a. BIBLE, 442
always There is a. something left to love HANSBERRY, LORRAINE, 1
am I A. THAT I AM BIBLE, 71
amateur a....artist who supports himself with outside jobs SHAHN, BEN, 1
amateurs a disease that afflicts a. CHESTERTON, G. K., 21
amaze How vainly men themselves a. MARVELL, ANDREW, 4
amazement look with a. on our audacity WRIGHT, ORVILLE, 1
amazing a. how nice people are ARLEN, MICHAEL, 2
ambassador a....honest man sent to lie abroad WOTTON, HENRY, 2
ambition A....a great man's madness WEBSTER, JOHN, 1
a great a. to die of exhaustion GROSSART, ANGUS, 1
A., in a private man a vice MASSINGER, PHILIP, 1
A. is the grand enemy of all peace POWYS, JOHN COWPER, 1
a. is the serious business of life SCOTT, SIR WALTER, 4
A man without a. is dead BAILEY, PEARL, 1
an a. to be a wag JOHNSON, SAMUEL, 52
a. of a Latin-American revolutionary BURKE, BILLIE, 1
A. should be made of sterner stuff SHAKESPEARE, WILLIAM, 314
Let not A. mock GRAY, THOMAS, 5
man in whom a....only suspended, the sentiments of religion CROMWELL, OLIVER, 1
Vaulting a., which o'er-leaps itself SHAKESPEARE, WILLIAM, 394
ambitious an a. man has as many masters LA BRUYÈRE, JEAN DE, 3
the very substance of the a. SHAKESPEARE, WILLIAM, 161
America A. as the paradigm of individualism FUKUYAMA, FRANCIS, 8
A....based on the dreams of spinsters RUSSELL, BERTRAND, 11

A. cannot be an ostrich WILSON, WOODROW, 20
A. died of the delusion she had moral leadership ROGERS, WILL, 12
A. does not consist of groups WILSON, WOODROW, 19
affection for A., but I hate her institution of slavery BROWN, WILLIAM WELLS, 2
A. found an absolute other...Nation of Islam ABUBAKER HADDAD, Y., 1
A....great inter-racial laboratory FAUSET, CRYSTAL BIRD, 1
A....has gone directly from barbarism to degeneration CLEMENCEAU, GEORGES, 10
A. has the best-dressed poverty HARRINGTON, MICHAEL, 1
A. is a hurricane MAILER, NORMAN, 4
A. is a vast conspiracy UPDIKE, JOHN, 14
A. is false to the past DOUGLASS, FREDERICK, 2
A. is not a young land BURROUGHS, WILLIAM S., 7
A. is the child society par excellence SHAPIRO, KARL, 2
A. is the greatest of opportunities SANTAYANA, GEORGE, 12
A. is the ultimate denial of the theory of man's continuous evolution BROWN, H. RAP, 1
A., I've given you all GINSBERG, ALLEN, 2
A. knows nothing of food, love...art DUNCAN, ISADORA, 3
A. must revive a nineteenth-century habit CLINTON, BILL, 16
A....nearer to the final triumph over poverty HOOVER, HERBERT, 6
A. needs a new approach to economics CLINTON, BILL, 13
A....never intended to be a nation ARMSTRONG, MICHAEL, 1
A. our nation has been beaten DOSTOYEVSKY, ANNA, 3
A....ourselves, with the Barbarians quite left out ARNOLD, MATTHEW, 17
A....prematurely old, as a fruit which rotted MILLER, HENRY, 9
A.'s freedom...the world expires BUSH, GEORGE, 12
A. should thank God for its gangsters BELLOW, SAUL, 7
A.'s neutrality is ineffectual WILSON, WOODROW, 7
A.'s present need is...normalcy HARDING, WARREN G., 3
A.'s really only a kind of Russia BURGESS, ANTHONY, 3
A. the beautiful...Burger King and Dairy Queen HUXTABLE, ADA LOUISE, 2
A. wants to establish reassurance through Imitation ECO, UMBERTO, 15
A. was discovered accidentally MORISON, SAMUEL ELIOT, 1
A., with all of its evils and faults GREGORY, DICK, 8
A....woven of many strands ELLISON, RALPH, 1
Being here in A. doesn't make you an American MALCOLM X, 6
come to pass in the heart of A. EISENHOWER, DWIGHT D., 15
don't measure A. by its achievement CHISHOLM, SHIRLEY, 1
Everybody in A. was supposed to grab VONNEGUT, KURT, 1
heart and mind of A....baseball BARZUN, JACQUES, 7
in A. anyone can be President FORD, GERALD, 4
In A....merger means: Increase our salaries CHEVALIER, MICHEL, 1
In A. possibilities always exist KLEIN, CALVIN, 3
in A. there are 20 million black people MALCOLM X, 9
Is it good for A. EISENHOWER, DWIGHT D., 24
I've come to look for A. SIMON, PAUL, 1
I wish for an A....alert HARDING, WARREN G., 4
Let A. be America again HUGHES, LANGSTON, 6
may A. awake from the apathy FORTEN, JAMES, 1
Men of A., the problem is plain DU BOIS, W. E. B., 11
most memorable epoch in the history of A. ADAMS, JOHN, 4
never again be able to show myself in A. HAMSUN, KNUT, 1
nothing wrong with A....right with America CLINTON, BILL, 21
spiritual and political loneliness of A. SNYDER, GARY, 8
terrible spirits, ghosts, in...A. LAWRENCE, D. H., 16
The Midwesterner...black American...certain they are the real A. ANGELOU, MAYA, 12
the true power and spirit of A. NORRIS, FRANK, 4
The true religion of A. has always been America MAILER, NORMAN, 24
They want an A. as good as its promise JORDAN, BARBARA, 1
things that will destroy A. ROOSEVELT, THEODORE, 7
Those who find A. an especially violent...country GENOVESE, EUGENE D., 1
to be willing to grant A. independence GEORGE III, 1
When A. is stronger...world is safer BUSH, GEORGE, 6
Why will A. not reach out...to Russia DUNCAN, ISADORA, 2
You cannot conquer A. PITT THE ELDER, WILLIAM, 12

American A. cinema...ruin French cinema GODARD, JEAN-LUC, 2
A. cities are like badger holes STEINBECK, JOHN, 18
a constant in the average A. imagination ECO, UMBERTO, 16
A. continents...not to be considered /as subjects for future colonization MONROE, JAMES, 2
A. corporations should abandon their old adversary FOX, HARRISON W., JR., 2
A. credit card...good as American gold BELLAMY, EDWARD, 3
A. democracy and the American economy FUKUYAMA, FRANCIS, 1
A. flag which Mrs. Peary gave me fifteen years ago PEARY, ROBERT EDWIN, 6
A. flag will gloat over CLARK, KENNETH (1850–1921), 1
A. freedom consists largely in talking nonsense HOWE, EDGAR WATSON, 3
A. heiress wants to buy a man MCCARTHY, MARY, 14
A. history...perceived...as a luxury DEGLER, CARL N., 2
A. leader class has really had it NIXON, RICHARD, 31
All modern A. literature TWAIN, MARK, 3
A. males must...have vasectomies BEALE, BETTY, 1
A. model...a form of state capitalism IGNATIEFF, MICHAEL, 1
An A. dialect will therefore be formed JEFFERSON, THOMAS, 23
An A. is either a Jew, or an anti-Semite SARTRE, JEAN-PAUL, 20
An A. town...amusing itself ANDERSON, SHERWOOD, 3
A. Nazis were all fanatics MAILER, NORMAN, 16
A. people will not stand up...rights VERONA, VIRGINIA, 1
a point of pride for the A. male COSBY, BILL, 5
A. society...half judaised and half negrified HITLER, ADOLF, 37
A. society has tried so hard GOODMAN, PAUL, 3
A. society is a...pond ADAMS, HENRY, 3
A. system of rugged individualism HOOVER, HERBERT, 7
average A. loves his family TWAIN, MARK, 2
A. Way is...essentially destructive KRONENBERGER, LOUIS, 3
A. way of looking at things MILLER, HENRY, 10
first A. to make sex funny LOOS, ANITA, 1
his twoness—an A., a Negro DU BOIS, W. E. B., 13
If I were an A., as I am an Englishman PITT THE ELDER, WILLIAM, 8
I hate A. simplicity JAMES, HENRY, 41
in love with A. names BENÉT, STEPHEN VINCENT, 1
In this country A. means white MORRISON, TONI, 29
I see an A. nightmare MALCOLM X, 5
I was born an A. WEBSTER, DANIEL, 5
one of my Goddamn precious A. rights UPDIKE, JOHN, 15
send A. boys nine or ten thousand miles JOHNSON, LYNDON BAINES, 10
the A. abroad STAPLEDON, OLAF, 1
The A. public...wants to be amused DUNBAR-NELSON, ALICE, 1
The great A. war chest O'BRIEN, TIM, 3

the greatest A. friend we have ever known CHURCHILL, WINSTON, 55
We A. blacks call that "soul." HIMES, CHESTER, 2
We are all A. at puberty WAUGH, EVELYN, 36
What then is the A. CRÈVECOEUR, JEAN DE, 5
When A. life is most American ELLISON, RALPH, 7
Without God...no A. form of government EISENHOWER, DWIGHT D., 26
You are living in A. society now CHANG, S. K., 1

American-Canadian the truth about A. relations MARTIN, CHESTER BAILEY, 1

American dream The A. is not dead JORDAN, BARBARA, 2
The A. turned belly up VONNEGUT, KURT, 4

Americanism hyphenated A. ROOSEVELT, THEODORE, 26

Americanized consider yourself A. MAUROIS, ANDRÉ, 4

American Negro The A. has changed his temper ROBESON, PAUL, 5

American Revolution A. had produced...Declaration of Independence MORISON, SAMUEL ELIOT, 3

Americans A. are people who prefer the Continent LUCAS, E. V., 1
A. are splendid while working SNYDER, GARY, 6
A. are the old inhabitants GOODMAN, PAUL, 5
A. cannot build airplanes GOERING, HERMANN, 2
A. expect to be loved SOYINKA, WOLE, 5
A. have a perfect right to exist BEERBOHM, MAX, 13
A. have been conditioned to respect newness UPDIKE, JOHN, 2
A. have plenty of everything KEATS, JOHN (b.1920), 1
A. love being conned REED, ISHMAEL, 2
A....projecting a pioneering spirit SAID, EDWARD W., 1
A....rather live next to a pervert BARRY, DAVE, 2
A. speaking their own language carefully PYNCHON, THOMAS, 9
A. think of themselves...as a huge rescue squad CLEAVER, ELDRIDGE, 7
A....weaker because of their vulnerability EINSTEIN, ALBERT, 17
A. were originally thrifty ZELDIN, THEODORE, 1
A. worship the almighty dollar TWAIN, MARK, 48
because A. won't listen to sense KEYNES, JOHN MAYNARD, 2
Black A. in West Africa ANGELOU, MAYA, 2
dear A., whip your horses WHITMAN, WALT, 50
Good A....go to Paris APPLETON, THOMAS GOLD, 1
Irish A....as Irish as Black Americans are African GELDOF, BOB, 3
more A. went to symphonies than...baseball KENNEDY, JOHN FITZGERALD, 37
the A. fought for souvenirs TRUMAN, HARRY S., 13
the matter with A. CHESTERTON, G. K., 23
We A. seem not to realize BAILEY, THOMAS A., 5
when good A. die they go to Paris WILDE, OSCAR, 17
When will A....encourage liberty BROWN, WILLIAM WELLS, 3

amiable It was an a. weakness SHERIDAN, RICHARD BRINSLEY, 5

amnesia a. is the most wished-for state GUARE, JOHN, 2

amo Odi et a. CATULLUS, 5

amplified I'm being a. by the mike CHESTERTON, G. K., 50

Amstrad At A. we want your money SUGAR, ALAN, 1

amused We are not a. VICTORIA, 8

amusement ancient a. of shooting the Christmas turkey COOPER, JAMES FENIMORE, 17

amusement park treating your body like an a. DAVID, LARRY, 1

amusements no a....but vice and religion! SMITH, SYDNEY, 25

amusing Any a. deaths lately BOWRA, MAURICE, 1

analogy a. is...the least misleading thing BUTLER, SAMUEL (1835–1902), 34

analysis a. of the effects of early disturbances KLEIN, MELANIE, 1

analyst a. thinks it "unscientific"...moral values HORNEY, KAREN, 10
suggestions of the a....never be proven MERLEAU-PONTY, MAURICE, 7

analysts Like all a....interested only in himself VIDAL, GORE, 6

analytical abandoned minute a. method LEHRER, KEITH, 1

anarchy partial training in a. CAGE, JOHN, 1

anathema a. to the name of France DESSALINES, JEAN JACQUES, 1

anatomists We a. are like the porters FONTENELLE, BERNARD LE BOVIER, 3

anatomy A. is destiny FREUD, SIGMUND, 26
in a....better to have learned and lost MAUGHAM, SOMERSET, 19
My a. is only part of an infinitely complex organisation CARTER, ANGELA, 6

ancestor I am my own a. JUNOT, ANDOCHE, DUC D'ABRANTÈS, 1

ancestors a. on either side of the Battle of Hastings LEE, HARPER, 2
a....the last people I should choose SHERIDAN, RICHARD BRINSLEY, 12
To acknowledge our a. means we are aware WALKER, ALICE, 17
when his half-civilized a. were hunting BENJAMIN, JUDAH, 2

ancestral A. voices prophesying war COLERIDGE, SAMUEL TAYLOR, 16

ancestry I can trace my a....primordial atomic globule GILBERT, W. S., 26

ancient a. as the sun BRYANT, WILLIAM CULLEN, 2
Let the a. serve the present MAO ZEDONG, 34
move beyond these a. texts NASREEN, TASLIMA, 1
the a. glory of your Rome FREDERICK I, 1

androids Do A. Dream of Electric Sheep DICK, PHILIP K., 5

anesthetics Three natural a. HOLMES, OLIVER WENDELL, 17

angel a....gazing at the violent abyss STEVENS, WALLACE, 11
a. to pass, flying slowly FIRBANK, RONALD, 1
contemplates an a. in his future self EMERSON, RALPH WALDO, 28
drive an a. from your door BLAKE, WILLIAM, 29
the a. of the Lord smote him BIBLE, 16
You may not be an a. DUBIN, AL, 1

angels A. can fly CHESTERTON, G. K., 30
a little lower than the a. MAP, WALTER, 2
as a. in some brighter dreams VAUGHAN, HENRY, 8
I told my desolation a. goodbye KEROUAC, JACK, 2
ne'er like a. till our passion dies DEKKER, THOMAS, 5
on the side of the a. DISRAELI, BENJAMIN, 44
on the side of the a. OPPENHEIMER, HARRY, 1

anger A. can be an effective negotiating tool MCCORMACK, MARK, 8
A. has no eyes PROVERBS, 62
A. is a momentary madness HORACE, 19
A. is an emotion that has some hope in it MINGUS, CHARLES, 5
A. is never without an argument SAVILE, SIR GEORGE, 2
A. is one of the sinews of the soul FULLER, THOMAS (1608–61), 3
A. makes dull men witty ELIZABETH I, 15
a. makes us all stupid SPYRI, JOHANNA, 2
A....policeman and a foul cunning slave AL-NAWAWI, MUHYID-DIN ABU ZAKARIYYA IBN SHARAF, 6
he that is slow to a. is better than the mighty BIBLE, 459
peculiar...a. women my age...feel SWARTLEY, ARIEL, 1
There is a sense of being in a. MORRISON, TONI, 25

angler in...scrupulous veracity...the experienced a. JEROME, JEROME K., 11

angles Not A., but angels GREGORY I, SAINT, 1

angling A. is somewhat like poetry WALTON, IZAAK, 2
say of a. as Dr. Boteler said of strawberries WALTON, IZAAK, 5

Anglo-Saxon Come in, you A. swine BEHAN, BRENDAN, 12

Anglo-Saxons A. have a love affair...manipulative ethos BENNIS, WARREN, 4
angry An a. man is always a stupid man ACHEBE, CHINUA, 1
a. with a man for loving himself BACON, FRANCIS (1561–1626), 57
A. Young Man PAUL, LESLIE, 1
cannot be a. at God BEAUVOIR, SIMONE DE, 3
gets a. at the right things ARISTOTLE, 18
I was a. with my friend BLAKE, WILLIAM, 21
not one of those "a. feminists" STEINEM, GLORIA, 7
Speak when you are a. PETER, LAURENCE J., 2
whenever you are a. PLUTARCH, 2
when very a., swear TWAIN, MARK, 30
anguish we are a. SARTRE, JEAN-PAUL, 5
world's a. is caused by people FAULKNER, WILLIAM, 10
animal a. capacity for happiness MASSON, JEFFREY, 3
A. life is biologically aesthetic HILLMAN, JAMES, 1
Any a....would...acquire a moral sense DARWIN, CHARLES, 9
"Are you a.—or vegetable—or mineral?" CARROLL, LEWIS, 49
fight against a. overpopulation BARDOT, BRIGITTE, 1
He was into a. husbandry LEHRER, TOM, 1
I'm like an a. trapped PASTERNAK, BORIS, 9
My a., my age MANDELSTAM, OSIP, 11
true to your a. instincts LAWRENCE, D. H., 51
animals A. are such agreeable friends ELIOT, GEORGE, 23
a. don't always speak with their mouths LOFTING, HUGH, 1
a....exist for their own reasons WALKER, ALICE, 32
All a. are equal ORWELL, GEORGE, 10
all a. were created...for the use of man PEACOCK, THOMAS LOVE, 7
But if we stop loving a. SOLZHENITSYN, ALEXANDER, 6
capturing a. and writing poems HUGHES, TED, 5
I could...live with a. WHITMAN, WALT, 33
love a. and children too much SARTRE, JEAN-PAUL, 32
Never work with a. or children MOTTOS AND SLOGANS, 25
The a. of the planet are in desperate peril WALKER, ALICE, 9
The a. went in one by one FOLK VERSE, 44
There are two things for which a. are...envied VOLTAIRE, 9
Wild a. never kill for sport FROUDE, J. A., 2
animate To a., in the precise sense GARCÍA LORCA, FEDERICO, 2
animated he was a. with the soul of a Briton VOLTAIRE, 1
Ankara A. might be able...drain the sea KEMAL, YASAR, 2
annihilating A. all that's made MARVELL, ANDREW, 5
annihilation I undertake to face the possibility of a. FANON, FRANTZ, 1
anniversaries More a. of national humiliation than...festivals BING XIN, 1
annuity Buy an a. cheap DICKENS, CHARLES, 50
annus it has turned out to be an "a. horribilis." ELIZABETH II, 1
anon A....was often a woman WOOLF, VIRGINIA, 5
answer a. a fool according to his folly BIBLE, 461
But a. came there none CARROLL, LEWIS, 34
I am here to a. YOUNG, BRIGHAM, 2
I can a. but for three things WASHINGTON, GEORGE, 10
If somebody yells "Hey stranger!" don't a. BRODSKY, JOSEPH, 5
I'll a. some of your questions SMITH, ROLAND, 1
right a. is the best answer MCNEALY, SCOTT, 1
There ain't no a. STEIN, GERTRUDE, 4
What *is* the a. STEIN, GERTRUDE, 14
answered They only a. "Little Liar!" BELLOC, HILAIRE, 14
antagonistic the most a. to the Victorian age DICKENS, CHARLES, 1
anthem national a. belongs to the eighteenth century SHAW, GEORGE BERNARD, 117
anthology a....a complete dispensary of medicine GRAVES, ROBERT, 6
a. is like all the plums and orange peel picked out of a cake RALEIGH, WALTER ALEXANDER, 1
anthropologists a. see...insanity is culturally defined PIRSIG, ROBERT T., 4
anticipate What we a. seldom occurs DISRAELI, BENJAMIN, 20
anti-communism The psychological impact of a. DAVIS, ANGELA, 4
antidote the a. to desire CONGREVE, WILLIAM, 25
anti-establishment I never tried to be a. GAULTIER, JEAN PAUL, 1
antipathy strong a. of good to bad POPE, ALEXANDER, 37
antiquity A....created to provide professors GONCOURT, EDMOND DE, 2
anti-Semitism A....a movement among civilized nations HERZL, THEODOR, 7
antiseptic Since the a. treatment LISTER, JOSEPH, 1
anti-slavery The history of a. begins APTHEKER, HERBERT, 3
antivivisectionists There are a few honest a. HALDANE, J. B. S., 4
anti-white not a., but anti-wrong KAUNDA, KENNETH DAVID, 5
ants closer to the a. than to the butterflies BRENAN, GERALD, 3
anxiety A. can be described as unresolved fear WOLPERT, LEWIS, 1
the Age of A., the age of the neurosis KRONENBERGER, LOUIS, 2
the a. of being a woman BEAUVOIR, SIMONE DE, 19
anxious a. to do the wrong thing correctly SAKI, 12
I am a....for the survival of Israel YEHOSHUA, A. B., 1
anyone a. here whom I have not insulted BRAHMS, JOHANNES, 3
a. who has worked for GM KELLER, MARYANN, 2
apart We have stood a., studiously neutral WILSON, WOODROW, 11
apartheid closed the book on a. DE KLERK, F. W., 1
I want a. destroyed, not reformed TUTU, DESMOND, 9
We don't want a. liberalized TUTU, DESMOND, 5
apathy where the a. is KENNEDY, FLORYNCE R., 1
ape having an a. for his grandfather HUXLEY, T. H., 2
How like us is...the a. ENNIUS, QUINTUS, 3
the a. from which he is descended WILBERFORCE, SAMUEL, 2
Apennines the A. once stood up in a sea LEONARDO DA VINCI, 16
apéritif a. is the evensong of the French MORAND, PAUL, 3
aphorists The great a. CANETTI, ELIAS, 13
apocalypse *A. Now* is not about Vietnam COPPOLA, FRANCIS FORD, 1
To prepare it...for another A. QASIM, SAMIH, 2
apologies A....do not alter DISRAELI, BENJAMIN, 2
apologize a good rule in life never to a. WODEHOUSE, P. G., 24
It's too late to a. TOSCANINI, ARTURO, 7
apophthegm The a. "Know thyself" is his THALES, 1
apoplexy A. is an affection of the head SMITH, SYDNEY, 5
apostle the a. of class-hatred MARX, KARL, 6
apparatus the transmitting a. of animals...more efficient LORENZ, KONRAD, 2
apparel a. oft proclaims the man SHAKESPEARE, WILLIAM, 150
apparition a. of these faces POUND, EZRA, 11
When I first beheld this a. POE, EDGAR ALLAN, 6
appear not wish to a. the best AESCHYLUS, 6
appearance secret of a successful a. SITWELL, EDITH, 7
appearances A. are deceptive PROVERBS, 140
A. are not...a clue to the truth COMPTON-BURNETT, IVY, 2

Keep up a. CHURCHILL, CHARLES, 4
appeaser An a. is one who feeds a crocodile CHURCHILL, WINSTON, 76
appendix mustn't take out a man's a. HEALEY, DENIS, 4
appetite A. comes with eating RABELAIS, FRANÇOIS, 1
appetites Subdue your a. my dears DICKENS, CHARLES, 58
applause A. is a receipt SCHNABEL, ARTUR, 4
Amid the a. of the West GORBACHEV, MIKHAIL, 3
I want to thank you for stopping the a. KISSINGER, HENRY, 17
seasoning of a play...the a. JONSON, BEN, 28
win the a. but lose the fight MOHAMAD, MAHATHIR BIN, 3
apple An a. a day PROVERBS, 131
as the a. of his eye BIBLE, 40
My a. trees will never...eat the cones FROST, ROBERT, 16
Apple A. has to be more pragmatic JOBS, STEVE, 2
apple pie a. and cheese FIELD, EUGENE, 1
apple-pie An a. without some cheese PROVERBS, 132
application a. is also learning MAO ZEDONG, 6
applied sciences There are no such things as a. PASTEUR, LOUIS, 3
appreciate never a. anything if you...hurry FITZGERALD, ELLA, 2
apprehend In reality we a. nothing for certain DEMOCRITUS, 2
apprehension The a. that one is someone else PAMUK, ORHAN, 3
approaching we are a. the limits of something SNYDER, GARY, 9
approved I never a....the errors of his book VOLTAIRE, 25
approves He who a. evil PROVERBS, 477
April A. is the cruellest month ELIOT, T. S., 49
A., /Laugh thy girlish laughter WATSON, WILLIAM, 1
And after A., when May follows BROWNING, ROBERT, 23
A. of your youth HERBERT, EDWARD, 1
Men are A. when they woo SHAKESPEARE, WILLIAM, 117
Sweet A. showers /Do spring May flowers TUSSER, THOMAS, 1
Aprill Whan that A. with his shoures soote CHAUCER, GEOFFREY, 14
apron an a. is merely tying himself with a rope TUTUOLA, AMOS, 1
Aquarius the dawning of the age of A. RADO, JAMES, 1
Arab like an A. stallion I smelled...rain QABBANI, NIZAR, 4
The A. who builds himself a hut FRANCE, ANATOLE, 4
Arabic A. language is not a foreign language HUSAYN, TAHA, 1
Arabs A. and the Jews...cousins in race FAISAL, 1
A. today...see a travesty of modernism KABBANI, RANA, 1
can a Westerner believe...A. have culture SHAYKH, HANAN AL-, 1
archaeologist An a. is the best husband CHRISTIE, AGATHA, 8
An a. of morning OLSON, CHARLES, 11
Archangel Gabriel If I were the A. MENZIES, ROBERT, 2
Archelaus A prating barber asked A. PLUTARCH, 1
archeologists A. dig up dirt on each other ADVERTISEMENTS, 3
arches a. in Rome...prototype of the billboard VENTURI, ROBERT, 3
Archimedes rather have the fame of A. ARCHIMEDES, 1
truths...A. would have sacrificed his life RENAN, ERNEST, 9
architect an a....should be not only correct, but entertaining RUSKIN, JOHN, 14
An a. should live as little in cities RUSKIN, JOHN, 18
An a.'s most useful tools WRIGHT, FRANK LLOYD, 4
a. of his own fate CLAUDIUS CAECUS, APPIUS, 1
A.: one who drafts a plan BIERCE, AMBROSE, 7
A....should...understand the principles of Geometry SERLIO, SEBASTIANO, 1
No person who is not a...painter can be an a. RUSKIN, JOHN, 2
architects Good a. nurture...psychological, mental, and spiritual needs HICKMAN, CRAIG R., 3
architecture A....art of how to waste space JOHNSON, PHILIP, 1
A. begins where engineering ends GROPIUS, WALTER, 1
A. completes nature DE CHIRICO, GIORGIO, 1
A. concerns itself only with those characters RUSKIN, JOHN, 19
A....*end* is to build well WOTTON, HENRY, 5
A. has its political use WREN, CHRISTOPHER, 1
A. in general is frozen music SCHELLING, FRIEDRICH WILHELM JOSEPH VON, 1
A. is inhabited sculpture BRANCUSI, CONSTANTIN, 2
A. is...life itself taking form WRIGHT, FRANK LLOYD, 2
A. is not in the empty building PELLI, CESAR, 1
A. is the most inescapable QUINTON, ANTHONY, 2
A....many notable Arts SERLIO, SEBASTIANO, 2
a. or revolution LE CORBUSIER, 3
A....play of masses brought together in light LE CORBUSIER, 2
Modern a. is the absence of style TERRY, QUINLAN, 1
modern, harmonic and lively a. GROPIUS, WALTER, 2
No a. is so haughty RUSKIN, JOHN, 13
Orthodox modern a. is progressive VENTURI, ROBERT, 1
Style in a....form that expression takes JONES, OWEN, 1
tin-can a. in a tin-horn culture ANONYMOUS, 29
Water is the wine of a. HUXTABLE, ADA LOUISE, 3
Argentina Don't Cry for me A. RICE, TIM, 1
arguing I am not a. with you WHISTLER, JAMES ABBOTT MCNEILL, 3
argument a. be intricate...to confound the court WYCHERLEY, WILLIAM, 3
All a. is against it, but all belief is for it BOSWELL, JAMES, 2
A man who criticizes the length...a. PLATO, 9
I have found you an a. JOHNSON, SAMUEL, 165
I love a., I love debate THATCHER, MARGARET, 31
power of *stating* an a. ELIOT, GEORGE, 2
some a. for suffrage MILLER, KELLY, 1
to get the best of an a. CARNEGIE, DALE, 1
arguments A. are to be avoided WILDE, OSCAR, 75
beware of long a. and long beards SANTAYANA, GEORGE, 8
though we have mastered...a. of Plato DESCARTES, RENÉ, 15
What's the point of...a. that prove nothing WITTGENSTEIN, LUDWIG, 14
aridity scorched a. of /the Mexican plateau WILLIAMS, WILLIAM CARLOS, 4
arise A., O Lord, plead Thine own cause LEO X, 1
I will a. and...go to Innisfree YEATS, W. B., 30
aristocracy An a. in a republic is like a chicken whose head has been cut off MITFORD, NANCY, 2
British a....jaundiced eye on its younger sons WODEHOUSE, P. G., 28
There is always an a. in art MIRÓ, JOAN, 3
aristocratic To be a. in Art MOORE, GEORGE, 7
aristocrats A. don't have...chips on their shoulders ATTALAH, NAIM, 1
Aristotle A. was but the rubbish of an Adam ARISTOTLE, 3
If A. had spoken Chinese MAUTHNER, FRITZ, 1
arithmetic foundations of a., seem to vanish RUSSELL, BERTRAND, 1
ark an a. of bulrushes BIBLE, 67
into the a., two and two BIBLE, 117
They shall make an a. of shittim wood BIBLE, 86
Arkansas I met a traveler from A. FROST, ROBERT, 13
ark of the covenant The priests brought in the a. BIBLE, 187
arm An a. /Rose up from...the lake TENNYSON, ALFRED, 17
Don't carry away that a. till I have...my ring RAGLAN, LORD, 2
taking the a. of an elm tree THOREAU, HENRY DAVID, 1

A work of a....has something which is anonymous WEIL, SIMONE, 1
bad a. is still art DUCHAMP, MARCEL, 1
become a work of a. myself...not an artist BERENSON, BERNARD, 3
excellence of every a. is its intensity KEATS, JOHN (1795–1821), 44
extremely important that a. be unjustifiable RAUSCHENBERG, ROBERT, 1
Fine a. is that in which the hand RUSKIN, JOHN, 22
function of a....not to illustrate a truth ROBBE-GRILLET, ALAIN, 2
goal of all a. is...to explain TARKOVSKY, ANDREY, 1
great...a. bears its meaning on its face JAMES, C. L. R., 12
I don't want a. for a few MORRIS, WILLIAM, 6
If a. is to confront AIDS more honestly WHITE, EDMUND, 1
if we go on, a. is labor DAY, CLARENCE SHEPARD, 5
I have loved A....better than myself HAYDON, BENJAMIN ROBERT, 1
I just wanna raise...a. and culture BEEFHEART, CAPTAIN, 1
In a., banality...becomes extraordinary BUREN, DANIEL, 1
In a. economy is always beauty JAMES, HENRY, 15
In a. there is liberation BERDYAEV, NIKOLAI, 1
Modern a. is what happens CIARDI, JOHN, 1
modern a. means...new ways to express yourself BOURGEOIS, LOUISE, 2
Modern a....where signs become symbols KANDINSKY, WASSILY, 1
nation's a....reflects...its people HOPPER, EDWARD, 1
Nothing important in high a. is happening PAGLIA, CAMILLE, 2
only a. that fully corresponds with...Christian belief WAGNER, RICHARD, 5
present role of a....powerlessness CHICAGO, JUDY, 1
Real a....to make us nervous SONTAG, SUSAN, 2
the a. of motorcycle maintenance PIRSIG, ROBERT T., 6
The a. world is a jungle HAMMER, ARMAND, 2
The difference between a. and life BUKOWSKI, CHARLES, 7
What is ugly in A. RODIN, AUGUSTE, 2
world of a....freedom and progress...main objectives BEETHOVEN, LUDWIG VAN, 5
you have to love your a. BONHEUR, ROSA, 1

Artful Dodger The A. DICKENS, CHARLES, 68

artificial a. wealth a masterpiece of human achievement BRAUDEL, FERNAND, 1
nothing so a. as sinning nowadays LAWRENCE, D. H., 45

artificial respiration He said it was a. BURGESS, ANTHONY, 5

artist a. has a tendency to reproduce...own likeness CARDUCHO, VICENTE, 1
a....must beware of the literary spirit CÉZANNE, PAUL, 2
a. must know how to convince PICASSO, PABLO, 16
a. must scorn...judgment CÉZANNE, PAUL, 3
an a. becomes...a woman he...painted ANONYMOUS, 47
An a....creature driven by demons FAULKNER, WILLIAM, 9
An a....has invented an artist ROSENBERG, HAROLD, 1
an a....having a limitless curiosity IMAMURA SHOHEI, 1
An a....produces things that people don't need WARHOL, ANDY, 9
an a. to taste a bit of madness ARMAH, AYI KWEI, 2
As an a., a man has no home NIETZSCHE, FRIEDRICH WILHELM, 13
a. who makes himself accessible is self-destructive BARKER, HOWARD, 2
Being an a. means ceasing ORTEGA Y GASSET, JOSÉ, 17
Being an a. now...question the nature of art KOSUTH, JOSEPH, 1
believe only what an a. does HOCKNEY, DAVID, 2
Beware of the a. who's an intellectual FITZGERALD, F. SCOTT, 21
classical a....recognized by his sincerity PÉGUY, CHARLES PIERRE, 15
Every a. who makes it big JOHN, ELTON, 2
Every a. writes his own autobiography ELLIS, HAVELOCK, 10
I do not believe any a. works in...fever GARCÍA LORCA, FEDERICO, 3
Like any a. with no art form she became dangerous MORRISON, TONI, 20
Never trust the a. LAWRENCE, D. H., 48
No a. is ahead of his time GRAHAM, MARTHA, 4
only one position for an a. anywhere THOMAS, DYLAN, 32
Remember I'm an a. CARY, JOYCE, 2
Show me any a. who wants to be respectable GRAHAM, MARTHA, 3
The aim of every a. FAULKNER, WILLIAM, 11
The a....is always an anarchist GARCÍA LORCA, FEDERICO, 6
The a. is like the hand that holds and moves the mirror NGUGI WA THIONGO, 1
The a., like the God of the creation JOYCE, JAMES, 9
The a.'s hand is more powerful PASTERNAK, BORIS, 2
The great a....conquers the romantic MILLER, HENRY, 3

artiste no...resignation for an a. in the music industry MICHAEL, GEORGE, 1

artistic more obdurate to a. treatment than...carnal FORSTER, E. M., 3
There never was an a. period WHISTLER, JAMES ABBOTT MCNEILL, 16

artists A common vice among a....mental cowardice MANZONI, PIERO, 1
a. dream...silence MURDOCH, IRIS, 14
A. go through periodic crises TÀPIES, ANTONI, 2
a. have become the most important people RICHTER, GERHARD, 1
A....live mainly in the red PEARCE, LORD, 1
A. often depend on the manipulation of symbols SERRANO, ANDRES, 1
Great a. have no country MUSSET, ALFRED DE, 4
I don't believe any real a. MORRISON, TONI, 10
Real a. ship JOBS, STEVE, 3
a. retired...British remained WHISTLER, JAMES ABBOTT MCNEILL, 13
The best a....*have* stood alone HESSE, EVA, 1

arts A. and sciences are not cast in a mold, but are formed and perfected MONTAIGNE, MICHEL DE, 13
a....attempts of the mind DEWEY, JOHN, 18
idleness has sent the a. to perdition PLINY THE ELDER, 13
If all the a. aspire to the condition of music SANTAYANA, GEORGE, 6
ignoble and degenerate offspring to the liberal a. MAP, WALTER, 3
liberal a. tend to soften our manners COLE, THOMAS, 1
secret of the a. is to correct nature VOLTAIRE, 29
The a. babblative and scribblative SOUTHEY, ROBERT, 7
The a. cannot thrive ROOSEVELT, FRANKLIN D., 17

art world painting...what goes on in the a. doesn't matter FRANKENTHALER, HELEN, 1

ashamed a. of confessing...I have nothing to confess BURNEY, FANNY, 3
a. of having been in love LA ROCHEFOUCAULD, FRANÇOIS, 1
Be a. to die MANN, HORACE, 1
If you're a. of being human GOLDEN, MARITA, 2
make a body a. of...human race TWAIN, MARK, 39

ashes A. fly back PROVERBS, 16
a. of an Oak...no epitaph DONNE, JOHN, 26
a. where once I was fire BYRON, LORD, 15

Asia if you're not in A., you're nowhere WELCH, JACK, 2
There is too much A....she is too old KIPLING, RUDYARD, 38

Asiatic an A. planet held to its orbit STEINBECK, JOHN, 1

ask a., and it shall be given BIBLE, 385
A. a silly question PROVERBS, 142

A. me no questions GOLDSMITH, OLIVER, 11
A. no one's view but your own PERSIUS, 1
A. no questions PROVERBS, 143
a. not what your country can do for you KENNEDY, JOHN FITZGERALD, 7
those things which we a. faithfully BOOK OF COMMON PRAYER, 5
asleep The devil is a. PEARY, ROBERT EDWIN, 1
a-smokin' a. of a whackin' white cheroot KIPLING, RUDYARD, 21
aspires a., however humbly, to the condition of art CONRAD, JOSEPH, 8
ass Ready to bite the a. of a bear GUTFREUND, JOHN, 1
assassin The greatest a. of life JIMÉNEZ, JUAN RAMÓN, 11
assassinate You may a. us...you won't intimidate us DE VALERA, EAMON, 1
assassinating I thought of a. many NASSER, GAMAL ABDEL, 3
assassination A. has never changed...history DISRAELI, BENJAMIN, 18
A....the extreme form of censorship SHAW, GEORGE BERNARD, 92
night before his a., Caligula dreamed SUETONIUS, 1
assassins A. have never changed history KENNEDY, ROBERT, 8
assembly proper office of a representative a. MILL, JOHN STUART, 13
asses seeking a. found a kingdom MILTON, JOHN, 105
assessment not interested in making an a. of myself BRANDO, MARLON, 8
asset I'm not a. stripping GOLDSMITH, JAMES, 5
assets Take my a....leave me my organization SLOAN, ALFRED P., JR., 2
association A general a. of nations WILSON, WOODROW, 23
assume A. a virtue, if you have it not SHAKESPEARE, WILLIAM, 201
assumption the a....you have lost your gall bladder you have also lost your mind KERR, JEAN, 2
assumptions a....blown to bits by global competition SMITH, RAYMOND W., 2
Astaire Anyone dancing...debt to A. ASTAIRE, FRED, 5
asthma A....same symptoms as passion PROVERBS, MODERN, 7
astonished a. at my own moderation CLIVE, ROBERT, 2
Astor Mrs. A., not some dowdy old lady ASTOR, BROOKE, 1
astrologer a. transacted his business by...a flare NARAYAN, R. K., 1
astrology serious rehabilitation of a. or palmistry NAIRN, TOM, 2
astronauts The a.!...Rotarians in outer space VIDAL, GORE, 14
astronomers A. and mathematicians...the most cheerful people SAYERS, DOROTHY L., 4
astronomy A. teaches the correct use LEACOCK, STEPHEN, 10
a. without knowing where the stars are WILSON, EDWARD O., 7
asunder When the sky is rent a. KORAN, 42
asylum An a. for the sane...empty in America SHAW, GEORGE BERNARD, 108
asylums a. can hold the sane people TWAIN, MARK, 56
a....the stately homes of England WOOLF, VIRGINIA, 17
ate I a. his liver with some...beans HOPKINS, ANTHONY, 4
atheism a....drastic uninterestingness as an intellectual position UPDIKE, JOHN, 20
honest a. for my money OTWAY, THOMAS, 1
the rock of a. BÜCHNER, GEORG, 4
atheist An a. is a man who has no invisible means of support FOSDICK, HENRY EMERSON, 1
Hardy became a sort of village a. CHESTERTON, G. K., 43
He was an embittered a. ORWELL, GEORGE, 13
he was no a. BURNET, GILBERT, 1
I am an a....thank God BUÑUEL, LUIS, 4
atheists a....citizens, nor...patriots BUSH, GEORGE, 13
Athens A. arose SHELLEY, PERCY BYSSHE, 33
A. holds sway over all Greece THEMISTOCLES, 2
a new A. might be created in the land of the Franks ALCUIN, 3
athlete great a. who died not knowing...pain BRADLEY, BILL, 1
athletes impossible for a. to grow up KING, BILLIE JEAN, 2
athletic only a. sport...backgammon JERROLD, DOUGLAS, 8
Atlanta people who settled...A. were a pushy people MITCHELL, MARGARET, 9
the "architecture" of A. is rococola GUNTHER, JOHN, 1
Atlantic cheaper to lower the A. GRADE, LEW, 2
atom That is how the a. is split CALDER, RITCHIE, 1
atom bomb The a. is a paper tiger MAO ZEDONG, 22
atomic every conceivable a. arrangement will come about DAVIES, PAUL, 2
The a. threat...brought us to the brink WOLF, CHRISTA, 6
The way to win an a. war BRADLEY, OMAR, 3
atomic age I was ten...when "the a." DIDION, JOAN, 3
atomic bomb a....made...future war unendurable OPPENHEIMER, J. ROBERT, 8
atomic war dangers of a. are underrated MCCORMICK, ROBERT RUTHERFORD, 1
atoms a. and other such dogma MACH, ERNST, 3
a. struggle and move in the void DEMOCRITUS, 3
atone a. for the sins of your fathers HORACE, 44
attached I never was a. to that great sect SHELLEY, PERCY BYSSHE, 29
attachment A. is embedded in the soul...animal magnetism HILLMAN, JAMES, 2
His a. to...his friends whom he could make useful JEFFERSON, THOMAS, 1
attacks Her frontal a. on old taboos STOPES, MARIE, 1
attainments rare a....but ...can she spin? JAMES I, 8
attempt The a. and not the deed, /Confounds us SHAKESPEARE, WILLIAM, 397
attend A. to yourself FICHTE, JOHANN, 1
attention Due a. to the inside of books CHESTERFIELD, LORD, 9
He did not draw your a. to how handsome he was KINCAID, JAMAICA, 3
He would take his a. away from the universe CRISP, QUENTIN, 3
I do not want a. centered on me ANDERSON, SHERWOOD, 5
If perticuliar...a. is not paid to the Ladies ADAMS, ABIGAIL, 5
It's easy to get people's a., what counts is getting their *interest* RANDOLPH, A. PHILIP, 2
attentive A clear a. mind /Has no meaning SNYDER, GARY, 7
always a. to the feelings of dogs ELIOT, GEORGE, 20
Attic A. wit PLINY THE ELDER, 3
Attila A. the Hen FREUD, CLEMENT, 1
attraction A. and Repulsion...are necessary to Human existence BLAKE, WILLIAM, 48
a. of the virtuoso for the public DEBUSSY, CLAUDE, 5
The chief a. of military service TOLSTOY, LEO, 11
attracts Nothing a. me like a closed door BOURKE-WHITE, MARGARET, 2
audacity a. of elected persons WHITMAN, WALT, 43
I had...shameful a. very much needed ASTOR, NANCY, 5
Auden A....has gradually turned into a rhetorical mill AUDEN, W. H., 8

A.'s most complacently self-indulgent idiosyncracy AUDEN, W. H., 7
greatest mind of the twentieth century...A. AUDEN, W. H., 5
The time is A....the place London MACNEICE, LOUIS, 1

audience Always make the a. suffer HITCHCOCK, ALFRED, 6
An a. is never wrong WILDER, BILLY, 2
a. was a disaster WILDE, OSCAR, 83
If an a. disrespects me SIMONE, NINA, 3
I know two kinds of a. SCHNABEL, ARTUR, 3
I'm draggin' the a. to hell LEWIS, JERRY LEE, 1
the a. thinks you are crying BERGMAN, INGRID, 3
the a. want to be surprised BERNARD, TRISTAN, 1
always think of the a. when I'm directing SPIELBERG, STEVEN, 7

audiences a. get bored so quickly FOSSE, BOB, 1
a. going mad with enthusiasm COWARD, NOEL, 4
A.? No, the plural is impossible BARRYMORE, JOHN, 1

auditors Who says a. are human? HAILEY, ARTHUR, 1

Augustan next A. age will dawn WALPOLE, HORACE, 2

aunt If my a. had bollocks she'd be me uncle BEHAN, BRENDAN, 1

aunts bad a. and good aunts WODEHOUSE, P. G., 20

Auschwitz a man can read Goethe...work at A. STEINER, GEORGE, 5

Austen A.'s novels...seem...vulgar AUSTEN, JANE, 2
Jane A.'s books, too, are absent from this library AUSTEN, JANE, 6
Miss A....most affected, husband-hunting butterfly AUSTEN, JANE, 5

Austerlitz There rises the sun of A. NAPOLEON I, 32

Australia So you're going to A. MELBA, NELLIE, 4

Australian I'm going to write the Great A. Novel WHITE, PATRICK, 4

Australians we A. inherited the British mentality PACKER, KERRY, 1

Austria A. is Switzerland...with history MORPURGO, J. E., 1
A. will astound the world SCHWARZENBERG, FELIX ZU, 1

authenticity If you seek a. for authenticity's sake SARTRE, JEAN-PAUL, 18

author a. was executed for murdering his publisher BARRIE, J. M., 4
a. who speaks about his own books DISRAELI, BENJAMIN, 43
Choose an a. as you choose a friend DILLON, WENTWORTH, 3
go to the a. to get at his meaning RUSKIN, JOHN, 7
He is the richest a. that ever grazed JOHNSON, SAMUEL, 145
No a. is...genius to his publisher HEINE, HEINRICH, 10
notion of "a." constitutes...individualization FOUCAULT, MICHEL, 7
you wish the a....was a terrific friend SALINGER, J. D., 13

authority a. be a stubborn bear SHAKESPEARE, WILLIAM, 669
A. compels...obedience...reason persuades RICHELIEU, CARDINAL, 2
A. forgets a dying king TENNYSON, ALFRED, 21
care to picture a. as weak MCCARTHY, MARY, 8

authorize to a. what you have yourself forbidden RICHELIEU, CARDINAL, 9

authors A. are easy to get on with JOSEPH, MICHAEL, 1
A., like coins, grow dear as they grow old POPE, ALEXANDER, 61
faults of great a....excellences carried to...excess COLERIDGE, SAMUEL TAYLOR, 53
let great a. have their due BACON, FRANCIS (1561–1626), 91
The trouble with our younger a. is MAUGHAM, SOMERSET, 12

autobiography a. is an obituary CRISP, QUENTIN, 4
A. is the poor man's history CARVER, RAYMOND, 10

autocracy intention of a....glory of the citizen, the state CATHERINE THE GREAT, 2
maintain the principle of a. NICHOLAS II, 2

autocrat be an a.: that's my trade CATHERINE THE GREAT, 4

automobile A....runs up hills and down pedestrians BIERCE, AMBROSE, 8
Money differs from an a., a mistress GALBRAITH, J. K., 23

automobiles A. are free of egotism O'ROURKE, P. J., 2

automobile traffic a....minutely unbalances the earth SIPLE, PAUL ALLMAN, 1

autonomy We offer you...a., self-government RABIN, YITZHAK, 5

autumn A....like Silence HOOD, THOMAS, 9
sobs of the violins of a. VERLAINE, PAUL, 3

avails What a. the classic bent KIPLING, RUDYARD, 63

avarice vanished before the a....the white man TECUMSEH, 1

average no great compliment...above the a. MAUGHAM, SOMERSET, 5
The a....adult gets up at seven-thirty in the morning KERR, JEAN, 3

a-waggle You must always be a. LAWRENCE, D. H., 49

awake A., arise, or be forever fallen MILTON, JOHN, 33
A., awake; put on thy strength, O Zion BIBLE, 219

awakening an a. of the imagination PINKER, STEVEN, 5

aware sufficiently a. to know all the evil he does LA ROCHEFOUCAULD, FRANÇOIS, 24
wasn't even a. of the Year of the Family DOYLE, RODDY, 3

away A.! away! for I will fly to thee KEATS, JOHN (1795–1821), 61

awe A. is composed of reverence and dread WOLF, CHRISTA, 3
live to be /In a. of...I myself SHAKESPEARE, WILLIAM, 297

aweary I gin to be a. of the sun SHAKESPEARE, WILLIAM, 419

awkward the a. squad BURNS, ROBERT, 54

axe An a. is sharp PROVERBS, 5
Lizzie Borden took an a. FOLK VERSE, 59

axioms A. in philosophy are not axioms KEATS, JOHN (1795–1821), 91

axis a. of the earth sticks out visibly HOLMES, OLIVER WENDELL, 24
This Berlin-Rome connection is...an a. MUSSOLINI, BENITO, 5

baa B., baa, black sheep CHILDREN'S VERSE, 50

Babbitt one thing wrong with the B. house LEWIS, SINCLAIR, 3

babbl'd a b. of green fields SHAKESPEARE, WILLIAM, 265

babe Come little b....father's shame, thy mother's grief BRETON, NICHOLAS, 2

Babel B....the Lord did there confound the language BIBLE, 122

Babelization B. of great capitals...sign of modernity GOYTISOLO, JUAN, 3

Babe Ruth thrill of watching B. play DIMAGGIO, JOE, 2

babies all b. look like me CHURCHILL, WINSTON, 84
B. are...obviously narcissistic FREUD, SIGMUND, 14
B. do more to women than make mothers GUY, ROSA, 1
b. don't come until...ready ELIZABETH II, 3
Other people's b.— /That's my life HERBERT, A. P., 1
You breed b. and you eat chips WESKER, ARNOLD, 2

baby A B. in an ox's stall BETJEMAN, JOHN, 7
b. born of woman, /if you'll only go to sleep MISTRAL, GABRIELA, 5
Don't throw the b. out PROVERBS, 188
Every b. born into the world DICKENS, CHARLES, 64
first b. laughed...beginning of fairies BARRIE, J. M., 9
hanging the b. on the clothes line to dry RUNYON, DAMON, 8
Holding my b....best drug COBAIN, KURT, 5
Hush-a-bye, b., on the tree top CHILDREN'S VERSE, 23
my b. at my breast SHAKESPEARE, WILLIAM, 94
no new b. in the womb of our society LAWRENCE, D. H., 37

Babylon B. in all its desolation DAVIES, SCROPE, 1

B. the great BIBLE, 472
How many miles to B.? CHILDREN'S VERSE, 39
Babylonish A B. dialect BUTLER, SAMUEL (1612–80), 5
Bacchus B., that first from out the purple grape MILTON, JOHN, 16
Bach the angels play only B. MOZART, WOLFGANG AMADEUS, 1
you play B. *your* way LANDOWSKA, WANDA, 1
bachelor A b....dies like a beggar LOWRY, L. S., 1
B.'s fare; bread and cheese, and kisses SWIFT, JONATHAN, 27
back Either b. us or sack us CALLAGHAN, JIM, 2
I'll be b. SCHWARZENEGGER, ARNOLD, 1
my b. goes out more than I DILLER, PHYLLIS, 3
sit with my b. to the future MCCAIG, NORMAN, 7
Sometimes I look b. on my life BROWN, JAMES, 1
background The b. reveals the true being JIMÉNEZ, JUAN RAMÓN, 13
backroom Boys in the B. Will Have LOESSER, FRANK, 3
backs With our b. to the wall HAIG, DOUGLAS, 1
backwardness B....recognized before it can be changed DENG XIAOPING, 9
bacon b....worth fifty thousand Methodist sermons COBBETT, WILLIAM, 4
Bacon asked B. /How many bribes BENTLEY, EDMUND CLERIHEW, 1
bad a b. man must have brains GORKY, MAKSIM, 1
A b. penny PROVERBS, 95
A b. woman always has...goodness TROUBRIDGE, LAURA, 1
b. man...with honors and social esteem PLATO, 20
If we believe a thing to be b. MILNER, ALFRED, 1
Nothing so b. but it might have been worse PROVERBS, 348
When b. men combine, the good must associate BURKE, EDMUND, 56
when she was b. she was horrid LONGFELLOW, HENRY WADSWORTH, 34
bad cause A b. will ever be supported PAINE, THOMAS, 6
badddDDD WE A b. PEOPLE SANCHEZ, SONIA, 1
Bad Lands the B....work of an evil child STEINBECK, JOHN, 24
badly If you want to do a thing b. USTINOV, PETER, 3
badness the b. of her badness BARRIE, J. M., 13
Bahamas they arrived at...B. COLUMBUS, CHRISTOPHER, 7
bakers B. and brewers, bouchers and cokes /...doth most harme LANGLAND, WILLIAM, 1
balance Between b. and unbalance, fall and recovery TERRY, WALTER, 2
b. of manpower and materials NAPOLEON I, 19
bald being b.—one can hear snowflakes DANIELS, R. G., 1
baldness a light form of premature b. FELLINI, FEDERICO, 1
There is more felicity on the far side of b. SMITH, LOGAN PEARSALL, 3
Balenciaga B.? He dresses women...like old Spaniards CHANEL, COCO, 8
ball doesn't bother me what b. I use NORMAN, GREG, 1
He never hit a b. out of the infield ELIOT, T. S., 2
ball-bearings b. where her pelvis should've been MEZZROW, MEZZ, 8
ballerina A b. must not be overly tall BROWNMILLER, SUSAN, 1
ballet b. dancer's mode of existence KIRSTEIN, LINCOLN, 4
it takes more than one to make a b. VALOIS, NINETTE DE, 1
ballets he liked to make b. for the women he loved BALANCHINE, GEORGE, 1
ballgame a great day for a b. BANKS, ERNIE, 2
I shall play such a b. with...French HENRY V, 3
ballot either the b. or the bullet MALCOLM X, 7
The b. is stronger than the bullet LINCOLN, ABRAHAM, 29
ball points B. belong to their age HANSBERRY, LORRAINE, 5
balm wash the b. from an anointed king SHAKESPEARE, WILLIAM, 516
baloney it's still b. SMITH, AL, 2
band a b. can really swing BASIE, COUNT, 1
My b. is my instrument ELLINGTON, DUKE, 11
the b. that turned everything around JONES, QUINCY, 4
bandages to walk around...with only a few light b. on RUNYON, DAMON, 4
bands b. don't think about the future ROTH, DAVID LEE, 1
bang bigger b. for a buck WILSON, CHARLES E., 2
bangs B. manes bouffants beehives WOLFE, TOM, 16
banishment bitter bread of b. SHAKESPEARE, WILLIAM, 514
banjo b. played chung, chung...smack on the beat MELLY, GEORGE, 6
bank A b....will lend you money HOPE, BOB, 2
don't trust a b. that would lend money BENCHLEY, ROBERT, 9
The b. that likes to say yes ADVERTISEMENTS, 22
the b. was mightier than the sword PLOMER, WILLIAM, 2
What's breaking into a b. BRECHT, BERTOLT, 24
bank balance better that a man should tyrannize over his b. KEYNES, JOHN MAYNARD, 12
banker woe betide the b. NASH, OGDEN, 19
banking B. is...cooperating in the morning WRISTON, WALTER B., 3
bankrupt Companies do not go b. GYLLENHAMMAR, PEHR G., 1
bankruptcy B. is a sacred state UPDIKE, JOHN, 10
banks b....in the business of collecting fees KELLY, PATRICK C., 1
Ye b. and braes BURNS, ROBERT, 37
banner A b. with the strange device, /Excelsior LONGFELLOW, HENRY WADSWORTH, 3
banners The b. of the king advance FORTUNATUS, 1
bar Back of the b., in a solo game, sat Dangerous Dan McGrew SERVICE, ROBERT W., 5
When I went to the B. as a very young man GILBERT, W. S., 12
Barabbas B. was a publisher CAMPBELL, THOMAS, 10
now B. was a robber BIBLE, 296
Barbara Allen For love of B. FOLK VERSE, 30
barbarian he had been a b., a beast CRANE, STEPHEN, 10
barbarians what will become of us without the b. CAVAFY, CONSTANTINE, 2
barbarism B. is the absence of standards ORTEGA Y GASSET, JOSÉ, 22
should the cloud of b....obscure...Europe JEFFERSON, THOMAS, 17
Barbarossa When B. commences HITLER, ADOLF, 42
barber It is like a b.'s chair SHAKESPEARE, WILLIAM, 51
barefoot b. and wearing coarse wool, he stood pitifully GREGORY VII, 2
I still go b. DYLAN, BOB, 5
barge Drag the slow b., or drive the rapid car DARWIN, ERASMUS, 3
The b. she sat in, like a burnish'd throne, Burn'd SHAKESPEARE, WILLIAM, 75
baritones b. are born villains in opera WARREN, LEONARD, 1
barking B. dogs PROVERBS, 154
b. mad about crime ROSS, NICK, 1
barn It's too late to shut the b. door PROVERBS, 283
Barnum the celebrated B.'s circus MACDONALD, RAMSAY, 2
barrel drowned in a b. of malmesey FABYAN, ROBERT, 1

out of the b. of a gun MAO ZEDONG, 23
barren A b. island with hardly a house PALMERSTON, LORD, 2
I am but a b. stock ELIZABETH I, 18
nothing encourageth a woman sooner to be b. PLINY THE ELDER, 1
Bartleby Ah, B.! Ah, humanity MELVILLE, HERMAN, 15
baseball A b. swing is a...finely tuned instrument JACKSON, REGGIE, 1
B. always comes first MITCHELL, LIZ, 1
B. can be trusted SAROYAN, WILLIAM, 1
b....greater impact on American life HOOVER, HERBERT, 11
B....greatest of American games EDISON, THOMAS ALVA, 2
B. has the great advantage over cricket SHAW, GEORGE BERNARD, 109
B. is a poker game ROBINSON, JACKIE, 2
B. is doomed MCLUHAN, MARSHALL, 1
b. is like writing MOORE, MARIANNE, 3
B. is ninety percent mental BERRA, YOGI, 2
B. is our national game COOLIDGE, CALVIN, 14
B. is the very symbol TWAIN, MARK, 6
B.: it breaks your heart GIAMATTI, A. BARTLETT, 2
B....most intellectual game KISSINGER, HENRY, 16
B....played by idiots for morons FITZGERALD, F. SCOTT, 25
B....poses as a sacred institution ROBINSON, JACKIE, 3
B....the literature of my boyhood ROTH, PHILIP, 4
B. was fun when I was in college JACKSON, BO, 1
Catherine...should prefer cricket, b. AUSTEN, JANE, 23
Close don't count in b. ROBINSON, FRANK, 2
I find b. fascinating COOKE, ALISTAIR, 3
no one who cared about b. could be an opportunist HOAGLAND, EDWARD, 1
Not making the b. team...greatest disappointments EISENHOWER, DWIGHT D., 27
baseball cap b. is just as valid as a felt hat JONES, STEPHEN, 1
basics time to get back to b. MAJOR, JOHN, 2
bastard Because I am a b. HEMINGWAY, ERNEST, 20
bastards The quickest way...to get the b. PATTON, GEORGE S., 2
bat I've got a b. AARON, HANK, 1
They came to see me b. GRACE, W. G., 2
bath B....to avoid being a public menace BURGESS, ANTHONY, 4
bathing b. in someone else's dirty water PROUST, MARCEL, 2
battering B. the gates of heaven TENNYSON, ALFRED, 62
batting the b. order of the New York Yankees THURBER, JAMES, 19
battle b. seen fought in the skies NOSTRADAMUS, 1
Go forward into b....do not shrink AL-MUFID, ABU ABDULLAH MUHAMMAD AL-HARITHI AL-BAGHDADI, 2
rather stand...in...b. than bear one child EURIPIDES, 10
The b. of Britain CHURCHILL, WINSTON, 31
battlefield the most beautiful b. NAPOLEON I, 15
battleground great b. for the defense KENNEDY, JOHN FITZGERALD, 26
battling b., inarticulate, /blindly making it DUNCAN, ROBERT, 4
Battling Bella They call me B. ABZUG, BELLA, 1
bauble that fool's b., the mace CROMWELL, OLIVER, 5
bayonets You can do everything with b. BISMARCK, PRINCE OTTO VON, 22
be Let them b. as they are or not CLEMENT XIII, 1
To b., or not to be—that is the question SHAKESPEARE, WILLIAM, 179
What...I shall b., /Venus, let me never see PRIOR, MATTHEW, 8
What must b., must be PROVERBS, 451
What will b., shall be MARLOWE, CHRISTOPHER, 3
beak Take thy b. from out my heart POE, EDGAR ALLAN, 15
beam B. us up, Mr. Scott STAR TREK, 1
beans plant my b. below the southern hill TAO QIAN, 4
The secret...growing more beans GOIZUETA, ROBERTO, 3
Beanz B. Meanz Heinz ADVERTISEMENTS, 12
bear a b. it would have bit you SWIFT, JONATHAN, 28
a B. of Very Little Brain MILNE, A. A., 20
Exit, pursued by a b. SHAKESPEARE, WILLIAM, 663
Never be on the b. side MORGAN, JOHN PIERPONT, 5
never...sell the b.'s skin LA FONTAINE, JEAN DE, 13
rather b. with you than bear you SHAKESPEARE, WILLIAM, 100
The b., the ponderous cinnamon STEVENS, WALLACE, 15
who could not b. another's misfortunes...like a Christian POPE, ALEXANDER, 53
bear-baiting b. was esteemed heathenish HUME, DAVID, 34
beard I nurse a b. PARKES, FRANCIS ERNEST KOBINA, 1
There was an Old Man with a b. LEAR, EDWARD, 1
bearded hard to hear...a b. man MANKIEWICZ, HERMAN J., 2
beards men wore their b., like they wear their neckties LAWRENCE, D. H., 43
bears And some of the bigger b. try to pretend MILNE, A. A., 15
beast A b. in civilization ELKIN, STANLEY, 1
B. gave beast as much YEATS, W. B., 50
"b.," "monster" and "sex fiend" are...used to describe the rapist CAMBRIDGE RAPE CRISIS CENTRE, 1
B., what is love BROWN, GEORGE MACKAY, 1
b....will be a monster computer ELLIS, BILL, 1
The b. with many heads SHAKESPEARE, WILLIAM, 124
the b. with two backs SHAKESPEARE, WILLIAM, 467
beastliness It is called in our schools "b." BADEN-POWELL, ROBERT, 3
beat b. the iron while it is hot DRYDEN, JOHN, 21
b. this face into submission CHER, 1
I'm going to b. it JOHNSON, "MAGIC," 1
make the b. keep time with short steps ANDERSEN, HANS CHRISTIAN, 5
We are b....Beat means beatific KEROUAC, JACK, 27
beaten All the best men...have been b. CAREY, MICHAEL S., 1
I was b. up by Quakers ALLEN, WOODY, 9
beating B. a way for the rising sun BONTEMPS, ARNA, 2
b. begins at home BEAUMONT & FLETCHER, 18
beatings the b. of the lonely heart FERRIER, SUSAN EDMONSTONE, 1
The dread of b....dread of games BETJEMAN, JOHN, 18
Beatles If we had a hundred B. MARSH, RICHARD, 2
The B. are second to none LEIBER, JERRY, 2
beats It b. as it sweeps as it cleans ADVERTISEMENTS, 1
beau When a B. goes in, /Into the drink EWART, GAVIN, 2
beautiful a b. ballet is nature herself NOVERRE, JEAN GEORGES, 1
Be b.! and be sad BAUDELAIRE, CHARLES, 15
b....for someone who could not read CHESTERTON, G. K., 56
b. is the symbol of...morally good KANT, IMMANUEL, 3
B....Magnificent desolation! ALDRIN, BUZZ, 1
b....pleases universally without a concept KANT, IMMANUEL, 4
I'm b. ROREM, NED, 3
more b. than thy first love YEATS, W. B., 29
most b. things...are the most useless RUSKIN, JOHN, 15
O b. for spacious skies BATES, KATHARINE LEE, 1
only the perception of the B. SCHILLER, FRIEDRICH VON, 13
She's more b. than the Brooklyn Bridge HAYES, HELEN, 3
The B. and the Damned FITZGERALD, F. SCOTT, 31

the most b. woman I've ever seen MARX, GROUCHO, 12
the name of which was B. BUNYAN, JOHN, 5
usually chose the b. WEYL, HERMANN, 1
What is most b. in virile men SONTAG, SUSAN, 9
What we find b. in a work of art LESSING, GOTTHOLD EPHRAIM, 2
when a woman isn't b. CHEKHOV, ANTON, 20

beautifully B. done SPENCER, STANLEY, 1

beauty A thing of b. is a joy for ever KEATS, JOHN (1795–1821), 83
author in the world /Teaches such b. SHAKESPEARE, WILLIAM, 376
B. alone makes all the world happy SCHILLER, FRIEDRICH VON, 15
B. and the lust for learning BEERBOHM, MAX, 20
b. draws us with a single hair POPE, ALEXANDER, 94
B....exists in the mind HUME, DAVID, 31
b. faded has no second spring PHILIPS, AMBROSE, 1
b....hath strange power MILTON, JOHN, 100
B. in distress BURKE, EDMUND, 33
B. is a gift of God SÉVIGNÉ, MADAME DE, 5
B. is all about us CASALS, PABLO, 3
B. is a shell /from the sea WILLIAMS, WILLIAM CARLOS, 9
B. is a social necessity GOLDSMITH, JAMES, 2
B. is...in the eye of the beholder HUNGERFORD, MARGARET WOLFE, 1
B. is momentary in the mind STEVENS, WALLACE, 3
B. is Nature's brag MILTON, JOHN, 20
B....isolating as genius, or deformity AVEDON, RICHARD, 1
b. is only sin deep SAKI, 13
B. is only skin-deep PROVERBS, 156
B. is our weapon against nature PAGLIA, CAMILLE, 11
B. is potent PROVERBS, 157
B. is the lover's gift CONGREVE, WILLIAM, 22
B. is truth, truth beauty KEATS, JOHN (1795–1821), 56
B. itself doth of itself persuade SHAKESPEARE, WILLIAM, 633
b. myth...more insidious WOLF, NAOMI, 2
b. of inflections /Or...of innuendoes STEVENS, WALLACE, 8
b. of these most beautiful...people PATER, WALTER, 3
b....perceived but not explained CAYLEY, ARTHUR, 1
B. stands /In the admiration ... of weak minds MILTON, JOHN, 103
b. that hath...strangeness in the proportion BACON, FRANCIS (1561–1626), 15
B. will be edible DALÍ, SALVADOR, 4
b. without a fortune FARQUHAR, GEORGE, 7
can't order the masses to love b. DEBUSSY, CLAUDE, 6
cruelly images of female b....weigh upon us WOLF, NAOMI, 3
delusion that b. is goodness TOLSTOY, LEO, 9
Everything has b. CONFUCIUS, 4
He hath a daily b. SHAKESPEARE, WILLIAM, 496
Helen, thy b. is to me /Like those Nicean barks of yore POE, EDGAR ALLAN, 8
her b. made /The bright world dim SHELLEY, PERCY BYSSHE, 39
Her b....silence in a cup of water DEVLIN, DENIS, 1
idea of b. does not descend into matter POUSSIN, NICOLAS, 3
I love b. above virtue SYMONDS, JOHN ADDINGTON, 2
its b. consists only in the agreement of numbers LEIBNIZ, GOTTFRIED WILHELM, 2
perceive real b. in a person as...get older AIMÉE, ANOUK, 1
Rigor of b. is the quest WILLIAMS, WILLIAM CARLOS, 5
Seirênês, crying b. /to bewitch men HOMER, 9
simple b....the best thing God invents BROWNING, ROBERT, 55
small b. of the forest OPPEN, GEORGE, 4
So much b....so much native good-breeding DE QUINCEY, THOMAS, 3
The b. of Moroccan palaces WHARTON, EDITH, 12
the b. of one blue hill in the distance WALKER, ALICE, 13
the power of b. will...transform honesty SHAKESPEARE, WILLIAM, 175
the world's b. becomes enough MORRISON, TONI, 22
'Tisn't b....just It KIPLING, RUDYARD, 64
walks in b., like the night BYRON, LORD, 13
Would you see true b. SAVONAROLA, GIROLAMO, 2

beauty-drunk a b. artist MAYAKOVSKY, VLADIMIR, 5

beaux Where none are b....vain to be a belle LYTTELTON, GEORGE, 1

because B. it is there MALLORY, GEORGE, 1

bed And so to b. PEPYS, SAMUEL, 15
"B.,"..."is the poor man's opera." HUXLEY, ALDOUS, 32
Come, let's to b. /Says Sleepy-head CHILDREN'S VERSE, 12
He didn't ought...to b. in boots HERBERT, A. P., 7
his b. was piled a foot high with books MAO ZEDONG, 2
in b. with a strange man O'BRIEN, EDNA, 3
It's just hard to get out of b. in the morning NAVRATILOVA, MARTINA, 1
Never go to b. mad DILLER, PHYLLIS, 2
Now deep in my b. I turn JENNINGS, ELIZABETH, 2
O b.! delicious bed HOOD, THOMAS, 19
The B. be blest ADY, THOMAS, 1
To b. SHAKESPEARE, WILLIAM, 411

Bedonebyasyoudid Mrs B. is coming KINGSLEY, CHARLES, 5

beds Will there be b. for me and all who seek? ROSSETTI, CHRISTINA, 10

bedside B. manners are no substitute SLOAN, ALFRED P., JR., 1
The b....true center of medical teaching HOLMES, OLIVER WENDELL, 15

bee How doth the little busy b. WATTS, ISAAC, 2
Where the b. sucks, There suck I SHAKESPEARE, WILLIAM, 651

beechen spare the b. tree CAMPBELL, THOMAS, 6

beef The roast b. of England FIELDING, HENRY, 14

Beelzebub When /Sir /B. called for his syllabub SITWELL, EDITH, 4

been It might have b. WHITTIER, JOHN GREENLEAF, 3
what has b., has been DRYDEN, JOHN, 50

beer all b. and skittles HUGHES, THOMAS, 1
Give us b. or brandy MACNEICE, LOUIS, 17
I'm only here for the b. ADVERTISEMENTS, 9

Beethoven B. came with music in his soul BEETHOVEN, LUDWIG VAN, 2
B. composed all his music without...the sea MICHAELS, ANNE, 1
B.'s Fifth Symphony is the most sublime noise FORSTER, E. M., 12
not B. lying here BEETHOVEN, LUDWIG VAN, 3

beetles inordinate fondness for b. HALDANE, J. B. S., 6

before I have been here b.. /But when or how I cannot tell ROSSETTI, DANTE GABRIEL, 2
One look b....two behind PROVERBS, 71

beggar a b. is still...an Englishman MORITZ, KARL PHILIPP, 1
The true b....is the true king LESSING, GOTTHOLD EPHRAIM, 5

beggars B. can't be choosers BEAUMONT & FLETCHER, 14
why should there be b. in...Israel PETERS, HUGH, 1

beggary b. in the love that can be reckon'd SHAKESPEARE, WILLIAM, 70

begin B., baby boy VIRGIL, 29
b. by committing ourselves to the truth NIXON, RICHARD, 32
b. with a calyx exulting towards...light AMICHAI, YEHUDA, 7
We b. in...carnal desire SCHOPENHAUER, ARTHUR, 19

beginning a b., a muddle, and an end LARKIN, PHILIP, 13
always a b. back of the beginning EGGLESTON, EDWARD, 1
bad b. makes a bad ending EURIPIDES, 2
b. and the ending BIBLE, 464

Begin at the b. CARROLL, LEWIS, 23
b. of a beautiful friendship BOGART, HUMPHREY, 6
b. of time according to our Chronologie USSHER, JAMES, 1
has a b., a middle, and an end ARISTOTLE, 21
In my b. is my end ELIOT, T. S., 17
in the b. God BIBLE, 101
In the b. was the Word BIBLE, 266
must be a b. of any great matter DRAKE, FRANCIS, 2
beginnings From small b. PROVERBS, 228
begins exception of the equator, everything b. somewhere FLEMING, PETER, 2
beguine When they begin the b. PORTER, COLE, 9
begun There is an old saying "well b. is half done" KEATS, JOHN (1795–1821), 28
To have b. is half the job HORACE, 18
wonder what I was b. for EPITAPHS, 2
behaved Have I b. badly LINDGREN, ASTRID, 1
behavior b....controlled by our genetic inheritance SAGAN, CARL, 19
b....may be *declared* to be a disease SZASZ, THOMAS, 3
behaviour observing the b....slimmer and the anorexic MACLEOD, SHEILA, 1
behaviourism B. "works". So does torture AUDEN, W. H., 19
behind Get thee b. me, Satan BIBLE, 358
behold B. her, single in the field WORDSWORTH, WILLIAM, 65
beige It's b.! My color DE WOLFE, ELSIE, 3
Beijing I...lived in B. too long LU XUN, 11
being A B., erect upon two legs DICKENS, CHARLES, 84
always at the edge of B. SPENDER, STEPHEN, 9
B.'s poem...is man HEIDEGGER, MARTIN, 3
that odd fork in B.'s road, /Eternity DICKINSON, EMILY, 9
The truth of B. and of Nothing HEGEL, G. W. F., 5
Beirut B. will be the Hanoi and Stalingrad ARAFAT, YASIR, 1
Belfast British troops were patrolling the streets of B. CROSSMAN, RICHARD, 1
belief b. is for it JOHNSON, SAMUEL, 164
Our b. in...natural law POPPER, KARL, 1
our pious b. in ghosts and witches HAZLITT, WILLIAM, 26
to speak of b. or unbelief...logically impossible AYER, A. J., 2
beliefs b. that mold great organizations WATSON, THOMAS, JR., 1
believe B. it or not RIPLEY, R. L., 1
B. me now, my Christian friends HAMMON, JUPITER, 1
B. nothing of what you hear PROVERBS, 159
b....what...the hierarchical Church so defines LOYOLA, IGNATIUS OF, 4
b. what we choose NEWMAN, JOHN HENRY, 1
except I...thrust my hand into his side, I will not b. BIBLE, 303
How can I b. in God ALLEN, WOODY, 16
I b. because it is impossible TERTULLIAN, 4
I b., first of all, in God BETHUNE, MARY MCLEOD, 3
I b. I am becoming a god VESPASIAN, 2
I b. in industry BRISTOW, ALAN, 1
I b. in the Church TEMPLE, WILLIAM, 4
I b. in the present ADAMS, FREDERICK UPHAM, 1
I b. so that I may understand ANSELM, SAINT, 3
I do not b. in moral issues WOODSWORTH, JAMES S., 1
I don't b. in an afterlife ALLEN, WOODY, 13
I don't b. in fairies BARRIE, J. M., 8
I don't b. in God GARCÍA MÁRQUEZ, GABRIEL, 7
I don't b. you. You're a liar DYLAN, BOB, 25
If you b., clap your hands BARRIE, J. M., 11
If you'll b. in me CARROLL, LEWIS, 46
inclined to b. those whom we do not know JOHNSON, SAMUEL, 35
It is hard to b. that a man is telling the truth MENCKEN, H. L., 27
I wish to b. in immortality KEATS, JOHN (1795–1821), 32
I would as soon b. /in paradise AMMONS, A. R., 2
only make b. that I love you HAMMERSTEIN, OSCAR, II, 8
The temerity to b. in nothing TURGENEV, IVAN, 3
To b. and to understand...not diverse things COLERIDGE, SAMUEL TAYLOR, 24
what we b. is not necessarily true BELL, CLIVE, 2
when you cease to b. you may cease to behave KRONENBERGER, LOUIS, 1
you must b. in God JOWETT, BENJAMIN, 1
believed All that b. were together BIBLE, 6
I've b....six impossible things CARROLL, LEWIS, 41
two things...be b. of any man TARKINGTON, BOOTH, 2
believer b. is high-spirited and speaks pleasantly JAMI, NUR AD-DIN ABD AR-RAHMAN IBN AHMAD, 1
believers Blessed are the b. KORAN, 26
believes if one person b. in me, I will try to move mountains ROSS, DIANA, 2
believing I stopped b. in Santa Claus BLACK, SHIRLEY TEMPLE, 1
bell B., book, and candle SHAKESPEARE, WILLIAM, 325
I'll b. the cat DOUGLAS, ARCHIBALD, 1
Once that b. rings LOUIS, JOE, 2
The b. strikes one...no note of time YOUNG, EDWARD, 6
Who will b. the cat DESCHAMPS, EUSTACHE, 1
Belle Dame sans Merci La B. /Hath Thee in thrall KEATS, JOHN (1795–1821), 15
bell jar The b. hung, suspended PLATH, SYLVIA, 12
bellow He who does not b. the truth PÉGUY, CHARLES PIERRE, 1
bells hawk's b. and glass beads COLUMBUS, CHRISTOPHER, 5
The b. of hell go ting-a-ling-a-ling FOLK VERSE, 13
belly Every man with a b. full of the classics MILLER, HENRY, 24
bellyful Rumble thy b. SHAKESPEARE, WILLIAM, 344
belongs Now he b. to the ages LINCOLN, ABRAHAM, 6
beloved cleave to your b. fatherland SCHILLER, FRIEDRICH VON, 24
Ben Adhem B.'s name led all the rest HUNT, LEIGH, 2
benefactors Our gratitude to most b. is the same as ...for dentists CHAMFORT, NICOLAS, 5
beneficiaries the b. of the established order PIRENNE, HENRI, 1
benefits B. make a man a slave PROVERBS, 17
great b. accruing...from true Christian tolerance JOSEPH II, 1
nature of men...bound by the b. they confer MACHIAVELLI, NICCOLÒ, 8
benevolence It is not...the b. of the butcher SMITH, ADAM, 4
benevolent only the b. man CONFUCIUS, 33
Bentley give every one a B. MARSH, RICHARD, 3
Bergman B. taught me how little you can do BERGMAN, INGMAR, 1
Berkeley Bishop B. said "there was no matter" BYRON, LORD, 72
Berlin B. meant Boys ISHERWOOD, CHRISTOPHER, 1
besiege When forty winters shall b. thy brow SHAKESPEARE, WILLIAM, 561
Bessie B....original in the way Armstrong was ARMSTRONG, LOUIS, 2
best b. men are moulded out of faults SHAKESPEARE, WILLIAM, 438

b. to slip over thoughts SÉVIGNÉ, MADAME DE, 2
I will do my b. BADEN-POWELL, ROBERT, 4
letting the b. be the enemy of the good JENKINS, ROY, 2
One of the b. ways to win MALONE, MICHAEL S., 2
Probably the b. lager in the world ADVERTISEMENTS, 5
The b. direction is...least visible RITT, MARTIN, 1
The b. is the enemy of the good VOLTAIRE, 19
the b. of all possible worlds LEIBNIZ, GOTTFRIED WILHELM, 3
the b. of all possible worlds VOLTAIRE, 15
The b. of friends PROVERBS, 394
the b. of times...worst of times DICKENS, CHARLES, 9
The b. that I can wish you JAMES II, 1
The b. thing others can do ROEPKE BAHAMONDE, GABRIELA, 1
the b. things are the most difficult PLUTARCH, 8
The b. things in life PROVERBS, 396

best-educated b. American people in the world QUAYLE, DAN, 3

bestow Let them b. on every airth a limb MONTROSE, JAMES GRAHAM, 1

bestride he doth b. the narrow world /Like a Colossus SHAKESPEARE, WILLIAM, 298

best-seller A b....because it was selling well BOORSTIN, DANIEL J., 4
A b. is the gilded tomb of a mediocre talent SMITH, LOGAN PEARSALL, 4

bet b. on a Baptist beating a Muslim ALI, MUHAMMAD, 10
b. you...he ain't in here DILLINGHAM, CHARLES BANCROFT, 1

Bethlehem a modern star of B. DAVIS, ADELLE, 1
O little town of B. BROOKS, PHILLIPS, 1

betray All a man can b. is his conscience CONRAD, JOSEPH, 10
b., you must first belong PHILBY, KIM, 1

betrayed first kid-napped and b. by some of my own complexion CUGOANO, OTTOBAH, 2
I have b. the innocent blood BIBLE, 440
the Son of man is b. BIBLE, 434

betraying if I had to choose between b. my country and betraying my friend FORSTER, E. M., 19

betroth I will b. thee unto me for ever BIBLE, 149

better any b. in Heaven, my friend Ford WILLIAMS, WILLIAM CARLOS, 17
b. for England we had never...born HATTON, CHRISTOPHER, 1
b. off when the Indians...running it DELORIA, VINE, 2
B. the occasional faults of a government ROOSEVELT, FRANKLIN D., 18
b. to be at the right place TAMERLANE, 1
b. to deal by speech than...letter BACON, FRANCIS (1561–1626), 48
b. to have loved and lost BUTLER, SAMUEL (1835–1902), 15
b. to marry than to burn BIBLE, 155
far, far, b. thing that I do DICKENS, CHARLES, 10
Give me b. wood...a better cabinet MACDONALD, JOHN A., 3
I am getting b. and better COUÉ, ÉMILE, 1
if you knows of a b. 'ole BAIRNSFATHER, BRUCE, 1
I had a b. year RUTH, BABE, 3
It is b. to be an artist PÉREZ GALDÓS, BENITO, 2
It is b. to be beautiful WILDE, OSCAR, 65
I've got to admit it's getting b. LENNON & MCCARTNEY, 12
never b. than when I am mad KYD, THOMAS, 1
no b. than you should be BEAUMONT & FLETCHER, 5
We have seen b. days SHAKESPEARE, WILLIAM, 677
what is b. than a good womman CHAUCER, GEOFFREY, 33
When you meet someone b....turn your thoughts to becoming his equal CONFUCIUS, 30
You're a b. man than I am, Gunga Din KIPLING, RUDYARD, 20

Beulah B., peel me a grape WEST, MAE, 6

beverage b. of hell YOUNG, GEORGE W., 1

Beverly Hills swivel the lights of B. BERRYMAN, JOHN, 2

beware "B. of the dog" PETRONIUS ARBITER, 1
B. of the man who does not return your blow SHAW, GEORGE BERNARD, 55
B. of those who are homeless by choice SOUTHEY, ROBERT, 11
B. the ides of March SHAKESPEARE, WILLIAM, 299
B. the Jabberwock CARROLL, LEWIS, 30

bewitched B., Bothered, and Bewildered HART, LORENZ, 3

bias Commodity, the b. of the world SHAKESPEARE, WILLIAM, 323
There is a b. in television journalism BIRT, JOHN, 1

Bible B. demands suspension of belief FRENCH, MARILYN, 1
B....in clear straightforward language GALBRAITH, J. K., 6
B....lowest stratum in the teaching of literature FRYE, NORTHROP, 5
I didn't write the B. DE MILLE, CECIL B., 2
I read the B. every night ELLINGTON, DUKE, 1
searching through the B. for loopholes FIELDS, W. C., 11
The English B. MACAULAY, THOMAS BABINGTON, 11

Bibles B. bound in Indian skin DAVENPORT, GUY, 2
Why do they put the Gideon B. MORLEY, CHRISTOPHER DARLINGTON, 5

big A b. man has no time FITZGERALD, F. SCOTT, 20
B. Brother is watching you ORWELL, GEORGE, 17
b. emotions come from b. words HEMINGWAY, ERNEST, 22
get what you are b. enough to take HOFFA, JIMMY, 1
not b. enough to lose...not big enough to win REUTHER, WALTER, 1
The b. print giveth and the fine print taketh away SHEEN, FULTON J., 1

bigger The b....the harder they fall PROVERBS, 488
The b. they come FITZSIMMONS, BOB, 1

big-league guy is...worth b. money EISNER, MICHAEL, 1

Bilbao We shall raze B. MOLA, EMILIO, 1

bill give me your b. of company SWIFT, JONATHAN, 22

billboard A b. lovely as a tree NASH, OGDEN, 6
When a man throws a b. across a view BROWN, PAT, 1

billionaire begin as a b. BRANSON, RICHARD, 6

bill of rights b. is what the people are entitled to JEFFERSON, THOMAS, 14

Billy B.... /Fell in the fire GRAHAM, HARRY, 3

biography all b. is ultimately fiction MALAMUD, BERNARD, 2
B. is about Chaps BENTLEY, EDMUND CLERIHEW, 2
hesitation in starting my b. too soon RUSSELL, BERTRAND, 3
how difficult it is to write b. WEST, REBECCA, 8
Read...nothing but b. DISRAELI, BENJAMIN, 11

biology b. and culture interpenetrate in an inextricable manner GOULD, STEPHEN JAY, 2
B....at least 50 more interesting years WATSON, JAMES DEWEY, 1
programmed...by b. or conditioning DALEY, JANET, 1

biotechnology B. has an ancient lineage YOXEN, EDWARD, 1

birch I'm all for bringing back the b. VIDAL, GORE, 19

bird a b. beating her wings against the cage of matrimony TOLSON, MELVIN, 1
A b. in the hand PROVERBS, 97
BIG B. SENSATION, MISSING LOCAL BOY PLOMER, WILLIAM, 1
b....instrument...according to a mathematical law LEONARDO DA VINCI, 15
Her prose is like a b. SPARK, MURIEL, 1
keep such a b. in a cage HENRY, PRINCE, 1

She's only a B. in a Gilded Cage LAMB, A. J., 1
The early b. who catches the worm MACDONALD, JOHN D., 1
birds All the b. of the air CHILDREN'S VERSE, 49
b....consider the muzzle of my gun SMITH, SYDNEY, 29
B. of a feather PROVERBS, 166
b. of this year CERVANTES, MIGUEL DE, 50
Dead b. don't fall out of their nests CHURCHILL, WINSTON, 85
I see all the b. are flown CHARLES I (1600–49), 7
Two little dicky b., /Sitting on a wall CHILDREN'S VERSE, 27
where...b. fly after the last sky DARWISH, MAHMOUD, 2
birth B., and copulation, and death ELIOT, T. S., 38
B. and death is a grave event FOLK VERSE, 57
B. counts for nothing MOLIÈRE, 2
b. had no meaning LEE, LAURIE, 3
B. may be a matter of a moment LEBOYER, FRÉDÉRICK, 1
b. of the Universe SMOOT, GEORGE, 1
From b. to eighteen, a girl needs good parents TUCKER, SOPHIE, 2
Our b. is but a sleep WORDSWORTH, WILLIAM, 52
The memory of b. FORSTER, E. M., 20
To hinder a b. is...speedier man-killing TERTULLIAN, 1
waiting for the miracle of b. HAMEL, GARY, 6
birthday is it my b. or am I dying ASTOR, NANCY, 10
Turning one hundred was the worst b. DELANY, ANNIE ELIZABETH "BESSIE," 1
birthdays they don't understand about b. CISNEROS, SANDRA, 2
birthright I cannot sell my b. MANDELA, NELSON, 7
biscuit Can't a fellow even enjoy a b. PORTLAND, DUKE OF, 1
bisexual I am b....it's the best thing BOWIE, DAVID, 3
bisexuality b....necessary factor in artistic production KOLLWITZ, KÄTHE, 1
bishop a b....must be blameless BIBLE, 235
How can a b. marry SMITH, SYDNEY, 13
Make him a b., and you will silence him CHESTERFIELD, LORD, 20
No B., no King JAMES I, 7
symbol of a b. is a crook DIX, GREGORY, 1
bisier he semed b. than he was CHAUCER, GEOFFREY, 19
bit He b. his lip in a manner PERELMAN, S. J., 4
bitch an old b. gone in the teeth POUND, EZRA, 15
deciding not to be a b. HEMINGWAY, ERNEST, 19
son of a b. isn't going...resign MACARTHUR, DOUGLAS, 1
bite b....if it prevents you from feeding SZASZ, THOMAS, 7
b. the hand that fed them BURKE, EDMUND, 52
b. the hand that feeds us ANONYMOUS, 73
will *b.* some of my other generals GEORGE II, 3
bites A dead woman b. not GRAY, LORD PATRICK, 1
when a man b. a dog that is news BOGART, JOHN B., 1
biting See what will happen...if you don't stop b. your fingernails ROGERS, WILL, 14
bitter it is b....it is my heart CRANE, STEPHEN, 3
I was b., blue and black BENNETT, LERONE, JR., 1
bittern He shall not hear the b. cry DAVIS, THOMAS, 1
bitterness B. is like cancer ANGELOU, MAYA, 18
You cannot be fuelled by b. BHUTTO, BENAZIR, 2
bivouac b. of the dead O'HARA, THEODORE, 1
black a B. choreographer talking to Black people AILEY, ALVIN, 1
a b. person's demanding equality in the Ku Klux Klan DALY, MARY, 2
A lady asked me why...I wore b. SITWELL, EDITH, 8
B. and beautiful HUGHES, LANGSTON, 8
b. and unknown bards of long ago JOHNSON, JAMES WELDON, 6
B. A, white E, red I...vowels RIMBAUD, ARTHUR, 4
b., black woman is our essential mother WALKER, ALICE, 7
Being b....is a reflection of a mental attitude BIKO, STEPHEN, 4
B. history began with Malcolm X CLEAVER, ELDRIDGE, 2
B. is a sacrament GIOVANNI, NIKKI, 2
B. is beautiful MOTTOS AND SLOGANS, 30
B. is beautiful when...a slum kid...enter college YOUNG, WHITNEY M., JR., 1
B. people are...bettering themselves COVEY, DONNA, 1
b. people possess the secret of joy WALKER, ALICE, 14
b. ram /Is tupping your white ewe SHAKESPEARE, WILLIAM, 465
British Government sees b. people as expendable TUTU, DESMOND, 2
B.'s not so black; nor white so very white CANNING, GEORGE, 2
B. tulips in my heart DARWISH, MAHMOUD, 4
every b. entrepreneur...lot of social worker TRAVIS, DEMPSEY J., 1
have it...in b. and white JONSON, BEN, 10
he leads his b. soldiers to death LOWELL, ROBERT, 11
I am a b. woman EVANS, MARI, 1
I am b. CONSTANTINE, LEARIE, 1
I am b. and I am beautiful JACKSON, JESSE, 2
I don't believe in b. majority rule SMITH, IAN, 1
If you are b., the only roads into the mainland of American life BARAKA, IMAMU AMIRI, 6
I have a b., a woman WATT, JAMES G., 1
I have seen b. hands /raised WRIGHT, RICHARD, 6
I'm B. and I'm Proud MOTTOS AND SLOGANS, 28
I'm b....It's like having a dick GOLDBERG, WHOOPI, 1
Kiss my happy, rich b. ass PRYOR, RICHARD, 1
Malcolm was...our living, b. manhood MALCOLM X, 1
My color is b., It stands for mourning ALEGRE, COSTA, 1
My major advice to young b. artists WALKER, ALICE, 4
No *sane* b. man really wants integration MALCOLM X, 19
People think we do not understand our b....countrymen BOTHA, ELIZE, 1
struggle for b. freedom...rivers of blood HARDING, VINCENT, 1
Take that b. box away TREE, HERBERT BEERBOHM, 1
That old b. magic MERCER, JOHNNY, 2
the white storyteller will not do full justice to the...b. race PICKENS, WILLIAM, 2
The world said you spelled b. with a capital nothing NAYLOR, GLORIA, 2
thou read'st b. where I read white BLAKE, WILLIAM, 35
To be b. and conscious in America BALDWIN, JAMES, 29
To like an individual because he's b. CUMMINGS, E. E., 23
we don't stand for b. majority rule MANDELA, NELSON, 5
we'll form a B. Nationalist army MALCOLM X, 17
What...should the B. dancer dance about THORPE, EDWARD, 1
Where is the b. man's Government GARVEY, MARCUS, 6
Who art as b. as hell, as dark as night SHAKESPEARE, WILLIAM, 589
Who can be born b. and not exult EVANS, MARI, 4
You b., you pore...you a woman WALKER, ALICE, 24
you do not do /Anymore, b. shoe PLATH, SYLVIA, 2
Black America B. in the nineties was a symphony of contradictions BENNETT, LERONE, JR., 2
blacker The b. the mantle the mightier the man DU BOIS, W. E. B., 8
you the b. devil SHAKESPEARE, WILLIAM, 497

black girl A little b. yearns for the blue eyes of a little white girl MORRISON, TONI, 24
black hole A b. has no hair WHEELER, JOHN ARCHIBALD, 1
black man The b. cannot protect a country TURNER, HENRY M., 1
blackness In b. there is some virtue ANTAR, 1
black people Imagine thinking that b. write only about being black WALKER, ALICE, 33
black power B....call for a black people TOURÉ, KWAME, 1
B. does not mean violence POWELL, ADAM CLAYTON, JR., 1
blacks They say things are better for B. in this country WONDER, STEVIE, 3
black woman Every B. in America LORDE, AUDRE, 1
black women Our history as B. MORRISON, TONI, 11
Blake B....presents only the essential BLAKE, WILLIAM, 1
blame b....the existence of humanity on women RICHARDSON, DOROTHY M., 1
blaming effective way of b. the victim STEINEM, GLORIA, 10
bland the b. lead the bland GALBRAITH, J. K., 12
blanket not a b. woven from one thread, one color, one cloth JACKSON, JESSE, 6
blasphemies To what extent would people tolerate b. AUSTER, PAUL, 7
blasphemous a b. frivolity BONHOEFFER, DIETRICH, 8
blasphemy b., Salman, can't be forgiven RUSHDIE, SALMAN, 9
blast the b. of war SHAKESPEARE, WILLIAM, 266
blessed b. are the poor in spirit BIBLE, 375
b. is he that cometh in the name of the Lord BIBLE, 419
B. is he who expects nothing FRANKLIN, BENJAMIN, 12
b. is the man that endureth temptation BIBLE, 241
B. rage for order STEVENS, WALLACE, 1
May you be b. with light FOLK VERSE, 10
blessing a b....very well disguised CHURCHILL, WINSTON, 66
b. of God Almighty BOOK OF COMMON PRAYER, 10
the b. of St. Peter's Master WALTON, IZAAK, 6
blessings b. in disguise HERVEY, JAMES, 1
B. on your young courage, boy VIRGIL, 22
blest B. is that nation JEFFERSON, THOMAS, 7
this b. man, let his just praise be given WALTON, IZAAK, 1
blew b. so much out /He couldn't think MITCHELL, ADRIAN, 3
blind A b. man in a dark room BOWEN, CHARLES, 2
B. Fortune still /Bestows her gifts JONSON, BEN, 11
b. in their own cause PROVERBS, MODERN, 18
How b. we are EKELÖF, GUNNAR, 1
If the b. lead the blind BIBLE, 406
It is not miserable to be b. MILTON, JOHN, 126
I wish all Americans...b. as you KELLER, HELEN, 1
Like so many b. people my grandfather...passionate sightseer VIDAL, GORE, 1
the b. receive their sight BIBLE, 398
whereas I was b., now I see BIBLE, 284
blinked the other fellow just b. RUSK, DEAN, 1
bliss b. in proof and proved...very woe SHAKESPEARE, WILLIAM, 584
b. /To go with you by train to Diss BETJEMAN, JOHN, 5
B. was it in that dawn to be alive WORDSWORTH, WILLIAM, 87
Follow your b. CAMPBELL, JOSEPH, 1
The b. of animals lies in this MACDONALD, GEORGE, 1
blithe Hail to thee, b. Spirit SHELLEY, PERCY BYSSHE, 24
blockhead bookful b., ignorantly read POPE, ALEXANDER, 24
No man but a b. ever wrote JOHNSON, SAMUEL, 105
blonde A b. to make a bishop kick a hole CHANDLER, RAYMOND, 2
springing from b....chamois of the Alps WODEHOUSE, P. G., 27
blondes B. have more fun ADVERTISEMENTS, 15
Gentlemen always seem to remember b. LOOS, ANITA, 3
blood be his b. on your own conscience CHARLES II, 14
B. is thicker than water PROVERBS, 167
B....moves the wheels of history MUSSOLINI, BENITO, 15
b. of the innocent will...rise MUSSORGSKY, MODEST, 1
b. of the martyrs...seed of the Church TERTULLIAN, 3
B. really is thicker than water PINKER, STEVEN, 2
B. sport is brought to its ultimate refinement INGHAM, BERNARD, 1
b., toil, tears and sweat CHURCHILL, WINSTON, 28
I am in b. /Stepp'd in so far SHAKESPEARE, WILLIAM, 405
Nothing like b., sir, in...men THACKERAY, WILLIAM MAKEPEACE, 10
shed his b. for the country ROOSEVELT, THEODORE, 12
There are two kinds of b. TUWIM, JULIAN, 1
We cannot go on spilling b. MAJOR, JOHN, 1
white in the b. of the Lamb BIBLE, 467
Who so sheddeth man's b. BIBLE, 118
You can't get b. PROVERBS, 465
bloody not half b. enough JEFFREYS, GEORGE, 1
Woe to the b. city BIBLE, 446
bloom a sort of b. on a woman BARRIE, J. M., 17
blossom Love's perfect b. PATMORE, COVENTRY, 2
blossoms B. and branches green to coffins WHITMAN, WALT, 48
blotted "Would he had b. a thousand" SHAKESPEARE, WILLIAM, 30
bloud I smell the b. of an English-man NASHE, THOMAS, 1
blow B., blow, thou winter wind SHAKESPEARE, WILLIAM, 108
I'd love to b. my own trumpet O'CASEY, SEAN, 1
bludgeoning the b. of the people WILDE, OSCAR, 69
blue Little Boy B., /Come blow your horn CHILDREN'S VERSE, 6
that little tent of b. WILDE, OSCAR, 35
The essence of any b. material RUE, DANNY LA, 1
The intense b. in the pool water DIDION, JOAN, 4
With the b. above and the blue below PROCTER, BRYAN WALLER, 1
blueeyed like your b. boy /Mister Death CUMMINGS, E. E., 20
blue jeans I wish I had invented b. SAINT LAURENT, YVES, 3
blues B. are the songs of despair JACKSON, MAHALIA, 1
b. came from the man farthest down HANDY, W. C., 3
Being a b. singer KING, B. B., 1
b. is an art of ambiguity ELLISON, RALPH, 8
B....not being at the centre SMITH, BESSIE, 1
No white man ever had the b. LEADBELLY, 1
People like their b. singers dead JOPLIN, JANIS, 5
person who sings only the b. JACKSON, MAHALIA, 2
Some days called for the b. MARSHALL, PAULE, 3
The b. would always be with us MOSLEY, WALTER, 10
When we sing the b. HURSTON, ZORA NEALE, 16
blue-vested short, b. people COREN, ALAN, 3
blunders b. usually do more to shape history than human wickedness TAYLOR, A. J. P., 4
blush a b. to the cheek of a young person DICKENS, CHARLES, 72
blushes Man is the only animal that b. TWAIN, MARK, 18
blushing I...take b....for a sign of guilt CONGREVE, WILLIAM, 20
BMW A B. can't hug and kiss you at night MCMILLAN, TERRY, 1

board I struck the b., and cried HERBERT, GEORGE, 17
boardroom Get me inside any b. BOND, ALAN, 1
I often get invited to b. lunches D'ABO, JENNIFER, 1
thrills and spills of a b. WHITEHORN, KATHARINE, 8
boast b. about their Brooklyn Bridge MCGONAGALL, WILLIAM, 1
boat Speed, bonny b., like a bird on the wing BOULTON, HAROLD EDWIN, 1
boats b. against the current FITZGERALD, F. SCOTT, 15
Boche drove the B. across the Rhine FOLK VERSE, 62
bodies B. devoid of mind...statues EURIPIDES, 6
well-developed b., fairly developed minds, and undeveloped hearts FORSTER, E. M., 6
what happens in our b....directed toward a useful end CANNON, WALTER BRADFORD, 1
bodily I had no b....or palpable presence POE, EDGAR ALLAN, 12
body a b. like mine ADVERTISEMENTS, 6
A b. seriously out of equilibrium SANTAYANA, GEORGE, 16
B. and mind...do not always agree to die OUSPENSKY, PETER, 1
b. exists for the sake of the eyes MORRISON, JIM, 7
b. of a man half my age FOREMAN, GEORGE, 1
b. of a weak and feeble woman ELIZABETH I, 12
b. that could melt a cheese sandwich ZUCKER, DAVID, 1
Gin a b. meet a body BURNS, ROBERT, 13
human b. remain nude and uncovered JOHN PAUL II, 3
If I had the use of my b. BECKETT, SAMUEL, 10
If the b. be feeble, the mind will not be strong JEFFERSON, THOMAS, 6
My b., eh. Friend Death, how now? JACKSON, HELEN HUNT, 1
My b. of a sudden blazed YEATS, W. B., 62
Our b. is a machine for living TOLSTOY, LEO, 13
pathways between b. and mind FREUD, ANNA, 4
She's got an amazing b....big tits SCHIFFER, CLAUDIA, 1
the b. is affected through the mind HOLMES, OLIVER WENDELL, 12
The b. is...kingdom of the self AL-NAWAWI, MUHYID-DIN ABU ZAKARIYYA IBN SHARAF, 7
The b. is not a permanent dwelling SENECA, "THE YOUNGER," 12
The b. is truly the garment of the soul HILDEGARDE OF BINGEN, 1
the b....medium for the mind and spirit PAVLOVA, ANNA, 2
The b. politic, like the human body, begins to die ROUSSEAU, JEAN-JACQUES, 18
The human b....indeed is like a ship MELVILLE, HERMAN, 9
The human b. is a machine LA METTRIE, JULIEN OFFROY DE, 2
the human b. is sacred WHITMAN, WALT, 25
The human b. is the best picture of the human soul WITTGENSTEIN, LUDWIG, 2
The human b....like a bakery SCHICK, BÉLA, 6
Thersites' b. is as good as Ajax' SHAKESPEARE, WILLIAM, 132
Well in b....sick in mind PLAUTUS, 3
your b. is your enemy ESCRIVÁ DE BALAGUER Y ALBAS, JOSÉ MARÍA, 1
bodyguards no use for b., but...accountants PRESLEY, ELVIS, 4
body-line B....was the violence...of our age expressing itself in cricket JAMES, C. L. R., 5
boets I hate all B. and Bainters GEORGE I, 2
Bogart B.'s a helluva nice guy till 11.30 p.m. CHAUSEN, DAVE, 1
Bognor Bugger B. GEORGE V, 3
bohemian B. elements have found...peculiar beatnik theories KEROUAC, JACK, 3
boil b. at different degrees EMERSON, RALPH WALDO, 43
Looks like he had a b. BURNS, ROBERT, 1
bold A b. bad man SPENSER, EDMUND, 7
He was a b. man PROVERBS, 251
boldness B., and again boldness DANTON, GEORGES JACQUES, 1
b. ever meets with friends POPE, ALEXANDER, 71
the b. to dream HART, MOSS, 2
Bolshevik the B. tyranny is the worst CHURCHILL, WINSTON, 19
bomb Ban the b. MOTTOS AND SLOGANS, 29
B. mark infinity a sudden furnace CORSO, GREGORY, 2
b. them into the Stone Age LEMAY, CURTIS EMERSON, 1
B....you're no crueller than cancer CORSO, GREGORY, 1
He carried up the b....let it fall WAIN, JOHN, 2
I said, "That was the B." FEYNMAN, RICHARD PHILLIPS, 3
piss us off we'll b. your cities WILLIAMS, ROBIN, 9
red b. that spouts...great white cloud DELILLO, DON, 5
bomber the b. will always get through BALDWIN, STANLEY, 6
bombers man the b. to kill the babies LE GUIN, URSULA, 1
bombs b. *are* unbelievable until they...fall WHITE, PATRICK, 1
Come, friendly b., and fall on Slough BETJEMAN, JOHN, 11
Whenever you drop b. GOLDWATER, BARRY, 2
Bonaparte B.'s whole life...was a fraud NAPOLEON I, 11
bond I want to be the b. market CARVILLE, JAMES, 1
make not a b. of love GIBRAN, KAHLIL, 2
the b. business had been the bedridden giant WOLFE, TOM, 5
Bond B....a cross, a privilege, a joke CONNERY, SEAN, 1
bondage Cassius from b. will deliver Cassius SHAKESPEARE, WILLIAM, 300
Of Human B. MAUGHAM, SOMERSET, 13
bondmen We were Pharaoh's b. in Egypt BIBLE, 34
bone b. to his bone BIBLE, 94
Fetiches may be fragments of b. POWELL, JOHN WESLEY, 1
The nearer the b. PROVERBS, 408
boneless no such thing as b. meat PROVERBS, 59
bones b. in his feet...like a bird's RAMBERT, DAME MARIE, 2
worth the healthy b. of a...Pomeranian grenadier BISMARCK, PRINCE OTTO VON, 15
bonfire The B. of the Vanities WOLFE, TOM, 23
bonnie for b. Annie Laurie DOUGLAS, WILLIAM, 1
My B. lies over the ocean FOLK VERSE, 40
Bonzo I thought B. would make a good change MACKENZIE, COMPTON, 4
boobies up to your b. in white satin HOLIDAY, BILLIE, 5
booby hatch a man who takes a woman to a b. GOLDMAN, WILLIAM, 3
book A b. by a great man...a compromise DELACROIX, EUGÈNE, 1
A b. is like a man STEINBECK, JOHN, 33
A b. may be amusing GOLDSMITH, OLIVER, 26
a b. that is a book flowers once LAWRENCE, D. H., 33
a b. to kill time MACAULAY, ROSE, 8
A classic b....survives the circumstances KAZIN, ALFRED, 1
age of the b. is almost gone STEINER, GEORGE, 2
A good b....a kind of absence PAMUK, ORHAN, 7
A good b. is the best of friends TUPPER, MARTIN FARQUHAR, 1
A good b. is the precious life-blood MILTON, JOHN, 11
Another damned, thick, square b. GLOUCESTER, WILLIAM, 1
A wonderful b. AKHMATOVA, ANNA, 8
bad b....as much a labour...as a good one HUXLEY, ALDOUS, 39
b. has much in common...your dress STOPPARD, TOM, 14
b. is not harmless merely ELIOT, T. S., 56
B. reading is a solitary...pursuit KEILLOR, GARRISON, 13

"B.!" repeated Hawkeye, with...disdain COOPER, JAMES FENIMORE, 8
b. that furnishes no quotations is...a plaything PEACOCK, THOMAS LOVE, 4
b. where men /May read strange matters SHAKESPEARE, WILLIAM, 389
b....your wife or your servants to read GRIFFITH-JONES, MERVYN, 1
Don't join the b. burners EISENHOWER, DWIGHT D., 22
each b. should be a new beginning HEMINGWAY, ERNEST, 5
Every b. must be chewed PROVERBS, 29
Everybody writes a b. too many RICHLER, MORDECAI, 2
everyone has it in him to write one b. MAUGHAM, SOMERSET, 42
God forbid...any b. should be banned WEST, REBECCA, 7
Go, little b., and wish to all STEVENSON, ROBERT LOUIS, 21
good of a b. lies in being read ECO, UMBERTO, 9
If a b. is worth reading RUSKIN, JOHN, 9
I have only read one b. MITFORD, NANCY, 3
moral or an immoral b. WILDE, OSCAR, 67
My B. and Heart FOLK VERSE, 42
My b....Thou, my God, art in't HERRICK, ROBERT, 13
never got around to reading the b. MARX, GROUCHO, 32
new b. is published, read an old one ROGERS, SAMUEL, 11
note it in a b., that it may be...for ever and ever BIBLE, 210
people will put anything in a b. MACKENZIE, COMPTON, 2
the b. cannot take the place of...*Practical Gamekeeping* LAWRENCE, D. H., 1
the b. that ran me down WALKER, ALICE, 31
The b. written against fame EMERSON, RALPH WALDO, 34
The possession of a b. BURGESS, ANTHONY, 7
This b. does me a *lot* of good JAMES, WILLIAM, 1
unprintable b. that is readable MILLER, HENRY, 2
What is the use of a b. CARROLL, LEWIS, 2
You can't tell a b. PROVERBS, 471

books A cool of b. /...a hot afternoon WILLIAMS, WILLIAM CARLOS, 7
against b. the Home Secretary is WAUGH, EVELYN, 31
All b. are divisible into two classes RUSKIN, JOHN, 11
All good b. are alike HEMINGWAY, ERNEST, 12
B. and friends PROVERBS, 168
B. are a load of crap LARKIN, PHILIP, 1
B. are made...like pyramids FLAUBERT, GUSTAVE, 1
b. are only words ZHUANGZI, 6
B....bloodless substitute for life STEVENSON, ROBERT LOUIS, 28
B. cannot always please CRABBE, GEORGE, 5
B. create eras and nations AMPÈRE, JEAN-JAQUES, 1
be not swallowed up in b. WESLEY, JOHN, 6
B., I don't know what you see in them USTINOV, PETER, 9
B. must follow sciences BACON, FRANCIS (1561–1626), 87
b....putting us to ignorance again BROWNING, ROBERT, 54
b....read by people who don't understand them LICHTENBERG, GEORG CHRISTOPH, 7
B. think for me LAMB, CHARLES, 20
B., we are told, propose to instruct or to amuse DE QUINCEY, THOMAS, 7
Few b. today are forgivable LAING, R. D., 12
Give me b., fruit, French wine and fine weather KEATS, JOHN (1795–1821), 34
He felt about b. as doctors...cynical but hopeful MACAULAY, ROSE, 3
If my b. had been any worse CHANDLER, RAYMOND, 12
I keep my b. at the British Museum BUTLER, SAMUEL (1835–1902), 8
No furniture so charming as b. SMITH, SYDNEY, 15
of making many b. there is no end BIBLE, 59
read...b. to find the juicy passages GREENE, GRAHAM, 2
Some b. are lies BURNS, ROBERT, 14
Some b. are to be tasted BACON, FRANCIS (1561–1626), 65
Some b. are undeservedly forgotten AUDEN, W. H., 30
think of all the b. I have read YEATS, W. B., 8
time to leave off b. and moanings COOPER, JAMES FENIMORE, 16
To read too many b. MAO ZEDONG, 12
two classes of b. are of universal appeal FORD, FORD MADOX, 1
We all know that b. burn ROOSEVELT, FRANKLIN D., 10

booksellers b....generous liberal-minded men JOHNSON, SAMUEL, 120

boot B., saddle, to horse, and away BROWNING, ROBERT, 12

Booth B. died blind LINDSAY, VACHEL, 1

boots If ever he went to school without any b. BULMER-THOMAS, IVOR, 1
look at his b. SHAW, GEORGE BERNARD, 77
These b. are made for walking HAZLEWOOD, LEE, 1
Very well, then I shall not take off my b. WELLINGTON, DUKE OF, 10

booze man shouldn't fool with b. until he's fifty FAULKNER, WILLIAM, 19

bo-peep Little B. has lost her sheep CHILDREN'S VERSE, 17

borderless In a b. world OHMAE, KENICHI, 8

bore A b., a bounder and a prig CHANNON, HENRY, 1
A healthy male adult b. UPDIKE, JOHN, 3
b. is a man who...tells you TAYLOR, BERT LESTON, 1
B....person who talks BIERCE, AMBROSE, 9
thou shalt not b. WILDER, BILLY, 5
you are...the club B.: I am the club Liar SAKI, 1

bored I wanted to be b. to death DE VRIES, PETER, 3
I wonder if he is b. SAINT LAURENT, YVES, 1
so b. with it all CHURCHILL, WINSTON, 63
When you're b. with yourself EDWARD VIII, 7

boredom B. is...a vital problem for the moralist RUSSELL, BERTRAND, 47
b....psychopathological phenomena FROMM, ERICH, 5
The effect of b. on a large scale INGE, WILLIAM RALPH, 18
Those who die of b....Sunday afternoon PRÉVERT, JACQUES, 3

bores he b. for England EDEN, ANTHONY, 1

boring a life so b....you are easily enchanted BRYSON, BILL, 9
I want a b. job PERLMAN, LAWRENCE, 2
Somebody's b. me, I think it's me THOMAS, DYLAN, 30
something curiously b. about...happiness HUXLEY, ALDOUS, 33
There is nothing as b. as the truth BUKOWSKI, CHARLES, 8
you ought to be ashamed...being b. HAILSHAM, LORD, 4

born Alas! and am I b. for this HORTON, GEORGE MOSES, 1
As soon as man is b. PROVERBS, 144
b. again, not of corruptible seed BIBLE, 191
b., bred, and hanged, all in the same parish EPITAPHS, 13
being b., to die DRUMMOND, WILLIAM, 1
Better mankind b. without mouths OLSEN, TILLIE, 1
b. in a duckyard ANDERSEN, HANS CHRISTIAN, 3
b....in the Baltic marshland BRODSKY, JOSEPH, 2
B. in the USA SPRINGSTEEN, BRUCE, 2
B. of the sun SPENDER, STEPHEN, 3
b. to obey COMPTON-BURNETT, IVY, 4
b. until I started to write HARE, DAVID, 3
Every moment...one sixteenth is b. TENNYSON, ALFRED, 2
except a man be b. again BIBLE, 271
I am not yet b. MACNEICE, LOUIS, 9
I was b. at the age of twelve GARLAND, JUDY, 1
I was b....because my mother needed a fourth at meals LILLIE, BEATRICE, 1

I was b. for a salesman MAMET, DAVID, 7
I was b. in 1896 ACKERLEY, J. R., 1
I was b. in a cellar CONGREVE, WILLIAM, 3
I was b. into big celebrity FISHER, CARRIE, 4
I was b. intoxicated Æ, 1
I was b. old and get younger TREE, HERBERT BEERBOHM, 3
I was b. on a day VALLEJO, CÉSAR, 2
I was b. to be...a writer OZICK, CYNTHIA, 1
I was b. when she kissed me BOGART, HUMPHREY, 7
I was not b. under a rhyming planet SHAKESPEARE, WILLIAM, 463
I who was B. a PAGAN and a SLAVE AFRICANUS, SCIPIO, 1
Man...hath but a short time to live BOOK OF COMMON PRAYER, 3
one of woman b. SHAKESPEARE, WILLIAM, 423
that which is b. of the flesh is flesh BIBLE, 272
to the manner b. SHAKESPEARE, WILLIAM, 154
We all are b. mad BECKETT, SAMUEL, 28

born-again b. people...wish they'd never been born WHITEHORN, KATHARINE, 9

borrow if you b. a million ANONYMOUS, 63
if you b., borrow big ONASSIS, ARISTOTLE, 2
Never b.! Something of freedom's lost IBSEN, HENRIK, 2
There are people who b. your watch TOWNSEND, ROBERT, 14
You b. money at a certain rate GOIZUETA, ROBERTO, 5

borrowed People who live on b. culture VITTACHI, VARINDRA TARZIE, 1

borrower Neither a b. nor a lender be SHAKESPEARE, WILLIAM, 152

borrowers b. of books LAMB, CHARLES, 18

borrowing He that goes a-b. goes a-sorrowing FRANKLIN, BENJAMIN, 16
we're b. from abroad VOLCKER, PAUL A., 3

bosom not a b. to repose upon DICKENS, CHARLES, 43

boss B. your boss CARNEGIE, ANDREW, 3
I'm the b.. I'm allowed to yell BOESKY, IVAN, 2
the b. shoots the arrow of...performance BUFFETT, WARREN, 3
working faithfully...you may eventually get to be a b. FROST, ROBERT, 24

Boston B. man...east wind made flesh APPLETON, THOMAS GOLD, 2
I have just returned from B. ALLEN, FRED, 1
In B. they ask, How much TWAIN, MARK, 45
not genuine B., I am Boston-plated ALDRICH, THOMAS BAILEY, 2
this is good old B. BOSSIDY, JOHN COLLINS, 1
We say the cows laid out B. EMERSON, RALPH WALDO, 57

botanical glorious b. and geological excursion MUIR, JOHN, 3

Botticelli If B. were alive today USTINOV, PETER, 8

bottinney b. means a knowledge of plants DICKENS, CHARLES, 59

bottom I'm the b. you're the top PORTER, COLE, 4

bottom line The b. is in heaven LAND, EDWIN HERBERT, 2

boudoir half-b., half-boardroom image...works best LAUDER, ESTÉE, 2

bough Loaf of Bread beneath the B. FITZGERALD, EDWARD, 5

bought The friend that can be b. PROVERBS, 72

bouillabaisse B....good because cooked by the French DOUGLAS, NORMAN, 2

Boulogne There was an old man of B. LIMERICKS, 4

bound Nobody is b. by obligation BETTI, UGO, 8
There is no one so b. MACHADO, ANTONIO, 8

boundary right to fix the b. of...a nation PARNELL, CHARLES STEWART, 4

boundaryless B. behavior is what integrates us WELCH, JACK, 8
Collocation...the ultimate b. behavior WELCH, JACK, 9

boundless b. fields of harvest in the West PIATT, JOHN JAMES, 1

bounty My b. is as boundless as the sea SHAKESPEARE, WILLIAM, 541
Your b. threatens me, Mandela SOYINKA, WOLE, 3

bouquet the b. is better than the taste POTTER, STEPHEN, 4
You set a b. of yellow flowers ablaze GOGH, VINCENT VAN, 1

bourgeois A b. careerist, intriguer LIN BIAO, 1
B....is an epithet HOPE, ANTHONY, 5
How beastly the b. is LAWRENCE, D. H., 30
The b. are other people RENARD, JULES, 12
The b. prefers comfort to pleasure HESSE, HERMANN, 3

bowels a good reliable set of b. is worth more to a man BILLINGS, JOSH, 4
a good reliable sett ov b. iz wurth more tu a man SHAW, HENRY WHEELER, 1
thirty yards of b. squeezed underneath that girdle ABERNETHY, JOHN, 3

bower-bird I'm a bit of a b. WHITE, PATRICK, 2

bowers to the b. of bliss conveyed TICKELL, THOMAS, 1

bowl inverted B. we call The Sky FITZGERALD, EDWARD, 13

box Your arm's too short to b. with God JOHNSON, JAMES WELDON, 4

boxer Every so often a b. dies ROBINSON, SUGAR RAY, 1

boxing B.'s just showbusiness with blood BRUNO, FRANK, 1
Professional b. is no longer worthy COSELL, HOWARD, 1

boy a nicens little b. named baby tuckoo JOYCE, JAMES, 4
at fourteen every b. should be in love NORMAN, BARRY, 1
every b. and every gal /That's born into the world alive GILBERT, W. S., 14
fair b. that had my heart entangled BARNFIELD, RICHARD, 7
like a b. playing on the sea-shore NEWTON, ISAAC, 8
Little B. kneels at the foot of the bed MILNE, A. A., 18
play the b....blubber in thy bosom OTWAY, THOMAS, 4
sit next to the b. you fancy LAMBERT, KIT, 1
Sometime a lovely b. in Dian's shape MARLOWE, CHRISTOPHER, 17
The b. stood on the burning deck HEMANS, FELICIA, 1
Try a b. for a change ORTON, JOE, 11
When I was a b. of 14 TWAIN, MARK, 49
When I was a little b. SINGER, ISAAC BASHEVIS, 2

boyhood from b. to manhood is a movable feast JOHNSON, JAMES WELDON, 3

boys B. and girls come out to play CHILDREN'S VERSE, 59
B. are capital fellows in their own way LAMB, CHARLES, 15
B. do not grow up gradually CONNOLLY, CYRIL, 8
b. plan for what they will achieve GILMAN, CHARLOTTE PERKINS, 3
had no relish of...fair fac'd b. DRYDEN, JOHN, 26
He hath his b., and beauteous girls JONSON, BEN, 14
Most b....wishing they could die gloriously ANDERSON, SHERWOOD, 4
three merry b. are we FLETCHER, JOHN, 5
We two b. together clinging WHITMAN, WALT, 45
Where are the b. of the Old Brigade WEATHERLY, FREDERIC EDWARD, 2
wild b. innocent as strawberries THOMAS, DYLAN, 15

bra Burn your b. MOTTOS AND SLOGANS, 4
I just told my mother I want a b. BLUME, JUDY, 1
pulled herself up by her b. straps MIDLER, BETTE, 1

bracelet diamond and sapphire b. lasts forever LOOS, ANITA, 6

braces Damn b. BLAKE, WILLIAM, 45

Brahms B....an extraordinary musician BRAHMS, JOHANNES, 2
do B. without knowing Schoenberg BRAHMS, JOHANNES, 1

brain a b....suited to our needs SMITH, ANTHONY, 2
b. is the means by which we think TUWIM, JULIAN, 2
b....my second favorite organ ALLEN, WOODY, 10
b....seat of, all our joys HIPPOCRATES, 5
b. the size of a planet ADAMS, DOUGLAS, 8
B....with which we think that we think BIERCE, AMBROSE, 10
depravement of the b....phlegm and bile HIPPOCRATES, 6
I can b. a Huron COOPER, JAMES FENIMORE, 7
It is good to rub and polish our b. MONTAIGNE, MICHEL DE, 2
keep his little b. attic stocked DOYLE, ARTHUR CONAN, 7
our b. is a mystery RAMÓN Y CAJAL, SANTIAGO, 1
part of...b. reliably devoted to sex STEINEM, GLORIA, 6
The b. has muscles for thinking LA METTRIE, JULIEN OFFROY DE, 1
the biggest b. of all the primates MORRIS, DESMOND, 5
The b. is a wonderful organ FROST, ROBERT, 26
The b. is not an organ to be relied upon BLOK, ALEKSANDR, 5
the human b. is a device to keep the ears from grating DE VRIES, PETER, 1
You've got the b. of a four-year-old boy MARX, GROUCHO, 21

brains a girl with b. ought to do something LOOS, ANITA, 4
A man's b. splattered ROSENBERG, ISAAC, 1
B. are...the core of organisations HANDY, CHARLES, 1
b. enough to make a fool of himself STEVENSON, ROBERT LOUIS, 24
b. were suitable for a woman MEAD, MARGARET, 2
sometimes his b. go to his head SMITH, F. E., 1
What good are b. to a man? WODEHOUSE, P. G., 17

branch Cut is the b. that might have grown MARLOWE, CHRISTOPHER, 14

Brando B. is always compulsive viewing BRANDO, MARLON, 1

brass bands B. are all very well...outdoors BEECHAM, THOMAS, 8

brave A b. world, Sir, full of religion BEHN, APHRA, 10
Any fool can be b. on a battle field MITCHELL, MARGARET, 4
I'm very b. generally CARROLL, LEWIS, 39
It is hard to be b. MILNE, A. A., 23
Many b. men...before Agamemnon's time HORACE, 52
None but the b. deserves the fair DRYDEN, JOHN, 22
Shall I ask the b. soldier MOORE, THOMAS, 14
The b. man thinks of himself...last SCHILLER, FRIEDRICH VON, 23
the b. poet is afraid to die GOSAIBI, GHAZI AL-, 2

Brazil In B. they throw flowers DIETRICH, MARLENE, 2

Brazilian handsome booted B. who is a wanted killer MATTHIESSEN, PETER, 7

breach Once more unto the b. SHAKESPEARE, WILLIAM, 267

breache lay the b. at their door ARLINGTON, HENRY BENNET, 1

bread b. and circuses JUVENAL, 16
B. is the staff of life PROVERBS, 169
I am the b. of life BIBLE, 279
Jesus took b., and blessed it BIBLE, 435
tasting a piece of good b. MILLER, HENRY, 4
The Royal slice of b. MILNE, A. A., 17

break B., break, break...O Sea TENNYSON, ALFRED, 39
Better...to b. sod as a farm hand HOMER, 8
I'll b. my staff SHAKESPEARE, WILLIAM, 653
Let's b. away from rationality MARINETTI, FILIPPO TOMMASO, 5

breakfast B. At Tiffanys CAPOTE, TRUMAN, 5
b. food...the leavings of carthorse nosebags MUIR, FRANK, 3
b. of champions ADVERTISEMENTS, 24
fragile, musaceous odor of B. PYNCHON, THOMAS, 2
Let's have b. at Tiffany's CLARKE, GERALD, 1

breakfast cereal Do you *know* what b. is made of DAHL, ROALD, 1

breakfasted I shall be b....I shall astonish you all HARDY, THOMAS, 7

breakthroughs three major b. in one year EINSTEIN, ALBERT, 6

break-up I felt the weight of the b. LENNON, JOHN, 3

breasts there are no b. in space FISHER, CARRIE, 1

breath b. of the wind sweeps through the harp FOLK VERSE, 47
in this harsh world draw thy b. in pain SHAKESPEARE, WILLIAM, 228
last b. be drawn through a pipe and exhaled in a pun LAMB, CHARLES, 10
the light b. of his dead host JAMES, HENRY, 32
with toil of b. COLERIDGE, SAMUEL TAYLOR, 12

breathed God...b. into his nostrils BIBLE, 107

breathes Who b. must suffer PRIOR, MATTHEW, 7

breathing Keep b. TUCKER, SOPHIE, 1

breathing-space b. in the architecture of your love FARAH, NURUDDIN, 6

bred B. en bawn in a brier-patch HARRIS, JOEL CHANDLER, 1

breeder a b. of sinners SHAKESPEARE, WILLIAM, 176

breeding Good b....concealing how much we think TWAIN, MARK, 26
rabbit-like in our unplanned b. of ourselves TOYNBEE, ARNOLD, 7

breeze The fair b. blew COLERIDGE, SAMUEL TAYLOR, 40

brevity B. is the soul of lingerie PARKER, DOROTHY, 35
B. is the soul of wit SHAKESPEARE, WILLIAM, 172
The b. of our life JOHN OF SALISBURY, 2

brewery never...bet my bladder against a b. KIRKLAND, LANE, 2

brews As he b., so shall he drink JONSON, BEN, 8

bribe a b. gives away...his own importance GREENE, GRAHAM, 4
The taking of a B. or Gratuity PENN, WILLIAM, 10
You cannot hope /to b. or twist WOLFE, HUMBERT, 1

brick found it b. and left it marble AUGUSTUS, 1
throw a b....hitting the niece of a bishop ORWELL, GEORGE, 36

bricks You can't make b. PROVERBS, 467

bride B., n. A woman with...happiness behind her BIERCE, AMBROSE, 11
I drew my b., beneath the moon PATMORE, COVENTRY, 4
remind your b....you gave up a throne EDWARD VIII, 8
the b. at every wedding ROOSEVELT, THEODORE, 4
The b. unrumples her white dress WHITMAN, WALT, 38

bride-bed I thought thy b. to have decked SHAKESPEARE, WILLIAM, 219

bridegroom A b. in my death SHAKESPEARE, WILLIAM, 80

brides All b. are beautiful PROVERBS, 495

bridge A B. Too Far RYAN, CORNELIUS, 1
Beautiful Railway B. of the Silv'ry Tay MCGONAGALL, WILLIAM, 8
I stood on the b. at midnight LONGFELLOW, HENRY WADSWORTH, 9
Like a b. over troubled water SIMON, PAUL, 2
over the B. of Sighs into eternity KIERKEGAARD, SØREN, 18

brief 'Tis b., my lord. /HAMLET As woman's love SHAKESPEARE, WILLIAM, 191

briefly lit b. by one another's light PATTEN, BRIAN, 2

briers how full of b. SHAKESPEARE, WILLIAM, 97

brigands B. demand your money BUTLER, SAMUEL (1835–1902), 39

bright All that 's b. must fade MOORE, THOMAS, 13
All things b. and beautiful ALEXANDER, C. F., 1
B. star, would I were steadfast as thou art KEATS, JOHN (1795–1821), 10
B. with names that men remember SWINBURNE, ALGERNON CHARLES, 10
Look on the b. side PROVERBS, 312

Sparkling and b. in liquid light HOFFMAN, CHARLES FENNO, 1
brighter Far b. scenes a future age FRENEAU, PHILIP, 1
Had I been b. ROONEY, MICKEY, 1
brilliant a far less b. pen than mine BEERBOHM, MAX, 12
most b. shower of Leonid meteors MOMADAY, N. SCOTT, 3
bring Why didn't you b. him with you CUNARD, LADY "EMERALD," 1
brink scared to go to the b. DULLES, JOHN FOSTER, 3
Britain a time when B. had a savage culture BANDA, HASTINGS, 1
B. has always been in private hands RIFKIND, MALCOLM, 1
B. has lived...on borrowed time CALLAGHAN, JIM, 5
B. is not...easily rocked by revolution HAMILTON, WILLIAM (b.1917), 1
B....where the ruling class does not rule MIKES, GEORGE, 1
Hath B. all the sun that shines SHAKESPEARE, WILLIAM, 131
In B., an attractive woman is somehow suspect LEIGH, VIVIEN, 1
When B. first, at heaven's command THOMSON, JAMES (1700–48), 1
When B. is at war, Canada is LAURIER, WILFRID, 9
British A B. subject I was born MACDONALD, JOHN A., 2
B....cowering on the very island BALLADUR, EDOUARD, 1
but we are B.—thank God MONTGOMERY OF ALAMEIN, SIR BERNARD LAW, 2
enjoy appearing before a B. audience HOPE, BOB, 3
fair play of the B. criminal law DOYLE, ARTHUR CONAN, 2
I would rather be B. than just PAISLEY, IAN, 3
last B. Prime Minister with jurisdiction in Ireland BLAIR, TONY, 1
no spectacle so ridiculous as the B. public MACAULAY, THOMAS BABINGTON, 7
seek...nothing more than B. subjects HOWE, JOSEPH, 1
the B. have more heritage than is good for them BRYSON, BILL, 1
We're B. and loyal /And love every royal COPE, WENDY, 1
when a B. Prime Minister sneezed LEVIN, BERNARD, 1
Yes, it is wonderful to be B.—until one comes to Britain BRAITHWAITE, EDWARD R., 2
British Empire "Can't" will be the epitaph of the B. MOSLEY, OSWALD, 1
the liquidation of the B. CHURCHILL, WINSTON, 15
British Isles This little speck, the B. HOLMES, OLIVER WENDELL, 27
British Museum in the B. an enormous mind WOOLF, VIRGINIA, 11
broad She is a smart old b. RUNYON, DAMON, 6
broadcasting b....lowest human capacity NICOLSON, HAROLD, 1
B....means of developing education DENG XIAOPING, 12
B....too important to be left to the broadcasters BENN, TONY, 2
We spend all day b. O'ROURKE, P. J., 1
Broadway Give me B., with the soldiers marching WHITMAN, WALT, 20
Give my regards to B. COHAN, GEORGE M., 1
broke If it ain't b., don't fix it LANCE, BERT, 1
We're really all of us bottomly b. KEROUAC, JACK, 10
broken He liked the sound of b. glass BELLOC, HILAIRE, 25
Bronx The B. /No thonx NASH, OGDEN, 16
brood There's something in his soul /O'er which his melancholy sits on b. SHAKESPEARE, WILLIAM, 181
brooding She didn't like...the b., introspective bit CARVER, RAYMOND, 8
Brooke B. got...a certain amount of...poetry BROOKE, RUPERT, 2
Brooklyn B. of ample hills was mine WHITMAN, WALT, 17
broth B. is the foundation of Cookery UDE, LOUIS EUSTACHE, 1
brothels B. with bricks of Religion BLAKE, WILLIAM, 43
brother B., can you spare a dime HARBURG, E. Y., 1
Be my b. or I kill you CHAMFORT, NICOLAS, 14
brotherhood b. of man under the fatherhood of God ROCKEFELLER, NELSON A., 1
brothers b. all /In honour WORDSWORTH, WILLIAM, 90
brought b. nothing into this world BIBLE, 238
brow I see a lily on thy b. KEATS, JOHN (1795–1821), 13
brown study you are in some b. LYLY, JOHN, 7
bruised places in us...that are b. forever LEVERTOV, DENISE, 3
Brussels B. is a madness GOLDSMITH, JAMES, 3
brute B. force, the law of violence, rules GRIMKÉ, SARAH MOORE, 1
Brute Et tu, B. SHAKESPEARE, WILLIAM, 305
Brutus B. is an honourable man SHAKESPEARE, WILLIAM, 312
You too, B. CAESAR, JULIUS, 6
buck A b. is important GREEN, AL, 1
The b. stops here TRUMAN, HARRY S., 17
bucket throw away the old b. PROVERBS, 476
Buckingham Palace changing guard at B. MILNE, A. A., 11
buckle One, two, /B. my shoe CHILDREN'S VERSE, 41
Buck Mulligan B. told his face in the mirror JOYCE, JAMES, 22
Stately, plump B. JOYCE, JAMES, 36
Buddha-spirit the B. appears in many manifestations TILLICH, PAUL, 8
Buddhism B. never conquered the principle of identity TILLICH, PAUL, 7
budget b. is a method of worrying PROVERBS, MODERN, 1
need a balanced b....discipline our politicians ARMSTRONG, MICHAEL, 6
you will not get your b. HOPPER, GRACE MURRAY, 1
buffalo b. is slowly killed for Durga Puja MATTHIESSEN, PETER, 11
give me a home where...b. roam HIGLEY, BREWSTER, 1
Over them wander the b. herds LONGFELLOW, HENRY WADSWORTH, 25
Buffalo Bill B.'s /defunct CUMMINGS, E. E., 19
buffaloes flower-fed b. of the spring LINDSAY, VACHEL, 5
bugs we said it had b. in it HOPPER, GRACE MURRAY, 3
building If I were b. a house MENCKEN, H. L., 42
the b. of a bridge FANON, FRANTZ, 11
Things have altered in the b. trade KIPLING, RUDYARD, 47
Yesterday's...fireproof b. material is today's carcinogen O'HARE, DEAN, 3
buildings b. are condemned...in advance SEIFERT, RICHARD, 1
bull Better send them a Papal B. CURZON, GEORGE NATHANIEL, 3
Brag, sweet tenor b. BUNTING, BASIL, 1
take the b. between the teeth GOLDWYN, SAMUEL, 11
When you take the b. by the horns RIDGE, WILLIAM PETT, 1
bullet b. that is to kill me NAPOLEON I, 14
Each b. has got its commission DIBDIN, CHARLES, 2
Every b. has its billet WILLIAM III, 4
put a b. through his head ROBINSON, EDWIN ARLINGTON, 6
bullets b. whistle...something charming in the sound WASHINGTON, GEORGE, 9
bullfighting B. is the only art HEMINGWAY, ERNEST, 11
bullfights put on some large b. TUCHOLSKY, KURT, 7
bulls the b. and the foxes live well ALGREN, NELSON, 2
bully let a b. come into your front yard JOHNSON, LYNDON BAINES, 20
man who has enjoyed his school...a b. MORLEY, ROBERT, 3
bump things that go b. in the night FOLK VERSE, 3
bums art and literature are left to...shabby b. LEWIS, SINCLAIR, 4
Bunbury an invaluable permanent invalid called B. WILDE, OSCAR, 43

bungalow proud of the position of the b....in the country WILSON, ANGUS, 1
bunk It was b. to *me* FORD, HENRY, 8
buns Hot cross b. CHILDREN'S VERSE, 8
Buñuel When B. was casting *Viridiana* BUÑUEL, LUIS, 1
Bunyan My word, B., you're a lucky fellow BUNYAN, JOHN, 2
Burbank beautiful downtown B. ROWAN AND MARTIN'S LAUGH-IN, 1
burden It's a b....to be human DOSTOYEVSKY, FYODOR, 1
The dreadful b. of having nothing to do BOILEAU, NICOLAS, 1
bureaucracy B....not an obstacle to democracy SCHUMPETER, JOSEPH ALOIS, 1
burgundy a naive domestic B., without any breeding THURBER, JAMES, 15
To treat a poor wretch with a bottle of B. BROWN, THOMAS, 3
buried She shall be b. by her Antony SHAKESPEARE, WILLIAM, 89
They all be b. at Wimble EPITAPHS, 6
Burlington Bertie I'm B. HARGREAVES, W. F., 1
Burma There's a B. girl a-settin' KIPLING, RUDYARD, 22
burn b. yourself with anger at yourself MCCAIG, NORMAN, 14
He would b. your house down CHAMFORT, NICOLAS, 2
We b. daylight SHAKESPEARE, WILLIAM, 627
burning Now is the time for the b. of the leaves BINYON, LAURENCE, 3
burr kind of b.; I shall stick SHAKESPEARE, WILLIAM, 436
burst She b. while drinking a Seidlitz powder EPITAPHS, 11
burthen the b. of the mystery...Is lightened WORDSWORTH, WILLIAM, 13
bury almost feel disposed to b. for nothing DICKENS, CHARLES, 51
B. my heart at Wounded Knee BENÉT, STEPHEN VINCENT, 2
B. the Great Duke /With...empire's lamentation TENNYSON, ALFRED, 31
We will b. you KHRUSHCHEV, NIKITA, 2
bus Waiting for a b....thrilling as fishing COURTAULD, GEORGE, 1
bush the b. burned with fire BIBLE, 69
Bush B....looking like Liberace BUSH, GEORGE, 1
business 21st century b....defies analysis ELKINGTON, JOHN, 1
A b. that makes nothing but money FORD, HENRY, 12
a delight...to be out of b. GOLDSMITH, JAMES, 1
a large b. is...survival of the fittest ROCKEFELLER, JOHN D., 4
All b....people selling to people PETERS, TOM, 1
B....accelerating our self-conscious awareness SCHWERIN, DAVID A., 1
b. at the speed of thought GATES, BILL, 6
b....can be reduced to three words IACOCCA, LEE, 2
b. community recognizes values SOLOMON, ROBERT C., 2
Big b. collectivism in industry ROOSEVELT, FRANKLIN D., 28
Big b....small business with...an extra nought HOLMES À COURT, ROBERT, 2
b. is successful in America SOLOMON, ROBERT C., 3
b. managers bring their experience JONES, REGINALD, 2
B....may bring money...friendship hardly ever does AUSTEN, JANE, 16
B. men with awkward hips BETJEMAN, JOHN, 12
B....most important engine for social change PERLMAN, LAWRENCE, 3
B....often about killing your favourite children HARVEY-JONES, JOHN, 7
b. of the wealthy man BELLOC, HILAIRE, 24
b. sagacity...a judicious use of sabotage VEBLEN, THORSTEIN BUNDE, 1
B....that's what I'm all about JACKSON, JANET, 1
b....in the hands of the youngest recruit MORITA AKIO, 5
b....the most fascinating kind of art WARHOL, ANDY, 8
b....will not yield a fair profit CARNEGIE, ANDREW, 6
Develop the b. around the people BRANSON, RICHARD, 3
everybody's b. is nobody's business WALTON, IZAAK, 3
I didn't get into this b. ROTH, DAVID LEE, 3
If everybody minded their own b. CARROLL, LEWIS, 7
In b. for yourself KROC, RAY, 2
In b. we cut...throats ONASSIS, ARISTOTLE, 1
long-term b. opportunities BARNEVIK, PERCY, 3
main problems of b. JONES, REGINALD, 1
more b. out there in small-town America WALTON, SAM, 1
No B. Like Show Business BERLIN, IRVING, 2
nonsense to refer to b....private sector PARKER, SIR PETER, 1
Our b. is the price of beans DOS PASSOS, JOHN, 8
send a clerk on b. IHARA SAIKAKU, 1
The b. of everybody MACAULAY, THOMAS BABINGTON, 8
The chief b. of the American people is b. COOLIDGE, CALVIN, 10
The Inner Game of B. MCCORMACK, MARK, 18
this b. is about selling CAMPBELL, NAOMI, 2
To b. that we love we rise betime SHAKESPEARE, WILLIAM, 78
we are each other's /b. BROOKS, GWENDOLYN, 2
well-run b. must have...ethics BRANSON, RICHARD, 2
we were allowed to be "b. czars" PETERS, TOM, 3
When a b. goes wrong DELL, MICHAEL, 3
When b. is bad DAY, GRAHAM, 4
Whenever you see a successful b. DRUCKER, PETER, 17
When two men in b. always agree WRIGLEY, WILLIAM, JR., 1
you have to kill your b. PLATT, LEWIS, 2
Your b. is to put me out of business EISENHOWER, DWIGHT D., 28
your b., when the wall next door HORACE, 25
businesses B. can be misread CARNEGIE, ANDREW, 1
businessman B. and businesswoman are mute BIRD, FREDERICK BRUCE, 2
b...."pillar of the community" SOLOMON, ROBERT C., 6
b....same fundamental psychology as the artist KNIGHT, FRANK HYNEMAN, 3
Every b. should have one day LAKER, FREDDIE, 2
I am a b., not a crusader TERRY, JESSE A., 1
successful b....essentially a dissenter GETTY, J. PAUL, 6
The b. makes money in America LUCE, HENRY R., 4
bust I'm going to have a b. made of them GOLDWYN, SAMUEL, 13
busy B., curious, thirsty fly OLDYS, WILLIAM, 1
not b. being born is...dying DYLAN, BOB, 20
too b. to take care of his health PROVERBS, 475
busyness b.! That's the eternal BÜCHNER, GEORG, 5
butlers b. and lady's maids do not reproduce their kind WELLS, H. G., 3
butter b....makes the temptation JERROLD, DOUGLAS, 1
b. wouldn't melt in her mouth LANCHESTER, ELSA, 1
not deny himself a pound of b. HITLER, ADOLF, 3
buttered B. bread...dry side up PROVERBS, 54
fell...on the b. side PAYN, JAMES, 1
butterfly Float like a b. ALI, MUHAMMAD, 12
The b....Preaches contentment KIPLING, RUDYARD, 31
the Flap of a B.'s Wings LORENZ, EDWARD, 1
buttocks Two b. of one bum MOORE, THOMAS STURGE, 1
button-cute B., rapier-keen PERELMAN, S. J., 10
buttons Our b. operate...in favor of our motions MACHADO DE ASSIS, JOAQUIM MARIA, 19

buy B. stocks like you buy your groceries BUFFETT, WARREN, 1
B. up the sunset PEAKE, MERVYN, 4
I b. when other people are selling GETTY, J. PAUL, 10
I could b. back my introduction MARX, GROUCHO, 23
I'm going to b. and sell people BOND, ALAN, 3
buying B. is a profound pleasure BEAUVOIR, SIMONE DE, 9
coming over here and b. the throne TAUBMAN, ALFRED, 2
bygones Let b. be bygones PROVERBS, 300
byrd That b. ys not honest SKELTON, JOHN, 6
Byron B. is dead BYRON, LORD, 1
B.'s technique is rotten BYRON, LORD, 5
B. was really a comedian DRYDEN, JOHN, 1
From the poetry of Lord B. BYRON, LORD, 4
Lord B....fervent mind penetrates BYRON, LORD, 2
When B.'s eyes were shut in death ARNOLD, MATTHEW, 6

cabin'd c., cribb'd, confin'd, bound in SHAKESPEARE, WILLIAM, 406
Caesar C.'s Laurel Crown BLAKE, WILLIAM, 8
C.'s wife must be above suspicion CAESAR, JULIUS, 4
Imperious C., dead and turn'd to clay SHAKESPEARE, WILLIAM, 221
Regions C. never knew COWPER, WILLIAM, 3
remember that I am C.'s daughter JULIA, 2
render...unto C. the things which are Caesar's BIBLE, 421
that C. might be great CAMPBELL, THOMAS, 3
You have seen C. in his tyranny SHAWQI, AHMAD, 1
caesium a lamb sips c. on a Welsh hill CLARKE, GILLIAN, 1
caged C. birds...flight is what they long for WILLIAMS, TENNESSEE, 5
I know why the c. bird sings DUNBAR, PAUL LAURENCE, 3
We think c. birds sing, when...they cry WEBSTER, JOHN, 11
cake art of dividing a c. ERHARD, LUDWIG, 1
certain sized c. to be divided up CRIPPS, STAFFORD, 1
Let them eat c. MARIE-ANTOINETTE, 2
cakes no more c. and ale SHAKESPEARE, WILLIAM, 697
Calais "C." lying in my heart MARY I, 2
calamities C....misfortune to ourselves BIERCE, AMBROSE, 12
the c. of life DEFOE, DANIEL, 4
calamity A happier c. never befell a people PARKMAN, FRANCIS, 1
C. is man's true touchstone BEAUMONT & FLETCHER, 2
calculator A good c. LAOZI, 1
Calcutta go to C. to get some relief BRYSON, BILL, 14
Oh, C. TYNAN, KENNETH, 6
Caledonia C.! stern and wild SCOTT, SIR WALTER, 26
calendar I've been on a c. MONROE, MARILYN, 9
calf a molten c. BIBLE, 87
but the c. won't get much sleep ALLEN, WOODY, 18
killed a c. he would do it in a high style SHAKESPEARE, WILLIAM, 1
California All scenery in C. requires distance TWAIN, MARK, 33
C.—a state so blessed FROST, ROBERT, 14
C....is a country by itself BRYCE, JAMES, 2
C. is a great place ALLEN, FRED, 9
C. is a tragic country ISHERWOOD, CHRISTOPHER, 2
C. is poor drinking country CHANDLER, RAYMOND, 5
C. is white, like washlines KEROUAC, JACK, 14
C....where we run out of continent DIDION, JOAN, 6
Ours was a C. summer STEVENSON, ROBERT LOUIS, 14
Whatever starts in C. CARTER, JIMMY, 8
Yes I have walked in C. LINDSAY, VACHEL, 3
call C. home the heart you gave DRAYTON, MICHAEL, 2
c. upon the best of all God gave you NAYLOR, GLORIA, 5
Let's C. the Whole Thing Off GERSHWIN, IRA, 6
what you c. /making me comfortable WILLIAMS, WILLIAM CARLOS, 13
calling I don't want anybody c. me Ms LANDERS, ANN, 2
calming A c. influence on the nervous system LINDNER, ROBERT, 1
calmness C. is great advantage HERBERT, GEORGE, 15
calumnies C. are answered best with silence JONSON, BEN, 24
Calvary the place, which is called C. BIBLE, 346
Calvinist That maniacal C. and coddled poet COWPER, WILLIAM, 1
Calvinistic C. creed...and an Arminian clergy PITT THE ELDER, WILLIAM, 11
came I c.; I saw; God conquered JAN III SOBIESKI, 2
I c., I saw, I conquered CAESAR, JULIUS, 5
it c. with a lass JAMES V, 1
camel the C. humphed himself KIPLING, RUDYARD, 35
Camelot there was a spot...known /As C. LERNER, ALAN JAY, 1
To many-tower'd C. TENNYSON, ALFRED, 65
camels the c. and the sand THOMAS, LOWELL, 1
camera c. is a sketchbook CARTIER-BRESSON, HENRI, 1
I am a c. ISHERWOOD, CHRISTOPHER, 4
I don't know how to use the c. BERTOLUCCI, BERNARDO, 1
I love the c. and it loves me BOGARDE, DIRK, 3
The c....an accessory to untruth EVANS, HAROLD, 1
The c....teaches people how to see LANGE, DOROTHEA, 1
camp C. is a vision of the world SONTAG, SUSAN, 4
C....lie that tells the truth CORE, PHILIP, 1
The pure examples of C. are unintentional SONTAG, SUSAN, 19
campaign whole c....a tragic case of mistaken identity MCGOVERN, GEORGE, 1
You c. in poetry CUOMO, MARIO, 1
can If I own a c. of tomato juice NOZICK, ROBERT, 1
If you think you c....you're probably right FORD, HENRY, 10
they c. because they think they can VIRGIL, 14
Canada All that C. owes to Great Britain CARTWRIGHT, RICHARD, 1
C....a vast hunting preserve WILSON, EDMUND, 4
C....blow to the old British Empire RIDDELL, WILLIAM RENWICK, 1
C....by-product of the United States MACMECHAN, ARCHIBALD, 1
C. has two official languages WHELAN, EUGENE, 1
C....secondary and second-rate country LOWER, A. R. M., 1
C.'s history is as dull as ditchwater HUTTON, MAURICE, 1
had C. been...anglicized in 1776 WRONG, GEORGE M., 4
In C., democracy...condition and less...theory LOWER, A. R. M., 2
In C. we have no revolutionary tradition UNDERHILL, FRANK H., 1
people of Upper C....the fag-end BROWN, GEORGE, 1
run the whole gamut...prejudices in C. LAURIER, WILFRID, 1
social and cultural freedom...hallmark of C. CLARK, JOE, 1
soul of C. is a dual personality CALL, FRANK OLIVER, 1
There are no ghosts in C. MOODIE, SUSANNA, 1
today C....portion of the British Empire CARTIER, GEORGE-ÉTIENNE, 1
what street C. is on CAPONE, AL, 4
Canadian a C. is an American who rejects the revolution FRYE, NORTHROP, 9
C. history can only be read TROTTER, REGINALD GEORGE, 1
take a seat in the C. Senate LEACOCK, STEPHEN, 21
Canadianism policy of true C., of moderation LAURIER, WILFRID, 7

Canadians C. have to protect themselves against...enemies PAPINEAU, LOUIS JOSEPH, 1
cancer c....close to the Presidency DEAN, JOHN, 1
C....due to the stagnation of...energy REICH, WILHELM, 3
chronic diseases more destructive to life than c. MAYO, CHARLES HORACE, 1
C.'s a Funny Thing HALDANE, J. B. S., 1
c. was the toughest competition I'd faced ZAHARIAS, BABE, 1
candidates C. should not attempt more than six BELLOC, HILAIRE, 36
Candid Camera Smile, you're on C. CANDID CAMERA, 1
candle blow out your c....to find your way DIDEROT, DENIS, 3
hold a c. to my shames SHAKESPEARE, WILLIAM, 605
light a c. to the sun SIDNEY, ALGERNON, 2
Like a c. in the wind TAUPIN, BERNIE, 1
My c. burns at both ends MILLAY, EDNA ST. VINCENT, 4
Thus hath the c. singed the moth SHAKESPEARE, WILLIAM, 608
When shall we...trim a c. LI SHANGYIN, 2
candles Night's c. are burnt out SHAKESPEARE, WILLIAM, 556
rather light c. than curse the darkness ROOSEVELT, ELEANOR, 1
cane cannot c. someone...painless YEO, GEORGE, 2
canker killing as the c. to the rose MILTON, JOHN, 118
The c. galls the infants of the spring SHAKESPEARE, WILLIAM, 148
canned music C. is like audible wallpaper COOKE, ALISTAIR, 2
Cannery Row C. in Monterey...is a poem STEINBECK, JOHN, 5
Cannes C. is where you lie on the beach REED, REX, 2
cannibalism c. would get him the votes ROOSEVELT, FRANKLIN D., 4
four thousand years of c. LU XUN, 15
Canossa We will not go to C. BISMARCK, PRINCE OTTO VON, 11
cant how full of c. you are FOLK VERSE, 51
Let them c. about decorum BURNS, ROBERT, 40
Cantonese ocean and hunger...made the C....explorers KINGSTON, MAXINE HONG, 3
capable always believe the other side is c. of doing anything it says REED, ISHMAEL, 4
capacity c. to admire others KISSINGER, HENRY, 14
c. to permit his ministers to serve him RICHELIEU, CARDINAL, 6
Our c. to retaliate must be...massive DULLES, JOHN FOSTER, 2
too much c. for sorrow AIDOO, AMA ATA, 2
capital As long as c....can move WRISTON, WALTER B., 1
C. as such is not evil GANDHI, MAHATMA, 8
C. is a result of labor GEORGE, HENRY, 1
C. is built in the past KEEN, PETER, 1
no intrinsic reasons for the scarcity of c. KEYNES, JOHN MAYNARD, 10
only irreplaceable c....knowledge and ability CARNEGIE, ANDREW, 8
The c. is taken DU FU, 3
The mobility of c. today NORBERG-HODGE, HELENA, 2
capitalism c....American girls turn into American women HAMPTON, CHRISTOPHER, 1
c. "inevitably" caused war LENIN, VLADIMIR ILYICH, 4
C. is an art form PAGLIA, CAMILLE, 12
C. is the exploitation of man PROVERBS, MODERN, 8
c....necessary condition for political freedom FRIEDMAN, MILTON, 4
c....quest for community and social justice BRUYN, SEVERYN, 2
C. tends to produce...multiplicity of petty dictators HUXLEY, ALDOUS, 21
C. was born out of an ethos MULGAN, GEOFF, 1
C., wisely managed KEYNES, JOHN MAYNARD, 18
C. without bankruptcy BORMAN, FRANK, 1
historic role of c....to destroy history BERGER, JOHN, 2
I am going to fight c. PANKHURST, SYLVIA, 3
irreligious c....defeat religious Communism KEYNES, JOHN MAYNARD, 4
Modern c. is absolutely irreligious KEYNES, JOHN MAYNARD, 5
not just here to manage c. BENN, TONY, 1
"Primitive c."...capitalism in a state of nature KEEGAN, WILLIAM, 2
We cannot remove the evils of c. KINNOCK, NEIL, 9
capitalist a c. system will be allowed DENG XIAOPING, 5
C. production begets...its own negation MARX, KARL, 14
Few ideas...as c. as profit-sharing SEMLER, RICARDO, 2
major c. countries resist Islam SAADAWI, NAWAL EL-, 2
The c. achievement...more silk stockings SCHUMPETER, JOSEPH ALOIS, 3
They're not the tools of any c. O'CONNOR, FRANK, 3
You show me a c., I'll show you a bloodsucker MALCOLM X, 11
capitalistic growth under a c. market economy BOOKCHIN, MURRAY, 1
capitalists C. are a self-nominating group LEKACHMAN, ROBERT, 1
With the c., class interests take precedence PADMORE, GEORGE, 3
capital punishment c. tend to the security of the people FRY, ELIZABETH, 1
C....treats...the human race BRENNAN, WILLIAM J., 2
capon The c. burns, the pig falls from the spit SHAKESPEARE, WILLIAM, 590
captain Captain's C. SHAKESPEARE, WILLIAM, 480
C. of the *Pinafore* GILBERT, W. S., 5
c. with the mighty heart TRUMAN, HARRY S., 1
I should be judged as a c. COLUMBUS, CHRISTOPHER, 2
captains C. of industry CARLYLE, THOMAS, 28
captive c. void of noble rage HALLAM, ARTHUR HENRY, 3
car c. for every purse and purpose SLOAN, ALFRED P., JR., 6
c. you will be found dead in GUINNESS, ALEC, 1
It's like driving a c. at night DOCTOROW, E. L., 6
The c. has become the carapace MCLUHAN, MARSHALL, 12
The c. industry used to be...Western KELLER, MARYANN, 3
Would you buy a used c. from this man NIXON, RICHARD, 7
carbon We cannot...manage the c. in the atmosphere DYSON, FREEMAN, 1
carbuncle Like a c. on the face of an old and valued friend CHARLES, PRINCE, 6
card man's idea in a c. game is war DUNNE, FINLEY PETER, 2
cardinal unbecoming for a c. to ski badly JOHN PAUL II, 8
cardinals He is like one...those old c. ADAMS, JOHN QUINCY, 2
cards I have not learned to play at c. JOHNSON, SAMUEL, 62
care c. intelligently for the future of England INGE, WILLIAM RALPH, 4
C. /Sat on his faded cheek MILTON, JOHN, 35
first C. in building of Cities ARBUTHNOT, JOHN, 1
I c. for nobody,... /If no one cares for me BICKERSTAFFE, ISAAC, 2
I don't c. anything about reasons JAMES, HENRY, 30
I don't c. for war NAPOLEON III, 4
I don't c. how long I live JACKSON, GEORGE, 6
I don't c. what you say MUMFORD, JAMES GREGORY, 2
Lord, put beneath Thy special c. BETJEMAN, JOHN, 16
take c. of the minutes CHESTERFIELD, LORD, 12
career A c. is born in public MONROE, MARILYN, 7
a c. that depends a lot on being tall and blonde DAVIES, SHARRON, 1
"C. commitment" is a euphemism PERLMAN, LAWRENCE, 1
c. in slavery DOUGLASS, FREDERICK, 11

c....wrecked if I became a "Black Muslim." ALI, MUHAMMAD, 8
Miss Madeleine Philips...was a c. WELLS, H. G., 4
nothing in his long c. which those...would wish otherwise EDWARD VII, 1
careers best c. advice to give to the young WHITEHORN, KATHARINE, 7
career woman A c. who has survived BIRD, CAROLINE, 1
careful Be c. when you're tired and angry SIMON, NEIL, 1
be very c. o' vidders DICKENS, CHARLES, 93
carefully I have lived c....I shall live long WAUGH, EVELYN, 6
careless C. talk costs lives MOTTOS AND SLOGANS, 5
cares Far from mortal c. retreating TAYLOR, JANE, 2
Who c. about great marks left behind BETTI, UGO, 14
Carling I'll bet he drinks C. Black Label ADVERTISEMENTS, 4
Carlyle good of God to let C....marry CARLYLE, THOMAS, 1
carping I am obnoxious to each c. tongue BRADSTREET, ANNE, 1
carrot single c....will set off a revolution CÉZANNE, PAUL, 5
carrying c. with them everywhere their home habits SEACOLE, MARY, 1
cars c....equivalent of the great Gothic cathedrals BARTHES, ROLAND, 2
giant finned c. nose forward LOWELL, ROBERT, 9
Carthage C. must be destroyed CATO THE ELDER, 1
cartography science of c. is limited BOLAND, EAVAN, 1
carver was the c. happy while he was about it RUSKIN, JOHN, 20
Cary Grant Old C. fine GRANT, CARY, 2
Casbah Come with me to the C. BOYER, CHARLES, 1
case good c. is not difficult PROVERBS, 1
cases Hard c. make bad law HAYES, GEORGE, 1
casey mighty C. has struck out THAYER, ERNEST LAWRENCE, 1
cash assess in terms of c....a familiar skyline BETJEMAN, JOHN, 14
take the C. in hand FITZGERALD, EDWARD, 6
cask A c. of wine PROVERBS, 73
cassowary If I were a c. WILBERFORCE, SAMUEL, 3
cast c. thy bread upon the waters BIBLE, 58
I c. actors from rock OSHIMA NAGISA, 1
I have set my life upon a c. SHAKESPEARE, WILLIAM, 536
she...did c. in all that she had BIBLE, 362
cast away The more he c., the more he had BUNYAN, JOHN, 16
caste measure the social c. of a person ALFONSO XIII, 1
castle A c. called Doubting Castle BUNYAN, JOHN, 4
castles C. in the air IBSEN, HENRIK, 18
I entered...c. of the heart PATIL, CHANDRASHEKHARA, 1
O c. RIMBAUD, ARTHUR, 10
the c. I have, are built with air JONSON, BEN, 7
cat A c. has nine lives PROVERBS, 99
A c. loves fish ANONYMOUS, 7
A c. may look PROVERBS, 100
a c. the size of a pig BULGAKOV, MIKHAIL, 6
best material model of a c. WIENER, NORBERT, 4
c. is a diagram and pattern of subtle air LESSING, DORIS, 2
For I will consider my C. Jeoffry SMART, CHRISTOPHER, 4
God tells him he's a good C. SMART, CHRISTOPHER, 6
he is a very fine c. JOHNSON, SAMUEL, 161
Hey diddle diddle, /The c. and the fiddle CHILDREN'S VERSE, 25
I am the c. that walks alone BEAVERBROOK, MAX AITKEN, LORD, 5
it's always a C. NASH, OGDEN, 20
More ways of killing a c. KINGSLEY, CHARLES, 7
pussy c., where have you been CHILDREN'S VERSE, 42
The C. in the Hat SEUSS, DR., 5
The mind of a c....inscrutable mystery THOMAS, LEWIS, 5
there wasn't room to swing a c. DICKENS, CHARLES, 26
When I play with my c. MONTAIGNE, MICHEL DE, 11
When the c.'s away PROVERBS, 456
which way the c. is jumping SULZBERGER, ARTHUR HAYS, 1
Yellow c., black cat DENG XIAOPING, 8
Catalans We C. believe MIRÓ, JOAN, 11
catalogs drop a million Sears...c. all over Russia BARTON, BRUCE, 1
catalyst To be a c. is the ambition ZELDIN, THEODORE, 7
catastrophe When a man confronts c. TURNBULL, MARGARET, 2
catch desperate to c. up BARYSHNIKOV, MIKHAIL, 1
Go, and c. a falling star DONNE, JOHN, 35
Catch-22 only one catch and that was C. HELLER, JOSEPH, 5
catchwords Man is a creature who lives...by c. STEVENSON, ROBERT LOUIS, 38
cathedral One c. is worth a hundred theologians BARNES, JULIAN, 2
the c. is a decorated shed VENTURI, ROBERT, 2
cathedrals the ancient c.—grand, wonderful, mysterious STANTON, ELIZABETH CADY, 2
Catherine the Great C....a great Prince MONTAGU, ELIZABETH, 2
Catholic cannot...be a C. and grown-up ORWELL, GEORGE, 11
C. must adopt the decision handed down ROUSSEAU, JEAN-JACQUES, 5
C. soul...Lutheran stomach ERASMUS, DESIDERIUS, 6
lawful for a C. woman to avoid pregnancy by...mathematics MENCKEN, H. L., 12
Catholicism C. frequently provokes madness FOUCAULT, MICHEL, 1
Catholics C. and Communists have committed great crimes GREENE, GRAHAM, 5
C....appetite for reading about gruesome diseases MCCARTHY, MARY, 5
my only proof that C. were human MACNEICE, LOUIS, 26
We know these new English C. LAWRENCE, D. H., 13
Cato What C. did...Cannot be wrong BUDGELL, EUSTACE, 1
cats All c. are gray PROVERBS, 119
A lotta c. copy the Mona Lisa ARMSTRONG, LOUIS, 14
C. are autocrats of naked self-interest PAGLIA, CAMILLE, 13
Naming of C. ELIOT, T. S., 24
what c. most appreciate in a human HOUSEHOLD, GEOFFREY, 1
caught I c. a tremendous fish BISHOP, ELIZABETH, 7
cauliflower C....cabbage with a college education TWAIN, MARK, 32
cause c. is like champagne BENNETT, ARNOLD, 4
c. of freedom versus tyranny ARENDT, HANNAH, 15
c. of the ailment before he can cure MOZI, 1
c. of the World...consciousness of...freedom HEGEL, G. W. F., 20
It's a blessing to die for a c. YOUNG, ANDREW (b.1932), 1
no other notion of c. and effect HUME, DAVID, 24
only connexion...that of c. and effect HUME, DAVID, 21
the c. that wit is in other men SHAKESPEARE, WILLIAM, 250
to attribute to a single c. that which is the product of several LIEBIG, JUSTUS, 1
causes Anything that, in happening, c. itself to happen ADAMS, DOUGLAS, 3
in its c. just DRYDEN, JOHN, 33
caustic Too c.? To hell with cost GOLDWYN, SAMUEL, 10
caution c. in love is perhaps the most fatal to true happiness RUSSELL, BERTRAND, 49

cautious how c. are the wise! POPE, ALEXANDER, 87
cavaliero a perfect c. BYRON, LORD, 20
cavaliers C. (Wrong but Wromantic) SELLAR, W. C., 3
cavalry Lord Raglan wishes the c. to advance rapidly RAGLAN, LORD, 1
caviare c. to the general SHAKESPEARE, WILLIAM, 166
cavity John Brown is filling his last c. EPITAPHS, 4
ceased Only when he has c. to need SADAT, ANWAR AL-, 2
celebrate I c. myself WHITMAN, WALT, 31
celebrity A c. is a person who...wears dark glasses ALLEN, FRED, 3
being a c. is...when you bore people KISSINGER, HENRY, 12
C....a marble bust with legs COCTEAU, JEAN, 2
owes his c. merely to his antiquity CHAUCER, GEOFFREY, 2
The c. is...known for his well-knownness BOORSTIN, DANIEL J., 3
celerity C. is never more admir'd SHAKESPEARE, WILLIAM, 77
celery two thousand people crunching c. SHAW, GEORGE BERNARD, 102
Celia Come, my C., let us prove JONSON, BEN, 26
celibacy c. is...a muddy horse-pond PEACOCK, THOMAS LOVE, 9
celluloid The minute frames of c. AYALA, FRANCISCO, 2
cement For without a c. of blood AUDEN, W. H., 44
The c. in our whole democracy IACOCCA, LEE, 4
cemetery c. in which nine of his daughters THURBER, JAMES, 5
censor only c. is the audience ECCLES, DAVID MCADAM, 2
censors C. are necessary MARQUIS, DON, 11
c....worry if a girl has cleavage MONROE, MARILYN, 11
censorship C....depraving and corrupting SMYTHE, TONY, 1
C. hurts pictures, it damages them HUSTON, JOHN, 4
official c....sign that speech is serious GOODMAN, PAUL, 6
Without c., things...get terribly confused WESTMORELAND, WILLIAM C., 2
censure All c. of a man's self JOHNSON, SAMUEL, 69
C....tax...for being eminent SWIFT, JONATHAN, 45
centralized Large, c. organizations foster alienation SEMLER, RICARDO, 4
central planning C. didn't work for Stalin or Mao BLOOMBERG, MICHAEL, 1
centre the c. cannot hold YEATS, W. B., 22
centuries c. are conspirators against...the soul EMERSON, RALPH WALDO, 17
CEO C.'s role...atmosphere that promotes knowledge sharing GATES, BILL, 4
CEOs the worst thing many C. do JENRETTE, RICHARD, 1
cerebration deep well of unconscious c. JAMES, HENRY, 17
ceremonial For any c. purposes...water, is unsuitable HERBERT, A. P., 8
certain Nothing is c. but death PROVERBS, 347
to be c....be sufficiently vague PEIRCE, C. S., 3
certainties begin with c....end in doubts BACON, FRANCIS (1561–1626), 90
certainty Absolute c. can never be faith POWELL, ADAM CLAYTON, JR., 3
c. of ideas...certainty of perception MERLEAU-PONTY, MAURICE, 12
Cervantes C. laughed chivalry out of fashion CERVANTES, MIGUEL DE, 2
chain A c. is no stronger PROVERBS, 101
I happen to be a c. breather SYLVESTER, ROBERT, 1
chains It's...safer to be in c. KAFKA, FRANZ, 5
Women's c. have been forged by men RAMEY, ESTELLE, 1
chairman c....shouldn't...second-guess successors JENRETTE, RICHARD, 3
I loathe being called "C." HARVEY-JONES, JOHN, 9
challenge c....prevailing assumptions with a single question OHMAE, KENICHI, 9
The c. in a start-up DELL, MICHAEL, 2
The c. is in the moment BALDWIN, JAMES, 10
chamber One need not be a C.—to be Haunted DICKINSON, EMILY, 14
Chamberlain a speech by C. is like...Woolworths CHAMBERLAIN, NEVILLE, 1
Like the sorry tapping of Neville C.'s umbrella CARTER, JIMMY, 2
chamber-of-commerce a C. Creationism SNYDER, GARY, 11
chamber pot We are in the c. BAZAINE, ACHILLE-FRANÇOIS, 1
chameleon A c. on plaid ROOSEVELT, FRANKLIN D., 1
champagne c. that has stood for five days ATTLEE, CLEMENT, 8
champion an undaunted c. of liberty SWIFT, JONATHAN, 7
chance c. and risk...history of painting FRANKENTHALER, HELEN, 2
c. favors only the prepared mind PASTEUR, LOUIS, 2
Grab a c. RANSOME, ARTHUR, 1
More is owing to...*c.* PRIESTLEY, JOSEPH, 1
no such thing as c. BOETHIUS, 2
Chanel Previous to C., clothes...designed for mature women BEATON, CECIL, 2
change Anyone...who thinks major c. is impossible KOTTER, JOHN P., 2
A single moment can c. all WIELAND, CHRISTOPH MARTIN, 1
c....established government by force of arms BROWN, GEORGE, 2
C. is the one constant in life GUY, ROSA, 5
c. is the very essence of life FRANCE, ANATOLE, 13
C....not made without inconvenience HOOKER, RICHARD, 3
C. your friends DE GAULLE, CHARLES, 23
do you want...to c. the world JOBS, STEVE, 5
for a c. I am going to be serious O'BRIEN, FLANN, 6
He who fears c. /More than disasters FRISCH, MAX, 2
Is there no c. of death in paradise STEVENS, WALLACE, 19
largest scope for c....men's attitude to women BRITTAIN, VERA, 2
Most of the c. we think we see FROST, ROBERT, 18
O the heavy c., now thou art gone MILTON, JOHN, 120
The biggest c. in the workplace ADAMS, SCOTT, 3
the pace of c. has accelerated KRUGMAN, PAUL, 3
They must often c. CONFUCIUS, 22
We cannot c. anything unless we accept it JUNG, CARL GUSTAV, 24
We c. the rules...to improve the quality HUTTON, WILL, 1
We meant to c. a nation...we changed a world REAGAN, RONALD, 19
we support c....then are swept away GORDIMER, NADINE, 1
without...c. there can be no Tao WATTS, ALAN, 9
changed All c., changed utterly YEATS, W. B., 20
Things...Are c. upon the blue guitar STEVENS, WALLACE, 22
changes c. in a state's constitution MACHIAVELLI, NICCOLÒ, 12
changing c. scenes of life TATE, NAHUM, 2
When you're through c., you're through BARTON, BRUCE, 3
chaos consider c. a gift CLARK, SEPTIMA POINSETTE, 1
C....provides us with a bridge DAVIES, PAUL, 1
C. umpire sits...more embroils the fray MILTON, JOHN, 45
To some...c. is a science of process GLEICK, JAMES, 2
chapels c. had been churches SHAKESPEARE, WILLIAM, 597
Chaplin C. is no business man GOLDWYN, SAMUEL, 16
chapter c. of accidents is the longest WILKES, JOHN, 3
c. of accidents...long one CHESTERFIELD, LORD, 18
You...are a mere c. ATTALI, JACQUES, 1
character a c. will never die PIRANDELLO, LUIGI, 13

c....the determination of incident JAMES, HENRY, 13
know...the c. of a man in...golf LLOYD-GEORGE, DAVID, 6
Loftiness of c....not essential to the comprehension of art MEIER-GRAEFE, JULIUS, 1
the c. of its womanhood BETHUNE, MARY MCLEOD, 1
three grades of c....superior, medium and inferior HAN YU, 1
Where the c. is not great ROLLAND, ROMAIN, 4
You can tell...a fellow's c. by the way he eats jelly beans REAGAN, RONALD, 34

character actor c....one who cannot act SHAW, GEORGE BERNARD, 105

characteristic Each age has its own c. depravity KIERKEGAARD, SØREN, 1

characteristics hard to retain...c. of one's sex COLETTE, 6
Three c. of top executives O'CONNOR, JOHNSON, 1

characterizes What c. a member of a minority MAILER, NORMAN, 7

characters c. are really alive before their author PIRANDELLO, LUIGI, 11
her c. are round, or capable of rotundity AUSTEN, JANE, 3
we are c. within a dream of industry MAMET, DAVID, 11

charge c. us no less on account of our sex STONE, LUCY, 1

Charing-Cross full tide of human existence...at C. JOHNSON, SAMUEL, 99

chariot a c....of fire BIBLE, 170

charity Cancel not your c. by reminders KORAN, 9
C. begins at home PROVERBS, 170
C....power of defending that which...indefensible CHESTERTON, G. K., 19
In c. there is no excess BACON, FRANCIS (1561–1626), 33

Charles cast out C. our Norman oppressor WINSTANLEY, GERRARD, 2

Charleston Old C. looks from roof, and spire TIMROD, HENRY, 1
Savannah and C. had...dignity of their years MITCHELL, MARGARET, 10

Charley's aunt I'm C. from Brazil THOMAS, BRANDON, 1

Charlie C. is my darling NAIRNE, CAROLINA, 2

charm C. is a product of the unexpected MARTÍ, JOSÉ, 1
Oozing c....He oiled his way LERNER, ALAN JAY, 8
That's the main c. of heaven TWAIN, MARK, 15
What constitutes the c. of our country BECKETT, SAMUEL, 7

charming c. people have something to conceal CONNOLLY, CYRIL, 7

charms c. reunite what common use...divided SCHILLER, FRIEDRICH VON, 1
C. strike the sight, but merit wins the soul POPE, ALEXANDER, 97

charter This c....constitutes an insult to the Holy See INNOCENT III, 5

chassis whole country's in a state o' c. O'CASEY, SEAN, 4

chaste C. as the icicle SHAKESPEARE, WILLIAM, 126
Nor ever c., except you ravish DONNE, JOHN, 17
to be c. a woman must not be clever DE JARS, MARIE, 1

chastity c....no more a virtue than malnutrition WALLER, EDMUND, 5
c....total orientation...towards a goal BONHOEFFER, DIETRICH, 4
Give me c. and continence AUGUSTINE OF HIPPO, SAINT, 3

Chaucer C. and Spenser are Normans CHAUCER, GEOFFREY, 4
C., with his...clasp of things divine CHAUCER, GEOFFREY, 1
I read C....with as much pleasure CHAUCER, GEOFFREY, 5

Chawcer pity that C....was so unedicated WARD, ARTEMUS, 5

cheap if you do things on the c. MILLIGAN, SPIKE, 2

cheaper c. to look for oil PICKENS, T. BOONE, JR., 1
it is c. to buy milk BUTLER, SAMUEL (1835–1902), 17
It was c. to do a new series COSBY, BILL, 7

cheats c. with an oath PLUTARCH, 4

check C. enclosed PARKER, DOROTHY, 46

checks c....drawn on destroyed banks UNITED STATES FEDERAL EMERGENCY MANAGEMENT AGENCY, 2

cheek C. to cheek and breast to breast ROSSETTI, CHRISTINA, 4
the c. that doth not fade KEATS, JOHN (1795–1821), 12

Cheevy Miniver C., child of scorn ROBINSON, EDWIN ARLINGTON, 7

Chekhov C.'s plays epitomize the disintegration of theater AKHMATOVA, ANNA, 7

chemical c. barrage has been hurled against the fabric of life CARSON, RACHEL, 2

chemists first c. seemed...hard-hearted and unpoetical SUMNER, W. G., 1

chequer-board a C. of Nights and Days FITZGERALD, EDWARD, 15

cherish I c. mental images DILLARD, ANNIE, 1

cherishing profound c. of free natural landscapes NAESS, ARNE, 1

cherries Those c. fairly do enclose CAMPION, THOMAS, 6
You can't pick c. MORGAN, JOHN PIERPONT, 6

cherry Before the c. orchard was sold CHEKHOV, ANTON, 11
C. ripe, ripe, ripe, I cry HERRICK, ROBERT, 4
c. ripe themselves do cry ALISON, RICHARD, 1

cherub A c.'s face, a reptile all the rest HERVEY, JOHN, 1
Fallen c. MILTON, JOHN, 28

chess I am...a victim of c. DUCHAMP, MARCEL, 3

chess-board c. is the world HUXLEY, T. H., 8

Chesterton C....a very witty...man CHESTERTON, G. K., 2
C. is like a vile scum on a pond CHESTERTON, G. K., 3

chestnut tree Under a spreading c. LONGFELLOW, HENRY WADSWORTH, 17

chewing gum C. for the eyes WRIGHT, FRANK LLOYD, 8

chic very *c.* for an atheist RUSSELL, BERTRAND, 41

Chicago In C. not only *your* vote counts GREGORY, DICK, 1
That astonishing C....achieving new impossibilities TWAIN, MARK, 22

chicken a c. in his pot every Sunday HENRY IV, 5

chickens count their c. ere they're hatched BUTLER, SAMUEL (1612–80), 15
Don't count your c. AESOP, 8

chicks you've got thousands of c. CLAPTON, ERIC, 1

chief C. of the Army NAPOLEON I, 30

chiefs my c., I am tired JOSEPH, CHIEF, 1

child A c. becomes an adult SZASZ, THOMAS, 6
A c. blown up by age BEAUVOIR, SIMONE DE, 18
A c. deserves the maximum respect JUVENAL, 19
a c. learn sooner than a song POPE, ALEXANDER, 50
A c.'s a plaything for an hour LAMB, MARY ANN, 1
A c. should always say what's true STEVENSON, ROBERT LOUIS, 2
a human c....taken over by the fairies DEANE, SEAMUS, 1
better...a poor and a wise c. BIBLE, 52
C.! do not throw this book BELLOC, HILAIRE, 33
c. her Mama hopes will anchor...Papa CISNEROS, SANDRA, 1
c. is...to be loved and respected SALINGER, J. D., 12
c. of five would understand this MARX, GROUCHO, 13
c.'s first year...an abyss of mysteries PIAGET, JEAN, 7
c.'s pleasure in listening to stories CALVINO, ITALO, 5
give her the living c. BIBLE, 186
Give me a c. for the first seven years PROVERBS, 233
Here a little c. I stand HERRICK, ROBERT, 10
If the c. is father of the man CARTER, ANGELA, 10
institute for the study of c. guidance KRUTCH, JOSEPH WOOD, 1
One stops being a c. PAVESE, CESARE, 5

spare the rod, and spoil the c. BUTLER, SAMUEL (1612–80), 18
The business of being a c. HOLLOWAY, DAVID, 1
The C. is Father of the Man WORDSWORTH, WILLIAM, 48
the c. should...meet the real experiences of life KEY, ELLEN, 3
The new-born c....through pain...understands...the body MAUGHAM, SOMERSET, 14
The nicest c. I ever knew BELLOC, HILAIRE, 11
The thing that best defines a c. COSBY, BILL, 1
two things a c. will share willingly SPOCK, BENJAMIN, 2
unto us a c. is born BIBLE, 201
With that the Wretched C. expires BELLOC, HILAIRE, 7

childbearing morality now treats c. as an aberration GREER, GERMAINE, 3

childbed A man may sympathize with a woman in c. SMITH, ADAM, 2

childbirth c., every woman has the same aura of isolation PASTERNAK, BORIS, 11

childhood C. is the kingdom where nobody dies MILLAY, EDNA ST. VINCENT, 1
I go carrying my c. MISTRAL, GABRIELA, 3
In my c. trees were green MACNEICE, LOUIS, 11
Is c. a necessary evil PIAGET, JEAN, 5
The c. shows the man MILTON, JOHN, 106
'tis the eye of c. /That fears a painted devil SHAKESPEARE, WILLIAM, 398

childish Sweet c. days WORDSWORTH, WILLIAM, 69

childlike develop the c. inclination for play EINSTEIN, ALBERT, 33

children a wicked man that comes after c. HOFFMANN, AMADEUS, 1
believe...c. are true judges of character AUDEN, W. H., 39
C. are not...yams to be counted NWAPA, FLORA, 1
C. aren't happy with nothing to ignore NASH, OGDEN, 13
C. are to be won...by...rational motives DEMOCRITUS, 1
c....born after their parents PIAGET, JEAN, 6
C. do not give up their innate imagination LAING, R. D., 8
c....figure out what it takes to succeed PINKER, STEVEN, 1
C....have no use for psychology. They detest sociology SINGER, ISAAC BASHEVIS, 1
C., in general, are overclothed and overfed CADOGAN, WILLIAM, 1
C. inherited by slums AUDEN, W. H., 46
C....never been very good at listening BALDWIN, JAMES, 1
c., obey your parents BIBLE, 63
Command your c. to perform ritual prayer IBN HANBAL, AHMAD, 1
C. should acquire...heroes...from fiction AUDEN, W. H., 9
c. should be born without parents HUGHES, LANGSTON, 17
C.'s talent to endure ANGELOU, MAYA, 6
C. sweeten labours BACON, FRANCIS (1561–1626), 51
C....taught to respect traditional moral values THATCHER, MARGARET, 16
c. were an unnatural strain on parents UPDIKE, JOHN, 25
c....when they cry MITFORD, NANCY, 7
C. with Hyacinth's temperament SAKI, 23
Despatch her scheming c. far and wide BYRON, LORD, 97
distinction between c. and adults...specious one BARTHELME, DONALD, 1
Do ye hear the c. weeping BROWNING, ELIZABETH BARRETT, 1
except ye...become as little c. BIBLE, 410
Far too good to waste on c. SHAW, GEORGE BERNARD, 95
fond of c. (except boys) CARROLL, LEWIS, 1
from theyr c. to spare the rod SKELTON, JOHN, 1
hates c. and dogs can't be all bad FIELDS, W. C., 3
Having c....fundamental duty of women TANG MIN, 1
Having no c....became a sadness BERTOLUCCI, BERNARDO, 2
He that has no c. PROVERBS, 245
He thought of c. dancing WEST, NATHANAEL, 3
In c. schizophrenia is less obvious KLEIN, MELANIE, 7
let his c. go unvaccinated HUXLEY, T. H., 10
Let our c. grow tall THATCHER, MARGARET, 19
make your c. *capable of honesty* RUSKIN, JOHN, 25
Mama exhorted her c....to "jump at de sun." HURSTON, ZORA NEALE, 5
my c....feed on bitter fruit BONTEMPS, ARNA, 1
Never have c. VIDAL, GORE, 13
Problem c. tend to grow up into problem adults FARRINGTON, DAVID, 1
There's a time when you have to explain to your c. why they're born SCOTT, HAZEL, 2
To bear many c. is considered...an investment GANDHI, INDIRA, 8
voices of c. are heard on the green BLAKE, WILLIAM, 31
We have no c., except me BEHAN, BRENDAN, 15
we have paid for our c.'s place in the world WILLIAMS, SHERLEY ANNE, 1
We want better reasons for having c. RUSSELL, DORA, 1
When c. of one family /Fall out WATTS, ISAAC, 4
Where are the c. I might have had LOWRY, MALCOLM, 2
You can do anything with c. BISMARCK, PRINCE OTTO VON, 24

chime to set a c. of words tinkling in...a few fastidious people SMITH, LOGAN PEARSALL, 19

Chimera a C. in my brain, troubles me DONNE, JOHN, 24

China C. can improve...by allowing populist politics LEE, KUAN YEW, 2
C. has a population of 1.1 billion LI PENG, 4
C. has never had citizens YU JIE, 1
C. is a vast country MAO ZEDONG, 7
Classical C....a civilization with a message GUO MORUO, 1
Contemporary C. has grown out of...the past MAO ZEDONG, 33
C. remains too important KISSINGER, HENRY, 9
foreigners coming to C. CIXI, 1
horrendous human rights situation there is in C. GERE, RICHARD, 1
If you want C. to beg DENG XIAOPING, 17
impossible for...C. to live on borrowed money DENG XIAOPING, 19
In C....one million people...a small sum DENG XIAOPING, 18
I wouldn't mind seeing C. LARKIN, PHILIP, 14
more we bring C. into the world CLINTON, BILL, 18
No foreign country can expect C. to be its vassal DENG XIAOPING, 6
not reward C. with improved trade status CLINTON, BILL, 17
On a slow boat to C. LOESSER, FRANK, 1
People's Republic of C....transformed China's image DENG XIAOPING, 16

Chinese C. Communist Party...must provide prosperity SOROS, GEORGE, 8
C. culture...values literature ZHAO, HENRY Y. H., 2
C. doctors were nothing more than quacks LU XUN, 12
C. have...pride in the Chinese nation DENG XIAOPING, 15
C....live by and for their bellies LO, VIVIENNE, 1
C. searches his memory for...suitable recipe LEVY, PAUL, 1
C....spelling with a foreign alphabet LU XUN, 8
C. want to sell their goods WU, HARRY, 2
C. Way is the way of man WANG TAO, 1
feed and clothe 1.2 billion C. LI PENG, 1

Imperialist aggression shattered...dreams of the C. MAO ZEDONG, 14
I was just like those patriotic C. DU MA, 1
more C. studying English than...Americans ARMSTRONG, MICHAEL, 5
Nothing ...can destroy the C. people BUCK, PEARL, 3
one out of every four people...C. HELLER, JOSEPH, 13
The C. feudal system is fragile JIN GUANTAO, 1
To the C. we have given /kerosene SANDBURG, CARL, 10
West...not totally alien to the C. HU SHI, 2

Chinese men C....are ruined by women LU XUN, 9

chintzy Oh! c., chintzy cheeriness BETJEMAN, JOHN, 13

chip Not merely a c. off the old "block" PITT THE YOUNGER, WILLIAM, 1

chivalry c....dispenses leniency ADLER, FREDA, 1
the age of c. is gone BURKE, EDMUND, 38

chlorine C. is a deadly poison gas SAGAN, CARL, 3

chocolate a c. cream soldier SHAW, GEORGE BERNARD, 17
I ate a whole c. bar SCHIFFER, CLAUDIA, 2

choice c....between bureaucracy and dilettantism WEBER, MAX, 6
No c. is also a choice PROVERBS, 506
the c. is...between...nonviolence or nonexistence KING, MARTIN LUTHER, JR., 22

choir We don't need a c. SCHNEIDER, FLORIAN, 1

choirs Bare ruin'd c., where...birds sang SHAKESPEARE, WILLIAM, 576
demented c. of wailing shells OWEN, WILFRED, 1

cholera If...an outbreak of c. INGE, WILLIAM RALPH, 11

choleric the captain's but a c. word SHAKESPEARE, WILLIAM, 431

choose c. people who offer us money MOHAMAD, MAHATHIR BIN, 4
C. your neighbor before...your house PROVERBS, 3
People don't c. their careers DOS PASSOS, JOHN, 10

choosers Beggars can't be c. PROVERBS, 158

Chopin awful gap between Dorothy and C. ADE, GEORGE, 3

chord I feel for the common c. BROWNING, ROBERT, 27
you can't write a c. ugly enough ZAPPA, FRANK, 5

chords amazing c. that mounted higher and higher KEROUAC, JACK, 6

choreography the struggle between music and c. STRAVINSKY, IGOR, 4

chosen a c. vessel BIBLE, 13
but few are c. BIBLE, 420

Christ Art thou the C., the Son of the Blessed? BIBLE, 364
C. called as his Apostles only men JOHN PAUL II, 2
C....established in the Church His kingdom INNOCENT III, 3
C....forgave the theft BROWNING, ROBERT, 72
C. himself was poor BURTON, ROBERT, 8
C. is all, and in all BIBLE, 24
C....is no longer male or female ZELL, KATHARINA, 1
C. with me PATRICK, SAINT, 1
C....would...have been arrested DE BLANK, JOOST, 1
Decide for C. GRAHAM, BILLY, 1
his face is half C. and half satyr STEINBECK, JOHN, 2
I beseech you, in the bowels of C. CROMWELL, OLIVER, 3
Jesus C....yesterday, and today, and for ever BIBLE, 147
like blaming Jesus C. for the Inquisition BENN, TONY, 3
Where did your C. come from TRUTH, SOJOURNER, 1
Who dreamed that C. has died in vain SITWELL, EDITH, 11

Christendom C....small part of the globe MAXIMILIAN I, 1
Of the two lights of C. PIUS II, 2

christened she c. her child, a girl, "Anaesthesia" LONGFORD, ELIZABETH, 1

Christian A C....feels /Repentance on a Sunday YBARRA, THOMAS RUSSELL, 1
Anyone who denies that he is a C. TRAJAN, 1
a sweet C. act of procreation BRUCE, LENNY, 6
C. American secretly loved...war in Vietnam MAILER, NORMAN, 17
Can any man be a C. EQUIANO, OLAUDAH, 1
C. church, in its attitude toward science MENCKEN, H. L., 18
centres of strong C. presence...kind of Walt Disney Theme Park CAREY, GEORGE, 1
C. glories in the death of a pagan BERNARD OF CLAIRVAUX, SAINT, 3
C. religion...attended with miracles HUME, DAVID, 3
C. religion...principle enemy of moral progress RUSSELL, BERTRAND, 54
C. resolution to find the world ugly NIETZSCHE, FRIEDRICH WILHELM, 30
C. should beware of mathematicians AUGUSTINE OF HIPPO, SAINT, 9
fount of all ugliness, C. humility ERNST, MAX, 1
horrified at hearing the C. religion doubted BUTLER, SAMUEL (1835–1902), 11
How very hard...To be a C. BROWNING, ROBERT, 8
in what peace a C. can die ADDISON, JOSEPH, 22
I write the wonders of...C. religion MATHER, COTTON, 1
Never...did I behold such squalid wretchedness...C. country BYRON, LORD, 14
Onward, C. soldiers BARING-GOULD, SABINE, 1
The C. ideal has not been tried CHESTERTON, G. K., 47
the honourable style of a C. BROWNE, THOMAS, 10
the manifest superiority of the C. revelation JUNG, CARL GUSTAV, 7
the rarity /Of C. charity HOOD, THOMAS, 10

Christianity C....a metaphysical system HUXLEY, ALDOUS, 30
C.,...but why journalism HARRIS, FRANK, 2
central symbol of C....psychological meaning JUNG, CARL GUSTAV, 8
C. has done a great deal for love FRANCE, ANATOLE, 6
C. has made even of death a terror OUIDA, 2
C. is part of the laws of England HALE, MATTHEW, 1
C....most materialistic of all great religions TEMPLE, WILLIAM, 2
counter to all C. for a thousand years LUTHER, MARTIN, 2
C....says that they are all fools CHESTERTON, G. K., 18
C. the one great curse NIETZSCHE, FRIEDRICH WILHELM, 27
decay of C. SAKI, 7
local thing called C. HARDY, THOMAS, 25
loving C. better than Truth COLERIDGE, SAMUEL TAYLOR, 25
much that is revolting about C. KIERKEGAARD, SØREN, 3
nothing in C. or Buddhism that quite matches SAKI, 21
objectively, C. has absolutely no existence KIERKEGAARD, SØREN, 2
prominent role played by C. during...two millennia JOHN PAUL II, 7

Christians C. have burnt each other BYRON, LORD, 41
none of us are C. BRADLEY, F. H., 1
See how these C. love one another TERTULLIAN, 2

Christian Science C. explains all...as mental EDDY, MARY BAKER, 1

Christmas C. should fall out in the Middle of Winter ADDISON, JOSEPH, 16
For C. comes but once a year TUSSER, THOMAS, 4
Happy C. to all MOORE, CLEMENT, 1
I'm dreaming of a white C. BERLIN, IRVING, 5
I must stop C. from coming SEUSS, DR., 2
no other reason than because it is C. FISHER, M. F. K., 1
perceive C. through its wrapping WHITE, E. B., 10

Christmas presents We always smash our C. KLEIN, MELANIE, 9

Christopher Robin C. /Has /Fallen /Down- /Stairs MORTON, J. C., 4
chronic c. flares and twitches JAMES, HENRY, 4
chronicler c. of her times BRITTAIN, VERA, 1
She is...the c. of contemporary Britain DRABBLE, MARGARET, 1
chrysanthemums c. fill the ground LI QINGZHAO, 2
Chrysler my new C. floated down...side streets MOSLEY, WALTER, 9
church Beware when you take on the C. of God TUTU, DESMOND, 1
c. and...movies...sacred and the profane SCORSESE, MARTIN, 3
Christian c. in South Africa...history of a faith betrayed TAMBO, OLIVER, 1
C. produced no geometers DRAPER, JOHN, 2
c. saves sinners, but science seeks to stop HUBBARD, ELBERT, 15
custom of the Roman C. GREGORY VII, 1
farther...from the c. of Rome WOTTON, HENRY, 6
he'd go to c., start a revolution—something MILLER, ARTHUR, 19
he goes to c....he goes to the bathroom BLYTHE, RONALD, 1
loud statement about...the C. DOWLER, HAROLD, 1
One of the problems I have with the Christian C. BOESAK, ALLAN, 1
She came to the village c. TENNYSON, ALFRED, 26
The c. and the rumshop! ... They're one and the same, you know MARSHALL, PAULE, 6
the c. he...did not attend was Catholic AMIS, KINGSLEY, 5
the c., it does provide a coherence WINTERSON, JEANETTE, 3
the C....never loses sight of the loaves PEACOCK, THOMAS LOVE, 6
There are many who stay away from c. MILLER, ARTHUR, 15
Unity cannot long continue in the C. LAUD, WILLIAM, 1
useful to the Holy C. of God ALCUIN, 4
churches c. are drowning with stars CUMMINGS, E. E., 16
thirty-seven c. /and no butcher shop KUMIN, MAXINE, 1
Churchill C....has...stuff of which tyrants are made CHURCHILL, WINSTON, 3
Mr. C. is proud of Britain's stand CHURCHILL, WINSTON, 6
She is trying to wear the trousers of Winston C. THATCHER, MARGARET, 4
churchman a species of person called a "Modern C." WAUGH, EVELYN, 17
No c. am I BURNS, ROBERT, 52
churchmen c. fain would kill their church TENNYSON, ALFRED, 29
Church of England C....fallen into danger LAUD, WILLIAM, 2
Church of Rome We Italians then owe to the C. MACHIAVELLI, NICCOLÒ, 3
chymists good understanding between the c. and...philosophers BOYLE, ROBERT, 2
Cicero C. /And many-minded Homer YEATS, W. B., 59
cigar It is like a c. WAVELL, ARCHIBALD PERCIVAL, 1
Sometimes a c. FREUD, SIGMUND, 62
the Man is Smoking a Five-Cent C. FIELD, EUGENE, 4
cigarette c....perfect pleasure WILDE, OSCAR, 64
cigars c....at my age I have to hold on to something BURNS, GEORGE, 5
Cincinnatians people...without amusement as the C. TROLLOPE, FRANCES, 1
cinder how dry a c. this world is DONNE, JOHN, 9
cinema c....experience without danger all the excitement JUNG, CARL GUSTAV, 28
c. is all about money GODARD, JEAN-LUC, 3
c. is not a slice of life HITCHCOCK, ALFRED, 3
C.'s...what's in the frame SCORSESE, MARTIN, 6
invent a new kind of c. KELBER, MICHEL, 1
our c. needs...a style, an idiom RAY, SATYAJIT, 3
saving grace of the c. RENOIR, JEAN, 3
The c. must be naturalistic PASOLINI, PIER PAOLO, 3
two kinds of c. WENDERS, WIM, 2
circle wheel is come full c. SHAKESPEARE, WILLIAM, 369
circumlocution the C. Office DICKENS, CHARLES, 40
circumstance the fell clutch of c. HENLEY, WILLIAM ERNEST, 2
circumstances men are products of c. and upbringing MARX, KARL, 24
circumstantial evidence Some c. is very strong THOREAU, HENRY DAVID, 14
cissies Some kids are c. by nature O'CONNOR, FRANK, 2
cities C. belong to human nature HILLMAN, JAMES, 4
c....built by the sound of music HAWTHORNE, NATHANIEL, 3
citizen first requisite of a good c. ROOSEVELT, THEODORE, 15
humblest c....stronger than all the hosts of error BRYAN, WILLIAM JENNINGS, 7
I am a c. of the world DIOGENES, 2
If a man be gracious...c. of the world BACON, FRANCIS (1561–1626), 32
I wished...c. of the world ERASMUS, DESIDERIUS, 1
Socrates...a c. of the world SOCRATES, 5
city A c. must be a place...seeking and developing MEAD, MARGARET, 11
A c....no need to wait MEAD, MARGARET, 13
A c. where everyone mutinies HERSHFIELD, HARRY, 1
c. is...a human zoo MORRIS, DESMOND, 4
c. is arrayed in squares just like a chessboard POLO, MARCO, 4
C. of Magnificent Distances...of Magnificent Intentions DICKENS, CHARLES, 7
C. of my birth...of my dreams OZ, AMOS, 1
C. of the Big Shoulders SANDBURG, CARL, 4
Come and show me another c. SANDBURG, CARL, 3
c. where you can see a sparrow fall O'BRIEN, CONOR CRUISE, 2
great c....has the greatest men and women WHITMAN, WALT, 42
most pleasant sight to see the C. PEPYS, SAMUEL, 13
not the walls that make the c., but the people GEORGE VI, 1
Take an harp, go about the c., thou harlot BIBLE, 206
The C. is of Night THOMSON, JAMES (1834–82), 1
the c. of perspiring dreams RAPHAEL, FREDERIC, 4
thing generally raised on c. land...taxes WARNER, CHARLES DUDLEY, 1
This is a c. of water MORRISON, TONI, 8
What is the c. but the people SHAKESPEARE, WILLIAM, 123
civil C. commitment and the insanity defense...Siamese twins SZASZ, THOMAS, 17
civil disobedience c....necessary to alert the organization SEMLER, RICARDO, 1
civilisation c....imprisoned in a linguistic contour FRIEL, BRIAN, 1
vast and complex c....intricate and rich NEEDHAM, JOSEPH, 1
civilisations All great c....based on success in war CLARK, KENNETH (1903–83), 1
civility C. costs nothing PROVERBS, 171
C. costs nothing...buys everything MONTAGU, MARY WORTLEY, 3
The reciprocal c. of authors JOHNSON, SAMUEL, 24
civilization A c. that proves incapable CÉSAIRE, AIMÉ, 1
As c. advances, poetry...declines MACAULAY, THOMAS BABINGTON, 13
C. advances by extending WHITEHEAD, A. N., 4
c. /always results in deserts MARQUIS, DON, 7
C. and profits go hand in hand COOLIDGE, CALVIN, 9

c. has a pattern of disease DUBOS, RENÉ, 1
c. is a bitch of a problem ZOSHCHENKO, MIKHAIL, 2
C. is a method of living ADDAMS, JANE, 3
C. is a movement, not a condition TOYNBEE, ARNOLD, 8
C. is an architecture of responses KANE, CHEIKH HAMIDOU, 1
c. is marked by...disregard MAUGHAM, SOMERSET, 20
C....not in man's heart DUHAMEL, GEORGES, 2
c. of Europe...completely materialistic SUN YAT-SEN, 3
C....progress toward a society of privacy RAND, AYN, 3
c....something to learn from the primitive ROUSSEAU, JEAN-JACQUES, 3
c....taught even the Devil tricks GOETHE, JOHANN WOLFGANG VON, 9
decline in c. ROWSE, A. L., 1
fighting in the quarrel of c. against barbarism ROOSEVELT, THEODORE, 17
How idiotic c. is MANSFIELD, KATHERINE, 1
I am the c. they are fighting to defend GARROD, HEATHCOTE WILLIAM, 1
If c. is to advance...women PANKHURST, EMMELINE, 4
little in c. to appeal to...Yeti HILLARY, EDMUND, 3
Our boasted c. is but a thin veneer CHESNUTT, CHARLES W., 2
You can't say c. don't advance ROGERS, WILL, 2

civilizations c. decay quite leisurely DURANT, WILL, 2

civilized c. language...Cambrianism of the proceedings NEWSPAPERS, 29
c. man cannot live without cooks OWEN, MEREDITH, 3

civil rights c....172 years late HUMPHREY, HUBERT H., 2

civil servant c. doesn't make jokes IONESCO, EUGÈNE, 9

civil servants the work...of wonderfully gifted c. CLARK, KENNETH (1903–83), 2

civil service British c....effective braking mechanism WILLIAMS, SHIRLEY, 2
The C. is profoundly deferential CROSSMAN, RICHARD, 2

civil war In a c., a general must know REED, HENRY, 2
In your hands...issue of c. LINCOLN, ABRAHAM, 14

civis *C. Romanus sum* PALMERSTON, LORD, 4

claim not c. the discovery as your own THALES, 3

claims no c. against fidelity to truth DOUGLASS, FREDERICK, 10

clap Don't c. too hard OSBORNE, JOHN, 10
You can't c. with one hand PROVERBS, 46

claret C. is the liquor for boys JOHNSON, SAMUEL, 80
drink a dozen of C. on my Tomb KEATS, JOHN (1795–1821), 26
look for the second cheapest c. POTTER, STEPHEN, 5

clarinet I could tickle the c. keys MEZZROW, MEZZ, 9

clarity C....politeness of the man of letters RENARD, JULES, 3

Clark Gable C....best ears of our lives GABLE, CLARK, 1

class Every c. is unfit to govern ACTON, LORD, 3
Without c. differences, England would cease...theatre it is BURGESS, ANTHONY, 8

classes I'm not interested in c. LEWIS, JOHN L., 2
two great c.: hosts and guests BEERBOHM, MAX, 8

classic c. attempt /at beauty WILLIAMS, WILLIAM CARLOS, 15

classical c. Canon and the multicultural cause FENTON, JAMES, 1
C. quotation is the *parole* JOHNSON, SAMUEL, 81
That's the c. mind at work PIRSIG, ROBERT T., 12

classical music The basic difference between c. and jazz PREVIN, ANDRÉ, 1

classicist C. in literature, royalist in politics ELIOT, T. S., 12

classics The c. are only primitive literature LEACOCK, STEPHEN, 2

classism C. and greed are making insignificant all other kinds of isms DEE, RUBY, 1

class struggles history of c. MARX, KARL, 18

clay Was it for this the c. grew tall OWEN, WILFRED, 7

clean Live c., think clean ATLAS, CHARLES, 1

clean air we can continue to enjoy c. SHAPIRO, ROBERT B., 6

cleanliness a different...degree of c. NIETZSCHE, FRIEDRICH WILHELM, 10
C. is...next to godliness WESLEY, JOHN, 5
c. lies in water supply NIGHTINGALE, FLORENCE, 3
secret of resistance to disease is c. PROVERBS, MODERN, 13

clear c....as the nose in a man's face BURTON, ROBERT, 18
C. days, feel so good and free PURIM, FLORA, 1
If I turn out to be particularly c. GREENSPAN, ALAN, 2

Cleopatra Each image of C. HUGHES-HALLETT, LUCY, 1
Had C.'s nose been shorter PASCAL, BLAISE, 12

clergy c. are men FIELDING, HENRY, 9
I never saw...c. were beloved SWIFT, JONATHAN, 43
the c. had first destroyed the Church CASTILLEJO, JOSÉ, 1

clergyman c. and...psychotherapist...join forces JUNG, CARL GUSTAV, 19
good enough to be a c. JOHNSON, SAMUEL, 75

clergymen three sexes—men, women, and c. SMITH, SYDNEY, 12

cleric C. before, and Lay behind BUTLER, SAMUEL (1612–80), 9

clericalism C.—there is the enemy GAMBETTA, LÉON, 1

clerk C. ther was of Oxenford also CHAUCER, GEOFFREY, 17
The best c. I ever fired EISENHOWER, DWIGHT D., 6

clerkes gretteste c. been noght wisest men CHAUCER, GEOFFREY, 32

clerks C. get into the damnedest wrangles BRENNAN, WILLIAM J., 1

clever c. man...came of...stupid people CARLYLE, THOMAS, 4
C. men are good CARLYLE, THOMAS, 17
I'm not c. but I'm always right BARRIE, J. M., 6
It's c., but is it Art KIPLING, RUDYARD, 25
never wise to try to appear...more c. WHITELAW, WILLIAM, 1
To be c. enough to get...money, one must be stupid CHESTERTON, G. K., 38

cleverest c. member of...the cleverest nation WEBB, BEATRICE, 2

cleverness height of c. is...to conceal it LA ROCHEFOUCAULD, FRANÇOIS, 23
When c. emerges /There is great hypocrisy LAOZI, 16

cliché poised between a c. and an indiscretion MACMILLAN, HAROLD, 6
The c. is dead poetry BRENAN, GERALD, 8

clichés Let's have some new c. GOLDWYN, SAMUEL, 4

client the c. buys someone else's luck BURROUGHS, WILLIAM S., 5

clients Avoid c. whose ethos is incompatible OGILVY, DAVID, 4

climate The c....of the Earth...optimal for life LOVELOCK, JAMES, 3

climate of opinion he is...Now but a c. FREUD, SIGMUND, 1

climb C. ev'ry mountain HAMMERSTEIN, OSCAR, II, 16
Don't c. a tree to look for fish PROVERBS, 27
Fain would I c., yet fear I to fall RALEIGH, WALTER, 11
The worst part of the c. BISHOP, ISABELLA, 1

climbed c. to the top of the greasy pole DISRAELI, BENJAMIN, 56

clime change their c., not their...mind HORACE, 24

cling c. to their own sex...less frightening THOMPSON, CLARA, 1

clinician If the c....wishes to see things as they really are CHARCOT, JEAN MARTIN, 2

Clinton Bill C., Boris Yeltsin and François Mitterrand; we all like to eat CLINTON, BILL, 3

C....philandering, pot-smoking draft dodger CLINTON, BILL, 4
cloathing c....a covering for shame FAWCONER, SAMUEL, 2
C....a thousand different forms FAWCONER, SAMUEL, 1
clock He turned and saw the accusing c. MACNEICE, LOUIS, 15
clocks Stop all the c., cut off the telephone AUDEN, W. H., 22
the c. were striking thirteen ORWELL, GEORGE, 19
close I have...regretted living so c. to Marie PROUST, MARCEL, 24
closed A c. mouth catches no flies CERVANTES, MIGUEL DE, 11
closed society from the..."c.,"...to the "open society" POPPER, KARL, 4
closets Out of the c. MOTTOS AND SLOGANS, 27
cloth make...c. give expression to the body WESTWOOD, VIVIENNE, 3
clothed she rode forth, c. on with chastity TENNYSON, ALFRED, 44
clothes Absolutely I wear my own c. HILFIGER, TOMMY, 1
C. do matter BAINBRIDGE, BERYL, 1
c. possess an influence ALCOTT, LOUISA MAY, 6
c....which fit us for society EBNER-ESCHENBACH, MARIE VON, 3
Fine c. are good JOHNSON, SAMUEL, 84
In c. there are no new fashions TAO QIAN, 6
I want to make c....women want GAULTIER, JEAN PAUL, 2
My c. are...ageless MIYAKE, ISSEY, 1
pay more for my c....you probably don't sleep in yours DARROW, CLARENCE, 6
The trouble with Yohji's c. ETHERINGTON-SMITH, MEREDITH, 1
clothes basket ever taken anything out of the c. WHITEHORN, KATHARINE, 12
clothing Our c. and our armor LOUIS IX, 1
cloud a c. received him out of their sight BIBLE, 1
bring away a patch of c. XU ZHIMO, 1
Every c. has a silver lining PROVERBS, 197
cloudes no weder warmer than after watery c. LANGLAND, WILLIAM, 4
clouds c. in my eyes TAUPIN, BERNIE, 2
clown Any c. can play with the ball ROWE, ARTHUR, 1
I remain...a c. CHAPLIN, CHARLIE, 10
clowns Send in the C. SONDHEIM, STEPHEN, 1
club I don't want to belong to any c. MARX, GROUCHO, 18
takes you so far from the c. house LINKLATER, ERIC, 4
the best c. in London DICKENS, CHARLES, 73
clubs played c....have a drink with...the audience MORRISON, VAN, 1
coach c. has turned into a pumpkin JOHNSON, LADY BIRD, 2
coal C. is a portable climate EMERSON, RALPH WALDO, 49
This island is almost made of c. and surrounded by fish BEVAN, ANEURIN, 3
though the whole world turn to c. HERBERT, GEORGE, 25
coaster Dirty British c. MASEFIELD, JOHN, 2
coat a c. of many colours BIBLE, 132
His c. resembles the snow WILLIAMS, WILLIAM CARLOS, 10
cobbler Let the c. stick PROVERBS, 302
rather be a c....than a physicist EINSTEIN, ALBERT, 52
Coca Colas Instead of drinking C. CURRIE, EDWINA, 3
cocaine C. is God's way of saying...too much money WILLIAMS, ROBIN, 7
C. isn't habit-forming BANKHEAD, TALLULAH, 9
c....separates you from your soul JONES, QUINCY, 1
C.—such a perfunctory, unintelligent drug VALENZUELA, LUISA, 4
still remains the c. bottle DOYLE, ARTHUR CONAN, 17
Without c., half a dozen couture houses would have gone ANONYMOUS, 65
cock before the c. crow, thou shalt deny me BIBLE, 436
c. has great influence on his own dunghill PUBLILIUS SYRUS, 5
Our c. won't fight EDWARD VIII, 1
we owe a c. to Aesculapius SOCRATES, 12
what it is the crowing c. foretells MANDELSTAM, OSIP, 18
cock-horse Ride a c. to Banbury Cross CHILDREN'S VERSE, 18
cockpit Can this c. hold SHAKESPEARE, WILLIAM, 278
cockroach to choose between him and a c. as a companion WODEHOUSE, P. G., 8
cocksure I wish I was as c. MELBOURNE, LORD, 4
cocktail parties c. of the geriatric set MACMILLAN, HAROLD, 7
coffee c., chocolate, cocoa...not good for man SMITH, JOSEPH, 4
C. for all MOTTOS AND SLOGANS, 8
c. that's too black...You integrate it with cream MALCOLM X, 12
Instant c. is just old beans SAUNDERS, JENNIFER, 1
Mr. Hayman never had a cup of c. BRAUTIGAN, RICHARD, 2
Some sunlight; c. and the papers SETH, VIKRAM, 3
coffee-house folly...echo of a London c. SWIFT, JONATHAN, 41
coffin C. after coffin /Seemed to float HEANEY, SEAMUS, 2
Get the c. ready and the man won't die PROVERBS, 30
Uncle Sol's c. lurched CUMMINGS, E. E., 11
coffins ignoring the price of c. BRAMAH, ERNEST, 1
stepping in to lift the c. HEANEY, SEAMUS, 6
cogito The C. depreciated the perception of others DESCARTES, RENÉ, 2
cognitive I have created a lot of c. dissonance CLINTON, HILLARY, 4
cohesive c. power of public plunder MCLAURIN, A. J., 1
coin realm cannot be rich whose c. CECIL, WILLIAM, 2
coinage one c. throughout the King's dominions ATHELSTAN, 1
coitus C. is punishment...for cowardice DWORKIN, ANDREA, 1
coke C. was a little like the Wizard of Oz SCULLEY, JOHN, 3
Happiness is like c. HUXLEY, ALDOUS, 44
cold As c. as cucumbers BEAUMONT & FLETCHER, 1
C. hands, warm heart PROVERBS, 172
It leapt straight past the common c. AYRES, PAM, 1
so c....the brandy was frozen PEARY, ROBERT EDWIN, 5
threat of a neglected c. is for doctors CHAMFORT, NICOLAS, 15
We called a c. a cold BENNETT, ARNOLD, 3
coldly c. she turns from their gaze, and weeps MOORE, THOMAS, 5
cold war we are...in the midst of a c. BARUCH, BERNARD MANNES, 2
Coliseum While stands the C., Rome shall stand BYRON, LORD, 35
collaboration C.—that's the word producers use SHEPARD, SAM, 1
Effective c. between government and business FOX, HARRISON W., JR., 5
Every sin is the result of a c. CRANE, STEPHEN, 1
collaborators they were never great c. LENNON, JOHN, 2
collage information about the origins of c. is misleading MEYER, MELISSA, 1
collections c. of verses or epigrams CHAMFORT, NICOLAS, 9
collector I am a sort of c. of religions SHAW, GEORGE BERNARD, 36
colonial a c. economy is...dishonest BERRY, WENDELL, 1
c. status...worn-out, by-gone thing LEACOCK, STEPHEN, 23
colonies C. are made to be lost MONTHERLANT, HENRI DE, 6
the C....are yet babes HARRINGTON, JAMES, 1

these United C. are,...free and independent states LEE, RICHARD HENRY, 1

colonize To remain a great nation...c. GAMBETTA, LÉON, 2

colony I have led...greatest c. into America PENN, WILLIAM, 2

color Any c., so long as it's black FORD, HENRY, 7
c. chose me or I chose color CHAGALL, MARC, 3
C....sensibility turned into matter KLEIN, YVES, 1
It's not c., it's like...sugar water over a roast HUSTON, JOHN, 1
the c. purple WALKER, ALICE, 25
Through c....I am truly free KLEIN, YVES, 2
Women think of all colors except the absence of c. CHANEL, COCO, 4

color bar how 'bout clearing the c. next GREGORY, DICK, 6

colored c. girls who have considered suicide SHANGE, NTOZAKE, 7
I'm a c., one-eyed Jew DAVIS, SAMMY, JR., 4

coloring spend...my free time c. my hair EVANGELISTA, LINDA, 1

colorless C. green ideas CHOMSKY, NOAM, 4

color-line the problem of the c. DU BOIS, W. E. B., 16

colors C. in painting are like allurements POUSSIN, NICOLAS, 1
five c. make a man's eyes blind LAOZI, 15

colour take the c. of his times HUXLEY, ALDOUS, 3

colour blindness an incurable disease—c. DE BLANK, JOOST, 2

coloured c. man can tell...whether a white man likes him MACINNES, COLIN, 1
see the c. counties HOUSMAN, A. E., 10

colours clashed his c. together like cymbals MATISSE, HENRI, 1
C....Will not look the same by day BROWNING, ELIZABETH BARRETT, 3

Coltrane C. sounds like...bore COLTRANE, JOHN, 1

Columbus C. did not seek a new route COLUMBUS, CHRISTOPHER, 1
C. didn't have a business plan GROVE, ANDREW S., 2

combat c. ceased from lack of combatants CORNEILLE, PIERRE, 7
single c. to decide...kingdom of England HAROLD II, 1

come I c. as a thief BIBLE, 470
O c. all ye faithful OAKELEY, FREDERICK, 1
Why don't you c. up sometime WEST, MAE, 14

comedian A c. can only last ROGERS, WILL, 1

comedy c. at the moment of deepest hysteria NAIPAUL, V. S., 2
C. in painting...ought to be allotted the first place HOGARTH, WILLIAM, 2
c. is like emotional hang-gliding WILLIAMS, ROBIN, 3
C. is medicine GRIFFITHS, TREVOR, 1
C. is tragedy CARTER, ANGELA, 9
C., like sodomy, is an unnatural act FELDMAN, MARTY, 1
c....public version of a private darkness THEROUX, PAUL, 3
C., we may say, is society PRIESTLEY, J. B., 4
fine c. this world would be DIDEROT, DENIS, 11
to make a c. CHAPLIN, CHARLIE, 7

comes Everything c. to him who waits PROVERBS, 207

comfort c. ye my people BIBLE, 212
I beg cold c. SHAKESPEARE, WILLIAM, 330
the safe c. of certainties BEAUVOIR, SIMONE DE, 2
Two loves I have, of c. and despair SHAKESPEARE, WILLIAM, 587
What a c. it was to see her pass NIGHTINGALE, FLORENCE, 1

comfortable The c. people in tight houses STEINBECK, JOHN, 12
to be baith grand and c. BARRIE, J. M., 15

comforted he refused to be c. BIBLE, 134

comforters miserable c. are ye all BIBLE, 260

comic so c. to hear oneself called old JAMES, ALICE, 3
The c....perception of the opposite ECO, UMBERTO, 13

coming cold c. they had of it ANDREWES, LANCELOT, 1
we're c. over MUMFORD, JAMES GREGORY, 1

command but to c. SHAKESPEARE, WILLIAM, 507
c. what you will AUGUSTINE OF HIPPO, SAINT, 4
I c. you: STOP THE REPRESSION ROMERO, OSCAR, 2

commanded He c. the most profound attention ADAMS, SAMUEL, 2

commerce C....art of exploiting...desire GONCOURT, EDMOND DE, 3
c. between master and slave JEFFERSON, THOMAS, 39
c....kind of transaction BIERCE, AMBROSE, 16
difficult business of c. CLARKE, KENNETH, 3
Let there be c. between us POUND, EZRA, 18

commercialism The crude c. of America WASHINGTON, GEORGE, 2

commercial tyranny great intangible machine of c. MORRIS, WILLIAM, 7

commissions If you pay c. MARCUS, BERNIE, 1

commit wouldn't c. himself to...time of day HOOVER, HERBERT, 1

committee A c. is a cul-de-sac BELLOC, HILAIRE, 26
A c. is an animal LE CARRÉ, JOHN, 1
A c. should consist of three men TREE, HERBERT BEERBOHM, 2
C....can do nothing ALLEN, FRED, 7
ideal c....committee of one STOKES, DONALD GRESHAM, 1

commodities C. all the way to the horizon BELLOW, SAUL, 22
Man does not only sell c. FROMM, ERICH, 19

commodity any c. necessitates the sacrifice of human life GOLDMAN, EMMA, 2
Their major c. was...people MO, TIMOTHY, 1
There is a c. in human experience WINFREY, OPRAH, 4

common c. notions in an individual way HORACE, 6
c. things...in an uncommon way CARVER, GEORGE WASHINGTON, 1
Do a c. thing in an uncommon way WASHINGTON, BOOKER T., 2
everywhere the c. people...get their due SUN, MADAME, 1
He nothing c. did or mean CHARLES I (1600–49), 1

common law C. of England HERBERT, A. P., 13

common-looking The Lord prefers c. people LINCOLN, ABRAHAM, 22

common man c....great protection against war BEVIN, ERNEST, 2
I have no concern for the c. WILSON, ANGUS, 2
we are entering...the century of the c. WALLACE, HENRY A., 1

commonplaces c. are the great poetic truths STEVENSON, ROBERT LOUIS, 15

commons The C., faithful to their system MACKINTOSH, JAMES, 2

common sense A man without c. BLYDEN, EDWARD WILMOT, 1
C....collection of prejudices EINSTEIN, ALBERT, 48
C. drives us to accept quantum theory ATKINS, P. W., 1
c. is suspect at high velocities SAGAN, CARL, 5
seldom attribute c. LA ROCHEFOUCAULD, FRANÇOIS, 28

communication C....most important form of marketing MORITA AKIO, 3
copper rigging and secular miracle of c. PYNCHON, THOMAS, 10
for c. to be effective MCMURRY, ROBERT N., 1

communications c., familiarity breeds apathy BERNBACH, WILLIAM, 1

communion They pluck't c. tables down JORDAN, THOMAS, 1

communism C....corruption of a dream of justice STEVENSON, ADLAI, 6
C. fits Germany...saddle does a cow STALIN, JOSEPH, 9
C. has...allied itself to...violence NEHRU, JAWAHARLAL, 3
C. has failed...capitalism has not succeeded KEEGAN, WILLIAM, 1
C. is like prohibition ROGERS, WILL, 11
C. is Soviet power plus the electrification LENIN, VLADIMIR ILYICH, 11

C. is Tsarist autocracy turned upside down HERZEN, ALEKSANDR IVANOVICH, 1
C....never be defeated by atomic bombs KING, MARTIN LUTHER, JR., 31
C....the completion of Socialism MORRIS, WILLIAM, 2
C. will not come...like an army with banners BEHAN, BRENDAN, 11
Every year humanity takes a step towards C. KHRUSHCHEV, NIKITA, 4
failure of c. as an economic system KEEGAN, WILLIAM, 3
Russian c. is the illegitimate child ATTLEE, CLEMENT, 2
the era of world c. will dawn MAO ZEDONG, 17
communist Calling somebody a C. JORDAN, JUNE, 10
"C." is just a term of abuse PADMORE, GEORGE, 7
Every c. has a fascist frown SPARK, MURIEL, 5
I'm a C. by day BEHAN, BRENDAN, 17
In c. society...society regulates...production MARX, KARL, 22
no nook...C. influence does not penetrate DULLES, JOHN FOSTER, 5
The C. plan for Hollywood REAGAN, RONALD, 39
communistic some sort of "c. fiction," ARENDT, HANNAH, 16
Communist Party joining the C. is the logical outcome PICASSO, PABLO, 11
The dictatorship of the C. TROTSKY, LEON, 9
communists looking under the beds for C. FOOT, MICHAEL, 4
The C. used to bring vodka DENISOVA, GALINA, 1
There are no C. in South Africa SOBUKWE, ROBERT MANGALISO, 3
communities We have exchanged our c. for jobs MILLER, STEVEN E., 5
community any c. cursed with crime DU BOIS, W. E. B., 14
Beware of the c....blasphemy does not exist MACHADO, ANTONIO, 4
No c. can...possess local self-government ALTGELD, JOHN PETER, 1
We are part of the c. of Europe GLADSTONE, WILLIAM EWART, 4
commuter C....riding to and from his wife WHITE, E. B., 2
companies Big c. are small companies TOWNSEND, ROBERT, 10
C. can't promise lifetime employment WELCH, JACK, 5
C. die because their managers focus DE GEUS, ARIE, 1
c. must offer something unique TICHY, NOEL M., 2
C. must re-envision and re-imagine themselves HAWKEN, PAUL, 2
C. pay too much attention to the cost of doing something KOTLER, PHILIP, 1
Modern c. collaborate to compete BLAIR, TONY, 4
The job for big c. WELCH, JACK, 3
companion God send the c. a better prince SHAKESPEARE, WILLIAM, 249
company A c....a portfolio of competencies HAMEL, GARY, 1
A c.'s ethical conduct ADAMS, WILLIAM, 1
Any c. whose stake in the past HAMEL, GARY, 3
c. of clever, well-informed people AUSTEN, JANE, 26
c. of their own sex BROOKNER, ANITA, 4
Considering the c. I keep MENZIES, ROBERT, 1
C., villainous company SHAKESPEARE, WILLIAM, 237
Even if the c. is not...exciting PETERS, TOM, 2
I have a great deal of c. THOREAU, HENRY DAVID, 39
I like to buy a c. LYNCH, PETER, 3
Making the c....self-sustaining institution GROVE, ANDREW S., 4
Tell me what c. thou keepest CERVANTES, MIGUEL DE, 38
You have your own c. NORRIS, STEVEN, 1
compare C. great things with small VIRGIL, 26
c. the great film with a horse race SCHULBERG, BUDD, 1
fit to c. to a candle FARADAY, MICHAEL, 1
Shall I c. thee to a summer's day SHAKESPEARE, WILLIAM, 565
comparison crude...as a c. of the penis BLACKWELL, ELIZABETH, 2
comparisons C. are odorous SHAKESPEARE, WILLIAM, 455
She, and c....odious DONNE, JOHN, 20
comparisouns C. doon offte gret greuaunce LYDGATE, JOHN, 3
compassion I have great c. for God DERSHOWITZ, ALAN, 3
I was speaking of c. BULGAKOV, MIKHAIL, 9
She had c. without condescension ADDAMS, JANE, 2
compelled Nor shall be c....be a witness CONSTITUTION OF THE UNITED STATES, 3
competencies c. that flow from self-awareness...self-regulation GOLEMAN, DANIEL, 4
competency only safe harbor is c. RODGERS, T. J., 1
competition C. is a performance stimulant KANTER, ROSABETH MOSS, 2
Free c. tends to give to labor CLARK, JOHN BATES, 2
competitors our c. get the profits CLINTON, BILL, 12
complacencies C. of the peignoir STEVENS, WALLACE, 5
complacency c. and satisfaction...of a new-married couple LAMB, CHARLES, 11
complain Never c. and never explain BALDWIN, STANLEY, 2
complaint always say...how is the old c. DISRAELI, BENJAMIN, 61
I want to register a c. MARX, GROUCHO, 24
complaints The imaginary c. of indestructible old ladies WHITE, E. B., 6
complexity C. and trust go together KEEN, PETER, 2
C. management...used to build unity HICKMAN, CRAIG R., 1
complies c. against his will BUTLER, SAMUEL (1612–80), 23
compose Never c. anything unless HOLST, GUSTAV, 1
painting...one can c. colors...motions CALDER, ALEXANDER, 1
composed When I c. that, I was...inspired by God BEETHOVEN, LUDWIG VAN, 9
composer A c. knows his work CAGE, JOHN, 2
c....must create the music COPLAND, AARON, 4
first requirement for a c....be dead HONEGGER, ARTHUR, 1
good c. does not imitate; he steals STRAVINSKY, IGOR, 6
never a great c. who left music COPLAND, AARON, 7
composers greatest c. were also the greatest thieves CASALS, PABLO, 5
Mozart...most reasonable of the world's greatest c. MOZART, WOLFGANG AMADEUS, 3
Not many c. have ideas GERSHWIN, GEORGE, 4
composing C....like making love to the future FOSS, LUKAS, 1
C....music is very feminine KOLB, BARBARA, 1
C.'s one thing, performing's another CAGE, JOHN, 4
George's method of c....nearest thing to playfulness GERSHWIN, GEORGE, 2
composition a nice c. of the two sexes HERVEY, JOHN, 2
comprehended c. two aspicious persons SHAKESPEARE, WILLIAM, 456
compromise an iota /Of c....the Cause fails DAY-LEWIS, CECIL, 1
C. is...on the same plane as fighting FOLLETT, MARY PARKER, 2
C. used to mean that half a loaf CHESTERTON, G. K., 45
compulsion seized by the stern hand of C. THURBER, JAMES, 1
compulsive C. drives are specifically neurotic HORNEY, KAREN, 3
computer C. networks...bring people together AGRE, PHILIP A., 1
c....programmed to enjoy modern concert music KINGTON, MILES, 1
C. technology...role in rebuilding community SCHULER, DOUGLAS, 1
c. which has some sort of personality SINCLAIR, CLIVE, 7
democratization of c. power ROSE, FRANK, 1
How come c. commands...come from keyboards PETERS, TOM, 5

the Macintosh c....is Catholic ECO, UMBERTO, 1
computers C. and art...bring out the worst NEGROPONTE, NICHOLAS, 1
c. are big...adding-machine-typewriters TOWNSEND, ROBERT, 1
C....not bastions of individual creativity ROSE, FRANK, 3
C. today are superhuman SINCLAIR, CLIVE, 2
c....wonderful tools for information processing DE BONO, EDWARD, 1
rise of c....forcing machinery to adapt STEWART, THOMAS A., 9
world market for about five c. WATSON, THOMAS J., 1
comrades C., leave me here a little TENNYSON, ALFRED, 50
Dear c., soldiers, sailors and workers LENIN, VLADIMIR ILYICH, 9
conceit C. is the finest armour JEROME, JEROME K., 1
conceited what man will do any good who is not c.? TROLLOPE, ANTHONY, 5
conceivable What is c. can happen too WITTGENSTEIN, LUDWIG, 1
conceive attempt to directly c. death...bound to fail SARTRE, JEAN-PAUL, 25
If I can c. it and believe it JACKSON, JESSE, 10
conceived Before I was 23...c. everything LINNAEUS, CAROLUS, 1
concentrate C. your energy, thought and capital CARNEGIE, ANDREW, 4
try to c. on concentrating NAVRATILOVA, MARTINA, 5
concentration camps c., by making death itself anonymous ARENDT, HANNAH, 23
concept not a single c. of which I am convinced EINSTEIN, ALBERT, 13
conception C. *is* capitalization YOXEN, EDWARD, 2
From...c....life...is to be respected PAUL VI, 3
concepts Physical c....creations of the human mind EINSTEIN, ALBERT, 39
conceptual art C....another kind of artistic style KOUNELLIS, JANNIS, 1
In C. the idea LEWITT, SOL, 1
concern C. for man himself...chief interest of all technical endeavors EINSTEIN, ALBERT, 47
deeper c. for his place in history NIXON, RICHARD, 1
concessions c. of the weak...concessions of fear BURKE, EDMUND, 27
conciliation Draw back the rifles...trust in c. BRIAND, ARISTIDE, 2
conclusion c. of your syllogism O'BRIEN, FLANN, 1
do not jump to the c. that you have found a lady LEBOWITZ, FRAN, 2
Concord Yes—around C. THOREAU, HENRY DAVID, 49
condemn c....man for what he cannot help PELAGIUS, 1
No man can justly censure or c. another BROWNE, THOMAS, 28
We...c. and rage against ourselves JUNG, CARL GUSTAV, 13
condemnation the dismal, ridiculous c. of Oscar Wilde WILDE, OSCAR, 4
condemned Man is c. to be free SARTRE, JEAN-PAUL, 8
the c....persist in surviving WIESEL, ELIE, 3
condemning anyone...c. it completely...know anything about it MACINNES, COLIN, 4
condition agreeable c. of doing nothing PLINY THE YOUNGER, 6
c. upon which God hath given liberty...eternal vigilance CURRAN, JOHN PHILPOT, 1
The c. of man...condition of war HOBBES, THOMAS, 9
the c. of our sex is so deplorable PANKHURST, EMMELINE, 2
thinks about...c. of her uterus LUCE, CLARE BOOTHE, 3
conditions Dese are de c. dat prevail DURANTE, JIMMY, 1
necessary and sufficient c. for knowing AYER, A. J., 5
no c. of life...cannot get accustomed TOLSTOY, LEO, 6
these are the c., now what happens FEYNMAN, RICHARD PHILLIPS, 6
condolence visit of c. to the Queen of England MONTPENSIER, DUCHESSE DE, 1
conducive anything c. to our national stability JIANG ZEMIN, 1
confess easy to make a man c....lies HOUSEHOLD, GEOFFREY, 2
only c. our little faults LA ROCHEFOUCAULD, FRANÇOIS, 26
We c. our bad qualities...out of fear BRENAN, GERALD, 4
confession no refuge from c. but suicide WEBSTER, DANIEL, 8
confessions I have never made written c. DIX, OTTO, 1
confidence C. and hope...more good than physic GALEN, 3
C. is a plant of slow growth PITT THE ELDER, WILLIAM, 4
c. of twenty-one JOHNSON, SAMUEL, 169
one cannot really have c. in doctors GOETHE, JOHANN WOLFGANG VON, 37
real sense of c. and optimism BLAIR, TONY, 11
confident There are two things which I am c. BOSWELL, JAMES, 4
conflagrations Great c....born of tiny sparks RICHELIEU, CARDINAL, 3
conflict c. between management and labor IVERSON, KEN, 6
Managing c. for mutual benefit TJOSVOLD, DEAN, 3
supposed "c."...between science and religion GOULD, STEPHEN JAY, 6
conform C. and be dull DOBIE, J. FRANK, 1
conformist c. is not born. He is made GETTY, J. PAUL, 4
No one can...get rich...being a c. GETTY, J. PAUL, 7
conformity mystique of c. is sapping...dynamic individualism GETTY, J. PAUL, 3
confronted c. primarily with a moral issue KENNEDY, JOHN FITZGERALD, 12
confuse c. the minds of others DISRAELI, BENJAMIN, 33
never c. elegance with snobbery SAINT LAURENT, YVES, 2
confused Anyone who isn't c....doesn't really understand ANONYMOUS, 89
you are hopelessly c. MONDALE, WALTER, 2
confusion C. is a word we have invented MILLER, HENRY, 28
nothing...except my own c. KEROUAC, JACK, 19
Spread c. in your wake PETERS, TOM, 10
What mazed c. CALDERÓN DE LA BARCA, PEDRO, 2
congenial Is a blue shirt without a tie c. enough? NEWSPAPERS, 7
connect Only c. FORSTER, E. M., 15
connected Everything is c. DELILLO, DON, 7
connection c. between history and nature ARENDT, HANNAH, 2
hidden c....stronger than an obvious one HERACLITUS, 4
connectivity c....equals competitiveness CRONIN, MARY J., 2
global c....technological breakthrough of our decade CRONIN, MARY J., 1
connoisseur c. of bad moments in the air MATTHIESSEN, PETER, 4
conquer Antony /Should c. Antony SHAKESPEARE, WILLIAM, 83
easier to c. it WALPOLE, HORACE, 4
I must not c. but liberate FRANCO, FRANCISCO, 2
They will c., but...not convince UNAMUNO Y JUGO, MIGUEL DE, 9
when we c. without danger CORNEILLE, PIERRE, 6
conquered I will be c.; I will not capitulate JOHNSON, SAMUEL, 147
conquering c. and elate humanity CRANE, STEPHEN, 2
See, the c. hero comes MORELL, THOMAS, 1
conquerors c. prefer enemies as fierce as tigers LU XUN, 7
The c. are kings PROVERBS, 40
conquers First man c. nature BELLOW, SAUL, 26
conquest c. and spoliation of the weaker nations DEBS, EUGENE VICTOR, 1
conscience A bad c. creates malignant behavior REICH, WILHELM, 2

a c. bypass KINNOCK, NEIL, 5
a good digestion depends upon a good c. DISRAELI, BENJAMIN, 38
A man has less c. when in love SCHOPENHAUER, ARTHUR, 1
a person's c. ain't got no sense TWAIN, MARK, 40
A quiet c. is not clearer DROSTE-HÜLSHOFF, ANNETTE ELISABETH VON, 2
A still and quiet c. SHAKESPEARE, WILLIAM, 281
C. and self-love...lead us the same way BUTLER, JOSEPH, 1
c. hath a thousand several tongues SHAKESPEARE, WILLIAM, 534
C. is a coward GOLDSMITH, OLIVER, 30
C. is...rejection of a particular wish FREUD, SIGMUND, 51
C. is the inner voice MENCKEN, H. L., 2
c....other people inside you PIRANDELLO, LUIGI, 1
cruelty with a good c. RUSSELL, BERTRAND, 34
c....weakest when he needs it most FROMM, ERICH, 2
I cannot...cut my c. to fit HELLMAN, LILLIAN, 5
Never do anything against c. EINSTEIN, ALBERT, 41
our own c. is asleep OSSIETZKY, CARL VON, 1
should not C. have *Vacation* BUTLER, SAMUEL (1612–80), 19
The disease of an evil c. GLADSTONE, WILLIAM EWART, 6
Thus c. does make cowards of us all SHAKESPEARE, WILLIAM, 178
what does c. say I *should* do MELVILLE, HERMAN, 14
conscious To be c. is an illness DOSTOYEVSKY, FYODOR, 3
consciousness All c. is consciousness *of* something SARTRE, JEAN-PAUL, 24
C. can neither be described nor defined DEWEY, JOHN, 8
c., her awful Mate DICKINSON, EMILY, 17
C. is an active process DEWEY, JOHN, 15
C....is an illegitimate birth JAMES, WILLIAM, 11
c. is...a state of nerves QUINE, WILLARD V., 2
c. is...consciousness of the object HEGEL, G. W. F., 10
C....is nothing jointed; it flows JAMES, WILLIAM, 12
common c. of the Power overseas AUSTIN, MARY, 3
C....teeming multiplicity of objects and relations JAMES, WILLIAM, 10
C....when nerve-processes are hesitant JAMES, WILLIAM, 13
delusion imprisons the c. that projects it FOUCAULT, MICHEL, 5
The state of our c. is peculiar JAMES, WILLIAM, 18
consequences do anything...take the c. MAUGHAM, SOMERSET, 26
conservation C. is a state of harmony LEOPOLD, ALDO, 1
conservatism c. is based upon the idea CHESTERTON, G. K., 29
The c. of to-morrow BIERCE, AMBROSE, 44
What is c.? LINCOLN, ABRAHAM, 27
conservative c....A statesman...enamored of existing evils BIERCE, AMBROSE, 17
the most c. thing is to be a revolutionary CAMBÓ, FRANCISCO, 2
which makes a man more c. KEYNES, JOHN MAYNARD, 15
Conservative Party the C. at prayer ROYDEN, MAUD, 1
consider c. your ways BIBLE, 140
When I c. how my light is spent MILTON, JOHN, 108
considerable to appear c. in his native place JOHNSON, SAMUEL, 173
consideration Devoid of c. for the selfishness BIERCE, AMBROSE, 47
considered Hast thou c. my servant Job BIBLE, 253
consistency C. is contrary to nature HUXLEY, ALDOUS, 20
c. is the hobgoblin of little minds EMERSON, RALPH WALDO, 16
consistent be c., do it all the time IBSEN, HENRIK, 8
conspicuous consumption C....is a means of reputability VEBLEN, THORSTEIN BUNDE, 3
conspiracy a vast, amorphous, unwitting, unconscious c. BENNIS, WARREN, 17
People of the same trade...conversation ends in a c. SMITH, ADAM, 5
Science...c. of brains against ignorance DYSON, FREEMAN, 3
constabulary When c. duty's to be done GILBERT, W. S., 39
constant A c. guest PROVERBS, 102
C. dripping wears away the stone PROVERBS, 173
constituents no formal c. to define the travel book RABAN, JONATHAN, 2
constitution c....first and second class citizens WILLKIE, WENDELL LEWIS, 1
c. is what the judges say HUGHES, CHARLES, 2
cling...actual c. of the thought JAMES, WILLIAM, 16
C. may be distinguished for...learning ADAMS, ABIGAIL, 6
c. or national army is totally out ALEXANDER II, 1
It is the genius of our c. JOHNSON, LYNDON BAINES, 8
The federal C....greatest of human experiments BRANDEIS, LOUIS D., 6
The people made the C. MARSHALL, JOHN, 1
The proposed C. MADISON, JAMES, 3
constitutional A c. king must learn to stoop LEOPOLD II, 1
I have no eyes but c. eyes LINCOLN, ABRAHAM, 38
constitutional heritage Our whole c....power to control men's minds MARSHALL, THURGOOD, 1
constitutions Some men look at c. JEFFERSON, THOMAS, 27
constraint arbitrariness of the c. STRAVINSKY, IGOR, 5
consult easier to c. than to manage TOFFLER, ALVIN, 7
consultant A c. solves other people's problems HANDY, CHARLES, 11
c. and client...using a common set of assumptions SCHEIN, EDGAR H., 2
c....mind uncluttered by any of the facts AUGUSTINE, NORMAN R., 1
C. specialists are a degree more remote FISHER, GEOFFREY, 1
c....takes your money and annoys your employees ADAMS, SCOTT, 1
hire a c. on snakes PEROT, H. ROSS, 2
The c.'s first obligation...to the patient HENDRICK, BURTON J., 1
consumed c. with this desire BROWNING, ROBERT, 1
consumer In a c. society there are...two kinds of slaves ILLICH, IVAN, 7
The c. isn't a moron OGILVY, DAVID, 3
The c....is the king SAMUELSON, P. A., 1
consumers C. resent it...company presumes to judge GROVE, ANDREW S., 1
Just before c. stop doing something POPCORN, FAITH, 1
Millions of c. and businesses...waiting in line MOUGAYAR, WALID, 1
consummatum c. est BIBLE, 502
consumption C....sole end and purpose of production SMITH, ADAM, 3
The c. explosion in the West AKHTER, FARIDA, 1
this c. of the purse SHAKESPEARE, WILLIAM, 251
contagion the strong c. of the gown JOHNSON, SAMUEL, 8
contained I have never been c. EVANS, MARI, 2
contemplation For c. he and valour formed MILTON, JOHN, 66
contemporary After the c. liberation MIRÓ, JOAN, 1
C. man has rationalized the myths PAZ, OCTAVIO, 4
I am no one's c.—ever MANDELSTAM, OSIP, 8
contempt C. mates well with pity NAYLOR, GLORIA, 1
their boundless c. for garlic ELLIS, ALICE THOMAS, 1
contender I could've been a c. BRANDO, MARLON, 4
content I have good reason to be c. SHAKESPEARE, WILLIAM, 31
To be c. with little is hard EBNER-ESCHENBACH, MARIE VON, 8
contented quite c. to have become an adjective FELLINI, FEDERICO, 4
contentment C. and fulfilment don't make...good fiction TROLLOPE, ANTHONY, 9

continence sexual perversion known as c. HUXLEY, ALDOUS, 13
continent this c....decide their own destiny POLK, JAMES KNOX, 1
continuing Here we have no c. city BIBLE, 148
continuous C. change is comfortable change HANDY, CHARLES, 9
contraception leave c. on the long finger LYNCH, JACK, 1
contraceptive best c. is a glass of cold water PROVERBS, MODERN, 23
Dr Marie Stopes made c. devices respectable STOPES, MARIE, 2
contraceptive pill c. may reduce the importance of sex BIRD, CAROLINE, 2
contraceptives People who use c....not understand love TERESA OF CALCUTTA, MOTHER, 10
Skullion had little use for c. SHARPE, TOM, 1
contract A verbal c. isn't worth the paper GOLDWYN, SAMUEL, 17
contradict Do I c. myself? WHITMAN, WALT, 36
contradiction c....basic law in materialist dialectics MAO ZEDONG, 13
c. in terms HOGARTH, WILLIAM, 1
contradictions C....can spark off the fires of invention ACHEBE, CHINUA, 2
c. that are pushing our society forward MAO ZEDONG, 28
contradicts One often c. an opinion NIETZSCHE, FRIEDRICH WILHELM, 20
contrariwise "C.," continued Tweedledee CARROLL, LEWIS, 35
contrary On the c. IBSEN, HENRIK, 19
contrive thy soul c. /Against thy mother aught SHAKESPEARE, WILLIAM, 157
control "c. of nature"...phrase conceived in arrogance CARSON, RACHEL, 4
impulse to c....essential element in obsessional neurosis KLEIN, MELANIE, 5
I must...c. the talking habit FRANK, ANNE, 6
When you c. a man's thinking WOODSON, CARTER G., 2
controlled events have c. me LINCOLN, ABRAHAM, 15
controlling By focussing...on c. their bodies DIANA, PRINCESS, 7
controversial It's altogether...less c. and more physical COE, SEBASTIAN, 1
controversies The most savage c. RUSSELL, BERTRAND, 53
controversy c. is either superfluous NEWMAN, JOHN HENRY, 5
convalescence I enjoy c. SHAW, GEORGE BERNARD, 19
convenient more c. to possess the ashes DESCARTES, RENÉ, 1
convent Benedictine c. is very close to the art world ANDERSON, LAURIE, 1
convention c. which says you must not make species extinct PHILIP, PRINCE, 4
conventionality C. has indeed curtailed feminine force BLACKWELL, ANTOINETTE LOUISA, 1
C. is not morality BRONTË, CHARLOTTE, 7
conversation C....art of never appearing a bore MAUPASSANT, GUY DE, 3
C. has a kind of charm SENECA, "THE YOUNGER," 3
c. must be an exchange of thought POST, EMILY, 1
Gleanings of good C. BEHN, APHRA, 11
happiest c. where there is no competition JOHNSON, SAMUEL, 119
many thousand subjects for elegant c. BRAMAH, ERNEST, 3
never-ending worldwide c. NEWSPAPERS, 9
no such thing as c. WEST, REBECCA, 5
reasonable c....frightens us in a madman FRANCE, ANATOLE, 12
spin c....out of thy own bowels JOHNSON, SAMUEL, 55
this c. is getting a little strange HOFFMAN, DUSTIN, 1
conversationalist the c. who adds "in other words" MORLEY, ROBERT, 1
convert We should easily c....the Turks CRANMER, THOMAS, 2
converted not c. a man because you have silenced him MORLEY, JOHN, 1
conviction loss of c....meaning of life NAGEL, THOMAS, 1
Unreasonable c. based on inadequate evidence PETERS, TOM, 16
convictions encompassed by a cloud of comforting c. RUSSELL, BERTRAND, 32
convicts C. are the best audience CASH, JOHNNY, 1
c. live like animals VARGAS LLOSA, MARIO, 8
cook a good c., as cooks go SAKI, 6
A good c. is like a sorceress SCHIAPARELLI, ELSA, 2
Any c. should be able to LENIN, VLADIMIR ILYICH, 22
c. that cannot lick his own fingers SHAKESPEARE, WILLIAM, 557
Learn how to c. CHILD, JULIA, 1
cookery C. cannot be done like pharmacy UDE, LOUIS EUSTACHE, 2
C....pandering which corresponds to medicine PLATO, 3
cooking C....combination of science, art, invention SPRY, CONSTANCE, 1
woman accepted c. as a chore POST, EMILY, 4
cooks great C....high Way of expressing themselves GLASSE, HANNAH, 1
Too many c. PROVERBS, 437
Too many c. spoil the broth...one to burn it CHILD, JULIA, 2
cool c., calm and elected MAJOR, JOHN, 6
Doth thy transparent, c., and watery wealth VAUGHAN, HENRY, 4
once c. but Mr. Gravity's been very unkind SAUNDERS, JENNIFER, 2
We real c.. /We /Left school. We /Lurk late. We /Strike straight BROOKS, GWENDOLYN, 4
Coolidge C. is a better example of evolution COOLIDGE, CALVIN, 5
Mr. C.'s genius for inactivity COOLIDGE, CALVIN, 1
Nero fiddled, but C. only snored COOLIDGE, CALVIN, 3
coordinating c. the talents...towards a certain goal DISNEY, WALT, 3
coot I come from haunts of c....hern TENNYSON, ALFRED, 34
copier A...c. of nature can never produce anything great REYNOLDS, SIR JOSHUA, 3
copies c. of my works are left behind BENCHLEY, ROBERT, 3
cops c....existential moment of making their bust MAILER, NORMAN, 15
c. in LA looked like handsome gigolos KEROUAC, JACK, 17
copulation The c. /of cats is harrowing PORTER, PETER, 2
copyright there's no c. on your own life MILES, SARAH, 1
cork Lighter than a c. I danced RIMBAUD, ARTHUR, 8
corn The c. is as high HAMMERSTEIN, OSCAR, II, 5
the meadows rich with c. WHITTIER, JOHN GREENLEAF, 2
Whoever could make two ears of c. SWIFT, JONATHAN, 20
coronets Kind hearts are more than c. TENNYSON, ALFRED, 46
corporate c. health falters...mobilize human potential DE GEUS, ARIE, 3
C. leaders...seeing their jobs as quasi-public FOX, HARRISON W., JR., 4
I'm a child of the c. struggle EISNER, MICHAEL, 5
power of c. teamwork and cooperation KANTER, ROSABETH MOSS, 5
corporation c....device for securing individual profit BIERCE, AMBROSE, 2
c. without a strategy TOFFLER, ALVIN, 5
one great c. working without friction CLARK, JOHN BATES, 1
the c. of the future HAAS, ROBERT, 5
corporations c. should be membership communities HANDY, CHARLES, 3
C....the dominant institution HAWKEN, PAUL, 5
U.S. c. are run like...Soviet economy OHMAE, KENICHI, 4

corpse buried the putrid c. of liberty MUSSOLINI, BENITO, 3
He'd make a lovely c. DICKENS, CHARLES, 52
One can't carry one's father's c. APOLLINAIRE, GUILLAUME, 1
The c. was dressed in a uniform CRANE, STEPHEN, 9
corpses battle-c....white skeletons of young men WHITMAN, WALT, 47
does not eat c. SHAW, GEORGE BERNARD, 107
when a hundred c. are lying together HIMMLER, HEINRICH, 2
corrupt All things...c. perverted minds OVID, 12
corrupted They had been c. by money GREENE, GRAHAM, 6
corruption c. /Never has been compulsory JEFFERS, ROBINSON, 1
C., the most infallible symptom of constitutional liberty GIBBON, EDWARD, 6
ERADICATION OF C. AWOLOWO, OBAFEMI, 2
I have said to c., thou art my father BIBLE, 261
cosmetics c. names seemed obscenely obvious JONG, ERICA, 4
cosmopolitan c....at home...in his own country JAMES, HENRY, 3
I was told I am a true c. VIZINCZEY, STEPHEN, 1
cosmos c. is about the smallest hole CHESTERTON, G. K., 25
cost The c. of a thing STEVENSON, ROBERT LOUIS, 7
the c. of paying people STEWART, THOMAS A., 1
Why so large c....upon thy fading mansion spend SHAKESPEARE, WILLIAM, 588
cost of living slaves to the c. DE JESÚS, CAROLINA MARIA, 1
costs C. merely register competing attractions KNIGHT, FRANK HYNEMAN, 2
That which c. little is less valued CERVANTES, MIGUEL DE, 3
Watch the c. ARISTOTLE, 9
cotton Hands that picked c....will pick a president JACKSON, JESSE, 1
couch when on my c. I lie WORDSWORTH, WILLIAM, 46
cough C.. A convulsion of the lungs JOHNSON, SAMUEL, 9
c. is something...everybody else does NASH, OGDEN, 27
counsel give me...c....you think best ELIZABETH I, 6
count c. your money you are not...rich man GETTY, J. PAUL, 9
I c. the votes TWEED, BOSS, 1
One has to be able to c. GORKY, MAKSIM, 4
counted the faster we c. our spoons EMERSON, RALPH WALDO, 58
countenance the Lord lift up his c. upon thee BIBLE, 448
counteracts he c. the powers of darkness SMART, CHRISTOPHER, 5
countries every man had two c. MURDOCH, RUPERT, 2
No two c. that...have a McDonald's FRIEDMAN, THOMAS L., 1
preferreth all c. before his own OVERBURY, THOMAS, 1
country A c....can never be morally free GANDHI, MAHATMA, 17
A c. governed by a despot JOHNSON, SAMUEL, 67
a c. of young men EMERSON, RALPH WALDO, 44
all these c. patriots BYRON, LORD, 94
A man should know...his own c. STERNE, LAURENCE, 15
a new c....with a castle of a House ADAMS, ABIGAIL, 1
Anyone who loves his c., follow me GARIBALDI, GIUSEPPE, 1
c. songwriter...cry-in-your-beer songs NELSON, WILLIE, 1
c. with thirty-two religions...one sauce TALLEYRAND, CHARLES MAURICE DE, 1
Every c. has the government it deserves MAISTRE, JOSEPH MARIE DE, 1
Every c. should realize JIMÉNEZ, JUAN RAMÓN, 9
Every c. that has caught up THUROW, LESTER, 1
good c. for all of us NIXON, RICHARD, 30
how shall I speak of my proud c.'s shame HARPER, FRANCES E. W., 7
How soon c. people forget MORRISON, TONI, 13
if a man takes away the character of the people of my c. NAIMBANNA, JOHN HENRY, 1
In the c. of the blind PROVERBS, 274
In the c., one excuse WHITE, E. B., 4
Know... thy native c. FULLER, THOMAS (1608–61), 10
Let our object be our c. WEBSTER, DANIEL, 1
love a c. that brings...people happiness CHEN DUXIU, 1
my c. /has known a thousand conquerors ZAYYAD, TAWFIQ, 2
My c. right or wrong CRITTENDEN, JOHN, 1
My c., 'tis of thee SMITH, SAMUEL FRANCIS, 1
my real c. is painting BOLTANSKI, CHRISTIAN, 1
My soul, there is a c. VAUGHAN, HENRY, 2
nothing good...in the c. HAZLITT, WILLIAM, 28
Our c. is the world GARRISON, WILLIAM LLOYD, 1
our c., right or wrong DECATUR, STEPHEN, 1
soil of our c.... scene of the fiercest fight MANDELA, NELSON, 14
suck'd on c. pleasures, childishly DONNE, JOHN, 42
That is no c. for old men YEATS, W. B., 37
the c....a kind of healthy grave SMITH, SYDNEY, 4
the c. demands bold, persistent experimentation ROOSEVELT, FRANKLIN D., 16
The c. was on the slide MO, TIMOTHY, 2
The undiscover'd c. SHAKESPEARE, WILLIAM, 177
this c. has given its least JORDAN, JUNE, 3
This c. needs...good plumbers NIXON, RICHARD, 28
This c., with its institutions, belongs to the people who inhabit it LINCOLN, ABRAHAM, 13
very fine c. to be acutely ill JOSEPH, KEITH, 3
We have a c. full of words DARWISH, MAHMOUD, 3
What's good for the c. WILSON, CHARLES E., 1
What this c. needs...5-cent cigar MARSHALL, THOMAS R., 1
What this c. needs...hard bloody war BIERCE, AMBROSE, 1
Who dare to love their c., and be poor POPE, ALEXANDER, 8
whole c....wild and savage hue BRADFORD, WILLIAM, 5
Why did my c....gateway /to hell TUQAN, FADWA, 1
your c....on the soles of your shoes BÜCHNER, GEORG, 3
Your King and C. Need You MOTTOS AND SLOGANS, 15
countryman the c. who looked for his ass while...mounted on his back CERVANTES, MIGUEL DE, 47
countryside A land whose c. would be bright DE VALERA, EAMON, 5
coup Pull off a c. and you're a...hero ARCHER, JEFFREY, 1
couple Splendid c.—slept with both of them BOWRA, MAURICE, 2
the perfect c....a mother and child ELLIS, ALICE THOMAS, 2
courage C. consists of staying at home MIRÓ, JOAN, 5
"C.!" he said, and pointed toward...land TENNYSON, ALFRED, 76
C. is the price...for granting peace EARHART, AMELIA, 3
C. mounteth with occasion SHAKESPEARE, WILLIAM, 321
C....think you I shall lose it MARIE-ANTOINETTE, 1
c. to love...courage to suffer TROLLOPE, ANTHONY, 7
good deal of physical c. to ride a horse LEACOCK, STEPHEN, 14
Let your c. rise with danger LUTHULI, ALBERT, 2
Lord...give us c. to recognize...the truth KAUNDA, KENNETH DAVID, 4
numberless diverse acts of c. KENNEDY, ROBERT, 2
takes a certain c....to be truly base ANOUILH, JEAN, 2
The Red Badge of C. CRANE, STEPHEN, 7
'Tis the c. you bring WALPOLE, HUGH, 1
two o'clock in the morning c. NAPOLEON I, 20
couragious Of hearte c., politique in counsaile MORE, THOMAS, 4

courted Better be c. and jilted CAMPBELL, THOMAS, 7
courtesy C....taken refuge in Great Britain DUHAMEL, GEORGES, 4
the Grace of God is in C. BELLOC, HILAIRE, 31
courting c. on the bed...customary throughout Wales RODENBERG, JULIUS, 2
When...c....an hour seems like a second EINSTEIN, ALBERT, 25
courtship C. to marriage CONGREVE, WILLIAM, 18
cousins Too many c. PROVERBS, 77
couture c. is an art POIRET, PAUL, 1
covenant a c. between me and the earth BIBLE, 119
age-old c. between man and dog LORENZ, KONRAD, 4
c. with death and an agreement with hell GARRISON, WILLIAM LLOYD, 3
I will make a new c. with the house of Israel BIBLE, 252
covenanted And they c. with him for thirty pieces of silver BIBLE, 433
covenants C. without the sword are but words HOBBES, THOMAS, 14
cover I...will c. thee with my hand BIBLE, 89
Never judge a c. by its book LEBOWITZ, FRAN, 4
cow A c. is a very good animal in the field JOHNSON, SAMUEL, 160
A c. is not an animal CLAUSEN, A. W., 1
c. is of the bovine ilk NASH, OGDEN, 7
Why buy a c. PROVERBS, 461
coward No c. soul is mine BRONTË, EMILY, 1
None but a c....has never known fear FOCH, FERDINAND, 3
Coward a very Noel C. sort of person TYNAN, KENNETH, 2
Cowardice guilty of Noel C. COWARD, NOEL, 1
cowards C. die many times SHAKESPEARE, WILLIAM, 302
C. in scarlet GRANVILLE, GEORGE, 1
that little god of talking c. WYCHERLEY, WILLIAM, 4
cows C. are my passion DICKENS, CHARLES, 30
Sacred c. make the tastiest hamburger HOFFMAN, ABBIE, 4
crack Blow, winds, and c. your cheeks SHAKESPEARE, WILLIAM, 342
cracks c. in the universe SMITH, SYDNEY, 28
cradle c. rocks above an abyss NABOKOV, VLADIMIR, 8
The hand that rocks the c. WALLACE, WILLIAM ROSS, 1
craft Between c. and credulity...reason is stifled BURKE, EDMUND, 7
C....what you can learn from other verse HEANEY, SEAMUS, 8
crafty She's too c....to invent a new lie MAUGHAM, SOMERSET, 30
crash-proof No c. system can be built ULLMAN, ELLEN, 1
crawl we cannot c. in the tracks of others MAO ZEDONG, 31
crawled something that...c. out of the sea NICHOLS, BEVERLEY, 1
crazy I became a bit c. BEETHOVEN, LUDWIG VAN, 4
I was c. and...he was drunk GRANT, ULYSSES S., 2
Orr was c. and could be grounded HELLER, JOSEPH, 4
Pound's c.. All poets are POUND, EZRA, 1
create c. good precedents...follow them BACON, FRANCIS (1561–1626), 36
The only things that c. wealth ROOKE, SIR DENIS, 1
created C. man out of a clot of blood KORAN, 44
Nothing can be c. out of nothing LUCRETIUS, 1
Thou hast c. us for Thyself AUGUSTINE OF HIPPO, SAINT, 2
We c. man from dry clay KORAN, 19
We c. you /From...a male and a female KORAN, 36
Yan'an has been c. by having guns MAO ZEDONG, 30
creating C. is harrowing business PROUST, MARCEL, 1
creation at the c., the earth was pure ANONYMOUS, 60
C. comes before distribution RAND, AYN, 4
c. comes out more beautiful GAUTIER, THÉOPHILE, 1
c. of a world...governed by justice ATTLEE, CLEMENT, 4
c. of the juridical entity of the citizen SCHAMA, SIMON, 1
man who talks about the "brute c." BARBELLION, W. N. P., 1
The C. state THORPE, THOMAS BANGS, 1
whole of C. /To produce my foot HUGHES, TED, 4
creations started more c. since Genesis ROOSEVELT, FRANKLIN D., 3
creative All men are c....few are artists GOODMAN, PAUL, 2
As c. retailers, our policy CONRAN, TERENCE, 3
c. act is not performed by the artist alone DUCHAMP, MARCEL, 2
C. imagination awakens early DAGERMAN, STIG, 1
no c. activity is possible ZAMYATIN, YEVGENY, 1
the c. process, inspiration is a mystery MITCHELL, JONI, 4
creativeness C....turning up what is already there FITZ-GIBBON, BERNICE, 1
creativity C. is a highfalutin word KROC, RAY, 4
c. is mastery of simplicity ZEEMAN, E.C., 1
Properly practiced c. BERNBACH, WILLIAM, 3
creator If one can call...C. to account LU XUN, 5
Man...hasn't been a c., only a destroyer CHEKHOV, ANTON, 19
the c....is apt to create *anything* DILLARD, ANNIE, 8
creature c. slipping in armed with a spear PU SONGLING, 1
Every c. is better alive than dead THOREAU, HENRY DAVID, 22
every c. of God is good BIBLE, 236
The c. hath a purpose KEATS, JOHN (1795–1821), 36
creatures little c....a thousand times smaller LEEUWENHOEK, ANTONI VAN, 1
credit not to mind who gets the c. JOWETT, BENJAMIN, 6
Remember...c. is money FRANKLIN, BENJAMIN, 5
creditor It is better to pay a c. ARISTOTLE, 8
creditors my oldest c. would hardly know me FOX, HENRY STEPHEN, 1
your c....beseech Almighty God RABELAIS, FRANÇOIS, 9
credulity C. is...the child's strength LAMB, CHARLES, 19
c....to think all men virtuous BURKE, EDMUND, 55
from c. to skepticism JEFFERSON, THOMAS, 9
creed His c. no parson ever knew DOYLE, FRANCIS, 1
creeds other c. and different nationalities...live amongst us HERZL, THEODOR, 6
creeps The man who c....may well arrive NYERERE, JULIUS KAMBARAGE, 7
creepy They're c. and they're kooky ADDAMS FAMILY, THE, 1
crème All my pupils are the c. de la crème SPARK, MURIEL, 7
Crete The people of C....make more history SAKI, 17
cricket c. is the greatest thing that God ever created PINTER, HAROLD, 4
c.... so very English BERNHARDT, SARAH, 2
The c. test TEBBIT, NORMAN, 1
this isn't no time for playin' /...this is c. BRATHWAITE, EDWARD KAMAU, 2
What do they know of c. JAMES, C. L. R., 4
cried I had never c. for my father's death PLATH, SYLVIA, 11
cries c. of men in meaningless debt...war HARDING, WARREN G., 2
crime C. always seems impossible in retrospect LEACOCK, STEPHEN, 19
c. and the criminal...perplexity of radical evil ARENDT, HANNAH, 13
C. has its heroes VOLTAIRE, 31
C., like virtue, has its degrees RACINE, JEAN, 20
c. pays. The hours are good ALLEN, WOODY, 11
c....repressed desire for aesthetic expression WAUGH, EVELYN, 18
C. which is prosperous...is called virtue SENECA, "THE YOUNGER," 13

duty to worship the sun...c. to examine...heat MORLEY, JOHN, 3
Every c. destroys more Edens HAWTHORNE, NATHANIEL, 13
From the one c. recognize them all as culprits VIRGIL, 11
He who secretly meditates c....guilty JUVENAL, 1
no man secures happiness by c. ALFIERI, VITTORIO, 1
study of c....knowledge of oneself MILLER, HENRY, 11
The atrocious c. of being a young man PITT THE ELDER, WILLIAM, 6
The worst c. is to leave a man's hands empty WALCOTT, DEREK, 3
worse than a c., it is a blunder BOULAY DE LA MEURTHE, ANTOINE, 1
worst c. is faking it COBAIN, KURT, 4

crimes capital c....Appear before us SHAKESPEARE, WILLIAM, 263
c. of this guilty land BROWN, JOHN, 6
C. of which a people is ashamed GENET, JEAN, 2
Successful c. alone are justified DRYDEN, JOHN, 46
The c. of extreme civilization BARBEY D'AUREVILLY, JULES-AMÉDÉE, 1

criminal To venerate an executed c. MINUCIUS FELIX, MARCUS, 1

criminals more c. out of jail than in jail GARVEY, MARCUS, 4

criterion c. for what is a fact PUTNAM, HILARY, 1

critic A c. is a man who TYNAN, KENNETH, 4
A c. should be a conduit MORRISON, TONI, 9
be a c....easier than... be an author PROVERBS, 60
c....historian who records FULLER, MARGARET, 2
c. is a bunch of biases BALLIETT, WHITNEY, 1
c. is a legless man POLLOCK, JACKSON, 5
c. is...the younger brother of genius FULLER, MARGARET, 6
drama c....surprises the playwright MIZNER, WILSON, 4
ever seen a dramatic c. in the daytime WODEHOUSE, P. G., 30
No one...a more severe c. of Margot than Margot FONTEYN, MARGOT, 1
Nor in the c. let the man be lost POPE, ALEXANDER, 13

critical nothing if not c. SHAKESPEARE, WILLIAM, 477

criticism A great deal of contemporary c. CHESTERTON, G. K., 10
As far as c. is concerned VORSTER, JOHN, 1
C. can talk...arts are dumb FRYE, NORTHROP, 2
c. is a letter to the public RILKE, RAINER MARIA, 3
C. is to art what...philosophy to wisdom FRYE, NORTHROP, 3
my own definition of c. ARNOLD, MATTHEW, 18
People ask you for c. MAUGHAM, SOMERSET, 17
The father of English c. DRYDEN, JOHN, 2
Writing c. is...hugging the shore UPDIKE, JOHN, 9

criticize Do not c. your government when out of the country CHURCHILL, WINSTON, 77
don't c. /What you can't understand DYLAN, BOB, 14

criticizing The pleasure of c. LA BRUYÈRE, JEAN DE, 13

critics c. are fueled by...failed ambitions REDFORD, ROBERT, 1
C. are more malicious about poetry JENNINGS, ELIZABETH, 1
c....desire our blood NIETZSCHE, FRIEDRICH WILHELM, 23
c....men who have failed DISRAELI, BENJAMIN, 27
C.!...Those cut-throat bandits BURNS, ROBERT, 55
heaves in the presence of c. FOWLER, GENE, 2
I had listened to the c. CHEKHOV, ANTON, 23
The greater part of c. are parasites PRIESTLEY, J. B., 8
There go the c., blinkin' eyes PARKER, CHARLIE, 2

crocodile How doth the little c. CARROLL, LEWIS, 4

Cromwell restless C. could not cease MARVELL, ANDREW, 1

crook I am not a c. NIXON, RICHARD, 12

crooked the c. timber of humanity KANT, IMMANUEL, 24
There was a c. man CHILDREN'S VERSE, 48
the shortest line...may be the c. one BRECHT, BERTOLT, 21

cross Don't c. the bridge PROVERBS, 182
find another c. if you flee PROVERBS, 88
never...a c. word with a man CARTLAND, BARBARA, 5
no c., no crown PENN, WILLIAM, 1
We can't always c. a bridge BARUCH, BERNARD MANNES, 5

cross-bow With my c. /I shot the Albatross COLERIDGE, SAMUEL TAYLOR, 39

crow I am but a c....in peacock feathers MONTESQUIEU, 1
I'd rather c. /And be a rooster FOLK VERSE, 56

crowd a c....brings a lump to my wallet WALLACH, ELI, 1
A c. is not company BACON, FRANCIS (1561–1626), 28
Far from the madding c. GRAY, THOMAS, 10
separate yourself from the c. NICKLAUS, JACK, 3
The c. are on the pitch WOLSTENHOLME, KENNETH, 1

crown c. o' the earth doth melt SHAKESPEARE, WILLIAM, 86
From the c....to the sole BEAUMONT & FLETCHER, 7

Crown influence of the C. has increased DUNNING, JOHN, 1

crowned He was my c. King HOWARD, THOMAS, 1
not a single c. head in Europe JEFFERSON, THOMAS, 31

Crown Jewels get the C....from the pawn-shop NAIRN, TOM, 3

crows some c., deceived...tried to alight on them PLINY THE ELDER, 11

crucified you might try getting c. TALLEYRAND, CHARLES MAURICE DE, 6

crucifixion Forget the c., remember the renaissance WEST, NATHANAEL, 5

cruel A c. story runs on wheels OUIDA, 4
be c. only to be kind SHAKESPEARE, WILLIAM, 202
How c. God would be LAMARTINE, ALPHONSE DE, 3
how much more c. the pen BURTON, ROBERT, 3

cruelties The c. of property and privilege JAMES, C. L. R., 10

cruelty C. is contagious in uncivilized communities JACOBS, HARRIET ANN, 2
inflict c....immediately before slaughter HIGGINS, ANDREW, 1
The c....is lack of imagination TUCHOLSKY, KURT, 3

cruising C....was a lot like hitchhiking MAUPIN, ARMISTEAD, 7

crumb I never wanted to be a c. LUCIANO, LUCKY, 1

crusaders one big target for the c. was the tango CASTLE, IRENE, 1

crush Either we do it, or they c. us STALIN, JOSEPH, 14
I've Got a C. on You GERSHWIN, IRA, 8

crust Even a c. is bread PROVERBS, 48

crustiness nothing...conquers John Bull's c. sooner than eating IRVING, WASHINGTON, 3

cry I c. all the way to the bank LIBERACE, 2
I often want to c. RHYS, JEAN, 1
the c. of him that ruleth among fools BIBLE, 56
when we c. to Thee WHITING, WILLIAM, 1

crying It is no use c. PROVERBS, 278

Cuban introduction to C. optimism GELLHORN, MARTHA, 1

cubic foot One c. less...would have constituted adultery PARKER, DOROTHY, 1

Cubists C....colored puzzle pictures of the Sunday newspapers ROOSEVELT, THEODORE, 23

cuckoo C.-echoing, bell-swarmèd, lark-charmèd HOPKINS, GERARD MANLEY, 2
C.! Shall I call thee bird WORDSWORTH, WILLIAM, 71

cucumber A c. should be well sliced JOHNSON, SAMUEL, 59

cucumbers project for extracting sun-beams out of c. SWIFT, JONATHAN, 21
they are but c. after all GRAY, THOMAS, 2
Cuernavaca in C. I learned more about the mind LEARY, TIMOTHY, 3
cuisine Every c. tells a story RODEN, CLAUDIA, 1
Culloden C....the symbol of the death LYNCH, MICHAEL, 4
culprits better to choose the c. PAGNOL, MARCEL, 5
cult a c....not enough...to make a minority ALTMAN, ROBERT, 2
brought their c. to California...everybody does HAMMETT, DASHIELL, 1
cultivate c. a few inhibitions LOOS, ANITA, 7
cultural c. health...is political MORGAN, EDWIN, 3
c. transmission is geared to learning BATESON, GREGORY, 1
great import of c. conditions on neuroses HORNEY, KAREN, 22
Cultural Revolution the C., an earthshaking disaster BO YANG, 1
culture A c. that values integrity O'HARE, DEAN, 1
C....abhors all simplification FANON, FRANTZ, 9
C....an instrument wielded by professors WEIL, SIMONE, 6
c. inebriated by noise and gregariousness STEINER, GEORGE, 3
"C." is simply how one lives BARAKA, IMAMU AMIRI, 5
C. is the passion for sweetness and light ARNOLD, MATTHEW, 23
C....perishing in overproduction KUNDERA, MILAN, 1
c. that...subscribes to the piratical ethic CLEAVER, ELDRIDGE, 3
c. that worships aggression STONE, OLIVER, 1
C., the acquainting ourselves with the best ARNOLD, MATTHEW, 24
ladies who pursue C. in bands WHARTON, EDITH, 14
path to c....through a man's specialism ASHBY, ERIC, 1
serious c. is being engulfed WANG MENG, 1
talk of C., I reach for my revolver GOERING, HERMANN, 3
cultures apt to leave his c. exposed FLEMING, ALEXANDER, 2
cunning Be as c. as a serpent and as harmless as a dove EMECHETA, BUCHI, 6
C. and deceit will every time serve a man better MACHIAVELLI, NICCOLÒ, 5
In saying...never choose c. OZICK, CYNTHIA, 5
cup Ah, fill the C. FITZGERALD, EDWARD, 11
between the c. and the lip BURTON, ROBERT, 9
Come, fill the C., and in the Fire of Spring FITZGERALD, EDWARD, 3
tak a c. o' kindness yet BURNS, ROBERT, 10
curate The c.; he was fatter than his cure TENNYSON, ALFRED, 42
curbing c. of minds to the government's will NABOKOV, VLADIMIR, 11
cur'd C....of my disease PRIOR, MATTHEW, 9
cure a c. that destroys the depression THOMAS, EDWARD, 5
best c. for depression...hope FANTHORPE, U. A., 2
It is part of the c. to wish to be cured SENECA, "THE YOUNGER," 15
most rational c....for...fear of death HAZLITT, WILLIAM, 24
no c. for birth and death SANTAYANA, GEORGE, 9
Nothing hinders a c. so much as frequent change of medicine SENECA, "THE YOUNGER," 4
"There is no c. for this disease." BELLOC, HILAIRE, 9
We all labour against our own c. BROWNE, THOMAS, 8
cured What can't be c. PROVERBS, 450
curfew C. shall not ring tonight THORPE, ROSE HARTWICK, 1
The C. tolls the knell of parting day GRAY, THOMAS, 4
curfews c. were declared illegal YÜCEL, CAN, 2
curing There is no c. a sick man AMIEL, HENRI FRÉDÉRIC, 2
curiosities these c. would be quite forgot AUBREY, JOHN, 1
curiosity C. conquers prejudice BARBELLION, W. N. P., 2
C. killed the cat PROVERBS, 174
C. will conquer fear STEPHENS, JAMES, 2
My c. was aroused to fever-pitch VERNE, JULES, 3
curious I am c. to see...the next world PERUGINO, 1
curiouser C. and curiouser CARROLL, LEWIS, 3
curly C. locks, /Wilt thou be mine CHILDREN'S VERSE, 20
currencies system of national c. WRISTON, WALTER B., 2
current we must take the c. when it serves SHAKESPEARE, WILLIAM, 316
curs'd c. be he that moves my bones SHAKESPEARE, WILLIAM, 14
curse c. God, and die BIBLE, 255
c....is eloquent men EMERSON, RALPH WALDO, 42
c. is on her if she stay TENNYSON, ALFRED, 67
c. of all the human race NAPOLEON I, 1
Don't c. the darkness PROVERBS, 28
make a c. sound like a caress BEVAN, ANEURIN, 2
O c. of marriage SHAKESPEARE, WILLIAM, 491
The c. of literacy MCCAIG, NORMAN, 1
The great c. of our modern society DAWSON, CHRISTOPHER, 1
cursed a dim remembering of a c. past VANZETTI, BARTOLOMEO, 2
curses C....come home to roost PROVERBS, 75
curst C. be the verse POPE, ALEXANDER, 45
curtain Behind the c.'s mystic fold HARTE, BRET, 1
Bring down the c. RABELAIS, FRANÇOIS, 19
cushion Like a c., he always bore the impress LLOYD-GEORGE, DAVID, 9
custom A c. loathsome to the eye JAMES I, 4
C. is almost a second nature PLUTARCH, 14
c. is the despot of mankind PUSHKIN, ALEXANDER, 1
C., that unwritten law DAVENANT, CHARLES, 1
what is done against c. PLUTARCH, 5
customer c....determines how many people are employed ROBENS, ALFRED, 2
If you love your c. to death DAY, GRAHAM, 1
The c. is always right SELFRIDGE, H. GORDON, 1
The c. is the most important part DEMING, W. EDWARDS, 4
customers c. have asked if...buried with me AL-FAYED, MOHAMED, 2
customs C. and convictions change UPDIKE, JOHN, 11
c. which treat us...as the vassals ADAMS, ABIGAIL, 7
cut c. its headquarters staff by 90 percent BARNEVIK, PERCY, 1
c. to the heart BIBLE, 10
Don't c. my throat STENGEL, CASEY, 1
Don't c. off your nose PROVERBS, 183
he c. his own throat and died SIMA QIAN, 2
I do not c. my life up JIMÉNEZ, JUAN RAMÓN, 10
Take him and c. him out in little stars SHAKESPEARE, WILLIAM, 554
cute How long can you be c. HAWN, GOLDIE, 1
cut off They...had been c. from people outside TAO QIAN, 1
Cybernetics field of control and communication theory...C. WIENER, NORBERT, 2
cyberspace C. does allow people to freely communicate KITCHIN, ROBERT, 1
C. is a topology, not a topography NEGROPONTE, NICHOLAS, 9
cycle c. of deprivation JOSEPH, KEITH, 2
this c. of good and bad days GOETHE, JOHANN WOLFGANG VON, 33
cyclone There is a c. fence between /ourselves FORCHÉ, CAROLYN, 3
cynic A c. is a man who MENCKEN, H. L., 45

cynical c. gestures of the poor SPENDER, STEPHEN, 8
public has become pretty c. IACOCCA, LEE, 3
cynicism C....unpleasant way of saying the truth HELLMAN, LILLIAN, 3
no little c., and every kind of con game VARGAS LLOSA, MARIO, 10
The worst c.: a belief in luck OATES, JOYCE CAROL, 1
Youthful c. is sad ANGELOU, MAYA, 11

dad d. is present at the conception ORTON, JOE, 2
Dadaists D. despised...art ARP, JEAN, 1
daddy D. daddy, you bastard, I'm through PLATH, SYLVIA, 1
My Heart Belongs to D. PORTER, COLE, 15
daffodils Fair d., we weep to see HERRICK, ROBERT, 12
I never saw d. so beautiful WORDSWORTH, DOROTHY, 1
dagger d. plunged in the name of Freedom MARTÍ, JOSÉ, 2
d. which I see before me SHAKESPEARE, WILLIAM, 396
daggers I will speak d. to her SHAKESPEARE, WILLIAM, 186
Daisy D., give me your answer, do DACRE, HARRY, 1
Dalhousie Lord and Lady D. are dead MCGONAGALL, WILLIAM, 6
dam not give a singel d. FLEMING, MARJORY, 1
damn D. the age; I'll write for Antiquity LAMB, CHARLES, 5
D. with faint praise ADDISON, JOSEPH, 2
D. you, England OSBORNE, JOHN, 1
I don't give a d. MITCHELL, MARGARET, 12
I don't give a d. for logic WILSON, WOODROW, 14
damnable d., deceitful woman OTWAY, THOMAS, 2
damn'd d. be him that first cries, "Hold, enough!" SHAKESPEARE, WILLIAM, 424
damned d. if you do...damned if you don't DOW, LORENZO, 1
one d. thing after another HUBBARD, ELBERT, 8
damner only good d. HAZLITT, WILLIAM, 1
damozel The blessèd d. leaned out ROSSETTI, DANTE GABRIEL, 3
damp Avoid d. beds and think of me EPITAPHS, 7
damper puts the d. on even a Yankee win RIZZUTO, PHIL, 1
dance a d. fever has gripped the public LIVINGSTONE, WILLIAM, 1
A d. is a measured pace BACON, FRANCIS (1561–1626), 92
A D. to the Music of Time POWELL, ANTHONY, 2
All I had to do was d. KELLY, GENE, 6
can we know the dancer from the d.? YEATS, W. B., 35
D. has to look like the music BALANCHINE, GEORGE, 6
d.—the sense of kinetic force KELLY, GENE, 1
I compare...d....to water CUNNINGHAM, MERCE, 1
I could d. with you till the cows come home MARX, GROUCHO, 15
if she d. on blood WILDE, OSCAR, 34
I have discovered the d. DUNCAN, ISADORA, 6
I must d. bare-foot on her wedding day SHAKESPEARE, WILLIAM, 636
Shall We D. HAMMERSTEIN, OSCAR, II, 14
The d.—the elephant-dance! KIPLING, RUDYARD, 55
the power of the d. RUMI, JALAL AL-DIN MUHAMMAD, 1
through d. I have experienced...joy of freedom PRIMUS, PEARL, 1
danced D. All Night LERNER, ALAN JAY, 4
I've always d. CUNNINGHAM, MERCE, 3
I've d. with a man FARJEON, HERBERT, 1
dancer A d. is rather like a nun POWELL, MICHAEL, 1
I don't want to become the oldest living d. ASTAIRE, FRED, 9
dancers d. have to be a little stupid CUNNINGHAM, MERCE, 2
Of d., 38 percent show anorexic behavior WOLF, NAOMI, 1
dancing D....a form of health insurance CAGNEY, JAMES, 3
D. disintegrates. Like a garden BALANCHINE, GEORGE, 5
d....from altar to gutter DE MILLE, AGNES, 2
d. is a primal urge coming to life CAGNEY, JAMES, 2
d., like youth, is wasted on the young LERNER, MAX, 2
D....most beautiful of the arts ELLIS, HAVELOCK, 12
d. on a volcano SALVANDY, COMTE DE, 1
how physically cruel d. really is FONTEYN, MARGOT, 2
My d. days are done BEAUMONT & FLETCHER, 15
that is how I began to learn d. CAGNEY, JAMES, 5
they rise on their d. shoes ASTAIRE, FRED, 3
want of skill in d. MOLIÈRE, 4
with her sister arts, shall d. claim JENYNS, SOAME, 1
Dane-geld if once you have paid...the D. /You never get rid of the Dane KIPLING, RUDYARD, 14
Danes D. were effeminately gay in their dress WALLINGFORD, JOHN OF, 1
danger D., the spur of all great minds CHAPMAN, GEORGE, 3
He who keeps d. in mind will rest safely CONFUCIUS, 40
only real d. that exists is man himself JUNG, CARL GUSTAV, 1
Out of this nettle, d. SHAKESPEARE, WILLIAM, 236
place of d. trusting in miracles PROVERBS, 19
The chief d....is *scholasticism* RAMSEY, FRANK, 1
The greatest d. for the mourner KLEIN, MELANIE, 4
there was a measure of d. EARHART, AMELIA, 2
dangerous A d. person to disagree with ELIOT, T. S., 37
d. to be playing a cooperative game KANTER, ROSABETH MOSS, 3
d. to...search an unknown coast BRADFORD, WILLIAM, 1
It is d. to be sincere SHAW, GEORGE BERNARD, 44
misery...caused by a single d. intimacy LACLOS, PIERRE CHODERLOS DE, 4
most d. creation of any society BALDWIN, JAMES, 6
dangers D. by being despised grow great BURKE, EDMUND, 21
Daniel A D. come to judgment SHAKESPEARE, WILLIAM, 618
brought D., and cast him into the den BIBLE, 33
Well-languaged D. BROWNE, WILLIAM, 2
Dante D.,...Hated wickedness that hinders loving BROWNING, ROBERT, 59
D. makes me sick DANTE ALIGHIERI, 1
Daphnis My lovely D. to my longing arms VIRGIL, 30
dappled Glory be to God for d. things HOPKINS, GERARD MANLEY, 5
dare to *d.* is the highest wisdom CHANNING, WILLIAM ELLERY, 2
You who d. MEREDITH, GEORGE, 6
dares Who d., wins MOTTOS AND SLOGANS, 2
daring only d. speculation can lead us EINSTEIN, ALBERT, 19
Darjeeling There was an old man from D. LIMERICKS, 3
dark D. as pitch BUNYAN, JOHN, 6
In a d. time...eye begins to see ROETHKE, THEODORE, 3
In a d. wood...several selves ROETHKE, THEODORE, 1
I will leave behind me the d. ravine MISTRAL, GABRIELA, 6
O d., dark, dark, amid the blaze of noon MILTON, JOHN, 95
The d. night of the soul JOHN OF THE CROSS, SAINT, 2
The D. World is going to submit DU BOIS, W. E. B., 6
What in me is d. /Illumine MILTON, JOHN, 24
darken days d. round me, and the years TENNYSON, ALFRED, 22
d. the Sunne...and remove the Moone LYLY, JOHN, 3
"Never d. my Dior again LILLIE, BEATRICE, 2
never d. my towels again MARX, GROUCHO, 14

darkest The d. hour PROVERBS, 397
darkness all depriving d. split now by crazy flashing JONES, DAVID, 2
Before us pass'd the door of D. FITZGERALD, EDWARD, 16
By this glass filled with d. MACHADO, ANTONIO, 12
instruments of d. tell us truths SHAKESPEARE, WILLIAM, 381
men loved d....because their deeds were evil BIBLE, 274
not frightened of the d. outside DELANEY, SHELAGH, 1
the people that walked in d. BIBLE, 200
To sit in d. here MILTON, JOHN, 48
darlin' he's a d. man O'CASEY, SEAN, 2
darling his d. popularity BURKE, EDMUND, 24
This d. of the Gods MARVELL, ANDREW, 10
Darwin D. discovered the law of evolution MARX, KARL, 3
Darwinism D., adorned...poorly comprehended Nietzscheanism LONDON, JACK, 1
dates no d. in this history LU XUN, 13
daughter d. of debate ELIZABETH I, 13
d. of Earth and Water SHELLEY, PERCY BYSSHE, 16
Don't Put Your D. on the Stage COWARD, NOEL, 31
My d.! O my ducats SHAKESPEARE, WILLIAM, 606
daughters The d. of England are too numerous NEWSPAPERS, 19
David D. danced before the Lord BIBLE, 176
Once in royal D.'s city ALEXANDER, C. F., 3
David Copperfield D. kind of crap SALINGER, J. D., 14
dawn by...d.'s early light KEY, FRANCIS SCOTT, 1
d. of knowledge is usually...false DEVOTO, BERNARD, 2
Rosy-fingered d. POPE, ALEXANDER, 81
day And make each d. a critic on the last POPE, ALEXANDER, 15
As I was saying the other d. LEÓN, LUIS PONCE DE, 1
Believe each d....your last HORACE, 20
Clear D. You Can See Forever LERNER, ALAN JAY, 12
d. must come when the nation's CHURCHILL, WINSTON, 24
d. Thou gavest, Lord, is ended ELLERTON, JOHN, 1
every dog has his d. BORROW, GEORGE HENRY, 3
first D.'s Night DICKINSON, EMILY, 15
Good morning to the d.: and, next, my gold JONSON, BEN, 23
I look upon every d. to be lost JOHNSON, SAMUEL, 114
let the d. perish wherein I was born BIBLE, 256
Now the d. is over BARING-GOULD, SABINE, 2
Our d. will come MOTTOS AND SLOGANS, 33
Sweet d., so cool, so calm HERBERT, GEORGE, 23
The bright d. is done SHAKESPEARE, WILLIAM, 93
The d. of glory has arrived ROUGET DE LISLE, CLAUDE-JOSEPH, 1
the hour of death and...the d. of judgement BOOK OF COMMON PRAYER, 29
though the d. be never so longe HAWES, STEPHEN, 1
thou knowest not what a d. may bring forth BIBLE, 462
What does one d. matter MACHADO, ANTONIO, 1
when the d. of Pentecost was fully come BIBLE, 4
daybreak D. /has that sadness of arriving JIMÉNEZ, JUAN RAMÓN, 1
days D. off TRACY, SPENCER, 3
sixteen consecutive d. of being scared stiff WEIDMAN, JEROME, 4
What are d. for? LARKIN, PHILIP, 18
dazzling O Hope! d. radiant Hope MCPHERSON, AIMEE SEMPLE, 1
dead A d. man oft is showered with praise FREIDANK, 1
better to be d....than to suffer NASH, OGDEN, 17
Come not, when I am d. TENNYSON, ALFRED, 41
d., but in the Elysian fields DISRAELI, BENJAMIN, 57
deal to be said /For being d. CLIVE, ROBERT, 1
D. men tell no tales PROVERBS, 175
d. will think the living are worth it MERWIN, W. S., 2
Either he's d. or my watch has stopped MARX, GROUCHO, 6
Home they brought her warrior d. TENNYSON, ALFRED, 89
I heard the d. cry ROETHKE, THEODORE, 9
let the d. bury their dead BIBLE, 391
more to say when I am d. ROBINSON, EDWIN ARLINGTON, 2
Nobody heard him, the d. man SMITH, STEVIE, 1
not d. yet, though in years WARREN, ROBERT PENN, 3
Now I'm d. in the grave MANDELSTAM, OSIP, 10
Once you are d....made for life HENDRIX, JIMI, 4
Over my d. body KAUFMAN, GEORGE S., 2
packed to its rafters with some d. Negro's grief MORRISON, TONI, 4
rather be d. than singing "Satisfaction" JAGGER, MICK, 7
simplify me when I'm d. DOUGLAS, KEITH, 1
That he's not d. any more MARCUS, GREIL, 1
The d. don't die LAWRENCE, D. H., 10
we are all d. KEYNES, JOHN MAYNARD, 1
When I am d., and laid in grave FOLK VERSE, 64
When I am d., my dearest ROSSETTI, CHRISTINA, 11
year d. for tax reasons ADAMS, DOUGLAS, 14
You're a long time d. OSBORNE, JOHN, 9
deadly There is a d. orgone energy REICH, WILHELM, 8
deaf None so d. HENRY, MATTHEW, 3
deal a billion dollars on a new d. KHASOGGI, ADNAN, 1
a new d. for the American people ROOSEVELT, FRANKLIN D., 25
good d. for men who own castles HOFFMAN, ABBIE, 2
dealing best anyone can do when d. with weakness GIOVANNI, NIKKI, 3
We are d. with Orientals BEVERIDGE, ALBERT J., 1
deals D. are my art form TRUMP, DONALD, 2
dear D. 338171 COWARD, NOEL, 32
death added another terror to d. LYNDHURST, JOHN SINGLETON COPLEY, 1
After the first d....no other THOMAS, DYLAN, 12
After your d. you will be SCHOPENHAUER, ARTHUR, 6
And D. put down his book AUDEN, W. H., 41
a short and violent d. MONTAIGNE, MICHEL DE, 1
A single d. is a tragedy STALIN, JOSEPH, 12
D....a friend that alone can bring the peace OUSPENSKY, PETER, 2
D. and grief are little things NORRIS, FRANK, 5
D. and taxes and childbirth MITCHELL, MARGARET, 7
D. be not proud DONNE, JOHN, 13
D. calls ye to the crowd SHIRLEY, JAMES, 1
D. came with friendly care COLERIDGE, SAMUEL TAYLOR, 13
D....comes at last SCOTT, SIR WALTER, 8
D. comes...like a gas bill one can't pay BURGESS, ANTHONY, 9
D. destroys a man FORSTER, E. M., 16
Dear, beauteous d. VAUGHAN, HENRY, 7
d....had been his next-door neighbour SCOTT, SIR WALTER, 27
D. has got something to be said for it AMIS, KINGSLEY, 2
D. hath so many doors FLETCHER, JOHN, 6
d. hath ten thousand several doors WEBSTER, JOHN, 4
D....haven't succeeded in completely vulgarizing HUXLEY, ALDOUS, 28
D. invented the phone HUGHES, TED, 1
D. is a delightful hiding-place HERODOTUS, 2
D. is an acquired trait ALLEN, WOODY, 20
D. is a punishment to some SENECA, "THE YOUNGER," 14
D. is better than disease LONGFELLOW, HENRY WADSWORTH, 22

D. is my neighbour now EVANS, EDITH, 1
D. is no more than an obituary DOCTOROW, E. L., 2
D. is not the greatest of ills SOPHOCLES, 3
D. is psychosomatic MANSON, CHARLES, 2
D. is still working like a mole HERBERT, GEORGE, 7
D. is the end of life TENNYSON, ALFRED, 74
D. is the greatest evil HAZLITT, WILLIAM, 4
D. is the greatest kick of all REISNER, ROBERT, 1
D. is the great leveler PROVERBS, 176
D. is the Messiah SINGER, ISAAC BASHEVIS, 6
D. is the mother of beauty STEVENS, WALLACE, 16
D. is the price paid by life TOYNBEE, ARNOLD, 6
D. is the privilege of human nature ROWE, NICHOLAS, 3
D. is the veil SHELLEY, PERCY BYSSHE, 38
d. itself must be...a mockery SHELLEY, PERCY BYSSHE, 21
D. kicks his way equally HORACE, 32
D.... kindly stopped for me DICKINSON, EMILY, 11
d....less hideous than explanations LEWIS, D. B. WYNDHAM, 1
d. looked lovely in her lovely face PETRARCH, 6
D. must be distinguished from dying SMITH, SYDNEY, 26
D. never comes too late PROVERBS, 70
D. never takes the wise man by surprise LA FONTAINE, JEAN DE, 2
d. of many...not wailed PROVERBS, 7
D....only for the mediocre JARRY, ALFRED, 1
Do not suppose that I do not fear d. JENNINGS, ELIZABETH, 3
D. or Liberty—one or tother I mean to have TUBMAN, HARRIET, 1
d....releases...aura of stupefaction FLAUBERT, GUSTAVE, 11
d.'s door...pardoned for mistaking her for its knocker GARFIELD, LEON, 1
D. Shall Have No Dominion THOMAS, DYLAN, 18
D....supreme festival on the road to freedom BONHOEFFER, DIETRICH, 2
D., the best of all mysteries DUNN, DOUGLAS, 1
d., the destroyer of worlds OPPENHEIMER, J. ROBERT, 5
d., the most terrifying of ills EPICURUS, 2
D., the poor man's dearest friend BURNS, ROBERT, 26
D., thou shalt die DONNE, JOHN, 15
D. took him by the heart OWEN, WILFRED, 3
D. to the young ANGELOU, MAYA, 9
D. was but /A scientific fact WILDE, OSCAR, 37
d., which has eclipsed the gaiety of nations GARRICK, DAVID, 1
D. will find you HAMMARSKJÖLD, DAG, 1
d. will have his day SHAKESPEARE, WILLIAM, 518
easy d. only to the just ALLILUYEVA, SVETLANA, 1
enormously improved by d. EMERSON, RALPH WALDO, 3
Even in...d., two and two TOLSTOY, LEO, 19
extract of what we assumed about d. BELLOW, SAUL, 11
follow my own d. step by step JOHN XXIII, 1
fynde D., turne up this croked way CHAUCER, GEOFFREY, 30
Go and try to disprove d. TURGENEV, IVAN, 4
Grim D. my son and foe MILTON, JOHN, 43
He has seen too much d. PLATH, SYLVIA, 14
He who pretends to look on d. without fear lies ROUSSEAU, JEAN-JACQUES, 14
I could not look on D. KIPLING, RUDYARD, 62
I do really think that d. will be marvellous SMITH, STEVIE, 5
Ignore d. up to the last moment HUXLEY, ALDOUS, 56
I had not thought d. had undone so many ELIOT, T. S., 51
I have never risked d. O'BRIEN, EDNA, 1
in d. we are in the midst of life ANONYMOUS, 69
in the teeth of d. we live OSBORNE, JOHN, 5
Into the jaws of D. TENNYSON, ALFRED, 38
I stare at d. in a mirror JOHNSON, ADAM, 1
it is not d., but dying, which is terrible FIELDING, HENRY, 3
I've been accused of every d. CAPONE, AL, 2
I want d. to find me planting my cabbages MONTAIGNE, MICHEL DE, 7
keep d. in my line of sight DIDION, JOAN, 1
Life is...d. /in small daily doses MODAYIL, ANNA SUJARTHA, 2
man fears...only the stroke of d. BACON, FRANCIS (1561–1626), 101
Man has given a false importance to d. WEISS, PETER, 1
Many men on the point of an edifying d. PAVESE, CESARE, 8
Men fear d., as children fear to go in the dark BACON, FRANCIS (1561–1626), 22
message of d. for our young men WILSON, WOODROW, 12
My name is d.; the last best friend SOUTHEY, ROBERT, 6
nothing can be said to be certain but d. and taxes FRANKLIN, BENJAMIN, 9
not so much afraid of d., as ashamed BROWNE, THOMAS, 20
O D., thou comest EVERYMAN, 1
O D., where is thy sting ROSS, RONALD, 3
one way to be prepared for d. MONTHERLANT, HENRI DE, 8
prefer d. to hopeless bondage DOUGLASS, FREDERICK, 12
report of my d. was an exaggeration TWAIN, MARK, 24
sentence of d....stay of execution CARSON, EDWARD, 1
Since the order of the world is shaped by d. CAMUS, ALBERT, 17
so natural...so universal as d. SWIFT, JONATHAN, 44
that...turneth the shadow of d. into the morning BIBLE, 22
the brother of d. exacteth a third part BROWNE, THOMAS, 2
the dull cold ear of d. GRAY, THOMAS, 7
the idea of d. as an individual KOESTLER, ARTHUR, 8
There is...no d. MALRAUX, ANDRÉ, 10
there's always d. NAPOLEON I, 27
The sense of d. is most in apprehension SHAKESPEARE, WILLIAM, 435
The stroke of d. is as a lover's pinch SHAKESPEARE, WILLIAM, 91
the struggle against d. HESSE, HERMANN, 4
the thousand doors that lead to d. BROWNE, THOMAS, 19
thought of d. came PARKER, DOROTHY, 18
We fear our d. DU BARTAS, GUILLAUME, 11
We have allowed d. to change its name JACKSON, JESSE, 14
Why fear d. FROHMAN, CHARLES, 1
world's an inn...d. the journey's end DRYDEN, JOHN, 34
deaths it is chiefly our own d. that we mourn BRENAN, GERALD, 5
These d. suit everybody MERCIER, LOUIS-SÉBASTIEN, 1
debasement force behind the d. of our culture MILLER, STEVEN E., 3
debasing I will not be a party to d. the currency KEYNES, JOHN MAYNARD, 20
debauch d. the currency KEYNES, JOHN MAYNARD, 3
debauchee D....who has so earnestly pursued pleasure BIERCE, AMBROSE, 18
debt A d. may get mouldy ACHEBE, CHINUA, 6
d. makes a man your debtor SENECA, "THE ELDER," 1
Lord forbid...I should be out of d. RABELAIS, FRANÇOIS, 11
debtor Not everyone is a d. RABELAIS, FRANÇOIS, 17
debts Small d....like small shot JOHNSON, SAMUEL, 22
When d. are not paid CELA, CAMILO JOSÉ, 2
decade We are now in the Me D. WOLFE, TOM, 3
decadence The difference between our d. and the Russians' THURBER, JAMES, 13

decades D. have a delusive edge MACAULAY, ROSE, 6
decay Bodily d. is gloomy in prospect JEFFERSON, THOMAS, 18
D. and disease are often beautiful THOREAU, HENRY DAVID, 13
D. turns me off DYLAN, BOB, 26
scent of d....fills those ancient buildings MERTON, THOMAS, 1
deceased I am a d. writer MACHADO DE ASSIS, JOAQUIM MARIA, 7
deceive D. boys with toys LYSANDER, 1
to d....at Harvard ELIOT, CHARLES WILLIAM, 1
To d. oneself is very easy PROVERBS, 434
Who could d. a lover VIRGIL, 13
deceived The world is still d. with ornament SHAKESPEARE, WILLIAM, 613
deceivers Men were d. ever SHAKESPEARE, WILLIAM, 449
Who are the greatest d. VOLTAIRE, 50
December D. 7, 1941...will live in infamy ROOSEVELT, FRANKLIN D., 20
decent D. without Indecent within DIPOKO, MBELLA SONNE, 2
minimum that a d. society provides MITCHELL, GEORGE, 1
the only d. thing...is to die at once BUTLER, SAMUEL (1835–1902), 38
decide d. how you're going to live BAEZ, JOAN, 1
decision Persuade the d. makers SHEA, MICHAEL, 2
decision-maker the d. must continually adjust TOFFLER, ALVIN, 6
decisions an environment in which others make d. SEMLER, RICARDO, 3
At a thousand feet we make quick d. JILES, PAULETTE, 1
d. are made through collective discussions DENG XIAOPING, 4
d. are seat-of-the-pants judgments MYHRVOLD, NATHAN, 3
d. should be made as low as possible TOWNSEND, ROBERT, 6
declaiming when you are d., declaim JOHNSON, SAMUEL, 138
Declaration of Independence D....eminently practical document WILSON, WOODROW, 26
the principles of the D. MARTINEAU, HARRIET, 7
decompose d. in a barrel of porter DONLEAVY, J. P., 5
decomposing d. in the eternity of print BRONTË, CHARLOTTE, 2
decompression the d. of the Western imagination STEINER, GEORGE, 4
decorative art mission of d....to adapt itself to the taste...of others BING, SIEGFRIED, 1
dedicate d. these pages to my Guardian Angel O'BRIEN, FLANN, 10
dedicated You must all grow up to be d. women SPARK, MURIEL, 13
deduction A d. is an argument ARISTOTLE, 32
deed a good d. in a naughty world SHAKESPEARE, WILLIAM, 625
a good d. to forget a poor joke BRACKEN, BRENDAN, 1
right d. for the wrong reason ELIOT, T. S., 22
The better day, the worse d. HENRY, MATTHEW, 2
The d. is all, and not the glory GOETHE, JOHANN WOLFGANG VON, 14
worth of a kind d. TALMUD, 6
deeds better d. /Shall be in water writ BEAUMONT, FRANCIS, 9
Our d. still travel with us ELIOT, GEORGE, 21
deep That sweet, d. sleep VIRGIL, 15
defeat a d. without a war CHURCHILL, WINSTON, 26
D. would be bad...victory...intolerable THOMPSON, HUNTER S., 6
In d. unbeatable CHURCHILL, WINSTON, 62
we are not interested in the possibilities of d. VICTORIA, 5
We are out to d. injustice KING, MARTIN LUTHER, JR., 23
defeated Down with the d. LIVY, 1
defect Chief D. of Henry King BELLOC, HILAIRE, 8
The most obvious d. MARTÍNEZ DE LA MATA, DON, 1
defects When the d. of others are perceived RENARD, JULES, 20
defence Never make a d. or apology CHARLES I (1600–49), 3
Preparing for suicide is not a...means of d. KENT, BRUCE, 1
The only d. is in offence BALDWIN, STANLEY, 5
defend D., O Lord, this thy Child BOOK OF COMMON PRAYER, 18
d. to...death your right to agree REAGAN, RONALD, 38
D. us IZETBEGOVIC, ALIJA, 1
Defender of Faith my title as D. CHARLES, PRINCE, 9
defense The best immediate d. of the United States ROOSEVELT, FRANKLIN D., 32
defiance The d. of established authority ARENDT, HANNAH, 5
deficit The d. is big enough REAGAN, RONALD, 33
defiles What a man does d. him GOLDING, WILLIAM, 4
define d. yourself...bite your own teeth WATTS, ALAN, 1
defined We have since d. Gaia LOVELOCK, JAMES, 5
defining d. on paper what I want to accomplish MCCORMACK, MARK, 17
deflation D. is the easiest thing to avoid FRIEDMAN, MILTON, 7
deflowered At last you are d. COWARD, NOEL, 33
deformity Another great Advantage of D. HAY, WILLIAM, 1
Degas D. purchased once /A fine El Greco DEGAS, EDGAR, 2
de Gaulle Foch, Clemenceau, d....the same thing CLEMENCEAU, GEORGES, 1
I, General d., now in London DE GAULLE, CHARLES, 5
degenerates everything d. in the hands of man ROUSSEAU, JEAN-JACQUES, 10
world d. and grows worse every day LUTHER, MARTIN, 9
degradation sense of...d. after an interview with a doctor JAMES, ALICE, 1
degree Observe d., priority, and place SHAKESPEARE, WILLIAM, 684
Take but d. away SHAKESPEARE, WILLIAM, 683
when d. is shak'd SHAKESPEARE, WILLIAM, 682
dehumanizing military-industrial drive toward...d. the workplace ROSZAK, THEODORE, 6
deil D. tak the hindmost BURNS, ROBERT, 46
deities the d. so kindly RABELAIS, FRANÇOIS, 13
déjà vu It was d. all over again BERRA, YOGI, 4
Delacroix The recipe for making a man like D. RENOIR, PIERRE AUGUSTE, 1
delay D....breeds danger CERVANTES, MIGUEL DE, 14
D. is the deadliest form of denial PARKINSON, CYRIL NORTHCOTE, 6
delays All d. are dangerous DRYDEN, JOHN, 51
delegate d. authority, and don't interfere REAGAN, RONALD, 30
If you don't d. CROSBY, PHILIP B., 1
deleted D. by French censor BENNETT, JAMES GORDON, JR., 1
deliberation D. is the work of many men DE GAULLE, CHARLES, 11
deliciously I am not d. saucy SIMPSONS, THE, 2
delight a degree of d. BURKE, EDMUND, 32
All for your d. /We are not here SHAKESPEARE, WILLIAM, 66
I d. in sinning SULPICIA, 1
She discovered with great d. GARCÍA MÁRQUEZ, GABRIEL, 9
sweet airs, that give d., and hurt not SHAKESPEARE, WILLIAM, 648
Teach us d. in simple things KIPLING, RUDYARD, 45
the fruit-trees...for you and for your cattle to d. in KORAN, 40
There is a land of pure d. WATTS, ISAAC, 8
delightful d., it's delicious, it's de-lovely PORTER, COLE, 18
What a d. thing this perspective is UCCELLO, PAOLO, 1
delirium d. that encounters despair and death CRANE, STEPHEN, 11

deliver if you don't d. the goods TRUMP, DONALD, 5
Lord, d. me from myself BROWNE, THOMAS, 27
deliverer their d. from Popish tyranny WILLIAM III, 1
Delphic oracle two sentences inscribed upon the D. PLUTARCH, 3
delude we d. ourselves if we think that humanity is becoming ever more civilised CHARLES, PRINCE, 7
deluge After us the d. POMPADOUR, MADAME DE, 1
delusion D....may well lead to hell ANONYMOUS, 48
delusions D....only things which render life tolerable STORR, ANTHONY, 3
Many people have d. of grandeur IONESCO, EUGÈNE, 3
demagogues the vilest specimens of human nature...found among d. MACAULAY, THOMAS BABINGTON, 20
demand Be realistic, d. the impossible MOTTOS AND SLOGANS, 21
democracies D....short in their lives MADISON, JAMES, 1
d....think that a stupid man is more likely to be honest RUSSELL, BERTRAND, 20
democracy A modern d. is a tyranny MAILER, NORMAN, 20
d. and academic freedom...important to...science ZHOU PEIYUAN, 1
D.! Bah! GINSBERG, ALLEN, 8
d. can be cured by more democracy SMITH, AL, 1
D. can't work HEINLEIN, ROBERT, 2
D....difficult kind of government KENNEDY, JOHN FITZGERALD, 21
Development requires d. AUNG SAN SUU KYI, 1
D. gives every man a right LOWELL, JAMES RUSSELL, 3
D....government by the uneducated CHESTERTON, G. K., 22
D. is a charming form of government PLATO, 25
D. is only an experiment in government INGE, WILLIAM RALPH, 1
D. is the theory that the common people know what they want MENCKEN, H. L., 3
D. is the wholesome and pure air GORBACHEV, MIKHAIL, 15
D. means choosing your dictators COREN, ALAN, 6
D. means government by discussion ATTLEE, CLEMENT, 3
D. passes into despotism PLATO, 26
d.... recognizes the subjecting of the minority LENIN, VLADIMIR ILYICH, 17
D. resumed her reign BELLOC, HILAIRE, 17
D. sometimes seems to be an end MAO ZEDONG, 18
D. substitutes election by the incompetent many SHAW, GEORGE BERNARD, 56
D....superior form of government KENNEDY, JOHN FITZGERALD, 33
D....worship of jackals by jackasses MENCKEN, H. L., 41
D....written into law DENG XIAOPING, 2
extreme d. or absolute oligarchy ARISTOTLE, 29
heroic example of d.'s solidarity IBÁRRURI, DOLORES, 2
I still can't see /Why D. means /Everybody but me HUGHES, LANGSTON, 5
supporters of D....obliged to attack Confucianism CHEN DUXIU, 4
there has never been a true d. ROUSSEAU, JEAN-JACQUES, 15
The technique of d. is group organization FOLLETT, MARY PARKER, 3
war wasn't fought about d. BUSH, GEORGE, 14
Western d....the seeds of death MERNISSI, FATIMA, 4
world must be safe for d. WILSON, WOODROW, 8
democratic A d. nation of persons...is an impossibility JORDAN, JUNE, 9
d. firms offer a spark of hope BRUYN, SEVERYN, 1
d. methods...work like dogs to justify...faith EISENHOWER, DWIGHT D., 17
d. system...people seeking favors FOX, HARRISON W., JR., 3
the ideal of a d. and free society MANDELA, NELSON, 4
thoroughly d. and patronise everybody SHAW, GEORGE BERNARD, 34
democratisation d....will be permanently stymied HUTTON, WILL, 2
demon fighting with a d. JAMES, HENRY, 35
demoniacal something d....discern a law THOREAU, HENRY DAVID, 7
demonstrations d. from Chengdu to Tiananmen Square JUNG CHANG, 3
denature easier to d. plutonium than...evil spirit of man EINSTEIN, ALBERT, 45
Denmark rotten in the state of D. SHAKESPEARE, WILLIAM, 153
dentist D.,...A prestidigitator who,..., pulls coins out BIERCE, AMBROSE, 19
like going to the d. MONROE, MARILYN, 5
dentists I have let d. ride roughshod over my teeth PERELMAN, S. J., 2
The thought of d. gave him just the same sick horror WELLS, H. G., 5
dentopedology D. is...opening your mouth PHILIP, PRINCE, 5
Denver D....like the Promised Land KEROUAC, JACK, 12
deny d. or delay, right or justice MAGNA CARTA, 2
D. yourself...the never-ending song GOETHE, JOHANN WOLFGANG VON, 7
let him d. himself BIBLE, 408
none d. there is a God BACON, FRANCIS (1561–1626), 13
depart lettest thou thy servant d. in peace BIBLE, 327
depend D. on none but yourself CHARLES V, 2
dependent too d. upon dachas YELTSIN, BORIS, 7
deplore d. in others...cannot accept in themselves STORR, ANTHONY, 4
depraved suddenly became d. JUVENAL, 5
depression best cures for d. SMITH, DODIE, 2
d. takes on...quality of physical pain STYRON, WILLIAM, 1
my d. felt worse than her death WOLPERT, LEWIS, 2
deprivation bear gently the d. of sight MILTON, JOHN, 131
D. is for me what daffodils were WORDSWORTH, WILLIAM, 7
total d. of it produces irritability BLACKWELL, ELIZABETH, 3
derivation d. of the religious attitude FREUD, SIGMUND, 54
derivative A d. is like a razor NEWSPAPERS, 6
derived we d....in a bolt of lightning THOMAS, LEWIS, 3
descend Never d. to the ways of those above you MALLABY, GEORGE, 1
descendants d., /Outnumber your friends NASH, OGDEN, 1
descended we are d. from barbarians DARWIN, CHARLES, 8
we are d....from monks HUBBARD, ELBERT, 3
desert d....gives compensation, deep breaths, deep sleep AUSTIN, MARY, 9
my own mind the d. of Chile ZURITA, RAUL, 1
The d., the abode of enforced sterility CARTER, ANGELA, 2
Use every man after his d. SHAKESPEARE, WILLIAM, 170
When you halt in the d. BRODSKY, JOSEPH, 6
deserts In the d. of the heart YEATS, W. B., 2
deserve don't d. this, but I have arthritis BENNY, JACK, 4
design d. clothes with...ideal woman in mind VERSACE, DONATELLA, 1
D. is not a philosophy MIYAKE, ISSEY, 2
D. occupies a unique space CONRAN, TERENCE, 2
D....the conscious effort to impose...order PAPANEK, VICTOR, 1
D....tribute art pays to industry FINCH, PAUL, 1
I d. for women ARMANI, GIORGIO, 1
I don't d. clothes, I design dreams LAUREN, RALPH, 1
If you d. something too well LOEWY, RAYMOND, 2

The d. of a pepper pot MACKINTOSH, MARGARET MACDONALD, 1
The two great rules for d. PUGIN, AUGUSTUS, 1
designer I didn't create the d. mystique LAUREN, RALPH, 2
spending too long in a d. chair SMITH, PAUL, 1
designers fashion d. who discover...fashion is dead VERSACE, GIANNI, 2
many d. like to be copied FAIRCHILD, JOHN B., 2
desire d. can again find a natural place SCHELL, JONATHAN, 5
D. is the very essence of man SPINOZA, BARUCH, 2
d. should so many years outlive performance SHAKESPEARE, WILLIAM, 254
d. the Happiness of others HUTCHESON, FRANCIS, 1
d. the things they failed to obtain MAUROIS, ANDRÉ, 1
d. we may be better strangers SHAKESPEARE, WILLIAM, 114
few things to d....many...to fear BACON, FRANCIS (1561–1626), 24
From fairest creatures we d. increase SHAKESPEARE, WILLIAM, 560
I d. their liberty and freedom CHARLES I (1600–49), 4
If you d. something more than their aroma MACHADO DE ASSIS, JOAQUIM MARIA, 14
It provokes the d. SHAKESPEARE, WILLIAM, 401
legitimate d. to have a child JOHN PAUL II, 5
object of the dreamer's d. MCEWAN, IAN, 1
The D. of Man being Infinite BLAKE, WILLIAM, 51
Those who restrain d. BLAKE, WILLIAM, 50
To d. anything...physical and metaphysical impossibility MILL, JOHN STUART, 20
When vain d. at last ROSSETTI, DANTE GABRIEL, 8
desires He who d....breeds pestilence BLAKE, WILLIAM, 40
So too with...all the d. PLATO, 13
desks Stick...to your d. and never go to sea GILBERT, W. S., 7
Des Moines I come from D. BRYSON, BILL, 5
prettiest girls...live in D. KEROUAC, JACK, 13
desolation the d. of an empty abundance HARRINGTON, MICHAEL, 2
despair D. and suicide...certain fatal situations NERVAL, GÉRARD DE, 1
D. is the one sin that cannot be forgiven NGUGI WA THIONGO, 3
Don't d., not even over...despair KAFKA, FRANZ, 2
In d. as in love, we are...alone GOLDEN, MARITA, 4
Now Giant D. had a wife BUNYAN, JOHN, 9
Utter d., impossible to pull myself together KAFKA, FRANZ, 4
despairs He who d. over an event is a coward CAMUS, ALBERT, 20
desperate Diseases d. grown /By desperate appliance are relieved SHAKESPEARE, WILLIAM, 209
D. situations PROVERBS, 177
despicable d....not always to be despised RETZ, CARDINAL DE, 2
despise do d. me! I 'm the prouder for it BICKERSTAFFE, ISAAC, 5
despised for he has d. God HIPPOLYTUS OF ROME, 1
heartily d. by a street boy HUXLEY, T. H., 6
He is d. and rejected of men BIBLE, 220
despises Whoever d. himself still respects himself NIETZSCHE, FRIEDRICH WILHELM, 11
woman d. a man for loving her STODDARD, ELIZABETH, 1
despoilers no matter what the d. of humanity APTHEKER, HERBERT, 2
Despond the slough was D. BUNYAN, JOHN, 13
despondent I am not d. of the future of my people HARPER, FRANCES E. W., 5
despotism *a little d. is absolutely necessary* HORTON, JAMES AFRICANUS BEALE, 1
D. accomplishes great things illegally BALZAC, HONORÉ DE, 7
d. tempered by casualness ADLER, VIKTOR, 1
princes head towards d....people towards servitude MARAT, JEAN PAUL, 2
dessert eat d. without eating her vegetables ALTHER, LISA, 1
destination The d. of all journeys CARTER, ANGELA, 4
destiny as if I were walking with d. CHURCHILL, WINSTON, 49
d. to be engulfed...Republical union MCGEE, THOMAS D'ARCY, 1
fulfilment of our manifest d. O'SULLIVAN, JOHN L., 2
We answer to a higher d. LAURIER, WILFRID, 10
destroy d. a bridge PROVERBS, 13
d....belief in immortality DOSTOYEVSKY, FYODOR, 4
d. large parts of the...countryside HANSON, LORD, 2
d. the eye of another man HAMMURABI, 1
He would like to d. his old diaries TOLSTOY, SOFYA, 1
Man's subliminal urge to d. ROY, ARUNDHATI, 3
necessary to d. the town...to save it NEWSPAPERS, 13
sought to d. institutions WHITMAN, WALT, 22
tried to d. the memory of Babi Yar YEVTUSHENKO, YEVGENY, 1
We will d. museums and libraries MARINETTI, FILIPPO TOMMASO, 2
destroys nation that d. its soil destroys itself ROOSEVELT, FRANKLIN D., 8
What d. one man preserves another CORNEILLE, PIERRE, 1
destruction prefer the d. of the whole world HUME, DAVID, 22
the d. of our "national essence" CHEN DUXIU, 2
urge for d. is also...creative BAKUNIN, MIKHAIL, 1
detective novel The d. is PRITCHETT, V. S., 1
detente D. is like the race CARRINGTON, LORD, 1
determined Nothing is d. in advance MILLER, HENRY, 27
detestable D. person but needs watching LAWRENCE, D. H., 4
detested D. sport COWPER, WILLIAM, 35
Detroit D. is weak on vitality and diversity JACOBS, JANE, 1
devaluation d. of the world of men MARX, KARL, 15
devastation d....of a large continent LYELL, CHARLES, 3
deviant you have to be a d. BURROUGHS, WILLIAM S., 12
deviates Shadwell never d. into sense SHADWELL, THOMAS, 1
deviation The secret equation...your twofold d. GOYTISOLO, JUAN, 2
devil d. and the deep blue sea RATTIGAN, TERENCE, 2
d. can cite Scripture SHAKESPEARE, WILLIAM, 598
d. doesn't exist either BULGAKOV, MIKHAIL, 5
D....is the author of confusion and lies BURTON, ROBERT, 22
D. only tempts men of genius BAUDELAIRE, CHARLES, 7
d. should have all the good tunes HILL, ROWLAND, 1
d.'s most devilish when respectable BROWNING, ELIZABETH BARRETT, 5
If the D. was devoted to destroying MAILER, NORMAN, 13
preserve me from the D. METTERNICH, 1
Renounce the d. BOOK OF COMMON PRAYER, 19
The d. finds some mischief MADAN, GEOFFREY, 1
The d. finds work PROVERBS, 398
The D., having nothing else to do BELLOC, HILAIRE, 28
The D.'s in her tongue BEHN, APHRA, 15
The d. will come MARLOWE, CHRISTOPHER, 10
three things the d. makes his mess FLORIO, JOHN, 3
To the d....those who published before us DONATUS, AELIUS, 1
we do sugar o'er /The d. himself SHAKESPEARE, WILLIAM, 184
what is got over the D.'s back is spent LESAGE, ALAIN RENÉ, 3
You are the d.'s gateway TERTULLIAN, 5
devils It is no good casting out d. LAWRENCE, D. H., 38
Many d....in dark pooly places LUTHER, MARTIN, 13

many d. would set on me in Worms LUTHER, MARTIN, 7
devise they d. an accusation...that we practice cannibalism TATIAN, 1
devotion d. of the Welsh to their land MORRIS, JAN, 1
diabetic Many a d. has stayed alive FISCHER, MARTIN H., 14
diagnosis D....physician's forecast of disease BIERCE, AMBROSE, 20
D. precedes treatment HOWARD, RUSSELL JOHN, 1
In d. think of the easy first FISCHER, MARTIN H., 12
no royal road to d. MORRIS, ROBERT TUTTLE, 4
dialect D. words...marks of the beast HARDY, THOMAS, 28
dialectics D. is the soul of Marxism STALIN, JOSEPH, 6
dialogue D....facilitates the process of change SCHEIN, EDGAR H., 1
D. is the oxygen of change MACLACHLAN, JIM, 1
the d. between Christianity and Buddhism TILLICH, PAUL, 5
diamond I'm like a d. in the mud LEONARD, SUGAR RAY, 1
diamonds D. Are A Girl's Best Friend ROBIN, LEO, 2
D. Are Forever FLEMING, IAN, 3
diaries Only good girls keep d. BANKHEAD, TALLULAH, 12
diary I never travel without my d. WILDE, OSCAR, 50
keep a d....keep you WEST, MAE, 4
What is a d. as a rule TERRY, ELLEN, 3
dice *He* is not playing d. EINSTEIN, ALBERT, 53
Dickens D.' world is not life-like CECIL, DAVID, 1
dictated not going to be d. to by fans GAYE, MARVIN, 2
dictator If I were a d. PINOCHET, AUGUSTO, 3
dictators D. ride to and fro upon tigers CHURCHILL, WINSTON, 61
dictatorship I believe in benevolent d. BRANSON, RICHARD, 1
the d. of the proletariat MARX, KARL, 8
dictionaries To make d. is dull work JOHNSON, SAMUEL, 15
dictionary A d. is a vocabulary restricted DAVENPORT, GUY, 1
d....record a language, not set its style GOVE, PHILIP BABCOCK, 1
this is the first time I ever made the d. WEST, MAE, 27
Dido When D. found Aeneas would not come PORSON, RICHARD, 1
die A man can d. PROVERBS, 128
And if I d., no soul will pity me SHAKESPEARE, WILLIAM, 533
A person doesn't d. GARCÍA MÁRQUEZ, GABRIEL, 10
As long as men are liable to d. LA BRUYÈRE, JEAN DE, 4
Because all died...I had to d. NEMEROV, HOWARD, 3
best not to d....no one remembers you MONTEJO, ESTEBAN, 1
better to d. on your feet than to live on your knees IBÁRRURI, DOLORES, 3
d. but once to serve our country ADDISON, JOSEPH, 9
don't d.! Stay alive for our children FRANCIS FERDINAND, 1
d. on the spot rather than give way JOFFRE, JOSEPH JACQUES CÉSAIRE, 1
D....the last thing I shall do! PALMERSTON, LORD, 1
easy ways to d. SHAKESPEARE, WILLIAM, 88
for...country 't is a bliss to d. POPE, ALEXANDER, 78
for me to d., for you to go on living SOCRATES, 9
Hope I d. before I get old TOWNSHEND, PETE, 1
How hard...that we have to d. TWAIN, MARK, 28
I d. a Christian CHARLES I (1600–49), 5
I d. because I do not die JOHN OF THE CROSS, SAINT, 1
I d. happy FOX, CHARLES JAMES, 4
I d.! I faint! I fail SHELLEY, PERCY BYSSHE, 19
I do not want to d. KOLLWITZ, KÄTHE, 2
If I should d., think only this of me BROOKE, RUPERT, 7
If we must d., let it not be like hogs MCKAY, CLAUDE, 3
I said I would d. a bachelor SHAKESPEARE, WILLIAM, 451
I shall not altogether d. HORACE, 49
I, too, will d. by violence MALCOLM X, 14
it was not easy for me to d. MAKARIOS III, 1
I will d. in the last ditch WILLIAM III, 2
I would d. for my country KINNOCK, NEIL, 4
learn how to d. by killing others CHATEAUBRIAND, RENÉ, 6
let me d. drinking in an inn MAP, WALTER, 1
Let us d. even as we rush into...battle VIRGIL, 8
Many people would sooner d. than think RUSSELL, BERTRAND, 59
Never say d. PROVERBS, 341
Now I've laid me down to d. STURGES, PRESTON, 1
Now...seems it rich to d. KEATS, JOHN (1795–1821), 63
people d. from pregnancy PAINTIN, DAVID, 1
she can't...d. in peace MURRAY, JOHN FISHER, 1
so afraid I will d. in the middle of shooting GIELGUD, JOHN, 1
sweet and seemly...to d. for one's country HORACE, 41
The d. is cast CAESAR, JULIUS, 2
these who d. as cattle OWEN, WILFRED, 2
those who are about to d. salute you ANONYMOUS, 81
to d., and go we know not where SHAKESPEARE, WILLIAM, 432
To d. for an idea FRANCE, ANATOLE, 9
to d.... /'Tis less than to be born BEAUMONT & FLETCHER, 4
to d., /'Twere now to be most happy SHAKESPEARE, WILLIAM, 479
To d. will be an awfully big adventure BARRIE, J. M., 10
To go away is to d. a little HARAUCOURT, EDMOND, 1
We must all d. SCHWEITZER, ALBERT, 2
We voted to d. with dignity ANONYMOUS, 59
when I d. IACOCCA, LEE, 5
When people d....fault of the harvest MENCIUS, 4
who d. /In a great cause BYRON, LORD, 91
with you be ready to d. HORACE, 46
died D. some...non "dulce" non "et decor." POUND, EZRA, 14
He d. as he lived—at sea MACDONALD, RAMSAY, 1
Hereabouts d. a very gallant gentleman ATKINSON, E. L., 1
I don't know when I d. BECKETT, SAMUEL, 14
I might have d....a failure VANZETTI, BARTOLOMEO, 1
people who d. of dropsies JOHNSON, SAMUEL, 66
She should have d. hereafter SHAKESPEARE, WILLIAM, 422
They d. /When time was open-eyed LOWELL, ROBERT, 24
dies Every moment d. a man TENNYSON, ALFRED, 80
It matters not how a man d. JOHNSON, SAMUEL, 101
nothing d. but something mourns BYRON, LORD, 63
One d. only once MOLIÈRE, 7
When a man d., the angels ask AL-MUFID, ABU ABDULLAH MUHAMMAD AL-HARITHI AL-BAGHDADI, 6
diet Doctor D., Doctor Quiet and Doctor Merryman SWIFT, JONATHAN, 36
knowledge of the principles of d....essential FARMER, FANNIE, 2
dieting Unnecessary d. is because...television and fashion ads BRACKEN, PEG, 1
dietitians The death of all d. FISCHER, MARTIN H., 7
Dieu D. et mon droit RICHARD I, 7
difference Because there is no d. THALES, 4
d. between a man and his valet FROST, ROBERT, 27
d. between fantasy and reality SCORSESE, MARTIN, 1
d. between intelligence and education KETTERING, CHARLES, 3
d. of sex...need to be forgotten ANTHONY, SUSAN B., 3
made the d. of forty thousand men NAPOLEON I, 12

more d. within the sexes than between them COMPTON-BURNETT, IVY, 3
the d. between Dante, Milton, and me SANDBURG, CARL, 11
There is all the d. GARBO, GRETA, 6
There is d., and there is power JORDAN, JUNE, 8
What sensible d....will its truth make JAMES, WILLIAM, 7
differences If we cannot now end our d. KENNEDY, JOHN FITZGERALD, 1
settle their d. like good Christians AUSTIN, WARREN ROBINSON, 1
different now for something completely d. MONTY PYTHON'S FLYING CIRCUS, 2
you would see some d. things ARMSTRONG, NEIL, 2
differently I would have done it d. WHISTLER, JAMES ABBOTT MCNEILL, 17
difficult D....I wish it were impossible JOHNSON, SAMUEL, 174
d. to speak, and impossible to be silent BURKE, EDMUND, 61
Nothing so d. as a beginning BYRON, LORD, 64
difficulty I feel...a certain d. in continuing to exist FONTENELLE, BERNARD LE BOVIER, 2
digestion d. is the great secret of life SMITH, SYDNEY, 1
the good or bad d. of a prime minister VOLTAIRE, 49
Diggers You noble D. all WINSTANLEY, GERRARD, 3
digital the d. age cannot be denied NEGROPONTE, NICHOLAS, 3
dignity as much d. in tilling a field as in writing a poem WASHINGTON, BOOKER T., 10
d. and greatness and peace again COWARD, NOEL, 10
man added to his d. by standing on it CHURCHILL, WINSTON, 79
Official d....in inverse ratio to ... importance HUXLEY, ALDOUS, 14
The d. of history BOLINGBROKE, HENRY ST. JOHN, 3
There is a d. in dying PROVERBS, MODERN, 29
there is no d. without freedom TOURÉ, SÉKOU, 1
Without d. there is no liberty LUMUMBA, PATRICE, 3
digressions D....the soul of reading STERNE, LAURENCE, 13
dikes our d....are ten feet deep WILHELMINA, 1
DiMaggio I would like to take the great D. fishing DIMAGGIO, JOE, 1
diminished Surely we have d. one another CARVER, RAYMOND, 5
dimple A d. in the chin, a devil within PROVERBS, 104
dine I d. at Blenheim once a week ANONYMOUS, 36
dined I d....with the Borgias BEERBOHM, MAX, 7
you have d. in every house in London HARRIS, FRANK, 3
diners Observe d. arriving at any restaurant MORRIS, DESMOND, 2
diners-out d. from whom we guard our spoons MACAULAY, THOMAS BABINGTON, 1
ding D. dong, bell, /Pussy's in the well CHILDREN'S VERSE, 24
dining where is the man that can live without d.? OWEN, MEREDITH, 2
dinner A d. lubricates business SCOTT, WILLIAM, 1
a good d. and feasting reconciles everybody PEPYS, SAMUEL, 9
a good d. upon his table JOHNSON, SAMUEL, 56
not a d. to *ask* a man to JOHNSON, SAMUEL, 128
our d. must have a limit PLINY THE YOUNGER, 1
dinner party best number for a d. is two GULBENKIAN, NUBAR SARKIS, 1
dinosaur The d. didn't know it was extinct either MCLUHAN, MARSHALL, 15
Diogenes D. lighted a candle in the daytime DIOGENES LÄERTIUS, 3
diplomacy D....game of chess KRAUS, KARL, 1
diplomat A d.... always remembers a woman's birthday FROST, ROBERT, 23
A real d....can cut his neighbor's throat LIE, TRYGVE, 2
d. these days is nothing but a head-waiter USTINOV, PETER, 10
diplomatic history of the d. service of England BLAKE, EDWARD, 1
diplomats aged d. to be bored AUSTIN, WARREN ROBINSON, 2
direct can't d. a Laughton picture HITCHCOCK, ALFRED, 10
I always d. the same film FELLINI, FEDERICO, 2
no director...can d....like an audience BRICE, FANNY, 1
To be d. and honest is not safe SHAKESPEARE, WILLIAM, 485
directing d....coming out of your individual loneliness HUSTON, JOHN, 3
D. her was like directing Lassie MONROE, MARILYN, 4
hardest part of d. is staying awake WINNER, MICHAEL, 1
director d. makes only one film in his life RENOIR, JEAN, 2
d. should listen...keep his mouth shut BERGMAN, INGMAR, 3
I have never been what is called a d. LUMIÈRE, LOUIS, 1
I still want to be a d. SPIELBERG, STEVEN, 5
working for a good d., you become...submissive SUTHERLAND, DONALD, 1
directors d....hand that lays the golden egg GOLDWYN, SAMUEL, 18
D....never in short supply of girlfriends FOSSE, BOB, 2
two kinds of d.—allies and judges HURT, JOHN, 1
dirt After the first four years the d. doesn't get any worse CRISP, QUENTIN, 11
Huddled in d. the reasoning engine lies ROCHESTER, 2ND EARL OF, 2
Throw enough d. PROVERBS, 430
dirty You d. double-crossing rat CAGNEY, JAMES, 1
dirtying-up I'm not through d. SIMON, NEIL, 6
dirty linen Airing one's d. never makes...masterpiece TRUFFAUT, FRANÇOIS, 1
disadvantage I saw it at a d. WINCHELL, WALTER, 1
disagree possible to d....about the ethics of non-violence HAMPTON, CHRISTOPHER, 6
disagreement absence of d....a developing discipline MERTON, ROBERT K., 1
disappoint I may not d. myself THOREAU, HENRY DAVID, 24
disarm Let no one expect us to d. unilaterally ANDROPOV, YURI, 1
disarmament d. by unilateral example BALDWIN, STANLEY, 4
Vertical d. makes a catastrophe SCHELL, JONATHAN, 7
disaster the imagination of d. KULYK KEEFER, JANICE, 1
disasters d. come at the same time MAHFOUZ, NAGUIB, 6
disbelief willing suspension of d. COLERIDGE, SAMUEL TAYLOR, 31
disciple A d....of the fiend JOHN OF LANCASTER, 1
The d. is not above his master BIBLE, 395
disciples here's to d. and Calvary JOYCE, JAMES, 24
discipline We must...d. ourselves to remember CALDWELL, SARAH, 2
Without d. true freedom cannot survive NKRUMAH, KWAME, 8
disco D. is the...quickest way to fame LEAR, AMANDA, 1
discomforts for...all the d. that will accompany my being blind PEPYS, SAMUEL, 14
discommendeth He who d. others obliquely BROWNE, THOMAS, 4
discontent astral d. with actual lives...touches beyond words DIDION, JOAN, 10
lent /To youth and age...—d. ARNOLD, MATTHEW, 15
Where does d. start STEINBECK, JOHN, 7
discontented We have produced a world of contented bodies and d. minds POWELL, ADAM CLAYTON, JR., 4
discourse d....cannot dominate absolutely DERRIDA, JACQUES, 2
public d....verbal equivalent of mud wrestling MOYERS, BILL, 1

their d. was about hunting PEPYS, SAMUEL, 5
discourses my d....are...good Scripture YOUNG, BRIGHAM, 3
discover not d. new lands GIDE, ANDRÉ, 5
When I d. who I am, I'll be free ELLISON, RALPH, 4
discovered d. something that he will die for KING, MARTIN LUTHER, JR., 5
in the morning we d. a bay COOK, JAMES, 1
We have d. the secret of life CRICK, FRANCIS, 3
discoverers ill d. that think there is no land BACON, FRANCIS (1561–1626), 97
discoveries d. are usually not made by one man alone SIGERIST, HENRY E., 2
My d....basis for a very grave philosophy FREUD, SIGMUND, 59
None of the great d. FISCHER, MARTIN H., 16
discovery d. is mathematical in form DARWIN, CHARLES, 13
I have just made a great d. PASTEUR, LOUIS, 6
discretion D. is the better part of reading MCCORMACK, MARK, 10
Perish d. when it interferes with duty MORE, HANNAH, 5
temper d. with deceit WAUGH, EVELYN, 9
the years of d. BOOK OF COMMON PRAYER, 17
discriminated Sometimes, I feel d. against HURSTON, ZORA NEALE, 17
discrimination d. based simply on race...barbarous DU BOIS, W. E. B., 1
discussion continue our d. in eternity SERVETUS, MICHAEL, 1
D. in class, which means NABOKOV, VLADIMIR, 5
If we had had more time for d. TROTSKY, LEON, 6
disdain my dear Lady D., are you yet living? SHAKESPEARE, WILLIAM, 440
disease All interest in d. and death MANN, THOMAS, 15
angel of d. is kith and kin HOLUB, MIROSLAV, 5
D. creates poverty SIGERIST, HENRY E., 6
desperate d. requires a dangerous remedy FAWKES, GUY, 1
D. is an image of thought externalized EDDY, MARY BAKER, 2
D. is...conflict between soul and mind BACH, EDWARD, 1
d. is connected only with immediate causes STEINER, RUDOLF, 1
d. is the result of sin PICKERING, GEORGE WHITE, 1
D. is very old CHARCOT, JEAN MARTIN, 1
D. makes men more physical MANN, THOMAS, 14
D., or sorrows strike him CLOUGH, ARTHUR HUGH, 11
D....social as well as physical...causes SIGERIST, HENRY E., 9
d....whole and entire within itself HAWTHORNE, NATHANIEL, 16
favourite d. FIELDING, HENRY, 16
For a desperate d. a desperate cure MONTAIGNE, MICHEL DE, 30
Have a chronic d. and take care HOLMES, OLIVER WENDELL, 34
he does not die from the d. alone PÉGUY, CHARLES PIERRE, 14
I have Bright's d. PERELMAN, S. J., 6
Nip d. in the bud PERSIUS, 2
remedy is worse than the d. BACON, FRANCIS (1561–1626), 60
strange d. of modern life ARNOLD, MATTHEW, 13
That d. is called Incubus AVICENNA, 2
The d. which must be cured METTERNICH, 4
the only d. you don't look forward to being cured of MANKIEWICZ, HERMAN J., 1
this long d., my life POPE, ALEXANDER, 43
when the cause of d. is discovered CICERO, 19
diseases D. are the tax on pleasures RAY, JOHN, 1
d....no less natural than the instincts which preserve SANTAYANA, GEORGE, 3
D. of their own Accord BUTLER, SAMUEL (1612–80), 1
D. of the soul are more dangerous CICERO, 16
In acute d....death or recovery HIPPOCRATES, 3
more or less numerous d. ROMAINS, JULES, 2
The cure of many d. is unknown PLATO, 2
disenchanting Is there anything...so d. as attainment? STEVENSON, ROBERT LOUIS, 12
disgrace a d. to our family name of Wagstaff MARX, GROUCHO, 22
d. for a woman to be sexually responsible HARRIS, JANET, 4
disgusted d. with literary men KEATS, JOHN (1795–1821), 20
disillusionments d. in the lives of the medieval saints SAKI, 4
disinclination d. to inflict pain upon oneself MEREDITH, GEORGE, 15
disinterested Difficulty in conceiving d. Desires HUTCHESON, FRANCIS, 2
D. intellectual curiosity...real civilisation TREVELYAN, G. M., 3
dislike I d. what I fancy I feel LIMERICKS, 1
dismal so d. and gloomy on these mountains RODENBERG, JULIUS, 1
the D. Science CARLYLE, THOMAS, 21
Who so beset him round /With d. stories BUNYAN, JOHN, 21
dismissed Shakespeare...is d. in a page carelessly HARRIS, FRANK, 4
Disney D....most significant figure in graphic art since Leonardo DISNEY, WALT, 1
disobedience Acts of d....postal service of disbelief AL-NAWAWI, MUHYID-DIN ABU ZAKARIYYA IBN SHARAF, 5
Of man's first d. MILTON, JOHN, 23
disorder A sweet d. in the dress HERRICK, ROBERT, 6
disparity A great d. subsists MAIMONIDES, 2
dispepsia d. is the apparatus of illusions MEREDITH, GEORGE, 9
disposed well d. towards those who are in interesting situations AUSTEN, JANE, 14
disposition I know the d. of women TERENCE, 5
dispute in any d. between a female...and a tradesman SOMERVILLE, EDITH, 3
Many a long d. among divines FRANKLIN, BENJAMIN, 18
disputes I hate religious d. MENDELSSOHN, MOSES, 1
dissatisfied better...d. than a pig satisfied MILL, JOHN STUART, 18
dissimulate how to d. is the knowledge of kings RICHELIEU, CARDINAL, 8
dissipated still keep looking so d. BENCHLEY, ROBERT, 2
dissipation other things than d....thicken the features WEST, REBECCA, 2
what time does the d. of energy begin KELVIN, WILLIAM THOMSON, 1
dissociation a d. of sensibility ELIOT, T. S., 36
dissolution d. of the feeling of individual responsibility MONTALE, EUGENIO, 3
dissolve d. the political bonds JEFFERSON, THOMAS, 35
distance D. sometimes endears friendship HOWELL, JAMES, 1
The d. doesn't matter DEFFAND, MARIE DU, 1
The shortest d. between two points LOBACHEVSKY, NIKOLAY, 1
distances D. are...the relation of space to time PROUST, MARCEL, 21
distills Pop d. whiskey and gin FOLK VERSE, 48
distinguish d. and divide /A hair BUTLER, SAMUEL (1612–80), 3
no longer d. direct experience from...television CALVINO, ITALO, 7
distinguished the d. thing JAMES, HENRY, 39
distinguishing d. fragrant flowers from poisonous weeds MAO ZEDONG, 3
distracted d. in his mind POPE, ALEXANDER, 67
distraction I will have less d. EULER, LEONHARD, 1
distress d. doesn't show on the face PROVERBS, 511

distrust d. of our senses CALVINO, ITALO, 2
D. that man who tells you to distrust WILCOX, ELLA WHEELER, 6
d. the familiar doctrine that age brings wisdom MENCKEN, H. L., 37
last fifty years...growing d....between black men and black women WALLACE, MICHELE, 1
shameful to d. one's friends LA ROCHEFOUCAULD, FRANÇOIS, 15
stay together, but we d. one another BRADBURY, MALCOLM, 8
distrustful most d....the greatest dupes RETZ, CARDINAL DE, 10
disturbance a great d. in the force GUINNESS, ALEC, 3
disturbed be not d....from any lawful recreation, such as...archery for men JAMES I, 5
ditchwater Is d. dull? CHESTERTON, G. K., 39
diversion d....an imitation of fighting SWIFT, JONATHAN, 47
diversity biological and cultural d. are now severely threatened GELL-MANN, MURRAY, 1
d. in the faculties of men MADISON, JAMES, 2
D. isn't a slogan TEETER, ROBERT M., 1
D. raises the intelligence of groups KLINE, NANCY, 2
legitimizing the d. of a multidimensional organization BARTLETT, CHRISTOPHER A., 2
divide D. and conquer PROVERBS, 178
D. not between Protestant and Papist WENTWORTH, THOMAS, 4
I shall d. and subdivide power PI Y MARGALL, FRANCISCO, 3
dividing d. one's own team is a grave sin FAYOL, HENRI, 1
divine attain to the d. perfection LONGFELLOW, HENRY WADSWORTH, 5
cannot d....conditions that will make happiness CATHER, WILLA, 7
domain where the d. is visible...art MALRAUX, ANDRÉ, 4
d. response, through the prophet's mind RAHMAN, FAZLUR, 1
I will make d. magnetic lands WHITMAN, WALT, 19
the d. sepulcher /Of life ASHBERY, JOHN, 1
Things d. are believed in HÖLDERLIN, FRIEDRICH, 1
To be discontented with the d. discontent KINGSLEY, CHARLES, 2
divine providence D. has granted this gift to man QUINTILIAN, 2
divine right The *d.* of husbands...may...be contested WOLLSTONECRAFT, MARY, 2
divinity a d....shapes our ends SHAKESPEARE, WILLIAM, 230
a piece of d. in us BROWNE, THOMAS, 29
D. is not playful DILLARD, ANNIE, 10
there is d. in odd numbers SHAKESPEARE, WILLIAM, 631
There's such d. doth hedge a king SHAKESPEARE, WILLIAM, 213
What is d....in silent shadows STEVENS, WALLACE, 17
division false d....into "feminine" and "masculine" STEINEM, GLORIA, 8
divorce d. between the producer of the text BARTHES, ROLAND, 3
d.... Blame our obsolete sex roles FRIEDAN, BETTY, 1
D.? Never. But murder often THORNDIKE, SYBIL, 1
Everyone should have a d. once REED, LOU, 4
not wanting to consent to the d. EDWARD VIII, 2
Suffer the women whom ye d. KORAN, 39
The great leveler nowadays is d. HOAGLAND, EDWARD, 6
divorced d. from his wife PLUTARCH, 22
divorces three d. and four wives to decide MAILER, NORMAN, 14
Dixie To live and die in D. EMMETT, DANIEL DECATUR, 1
Way down South in D. HUGHES, LANGSTON, 4
DNA if all the D....were stretched out JONES, STEVE, 1
do All that I d., I do quickly MORAND, PAUL, 2
D. as you would be done by PROVERBS, 180
D. other men...they would do you DICKENS, CHARLES, 49
d. what the mob do DICKENS, CHARLES, 92
what d. I do with *this* EDWARD VIII, 9
Doasyouwouldbedoneby her name is Mrs D. KINGSLEY, CHARLES, 6
doctor A country d. needs more brains to do his work PITKIN, WALTER B., 1
A d....is a patient half-cured PROUST, MARCEL, 11
A d. must work eighteen hours a day FISCHER, MARTIN H., 1
D. Foster went to Gloucester CHILDREN'S VERSE, 45
d. says...have to keep cutting yourself NAKHLA, FAYED, 1
duty of a d. to prolong life HORDER, THOMAS, 1
Foolish the d. who despises the knowledge HIPPOCRATES, 7
Give me a d. partridge-plump AUDEN, W. H., 49
He has been a d. a year now TWAIN, MARK, 51
I am like a d. PÉREZ DE CUÉLLAR, JAVIER, 1
I'm more a...d. for women's problems KARAN, DONNA, 2
Knocked down a d. SIMPSON, N. F., 1
Make it compulsory for a d. using a brass plate SHAW, GEORGE BERNARD, 90
no one ever considered the d. a gentleman MAUGHAM, SOMERSET, 15
no point in calling a d. CICERO, 3
People pay the d. for his trouble SENECA, "THE YOUNGER," 5
The D. fared even better BUNNER, HENRY CUYLER, 1
There is not a d. who desires...health PHILEMON, 1
"What sort of d. is he?" DU MAURIER, GEORGE, 1
When a d. does go wrong DOYLE, ARTHUR CONAN, 10
doctors a meeting of d. MAYO, WILLIAM JAMES, 1
Call in three good d. and play bridge BENCHLEY, ROBERT, 4
D. are just the same as lawyers CHEKHOV, ANTON, 7
D. bury their mistakes PROVERBS, MODERN, 9
D....know men as thoroughly as if they had made them SARTRE, JEAN-PAUL, 16
D....preserve our health DIDEROT, DENIS, 13
d....simple trusting folk OSLER, WILLIAM, 14
sitting in the midst of the d. BIBLE, 328
The d. allow one to die LA BRUYÈRE, JEAN DE, 11
The d. are always changing their opinions LLOYD-GEORGE, DAVID, 11
The d. were very brave about it PARKER, DOROTHY, 25
The great d. all got their education off dirt pavements FISCHER, MARTIN H., 19
There are only two classes...d. and patients KIPLING, RUDYARD, 3
doctrine We lov'd the d. for the teacher's sake DEFOE, DANIEL, 3
doctrines false d. and bad institutions MILL, JOHN STUART, 4
makes all d. plain and clear BUTLER, SAMUEL (1612–80), 21
document historic d....towards entering Europe YELTSIN, BORIS, 3
dodgers The dodgerest of the d. DICKENS, CHARLES, 76
dodo The D. never had a chance CUPPY, WILL, 1
dog A d. starv'd at his Master's Gate BLAKE, WILLIAM, 5
a truly faithful d. LORENZ, KONRAD, 3
cat will mew...d. will have his day SHAKESPEARE, WILLIAM, 222
curious incident of the d. in the night-time DOYLE, ARTHUR CONAN, 14
ever d. that praised his fleas YEATS, W. B., 28
Every d. has his day PROVERBS, 198
Every d. is allowed PROVERBS, 199
Give a d. a bad name PROVERBS, 230
I am His Highness' d. at Kew POPE, ALEXANDER, 5
If a d. jumps onto your lap WHITEHEAD, A. N., 5
Let the d. return to his vomit HOWE, JOSEPH, 2
Shall the d. lie where the deer GWYN, NELL, 2

something about being a d. MASSON, JEFFREY, 2
The d. barks but the caravan passes AL-FAYED, MOHAMED, 1
The d. in the kennel PROVERBS, 41
The d. it was that died GOLDSMITH, OLIVER, 31
the d. truly loves us MASSON, JEFFREY, 1
The d.…Went mad and bit the man GOLDSMITH, OLIVER, 32
The great pleasure of a d. BUTLER, SAMUEL (1835–1902), 32
We do need the d. LORENZ, KONRAD, 5
Why should a d., a horse, a rat have life SHAKESPEARE, WILLIAM, 371

doggerel In d. and stout...honour this country MACNEICE, LOUIS, 10

doggie The d. in front has suddenly gone blind COWARD, NOEL, 27

dogma D. is credulous MARTIN, GRAHAM DUNSTAN, 1
d. of women's...subjugation to men BEARD, MARY RITTER, 3
no d., no Dean DISRAELI, BENJAMIN, 55
You can't teach an old d. PARKER, DOROTHY, 32

dogmas these d. or goals are in doubt PIRSIG, ROBERT T., 8

dogs d.…animated when...in a pack HUME, DAVID, 11
d. delight to bark and bite WATTS, ISAAC, 3
D., easily won to fawn on any man SHAKESPEARE, WILLIAM, 517
D., like horses, are quadrupeds MUIR, FRANK, 5
D. show us their tongues GÓMEZ DE LA SERNA, RAMÓN, 3
let slip the d. of war SHAKESPEARE, WILLIAM, 306
Stop running those d. on your page HEARST, WILLIAM RANDOLPH, 3

doing Anything...worth d. has been done frequently BEERBOHM, MAX, 9
Anything worth d. is worth doing poorly DOWNEY, ROBERT, JR., 1
D. is better than saying PROVERBS, 181

doings All our d. without charity BOOK OF COMMON PRAYER, 8

doll worthier than the d. in the doll's house DICKENS, CHARLES, 75

dollar A d. that stays 100 cents FORD, HENRY, 4
Nothing that costs only a d. ARDEN, ELIZABETH, 1
The almighty d., that great object of universal devotion IRVING, WASHINGTON, 9

dolmens Like d. round my childhood, the old people MONTAGUE, JOHN, 3

dolphin Irish d., swift and single SETH, VIKRAM, 1
That d.-torn, that gong-tormented sea YEATS, W. B., 53

domestic d. bliss PATMORE, COVENTRY, 1
D. happiness, thou only bliss COWPER, WILLIAM, 32

dominated Nobody ever d. a theater like Jolson JOLSON, AL, 1

dominoes You have a row of d. EISENHOWER, DWIGHT D., 20

done d. anything that could be recalled DISRAELI, BENJAMIN, 28
D. because we are too menny HARDY, THOMAS, 12
If it were done when 'tis d. SHAKESPEARE, WILLIAM, 393
well d.…done soon enough DU BARTAS, GUILLAUME, 5
What's d. cannot be undone PROVERBS, 452
What you do not want d. to yourself CONFUCIUS, 28

dong The D. with a luminous Nose LEAR, EDWARD, 2

Donne Dr D.'s verses are like the peace of God DONNE, JOHN, 4
D.'s Body only, lyes below DONNE, JOHN, 3
John D., Anne Donne, Un-done DONNE, JOHN, 5

donsmanship D.…the art of criticizing POTTER, STEPHEN, 2

don't D. let anyone bomb me BETJEMAN, JOHN, 9
D. view me with a critic's eye EVERETT, DAVID, 1

don't-knows One day the d. will get in MILLIGAN, SPIKE, 12

door A d. is what a dog NASH, OGDEN, 23
Behold, I stand at the d. and knock BIBLE, 465
keep ajar the d. that leads to madness MORLEY, CHRISTOPHER DARLINGTON, 2
the d.…opens like a wound QASIM, SAMIH, 3
When one d. shuts PROVERBS, 455

doorkeeper d. of a bordello TOSCANINI, ARTURO, 2

doors Men shut their d. against a setting sun SHAKESPEARE, WILLIAM, 675
the d. of perception were cleansed BLAKE, WILLIAM, 37

dormice Stuff the d. with minced pork APICIUS, MARCUS GAVIUS, 1

dote I d. on myself WHITMAN, WALT, 30

dots those damned d. CHURCHILL, RANDOLPH (1849–95), 3

double I was d. their age SWIFT, JONATHAN, 8
You might make that a d. HEATH, NEVILLE GEORGE, 1

double bed down the grass-green gooseberried d. THOMAS, DYLAN, 21

double bogey Last week I made a d. NICKLAUS, JACK, 2

doublethink *D.* means...holding two contradictory beliefs ORWELL, GEORGE, 22

doubt a life of d. diversified by faith BROWNING, ROBERT, 50
Attempt the end, and never...d. HERRICK, ROBERT, 11
d.…an art...acquired with difficulty PEIRCE, C. S., 1
D.…necessary precondition to meaningful action BARTHELME, DONALD, 2
never d. /What nobody is sure BELLOC, HILAIRE, 21
Through the night of d. and sorrow BARING-GOULD, SABINE, 3
To d. everything or...believe everything POINCARÉ, JULES HENRI, 4
When a man is in d. about... his writing BUTLER, SAMUEL (1835–1902), 37
When in d., don't call a meeting MCCORMACK, MARK, 5

doubter I am a d.…a skeptic BURBANK, LUTHER, 2

doubtful d. of his dinner JOHNSON, SAMUEL, 25

doubting d. in order to philosophize KIERKEGAARD, SØREN, 16
Everyone who observes himself d. AUGUSTINE OF HIPPO, SAINT, 10
The game of d. itself presupposes certainty WITTGENSTEIN, LUDWIG, 22

doubts d.…dissolved like a piece of thawing ice WATTS, ALAN, 7

doughty The d. knight of the stuffed cravat ADAMS, JOHN QUINCY, 8

Dove Cottage No visit to D., Grasmere, is complete COREN, ALAN, 1

doves The moans of d. in immemorial elms TENNYSON, ALFRED, 88

Dowel D., Dobet and Dobest LANGLAND, WILLIAM, 2

down D. among the dead men DYER, JOHN, 1
He that is d. BUNYAN, JOHN, 24
I brought myself d. NIXON, RICHARD, 25
When you are d. and out WELLES, ORSON, 5
Yes, and they went d. very well too WELLINGTON, DUKE OF, 6

Downing Street the first comic genius...in D. DISRAELI, BENJAMIN, 1

downsizing D. suddenly became news KRUGMAN, PAUL, 2
Tactics of open-ended d. ROACH, STEPHEN S., 1

Dracula I hope never to hear...D. again LUGOSI, BELA, 2

Drake D. he's in his hammock NEWBOLT, HENRY, 2

drama d. is when the audience cries CAPRA, FRANK, 1
D. never changed anybody's mind MAMET, DAVID, 12
d. of people struggling BAILYN, BERNARD, 3
d.…people dealing nobly with...misery STEVENSON, JULIET, 1
essence and d. of history BAILYN, BERNARD, 1
We respond to a d. MAMET, DAVID, 13

drama critic d.…perceives what is not happening TYNAN, KENNETH, 5

dramatist the d. only wants more liberties JAMES, HENRY, 18

dramatize D. it, dramatize it JAMES, HENRY, 16
drat Drat and triple d. WACKY RACES, 1
draught O, for a d. of vintage KEATS, JOHN (1795–1821), 60
draw I d. what I feel in my body HEPWORTH, BARBARA, 2
drawing D. is the true test INGRES, JEAN-AUGUSTE DOMINIQUE, 1
good d....makes figures beautiful TITIAN, 1
drawing board back to the old d. ARNO, PETER, 2
drawing rooms d....spoiled more poets BEER, THOMAS, 1
dream A d. can be the highest point of a life OKRI, BEN, 2
A d. is a scripture ECO, UMBERTO, 10
a d. of perfect bliss BAYLY, THOMAS HAYNES, 1
All men d.: but not equally LAWRENCE, T. E., 3
All that we see...Is but a d. POE, EDGAR ALLAN, 9
A sight to d. of COLERIDGE, SAMUEL TAYLOR, 8
awakened from the d. of life KEATS, JOHN (1795–1821), 6
behold it was a d. BUNYAN, JOHN, 10
every d. I...dreamed has come true PRESLEY, ELVIS, 2
God pity a one-d. man GODDARD, ROBERT, 1
his d....turn the age to gold JONSON, BEN, 15
I d. things that never were KENNEDY, ROBERT, 3
I d. when I am awake CALDERÓN DE LA BARCA, PEDRO, 4
If you can d. it you can do it DISNEY, WALT, 5
I have a d. KING, MARTIN LUTHER, JR., 9
I have had a d., past the wit of man SHAKESPEARE, WILLIAM, 61
In a d. I walked with God HAMMARSKJÖLD, DAG, 3
in a d. she had come to him after her death JOYCE, JAMES, 28
In a d. you are never eighty SEXTON, ANNE, 1
Over the gulfs of d. ROETHKE, THEODORE, 8
The d. is real, my friends BAMBARA, TONI CADE, 3
the fondest d. of Phallic science EHRENREICH, BARBARA, 2
What happens to a d. deferred HUGHES, LANGSTON, 7
What is a d.? /What is reality XU YUNUO, 1
what my d. was SHAKESPEARE, WILLIAM, 62
dreamed I d. of a white saucepan VOINOVICH, VLADIMIR, 1
dreamer that prophet, or...d. of dreams BIBLE, 37
this d. cometh BIBLE, 133
dreamin Last night I d. dat de sun MATTHIESSEN, PETER, 1
dreaming a man d. I was a butterfly ZHUANGZI, 9
d. in America is no cinch BELLOW, SAUL, 12
dreams D. /are cages WANTLING, WILLIAM, 2
D. are necessary to life NIN, ANAÏS, 4
d....imagination informs the understanding SCOT, REGINALD, 1
do we not live in d. TENNYSON, ALFRED, 85
D. release the soul's love urge DROSTE-HÜLSHOFF, ANNETTE ELISABETH VON, 1
d. to come true, don't sleep PROVERBS, 501
Even in d. good works are not wasted CALDERÓN DE LA BARCA, PEDRO, 3
For one person who d. of making fifty thousand pounds MILNE, A. A., 2
Ground not upon d. MIDDLETON, THOMAS, 6
He lived as one d. of living COCTEAU, JEAN, 10
I arise from d. of thee SHELLEY, PERCY BYSSHE, 18
I like the d. of the future JEFFERSON, THOMAS, 43
In d. begins responsibility YEATS, W. B., 25
in My D. KAHN, GUS, 1
My d. were all my own SHELLEY, MARY WOLLSTONECRAFT, 1
notion of d. as transparently meaningful FREUD, SIGMUND, 8
Our d. are our real life FELLINI, FEDERICO, 3
Our d. are tales /Told in dim Eden DE LA MARE, WALTER, 5
power of d....multiformity of animals CANETTI, ELIAS, 11
sick men's d....out of the ivory gate BROWNE, THOMAS, 3
The d. are over BARTH, KARL, 2
We are such stuff /As d. are made on SHAKESPEARE, WILLIAM, 650
We cast away priceless time in d. GARLAND, JUDY, 2
dreamt d. that I was making a speech CAVENDISH, SPENCER COMPTON, 1
dress A d. has no life of its own SCHIAPARELLI, ELSA, 1
distinctive d....stimulate...sexual instinct FLÜGEL, J. C., 1
Englishman's d. is like a traitor's body DEKKER, THOMAS, 3
I have no d. except the one I wear CURIE, MARIE, 2
put on a d. of guilt MCGOUGH, ROGER, 1
the d. was drawing attention BLOOMER, AMELIA JENKS, 1
There is no one left to d. BALENCIAGA, CRISTÓBAL, 1
Those who make their d....themselves HAZLITT, WILLIAM, 23
why do you d. me /In borrow'd robes SHAKESPEARE, WILLIAM, 384
dress code d. violations...charm bracelets, long dangling earrings FISCHER-MIRKIN, TOBY, 2
dress'd man /D. in a little brief authority SHAKESPEARE, WILLIAM, 430
dress designers they turned to the d. WOLFE, TOM, 12
dress designing D....not a profession but an art SCHIAPARELLI, ELSA, 3
dressed All d. up, with nowhere to go WHITE, WILLIAM ALLEN, 1
d. to meet my father's eyes JULIA, 1
dresses d. that crawl and dresses that fly CHANEL, COCO, 3
long d....cover a multitude of shins WEST, MAE, 18
dressmaking D. is a technique...trade CHANEL, COCO, 2
Dreyfus It is the revenge of D. MAURRAS, CHARLES, 1
drink A good d. PROVERBS, 110
A little in d. STEELE, RICHARD, 1
And if I d. oblivion MEREDITH, GEORGE, 2
Another little d. SITWELL, EDITH, 3
D.! for you know not whence you came FITZGERALD, EDWARD, 17
D. the first. Sip the second ROCKNE, KNUTE, 2
D. to-day, and drown all sorrow FLETCHER, JOHN, 4
D. to me only with thine eyes JONSON, BEN, 2
First you take a d....then the drink takes you FITZGERALD, F. SCOTT, 23
He who is given to d. PERSIUS, 4
I d. no more than a sponge RABELAIS, FRANÇOIS, 3
I d....sometimes when I have no occasion CERVANTES, MIGUEL DE, 41
may d. and no be drunk BURNS, ROBERT, 43
never...d. by daylight MENCKEN, H. L., 9
no one has yet found a way to d. for a living KERR, JEAN, 5
One more d. and I'd be under the host PARKER, DOROTHY, 36
One reason I don't d. ASTOR, NANCY, 8
soft d. at a party CURRIE, EDWINA, 2
There are five reasons we should d. ALDRICH, HENRY, 1
We d. one another's health JEROME, JEROME K., 6
drinker The d. of wine...spreads calumnies AL-MUFID, ABU ABDULLAH MUHAMMAD AL-HARITHI AL-BAGHDADI, 5
drinkers written by d. of water HORACE, 26
drinking D....and making love all year round BEAUMARCHAIS, PIERRE-AUGUSTIN CARON DE, 5
I have been d. it for sixty-five years and I am not dead yet VOLTAIRE, 53
much d., little thinking SWIFT, JONATHAN, 23
no d. after death FLETCHER, JOHN, 3

there's nothing like d. DIBDIN, CHARLES, 4
'Tis not the d....but the excess SELDEN, JOHN, 7
two reasons for d. PEACOCK, THOMAS LOVE, 8
drinks He who d. a little too much PROVERBS, 252
drip long d. of human tears HARDY, THOMAS, 24
dripping Constant d. hollows out a stone LUCRETIUS, 3
driven d. /Into a desperate strait MASSINGER, PHILIP, 4
driving busy d. cabs and cutting hair BURNS, GEORGE, 7
d. alone...exhilarates some people DIDION, JOAN, 2
spend ...life...d. briskly in a post-chaise JOHNSON, SAMUEL, 94
drollery fatal d....representative government DISRAELI, BENJAMIN, 34
drop a single d. of human blood O'CONNELL, DANIEL, 4
D. 30 per cent of your Latinisms WHARTON, EDITH, 2
people ...one should like...to d. MONTAGU, ELIZABETH, 1
dross lovest well remains, /the rest is d. POUND, EZRA, 19
drought As the d. continued, prayer was abandoned LEE, LAURIE, 1
drown d. in their own blood HUSSEIN, SADDAM, 1
Don't d. the man PROVERBS, 184
drowned d. in the muck of poverty DAVIS, ANGELA, 2
drowning A d. man PROVERBS, 105
If I rescued a child from d. BENN, TONY, 4
drowsy A d. frowzy poem WORDSWORTH, WILLIAM, 3
drudge a harmless d. JOHNSON, SAMUEL, 11
drudgery We must drive out d. FORD, HENRY, 5
drug A d....when injected into a rat, will produce a scientific report PROVERBS, MODERN, 2
A miracle d. HODGINS, ERIC, 1
D. misuse is not a disease DICK, PHILIP K., 1
Ether...the perfect d. for Las Vegas THOMPSON, HUNTER S., 2
No d....causes the...ills of society O'ROURKE, P. J., 3
drugging Imperative d....the chief function of the doctor OSLER, WILLIAM, 3
drugs D. are the greatest threat JACKSON, JESSE, 13
Half the modern d. could well be thrown out the window FISCHER, MARTIN H., 8
how do d., hygiene, and animal magnetism heal EDDY, MARY BAKER, 5
I didn't take d. MARADONA, DIEGO, 1
if you're on d. then you're in trouble CHRISTIE, LINFORD, 1
There is only one reason why men become addicted to d. FISCHER, MARTIN H., 20
drum Not a d. was heard WOLFE, CHARLES, 1
drum major say that I was a d. for justice KING, MARTIN LUTHER, JR., 1
drummer d....kicking his drums to the cellar KEROUAC, JACK, 5
drums "Thin red line of 'eroes" when the d. begin to roll KIPLING, RUDYARD, 26
You're not supposed to *rape* the d. HIGGINS, BILLY, 1
drunk have d. a lot...if I'd lost NAVRATILOVA, MARTINA, 4
I was very d. BURROUGHS, WILLIAM S., 13
Lord George Brown d. is a better man WILSON, HAROLD, 1
Man, being reasonable, must get d. BYRON, LORD, 50
not so think as you d. SQUIRE, J. C., 1
partly she was d. BURNS, ROBERT, 42
this meeting is d. DICKENS, CHARLES, 98
What, when d., one sees...other women GARBO, GRETA, 3
drunkard A d. clasp his teeth TOURNEUR, CYRIL, 1
drunken What shall we do with the d. sailor FOLK VERSE, 27
drunkenness A branch of the sin of d. JAMES I, 3
D. is never anything but a substitute for happiness GIDE, ANDRÉ, 1
D. is simply voluntary insanity SENECA, "THE YOUNGER," 9
D. is temporary suicide RUSSELL, BERTRAND, 43
D....spoils health PENN, WILLIAM, 6
D., the ruin of reason BASIL THE GREAT, SAINT, 1
d....the supremely valid human experience JAMES, WILLIAM, 27
that d. which is stupid, maudlin NORRIS, FRANK, 3
there is more drinking...less d. BOOTH, CHARLES, 1
dry nothing sooner d. than women's tears WEBSTER, JOHN, 9
O ye d. bones BIBLE, 93
Dublin D....not so bad as Iceland JOHNSON, SAMUEL, 23
D....paved with great affectations GOGARTY, OLIVER ST. JOHN, 3
first day in D....your worst BERRYMAN, JOHN, 4
When I die, D. will be written on my heart JOYCE, JAMES, 42
Duce The D. is always right MUSSOLINI, BENITO, 1
duchess That's my last D. BROWNING, ROBERT, 15
duck I forgot to d. REAGAN, RONALD, 36
I just forgot to d. DEMPSEY, JACK, 2
looks like a d. MCCARTHY, JOSEPH (1909–57), 3
ducks go about the country stealing d. ARABIN, WILLIAM ST. JULIEN, 1
dues Many d. imposed by law are hostile ANTIPHON, 1
duke A...D. costs as much...as two Dreadnoughts LLOYD-GEORGE, DAVID, 4
married the D....not for lunch SIMPSON, WALLIS, 2
dull as d. as ditch water DICKENS, CHARLES, 74
He was d. in a new way GRAY, THOMAS, 1
not only d. in himself FOOTE, SAMUEL, 4
The prospect of a lot /Of d. MPs GILBERT, W. S., 15
dullard The d.'s envy of brilliant men BEERBOHM, MAX, 14
dumb D. as a drum vith a hole in it DICKENS, CHARLES, 81
so d. that he can't fart and chew FORD, GERALD, 2
think I'm a d. blonde...then they're dumber PARTON, DOLLY, 1
Dundee year I intend to leave D. MCGONAGALL, WILLIAM, 2
dungeon A d. horrible, on all sides round MILTON, JOHN, 26
What other d....dark as one's own heart HAWTHORNE, NATHANIEL, 8
dungeons d. deep and caverns old TOLKIEN, J. R. R., 3
dupe d. of friendship...the fool of love HAZLITT, WILLIAM, 27
dust A heap of d. alone remains POPE, ALEXANDER, 33
d. thou art BIBLE, 113
like d., I'll rise ANGELOU, MAYA, 3
not worth the d. SHAKESPEARE, WILLIAM, 356
pile your d. upon the quick and dead SHAKESPEARE, WILLIAM, 224
raised a d....complain we cannot see BERKELEY, BISHOP, 3
shake off the d. under your feet as a testimony against them BIBLE, 356
The d. upon the paper eye DOUGLAS, KEITH, 2
They shook off the d. of their feet BIBLE, 17
This d. was once the man LINCOLN, ABRAHAM, 8
To sweep the d. behind the door SHAKESPEARE, WILLIAM, 65
Dutch my dear old D. CHEVALIER, ALBERT, 1
duties the d. of a physician ANONYMOUS, 23
duty a stupid man...always declares that it is his d. SHAW, GEORGE BERNARD, 22
D. cannot be contrasted with pleasure MASLOW, ABRAHAM, 2
Do the d. which lies nearest thee CARLYLE, THOMAS, 36
Do your d. and leave the rest to the Gods CORNEILLE, PIERRE, 4

Do your d....history will do you justice TRUMAN, HARRY S., 15
give my d. to the Queen MARLBOROUGH, JOHN CHURCHILL, 1
It is a d. of humanity MARIANA, JUAN DE, 2
my d. to make money ROCKEFELLER, JOHN D., 1
No higher d....maintaining this constitutional shield BLACK, HUGO LAFAYETTE, 3
O D.! if that name thou love WORDSWORTH, WILLIAM, 58
our sacred d. to marry and procreate RAY, SATYAJIT, 1
owe a d., where I cannot love BEHN, APHRA, 9
the d. of being happy STEVENSON, ROBERT LOUIS, 30
thing of d. is a boy O'BRIEN, FLANN, 8
dwarf d....on the shoulders of a giant BURTON, ROBERT, 27
d. sees farther than the giant COLERIDGE, SAMUEL TAYLOR, 62
dwarfs We are like d. BERNARD OF CHARTRES, 1
dwell d. among scorpions BIBLE, 90
dwelt She d. among the untrodden ways WORDSWORTH, WILLIAM, 30
dying D. for an idea LEWIS, WYNDHAM, 1
d. for their country RUSSELL, BERTRAND, 63
D. /is an art PLATH, SYLVIA, 3
D. is a very dull, dreary affair MAUGHAM, SOMERSET, 43
d. is more the survivors' affair MANN, THOMAS, 16
d. is nothing. So start by living ANOUILH, JEAN, 8
d. /On a log, /Expiring frog DICKENS, CHARLES, 79
He had been...an unconscionable time d. CHARLES II, 9
I am d., Egypt, dying SHAKESPEARE, WILLIAM, 82
If this is d. STRACHEY, LYTTON, 1
O life of earth! O d. age MANDELSTAM, OSIP, 9
since d. came into fashion PROVERBS, MODERN, 10
those poor devils are d. PHILIP, JOHN WOODWARD, 1
'Tis not the d. for a faith THACKERAY, WILLIAM MAKEPEACE, 4
Up north they were d. in...mud DOS PASSOS, JOHN, 16
We're d. from not knowing...our past BAINVILLE, JACQUES, 1
dying industry victim of the whole d. LEARY, TIMOTHY, 5
dyke never said I was a d. JOHNSTON, JILL, 1
Dylan D. made...our contemporaries seem small THOMAS, DYLAN, 1
Dylan Thomas D. is very Welsh THOMAS, DYLAN, 4
first time I saw D. THOMAS, DYLAN, 5
dynamic d. network...accommodates constant and accelerating change HICKMAN, CRAIG R., 5

eagle the E. has landed ARMSTRONG, NEIL, 1
ear hearing e....close to the speaking tongue EMERSON, RALPH WALDO, 5
more is meant than meets the e. MILTON, JOHN, 110
early E. to bed and early to rise PROVERBS, 190
E. to rise and early to bed THURBER, JAMES, 4
The e. bird PROVERBS, 399
earn I e. that I eat, get that I wear SHAKESPEARE, WILLIAM, 112
I wasn't satisfied...e. a good living TRUMP, DONALD, 4
prefer to e. a thousand ANDERSON, ELIZABETH GARRETT, 1
this is the week I e. my salary KENNEDY, JOHN FITZGERALD, 13
earnest I am in e.—I will not equivocate GARRISON, WILLIAM LLOYD, 2
earnestly striven long and e. to become a man ANTHONY, SUSAN B., 2
earnings gap between men's and women's e. O'CONNOR, SANDRA DAY, 2
regular e. for Ziggy Stardust dolls BOWIE, DAVID, 2
ears e. make him look like a taxi GABLE, CLARK, 2
e. to hear, let him hear BIBLE, 399
now the e. of my ears awake CUMMINGS, E. E., 22
the seven thin e. BIBLE, 136
earth After e. has stopped the ears HOUSMAN, A. E., 20
As the e. darkens when...sun departs RICHARD I, 1
But did thee feel the e. move HEMINGWAY, ERNEST, 13
e....blue like an orange ÉLUARD, PAUL, 3
e. doesn't have a cleaning woman PICASSO, PABLO, 4
E. felt the wound MILTON, JOHN, 86
E. has not anything to show more fair: WORDSWORTH, WILLIAM, 40
E. hath no sorrow...heaven cannot heal MOORE, THOMAS, 16
e. is the mother of all people JOSEPH, CHIEF, 2
E....laughs with a harvest JERROLD, DOUGLAS, 4
E., receive an honoured guest YEATS, W. B., 1
E....too small and fragile a basket HEINLEIN, ROBERT, 1
E. was bountiful...the Great Mystery STANDING BEAR, LUTHER, 2
God called the dry land E. BIBLE, 102
If all the e. were paper white LYLY, JOHN, 12
lay /Lightly gently e. BEAUMONT & FLETCHER, 9
let all the e. keep silence before him BIBLE, 139
Lie heavy on him, E. EVANS, ABEL, 1
make the E. appear a bit less whimsical OFFICER, CHARLES B., 1
Spaceship E.—an instruction book didn't come with it FULLER, R. BUCKMINSTER, 4
The e. and sun were to me...flesh and blood JEFFERIES, RICHARD, 3
The e. does not argue WHITMAN, WALT, 16
The e. is as full of brutality LONDON, JACK, 17
the e. is barren as the moon MARQUIS, DON, 6
the E. is perfectly suitable for life SAGAN, CARL, 6
the e. is the Lord's, and the fulness BIBLE, 160
the e. seems...a step-dame DU BARTAS, GUILLAUME, 10
the e. was the road /Of the body JIMÉNEZ, JUAN RAMÓN, 2
this e....a mote...in the abyss JEFFERIES, RICHARD, 1
What if e. /Be but the shadow of heaven MILTON, JOHN, 67
When people thought the E. was flat ASIMOV, ISAAC, 4
earthquake Not by the e. daunted LINDSAY, VACHEL, 4
Small e. in Chile COCKBURN, CLAUD, 1
earth-secrets They know E. that know not I HARDY, THOMAS, 19
ease What infinite heart's e. /Must kings neglect SHAKESPEARE, WILLIAM, 273
easier E. said than done PROVERBS, 191
much e. to point out the problem GALBRAITH, J. K., 5
easiest e. way of life is the best MELVILLE, HERMAN, 11
East E. is East, and West is West KIPLING, RUDYARD, 24
E., west, home's best PROVERBS, 192
hold the gorgeous E. in fee WORDSWORTH, WILLIAM, 61
Neither E. nor West KHOMEINI, RUHOLLAH, 13
The wind from the E. prevails MAO ZEDONG, 27
East End look the E. in the face ELIZABETH, 1
eastertide I love the gay E. BORN, BERTRAN DE, 1
eastwards E. goes the great river SU DONGPO, 1
easy E. come, easy go PROVERBS, 193
It is e. to bear the misfortunes PROVERBS, 276
It is e. to be wise PROVERBS, 277
It's either e. or impossible DALÍ, SALVADOR, 6
not e. to get a...productive spirit to read KRAUS, KARL, 15
eat e. and drink SOCRATES, 4
e. moderately...and don't worry HUTCHISON, ROBERT, 2

E. not to dullness FRANKLIN, BENJAMIN, 29
E. slowly: only men in rags RALEIGH, WALTER ALEXANDER, 2
e. the soup they...brewed for us LUDENDORFF, ERICH VON, 1
E. to live PROVERBS, 194
e. to live and live to eat FIELDING, HENRY, 1
e. to live, and not live to eat MOLIÈRE, 25
I e. to live GANDHI, MAHATMA, 25
I e. well, and I drink well MORTON, THOMAS, 1
Let them e. the lie CERVANTES, MIGUEL DE, 25
let us e. and drink; for tomorrow we...die BIBLE, 205
Never e. at a place called Mom's ALGREN, NELSON, 1
So I did sit and e. HERBERT, GEORGE, 10
that must e. with the devil SHAKESPEARE, WILLIAM, 593
they know I don't e. babies HAUGHEY, CHARLES, 1
To e. well in England...breakfast three times MAUGHAM, SOMERSET, 44
what you e....what you are BRILLAT-SAVARIN, ANTHELME, 1

eaten e. me out of house and home SHAKESPEARE, WILLIAM, 253

eating E. cannot be a solitary affair LO, VIVIENNE, 2
E. people is wrong FLANDERS, MICHAEL, 1
E.'s going to be a whole new ball game PIGGOTT, LESTER, 1
e. should be a pleasure PORTER, MARK, 1
E. the flesh that she herself hath bred SHAKESPEARE, WILLIAM, 680
I drew near...e. from the tree AL-NAWAWI, MUHYID-DIN ABU ZAKARIYYA IBN SHARAF, 4

eats The thing that e. the heart KUNITZ, STANLEY, 3

ecclesiastical lay interest in e. matters...often a prelude to insanity WAUGH, EVELYN, 15

echo e. is the soul of the voice SMART, CHRISTOPHER, 7

Echo E....call her and she will call you AI QING, 1

echoes e....Ring from their marble caves DRUMMOND, WILLIAM, 3

ecologist I became an e. MENDES, CHICO, 1

ecologists e....the ultimate accountants UDALL, STEWART L., 1

ecology E....compulsory subject for all economists SCHUMACHER, E. F., 2
The restorative economy unites e. and commerce HAWKEN, PAUL, 4

economic cold metal of e. theory SCHUMPETER, JOSEPH ALOIS, 4
E. activity should...be socially just BENNIS, WARREN, 1
e. and military unification...not brought peace BERGER, JOHN, 1
e. crisis of the 1930s JOHNSON, RICHARD W., 4
E. growth...a curse rather than a good ARENDT, HANNAH, 14
e. wisdom...know what you do not know GALBRAITH, J. K., 22
modern e. life...minimum level of informal trust FUKUYAMA, FRANCIS, 4
Modern e. thinking...consider the long term SCHUMACHER, E. F., 3
the return of normal e. health MARSHALL, GEORGE, 4

economic modernization E....spawns indigenous types of capitalism GRAY, JOHN, 1

economics attempt to isolate e. from other disciplines HUTTON, WILL, 3
E....as much a study in fantasy ROSZAK, THEODORE, 8
e. forecast may well affect the economy MASON, JOHN, 1
e. is a lot like pissing JOHNSON, LYNDON BAINES, 21
E. is a subject that KHRUSHCHEV, NIKITA, 10
E....must be a mathematical science JEVONS, WILLIAM STANLEY, 1
E....theory of maximum possible welfare LUTZ, MARK, 1
E. without ethics SOLOMON, ROBERT C., 1
Good e. is good politics KEATING, PAUL, 1
good e....not everyone believes RUBIN, ROBERT E., 1
I am not prepared to accept the e. of a housewife THATCHER, MARGARET, 6
mistake to equate e. with real life MIDDLETON, PETER, 1
nobler e....not afraid to discuss spirit ROSZAK, THEODORE, 13
sense of history...divides good e. from bad GALBRAITH, J. K., 19
Studying e. is not a good preparation SOROS, GEORGE, 7
The first law of e. YAMANI, SHEIKH, 3

economic system A mature e. HAWKEN, PAUL, 1

economies emerging e....entire industrial revolution SHAPIRO, ROBERT B., 3
most successful e....harness their brain power LONG, CLARISA, 3
successful e....generating and disseminating knowledge BLAIR, TONY, 6

economist An e....expert who will know tomorrow PETER, LAURENCE J., 6
e....knows 100 ways of making love BUCHWALD, ART, 1

economists All races have...e., with the exception of the Irish GALBRAITH, J. K., 17
If all e. were laid end to end SHAW, GEORGE BERNARD, 111
If e. were good at business KERKONIAN, KIRK, 1

economy Do we want...e. dominated by the mafia ATTALI, JACQUES, 2
e....description of the career of money BERRY, WENDELL, 4
E. is going without HOPE, ANTHONY, 1
E....Purchasing the barrel of whiskey BIERCE, AMBROSE, 21
understand the workings of the e. SIMPSON, DAVID, 1
whole e. is based on planned obsolescence STEVENS, BROOKS, 1
world e. will shift to the Asia-Pacific YEO, GEORGE, 3

ecstasy e. of striking matches in the dark JONG, ERICA, 7

ecstatic It isn't the e. leap ANONYMOUS, 88

ecu You can call an e. a pound HESELTINE, MICHAEL, 1

Edison E....wasn't...a scientist EDISON, THOMAS ALVA, 1

edited e. for the old lady from Dubuque ROSS, HAROLD W., 4

editor E.: a person employed...to see that chaff is printed HUBBARD, ELBERT, 10
e....separates the wheat from the chaff STEVENSON, ADLAI, 11
e. should have a pimp for a brother FOWLER, GENE, 1

editorial the nineteenth century...age of the e. chair MCLUHAN, MARSHALL, 13

educate e. a woman you educate a family MANIKAN, RUBY, 1
E., Inform, Entertain REITH, LORD, 2
e. with the head instead of with the hand KEY, ELLEN, 4
got to e. him first SAKI, 15

educated Most Americans aren't e. to American culture REED, ISHMAEL, 5

education All e. is bad DAVIES, ROBERTSON, 2
combining e. with productive labor DENG XIAOPING, 14
difference between e. and entertainment MCLUHAN, MARSHALL, 2
do not know what e. can do HUTCHINS, ROBERT M., 2
E....an admirable thing WILDE, OSCAR, 76
E....a vast population able to read TREVELYAN, G. M., 2
E....formation of character SPENCER, HERBERT, 7
E. forms the common mind POPE, ALEXANDER, 41
E. in music is most sovereign PLATO, 11
e....inspire people to live more abundantly WOODSON, CARTER G., 1
e. is a leading out of what is...in the pupil's soul SPARK, MURIEL, 12
E. is that which remains EINSTEIN, ALBERT, 29
E. is...the soul of a society CHESTERTON, G. K., 24

E. is what survives SKINNER, B. F., 4
E. made us what we are HELVÉTIUS, CLAUDE ADRIEN, 1
e....makes a straight cut ditch THOREAU, HENRY DAVID, 17
e....one who INSISTS on knowing POUND, EZRA, 6
e....reverent joining of the past to...the present PESTALOZZI, JOHANN HEINRICH, 9
e. was an ornament in prosperity DIOGENES LÄERTIUS, 1
Higher e. in America LEACOCK, STEPHEN, 16
if e. is...a mere transmission of knowledge MONTESSORI, MARIA, 1
make all this fuss about e. MELBOURNE, LORD, 7
Medical e. is not completed at the medical school WELCH, WILLIAM H., 1
one of the ultimate advantages of an e. SKINNER, B. F., 5
Our e. system has largely failed BRANSON, RICHARD, 5
philosophic aim of e. GOODMAN, PAUL, 1
Soap and e....are more deadly TWAIN, MARK, 9
The e. of the doctor BILLINGS, JOHN SHAW, 1
traditions of e. have emphasized knowledge DE BONO, EDWARD, 7
Twelve years of formal e. NEWTON, HUEY P., 1
Upon...e....this country depends DISRAELI, BENJAMIN, 5
When a man's e. is finished FILENE, E. A., 1
with e. and whisky the price it is WAUGH, EVELYN, 14

educational e. process...is its own end DEWEY, JOHN, 5
Separate e. facilities are inherently unequal SUPREME COURT OF THE UNITED STATES, 1

educator task of the e. of young children MONTESSORI, MARIA, 3

effective more e. to get a 20% solution ELKINGTON, JOHN, 2

effeminate it is an e. business KELLY, GENE, 4

efficiency lack of e....scientific achievements for economic needs GORBACHEV, MIKHAIL, 13

efforts Wherever man would not...spend his e. O'NEILL, HUGH, 1

effrontery e. to kiss me on the lips CARTER, JIMMY, 1

effulgence When thou sheddest thy e. MCGONAGALL, WILLIAM, 4

egalitarian For all its e. promise STOLL, CLIFFORD, 3

egalitarianism E. in Islam is more pronounced AHMED, AKBAR, 1
The majestic e. of the law FRANCE, ANATOLE, 8

egg Everything from an e. HARVEY, WILLIAM, 2
Only as an e.... are we all equal FALLACI, ORIANA, 1
throw an e. into an electric fan HERFORD, OLIVER, 3

egghead E. WEDS HOURGLASS MILLER, ARTHUR, 1

eggs Don't put all your e. in one basket PROVERBS, 187
Green E. and Ham SEUSS, DR., 4
putting all my e. in one bastard PARKER, DOROTHY, 43

ego Avoid having your e. so close to your position POWELL, COLIN, 4
E. is a treacherous and debilitating force HIATT, ARNOLD, 1
e. is that part of the id FREUD, SIGMUND, 34
e. locks the muse WILLIAMS, ROBIN, 6
e. represents what we call reason...sanity FREUD, SIGMUND, 35
male e....is elephantine DAVIS, BETTE, 6
The human e. is like an insatiable tick LESTER, JULIUS, 3

egoist E....more interested in himself than in me BIERCE, AMBROSE, 22

egos An aggregate of e....a mob FRYE, NORTHROP, 8

egotism E....dulls the pains of stupidity LEAHY, FRANK, 1

Egypt I will to E. SHAKESPEARE, WILLIAM, 69
link E. with...advance of human progress MAHFOUZ, NAGUIB, 9

Egyptian E. politicians...aimed...at the instincts NASSER, GAMAL ABDEL, 1

Egyptians Ancient E....contemporary man all have a kinship HERZBERG, FREDERICK, 1
the E. worshipped an insect RUSSELL, LORD, 1

Eiffel Tower E....representing the world's age WALLACE, ALFRED RUSSEL, 2

eighteen I knew almost as much at e. JOHNSON, SAMUEL, 98
I've had e. straight whiskies THOMAS, DYLAN, 34
she speaks e. languages PARKER, DOROTHY, 30

Eightfold Path E....Right view, right aim, right speech BUDDHA, 4

Einstein E.'s space is no closer to reality than Van Gogh's sky KOESTLER, ARTHUR, 5
E.—the greatest Jew since Jesus EINSTEIN, ALBERT, 3
E. was right. The world is crazy EINSTEIN, ALBERT, 2
Let E. be! SQUIRE, J. C., 2
Mr. E. doesn't like the natural laws BENCHLEY, ROBERT, 6
The genius of E. leads to Hiroshima EINSTEIN, ALBERT, 5

Eisenhower E. proved we don't need a president EISENHOWER, DWIGHT D., 1

ejected e. from all *decent* society BEHN, APHRA, 1

elder the idea of e. wisdom UPDIKE, JOHN, 12

elderly distinguished but e. scientist states CLARKE, ARTHUR C., 3
see it as an e. lady CAREY, GEORGE, 3

elect The e....die dishevelled and soft LOWELL, ROBERT, 13

elected e. ex-president by such a large majority WILSON, WOODROW, 4

electric E. lighting is no great boon SCHUMPETER, JOSEPH ALOIS, 2
That's an e. doughnut WOLFE, TOM, 8
the e. message came AUSTIN, ALFRED, 2

electrical e. charge...exerts electric force EDDINGTON, ARTHUR, 2

electricity by means of e., the world of matter HAWTHORNE, NATHANIEL, 5
e. was dripping invisibly THURBER, JAMES, 8

electronic "E. democracy"...open new doors for participation SCHULER, DOUGLAS, 2
They are e. lice BURGESS, ANTHONY, 1

electronic commerce E....redefine many basics of business KEEN, PETER, 5

electronic highway e....redefining business in America CRONIN, MARY J., 3

electronics cost of the e. in a modern car NEGROPONTE, NICHOLAS, 6

elegant If you can't be e....be extravagant MOSCHINO, FRANCO, 1

elemental The smack and tang of e. things LINCOLN, ABRAHAM, 5

elementary "E.," said he DOYLE, ARTHUR CONAN, 12
the use of e. shapes. A sane morality LE CORBUSIER, 5

elephant African e.'s ear /...the shape of Africa WILLIAMS, HEATHCOTE, 2
An e.'s faithful SEUSS, DR., 1
I shot an e. in my pajamas MARX, GROUCHO, 11
I think I am an E. MILNE, A. A., 4
Nonsense, they couldn't hit an e. at this dist— SEDGWICK, JOHN, 1
teaching an e. to tap dance PEROT, H. ROSS, 1

elephants the e. in Africa /Have been massacred WILLIAMS, HEATHCOTE, 1

elevate difficult to e. the poor SENIOR, NASSAU WILLIAM, 1
E. them guns a little lower JACKSON, ANDREW, 5

elf Here's not a modest maiden e. HARDY, THOMAS, 6

Elijah I will send you E. the prophet BIBLE, 349

eliminate e....members of that family because profits are down MORITA AKIO, 4

Eliot Funny, ain't it. T. S. E. likes rain PYNCHON, THOMAS, 12
elites new e....rise up...and then fall PARETO, VILFREDO, 1
Elizabethan E. age...beginning of the smoking era BARRIE, J. M., 5
Ellington we came here to hear E. ELLINGTON, DUKE, 9
elopement an e. would be preferable ADE, GEORGE, 4
eloquence e. offers...great avenue to popular favor COOPER, JAMES FENIMORE, 4
Elton John E....became my real name JOHN, ELTON, 3
Elvis E. Presley, in his spare time QUEENAN, JOE, 2
E. was the greatest...I'm the best LEWIS, JERRY LEE, 2
Elysian The immortals will send you...E. plain HOMER, 4
emancipate E. yourselves from mental slavery MARLEY, BOB, 5
one of these days we'll e. *you*! WILKINS, ROY, 1
emancipating woman is...e. herself from emancipation GOLDMAN, EMMA, 3
emancipation After e....they needed the music more BECHET, SIDNEY, 1
All e. is from within GARVEY, MARCUS, 7
The e. of women...the greatest egoistic movement KEY, ELLEN, 2
When the history of the e. movement DOUGLASS, FREDERICK, 25
embalmed I am e. in a book JAMES, HENRY, 5
embalmer A triumph of the e.'s art REAGAN, RONALD, 13
embarrassment blushing with e. for...every ridiculous sentence SALINGER, J. D., 1
embrace e. tenderly in a darkened room YEVTUSHENKO, YEVGENY, 2
I e. the purpose of God TENNYSON, ALFRED, 30
embraced e. the summer dawn RIMBAUD, ARTHUR, 5
embroidered two blankets e. with smallpox MULDOON, PAUL, 2
embryo This e. capital, where Fancy sees MOORE, THOMAS, 12
emerald A livelier e. twinkles in the grass TENNYSON, ALFRED, 27
Emerson I could...see in E. a gaping flaw EMERSON, RALPH WALDO, 2
émigré An inner é., grown long-haired HEANEY, SEAMUS, 5
eminence E. engenders enemies JAMES, C. L. R., 7
emotion e. in...art...an "objective correlative" ELIOT, T. S., 46
emotional seven constituents of e. make-up HAN YU, 2
emotional intelligence E....more weight than IQ GOLEMAN, DANIEL, 3
emotionally When an e. exciting object stimulates WATSON, JOHN B., 2
emotions E. are the lowest form of consciousness LEARY, TIMOTHY, 7
e.! Don't leave them on the road GOGOL, NIKOLAY, 7
She ran...e. from A to B PARKER, DOROTHY, 47
Strong e. and passions SUSRUTA, 1
emperor An e.'s word may no man wrest BÜRGER, GOTTFRIED AUGUST, 1
Be the E., be Peter the Great ALEXANDRA, EMPRESS, 1
E. of Russia...crossed over the bridge ALEXANDER I, 2
For...big stealin' dey makes you e. O'NEILL, EUGENE, 5
I am the e., and I want dumplings FERDINAND I (1793–1875), 1
Name me an e. CHARLES V, 1
None of the E.'s clothes ANDERSEN, HANS CHRISTIAN, 1
the e. of ice-cream STEVENS, WALLACE, 6
You are e....yet you weep RACINE, JEAN, 9
empire a more powerful or a more united e. CARSON, GEORGE NATHANIEL, 1
An e. founded by war MONTESQUIEU, 2
e. is...power in trust DRYDEN, JOHN, 17
How is the E. GEORGE V, 2
Mother E. stands splendidly isolated in Europe FOSTER, GEORGE E., 1
the downfall of the British E. CHURCHILL, WINSTON, 20
The E. means Peace NAPOLEON III, 3
To found a great e....for a nation of shopkeepers SMITH, ADAM, 9
empiricist e. view...has the character of a superstition CHOMSKY, NOAM, 5
employee e. and...tools of production are interdependent DRUCKER, PETER, 10
every e....rise to his level of incompetence PETER, LAURENCE J., 3
keep the e. happy WATSON, THOMAS J., 2
employees e. of the government TOOLE, JOHN KENNEDY, 2
employer an e. should...pursue the best...relationship with the community SIEFF, MARCUS, 2
ideal of the e....production without employees SCHUMACHER, E. F., 5
What must I do for my e. CARNEGIE, ANDREW, 5
employment E....essential to human happiness GALEN, 4
empty An e. house can gain centuries WHITTEMORE, REED, 2
Bring on the e. horses CURTIZ, MICHAEL, 1
e. and awake...emptiness and awakedness of everything KEROUAC, JACK, 24
E. vessels PROVERBS, 195
enamour'd Methought I was e. of an ass SHAKESPEARE, WILLIAM, 63
enchanted e. by his own ugliness HAMMARSKJÖLD, DAG, 4
enchantment distance lends e. to the view CAMPBELL, THOMAS, 2
encomium e. in Greek has a marvelous effect MOLIÈRE, 20
encounter I will e. darkness as a bride SHAKESPEARE, WILLIAM, 433
encounters Close E. of the Third Kind SPIELBERG, STEVEN, 8
encyclopedia The E. Britannica devotes many columns to...love MENNINGER, KARL, 1
end And now the e. is near ANKA, PAUL, 2
an e. to the beginnings of all wars ROOSEVELT, FRANKLIN D., 35
beginning of the e. when you...have style HAMMETT, DASHIELL, 4
e. is where we start from ELIOT, T. S., 21
e. of all we do...free from pain EPICURUS, 1
Here is my journey's e. SHAKESPEARE, WILLIAM, 498
In my e. is my beginning MARY, QUEEN OF SCOTS, 1
looks like the e. of the world ROWLAND, SHERWOOD, 1
makes me e., where I begun DONNE, JOHN, 32
man awaits his e. /Dreading and hoping YEATS, W. B., 55
the e. begins to come into view WESTMORELAND, WILLIAM C., 1
the e. is not yet BIBLE, 424
The e. justifies the means PROVERBS, 400
The e. must justify the means PRIOR, MATTHEW, 4
the e. of the beginning CHURCHILL, WINSTON, 16
The first sign of his approaching e. GREENE, GRAHAM, 11
the same thing at the e. BROWNING, ROBERT, 45
This is...an e. of all wars SEYMOUR, EDWARD, 1
what e. the gods have in store HORACE, 35
Who knows but the world may e. to-night BROWNING, ROBERT, 60
ende a good e. he winneth GOWER, JOHN, 1
endeavor Human e....betrays /Humanity HECHT, ANTHONY, 1
Through e. to the stars MOTTOS AND SLOGANS, 19
To e. to forget anyone LA BRUYÈRE, JEAN DE, 19
endeavors in great e....the will is enough PROPERTIUS, SEXTUS, 2
endings E. are elusive, middles are nowhere BARTHELME, DONALD, 3
endless there are e. histories, overlapping and contradicting BARZUN, JACQUES, 4
end of the world stay on until the e. TURNER, TED, 4
ends I want to see how it e. WILDE, OSCAR, 74

Let all the e.... be thy country's SHAKESPEARE, WILLIAM, 282
the best e. by the best means HUTCHESON, FRANCIS, 3
endurance the overwhelming beauty of e. HARDWICK, ELIZABETH, 1
endure e. my own despair WALSH, WILLIAM, 1
endures only thing that e. is character SIMPSON, O. J., 2
enemies Better a thousand e. outside PROVERBS, 18
He could not make e. SHERIDAN, RICHARD BRINSLEY, 2
my e. have a point RUSHDIE, SALMAN, 10
Of the e. of the soul MISTRAL, GABRIELA, 4
The e. of Freedom INGE, WILLIAM RALPH, 17
we have been mortal e. ever since LESAGE, ALAIN RENÉ, 4
enemy despise your e. strategically...respect him tactically MAO ZEDONG, 36
discover what your e. fears most HOFFER, ERIC, 5
e. of clear language is insincerity ORWELL, GEORGE, 28
Every man is his own worst e. PROVERBS, 204
I am the e. you killed OWEN, WILFRED, 9
I cannot get any sense of an e. LAWRENCE, D. H., 9
It takes your e. and...friend TWAIN, MARK, 20
no more sombre e. of good art CONNOLLY, CYRIL, 6
the e. halts, we harass MAO ZEDONG, 29
the e. who can...teach us DALAI LAMA, 8
We have met the e., and they are ours PERRY, OLIVER HAZARD, 1
energy E. is Eternal Delight BLAKE, WILLIAM, 49
exhausted my e. in tirades against fate BASHKIRTSEFF, MARIE, 1
It takes too much e. *not* to care HANSBERRY, LORRAINE, 4
engaged we are e. in nation building GARVEY, MARCUS, 5
engineer the e. assumed accountability for his work ARMSTRONG, MICHAEL, 4
engineers e....end up with the atomic bomb PAGNOL, MARCEL, 3
England Be E. what she will CHURCHILL, CHARLES, 5
E.—a happy land we know CHURCHILL, CHARLES, 6
E., ah, faithless England BOSSUET, JACQUES-BÉNIGNE, 3
E....a nation of pimps ZELDIN, THEODORE, 8
E. and I first set foot on each other MIKES, GEORGE, 8
earth of E. is in my two hands WILLIAM THE CONQUEROR, 1
E. elects a Labour Government ROGERS, WILL, 9
E. expects NELSON, HORATIO, 6
E. invented the phrase, "Her Majesty's Opposition" BAGEHOT, WALTER, 2
E. is a nation of shopkeepers NAPOLEON I, 26
E. is an empire MICHELET, JULES, 1
E. is the paradise of individuality SANTAYANA, GEORGE, 7
E. is the paradise of women FLORIO, JOHN, 2
E., my England HENLEY, WILLIAM ERNEST, 4
E....neck wrung like a chicken WEYGAND, MAXIME, 1
E....racist, homophobic, narrow-minded, authoritarian rat-hole KUREISHI, HANIF, 1
E.'s chief defense depends upon the navy PHILIP II (1527–98), 1
E.'s on the anvil—hear the hammers ring KIPLING, RUDYARD, 6
E.'s trousers falling down MITCHELL, ADRIAN, 2
E....the envy of less happy lands DENNING, LORD, 2
E....will understand our aspirations HERZL, THEODOR, 3
E., with all thy faults COWPER, WILLIAM, 28
Hating E....a form of self-defense MAHFOUZ, NAGUIB, 7
In E. even the poorest...have rights HEGEL, G. W. F., 4
in E. people have good table manners MIKES, GEORGE, 6
In E....people so desirous of titles GOGARTY, OLIVER ST. JOHN, 4
In E., pop art and fine art MACINNES, COLIN, 3
In E. there is only silence or scandal MAUROIS, ANDRÉ, 3
In E....uneducated people show off their knowledge MIKES, GEORGE, 4
In E. you worship two goddesses EMECHETA, BUCHI, 7
King of E., who lacks nothing LOUIS VII, 1
Living in E....like being married HALSEY, MARGARET, 3
no man in E. will take away my life CHARLES II, 12
Oh, to be in E. BROWNING, ROBERT, 24
Old E. is lost JOHNSON, SAMUEL, 115
open my legs and think of E. HILLINGDON, ALICE, 1
Rule all E. under a hog COLLINGBOURNE, WILLIAM, 1
The only E. he had known was...passionate in incest with its past LAMMING, GEORGE, 2
this generation...found E. a land of beauty JOAD, C. E. M., 1
this is E.'s greatest son TENNYSON, ALFRED, 33
When people say E. MIKES, GEORGE, 7
You cannot leave E. PORTER, PETER, 4
You poison E. at her roots BOTTOMLEY, GORDON, 1
English Acting in E....I'm like a blind man DEPARDIEU, GÉRARD, 1
attitude of the E....toward English history HALSEY, MARGARET, 4
Correct E. is the slang of prigs ELIOT, GEORGE, 17
E....admire any man who has no talent AGATE, JAMES, 3
E. are polite by telling lies BRADBURY, MALCOLM, 5
E....are rather a foul-mouthed nation HAZLITT, WILLIAM, 18
E. bohemianism more sordid than other kinds EMPSON, WILLIAM, 1
E. character...iron force of the Latins FULLER, MARGARET, 4
E. drunkard made the rolling English road CHESTERTON, G. K., 7
E....have the most rigid code of immorality BRADBURY, MALCOLM, 2
E. is the language of the fox VÉLIZ, CLAUDIO, 1
E. kept history...Irish kept it in mind BOWEN, ELIZABETH, 1
E. kill themselves without any...reason MONTESQUIEU, 10
E. may not like music—but...love the noise BEECHAM, THOMAS, 6
E. soldiers fight like lions HOFFMANN, MAX, 1
E. style...key is understatement AMIES, HARDY, 1
E....the language of the world ADAMS, JOHN, 5
E. think cricket is a game MIKES, GEORGE, 5
E. think...opinion as something...to hide HALSEY, MARGARET, 5
E. tongue a gallimaufry or hodgepodge SPENSER, EDMUND, 12
E....very little...inferior to the Scotch NORTH, CHRISTOPHER, 1
E. winter—ending in July BYRON, LORD, 78
E. women are elegant MITFORD, NANCY, 6
Except for the fact that they all speak E. O'ROURKE, P. J., 6
give him seven feet of E. ground HAROLD II, 2
learn E....in thirty hours TWAIN, MARK, 13
Nothing unites the E. like war MILLS, HUGH, 1
one E. book and one only ARNOLD, MATTHEW, 7
range of the E. longbows MULDOON, PAUL, 1
The baby doesn't understand E. KNOX, RONALD, 2
The E. are busy MONTESQUIEU, 9
the E. have hot-water bottles MIKES, GEORGE, 3
The E. have no respect for their language SHAW, GEORGE BERNARD, 80
The E. sentence is just as difficult STEINBECK, JOHN, 31
The E. take their pleasures sadly SULLY, MAXIMILIEN DE BÉTHUNE, 1
the E. would manage to meet and dine JERROLD, DOUGLAS, 9
This is the sort of E. CHURCHILL, WINSTON, 68
To Americans E. manners are...frightening JARRELL, RANDALL, 3
we E. have sex on the brain MUGGERIDGE, MALCOLM, 3
English language E. restricts YEO, GEORGE, 1

if I created the E. BRUCE, LENNY, 5
If the E. had been properly organized MILNE, A. A., 6
master of the E. HAILSHAM, LORD, 2
mobilized the E. CHURCHILL, WINSTON, 7

Englishman An E. afraid to support a friend COOPER, JAMES FENIMORE, 10
An E....forms an orderly queue of one MIKES, GEORGE, 2
an E....he'll come sleep in your closet CAPOTE, TRUMAN, 3
An E. is never so natural JAMES, HENRY, 28
An E.'s home PROVERBS, 133
An E.'s way of speaking LERNER, ALAN JAY, 5
born an E. and remained one BEHAN, BRENDAN, 6
E. does not joke VERNE, JULES, 2
E. never enjoys himself HERBERT, A. P., 10
E. thinks he is moral SHAW, GEORGE BERNARD, 51
every E. is an island NOVALIS, 4
in spite of all temptations /...He remains an E. GILBERT, W. S., 9
Remember that you are an E. RHODES, CECIL, 1
the E. can't feel FORSTER, E. M., 5
The last great E. is low TENNYSON, ALFRED, 32

Englishmen E. must take business...seriously MARSHALL, ALFRED, 1
Mad dogs and E. COWARD, NOEL, 6
to see the absurd nature of E. PEPYS, SAMUEL, 1

English rose I'm not what you'd call...the typical E. CAMPBELL, NAOMI, 1

Englishwoman This E. is so refined SMITH, STEVIE, 2

enjoy Better to e. and suffer LEE, JENNIE, 1
e. being a highly overpaid actor MOORE, ROGER, 2
You never e. the world aright TRAHERNE, THOMAS, 1

enjoyment a capacity for e. HEMINGWAY, ERNEST, 4
E. is *not* a goal GOODMAN, PAUL, 4

enlarged condensed and e. in New York BELLOW, SAUL, 29

enmity The e. of the community WHITE, THEODORE H., 1
Walls of e. have fallen, borders...disappeared RABIN, YITZHAK, 2

ennui to produce e. in an Englishman HALSEY, MARGARET, 2

enough E. is as good as a feast HEYWOOD, JOHN, 5
E. is equal to a feast FIELDING, HENRY, 13
E. lives have been sacrificed LINCOLN, ABRAHAM, 32
It is e. YOUNG, BRIGHAM, 8
it is not e. /to be pause BRATHWAITE, EDWARD KAMAU, 1
Why, then, have we not e. JEFFERIES, RICHARD, 2

entered I should never have e. the church on that day CHARLEMAGNE, 2

enterprise If E. is afoot, Wealth accumulates KEYNES, JOHN MAYNARD, 19
Mrs Thatcher's emphasis on e. THATCHER, MARGARET, 3
Pushing a new e....bordering on monomania ANDERSON, KYE, 1
There's no resting place for an e. SLOAN, ALFRED P., JR., 4

enterprises Beware of...e. that require new clothes THOREAU, HENRY DAVID, 35
Speaking about commercial e....application of intellectual capital IMPARATO, NICHOLAS, 2

entertained have e. angels unawares BIBLE, 146
three unhappy women...e. within an inch of their lives SOMERVILLE, EDITH, 1

entertainers people think that e. see the world WONDER, STEVIE, 4

entertainment E....turns soft when times turn tough COHN, NIK, 1

enthusiasm Nothing is so contagious as e. LYTTON, BULWER, 5
When e. and commitment take root SIEGER, ROBIN, 2

enthusiasts so few e. can be trusted BALFOUR, ARTHUR, 2

entities E. should not be multiplied OCKHAM, WILLIAM OF, 1

entrances story of my life is about back e. and side doors GARBO, GRETA, 8

entrapment e. in sterile, bureaucratic corporate slots POSTE, GEORGE, 1

entrepreneurs E. should be able to spend IVERSON, KEN, 5

entrepreneurship E. will become a core skill BLAIR, TONY, 2

envied Better be e. PROVERBS, 163

envious An e. heart makes a treacherous ear HURSTON, ZORA NEALE, 13
e. of chess players MANDELSTAM, OSIP, 6

environment a standing-room-only e. UDALL, STEWART L., 4
create an e. that relaxes morality DILEONARDO, ROBERT, 1
grateful e. is a substitute for happiness SANTAYANA, GEORGE, 18
The e. can act on the subject SARTRE, JEAN-PAUL, 6
The e. is man's first right SARO-WIWA, KEN, 2
won't have a society...destroy the e. MEAD, MARGARET, 17

envision I can e. a small cottage somewhere VAN DE GEER, RICHARD, 1

envy e. is a kind of praise GAY, JOHN, 8
not through e. of thy happy lot KEATS, JOHN (1795–1821), 58
real genuine, hard-working e. EDEN, EMILY, 2

ephemeral all /The lessons are e. BARKER, GEORGE, 1
e. stuff—wives, kids, diapers, death BELLOW, SAUL, 25

epic e. disappeared along with...heroism RENAN, ERNEST, 2

epidemic living this e. every minute KRAMER, LARRY, 1

epidemics E....more influential than statesmen and soldiers DUBOS, RENÉ, 2

epigram What is an E. COLERIDGE, SAMUEL TAYLOR, 11

epileptics I have myself seen...e. and insane DIX, DOROTHEA, 1

Epipsychidion understand *E.* best when you are in love SHELLEY, PERCY BYSSHE, 4

epitaph Be my e. writ on my country's mind DAVIS, THOMAS, 3
Let no man write my e. EMMET, ROBERT, 1
my e..../*She Paid the Bills* SWANSON, GLORIA, 2

epoch a new e. in the history of the world GOETHE, JOHANN WOLFGANG VON, 34
Every e. bears its own ending FORCHÉ, CAROLYN, 1

Epsom salts Had we but stuck to E. FOLK VERSE, 31

Epstein If people...a thousand years hence...found E.'s statues EPSTEIN, JACOB, 1

equal All men are e. FORSTER, E. M., 13
all men are e. is a proposition HUXLEY, ALDOUS, 46
all were created e. by nature BALL, JOHN, 1
Everybody should have an e. chance WILSON, HAROLD, 3
E. wealth and opportunities of culture BELLAMY, EDWARD, 4

equality e. is an ethical aspiration PAZ, OCTAVIO, 1
E....is the thing PEAKE, MERVYN, 5
E. may perhaps be a right BALZAC, HONORÉ DE, 4
E. must yield BENTHAM, JEREMY, 5
e. of the white and black races LINCOLN, ABRAHAM, 28
e. pulls everyone down MURDOCH, IRIS, 5
E., this chimera of the peasantry BARBEY D'AUREVILLY, JULES-AMÉDÉE, 3
e....with our superiors BECQUE, HENRY, 1
Human e....contingent fact of history GOULD, STEPHEN JAY, 12
never be e. in the servants' hall BARRIE, J. M., 14
never will be...e. until women...make laws ANTHONY, SUSAN B., 5
pushes for e....is declared "PC" ALIBHAI-BROWN, YASMIN, 1

equalize I've always wanted to e. things KING, BILLIE JEAN, 1
equanimity an e. bordering on indifference GILBERT, W. S., 44
equipping e. us with a neck KOESTLER, ARTHUR, 3
eras When e. die...left to strange police DAY, CLARENCE SHEPARD, 6
erection Then we must rate the cost of the e. SHAKESPEARE, WILLIAM, 252
erections E.—not mentioned FLAUBERT, GUSTAVE, 6
Eros capitalist society has converted E. into an employee PAZ, OCTAVIO, 2
Unarm, E. SHAKESPEARE, WILLIAM, 81
erotic E. practices have been diversified BELLOW, SAUL, 16
erotica E. is about sexuality STEINEM, GLORIA, 5
eroticism E. has its own moral justification VARGAS LLOSA, MARIO, 6
erotics e. is a...respectable function of medicine AVICENNA, 1
err to e. in opinion...is at least human PLUTARCH, 17
To e. is human, not to, animal FROST, ROBERT, 7
To e. is human; to forgive, divine POPE, ALEXANDER, 14
error a political e. to practice deceit FREDERICK II (1712–86), 3
e....man's life takes place inside himself ORTEGA Y GASSET, JOSÉ, 16
show a man that he is in an e. LOCKE, JOHN, 5
errors e. do not count as failures in science GOULD, STEPHEN JAY, 5
e. in religion are dangerous HUME, DAVID, 12
E., like Straws, upon the surface DRYDEN, JOHN, 4
The E. of a Wise Man BLAKE, WILLIAM, 17
Esau E....a hairy man BIBLE, 129
Escort bit like an old, battered E. BOTHAM, IAN, 1
ESP the heading E....Error Some Place WALTON, SAM, 3
Esperance Now, E.! Percy! and set on SHAKESPEARE, WILLIAM, 242
esse Their *e.* is *percipi* BERKELEY, BISHOP, 2
essence Become the e., man ANGELUS SILESIUS, 3
establishment the e....united...always wrong MACMILLAN, HAROLD, 3
to refer to your friend's country e. as a "cottage" POTTER, STEPHEN, 1
estate stand so highly in our e. royal HENRY VIII, 10
estimate e. what we do...from instinct PIRANDELLO, LUIGI, 3
etcetera my sweet old e. CUMMINGS, E. E., 17
eternal But thy e. summer shall not fade SHAKESPEARE, WILLIAM, 566
e. couple of the criminal and...saint GENET, JEAN, 1
of e. importance, like baseball LEWIS, SINCLAIR, 2
real, true, e. love BULGAKOV, MIKHAIL, 7
The e.... makes for righteousness ARNOLD, MATTHEW, 22
We feel...we are e. SPINOZA, BARUCH, 4
eternally He who is e. without desire LAOZI, 5
eternity All things from e....come round in a circle MARCUS AURELIUS, 3
E.'s a terrible thought STOPPARD, TOM, 10
E. was in that moment CONGREVE, WILLIAM, 16
I saw E. the other night VAUGHAN, HENRY, 5
PRESENT,...part of e. dividing BIERCE, AMBROSE, 43
Tears of e., and sorrow HOUSMAN, A. E., 25
Who can speak of e. without a solecism BROWNE, THOMAS, 14
ethereal E. minstrel WORDSWORTH, WILLIAM, 79
ethic e. of personal responsibility gains appeal TICHY, NOEL M., 3
e. of progress...an anti-evolutionary ethic GOLDSMITH, EDWARD, 1
ethical e. behavior should be based...on sympathy EINSTEIN, ALBERT, 28
e. leadership...integration of corporate self-interest HICKMAN, CRAIG R., 6
E. standards, set by top management AGUILAR, FRANCIS J., 1
E. traps are more common now KOTTER, JOHN P., 4
I lost my e. compass MAGRUDER, JEB, 1
ethics E. and Science need to shake hands CABOT, RICHARD CLARKE, 1
Is this kind of e. individualistic BEAUVOIR, SIMONE DE, 6
The condition of all human e. TUCHOLSKY, KURT, 2
Ethiopians E. say that their gods XENOPHANES, 1
ethnic cleansing undergoing e. NEWSPAPERS, 27
Eton the playing fields of E. WELLINGTON, DUKE OF, 7
eugenics E....affects the success of the state CHEN MUHUA, 1
eureka E. ARCHIMEDES, 4
I have found it! E.! ARCHIMEDES, 2
It was a flash of e. SCHREIBER, STUART L., 1
Europe another war in E. BISMARCK, PRINCE OTTO VON, 8
any other E. than...Europe of states DE GAULLE, CHARLES, 4
countries of E....spurring one another on LIANG QICHAO, 1
countries of western E.... no longer... protect themselves ADENAUER, KONRAD, 2
E....a conglomeration of mistakes ENZENSBERGER, HANS, 2
E. had...art and America had...money BEHRMAN, S. N., 1
E. is a state of mind DELORS, JACQUES, 2
E. is not a boxing match DELORS, JACQUES, 5
E. is the unfinished negative MCCARTHY, MARY, 13
E. made the revolution...to conquer liberty SUN YAT-SEN, 2
E. needs tolerance...freedom of thought BRANDT, WILLY, 1
E. of the ancient parapets RIMBAUD, ARTHUR, 7
E....plunging into a Cold Peace YELTSIN, BORIS, 4
E. should not unite against something BRANDT, WILLY, 5
I always hear the word "E." BISMARCK, PRINCE OTTO VON, 5
In E. people have thought...about the war TUCHOLSKY, KURT, 6
I've come to think of E. DELILLO, DON, 3
lamps are going out over all E. GREY, EDWARD, 2
raided E. and brought white slaves over RUHLEN, MERRITT, 1
That E.'s nothin' on earth WILLIAMS, TENNESSEE, 9
United States of E. CHURCHILL, WINSTON, 37
We do not live alone in E. BISMARCK, PRINCE OTTO VON, 3
Western E....now only small countries LEFÈVRE, THÉO, 1
world is covered over with...E. ARMAH, AYI KWEI, 4
European A E. war must come MOLTKE, HELMUTH JOHANNES VON, 1
the realization of E. unification KOHL, HELMUT, 1
to shoot down a E. SARTRE, JEAN-PAUL, 34
Europeanism Their E....imperialism with an inferiority complex HEALEY, DENIS, 3
European tour The time to enjoy a E. ADE, GEORGE, 1
euthanasia E. is a long, smooth-sounding word BUCK, PEARL, 6
evading the first way of e. responsibility MANDELSTAM, NADEZHDA, 1
Evangeline E. wept bitter tears LONG, HUEY, 1
evaporates A man e. without an eye-witness SARTRE, JEAN-PAUL, 28
eve on the e. of a new era GRANT, ULYSSES S., 7
Eve Since E. ate apples BYRON, LORD, 80
When E. ate this particular apple LAWRENCE, D. H., 21
evening Here is the charming e., the criminal's friend BAUDELAIRE, CHARLES, 14
In the e., on the blue lagoon WEST, NATHANAEL, 8
It is a beauteous e., calm and free WORDSWORTH, WILLIAM, 42
Now came still e. on MILTON, JOHN, 57

evening star The e., /Love's harbinger MILTON, JOHN, 89
event greatest e....that ever happened FOX, CHARLES JAMES, 1
events all great e. and personalities...reappear HEGEL, G. W. F., 1
many e. in the womb of time SHAKESPEARE, WILLIAM, 473
ever e. shall be: world without end BOOK OF COMMON PRAYER, 15
Everest summit of E. was hardly the place HILLARY, EDMUND, 1
every E. man to count for one BERLIN, ISAIAH, 1
everybody 18 means that e. gets the girl DOUGLAS, MICHAEL, 1
E. has got to die SAROYAN, WILLIAM, 3
E. is an artist until he begins to learn LIYONG, TABAN LO, 4
E. is...in favour of general economy EDEN, ANTHONY, 4
E. is sleeping with everybody else JOEL, BILLY, 1
E. wants to do something to help BAILEY, PEARL, 2
E. was up to something COWARD, NOEL, 12
everyman E. has his own destiny MILLER, HENRY, 14
E., I will go with thee, and be thy guide EVERYMAN, 3
E.'s an Angel GINSBERG, ALLEN, 9
everyone E. dreams the thing he is CALDERÓN DE LA BARCA, PEDRO, 5
He wanted e. with him JOHNSON, LYNDON BAINES, 1
What concerns e. DÜRRENMATT, FRIEDRICH, 3
everything E. WEST, MAE, 28
E....endeavors to persist SPINOZA, BARUCH, 7
E. has been said LA BRUYÈRE, JEAN DE, 5
E. has been said already LEC, STANISLAW, 4
e. is a luxury...the world PAVESE, CESARE, 7
E. is funny ROGERS, WILL, 10
E. is only for a day MARCUS AURELIUS, 6
E. may happen SENECA, "THE YOUNGER," 8
E. must be like something FORSTER, E. M., 7
E. necessarily is or is not ARISTOTLE, 5
E. passes PROVERBS, 50
E. that has been will be IONESCO, EUGÈNE, 2
e. that lives is holy BLAKE, WILLIAM, 10
In e. there is...everything except Mind ANAXAGORAS, 1
Not e.'s for everyone CRUMB, R., 1
one gets used to e....learning process ENZENSBERGER, HANS, 4
We can't all do e. VIRGIL, 32
everywhere I am e. and of all times STRINDBERG, AUGUST, 4
evidence let them see and...smell the e. BELLI, MELVIN, 1
men...give e. against their own understanding HALIFAX, GEORGE SAVILE, 4
no e....no history HANDLIN, OSCAR, 2
Where e. takes a supernatural character GASKELL, ELIZABETH, 1
evil belief in a supernatural source of e. CONRAD, JOSEPH, 12
city reaped the e. fruit...bad man HESIOD, 1
E. be to him who evil thinks ANONYMOUS, 6
E. comes...like the disease; good...like the doctor CHESTERTON, G. K., 40
e. communications corrupt good manners BIBLE, 162
E. denotes the absence of Good AQUINAS, THOMAS, 11
e. for a man...despise his brother MUHAMMAD, 13
E. has encircled man from all sides MAHFOUZ, NAGUIB, 4
e. in theory...in practice excellent BURKE, EDMUND, 18
e. is nothing BOETHIUS, 4
e. is wrought by want of thought HOOD, THOMAS, 12
e. men and seducers BIBLE, 179
E. societies always kill their consciences FARMER, JAMES, 1
E. visited us yesterday TAYLOR, RON, 1
focus of e....an evil empire REAGAN, RONALD, 23
He who passively accepts e. KING, MARTIN LUTHER, JR., 19
how can ye, being e., speak good BIBLE, 400
Men never do e. so completely PASCAL, BLAISE, 8
oldest and best known e. was...more supportable MONTAIGNE, MICHEL DE, 25
recognition of some e....sum of human suffering BARTON, CLARA, 1
the eternal cycle of e. SOYINKA, WOLE, 12
the e. that may spring from good PIRANDELLO, LUIGI, 8
The e. that men do lives after them SHAKESPEARE, WILLIAM, 311
the e. work under the sun BIBLE, 49
The fearsome...banality of e. ARENDT, HANNAH, 9
The greatest e. is physical pain AUGUSTINE OF HIPPO, SAINT, 14
The purpose of e. was to survive it MORRISON, TONI, 21
These e. spirits accomplish some wondrous feats WEYER, JOHANN, 1
Touch for the E. according to costome EVELYN, JOHN, 5
whence then is e. HUME, DAVID, 27
evilly e. disposed people stir up strife SIMA QIAN, 1
evils Don't let us make imaginary e. GOLDSMITH, OLIVER, 21
e. are equal when they are extreme CORNEILLE, PIERRE, 3
least likely to meet these necessary e. JOYCE, JAMES, 34
men do not live only by fighting e. BERLIN, ISAIAH, 4
Of two e. I have chose the least PRIOR, MATTHEW, 13
There exist some e. so terrible LA BRUYÈRE, JEAN DE, 16
To great e. we submit HAZLITT, WILLIAM, 25
two e., the lesser is always to be chosen KEMPIS, THOMAS À, 9
Whenever I'm caught between two e. WEST, MAE, 10
evocative e. of her African heritage CAGE, JOHN, 10
evolution E....a matter of days well-lived HOAGLAND, EDWARD, 8
E....inference from thousands of independent sources GOULD, STEPHEN JAY, 4
The e. of the human race DARWIN, CHARLES GALTON, 1
The secrets of e....death and time SAGAN, CARL, 8
The tide of e. carries everything before it SANTAYANA, GEORGE, 5
evolutionary From an e. point...man has stopped TEILHARD DE CHARDIN, PIERRE, 1
exactitude E. is not truth MATISSE, HENRI, 4
exalted May you be e., O my God HUSAIN, 2
examinations E. are formidable COLTON, CHARLES, 1
examine E. the contents TALMUD, 2
One should e. oneself...before...condemning others MOLIÈRE, 15
example An e. is no proof PROVERBS, 496
excel To e. the past ORTEGA Y GASSET, JOSÉ, 14
excellence acute limited e. at twenty-one FITZGERALD, F. SCOTT, 16
excellent So e. a king SHAKESPEARE, WILLIAM, 145
exception The e. proves the rule PROVERBS, 401
excess Anything worth doing is worth doing to e. LAND, EDWIN HERBERT, 1
E. of wealth is cause of covetousness MARLOWE, CHRISTOPHER, 24
Nothing in e. ANONYMOUS, 83
Nothing in e. SOLON, 1
Nothing succeeds like e. WILDE, OSCAR, 20
excessive One man's definition of e. ASHCROFT, JOHN, 2
exchanged e....Washingtonian dignity for the Jeffersonian simplicity POTTER, HENRY CODMAN, 1
excited e. by the dance...graceful or not SELDES, GILBERT, 1

extermination camps e....turn man into a beast MALRAUX, ANDRÉ, 3
extinction threat of universal e. BALDWIN, JAMES, 23
extraordinary How e. ordinary /things are MCCAIG, NORMAN, 15
this is an e. man BURKE, EDMUND, 2
extras No e., no vacations, and diet unparalleled DICKENS, CHARLES, 56
extravagance e....thrift and adventure seldom go hand in hand CHURCHILL, JENNIE, 4
extraversion In e. and introversion GOETHE, JOHANN WOLFGANG VON, 2
extreme E. justice is extreme injury VOLTAIRE, 36
E. justice is extreme injustice CICERO, 7
E. remedies...for extreme diseases HIPPOCRATES, 1
leave one e....rush into the opposite REID, THOMAS, 3
extremes The two e. appear like man and wife CHURCHILL, CHARLES, 11
extremism e....defense of liberty is no vice GOLDWATER, BARRY, 3
extremists what is dangerous about e. is...they are intolerant KENNEDY, ROBERT, 5
exuberance E. is Beauty BLAKE, WILLIAM, 46
e. of his own verbosity GLADSTONE, WILLIAM EWART, 1
exult How you'd e. if I could put you back BROWNING, ROBERT, 51
exultantly Walk not on the earth e. KORAN, 20
eye all looks yellow to the jaundiced e. POPE, ALEXANDER, 23
an e. for an eye leaves everybody blind KING, MARTIN LUTHER, JR., 32
Beauty is in the e. PROVERBS, 155
e. for eye BIBLE, 81
e. hath not seen BIBLE, 152
He had but one e. DICKENS, CHARLES, 57
I have only one e. NELSON, HORATIO, 4
less in this than meets the e. BANKHEAD, TALLULAH, 7
My e....woke me AL-KHANSA, 1
neither e. to see, nor tongue to speak LENTHALL, WILLIAM, 1
the e....shall see me no more BIBLE, 257
the sort of e....open an oyster WODEHOUSE, P. G., 19
eyeless E. in Gaza MILTON, JOHN, 94
eyes bein' only e....my vision's limited DICKENS, CHARLES, 101
Dry your e. KEATS, JOHN (1795–1821), 90
e. of the world are upon you EISENHOWER, DWIGHT D., 31
e. were the brown gold of pebbles LEVERTOV, DENISE, 1
His e. flamed red with devilish passion STOKER, BRAM, 2
I close my e. and I see stars DILLARD, ANNIE, 2
I gave her e. my own eyes to take BROWNING, ROBERT, 41
I was e. to the blind BIBLE, 264
keep my e. clear and hit 'em KEELER, WILLIAM, 1
Look not in my e. HOUSMAN, A. E., 6
Mine e. have seen the glory HOWE, JULIA WARD, 1
Open your e. and look within MARLEY, BOB, 3
Our e. are sentinels unto our judgments MIDDLETON, THOMAS, 4
People who shut their e. to reality BALDWIN, JAMES, 18
still e. in the white face H. D., 1
The e. and the hand of Picasso PICASSO, PABLO, 1
The e. are the windows PROVERBS, 402
The e. of all people are upon us WINTHROP, JOHN, 1
The e. of a lover tell lies ABRAHAMS, PETER, 1
the e. of the blind shall be opened BIBLE, 211
voice of your e....deeper than all roses CUMMINGS, E. E., 4
Your e. shine like the pants MARX, GROUCHO, 29
Ezra pretends to be E. ELIOT, T. S., 5
Fabians A good man fallen among F. SHAW, GEORGE BERNARD, 9
fable The f. is the best storytelling device DISNEY, WALT, 2
fables Man is fed with f. through life JEFFERSON, THOMAS, 28
fabulous How f., in a bathtub, in Paris REED, LOU, 8
fabulously man believes himself f. capable of creation ORTEGA Y GASSET, JOSÉ, 30
face A good f. PROVERBS, 111
a gross and repulsive f. TROLLOPE, ANTHONY, 1
At 50...the f. he deserves ORWELL, GEORGE, 2
f. looks like a wedding cake AUDEN, W. H., 54
from whose f. the earth and the heaven fled BIBLE, 475
her f. in speech...a lighted window JAMES, HENRY, 37
I have looked upon the f. of Agamemnon SCHLIEMANN, HEINRICH, 1
Look in my f.; my name is Might-have-been ROSSETTI, DANTE GABRIEL, 6
My f. and rump were famous BAKER, JOSEPHINE, 3
My f. is my fortune, sir, she said CHILDREN'S VERSE, 4
The f. distorted in a jungle pool LEWIS, ALUN, 1
The f. of "evil"...face of...need BURROUGHS, WILLIAM S., 10
the f. that launch'd a thousand ships MARLOWE, CHRISTOPHER, 8
The loveliest f....will not please BEERBOHM, MAX, 15
The more serious the f. CHATEAUBRIAND, RENÉ, 8
Who has seen the f. of the God MACHADO, ANTONIO, 2
faces cover their f. or burst into laughter KNIGHT, FRANK HYNEMAN, 1
proud, seamed f....mercy and murder hinting BROOKS, GWENDOLYN, 6
the old familiar f. LAMB, CHARLES, 9
they have the f. of angels BEDE, 2
fact A f. is like a sack PIRANDELLO, LUIGI, 6
a physical f. denotes a state of consciousness SCHNABEL, JULIAN, 1
factory In the f. we make cosmetics REVSON, CHARLES, 1
facts begin from a good body of f....not...a principle DARWIN, CHARLES, 3
All we want is the f. DRAGNET, 1
But f. are facts and flinch not BROWNING, ROBERT, 71
F. alone are wanted in life DICKENS, CHARLES, 38
F. are not science FISCHER, MARTIN H., 6
F. are piffle CARR, JOHN DICKSON, 1
F. are ventriloquists' dummies HUXLEY, ALDOUS, 54
F. do not cease to exist HUXLEY, ALDOUS, 45
F. do not make history BANKS, RUSSELL, 1
F. influence SHEA, MICHAEL, 1
f. must never get in the way of truth CAMERON, JAMES, 1
F. speak louder than statistics STREATFIELD, GEOFFREY, 1
F. to be dealt with, as the sea OLSON, CHARLES, 6
get twelve people to listen to all the f. SIMPSON, O. J., 3
People who mistake f. for ideas...gossips OZICK, CYNTHIA, 6
The f. are to blame, my friend PIRANDELLO, LUIGI, 19
The f. at hand...speak for themselves SALINGER, J. D., 10
treat your f. with imagination BURROUGHS, JOHN, 1
fading How f. are the joys NORRIS, JOHN, 1
fail I f....less than everyone else NICKLAUS, JACK, 7
I would sooner f. than not be among the greatest KEATS, JOHN (1795–1821), 47
The LA Skytrain can't possibly f. LAKER, FREDDIE, 1
to f. conventionally KEYNES, JOHN MAYNARD, 11
failing f....greatest arts in the world KETTERING, CHARLES, 2
F. is good EISNER, MICHAEL, 2

worse than any loss of limb...f. mind JUVENAL, 14
failings even his f. leaned to virtue's side GOLDSMITH, OLIVER, 17
man's greatest f....excuse in the misfortune RETZ, CARDINAL DE, 5
fails If thy heart f....climb not ELIZABETH I, 23
failure F. and success have no fixed abodes TAO QIAN, 2
F. is inevitable SPIELBERG, STEVEN, 2
F. is success's only launching pad PETERS, TOM, 8
F....not our only punishment for laziness RENARD, JULES, 5
f....only thing that worked predictably HELLER, JOSEPH, 14
greatest f. for any man is to fail with a woman HIMES, CHESTER, 3
spent the rest of the century looking on itself as a dismal f. BRYSON, BILL, 4
The triumph of f. RYAN, DESMOND, 1
utterly unspoiled by f. CHURCHILL, RANDOLPH (1911–68), 1
failures f....an explosion of virulent cells PROULX, E. ANNIE, 3
f....arise from pulling in one's horse HARE, JULIUS, 1
f. married white women EMECHETA, BUCHI, 5
We don't publicize our f. IVERSON, KEN, 3
fainted He f. on his vengefulness MEREDITH, GEORGE, 4
fair All is f. in love and war PROVERBS, 121
all's f. in love and war FORREST, NATHAN BEDFORD, 2
F. be their wives DUNBAR, WILLIAM, 2
F. stood the wind for France DRAYTON, MICHAEL, 6
She f., divinely fair MILTON, JOHN, 84
so excellently f. COLERIDGE, SAMUEL TAYLOR, 10
Too f. to worship MILMAN, HENRY HART, 2
were she pitiful as she is f. GREENE, ROBERT, 1
Who'd see the F. JONSON, BEN, 5
fair deal a right to expect...a f. TRUMAN, HARRY S., 6
fairer thou art f. than the evening's air MARLOWE, CHRISTOPHER, 7
fairest f. of creation MILTON, JOHN, 87
The f. things have fleetest end THOMPSON, FRANCIS, 3
the f. things have the worst fate MALHERBE, FRANÇOIS DE, 2
fairies rewards and F. CORBETT, RICHARD, 1
There are f. at the bottom of our garden FYLEMAN, ROSE, 1
fairy tales F....temporary and permanent solutions BETTELHEIM, BRUNO, 2
faith Being justified by f., we have peace with God BIBLE, 480
But F., fanatic Faith MOORE, THOMAS, 2
by f. the walls of Jericho fell down BIBLE, 145
F....a charisma not granted to all JUNG, CARL GUSTAV, 6
F....an illogical belief MENCKEN, H. L., 38
F....believing...beyond the power of reason VOLTAIRE, 38
F. is necessary to victory HAZLITT, WILLIAM, 2
f. is the substance of things hoped for BIBLE, 144
F. will move mountains PROVERBS, 211
f. will soon return ALEMBERT, JEAN LE ROND D', 3
Have f. in the Yankees HEMINGWAY, ERNEST, 17
If ye have f. as a grain of mustard seed BIBLE, 409
In this f. I wish to live and die VILLON, FRANÇOIS, 4
no need for any other f. than...in human beings BUCK, PEARL, 5
Nothing in life is more wonderful than f. OSLER, WILLIAM, 13
short sight to limit our f. in laws EMERSON, RALPH WALDO, 60
There can be no scientific dispute with respect to f. VIRCHOW, RUDOLF, 1
there is a component of f. to science NATIONAL ACADEMY OF SCIENCES, 1
thy f. hath saved thee BIBLE, 332
To believe only possibilities, is not f. BROWNE, THOMAS, 22
we walk by f., not by sight BIBLE, 164
Without f. nothing is possible BETHUNE, MARY MCLEOD, 2
faithful f. in love...dauntless in war SCOTT, SIR WALTER, 10
if you had been f. RACINE, JEAN, 3
man is not f. to his God THEODORIC, 1
we must be f....to our country ANONYMOUS, 54
faithfully All these things shall I keep f. HENRY III, 2
faithless F. is he that says farewell TOLKIEN, J. R. R., 5
fake fur Real people wear f. ADVERTISEMENTS, 19
falcon Soaring f., noble Poet, come to my aid GOYTISOLO, JUAN, 1
Falklands F....a fight between two bald men BORGES, JORGE LUIS, 6
fall If I f. take my place ARAFAT, YASIR, 2
I f. upon the thorns of life SHELLEY, PERCY BYSSHE, 7
Whenever you f., pick up something AVERY, OSWALD THEODORE, 1
fallacy a falseness in all our impressions...the "Pathetic F." RUSKIN, JOHN, 5
great f. is that the game is... about winning BLANCHFLOWER, DANNY, 1
falling I have a feeling I'm f. FERLINGHETTI, LAWRENCE, 3
We were f. women ATWOOD, MARGARET, 1
falls Where he f. short, 'tis Nature's fault alone CHURCHILL, CHARLES, 12
false beware of f. prophets BIBLE, 386
F. face must hide what the false heart SHAKESPEARE, WILLIAM, 391
f. to his friends...true to the public BERKELEY, BISHOP, 4
In a f. quarrel there is no true valour SHAKESPEARE, WILLIAM, 460
falsehood Let her and F. grapple MILTON, JOHN, 12
One f. spoils a thousand truths PROVERBS, 2
unmask f., and bring truth to light SHAKESPEARE, WILLIAM, 634
falsehoods Avoid f. like the plague MORELLI, GIOVANNI, 1
false teeth f....hurling them at his wife DOYLE, ARTHUR CONAN, 5
falsifying f....my life made me feel phoney STEINEM, GLORIA, 4
Falstaff F....lards the lean earth SHAKESPEARE, WILLIAM, 235
fame F. and tranquility can never be bedfellows MONTAIGNE, MICHEL DE, 9
F. creates its own standard DAVIS, SAMMY, JR., 2
F. is a food DOBSON, AUSTIN, 1
F. is a powerful aphrodisiac GREENE, GRAHAM, 3
F. is no good ANDERSON, SHERWOOD, 6
F. is sometimes like unto a...mushroom FULLER, THOMAS (1608–61), 4
F. is the spur MILTON, JOHN, 123
F., like water, bears up the lighter things CALDERÓN DE LA BARCA, PEDRO, 9
I handle f. by not being famous MARLEY, BOB, 9
I owe my f. only to myself CORNEILLE, PIERRE, 11
Love of f. is the last thing TACITUS, 4
One of the drawbacks of F. MELBA, NELLIE, 2
one whom f. has not corrupted CURIE, MARIE, 1
What is f. GRAINGER, JAMES, 1
What is the end of f. BYRON, LORD, 46
You never feel you have f. HEPBURN, KATHARINE, 3
familiarity F. breeds contempt PROVERBS, 212
F. breeds contempt—and children TWAIN, MARK, 25
f....has bred contempt CERVANTES, MIGUEL DE, 8
I like f. STEIN, GERTRUDE, 12
families All happy f. resemble one another TOLSTOY, LEO, 2
Be true to your f., loyal to them MCKAY, DAVID O., 1

F. ain't just born HUNT, MARSHA, 1
F. aren't dying BOMBECK, ERMA, 2
Good f. are generally worse HOPE, ANTHONY, 8
There are only two f. in the world CERVANTES, MIGUEL DE, 35
family A f. with the wrong members in control ORWELL, GEORGE, 31
Ambivalence about f. responsibilities KANTER, ROSABETH MOSS, 1
as if they took the f. to the laundry IRVING, JOHN, 1
f....a kind of hothouse of obligations KEENAN, BRIAN, 2
f. always creeps back MEAD, MARGARET, 15
F. is a mixed blessing PRYOR, RICHARD, 2
f....most ridiculous and least respectable BETTI, UGO, 12
I am the f. face HARDY, THOMAS, 18
if a f. is held together...it's the woman DOYLE, RODDY, 2
my f. begins with me IPHICRATES, 1
preservation of f. and community values CLINTON, HILLARY, 1
The f. is strongest where objective reality DELILLO, DON, 9
the f....source of all our discontents LEACH, EDMUND, 1
The f., that...octopus...we never quite escape SMITH, DODIE, 1
The f. that prays together PROVERBS, 403
There's a wonderful f. called Stein LIMERICKS, 7
family tree It is hazardous to shake a f. TOLSON, MELVIN, 2
famine f. was sore in the land BIBLE, 137
They...die by f. die by inches HENRY, MATTHEW, 4
you look as if there were f. in the land SHAW, GEORGE BERNARD, 113
famous awoke one morning...found myself f. BYRON, LORD, 90
everyone will be f. for 15 minutes WARHOL, ANDY, 3
f. men have the whole earth PERICLES, 2
F. remarks are seldom quoted correctly STRUNSKY, SIMEON, 1
I don't care if I'm...f. ZAPPA, FRANK, 1
I'll make thee f. by my pen SCOTT, SIR WALTER, 28
I'm never going to be f. PARKER, DOROTHY, 17
In fifteen minutes everybody will be f. WARHOL, ANDY, 4
so f., that it would permit me...to break wind BALZAC, HONORÉ DE, 12
To f. men all the earth...sepulcher THUCYDIDES, 4
What are you f. *for* MURDOCH, IRIS, 8
Why am I so f. STREISAND, BARBRA, 2
fanatic f....does what he thinks DUNNE, FINLEY PETER, 4
f....over-compensates a secret doubt HUXLEY, ALDOUS, 37
fanatical F. enthusiasm...mark of the real man THUCYDIDES, 3
fanaticism They charge me with f. WILBERFORCE, WILLIAM, 1
fanatics F. have their dreams KEATS, JOHN (1795–1821), 89
fancy Ever let the f. roam KEATS, JOHN (1795–1821), 11
F. is...a mode of memory COLERIDGE, SAMUEL TAYLOR, 28
fan-mail F. from foreign countries BERRYMAN, JOHN, 7
fantasies A thousand f....throng into my memory MILTON, JOHN, 18
fantasy A f. can be equivalent JIMÉNEZ, JUAN RAMÓN, 15
a solitary f. can totally transform ANGELOU, MAYA, 10
live in a f. world MURDOCH, IRIS, 13
far As f. as we can see WILKINS, JAMES, 1
F. off his coming shone MILTON, JOHN, 72
F. off thou art, but ever nigh TENNYSON, ALFRED, 24
Faraday remain plain Michael F. to the last FARADAY, MICHAEL, 2
farce But not as hard as f. GWENN, EDMUND, 1
F. is the essential theatre CRAIG, EDWARD GORDON, 1
f. or a comedy is best played LINCOLN, ABRAHAM, 23
There is no greater f. than...democracy BOURASSA, HENRI, 2
You just can't have a leisurely f. SIMON, NEIL, 15
farewell F., a long farewell, to all my greatness SHAKESPEARE, WILLIAM, 283
F. and adieu to you, Ladies of Spain FOLK VERSE, 14
F. my Piers, my lovely Gaveston DRAYTON, MICHAEL, 1
F., my poor hands RACHMANINOV, SERGEI VASILYEVICH, 3
F.! thou art too dear for my possessing SHAKESPEARE, WILLIAM, 578
F. to Lochaber RAMSAY, ALLAN, 1
F. to the Highlands BURNS, ROBERT, 27
farewells f. should be sudden BYRON, LORD, 92
farmer good f. is ... a handy man WHITE, E. B., 8
This is the f. sowing his corn CHILDREN'S VERSE, 34
farmers f., flourish and complain CRABBE, GEORGE, 6
farms take from f. and give to arms REAGAN, RONALD, 4
farthest down the "man f." LOCKE, ALAIN LE ROY, 1
farthing burning a f. candle at Dover SHERIDAN, RICHARD BRINSLEY, 3
farts Without f., there are no flowers JONG, ERICA, 8
fascism F. is a religion HITLER, ADOLF, 7
F. is not an article for export MUSSOLINI, BENITO, 2
F. is...the future refusing to be born BEVAN, ANEURIN, 12
F. is the open, terrorist dictatorship ANONYMOUS, 37
f....means to re-establish national equilibrium MUSSOLINI, BENITO, 12
For F. the State is absolute MUSSOLINI, BENITO, 7
F. recognizes women...life force of the country CASTELLANI, MARIA, 1
F. was a fairly popular political philosophy VONNEGUT, KURT, 2
If f. has been a criminal association MUSSOLINI, BENITO, 6
fascists f. and social democrats...national economic autonomy JOHNSON, RICHARD W., 6
fashion a dedicated follower of f. DAVIES, RAY, 1
Every man after his f. PROVERBS, 202
F.—a word which knaves and fools may use CHURCHILL, CHARLES, 13
f....creating authority through provocation GLASER, MILTON, 1
f. designers...sell a lifestyle DE LA RENTA, OSCAR, 1
F....image of an age LAGERFELD, KARL, 1
F. is about profit and expansion SMITH, PAUL, 2
F. is a high-risk investment MELTZER, JAY, 1
F....is a language MCGRATH, CHARLES, 1
F. is architecture CHANEL, COCO, 6
f. is born by small facts SCHIAPARELLI, ELSA, 4
F. is made to become unfashionable CHANEL, COCO, 1
F.'s job...combat the tedium of routine DONOVAN, CARRIE, 1
F....sub-art and...not intellectual FAIRCHILD, JOHN B., 1
f. was...brutal, nostalgic and sometimes vulgar ARMANI, GIORGIO, 2
f....wear what suits you POIRET, PAUL, 2
I pay no attention to f. FARHI, NICOLE, 1
love of f. makes the economy go TILBERIS, LIZ, 1
Modern f. is about freedom, democracy...individualism ARMANI, GIORGIO, 3
One cannot f. a credible deterrent MCNAMARA, ROBERT, 3
only reason I ever did f....girls BAILEY, DAVID, 1
she has groped her way from the f. nadir THATCHER, MARGARET, 11
Stop the f. system MOSCHINO, FRANCO, 2
fashionable an idea...to be f. is ominous SANTAYANA, GEORGE, 20
fashion-mad I saw a lot of f. people GREER, GERMAINE, 1
fashions Every man f. and stays with the gods MPHAHLELE, ES'KIA, 1
F.,...are only induced epidemics SHAW, GEORGE BERNARD, 89
F. in sin change HELLMAN, LILLIAN, 4
faster F. than a speeding bullet SIEGEL, JERRY, 1

f. you go, the worse it is ASIMOV, ISAAC, 3
Will you walk a little f.? CARROLL, LEWIS, 19
fasting F. is a medicine CHRYSOSTOM, SAINT JOHN, 1
fat f. content of an avocado YOUNG, MARY EVANS, 1
F., fair and forty O'KEEFFE, JOHN, 1
F., fair, and forty SCOTT, SIR WALTER, 19
f. is sexy BRAND, JO, 1
Jack Sprat could eat no f. CHILDREN'S VERSE, 35
Let me have men about me that are f. SHAKESPEARE, WILLIAM, 295
Outside every f. man...an even fatter man AMIS, KINGSLEY, 4
the f. of the land BIBLE, 138
till the f. lady sings COOK, DANIEL JOHN, 1
fatal f. question...the meaning of their lives JUNG, CARL GUSTAV, 21
fate f. and character are the same conception HARDENBERG, FRIEDRICH LEOPOLD VON, 1
F. cannot harm me, I have dined to-day SMITH, SYDNEY, 19
F. chooses your relations DELILLE, JACQUES, 1
F. has not been kind to Mrs. Browning WOOLF, VIRGINIA, 19
Fixed f., free will, foreknowledge absolute MILTON, JOHN, 49
F. sits on these dark battlements RADCLIFFE, ANN, 2
He either fears his f. too much MONTROSE, JAMES GRAHAM, 2
I have a bone to pick with F. NASH, OGDEN, 12
It is F. that draws the plan SHAKESPEARE, WILLIAM, 19
it is...our f....to lose innocence BOWEN, ELIZABETH, 8
The f. of a nation was riding that night LONGFELLOW, HENRY WADSWORTH, 7
We may become the makers of our f. POPPER, KARL, 6
when F. summons, Monarchs must obey DRYDEN, JOHN, 31
fated We have been f. to live together RABIN, YITZHAK, 4
father As my poor f. used to say HERBERT, A. P., 3
a wise f. that knows his own child SHAKESPEARE, WILLIAM, 602
easier for a f. to have children JOHN XXIII, 3
F., all things are possible unto thee BIBLE, 363
F....come home with me now WORK, HENRY CLAY, 1
f., Harry, to that thought SHAKESPEARE, WILLIAM, 261
F. is rather vulgar, my dear DICKENS, CHARLES, 44
Full fathom five thy f. lies SHAKESPEARE, WILLIAM, 642
f. whose son raises...hand against him PÉGUY, CHARLES PIERRE, 11
How many a f. have I seen HALLAM, ARTHUR HENRY, 7
in my F.'s house are many mansions BIBLE, 290
In serving your f. and mother CONFUCIUS, 35
I wish either my f. or...mother STERNE, LAURENCE, 10
Like f., like son PROVERBS, 307
My f. didn't create you to arrest me PEEL, ARTHUR WELLESLEY, 1
My f. has no older son FOLK VERSE, 17
my f. moved through dooms of love CUMMINGS, E. E., 9
My f. was an immigrant from Austria WEIDMAN, JEROME, 3
My f. was a slave ROBESON, PAUL, 1
No man is responsible for his f. TURNBULL, MARGARET, 1
Our F....in heaven /Stay there PRÉVERT, JACQUES, 2
Our F....Stop thinking about us PARRA, NICANOR, 1
father figures constantly searching for f. WALKER, ALICE, 11
fatherland One F., One State, One Leader FRANCO, FRANCISCO, 6
the filth of my f. HEINE, HEINRICH, 3
fathers f. in Western civilization...military origin WAKOSKI, DIANE, 1
f., provoke not your children BIBLE, 26
Our f. were Englishmen BRADFORD, WILLIAM, 7
we could become the f. of nations LONDON, JACK, 16
Father William You are old, F. SOUTHEY, ROBERT, 5
fatiguing Total commitment...possible, but f. FOX, MURIEL, 1
Faulkner F.'s hallucinatory tendencies...not unworthy of Shakespeare FAULKNER, WILLIAM, 1
fault Condemn the f. and not the actor SHAKESPEARE, WILLIAM, 427
f. confessed is half redressed PROVERBS, 10
never commit a f. PLUTARCH, 25
only f. is that he has no fault PLINY THE YOUNGER, 7
faultless F. to a fault BROWNING, ROBERT, 73
Whoever thinks a f. piece to see POPE, ALEXANDER, 12
faults by pointing out...the f. of his mistress PROUST, MARCEL, 8
If we had no f. of our own LA ROCHEFOUCAULD, FRANÇOIS, 8
When you have f. CONFUCIUS, 29
favela the *f.* is the back yard DE JESÚS, CAROLINA MARIA, 2
favor those who f. fire FROST, ROBERT, 10
favorite These are a few of my f. things HAMMERSTEIN, OSCAR, II, 17
favour every man...enjoying his special f. HENRY VIII, 4
favoured thou that art highly f. BIBLE, 318
fav'rite A f. has no friend GRAY, THOMAS, 15
FBI the F....a church for the mediocre MAILER, NORMAN, 21
fear f. and deny the reality of death KÜBLER-ROSS, ELISABETH, 2
f. clawed at my mind and body FRANK, ANNE, 7
f. God, and keep his commandments BIBLE, 60
F. has many eyes CERVANTES, MIGUEL DE, 21
f. in a handful of dust ELIOT, T. S., 48
f. in passing judgment BRUNO, GIORDANO, 1
F. is an important feeling SENNA, AYRTON, 3
F. is of being in the world SARTRE, JEAN-PAUL, 4
F. is the parent of cruelty FROUDE, J. A., 4
F. is very exciting MORRISON, JIM, 4
F. lent wings to his feet VIRGIL, 20
F. no more the heat o' the sun SHAKESPEARE, WILLIAM, 134
F. of death PROVERBS, 213
f. of one evil leads us into a worse BOILEAU, NICOLAS, 4
F. prophets...and those prepared to die ECO, UMBERTO, 11
F. tastes like a rusty knife CHEEVER, JOHN, 2
f. weakens judgment most RETZ, CARDINAL DE, 4
I f. God...and I have no other fear RACINE, JEAN, 4
I learned not f. infinity ROETHKE, THEODORE, 6
In Place of F. BEVAN, ANEURIN, 6
It was the f. of himself ACHEBE, CHINUA, 8
methods of f....produces a subservient subject EINSTEIN, ALBERT, 22
only thing we have to f. is fear itself ROOSEVELT, FRANKLIN D., 23
raised to f. the *yes* within ourselves, our deepest cravings LORDE, AUDRE, 3
the f. of being ourselves PORCHIA, ANTONIO, 1
those who f. are always in the majority HEAD, BESSIE, 7
Three years...spent between f. and hope MAHFOUZ, NAGUIB, 2
feared It is better to be f. than loved MACHIAVELLI, NICCOLÒ, 7
neither f. nor flattered KNOX, JOHN, 1
fearful Nothing gives a f. man more courage ECO, UMBERTO, 8
fears A man who f. suffering MONTAIGNE, MICHEL DE, 19
f. that I may cease to be KEATS, JOHN (1795–1821), 79
feast f. for years on shots from this picture KAUFFMANN, STANLEY, 1
feasting It was like f. with panthers WILDE, OSCAR, 10
feather a f. for each wind SHAKESPEARE, WILLIAM, 659
feathers Fine f. PROVERBS, 216

not only fine f....make fine birds AESOP, 5
February F., fill the dyke TUSSER, THOMAS, 2
fed I have f. purely upon ale FARQUHAR, GEORGE, 4
feed Feed yourself...f. others MOREAU, JEANNE, 3
F. the World GELDOF, BOB, 1
he shall f. his flock BIBLE, 214
You cannot f. the hungry on statistics LLOYD-GEORGE, DAVID, 2
feedeth he f. among the lilies BIBLE, 494
feel he can f. that he is dying SUETONIUS, 2
how you really f. about someone SCHOPENHAUER, ARTHUR, 10
I f. like a baseball team ROOSEVELT, FRANKLIN D., 33
feeling a f. akin to disappointment TOLSTOY, LEO, 5
A man gets tired of f. too much SOYINKA, WOLE, 11
F. is the subjective side of consciousness DEWEY, JOHN, 9
personal f. is the main thing MODERSOHN-BECKER, PAULA, 1
feelings First f. are always the most natural LOUIS XIV, 8
f. time cannot benumb BYRON, LORD, 33
feet Alan will always land on somebody's f. PARKER, DOROTHY, 44
don't use both f. PROVERBS, 44
her f. are as precise as pens BUCKLE, RICHARD, 1
her f. be pared down to ethereal points PAVLOVA, ANNA, 1
Her f....Like little mice stole in SUCKLING, JOHN, 1
Her pretty f., like snails, did creep HERRICK, ROBERT, 15
my f....little time on the ground OWENS, JESSE, 1
My f., so deep in the earth JIMÉNEZ, JUAN RAMÓN, 4
those f. in ancient time BLAKE, WILLIAM, 18
feign I f. no hypotheses NEWTON, ISAAC, 7
felicity f. consists not in the outward and visible PLUTARCH, 15
fell f. among thieves BIBLE, 335
f. *dead-born from the press* HUME, DAVID, 29
Fellini I can understand F. KIESLOWSKI, KRZYSZTOF, 2
fellow if a f. really likes potatoes MILNE, A. A., 3
fellowship such a f. of good knights MALORY, THOMAS, 5
felt I f....there must be something for me DIX, DOROTHEA, 2
female a f. goes over the boundary from childhood DOLSON, HILDEGARDE, 1
F. artists are no longer accepting tokenization MCDONNELL, EVELYN, 1
image of the f....all boobs and buttocks GREER, GERMAINE, 7
movement which passes by the f....ephemeral CRUMMELL, ALEXANDER, 1
not one f. comic who was beautiful RIVERS, JOAN, 1
our f. friends WELDON, FAY, 1
Our great poet-teacher, has given us 126...f. characters SHAKESPEARE, WILLIAM, 8
see the F. Eunuch the world over GREER, GERMAINE, 8
Some...have called me quite a f. Ulysses SEACOLE, MARY, 2
the f. of the species is more deadly than the male KIPLING, RUDYARD, 13
The fundamental fault of the f. character SCHOPENHAUER, ARTHUR, 5
The seldom f. PITTER, RUTH, 1
What f. heart can gold despise GRAY, THOMAS, 14
females F. get hired along procreative lines FISHER, CARRIE, 3
Why should human f. become sterile HUXLEY, ALDOUS, 6
feminine f. traits: incapacity to destroy NIN, ANAÏS, 1
I know I'm f., damnably feminine AUSTIN, MARY, 5
femininity where in the world did I put my f. GIROUD, FRANÇOISE, 2
feminism F. is an entire world view BUNCH, CHARLOTTE, 1
violent backlash against f. WOLF, NAOMI, 4
feminist f. change is both irresistible and irreversible NORTON, ELEANOR HOLMES, 1
f. movement will...rise from...Arab lands SAADAWI, NAWAL EL-, 1
I am a f. JORDAN, JUNE, 2
I'm not a f. MITCHELL, JONI, 7
the best home for a f. WATSON, JAMES DEWEY, 2
The f. of the *fin de siècle* PAGLIA, CAMILLE, 9
feminists f....dug themselves into their own grave DOUGLAS, MICHAEL, 2
feminization the f. of the white European and American is already far advanced LEWIS, WYNDHAM, 2
feminized She f. corporate attire KARAN, DONNA, 1
fences Good f. make good neighbors PROVERBS, 238
fertility The management of f. GREER, GERMAINE, 4
fervor F. is the weapon of choice of the impotent FANON, FRANTZ, 2
festivals All f. are bunk BEECHAM, THOMAS, 7
fetish Do not make a f. of truffles ANONYMOUS, 49
fetus A f. is a benign tumor PAGLIA, CAMILLE, 10
fever f. called "living" /Is conquered at last POE, EDGAR ALLAN, 11
"The f....has just left me." PLUTARCH, 30
few we happy f., we band of brothers SHAKESPEARE, WILLIAM, 275
fiber Every f. of me is thrilling LONDON, JACK, 12
fiction f. is made of that which is real ELLISON, RALPH, 6
f. which...put out boundaries WOOLF, VIRGINIA, 1
no longer any such thing as f. DOCTOROW, E. L., 4
She regarded me as a piece of f. WEST, REBECCA, 1
fidelity Your idea of f. is not having more than one man in the bed RAPHAEL, FREDERIC, 1
field What though the f. be lost MILTON, JOHN, 27
fiend forgive the f. for becoming a torrent NAPOLEON I, 8
fier You k'n hide de f. HARRIS, JOEL CHANDLER, 5
fierce I rav'd and grew more f. and wild HERBERT, GEORGE, 18
fifteen At f. I set my heart on learning CONFUCIUS, 31
F. men on the dead man's chest STEVENSON, ROBERT LOUIS, 18
fifth One f. of the people are against everything KENNEDY, ROBERT, 4
fifth column The F. MOLA, EMILIO, 2
fifty You'll see, when you're f. SATIE, ERIK, 1
fifty-fifty There can be no f. Americanism ROOSEVELT, THEODORE, 24
fifty-four F. forty or fight ALLEN, WILLIAM, 1
fig A f. for those by law protected BURNS, ROBERT, 39
fight do not f. with the world BUDDHA, 2
don't want to f., but, by jingo HUNT, GEORGE WILLIAM, 1
easier to f. for one's principles ADLER, ALFRED, 7
f. all my life to survive COBB, TY, 2
F. fire with fire PROVERBS, 214
f. in your own cause...committed to winning MORGAN, ROBIN, 1
f. it out on this line GRANT, ULYSSES S., 3
f. like hell for the living JONES, MOTHER, 1
f. the good fight BIBLE, 240
F. the good fight with all thy might MONSELL, JOHN, 1
f....to record what you want HOLIDAY, BILLIE, 4
f. to save wild beauty...democracy TEALE, EDWIN WAY, 2
If we must f. ERASMUS, DESIDERIUS, 3
If you f. against all your sensations EPICURUS, 3
I have not yet begun to f. JONES, JOHN PAUL, 1
Never f. fair with a stranger MILLER, ARTHUR, 8

Our business in the field of f....to prove our might POPE, ALEXANDER, 79
The only time...ever put up a f. CLEMENCEAU, GEORGES, 9
There'll be a hard f. tomorrow SAKHAROV, ANDREI, 1
We f....to set a country free PAINE, THOMAS, 8
we shall f. on the beaches CHURCHILL, WINSTON, 29
fighting f. in the street JAGGER, MICK, 3
F. is like champagne MITCHELL, MARGARET, 5
not fifty ways of f....only one MALRAUX, ANDRÉ, 8
What are we f. for SERVICE, ROBERT W., 2
You know I hate f. ALI, MUHAMMAD, 4
fights He that f. and runs away FOLK VERSE, 39
he who f. and runs away GOLDSMITH, OLIVER, 13
not the f. but the fights to get those fights JOHNSON, JACK, 1
figure f. that out BUSH, GEORGE, 10
in did come the strangest f. BROWNING, ROBERT, 21
figures don't have to be good with f. DIDDLEY, BO, 1
file my f....lost...means my disappearance MOU SEN, 2
Filipinos educate the F....and Christianize them MCKINLEY, WILLIAM, 2
filling F. her compact & delicious body BERRYMAN, JOHN, 8
film A f....begins with something very vague BERGMAN, INGMAR, 2
F. dancing will always be a problem KELLY, GENE, 2
F....dust and heat and noise MCEWAN, IAN, 2
f. is made under the commercial umbrella PARKER, ALAN, 1
F. people find it difficult to *place* me GIELGUD, JOHN, 2
f....petrified fountain of thought COCTEAU, JEAN, 1
good f....babysitter was well worth it HITCHCOCK, ALFRED, 8
I like a f. to have a beginning GODARD, JEAN-LUC, 5
My first f. will be a very simple one WILLIAMS, ROBIN, 4
No matter if the f. is banned WONG KAR WAI, 1
you want to make the greatest f. COPPOLA, FRANCIS FORD, 4
filmmaker A f. isn't supposed to say things HITCHCOCK, ALFRED, 5
films All f. are subversive CRONENBERG, DAVID, 1
all f. are surrealist POWELL, MICHAEL, 2
best f. are the best POLANSKI, ROMAN, 2
good European f....turning...into very bad American DOYLE, RODDY, 1
hope to build...house with my f. FASSBINDER, RAINER WERNER, 1
I feel like...father towards my old f. ANTONIONI, MICHELANGELO, 3
I seldom go to *f*....too exciting ELIOT, T. S., 1
making f. for...something to do MALLE, LOUIS, 2
modern f....close-ups of people's feet GISH, LILLIAN, 1
my f....four minutes of real cinema KUROSAWA, AKIRA, 1
film script A good f....without dialogue MAMET, DAVID, 8
filths F. savour but themselves SHAKESPEARE, WILLIAM, 355
final solution The f. of the Jewish problem HITLER, ADOLF, 39
finance F....art of passing currency SARNOFF, ROBERT W., 1
F....science of managing revenues and resources BIERCE, AMBROSE, 3
F....stomach of the country GLADSTONE, WILLIAM EWART, 9
financial markets F....resent...government interference SOROS, GEORGE, 2
find f. a kingdom between midday and midnight MAUNICK, EDOUARD J., 1
finders F. keepers PROVERBS, 215
fine another f. mess HARDY, OLIVER, 1
fine art F. can only be...exclusive REINHARDT, AD, 2
F. has its own...tradition REINHARDT, AD, 3
finest their f. hour CHURCHILL, WINSTON, 32
finger a f. in every pie CERVANTES, MIGUEL DE, 37
finger-lickin' It's f. good ADVERTISEMENTS, 14
fingers Fat f. as oily as maggots MANDELSTAM, OSIP, 19
f. of a man's hand, and wrote BIBLE, 31
F. were made before forks PROVERBS, 217
Just as my f....Make music STEVENS, WALLACE, 4
our f. are circumcised PERLMAN, ITZHAK, 1
fings F. Ain't Wot They Used T'Be NORMAN, FRANK, 1
finished it is f. BIBLE, 299
I've f. my war book now VONNEGUT, KURT, 7
finite All f. things reveal infinitude ROETHKE, THEODORE, 2
We are f. beings NAGEL, THOMAS, 3
fire Anyone using f. depends on the wind LUO GUANZHONG, 2
bound /Upon a wheel of f. SHAKESPEARE, WILLIAM, 365
falsely shouting "F.!" in a theater HOLMES, OLIVER WENDELL, JR., 2
f. in his eye...fever in his blood SHELLEY, PERCY BYSSHE, 3
f. near Fish Street in London EVELYN, JOHN, 4
F. the whole purchasing department TOWNSEND, ROBERT, 11
F.—without hatred PRIMO DE RIVERA, JOSÉ ANTONIO, 1
Great Balls of F. BLACKWELL, OTIS, 1
I didn't f. him MACARTHUR, DOUGLAS, 2
If you play with f. PROVERBS, 270
I live between...f. and the plague ADONIS, 1
Look not for f. in Hell KEMAL, YASAR, 1
tenement f. curdling in the brain WOLFE, TOM, 13
The beauty of f. from... embers MASEFIELD, JOHN, 7
You may f. when you are ready DEWEY, GEORGE, 1
firebell a f. in the night JEFFERSON, THOMAS, 21
fire-breathing I was a f. Catholic LOWELL, ROBERT, 14
fired Get f. PETERS, TOM, 6
If we get f., it's not a failure O'ROURKE, P. J., 5
fires Big f. flare up FRANCIS DE SALES, SAINT, 1
burning f....threatening to consume WHITMAN, WALT, 7
fireside no f., howsoe'er defended, /But has one vacant chair LONGFELLOW, HENRY WADSWORTH, 20
firm f.'s IQ is determined...IT infrastructure connects HAECKEL, STEVE H., 1
not a family; we're a f. GEORGE VI, 2
Nothing stays f. forever...everything vanishes HE QIFANG, 1
first always a f. time PROVERBS, 489
F. come, first served PROVERBS, 218
F. impressions PROVERBS, 219
F. in war WASHINGTON, GEORGE, 1
F. things first PROVERBS, 220
I had rather be the f. in this town PLUTARCH, 29
many that are f. shall be last BIBLE, 418
what to put f. PASCAL, BLAISE, 10
first-aid His ideas of f. WODEHOUSE, P. G., 9
firstfruits first of the f. BIBLE, 83
first light I lie and imagine a f. gleam MAHON, DEREK, 1
first night Cannot make f. SHAW, GEORGE BERNARD, 5
first-rate to mistake for the f., the fecund rate PARKER, DOROTHY, 31
First World War We mutually agreed to call it *The F.* REPINGTON, CHARLES À COURT, 1
fish a great f. to swallow up Jonah BIBLE, 306
F. and guests PROVERBS, 221

F. die belly-upward GIDE, ANDRÉ, 2
F. fuck in it FIELDS, W. C., 9
neither f. nor beast is the otter HUGHES, TED, 3
Rotten f. is a Malagasy delicacy MURPHY, DERVLA, 4
sliver-like little f. of wretched bent MATTHIESSEN, PETER, 3
There's a f. that *talks* /In the frying-pan DE LA MARE, WALTER, 2
fisher gallant f.'s life CHALKHILL, JOHN, 1
fishers f. of men BIBLE, 374
fishes f. live in the sea SHAKESPEARE, WILLIAM, 505
F., that tipple in the deep, /Know no such liberty LOVELACE, RICHARD, 1
fishing I hate his f., though HEMINGWAY, ERNEST, 1
fish knives Phone for the f. Norman BETJEMAN, JOHN, 3
fission F. is like kissing your wife MACAULAY, ROBERT B., 1
fit taen the f. o' rhyme BURNS, ROBERT, 16
The f.'s upon me now BEAUMONT & FLETCHER, 19
fitly more f. to come to me than I to him RICHARD, DUKE OF YORK, 1
fittest the f. would survive WALLACE, ALFRED RUSSEL, 3
Fitzgerald F. was an alcoholic FITZGERALD, F. SCOTT, 1
Fitzgeralds The F....were the sights FITZGERALD, F. SCOTT, 3
five o'clock At exactly f. in the afternoon GARCÍA LORCA, FEDERICO, 7
five-pound note get a f. as one got a light for a cigarette JAMES, HENRY, 23
five-year-old real menace in dealing with a f. KERR, JEAN, 4
fixed God deliver you...from a f. idea MACHADO DE ASSIS, JOAQUIM MARIA, 6
Nothing to be f. except COWARD, NOEL, 24
flag f. of our Union forever MORRIS, GEORGE POPE, 2
F. of the free heart's hope and home DRAKE, JOSEPH RODMAN, 1
room...this country for but one f. ROOSEVELT, THEODORE, 9
the f. to which you have pledged allegiance BALDWIN, JAMES, 27
The people's f. is deepest red CONNELL, JAMES, 2
flags frayed f. /quilt the graveyards LOWELL, ROBERT, 16
Planting f....not a strategy for success KELLER, MARYANN, 1
Flanders In F. fields MCCRAE, JOHN, 1
You have sent me a F. mare HENRY VIII, 9
flats high f....an architectural representation of a filing cabinet REID, JIMMY, 1
flatter F. the mountain-tops with sovereign eye SHAKESPEARE, WILLIAM, 571
not f. me CROMWELL, OLIVER, 7
We f. those we scarcely know WILCOX, ELLA WHEELER, 1
flattered Being f., is a lamb; threatened, a lion CHAPMAN, GEORGE, 2
He that loves to be f. is worthy o' the flatterer SHAKESPEARE, WILLIAM, 673
flatterers f. live at the expense of those who listen LA FONTAINE, JEAN DE, 6
flattering f. some men to endure them HALIFAX, GEORGE SAVILE, 3
talent of f. with delicacy AUSTEN, JANE, 33
flattery A little f. will support a man MONROE, JAMES, 3
consider whether...your f. is worth his having JOHNSON, SAMUEL, 51
Everyone likes f. DISRAELI, BENJAMIN, 52
f. hurts no one...if he doesn't inhale STEVENSON, ADLAI, 7
f.'s the food of fools SWIFT, JONATHAN, 6
Imitation is the sincerest form of f. COLTON, CHARLES, 2
None are more taken in with f. than the proud, who wish to be the first and are not SPINOZA, BARUCH, 3
flaunt if you've got it, f. it BROOKS, MEL, 3
flautists f....know something we don't know JENNINGS, PAUL, 1
flea with a f. in's ear FLETCHER, JOHN, 9
fleas The f. that tease BELLOC, HILAIRE, 4
these have smaller f. to bite 'em SWIFT, JONATHAN, 12
fled I f. Him, down the nights THOMPSON, FRANCIS, 1
flee They f. from me WYATT, THOMAS, 4
flees He who f. will fight again TERTULLIAN, 6
Fleming had F. not possessed immense knowledge FLEMING, ALEXANDER, 3
flesh f. and blood so cheap HOOD, THOMAS, 14
I, born of f. and ghost THOMAS, DYLAN, 6
I have more f. than another man SHAKESPEARE, WILLIAM, 238
I wants to make your f. creep DICKENS, CHARLES, 78
O! that this too too solid f. would melt SHAKESPEARE, WILLIAM, 144
The f....is wearied MALLARMÉ, STÉPHANE, 1
the f. lusteth against the Spirit BIBLE, 98
the way of all f....towards the kitchen WEBSTER, JOHN, 14
'Tis the way of all f. SHADWELL, THOMAS, 5
flextime F. is the essence of respect PACKARD, DAVID, 1
flies As f. to wanton boys SHAKESPEARE, WILLIAM, 354
f. around from hotel to hotel STOPPARD, TOM, 7
flight attendant now possible for a f. FERRIS, RICHARD J., 1
fling I'll have a f. BEAUMONT, FRANCIS, 2
flirt f. with their own husbands WILDE, OSCAR, 46
flirtation Merely innocent f. BYRON, LORD, 74
floats Before me f. an image YEATS, W. B., 52
when a line just f. into your head, don't pay attention BROOKS, GWENDOLYN, 8
flocks My f. feed not BARNFIELD, RICHARD, 4
flog f. the rank and file ARNOLD, THOMAS, 1
flogging less f. in our great schools JOHNSON, SAMUEL, 127
flood I am a f. AMERGIN, 1
Florida F. bear may be fat and sweet RAWLINGS, MARJORIE, 1
F. carried the message of warmth and ease STEINBECK, JOHN, 19
F. was weighted down with regret OZICK, CYNTHIA, 3
I will not sell land in F. SIMPSONS, THE, 3
flourishing f. in an immortal youth BARROW, ISAAC, 1
flow F. gently, sweet Afton, disturb not her dream BURNS, ROBERT, 7
flower A lovelier f....was never sown WORDSWORTH, WILLIAM, 35
f. is born to blush unseen GRAY, THOMAS, 8
flowers colours of the f. /Have faded KOMACHI, 1
Gather the f., but spare the buds MARVELL, ANDREW, 11
Here among f....with no close friends LI BAI, 3
I cannot see what f. are at my feet KEATS, JOHN (1795–1821), 62
I have...made up a bunch...f. MONTAIGNE, MICHEL DE, 24
Letting a hundred f. blossom MAO ZEDONG, 21
The f. of the forest ELLIOT, JANE, 1
The f. that bloom in the spring GILBERT, W. S., 30
Where have all the f. gone? SEEGER, PETE, 1
flower vases Never have high f. DE WOLFE, ELSIE, 2
flows Everything f. and nothing stays HERACLITUS, 1
I love everything that f. MILLER, HENRY, 21
flushpots The f. of Euston JOYCE, JAMES, 15

fluttered still he f. pulses ROBINSON, EDWIN ARLINGTON, 5
fly A f., Sir, may sting a stately horse JOHNSON, SAMUEL, 144
Do not remove a f....with a hatchet PROVERBS, 26
f....said, what a dust do I raise BACON, FRANCIS (1561–1626), 76
I heard a F. buzz—when I died DICKINSON, EMILY, 8
small gilded f. /Does lecher SHAKESPEARE, WILLIAM, 360
those that f. may fight again BUTLER, SAMUEL (1612–80), 24
fly fronts F. with buttons...encourage...forgetfulness BARNEY, SYDNEY D., 1
flying When it comes to f. AMIS, MARTIN, 3
Flying Dutchman F....furls his shadowy sail IRVING, WASHINGTON, 5
flying machines He ought to have stuck to his f. LEONARDO DA VINCI, 2
flying saucer interior of a f. ADAMS, DOUGLAS, 5
foe he is the sworn f. of our nation CAMPBELL, THOMAS, 11
my deadly f., no worse /Than want of friends BRETON, NICHOLAS, 1
rushed to meet the insulting f. FRENEAU, PHILIP, 3
foeman When the f. bares his steel GILBERT, W. S., 38
foes judge of a man by his f. CONRAD, JOSEPH, 7
fog natural f. of the good man's mind BROWNING, ROBERT, 9
The f. comes SANDBURG, CARL, 1
yellow f....upon the window panes ELIOT, T. S., 35
foggy Just to save her from the f., foggy dew FOLK VERSE, 26
folk music I don't know no other kind of music *but* f. ARMSTRONG, LOUIS, 13
folks F. don't like...somebody around knowin' more LEE, HARPER, 5
Only ways you can keep f. hating WALKER, MARGARET, 2
follies count their youthful f. o'er SCOTT, SIR WALTER, 18
f. of the town crept...among us GOLDSMITH, OLIVER, 8
The f. which a man regrets ROWLAND, HELEN, 3
follow I have to f. them, I am their leader LEDRU-ROLLIN, ALEXANDRE AUGUSTE, 1
folly foe was f....his weapon wit GILBERT, W. S., 1
He who is aware of his f. PROVERBS, 500
It is a f. to expect men to do all WHATELY, RICHARD, 3
One man's f. ROWLAND, HELEN, 2
shielding men from the effects of f. SPENCER, HERBERT, 3
The final and funniest f. BIERCE, AMBROSE, 36
the slightest f. /That ever love did make SHAKESPEARE, WILLIAM, 102
two kinds of f....madness and...ignorance PLATO, 29
When lovely woman stoops to f. GOLDSMITH, OLIVER, 33
fond Ae f. kiss, and then we sever BURNS, ROBERT, 5
very f. of making things HOPE, ANTHONY, 6
food do not draw any distinction between f. and medicine LIN YUTANG, 1
f. in America travels 1,200 miles NORBERG-HODGE, HELENA, 1
f. is, actually, very beautiful SMITH, DELIA, 1
F. is an important part of a balanced diet LEBOWITZ, FRAN, 1
f. is not necessarily essential WHITEHORN, KATHARINE, 1
F. is the beginning of wisdom FEUERBACH, LUDWIG ANDREAS, 2
F....our common ground, a universal experience BEARD, JAMES, 1
f. to one man is bitter poison to others LUCRETIUS, 8
I luuuuuuv f. WINFREY, OPRAH, 2
nursery f. was so disgusting KEANE, MOLLY, 1
respect ought to be paid to f. SPRY, CONSTANCE, 3
Yielding more wholesome f. DU BARTAS, GUILLAUME, 13
fool a f. among fools or a fool alone WILDER, THORNTON, 5
A f. and his money PROVERBS, 106
A F. and his words are soon parted SHENSTONE, WILLIAM, 1
A f. at forty PROVERBS, 107
A f. believes everything PROVERBS, 108
A f. bolts pleasure ANTRIM, MINNA, 1
A F. lies here who tried to hustle the East KIPLING, RUDYARD, 39
A f. sees not the same tree BLAKE, WILLIAM, 42
a f. who lets slip a bird in the hand PLUTARCH, 6
Better be a f. than a knave PROVERBS, 161
don't let me make...f. of myself BANKHEAD, TALLULAH, 5
fool always finds a greater f. to admire him BOILEAU, NICOLAS, 2
f. walketh in darkness BIBLE, 47
f. who thinks by force or skill TUKE, SAMUEL, 1
How every f. can play upon the word SHAKESPEARE, WILLIAM, 614
knowledgeable f. is a greater fool MOLIÈRE, 19
more of the f. than of the wise BACON, FRANCIS (1561–1626), 17
One f....in every married couple FIELDING, HENRY, 5
The f. is happy that he knows no more POPE, ALEXANDER, 28
The haste of a f. SHADWELL, THOMAS, 2
There's no f. like an old fool PROVERBS, 419
The wisest f. in Christendom HENRY IV, 6
You can f. some of the people all the time LINCOLN, ABRAHAM, 37
You can f. too many...people THURBER, JAMES, 3
foolery a little f. governs the world SELDEN, JOHN, 12
foolish A knavish speech sleeps in a f. ear SHAKESPEARE, WILLIAM, 207
a very f., fond old man SHAKESPEARE, WILLIAM, 364
did anything very f. except from...principle MELBOURNE, LORD, 5
f. enough to be contented JEROME, JEROME K., 2
Looking f. does the spirit good UPDIKE, JOHN, 18
more f. when he had not a pen in his hand GOLDSMITH, OLIVER, 2
These f. things MASCHWITZ, ERIC, 1
You must not think me...f. because I am facetious SMITH, SYDNEY, 2
foolishness by the f. of preaching BIBLE, 151
little f. with your serious plans HORACE, 54
fools F. are in a terrible, overwhelming majority IBSEN, HENRIK, 4
F. give you reasons HAMMERSTEIN, OSCAR, II, 11
F. live poor PROVERBS, 222
f. rush in where angels fear to tread POPE, ALEXANDER, 16
I am two f. DONNE, JOHN, 46
it leaves 'em still two f. CONGREVE, WILLIAM, 9
many fond f. serve mad jealousy SHAKESPEARE, WILLIAM, 592
To suckle f. SHAKESPEARE, WILLIAM, 478
what f. these mortals be SHAKESPEARE, WILLIAM, 60
foot caught my f. in the mat GROSSMITH, GEORGE, 2
football F....causeth fighting, brawling, contention STUBBES, PHILIP, 2
F....hatred for your opponent REAGAN, RONALD, 44
f. is a matter of life and death SHANKLY, BILL, 1
F....is a species of fighting ORWELL, GEORGE, 3
spontaneity is fundamental in art and f. CANTONA, ERIC, 1
footballers f. being ignorant is rubbish WELCH, RAQUEL, 2
footfalls F. echo in the memory ELIOT, T. S., 13
footloose When you're f. and collar-free TRAMP, THE, 1
footprints F. across an artificial reality STOLL, CLIFFORD, 1
F. on the sands of time PROVERBS, 223
the f. of a gigantic hound DOYLE, ARTHUR CONAN, 11
you can have my f. MARX, GROUCHO, 8
footsteps I tread in...f. of illustrious men JACKSON, ANDREW, 3
foppery the excellent f. of the world SHAKESPEARE, WILLIAM, 334

for who's f. you and who's against you JOHNSON, LYNDON BAINES, 23
forbearance f. ceases to be a virtue BURKE, EDMUND, 14
Forbes "F." list of the richest people ORBEN, ROBERT, 1
forbidden F. fruit PROVERBS, 224
f. to eat that which dieth of itself KORAN, 13
force best way of using f....show it ANNAN, KOFI, 1
f. alone is but *temporary* BURKE, EDMUND, 28
F. and fraud...the two cardinal virtues HOBBES, THOMAS, 12
F., if unassisted by judgment HORACE, 43
F. is not a remedy BRIGHT, JOHN, 2
May the F. be with you GUINNESS, ALEC, 2
no f. however great can stretch a cord WHEWELL, WILLIAM, 1
force-feeding This universal, obligatory f. with lies SOLZHENITSYN, ALEXANDER, 2
forces one of the f. of nature DUMAS, ALEXANDRE, 1
Ford Before the time of our F. HUXLEY, ALDOUS, 15
F., not a Lincoln FORD, GERALD, 3
Henry F. declared...history was bunk FORD, HENRY, 1
more about the F. coil than the clitoris STEINBECK, JOHN, 3
when Gerald F. was king STRAUSS, BILL, 1
forefathers Think of your f. ADAMS, JOHN QUINCY, 7
foreign F. places help your mind...float free KEILLOR, GARRISON, 10
pronounce f. names as he chooses CHURCHILL, WINSTON, 46
foreigner f. should...be wiser than ourselves TROLLOPE, ANTHONY, 4
foreigners f. take too active a hand YELTSIN, BORIS, 6
foreign policy f...."meddle" and "muddle STANLEY, EDWARD GEOFFREY SMITH, 2
My dog Millie knows more about f. CLINTON, BILL, 1
foreign secretary you will send a F....naked BEVAN, ANEURIN, 5
foreparents f. came to America in slave ships JACKSON, JESSE, 3
forests Only You Can Prevent F. ANONYMOUS, 45
forever Even f. comes to an end GUY, ROSA, 2
forewarned F. is forearmed PROVERBS, 225
forget Better by far you should f. and smile ROSSETTI, CHRISTINA, 7
f. the human race BYRON, LORD, 36
I f. what I was taught WHITE, PATRICK, 3
I never f. a face, but I'll make an exception in your case MARX, GROUCHO, 19
nor f....she had to forgive WEST, JESSAMYN, 1
Old men f. SHAKESPEARE, WILLIAM, 274
three things I always f. SVEVO, ITALO, 1
Were it not better to f. LANDON, LETITIA ELIZABETH, 1
forgetfulness F....condition of the memory JARRY, ALFRED, 2
forgive F. and forget PROVERBS, 226
Father, f. them BIBLE, 347
F. me and forget me BULGAKOV, MIKHAIL, 8
f. my enemies...had them all shot NARVÁEZ, RAMÓN MARÍA, 2
f. your enemies—but never forget their names KENNEDY, ROBERT, 7
how oft shall...I f. him BIBLE, 413
I f. nobody BECKETT, SAMUEL, 11
lambs could not f....nor worms forget DICKENS, CHARLES, 55
Lord, f. them, for they know what they do KRAUS, KARL, 25
Lord God, f. white Europe SENGHOR, LÉOPOLD, 2
Men will f. a man CHURCHILL, WINSTON, 9
we ought to f. our friends BACON, FRANCIS (1561–1626), 4
forgiving act of f. can never be predicted ARENDT, HANNAH, 20
forgot When the lips have spoken...accents are soon f. SHELLEY, PERCY BYSSHE, 25
forgotten f. nothing and learned nothing LOUIS XVIII, 1
f. when it is convenient to remember DISRAELI, BENJAMIN, 60
If you have f. my kisses SWINBURNE, ALGERNON CHARLES, 6
I want to be f. even by God BROWNING, ROBERT, 66
The f. man ROOSEVELT, FRANKLIN D., 12
We'll be f.. Such is our fate CHEKHOV, ANTON, 15
fork he had a f. LEVERSON, ADA, 2
When you come to a f. in the road BERRA, YOGI, 5
forlorn F.! the very word is like a bell KEATS, JOHN (1795–1821), 65
form A f. is never something abstract MIRÓ, JOAN, 10
one loves f. only OLSON, CHARLES, 8
significant f. BELL, CLIVE, 1
The f. most contradictory ORTEGA Y GASSET, JOSÉ, 25
formidable so f. an effort...the people CASTLEREAGH, LORD, 2
formula The f. "Two and two make five DOSTOYEVSKY, FYODOR, 2
Formula One There's nothing natural about F. PROST, ALAIN, 2
when you get into F. PROST, ALAIN, 1
fornicated f. and read the papers CAMUS, ALBERT, 9
fornication F.: but that was in another country MARLOWE, CHRISTOPHER, 25
fortunate Hold him alone truly f. AESCHYLUS, 1
fortune F. always favours fools GAY, JOHN, 6
F. favors the bold VIRGIL, 23
F. favors the brave TERENCE, 2
F. flatters...to betray PUBLILIUS SYRUS, 3
F. is for all AESCHYLUS, 4
F. is not on the side of the faint-hearted SOPHOCLES, 9
F. leaves always some door open CERVANTES, MIGUEL DE, 51
fools of f., trencher-friends SHAKESPEARE, WILLIAM, 676
F., that favours fools JONSON, BEN, 16
F....though she be blind BACON, FRANCIS (1561–1626), 27
Ill f. seldom comes alone DRYDEN, JOHN, 6
make no effort to increase f. CARNEGIE, ANDREW, 12
Man's greatest...f. is to...defeat his enemy GENGHIS KHAN, 3
not now in f.'s power BUTLER, SAMUEL (1612–80), 12
O! I am F.'s fool SHAKESPEARE, WILLIAM, 551
people of f....indulge in...delinquencies ELIOT, GEORGE, 22
The shortest and best way to make your f. LA BRUYÈRE, JEAN DE, 18
Whom F. wishes to destroy...makes mad PUBLILIUS SYRUS, 13
fortunes you'll ne'er mend your f....By breaking...laws MORE, HANNAH, 1
forty By age f....a million a year WOLFE, TOM, 10
f. days and forty nights BIBLE, 371
f., half of you belongs to the past ANOUILH, JEAN, 11
I am just turning f. LLOYD, HAROLD, 1
forty-three She may very well pass for f. GILBERT, W. S., 42
forty-two "F.," said Deep Thought ADAMS, DOUGLAS, 9
forward It's looking f. or it's looking back MAMET, DAVID, 6
looking f. to the past OSBORNE, JOHN, 3
those behind cried "F.!" MACAULAY, THOMAS BABINGTON, 24
fought better to have f. and lost CLOUGH, ARTHUR HUGH, 1
We f. ourselves SHEEN, CHARLIE, 1
what they f. each other for SOUTHEY, ROBERT, 2
foul Fair is f., and foul is fair SHAKESPEARE, WILLIAM, 380
So f. and fair a day SHAKESPEARE, WILLIAM, 383

F. is the oxygen without which science SARNOFF, DAVID, 1
F. is the right to be wrong DIEFENBAKER, JOHN, 1
F. is the right to tell people ORWELL, GEORGE, 32
fit to use their f. MACAULAY, THOMAS BABINGTON, 14
F. lives only in...dreams SCHILLER, FRIEDRICH VON, 6
F....never voluntarily given up KING, MARTIN LUTHER, JR., 7
F. of men under government LOCKE, JOHN, 7
f. of person JEFFERSON, THOMAS, 4
f. of speech, freedom of conscience TWAIN, MARK, 17
F. of the press in Britain SWAFFER, HANNEN, 1
F.'s just another word KRISTOFFERSON, KRIS, 1
F....the disciplined overcoming of self MURDOCH, IRIS, 11
f. without discipline is anarchy; discipline without freedom is tyranny NYERERE, JULIUS KAMBARAGE, 5
giving f. to the slave LINCOLN, ABRAHAM, 24
He who believes in f. of the will EBNER-ESCHENBACH, MARIE VON, 5
How good can f. be VALENZUELA, LUISA, 1
I am free, deliver me from f. CLAUDEL, PAUL, 2
idea that we should expect sudden f. MAO YUSHI, 1
If f. were not so economically efficient FRIEDMAN, MILTON, 2
I gave my life for f. EWER, WILLIAM NORMAN, 1
Me this unchartered f. tires WORDSWORTH, WILLIAM, 59
more f....where it is not your natural language AGASSI, ANDRE, 1
None can love f. heartily, but good men MILTON, JOHN, 129
only f. can make security secure POPPER, KARL, 7
our f. to determine our own future NYERERE, JULIUS KAMBARAGE, 6
right to be let alone...beginning of all f. DOUGLAS, WILLIAM ORVILLE, 1
So greatly did she care for f. that she died for it PANKHURST, CHRISTABEL, 4
The cause of F. is the cause of God BOWLES, WILLIAM LISLE, 1
The fight is for f., not whiteness BROWN, H. RAP, 3
The f. of the press MASON, GEORGE, 3
the idea of F. PARKER, THEODORE, 1
The price of f. can never be too high NKOMO, JOSHUA, 2
There is no easy walk to f. anywhere MANDELA, NELSON, 21
This f., this liberty, this beautiful /...thing HAYDEN, ROBERT E., 1
Those who deny f. to others LINCOLN, ABRAHAM, 18
to reap the blessings of f. PAINE, THOMAS, 7
two kinds of f. AHRENDS, MARTIN, 2
what is F. COLERIDGE, HARTLEY, 1
When f. came WASHINGTON, BOOKER T., 9
Who ever walked behind anyone to f.? SCOTT, HAZEL, 3
yearning for f....suppressed but never destroyed GROSSMAN, VASILY, 2
You only get your f. by sweating MIRÓ, JOAN, 7
Your f. and mine cannot be separated MANDELA, NELSON, 25
You took my f. away a long time ago SOLZHENITSYN, ALEXANDER, 13
freedoms few remaining f....the blank page KELMAN, JAMES, 1
four essential human f. ROOSEVELT, FRANKLIN D., 26
free enterprise F. is a rough and competitive game REAGAN, RONALD, 26
freeloader A f. is a confirmed guest RUNYON, DAMON, 9
free lunch no such thing as a f. ANONYMOUS, 85
freeman No f. shall be taken...or outlawed MAGNA CARTA, 1
free market The trouble with a f. economy ASCHERSON, NEAL, 1
free-market our f. system was not nature GREENSPAN, ALAN, 4
free men All f....are citizens of Berlin KENNEDY, JOHN FITZGERALD, 28
live at last as f. HERZL, THEODOR, 15
Only f. can negotiate MANDELA, NELSON, 6
freemen rather *die f., than live to be slaves* GARNET, HENRY HIGHLAND, 1
free society control a f. by force MARK, ROBERT, 1
f....safe to be unpopular STEVENSON, ADLAI, 2
free speech f. will be extinguished NIXON, RICHARD, 27
free thought a horrible example of f. JOYCE, JAMES, 35
free trade F. policies work NORBERG-HODGE, HELENA, 3
free will F. and Predestination CHURCHILL, WINSTON, 42
We have to believe in f.. We've got no choice SINGER, ISAAC BASHEVIS, 7
free-will f. as a subjective illusion BORN, MAX, 1
French F....big in the culture business BELLOW, SAUL, 14
fear that the F. would invade BYNG, GEORGE, 1
F. Guard, fire first HAY, LORD CHARLES, 1
F. language...language of humanity RIVAROL, ANTOINE DE, 1
Food isolates the F. ZELDIN, THEODORE, 9
F. rhetorical models are too narrow PAGLIA, CAMILLE, 14
F. want no one to be their *superior* TOCQUEVILLE, ALEXIS DE, 4
Imagine the Lord talking F. DAY, CLARENCE SHEPARD, 1
The F. are nice people MAZARIN, JULES, 1
The F., for all their slogans, are becoming modern WILLIAMS, JOHN A., 2
The F. took three years of struggle ALCALA GALIANO, JUAN VALERA, 1
The F....united under the threat of danger DE GAULLE, CHARLES, 3
the F....with strange habit DU BARTAS, GUILLAUME, 6
Those goddam F. are so degenerate DOS PASSOS, JOHN, 6
to the F. the empire of the land RICHTER, JEAN PAUL, 1
What is not clear is not F. RIVAROL, ANTOINE DE, 3
worthy of the confidence of the F. LOUIS XVI, 2
French Canada F. is...preserved by isolation SMITH, GOLDWIN, 2
French Canadian F. father...learn English LAURIER, WILFRID, 8
Frenchman F. must be always talking JOHNSON, SAMUEL, 68
F. needs...to feel his neighbor's elbow CHEVALIER, MICHEL, 2
Frenchmen F. drink wine just like LARDNER, RING, 2
For all of us F., the guiding rule DE GAULLE, CHARLES, 9
French Revolution F....witness in favor of Woman FULLER, MARGARET, 9
too early...judgement on the F. TREVELYAN, G. M., 1
freshness The glory and the f. of a dream WORDSWORTH, WILLIAM, 49
fret Best, to forget! /Living, we f. BROWNING, ROBERT, 38
Freud Every reader of F....his first impressions FREUD, SIGMUND, 9
F....agreed in principle to...sexual health FREUD, SIGMUND, 16
F. and Jung...proscribed by the Nazis FREUD, SIGMUND, 18
F....destroy sex in America forever FREUD, SIGMUND, 3
F....genuinely believed in reason FREUD, SIGMUND, 4
F. is all nonsense FREUD, SIGMUND, 13
F. is constantly claiming to be scientific FREUD, SIGMUND, 19
F. is midwife to the soul FREUD, SIGMUND, 7
F. is the father of psychoanalysis GREER, GERMAINE, 12
For F. the ultimate psychological reality FREUD, SIGMUND, 10
F....progressive free thinker and...gentleman professor FREUD, SIGMUND, 17
F....propound a new myth FREUD, SIGMUND, 21
Freudian F. research will...be too easily accepted FREUD, SIGMUND, 11
Freudianism F....a means of transportation AUDEN, W. H., 2
friars We cannot all be f. CERVANTES, MIGUEL DE, 31
Friday I takes my man F. DEFOE, DANIEL, 5
friend a f. can't take a mother's place FRANK, ANNE, 3
a f. in need PLAUTUS, 4
A f. in need PROVERBS, 109

A f. in power ADAMS, HENRY, 5
A f. should bear his friend's infirmities SHAKESPEARE, WILLIAM, 315
A F....the masterpiece of Nature EMERSON, RALPH WALDO, 8
A f. you have to buy PROVERBS, 494
a good f., but bad acquaintance BYRON, LORD, 53
A good f. is my nearest relation PROVERBS, 112
being a f....mastering the art of timing NAYLOR, GLORIA, 6
Each f. represents a world in us NIN, ANAÏS, 3
F. after friend departs MONTGOMERY, JAMES, 1
f....enough to tell him disagreeable truths LYTTON, BULWER, 4
f. in the market...better than money FULLER, THOMAS (1654–1734), 1
f. is another self ARISTOTLE, 15
f. of every country but his own CANNING, GEORGE, 1
f. of virtue and not of fortune SCANDERBEG, 1
He makes no f. TENNYSON, ALFRED, 10
In the death of every f. we lose a part of ourselves POPE, ALEXANDER, 6
no f. like a sister ROSSETTI, CHRISTINA, 3
the f. of all humanity is not my friend MOLIÈRE, 12
Was it a f. or foe that spread these lies ROSSETTI, DANTE GABRIEL, 1
What trusty treasure...can countervail a f. GRIMALD, NICHOLAS, 1
When a f. dies out on us MACNEICE, LOUIS, 22
Whenever a f. succeeds VIDAL, GORE, 9
You've got a f. KING, CAROLE, 1

friendliness F. and easy hospitality SPRY, CONSTANCE, 2

friends better to drop thy f. CALVERLEY, C. S., 2
better to make f. at home PLUTARCH, 28
cherish our f. not for...ability to amuse us WAUGH, EVELYN, 39
Don't tell your f. their social faults SMITH, LOGAN PEARSALL, 1
easier to visit your f. than...live with them PROVERBS, 33
F. and good manners will carry you where money won't go WALKER, MARGARET, 1
F. are God's apology for relations KINGSMILL, HUGH, 2
F., carve a monument /out of dream stone GARCÍA LORCA, FEDERICO, 1
F. depart, and memory takes them BAYLY, THOMAS HAYNES, 4
God defend me from my f. PROVERBS, 234
Good thoughts his only f. CAMPION, THOMAS, 3
Have no f. not equal CONFUCIUS, 6
He who has a thousand f. TALEB, ALI BEN ABI, 1
How to Win F. CARNEGIE, DALE, 3
I cannot forgive my f. for dying SMITH, LOGAN PEARSALL, 17
If you want to know who your f. are BUKOWSKI, CHARLES, 6
I have my f. MILNE, A. A., 24
I let down my f. NIXON, RICHARD, 29
I thank the Lord for f. GOLDEN, MARITA, 7
keep clear who your f. are MAMET, DAVID, 3
Mr O'Connor and I are old f. O'BRIEN, FLANN, 5
My f....dislike me or hate me LEVANT, OSCAR, 2
my glory was I had such f. YEATS, W. B., 23
not be four f. in the world PASCAL, BLAISE, 3
not so much our f.' help EPICURUS, 7
Old f. are best SELDEN, JOHN, 5
Old f....refuge of unsociable persons BEERBOHM, MAX, 25
remember those f. who were absent as well as...present THALES, 2
treat your f. a little better HOWE, EDGAR WATSON, 4
why one's f. chose to marry WYNDHAM, JOHN, 2
You are honored by your f....distinguished by your enemies HOOVER, J. EDGAR, 2

friendship A generous f. no cold medium knows POPE, ALEXANDER, 72
f. founded on business is better ROCKEFELLER, JOHN D., 3
F. has splendors that love knows not BÂ, MARIAMA, 2
F. is a disinterested commerce between equals GOLDSMITH, OLIVER, 19
F. is constant in all other things SHAKESPEARE, WILLIAM, 447
F. is Love without his wings BYRON, LORD, 10
F. is unnecessary LEWIS, C. S., 4
If I speak to thee in f.'s name MOORE, THOMAS, 15
keep his f. in *constant repair* JOHNSON, SAMUEL, 93
Learn to reject f. WEIL, SIMONE, 3
Men seem to kick f. around like a football LINDBERGH, ANNE MORROW, 2
Most f. is feigning SHAKESPEARE, WILLIAM, 109
To like...the same things, that is...true f. SALLUST, 1
true bond of f. MORRIS, DESMOND, 3

friendships F. begin with liking ELIOT, GEORGE, 13
F. made o'er wine are slight LOGAU, FRIEDRICH VON, 4

frighted f. out of my...senses CERVANTES, MIGUEL DE, 10

frighten by God, they f. me WELLINGTON, DUKE OF, 8

frightened I was f. but I fought MOSLEY, WALTER, 6

frightful it is f. not to live HUGO, VICTOR, 7

frills f. round the cutlets can wait BETJEMAN, JOHN, 2

Frisco F.—long, bleak streets with trolley wires KEROUAC, JACK, 15

frocks f. are built in Paris SAKI, 10

frog A f. he would a-wooing go CHILDREN'S VERSE, 21

frogs F. and snails /And puppy-dogs' tails CHILDREN'S VERSE, 33

frontier We stand today on the edge of a new f. KENNEDY, JOHN FITZGERALD, 18

frown a f. on a customer's face PETERS, TOM, 13

frowns her very f. are fairer far, /Than smiles COLERIDGE, SAMUEL TAYLOR, 21

fruit every good tree bringeth forth good f. BIBLE, 387
the f. of the Spirit is love, joy, peace BIBLE, 99
the f. which I bore was the sun PROCLUS, 1
Too late for f., too soon for flowers DE LA MARE, WALTER, 10

fruitful Be f. and multiply INGE, WILLIAM RALPH, 6

fruits In no nation are...f. of accomplishment HOOVER, HERBERT, 4

frustration sign of f. is putting on weight TOWNSEND, ROBERT, 9

fuck They f. you up, your mum and dad LARKIN, PHILIP, 9
The zipless f. is the purest thing JONG, ERICA, 3

fucking all this cold-hearted f. LAWRENCE, D. H., 26
too f. busy—or vice versa PARKER, DOROTHY, 41

fuel adding f. to the flame MILTON, JOHN, 101

fugitive f. from th' law of averages MAULDIN, BILL, 1

full f. of new wine BIBLE, 5

fun f. to be in the same decade ROOSEVELT, FRANKLIN D., 30
had enough f....time you were off HORACE, 29
It was great f. PORTER, COLE, 11
most f. I've had since I've been black GILLESPIE, DIZZY, 2
People must not do things for f. HERBERT, A. P., 11
the most f. I ever had without laughing ALLEN, WOODY, 3
What f. it would be to be poor ANOUILH, JEAN, 7
Work is much more f. than fun COWARD, NOEL, 16

function principal f. of ritual, religion...culture OPPENHEIMER, J. ROBERT, 7

fundamentalism F....specter that is stalking the globe KABBANI, RANA, 4

funeral At the f. of the marriage DURCAN, PAUL, 2
The f. bak'd-meats SHAKESPEARE, WILLIAM, 146
funerals If you don't go to other men's f. DAY, CLARENCE SHEPARD, 2
I like f.. All those flowers BAINBRIDGE, BERYL, 6
Many f. discredit a physician JONSON, BEN, 29
They say such nice things...f. KEILLOR, GARRISON, 4
funniest f. when he said nothing BENNY, JACK, 1
funny F. noises are not funny SIMPSONS, THE, 1
F.-peculiar or funny-ha-ha HAY, IAN, 1
F. without being vulgar GILBERT, W. S., 45
hard to be f. when you have to be clean WEST, MAE, 20
Isn't it f. /How a bear likes honey MILNE, A. A., 19
It's a f. thing about that bust SHAW, GEORGE BERNARD, 98
What a f. little man you are DOUGLAS, ALFRED, 1
furnace Heat not a f. for your foe SHAKESPEARE, WILLIAM, 279
heat the f. one seven times more BIBLE, 29
furniture good...f. for a yacht ASTOR, BROOKE, 2
re-arrange the f....of the Titanic MORTON, ROGERS, 1
further f. one goes, the less one knows LAOZI, 19
f. you get away from any period DUNNE, FINLEY PETER, 6
fury F. at failure to...achieve a desired status KIRSTEIN, LINCOLN, 2
no f. like an ex-wife searching for a new lover CONNOLLY, CYRIL, 20
nothing but beastly f. and extreme violence ELYOT, THOMAS, 1
the F. of a Patient Man DRYDEN, JOHN, 11
fuse force that through the green f. THOMAS, DYLAN, 8
fusillade F....only way to silence Parisians FLAUBERT, GUSTAVE, 7
fuss All this f. about sleeping together WAUGH, EVELYN, 33
fustest I got there f. with the mostest FORREST, NATHAN BEDFORD, 1
future all f. plunges to the past JOYCE, JAMES, 31
F. contingents cannot be certain AQUINAS, THOMAS, 5
f....struggle against...our intelligence WIENER, NORBERT, 3
f....the faith of our age AMPÈRE, JEAN-JAQUES, 2
f. through a rearview mirror LYNCH, PETER, 2
F....time in which our affairs prosper BIERCE, AMBROSE, 23
f. will one day be the present MAUGHAM, SOMERSET, 41
f. winds no garlands for the actor SCHILLER, FRIEDRICH VON, 22
guide to the f....lessons of the past HARDING, WARREN G., 5
If...f. and the past do exist AUGUSTINE OF HIPPO, SAINT, 7
I have seen the f....it works STEFFENS, LINCOLN, 2
The architecture of our f. is not only unfinished; the scaffolding has hardly gone up LAMMING, GEORGE, 1
the f....a boot stamping ORWELL, GEORGE, 23
The f. belongs to Russia BETHMANN HOLLWEG, THEOBALD VON, 3
the f....belongs to the brave BERNBACH, WILLIAM, 8
the f....comes soon enough EINSTEIN, ALBERT, 20
The f. is...black BALDWIN, JAMES, 20
The f. is like heaven—everyone exalts it but no one wants to go there now BALDWIN, JAMES, 9
The f. is made of the same stuff WEIL, SIMONE, 4
The f. is the only kind of property CAMUS, ALBERT, 24
the f....makes cowards of us DIX, DOROTHY, 2
The f. of humanity is uncertain LEVI, PRIMO, 1
the f. of my kind of writing SIMAK, CLIFFORD D., 2
the f....what you make of it MOSLEY, WALTER, 1
Those who talk about...f. are scoundrels CÉLINE, LOUIS-FERDINAND, 2
to look at the f. being digital NEGROPONTE, NICHOLAS, 5
with a great f. behind him JOYCE, JAMES, 19
You cannot fight against the f. GLADSTONE, WILLIAM EWART, 8
fuzzy-looking What are all those /f. things WILLIAMS, WILLIAM CARLOS, 14
fuzzy-wuzzy to you, F. KIPLING, RUDYARD, 17

Gaels For the great G. of Ireland CHESTERTON, G. K., 5
gai toujours g. is my motto MARQUIS, DON, 5
gaiety the only concession to g....striped shroud THOMAS, GWYN, 1
gain Let him think to g. many to Christ imperceptibly BUSHNELL, HORACE, 1
would be a g. to the country NEWMAN, JOHN HENRY, 2
gainful have to seek...g. employment ACHESON, DEAN, 2
gains Chief among our g....possibility of choice MEAD, MARGARET, 4
gal a g. to answer the phone HUMPHREY, HUBERT H., 1
galaxy A g....billions upon billions of stars SAGAN, CARL, 10
A long time ago in a g. STAR WARS, 1
Galileo G. was no idiot GALILEO, 1
If G. had said in verse HARDY, THOMAS, 33
What G. and Newton were to the seventeenth century GALILEO, 2
gallant a g., civilised and democratic people betrayed ATTLEE, CLEMENT, 5
gallantry What men call g. BYRON, LORD, 40
gallows make the g. glorious BROWN, JOHN, 3
see nothing but the g. BURKE, EDMUND, 42
You will die...g., or of the pox WILKES, JOHN, 2
gallows-maker The g. SHAKESPEARE, WILLIAM, 218
galvanize I come to g. the political corpse CÁNOVAS DEL CASTILLO, ANTONIO, 1
gambling primary notion...of most g. is the excitement KENNEDY, JOSEPH, 2
game aesthetic g....played by these connoisseurs PICASSO, PABLO, 9
g. enough to take a wicked amount of punishment GIBSON, ALTHEA, 2
He no play-a da g. BUTZ, EARL, 1
It's a g....winning is everything KLEIN, ALLEN, 1
more than a g....an institution HUGHES, THOMAS, 2
Play the g., but don't believe in it ELLISON, RALPH, 2
time to win this g., and to thrash the Spaniards DRAKE, FRANCIS, 4
gameboy g. down a well COSTELLO, ELVIS, 2
gamekeeper would you allow your g. to read it ANONYMOUS, 87
games G. People Play BERNE, ERIC, 2
gamesmanship G. or The Art of Winning Games POTTER, STEPHEN, 6
game theory G. for managers GILBERT, DANIEL J., JR., 2
gaming Man is a g. animal LAMB, CHARLES, 14
gammon a world of g. and spinnage DICKENS, CHARLES, 24
gander Goosey, goosey g., /Whither shall I wander CHILDREN'S VERSE, 13
Gandhi G. was very keen on sex GANDHI, MAHATMA, 4
gandy dancers the tales of the g. BOX-CAR BERTHA, 1
gangster I always wanted to be a g. LIOTTA, RAY, 1
gangsterism g....important avenue into mainstream society DOCTOROW, E. L., 3
gaps patches up the g. in...the universe FREUD, SIGMUND, 30
Garbo face of G. is an Idea GARBO, GRETA, 1
G. Talks ADVERTISEMENTS, 25

not another Greta G. BLEASDALE, ALAN, 2
garden a g. in her face CAMPION, THOMAS, 5
A g. is a lovesome thing BROWN, THOMAS EDWARD, 1
Come into the g., Maud TENNYSON, ALFRED, 28
God the first g. made COWLEY, ABRAHAM, 4
I have a g. of my own MARVELL, ANDREW, 9
My beloved is gone down into his g. BIBLE, 497
the g. of Eden BIBLE, 108
There is a g. in her face ALISON, RICHARD, 2
Who loves a g. loves a greenhouse too COWPER, WILLIAM, 31
gardener I work like a g. or a wine grower MIRÓ, JOAN, 12
gardens closing time in the g. of the West CONNOLLY, CYRIL, 12
These are the g. of the Desert BRYANT, WILLIAM CULLEN, 6
garlands gather g. there SCOTT, SIR WALTER, 17
garret living in a g. FOOTE, SAMUEL, 2
garrulous That g. monk HITLER, ADOLF, 8
Garter I like the G. MELBOURNE, LORD, 3
gas All is g. and gaiters DICKENS, CHARLES, 65
gather Birds of a feather...g. together BURTON, ROBERT, 11
g. thyself together KEMPIS, THOMAS À, 1
G. ye rosebuds while ye may HERRICK, ROBERT, 16
gathered where a number of men g. together STEINBECK, JOHN, 11
where two or three are g. together BIBLE, 412
gatherer g. and disposer of other men's stuff WOTTON, HENRY, 4
Gaul G. is divided into three CAESAR, JULIUS, 3
Gaullist G. only little by little DE GAULLE, CHARLES, 15
gay g. characters are on exactly the same footing as the straight MAUPIN, ARMISTEAD, 3
g. people...get into right-wing politics MAUPIN, ARMISTEAD, 2
gays G. grow up...watching heterosexual movies FIERSTEIN, HARVEY, 3
there have always been g. in the military CLINTON, BILL, 9
wouldn't be discriminating against g. and lesbians LOYDEN, EDDIE, 1
gazed still they g....the wonder grew GOLDSMITH, OLIVER, 18
gazelle never nurs'd a dear g. MOORE, THOMAS, 1
geese heard /The great g. hoot northward WARREN, ROBERT PENN, 1
gelded successfully if /delicately g....gentlemen CUMMINGS, E. E., 3
geldyng I trow he were a g. CHAUCER, GEOFFREY, 8
gender Undoubtedly g. does play an important part BISHOP, ELIZABETH, 3
gender-related g. movement BROWNMILLER, SUSAN, 2
gene g. replacement therapy for...management HAMEL, GARY, 9
g. that makes us human JONES, STEVE, 2
general No g....has a great discussion OWEN, DAVID, 1
generalizations All g. are dangerous DUMAS, ALEXANDRE, 5
generalize One should always g. JACOBI, KARL GUSTAV JAKOB, 1
To g. is to be an idiot BLAKE, WILLIAM, 52
generals at the age of four with paper hats and wooden swords we're all G. USTINOV, PETER, 11
It is not the business of g. to shoot one another WELLINGTON, DUKE OF, 9
General Staff The G. tells me nothing WILLIAM II, 1
generation a g. that don't spend THATCHER, MARGARET, 26
Each g. imagines itself...more intelligent ORWELL, GEORGE, 42
each g. will become more digital NEGROPONTE, NICHOLAS, 8
Eamon de Valera g....changed the occasional nappy O'CONNOR, JOSEPH, 2
Every g. revolts against its fathers MUMFORD, LEWIS, 1
this g....determination to act ARENDT, HANNAH, 8
We're a *beat* g. KEROUAC, JACK, 26
Ye are a chosen g. BIBLE, 192
You are all a lost g. STEIN, GERTRUDE, 13
generations g....pass in a short time LUCRETIUS, 5
To some g. much is given ROOSEVELT, FRANKLIN D., 14
generosity nothing more praiseworthy than g. RETZ, CARDINAL DE, 11
Unasked-for g. FARAH, NURUDDIN, 3
genius A genius! For thirty-seven years I've practiced...and now they call me a g. SARASATE, PABLO DE, 1
a g. for backing into the limelight LAWRENCE, T. E., 1
A g....somebody a computer cannot programme LIYONG, TABAN LO, 2
Almost everyone is born a g. BUKOWSKI, CHARLES, 2
a spark of g. in the leadership BENNIS, WARREN, 9
Everyone denies I am a g. WELLES, ORSON, 11
function of g. is to furnish...ideas ARAGON, LOUIS, 2
g....adulterates philosophy REID, THOMAS, 1
G. does what it must OWEN, MEREDITH, 1
G. hath electric power CHILD, LYDIA MARIA, 6
G. is an infinite capacity PROVERBS, 229
G. is of no country CHURCHILL, CHARLES, 9
G. is one per cent inspiration EDISON, THOMAS ALVA, 4
G. is only a greater aptitude for patience BUFFON, COMTE DE, 2
g. with the IQ of a moron WARHOL, ANDY, 2
identified g. with immunity SHAW, GEORGE BERNARD, 8
I'm a g. BEEFHEART, CAPTAIN, 2
no great g. without a tincture of madness SENECA, "THE YOUNGER," 2
Nothing, except my g. WILDE, OSCAR, 86
Since when was g....respectable BROWNING, ELIZABETH BARRETT, 4
takes...time to be a g. STEIN, GERTRUDE, 5
there is too much g., not enough talent PRIESTLEY, J. B., 7
Three fifths...g. and two fifths sheer fudge POE, EDGAR ALLAN, 2
true g. is a mind of large...powers JOHNSON, SAMUEL, 26
True g. walks along a line GOLDSMITH, OLIVER, 14
what a g. I had SWIFT, JONATHAN, 53
When a true g. appears SWIFT, JONATHAN, 50
geniuses G. are wonks PINKER, STEVEN, 3
G. don't die DALÍ, SALVADOR, 3
genteel A man...is not g. when he gets drunk BOSWELL, JAMES, 3
G. in personage CAREY, HENRY, 5
Gentile There is neither G. nor Jew AGOBARD, SAINT, 1
Gentiles G. shall come to thy light BIBLE, 223
gentle A g. knight was pricking on the plain SPENSER, EDMUND, 5
Be g. to all and stern with yourself TERESA OF ÁVILA, SAINT, 3
Do not go g. into...good night THOMAS, DYLAN, 16
gentleman a g....isn't easy PIRANDELLO, LUIGI, 15
A g. need not know Latin MATTHEWS, BRANDER, 1
a g....never inflicts pain NEWMAN, JOHN HENRY, 6
a g., though spoiled i' the breeding BROME, RICHARD, 1
A g....who could calculate an eclipse JEFFERSON, THOMAS, 3
Every other inch a g. ARLEN, MICHAEL, 1
g.....robbing the poor SHAW, GEORGE BERNARD, 52
g. to haul...with the mariner DRAKE, FRANCIS, 5
g. who has lost his nose GOGOL, NIKOLAY, 2
last g. in Europe WILDE, OSCAR, 3
such a nice old g. CHAMBERLAIN, NEVILLE, 2
the g. is not in your books SHAKESPEARE, WILLIAM, 443

the g. was an *attorney* JOHNSON, SAMUEL, 87
The g. was a sweet LONGFELLOW, HENRY WADSWORTH, 1
gentlemen Good-morning, g. both ELIZABETH I, 21
written by g. for gentlemen THACKERAY, WILLIAM MAKEPEACE, 7
gentleness G. was considered "bourgeois" JUNG CHANG, 2
gentler sex fell short of the g. CAO XUEQIN, 1
gentlewoman a g. made ready STUBBES, PHILIP, 1
gentry g....act like the common people STRINDBERG, AUGUST, 5
genuine a place for the g. MOORE, MARIANNE, 4
genuinely g. bogus HASSALL, CHRISTOPHER, 1
genuineness G. only thrives in the dark HUXLEY, ALDOUS, 53
geographers g....crowd into...maps PLUTARCH, 16
geography A man should know a little of G.—History, nothing more useful, or pleasant SANCHO, IGNATIUS, 2
G. is...the art of war SAID, EDWARD W., 4
geometricians we are g. only by chance JOHNSON, SAMUEL, 27
geometry G. HOBBES, THOMAS, 8
G. enlightens the intellect IBN KHALDUN, 1
G., without which no one can...become an...artist DÜRER, ALBRECHT, 2
One g. cannot be more true PIRSIG, ROBERT T., 9
There is no "royal road" to g. EUCLID, 2
Where there is matter...g. KEPLER, JOHANNES, 2
George G. III was a kind of "consecrated obstruction" BAGEHOT, WALTER, 9
G. the First knew nothing JOHNSON, SAMUEL, 85
G. the First was always reckoned /Vile LANDOR, WALTER SAVAGE, 4
G. the Third /Ought never BENTLEY, EDMUND CLERIHEW, 5
King G. will be able to read that HANCOCK, JOHN, 1
George Bush G....tweedier version of Ronald Reagan ANDERSON, JOHN B., 1
Georgia glimpse some hill my G. high uprears LANIER, SIDNEY, 1
in north G., a lack of the niceties MITCHELL, MARGARET, 2
Georgian We've given up the G. poets EWART, GAVIN, 1
Georgie Porgie G., pudding and pie CHILDREN'S VERSE, 46
German After the war...G. entertainment was destroyed HÜTTER, RALF, 1
a G. and a genius! a prodigy SWIFT, JONATHAN, 54
A good G. cannot be a nationalist BRANDT, WILLY, 2
A G....someone who cannot tell a lie ADORNO, THEODOR, 1
another...century of G. music BEECHAM, THOMAS, 5
Are there G. philosophers BISMARCK, PRINCE OTTO VON, 1
G. misery must be broken...German steel HITLER, ADOLF, 35
history of the G. nation-state is at an end JASPERS, KARL, 1
isn't going to be...G. reunification LEWIS, FLORA, 1
It says /a lot about G. morals /that we stick to this...custom HEINE, HEINRICH, 6
no better place...G. bed of feathers HEINE, HEINRICH, 5
People don't understand G. KRAUS, KARL, 18
start a sentence in G....end it in English ATKINS, P. W., 2
The G. is the eternal student MANN, THOMAS, 5
The G.'s revolutions are the puppet shows of world history MANN, THOMAS, 6
the G. text of French operas WHARTON, EDITH, 8
the literary G. dives into a sentence TWAIN, MARK, 8
Those perfect G. Orientalists YEHOSHUA, A. B., 3
German Reich the criminal pride of the G. ANONYMOUS, 20
German Republic Long live the great G. SCHEIDEMANN, PHILIPP, 1
Germans Don't Let's Be Beastly to the G. COWARD, NOEL, 30
G. have a normality bordering on the tedious ENZENSBERGER, HANS, 5
G....learn not to regard the Jew HIMMLER, HEINRICH, 1
G....not brave enough to be afraid GRASS, GÜNTER, 5
G....prepare for the last war TUCHMAN, BARBARA, 1
G....will end by ruining our idea HITLER, ADOLF, 5
How appallingly thorough these G. HUXLEY, ALDOUS, 55
no people more dismembered than the G. HÖLDERLIN, FRIEDRICH, 2
The G. are exceedingly fond of Rhine wines TWAIN, MARK, 11
The G....are going to be squeezed GEDDES, ERIC, 1
The G. are praised KANT, IMMANUEL, 25
the G. seem a philosophical people MANN, GOLO, 1
The G....will never pose a threat KOHL, HELMUT, 4
three very powerful nations of the G. BEDE, 3
We G. fear God and nothing else BISMARCK, PRINCE OTTO VON, 17
Germany arbitrary division of G....senseless DUMAS, ROLAND, 1
A reunited G. would be a colossus GRASS, GÜNTER, 2
every country except G. was afraid GREY, EDWARD, 1
G. calling JOYCE, WILLIAM, 1
G., Germany before all else HOFFMANN VON FALLERSLEBEN, HEINRICH, 1
G. is our fatherland KOHL, HELMUT, 3
G. is winning...help Russia TRUMAN, HARRY S., 9
G....linked with...sign of pacifism OSSIETZKY, CARL VON, 4
G....no tradition of liberty OSSIETZKY, CARL VON, 5
G.'s greatest power...economic impotence FOLLETT, MARY PARKER, 1
G....taken seriously Shelley's famous dictum GAY, PETER, 1
G. was the cause of Hitler HITLER, ADOLF, 15
G., when it mobilizes against Russia MOLTKE, HELMUTH JOHANNES VON, 3
G....where the hands of the men are better cared for COLLIER, PRICE, 1
G. will be...a world power HITLER, ADOLF, 34
G....wrecked by...idea of power OSSIETZKY, CARL VON, 3
history of G....history of wars HAMILTON, ALEXANDER, 5
Let us put G....in the saddle BISMARCK, PRINCE OTTO VON, 18
relationship of G. to the family of European peoples HAVEL, VACLAV, 1
Their aim is to reduce G. to ruins HITLER, ADOLF, 18
what will become of G. ADENAUER, KONRAD, 1
germ plasm pool of human g....is deteriorating PAULING, LINUS, 1
germs the g. of a success that will blossom in time HARPER, FRANCES E. W., 1
Gershwin George G. died last week GERSHWIN, GEORGE, 3
Gertrude Stein G....unreadable at times BORGES, JORGE LUIS, 2
gestalt therapy G....guilt...much simpler PERLS, FRITZ, 1
gesture an unconscious g. of television-enforced democracy ROY, ARUNDHATI, 1
gestures dancer's g. are signs of things AUGUSTINE OF HIPPO, SAINT, 15
get a round of G. the Guests ALBEE, EDWARD, 3
can't always g. what you want JAGGER, MICK, 4
gets off he g. with women because he can't get on FLEMING, IAN, 1
getting up g....not so easy /...as lying HOOD, THOMAS, 7
ghetto A g. can be improved BALDWIN, JAMES, 11
ghost g....I haven't got the smell for 'em ELIOT, GEORGE, 24
g. /That eats handkerchiefs MORGENSTERN, CHRISTIAN, 1
please my g....and wink...at some homely girl MENCKEN, H. L., 39
the G. in the Machine DESCARTES, RENÉ, 3

You've obviously never spoken to a g. KAFKA, FRANZ, 1
ghosts g. went...electric light came in WHARTON, EDITH, 3
ghost stories g....spiritualized essence of fear WOOLF, VIRGINIA, 23
ghost story the "g."...form of the fairy tale JAMES, HENRY, 14
GI Every G. in Europe...lost one of his best friends EISENHOWER, DWIGHT D., 29
Giaconda a G. /that had to be stolen MAYAKOVSKY, VLADIMIR, 8
Gianni G....was glitz, glitz, glitz VERSACE, GIANNI, 1
giant it is excellent /To have a g.'s strength SHAKESPEARE, WILLIAM, 429
giants not g. but windmills CERVANTES, MIGUEL DE, 18
Giants G. three, Dodgers nothing ROOSEVELT, FRANKLIN D., 29
gibberish Whenever a poet...spouts g. ECO, UMBERTO, 2
gift first great g. we can bestow MORELL, THOMAS, 2
for this g. I feel blest COBAIN, KURT, 2
most fateful g....knowledge without skill PESTALOZZI, JOHANN HEINRICH, 6
gift horse Never look a g. PROVERBS, 339
gift-horse look a g. in the mouth BUTLER, SAMUEL (1612–80), 7
gifts Give g. to those who should know love SHANGE, NTOZAKE, 4
g. persuade even the gods EURIPIDES, 11
Rich g. wax poor when givers prove unkind SHAKESPEARE, WILLIAM, 182
gig We'd...go anywhere to play a g. GALLAGHER, NOEL, 1
gild To g. refined gold, to paint the lily SHAKESPEARE, WILLIAM, 328
gin G. was mother's milk SHAW, GEORGE BERNARD, 76
stronger than g. before breakfast FIELDS, W. C., 2
gin joints Of all the g. in all the towns in all the world BOGART, HUMPHREY, 4
Giotto G....as a beginner he painted flies FILARETE, 1
girdle I'll put a g. round about the earth SHAKESPEARE, WILLIAM, 57
girl a g. of thirty is virtually on the shelf ZHANG JIE, 1
Any g. can be glamorous LAMARR, HEDY, 1
Any g. who was a lady LOOS, ANITA, 5
Every little g. knows about love SAGAN, FRANÇOISE, 1
Give me a g. at an impressionable age SPARK, MURIEL, 8
g....raped by a brute SAND, GEORGE, 5
How can I, that g....My attention fix YEATS, W. B., 13
in a little g....threat of a woman DUMAS, ALEXANDRE, 6
little g. /Who had a little curl MILLER, MAX, 1
One g. can be pretty FITZGERALD, F. SCOTT, 18
the only g. in the world GROSSMITH, GEORGE, 1
this g. with...hopes to the woman O'BRIEN, EDNA, 2
What can you say about a 25-year-old g. who died SEGAL, ERICH, 2
girls always...new g. in town WARHOL, ANDY, 5
G. are so queer ALCOTT, LOUISA MAY, 4
g....had to behave like little ladies WILDER, LAURA INGALLS, 2
Good g. go to heaven BROWN, HELEN GURLEY, 1
if ever I was to have a dozen g., I'd call 'em all Jane WELLS, H. G., 6
life with g. has ended HORACE, 47
one of the nicest g....ever engaged WODEHOUSE, P. G., 16
prevent g. from being girls HOPE, ANTHONY, 4
pubescent g. have any inclination toward dancing DE MILLE, AGNES, 1
send little g. to school CHRISTINE DE PISAN, 1
Thank heaven for little g. LERNER, ALAN JAY, 3
Two g. in silk kimonos YEATS, W. B., 57
When you see what some g. marry ROWLAND, HELEN, 5
give For God's sake, please g. it up BOLYAI, FARKAS, 1
G. every man thy ear...few thy voice SHAKESPEARE, WILLIAM, 151
G. me my scallop-shell of quiet RALEIGH, WALTER, 6
G. the lady what she wants FIELD, MARSHALL, 1
Say will you g. me a lift? DOS PASSOS, JOHN, 9
To g. and not to count the cost LOYOLA, IGNATIUS OF, 2
given I would have g. you another JARRY, ALFRED, 3
unto every one that hath shall be g. BIBLE, 429
gives He g. twice who gives promptly PUBLILIUS SYRUS, 17
giving The manner of g. CORNEILLE, PIERRE, 8
glacier tug the g. backwards PROVERBS, 478
glad g. if I had written it PIRON, ALEXIS, 1
glamor G....makes a man ask for your telephone number DACHÉ, LILLY, 1
kind of g., a purple-gold glamor MCCARTHY, MARY, 2
glamorize g. addiction to sell clothes CLINTON, BILL, 8
glances piercing g. into the life of things MOORE, MARIANNE, 7
glands determined by...ductless g. and our viscera HUXLEY, ALDOUS, 36
glass A double g. o' the inwariable DICKENS, CHARLES, 82
g. I drink from is not large MUSSET, ALFRED DE, 1
The g. is falling hour by hour MACNEICE, LOUIS, 5
glittering The world continues to offer g. prizes SMITH, F. E., 2
glitters All that g. is not gold PROVERBS, 125
global g. business community...becoming a learning community SENGE, PETER M., 4
G. democratic capitalism is...unrealizable GRAY, JOHN, 2
global economy In the...g., everything is mobile CLINTON, BILL, 14
prospering in the g. CLINTON, BILL, 15
global markets Nothing disrupts g. KRUGMAN, PAUL, 5
global village no such thing as a g. MURDOCH, RUPERT, 3
global warming g. is a rock-solid certainty RAYMOND, LEE R., 2
gloom radiating g. he acts as a depressant HORNEY, KAREN, 16
gloomy g., hare-brained enthusiast HUME, DAVID, 4
glorious A g. age, a glorious age WOLFE, TOM, 15
a g. thing GILBERT, W. S., 36
I'll make thee g. by my pen MONTROSE, JAMES GRAHAM, 3
glory Another g. awaits us in heaven PETRARCH, 4
chief g. of every people...its authors JOHNSON, SAMUEL, 19
g. and the nothing of a name BYRON, LORD, 7
greatest g. is not in never falling CONFUCIUS, 14
g. to God in the highest BIBLE, 325
G. to Man in the highest SWINBURNE, ALGERNON CHARLES, 1
how quickly the g. of the world passes KEMPIS, THOMAS À, 3
I go to g. DUNCAN, ISADORA, 12
know what you mean by 'g.' CARROLL, LEWIS, 28
Let us not scorn g. too much CHATEAUBRIAND, RENÉ, 3
passed away a g. from the earth WORDSWORTH, WILLIAM, 50
paths of g. lead...to the grave GRAY, THOMAS, 6
resounding g. of eras to come MANDELSTAM, OSIP, 3
So passes the g. of the world ANONYMOUS, 18
'Twas my one G. DICKINSON, EMILY, 12
What price G. ANDERSON, MAXWELL, 2
glotoun A g. of wordes LANGLAND, WILLIAM, 6
glove that I were a g. upon that hand SHAKESPEARE, WILLIAM, 547
gluttony G. is an emotional escape DE VRIES, PETER, 2
GNP Man does not live by G. alone SAMUELSON, P. A., 2

go g., and do thou likewise BIBLE, 337
Let us g. then, you and I ELIOT, T. S., 33
shall we g. BECKETT, SAMUEL, 30
goal G. setting...manifestation of creative imagination COVEY, STEPHEN R., 1
My personal g....last 10 years KELLY, PATRICK C., 2
goat plucking the wild g. by the beard WOOLF, VIRGINIA, 9
god i found g. in myself /& i loved her /i loved her fiercely SHANGE, NTOZAKE, 1
What g. would be hanging around Terminal Two ADAMS, DOUGLAS, 10
You are your own g. HAMMARSKJÖLD, DAG, 9
God A G. of the Gaps SAGAN, CARL, 17
A G. who let us prove his existence BONHOEFFER, DIETRICH, 1
All men...come close to G. BUBER, MARTIN, 1
All service ranks the same with G. BROWNING, ROBERT, 67
A most just and good G. WEYER, JOHANN, 2
An honest G. INGERSOLL, ROBERT G., 5
Any G. I ever felt in church WALKER, ALICE, 20
Are G. and Nature then at strife HALLAM, ARTHUR HENRY, 10
Batter my heart, three person'd G. DONNE, JOHN, 23
Be concerned only with how you appear to G. UNAMUNO Y JUGO, MIGUEL DE, 3
better to have no opinion of G. BACON, FRANCIS (1561–1626), 68
didn't love G., he just fancied AUDEN, W. H., 1
Even a G. cannot change the past AGATHON, 1
even G. was born /too late LOWELL, ROBERT, 8
Every man thinks G. is on his side ANOUILH, JEAN, 9
Fear G., and take your own part BORROW, GEORGE HENRY, 5
final proof of G.'s omnipotence DE VRIES, PETER, 7
find a G. by five o'clock JOWETT, BENJAMIN, 7
For where G. built a church LUTHER, MARTIN, 11
G. a bad time for making him bald SINATRA, FRANK, 1
G....a cosmic Cheshire cat HUXLEY, JULIAN, 2
G. all-bounteous, all creative SMART, CHRISTOPHER, 3
G. Almighty first planted a garden BACON, FRANCIS (1561–1626), 31
G. alone deserves to be loved SAND, GEORGE, 3
G. as a working hypothesis BONHOEFFER, DIETRICH, 6
G. be in my head FOLK VERSE, 45
G. be thanked who has matched us with His hour BROOKE, RUPERT, 3
G. bless...God damn THURBER, JAMES, 20
G. bless the child that's got his own HOLIDAY, BILLIE, 1
"G. bless us every one!" DICKENS, CHARLES, 2
G. blew and they were scattered ANONYMOUS, 19
G....caught his eye KAUFMAN, GEORGE S., 3
G....cause of all time and eternity DIONYSIUS THE AREOPAGITE, 1
G. changes not what is in a people KORAN, 16
G....corrected his mistakes and made Wales HEPBURN, KATHARINE, 4
G. did send me JOAN OF ARC, SAINT, 1
G. does arithmetic GAUSS, CARL FRIEDRICH, 5
G. does nothing to stop...nefarious activity JUNG, CARL GUSTAV, 11
G. does not live in buildings SACKS, JONATHAN, 1
G. does not want to be believed BUBER, MARTIN, 4
G....doesn't even need to exist BAUDELAIRE, CHARLES, 4
G. exists since mathematics is consistent WEIL, ANDRÉ, 1
G. gave us our memories BARRIE, J. M., 1
G. has been replaced BARAKA, IMAMU AMIRI, 12
G. has foreknowledge of what all men will do JUSTIN MARTYR, SAINT, 1
G. has forgotten me CALMENT, JEANNE, 1
G. has no religion GANDHI, MAHATMA, 24
G. has not...power of a malicious woman WEYER, JOHANN, 3
G. has pity on kindergarten children AMICHAI, YEHUDA, 6
G. has touch'd him! Why should we WHITTIER, JOHN GREENLEAF, 4
G. has written all the books BUTLER, SAMUEL (1835–1902), 20
G. heals, and the doctor PROVERBS, 235
G. helps those PROVERBS, 236
G....integrates empirically EINSTEIN, ALBERT, 50
G. is a gentleman ORTON, JOE, 6
G. is always on the side PROVERBS, 237
G. is always on the side of the heaviest battalions VOLTAIRE, 13
G. is a mathematician DIRAC, PAUL, 1
G. /is an absentee landlord MCCAIG, NORMAN, 13
G....is a verb FULLER, R. BUCKMINSTER, 2
G. is but a word LAMARTINE, ALPHONSE DE, 6
G. is dead NIETZSCHE, FRIEDRICH WILHELM, 29
G. is dead! Heaven is empty NERVAL, GÉRARD DE, 4
G. /Is distant, difficult HILL, GEOFFREY, 1
G. is in the details MIES VAN DER ROHE, LUDWIG, 2
G. is like a...Geometrician BROWNE, THOMAS, 17
G. is love, but get it in writing LEE, GYPSY ROSE, 1
G. is man idealized BARAKA, IMAMU AMIRI, 8
G. is no respecter of persons BIBLE, 15
G. is not a word...but a consciousness RADHAKRISHNAN, SARVEPALLI, 5
G. is nothing more than an exalted father FREUD, SIGMUND, 25
G. is not in the habit of coming down from heaven BIKO, STEPHEN, 3
G. is really only another artist PICASSO, PABLO, 10
G. is subtle but he is not malicious EINSTEIN, ALBERT, 46
G. is the friend of silence TERESA OF CALCUTTA, MOTHER, 8
G. is the perfect poet BROWNING, ROBERT, 64
G. is the...refuge of the incompetent MENCKEN, H. L., 11
G. is thy law, thou mine MILTON, JOHN, 58
G....just like all the other mens WALKER, ALICE, 21
G. knows in advance the possibilities GERSONIDES, 1
G....loves His world so much BROWNING, ROBERT, 69
G. made everything out of nothing VALÉRY, PAUL, 3
G. made the country COWPER, WILLIAM, 26
G. made the woman for the man TENNYSON, ALFRED, 43
G. made us from the waist down O'CASEY, SEAN, 8
G....meant everyone to be in bed KEILLOR, GARRISON, 5
G....moral source of all slavery BAKUNIN, MIKHAIL, 2
G. moves in a mysterious way COWPER, WILLIAM, 24
G. never shut one door...closed another PLUNKETT, JAMES, 2
G. not only plays dice HAWKING, STEPHEN, 5
G....personified incomprehensibility LICHTENBERG, GEORG CHRISTOPH, 8
G. rest you merry, gentlemen FOLK VERSE, 35
G., Satan, Paradise and Hell all vanished one day RUSHDIE, SALMAN, 3
G. seems to have left the receiver off the hook KOESTLER, ARTHUR, 6
G. sent me down to kiss FISHER, CARRIE, 2
G.'s gifts put man's best gifts to shame BROWNING, ELIZABETH BARRETT, 7
G. should go before such villains SHAKESPEARE, WILLIAM, 459
G....shown me...spot to locate His people YOUNG, BRIGHAM, 5
G. shows his contempt for wealth O'MALLEY, AUSTIN, 1

G....taking, literally, a hell of a risk MACKIE, J. L., 2
G. tempers the wind STERNE, LAURENCE, 3
G.! There is no god but he KORAN, 8
G. will bring forth...believers in the graves AL-MUFID, ABU ABDULLAH MUHAMMAD AL-HARITHI AL-BAGHDADI, 10
G. will pardon me...is His trade HEINE, HEINRICH, 8
G. wrote it. I merely did his dictation STOWE, HARRIET BEECHER, 7
G., You who are somewhere BERGMAN, INGMAR, 8
Had I but served G. as diligently WOLSEY, THOMAS, 1
hand folks over to G.'s mercy ELIOT, GEORGE, 10
Has G. then forgotten LOUIS XIV, 10
have one G. only CLOUGH, ARTHUR HUGH, 5
honest G.'s the noblest work of man BUTLER, SAMUEL (1835–1902), 6
I could prove G. statistically GALLUP, GEORGE, 1
I do not believe in a personal G. EINSTEIN, ALBERT, 11
If G. be for us who can be against us? TUTU, DESMOND, 3
If G. did not exist VOLTAIRE, 28
If G. exists, all depends on him CAMUS, ALBERT, 14
If G. hadn't rested on Sunday GARCÍA MÁRQUEZ, GABRIEL, 14
if G. had wanted us to share our homes BARRY, DAVE, 3
If G. made us in His image VOLTAIRE, 34
If the concept of G. has...validity BALDWIN, JAMES, 21
If you talk to G., you are praying SZASZ, THOMAS, 12
I have always declared G. to be...distinct SMITH, JOSEPH, 3
I have found G., but he is insufficient MILLER, HENRY, 19
I neglect G. and his angels DONNE, JOHN, 25
in the aftermath of the death of G. RUSHDIE, SALMAN, 8
In the name of G., Most Gracious KORAN, 1
I see G. in...shoes LANG, K.D., 1
I see the marks of G. CHANNING, WILLIAM ELLERY, 3
it pisses G. off if you walk by the color purple WALKER, ALICE, 26
I wish...G. had not given me what I prayed for SPYRI, JOHANNA, 1
know where G. is, ask a drunk BUKOWSKI, CHARLES, 5
man destroys G. GOLDBLUM, JEFF, 1
Many people believe that they are attracted by G. INGE, WILLIAM RALPH, 7
May G. deny you peace UNAMUNO Y JUGO, MIGUEL DE, 7
My G., my Father, and my Friend DILLON, WENTWORTH, 2
"My G.," said God SQUIRE, J. C., 3
nearest thing I can do to being G. STEIGER, ROD, 1
no G....try getting a plumber ALLEN, WOODY, 5
Nothing that G. ever made HURSTON, ZORA NEALE, 6
not to pare down G.'s omnipotence JUNG, CARL GUSTAV, 10
One G., one law, one element HALLAM, ARTHUR HENRY, 17
One on G.'s side is a majority PHILLIPS, WENDELL, 2
only acceptable form...G. can...appear is...promise of food GANDHI, MAHATMA, 16
only...G. and angels...be lookers on BACON, FRANCIS (1561–1626), 93
only G. can make a tree KILMER, JOYCE, 2
Our G. and soldiers we alike adore QUARLES, FRANCIS, 1
Our G., our help in ages past WATTS, ISAAC, 10
Ours is the one G. ATHENAGORAS, 2
People think pleasing G. WALKER, ALICE, 27
pray to G. that He absolve VILLON, FRANÇOIS, 3
Put your trust in G., my boys BLACKER, VALENTINE, 1
relation to G....billboards did to Coca-Cola UPDIKE, JOHN, 1
sneak a look at G.'s cards EINSTEIN, ALBERT, 12
thanked G. for...bite of raw dog PEARY, ROBERT EDWIN, 4
Thank G. men cannot as yet fly THOREAU, HENRY DAVID, 15
The Direction of G. is the true direction KORAN, 2
The G. of distance and of absence MACHADO, ANTONIO, 11
The G. of love my Shepherd is HERBERT, GEORGE, 14
the hands of the living G. BIBLE, 143
the highest praise of G. consists in...denial PROUST, MARCEL, 16
the idea...G. will not help MENCKEN, H. L., 13
The immortal G. JAN III SOBIESKI, 1
There, but for the Grace of G., goes God WELLES, ORSON, 2
There's something wrong with G. HEAD, BESSIE, 1
The true G....is the God of ideas VIGNY, ALFRED DE, 1
The whole world is a name of G. KHOMEINI, RUHOLLAH, 9
the wind /scouring G.'s world BLOK, ALEKSANDR, 3
To know G.'s nature ALBO, JOSEPH, 1
to obstruct the way of G. KORAN, 3
To the greater glory of G. MOTTOS AND SLOGANS, 18
understand G.'s thoughts...study statistics NIGHTINGALE, FLORENCE, 6
We are G.'s bouquet LITTLE RICHARD, 1
We believe in G. and the revelation KORAN, 5
we cannot know what G. is AQUINAS, THOMAS, 7
we would know the mind of G. HAWKING, STEPHEN, 4
What G. does, He does well LA FONTAINE, JEAN DE, 7
what G. would have done...the money HART, MOSS, 1
What sort of G. are we portraying JENKINS, DAVID, 1
What was G. doing AUGUSTINE OF HIPPO, SAINT, 5
When G. gives you a rash, he also gives you nails to scratch it with NWAPA, FLORA, 4
When G....unsaid all his sacred books QABBANI, NIZAR, 5
When I found out...that G. was white WALKER, ALICE, 30
Where G. hath a temple BURTON, ROBERT, 24
Wherever G. erects a house of prayer DEFOE, DANIEL, 10
whom G. to ruin has designed DRYDEN, JOHN, 41
Whom G. would destroy DUPORT, JAMES, 1
with G. he passed the days PARNELL, THOMAS, 1
yearning like a G. in pain KEATS, JOHN (1795–1821), 71

goddam it's the g. lousy system DOS PASSOS, JOHN, 15

goddess She moves a g., and she looks a queen POPE, ALEXANDER, 69
the g. who belched KIRSTEIN, LINCOLN, 1
who could see the passage of a g. HOMER, 7

god-forsaken This g. city BEECHAM, THOMAS, 4

Godot We're waiting for G. BECKETT, SAMUEL, 24

gods all G. dead, all wars fought FITZGERALD, F. SCOTT, 14
All the g. are dead CLEAVER, ELDRIDGE, 5
By the nine g. he swore MACAULAY, THOMAS BABINGTON, 21
Concerning the g. I have no means PROTAGORAS, 1
g....Make instruments to plague us SHAKESPEARE, WILLIAM, 367
no other g. before me BIBLE, 80
So many g., so many creeds WILCOX, ELLA WHEELER, 4
The g....myopia makes all error mortal LOWELL, ROBERT, 19
The G., that wanton in the air, /Know no such liberty LOVELACE, RICHARD, 2
The G. themselves cannot recall their gifts TENNYSON, ALFRED, 8
use the g.' gifts wisely HORACE, 53
Whom the g. love dies young MENANDER, 1
whom the g. love dies young PLAUTUS, 1
Whom the g. wish to destroy CONNOLLY, CYRIL, 5

god-step g. at the margins of thought DUNCAN, ROBERT, 1

goe To morowe longe I to g. to God MORE, THOMAS, 1

Goebbels G. decreed..."Judeo-Negroid" swing sounds...potentially harmful CAMPBELL, JAMES, 1
Goethe Official Germany celebrated G....as opium GOETHE, JOHANN WOLFGANG VON, 3
Gog G. and Magog BIBLE, 474
going am I g. to my bed MUNRO, NEIL, 2
I am just g. outside OATES, LAWRENCE, 1
Where are you g. to, my pretty maid CHILDREN'S VERSE, 3
gold all the g. that the goose could give AESOP, 4
cursed /craving for g. VIRGIL, 12
For g. in phisik is a cordial CHAUCER, GEOFFREY, 20
g....God of our time HEINE, HEINRICH, 9
G. is for the mistress KIPLING, RUDYARD, 48
G. that buys health WEBSTER, JOHN, 15
If g. ruste, what shall iren do CHAUCER, GEOFFREY, 13
Nothing melts a Woman's heart like g. CENTLIVRE, SUSANNAH, 1
picking g....dunghills of old Roman writers VIRGIL, 2
stand a great deal of g. JAMES, HENRY, 40
To a shower of g. CARLYLE, THOMAS, 38
turn his g. into smoke ELIZABETH I, 20
golde All is not g. that outward shewith bright LYDGATE, JOHN, 1
golden all my G. Money /on...Silver Shoes ANONYMOUS, 51
G. chalices, wooden priests FOLK VERSE, 5
No g. weights can turn the scale HARPER, FRANCES E. W., 4
the g. mean HORACE, 38
there are no g. rules SHAW, GEORGE BERNARD, 66
golden age your future G. that displeases me LU XUN, 17
gold rush A g. is what happens when WEST, MAE, 9
Goldsmith Here lies Nolly G. GOLDSMITH, OLIVER, 1
Goldwyn knew where you were with G. GOLDWYN, SAMUEL, 1
golf bestowed upon the games of g. and bridge EISENHOWER, DWIGHT D., 4
G. is a game whose aim CHURCHILL, WINSTON, 78
G. is a good walk spoiled TWAIN, MARK, 50
G. is not...a fair game NICKLAUS, JACK, 6
G. may be played on Sunday LEACOCK, STEPHEN, 18
impossible to remember how tragic...playing g. LYND, ROBERT, 2
I wasn't this nervous playing g. when I was drinking DALY, JOHN, 1
more satisfying to be a bad player at g. GULBENKIAN, NUBAR SARKIS, 2
Television controls the game of g. NICKLAUS, JACK, 5
golf clubs g....and a beautiful partner BENNY, JACK, 3
G.O.M. The G., when his life ebbs out GLADSTONE, WILLIAM EWART, 2
Gomorrahs wooden-walled G. of the deep MELVILLE, HERMAN, 16
gone G. before /To that unknown and silent shore LAMB, CHARLES, 3
G. with the Wind MITCHELL, MARGARET, 1
It will be g. by June NEWSPAPERS, 32
good A G. Time Was Had by All SMITH, STEVIE, 6
All things work together for g. BIBLE, 482
Anybody can be g. in the country WILDE, OSCAR, 66
as gods, knowing g. and evil BIBLE, 112
Being g. is good business RODDICK, ANITA, 2
Do all the g. you can WESLEY, JOHN, 3
Do g. by stealth POPE, ALEXANDER, 36
doing g. to base fellows CERVANTES, MIGUEL DE, 23
G. and ill...are entirely relative HUME, DAVID, 33
G. at a fight SHERIDAN, RICHARD BRINSLEY, 1
G., but not religious-good HARDY, THOMAS, 30
G. can imagine Evil AUDEN, W. H., 11
g. in everything SHAKESPEARE, WILLIAM, 98
G. isn't the word GILBERT, W. S., 46
g. is: to forgive evil PORCHIA, ANTONIO, 10
G. things, when short, are twice as good GRACIÁN, BALTASAR, 1
g. without qualification...good will KANT, IMMANUEL, 23
G. wood is better than good paint PROVERBS, 491
He tried the luxury of doing g. CRABBE, GEORGE, 2
He who would do g....do it in Minute Particulars BLAKE, WILLIAM, 12
I also say it is g. to fall WHITMAN, WALT, 32
If you can't be g. PROVERBS, 268
In doing g....afraid of being...right BURKE, EDMUND, 17
it cannot come to g. SHAKESPEARE, WILLIAM, 143
It's wiser being g. than bad BROWNING, ROBERT, 30
I was just as g. when I was poor MARLEY, BOB, 4
I will be g. VICTORIA, 6
Men have never been g. BARTH, KARL, 1
Nothing is so g. as it seems ELIOT, GEORGE, 25
Only the g. die young PROVERBS, 358
point is to be g....and sincere PRIESTLEY, J. B., 11
Say not that the g. die CALLIMACHUS, 1
She was g. as she was fair ROGERS, SAMUEL, 1
the g. are always the merry YEATS, W. B., 46
The g. are better made by ill ROGERS, SAMUEL, 2
The g. die early, and the bad die late DEFOE, DANIEL, 2
the g. die first WORDSWORTH, WILLIAM, 81
The G. he scorn'd BLAIR, ROBERT, 3
The g. is...an immense landscape ORTEGA Y GASSET, JOSÉ, 7
The g. is the beautiful PLATO, 7
The g. of the people CICERO, 6
The greatest g. CICERO, 8
the g. things...in our own tradition APPELFIELD, AHARON, 1
There are g. women and good men HEAD, BESSIE, 6
There is no man so g. MONTAIGNE, MICHEL DE, 26
thou g. and faithful servant BIBLE, 428
Understanding the g. is fundamental ZHU XI, 1
we shall never be "beyond g. and evil" JUNG, CARL GUSTAV, 5
we trust that...g. /Will be the final goal of ill HALLAM, ARTHUR HENRY, 8
When I'm g. I'm very good WEST, MAE, 8
Whoso hath this world's g. BIBLE, 181
You Never Had It So G. MOTTOS AND SLOGANS, 3
You shouldn't say it is not g. WHISTLER, JAMES ABBOTT MCNEILL, 12
goodby G. to childhood MERRILL, JAMES, 1
goodbye G. to All That GRAVES, ROBERT, 2
science of saying g. MANDELSTAM, OSIP, 17
So g., dear, and amen PORTER, COLE, 12
good bye We have begun to say g. OPPEN, GEORGE, 3
goodbyes never any good dwelling on g. BIBESCU, ELIZABETH CHARLOTTE LUCY, 1
good deed If one g. in all my life SHAKESPEARE, WILLIAM, 679
good example if the lower orders don't set us a g. WILDE, OSCAR, 45
good heart people...took plenty of advantage of Louis' g. ARMSTRONG, LOUIS, 5
good-looking live fast, die young, and have a g. corpse HEAD, BESSIE, 5
goodly they left the g....pleasant city BRADFORD, WILLIAM, 4
good man Nothing can harm a g. SOCRATES, 6
You was a g. HARDY, THOMAS, 29

goodness G. does not...make men happy LANDOR, WALTER SAVAGE, 2
G. had nothing to do with it, dearie WEST, MAE, 11
g. is imprinted deeply in...man BACON, FRANCIS (1561–1626), 34
goodnight G., my darlings COWARD, NOEL, 25
goods All social primary g....distributed equally RAWLS, JOHN, 1
Good Samaritan No one would have remembered...G. THATCHER, MARGARET, 20
good will A g. is...good in itself KANT, IMMANUEL, 22
goose g. that lays the golden egg PROVERBS, 185
Lone g....yearns for the flock DU FU, 1
Goose Green leave theirs on the ground at G. KINNOCK, NEIL, 2
gorilla like a g. but less timid MCCAIG, NORMAN, 6
gormed I'm G. DICKENS, CHARLES, 27
gospel Either this is not the g. LINACRE, THOMAS, 1
preach the g. to every creature BIBLE, 366
The g. is meant to...afflict the comfortable KEILLOR, GARRISON, 8
gospels literal adherence to...the G. would mean sudden death WHITEHEAD, A. N., 1
We had no use for the policy of the G. KHRUSHCHEV, NIKITA, 6
gossip Men...detested women's g. JONG, ERICA, 1
gossips No one g. about...secret virtues RUSSELL, BERTRAND, 24
got Them's that g., lose GUY, ROSA, 3
gotcha G. NEWSPAPERS, 25
Gothic G. is...the only rational architecture RUSKIN, JOHN, 12
principle of the G. architecture COLERIDGE, SAMUEL TAYLOR, 58
gout drink wine you have the g. SYDENHAM, THOMAS, 1
g. /Had taken him in toe HOOD, THOMAS, 6
G. is not relieved by a fine shoe PLUTARCH, 18
I refer to g. ELLIS, HAVELOCK, 1
the pleasant titillation of the g. HAWTHORNE, NATHANIEL, 1
what is a cure for g. ABERNETHY, JOHN, 1
When I have the g....I was walking on my eyeballs SMITH, SYDNEY, 9
govern g. kingdoms with maxims found in books RICHELIEU, CARDINAL, 1
He that would g. others MASSINGER, PHILIP, 2
I will g. according to the common weal JAMES I, 6
Let the people think they g. PENN, WILLIAM, 7
Let those g. who prevent MAURA, ANTONIO, 3
No man is good enough to g. another man LINCOLN, ABRAHAM, 30
They'd rather even g. themselves badly VAN DER POST, LAURENS, 3
governed not so well g. as they ought HOOKER, RICHARD, 1
not willing to be g. by laws...no voice in making GRIMKÉ, ANGELINA EMILY, 1
governing the right of g. was not property but a trust FOX, CHARLES JAMES, 3
government admit of no g. by divine right HARRISON, WILLIAM HENRY, 2
A g. agency is the nearest thing to eternal life REAGAN, RONALD, 46
a g. organization could do it that quickly CARTER, JIMMY, 7
all g. is evil O'SULLIVAN, JOHN L., 1
All g....is founded on compromise and barter BURKE, EDMUND, 26
art of g. is to deal with threats KISSINGER, HENRY, 8
benevolent g. towards the people MENCIUS, 1
Every g. degenerates JEFFERSON, THOMAS, 37
free g. is...what the people think BURKE, EDMUND, 8
function of a g....to calm PALMERSTON, LORD, 6
function of g....easy for us to do good CARTER, JIMMY, 3
g....big enough to give you all you want GOLDWATER, BARRY, 5
g....built upon the rights of the people SUN YAT-SEN, 1
g. by crony ICKES, HAROLD L., 1
G. cannot close its eyes to the pollution ROOSEVELT, FRANKLIN D., 38
g. cannot endure...half slave LINCOLN, ABRAHAM, 31
G. exists to protect us REAGAN, RONALD, 18
G. gives me a count of corpses VONNEGUT, KURT, 11
g. gives us is charity at election time MARCOS, SUBCOMANDANTE, 1
g....greatest of all reflections...human nature MADISON, JAMES, 4
G. has no other end but the preservation of property LOCKE, JOHN, 8
g. has not been all that I had hoped DUVALIER, FRANÇOIS, 2
G....instituted for the common benefit MASON, GEORGE, 1
G. intervention...benefit of economic progress BLAIR, TONY, 3
G. is a contrivance of human wisdom BURKE, EDMUND, 40
G. is a referee REAGAN, RONALD, 47
g. is best in which every man ARISTOTLE, 26
g. is best which governs not at all THOREAU, HENRY DAVID, 20
G.,...is but a necessary evil PAINE, THOMAS, 1
G. is not the solution...government is the problem REAGAN, RONALD, 48
G. is the common enemy BERKMAN, ALEXANDER, 1
g....leader in the use of technology GATES, BILL, 2
g. officials have contempt for innocence MOSLEY, WALTER, 3
good g....less, not more, democracy MAHBUBANI, KISHORE, 1
G....organized benevolence or organized madness UPDIKE, JOHN, 4
G.'s purposes are beneficent BRANDEIS, LOUIS D., 3
No G....long secure without...Opposition DISRAELI, BENJAMIN, 6
no necessary evils in g. JACKSON, ANDREW, 4
one form of g. rather than another JOHNSON, SAMUEL, 102
people's g. WEBSTER, DANIEL, 4
the g. and the governed in opposition KENYATTA, JOMO, 3
The g. burns down whole cities MAO ZEDONG, 37
The g. must always be in advance of the public opinion ARNIM-BOYTZENBURG, ADOLF HEINRICH VON, 1
The g. of the absolute majority CALHOUN, JOHN C., 4
The important thing for G. KEYNES, JOHN MAYNARD, 17
The object of g....is not the glory of rulers BEVERIDGE, WILLIAM HENRY, 4
the things which g. does...social progress WARREN, EARL, 1
The worst g. is the most moral MENCKEN, H. L., 21
Things continue in g. VOLCKER, PAUL A., 1
We live under a g. of men PHILLIPS, WENDELL, 5
workings of g. that led...Vietnam War BLACK, HUGO LAFAYETTE, 1
government officials I think certain g., industrialists MEAD, MARGARET, 9
governments all G. are selfish ECCLES, DAVID MCADAM, 1
g....mainly engaged in kicking people around STEVENSON, ADLAI, 9
G. need...both shepherds and butchers VOLTAIRE, 40
g. to choose only *between* evils NYERERE, JULIUS KAMBARAGE, 1
G. will...let them have peace EISENHOWER, DWIGHT D., 10
governor g., much less president REAGAN, RONALD, 6
grab G. this land MORRISON, TONI, 16
grace but for the g. of God, goes BRADFORD, JOHN, 1
By g. are ye saved through faith BIBLE, 61
g. and virtue are within /Prohibited degrees BUTLER, SAMUEL (1612–80), 13
G. is given of God CLOUGH, ARTHUR HUGH, 12
G. under pressure HEMINGWAY, ERNEST, 21
Lord, I ascribe it to Thy g. WATTS, ISAAC, 5
she obtained g. and favour BIBLE, 65

The g. of the Lord Jesus Christ BIBLE, 169
gracehoper G. was always jigging ajog JOYCE, JAMES, 13
Graces the G. do not seem...natives of Great Britain CHESTERFIELD, LORD, 13
grades Neither in high or low g....hereditary succession BOOK OF LORD SHANG, 1
gradualism "G." is a mighty long road ROBESON, PAUL, 2
graduate G. students...grimly trained to be technicians PAGLIA, CAMILLE, 4
graduating g. with a "spinster of arts" degree STEINEM, GLORIA, 3
grail g. of laughter of an empty ash can CRANE, HART, 1
going to do with the G. BEERBOHM, MAX, 2
grain A g....generally given to horses JOHNSON, SAMUEL, 13
grammar G., which can govern even kings MOLIÈRE, 16
I am...above g. SIGISMUND, 2
Why care for g. WARD, ARTEMUS, 2
grammar school more fit for a g. than a Court of Parliament SALISBURY, LORD, 1
grammatical refine our language to g. purity JOHNSON, SAMUEL, 43
grammere G., that grounde is of al LANGLAND, WILLIAM, 3
grand A "G. Old Man" LEACOCK, STEPHEN, 17
Grand Canyon coming across him at the G. SHAW, GEORGE BERNARD, 10
Grand Central Station By G. I Sat Down and Wept SMART, ELIZABETH, 1
grandeur beauty and g. of The One State ZAMYATIN, YEVGENY, 4
charged with the g. of God HOPKINS, GERARD MANLEY, 3
g. of the dooms KEATS, JOHN (1795–1821), 82
grandfather g.'s clock WORK, HENRY CLAY, 3
I don't know who my g. was LINCOLN, ABRAHAM, 40
grandson g. of the one who brought the good news HUSAIN, 3
grant O g. me, Heaven, a middle state MALLET, DAVID, 1
grapes I am sure the g. are sour AESOP, 3
grapeshot A whiff of g. CARLYLE, THOMAS, 39
grass goes to g. BEAUMONT, FRANCIS, 6
g. will grow in the streets HOOVER, HERBERT, 9
grasshoppers G....are exceptionally nutritious food FARB, PETER, 1
grateful The g. dead ANONYMOUS, 38
gratification I have had no real g....more than my neighbor VANDERBILT, WILLIAM HENRY, 1
gratitude g....a secret hope for greater favors LA ROCHEFOUCAULD, FRANÇOIS, 25
G. is cowardice DUVALIER, FRANÇOIS, 1
G., like love, is never...dependable ALSOP, JOSEPH, 1
gratuities g. rather than any direct bribe FOX, HARRISON W., JR., 8
grave Dig the g. both wide and deep FERGUSON, SAMUEL, 1
g....like a ditch from...Hell AL-TIRMIDHI, 1
G.,...place in which the dead are laid BIERCE, AMBROSE, 24
I shall soon be laid in the quiet g. KEATS, JOHN (1795–1821), 19
most still, most secret, and most g. SHAKESPEARE, WILLIAM, 205
O g.! where is thy victory? /O death! where is thy sting? POPE, ALEXANDER, 66
one foot already in the g. PLUTARCH, 9
The g.'s a fine and private place MARVELL, ANDREW, 14
They give birth astride of a g. BECKETT, SAMUEL, 26
To that dark inn, the g. SCOTT, SIR WALTER, 29
graveyards I have no bone to pick with g. BECKETT, SAMUEL, 6
one of the healthiest g. in Dublin BEHAN, BRENDAN, 5
gravitation g....by the fall of an apple NEWTON, ISAAC, 4
gravity alters the...g. of the universe CARLYLE, THOMAS, 29
gravy Davy /Abominated g. BENTLEY, EDMUND CLERIHEW, 4
gray hairs G. are death's blossoms PROVERBS, 239
great Almost everything that is g. DISRAELI, BENJAMIN, 8
g., ere fortune made him CROMWELL, OLIVER, 2
G. I call the elusive LAOZI, 4
G. men are but life-sized BEERBOHM, MAX, 6
g. ones have a little something extra ATKINSON, BROOKS, 1
G. White Way PAINE, ALBERT BIGELOW, 1
made me too g. for my house ELIZABETH I, 1
No g. man lives in vain CARLYLE, THOMAS, 25
Nothing g....without enthusiasm EMERSON, RALPH WALDO, 7
On earth...nothing g. but man HAMILTON, WILLIAM (1788–1856), 2
Really g. people always see the best in others COLERIDGE-TAYLOR, SAMUEL, 1
The g. man...walks across his century LEACOCK, STEPHEN, 15
those who were truly g. SPENDER, STEPHEN, 4
To be g. is to be misunderstood EMERSON, RALPH WALDO, 18
great-aunt A person may be indebted...a g. HAZLITT, WILLIAM, 9
Great Britain G. has lost an Empire ACHESON, DEAN, 1
G. is going to make war BETHMANN HOLLWEG, THEOBALD VON, 1
Great Depression went through...G. without missing a meal ASIMOV, ISAAC, 1
greater g. love hath no man BIBLE, 293
g. than the *Iliad* PROPERTIUS, SEXTUS, 3
Something...which nothing g. can be thought ANSELM, SAINT, 4
The g. the power BURKE, EDMUND, 23
greatest I liv'd the g. prince o' the world SHAKESPEARE, WILLIAM, 84
I'm the g. ALI, MUHAMMAD, 13
greatness get out with my g. intact ALI, MUHAMMAD, 3
g. in goodness ATHENAEUS, 1
G. knows itself SHAKESPEARE, WILLIAM, 239
measure g....from the manger up JACKSON, JESSE, 9
Men who have g....don't go in for politics CAMUS, ALBERT, 4
some have g. thrust upon 'em SHAKESPEARE, WILLIAM, 702
Great Spirit May...G. shed light on yours BLACK HAWK, 2
Great Wall On the G....miles of moonlight LI HE, 1
Greece G....brought the arts HORACE, 27
G.! sad relic BYRON, LORD, 25
greed G....bottomless pit which exhausts FROMM, ERICH, 1
G. is all right BOESKY, IVAN, 1
G. is essential to the proper functioning DIMMA, WILLIAM, 1
Greek G. thought...is essential to high culture NORTON, CHARLES ELIOT, 1
it was G. to me SHAKESPEARE, WILLIAM, 296
mixture of smells...anthology of a G. holiday DURRELL, LAWRENCE, 5
Greeks G....did not even call thinking...philosophy HEIDEGGER, MARTIN, 1
G. Had a Word AKINS, ZOË, 1
G....practical and open-minded DAVIES, NORMAN, 1
Let G. be Greeks, and Women what they are BRADSTREET, ANNE, 2
where the G. had modesty, we have cant PEACOCK, THOMAS LOVE, 3
which came first, the G. or the Romans DISRAELI, BENJAMIN, 62
green G. grow the rushes O FOLK VERSE, 19
not quite so g. KIPLING, RUDYARD, 42
There is a g. hill far away ALEXANDER, C. F., 4
greenest the g. place I've never seen MOORE, MARIANNE, 5

Greenland great G. ice cap, silent, eternal, immeasurable PEARY, ROBERT EDWIN, 3
green politics G. is not...far left or far right ICKE, DAVID, 1
Greensleeves G. was all my joy FOLK VERSE, 28
greenwood Under the g. tree SHAKESPEARE, WILLIAM, 104
greetings g. where no kindness is WORDSWORTH, WILLIAM, 18
perhaps the g. are intended for me BEETHOVEN, LUDWIG VAN, 10
grey hair There is only one cure for g.....the guillotine WODEHOUSE, P. G., 25
grief A g. too much to be told VIRGIL, 9
between g. and nothing I will take grief FAULKNER, WILLIAM, 15
From perfect g. there need not be /Wisdom or even memory ROSSETTI, DANTE GABRIEL, 5
G. and disappointment give rise to anger HUME, DAVID, 13
G. has turned her fair WILDE, OSCAR, 84
G. never mended no broken bones DICKENS, CHARLES, 87
heart which g. hath cankered...remedy—the Tankard CALVERLEY, C. S., 1
My g. and my smile MISTRAL, GABRIELA, 2
No man can cause more g. FAULKNER, WILLIAM, 5
When one g. afflicts us we choose a sharper grief WALCOTT, DEREK, 4
you...must first feel g. HORACE, 5
griefs my g.; still am I king of those SHAKESPEARE, WILLIAM, 521
grievance a g. is...a purpose in life HOFFER, ERIC, 1
grievances redress of the g. of the vanquished CHURCHILL, WINSTON, 48
grieve G. not that I die young HASTINGS, FLORA, 1
grieving Margaret, are you g. HOPKINS, GERARD MANLEY, 6
grin ending with the g., which remained some time CARROLL, LEWIS, 11
grist All's g. that comes to the mill PROVERBS, 123
groaning hear the g. of oppressed people OZ, AMOS, 2
grope they g. in the dark BIBLE, 258
Groucho No, G. is not my real name MARX, GROUCHO, 3
ground a bit of g....call his own WARNER, CHARLES DUDLEY, 2
The fruitful g., the quiet mind SURREY, HENRY HOWARD, 1
group A g. of closely related persons MACAULAY, ROSE, 5
groupies We don't get g. STIPE, MICHAEL, 2
grovelled g. before...and my-lorded him THACKERAY, WILLIAM MAKEPEACE, 9
grow Green g. the rashes O BURNS, ROBERT, 20
growing Be not afraid of g. slowly PROVERBS, 24
one can't help g. older CARROLL, LEWIS, 8
growing up I wasn't good /At g. FANTHORPE, U. A., 1
So much of g. is an unbearable waiting SANCHEZ, SONIA, 2
growl a fellow...who does nothing...but...g. JOHNSON, SAMUEL, 95
grown-up If we are...a g. nation KENNAN, GEORGE F., 1
grown-ups g....have forgotten what it is like to be a child JARRELL, RANDALL, 4
grows Nothing g. in our garden THOMAS, DYLAN, 25
Nothing g. well in the shade BRANCUSI, CONSTANTIN, 1
growth G. does not always lead a business BRANSON, RICHARD, 4
G. is a greater mystery than death MAILER, NORMAN, 3
grub First comes the g., then...morals BRECHT, BERTOLT, 25
grudges I don't hold...g. more'n five years KENNEDY, WILLIAM, 1
grumbler I have always been a g. PRIESTLEY, J. B., 5
gruntled he was far from being g. WODEHOUSE, P. G., 18
guarantee No one can g. success in war CHURCHILL, WINSTON, 52
guard But who is to g. the guards themselves JUVENAL, 10
guardian angel A g. o'er his life presiding ROGERS, SAMUEL, 3
guerilla in g. warfare FANON, FRANTZ, 10
guerrilla g. fights the war of the flea TABER, ROBERT, 1
guess g. what a million people will like HUSTON, JOHN, 6
guests the g. must be chosen as carefully as the wine SAKI, 16
guided missiles We have g. and misguided men KING, MARTIN LUTHER, JR., 15
guiding A little onward lend thy g. hand MILTON, JOHN, 99
guilt g. of having a nice body DRABBLE, MARGARET, 2
g. to make you turn pale HORACE, 13
I have no sense of g. PANKHURST, EMMELINE, 3
guilty are you not as g....as I MIDDLETON, THOMAS, 5
better that ten g. persons escape BLACKSTONE, WILLIAM, 5
feel...g. about laughing WATERS, JOHN, 1
g. conscience needs no accuser PROVERBS, 93
"I feel so g.." UPDIKE, JOHN, 17
If...persons g. of Oscar Wilde's offences STEAD, W. I., 1
It is quite gratifying to feel g. ARENDT, HANNAH, 10
Let g. men remember their black deeds WEBSTER, JOHN, 12
Let no g. man escape GRANT, ULYSSES S., 9
guinea pig monstrous to introduce under the skin of a g. LISTER, JOSEPH, 2
guinea pigs Laboratory g. say to themselves GÓMEZ DE LA SERNA, RAMÓN, 4
We're all of us g. in the laboratory of God WILLIAMS, TENNESSEE, 6
guineas I have only five g. in my pocket PETERBOROUGH, 3RD EARL OF, 1
guitar his g....whole back-country of melancholy LARKIN, PHILIP, 10
I do not play the g. for applause PARRA, VIOLETA, 1
Gulf War G....peoples terrorized by...destruction MERNISSI, FATIMA, 3
G....surprised to find yourself singing MERNISSI, FATIMA, 2
gun Every g....theft from those who hunger EISENHOWER, DWIGHT D., 21
g. is the ideal weapon MOSLEY, OSWALD, 3
have a man come through a door with a g. in his hand CHANDLER, RAYMOND, 11
hear the word "culture"...reach for my g. JOHST, HANNS, 1
I have no g., but I can spit AUDEN, W. H., 50
looks like he's carrying a g. FISHER, CARRIE, 5
she...fired her g. STANTON, ELIZABETH CADY, 1
The difference between a g. and a tree POUND, EZRA, 9
gunpowder G., Printing, and the Protestant Religion CARLYLE, THOMAS, 15
guns g. in the jungle stew SMITH, STEVIE, 3
g. on the slope roared out a message CRANE, STEPHEN, 13
G. will make us powerful GOERING, HERMANN, 1
I do not foresee meson g. FRISCH, O.R., 1
O charioteers, above your dormant g. HEANEY, SEAMUS, 3
Such a lot of g....so few brains BOGART, HUMPHREY, 9
guts progress through the g. of a beggar SHAKESPEARE, WILLIAM, 208
gutter We are all in the g. WILDE, OSCAR, 31
guy G.'s Only Doin' it for Some Doll LOESSER, FRANK, 6
guys The g. with that humble pouch WAX, RUBY, 1
guys and dolls G. RUNYON, DAMON, 11
gymnasium I was sitting in the g. writing MINGUS, CHARLES, 3

gypsies Play with the g. in the wood CHILDREN'S VERSE, 9
gypsy g. passion for separation TSVETAEVA, MARINA, 7

habit A h. the pleasure of which increases ADAMS, ABIGAIL, 2
H. is a great deadener BECKETT, SAMUEL, 25
H. with him was all the test of truth CRABBE, GEORGE, 4
Powerful indeed is the empire of h. PUBLILIUS SYRUS, 4
some h. of which he is...ashamed CRISP, QUENTIN, 1
habitation Let his h. be desolate BIBLE, 3
to airy nothing /A local h. SHAKESPEARE, WILLIAM, 68
habits Cultivate only the h. HUBBARD, ELBERT, 14
Curious things, h. CHRISTIE, AGATHA, 7
Ill h. gather by unseen degrees OVID, 10
Old h. die hard PROVERBS, 352
reconciling my gross h. with my net income FLYNN, ERROL, 3
hack Do not h. me MONMOUTH, JAMES SCOTT, 1
had you h. it in you PARKER, DOROTHY, 6
Hadrian's Wall pace /the H. /of her shoulder HEANEY, SEAMUS, 4
hag The H. is astride, /The night for to ride HERRICK, ROBERT, 1
Hagia Sophia H. MANDELSTAM, OSIP, 12
hags unnatural h., /I will have such revenges on you SHAKESPEARE, WILLIAM, 341
hail H. fellow, well met SWIFT, JONATHAN, 11
the flail of the lashing h. SHELLEY, PERCY BYSSHE, 17
hair A h. in the head HERFORD, OLIVER, 2
All her h. /In one long yellow string I wound BROWNING, ROBERT, 16
He may have h. upon his chest PORTER, COLE, 14
Her h....Was yellow like ripe corn ROSSETTI, DANTE GABRIEL, 4
like a h. across your cheek ANDERSON, MARIAN, 1
long gray h. on Kevin's jacket SIMON, NEIL, 3
Take a h. of the dog PROVERBS, 390
there shall not one h. of his head fall BIBLE, 226
half H. a loaf PROVERBS, 242
The h. is greater than the whole HESIOD, 5
half-cent worth a h. to kill a "nigger," DOUGLASS, FREDERICK, 20
halitosis h. of the intellect LONG, RUSSELL B., 1
Halloween Nobody writes H. stories ZOSHCHENKO, MIKHAIL, 1
halters talk of h. in the hanged man's house CERVANTES, MIGUEL DE, 26
halves Never do things by h. PROVERBS, 337
hamburger British h. JAMES, CLIVE, 2
Why have h. out NEWMAN, PAUL, 1
Hamelin H. Town's in Brunswick BROWNING, ROBERT, 17
Hamlet H. was just a badly conditioned rat LAING, R. D., 14
the tragedy of H. SHAKESPEARE, WILLIAM, 45
hammer h. your iron when it is...hot PUBLILIUS SYRUS, 2
If I Had a H. SEEGER, PETE, 3
Hampden Some village H. GRAY, THOMAS, 9
hamster h....for...animal lover in the city LORENZ, KONRAD, 1
hand a little bit by the h. of God MARADONA, DIEGO, 2
bringing me up by h. DICKENS, CHARLES, 33
h. that signed the treaty bred...fever THOMAS, DYLAN, 20
Our h. will not tremble STALIN, JOSEPH, 11
shook his h....tore my heart HOUSMAN, A. E., 28
The h. that held the dagger ROOSEVELT, FRANKLIN D., 15
The H. that made us is divine ADDISON, JOSEPH, 19
The h. that rocks the cradle PROVERBS, 405
This was the h. that wrote it CRANMER, THOMAS, 3
handicaps Of my two "h.," being female CHISHOLM, SHIRLEY, 2
hand in hand When people walk h. there's neither overtaking nor meeting CONGREVE, WILLIAM, 11
handiwork the h. you give to God MARKHAM, EDWIN, 1
handle I polished up the h. of the big front door GILBERT, W. S., 8
hands don't raise your h....I am...nearsighted AUDEN, W. H., 51
He hath shook h. with time FORD, JOHN (1586–1640?), 3
he shakes h. with people's hearts BEAVERBROOK, MAX AITKEN, LORD, 8
h. of science must ever be at work EINSTEIN, ALBERT, 23
into thy h. I commend my spirit BIBLE, 348
I want a pair of h. FORD, HENRY, 11
Many h. make light work PROVERBS, 324
no more of her than...the palms of her h. BIBLE, 172
To be played with both h. in the pocket SATIE, ERIK, 3
With my own h. I had done LONDON, JACK, 13
You cannot shake h. with a clenched fist GANDHI, INDIRA, 3
handsome H. is as handsome does PROVERBS, 243
H. is that handsome does GOLDSMITH, OLIVER, 27
not as h. as his photographs ARNOLD, MATTHEW, 1
handsome man I dig up a h. NAYLOR, GLORIA, 7
hang Here they h. a man first MOLIÈRE, 23
h. me from a flowering tree PARKER, DOROTHY, 9
H. yourself, brave Crillon HENRY IV, 1
I am worth inconceivably more to h. BROWN, JOHN, 5
They h. us now in Shrewsbury HOUSMAN, A. E., 14
to h. one another FARQUHAR, GEORGE, 8
we like to h. people to make the Americans sit up LEACOCK, STEPHEN, 7
We must indeed all h. together FRANKLIN, BENJAMIN, 28
hanged being h. in all innocence STEVENSON, ROBERT LOUIS, 16
h. in a fortnight...concentrates his mind JOHNSON, SAMUEL, 155
live to be h....cutting a purse JONSON, BEN, 6
hanging H. and marriage...destiny FARQUHAR, GEORGE, 13
H. and wiving goes by destiny SHAKESPEARE, WILLIAM, 607
H. is too good for him BUNYAN, JOHN, 7
H....makes murderers DARROW, CLARENCE, 4
H. of his cat...killing of a mouse on Sunday BRATHWAITE, RICHARD, 1
h. prevents a bad marriage SHAKESPEARE, WILLIAM, 695
hangman noose naked to the h. HOUSMAN, A. E., 13
hapless H. are the favorites of heaven MELVILLE, HERMAN, 18
H. Nation! hapless Land DRENNAN, WILLIAM, 1
happen Can't H. Here LEWIS, SINCLAIR, 6
You let this thing h., you people AUSTIN, MARY, 4
happening something is h. here DYLAN, BOB, 3
happens Everything that h. happens as it should MARCUS AURELIUS, 13
Nothing h. BECKETT, SAMUEL, 21
happiest He is h. of whom the world says least JEFFERSON, THOMAS, 19
happiness A lifetime of h....hell on earth SHAW, GEORGE BERNARD, 47
fail to find h. in theatrical life PAVLOVA, ANNA, 3
H.: a good bank account, a good cook, a good digestion ROUSSEAU, JEAN-JACQUES, 22
H....good cigar, a good meal BURNS, GEORGE, 1
h. in the dedication of his life ELIOT, GEORGE, 3
H. is a mystery like religion CHESTERTON, G. K., 17
H. is an imaginary condition SZASZ, THOMAS, 9

H. is a Warm Gun LENNON & MCCARTNEY, 17
H. is beneficial for the body PROUST, MARCEL, 19
h. is despised nowadays BARNES, JULIAN, 1
H. is like a butterfly PAVLOVA, ANNA, 5
H. is no laughing matter WHATELY, RICHARD, 1
h. is no longer a possibility RUSSELL, BERTRAND, 60
H. is not an ideal of reason KANT, IMMANUEL, 19
H. is not best achieved RUSSELL, BERTRAND, 18
h. is produced...by a good tavern JOHNSON, SAMUEL, 126
H. is the only sanction of life SANTAYANA, GEORGE, 13
h. never occurs in the creation of a work of art FREUD, LUCIEN, 1
h. of man that he be mentally faithful PAINE, THOMAS, 3
h. of the wicked RACINE, JEAN, 6
h. through another man's eyes SHAKESPEARE, WILLIAM, 119
H. was born a twin BYRON, LORD, 48
Let no one trust the h. of the moment MACHADO DE ASSIS, JOAQUIM MARIA, 9
man's h. is his income RUSSELL, BERTRAND, 29
not the h. of all men VIAN, BORIS, 1
only real h. a ballplayer has LARDNER, RING, 4
secret of h. is to admire without desiring BRADLEY, F. H., 5
supreme h. of life...we are loved HUGO, VICTOR, 10
the greatest h. for the greatest numbers HUTCHESON, FRANCIS, 4
the greatest h. of the whole PLATO, 21
the outward...signs...of h. and success MANN, THOMAS, 4
We all seek h. and...avoid suffering DALAI LAMA, 3
Were...h....apprehended...it were a martyrdom to live BROWNE, THOMAS, 37
you'll give h. and joy to many BEETHOVEN, LUDWIG VAN, 8

happy all who are h., are equally happy JOHNSON, SAMUEL, 118
Ask...whether you are h. MILL, JOHN STUART, 5
be h. later...but it's much harder BEAUVOIR, SIMONE DE, 4
Few people can be h. unless they hate RUSSELL, BERTRAND, 61
h. as a result of one's own efforts SAND, GEORGE, 2
H. beings...carry their happiness cautiously BARBEY D'AUREVILLY, JULES-AMÉDÉE, 2
H. Days Are Here Again ROOSEVELT, FRANKLIN D., 6
H. he who like Ulysses DU BELLAY, JOACHIM, 2
h. in the arms of a chambermaid JOHNSON, SAMUEL, 130
H. in the monotony of boats MURPHY, RICHARD, 1
H. is the people ALCUIN, 1
h. life, /To be no better than a homely swain SHAKESPEARE, WILLIAM, 291
How h. are the dead SCHILLER, FRIEDRICH VON, 5
H. that Nation, fortunate that age FRANKLIN, BENJAMIN, 14
H. the people whose annals are blank CARLYLE, THOMAS, 23
h. they that never saw the court WEBSTER, JOHN, 13
h. who does not think himself so PUBLILIUS SYRUS, 8
If one only wished to be h. MONTESQUIEU, 11
Let us all be h., and live within our means WARD, ARTEMUS, 3
Made h. by compulsion COLERIDGE, SAMUEL TAYLOR, 23
make a h. fire-side clime BURNS, ROBERT, 15
never so h. nor so unhappy LA ROCHEFOUCAULD, FRANÇOIS, 10
No man is genuinely h., married MENCKEN, H. L., 32
Oh, this *is* a h. day BECKETT, SAMUEL, 8
only really h. people MENCKEN, H. L., 50
that h. garden-state MARVELL, ANDREW, 6
This h. breed of men, this little world SHAKESPEARE, WILLIAM, 512
We are so h. to advise others RENARD, JULES, 17
you don't know how truly h. you were SIMONE, NINA, 4

harbor Being thus arrived in a good h. BRADFORD, WILLIAM, 3

hard better for h. words to be on paper FRANK, ANNE, 1
It's been a h. day's night LENNON & MCCARTNEY, 5

hardboiled I've met a lot of h. eggs WILDER, BILLY, 1

hardest h. to confess...ridiculous and shameful ROUSSEAU, JEAN-JACQUES, 4

hare Happy the h. at morning AUDEN, W. H., 26
He finds it hard... to shoot the h. HOFFMAN, HEINRICH, 6
I mean not to run with the H. LYLY, JOHN, 6

hares If you chase two h. PROVERBS, 9

Harlem H. was Seventh Heaven MALCOLM X, 16

harlot how is the faithful city become an h. BIBLE, 196

harm I didn't want to h. the man CAPOTE, TRUMAN, 2
No people do...h. CREIGHTON, MANDELL, 1

harmless Mostly h. ADAMS, DOUGLAS, 6

harmony for h....both the black and the white AGGREY, JAMES EMMAN KWEGYIR, 3
h. in bad taste...height of elegance GENET, JEAN, 3
in h. with the mysteries of religion KEBLE, JOHN, 1
Inner h. is attained...with the environment DEWEY, JOHN, 3
our country...h. between God and man ANONYMOUS, 30

harp The h. that once MOORE, THOMAS, 6

harpoon exploding h. in the guts ELTON, BEN, 1

harpsichord h. resembles...a bird-cage played with toasting-forks BEECHAM, THOMAS, 9

Harrison Major-general H. hanged PEPYS, SAMUEL, 4

Harry God for H.! England and Saint George SHAKESPEARE, WILLIAM, 268

hart a young h. upon the mountains of spices BIBLE, 498

Harvard I didn't go to H. JOHNSON, LYNDON BAINES, 24

has beens one of the h. HONE, WILLIAM, 1

Hasta La Vista H., baby SCHWARZENEGGER, ARNOLD, 2

haste always in h....never in a hurry WESLEY, JOHN, 1
Art thou gone in h. ROWLEY, WILLIAM, 1
H. makes waste PROVERBS, 244
Make h. slowly AUGUSTUS, 2
Marry'd in h. CONGREVE, WILLIAM, 17
More h., less speed PROVERBS, 333

hat a h. that lets the rain in FREDERICK II (1712–86), 4
He forbade me to put off my h. FOX, GEORGE, 1
Where did you get that h. ANONYMOUS, 93

hate h. a Frenchman as you hate the devil NELSON, HORATIO, 3
h. anybody and hope to see God's face HAMER, FANNIE LOU, 1
H. has no medicine PROVERBS, 6
H. is also creative DUMAS, HENRY, 2
h. that which we often fear SHAKESPEARE, WILLIAM, 71
h. the man you have hurt TACITUS, 2
If you h. a person, you hate...yourself HESSE, HERMANN, 1
I h. her, she despises me AKHTAR-UL-IMAN, 1
I h. that dreadful hollow TENNYSON, ALFRED, 25
men h. one another so damnably MELBOURNE, LORD, 6
now I h. her guts CARVER, RAYMOND, 9
scarcely h. any one that we know HAZLITT, WILLIAM, 19
they h. the English with good reason HUMPHRIES, ROLFE, 2
we dancers h. him ASTAIRE, FRED, 2

hated h. of all men for my name's sake BIBLE, 394
h. the ruling few BENTHAM, JEREMY, 7
I never h. a man enough GABOR, ZSA ZSA, 3
to be h. is to achieve distinction ANTRIM, MINNA, 4
hates Everybody h. me DE VRIES, PETER, 11
It does not matter...what a man h. BUTLER, SAMUEL (1835–1902), 23
hating The price of h. other human beings is loving oneself less CLEAVER, ELDRIDGE, 6
hatred An intellectual h. is the worst YEATS, W. B., 19
H. is a feeling ORTEGA Y GASSET, JOSÉ, 1
H. is a tonic...inspires vengeance BALZAC, HONORÉ DE, 6
h. is by far the longest pleasure BYRON, LORD, 75
h. of other races that I prosecute CÉSAIRE, AIMÉ, 3
H., too, is a precious habit ENZENSBERGER, HANS, 3
hats H. divide...into three classes WHITEHORN, KATHARINE, 13
I don't like to wear top h. ASTAIRE, FRED, 11
haunting h. the house I am the house DUNCAN, ROBERT, 2
have All I h., I would have given JOHNSON, LYNDON BAINES, 5
To h. and to hold BOOK OF COMMON PRAYER, 21
Hawaii H....paradise for the well to do LONDON, JACK, 6
hay h....allowed...civilizations to flourish DYSON, FREEMAN, 2
make h. while the sun shines CERVANTES, MIGUEL DE, 13
Make h. while the sun shines PROVERBS, 319
that's what h. looks like MARY OF TECK, 2
hazard an occupational h. of being a wife ANNE, PRINCESS, 1
The greatest h....losing one's self KIERKEGAARD, SØREN, 17
he every h. has got him a she FOLK VERSE, 32
head a moment to remove his h. LAGRANGE, JOSEPH LOUIS, 1
call that thing under your hat...h. HOLBERG, LUDVIG, 1
cuts the wrong man's h. off DICKENS, CHARLES, 95
h. downwards between cliffs of bone BAGNOLD, ENID, 1
h. so high it'll strike the stars HORACE, 31
h. to contrive...any mischief CLARENDON, EDWARD HYDE, 2
I've a h. like a concertina KIPLING, RUDYARD, 16
John Baptist's h. in a charger BIBLE, 404
moment when a man's h. drops off HAWTHORNE, NATHANIEL, 20
Off with his h. CARROLL, LEWIS, 15
shorter by a h. ELIZABETH I, 19
show my h. to the people DANTON, GEORGES JACQUES, 2
sleeping h....on my faithless arm AUDEN, W. H., 15
Uneasy lies the h. that wears a crown SHAKESPEARE, WILLIAM, 255
When the h. aches CERVANTES, MIGUEL DE, 29
headmasters H. have powers CHURCHILL, WINSTON, 41
headmistress a h....wearing calico knickers THATCHER, MARGARET, 13
heads H. I win CROKER, JOHN WILSON, 1
h. to get money...hearts to spend FARQUHAR, GEORGE, 6
Seen better h. on a mop BLEASDALE, ALAN, 3
Two h. are better than one PROVERBS, 442
headstone His h. said /FREE AT LAST, FREE AT LAST GIOVANNI, NIKKI, 1
headstrong h. as an allegory SHERIDAN, RICHARD BRINSLEY, 10
healers The best of h. is good cheer PINDAR, 1
healing H. is a matter of time HIPPOCRATES, 8
health All h. is better than wealth SCOTT, SIR WALTER, 3
A person...returns to h. much disappointed CANETTI, ELIAS, 4
Attention to h. is the greatest hindrance to life PLATO, 32
do always in h. what you have often promised to do SIGISMUND, 1
Effective h. care depends on self care ILLICH, IVAN, 4
Give me h. and a day EMERSON, RALPH WALDO, 38
Good h....essential to happiness MAYO, CHARLES HORACE, 5
H. and cheerfulness mutually beget each other ADDISON, JOSEPH, 17
He destroys his h. by laboring to preserve it VIRGIL, 25
H. indeed is a precious thing BURTON, ROBERT, 13
H. is a precious thing MONTAIGNE, MICHEL DE, 10
H. is a relative term ELIOT, T. S., 41
H. is beauty SHENSTONE, WILLIAM, 2
H. is the first muse EMERSON, RALPH WALDO, 63
H. is the first of all liberties AMIEL, HENRI FRÉDÉRIC, 1
h.! the blessing of the rich JONSON, BEN, 25
I'd make h. catching instead of disease INGERSOLL, ROBERT G., 7
In a disordered mind...soundness of h. is impossible CICERO, 17
Look to your h. WALTON, IZAAK, 8
Nothing is more fatal to *H.*, than an *over Care* of it FRANKLIN, BENJAMIN, 20
preservation of h. is a duty SPENCER, HERBERT, 9
Safeguard the h....of body and soul CLEOBULUS, 1
Talk h....dreary, never-ending tale WILCOX, ELLA WHEELER, 5
The h. of the people DISRAELI, BENJAMIN, 3
the quadrangle of h. OSLER, WILLIAM, 10
They pay this price for h. TWAIN, MARK, 55
Too much h., the cause of illness FLAUBERT, GUSTAVE, 5
To preserve one's h. by too strict a regime LA ROCHEFOUCAULD, FRANÇOIS, 21
Use your h. SHAW, GEORGE BERNARD, 91
What have I gained by h. LAMB, CHARLES, 8
Without h. life is not life RABELAIS, FRANÇOIS, 14
Your h., Master Yew MACNEICE, LOUIS, 25
healths Urge no h. CHARLES I (1600–49), 8
healthy Blessed is the h. nature CARLYLE, THOMAS, 24
how h....to play "Da Do Ron Ron" EVERETT, KENNY, 1
H. people...live in healthy homes ILLICH, IVAN, 5
'Tis h. to be sick sometimes THOREAU, HENRY DAVID, 47
hear H. before you blame PROVERBS, 483
h. someone accidentally whistle something of mine BERNSTEIN, LEONARD, 1
if I hadn't been able to h. CHARLES, RAY, 3
I h. it in the deep heart's core YEATS, W. B., 31
heart A gen'rous h. repairs a sland'rous tongue POPE, ALEXANDER, 83
A good h. will help you to a bonny face BRONTË, EMILY, 2
a h....too soon made glad BROWNING, ROBERT, 14
A woman's h. always has a burned mark LABÉ, LOUISE, 1
Counting the slow h. beats GRAVES, ROBERT, 7
give me back my h. BYRON, LORD, 11
h. as willing /As bondage e'er of freedom; here's my hand SHAKESPEARE, WILLIAM, 647
His h. is dead BLACK HAWK, 1
h. of man is the place the Devil's in BROWNE, THOMAS, 23
Home is where the h. is PROVERBS, 484
h. to a dog to tear KIPLING, RUDYARD, 9
I Left My H. in San Francisco CROSS, DOUGLAS, 1
I love thee for a h. that's kind DAVIES, W. H., 4
In a full h....room for everything PORCHIA, ANTONIO, 5
look in thy h. and write SIDNEY, PHILIP, 2
My h. aches, and a drowsy numbness pains KEATS, JOHN (1795–1821), 59
my h....dictates my decision NASH, OGDEN, 18

my h. has learn'd to glow /For others' good POPE, ALEXANDER, 91
My h. is a lonely hunter SHARP, WILLIAM, 1
My h. is like a singing bird ROSSETTI, CHRISTINA, 1
My h. shall be thy garden MEYNELL, ALICE, 2
My h. sings, full of sadness SIBELIUS, JEAN, 1
my h. was...only for my subjects' good ELIZABETH I, 10
my shrivelled h. HERBERT, GEORGE, 20
No, the h. that has truly lov'd never forgets MOORE, THOMAS, 4
Now my h. turns to and fro HATSHEPSUT, 1
One's fancy chuckle, while his h. doth ache BUNYAN, JOHN, 20
Out-worn h., in a time out-worn YEATS, W. B., 45
So the h. be right RALEIGH, WALTER, 10
take heed...that your h. be not deceived BIBLE, 36
That...from the h. can be written MUSSET, ALFRED DE, 3
that mighty h. is lying still WORDSWORTH, WILLIAM, 41
The h. has its reasons PASCAL, BLAISE, 13
The H. Is a Lonely Hunter MCCULLERS, CARSON, 1
The h. is deceitful above all things BIBLE, 250
The h. of a woman falls back JOHNSON, GEORGIA DOUGLAS, 2
the motions and uses of the h. HARVEY, WILLIAM, 1
We had fed the h. on fantasies YEATS, W. B., 36
What comes from the h. COLERIDGE, SAMUEL TAYLOR, 59
when every lusty h. beginneth to blossom MALORY, THOMAS, 3

heartbeat h. of the country BUSH, GEORGE, 16

heartbreak h., struggle...for being black CHARLES, RAY, 1

heartless It is h. and it is mindless MCGAHERN, JOHN, 1

hearts False h. and broken vows ROCHESTER, 2ND EARL OF, 3
h. of Men...seek beyond the world TOLKIEN, J. R. R., 7
live in h. we leave...not to die CAMPBELL, THOMAS, 9
Our h. are surviving at the poverty level MCMILLAN, TERRY, 2

hearty he is so h., so straightforward, outspoken ROOSEVELT, THEODORE, 5

heat H., ma'am SMITH, SYDNEY, 16
If you can't take the h. PROVERBS, 269

Heathcliff My love for H. resembles the eternal rocks BRONTË, EMILY, 4

heathenism H. and Liberty DELANY, MARTIN ROBINSON, 1

heat waves The h. are solidifying WOLFE, TOM, 14

heaven All this and h. too HENRY, MATTHEW, 5
flat road to h. SANTAYANA, GEORGE, 1
for the unbelievers a gate in h. KORAN, 18
H. affords /unlimited accommodation THOMAS, R. S., 1
H. and earth are ruthless LAOZI, 13
h. and earth shall pass away BIBLE, 426
H. and hell /Are words KRISHNAMURTI, JIDDU, 2
H. bred in me talents LI BAI, 2
H. has granted me no offspring WHISTLER, JAMES ABBOTT MCNEILL, 14
H. has its material for slaughter WANG SHIDUO, 1
H. has its seasons...Man...government XUNZI, 2
H....is a place so inane, so dull SHAW, GEORGE BERNARD, 70
H. is full of answers to prayers GRAHAM, BILLY, 2
h. make me poor JONSON, BEN, 17
h. on earth MILTON, JOHN, 53
H.'s last best gift, my ever new delight MILTON, JOHN, 69
If this belief from h. be sent WORDSWORTH, WILLIAM, 19
In h. an angel is nobody in particular SHAW, GEORGE BERNARD, 60
I want to know...way to h. WESLEY, JOHN, 4
I wouldn't go to h....free ticket O'CASEY, SEAN, 7
key to the gate of h. FEYNMAN, RICHARD PHILLIPS, 5
knockin' on H.'s door DYLAN, BOB, 7
more things in h. and earth SHAKESPEARE, WILLIAM, 159
near to h. by sea as by land GILBERT, HUMPHREY, 1
no invention came more easily to man than H. LICHTENBERG, GEORG CHRISTOPH, 4
steep and thorny way to h. SHAKESPEARE, WILLIAM, 149
the starry h. above...the moral law within KANT, IMMANUEL, 6
trouble deaf h. with my bootless cries SHAKESPEARE, WILLIAM, 569
We are all going to H. GAINSBOROUGH, THOMAS, 2
We shall roll up...h. like a scroll KORAN, 24
What they do in h. we are ignorant of SWIFT, JONATHAN, 51
who has once strayed into H. ALAIN-FOURNIER, 1

heavenly Such h. touches ne'er touched earthly faces SHAKESPEARE, WILLIAM, 564

heavens vault of the h....history is written RACINE, JEAN, 12

heaventree The h. of stars JOYCE, JAMES, 30

heavier you who have borne even h. things VIRGIL, 3

Hebrew H. and Arabic...stones on the tongue AMICHAI, YEHUDA, 2
the H. word...*timshel*—"Thou mayest"...gives a choice STEINBECK, JOHN, 6

Hebrews See H. 13:8 BENCHLEY, ROBERT, 10

hedgehog a h. rolled up the wrong way HOOD, THOMAS, 18
My Darling, prickly h. of the hearth LOWELL, ROBERT, 20

hedgehogs If you start throwing h. under me KHRUSHCHEV, NIKITA, 7

heel to bring a man to h. BROOKNER, ANITA, 2

height It has been observed that the h. of a man PLINY THE ELDER, 8

heights The h. by great men reached LONGFELLOW, HENRY WADSWORTH, 12

heill I that in h. wes and gladnes DUNBAR, WILLIAM, 1

Heineken H. refreshes the parts ADVERTISEMENTS, 11

heiresses All h. are beautiful DRYDEN, JOHN, 28

helicopters they are all my h. JOHNSON, LYNDON BAINES, 25

hell A firm conviction of the material reality of H. HUXLEY, ALDOUS, 49
all h. broke loose MILTON, JOHN, 63
All place...be h. that is not heaven MARLOWE, CHRISTOPHER, 6
Down, down to h. SHAKESPEARE, WILLIAM, 293
H. has three gates BHAGAVAD-GITA, 1
H. is a city much like London SHELLEY, PERCY BYSSHE, 13
H. is oneself; /Hell is alone ELIOT, T. S., 40
H. is other people SARTRE, JEAN-PAUL, 9
H....is to love no more BERNANOS, GEORGES, 1
H. no, we won't go MOTTOS AND SLOGANS, 38
h....small chat to the babbling of Lethe BECKETT, SAMUEL, 1
H. the Shadow of a Soul on fire FITZGERALD, EDWARD, 18
h. upon earth...a melancholy man's heart BURTON, ROBERT, 1
H. was right now NAYLOR, GLORIA, 3
I believe I am in h. RIMBAUD, ARTHUR, 11
I never give them h. TRUMAN, HARRY S., 8
I shall move H. VIRGIL, 19
I will make all h. howl NATION, CARRY, 2
make...h. of this world BECKFORD, WILLIAM, 1
My idea of h. BOGARDE, DIRK, 2
the filth of H. is fouled by his foul presence PARIS, MATTHEW, 1
The road to h. is paved PROVERBS, 426
The road to h....works-in-progress ROTH, PHILIP, 5
Ugly h., gape not MARLOWE, CHRISTOPHER, 13

way down to H. is easy VIRGIL, 17
Why this is h. MARLOWE, CHRISTOPHER, 5
hell-broth Like a h. boil and bubble SHAKESPEARE, WILLIAM, 408
hell-fire There shall come out of H. MUHAMMAD, 5
help God helps those who h. themselves SIDNEY, ALGERNON, 1
gods h. them that help themselves AESOP, 1
H. me down Cemetery Road LARKIN, PHILIP, 21
h., not succession EISNER, MICHAEL, 3
h. one...by trampling down a dozen BRECHT, BERTOLT, 19
h. those we love to escape from us HÜGEL, FRIEDRICH, 1
H. thyself LA FONTAINE, JEAN DE, 1
past my h. is past my care BEAUMONT & FLETCHER, 6
Whoever is unwilling to h. himself PESTALOZZI, JOHANN HEINRICH, 10
with a little h. from my friends LENNON & MCCARTNEY, 4
you will find light and h. and human kindness SCHWEITZER, ALBERT, 1
hen a broody h. sitting on a china egg FOOT, MICHAEL, 1
A h....an egg's way of making another egg BUTLER, SAMUEL (1835–1902), 7
A h. stares at nothing with one eye MCCAIG, NORMAN, 10
Henry Junker H. means to be God HENRY VIII, 2
Henry James The work of H....seemed divisible GUEDALLA, PHILIP, 2
Henry VIII pig of a H. WINDEBANK, FRANCIS, 1
herb an excellent h. to our fathers of old KIPLING, RUDYARD, 65
heredity law of h. is that all undesirable traits PROVERBS, MODERN, 25
heresy h. of one age becomes...orthodoxy KELLER, HELEN, 5
heretic h....he who has a particular opinion BOSSUET, JACQUES-BÉNIGNE, 2
h. that makes the fire SHAKESPEARE, WILLIAM, 660
I shall never be a h. LUTHER, MARTIN, 4
heretics Modern h....are relegated to backwaters KLEINER, ART, 1
heritage Our h. the sea CUNNINGHAM, ALLAN, 1
hero a h. with coward's legs MILLIGAN, SPIKE, 5
a h....would argue with Gods MAILER, NORMAN, 19
Being a h. ROGERS, WILL, 3
Every h. becomes a bore EMERSON, RALPH WALDO, 39
h. and I will write you a tragedy FITZGERALD, F. SCOTT, 9
h....one who does what he can ROLLAND, ROMAIN, 1
h. to his wife's psychiatrist BERNE, ERIC, 3
irrelevant...conception of the h. as a morally worthy man HOOK, SIDNEY, 2
No man is a h. to his valet CORNUEL, ANNE-MARIE BIGOT DE, 1
The H. can be Poet CARLYLE, THOMAS, 27
Today's h., the urban animal GOYTISOLO, JUAN, 4
Herod H....saw that he was mocked BIBLE, 369
heroes H. cannot stand side by side PROVERBS, 78
if h. were never afraid DAUDET, ALPHONSE, 2
setting up of h., mainly bogus MENCKEN, H. L., 28
There are few h. or villains SHOSTAKOVICH, DMITRI, 1
heroic h. element in the soldier's work RUSKIN, JOHN, 16
heroin People were offended...song called "H." REED, LOU, 3
hesitate Never h. to say what ought to be said VIEIRA, ANTÓNIO, 1
hesitates He who h. is lost PROVERBS, 253
Hesperus the schooner H. LONGFELLOW, HENRY WADSWORTH, 18
heterosexual artificial categories "h." and "homosexual" YOUNG, ALLEN, 1
lived my entire life with h. hatred FIERSTEIN, HARVEY, 1
heterosexuality failed to convert me to h. MCKELLEN, IAN, 2
hewers h. of wood BIBLE, 309
hidden wot's h. in each other's hearts DICKENS, CHARLES, 54
hide H. nothing from the masses of our people CABRAL, AMILCAR, 1
hierarchy in a h. people can be equal KLINE, NANCY, 3
high ye'll tak' the h. road FOLK VERSE, 18
highbrow What is a h. WALLACE, EDGAR, 1
Highlands My heart's in the H. BURNS, ROBERT, 28
highlights h. and shadows of our history GENSCHER, HANS-DIETRICH, 1
highness attend your H. upon your landing ANONYMOUS, 5
high school h. is the place where the band practices HUTCHINS, ROBERT M., 1
high tech H....needs to be planned into existence ROSZAK, THEODORE, 1
high-technology successful h. company SCULLEY, JOHN, 1
highwayman The h. came riding NOYES, ALFRED, 2
hill H. and house should live together WRIGHT, FRANK LLOYD, 1
hills a fine thing to be out on the h. alone KILVERT, FRANCIS, 2
after climbing a great hill...many more h. to climb MANDELA, NELSON, 13
And o'er the h., and far away TENNYSON, ALFRED, 63
H. sink to plains...man returns to dust FRENEAU, PHILIP, 5
Over the h. and far away GAY, JOHN, 16
The h. are alive...sound of music HAMMERSTEIN, OSCAR, II, 18
those blue remembered h. HOUSMAN, A. E., 18
him avoid making H. set the world in motion PASCAL, BLAISE, 11
himself Every man for h. PROVERBS, 203
None but h. can be his parallel THEOBALD, LEWIS, 1
Therein the patient /Must minister to h. SHAKESPEARE, WILLIAM, 416
hinder h. the reception of every work JOHNSON, SAMUEL, 45
hindsight H. is always twenty-twenty WILDER, BILLY, 4
Hinduism H....emphasizes Divine Immanence RADHAKRISHNAN, SARVEPALLI, 6
hip H....sophistication of the wise primitive MAILER, NORMAN, 25
Hippocleides H. doesn't care HIPPOCLEIDES, 1
hippopotamus I shoot the H. BELLOC, HILAIRE, 5
hire H. people smarter than you SCHULTZE, HOWARD, 1
h. people who bring new talents MYHRVOLD, NATHAN, 2
If you were to h. household staff NEGROPONTE, NICHOLAS, 7
Hiroshima H., the flower, petaled off into extinction HÜSNÜ DAG IARCA, FAZIL, 1
histhry I know h. isn't thrue DUNNE, FINLEY PETER, 8
historian A h. is a prophet in reverse SCHLEGEL, FRIEDRICH VON, 1
h. is doomed...writing in the sand CRAVEN, AVERY O., 1
h. must re-tell, with a new richness BAILYN, BERNARD, 4
h....performs an act of faith BEARD, CHARLES, 7
h....trying to do in time BERKHOFER, ROBERT FREDERICK, JR., 1
If an h. were to relate truthfully BAYLE, PIERRE, 1
If the h. could indeed separate himself BECKER, CARL, 5
modern h. admits that there were lies BECKER, CARL, 9
No effective h....can be innocent of statistics BAILYN, BERNARD, 2
No h. achieves the highest excellence TAYLOR, A. J. P., 2
The h. must not try to know what is truth ADAMS, HENRY, 13
The h. must resist all pleas HANDLIN, OSCAR, 1
The h. who attempts to interpret the past BAILEY, THOMAS A., 3
the profession of h. fits a man for psychological analysis SARTRE, JEAN-PAUL, 10

h. of a civilization...instrument of civilization BEARD, CHARLES, 4
H. offers no comfort GRASS, GÜNTER, 1
H. offers some consolation DURANT, WILL, 7
h. of free men...never really written by chance but...choice EISENHOWER, DWIGHT D., 9
h. of man...nine months preceding his birth COLERIDGE, SAMUEL TAYLOR, 63
h. of nations...is often best studied MACAULAY, THOMAS BABINGTON, 4
h. of scholarship is a record of disagreements HUGHES, CHARLES, 1
h. of the progress of human liberty DOUGLASS, FREDERICK, 24
H....organized memory COMMAGER, HENRY STEELE, 6
h. pays its way CRAVEN, AVERY O., 2
H. repeats itself PROVERBS, 258
H....science in technique...art in interpretation HAMEROW, THEODORE S., 1
H. shows you prospects by starlight CHOATE, RUFUS, 1
H. smiles at all attempts DURANT, WILL, 9
H. subverts the stereotype of science GOULD, STEPHEN JAY, 11
H. teaches perhaps few lessons CARTER, JIMMY, 4
H. tells how it was ANDERSCH, ALFRED, 1
H., that excitable and lying old lady MAUPASSANT, GUY DE, 4
H. that ignores the...altar PRIESTLEY, J. B., 10
h. that lies inert in unread books BECKER, CARL, 3
H....the conflict of minorities DURANT, WILL, 3
H....things that could have been avoided ADENAUER, KONRAD, 4
H., too, has its uses BENNETT, EDWARD W., 2
Human h....a brief spot in space DURANT, WILL, 10
h....value to the present hour EMERSON, RALPH WALDO, 46
H., without moral philosophy SMITH, GOLDWIN, 1
H....working of the spirit of man WRONG, GEORGE M., 3
H....written by the winners HALEY, ALEX, 2
if h. relates good things of good men BEDE, 1
If men could learn from h. COLERIDGE, SAMUEL TAYLOR, 54
If the h. of a people BEARD, CHARLES, 3
If the whole of h. is in one man EMERSON, RALPH WALDO, 10
I like h. because my reading LLOYD, CECIL FRANCIS, 1
In analyzing h. do not be too profound EMERSON, RALPH WALDO, 30
In h....man sees himself CALLCOTT, GEORGE H., 1
In the modern age h. ARENDT, HANNAH, 1
I see h. as a book with many pages BUSH, GEORGE, 8
It is impossible to write ancient h. PÉGUY, CHARLES PIERRE, 10
lack of a sense of h. could have mortal consequences HUMPHREY, HUBERT H., 5
Let the h. of the past FORTUNE, TIMOTHY THOMAS, 1
minute hand of h. MACCARTHY, DESMOND, 3
morsel of genuine h....thing so rare JEFFERSON, THOMAS, 16
Most h. is guessing...the rest is prejudice DURANT, WILL, 11
most interesting thing about h....its invention CANETTI, ELIAS, 9
no h.; only biography EMERSON, RALPH WALDO, 12
no h. without...knowing what to leave out BARZUN, JACQUES, 2
one of these is the h. of political power POPPER, KARL, 5
People are trapped in h. and history is trapped in them BALDWIN, JAMES, 17
problem of h....problem of consciousness DIGGINS, JOHN P., 2
real makers of h. are the ordinary men and women MANDELA, NELSON, 17
riddle of h. is not in Reason but in Desire BROWN, NORMAN O., 3
shallow village tale our so-called h. is EMERSON, RALPH WALDO, 13
study of h....the playground of patriotism WRONG, GEORGE M., 5
That great dust-heap called "h." BIRRELL, AUGUSTINE, 1
That is the triumph of h. BARZUN, JACQUES, 6
the case for a sense of h. MACDOUGALL, DONALD, 1
The good things in h. ARENDT, HANNAH, 12
The h. of every country begins in the heart CATHER, WILLA, 4
The h. of the World is the World's court SCHILLER, FRIEDRICH VON, 11
The h. of what the law has been HOLMES, OLIVER WENDELL, JR., 4
The study of h. ADAMS, HENRY, 15
the whole subsequent h. of civilisation takes its rise LUTHER, MARTIN, 1
This is the h. of a human heart DU BOIS, W. E. B., 17
Those who mill around...crossroads of h. BOREN, DAVID L., 1
treat world h. as a mathematician HESSE, HERMANN, 5
we are not helpless prisoners of h. EISENHOWER, DWIGHT D., 14
We have constantly to check ourselves in reading h. BOURNE, RANDOLPH S., 1
We have need of h. ORTEGA Y GASSET, JOSÉ, 29
We have wasted H. like a bunch of drunks BUKOWSKI, CHARLES, 9
What, then, are the criteria of h. BARZUN, JACQUES, 3
why write h. at all CANETTI, ELIAS, 7
world's h....divine poem GARFIELD, JAMES A., 6
writing of h. is, like the preaching of a sermon BRINTON, CRANE, 1

hit Getting h. ROBINSON, SUGAR RAY, 3
how many people...write a h. song NEWMAN, RANDY, 1
h. you before God gets the news ALI, MUHAMMAD, 1
if a man h. you, you could shoot him BRAND, JO, 3
If you would h. the mark LONGFELLOW, HENRY WADSWORTH, 23
I had h. the big time ARMSTRONG, LOUIS, 9
I think I can tell a h. record YETNIKOFF, WALTER, 1
made a h. as a *human being* LAHR, BERT, 1
never h. softly ROOSEVELT, THEODORE, 19
You write a h. the same way you write a flop LERNER, ALAN JAY, 13

Hitler Adolf H. was *sui generis* HITLER, ADOLF, 2
every time H. occupies a country HITLER, ADOLF, 6
H. and Signor Mussolini...been at Oxford HALIFAX, LORD, 1
H. has missed the bus CHAMBERLAIN, NEVILLE, 5
H. /Has only got one ball FOLK VERSE, 63
H.'s cognitive dissonance that enabled him HITLER, ADOLF, 14
H. showed surprising loyalty to Mussolini BULLOCK, ALAN, 2
H.'s rule does not...historical process HITLER, ADOLF, 11
H. was a nuisance HITLER, ADOLF, 4
I deny H.'s right BEVIN, ERNEST, 1
If we can stand up to H. CHURCHILL, WINSTON, 30
I wouldn't believe H. was dead HITLER, ADOLF, 13
one purpose, the destruction of H. HITLER, ADOLF, 1
The people H. never understood BULLOCK, ALAN, 1
we...pushed H. so far...he'll squeak HITLER, ADOLF, 10

hits H. are like babies HANDY, W. C., 1

ho "What h.!" I said WODEHOUSE, P. G., 6

hobbit In a hole in the ground there lived a h. TOLKIEN, J. R. R., 2

hobbled We may be a h. tiger BECKETT, TERENCE, 1

hobby-horse a man rides his *H.* peaceably STERNE, LAURENCE, 11

hobbyists h....connected...with the music BARAKA, IMAMU AMIRI, 3

Hofstadter H.'s Law HOFSTADTER, DOUGLAS R., 1

hog get the h. out of the spring PROVERBS, 272

hokies By the h., there was a man O'CONNOR, FRANK, 4

hold h. fast that which is good BIBLE, 233

H. the fort, for I am coming BLISS, PHILIP PAUL, 1
h. the most adorable creature in one's arms GOETHE, JOHANN WOLFGANG VON, 29
h. to the things which are reliable LAOZI, 8
I Want to H. Your Hand LENNON & MCCARTNEY, 18
holders H. of one position, wrong for years AUDEN, W. H., 25
holds h. him with his glittering eye COLERIDGE, SAMUEL TAYLOR, 36
hole A h. is the accident...a darn is...poverty SHUTER, EDWARD, 1
Dig a h., cover it with...doors JONES, THOMAS K., 1
out of a black h. into glaring light MCCARTHY, JOHN, 1
the h. when the cheese is gone BRECHT, BERTOLT, 13
When...in a h., stop digging HEALEY, DENIS, 1
holes h. in our trousers were palace windows BÜCHNER, GEORG, 10
holiday it's a regular h. to them DICKENS, CHARLES, 85
Holiday Inns spend...two years in H. MONDALE, WALTER, 1
holidays H. /Have no pity MONTALE, EUGENIO, 5
holiness the h. of the heart's affections KEATS, JOHN (1795–1821), 23
Holland H....saved by being dammed HOOD, THOMAS, 20
New H....most barren country BANKS, JOSEPH, 1
hollers somebody jumps up and h....raises cain GUTHRIE, WOODY, 3
hollow We are the h. men ELIOT, T. S., 44
holly The h. and the ivy FOLK VERSE, 20
Hollywood All H. corrupts WILSON, EDMUND, 3
Everyone in H. is looking for the blockbuster SIMON, NEIL, 13
H. is a corporate mentality KONCHALOVSKY, ANDREI, 1
H....men get younger...women get older BARRYMORE, LIONEL, 1
H....the personality of a paper cup CHANDLER, RAYMOND, 14
H....they'll pay you...fifty cents for your soul MONROE, MARILYN, 6
H....where everything is incredibly expensive MAMET, DAVID, 14
H....where people from Iowa ALLEN, FRED, 4
H. will rot on...windmills of Eternity GINSBERG, ALLEN, 3
In H., if you don't have happiness REED, REX, 1
It is H. who originated...hip hop GEORGE, NELSON, 2
Strip the phony tinsel off H. LEVANT, OSCAR, 3
holy If you become h. HUME, BASIL, 1
They never poured h. water PLUNKETT, JAMES, 1
holy land As you came from the h. RALEIGH, WALTER, 1
Holy Roman Empire the H. was neither holy, nor Roman, nor an empire VOLTAIRE, 30
Holy Spirit It is the H.'s intention GALILEO, 5
homage h. vain /...with hypocritic tear EVERETT, EDWARD, 1
the h. paid by vice to virtue LA ROCHEFOUCAULD, FRANÇOIS, 22
home An exile from h. splendor dazzles PAYNE, JOHN HOWARD, 1
Curses...always come h. to roost SOUTHEY, ROBERT, 9
don't do this at h. LETTERMAN, DAVID, 2
h....a tavern for his friends DOUGLAS, NORMAN, 3
H. is home CLARKE, JOHN, 1
H. is so sad LARKIN, PHILIP, 2
H. is the place where FROST, ROBERT, 19
H. is what I fled from PEAKE, MERVYN, 2
H., the spot of earth supremely blest MONTGOMERY, ROBERT, 1
H....when you have nothing better THATCHER, MARGARET, 34
H....where they understand you MORGENSTERN, CHRISTIAN, 2
H....you never leave it NAYLOR, GLORIA, 4
I want to go h. MCCARTHY, JOHN, 2
Life in the h....faults and calamities ANONYMOUS, 46
My h. is not in this world MILLER, HENRY, 26
My only concern was to get h. after a hard day's work PARKS, ROSA, 1
There's no place like h. PROVERBS, 420
they come h. talking dirty O'BRIEN, TIM, 2
value h....go abroad for a while HALIBURTON, THOMAS CHANDLER, 1
What's the good of a h. GROSSMITH, GEORGE, 3
you can't go h. again BRYSON, BILL, 8
home fires Keep the H. Burning NOVELLO, IVOR, 1
home-making h....art and a profession HALE, SARAH JOSEPHA, 1
homeopathy H....a mingled mass of perverse ingenuity HOLMES, OLIVER WENDELL, 11
H....insignificant as an act of healing EMERSON, RALPH WALDO, 24
Homer even excellent H. nods HOMER, 1
H. is new this morning PÉGUY, CHARLES PIERRE, 13
H. sometimes sleeps WORDSWORTH, WILLIAM, 4
Seven cities warr'd for H., being dead HEYWOOD, THOMAS, 1
The author of that poem is either H. HOMER, 2
home rulers We are all H. today NEWSPAPERS, 28
home run Why didn't you hit a h. BENNY, JACK, 2
homesickness feeling weepy with h. GELLHORN, MARTHA, 2
H. is...absolutely nothing CHEEVER, JOHN, 1
H....long exposed weariness TSVETAEVA, MARINA, 4
H. starts with food GARCÍA MÁRQUEZ, GABRIEL, 1
home-sickness In h. you must keep moving STACPOOLE, HENRY DE VERE, 1
homeward Look H., Angel WOLFE, THOMAS, 1
homo The "h." is the legitimate child LEWIS, WYNDHAM, 3
homogeneity H. is a form of denial KLINE, NANCY, 4
homos one of the stately h. of England CRISP, QUENTIN, 5
homo sapiens *H*....interest in its distant origins WILFORD, JOHN NOBLE, 1
homosexual never met a h. in his life LANCASTER, OSBERT, 1
the h. urge BENKERT, KAROLY MARIA, 1
homosexuality I will resist...government endorsement of h. REAGAN, RONALD, 22
homosexuals problem which confronts h. CRISP, QUENTIN, 10
honest An h. broker BISMARCK, PRINCE OTTO VON, 20
An h. man 's the noblest work of God POPE, ALEXANDER, 31
An h. man's word PROVERBS, 134
be h. without a thought of heaven or hell BROWNE, THOMAS, 21
h. tale SHAKESPEARE, WILLIAM, 531
I am as h. as any man living SHAKESPEARE, WILLIAM, 457
life of an h. man...perpetual infidelity PÉGUY, CHARLES PIERRE, 8
preferred an h. man...before a rich man THEMISTOCLES, 1
so h. about music...kernel of creativity DAVIS, MILES, 1
Though I am not naturally h. SHAKESPEARE, WILLIAM, 667
too h. to live above his means JACKSON, ANDREW, 2
twelve h. men have decided the cause PULTENEY, WILLIAM, 1
honestly be h. wealthy, than miserably poor GARVEY, MARCUS, 9
If possible h....make money HORACE, 14
honesty H. is the best policy PROVERBS, 259
H. is the best policy WHATELY, RICHARD, 2
what a fool H. is SHAKESPEARE, WILLIAM, 665
honey'd the h. middle of the night KEATS, JOHN (1795–1821), 70
Hong Kong worst fears of the H. people CHOW, SELINA, 1
hongry H. rooster don't cackle HARRIS, JOEL CHANDLER, 3
honky-tonk a rambling h. hitter GUTHRIE, WOODY, 4

h. to fortune BACON, FRANCIS (1561–1626), 43
moral and emotional responsibility...remaining h. KEENAN, BRIAN, 1
Ten h. is terrorism; /A million...strategy SETH, VIKRAM, 5
hostesses the dread of h. CHURCHILL, RANDOLPH (1911–68), 2
hostile I'm h. to cats...afraid of horses MAILER, NORMAN, 22
hostilities controlled h....the normal condition of mankind HAMPSHIRE, STUART, 1
h. unmistakably to England and France HITLER, ADOLF, 17
hostility I've noticed your h. towards him BRADBURY, MALCOLM, 9
hot blow h. and cold with the same breath AESOP, 7
Houdini Robert H. who...invented the vanishing bird-cage trick WELLES, ORSON, 8
hound dog You ain't nothin' but a h. LEIBER, JERRY, 1
hour An h. in the morning PROVERBS, 135
from hour to h., we rot and rot SHAKESPEARE, WILLIAM, 106
In the h. of distress, a vow PROVERBS, 55
mine h. is not yet come BIBLE, 269
No h. is ever eternity HURSTON, ZORA NEALE, 14
one bare h. to live MARLOWE, CHRISTOPHER, 9
One h.'s sleep before midnight PROVERBS, 355
Some people...stay longer in an h. HOWELLS, WILLIAM DEAN, 2
tell what h....The clock does strike BUTLER, SAMUEL (1612–80), 6
The h. I have long wished for TERESA OF ÁVILA, SAINT, 7
The h. is come, but not the man SCOTT, SIR WALTER, 23
This is the H. of Lead DICKINSON, EMILY, 6
hours golden h....set with sixty diamond minutes MANN, HORACE, 2
The h. we waste in work MARQUIS, DON, 12
There are only twenty-four h. in the day PROVERBS, 409
house a fair h. built upon another man's ground SHAKESPEARE, WILLIAM, 628
A h. can be haunted MACNEICE, LOUIS, 13
a h. divided ...cannot stand JOHNSON, LYNDON BAINES, 17
A h. is a machine for living in LE CORBUSIER, 1
A H. Is Not a Home ADLER, POLLY, 1
Always pick a h. with baby-clothes BRODSKY, JOSEPH, 4
Cleaning your h. while your kids DILLER, PHYLLIS, 1
Every man's h. will be fair and decent MORRIS, WILLIAM, 5
get thee out...from thy father's h. BIBLE, 123
h. as nigh heaven as my own MORE, THOMAS, 6
heap o' livin' in a h. GUEST, EDGAR A., 1
h. we all had in common CARTER, ANGELA, 13
h. which is not opened for charity TALMUD, 5
In every h. of marriage KUNITZ, STANLEY, 1
Is this h....become a den of robbers BIBLE, 247
My h. shall be called...the house of prayer BIBLE, 361
The h. of every one is to him as his castle COKE, EDWARD, 3
Thine h. and thy kingdom BIBLE, 177
this H....a place of free speech WENTWORTH, PETER, 1
When h. and land are gone and spent FOOTE, SAMUEL, 1
household your h. is short of...righteousness ZHANGUO CE, 1
housekeeping H. ain't no joke ALCOTT, LOUISA MAY, 2
House of God He...said:...This is the H. ALEXANDER THE GREAT, 1
House of Lords Every man has a H. in his own head LLOYD-GEORGE, DAVID, 3
naked Duke...addressing a naked H. CARLYLE, THOMAS, 33
The H....kept efficient by...persistent absenteeism SAMUEL, HERBERT, 4
houses All h....Are haunted houses LONGFELLOW, HENRY WADSWORTH, 4
Enter not h. /other than your own KORAN, 28
falling h. thunder on your head JOHNSON, SAMUEL, 4
H. are built to live in BACON, FRANCIS (1561–1626), 19
H. are like sentinels in the plain MOMADAY, N. SCOTT, 1
How few of his friends' h. JOHNSON, SAMUEL, 89
h. will be turned inside out ÉLUARD, PAUL, 4
Old h. mended CIBBER, COLLEY, 4
housewives H. and mothers seldom...strike MORGAN, ELAINE, 3
h., tend to think in lists JACKSON, SHIRLEY, 1
housework H. isn't bad in itself LOUD, PAT, 1
Housman His opinion of H. is very low FROST, ROBERT, 1
Houston H., we have a problem LOVELL, JAMES, 1
how ask h. and why LEONARDO DA VINCI, 1
H. can I know what I think till I see what I say WALLAS, GRAHAM, 1
howls there are going to be h. of anguish HEALEY, DENIS, 2
Hugo H.—hélas HUGO, VICTOR, 2
human Adam was but h. TWAIN, MARK, 31
a h. being, and a terrible thing is happening to him MILLER, ARTHUR, 7
A h. being...a pun made by God MORLEY, CHRISTOPHER DARLINGTON, 1
All h. beings seek to locate themselves DEGLER, CARL N., 1
all h. life is there JAMES, HENRY, 26
being h....one does not seek perfection ORWELL, GEORGE, 29
between...*closest* h. beings infinite distances continue RILKE, RAINER MARIA, 4
equality was created by taking the h. rights away KRAUS, KARL, 24
every h. creature...secret and mystery DICKENS, CHARLES, 8
force h. beings to despise themselves...hell MALRAUX, ANDRÉ, 2
greatest moments of the h. spirit...in music COPLAND, AARON, 2
h. being is a collection of ideas PIRSIG, ROBERT T., 5
h. beings are heroic ORWELL, GEORGE, 16
H. beings are like timid punctuation marks GIRAUDOUX, JEAN, 1
H. beings are more alike than unalike ANGELOU, MAYA, 15
h. beings...besides...one's own set HOWELLS, WILLIAM DEAN, 1
h. beings...taking things for granted HUXLEY, ALDOUS, 50
H. beings were invented by water ROBBINS, TOM, 1
held the H. race in Scorn BELLOC, HILAIRE, 12
h. flesh is made of stardust CALDER, NIGEL, 1
H. folly is international TUCHOLSKY, KURT, 1
H. life is...much is to be endured JOHNSON, SAMUEL, 29
h. race...cancer of the planet HUXLEY, JULIAN, 3
h. race has...means for annihilating itself BORN, MAX, 2
h. race...heart's in the right place MAUGHAM, SOMERSET, 36
h. race may well become extinct RUSSELL, BERTRAND, 27
h. spirit thrives...music in some living form COPLAND, AARON, 1
h. tendency to search for panaceas KEEGAN, WILLIAM, 4
I am a h. being MOTTOS AND SLOGANS, 16
If h. beings could be propagated HALDANE, J. B. S., 5
It is not h. to feel safely placed EMPSON, WILLIAM, 3
I wish I loved the H. Race; RALEIGH, WALTER ALEXANDER, 3
leveling all h. activities...securing the necessities ARENDT, HANNAH, 17
No h. being...so free as a fish RUSKIN, JOHN, 23
Nothing defines h. beings better ADAMS, SCOTT, 2
nothing to distinguish h. society from the farm-yard SHAW, GEORGE BERNARD, 27
nuclear warfare...might well destroy the entire h. race WODEHOUSE, P. G., 2

only good h....a dead one ORWELL, GEORGE, 8
The h. body is private property MILLER, JONATHAN, 4
The h. face is...a whole cluster of faces PROUST, MARCEL, 6
the h. race does command its own destiny HANSBERRY, LORRAINE, 6
The h. race...knows it must die VOLTAIRE, 44
There is nothing h. in nature JEFFERIES, RICHARD, 5
We tolerate shapes in h. beings INGE, WILLIAM RALPH, 19

human condition h....pain and effort ARENDT, HANNAH, 21

humane There may be h. masters NORTHUP, SOLOMON, 2

humanism H....is not sufficiently human LEVINAS, EMMANUEL, 1

humanitarianism h. bred of Enlightenment hope DAVENPORT, GUY, 3

humanity Christians...h. without race SARTRE, JEAN-PAUL, 3
h....a series of learned behaviors MEAD, MARGARET, 8
h. does not know where to go PORCHIA, ANTONIO, 7
H. i love you CUMMINGS, E. E., 18
interests of h. in his breast PESTALOZZI, JOHANN HEINRICH, 2
no h. before that which starts with yourself GARVEY, MARCUS, 2
Oh wearisome condition of h. GREVILLE, FULKE, 2
quest for true h. BIKO, STEPHEN, 1
the fine h....generous humor of Burns BURNS, ROBERT, 3
We have h. and justice LAOZI, 7

human nature disappointed in h. DONLEAVY, J. P., 1
h. changes with geological leisureliness DURANT, WILL, 8
h....reaction to the restraints BOAS, FRANZ, 1
H. will not flourish HAWTHORNE, NATHANIEL, 18
there is something in h. which always makes an individual...reward merit WASHINGTON, BOOKER T., 6

humans all h. are born American GRAY, JOHN, 3
H....fortuitous and contingent outcome GOULD, STEPHEN JAY, 8
H. regard animals differently than animals HILLMAN, JAMES, 5
h. should have the...earth to themselves LAGERLÖF, SELMA, 1

humble go and h. myself to a nigger TWAIN, MARK, 38
It is difficult to be h. DOBRÉE, BONAMY, 1
it's hard to be h. ALI, MUHAMMAD, 14
One may be h. out of pride MONTAIGNE, MICHEL DE, 17

humbug connection between h. and politics BELL, RONALD, 1
Yes we have. H. PALMERSTON, LORD, 8

humiliation h. is...when the spirit is proudest PANKHURST, CHRISTABEL, 1
the last h. of an aged scholar COLLINGWOOD, R. G., 1

humility H. is a virtue SELDEN, JOHN, 6
H. is not...self-effacement MURDOCH, IRIS, 12
H. must always be doing its work TERESA OF ÁVILA, SAINT, 1
royal incognito of h. CUMMINGS, E. E., 13

humor Good h....philosophic state of mind RENAN, ERNEST, 6
Good h....seasoning of truth PESTALOZZI, JOHANN HEINRICH, 1
H. is emotional chaos remembered in tranquility THURBER, JAMES, 12
H....is to Americans KEILLOR, GARRISON, 14
H. is your own smile surprising you in the mirror HUGHES, LANGSTON, 14
H....laughing at what you haven't got HUGHES, LANGSTON, 15
we have no sense of h. WEISSTEIN, NAOMI, 1

humorist There is no h. like history DURANT, WILL, 14

humour H....first of the gifts to perish WOOLF, VIRGINIA, 15

Humphrey Bogart H. was a brilliant smoker BOGART, HUMPHREY, 1

Humpty Dumpty H. sat on a wall CHILDREN'S VERSE, 14

Hun The H. is at the gate KIPLING, RUDYARD, 4

hundreds h. of people waiting to abuse me MURRAY, BILL, 1

Hungarian It's not enough to be H. KORDA, ALEXANDER, 1

hunger banish h. by rubbing the belly DIOGENES, 1
H. and satisfaction...intense states of consciousness DEWEY, JOHN, 10
H. for fellowship, hunger for righteousness HAMMARSKJÖLD, DAG, 2
h. for love is much more difficult TERESA OF CALCUTTA, MOTHER, 4
H. is the best sauce PROVERBS, 261
H. will make a monkey PROVERBS, 53
The only power poor people have is their h. OKRI, BEN, 3
The war against h. KENNEDY, JOHN FITZGERALD, 19

hungover a h. poet rustling his paper DONLEAVY, J. P., 3

hungred h., and ye gave me meat BIBLE, 431

hungry A ball player's got to be kept h. DIMAGGIO, JOE, 3
a h. lean-fac'd villain SHAKESPEARE, WILLIAM, 595
A h. stomach has no ears LA FONTAINE, JEAN DE, 10

Hungry Joe H. collected lists of fatal diseases HELLER, JOSEPH, 8

hunt people who h. are the right people SHAW, GEORGE BERNARD, 28

hunting a passion for h. DICKENS, CHARLES, 69
daren't go a-h. ALLINGHAM, WILLIAM, 1

hurrah H.! hurrah! we bring the Jubilee WORK, HENRY CLAY, 4

hurricane h. on the way FISH, MICHAEL, 1
no h....so disastrous...as a ruthlessly humanitarian woman STOWE, HARRIET BEECHER, 1

hurry He sows h. and reaps indigestion STEVENSON, ROBERT LOUIS, 29
H.!...I have no time to hurry STRAVINSKY, IGOR, 8
So who's in a h. BENCHLEY, ROBERT, 12

hurt do not h. her...she is mad GEORGE III, 2
h. a man...strike at his self-love WALLACE, LEW, 2
I can h. anybody ROBINSON, SUGAR RAY, 2
It doesn't h. to lose my crown GRAF, STEFFI, 1
it h. too much to laugh LINCOLN, ABRAHAM, 7
Those have most power to h....we love BEAUMONT & FLETCHER, 10

husband A h. is better than talent MOORE, GEORGE, 1
A h. is what is left of the lover ROWLAND, HELEN, 1
Being a h. is a whole-time job BENNETT, ARNOLD, 5
h. and the wife will be equal MOTT, LUCRETIA, 1
Her h....for life NORRIS, FRANK, 1
Let your h. be content with you MSHAM, MWANA KUPONA BINTI, 1
My h. and I ELIZABETH II, 2
My h. is dead MARX, GROUCHO, 16
Never trust a h. too far ROWLAND, HELEN, 6
So sways she level in her h.'s heart SHAKESPEARE, WILLIAM, 700
that monstrous animal a h. and wife FIELDING, HENRY, 20
trust my h. not to fall asleep THATCHER, MARGARET, 23
what h. ever forgave the faithlessness NAVARRE, MARGARET OF, 1
Who would not make her h. a cuckold SHAKESPEARE, WILLIAM, 494
You may have my h., but not my horse LAWRENCE, D. H., 47

husbands a little more respeckt for h. LOOS, ANITA, 2
h. and wives...belong to different sexes DIX, DOROTHY, 4
h. and wives make shipwreck DIX, DOROTHY, 1
H. are like fires GABOR, ZSA ZSA, 2
h., love your wives BIBLE, 25
that h. and wives should have children HOUSMAN, LAURENCE, 1

hush a breathless h. in the Close tonight NEWBOLT, HENRY, 3
somebody ought to have said "h." SHAW, GEORGE BERNARD, 2

husks the h. that the swine did eat BIBLE, 340

hussy a brazen h. of a speech CHURCHILL, WINSTON, 65

hustle all he needed was a h. MONK, THELONIOUS, 1

hybridity h. is heresy, to blaspheme is to dream BHABA, HOMI, 1
Hyde Park Beyond H. all is a desert ETHEREGE, GEORGE, 1
hydrogen All things come from h. MAMET, DAVID, 9
hygiene H. is the corruption of medicine by morality MENCKEN, H. L., 33
hymen the h. is often relaxed in virgins BELL, T., 1
hypnotize I could h. with music MINGUS, CHARLES, 2
hypochondria H. torments us not only with causeless irritation SCHOPENHAUER, ARTHUR, 8
hypochondriac h. affection in men...hysteric in women HEBERDEN, WILLIAM, 1
hypochondriacs H. squander large sums of time OUSPENSKY, PETER, 3
hypocrisy H. is the most...nerve-racking vice MAUGHAM, SOMERSET, 9
neither man nor angel can discern /H. MILTON, JOHN, 50
hypocrite No man is a h. in his pleasures CAMUS, ALBERT, 11
hypocritical Man...learns by being h. KERR, JEAN, 1
hypodermic man who cannot work without his h. needle FISCHER, MARTIN H., 3
hypotheses Questions, h., call them that BECKETT, SAMUEL, 19
hypothesis discard a pet h. every day LORENZ, KONRAD, 7
Factual evidence can never "prove" a h. FRIEDMAN, MILTON, 6
slaying of a beautiful h. HUXLEY, T. H., 3
hysteria H. is a natural phenomenon...female nature WILLIAMS, TENNESSEE, 16
h....snake whose scales are tiny mirrors WEST, NATHANAEL, 6

I I. am not what I am SHAKESPEARE, WILLIAM, 464
I. am the way I am PRÉVERT, JACQUES, 1
I. is somebody else RIMBAUD, ARTHUR, 2
ice A Shape of I. HARDY, THOMAS, 20
green i. /Of envy's mean gaze ROETHKE, THEODORE, 7
The i. was here, the ice was there COLERIDGE, SAMUEL TAYLOR, 38
ice cream just enjoy your i. while it's on your plate WILDER, THORNTON, 7
iceman The I. Cometh O'NEILL, EUGENE, 7
icicles When i. hang by the wall SHAKESPEARE, WILLIAM, 378
id put the i. back in yid ROTH, PHILIP, 8
the care of the i. by the odd PROVERBS, MODERN, 26
Idaho smell of a roasting I....so cozy TYLER, ANNE, 1
idea An i. does not pass from one language UNAMUNO Y JUGO, MIGUEL DE, 6
An i. isn't responsible for the people MARQUIS, DON, 9
best way to kill an i. PROVERBS, MODERN, 24
do in the hope of an i. FABRE, JEAN HENRI, 1
entertain an i. of committing suicide HAWTHORNE, NATHANIEL, 19
intensity of an i. depends...somatic excitation REICH, WILHELM, 7
i. of a person as a marionette HAAS, ROBERT, 1
i.'s worth having once STOPPARD, TOM, 4
I think it would be a good i. GANDHI, MAHATMA, 26
live in the shadow of an i. without grasping it BOWEN, ELIZABETH, 5
Nothing is more dangerous than an i. ALAIN, 1
to possess but one i. JOHNSON, SAMUEL, 142
idea-intensive i., interdependent network environment SCULLEY, JOHN, 6
ideal i. of a man of science DARWIN, CHARLES, 1
my i. the life of Jesus NIXON, RICHARD, 34
The i. universe for us SAGAN, CARL, 1
idealism What an extraordinary mixture of i. and lunacy LLOYD-GEORGE, DAVID, 10
idealist An i....on noticing...a rose smells better than a cabbage MENCKEN, H. L., 44
true i....true realist DELORS, JACQUES, 1
ideals Away with all i. LAWRENCE, D. H., 35
ideas Great i. are not charitable MONTHERLANT, HENRI DE, 7
I. are a commodity DELL, MICHAEL, 1
i. are of more importance than values BRENAN, GERALD, 6
i. grow better when transplanted HOLMES, OLIVER WENDELL, JR., 7
i. simply pass through him BRADLEY, F. H., 7
I. that enter...mind under fire remain TROTSKY, LEON, 7
Keep on the lookout for novel i. EDISON, THOMAS ALVA, 3
Learn our i., or otherwise get out LESSING, DORIS, 4
no i., no information ROSZAK, THEODORE, 3
Old i. give way slowly DEWEY, JOHN, 1
she's only got two i. in her head LINKLATER, ERIC, 2
simple i....derived from simple impressions HUME, DAVID, 7
We are constantly hatching...false i. PIAGET, JEAN, 2
Whenever i. fail, men invent words FISCHER, MARTIN H., 23
identity Before national i., before local affiliation OHMAE, KENICHI, 2
The i. crisis...occurs in that period ERIKSON, ERIK, 2
ideology the i. is not the private sector DAY, GRAHAM, 2
ides The i. of March PLUTARCH, 23
idiocy between the i. of infancy and the folly of youth BIERCE, AMBROSE, 14
idiom the i. of words very little she heeded PRIOR, MATTHEW, 6
idiot he is a sort of *i. savant* of language THOMAS, DYLAN, 3
The i. who praises...every country but his own GILBERT, W. S., 24
idiots How many i....make up a public BEAUMARCHAIS, PIERRE-AUGUSTIN CARON DE, 6
idle As i. as a painted ship COLERIDGE, SAMUEL TAYLOR, 41
I am happiest when I am i. WARD, ARTEMUS, 4
We would all be i. JOHNSON, SAMUEL, 131
idleness i. and crime...deferring of our hopes EMERSON, RALPH WALDO, 25
I. begets ennui JEFFERSON, THOMAS, 25
I. is the parent of all psychology NIETZSCHE, FRIEDRICH WILHELM, 34
I., sorrow, a friend, and a foe PARKER, DOROTHY, 11
I....the refuge of weak minds CHESTERFIELD, LORD, 11
round of strenuous i. WORDSWORTH, WILLIAM, 93
idling It is impossible to enjoy i. JEROME, JEROME K., 4
idolatry no i. in the Mass JOHNSON, SAMUEL, 125
idols We shouldn't touch our i. FLAUBERT, GUSTAVE, 10
if I. you can make one heap of all your winnings KIPLING, RUDYARD, 51
I. you had been mine when you were seven SPARK, MURIEL, 11
ifs If i. and ands PROVERBS, 265
ignoramus i....person unacquainted with ...knowledge familiar to yourself BIERCE, AMBROSE, 27
ignorance a real i. of anything American MACNEICE, LOUIS, 2
even the learned i. of a nomenclature HOLMES, OLIVER WENDELL, 20
From i. our comfort flows PRIOR, MATTHEW, 11
he knew nothing, except...his i. SOCRATES, 3
his chosen mode of i. HUBBARD, ELBERT, 16

His i. was an Empire State Building of ignorance ROSS, HAROLD W., 1
I....a delicate exotic fruit WILDE, OSCAR, 42
I., arrogance, and racism have bloomed as Superior Knowledge in all too many universities WALKER, ALICE, 6
i....causes most mistakes TRUMAN, HARRY S., 16
I. is an evil weed BEVERIDGE, WILLIAM HENRY, 1
I. is not innocence but sin BROWNING, ROBERT, 6
I. is preferable to error JEFFERSON, THOMAS, 38
"i. is the mother of devotion," BURTON, ROBERT, 20
I. is the mother of devotion TAYLOR, JEREMY, 3
I., madam, pure ignorance JOHNSON, SAMUEL, 139
I. of the law excuses SELDEN, JOHN, 8
i. of the law is not punished BENTHAM, JEREMY, 8
i. of...true laws of social life COMTE, AUGUSTE, 2
i....the source of our anguish RADHAKRISHNAN, SARVEPALLI, 1
knowledge increases...i. unfolds KENNEDY, JOHN FITZGERALD, 22
Let us all honestly own our i. DENG TO, 1
Our age has robbed millions of the simplicity of i. DAVIES, ROBERTSON, 4
Somebody else's i. is bliss VANCE, JACK, 1
Your i. cramps my conversation HOPE, ANTHONY, 7

ignorant conscious that you are i....step to knowledge DISRAELI, BENJAMIN, 29
Have the courage to be i. SMITH, SYDNEY, 8
The i. man always adores LOMBROSO, CESARE, 1

ill being i. as one of the greatest pleasures of life BUTLER, SAMUEL (1835–1902), 16
human i. does not...seem...an alternative WILDER, THORNTON, 1
I. can he rule the great SPENSER, EDMUND, 9
If ...someone is speaking i. of you EPICTETUS, 1
means to do i. deeds SHAKESPEARE, WILLIAM, 327
One who is i....duty to seek medical aid MAIMONIDES, 3
seal up the avenues of i. EMERSON, RALPH WALDO, 36

illegitimate There are no i. children YANKWICH, LÉON R., 1

ill-fated Oh! i. bridge of the Silv'ry Tay MCGONAGALL, WILLIAM, 9

ill-fed i., ill-killed, ill-kept JOHNSON, SAMUEL, 136

ill-housed one-third of a nation i. ROOSEVELT, FRANKLIN D., 24

illiteracy To deliver the nation from i. ATATURK, KEMAL, 3

illiterate An i. king is a crowned ass HENRY I, 2

illiterates I. have to dictate LEC, STANISLAW, 5

ill-luck I....seldom comes alone CERVANTES, MIGUEL DE, 9

illness A long i....between life and death LA BRUYÈRE, JEAN DE, 1
Considering how common i. is WOOLF, VIRGINIA, 20
I. is in part what the world has done to a victim MENNINGER, KARL, 2
I. isn't...thing that spoils the appetite TURGENEV, IVAN, 1
I. makes a man a scoundrel JOHNSON, SAMUEL, 3
in i....never to lose heart LENIN, VLADIMIR ILYICH, 24
In i. the physician is a father PROVERBS, 66
in moments of i....we live not alone PROUST, MARCEL, 17

illnesses "i. of the body...of the mind" FOUCAULT, MICHEL, 3

ill-treated This is for all i. fellows HOUSMAN, A. E., 26

illuminate They i. our whole country GROSSETESTE, ROBERT, 1

ill-usage complaints of i. contemptible EDEN, EMILY, 1

illustrious This i. man, the largest and most spacious intellect COLERIDGE, SAMUEL TAYLOR, 4

image an i. of the Cosmos STRINDBERG, AUGUST, 8
fall down and worship the golden i. BIBLE, 28
i. is one thing...human being...another PRESLEY, ELVIS, 5
I made my own i. HARRY, DEBORAH, 3

imagery the loveliest i. and...eloquent expressions KEATS, JOHN (1795–1821), 4

images A heap of broken i. ELIOT, T. S., 52
i. convey a deeper wisdom SHAKESPEARE, WILLIAM, 40
the good that holy i. do PACHECO, FRANCISCO, 1

imaginary no other way to conceive an i. world VIZINCZEY, STEPHEN, 2

imagination An i. sublimated and eccentric ADAMS, JOHN, 1
I. alone never did...produce works CONSTABLE, JOHN, 1
I. and fiction make up...our real life WEIL, SIMONE, 2
if your i. had to sin GARBO, GRETA, 2
i. in a mathematician ALEMBERT, JEAN LE ROND D', 1
I....I put it first years ago TERRY, ELLEN, 2
i. is a necessary ingredient of perception KANT, IMMANUEL, 11
I....is the irrepressible revolutionist STEVENS, WALLACE, 23
indebted to his...i. for his facts SHERIDAN, RICHARD BRINSLEY, 17
I....not an empirical...power of consciousness SARTRE, JEAN-PAUL, 27
lack of i. that makes us come BISHOP, ELIZABETH, 10
no i. and... no compassion THATCHER, MARGARET, 10
no i., dying doesn't mean much CÉLINE, LOUIS-FERDINAND, 4
The i. is the only genius STEVENS, WALLACE, 25
The primary i. COLERIDGE, SAMUEL TAYLOR, 29
Using one's i. avoids many misfortunes MARIAS, JAVIER, 2
where the i....is rich and living SYNGE, J. M., 4

imaginative an i. creation, a personal possession BECKER, CARL, 4

imagine I. six apartments LENNON, JOHN, 1
I. there's no heaven LENNON, JOHN, 6
Why...i. Others to be Fools AIDOO, AMA ATA, 4

Imam an I. while still in...childhood AL-MUFID, ABU ABDULLAH MUHAMMAD AL-HARITHI AL-BAGHDADI, 9

imbecility i....lowered the character of Great Britain COOPER, JAMES FENIMORE, 13

imitate Those who do not...i....produce nothing DALÍ, SALVADOR, 1

imitation An i. rough diamond ASQUITH, MARGOT, 1
I. is not inspiration RYDER, ALBERT PINKHAM, 1
Man...is an i. OUSPENSKY, PETER, 4
pleasure of i....most innate ECO, UMBERTO, 14

Immaculate Conception the I. was spontaneous combustion PARKER, DOROTHY, 34

immature i. man...wants to die nobly STEKEL, WILHELM, 1

immaturity common symptom of i. WHARTON, EDITH, 11

immediacy I. can be accomplished in a picture KLINE, FRANZ, 1

immediate I call for his i. resignation GORBACHEV, MIKHAIL, 4
I distrust an i. morality SARTRE, JEAN-PAUL, 17

immersed We all become so i. in the habits of American culture that...we mistake them for life itself MANLEY, MICHAEL, 2

immigrant Every i....should...learn English or leave ROOSEVELT, THEODORE, 22

immodesty towering i.... of his self love AMIS, MARTIN, 2

immoral Call a thing i. or ugly SCHUMACHER, E. F., 1
either i., illegal, or fattening WOOLLCOTT, ALEXANDER, 2
worse than i. ACHESON, DEAN, 4

immorality I....found support in religion FREUD, SIGMUND, 45

immortal I have left no i. work KEATS, JOHN (1795–1821), 30
I.! William Shakespeare SHAKESPEARE, WILLIAM, 38
there shall wait on them i. youths KORAN, 37

independence Complete i. through truth and non-violence GANDHI, MAHATMA, 18
cultural and political i. and economic integration DRUCKER, PETER, 4
Genuine i. can only come out of the barrel of a gun MUGABE, ROBERT, 2
independent I., we could not survive LEACOCK, STEPHEN, 1
indestructible In your 20s, you feel like you're i. BELUSHI, JOHN, 2
indexes He writes i. to perfection GOLDSMITH, OLIVER, 4
India diseases that people get in I....purely psychic JHABVALA, RUTH PRAWER, 1
Establish...sure English dominion in I. ANONYMOUS, 15
If I. won her freedom through truth GANDHI, MAHATMA, 19
I. is a geographical term CHURCHILL, WINSTON, 18
In I., human misery seems so pervasive MATTHIESSEN, PETER, 9
I....the strength and the greatness of England CURZON, GEORGE NATHANIEL, 1
message of I. FORSTER, E. M., 9
midnight hour, I. will awake to...freedom NEHRU, JAWAHARLAL, 2
no need...to I....to find peace KÜBLER-ROSS, ELISABETH, 1
no politician in I. daring enough GANDHI, INDIRA, 7
Indian Everything an I. does is in a circle BLACK ELK, 1
I. wars have had their origin in broken promises HAYES, RUTHERFORD B., 2
I. woman of today NAIDU, SAROJINI, 1
lay out ten to see a dead I. SHAKESPEARE, WILLIAM, 646
Indiana I....more first-rate second-class men MARSHALL, THOMAS R., 2
Mooresville, I....John Dillinger capital of America BRAUTIGAN, RICHARD, 7
Indian corn I....most agreeable grains FRANKLIN, BENJAMIN, 11
indians ain't /no mo /i. blowing /custer's mind SANCHEZ, SONIA, 3
Indians The only good I. I ever saw were dead SHERIDAN, PHILIP HENRY, 1
We'll be the I. MCMURTRY, LARRY, 1
indication an i. of truth's jealousy MAHFOUZ, NAGUIB, 1
indifference and cold i. came ROWE, NICHOLAS, 1
enormous amount of i. to all religions TILLICH, PAUL, 3
i. closely bordering on aversion STEVENSON, ROBERT LOUIS, 13
indifferent An i. spectator like myself BAROJA, PÍO, 4
indigestion I. is charged by God HUGO, VICTOR, 8
indignation i. makes an excellent speech EMERSON, RALPH WALDO, 67
i. makes me write verse JUVENAL, 4
My heart burned...with i. and grief LINCOLN, ABRAHAM, 2
indignity ultimate i. is to be given a bedpan KUHN, MAGGIE, 1
indiscreet people so i. in appearing to know BOCCACCIO, GIOVANNI, 4
indiscretion contain at least one blazing i. MORLEY, LORD, 1
indispensable There is no i. man WILSON, WOODROW, 13
indispensables She was one of those i. HUXLEY, ALDOUS, 35
individual each i., regardless of their heritage BUSH, GEORGE W., 1
i.'s desire to dominate his environment VIDAL, GORE, 3
Over himself...the i. is absolute MILL, JOHN STUART, 6
the i. now threatens the rest of society LEE, KUAN YEW, 5
individualist Be an i.—and an individual GETTY, J. PAUL, 2
individuality i. lies in...universal element of mind HEGEL, G. W. F., 15
Untalented i. is...useless GONCHAROVA, NATALIA, 2
individuals i. need to accept our past HANDY, CHARLES, 7
I. pass like shadows BURKE, EDMUND, 15
Indonesia in I....a male may...run amok VAN DER POST, LAURENS, 4
industrial roots of the i. world AYALA, FRANCISCO, 1
industrial age Goodbye i. RODIN, ROBERT, 1
industrial design i....on a mass-production basis PAPANEK, VICTOR, 2
industrialized i. nation consumes...energy and raw materials STRONG, MAURICE F., 1
industrial organization optimal form of i....network structures FUKUYAMA, FRANCIS, 3
industrial relations I. are like sexual relations FEATHER, VIC, 1
industry an i. like the railroads EISNER, MICHAEL, 6
development of i....new sources of danger SIGERIST, HENRY E., 5
Every time the i. gets powerful SIMON, PAUL, 5
first honesty, then i., then concentration CARNEGIE, ANDREW, 10
I. is...like the human body HARVEY-JONES, JOHN, 3
i. is...rife with jealousy MORRISSEY, 5
i. with a low level of competitiveness KOTTER, JOHN P., 1
inelegance a continual state of i. AUSTEN, JANE, 10
inequalities i....begin in the mind HAWKES, JACQUETTA, 1
inequality i. that has no special utility...injustice BENTHAM, JEREMY, 6
saddest sight that fortune's i. exhibits CARLYLE, THOMAS, 7
inevitability The i. of gradualness WEBB, SIDNEY, 1
There is no i. in history FRANKFURTER, FELIX, 1
inevitable Nothing is i. until it happens TAYLOR, A. J. P., 1
inexhaustible i. bodies that...feed the grass TATE, ALLEN, 1
inexperience I....makes a young man do...impossible PROCHNOW, HERBERT V., 1
infallible No man is i. PROVERBS, 345
infamous I have got an i. army WELLINGTON, DUKE OF, 2
infancy between i. and adultery ANONYMOUS, 86
i., childhood, adolescence, and obsolescence LINKLETTER, ART, 2
I....Heaven lies about us BIERCE, AMBROSE, 29
infant a mixed i. BEHAN, BRENDAN, 9
An i. crying in the night HALLAM, ARTHUR HENRY, 9
Have you ever watched an i. BRYSON, BILL, 12
infantryman An i. 's heart...grows horny ROTH, PHILIP, 1
infection gazing into that happy future when the i. will be banished SEMMELWEIS, IGNAZ, 1
inferior greatest possible number of i. beings BRADLEY, F. H., 2
No one can make you feel i. without your consent ROOSEVELT, ELEANOR, 4
inferiority i. complex...readily developed in Hollywood LAHR, BERT, 2
i. of all...who were not white COOPER, JAMES FENIMORE, 3
Wherever an i. complex exists, there is ...reason JUNG, CARL GUSTAV, 2
inferiors I. revolt...that they may be equal ARISTOTLE, 30
inferno the i. of his passions JUNG, CARL GUSTAV, 15
infidel an i. pronounces the Twin Blessings KHOMEINI, RUHOLLAH, 3
infidelity i. against the authority of his instructors JEFFERSON, THOMAS, 11
infinite delivered i. babies, in one great birth WILLIAMS, WILLIAM CARLOS, 1
i. number of possible universes LEIBNIZ, GOTTFRIED WILHELM, 7
i. sadness at the core of his consciousness BOWLES, PAUL, 1
The sight...gave me i. pleasure PARK, MUNGO, 1
infinity i. torments me MUSSET, ALFRED DE, 2
inflammation i. of his weekly bills BYRON, LORD, 58

inflation i. can hamper economic performance GREENSPAN, ALAN, 3
i. caused by excessive money supply JOSEPH, KEITH, 1
I. is as violent as a mugger REAGAN, RONALD, 32
I. is never ultimately tamed GREENSPAN, ALAN, 1
I. is the one form of taxation FRIEDMAN, MILTON, 8
I....prosperity with high blood pressure NEWSPAPERS, 35
little i....like being a little pregnant HENDERSON, LEON, 1
no stable trade-off between i. and unemployment FRIEDMAN, MILTON, 1
Nothing so weakens a government as...i. GALBRAITH, J. K., 9
one place where i. is made...Washington FRIEDMAN, MILTON, 9
inflationary i. policies led...to economic stagnation FRIEDMAN, MILTON, 3
influence i....accumulation of a lifetime's thoughts WILDER, THORNTON, 9
proper time to i. the character of a child INGE, WILLIAM RALPH, 9
unwarranted i....by the military-industrial complex EISENHOWER, DWIGHT D., 11
influenced I am easily i. ADAMS, FRANKLIN P., 3
information A world awash in i. KRUGMAN, PAUL, 1
computerized i. services...democratic society ROSZAK, THEODORE, 2
I. about money WRISTON, WALTER B., 5
I. and knowledge are...weapons STEWART, THOMAS A., 3
I. flow...lifeblood of your company GATES, BILL, 3
I. is not knowledge ZAPPA, FRANK, 2
I only ask for i. DICKENS, CHARLES, 23
rise of the i. economy in America ROSZAK, THEODORE, 7
Withholding i....act of intellectual imperialism KLINE, NANCY, 9
information-based right model for the i. organization DRUCKER, PETER, 9
information technology Today's i. SMITH, RAYMOND W., 3
informed far better i. SMITH, F. E., 5
infuriate pleasant /to i. a clumsy foe PUSHKIN, ALEXANDER, 3
infusion The i. of a China plant ADDISON, JOSEPH, 14
Inglan I. is a bitch JOHNSON, LINTON KWESI, 1
ingratitude I hate i. more in a man SHAKESPEARE, WILLIAM, 710
I., thou marble-hearted fiend SHAKESPEARE, WILLIAM, 337
ingredients three i. in the good life MORLEY, CHRISTOPHER DARLINGTON, 3
ingress man's i....naked and bare EDWIN, JOHN, 1
Our i....Was naked and bare LONGFELLOW, HENRY WADSWORTH, 28
inhabitable the i. world is not worth...two monarchs TAMERLANE, 2
inherit It's not just what we i. IBSEN, HENRIK, 10
inherited as if he had i. it GRANT, ULYSSES S., 1
inhumanity Man's i. to man BURNS, ROBERT, 24
iniquity purchased a field with the reward of i. BIBLE, 2
Injun I.'s natur' to be found where...least expected COOPER, JAMES FENIMORE, 14
injunction About the i. of the Apostle Paul TERESA OF ÁVILA, SAINT, 8
injury An i. is much sooner forgotten CHESTERFIELD, LORD, 6
If an i. has to be done MACHIAVELLI, NICCOLÒ, 6
injustice I....a threat to justice KING, MARTIN LUTHER, JR., 4
I cry I.! Let Earth be moved GUAN HANQING, 1
i. done to an individual JUNIUS, 1
i. is always in the right hands LEC, STANISLAW, 2
I., swift, erect, and unconfin'd POPE, ALEXANDER, 73
I. which lasts for three long centuries WRIGHT, RICHARD, 2
mortgage his i....for his fidelity BURKE, EDMUND, 48
National i....national downfall GLADSTONE, WILLIAM EWART, 7
No i. is done ULPIAN, 1
threatened with a great i. CARLYLE, JANE, 3
what you still have planned...shows the...i. in your death CANETTI, ELIAS, 12
injustices thought only to justify their i. VOLTAIRE, 20
ink he hath not drunk i. SHAKESPEARE, WILLIAM, 375
i. of the scholar MUHAMMAD, 16
in-laws i. was that they were outlaws MALCOLM X, 15
innocence I. is a kind of insanity GREENE, GRAHAM, 8
i. that is full and experience...empty PÉGUY, CHARLES PIERRE, 2
my i. begins to weigh me down RACINE, JEAN, 2
Ralph wept for the end of i. GOLDING, WILLIAM, 1
sensitive i. which Holden Caulfield retained SALINGER, J. D., 3
innocent An i. man is a sin before God MORRISON, TONI, 23
Everyone is i. PROVERBS, 205
i. creatures should come to no harm HARDY, THOMAS, 16
not...without distress...killed an i. animal MONTAIGNE, MICHEL DE, 29
The i....no enemy but time YEATS, W. B., 58
innocently i. employed...getting money JOHNSON, SAMUEL, 122
innocuous There is nothing i. left ADORNO, THEODOR, 5
innovate ability to i....source of competitive success BARTLETT, CHRISTOPHER A., 1
To i. is not to reform BURKE, EDMUND, 3
innovation every i. is a going astray MUHAMMAD, 11
I., everyday entrepreneurship, and creativity KEEN, PETER, 3
I. is a low-odds business PETERS, TOM, 7
I....necessary condition for business success TOBIAS, RANDALL L., 1
i. occurs when...new idea is adopted ROGERS, EVERETT, 1
innovations i....are the births of time BACON, FRANCIS (1561–1626), 37
insane i. person...running a private unapproved film PIRSIG, ROBERT T., 3
Man is quite i. MONTAIGNE, MICHEL DE, 14
Ordinarily he is i. HEINE, HEINRICH, 2
the i. take themselves...seriously BEERBOHM, MAX, 23
This fellow isn't i....only doing philosophy WITTGENSTEIN, LUDWIG, 21
you want to get out...i. asylum PIRSIG, ROBERT T., 1
insanities I've always been interested...i. of people HIRSCHFELD, AL, 1
insanity I....disorder of brain producing disorder of mind MAUDSLEY, HENRY, 1
I. in individuals is something rare NIETZSCHE, FRIEDRICH WILHELM, 3
I....logic of an accurate mind overtaxed HOLMES, OLIVER WENDELL, 22
insecurity the i. outside the human economy JUNG, CARL GUSTAV, 4
insensitivity show some i. to your past GOIZUETA, ROBERTO, 1
insert i....certain genes into subsequent generations WILSON, EDWARD O., 5
insider I was an i. and an outsider LORD, BETTY BAO, 1
insight moment's i. is...worth a life's experience HOLMES, OLIVER WENDELL, 32
insolence i. is not invective DISRAELI, BENJAMIN, 19
insomnia every man's i. is as different from his neighbor's FITZGERALD, F. SCOTT, 11
for i....get an opera score HORNE, MARILYN, 2
I. troubles only those who can sleep HUBBARD, ELBERT, 9
inspiration He who...is waiting for...i. REYNOLDS, SIR JOSHUA, 6
Ninety percent of i. PROVERBS, 343

inspired i. by the abusive hopelessness of everything MILLER, HENRY, 17
instant considered an i. classic CAPOTE, TRUMAN, 1
instinct Permanence of i....permanence of form FABRE, JEAN HENRI, 3
triple blow...science of i. FABRE, JEAN HENRI, 2
instincts Our i. are at war LEWIS, C. S., 2
institution An i....lengthened shadow of one man EMERSON, RALPH WALDO, 9
If an i. wants to be adaptive SHAPIRO, ROBERT B., 2
No i. can...survive DRUCKER, PETER, 15
She cannot see an i. without hitting it THATCHER, MARGARET, 9
institutionalize The minute you i. a problem GIOVANNI, NIKKI, 4
institutions In the best i., promises are kept OGILVY, DAVID, 1
working of great i. is...sheer mistake SANTAYANA, GEORGE, 10
instructions i. for being a pigeon BRYSON, BILL, 2
insubordination price of i. and insurrection MCGREGOR, IAN, 1
insularity fundamental i. of outlook NEEDHAM, JOSEPH, 3
insulin method to counter the increasing doses of i. ANONYMOUS, 70
insult adding i. to injuries MOORE, EDWARD, 1
I like Frenchmen...even when they i. you BAKER, JOSEPHINE, 5
i. the river god PROVERBS, 36
man should not i. his wife publicly THURBER, JAMES, 14
insupportable i. labour of doing nothing STEELE, RICHARD, 2
insurance I....ingenious modern game of chance BIERCE, AMBROSE, 30
one of the answers is—i. WHITEHORN, KATHARINE, 3
insurrection I. is an art TROTSKY, LEON, 5
integrated a totally i. world culture SNYDER, GARY, 1
Do I really *want* to be i. BALDWIN, JAMES, 25
integrity I. without knowledge is weak JOHNSON, SAMUEL, 31
intellect A towering i., grand in its achievements HARPER, FRANCES E. W., 2
Go! put off Holiness, /"And put on I." BLAKE, WILLIAM, 13
I. is invisible SCHOPENHAUER, ARTHUR, 2
Our meddling i. WORDSWORTH, WILLIAM, 22
take care not to make the i. our god EINSTEIN, ALBERT, 35
The i. is part of life TUCHOLSKY, KURT, 4
The i. of man...forced to choose YEATS, W. B., 61
The voice of the i. is a soft one FREUD, SIGMUND, 39
intellects highest i., like the tops of mountains MACAULAY, THOMAS BABINGTON, 17
intellectual An i....says a simple thing BUKOWSKI, CHARLES, 3
called many things, but never an i. BANKHEAD, TALLULAH, 4
demand for i. honesty is itself dishonest ADORNO, THEODOR, 3
Every i. attitude is latently political MANN, THOMAS, 18
Every i....ought to refuse to testify EINSTEIN, ALBERT, 27
I. ...A man who's untrue to his wife AUDEN, W. H., 16
i. community...stand up for freedom of the imagination RUSHDIE, SALMAN, 2
I. courage is extremely important GOIZUETA, ROBERTO, 4
i....doesn't know how to park a bike AGNEW, SPIRO T., 5
i. excitement...the driving force of science NELSON, DAVID R., 1
i. has been...an outsider, a servant HOFSTADTER, RICHARD, 1
I. honesty...more than what's legislated SANFORD, CHARLES, JR., 2
i....I found it too difficult SCHWEITZER, ALBERT, 6
I. virtue owes...its growth to teaching ARISTOTLE, 12
The i. rigour of Marxism MARX, KARL, 1
intellectual capital I. is...competitive edge STEWART, THOMAS A., 4
i. measurement...first universal measurement tool MALONE, MICHAEL S., 1
social architecture...generates i. BENNIS, WARREN, 13
intellectual property I. must adapt to the globalization LONG, CLARISA, 1
intellectuals I.' Betrayal BENDA, JULIEN, 2
i.' chief cause of anguish BARZUN, JACQUES, 8
i....out to destroy faith and fatherland FLANAGAN, OLIVER J., 2
vanishing race...the i. SHERWOOD, ROBERT E., 1
intellectual slavery I. masquerading as sophistication NGUGI WA THIONGO, 2
intelligence I. becomes an asset STEWART, THOMAS A., 5
I. begins with the external DEWEY, JOHN, 12
i. cannot be hidden; like a cough DAVIES, ROBERTSON, 5
i. consists in identifying the apparently unlike DEWEY, JOHN, 11
I. is almost useless CARREL, ALEXIS, 1
I. is...a natural incomprehension of life BERGSON, HENRI-LOUIS, 2
I. is quickness to apprehend WHITEHEAD, A. N., 8
i. is the great polluter SIMAK, CLIFFORD D., 1
i. of the American people MENCKEN, H. L., 49
i....recognize it when we see it PINKER, STEVEN, 7
let the i. of...individuals unfold XU WENLI, 3
No tool is more beneficial than i. AL-MUFID, ABU ABDULLAH MUHAMMAD AL-HARITHI AL-BAGHDADI, 3
The more i. one has PASCAL, BLAISE, 9
intelligent an i. man at the point of death AMR IBN AL-'AS, 1
appeal to "Every i. voter" ADAMS, FRANKLIN P., 1
English Law...one i., one stupid CONNOLLY, CYRIL, 10
i. man feels what other men...know MONTESQUIEU, 3
i. people...are socialists BENNETT, ALAN, 2
Is an i. human being likely ROTH, PHILIP, 9
most i. people...people of doing without MUHAMMAD, 12
The i. are to the intelligentsia BALDWIN, STANLEY, 8
The i. man...must not exert himself AL-NAWAWI, MUHYID-DIN ABU ZAKARIYYA IBN SHARAF, 1
intelligible aim at being i. HOPE, ANTHONY, 3
intention call the i. good ABELARD, PETER, 2
i., ability, success, and correctness HUSAIN, 1
I....measure for rendering actions true AL-NAWAWI, MUHYID-DIN ABU ZAKARIYYA IBN SHARAF, 2
slightest i. of honouring that Declaration CONSTANTINE, LEARIE, 2
There is less i. in history EMERSON, RALPH WALDO, 48
interaction the most direct i. with the earth LAPPÉ, FRANCES MOORE, 1
intercourse i. is...a social act DWORKIN, ANDREA, 3
interest How can I take an i. in my work BACON, FRANCIS (1909–92), 1
interested always been i. in people MAUGHAM, SOMERSET, 11
i. in a woman who is interested in him DIETRICH, MARLENE, 4
interests i. are eternal and perpetual PALMERSTON, LORD, 3
interior decorators I....rather die than agree BARRY, DAVE, 4
intermarriage By i. and by every means in his power HENRY I, 1
intermediary everybody can be an i. ZELDIN, THEODORE, 3
international i. financial system...meltdown process SOROS, GEORGE, 10
Internet I....can be compared to the Mediterranean Sea MOUGAYAR, WALID, 4
I.-driven electronic commerce EDELMAN, ROBERT, 1
I....giving us new dreams of success MOUGAYAR, WALID, 3
I. is becoming the town square GATES, BILL, 5
Is the I. a typhoon force GROVE, ANDREW S., 3

I....technology in search of a strategy CRONIN, MARY J., 4
new rule for business...I. changes everything GATES, BILL, 1
The glory of the I. TUCKER, LAURIE, 1
the I....opportunity or a rat hole JONES, CHRIS, 1
interpretation i....not to play what is written CASALS, PABLO, 2
I....revenge of...intellect upon art SONTAG, SUSAN, 1
interpreter I'm an i., a...tool DEPARDIEU, GÉRARD, 3
interviewer gain...as an i. access to both sexes MOSSELL, MRS. N. F., 2
interviewing i. a faded female in a...basement HARDING, GILBERT, 1
intimate an i. night /In a strange room FENG ZHI, 1
intimidation Years of i. and violence could not stop us MANDELA, NELSON, 3
intolerably I would grow i. conceited WHISTLER, JAMES ABBOTT MCNEILL, 9
intoxicating liquors the manufacture, sale, or transportation of i. CONSTITUTION OF THE UNITED STATES, 5
intricate that marvelously i. step, the Peabody CAGNEY, JAMES, 4
introductions I. inhibit pleasure LEE, HARPER, 1
intrusions i. of the state into the private PAGLIA, CAMILLE, 8
intuition with woman the powers of i....more strongly marked than in man DARWIN, CHARLES, 6
invasion One...cannot resist the i. of ideas HUGO, VICTOR, 6
the long-promised i. CHURCHILL, WINSTON, 12
invent I just i., then wait FULLER, R. BUCKMINSTER, 6
make an apple pie...i. the universe SAGAN, CARL, 9
invention his own greatest i. COWARD, NOEL, 2
i.... arises directly from idleness CHRISTIE, AGATHA, 1
I....is the most essential part of painting BOSCHINI, MARCO, 1
I. is the mother of necessity VEBLEN, THORSTEIN BUNDE, 4
resorted to elaborate i. only after...simple falsehood MACHADO DE ASSIS, JOAQUIM MARIA, 8
inventions All one's i. are true FLAUBERT, GUSTAVE, 2
my i. go to the wrong hands WEINER, NORBERT, 1
inventor i. is not just someone...with ideas SINCLAIR, CLIVE, 1
i....makes an ingenious arrangement...believes it civilization BIERCE, AMBROSE, 6
inverted commas absence of i. guarantees...originality FADIMAN, CLIFTON, 1
invest Never i. in any idea LYNCH, PETER, 1
Never i....in anything that eats ROSE, BILLY, 1
investment opportunities for the profitable i. of resources KNIGHT, FRANK HYNEMAN, 4
There is no finer i. CHURCHILL, WINSTON, 72
where is your i. WALESA, LECH, 3
investors Most of the truly great i. HELLER, ROBERT, 5
inviolability an i. founded on justice RAWLS, JOHN, 2
invisible I am an i. man...people refuse to see me ELLISON, RALPH, 5
invitation accept my i....and never come PLINY THE YOUNGER, 2
invited People were not i.—they went there FITZGERALD, F. SCOTT, 17
involuntary It was i.. They sank my boat KENNEDY, JOHN FITZGERALD, 34
involvement spirit of i. and partnership SEMLER, RICARDO, 5
IRA I. would think me a worthwhile target MOUNTBATTEN, LORD, 3
Iraq Our goal is not the conquest of I. BUSH, GEORGE, 17
support of I....defiance against the West AHMED, AKBAR, 2
Ireland And I....A Nation once again DAVIS, THOMAS, 2
brought back to I. her full rights GRIFFITH, ARTHUR, 1
delivered I. from plunder and oppression SWIFT, JONATHAN, 2
English should give I. home rule ROGERS, WILL, 7
government of I....rests on restraint CASEMENT, ROGER, 3
How's poor ould I. ANONYMOUS, 12
I am of I. FOLK VERSE, 53
I believe in the freedom of I. O'CASEY, SEAN, 6
If factories close in I. ROOSEVELT, FRANKLIN D., 9
I. has no blood to give CASEMENT, ROGER, 4
I. is a little Russia MOORE, GEORGE, 2
I. is a woman risen again FOLK VERSE, 7
I. is being treated...a convicted criminal CASEMENT, ROGER, 2
I. is the old sow JOYCE, JAMES, 7
I....knocking at the English door PARNELL, CHARLES STEWART, 5
In I. alone...loyalty held to be a crime CASEMENT, ROGER, 1
I. remains a glowingly sweet emerald vision DONLEAVY, J. P., 2
I. shall get her freedom PARNELL, CHARLES STEWART, 3
I....strikes for her freedom PEARSE, PATRICK, 5
I....strikes for her freedom PROVISIONAL GOVERNMENT OF THE IRISH REPUBLIC, 1
I. unfree shall never be at peace PEARSE, PATRICK, 3
I would have liked to go to I. VICTORIA, 3
Men have been dying for I. MCCOURT, FRANK, 1
no sex in I. before television FLANAGAN, OLIVER J., 3
Now I. has her madness AUDEN, W. H., 12
One of I.'s many tricks MOORE, GEORGE, 3
Out of I....Great hatred, little room YEATS, W. B., 60
split I. from top to bottom BRUGHA, CATHAL, 1
the problem with I....named after someone O'CONNOR, JOSEPH, 3
They are part of I. DE VALERA, EAMON, 4
Think—what have I got for I. COLLINS, MICHAEL, 1
Whatever I have said...on the subject of I. TONE, WOLFE, 1
Would to God this was shed for I. SARSFIELD, PATRICK, 1
iris I, when the i. blooms, /Remember COLERIDGE, MARY, 1
Irish answer to the I. question SELLAR, W. C., 6
begun to get back our I. ways COLLINS, MICHAEL, 4
I. blunders...never blunders of the heart EDGEWORTH, MARIA, 1
I look forward to...when I. patriotism BALFOUR, ARTHUR, 3
I. might do very good Service WENTWORTH, THOMAS, 1
I. that the Irish themselves detest BEHAN, BRENDAN, 4
It is not an I. rebellion BIRRELL, AUGUSTINE, 2
I wanted to know what the I....wanted DE VALERA, EAMON, 7
majority of...I. parliament are professional politicians O'BRIEN, FLANN, 12
Politics is the chloroform of the I. GOGARTY, OLIVER ST. JOHN, 2
struggle for I. national freedom...Oedipal terms O'CONNOR, JOSEPH, 1
task of reviving I....hard O'BRIEN, FLANN, 7
The I. are a FAIR PEOPLE JOHNSON, SAMUEL, 121
the I. are great lickers of wounds DEVLIN, POLLY, 1
The I....are needed in this cold age CHILD, LYDIA MARIA, 2
The I. don't know what they want LITTLEWOOD, SYDNEY, 1
To marry the I. DONLEAVY, J. P., 4
Volunteers would have to wade through I. blood DE VALERA, EAMON, 6
We I. are always...looking backwards MURPHY, DERVLA, 1
Irishman stage I....my vocation...to abolish BOUCICAULT, DION, 1
Irishmen We I., Protestant and Catholic MCGEE, THOMAS D'ARCY, 2
iron An i. curtain CHURCHILL, WINSTON, 8
i. curtain...veil of indifference CLINTON, BILL, 7
I. Curtain has been demolished ANTALL, JOZSEF, 1

I. Lady of British politics THATCHER, MARGARET, 1
If I didn't act with an i. hand FRANCO, FRANCISCO, 4
There is an i. curtain across Europe TROUBRIDGE, T. ST VINCENT, 1
irons Many i. in the fire PROVERBS, 325
irony a mass of i....Washington, D.C. SCOTT-HERON, GIL, 1
everyone gets i. nowadays WATERS, JOHN, 2
I....humanity's sense of propriety RENARD, JULES, 9
I. is the very substance of Providence BALZAC, HONORÉ DE, 2
treat everything with i. SHOSTAKOVICH, DMITRI, 3
irrational Man stands face to face with...i. CAMUS, ALBERT, 15
irresolution i....nothing is more uncertain RETZ, CARDINAL DE, 7
irresponsible better to be i. and right CHURCHILL, WINSTON, 10
irritates Everything you do i. me SIMON, NEIL, 12
Irving Berlin I. *is* American music BERLIN, IRVING, 1
Islam God Almighty. The Sacred Legislator of I. KHOMEINI, RUHOLLAH, 10
I....allowed blacks the ultimate protest MCCLOUD, BEVERLEY THOMAS, 1
I....a transient ruler of the world HOURANI, ALBERT, 1
I....devotion, subjection to the divine order TILLICH, PAUL, 12
I. is the religion of militant individuals KHOMEINI, RUHOLLAH, 11
In order to appreciate I., Europe AHMED, AKBAR, 3
I owe a great deal to I. BURROUGHS, WILLIAM S., 2
I....religion the West loves to hate KABBANI, RANA, 5
I....tolerance, compassion and love are at its very heart RUSHDIE, SALMAN, 7
I. unashamedly came with a sword RUNCIMAN, STEVEN, 1
part of...excellence of a man's I. MUHAMMAD, 9
religion for me has always meant I. RUSHDIE, SALMAN, 6
they say...I., was a "race hate" religion ALI, MUHAMMAD, 6
Islamic I. idea of the justice of God HOURANI, ALBERT, 2
island i....devoted to the pursuit of lunch SOKOLOV, RAYMOND, 1
It is not easy to shake off the spell of i. life CONRAD, JOSEPH, 14
right little, tight little I. DIBDIN, CHARLES, 5
wealth of our i. may be diminished DAVY, HUMPHRY, 1
We got one little i....it is hard LEE, KUAN YEW, 1
isle A green i. in the sea, love POE, EDGAR ALLAN, 13
isolation central theme is the theme of spiritual i. MCCULLERS, CARSON, 2
We must overcome the sense of i. RABIN, YITZHAK, 3
Israel I say to I., the Lord WOODRUFF, WILFORD, 1
I....space we make for God SACKS, JONATHAN, 2
new I. is not...kingdom of David OZ, AMOS, 4
Spirit of I....no more...the synthetic BUBER, MARTIN, 6
Israelis I. are now...enemy-friends MACAULAY, ROSE, 7
issues I. affecting women are not soft or marginal CLINTON, HILLARY, 2
i. of intolerance and exclusivity go unexamined SMITH, RAYMOND W., 5
it Do I. in the Road LENNON & MCCARTNEY, 20
Italian a vigorous, I. sort of pessimism PYNCHON, THOMAS, 11
I. in its particular institutions MUSSOLINI, BENITO, 10
no nation...can perfectly attain...I. manner of painting HOLANDA, FRANCISCO DE, 1
The I. navigator...reached the New World FERMI, ENRICO, 2
Italy I. has managed, with characteristic artistry VIDAL, GORE, 11
I. is a geographical expression METTERNICH, 3
I. will do it alone CHARLES ALBERT, 1
Thou Paradise of exiles, I. SHELLEY, PERCY BYSSHE, 35
itch an i. is now an allergy PROVERBS, MODERN, 31
i. of disputing...scab of churches WOTTON, HENRY, 3
The Seven Year I. AXELROD, GEORGE, 1
itself For nothing is really i. anymore AUSTER, PAUL, 3
Jabberwock And hast thou slain the J. CARROLL, LEWIS, 29
Jack J. and Jill went up the hill CHILDREN'S VERSE, 26
J. of all trades PROVERBS, 289
J. shall have Jill SHAKESPEARE, WILLIAM, 59
Jack Benny When J. has a party BURNS, GEORGE, 4
jacket snakeskin j. is a symbol of...individuality CAGE, NICOLAS, 1
Jack Horner Little J. /Sat in the corner CHILDREN'S VERSE, 31
Jackson J....standing like a stone wall BEE, BARNARD, 1
Jack the Ripper J.'s dead FOLK VERSE, 52
jail you cannot j. the revolution SEALE, BOBBY, 2
jam The rule is, j. tomorrow and jam yesterday CARROLL, LEWIS, 40
James Henry J. has a mind so fine JAMES, HENRY, 1
J. James /Morrison Morrison MILNE, A. A., 12
James Joyce J....Nothing but...cabbage stumps of quotations JOYCE, JAMES, 3
Jane Eyre J. strikes us as a personage LORIMER, JAMES, 1
January dreadful pictures of J. and February TROLLOPE, ANTHONY, 2
Japan Defeat of Germany means the defeat of J. ROOSEVELT, FRANKLIN D., 31
In J., projects have direction SCULLEY, JOHN, 4
In J., we live life with no guns HATTORI, MASAICHI, 1
J. /...a bright design upon a fan HECHT, ANTHONY, 2
nothing J. really wants to buy INAYAMA, YOSHIHIRO, 1
not necessarily to J.'s advantage HIROHITO, 1
There was a young man of J. LIMERICKS, 6
Japanese A J. teacher...was like a whirlwind JUNG CHANG, 1
glory and the nemesis of J. business MORITA AKIO, 2
the ferocious competition of the J. HELLER, ROBERT, 7
The J. have perfected good manners THEROUX, PAUL, 9
jargon Murder with j. where his medicine fails GARTH, SAMUEL, 1
The j. of scientific terminology FISCHER, MARTIN H., 25
jaw-jaw To j. is better than to war-war CHURCHILL, WINSTON, 36
jaws In the j. of death DU BARTAS, GUILLAUME, 12
jazz As for my j. ability TERRY, CLARK, 1
City of J....citizens...concerned with what they like ELLINGTON, DUKE, 5
equation between j. and freedom in...history CAMPBELL, JAMES, 2
great j. giants whom I have heard LYTTELTON, HUMPHREY, 3
history of j. as a picture WELLES, ORSON, 1
I usually don't buy j. records DAVIS, MILES, 2
J....and its sources were *secret* BARAKA, IMAMU AMIRI, 2
J....an international music ELLINGTON, DUKE, 2
J. is an impure art MELLY, GEORGE, 4
J. isn't *what* you do, it's *how* you do it WALLER, FATS, 1
J. musicians can be great teachers KAO, JOHN J., 1
J. music is a style, not compositions MORTON, JELLY ROLL, 1
J....music...perpetually in motion PANASSIE, HUGUES, 2
J....only form of art existing today BRUBECK, DAVE, 1
j. people did not achieve respectability SHEPP, ARCHIE, 1
J....people hear it through their feet SOUSA, JOHN PHILIP, 1
J....spontaneous urge of a whole people PANASSIE, HUGUES, 1

J....what it means to be American MARSALIS, WYNTON, 1
King J. was moving in MEZZROW, MEZZ, 7
Modern j....like the Roman Catholic Church MELLY, GEORGE, 3
saintly goof in whom...history of j. KEROUAC, JACK, 8
some cats playing j. at...Tokyo Hilton ELLINGTON, DUKE, 6
that beautiful cry of j. music PANASSIE, HUGUES, 3
that's the death of j. MELLY, GEORGE, 2
the J. Age...became less and less an affair of youth FITZGERALD, F. SCOTT, 5
tired faces in...dawn of J. America KEROUAC, JACK, 4
voice of j. making itself heard MEZZROW, MEZZ, 5
what rich punks think...about j. MINGUS, CHARLES, 1
You had your Shakespeare...we came up with *j.* MINGUS, CHARLES, 4

jazzmen j....cuddly as man-eating tigers LYTTELTON, HUMPHREY, 2
j....rogues and vagabonds LYTTELTON, HUMPHREY, 1

jealous j. for they are jealous SHAKESPEARE, WILLIAM, 493

jealousy It is with j. as with the gout FIELDING, HENRY, 15
J. in romance...like salt in food ANGELOU, MAYA, 14
J. is all the fun you *think* they had JONG, ERICA, 5
j.; /It is the green-ey'd monster SHAKESPEARE, WILLIAM, 484
To j., nothing...more frightful than laughter SAGAN, FRANÇOISE, 2

jeepers J. Creepers MERCER, JOHNNY, 1

Jeeves J. coughed one soft, low, gentle cough WODEHOUSE, P. G., 22

Jehovah Great J. and the Continental Congress ALLEN, ETHAN, 1

jelly even j. breaks your tooth PROVERBS, 67
Out vile j. SHAKESPEARE, WILLIAM, 352

Jerusalem absence from J. of a lunatic asylum ELLIS, HAVELOCK, 2
J. the golden NEALE, JOHN MASON, 3
J....the mother of us all BIBLE, 97
Priests at J. sell...tickets for heaven MELVILLE, HERMAN, 19
steadfastly set his face to go to J. BIBLE, 333

jest A j.'s prosperity lies in the ear SHAKESPEARE, WILLIAM, 377

Jesus At the name of J. NOEL, CAROLINE M., 1
From the days of J. NAHMANIDES, 1
Gentle J. WESLEY, CHARLES, 1
If J. Christ were to come to-day CARLYLE, THOMAS, 45
J.' most deep-seated Judaism BUBER, MARTIN, 15
J. picked...men from the bottom ranks BARTON, BRUCE, 2
J. was...a first-rate political economist SHAW, GEORGE BERNARD, 15
J. was no more than a mortal KORAN, 33
J. was not...marrying sort MONTEFIORE, HUGH, 1
my name is J. DURCAN, PAUL, 3
None speaks of...the intellect of J. CHILD, LYDIA MARIA, 1
stand up for J. DUFFIELD, GEORGE, 1
We are all making a crown for J. MCPHERSON, AIMEE SEMPLE, 2
when J. was born in Bethlehem of Judaea BIBLE, 367
Ye seek J. of Nazareth, which was crucified BIBLE, 365

Jew A French J., of...French ancestors BLUM, LÉON, 1
difficult for a J. to be converted HEINE, HEINRICH, 11
German J....a second-class citizen RATHENAU, WALTHER, 1
I am a J. to Catholics GOLDSMITH, JAMES, 6
I decide who is a J. LUEGER, KARL, 1
I'm not really a J.; just Jew-ish MILLER, JONATHAN, 2
J. dies on a Christian bosom BARNES, DJUNA, 6
J....most obvious antithesis of the Greek BUBER, MARTIN, 11
J. of antiquity...world is not divided BUBER, MARTIN, 3
no intellectual society...where a J. feels...uneasy JOHNSON, PAUL, 1
The J....sees the forest more truly BUBER, MARTIN, 12
To be a J. is a destiny BAUM, VICKI, 2

jewelry Don't ever wear artistic j. COLETTE, 3

jewels Bright j. of the mine HEMANS, FELICIA, 2

Jewish A J. community...lost its *edah* SACKS, JONATHAN, 7
A J. man with parents alive is a fifteen-year-old boy ROTH, PHILIP, 7
best that is in the J. blood LAWRENCE, D. H., 24
I founded the J. State HERZL, THEODOR, 5
image of the J. woman as a mother SACKS, JONATHAN, 10
I'm J., aren't all the best people REED, LOU, 6
J. life has moved from Europe SACKS, JONATHAN, 6
J. migration...in accordance with scientific principles HERZL, THEODOR, 12
J. tradition...don't die very well NEUBERGER, JULIA, 1
only half-J. MARX, GROUCHO, 27
spit upon my J. gaberdine SHAKESPEARE, WILLIAM, 600

Jews choose /A Jewish God, /But spurn the J. BROWNE, CECIL, 1
don't be seen with J. or Socialists DOS PASSOS, JOHN, 11
J. have produced only three originative geniuses STEIN, GERTRUDE, 11
J. may not be immediately likeable BLUE, LIONEL, 1
J. need to know that...our character BUBER, MARTIN, 16
the fat of rendered J. and Gypsies VONNEGUT, KURT, 8
The J. were...the mythless people BUBER, MARTIN, 13
The murder of the European J. OZ, AMOS, 7
to share the fate of other J. OZ, AMOS, 3
We are going to destroy the J. HITLER, ADOLF, 20

Jezebel J....painted her face BIBLE, 171

jihad j....monasticism of believers MUHAMMAD, 10

jo John Anderson, my j. BURNS, ROBERT, 22

job Any j. will expand or shrink SPAULDING, ASA T., 1
Choose a j. you love CONFUCIUS, 2
cleaning the floor and no j. at all DAY, GRAHAM, 5
I wasn't looking for this j. PINOCHET, AUGUSTO, 2
just a j....I beat people up ALI, MUHAMMAD, 2
only j....no woman...can be qualified is sperm donor HEIDE, WILMA SCOTT, 1
We have finished the j. HAILE SELASSIE I, 1
We've replaced...concept of having a j. MEYERS, JOHN, 1
When your neighbor loses his j. ANONYMOUS, 66

Job Could J. have been thinking of Chicago ANONYMOUS, 64
J. endured everything—until his friends came KIERKEGAARD, SØREN, 6

J.O.B. Unfortunately, they don't have a J. DOMINO, "FATS," 1

joblillies J. FOOTE, SAMUEL, 3

jobs few j....require a penis or vagina KENNEDY, FLORYNCE R., 3
I've got thousands of j. IACOCCA, LEE, 1

John Barleycorn Inspiring bold J. BURNS, ROBERT, 34

John Brown J.'s body HALL, CHARLES SPRAGUE, 1
When J. stretched forth his arm BROWN, JOHN, 2

Johnny Head-in-Air Little J. HOFFMAN, HEINRICH, 3

Johnny Keats Here is J.' piss-a-bed poetry KEATS, JOHN (1795–1821), 2

John Peel D'ye ken J. GRAVES, JOHN WOODCOCK, 1

Johnson Dr. J. condemns whatever he disapproves BURNEY, FANNY, 1
J. made the most brutal speeches JOHNSON, SAMUEL, 2

John Thomas J. says good-night to Lady Jane LAWRENCE, D. H., 28

John Wayne I play J. in every picture WAYNE, JOHN, 2
J. is dead ANONYMOUS, 17

join He's gone to j. the majority PETRONIUS ARBITER, 5

joined what...God hath j. together, let not man put asunder BIBLE, 414
joke A j.'s a very serious thing CHURCHILL, CHARLES, 8
a j. with a double meaning BARKER, RONNIE, 1
jokes different taste in j....strain on the affections ELIOT, GEORGE, 12
Forgive...my little j. on Thee FROST, ROBERT, 11
I don't make j. ROGERS, WILL, 4
joking J....third best method of hoodwinking people FRISCH, MAX, 3
My way of j. is to tell the truth SHAW, GEORGE BERNARD, 33
jolly And who gave thee that j. red nose? RAVENSCROFT, THOMAS, 1
Joseph Here lies J., who failed JOSEPH II, 2
jot one j. or one tittle BIBLE, 377
journalism British j. will not suffer MURDOCH, RUPERT, 4
J....challenge of filling the space WEST, REBECCA, 3
J....consists of saying "Lord Jones is dead" CHESTERTON, G. K., 52
j....in touch with the ignorance of the community WILDE, OSCAR, 25
J. is the only job that requires no degrees CAMPBELL, PATRICK, 1
The farmers of j. WOLFE, TOM, 19
journalist A j. is stimulated by a deadline KRAUS, KARL, 7
Good taste...dispensable part of...j.'s equipment HOGG, MICHAEL, 1
j.: no ideas and the ability to express them KRAUS, KARL, 10
life of the j. is poor, nasty GIBBONS, STELLA, 5
the functions of the modern j. CURZON, GEORGE NATHANIEL, 2
journalists J. belong in the gutter PRIESTLAND, GERALD, 1
no j. is even better BENTLEY, NICOLAS, 1
journey A j. is a person in itself STEINBECK, JOHN, 15
A j. is like a marriage STEINBECK, JOHN, 17
A j. of a thousand miles LAOZI, 18
begin a j. on Sundays SWIFT, JONATHAN, 33
dawn speeds a man on his j. HESIOD, 3
How like /Is a j. by sea JIMÉNEZ, JUAN RAMÓN, 3
I prepare for a j....as though for death MANSFIELD, KATHERINE, 3
J....the universe in a map CERVANTES, MIGUEL DE, 52
longest part of the j. VARRO, MARCUS TERENTIUS, 2
long j....must bid the company farewell RALEIGH, WALTER, 9
pleasantest things...going on a j. HAZLITT, WILLIAM, 20
The j. began one day long ago MOMADAY, N. SCOTT, 5
worst time of the year /For a j. ELIOT, T. S., 11
journeys Bad j....lead straight to the confession box FRASER, KEATH, 1
joy brief moments of j....unforgettable sorrows ROBERT, YVES, 1
Do anything, but let it produce j. MILLER, HENRY, 18
greater j. is to ride a bicycle XU ZHIMO, 3
he who kisses the j. as it flies BLAKE, WILLIAM, 16
J. and Temperance and Repose LOGAU, FRIEDRICH VON, 1
J. is the sweet voice COLERIDGE, SAMUEL TAYLOR, 9
J. shivers in the corner ROBINSON, EDWIN ARLINGTON, 4
One inch of j. surmounts of grief a span RABELAIS, FRANÇOIS, 16
One j. scatters a hundred griefs PROVERBS, 37
Phyllis is my only j. SEDLEY, CHARLES, 1
The melancholy j. of evils past POPE, ALEXANDER, 89
ther ys j. in hevene and peyne in helle CHAUCER, GEOFFREY, 36
we're all owed j. /sooner or later DUFFY, CAROL ANN, 1
Joyce That bloody J. JOYCE, JAMES, 1
joyous j. Time will not be staid SPENSER, EDMUND, 3
joys Great j., like griefs, are silent MARMION, SHACKERLEY, 1
Of j. departed BLAIR, ROBERT, 2
One of the j. of being a judge LAING, B. KOJO, 1
present j. are more to flesh DRYDEN, JOHN, 42
redoubleth j., and cutteth griefs BACON, FRANCIS (1561–1626), 29
the j. of sense, /Lie in three words, health, peace, and competence POPE, ALEXANDER, 30
jubilation day of j., a day of remembrance GENSCHER, HANS-DIETRICH, 2
Judaism For J., God is not a Kantian idea BUBER, MARTIN, 2
J. has a morally ambivalent God JUNG, CARL GUSTAV, 3
J. makes my third great religion ROTH, PHILIP, 6
religious reality...manifest in and through J. BUBER, MARTIN, 14
striving for unity...makes J. a phenomenon BUBER, MARTIN, 7
judge A j. is not supposed to know PARKER, HUBERT LISTER, 1
A j. knows nothing PROVERBS, 115
Do not j....never be mistaken ROUSSEAU, JEAN-JACQUES, 12
duty of a j....administer justice LA BRUYÈRE, JEAN DE, 21
It is fair to j. people DAY, CLARENCE SHEPARD, 4
j. in his own cause ANONYMOUS, 41
j. is a law student MENCKEN, H. L., 46
j. not me CAMDEN, WILLIAM, 1
j. not, that ye be not judged BIBLE, 384
j. one black person EMECHETA, BUCHI, 4
Never j. from appearances PROVERBS, 338
others j. us by what we have...done LONGFELLOW, HENRY WADSWORTH, 27
shallow people...do not j. by appearances WILDE, OSCAR, 60
the j. standeth before the door BIBLE, 244
judged j. on how much sex you've had FIERSTEIN, HARVEY, 2
judgement For j. I am come into this world BIBLE, 285
judges a shortage...of good j. and...beautiful women RAPHAEL, 1
J. are the weakest link in...justice DERSHOWITZ, ALAN, 1
judging no way of j. the future but by the past HENRY, PATRICK, 3
judgmatical a j. rap over the head COOPER, JAMES FENIMORE, 12
judgment all right j. of any man CARLYLE, THOMAS, 18
I expect a j. DICKENS, CHARLES, 15
in my j., hindsight proves us wrong MCNAMARA, ROBERT, 1
I was green in j. SHAKESPEARE, WILLIAM, 72
j....how to choose between two disadvantages RETZ, CARDINAL DE, 3
J. is the typical act of intelligence DEWEY, JOHN, 13
One cool j....a thousand hasty councils WILSON, WOODROW, 18
the j. of the great whore BIBLE, 471
What j. shall I dread SHAKESPEARE, WILLIAM, 619
judgments false and true j....equally psychological processes DEWEY, JOHN, 17
'Tis with our j. as our watches POPE, ALEXANDER, 11
Value j....founded on the study of literature FRYE, NORTHROP, 1
Jumblies far and few, /Are the lands where the J. live LEAR, EDWARD, 15
jump I don't look to j. over 7-foot bars BUFFETT, WARREN, 5
I will not j. with common spirits SHAKESPEARE, WILLIAM, 609
We'd j. the life to come SHAKESPEARE, WILLIAM, 395
junk J....the ultimate merchandise BURROUGHS, WILLIAM S., 9
Jupiter J....turned into a satyr...for love BURTON, ROBERT, 15
Oh if only J. would give me back my past years VIRGIL, 21
jury Trial by j....will be a delusion DENMAN, THOMAS, 1
just Be j. before you are generous SHERIDAN, RICHARD BRINSLEY, 15
In a j. cause the weak o'ercome the strong SOPHOCLES, 5
j. and merciful as Nero ELIZABETH I, 5
the true place for a j. man is also a prison THOREAU, HENRY DAVID, 21
When a j. cause reaches its flood-tide CATT, CARRIE CHAPMAN, 3

justice American j....not telling the whole truth DERSHOWITZ, ALAN, 2
capacity for j. makes democracy possible NIEBUHR, REINHOLD, 1
Extreme j. is often injustice RACINE, JEAN, 13
I have loved j....I die in exile GREGORY VII, 3
It might help...if J. would take off that blindfold LESTER, JULIUS, 1
J....allowed to do whatever I like BUTLER, SAMUEL (1835–1902), 25
J.! Custodian of the world BETTI, UGO, 10
J. is a certain rectitude of mind AQUINAS, THOMAS, 3
J. is a human illusion BAROJA, PÍO, 2
J. is not to be taken by storm CARDOZO, BENJAMIN, 1
J. is open to all MATHEW, JAMES, 1
J. is such a fine thing LESAGE, ALAIN RENÉ, 1
J....limps along GARCÍA MÁRQUEZ, GABRIEL, 3
J. means "just-us-white-folks." BROWN, H. RAP, 2
j. must be...more or less done STOPPARD, TOM, 5
J. must...be seen to be believed MORTON, J. C., 7
J. should...be seen to be done HEWART, GORDON, 1
j....the pressure of necessity is equal THUCYDIDES, 1
J., though she's painted blind BUTLER, SAMUEL (1612–80), 25
"J." was done HARDY, THOMAS, 23
J....will be pursued HAMILTON, ALEXANDER, 3
J. without force is impotent PASCAL, BLAISE, 5
know what j. is...ask your reason KHOMEINI, RUHOLLAH, 8
Let j. be done FERDINAND I (1503–64), 1
one must start from an absolute principle of *j.* BÜCHNER, GEORG, 9
Only J. Can Stop a Curse WALKER, ALICE, 5
Recompense injury with j. CONFUCIUS, 16
Revenge is a kind of wild j. BACON, FRANCIS (1561–1626), 56
She's like the old line about j. OSBORNE, JOHN, 13
The love of j....is...the fear of...injustice LA ROCHEFOUCAULD, FRANÇOIS, 13
the only j. is in the halls BRUCE, LENNY, 4
The place of j. is...hallowed BACON, FRANCIS (1561–1626), 39
There is a j....behind injustice RENARD, JULES, 14
We have chosen to accept human j. CAMUS, ALBERT, 27
we must do j. upon ourselves IBSEN, HENRIK, 16
what stings is j. MENCKEN, H. L., 26
When...they close the doors of j. SAGASTA, PRÁXEDES, 1
which is the j., which is the thief SHAKESPEARE, WILLIAM, 357
withers...like j. and truth...patriotic passion MENCKEN, H. L., 25
your j. would freeze beer MILLER, ARTHUR, 16
You want j....you want to pay BRECHT, BERTOLT, 16

justified life of one man can only be j. ROSEWARNE, V. A., 1
No man is j. in doing evil ROOSEVELT, THEODORE, 25

justifies something that j. the end TROTSKY, LEON, 12

justify Everything must j. its existence ENGELS, FRIEDRICH, 3
If we j. war BENEDICT, RUTH, 3

K K. = (P+I)S MOTTOS AND SLOGANS, 9

kamikaze a k. pilot who keeps apologizing NIXON, RICHARD, 6

Kansas K. and Nebraska the best corn country CATHER, WILLA, 3
farmers of K....raise less corn and more Hell LEASE, MARY ELIZABETH, 1
This doesn't look like K., Toto BAUM, L. FRANK, 1

karaoke running against the K. Kids CLINTON, BILL, 2

karma man's K. travels with him WATTS, ALAN, 2

Katy K-K-K-K., beautiful Katy O'HARA, GEOFFREY, 1

Keats Mister John K. five feet high KEATS, JOHN (1795–1821), 25
Who killed John K. KEATS, JOHN (1795–1821), 1

keep If you can k. your head KIPLING, RUDYARD, 50
k. on saying it...it will be true BENNETT, ARNOLD, 6

keeping up K. with the Joneses was a full-time job CRISP, QUENTIN, 7

Kelly Has anybody here seen K. MURPHY, C. W., 1
K. isn't a winged dancer—he's a hoofer and a man ASTAIRE, FRED, 4

Kelt mounted K. is irresistible ANNA COMNENA, 1

Kennedy K. promised, Johnson delivered JOHNSON, LYNDON BAINES, 3

Kennedys I don't feel the attraction of the K. MCCARTHY, MARY, 10

Kent everybody knows K.—apples, cherries, hops and women DICKENS, CHARLES, 91

kept He k. us out of war GLYNN, MARTIN H., 1

Kerouac Jack K. sat beside me KEROUAC, JACK, 1

kettle *this* is a pretty k. of fish MARY OF TECK, 1

key anybody know what k. that is GLOVER, JANE, 1
Turn the k. deftly KEATS, JOHN (1795–1821), 68

keynote the k. of Burns' verse BURNS, ROBERT, 2

keys all the k. should hang from the belt of one woman BRINTON, THOMAS, 1
don't go around hitting too many white k. BLAKE, EUBIE, 2

kick I get no k. from champagne PORTER, COLE, 3
k. a fellow when he's down PROVERBS, 480
K. is seeing things from a special angle BURROUGHS, WILLIAM S., 6
why did you k. me downstairs BICKERSTAFFE, ISAAC, 1

kicked never knew any k. up stairs before HALIFAX, GEORGE SAVILE, 1

kicks Get your k. on Route 66 TROUP, BOBBY, 1

kid keep a k. at home EDELMAN, MARIAN WRIGHT, 1

kidder Everyone likes a k. MILLER, ARTHUR, 5

kids Do something for his k. MCCORMACK, MARK, 11
K. haven't changed much LEACH, PENELOPE, 1
what my k. leave over from lunch SIMON, NEIL, 7

kill all arranged to k. my grandmother O'CONNOR, FRANK, 1
As soon as one does not k. oneself CAMUS, ALBERT, 2
can't...k. a woman...bit unchivalrous BENCHLEY, ROBERT, 1
First...cut it off, and then...*k.* it POWELL, COLIN, 6
How many people have wanted to k. themselves RENARD, JULES, 6
if you want to k. a picture PICASSO, PABLO, 12
I'll k. you if you quote it BURGESS, GELETT, 1
K. a man, and you are a murderer ROSTAND, JEAN, 3
k. a wife with kindness SHAKESPEARE, WILLIAM, 638
K. the brave ones JACKSON, STONEWALL, 2
K. the other guy before he kills you DEMPSEY, JACK, 1
Let's go out and k. SCORSESE, MARTIN, 5
let's k. all the lawyers SHAKESPEARE, WILLIAM, 288
Next week...I'll k. myself RHYS, JEAN, 2
To k. a human being JAMES, HENRY, 9
To k. a man is to merit a woman GIRAUDOUX, JEAN, 3
We k. time; time buries us MACHADO DE ASSIS, JOAQUIM MARIA, 13
When you have to k. a man CHURCHILL, WINSTON, 50

killed He must have k. a lot of men MOLIÈRE, 8
I haven't k. anybody for years BANKS, IAIN, 1
Oh my God, they k. Kenny SOUTH PARK, 1
ten to twenty million people k. SCOTT, GEORGE C., 1
Who k. Cock Robin CHILDREN'S VERSE, 56

killer a good k., one of our best HERR, MICHAEL, 2

the first trained k. to be a party leader ARCHER, GILBERT, 1
killin' a hell of a thing k. a man EASTWOOD, CLINT, 4
killing K. is the lowest form of survival CANETTI, ELIAS, 1
K. /Is the ultimate simplification of life MACDIARMID, HUGH, 1
K. myself to die upon a kiss SHAKESPEARE, WILLIAM, 499
k. time /...kills us SITWELL, OSBERT, 1
medal for k....a discharge for loving MATLOVICH, LEONARD, 1
no difference between...k. and making decisions MEIR, GOLDA, 8
sullen k. continues WILLIAMS, HEATHCOTE, 4
killing time The man is k. LOWELL, ROBERT, 3
kills Who k. a man kills a reasonable creature MILTON, JOHN, 13
Yet each man k. the thing he loves WILDE, OSCAR, 36
kilt The k....an unrivalled garment for fornication MASTERS, JOHN, 1
kin k. and kith /Were more fun NASH, OGDEN, 14
less than "k.", and rather more than "kind" BARHAM, RICHARD HARRIS, 1
more than k., and less than kind SHAKESPEARE, WILLIAM, 140
kind a k. parent...or a merciless step-mother PLINY THE ELDER, 4
Do not ask me to be k. RENARD, JULES, 4
k. as kings DRYDEN, JOHN, 39
One k. word can warm PROVERBS, 81
kindle k. a light in the darkness of mere being JUNG, CARL GUSTAV, 16
kindness A man...has seldom an offer of k. STERNE, LAURENCE, 7
if your k. is rewarded with ingratitude MACHADO DE ASSIS, JOAQUIM MARIA, 5
its unembarrassed k., its insight into life PAGET, STEPHEN, 2
the k. of strangers WILLIAMS, TENNESSEE, 3
True k....imagining as one's own the suffering...others GIDE, ANDRÉ, 4
king a k....cannot make a gentleman BURKE, EDMUND, 12
A k. is a thing SELDEN, JOHN, 10
A k. of shreds and patches SHAKESPEARE, WILLIAM, 199
a new k. over Egypt BIBLE, 66
A worse k. never left a realm undone BYRON, LORD, 99
behold, thy K. cometh unto thee BIBLE, 500
better have one K. than five hundred CHARLES II, 8
every inch a k. SHAKESPEARE, WILLIAM, 358
God save our Gracious K. CAREY, HENRY, 2
harm that cometh of a k.'s poverty FORTESCUE, JOHN, 1
He played the K. as though ...someone else was about to play the ace FIELD, EUGENE, 5
he was a k.'s son JOHN OF GAUNT, 1
if I were not k., I should lose my temper LOUIS XIV, 7
impossible for the K....as cheap as other men PEPYS, SAMUEL, 3
Is it not passing brave to be...k. MARLOWE, CHRISTOPHER, 22
I think the K. is but a man SHAKESPEARE, WILLIAM, 271
I wanted to be an up-to-date k. EDWARD VIII, 5
I will that a k. succeed me JAMES I, 1
k., and his faithful subjects, the lords BURKE, EDMUND, 4
K....commonly known in America as a "crowned head" BIERCE, AMBROSE, 31
K. James is...the most incompetent man ORLÉANS, DUCHESS OF, 1
K. of England changes his ministers FREDERICK II (1712–86), 7
k. of France...never did a Christian thing HENRY VIII, 3
K. of Scots was named to succeed her CAREY, ROBERT, 1
K. of the Road MILLER, ROGER, 1
k.'s council...chosen of the great princes FORTESCUE, JOHN, 2
k....will allow the fixed laws HENRY VIII, 7
lessened my esteem of a k. PEPYS, SAMUEL, 2
Let a k. recall ERASMUS, DESIDERIUS, 4
more than a k....intolerable tyrant WILLIAM OF NEWBURGH, 1
Never alone /did the k. sigh, but with a general groan SHAKESPEARE, WILLIAM, 197
not become K. to live...in a wardrobe RUDOLF I, 1
often seen the K. consume LOUIS XIV, 1
the k. can do no wrong BLACKSTONE, WILLIAM, 4
The k. has been very good to me BOLEYN, ANNE, 1
The k. never dies BLACKSTONE, WILLIAM, 2
The K., observing with judicious eyes GEORGE I, 1
The K. over the Water ANONYMOUS, 84
The k. sits in Dunfermline toon FOLK VERSE, 12
What is a K. PRIOR, MATTHEW, 16
When a K. has Dethron'd himself LOCKE, JOHN, 9
King Cole Old K. /Was a merry old soul CHILDREN'S VERSE, 60
kingdom If a k. be divided against itself BIBLE, 352
I'm going to try for the k. REED, LOU, 1
k. and the priesthood...together by divine mystery DAMIAN, PETER, 1
K. of God is within us RADHAKRISHNAN, SARVEPALLI, 4
No k. has...had as many...wars as the kingdom of Christ MONTESQUIEU, 6
Our k....we place at your disposal HENRY II, 2
the k. of God is not in word, but in power BIBLE, 153
the k. of God is within you BIBLE, 343
kingfish I'm the K. LONG, HUEY, 4
King John K. was not a good man MILNE, A. A., 5
King Kong We play like K. one day KENNEDY, TERRY, 1
kings Change k., and we will fight it over SARSFIELD, PATRICK, 2
function of k....using good sense LOUIS XIV, 2
K....are just as funny ROOSEVELT, THEODORE, 27
K....are made by artificial hallucination SHAW, GEORGE BERNARD, 45
k. enough in England GEORGE II, 1
K. govern by ...assemblies only when FOX, CHARLES JAMES, 2
k. of England...never had any superior but God HENRY VIII, 8
K....slaves of their own position SCHILLER, FRIEDRICH VON, 12
K. will be tyrants...when subjects are rebels BURKE, EDMUND, 43
the K. of England, Diamonds, Hearts, Spades, and Clubs FAROUK I, 1
There were three k. into the east BURNS, ROBERT, 23
To k. that fear their subjects' treachery SHAKESPEARE, WILLIAM, 290
'Twixt k. and tyrants there's this difference HERRICK, ROBERT, 8
kingship Whenever k. approaches tyranny NICOLE D'ORESME, 1
King Wenceslas Good K. looked out NEALE, JOHN MASON, 2
kinquering K. Congs their titles take SPOONER, WILLIAM ARCHIBALD, 2
kinship k. with the stars MEREDITH, GEORGE, 5
Kipling K. tries so hard to...justify true authority KIPLING, RUDYARD, 1
kiss A k. is but a k. now MEREDITH, GEORGE, 1
a k. without a moustache CAWEIN, MADISON, 1
A k. without a mustache SARTRE, JEAN-PAUL, 29
come let us k. and part DRAYTON, MICHAEL, 3
K. me, Hardy NELSON, HORATIO, 5
K. me Kate, we will be married SHAKESPEARE, WILLIAM, 637
k. the *Image* of my *Death* DRUMMOND, WILLIAM, 2
K. till the cow comes home BEAUMONT & FLETCHER, 11
'Scuse me while I k. the sky HENDRIX, JIMI, 1
spend that k. /Which is my heaven to have SHAKESPEARE, WILLIAM, 95

stop his mouth with a k. SHAKESPEARE, WILLIAM, 444
tell him he can k. my arse GOETHE, JOHANN WOLFGANG VON, 18
Therewith all sweetly did me k. WYATT, THOMAS, 3
The words, "K. Kiss Bang Bang" KAEL, PAULINE, 3
waste his whole heart in one k. TENNYSON, ALFRED, 61
Whenever you k. a man SARIEGOS, QUENTIN DE, 1
will not k. your f.king flag CUMMINGS, E. E., 1
you must not k. and tell CONGREVE, WILLIAM, 4
You must remember this; /A k. is still a kiss HUPFELD, HERMAN, 1
kissed hail, master; and k. him BIBLE, 438
He k. me...I am someone else MISTRAL, GABRIELA, 1
I k. her little sister MONTROSE, PERCY, 1
Wherever one wants to be k. CHANEL, COCO, 7
kisses Dear as remember'd k. after death TENNYSON, ALFRED, 92
more than k., letters mingle souls DONNE, JOHN, 8
kissin' K. wears out. Cookin' don't PROVERBS, 91
kissing it was made /For k. SHAKESPEARE, WILLIAM, 528
k. behind ash pits and telephone poles WILLIAMS, TENNESSEE, 14
K. don't last MEREDITH, GEORGE, 13
President spends most of his time k. TRUMAN, HARRY S., 12
when the k. had to stop BROWNING, ROBERT, 46
Kissinger K. brought peace to Vietnam KISSINGER, HENRY, 1
kitchen made in the k. started from scratch WELTY, EUDORA, 2
kittens Cute k. turn into scraggly cats KIRSTEIN, LINCOLN, 3
knaves He calls the k., Jacks DICKENS, CHARLES, 32
kneaded k. out of the same dough PROVERBS, 499
knee at the name of Jesus every k. should bow BIBLE, 450
knell The k. of private property sounds MARX, KARL, 13
knew I k. all her ways HOUSMAN, A. E., 23
k. I would never be so happy FITZGERALD, F. SCOTT, 12
K. only...that he knew nothing BEHN, APHRA, 5
O! that she k. she were SHAKESPEARE, WILLIAM, 545
knight K. of the Doleful Countenance CERVANTES, MIGUEL DE, 20
knits Nothing k. man to man, the Manchester School wisely taught, like...cash SICKERT, WALTER, 1
knitter a beautiful little k. WOOLF, VIRGINIA, 2
knitting you should stick to your k. MYHRVOLD, NATHAN, 1
knock k. him down first...pity him afterwards JOHNSON, SAMUEL, 92
knocked k. everything but...knees of the chorus HAMMOND, PERCY, 1
we k. the bastard off HILLARY, EDMUND, 2
knocking k. at Preferment's door ARNOLD, MATTHEW, 14
know Can we k....a grain of salt SAGAN, CARL, 2
How do they k. COOLIDGE, CALVIN, 4
I do not k. myself GOETHE, JOHANN WOLFGANG VON, 30
I don't k. everything, I just do everything MORRISON, TONI, 19
I happen to k. quite a bit about the South GREGORY, DICK, 3
I k. everything except myself VILLON, FRANÇOIS, 2
I k. I am God BARNES, PETER, 1
I k. not where I am going RACINE, JEAN, 19
I k. that my redeemer liveth BIBLE, 262
I k. what I have given you PORCHIA, ANTONIO, 4
K. then thyself, presume not God to scan POPE, ALEXANDER, 27
k. the various races of men POLO, MARCO, 2
K. thyself PROVERBS, 294
Never k. what you made of GOLDEN, MARITA, 8
No one can really *k.* the life BECK, EARL R., 3
Not many people k. that CAINE, MICHAEL, 3
Not to k. is bad PROVERBS, 351
occupy our minds only with what we...k. SAINTE-BEUVE, CHARLES AUGUSTIN, 1
one thing to k. virtue HUME, DAVID, 23
ready to say...I do not k. OSLER, WILLIAM, 2
say "I do not k." MAIMONIDES, 4
saying you want to k., you know DICKENS, CHARLES, 41
Those who k. are silent BO JUYI, 1
To k. how to say what others only...think CHARLES, ELIZABETH, 1
To k.... to love, and then to part COLERIDGE, SAMUEL TAYLOR, 18
We all *k.* what light is JOHNSON, SAMUEL, 162
We k. more about...primitive peoples LEWIS, ROY, 1
What canst thou k. of freedom KRISHNAMURTI, JIDDU, 1
What do I k.? MONTAIGNE, MICHEL DE, 16
What we k. is not much LAPLACE, PIERRE SIMON, 2
What you don't k. PROVERBS, 453
What you don't k....make a great book SMITH, SYDNEY, 20
knowest thou k. all things BIBLE, 305
knowing K. me, knowing you ANDERSSON, BENNY, 1
k. what you *cannot* do...good taste BALL, LUCILLE, 2
K. who you are O'CONNOR, FLANNERY, 5
knowledge All k. is...of some value JOHNSON, SAMUEL, 70
all k. to be my province BACON, FRANCIS (1561–1626), 2
all our k. is ourselves to know POPE, ALEXANDER, 32
civilizations...abandon the quest for k. LOVELL, BERNARD, 2
compelled to drive toward total k. WILSON, EDWARD O., 4
deny *k.*...to make room for *faith* KANT, IMMANUEL, 16
enthused by...attraction of k. YANG WENZHI, 1
genuine k. originates in direct experience MAO ZEDONG, 16
I am the city of k. AL-MUFID, ABU ABDULLAH MUHAMMAD AL-HARITHI AL-BAGHDADI, 7
If a little k. is dangerous HUXLEY, T. H., 12
if a little k. was a dangerous thing SHARPE, TOM, 2
I have no *k.* of myself KANT, IMMANUEL, 17
K. advances by steps MACAULAY, THOMAS BABINGTON, 10
k. and capability...keys to success PFEFFER, JEFFREY, 1
k....antiquarian lore...most unwomanly HALE, SARAH JOSEPHA, 3
k....bounds of possible experience KANT, IMMANUEL, 12
K. can be communicated but not wisdom HESSE, HERMANN, 2
k. gained by reason from concepts KANT, IMMANUEL, 14
k. if out of proportion...is invalid ADORNO, THEODOR, 2
K....is becoming dispensable TOFFLER, ALVIN, 3
K. is Life with wings GIBRAN, KAHLIL, 7
K. is of two kinds JOHNSON, SAMUEL, 103
K. is power PROVERBS, 292
"K. is power"...finest idea RENAN, ERNEST, 1
K. is the mother of all virtue PROVERBS, 293
K. itself is power BACON, FRANCIS (1561–1626), 82
k. of science...outstripped our capacity to control BRADLEY, OMAR, 1
k. of the limits of human understanding VOLTAIRE, 3
k. of the other world can be obtained KANT, IMMANUEL, 1
K. of the tragic dimension of history COOK, SAMUEL D., 2
k. passes...through three different theoretical states COMTE, AUGUSTE, 4
k. puffeth up BIBLE, 157
k....understood in human and political terms SAID, EDWARD W., 2
make k. productive...exploitation of opportunities for change DRUCKER, PETER, 11

much richer in k. and experience GIBSON, ALTHEA, 1
non-productivity of its k....British economy DRUCKER, PETER, 8
Our k. can only be finite POPPER, KARL, 2
Our k. forms an enormous system WITTGENSTEIN, LUDWIG, 24
province of k. to speak HOLMES, OLIVER WENDELL, 30
Real k....one's ignorance CONFUCIUS, 15
Shall I teach you what k. is CONFUCIUS, 39
so little k....such great account SHAKESPEARE, WILLIAM, 12
the k. of a lifetime WHISTLER, JAMES ABBOTT MCNEILL, 6
The k. of the world CHESTERFIELD, LORD, 15
true lover of k....strives for truth PLATO, 19
we swallow a k. of ourselves BAILEY, PEARL, 3
What is all our k. AUERBACH, BERTHOLD, 1
What use is it that k. mounts LOGAU, FRIEDRICH VON, 5

knowledge-based a k. economy PFEFFER, JEFFREY, 3

known apart from the k. and the unknown PINTER, HAROLD, 7
going from the k. to the unknown BERNARD, CLAUDE, 1
I am k....never heard of Jesus CHAPLIN, CHARLIE, 11
Once upon a time she had k. more and wanted to MORRISON, TONI, 5
Which of us has k. his brother WOLFE, THOMAS, 2

knows He that k. little PROVERBS, 247
He that k. nothing PROVERBS, 248
he thinks he k. everything SHAW, GEORGE BERNARD, 37
how little one k. oneself DE GAULLE, CHARLES, 10
k. too much...hard not to lie WITTGENSTEIN, LUDWIG, 15
Nobody k. you when you're down and out SMITH, BESSIE, 3
one k. more at forty VIDAL, GORE, 7
She k. wot's wot, she does DICKENS, CHARLES, 103
who k. only his own...case knows little MILL, JOHN STUART, 8

knyght a verray, parfit gentil k. CHAUCER, GEOFFREY, 9
K. ther was and that a worthy man CHAUCER, GEOFFREY, 15

Kool-art I am for K....Pepsi-art OLDENBURG, CLAES, 2

Koran I know the K. and its interpretation ALI, 1
Recite the K. and weep IBN MAJA, YAZID AL-RABA AL-QAZWINI, 1
The K. becomes prosaic in any tongue KABBANI, RANA, 2
Touching the writings of the K. KHOMEINI, RUHOLLAH, 7
verses of the K....value of sunlight AL-GHAZALI, 4

Kremlin We cannot allow anyone spitting...on the K. LEBED, ALEXANDER, 2

Kublai words of the lad K....worth attention GENGHIS KHAN, 1

Ku Klux Klan who don't know what the K. is GREGORY, DICK, 2

kulfi-seller A k. set up his cart CHANDRA, VIKRAM, 1

Kurdish Have the K. people committed such crimes BARZANI, MUSTAFA, 2

Kurtz Mistah K.—he dead CONRAD, JOSEPH, 4

Kuwait If K....sold bananas NYERERE, JULIUS KAMBARAGE, 8

Kuwaitis K. enjoy a crisis AL-TAKRITI, BARZAN, 1

LA L....most brutal of American cities KEROUAC, JACK, 16

L.A. there's so much smog in L. CAMPBELL, GLEN, 1

label Putting a l. on a patient MITCHELL, ALEXANDER, 1
The only l. she wears is "drip dry" SAUNDERS, JENNIFER, 3

labor A man who will not l. to gain his rights DOUGLASS, FREDERICK, 21
British l. movement...narrow circle of strikes ENGELS, FRIEDRICH, 1
Man...can only find relaxation from...l. FRANCE, ANATOLE, 5
Poorly paid labor is inefficient l. GEORGE, HENRY, 2
visible l. and...invisible labor HUGO, VICTOR, 9

laboratory A first-rate l. is one BLACKETT, PATRICK M. S., 1
All the world is a l. FISCHER, MARTIN H., 2

labor relations L. have to be war ANONYMOUS, 8

labour l. of love BIBLE, 231
L. without joy is base RUSKIN, JOHN, 24
nothing but their l. for their pains CERVANTES, MIGUEL DE, 6
The natural price of l. RICARDO, DAVID, 2
We l. soon, we labour late BURNS, ROBERT, 44
wish you were here to upstage my...l. MAHON, DEREK, 2

Labour I vote L., but my butler's a Tory MOUNTBATTEN, LORD, 4
L. is not fit to govern CHURCHILL, WINSTON, 70
L. isn't working MOTTOS AND SLOGANS, 1

labouring I'm a l. man HARDY, THOMAS, 3

Lacedaemonians Go, stranger, and tell the L. that here we lie LEONIDAS, 1

lack l. of power corrupts absolutely ACTON, LORD, 1

lad A Grecian l....that many loved HOUSMAN, A. E., 4

ladder behold a l. set up on earth BIBLE, 130
make...a l. out of our vices AUGUSTINE OF HIPPO, SAINT, 13
Now that my l.'s gone YEATS, W. B., 16

ladies I want no delicate l. or king's majesties COOPER, JAMES FENIMORE, 15
L. never move CURZON, GEORGE NATHANIEL, 5
several other old l. of both sexes DICKENS, CHARLES, 42
Young l. are delicate plants AUSTEN, JANE, 17

lads Lovely l. and dead and rotten HOUSMAN, A. E., 16

lady A l. always does AUSTEN, JANE, 18
a l. says no...means perhaps DENNING, LORD, 1
a l. turns her when she dances DANTE ALIGHIERI, 7
And when a l.'s in the case GAY, JOHN, 7
First L....sounds like a saddle horse ONASSIS, JACQUELINE KENNEDY, 1
I met a l. in the meads KEATS, JOHN (1795–1821), 14
impossible...single l. to travel without injury ADAMS, ABIGAIL, 3
l. doth protest too much SHAKESPEARE, WILLIAM, 192
l. of a "certain age" BYRON, LORD, 71
l. of Christ's College MILTON, JOHN, 1
She ain't no l.; she's my wife WEBER, JOSEPH, 1
the L. is a Tramp HART, LORENZ, 2
The L.'s Not for Burning FRY, CHRISTOPHER, 11
the l. with the lapdog CHEKHOV, ANTON, 4
There is a l. sweet and kind FOLK VERSE, 8
There was a young l. of Riga LIMERICKS, 5
young l. named Bright BULLER, ARTHUR HENRY REGINALD, 1

lady barber one l. that made good WEST, MAE, 5

ladybird L., ladybird, /Fly away home CHILDREN'S VERSE, 52

Lady Chatterley *L.'s Lover*...Christians might read with profit LAWRENCE, D. H., 5

Lafayette L., we are here STANTON, CHARLES E., 1

lag-end entertain the l. of my life SHAKESPEARE, WILLIAM, 241

lagging Four l. winters and four wanton springs SHAKESPEARE, WILLIAM, 509

Lake Wobegon the news from L. KEILLOR, GARRISON, 1
The town of L., Minnesota KEILLOR, GARRISON, 3

lamb as a l. to the slaughter BIBLE, 221
Did he who made the L. make thee BLAKE, WILLIAM, 28

l. for a burnt BIBLE, 127
Little L., who made thee BLAKE, WILLIAM, 34
L. of God, I come ELLIOTT, CHARLOTTE, 1
l....without blemish BIBLE, 73
the L. of God BIBLE, 268
Lambeth doin' the L. walk FURBER, DOUGLAS, 1
lambs send you forth as l. among wolves BIBLE, 334
lame still a l. dog NEWMAN, ERNEST, 2
lament l. the past...conceive extravagant hopes of the future BURKE, EDMUND, 54
lamented I l. the hairs that had fallen BAI JUYI, 1
l'amour Vive l.! et vive la bagatelle STERNE, LAURENCE, 5
lamp A Lady with a L. shall stand NIGHTINGALE, FLORENCE, 2
To keep a l. burning TERESA OF CALCUTTA, MOTHER, 7
lamplit mysterious l. evenings, here in the galaxy DILLARD, ANNIE, 3
lamp-post I'm leaning on a l. FORMBY, GEORGE, 1
lamps new l. for old ones ARABIAN NIGHTS, THE, 1
Lancelot L. mused a little space TENNYSON, ALFRED, 72
"Tirra lirra," by the river /Sang Sir L. TENNYSON, ALFRED, 69
lancet The l. was the magician's wand HOLMES, OLIVER WENDELL, 16
land a l. flowing with milk and honey BIBLE, 70
Al was this l. fulfild of fayerye CHAUCER, GEOFFREY, 34
Does the l. wait the sleeping lord JONES, DAVID, 3
God said this is our l. KENYATTA, JOMO, 1
Ill fares the l. GOLDSMITH, OLIVER, 15
It is my l., my home GERONIMO, 1
l., like women...meant to be possessed GINSBURG, RUTH BADER, 1
L. of Hope and Glory BENSON, A. C., 1
L. of lost gods and godlike men BYRON, LORD, 28
l.'s sharp features seemed...Century's corpse HARDY, THOMAS, 4
l., ten miles square on the Potomac NEWSPAPERS, 10
l. was ours...a hundred years FROST, ROBERT, 8
The l. is a mother PROVERBS, 86
The l. of my fathers THOMAS, DYLAN, 10
this l....is very great COLUMBUS, CHRISTOPHER, 3
This l. is your land GUTHRIE, WOODY, 1
Thou l. of blood, and crime, and wrong WHITFIELD, JAMES M., 1
We abuse l....regard it as a commodity LEOPOLD, ALDO, 3
wonderful l. and a faithless one RICHARD II, 1
Yet, who can help loving the l. that has taught us MOORE, THOMAS, 3
landlady The l....is a parallelogram LEACOCK, STEPHEN, 11
landlord Come l., fill the flowing bowl FOLK VERSE, 6
The interest of the l. is always opposed to...every other class RICARDO, DAVID, 1
lands l....where deep seas once prevailed LYELL, CHARLES, 2
landscape By avarice and selfishness...the l. is deformed THOREAU, HENRY DAVID, 41
get the l. right, the characters PROULX, E. ANNIE, 4
half the l....covered by useless water DOUGLAS, NORMAN, 1
The l. should belong to the people who see it all the time BARAKA, IMAMU AMIRI, 9
The whole l. a manuscript MONTAGUE, JOHN, 1
When will the l. tire the view DYER, JOHN, 3
landscapist The great l. has his own...obsession DIDEROT, DENIS, 10
landsman a l. beginning a sailor's life DANA, RICHARD HENRY, 2
language don't confound the l. of the nation FRERE, JOHN HOOKHAM, 1
Finding l. that will allow STEINEM, GLORIA, 13
I master the l. of others KRAUS, KARL, 2
In a logically perfect l. RUSSELL, BERTRAND, 10
It survived, this stubborn l. ATXAGA, BERNARDO, 3
L. and *knowledge* are indissolubly connected SULLIVAN, ANNE, 2
L. can only deal meaningfully STEINER, GEORGE, 8
L....created...by talking to oneself SONG LIN, 2
L. did not emerge from...ratiocination WITTGENSTEIN, LUDWIG, 20
L. grows out of life SULLIVAN, ANNE, 3
L. has created the word loneliness TILLICH, PAUL, 11
L. is a form of human reason LÉVI-STRAUSS, CLAUDE, 1
L. is called the garment of thought CARLYLE, THOMAS, 34
L. is not an excrescence of mind DEWEY, JOHN, 14
L. is the autobiography of the human mind MÜLLER, MAX, 1
"*L.*, man!"...it's LITERATURE WELLS, H. G., 7
l.'s /desire to enclose the loved world WALCOTT, DEREK, 2
l. that would make your hair curl GILBERT, W. S., 20
L....to describe the infant phenomenon DICKENS, CHARLES, 63
my native l., its milky call TSVETAEVA, MARINA, 5
no l....foreign to this history DERRIDA, JACQUES, 5
oppress...one l....render it inferior MACDONALD, JOHN A., 1
our existence as l. users THOMAS, LEWIS, 4
separated by the same l. SHAW, GEORGE BERNARD, 120
speak a l. of their own SWIFT, JONATHAN, 13
The l. in which we are speaking is his JOYCE, JAMES, 5
the l. of pioneer women of the air EARHART, AMELIA, 1
The only living l. MACHADO, ANTONIO, 7
the past embodied in l. FRIEL, BRIAN, 2
the whole earth was of one l. BIBLE, 121
To speak a l. is to take on a world FANON, FRANTZ, 8
Understanding l. is more like understanding cricket RUSSELL, BERTRAND, 36
when his l. performs what is required...without shyness CONNOLLY, CYRIL, 2
languages I know of only four l. O'BRIEN, FLANN, 4
keeping up with two spoken l. without trying to invent slang LEACOCK, STEPHEN, 5
l. are the pedigree of nations JOHNSON, SAMUEL, 61
working in the graves of deceased l. DICKENS, CHARLES, 28
lap-dogs when l. breathe their last POPE, ALEXANDER, 96
lapidary l. inscriptions...not upon oath JOHNSON, SAMUEL, 97
laptop Instead of carrying your l., wear it NEGROPONTE, NICHOLAS, 2
lard l. their lean books BURTON, ROBERT, 29
largesse allotting l. to the Lost BROOKS, GWENDOLYN, 7
lark We rise with the l. and go to bed with the lamb BRETON, NICHOLAS, 3
lass gie me the l. that has acres o' charms BURNS, ROBERT, 21
lassie I Love a L. LAUDER, HARRY, 2
last in the l. days...the Lord's house shall be established BIBLE, 197
l. blossom is the first blossom MACNEICE, LOUIS, 18
l. time...I...take part as an amateur AUBER, DANIEL FRANÇOIS ESPRIT, 1
l. twice as long and...as noisy COWARD, NOEL, 35
The L. Hurrah O'CONNOR, EDWIN, 1
the l. monarch of the old school FRANCIS JOSEPH I, 2
The l. straw PROVERBS, 406
the l. territorial claim...in Europe HITLER, ADOLF, 26
we are all on our l. cruise STEVENSON, ROBERT LOUIS, 31
We have had our l. chance MACARTHUR, DOUGLAS, 5
Last Judgement Don't wait for the L. CAMUS, ALBERT, 10

Las Vegas Fear and Loathing in L. THOMPSON, HUNTER S., 12
late Better l. than never PROVERBS, 165
come too l. into a world too old MUSSET, ALFRED DE, 6
in...six and three-quarter minutes...damned fella will be l. MITFORD, NANCY, 1
It's never too l. to learn PROVERBS, 282
It was l., late in the evening AUDEN, W. H., 35
often come too *l.* FANE, VIOLET, 1
later It is l. than you think SERVICE, ROBERT W., 1
lateral thinking L....a way of using information DE BONO, EDWARD, 2
Latin Ah bloody can't ah've gorra L. prose HARRISON, TONY, 2
learning L. by so tedious a grammar BURNET, GILBERT, 2
Thou hadst small L., and less Greek SHAKESPEARE, WILLIAM, 29
was no L. word for tea BELLOC, HILAIRE, 35
Latin America L....fond of the word "hope." NERUDA, PABLO, 2
laudanum L. gave me repose, not sleep COLERIDGE, SAMUEL TAYLOR, 65
laugh castle's strength /Will l. a siege to scorn SHAKESPEARE, WILLIAM, 418
if I l....I may not weep BYRON, LORD, 65
I make myself l. at everything BEAUMARCHAIS, PIERRE-AUGUSTIN CARON DE, 1
L. and the world laughs PROVERBS, 485
L., and the world laughs with you WILCOX, ELLA WHEELER, 3
L. before breakfast PROVERBS, 295
l. before one is happy LA BRUYÈRE, JEAN DE, 9
let your full lips l. at Fate BENNETT, GWENDOLYN, 1
Make 'em l. READE, CHARLES, 1
To l., if but for an instant only PLINY THE ELDER, 5
We are in the world to l. RENARD, JULES, 16
When the green woods l. BLAKE, WILLIAM, 30
laughed I l. all the time COWARD, NOEL, 26
No man who has once...l. CARLYLE, THOMAS, 30
Spirit of the River l. for joy ZHUANGZI, 4
laughing cannot be always l. at a man AUSTEN, JANE, 35
read the death of Little Nell without l. WILDE, OSCAR, 9
laughs who l. on Friday...cry on Sunday RACINE, JEAN, 14
laughter I was convulsed with l. MARX, GROUCHO, 30
l. and the love of friends BELLOC, HILAIRE, 32
L. is an affection KANT, IMMANUEL, 2
L. is as ridiculous as...deceptive VERLAINE, PAUL, 2
L. is nothing else but sudden glory HOBBES, THOMAS, 2
L. is pleasant PEACOCK, THOMAS LOVE, 11
L. is the best medicine PROVERBS, 296
l. is weakness ECO, UMBERTO, 6
Launcelot Sir L. saw her visage MALORY, THOMAS, 6
laundry Give me a l.-list ROSSINI, GIOACCHINO, 1
The general idea,...in any first-class l. LEACOCK, STEPHEN, 24
laurels Nothing is harder on your l. PROVERBS, MODERN, 19
once more, O ye l. MILTON, JOHN, 119
lavatory if you have to keep the l. door shut BANKS-SMITH, NANCY, 1
law a higher l. than the Constitution SEWARD, WILLIAM HENRY, 2
A man's respect for l. and order POWELL, ADAM CLAYTON, JR., 2
Any l. which violates the...rights of man...is not a law at all ROBESPIERRE, MAXIMILIEN, 2
Every l. is a contract SELDEN, JOHN, 1
every l. is an infraction of liberty BENTHAM, JEREMY, 4
good l. must...mean good order ARISTOTLE, 31
great l. of culture CARLYLE, THOMAS, 12
How can l. contradict the lives of millions WRIGHT, RICHARD, 1
Human l....flows from Eternal law AQUINAS, THOMAS, 2
I don't want to know...the l. COHN, ROY, 1
I have forgotten more l. than you ever knew MAYNARD, JOHN, 1
L. and equity...man hath put asunder COLTON, CHARLES, 3
"l. and order"...a code phrase VIDAL, GORE, 18
l. cannot make a man love me KING, MARTIN LUTHER, JR., 25
L....effort of men to organize Society BEECHER, HENRY WARD, 1
L....founded not on theory CICERO, 4
L. grinds the poor GOLDSMITH, OLIVER, 24
life of the l....has been experience HOLMES, OLIVER WENDELL, JR., 5
l. isn't justice...a very imperfect mechanism CHANDLER, RAYMOND, 8
l. is the only aristocratic element TOCQUEVILLE, ALEXIS DE, 3
l. of life...do evil and good MAMET, DAVID, 2
l. of reaction between force and force ADAMS, HENRY, 17
L....ordinance of reason AQUINAS, THOMAS, 9
l....witness...of our moral life HOLMES, OLIVER WENDELL, JR., 1
Man's first l....his own preservation ROUSSEAU, JEAN-JACQUES, 16
Necessity knows no l. PUBLILIUS SYRUS, 18
No brilliance is needed in the l. MORTIMER, JOHN, 1
nothing is l. that is not reason POWELL, JOHN, 1
one general l. of communication HANDY, CHARLES, 10
one l....requires unanimous assent ROUSSEAU, JEAN-JACQUES, 20
People crushed by l. have no hopes but from power BURKE, EDMUND, 5
regard the l. courts...as a casino INGRAMS, RICHARD, 2
Religious l. is like the grammar of a language SACKS, JONATHAN, 9
remember, please, the L. by which we live KIPLING, RUDYARD, 10
Rigorous l. is often rigorous injustice TERENCE, 8
That l. preserves the earth a sphere ROGERS, SAMUEL, 9
the greater part of the l. is learning to tolerate fools LESSING, DORIS, 1
The l.-courts of England are open to all men DARLING, CHARLES JOHN, 6
The l. does not concern itself PROVERBS, 407
the l. is a ass DICKENS, CHARLES, 71
The L. is...everything that's excellent GILBERT, W. S., 13
The L. of England is a very strange one DARLING, CHARLES JOHN, 5
The L. of the Jungle KIPLING, RUDYARD, 57
The l. of the realm COKE, EDWARD, 2
the L. of the Yukon SERVICE, ROBERT W., 4
The L. of Triviality PARKINSON, CYRIL NORTHCOTE, 1
The l. regards man as man HARLAN, JOHN MARSHALL, 1
There can be no l. EISENHOWER, DWIGHT D., 19
The regnant l. of the life of political parties RANDOLPH, A. PHILIP, 1
There is but one l. BURKE, EDMUND, 59
There's one l. for the rich PROVERBS, 423
The ultimate expression of l. JACKSON, GEORGE, 2
they are a l. unto themselves BIBLE, 479
this is the L. of the Jungle KIPLING, RUDYARD, 58
th' windy side of the l. SHAKESPEARE, WILLIAM, 708
lawfulness l. of telling a lie to a sick man JOHNSON, SAMUEL, 91
lawless consummation of their l. pleasure CAVAFY, CONSTANTINE, 1
lawlessness Yours the l. /of something simple LOWELL, ROBERT, 1
Lawrence Mr L. has penned another novel LAWRENCE, D. H., 3
laws Bad l. are the worst sort of tyranny BURKE, EDMUND, 60
good l. to restrain bad people CHESTERTON, G. K., 11

I know not whether L. be right WILDE, OSCAR, 40
iron l. of tradition and law CRANE, STEPHEN, 8
l. and institutions require to be adapted MILL, JOHN STUART, 17
L. are like cobwebs SWIFT, JONATHAN, 3
L. are like spiders' webs SOLON, 3
L. are not masters but servants BEECHER, HENRY WARD, 4
L. can be unjust AQUINAS, THOMAS, 10
L., like houses, lean on one another BURKE, EDMUND, 58
L....must be occasionally cleansed BEECHER, HENRY WARD, 2
l. of physical science have all been discovered MICHELSON, ALBERT A., 1
L. of thermodynamics ANONYMOUS, 68
l. were like cobwebs BACON, FRANCIS (1561–1626), 6
L. were made to be broken NORTH, CHRISTOPHER, 3
nothing to do with the l. but to obey HORSLEY, SAMUEL, 1
scarcely a man learned in the l....who is not noble FORTESCUE, JOHN, 3
The best L. without Money LAW, JOHN, 2
The l. of history ADAMS, HENRY, 14
the l. of poetic truth and poetic beauty ARNOLD, MATTHEW, 19
there *are* l. of nature SAGAN, CARL, 4
there cannot be good l. where there are not good arms MACHIAVELLI, NICCOLÒ, 10
the repeal of bad or obnoxious l. GRANT, ULYSSES S., 4
to interpret l. is...to corrupt them VOLTAIRE, 21
Where l. end, tyranny begins WILKES, JOHN, 1
you do not make the l. GRIMKÉ, ANGELINA EMILY, 2
lawsuit Win your l. and lose your money PROVERBS, 45
lawyer A l.'s opinion PROVERBS, 116
a l.? /Where be his quiddities now SHAKESPEARE, WILLIAM, 223
A l. who has not studied economics BRANDEIS, LOUIS D., 4
A l. with his briefcase can steal O'HARA, THEODORE, 2
as freely as a l. interprets...truth GIRAUDOUX, JEAN, 5
Behold a l., an honest man FRANKLIN, BENJAMIN, 33
class the l. in...history of monsters KEATS, JOHN (1795–1821), 41
don't know as I want a l. MORGAN, JOHN PIERPONT, 4
He that is his own l. PROVERBS, 246
hire a l. to keep from...other lawyers BUTLER, SAMUEL (1612–80), 26
l. has no business with...justice or injustice JOHNSON, SAMUEL, 60
l. with his briefcase can steal more PUZO, MARIO, 1
lawyers influence of the l. in public business TOCQUEVILLE, ALEXIS DE, 2
L. are...civil delinquents COLTON, CHARLES, 4
L. earn a living HUNEKER, JAMES GIBBONS, 2
no bad people...no good l. DICKENS, CHARLES, 89
the trade of l. to question everything JEFFERSON, THOMAS, 41
woe unto you, l. BIBLE, 338
laxative be afraid...castor oil is a l. FLAMMARION, CAMILLE, 1
lay Now I l. me down to sleep FOLK VERSE, 43
lays l. it on with a trowel CONGREVE, WILLIAM, 10
Lazarus L....laid at his gate, full of sores BIBLE, 342
L. was not /Questioned about after-lives JENNINGS, ELIZABETH, 4
lazy always the option of being emotionally l. DE BOTTON, ALAIN, 1
LBJ L., How many kids did you kill today MOTTOS AND SLOGANS, 11
lead L., kindly Light NEWMAN, JOHN HENRY, 7
l. us out of this recovery REAGAN, RONALD, 9
You don't l. by...telling people KESEY, KEN, 1
leader A l. who doesn't hesitate MEIR, GOLDA, 6
l. of a technological youth cult JOBS, STEVE, 1
l....the ability to get other people TRUMAN, HARRY S., 14
No man will make a great l. CARNEGIE, ANDREW, 9
one man in a thousand is a l. of men MARX, GROUCHO, 33
Take me to your l. ANONYMOUS, 80
the L. and the Idea are one HITLER, ADOLF, 16
The l.'s unending responsibility WELCH, JACK, 1
The most effective l....satisfies...psychological needs OGILVY, DAVID, 7
leaders Businessmen...seen as l. and possible saviours JOHNSON, RICHARD W., 3
I have worked with l. HARVEY-JONES, JOHN, 2
L. are psychologists TJOSVOLD, DEAN, 1
L. do things right BENNIS, WARREN, 15
L. learn by leading BENNIS, WARREN, 12
L. must be seen to be up front SIEFF, MARCUS, 1
L. should leave behind them assets DE PREE, MAX, 1
The best l....have a...component of unorthodoxy OGILVY, DAVID, 6
leadership L....consists of telling the truth ROBENS, ALFRED, 1
l. is saying no BLAIR, TONY, 10
L. is the art of accomplishing more POWELL, COLIN, 3
L. is the priceless gift HARVEY-JONES, JOHN, 8
l....(Managing by Wandering Around) PETERS, TOM, 4
l. of western man...coming to an end QUTB, SAYYID, 1
l....on the lunatic fringe WELCH, JACK, 4
men do not approach to l. BEVERIDGE, WILLIAM HENRY, 3
Ninety percent of l. FEINSTEIN, DIANNE, 1
Successful l. is not dependent on...abilities MACGREGOR, DOUGLAS, 1
The aim of l. DEMING, W. EDWARDS, 2
The only l. I can respect JORDAN, JUNE, 1
True l....benefit of the followers TOWNSEND, ROBERT, 2
leaf The last red l. is whirl'd away HALLAM, ARTHUR HENRY, 2
Turn over a new l. DEKKER, THOMAS, 6
league half a l., /Half a league onward TENNYSON, ALFRED, 36
Leah L. was tender eyed BIBLE, 131
lean grow l. /in loneliness NANNAKAIYAR, KACCIPETTU, 1
leaned l. on each other and laughed CARVER, RAYMOND, 4
leap a great l. in the dark HOBBES, THOMAS, 19
A l. over the hedge CERVANTES, MIGUEL DE, 22
l. up to my God MARLOWE, CHRISTOPHER, 11
Lear How pleasant to know Mr L. LEAR, EDWARD, 11
the L. of Shakespeare cannot be acted SHAKESPEARE, WILLIAM, 33
learn always ready to l. CHURCHILL, WINSTON, 45
Beware...the man who works hard to l. VONNEGUT, KURT, 3
In the 1950s we went to l., now we go to teach WILLIAMS, ERIC, 1
know enough who know how to l. ADAMS, HENRY, 16
l. about money WHITEHORN, KATHARINE, 2
L., compare, collect the facts PAVLOV, IVAN PETROVICH, 1
l. from mistakes, not from example HOYLE, FRED, 1
l. playing in a fraternity band POP, IGGY, 1
L. the fundamentals COBB, TY, 1
l. the simplest things /last OLSON, CHARLES, 9
l. to play...within a week KAYE, LENNY, 1
L. to write well SHEFFIELD, JOHN, 1
We could never l. to be brave...if there were only joy KELLER, HELEN, 3
We l. best from experience SENGE, PETER M., 6
we l. by doing ARISTOTLE, 16
We l. so little and forget so much DAVIES, JOHN, 1
You never l. from success YOUNG, DAVID IVOR, 1
learned A l. man is an idler SHAW, GEORGE BERNARD, 43

l. man who is not cleansed KHOMEINI, RUHOLLAH, 1
Soon l. PROVERBS, 384
They have l. nothing, and forgotten nothing TALLEYRAND, CHARLES MAURICE DE, 2
What I have l. I no longer know CHAMFORT, NICOLAS, 8
learning adds not to his l. TALMUD, 3
A little l. is a dangerous thing POPE, ALEXANDER, 19
I got more said than any l. SYNGE, J. M., 5
I thought that I was l. how to live LEONARDO DA VINCI, 12
I've been l. how to give TURNER, TED, 3
l....grants the greatest enjoyment GAUSS, CARL FRIEDRICH, 2
L. had made us not more human CAREW, JAN, 1
L. hath gained most FULLER, THOMAS (1608–61), 5
L. is a common journey TJOSVOLD, DEAN, 2
L. is a treasure PROVERBS, 34
L. is good in and of itself BUSH, GEORGE, 3
L. is not worth a penny PESTALOZZI, JOHANN HEINRICH, 3
L. organizations are possible SENGE, PETER M., 2
L. organizations...evolution of intelligence SENGE, PETER M., 3
L., that cobweb of the brain BUTLER, SAMUEL (1612–80), 14
l....the growth of cognitive structures CHOMSKY, NOAM, 3
L. will be cast into the mire BURKE, EDMUND, 44
L. without thought is labor lost CONFUCIUS, 11
neglects l. in his youth EURIPIDES, 12
scraps of l. dote YOUNG, EDWARD, 1
Their l. is like bread JOHNSON, SAMUEL, 146
Whence is thy l. GAY, JOHN, 5
learns one l. from others CONFUCIUS, 32
learnt l. my twelve times table HOYLE, FRED, 3
More can be l. from Miss Austen AUSTEN, JANE, 1
When you have l. all that Oxford can teach CAIRD, EDWARD, 1
least L. said soonest mended PROVERBS, 297
l. thing contains something unknown MAUPASSANT, GUY DE, 2
l. things...more telling than the greatest RETZ, CARDINAL DE, 8
the l. of these my brethren BIBLE, 432
leave How I l. my country PITT THE YOUNGER, WILLIAM, 6
l. his country as...he had found it COBBETT, WILLIAM, 3
L. well enough alone PROVERBS, 298
They l. it on the dresser MACLAINE, SHIRLEY, 1
We will not l. the monster NAPOLEON I, 10
leaves After the l. have fallen STEVENS, WALLACE, 2
before the l. have fallen WILLIAM II, 3
cool as...l. /of lily-of-the-valley POUND, EZRA, 10
Though l. are many...root is one YEATS, W. B., 27
leaving L. reminds us what we can part with FORD, RICHARD, 1
She's l. home LENNON & MCCARTNEY, 15
lecture given the same l. several times LITTLEWOOD, JOHN, 2
lectures l. or a little charity WHITMAN, WALT, 34
Lee surrendering of L.'s sword GRANT, ULYSSES S., 8
leeches l. have red blood CUVIER, GEORGES, 1
leene As l. was his hors as is a rake CHAUCER, GEOFFREY, 12
left better to be l. than never to have been loved CONGREVE, WILLIAM, 21
let not thy l. hand know what thy right hand doeth BIBLE, 380
legacy l. should be...you made it better IACOCCA, LEE, 9
legal give him a little l. experience KENNEDY, JOHN FITZGERALD, 32
Legion My name is L.: for we are many BIBLE, 354
legs apart from having two good l. CURRIE, EDWINA, 1
born with your l. apart ORTON, JOE, 10
Break the l. of an evil custom PROVERBS, 74
four bare l. in a blanket DAVIES, ROBERTSON, 1
Four l. good, two legs bad ORWELL, GEORGE, 7
His l. bestrid the ocean SHAKESPEARE, WILLIAM, 90
l. which prevents his holding a pen DICKENS, CHARLES, 61
On his last l. MIDDLETON, THOMAS, 8
the longest of l. to the smallest of ideas MACHADO DE ASSIS, JOAQUIM MARIA, 3
leisure I am interested in l. PHILIP, PRINCE, 6
lend L. only that PROVERBS, 299
Lenin L....influenced by the scholarship of Marx LENIN, VLADIMIR ILYICH, 1
L.'s method leads to this LENIN, VLADIMIR ILYICH, 5
transported L....like a plague bacillus CHURCHILL, WINSTON, 59
leopard or the l. his spots BIBLE, 249
Leopold Bloom Mr L. ate with relish the inner organs of beasts and fowls JOYCE, JAMES, 27
leprosy It is full of l. DAMIEN, FATHER, 1
lerne gladly wolde he l. CHAUCER, GEOFFREY, 18
lesbian I was not interested in being...l. MCCARTHY, MARY, 9
lesbianism l. makes a woman virile WOLFF, CHARLOTTE, 2
lesbians most l.... cultivate the treasures of their femininity BEAUVOIR, SIMONE DE, 13
less L. and less are we able to locate our lives HEILBRONER, ROBERT, 1
L. is a bore VENTURI, ROBERT, 4
L. is more MIES VAN DER ROHE, LUDWIG, 1
l. you do...better you do it MASTROIANNI, MARCELLO, 1
lesson a l. which all history teaches EMERSON, RALPH WALDO, 37
l. of history...rarely learned GARFIELD, JAMES A., 5
This taught me a l. MCENROE, JOHN, 1
lessons l. of historical experience KISSINGER, HENRY, 6
l. were...given up to natural history DURRELL, GERALD, 1
Ma, I want l. BERNSTEIN, LEONARD, 2
let L. It Be LENNON & MCCARTNEY, 19
L. my people go FOLK VERSE, 61
L. there be light BIBLE, 501
letter I have made this l. longer PASCAL, BLAISE, 1
I just got your beautiful l. SALINGER, J. D., 8
Someone...wants a l. from you MOTTOS AND SLOGANS, 14
Whenever you receive a l. from a creditor BAUDELAIRE, CHARLES, 3
letters Don't you like writing l. HEMINGWAY, ERNEST, 6
lettuce l....Americans call it *lactuca* GOETHE, JOHANN WOLFGANG VON, 20
l. has been fattening all along BOMBECK, ERMA, 1
level-headed remember to stay l. HORACE, 37
levellers l. wish to level *down* JOHNSON, SAMUEL, 135
Leviathan There is a fish, called the L. ZHUANGZI, 8
Levin When L. puzzled over what he was TOLSTOY, LEO, 8
lexicographer a poet doomed...to wake a l. JOHNSON, SAMUEL, 16
liar A l. is always lavish of oaths CORNEILLE, PIERRE, 9
A l. is worse than a thief PROVERBS, 117
A l. of magnitude BENTON, THOMAS HART, 1
A l. should have a good memory QUINTILIAN, 1
even if I am a l. and a poisoner MILLER, HENRY, 25
liars It has made more l. ROGERS, WILL, 6

libel worst l. is the truth PROVERBS, 509
writs for l. and slander PROFUMO, JOHN, 2
Liberace L. has always been my total hero LIBERACE, 1
liberal A l. is a conservative who has been arrested WOLFE, TOM, 6
a l....tells other people what to do with their money BARAKA, IMAMU AMIRI, 11
I am a l. of the British school BOURASSA, HENRI, 1
l. dreams of a better world VARGAS LLOSA, MARIO, 7
Modern l. political and economic institutions FUKUYAMA, FRANCIS, 5
To be a l. you have to be white MPHAHLELE, ES'KIA, 2
When a l. is abused, he says LENIN, VLADIMIR ILYICH, 14
liberalism L. is a manifestation of opportunism MAO ZEDONG, 8
liberality L. lies less in giving liberally LA BRUYÈRE, JEAN DE, 8
liberals L. think that goats are just sheep BRADBURY, MALCOLM, 6
liberate l. themselves from the fear of man LIN YUTANG, 2
liberation L. is an evershifting horizon HUFFINGTON, ARIANNA, 2
l. of women...time of freedom FRASER, ANTONIA, 2
L. will only arrive ROMERO, OSCAR, 1
The l. of language DALY, MARY, 1
whole point of l. FONDA, JANE, 2
liberationists I'm furious about the Women's L. LOOS, ANITA, 8
liberties Freedom, what l. are taken GEORGE, DANIEL, 1
people never give up their l. BURKE, EDMUND, 16
protect all l. but one DÍAZ ORDAZ, GUSTAVO, 1
liberty A man is master of his l. SHAKESPEARE, WILLIAM, 591
an hour, of virtuous l. ADDISON, JOSEPH, 4
Climb ye the heights of l. GARVEY, MARCUS, 12
give me l. or give me death HENRY, PATRICK, 2
It is true that l. is precious LENIN, VLADIMIR ILYICH, 21
l. connected with order BURKE, EDMUND, 20
L., Equality, Fraternity...peace LAMARTINE, ALPHONSE DE, 1
l. for one person is constrained only ILLICH, IVAN, 6
L. is so much latitude as the powerful HAND, LEARNED, 1
L. is the hardest test VALÉRY, PAUL, 6
L. is the right to do everything MONTESQUIEU, 4
L. is to Science what air is POINCARÉ, JULES HENRI, 1
L. is won with the edge of the machete MACEO, ANTONIO, 1
L. means responsibility SHAW, GEORGE BERNARD, 112
l....measured...by the paucity of restraints SPENCER, HERBERT, 8
L....not...mere declarations of the rights of man WILSON, WOODROW, 16
L. of action, liberty of movement GOURNAY, JEAN-CLAUDE-MARIE-VINCENT DE, 1
love of l....the love of others HAZLITT, WILLIAM, 30
L. plucks justice by the nose SHAKESPEARE, WILLIAM, 425
L....right of any person to...say anything STEFFENS, LINCOLN, 1
L.'s in every blow BURNS, ROBERT, 30
L....the absence of coercion BENTHAM, JEREMY, 9
l. /...with right reason dwells MILTON, JOHN, 90
Oh l.!...What crimes are committed in thy name ROLAND, MADAME, 1
price of l. is...eternal dirt ORWELL, GEORGE, 35
price of L. is eternal vigilance DOUGLASS, FREDERICK, 9
The L. of Man, in Society LOCKE, JOHN, 12
The l. of the individual...limited MILL, JOHN STUART, 11
The tree of l. must be refreshed JEFFERSON, THOMAS, 30
When the People contend for their L. HALIFAX, GEORGE SAVILE, 6
yelps for l. among the drivers of Negroes JOHNSON, SAMUEL, 33
libraries I thank the...Westminster /Public L. PORTER, PETER, 5
library A l. is thought in cold storage SAMUEL, HERBERT, 2
half a l. to make one book JOHNSON, SAMUEL, 76
licence L. my roving hands DONNE, JOHN, 21
licker L. talks mighty loud HARRIS, JOEL CHANDLER, 4
lie allowed to l. for the good of the State PLATO, 17
a l. plausible enough to believe WILLIAMS, JOHN A., 1
A l....very present help in trouble STEVENSON, ADLAI, 5
a l. which is part a truth TENNYSON, ALFRED, 7
Better a l. that heals PROVERBS, 160
can't come. L. follows by post BERESFORD, CHARLES WILLIAM DE LA POER, 1
Father, I cannot tell a l. WASHINGTON, GEORGE, 8
Here l. I by the chancel door EPITAPHS, 3
He who does not...l. is proud NIETZSCHE, FRIEDRICH WILHELM, 24
if a l. may do thee grace SHAKESPEARE, WILLIAM, 248
l. down quietly forever, on linen PEAKE, MERVYN, 3
l. that sinketh in...doth the hurt BACON, FRANCIS (1561–1626), 72
man...should never...l. MONTAIGNE, MICHEL DE, 5
mixture of a l. doth...add pleasure BACON, FRANCIS (1561–1626), 71
more easily fall victim to a big l. HITLER, ADOLF, 33
no worse l. than a truth misunderstood JAMES, WILLIAM, 30
old L.: Dulce et decorum OWEN, WILFRED, 5
people...tell a l. with their last gasp MONTHERLANT, HENRI DE, 2
Stamps God's own name upon a l. COWPER, WILLIAM, 14
the l. has become...a pillar of the State SOLZHENITSYN, ALEXANDER, 11
The l. has...lost its honest function ADORNO, THEODOR, 4
The l. that flatters I abhor the most COWPER, WILLIAM, 13
we'll l. quite still, nor listen nor look MACAULAY, ROSE, 1
Whoever would l. usefully HERVEY, JOHN, 3
who has lived a l. loves the truth BERGMAN, INGMAR, 6
Yes, lad, I l. easy HOUSMAN, A. E., 11
lied because our fathers l. KIPLING, RUDYARD, 33
Who l. in the chapel /Now lies in the Abbey BYRON, LORD, 9
lie down I could l. like a tired child SHELLEY, PERCY BYSSHE, 15
lies believing their own l. ARBUTHNOT, JOHN, 3
enough white l. to ice a wedding cake ASQUITH, MARGOT, 6
Father of L. HERODOTUS, 1
He l. like an eyewitness PROVERBS, 472
Here l. my wife EPITAPHS, 5
If we live all our lives under l. BARAKA, IMAMU AMIRI, 7
l. and evil come from letting people off MURDOCH, IRIS, 2
l., damned lies and statistics DISRAELI, BENJAMIN, 51
l., injustice...are a part of every ordinary community LARSEN, NELLA, 3
Matilda told such Dreadful L. BELLOC, HILAIRE, 15
only l. can get the truth ROTH, PHILIP, 2
The cruellest l. are...told in silence STEVENSON, ROBERT LOUIS, 40
Without l. humanity would perish FRANCE, ANATOLE, 3
life a busy l., a just mind and a timely death HURSTON, ZORA NEALE, 3
A l. is not important ROBINSON, JACKIE, 4
All l.'s answers are on TV GROENING, MATT, 1
all my l. to learn what not to play GILLESPIE, DIZZY, 1
All my l....trouble with women WATERS, MUDDY, 1
All the best days of l. slip away from us poor mortals first VIRGIL, 36
A man's l....is a continual allegory KEATS, JOHN (1795–1821), 37
As our l. is very short TAYLOR, JEREMY, 2
At 70...you take l. more calmly ROOSEVELT, ELEANOR, 6
because all l. has the same root YEATS, W. B., 10

believe in the l. to come BECKETT, SAMUEL, 3
brief is l. but love is long TENNYSON, ALFRED, 90
but one l. and one death BROWNING, ROBERT, 56
certain, that L. flies FITZGERALD, EDWARD, 10
each time of l. has its appropriate rewards ALLEN, WOODY, 17
Every l. is...a ruin ORTEGA Y GASSET, JOSÉ, 9
Every l. is many days JOYCE, JAMES, 20
few things in l. more agreeable JAMES, HENRY, 27
finding l. too easy ORTEGA Y GASSET, JOSÉ, 11
her l. to a clod of wayward marl SHAKESPEARE, WILLIAM, 445
human l....a maimed happiness RENAN, ERNEST, 7
Human l. is...filling in time until...death BERNE, ERIC, 1
human l. is...like a froward child TEMPLE, SIR WILLIAM, 1
I have a l. that...stopped AMMONS, A. R., 1
I might give my l. for my friend SMITH, LOGAN PEARSALL, 18
in l., you get moments AYCKBOURN, ALAN, 7
In real l....it is the hare who wins BROOKNER, ANITA, 3
intelligently, lay down his l. for his country DOUGLASS, FREDERICK, 3
Into each l. some rain must fall LONGFELLOW, HENRY WADSWORTH, 21
Is l. a boon GILBERT, W. S., 40
Is l. worth living BUTLER, SAMUEL (1835–1902), 22
isn't l. a terrible thing THOMAS, DYLAN, 26
Is there another l.? Shall I...find all this a dream? KEATS, JOHN (1795–1821), 29
It's as large as l. CARROLL, LEWIS, 48
It takes l. to love life MASTERS, EDGAR LEE, 1
I've had a happy l. HAZLITT, WILLIAM, 31
I've looked at l. from both sides now MITCHELL, JONI, 3
L....a battle...between Bad and Worse BRODSKY, JOSEPH, 3
l. always produces a "third" JUNG, CARL GUSTAV, 12
L. and the Maiden DUNCAN, ISADORA, 9
L. as a therapist is ruthless HORNEY, KAREN, 14
l....a series of arrivals THEROUX, PAUL, 17
L....a very effective therapist HORNEY, KAREN, 6
law of l....complete negation of repetition BERGSON, HENRI-LOUIS, 3
lay down my l. for the British female? CLOUGH, ARTHUR HUGH, 8
l....basis of teaching and education PESTALOZZI, JOHANN HEINRICH, 5
L. begins at forty PROVERBS, 303
l....being content to accept many things WITTGENSTEIN, LUDWIG, 23
L. consists with wildness THOREAU, HENRY DAVID, 8
l. deserves the protection of society GRASSO, ELLA, 1
L. does not suit me CHATEAUBRIAND, RENÉ, 9
L. exists...because the carbon atom JEANS, JAMES, 1
l. exists more fully WOOLF, VIRGINIA, 18
L....few pleasanter prospects than...well-provisioned breakfast-table HAWTHORNE, NATHANIEL, 10
L. for the living...rest for the dead ARNOLD, GEORGE, 1
L., friends, is boring BERRYMAN, JOHN, 11
l....goes so fast BELLOW, SAUL, 27
l....happens almost exclusively in newspapers ANOUILH, JEAN, 10
L....happens ...while you're busy making other plans LENNON, JOHN, 4
L. has different laws in here SOLZHENITSYN, ALEXANDER, 16
L. has its tale in its mouth FERLINGHETTI, LAWRENCE, 4
L. in itself is short enough PETRARCH, 2
L. is...a bad dream O'NEILL, EUGENE, 3
L. is a disease SHAW, GEORGE BERNARD, 21
l. is a dream HOPKINS, ANTHONY, 2
L. is a fatal complaint HOLMES, OLIVER WENDELL, 31
l. is a foreign country KEROUAC, JACK, 28
L. is a foreign language MORLEY, CHRISTOPHER DARLINGTON, 4
L. is a gamble, at terrible odds STOPPARD, TOM, 12
L. is a great surprise NABOKOV, VLADIMIR, 3
L. is a horizontal fall COCTEAU, JEAN, 6
L. is a jest GAY, JOHN, 3
L. is a kiln FARAH, NURUDDIN, 5
L. is a maze in which we take the wrong turning CONNOLLY, CYRIL, 16
L. is an incurable disease COWLEY, ABRAHAM, 1
L. is an offensive WHITEHEAD, A. N., 2
L. is a partial,... interactive self-realization BERNAL, JOHN DESMOND, 1
L. is a petty thing ORTEGA Y GASSET, JOSÉ, 18
L. is a school of probability BAGEHOT, WALTER, 13
L. is a short day MORE, HANNAH, 4
L. is...a solitary cell O'NEILL, EUGENE, 1
L. is as tedious as a twice-told tale SHAKESPEARE, WILLIAM, 326
L. is as the sea ELLISON, RALPH, 9
L. is a...stinking, treacherous game DREISER, THEODORE, 1
L. is a system of half-truths and lies HUGHES, LANGSTON, 3
L. is a tragedy...in close-up CHAPLIN, CHARLIE, 3
L. is doubt UNAMUNO Y JUGO, MIGUEL DE, 5
L. is...drawing...conclusions from insufficient premises BUTLER, SAMUEL (1835–1902), 27
l. is extinct on other planets KENNEDY, JOHN FITZGERALD, 14
l. is frittered away by detail THOREAU, HENRY DAVID, 43
L. is full of infinite absurdities PIRANDELLO, LUIGI, 10
l. is given to none freehold LUCRETIUS, 7
L. is good for only two things POISSON, SIMÉON-DENIS, 1
L. is Just a Bowl of Cherries BROWN, LEW, 2
L. is just a bowl of cherries PROVERBS, 304
l. is like a box of chocolates HANKS, TOM, 1
L. is like a sewer LEHRER, TOM, 2
L. is...living in health MARTIAL, 2
L. is made of marble and mud HAWTHORNE, NATHANIEL, 9
L. is made up of sobs HENRY, O., 3
L. is mostly froth and bubble GORDON, ADAM LINDSAY, 1
L. is much easier, being an Earl ARRAN, 1
L. is not all peaches PROVERBS, 305
L. is not a spectacle or a feast SANTAYANA, GEORGE, 24
L. is not the highest blessing SCHILLER, FRIEDRICH VON, 7
l. is of a mingled yarn SHAKESPEARE, WILLIAM, 53
l. is one damn thing after another MILLAY, EDNA ST. VINCENT, 3
L. is...process of getting tired BUTLER, SAMUEL (1835–1902), 26
L. is short and so is money BRECHT, BERTOLT, 22
L. is so beautiful MACHADO DE ASSIS, JOAQUIM MARIA, 1
L. is something to do LEBOWITZ, FRAN, 3
L. is the eternal text ORTEGA Y GASSET, JOSÉ, 5
L. is the...functions that resist death BICHAT, MARIE FRANÇOIS, 1
L. is the game ROBINSON, EDWIN ARLINGTON, 1
L. is the only art MUMFORD, LEWIS, 3
l. is the thing...I prefer reading SMITH, LOGAN PEARSALL, 11
L. is too short to do anything for oneself MAUGHAM, SOMERSET, 39
L. is water that is being drawn off TOOMER, JEAN, 2
L. itself is but the shadow of death BROWNE, THOMAS, 34
L. levels all men SHAW, GEORGE BERNARD, 62
L....like boarding-house wallpaper MARLOWE, DEREK, 1
L....little more than a loan shark PIRANDELLO, LUIGI, 16
l. lived on top of a nuclear stockpile SCHELL, JONATHAN, 3

L....mystery which defies solution MORTIMER, JOHN, 5
l. on the whole is far from gay LEAR, EDWARD, 5
L....our reaction to the basic insecurity ORTEGA Y GASSET, JOSÉ, 10
L. protracted is protracted woe JOHNSON, SAMUEL, 6
L.'s a tough proposition MIZNER, WILSON, 6
l.'s dime-thin...two-faced coin WARREN, ROBERT PENN, 4
l. shouldn't be printed on dollar bills ODETS, CLIFFORD, 1
L.'s Little Ironies HARDY, THOMAS, 15
l....solitary, poor, nasty, brutish, and short HOBBES, THOMAS, 13
l. so short, the craft so long HIPPOCRATES, 2
L.'s short span forbids...hopes HORACE, 33
L.'s too short for chess BYRON, HENRY JAMES, 1
L....the leavings of many deaths WHITMAN, WALT, 14
L., the permission to know death BARNES, DJUNA, 1
L., the Universe and Everything ADAMS, DOUGLAS, 4
L....too short to be taken seriously BENTLEY, NICOLAS, 2
l....too short...to bore ourselves? NIETZSCHE, FRIEDRICH WILHELM, 4
L. was a funny thing CRISP, QUENTIN, 8
l. was but a battle SCHILLER, FRIEDRICH VON, 17
L. with him was a life without him MANDELA, NELSON, 2
L. without industry is guilt RUSKIN, JOHN, 3
L. would be tolerable LEWIS, GEORGE CORNEWALL, 1
Madam, L.'s a piece in bloom HENLEY, WILLIAM ERNEST, 3
Man's l. is cheap as beast's SHAKESPEARE, WILLIAM, 340
Man's l. is like...a winter's day HENSHAW, JOSEPH, 1
meaninglessness of l. forces man to create KUBRICK, STANLEY, 2
measured out my l. with coffee spoons ELIOT, T. S., 30
Men deal with l. as children with their play COWPER, WILLIAM, 11
my l. a cause for singing IBSEN, HENRIK, 14
My l. closed twice before its close DICKINSON, EMILY, 13
my l. had been dominated by a sign ABRAHAMS, PETER, 3
My l. has been one great big joke ANGELOU, MAYA, 7
neglected...l. for the sake of love LU XUN, 3
Nobody loves l. like an old man SOPHOCLES, 1
No l. that breathes with human breath TENNYSON, ALFRED, 79
Not everyone's l. is what they make it WALKER, ALICE, 34
Nothing in his l. /Became him like the leaving SHAKESPEARE, WILLIAM, 386
on balance l. is suffering ORWELL, GEORGE, 25
one l. to lose for my country HALE, NATHAN, 1
Our l. goes at such a fearful pace BIERMANN, WOLF, 1
real l. process...development of the ideological reflexes MARX, KARL, 23
show l. neither as it is nor as it ought to be CHEKHOV, ANTON, 13
The art of l....avoiding pain JEFFERSON, THOMAS, 24
The Book of L. begins WILDE, OSCAR, 16
The examined l. has always been...confined to a privileged class FRIEDENBERG, EDGAR Z., 1
The L. and Soul, the man who will never go home WHITEHORN, KATHARINE, 15
the l. her husband makes ELIOT, GEORGE, 18
The l. of man passes...galloping horse ZHUANGZI, 3
the long littleness of l. BROOKE, RUPERT, 1
The May of l. blooms once SCHILLER, FRIEDRICH VON, 2
The payment for l. is death JACKSON, GEORGE, 8
therefore choose l. BIBLE, 38
There is no wealth but l. RUSKIN, JOHN, 27
the tree of l. MILTON, JOHN, 65
The whole l. of man is but a point of time PLUTARCH, 20
The Wine of L. keeps oozing FITZGERALD, EDWARD, 4
Those who have likened our l. to a dream MONTAIGNE, MICHEL DE, 15
Till l. forget and death remember SWINBURNE, ALGERNON CHARLES, 2
To live a l. half dead MILTON, JOHN, 96
trouble with l....so many answers BENEDICT, RUTH, 1
two things to aim at in l. SMITH, LOGAN PEARSALL, 10
value l. less than sport ROSS, PAMELA, 1
We know l. is futile DARROW, CLARENCE, 1
We pay the first cost on all human l. SCHREINER, OLIVE, 1
what an everyday business l. is LAFORGUE, JULES, 1
what a queer thing L. is! WODEHOUSE, P. G., 12
What is l.? A frenzy CALDERÓN DE LA BARCA, PEDRO, 7
What is l. like with another TSVETAEVA, MARINA, 2
what is l. /Like with a woman TSVETAEVA, MARINA, 3
What is l. without dreams ROSTAND, EDMOND, 2
When he can keep l. no longer in FULLER, THOMAS (1608–61), 8
While there is l., there's hope GAY, JOHN, 10
While there's l. PROVERBS, 459
your whole l. shows in your face BACALL, LAUREN, 1

lifeboat haggle over the price...invited to climb onto a l. CROWTHER, GEOFFREY, 2

life-insurance I detest l. agents LEACOCK, STEPHEN, 13

life style l....destructive of the individual HARVEY-JONES, JOHN, 1

lifestyle l. that doesn't require my presence TRUDEAU, GARRY, 2
We're all in the l. game now LACROIX, CHRISTIAN, 2
we sell a l. LAUREN, RALPH, 4

life-style your l. a Crime in Progress THOMPSON, HUNTER S., 9

lifted I would never have l. a finger EINSTEIN, ALBERT, 44

light a l. so dim he would not have chosen a suit by it CHEVALIER, MAURICE, 2
I am the l. of the world BIBLE, 282
I got to l. out for the Territory TWAIN, MARK, 41
L.... a principal beauty in building FULLER, THOMAS (1608–61), 9
L. breaks where no sun shines THOMAS, DYLAN, 7
l. my fire MORRISON, JIM, 2
L. of Lights /Looks always on...motive YEATS, W. B., 5
l. that fills the world ANONYMOUS, 35
More l. GOETHE, JOHANN WOLFGANG VON, 4
No one is a l. unto himself PORCHIA, ANTONIO, 6
Put out the l. SHAKESPEARE, WILLIAM, 500
The l. has gone out GANDHI, MAHATMA, 3
the l. of an oncoming train LOWELL, ROBERT, 7
The L. that Failed KIPLING, RUDYARD, 56
the l. that led astray BURNS, ROBERT, 45
weak, yellow l....the corpselike face NIEDERMAN, ANDREW, 1
what l. through yonder window breaks SHAKESPEARE, WILLIAM, 544

Light Brigade Forward the L. TENNYSON, ALFRED, 37

light bulb I can't stand a naked l. WILLIAMS, TENNESSEE, 2
like a l. HOFF, TED, 1

lighten L. our darkness BOOK OF COMMON PRAYER, 9

lightning Bring in the bottled l. DICKENS, CHARLES, 66
Here lies a man who was killed by l. EPITAPHS, 8
snatched the l. shaft from heaven FRANKLIN, BENJAMIN, 4
the l. flashes of the mental circuits CALVINO, ITALO, 6
vain to look for...defense against l. PUBLILIUS SYRUS, 10

lightning rod be a l. than a seismograph KESEY, KEN, 4

lights God made two great l. BIBLE, 103

We live in...day of l. noses WHARTON, EDITH, 5
Little Buttercup I'm called L. GILBERT, W. S., 6
little girls l....slamming doors BELLOC, HILAIRE, 10
Little Nell combination of L. and Lady Macbeth PARKER, DOROTHY, 3
liv'd I have l. long enough SHAKESPEARE, WILLIAM, 417
live Better a l. beggar than a dead king PROVERBS, 25
better not to l....than to live disgraced SOPHOCLES, 8
Come l. with me, and be my love MARLOWE, CHRISTOPHER, 1
Do you want to l. forever? DALY, DANIEL, 1
feel content to l. dangerously BARBELLION, W. N. P., 3
How may I l. without my name MILLER, ARTHUR, 18
in him we l....and have our being BIBLE, 19
It matters not how long you l. PUBLILIUS SYRUS, 9
known I was gonna l. this long BLAKE, EUBIE, 1
l. all the days of your life SWIFT, JONATHAN, 34
L. all you can; it's a mistake not to JAMES, HENRY, 19
L. among men as if God beheld you SENECA, "THE YOUNGER," 6
L. and learn PROVERBS, 309
l. dangerously NIETZSCHE, FRIEDRICH WILHELM, 31
l. for ever...die in the attempt HELLER, JOSEPH, 2
l. in the cities...sick with unused self HECHT, BEN, 1
l. long enough...venerability factor creeps in STONE, I. F., 1
L. Now, Pay Later STORY, JACK TREVOR, 1
L. or die, sink or swim PEELE, GEORGE, 1
l. with me, and be my love DONNE, JOHN, 7
L. with the gods MARCUS AURELIUS, 10
Men cannot l....explain the universe BERLIN, ISAIAH, 2
not fit to l. on land JOHNSON, SAMUEL, 133
now I go where I shall l....with Him BUNYAN, JOHN, 23
One cannot l. with sighted eyes HANSBERRY, LORRAINE, 7
One can't l. on love alone TOLSTOY, SOFYA, 3
Teach me to l. KEN, THOMAS, 2
They l. ill who expect...live always PUBLILIUS SYRUS, 12
This is the urgency: L. BROOKS, GWENDOLYN, 5
Those who can't find anything to l. for WELCH, LEW, 1
Those who l. by...a lie HAMPTON, CHRISTOPHER, 5
To l. is like love BUTLER, SAMUEL (1835–1902), 35
To l. is to be slowly born SAINT-EXUPÉRY, ANTOINE DE, 2
To l. is to choose TUCHOLSKY, KURT, 5
trying to l. without friends HURSTON, ZORA NEALE, 2
We do not l. to think ORTEGA Y GASSET, JOSÉ, 15
We l. and learn POMFRET, JOHN, 1
we l. in details WHITEHEAD, A. N., 19
We l. in our own world THOMAS, R. S., 2
We l. in stirring times ISHERWOOD, CHRISTOPHER, 5
We l. our lives, for ever taking leave RILKE, RAINER MARIA, 2
wish to l....first attend your own funeral MANSFIELD, KATHERINE, 4
you will l. to ninety-nine FOLK VERSE, 50
lived I have l. in this house many years ADAMS, HENRY, 4
Never to have l. is best YEATS, W. B., 24
to have l....unnecessary and unaccommodated NAIPAUL, V. S., 1
You l. aloof, maintaining...your magnificent disdain BULGAKOV, MIKHAIL, 1
liver the positions of the l. and the heart MOLIÈRE, 10
lives He that l. long PROVERBS, 249
He who l. by the sword PROVERBS, 254
he who lives more l. than one WILDE, OSCAR, 39
L. of great men all remind us LONGFELLOW, HENRY WADSWORTH, 2
many l. are needed...to make one MONTALE, EUGENIO, 1
Our l. are...strange dark interludes O'NEILL, EUGENE, 4
The l. of small men are like spiders' webs MARECHERA, DAMBUDZO, 2
We spend our l. talking about...mystery RENARD, JULES, 19
Who l. medically lives miserably ANONYMOUS, 43
living A l. doll PLATH, SYLVIA, 5
A l. is made...by selling something that everybody needs WILDER, THORNTON, 2
every l. being has an intrinsic value NAESS, ARNE, 2
habit of l. indisposeth us for dying BROWNE, THOMAS, 39
l. ad interim SCHOPENHAUER, ARTHUR, 12
l. company exists primarily...own survival DE GEUS, ARIE, 4
l. doll BART, LIONEL, 1
let the earth bring forth the l. creature BIBLE, 104
L. is abnormal IONESCO, EUGÈNE, 5
L. is an illness CHAMFORT, NICOLAS, 10
L. is like...one long addition sum PAVESE, CESARE, 1
L. is my job and my art MONTAIGNE, MICHEL DE, 12
L....sleeping with an elephant TRUDEAU, PIERRE, 2
L.? The servants will do that VILLIERS DE L'ISLE-ADAM, AUGUSTE, 1
l. together...suggests a lack of spirit HERBERT, A. P., 5
L. well and beautifully and justly SOCRATES, 10
one guy...l. out his own fantasies HEFNER, HUGH, 1
start l....first got to redeem our past CHEKHOV, ANTON, 10
strange making a l. out of yourself TAYLOR, JAMES, 1
take me as a l. person ZHANG XIANLIANG, 1
The l. need charity ARNOLD, GEORGE, 2
The l....the dead on vacation MAETERLINCK, MAURICE, 1
There are l. systems MONOD, JACQUES LUCIEN, 2
We, who are the l., possess the past FARMER, JAMES, 2
living standard Our l....maintained by foreign capital SACHS, JEFFREY, 1
Livingstone Dr. L., I presume STANLEY, HENRY MORTON, 1
llama a female l. surprised in her bath DE GAULLE, CHARLES, 1
L....Like an unsuccessful literary man BELLOC, HILAIRE, 20
Lloyd George L. could not see a belt ASQUITH, MARGOT, 5
L. spoke for a hundred and seventeen minutes BENNETT, ARNOLD, 9
loafed better to have l. and lost THURBER, JAMES, 2
loath l. to lay out money on a rope BURTON, ROBERT, 7
loathe I l. people who keep dogs STRINDBERG, AUGUST, 1
loathings My l. are simple NABOKOV, VLADIMIR, 15
loathsome l. canker lives in sweetest bud SHAKESPEARE, WILLIAM, 572
loaves five barley l., and two small fishes BIBLE, 278
lobotomies more subtle l. and tranquillizers LAING, R. D., 6
lobster l....more ridiculous than a dog NERVAL, GÉRARD DE, 5
Lochinvar young L. SCOTT, SIR WALTER, 9
loftiest The l. interests of man COOPER, JAMES FENIMORE, 2
log-cabin L. to White House GARFIELD, JAMES A., 1
logic L. and sermons never convince WHITMAN, WALT, 12
L. is...a dodge JOWETT, BENJAMIN, 4
L., like whiskey, loses its...effect DUNSANY, LORD, 1
L. must take care of itself WITTGENSTEIN, LUDWIG, 8
L....the art of going wrong KLINE, MORRIS, 2
L....The art of thinking and reasoning BIERCE, AMBROSE, 32
L....the last scientific ingredient of Philosophy CARNAP, RUDOLF, 1
the l. of our times DAY-LEWIS, CECIL, 3
The principles of l. and metaphysics are true AYER, A. J., 3

logical L. activity...not the whole of intelligence PIAGET, JEAN, 1
logo A l. is like a man's name BERNBACH, WILLIAM, 6
Logos the seed of the L. implanted in all mankind JUSTIN MARTYR, SAINT, 2
loitered I l. my life away, reading books HAZLITT, WILLIAM, 8
Lolita L., light of my life NABOKOV, VLADIMIR, 1
London a L. particular...A fog DICKENS, CHARLES, 14
dominate a L. dinner-table WILDE, OSCAR, 72
He who drinks a tumbler of L. water SMITH, SYDNEY, 3
I would sell L. RICHARD I, 6
L.: a nation, not a city DISRAELI, BENJAMIN, 23
L. burnt by fire NOSTRADAMUS, 2
L. doesn't love the latent JAMES, HENRY, 24
L. is a modern Babylon DISRAELI, BENJAMIN, 37
lowest and vilest alleys of L. DOYLE, ARTHUR CONAN, 6
L., that great cesspool DOYLE, ARTHUR CONAN, 1
L. was a city not to be visited JOHNSON, JAMES WELDON, 1
MPs never see the L....beyond the wine bars LIVINGSTONE, KEN, 1
Nobody is healthy in L. AUSTEN, JANE, 13
tired of L....tired of life JOHNSON, SAMUEL, 132
loneliness a reflection of my own...l. HOPPER, EDWARD, 2
Beside the clock's l. HUGHES, TED, 7
each of us must live with...l. HARRISON, JIM, 1
l. may spur you into finding something...great enough to die for HAMMARSKJÖLD, DAG, 7
l. of my country and my God SHAW, GEORGE BERNARD, 82
L....the great American disease CORRY, JOHN, 1
L....the most terrible poverty TERESA OF CALCUTTA, MOTHER, 5
lonely All the l. people LENNON & MCCARTNEY, 1
l. while eating spaghetti MORLEY, ROBERT, 2
She left l. for ever ARNOLD, MATTHEW, 12
So l. am I /My body is a floating weed KOMACHI, 2
lonely heart None But the L. LLEWELLYN, RICHARD, 1
lonesome A l. man...who does not know how to read FRANKLIN, BENJAMIN, 32
one, that on a l. road COLERIDGE, SAMUEL TAYLOR, 48
long L. is the way /And hard MILTON, JOHN, 39
So l. had life together been BRODSKY, JOSEPH, 1
You've come a l. way, baby ADVERTISEMENTS, 23
longer wished l. by its readers BUNYAN, JOHN, 1
longevity L. is the revenge of talent CONNOLLY, CYRIL, 11
L., n. Uncommon extension BIERCE, AMBROSE, 33
longing L....is what makes history DELILLO, DON, 6
Long Island L. represents the American's idea FLEMING, PETER, 1
long life Man...prays for a l. PROVERBS, 35
longueurs Very good, but it has its *l.* RIVAROL, ANTOINE DE, 7
look A "l." can so easily become weak QUANT, MARY, 1
How do I l. ROREM, NED, 2
I love the l., austere, immaculate WYLIE, ELINOR, 1
It costs nothing to l. PROVERBS, 502
It is said we all l. alike REMOND, CHARLES LENOX, 2
I want to l. like...American Voltaire ADAMS, HENRY, 19
l. at him! He might be Stalin DE GAULLE, CHARLES, 2
L. before you leap PROVERBS, 311
Let him l. to his bond SHAKESPEARE, WILLIAM, 611
L. for me by moonlight NOYES, ALFRED, 1
L. thy last on all things lovely DE LA MARE, WALTER, 6
see what I l. like from the *side* PEAKE, MERVYN, 6
the L. isn't...garments you wear QUANT, MARY, 2
looked better to be l. over than overlooked WEST, MAE, 19
I l. like a bowl of kraut MCGHEE, HOWARD, 1
looker-on sit thou a patient l. QUARLES, FRANCIS, 4
looking Here's l. at you, kid BOGART, HUMPHREY, 5
l. for a man's foot-print BEERBOHM, MAX, 16
The art of l. for trouble BENN, ERNEST, 1
looking glass The cracked l. of a servant JOYCE, JAMES, 26
looks A man who l. a part MAUPASSANT, GUY DE, 1
l. commercing with the skies MILTON, JOHN, 111
man who l. you...in the eye FADIMAN, CLIFTON, 2
never had the l. to lose CARTER, ANGELA, 12
No man ever l....with pristine eyes BENEDICT, RUTH, 2
Well, he l. like a man WHITMAN, WALT, 3
Your l. looked after you GUNN, THOM, 3
loosed For l. till dawn are we KIPLING, RUDYARD, 54
lord a L. among wits CHESTERFIELD, LORD, 1
drunk as a l. RUSSELL, BERTRAND, 56
God bless our L. the King HOGG, JAMES, 2
L. of himself, though not of lands WOTTON, HENRY, 1
l. of lycht and lamp of day DOUGLAS, GAWIN, 1
Lord Alas, O L., to what a state TERESA OF ÁVILA, SAINT, 6
good L. take a liking to you ROGERS, ROY, 1
L., I have set my hopes ANONYMOUS, 10
L.,! Lay not on us a burden KORAN, 10
L.! thou knowest how busy ASTLEY, JACOB, 1
The L. descended from above STERNHOLD, THOMAS, 1
The L....has begotten a son KORAN, 23
the L. is a man of war BIBLE, 77
the L. looketh on the heart BIBLE, 227
the L. should deport him to Hell MACKENZIE, COMPTON, 5
The L. survives the rainbow of His will LOWELL, ROBERT, 25
the Son of man is L. also of the sabbath BIBLE, 350
thy L. shall give thee a reward KORAN, 43
lordlike what makes men walk l....love of women ROUTSONG, ALMA, 1
lords Great l. have their pleasures MONTESQUIEU, 8
None ought to be l. or landlords over another WINSTANLEY, GERRARD, 1
lordships good enough for their l. ANONYMOUS, 72
Los Angelean To qualify for a L. CAINE, MICHAEL, 1
Los Angeles L....you've got to be an actor FORD, HARRISON, 1
the vast, blind-eyed reservation of L. JACOBS, JANE, 2
To live sanely in L. ISHERWOOD, CHRISTOPHER, 3
lose A man who does not l. his reason LESSING, GOTTHOLD EPHRAIM, 1
don't l. it again ZEC, PHILIP, 1
I hate to l. ROBINSON, JACKIE, 1
I hate to l. more than...win CONNORS, JIMMY, 1
I shall l. no time in reading it DISRAELI, BENJAMIN, 50
No man can l. WALTON, IZAAK, 7
nothing to l. but our aitches ORWELL, GEORGE, 39
to l. our teeth...keep on growing thinner LEAR, EDWARD, 6
What you l. on the swings PROVERBS, 454
You l. COOLIDGE, CALVIN, 19
loser Show me a good and gracious l....show you a failure ROCKNE, KNUTE, 1
Show me a good l....an idiot DUROCHER, LEO, 1

losers L. must have leave to speak CIBBER, COLLEY, 5
loses no man l. any other life MARCUS AURELIUS, 4
losing art of l. isn't hard to master BISHOP, ELIZABETH, 5
loss better to incur l. than to make gain PLAUTUS, 2
People...encouraging about a terrible l. KEILLOR, GARRISON, 9
lost girl is l....burnt flesh ECO, UMBERTO, 7
he was l., and is found BIBLE, 341
I can't say I was ever l. BOONE, DANIEL, 1
I've l. one...my children this week TURNER, J. M. W., 1
My friends, I have l. a day SUETONIUS, 3
There will always be a l. dog ANOUILH, JEAN, 6
you've l. your true self O'NEILL, EUGENE, 2
loudest l. complainers for the public BURKE, EDMUND, 13
Louis Son of Saint L. EDGEWORTH DE FIRMONT, ABBÉ, 1
lousy only one fault. It was...l. THURBER, JAMES, 22
louts oafish l. remember Mum BETJEMAN, JOHN, 1
lov'd Of one that l. not wisely, but too well SHAKESPEARE, WILLIAM, 502
She l. me for the dangers SHAKESPEARE, WILLIAM, 475
love a comfort in the strength of l. WORDSWORTH, WILLIAM, 28
all for l. and a little for the bottle DIBDIN, CHARLES, 1
all for l., and nothing for reward SPENSER, EDMUND, 8
all the world and l. were young RALEIGH, WALTER, 5
All You Need Is L. LENNON & MCCARTNEY, 7
A man in l. is incomplete until...married GABOR, ZSA ZSA, 1
a man in l. with a dimple LEACOCK, STEPHEN, 9
Any scientist who has ever been in l. LONSDALE, KATHLEEN, 1
believe in...true l....after the first attack EBNER-ESCHENBACH, MARIE VON, 2
Benedick, l. on; I will requite thee SHAKESPEARE, WILLIAM, 452
better to l. a woman as a woman NAVARRE, MARGARET OF, 3
breeze of l. blows for an hour MAHFOUZ, NAGUIB, 5
Could l. you for yourself alone YEATS, W. B., 56
Could we forbear dispute and practise l. WALLER, EDMUND, 3
difficult...to lay aside a long-cherished l. CATULLUS, 8
Do not l. your neighbour as yourself SHAW, GEORGE BERNARD, 58
Every l. is the love before PARKER, DOROTHY, 8
Falling in Love with L. HART, LORENZ, 4
Falling out of l. is very enlightening MURDOCH, IRIS, 4
For l. deceives the best of womankind POPE, ALEXANDER, 90
For the l. of a lousy buck DYLAN, BOB, 16
from l. to matrimony in a moment AUSTEN, JANE, 31
Give me l., /or nothing WALKER, ALICE, 1
give...your l. but not your thoughts GIBRAN, KAHLIL, 4
God is l. BIBLE, 182
Hail wedded l., mysterious law MILTON, JOHN, 59
He that falls in l. with himself...no rivals FRANKLIN, BENJAMIN, 15
he told men to l. their neighbor BRECHT, BERTOLT, 8
How alike are the groans of l. to those of the dying LOWRY, MALCOLM, 3
how did you l. my picture GOLDWYN, SAMUEL, 6
How do I l. thee BROWNING, ELIZABETH BARRETT, 8
How they l. money, thought Wilhelm BELLOW, SAUL, 20
I consider l. higher than art DUNCAN, ISADORA, 7
I do l. nothing in the world so well as you SHAKESPEARE, WILLIAM, 458
I do not l. thee, Doctor Fell BROWN, THOMAS, 1
I do not l. the money ARMOUR, PHILIP D., 1
I don't know much about l. GOLDEN, MARITA, 1
I fell in l. with a patient REICH, WILHELM, 4
If the heart bleeds l. MCGOUGH, ROGER, 2
I hate all that don't l. me FARQUHAR, GEORGE, 10
I l. all my children CARTER, LILLIAN, 1
I l. all waste SHELLEY, PERCY BYSSHE, 34
I l. my rags MOLIÈRE, 18
I l. thee with the breath...of all my life BROWNING, ELIZABETH BARRETT, 9
I l. the road BASIE, COUNT, 2
I'm tired of L. BELLOC, HILAIRE, 1
I never was in l. KEATS, JOHN (1795–1821), 49
in l., and in debt, and in drink BROME, ALEXANDER, 1
in l. with the whole world ERDRICH, LOUISE, 2
I pursued...origin and course /Of l. STEVENS, WALLACE, 13
Is thy l. a plant /Of such weak fibre WORDSWORTH, WILLIAM, 92
I want to l. first, and live incidentally FITZGERALD, ZELDA, 1
I will confess /I l. this cultured hell that tests my youth MCKAY, CLAUDE, 2
I would *l.* infinitely, and be loved BROWNING, ROBERT, 63
Kind souls, you wonder why, I l. you PATMORE, COVENTRY, 3
l.—all the wretched cant of it GREER, GERMAINE, 10
L. and all his pleasures CAMPION, THOMAS, 7
L. and compassion...essence of all religion DALAI LAMA, 9
l. and marriage...like a horse and carriage CAHN, SAMMY, 1
l. and marriage rarely can combine BYRON, LORD, 55
l. and murder will out CONGREVE, WILLIAM, 12
L. bade me welcome HERBERT, GEORGE, 9
L. built on beauty... dies DONNE, JOHN, 19
L. ceases to be a pleasure BEHN, APHRA, 7
l....clearer in his absence GIBRAN, KAHLIL, 3
L. comes from blindness, friendship from knowledge BUSSY-RABUTIN, 2
L. conquers all PROVERBS, 314
L. conquers all...except poverty and toothache WEST, MAE, 24
L. conquers all things VIRGIL, 34
L., curiosity, freckles, and doubt PARKER, DOROTHY, 12
L. divine, all loves excelling WESLEY, CHARLES, 2
L. does not consist in gazing at each other SAINT-EXUPÉRY, ANTOINE DE, 8
l. dwells in gorgeous palaces BOCCACCIO, GIOVANNI, 3
let's fall in l. PORTER, COLE, 17
L. feels no burden, thinks nothing of trouble KEMPIS, THOMAS À, 8
L. goes toward love SHAKESPEARE, WILLIAM, 546
L. has never turned aside the...bullet JACKSON, GEORGE, 10
l....has one arch-enemy...life ANOUILH, JEAN, 4
L. I did the fairest boy BARNFIELD, RICHARD, 3
L., I find is like singing HURSTON, ZORA NEALE, 4
L. in a hut KEATS, JOHN (1795–1821), 16
L.?...I never talk about it PROUST, MARCEL, 12
L. is above the laws STAËL, MADAME DE, 5
L. is a growing...constant light DONNE, JOHN, 30
L. is a king uncrowned HEATH-STUBBS, JOHN, 1
L. is a sickness...All remedies refusing DANIEL, SAMUEL, 2
L. is a spirit all compact of fire SHAKESPEARE, WILLIAM, 713
L....is a strange disease HANDY, W. C., 7
l. is a thing that can never go wrong PARKER, DOROTHY, 10
L. is based on a view of women MENCKEN, H. L., 48
l. is blind SHAKESPEARE, WILLIAM, 604
L. is blind PROVERBS, 315
L. is Here to Stay GERSHWIN, IRA, 7

L. is...like a coconut BRECHT, BERTOLT, 3
L. is like linen FLETCHER, PHINEAS, 1
L. is like quicksilver PARKER, DOROTHY, 45
L. is like the measles JEROME, JEROME K., 5
l. is maister GOWER, JOHN, 2
L. is moral even without...marriage KEY, ELLEN, 5
L. is my religion KEATS, JOHN (1795–1821), 33
L. is not consolation, it is light WEIL, SIMONE, 9
l. is...not individual BRADLEY, F. H., 3
L. is not love /Which alters SHAKESPEARE, WILLIAM, 581
L....is not only apolitical but antipolitical ARENDT, HANNAH, 19
L. isn't like a reservoir CANTOR, EDDIE, 1
L. is our Lord's meaning JULIAN OF NORWICH, 1
l. is such a mystery SUCKLING, JOHN, 2
L. is the difficult realization MURDOCH, IRIS, 3
L....is...the exchange of two fantasies CHAMFORT, NICOLAS, 11
L. is...the gift of oneself ANOUILH, JEAN, 3
L. is the lesson which the Lord us taught SPENSER, EDMUND, 2
L. is the wisdom of the fool JOHNSON, SAMUEL, 57
L. is wonderful; but if I could not have both, I would prefer respect MAYS, BENJAMIN E., 1
L. iz like the meazles BILLINGS, JOSH, 3
L....known by him who hopelessly persists SCHILLER, FRIEDRICH VON, 10
L. leaped out BULGAKOV, MIKHAIL, 4
l., like a running brook, is disregarded GIBRAN, KAHLIL, 6
l. like other arts requires experience LAMB, CAROLINE, 1
l....looks more like hatred than like friendship LA ROCHEFOUCAULD, FRANÇOIS, 12
L. looks not with the eyes SHAKESPEARE, WILLIAM, 56
L. makes the world PROVERBS, 316
L. means never having to say SEGAL, ERICH, 1
l. me...for love's sake only BROWNING, ELIZABETH BARRETT, 6
L. me little, love me long FOLK VERSE, 37
l. me little...love me long HERRICK, ROBERT, 9
L. me, love my dog PROVERBS, 317
L. of honour SIDNEY, PHILIP, 5
l. of money is the root of all evil BIBLE, 239
L. of self and kind JACKSON, GEORGE, 7
l. oneself...lifelong romance WILDE, OSCAR, 14
l. one's neighbor as one's self CHAMFORT, NICOLAS, 4
l....pleasure in the perfection of another LEIBNIZ, GOTTFRIED WILHELM, 5
L....rarer than genius PÉGUY, CHARLES PIERRE, 7
l.—reveals us in our nakedness PAVESE, CESARE, 2
l. robs those who have it of their wit DIDEROT, DENIS, 5
L.'s but a frailty of the mind CONGREVE, WILLIAM, 23
L. seeketh not itself to please BLAKE, WILLIAM, 22
L. seeketh only Self to please BLAKE, WILLIAM, 23
L. seldom haunts the breast where learning lies POPE, ALEXANDER, 98
L.'s like the measles JERROLD, DOUGLAS, 5
L....sole and everlasting foundation PESTALOZZI, JOHANN HEINRICH, 4
L....someone to call you darling after sex BARNES, JULIAN, 5
L. sought is good SHAKESPEARE, WILLIAM, 704
L.'s pleasure lasts but a moment FLORIAN, JEAN-PIERRE CLARIS DE, 1
l.'s the noblest frailty DRYDEN, JOHN, 43
L. that dare not speak its name DOUGLAS, ALFRED, 2
L. that dare not speak its name WILDE, OSCAR, 11
L. that's wise ROBINSON, EDWIN ARLINGTON, 3
l....the dirty trick MAUGHAM, SOMERSET, 4
l....the fear that tenderness always has an end DIPOKO, MBELLA SONNE, 1
l. the Lord thy God with all thy heart BIBLE, 422
L.-thirty, love-forty, oh! weakness of joy BETJEMAN, JOHN, 6
L., thou art...Lord CRASHAW, RICHARD, 1
"L.", till its incantation MCCAIG, NORMAN, 2
L....to make sure of the legitimacy of the children RUSSELL, BERTRAND, 12
L. truth VOLTAIRE, 39
l....was not as love is nowadays MALORY, THOMAS, 4
l. we give away...we keep HUBBARD, ELBERT, 7
l....with a twined thread BURTON, ROBERT, 17
Make l. not war MOTTOS AND SLOGANS, 10
make l. to you at five o'clock BANKHEAD, TALLULAH, 8
make us l. your goodly gifts SHAKESPEARE, WILLIAM, 506
making l. is child's play MITFORD, NANCY, 4
Making l. is the sovereign remedy for anguish LEBOYER, FRÉDÉRICK, 2
Maybe l. will come GINSBERG, ALLEN, 4
most wonderful kind of delirium is...l. ZAMYATIN, YEVGENY, 3
Murmur, a little sadly, how L. fled YEATS, W. B., 34
My L. in her attire doth show her wit FOLK VERSE, 38
my l. is forever gone LI QINGZHAO, 5
My l. is of a birth as rare MARVELL, ANDREW, 2
My l. is the maïd ov all maïdens BARNES, WILLIAM, 1
my l. swears that she is made of truth SHAKESPEARE, WILLIAM, 586
my real l....sleep that rescued me PIRANDELLO, LUIGI, 18
Never l. with all your heart CULLEN, COUNTEE, 7
No l. like the first love PROVERBS, 344
No l....spared that BECKETT, SAMUEL, 13
no man dies for l., but on the stage DRYDEN, JOHN, 25
no such...l. since humanity was divided into classes MAO ZEDONG, 25
Nothing is too much trouble for l. TUTU, DESMOND, 10
Now I know what L. is VIRGIL, 31
Now what is l. RALEIGH, WALTER, 7
Oh mighty l. HERBERT, GEORGE, 11
Oh, when I was in l. with you HOUSMAN, A. E., 7
old l. of going returns upon them MOMADAY, N. SCOTT, 2
O L.! has she done this to thee LYLY, JOHN, 2
only l. sprung from my only hate SHAKESPEARE, WILLIAM, 539
Only our l. hath no decay DONNE, JOHN, 38
O tell me the truth about l. AUDEN, W. H., 24
Our l....does not lead to extravagance PERICLES, 1
People Will Say We're in L. HAMMERSTEIN, OSCAR, II, 3
secure the l. of your neighbor PLINY THE ELDER, 14
She makes l. just like a woman DYLAN, BOB, 6
She whom I l. is hard to catch MEREDITH, GEORGE, 8
Something to l. /He lends us TENNYSON, ALFRED, 82
So true a fool is l. SHAKESPEARE, WILLIAM, 574
Such ever was l.'s way BROWNING, ROBERT, 29
Sweetest l., I do not go DONNE, JOHN, 37
sweet l. remembered SHAKESPEARE, WILLIAM, 568
sweet L.!, was thought a crime BLAKE, WILLIAM, 20
Ten men l. what I hate BROWNING, ROBERT, 35
The difficult part of l. /Is being selfish LARKIN, PHILIP, 3
the expression of l. CASANOVA, GIOVANNI GIACOMO, 1
The girl I l. is beautiful BOUCICAULT, DION, 2
the l. machine would appear a natural development MCLUHAN, MARSHALL, 4
The l. of life is necessary to...any undertaking JOHNSON, SAMUEL, 44

The loss of l. is a terrible thing CULLEN, COUNTEE, 6
the one I l. most lay sleeping WHITMAN, WALT, 46
Therefore l. moderately SHAKESPEARE, WILLIAM, 550
Therefore the l. which does us bind MARVELL, ANDREW, 3
They sin who tell us l. can die SOUTHEY, ROBERT, 8
They that l. beyond the world PENN, WILLIAM, 4
Those who l. everything are despised BARNES, DJUNA, 5
thought that l. would last for ever: I was wrong AUDEN, W. H., 23
To fear l. is to fear life RUSSELL, BERTRAND, 15
to l. and be loved SAND, GEORGE, 1
To l. a thing CONFUCIUS, 25
to l. her is a liberal education STEELE, RICHARD, 5
To l. without suffering is impossible EKELÖF, GUNNAR, 2
To l. you was pleasant enough MOORE, THOMAS, 10
True L....differs from gold and clay SHELLEY, PERCY BYSSHE, 31
True l.'s the gift...God has given /To man SCOTT, SIR WALTER, 24
Try thinking of l. FRY, CHRISTOPHER, 1
want to l. a strong young man FORSTER, E. M., 4
We all l. a pretty girl under the rose BICKERSTAFFE, ISAAC, 3
We all l. each other, right REDDING, OTIS, 1
weight of the world /is l. GINSBERG, ALLEN, 5
We l. being in love THACKERAY, WILLIAM MAKEPEACE, 3
We must l. one another or die AUDEN, W. H., 38
Were you ever in l., Beach WODEHOUSE, P. G., 15
what a mischievous devil L. is BUTLER, SAMUEL (1835–1902), 21
What is commonly called l. FIELDING, HENRY, 18
What is l.? 'Tis not hereafter SHAKESPEARE, WILLIAM, 699
What kills l. is words SEMBÈNE, OUSMANE, 2
what l. was worth /in the end DAS, KAMALA, 2
What thing is l....it is a sting PEELE, GEORGE, 3
When I imagine a faultless l. AUDEN, W. H., 14
when I l. thee not, /Chaos is come SHAKESPEARE, WILLIAM, 492
When...man is abandoned by /his l. AMICHAI, YEHUDA, 5
When you are in l. with humanity PIRANDELLO, LUIGI, 2
Where l. is absent...no woman SAND, GEORGE, 4
where the course of true l. may...run smooth MARTINEAU, HARRIET, 5
whom to look at was to l. TENNYSON, ALFRED, 52
Why L. must needs be blind COLERIDGE, SAMUEL TAYLOR, 19
why should l. stop at the border CASALS, PABLO, 4
Wilt thou l. her, comfort her BOOK OF COMMON PRAYER, 22
With a l. that the winged seraphs POE, EDGAR ALLAN, 4
you should l. your enemies SCHWARZKOPF, NORMAN, 2

love affairs One must keep l. quiet SIMPSON, WALLIS, 1

loved Aim at being l. without being admired WITTGENSTEIN, LUDWIG, 12
Had we never l. BURNS, ROBERT, 6
He l. me, and 'twas right that he should CHRISTINE DE PISAN, 4
I have not l. the world BYRON, LORD, 32
I l. much, I never loved long BOLINGBROKE, HENRY ST. JOHN, 1
I...l. my english teacher miss laha DAS, KAMALA, 1
l. him too much to feel no hate RACINE, JEAN, 1
Only one who has l. knows HU SHI, 1
seems to me that he has never l. DOSTOYEVSKY, ANNA, 2
She who has never l. has never lived GAY, JOHN, 19
Those that he l. so long and sees no more ROGERS, SAMUEL, 7
'Tis better to have l. and lost HALLAM, ARTHUR HENRY, 4
To be l....very demoralizing HEPBURN, KATHARINE, 2
Who...l. that loved not at first sight MARLOWE, CHRISTOPHER, 20

lovelies Fifty l. in the rude THOMAS, DYLAN, 17

love life l. of...average middle class American AUSTIN, MARY, 6

loveliness A woman of so shining l. YEATS, W. B., 48
when I approach /her l. MILTON, JOHN, 79

lovely All l. things will have an ending AIKEN, CONRAD, 1
l. and pleasant in their lives BIBLE, 175
My l. living boy DU BARTAS, GUILLAUME, 14

love-quarrels L. oft in pleasing concord end MILTON, JOHN, 97

lover All the world loves a l. PROVERBS, 126
A l. without indiscretion is no lover HARDY, THOMAS, 27
easier to be a l. than a husband BALZAC, HONORÉ DE, 13
If you wanna be my l. SPICE GIRLS, THE, 2
my fause l. stole my rose BURNS, ROBERT, 36
One l. is always more moved BELLOW, SAUL, 4
satisfied with her l.'s mind TROLLOPE, ANTHONY, 8
talk with some old l.'s ghost DONNE, JOHN, 29

lovers Daddy and I were l. DURCAN, PAUL, 1
Hello young l., wherever you are HAMMERSTEIN, OSCAR, II, 15
l. fled away into the storm KEATS, JOHN (1795–1821), 75
l. run into strange capers SHAKESPEARE, WILLIAM, 101
L. will find /A hedge-school CLARKE, AUSTIN, 1
Sweet l. love the spring SHAKESPEARE, WILLIAM, 120
two young l. lately wed TENNYSON, ALFRED, 68

loves A woman must marry the man who l. her BÂ, MARIAMA, 1
Every man l. what he is good at SHADWELL, THOMAS, 3
He l. his bonds HERRICK, ROBERT, 14
He that l. a rosy cheek CAREW, THOMAS, 1
He that l. not his wife and children TAYLOR, JEREMY, 4
one that l. his fellow-men HUNT, LEIGH, 3
real l., real revolts, real desires BEAUVOIR, SIMONE DE, 5
She L. You, Yeh, Yeh, Yeh LENNON & MCCARTNEY, 3
very rarely that a man l. MACDIARMID, HUGH, 2
When one l. somebody GORKY, MAKSIM, 5
Who l. ya, baby SAVALAS, TELLY, 1

loveth God l. a cheerful giver BIBLE, 165

lovin' You've Lost That L. Feelin' SPECTOR, PHIL, 2

low Begin l., speak slow ANONYMOUS, 75

lower l. classes had such white skins CURZON, GEORGE NATHANIEL, 4

lowliness l. is young ambition's ladder SHAKESPEARE, WILLIAM, 301

Lowry Malcolm L. /Late of the Bowery LOWRY, MALCOLM, 1

loyalty An ounce of l. HUBBARD, ELBERT, 4
l....possible only when fidelity is emptied ARENDT, HANNAH, 22
Party l. lowers the greatest of men LA BRUYÈRE, JEAN DE, 10

lucid L. intervals and happy pauses BACON, FRANCIS (1561–1626), 100

Lucifer L. legend is in no sense...absurd JUNG, CARL GUSTAV, 9
Unhappy spirits that fell with L. MARLOWE, CHRISTOPHER, 4

luck bring down a man...l. went bad CARVER, RAYMOND, 2
for bad l. you need luck PROVERBS, 498
it brings you l. whether you believe...or not BOHR, NIELS, 2
L. be a Lady Tonight LOESSER, FRANK, 4
l. in our methodology of science MEDAWAR, PETER, 2
L. is only important...right moment SINATRA, FRANK, 3
l.,... the harder I work the more I have LEACOCK, STEPHEN, 8
L. to me is...hard work BALL, LUCILLE, 3
Some l. lies in not getting what KEILLOR, GARRISON, 6
sure thing about l....change MIZNER, WILSON, 9
Tell the boys I've got the L. HARTE, BRET, 2
The only sure thing about l. HARTE, BRET, 4

lucke for good l., cast an old shooe HEYWOOD, JOHN, 3
lucky "Do I feel l....do ya, punk? EASTWOOD, CLINT, 1
L. at cards PROVERBS, 318
l. enough to get to Corinth HORACE, 22
L. is he who could understand the causes of things VIRGIL, 35
Third time l. PROVERBS, 429
we have only to be l. once ANONYMOUS, 9
we only have to be l. once THATCHER, MARGARET, 12
ludicrous He has no sense of the l. BLAKE, WILLIAM, 2
Luftwaffe L.—...knocked down our buildings CHARLES, PRINCE, 5
lukewarm not the...l. who make history HITLER, ADOLF, 24
lumberjack I'm a l. and I'm OK MONTY PYTHON'S FLYING CIRCUS, 6
lunatic fringe There is apt to be a l. ROOSEVELT, THEODORE, 29
lunatics All are l. BIERCE, AMBROSE, 49
No vote can be given by l.... females BLACKSTONE, WILLIAM, 1
lunch L. kills half of Paris MONTESQUIEU, 12
no such thing as a free l. FRIEDMAN, MILTON, 10
lungs even my l. are affected BEARDSLEY, AUBREY, 1
lust Delight of l. is gross and brief PETRONIUS ARBITER, 6
l. in action; and till action, lust SHAKESPEARE, WILLIAM, 583
O wicked wit and gifts...won to his shameful l. SHAKESPEARE, WILLIAM, 156
lust'st Thou hotly l. to use her in that kind SHAKESPEARE, WILLIAM, 361
lute It is the little rift within the l. TENNYSON, ALFRED, 13
My l., be still, for I have done WYATT, THOMAS, 1
When to her l. Corinna sings CAMPION, THOMAS, 2
luve My l.'s like a red red rose BURNS, ROBERT, 8
luxuries Give me the l. of life WRIGHT, FRANK LLOYD, 6
Give us the l. of life MOTLEY, JOHN LOTHROP, 1
I have two l....your loveliness and...my death KEATS, JOHN (1795–1821), 31
luxury Every l. was lavished on you ORTON, JOE, 5
The saddest thing...to get used to l. CHAPLIN, CHARLIE, 6
lyf That l. so short CHAUCER, GEOFFREY, 37
lying how this world is given to l. SHAKESPEARE, WILLIAM, 244
L. is the beginning of fiction KINCAID, JAMAICA, 4
One of you is l. PARKER, DOROTHY, 24
this vice of l. SHAKESPEARE, WILLIAM, 258
lynch Here is a state that used to l. people like me CHARLES, RAY, 2
They never l. children BECKETT, SAMUEL, 17
lynching he could have attended a l. every day SMITH, THORNE, 1
It is a hi-tech l. for uppity blacks THOMAS, CLARENCE, 1
Lyndon L. acts like there was never going to be a tomorrow JOHNSON, LADY BIRD, 3
lyrics heroines of her l. are Amazonian ARMSTRONG, LOUIS, 1

Macavity M. WASN'T THERE ELIOT, T. S., 23
Macbeth M. doth murder sleep SHAKESPEARE, WILLIAM, 399
McCarthyism M. is Americanism MCCARTHY, JOSEPH (1909–57), 2
McDonald I believe in God, family, and M.'s KROC, RAY, 3
McGregor Don't go into Mr M.'s garden POTTER, BEATRIX, 1
Machiavel We are much beholden to M. BACON, FRANCIS (1561–1626), 89
machine a m....do a mental task SINCLAIR, CLIVE, 3
a m....that is...intelligent SINCLAIR, CLIVE, 4
cannot endow...m. with initiative LIPPMANN, WALTER, 3
how strange it seemed...that magical m. KEMBLE, FANNY, 2
m....work of fifty ordinary men HUBBARD, ELBERT, 2
machines M....keep free men in subjection CLARK, KENNETH (1903–83), 3
M. need to talk easily to one another NEGROPONTE, NICHOLAS, 4
M....produce of the mind of man COBBETT, WILLIAM, 1
no reason to suppose that these m....general use WELLINGTON, DUKE OF, 4
whether m. think SKINNER, B. F., 3
Macintosh M. was an artificial arrangement ROSE, FRANK, 2
McKinley face of M.'s, this...unchipped mask MCKINLEY, WILLIAM, 1
MacWonder M. one moment and MacBlunder the next MACMILLAN, HAROLD, 5
mad A knight errant who turns m. for a reason CERVANTES, MIGUEL DE, 24
All of us are m. BETTI, UGO, 7
Don't get m., get even KENNEDY, JOSEPH, 1
Don't get m.. Get smart DIXON, WILLIE, 1
Every one is...m. on one point KIPLING, RUDYARD, 40
Get m., then get over it POWELL, COLIN, 5
he ceased to be m. he became merely stupid PROUST, MARCEL, 13
He's m. that trusts...a boy's love SHAKESPEARE, WILLIAM, 350
I feel certain...I am going m. WOOLF, VIRGINIA, 4
I must be m., or very tired LOWELL, AMY, 1
less harm...in being m. among madmen DIDEROT, DENIS, 8
M. about the boy COWARD, NOEL, 5
"M."...a man...obsessed with one idea BETTI, UGO, 3
m. as a March hare CERVANTES, MIGUEL DE, 40
M. as the sea and wind when both contend /Which is the mightier SHAKESPEARE, WILLIAM, 206
M., bad, and dangerous to know BYRON, LORD, 3
Men are so necessarily m. PASCAL, BLAISE, 6
m. north-north-west SHAKESPEARE, WILLIAM, 163
M. world! mad kings! mad composition SHAKESPEARE, WILLIAM, 322
rather be m. than delighted DIOGENES, 5
The insane, the m., the frenzied ANONYMOUS, 2
the only people for me are the m. ones KEROUAC, JACK, 9
Though they go m....shall be sane THOMAS, DYLAN, 19
We want a few m. people now SHAW, GEORGE BERNARD, 83
When we remember...we are all m. TWAIN, MARK, 57
Who e're is m....had Wit to lose CARKESSE, JAMES, 1
Whom God wishes to destroy...makes m. EURIPIDES, 14
Madagascar M.'s pervasive taboos MURPHY, DERVLA, 3
madam M. I may not call you ELIZABETH I, 14
M., we must live in the same room IONESCO, EUGÈNE, 7
madame Call me m. PERKINS, FRANCES, 1
M., you must really be more careful PLESSIS, ARMAND-EMMANUEL DU, 1
Madame Bovary All I could think of... was: *M.* MCCARTHY, MARY, 11
made Don't you think I was m. for you? FITZGERALD, ZELDA, 2
Do you know who m. you STOWE, HARRIET BEECHER, 4
My father m....you...out of nothing MARY I, 1
Nothing should be m....which is not worth making MORRIS, WILLIAM, 8
Madeira We're from M. SHAW, GEORGE BERNARD, 93
mademoiselle A m. from Armenteers ROWLAND, EDWARD, 1
madman The m. ...has lost everything except his reason CHESTERTON, G. K., 26
The m. thinks...the world crazy PUBLILIUS SYRUS, 11

madmen M....lost the faculty of reasoning LOCKE, JOHN, 2
madness Could it be M.—this DICKINSON, EMILY, 16
destroyed by m., starving hysterical naked GINSBERG, ALLEN, 7
Like m. is the glory of this life SHAKESPEARE, WILLIAM, 674
M. in great ones SHAKESPEARE, WILLIAM, 180
M. is a final distillation of self DELILLO, DON, 4
m. is the only freedom BALLARD, J. G., 1
M. need not be all breakdown LAING, R. D., 11
model of m....believe oneself to be God FOUCAULT, MICHEL, 2
Much M. is divinest Sense DICKINSON, EMILY, 7
m., yet there is method in't SHAKESPEARE, WILLIAM, 173
opinions...concerning the cause of m. HOBBES, THOMAS, 6
Our occasional m. is less wonderful SANTAYANA, GEORGE, 21
saved from m. by a...fox terrier CRICHTON-BROWNE, JAMES, 1
streak of m. in the family BOWIE, DAVID, 1
That I essentially am not in m., /But mad in craft SHAKESPEARE, WILLIAM, 203
that way m. lies SHAKESPEARE, WILLIAM, 346
The great proof of m. NAPOLEON I, 24
There be iiii kyndes of m. BOORDE, ANDREW, 1
What is m. VOLTAIRE, 24
What is m. /To those who only observe FRY, CHRISTOPHER, 3
What's m. but nobility of soul ROETHKE, THEODORE, 4
madnesse another kinde of m. named lunaticus BOORDE, ANDREW, 2
maestro You can't teach the old m. a new tune KEROUAC, JACK, 11
Maggie ain't gonna work on M.'s farm DYLAN, BOB, 10
Magi of the ancient race of those M. OTTO OF FREISING, 1
magic If this be m., let it be an art SHAKESPEARE, WILLIAM, 672
m., prayers, trickery...Irish politics" O'BRIEN, FLANN, 11
There is not enough m. in a bloodline JONES, JAMES EARL, 1
magistrates m. /Want no comic-singers in town BROWN, GEORGE MACKAY, 2
magnanimity M. in politics...the truest wisdom BURKE, EDMUND, 22
magnet-south O M. WHITMAN, WALT, 27
magnificent It is m., but it is not war BOSQUET, PIERRE, 1
It's more than m.— it's mediocre GOLDWYN, SAMUEL, 22
some m. myth PLATO, 23
that m. instrument between your legs TOSCANINI, ARTURO, 5
Mahomet M. will go to the hill BACON, FRANCIS (1561–1626), 18
maid Being an old m. is like death by drowning FERBER, EDNA, 3
I once was a m. BURNS, ROBERT, 41
Much better to play a m. than to be one MCDANIEL, HATTIE, 1
The m....lies to me LI QINGZHAO, 3
Maid await news of the M. JOAN OF ARC, SAINT, 3
maiden A simple m. in her flower TENNYSON, ALFRED, 45
I pursued a m. and clasped a reed SHELLEY, PERCY BYSSHE, 5
this m. she lived...to...be loved by me POE, EDGAR ALLAN, 10
maidens M. aspiring to godheads STOPPARD, TOM, 9
M., like moths...caught by glare BYRON, LORD, 23
Maine M. and Texas...nothing important to communicate THOREAU, HENRY DAVID, 46
mainstream pallid m. of American life KILLENS, JOHN OLIVER, 3
majesty Her M. is not a subject DISRAELI, BENJAMIN, 63
her M....must not...look upon me as a source of income KEMBLE, CHARLES, 1
more serious...offend the divine m. INNOCENT III, 1
major-general very model of a modern M. GILBERT, W. S., 37
majority doesn't abide by m. rule...conscience LEE, HARPER, 4
great changes occur in history... the m. are wrong DEBS, EUGENE VICTOR, 2
m. is...the best repartee DISRAELI, BENJAMIN, 36
One with the law is a m. COOLIDGE, CALVIN, 11
The m. has the might IBSEN, HENRIK, 5
make Go ahead, m. my day EASTWOOD, CLINT, 3
make-believe used...m. with a certain desperation BENEDICT, RUTH, 6
maker Whether my M. is ready for...meeting me CHURCHILL, WINSTON, 74
makes either m. me or fordoes me quite SHAKESPEARE, WILLIAM, 495
makin' M. Whoopee KAHN, GUS, 2
maladies Medical men...call all sorts of m....by one name CARLYLE, JANE, 2
malady a single m. is more easily cured JOHNSON, SAMUEL, 37
It is the m. of our age HOFFER, ERIC, 6
not only the m....also...habits when in health CICERO, 9
male only a m. can represent Christ CAREY, GEORGE, 2
peculiar situation of the human m. BEAUVOIR, SIMONE DE, 7
standing out against m. assumption AUSTIN, MARY, 10
the m. artist approximates...to the psychology of woman HINKLE, BEATRICE, 1
the m. equivalent of childbirth ACLAND, RICHARD, 1
The m. is a biological accident SOLANAS, VALERIE, 1
male domination M. has not destroyed the longing HOOKS, BELL, 1
malefactions They have proclaim'd their m. SHAKESPEARE, WILLIAM, 164
Malherbe At last came M. MALHERBE, FRANÇOIS DE, 1
malice M. is like a game of poker SPIEL, HILDE, 1
M. is of a low stature SAVILE, SIR GEORGE, 3
M. of Inanimate Objects JAMES, M. R., 1
Yet m. never was his aim SWIFT, JONATHAN, 17
malign rather m. oneself LA ROCHEFOUCAULD, FRANÇOIS, 19
Malraux M., like Sartre, has read Freud FREUD, SIGMUND, 12
malt m. does more than Milton can MILTON, JOHN, 3
mama the m. of dada STEIN, GERTRUDE, 1
mammy Your m....Brought forth a goodly baby SKELTON, JOHN, 4
man A dear old m. with his...somewhat toothless smile GANDHI, MAHATMA, 1
ain't nothin' an ol' m. can do MABLEY, JACKIE, 1
a m. after his own heart BIBLE, 225
a m. can die but once SHAKESPEARE, WILLIAM, 259
A m. can't help his feelings sometime MARSHALL, PAULE, 4
A m....chooses to be happy SOLZHENITSYN, ALEXANDER, 4
a m....his blood is sea water PEATTIE, DONALD CULROSS, 1
a m. in my position MCCAIG, NORMAN, 3
A m. in the house is worth two WEST, MAE, 3
A m. is always resident in the castle of his skin LAMMING, GEORGE, 4
A m. is as old as he feels PROVERBS, 129
A m. is either free or he is not BARAKA, IMAMU AMIRI, 10
A m. is only as old as the woman he feels MARX, GROUCHO, 2
A m....is *so* in the way GASKELL, ELIZABETH, 2
A m. knows when he is growing old GARCÍA MÁRQUEZ, GABRIEL, 5
a m. might think ill of women CHAMFORT, NICOLAS, 3
A m. of the hour MARTIN, JOHN, 1
A m.'s greatest battles...he fights within himself OKRI, BEN, 1
A m. should never put on his best trousers IBSEN, HENRIK, 7

A m. should not strive to eliminate his complexes FREUD, SIGMUND, 60
A m. should...own he has been in the wrong POPE, ALEXANDER, 52
A m. should wake up in his own bed ACHEBE, CHINUA, 3
A m. that looks on glass HERBERT, GEORGE, 19
a m. who never tried an experiment DARWIN, ERASMUS, 4
A m. with God KNOX, JOHN, 2
A sick m. is as wayward as a child MITFORD, MARY RUSSELL, 1
'A was a m., take him for all in all SHAKESPEARE, WILLIAM, 147
Beware of the m. of one book PROVERBS, 84
broken m. writing dull English NABOKOV, VLADIMIR, 13
but you are not a m. MERCOURI, MELINA, 1
cannot make a m. by standing a sheep BEERBOHM, MAX, 21
credit goes to the m. who convinces the world DARWIN, FRANCIS, 1
dare do all that may become a m. SHAKESPEARE, WILLIAM, 392
deviation of m. from...nature JENNER, EDWARD, 1
Different m., different land, but de same outlook LAMMING, GEORGE, 3
dumb, dark...belly-tension between...m. and woman LAWRENCE, D. H., 2
Each coming together of m. and wife STOPES, MARIE, 6
each m....amplification of one organ EMERSON, RALPH WALDO, 65
each m. has a...sphere of activity MARX, KARL, 21
Every m. a king LONG, HUEY, 2
Every m. carries the entire form of human condition MONTAIGNE, MICHEL DE, 27
every m. did that which was right in his own eyes BIBLE, 314
every m. for himself CERVANTES, MIGUEL DE, 12
Every m. for himself BURTON, ROBERT, 12
Every m. has a sane spot somewhere STEVENSON, ROBERT LOUIS, 41
Every m. has a wild beast within him FREDERICK II (1712–86), 1
every m....his hand on his heart WENTWORTH, THOMAS, 3
Every m. is as Heaven made him CERVANTES, MIGUEL DE, 30
Every m. is wanted EMERSON, RALPH WALDO, 23
every m. lives...by love TOLSTOY, LEO, 7
Every m. meets his Waterloo PHILLIPS, WENDELL, 1
Every m. over forty is a scoundrel SHAW, GEORGE BERNARD, 53
Every m.'s a chasm BÜCHNER, GEORG, 6
for a m. to go about unlabelled HUXLEY, T. H., 7
Funny how a m. who can stay decent HEARNE, JOHN, 2
"Give me," says Lamb, "m. as he is not to be" LAMB, CHARLES, 1
Have you become a m. this morning MARTIAL, 3
He is a m. of brick UPDIKE, JOHN, 16
He was her m., but he done her wrong FOLK VERSE, 34
how infirm m. is KLEIST, HEINRICH VON, 1
I am a m....nothing human foreign to me TERENCE, 7
I am a m. of reserved, cold ADAMS, JOHN QUINCY, 3
I—am—a m....you—are—another JACKSON, ANDREW, 1
If a m. have not a friend BACON, FRANCIS (1561–1626), 103
If a m. stays away from his wife DARLING, CHARLES JOHN, 2
If any m. should buy another man CUGOANO, OTTOBAH, 1
If I could have a m. like that LUO GUANZHONG, 1
if I were a m., I would be at the battlefront KIEKO, YAMAMURO, 1
If m. does find...solution for world peace MARSHALL, GEORGE, 2
I met a m. with seven wives CHILDREN'S VERSE, 30
Indeed, m. was created impatient KORAN, 41
in every m....two simultaneous postulations BAUDELAIRE, CHARLES, 8
I rather a m. be anything WELTY, EUDORA, 1
I sit on a m.'s back, choking him TOLSTOY, LEO, 16
I think any m....mad or stupid WESTWOOD, VIVIENNE, 1
It is the lot of m. but once to die QUARLES, FRANCIS, 3
It takes...twenty years to make a m. ROWLAND, HELEN, 4
Let each m. make himself LIYONG, TABAN LO, 3
let no m. put asunder BOOK OF COMMON PRAYER, 26
life of m....of no greater importance HUME, DAVID, 30
lot of m....ceaseless labour ELIOT, T. S., 45
M....a certain number of teeth, hair, and ideas VOLTAIRE, 22
M....a cog in an intricate social system HORNEY, KAREN, 7
m. after his deeth CHAUCER, GEOFFREY, 25
make m. in our own image BIBLE, 105
M. alone at the very moment of his birth PLINY THE ELDER, 6
m. alone builds up...the past WRONG, GEORGE M., 6
m. alone leaves traces of what he created BRONOWSKI, JACOB, 1
M. always dies before he is fully born FROMM, ERICH, 3
M....animal so lost in rapturous contemplation BIERCE, AMBROSE, 34
M. appears to be the missing link LORENZ, KONRAD, 8
M. arrives as a novice at each age of his life CHAMFORT, NICOLAS, 1
m....at the gate of the year HASKINS, MINNIE LOUISE, 1
M. becomes what he eats GANDHI, MAHATMA, 9
m., by possessing consciousness, is...a diseased animal UNAMUNO Y JUGO, MIGUEL DE, 8
m. can be destroyed but not defeated HEMINGWAY, ERNEST, 16
m. can brave an opinion STAËL, MADAME DE, 4
M....can neither repeat his past AUDEN, W. H., 28
M....consumes without producing ORWELL, GEORGE, 6
m....decides, not heaven CHEN YI, 1
M. does not live by words alone STEVENSON, ADLAI, 12
M. dreams of fame TENNYSON, ALFRED, 14
M....explicable by...his history EMERSON, RALPH WALDO, 11
m. fell into his anecdotage DISRAELI, BENJAMIN, 24
M. follows only phantoms LAPLACE, PIERRE SIMON, 1
M. for the field and woman...hearth TENNYSON, ALFRED, 86
m. goes far to find...what he is ROETHKE, THEODORE, 5
M....greatest miracle and the greatest problem SARNOFF, DAVID, 3
M....greatness and animal fused together BÂ, MARIAMA, 3
M....grows beyond his work STEINBECK, JOHN, 9
M. hands on misery to man LARKIN, PHILIP, 12
M. has his will HOLMES, OLIVER WENDELL, 26
M. has...limited biological capacity for change TOFFLER, ALVIN, 1
M. has never been the same since God died MILLAY, EDNA ST. VINCENT, 2
m....his universal malady BARNES, DJUNA, 2
M. is a beautiful machine MENCKEN, H. L., 14
m. is a dangerous creature ADAMS, ABIGAIL, 4
M. is a dupable animal SOUTHEY, ROBERT, 12
M....is alone in...the Universe MONOD, JACQUES LUCIEN, 3
M. is a machine GURDJIEFF, G. I., 1
m. is a man for...much longer BALZAC, HONORÉ DE, 9
M. is a master of contradictions MANN, THOMAS, 12
M. is a masterpiece of creation LICHTENBERG, GEORG CHRISTOPH, 2
M. is a museum of diseases TWAIN, MARK, 54
M. is an...everlasting contradiction HAZLITT, WILLIAM, 3
M. is a noble animal BROWNE, THOMAS, 38
M. is a rope NIETZSCHE, FRIEDRICH WILHELM, 39
M. is a social animal SPINOZA, BARUCH, 5
m. is as old as his arteries SYDENHAM, THOMAS, 4
M. is ...a thing of shreds and patches EMERSON, RALPH WALDO, 51
m. is a thinking erratum MACHADO DE ASSIS, JOAQUIM MARIA, 10

M. is a tool-making animal FRANKLIN, BENJAMIN, 31
M. is a tool-using animal CARLYLE, THOMAS, 31
M. is but the place where I stand THOREAU, HENRY DAVID, 10
M. is by his constitution a religious animal BURKE, EDMUND, 46
M. is created free SCHILLER, FRIEDRICH VON, 8
M. is defined as a human being BEAUVOIR, SIMONE DE, 11
m. is designed to walk three miles WOOD, VICTORIA, 1
M. is developed from an ovule DARWIN, CHARLES, 10
M. is different from animals...he speculates HOAGLAND, EDWARD, 2
M. is exceedingly contentious KORAN, 22
M. is...great when he acts from the passions DISRAELI, BENJAMIN, 10
M....is halfway between an ape and a god INGE, WILLIAM RALPH, 12
M. is Heaven's masterpiece QUARLES, FRANCIS, 2
m. is man...master of his fate TENNYSON, ALFRED, 16
M. is Nature's sole mistake GILBERT, W. S., 17
M. is...nearer to the atom than the stars EDDINGTON, ARTHUR, 1
M. is neither good nor bad BALZAC, HONORÉ DE, 3
M. is not merely the sum of his masks PAGLIA, CAMILLE, 6
M. is...not only of necessity BERDYAEV, NIKOLAI, 2
M. is not the creature of circumstances DISRAELI, BENJAMIN, 49
M. is only a reed PASCAL, BLAISE, 4
M., ... is the best of animals ARISTOTLE, 28
M. is the hunter; woman...his game TENNYSON, ALFRED, 87
M. is the only one that knows nothing PLINY THE ELDER, 7
M. is the shepherd of Being HEIDEGGER, MARTIN, 2
M. is what he does MALRAUX, ANDRÉ, 5
m....left by nature a functionless being ARISTOTLE, 11
M. makes holy what he believes RENAN, ERNEST, 5
m. must be a nonconformist EMERSON, RALPH WALDO, 19
m....nature does not regard him as important CRANE, STEPHEN, 6
m....noblest of all creatures LICHTENBERG, GEORG CHRISTOPH, 5
m....not wholly in control of...productive process SCHUMACHER, E. F., 4
m. of sixty...twenty years in bed BENNETT, ARNOLD, 11
M....on friendly terms with the victims...he eats BUTLER, SAMUEL (1835–1902), 28
M. proposes KEMPIS, THOMAS À, 5
M. proposes, God disposes PROVERBS, 322
M. rushes to woman like the stag to the spring BINGEN, HILDEGARD OF, 1
M.'s chief goal...stay human HOFFER, ERIC, 3
m.'s eagerness for power CRUMMELL, ALEXANDER, 2
m.'s fear of women's creative energy BUCK, PEARL, 9
M.'s goodness is a flame that can be hidden but never extinguished MANDELA, NELSON, 12
m.'s greatest crime...to have been born CALDERÓN DE LA BARCA, PEDRO, 1
m. should be...hoarser than his wife HOWE, EDGAR WATSON, 1
m. should live only for the present SOPHOCLES, 7
M.'s love is of man's life a thing apart BYRON, LORD, 45
M.'s main task in life is to give *birth* to himself FROMM, ERICH, 4
m.'s place to rule...woman's to yield SEWELL, SARAH ANN, 1
m. that hath no music in himself SHAKESPEARE, WILLIAM, 622
m. that is born of a woman BIBLE, 259
m. was made to mourn BURNS, ROBERT, 25
m. who can own up to his error RETZ, CARDINAL DE, 9
m. who doesn't spend time with...family BRANDO, MARLON, 6
m. who doesn't trust himself RETZ, CARDINAL DE, 1
m. who has never made a woman angry MORLEY, CHRISTOPHER DARLINGTON, 6
m. who obeys is nearly always better RENAN, ERNEST, 4
m. who reads...belongs to the species YOURCENAR, MARGUERITE, 1
m. whose second thoughts are good BARRIE, J. M., 19
M....will end by destroying the earth SCHWEITZER, ALBERT, 5
m. will not merely endure; he will prevail...because he has a soul FAULKNER, WILLIAM, 2
m. with all his noble qualities DARWIN, CHARLES, 12
m. within me...rebukes, commands, and dastards me BROWNE, THOMAS, 7
No m....be friends with a woman CRYSTAL, BILLY, 1
No m. can be a Politician HARRINGTON, JAMES, 2
no m....hath lived better than I MALORY, THOMAS, 2
No m. is an Island DONNE, JOHN, 12
No m. is born unto himself alone QUARLES, FRANCIS, 6
No m. is himself...sum of his past FAULKNER, WILLIAM, 16
no...reason to believe that m. descended BRYAN, WILLIAM JENNINGS, 4
Nothing happens to any m. MARCUS AURELIUS, 9
No young m. believes he shall...die HAZLITT, WILLIAM, 10
Of all...created things, m. is but one ZHUANGZI, 2
one m. pick'd out of ten thousand SHAKESPEARE, WILLIAM, 169
place where a m. can feel...secure GREER, GERMAINE, 11
proper function of m. is to live LONDON, JACK, 3
Put a m. aboard a horse WAYNE, JOHN, 1
say to all the world "This was a m." SHAKESPEARE, WILLIAM, 318
She is clearly the best m. among them THATCHER, MARGARET, 5
Since M. with that inconstancy BEHN, APHRA, 4
Such a little m....a big depression HOOVER, HERBERT, 3
such a m. is from another planet SMITH, ANTHONY, 1
superior m. is distressed by his want of ability CONFUCIUS, 20
the honest m. who married GOLDSMITH, OLIVER, 29
The m. dies...silent in the face of tyranny SOYINKA, WOLE, 10
the m. of the Revolution ADAMS, SAMUEL, 1
The m. who makes no mistakes PHELPS, EDWARD JOHN, 1
The m. who once cursed his fate GARDNER, JOHN W., 3
The M. with the Golden Arm ALGREN, NELSON, 4
The noblest work of God? M. TWAIN, MARK, 14
There once was a m. who said, "God..." KNOX, RONALD, 4
The small m. understands what is profitable CONFUCIUS, 34
The true...study of m. is man CHARRON, PIERRE, 1
The worth of a m. TRESCKOW, HENNING VON, 1
thing...differentiates m. from animals is money STEIN, GERTRUDE, 10
This m....is a poor fish DENNIS, NIGEL, 2
Though m. may endure...like Sisyphus DJILAS, MILOVAN, 1
'Tis strange what a m. may do THACKERAY, WILLIAM MAKEPEACE, 5
To be a great m. and a saint BAUDELAIRE, CHARLES, 10
To preserve a m. alive TAYLOR, JEREMY, 1
Treat the m. who is sick JACOBI, ABRAHAM, 1
were m. /But constant SHAKESPEARE, WILLIAM, 657
What a m. wants is a mate PLATH, SYLVIA, 9
what a m. would like to be true BACON, FRANCIS (1561–1626), 84
What a piece of work is a m. SHAKESPEARE, WILLIAM, 171
What is it in m. that lies, murders, steals BÜCHNER, GEORG, 12
What is m. anyhow? what am I WHITMAN, WALT, 39
What's a m.'s first duty IBSEN, HENRIK, 15
When a m. is in love NIETZSCHE, FRIEDRICH WILHELM, 25
When is m. strong until he feels alone? BROWNING, ROBERT, 11
While m. is other than...beast DEWEY, JOHN, 4
you'll be a M. my son KIPLING, RUDYARD, 49

You may give a m. an office FRANKLIN, BENJAMIN, 21
manage dull m. of a servile house FINCH, ANNE, 2
two successful ways to m....employees IVERSON, KEN, 2
You don't m. people...You lead people HOPPER, GRACE MURRAY, 4
management best m....based on covenantal relationships DE PREE, MAX, 3
Good m. consists in showing average people ROCKEFELLER, JOHN D., 5
m....a chasm between ambition and resources HAMEL, GARY, 4
M. and union...serpent of the fables DRUCKER, PETER, 12
M. democracy is everybody agreeing ASHCROFT, JOHN, 3
M....efficiency in the ladder of success COVEY, STEPHEN R., 2
M. is doing things right DRUCKER, PETER, 14
M. is the generic organ DRUCKER, PETER, 2
m. must know...employees' working conditions SIEFF, MARCUS, 3
"Professional m." is the great invention MINTZBERG, HENRY, 1
The central problem in m. DEMING, W. EDWARDS, 3
the m. of change DRUCKER, PETER, 5
Traditional m. structures SMITH, RAYMOND W., 4
manager Every m. is a sales manager ASHCROFT, JOHN, 1
m. of the Cleveland Indians ROBINSON, FRANK, 1
m.'s ability to turn meetings...thinking environment KLINE, NANCY, 1
m.'s job...Define, Nurture, Allocate STEWART, THOMAS A., 6
m.'s job...thrive in a chaotic world ZELDIN, THEODORE, 4
No m. ever thinks he got a break ODOM, JIM, 1
no m. more lucid...than a poet GARCÍA MÁRQUEZ, GABRIEL, 6
Someone once defined the m. MINTZBERG, HENRY, 3
The extraordinary m. operates...spiritual resources BENNIS, WARREN, 7
managerial There is no science in m. work MINTZBERG, HENRY, 2
managers kinds of m....growing and the obsolete CROSBY, PHILIP B., 3
m. and workers in a lord-liege relationship HAMMER, MICHAEL, 3
M....eyes on the bottom line BENNIS, WARREN, 10
m. must learn to revere...ideas MCCORMACK, MARK, 2
M....too much time managing the present HAMEL, GARY, 5
M. who have no beliefs...are modern-day eunuchs DE PREE, MAX, 2
The first "m." assumed THORNELY, NICK, 1
Young m. in the 1960s and 1970s GOLZEN, GODFREY, 1
managing m. a business is managing its processes HAMMER, MICHAEL, 4
men capable of m. business efficiently KNIGHT, FRANK HYNEMAN, 5
M....getting paid for home runs STENGEL, CASEY, 2
M. intellectual assets STEWART, THOMAS A., 7
Manchester The shortest way out of M. is...gin BOLITHO, WILLIAM, 1
Mandela Mr M. has walked a long road MANDELA, NELSON, 1
Manderley I dreamt I went to M. again DU MAURIER, DAPHNE, 1
man-governed nothing worse than a m. world ASTOR, NANCY, 3
Manhattan I like to walk around M. STOUT, REX, 2
Stand up, tall masts of M. WHITMAN, WALT, 18
mania m. and the world laughs with you ASHER, RICHARD, 1
manipulation basic tool for the m. of reality DICK, PHILIP K., 4
mankind All m. love a lover EMERSON, RALPH WALDO, 14
difficult to love m. unless one has a...private income KINGSMILL, HUGH, 1
Ideal m. would abolish death LAWRENCE, D. H., 42
I dislike m. KEATS, JOHN (1795–1821), 46
If all m....were of one opinion MILL, JOHN STUART, 9
In the center stands /m. KUNZE, REINER, 1
know more of m....expect less JOHNSON, SAMUEL, 77
love all m., *except an American* JOHNSON, SAMUEL, 90
M. are always happy for having been happy SMITH, SYDNEY, 6
mass of m. is divided into two classes CERVANTES, MIGUEL DE, 1
M....begins by feeding at the breast MERCIER, LOUIS-SÉBASTIEN, 2
M. is a closed society SCHUMACHER, E. F., 7
M. is not a tribe of animals CHESTERTON, G. K., 12
M. is resilient HELLER, JOSEPH, 15
proper study of m. is books HUXLEY, ALDOUS, 18
We should expect the best and the worst from m. VAUVENARGUES, MARQUIS DE, 3
wished that m. were propagated like trees BROWNE, THOMAS, 1
man-like M. is it to fall into sin LOGAU, FRIEDRICH VON, 2
manly m., moral, regulated liberty BURKE, EDMUND, 41
manna Exalted m. HERBERT, GEORGE, 13
manner M. is all in all COWPER, WILLIAM, 15
The m. in which one endures ACHESON, DEAN, 5
manners don't like my m....don't like 'em myself BOGART, HUMPHREY, 8
M. maketh man PROVERBS, 321
M....the need of the plain WAUGH, EVELYN, 21
the m. of a Marquis GILBERT, W. S., 19
manpower We have limitless m....unlimited time CHIA, THYE POH, 1
manufacturing surest foundation of a m. concern CARNEGIE, ANDREW, 11
manuscripts M. don't burn BULGAKOV, MIKHAIL, 10
Mao I was one of Chairman M.'s children WU, HARRY, 3
M. is our supreme commander MOTTOS AND SLOGANS, 23
map Roll up that m. PITT THE YOUNGER, WILLIAM, 5
The world is like a m. of antipathies JIMÉNEZ, JUAN RAMÓN, 12
maples scarlet of the m. can shake me CARMAN, BLISS, 1
marble Not m., nor the gilded monuments /Of princes SHAKESPEARE, WILLIAM, 573
march m. into battle together with the men IBÁRRURI, DOLORES, 6
"M. on Rome"...a comfortable train ride MACK SMITH, DENIS, 1
March M. comes in like a lion PROVERBS, 326
M. winds and April showers PROVERBS, 327
marching Twelve men are m. BLOK, ALEKSANDR, 4
Marconi M.'s most cherished possession ANONYMOUS, 14
marijuana I experimented with m. CLINTON, BILL, 20
M. is...self-punishing O'ROURKE, P. J., 4
Marilyn M....every man's love affair with America MONROE, MARILYN, 2
M. Monroe committed suicide KENNEDY, ROBERT, 1
mariner It is an ancient M. COLERIDGE, SAMUEL TAYLOR, 35
marionette same m. you are with other directors ALTMAN, ROBERT, 1
mark the m....of the beast BIBLE, 469
market Each m. need entering the innovation cycle KLINE, STEPHEN, 1
m. came with the dawn of civilization GORBACHEV, MIKHAIL, 10
M. fundamentalism undermines the democratic...process SOROS, GEORGE, 5
m. that has gone to the moon ROACH, STEPHEN S., 2
The m. is not a panacea YELTSIN, BORIS, 2
We want to create a home m. BARNEVIK, PERCY, 2
Market Harborough Am in M. CHESTERTON, G. K., 49
marketing No great m. decisions...on quantitative data SCULLEY, JOHN, 7
markets M. are not created by God DRUCKER, PETER, 13
M. are superb at setting prices HAWKEN, PAUL, 3
M. can be adaptive and flexible MILLER, STEVEN E., 1

marvel To m. at nothing HORACE, 21
Marx had M. been Groucho instead of Karl MARX, GROUCHO, 1
M. here tells me Jews...pushy ROTH, PHILIP, 3
not even M. is more precious...than the truth MARX, KARL, 7
Marxian Socialism M. must always remain a portent KEYNES, JOHN MAYNARD, 16
Marxism M. and communism should serve the black people CÉSAIRE, AIMÉ, 5
M....integrated with Chinese conditions DENG XIAOPING, 1
M. is like a classical building MACMILLAN, HAROLD, 4
Marxist Ask anyone committed to M. analysis DIDION, JOAN, 9
I am not a M. MARX, KARL, 28
wasn't a M. all the time FOOT, MICHAEL, 3
Mary blustering windy weather of Queen M. ELIZABETH I, 3
Hail M., full of grace ANONYMOUS, 3
Mary, M., quite contrary CHILDREN'S VERSE, 54
M. had a little lamb HALE, SARAH JOSEPHA, 2
masculine Fighting is essentially a m. idea GINGOLD, HERMIONE, 1
It makes me feel m. HELLMAN, LILLIAN, 6
There is an absolute human type...m. BEAUVOIR, SIMONE DE, 16
There is no m. power or privilege PAGLIA, CAMILLE, 7
The usual m. disillusionment MITCHELL, MARGARET, 11
When you hear strong m. music like this IVES, CHARLES, 2
mask how to wear his m. PIRANDELLO, LUIGI, 5
No m. like open truth to cover lies CONGREVE, WILLIAM, 13
wearing a m. of morality in public CAO YU, 1
We wear the m. that grins and lies DUNBAR, PAUL LAURENCE, 4
masks to use the m. BOWIE, DAVID, 4
masochistic He suffered from severe m. attacks ADLER, ALFRED, 6
Mason and Dixon country south of M.'s line RANDOLPH, JOHN, 1
mass After two thousand years of m. HARDY, THOMAS, 32
masses Give me...your poor, /Your huddled m. LAZARUS, EMMA, 1
give me your tired, your poor, your huddled m. JACKSON, JESSE, 7
It is what the m. endure APTHEKER, HERBERT, 1
I will back the m. against the classes GLADSTONE, WILLIAM EWART, 5
m. will stand...the side of kingship BISMARCK, PRINCE OTTO VON, 7
mass production M. couldn't sell its goods CHANDLER, RAYMOND, 6
master A m. is dead WAGNER, RICHARD, 1
Betty from her m.'s bed had flown SWIFT, JONATHAN, 4
He must m. or be mastered LONDON, JACK, 10
I am M. of this college BEECHING, H. C., 1
In order to m. the unruly torrent ORTEGA Y GASSET, JOSÉ, 4
m. of every nook and cranny...Baltic OXENSTIERNA, AXEL, 2
The m. has gone to pick herbs JIA DAO, 1
the m. who had coupled with his slave BALDWIN, JAMES, 5
Thou are my m. and my author VIRGIL, 1
You must be m. and win, or serve and lose GOETHE, JOHANN WOLFGANG VON, 6
masterpiece tamper with a m. WILDE, OSCAR, 85
masterpieces I have no quarrel with m. COPLAND, AARON, 6
masters Assistant m....liked little boys WAUGH, EVELYN, 4
blind fetishism...puts..."the m." above the living, breathing artist GARLAND, HAMLIN, 1
future m. to learn their letters LOWE, ROBERT, 1
no man can serve two m. BIBLE, 383
old m....better price than old mistresses BEAVERBROOK, MAX AITKEN, LORD, 7
people are the m. BURKE, EDMUND, 29
master tools The M. LORDE, AUDRE, 2
masturbating man m....snuff film...not actually raping ENGLISH, DEIRDRE, 1
masturbation M. is the thinking man's television HAMPTON, CHRISTOPHER, 3
m....I thought I invented it POLANSKI, ROMAN, 1
M.: the primary sexual activity of mankind SZASZ, THOMAS, 14
match first throws...m. into the powder keg MOLTKE, HELMUTH JOHANNES VON, 4
matches with our m. and our necklaces, we shall liberate this country MANDELA, WINNIE, 2
material put...most m. in the postscript BACON, FRANCIS (1561–1626), 21
material comforts Increase of m....conduce to moral growth GANDHI, MAHATMA, 10
materialistic most m. age...history of the world ANDERSON, SHERWOOD, 1
materials m. of city planning LE CORBUSIER, 7
maternity M....an unsocial experience MALLET, DAVID, 2
mathematical entire world...of m. truths HERMITE, CHARLES, 1
good m. joke is better LITTLEWOOD, JOHN, 1
m. theory of ignorance KLINE, MORRIS, 3
reduc'd to a M. Reasoning ARBUTHNOT, JOHN, 2
mathematician A m. is great or...nothing ADLER, ALFRED, 8
life of a m. is short ADLER, ALFRED, 9
m....highest rung...human thought ELLIS, HAVELOCK, 5
union of the m. with the poet JAMES, WILLIAM, 3
mathematicians better...if there were no m. BERNOULLI, DANIEL, 1
m. do not know mathematics OPPENHEIMER, J. ROBERT, 2
M. go mad CHESTERTON, G. K., 27
m. have invaded...relativity EINSTEIN, ALBERT, 42
m. have to shoot somebody NICELY, THOMAS R., 1
mathematics all M. is Symbolic Logic RUSSELL, BERTRAND, 28
All science requires m. BACON, ROGER, 3
As...laws of m. refer to reality EINSTEIN, ALBERT, 54
How are you at M. MILLIGAN, SPIKE, 10
I like m. because it is *not* human SPINOZA, BARUCH, 1
In m. you don't understand VON NEUMANN, JOHN, 1
Let no one ignorant of m. enter PLATO, 30
m....a creative art HARDY, GODFREY HAROLD, 3
M....art of giving the same name POINCARÉ, JULES HENRI, 6
m....best remedy against...lusts MANN, THOMAS, 11
m....can say as little as the physicist RUSSELL, BERTRAND, 51
m....doesn't make life any sweeter KELLER, HELEN, 8
M....draws necessary conclusions PEIRCE, BENJAMIN, 1
m., may it never be of...use SMITH, HENRY JOHN STEPHEN, 1
m....most inhuman of...activities ELLIS, HAVELOCK, 9
M....never know what we are talking about RUSSELL, BERTRAND, 30
M....no hypocrisy and no vagueness STENDHAL, 3
M....possesses not only truth, but supreme beauty RUSSELL, BERTRAND, 25
M....science of what is clear JACOBI, KARL GUSTAV JAKOB, 2
M....sphere of complete abstraction WHITEHEAD, A. N., 13
no...place...for ugly m. HARDY, GODFREY HAROLD, 2
The longer m. lives BELL, ERIC TEMPLE, 1
things...cannot be made known without...m. BACON, ROGER, 4
maths m....to carry out science is pretty straightforward DE BONO, EDWARD, 6

matrimonial cares for m. cooings BYRON, LORD, 56
matrimonie m....dignified and commodious sacrament ELIOT, T. S., 18
matrimony critical period in m. is breakfast-time HERBERT, A. P., 12
in m....begin with a little aversion SHERIDAN, RICHARD BRINSLEY, 9
m....a highly overrated performance DUNCAN, ISADORA, 11
m....a legalized way of committing assault EMECHETA, BUCHI, 3
m. at its lowest STEVENSON, ROBERT LOUIS, 34
matter Does it...m. whose story this is BUNIN, IVAN, 1
M....a convenient formula RUSSELL, BERTRAND, 7
Matthew M., Mark, Luke, and John FOLK VERSE, 2
mature he acts like a man of m. years CHEN DUXIU, 3
I'm too m. to be angry JACKSON, JESSE, 15
maturity m. is only a short break in adolescence FEIFFER, JULES, 1
mausoleums designing m. for his enemies LINKLATER, ERIC, 1
maverick m. who enjoys...creating a little anarchy WALTON, SAM, 2
maxim A new m. is often a brilliant error MALESHERBES, CHRÉTIEN DE, 1
Nothing is so useless as a general m. MACAULAY, THOMAS BABINGTON, 12
We have a m....House of Commons COKE, EDWARD, 1
Maxim gun got /The M., and they have not BELLOC, HILAIRE, 16
maximum M. meaning—minimum means GAMES, ABRAM, 1
May as fresh as is the month of M. CHAUCER, GEOFFREY, 10
In the merry month of M. BARNFIELD, RICHARD, 5
More matter for a M. morning SHAKESPEARE, WILLIAM, 707
Mayakovsky M. is deafeningly novel MAYAKOVSKY, VLADIMIR, 1
maybe I'll give you a definite m. GOLDWYN, SAMUEL, 7
M.D.s Weighed down by B.A.s and M. LIMERICKS, 2
me I gotta be m. DAVIS, SAMMY, JR., 3
on m. PARKER, DOROTHY, 42
used to be a m. behind the mask SELLERS, PETER, 3
meadow Often I am permitted to return to a m. DUNCAN, ROBERT, 3
meal A m. without flesh PROVERBS, 65
the perfect m. is the short meal DE WOLFE, ELSIE, 1
mean Down these m. streets CHANDLER, RAYMOND, 10
it means just what I choose it to m. CARROLL, LEWIS, 44
"Then you should say what you m.," the March Hare went on CARROLL, LEWIS, 13
whatever that may m. CHARLES, PRINCE, 10
meaning answer to...the m. of our life TILLICH, PAUL, 2
as m. does with words MCCAIG, NORMAN, 5
displace the conventional m....image usually carries KRUGER, BARBARA, 1
M. implies that something is happening JOHNS, JASPER, 1
The least of things with a m. JUNG, CARL GUSTAV, 20
to "give a m." to the world CARTIER-BRESSON, HENRI, 2
What's the...m. of this long harangue SCHILLER, FRIEDRICH VON, 16
meannesses some m....too mean even for man THACKERAY, WILLIAM MAKEPEACE, 1
means Increased m. and increased leisure DISRAELI, BENJAMIN, 46
We are living beyond our m. MEAD, MARGARET, 12
meant m. well, tried a little, failed much STEVENSON, ROBERT LOUIS, 4
what comes out isn't what I m. DOYLE, RODDY, 4
measle More than One M. at a time FIELD, EUGENE, 3
measure Man is the m. of all things PROTAGORAS, 3
M. still for Measure SHAKESPEARE, WILLIAM, 437
M. what is measurable GALILEO, 10
Never m. the height of a mountain HAMMARSKJÖLD, DAG, 6
The ultimate m. of a man KING, MARTIN LUTHER, JR., 16
measured you're m. not by how much you undertake TRUMP, DONALD, 3
meat man loves the m. in his youth SHAKESPEARE, WILLIAM, 450
My m. is to do the will of him that sent me BIBLE, 275
One man's m. PROVERBS, 356
meats m. for the belly BIBLE, 154
mechanics M....paradise of the mathematical sciences LEONARDO DA VINCI, 8
mechanisms ancient...m. persisting in modern man DUBOS, RENÉ, 3
meddling He was m. too much in my private life WILLIAMS, TENNESSEE, 19
media M....has come to mean bad journalism GREENE, GRAHAM, 15
purpose of the m....sell us shit HOFFMAN, ABBIE, 3
The m....a convention of spiritualists STOPPARD, TOM, 6
medical Alarmed...by every fashionable m. terror EDGEWORTH, MARIA, 3
A m. revolution has extended the life of our elder citizens KENNEDY, JOHN FITZGERALD, 17
m. attention—a dog licked me SIMON, NEIL, 4
the cost of m. care KENNEDY, JOHN FITZGERALD, 4
the dead hand of m. tradition HOLMES, OLIVER WENDELL, 7
two objects of m. education MAYO, CHARLES HORACE, 3
medical practice essential unit of m....advice SPENCE, JAMES CALVERT, 1
M....must be inspired MAIMONIDES, 1
medical profession m. is reaching near-paralysis JOHNSON, LUKE, 1
medical student teaching the m....keep him awake JACKSON, CHEVALIER, 1
medical students I taught m. in the wards OSLER, WILLIAM, 5
medicine Advances in m. and agriculture SAGAN, CARL, 11
Among the arts, m....hold the highest place BUCKLE, HENRY THOMAS, 1
art of m. consists of VOLTAIRE, 48
basis of m. is sympathy PAYNE, FRANK, 1
By m. life may be prolonged SHAKESPEARE, WILLIAM, 137
educate the masses not to take m. OSLER, WILLIAM, 9
history of m....history of the people MUMFORD, JAMES GREGORY, 3
I wasn't driven into m. by a social conscience MILLER, JONATHAN, 3
M. absorbs the physician's whole being GOETHE, JOHANN WOLFGANG VON, 38
M....a noble profession ROLLESTON, HUMPHREY, 2
M....an occupation for slaves RUSH, BENJAMIN, 1
m....a question of time OVID, 11
m. becomes a heroic art EMERSON, RALPH WALDO, 64
M....deals with the very processes of life PARACELSUS, 1
M. for the dead is too late QUINTILIAN, 3
M. is a conjectural art CORVISART DES MARETS, JEAN NICOLAS, 1
M. is an art PLATO, 4
m....is as sensitive to outside influences HOLMES, OLIVER WENDELL, 10
M. is for the patient MERCK, GEORGE, 1
M. is not a lucrative profession LETTSOM, JOHN COAKLEY, 1
m....learned only from its practice SYDENHAM, THOMAS, 3
M. makes sick patients LUTHER, MARTIN, 17
m. midway between Allopathy and Christian Science BIERCE, AMBROSE, 26
M. sometimes snatches away health OVID, 13
M....strange mixture of speculation and action LATHAM, PETER MERE, 2
m....the knowledge of the...desires of the body PLATO, 10
M....the only profession that labours incessantly BRYCE, JAMES, 1

M....the show is stripped of the human drama FISCHER, MARTIN H., 15
M., to produce health, has to examine disease PLUTARCH, 21
M....tune this curious harp of man's body BACON, FRANCIS (1561–1626), 96
M. would be the ideal profession ADAMS, SAMUEL HOPKINS, 1
never read a patent m. advertisement JEROME, JEROME K., 8
No families take so little m. HOLMES, OLIVER WENDELL, 5
not the truths most commonly met with in m. LATHAM, PETER MERE, 3
sure foundations of m. JEFFERSON, THOMAS, 12
technology of m. has outrun its sociology SIGERIST, HENRY E., 8
The aim of m. is...not to make men virtuous MENCKEN, H. L., 34
The aim of m. is to prevent disease MAYO, WILLIAM JAMES, 5
The art of m. is my discovery OVID, 7
the experimental part of m. BACON, FRANCIS (1561–1626), 85
The foundation of the study of M. GULL, WILLIAM WITHEY, 2
The great glory of modern m. HENDRICK, BURTON J., 2
The...popular hunting for "Fathers" of every branch of m. SIGERIST, HENRY E., 1
The practice of m. is a thinker's art FISCHER, MARTIN H., 26
This is m., not poison that I bring LESSING, GOTTHOLD EPHRAIM, 4
Truth in m. is an unattainable goal AL-RAZI, 1
unnecessary...in m. to be too clever HUTCHISON, ROBERT, 1
medicines M. are nothing in themselves HEROPHILUS, 1
m. when well used restore health to the sick LEONARDO DA VINCI, 10
the best m. for an afflicted mind LESLIE, ELIZA, 1
medics at night the m. gave you pills HERR, MICHAEL, 4
medieval M. education was supposed to fit people to die LEACOCK, STEPHEN, 22
you m. dickweed REEVES, KEANU, 1
mediocre All I'm after is...a m. brain TURING, ALAN, 1
m. are always at their best GIRAUDOUX, JEAN, 6
Some men are born m. HELLER, JOSEPH, 7
The most m. of males BEAUVOIR, SIMONE DE, 15
Women want m. men MEAD, MARGARET, 10
mediocrity It isn't evil...ruining the earth, but m. ROREM, NED, 1
m....always at its best BEERBOHM, MAX, 22
supreme expression of the m....Stalin TROTSKY, LEON, 8
meditation M. is not a means to an end KRISHNAMURTI, JIDDU, 3
Mediterranean All my wife has ever taken from the M. SHAFFER, PETER, 2
medium The m. is the message MCLUHAN, MARSHALL, 11
The m. is too powerful and important PUTTNAM, DAVID, 1
medley a m. of your hit LEVANT, OSCAR, 4
meek I am m. and gentle with these butchers SHAKESPEARE, WILLIAM, 307
m. are thirsting for blood ORTON, JOE, 4
The m. do not inherit the earth LASKI, HAROLD, 1
The m.... not the mineral rights GETTY, J. PAUL, 11
meet Let's m. BEAUMONT & FLETCHER, 8
M. on the stairs PROVERBS, 330
meeting A m. is an arrangement VOINOVICH, VLADIMIR, 6
a m....to discuss work-life balance PLATT, LEWIS, 1
as if I was a public m. GLADSTONE, WILLIAM EWART, 3
meetings m. should be long and leisurely TOWNSEND, ROBERT, 13
megalomaniac m. differs from the narcissist RUSSELL, BERTRAND, 45
megaphone M. diplomacy HOWE, GEOFFREY, 1
melancholia little about m. that he didn't know TENNYSON, ALFRED, 1
M....an affection of the brain MONTANUS, 1
melancholic the fancy of a m. person SCOT, REGINALD, 2
melancholy characteristic m. music of my race ELLINGTON, DUKE, 12
Full of spirit's m. /And eternity's despair BROWNING, ELIZABETH BARRETT, 2
I can suck m. out of a song SHAKESPEARE, WILLIAM, 103
M. is a humour, boystrous & thycke BARTHOLOMAEUS ANGLICUS, 1
m....merely the work of the devil LUTHER, MARTIN, 8
Naught so sweet as M. BURTON, ROBERT, 25
The m. days are come BRYANT, WILLIAM CULLEN, 5
melodies And as I sang these lovely m. ROBESON, PAUL, 3
Heard m. are sweet, but those unheard /Are sweeter KEATS, JOHN (1795–1821), 54
melody The heart of the m. CASALS, PABLO, 1
melting pot not a m. but a beautiful mosaic CARTER, JIMMY, 5
that m. stuff...we haven't melted JACKSON, JESSE, 11
Melville M....a creator of myths MELVILLE, HERMAN, 1
M.'s...books...obvious and obscure MELVILLE, HERMAN, 2
memoirs These are not m. about myself SHOSTAKOVICH, DMITRI, 2
write one's m....speak ill of everybody PÉTAIN, HENRI PHILIPPE, 2
memorandum m. is written...to protect the writer ACHESON, DEAN, 3
memorial m. longer lasting than bronze HORACE, 48
m. to all the victims of...terror AKHMATOVA, ANNA, 1
Your m. will be...the children ALEXANDER THE GREAT, 2
memories M. are like mulligatawny soup WODEHOUSE, P. G., 5
M. are like stones BETTI, UGO, 1
more m. than if I were a thousand BAUDELAIRE, CHARLES, 16
The nice thing about having m. TREVOR, WILLIAM, 2
memory a grand m. for forgetting STEVENSON, ROBERT LOUIS, 9
dark m....noise of /Playing children AMICHAI, YEHUDA, 4
Everyone complains of his m. LA ROCHEFOUCAULD, FRANÇOIS, 16
flesh out the m. of the poet FORCHÉ, CAROLYN, 4
good m. is needed after one has lied CORNEILLE, PIERRE, 10
I got a long m. CLIFTON, LUCILLE, 2
"I have done that," says my m. NIETZSCHE, FRIEDRICH WILHELM, 2
It has m.'s ear MOORE, MARIANNE, 9
M. believes before knowing remembers FAULKNER, WILLIAM, 7
m. images...stored in different parts of the brain IGNATIEFF, MICHAEL, 2
M. is not an act of will AUSTER, PAUL, 4
m....more loyal than my best friends DAI WANGSHU, 1
M....often the attribute of stupidity CHATEAUBRIAND, RENÉ, 5
M....the thread of personal identity HOFSTADTER, RICHARD, 3
rather be a brilliant m. EAMES, EMMA, 1
Sweet M.! wafted by thy gentle gale ROGERS, SAMUEL, 8
Thanks for the M. ROBIN, LEO, 1
The chain of m. is resurrection OLSON, CHARLES, 3
What a strange thing is m., and hope GRANDMA MOSES, 2
worst happenings...acquire a sweetness in the m. ARMAH, AYI KWEI, 3
men All m. are born equal MANCROFT, STORMONT SAMUEL, 2
all m., black and brown and white, are brothers DU BOIS, W. E. B., 3
all m....just seven years old WATERS, JOHN, 3
all m. naturally were born free MILTON, JOHN, 128
always find m. subject to three codes DIDEROT, DENIS, 7
becoming the m. we wanted to marry STEINEM, GLORIA, 2
Bloody m. are like bloody buses COPE, WENDY, 5
both m. and women are wretched NEEL, ALICE, 1

By this shall all m. know that ye are my disciples BIBLE, 289
depict m. as they ought to be EURIPIDES, 1
For m. may come TENNYSON, ALFRED, 35
Great m. can't be ruled RAND, AYN, 5
If m. had to have babies DIANA, PRINCESS, 4
If m. knew...women pass the time HENRY, O., 2
I grew up thinking m. were...wonderful GOLDEN, MARITA, 3
It is m. who face the biggest problems FORD, ANNA, 2
It's not the m. in my life that count WEST, MAE, 7
It was...year of Trouble for M. HOLLINGHURST, ALAN, 1
M. and women...ranked with horses DOUGLASS, FREDERICK, 19
many m., many women, and many children JOHNSON, SAMUEL, 168
M. are boring to women NICHOLSON, JACK, 1
M. are but gilded loam or painted clay SHAKESPEARE, WILLIAM, 508
M. are good in one way ARISTOTLE, 13
M. are like plants CRÈVECOEUR, JEAN DE, 2
M. are never so good or so bad as their opinions MACKINTOSH, JAMES, 1
M. are we, and must grieve WORDSWORTH, WILLIAM, 63
M. come of age at sixty STEPHENS, JAMES, 1
M....deceive themselves in big things MACHIAVELLI, NICCOLÒ, 9
m. determine, the gods doo dispose GREENE, ROBERT, 2
m. devote the greater part of their lives LA BRUYÈRE, JEAN DE, 12
M. do kill women SACKVILLE-WEST, VITA, 1
M. don't understand anything about women GASSMAN, VITTORIO, 1
M. fear death as if unquestionably the greatest evil MITFORD, WILLIAM, 1
M. have structured society...woman feel guilty WEST, MAE, 16
m. in the back rooms BEAVERBROOK, MAX AITKEN, LORD, 2
m. in their torment must be mute GOETHE, JOHANN WOLFGANG VON, 27
m....judge by appearances GLASGOW, ELLEN, 1
M. know they are sexual exiles PAGLIA, CAMILLE, 15
M. know...women are an overmatch for them BOSWELL, JAMES, 1
m. lead lives of quiet desperation THOREAU, HENRY DAVID, 37
m., like satyrs grazing on the lawns MARLOWE, CHRISTOPHER, 16
m. look like frogs to me WALKER, ALICE, 28
M....more careful of the breed of their...dogs than of their children PENN, WILLIAM, 9
M. of few words are the best men SHAKESPEARE, WILLIAM, 269
Most m. admire /Virtue MILTON, JOHN, 102
Most m. in this world are colored DU BOIS, W. E. B., 10
m. ought not to investigate things from words DIOGENES LÄERTIUS, 4
M. peak at age nineteen KEILLOR, GARRISON, 11
M. shout as they die DELILLO, DON, 8
m. succeeded...in swindling themselves GALBRAITH, J. K., 20
M....the protectors and maintainers of women KORAN, 12
m. think all...mortal, but themselves YOUNG, EDWARD, 5
m. today make...sport out of shopping KALENDARIAN, TOM, 1
m. who remain at home...when married MOSSELL, MRS. N. F., 1
m. who think as men of action and act as men of thought NKRUMAH, KWAME, 1
M. will always be mad VOLTAIRE, 6
M. will say (and accept) anything JAMES, C. L. R., 9
M. with secrets DELILLO, DON, 1
m. with the muckrakes are often indispensable ROOSEVELT, THEODORE, 18
Nature has given m. proud and high spirits BOCCACCIO, GIOVANNI, 1
not so many m. of large fortune AUSTEN, JANE, 20
Not that which m. do worthily BEECHER, HENRY WARD, 3
So many m., so many opinions TERENCE, 3
The many m., so beautiful COLERIDGE, SAMUEL TAYLOR, 44
The more I see of m., the more I admire dogs SÉVIGNÉ, MADAME DE, 4
The most positive m. are the most credulous POPE, ALEXANDER, 55
The m. that women marry LONGFELLOW, HENRY WADSWORTH, 6
the m. who *borrow*, and *the men who lend* LAMB, CHARLES, 17
the race of m. is almost extinct in Europe LAWRENCE, D. H., 40
There was no question that they were truly m. MARSHALL, PAULE, 2
the tongues of m. and of angels BIBLE, 161
think m. and women...different animals DORS, DIANA, 1
those m. have their price WALPOLE, SIR ROBERT, 3
Those m. of faction QU YUAN, 3
Twenty-eight young m. bathe by the shore WHITMAN, WALT, 37
Unfortunately, most m. are deaf MCMILLAN, TERRY, 10
until m. are prepared to kill each other SHAW, GEORGE BERNARD, 39
Why don't the m. propose BAYLY, THOMAS HAYNES, 7
wise m. don't say "I shall live to do that" MARTIAL, 1
with m. as it is with plants CRÈVECOEUR, JEAN DE, 3

menstrual period history of a missed m. MORRISON, RUTHERFORD, 2

menstruation m. would become...masculine event STEINEM, GLORIA, 1

mental A m. stain can neither be blotted out CICERO, 5
Every m. act is conscious BRENTANO, FRANZ, 1
every "m." symptom...veiled cry of anguish SZASZ, THOMAS, 18
how the m. apparatus is constructed FREUD, SIGMUND, 56
M. disease...no different to bodily disease VINCENT DE PAUL, SAINT, 1
When a man lacks m. balance in pneumonia FISCHER, MARTIN H., 22

mental illness consider m. an excusing condition SZASZ, THOMAS, 2

mental reflection M....more interesting than T.V. PIRSIG, ROBERT T., 7

mention The m. of Greece MONROE, JAMES, 1

mentoring M. requires special skills PRAHALAD, C. K., 1

Mercedes-Benz Lord...buy me a M. JOPLIN, JANIS, 2

merchant name of...m. never degrades the gentleman LILLO, GEORGE, 1
the m. and monied man LOCKE, JOHN, 11

mercy For M. has a human heart BLAKE, WILLIAM, 33
Increase and multiply upon us thy m. BOOK OF COMMON PRAYER, 7
May the Lord have m. on your soul CHAPLIN, CHARLIE, 4
m. shown /To every failing but their own BYRON, LORD, 98
m. unto you...be multiplied BIBLE, 310
quality of m. is not strain'd SHAKESPEARE, WILLIAM, 617
sentiments of m....a woman's heart MEDICI, CATHERINE DE', 1
Whereto serves m. /But to confront the visage of offence SHAKESPEARE, WILLIAM, 196

merit m. Heaven by making earth a Hell BYRON, LORD, 21
m. of this gentleman is certainly great WASHINGTON, GEORGE, 7
M. will win...promised by baseball GIAMATTI, A. BARTLETT, 1
What is m. PALMERSTON, LORD, 7

meritocracies All m. are limited MOHAMAD, MAHATHIR BIN, 2

meritocracy The Rise of the M. YOUNG, MICHAEL, 1

Mermaid things have we seen /Done at the M. BEAUMONT, FRANCIS, 1

merrily M. We Roll Along KAUFMAN, GEORGE S., 1

merry m. click of the two-base lick NEWSPAPERS, 22
never m. when I hear sweet music SHAKESPEARE, WILLIAM, 620

merry-go-round where to put us on the m. GREGORY, DICK, 4

merry monarch A m. CHARLES II, 4

Merry Widow M. black lace bras MADONNA, 1

Mersey quality of M. is not strained NEWSPAPERS, 23

mesa The m. plain had an appearance of...incompleteness CATHER, WILLA, 2
mesas From the...sand rose great rock m. CATHER, WILLA, 1
message take a m. to Albert DISRAELI, BENJAMIN, 54
Messiah He was the M. of the new age WILSON, WOODROW, 3
M. will come...much less probable FREUD, SIGMUND, 41
Messianism M. is Judaism's...original idea BUBER, MARTIN, 8
messing about m. in boats GRAHAME, KENNETH, 3
met I m. a man who wasn't there MEARNS, HUGHES, 1
We have m. too late YEATS, W. B., 3
metaphor hunt down a tired m. BYRON, LORD, 77
m. is...the most fertile power ORTEGA Y GASSET, JOSÉ, 19
Science is all m. LEARY, TIMOTHY, 1
Through m. to reconcile WILLIAMS, WILLIAM CARLOS, 16
metaphysical the world...m. brothel for emotions KOESTLER, ARTHUR, 2
metaphysics M....an attempt to prove the incredible MENCKEN, H. L., 15
M....bad reasons for what we believe BRADLEY, F. H., 6
M....ends by confirming...despair KRUTCH, JOSEPH WOOD, 5
m....speaks the language of Plato HEIDEGGER, MARTIN, 4
The unrest which keeps...m. going JAMES, WILLIAM, 8
metaquizzical The great M. poet WORDSWORTH, WILLIAM, 2
method Napoleon had the best m.. He dissolved all representative institutions NAPOLEON I, 9
You know my m. DOYLE, ARTHUR CONAN, 8
method-acting term m. is so much nonsense STRASBERG, SUSAN, 1
methods By different m. different men excel CHURCHILL, CHARLES, 2
Methuselah all the days of M. BIBLE, 115
metre without...understanding what m. is TENNYSON, ALFRED, 3
metric M. derives from the dance DAVENPORT, GUY, 4
Metro M.'s going to keep me for life LAHR, BERT, 3
metropolis steam-heated, air-conditioned m. PARMENTER, ROSS, 1
the m. of the empire COBBETT, WILLIAM, 5
Mexico Poor M....so near to the United States DÍAZ, PORFIRIO, 1
Mezzrow M....by far the greatest jazz clarinettist MEZZROW, MEZZ, 1
mice Three blind m., see how they run CHILDREN'S VERSE, 10
Michelangelo If M. had been straight TYLER, ROBIN, 1
Michigan M. is...like an oven mitt BRYSON, BILL, 15
Mickey Mouse I love M. more than any woman DISNEY, WALT, 4
microbe The M. is so very small BELLOC, HILAIRE, 22
microbes There are more m. *per person* BENNETT, ALAN, 7
microscope It is only in the m. that our life looks so big SCHOPENHAUER, ARTHUR, 11
middle people who stay in the m. of the road BEVAN, ANEURIN, 7
middle age m....all you exercise is caution PROVERBS, MODERN, 33
M....every new person...reminds you of someone NASH, OGDEN, 26
m. is the best time INGE, WILLIAM RALPH, 8
M. is when your age starts to show HOPE, BOB, 4
M. snuffs out more talent HUGHES, RICHARD, 2
M....youth without its levity DEFOE, DANIEL, 16
One of the pleasures of m. POUND, EZRA, 5
the dead center of m. ADAMS, FRANKLIN P., 2
Middle Ages In the M. they would have burned me FREUD, SIGMUND, 22
middle class the ease...move into the m. THATCHER, MARGARET, 27
middle-class the healthy type that was essentially m. FITZGERALD, F. SCOTT, 19
Middle East complex problems that face the M. WAITE, TERRY, 3
not possible to create peace...M. BEVAN, ANEURIN, 4
Our region is not the M. YEHOSHUA, A. B., 2
middle income M....if you steal, you can pay the rent CAMBRIDGE, GODFREY, 1
Middlemarch *M*....for grown up people WOOLF, VIRGINIA, 16
middle years In a man's m. there is scarcely a part of the body WHITE, E. B., 11
midnight It came upon the m. clear SEARS, E. H., 1
M. brought on the dusky hour MILTON, JOHN, 68
Once upon a m. dreary POE, EDGAR ALLAN, 7
mid-point The m. being passed O'DONOGHUE, BERNARD, 1
midst In the m. of life we are in death BOOK OF COMMON PRAYER, 2
mid-stream best not to swap horses in m. LINCOLN, ABRAHAM, 33
midsummer this is very m. madness SHAKESPEARE, WILLIAM, 709
midway M. along the path DANTE ALIGHIERI, 2
midwife Like a m....my living...new advertising campaigns OGILVY, DAVID, 2
mid-winter In the bleak m. ROSSETTI, CHRISTINA, 5
might We m. have been LANDON, LETITIA ELIZABETH, 3
mighty a m. man...the humblest of creatures AL-MUFID, ABU ABDULLAH MUHAMMAD AL-HARITHI AL-BAGHDADI, 4
m. things from small beginnings DRYDEN, JOHN, 5
migrating like two m. birds, male and female CHEKHOV, ANTON, 5
Mike Tyson see M. a free man again JORDAN, JUNE, 5
militarism M....is one of the chief bulwarks of capitalism KELLER, HELEN, 7
military The m. knows what to choose KALASHNIKOV, MIKHAIL, 1
When the m. man approaches SHAW, GEORGE BERNARD, 119
your m. genius...has inspired my sword PETER THE GREAT, 3
militia A well-regulated m....security of a free state CONSTITUTION OF THE UNITED STATES, 2
milk between the m. and the yoghurt MORTIMER, JOHN, 2
the hills shall flow with m. BIBLE, 265
too full o' th' m. of human kindness SHAKESPEARE, WILLIAM, 388
Mill M. /By a mighty effort of will MILL, JOHN STUART, 1
Miller M. is...a non-stop talker MILLER, HENRY, 1
million man who has a m. dollars ASTOR, JOHN JACOB, 1
Son, here's a m. dollars NIVEN, LARRY, 1
We are living a m. lives MILLER, HENRY, 23
millionaire "He must be a m." GILBERT, FRED, 1
I am a m.. That is my religion SHAW, GEORGE BERNARD, 35
Who Wants to Be a M. PORTER, COLE, 20
millions M. long for immortality ERTZ, SUSAN, 1
mills m. of God grind slowly LOGAU, FRIEDRICH VON, 3
Milton M. almost requires a solemn service MILTON, JOHN, 5
M., Madam, was a genius MILTON, JOHN, 4
M.'s Devil...far superior to his God MILTON, JOHN, 6
M. the prince of poets BYRON, LORD, 62
M.! thou shouldst be living at this hour MILTON, JOHN, 7
mind a m. of winter STEVENS, WALLACE, 7
a m. to kill HOBBES, THOMAS, 18
an unseemly exposure of the m. HAZLITT, WILLIAM, 14
a prodigious quantity of m. TWAIN, MARK, 42
a sound m. in a sound body JUVENAL, 17
A sound m. in a sound body LOCKE, JOHN, 10

clap your padlock—on her m. PRIOR, MATTHEW, 1
clear your *m.* of cant JOHNSON, SAMUEL, 104
force of m. is only as great HEGEL, G. W. F., 16
his m. is in perfect tranquillity VOLTAIRE, 2
His m. moves upon silence YEATS, W. B., 12
His m. was like a soup dish BRYAN, WILLIAM JENNINGS, 2
human m....created celestial and terrestrial physics COMTE, AUGUSTE, 3
human m. *has* to ask...why am I LAING, R. D., 15
human m. invents its Puss-in-Boots MALRAUX, ANDRÉ, 1
human m. treats a new idea MEDAWAR, PETER, 4
I call the...m. thinking substance ARNAULD, ANTOINE, 1
I don't m. being different BETHUNE, MARY MCLEOD, 4
if anything...the matter with your m. HORACE, 17
inability of the human m. to correlate LOVECRAFT, H. P., 1
I took my m. a walk MCCAIG, NORMAN, 4
it's all in the m. WOLFE, THOMAS, 3
m....an erogenous zone WELCH, RAQUEL, 1
m. cannot be...something completely rigid HEGEL, G. W. F., 14
Measure your m.'s height by the shade it casts BROWNING, ROBERT, 65
m. grows sicker than the body OVID, 14
m. has added nothing to human nature STEVENS, WALLACE, 28
m. has mountains HOPKINS, GERARD MANLEY, 4
M. is ever the ruler of the universe PLATO, 8
m. is utterly indivisible DESCARTES, RENÉ, 13
m....not one that shuns death HEGEL, G. W. F., 17
m., once expanded to...larger ideas HOLMES, OLIVER WENDELL, 33
M....process of becoming an other HEGEL, G. W. F., 12
m. that makes the body rich SHAKESPEARE, WILLIAM, 639
M....the great lever of all things WEBSTER, DANIEL, 2
m. thinks, not with data, but...ideas ROSZAK, THEODORE, 5
my m. is clouded with a doubt TENNYSON, ALFRED, 23
My m. is not a bed AGATE, JAMES, 2
M. your own business PROVERBS, 331
natural tendency of...m. is to dichotomise STEVENS, ANTHONY, 4
never to ransack any m. but his own REYNOLDS, SIR JOSHUA, 4
No m. is thoroughly well organized COLERIDGE, SAMUEL TAYLOR, 56
not enough to have a good m. DESCARTES, RENÉ, 5
not to have a m. is very wasteful QUAYLE, DAN, 2
open m., too much...likely to fall BARNEY, NATALIE CLIFFORD, 1
out of my m., it's all right BELLOW, SAUL, 6
sick m. cannot endure any harshness OVID, 4
someone whose m. watches itself CAMUS, ALBERT, 1
suppose the M....void of all Characters LOCKE, JOHN, 1
that m. free which...guards its intellectual rights CHANNING, WILLIAM ELLERY, 1
The conscious m. may be compared to a fountain FREUD, SIGMUND, 52
the creations of our m. shall be a blessing EINSTEIN, ALBERT, 7
The highest function of *m.* LAWRENCE, D. H., 22
The human m. is finite ARGYRIS, CHRIS, 1
the man...chang'd his m. POPE, ALEXANDER, 42
The m. /...as though blind MOORE, MARIANNE, 8
The m. cannot picture...thing without form ZHUANGZI, 1
The m. has great influence over the body MOLIÈRE, 11
The M. is an Enchanting Thing MOORE, MARIANNE, 2
The m. is an iceberg FREUD, SIGMUND, 53
The m. is its own place MILTON, JOHN, 30
The m. like a sick body can be healed LUCRETIUS, 6
The m. longs for certainty BARNES, JULIAN, 3
the m....makes the man OVID, 8
The m. of man is less perturbed MAMET, DAVID, 10
The tendency of the casual m. LIPPMANN, WALTER, 4
To a m. of sufficient intellectual power RUSSELL, BERTRAND, 17
To know the *m.* of a woman LAWRENCE, D. H., 8
Whatsoever the M. perceives...I call *Idea* LOCKE, JOHN, 3

minds greatest m. are capable of...greatest vices DESCARTES, RENÉ, 7
Great m. think alike PROVERBS, 240
Little m. are interested in the extraordinary HUBBARD, ELBERT, 1
m. carry an immense horizon with them JAMES, WILLIAM, 26
M. like beds always made up WILLIAMS, WILLIAM CARLOS, 8
M. like bodies, will often fall DICKENS, CHARLES, 11
m. need relaxation MOLIÈRE, 26
m. remain open...for the truth...to enter KENNY, ELIZABETH, 2
Our m. are lazier than our bodies LA ROCHEFOUCAULD, FRANÇOIS, 30

mine Thou art m., I am thine FOLK VERSE, 46

miner In a cavern...Dwelt a m., Forty-niner MONTROSE, PERCY, 2

miners m. sweat their guts out ORWELL, GEORGE, 34

Minerva owl of M. spreads its wings HEGEL, G. W. F., 26

mines Lord Stafford m. for coal and salt HALLECK, FITZ-GREENE, 1

mining M....a search-and-destroy mission UDALL, STEWART L., 2

minister a m. given by the people to the King JOHNSON, SAMUEL, 129
m. kiss'd the fiddler's wife BURNS, ROBERT, 29
m. of a prince...not the favorite RETZ, CARDINAL DE, 12

ministers I don't mind how much...m. talk THATCHER, MARGARET, 30

mink The trick of wearing m. BALMAIN, PIERRE, 1

Minnehaha M., Laughing Water LONGFELLOW, HENRY WADSWORTH, 30

minorities A record of the power of m. EMERSON, RALPH WALDO, 35
M....almost always in the right SMITH, SYDNEY, 24

minority The m....has the schools and press EINSTEIN, ALBERT, 15
the right of a m....to opt out LYNCH, JACK, 2

minstrel A wandering m. I GILBERT, W. S., 25
The M. Boy to the war is gone MOORE, THOMAS, 7

minuteness our m. and our impotence...cosmic forces RUSSELL, BERTRAND, 21

minutes Some of them are about ten m. long DYLAN, BOB, 27

miracle A m. is an event which creates faith SHAW, GEORGE BERNARD, 81
a m. of rare device COLERIDGE, SAMUEL TAYLOR, 17
If a man does...a m. KHASOGGI, ADNAN, 3
I weigh...one m. against the other HUME, DAVID, 16
m. cannot fix LEVANT, OSCAR, 1
One m. is just as easy to believe BRYAN, WILLIAM JENNINGS, 5
quiet m. of a normal life CLINTON, BILL, 19

miracles M. are instantaneous PORTER, KATHERINE ANNE, 1
M. are laughed at DUNNE, FINLEY PETER, 3
There are as many m. JOHN XXII, 1

mirror I'll Be Your M. REED, LOU, 10
Smashing a m....social problems evaporate LIU BINYAN, 1
The m. crack'd from side to side TENNYSON, ALFRED, 71

mirrors M....ices which do not melt MORAND, PAUL, 4
M. should think longer COCTEAU, JEAN, 8
Never believe in m. or newspapers OSBORNE, JOHN, 11

mirth Far from all resort of m. MILTON, JOHN, 113
I commended m....to eat...to drink, and to be merry BIBLE, 53
love such m. as does not make friends ashamed WALTON, IZAAK, 4
M., admit me of thy crew MILTON, JOHN, 116

mischief make m....work on my papers BEAVERBROOK, MAX AITKEN, LORD, 4
thou little knowest the m. NEWTON, ISAAC, 9
misconduct many forms of m....fatal to married happiness RUSSELL, BERTRAND, 55
miserable Me m.! which way shall I fly MILTON, JOHN, 51
The m. have no other medicine SHAKESPEARE, WILLIAM, 434
The secret of being m. is to have leisure SHAW, GEORGE BERNARD, 72
miseries Take away the m. BAMBARA, TONI CADE, 2
misery Can there be m. BECKETT, SAMUEL, 2
greatest m. is a battle gained WELLINGTON, DUKE OF, 5
Half the m....caused by ignorance THOMPSON, BONAR, 1
M. acquaints a man with strange bedfellows SHAKESPEARE, WILLIAM, 645
M. generates hate BRONTË, CHARLOTTE, 9
m. of an old man HUGO, VICTOR, 11
much greater m. of the people WOODCOCK, GEORGE, 1
misfortune In the m. of our best friends LA ROCHEFOUCAULD, FRANÇOIS, 17
m. of an old man CARY, JOYCE, 3
The Army of M. HAMMARSKJÖLD, DAG, 11
the m. of knowing anything AUSTEN, JANE, 25
the most unhappy sort of m. is to have been happy BOETHIUS, 3
worst m....an extraordinary father O'MALLEY, AUSTIN, 2
worst m. was his birth LENIN, VLADIMIR ILYICH, 2
misfortunes Few m. can befall a boy...really affectionate mother MAUGHAM, SOMERSET, 3
if a man talks of his m. JOHNSON, SAMUEL, 82
mislead One to m. the public, another...the Cabinet ASQUITH, HERBERT HENRY, 1
misquotation M. is the pride and privilege of the learned PEARSON, HESKETH, 1
misquotations M. are...never misquoted PEARSON, HESKETH, 2
misread no surer way to m. a document HAND, LEARNED, 2
misry He gave to M. all he had GRAY, THOMAS, 13
miss A m. is as good as a mile PROVERBS, 130
mission I have a m. only, no opinions SCHILLER, FRIEDRICH VON, 20
missionaries First, the traders and the m. TEWODROS II, 1
Mississippi Like the M., it just keeps rolling CHURCHILL, WINSTON, 33
Miss Lonelyhearts Write to M. WEST, NATHANAEL, 1
Miss Martin Two things, M., /I cannot stand HUGHES, LANGSTON, 12
Miss Muffet Little M. /Sat on a tuffet CHILDREN'S VERSE, 40
Miss Otis M. regrets PORTER, COLE, 7
Missouri River M....boundary between east and west STEINBECK, JOHN, 25
Miss T whatever M. eats DE LA MARE, WALTER, 3
misstatements I stand by all the m. QUAYLE, DAN, 6
mistake A man who has committed a m....another mistake CONFUCIUS, 1
he who never made a m. never made a discovery SMILES, SAMUEL, 1
m....not to die in office DULLES, JOHN FOSTER, 1
m....to put...creativity first WESTWOOD, VIVIENNE, 2
My big m. was love PYNCHON, THOMAS, 8
The biggest m. BIKO, STEPHEN, 6
The core reductive m....single fundamental explanation MIDGLEY, MARY, 2
The proactive approach to a m. COVEY, STEPHEN R., 3
worst m. a boss can make ASHCROFT, JOHN, 4
mistakes Great men too make m. LICHTENBERG, GEORG CHRISTOPH, 1
make all the same m.—only sooner BANKHEAD, TALLULAH, 10
who makes no m., never makes...progress WINKLER, PAUL, 1
mistress marry your m....create a job vacancy GOLDSMITH, JAMES, 8
m. should be like a...country retreat WYCHERLEY, WILLIAM, 2
My m.' eyes are nothing like the sun SHAKESPEARE, WILLIAM, 585
why and how I became...m. of the Earl of Craven WILSON, HARRIETTE, 2
mistresses No, I shall have m. GEORGE II, 2
mistrust M. first impulses TALLEYRAND, CHARLES MAURICE DE, 8
mists Season of m. and mellow fruitfulness KEATS, JOHN (1795–1821), 77
misunderstood Being m. by everyone is tragedy LIU SHAHE, 1
Mithras M., God of the Morning KIPLING, RUDYARD, 44
Mitty Walter M., the undefeated THURBER, JAMES, 9
mix I m. them with my brains OPIE, JOHN, 1
moanday m., tearsday, wailsday JOYCE, JAMES, 11
mob From this amphibious ill-born m....an Englishman DEFOE, DANIEL, 11
mob-hearted m., lynching, relenting, repenting millions LINDSAY, VACHEL, 2
mock M. on, Mock on, Voltaire, Rousseau BLAKE, WILLIAM, 15
mockery m. to allow women to baptise CALVIN, JOHN, 1
mockingbird it's a sin to kill a m. LEE, HARPER, 3
mocks heaven m. itself SHAKESPEARE, WILLIAM, 489
models m. and data...based on "soft" assumptions TOFFLER, ALVIN, 4
M. are the apex of consumer society MCINERNEY, JAY, 1
My m....the life of my dresses DIOR, CHRISTIAN, 2
moderation m. even in excess DISRAELI, BENJAMIN, 47
M. in all things PROVERBS, 332
m....is a sort of treason BURKE, EDMUND, 9
M. is a virtue only in those KISSINGER, HENRY, 11
still for m. and will govern by it ANNE, 1
modern It is so stupid of m. civilization KNOX, RONALD, 1
M. dance dates so quickly GRAHAM, MARTHA, 1
m. delusion...we know enough facts TAYLOR, A. J. P., 6
M. man...is a means MORAVIA, ALBERTO, 2
One must be absolutely m. RIMBAUD, ARTHUR, 9
modern dance M. in the 1930s had few followers TERRY, WALTER, 1
modernism m. is the secularization of culture TÀPIES, ANTONI, 1
modernity M. desacralized the human body PAZ, OCTAVIO, 3
modernization m. of science and technology DENG XIAOPING, 10
modest Be m.! It is the kind of pride least likely to offend RENARD, JULES, 1
modesty I have often wished I had time to cultivate m. SITWELL, EDITH, 5
She just wore /Enough for m. BUCHANAN, ROBERT WILLIAMS, 1
There is false m., but there is no false pride RENARD, JULES, 15
Mofass M. didn't trust his own mother MOSLEY, WALTER, 2
Mohammad M. wanted equality for women ALI, ZEENAT, 1
Mohammed M.'s revelations all...from the subconscious sphere JAMES, WILLIAM, 28
We have taught M. no poetry KORAN, 31
Mohicans The Last of the M. COOPER, JAMES FENIMORE, 6
molecule m. of hydrogen...executes its vibrations MAXWELL, JAMES CLERK, 1
moment a m. of time ELIZABETH I, 24

A m. of time may make us unhappy for ever GAY, JOHN, 17
in a m. of time BIBLE, 329
make of the m. a topiary DOVE, RITA, 4
m. of my greatness flicker ELIOT, T. S., 31
moments m. when everything goes well RENARD, JULES, 13
One should leave m. alone BÖLL, HEINRICH, 1
Mona Lisa the portrait of his wife M. LEONARDO DA VINCI, 3
Mona Lisas several original M. MILLIGAN, SPIKE, 3
monarch every hereditary m. was insane BAGEHOT, WALTER, 4
m. of all I survey COWPER, WILLIAM, 23
monarchy characteristic of the English M. BAGEHOT, WALTER, 7
decide the fate of the m. MIRABEAU, COMTE DE, 1
M. is a strong government BAGEHOT, WALTER, 6
m. is part of the fabric of the country PHILIP, PRINCE, 7
m. is the supremest thing upon earth JAMES I, 2
m....merchantman which sails well AMES, FISHER, 1
sitting at the Helm of this Imperiall M. DEE, JOHN, 1
The m....oldest profession in the world CHARLES, PRINCE, 11
They that are discontented under *m.* HOBBES, THOMAS, 16
Monday M.'s child is fair of face CHILDREN'S VERSE, 58
monetary When the m. damages are smaller O'HARE, DEAN, 2
money all the m. I've spent on drink STANSHALL, VIVIAN, 1
always try to rub up against m. RUNYON, DAMON, 3
a man who doesn't know how to handle m. SHAW, GEORGE BERNARD, 30
art...of draining m. SMITH, ADAM, 8
Can a bag of m. go for an errand for you NWAPA, FLORA, 2
don't have any m., the problem is food DONLEAVY, J. P., 6
find m. in a desk BALZAC, HONORÉ DE, 14
from a m.-centred world to a human-centred world PETTIFOR, ANN, 1
Half the m. I spend on advertising LEVERHULME, WILLIAM HESKETH LEVER, 1
He knew the value of m. HEATH, ROY A. K., 2
He that wants m., means, and content SHAKESPEARE, WILLIAM, 111
hired the m. COOLIDGE, CALVIN, 17
I am only interested in m. SHAW, GEORGE BERNARD, 103
I don't know how much m. I've got LENNON, JOHN, 11
I don't want to make m. MONROE, MARILYN, 8
If you give m., spend yourself THOREAU, HENRY DAVID, 29
I have no m., no resources, no hopes MILLER, HENRY, 20
I have seen so little happiness come of m. DICKENS, CHARLES, 39
I must say I hate m. MANSFIELD, KATHERINE, 5
I only take m. from sick people BRETONNEAU, PIERRE, 1
it's one for the m. PERKINS, CARL, 1
I went into the business for the m. CHAPLIN, CHARLIE, 12
Lack of m....root of all evil SHAW, GEORGE BERNARD, 61
Let the other fellow make some m. GETTY, J. PAUL, 8
M. and time...the heaviest burdens JOHNSON, SAMUEL, 38
man receives m. MELVILLE, HERMAN, 6
m. answereth all things BIBLE, 57
M. can't buy friends MILLIGAN, SPIKE, 6
m. can't buy me love LENNON & MCCARTNEY, 6
m. Cause of all evil FLAUBERT, GUSTAVE, 8
M....closest to God that I've seen MOSLEY, WALTER, 8
M. demands that you sell RAND, AYN, 1
M. doesn't make you happy SCHWARZENEGGER, ARNOLD, 3
meaning of m....remains to be popularly explained DREISER, THEODORE, 3
M....Fat of the Body-politick PETTY, SIR WILLIAM, 1
m....from clients and...from gambling DING LING, 1
M. goes to money PROVERBS, 505
M. grows on the tree of patience PROVERBS, 79
M. has no smell VESPASIAN, 1
m. has something to do with life LARKIN, PHILIP, 4
M....has two properties CROWTHER, GEOFFREY, 1
M....instrument by which men's wants are supplied MADISON, JAMES, 5
m. in the stomachs of the poor JEROME, SAINT, 1
M. is a poor man's credit card MCLUHAN, MARSHALL, 16
m. I saved on aspirins ALLEN, FRED, 6
M. is better than poverty ALLEN, WOODY, 14
M. is good for bribing yourself REINHARDT, GOTTFRIED, 1
M. is like a sixth sense MAUGHAM, SOMERSET, 18
M. is like manure MURCHISON, CLINT, 1
M. is like muck BACON, FRANCIS (1561–1626), 58
M. is...only the instrument HUME, DAVID, 1
M. is power SANDBURG, CARL, 8
M. is the external, universal means MARX, KARL, 26
M. is the most important thing in the world SHAW, GEORGE BERNARD, 42
M. is the seed of money ROUSSEAU, JEAN-JACQUES, 8
M. is the sinews of love FARQUHAR, GEORGE, 1
M....like an arm or a leg FORD, HENRY, 6
m. ...more fundamental than sex DENNIS, NIGEL, 1
M....not one particular type of wealth HEGEL, G. W. F., 23
M., of course, is never just money AUSTER, PAUL, 2
m.; psychiatrists give us a place to spend it BLOOM, ALLAN, 1
M.'s a horrid thing to follow JAMES, HENRY, 31
M. saves me the trouble of being dishonest MARX, KARL, 27
m.: Save...when you need it least MODIGLIANI, FRANCO, 1
M. speaks sense BEHN, APHRA, 14
M., the life-blood of the nation SWIFT, JONATHAN, 26
m. the sinews of the state PLUTARCH, 24
M....was exactly like sex BALDWIN, JAMES, 4
Once one has got the m. habit GOLZEN, GODFREY, 2
pays your m....takes your choice ANONYMOUS, 39
pleasant it is to have m. CLOUGH, ARTHUR HUGH, 9
power to make m. is a gift of God ROCKEFELLER, JOHN D., 2
Put m. in thy purse SHAKESPEARE, WILLIAM, 472
Put not your trust in m. HOLMES, OLIVER WENDELL, 23
She had m. and she had connections CARVER, RAYMOND, 7
Some people's m. is merited NASH, OGDEN, 8
spend m. just to stay in business SLOAN, ALFRED P., JR., 3
spiritual snobbery...happy without m. CAMUS, ALBERT, 3
sums of m....vary HUXLEY, JULIAN, 1
The earning of m. WEBER, MAX, 3
the love of m. is the root of all evil BUTLER, SAMUEL (1835–1902), 4
The man who leaves m. to charity in his will VOLTAIRE, 8
The more m. you have MADONNA, 5
The one real thing that m. buys BONNER, MARITA, 2
the question of m....good nature ends HANSEMANN, DAVID, 1
there was nothing our m. could buy KIPLING, RUDYARD, 8
The working classes are never embarrassed by m. LIVINGSTONE, KEN, 2
To make m....one must be really interested HUXLEY, ALDOUS, 10
We haven't got the m., so we've got to think RUTHERFORD, ERNEST, 1
we should have M. in proportion LAW, JOHN, 3

what the Lord God thinks of m. BARING, MAURICE, 1
When m. is at stake YAMANI, SHEIKH, 2
Where large sums of m. are concerned...trust nobody CHRISTIE, AGATHA, 3
Where there is m., there is fighting ANDERSON, MARIAN, 2
"*Why* should m. be made out of men?" WEBER, MAX, 2
Would you know what m. is HERBERT, GEORGE, 2
You can't be too ambiguous for m. DELAUNAY, SONIA, 2
You've heard m. talking MCLUHAN, MARSHALL, 8

monk That m. shall have...Twelve new wives FOLK VERSE, 54

Monk asked to bring a new M. tune MONK, THELONIOUS, 4

monkey accomplished m. cannot draw a monkey LICHTENBERG, GEORG CHRISTOPH, 6
a performing m. CHARLES, PRINCE, 8
I could never look long upon a M., without very Mortifying Reflections CONGREVE, WILLIAM, 1
m. became man /who...split the atom QUENEAU, RAYMOND, 1
no reason to attack the m. when the organ-grinder is present MACMILLAN, HAROLD, 1

monogamy M....one wife and hardly any mistresses SAKI, 24
serial m. CARTER, ANGELA, 14

monologue A m. is not a decision ATTLEE, CLEMENT, 7

monotheism hot and rigid m. of...Arab mind JAMES, WILLIAM, 31

monotony In Victor's life, m. and boredom VALENZUELA, LUISA, 2

Monroe Doctrine adherence...to the M. ROOSEVELT, THEODORE, 6

monster as a m. he was superb NEWTON, ISAAC, 3
m. in his thought SHAKESPEARE, WILLIAM, 486
The "Green-Eyed M." ANTRIM, MINNA, 3
the m. hiding in a child's dark room PATTEN, BRIAN, 1
The m. was indeed the best friend KARLOFF, BORIS, 1

monsters transform /Men into m. FORD, JOHN (1586–1640?), 4

mons Veneris treating the *m.* as...Mount Everest HUXLEY, ALDOUS, 27

Montana I am in love with M. STEINBECK, JOHN, 23
M....what a small boy would think Texas is STEINBECK, JOHN, 14

Monte Carlo What they wanted was M. MENDELSON, STUART, 1

Monterey M....long and brilliant literary tradition STEINBECK, JOHN, 4

monument The m. sticks like a fishbone LOWELL, ROBERT, 12

monuments M. last much longer than words JOHNSON, PHILIP, 2

moon a dancing spectre seems the m. MEREDITH, GEORGE, 3
A trip to the m. on gossamer wings PORTER, COLE, 10
Beautiful M., with thy silvery light MCGONAGALL, WILLIAM, 7
could Uncle M. ever be the same RAY, SATYAJIT, 4
Do I carry the m. in my pocket BROWNING, ROBERT, 57
Don't let's ask for the m. DAVIS, BETTE, 1
hadn't put a man on the m. SCULLEY, JOHN, 5
I see the m., /And the moon sees me CHILDREN'S VERSE, 16
Just as the m. receives its light INNOCENT III, 4
landing a man on the M. KENNEDY, JOHN FITZGERALD, 5
m. is full I turn into a wolf COSTELLO, LOU, 1
on the m. as in Imperial Russia CHEKHOV, ANTON, 1
The lilac m. of the earth's backyard OLSON, CHARLES, 4
The m. is nothing /But a circumambulating aphrodisiac FRY, CHRISTOPHER, 6
the M. is not perfectly smooth GALILEO, 8
the m. is...there as a stepping stone TOMLINSON, RICK, 1
the m. landing...had never really happened AUSTER, PAUL, 6
the m.'s /a balloon CUMMINGS, E. E., 12
the m. /Walks the night DE LA MARE, WALTER, 4
What good is the m. BOESKY, IVAN, 3

moonshine nearest thing to good m. FAULKNER, WILLIAM, 18

Moor M. and Spaniard are more brothers PÉREZ GALDÓS, BENITO, 7

moral a m. duty to speak one's mind WILDE, OSCAR, 51
A m., sensible, and well-bred man COWPER, WILLIAM, 6
basis of the m. life must be spontaneity, that is, the immediate SARTRE, JEAN-PAUL, 19
bestow the m. salvation of work HERZL, THEODOR, 11
Everything's got a m. CARROLL, LEWIS, 16
general numbness of m. perception has developed HORNEY, KAREN, 2
Human m. capacities...expected to evolve MIDGLEY, MARY, 1
Let us be m....contemplate existence DICKENS, CHARLES, 48
m. centaur, man and wife BYRON, LORD, 69
M....cleanliness is not acquired once OCAMPO, VICTORIA, 1
m. is what you feel good after HEMINGWAY, ERNEST, 10
profoundly m. and packed with deep spiritual significance LANCASTER, OSBERT, 2
putting him into a m. Coventry PARNELL, CHARLES STEWART, 6
quality of m. behaviour varies HUXLEY, ALDOUS, 31
The highest possible stage in m. culture DARWIN, CHARLES, 11
The m. problem of our age KEYNES, JOHN MAYNARD, 6
there are no m. actions NIETZSCHE, FRIEDRICH WILHELM, 12
There is no such thing as a m. dress CHURCHILL, JENNIE, 2
woman can look both m. and exciting FERBER, EDNA, 2

morale It is m. that wins the victory MARSHALL, GEORGE, 3

moralist m....must be truly wretched BLACKMORE, R. D., 3
no sterner m. than Pleasure BYRON, LORD, 59

morality master m. and slave morality NIETZSCHE, FRIEDRICH WILHELM, 8
m. comes up against profit CHISHOLM, SHIRLEY, 4
M. consists in suspecting SHAW, GEORGE BERNARD, 88
M....is an invented structure RULE, JANE, 1
m. is determined by sentiment HUME, DAVID, 6
M....is herd-morality NIETZSCHE, FRIEDRICH WILHELM, 5
m....is what the majority...happen to like WHITEHEAD, A. N., 6
M.'s not practical BOLT, ROBERT, 1
M. transcends not only markets SOLOMON, ROBERT C., 5
M. which is based on ideas LAWRENCE, D. H., 20
new m....the old immorality condoned SHAWCROSS, LORD, 1
no scientific m....neither can science be immoral POINCARÉ, JULES HENRI, 2
The triumph of m. KRAUS, KARL, 21
two kinds of m....one which we preach RUSSELL, BERTRAND, 33

moral judgment m. made about one situation HARE, R. M., 1

moral judgments m....intended to guide our conduct HARE, R. M., 2

morally I am m. bound to perform MOORE, G. E., 1

moral principles All universal m. are idle fancies SADE, MARQUIS DE, 1
M. have lost their distinctiveness KING, MARTIN LUTHER, JR., 13

moral resistance people of good will...support women's m. MAMONOVA, TATYANA, 1

morals basing m. on myth SAMUEL, HERBERT, 1
m. and sex taboos and homosexuality COWARD, NOEL, 3
M. are an acquirement TWAIN, MARK, 34
M. excite passions HUME, DAVID, 17
m. in art...legislature in sex NATHAN, G. J., 1
m. is simply blind obedience ELLIS, HAVELOCK, 8
m. make you dreary STEVENSON, ROBERT LOUIS, 3

They teach the m. of a whore CHESTERFIELD, LORD, 2
mordre M. wol out CHAUCER, GEOFFREY, 29
more M. than Somewhat RUNYON, DAMON, 12
m. we get out of the world WIENER, NORBERT, 6
M. WILL MEAN WORSE AMIS, KINGSLEY, 3
Mormon Book of M....keystone of our religion SMITH, JOSEPH, 1
morn From m. /To noon he fell MILTON, JOHN, 38
get up for shame, the blooming m. HERRICK, ROBERT, 5
mornin' Oh, what a beautiful m. HAMMERSTEIN, OSCAR, II, 4
morning always m. somewhere HORNE, RICHARD HENRY, 1
Early one m., just as the sun was rising FOLK VERSE, 33
I caught this morning m.'s minion HOPKINS, GERARD MANLEY, 8
If it *is* a good m. MILNE, A. A., 22
It's m. again in America RINEY, HAL, 1
M. in the Bowl of Night FITZGERALD, EDWARD, 2
straight on till m. BARRIE, J. M., 7
moronic m. inferno had caught up with me BELLOW, SAUL, 15
morrow good m. to our waking souls DONNE, JOHN, 43
mortal I was not unaware...begotten a m. GOETHE, JOHANN WOLFGANG VON, 35
So blind am I to my m. entanglement QUEVEDO Y VILLEGAS, FRANCISCO GÓMEZ DE, 1
mortals not in m. to command success ADDISON, JOSEPH, 5
We m. cross the ocean BROWNING, ROBERT, 48
mortgaged m. to the devil SMITH, STEVIE, 4
Moscow nowhere in the world like M. CHEKHOV, ANTON, 16
Moses M. tells the Israelites to "Choose life" SACKS, JONATHAN, 3
sent forth M....with our signs to Pharaoh KORAN, 15
mosquitoes something very promising...in my...m. ROSS, RONALD, 2
most The M. may err as grossly DRYDEN, JOHN, 15
moth like a m., the simple maid /...the flame GAY, JOHN, 14
The desire of the m. for the star JOYCE, JAMES, 39
mother A m.! What are we worth really STEAD, CHRISTINA, 2
an unmarried m., simply disappears for a while from her community BUCK, PEARL, 2
Don't tell my m. I'm in politics ANONYMOUS, 92
English girl hates...her m. SHAW, GEORGE BERNARD, 49
I am old enough to be...your m. MILNE, A. A., 1
importance of bondage between...m. and child QUAYLE, DAN, 5
It is not that I half knew my m. O'BRIEN, FLANN, 13
I wished to be near my m. WHISTLER, JAMES ABBOTT MCNEILL, 18
May you be the m. of a bishop BEHAN, BRENDAN, 18
m. bids me bind my hair HUNTER, ANNE, 1
M. doesn' t cook TOOLE, JOHN KENNEDY, 1
m. is a mother still COLERIDGE, SAMUEL TAYLOR, 22
m. is a noble status KENNEDY, FLORYNCE R., 5
M. is far too clever BENNETT, ARNOLD, 7
M....the dead heart of the family GREER, GERMAINE, 6
My m. only ever said two things. BRYSON, BILL, 6
my m. picked Doreen BLEASDALE, ALAN, 1
My m.'s life made me a man MASEFIELD, JOHN, 6
Never throw stones at your m. BEHAN, BRENDAN, 7
Nobody loves me but my m. KING, B. B., 2
role of a m....most important career RILEY, JANET MARY, 1
That great m. of sciences BACON, FRANCIS (1561–1626), 86
The m.-child relationship is paradoxical FROMM, ERICH, 21
The m. of battles HUSSEIN, SADDAM, 2
the m. of parliaments BRIGHT, JOHN, 1
Thou art thy m.'s glass SHAKESPEARE, WILLIAM, 562
what m. and daughter understand each other ANGELOU, MAYA, 5
"Who was your m.?" "Never had none!" STOWE, HARRIET BEECHER, 6
motherhood M. meant I have written four fewer books BYATT, A. S., 1
m....most important of all the professions STANTON, ELIZABETH CADY, 3
The best thing that could happen to m. BILLINGS, VICTORIA, 1
Mother Hubbard Old M. /Went to the cupboard CHILDREN'S VERSE, 43
mother-in-law a marvellous place to drop one's m. FOCH, FERDINAND, 4
as the man said when his m. died JEROME, JEROME K., 9
mother love M....is a highly respected and much publicised emotion COWARD, NOEL, 13
mothers M.? Hell, they seldom die MARSHALL, PAULE, 1
Our m. were...sans freezer, sans blender WELTY, EUDORA, 3
mothers-in-law Two m. RUSSELL, LORD, 4
Mother Teresa M....remarkable only for her ordinariness TERESA OF CALCUTTA, MOTHER, 1
mother-tongue The m....relegated to the kitchen VITTACHI, VARINDRA TARZIE, 3
motion At worst one is in m. GUNN, THOM, 5
God order'd m., but ordain'd no rest VAUGHAN, HENRY, 1
M. being eternal, the first mover ARISTOTLE, 20
m. matched with motion DANTE ALIGHIERI, 6
The poetry of m. GRAHAME, KENNETH, 4
Whatever is in m. must be moved AQUINAS, THOMAS, 8
motivation m....writing all these songs are revenge COSTELLO, ELVIS, 1
motive My m. is to expose the illness LU XUN, 14
motives m. meaner than your own BARRIE, J. M., 3
motorcycles On m. up the road they come GUNN, THOM, 6
motorists M....for their benefit homicide was legalised HARTLEY, L. P., 1
mould If you cannot m. yourself KEMPIS, THOMAS À, 2
mountain A m. in labor shouted so loud LA FONTAINE, JEAN DE, 3
I don't much care if I never see another m. LAMB, CHARLES, 7
See...one m., one sea, one river, and see all BURTON, ROBERT, 5
mountains Climb the m....get their good tidings MUIR, JOHN, 10
I have climbed highest m. U2, 1
M. interposed /Make enemies of nations COWPER, WILLIAM, 27
m. look on Marathon BYRON, LORD, 60
m. rising...from the lowest valleys DEFOE, DANIEL, 15
M....the beginning and the end of all natural scenery RUSKIN, JOHN, 6
M. will heave in childbirth HORACE, 7
The m....appear airy masses DIOGENES, 3
Mount Everest skied down M. in the nude MCKINNEY, JOYCE, 1
mourn M. O Ye Angels of the Left Wing WILLIAMS, WILLIAM CARLOS, 2
To m. a mischief that is past SHAKESPEARE, WILLIAM, 471
mourning I'm in m. for my life CHEKHOV, ANTON, 12
we do not call m. an illness KLEIN, MELANIE, 3
What we call m. for our dead MANN, THOMAS, 13
with my m....and new periwig PEPYS, SAMUEL, 10
mouse Consider the little m., how sagacious PLAUTUS, 9
leave room for the m. SAKI, 3
m. that always trusts to one poor hole POPE, ALEXANDER, 100
The m. ran up the clock CHILDREN'S VERSE, 51
mouse-trap make a better m. EMERSON, RALPH WALDO, 66

mouth He hath made my m. like a sharp sword BIBLE, 218
Keep your m. shut and your eyes open PROVERBS, 291
Sweet red splendid kissing m. SWINBURNE, ALGERNON CHARLES, 9
mouths I stuffed their m. with gold BEVAN, ANEURIN, 13
move M. him into the sun OWEN, WILFRED, 6
moved Once I m. like the wind GERONIMO, 2
movement I want to be a m. MITCHELL, ADRIAN, 1
Our m. and people are being destroyed BARZANI, MUSTAFA, 1
moves Yet it m. GALILEO, 6
movie don't like his m., you're dead VON STERNBERG, JOSEF, 2
don't make a m....movie makes you GODARD, JEAN-LUC, 4
In a...m. the sound could go off HITCHCOCK, ALFRED, 7
looks like the guy in a science fiction m. FORD, GERALD, 1
This is a m., not a lifeboat TRACY, SPENCER, 2
Woody makes a m. ALLEN, WOODY, 1
movie audience It takes a M. years ROGERS, WILL, 13
movie-making M. is...turning money into light BOORMAN, JOHN, 1
movies Good m. make you care KAEL, PAULINE, 1
I don't watch funny m. ALLEN, WOODY, 12
M. are an inherently stupid art form QUEENAN, JOE, 1
m. become the tool of their experience SCHULBERG, BUDD, 2
M. for me are a heightened reality SPIELBERG, STEVEN, 9
My own start in m. was...lucky one WELLES, ORSON, 3
Thanks to the m., gunfire has always sounded unreal USTINOV, PETER, 2
we make m., American movies SHEPARD, SAM, 4
What's history going to say about...m.? MITCHUM, ROBERT, 1
Why...pay money to see bad m. GOLDWYN, SAMUEL, 5
moving m. Moon went up the sky COLERIDGE, SAMUEL TAYLOR, 45
The M. Finger writes FITZGERALD, EDWARD, 13
Mozart From M. I learned to say important things MOZART, WOLFGANG AMADEUS, 7
He was simply the M. of conversation BELLOW, SAUL, 8
M....happily married—but his wife wasn't MOZART, WOLFGANG AMADEUS, 2
M. would have written...while awaiting a transplant HOLUB, MIROSLAV, 4
the M. idea—simplicity in composition MOZART, WOLFGANG AMADEUS, 4
The sonatas of M. are unique MOZART, WOLFGANG AMADEUS, 6
when M. was my age MOZART, WOLFGANG AMADEUS, 5
Mrs. Robinson Here's to you, M. SIMON, PAUL, 3
MTV M. trying to visualize the music YOUNG, NEIL, 1
much He who requires m....the object of resentment CONFUCIUS, 7
m. might be said on both sides ADDISON, JOSEPH, 15
so m. owed by so many to so few CHURCHILL, WINSTON, 34
Too m. of a good thing CERVANTES, MIGUEL DE, 7
muchness Much of a m. VANBRUGH, JOHN, 3
muckrake A man...with a m. in his hand BUNYAN, JOHN, 15
mud liquid m. up to our knees MCGREGOR, PETER, 1
One sees the m., and one the stars LANGBRIDGE, FREDERICK, 1
The m. that you throw PROVERBS, 68
muddled somewhere in the m. middle PRIESTLEY, J. B., 1
muddle-headed He's a m. fool CERVANTES, MIGUEL DE, 34
Muhammad Ali M. was so quick FOREMAN, GEORGE, 2
mule smelt a lot of m. manure WILLIAMS, HANK, 1
that ol' m. fartin' in my face ARMSTRONG, LOUIS, 11
mules The m. that angels ride come slowly STEVENS, WALLACE, 12
multicultural The arrival of m. companies MICKLETHWAIT, JOHN, 1
multitude a m. of sins BIBLE, 245
The m. of the sick EMERSON, RALPH WALDO, 59
the m., the *hoi polloi* DRYDEN, JOHN, 10
This many-headed monster, M. DANIEL, SAMUEL, 3
mum M.'s the word COLMAN, GEORGE, 1
munch So m. on, crunch on...dinner, luncheon BROWNING, ROBERT, 22
Munich Glory to God for M. MACNEICE, LOUIS, 20
murder I knew nothing of your m. O'CONNELL, EIBHLIN DUBH, 1
lest we become privy to...m. THEOPHILUS, 1
m. can be justified BONHOEFFER, DIETRICH, 7
M. Considered as One of the Fine Arts DE QUINCEY, THOMAS, 1
M....had a mask like Castlereagh CASTLEREAGH, LORD, 1
m....its rightful setting—in the home HITCHCOCK, ALFRED, 1
M., like talent, seems...to run in families LEWES, GEORGE HENRY, 2
M. most foul SHAKESPEARE, WILLIAM, 155
m. shrieks out WEBSTER, JOHN, 5
Sooner m. an infant in its cradle BLAKE, WILLIAM, 47
stick to m....leave art to us EPSTEIN, JACOB, 2
murdered I m. my grandmother this morning ROOSEVELT, FRANKLIN D., 27
The man who m. his parents LINCOLN, ABRAHAM, 35
murderer I have never yet heard of a m. CURRAN, JOHN PHILPOT, 2
murderers M....are people who are consistent BETTI, UGO, 4
Murree To M. or Chakrata TROLLOPE, JOANNA, 1
muse O for a M. of fire SHAKESPEARE, WILLIAM, 277
the M. gave native wit HORACE, 8
mushroom a supramundane m. LAURENCE, WILLIAM L., 1
I am a m. FORD, JOHN (1586–1640?), 1
mushrooms Like m., they look enticing GENEEN, HAROLD, 1
music a m. with strong rhythmic foundations LYTTELTON, HUMPHREY, 4
Beauty in m. is too often confused IVES, CHARLES, 3
better to make...m. than to perform CAGE, JOHN, 5
Can m. be something more than shadows SILES, JAIME, 1
God tells me how...this m. played TOSCANINI, ARTURO, 1
good m., people don't listen WILDE, OSCAR, 77
hear m. in the heart of noise GERSHWIN, GEORGE, 5
I always thought my m. was pretty much hollering FITZGERALD, ELLA, 1
I don't write modern m. STRAVINSKY, IGOR, 1
If I liked the m. SIMON, PAUL, 6
If m. be the food of love SHAKESPEARE, WILLIAM, 693
I hear m., I fear no danger THOREAU, HENRY DAVID, 12
I like most m. unless it's wrong HAWKINS, COLEMAN, 1
I love m. passionately DEBUSSY, CLAUDE, 7
Is there a meaning to m. COPLAND, AARON, 8
It is only in his m. BALDWIN, JAMES, 16
I was too interested in my m. ARMSTRONG, LOUIS, 8
love of m. in our bones ARMSTRONG, LOUIS, 7
luckily, one of his pleasures was m. PARKER, CHARLIE, 6
m....affects your nerves LENIN, VLADIMIR ILYICH, 23
m. and sweet poetry BARNFIELD, RICHARD, 2
M. and women I cannot but give way to PEPYS, SAMUEL, 6
M. begins to atrophy POUND, EZRA, 7
M....best means we have of digesting AUDEN, W. H., 52
M....cannot do without CONFUCIUS, 13

M....certain effect on the moral character ARISTOTLE, 24
M....confirm human loneliness DURRELL, LAWRENCE, 2
M. creates order out of chaos MENUHIN, YEHUDI, 1
M. goes on forever MARLEY, BOB, 11
M....in a continual state of becoming COPLAND, AARON, 3
m. in the air ELGAR, EDWARD, 2
M. is a beautiful opiate MILLER, HENRY, 12
M. is going to break the way HENDRIX, JIMI, 3
M. /...is invisible, /And does not smell AUDEN, W. H., 13
m....is made up of colors DEBUSSY, CLAUDE, 2
M. is mathematics STOCKHAUSEN, KARLHEINZ, 1
M. is my mistress ELLINGTON, DUKE, 3
M. is not written in red, white and blue MELBA, NELLIE, 1
M. is spiritual...music business is not MORRISON, VAN, 2
M. is the arithmetic of sounds DEBUSSY, CLAUDE, 8
M. is the crystallization of sound THOREAU, HENRY DAVID, 11
M. is the language of love PROVERBS, 334
M. is the pleasure...from counting LEIBNIZ, GOTTFRIED WILHELM, 12
M. is your own experience PARKER, CHARLIE, 7
M., Maestro, Please MAGIDSON, HERBERT, 1
M. must never offend the ear MOZART, WOLFGANG AMADEUS, 8
M., not sex, got me aroused GAYE, MARVIN, 1
M....one of the attributes of matter MUIR, JOHN, 2
m....People should die for it REED, LOU, 7
M. proclaimed an orderly universe HUNNICUTT, ELLEN, 1
M. revives the recollections STAËL, MADAME DE, 1
M....sets the soul in operation CAGE, JOHN, 6
M....sum total of scattered forces DEBUSSY, CLAUDE, 4
m. that changed a man's decision SCHNABEL, ARTUR, 2
M. that gentlier on the spirit lies TENNYSON, ALFRED, 73
M., the greatest good ADDISON, JOSEPH, 3
M....the source of the mystery NORMAN, MARSHA, 3
M....the speech of angels CARLYLE, THOMAS, 43
m. throatily and palpitatingly sexual HUXLEY, ALDOUS, 8
M. to me is a sound sensation ELLINGTON, DUKE, 4
M....Vibrates in the memory SHELLEY, PERCY BYSSHE, 22
M....ways God has of beating IVES, CHARLES, 1
M....with you was more than music AIKEN, CONRAD, 2
My m. made your liver quiver LITTLE RICHARD, 2
My m....understood by children and animals STRAVINSKY, IGOR, 3
New m., new listening CAGE, JOHN, 7
No one really understood m. unless he was a scientist BUCK, PEARL, 7
Nothing is...well set to m. ADDISON, JOSEPH, 13
play his m. and be whistled at DORATI, ANTAL, 1
Talking about m....like dancing about architecture MARTIN, STEVE, 1
the connection between m. and violence JAGGER, MICK, 5
The day the m. died MCLEAN, DON, 1
the m....lovelier than men's cursing voices WEN YIDUO, 1
The m. of what happens FIONN MACCOOL, 1
This m. won't do...not enough sarcasm GOLDWYN, SAMUEL, 24
three important ways...m. helps a picture COPLAND, AARON, 5
took my m....gave me my name JAGGER, MICK, 1
Too many pieces of m. STRAVINSKY, IGOR, 7
We are the m. makers O'SHAUGHNESSY, ARTHUR WILLIAM EDGAR, 1
what is the purpose of writing m. CAGE, JOHN, 3
where the speech of man stops...M.'s reign begins WAGNER, RICHARD, 4
why...explain the beauty of m. EINSTEIN, ALBERT, 1
write me some m. about /Daybreak in Alabama HUGHES, LANGSTON, 9
write m. like Wagner, only louder GOLDWYN, SAMUEL, 27

musical m. is the victim of changing times KELLY, GENE, 7
Most m., most melancholy MILTON, JOHN, 112
M. people are so very unreasonable WILDE, OSCAR, 12

musical composition no rules...m. except rules of thumb SHAW, GEORGE BERNARD, 74

musical instruments deliver all our m. to...Gestapo VOGEL, ERIC, 1

musical theater M....highest...form of theater WEILL, KURT, 2

music business in the m., someone's gonna rip you anyway WATERS, MUDDY, 2

music critics m....rodent-like with padlocked ears STRAVINSKY, IGOR, 2

music-hall M. songs provide...wit MAUGHAM, SOMERSET, 6

musician A m., if he's a messenger, is like a child HENDRIX, JIMI, 2
A m. must make music MASLOW, ABRAHAM, 1

musicians assumed that a lot of m....underprivileged BYRNE, DAVID, 1
M. don't retire ARMSTRONG, LOUIS, 6

music-lovers Thank-you, m. JONES, SPIKE, 1

musicologist m....can read music but can't hear it BEECHAM, THOMAS, 2

music people M. never wanted ordinary drinks JOPLIN, JANIS, 1

Muslim A M. will inherit from an infidel KHOMEINI, RUHOLLAH, 2
I was a M....didn't hate nobody ALI, MUHAMMAD, 9
M. men...suppression of women MALCOLM X, 4
M. peoples...Come to our aid KHOMEINI, RUHOLLAH, 12
M. women...we are not sex symbols KABBANI, RANA, 6

Muslims M....most part too poor and insecure KABBANI, RANA, 3

Mussolini a still more swollen M. of the soul WEST, NATHANAEL, 7

must Is *m.* a word to be addressed to princes ELIZABETH I, 16

mustache a man outside with a big black m. MARX, GROUCHO, 20

muttering the m. grew to a grumbling BROWNING, ROBERT, 18

myrrh gathered my m. with my spice BIBLE, 496

myself A violinist had his violin...All I had was m. BAKER, JOSEPHINE, 1
I am m. plus my circumstance ORTEGA Y GASSET, JOSÉ, 3
I follow but m. SHAKESPEARE, WILLIAM, 466
I have always disliked m. CONNOLLY, CYRIL, 9
I know m. FITZGERALD, F. SCOTT, 22
I m. also am a man BIBLE, 14
I m. am hell LOWELL, ROBERT, 15
m. as the imaginary possessor MOORE, MARIANNE, 6
true feeling of m. only when...unbearably unhappy KAFKA, FRANZ, 3

mysteries Talk of m. THOREAU, HENRY DAVID, 23
those wingy m. in divinity BROWNE, THOMAS, 13

mystery don't destroy the m. of a rainbow MCLAREN, ANNE, 1
you would pluck out the heart of my m. SHAKESPEARE, WILLIAM, 190

mystic No m. wonders fired his mind FRENEAU, PHILIP, 6
The m. sees the ineffable MAUGHAM, SOMERSET, 31

mystical The m. and the ethical...no living religion TILLICH, PAUL, 6

mysticism I regard m. as a state of mind TÀPIES, ANTONI, 3

mystics M. always hope that science TARKINGTON, BOOTH, 1

mystify m., mislead, and surprise the enemy JACKSON, STONEWALL, 1

myth A m. is, of course, not a fairy story RYLE, GILBERT, 1
At the centre of every m. is another FARAH, NURUDDIN, 1
"m." a form of expression TOYNBEE, ARNOLD, 3
M. deals in false universals CARTER, ANGELA, 7

mythical m. places with strange men ADAMS, DOUGLAS, 11
myths A people needs legends, heroes, m. KILLENS, JOHN OLIVER, 1
M. and legends die hard in America THOMPSON, HUNTER S., 11
m....products of the human mind CARTER, ANGELA, 1
old m. never die BAILEY, THOMAS A., 2

nabobs nattering n. of negativism AGNEW, SPIRO T., 3
nail Hit the n. on the head FLETCHER, JOHN, 8
nails gold n. in temples...hang trophies on EMERSON, RALPH WALDO, 1
naked A n. thinking heart DONNE, JOHN, 39
Half n., loving, natural, and Greek BYRON, LORD, 51
N. came I out of my mother's womb BIBLE, 254
To see you n. is to recall the Earth GARCÍA LORCA, FEDERICO, 4
Unaccustomed to seeing an almost n. body DUNCAN, ISADORA, 1
naked ape The exception is a n. MORRIS, DESMOND, 6
name A good n. is better than riches CERVANTES, MIGUEL DE, 39
He called me by n. SMITH, JOSEPH, 2
I don't like your Christian n. BEECHAM, THOMAS, 11
I have no middle n. SELZNICK, DAVID O., 2
I remember your n. perfectly SPOONER, WILLIAM ARCHIBALD, 3
like putting a n. on the universe WHITMAN, WALT, 51
my n. and memory, I leave BACON, FRANCIS (1561–1626), 81
n.: I'm a Cablinasian WOODS, TIGER, 1
no n. on the door SELFRIDGE, H. GORDON, 2
pleasant, sure, to see one's n. in print BYRON, LORD, 85
signing his n....forgetting to write the letter BEECHER, HENRY WARD, 6
So-and-so, whose other n. was so-and-so LU XUN, 6
that was the n. thereof BIBLE, 109
Their n., their years GRAY, THOMAS, 11
To *n.* an object is to destroy MALLARMÉ, STÉPHANE, 4
What's in a n. SHAKESPEARE, WILLIAM, 548
With a n. like yours CARROLL, LEWIS, 45
name-dropper One must not be a n. STEVAS, NORMAN ST. JOHN, 1
names All the n. that I gave JIMÉNEZ, JUAN RAMÓN, 5
N. should be charms WHITE, PATRICK, 5
There is no counting the n., that surgeons and anatomists give MELVILLE, HERMAN, 10
naming The act of n....consolation of mankind CANETTI, ELIAS, 8
Today we have n. of parts REED, HENRY, 1
nanny The n. state MACLEOD, IAIN, 3
nanoo N. nanoo! WILLIAMS, ROBIN, 1
Nantucket You could cut the brackish winds...in N. LOWELL, ROBERT, 21
napkins table n. but no food SCHELL, JONATHAN, 4
Naples See N. and die PROVERBS, 380
Napoleon friendship afforded me by the Emperor N. NAPOLEON I, 2
N. has not been conquered by men NAPOLEON I, 7
N. is a dangerous man...tyrant NAPOLEON I, 4
N. is always right ORWELL, GEORGE, 5
N. is a torrent KUTUZOV, MIKHAIL ILARIONOVICH, 1
N.—mighty somnambulist NAPOLEON I, 6
N. never wished to be justified NAPOLEON I, 5
N.'s armies...march on their stomachs SELLAR, W. C., 5
N. thinks I am a fool ALEXANDER I, 1
the N. of crime DOYLE, ARTHUR CONAN, 13
narcissism N....earliest stage of human development FROMM, ERICH, 14
narcissist n. is someone better looking VIDAL, GORE, 17
narcissistic n. orientation...phenomena in the outside world FROMM, ERICH, 17
narcotics Two...European n., alcohol and Christianity NIETZSCHE, FRIEDRICH WILHELM, 36
nastier she could have found anything n. to say SAYERS, DOROTHY L., 1
nation A mighty n. moving west MILLER, JOAQUIN, 1
A n....adrift without purpose JOHNSON, LYNDON BAINES, 18
a n. can win freedom without its people becoming free NKOMO, JOSHUA, 1
A n. is not in danger of financial disaster MELLON, ANDREW, 1
A n. is the universality of citizens MAZZINI, GIUSEPPE, 1
A n. must...look dispassionately at its own history BRANDT, WILLY, 4
A N. spoke to a Nation KIPLING, RUDYARD, 52
dedicate this n. to the policy of the good neighbor ROOSEVELT, FRANKLIN D., 22
Every n. for itself...God for us CANNING, GEORGE, 5
In a n. ruled by swine THOMPSON, HUNTER S., 10
Is every modern n. like the tower YEATS, W. B., 51
n. has character only when...free STAËL, MADAME DE, 3
n. is no longer able to act alone DELORS, JACQUES, 6
No n. can be competitive in...everything PORTER, MICHAEL E., 1
n. refreshed by freedom BUSH, GEORGE, 7
N. shall speak peace RENDALL, MONTAGUE JOHN, 1
one day this n. will rise up KING, MARTIN LUTHER, JR., 11
Our n. is moving towards two societies KERNER, OTTO, JR., 1
the kind of n. ...President Kennedy died for JOHNSON, LYNDON BAINES, 12
The n....ceasing to be...defining unit of society FRYE, NORTHROP, 7
The n. guarantees the nurture BELLAMY, EDWARD, 2
The n. had the lion's heart CHURCHILL, WINSTON, 22
The n. has been deeply stirred WILSON, WOODROW, 10
Think of what our N. stands for BETJEMAN, JOHN, 10
This n. openly...legalizes the very abuses BURROUGHS, NANNIE HELEN, 1
ventured my life in defence of this n. JAMES II, 2
we are a n., a new breed STEINBECK, JOHN, 22
We are not a n., but a union CALHOUN, JOHN C., 1
national N. in form, socialist in content STALIN, JOSEPH, 5
n. repugnances do not touch me BROWNE, THOMAS, 30
Our long n. nightmare is over FORD, GERALD, 5
There is no n. science CHEKHOV, ANTON, 22
national debt The N. is a very Good Thing SELLAR, W. C., 4
national emblem The decoration on the front of the Mercedes has almost become our n. KAUNDA, KENNETH DAVID, 6
nationalism N. and Communism...man's self-centred worship TOYNBEE, ARNOLD, 1
N. is a form of lack of culture VARGAS LLOSA, MARIO, 2
N. isolates people from...good PAUL VI, 2
N. is...the measles of mankind EINSTEIN, ALBERT, 43
wind of n. and freedom blowing BALDWIN, STANLEY, 3
nationalities keep all the n....well-modulated dissatisfaction TAAFFE, EDUARD VON, 1
nationality Other people have a n. BEHAN, BRENDAN, 3
national pastime The n. in this country is...lying COSBY, BILL, 8
national resources He smote the rock of...n. HAMILTON, ALEXANDER, 1
national security The n. state controls the President MOYNIHAN, DANIEL PATRICK, 2

national socialism N....imposed on the German people MANN, THOMAS, 2
nations all n....melted into a new race CRÈVECOEUR, JEAN DE, 1
men and n. behave wisely EBAN, ABBA, 1
N....always managed to find...ideological reasons for murdering MANN, GOLO, 2
N., like men, have their infancy BOLINGBROKE, HENRY ST. JOHN, 2
N. that cheat innovators LONG, CLARISA, 2
N. touch at their summits BAGEHOT, WALTER, 5
n. which have put...posterity...in their debt INGE, WILLIAM RALPH, 14
The day of small n. has long passed away CHAMBERLAIN, JOSEPH, 1
The great n. have always acted like gangsters KUBRICK, STANLEY, 1
Two n.; between whom...no intercourse DISRAELI, BENJAMIN, 31
two n....The good, the bad MARVELL, ANDREW, 7
native my own, my n. land SCOTT, SIR WALTER, 25
threads of the n. life WHARTON, EDITH, 13
natural In him...'twas N. to please DRYDEN, JOHN, 16
natural selection I have called this principle...by the term N. SPENCER, HERBERT, 1
making so much of n. STEVENSON, ROBERT LOUIS, 42
n. is...scrutinizing...every variation DARWIN, CHARLES, 4
nature All N. wears one universal grin FIELDING, HENRY, 21
Auld N. swears, the lovely dears BURNS, ROBERT, 19
Divine n. gave the fields VARRO, MARCUS TERENTIUS, 1
drive out n. with a pitchfork HORACE, 23
go into partnership with n. FISCHER, MARTIN H., 9
I am...concerned about being in tune with n. BRAQUE, GEORGES, 3
I have learned /To look on n. WORDSWORTH, WILLIAM, 15
I love n. but not its substitutes ARP, JEAN, 2
In n. one thing just happens AYER, A. J., 4
In n. there are no rewards VACHELL, HORACE ANNESLEY, 1
irregular side of n....puzzles to science GLEICK, JAMES, 1
I watched what method N. might take SYDENHAM, THOMAS, 2
Let N. be your Teacher WORDSWORTH, WILLIAM, 20
list /To N.'s teachings BRYANT, WILLIAM CULLEN, 3
Man has wrested from n. STEVENSON, ADLAI, 3
Man's dominion /Has broken N.'s social union BURNS, ROBERT, 48
man's n. runs...to herbs, or...weeds BACON, FRANCIS (1561–1626), 46
N. abhors a vacuum RABELAIS, FRANÇOIS, 4
N. admits no lie CARLYLE, THOMAS, 22
N. can do more than physicians CROMWELL, OLIVER, 8
N. contains the elements...of all pictures WHISTLER, JAMES ABBOTT MCNEILL, 4
N....convulsed by a great unending scream MUNCH, EDVARD, 1
N. did me that honour BOUCICAULT, DION, 4
new sights of N. made me rejoice CURIE, MARIE, 7
N. exists primarily for her face MACDONALD, GEORGE, 4
N. forms us for ourselves MONTAIGNE, MICHEL DE, 18
N. gave me the form of a woman SEMIRAMIS, 1
N. has always had more power than education VOLTAIRE, 41
N. has left this tincture DEFOE, DANIEL, 8
N. has no cure for this sort of madness SMITH, F. E., 4
N. has provided pleasures for every state MONTAGU, MARY WORTLEY, 5
N., in medical language HOLMES, OLIVER WENDELL, 8
n....intended greatness for men ELIOT, GEORGE, 19
N. is a benevolent old hypocrite HOLMES, OLIVER WENDELL, 18
n. is a conjugation of the verb to eat INGE, WILLIAM RALPH, 10
N. is all very well in her place GIBBONS, STELLA, 2
N. is amoral, not immoral GOULD, STEPHEN JAY, 7
N. is but a name for an effect COWPER, WILLIAM, 34
N. is...conformable NEWTON, ISAAC, 6
N. is creeping up WHISTLER, JAMES ABBOTT MCNEILL, 11
N. is not easy to live with BERRY, WENDELL, 3
N. is often hidden BACON, FRANCIS (1561–1626), 47
N. is that which the physician must read PARACELSUS, 2
n. is the art of God BROWNE, THOMAS, 16
N. is usually wrong WHISTLER, JAMES ABBOTT MCNEILL, 5
N. made him...then broke the mold ARIOSTO, LUDOVICO, 1
n. makes no leaps LEIBNIZ, GOTTFRIED WILHELM, 11
N.... meant to shew all DRAYTON, MICHAEL, 5
N. must produce a man HUME, DAVID, 32
N. never did betray WORDSWORTH, WILLIAM, 17
n. of...man as he grows older STEINBECK, JOHN, 20
N. remains WHITMAN, WALT, 49
N.'s attempt...get rid of soft boys FITZGERALD, F. SCOTT, 30
N.'s laws lay hid in night POPE, ALEXANDER, 47
N. tells every secret once EMERSON, RALPH WALDO, 52
N....this world to rise above HEPBURN, KATHARINE, 1
N., time and patience are the three great physicians PROVERBS, 335
N., to be commanded, must be obeyed BACON, FRANCIS (1561–1626), 83
N. uses as little as possible KEPLER, JOHANNES, 1
N....wasteful of promising young men HUGHES, RICHARD, 3
operations in n....effected insensibly LYELL, CHARLES, 4
passing from...n. to the civil society ROUSSEAU, JEAN-JACQUES, 19
some are by n. free, others...slaves ARISTOTLE, 25
the idea of blind n. HUME, DAVID, 28
The n. of our meal and its purpose TERTULLIAN, 7
the problem of interference with the wisdom of n. HOLUB, MIROSLAV, 3
They perfect n. BACON, FRANCIS (1561–1626), 67
To look n. in the face MIRÓ, JOAN, 4
truth about n....more beautiful LORENZ, KONRAD, 6
Whatever N. has in store for mankind FERMI, ENRICO, 3
Where N.'s wildest genius FRENEAU, PHILIP, 2
natures Men's n. are alike CONFUCIUS, 12
naught I tell you n. for your comfort CHESTERTON, G. K., 6
navy joined the N. to see the world BERLIN, IRVING, 4
N. continues to bomb...the land sings KINGSTON, MAXINE HONG, 4
The royal n. of England...its greatest defence and ornament BLACKSTONE, WILLIAM, 3
upon the n....safety, honour, and welfare...chiefly attend CHARLES II, 15
Nazi If I'd been a real N. I'd have chosen Jung FREUD, SIGMUND, 15
Nazi Germany N. had become a menace NEVINS, ALLAN, 1
Nazism I think he took N. personally AUDEN, W. H., 3
radicalized and demoniacal quasi-religions—N. TILLICH, PAUL, 4
near Be n. me when my light is low HALLAM, ARTHUR HENRY, 6
nearer N., my God, to thee ADAMS, SARAH FLOWER, 1
Nebraska headed for N. BRYSON, BILL, 16
Nebuchadnezzar N....did eat grass as oxen BIBLE, 30
necessarily It ain't n. so GERSHWIN, IRA, 5
necessary He had a n. trade...a baker CARVER, RAYMOND, 1
I am the n. angel of earth STEVENS, WALLACE, 10
it is n. not to change FALKLAND, LUCIUS CARY, 1
n. to assume something which is necessary AQUINAS, THOMAS, 6

What is n. is never a risk RETZ, CARDINAL DE, 13
necessity If...a n., then...not a sin PELAGIUS, 2
N. hath no law CROMWELL, OLIVER, 6
N. is the mother PROVERBS, 336
N. is the mother of futile dodges WHITEHEAD, A. N., 17
N. is the plea for every infringement of human freedom PITT THE YOUNGER, WILLIAM, 2
N. knows no law FORTUNE, TIMOTHY THOMAS, 2
N. makes an honest man a knave DEFOE, DANIEL, 9
n. of making good on his own AUSTIN, MARY, 2
n., /The tyrant's plea MILTON, JOHN, 55
n., which is the mother of invention PLATO, 18
neck A short n. denotes a good mind SPARK, MURIEL, 3
necking Whoever named it n. MARX, GROUCHO, 5
need deepest n. of man...to overcome his separateness FROMM, ERICH, 16
I had no n. of that hypothesis LAPLACE, PIERRE SIMON, 3
Lord, forgive me if my n. CULLEN, COUNTEE, 2
Thy n. is yet greater than mine SIDNEY, PHILIP, 1
you might n. the Pope KHASOGGI, ADNAN, 2
needle The n. went rasp rasp DOS PASSOS, JOHN, 13
needs He n....cutting and pruning BANCROFT, GEORGE, 1
n. go whom the Devil drives CERVANTES, MIGUEL DE, 15
Negative Capability N. KEATS, JOHN (1795–1821), 43
neglect A little n. may breed mischief FRANKLIN, BENJAMIN, 26
negotiate never fear to n. KENNEDY, JOHN FITZGERALD, 9
negotiating n. attitude...*question everything* and *think big* MCCORMACK, MARK, 6
N. with de Valera...mercury with a fork DE VALERA, EAMON, 3
negotiation you know who's going to win a n. HOLMES À COURT, ROBERT, 1
negotiator If you choose to be a n. ZELDIN, THEODORE, 2
Negritude N. is the sum total of the values of the civilization of the African world SENGHOR, LÉOPOLD, 1
Negro a N. in Mississippi cannot vote KING, MARTIN LUTHER, JR., 10
Bad taste...kept the best N. music BARAKA, IMAMU AMIRI, 1
being a N. doesn't qualify you GREGORY, DICK, 5
Being a N. in America KING, MARTIN LUTHER, JR., 28
Especially do I believe in the N. Race DU BOIS, W. E. B., 2
history of the American N....strife DU BOIS, W. E. B., 15
I had rather be...a member of the N. race WASHINGTON, BOOKER T., 4
no national boundary where the N. is concerned GARVEY, MARCUS, 8
N. race...to be saved by its exceptional men DU BOIS, W. E. B., 12
N. wants to be everything but himself MUHAMMAD, ELIJAH, 1
Of the many mysteries of N. history COOK, SAMUEL D., 3
One of the things that makes a N. unpleasant MENCKEN, H. L., 16
Please stop using the word "N." TERRELL, MARY CHURCH, 1
root of the American N. problem BALDWIN, JAMES, 15
The new N. history FRANKLIN, JOHN HOPE, 1
the N. is America's metaphor POWELL, COLIN, 1
The N. is America's metaphor WRIGHT, RICHARD, 5
The N. is not free ABRAHAMS, PETER, 2
the N. man being a coward MEREDITH, JAMES, 2
the N. should work with his hands DUNBAR, PAUL LAURENCE, 1
The world should not pass judgment upon the N. WASHINGTON, BOOKER T., 8
tired of working like a N. all week HUGHES, LANGSTON, 11
Who will uninvent the N. KILLENS, JOHN OLIVER, 2
Negroes All N. are angry MALCOLM X, 20
N. ALLOWED IN NEWSPAPERS, 12
N....to have a little more democracy HUGHES, LANGSTON, 1
N. used to brand...Caucasian jazz players TERRY, CLARK, 2
There are a million N. in Mississippi MEREDITH, JAMES, 1
neighbor A bad n. is...a misfortune HESIOD, 2
neighborhood n....out of it, you get beat ANONYMOUS, 42
neighbour they helped every one his n. BIBLE, 215
Whenever our n.'s house is on fire BURKE, EDMUND, 51
neighbours fear of what the n. might say CONNOLLY, CYRIL, 19
neither better if n. of us had been born ROUSSEAU, JEAN-JACQUES, 2
N. am I COOK, PETER, 3
Nell Pretty witty N. PEPYS, SAMUEL, 12
Nelly Let not poor N. starve CHARLES II, 16
neo-biological A n. technology KELLY, KEVIN, 1
neon signs practical use in something like n. UREY, HAROLD C., 1
Neopolitan N. not only enjoys his food GOETHE, JOHANN WOLFGANG VON, 21
nerves destroys one's n. to be amiable DISRAELI, BENJAMIN, 39
nerve specialist called a n....it sounds better WODEHOUSE, P. G., 21
nervous system you're being attacked by the n. HOBAN, RUSSELL, 1
Net The N. still resembles a congested street NEWSPAPERS, 4
nettle Tender-handed stroke a n. HILL, AARON, 2
networks If n. are to be more efficient FUKUYAMA, FRANCIS, 2
n....pervasive community spirit that invigorates COATE, JOHN, 1
n., rather than hierarchies STEWART, THOMAS A., 2
N....subvert managerial authority STEWART, THOMAS A., 8
Our n....cooperative communities STOLL, CLIFFORD, 4
neurosis by accepting the universal n. he is spared ...a personal neurosis FREUD, SIGMUND, 47
Modern n. began with the discoveries of Copernicus MCCARTHY, MARY, 15
N....always a substitute for legitimate suffering JUNG, CARL GUSTAV, 25
N....avoiding non-being by avoiding being TILLICH, PAUL, 10
N....battle between two tendencies FROMM, ERICH, 8
N. has an absolute genius for malingering PROUST, MARCEL, 18
neurotic All the pretenses to which...n. resorts HORNEY, KAREN, 1
n....airplane directed by remote control HORNEY, KAREN, 4
nature of a n....feeling of inferiority ADLER, ALFRED, 1
N. conflicts cannot be resolved...rational decision HORNEY, KAREN, 8
n....dread of that grim certainty MILLER, HENRY, 7
N. girls cannot love a "weak" man HORNEY, KAREN, 17
n....in a cellar with many doors HORNEY, KAREN, 20
n. individual is the typical killjoy ADLER, ALFRED, 3
N....not as sensible as I am MENNINGER, KARL, 3
N. nuclei...in the minds of normal FREUD, ANNA, 2
n. person is not free to choose HORNEY, KAREN, 13
N. persons...behave as if their existence HORNEY, KAREN, 18
N. suffering...what he pays HORNEY, KAREN, 19
someone nice & n. in...White House EISENHOWER, DWIGHT D., 3
the n. ills of an entire generation LAWRENCE, T. E., 2
The n. striving for power HORNEY, KAREN, 21
neurotics A mistake which is commonly made about n. CONNOLLY, CYRIL, 13
Everything great in the world is done by n. PROUST, MARCEL, 14

neutral United States must be n. WILSON, WOODROW, 17
neutrality "positive n." is a contradiction in terms MENON, V. K. KRISHNA, 1
The cold n. of an impartial judge BURKE, EDMUND, 57
neutralize White shall not n. the black BROWNING, ROBERT, 74
neutrinos N....enter at Nepal UPDIKE, JOHN, 24
N., they are very small UPDIKE, JOHN, 23
never Better n. than late SHAW, GEORGE BERNARD, 104
I have n. left the army LOYOLA, IGNATIUS OF, 3
n. go down to the end of the town MILNE, A. A., 13
new a n. heaven and a new earth BIBLE, 476
A n. type of woman...a career woman JAMES, C. L. R., 1
doing something impossibly n....an illusion THARP, TWYLA, 1
The n. always happens against...overwhelming odds ARENDT, HANNAH, 18
The n. man is born too old MONTALE, EUGENIO, 4
there is no n. thing under the sun BIBLE, 43
they should adopt n. processes SANFORD, CHARLES, JR., 3
new-born What is the use of a n. child FRANKLIN, BENJAMIN, 30
New England I first drew in N.'s air LOWELL, JAMES RUSSELL, 1
most serious charge...against N....February KRUTCH, JOSEPH WOOD, 7
N....never really developed a civilization MENCKEN, H. L., 36
N....will be the noblest country KEMBLE, FANNY, 1
praise the climate of N. MARTINEAU, HARRIET, 2
The natural N. taciturnity STEINBECK, JOHN, 21
variety about the N. weather TWAIN, MARK, 47
newmoon n. new in all /the ancient sky OLSON, CHARLES, 1
newness There isn't much n. in *man* LAWRENCE, D. H., 23
New Orleans N., through which the produce...pass to market JEFFERSON, THOMAS, 26
The air was so sweet in N. KEROUAC, JACK, 20
news Bad n. travels fast PROVERBS, 153
evil n. rides post MILTON, JOHN, 98
good n. from a far country BIBLE, 460
Ill n. goes quick PLUTARCH, 7
Ill n. hath wings DRAYTON, MICHAEL, 4
No n. is good news PROVERBS, 346
Nothing is n. until it has appeared in *The Times* DEAKIN, RALPH, 1
n. that's fit to print OCHS, ADOLPH SIMON, 1
only n. until he's read it. After that it's dead WAUGH, EVELYN, 26
newspaper A n. is a court CRANE, STEPHEN, 15
good n....is a nation talking to itself MILLER, ARTHUR, 12
good n. is never nearly good enough KEILLOR, GARRISON, 2
Moses...n. rates for the Ten Commandments SINGER, ISAAC BASHEVIS, 3
Once a n. touches a story, the facts are lost MAILER, NORMAN, 18
Reading someone else's n. BRADBURY, MALCOLM, 3
yesterday's n. and today's garbage LUCE, HENRY R., 1
newspapers I read the n. avidly BEVAN, ANEURIN, 9
N. always excite curiosity LAMB, CHARLES, 21
n....filled with good news MOYNIHAN, DANIEL PATRICK, 3
n.!...they are the most villainous SHERIDAN, RICHARD BRINSLEY, 6
New Testament the N. is a divinely inspired book BIERCE, AMBROSE, 15
The N....the soul of man CHAPMAN, JOHN JAY, 1
newts get rid of all them n. and saveloys ARMSTRONG, LOUIS, 12
new wave N. literature is...fashionable ZHAO, HENRY Y. H., 1
New World N....crime of its destruction LÉVI-STRAUSS, CLAUDE, 3
we may rightly call a N. VESPUCCI, AMERIGO, 1
New Year Meretricious and a Happy N. VIDAL, GORE, 21
New-year happiest time of all the glad N. TENNYSON, ALFRED, 77
New York away from N. too long ANDERSON, SHERWOOD, 7
in N., everything is torn down MERRILL, JAMES, 2
mutter the great lights of N. BERRYMAN, JOHN, 3
N. is a small place WODEHOUSE, P. G., 13
N. is the most fatally fascinating thing JOHNSON, JAMES WELDON, 7
N. let black blood flow into your blood SENGHOR, LÉOPOLD, 3
N. makes one think...collapse of civilization BELLOW, SAUL, 19
N., New York—a helluva town COMDEN, BETTY, 1
N....squalid barbarism and reckless extravagance KIPLING, RUDYARD, 34
N....that unnatural city GILMAN, CHARLOTTE PERKINS, 2
N....the mad dream KEROUAC, JACK, 18
One belongs to N. instantly WOLFE, THOMAS, 4
Outside of N. there's nothing WEIDMAN, JEROME, 1
subway is N. City's best hope THEROUX, PAUL, 2
The present in N. is so powerful CHAPMAN, JOHN JAY, 2
This is the gullet of N. MILLER, ARTHUR, 2
'tis now called N. CHARLES II, 6
two million interesting people in N. SIMON, NEIL, 5
nice Be n. to people on your way up MIZNER, WILSON, 3
If you haven't anything n. to say about anyone LONGWORTH, ALICE LEE, 1
N. guys. Finish last DUROCHER, LEO, 2
very n. if there were a God FREUD, SIGMUND, 42
Nicely-Nicely what N. dies of will be over-feeding RUNYON, DAMON, 10
nickel I don't care if it doesn't make a n. GOLDWYN, SAMUEL, 12
nickname n. is the heaviest stone HAZLITT, WILLIAM, 12
n. the neighbours stuck upon him was Handy Andy LOVER, SAMUEL, 1
nicknames N....give away the whole drama of man BARNES, DJUNA, 7
nicotinic acid N. cures pellagra SIGERIST, HENRY E., 4
Nietzsche To understand N....envisage a new race MUSSOLINI, BENITO, 8
nigger if a man calls me a n. LARSEN, NELLA, 1
We're the wrong kind of n. KING, DON, 1
night at n. things live DAUDET, ALPHONSE, 1
By n....atheist half believes a God YOUNG, EDWARD, 8
Dear N.! this world's defeat VAUGHAN, HENRY, 3
eldest N. /And Chaos MILTON, JOHN, 44
Good n., sweet Prince SHAKESPEARE, WILLIAM, 233
How long a n. can last MICHITSUNA NO HAHA, 1
In the n. reason disappears SAINT-EXUPÉRY, ANTOINE DE, 7
It ain't a fit n. out FIELDS, W. C., 1
Last n. the moon...fell on me TRUMAN, HARRY S., 5
N. and day PORTER, COLE, 19
N. and Fog HITLER, ADOLF, 19
N. hath a thousand eyes LYLY, JOHN, 10
N. of the Long Knives HITLER, ADOLF, 40
N. sank upon the dusky beach MACAULAY, THOMAS BABINGTON, 5
n. was made for loving BYRON, LORD, 17
O thievish N. MILTON, JOHN, 17
real dark n. of the soul FITZGERALD, F. SCOTT, 13
Spread thy close curtain, love-performing n. SHAKESPEARE, WILLIAM, 553
The n. has a thousand eyes...day but one BOURDILLON, FRANCIS WILLIAM, 1

The n. roared like a lion KING, STEPHEN, 1
This is the n. mail crossing AUDEN, W. H., 37
'Twas the n. before Christmas MOORE, CLEMENT, 2
What hath n. to do with sleep MILTON, JOHN, 14
nightingale N.!...creature of a "fiery heart" WORDSWORTH, WILLIAM, 60
n. dies for shame BURTON, ROBERT, 2
The n. does sit so late MARVELL, ANDREW, 8
nightingales The n. are singing ELIOT, T. S., 26
night watchman only one man...can count on steady work—the n. BANKHEAD, TALLULAH, 2
nihilism what is coming...the rise of n. NIETZSCHE, FRIEDRICH WILHELM, 41
nihilist a part-time n. CAMUS, ALBERT, 23
nihilists The n. say it is the end FAULKNER, WILLIAM, 4
Nile as well dam ...the N. with bulrushes CHILD, LYDIA MARIA, 5
Nimrod N. the mighty hunter BIBLE, 120
ninepence I have but n. in ready money ADDISON, JOSEPH, 23
ninety n.-odd years is gradual enough MARSHALL, THURGOOD, 2
Nineveh Quinquireme of N. MASEFIELD, JOHN, 1
Nixon If Richard N. was second-rate NIXON, RICHARD, 3
N. is a shifty-eyed goddam liar NIXON, RICHARD, 10
N. is the kind of politician NIXON, RICHARD, 8
N.'s motto was, if two wrongs NIXON, RICHARD, 2
N. was still the spirit of television NIXON, RICHARD, 5
Richard N....Gerald Ford as his revenge ABZUG, BELLA, 2
standing between N. and the White House NIXON, RICHARD, 4
Under N. the great corporations became drunk BELLOW, SAUL, 13
won't have N. to kick around NIXON, RICHARD, 13
nobility leave us still our old n. MANNERS, LORD JOHN, 1
New n....the act of power BACON, FRANCIS (1561–1626), 49
N....graceful ornament to the civil order BURKE, EDMUND, 47
N. has its own obligations LÉVIS, PIERRE MARC GASTON DE, 1
N. of birth commonly abateth industry BACON, FRANCIS (1561–1626), 50
Real n. is based on scorn CAMUS, ALBERT, 5
The n. of England,...snored through the Sermon BOLT, ROBERT, 2
noble N. values...are always overcome MONTHERLANT, HENRI DE, 5
O, what a n. mind is here o'erthrown! SHAKESPEARE, WILLIAM, 183
The n. living and the noble dead WORDSWORTH, WILLIAM, 89
noblest n. mind the best contentment has SPENSER, EDMUND, 6
the two n. of things...sweetness and light SWIFT, JONATHAN, 39
nobody n. around has any sexual relevance PYNCHON, THOMAS, 7
n. ever changes for a woman MCCARTHY, MARY, 3
N. ever tells me anything GALSWORTHY, JOHN, 2
N. knows anything GOLDMAN, WILLIAM, 2
n. walks much faster CARROLL, LEWIS, 47
What will we do /when there is n. left /to kill JORDAN, JUNE, 4
When n. wants something ICAHN, CARL, 2
nod a n. from a person who is esteemed PLUTARCH, 27
A n. is as good as a wink PROVERBS, 136
no go It's n. the picture palace MACNEICE, LOUIS, 4
noise A loud n. at one end KNOX, RONALD, 3
the n....and the people ANONYMOUS, 78
the n. of the shout of joy BIBLE, 96
Those people...are making such a n. PARKER, HENRY TAYLOR, 1
noisy A n. man is always in the right COWPER, WILLIAM, 5
nominate n. a spade a spade JONSON, BEN, 19
non-commissioned backbone of the Army is the N. man KIPLING, RUDYARD, 59
nonconformity N. and lust stalking hand in hand WAUGH, EVELYN, 13
non-existent You're entering a n. universe STOLL, CLIFFORD, 2
nonsense Even God has been defended with n. LIPPMANN, WALTER, 1
little n. now and then is treasured DONAHUE, PHIL, 1
nonviolence N. is a powerful and just weapon KING, MARTIN LUTHER, JR., 30
non-violence N....law of our species GANDHI, MAHATMA, 15
N....not a garment to be put on GANDHI, MAHATMA, 12
nonviolent I'm n. with those who are nonviolent MALCOLM X, 21
N. direct action seeks to create KING, MARTIN LUTHER, JR., 3
Norma Jean Goodbye N. DIANA, PRINCESS, 2
normal I've had a n. life SAMPRAS, PETE, 1
normal guy I'm just a n. with heart TYSON, MIKE, 4
north N. is sad /and the endless Yellow River AI QING, 5
North America The history of much of N. LOWER, A. R. M., 3
Northern Ireland consent of a majority...of N. ANONYMOUS, 13
politics of N....macho in style MCWILLIAMS, MONICA, 1
nose Any n. /May ravage... a rose BROWNING, ROBERT, 70
could not blow his n. without moralising ORWELL, GEORGE, 1
Entuned in hir n. ful semely CHAUCER, GEOFFREY, 16
My n. is huge! ROSTAND, EDMOND, 1
N., nose, jolly red nose BEAUMONT, FRANCIS, 3
see farther than his own n. LA FONTAINE, JEAN DE, 11
noses Hold their n. to the grindstone MIDDLETON, THOMAS, 2
nostalgia n....a hypertrophied sense of lost childhood NABOKOV, VLADIMIR, 9
N. isn't what it used to be ANONYMOUS, 82
not n. one...who left their land AKHMATOVA, ANNA, 3
note The world will little n., nor long remember LINCOLN, ABRAHAM, 12
notes N....are necessary evils JOHNSON, SAMUEL, 28
thinks two n. a song DAVIES, W. H., 2
not guilty I am one hundred percent n. SIMPSON, O. J., 1
nothin' N. Like a Dame HAMMERSTEIN, OSCAR, II, 10
You ain't heard n. yet JOLSON, AL, 2
nothing Adapt the n. therein to the purpose LAOZI, 14
Certainly n. is unnatural SHERIDAN, RICHARD BRINSLEY, 7
doing n. for each other HOPE, BOB, 1
Doing n. is...wrong RUBIN, ROBERT E., 2
do n. and get something...a boy's ideal DISRAELI, BENJAMIN, 30
from n. to a state of extreme poverty MARX, GROUCHO, 25
I believe in n....everything is absurd CAMUS, ALBERT, 22
I'm going to do n. for ever and ever EPITAPHS, 1
knows n. and understands everything BRIAND, ARISTIDE, 1
N. LOUIS XVI, 3
N. begins and nothing ends THOMPSON, FRANCIS, 4
n. can be known BYRON, LORD, 24
N. can be produced out of nothing DIOGENES LÄERTIUS, 2
n. can bring back the hour WORDSWORTH, WILLIAM, 56
n. deep down inside us RORTY, RICHARD, 1
n. either good or bad SHAKESPEARE, WILLIAM, 168
n....except empty curved space WHEELER, JOHN ARCHIBALD, 2
N. for nothing...my door stayed shut RACINE, JEAN, 16
N. happens to the very rich MCCARTHY, MARY, 4
N. has been spared in this world FRANCIS JOSEPH I, 1

N. in the world is single SHELLEY, PERCY BYSSHE, 6
N. in the world matters KEROUAC, JACK, 25
n. is had for nothing CLOUGH, ARTHUR HUGH, 13
N. is indifferent, nothing is powerless NERVAL, GÉRARD DE, 2
n. is often a good thing to do DURANT, WILL, 17
N. is small, nothing is great MUNCH, EDVARD, 2
N. is won forever in human affairs MITTERRAND, FRANÇOIS, 2
N. lasts long enough to make any sense MARECHERA, DAMBUDZO, 1
N., like something, happens anywhere LARKIN, PHILIP, 19
N. matters very much BALFOUR, ARTHUR, 7
N....said that's not been said before TERENCE, 6
n. should ever be done for the first time CORNFORD, F. M., 1
N. very much happens in her books AUSTEN, JANE, 4
n. when the ado is about himself TROLLOPE, ANTHONY, 6
N. will come of nothing SHAKESPEARE, WILLIAM, 333
People don't resent having n. COMPTON-BURNETT, IVY, 1
Says little, thinks less...does—n. FARQUHAR, GEORGE, 3
there is n. else here to enjoy SHAW, GEORGE BERNARD, 100
There is n. from without a man BIBLE, 357
there is n., nothing /yet I still pray WANTLING, WILLIAM, 1
There is n. to be said in mitigation
INTERNATIONAL MILITARY TRIBUNAL OF THE NUREMBERG TRIALS, 2
To whom n. is given FIELDING, HENRY, 10
very good, sometimes, to have n. THOMAS, DYLAN, 29
We are n.; less than nothing, and dreams LAMB, CHARLES, 12
When you have n. to say, say nothing COLUMBUS, CHRISTOPHER, 8
Who lendeth n. is an ugly...creature RABELAIS, FRANÇOIS, 12
nothingness n. between me and the light DILLARD, ANNIE, 5
Those who...have a taste for n. CHAR, RENÉ, 3
notice n. whether it's summer or winter CHEKHOV, ANTON, 18
noticed You just have to be n. BURNETT, LEO, 1
notices One never n. what has been done CURIE, MARIE, 3
nought N.'s had, all's spent SHAKESPEARE, WILLIAM, 402
N.'s permanent BYRON, LORD, 73
nourisher a n. of thine old age BIBLE, 489
nourishment turn...n....into a painful attack DIANA, PRINCESS, 6
Nouvelle Vague The dream of the N. GODARD, JEAN-LUC, 1
novel A good n. tells us the truth CHESTERTON, G. K., 20
a n. about this astonishing metropolis WOLFE, TOM, 1
A n. is a mirror STENDHAL, 5
A n. is a river OKRI, BEN, 4
A n. is a static thing TYNAN, KENNETH, 1
In the n. as in literature BAROJA, PÍO, 5
no more beautiful mission than...the free n.
GÓMEZ DE LA SERNA, RAMÓN, 1
No one says a n. has to be one thing REED, ISHMAEL, 3
not a n. to be tossed aside lightly PARKER, DOROTHY, 33
only obligation to which...we may hold a n. JAMES, HENRY, 11
the last fashionable n. on the tables of young ladies
MACAULAY, THOMAS BABINGTON, 2
The n. being dead VIDAL, GORE, 5
The n. is an art form O'CONNOR, FLANNERY, 4
The n. is a way of life BAMBARA, TONI CADE, 4
the n. is...the retail business NEMEROV, HOWARD, 2
the n....none of our culture's business PAMUK, ORHAN, 8
the n. tells a story FORSTER, E. M., 10
to read a n. I write one DISRAELI, BENJAMIN, 58
novelist a n. hot as a firecracker BERRYMAN, JOHN, 10
A n. is, like all mortals NABOKOV, VLADIMIR, 12
being a n., I consider myself superior to the saint, the scientist
LAWRENCE, D. H., 39
n. is the historian of the present DUHAMEL, GEORGES, 1
n. sits over his work like...god MAILER, NORMAN, 2
n. who writes nothing for 10 years PRIESTLEY, J. B., 6
novelists if a third of all the n....dropped dead OSBORNE, CHARLES, 1
There are many reasons why n. write FOWLES, JOHN, 1
novels If anything I do, in the way of writing n. MORRISON, TONI, 27
only women...have time to write n. WAUGH, AUBERON, 1
The lies of n. are never gratuitous VARGAS LLOSA, MARIO, 4
novelty not in n. but in habit...pleasure RADIGUET, RAYMOND, 2
N., novelty, novelty HOOD, THOMAS, 16
November No warmth, no cheerfulness...N. HOOD, THOMAS, 8
Thirty days hath N. GRAFTON, RICHARD, 1
now Right N....better than the Good Old Days BINCHY, MAEVE, 1
nowhere He's a real N. Man LENNON & MCCARTNEY, 9
nuclear discovery of n. chain reactions...destruction of mankind
EINSTEIN, ALBERT, 18
Following a n. attack on...United States
UNITED STATES FEDERAL EMERGENCY MANAGEMENT AGENCY, 1
n. sword of Damocles KENNEDY, JOHN FITZGERALD, 24
rival n. revels rumble round the globe BANDYOPADHYAY, PRANAB, 1
nuclear disarmament adopt n. PENHALIGON, DAVID, 1
nuclear family Nobody has ever before asked the n.
MEAD, MARGARET, 14
nuclear fission n....natural process LOVELOCK, JAMES, 1
nuclear power plant waste...from a n. REAGAN, RONALD, 28
nuclear weapons a market in...portable n. SUGAR, ALAN, 3
What is wrong with n. JAMES, C. L. R., 6
nude The trouble with n. dancing HELPMANN, ROBERT, 1
nudge N., nudge, wink, wink MONTY PYTHON'S FLYING CIRCUS, 3
nudity you don't need the n. WEST, MAE, 12
nuisances a change of n. is as good as a vacation
LLOYD-GEORGE, DAVID, 13
number a very interesting n. RAMANUJAN, SRINIVASA, 1
N. theorists are like lotus-eaters KRONECKER, LEOPOLD, 1
number one Look after n. PROVERBS, 310
numbers N....only universal language WEST, NATHANAEL, 4
Round n. are always false JOHNSON, SAMUEL, 112
numerous N. words show scanty wares PROVERBS, 80
nuns Ha! Easy for n. to talk KEILLOR, GARRISON, 7
The n. who never take a bath RUSSELL, BERTRAND, 42
nuptial N. love maketh mankind BACON, FRANCIS (1561–1626), 41
nuptials prone to any iteration of n. CONGREVE, WILLIAM, 24
Nuremberg Rally I know it's like a N. MAY, BRIAN, 1
nurse A good n....more importance than a physician
LEE, HANNAH FARNHAM, 2
Always keep a-hold of N. BELLOC, HILAIRE, 13
n....one of the great blessings OSLER, WILLIAM, 4
n. should be..."devoted and obedient." NIGHTINGALE, FLORENCE, 5
N. unupblown WAUGH, EVELYN, 38
the n. was shaking /her head PASTERNAK, BORIS, 5
The trained n....the divine touch MAYO, CHARLES HORACE, 4
nursing mother The n. of half a continent NEWSPAPERS, 31
nuts Here we come gathering n. in May CHILDREN'S VERSE, 63

nuttin' I got plenty o' n. GERSHWIN, IRA, 3
nut tree I had a little n. CHILDREN'S VERSE, 32
nymphomaniac n. who...imagines herself unsatiated ADLER, ALFRED, 4

Oakland O....there isn't any there there STEIN, GERTRUDE, 7
oaks Great o. PROVERBS, 241
oath No o. too binding for a lover SOPHOCLES, 10
oaths O. are but words BUTLER, SAMUEL (1612–80), 17
o. are straws SHAKESPEARE, WILLIAM, 264
obedience O. is the mother of success AESCHYLUS, 7
O....woman's duty on earth SCHILLER, FRIEDRICH VON, 18
obey not o. the laws too well EMERSON, RALPH WALDO, 26
obituaries I begin each day with coffee and o. COSBY, BILL, 6
object An o. in possession PLINY THE YOUNGER, 5
don't o. if I'm sick BEECHAM, THOMAS, 12
Every o. is the mirror MERLEAU-PONTY, MAURICE, 1
I have no o....superficial one ADAMS, HENRY, 1
My o. all sublime /I shall achieve GILBERT, W. S., 32
o. may exist...yet be no where HUME, DAVID, 9
o. of...civil government is the improvement ADAMS, JOHN QUINCY, 5
o. of painting is not to make a picture HENRI, ROBERT, 1
o. the sum of its complications STEVENS, WALLACE, 30
she was only an o. of contempt AUSTEN, JANE, 19
objective by losing himself in the o. GOODMAN, PAUL, 7
live with the o. of being happy FRANK, ANNE, 5
o. indices so dear to...the psychologist LEARY, TIMOTHY, 4
O. knowing is alienated knowing ROSZAK, THEODORE, 12
objects o. bring renown...to an entire nation CARDUCHO, VICENTE, 2
o. must conform to our knowledge KANT, IMMANUEL, 8
Our...World has been overrun by...art o. KIESLER, FREDERICK, 1
What o. may be in themselves KANT, IMMANUEL, 9
oblige One should o. everyone to...one's ability LA FONTAINE, JEAN DE, 8
oblivion formless ruin of o. SHAKESPEARE, WILLIAM, 689
obnoxious as o. as a physical servitude DELANY, MARTIN ROBINSON, 2
obscenity O. is such a tiny kingdom BROUN, HEYWOOD, 2
"o."...not a term capable of exact legal definition RUSSELL, BERTRAND, 35
obscurely Content thyself to be o. good ADDISON, JOSEPH, 7
observation From his close o. of life VOINOVICH, VLADIMIR, 3
O. is an aggressive act MCCORMACK, MARK, 14
o. of nature...an artist's life MOORE, HENRY, 3
observations Don't make o. on cats and dogs PAMUK, ORHAN, 6
To o. which ourselves we make POPE, ALEXANDER, 59
observe Whenever you o. an animal closely CANETTI, ELIAS, 14
obsession O. of all the beds...pigeonhole bedrooms DOS PASSOS, JOHN, 4
obstacles many o. and difficulties...of revolution MAO ZEDONG, 35
obvious the analysis of the o. WHITEHEAD, A. N., 12
occasions all o. do inform against me SHAKESPEARE, WILLIAM, 210
Great o. make great men PROVERBS, 482
occupation I doubt...any o....more...demeaned PROXMIRE, WILLIAM, 1
occupations worse o....than feeling a woman's pulse STERNE, LAURENCE, 6
occupied Although they are an o. nation HEANEY, SEAMUS, 9
occurred X o. and Y occurred MACKIE, J. L., 1
ocean A life on the o. wave SARGENT, EPES, 1
an immense o....unlimited gleaming white XU ZHIMO, 2
o. is a place of paradoxes CARSON, RACHEL, 1
ocean people O. are different from land people KINGSTON, MAXINE HONG, 1
odd How o. /Of God EWER, WILLIAM NORMAN, 2
It's o. how people waiting for you GIRAUDOUX, JEAN, 4
Odysseus Like O., he looked wiser when seated WILSON, WOODROW, 1
Odyssey O. and...Exodus...early travel books RABAN, JONATHAN, 1
Oedipus complex mother...the O. FREUD, SIGMUND, 36
Oedipuses a tense and peculiar family, the O. BEERBOHM, MAX, 24
offence dire o. from am'rous causes springs POPE, ALEXANDER, 93
greatest o. against virtue HAZLITT, WILLIAM, 13
offend don't o. the cook PROVERBS, 32
offended This hath not o. the king MORE, THOMAS, 2
offends o....a new type of money LYND, ROBERT, 1
offense A good o. is the best PROVERBS, 113
o. of the political prisoner...political boldness DAVIS, ANGELA, 6
offensive o. letter follows ANONYMOUS, 11
You are extremely o., young man SMITH, F. E., 3
offer an o. he can't refuse O'HARA, THEODORE, 3
make him an o. he can't refuse PUZO, MARIO, 2
office in o. but not in power LAMONT, NORMAN, 2
tall modern o. building is the machine WRIGHT, FRANK LLOYD, 7
wouldn't have gone to the o. at all GOGOL, NIKOLAY, 1
officials o. are held accountable as dupes STEVENSON, ADLAI, 8
official secret the "o." is bureaucracy's specific invention WEBER, MAX, 1
off-shore O., by islands hidden in the blood OLSON, CHARLES, 7
often Do you come here o. MILLIGAN, SPIKE, 8
Ogoni O. people...confront their tormentors SARO-WIWA, KEN, 1
Ohio In O. seasons are theatrical MORRISON, TONI, 2
Why did I ever leave O. GREEN, ADOLPH, 1
Winter in O. was especially rough MORRISON, TONI, 7
oil no sense owning o. companies LYNCH, PETER, 7
O., despite its vital...importance YAMANI, SHEIKH, 1
oil olive a land of o., and honey BIBLE, 35
oily I want that...o. art /To speak SHAKESPEARE, WILLIAM, 331
Okie O. use' ta mean...from Oklahoma STEINBECK, JOHN, 10
Oklahoma To the red country...O., the last rains STEINBECK, JOHN, 8
Oklahoma City O. with its towers STEIN, GERTRUDE, 6
old an o. man decayed in his intellects JOHNSON, SAMUEL, 124
an o. man is twice a child SHAKESPEARE, WILLIAM, 174
being o. is having lighted rooms LARKIN, PHILIP, 7
Better be an o. man's darling PROVERBS, 162
Don't grow o. without money, honey HORNE, LENA, 1
few...grow o. with a good grace STEELE, RICHARD, 4
getting o....about losing people you love OATES, JOYCE CAROL, 2
getting o. when the gleam in your eyes...bifocals PROVERBS, MODERN, 32
grew o. first...in other people's eyes BARNES, JULIAN, 4
Growing o. is...a bad habit MAUROIS, ANDRÉ, 2
Grow o. along with me BROWNING, ROBERT, 33
If you want to be a dear o. lady at seventy ROYDEN, MAUD, 2
I love everything that's o. GOLDSMITH, OLIVER, 7
I see thee o. and formal TENNYSON, ALFRED, 54

natural that o. people would have to go MOHAMAD, MAHATHIR BIN, 1
nicest o. ladies I ever met JAMES, HENRY, 2
Nobody hears o. people complain ALBEE, EDWARD, 1
No matter how o. a mother is SCOTT-MAXWELL, FLORIDA, 1
o. and ill and terrified and tight BETJEMAN, JOHN, 4
o., but I'm not cold CHRISTIE, LINFORD, 2
O. deeds for old people...new deeds for new THOREAU, HENRY DAVID, 28
O. men and comets have been reverenced SWIFT, JONATHAN, 48
O. men are dangerous SHAW, GEORGE BERNARD, 29
O. men are twice children PROVERBS, 52
O. men...children for a second time ARISTOPHANES, 2
O. people are like old trees DELANEY, LUCY A., 2
o. repeat themselves...young have nothing to say BAINVILLE, JACQUES, 2
terrible thing for an o. woman to outlive her dogs WILLIAMS, TENNESSEE, 7
That o. monkish place VICTORIA, 7
The o. are always serious KIRKUP, JAMES, 1
the o. great ones /leave us alone LEVERTOV, DENISE, 2
the o. have rubbed it into the young MAUGHAM, SOMERSET, 10
There are no o. men any more USTINOV, PETER, 6
They shall grow not o. BINYON, LAURENCE, 2
thought the o. man...had so much blood in him SHAKESPEARE, WILLIAM, 412
Tidy the o. into tall flats BENNETT, ALAN, 3
To be o. is to be part of a...multitude BLYTHE, RONALD, 3
too o. to go again to my travels CHARLES II, 7
very o. before...amused rather than shocked BUCK, PEARL, 4
We grow o. more through indolence CHRISTINA, 1
What can an o. man do but die HOOD, THOMAS, 3
Whatever is o. corrupts EMERSON, RALPH WALDO, 47
What makes o. age hard to bear MAUGHAM, SOMERSET, 22
When I am an o. woman I shall wear purple JOSEPH, JENNY, 1
When one is too o. for love HURSTON, ZORA NEALE, 12
When you are o. and grey YEATS, W. B., 33
When you are very o., and sit in the candle-light RONSARD, PIERRE DE, 1
why wasn't I born o. and ugly DICKENS, CHARLES, 13
You are o., Father William CARROLL, LEWIS, 5
you grow o. beautifully MAUGHAM, SOMERSET, 25
You have lived to be an o. man PAUSANIAS, 1
You're Only O. Once SEUSS, DR., 6

old age desire o. ...prolonged infirmity AUGUSTINE OF HIPPO, SAINT, 1
fatal period when o. must be endured SÉVIGNÉ, MADAME DE, 1
first sign of o. HICKS, SEYMOUR, 1
Forty is the o. of youth PROVERBS, MODERN, 12
I prefer o. to the alternative CHEVALIER, MAURICE, 1
O. and...time teach many things SOPHOCLES, 12
O....an island surrounded by death MONTALVO, JUAN, 1
O. brings...the comfort EMERSON, RALPH WALDO, 32
o....chewing...over the past HURST, FANNIE, 1
O. comes on apace BEATTIE, JAMES, 1
O. is a disease SENECA, "THE YOUNGER," 11
O. is a shipwreck DE GAULLE, CHARLES, 19
O. is...crossed off names in an address book BLYTHE, RONALD, 2
o. is...fifteen years older than I BARUCH, BERNARD MANNES, 4
O. is the most unexpected TROTSKY, LEON, 1
O. puts more wrinkles in our minds MONTAIGNE, MICHEL DE, 28
o., serene and bright, /And lovely as a Lapland night WORDSWORTH, WILLIAM, 70
O. takes away from us what we have inherited BRENAN, GERALD, 7
remember till o. age...our brilliant youth SAPPHO, 2
The greatest problem about o. TAYLOR, A. J. P., 3
The secret of good o. GARCÍA MÁRQUEZ, GABRIEL, 12

old-age O., a second child CHURCHILL, CHARLES, 3

older As you get o. you become more boring RAVEN, SIMON, 1
He was o. than the days LONDON, JACK, 11
I want...to go on getting o. ADENAUER, KONRAD, 5
I was so much o. then DYLAN, BOB, 17
make way for an o. man MAUDLING, REGINALD, 2
O. men declare war HOOVER, HERBERT, 8
o. than the rocks among which she sits PATER, WALTER, 1
The o. one grows...one likes indecency WOOLF, VIRGINIA, 3

old-fashioned I want an o. house FISHER, MARVE, 1
o. respect for the young WILDE, OSCAR, 47

old friend I'm having an o. for dinner HOPKINS, ANTHONY, 5

oligarchy O. was established by men PLATO, 27

Oliver Twist O. has asked for more DICKENS, CHARLES, 67

Olympic Games The most important thing in the O. COUBERTIN, PIERRE DE, 1

Olympus fling /Ossa upon O. BRYANT, WILLIAM CULLEN, 7
O....ever unchanging HOMER, 5

Omaha around O.—the farmers /haul tanks of cream SANDBURG, CARL, 7
O. is a little like Newark RIVERS, JOAN, 2
O., the roughneck feeds armies SANDBURG, CARL, 6

omelette You can't make an o. PROVERBS, 466

omniscient O. am I not, but well-informed GOETHE, JOHANN WOLFGANG VON, 10

Onan O. knew that the seed should not be his BIBLE, 135

Onaway O.! Awake, beloved LONGFELLOW, HENRY WADSWORTH, 32

one if we knew o., we knew two EDDINGTON, ARTHUR, 4
O. Realm, One People, One Leader MOTTOS AND SLOGANS, 32
to try to be o. of three BISMARCK, PRINCE OTTO VON, 10
What man...content with o. crime JUVENAL, 2

one-and-twenty When I was o. HOUSMAN, A. E., 5

one-eyed A little o., blinking sort o' place HARDY, THOMAS, 21

one-handed Give me a o. economist TRUMAN, HARRY S., 18

oneness o. of our resources...chain of life UDALL, STEWART L., 5

one up How to be o. POTTER, STEPHEN, 3

online O. conversation...talking by writing COATE, JOHN, 2

on the spot those fellows we put o. COLLINS, MICHAEL, 3

oon O. ere it herde CHAUCER, GEOFFREY, 39

ope o. /His mouth...out there flew a trope BUTLER, SAMUEL (1612–80), 4

open I declare this thing o.—whatever it is PHILIP, PRINCE, 10
I o. my eyes and exist BETTI, UGO, 11
O. Sesame ARABIAN NIGHTS, THE, 2

openmindedness O. should not be fostered...Truth is great RORTY, RICHARD, 2

opera an o. without an interval NEWMAN, ERNEST, 1
approach an o. as...didn't know it CALDWELL, SARAH, 1
first rule in o....first rule in life MELBA, NELLIE, 3
German o., too long and too loud WAUGH, EVELYN, 40

Going to the o....a sin that carries its own punishment MORE, HANNAH, 2
No good o. plot can be sensible AUDEN, W. H., 40
O. in English...as sensible as baseball in Italian MENCKEN, H. L., 43
o. isn't what it used to be COWARD, NOEL, 11
O. is when a guy gets stabbed in the back GARDNER, ED, 1
what language an o. is sung in APPLETON, EDWARD VICTOR, 1
operas Our mistake...write interminable large o. VERDI, GIUSEPPE, 1
operate I don't o. often BERRYMAN, JOHN, 9
operating o. jointly on me for years YOUNG, COLEMAN, 1
operation Before undergoing a surgical o. GOURMONT, RÉMY DE, 1
Exploratory o.: a remunerative reconnaissance PROVERBS, MODERN, 11
o. was successful...patient died PROVERBS, MODERN, 27
The feasibility of an o. COHEN, HENRY, 1
operations I am of the opinion my o. rather kept down my practice COOPER, ASTLEY, 2
the king of all topics is o. COBB, IRVIN S., 1
opinion fact that an o. has been widely held RUSSELL, BERTRAND, 14
give him my o.. You know it DICKENS, CHARLES, 17
good o. of the law TRUMBULL, JOHN, 1
I agree with no man's o. TURGENEV, IVAN, 2
I am...of the o. with the learned CONGREVE, WILLIAM, 2
man's o. on tramcars matters CHESTERTON, G. K., 13
o. of those we don't care for EBNER-ESCHENBACH, MARIE VON, 1
They that approve...call it o. HOBBES, THOMAS, 11
opinion poll public-o....no substitute for thought BUFFETT, WARREN, 4
opinions I have o. of my own BUSH, GEORGE, 18
New o. are always suspected LOCKE, JOHN, 6
only o., some...preferable to others ECO, UMBERTO, 3
The average man's o. RUSSELL, BERTRAND, 38
the proper o. for the time of year AUDEN, W. H., 17
the same o. have arisen...in cycles ARISTOTLE, 7
when o. universally prevail WOOLF, VIRGINIA, 14
opium O. gives and takes away DE QUINCEY, THOMAS, 5
O....the Creator himself seems to prescribe HOLMES, OLIVER WENDELL, 9
the story of Coleridge without the o. COLERIDGE, SAMUEL TAYLOR, 7
Thou hast the keys of Paradise...mighty o. DE QUINCEY, THOMAS, 6
opportunist rather be an o. and float BALDWIN, STANLEY, 11
opportunities O. are usually disguised as hard work LANDERS, ANN, 3
One can present people with o. LEHMANN, ROSAMOND, 1
opportunity Equality of o. MACLEOD, IAIN, 4
O. makes a thief BACON, FRANCIS (1561–1626), 104
O. seldom knocks twice PROVERBS, 359
o. to relieve yourself EDWARD VIII, 3
the o. to move...upward to the Great Society JOHNSON, LYNDON BAINES, 19
windows of o. open and close MCCORMACK, MARK, 3
oppose o. everything, and propose nothing STANLEY, EDWARD GEOFFREY SMITH, 1
We set out to o. Tyranny CLARK, ABRAHAM, 1
opposed hold two o. ideas in the mind FITZGERALD, F. SCOTT, 27
I even o. the death penalty KENNEDY, EDWARD M., 2
opposite o. is also a great truth MANN, THOMAS, 8
opposition I have spent many years...in o. ROOSEVELT, ELEANOR, 2
The duty of an o. CHURCHILL, RANDOLPH (1849–95), 1
oppressed O. people...oppressive when first liberated KENNEDY, FLORYNCE R., 8
oppression a system of o. has become institutionalized KENNEDY, FLORYNCE R., 9
o. did...make the Irish a craftie people DAVIES, JOHN, 2
O. makes the wise man mad BROWNING, ROBERT, 39
so likewise shall we...render sinewless...o. LAWRENCE, GEORGE, 1
To overthrow o. has been sanctioned by humanity MANDELA, NELSON, 20
oppressive We live in o. times MAMET, DAVID, 18
oppressors We cannot have the o. telling the oppressed how to rid themselves TOURÉ, KWAME, 2
optimism o.: A kind of heart stimulant HUBBARD, ELBERT, 13
O. is an alienated form of faith FROMM, ERICH, 9
O. is the content of small men FITZGERALD, F. SCOTT, 26
o. most flourishes...lunatic asylum ELLIS, HAVELOCK, 6
optimist an o....fills up his crossword puzzle in ink SHORTER, CLEMENT KING, 1
an o. is a guy /that never had /much experience MARQUIS, DON, 2
an o. who carries a raincoat WILSON, HAROLD, 4
I am an o., unrepentant and militant USTINOV, PETER, 5
I am not an o. but a meliorist ELIOT, GEORGE, 28
o., in the atomic age CROUSE, RUSSELL M., 1
The o. proclaims...best of all possible worlds CABELL, JAMES BRANCH, 3
optimistic O. lies SHAW, GEORGE BERNARD, 71
oracle I am Sir O. SHAKESPEARE, WILLIAM, 596
oracular the use of my o. tongue SHERIDAN, RICHARD BRINSLEY, 11
oral contraception a terrific story about o. ALLEN, WOODY, 24
oral sex worst thing about o. LIPMAN, MAUREEN, 1
orange bowler hats...O. sashes, polished boots MURPHY, RICHARD, 2
Orangeman O. with a rifle...ridiculous figure PEARSE, PATRICK, 2
oranges O. and lemons CHILDREN'S VERSE, 57
orange-tree Oh that I were an o. HERBERT, GEORGE, 6
orangutan an o. trying to play the violin BALZAC, HONORÉ DE, 10
oration a magnificent o. by Agrippa PLINY THE ELDER, 12
orators What o. lack in depth MONTESQUIEU, 13
oratory object of o....persuasion MACAULAY, THOMAS BABINGTON, 26
Rhetorical o. is the foundation JOHNSON, JAMES WELDON, 2
orchestra golden rules for an o.: start...and finish together BEECHAM, THOMAS, 3
o. whirls me wider than Uranus flies WHITMAN, WALT, 41
orchid o....bore me no fruit QU YUAN, 2
orchids many colored shining o. DUNCAN, ISADORA, 10
ordained He o. twelve BIBLE, 351
o. for the procreation of children BOOK OF COMMON PRAYER, 23
order All things began in o., so shall they end BROWNE, THOMAS, 35
Good o. is the foundation BURKE, EDMUND, 39
o. and beauty...and sensual indulgence BAUDELAIRE, CHARLES, 13
o. imposes itself on things RADIGUET, RAYMOND, 1
O. is heaven's first law POPE, ALEXANDER, 29
o. of the acts is planned PASTERNAK, BORIS, 4
Stand not upon the o. of your going SHAKESPEARE, WILLIAM, 404
The old o. changeth TENNYSON, ALFRED, 18
"They o....this matter better in France" STERNE, LAURENCE, 1
ordering better o. of the universe ALFONSO X, 1
orderly I am an o. man BOGARDE, DIRK, 1
so o. in his way of life SOCRATES, 2

orders final o. given him by his master VERNE, JULES, 1
ordinary don't pretend to be an o. housewife TAYLOR, ELIZABETH, 5
I can with ease become an o. fool THOMAS, DYLAN, 33
Stella, an o. American, indistinguishable OZICK, CYNTHIA, 4
Oregon green damp England of O. COOKE, ALISTAIR, 1
organ Seated...at the o. PROCTER, ADELAIDE ANN, 1
The only bodily o. which is really regarded as inferior FREUD, SIGMUND, 32
organic O. life...from the protozoon to the philosopher RUSSELL, BERTRAND, 19
organisation an o. that is not a machine HANDY, CHARLES, 4
o....protective against mental illness STORR, ANTHONY, 1
organisations Most o. are not designed HANDY, CHARLES, 2
organiser deviationingist old o. of futility GOLDMAN, EMMA, 1
organisms All o....influenced by the consequences SKINNER, B. F., 1
complete o. don't need to drink DOS PASSOS, JOHN, 5
organization An o. can develop a strong...conscience BIRD, FREDERICK BRUCE, 1
contrary to the o. of the mind NAPOLEON I, 21
Everybody in an o. has to believe IACOCCA, LEE, 7
o....grounded in the idea of exclusion MILLER, ARTHUR, 14
o. that...operates like a smaller business KOTTER, JOHN P., 5
things that evolve...in an o. DRUCKER, PETER, 16
organizations Failing o. are usually over-managed BENNIS, WARREN, 16
Modern o....built on making conflict constructive DRUCKER, PETER, 3
O. are becoming like insects MULGAN, GEOFF, 2
O....less heavily structured through internal architectures MULGAN, GEOFF, 3
o. now must compete in two marketplaces MOUGAYAR, WALID, 2
o....require a high degree of social cooperation FUKUYAMA, FRANCIS, 10
people in o. may have vision BENNIS, WARREN, 14
winning o....a pack of wolves HAMEL, GARY, 2
organize O. for the next day MCCORMACK, MARK, 15
organized an o. hypocrisy DISRAELI, BENJAMIN, 17
Who o. this standing ovation STALIN, JOSEPH, 8
orgasm absence of the vaginal o. FREUD, SIGMUND, 50
The o. has replaced the Cross MUGGERIDGE, MALCOLM, 5
orgies City of o. WHITMAN, WALT, 8
orgy An o. looks particularly alluring MUGGERIDGE, MALCOLM, 4
you *need* an o., once in a while NASH, OGDEN, 22
orient o....vacillates between the West's contempt SAID, EDWARD W., 3
Orientals If we heard it said of O. LA BRUYÈRE, JEAN DE, 7
origin The o. of action...is choice ARISTOTLE, 14
The o. of the leisure society ZELDIN, THEODORE, 5
original An o. writer...nobody can imitate CHATEAUBRIAND, RENÉ, 1
A thought is often o. HOLMES, OLIVER WENDELL, 21
Behold the bright o. appear GAY, JOHN, 1
I have nothing o. in me— /Excepting Original Sin CAMPBELL, THOMAS, 8
o. is unfaithful to the translation BORGES, JORGE LUIS, 1
she's the o. good time that was had by all DAVIS, BETTE, 4
originality All good things...are the fruits of o. MILL, JOHN STUART, 10
O. is the essence of true scholarship AZIKIWE, NNAMDI, 1
original sin Mona did researches in o. PLOMER, WILLIAM, 4
originators Every people should be the o. DELANY, MARTIN ROBINSON, 3
We were the o. of...this stuff DIDDLEY, BO, 2
ornament An o. to her profession BUNYAN, JOHN, 17
orthodoxy O. is my doxy WARBURTON, WILLIAM, 1
"o."...no longer means being right CHESTERTON, G. K., 15
O. or My-doxy CARLYLE, THOMAS, 41
To overturn o....no easier in science HUBBARD, RUTH, 1
Oscar Nothing would disgust me more...winning an O. BUÑUEL, LUIS, 6
We all assume that O. said it WILDE, OSCAR, 6
ostrich the wings of an o. DRYDEN, JOHN, 3
Othello I felt like O. THOMPSON, HUNTER S., 1
role of O. is the biggest strain OLIVIER, LAURENCE, 2
other Hear the o. side AUGUSTINE OF HIPPO, SAINT, 8
it did a lot of o. things JOYCE, JAMES, 41
O. people are quite dreadful WILDE, OSCAR, 13
others Do not do that which o. can do as well WASHINGTON, BOOKER T., 7
live for o....middle class morality SHAW, GEORGE BERNARD, 79
ouch "O." is a one-word sentence QUINE, WILLARD V., 5
ought those things we o. not to have done BOOK OF COMMON PRAYER, 14
ounce An o. of a man's own wit STERNE, LAURENCE, 8
ourselves It is always o. we love BAINBRIDGE, BERYL, 2
We never are but by o. betrayed CONGREVE, WILLIAM, 15
out It will all come o. in the wash PROVERBS, 287
outcast us put-down, o. makers of jazz MONK, THELONIOUS, 3
outcome the o. serves as a reality check SOROS, GEORGE, 4
outhouse And there's the o. poet ROSTEN, NORMAN, 1
outing O....nasty word for telling the truth MAUPIN, ARMISTEAD, 1
outlook O.: Dry and warm BRYSON, BILL, 3
outright we gave ourselves o. FROST, ROBERT, 9
outside live o. the law DYLAN, BOB, 18
outsiders Spend 50 per cent of your time with "o." PETERS, TOM, 9
outspoken O. by whom PARKER, DOROTHY, 48
outworn O. organizations are not half as malignant CLEAVER, ELDRIDGE, 1
over It ain't o. 'til it's over BERRA, YOGI, 1
overcome We Shall O. SEEGER, PETE, 2
overcomes Who o. /By force MILTON, JOHN, 37
overeducated o. broads with the soft heads PYNCHON, THOMAS, 5
over-educated I've o. myself in all the things COWARD, NOEL, 14
overlord o. of the M5 HILL, GEOFFREY, 2
overpaid o., overfed, oversexed...over here TRINDER, TOMMY, 1
overpaying o. him but he's worth it GOLDWYN, SAMUEL, 26
overrefines Who o. his argument brings himself to grief PETRARCH, 1
overshadowed o. by his overdressed...wife STOPES, MARIE, 7
overspending o. is not money management CROSBY, PHILIP B., 2
overstatement the only kind of statement worth making is an o. LEACOCK, STEPHEN, 20
overtakers o. who keep the undertakers busy PITTS, WILLIAM EWART, 1
overtures I tried to resist his o. PERELMAN, S. J., 5
overworked he rarely used...now o. technical terms, invented by himself FREUD, SIGMUND, 5
Ovid O., the soft philosopher of love DRYDEN, JOHN, 30
owe as we o. everything to him SHAKESPEARE, WILLIAM, 23
I don't o. a penny to a single soul WODEHOUSE, P. G., 10

If there's anyone listening to whom I o. money FLYNN, ERROL, 2
I o. nothing to Women's Lib THATCHER, MARGARET, 24
O. no man anything, but to love one another BIBLE, 486
owl The O. and the Pussy-Cat went to sea LEAR, EDWARD, 16
ox This dumb o. will fill the whole world AQUINAS, THOMAS, 1
Oxford might have been to O. twice DOUGLAS-HOME, ALEC, 1
O. is...more attractive than Cambridge BAEDEKER, KARL, 1
The clever men at O. GRAHAME, KENNETH, 5
oxygen the o. of publicity THATCHER, MARGARET, 17
oyster He was a bold man that first ate an o. SWIFT, JONATHAN, 32
o....more reasoning power than a scientist WALLACE, ALFRED RUSSEL, 1
Ozymandias My name is O. SHELLEY, PERCY BYSSHE, 10

pace man does not keep p. with...companions THOREAU, HENRY DAVID, 31
pacifism Extreme p....getting yourself slaughtered AMICHAI, YEHUDA, 8
My p. is not based on...intellectual theory EINSTEIN, ALBERT, 59
pacifist p. revolutionary...akin to a vegetarian lion PERÓN, JUAN DOMINGO, 2
The quietly p. peaceful /always die WALKER, ALICE, 18
packed My bag is always p. XU WENLI, 1
padded shoulders P. are an abomination POST, EMILY, 3
paddle every man p. his own canoe MARRYAT, FREDERICK, 2
P. your own canoe PROVERBS, 487
pagan A P. suckled in a creed outworn WORDSWORTH, WILLIAM, 67
page if p. 534 finds us...in the second chapter DOYLE, ARTHUR CONAN, 19
p. of history...worth a volume of logic HOLMES, OLIVER WENDELL, JR., 3
pages spring from the p. into your arms WHITMAN, WALT, 29
pain After great p., a formal feeling DICKINSON, EMILY, 18
A mighty p. to love it is COWLEY, ABRAHAM, 2
But p. is perfect misery MILTON, JOHN, 71
I have no p., dear mother, now FARMER, EDWARD, 1
Man endures p. as an undeserved punishment PROVERBS, MODERN, 17
Much of your p. is self-chosen GIBRAN, KAHLIL, 5
not...bear p. unless there is hope EDWARDES, MICHAEL, 1
P. and death are a part of life ELLIS, HAVELOCK, 4
P.—has an Element of Blank DICKINSON, EMILY, 10
P. is life LAMB, CHARLES, 4
P. is unjust RACINE, JEAN, 11
P. of mind...pain of body PUBLILIUS SYRUS, 16
P. with the thousand teeth WATSON, WILLIAM, 2
Remember that p. has this most excellent quality SENECA, "THE YOUNGER," 10
Significant p. isolates you BANKS, RUSSELL, 3
The least p. in our little finger HAZLITT, WILLIAM, 6
The p. passes, but the beauty remains. RENOIR, PIERRE AUGUSTE, 4
pained greatly p. at how little he was pained WAUGH, EVELYN, 19
pains too much p. to think otherwise HUME, DAVID, 15
With what shift and p. we come into the World BROWNE, THOMAS, 6
paint He best can p. them who can feel them Most POPE, ALEXANDER, 4
I could not p. fast enough MÜNTER, GABRIELE, 1
I p. objects as I think them PICASSO, PABLO, 8
I p....to be very intimate and human ROTHKO, MARK, 1
I p. with the stubbornness I need VALADON, SUZANNE, 2
My business is to p....I see TURNER, J. M. W., 2
nothing more difficult...than to p. a rose MATISSE, HENRI, 3
p. a world of resounding power ZHANG YIMOU, 1
p. me as a ruler of men LAURIER, WILFRID, 2
Some people p. Picassos and some...fingerpaint ROTH, DAVID LEE, 2
Sometimes I see it and then p. it JOHNS, JASPER, 2
'Tis labor in vain to p....midday light DU FRESNOY, CHARLES-ALPHONSE, 2
To p. well is to express one's own time CÉZANNE, PAUL, 4
You p. *from* your subject O'KEEFFE, GEORGIA, 1
paintbrush I...cannot stand the sight of a p. ROSA, SALVATOR, 1
painted He p....firm insolent /Young whore GUNN, THOM, 1
I p. Our Lord as a boy LEONARDO DA VINCI, 14
p. /women under the gas lamps SANDBURG, CARL, 5
painter A p. should not paint what he sees VALÉRY, PAUL, 2
Every good p. who aspires...should...marry my wife DALÍ, SALVADOR, 5
I could have become a real p. HOKUSAI, 1
never been a boy p. CONSTABLE, JOHN, 3
the p., is he the creator or maker PLATO, 28
The p. Orbaneja of Ubeda, if he chanced to draw a cock CERVANTES, MIGUEL DE, 4
Whatever exists...p. has first in his mind LEONARDO DA VINCI, 13
painters Do it like the p. used to SCORSESE, MARTIN, 2
Good p. imitate nature CERVANTES, MIGUEL DE, 53
most worthy p....have aided nature with art AGUCCHI, GIOVANNI BATTISTA, 1
P. and poets...license to dare HORACE, 1
P. and Sculptors...exceed and remain superior to nature BELLORI, GIOVANNI PIETRO, 2
P. and Sculptors, imitating that first maker BELLORI, GIOVANNI PIETRO, 1
p., poets and builders have very high flights CHURCHILL, SARAH, 1
p. who transform the sun into a yellow spot PICASSO, PABLO, 17
P....worker priests of the cult of man MARDEN, BRICE, 1
p. work from...within POLLOCK, JACKSON, 4
why the old p. were so...superior MILL, JOHN STUART, 16
painting a great difference between p. a face FULLER, THOMAS (1608–61), 1
Any p. is an object STELLA, FRANK, 1
A p.'s meaning lies...in its destination LEVINE, SHERRIE, 1
Between me and p. there is nothing DELAUNAY, SONIA, 1
delineation of a sphere on a flat plane...similar to p. GREGORAS, NICEPHORUS, 1
first virtue of a p. DELACROIX, EUGÈNE, 4
form of my p. is the content KELLY, ELLSWORTH, 1
how I started p. money WARHOL, ANDY, 6
I can...literally be "in" the p. POLLOCK, JACKSON, 3
idea of an isolated American p....seems absurd POLLOCK, JACKSON, 1
If I didn't start p....raised chickens GRANDMA MOSES, 3
If people only knew...about p. LANDSEER, EDWIN HENRY, 1
I just keep p. till I feel like pinching RENOIR, PIERRE AUGUSTE, 3
Is she not more than p. can express ROWE, NICHOLAS, 2
Love and delight...teachers of...P. DÜRER, ALBRECHT, 1
no such thing as good p. about nothing ROTHKO, MARK, 2
of importance in p. is paint OLITSKI, JULES, 1
P....a cruel jilt to me MORSE, SAMUEL, 1
p....a form of drawing KLINE, FRANZ, 2
P....art of protecting flat surfaces BIERCE, AMBROSE, 37

P....Uncrowned King of Ireland PARNELL, CHARLES STEWART, 2
parrot There is a p. imitating spring DOVE, RITA, 1
This p. is no more MONTY PYTHON'S FLYING CIRCUS, 5
to sell the family p. ROGERS, WILL, 15
parson P. might preach, & drink, & sing BLAKE, WILLIAM, 24
part a little flesh and breath, and the ruling p. MARCUS AURELIUS, 1
If you're not p. of the solution PROVERBS, MODERN, 14
p. at last without a kiss MORRIS, WILLIAM, 3
play the same p. all...your life ABBOTT, GEORGE, 2
p. never calls for it MIRREN, HELEN, 2
p. of Quoyle that was wonderful PROULX, E. ANNIE, 1
read p. of it all the way GOLDWYN, SAMUEL, 8
We only p. to meet again GAY, JOHN, 4
partial no such thing as p. independence SAID, EDWARD W., 5
parties it is always like that at p. PROUST, MARCEL, 22
one of those p., got out of hand, you know BRUCE, LENNY, 2
parting Every p. gives a foretaste of death SCHOPENHAUER, ARTHUR, 4
P. is such sweet sorrow SHAKESPEARE, WILLIAM, 540
P. is the younger sister of death MANDELSTAM, OSIP, 5
P.'s well-paid with soon again to meet PATMORE, COVENTRY, 7
partisanship P. is our great curse ROBINSON, JAMES HARVEY, 1
partners Mr. Morgan buys his p. MORGAN, JOHN PIERPONT, 1
partridge p. in a pear tree CHILDREN'S VERSE, 22
parts It is seldom...one p. on good terms PROUST, MARCEL, 10
P. of it are excellent NEWSPAPERS, 2
three p. iced over ARNOLD, MATTHEW, 4
party A great p. is not to be brought down HAILSHAM, LORD, 1
A p. of order...necessary elements...of political life MILL, JOHN STUART, 7
Every p. in Ireland...founded on the gun HUME, JOHN, 1
Heard there was a p.. Came LILLIE, BEATRICE, 3
In our p., being a woman is no problem DO CARMO, ISABEL, 1
It's my p. and I'll cry WEINER, HERB, 1
never belonged to any political p. LA GUARDIA, FIORELLO, 2
new p....not be allowed to exist LI PENG, 2
No p. has a monopoly over...right GORBACHEV, MIKHAIL, 5
P. honesty is party expediency CLEVELAND, GROVER, 2
p. is a political evil BOLINGBROKE, HENRY ST. JOHN, 4
P. is organized opinion DISRAELI, BENJAMIN, 42
p. member must cultivate...style of work DENG XIAOPING, 7
p. which takes credit for the rain MORROW, DWIGHT WHITNEY, 2
sooner every p. breaks up the better AUSTEN, JANE, 15
Then none was for a p. MACAULAY, THOMAS BABINGTON, 23
The p. has already drawn...correct conclusion LI PENG, 3
we are the p. of the community BLAIR, TONY, 8
Well, did you evah! What a swell p. PORTER, COLE, 8
without p....government is impossible DISRAELI, BENJAMIN, 45
Pasadena P., where the stuffy millionaires holed up CHANDLER, RAYMOND, 7
pass They shall not p. IBÁRRURI, DOLORES, 5
They shall not p. PÉTAIN, HENRI PHILIPPE, 1
passage a p. which...is particularly fine, strike it out JOHNSON, SAMUEL, 141
passages For the sake of a few fine...p. WORDSWORTH, WILLIAM, 6
passed p. from death unto life BIBLE, 277
That p. the time BECKETT, SAMUEL, 22
the people were p. clean over Jordan BIBLE, 307
We have all p. a lot of water GOLDWYN, SAMUEL, 25
passes Men seldom make p. PARKER, DOROTHY, 4
what *is* p....into what *was* OATES, JOYCE CAROL, 3
passing They are p., posthaste...the gliding years NABOKOV, VLADIMIR, 10
passion Before I felt p. for any woman RIVERA, JOSÉ EUSTASIO, 1
cheated into p....reasoned into truth DRYDEN, JOHN, 35
May I govern my p. with absolute sway POPE, WALTER, 1
p. and desire...not the same as truth WILSON, EDWARD O., 1
p. for the name of "Mary" BYRON, LORD, 68
P. is like genius: a miracle ROLLAND, ROMAIN, 3
p....moved into his body like a stranger MILLER, ARTHUR, 4
P. too deep seems like none DU MU, 2
remark any p. or principle HUME, DAVID, 25
So I triumph'd ere my p. TENNYSON, ALFRED, 55
Strange fits of p. have I known WORDSWORTH, WILLIAM, 33
that man /That is not p.'s slave SHAKESPEARE, WILLIAM, 185
The ruling p. conquers reason still POPE, ALEXANDER, 40
passionate As far as the p. spirit MIRÓ, JOAN, 9
passions basest p. have roused...my nature HALLAM, ARTHUR HENRY, 19
In men, we various ruling p. find; /In women, two POPE, ALEXANDER, 39
man who is master of his p. CONNOLLY, CYRIL, 22
P. are less mischievous than boredom BARBEY D'AUREVILLY, JULES-AMÉDÉE, 4
p. are most like to floods and streams RALEIGH, WALTER, 2
P. fade when one removes them FLAUBERT, GUSTAVE, 9
Three p....have governed my life RUSSELL, BERTRAND, 40
passover it is the Lord's p. BIBLE, 74
past Each has his p. shut in him WOOLF, VIRGINIA, 10
Man has truly a p. only...conscious ARON, RAYMOND, 1
p....only dead thing that smells sweet THOMAS, EDWARD, 2
p....product of all the present BECKER, CARL, 6
p....prophecy of the present HAWTHORNE, NATHANIEL, 6
putting the p. to bed HANDY, CHARLES, 6
quite true that the p. *haunts* us ARENDT, HANNAH, 26
Study the p. CONFUCIUS, 18
The p. is a foreign country HARTLEY, L. P., 3
The p. is a kind of screen BECKER, CARL, 10
The p. is a rich resource on which we can draw in order to make decisions for the future MANDELA, NELSON, 18
The p. is never dead FAULKNER, WILLIAM, 17
The p....is secure WEBSTER, DANIEL, 3
The P. lies upon the Present HAWTHORNE, NATHANIEL, 7
the p. must yield to...the future BENNETT, ARNOLD, 1
The p. was nothing...The future was a mystery CHOPIN, KATE, 2
The p. will provide...any fate BECKER, CARL, 11
What is p. is not dead WOLF, CHRISTA, 2
what's p. help /Should be past grief SHAKESPEARE, WILLIAM, 661
What we know of the p....not worth knowing INGE, WILLIAM RALPH, 5
Who can afford to live in the p. PINTER, HAROLD, 6
Who controls the p. controls...the future ORWELL, GEORGE, 21
Why doesn't the p. decently bury itself LAWRENCE, D. H., 46
Pasternak poems of P....cure for tuberculosis PASTERNAK, BORIS, 1
Pasteur Louis P. was the greatest Frenchman ANONYMOUS, 67
pastoral investiture by the gift of the p. staff EADMER, 1
p....an aesthetic category for aristocrats HOLUB, MIROSLAV, 2
pat-a-cake p., baker's man CHILDREN'S VERSE, 64

Patagonia the train to P. THEROUX, PAUL, 15
patch P. grief with proverbs SHAKESPEARE, WILLIAM, 462
pate You beat your p. POPE, ALEXANDER, 35
paternal dear and kindly p. image DANTE ALIGHIERI, 3
paternalism P. has become a nasty word MCGREGOR, DOUGLAS M., 2
path p. followed by the brain in materializing a dream PICASSO, PABLO, 14
pathetic nothing more p. than...laughter of people WESKER, ARNOLD, 3
patience He that has p. may compass anything RABELAIS, FRANÇOIS, 7
like P. on a monument SHAKESPEARE, WILLIAM, 701
P. and passage of time LA FONTAINE, JEAN DE, 9
P....form of despair, disguised as a virtue BIERCE, AMBROSE, 38
P. is a virtue PROVERBS, 361
P. is the best medicine FLORIO, JOHN, 1
P. is the best remedy PLAUTUS, 6
Talk of the p. of Job, said a Hospital nurse PAGET, STEPHEN, 1
There is a p. of the wild LONDON, JACK, 9
the years teach us p. TAYLOR, ELIZABETH, 2
Though p. be a tired mare SHAKESPEARE, WILLIAM, 262
we through p....might have hope BIBLE, 487
patient An unruly p. makes a harsh physician PUBLILIUS SYRUS, 14
a p. of sense HOLMES, OLIVER WENDELL, 19
cure their p. and lose their fee RUSKIN, JOHN, 17
God help the p. MANSFIELD, WILLIAM MURRAY, 3
if the p. can keep awake TROTTER, WILFRED, 1
In treating a p....strengthen his natural vitality AL-RAZI, 2
It is the p. rather than the case which requires treatment MORRIS, ROBERT TUTTLE, 1
Keep up the spirits of your p. MONDEVILLE, HENRI DE, 1
The safest thing for a p. MAYO, CHARLES HORACE, 7
we cannot cut the p. in half SCHICK, BÉLA, 5
what a p. tells you his doctor has said JENNER, WILLIAM, 1
What I call a good p. HOLMES, OLIVER WENDELL, 3
patients a small number of p. with peptic ulcer MAYO, WILLIAM JAMES, 2
p. being willing to steal MORRIS, ROBERT TUTTLE, 2
p....had no name FRAME, JANET, 1
Private p....can go elsewhere ABERNETHY, JOHN, 2
patriarch I am just as much the P. in my art as he DONATELLO, 1
patriarchal Within p. society, women...victimized by male violence HOOKS, BELL, 2
patriot He was a great p....provided...that he really is dead VOLTAIRE, 52
"My country, right or wrong"...no p. would think of saying CHESTERTON, G. K., 34
Never was p....but was a fool DRYDEN, JOHN, 18
patriotism knock the p. out of the human race SHAW, GEORGE BERNARD, 75
p....fulfils our worst wishes HUXLEY, ALDOUS, 24
p. had to be proved in blood NEWSPAPERS, 3
P....is a revolutionary duty TROTSKY, LEON, 11
p. is like charity JAMES, HENRY, 29
p. is not enough CAVELL, EDITH, 1
P. is often an arbitrary veneration NATHAN, G. J., 2
P. is the last refuge JOHNSON, SAMUEL, 109
P. is the last refuge of the sculptor PLOMER, WILLIAM, 5
P....looking out for yourself while COOLIDGE, CALVIN, 15
P....the first bolt-hole of the hypocrite BRAGG, MELVYN, 1
p. which consists in hating all other nations GASKELL, ELIZABETH, 4
The religion of Hell is p. CABELL, JAMES BRANCH, 2
True p. is of no party SMOLLETT, TOBIAS, 2
patron a P....looks with unconcern on a man JOHNSON, SAMUEL, 172
patronizing p. disposition ...has its meaner side ELIOT, GEORGE, 6
patron saint p. of the peripheral MEAD, MARGARET, 1
patter particularly rapid, unintelligible p. GILBERT, W. S., 21
paucity the p. of human pleasures JOHNSON, SAMUEL, 48
paunch his p. grew mutinous BROWNING, ROBERT, 20
man...must wear his belt under...p. DE VRIES, PETER, 4
pause Now I'll have *eine kleine* P. FERRIER, KATHLEEN, 1
pauses the p. between the notes SCHNABEL, ARTUR, 1
pave we could p. the whole country REAGAN, RONALD, 31
pay A man may p....for his livelihood THOREAU, HENRY DAVID, 3
Can't P.!...Won't Pay! FO, DARIO, 1
not my interest to p. the principal SHERIDAN, RICHARD BRINSLEY, 21
p....with money...they have not got HURST, GERALD, 1
pays He that dies p. all debts SHAKESPEARE, WILLIAM, 649
He who p. the piper PROVERBS, 255
peace a just and lasting p. among ourselves LINCOLN, ABRAHAM, 25
all her paths are p. SPRING-RICE, CECIL ARTHUR, 1
And who will bring white p. LINDSAY, VACHEL, 6
a period of cold p. LIE, TRYGVE, 1
Arms alone are not enough to keep the p. KENNEDY, JOHN FITZGERALD, 29
days of p. and slumberous calm KEATS, JOHN (1795–1821), 86
forbidden...to make p. with a monarch GENGHIS KHAN, 2
For I must go where lazy P. DAVENANT, WILLIAM, 1
Give P. a Chance LENNON, JOHN, 5
He accepted p. WELLINGTON, DUKE OF, 1
If p. cannot be maintained with honour RUSSELL, LORD, 2
I live in p. with men MACHADO, ANTONIO, 3
I'm no p.-creep BARGER, SONNY, 1
in time of p....prepare for war BARTON, CLARA, 2
I want p....I'm willing to fight TRUMAN, HARRY S., 2
Knowledge of p. /passes...like children's games AMICHAI, YEHUDA, 3
Let him who desires p., prepare for war VEGETIUS, 1
Let us have p. GRANT, ULYSSES S., 5
My p. is gone, /My heart is heavy GOETHE, JOHANN WOLFGANG VON, 12
never was a good war or a bad p. FRANKLIN, BENJAMIN, 10
no p....unto the wicked BIBLE, 217
Nothing is more conducive to p. of mind LICHTENBERG, GEORG CHRISTOPH, 3
not to send p., but a sword BIBLE, 396
no way to p.. Peace is the way MUSTE, A. J., 1
now we have to win the p. CLEMENCEAU, GEORGES, 7
Only p. will emanate from German soil KOHL, HELMUT, 2
Open covenants of p. WILSON, WOODROW, 24
p. and propagation WALPOLE, HORACE, 5
p. at that price would be a humiliation LLOYD-GEORGE, DAVID, 8
P., Bread and Land MOTTOS AND SLOGANS, 36
P. cannot be built on exclusion ADAMS, GERRY, 2
P., commerce, and honest friendship JEFFERSON, THOMAS, 5
Perpetual p. is a dream MOLTKE, HELMUTH JOHANNES VON, 2
P. goes into the making of a poem NERUDA, PABLO, 1
p. has broken out BRECHT, BERTOLT, 14
P. hath her victories MILTON, JOHN, 22

p. I hope with honour DISRAELI, BENJAMIN, 40
p. in being what one is BETTI, UGO, 2
P. is indivisible LITVINOV, MAXIM MAXIMOVICH, 1
P. is made with yesterday's enemies PERES, SHIMON, 1
P. is much more precious than...land SADAT, ANWAR AL-, 3
P....is no original state BRANDT, WILLY, 3
P. is not only better than war SHAW, GEORGE BERNARD, 32
plant p....I do not want discord ANGELOU, MAYA, 13
P....period of cheating BIERCE, AMBROSE, 39
P. took them all prisoner HUGHES, TED, 2
Public p. is the act of public trust WRIGHT, RICHARD, 4
p. with honour. I believe it is peace for our time CHAMBERLAIN, NEVILLE, 9
seek the true meaning of p. DALAI LAMA, 5
The Bomb brought p. but man alone CHURCHILL, WINSTON, 35
the miasma of p. seems more suffocating STEINER, GEORGE, 1
the p. of God, which passeth all understanding BIBLE, 452
The pursuit of p. KISSINGER, HENRY, 4
There can be no p. of mind in love PROUST, MARCEL, 7
there is nothing...meaning of p. BETTI, UGO, 9
We wanted p. on earth MCCARTNEY, PAUL, 1
When p. has been broken anywhere ROOSEVELT, FRANKLIN D., 21
You may either win your p. or buy it RUSKIN, JOHN, 1

peaceful Be p., be courteous, obey the law MALCOLM X, 10

peace process p. will be irreversible ADAMS, GERRY, 5

peach dare to eat a p. ELIOT, T. S., 34
ripest p. is highest on the tree RILEY, JAMES WHITCOMB, 1

peaches With p. and women OUIDA, 1

peak you have to p. ten times THOMPSON, DALEY, 1

peanuts If you pay p., you get monkeys GOLDSMITH, JAMES, 7

pearls P. before swine PARKER, DOROTHY, 38

peas I eat my p. with honey FOLK VERSE, 9

peasant humblest p. is as free...as the proudest monarch GARNET, HENRY HIGHLAND, 3
O what a rogue and p. slave am I! SHAKESPEARE, WILLIAM, 165

peasants better that...these p. should be killed LUTHER, MARTIN, 5
How do p. die TOLSTOY, LEO, 18

pease As lyke as one p. is to another LYLY, JOHN, 5

pebbles change the p. of our puddly thought DU BARTAS, GUILLAUME, 16

peck picked a p. of pickled pepper CHILDREN'S VERSE, 36

pedantic I acquired a certain p. presumption PÉREZ GALDÓS, BENITO, 3

peer A life p. is like a mule SHACKLETON, LORD, 1
a p. can make a bit of extra money NEWSPAPERS, 24

peerage When I want a p., I shall buy one NORTHCLIFFE, LORD, 1

Peking P.'s food...part of the city's life LO, KENNETH H., 1

pelican A wonderful bird is the p. MERRITT, DIXON LANIER, 1

pen I cannot put p. to paper ISHERWOOD, CHRISTOPHER, 6
p. is mightier than the sword LYTTON, BULWER, 2
p. is the tongue CERVANTES, MIGUEL DE, 33
The squat p. rests HEANEY, SEAMUS, 1

penance The man hath p. done COLERIDGE, SAMUEL TAYLOR, 47

pendulum The p. of the mind JUNG, CARL GUSTAV, 14

Penelope P....no more meant for a baker FULLER, MARGARET, 7

pennies P. do not come from heaven THATCHER, MARGARET, 28
P. from Heaven BURKE, JOHNNY, 1
Take care of the p. PROVERBS, 391

penny A p. for your thoughts SWIFT, JONATHAN, 38
A p. saved PROVERBS, 139
In for a p. PROVERBS, 273
P. saved is a penny got FIELDING, HENRY, 2
P. wise PROVERBS, 362

pennyworth bought a p. of life DE LA MARE, WALTER, 7

pens Let other p. dwell on guilt and misery AUSTEN, JANE, 22

people all God's p....like to play MUIR, JOHN, 8
A lot of p. are disappointed LEE, SPIKE, 2
A p. not prepared to face its own history HANSEN, KARL-HEINZ, 1
A p....rise to the completer life of one BROWNING, ROBERT, 40
Every p. should be left free WILSON, WOODROW, 5
For a p. to be without History COMMAGER, HENRY STEELE, 5
forget that ...p. are human HUXLEY, ALDOUS, 52
How do p. go to sleep PARKER, DOROTHY, 16
I am for p. CHAPLIN, CHARLIE, 9
I didn't think p. invented anymore PYNCHON, THOMAS, 6
If p. behaved...the way nations do WILLIAMS, TENNESSEE, 18
if the p....can be reached with the truth ROOSEVELT, ELEANOR, 5
I like the kind to which I belong: p. BÖLL, HEINRICH, 2
I love the p. with their straightforward minds BRECHT, BERTOLT, 15
It is with...p. as with...bottles POPE, ALEXANDER, 54
make p. think they're thinking MARQUIS, DON, 1
Most p. seek...they do not possess SADAT, ANWAR AL-, 1
my p. *is* my soul BUBER, MARTIN, 9
never has a p. felt more deceived BOORSTIN, DANIEL J., 2
not one...who think...the p. are never...wrong BURKE, EDMUND, 53
Once the p. begin to reason VOLTAIRE, 11
p. annoy me...talking about...dumb animals LOFTING, HUGH, 2
P. are either charming or tedious WILDE, OSCAR, 29
P. are inexterminable FROST, ROBERT, 20
P. are our most valuable capital STALIN, JOSEPH, 13
P. are people...not personnel PETERS, TOM, 14
P. are prone to build a statue HURSTON, ZORA NEALE, 7
p....complained of the long voyage COLUMBUS, CHRISTOPHER, 4
p....creatures of emotion CARNEGIE, DALE, 2
P. don't do such things IBSEN, HENRIK, 12
P. don't start wars, governments do REAGAN, RONALD, 37
P. don't want to like you TURLINGTON, CHRISTIE, 1
P. either think I'm famous MAUPIN, ARMISTEAD, 4
p. give out of the goodness of their hearts FALL, AMINATA SOW, 1
P. have power when people think they have FOWLER, WILLIAM WYCHE, 1
Pleasant p. are just as real as horrible people BRAINE, JOHN, 2
P....lives riding iron bicycles O'BRIEN, FLANN, 9
p. may be made to follow a course of action CONFUCIUS, 19
P. must help one another LA FONTAINE, JEAN DE, 5
p....strongest links in our networks GOLEMAN, DANIEL, 5
P....taking care of their health STERNE, LAURENCE, 16
p. under suspicion are better moving KAFKA, FRANZ, 6
p....usually imitate each other HOFFER, ERIC, 2
P. who can see, often don't WONDER, STEVIE, 2
P. who can't talk...who can't read ZAPPA, FRANK, 3
p. who do things MORROW, DWIGHT WHITNEY, 1
P. who like this sort of thing LINCOLN, ABRAHAM, 34
p. who love to tell us what to do MACINNES, COLIN, 2
P. who need people are the luckiest MERRILL, BOB, 1
P. who never get carried away FORBES, STEVE, 1
p. whose company is coveted MACCARTHY, DESMOND, 1

P. will perform at their potential SEMLER, RICARDO, 6
p. will see, tremble, and groan LENIN, VLADIMIR ILYICH, 6
P. will swim through shit SELLERS, PETER, 1
Some p. are...turned on by money VAN BUREN, ABIGAIL, 3
suppose the p. good, and the magistrate corruptible ROBESPIERRE, MAXIMILIEN, 1
Takes all kinds to make my p. WIDEMAN, JOHN EDGAR, 1
talk of p. trying to convince themselves SNYDER, GARY, 2
the only p. who like to be told how bad things CHURCHILL, WINSTON, 75
The p. are at bay LEASE, MARY ELIZABETH, 2
The p. are unreal BARRYMORE, ETHEL, 1
The p.—could you patent the sun? SALK, JONAS E., 1
The p. have lost confidence in themselves BEAVERBROOK, MAX AITKEN, LORD, 1
the p. we should have been seen dead with WEST, REBECCA, 10
The p. would be just as noisy CROMWELL, OLIVER, 4
These p. have no religion COLUMBUS, CHRISTOPHER, 6
thy p. shall be my people BIBLE, 488
Too many p. grow up DISNEY, WALT, 6
two kinds of p. in the world ARGYLL, 12TH DUKE OF, 1
two p. entitled to refer to themselves as "we" NYE, BILL, 1
we are not a small p. HEATH, EDWARD, 1
we as p. will get to the promised land KING, MARTIN LUTHER, JR., 2
We'll pretend the p. cannot see you BARAKA, IMAMU AMIRI, 13
we need...p. who can think strategically OHMAE, KENICHI, 7
We, the p....a very eloquent beginning JORDAN, BARBARA, 3
what p. say of us is true SMITH, LOGAN PEARSALL, 8
When p....talk...of their aspirations SMITH, LOGAN PEARSALL, 15
When the p. are too comfortable RICHELIEU, CARDINAL, 10

people's will mightiest river of all the p. for peace and freedom ROBESON, PAUL, 4
perception Organized p....what art is all about LICHTENSTEIN, ROY, 2
perceptions All the p. of the human mind HUME, DAVID, 8
perestroika essence of p. GORBACHEV, MIKHAIL, 14
"p." has easily entered the international lexicon GORBACHEV, MIKHAIL, 12
perfect No one is p. in this imperfect world LUMUMBA, PATRICE, 2
P. behavior is born of complete indifference PAVESE, CESARE, 3
p. love casteth out fear BIBLE, 183
the most p. actual world which is possible LEIBNIZ, GOTTFRIED WILHELM, 1
the p. and unique cause of all things DIONYSIUS THE AREOPAGITE, 2
perfection P. has one grave defect MAUGHAM, SOMERSET, 40
P. is the child of Time HALL, JOSEPH, 1
p. of form and beauty is contained in the sum of all men DÜRER, ALBRECHT, 3
The pursuit of p. ARNOLD, MATTHEW, 16
perfectionism The p. of obsessional neurotics STEVENS, ANTHONY, 1
performance The only true p. JAGGER, MICK, 6
performances p. where the public is...without talent JOUVET, LOUIS, 1
performing p. gives...a place where I hide MORRISON, JIM, 5
perfumes All the p. of Arabia will not sweeten SHAKESPEARE, WILLIAM, 410
No p., but very fine linen BRUMMELL, "BEAU," 1
perfuming P. him and bathing him MSHAM, MWANA KUPONA BINTI, 3
perhaps I am going in search of a great p. RABELAIS, FRANÇOIS, 18
The grand P. BROWNING, ROBERT, 49
perils p. both of wind and limb BUTLER, SAMUEL (1612–80), 11
perish P. the Universe CYRANO DE BERGERAC, SAVINIEN, 1
perished If all else p., and he remained BRONTË, EMILY, 3
perjury P. is...bold and open DARLING, CHARLES JOHN, 4
permanence love p. more than...beauty CASSON, HUGH, 1
permissive society The p. has...become a dirty phrase JENKINS, ROY, 1
pernicious most p. race of little odious vermin SWIFT, JONATHAN, 19
Perón If I had not been born P. PERÓN, JUAN DOMINGO, 1
perpendicular p. expression of a horizontal desire SHAW, GEORGE BERNARD, 101
perpetrate p. thirty bad novels HUXLEY, ALDOUS, 1
perpetuate To p. was the task of life LONDON, JACK, 2
perpetuation Why should I consent to the p. of the image PLOTINUS, 2
persecutest Saul, why p. thou me BIBLE, 11
persecution P. is a bad...way to plant religion BROWNE, THOMAS, 18
P. produced its natural effect MACAULAY, THOMAS BABINGTON, 18
Religious p. may shield itself BURKE, EDMUND, 19
perseverance p. in a good cause STERNE, LAURENCE, 12
person A p. can run for years MARSHALL, PAULE, 5
I am not...the sort of p. CARLYLE, JANE, 1
If you give a p. a fish QUAYLE, DAN, 4
most important p. in the operating theatre HOWARD, RUSSELL JOHN, 3
only p....I should like to know WILDE, OSCAR, 30
"p.,"...individual substance of a rational nature BOETHIUS, 1
p....most likely to kill you is yourself YOUNG, JOCK, 1
the only thing that can exist is an uninterested p. CHESTERTON, G. K., 14
We know what a p. thinks SINGER, ISAAC BASHEVIS, 5
personal don't have a warm p. enemy left LUCE, CLARE BOOTHE, 1
p. things people sometimes do...alone in railway carriages MILLER, JONATHAN, 1
personality disturbance of the p....psychic illness HORNEY, KAREN, 15
personnel p. man with his arm around an employee TOWNSEND, ROBERT, 7
persons p. who lived...rich emotional life GIBBONS, STELLA, 1
Such p. are often good HUME, BASIL, 3
persuade P. your neighbors to compromise LINCOLN, ABRAHAM, 20
p. you that things are too difficult BADER, DOUGLAS, 1
Peruvians we P. lie, invent, dream VARGAS LLOSA, MARIO, 9
perverse p. nature can be stimulated by anything BURGESS, ANTHONY, 2
perversity P. is not very inventive PÉREZ GALDÓS, BENITO, 5
P. is the muse of modern literature SONTAG, SUSAN, 3
pessimism P....as agreeable as optimism BENNETT, ARNOLD, 10
P. is a luxury that a Jew never can allow himself MEIR, GOLDA, 3
p. is a mark of superior intellect GALBRAITH, J. K., 8
pessimist A p....looks both ways PETER, LAURENCE J., 1
p.... believes things couldn't possibly be worse BUKOVSKY, VLADIMIR, 1
Scratch a p. BEVERIDGE, WILLIAM HENRY, 2
pessimistic Nothing makes me more p. IONESCO, EUGÈNE, 10
pessimists p. end up...desiring the things they fear MALLET, ROBERT, 1
Peter see Shock-headed P. HOFFMAN, HEINRICH, 4
thou art P. BIBLE, 407
Petersburg live in P....sleep in a grave MANDELSTAM, OSIP, 7
petrifactions p. of a plodding brain BYRON, LORD, 88

petty P. intrigues and dramatic scenes among the relatives MPHAHLELE, ES'KIA, 3
pews Talk about the p. and steeples CHESTERTON, G. K., 31
phantoms P....trifling disorders of the spirit PIRANDELLO, LUIGI, 4
phenomena all tangible p....based on material processes WILSON, EDWARD O., 2
eight...p....worth talking about DILLARD, ANNIE, 4
p. must be *discerned, discriminated, classified* POWELL, JOHN WESLEY, 2
phenomenology P....a transcendental philosophy MERLEAU-PONTY, MAURICE, 2
P. permits psychoanalysis to recognize MERLEAU-PONTY, MAURICE, 9
P. proceeds by...distinguishing meanings HUSSERL, EDMUND, 1
Philadelphia I'd rather be in P. FIELDS, W. C., 10
I went to P., but it was closed FIELDS, W. C., 7
P....City of Bleak November Afternoons PERELMAN, S. J., 1
P.—most colonial of our true Colonial Dames DALY, T. A., 1
Philadelphian The religious severity of P. manners TROLLOPE, FRANCES, 2
philanthropist Suspicion...necessary for the p. RUSSELL, BERTRAND, 44
Philippi thou shalt see me at P. SHAKESPEARE, WILLIAM, 317
Philippines People of the P. MACARTHUR, DOUGLAS, 4
Philistine smote the P. in his forehead BIBLE, 229
philosopher Be a p....be still a man HUME, DAVID, 10
Once: a p.; twice: a pervert VOLTAIRE, 55
p....doesn't think in a vacuum WHITEHEAD, A. N., 10
p. no circumstance...is too minute GOLDSMITH, OLIVER, 5
p....redefines his subject GELLNER, ERNEST, 2
p.'s treatment of a question...illness WITTGENSTEIN, LUDWIG, 3
p. /That could endure the toothache SHAKESPEARE, WILLIAM, 461
philosophers P. are as jealous as women SANTAYANA, GEORGE, 2
p. have only interpreted the world MARX, KARL, 25
p. intent on forcing others NOZICK, ROBERT, 2
p....need not bother...about issues NOVALIS, 3
P. never balance between profit and honesty HUME, DAVID, 19
P. use a language...deformed WITTGENSTEIN, LUDWIG, 13
serious p....looking forward to the pension QUINTON, ANTHONY, 1
The great p. are poets MACHADO, ANTONIO, 6
till p. become kings PLATO, 24
philosophic the p. anarchists of the North PEARY, ROBERT EDWIN, 2
philosophical European p. tradition...footnotes to Plato PLATO, 1
proof of p. mediocrity PROUDHON, PIERRE JOSEPH, 1
philosophizing two main requirements for p. SCHOPENHAUER, ARTHUR, 16
philosophy a great advantage for...p. to be...true SANTAYANA, GEORGE, 19
great p. is...a fearless one PÉGUY, CHARLES PIERRE, 12
history is p. teaching by examples DIONYSIUS OF HALICARNASSUS, 1
How charming is divine p. MILTON, JOHN, 19
knowing its limits...p. consists KANT, IMMANUEL, 15
mere touch of cold p. KEATS, JOHN (1795–1821), 18
Method...in...p....shortest way of finding effects HOBBES, THOMAS, 1
modern p. holds passion in contempt KIERKEGAARD, SØREN, 4
new P. calls all in doubt DONNE, JOHN, 10
Not to care for p. PASCAL, BLAISE, 14
p. and vain deceit BIBLE, 23
P. does not exist LAING, R. D., 1
P....is a fight against...fascination WITTGENSTEIN, LUDWIG, 4
P. is...like Russia NIMIER, ROGER, 2
P. is not a theory WITTGENSTEIN, LUDWIG, 7
P. is the childhood of the intellect NAGEL, THOMAS, 2
P. is the product of wonder WHITEHEAD, A. N., 11
P., like medicine, has plenty of drugs CHAMFORT, NICOLAS, 6
P....living voluntarily among ice NIETZSCHE, FRIEDRICH WILHELM, 16
p. ought to...unravel people's mental blocks RAPHAEL, FREDERIC, 3
p....the personal confession of its author NIETZSCHE, FRIEDRICH WILHELM, 1
P. triumphs...over past evils LA ROCHEFOUCAULD, FRANÇOIS, 5
simple p....scratch where it itches LONGWORTH, ALICE LEE, 2
The goal of p....men to understand themselves BERLIN, ISAIAH, 3
The point of p. is to start with something...simple RUSSELL, BERTRAND, 9
Phoebus And P. 'gins arise SHAKESPEARE, WILLIAM, 127
phoenixes bade my p. mount up in flight QU YUAN, 1
phone E. T. p. home E. T., 1
phone box don't...know how to use...a p. DIANA, PRINCESS, 8
phone call p....a rude metal double-fart PYNCHON, THOMAS, 3
the most historic p. ever made NIXON, RICHARD, 21
phony a p. war DALADIER, ÉDOUARD, 1
You're p.. Everything about you is ANONYMOUS, 91
photograph A p. is not an accident, it is a concept ADAMS, ANSEL, 1
A p. is not only an image SONTAG, SUSAN, 15
one criterion for a good p....unforgettable BRASSAÏ, 1
p. guards the memory of a man BRAUTIGAN, RICHARD, 3
she took down the signed p. of the Kaiser WAUGH, EVELYN, 32
things nobody would see...didn't p. them ARBUS, DIANE, 1
photography P. can never grow up if it imitates some other medium ABBOTT, BERENICE, 1
p. is a...lifetime of pleasure BENN, TONY, 5
p....the "art form" of the untalented VIDAL, GORE, 10
physic practice of p....jostled by quacks LATHAM, PETER MERE, 1
physical a right p. size for every idea MOORE, HENRY, 4
man thinks about his p. or moral state GOETHE, JOHANN WOLFGANG VON, 24
physical laws no right to assume that any p. exist PLANCK, MAX, 2
physician A p. can...parry the scythe of death PIOZZI, HESTER LYNCH, 1
A p. is...a consoler of the mind PETRONIUS ARBITER, 2
A p. is one who pours drugs VOLTAIRE, 47
A p....obligated to consider more CUSHING, HARVEY, 2
A p. ought to be...watchful against covetousness GISBORNE, THOMAS, 1
fond of...their p. MORE, HANNAH, 3
from the point of view of...the p. BILLINGS, JOHN SHAW, 2
one well-trained p. of the highest type MAYO, WILLIAM JAMES, 6
p....has a fool for a patient OSLER, WILLIAM, 8
p., heal thyself BIBLE, 330
P., n. One upon whom we set our hopes BIERCE, AMBROSE, 40
Prevention of disease...the goal of every p. SIGERIST, HENRY E., 7
p.'s best remedy...*Tincture of Time* SCHICK, BÉLA, 3
See, one p., like a sculler plies GARTH, SAMUEL, 2
That p. will hardly be thought very careful GALEN, 1
The examining p. often hesitates to make the necessary examination MAYO, WILLIAM JAMES, 3
The first qualification for a p. is hopefulness LITTLE, JAMES, 1
The p. cannot prescribe by letter SENECA, "THE YOUNGER," 7
The p....the flower...of our civilization STEVENSON, ROBERT LOUIS, 20
young p. fattens the churchyard PROVERBS, 152

physicians P....are best when they are old FULLER, THOMAS (1608–61), 7
P. are inclined to engage in hasty generalizations PASTEUR, LOUIS, 4
P. are like kings WEBSTER, JOHN, 6
p. are the class of people who kill other men JOHN OF SALISBURY, 1
P. must discover the weaknesses of the human mind COLTON, CHARLES, 6
P. of all men are most happy QUARLES, FRANCIS, 7
P. think they do a lot for a patient KANT, IMMANUEL, 26
The crowd of p. has killed me HADRIAN, 2
the help of too many p. ALEXANDER THE GREAT, 6
The most dangerous p. NIETZSCHE, FRIEDRICH WILHELM, 21
two p. cure you of the medicine ANONYMOUS, 24
physicist If I were not a p....musician EINSTEIN, ALBERT, 36
physicists P....ahead of practical applications FRISCH, O.R., 2
The p. have known sin OPPENHEIMER, J. ROBERT, 1
physics Classical p....superseded by quantum theory WEIZSÄCKER, CARL FRIEDRICH VON, 1
p. is the concern of physicists DÜRRENMATT, FRIEDRICH, 2
P....the greatest collective work of science BRONOWSKI, JACOB, 3
P....too hard for physicists HILBERT, DAVID, 1
theoretical p....is all in the mind HAWKING, STEPHEN, 2
The pope of P. has moved EINSTEIN, ALBERT, 4
There is no democracy in p. FERMI, ENRICO, 1
physiology Of p....I sing WHITMAN, WALT, 24
pianist the only p....who did not grimace RACHMANINOV, SERGEI VASILYEVICH, 2
piano I hit the p. with my elbow MONK, THELONIOUS, 5
notes lying around on that old p. COLE, NAT KING, 1
that prodding, unseductive p. style MONK, THELONIOUS, 2
pianoforte p....most important of all musical instruments SHAW, GEORGE BERNARD, 26
Picasso There's no such thing as a bad P. PICASSO, PABLO, 7
Piccadilly Circus Crossing P. THOMSON, JOSEPH, 1
pick p. a good one and sock it RUTH, BABE, 1
picnic p. is the Englishman's grand gesture BATTISCOMBE, GEORGINA, 1
Picts the P. can be likened to a mystery LYNCH, MICHAEL, 5
picture A p....tissue of quotations LEVINE, SHERRIE, 2
A well-painted p. gives us a pleasure PETRARCH, 5
Every p. tells a story PROVERBS, 206
Every time I make a p. DE MILLE, CECIL B., 1
nature sitting for her p. GAINSBOROUGH, THOMAS, 1
pictures dearth of bad p. GOLDWYN, SAMUEL, 23
greatly moved by the sight of such p. CHRYSOLORAS, EMANUEL, 1
It's the p. that got small SWANSON, GLORIA, 1
Only two things...good p. and bad VALADON, SUZANNE, 1
p....determine most of our philosophical convictions RORTY, RICHARD, 4
p. for people, not for critics DE MILLE, CECIL B., 3
P. should not be given approbation VITRUVIUS, MARCUS, 1
picturesque I distinguish the p. and the beautiful PEACOCK, THOMAS LOVE, 5
pidgin-English I include "p." PHILIP, PRINCE, 2
pie p. in the sky when you die HILL, JOE, 1
You don't want no p. in the sky ALI, MUHAMMAD, 15
piece A p. of us is in every person KING, STEPHEN, 3
When a p. gets difficult make faces SCHNABEL, ARTUR, 5
pieces of eight P. STEVENSON, ROBERT LOUIS, 19
Pierre Cardin a name as important as P. CARDIN, PIERRE, 1
piety P....honor truth over our friends ARISTOTLE, 10
pigeon-liver'd But I am p., and lack gall SHAKESPEARE, WILLIAM, 162
piggy This little p. went to market CHILDREN'S VERSE, 44
piggy-wig a P. stood /With a ring at the end of his nose LEAR, EDWARD, 19
pigs P. might fly PROVERBS, 363
Pilate P....washed his hands BIBLE, 441
What is truth said jesting P. BACON, FRANCIS (1561–1626), 74
pile P. it high, sell it cheap COHEN, JACK, 1
pill The P. has so much bad press PAINTIN, DAVID, 2
pillar a p. of a cloud BIBLE, 75
a p. of salt BIBLE, 126
pillars The four p. of government BACON, FRANCIS (1561–1626), 59
pillow I wish that I his p. were BARNFIELD, RICHARD, 8
like a p. on a bed DONNE, JOHN, 41
no-sooner-have-I-touched-the-p. people PRIESTLEY, J. B., 2
pills It is an age of p. MUGGERIDGE, MALCOLM, 2
pin like a p., but without...head or...point JERROLD, DOUGLAS, 10
See a p. and pick it up PROVERBS, 378
pinball deaf, dumb and blind kid...plays a mean p. TOWNSHEND, PETE, 2
pink The very p. of perfection GOLDSMITH, OLIVER, 9
pint A P. OF PLAIN IS YOUR ONLY MAN O'BRIEN, FLANN, 2
pin-up p., the centerfold, the poster DWORKIN, ANDREA, 4
pioneering The two p. forces of modern sensibility SONTAG, SUSAN, 8
pious A p. man...would be an atheist if the king were LA BRUYÈRE, JEAN DE, 2
It was certainly a p. fraud JEFFERSON, THOMAS, 8
pipe Marston...broke his p. SPENDER, STEPHEN, 5
pipers a hundred p. an' a' NAIRNE, CAROLINA, 3
Pirandello reduced to putting on plays by P. PIRANDELLO, LUIGI, 12
pissing inside my tent p. out HOOVER, J. EDGAR, 1
pistol Somebody leaves a p. in the drawer NIXON, RICHARD, 33
pitee For p. renneth soone in gentil herte CHAUCER, GEOFFREY, 22
pits You are the p. MCENROE, JOHN, 3
Pittsburgh P. is like Birmingham in England DICKENS, CHARLES, 6
pity A p. beyond all telling YEATS, W. B., 32
It is essential to banish p. RICHELIEU, CARDINAL, 4
P....arrests the mind JOYCE, JAMES, 8
p. is...a sign of contempt NIETZSCHE, FRIEDRICH WILHELM, 37
P.'s akin to love SOUTHERNE, THOMAS, 1
p....the brevity of human life XERXES I, 1
p. this busy monster, manunkind, /not CUMMINGS, E. E., 7
place always one p. remembered above the rest CATHER, WILLA, 8
A p. for everything SMILES, SAMUEL, 2
certain p., which 'tis not good manners to mention BROWN, THOMAS, 2
out of p., out of season JACKSON, GEORGE, 5
People like to p. you and your desires BONNER, MARITA, 3
The biggest little p. in America JAMES, HENRY, 22
there was no p. in particular to go O'BRIEN, TIM, 6
this is an awful p. SCOTT, CAPTAIN, 2
places I have lived in important p. KAVANAGH, PATRICK, 2
plagiarism P. has many advantages ATXAGA, BERNARDO, 1

plague A p. o' both your houses SHAKESPEARE, WILLIAM, 552
I watch the progress of the p. GUNN, THOM, 2
P. still increasing EVELYN, JOHN, 2
plagues of all p. with which mankind are curst DEFOE, DANIEL, 12
two main p....wine and women BURTON, ROBERT, 4
plain be p. and simple BUNYAN, JOHN, 3
making things p. to uninstructed people HUXLEY, T. H., 9
plan This p....reserve against more evil days HERZL, THEODOR, 2
plane only two emotions in a p.: boredom and terror WELLES, ORSON, 6
planet lived some thirty years on this p. THOREAU, HENRY DAVID, 36
Our p. alone has death DILLARD, ANNIE, 9
Our p....consists...of lumps of fall-out LOVELOCK, JAMES, 2
Pity the p., all joy gone LOWELL, ROBERT, 18
planets The p. in their station listening stood MILTON, JOHN, 74
planning P....natural to the process of success SIEGER, ROBIN, 1
plans The finest p. have always been spoiled BRECHT, BERTOLT, 11
plant A p. in the world is an event MANDELSTAM, OSIP, 4
plantation After the coming of freedom...leave the old p. WASHINGTON, BOOKER T., 3
plantations P. didn't have any wire BARAKA, IMAMU AMIRI, 14
plants p. left over from the Edwardian Wilderness OSBORNE, JOHN, 4
plastic No p. expression...residue of an experience MAN RAY, 3
plate eat offa' p. with...Idaho starin' ya' SHEPARD, SAM, 2
platitude p. is...a truth repeated BALDWIN, STANLEY, 7
Plato P. is dear...dearer still is truth ARISTOTLE, 33
platonic I know nothing about p. love JEPSON, EDGAR, 1
play a good p. needs no epilogue SHAKESPEARE, WILLIAM, 122
a p. without a woman KYD, THOMAS, 3
Better than a p. CHARLES II, 17
Did that p. of mine send out YEATS, W. B., 14
"haircut" guys can't just p. COODER, RY, 1
If she can stand it I can. P. it BOGART, HUMPHREY, 3
In a good p. every speech...fully flavoured SYNGE, J. M., 3
I p. from desire BERRY, CHUCK, 1
Knowing how to p....the barest superficiality BARAKA, IMAMU AMIRI, 4
p. is an expression of the highest seriousness GADAMER, HANS-GEORG, 1
P. It Again, Sam ALLEN, WOODY, 22
p. my fortieth fallen female STANWYCK, BARBARA, 1
P. off everyone against each other HUGHES, HOWARD, 1
structure of a p....always the story MILLER, ARTHUR, 11
The p. is memory WILLIAMS, TENNESSEE, 13
The p.'s the thing SHAKESPEARE, WILLIAM, 167
This is a p....men admire...most women dislike SHAKESPEARE, WILLIAM, 22
this may be p. to you, 'tis death to us L'ESTRANGE, ROGER, 1
this p. might well have stuck MILLER, ARTHUR, 21
unless the p. is stopped, the child cannot...go on KEMBLE, JOHN PHILIP, 1
Why shouldn't I p. God BURNS, GEORGE, 8
playboy the only p. of the western world SYNGE, J. M., 2
played I've p. everything but the harp BARRYMORE, LIONEL, 2
players I like my p....married and in debt BANKS, ERNIE, 1
playing guy came along p. a coke bottle BRADFORD, BOBBY, 1
p. him could never entirely do him justice SHAKESPEARE, WILLIAM, 2
plays *no* first p. are any good ABBOTT, GEORGE, 1
p. about rape, sodomy and drug addiction COOK, PETER, 2
p. are sinfull, heathenish...Spectacles PRYNNE, WILLIAM, 3
p. are suited to incoherent argument BENNETT, ALAN, 6
Some of my p. peter out BARRIE, J. M., 22
playthings p. of blind chance BETTI, UGO, 5
playwright a p....void of dramatic interest SARTRE, JEAN-PAUL, 1
nothing but a lousy p. MARQUIS, DON, 4
playwrights p. and novelists sneak up the back stairs BENNETT, ALAN, 5
plead We p. with you fathers KIMBALL, SPENCER W., 1
pleasant How p. to know Mr Lear LEAR, EDWARD, 10
If we do not find anything p. VOLTAIRE, 16
p. to be urged to do something SANTAYANA, GEORGE, 23
We meet thee, like a p. thought WORDSWORTH, WILLIAM, 74
please Nothing can permanently p. COLERIDGE, SAMUEL TAYLOR, 30
You can't p. everyone PROVERBS, 468
pleasing art of p. consists in being pleased HAZLITT, WILLIAM, 29
no thought of p. you when she was christened SHAKESPEARE, WILLIAM, 113
surest method...of p. CHESTERFIELD, LORD, 8
pleasure admit the Muse of sweet p. PLATO, 12
as much p. in the reading QUARLES, FRANCIS, 5
breathe the p. of natural freedom FITZNIGEL, RICHARD, 1
did p. me in his top-boots CHURCHILL, SARAH, 2
Everyone is dragged on by their favorite p. VIRGIL, 27
He that will do anything for...p. HOBBES, THOMAS, 5
P. after all is a safer guide BUTLER, SAMUEL (1835–1902), 12
p. for the senses, and let the devil PÉREZ GALDÓS, BENITO, 1
p....In being mad DRYDEN, JOHN, 47
P. is a lovely flame CALDERÓN DE LA BARCA, PEDRO, 8
P. is labour too COWPER, WILLIAM, 10
P. is ... seldom found where it is sought JOHNSON, SAMUEL, 34
p. is the goal EPICURUS, 6
P. is...the intermission of pain SELDEN, JOHN, 11
P....knowledge or feeling of perfection LEIBNIZ, GOTTFRIED WILHELM, 4
p. requires an aristocratic setting SANTAYANA, GEORGE, 17
P.'s a sin BYRON, LORD, 44
p....the criterion of every good thing EPICURUS, 4
The p. is momentary CHESTERFIELD, LORD, 19
the p. of offering my seat to three ladies CHESTERTON, G. K., 48
There is a p. in poetic pains COWPER, WILLIAM, 29
pleasures interfering with the p. of others RUSSELL, BERTRAND, 31
Look not on p. HERBERT, GEORGE, 16
Mid p. and palaces though we may roam PAYNE, JOHN HOWARD, 2
None other knows what p. man YEATS, W. B., 15
one of the p. of having a rout HOOD, THOMAS, 17
P. are all alike SELDEN, JOHN, 3
p. are plenty...troubles are two HOUSMAN, A. E., 3
p. are their only care COWPER, WILLIAM, 19
P. newly found are sweet WORDSWORTH, WILLIAM, 75
seize the p. of the present day DODDRIDGE, PHILIP, 1
Pledge of Allegiance P....Hail Satan SIMPSONS, THE, 4
plot p....means to get at the behavior of the characters CHABROL, CLAUDE, 1
P. me no plots BEAUMONT, FRANCIS, 5
p. was to have blown up the King HOBY, EDWARD, 1
some universal p....hatched by men GIROUD, FRANÇOISE, 3
the p. thickens BUCKINGHAM, DUKE OF, 2
Those blessed structures, p. and rhyme LOWELL, ROBERT, 5

plots there are only six basic p. HALLIWELL, LESLIE, 1
plow man who pulls the p. gets...plunder LONG, HUEY, 3
those who hold the p. are few HAN FEI, 3
pluck if thy right eye offend thee, p. it out BIBLE, 378
p. till time and times are done YEATS, W. B., 49
plucked p. my nipple from his boneless gums SHAKESPEARE, WILLIAM, 390
plums p. /that were in /the icebox WILLIAMS, WILLIAM CARLOS, 11
plunder Let no man stop to p. MACAULAY, THOMAS BABINGTON, 25
plural in the p. and they bounce LUTYENS, EDWIN LANDSEER, 1
plutography p.: depicting the acts of the rich WOLFE, TOM, 20
PM But he ended P. ATTLEE, CLEMENT, 1
poacher a p. a keeper turned inside out KINGSLEY, CHARLES, 4
pobble The P. who has no toes LEAR, EDWARD, 3
Podduyev life had prepared P. for living SOLZHENITSYN, ALEXANDER, 5
poem A good p. about failure...a success LARKIN, PHILIP, 16
A long p. is a test of invention KEATS, JOHN (1795–1821), 22
A p. is energy transferred OLSON, CHARLES, 10
A p. is never finished VALÉRY, PAUL, 1
A p. lovely as a tree KILMER, JOYCE, 1
a pretty p., Mr Pope POPE, ALEXANDER, 2
a p. shd happen to you like cold water or a kiss SHANGE, NTOZAKE, 3
A P. should be palpable and mute MACLEISH, ARCHIBALD, 1
A p. should not mean /But be MACLEISH, ARCHIBALD, 2
bathed in the P. /Of the Sea RIMBAUD, ARTHUR, 6
don't make a p. with thoughts COCTEAU, JEAN, 9
I do not think this p. will reach its destination VOLTAIRE, 54
P. me no poems MACAULAY, ROSE, 4
p....not made up of these letters CLAUDEL, PAUL, 1
The p. /feeds upon thought DUNCAN, ROBERT, 5
the p. wants to glorify suffering FISHER, ROY, 1
the visible p. of the world EBERHART, RICHARD, 1
poems all the p. that ever were invented CARROLL, LEWIS, 42
Most of my p. are written to women SMITH, PATTI, 1
My p. are hymns of praise SITWELL, EDITH, 2
The few bad p....created during abstinence REICH, WILHELM, 1
These p., with all their crudities, doubts, and confusions THOMAS, DYLAN, 11
They're just people that write p. SALINGER, J. D., 7
We all write p. FOWLES, JOHN, 4
poet a good p.'s made SHAKESPEARE, WILLIAM, 26
All the p. can do today is to warn OWEN, WILFRED, 11
a modern p.'s fate HOOD, THOMAS, 22
A p. is an unhappy being KIERKEGAARD, SØREN, 5
A p. is not a public figure DAY-LEWIS, CECIL, 2
A p. is...unpoetical KEATS, JOHN (1795–1821), 52
A p. like a pale candle MACNEICE, LOUIS, 7
a p. past thirty-five...seems somehow unnatural MENCKEN, H. L., 31
A p.'s mouth be silent YEATS, W. B., 40
A p., starving in a garret SWIFT, JONATHAN, 15
a p. who writes with a knife QABBANI, NIZAR, 1
a semi-talented p. on the Left Bank JOBS, STEVE, 4
A true p. does not bother to be poetical COCTEAU, JEAN, 7
But the p.'s job DEUTSCH, BABETTE, 1
For now the P. cannot die TENNYSON, ALFRED, 81
godly p. must be chaste himself CATULLUS, 2
he was a smash of a p. ELIOT, T. S., 3
How does the p. speak CARLYLE, THOMAS, 16
I expected every p. to have a spare wife GOGARTY, OLIVER ST. JOHN, 1
lunatic, the lover, and the p. SHAKESPEARE, WILLIAM, 67
No man was ever yet a great p....profound philosopher COLERIDGE, SAMUEL TAYLOR, 32
no person can be a p....without...unsoundness of mind MACAULAY, THOMAS BABINGTON, 15
No p....has his complete meaning alone ELIOT, T. S., 9
not possible for a p....to protect BOGAN, LOUISE, 2
p. can earn much more money...talking AUDEN, W. H., 27
p....do as the imagination bids STEVENS, WALLACE, 27
p. is like the prince of the clouds BAUDELAIRE, CHARLES, 12
p. like an acrobat /climbs on rime FERLINGHETTI, LAWRENCE, 1
p. may be used as the barometer TRILLING, LIONEL, 1
p....medium /of Nature GARCÍA LORCA, FEDERICO, 9
p....priest of the invisible STEVENS, WALLACE, 9
p., prying locksmith of invisible things FAZIL, NECIP, 1
p. ranks far below the painter LEONARDO DA VINCI, 11
p. without love CARLYLE, THOMAS, 8
She is a p. /she don't have no sense CLIFTON, LUCILLE, 1
The most original p. now living WORDSWORTH, WILLIAM, 5
The p. and the dreamer are distinct KEATS, JOHN (1795–1821), 88
The p. begins where the man ends ORTEGA Y GASSET, JOSÉ, 20
The p. gives us his essence WOOLF, VIRGINIA, 13
The p....like the lover DEUTSCH, BABETTE, 2
The p. lives by exaggeration CANETTI, ELIAS, 10
The P. of Immortal Youth KEATS, JOHN (1795–1821), 8
the room of the p. in disgrace MANDELSTAM, OSIP, 1
To be a p. and not to know the trade KAVANAGH, PATRICK, 1
To be a p. is a condition GRAVES, ROBERT, 3
To make a p. black, and bid him sing CULLEN, COUNTEE, 5
What p. would not grieve to see SWIFT, JONATHAN, 16
You should have been a p. BECKETT, SAMUEL, 23
poetic p. effect...generate different readings ECO, UMBERTO, 5
poetical As to the p. character KEATS, JOHN (1795–1821), 53
poetic license P.. There's no such thing BANVILLE, THÉODORE DE, 1
poetry All p. /is a journey MAYAKOVSKY, VLADIMIR, 2
can't ignore p....into the Top Ten DYLAN, BOB, 1
complexities of p....destroyed by the media BARKER, HOWARD, 3
essential elements of our p....courage, audacity MARINETTI, FILIPPO TOMMASO, 1
If P. comes not...as Leaves to a tree KEATS, JOHN (1795–1821), 51
I've never gone in much for p. MACKENZIE, COMPTON, 3
I would define...p.... as the rhythmical creation of Beauty POE, EDGAR ALLAN, 14
Most wretched men /Are cradled into p. SHELLEY, PERCY BYSSHE, 36
motive of p. OPPEN, GEORGE, 2
no man ever talked p. DICKENS, CHARLES, 99
p. after Auschwitz is barbaric ADORNO, THEODOR, 6
P. and painting...same way you make love MIRÓ, JOAN, 6
P....cat concert under the window SIMIC, CHARLES, 1
p. had the strength to rival...narcotics BELLOW, SAUL, 28
P. is a comforting piece of fiction MENCKEN, H. L., 35
p. is...more philosophical...than history ARISTOTLE, 22
P. is not a turning loose of emotion ELIOT, T. S., 10
P. is opposed to science COLERIDGE, SAMUEL TAYLOR, 34
p. is reflective AUDEN, W. H., 29
P. is the record of the...happiest moments SHELLEY, PERCY BYSSHE, 26

P. is the revelation of a feeling QUASIMODO, SALVATORE, 1
P. is the supreme fiction STEVENS, WALLACE, 20
P. is the voice of a poet DAVENPORT, GUY, 5
P. is to prose WAIN, JOHN, 1
P. is what gets lost in translation FROST, ROBERT, 22
P. makes things happen NEMEROV, HOWARD, 1
P. ...man explores his own amazement FRY, CHRISTOPHER, 8
p. of dramatic representation PLATO, 16
p....religion represents the world as a man KRUTCH, JOSEPH WOOD, 6
P....spontaneous overflow of powerful feelings WORDSWORTH, WILLIAM, 25
P., "The Cinderella of the Arts" MONROE, HARRIET, 1
P....the synthesis of hyacinths and biscuits SANDBURG, CARL, 2
p....to me it's the oil of life BETJEMAN, JOHN, 15
P. was the maiden I loved HOWE, JOSEPH, 3
P. will steal death from me CHAR, RENÉ, 1
resuscitate the dead art /Of p. POUND, EZRA, 13
show me...great work that does not have...p. CHAGALL, MARC, 2
The difference between genuine p. ARNOLD, MATTHEW, 20
The Fleshly School of P. BUCHANAN, ROBERT WILLIAMS, 2
the fusion of p., truth and character BARTON, JOHN, 1
The thing that makes p. different MERWIN, W. S., 3
Things in p. AKHMATOVA, ANNA, 4
Today's p....poetry of strife MAYAKOVSKY, VLADIMIR, 6
To search the heart is p.'s lifeblood CAI QIJIAO, 1
truest p. is the most feigning SHAKESPEARE, WILLIAM, 116
unseeing to ask what is the *use* of p. SITWELL, EDITH, 10
We hate p. that has a palpable design upon us KEATS, JOHN (1795–1821), 48

poets All p. are mad BURTON, ROBERT, 26
among the English P. after my death KEATS, JOHN (1795–1821), 38
A new art colour for our Irish p. JOYCE, JAMES, 29
excellent p. that have never versified SIDNEY, PHILIP, 4
For p., language is a maze SONG LIN, 1
Immature p. imitate ELIOT, T. S., 47
I must have wanton p., pleasant wits MARLOWE, CHRISTOPHER, 15
Irish p., learn your trade YEATS, W. B., 17
Modern p....more wonderful material than Homer BELLOW, SAUL, 9
Most p. are dead by their late twenties GRAVES, ROBERT, 4
Oh, where's my name /among the p. DU FU, 2
P. are...the trumpets which sing SHELLEY, PERCY BYSSHE, 28
p. being second-rate HORACE, 9
P....followed by none save erring men KORAN, 30
P....like baseball pitchers FROST, ROBERT, 25
P. lose half the praise WALLER, EDMUND, 4
Popular p. are the parish priests SANTAYANA, GEORGE, 15
P. should never marry GONNE, MAUD, 1
p. steal from Homer BURTON, ROBERT, 30
The p. and philosophers... have discovered the unconscious FREUD, SIGMUND, 57
three great p., each one a prize son of a bitch BRECHT, BERTOLT, 1
Why do some p....get by THOMAS, DYLAN, 2

point of view A p. can be a dangerous luxury MCLUHAN, MARSHALL, 6

poison a subtile p. from ordinary trifles HAWTHORNE, NATHANIEL, 15
coward's weapon, p. FLETCHER, PHINEAS, 2
pellet with the p.'s KAYE, DANNY, 1
Sweet, sweet, sweet p. SHAKESPEARE, WILLIAM, 320
the p. is in the sugar LEC, STANISLAW, 1
The surest p. is time EMERSON, RALPH WALDO, 40

poisons p. are our principal medicines EMERSON, RALPH WALDO, 50
P. more deadly than a mad dog's tooth SHAKESPEARE, WILLIAM, 594

poker I'm at a p. table with five guys COPPOLA, FRANCIS FORD, 2
P. shouldn't be played...house with women WILLIAMS, TENNESSEE, 1

Poland P. is in the position...I wanted her HITLER, ADOLF, 22

pole One step beyond the p. PEARY, ROBERT EDWIN, 7

police People's p. have the love of the people MOTTOS AND SLOGANS, 7
The p. are the only 24-hour social service MARNOCH, ALEX, 1

policeman a situation so dismal... p. couldn't make it worse BEHAN, BRENDAN, 16
p.'s ballbearing eyes searched his face DOS PASSOS, JOHN, 2
The p. isn't there to *create* disorder DALEY, RICHARD, 1

policemen P....must be protected ORTON, JOE, 7
P. so cherish their status MAMET, DAVID, 19

policy if the p. isn't hurting, it isn't working MAJOR, JOHN, 3
My home p.? I wage war CLEMENCEAU, GEORGES, 5
Our p. is directed...against hunger MARSHALL, GEORGE, 1

Polish any action which clearly threatened P. independence CHAMBERLAIN, NEVILLE, 6

politeness P. and amiability breed wealth LU XUN, 1
P. is organized indifference VALÉRY, PAUL, 7

political absence of p. competence within...business FOX, HARRISON W., JR., 6
All p. lives...end in failure POWELL, ENOCH, 3
a man...enough to have discovered a p. theory CASTRO, FIDEL, 2
little place in the p. scheme of things CHISHOLM, SHIRLEY, 3
Man is by nature a p. animal ARISTOTLE, 27
no p. or ideological difference KENNAN, GEORGE F., 3
p. authority of the state dies out ENGELS, FRIEDRICH, 6
p. chaos...decay of language ORWELL, GEORGE, 27
P. genius...identifying oneself with a principle HEGEL, G. W. F., 3
P. morality...a long way from church YOUNG, ANDREW (b.1932), 2
p. speech...defence of the indefensible ORWELL, GEORGE, 26
p. succession belongs to us MUSSOLINI, BENITO, 9
schemes of p. improvement are...laughable JOHNSON, SAMUEL, 134
Seek ye first the p. kingdom NKRUMAH, KWAME, 7
we are not p. whores MUSSOLINI, BENITO, 13
When p. ammunition runs low STEVENSON, ADLAI, 4

political philosophy collection of prejudices...called p. RUSSELL, BERTRAND, 23

political science new world demands a new p. TOCQUEVILLE, ALEXIS DE, 1

political systems To model our p. upon speculations HAMILTON, ALEXANDER, 6

politician a bit of a murderer, to be a p. MILLER, HENRY, 29
A p....can give away...his soul MAILER, NORMAN, 9
a p. is an arse CUMMINGS, E. E., 5
a p. never believes what he says DE GAULLE, CHARLES, 21
A p. rises on the backs HUGHES, RICHARD, 1
career p....bull elk in the rut THOMPSON, HUNTER S., 5
carefully packaged persona of today's p. REAGAN, RONALD, 11
like a scurvy p. SHAKESPEARE, WILLIAM, 359
p....approaches every question with...open mouth STEVENSON, ADLAI, 10
p. is a man who understands government TRUMAN, HARRY S., 10
p. is the devil's quilted anvil WEBSTER, JOHN, 3
p. ought to be born a foundling JOHNSON, LADY BIRD, 1

p. who steals...worse than...thief PLUNKITT, GEORGE WASHINGTON, 1
p. will...even become a patriot HEARST, WILLIAM RANDOLPH, 2
p....with whose politics you did not agree LLOYD-GEORGE, DAVID, 7
The p. is an acrobat BARRÈS, MAURICE, 1
the p. poses as the servant DE GAULLE, CHARLES, 20
The proper memory for a p. MORLEY, JOHN, 2
unfair to expect a p. to live in private MAUGHAM, SOMERSET, 24

politicians all the p. I ever saw BELLOC, HILAIRE, 3
a pity...more p. are not bastards WHITEHORN, KATHARINE, 6
more sensible than p. or the press CLARKE, KENNETH, 1
Old p....revive in the limelight MUGGERIDGE, MALCOLM, 9
P. are the same all over KHRUSHCHEV, NIKITA, 3
P. can forgive almost anything WAUGH, AUBERON, 2
P....get respectable if they last HUSTON, JOHN, 2
p. have promised the moon NIXON, RICHARD, 36
P. neither love nor hate DRYDEN, JOHN, 13
P....order more tunnel QUINTON, SIR JOHN, 1
P. tend to live *in character* LIPPMANN, WALTER, 2
p. will always be there MOTTOS AND SLOGANS, 39
There is just one rule for p. GALSWORTHY, JOHN, 1

politicks P. are...a means of rising JOHNSON, SAMUEL, 110

politics can't adopt p....and remain honest HOWE, LOUIS MCHENRY, 1
Confound their p. CAREY, HENRY, 1
didn't care for domestic p. BUSH, GEORGE, 2
don't play p. with people's jobs KINNOCK, NEIL, 3
first part of p.? Education MICHELET, JULES, 5
first rule of p. is not to lie LONG, RUSSELL B., 2
first thing that one loses in p. MACHADO DE ASSIS, JOAQUIM MARIA, 16
I am not made for p. CAMUS, ALBERT, 21
I don't want p.. I want impartiality MANN, THOMAS, 9
In p....ask a woman THATCHER, MARGARET, 36
in p. there is no heart NAPOLEON I, 31
It is p. which begets war CLAUSEWITZ, KARL MARIE VON, 1
It is the nature of p. HOFSTADTER, RICHARD, 2
making p. Christian VAN DER POST, LAURENS, 2
never get on in p. WILLIAMS, SHIRLEY, 1
Never judge a country by its p. HITCHCOCK, ALFRED, 4
Nothing doing on p. HOOVER, HERBERT, 2
p....art of staying /out of jail YÜCEL, CAN, 1
P....between the disastrous and the unpalatable GALBRAITH, J. K., 3
P. come from man. Mercy WAITE, TERRY, 2
P. does work better when citizens SOROS, GEORGE, 6
peculiar contribution...to make p. boring EISENHOWER, DWIGHT D., 7
p. in the East...dissimulation DISRAELI, BENJAMIN, 12
P. is a blood sport BEVAN, ANEURIN, 11
P. is a profession EISENHOWER, DWIGHT D., 16
p. is for the present EINSTEIN, ALBERT, 40
P. is just like show business REAGAN, RONALD, 45
P. is not an exact science BISMARCK, PRINCE OTTO VON, 13
P. is not a science...but an art BISMARCK, PRINCE OTTO VON, 19
P. is opposed to morality LEVINAS, EMMANUEL, 2
P. is supposed to be the second oldest profession REAGAN, RONALD, 43
P. is the art of preventing people from taking part VALÉRY, PAUL, 8
P. is the art of the possible BISMARCK, PRINCE OTTO VON, 21
p. is the bow of idealism MOYERS, BILL, 2
p. is too serious...to be left to the politicians DE GAULLE, CHARLES, 16
p. is...undignified contest between groups MANLEY, MICHAEL, 1
p....makes a fool of a man GLASGOW, ELLEN, 2
p....makes men arrogant MANN, THOMAS, 10
p. of the East...economics of the future MEAD, WALTER RUSSELL, 1
P....only profession for which no preparation STEVENSON, ROBERT LOUIS, 8
Practical p....ignoring facts ADAMS, HENRY, 11
P....reflex of the business and industrial GOLDMAN, EMMA, 4
P....the systematic organization of hatreds ADAMS, HENRY, 10
that men enter local p. PARKINSON, CYRIL NORTHCOTE, 5
That's why p. is such a sad thing HEARNE, JOHN, 1
The more you read and observe about this p. ROGERS, WILL, 5
The P. of Joy HUMPHREY, HUBERT H., 4
times in p. when you must...lose GALBRAITH, J. K., 7
We cannot safely leave p. to politicians GEORGE, HENRY, 4

polling booth Now we can go to the p. without a bad conscience BOTHA, P. W., 3

pollution 80% of our air p. stems from...vegetation REAGAN, RONALD, 35

Polly P. put the kettle on CHILDREN'S VERSE, 65

polygamy I am tired to death of p. MACNEICE, LOUIS, 6
the sons of Gods...enter into p. YOUNG, BRIGHAM, 7

pomp Pride, p., and circumstance SHAKESPEARE, WILLIAM, 487

pompous A p. woman...complaining that the head-waiter SITWELL, EDITH, 9

pondered Mary...p. them in her heart BIBLE, 326

pontiff Nothing...escape the notice...supreme p. INNOCENT III, 2

poodle small p. tries to walk through KOZYREV, ANDREY VLADIMIROVICH, 1

Pooh P. began to feel a little more comfortable MILNE, A. A., 7
Supposing P....a tree fell on us MILNE, A. A., 8

pool a p. of freely flowing, formless water FENG ZHI, 2

poor A p. man is despised JEROME, JEROME K., 3
A p. relation LAMB, CHARLES, 22
ask of the p. that they...act HARRINGTON, MICHAEL, 3
being p....takes up all your time DE KOONING, WILLEM, 1
Few, save the p., feel for the poor LANDON, LETITIA ELIZABETH, 2
give to the p. BIBLE, 416
how p. a thing is man DANIEL, SAMUEL, 1
I am...on the side of the p. GARCÍA LORCA, FEDERICO, 10
I, being p., have only my dreams YEATS, W. B., 44
I can dare to be p. GAY, JOHN, 12
If a free society cannot help the...p. KENNEDY, JOHN FITZGERALD, 15
If there were no p. GUY, ROSA, 4
it is p. grub, poor pay, and easy work LONDON, JACK, 14
let the p....starve at door HERBERT, GEORGE, 22
many a p. man...relieved and helped by him LANGTON, THOMAS, 1
Nobody but p. folks get happy in church WRIGHT, RICHARD, 3
not be a p. man...Tsardom GODUNOV, BORIS, 1
one has to go there p. MOORE, GRACE, 1
only the p....are forbidden to beg FRANCE, ANATOLE, 1
only the p. who pay cash FRANCE, ANATOLE, 10
p. and black was normal...poor and white was a tragedy MANDELA, NELSON, 11
p. have no right to the property of the rich RUSKIN, JOHN, 26
"P. old Joe..." FOSTER, STEPHEN, 4
P. people want change MAO ZEDONG, 32
relation between the p. and the rich...only revolutionary element BÜCHNER, GEORG, 11
Resolve not to be p. JOHNSON, SAMUEL, 171

spoke like a p. man...walked like a king MALCOLM X, 2
The p. are Europe's blacks CHAMFORT, NICOLAS, 13
The p. are our brothers and sisters TERESA OF CALCUTTA, MOTHER, 6
The p. don't rest DE JESÚS, CAROLINA MARIA, 3
The p....function...to exercise our generosity SARTRE, JEAN-PAUL, 31
the p. person has hope. He thinks money would help KERR, JEAN, 6
The voice of the p. has no poetry DE JESÚS, CAROLINA MARIA, 4
Though I be p., I'm honest MIDDLETON, THOMAS, 9
to be a p. man's slave DOUGLASS, FREDERICK, 13
To be p. and independent...an impossibility COBBETT, WILLIAM, 2
train to accept being p. HORACE, 30
very p. are unthinkable FORSTER, E. M., 11

poorest p....hath a life to live as the greatest RAINBOROWE, THOMAS, 1
p. man may...bid defiance to...the Crown PITT THE ELDER, WILLIAM, 3
Think of the p. person GANDHI, MAHATMA, 5

pop P. is the perfect religious vehicle DONOVAN, 1
P. music is...lots of drugs MAMA CASS, 1
P. was...the new Art WARHOL, ANDY, 14

pop art P. "American" painting...actually industrial painting LICHTENSTEIN, ROY, 1

popcorn P. peanuts clams and gum MACNEICE, LOUIS, 21

pop culture P. is still the one way STIPE, MICHAEL, 1

pope Anybody can be P. JOHN XXIII, 2
a p.'s theoretically infallible KÜNG, HANS, 1
His Holiness, the P. yesterday received GOGARTY, OLIVER ST. JOHN, 5
I wake up...remember I am the P. JOHN XXIII, 4
look upon p. and emperor...as names PIUS II, 1
The P.! How many divisions STALIN, JOSEPH, 10
Women, children and lunatics can't be P. CHURCHILL, CARYL, 1

poplars The p. are fell'd COWPER, WILLIAM, 17

popped P. in between th'election and my hopes SHAKESPEARE, WILLIAM, 227

popular a p. politics reconciling themes BLAIR, TONY, 5
We're more p. than Jesus Christ LENNON, JOHN, 9

popular culture p. saves its adulation LYNCH, PETER, 5

popularity P.?...glory's small change HUGO, VICTOR, 13
P. is a crime HALIFAX, GEORGE SAVILE, 2
P. is exhausting MIZNER, WILSON, 7

popular music I am merely fond of p. MENCIUS, 3

population P. growth...environmental damage COUSTEAU, JACQUES, 1
P....increases in a geometrical ratio MALTHUS, THOMAS, 1
starving p....absentee aristocracy...alien Church DISRAELI, BENJAMIN, 16
The purpose of p....is to fill heaven LEONARD, GRAHAM, 1

populism P....threatens to pollute democracy DELORS, JACQUES, 4

porcelain precious p. of human clay BYRON, LORD, 66

pornographers P. are the enemies of women CARTER, ANGELA, 5
P. subvert this last, vital privacy STEINER, GEORGE, 7

pornography p. is really about...death SONTAG, SUSAN, 17
P. is the attempt to insult sex LAWRENCE, D. H., 34
p. ...it is terribly, terribly boring COWARD, NOEL, 15
show that gives p. a bad name BARNES, CLIVE, 1
what p. says about women DWORKIN, ANDREA, 5

port Any p. in a storm PROVERBS, 137
In every p. a wife DIBDIN, CHARLES, 3
In every p. he finds a wife BICKERSTAFFE, ISAAC, 6
It would be p. if it could BENTLEY, RICHARD, 1

portentous p. phrase, "I told you so." BYRON, LORD, 82

porter Oh, mister p., what shall I do LLOYD, MARIE, 1

portion best p. of a good man's life WORDSWORTH, WILLIAM, 12

portrait Every time I paint a p. I lose a friend SARGENT, JOHN SINGER, 1
I do not paint a p. to look like the subject DALÍ, SALVADOR, 2
p. painters suffer from the vanity CLARK, KENNETH (1903–83), 6
p....something wrong with the mouth SPEICHER, EUGENE, 1
two styles of p. painting DICKENS, CHARLES, 60

portraits P. of famous bards and preachers THOMAS, DYLAN, 28
When p. are good...reflect the culture NEEL, ALICE, 2

portrayal My task...p. of human beings IBSEN, HENRIK, 1

posed I have a horror of p. shots BUÑUEL, LUIS, 3

position p. warranted by the history of mankind HAMILTON, ALEXANDER, 2

positive P., adj. Mistaken at the top of one's voice BIERCE, AMBROSE, 41

positive thinking Power of P. PEALE, NORMAN VINCENT, 1

positivism P. becomes...a religion COMTE, AUGUSTE, 1

possess We p. nothing certainly except the past WAUGH, EVELYN, 5

possessed divinely p. by his science ARCHIMEDES, 3

possession best p. is a sympathetic wife EURIPIDES, 5
P. is eleven points in the law CIBBER, COLLEY, 7
P. is nine tenths of the law PROVERBS, 364

possessions Why grab p. like thieves BARNEY, NATALIE CLIFFORD, 2

possibilities P. do not add up. They multiply ROMER, PAUL M., 1

possibility How great a p. COLERIDGE, SAMUEL TAYLOR, 3

possible all things are p. to him that believeth BIBLE, 360
The only way of finding the limits of the p. CLARKE, ARTHUR C., 5

Possum P.'s hommage to Milton ELIOT, T. S., 4

postcards I sent p. that never arrived YUSUF, SA'DI, 2

post-entrepreneurial P. organizations KANTER, ROSABETH MOSS, 4

posterity always doing something for p. ADDISON, JOSEPH, 21
down to p. talking bad grammar DISRAELI, BENJAMIN, 53
looked upon by p. as a brave, bad man CLARENDON, EDWARD HYDE, 1
People will not look forward to p. BURKE, EDMUND, 49
P....wrong as anybody else BROUN, HEYWOOD, 1
What has p. done for us ROCHE, BOYLE, 1

postman The P. Always Rings Twice CAIN, JAMES M., 1

posture things spoken by means of p. and gesture PLATO, 31

posy I made a p. while the day ran HERBERT, GEORGE, 8

pot The p. calls the kettle black CERVANTES, MIGUEL DE, 44

potent He is the most p. man POLO, MARCO, 3
how p. cheap music is COWARD, NOEL, 20

Potomac All quiet along the P. MCCLELLAN, GEORGE, 1

Potsdam What could I have done at P. DE GAULLE, CHARLES, 13

potter Who *is* the P. FITZGERALD, EDWARD, 14

pounds I only ask you for twenty-five p. SHERIDAN, RICHARD BRINSLEY, 19

poverty Do you call p. a crime? SHAW, GEORGE BERNARD, 40
For every talent that p. has stimulated GARDNER, JOHN W., 1
If p. is the mother of crime, stupidity is its father LA BRUYÈRE, JEAN DE, 6
p. and oysters always seem to go together DICKENS, CHARLES, 94
p. crosses the threshold love flies out PROVERBS, 15
P. is an anomaly to rich people BAGEHOT, WALTER, 12
P....is confoundedly inconvenient SMITH, SYDNEY, 22
P. is not a crime PROVERBS, 365

P. iz the stepmother ov genius BILLINGS, JOSH, 2
P. of goods is easily cured MONTAIGNE, MICHEL DE, 21
p.'s catching BEHN, APHRA, 12
P., therefore, was comparative DRABBLE, MARGARET, 6
P. works like a steam roller WATERS, ETHEL, 1
The misfortunes of p. JUVENAL, 6
the p. of my...experience JAMES, ALICE, 2
unconditional war on p. in America JOHNSON, LYNDON BAINES, 16
We don't need a War on P. CLEAVER, ELDRIDGE, 8
well governed p. is something to be ashamed of CONFUCIUS, 8
Where p. is mocked by extravagance MANLEY, MICHAEL, 3
world p....problem of two million villages SCHUMACHER, E. F., 6

power all p. is a trust DISRAELI, BENJAMIN, 48
Concentrated p. means no freedom DE GEUS, ARIE, 2
concentration of p. in the heart of Europe GRASS, GÜNTER, 3
confer all their p....upon one man HOBBES, THOMAS, 15
corridors of p. SNOW, C. P., 1
Every man who has p. PI Y MARGALL, FRANCISCO, 1
greatest p. available to man ECKHART, MEISTER, 1
It is not in...p. of professors GALILEO, 4
life depends on your p. to master words SCARGILL, ARTHUR, 1
love of p....apt to inflict pain RUSSELL, BERTRAND, 4
Men of p. have not time to read FOOT, MICHAEL, 2
not in our p. to love, or hate MARLOWE, CHRISTOPHER, 18
P....and Liberty...seldom upon good Terms HALIFAX, GEORGE SAVILE, 5
P. and violence are opposites ARENDT, HANNAH, 6
P. at its best is love...justice KING, MARTIN LUTHER, JR., 29
P. buries those who wield it TALMUD, 4
P. concedes nothing without demand DOUGLASS, FREDERICK, 6
P. doesn't have to show off ELLISON, RALPH, 3
p. has been the vice of the ascetic RUSSELL, BERTRAND, 22
p. is apt to corrupt PITT THE ELDER, WILLIAM, 10
P. is my mistress NAPOLEON I, 22
P. is not merely shouting aloud NASSER, GAMAL ABDEL, 4
p. is the law of man EDGEWORTH, MARIA, 2
P. is the only argument GARVEY, MARCUS, 11
P. is the ultimate aphrodisiac KISSINGER, HENRY, 10
P. is where power goes JOHNSON, LYNDON BAINES, 13
P.?...like a dead sea fruit MACMILLAN, HAROLD, 9
p....makes people so utterly boring ACHEBE, CHINUA, 4
P. must always be balanced by responsibility DRUCKER, PETER, 7
P. never takes a back step MALCOLM X, 18
p. of the people...greater potential for violence JACKSON, GEORGE, 1
p. of the spirit GANDHI, MAHATMA, 2
p. over men WOLLSTONECRAFT, MARY, 4
p. pressed too far...relaxed too much BACON, FRANCIS (1561–1626), 25
p. should always be distrusted JONES, WILLIAM, 1
P. to the People SEALE, BOBBY, 1
p. without responsibility BALDWIN, STANLEY, 10
P. without responsibility KIPLING, RUDYARD, 66
seek p. and...lose liberty BACON, FRANCIS (1561–1626), 35
terrible p. of the things they carried O'BRIEN, TIM, 4
that life and p. that took away... wars FOX, GEORGE, 2
The balance of p. WALPOLE, SIR ROBERT, 1
The cold reality of p. SOYINKA, WOLE, 9
The p. of kings and magistrates MILTON, JOHN, 130
There is no p. but of God BIBLE, 484
The self-sufficing p. of Solitude WORDSWORTH, WILLIAM, 86
When p. narrows the areas of man's concern KENNEDY, JOHN FITZGERALD, 2
You only have p. over people SOLZHENITSYN, ALEXANDER, 12

powerful A "p." office is...a very big one MCCORMACK, MARK, 9
P. people never teach powerless people CLARKE, JOHN HENRIK, 4
Who is all-p....fear all things CORNEILLE, PIERRE, 2

power politics P....the law of the jungle CULBERTSON, ELY, 1

powers P....of themselves our minds impress WORDSWORTH, WILLIAM, 11

power saw a p. can fell a tree TEALE, EDWIN WAY, 1

Powhatan if P. should know it, she were...dead SMITH, JOHN, 4
P....told him now they were friends SMITH, JOHN, 3
Two great stones were brought before *P.* SMITH, JOHN, 2

pow'r O wad some P. the giftie gie us BURNS, ROBERT, 47

practical Nothing...so p. as a good theory LEVIN, KURT, 1
P. efficiency is common ROOSEVELT, THEODORE, 21
P. men,...are usually the slaves of some defunct economist KEYNES, JOHN MAYNARD, 13

practicality Alone, p. becomes dangerous BERRY, WENDELL, 2

practical religion One ounce of p. is worth all...the Stoics wrote SANCHO, IGNATIUS, 1

practice I p. a lot when I'm on my own ALLEN, WOODY, 6
P. makes perfect PROVERBS, 366
P. should always be based upon a sound knowledge of theory LEONARDO DA VINCI, 9
P. what you preach PROVERBS, 367

practising p. the hundredth psalm BYRON, LORD, 100

prairie There was only the enormous, empty p. WILDER, LAURA INGALLS, 3

prairies The wondrous, beautiful p. LONGFELLOW, HENRY WADSWORTH, 24

praise how a man takes p. BURKE, THOMAS, 1
no such whetstone...as is p. ASCHAM, ROGER, 2
P. and blame are much the same WINTERSON, JEANETTE, 1
p. any man that will praise me SHAKESPEARE, WILLIAM, 76
P. from a friend, or censure from a foe POPE, ALEXANDER, 75
p. is given to many...without perspective FRANCESCA, PIERO DELLA, 1
P. the Lord and pass the ammunition FORGY, HOWELL MAURICE, 1
to refuse p. reveals a desire to be praised LA ROCHEFOUCAULD, FRANÇOIS, 20
The man worthy of p. HORACE, 51
The moment you p. a book...awaken resistance MILLER, HENRY, 13
we but p. ourselves in other men POPE, ALEXANDER, 22

praises He who p. everybody JOHNSON, SAMUEL, 88

pram the bliss of my p. LANCASTER, OSBERT, 3

pray Common people do not p. SHAW, GEORGE BERNARD, 69
Do you p. for the senators HALE, EDWARD EVERETT, 1
Let no man p....Brown be spared BROWN, JOHN, 1
p. for you at St Paul's SMITH, SYDNEY, 27
P. to God and say the lines DAVIS, BETTE, 8
We can p. over the cholera victim SAGAN, CARL, 16
when ye p., use not vain repetitions BIBLE, 381
You can't p. a lie TWAIN, MARK, 36

prayer cravings...do not become a p. HAMMARSKJÖLD, DAG, 10
More things are wrought by p. TENNYSON, ALFRED, 20
most odious of ...narcissisms—p. FOWLES, JOHN, 2
My final p. FANON, FRANTZ, 7
person who does not heed p. KHOMEINI, RUHOLLAH, 6
p. is answered MEREDITH, GEORGE, 11
The p. that...heals the sick EDDY, MARY BAKER, 6

prayeth He p. best, who loveth best COLERIDGE, SAMUEL TAYLOR, 51
prays man p....for a miracle TURGENEV, IVAN, 5
When a man p. BETTI, UGO, 6
preached p....as a dying man to dying men BAXTER, RICHARD, 1
preacher The British churchgoer prefers a severe p. SHAW, GEORGE BERNARD, 116
preachers P. say, Do as I say, not as I do SELDEN, JOHN, 13
precautions the necessary p. to avoid having parents CRISP, QUENTIN, 6
precedency p. between a louse and a flea SMART, CHRISTOPHER, 1
precept for p. must be upon precept BIBLE, 209
precious Where iss it...my P. TOLKIEN, J. R. R., 6
precisely thinking too p. on th' event SHAKESPEARE, WILLIAM, 212
predatory real world calls for a p. man's brand of thinking JACKSON, GEORGE, 11
predict only p. things after they've happened IONESCO, EUGÈNE, 6
prediction seldom does p. fail, when evil CALDERÓN DE LA BARCA, PEDRO, 6
predictions cut back on p. O'BRIEN, CONOR CRUISE, 1
prefer Let us p. to be human RADHAKRISHNAN, SARVEPALLI, 2
preferable It is p. to change the world HEAD, BESSIE, 2
pregnancy P. is not a disease SCHARLIEB, DAME MARY ANN DACOMB, 1
pregnant If men could get p. KENNEDY, FLORYNCE R., 6
prehistoric a truly p. and beautiful pose RAMBERT, DAME MARIE, 1
find themselves...in p. fields PASOLINI, PIER PAOLO, 2
prejudge I do not...p. the past WHITELAW, WILLIAM, 2
prejudice I am free of all p. FIELDS, W. C., 5
p....associated with the white...cultural mainstream THORPE, EDWARD, 2
P. is planted in childhood BAINBRIDGE, BERYL, 3
P...., the brand of the white man REMOND, CHARLES LENOX, 1
We cannot, through ignorant p., afford to under-use the talents MBOYA, TOM, 2
You can never beat p. by a frontal attack AGGREY, JAMES EMMAN KWEGYIR, 4
prejudices p. swell like varicose veins HUNEKER, JAMES GIBBONS, 1
to rearrange one's p. LUCE, CLARE BOOTHE, 4
premature A p. announcement...unsettles TOWNSEND, ROBERT, 8
preparation Begin the p. for your death YEATS, W. B., 6
p. for war...best security MADISON, JAMES, 6
The best p. for good work HUBBARD, ELBERT, 6
prepared Be P. BADEN-POWELL, ROBERT, 2
p....from all eternity MARCUS AURELIUS, 12
preppies P. are dressed for it BIRNBACH, LISA, 1
presbyter *P.* is but old *Priest* writ large MILTON, JOHN, 107
Presbyterian The nature of P. government CHARLES I (1600–49), 2
presence We are in the p. of the contradiction ORTEGA Y GASSET, JOSÉ, 28
present All p. and correct ANONYMOUS, 25
don't run down the p., pursue it DILLARD, ANNIE, 7
employ /The p. well, and e'en the past enjoy POPE, ALEXANDER, 48
Only the p. is real BELLOW, SAUL, 21
p. contains nothing more than the past BERGSON, HENRI-LOUIS, 1
P. has latched its postern HARDY, THOMAS, 17
p....movie of what happened in the past KESEY, KEN, 3
p. was too brutal and too formless RILKE, RAINER MARIA, 1
The P. Is a Dangerous Place to Live KGOSITSILE, KEORAPETSE, 1
The p. is the past rolled up DURANT, WILL, 13
The p....merely a nation's skin DEGLER, CARL N., 4
this p....world's last night DONNE, JOHN, 16
We p. you with this Book ANONYMOUS, 16
When the p. is intolerable SOYINKA, WOLE, 4
presentiment P.—is that long Shadow DICKINSON, EMILY, 20
presidency The p. is...a daily fight GORE, AL, 1
president American...prepared to run for P. VIDAL, GORE, 20
anybody could become P. DARROW, CLARENCE, 7
a p. without a people GORBACHEV, MIKHAIL, 2
aspired to become the least P. COOLIDGE, CALVIN, 6
being P.—nobody can tell you when to sit EISENHOWER, DWIGHT D., 25
Even the p....must...stand naked DYLAN, BOB, 19
I don't mind not being P. KENNEDY, EDWARD M., 1
if your own P. had never left Brooklyn DE VALERA, EAMON, 2
I'm not running for p. TRUMP, DONALD, 1
I never think of anyone as...P. TRUMAN, HARRY S., 3
Mothers all want their sons...to become p. KENNEDY, JOHN FITZGERALD, 39
not choose to run for P. in 1928 COOLIDGE, CALVIN, 7
p. used the third derivative ROSSI, HUGO, 1
that damned cowboy is P. ROOSEVELT, THEODORE, 1
the P. is dead, but the Government lives GARFIELD, JAMES A., 4
To be perfect for television is all a P. has to be REAGAN, RONALD, 12
We are all the P.'s men KISSINGER, HENRY, 13
What would be the first thing I'd do if I were p.? MURPHY, EDDY, 1
When the P. does it NIXON, RICHARD, 24
press Facing the p....difficult TERESA OF CALCUTTA, MOTHER, 9
If the P.... be a foe to the tyrant CORNISH, SAMUEL ELI, 1
would not say that our P. is obscene LONGFORD, LORD, 2
pretend I could not...p. that I did not exist DESCARTES, RENÉ, 8
pretending p. to be wicked WILDE, OSCAR, 49
pretense not make a p. of doing philosophy EPICURUS, 5
pretentious p. ballet finales of fifties musicals KAEL, PAULINE, 4
P.? *Moi?* CLEESE, JOHN, 1
pretty anyone lived in a p. how town CUMMINGS, E. E., 8
a p. flim-flam BEAUMONT, FRANCIS, 4
a p. girl...naked CUMMINGS, E. E., 10
There's only one p. child PROVERBS, 424
prevent you will not p. us...being pleasant BEUGNOT, COUNT, 1
prevention The p. of disease today is...important MAYO, CHARLES HORACE, 2
preventive p. for the maladies...death CUSHING, HARVEY, 1
prey the p. goes to the hunter PROVERBS, 69
price Everything has its p. PROVERBS, 481
One person's p. is another person's income HELLER, WALTER W., 1
P. of Herald three cents daily HEARST, WILLIAM RANDOLPH, 1
p. which is too great to pay for peace WILSON, WOODROW, 21
The p....for pursuing any profession BALDWIN, JAMES, 7
the p. of everything...the value of nothing WILDE, OSCAR, 32
Who never knew the p. of happiness YEVTUSHENKO, YEVGENY, 4
prices High p. and heavy taxation CHANDLER, RAYMOND, 13
prick If you p. us, do we not bleed SHAKESPEARE, WILLIAM, 610
pride dark flame of his male p. GIBBONS, STELLA, 3
P. and arrogancy...the master sins ELAW, ZILPHA, 1
p. goeth before destruction BIBLE, 458
p. is a word often on women's lips CHRISTIE, AGATHA, 6
P. is like a perfume WONDER, STEVIE, 1

P. is My cloak...greatness My robe MUHAMMAD, 3
p. that apes humility SOUTHEY, ROBERT, 3
P., the never-failing vice of fools POPE, ALEXANDER, 9
priest A p. sees people at their best PROVERBS, 141
For a p. to turn a man when he lies a-dying SELDEN, JOHN, 2
the p. looked on the women MOORE, GEORGE, 6
priests All things, oh p., are on fire BUDDHA, 1
gay p. HARE, DAVID, 1
like to associate with...p. BELLOC, HILAIRE, 2
p....saw that the Temple was destroyed BIN GORION, MICHA JOSEPH, 2
We shall keep our p. within...temples HERZL, THEODOR, 10
ye shall be unto me a kingdom of p. BIBLE, 78
prima donnas hard...to deal with other p. ROSS, DIANA, 1
They are for p. or corpses TOSCANINI, ARTURO, 6
primal therapy P. shuts off any transference JANOV, ARTHUR, 1
prime having lost but once your p. HERRICK, ROBERT, 17
One's p. is elusive SPARK, MURIEL, 9
prime minister I would not wish to be P. THATCHER, MARGARET, 33
the best p. we have BUTLER, RAB, 1
primitive peoples all p....reverence for lifegiving earth UDALL, STEWART L., 3
primitive religion P. is concerned...with practice TOYNBEE, ARNOLD, 4
primrose A p. by a river's brim WORDSWORTH, WILLIAM, 37
prince a p. must be able to act just like a beast MACHIAVELLI, NICCOLÒ, 4
p. can make a belted knight BURNS, ROBERT, 17
p. of royal courage HENRY VIII, 6
p.'s power makes all his actions virtue JONSON, BEN, 13
p. who desires to maintain his position MACHIAVELLI, NICCOLÒ, 1
The p. of darkness is a gentleman SUCKLING, JOHN, 3
Prince of Aquitaine The P., with the blasted tower NERVAL, GÉRARD DE, 3
Prince of Wales first P....not to have a mistress CHARLES, PRINCE, 3
princes p. learn no art truly, but ...horsemanship JONSON, BEN, 22
princess advantage about marrying a p. CHARLES, PRINCE, 12
she was a real p. ANDERSEN, HANS CHRISTIAN, 2
principle first p. of all human knowledge FICHTE, JOHANN, 3
original, inherent p. or order HUME, DAVID, 26
the most useful thing about a p. MAUGHAM, SOMERSET, 29
the p. seems the same CHURCHILL, WINSTON, 39
There is only *one*...p.: *anything goes* FEYERABEND, PAUL K., 1
principles If one sticks too rigidly to one's p. CHRISTIE, AGATHA, 5
The p. of a free constitution GIBBON, EDWARD, 4
Whenever two people argue over p. EBNER-ESCHENBACH, MARIE VON, 9
Prinney So poor P. is really dead GEORGE IV, 1
print Some said, "John, p. it;" others said, "Not so." BUNYAN, JOHN, 11
priorities The language of p. is BEVAN, ANEURIN, 8
priority the need to set...p. HARVEY-JONES, JOHN, 4
prison an extraordinarily pleasant p. BURCHFIELD, ROBERT, 1
Any event is welcome in p. SOYINKA, WOLE, 7
half of the world...p. guard to the other half DUHAMEL, GEORGES, 3
no p. like a guilty conscience PROVERBS, 493
P. kills everything SEMBÈNE, OUSMANE, 1
P....start sending a better class of people PETER, LAURENCE J., 7
the p. of our mind USTINOV, PETER, 7
The world is a p. KRAUS, KARL, 22
They're not in p. LEE, KUAN YEW, 3
prisoner p. sees the door of his dungeon open he dashes SHAW, GEORGE BERNARD, 18
prisoners of war only way...to get our p. back NIXON, RICHARD, 15
prisons Jails and p. are designed to break human beings DAVIS, ANGELA, 1
not enough p....in Palestine to hold...the Jews MEIR, GOLDA, 1
privacy a right to share your p. in a public place USTINOV, PETER, 12
That should assure us of...undisturbed p. PARKER, DOROTHY, 26
private P. faces in public places AUDEN, W. H., 48
P. practice and marriage BROCA, PAUL, 1
private parts They didn't...take much interest in my p. BECKETT, SAMUEL, 15
privilege p. I claim for my own sex AUSTEN, JANE, 28
P....the greatest enemy of right EBNER-ESCHENBACH, MARIE VON, 7
the p. of knocking down any man O'CONNELL, DANIEL, 2
this p. of education NYERERE, JULIUS KAMBARAGE, 9
privileged only p. persons...are the children PERÓN, EVA, 2
p. man...depraved in mind and heart BAKUNIN, MIKHAIL, 3
privileges values its p. above its principles EISENHOWER, DWIGHT D., 12
prize first p. was a woman skilled in graceful handicraft HOMER, 10
the p. of truth SCHILLER, FRIEDRICH VON, 4
prizes miss the p. at the flower show BRONOWSKI, JACOB, 5
ready to receive p. as...thrown into prison WALESA, LECH, 1
prizing Not p. hard-to-get valuables LAOZI, 6
probable P. impossibilities are...preferred ARISTOTLE, 23
problem any p., however complicated ANDERSON, POUL, 1
my biggest p. all my life...men DAVIS, BETTE, 3
Not every p. someone has with his girlfriend MARCUSE, HERBERT, 1
p. as I see it at this moment CHARLES, PRINCE, 2
p. difficult at night...committee of sleep STEINBECK, JOHN, 34
to solve any p. is to remove its cause KING, MARTIN LUTHER, JR., 21
your p. or part of your solution MURDOCH, RUPERT, 6
problems all p. begin to look like nails MASLOW, ABRAHAM, 3
I solve my p. with...movies SPIELBERG, STEVEN, 6
P. are the price of progress KETTERING, CHARLES, 1
People create p. by not trusting MARCUS, BERNIE, 2
p. when I came into office KENNEDY, JOHN FITZGERALD, 35
the many p. which beset the novelist SACKVILLE-WEST, VITA, 4
two p. in my life DOUGLAS-HOME, ALEC, 2
process a cosmic-historical p. of Change YAN FU, 1
procession torchlight p....down your throat O'SULLIVAN, JOHN L., 3
proclamation The p. and repetition of first principles MAMET, DAVID, 16
Thou art the p. DONNE, JOHN, 27
procrastination After a fatal p. BURGOYNE, JOHN, 1
p. is the art of keeping up with yesterday MARQUIS, DON, 3
P. is the thief of time YOUNG, EDWARD, 4
procreate I could be content that we might p. like trees BROWNE, THOMAS, 32
procreation Excluded is every action...to render p. impossible PAUL VI, 1
trivialization of the act of p. COGGAN, DONALD, 1
unless there's a spurt in p. MERRIMAN, BRIAN, 1
procurer common p. of people and nations MARX, KARL, 17
produce P. or get out KAUFFMAN, EWING M., 1
producer p. must be a prophet and...general LASKY, JESSE L., 1
produces He p. but does not own LAOZI, 3

product p. of every other black woman before me WINFREY, OPRAH, 1
The p. of the artist MAMET, DAVID, 15
products Between two p., equal in function LOEWY, RAYMOND, 1
try to picture what the p. will be SCULLEY, JOHN, 2
profanation P. and violation are part of...sex PAGLIA, CAMILLE, 16
profession no p....less...contentment than in painting RIDOLFI, CARLO, 1
p. where you can gain great eminence MEANY, GEORGE, 1
professional I never use p. actors nowadays BRESSON, ROBERT, 1
professions All p., achievements...thrown up to compete MAMET, DAVID, 1
professor A p....talks in someone else's sleep AUDEN, W. H., 55
p. of poetry...like...a Kentucky colonel AUDEN, W. H., 56
The old P....Hercules struggling with death FREUD, SIGMUND, 6
professors American p. like their literature clear and cold and pure and very dead LEWIS, SINCLAIR, 7
p. of philosophy but not philosophers THOREAU, HENRY DAVID, 38
profile P. and contour...touchstone of the Architect LE CORBUSIER, 4
profit count...p. every day...Fate allows HORACE, 34
In a p. squeeze TOWNSEND, ROBERT, 12
No p. grows where is no pleasure SHAKESPEARE, WILLIAM, 635
p. by the folly of others PLINY THE ELDER, 15
their aime was nothing but present p. SMITH, JOHN, 1
To whose p. CICERO, 15
trouble with the p. system WHITE, E. B., 13
what shall it p. a man BIBLE, 359
profitability to extrapolate p. into the future HELLER, ROBERT, 3
profiteering p., profiteering! Strike hard against it MOTTOS AND SLOGANS, 6
profits You must deodorise p. PARKER, SIR PETER, 3
progeny p. of this parent cell...take our looks THOMAS, LEWIS, 2
programming P. used to be...arcane matter SINCLAIR, CLIVE, 5
progress All p. is based upon...desire BUTLER, SAMUEL (1835–1902), 19
apply p. and education to one half ATATURK, KEMAL, 1
human p....a purely intellectual affair BERTALANFFY, LUDWIG VON, 1
Man's "p." is but a gradual discovery SAINT-EXUPÉRY, ANTOINE DE, 6
Much of our American p. HUMPHREY, HUBERT H., 3
P....depends on retentiveness SANTAYANA, GEORGE, 14
p....exchange of one nuisance for another ELLIS, HAVELOCK, 3
P. has gone full circle to regress LIYONG, TABAN LO, 1
P. in civilization...progress in cookery FARMER, FANNIE, 1
"p." is simply a comparative CHESTERTON, G. K., 16
Praise p....a moving target DAVIS, BOB, 1
P....The law of life BROWNING, ROBERT, 62
P. toward a global environment IMPARATO, NICHOLAS, 1
stopped believing in p. BORGES, JORGE LUIS, 7
The p. of freedom COBDEN, RICHARD, 2
There can be no p. KENNEDY, JOHN FITZGERALD, 23
thievish p. SHAKESPEARE, WILLIAM, 577
progression Nothing in p. can rest BURKE, EDMUND, 10
prohibit *One thing they cannot p. /*...The strong men gittin' stronger BROWN, STERLING, 1
project the p. will enjoy perpetual funding MAHONEY, RICHARD J., 1
proletarian p....helping to bolster up the capitalist system WAUGH, EVELYN, 27
substitution of the p. for the bourgeois state LENIN, VLADIMIR ILYICH, 16
proletarianization p. and mystification CÉSAIRE, AIMÉ, 2
proletariat The p. seizes the public power ENGELS, FRIEDRICH, 7
we become a revolutionary p. HERZL, THEODOR, 13
prologues P. precede the piece GARRICK, DAVID, 2
prolonging p. life rather than diminishing human suffering KÜBLER-ROSS, ELISABETH, 3
promise A p. made is a debt unpaid SERVICE, ROBERT W., 3
Never p. more than you can perform PUBLILIUS SYRUS, 7
Promised Land P., where...can have hooked noses HERZL, THEODOR, 8
promises not enough p. to go round REAGAN, RONALD, 21
P. and pie-crust...made to be broken SWIFT, JONATHAN, 30
P. are like pie-crust PROVERBS, 368
P....human way of ordering the future ARENDT, HANNAH, 4
young man of p. CHURCHILL, WINSTON, 2
promote P. the Causes of Reform and Modernization NEWSPAPERS, 16
promotion All to have p....their whole devotion SKELTON, JOHN, 2
pronunciation To correct an Englishman's p. SHAW, GEORGE BERNARD, 121
proof I have...found an admirable p. FERMAT, PIERRE DE, 1
only p....that an object is visible MILL, JOHN STUART, 19
Science has p. without any certainty MONTAGU, ASHLEY, 1
proofs All p. or disproofs that we tender AUDEN, W. H., 43
propaganda If p. worked we'd be straight MAUPIN, ARMISTEAD, 5
making p. for one style of thinking WITTGENSTEIN, LUDWIG, 19
P....consists in nearly deceiving your friends CORNFORD, F. M., 2
proper He never does a p. thing without...an improper reason SHAW, GEORGE BERNARD, 38
P. words in proper places SWIFT, JONATHAN, 9
property Get hold of portable p. DICKENS, CHARLES, 35
give me a little snug p. EDGEWORTH, MARIA, 4
It is for our p....our liberty...our independence PITT THE YOUNGER, WILLIAM, 3
P. has its duties DRUMMOND, THOMAS, 1
P. is organised robbery SHAW, GEORGE BERNARD, 41
P. is theft PROUDHON, PIERRE JOSEPH, 2
prophecy Among all forms of mistake, p. ELIOT, GEORGE, 16
prophet a p. is not without honour BIBLE, 403
every P. knows the convulsion of truth KEROUAC, JACK, 23
I'm the P. of the Utterly Absurd KIPLING, RUDYARD, 61
not...a p. but...a humble servant MANDELA, NELSON, 23
sons of the p. were brave FOLK VERSE, 1
The P. said to Gabriel AL-GHAZALI, 3
The p. who fails to present...alternative MEAD, MARGARET, 6
there arose not a p....like unto Moses BIBLE, 41
the sole qualification to be a p. CHURCHILL, WINSTON, 25
proportion p....Musicke is measured by it GIBBONS, ORLANDO, 1
proportional representation P....is fundamentally counter-democratic KINNOCK, NEIL, 6
proposition Every p. which we can understand RUSSELL, BERTRAND, 50
important that a p. be interesting WHITEHEAD, A. N., 16
propositions resolve the p. of a lover SHAKESPEARE, WILLIAM, 110
prose All that is not p. is verse MOLIÈRE, 5
a p. which knows no reason KIPLING, RUDYARD, 2
a sort of p. home movie SALINGER, J. D., 9
difference between...p. and metrical composition WORDSWORTH, WILLIAM, 24
good p. is an affair of good manners MAUGHAM, SOMERSET, 34
good p. should resemble...conversation MAUGHAM, SOMERSET, 37

I can only write p. today YEATS, W. B., 63
I have been talking p. for over forty years MOLIÈRE, 6
most beautiful p. paragraph yet written TWAIN, MARK, 1
P....can bear a great deal of poetry LANDOR, WALTER SAVAGE, 1
p. = words in their best order COLERIDGE, SAMUEL TAYLOR, 55
the cradle of English p. LITTLE, A. G., 1

prospect what a p. this opens DICKENS, CHARLES, 70

prospects cannot live on p. PROVERBS, 486
p. of the world population SHAPIRO, ROBERT B., 1

prosperity don't die waiting for p. IACOCCA, LEE, 6
In p. men friends may find EVERYMAN, 2
I wish you all sorts of p. LESAGE, ALAIN RENÉ, 2
P. doth best discover vice BACON, FRANCIS (1561–1626), 10
P. is only an instrument COOLIDGE, CALVIN, 8
P. is the blessing of the Old Testament BACON, FRANCIS (1561–1626), 11
P. or egalitarianism—you have to choose VARGAS LLOSA, MARIO, 5

prosperous Oh! ye p. DELANEY, LUCY A., 1

prostitute every p. an accusing finger pointing firmly at society SANKARA, THOMAS, 2
I don't think a p. is more moral PHILIP, PRINCE, 3
I will not p. myself BALENCIAGA, CRISTÓBAL, 2

prostitution P....a blight on the human race TRISTAN, FLORA, 1
P....an opportunity to meet people HELLER, JOSEPH, 11

protect Every man I meet wants to p. me WEST, MAE, 23
To p. workers in their inalienable rights GOMPERS, SAMUEL, 1

protection entitled to the p. of the English law MANSFIELD, WILLIAM MURRAY, 1
P. is not a principle DISRAELI, BENJAMIN, 4
p. of the father, mother, God, alcoholism ADLER, ALFRED, 5

protections several good p. against temptations TWAIN, MARK, 19

protest an earnest p. against golf GRACE, W. G., 1
open, unorganized p. against empty stomachs POWELL, ADAM CLAYTON, JR., 5
voice of p....is never more needed NORTON, CHARLES ELIOT, 2

Protestant one of my favorite activities is P. spotting BROOKS, MEL, 2
P....can only go to his solicitor DISRAELI, BENJAMIN, 22
P. women may take the Pill THOMAS, IRENE, 1

Protestantism The chief contribution of P. to human thought MENCKEN, H. L., 17

Protestants God knows how...P....have any sense of direction WILSON, ANGUS, 3

protons p. in the universe...same number of electrons EDDINGTON, ARTHUR, 3

proud p. in humility BURTON, ROBERT, 6
Yes; I am p. POPE, ALEXANDER, 38

prouder P. than rustling in unpaid-for silk SHAKESPEARE, WILLIAM, 130

proudest The thing I am p. of GREEN, HETTY, 1

Proust Where is the P. of Papua BELLOW, SAUL, 1

prov'd For he was...p. most royal SHAKESPEARE, WILLIAM, 226

prove p. anything by figures CARLYLE, THOMAS, 9
p. that your diagnosis was correct MELTZER, SAMUEL J., 1
p....they are first of the litter LLOYD-GEORGE, DAVID, 1

proved What is now p. was...imagin'd BLAKE, WILLIAM, 44
Which was to be p. EUCLID, 1

proverb A p. is much matter FULLER, THOMAS (1608–61), 2
p. is one man's wit...all men's wisdom RUSSELL, LORD, 3

provided Add: "p. he is really dead" LA BRUYÈRE, JEAN DE, 17

Providence a kind of P. will...end...the acts of God DE VRIES, PETER, 8
happy P. kept it from being...worse HARDY, THOMAS, 9
I go the way that P. dictates HITLER, ADOLF, 27
P. had sent a few men RUMBOLD, RICHARD, 1

provinces the p....overturned the liberties of Rome CLAY, HENRY, 2
The reluctant obedience of distant p. MACAULAY, THOMAS BABINGTON, 6

provincial worse than p.... parochial THOREAU, HENRY DAVID, 2

provision make p. for...your return to God AL-MUFID, ABU ABDULLAH MUHAMMAD AL-HARITHI AL-BAGHDADI, 1

provoke p. /The years to bring the inevitable yoke WORDSWORTH, WILLIAM, 53

prudence P....the virtue which must be preferred LACLOS, PIERRE CHODERLOS DE, 2

prudery P. is a kind of avarice STENDHAL, 1

Prussia P. merges into Germany FREDERICK WILLIAM IV, 1
P....only the kings who make revolution BISMARCK, PRINCE OTTO VON, 9

pseudonym use a p. during publication years SALINGER, J. D., 4

pseudoscience P. is easier to contrive than science SAGAN, CARL, 12
P. is embraced SAGAN, CARL, 13

psyche through lands, caves of the p., doctrines, creeds AUDEN, W. H., 4

psychedelic drugs Pursuing the religious life today...using p. LEARY, TIMOTHY, 9

psychedelics discovery of p. HUXLEY, ALDOUS, 2

psychiatrist Any man who goes to a p. GOLDWYN, SAMUEL, 14
need to retain a first-rate p. BAKER, RUSSELL, 1
p. has learned...first single phrases FREUD, ANNA, 5
p. is the obstetrician of the mind PROVERBS, MODERN, 28
p....man who goes to the Folies-Bergère STOCKWOOD, MERVYN, 1
p....may not be a mental healer LAING, R. D., 13
p. now animalizes man SZASZ, THOMAS, 1

psychiatrists p....delighted in compiling lists of phobias STEVENS, ANTHONY, 3

psychiatry p. responsible for the damage it inflicts BREGGIN, PETER R., 2
P. will fight...any kind of reform BREGGIN, PETER R., 3

psychic p. development of the individual FREUD, SIGMUND, 29
the p. invalid throws away his crutches MILLER, HENRY, 8
We use p. bullets...kill each other MAILER, NORMAN, 23

psychoanalysis essential to p....to remain...disreputable MERLEAU-PONTY, MAURICE, 15
goal of p....cultural achievement FREUD, SIGMUND, 61
I had read a good deal about p. MUIR, EDWIN, 2
Like Communism and Christianity, p....revered orthodoxy LEARY, TIMOTHY, 2
not the task of p. to save REICH, WILHELM, 5
p....an end product...like a dinosaur MEDAWAR, PETER, 3
P....as...medical psychology FREUD, ANNA, 3
P. cannot be considered a method of education JUNG, CARL GUSTAV, 27
P. can provide a theory of "progress," BROWN, NORMAN O., 2
P. does not make freedom impossible MERLEAU-PONTY, MAURICE, 10
P....essentially a theory of unconscious strivings FROMM, ERICH, 11
p....has returned our myths to us MERLEAU-PONTY, MAURICE, 8
P....in essence a cure through love FREUD, SIGMUND, 28
P. is a permanent fad DE VRIES, PETER, 5
P. is confession CHESTERTON, G. K., 54

P. is...embryology of the personality PIAGET, JEAN, 3
P. is spending 40 dollars an hour CONNELL, JAMES, 1
p....not a matter of discovery WITTGENSTEIN, LUDWIG, 17
P....raised understanding to an art LINDNER, ROBERT, 3
Reaction to p. is different in...childhood KLEIN, MELANIE, 6
The aim of p. is very daring PIAGET, JEAN, 4
psychoanalyst A p....pretends he doesn't know everything PROVERBS, MODERN, 6
psychoanalysts P. are father confessors KRAUS, KARL, 3
P....believe in...cerebral intestine BERENSON, BERNARD, 2
psychoanalytic P. concepts...have lost their enigmas MERLEAU-PONTY, MAURICE, 11
psycho-linguistics the p. of racism JACKSON, JESSE, 12
psychological p. observer ought to be more agile KIERKEGAARD, SØREN, 12
There is no such thing as p. SARTRE, JEAN-PAUL, 33
psychologically P., the bond of union...is love DEWEY, JOHN, 16
psychologist animal p....pulls habits out of rats PROVERBS, MODERN, 5
snare of the p. is...confusion JAMES, WILLIAM, 19
psychology banish concepts like meaning...value from p. KOFFKA, KURT, 1
Modern p....does not like to see LEARY, TIMOTHY, 8
My tyrant is p. FREUD, SIGMUND, 24
P. as a science has its limitations FROMM, ERICH, 15
P. as the behaviorist views it WATSON, JOHN B., 1
p....a sublimated spiritualism SONTAG, SUSAN, 13
P. can never tell...truth about madness FOUCAULT, MICHEL, 4
P....delineates sin KIERKEGAARD, SØREN, 8
P....describes a bump on the bump QUINE, WILLARD V., 4
P. has a long past EBBINGHAUS, HERMANN, 1
p. has the right to postulate JAMES, WILLIAM, 21
p. of women...greater orientation toward relationships GILLIGAN, CAROL F., 1
Popular p. is a mass of cant DEWEY, JOHN, 20
p....question how sin came into existence KIERKEGAARD, SØREN, 11
P. which explains everything MOORE, MARIANNE, 1
studying p....there is something unsatisfactory WITTGENSTEIN, LUDWIG, 18
The object of p. is to give us a totally different idea VALÉRY, PAUL, 9
There is no p. SZASZ, THOMAS, 11
treating p. *like* a natural science JAMES, WILLIAM, 2
psychopath treat a p....onerous and unrewarding job LINDNER, ROBERT, 2
psychopathologist The greatest p. has been Freud LAING, R. D., 2
psychosis All forms of p....inability to be objective FROMM, ERICH, 13
psycho-therapeutic defining life's problems in p. categories KOVEL, JOEL, 1
psychotherapy caring, understanding relationship...essence of p. BREGGIN, PETER R., 1
old-fashioned horsehair sofa...instrument of...p. H. D., 2
P....is useless when forced VAN BUREN, ABIGAIL, 1
psychotic Freud...compared *p.* patients to crystals FREUD, ANNA, 1
puberty P. is the cradle of love EGBUNA, OBI, 1
public give the p. what they want COHN, HARRY, 1
mean, stupid...ungrateful animal than the p. HAZLITT, WILLIAM, 22
Not even a p. figure BALDWIN, STANLEY, 1
P. business ought to be the business of the public FANON, FRANTZ, 12
p. buys its opinions as it buys its meat BUTLER, SAMUEL (1835–1902), 33
p. history...is but a sort of mask ADAMS, JOHN QUINCY, 4
P. participation...essence of democracy JOHNSON, LYNDON BAINES, 9
The p. be damned. I am working for my stockholders VANDERBILT, WILLIAM HENRY, 2
The P. is an old woman CARLYLE, THOMAS, 20
you owe the p....a good performance BOGART, HUMPHREY, 11
public bath great p....*New York Times* WOLFE, TOM, 18
public expenditure You can cut any p. MARSH, RICHARD, 4
publicity Any p. is good publicity PROVERBS, 138
no such thing as bad p. BEHAN, BRENDAN, 13
With p. comes humiliation JANOWITZ, TAMA, 1
public opinion One should...respect p. RUSSELL, BERTRAND, 48
P....always in advance of the law GALSWORTHY, JOHN, 3
rather follow p. ROOSEVELT, FRANKLIN D., 2
public property consider himself as p. JEFFERSON, THOMAS, 32
public school p., where...learning was painfully beaten into him PEACOCK, THOMAS LOVE, 10
public-school the p. system all over WAUGH, EVELYN, 10
public schools P. are the nurseries of all vice FIELDING, HENRY, 11
P. 'tis public folly feeds COWPER, WILLIAM, 21
public transport more money spent on p. GUMMER, JOHN SELWYN, 1
publish I'll p., right or wrong BYRON, LORD, 84
P. and be damned WILSON, HARRIETTE, 1
p. and be sued INGRAMS, RICHARD, 1
To p. a book is to talk MONTHERLANT, HENRI DE, 1
publishers American p. are not interested in black writers HIMES, CHESTER, 1
publishing p. faster than you think PAULI, WOLFGANG, 1
pun A p. is a pistol let off at the ear LAMB, CHARLES, 23
make so vile a p. DENNIS, JOHN, 1
punch I'd p. him in the snoot GEORGE V, 1
p. the other guy's bone into his brain TYSON, MIKE, 3
Punch *P.*—the official journal NEWSPAPERS, 18
punches P. did not often hurt MAILER, NORMAN, 10
punctuality P. is the politeness PROVERBS, 369
P. is the politeness of kings LOUIS XVIII, 2
P. is the soul of business HALIBURTON, THOMAS CHANDLER, 2
P. is the virtue of the bored WAUGH, EVELYN, 35
punctuation The p. of anniversaries is terrible LINDBERGH, ANNE MORROW, 1
punish I shall p. him and escape TOLSTOY, LEO, 3
punished Am I not p. enough in not being born an Englishman? VOLTAIRE, 51
punishment All p. is mischief BENTHAM, JEREMY, 3
No p. has ever...power of deterrence ARENDT, HANNAH, 11
P....art of unsupportable sensations FOUCAULT, MICHEL, 6
P. is not for revenge FRY, ELIZABETH, 2
power of p. is to silence JOHNSON, SAMUEL, 32
punishments In nature there are neither rewards nor p. INGERSOLL, ROBERT G., 4
punk P....a musical movement without music MORRISSEY, 1
p. music...I found my calling COBAIN, KURT, 3
P. rock promoted blatantly the word chaos MCLAREN, MALCOLM, 1
purchasers a pattern to encourage p. SWIFT, JONATHAN, 42
pure All those who are not racially p. HITLER, ADOLF, 31

a p. river of water of life BIBLE, 477
No man can be a p. specialist SHAW, GEORGE BERNARD, 114
p. as the driven slush BANKHEAD, TALLULAH, 6
P....to mount unto the stars DANTE ALIGHIERI, 8
Unto the p. all things are pure BIBLE, 499
purgatory no other p. but a woman BEAUMONT & FLETCHER, 12
P. is a pawnshop MACHADO DE ASSIS, JOAQUIM MARIA, 2
puritan A p.'s a person who pours righteous indignation CHESTERTON, G. K., 51
Puritan The P. hated bear-baiting MACAULAY, THOMAS BABINGTON, 19
To the P. all things are impure LAWRENCE, D. H., 17
Puritanism hearty P....pervades the instrument of 1787 BRYCE, JAMES, 3
P.—the haunting fear that someone...may be happy MENCKEN, H. L., 4
Puritans P....ceased to...find pleasure in ritual AUSTIN, MARY, 7
purple I never saw a p. cow BURGESS, GELETT, 2
purpose main p. of science is simplicity TELLER, EDWARD, 1
My p. is, indeed, a horse SHAKESPEARE, WILLIAM, 696
my real p. is for being here JACKSON, MICHAEL, 2
P. is the central ingredient of power EISNER, MICHAEL, 4
P. is the keystone ALLEN, JAMES, 1
p. of human life...to show compassion SCHWEITZER, ALBERT, 4
p. of its own /And measured motion WORDSWORTH, WILLIAM, 85
p. of our life is not suffering SCHOPENHAUER, ARTHUR, 9
p. of our lives...is beyond all human wisdom PATON, ALAN STEWART, 1
sense of p....get it from their archbishop MACMILLAN, HAROLD, 8
supreme p. of history...better world HOOVER, HERBERT, 10
The final p. of art MAILER, NORMAN, 26
The p. of studying economics ROBINSON, JOAN, 1
ultimate p. of the world HEGEL, G. W. F., 9
You seem to have no real p. in life CHURCHILL, JENNIE, 1
purposes the great p. of the Park OLMSTED, FREDERICK LAW, 1
purse the longest p. finally wins GANDHI, MAHATMA, 6
pussy P. said to the Owl LEAR, EDWARD, 18
What a beautiful p. you are LEAR, EDWARD, 17
putsch none but I...can make a p. SEECKT, HANS VON, 1
pygmies P....on the shoulders of giants LUCAN, 1
pylons P., those pillars SPENDER, STEPHEN, 6
pyramid After seeing the p., all other architecture MELVILLE, HERMAN, 23
p....organizational principle of the modern organization SEMLER, RICARDO, 8
we taper up like a p. MANN, HEINRICH, 1
pyramids summit of these p., forty centuries look down NAPOLEON I, 18
The heart of the eternal p. MELVILLE, HERMAN, 13
Pyrenees I see the P. MARAGALL, JOAN, 1
There are no more P. LOUIS XIV, 5
quacks Q. are the greatest liars in the world FRANKLIN, BENJAMIN, 34
quaffing Long q. maketh a short lyfe LYLY, JOHN, 8
Quaker A philosophical Q. full of...maxims FRANKLIN, BENJAMIN, 3
quaking The q. of the earth...rushing torrent WILLIAMS, VELINA, 1
qualifications q....an enormous nose, disappointment in love MAHFOUZ, NAGUIB, 10
qualities display q. which he does not possess JOHNSON, SAMUEL, 41
q. as would wear well GOLDSMITH, OLIVER, 28
quality The q. of your attention KLINE, NANCY, 7
quarks Three q. for Muster Mark JOYCE, JAMES, 17
quarrel a q. in the streets is...to be hated KEATS, JOHN (1795–1821), 40
a very pretty q. as it stands SHERIDAN, RICHARD BRINSLEY, 13
find q. in a straw /When honour's at the stake SHAKESPEARE, WILLIAM, 211
I never q....But sometimes I fight BENTON, THOMAS HART, 2
It takes...one to make a q. INGE, WILLIAM RALPH, 13
Out of the q....we make rhetoric YEATS, W. B., 9
q. between painters and *littérateurs* will...never be healed JAMES, HENRY, 25
q. with my bread and butter SWIFT, JONATHAN, 29
quarreled I did not know that we had ever q. THOREAU, HENRY DAVID, 50
quarrelled I have q. with my wife PEACOCK, THOMAS LOVE, 12
quarrels q. of lovers...the renewal of love TERENCE, 1
Q. would not last so long LA ROCHEFOUCAULD, FRANÇOIS, 31
quart one cannot put a q. in a pint cup GILMAN, CHARLOTTE PERKINS, 1
Quebec Q. does not have opinions LAURIER, WILFRID, 11
Q. remained British because it was French WRONG, GEORGE M., 1
queen a screaming q. or a tired fairy CROWLEY, MART, 1
I am your anointed Q. ELIZABETH I, 11
I'll q. it no inch farther SHAKESPEARE, WILLIAM, 671
isn't a bad bit of goods, the Q. CERVANTES, MIGUEL DE, 28
I would not be a q. SHAKESPEARE, WILLIAM, 280
Most Gracious Q., we thee implore ANONYMOUS, 33
q. did fish for men's souls ELIZABETH I, 2
The q. of curds and cream SHAKESPEARE, WILLIAM, 668
the q. of Sheba BIBLE, 188
Queen Anne Q.'s dead COLMAN, GEORGE, 2
queene (That greatest Glorious Q. of Faery lond) ELIZABETH I, 4
queenly She keeps on being Q. WHARTON, EDITH, 9
Queen Mab Q. hath been with you SHAKESPEARE, WILLIAM, 537
Queen of Hearts The Q. CARROLL, LEWIS, 22
The Q. /She made some tarts CHILDREN'S VERSE, 11
Queen Victoria a parlourmaid as ignorant as Q. VICTORIA, 1
queer I'm putting my q. shoulder to the /wheel GINSBERG, ALLEN, 1
the q. old Dean SPOONER, WILLIAM ARCHIBALD, 4
There's nought so q. PROVERBS, 422
question A timid q. will...receive a confident answer DARLING, CHARLES JOHN, 1
Every q....the mask of another question FERRIER, JAMES F., 1
If a q. can be framed...answer it WITTGENSTEIN, LUDWIG, 5
man who sees both sides of a q. WILDE, OSCAR, 24
No q. is ever settled WILCOX, ELLA WHEELER, 2
On this q. of principle WEBSTER, DANIEL, 6
q....which I have not been able to answer FREUD, SIGMUND, 23
The q. of the ultimate meaning of life TILLICH, PAUL, 9
the q. that we do not know MACLEISH, ARCHIBALD, 3
Whatever q. there may be of his talent JAMES, HENRY, 8
questioning Q....not the mode of conversation among gentlemen JOHNSON, SAMUEL, 111
questionings obstinate q. /Of sense and outward things WORDSWORTH, WILLIAM, 54
questions Real q. to the dead BELLOW, SAUL, 10

quick the q....listed among the dead STEWART, JACKIE, 1
quickies q. in hot showers or behind...bushes NORSE, HAROLD, 1
quickly Desire to have things done q. CONFUCIUS, 3
quickness my q. was fear LEONARD, SUGAR RAY, 2
quid pro quo These days, for a q. AMIS, KINGSLEY, 7
quiet All q. along the Potomac to-night BEERS, ETHEL LYNN, 1
Anythin' for a q. life DICKENS, CHARLES, 104
Anything for a Q. Life MIDDLETON, THOMAS, 1
quits A man is...finished when he q. NIXON, RICHARD, 35
quitter I'm not a q. NIXON, RICHARD, 22
quixotic One may be q. BAROJA, PÍO, 3
quotable better to be q. than...honest STOPPARD, TOM, 3
quotation Every q. contributes something JOHNSON, SAMUEL, 20
q. at the right moment TALMUD, 1
q. covers the absence of original thought SAYERS, DOROTHY L., 3
q. is a national vice WAUGH, EVELYN, 28
the great spring of happy q. MONTAGUE, C. E., 1
To say that anything was a q. SAKI, 18
quotations It needs no dictionary of q. BEERBOHM, MAX, 17
uneducated man to read books of q. CHURCHILL, WINSTON, 43
quote can q. Shakespeare in an economic crisis SHAKESPEARE, WILLIAM, 43
good q., I'd be wearing it DYLAN, BOB, 22

rabbi hung a sign, "Chief R. of America" SACKS, JONATHAN, 8
R.'s daughter is forbidden PROVERBS, 508
rabbit The r. has a charming face FOLK VERSE, 22
white r....have the Asiatic cholera COBB, IRVIN S., 3
rabbits a tale of four little r. POTTER, BEATRIX, 2
Rabelais R. is the wondrous mask of ancient comedy HUGO, VICTOR, 14
race All is r....no other truth DISRAELI, BENJAMIN, 35
in a r. run all, but one receiveth the prize BIBLE, 158
loftier r. /Than...the world hath known SYMONDS, JOHN ADDINGTON, 1
My r. began as the sea began WALCOTT, DEREK, 6
No r. holds the monopoly of beauty CÉSAIRE, AIMÉ, 4
no r. is civilized until it produces a literature TOLSON, MELVIN, 4
Nothing is more narrow-minded than...r. hatred KRAUS, KARL, 17
r. is not to the swift BIBLE, 55
r. question is subsidiary to the class question JAMES, C. L. R., 11
Some view our sable r. with scornful eye WHEATLEY, PHILLIS, 1
race relations God is trying to solve the r. problem COSBY, BILL, 3
Rachel R. weeping for her children BIBLE, 251
racial R. oppression of black people in America NORTON, ELEANOR HOLMES, 2
We do not want the r. antipathies BORAH, WILLIAM E., 1
racism modern r....traced to...conquest CLARKE, JOHN HENRIK, 5
R....everyone...today is exposed BENEDICT, RUTH, 4
r.—is a device HANSBERRY, LORRAINE, 2
R....is a weapon used by the wealthy DAVIS, ANGELA, 3
r....more serious than sexism KENNEDY, FLORYNCE R., 4
racist the r. who creates his inferior FANON, FRANTZ, 6
rack r. of this tough world SHAKESPEARE, WILLIAM, 370
radiance Life...Stains the white r. of eternity KEATS, JOHN (1795–1821), 7
There is r. in the darkness, if we could but see AWOLOWO, OBAFEMI, 1
radiation r....much in mind these days LOVELOCK, JAMES, 4
r.'s...laws /Impel us into common cause SETH, VIKRAM, 4
radical A r. is a man with both feet...in the air ROOSEVELT, FRANKLIN D., 13
I never dared be r. when young FROST, ROBERT, 6
r. invents the views...the conservative adopts TWAIN, MARK, 27
radical chic R....only radical in style WOLFE, TOM, 4
radio I had the r. on MONROE, MARILYN, 10
R. and television have lawful intellectual benefits KHOMEINI, RUHOLLAH, 4
radio 4 What do we want? R. NEWSPAPERS, 8
radioactive one's clothes all become r. CURIE, MARIE, 6
radioactivity R....is a horror HOLUB, MIROSLAV, 1
radium substance contains a new element...R. CURIE, MARIE, 5
Raffles They have not forgiven us Stamford R. yet VAN DER POST, LAURENS, 6
rage R. can only with difficulty BALDWIN, JAMES, 19
rags deal in r. and dress in velvet PROVERBS, 513
rails he r. at those things...he wants WEBSTER, JOHN, 2
rain A Hard R.'s A-Gonna Fall DYLAN, BOB, 2
Caught by the r. far from shelter BECKETT, SAMUEL, 9
drop of r. maketh a hole in the stone LATIMER, HUGH, 1
R. is grace UPDIKE, JOHN, 19
R., rain, go away CHILDREN'S VERSE, 62
r. will...wash all this scum DE NIRO, ROBERT, 1
Still falls the R. SITWELL, EDITH, 1
rainbow Somewhere over the r. HARBURG, E. Y., 5
the R. gave thee birth DAVIES, W. H., 3
raineth it r. on the just BOWEN, CHARLES, 1
rains It never r. but it pours PROVERBS, 279
rainy Save something for a r. day PROVERBS, 374
Rainy Mountain way to R. is...an idea MOMADAY, N. SCOTT, 4
raise If you do not r. your eyes PORCHIA, ANTONIO, 3
R. the stone...thou shalt find me ANONYMOUS, 56
ram a r. caught in a thicket BIBLE, 128
Ramadan month of R. shall ye fast KORAN, 4
Rambo I love *R.* SPIELBERG, STEVEN, 4
rampage On the R., Pip DICKENS, CHARLES, 34
ranches eight r. and three plantations TURNER, TED, 2
rank O! my offence is r., it smells SHAKESPEARE, WILLIAM, 195
r. is but the guinea's stamp BURNS, ROBERT, 18
rap R. music is information D, CHUCK, 1
rapacious r. and licentious soldiery BURKE, EDMUND, 25
rape R....form of mass terrorism GRIFFIN, SUSAN, 1
r. is one of the least-reported crimes ADLER, FREDA, 2
raped been r. and speaks English ANONYMOUS, 90
Raphael When I was their age, I could draw like R. PICASSO, PABLO, 13
rapist a rapist remains a r. LANE, GEOFFREY DAWSON, 1
rapists All men are r. FRENCH, MARILYN, 2
rapture There is a r. on the lonely shore BYRON, LORD, 37
Though r. brings us delight TERESA OF ÁVILA, SAINT, 5
rare as r. things will, it vanished BROWNING, ROBERT, 58
neither r. nor well done KOVACS, ERNIE, 1
O R. Ben Jonson JONSON, BEN, 1
rarer A r. spirit never /Did steer humanity SHAKESPEARE, WILLIAM, 87

rascals R., would you live for ever? FREDERICK II (1712–86), 6
rat even a r. becomes a tiger PROVERBS, 82
you can r., but you can't re-rat CHURCHILL, WINSTON, 13
rational could an entirely r. being speak of LEVINAS, EMMANUEL, 3
there is that which is r. DEANE, SEAMUS, 2
What is r. is actual HEGEL, G. W. F., 25
yet to meet the famous R. Economic Man SANFORD, CHARLES, JR., 1
rationality r....factors governing human behavior GELL-MANN, MURRAY, 2
rationalization *R....self-deception by reasoning* HORNEY, KAREN, 9
rats I see some r. have got in LLOYD-GEORGE, DAVID, 12
R.! /They fought the dogs BROWNING, ROBERT, 19
rattle r. the saber at every diplomatic entanglement BETHMANN HOLLWEG, THEOBALD VON, 2
the rest of you...r. your jewellery LENNON, JOHN, 7
rattlesnake After God had finished the r. LONDON, JACK, 4
ravages the r. of time HORACE, 45
raven r. himself is hoarse SHAKESPEARE, WILLIAM, 387
ravens There were three r. sat on a tree FOLK VERSE, 25
ravish You can't r. a tin of sardines LAWRENCE, D. H., 27
ravished He...r. this fair creature FIELDING, HENRY, 8
raznochinetz *r.* needs no memory MANDELSTAM, OSIP, 16
razors R. pain you PARKER, DOROTHY, 21
reach a man's r. should exceed his grasp BROWNING, ROBERT, 44
When you r. the top CAINE, MICHAEL, 2
reactionaries r. are paper tigers MAO ZEDONG, 24
r. of 1815 hid...name of revolution BLOCH, MARC, 1
reactors R. breed plutonium /bloodcells pay their dues CORTEZ, JAYNE, 1
read do *you* r. books *through*? JOHNSON, SAMUEL, 83
I have never r. it CLARKE, KENNETH, 2
I've just r. that I am dead... KIPLING, RUDYARD, 67
Men who r. Lenin...don't riot, "they mass" JACKSON, GEORGE, 9
never r. a book before reviewing it SMITH, SYDNEY, 23
O, learn to r. what silent love hath writ SHAKESPEARE, WILLIAM, 567
R. in order to live FLAUBERT, GUSTAVE, 3
r. just as inclination leads him JOHNSON, SAMUEL, 72
R., mark, learn and inwardly digest BOOK OF COMMON PRAYER, 6
R....to weigh and consider BACON, FRANCIS (1561–1626), 64
Something that everybody wants to have r. TWAIN, MARK, 23
The man who in himself can r. FREIDANK, 3
Who r. to doubt, or...scorn SCOTT, SIR WALTER, 31
Wrap...in a blanket and...r. SNYDER, GARY, 10
reader A good r. has imagination NABOKOV, VLADIMIR, 14
A r. seldom peruses a book with pleasure ADDISON, JOSEPH, 11
Hypocrite r....my brother BAUDELAIRE, CHARLES, 11
ideal r.... ideal insomnia JOYCE, JAMES, 12
R., I married him BRONTË, CHARLOTTE, 6
r. read a novel...for the moral O'CONNOR, FLANNERY, 2
The r. of the novel UNAMUNO Y JUGO, MIGUEL DE, 4
readers r. and writers...bereft when criticism remains too polite MORRISON, TONI, 15
R. may be divided into four classes COLERIDGE, SAMUEL TAYLOR, 64
reading art of r. is to skip judiciously HAMERTON, PHILIP GILBERT, 1
half learned the art of r. BALFOUR, ARTHUR, 5
no society can exist without r. MANGUEL, ALBERTO, 2
R....good way to define pleasure FORD, RICHARD, 2
r....is like a conversation DESCARTES, RENÉ, 9
R. isn't an occupation we encourage ORTON, JOE, 8
R....is simply the expansion of one's mind SHANGE, NTOZAKE, 6
R. is to the mind STEELE, RICHARD, 6
R. maketh a full man BACON, FRANCIS (1561–1626), 63
There are two motives for r. a book RUSSELL, BERTRAND, 46
ready necessity of being *r.* increases LINCOLN, ABRAHAM, 16
ready-made a better word than "prefabricated"..."r." CHURCHILL, WINSTON, 38
reaffirm to r. to ourselves our basic irresponsibility DOCTOROW, E. L., 1
Reagan disastrous fire in President R.'s library REAGAN, RONALD, 5
R. is the most popular REAGAN, RONALD, 8
Reaganomics R....a rising tide lifts all yachts REAGAN, RONALD, 7
R. consists of rearming the United States REAGAN, RONALD, 1
real abyss that separates...r. from the imaginary SARTRE, JEAN-PAUL, 23
Everything r. must be experienceable JAMES, WILLIAM, 4
It's the r. thing ADVERTISEMENTS, 8
Nothing ever becomes r. till it is experienced KEATS, JOHN (1795–1821), 39
Nothing...r. unless it happens on television BOORSTIN, DANIEL J., 1
R....was happening to me right then MOSLEY, WALTER, 5
There are R. things PEIRCE, C. S., 4
whether Zelda and I are r. FITZGERALD, F. SCOTT, 24
real estate act of r. rather than...God HUXTABLE, ADA LOUISE, 1
realism necessity of r. in art DE WYZEWA, TÉODOR, 1
realist R....Idealist who knows nothing of himself NOVALIS, 2
realistic "a r. decision,"...to do something bad MCCARTHY, MARY, 12
reality Cannot bear very much r. ELIOT, T. S., 14
He had surrendered all r. FAULKNER, WILLIAM, 8
I was testing the bounds of r. MORRISON, JIM, 6
may always be another r. FRY, CHRISTOPHER, 4
r. and his brain came into contact WILBERFORCE, SAMUEL, 1
r....brought forth solely by the imagination FICHTE, JOHANN, 2
R. is that which...doesn't go away DICK, PHILIP K., 2
r. of yesterday...illusion tomorrow PIRANDELLO, LUIGI, 14
R....something you rise above MINNELLI, LIZA, 1
She simply inhabits r. ADDAMS, JANE, 1
speak *excessively* of r. BARTHES, ROLAND, 1
realization There can be no...complete r. of utility without beauty LEACH, BERNARD, 1
realm I came not into this r. as merchandise CATHERINE OF ARAGÓN, 1
reap sown the wind...r. the whirlwind BIBLE, 150
reaper a R. whose name is Death LONGFELLOW, HENRY WADSWORTH, 14
rears Of *R.* and *Vices*, I saw enough AUSTEN, JANE, 21
reason contrary to r....that there is a vacuum DESCARTES, RENÉ, 14
Cultivate a superiority to r. COLLINS, WILKIE, 1
hearts must know the world of r. BETTELHEIM, BRUNO, 1
Human r. won. Mankind won KHRUSHCHEV, NIKITA, 9
let us r. together JOHNSON, LYNDON BAINES, 26
R. cannot be forced into belief CRESCAS, HASDAI BEN ABRAHAM, 1
R. has ruled...the world's history HEGEL, G. W. F., 19
R. is itself a matter of faith CHESTERTON, G. K., 28
R. is nothing but...unintelligible instinct HUME, DAVID, 20
R. is the Sovereign of the World HEGEL, G. W. F., 21
R. must be awake and reflection applied HEGEL, G. W. F., 7
r. must be consider'd...kind of cause HUME, DAVID, 18
R. must sit at...knee of instinct SCHELL, JONATHAN, 2
R., Observation, and Experience INGERSOLL, ROBERT G., 6

R....one out of a thousand possibilities JAMES, WILLIAM, 17
R. to rule...mercy to forgive DRYDEN, JOHN, 40
wanted to be the r. for everything BARNES, DJUNA, 4
reasonable We are r. PAISLEY, IAN, 2
reasoning R. draws a conclusion BACON, ROGER, 2
reasons greatest r. why so few people understand themselves MANDEVILLE, BERNARD, 1
man always has two r. MORGAN, JOHN PIERPONT, 2
never give your r. MANSFIELD, WILLIAM MURRAY, 2
R. are not like garments DEVEREUX, ROBERT, 1
r. for not printing any list of subscribers JOHNSON, SAMUEL, 153
rebel go on being a r. too long DURRELL, LAWRENCE, 1
What is a r. CAMUS, ALBERT, 26
rebell R. and Atheist too DONNE, JOHN, 34
rebellion A little r. now and then JEFFERSON, THOMAS, 15
little r....shirt undone LENNON, JOHN, 12
reborn If I must be r. CHANDRA, VIKRAM, 3
I know I will be r. CHANDRA, VIKRAM, 4
rebukes If he r. you, do not answer back MSHAM, MWANA KUPONA BINTI, 2
recall machinery of r....machinery of association JAMES, WILLIAM, 20
receipts How were the r....in Madison Square BARNUM, P. T., 2
receive R. from me this city MANDELSTAM, OSIP, 2
whoso shall r. one such little child BIBLE, 411
received freely ye have r., freely give BIBLE, 393
recession effects of r....underclass of the unemployed JOHNSON, RICHARD W., 1
r....far from producing new fascist states JOHNSON, RICHARD W., 5
R. isn't the fault of the workers MORITA AKIO, 1
R....the social power of the rich JOHNSON, RICHARD W., 2
r....when your neighbor loses his job REAGAN, RONALD, 42
r. when your neighbor loses his job TRUMAN, HARRY S., 11
R....you have to tighten the belt PANKIN, BORIS, 1
recessions every government...promises...to cure r. DRUCKER, PETER, 6
recipe r....like writing a little short story CHILD, JULIA, 3
reckoning No man gets away from his r. GUNN, NEIL, 1
reconcile How r. this world...with...my imagining KELLER, HELEN, 6
record I was...at a major r. company DAVIS, CLIVE, 1
To r. the manners...that is my aim COURBET, GUSTAVE, 1
record companies All r. prefer third-rate talents SIMONE, NINA, 1
recorded What is not r. is not remembered BHUTTO, BENAZIR, 1
recording When I'm r. I could have orgasm PRINCE, 1
recreations R.: listening to music, silence SITWELL, EDITH, 12
rectitude the r. of which you are in doubt PLINY THE YOUNGER, 3
red asking for...r. piece of green chalk FEATHER, LEONARD G., 1
a small packet of r. earth MURPHY, DERVLA, 5
Better r. than dead MOTTOS AND SLOGANS, 31
good Tray grew very r. HOFFMAN, HEINRICH, 1
R. sky at night PROVERBS, 370
That man is a R....a Communist HAGUE, FRANK, 1
red-handed R. with the silver FRY, CHRISTOPHER, 2
Red-Hot Mamas The Last of the R. TUCKER, SOPHIE, 3
Red Sea I will set thy bounds from the R. BIBLE, 84
reduce more we r. ourselves to machines BRACKETT, ANNA C., 1
redundance r. of blood MANGAN, JAMES CLARENCE, 1
reek you and your Senate r. with French blood NAPOLEON I, 23
reeling R. and Writhing CARROLL, LEWIS, 17
referendum R....popular vote to learn the nonsensus BIERCE, AMBROSE, 45
refined I'll never be r. if I twitch THOMAS, DYLAN, 27
One of those r. people COLETTE, 7
reflection The man of r. discovers Truth PÉREZ GALDÓS, BENITO, 4
The r. in my shaving mirror ROEPKE BAHAMONDE, GABRIELA, 2
reform All r....will prove unavailing CARLYLE, THOMAS, 10
Beginning r. is beginning revolution WELLINGTON, DUKE OF, 3
Every r. movement ROOSEVELT, THEODORE, 20
R. never comes to a class or a people CASELY-HAYFORD, JOSEPH EPHRAIM, 1
r....will be when the milk isn't sour NEWSPAPERS, 30
reformation Every r. must have its victims SAKI, 9
reformer A r....rides through a sewer WALKER, JIMMY, 1
reforms point of all r....human liberation XU WENLI, 2
refrain R. from these men BIBLE, 9
refrigerator His r.'s been broken SIMON, NEIL, 10
refusal r. to act, not of inability MENCIUS, 2
refuse do not always r. to believe in others MACHADO DE ASSIS, JOAQUIM MARIA, 4
r. to cooperate with an evil system KING, MARTIN LUTHER, JR., 20
r. to give the title of art PLATO, 5
Should I r. a good dinner HEAVISIDE, OLIVER, 1
those who collect the r. of the public streets BRAMAH, ERNEST, 2
refused She r. to begin the "Beguine COWARD, NOEL, 21
refute I r. it *thus* JOHNSON, SAMUEL, 159
regard r. and affection for a young man WILLIAM III, 3
regardless R. of what they say NIXON, RICHARD, 26
reggae R. is a music that has plenty fight MARLEY, BOB, 10
r. music...carry earth force, people rhythm MARLEY, BOB, 7
regime No r. has ever loved great writers SOLZHENITSYN, ALEXANDER, 15
regimen R. is superior to medicine VOLTAIRE, 26
regiment led his r. from behind GILBERT, W. S., 22
region states R.'...primary linkage...global economy OHMAE, KENICHI, 1
regret I r. only two things HENRY IV, 3
little more r. and a little less satisfaction BEECHAM, THOMAS, 10
my r. /Becomes an April violet HALLAM, ARTHUR HENRY, 16
place...endless r. or secret happiness JEWETT, SARAH ORNE, 1
R. is an appalling waste of energy MANSFIELD, KATHERINE, 6
regrets I have no r. BERGMAN, INGRID, 2
No, I have no r. VAUCAIRE, MICHEL, 1
no r. over anything left undone MENCIUS, 5
re-gu-la-ri-ty the r. of our experiences PIRANDELLO, LUIGI, 17
regulate We must either r....own, or destroy LLOYD, HENRY DEMAREST, 1
rehearsing R. a play is making the word flesh SHAFFER, PETER, 1
reign Better to r. in hell, than serve in heaven MILTON, JOHN, 31
we r. unchallenged in the realm /of...abstract notions HEINE, HEINRICH, 4
reigned I have r. with your loves ELIZABETH I, 9
r. a virgin and died a virgin" ELIZABETH I, 22
reject r. me on account of my religion BELLOC, HILAIRE, 34
rejection accept r. and reject acceptance BRADBURY, RAY, 1
rejoice r. in the Lord alway BIBLE, 451
relations great men have their poor r. DICKENS, CHARLES, 18
I maintain very happy r....my mistress ELLINGTON, DUKE, 8
Personal r.... important thing FORSTER, E. M., 14

The sum total of these r. of production MARX, KARL, 11

relationships don't ever sever r. LAUDER, ESTÉE, 1
new r. between the individual and...corporation TICHY, NOEL M., 1

relatives nice thing about having r.' kids RICHARD, CLIFF, 1

relativism Conceptual r. is a heady...exotic doctrine DAVIDSON, DONALD, 1

relaxing R. your brain is fatal MOSS, STIRLING, 1

released Nothing is more desirable than to be r. from an affliction BALDWIN, JAMES, 8

relics With Crosses, R., Crucifixes BUTLER, SAMUEL (1612–80), 22

relief For this r. much thanks SHAKESPEARE, WILLIAM, 139
There is a certain r. in change IRVING, WASHINGTON, 4
thou wilt give thyself r. MARCUS AURELIUS, 2

religion And what is r. BAMBARA, TONI CADE, 1
As far as R., I'm a Baptist ARMSTRONG, LOUIS, 10
As if r. was intended BUTLER, SAMUEL (1612–80), 10
Congress shall make no law respecting...r. CONSTITUTION OF THE UNITED STATES, 1
consolations of r. or philosophy HUXLEY, ALDOUS, 17
foundation of r....acts of men WOLLASTON, WILLIAM, 1
I am of the same r. as all those who are brave and true HENRY IV, 2
just enough r. to make us hate SWIFT, JONATHAN, 49
Many people think they have r. INGERSOLL, ROBERT G., 3
Men will wrangle for r. COLTON, CHARLES, 5
missionary r....experimental economic technique KEYNES, JOHN MAYNARD, 7
narrow the meaning of r. to the *cultus deorum* TILLICH, PAUL, 1
no reason to bring r. into it O'CASEY, SEAN, 5
Not a r. for gentlemen CHARLES II, 10
Nothing is so fatal to r. as indifference BURKE, EDMUND, 11
One r. is as true as another BURTON, ROBERT, 21
r. cannot be concerned with politics TUTU, DESMOND, 8
R. circumscribes...choice and adaptation FREUD, SIGMUND, 55
r....duty of government to protect all conscientious professors PAINE, THOMAS, 2
R. had, after all, its uses LARSEN, NELLA, 2
R. /Has made an honest woman of the supernatural FRY, CHRISTOPHER, 5
r. has many lives, and a habit of resurrection DURANT, WILL, 12
r., I mean... the Church of England FIELDING, HENRY, 17
R. is an illusion FREUD, SIGMUND, 31
R. is a support...ruins the edifice DIDEROT, DENIS, 12
R. is by no means a proper subject CHESTERFIELD, LORD, 4
R. is love WEBB, BEATRICE, 1
R. is... the opium of the people MARX, KARL, 12
R., like water, may be free VAN BUREN, ABIGAIL, 2
r....must also be concerned about man's social conditions KING, MARTIN LUTHER, JR., 18
R.'s in the heart JERROLD, DOUGLAS, 2
R....the dream of the human mind FEUERBACH, LUDWIG ANDREAS, 1
R....the wound, not the bandage POTTER, DENNIS, 1
R. was my protection against pain HARE, DAVID, 2
r. without a prelate BANCROFT, GEORGE, 2
r....yours is Success BARRIE, J. M., 16
The equation of r. with belief TOYNBEE, ARNOLD, 5
The true meaning of r. ARNOLD, MATTHEW, 21
To become a popular r. INGE, WILLIAM RALPH, 2
To die for a r. is easier than to live it absolutely BORGES, JORGE LUIS, 4
when r. is allowed to invade...private life MELBOURNE, LORD, 1
when r. was strong...men mistook magic for medicine SZASZ, THOMAS, 13
Where questions of r. are concerned FREUD, SIGMUND, 44

religions all r. are on a tottering foundation BURBANK, LUTHER, 1
r. we call false were once true EMERSON, RALPH WALDO, 21
sixty different r., and only one sauce CARACCIOLO, FRANCESCO, 1

religious first, r. and moral principles ARNOLD, THOMAS, 2
If there were no r. reality BUBER, MARTIN, 5
My relationship with formal r. belief...chequered RUSHDIE, SALMAN, 4
O ye R. BLAKE, WILLIAM, 14
R. cultures produce poetry VARGAS LLOSA, MARIO, 3
R. ideas...sprung from the same need FREUD, SIGMUND, 40
R. insanity, fantasies...infantile megalomaniac ideas ADLER, ALFRED, 2
r. outlook on life JUNG, CARL GUSTAV, 18
the r. union of all people MACKENZIE, COMPTON, 8

religious doctrines historical value of certain r. FREUD, SIGMUND, 46
R....are all illusions FREUD, SIGMUND, 43

reluctant He who is r. to recognize me FANON, FRANTZ, 3

remain Who should r. alive and praised PASTERNAK, BORIS, 10

remarks no one hears his own r. as prose AUDEN, W. H., 21
R. are not literature STEIN, GERTRUDE, 3

remedies If you are too fond of new r. COOPER, ASTLEY, 3
Most men die of their r....not...illnesses MOLIÈRE, 9
Our r. oft in ourselves do lie SHAKESPEARE, WILLIAM, 50
r....suggested for a disease CHEKHOV, ANTON, 9

remedy a r. for everything except death CERVANTES, MIGUEL DE, 32
I never think of finding a r. PASTEUR, LOUIS, 1
'Tis a sharp r., but a sure one RALEIGH, WALTER, 8

remember I can never r. whether it snowed THOMAS, DYLAN, 9
I don't r....tournaments I lose NICKLAUS, JACK, 1
I r., I remember /How my childhood PRAED, WINTHROP, 1
I r. it well LERNER, ALAN JAY, 2
I r., /The house HOOD, THOMAS, 5
I r. the way we parted SWINBURNE, ALGERNON CHARLES, 5
one man to r. me RUNYON, DAMON, 1
r. Lot's wife BIBLE, 344
R. me when I am gone away, ROSSETTI, CHRISTINA, 8
r. sweet Alice, Ben Bolt ENGLISH, THOMAS DUNN, 1
R. to be on your guard MÉRIMÉE, PROSPER, 1
things I r....may never have happened PINTER, HAROLD, 5
we shall be glad to r. even these hardships VIRGIL, 6
Who will r....The unheroic dead SASSOON, SIEGFRIED, 3

remembered I really do want to be r. MORRISSEY, 4
we shall be r. by posterity PEARSE, PATRICK, 1

remembering r. my good friends SHAKESPEARE, WILLIAM, 513

remembrance Praising what is lost /Makes the r. dear SHAKESPEARE, WILLIAM, 54
R....secret of reconciliation SCHARPING, RUDOLF, 1
there is no r. of former things BIBLE, 44

remorse R.: beholding heaven and feeling hell MOORE, G. E., 3
r. for what you have thought about your wife ROSTAND, JEAN, 2
R. is nothing but the wry face MACHADO DE ASSIS, JOAQUIM MARIA, 11
r. is the poison of life BRONTË, CHARLOTTE, 3

R. sleeps during a prosperous period ROUSSEAU, JEAN-JACQUES, 6
R., the fatal egg by pleasure laid COWPER, WILLIAM, 18
remote R. and ineffectual Don CHESTERTON, G. K., 1
remove R. the document...you remove the man BULGAKOV, MIKHAIL, 11
Renaissance R....architects were artists CLARK, KENNETH (1903–83), 5
R....mere ripple on the surface of literature LEWIS, C. S., 3
R....the green end of one of civilization's hardest winters FOWLES, JOHN, 3
renaissances we have spoken of r. before MORRISON, TONI, 12
render r. to everyone his due JUSTINIAN I, 1
rendezvous a r. with Death SEEGER, ALAN, 1
rent I r. everything, other than...life itself KOSINSKI, JERZY, 1
you can't r. a heart MCCORMACK, MARK, 4
reorganizing we tend to meet any new situation by r. PETRONIUS ARBITER, 3
repair r. the irreparable ravages of time RACINE, JEAN, 5
The time to r. the roof KENNEDY, JOHN FITZGERALD, 25
repartee R....what you wish you'd said BROUN, HEYWOOD, 3
repast A new r., or an untasted spring ADDISON, JOSEPH, 6
repeat r. that on the Golden Floor HOUSMAN, A. E., 30
repent Chang E must surely r. /...theft of that magic herb LI SHANGYIN, 1
Do you...my Love, r. PATMORE, COVENTRY, 6
I hardly ever r. NASH, OGDEN, 5
r.: for the kingdom of heaven is at hand BIBLE, 373
truly and earnestly r. you of your sins BOOK OF COMMON PRAYER, 11
repentance no r. in the grave WATTS, ISAAC, 6
Our r. is not so much regret for the ill we have done LA ROCHEFOUCAULD, FRANÇOIS, 3
R....virtue of weak minds DRYDEN, JOHN, 44
with the morning cool r. SCOTT, SIR WALTER, 15
repented it r. the Lord that he had made man BIBLE, 116
never r. that he held his tongue PLUTARCH, 13
repents a man r., stop reminding him PROVERBS, 56
repetition constant r. will finally succeed HITLER, ADOLF, 32
replace no one can r. him FRANKLIN, BENJAMIN, 2
reporter I am a r. GREENE, GRAHAM, 9
r....has renounced everything MURRAY, DAVID, 1
representative Your r. owes you...his judgement BURKE, EDMUND, 31
reproach r. to religion and government PENN, WILLIAM, 8
reproduce impossible to r. what one sees GIACOMETTI, ALBERTO, 1
reproduction The r. of mankind is a great marvel and mystery LUTHER, MARTIN, 18
republic founding the R. of Equals BABEUF, FRANÇOIS NOËL, 1
In a R. in which some MARIANA, JUAN DE, 1
make the...r. into a collective farm PLATONOV, ANDREI, 1
r. or monarchy is well constituted MACHIAVELLI, NICCOLÒ, 2
we are talking of a r....yet Louis lives! LOUIS XVI, 1
republican r. liberty...God deliver us from it PAUL, NATHANIEL, 1
The R. form of Government is the highest SPENCER, HERBERT, 4
Republicans a lot of damn fool R. EISENHOWER, DWIGHT D., 8
Please assure me that you are all R. REAGAN, RONALD, 41
republication Every twenty years...r. of...same ideas SCHICK, BÉLA, 4
repulsive The most r. thing...inside of a camel's mouth BRANDO, MARLON, 5
reputation 20 years to build a r. BUFFETT, WARREN, 6
a r. for being a creative genius OGILVY, DAVID, 9
endowed with the r. of a magician SOROS, GEORGE, 3
good r. is more valuable than money PUBLILIUS SYRUS, 1
My r. grew with every failure SHAW, GEORGE BERNARD, 96
R., reputation, reputation! SHAKESPEARE, WILLIAM, 481
Until you've lost your r., you never realize MITCHELL, MARGARET, 3
written out of r. but by himself POPE, ALEXANDER, 1
requests in thy Name thou wilt grant their r. BOOK OF COMMON PRAYER, 16
requirements r. that go with MBWA PACKARD, DAVID, 2
requisite The first r. for the happiness MARX, KARL, 9
research In r. the horizon recedes PATTISON, MARK, 1
R.! A mere excuse for idleness JOWETT, BENJAMIN, 5
R. has been called good business FISCHER, MARTIN H., 17
R. is formalized curiosity HURSTON, ZORA NEALE, 8
R. is fundamentally a state of mind SMITH, THEOBALD, 1
steal from many, it's r. MIZNER, WILSON, 2
The aim of r. is the discovery of...equations MACH, ERNST, 1
The outcome of any serious r. VEBLEN, THORSTEIN BUNDE, 2
resembled Had he not r. /My father SHAKESPEARE, WILLIAM, 400
resent I don't r. his popularity FLYNN, ERROL, 1
resentment difficult to get up r. NEWMAN, JOHN HENRY, 3
r. against the "minimum gender" rule BRUNDTLAND, GRO HARLEM, 1
reservoir a gigantic r. of good will WILLKIE, WENDELL LEWIS, 2
resist r....doctrines and hypotheses BEAUMONT, WILLIAM, 1
r. everything except temptation WILDE, OSCAR, 28
r. the devil, and he will flee BIBLE, 243
strength to r....renders acting powerful MAMET, DAVID, 5
resistance "R. to tyranny is obedience to God." ANTHONY, SUSAN B., 4
resolve R. to be thyself ARNOLD, MATTHEW, 9
resolves He that r. to deal with none but honest men FULLER, THOMAS (1654–1734), 2
resources As long as I have enough r. DAY, GRAHAM, 3
respect I can't get no r. DANGERFIELD, RODNEY, 1
I have too much r. for...faith LAURIER, WILFRID, 6
I r. only those who resist me DE GAULLE, CHARLES, 14
now I don't have to r. *anybody* BURNS, GEORGE, 3
only three beings worthy of r. BAUDELAIRE, CHARLES, 9
r. that is only bought by gold HARPER, FRANCES E. W., 3
There is no r. of persons with God BIBLE, 478
We must r. the other fellow's religion MENCKEN, H. L., 23
We owe r. to the living VOLTAIRE, 37
When people do not r. us TWAIN, MARK, 21
respectable R. means rich PEACOCK, THOMAS LOVE, 2
r., middle-class...lady RATTIGAN, TERENCE, 1
responsibility first r. of a leader...define reality DE PREE, MAX, 4
Moral r. is what is lacking in a man KRAUS, KARL, 16
the biggest r. of any corporation IACOCCA, LEE, 8
responsible every man is r. for his face CAMUS, ALBERT, 8
You become r., forever, for what you have tamed SAINT-EXUPÉRY, ANTOINE DE, 5
rest I ask but r. and quiet COTTER, JOSEPH SEAMON, JR., 1
I have nothing; the r. I leave to the poor RABELAIS, FRANÇOIS, 20
r. and sleep...thy pictures be DONNE, JOHN, 14
Seek home for r. TUSSER, THOMAS, 3
The Lord shall give thee r. from thy sorrow BIBLE, 204

restaurants Great r. are...nothing but mouth-brothels RAPHAEL, FREDERIC, 2
rested God...r. on the seventh day BIBLE, 106
restless He was r.. He loved upheavals MAO ZEDONG, 1
restrictions two kinds of r. upon human liberty CATT, CARRIE CHAPMAN, 1
restructuring three forces driving r. TOWNLEY, PRESTON, 1
rests Here r....upon the lap of Earth GRAY, THOMAS, 12
results had my r. for a long time GAUSS, CARL FRIEDRICH, 4
not getting the fullest r. for your efforts NARAYAN, R. K., 2
resurrection I am the r., and the life BIBLE, 286
retain To expect a man to r. everything...ever read SCHOPENHAUER, ARTHUR, 17
reticulated Anything r. or decussated at equal distances JOHNSON, SAMUEL, 12
retire r. relatively young CASTRO, FIDEL, 3
retirement On my r. I became a consultant BUTLIN, BILLY, 1
R. is an illusion BELLOW, SAUL, 23
R....is like giving up smoking GIGLI, BENIAMINO, 1
R.... is not a good idea CHARLES, PRINCE, 1
retires When a man r. SHERRIFF, R. C., 1
retrace r. with certainty...footsteps of my soul YE SI, 1
retreat r. than in his own soul MARCUS AURELIUS, 5
return I shall r. MACARTHUR, DOUGLAS, 8
returns Each thing that goes away r. ARMAH, AYI KWEI, 1
reunion r. at a Washington party...of...Evil DOLE, BOB, 1
reveng'd r. on the whole pack of you SHAKESPEARE, WILLIAM, 712
revenge A man that studieth r. BACON, FRANCIS (1561–1626), 55
good, old-fashioned, bloodcurdling r. AYCKBOURN, ALAN, 3
R., at first though sweet MILTON, JOHN, 82
R. is a dish PROVERBS, 371
R. is sweet PROVERBS, 372
Sweet is r....to women BYRON, LORD, 43
revenue how much r. companies are extracting from the Internet PETZINGER, THOMAS, JR., 1
reverence a great r. for all things living DALAI LAMA, 1
How much r....for a Supreme Being HELLER, JOSEPH, 9
Just a little more r....and not so much astonishment SARGENT, MALCOLM, 1
Kill r. and you've killed the hero RAND, AYN, 6
rudiments of r. for the human body HOFFER, ERIC, 4
review We r. the past COOLIDGE, CALVIN, 13
review copy In the beginning was the r. KRAUS, KARL, 13
reviewer Unless a r. has the courage...ignore the bastard GALBRAITH, J. K., 1
reviewers R....a most stupid and malignant race SHELLEY, PERCY BYSSHE, 40
R. are usually people who would have been poets COLERIDGE, SAMUEL TAYLOR, 20
reviews r. are...for people who still read WILLIS, BRUCE, 1
re-vision R....is an act of survival RICH, ADRIENNE, 1
revolt interested in anything about r. MORRISON, JIM, 1
right to r....deep in our history DOUGLAS, WILLIAM ORVILLE, 2
r. into a style GUNN, THOM, 4
revolution A r. is not a dinner party MAO ZEDONG, 5
don't suppose...r. is going to bring liberty HUXLEY, ALDOUS, 9
Ground for a r. is always fertile BIKO, STEPHEN, 5
I want a r....in Crotonville WELCH, JACK, 7
no such thing as an orderly r. OSBORNE, JOHN, 6
R. by its very nature TROTSKY, LEON, 2
R....delightful in the preliminary stages HUXLEY, ALDOUS, 25
r....devours its own children BÜCHNER, GEORG, 1
R....ecstasy of history MOTTOS AND SLOGANS, 22
R....intellectually acceptable form of modern war KAUNDA, KENNETH DAVID, 2
r. is a struggle to the death CASTRO, FIDEL, 1
"r." is a word for which you kill WEIL, SIMONE, 5
R....is the idea of justice PI Y MARGALL, FRANCISCO, 2
R. is...the setting-up of a new order ORTEGA Y GASSET, JOSÉ, 24
R....not a nursery of future revolutions BURKE, EDMUND, 45
r. of 1917...defined...the contemporary world FIGES, ORLANDO, 1
R....on the basis of...material benefit DENG XIAOPING, 3
spirit of r....radically opposed to liberty GUIZOT, FRANÇOIS, 1
The history of our r. ADAMS, JOHN, 3
The r. and women's liberation go together SANKARA, THOMAS, 1
The r. does not choose its paths TROTSKY, LEON, 3
The r. eats its own RICHLER, MORDECAI, 1
the r. made us BÜCHNER, GEORG, 2
the R. may...devour each of her children VERGNIAUD, PIERRE-VICTURNIEN, 1
The whole cause of world r. LIN BIAO, 2
They are not the leaders of a r.. They are its victims CONRAD, JOSEPH, 13
to export r. is nonsense STALIN, JOSEPH, 4
trace r. beneath her woolly hair NICHOLS, GRACE, 1
We invented the R. WEISS, PETER, 2
What is wrong with a r....natural GOLDING, WILLIAM, 2
revolutionary all r. wars are just MAO ZEDONG, 9
A r. woman FONDA, JANE, 1
Every r. movement also liberates language WOLF, CHRISTA, 1
fierce and r. in a bathroom LINKLATER, ERIC, 3
I stand here as a r. HITLER, ADOLF, 28
R. spirits of my father's generation ROSZAK, THEODORE, 9
the r. is he who cries for those he has killed LESTER, JULIUS, 4
revolutions All modern r. have ended CAMUS, ALBERT, 19
I've seen all sorts of r. CUMMINGS, E. E., 15
R. are always verbose TROTSKY, LEON, 4
R. are not made PHILLIPS, WENDELL, 3
R. are not made for export KHRUSHCHEV, NIKITA, 5
R. aren't made by gadgets and technology WRISTON, WALTER B., 4
R....like a water wheel PESTALOZZI, JOHANN HEINRICH, 7
R. never go backward PHILLIPS, WENDELL, 4
We now live in two r. NASSER, GAMAL ABDEL, 6
reward don't expect r. HUA GUOFENG, 1
he shall in no wise lose his r. BIBLE, 397
r. of a thing well done EMERSON, RALPH WALDO, 22
r. the good...forgive the bad HANDY, CHARLES, 5
rewarded Men are r. and punished SZASZ, THOMAS, 5
rewarding r. sense of total creation...multiple monotonous chores STERN, EDITH MENDEL, 1
rewards r....disproportionate to their usefulness to the community RUSSELL, LORD, 5
rheumatism never have occurred to me to complain of r. SAKI, 22
rhyme A r.'s /a bill of exchange MAYAKOVSKY, VLADIMIR, 3

it was neither r. nor reason MORE, THOMAS, 5
received nor r. nor reason SPENSER, EDMUND, 13
R....the invention of a barbarous age MILTON, JOHN, 92
though my r. be ragged, /Tattered and jagged SKELTON, JOHN, 3
rhyming troublesome...bondage of r. MILTON, JOHN, 93
rhythm I got r., /I got music GERSHWIN, IRA, 2
rib the r....made he a woman BIBLE, 110
ribband Give me but what this r. bound WALLER, EDMUND, 2
rice pudding lovely r. for dinner again MILNE, A. A., 16
rich a r. man cannot imagine poverty PÉGUY, CHARLES PIERRE, 3
a r. man shall hardly enter into...heaven BIBLE, 417
Do you sincerely want to be r. CORNFELD, BERNARD, 1
Eat with the r. SMITH, LOGAN PEARSALL, 6
everybody thinks they can get r. quick SCORSESE, MARTIN, 4
Few r. men own their property INGERSOLL, ROBERT G., 1
If one's r. and one's a woman GRAHAM, KATHARINE, 1
I think people still want to marry r. GRAHAM, SHEILAH, 1
only the extremely r....escape other people MULGAN, GEOFF, 4
Only the r. have distant relatives PROVERBS, 38
Poor Little R. Girl COWARD, NOEL, 17
r. Americans can...look at them VONNEGUT, KURT, 5
r. are different from us FITZGERALD, F. SCOTT, 8
r. beyond the dreams of avarice MOORE, EDWARD, 2
r....distinguishing themselves from the poor ROUSSEAU, JEAN-JACQUES, 9
r. man in his castle ALEXANDER, C. F., 2
r. man...isn't afraid to ask the salesman ANONYMOUS, 26
r. man's joys increase...poor's decay GOLDSMITH, OLIVER, 16
R. men's houses are seldom beautiful ASQUITH, MARGOT, 2
r....possess what they rightly acquire EDGAR, 1
that art most r., being poor SHAKESPEARE, WILLIAM, 332
The r. add riches to riches PROVERBS, 42
The r. are the scum of the earth CHESTERTON, G. K., 37
The r. have become richer SHELLEY, PERCY BYSSHE, 27
the wretchedness of being r. SMITH, LOGAN PEARSALL, 7
whether to be r. in things ILLICH, IVAN, 2
why aren't you r. ANONYMOUS, 21
Richelieu R. leaned to the good RETZ, CARDINAL DE, 6
richer not right to seem r. than one really is LESSING, GOTTHOLD EPHRAIM, 3
riches exchange my Sabine valley for r. HORACE, 40
R. and poverty PLATO, 22
R. are a good handmaid BACON, FRANCIS (1561–1626), 8
R. are for spending BACON, FRANCIS (1561–1626), 26
R. have wings COWPER, WILLIAM, 30
R. without law are...dangerous BEECHER, HENRY WARD, 5
the chief employment of r. consists in the parade of riches SMITH, ADAM, 6
rich man A r.'s joke is always funny BROWN, THOMAS EDWARD, 2
Richmond Hill On R. there lives a lass MACNALLY, LEONARD, 1
richness r. of life...memories we have forgotten PAVESE, CESARE, 4
riddle a r. wrapped in a mystery inside an enigma CHURCHILL, WINSTON, 71
R. of destiny LAMB, CHARLES, 27
ride R. on! ride on in majesty MILMAN, HENRY HART, 1
Sweet to r. forth at evening FLECKER, JAMES ELROY, 3
ridicule he who endeavors to r. other people BOCCACCIO, GIOVANNI, 2
R. often checks what is absurd SCOTT, SIR WALTER, 14
ridiculous At the heart of the r., the sublime MAHON, DEREK, 3
Look for the r....you will find it RENARD, JULES, 10
r. to call this an industry KROC, RAY, 1
sense of the r. ALBEE, EDWARD, 6
right Always do r. TWAIN, MARK, 5
An insignificant r. becomes important when it is assailed PICKENS, WILLIAM, 1
a r. to utter...truth JOHNSON, SAMUEL, 96
believe that they are...in the r. HUXLEY, ALDOUS, 47
do a great r., do a little wrong SHAKESPEARE, WILLIAM, 615
For r. is right, since God is God FABER, FREDERICK WILLIAM, 1
have a r. to censure, that...help PENN, WILLIAM, 3
have faith that r. makes might LINCOLN, ABRAHAM, 11
His r. was clear, his will was strong EPITAPHS, 14
I am not...a man of the r. MOSLEY, OSWALD, 2
I'd rather be r. than president THOMAS, NORMAN, 1
I may not always be r. GOLDWYN, SAMUEL, 19
It's the r. one ADVERTISEMENTS, 18
I worry about if and when I'll ever find the *r.* man MCMILLAN, TERRY, 9
Keep R. on to the End of the Road LAUDER, HARRY, 3
R. and truth are greater than any power WHICHCOTE, BENJAMIN, 1
r. and wrong in...arts and sciences MAO ZEDONG, 19
rather be r. than be President CLAY, HENRY, 1
R. is of no sex DOUGLASS, FREDERICK, 23
r. of all,...duty of some QUINCY, JOSIAH, 1
r. of the citizens...not be denied...on account of race CONSTITUTION OF THE UNITED STATES, 7
r. to bear fruit /will never die ZAYYAD, TAWFIQ, 1
The more you are in the r. ORWELL, GEORGE, 33
The R. Divine of Kings to govern wrong POPE, ALEXANDER, 65
The r. of a man to stand upright...in his own country NYERERE, JULIUS KAMBARAGE, 4
The R. Stuff WOLFE, TOM, 22
the r. stuff in the right place SUGAR, ALAN, 4
the r. to be plainly dressed NAPOLEON I, 25
the r. to criticize Shakespeare SHAKESPEARE, WILLIAM, 46
the r. wing of the middle of the road BENN, TONY, 6
To see what is r., and not do it CONFUCIUS, 26
you know he's r. GOLDWATER, BARRY, 1
righteous I have seen the r. forsaken BLUNDEN, EDMUND, 1
leave r. ways behind BUDDHA, 5
r. people who anger slowly JACKSON, GEORGE, 3
the r. perisheth, and no man layeth it to heart BIBLE, 222
righteousness in r. he doth judge and make war BIBLE, 473
it is r. to believe in God KORAN, 6
rightful we claim our r. place within this Empire ARCHER, JOHN RICHARD, 1
right hand this r. shall work it all off SCOTT, SIR WALTER, 32
rights I do not ask for my r. NORTON, CAROLINE, 2
interpretation of women's r. in Islam NASREEN, TASLIMA, 2
men their r. and nothing more ANTHONY, SUSAN B., 6
quest for r....emphasis on their wrongs BEARD, MARY RITTER, 1
r. and interests of the laboring man BAER, GEORGE FREDERICK, 1
R. that depend on the sufferance LA FOLLETTE, SUZANNE, 1
Stand up for your r. MARLEY, BOB, 2
The question of the r. of women WILLEBRANDS, CARDINAL, 1

The R. of woman merit some attention BURNS, ROBERT, 4
right to strike confers the absolute r. BRANDEIS, LOUIS D., 1
ring One R. to rule them all TOLKIEN, J. R. R., 4
R.-a-ring o'roses CHILDREN'S VERSE, 28
R. out, wild bells HALLAM, ARTHUR HENRY, 15
The r. so worn...is yet of gold CRABBE, GEORGE, 1
With this R. I thee wed BOOK OF COMMON PRAYER, 27
riot A r. is...the language of the unheard KING, MARTIN LUTHER, JR., 27
riots Urban r....a durable social phenomenon KING, MARTIN LUTHER, JR., 24
ripeness R. is all SHAKESPEARE, WILLIAM, 366
rip-tooth A r. of the sky's acetylene CRANE, HART, 3
rise able to r. above the brutes HUXLEY, ALDOUS, 5
nobody who does not r. early JOHNSON, SAMUEL, 63
R. with the lark HURDIS, JAMES, 1
risk r. of producing more technology HUTCHESON, DAN, 2
r. one's life in the...city HOAGLAND, EDWARD, 9
risk-averse r. environments are career killers KOTTER, JOHN P., 3
risks He who doesn't take r. LEBED, ALEXANDER, 1
There are r. everywhere HARRIS, WILSON, 2
risk-taking R....intrinsic part of success FORBES, MALCOLM S., 1
Rita Lovely R. Meter Maid LENNON & MCCARTNEY, 13
rites where do r. and justice spring from XUNZI, 3
river cannot step into the same r. twice ARISTOTLE, 6
Ol' man r. HAMMERSTEIN, OSCAR, II, 7
This yellow r....bred a nation SU XIAOKANG, 1
riverrun r., past Eve and Adam's JOYCE, JAMES, 16
rivers By r....at odds with life I journeyed DU MU, 1
River Tiber the R. foaming with much blood POWELL, ENOCH, 1
roach Timid r., why be so shy MORLEY, CHRISTOPHER DARLINGTON, 9
road A broad and ample r., whose dust is gold MILTON, JOHN, 80
Does the r. wind up-hill ROSSETTI, CHRISTINA, 9
There is a r. from the eye to the heart CHESTERTON, G. K., 36
wrong r., if it is your own PORCHIA, ANTONIO, 9
roads All r. lead to Rome PROVERBS, 122
How many r. must a man walk down DYLAN, BOB, 4
New r.: new ruts CHESTERTON, G. K., 53
No more r., no more relief DEVI, MAHASWETA, 1
These r. have no corners MURPHY, DERVLA, 2
Two r. diverged in a wood FROST, ROBERT, 12
roamin' R. in the gloamin' LAUDER, HARRY, 1
rob R. Peter, and pay Paul BURTON, ROBERT, 28
robb'd He that is r., not wanting what is stol'n SHAKESPEARE, WILLIAM, 488
robbed Terrible place to be r. or murdered MELVILLE, HERMAN, 21
We wuz r. JACOBS, JOE, 1
Robbins President R....adjusted to his environment JARRELL, RANDALL, 2
robin A R. Red breast in a Cage BLAKE, WILLIAM, 4
Robinson Crusoe live like R., shipwrecked LEMMON, JACK, 1
robot Where r. mice and robot men BRADBURY, RAY, 2
rock he smote the r. twice BIBLE, 449
r. concert...inside my head MORRISON, JIM, 8
R. criticism is more...male than rock DURBIN, KAREN, 1
r....immature and totally macho-orientated COSTELLO, ELVIS, 3
R. of ages, cleft for me TOPLADY, AUGUSTUS MONTAGUE, 1
rock and roll R. is phony and false SINATRA, FRANK, 2
R....trying to convince girls HELL, RICHARD, 1
rock and roller r....a rather foolish, empty-headed figure MORRISSEY, 2
rocket A r. man TAUPIN, BERNIE, 3
rocking r. the cradle...rocked the system ROBINSON, MARY, 1
rocking horse They sway'd about upon a r. KEATS, JOHN (1795–1821), 67
Rockin' the Boat Sit Down, You're R. LOESSER, FRANK, 5
rock 'n' roll no more r., it's an imitation DYLAN, BOB, 24
people who listen to r. REED, LOU, 5
"r....jazz *before* getting this name PANASSIE, HUGUES, 4
R. man...the Voice of America SPRINGSTEEN, BRUCE, 1
R. stars look dangerous JONES, MABLEN, 1
R. was not fun anymore LENNON, JOHN, 10
young woman who seeks...a r. group ANONYMOUS, 58
rod spare the r., and spoyle the child VENNING, RALPH, 1
spoils the r....never spares the child HOOD, THOMAS, 11
We spared the r. WOLF, L. J., 1
rode You r. up on your bamboo steed LI BAI, 4
role She was...cast for a great r. PANKHURST, EMMELINE, 1
roll a r. big enough to choke on FEINSTEIN, ELAINE, 1
rolling stone Like a r. DYLAN, BOB, 8
Rolls-Royce loudest noise in this new R....electric clock ADVERTISEMENTS, 2
Roman more antique R. than a Dane SHAKESPEARE, WILLIAM, 232
noblest R. of them all SHAKESPEARE, WILLIAM, 319
R. generals during their triumphs HELLER, ROBERT, 6
the R. people had but one neck CALIGULA, 1
Roman Catholic Waugh...like you, your Holiness, is a R. WAUGH, EVELYN, 2
Roman Catholics if you give R. a good job O'NEILL, TERENCE, 1
Roman Conquest The R. was, however, a *Good Thing* SELLAR, W. C., 1
Romanism rum, R., and rebellion BURCHARD, SAMUEL DICKINSON, 1
Romans Are you not my own R. OTTO III, 1
Friends, R., countrymen SHAKESPEARE, WILLIAM, 309
The ancient R. built their greatest masterpieces VOLTAIRE, 14
The R. and Greeks found everything human LAWRENCE, D. H., 19
romantic mustn't be r. about money SHAW, GEORGE BERNARD, 50
Romantic In the R. age, history...was more real than reality CALLCOTT, GEORGE H., 2
Romanticism R. is...the greatest possible pleasure STENDHAL, 4
Rome at R., do as they do at Rome CERVANTES, MIGUEL DE, 45
I lov'd R. more SHAKESPEARE, WILLIAM, 313
In R. you long for the country HORACE, 55
R. has spoken AUGUSTINE OF HIPPO, SAINT, 12
R. shall perish COWPER, WILLIAM, 2
R.'s just a city like anywhere else SHAKESPEARE, WILLIAM, 7
R. was not built PROVERBS, 373
That man goes to R.—to death KEATS, JOHN (1795–1821), 3
The R....of the 20th century WOLFE, TOM, 9
When in R., live as the Romans AMBROSE, SAINT, 1
When they are at R. BURTON, ROBERT, 23
without R. Italy cannot be constituted CAVOUR, CAMILLO BENSO, 2
Romeo R.! wherefore art thou Romeo SHAKESPEARE, WILLIAM, 542
room All I want is a r. somewhere LERNER, ALAN JAY, 6
There's always r. at the top PROVERBS, 416
room-mates A world full of r. SIMON, NEIL, 11
rooms r. we cannot die in DICKEY, JAMES, 1

Roosevelt I've always voted for R. ROOSEVELT, THEODORE, 2
R. were alive...turn in his grave GOLDWYN, SAMUEL, 21
roots people digging...own r. HALEY, ALEX, 1
What good is r. if you can't go back to 'em? MCMILLAN, TERRY, 6
rope the end of your r., tie a knot ROOSEVELT, FRANKLIN D., 39
the r. stood straight up in the air PU SONGLING, 3
rose An unofficial English r. BROOKE, RUPERT, 6
A R. is sweeter in the budde LYLY, JOHN, 4
a r. should shut, and be a bud again KEATS, JOHN (1795–1821), 73
budding r. above the rose full blown WORDSWORTH, WILLIAM, 88
do you call that a r. AYCKBOURN, ALAN, 5
Go, lovely r. WALLER, EDMUND, 1
He r. renewed renamed MALCOLM X, 3
I r. the wrong way to-day BEHN, APHRA, 16
not the r. for me BAYLY, THOMAS HAYNES, 6
O R., thou art sick BLAKE, WILLIAM, 25
R. is a rose STEIN, GERTRUDE, 8
r....prized beyond the sculptured flower BRYANT, WILLIAM CULLEN, 1
R....where some buried Caesar bled FITZGERALD, EDWARD, 8
the last r. of summer MOORE, THOMAS, 8
The r. is fairest SCOTT, SIR WALTER, 5
Through what wild centuries /Roves back the r. DE LA MARE, WALTER, 9
rose garden I Never Promised You a R. GREEN, HANNAH, 1
rosemary There's r., that's for remembrance SHAKESPEARE, WILLIAM, 215
Rosencrantz R. and Guildenstern are dead SHAKESPEARE, WILLIAM, 225
roses Everything's Coming up R. SONDHEIM, STEPHEN, 2
Flung r., roses, riotously DOWSON, ERNEST, 1
hand that gives you r. PROVERBS, 21
It was r., roses, all the way BROWNING, ROBERT, 61
I will make thee beds of r. MARLOWE, CHRISTOPHER, 2
I would like my r. to see you SHERIDAN, RICHARD BRINSLEY, 20
R. are flowering in Picardy WEATHERLY, FREDERIC EDWARD, 1
R. at first were white HERRICK, ROBERT, 7
Send two dozen r. to Room 424 MARX, GROUCHO, 10
When r. are fresh MACHADO DE ASSIS, JOAQUIM MARIA, 18
rots It r. a writer's brain UPDIKE, JOHN, 13
Rouen forcing R. into submission by starvation HENRY V, 2
rough a little r. to begin with GOETHE, JOHANN WOLFGANG VON, 36
round At the r. earth's imagin'd corners DONNE, JOHN, 22
rounded r. and orbicular sound to it MELVILLE, HERMAN, 12
Rousseau self-torturing sophist, wild R. BYRON, LORD, 31
roving we'll go no more a r. BYRON, LORD, 16
row Row upon r. with strict impunity TATE, ALLEN, 2
royal thus the r. mandate ran BURNS, ROBERT, 32
trying not to be...r. MOUNTBATTEN, LORD, 2
Royal Family Loss of the R.'s symbolism CHOMSKY, NOAM, 1
royalty something of r. in his demeanor HENRY VIII, 1
rub-a-dub-dub R., /Three men in a tub CHILDREN'S VERSE, 66
rubbish What r. BLÜCHER, GEBHARD LEBERECHT VON, 1
rude manner r. and wild /Is common BELLOC, HILAIRE, 29
The right people are r. MAUGHAM, SOMERSET, 21
rudeness confused r. with blunt speech JAMES, CLIVE, 1
Rudolph R. The Red-Nosed Reindeer MARKS, JOHNNY, 1
rue With r. my heart is laden HOUSMAN, A. E., 19
ruin I am inclined to notice the r. in things MILLER, ARTHUR, 3
She's not so pretty anyone would want to r. her BRECHT, BERTOLT, 5
With hideous r. and combustion down MILTON, JOHN, 25
ruined r. on the side of their natural propensities BURKE, EDMUND, 36
rule A little r., a little sway DYER, JOHN, 2
few men are wise enough to r. RAND, AYN, 2
How shall I be able to r. over others RABELAIS, FRANÇOIS, 5
I must r. after my own fashion CATHERINE THE GREAT, 1
I was born to r. IVAN IV, 1
r. by fettering the mind HYPATIA, 3
That's not a regular r. CARROLL, LEWIS, 25
the greatest r. of all...to give pleasure MOLIÈRE, 3
they who r. industrially will rule politically CONNOLLY, JAMES, 1
ruler A r. has to examine the dark side of human life HEAD, BESSIE, 3
a r. may be wise as a sage SIMA GUANG, 1
out of thee shall he come forth...r. in Israel BIBLE, 444
The r. firmly bars his inner door HAN FEI, 2
rules I would make my own r. WEST, MAE, 15
R. and models destroy genius and art HAZLITT, WILLIAM, 17
r. for becoming more alive SONTAG, SUSAN, 12
R. freeze companies inside a glacier SEMLER, RICARDO, 7
R. serve no purpose ZUCCARO, FEDERICO, 1
Systems governed by...one set of r. MULGAN, GEOFF, 5
the r. of the universe be annulled BIERCE, AMBROSE, 42
rum r., sodomy, and the lash CHURCHILL, WINSTON, 64
run Gwine to r. all night FOSTER, STEPHEN, 1
He can r., but he can't hide LOUIS, JOE, 1
r. about the braes BURNS, ROBERT, 11
r. scared and never think WATSON, THOMAS, JR., 2
to r. the world FELKER, CLAY S., 1
You cannot r. with the hare PROVERBS, 464
runcible He weareth a r. hat LEAR, EDWARD, 12
running r....to keep in the same place CARROLL, LEWIS, 31
you been r. through my mind *all* day SMITH, WILL, 1
rupee a full 12 annas for his r. MAXWELL, ROBERT, 3
Rupert R. is the only man I know MURDOCH, RUPERT, 1
rush hour *R....traffic...at a standstill* MORTON, J. C., 3
Russell R.'s beautiful mathematical mind RUSSELL, BERTRAND, 2
Russia For us in R. communism is a dead dog SOLZHENITSYN, ALEXANDER, 10
I have signed legislation which outlaws R. REAGAN, RONALD, 40
R. has entered the family of civilized nations POPOV, GAVRIL, 1
R. has not attacked...we can outproduce GOLDWATER, BARRY, 4
R. has thrown a firebrand BETHMANN HOLLWEG, THEOBALD VON, 5
R. has two generals NICHOLAS I, 2
R. is a sphinx BLOK, ALEKSANDR, 2
R. is our Africa HITLER, ADOLF, 36
R. is such an amazing country GOGOL, NIKOLAY, 4
R. will certainly inherit the future LAWRENCE, D. H., 36
salvaged from R.—her language NABOKOV, VLADIMIR, 7
The moment R. mobilizes, Germany will...mobilize MOLTKE, HELMUTH JOHANNES VON, 5
there is no democracy in R. SOLZHENITSYN, ALEXANDER, 9
What hope is there for R. LENIN, VLADIMIR ILYICH, 3
Russian hated /by every anti-Semite /...I am a R. YEVTUSHENKO, YEVGENY, 3
like any honest R....a terrible drunkard GOGOL, NIKOLAY, 3
Scratch the R. and...find the Tartar MAISTRE, JOSEPH MARIE DE, 2

The autocracy of this R. kingdom IVAN IV, 2
Russians R. do not possess...self-restraint BISMARCK, PRINCE OTTO VON, 2
test the R., not the bombs GAITSKELL, HUGH, 2
rye When as the r. reach to the chin PEELE, GEORGE, 2

Sabbath never broke the S., but for Gain DRYDEN, JOHN, 12
sacred s. hunger of ambitious minds SPENSER, EDMUND, 10
The idea of the s....most conservative notions RUSHDIE, SALMAN, 5
sacrifice Too long a s. YEATS, W. B., 21
Who are these coming to the s. KEATS, JOHN (1795–1821), 55
sacrificed I have s. everything NIXON, PATRICIA, 1
sacrifices s....to achieve law and order AMIN, IDI, 2
sad A s. tale's best for winter SHAKESPEARE, WILLIAM, 658
How s. and bad and mad it was BROWNING, ROBERT, 32
I love this s. land of my country AI QING, 4
our s. bad glad mad brother's name VILLON, FRANÇOIS, 1
s., /Because it makes us smile BYRON, LORD, 76
So s....days that are no more TENNYSON, ALFRED, 91
So why be s.?...Take another wife RAY, SATYAJIT, 2
tell s. stories of the death of kings SHAKESPEARE, WILLIAM, 515
sadder A s. and a wiser man COLERIDGE, SAMUEL TAYLOR, 52
saddle A lot depends who's in the s. BACALL, LAUREN, 2
sadist A s. is always...a masochist FREUD, SIGMUND, 27
s....exploitation becomes a kind of passion HORNEY, KAREN, 5
sadists repressed s. are supposed to become policemen or butchers CONNOLLY, CYRIL, 3
sadness Farewell s. ÉLUARD, PAUL, 1
may there be no s. of farewell TENNYSON, ALFRED, 6
S. is...but a form of fatigue GIDE, ANDRÉ, 3
safari I want you to accompany me on the s. MILLIGAN, SPIKE, 11
safe Better be s. than sorry PROVERBS, 164
see me s. up MORE, THOMAS, 3
The only way to be absolutely s. INGRES, JEAN-AUGUSTE DOMINIQUE, 2
safer s. to obey than to rule KEMPIS, THOMAS À, 4
safety s. of the nation lies in...conciliation JOHNSON, ANDREW, 1
There is s. in numbers PROVERBS, 415
saga Hearing one s., we enact the next DAVIE, DONALD, 1
sage The s....practices...teaching that uses no words LAOZI, 11
said Little s. is soonest mended WITHER, GEORGE, 1
'Tis s....some have died for love WORDSWORTH, WILLIAM, 36
what you've s. can't be stopped HORACE, 10
When a thing has been s. and said well FRANCE, ANATOLE, 11
sailor any sane man can be a s. EMERSON, RALPH WALDO, 6
I always go to sea a s. MELVILLE, HERMAN, 5
Our Handsome S. had...masculine beauty MELVILLE, HERMAN, 3
sailors like s. who must rebuild their ship NEURATH, OTTO, 1
saint s....dead sinner revised and edited BIERCE, AMBROSE, 46
seem a s. when most I play the devil SHAKESPEARE, WILLIAM, 530
saintliness S. is also a temptation ANOUILH, JEAN, 5
Saint Preux S. never kicked the fireirons CARLYLE, THOMAS, 2
saints All are not s. PROVERBS, 118
salary The s. of the chief executive GALBRAITH, J. K., 4
sales S. techniques...include getting irritated WHITEHORN, KATHARINE, 4
Today's s. should be better than yesterday's PROVERBS, MODERN, 30
salesman A s. has got to dream MILLER, ARTHUR, 9
best s. we ever heard of PROCHNOW, HERBERT V., 2
For a s....no rock bottom MILLER, ARTHUR, 10
I am the world's worst s. WOOLWORTH, FRANK W., 1
The s. that always gets the sale HARVEY-JONES, JOHN, 6
salesmen 20% of any group of s. TOWNSEND, ROBERT, 4
Salinger S. was the perfect *New Yorker* SALINGER, J. D., 2
Sally There's none like pretty S. CAREY, HENRY, 4
salmon s. move /out from the river CARVER, RAYMOND, 3
salon André came to London to start a s. WILDE, OSCAR, 70
salt nobody likes...s. rubbed into their wounds WEST, REBECCA, 6
the s. of the earth BIBLE, 376
Salt Lake City lights of S. infinitesimally glimmering KEROUAC, JACK, 22
salvation deeds of lasting merit...hold...a greater hope of s. KORAN, 21
S. doesn't do them the same good WAUGH, EVELYN, 30
s. lies in the...creatively maladjusted KING, MARTIN LUTHER, JR., 12
There is no s. outside the church AUGUSTINE OF HIPPO, SAINT, 11
The s. of mankind SOLZHENITSYN, ALEXANDER, 3
Sam Play it, S. BOGART, HUMPHREY, 2
Samaritan But a certain S....had compassion on him BIBLE, 336
Samarkand the Golden Journey to S. FLECKER, JAMES ELROY, 4
same all the s. a hundred years hence DICKENS, CHARLES, 47
It will be all the s. PROVERBS, 288
The s. as usual BECKETT, SAMUEL, 4
the s. is my brother BIBLE, 401
we're all made the s. COWARD, NOEL, 22
Samuel Johnson Cham of Literature, S. JOHNSON, SAMUEL, 1
sanction There is a s. like...religion HAY, JOHN, 1
sanctions S....ultimate "feel-good" foreign policy ARMSTRONG, MICHAEL, 3
sanctuary No s. GALVIN, ROBERT W., 1
sand s. of the desert is sodden red NEWBOLT, HENRY, 4
San Domingo you have cut down in S. only the trunk of the tree of liberty TOUSSAINT L'OUVERTURE, 2
sane Show me a s. man JUNG, CARL GUSTAV, 22
"s." man...not the one who has eliminated all contradictions MERLEAU-PONTY, MAURICE, 6
s. person...feels isolated in the insane society FROMM, ERICH, 7
to *play at being s.* LAING, R. D., 4
San Francisco S....most European of all American cities BEATON, CECIL, 1
S. supplemented...anti-Chinese state laws KINGSTON, MAXINE HONG, 2
sanitary towel Golden S. Award Presentation OSBORNE, JOHN, 12
sanity pursuit of s....a form of madness BELLOW, SAUL, 2
S. is a cozy lie SONTAG, SUSAN, 6
S. is an unknown room BARNES, DJUNA, 3
S. is madness put to good uses SANTAYANA, GEORGE, 25
S. is not truth. Sanity is conformity PIRSIG, ROBERT T., 2
S. is very rare EMERSON, RALPH WALDO, 33
Too much s. may be madness CERVANTES, MIGUEL DE, 5
San Narciso S. lay further south, near L.A. PYNCHON, THOMAS, 4
sans S. teeth, sans eyes, sans taste, sans every thing SHAKESPEARE, WILLIAM, 107
Sappho S. survives...we sing her songs SAPPHO, 1
sarcasm S....the language of the devil CARLYLE, THOMAS, 35
sardines Life is...like a tin of s. BENNETT, ALAN, 1

Sartre ineptitude of M. S.'s political performance SARTRE, JEAN-PAUL, 2
sat The...gentleman has s. so long on the fence LLOYD-GEORGE, DAVID, 14
Satan Incensed with indignatio S. stood MILTON, JOHN, 42
S. comes as a man of peace DYLAN, BOB, 11
S. finds...mischief...For idle hands WATTS, ISAAC, 1
S. had come around with sweet corn KEILLOR, GARRISON, 12
Satanic Verses The author of the S....against Islam, the Prophet and the Koran RUSHDIE, SALMAN, 1
satire hard not to write s. JUVENAL, 3
S. died...Kissinger the Nobel Peace Prize KISSINGER, HENRY, 2
S. is alive and well REAGAN, RONALD, 14
S. is a sort of glass SWIFT, JONATHAN, 40
S....like a polished razor keen MONTAGU, MARY WORTLEY, 4
S. picks a one-sided fight TRUDEAU, GARRY, 1
Through my s. I make little people so big KRAUS, KARL, 5
satisfaction I am a source of s. to him TOLSTOY, SOFYA, 2
I can't get no s. JAGGER, MICK, 2
work *gives* s. FRANK, ANNE, 2
satisfied Don't be s....just selling a song D, CHUCK, 2
The superior man is s. CONFUCIUS, 21
sauce Make not the s. PROVERBS, 320
Saul S. hath slain his thousands BIBLE, 230
savage I will take some s. woman TENNYSON, ALFRED, 49
s. place! as holy and enchanted COLERIDGE, SAMUEL TAYLOR, 15
The s. is a positive man POWELL, JOHN WESLEY, 4
The young man who has not wept is a s. SANTAYANA, GEORGE, 4
savages two thousand raving s. broke from...forest COOPER, JAMES FENIMORE, 11
save Christ Jesus came into the world to s. sinners BIBLE, 234
I know that I can s. this country PITT THE ELDER, WILLIAM, 2
s. a man's life against his will HORACE, 11
S. me...from the candid friend CANNING, GEORGE, 3
S. us, save us, they seem to say MAHON, DEREK, 4
S. your breath PROVERBS, 375
saviour Tommy..."S. of 'is country" KIPLING, RUDYARD, 27
saw I s. it, but I did not realize it PEABODY, ELIZABETH, 1
O s. ye bonnie Lesley BURNS, ROBERT, 12
sawdust Have you ever tried to split s. MCCARTHY, EUGENE J., 1
sax learned to play the s. in Pontiac Reformatory MEZZROW, MEZZ, 2
saxophonest the s. blowinest man MEZZROW, MEZZ, 6
say and you s. "Oh, nothing" MILNE, A. A., 9
cannot s. what you have to say in twenty minutes BRABAZON, DEREK, 1
Do as I s. PROVERBS, 179
how can I s. anything WHITMAN, WALT, 15
if we s. that we have no sin, we deceive BIBLE, 180
I have nothing to s., I am saying it CAGE, JOHN, 11
people who s. nothing SOLZHENITSYN, ALEXANDER, 7
S. it ain't so, Joe ANONYMOUS, 74
S. it with flowers O'KEEFE, PATRICK, 1
The great consolation...is to s. what one thinks VOLTAIRE, 7
they do not know what they are going to s. CHURCHILL, WINSTON, 23
whatever you s., you say nothing HEANEY, SEAMUS, 7
saying S. is one thing PROVERBS, 376
something is not worth s....sing it BEAUMARCHAIS, PIERRE-AUGUSTIN CARON DE, 2
sayings His s. are generally like women's letters LAMB, CHARLES, 2
scab A s. is a two-legged animal LONDON, JACK, 5
scalping s....no more the true picture of savagery POWELL, JOHN WESLEY, 5
scandal It is a public s. that gives offense MOLIÈRE, 24
There is no s. like rags FARQUHAR, GEORGE, 5
The s. is what's legal KINSLEY, MICHAEL, 1
scandalous We must prevent these s. practices LIVERPOOL, LORD, 1
scandals no s. in this administration CLINTON, BILL, 11
scarce S., sir. Mighty scarce TWAIN, MARK, 61
scare A good s. is worth more PROVERBS, 114
Don't let them s. you DAVIS, ELMER, 1
scarecrow a s. of the law SHAKESPEARE, WILLIAM, 426
scarecrows s. of fools...beacons of wise men HUXLEY, T. H., 13
scared I'm s. I might kill LOUIS, JOE, 3
What difference...if the thing you s. of is real or not? MORRISON, TONI, 17
scattered s. the proud BIBLE, 320
scenery s. habit in its most artificial forms MUIR, JOHN, 6
S. is fine—but human nature is finer KEATS, JOHN (1795–1821), 21
sceptic I am too much of a s. HUXLEY, T. H., 1
scepticism tolerant s....a good test of maturity STORR, ANTHONY, 2
schemes best laid s. o' mice an' men BURNS, ROBERT, 49
schhh S....you know who ADVERTISEMENTS, 20
schizophrenia No one *has* s., like having a cold LAING, R. D., 3
S....the price...for language CROW, TIM J., 1
schizophrenic S. behaviour is a special strategy LAING, R. D., 9
the s. imagines so many amorous scenes SARTRE, JEAN-PAUL, 26
scholar The s.—a decadent NIETZSCHE, FRIEDRICH WILHELM, 15
scholars great men...not commonly been great s. HOLMES, OLIVER WENDELL, 25
S. dispute HORACE, 4
school If every day in the life of a s. LEACOCK, STEPHEN, 3
it don't take s. stuff to help a fella play ball JACKSON, SHOELESS JOE, 1
never gone to s. may steal from a freight car ROOSEVELT, FRANKLIN D., 36
nothing on earth...so horrible as a s. SHAW, GEORGE BERNARD, 73
s....most important means of transferring EINSTEIN, ALBERT, 26
they went to the grammar s. little children ASCHAM, ROGER, 1
schoolboys s....educate my son EMERSON, RALPH WALDO, 31
schooling formal s. is an important advantage KROC, RAY, 5
s. interfere with my education TWAIN, MARK, 52
schoolmaster last resort of feeble minds with classical educations...s. HUXLEY, ALDOUS, 11
s. should have...awe BAGEHOT, WALTER, 11
The average s. is...essentially an ass MENCKEN, H. L., 8
schoolmasters Let s. puzzle their brain GOLDSMITH, OLIVER, 10
most s. are idiots PEARSON, HESKETH, 3
schoolrooms Better build s. for "the boy" COOK, ELIZA, 1
schoolteacher s....underpaid as a childminder OSBORNE, JOHN, 8
science A man of true s....uses but few hard words MELVILLE, HERMAN, 17
American s. is a thing of the future ROWLAND, HENRY AUGUSTUS, 1
A s. is said to be useful HARDY, GODFREY HAROLD, 1
A s. which hesitates to forget WHITEHEAD, A. N., 15
do not need s. and philosophy KANT, IMMANUEL, 20

drawback that s. was invented after I left school CARRINGTON, LORD, 2
Every s. has been an outcast INGERSOLL, ROBERT G., 2
Experimental s. is the mistress of...sciences BACON, ROGER, 1
extraordinary if...s. was *not* applied in warfare DANDO, MALCOLM, 1
fundamental ideas of s. are essentially simple EINSTEIN, ALBERT, 38
goal of s....seek naturalistic explanations for phenomena COMMITTEE ON SCIENCE AND CREATIONISM, NATIONAL ACADEMY OF SCIENCES, 1
Go on, fair s....Shall nature yield HOLMES, OLIVER WENDELL, 28
history of s....conflict of two contending powers DRAPER, JOHN, 1
human s. is at a loss CHOMSKY, NOAM, 2
If s. produces no better fruits than tyranny JEFFERSON, THOMAS, 20
If th' Christyan Scientists had some s. DUNNE, FINLEY PETER, 5
If we take s. as our sole guide BURROUGHS, JOHN, 2
In discussing extremes of unorthodoxy in s. GARDNER, MARTIN, 2
In everything that relates to s. LAMB, CHARLES, 16
In s. one tries to tell DIRAC, PAUL, 2
In s. the excellent is...all that matters U.S. PRESIDENT'S SCIENCE ADVISORY COMMITTEE, 1
invoke the wonders of s. instead of its terrors KENNEDY, JOHN FITZGERALD, 8
Man lives for s. as well as bread JAMES, WILLIAM, 35
man of s. and the man of art OPPENHEIMER, J. ROBERT, 4
man of s. is a poor philosopher EINSTEIN, ALBERT, 32
men only care for s....get a living GOETHE, JOHANN WOLFGANG VON, 32
modern s....securing a more abundant life COMPTON, KARL TAYLOR, 1
Natural s....outstripped moral and political science DULLES, JOHN FOSTER, 4
negative cautions of s. are never popular MEAD, MARGARET, 5
No one should approach the temple of s. BROWNE, THOMAS, 40
not s....who has destroyed man LERNER, MAX, 1
One s. only will one genius fit POPE, ALEXANDER, 17
O star-eyed S. CAMPBELL, THOMAS, 4
problems of s. are close enough PINKER, STEVEN, 6
real accomplishment of modern s. and technology GALBRAITH, J. K., 21
reason s. works...built-in error-correcting SAGAN, CARL, 15
s....achieved its most spectactular triumphs RUSSELL, BERTRAND, 5
S....all those things which are confirmed GOULD, STEPHEN JAY, 1
S....a minimal problem MACH, ERNST, 2
S. and art...superior kind of dope HUXLEY, ALDOUS, 23
s....a refinement of everyday thinking EINSTEIN, ALBERT, 34
S....attempt to make the chaotic diversity EINSTEIN, ALBERT, 31
s. begins as philosophy...ends as art DURANT, WILL, 1
S. can purify religion JOHN PAUL II, 6
s. can wait, research can wait SCHICK, BÉLA, 1
S....changed the condition of human life FULBRIGHT, J. WILLIAM, 2
S. conducts us...through the whole range of creation MARGARET OF VALOIS, 1
S....far from a perfect instrument SAGAN, CARL, 14
S....feeds on its own decay JAMES, WILLIAM, 34
S....given us light, truth BURBANK, LUTHER, 4
S. has a simple faith...transcends utility BUSH, VANNEVAR, 1
S. has "explained" nothing HUXLEY, ALDOUS, 7
S. has nothing to be ashamed of BRONOWSKI, JACOB, 6
S., history, politics...within his compass WELLS, H. G., 2
Should we force s. down the throats PORTER, GEORGE, 1
S....impact on many ideas associated with religion FEYNMAN, RICHARD PHILLIPS, 4
S. is a first-rate piece of furniture HOLMES, OLIVER WENDELL, 29
S. is always wrong SHAW, GEORGE BERNARD, 115
S. is an integral part of culture GOULD, STEPHEN JAY, 3
S. is built up of facts POINCARÉ, JULES HENRI, 3
s. is either physics or stamp collecting RUTHERFORD, ERNEST, 2
s. is...international CURIE, MARIE, 4
s. is...neither a potential for good nor for evil SEABORG, GLENN, 1
S. is not...a storehouse of facts GREGORY, RICHARD ARMAN, 1
S. is...organized common sense HUXLEY, T. H., 4
S. is organized knowledge SPENCER, HERBERT, 2
S. is the great antidote SMITH, ADAM, 7
S. is the search for truth PAULING, LINUS, 2
S. is the topography of ignorance HOLMES, OLIVER WENDELL, 6
S. is what you know RUSSELL, BERTRAND, 64
S....kind of cosmic apple juice BRANSCOMB, LEW, 1
S. moves, but slowly slowly TENNYSON, ALFRED, 48
S. must begin with myths POPPER, KARL, 9
S....nonaggression with the rest of society PRICE, DON K., 1
S. robs men of wisdom UNAMUNO Y JUGO, MIGUEL DE, 1
S. says: "We must live," UNAMUNO Y JUGO, MIGUEL DE, 2
S. should leave off making pronouncements JEANS, JAMES, 2
s. swarms with...outright fakery GARDNER, MARTIN, 1
S....system of statements based on...experience CARNAP, RUDOLF, 2
s. teaches us...be our own saviors BURBANK, LUTHER, 6
S....the art of systematic over-simplification POPPER, KARL, 3
S....the Differential Calculus of the mind ROSS, RONALD, 4
S....the great instrument of social change BALFOUR, ARTHUR, 4
s....the interplay between nature and ourselves HEISENBERG, WERNER, 2
S., unlike theology, never leads to insanity BURBANK, LUTHER, 5
S. will be the master of man ADAMS, HENRY, 2
S. without conscience RABELAIS, FRANÇOIS, 8
S. without religion is lame EINSTEIN, ALBERT, 37
The effort to reconcile s. and religion MENCKEN, H. L., 19
the essence of s.: ask an impertinent question BRONOWSKI, JACOB, 2
The extraordinary development of modern s. OSLER, WILLIAM, 1
the god of s....has given us the atomic bomb KING, MARTIN LUTHER, JR., 17
The term S. should not be given to anything VALÉRY, PAUL, 5
What s. can measure...man can know ROSZAK, THEODORE, 11

science fiction S. is no more written for scientists ALDISS, BRIAN, 2
S. is the search for a definition ALDISS, BRIAN, 3
S. writers, I am sorry DICK, PHILIP K., 3

sciences exact s....last to suffer under despotisms DANA, RICHARD HENRY, 1
S. may be learned by rote STERNE, LAURENCE, 9
s....prepared by magicians, alchemists, astrologers, and witches NIETZSCHE, FRIEDRICH WILHELM, 28
s. were transmitted into the Arabic language AL-BIRUNI, 1

scientific A new s. truth does not triumph PLANCK, MAX, 1
A s. society is based on respect HOLUB, MIROSLAV, 6
level of s. knowledge unapproached in the west NEEDHAM, JOSEPH, 2
S. activity is...cumulative and progressive SARTON, GEORGE, 1
sad s. facts...usually not thrue DUNNE, FINLEY PETER, 1
s. faith's absurd BROWNING, ROBERT, 10
s. truth goes through three stages AGASSIZ, LOUIS RODOLPHE, 1
The s. revolution has finished its role QUTB, SAYYID, 2
very s. if...derived from twitching of frogs' legs JAMES, WILLIAM, 6

where we do our s. work...place of prayer NEEDHAM, JOSEPH, 4
scientific illiteracy The consequences of s. SAGAN, CARL, 18
scientific knowledge frontiers of s. MAHONEY, RICHARD J., 3
scientific method Traditional s....20–20 hindsight PIRSIG, ROBERT T., 10
scientific research great revolutions brought about by s. MEDAWAR, PETER, 1
scientific work measure the importance of a s. HILBERT, DAVID, 2
scientist degradation of the position of the s. WIENER, NORBERT, 1
good s....perennial curiosity lingers on SEITZ, FREDERICK, 1
have more faith in the s. SARNOFF, DAVID, 2
He had...qualities that make a great s. FLEMING, ALEXANDER, 1
independent s....has a consecration WIENER, NORBERT, 5
s. is a lover of truth BURBANK, LUTHER, 7
s. never loses the faculty of amazement SELYE, HANS, 1
s.'s aim...to clarify SZILARD, LEO, 1
s.'s sense of wonder has not diminished WEINBERG, STEVEN, 1
s. takes off from...observations of predecessors ZINSSER, HANS, 1
s. who yields anything to theology MENCKEN, H. L., 20
tension between the s.'s laws and...breaches of them QUINE, WILLARD V., 3
Touch a s....touch a child BRADBURY, RAY, 3
scientists great s. have been occupied with values WILSON, EDMUND, 1
in the company of s., I feel like a...curate AUDEN, W. H., 32
S. are treated like gods HOWATCH, SUSAN, 1
scissor The great, long, red-legged s.-man HOFFMAN, HEINRICH, 5
Scooby Dooby Doo S. SCOOBY DOO, 1
scorched maybe we might have s. the moon ELLINGTON, DUKE, 10
scored They s.. We didn't. That's it BLUE, VIDA, 1
scorer when the One Great S. comes RICE, GRANTLAND, 1
scorn s. ride sparkling in her eyes SHAKESPEARE, WILLIAM, 453
scornful dart not s. glances from those eyes SHAKESPEARE, WILLIAM, 640
Scorpus I am S., the glory of the roaring circus MARTIAL, 4
Scotchman A S. must be a very sturdy moralist JOHNSON, SAMUEL, 21
Much may be made of a S. JOHNSON, SAMUEL, 150
S....a man of sense LOCKIER, FRANCIS, 1
the noblest prospect which a S. ever sees JOHNSON, SAMUEL, 107
what...makes a S. happy JOHNSON, SAMUEL, 65
Scotia old S.'s grandeur BURNS, ROBERT, 38
O S.! my dear, my native soil BURNS, ROBERT, 53
Scotland I...come from S., but...cannot help it JOHNSON, SAMUEL, 79
patriotism has no...persona in S. NAIRN, TOM, 1
Politics and government in Victorian S. LYNCH, MICHAEL, 1
S....a worse England JOHNSON, SAMUEL, 113
S., I rush towards you MCCAIG, NORMAN, 9
S....most important centres of intellectual culture LYNCH, MICHAEL, 2
the English politician's view of S. MORGAN, EDWIN, 2
Scots blow the S. back again into Scotland FAWKES, GUY, 2
S., wha hae wi' Wallace bled BURNS, ROBERT, 31
Scotsman S....do nothing which might damage his career BARRIE, J. M., 18
Scottish few decisive battles in S. history LYNCH, MICHAEL, 3
scoundrels pack of s. /...Order of the State KUNITZ, STANLEY, 2
scout A S. smiles and whistles BADEN-POWELL, ROBERT, 1
scowl Rachmaninov's immortalizing totality was his s. RACHMANINOV, SERGEI VASILYEVICH, 1
scratch S. my back PROVERBS, 377
scream I have to s. a spring scream LINDGREN, ASTRID, 2
screech-owls when s. cry, and ban-dogs howl SHAKESPEARE, WILLIAM, 287
screenplays S. are not works of art SCHRADER, PAUL, 2
screenwriter behind every successful s. MARX, GROUCHO, 34
screw Don't s. around and don't smoke CURRIE, EDWINA, 5
scribbling My s. pays me zero francs per line ROCHEFORT, HENRI, 1
script don't look at a s. during...filming CASSAVETES, JOHN, 1
If it's a good s., I'll do it BURNS, GEORGE, 2
scriptures I believe...the holy S. ERASMUS, DESIDERIUS, 2
We gave the S. to the Israelites KORAN, 34
Scrooge "I do," said S.. "I must." DICKENS, CHARLES, 5
scrutamini scripturas S....These two words have undone the world SELDEN, JOHN, 4
sculptor S....asked not to leave any holes MOORE, HENRY, 1
sculpture S. cannot translate...emotion GONCHAROVA, NATALIA, 1
S. museums are places where parents hear their children GÓMEZ DE LA SERNA, RAMÓN, 5
S. to me is like poetry LIN, MAYA, 1
S.: You began in shadow JÁUREGUI, JUAN DE, 1
You can't make a s....without involving your body HEPWORTH, BARBARA, 1
You make s. because...wood allows you to express something BOURGEOIS, LOUISE, 3
sea A singular disadvantage of the s. CRANE, STEPHEN, 4
Bobby Shafto's gone to s. CHILDREN'S VERSE, 38
For all at last return to the s. CARSON, RACHEL, 5
forth on the godly s. POUND, EZRA, 21
I have known the s. too long CONRAD, JOSEPH, 2
I loved the great s. more and more PROCTER, BRYAN WALLER, 2
Learn the secret of the s. LONGFELLOW, HENRY WADSWORTH, 15
s. is English by inclination MICHELET, JULES, 2
s., trembling with a long line of radiance RADCLIFFE, ANN, 1
the midst of the s. upon dry ground BIBLE, 76
The s. is the universal sewer COUSTEAU, JACQUES, 2
The s.! the sea! XENOPHON, 1
The voice of the s. speaks to the soul CHOPIN, KATE, 1
seafarers S. tell of the Fairy Isles LI BAI, 1
seamen the s. were not gentlemen CHARLES II, 3
Sean O'Casey Last year it was all S. HOLLOWAY, JOSEPH, 1
search s. the land of living men SCOTT, SIR WALTER, 7
searched s....for snakes, tarantulas, and scorpions MATTHIESSEN, PETER, 8
seas I must down to the s. again MASEFIELD, JOHN, 4
West of these out to s....I must go FLECKER, JAMES ELROY, 1
season always the s. for...old to learn AESCHYLUS, 3
ghastly s....for you Spanish dancers BANKHEAD, TALLULAH, 11
I remember the last s. I played MAYS, WILLIE, 1
to every thing there is a s. BIBLE, 48
seasons a man for all s. WHITTINGTON, ROBERT, 1
In this country...only two s. DELANEY, SHELAGH, 3
seatbelts Fasten your s. DAVIS, BETTE, 2
Seattle I remembered S. as a town STEINBECK, JOHN, 26
seceded Say to the s. states SCOTT, WINFIELD, 1
second-rate an infallible sign of the s. LEVERSON, ADA, 1
second time I will not point it out...a s. CONFUCIUS, 37

secrecy S. is the first essential RICHELIEU, CARDINAL, 7
secret a s. in the Oxford sense FRANKS, OLIVER, 1
deepest s. of spiritual life is hidden RADHAKRISHNAN, SARVEPALLI, 3
I know that's a s. CONGREVE, WILLIAM, 5
most difficult s. for a man PAGNOL, MARCEL, 1
s. as the grave CERVANTES, MIGUEL DE, 48
s. hidden since the world began ROSS, RONALD, 1
s. of a successful life FORD, HENRY, 3
tell...s. of my nights and days WHITMAN, WALT, 23
Three may keep a s. FRANKLIN, BENJAMIN, 23
secretary call in a s....chew him out JOHNSON, LYNDON BAINES, 22
secrets s. are edged tools DRYDEN, JOHN, 36
s. of the structure...human body FONTENELLE, BERNARD LE BOVIER, 1
sects men have divided themselves into different s. KORAN, 25
no s. in geometry VOLTAIRE, 45
security S. is...the first essential HOBSON, JOHN, 1
s. we...seek in foreign adventures KING, MARTIN LUTHER, JR., 6
There is no s....there is only opportunity MACARTHUR, DOUGLAS, 7
seditions prevent s....take away the matter BACON, FRANCIS (1561–1626), 61
seditious s. person is an outlaw before God LUTHER, MARTIN, 3
seducer Thou strong s., opportunity DRYDEN, JOHN, 38
seduction Rough s. /Delights them OVID, 2
see eyes to s., and see not BIBLE, 92
I'll s. you at four MAYAKOVSKY, VLADIMIR, 7
I s. but as one sees after an operation CARRIERA, ROSALBA, 1
I s. the steady gain of man WHITTIER, JOHN GREENLEAF, 6
people really s. the world upside down JERSILD, P. C., 1
Shall never s. so much or live so long SHAKESPEARE, WILLIAM, 368
Something I cannot s....libidinous prongs WHITMAN, WALT, 40
s. others as they see themselves HUXLEY, ALDOUS, 57
there shall no man s. me, and live BIBLE, 88
We s. only the appearances...of things BERKELEY, BISHOP, 1
seed he spills his s. on the ground PARKER, DOROTHY, 39
seed time In s. learn, in harvest teach BLAKE, WILLIAM, 38
seed-time Fair s. had my soul WORDSWORTH, WILLIAM, 83
seeing S. is believing PROVERBS, 379
Worth s....but not worth going to see JOHNSON, SAMUEL, 156
seek s. him here...seek him there ORCZY, BARONESS, 1
S. roses in December BYRON, LORD, 89
We s. it, ere it come to light, /In ev'ry cranny but the right COWPER, WILLIAM, 20
seeming beguile /The thing I am by s. SHAKESPEARE, WILLIAM, 476
seen He who has s. little marvels much PROVERBS, 31
I have s. Voltaire VOLTAIRE, 4
s. one ant...not seen them all WILSON, EDWARD O., 6
they that have not s., and yet have believed BIBLE, 304
seer one must be a *s.* RIMBAUD, ARTHUR, 3
see-saw S., Margery Daw CHILDREN'S VERSE, 29
segregation s. now, segregation tomorrow, segregation forever WALLACE, GEORGE, 1
seize S. the day HORACE, 36
sekret A s....iz like a dollar bill BILLINGS, JOSH, 1
selected s. my collaborators...not on...their grandmothers HABER, FRITZ, 1
self dearer to anyone than his own s. BUDDHA, 3
perhaps within a few days I should dissent my s. BROWNE, THOMAS, 12
S. under self, a pile of selves MCCAIG, NORMAN, 11
The s. posits self FICHTE, JOHANN, 4
The s., what a brute it is WHITTEMORE, REED, 1
where the s. that was no self made its home MORRISON, TONI, 6
self-belief s. and a sense of proportion BECKER, BORIS, 1
self-censorship serious game of s. MAUPIN, ARMISTEAD, 8
self-consciousness s....divides us from our fellow creatures DILLARD, ANNIE, 6
self-contemplation S. is...the symptom of disease CARLYLE, THOMAS, 6
self-delusion Nothing causes s....so readily as power LIU BINYAN, 2
self-denial S. is not a virtue SHAW, GEORGE BERNARD, 64
self-destruction S. is the effect of cowardice in the highest extreme DEFOE, DANIEL, 1
self-determination S. is not a mere phrase WILSON, WOODROW, 6
self-disgust I asked for s. SOYINKA, WOLE, 2
self-employed I'm s. PHILIP, PRINCE, 9
self-esteem healthy s....based on *deserved* respect MASLOW, ABRAHAM, 4
nothing profits more /Than s. MILTON, JOHN, 77
self-government s. and self-determination...no turning back PADMORE, GEORGE, 6
We prefer s. with danger to servitude in tranquility NKRUMAH, KWAME, 4
self-indulgence write an essay on "s." WAUGH, EVELYN, 12
self-interest s....irreversible force behind the markets' opening ARMSTRONG, MICHAEL, 2
S. speaks all sorts of tongues LA ROCHEFOUCAULD, FRANÇOIS, 9
selfish How s. soever man may be supposed SMITH, ADAM, 1
the s. propriety of civilized man MUIR, JOHN, 1
self-knowledge S. is a dangerous thing SHAPIRO, KARL, 1
self-made man A s....believes in luck STEAD, CHRISTINA, 1
s....owed his lack of success HELLER, JOSEPH, 3
self-parody S....the first portent of age MCMURTRY, LARRY, 2
self-pity S....as snug as a feather mattress ANGELOU, MAYA, 4
self-praise S. is no recommendation PROVERBS, 381
self-preservation gifted with...instinct for s. WAUGH, EVELYN, 24
S. is the first of Laws DRYDEN, JOHN, 48
self-reflection S. is the school of wisdom GRACIÁN, BALTASAR, 2
self-respect S.—the secure feeling that no one...is suspicious MENCKEN, H. L., 6
self-revelation terrible *fluidity of s.* JAMES, HENRY, 21
self-rule Never...has an alien ruler granted s. NKRUMAH, KWAME, 6
self-sacrifice S. enables us to sacrifice SHAW, GEORGE BERNARD, 65
self-sufficient know how to be s. MONTAIGNE, MICHEL DE, 4
sell Everything we s., we sell on image GOIZUETA, ROBERTO, 6
I s....what all the world desires BOULTON, MATTHEW, 1
S. a country HARRISON, WILLIAM HENRY, 1
s. a murky trout stream here BRAUTIGAN, RICHARD, 5
selling Every one lives by s. something STEVENSON, ROBERT LOUIS, 5
the s. of cars in Great Portland Street COWARD, NOEL, 36
semantic S. inflation SZASZ, THOMAS, 16
semi-apes We are...changed /From the s. KIPLING, RUDYARD, 30
senator S., you're no Jack Kennedy QUAYLE, DAN, 1
senility S. is looking back with nostalgia MARTIN, AGNES, 1

sensations S. rather than of Thoughts KEATS, JOHN (1795–1821), 27
sense Good s. is the best distributed thing DESCARTES, RENÉ, 4
Horse s. is a good judgment FIELDS, W. C., 4
Let's talk s. to the American people STEVENSON, ADLAI, 1
Take care of the s. CARROLL, LEWIS, 18
sense of humour God withheld the s. from women CAMPBELL, MRS. PATRICK, 1
senses The five s. are as spies MUHAMMAD, 15
the s. do not err KANT, IMMANUEL, 13
sensible S. men are all of the same religion DISRAELI, BENJAMIN, 14
s. people are selfish EMERSON, RALPH WALDO, 53
sensitivity You must have...s.—a cutting edge OLIVIER, LAURENCE, 1
sensual the average s. man impassioned HUGO, VICTOR, 1
The only s. pleasure without vice JOHNSON, SAMUEL, 54
sensuality S....a synonym of sexuality VARGAS LLOSA, MARIO, 1
sentence S. first—verdict afterwards CARROLL, LEWIS, 24
simple declarative s. with seven grammatical errors HARDING, WARREN G., 1
Whatever s....bear to be read twice THOREAU, HENRY DAVID, 26
sentences attractive s. are not perhaps the wisest THOREAU, HENRY DAVID, 16
Backward ran s. GIBBS, WOLCOTT, 1
S. which simply express moral judgements AYER, A. J., 1
sentimental s. cheats of the movie screen MAILER, NORMAN, 6
sentimentality S. is a superstructure JUNG, CARL GUSTAV, 23
S. is...emotional promiscuity MAILER, NORMAN, 8
S. is only sentiment MAUGHAM, SOMERSET, 8
sentiments s. that no legislature can manufacture BAGEHOT, WALTER, 3
separation We go for s. MALCOLM X, 8
Septuagint The S. minus the Apostles VERRALL, ARTHUR WOOLLGAR, 1
sepulchre a new s., wherein was never man yet laid BIBLE, 300
sepulchres whited s. BIBLE, 423
serene With s. regularity...bullets buffed into men CRANE, STEPHEN, 12
serf No man should be a s. TYLER, WAT, 1
serfdom better to...abolish s. from above ALEXANDER II, 2
Sergeant Pepper S.'s Lonely Hearts Club Band LENNON & MCCARTNEY, 11
seriously Everything must be taken s., nothing tragically THIERS, ADOLPHE, 1
one must do...work s. and must be independent CURIE, IRÈNE, 1
serpent my s. of old Nile SHAKESPEARE, WILLIAM, 73
sharper than a s.'s tooth SHAKESPEARE, WILLIAM, 336
The s. subtlest beast of all the field MILTON, JOHN, 81
the s. was more subtil BIBLE, 111
servant A s.'s too often a negligent elf BARHAM, RICHARD HARRIS, 2
Behold my s., whom I uphold BIBLE, 216
good s. does not all commands SHAKESPEARE, WILLIAM, 135
good s. is a real godsend LUTHER, MARTIN, 16
the hired s. of Ireland O'CONNELL, DANIEL, 1
servants both were *S.*...both *Princes* COWLEY, ABRAHAM, 3
he wouldn't have white s. PARKER, DOROTHY, 7
S. should not be ill COOPER, LADY DIANA, 1
serv'd Had I but s. my God SHAKESPEARE, WILLIAM, 284
serve s. his time to every trade BYRON, LORD, 86
to s., to heal the wounds and give love DE KLERK, MARIKE, 1
serves He serves me most who s. his country best POPE, ALEXANDER, 74
He s. his party best HAYES, RUTHERFORD B., 1
service life goes in the s. of the nation GANDHI, INDIRA, 6
S. is not a kind of blackmail LUCE, HENRY R., 2
S. is the rent...you pay CHISHOLM, SHIRLEY, 5
S. is what the typical American businessman LUCE, HENRY R., 3
Small s. is true service WORDSWORTH, WILLIAM, 10
s. to mankind ennobles...his labor LOWELL, A. LAWRENCE, 1
service economy a microelectronic-driven s. KRUGMAN, PAUL, 4
serving S. the customer...not a mechanical act HAMMER, MICHAEL, 2
set s. thine house in order BIBLE, 173
setter up Proud s. and puller down of kings SHAKESPEARE, WILLIAM, 292
settled Thank God, that's s. SHERIDAN, RICHARD BRINSLEY, 18
settlers s....frequently become slatterns FULLER, MARGARET, 5
When white s. come...Indians have to move WILDER, LAURA INGALLS, 4
Seventh Avenue S., the battlements of...office buildings GINSBERG, ALLEN, 10
seventy Being over s. is like being engaged in a war SPARK, MURIEL, 2
Being s. is not a sin MEIR, GOLDA, 4
Oh, to be s. again HOLMES, OLIVER WENDELL, JR., 6
sewage piped growing volumes of s. into the sea CECIL, ROBERT, 2
sewer A trip through a s. MIZNER, WILSON, 1
sex Ah, the s. thing GARBO, GRETA, 7
a s. story in biblical garb ZANUCK, DARRYL F., 1
Being the inventor of s. KRUTCH, JOSEPH WOOD, 3
both of them were extremely interested in s. LODGE, DAVID, 2
Everything You Always Wanted to Know About S. REUBEN, DAVID, 1
His excessive emphasis on s. LAWRENCE, D. H., 7
How can I...dislike a s. to which Your Majesty belongs? RHODES, CECIL, 3
If God...meant us to have group s. BRADBURY, MALCOLM, 10
if s. isn't the most important thing DRABBLE, MARGARET, 3
If s. is such a natural phenomenon MIDLER, BETTE, 2
Is s. dirty ALLEN, WOODY, 4
Is S. Necessary WHITE, E. B., 12
it's s. with someone you love ALLEN, WOODY, 2
No more about s., it's too boring DURRELL, LAWRENCE, 6
normal man's s. needs STOPES, MARIE, 4
No s. is better than bad sex GREER, GERMAINE, 14
No s. without responsibility LONGFORD, LORD, 1
Personally I know nothing about s. GABOR, ZSA ZSA, 4
popular...talk of s., divorce and drugs FLANAGAN, OLIVER J., 1
pseudo-sophistication of twentieth-century s. theory GREER, GERMAINE, 13
S. & Drugs & Rock & Roll DURY, IAN, 1
s....a very private, secretive activity SZASZ, THOMAS, 15
S. between a man and a woman ALLEN, WOODY, 25
S., consolation for misery PASOLINI, PIER PAOLO, 1
S....Every bit as interesting as agriculture SPARK, MURIEL, 6
s. for the students, athletics for the alumni KERR, CLARK, 1
S. had to be brought out of the Victorian closet CALDERONE, MARY, 1
she is s.—absolute sex BEAUVOIR, SIMONE DE, 10
S. is a fact of life BLACK, HUGO LAFAYETTE, 2
s. is...a form of holy communion LAWRENCE, D. H., 6
S. is like money UPDIKE, JOHN, 7
s. is not a relationship NILSEN, DENNIS, 1
S. is one of the nine reasons for reincarnation MILLER, HENRY, 6

S. is something I really don't understand SALINGER, J. D., 15
S. is the biggest nothing WARHOL, ANDY, 11
S. is the curse of life FULLER, MARGARET, 1
S....is the gateway to life HARRIS, FRANK, 1
S. is the tabasco sauce WINN, MARY DAY, 1
S. is to women's history DEGLER, CARL N., 3
s....more important...in the life of woman SIGERIST, HENRY E., 3
s....must itself be subject...to evolution BLACKWELL, ANTOINETTE LOUISA, 2
Some people like s. more than others COPE, WENDY, 3
the s. novel is now normal SHAW, GEORGE BERNARD, 84
To defend society from s. is no one's business BROPHY, BRIGID, 1
You mustn't think I advocate perpetual s. LAWRENCE, D. H., 12
your s. are naturally tyrannical ADAMS, ABIGAIL, 8

s-e-x if S. ever rears its ugly head AYCKBOURN, ALAN, 2

sexes motive force behind the union of the s. LACLOS, PIERRE CHODERLOS DE, 3
the intellectual powers of the two s. DARWIN, CHARLES, 7

sex-life s....gladly...am I rid of it all SOPHOCLES, 13

sexual avowed purpose is to excite s. desire MUGGERIDGE, MALCOLM, 7
Civilized people cannot fully satisfy their s. instinct RUSSELL, BERTRAND, 16
explicit s. statement...crash down around you WESTWOOD, VIVIENNE, 4
Mailer's s. journalism MAILER, NORMAN, 1
S. pleasure...discharge of nervous energy ORTEGA Y GASSET, JOSÉ, 6
surest guarantee of s. success AMIS, MARTIN, 1
The discussion of the s. problem JUNG, CARL GUSTAV, 29

sexual feeling s. is unwomanly and intolerable SCHARLIEB, DAME MARY ANN DACOMB, 2

sexual intercourse appetite for s....softens the heart AL-NAWAWI, MUHYID-DIN ABU ZAKARIYYA IBN SHARAF, 3
S. began /In nineteen sixty-three LARKIN, PHILIP, 11

sexuality difficulties with their s. MCKELLEN, IAN, 4
man's s....ultimate pinnacle of his spirit NIETZSCHE, FRIEDRICH WILHELM, 7
My s. has never been a problem SPRINGFIELD, DUSTY, 1
My s. struck me like...thunder BERGMAN, INGMAR, 5
S. is the lyricism of the masses BAUDELAIRE, CHARLES, 2
s. was utterly irrelevant MAUPIN, ARMISTEAD, 6
There is no essential s. WALLACE, NAOMI, 1

sex-war In the s. thoughtlessness is the weapon of the male CONNOLLY, CYRIL, 15

sexy I don't know any guy more s. GUCCIONE, BOB, 1
I never meant...to be s. WEST, MAE, 17

shade a s. uncast, a light unshed...vain entelechies BECKETT, SAMUEL, 31
we desire to throw no one into the s. BÜLOW, BERNHARD VON, 1

shadow I am no s....I am a wife PLATH, SYLVIA, 15
Me and My S. ROSE, BILLY, 3
Those who live in the s. ENZENSBERGER, HANS, 1

shadows s. to-night /Have struck more terror SHAKESPEARE, WILLIAM, 532

shady Deep in the s. sadness of a vale KEATS, JOHN (1795–1821), 85

shake I will s. my little finger—and there will be no more Tito STALIN, JOSEPH, 15

shaken S. and not stirred FLEMING, IAN, 4

Shakespeare after S. and Milton are forgotten SOUTHEY, ROBERT, 1
A strange, horrible business...good enough for S.'s day SHAKESPEARE, WILLIAM, 49
a wonderful fellow is old S. SHAKESPEARE, WILLIAM, 35
Besides S. and me SHAKESPEARE, WILLIAM, 47
Brush Up Your S. SHAKESPEARE, WILLIAM, 44
I despise S. HOMER, 3
I don't really like words by S. SHAKESPEARE, WILLIAM, 37
myriad-minded S. COLERIDGE, SAMUEL TAYLOR, 33
Nature proclaims her wisdom through S. GOETHE, JOHANN WOLFGANG VON, 5
People are engrossed in S. SHAKESPEARE, WILLIAM, 36
reading S. by flashes of lightning COLERIDGE, SAMUEL TAYLOR, 60
S. absolutely belongs to everyone SHAKESPEARE, WILLIAM, 42
S. enjoyed...living in a creative age SHAKESPEARE, WILLIAM, 17
S....fearless, high-spirited, resolute, and intelligent heroines SHAKESPEARE, WILLIAM, 48
S. has no heroes SHAKESPEARE, WILLIAM, 25
S., I come DREISER, THEODORE, 4
S....incarnates "Merry England" MARCUS, LEAH S., 1
S., in your threefold, fourfold tomb SHAKESPEARE, WILLIAM, 3
S....is great literature SHAKESPEARE, WILLIAM, 11
S. never had six lines together without a fault SHAKESPEARE, WILLIAM, 24
S....only biographer of Shakespeare SHAKESPEARE, WILLIAM, 13
S.'s language is "the best" SHAKESPEARE, WILLIAM, 15
S.'s so bloody difficult SHAKESPEARE, WILLIAM, 21
S.'s verbal imagination SHAKESPEARE, WILLIAM, 16
S.'s works...one great bubbling fair SHAKESPEARE, WILLIAM, 18
S....the eye of God SHAKESPEARE, WILLIAM, 41
S. was something of an Establishment creep SHAKESPEARE, WILLIAM, 5
S. wrote for the masses SHAKESPEARE, WILLIAM, 39
The remarkable thing about S. SHAKESPEARE, WILLIAM, 20
tried lately to read S. SHAKESPEARE, WILLIAM, 9
When I read S. I am struck SHAKESPEARE, WILLIAM, 34

Shakespeares a committee of S. SHAKESPEARE, WILLIAM, 32

sham when he is a...S. JOYCE, JAMES, 14

shame In that land...s. resides CANETTI, ELIAS, 2
Put off your s. with your clothes THEANO, 1
s. of being a tourist GARCÍA MÁRQUEZ, GABRIEL, 2
S. on you, woman of Satan STRINDBERG, AUGUST, 7

shape The S. of Things to Come WELLS, H. G., 9

share s. in the good fortunes of the mighty BRECHT, BERTOLT, 17
s. your friend's crime PUBLILIUS SYRUS, 15

shared s. vision is not an idea SENGE, PETER M., 1

shareholders the s. are the owners MAKIHARA, MINORU, 1

shark the s. has pretty teeth BRECHT, BERTOLT, 26

shatter You may s. us at the canon's mouth GANDHI, MAHATMA, 23

shaven This is THE MAN...all s. and shorn GEORGE IV, 2

Shaw Bernard S. is greatly improved by music SHAW, GEORGE BERNARD, 7
George Bernard S. is sadly miscast SHAW, GEORGE BERNARD, 12
Mr S....has never written any poetry SHAW, GEORGE BERNARD, 4
S....is intensely disliked by all his friends SHAW, GEORGE BERNARD, 13
S. relished every opportunity SHAW, GEORGE BERNARD, 6
S. replied, "I'll wait for you to grow up" SHAW, GEORGE BERNARD, 3
S.'s judgements are often scatterbrained SHAW, GEORGE BERNARD, 1
S.'s mind...better than anyone else's SHAW, GEORGE BERNARD, 14

shazbot S.! WILLIAMS, ROBIN, 2
she S.-who-must-be-obeyed HAGGARD, H. RIDER, 1
Sheba the queen of S. had seen all Solomon's wisdom BIBLE, 189
shedding without s. of blood is no remission BIBLE, 142
sheep as a shepherd divideth his s. from the goats BIBLE, 430
like lost s. BOOK OF COMMON PRAYER, 13
s. are born carnivores ROUSSEAU, JEAN-JACQUES, 1
s. had already made its statement HIRST, DAMIEN, 1
S. speckle the mountainside GINSBERG, ALLEN, 6
We are accounted as s. for the slaughter BIBLE, 483
shell How the s. came off the almond FLECKER, JAMES ELROY, 5
one s. to the soul of man SOYINKA, WOLE, 1
Shelley S...."a beautiful and ineffectual angel" SHELLEY, PERCY BYSSHE, 1
S. and Keats...their chemical knowledge SHELLEY, PERCY BYSSHE, 2
Shenandoah O, S., I long to hear you FOLK VERSE, 11
shepherd Lord delights at a s. who...prays MUHAMMAD, 8
shepherds s. abiding in the field BIBLE, 324
s. watch'd their flocks TATE, NAHUM, 3
Sherard Blaw S....who had discovered himself SHAW, GEORGE BERNARD, 11
Sherlock Holmes S. *is* literature WILSON, EDMUND, 2
sherry With first-rate s. flowing into second-rate whores PLOMER, WILLIAM, 3
shilling you don't happen to have the s....do you? SHERIDAN, RICHARD BRINSLEY, 4
shimmy s. and the snake-hip ASTAIRE, FRED, 10
shine s. on, harvest moon NORWORTH, JACK, 1
ship A s. comes into the harbor BRADFORD, WILLIAM, 2
being in a s. is being in a jail JOHNSON, SAMUEL, 106
Don't give up the s. LAWRENCE, JAMES, 1
I have not been on a s....still call me "Admiral" PERÓN, EVA, 1
It was so old a s. FLECKER, JAMES ELROY, 2
places his s. alongside that of an enemy NELSON, HORATIO, 2
S. me somewheres east of Suez KIPLING, RUDYARD, 23
The s. follows Soviet custom THEROUX, PAUL, 11
The s. has weathered every rack WHITMAN, WALT, 26
They did not...so much as sink...one s. ANONYMOUS, 71
ship of state sail on, O S. LONGFELLOW, HENRY WADSWORTH, 11
ships And the stately s. go on TENNYSON, ALFRED, 40
I spied three s. come sailing by FOLK VERSE, 29
Like s., that sailed for sunny isles HERVEY, THOMAS K., 1
My experience of s....one makes an interesting discovery about the world BRADBURY, MALCOLM, 4
not what s. are built for HOPPER, GRACE MURRAY, 2
Our s. have been salvaged HALSEY, WILLIAM, 1
something wrong with our bloody s. BEATTY, DAVID, 1
S. that pass in the night LONGFELLOW, HENRY WADSWORTH, 29
shipwreck s. /Of the singular OPPEN, GEORGE, 1
shipwrecks S. are *apropos* of nothing CRANE, STEPHEN, 5
shirt-sleeves from s. to shirt-sleeves BUTLER, NICHOLAS MURRAY, 1
shit I don't give a s. what happens NIXON, RICHARD, 16
you're so full of s. VONNEGUT, KURT, 6
shock Anybody can s. a baby STERN, RICHARD G., 1
a short, sharp s. GILBERT, W. S., 33
deliberately set out to s. OSBORNE, JOHN, 7
shoe If the s. doesn' t fit STEINEM, GLORIA, 12
my own s. pinches CERVANTES, MIGUEL DE, 16
shoemaker The s.'s son PROVERBS, 427
shoes carry about six or eight pairs of s. HAMMOND, CELIA, 1
I take my s. from the shoemaker GOLDSMITH, OLIVER, 34
shook s. me like...end of the world PLATH, SYLVIA, 10
shoot do not s. the pianist WILDE, OSCAR, 73
S....this old gray head WHITTIER, JOHN GREENLEAF, 1
they could s. me in my absence BEHAN, BRENDAN, 10
They s. folks here somewhat WARD, ARTEMUS, 1
They S. Horses Don't They MCCOY, HORACE, 1
shooting A bit of s. takes your mind off BEHAN, BRENDAN, 14
S. is really a bore BUÑUEL, LUIS, 2
s....not such a...spectacle as...decapitation LU XUN, 10
shop A man should keep for himself a little back s. MONTAIGNE, MICHEL DE, 8
shopkeeper The s.'s view of nature SNYDER, GARY, 3
shop-keepers A nation of s. ADAMS, SAMUEL, 3
shore By the s. of Gitche Gumee LONGFELLOW, HENRY WADSWORTH, 31
From that s. below the mountain STAFFORD, WILLIAM, 1
On the Black Lake's s. DU FU, 5
shortest I never realized that I'd end up being the s. knight of the year RICHARDS, GORDON, 1
the s. works are always the best LA FONTAINE, JEAN DE, 12
shot S.? so quick HOUSMAN, A. E., 8
think up a s. in five seconds SCHRADER, PAUL, 1
shots They really are bad s. DE GAULLE, CHARLES, 18
should S. I get married...be good? CORSO, GREGORY, 4
shoulder-blade I have a left s. GILBERT, W. S., 28
shoulders standing on the s. of giants NEWTON, ISAAC, 5
shout get to s. at people PALIN, MICHAEL, 2
shouting people leaning out of car windows and s. obscenities MINOGUE, KYLIE, 1
show kind of s. where...girls are not auditioned THOMAS, IRENE, 2
The s. was like eating a banana nut Brillopad CROSBY, DAVID, 1
show business I went into s....from hunger CAGNEY, JAMES, 6
S. offers more...promises than Catholicism GUARE, JOHN, 1
shower s. with a friend MOTTOS AND SLOGANS, 24
shows All my s. are great GRADE, LEW, 1
shrimp a s. learns to whistle KHRUSHCHEV, NIKITA, 12
shrine practically a national s. ZINSSER, WILLIAM, 1
shrink those who s. from the ultimate sacrifice PEARSE, PATRICK, 4
shuttlecock Battledore and s.'s a wery good game DICKENS, CHARLES, 80
shyness S. is just egotism KEITH, PENELOPE, 1
S....Self-consciousness it was always called TAYLOR, ELIZABETH, 4
Sibyl I saw the S. at Cumae PETRONIUS ARBITER, 4
sick Are you s., or...sullen JOHNSON, SAMUEL, 170
better to be s. than nurse the sick EURIPIDES, 9
have on our hands a s. man NICHOLAS I, 1
If you are physically s. FISCHER, MARTIN H., 11
I'm never, never s. at sea GILBERT, W. S., 3
I'm s. of just liking people SALINGER, J. D., 6
make any man s. to hear her PEPYS, SAMUEL, 11
s. are the greatest danger for the healthy NIETZSCHE, FRIEDRICH WILHELM, 17

s. man is a parasite of society NIETZSCHE, FRIEDRICH WILHELM, 35
so many poor s. people in the streets PEPYS, SAMUEL, 16
the man who does not know s. women MITCHELL, S. WEIR, 1
To be s. is to enjoy monarchal prerogatives LAMB, CHARLES, 24
While the s. man has life, there is hope CICERO, 11
sickle She was the s....I, the rake ROETHKE, THEODORE, 11
sickness greatest misery of s. is *solitude* DONNE, JOHN, 49
His s. has created atrocities PICASSO, PABLO, 3
S., sin and death...do not originate in God EDDY, MARY BAKER, 3
Study s. while you are well FULLER, THOMAS (1654–1734), 3
The problem of economic loss due to s. ROOSEVELT, FRANKLIN D., 34
The s. of our times MAILER, NORMAN, 27
weary thing is s. EURIPIDES, 8
sideburn The S. Fairy...visiting young groovies WOLFE, TOM, 2
sieve They went to sea in a s. LEAR, EDWARD, 14
sigh I often s. still /for the dark LOWELL, ROBERT, 10
sigh'd s. to many...loved but one BYRON, LORD, 22
sight Out of s., out of mind PROVERBS, 360
s. is the most perfect...of all our senses ADDISON, JOSEPH, 18
s. to make an old man young TENNYSON, ALFRED, 64
when he is out of s., quickly...out of mind KEMPIS, THOMAS À, 6
sightless clapped the glass to his s. eye NEWBOLT, HENRY, 1
sign Never s. a walentine DICKENS, CHARLES, 83
the s. "Members Only" MILLIGAN, SPIKE, 7
signature s....ending a war when we did not win CLARK, MARK, 1
signatures S. of all things I am here to read JOYCE, JAMES, 25
signed There, I've s. it YELTSIN, BORIS, 8
significance What is the s. of Man? BECKER, CARL, 12
sign language S. is the equal of speech SACKS, OLIVER, 1
silence A great s. has fallen DU BOIS, W. E. B., 7
a minute's s. like that DIANA, PRINCESS, 1
Come to me in the s. of the night ROSSETTI, CHRISTINA, 2
Hinge of s. MONTAGUE, JOHN, 2
His s....ought to be seductive KIERKEGAARD, SØREN, 14
impression that their normal condition is s. SARTRE, JEAN-PAUL, 15
I need a circumference of s. BARBER, SAMUEL, 1
It will be s. BECKETT, SAMUEL, 18
looking for the s. in somebody CARTIER-BRESSON, HENRI, 3
occasional flashes of s. SMITH, SYDNEY, 18
S. alone is great VIGNY, ALFRED DE, 2
s. be good for the wise PROVERBS, 266
S....full of potential wisdom HUXLEY, ALDOUS, 41
S. is become his mother tongue GOLDSMITH, OLIVER, 23
S. is golden PROVERBS, 382
S. is talk too PROVERBS, 4
S. is the best tactic LA ROCHEFOUCAULD, FRANÇOIS, 14
S. is the perfectest herald of joy SHAKESPEARE, WILLIAM, 448
S. is the...perfect expression of scorn SHAW, GEORGE BERNARD, 20
Speech is the small change of S. MEREDITH, GEORGE, 14
s. sank /Like music COLERIDGE, SAMUEL TAYLOR, 49
That man's s. is wonderful to listen to HARDY, THOMAS, 31
The rest is s. SHAKESPEARE, WILLIAM, 231
the s. of astounded souls PLATH, SYLVIA, 6
Try...to make a s., we cannot CAGE, JOHN, 8
when...even s., is spray-gunned OLSON, CHARLES, 5
silences S. have a climax BOWEN, ELIZABETH, 6
There are two s. PINTER, HAROLD, 2
silent man who...s. in several languages HARBORD, JAMES GUTHRIE, 1
s. era cannot be...noisy LIU BINYAN, 3
s. shadows turned...pale faces towards me BERGMAN, INGMAR, 7
silent majority great s. of my fellow Americans NIXON, RICHARD, 18
silicon Had s. been a gas WHISTLER, JAMES ABBOTT MCNEILL, 8
silk s., too often hides eczema CAMUS, ALBERT, 12
silken a fine s. thing which I spied EVELYN, JOHN, 6
silks Whenas in s. my Julia goes HERRICK, ROBERT, 18
silk stocking s.'s hanging down SELLAR, W. C., 2
silly A s. remark can be made in Latin CERVANTES, MIGUEL DE, 54
there is nothing sillier than a s. laugh CATULLUS, 4
silver no s. linings without a cloud CARTER, ANGELA, 8
S. and gold have I none BIBLE, 7
S. threads among the gold REXFORD, EBEN, 1
Silvia Who is S.? What is she SHAKESPEARE, WILLIAM, 656
similes s. are true...most metaphors are false DAVIDSON, DONALD, 2
simple as s. as possible, but not simpler EINSTEIN, ALBERT, 56
less s. than "it oozes" HALDANE, J. B. S., 2
Simple Simon S. met a pieman CHILDREN'S VERSE, 7
simpletons The world is...full of s. and madmen GOETHE, JOHANN WOLFGANG VON, 31
simplicity greater s. in nature than there really is REID, THOMAS, 2
O holy s. HUSS, JOHN, 1
Seek s., and distrust it WHITEHEAD, A. N., 18
S. is the soul of efficiency FREEMAN, RICHARD AUSTIN, 1
takes a long time to learn s. MALLE, LOUIS, 1
simplify ability to s....eliminate the unnecessary HOFMANN, HANS, 1
S. and simplify LAOZI, 20
simplifying s. something by destroying nearly everything CHESTERTON, G. K., 9
sin A private s. is not so prejudicial CERVANTES, MIGUEL DE, 36
Be a sinner and s. strongly LUTHER, MARTIN, 10
biggest s. is sitting on your ass KENNEDY, FLORYNCE R., 2
committing the s. against the Holy Ghost DOS PASSOS, JOHN, 12
Don't tell...mother I'm living in s. HERBERT, A. P., 4
go, and s. no more BIBLE, 281
Grant that this day we fall into no s. BOOK OF COMMON PRAYER, 12
he that is without s....let him first cast a stone BIBLE, 280
How shall I lose the s., yet keep the sense POPE, ALEXANDER, 34
If it be s. to love a...lad BARNFIELD, RICHARD, 6
if there is such a thing as s. WAUGH, EVELYN, 7
no s. but to be rich SHAKESPEARE, WILLIAM, 324
one s. will destroy a sinner BUNYAN, JOHN, 19
people who can s. with a grin NASH, OGDEN, 4
S. brought death EDDY, MARY BAKER, 4
S., Death...Hell that was to him a terror BUNYAN, JOHN, 18
s. no more, lest a worse thing come unto thee BIBLE, 276
S....not a theme for psychological interest KIERKEGAARD, SØREN, 9
S. should not be effortless CLIFF, MICHELLE, 1
s....taken out of man SMITH, SYDNEY, 21
S....ugly but passé MCGINLEY, PHYLLIS, 2
The wages of s. is death BIBLE, 481
without s. jail the first Stone ANONYMOUS, 57
Sinai S. was...on a smoke BIBLE, 79
sincere Be s., be brief, be seated ROOSEVELT, FRANKLIN D., 37
He is *absolutely* s. BRYAN, WILLIAM JENNINGS, 3
I am not s. RENARD, JULES, 7

Mr. Spender...looked so s. SPENDER, STEPHEN, 1
Some of the worst men...are s. HAILSHAM, LORD, 3
sincerity A little s....a dangerous thing WILDE, OSCAR, 22
S. is...modern heresy DRIBERG, TOM, 1
sinews twist the s. of thy heart BLAKE, WILLIAM, 27
sing cannot s. the old songs BARNARD, CHARLOTTE ALINGTON, 1
I can't stand to s. the same song the same way HOLIDAY, BILLIE, 2
s. as he tackled GUEST, EDGAR A., 2
S. a song full of the faith JOHNSON, JAMES WELDON, 5
s. to please someone...prostituting yourself BREL, JACQUES, 1
When you have nothing to say, s. it OGILVY, DAVID, 8
Singapore S. had to be better organised LEE, KUAN YEW, 4
singed s. the Spanish king's beard DRAKE, FRANCIS, 3
singer I was a s. in a jazz band MELLY, GEORGE, 1
singers s. today...don't breathe right HORNE, MARILYN, 1
singin' s. in the rain FREED, ARTHUR, 1
single A s. life doth well with churchmen BACON, FRANCIS (1561–1626), 42
being a s. female...having power MADONNA, 2
S. men...are *terribly* desirable WOLFE, TOM, 17
sings no one who s....ever treated fairly REEVES, MARTHA, 1
sink The s. is the great symbol...of family life BARRY, DAVE, 1
sinn'd More s. against than sinning SHAKESPEARE, WILLIAM, 343
sinned I have s. NAPIER, CHARLES JAMES, 1
sinner goodness in the s....condemn the law WELLS, H. G., 11
Oh, who is that young s. HOUSMAN, A. E., 29
When I found out that I was a great s. PRINCE, MARY, 1
sinners At such an hour the s. are still in bed RUNYON, DAMON, 7
sins All s. shall be forgiven BIBLE, 353
Commit /The oldest s. SHAKESPEARE, WILLIAM, 260
none s. unless he stands to profit TALMUD, 7
Our s. are tawdry Ó'FAOLÁIN, SEAN, 1
reheat his s. for breakfast DIETRICH, MARLENE, 1
s. were scarlet...books were read BELLOC, HILAIRE, 18
the s. of the fathers EURIPIDES, 13
the s. they love to act SHAKESPEARE, WILLIAM, 504
though your s. be as scarlet BIBLE, 195
sip can't be tasted in a s. DICKENS, CHARLES, 90
sirens Blest pair of s. MILTON, JOHN, 109
sister My s., Life PASTERNAK, BORIS, 7
Sidney's s., Pembroke's mother BROWNE, WILLIAM, 1
sisterhood S. is Powerful MORGAN, ROBIN, 2
sisters so do his s., and his cousins GILBERT, W. S., 2
sit I would rather s. on a pumpkin THOREAU, HENRY DAVID, 42
situation s. excellent. I shall attack FOCH, FERDINAND, 2
six s. of one and half-a-dozen of the other MARRYAT, FREDERICK, 3
sixpence I love s., jolly little sixpence CHILDREN'S VERSE, 15
sixpences two-and-forty s....to one guinea JOHNSON, SAMUEL, 49
sixteen S. tons TRAVIS, MERLE, 1
sixties If you can remember the s. NEWSPAPERS, 34
The s. ended abruptly MANSON, CHARLES, 1
sixty-four When I'm s. LENNON & MCCARTNEY, 16
sixty minutes at the rate of s. an hour LEWIS, C. S., 6
size S. determines an object SMITHSON, ROBERT, 1
S. is not a deterrent to success GERSTNER, LOUIS, JR., 1
skating In s. over thin ice EMERSON, RALPH WALDO, 15
skeleton a s. in the closet PROVERBS, 200
skepticism healthy s. of the powers of government MOYNIHAN, DANIEL PATRICK, 1
only her s. kept her from being an atheist SARTRE, JEAN-PAUL, 30
S. about what is unproven ADORNO, THEODOR, 7
sketch A s. is generally more spirited than a picture DIDEROT, DENIS, 9
skill No s. or art is needed to grow old GOETHE, JOHANN WOLFGANG VON, 39
S. without imagination is craftsmanship STOPPARD, TOM, 2
skin Her s. is like the dusk on the eastern horizon TOOMER, JEAN, 1
I've Got You Under My S. PORTER, COLE, 5
my s. bristles...razor ceases to act HOUSMAN, A. E., 2
S. is like wax paper LINKLETTER, ART, 1
There is more than one way to s. a cat PROVERBS, 411
Your s. like dawn /Mine like dusk ANGELOU, MAYA, 8
skinning When you are s. your customers KHRUSHCHEV, NIKITA, 8
skins Like the s. of some small mammal PINERO, ARTHUR, 1
skunk what a guilty s. she made me O'NEILL, EUGENE, 6
sky I saw the s. descending, black and white LOWELL, ROBERT, 26
s. is brighter than the earth KELLER, HELEN, 4
s. is darkening like a stain AUDEN, W. H., 18
s., red as the Marseillaise MAYAKOVSKY, VLADIMIR, 9
The s. opens...soil turns into books ADONIS, 2
The s. was so low ERDRICH, LOUISE, 1
slander S. away...something will always stick BEAUMARCHAIS, PIERRE-AUGUSTIN CARON DE, 3
something always sticks when people...s. BACON, FRANCIS (1561–1626), 88
S. will go on...slander of love REICH, WILHELM, 6
slang All s. is metaphor CHESTERTON, G. K., 33
I know only two words of American s. PRIESTLEY, J. B., 12
The one...poetry...continually flowing is s. CHESTERTON, G. K., 35
slate S. I picked from a nettlebed MURPHY, RICHARD, 3
slave Be not the s. of Words CARLYLE, THOMAS, 32
Hath not a s. feelings WEDDERBURN, ROBERT, 1
If a s. has a bad master DOUGLASS, FREDERICK, 4
The s. begins by demanding justice CAMUS, ALBERT, 25
the s. of every second PASTERNAK, BORIS, 8
the s. of the Slavery FANON, FRANTZ, 5
Whatever day /Makes man a s., takes half his worth away POPE, ALEXANDER, 92
you shall see how a s. was made a man DOUGLASS, FREDERICK, 15
slave girl the history of a s. DRUMGOOLD, KATE, 1
slave-holding entirely a s. nation, or entirely a free-labor nation SEWARD, WILLIAM HENRY, 1
slavery cursed and ruined by American s. GARNET, HENRY HIGHLAND, 2
how heavily the weight of s. pressed upon me then NORTHUP, SOLOMON, 1
Neither s. nor...servitude...within the United States CONSTITUTION OF THE UNITED STATES, 4
s....brands your republicanism as a sham DOUGLASS, FREDERICK, 22
S. has been abandoned CONSTANTINE, LEARIE, 3
S. is damnable JACOBS, HARRIET ANN, 1
S....supported by local police DOUGLAS, STEPHEN A., 1
The prolonged s. of women STANTON, ELIZABETH CADY, 6
The trouble with our people...s. WALKER, ALICE, 29

they hold us in their infernal chains of s. WALKER, DAVID, 1
slaves forced to continue the employment of his s. CHRISTY, DAVID, 1
Numerousness of S....in the Province SEWALL, SAMUEL, 1
S....imbibe prejudices...common to others DOUGLASS, FREDERICK, 18
S. sing most when...unhappy DOUGLASS, FREDERICK, 17
the real s....those who will accept it SEMBÈNE, OUSMANE, 4
voluntarily to submit to be s. PITT THE ELDER, WILLIAM, 5
When you make men s. EQUIANO, OLAUDAH, 3
slave trade suppression of the S. WILBERFORCE, WILLIAM, 2
sleep Better s. with a sober cannibal than a drunken Christian MELVILLE, HERMAN, 8
Blessings on him who invented s. CERVANTES, MIGUEL DE, 49
Can s. so soundly as the wretched slave SHAKESPEARE, WILLIAM, 272
Come, S.!...The poor man's wealth SIDNEY, PHILIP, 3
don't s. with happily married men EKLAND, BRITT, 1
Every time you s. with a boy MOTTOS AND SLOGANS, 13
haven't been to s. for...a year WAUGH, EVELYN, 16
I have come to the borders of s. THOMAS, EDWARD, 3
I make the s....my sword WATTS, ALAN, 6
make s. not so sound, as sweet HERRICK, ROBERT, 2
O s., O gentle sleep, / Nature's soft nurse SHAKESPEARE, WILLIAM, 256
S. and watchfulness...when immoderate, constitute disease HIPPOCRATES, 4
S., Death's twin-brother, knows not Death HALLAM, ARTHUR HENRY, 12
S. is a death BROWNE, THOMAS, 33
S. is good, death is better HEINE, HEINRICH, 1
S.! it is a gentle thing COLERIDGE, SAMUEL TAYLOR, 46
s. like a glass of water DOVE, RITA, 2
S., my body, sleep, my ghost MACNEICE, LOUIS, 19
s. of kings is on an anthill PROVERBS, 90
S. on /Blest pair MILTON, JOHN, 60
S. on, my Love, in thy cold bed KING, HENRY, 1
s. required...five minutes more PROVERBS, MODERN, 22
S.'s the only medicine that gives ease SOPHOCLES, 11
S....ties health and our bodies together DEKKER, THOMAS, 4
still she slept an azure-lidded s. KEATS, JOHN (1795–1821), 74
s., when...channels of perception are shut HERACLITUS, 8
s. with one form of economic system GORBACHEV, MIKHAIL, 16
There'll be time enough to s. HOUSMAN, A. E., 12
to s. with the same woman forever MORRISON, TONI, 26
sleeping all, are s. on the hill MASTERS, EDGAR LEE, 2
Let s. dogs lie PROVERBS, 301
s. and dreaming...perform vital biological functions STEVENS, ANTHONY, 5
There will be s. enough PROVERBS, 425
sleeping giant we have only awakened a s. YAMAMOTO ISOROKU, 1
sleeplessness S.. Homer. The sails tight MANDELSTAM, OSIP, 14
sleeps She s. alone at last BENCHLEY, ROBERT, 11
slepe S....nouryshment...of a sucking child PHAER, THOMAS, 1
slept David s. with his fathers BIBLE, 185
She...s. all night upon the money NORRIS, FRANK, 2
slepyng It is nought good a s. hound to wake CHAUCER, GEOFFREY, 38
slight Straight and s. as a young larch tree MARLOWE, CHRISTOPHER, 27
sling his s. was in his hand BIBLE, 228
slip There's many a s. PROVERBS, 418
slippers Same old s. LAMPTON, WILLIAM JAMES, 1
slitting When you dream of s. his throat COPE, WENDY, 2
slob just a lucky s. from Ohio GABLE, CLARK, 3
slogan democracy is just a s. GORBACHEV, MIKHAIL, 11
slogans If you feed people just with revolutionary s. KHRUSHCHEV, NIKITA, 11
Slough There was an old person of S. LEAR, EDWARD, 8
slow S. but sure PROVERBS, 383
slum if you've seen one city s. AGNEW, SPIRO T., 1
slumber A s. did my spirit seal WORDSWORTH, WILLIAM, 26
slumbers Golden s. kiss your eyes DEKKER, THOMAS, 2
s. of the virtuous man ADDISON, JOSEPH, 10
slumbr'ed s. here /While these visions did appear SHAKESPEARE, WILLIAM, 64
slums man in the s....is a man VARMA, MONIKA, 1
small It's a s. world PROVERBS, 281
misconception that s. is always more beautiful GERSTNER, LOUIS, JR., 2
The best things come in s. packages PROVERBS, 395
The known world was too s. for Alexander ALEXANDER THE GREAT, 3
small-company s. soul...inside our big company WELCH, JACK, 10
smallest a s. part of what is small ANAXAGORAS, 2
small pox take the S....by way of diversion MONTAGU, MARY WORTLEY, 2
small-talking Where in this s. world FRY, CHRISTOPHER, 7
smart He's not a particularly s. fish BRAUTIGAN, RICHARD, 4
I'm not s.. I try to observe BARUCH, BERNARD MANNES, 3
smattering s. of everything...knowledge of nothing DICKENS, CHARLES, 86
smell enjoy the s. of their own farts AUDEN, W. H., 33
I miss the s. of teargas THOMPSON, HUNTER S., 7
Nothing recalls the past so potently as a s. CHURCHILL, WINSTON, 40
smile And he smiled a kind of sickly s. HARTE, BRET, 3
a s. I could feel in my hip pocket CHANDLER, RAYMOND, 3
A s. that floated without support PROUST, MARCEL, 3
A s. that snapped back LEWIS, SINCLAIR, 8
nice s., but...iron teeth GORBACHEV, MIKHAIL, 1
one vast substantial s. DICKENS, CHARLES, 3
s. at perils past SCOTT, SIR WALTER, 22
S. if it kills you PETERS, TOM, 11
s. of a woman...dined off her husband DURRELL, LAWRENCE, 7
smiled He s. bunching his fat cheeks WEST, NATHANAEL, 2
smiles odd s. of most of the dead HOAGLAND, EDWARD, 7
robb'd that s. steals something from the thief SHAKESPEARE, WILLIAM, 470
s. that are worse than griefs FOLK VERSE, 55
smiling S. encouragement MANSFIELD, KATHERINE, 2
S. the boy fell dead BROWNING, ROBERT, 13
smite whosoever shall s. thee on thy right cheek BIBLE, 379
Smith Bessie S. shared with Louis Armstrong ARMSTRONG, LOUIS, 4
smoke I only s. on special occasions ANONYMOUS, 79
S. Gets in Your Eyes HAMMERSTEIN, OSCAR, II, 6
S., my friend SATIE, ERIK, 2
Ther can no great s. arise LYLY, JOHN, 9
There's no s. without fire PROVERBS, 421
when I don't s. I scarcely feel HOBAN, RUSSELL, 2
smokers S....inject and excuse idleness COLETTE, 2
smoking cease s....easiest thing I ever did TWAIN, MARK, 60
resolve to give up s., drinking and loving FREUD, CLEMENT, 2
s. can play a valuable role MORRIS, DESMOND, 1

s. cigars and...during all meals CHURCHILL, WINSTON, 57
s. does not cause lung cancer LEWIS, DREW, 1
S....is a shocking thing JOHNSON, SAMUEL, 64
S. kills SHIELDS, BROOKE, 1
What a blessing this s. is HELPS, ARTHUR, 1
smooth S. seas do not make skillful sailors PROVERBS, 14
smote they s. the city with the edge of the sword BIBLE, 311
smug insufferably s. pair of characters HAMMETT, DASHIELL, 5
smylere The s. with the knyf CHAUCER, GEOFFREY, 23
snake A s. came to my water-trough LAWRENCE, D. H., 15
bitten by a s. fears...string PROVERBS, 92
If a s. bites your neighbor PROVERBS, 12
There's a s. hidden in the grass VIRGIL, 28
The S. is living yet BELLOC, HILAIRE, 23
snapper-up s. of unconsidered trifles SHAKESPEARE, WILLIAM, 664
snare a s. in which the feet of women ADDAMS, JANE, 4
world's great s. SHAKESPEARE, WILLIAM, 79
Snark For the S. *was* a Boojum CARROLL, LEWIS, 26
sneer Who can refute a s. PALEY, WILLIAM, 1
sneeze s. in English...harbinger of misery DURRELL, GERALD, 2
sneezed Not to be s. at COLMAN, GEORGE, 4
sniffing S. the trees, /just another dog WILLIAMS, WILLIAM CARLOS, 6
sniper Then the s. turned over the dead body O'FLAHERTY, LIAM, 1
snob a s. in search of a class WAUGH, EVELYN, 3
He who...admires mean things is a S. THACKERAY, WILLIAM MAKEPEACE, 2
Indian s. reasons...calling an English person by his Christian name SCOTT, PAUL, 1
no s. welcomes another WAUGH, EVELYN, 1
snobbery that school of S. with Violence BENNETT, ALAN, 8
snobbish Don't be s., we seek to abolish LOGUE, CHRISTOPHER, 1
snobs His hatred of s. PROUST, MARCEL, 15
impudent s. who characterize themselves as intellectuals AGNEW, SPIRO T., 4
snore s. and you sleep alone BURGESS, ANTHONY, 6
snorer can't hear himself s. TWAIN, MARK, 44
snotgreen The s. sea JOYCE, JAMES, 32
snow both its national products, s. and chocolate, melt COREN, ALAN, 5
Like an army defeated /The s. hath retreated WORDSWORTH, WILLIAM, 78
S. was general all over Ireland JOYCE, JAMES, 10
The first fall of s. PRIESTLEY, J. B., 3
snows the s. of yesteryear VILLON, FRANÇOIS, 5
Snow White I used to be S. WEST, MAE, 21
snowy S., Flowy, Blowy ELLIS, GEORGE, 1
snubbed s. if an epidemic overlooks them HUBBARD, FRANK MCKINNEY, 1
snuff enjoy another pinch of s. BAILLY, JEAN SYLVAIN, 1
snug s. /As a bug /In a rug FRANKLIN, BENJAMIN, 8
soap S....and common sense are the best disinfectants OSLER, WILLIAM, 11
soap operas s. are...popular with...housebound women STEINEM, GLORIA, 14
soar S. not too high to fall MASSINGER, PHILIP, 3
sober as s. as a Judge FIELDING, HENRY, 6
England should be compulsorily s. MAGEE, WILLIAM CONNOR, 1
he that will go to bed s. FLETCHER, JOHN, 2
How do you look when I'm s. LARDNER, RING, 1
neither ingenious, s., nor kind EPITAPHS, 12
No s. man dances CICERO, 18
soccer s. is a grey game MARSH, RODNEY, 1
sociable I am a s. worker BEHAN, BRENDAN, 8
social a great s. and economic experiment HOOVER, HERBERT, 5
common core of personal and s. abilities GOLEMAN, DANIEL, 1
s. consequences of my actions SOROS, GEORGE, 1
S. event as an extension of business ANONYMOUS, 55
S. intercourse...a great power BLACKWELL, ELIZABETH, 1
Who is it that exercises s. power ORTEGA Y GASSET, JOSÉ, 31
social capital S. is critical to prosperity FUKUYAMA, FRANCIS, 6
S. is like a ratchet FUKUYAMA, FRANCIS, 7
social engineering s. resembles physical engineering POPPER, KARL, 8
socialism nothing in S....money will not cure DURANT, WILL, 18
Only s. would put up with it GORBACHEV, MIKHAIL, 9
Real s. is inside man MARX, KARL, 4
S....a finitizing of the Messianic ideal BUBER, MARTIN, 10
s....as a whole is threatened BREZHNEV, LEONID, 1
S. does not mean...more than better wages ORWELL, GEORGE, 38
s....must be about...smoked salmon MARSH, RICHARD, 1
S....must function again for a new generation DUBČEK, ALEXANDER, 1
s. with Chinese characteristics DENG XIAOPING, 20
s. would not lose its human face DUBČEK, ALEXANDER, 2
Under s. *all* will govern LENIN, VLADIMIR ILYICH, 20
socialist a s. manager...a Christian mathematician PARKER, SIR PETER, 2
A s. state in Germany is absolutely necessary HEYM, STEFAN, 1
construct the s. order LENIN, VLADIMIR ILYICH, 8
s. party...sole prospect of maintaining peace JAURÈS, JEAN, 3
today I shall cease being a s. LENIN, VLADIMIR ILYICH, 7
socialist revolution Hail the worldwide s. LENIN, VLADIMIR ILYICH, 10
socialists what are you s. going to do about me MACDONALD, RAMSAY, 3
social justice meet demands for s. with violence PALME, OLOF, 2
social science dark mass of s. BRADBURY, MALCOLM, 7
societies history of s....different political elites HOOK, SIDNEY, 1
range of human s. in time, the other in space LÉVI-STRAUSS, CLAUDE, 2
society a nonracial s. in a multiracial country DE KLERK, F. W., 2
a s. full of responsible men DELORS, JACQUES, 3
A s. in which women are taught HUBBARD, L. RON, 1
A s....of individuals...all capable of original thought MENCKEN, H. L., 10
A s. which is clamoring for choice MEAD, MARGARET, 3
can you go in s. and scream LAING, R. D., 16
human s. dared to think of...health TOYNBEE, ARNOLD, 9
in s. comfort, use, and protection BACON, FRANCIS (1561–1626), 94
It was an old s....long memory THEROUX, PAUL, 12
Man was formed for s. BLACKSTONE, WILLIAM, 6
modern man and...s. are completely dishonest LEARY, TIMOTHY, 6
Never speak disrespectfully of S. WILDE, OSCAR, 55
no such thing as S. THATCHER, MARGARET, 35
open s....unrestricted access to knowledge OPPENHEIMER, J. ROBERT, 3
S....can certainly do without ballplayers GARVEY, STEVE, 1
s. can crave lethal weapons BENNIS, WARREN, 3
S. damned the pulsing blood MU DAN, 1
S....deprives the more responsible Negro leaders RUSTIN, BAYARD, 1
seeking a Great S. in America JOHNSON, LYNDON BAINES, 4

S. goes on and on and on MACDONALD, RAMSAY, 4
S. has resembled a pyramid...turned upside down NAPOLEON III, 1
S. is an organism, not a machine GEORGE, HENRY, 3
s. is in the room DWORKIN, ANDREA, 2
S. is no comfort /To one not sociable SHAKESPEARE, WILLIAM, 133
S. is now one polish'd horde BYRON, LORD, 79
S. needs to condemn a little MAJOR, JOHN, 5
S....prepares crimes QUÉTELET, LAMBERT ADOLPHE JACQUES, 1
s. which acts as one big family SADAT, ANWAR AL-, 4
The great s. JOHNSON, LYNDON BAINES, 11
the sort of s. we're creating SINCLAIR, CLIVE, 6
the vanilla of s. SMITH, SYDNEY, 11
which s....is beneficial for all life NAESS, ARNE, 3
sociology S. is the science of talk KNIGHT, FRANK HYNEMAN, 6
S....the science with the greatest number of methods POINCARÉ, JULES HENRI, 5
Socrates S. is a doer of evil SOCRATES, 7
S. was the first to call philosophy down SOCRATES, 1
sod I'm a fat old s....untalented bastard JOHN, ELTON, 1
Sodom S. and...Gomorrah BIBLE, 125
the men of S. were wicked BIBLE, 124
sofa rather lie on a s. than sweep beneath it CONRAN, SHIRLEY, 2
soft landing so s. that it wouldn't break eggs BALANCHINE, GEORGE, 2
the s., delicious functions of nature STERNE, LAURENCE, 17
soil our record for s. destruction WALLACE, HENRY A., 2
Untilled s....thistles and thorns TERESA OF ÁVILA, SAINT, 4
solar s. and stellar systems could only kill you once CARLYLE, THOMAS, 3
sold *We* never s. no sex or sideburns HALEY, BILL, 1
soldier a s. among sovereigns SCOTT, SIR WALTER, 6
Ben Battle was a s. bold HOOD, THOMAS, 21
glazed eyes of a s. will think...before starting a war BISMARCK, PRINCE OTTO VON, 14
I never expect a s. to think SHAW, GEORGE BERNARD, 86
Like the old s. of the ballad MACARTHUR, DOUGLAS, 3
O mighty s., O man of war BERNARD OF CLAIRVAUX, SAINT, 2
s. who hated war RABIN, YITZHAK, 1
The s.'s body...a stock of accessories SAINT-EXUPÉRY, ANTOINE DE, 1
the s.'s greatest fear O'BRIEN, TIM, 5
worse the man the better the s. NAPOLEON I, 28
soldiers Old s. never die PROVERBS, 353
S. are citizens of death's grey land SASSOON, SIEGFRIED, 2
S. in peace are like CECIL, WILLIAM, 1
solemn great s. guns leisurely manipulated JONES, DAVID, 1
solicitor s. is a man who BATESON, DINGWALL, 1
whose s. has given me my brief GILBERT, W. S., 43
solid How...s. the best work still seems HEMINGWAY, ERNEST, 2
Solidarity s. was born...when the shipyard strike evolved WALESA, LECH, 2
solitary heard among the s. hills /Low breathings WORDSWORTH, WILLIAM, 84
He lived the life of a s. NEWTON, ISAAC, 2
Only s. men know the full joys of friendship CATHER, WILLA, 5
solitude In s. /What happiness MILTON, JOHN, 78
One can acquire everything in s. STENDHAL, 2
S. and melancholy CARTER, ANGELA, 3
s....a wild beast or a god BACON, FRANCIS (1561–1626), 30
S....is not humanity's highest state SACKS, JONATHAN, 4
S. is the playfield of Satan NABOKOV, VLADIMIR, 2
S. is un-American JONG, ERICA, 2
so companionable as s. THOREAU, HENRY DAVID, 40
s. sometimes is best society MILTON, JOHN, 83
s. was what I hoped for DE GAULLE, CHARLES, 12
worst s....destitute of sincere friendship BACON, FRANCIS (1561–1626), 9
You find in s. JIMÉNEZ, JUAN RAMÓN, 6
solo sweet, fairy-tale s. on an alto KEROUAC, JACK, 7
Solomon S. of saloons BROWNING, ROBERT, 4
Solomon Grundy S., /Born on Monday CHILDREN'S VERSE, 47
solve If I can't s. something GENEEN, HAROLD, 3
We do not s. them DEWEY, JOHN, 2
some S. have too much DYER, EDWARD, 1
someone Getting s. to do something for you SANFORD, CHARLES, JR., 4
somer In a s. seson LANGLAND, WILLIAM, 5
something difference...between having s. to say DEWEY, JOHN, 6
gentlemen, let us do s. today COLLINGWOOD, CUTHBERT, 1
I too hope to become "s." HITLER, ADOLF, 30
S. and Nothing produce each other LAOZI, 12
son An only s....might expect more indulgence GOLDSMITH, OLIVER, 20
examined your s.'s head...there's nothing there MUIR, FRANK, 1
I'm the s. of a painter RENOIR, JEAN, 4
O wonderful s., that can so 'stonish a mother! SHAKESPEARE, WILLIAM, 187
the S. of man coming...with power BIBLE, 425
what's a s. KYD, THOMAS, 2
song good s. about a whorehouse GUTHRIE, WOODY, 2
I have a s. to sing O GILBERT, W. S., 41
said what I need...in a s. DYLAN, BOB, 23
Sing a s. of sixpence CHILDREN'S VERSE, 55
s. of power came...I sang it ANONYMOUS, 62
s. that has sold half a million PORTER, COLE, 1
the s. that is sung in our hearts OUIDA, 3
without a s....road would never bend PRESLEY, ELVIS, 1
You have interrupted the old s. which lulled human misery JAURÈS, JEAN, 2
songs all our pretty s. COBAIN, KURT, 1
I liked to do the s. GERSHWIN, GEORGE, 1
Our sweetest s. are those that tell of saddest thought SHELLEY, PERCY BYSSHE, 23
Simple s., one-line lyrics, gimmicks COHN, NIK, 2
The Lord holds copyright on all s. DOYLE, RODDY, 5
The s. of the slave DOUGLASS, FREDERICK, 14
Where are the s. of Spring KEATS, JOHN (1795–1821), 78
son-in-law The s. also rises SELZNICK, DAVID O., 1
sonnet make my life as slick as a s. BANKHEAD, TALLULAH, 3
s. is a moment's monument ROSSETTI, DANTE GABRIEL, 7
son-of-a-bitch poor s. FITZGERALD, F. SCOTT, 2
s. named George Patton PATTON, GEORGE S., 3
sons of bitches Now we are all s. BAINBRIDGE, KENNETH T., 1
sophistry s. which insane remorse...no dialectic KIERKEGAARD, SØREN, 13
sorrow Down, thou climbing s. SHAKESPEARE, WILLIAM, 339
hang s., care'll kill a cat JONSON, BEN, 9
Much in s., oft in woe WHITE, HENRY KIRKE, 1
One scene of s. and of pain EQUIANO, OLAUDAH, 2
O S., wilt thou live with me HALLAM, ARTHUR HENRY, 11

Pure and complete s. is as impossible TOLSTOY, LEO, 14
S. and silence are strong LONGFELLOW, HENRY WADSWORTH, 26
s. is remembering happier things TENNYSON, ALFRED, 53
S. is tranquillity remembered in emotion PARKER, DOROTHY, 15

sorrowing the s. are nomads MCMURTRY, LARRY, 3

sorrows When s. come, they come not single spies SHAKESPEARE, WILLIAM, 214

sorry being s. & colored...redundant in the modern world SHANGE, NTOZAKE, 2
s. for all those who have lost THATCHER, MARGARET, 21

sought I s. them far and found them HOUSMAN, A. E., 24

soul a single human s. who cannot be matched DU BOIS, W. E. B., 5
become a living s. WORDSWORTH, WILLIAM, 14
gods approve /The depth...of the s. WORDSWORTH, WILLIAM, 38
Go, S., the body's guest RALEIGH, WALTER, 4
Hang there like fruit, my s. SHAKESPEARE, WILLIAM, 138
Heaven take my s., and England my bones SHAKESPEARE, WILLIAM, 329
highly dishonourable for a Reasonable S. BOYLE, ROBERT, 1
I am positive I have a s. STERNE, LAURENCE, 4
I have too great a s. BOOTH, JOHN WILKES, 1
I must place a motor in my s. DUNCAN, ISADORA, 5
It's good for one's s. to sit CATHER, WILLA, 6
life...in which the s. is in a ferment KEATS, JOHN (1795–1821), 84
man who says...lost his s. LAING, R. D., 5
my s. doth magnify the Lord BIBLE, 319
Never mind about my s....get my tie right JOYCE, JAMES, 40
Nobody can have the s. of me LAWRENCE, D. H., 29
O s., be changed into little water MARLOWE, CHRISTOPHER, 12
Part of My S. Went With Him MANDELA, WINNIE, 3
possessive outrage done to a free solitary human s. POWYS, JOHN COWPER, 2
s. descends...To accept the waking body WILBUR, RICHARD, 1
s. follows its own laws LEIBNIZ, GOTTFRIED WILHELM, 10
s....habitation of the devil EDWARDS, JONATHAN, 1
sigh'd his s. toward the Grecian tents SHAKESPEARE, WILLIAM, 623
S....individuality of each personal consciousness JAMES, WILLIAM, 15
S. is the rhythm o' sex DOYLE, RODDY, 6
s. of Ovid lives in...Shakespeare OVID, 1
S. of the Age JONSON, BEN, 3
Steel'd was that s. and by no misery mov'd WHEATLEY, PHILLIS, 2
the...essence of a human s. CARLYLE, THOMAS, 44
the s....a republic or commonwealth HUME, DAVID, 14
The s....has an interpreter...in the eye BRONTË, CHARLOTTE, 5
The s. is characterized by these capacities ARISTOTLE, 4
the s. is not more than the body WHITMAN, WALT, 35
The s. of music slumbers in the shell ROGERS, SAMUEL, 4
The s....remains as much *outside* ORTEGA Y GASSET, JOSÉ, 12
The s. selects her own Society DICKINSON, EMILY, 21
The voyage of the s. WHITMAN, WALT, 21
This grey, monotonous s. in the water LAWRENCE, D. H., 14
thou hast heard, O my s., the sound of the trumpet BIBLE, 246
Thy s. was like a star WORDSWORTH, WILLIAM, 47
turn'st mine eyes into my very s. SHAKESPEARE, WILLIAM, 198

souls every two s. are absolutely different GIBRAN, KAHLIL, 8
Most people sell their s. SMITH, LOGAN PEARSALL, 14
Our s. have sight of...immortal sea WORDSWORTH, WILLIAM, 55
People have invented s. GU CHENG, 1
s. originally one...seeks the half it lost CHILD, LYDIA MARIA, 3
the s. of five hundred...Newtons NEWTON, ISAAC, 1
Tis an awkward thing to play with s. BROWNING, ROBERT, 42
Two s. dwell, alas! in my breast GOETHE, JOHANN WOLFGANG VON, 17
Two s. in one DU BARTAS, GUILLAUME, 9
Two s. with but a single thought HALM, FRIEDRICH, 1
Two s. with but a single thought LOVELL, MARIA, 1

sound A s. mind in a sound body LOYOLA, IGNATIUS OF, 1
s....scared the shit out of people WILMER, VALERIE, 1
The last s. on the worthless earth FAULKNER, WILLIAM, 3

sounded last one s. kinda high RUTH, BABE, 2

sounds deep s. from the stomach CHURCHILL, WINSTON, 81
Until I die there will be s. CAGE, JOHN, 9
When it s. good ELLINGTON, DUKE, 7

soup I live on good s., not fine words MOLIÈRE, 17
serve people s....believe it is chocolate GRAPPELLI, STEPHANE, 1
S. of the evening, beautiful Soup CARROLL, LEWIS, 21

sour How s. sweet music is SHAKESPEARE, WILLIAM, 523

south Behold the spirit of the musky S. LAZARUS, EMMA, 2
go s. in the winter ELIOT, T. S., 50
I faced the S. with dread STEINBECK, JOHN, 27
The S. creates the civilizations DURANT, WILL, 15
the S. is...certainly Christ-haunted O'CONNOR, FLANNERY, 3

South Africa racial policy of the Union of S. HITLER, ADOLF, 9
S., renowned both far and wide CAMPBELL, ROY, 1
S. will not allow the double standards BOTHA, P. W., 1
the greatest waste of time in S. BIKO, STEPHEN, 2
The paradox in S. TUTU, DESMOND, 7
The spectre of Belsen...is haunting S. MANDELA, NELSON, 19
victory for all the people of S. MANDELA, NELSON, 9
you have mandated us to change S. MANDELA, NELSON, 8

South Africans force S. to commit national suicide BOTHA, P. W., 2
White S. are not demons TUTU, DESMOND, 11

southern S. life is...more grotesque O'CONNOR, FLANNERY, 1
the workings of the S. mind BRYSON, BILL, 11

Southerners S. could despise blacks BRYSON, BILL, 10

sovereign Here lies our s. lord the King ROCHESTER, 2ND EARL OF, 1
That s. of insufferables WILDE, OSCAR, 2
The S. has...three rights BAGEHOT, WALTER, 8
The s. is absolute CATHERINE THE GREAT, 3
two s. masters, *pain* and *pleasure* BENTHAM, JEREMY, 2

Soviet S. citizen...state of permanent inner dialogue BUKOVSKY, VLADIMIR, 2
S. people want full-blooded...democracy GORBACHEV, MIKHAIL, 6

Soviets All Power to the S. MOTTOS AND SLOGANS, 37

Soviet Union S. was forced to recognize reality THATCHER, MARGARET, 14
the three ugly sisters...in the S. HURD, DOUGLAS, 1
when asked to leave, the S. has always left NKOMO, JOSHUA, 3

sow that man hath the s. by the...ear CRANMER, THOMAS, 1

soweth whatsoever a man s., that shall he also reap BIBLE, 100

space annihilate but s. and time POPE, ALEXANDER, 63
Empty s. and points of light WINTERSON, JEANETTE, 4
Outer s. is no place BONHAM-CARTER, LADY VIOLET, 1
S....is big. Really big ADAMS, DOUGLAS, 7
S. isn't remote at all HOYLE, FRED, 2
S.—the final frontier STAR TREK, 2
s....the uncontrollable mystery MCLUHAN, MARSHALL, 9
s. will treat you kindly VON BRAUN, WERNHER, 1

spaceship passenger on the s., Earth FULLER, R. BUCKMINSTER, 3
spade never so merely a s. as the word FRY, CHRISTOPHER, 9
When I see a s. I call it a spade WILDE, OSCAR, 48
spades S. take up leaves FROST, ROBERT, 2
Spain Beware S., of your own Spain VALLEJO, CÉSAR, 1
I have the most evil memories of S. ORWELL, GEORGE, 14
I prefer a Red S. CALVO SOTELO, JOSÉ, 1
S....a country in search of an ideology BRENAN, GERALD, 1
S....appearance of a constitutional democratic regime CAMBÓ, FRANCISCO, 1
S. will either win as a free democratic country IBÁRRURI, DOLORES, 1
spam wonderful s. MONTY PYTHON'S FLYING CIRCUS, 4
Spaniards S. are those people CÁNOVAS DEL CASTILLO, ANTONIO, 2
The time has come for S. NARVÁEZ, RAMÓN MARÍA, 1
Spanish I speak S. to God CHARLES V, 4
Nothing is so like a rising of S. revolutionaries PÉREZ GALDÓS, BENITO, 8
The S. are rarely sentimental about suffering MATTHIESSEN, PETER, 5
spare I can't s. this man; he fights LINCOLN, ABRAHAM, 39
S. all I have FARQUHAR, GEORGE, 9
S. the rod PROVERBS, 385
S. your ships ARTEMISIA, 1
spared I have not s....my life PETER THE GREAT, 2
spareth he that s. his rod hateth his son BIBLE, 457
spark that little s. of celestial fire...conscience WASHINGTON, GEORGE, 6
sparkle That youthful s. in his eyes is caused by his contact lenses REAGAN, RONALD, 3
sparrow a s. alight upon my shoulder THOREAU, HENRY DAVID, 45
sparrowhawks S., Ma'am VICTORIA, 2
spasm a lonely s. of helpless agony JAMES, WILLIAM, 29
spat Today I s. in the Seine PATTON, GEORGE S., 4
speak as we s....we find our ideas IONESCO, EUGÈNE, 8
I'll s. for the man NIXON, RICHARD, 38
let him now s. BOOK OF COMMON PRAYER, 24
Never s. ill of the dead PROVERBS, 342
Never s. of yourself...art of pleasing GONCOURT, EDMOND DE, 1
S. in French when you can't think of the English CARROLL, LEWIS, 32
some...s....before they think LA BRUYÈRE, JEAN DE, 15
S. roughly to your little boy CARROLL, LEWIS, 9
S. softly and carry a big stick ROOSEVELT, THEODORE, 11
s. to everyone you meet BISHOP, ELIZABETH, 9
s....to your silent ashes CATULLUS, 7
S. up for yourself, or...end up a rug WEST, MAE, 25
S. when you are spoken to PROVERBS, 386
"S. when you're spoken to!" the Red Queen...interrupted CARROLL, LEWIS, 50
Whereof one cannot s. WITTGENSTEIN, LUDWIG, 9
speaks no one...s....except the scientists ROSZAK, THEODORE, 10
spear His s....were but a wand MILTON, JOHN, 32
spearmint Does the S. Lose Its Flavor ROSE, BILLY, 2
specialist Choose your s....choose your disease NEWSPAPERS, 33
S.—A man who knows more...about less MAYO, WILLIAM JAMES, 4
s....One who knows everything about something BIERCE, AMBROSE, 48
The s. is a man who fears the other subjects FISCHER, MARTIN H., 21
specialists s....tend to think in grooves MORGAN, ELAINE, 1
speciality s. of the happy journey MORRIS, JAN, 3
special relationship a s. CHURCHILL, WINSTON, 14
species s. cannot be immortal LYELL, CHARLES, 1
s. I wouldn't mind seeing vanish BENNETT, ALAN, 4
spectacles Putting on the s. of science DOBIE, J. FRANK, 2
spectator rather as a S. of mankind ADDISON, JOSEPH, 12
specter A s. is haunting Europe...communism MARX, KARL, 20
speculator s....observes the future, and acts BARUCH, BERNARD MANNES, 6
speech A s. is like a love affair MANCROFT, STORMONT SAMUEL, 3
disturbing influence of something outside...intended s. FREUD, SIGMUND, 33
Giving the s. is fun MEYER, LAWRENCE H., 1
his bodily presence is weak, and his s. contemptible BIBLE, 166
I have strange power of s. COLERIDGE, SAMUEL TAYLOR, 50
large tracts of human s. are nothing JAMES, WILLIAM, 25
S. is civilization itself MANN, THOMAS, 17
Speak the s., I pray you SHAKESPEARE, WILLIAM, 188
s....seasoned with salt BIBLE, 27
S. was given...to disguise his thoughts TALLEYRAND, CHARLES MAURICE DE, 5
S. was not given to man ARAGON, LOUIS, 1
The most precious things in s. RICHARDSON, RALPH, 2
The true use of s....to conceal GOLDSMITH, OLIVER, 6
speeches he tries on s. like a man trying on ties CHURCHILL, WINSTON, 5
more than whisky into my s. CHURCHILL, WINSTON, 83
solved by s. and majority votes BISMARCK, PRINCE OTTO VON, 12
speechmaker fellow who says, "I'm no s." HUBBARD, FRANK MCKINNEY, 3
speed enjoy s. to the absolute limit MOSS, STIRLING, 2
S. in operating...the achievement HOWARD, RUSSELL JOHN, 4
S. is a great asset COBB, TY, 3
The splendor...the beauty of s. MARINETTI, FILIPPO TOMMASO, 4
spell s. it Vinci and pronounce it Vinchy TWAIN, MARK, 43
speller depends upon the...fancy of the s. DICKENS, CHARLES, 100
spend Let's S. the Night Together JAGGER, MICK, 8
s. a single day really well KEMPIS, THOMAS À, 7
s. your way out of a recession CALLAGHAN, JIM, 3
Spender S....an open...and simple-minded poet SPENDER, STEPHEN, 2
spermatozoa A million million s....one poor Noah HUXLEY, ALDOUS, 29
spheres Fifty-five crystal s. geared...God's crankshaft STOPPARD, TOM, 8
spice S. up your life SPICE GIRLS, THE, 1
Variety's the very s. of life COWPER, WILLIAM, 36
spider almost like a s. DU BARTAS, GUILLAUME, 8
spiders I saw the s. marching through the air LOWELL, ROBERT, 2
spinach s., and I say the hell with it WHITE, E. B., 7
spirit bound in the s. BIBLE, 20
essence of S. is Freedom HEGEL, G. W. F., 8
Give me the s. SHAKESPEARE, WILLIAM, 257
human s. is in prison BERDYAEV, NIKOLAI, 3
my s. found outlet in the air JOHNSON, AMY, 1
Oh, empty s. and full soul MACHADO, ANTONIO, 13
O that the s. could remain LOWELL, ROBERT, 17
S. is dreaming in man KIERKEGAARD, SØREN, 10
There's nought...so much the s. calms BYRON, LORD, 47
The s. burning but unbent BYRON, LORD, 95
The s. of the Lord God is upon me BIBLE, 224

the s. that always denies GOETHE, JOHANN WOLFGANG VON, 16
spirits Houses of any antiquity...possessed with s. HAWTHORNE, NATHANIEL, 2
Ill s. walk in white DONNE, JOHN, 28
in good s....when he's well dressed DICKENS, CHARLES, 45
s. are enslaved which serve...evil SHELLEY, PERCY BYSSHE, 37
S. when they please /Can either sex assume MILTON, JOHN, 34
Those who cannot see the s....dead CHANDRA, VIKRAM, 2
white s. and black spirits engaged in battle TURNER, NAT, 1
spirituality Pure s....soil of science, is thinking HEGEL, G. W. F., 13
spiritually one man gains s....whole world gains GANDHI, MAHATMA, 20
Spiro Agnew S. is not a household name AGNEW, SPIRO T., 2
spite Hold no man's actions up to s. FREIDANK, 2
S. will make a woman NAVARRE, MARGARET OF, 2
spits Who s. against the wind PROVERBS, 460
spleen S. can subsist on any...food HAZLITT, WILLIAM, 7
splendid Ours was a kind of s. isolation KELLY, GENE, 3
splendour small line of inconceivable s. RADCLIFFE, ANN, 3
split When I s. an infinitive CHANDLER, RAYMOND, 1
spoil s. a painting to finish it DELACROIX, EUGÈNE, 2
spoke He s., and loos'd our heart in tears WORDSWORTH, WILLIAM, 1
She s., and turned away VIRGIL, 4
spokespersons s. for all the oppressed DAVIS, ANGELA, 7
spontaneous set a high value on s. kindness JOHNSON, SAMUEL, 71
spoon S. feeding ...teaches us nothing but the shape of the spoon FORSTER, E. M., 17
sport In love as in s., the amateur status GRAVES, ROBERT, 5
no way s. is so important OVETT, STEVE, 1
s....a foreigner is least likely to take to HALBERSTAM, DAVID, 1
Serious s....is war minus the shooting ORWELL, GEORGE, 30
S. is cut and dried DAVIS, STEVE, 1
s. with Amaryllis in the shade MILTON, JOHN, 122
to make s. for our neighbors AUSTEN, JANE, 37
sports "s. and politics don't mix" BARNES, STUART, 1
S. figures are to the '70s WARHOL, ANDY, 10
the childish nature will require s. PLATO, 6
sportsman When a man wantonly destroys...call him a s. KRUTCH, JOSEPH WOOD, 8
spot Out, damned s. SHAKESPEARE, WILLIAM, 413
spouse good s. but a bad husband GARCÍA MÁRQUEZ, GABRIEL, 4
spring Away from thee did I s. NIETZSCHE, FRIEDRICH WILHELM, 40
bad-cinema s. PYNCHON, THOMAS, 1
can S. be far behind SHELLEY, PERCY BYSSHE, 8
hounds of s. are on winter's traces SWINBURNE, ALGERNON CHARLES, 4
I hear s. is nice LI QINGZHAO, 4
In the S. a young man's fancy TENNYSON, ALFRED, 47
It is s., moonless night in the small town THOMAS, DYLAN, 23
It Might as Well Be S. HAMMERSTEIN, OSCAR, II, 12
S. /Flow down the woods SACKVILLE-WEST, VITA, 5
S. has returned. RILKE, RAINER MARIA, 5
S. is come home THOMPSON, FRANCIS, 6
S. is not on the willow tips LI JINFA, 1
s. now comes unheralded by the return of the birds CARSON, RACHEL, 3
Sweet s. HERBERT, GEORGE, 24
S. /Will be a little late this year LOESSER, FRANK, 2
there would be S. no more HALLAM, ARTHUR HENRY, 13
The year's at the s. BROWNING, ROBERT, 68
sprite gentle, fleeting, wav'ring s. HADRIAN, 1
square deal I stand for the s. ROOSEVELT, THEODORE, 16
squire Bless the s. and his relations DICKENS, CHARLES, 88
stage All the world's a s. SHAKESPEARE, WILLIAM, 105
I have come on s. PASTERNAK, BORIS, 3
Once you get on s., everything is right PRICE, LEONTYNE, 2
On s. I have to make love JOPLIN, JANIS, 4
The s. is my best medicine BAKER, JOSEPHINE, 4
this great s. of fools SHAKESPEARE, WILLIAM, 363
stagflation a sort of "s." situation MACLEOD, IAIN, 1
St. Agnes S.' Eve—Ah, bitter chill it was KEATS, JOHN (1795–1821), 69
stains Placed on our backs indelible s. JACKSON, MATTIE J., 1
S. are not seen at night PROVERBS, 57
stairs Halfway down the s. MILNE, A. A., 14
Stalin I like old Joe S. STALIN, JOSEPH, 3
S. hates...all your top people STALIN, JOSEPH, 1
stamp to order a new s. ...with my face on it CHARLES I (1887–1922), 1
stand a firm place to s. ARCHIMEDES, 5
here I s. /in...this small garden TANG XIANZU, 1
Here s. I LUTHER, MARTIN, 6
no time to s. and stare DAVIES, W. H., 7
S. by Your Man SHERRILL, BILLY, 1
S. on two phone books BRYSON, BILL, 7
S. your ground...if they mean to have a war PARKER, JOHN, 1
standard a s. of rebellion JAMES II, 3
Stanislavsky S....said was: "Avoid generalities." HOPKINS, ANTHONY, 1
staphococcal colonies s. were undergoing lysis FLEMING, ALEXANDER, 5
star Any little pinhead...is called a "s." BOGART, HUMPHREY, 10
Being a s. has made it possible DAVIS, SAMMY, JR., 1
It's far easier to become a s. again BAKER, JOSEPHINE, 6
one s. differeth from another...in glory BIBLE, 163
relate the life of a s. to...a man CLARKE, ARTHUR C., 1
Remember you are a s. DE MILLE, CECIL B., 4
small s. shines in the darkness PROVERBS, 49
s....spell your name in Karachi MOORE, ROGER, 1
Sunset and evening s. TENNYSON, ALFRED, 5
the company really has only one s. BALANCHINE, GEORGE, 3
the s. moves not but in his sphere SHAKESPEARE, WILLIAM, 216
Star-Chamber I will make a S. matter of it SHAKESPEARE, WILLIAM, 626
star-cross'd pair of s. lovers SHAKESPEARE, WILLIAM, 559
stardom achieve s. and...you can relax EVERLY, PHIL, 1
Getting s. and, once you've got it, keeping it SIMONE, NINA, 2
staring I don't know what I'm s. at GOODMAN, BENNY, 1
starry Under the wide and s. sky STEVENSON, ROBERT LOUIS, 23
stars empty spaces /Between s. FROST, ROBERT, 5
falling s....excrements of dirty little star-gods POWELL, JOHN WESLEY, 3
I am greater than the s. TEMPLE, WILLIAM, 3
it was near the s. RAMBERT, DAME MARIE, 3
Look at the s. HOPKINS, GERARD MANLEY, 7
S. lay like yellow pollen YOUNG, ANDREW (1885–1971), 1
s. /Regard me sadly PLATH, SYLVIA, 4
S....robbed men of their souls ASIMOV, ISAAC, 2
Tempt not the s. FORD, JOHN (1586–1640?), 2
the field of the s. is so vast FRANCE, ANATOLE, 7
The s. grew bright in the winter sky MASEFIELD, JOHN, 3
the s. in their courses BIBLE, 312

The s. will still remain BULGAKOV, MIKHAIL, 12
three s....moving about Jupiter GALILEO, 9
We are...the s.' tennis-balls WEBSTER, JOHN, 7
what is the s. O'CASEY, SEAN, 3
stars and stripes They wrapped me in...s. DOS PASSOS, JOHN, 14
star-spangled banner that s. yet wave KEY, FRANCIS SCOTT, 2
start s. again, somewhere else MAJOR, JOHN, 4
starvation underscored his demand for s. BALANCHINE, GEORGE, 4
starve good men s. for want of impudence DRYDEN, JOHN, 7
He helped to bury whom he helped to s. POPE, ALEXANDER, 44
otherwise I would s., naked HAYES, HELEN, 2
To s. is to be of media interest FARAH, NURUDDIN, 2
starving Why is he s. to death GELDOF, BOB, 2
state a s. in the proper sense of the word LENIN, VLADIMIR ILYICH, 18
A s. is then well constituted HEGEL, G. W. F., 18
A s. without the means of...change BURKE, EDMUND, 37
In a s. worthy of the name there is no liberty LENIN, VLADIMIR ILYICH, 15
not good enough to have just any old s. ASHRAWI, HANAN, 1
One man...put the s. to rights ENNIUS, QUINTUS, 2
Our s. cannot be severed MILTON, JOHN, 88
s. has no business in the bedrooms TRUDEAU, PIERRE, 1
s. is not only a necessary institution BISMARCK, PRINCE OTTO VON, 16
Star for every S. WINTHROP, ROBERT CHARLES, 1
That s. is a state of slavery GILL, ERIC, 1
The s. is the march of God HEGEL, G. W. F., 24
The s....withers away ENGELS, FRIEDRICH, 4
The s. with the prettiest name BISHOP, ELIZABETH, 6
where's the s. beneath the firmament DU BARTAS, GUILLAUME, 2
While the s. exists there can be no freedom LENIN, VLADIMIR ILYICH, 19
state education S. in Spain MADARIAGA Y ROGO, SALVADOR DE, 1
stately homes go back to thy s. of England LAWRENCE, D. H., 25
statement Any general s. is like a check POUND, EZRA, 3
states S. as great engines move slowly BACON, FRANCIS (1561–1626), 95
Thirteen S....erecting one great American system HAMILTON, ALEXANDER, 4
statesman abroad you're a s. MACMILLAN, HAROLD, 2
A s. is a politician POMPIDOU, GEORGES, 1
s. thinks of us and tomorrow EISENHOWER, DWIGHT D., 23
statesmen If only s. had hearts as sincere as their words BAKER, JOSEPHINE, 2
S. are far too busy making speeches RUSSELL, BERTRAND, 57
s. of the world who...have Doomsday weapons LAING, R. D., 7
static class people as s. and dynamic WAUGH, EVELYN, 20
station A s. like the herald Mercury /New lighted... SHAKESPEARE, WILLIAM, 200
statistics Politicians use s....drunken man uses lamp-posts LANG, ANDREW, 1
S. will prove anything MOYNIHAN, NOËL, 1
There are two kinds of s. STOUT, REX, 1
The s. of suicide INGE, WILLIAM RALPH, 16
unrewarded millions without whom S....a bankrupt science SMITH, LOGAN PEARSALL, 16
We are just s., born to consume HORACE, 16
statue No s....put up to a critic SIBELIUS, JEAN, 3
s. of the onehandled adulterer Nelson JOYCE, JAMES, 37
statues bodies...melted down to pay for political s. OWEN, WILFRED, 4
stature man of giant s. NEHRU, JAWAHARLAL, 1
status quo Challenging the s. HAMEL, GARY, 7
Don't keep... defending the s. MCLUHAN, MARSHALL, 14
staunch Nothing can still or s. BUSTA, CHRISTINE, 1
stay s. me with flagons BIBLE, 490
stay-at-home Sweet S. DAVIES, W. H., 5
steak he wanted s. and they offered spam MALAMUD, BERNARD, 1
steal A man who will s. *for* me ROOSEVELT, THEODORE, 28
if we're smart...s. from great directors KIESLOWSKI, KRZYSZTOF, 1
Thou shalt not s.; an empty feat CLOUGH, ARTHUR HUGH, 4
To s. from the rich is...sacred RUBIN, JERRY, 1
stealing s. an office and stealing a purse ROOSEVELT, THEODORE, 14
s. bases on their bellies TWAIN, MARK, 7
steals s. the common from the goose FOLK VERSE, 58
Who s. my purse steals trash SHAKESPEARE, WILLIAM, 483
stealth greatest pleasure I know, is to do a good action by s. LAMB, CHARLES, 25
steel Don't waste good s. SASSOON, SIEGFRIED, 5
Give them the cold s. ARMISTEAD, LEWIS ADDISON, 1
steer s. and avoid death WHITE, E. B., 5
stem a rod out of the s. of Jesse BIBLE, 202
step For your s. following and damned if I look back JOYCE, JAMES, 2
One s. forward, two steps back LENIN, VLADIMIR ILYICH, 13
one small s. for man ARMSTRONG, NEIL, 3
s. into the same rivers HERACLITUS, 6
Take a s. forward, lads CHILDERS, ERSKINE, 1
The first s. PROVERBS, 404
While others make one s., we make ten NEWSPAPERS, 15
stereotype The resort to s....chief strategy of the bigot RUSTIN, BAYARD, 2
stereotypes abandon established s. and outdated views GORBACHEV, MIKHAIL, 7
stew It's like s....cook it properly ADAMS, GERRY, 4
w'en de s. is smokin' hot DUNBAR, PAUL LAURENCE, 2
stick When my s. touches the air KOUSSEVITZKY, SERGE, 1
sticks S. and stones may break my bones PROVERBS, 387
stigma Any s....to beat a dogma GUEDALLA, PHILIP, 1
still a s. small voice BIBLE, 190
A s. tongue PROVERBS, 145
s. point of the turning world ELIOT, T. S., 16
S. waters run deep PROVERBS, 388
still lifes Painting s....like contemplation or meditation FISH, JANET, 1
stilly Oft in the s. night MOORE, THOMAS, 11
stirring s. times we live in HARDY, THOMAS, 10
stitch A s. in time PROVERBS, 146
St. Louis Meet me in S....at the fair STERLING, ANDREW B., 1
stocking a glimpse of s. /Was...something shocking PORTER, COLE, 2
stock market fear the tyranny of a s. CHERNOW, RON, 1
s. adopts a thesis and tests it SOROS, GEORGE, 9
stoic man is...either a s. or a satyr PINERO, ARTHUR, 2
stole She s. everything but the cameras WEST, MAE, 2
stolen S. sweets are always sweeter HUNT, LEIGH, 4
S. sweets are best CIBBER, COLLEY, 6
s. waters are sweet BIBLE, 456

stomach The s. is a bottomless pit AUSTER, PAUL, 5
The way to a man's heart is through his s. FERN, FANNY, 1
stone A rolling s. gathers no moss PUBLILIUS SYRUS, 6
Fling but a s., the giant dies GREEN, MATTHEW, 1
if someone throws a s....respond with food ANONYMOUS, 53
Leave no s. unturned ANONYMOUS, 50
the s. Christ leaned against MELVILLE, HERMAN, 20
the s. taken away from the sepulchre BIBLE, 301
the s. word fell AKHMATOVA, ANNA, 5
This is the s. which was set at nought BIBLE, 8
stones s. kissed by the English dead OWEN, WILFRED, 8
the s. would immediately cry out BIBLE, 345
stony fell upon s. places BIBLE, 402
stop s. everyone from doing it HERBERT, A. P., 2
S. the World, I Want to Get Off NEWLEY, ANTHONY, 1
s. upon the shores of Fusang TAO QIAN, 5
The way to s. the spread of HIV MCKELLEN, IAN, 3
stopped it s. short—never to go again WORK, HENRY CLAY, 2
stories She likes s. that make her cry KELLER, HELEN, 2
tell ourselves s. in order to live DIDION, JOAN, 7
The seaman tells s. of winds PROPERTIUS, SEXTUS, 1
stork I wish I were a s. MARTIN IV, 1
storm a mighty s....to freshen us up CHEKHOV, ANTON, 17
S. and Stress KLINGER, FRIEDRICH MAXIMILIAN VON, 1
S. in a Teacup BERNARD, W. B., 1
story a s. in the likeness of my life BECKETT, SAMUEL, 16
A s. is a formula for extracting meaning from chaos WIDEMAN, JOHN EDGAR, 3
For never was a s. of more woe SHAKESPEARE, WILLIAM, 558
Not that the s. need be long THOREAU, HENRY DAVID, 4
S. is just the spoiled child of art JAMES, HENRY, 20
s. that starts with an earthquake GOLDWYN, SAMUEL, 9
that a true s....It is now WENDERS, WIM, 1
That's the s. of our life VOINOVICH, VLADIMIR, 5
The s. is like the wind VAN DER POST, LAURENS, 1
To write a s. in just five minutes ATXAGA, BERNARDO, 2
storys S. to rede ar delitabill BARBOUR, JOHN, 1
storyteller good s....has a good memory COBB, IRVIN S., 2
storytelling S. and copulation...amusement in the South WARREN, ROBERT PENN, 2
s....a public art O'CONNOR, FRANK, 5
stoutness I see no objection to s. GILBERT, W. S., 11
St. Paul's Say I am designing S. BENTLEY, EDMUND CLERIHEW, 3
St. Petersburg the final stone...in the foundation of S. PETER THE GREAT, 1
Strabismus Dr S. (Whom God Preserve) of Utrecht MORTON, J. C., 1
straight S. down the Crooked Lane HOOD, THOMAS, 1
straightforwardness S., without...propriety, becomes rudeness CONFUCIUS, 17
strait It matters not how s. the gate HENLEY, WILLIAM ERNEST, 1
straitened face s. circumstances at home JUVENAL, 7
stranded s. in a hungerland /of great prosperity JORDAN, JUNE, 7
strange it's a jolly s. world BENNETT, ARNOLD, 8
strangeness The saturating s. of the place HERR, MICHAEL, 5
stranger a s. in a strange land BIBLE, 68
S....ask thyself the question DICKENS, CHARLES, 31
strangers among s....preserve appearances EMERSON, RALPH WALDO, 68
strategic maximize one's s. degrees of freedom OHMAE, KENICHI, 5
s. repositioning...a way of life ANSOFF, IGOR, 1
strategies s. fail because they are overripe OHMAE, KENICHI, 3
strategy S. is buying a bottle of fine wine MUIR, FRANK, 6
think about s. as revolution PRAHALAD, C. K., 2
Stratford S....suggests powdered history HALSEY, MARGARET, 1
strawberry I'm not a s. EDWARD VII, 2
Like s. wives BACON, FRANCIS (1561–1626), 7
straying s. away from the church BRUCE, LENNY, 1
stream s. of our thought...like a river JAMES, WILLIAM, 23
Still glides the S. WORDSWORTH, WILLIAM, 91
street don't do it in the s. CAMPBELL, MRS. PATRICK, 2
S. Fighting Man JAGGER, MICK, 9
the s. which is called Straight BIBLE, 12
streets s. are paved with gold COLMAN, GEORGE, 3
S. full of water BENCHLEY, ROBERT, 7
Where the s. have no name U2, 2
strength all our s. and all /Our sweetness MARVELL, ANDREW, 15
My s....as the strength of ten TENNYSON, ALFRED, 59
S. and a gift for physical feats HOAGLAND, EDWARD, 10
We are not now that s. TENNYSON, ALFRED, 84
strenuous doctrine of the s. life ROOSEVELT, THEODORE, 13
stress an exaggerated s. on not changing one's mind MAUGHAM, SOMERSET, 16
s. and...violence is worse at home STEINEM, GLORIA, 9
stretched things which he s. TWAIN, MARK, 35
strike A s. has to reach a climax BJELKE-PETERSEN, JOHANNES, 1
difficult to go on s. GEORGE-BROWN, LORD, 1
no right to s. against the public safety COOLIDGE, CALVIN, 16
S. while the iron is hot PROVERBS, 389
twenty-four-hour s....lasting at least five days MUIR, FRANK, 4
strikes I cannot tolerate s. BOND, ALAN, 2
s. where it doth love SHAKESPEARE, WILLIAM, 503
strings I had two s. to my bow FIELDING, HENRY, 12
There are s....in the human heart DICKENS, CHARLES, 12
stripling yon pale s. SCOTT, SIR WALTER, 16
strive Always s. to excel RORTY, RICHARD, 3
I s. to be brief HORACE, 2
men should s. to learn THURBER, JAMES, 16
needst not s. /...to keep alive CLOUGH, ARTHUR HUGH, 6
striven s. not to laugh at human actions SPINOZA, BARUCH, 6
strives s. to touch the stars SPENSER, EDMUND, 11
striving what are we actually s. for DE JOUVENEL, BERTRAND, 1
strivings parcel of vain s. THOREAU, HENRY DAVID, 25
stroke To s. a platitude until it purrs MARQUIS, DON, 10
You can s. people with words FITZGERALD, F. SCOTT, 29
strokes Different s. for different folks PROVERBS, 479
strong be s. and of a good courage BIBLE, 39
disarm the s. and arm the weak FRANCE, ANATOLE, 2
s. enough to bear the misfortunes of others LA ROCHEFOUCAULD, FRANÇOIS, 4
The s. demand, contend, prevail JOHNSON, GEORGIA DOUGLAS, 1
waxed s. in spirit BIBLE, 321
strongest S. minds /Are often those WORDSWORTH, WILLIAM, 80
the s. man...stands most alone IBSEN, HENRIK, 3

I don't think s. is harmful...indispensable to talent MOREAU, JEANNE, 1
I was never affected by...s. MEIR, GOLDA, 7
Man owes his s. to his creativity DE BONO, EDWARD, 3
Never let s. hide its emptiness HAMMARSKJÖLD, DAG, 5
no s. like failure DYLAN, BOB, 9
Nothing fails like s. MCGINLEY, PHYLLIS, 1
real s. is...a good day's work FORTE, CHARLES, 1
s. and miscarriage are empty sounds JOHNSON, SAMUEL, 18
s....Beyond the dreams of avarice BELLOC, HILAIRE, 19
S. can deaden an organization's responses TICHY, NOEL M., 4
s. comes from ignoring the obvious HOLDSWORTH, TREVOR, 1
s. depends...upon individual initiative and exertion PAVLOVA, ANNA, 4
secret of my s. MAXWELL, ELSA, 1
S....first three-piece suit, first lawsuit WILLIAMS, ROBIN, 5
S., for women...partly failure JONG, ERICA, 6
S.. Four flights Thursday morning WRIGHT, WILBUR, 1
s. in ad writing is the product BERNBACH, WILLIAM, 7
S. is counted sweetest DICKINSON, EMILY, 3
S....is having ten honeydew melons STREISAND, BARBRA, 1
S. is man's god AESCHYLUS, 8
S. is relative ELIOT, T. S., 42
s. is to be measured...by the obstacles WASHINGTON, BOOKER T., 5
s. leads to complacency HELLER, ROBERT, 1
S. never satisfies me GARCÍA LORCA, FEDERICO, 8
s....nothing like we had anticipated INGE, WILLIAM, 1
S....sole...judge of right and wrong HITLER, ADOLF, 29
s. will depend...each unique stakeholder HICKMAN, CRAIG R., 7
S....you have to recover from NORMAN, MARSHA, 2
The penalty of s. ASTOR, NANCY, 4
The Sweet Smell of S. LEHMAN, ERNEST, 1
'Tis...Heaven's to give s. POPE, ALEXANDER, 70
you probably don't care enough about s. MCCORMACK, MARK, 13

successes Observing your own and your competitors' s. LAUDER, ESTÉE, 3

successful He who is s. is good ECO, UMBERTO, 4
I'm s....because I'm a good businesswoman MADONNA, 4
It was very s. VON BRAUN, WERNHER, 2
two reasons why I am s. GRABLE, BETTY, 1
we do everything we can to appear s. LA ROCHEFOUCAULD, FRANÇOIS, 11

sucker s. an even break FIELDS, W. C., 8
There's a s. born every minute BARNUM, P. T., 1

sudden you shouldn't make a s. move LETTERMAN, DAVID, 1

sue If they get you...s. the bastards LAKER, FREDDIE, 3
I won't s. you...I'll ruin you VANDERBILT, CORNELIUS, 1

Suez Canal S....flowing through my drawing room EDEN, CLARISSA, 1

suffer Can they *s.* BENTHAM, JEREMY, 1
Do not s....wickedness YOUNG, BRIGHAM, 4
easier to s. in obedience to a human command BONHOEFFER, DIETRICH, 3
let's s. on the heights HUGO, VICTOR, 5
none of you s. for your opinions or religion CHARLES II, 13
Rather s. than die LA FONTAINE, JEAN DE, 4
s. fools gladly BIBLE, 167
s. me not...see thy holy city RICHARD I, 4

sufferance s. is the badge of all our tribe SHAKESPEARE, WILLIAM, 599

suffered love a place the less for having s. AUSTEN, JANE, 27

suffering About s....never wrong, /The Old Masters AUDEN, W. H., 36
accept s. as part of...life with Christ AQUINO, CORAZON, 1
alleviate s....not to prolong life BARNARD, CHRISTIAAN, 1
attained the title of /"s. humanity" FERLINGHETTI, LAWRENCE, 2
He preferred s. in freedom LONDON, JACK, 15
I love the majesty of human s. VIGNY, ALFRED DE, 4
s. did not ennoble MAUGHAM, SOMERSET, 35
the appalling total of human s. BORGES, JORGE LUIS, 5

suffragettes we s. aspire to be...ambassadors of freedom to women PANKHURST, CHRISTABEL, 2

suggestion take s. as a cat laps milk SHAKESPEARE, WILLIAM, 644

suicide a s. hung from every rafter MELVILLE, HERMAN, 22
commits s. when it adopts a creed HUXLEY, T. H., 5
committed s. 25 years after his death BEAVERBROOK, MAX AITKEN, LORD, 3
committed s....failure to realize their passions FROMM, ERICH, 10
dallied with the thought of s. JAMES, WILLIAM, 36
If you must commit s. BORROW, GEORGE HENRY, 1
No one ever lacks a good reason for s. PAVESE, CESARE, 6
nothing ever interfered with...National S. Day MORRISON, TONI, 18
one truly serious philosophical problem...s. CAMUS, ALBERT, 16
s. as a regulator of nature LUDWIG, EMIL, 1
s. in this man's town RUNYON, DAMON, 2
s. is a test of height in civilization ELLIS, HAVELOCK, 7
s. is God's best gift to man PLINY THE ELDER, 2
S. is not a remedy GARFIELD, JAMES A., 2
s. really *validates*...the life VIDAL, GORE, 2
the s. braves death ARISTOTLE, 17
thought of s. is a...comfort NIETZSCHE, FRIEDRICH WILHELM, 9

suicides There are desperate s. and crafty suicides HOAGLAND, EDWARD, 3

suit My s. is pale yellow. My nationality is French WILLIAMS, TENNESSEE, 4

suits I live for meeting with the S. MADONNA, 3

sumer S. is icumen FOLK VERSE, 4

summer Now the peak of s.'s past DAY-LEWIS, CECIL, 4
S. afternoon...two most beautiful words JAMES, HENRY, 38
The Long, Hot S. RAVETCH, IRVING, 1
the s. is ended, and we are not saved BIBLE, 248
'Tis now the s. of your youth MOORE, EDWARD, 3

summertime S. /And the livin' is easy GERSHWIN, IRA, 4

sun before you let the s. in THOMAS, DYLAN, 24
better for s. and moon to drop NEWMAN, JOHN HENRY, 4
between me and the s. DIOGENES, 4
Busy old fool, unruly S. DONNE, JOHN, 44
enjoy'd the s....lived light in the spring ARNOLD, MATTHEW, 3
Follow thy fair s. CAMPION, THOMAS, 4
got the s. in the mornin' and the moon at night BERLIN, IRVING, 3
I loved the s. WORDSWORTH, WILLIAM, 82
let not the s. go down upon your wrath BIBLE, 62
Lovely day: s....weed-killer ELGAR, EDWARD, 1
Mother, give me the s. IBSEN, HENRIK, 11
Neither...s. nor death can be looked at LA ROCHEFOUCAULD, FRANÇOIS, 7
on which the s. never sets NORTH, CHRISTOPHER, 2
s. came dazzling thro' the leaves TENNYSON, ALFRED, 70
s. destroys /The interest of what's happening LARKIN, PHILIP, 8
self-same s. that shines upon his court SHAKESPEARE, WILLIAM, 670
shadow'd livery of the burnish'd s. SHAKESPEARE, WILLIAM, 601
s. had risen to hear him crow ELIOT, GEORGE, 7
s. is...rising on America CLINTON, BILL, 5

sit out in the s. to become darker JACKSON, MICHAEL, 1
S. remains fixed in the centre GALILEO, 3
S. shrinks to a dull red dwarf CLARKE, ARTHUR C., 2
s. turns the heart's agitation into tranquility MA LIHUA, 1
Thank heavens the s. has gone in SMITH, LOGAN PEARSALL, 12
The S. Also Rises HEMINGWAY, ERNEST, 23
The S. came up upon the left COLERIDGE, SAMUEL TAYLOR, 37
The s. has only memory of flame MODAYIL, ANNA SUJARTHA, 1
The s. in my dominion never sets SCHILLER, FRIEDRICH VON, 9
The s. is coming down to earth MEREDITH, GEORGE, 12
the s. is high LI QINGZHAO, 1
The s. shone, having no alternative BECKETT, SAMUEL, 12
Till the s. grows cold TAYLOR, BAYARD, 1
sunbeams That's the only s., money BELLOW, SAUL, 18
sunbonnet the s. as well as the sombrero has helped to settle this...land FERBER, EDNA, 1
sunburn S. is very becoming COWARD, NOEL, 23
Sunday And O she was the S. CLARKE, AUSTIN, 2
It was a S. afternoon, wet and cheerless DE QUINCEY, THOMAS, 4
The feeling of S. is the same everywhere, RHYS, JEAN, 4
sundial s., and I make a botch BELLOC, HILAIRE, 27
sung I have s. women in three cities POUND, EZRA, 2
sunglasses It's dark...we're wearing s.. Hit it BELUSHI, JOHN, 1
sunlight s. as a kind of cosmetic effulgence WYNDHAM, JOHN, 1
The s. on the garden MACNEICE, LOUIS, 23
sunny side Keep your s. up BROWN, LEW, 1
suns The mass starts into a million s. DARWIN, ERASMUS, 2
sunsets I have a horror of s. PROUST, MARCEL, 23
sunshine Flaunt of the s. WHITMAN, WALT, 13
superfluity S. of Good Things ALLAINVAL, ABBÉ D', 1
superior s....because one sees the world in an odious light CHATEAUBRIAND, RENÉ, 10
the s. officers were white MOSLEY, WALTER, 7
What the s. man seeks CONFUCIUS, 27
superiority S. we've always had...ask is equality ASTOR, NANCY, 9
The s. of one man's opinion JAMES, HENRY, 33
superiors In America everybody...has no...s. RUSSELL, BERTRAND, 52
super-Jew I'm S. BRUCE, LENNY, 3
superlative wouldn't touch a s....with an umbrella PARKER, DOROTHY, 19
Superman I teach you the S. NIETZSCHE, FRIEDRICH WILHELM, 38
S. comics...deep cry for help MAMET, DAVID, 4
supermodel I don't like the word s. CAMPBELL, NAOMI, 3
supernatural Some element of the s....poetry WOOLF, VIRGINIA, 22
superstition Men will fight for s. HYPATIA, 2
s. has ...received much ruder shocks BURKE, EDMUND, 34
s. in avoiding superstition BACON, FRANCIS (1561–1626), 69
S. is the poetry of life GOETHE, JOHANN WOLFGANG VON, 23
S. is the religion of feeble minds BURKE, EDMUND, 50
S. may be defined as constructive religion TYNDALL, JOHN, 1
S. sets the whole world in flames VOLTAIRE, 27
superstitions s. of the human mind VOLTAIRE, 46
supervisor the s. has the power to compel PFEFFER, JEFFREY, 2
support s. me when I am...wrong MELBOURNE, LORD, 2
s. of...the decent opinion of mankind MCCARTHY, EUGENE J., 2
supposing s. him to be the gardener BIBLE, 302
suppress No, don't s. BULGAKOV, MIKHAIL, 2
suppressed s. animation which played over her face TOLSTOY, LEO, 4
supreme only s. /in misery MILTON, JOHN, 64
Our s. governors, the mob WALPOLE, HORACE, 3
sups He who s. with the devil PROVERBS, 257
sure Be always s. you're right CROCKETT, DAVY, 1
nothing is s., everything is possible DRABBLE, MARGARET, 5
surgeon first attribute of a s....curiosity HOWARD, RUSSELL JOHN, 2
good s. operates with his hand DUMAS, ALEXANDRE, 4
one little touch of a s.'s lancet MONTAIGNE, MICHEL DE, 32
s....sawes off th'infested part DU BARTAS, GUILLAUME, 7
s....tempted to supplant...Nature MAUDSLEY, HENRY, 2
the best s....is he who makes the fewest mistakes COOPER, ASTLEY, 1
vain s. is like a milking stool MORRIS, ROBERT TUTTLE, 5
wounded s. plies the steel ELIOT, T. S., 19
surgeons S. and anatomists see no beautiful women TWAIN, MARK, 10
S. must be very careful DICKINSON, EMILY, 4
surgery S. is the ready motion...experienced hands GALEN, 2
ways for avoiding s. MORRIS, ROBERT TUTTLE, 3
surgical The s. cycle in woman OSLER, WILLIAM, 12
surly I have slipped the s. bonds of earth MAGEE, JOHN GILLESPIE, 1
surpass s....advanced countries in science and technology DENG XIAOPING, 13
surprise The Sound of S. BALLIETT, WHITNEY, 2
surprised it is *I* who am s.; you are merely astonished WEBSTER, NOAH, 1
S. by joy WORDSWORTH, WILLIAM, 39
surprising a combination of the s. and the beautiful BEETHOVEN, LUDWIG VAN, 7
s....a man who could write it would LITTLEWOOD, JOHN, 3
surrender if you s. your personality BLYDEN, EDWARD WILMOT, 2
No terms except unconditional and immediate s. GRANT, ULYSSES S., 6
Nothing less than the unconditional s. ROOSEVELT, FRANKLIN D., 19
we will never s. our heritage PAISLEY, IAN, 1
survey When I s. the wondrous Cross WATTS, ISAAC, 9
survival s. of the European order in jeopardy BISMARCK, PRINCE OTTO VON, 4
S. of the fittest SPENCER, HERBERT, 5
the s. of the unfittest ICAHN, CARL, 1
We are s. machines DAWKINS, RICHARD, 1
survive obligation to s. is owed...to that cosmos SAGAN, CARL, 7
One can s. everything...except death WILDE, OSCAR, 18
What will s. of us is love LARKIN, PHILIP, 20
survived I s. SIEYÈS, ABBÉ, 2
Susanna O, S. FOSTER, STEPHEN, 3
suspect I rather s. her of being in love CHURCHILL, JENNIE, 3
suspense This s. is terrible WILDE, OSCAR, 57
suspicion S. always haunts the guilty mind SHAKESPEARE, WILLIAM, 294
S....haunts the guilty mind PROVERBS, 94
sustainability world cannot avoid needing s. SHAPIRO, ROBERT B., 5
sustainable development policy challenge of s. NORGAARD, RICHARD, 2
S. challenges...industrial and commercial system BENNIS, WARREN, 6
swagman Once a jolly s. camped by a billy-bong PATERSON, A. B., 1
swallow One s. does not make a summer PROVERBS, 357
swallowe One s. prouveth not that summer NORTHBROOKE, JOHN, 1

swallow-flights Short s. of song HALLAM, ARTHUR HENRY, 5
swallows I hate a man who s. it LAMB, CHARLES, 13
S. certainly sleep all winter JOHNSON, SAMUEL, 117
swamp fellow with the s. shanty...cabbagey acres HOAGLAND, EDWARD, 5
That Indian s. in the wilderness JEFFERSON, THOMAS, 44
swan s. in the evening moves over the lake COLUM, PADRAIG, 1
What time's the next s. SLEZAK, LEO, 1
Swanee 'Way down upon the S. River FOSTER, STEPHEN, 5
swans s. seem whiter if...crowes be by DU BARTAS, GUILLAUME, 3
S. sing before they die COLERIDGE, SAMUEL TAYLOR, 61
swarm A s. of high and low agents MAURA, ANTONIO, 1
swear s. not by the moon SHAKESPEARE, WILLIAM, 543
swearword A foreign s. is THEROUX, PAUL, 6
sweat we haven't gone through this s. for nothing FITZGERALD, F. SCOTT, 7
Sweden S. should be...the people's home HANSSON, PER ALBIN, 1
suddenly anything seemed possible in S. PALME, OLOF, 1
sweet A s. attractive kind of grace ROYDON, MATTHEW, 1
How s. are looks that ladies bend TENNYSON, ALFRED, 60
How s. the moonlight sleeps SHAKESPEARE, WILLIAM, 621
How s. the name of Jesus NEWTON, JOHN, 1
S. is pleasure after pain DRYDEN, JOHN, 23
so dainty s. as lovely melancholy BEAUMONT, FRANCIS, 8
S. Swan of Avon SHAKESPEARE, WILLIAM, 28
S. things are bad for the teeth SWIFT, JONATHAN, 35
s. will be the flow'r COWPER, WILLIAM, 25
sweeter what is s. than honey BIBLE, 313
sweetes' S. li'l' feller STANTON, FRANK L., 1
sweetest The s. thing that ever grew WORDSWORTH, WILLIAM, 27
sweets I sing the s....of Hasty-Pudding BARLOW, JOEL, 1
S. with sweets war not SHAKESPEARE, WILLIAM, 563
swell a s. is nothing but a phonus bolonus RUNYON, DAMON, 5
swimming S. for his life GLADSTONE, WILLIAM EWART, 10
swine a s. to show you where the truffles are ALBEE, EDWARD, 7
swing S. low sweet chariot FOLK VERSE, 16
Swiss if the S. had designed these mountains THEROUX, PAUL, 10
The S....are not a people so much as a...business FAULKNER, WILLIAM, 6
Swithin St. S.'s Day, if thou dost rain FOLK VERSE, 60
Switzerland S....five hundred years of democracy and...The cuckoo clock WELLES, ORSON, 7
S. only seems small KINNOCK, NEIL, 7
sword draw the s. with a clear conscience WILLIAM II, 2
his sore and great and strong s. BIBLE, 208
Joan of Arc resisting a s....piercing her chest GRAHAM, MARTHA, 2
My s....shall succeed me BUNYAN, JOHN, 25
s....responsible for more misery...than opium GANDHI, MAHATMA, 14
they that take the s. shall perish with the sword BIBLE, 439
Whoso pulleth out this s. of this stone MALORY, THOMAS, 1
Without a sign his s. the brave man draws POPE, ALEXANDER, 76
swords beat their s. into plowshares BIBLE, 198
Keep up your bright s. SHAKESPEARE, WILLIAM, 468
s. shall play the orators for us MARLOWE, CHRISTOPHER, 21
s. taller than ourselves QABBANI, NIZAR, 2
They shall beat their s. into plowshares BIBLE, 443
sworn I am s. brother, sweet, /To grim Necessity SHAKESPEARE, WILLIAM, 522
symbol a...s. of commitment and surrender ABRAHAMS, PETER, 4
symbols night's starr'd face, /Huge cloudy s. of a high romance KEATS, JOHN (1795–1821), 80
sympathetic To be s. without discrimination FIRBANK, RONALD, 3
sympathize s. with everything, except suffering WILDE, OSCAR, 62
sympathy S. for the Devil JAGGER, MICK, 10
S....lay over the gathering like a woolly blanket BRADBURY, MALCOLM, 1
the modern s. with invalids WILDE, OSCAR, 44
symphony s. means slavery in any jazzman's dictionary MEZZROW, MEZZ, 3
The s. must be like the world SIBELIUS, JEAN, 2
synergy S. takes place best in structure KLINE, NANCY, 5
syngen to seyn, to s. and to rede CHAUCER, GEOFFREY, 31
syringe a hypodermic s. of my own BISHOP, ELIZABETH, 1
system present s....subordinates the weaker sex MILL, JOHN STUART, 14
systematic enormous s. buildings KIERKEGAARD, SØREN, 15
s. occupation of territory FRANCO, FRANCISCO, 3
systems Our little s. have their day HALLAM, ARTHUR HENRY, 18
Simple s. give rise to complex behavior GLEICK, JAMES, 3

t The "t." is silent ASQUITH, MARGOT, 4
table put them at a t. together CHURCHILL, WINSTON, 69
tables t. of stone, and a law BIBLE, 85
taboos inroads against the t....lowering her neckline WEST, MAE, 1
taciturn You came, t., with nothing to give WHITMAN, WALT, 28
tact t. is making...feel at home PROVERBS, MODERN, 21
tactful Being t. in audacity COCTEAU, JEAN, 4
tail A case of the t. dogging the wag PERELMAN, S. J., 8
taint I cannot t. with fear SHAKESPEARE, WILLIAM, 415
tainted the supply is not t. SCOTT, C. P., 1
take You can't t. it with you PROVERBS, 469
takeover the downside risk on a t. HANSON, LORD, 1
takeovers The...best t. are...hostile GOLDSMITH, JAMES, 4
takes It t. all sorts PROVERBS, 284
tale A t. never loses PROVERBS, 147
A t. should be judicious, clear, succinct COWPER, WILLIAM, 7
t. to tell of the hardihood...of my companions SCOTT, CAPTAIN, 1
talent A t. to amuse COWARD, NOEL, 8
man has t. and cannot use it WOLFE, THOMAS, 5
no...great t. without great willpower BALZAC, HONORÉ DE, 5
no substitute for t. HUXLEY, ALDOUS, 43
T. alone cannot make a writer GOETHE, JOHANN WOLFGANG VON, 1
T. develops in quiet places GOETHE, JOHANN WOLFGANG VON, 26
the difference between t. and genius ALCOTT, LOUISA MAY, 5
the most extraordinary collection of t. KENNEDY, JOHN FITZGERALD, 16
t. instantly recognizes genius DOYLE, ARTHUR CONAN, 18
t. is...good stories about lawyers GRISHAM, JOHN, 1
T. wins games...teamwork wins championships JORDAN, MICHAEL, 1
unless they...have t., and are crippled GRANDMA MOSES, 1
Wherever did you get your t. from HARRISON, TONY, 1
Why hast thou /held t. above my head PORTER, PETER, 1

talents If you have great t., industry will improve them REYNOLDS, SIR JOSHUA, 2
We need t. more than the intellect HANDY, CHARLES, 8
tales t....so dear BAYLY, THOMAS HAYNES, 2
talk first t. is of the weather JOHNSON, SAMUEL, 36
If you want me to t. for ten minutes WILSON, WOODROW, 28
I t. it best through an interpreter TWAIN, MARK, 12
It would t.: /Lord how it talk't BEAUMONT & FLETCHER, 13
I want to t. like a lady SHAW, GEORGE BERNARD, 78
T. doesn't cook rice PROVERBS, 39
T. had feet...gossip had wings WALKER, MARGARET, 3
the need to t. is a primary impulse CERVANTES, MIGUEL DE, 27
the t. slid north...the talk slid south KIPLING, RUDYARD, 15
They...t. who never think PRIOR, MATTHEW, 12
T. of the devil PROVERBS, 392
t. well but not too wisely MAUGHAM, SOMERSET, 2
Two may t....yet never really meet CATHERWOOD, MARY, 1
we never t. about anything except me WILDE, OSCAR, 7
talk'd So much they t. CHURCHILL, CHARLES, 10
talked He t. on for ever COLERIDGE, SAMUEL TAYLOR, 5
one thing...worse than being t. about WILDE, OSCAR, 59
The more you are t. about RUSSELL, BERTRAND, 8
talker good t.—learn to listen MORLEY, CHRISTOPHER DARLINGTON, 8
talkers fluent t....not always the justest thinkers HAZLITT, WILLIAM, 15
talking Everyone knows of the t. artists ANDERSON, SHERWOOD, 2
for thirty-five years he had not stopped t. CRICK, FRANCIS, 1
if you ain't t. about him, ain't listening BRANDO, MARLON, 3
I wouldn't be ...t. to someone like you CARTLAND, BARBARA, 6
People t. without speaking SIMON, PAUL, 4
T. and eloquence are not the same JONSON, BEN, 21
T.'s something you can't do judiciously HAMMETT, DASHIELL, 2
Tallulah Bankhead T. barged down the Nile BROWN, JOHN MASON, 2
tambourine Hey! Mr T. Man DYLAN, BOB, 12
tamed I have t. men of iron ALBA, DUKE OF, 1
tangerine t. trees and marmalade skies LENNON & MCCARTNEY, 14
tango this t.-dancing female O'CONNELL, WILLIAM HENRY, 1
tank leading from the top of a t. YELTSIN, BORIS, 1
tanks I was interested in t. USTINOV, PETER, 4
tanned getting more t. and more tired PEGLER, WESTBROOK, 1
tap Some people t. their feet PRESLEY, ELVIS, 3
tar-baby T. ain't sayin' nuthin' HARRIS, JOEL CHANDLER, 2
tarmac t. over the whole of England CHANNON, PAUL, 1
Tarzan Me T. BURROUGHS, EDGAR RICE, 1
task a really difficult t. for a nation OSSIETZKY, CARL VON, 2
Our t....to defend the Holy Church CHARLEMAGNE, 1
the t....one dare not start BAUDELAIRE, CHARLES, 5
tasks best ways of avoiding necessary and even urgent t. GALBRAITH, J. K., 10
Tasmanians the T., who never committed adultery, are now extinct MAUGHAM, SOMERSET, 23
taste 60s contributed to...incredible malaise of t. FLUSSER, ALAN, 1
bad t. is better than no taste BENNETT, ARNOLD, 2
go on about...good t. ORTON, JOE, 12
great common sense and good t. CAESAR, JULIUS, 1
If you want to see bad t. LE CORBUSIER, 6
Matters of t. must be felt JEKYLL, LADY, 1
no t. when you married me SHERIDAN, RICHARD BRINSLEY, 14
satisfy t....satisfy the demands of utility CHESNEAU, ERNEST, 1
T. all...hand the knowledge down SNYDER, GARY, 12
T. does not come by chance REYNOLDS, SIR JOSHUA, 5
T. has no systems and no proofs SONTAG, SUSAN, 7
The t. was that of the little crumb of madeleine PROUST, MARCEL, 9
Things sweet to t. prove in digestion sour SHAKESPEARE, WILLIAM, 511
T. is the best judge CÉZANNE, PAUL, 1
T. is the feminine of genius FITZGERALD, EDWARD, 1
willing to t. any drink once CABELL, JAMES BRANCH, 1
worse t., than in a churchyard JOWETT, BENJAMIN, 2
tasted never t. what is bitter PROVERBS, 51
Sir, you have t. two whole worms SPOONER, WILLIAM ARCHIBALD, 5
tastes cater to...pubescent t. of the public WEXLER, JERRY, 1
Our t. greatly alter JOHNSON, SAMUEL, 108
There is no accounting for t. PROVERBS, 412
t. may not be the same SHAW, GEORGE BERNARD, 57
tatter'd Through t. clothes small vices do appear SHAKESPEARE, WILLIAM, 362
taught You t. me language SHAKESPEARE, WILLIAM, 643
tavern A t. chair is the throne JOHNSON, SAMUEL, 58
There is a t. in the town FOLK VERSE, 24
tavernes knew the t. wel in every toun CHAUCER, GEOFFREY, 11
tax A hateful t. JOHNSON, SAMUEL, 10
An Englishman's home is his t. haven NEWSPAPERS, 5
a t. on pianos for the incompetent SITWELL, EDITH, 6
immoral and outrageous act to t. me STOPES, MARIE, 3
It is better to t. 25 per cent BJELKE-PETERSEN, JOHANNES, 2
one thing to say to the t. increasers REAGAN, RONALD, 24
power to t. involves...power to destroy MARSHALL, JOHN, 2
To t. and to please...is not given BURKE, EDMUND, 62
taxation No t. without respiration SCHAFFER, BOB, 1
T. and representation are inseparably united PRATT, SIR CHARLES, 1
T. without representation is tyranny OTIS, JAMES, 1
taxes collect legal t. from illegal money CAPONE, AL, 1
read my lips: no new t. BUSH, GEORGE, 4
The avoidance of t....still carries...reward KEYNES, JOHN MAYNARD, 21
The little people pay t. HELMSLEY, LEONA, 1
t. now prove /...love for the people MORRIS, CHARLES, 1
taxi driver When a t. recognizes me FORTE, CHARLES, 2
taxpayer The t. is someone who works for the federal government REAGAN, RONALD, 49
tea is there honey still for t. BROOKE, RUPERT, 5
it is just like having a cup of t. PAYNE, CYNTHIA, 1
Take some more t. CARROLL, LEWIS, 12
T. for two, and two for tea HARBACH, OTTO, 1
When I makes t. I makes tea JOYCE, JAMES, 33
teach For every person wishing to t. SELLAR, W. C., 8
He who shall t. the Child to Doubt BLAKE, WILLIAM, 7
He who wishes to t. ORTEGA Y GASSET, JOSÉ, 2
He who would t. men to die MONTAIGNE, MICHEL DE, 6
I'd like to t. the world to sing ADVERTISEMENTS, 7
no matter what you t. them first JOHNSON, SAMUEL, 154
Nothing is easier to t. ADAMS, HENRY, 9
private master comes to t. us DICKENS, CHARLES, 62
T. him to think for himself WOLLSTONECRAFT, MARY, 5
To t. how to live without certainty RUSSELL, BERTRAND, 6

To t. well is to be a lifelong student COLE, JOHNETTA BETSCH, 1
t. taste or genius by rules REYNOLDS, SIR JOSHUA, 1
t. them in the city VOINOVICH, VLADIMIR, 4
T. us to care ELIOT, T. S., 7
t. you how to make strawberry jam MITCHELL, JULIAN, 1
You can't t. an old dog PROVERBS, 470

teacher art of the t. to awaken joy EINSTEIN, ALBERT, 16
good clinical t. is...a Medical School HOLMES, OLIVER WENDELL, 13
I did not become a t....sense of vocation BRAITHWAITE, EDWARD R., 1
t. affects eternity ADAMS, HENRY, 6
t....have maximal authority and minimal power SZASZ, THOMAS, 8
t....is a senior student OSLER, WILLIAM, 7
t. is one who...admired teachers MENCKEN, H. L., 47
true t. defends his pupils ALCOTT, BRONSON, 1

teachers give the t. stipends worthy of the pains LATIMER, HUGH, 2
We t. can only help...as servants MONTESSORI, MARIA, 2

teaches He who cannot, t. SHAW, GEORGE BERNARD, 59

teaching T. has ruined more American novelists VIDAL, GORE, 16
T. is like turning a grindstone ELGAR, EDWARD, 3

team Form a t., not a committee MCCORMACK, MARK, 1
the other t. usually beats itself WILLIAMS, DICK, 1
women...better t. members than men DORRINGTON, SUE, 1

teams T....primary force of organizations KLINE, NANCY, 6

teamwork T. doesn't appear magically RILEY, PAT, 1
T. is a constant balancing act CAMPBELL, SUSAN M., 1

tears His big t., for he wept full well SHELLEY, PERCY BYSSHE, 20
I ain't got no t....spent them WILSON, AUGUST, 1
I forbid my t. SHAKESPEARE, WILLIAM, 217
If you have t., prepare to shed them SHAKESPEARE, WILLIAM, 310
in a flood of t. and a Sedan chair DICKENS, CHARLES, 102
launched into this vale of t. BLACKMORE, R. D., 4
No more t. now MARY, QUEEN OF SCOTS, 2
No t. in the writer FROST, ROBERT, 3
T. fall in my heart /As rain falls VERLAINE, PAUL, 5
The bitterest t. shed over graves STOWE, HARRIET BEECHER, 3
the land of t. SAINT-EXUPÉRY, ANTOINE DE, 4
T., idle tears TENNYSON, ALFRED, 93
T. left unshed /turn to poison /in the ducts WALKER, ALICE, 2
T. such as angels weep MILTON, JOHN, 36
T. were to me CRISP, QUENTIN, 9
view the world as a vale of t. BROWNING, ROBERT, 31

teas T., /Where small talk dies SHELLEY, PERCY BYSSHE, 12

tease He who attempts to t. the cobra NASH, OGDEN, 3

technical prowess t. of nations such as India GATES, BILL, 7

technique perfect t....not noticed at all CASALS, PABLO, 6

techniques the t. gradually became common KELLY, GENE, 5

technological a t. assault is being prepared YOXEN, EDWARD, 3
t. equivalent of unsafe sex DUDLEY EDWARDS, RUTH, 1

technologies As we push our t. NORGAARD, RICHARD, 1

technology For a successful t., reality must take precedence FEYNMAN, RICHARD PHILLIPS, 2
T. feeds on itself TOFFLER, ALVIN, 2
The development of t. will leave only one problem KRAUS, KARL, 4
t....important to modern man COPPOLA, FRANCIS FORD, 3
t....indistinguishable from magic CLARKE, ARTHUR C., 4
T. is reshaping this economy DALEY, WILLIAM, 1
T. is the knack FRISCH, MAX, 1
T. travels with people GESCHKE, CHUCK, 1

tedious t. as a twice-told tale POPE, ALEXANDER, 85

teeming city of t. millions and multi-millionaires BANERJEE, SUDHANSU MOHAN, 1

teenage T. boys, goaded by their surging hormones PAGLIA, CAMILLE, 1

teenagers t. sitting around...I'd rather be dancing MITCHELL, JONI, 5

teeth I had braces on my t. and got high marks MACDONALD, BETTY, 1
I'll dispose of my t. as I see fit PERELMAN, S. J., 3
It is necessary to clean the t. frequently JEAN BAPTIST DE LA SALLE, 1
peculiarly sharp white t. STOKER, BRAM, 1
Removing the t. will cure something PROVERBS, MODERN, 20
Show not your t. PROVERBS, 87
to lose one's t....a catastrophe WHEELER, HUGH, 1

teething Adam and Eve...escaped t. TWAIN, MARK, 29

teetotaller a beer t., not a champagne teetotaller SHAW, GEORGE BERNARD, 23

teetotallers T. lack the sympathy DAVIES, W. H., 6

Teflon like a T. frying pan: nothing sticks REAGAN, RONALD, 10

telephone He really needs to t. PARKER, DOROTHY, 40

television amazed that people will actually choose to sit in front of the t. WALKER, ALICE, 35
Everybody watching the t. PLÀ, JOSEP, 1
I hate t....as much as peanuts WELLES, ORSON, 4
no plain women on t. FORD, ANNA, 1
T. brought the brutality of war into...the living room MCLUHAN, MARSHALL, 3
T....half Greek and half Latin SCOTT, C. P., 2
T. is for appearing on COWARD, NOEL, 34
T....permits you to be entertained in your living room FROST, DAVID, 1
t. programs are...chewing gum for the eyes BROWN, JOHN MASON, 1
T.—the drug of the nation DISPOSABLE HEROES OF HIPHOPRISY, 1
T. was the ultimate evidence of cultural anemia HEATH, ROY A. K., 3

television commercial country...turned into a gigantic t. EISENHOWER, DWIGHT D., 2

tell always t. what one sees PÉGUY, CHARLES PIERRE, 5
I t. for precisely what it is WHITMAN, WALT, 11
T. me whom you live with CHESTERFIELD, LORD, 16
you never can t.. That's a principle SHAW, GEORGE BERNARD, 94

tells man never t. you anything SHAW, GEORGE BERNARD, 106

temper A tart t. never mellows with age IRVING, WASHINGTON, 6
Never lose your t. with the Press PANKHURST, CHRISTABEL, 5

temperament He who lacks t. must...ornament KRAUS, KARL, 26

temperance She belongs to a T. Society TAYLOR, ELIZABETH, 1
T. and labor are the two real physicians of man ROUSSEAU, JEAN-JACQUES, 11
T. is the love of health LA ROCHEFOUCAULD, FRANÇOIS, 32
T. is the nurse of chastity WYCHERLEY, WILLIAM, 1

temple go into the t. to save his life BIBLE, 447
in the very t. of delight KEATS, JOHN (1795–1821), 57

temples t. made with hands BIBLE, 18

tempt thou shalt not t. the Lord thy God BIBLE, 372

temptation best way to get the better of t. GRAHAM, CLEMENTINA STIRLING, 1
he resisted every t. to magical thought FREUD, SIGMUND, 49
I never resist t. SHAW, GEORGE BERNARD, 85
Many a dangerous t....fine gay colours HENRY, MATTHEW, 1

not over-fond of resisting t. BECKFORD, WILLIAM, 2
only way to get rid of a t. WILDE, OSCAR, 61
The great t. in these difficult days JACKSON, JESSE, 5
tempter The t. or the tempted, who sins most SHAKESPEARE, WILLIAM, 428
tempts Not all that t....is lawful prize GRAY, THOMAS, 16
ten about t. minutes WELLINGTON, DUKE OF, 11
only t. NORTHCLIFFE, LORD, 2
T. Days that Shook the World REED, JOHN, 1
Ten Commandments The good Lord needed only T. CLEMENCEAU, GEORGES, 2
tender T. Is the Night FITZGERALD, F. SCOTT, 32
tenderness its t., its joys and fears WORDSWORTH, WILLIAM, 57
Tennessee in T., they chatta nougat NASH, OGDEN, 24
I placed a jar in T. STEVENS, WALLACE, 21
tennis Anyone for t. ANONYMOUS, 76
Tennyson T. was not Tennysonian TENNYSON, ALFRED, 4
tension transformation of the t. of the line MONDRIAN, PIET, 1
tents Those who have never dwelt in t. SACKVILLE-WEST, VITA, 6
terrible t. thing for a man to find out WILDE, OSCAR, 54
terrifying In a world we find t. MAMET, DAVID, 17
terror T. is the fiercest nurse of cruelty HENSON, JOSIAH, 1
T. just before death BLY, ROBERT, 1
terrorism t. inflicted on society by crime figures RUNCIMAN OF DOXFORD, LADY, 1
terrorist The t. and the policeman CONRAD, JOSEPH, 9
terrorists All t....end up with drinks at the Dorchester GAITSKELL, DORA, 1
terrorize No one can t. a whole nation MCCARTHY, JOSEPH (1909–57), 1
test t. the reality /Of misty fields STEVENS, WALLACE, 18
testaments T. are full of pundits...favorite *sons* SALINGER, J. D., 11
tether Nae man can t. time or tide BURNS, ROBERT, 33
Texan The T. turned out to be good-natured HELLER, JOSEPH, 1
Texas If I owned T. and Hell SHERIDAN, PHILIP HENRY, 2
T. could wear Rhode Island NEFF, PAT, 1
T....forever to get out STEINBECK, JOHN, 28
T....good place to be rich in HOAGLAND, EDWARD, 4
T.. Its unity lies in the mind STEINBECK, JOHN, 29
T.. Texas HOUSTON, SAM, 1
Writers facing the problem of T. STEINBECK, JOHN, 30
text The conscious t. is...not a transcription DERRIDA, JACQUES, 4
Thames know how far T. doth outgo DRAYTON, MICHAEL, 7
Sweet T.! run softly SPENSER, EDMUND, 1
What is there...in the T. DOUGLAS, WILLIAM, 2
thank i t. You God for...this amazing /day CUMMINGS, E. E., 21
not going to t. anybody MILLIGAN, SPIKE, 1
Now t. we all our God WINKWORTH, CATHERINE, 1
T. me no thankings SHAKESPEARE, WILLIAM, 555
T. you for not killing me BRYSON, BILL, 13
thanks glad...he t. God for anything JOHNSON, SAMUEL, 137
thanksgiving With proud t. BINYON, LAURENCE, 1
that 1066 And All T. SELLAR, W. C., 9
Thatcherism T....reversion to the idea of nature BARKER, HOWARD, 1
theater The t. is like a faithful wife BERGMAN, INGMAR, 9
the t. the critics have permitted us MILLER, ARTHUR, 20
T. is the first serum BARRAULT, JEAN-LOUIS, 1
t....school of the moral LESSING, GOTTHOLD EPHRAIM, 6
theatre For the t. one needs long arms BERNHARDT, SARAH, 1
nobody goes to the t. unless he...has bronchitis AGATE, JAMES, 1
Theatre of the Absurd T....senselessness...human condition ESSLIN, MARTIN, 1
theatres Most t. are still controlled by men CHURCHILL, CARYL, 2
theft A clever t....praiseworthy...amongst Christians SPENCER, HERBERT, 6
theology T. and Absolute Ethics...no real objects RAMSEY, FRANK, 2
theorems About binomial t. GILBERT, W. S., 34
theories In making t....keep a window open SCHICK, BÉLA, 2
theorist I'm not a t. PINTER, HAROLD, 1
theorists mortmain of t. extinct in science HOLMES, OLIVER WENDELL, 2
theory Don't confuse *hypothesis* and *t.* FISCHER, MARTIN H., 4
more important...t. to be shapely HAMPTON, CHRISTOPHER, 4
physical t. is not an explanation DÜHEM, PIERRE, 1
t. is all gray GOETHE, JOHANN WOLFGANG VON, 15
T. like mist on eyeglasses. Obscure facts BIGGERS, EARL DERR, 1
theory of relativity If my t. is proven correct EINSTEIN, ALBERT, 8
therapeutic formulation of t....striving for *wholeheartedness* HORNEY, KAREN, 11
The most important t. step HORNEY, KAREN, 12
therapy I go to t. FERGUSON, SARAH, 1
prayer, amulets, baths, and poultices...valuable t. FISCHER, MARTIN H., 18
Thermopylae There was an old man of T. LEAR, EDWARD, 7
thief as a t. in the night BIBLE, 232
Give a t. enough rope PROVERBS, 231
He that first cries out stop t. CONGREVE, WILLIAM, 6
If you give to a t. he cannot steal SAROYAN, WILLIAM, 2
What is a man if he is not a t. GANDHI, MAHATMA, 13
thieves One of the t. was saved BECKETT, SAMUEL, 27
There is no honor among t. PROVERBS, 413
the worst of the lot, and the boldest t., be Yank KIPLING, RUDYARD, 60
T. respect property CHESTERTON, G. K., 42
thin Enclosing every t. man, there's a fat man WAUGH, EVELYN, 22
One can never be too t. SIMPSON, WALLIS, 3
Outside every t. girl WHITEHORN, KATHARINE, 17
The one way to get t. CONNOLLY, CYRIL, 17
The T. Man HAMMETT, DASHIELL, 6
t. man inside every fat man ORWELL, GEORGE, 12
thing If a t. is worth doing CHESTERTON, G. K., 46
put a t. for the first time MCCAIG, NORMAN, 12
something between a t. and a thought PALMER, SAMUEL, 1
T. One and Thing Two SEUSS, DR., 3
when the t. itself is missing MONTHERLANT, HENRI DE, 3
thing-in-itself The t., the will-to-live SCHOPENHAUER, ARTHUR, 15
things all t. are one HERACLITUS, 7
be without some of the t. you want RUSSELL, BERTRAND, 65
T. are always best seen CELA, CAMILO JOSÉ, 1
T. are entirely what they appear to be SARTRE, JEAN-PAUL, 13
T. are not always what they seem PROVERBS, 428
T. are seldom what they seem GILBERT, W. S., 10
T....are what they are BUTLER, JOSEPH, 2
There are no t., only processes BOHM, DAVID, 1
T....value that we give them MOLIÈRE, 22

Two t. are certain CARVER, RAYMOND, 6
uncomfortable feeling of "t." in the head BISHOP, ELIZABETH, 4
think can't t. without his hat BECKETT, SAMUEL, 20
How can you t. and hit BERRA, YOGI, 3
I must not t. of thee MEYNELL, ALICE, 1
I t. that I think BIERCE, AMBROSE, 13
I t., therefore I am DESCARTES, RENÉ, 11
I t. with my hands HODGKIN, DOROTHY, 1
let us t. that we build for ever RUSKIN, JOHN, 21
t. him so, because I think him so SHAKESPEARE, WILLIAM, 655
time to t. before I speak DARWIN, ERASMUS, 1
T. no more of it, John RICHARD I, 5
T. nothing done while aught remains to do ROGERS, SAMUEL, 5
To t. is to differ DARROW, CLARENCE, 3
Under all that we t. MACHADO, ANTONIO, 9
You can't t. rationally on an empty stomach REITH, LORD, 1
you used to t. my trifles were worth something CATULLUS, 1
thinking action of the t. power called an idea JEFFERSON, THOMAS, 13
effort to prevent oneself t. HUXLEY, ALDOUS, 34
I am t., therefore I exist DESCARTES, RENÉ, 6
In order to draw a limit to t. WITTGENSTEIN, LUDWIG, 10
its disease of t. RUSKIN, JOHN, 4
my t. time isn't worth anything LEONARDO DA VINCI, 4
Only the t. man lives his life EBNER-ESCHENBACH, MARIE VON, 6
Plain living and high t....no more WORDSWORTH, WILLIAM, 77
T. is the desire to gain reality ORTEGA Y GASSET, JOSÉ, 21
T. is to me the greatest fatigue in the world VANBRUGH, JOHN, 5
t. makes /it less tangible CREELEY, ROBERT, 1
T....most unhealthy thing in the world WILDE, OSCAR, 27
t....thought in retreat or in reply MERLEAU-PONTY, MAURICE, 14
t., weeping, and high contemplation KEMPE, MARGERY, 1
We are t. beings JAMES, WILLIAM, 33
when things become unthinkable, t. stops FULBRIGHT, J. WILLIAM, 1
thinks A thing that t. DESCARTES, RENÉ, 12
man who says what he t. is finished HOCHHUTH, ROLF, 1
thin red line *t. tipped with steel* RUSSELL, WILLIAM HOWARD, 1
Third Estate the T. contains...a nation SIEYÈS, ABBÉ, 1
third sex if there was a t. VAIL, AMANDA, 1
That's the t., my lord BALZAC, HONORÉ DE, 1
Third World T....not a reality but an ideology ARENDT, HANNAH, 7
thirst And pines with t. amidst a sea of waves POPE, ALEXANDER, 84
the t. to come RABELAIS, FRANÇOIS, 2
thirsty He that goes to bed t. rises healthy HERBERT, GEORGE, 1
I'm t., not dirty LEWIS, JOE E., 1
thirty T. days hath September FOLK VERSE, 15
thistle plucked a t. and planted a flower LINCOLN, ABRAHAM, 36
Thomas Edison If T. had gone to business school MCCORMACK, MARK, 12
thorn a t. in the flesh BIBLE, 168
thoroughness with the t. of a mind that reveres details LEWIS, SINCLAIR, 5
thought a t. came like a full-blown rose KEATS, JOHN (1795–1821), 72
conscious utterance of t....is Art EMERSON, RALPH WALDO, 62
formal t....direct consequence of puberty PIAGET, JEAN, 8
I prefer t. to action BALZAC, HONORÉ DE, 11
My t. is *me* SARTRE, JEAN-PAUL, 12
Stung by the splendour of a sudden t. BROWNING, ROBERT, 28
the slow, assiduous, corrosive worm of t. MONTALE, EUGENIO, 2
T. is not a gift ORTEGA Y GASSET, JOSÉ, 13
T. is only a flash POINCARÉ, JULES HENRI, 7
T....labor of the intellect HUGO, VICTOR, 12
T. must be divided against itself HUXLEY, ALDOUS, 19
To give a...perfect form to...t. DAVID, JACQUES-LOUIS, 1
transition between one t. and another JAMES, WILLIAM, 24
t....stamped with the brand of a class MAO ZEDONG, 15
t. which saddens while it soothes BROWNING, ROBERT, 26
What was once t. DÜRRENMATT, FRIEDRICH, 4
thoughtcrime T. was not a thing...concealed ORWELL, GEORGE, 18
thoughtless t. words...Let them eat cake ROUSSEAU, JEAN-JACQUES, 7
thoughts Great t. come from the heart VAUVENARGUES, MARQUIS DE, 1
Heavy t. bring on physical maladies LUTHER, MARTIN, 12
His t....borne on the gusts of genius COLERIDGE, SAMUEL TAYLOR, 6
His t....lay silent MILLIGAN, SPIKE, 4
my t. remain below SHAKESPEARE, WILLIAM, 194
relation between t. and the brain SHERRINGTON, CHARLES SCOTT, 1
T. that are at peace WITTGENSTEIN, LUDWIG, 16
t....value for him who thinks them SCHOPENHAUER, ARTHUR, 14
T. without content are empty KANT, IMMANUEL, 10
thousand t. years scarce serve to form a state BYRON, LORD, 27
What's a t. dollars MARX, GROUCHO, 28
three There are only t. events in a man's life LA BRUYÈRE, JEAN DE, 14
there are only t. things to see ROSS, HAROLD W., 2
T. little maids from school are we GILBERT, W. S., 27
t. men who have ever understood it PALMERSTON, LORD, 5
t. of us in this marriage DIANA, PRINCESS, 5
t. species: first, the servile American FULLER, MARGARET, 3
T. things ruin a man TRUMAN, HARRY S., 7
When shall we t. meet again SHAKESPEARE, WILLIAM, 379
three-dimensional a t. drawing HIRSCHFELD, AL, 2
threefold a t. cord is not quickly broken BIBLE, 51
three o'clock T. is always too late or too early SARTRE, JEAN-PAUL, 14
three-pipe problem a t. DOYLE, ARTHUR CONAN, 9
thrift T. has nearly killed her DRABBLE, MARGARET, 7
thriller *T.*, which was mind-boggling JONES, QUINCY, 2
throat I took by the t. the circumcised dog SHAKESPEARE, WILLIAM, 501
throats cutting each other's t. CARLYLE, THOMAS, 48
fished down their t. with a spanner BETJEMAN, JOHN, 8
throne A man may build...a t. of bayonets INGE, WILLIAM RALPH, 15
High on a t. of royal state MILTON, JOHN, 46
no middle course between the t. and the scaffold CHARLES X, 1
something behind the t. PITT THE ELDER, WILLIAM, 9
throwaway society ultimate in the t....disposable woman HARRIS, JANET, 1
throw up people to t. at board meetings WAGNER, JANE, 1
thrush That's the wise t. BROWNING, ROBERT, 25
thunder-cloud big bossy, well-charged t. MUIR, JOHN, 5
thusness What is the reason of this t. WARD, ARTEMUS, 6
thyself Be so true to t. BACON, FRANCIS (1561–1626), 79
Tiananmen Square few people were killed in T. WU, HARRY, 1
Tiberius Had T. been a cat ARNOLD, MATTHEW, 8
Tibet Any relationship between T. and China DALAI LAMA, 2
Tibetan finding a solution to the T. issue DALAI LAMA, 10
Tibetans T....the list of endangered peoples DALAI LAMA, 6
ticker tape T. ain't spaghetti LA GUARDIA, FIORELLO, 1

ticket I don't buy a t. HEMINGWAY, ERNEST, 7
ticky-tacky they're all made out of t. REYNOLDS, MALVINA, 1
tide T. and wind stay no man's pleasure SOUTHWELL, ROBERT, 1
there is a t. in the affairs of men LOWELL, JAMES RUSSELL, 2
t. is eventually coming in MACAULAY, THOMAS BABINGTON, 16
tie A man's t. is a penis symbol HARRAGAN, BETTY LEHAN, 1
tied I am t. to the stake SHAKESPEARE, WILLIAM, 351
tiger catch t. cubs...entering the tiger's lair BANCHAO, 1
He who rides a t. PROVERBS, 256
man wants to murder a t. he calls it sport SHAW, GEORGE BERNARD, 118
O t.'s heart wrapp'd in a woman's hide SHAKESPEARE, WILLIAM, 289
Put a t. in your tank ADVERTISEMENTS, 10
This t. has other ideas KHRUSHCHEV, NIKITA, 1
tiggers T. always eat thistles MILNE, A. A., 10
tight T. boots are one of the greatest goods MACHADO DE ASSIS, JOAQUIM MARIA, 12
tightrope You may reasonably expect a man to walk a t. RUSSELL, BERTRAND, 58
tiller a t. of the ground BIBLE, 114
timber replacing some of the t. used up by my books INNES, HAMMOND, 1
time a comfortable t. lag...between...perception WELLS, H. G., 12
And t....Must have a stop SHAKESPEARE, WILLIAM, 246
Ask him the t. REAGAN, RONALD, 15
Be ruled by t. PLUTARCH, 26
bid t. return SHAKESPEARE, WILLIAM, 519
But what is t. AUGUSTINE OF HIPPO, SAINT, 6
could kill t. without injuring eternity THOREAU, HENRY DAVID, 34
do not squander t. FRANKLIN, BENJAMIN, 13
Even such is T. RALEIGH, WALTER, 3
Fly, envious T. MILTON, JOHN, 10
haven't the t. to take our time IONESCO, EUGÈNE, 4
I am T....night and the day MUHAMMAD, 7
I have t. enough in fourteen years KICKHAM, CHARLES JOSEPH, 1
inaudible and noiseless foot of T. SHAKESPEARE, WILLIAM, 55
irretrievable t. is flying VIRGIL, 37
I say t. is a crook LORRE, PETER, 1
It is only t. that weighs PLATH, SYLVIA, 16
It is time to make the t. DUMAS, HENRY, 1
Keeping t....In a sort of Runic rhyme POE, EDGAR ALLAN, 5
Men talk of killing t. BOUCICAULT, DION, 3
My t. has not yet come NIETZSCHE, FRIEDRICH WILHELM, 14
Never before have we had so little t. ROOSEVELT, FRANKLIN D., 11
nothing but t. destroys us KORAN, 35
now doth t. waste me SHAKESPEARE, WILLIAM, 524
O aching t. KEATS, JOHN (1795–1821), 87
Oh T., oh Still and Now MACHADO, ANTONIO, 10
O T.! arrest your flight LAMARTINE, ALPHONSE DE, 4
Our t. has come JACKSON, JESSE, 8
Redeem thy mis-spent t. KEN, THOMAS, 1
So it is with T. in one's life PROUST, MARCEL, 5
T. and the hour runs through SHAKESPEARE, WILLIAM, 382
T. and tide PROVERBS, 431
t. as a tool, not as a couch KENNEDY, JOHN FITZGERALD, 31
T. carries all things VIRGIL, 33
T. driveth onward fast TENNYSON, ALFRED, 75
T. drops in decay YEATS, W. B., 47
T. flies, death urges YOUNG, EDWARD, 3
T. for a little something MILNE, A. A., 21
T. goes by: reputation increases, ability declines HAMMARSKJÖLD, DAG, 8
T. had robbed her of her personal charms LEE, HANNAH FARNHAM, 1
T. hath, my lord, a wallet at his back SHAKESPEARE, WILLIAM, 688
That old bald cheater, T. JONSON, BEN, 18
that old common arbitrator, T. SHAKESPEARE, WILLIAM, 690
T. heals what reason cannot SENECA, "THE YOUNGER," 1
T. held me green and dying THOMAS, DYLAN, 14
the noise and germination of t. MANDELSTAM, OSIP, 15
There is a t. and place PROVERBS, 410
There is no t. like the present PROVERBS, 414
The study of t. and history COOK, SAMUEL D., 4
The supreme reality of our t. KENNEDY, JOHN FITZGERALD, 6
"The t. has come," the Walrus said CARROLL, LEWIS, 37
the ticking luggage of God's t. SACHS, NELLY, 1
The t. is out of joint SHAKESPEARE, WILLIAM, 160
the t. will come when you will hear me DISRAELI, BENJAMIN, 15
the whirligig of t. SHAKESPEARE, WILLIAM, 711
t. imposes on us its evolution NASSER, GAMAL ABDEL, 2
T. is a great healer PROVERBS, 432
T. is a great teacher BERLIOZ, HECTOR, 1
T. is a physician DIPHILUS, 1
T. is as Eternity is ANGELUS SILESIUS, 4
T. is a traitor MARTÍNEZ-SARRIÓN, ANTONIO, 1
T. is but the shadow of the world JEROME, JEROME K., 7
T. is dead as long as FAULKNER, WILLIAM, 14
T. is like a river made up of...events MARCUS AURELIUS, 8
T. is man's angel SCHILLER, FRIEDRICH VON, 21
t. is money FRANKLIN, BENJAMIN, 6
T. is money...vulgarest saw GISSING, GEORGE, 1
t. is now propitious, as he guesses ELIOT, T. S., 53
T. is now writing AKHMATOVA, ANNA, 6
t. is the greatest innovator BACON, FRANCIS (1561–1626), 38
T. is the great physician DISRAELI, BENJAMIN, 21
T. is the only critic without ambition STEINBECK, JOHN, 32
T., like a loan from the bank BRAINE, JOHN, 3
T. makes love pass ANONYMOUS, 1
To choose t. is to save time BACON, FRANCIS (1561–1626), 23
t. of life is short SHAKESPEARE, WILLIAM, 243
To manage t. well MCCORMACK, MARK, 19
To take t. to think KLINE, NANCY, 8
to waste my t. making money AGASSIZ, LOUIS RODOLPHE, 2
T. present and time past ELIOT, T. S., 15
T. presupposes a view of time MERLEAU-PONTY, MAURICE, 4
T....prevents everything from happening WHEELER, JOHN ARCHIBALD, 3
T. stays, *we* go DOBSON, AUSTIN, 2
T....stream I go a-fishing in THOREAU, HENRY DAVID, 44
T.'s wheel runs back or stops BROWNING, ROBERT, 36
T.'s wingèd chariot hurrying near MARVELL, ANDREW, 13
T., teach us the art MUIR, EDWIN, 1
T. the devourer OVID, 9
t....the longest distance between two places WILLIAMS, TENNESSEE, 15
T. was away and somewhere else MACNEICE, LOUIS, 8
T. waste differs from material waste FORD, HENRY, 9
t....we lose it CLAUDEL, PAUL, 5
T. will tell PROVERBS, 433
T. will walk behind you JIMÉNEZ, JUAN RAMÓN, 16

T. with a gift of tears SWINBURNE, ALGERNON CHARLES, 3
T. would pass JAMES, C. L. R., 3
T. wounds all heels MARX, GROUCHO, 4
What a long t. life takes PEAKE, MERVYN, 1
Will T. say nothing but I told you so AUDEN, W. H., 45
times all t. when old are good BYRON, LORD, 93
T. go by turns SOUTHWELL, ROBERT, 2
there are good t. and bad times RENARD, JULES, 2
These are the t. that try men's souls PAINE, THOMAS, 5
the true old t. are dead TENNYSON, ALFRED, 19
The T. They Are A-Changin' DYLAN, BOB, 15
t....shift, each thing his turn does hold HERRICK, ROBERT, 3
What t.! What customs CICERO, 12
Times one copy of *The T.* COBDEN, RICHARD, 1
time-table I would sooner read a t. MAUGHAM, SOMERSET, 38
timing T....everything in selling an idea FOX, HARRISON W., JR., 7
T.! My mother gave me that CHAPLIN, CHARLIE, 13
tinker T., /Tailor, /Soldier, /Sailor CHILDREN'S VERSE, 37
tinkers T. may work, quacks may prescribe HILL, BENJAMIN H., 1
tipping Do they allow t. on the boat MARX, GROUCHO, 7
tiptoe T. through the tulips DUBIN, AL, 2
tiptoes He who t. cannot stand LAOZI, 17
tire spare t. on the automobile of government GARNER, JOHN NANCE, 1
tired I haven't got time to be t. WILLIAM I, 1
T. of making himself loved RACINE, JEAN, 10
T. people make bad decisions JENRETTE, RICHARD, 2
title Because of my t., I was the first ALENÇON, SOPHIE-CHARLOTTE, DUCHESSE D', 1
does he feel his t. /Hang loose about him SHAKESPEARE, WILLIAM, 414
never think of a t. first FELLINI, FEDERICO, 5
quiet life is...helped by not having a t. PHILLIPS, MARK, 1
t. from a better man I stole STEVENSON, ROBERT LOUIS, 22
t. means exactly what the words say BURROUGHS, WILLIAM S., 11
title-page a t. to a great tragic volume ADAMS, JOHN QUINCY, 6
titles T. are a form of psychic compensation TOWNSEND, ROBERT, 15
T. are shadows, crowns are empty things DEFOE, DANIEL, 13
T. distinguish the mediocre SHAW, GEORGE BERNARD, 67
t....get one into disreputable company SHAW, GEORGE BERNARD, 97
thy other t. thou hast given away SHAKESPEARE, WILLIAM, 335
tits T. and sand...sex and violence in Hollywood LANCASTER, BURT, 1
titwillow a little tom-tit /Sang "Willow, t., titwillow GILBERT, W. S., 31
toad Squat like a t. MILTON, JOHN, 61
the t. has a very spiritual look ORWELL, GEORGE, 41
toads t. as big as your hat BISHOP, ELIZABETH, 2
toasted t. and buttered on both sides JACKSON, JESSE, 4
tobacco divine, rare, superexcellent t. BURTON, ROBERT, 10
For thy sake, T., I /Would do any thing but die LAMB, CHARLES, 26
I am going to leave off t. LAMB, CHARLES, 6
never since have I wasted...time on t. TOSCANINI, ARTURO, 3
T. drieth the brain VENNER, TOBIAS, 1
that tawney weed t. JONSON, BEN, 4
The t. business is a conspiracy against womanhood KELLOGG, JOHN HARVEY, 1
This is the t. he kills with ANONYMOUS, 28
T. surely was designed /To poison FRENEAU, PHILIP, 4
what pleasure...they have in...t. JONSON, BEN, 12
today Gone t., here tomorrow KNOPF, ALFRED A., 1
That virgin, vital, fine day: t. MALLARMÉ, STÉPHANE, 2
to-day here t., and gone tomorrow BEHN, APHRA, 8
the Cup that clears /T. of past Regrets FITZGERALD, EDWARD, 9
toes Pobbles are happier without their t. LEAR, EDWARD, 4
together we grew t., /Like to a double cherry SHAKESPEARE, WILLIAM, 58
toil T., envy, want, the patron, and the jail JOHNSON, SAMUEL, 5
The t. of everyday supplied JOHNSON, SAMUEL, 40
t. /That goes like blood to...poem CHAUCER, GEOFFREY, 6
toilets *T....women couldn't become engineers* WEST, REBECCA, 9
token I was a t....a happy, paid token WINFREY, OPRAH, 3
told I have not t. half of what I saw POLO, MARCO, 1
tolerance T. is not acceptance MCWILLIAMS, CAREY, 1
toleration t. produced...religious concord GIBBON, EDWARD, 3
We have learned t. in Europe HERZL, THEODOR, 9
toll'd The sexton t. the bell HOOD, THOMAS, 4
Tolstoy I like Leo T. enormously DOSTOYEVSKY, FYODOR, 5
Their teacher had advised them not to read T. novels SOLZHENITSYN, ALEXANDER, 14
Tom T., he was a piper's son CHILDREN'S VERSE, 1
T. went howling down the street CHILDREN'S VERSE, 2
tomb May never come ...This side the t. DAVIES, W. H., 1
tombstone Know what I want...on my t. TURNER, TED, 1
Tommy Oh, it's T. this, an' Tommy that KIPLING, RUDYARD, 28
Tommy Tucker Little T., /Sings for his supper CHILDREN'S VERSE, 53
tomorrow about t. there's no knowing MEDICI, LORENZO DE', 1
Never put off till t. PROVERBS, 340
T., and tomorrow, and tomorrow SHAKESPEARE, WILLIAM, 421
T. do thy worst...have liv'd today DRYDEN, JOHN, 49
t. is another day MITCHELL, MARGARET, 8
T. is another day PROVERBS, 435
t. is ours to win or lose JOHNSON, LYNDON BAINES, 6
T. never comes PROVERBS, 436
T. to fresh woods, and pastures new MILTON, JOHN, 124
to-morrow Defer not till t. to be wise CONGREVE, WILLIAM, 26
Never leave...till t. FRANKLIN, BENJAMIN, 19
not too late t. to be brave ARMSTRONG, JOHN, 2
T. let us do or die CAMPBELL, THOMAS, 1
tone Take the t. of the company CHESTERFIELD, LORD, 14
tongue hold your t. and let me love DONNE, JOHN, 40
One t. is sufficient for a woman MILTON, JOHN, 132
The t. in the ear MARIAS, JAVIER, 1
The t. is harder than the stick PROVERBS, 8
The t. is like a sharp knife PROVERBS, 43
t....so much refined since Shakespeare's time SHAKESPEARE, WILLIAM, 10
Toni Morrison T. doesn't watch TV MORRISON, TONI, 1
too You can have t. much PROVERBS, 462
took I t. thee for thy better SHAKESPEARE, WILLIAM, 204
tools Give us the t. CHURCHILL, WINSTON, 11
tooth Every t. in a man's head CERVANTES, MIGUEL DE, 17
have a t. pulled for five FISCHER, MARTIN H., 10
toothache He that sleeps feels not the t. SHAKESPEARE, WILLIAM, 136
The man with t. thinks everyone happy SHAW, GEORGE BERNARD, 46
toothbrush Only a t. is really indispensable COURTAULD, GEORGE, 2
top I started at the t....worked my way down WELLES, ORSON, 12
People at the t. of the tree USTINOV, PETER, 13

There is always room at the t. WEBSTER, DANIEL, 9
Torah The T. is not meant for angels SACKS, JONATHAN, 5
torch t. has been passed to a new generation KENNEDY, JOHN FITZGERALD, 10
torches she doth teach the t. to burn bright SHAKESPEARE, WILLIAM, 538
torment I have mislaid the t. and the fear EMPSON, WILLIAM, 4
torments Our t. also may...Become our elements MILTON, JOHN, 47
torrent t. sweeps a man against a boulder STEVENSON, ROBERT LOUIS, 26
tortoise He was the great t. EISENHOWER, DWIGHT D., 5
would this t. rather be dead...or be alive ZHUANGZI, 5
Tory attached to what is called the T....party CROKER, JOHN WILSON, 2
I am a T. Anarchist BEERBOHM, MAX, 26
T. men and Whig measures DISRAELI, BENJAMIN, 7
Toscanini How much does T. get GOODMAN, BENNY, 2
totalitarian common failing of t. regimes JOHNSON, LYNDON BAINES, 14
Our fierce t. will MUSSOLINI, BENITO, 11
t. past...civilised future YELTSIN, BORIS, 5
t. state...truth in chains LÉVY, BERNARD HENRI, 1
totalitarianism T. cannot renounce violence GROSSMAN, VASILY, 3
T. is not so good at industrial innovation KEEGAN, WILLIAM, 5
touch He had been to t....great death CRANE, STEPHEN, 14
not as closely in t. with modern life GRENFELL, JOYCE, 1
t. of earth TENNYSON, ALFRED, 11
We t. our caps ANTHONY, SUSAN B., 1
touchy No one's more t. than...government departments GOGOL, NIKOLAY, 5
tough Of course, we had it t. MONTY PYTHON'S FLYING CIRCUS, 1
You don't have to be t. to survive HARRY, DEBORAH, 1
toughness T. doesn't have to come FEINSTEIN, DIANNE, 2
tourism T. is the march of stupidity DELILLO, DON, 2
T. is whorism CLIFF, MICHELLE, 2
tourist A t. is an ugly human being KINCAID, JAMAICA, 2
the most noxious is a t. KILVERT, FRANCIS, 1
tourists people were t. because of their religion RUNCIE, ROBERT, 2
t....take in the Monarchy...with...the pigeons HAMILTON, WILLIAM (b.1917), 2
towels Snappin' t. at each others' privates SHEPARD, SAM, 3
Tower of Babel God made a mistake...at the T. CANETTI, ELIAS, 5
town the t. depends on contraband for its economy MATTHIESSEN, PETER, 2
The t. was roaring MITCHELL, MARGARET, 6
This t. was made to make money in CONNOLLY, BILLY, 1
towns Some little t. get on the map HEAT-MOON, WILLIAM LEAST, 1
toxic waste t. in the lowest wage country SUMMERS, LAWRENCE H., 2
toy but a childish t. MARLOWE, CHRISTOPHER, 26
trace confronted with the t. instead of...memory PAMUK, ORHAN, 4
ineffaceable t. is not a trace DERRIDA, JACQUES, 3
trade Free t....is in almost every country unpopular MACAULAY, THOMAS BABINGTON, 3
no t. more profitable...selling of dreams MAHFOUZ, NAGUIB, 3
T. depends on Money LAW, JOHN, 1
the heart of this nation is t. CHARLES II, 5
T. in general is built upon DEFOE, DANIEL, 14
when you t. for the Fed VOLCKER, PAUL A., 2
trade-unionists There are the *T.* KEYNES, JOHN MAYNARD, 14
trading t. on the blood of my men LEE, ROBERT E., 2
tradition It is a t. in our country MAURA, ANTONIO, 2
Our t....beginning in the teachings of Plato and Aristotle ARISTOTLE, 1
With the loss of t....lost the thread ARENDT, HANNAH, 25
traditionalists T....pessimists about the future MUMFORD, LEWIS, 4
tragedie T. is to seyn a certeyn storie CHAUCER, GEOFFREY, 28
tragedies t. are finish'd by a death BYRON, LORD, 57
There are two t. in life SHAW, GEORGE BERNARD, 54
tragedy a t. and therefore not worth reading AUSTEN, JANE, 11
brooding t. and its dark shadows can be lightened GANDHI, INDIRA, 2
Men play at t. ORTEGA Y GASSET, JOSE, 23
Real t. is never resolved ACHEBE, CHINUA, 7
t. ends /People return to their homes WU YINGTAO, 1
the composition of a t. requires testicles VOLTAIRE, 43
The t. of life...heroes lose their glamour WODEHOUSE, P. G., 14
t. is an experience of hyperinvolvement SONTAG, SUSAN, 5
T. is if I cut my finger BROOKS, MEL, 1
T. represents the life of princes AUBIGNAC, FRANÇOIS, 1
we have conceived life as a t. YEATS, W. B., 7
We participate in a t. HUXLEY, ALDOUS, 48
tragic The most t. thing in the world is a sick doctor SHAW, GEORGE BERNARD, 87
train a t. pulls into a great city GREENE, GRAHAM, 12
God helps those who t. themselves YOUNG, DAVID IVOR, 2
If you board the wrong t. BONHOEFFER, DIETRICH, 5
If your t.'s on the wrong track MALAMUD, BERNARD, 3
I have seldom heard a t. go by THEROUX, PAUL, 7
The best way to really t. people PETERS, TOM, 15
The only way...of catching a t. CHESTERTON, G. K., 55
T. up a fig-tree DICKENS, CHARLES, 29
You can't t. anybody HAAS, ROBERT, 4
train set the biggest electric t. WELLES, ORSON, 9
traitor I find myself a t. with the rest SHAKESPEARE, WILLIAM, 520
traitors t. rose against him ANGLO-SAXON CHRONICLE, 1
tramp A t....hopeful of romance CHAPLIN, CHARLIE, 8
It's hard to call a lousy t. your brother TOLSON, MELVIN, 6
little t. turned around and killed him CHAPLIN, CHARLIE, 1
tranquilisers lot of t. and my mother THOMPSON, EMMA, 1
tranquilizers What is dangerous about the t. LERNER, MAX, 3
tranquillity no intention of buying an illusory t. KISSINGER, HENRY, 3
T. comes with years FREUD, SIGMUND, 2
T. is now restored to the capital JEFFERSON, THOMAS, 22
tranquillizers t....bought as easily...as aspirin HUXLEY, ALDOUS, 16
transcendent t. capacity of taking trouble CARLYLE, THOMAS, 19
transcendental *t....mode of our knowledge of objects* KANT, IMMANUEL, 7
transform t. society...transform business PERLMAN, LAWRENCE, 4
transformation t....imagination and memory work together DEGAS, EDGAR, 6
We are living through a t. REICH, ROBERT B., 1
transformed man can be t....by will IBSEN, HENRIK, 9
transition A permanent state of t. JIMÉNEZ, JUAN RAMÓN, 8
transitory t. will...succeed the eternal PETRARCH, 3
translate such as cannot write, t. DENHAM, JOHN, 1
translated A linguistic work t. into another language KRAUS, KARL, 8
translating T. is the ultimate act of comprehending MANGUEL, ALBERTO, 1

translator A t. is to be like his author JOHNSON, SAMUEL, 46
transnational The strategic challenge for the t. corporation BARTLETT, CHRISTOPHER A., 3
transsexual small talk to a t. bird cage BELL, MARTIN, 1
transubstantiation weeds...popish doctrine of t. CRANMER, THOMAS, 4
trap the t. you set for yourself CHANDLER, RAYMOND, 9
trapeze daring young man on the flying t. LEYBOURNE, GEORGE, 1
trash The lowest action t. is preferable KAEL, PAULINE, 2
travaille Myn be the t. CHAUCER, GEOFFREY, 24
travel classes of t.—first class...with children BENCHLEY, ROBERT, 5
he must fly rather than t. HENRY II, 1
men t. first class...literature goes as freight GARCÍA MÁRQUEZ, GABRIEL, 13
Men who t. should leave their prejudices DOUGLASS, FREDERICK, 7
Never seen /a man /t. more BRATHWAITE, EDWARD KAMAU, 3
never t. disagreeably again MORRIS, JAN, 2
passion for t. for travel's sake TROLLOPE, JOANNA, 2
Principles of t. MORRIS, JAN, 4
T. broadens the mind PROVERBS, 438
t. from Dan to Beersheba STERNE, LAURENCE, 2
those who do not t. AUGUSTINE OF HIPPO, SAINT, 16
t. in the direction of our fear BERRYMAN, JOHN, 5
tired with labor of far t. CATULLUS, 3
T....is a part of education BACON, FRANCIS (1561–1626), 70
T. is a vanishing act THEROUX, PAUL, 16
T. is glamorous only in retrospect THEROUX, PAUL, 5
T. is the most private of pleasures SACKVILLE-WEST, VITA, 3
T. light JUVENAL, 15
t. not to go anywhere, but...go STEVENSON, ROBERT LOUIS, 17
To t. hopefully...a better thing than to arrive STEVENSON, ROBERT LOUIS, 32
To t. /is to return /to strangers SCOTT, DENNIS, 1
T. still suggests "travail" FRASER, KEATH, 2
universal test of t.; boredom GELLHORN, MARTHA, 5
Whoever claimed that t....home FRASER, KEATH, 3
travel book A t....the simplest sort of narrative THEROUX, PAUL, 14
traveler t. need have no scruple in limiting BAEDEKER, KARL, 2
traveling Extensive t. includes a feeling of encapsulation THEROUX, PAUL, 8
T....like talking with men of other centuries DESCARTES, RENÉ, 10
travell'd Much have I t. in the realms of gold KEATS, JOHN (1795–1821), 66
travelled He t. in order to come home TREVOR, WILLIAM, 1
I t. among unknown men WORDSWORTH, WILLIAM, 44
traveller a t. from an antique land SHELLEY, PERCY BYSSHE, 11
Now spurs the lated t. apace SHAKESPEARE, WILLIAM, 403
T., /Knocking on the moonlit door DE LA MARE, WALTER, 8
travelling my practice in t. to make my arrangements very carefully BISHOP, ISABELLA, 2
The grand object of t. JOHNSON, SAMUEL, 74
T. is the ruin of all happiness BURNEY, FANNY, 2
t. post from Tiflis LERMONTOV, MIKHAIL, 1
travels A man t. the world MOORE, GEORGE, 5
aspect of our t....disaster GELLHORN, MARTHA, 4
He t. fastest PROVERBS, 250
He t. the fastest who travels alone KIPLING, RUDYARD, 11
Like him that t., I return again SHAKESPEARE, WILLIAM, 580
motives of our t....are often overlooked PLINY THE YOUNGER, 8
treachery service rendered to the temporal king...act of t. LANGTON, STEPHEN, 1
t. and chicanery of the Natives SANCHO, IGNATIUS, 3
Weakness is not t. NICHOLAS II, 1
treason If *this* be t., make the most of it HENRY, PATRICK, 4
T. doth never prosper HARINGTON, JOHN, 1
treasures lay not up...t. upon earth BIBLE, 382
treated didn't want to be t. alphabetically MACDONAGH, DONAGH, 1
should I alone be t. so well BAI JUYI, 2
treaties T. are like roses and young girls DE GAULLE, CHARLES, 7
tree A t. is a tree REAGAN, RONALD, 27
I read...wish I were a t. HERBERT, GEORGE, 4
I shall be like that t. SWIFT, JONATHAN, 52
trees By the river...shall grow all t. for meat BIBLE, 95
God has cared for these t. MUIR, JOHN, 7
Loveliest of t., the cherry HOUSMAN, A. E., 9
T. are poems...earth writes upon the sky GIBRAN, KAHLIL, 1
The t. are in their autumn beauty YEATS, W. B., 41
tremble I t. for my country JEFFERSON, THOMAS, 40
trenches digging t. and trying on gas-masks CHAMBERLAIN, NEVILLE, 8
trench warfare In t. five things are important ORWELL, GEORGE, 15
trends Extreme t. are breeding grounds ROACH, STEPHEN S., 3
trial on t....moment of excessive good fortune WALLACE, LEW, 1
triangles if t. invented a god MONTESQUIEU, 5
triangular generally...the t. person has got into the square hole SMITH, SYDNEY, 7
tribalism T. is the strongest force at work DELORIA, VINE, 1
tribe may his t. increase HUNT, LEIGH, 1
tribulations the great t. of someone else LUCRETIUS, 4
tribunal a new t.... the educated man's BROWNING, ROBERT, 75
tribute receives...t. of all the riches TROLLOPE, FRANCES, 3
t. to whom tribute is due BIBLE, 485
trick A t. is clever only once PROVERBS, 497
t. is to love somebody BALDWIN, JAMES, 30
When in doubt, win the t. HOYLE, EDMOND, 1
tricks t. /Should flourish in a child of six BELLOC, HILAIRE, 6
tricolour the t. of the Irish Free State JORDAN, NEIL, 1
trimmer This innocent word "T." signifies...this SAVILE, SIR GEORGE, 1
trip don't t. over the furniture COWARD, NOEL, 7
t....the light fantastic toe MILTON, JOHN, 115
triumph T. cannot help being cruel ORTEGA Y GASSET, JOSÉ, 8
triumphant something gloriously t. will prevent the worst ATKINSON, BROOKS, 2
triumphs Are all thy conquests, glories, t., spoils, /Shrunk SHAKESPEARE, WILLIAM, 304
trivial pursuit of the t. and... the third rate ANDERSON, ERIC, 1
trod t. upon eggs BURTON, ROBERT, 14
tropics The nuisance of the t. BELLOC, HILAIRE, 30
trouble a lot of t. in his life CHURCHILL, WINSTON, 53
A t. shared PROVERBS, 148
Find out how they like it...you'll have no t. WATERS, ETHEL, 2
saves me the t. of liking them AUSTEN, JANE, 7
to have your t. doubled DEFOE, DANIEL, 7
took the t. to be born BEAUMARCHAIS, PIERRE-AUGUSTIN CARON DE, 4
you're in t. when you need...supercomputer LYNCH, PETER, 4

T....Let us economize it TWAIN, MARK, 16
t. lies on...far side of madness DIDION, JOAN, 8
t. lies somewhere COWPER, WILLIAM, 12
T., like a torch HAMILTON, WILLIAM (1788–1856), 1
T. made you a traitor HELLMAN, LILLIAN, 2
T....never comes into the world MILTON, JOHN, 127
T. never turns tail FARAH, NURUDDIN, 8
T....no road to fortune ROUSSEAU, JEAN-JACQUES, 21
T....not compatible with the defence of the realm SHAW, GEORGE BERNARD, 31
t. of a proposition ANSELM, SAINT, 1
t. of religious doctrines...dependent on an inner experience FREUD, SIGMUND, 38
T. often suffers...by the heat of its defenders PENN, WILLIAM, 5
to make t. laugh ECO, UMBERTO, 12
T....psychological standpoint, is agreement of relations DEWEY, JOHN, 19
"t."..."rightness" perceptible by the mind alone ANSELM, SAINT, 2
T. should not be forced UPDIKE, JOHN, 22
T., Sir, is a cow JOHNSON, SAMUEL, 152
T. sits upon the lips of dying men ARNOLD, MATTHEW, 10
t. were self-evident, eloquence would be unnecessary CICERO, 10
t. which makes men free AGAR, HERBERT, 1
T. will come to light SHAKESPEARE, WILLIAM, 603
T. will out PROVERBS, 441
Two half-truths do not make a t. KOESTLER, ARTHUR, 7
We know the t., not...by the reason PASCAL, BLAISE, 15
what is t. BIBLE, 295
When I tell any T. BLAKE, WILLIAM, 9
When t. is discovered by someone else SOLZHENITSYN, ALEXANDER, 8
You can only find t. with logic CHESTERTON, G. K., 41
truthfulness Learn first to perceive with t. DURAND, ASHER B., 1
T. so often goes with ruthlessness SMITH, DODIE, 3
truths All great t. begin as blasphemies SHAW, GEORGE BERNARD, 16
all t. are half-truths WHITEHEAD, A. N., 7
He was a man of two t. MURDOCH, IRIS, 10
hold these t. to be sacred and undeniable JEFFERSON, THOMAS, 34
Irrationally held t....reasoned errors HUXLEY, T. H., 14
new t....begin as heresies HUXLEY, T. H., 15
T. are illusions NIETZSCHE, FRIEDRICH WILHELM, 32
The only t. which are universal VALÉRY, PAUL, 4
There are no new t. MCCARTHY, MARY, 16
There are two kinds of t. LEIBNIZ, GOTTFRIED WILHELM, 8
two t. in this world RIVAROL, ANTOINE DE, 4
We hold these t. to be self-evident JEFFERSON, THOMAS, 33
try Many things...are done worst when we t. hardest LEWIS, C. S., 1
T. to be one of the people JAMES, HENRY, 12
t. to win all the way TOWNSEND, ROBERT, 3
tsar THE SKIBBEREEN EAGLE HAS ITS EYE ON THE T. NEWSPAPERS, 21
tubby a t. little chap WODEHOUSE, P. G., 26
Tucson T....one great big construction job KEROUAC, JACK, 21
tune There's many a good t. PROVERBS, 417
turbot would give the price of a large t. for it RUSKIN, JOHN, 8
turbulent rid me of this t. priest HENRY II, 3
turkey It was a t. DICKENS, CHARLES, 4
Turks the royal turban of the T. DUCAS, 1
turn One good t. deserves another PROVERBS, 354
turned in case anything t. up DICKENS, CHARLES, 19
turnip rather /Have a t. than his father JOHNSON, SAMUEL, 47
turn on T., tune in, drop out LEARY, TIMOTHY, 10
turtles t. are good to eat CRÈVECOEUR, JEAN DE, 4
TV T....our latest medium ACE, GOODMAN, 1
Twain I could not say, as Mark T. did ASHE, ARTHUR, 1
T. and I are in the same position TWAIN, MARK, 4
twang the triumphant t. of a bedspring PERELMAN, S. J., 9
Tweedledum T. and Tweedledee /Agreed to have a battle CARROLL, LEWIS, 33
twelve Why only t. GOLDWYN, SAMUEL, 28
twenties great to be 20 in the t. COPLAND, AARON, 9
twentieth century t. shall be filled by Canada LAURIER, WILFRID, 4
twenty first t. years...longest half of your life SOUTHEY, ROBERT, 13
twenty-four hour t. day has come to stay BEERBOHM, MAX, 4
twice T. is quite enough CONFUCIUS, 36
You can't step t. into the same river HERACLITUS, 2
twinkle T., twinkle, little bat CARROLL, LEWIS, 14
T., twinkle, little star TAYLOR, JANE, 1
twist last t. of the knife ELIOT, T. S., 28
Let him t. slowly...in the wind EHRLICHMAN, JOHN D., 1
two It takes t. PROVERBS, 285
It takes t. to tango PROVERBS, 286
T....an army against one PROVERBS, 64
T. of a trade can ne'er agree GAY, JOHN, 9
what can t. do against so many? SHAW, GEORGE BERNARD, 99
two and two t. would...make four WHISTLER, JAMES ABBOTT MCNEILL, 7
two-faced I grant you that he's not t. SNOW, C. P., 2
tycoon the t. depends on...warders and hangman HELLER, ROBERT, 2
tyger T.! Tyger! burning bright BLAKE, WILLIAM, 26
typewriters I keep these t. HAMMETT, DASHIELL, 3
typhoid Not...t. fever, but a typhoid man GULL, WILLIAM WITHEY, 1
typographical error but for a t. PARKER, DOROTHY, 37
tyrannical t. sultan...better than...anarchy PROVERBS, 47
tyrannies the t. of minorities ROOSEVELT, THEODORE, 10
tyranny resumption of t. LINCOLN, ABRAHAM, 26
root from which t. springs PLATO, 15
T....always better organized than freedom PÉGUY, CHARLES PIERRE, 9
t....easier to act than think ARENDT, HANNAH, 24
the t. of the majority ACTON, LORD, 4
tyrant professed t. to their sex SHAKESPEARE, WILLIAM, 441
put himself above everyone else and become a t. NAPOLEON I, 3
Tyson I'm "Mike T.," everyone likes me now TYSON, MIKE, 1
Sometimes it's not easy being Mike T. TYSON, MIKE, 2

U U. and Non-U ROSS, ALAN STRODE CAMPBELL, 1
ugliest u. of trades...moments of pleasure JERROLD, DOUGLAS, 6
ugliness the reason for the u. of adults ORWELL, GEORGE, 4
U. could only be cured with gold HEATH, ROY A. K., 4
U. is a point of view O'MALLEY, AUSTIN, 3
ugly an u., affected, disgusting fellow GIBBON, EDWARD, 1
an u. *woman* is a blot on...creation BRONTË, CHARLOTTE, 4
better to be first with an u. woman BUCK, PEARL, 8
I'm obsessed by...u. and sordid BREL, JACQUES, 2

I'm...u. enough to succeed on my own ALLEN, WOODY, 8
It's nothing to be born u. COLETTE, 4
There is nothing u. CONSTABLE, JOHN, 2
you, madam, are u. CHURCHILL, WINSTON, 82
ugly duckling The U. ANDERSEN, HANS CHRISTIAN, 4
U.K. century of the U. ROGERS, JIM, 1
ulcers I don't have u.; I give them COHN, HARRY, 2
Ulster preparing an U. fry for breakfast LONGLEY, MICHAEL, 1
problem in U....believed in an after-life THEROUX, PAUL, 13
U. is asking to be let alone CARSON, EDWARD, 2
U. will fight; Ulster will be right CHURCHILL, RANDOLPH (1849–95), 2
'umble a very 'u. person DICKENS, CHARLES, 21
We are so very 'u. DICKENS, CHARLES, 22
unaccommodated u. man is...a poor, bare, forked animal SHAKESPEARE, WILLIAM, 349
unanswerable the u. tear BYRON, LORD, 96
unapt u. to serve the world ASCHAM, ROGER, 3
unartificial insemination Surely you don't mean by u. THURBER, JAMES, 21
unassuming u. common-place /Of Nature WORDSWORTH, WILLIAM, 73
unawares happened u. to look at her husband AUSTEN, JANE, 8
unbaptized Frazer...left his children u. WOOLF, VIRGINIA, 12
unbecoming There is nothing more u. a man of quality than to laugh CONGREVE, WILLIAM, 8
u. the character of an officer ANONYMOUS, 44
un-birthday an u. present CARROLL, LEWIS, 43
unborn Better u. than untaught PROVERBS, 473
uncertainly I have known u. BORGES, JORGE LUIS, 3
Without measureless and perpetual u. CHURCHILL, WINSTON, 47
unclean spirits the u. went out, and entered into the swine BIBLE, 355
unclubbable A very u. man JOHNSON, SAMUEL, 151
unconfessable u. things...secrecy of his own heart PIRANDELLO, LUIGI, 7
unconscious concept of the u....theory of repression FREUD, SIGMUND, 37
uncreated the u. conscience of my race JOYCE, JAMES, 6
undeceived We are only u. ELIOT, T. S., 20
underemployed necessary to be slightly u. WATSON, JAMES DEWEY, 3
underestimate they u. the cumulative effect WHITEHORN, KATHARINE, 5
undersexed he was somewhat u. CHEKHOV, ANTON, 2
undersold Never knowingly u. ADVERTISEMENTS, 13
understand half of the world cannot u. the pleasures AUSTEN, JANE, 12
I don't u. life at all RENARD, JULES, 8
if he could make *me* u....it would be clear to all ROOSEVELT, FRANKLIN D., 5
I u. only because I love TOLSTOY, LEO, 12
never u. everything ANDERSON, P. W., 1
Nobody can u. Tibet DALAI LAMA, 7
The effort to u. the universe WEINBERG, STEVEN, 2
they are said to u. one another CHAMFORT, NICOLAS, 12
We don't u. life any better RENARD, JULES, 18
You suddenly u. something...in a new way LESSING, DORIS, 3
understanding friendly u....between my government and hers LOUIS-PHILIPPE, 1
Perfect u. will...extinguish pleasure HOUSMAN, A. E., 1
ten cents' worth of human u. FISCHER, MARTIN H., 13
To be...u. makes one...indulgent STAËL, MADAME DE, 2
understood Only one man ever u. me HEGEL, G. W. F., 2
What has been u. no longer exists ÉLUARD, PAUL, 2
undertakers I have nothing against u. personally MITFORD, JESSICA, 1
undertaking no such u. has been received CHAMBERLAIN, NEVILLE, 4
under water if I were u. I would scarcely kick KEATS, JOHN (1795–1821), 24
underwear Show the u. on a clothesline KLEIN, CALVIN, 1
unemployment Here is hard-core u. CALDWELL, ERSKINE, 1
more than attack the scourge of u. BLAIR, TONY, 9
Rising u. and the recession have been the price LAMONT, NORMAN, 1
u. is...getting off your backside ARCHER, JEFFREY, 3
unequal Men are made by nature u. FROUDE, J. A., 1
unexamined The u. life SOCRATES, 8
unexplained number of u. cures has dropped MANGIPAN, THEODORE, 1
unfaithful a far more concentrated woman...to be u. COWARD, NOEL, 19
better to be u. than faithful BARDOT, BRIGITTE, 3
unfortunate I am learning to care for the u. VIRGIL, 7
ungain'd Men prize the thing u. more SHAKESPEARE, WILLIAM, 681
ungovernable An absolute u. curiosity KING, LARRY, 2
ungrateful one u....and a hundred with a grievance LOUIS XIV, 6
unhappier I don't suppose I'm u. there LARKIN, PHILIP, 17
unhappily The bad end u. STOPPARD, TOM, 11
unhappiness not what isn't...that makes u. JOPLIN, JANIS, 3
U. is...the difference DE BONO, EDWARD, 4
u....will be ordinary, and not neurotic GELLNER, ERNEST, 1
unhappy an u. person who was happy BAINBRIDGE, BERYL, 4
don't believe one can ever be u. for long WAUGH, EVELYN, 11
It is better that some should be u. JOHNSON, SAMUEL, 100
one is u. one becomes moral PROUST, MARCEL, 4
the instinct for being u. SAKI, 20
those who are u. are mad MORAVIA, ALBERTO, 1
U. the land that has no heroes BRECHT, BERTOLT, 20
unhoming Men move u., and eternally FRY, CHRISTOPHER, 10
uniform The u. 'e wore KIPLING, RUDYARD, 19
uniformity U. isn't bad HARTLEY, L. P., 2
unimpeachably u. right-looking girl SALINGER, J. D., 5
uninvented An u. past can never be used BALDWIN, JAMES, 24
union indestructible U. composed of indestructible States CHASE, SALMON P., 1
sacred u. materialized...by magic POINCARÉ, RAYMOND, 1
The U....was a crime O'CONNELL, DANIEL, 3
To make a u. with Great Britain PÉTAIN, HENRI PHILIPPE, 3
u. there is strength PROVERBS, 275
unionists U. would still find we are...dishonest HAUGHEY, CHARLES, 2
unique something as u. and remote as Undine DICKINSON, EMILY, 1
united U. we stand PROVERBS, 444
united mass action Between the anvil of u....crush apartheid MANDELA, NELSON, 16
United Nations U. is not...the rule of law EDEN, ANTHONY, 3
United States More die in the U. of too much food GALBRAITH, J. K., 14
people who have sunk themselves as low...people of the U. BROWN, WILLIAM WELLS, 1
The U. has to move very fast KENNEDY, JOHN FITZGERALD, 30
The U. is blessed with four elements LYNCH, PETER, 6
the U....speak...better English COOPER, JAMES FENIMORE, 1
The U....the melting pot of the world MARSHALL, THURGOOD, 3

the U. will never again seek one additional foot of territory by conquest WILSON, WOODROW, 22
U....fifty or sixty nations of equals WHITMAN, WALT, 10
U. is the best and fairest...nation BUSH, GEORGE, 9
U....more space where nobody is STEIN, GERTRUDE, 9
U....surmount the gorgeous history of feudalism WHITMAN, WALT, 9
U...vast prison house for Poe POE, EDGAR ALLAN, 1
U. will be up for sale VIDAL, GORE, 8
With the U., history...a creation COMMAGER, HENRY STEELE, 1

uniting By u. we stand, by dividing...fall DICKINSON, JOHN, 1

unity U. in a movement situation is overrated KENNEDY, FLORYNCE R., 7

universe a hell of a good u. next door CUMMINGS, E. E., 6
But the u. exists MONOD, JACQUES LUCIEN, 1
created a strange new u. BOLYAI, JÁNOS, 1
discovers exactly what the U. is for ADAMS, DOUGLAS, 12
I accept the u. CARLYLE, THOMAS, 46
I don't pretend to understand the U. CARLYLE, THOMAS, 47
In this unbelievable u....no absolutes BUCK, PEARL, 1
I regarded the u. as an open book KOESTLER, ARTHUR, 1
more the u. seems comprehensible WEINBERG, STEVEN, 3
no reason to assume...u. has the slightest interest CLARKE, ARTHUR C., 6
nothing waste...nothing dead in the u. LEIBNIZ, GOTTFRIED WILHELM, 9
that's how the u. designs itself FULLER, R. BUCKMINSTER, 1
the immense and alien power of the u. HARRIS, WILSON, 3
the u. and all that surrounds it COOK, PETER, 1
The u. is a machine BERGSON, HENRI-LOUIS, 4
the u. is expanding and contracting DE VRIES, PETER, 6
The u. is not hostile HOLMES, JOHN HAYNES, 1
The u. is transformation MARCUS AURELIUS, 7
The u....like a great thought JEANS, JAMES, 3
The u. ought to be presumed too vast PEIRCE, C. S., 2
the u....queerer than we *can* suppose HALDANE, J. B. S., 3
u. go to...the bother of existing HAWKING, STEPHEN, 3
u. has not yet come to an end MACHADO DE ASSIS, JOAQUIM MARIA, 17
u. was dictated but not signed MORLEY, CHRISTOPHER DARLINGTON, 7
What is it that breathes fire into the...u. HAWKING, STEPHEN, 1

universes Out of all possible u. LOVELL, BERNARD, 1

universities U. are the cathedrals of the modern age LODGE, DAVID, 3
U. hire professors...others will admire KLINE, MORRIS, 1
U. incline wits to sophistry BACON, FRANCIS (1561–1626), 102

university Any attempt to reform the u. ILLICH, IVAN, 1
it is necessary to go to a u. BRITTAIN, VERA, 3
no u. has had any justification WHITEHEAD, A. N., 3
The u.'s characteristic state GRAY, HANNA, 1
true U....collection of books CARLYLE, THOMAS, 26
u. is traditionally...a psychosocial moratorium HOFFMAN, ABBIE, 1

unjust nothing can be u. HOBBES, THOMAS, 7
u. to possess a woman exclusively SADE, MARQUIS DE, 2

unknown She lived u. WORDSWORTH, WILLIAM, 32
Whatever is u. is taken for marvelous TACITUS, 3

unlettered An u. king is a crowned ass PROVERBS, 83

unlucky person born /who is so u. MARQUIS, DON, 8

unmixed Nothing is an u. blessing HORACE, 39

unmoral It is by becoming u. that history serves BEARD, CHARLES, 2

unmotivated The u. action GIDE, ANDRÉ, 6

unnatural nothing so u. as the commonplace DOYLE, ARTHUR CONAN, 3

unnecessary It is u. for a man RICHELIEU, CARDINAL, 5
u. for me to bend...my reason MONTAIGNE, MICHEL DE, 31

unparticular A nice u. man HARDY, THOMAS, 8

unpreparedness consequences of...u. and feeble counsel AMERY, JULIAN, 1

unreliability The felt u. of human experience SONTAG, SUSAN, 10

unrest Take a Clear-Cut Stand against U. NEWSPAPERS, 14

unscrupulous It is an u. intellect ERASMUS, DESIDERIUS, 5

unseen an u. world KING, STEPHEN, 2
We keep passing u. PIRSIG, ROBERT T., 11

unspellables u. killing the unpronouncables O'ROURKE, P. J., 7

unstable u. pact to commit...total mutual suicide BRZEZINSKI, ZBIGNIEW, 1

unthinkable Think the u....wear a dark suit WHITEHORN, KATHARINE, 11

untrue he never was u. PARKER, DOROTHY, 14
not u. and not unkind LARKIN, PHILIP, 6

unwashed The great U. BROUGHAM, HENRY PETER, 1

unwelcoming u. outpost of the American way of life KIRKUP, JAMES, 2

upper classes the u. /Have still the upper hand COWARD, NOEL, 18

upright man of life u. CAMPION, THOMAS, 1

uproar u.'s your only music KEATS, JOHN (1795–1821), 45

uranium u....new and important source of energy EINSTEIN, ALBERT, 14

urban The u. man is an uprooted tree JIMÉNEZ, JUAN RAMÓN, 7

US U. is a truly monstrous force PINTER, HAROLD, 3

U.S. U. foreign policy...is to bring Canada KING, W. L. MACKENZIE, 1

usage u....with whom resides the decision HORACE, 3

used words...already been u. by Barbara Cartland CARTLAND, BARBARA, 1

useful A u. life by sacred wisdom crowned PAYNE, DANIEL ALEXANDER, 1
nothing...you do not know to be u. MORRIS, WILLIAM, 4

useless A u. life is an early death GOETHE, JOHANN WOLFGANG VON, 19
no man is u. while...a friend STEVENSON, ROBERT LOUIS, 6
U. each without the other LONGFELLOW, HENRY WADSWORTH, 33

uselessness spirit of u. /which delights them WILLIAMS, WILLIAM CARLOS, 12

USSR Am I conceivable in the U. BULGAKOV, MIKHAIL, 3

usual Business as u. CHURCHILL, WINSTON, 17

usura U. rusteth the chisel POUND, EZRA, 20

utility *u.*...the chief part of morals HUME, DAVID, 5

Utopia this U. is far less attractive HERZL, THEODOR, 14

utopian it is "u." to want to survive SCHELL, JONATHAN, 1

vaccination V....corresponding to baptism BUTLER, SAMUEL (1835–1902), 36

vacuum A v. can only exist,... by the things which enclose it FITZGERALD, ZELDA, 3
v. is a hell of a lot better WILLIAMS, TENNESSEE, 8

vacuums most dreaded v. in all of mapdom MATTHIESSEN, PETER, 6

vagina The v. walls are quite insensitive KINSEY, ALFRED, 1

vaguery For V. in the Field OSBORNE, JOHN, 2

vain He is v., irritable ADAMS, JOHN, 2
V. man is apt to think WOOLLEY, HANNAH, 2

vale ave atque v. CATULLUS, 6
There lies a v. in Ida TENNYSON, ALFRED, 58

Victoria the way Queen V. treats her prisoners WILDE, OSCAR, 79
victory A v. is twice itself SHAKESPEARE, WILLIAM, 442
declare v. and leave AIKEN, GEORGE, 1
every v. turns into a defeat BEAUVOIR, SIMONE DE, 1
greatest v. a man can win PESTALOZZI, JOHANN HEINRICH, 8
let there be v., before the Americans HAIG, DOUGLAS, 2
moment of v. is much too short NAVRATILOVA, MARTINA, 2
no substitute for v. MACARTHUR, DOUGLAS, 6
Such another v. and we are ruined PYRRHUS, 1
This is *your* v. CHURCHILL, WINSTON, 21
V. at all costs CHURCHILL, WINSTON, 27
v. filled up /the little rented boat BISHOP, ELIZABETH, 8
v. finds a hundred fathers CIANO, GALEAZZO, 1
V. has a thousand fathers KENNEDY, JOHN FITZGERALD, 40
Viet Cong no quarrel with the V. ALI, MUHAMMAD, 7
Vietnam Nobody heard of V. until there was a war ALI, MUHAMMAD, 11
To win in V., we will have to exterminate a nation SPOCK, BENJAMIN, 1
V., man, bomb 'em and feed 'em HERR, MICHAEL, 1
war in V. destroyed three ancient civilizations GELLHORN, MARTHA, 3
Viet Nam We didn't wake up with V. JOHNSON, LYNDON BAINES, 7
vigilance Eternal v....price of sexual confidence TIGER, LIONEL, 1
I never could mix v. and sex BURROUGHS, WILLIAM S., 4
vigilantes goose-stepping v. or Bible-babbling mob LEWIS, JOHN L., 1
vile make v. things precious SHAKESPEARE, WILLIAM, 345
vilest two paces of the v. earth /Is...enough SHAKESPEARE, WILLIAM, 247
villain I am determined to prove a v. SHAKESPEARE, WILLIAM, 525
O v., villain, smiling, damned villain SHAKESPEARE, WILLIAM, 158
villainy so hackneyed in v. WASHINGTON, GEORGE, 4
vine I am the v., ye are the branches BIBLE, 292
With v. leaves in his hair IBSEN, HENRIK, 13
violate men never v. the laws of God CHILD, LYDIA MARIA, 4
violation v. of the medium...most perfect assurance MAN RAY, 2
violence If v. is as American as apple pie REED, ISHMAEL, 1
Keep v. in the mind ALDISS, BRIAN, 1
prisoners of the idea of v. TAMBO, OLIVER, 2
reduce...v. to...an acceptable level MAUDLING, REGINALD, 1
remake the v. of reality itself BACON, FRANCIS (1909–92), 2
Take away the v. HANSBERRY, LORRAINE, 3
tension and v....rise when compromise is in the air AHERN, BERTIE, 1
The gains of v. are transient NKRUMAH, KWAME, 3
through v. that one must achieve liberty MARAT, JEAN PAUL, 1
v. can only breed more violence DALAI LAMA, 4
v. in the movies can be cool TARANTINO, QUENTIN, 1
V. is American as apple pie TOURÉ, KWAME, 3
V. is as American as cherry pie BROWN, H. RAP, 4
v. is a totally aesthetic subject TARANTINO, QUENTIN, 2
V. is like money in the bank GIOVANNI, NIKKI, 5
V. is the repartee of the illiterate BRIEN, ALAN, 2
v. is the rhetoric ORTEGA Y GASSET, JOSÉ, 27
v. masquerading as love LAING, R. D., 10
violent better to be v....to cover impotence GANDHI, MAHATMA, 11
I expect no very v. transition SEDGWICK, CATHARINE MARIA, 1
violet A v. by a mossy stone WORDSWORTH, WILLIAM, 31
Violet Elizabeth V. dried her tears CROMPTON, RICHMAL, 1
violets Good God, I forgot the v. LANDOR, WALTER SAVAGE, 5
virgin a v. shall conceive BIBLE, 199
fashionable...to be a v. CARTLAND, BARBARA, 3
I started fresh—a "v." BRANSON, RICHARD, 7
Lillian, you should have stayed a v. CARTER, LILLIAN, 2
Virginia V., where charm is laid on GOLDING, WILLIAM, 5
Virginian I am not a V., but an American HENRY, PATRICK, 1
virginity holding v. not to be preferable to marriage AQUINAS, THOMAS, 4
In my first year...I lost my v. MCCARTHY, MARY, 7
my v., /When I lose that PRIOR, MATTHEW, 2
V....a state of mind ANDERSON, MAXWELL, 1
Virginny old V., the state where I was born BLAND, JAMES A., 1
virgins Are there still v. GIROUD, FRANÇOISE, 1
everyone is back to v. again CARTLAND, BARBARA, 4
virtual Sometimes v. crimes lie dormant MACHADO DE ASSIS, JOAQUIM MARIA, 15
Within a v. market MULGAN, GEOFF, 6
virtually v. speaking, it wasn't very small MCGONAGALL, WILLIAM, 3
virtue A minimum of comfort is necessary for...v. LUMUMBA, PATRICE, 1
follow v. and knowledge DANTE ALIGHIERI, 4
kindled his fire but extinguished his v. GERALD OF WALES, 1
Let them recognize v. and rot for having lost it PERSIUS, 3
Loss of v. in a female is irretrievable AUSTEN, JANE, 36
Love v., she alone is free MILTON, JOHN, 21
Make a v. of necessity BURTON, ROBERT, 19
much v. in "If" SHAKESPEARE, WILLIAM, 121
My v.'s still far too small COLETTE, 1
next to impossible is the exercise of v. GOLDING, WILLIAM, 3
no distinction between v. and vice JOHNSON, SAMUEL, 143
no road or ready way to v. BROWNE, THOMAS, 24
no v. like necessity SHAKESPEARE, WILLIAM, 510
Our king does not desire gold...but v. HENRY VIII, 5
to practice five things...constitutes perfect v. CONFUCIUS, 23
V.! a fig! 'tis in ourselves SHAKESPEARE, WILLIAM, 474
V. consisted in CECIL, ROBERT, 1
V....habit of acting according to wisdom LEIBNIZ, GOTTFRIED WILHELM, 6
v. in the creator STAPLEDON, OLAF, 2
V. is its own punishment BEVAN, ANEURIN, 10
V. is its own reward PRIOR, MATTHEW, 14
V. is like a rich stone BACON, FRANCIS (1561–1626), 16
V. is like precious odours BACON, FRANCIS (1561–1626), 12
v. is no longer considered a virtue ANGELOU, MAYA, 16
V. is the fount whence honour springs MARLOWE, CHRISTOPHER, 23
V. is to herself the best reward MORE, HENRY, 1
V. may be assailed, but never hurt MILTON, JOHN, 15
V....own fairest reward SILIUS ITALICUS, 1
v....will keep me warm DRYDEN, JOHN, 27
What is it that constitutes v. BRONTË, ANNE, 1
virtues a world to hide v. in SHAKESPEARE, WILLIAM, 694
greater v. to sustain good fortune LA ROCHEFOUCAULD, FRANÇOIS, 6
social v....virtue of pigs in a litter THOREAU, HENRY DAVID, 18
v. and vices couple with one another HALIFAX, GEORGE SAVILE, 8
v. are...vices in disguise LA ROCHEFOUCAULD, FRANÇOIS, 2
v. /We write in water SHAKESPEARE, WILLIAM, 285
Whenever there are tremendous v. BRECHT, BERTOLT, 7
virtuous more v. man...does not exist JEFFERSON, THOMAS, 29
Tarry Flynn loved v. girls KAVANAGH, PATRICK, 3
the v. poor WILDE, OSCAR, 68

who can find a v. woman BIBLE, 463
virus cross between...severe v. and getting married THOMPSON, EMMA, 2
vision a v. has to be...shared BENNIS, WARREN, 2
his v....remained singularly a collective vision VAN DER POST, LAURENS, 5
V. is the art of seeing things invisible SWIFT, JONATHAN, 14
"V." is what...the Japanese have HELLER, ROBERT, 4
V. paints the picture...want to create SENGE, PETER M., 5
With a v., the executive provides the...bridge BENNIS, WARREN, 8
visionary Thin, airy shoals of v. ghosts POPE, ALEXANDER, 80
Whither is fled the v. gleam WORDSWORTH, WILLIAM, 51
visions actual v. & actual prisons BURROUGHS, WILLIAM S., 1
visit always ready to v. a new place GREENE, GRAHAM, 10
time to go v. with the grandchildren ANONYMOUS, 34
visiting like v. another country BAINBRIDGE, BERYL, 5
visitors V.' footfalls are like medicine PROVERBS, 446
viskey Gimme a v....And don't be stingy GARBO, GRETA, 4
vitalism As long as v. and spiritualism are open questions VIRCHOW, RUDOLF, 2
the desire...to refute v. CRICK, FRANCIS, 2
vitality The lower one's v. BEERBOHM, MAX, 10
vitamins the right proteins and v. CARTLAND, BARBARA, 2
vivisect We v. the nightingale ALDRICH, THOMAS BAILEY, 1
vivisection V....is justifiable for real investigations DARWIN, CHARLES, 2
vixen strong-footed, but sore-eyed v. HAMILTON, SIR WILLIAM ROWAN, 1
vocabulary v. needs constant fertilisation WAUGH, EVELYN, 34
vocation The test of a v....drudgery it involves SMITH, LOGAN PEARSALL, 5
voice A still small v. spake unto me TENNYSON, ALFRED, 78
At once a v. arose HARDY, THOMAS, 5
God sent a v. to guide me JOAN OF ARC, SAINT, 2
Her v. was ever soft SHAKESPEARE, WILLIAM, 373
higher the v....smaller the intellect NEWMAN, ERNEST, 3
If you'll be my v. today CLINTON, BILL, 6
Let no v. but your own speak to you GARVEY, MARCUS, 1
so pleasing on their ear /His v. POPE, ALEXANDER, 86
The melting v. through mazes running MILTON, JOHN, 117
the v. of my beloved BIBLE, 491
the v. of the turtle is heard BIBLE, 492
v. of the people is the voice of God ALCUIN, 2
v. of the people...voice of God ATATURK, KEMAL, 4
v. of the sluggard WATTS, ISAAC, 7
v. on the ruins of another voice QASIM, SAMIH, 1
v....sways the soul PLINY THE YOUNGER, 4
voices Other V., Other Rooms CAPOTE, TRUMAN, 6
Two v....sea...mountains WORDSWORTH, WILLIAM, 68
Voltaire V.—poison and antidote VOLTAIRE, 5
voluntary v. act...guided by idea, perception JAMES, WILLIAM, 9
volunteers V. usually fall into two groups NIVEN, DAVID, 1
Volvox V....demonstrated its superb fitness KRUTCH, JOSEPH WOOD, 4
voodoo V. economics REAGAN, RONALD, 2
vote Nothing would induce me to v. for...women CHURCHILL, WINSTON, 80
One man shall have one v. CARTWRIGHT, JOHN, 1
right of citizens of the United States to v. CONSTITUTION OF THE UNITED STATES, 6
v. is the most powerful instrument JOHNSON, LYNDON BAINES, 15
v....means nothing to women O'BRIEN, EDNA, 4
voted I always v. at my party's call GILBERT, W. S., 4
votes Five v. can do anything around here BRENNAN, WILLIAM J., 3
V. for Women MOTTOS AND SLOGANS, 35
vow I v. to thee, my country SPRING-RICE, CECIL ARTHUR, 2
V. me no vows BEAUMONT & FLETCHER, 16
vulgar It's v. to be famous PASTERNAK, BORIS, 6
the sign of a v. mind CAMUS, ALBERT, 6
v....a gold toothpick KRONENBERGER, LOUIS, 4
v. flight of common souls MURPHY, ARTHUR, 1
vulgarity love...v. for its own sake HUXLEY, ALDOUS, 38
v. begins at home WHISTLER, JAMES ABBOTT MCNEILL, 1
vulture a v. can't stand...a glass eye HUBBARD, FRANK MCKINNEY, 2
I eat like a v. MARX, GROUCHO, 31
vulva To the Blameless V. WALKER, ALICE, 16

wafer applying /W. and wine to...human wound BERRYMAN, JOHN, 1
wage One man's w. rise...another man's price increase WILSON, HAROLD, 2
wager w. that he does exist PASCAL, BLAISE, 7
waggle can you w. your ears BARRIE, J. M., 21
Wagner I can't listen to that much W. ALLEN, WOODY, 7
I like W.'s music better than anybody's WAGNER, RICHARD, 3
W. has lovely moments WAGNER, RICHARD, 2
W. is the Puccini of music MORTON, J. C., 8
wagon Hitch your w. to a star EMERSON, RALPH WALDO, 41
wagons The din of w.! Whinnying horses DU FU, 4
waif I'm going to be called a w. MOSS, KATE, 1
wailers Name w. from the Bible MARLEY, BOB, 8
waistcoats flannel w. and moral pocket handkerchiefs DICKENS, CHARLES, 97
wait ability to w....requisite of practical policy BISMARCK, PRINCE OTTO VON, 6
I almost had to w. LOUIS XIV, 3
I can w. SCHOENBERG, ARNOLD, 2
told you to w. in the car BANKHEAD, TALLULAH, 13
waiting We've been w. 700 years COLLINS, MICHAEL, 2
W. for the end, boys EMPSON, WILLIAM, 2
w....most uninspired form of death VALENZUELA, LUISA, 3
Wakan W. comes from the wakan beings ANONYMOUS, 61
wake If you w. at midnight, and hear a horse's feet KIPLING, RUDYARD, 43
I w. to sleep ROETHKE, THEODORE, 10
waking w. from a troubled dream HAWTHORNE, NATHANIEL, 4
Wales different material to England's robe of state, W. DAVIES, RHYS, 1
in W....a harpist sits in...every inn MENDELSSOHN, FELIX, 1
Shut the door, W. BRUMMELL, "BEAU," 2
W., which I have never seen HUMPHRIES, ROLFE, 1
walk A W. on the Wild Side ALGREN, NELSON, 3
I want to get up and w. out ASTAIRE, FRED, 7
I w. down the Strand HARGREAVES, W. F., 2
learn to w. before we can run PROVERBS, 449
not once...have I gone...for a w. BEERBOHM, MAX, 3

walked He w. by himself KIPLING, RUDYARD, 36
walking idea of w. through walls ADAMS, DOUGLAS, 2
I'm w. backwards till Christmas MILLIGAN, SPIKE, 9
Jesus...w. on the sea BIBLE, 405
w. round him has always tired me MORRIS, WILLIAM, 1
wall a lamentably thick w. had grown LU XUN, 4
an outside w. after wars and devastations AMICHAI, YEHUDA, 1
Something... doesn't love a w. FROST, ROBERT, 17
the w. fell down flat BIBLE, 308
W. of Sound SPECTOR, PHIL, 1
wallflower call me a w. ASTAIRE, FRED, 8
wallis Strong be thy w. that about thee standis DUNBAR, WILLIAM, 3
Wall of China The Great W.: a wonder LU XUN, 16
wallpaper Either that w. goes, or I do WILDE, OSCAR, 82
w. with which the men of science MILLER, HENRY, 22
walls No part of the w. is left undecorated PEVSNER, NIKOLAUS, 1
Stone w. do not a prison make LOVELACE, RICHARD, 3
w....covered with gold and silver POLO, MARCO, 5
W. have ears PROVERBS, 447
Wall Street a generation...thinking of W. as anathema BROOKS, JOHN, 1
hedge funds...W.'s last bastions of secrecy BROOKS, JOHN, 2
W....last bastion of...male supremacy BROOKS, JOHN, 3
W. Lays An Egg SILVERMAN, SIME, 1
W....Masters of the Universe WOLFE, TOM, 7
walrus "I weep for you," the W. said CARROLL, LEWIS, 36
The W. and the Carpenter CARROLL, LEWIS, 38
The w. was Paul LENNON & MCCARTNEY, 2
wandered I've w. east...wandered west MOTHERWELL, WILLIAM, 1
I w. lonely as a cloud WORDSWORTH, WILLIAM, 45
wandering Poor w. one GILBERT, W. S., 35
W. between two worlds ARNOLD, MATTHEW, 11
wankers We're all w. underneath ELTON, BEN, 2
want a hidden w....science cannot supply OSLER, WILLIAM, 6
For w. of a nail PROVERBS, 227
If there's anything that you w. LENNON & MCCARTNEY, 8
If you w. a thing well done PROVERBS, 271
I w. to be at the table MURDOCH, RUPERT, 5
The w. of a thing is perplexing enough VANBRUGH, JOHN, 1
to w. is what bodies do TSVETAEVA, MARINA, 6
wanting Always leave them w. less WARHOL, ANDY, 12
stop w. something you get it WARHOL, ANDY, 15
wanton w. and effeminate sound JOHN OF SALISBURY, 3
wants Man w. but little YOUNG, EDWARD, 7
war abolish w. or war will abolish mankind MAYS, BENJAMIN E., 2
advocate w. out of irritability KENNEDY, JOHN FITZGERALD, 27
As long as w. is regarded as wicked WILDE, OSCAR, 23
average men and women were delighted at...w. RUSSELL, BERTRAND, 37
A w....left nothing to be desired BRECHT, BERTOLT, 10
A w....must shatter the foundations of thought and re-create SOYINKA, WOLE, 8
better to have a w. for justice PÉGUY, CHARLES PIERRE, 6
desire of our two peoples never to go to w. CHAMBERLAIN, NEVILLE, 10
Don't mention the w. CLEESE, JOHN, 2
easier to make w. than CLEMENCEAU, GEORGES, 4
every w. is against the world and...is lost WALKER, ALICE, 15
first casualty when w. comes is truth JOHNSON, HIRAM W., 1
glorify w.—the world's only hygiene MARINETTI, FILIPPO TOMMASO, 3
Grim-visag'd w. hath smooth'd his wrinkl'd front SHAKESPEARE, WILLIAM, 526
he came hiccupping to the w. WILLIAM OF MALMESBURY, 1
he knew as much about w. BENJAMIN, JUDAH, 1
I believe that the W. is being deliberately prolonged SASSOON, SIEGFRIED, 6
I'd like...government get out of w. HELLER, JOSEPH, 10
If we lose this w. DAYAN, MOSHE, 2
I have loved w. too much LOUIS XIV, 9
I look upon w. with horror SHERMAN, WILLIAM TECUMSEH, 3
I make w. on the living CHARLES V, 5
In every w. someone puts the cigarette FORCHÉ, CAROLYN, 2
In starting and waging a w. HITLER, ADOLF, 41
into w. on the command of gold NORRIS, GEORGE W., 1
In w., resolution; in defeat, defiance CHURCHILL, WINSTON, 56
In w....there are no winners CHAMBERLAIN, NEVILLE, 3
Is it that w. is a luxury COBDEN, RICHARD, 3
It is a very important w. MCNAMARA, ROBERT, 2
It is well that w. is so terrible LEE, ROBERT E., 3
I wanted the experience of w. CARY, JOYCE, 4
just w....better for a nation's soul ROOSEVELT, THEODORE, 8
Let me have w., say I; it exceeds peace SHAKESPEARE, WILLIAM, 125
makes a good w. makes a good peace HERBERT, GEORGE, 3
no more win a w. than...an earthquake RANKIN, JEANNETTE, 1
nothing that w. has ever achieved ELLIS, HAVELOCK, 11
Our w. is...a Crusade FRANCO, FRANCISCO, 5
quickest way of ending a w. ORWELL, GEORGE, 24
seek by all means...to avoid w. CHAMBERLAIN, NEVILLE, 7
subject is W....the pity OWEN, WILFRED, 10
tell how much w. he has seen MAULDIN, BILL, 2
there was w. in heaven BIBLE, 468
the second rule of w. MONTGOMERY OF ALAMEIN, SIR BERNARD LAW, 1
The W. between Men and Women THURBER, JAMES, 10
The w....four years of long vacation RADIGUET, RAYMOND, 3
the w. of the giants is over CHURCHILL, WINSTON, 60
The wrong w., at the wrong place BRADLEY, OMAR, 2
The W. That Will End War WELLS, H. G., 10
The w. wasn't the worst thing GLASGOW, ELLEN, 3
The w. we have just been through WILSON, WOODROW, 27
they'll give a w. and nobody will come SANDBURG, CARL, 9
This w....is a war to end war LLOYD-GEORGE, DAVID, 15
This w. is not as in the past STALIN, JOSEPH, 7
this w....which did not justify the sacrifice PANKHURST, SYLVIA, 2
Those who can win a w. well CHURCHILL, WINSTON, 44
To w. and arms I fly LOVELACE, RICHARD, 4
twenty seconds of w. to destroy BAUDOUIN I, 1
W....a continuation of politics CLAUSEWITZ, KARL MARIE VON, 3
w....antiquated as a duel GOOCH, GEORGE PEABODY, 1
w....an unlimited world catastrophe BETHMANN HOLLWEG, THEOBALD VON, 4
W. becomes an awful bore NIMIER, ROGER, 1
W. belongs...to the province of social life CLAUSEWITZ, KARL MARIE VON, 2
w. can only be abolished through war MAO ZEDONG, 4
We are having one hell of a w. PATTON, GEORGE S., 1
We are not at w. with Egypt EDEN, ANTHONY, 2
We have all lost the w. LAWRENCE, D. H., 50
We prepare for w. like ferocious giants PEARSON, LESTER, 1

W....essentially an evil thing INTERNATIONAL MILITARY TRIBUNAL OF THE NUREMBERG TRIALS, 1

We want w. RIBBENTROP, JOACHIM VON, 1

w....forces men collectively to commit acts KEY, ELLEN, 7

what can w., but endless war still breed MILTON, JOHN, 9

What factors caused the outbreak of w. TAYLOR, A. J. P., 5

W. hath no fury like a non-combatant MONTAGUE, C. E., 2

What made w. inevitable...growth of Athenian power THUCYDIDES, 2

What they could do with...is a good w. BRECHT, BERTOLT, 6

When a w. breaks out CAMUS, ALBERT, 18

When the rich wage w. SARTRE, JEAN-PAUL, 22

When you're at w. you think about a better life WILDER, THORNTON, 8

Who...believes we can win the w. MORRISON, DANNY, 1

Who live under the shadow of a w. SPENDER, STEPHEN, 7

W....imposes the stamp of nobility MUSSOLINI, BENITO, 14

W. is a great accelerator of events NIVEN, DAVID, 2

W. is an essential part of capitalism PADMORE, GEORGE, 2

W. is an extreme of political action MONDLANE, EDUARDO CHIVAMBO, 1

W. is an organized bore HOLMES, OLIVER WENDELL, JR., 8

W....is a violent schoolmaster THUCYDIDES, 6

W. is capitalism with the gloves off STOPPARD, TOM, 13

w. is declared with a numerous and bold enemy NAPIER, CHARLES JAMES, 2

W. is hell SHERMAN, WILLIAM TECUMSEH, 1

W. is just like bush-clearing KAUNDA, KENNETH DAVID, 3

W. is like love BRECHT, BERTOLT, 12

W. is never cheap or easy BUSH, GEORGE, 15

W. is not an adventure SAINT-EXUPÉRY, ANTOINE DE, 3

W. is not for...children SFORZA, CATERINA, 1

W. is Peace ORWELL, GEORGE, 20

W. is the best university MACHEL, SAMORA, 1

W. is the continuation of politics MAO ZEDONG, 20

W. is the highest form of struggle MAO ZEDONG, 10

W. is the trade of kings DRYDEN, JOHN, 29

W. is too important CLEMENCEAU, GEORGES, 8

W. its thousands slays PORTEUS, BEILBY, 1

W. lays a burden on the reeling state COWPER, WILLIAM, 8

W. makes rattling good history HARDY, THOMAS, 26

W....one of the constants of history DURANT, WILL, 16

w. regarded as inevitable...even probable KENNAN, GEORGE F., 2

W. should belong to the tragic past JOHN PAUL II, 1

W. should be...only study of a prince MACHIAVELLI, NICCOLÒ, 11

W....the hope that one will be better off KRAUS, KARL, 6

W., this monster of mutual slaughter MAO ZEDONG, 11

W....too serious...to be left to military men TALLEYRAND, CHARLES MAURICE DE, 7

W. to the knife PALAFOX, JOSÉ, 1

W. will never cease MENCKEN, H. L., 22

You can tell when a w. starts WOLF, CHRISTA, 4

ward as if I were locked up in a w. too CHEKHOV, ANTON, 3

Ware There was an old person of W. LEAR, EDWARD, 9

Warhol I love Andy W. WARHOL, ANDY, 1

warld half of the w. thinks the tither daft SCOTT, SIR WALTER, 30

warm Be w., but pure BYRON, LORD, 87

warmth w. is the vital element...for the soul of the child JUNG, CARL GUSTAV, 26

warn I w. you not to fall ill KINNOCK, NEIL, 1

warrior Here lies a valiant w. /Who never drew a sword EPITAPHS, 9

w. in the time of women JOHNSON, SONIA, 1

warriors w., never tired of...battle of life ANONYMOUS, 31

wars All w. are planned by old men RICE, GRANTLAND, 2

military don't start w. WESTMORELAND, WILLIAM C., 3

Still w. and lechery SHAKESPEARE, WILLIAM, 691

Suppose those /who made /w. MADHUBUTI, HAKI R., 1

W. are not won by evacuations CHURCHILL, WINSTON, 54

w. are popular for the first thirty days SCHLESINGER, ARTHUR, JR., 1

W. cannot be fought with nuclear weapons MOUNTBATTEN, LORD, 1

W., conflict, it's all business CHAPLIN, CHARLIE, 5

w....everybody knew would never happen POWELL, ENOCH, 2

w., horrible wars VIRGIL, 16

W....not enough people...afraid SCHONFIELD, HUGH JOSEPH, 1

wartime w....occasion to play about with letters ATATURK, KEMAL, 5

wash Don't w. your dirty linen PROVERBS, 189

I do...also w. and iron them THATCHER, DENIS, 1

wish you wouldn't w. your dirty Lenin MACKENZIE, COMPTON, 1

W. That Man Right Out of My Hair HAMMERSTEIN, II, OSCAR, 9

ye also ought to w. one another's feet BIBLE, 288

washed w. himself with oriental scrupulosity SWIFT, JONATHAN, 1

w. me out of the turret JARRELL, RANDALL, 1

washing Always w., and never getting finished HARDY, THOMAS, 22

Washington A basic truism in W. FOX, HARRISON W., JR., 1

Every man who takes office inW....grows or swells WILSON, WOODROW, 15

W. *en petit*...through a reversed glass OLMSTED, FREDERICK LAW, 3

W....everyone has been too long away EISENHOWER, DWIGHT D., 18

W. is like a self-sealing tank ACHESON, DEAN, 6

W....southern efficiency and northern charm KENNEDY, JOHN FITZGERALD, 36

waste biggest w. of water PHILIP, PRINCE, 1

W. not, want not PROVERBS, 448

wasted gonna get w., get wasted elegantly RICHARDS, KEITH, 1

most w. of all days CHAMFORT, NICOLAS, 7

w. 30 years of his life ALI, MUHAMMAD, 5

watch The W. on the Rhine SCHNECKENBURGER, MAX, 1

w. and pray BIBLE, 437

why not carry a w. TREE, HERBERT BEERBOHM, 5

watched A w. clock never moves MACNEICE, LOUIS, 14

A w. pot PROVERBS, 149

watchmaker I should have become a w. EINSTEIN, ALBERT, 49

watchman Son of man, I have made thee a w. BIBLE, 91

water man...drinks only w. has a secret BAUDELAIRE, CHARLES, 1

Much w. goeth by the mill HEYWOOD, JOHN, 4

No more w., the fire next time BALDWIN, JAMES, 22

no w. in oxygen, no water in hydrogen MACDONALD, GEORGE, 3

the w. that was made wine BIBLE, 270

w. continually dropping will wear hard rocks hollow PLUTARCH, 11

W. far away cannot put out...fire nearby HAN FEI, 1

w. flowed like champagne EVARTS, WILLIAM M., 1

w. hollow out a stone OVID, 5

W. in motion...precise and sharp SNYDER, GARY, 5

W. is H2O, hydrogen two parts, oxygen one LAWRENCE, D. H., 32

W....only drink for a wise man THOREAU, HENRY DAVID, 27

W., water, every where COLERIDGE, SAMUEL TAYLOR, 42

water-buffalo more trouble for killing a w. CHILDERS, LEE, 1
waterfront I've covered the w. WILLIAMS, TENNESSEE, 17
watering a-w. the last year's crop ELIOT, GEORGE, 8
watermelon my life is done in w. sugar BRAUTIGAN, RICHARD, 1
waters w. flowed over mine head BIBLE, 317
Watson Mr W., come here; I want you BELL, ALEXANDER GRAHAM, 1
waves w. make towards the pebbled shore SHAKESPEARE, WILLIAM, 575
way I am the w., the truth, and the life BIBLE, 291
I did it my w. ANKA, PAUL, 1
longest w. round...the shortest way home BOHN, HENRY GEORGE, 1
shortest w. is the best PROVERBS, 490
simple w. of saying complicated things COCTEAU, JEAN, 5
That's the w. for Billy and me HOGG, JAMES, 1
that's the w. it is CRONKITE, WALTER, 1
The w....Is not the constant way LAOZI, 10
w. up and the way down HERACLITUS, 5
ways We have w. of making men talk ANONYMOUS, 27
wayside If you see anybody fallen by the w. SHEPPARD, DICK, 1
we the people like us are W....every one else is They KIPLING, RUDYARD, 29
weak I inhabit a w., frail, decayed tenement ADAMS, JOHN QUINCY, 9
The w....always prevail over the strong NIETZSCHE, FRIEDRICH WILHELM, 33
The w. have one weapon BIDAULT, GEORGES, 1
When men are w., they become moral TOLSON, MELVIN, 5
weakness Men rail at w. themselves create WARREN, MERCY, 1
universe of physical w. and mental decay HUXLEY, ALDOUS, 51
weaknesses Never support two w. WILDER, THORNTON, 4
touch his w. with a delicate hand GOLDSMITH, OLIVER, 22
wealth absentee w. and resident poverty HOAGLAND, EDWARD, 11
new w. comes from creative engineering HUTCHESON, DAN, 1
so much w....unmindful of the poor SITTING BULL, 1
Superfluous w. can buy superfluities only THOREAU, HENRY DAVID, 32
temptations which w. subjects them to CARNEGIE, ANDREW, 7
the insolence of w. JOHNSON, SAMUEL, 116
w. brings so little happiness FREUD, SIGMUND, 58
W. covers sin KASSIA, 1
w. had rendered her helpless BROOKNER, ANITA, 1
W. has in it...not anything...that is good LUTHER, MARTIN, 14
W. has never been a sufficient source of honor GALBRAITH, J. K., 13
Where w. and freedom reign, contentment fails GOLDSMITH, OLIVER, 25
W. I seek not; hope nor love STEVENSON, ROBERT LOUIS, 11
W. is like seawater SCHOPENHAUER, ARTHUR, 18
W. is not without its advantages GALBRAITH, J. K., 11
W. is the smallest thing LUTHER, MARTIN, 15
w. only the fear of losing it RIVAROL, ANTOINE DE, 6
weaned w. on a pickle COOLIDGE, CALVIN, 2
weapon anybody who wanted...w. could have one VONNEGUT, KURT, 10
Her w. is the snub GANDHI, INDIRA, 1
weapons If sunbeams were w. PORTER, GEORGE, 2
w. of the child's primary sadism KLEIN, MELANIE, 2
W. speak to the wise PINDAR, 2
wear w. what the movie star was wearing LAUREN, RALPH, 3
weariest The w. nights, the longest days ORCZY, BARONESS, 2
wears w. her clothes...with a pitchfork SWIFT, JONATHAN, 31
weary Art thou w....sore distressed? NEALE, JOHN MASON, 1
weasel w. under the cocktail cabinet PINTER, HAROLD, 8
weather A funny thing w. DOS PASSOS, JOHN, 1
I like the w. BYRON, LORD, 19
Stormy w. KOEHLER, TED, 1
The w. veers from dull to foul HUMPHRIES, ROLFE, 3
This is the w. the cuckoo likes HARDY, THOMAS, 13
This is the w. the shepherd shuns HARDY, THOMAS, 14
weather-eye Keep a w. open PROVERBS, 290
weather forecast even the w. seemed to be some kind of spoof LODGE, DAVID, 1
weather man You don't need a w. DYLAN, BOB, 13
weather-wise Some are w. FRANKLIN, BENJAMIN, 22
weavers The hard-pressed w. of Northern England ROSZAK, THEODORE, 4
web what a tangled w. we weave SCOTT, SIR WALTER, 11
Webster W....much possessed by death ELIOT, T. S., 27
Webster's Dictionary Like W. /We're Morocco bound BURKE, JOHNNY, 2
wedding Let's have a w. DICKENS, CHARLES, 37
lose our heads...mention of a w. CHITTY, SUSAN, 1
O God, and the w. CORSO, GREGORY, 3
W. is destiny...hanging likewise HEYWOOD, JOHN, 2
wedding-ring how many torments lie in the small circle of a w. CIBBER, COLLEY, 3
weddings w. is sadder than funerals BEHAN, BRENDAN, 2
wee W., sleekit, cow'rin', tim'rous beastie BURNS, ROBERT, 50
weed w....plant whose virtues EMERSON, RALPH WALDO, 27
week a w. from tomorrow ev-e-nink LUGOSI, BELA, 1
A w. is a long time in politics WILSON, HAROLD, 5
greatest w. in the history of the world NIXON, RICHARD, 37
Of all the days that's in the w. CAREY, HENRY, 3
weep wilt thou w. when I am low BYRON, LORD, 6
W. no more, my lady FOSTER, STEPHEN, 2
W. not, oh my well-sheltered sisters HARPER, FRANCES E. W., 6
weeping How often we sit w. BLOK, ALEKSANDR, 1
O Muse of w. AKHMATOVA, ANNA, 2
So stop your w. now O'CONNELL, EIBHLIN DUBH, 2
w. and gnashing of teeth BIBLE, 390
Why are you w.? Did you imagine that I was immortal? LOUIS XIV, 4
Wee Willie Winkie W. runs through the town CHILDREN'S VERSE, 61
weigh w. this song with the great YEATS, W. B., 43
weighed thou art w. in the balances, and art found wanting BIBLE, 32
weight deadly w. of the terrible tradition of a dialogue MANDELA, NELSON, 10
remove w. from the structure of stories CALVINO, ITALO, 3
the w. of rages SPOONER, WILLIAM ARCHIBALD, 1
weirdo not the w. people think he is JONES, QUINCY, 3
welcome I believe my arrival was most w. NELSON, HORATIO, 1
Thrice w., darling of the Spring WORDSWORTH, WILLIAM, 72
welfare-state led to that of the W. TEMPLE, WILLIAM, 1
well All's w. that ends well ANONYMOUS, 52
At last I am going to be w. SCARRON, PAUL, 1
do not speak w. of yourself PASCAL, BLAISE, 2
Every man who feels w. is a sick man ROMAINS, JULES, 1

gets w. in spite of the medicine JEFFERSON, THOMAS, 10
I am not w.; pray get me...brandy GEORGE IV, 3
Is getting w. ever an art LOWELL, ROBERT, 4
the kingdom of the w. SONTAG, SUSAN, 14
We never do anything w. HAZLITT, WILLIAM, 16
Who w. lives, long lives DU BARTAS, GUILLAUME, 15

well-being W. and happiness never appeared...an absolute aim EINSTEIN, ALBERT, 55

well-dressed The sense of being w. FORBES, MISS C. F., 1
You may be a w. animal KOCH, ED, 1

Wells Whatever W. writes is not only alive WELLS, H. G., 1

well-written A w. Life CARLYLE, THOMAS, 13

Welsh English are striving for power...W. for freedom GERALD OF WALES, 2
The W. are all actors BURTON, RICHARD, 2
The W. peasants have the reputation COSTELLO, LOUISA, 1
the W. were punished by God GERALD OF WALES, 3
whole of the W. nation FAIRFIELD, JOHN, 1
W. people...surest of all retreats...language MORTON, H. V., 1

Welshmen Most W. are worthless, /an inferior breed ABSE, DANNIE, 1

Wenlock Edge On W. the wood's in trouble HOUSMAN, A. E., 17

wept I have sometimes w. MUSSET, ALFRED DE, 5
I w. and I believed CHATEAUBRIAND, RENÉ, 2
Jesus w. BIBLE, 287

west Can the W. realize its ideal MERNISSI, FATIMA, 1
Go W., young man GREELEY, HORACE, 1
Go W., young man SOULE, JOHN LANE BABSONE, 1
In the W....past is very close MASTERS, JOHN, 2
The W....wake of the Soviet collapse SCHELL, JONATHAN, 6

western our W. lore is exaggerated and distorted STEWART, JIMMY, 1
W. women...often had to struggle GANDHI, INDIRA, 5

Western Front All Quiet on the W. REMARQUE, ERICH MARIA, 1

westerns W. are closer to art WAYNE, JOHN, 3

whale Very like a w. SHAKESPEARE, WILLIAM, 193
When the w. comes to the surface WEINBERG, JOHN LIVINGSTON, 1
When the w.'s viscera go LOWELL, ROBERT, 23
w.-steak must be tough MELVILLE, HERMAN, 7

whaleroad end of the w. and the whale LOWELL, ROBERT, 22

whale ship A w. was my Yale College MELVILLE, HERMAN, 4

whaling boats When w. have been overturned WILLIAMS, HEATHCOTE, 3

what W. and Why and When KIPLING, RUDYARD, 37
W. have they done to the earth MORRISON, JIM, 3
"W. is there...Everything" QUINE, WILLARD V., 1
W. is the will of the people PITT THE YOUNGER, WILLIAM, 4
W. the dickens HEYWOOD, THOMAS, 4

what's up W., Doc BUGS BUNNY, 1

wheat the origin of w. FABRE, JEAN HENRI, 4

wheelbarrow So much depends /upon /a red w. WILLIAMS, WILLIAM CARLOS, 3

wheels a spoke among your w. BEAUMONT, FRANCIS, 7
our w. grazed his dead face ROSENBERG, ISAAC, 2

where That depends...on w. you want to get to CARROLL, LEWIS, 10
W. did it all go wrong BERRYMAN, JOHN, 13
W. does she find them PARKER, DOROTHY, 27
W. does this tenderness come from TSVETAEVA, MARINA, 8

Whig Sir, I perceive you are a vile W. JOHNSON, SAMUEL, 166

whim The strangest w. CHESTERTON, G. K., 4

whipping A w. never hurts HOWE, EDGAR WATSON, 2
take great pleasure in w. a slave DOUGLASS, FREDERICK, 16
W. and abuse are like laudanum STOWE, HARRIET BEECHER, 5

whiskey contraband w. in women's underwear MENCKEN, H. L., 30
w. fumes...out of that beat-up old cornet MEZZROW, MEZZ, 4

whisky A good gulp of hot w. at bedtime FLEMING, ALEXANDER, 4
Fancy the Government running out of w. MACKENZIE, COMPTON, 7
That w. priest GREENE, GRAHAM, 7

whispering w. in her mouth MARX, CHICO, 1
w. "I will ne'er consent"—consented BYRON, LORD, 42

whistle I W. a Happy Tune HAMMERSTEIN, OSCAR, II, 13
W. and she'll come to you BEAUMONT & FLETCHER, 17
You know how to w....Steve BACALL, LAUREN, 3

whistling W. aloud to bear his Courage up BLAIR, ROBERT, 1
W. to keep...from being afraid DRYDEN, JOHN, 24

white as w. as driven snow SHAKESPEARE, WILLIAM, 666
Every fork like a w. web-foot HARDY, THOMAS, 11
'E was w., clear white, inside KIPLING, RUDYARD, 18
important to the w. man as to the Negro DUNHAM, KATHERINE, 1
It is for the w. man to save himself...that I plead WASHINGTON, BOOKER T., 1
I want to be the w. man's brother KING, MARTIN LUTHER, JR., 8
no "w." or "colored" signs on...foxholes KENNEDY, JOHN FITZGERALD, 11
only thing w. people have that black people need BALDWIN, JAMES, 26
show the w. man the hell he comes to make! TOUSSAINT L'OUVERTURE, 3
so-called w. races FORSTER, E. M., 8
Take up the W. Man's burden— /And reap KIPLING, RUDYARD, 12
Take up the W. Man's burden— /Send forth KIPLING, RUDYARD, 53
Them w. men is always fightin' MOSLEY, WALTER, 4
the w. American is even more unprepared KING, MARTIN LUTHER, JR., 26
The w. man knows how to make everything SITTING BULL, 2
The W. Protestant's ultimate sympathy MAILER, NORMAN, 5
Under the w. man's menace, out of time MCKAY, CLAUDE, 1
w. Americans find it hard...truth about colored people DOUGLASS, FREDERICK, 8
"W. folks is white," says uncle Jim CULLEN, COUNTEE, 4
When a w. man in Africa LESSING, DORIS, 5
When the w. man came we had the land GEORGE, DAN, 1
Why should I want to be w. HUGHES, LANGSTON, 16
W. in the moon the long road HOUSMAN, A. E., 21
w. is not *all* that's beautiful COSBY, BILL, 4
W. is ugly when it oppresses blacks YOUNG, WHITNEY M., JR., 2
w. man can dress like a black pimp WILLIAMS, ROBIN, 8
w. man...does not understand America STANDING BEAR, LUTHER, 1
W. man fret and worry and kill hisself HURSTON, ZORA NEALE, 11
W. people have often confused MBOYA, TOM, 1
w. people...indiscriminately viewed as the enemy DAVIS, ANGELA, 5
w. people ought to be transformed into Negroes AGGREY, JAMES EMMAN KWEGYIR, 2
W. people...underestimate all blacks JACKSON, GEORGE, 4
w. teenagers in the Midwest COKER, CHEO HODARI, 1
You gotta say this for the w. race GREGORY, DICK, 7

whitecaps Bay crawled with w. like maggots PROULX, E. ANNIE, 2

white folks These w. didn't actually hate colored people MCMILLAN, TERRY, 5

Whitehall came into W. laughing and jolly EVELYN, JOHN, 3
Members rise from CMG (known...in W. as "Call me God") SAMPSON, ANTHONY, 1
the gentleman in W. really does know better JAY, DOUGLAS, 1
White House Since I came to the W. REAGAN, RONALD, 25
white liberal the w....more white than liberal whenever blacks assert themselves LESTER, JULIUS, 2
white man a living symbol of the w.'s fear MANDELA, WINNIE, 1
whiteness the flood of w. and maleness that diluted...black art HURSTON, ZORA NEALE, 1
There can be no whiter w....An insurance man's shirt BROOKS, GWENDOLYN, 3
whites because the w. oppressed us yesterday MUGABE, ROBERT, 1
the w. of their eyes PRESCOTT, WILLIAM, 1
whitewash no w. at the White House NIXON, RICHARD, 23
Whitman Walt W., childless, lonely old grubber WHITMAN, WALT, 1
Walt W. who laid end to end words WHITMAN, WALT, 4
Where are we going, Walt W. WHITMAN, WALT, 2
W....like a new Adam WHITMAN, WALT, 5
who I do not know w....I am SELLERS, PETER, 2
If you have to tell them w. you are PECK, GREGORY, 1
W. am I? Why am I here STOCKDALE, JAMES B., 1
W.'s Nureyev LAMBERT, JACK, 1
whole They that be w. need not a physician BIBLE, 392
wholesome w., manly, simple ideals of English life WILDE, OSCAR, 1
whom "W. are you?" said he ADE, GEORGE, 2
whore I am the Protestant w. GWYN, NELL, 1
'Tis Pity She's a W. FORD, JOHN (1586–1640?), 5
w., and the whoremonger, shall ye scourge KORAN, 29
w....of Boston, no Church of Christ HUTCHINSON, ANNE, 1
You can lead a w. to culture PARKER, DOROTHY, 5
you must be ...w. in the bedroom HALL, JERRY, 1
whorehouses virgin territory for w. CAPONE, AL, 3
whortleberrying Ye Gods! w. on Olympus MELVILLE, HERMAN, 24
why For every w. he had a wherefore BUTLER, SAMUEL (1612–80), 2
w. and wherefore SHAKESPEARE, WILLIAM, 276
W. should I go? She won't be there MONROE, MARILYN, 3
W. was this world created JOHNSON, SAMUEL, 123
wicked A horrid w. boy was he HOFFMAN, HEINRICH, 2
The w. can have only accomplices VOLTAIRE, 23
w. always have recourse to perjury RACINE, JEAN, 18
wickedness so monstrous a w. should be found CORNWALLIS, CHARLES, 1
The w. of the world BRECHT, BERTOLT, 23
w. of the world is print to him DICKENS, CHARLES, 53
wide screen A w....bad film twice as bad GOLDWYN, SAMUEL, 2
widow a w....a kind of sinecure WYCHERLEY, WILLIAM, 5
better to be the w. of a hero than the wife of a coward IBÁRRURI, DOLORES, 4
to comfort a young w. PROVERBS, 512
widows do as other w. GAY, JOHN, 18
When w. exclaim loudly against second marriages FIELDING, HENRY, 4
wife a fellow's weak point in his w. JOYCE, JAMES, 18
a Japanese w., a French mistress...a Chinese cook LIN YUTANG, 3
A loving w. will do anything PRIESTLEY, J. B., 9
A w. who preaches in her gown HOOD, THOMAS, 15
he knows your w. MOTTOS AND SLOGANS, 12
his...w....a wider circulation than both papers ASTOR, NANCY, 1
his w., or himself must be dead AUSTEN, JANE, 9
I'd have no w. CRASHAW, RICHARD, 2
If you don't give a w. the last word HUGHES, LANGSTON, 10
If you were my w., I'd drink it CHURCHILL, WINSTON, 67
killed his w....salted her WILLISON, GEORGE F., 1
light w. doth make a heavy husband SHAKESPEARE, WILLIAM, 624
marvellous to have a w. HUME, BASIL, 2
My w....had taken my child MOSLEY, WALTER, 11
My w. hath something in her gizzard PEPYS, SAMUEL, 7
Taking a w.?...better to sleep with a pretty boy JUVENAL, 8
that a man lay down his w. for a friend JOYCE, JAMES, 21
the titles of w. and mother...are transitory and accidental LIVERMORE, MARY ASHTON, 2
the w....the weaker vessel BIBLE, 194
They took me from my w. CLARE, JOHN, 1
uncumber'd with a w. DRYDEN, JOHN, 8
When a man opens the car door for his w. PHILIP, PRINCE, 8
Whose w. shall it be TOOKE, HORNE, 1
Whosoever shall put away his w. BIBLE, 415
Widowed w., and married maid SCOTT, SIR WALTER, 20
w....is a receiver of stolen goods JOHNSON, SAMUEL, 140
with a w. to tell him what to do MANCROFT, STORMONT SAMUEL, 1
wifehood Meek w. is no part of my profession BRITTAIN, VERA, 4
wig Can you imagine that I...could ever tolerate a w.? VIGÉE-LEBRUN, ÉLISABETH, 1
wild Walk on the W. Side REED, LOU, 9
w. creatures...integral part of our natural resources NYERERE, JULIUS KAMBARAGE, 2
W. things...taken for granted until progress LEOPOLD, ALDO, 2
Wilde W.'s...persecutors were...the *Daily Telegraph* PARRIS, MATTHEW, 1
wilderness make a w. and call it peace TACITUS, 1
the voice of one crying in the w. BIBLE, 370
the w. of this world BUNYAN, JOHN, 14
wildernesses His stride is w. of freedom HUGHES, TED, 6
wildness w....preservation of the world THOREAU, HENRY DAVID, 9
wild thing never saw a w. /Sorry for itself LAWRENCE, D. H., 31
will committed themselves to the w. of God BRADFORD, WILLIAM, 6
Do what you w. RABELAIS, FRANÇOIS, 6
general w. rules in society ROBESPIERRE, MAXIMILIEN, 3
His W.'s the law FAIRFAX, LORD, 1
In His w. is our peace DANTE ALIGHIERI, 5
It is my w. to go with the man I love BRECHT, BERTOLT, 18
let my w. replace reasoned judgment JUVENAL, 11
one man's w....cause of all men's misery HOOKER, RICHARD, 2
take the w. for the deed SWIFT, JONATHAN, 37
the w. is infinite, and the execution confin'd SHAKESPEARE, WILLIAM, 687
The w. /...of all-ruling heaven MILTON, JOHN, 29
W. and wisdom are both mighty leaders DAY, CLARENCE SHEPARD, 3
w. does not choose...good and evil JASPERS, KARL, 4
Where there's a w. PROVERBS, 458
Where there's a w., there's a lawsuit MIZNER, ADDISON, 1
W. is always Evil BLAKE, WILLIAM, 11
With all my w....We two now part PATMORE, COVENTRY, 5
W. ye no come back again? NAIRNE, CAROLINA, 1

w. you join the dance CARROLL, LEWIS, 20
You w., Oscar, you will WILDE, OSCAR, 8
willingly Most w. and cheerfully MCGONAGALL, WILLIAM, 5
willow All a green w. is my garland HEYWOOD, JOHN, 1
willows W. whiten, aspens quiver TENNYSON, ALFRED, 66
Wilson I choose neither W. nor Lenin JAURÈS, JEAN, 1
Mr W.... is the 14th Mr Wilson DOUGLAS-HOME, ALEC, 3
W....noble failure and a Biblical prophet WILSON, WOODROW, 2
Wimbledon phoniness...a lot of it at W. MCENROE, JOHN, 2
win I can no longer w. NICKLAUS, JACK, 4
If we w. here we will win everywhere HEMINGWAY, ERNEST, 14
we will w....God's on our side LOUIS, JOE, 4
When you w., nothing hurts NAMATH, JOE, 1
whether you w. or lose NAVRATILOVA, MARTINA, 6
W. or lose, I'll be going out in style NAVRATILOVA, MARTINA, 3
wind a roaring in the w. all night WORDSWORTH, WILLIAM, 64
Come w., come weather BUNYAN, JOHN, 22
How slow the W. DICKINSON, EMILY, 19
if, as I suspect, it's only w. HEWART, GORDON, 2
It's an ill w. PROVERBS, 280
O wild West W. SHELLEY, PERCY BYSSHE, 9
The roaring of the w. is my wife KEATS, JOHN (1795–1821), 42
When the w. blows the cradle will rock BLAKE, CHARLES DUPEE, 1
Who has seen the w. ROSSETTI, CHRISTINA, 12
winding sheet The waters were his w. BARNFIELD, RICHARD, 1
window the broken w. pane is the most valuable argument PANKHURST, EMMELINE, 6
you can't help w. shopping AYCKBOURN, ALAN, 4
windows only way to get your w. cleaned AIREY, LAWRENCE, 1
wine A man may...be allowed to take a glass of w. SHERIDAN, RICHARD BRINSLEY, 16
And w. can...the wise beguile POPE, ALEXANDER, 88
days of w. and roses DOWSON, ERNEST, 2
good w. is a good familiar creature SHAKESPEARE, WILLIAM, 482
It wasn't the w....It was the salmon DICKENS, CHARLES, 77
no man...having drunk old w. straightway desireth new BIBLE, 331
the w. is in, the wit is out BECON, THOMAS, 1
they shall not drink w. with a song BIBLE, 207
This w. is too good for toast-drinking HEMINGWAY, ERNEST, 18
turning... w. of Shiraz into urine DINESEN, ISAK, 1
use a little w. for thy stomach's sake BIBLE, 237
w. and women, mirth and laughter BYRON, LORD, 49
W. comes in at the mouth YEATS, W. B., 26
when I touch w., it turns into water AGA KHAN III, SIR, 1
When the w. is in PROVERBS, 457
white w. came up with the fish MANKIEWICZ, HERMAN J., 3
Who loves not w., woman and song LUTHER, MARTIN, 19
W. in, secret out PROVERBS, 61
w. is mightier than the king BIN GORION, MICHA JOSEPH, 1
W. is the most healthful...of beverages PASTEUR, LOUIS, 5
w....should be drunk PAGNOL, MARCEL, 2
W....show the mind of man THEOGNIS OF MEGARA, 1
wines W....and girls are good LYLY, JOHN, 11
wing Comin' in on a W. and a Prayer ADAMSON, HAROLD, 1
wings gift of w., and you learn...that you will not fall WINTERSON, JEANETTE, 2
man with w. large enough and duly attached LEONARDO DA VINCI, 7
to walk on w., and tread in air POPE, ALEXANDER, 77
wink a w. behind everything I do MADONNA, 6
winners The only people who are remembered are the w. CHRISTIE, LINFORD, 3
winning W. isn't everything, but wanting to win is LOMBARDI, VINCE, 1
winston It hasn't taken W. long CHURCHILL, WINSTON, 1
winter From w....good lord, deliver us NASHE, THOMAS, 2
Many...say that they enjoy the w. ADAMS, RICHARD, 1
No one thinks of w. KIPLING, RUDYARD, 46
The swift red flesh, a w. king CRANE, HART, 2
W. is icummen in POUND, EZRA, 17
w. of our discontent SHAKESPEARE, WILLIAM, 527
winter-time Through w. we call on spring YEATS, W. B., 39
Wisconsin little girl lived in...Big Woods of W. WILDER, LAURA INGALLS, 1
wisdom by disposition is w. acquired PLAUTUS, 8
give my w. and experience to animals BARDOT, BRIGITTE, 2
If one is too lazy to think...never attain w. CONNOLLY, CYRIL, 14
in much w. is much grief BIBLE, 46
It is a point of w. to be silent PLUTARCH, 12
more w. in your body NIETZSCHE, FRIEDRICH WILHELM, 22
one dispensing w. rather than seeking it MCCORMACK, MARK, 7
The highest w. has but one science TOLSTOY, LEO, 10
the price of w. is above rubies BIBLE, 263
Vain w. all, and false philosophy MILTON, JOHN, 40
w....beyond the rules of physic BACON, FRANCIS (1561–1626), 54
W. has taught us to be calm HOLMES, OLIVER WENDELL, 4
w....hath hewn out her seven pillars BIBLE, 455
W. is humble COWPER, WILLIAM, 33
W. is something...never expect from Freud FREUD, SIGMUND, 20
with how little w. the world is governed OXENSTIERNA, AXEL, 1
w. not to kick away the...step GANDHI, MAHATMA, 7
W., with tear-filled eyes CHAR, RENÉ, 2
wise a little w. the best fools be DONNE, JOHN, 45
Be lowly w. MILTON, JOHN, 75
Be w. with speed YOUNG, EDWARD, 2
If you are w., be wise PLAUTUS, 7
Many have been the w. speeches of fools FULLER, THOMAS (1608–61), 6
Neither a w. man nor a brave man EISENHOWER, DWIGHT D., 30
not a w. question...to answer EDEN, ANTHONY, 5
No w. man ever wished to be younger SWIFT, JONATHAN, 25
See nations slowly w. and meanly just JOHNSON, SAMUEL, 7
Some folk are w....some are otherwise SMOLLETT, TOBIAS, 1
The most w. speech is not as holy VEGA, LOPE DE, 1
To be w. and love SHAKESPEARE, WILLIAM, 685
w. enough to play the fool SHAKESPEARE, WILLIAM, 705
w. man...built his house upon a rock BIBLE, 388
w. man...make more opportunities BACON, FRANCIS (1561–1626), 20
w. man makes his own decisions PROVERBS, 23
wiser Be w. than other people CHESTERFIELD, LORD, 7
w. than thou art ware of SHAKESPEARE, WILLIAM, 99
w. than we know EMERSON, RALPH WALDO, 20
wisest only the w. and the stupidest CONFUCIUS, 10
The w. invention in the world GÓMEZ DE LA SERNA, RAMÓN, 2
wish Someday I'll w. upon a star HARBURG, E. Y., 4
The w. to hurt BRONOWSKI, JACOB, 4
The w. to spread... opinions BUTLER, SAMUEL (1835–1902), 5
w. a snow in May's newfangled shows SHAKESPEARE, WILLIAM, 374

for a w. to get her Ph.D. she's gotta pass Men MCMILLAN, TERRY, 7
genius of W....electrical in movement FULLER, MARGARET, 8
God created W. NIETZSCHE, FRIEDRICH WILHELM, 26
greatest glory of a w. PERICLES, 3
hell a fury like a w. scorned CONGREVE, WILLIAM, 14
help and support of the w. I love EDWARD VIII, 6
I am a w. and a woman of Africa EMECHETA, BUCHI, 1
I am a w. first of all NIN, ANAÏS, 2
I am a w. meant for a man DAVIS, BETTE, 5
I could be a good w. if I had five thousand THACKERAY, WILLIAM MAKEPEACE, 11
If a w. is strong BAI FENGXI, 1
if a w. leaves her lawful husband TOLSTOY, LEO, 1
if a w. no longer wants you in her arms HUGHES, LANGSTON, 13
If de fust w. God ever made...turn the world upside down TRUTH, SOJOURNER, 3
If I had been a w. MAXWELL, ROBERT, 2
I had become a w. of...character DOSTOYEVSKY, ANNA, 1
I have nothing /Of w. in me SHAKESPEARE, WILLIAM, 92
It is a great glory in...w. THUCYDIDES, 5
I will not admit that a w. can draw so well DEGAS, EDGAR, 3
knew... ills enow /To be a w. DONNE, JOHN, 48
Last week I saw a w. flayed SWIFT, JONATHAN, 18
Let us look for the w. DUMAS, ALEXANDRE, 2
love is the natural impulse of a w. FICHTE, JOHANN, 5
lovely w. in a rural spot HUNT, LEIGH, 5
lovely w.! Nature made thee OTWAY, THOMAS, 3
never trust a w. WILDE, OSCAR, 19
no fiend in hell can match the fury of a disappointed w. CIBBER, COLLEY, 2
no more a w. /than Christ...a man SEXTON, ANNE, 2
none of w. born /Shall harm Macbeth SHAKESPEARE, WILLIAM, 407
no such thing as an old w. MICHELET, JULES, 4
not in my time—before a w. THATCHER, MARGARET, 15
No w. can call herself free SANGER, MARGARET, 1
No where /Lives a w. true DONNE, JOHN, 36
No w. should...be...accurate about her age WILDE, OSCAR, 56
no w. should marry a teetotaller STEVENSON, ROBERT LOUIS, 33
No w. so naked as...underneath her clothes FRAYN, MICHAEL, 1
Old age is w.'s hell LENCLOS, NINON DE, 1
old w....uncontrollable by any earthly force SAYERS, DOROTHY L., 2
Once a w. has given you her heart VANBRUGH, JOHN, 4
One is not born a w. BEAUVOIR, SIMONE DE, 12
one w. who is a perfect angel FIELDING, SARAH, 1
only three things to be done with a w. DURRELL, LAWRENCE, 3
O W.! in our hours of ease SCOTT, SIR WALTER, 12
role of the mature w. in the media...negative HARRIS, JANET, 2
She floats, she hesitates; in a word, she's a w. RACINE, JEAN, 7
She is a w. therefore may be won SHAKESPEARE, WILLIAM, 678
She may be a w. but she isn't a sister THATCHER, MARGARET, 7
Should a w. /...lie down with grammarians QABBANI, NIZAR, 3
Society...decrees that w. is inferior BEAUVOIR, SIMONE DE, 14
some w....he knew in the past SEI SHONAGON, 1
still be a w. to you PARNELL, THOMAS, 2
surest way to hit a w.'s heart JERROLD, DOUGLAS, 3
thanks God for not making him a w. NEUBERGER, JULIA, 2
Than to ever let a w. in my life LERNER, ALAN JAY, 7
the figure of a solitary W....in white garments COLLINS, WILKIE, 2
There was an old w. who lived in a shoe CHILDREN'S VERSE, 19
The silliest w. can manage a clever man KIPLING, RUDYARD, 41
the sort of w. who lives for others LEWIS, C. S., 7
The w.'s a whore JOHNSON, SAMUEL, 149
The w. that deliberates is lost ADDISON, JOSEPH, 8
This is a w.'s industry JONES, AMANDA THEODOSIA, 1
To be a w....a peculiarity BEAUVOIR, SIMONE DE, 17
'Twere more than w. to be wise MOORE, THOMAS, 9
w. behaves like a man EVANS, EDITH, 2
w., behold thy son BIBLE, 298
w. can go skiing in pearls LACROIX, CHRISTIAN, 1
w. discovered the orgasm FIGES, EVA, 2
W. does not love STRINDBERG, AUGUST, 3
w. feels...the injustice of disfranchisement STANTON, ELIZABETH CADY, 7
w. governs America MADARIAGA Y ROGO, SALVADOR DE, 2
W....greater respect for life than man KEY, ELLEN, 6
What w. was not susceptible to flattery NWAPA, FLORA, 3
When a W. appears in the World COCKBURN, CATHERINE, 1
When a w. gives her opinion she's a bitch DAVIS, BETTE, 7
When w. complains...about...inequality ROUSSEAU, JEAN-JACQUES, 13
Where there is a w. there is magic SHANGE, NTOZAKE, 5
Whether a pretty w. grants...her favors OVID, 3
Why can't a w. be more like a man? LERNER, ALAN JAY, 10
Why...was I born a w. NOGAROLA, ISOTTA, 1
will not stand...being called a w. in my own house WAUGH, EVELYN, 25
w. in her middle years does not...look too closely GIBBONS, STELLA, 6
w. in this age is considered learned WOOLLEY, HANNAH, 1
w. in this humour woo'd SHAKESPEARE, WILLIAM, 529
w. is a slave...beast of burden SCHIRMACHER, KÄTHE, 1
w. is dependent...self-image PERRY, ELEANOR, 1
W. is the lesser man TENNYSON, ALFRED, 56
W. is unrivaled as a wet nurse TWAIN, MARK, 58
W. is woman's natural ally EURIPIDES, 3
w. loves her lover BYRON, LORD, 54
W....must...protect herself ANTHONY, SUSAN B., 8
"W."...no less capable...than "Man" ASTELL, MARY, 1
w. of common views but uncommon abilities CRITCHLEY, JULIAN, 1
w. of education VANBRUGH, JOHN, 2
w. oweth to her husband SHAKESPEARE, WILLIAM, 641
W. puts us back into communication RENAN, ERNEST, 10
w. really succeeds in changing a man WOOD, NATALIE, 1
W.'s at best a contradiction POPE, ALEXANDER, 57
w.'s business...preparation...of food and wine CONFUCIUS, 38
w. seldom asks advice ADDISON, JOSEPH, 20
W. seldom Writes her Mind STEELE, RICHARD, 3
W.'s faith, and woman's trust SCOTT, SIR WALTER, 21
w. should always stand by a woman EURIPIDES, 7
w.'s...life is a history of the affections IRVING, WASHINGTON, 7
w. smiles her dress must smile too VIONNET, MADELEINE, 1
W.'s Pen present you with a Play BOOTHBY, FRANCES, 1
W., stick to your spinning ARISTOPHANES, 1
W.'s virtue...man's greatest invention SKINNER, CORNELIA OTIS, 1
w. then go on MOTT, LUCRETIA, 2
w. to dress like her male colleagues FISCHER-MIRKIN, TOBY, 1
w. was made...to be his equall SPEGHT, RACHEL, 1
W.! when I behold thee flippant, vain KEATS, JOHN (1795–1821), 81
w. who is chic...a little different POST, EMILY, 2
w. who is loved always has success BAUM, VICKI, 3
w. who is really kind to dogs BEERBOHM, MAX, 19

w. who reads the marriage contract DUNCAN, ISADORA, 4
w. who's committed to her own development NORTON, ELEANOR HOLMES, 3
w. who...would start rearranging the pictures THATCHER, MARGARET, 2
W. will be the last thing civilized by Man MEREDITH, GEORGE, 10
w. with an actively male soul TSVETAEVA, MARINA, 1
w. with cut hair...a monster PRYNNE, WILLIAM, 1
w. without a man is like a fish STEINEM, GLORIA, 16
w. would rather visit her own grave HARRIS, CORRA MAY, 1
w....wrote the book that made this...war LINCOLN, ABRAHAM, 21
You ask whether w. possesses any natural intelligence CHRISTINE DE PISAN, 2
You're a fine w., Lou WEST, MAE, 13

womanhood All w. is hampered today DU BOIS, W. E. B., 4
ideal of an intellectual and emancipated w. PANKHURST, SYLVIA, 1
W....the great fact in her life STANTON, ELIZABETH CADY, 8

womankind With w., the less we love PUSHKIN, ALEXANDER, 2

woman-kind whole race of w. is...made subject to man BOCCACCIO, GIOVANNI, 5

womanliness W. means only motherhood BROWNING, ROBERT, 7

woman's emancipation greatest stumbling block in the way of w. STANTON, ELIZABETH CADY, 4

woman's rights this mad, wicked folly...W. VICTORIA, 4

womb think with our w., why...a brain LUCE, CLARE BOOTHE, 2

wombs when they feel the life of a child in their w. BRIDGET OF SWEDEN, 1

women a few w. told me...it was sex HARRIS, JANET, 3
all men and w. are created equal STANTON, ELIZABETH CADY, 9
all W. are born slaves ASTELL, MARY, 2
American w. expect to find in their husbands MAUGHAM, SOMERSET, 1
Arab w.'s unity and solidarity...important weapons SAADAWI, NAWAL EL-, 3
a tide in the affairs of w. BYRON, LORD, 70
beautiful w. never last BUKOWSKI, CHARLES, 4
Between w. love is contemplative BEAUVOIR, SIMONE DE, 8
Changeable w. are more endurable SHAW, GEORGE BERNARD, 110
Does anybody wonder so many w. die CHESNUT, MARY, 1
Ef w. want any rights TRUTH, SOJOURNER, 2
few w. can bear being laughed at RUSSELL, ANNA, 1
Few w. care to be laughed at AYCKBOURN, ALAN, 6
few w. ever pass forty DIOR, CHRISTIAN, 1
for w....still room to advance O'CONNOR, SANDRA DAY, 1
For w., writing is a medium WOLF, CHRISTA, 5
Give w. scope and opportunity PLASCHKINA, NELLY, 1
Give w. the vote SHAW, GEORGE BERNARD, 68
God, why didn't you make w. first MONTAND, YVES, 1
I am not for w. but against men KRAUS, KARL, 9
If w. be proud TATTLEWELL, MARY, 1
If w....cease producing cannon fodder GREER, GERMAINE, 5
If w. didn't exist ONASSIS, ARISTOTLE, 3
if weak w. went astray, /Their stars PRIOR, MATTHEW, 3
I hate w. THURBER, JAMES, 18
Impossible to know...with w. STRINDBERG, AUGUST, 2
Intimacies between w. often go backwards BOWEN, ELIZABETH, 3
in w....abdominal swellings MORRISON, RUTHERFORD, 1
It was hell for w. architects then KERBIS, GERTRUDE LEMPP, 1
made love to ten thousand w. SIMENON, GEORGES, 2
man...driving w. round the bend for generations COPE, WENDY, 4
Most good w. are hidden treasures PARKER, DOROTHY, 20
Most w. set out to try to change a man DIETRICH, MARLENE, 3
no one ever asks the w. and children what they think SCHROEDER, PATRICIA, 1
not denyin' the w. are foolish ELIOT, GEORGE, 11
Older w. are best FLEMING, IAN, 6
one physical performance possible to w. DE MILLE, AGNES, 3
Only w. have children STRINDBERG, AUGUST, 6
Powerful w....succeed in spite of their husbands LEE-POTTER, LINDA, 1
proper function of w. ELIOT, GEORGE, 26
saluting strange w. and grandfather clocks NASH, OGDEN, 25
several young w....would render the Christian life intensely difficult LEWIS, C. S., 5
So few grown w. like their lives GRAHAM, KATHARINE, 2
some w....should only be caressed DEGAS, EDGAR, 7
than keeping w. in a state of ignorance KNOX, VICESIMUS, 1
The fates of w. mold her GOETHE, JOHANN WOLFGANG VON, 11
The happiest w.,...have no history ELIOT, GEORGE, 27
the more I see of w....law WODEHOUSE, P. G., 31
There are two kinds of w. PICASSO, PABLO, 18
the w. come and go ELIOT, T. S., 32
this movement represented...protests of individual w. CATT, CARRIE CHAPMAN, 2
to fit w....masculine pattern of attitudes HUFFINGTON, ARIANNA, 1
to w.'s beauty would submit BEHN, APHRA, 6
w. and minorities striving to move up MAHONEY, RICHARD J., 2
W. and music should never be dated GOLDSMITH, OLIVER, 12
W. and Revolution...epics of courage YANG PING, 1
W....architects of society STOWE, HARRIET BEECHER, 2
w. are a sex by themselves BEERBOHM, MAX, 5
w. are attracted by power and money CONRAN, TERENCE, 1
W. are dirt searchers KENNEDY, FLORYNCE R., 10
W....are either better or worse than men LA BRUYÈRE, JEAN DE, 20
W. are entitled to dress attractively ROUGIER, RICHARD, 1
W. are equal because... not different FROMM, ERICH, 18
W. are learning...genius has no sex. BRYAN, MARY E., 1
W. are like banks ORTON, JOE, 3
W. are like tricks by slight of hand CONGREVE, WILLIAM, 7
W. are like water BALDWIN, JAMES, 2
W. are...much nicer than men AMIS, KINGSLEY, 1
W. are no longer...veiled and silent MERNISSI, FATIMA, 5
W. are not the moon BAI FENGXI, 2
W. are so opinionated SAKI, 11
w. become like their mothers WILDE, OSCAR, 41
w. be educated to dependence WOLLSTONECRAFT, MARY, 1
W....be obscene and not heard LENNON, JOHN, 13
w. can do nothing except love MAUGHAM, SOMERSET, 33
W. can do nothing that has permanence LAGERLÖF, SELMA, 2
w. can live their whole lives and not know the law FAISAL, TAUJAN, 1
W. cannot be part of the Institute of France AMAGAT, EMILE HILAIRE, 1
W. can't forgive failure CHEKHOV, ANTON, 14
W....care fifty times more for a marriage BAGEHOT, WALTER, 10
W. complain about sex LANDERS, ANN, 1
W. confide in other women MORRIS, MARY, 1
W....content with...easily broken ties LEWES, GEORGE HENRY, 1
w. defend themselves so poorly LACLOS, PIERRE CHODERLOS DE, 1
w. dislike his books CONRAD, JOSEPH, 1
We are here to claim our rights as w. PANKHURST, CHRISTABEL, 3

W....emancipated on condition...don't upset men ROVER, CONSTANCE, 1
w....embarrassed to talk about money MIRMAN, SOPHIE, 1
Were w. never so fair, men would be false LYLY, JOHN, 1
W. exist...solely for the propagation of the species SCHOPENHAUER, ARTHUR, 21
W. fail to understand...men hate them GREER, GERMAINE, 9
W....find it extremely difficult to behave like gentlemen MACKENZIE, COMPTON, 6
what most w. think about anything AYCKBOURN, ALAN, 1
W. have always fought for men PANKHURST, EMMELINE, 5
w. have been presented as devils or angels DUNAYEVSKAYA, RAYA, 1
W. have been...queens for a long time ALCOTT, LOUISA MAY, 1
W. have done well in wartime FRASER, ANTONIA, 1
w. have fewer teeth than men ARISTOTLE, 2
W. have no wilderness in them BOGAN, LOUISE, 1
w. have often been handicapped...by a fear of success RUDIKOFF, SONYA, 1
W. have served...as looking-glasses WOOLF, VIRGINIA, 8
When w. are the advisers ALCOTT, LOUISA MAY, 3
When w. go wrong WEST, MAE, 22
When w. kiss...prize-fighters shaking hands MENCKEN, H. L., 5
When W. write, the Criticks...damn their Plays DAVYS, MARY, 1
Where do all the w....get the heroism KOLLWITZ, KÄTHE, 3
Why are w....interesting to men WOOLF, VIRGINIA, 7
Will never understand what w. want BELLOW, SAUL, 5
w....ill-using them and then confessing TROLLOPE, ANTHONY, 3
w. inch forward ROOSEVELT, ELEANOR, 3
w....know that life is messy NORMAN, MARSHA, 1
w....little sisters to all the world DIX, DOROTHY, 3
w....live like human beings...outside the religion NASREEN, TASLIMA, 3
w. must be half-workers SHAKESPEARE, WILLIAM, 128
w....must do twice as well WHITTON, CHARLOTTE, 1
w. need kindness more than love CHILDRESS, ALICE, 2
W. never have young minds DELANEY, SHELAGH, 2
Wonderful w. TERRY, ELLEN, 1
w....perceive their bodies in their entirety WITTIG, MONIQUE, 1
w. possess but one class of physical organs LIVERMORE, MARY ASHTON, 1
W. receive /the insults of men /with tolerance LAING, DILYS, 1
W. rule the world DYLAN, BOB, 21
W.'s history...tool for women's emancipation LERNER, GERDA, 1
w. should cultivate...ability to make money DEMAREST, ELLEN, 1
w. should talk an hour BEAUMONT & FLETCHER, 3
W....the guardians of wisdom and humanity WOLFF, CHARLOTTE, 1
W....the mothers of all mischief BLACKMORE, R. D., 1
W....triumph of matter over mind WILDE, OSCAR, 63
w. use but half their strength MARLOWE, CHRISTOPHER, 19
W., we need you to give us back our faith in humanity TUTU, DESMOND, 12
W. were not supposed to be so soft BONNER, MARITA, 1
w. who have done something with their lives GILOT, FRANÇOISE, 1
W. who live by the goodwill of men WELDON, FAY, 2
W. who love the same man BEERBOHM, MAX, 18
W. who marry...happiest years...giving life ROOSEVELT, EDITH CAROW, 1
w. working in the factories stopped JOFFRE, JOSEPH JACQUES CÉSAIRE, 2
W. would rather be right NASH, OGDEN, 2
You asked me if I knew w. ALBEE, EDWARD, 4

women's lib w. movement came from the war WOLFARD, MARY, 1

women's liberation W. is...foolishness MEIR, GOLDA, 2
W. is the liberation of the feminine in the man KENT, CORITA, 1

women's rights battle for w....been largely won THATCHER, MARGARET, 22
The extension of w. FOURIER, CHARLES, 1

womman worthy w. al hir lyve CHAUCER, GEOFFREY, 21

wommen W. desiren to have sovereynetee CHAUCER, GEOFFREY, 35

won I w. the count SOMOZA DEBAYLE, ANASTASIO, 1
When I w. my first one FIELD, SALLY, 1

wonder I never w. to see men wicked SWIFT, JONATHAN, 46
Many a man...a w. to the world MONTAIGNE, MICHEL DE, 23
Men love to w....seed of our science EMERSON, RALPH WALDO, 45
The chief w. of education ADAMS, HENRY, 12

wonderful If...work were such a w. thing KIRKLAND, LANE, 1
I've had a w. life PORTER, PETER, 3
none is more w. than man SOPHOCLES, 2
w. to see persons of the best sense ADDISON, JOSEPH, 24

wonders We carry within us the w. BROWNE, THOMAS, 15

wood about the dreadful w. /Of conscious evil AUDEN, W. H., 42
therefore to be w. SHAKESPEARE, WILLIAM, 286
w. is also sawing the saws LIU SHAHE, 2

woodman W., spare that tree MORRIS, GEORGE POPE, 1

woods Thee Shepherd, thee the w., and desert caves MILTON, JOHN, 121
The w. are lovely FROST, ROBERT, 15
the w. decay and fall TENNYSON, ALFRED, 9
We'll to the w. no more HOUSMAN, A. E., 22

woodshed Something nasty in the w. GIBBONS, STELLA, 4

wool go out for w. CERVANTES, MIGUEL DE, 42
W...."survival of the fittest" clothing material JAEGER, GUSTAV, 1

woord W. is but wynd LYDGATE, JOHN, 2

word Better one w. less PROVERBS, 85
but a w. and a blow BUNYAN, JOHN, 12
every w. stabs SHAKESPEARE, WILLIAM, 446
I would never use a long w. HOLMES, OLIVER WENDELL, 14
Man's w. is God in man TENNYSON, ALFRED, 15
Stevenson seemed to pick the right w. STEVENSON, ROBERT LOUIS, 1
the w. no longer belongs to the speaker HEINE, HEINRICH, 7
the w. of God is...sharper than any two-edged sword BIBLE, 141
use a w. that might send a reader to the dictionary HEMINGWAY, ERNEST, 3
w. connects the visible...with the invisible CALVINO, ITALO, 4
w....not the same with one writer PÉGUY, CHARLES PIERRE, 4
w., which tells us nothing...calms us PIRANDELLO, LUIGI, 9

Word He was the W., that spake it DONNE, JOHN, 18
The W. was made flesh BIBLE, 267

Word of God most precious jewel, the W. HENRY VIII, 11

words All w., /And no performance MASSINGER, PHILIP, 5
But w. are words SHAKESPEARE, WILLIAM, 469
Fine w. and an insinuating appearance CONFUCIUS, 5
For w., like Nature, half reveal HALLAM, ARTHUR HENRY, 1
His w....trip about him at command MILTON, JOHN, 8
how can w. say it *for* the music COLTRANE, JOHN, 2
If w. spoken to friends...treason WENTWORTH, THOMAS, 2
I learned w.: but half of them /died MCCAIG, NORMAN, 8
I put the w. down WAUGH, EVELYN, 37
I've gotta use w. when I talk to you ELIOT, T. S., 39
learn the use of living w. DE LA MARE, WALTER, 1
my w. are idle WEBSTER, JOHN, 8

my w. are my own CHARLES II, 11
Of every four w....I strike out three BOILEAU, NICOLAS, 7
Our w. are dead /like...tyrant's conscience GOSAIBI, GHAZI AL-, 1
She shrank from w. TAYLOR, ELIZABETH, 3
text consists not of a line of w. BARTHES, ROLAND, 4
The use...of w....sensible marks of ideas LOCKE, JOHN, 4
the very simplest w. /Must be enough BRECHT, BERTOLT, 2
the w. you use should be your own MORRISSEY, 3
use the most common...w. WESLEY, JOHN, 7
w. and what they described were intermingled PAMUK, ORHAN, 1
W. are but empty thanks CIBBER, COLLEY, 8
w. are but the shadows of actions PLUTARCH, 10
W....are great foes of reality CONRAD, JOSEPH, 11
W. are like leaves POPE, ALEXANDER, 18
W. are men's daughters MADDEN, SAMUEL, 1
w. are the daughters of earth JOHNSON, SAMUEL, 17
W. are...the most powerful drug KIPLING, RUDYARD, 5
W. are the tokens BACON, FRANCIS (1561–1626), 98
w. are things BYRON, LORD, 61
W. can be deceitful MARCEAU, MARCEL, 1
W. can destroy KIRKPATRICK, JEANE JORDAN, 2
W. cannot explain...there is some mysterious art ZHUANGZI, 7
W. do not pay for...dead people JOSEPH, CHIEF, 3
W. gave her clarity, brought reason ONDAATJE, MICHAEL, 1
W. may be false and full of art SHADWELL, THOMAS, 4
w. once spoke...never be recall'd. DILLON, WENTWORTH, 1
W....physicians of a mind diseased AESCHYLUS, 5
w. /retain a man's imprint SEFERIS, GEORGE, 1
W....saturated with lies or atrocity STEINER, GEORGE, 6
W. sweet as honey from his lips distill'd POPE, ALEXANDER, 68
w. take the place of actions BRYAN, WILLIAM JENNINGS, 1
W....the small change of thought RENARD, JULES, 21
W., words, mere words SHAKESPEARE, WILLIAM, 692
W., words, or I shall burst FARQUHAR, GEORGE, 12

Wordsworth Mr. W., a stupid man, with a...gift WORDSWORTH, WILLIAM, 8
simple W. chime his childish verse COLERIDGE, SAMUEL TAYLOR, 1
W. is never interrupted KEATS, JOHN (1795–1821), 9
W....never was a lake poet WORDSWORTH, WILLIAM, 9
W.'s healing power ARNOLD, MATTHEW, 5

work After hard w., the biggest determinant BLOOMBERG, MICHAEL, 2
All w. and no play PROVERBS, 127
All your w. is done on paper DIDEROT, DENIS, 1
By the w. one knows the workman LA FONTAINE, JEAN DE, 14
can't call yourself a great w. of nature WHISTLER, JAMES ABBOTT MCNEILL, 15
dignity in w. CAMUS, ALBERT, 7
Eight hours of hard w. BERGMAN, INGMAR, 4
Every man's w.... is always a portrait of himself BUTLER, SAMUEL (1835–1902), 10
Every w....is a system BUTLER, JOSEPH, 3
few people...w. without praise or recognition VITTACHI, VARINDRA TARZIE, 2
For men must w., and women must weep KINGSLEY, CHARLES, 1
harder you w. PLAYER, GARY, 1
Hard w.. There is no short cut SLOAN, ALFRED P., JR., 5
her w. has been described as applied art ARP, JEAN, 3
I do most of my w. sitting down BENCHLEY, ROBERT, 8
I don't w. from a written script ANTONIONI, MICHELANGELO, 2
if any would not w., neither should he eat BIBLE, 178
I like w.; it fascinates me JEROME, JEROME K., 10
In w. consciousness becomes aware of itself HEGEL, G. W. F., 11
Let there be w.... for all MANDELA, NELSON, 15
most important motive...is pleasure in w. EINSTEIN, ALBERT, 24
My w. is done EASTMAN, GEORGE, 1
Nice W. If You Can Get It GERSHWIN, IRA, 1
Nothing to do but w. KING, BENJAMIN FRANKLIN, 1
not real w....doing something else BARRIE, J. M., 2
no w., nor device, nor knowledge...in the grave BIBLE, 54
People w. better...experience beautiful shapes KEY, ELLEN, 1
salvation, to which w....is the door BLUE, LIONEL, 2
the w. is negligible GRAHAME, KENNETH, 1
They say hard w. never hurt anybody REAGAN, RONALD, 50
To him, /w. is a narrow grief DOVE, RITA, 3
to w. early...to make shareholders rich HAMMER, MICHAEL, 1
W. and love—these are the basics REIK, THEODOR, 1
W. banishes those three great evils VOLTAIRE, 18
w. becomes more complex and collaborative GOLEMAN, DANIEL, 2
W....by those employees PETER, LAURENCE J., 4
W....curse of the drinking classes WILDE, OSCAR, 78
W. expands so as to fill the time PARKINSON, CYRIL NORTHCOTE, 4
When a man says he wants to w. WHATELY, RICHARD, 4
When I w. 14 hours a day HAMMER, ARMAND, 1
When...people are unable to find w. COOLIDGE, CALVIN, 12
Which of us...is to do the hard and dirty w. RUSKIN, JOHN, 10
W. is a dull way to get rich ASCHERSON, NEAL, 2
w. is a pleasure, life is a joy GORKY, MAKSIM, 3
W. is more fun than fun RODDICK, ANITA, 3
W. is necessary for man PICASSO, PABLO, 19
w. is perceived as...form of punishment MCGREGOR, DOUGLAS M., 1
w. is still done by the women WICKS, MALCOLM, 1
W. is the grand cure CARLYLE, THOMAS, 5
W. Makes One Free MOTTOS AND SLOGANS, 26
world's w....is done by men who do not feel...well MARX, KARL, 5
w. to a state of statistical control DEMING, W. EDWARDS, 1
W. to me is a sacred thing BOURKE-WHITE, MARGARET, 1
w. well done, select a busy man HUBBARD, ELBERT, 5
Your w. and your life...one existence WESKER, ARNOLD, 1

worked what w. once must always work HELLMAN, LILLIAN, 1
w. just long enough...didn't like it THEROUX, PAUL, 4

worker a standardized w. with interchangeable parts GIRAUDOUX, JEAN, 2
good w. loves the board BERRY, WENDELL, 5
The w. becomes an ever cheaper commodity MARX, KARL, 16

workers don't agree with w.' control of industry NADER, RALPH, 1
trouble with the w....don't know nothin' DOS PASSOS, JOHN, 7
used to dealing with estate w. DOUGLAS-HOME, CAROLINE, 1
w....nothing to lose but their chains MARX, KARL, 19
w. reassert their responsibility for themselves CLINTON, HILLARY, 3

work force discontented w....inferior product MORGAN, ELAINE, 2

workforce lay off half your w. IVERSON, KEN, 4

workhouse "The W."—always a word of shame LEE, LAURIE, 4

working If you keep w., you'll last longer GENEEN, HAROLD, 2
w. Americans...forgotten Americans NIXON, RICHARD, 20
What's the need of w. if it doesn't get you anywhere? BONNER, MARITA, 4

working-class w. became...psychic dumping-ground EHRENREICH, BARBARA, 1

working classes No writer before the...19th century wrote about the w. WAUGH, EVELYN, 23
worst fault of the w. MORTIMER, JOHN, 3

working class hero w. is something to be LENNON, JOHN, 8

working group The number...in any w. tends to increase PARKINSON, CYRIL NORTHCOTE, 2

workman A bad w. PROVERBS, 96

works cast away the w. of darkness BOOK OF COMMON PRAYER, 4
great w....awaken our spirit CÉLINE, LOUIS-FERDINAND, 1
W. of the Lord BOOK OF COMMON PRAYER, 1
w. published...by real lunatics JAMES, WILLIAM, 22

world all the w. should be taxed BIBLE, 322
a man for whom the outside w. exists GAUTIER, THÉOPHILE, 2
Any w. which did not have a place for me LORDE, AUDRE, 5
as good be out of the w. CIBBER, COLLEY, 1
a W. in a Grain of Sand BLAKE, WILLIAM, 3
a w. of vile ill-favour'd faults SHAKESPEARE, WILLIAM, 630
beauty of the w., 't is but skin deep VENNING, RALPH, 2
brave new w. /That has such people in't SHAKESPEARE, WILLIAM, 652
Charity begins at home...voice of the w. BROWNE, THOMAS, 31
Dear W., I am leaving you because I am bored SANDERS, GEORGE, 1
fill his w. with phantoms PORCHIA, ANTONIO, 2
God so loved the w. BIBLE, 273
gone into the w. of light VAUGHAN, HENRY, 6
Had we but w. enough, and time MARVELL, ANDREW, 12
He pleases all the w. MOLIÈRE, 1
Here, where the w. is quiet SWINBURNE, ALGERNON CHARLES, 8
I believe the w. is going to end WEINBERGER, CASPAR, 1
I called the New W. into existence CANNING, GEORGE, 4
If all the w. were paper FOLK VERSE, 36
If the w. should break HORACE, 42
If the w. were a well-tuned instrument ATHENAGORAS, 1
if you cannot turn the w....at least get out of the way MAKEBA, MIRIAM, 1
I have...been all round the w. BEECHAM, THOMAS, 1
I...pass through this w. but once GRELLET, STEPHEN, 1
It is not the w. that confines you ANGELUS SILESIUS, 2
know the w., not love her YOUNG, EDWARD, 9
Let all the w. in every corner sing HERBERT, GEORGE, 5
Let the great w. spin forever TENNYSON, ALFRED, 57
Looks the whole w. in the face LONGFELLOW, HENRY WADSWORTH, 16
Most people are on the w., not in it MUIR, JOHN, 9
Of the w....one cannot be enough afraid ADORNO, THEODOR, 8
one being is lacking...w. is empty LAMARTINE, ALPHONSE DE, 5
One w. at a time THOREAU, HENRY DAVID, 48
O w. invisible THOMPSON, FRANCIS, 5
she ain't long for this w. WALKER, ALICE, 23
There is another and a better w. KOTZEBUE, AUGUST FRIEDRICH FERDINAND VON, 1
The true system of the W. has been recognized ALEMBERT, JEAN LE ROND D', 2
The w. befriends the elephant PROVERBS, 63
The w. breaks everyone HEMINGWAY, ERNEST, 8
The w....gray-bearded and wrinkled HAWTHORNE, NATHANIEL, 11
the w. is...a fine book MALLARMÉ, STÉPHANE, 3
The w. is a wheel DISRAELI, BENJAMIN, 13
The w. is becoming like a lunatic asylum LLOYD-GEORGE, DAVID, 5
The w....is but a large prison RALEIGH, WALTER, 12
The w. is disgracefully managed FIRBANK, RONALD, 2
The w. is everything that is the case WITTGENSTEIN, LUDWIG, 6
The w. is made up...of fools and knaves BUCKINGHAM, DUKE OF, 1
The w. is out of order BÜCHNER, GEORG, 7
the w. is that which we perceive MERLEAU-PONTY, MAURICE, 5
The w. is too much with us WORDSWORTH, WILLIAM, 66
The w. owes all its onward impulse HAWTHORNE, NATHANIEL, 12
The w.'s a stage DU BARTAS, GUILLAUME, 4
The w.'s a theatre...earth a stage HEYWOOD, THOMAS, 2
the w.'s mine oyster SHAKESPEARE, WILLIAM, 629
The w. soon kills /what it cannot suffer WANTLING, WILLIAM, 3
the w., the flesh, and the devil BOOK OF COMMON PRAYER, 28
The w. visits his dinners MOLIÈRE, 27
The w. wants to be deceived FRANCK, SEBASTIAN, 1
The w. was all before them MILTON, JOHN, 91
the w. was headed for sorrow SZILARD, LEO, 2
the w. were good for...speculation HAZLITT, WILLIAM, 5
The W. would be a safer place HARBURG, E. Y., 6
the w. would not be the same OPPENHEIMER, J. ROBERT, 6
This w....isn't safe GOLDEN, MARITA, 6
This w. is very odd we see CLOUGH, ARTHUR HUGH, 10
This w. nys but a thurghfare CHAUCER, GEOFFREY, 26
To save your w....asked this man to die AUDEN, W. H., 10
visible w....abstract and mysterious enough GUSTON, PHILIP, 1
w....a global village MCLUHAN, MARSHALL, 7
w....a school of inquiry MONTAIGNE, MICHEL DE, 22
way the w. ends ELIOT, T. S., 43
w. belongs to the man with guts HITLER, ADOLF, 23
w. be made fit and safe to live in WILSON, WOODROW, 25
When all the w. is young, lad KINGSLEY, CHARLES, 3
w. is a beautiful place FERLINGHETTI, LAWRENCE, 5
w. is a bundle of hay BYRON, LORD, 8
w. is a comedy to those who think WALPOLE, HORACE, 1
w. is a vale of tears MORAND, PAUL, 1
W. is crazier...than we think MACNEICE, LOUIS, 24
w. is made...of morons and natural tyrants DARROW, CLARENCE, 5
w. is not made on a human scale MALRAUX, ANDRÉ, 6
W. is suddener than we fancy it MACNEICE, LOUIS, 12
w. is...what I live through MERLEAU-PONTY, MAURICE, 3
With the w. a war began MICHELET, JULES, 3
w. of their own thoughts STEVENS, WALLACE, 26
w. only gives itself to Man WEIL, SIMONE, 7
w. to be but as a stage DU BARTAS, GUILLAUME, 1
W. with its smells hints its follies CUMMINGS, E. E., 14

world-famous It is rare that one *likes* a w. man BALDWIN, JAMES, 3

world-historical W. men...clear-sighted ones HEGEL, G. W. F., 22

worlds So many w., so much to do HALLAM, ARTHUR HENRY, 14
Zwicky wants to make a hundred *new* w. WHITE, E. B., 3

World War II W. began last week NEWSPAPERS, 26

World War III W....the mathematicians' war DAVIS, PHILIP J., 1

worm a w. at one end and a fool at the other JOHNSON, SAMUEL, 53
Even a w. will turn PROVERBS, 196
The cut w. forgives the plow BLAKE, WILLIAM, 41
To tread by chance upon a w. PARKER, DOROTHY, 23

worms the most exclusive w. PARKER, DOROTHY, 22
w. have eaten them, but not for love SHAKESPEARE, WILLIAM, 118

wormwood her end is bitter as w. BIBLE, 454
the w. and the gall BIBLE, 315
worries secret of not having w....ideas DELACROIX, EUGÈNE, 5
worry time to w....when everybody likes you ANT, ADAM, 1
W. affects circulation, the heart, and the glands MAYO, CHARLES HORACE, 8
worrying W. about the past ADAMS, JOEY, 1
W....most natural and spontaneous THOMAS, LEWIS, 1
worse Let it be w. PROVERBS, 503
only thing w. than...give gratitude constantly FAULKNER, WILLIAM, 13
The w. I do, the more popular I get KENNEDY, JOHN FITZGERALD, 38
things get w. for the better MARLEY, BOB, 6
worship external public w. of God,... might be preserved LAUD, WILLIAM, 3
So long as men w. the Caesars HUXLEY, ALDOUS, 22
worst His w. is better than...person's best SCOTT, SIR WALTER, 2
no surer way of calling the w. BENSON, E. F., 1
the w. is yet to come JOHNSON, PHILANDER CHASE, 1
The w. of doing one's duty WHARTON, EDITH, 7
we can say "This is the w." SHAKESPEARE, WILLIAM, 353
w. thing...important problem...discuss GRAY, SIMON, 1
You do your w. CHURCHILL, WINSTON, 73
worth If a job's w. doing PROVERBS, 262
The w. of a State MILL, JOHN STUART, 12
Whatever is w. doing CHESTERFIELD, LORD, 17
worthy Lord, I am not w. BIBLE, 389
w. man...not mindful of past injuries EURIPIDES, 4
would He w., wouldn't he? RICE-DAVIES, MANDY, 1
wound We are...a w. that fights DARWISH, MAHMOUD, 1
wounds Bind up their w. GILBERT, W. S., 18
Millions have died of medicable w. ARMSTRONG, JOHN, 1
What deep w. ever closed without a scar BYRON, LORD, 30
W. inflicted by the sword RICHELIEU, CARDINAL, 11
wrapped w. him in swaddling clothes BIBLE, 323
wrath eternal w. /Burnt after them MILTON, JOHN, 73
slow to w. BIBLE, 242
the children of w. CALLAGHAN, JIM, 1
To the w. of my enemies VARGAS, GETÚLIO, 1
wreath She wore a w. of roses BAYLY, THOMAS HAYNES, 3
wrestle beautiful...see man w. with his illusions MAHFOUZ, NAGUIB, 8
we w....against the rulers of the darkness BIBLE, 64
wrestled w. with a self-adjusting card table THURBER, JAMES, 6
wrestling Talk w. KING, LARRY, 1
wretch a w. who supports with insolence JOHNSON, SAMUEL, 14
I w. lay wrestling with /...my God HOPKINS, GERARD MANLEY, 1
wretches feel what w. feel SHAKESPEARE, WILLIAM, 348
Poor naked w. SHAKESPEARE, WILLIAM, 347
poor w. have got it into their heads LUCIAN, 1
w. hang that jury-men may dine POPE, ALEXANDER, 95
wrinkles Having w. is...strange and exciting STREEP, MERYL, 1
When the first few w. appear JUVENAL, 9
writ Here lies one whose name was w. in water KEATS, JOHN (1795–1821), 92
I never w., nor no man ever lov'd SHAKESPEARE, WILLIAM, 582
What is w. is writ BYRON, LORD, 38
write Do not...w. on both sides of the paper at once SELLAR, W. C., 7
healthier...to w. for the adults WALKER, ALICE, 10
I like to w. when I feel spiteful LAWRENCE, D. H., 11
I w. for today WEILL, KURT, 1
learn to w. as he would talk STEFFENS, LINCOLN, 3
To w. is an act of love COCTEAU, JEAN, 3
w. and read comes by nature SHAKESPEARE, WILLIAM, 454
w. and /rewrite till...right AMMONS, A. R., 3
W. and risk damnation NGUGI WA THIONGO, 5
w. for children...as you do for adults GORKY, MAKSIM, 6
writer A great w. creates a world of his own CONNOLLY, CYRIL, 1
Asking a working w....about critics HAMPTON, CHRISTOPHER, 2
A w. depicting humdrum realities FARAH, NURUDDIN, 7
A w. is a writer EMECHETA, BUCHI, 9
a w....knows how to explain his ideas clearly PALEOTTI, GABRIELE, 1
a w. who drank LEWIS, SINCLAIR, 1
Becoming a w....not a "career decision" AUSTER, PAUL, 1
best way to become a successful w. FOWLER, GENE, 3
essential gift for any w....shit detector HEMINGWAY, ERNEST, 15
Every great and original w. WORDSWORTH, WILLIAM, 23
good for a w. to think he's dying WILLIAMS, TENNESSEE, 11
prolific w. of notes of condolence DICKINSON, EMILY, 2
should have been a more famous w. FORSTER, E. M., 1
The true w. has nothing to say ROBBE-GRILLET, ALAIN, 1
The w. or the reader DIDEROT, DENIS, 4
the w. who is the impregnator WHITE, E. B., 9
understand a w.'s ignorance COLERIDGE, SAMUEL TAYLOR, 27
w.'s only responsibility is to his art FAULKNER, WILLIAM, 12
writers American w. want to be...great VIDAL, GORE, 12
Clear w....do not seem so deep as they are LANDOR, WALTER SAVAGE, 3
Creative w. are...greater than the causes...they represent FORSTER, E. M., 18
many historical w. are the votaries of cults BAILEY, THOMAS A., 4
The only way for w. to meet CONNOLLY, CYRIL, 18
things...that w. are there to overhear BEATTIE, ANN, 1
w. against religion...oppose every system BURKE, EDMUND, 35
W. are always selling somebody out DIDION, JOAN, 5
W....are divided into incisors and grinders BAGEHOT, WALTER, 1
w. are made to look like schoolboys by history BÜCHNER, GEORG, 8
W. are witnesses DOCTOROW, E. L., 5
W. can't back off from realism WOLFE, TOM, 21
W. don't give prescriptions ACHEBE, CHINUA, 5
W....file reports BURROUGHS, WILLIAM S., 8
w. have nearly all been fortunate in escaping regular education MACDIARMID, HUGH, 3
w. who can express in as little as twenty pages KRAUS, KARL, 20
writes He w. as fast as they...read SCOTT, SIR WALTER, 1
writing Against the disease of w. ABELARD, PETER, 3
All good w. FITZGERALD, F. SCOTT, 6
Charlotte has been w. a book BRONTË, CHARLOTTE, 1
fine w. is next to fine doing KEATS, JOHN (1795–1821), 50
Good w. is like a bomb FARAH, NURUDDIN, 4
greater want of skill...in w. POPE, ALEXANDER, 10
I accept no responsibility for the w. process PÉREZ GALDÓS, BENITO, 6
If I could...I'd do no w. AGEE, JAMES, 1
I loathe w. PERELMAN, S. J., 7
I suffer from the disease of w. MONTESQUIEU, 7
it was a woman's w. ELIOT, GEORGE, 1
left scarcely any style of w. untouched GOLDSMITH, OLIVER, 3

My father is w. in Irish SWEENEY, MATTHEW, 1
my own w....is a useful thing WALKER, ALICE, 8
That's not w., that's typing CAPOTE, TRUMAN, 7
the incurable disease of w. JUVENAL, 12
The point of good w. MONTGOMERY, L. M., 1
True ease in w. comes from art POPE, ALEXANDER, 21
W. always means hiding something CALVINO, ITALO, 1
W....a vocation of unhappiness SIMENON, GEORGES, 1
W. books is the closest...to childbearing MAILER, NORMAN, 28
w. briefly takes far more time GAUSS, CARL FRIEDRICH, 3
W....but a different name for conversation STERNE, LAURENCE, 14
What is w. a novel like WHARTON, EDITH, 1
W. is a form of therapy GREENE, GRAHAM, 14
w. is a labor of love CHILDRESS, ALICE, 1
W. is like getting married MURDOCH, IRIS, 7
W. is turning one's worst moments into money DONLEAVY, J. P., 7
W....no one considers you ridiculous RENARD, JULES, 23
W. saved me from the sin...violence WALKER, ALICE, 12
W....talking without being interrupted RENARD, JULES, 22
w. to my conscience...according to command ZAMYATIN, YEVGENY, 2
written No one has w. worse English HARDY, THOMAS, 2
no-one's w. what you want to read LARKIN, PHILIP, 15
rather have w. those lines than take Quebec GRAY, THOMAS, 3
she has w....moments of human experience PARKER, DOROTHY, 2
w....for the sake of "self-expression" HARDY, THOMAS, 1
what I have w. I have written BIBLE, 297
w. without effort...read without pleasure JOHNSON, SAMUEL, 50
wrong If anything can go w. PROVERBS, 263
if I called the w. number THURBER, JAMES, 11
If...w., I shall never win LINNAEUS, CAROLUS, 2
I may be w. RUSSELL, BERTRAND, 66
I was 90% w. KRUGMAN, PAUL, 6
Only the man who finds everything w. GALBRAITH, J. K., 18
So much w. could religion induce LUCRETIUS, 2
the w. man...at the wrong time JOHNSON, LYNDON BAINES, 2
To be w. is nothing CONFUCIUS, 24
w. about what it explicitly asserts DERRIDA, JACQUES, 1
What's w. with it is money, honey WALKER, MARGARET, 4
When everyone is w., everyone is right LA CHAUSSÉE, NIVELLE DE, 1
who does no w. needs no law MENANDER, 2
w. side of the tracks CARTER, ANGELA, 15
w. sort of people...always in power WYNNE-TYSON, JON, 1
w. to have *thought* that I was wrong DULLES, JOHN FOSTER, 6
w. with wanton cruelty...don't like it RUSSELL, BERTRAND, 26
You rose o' the w. side to-day BROME, RICHARD, 2
wrongdoing W. can only be avoided SOLON, 2
wrongs Two w. do not make a right PROVERBS, 443
wrote I w. her name upon the strand SPENSER, EDMUND, 4
I w. my first novel because I wanted to read it MORRISON, TONI, 28
wuth I's w. eight hund'd dollars TWAIN, MARK, 37
Wynken W., Blynken, and Nod FIELD, EUGENE, 2
wynne to w. his spurres EDWARD III, 2
Wyoming Dryness is the common denominator in W. EHRLICH, GRETEL, 1

Xanadu In X. did Kubla Khan COLERIDGE, SAMUEL TAYLOR, 14
x-rays I shall call them "X." ROENTGEN, WILHELM CONRAD, 1
x....see through almost anything BUTLER, SAMUEL (1835–1902), 18

yabba Y. Dabba Do FLINTSTONES, THE, 1
yacht annual upkeep of a y. MORGAN, JOHN PIERPONT, 3
I had to sink my y. to make my guests go home FITZGERALD, F. SCOTT, 10
on the y. of a Greek oil millionaire DE GAULLE, CHARLES, 22
yachts I don't go in for owning y. MAXWELL, ROBERT, 1
yaks a lot of y. jumping about BEETHOVEN, LUDWIG VAN, 1
Yale young ladies who attended the Y. promenade PARKER, DOROTHY, 28
Yank another Y. half a step behind CLINTON, BILL, 10
Yankee don't hang back like a Y. lawyer COOPER, JAMES FENIMORE, 5
what good Y. stuff is made on COOPER, JAMES FENIMORE, 18
Yankee Doodle I'm a Y. Dandy COHAN, GEORGE M., 2
Y. came to town BANGS, EDWARD, 1
yawns a day that y. like a caesura MANDELSTAM, OSIP, 13
year all the y. were playing holidays SHAKESPEARE, WILLIAM, 234
Every y....I have passed the day MERWIN, W. S., 1
One y. was like another year BOWLES, PAUL, 2
'Tis the y.'s midnight DONNE, JOHN, 31
yearn To y. for a single...explanation...immaturity COMMAGER, HENRY STEELE, 4
years he that cuts off twenty y. of life SHAKESPEARE, WILLIAM, 303
Lost y....lost dollars PROVERBS, 504
meet thee /After long y. BYRON, LORD, 18
The y. that a woman subtracts DIANE DE POITIERS, 1
twelve y.; that's progress TELLER, EDWARD, 2
y. between fifty and seventy ELIOT, T. S., 55
Y. following years steal something every day POPE, ALEXANDER, 62
Yeats In Drumcliff churchyard Y. is laid YEATS, W. B., 18
Y., a poet twoice the soize YEATS, W. B., 4
yellow Pale y. ties...insignia of the worker WOLFE, TOM, 11
yellow badge Wear it with pride, the y. WELTSCH, ROBERT, 1
yellow brick road...is paved with y. BAUM, L. FRANK, 2
Yellow Brick Road Goodbye Y. TAUPIN, BERNIE, 4
the Y. HARBURG, E. Y., 3
yeoman y. every inch of me BLACKMORE, R. D., 2
yes She didn't say y. HARBACH, OTTO, 2
y. I said yes I will Yes JOYCE, JAMES, 38
yes-men I don't want any y. around me GOLDWYN, SAMUEL, 20
yesterday but y. a King BYRON, LORD, 12
Y., all my troubles LENNON & MCCARTNEY, 10
Y. you told me...world is joyful BING XIN, 2
Yiddish Y. is a household tongue OZICK, CYNTHIA, 2
yield y. to temptation...somebody must HOPE, ANTHONY, 2
YMCA It's fun to stay at the Y. VILLAGE PEOPLE, 1
yoke good...that he bear the y. in his youth BIBLE, 316
Yorick Alas, poor Y. SHAKESPEARE, WILLIAM, 220
Yorkshire My living in Y. SMITH, SYDNEY, 14
you If y. are as happy BUCHANAN, JAMES, 1
It could be y. ADVERTISEMENTS, 21
Maybe y. both, /like most of we BERRYMAN, JOHN, 6
You are not y. without me FULLER, R. BUCKMINSTER, 5

young All that the y. can do for the old SHAW, GEORGE BERNARD, 25
a man of about a hundred and fifty who was rather y. WODEHOUSE, P. G., 29
A man that is y. in years BACON, FRANCIS (1561–1626), 80
a very few years to be y. SWIFT, JONATHAN, 10
a y. man's fancy GRANT, CARY, 1
I'll die y., but it's like kissing God BRUCE, LENNY, 7
I'm a y. woman...runnin' aroun' SMITH, BESSIE, 2
look y. till forty DRYDEN, JOHN, 45
man's friends begin to compliment him about looking y. IRVING, WASHINGTON, 2
Most women are not so y. as they are painted BEERBOHM, MAX, 11
Now as I was y. and easy under the apple boughs THOMAS, DYLAN, 13
One starts to get y. at the age of sixty PICASSO, PABLO, 5
so y. a body with so old a head SHAKESPEARE, WILLIAM, 616
staying y....lie about your age BALL, LUCILLE, 1
stay y. as long as you...learn EBNER-ESCHENBACH, MARIE VON, 10
The denunciation of the y. SMITH, LOGAN PEARSALL, 2
The y. always have the same problem CRISP, QUENTIN, 12
The y. have aspirations SAKI, 5
What can a y. lassie do wi' an auld man BURNS, ROBERT, 51
Y. fellows will be young fellows BICKERSTAFFE, ISAAC, 4
y. healthy child...a most delicious...food SWIFT, JONATHAN, 5
Y. men make great mistakes JOWETT, BENJAMIN, 3
Y. men should prove theorems HARDY, GODFREY HAROLD, 4
Y. men think old men are fools CHAPMAN, GEORGE, 1
You can be y. without money WILLIAMS, TENNESSEE, 10
y. people...develop mental arteriosclerosis HUXLEY, ALDOUS, 4
y. people...distinctive brand of entertainment GEORGE, NELSON, 1
Y. people ought not to be idle THATCHER, MARGARET, 32
yours 'Tain't y., and 'tain't mine TWAIN, MARK, 59
yourself Better to write for y. CONNOLLY, CYRIL, 21
to be y....be somebody LEC, STANISLAW, 6
youth and y. stone dead SASSOON, SIEGFRIED, 1
high-water mark of my y. THURBER, JAMES, 7
Home-keeping y. have ever homely wits SHAKESPEARE, WILLIAM, 654
I am not going to exploit...my opponent's y. and inexperience REAGAN, RONALD, 20
I am very close to y. CARLOS I, JUAN, 1
If only y. knew ESTIENNE, HENRI, 1
"In my y.," Father William replied CARROLL, LEWIS, 6
In the days of my y. I remembered my God SOUTHEY, ROBERT, 4
In the y. of a state BACON, FRANCIS (1561–1626), 77
In y. and beauty wisdom is but rare! POPE, ALEXANDER, 82
Let age approve of y. BROWNING, ROBERT, 37
long sad years of y. ELIOT, GEORGE, 4
my black interim, my y. and age LEWIS, ALUN, 2
nourishing a y. sublime TENNYSON, ALFRED, 51
She's neither or either, but...Cheating y. MIDDLETON, THOMAS, 3
Sweet wine of y.; gave up the years BROOKE, RUPERT, 4
the lexicon of y., which Fate reserves LYTTON, BULWER, 3
time the subtle thief of y. MILTON, JOHN, 125
We hold...y. sacred to education BELLAMY, EDWARD, 1
What Y. deemed crystal BROWNING, ROBERT, 3
Y. has vision! Old age, dreams TOLSON, MELVIN, 3
Y. is a blunder...Old Age a regret DISRAELI, BENJAMIN, 9
Y. is a malady MUSSOLINI, BENITO, 16
y. is but a frost of cares TICHBORNE, CHIDIOCK, 1
y. is cruel, and has no remorse ELIOT, T. S., 8
Y. is full of pleasure SHAKESPEARE, WILLIAM, 632
Y. is in itself so amiable SÉVIGNÉ, MADAME DE, 3
Y. is something very new CHANEL, COCO, 5
Y. is the season of credulity PITT THE ELDER, WILLIAM, 7
Y....nothing to do with political history MANN, THOMAS, 7
y. now in England... be set to learn ALFRED, 1
y. to whom was given /So much WORDSWORTH, WILLIAM, 29
Y. will come...beat on my door IBSEN, HENRIK, 17
y. would sleep out the rest SHAKESPEARE, WILLIAM, 662
youths y. dancing, and maidens...hands upon one another's wrists HOMER, 6
Yugoslav I am the only Y. TITO, 1

Zadok Z. the priest took an horn of oil BIBLE, 184
zeal not too much z. TALLEYRAND, CHARLES MAURICE DE, 4
stir up the z. of women MILL, JOHN STUART, 2
zebra z. is a light-colored animal with dark stripes AMERICAN MUSEUM OF NATURAL HISTORY, 1
zed whoreson z. SHAKESPEARE, WILLIAM, 338
Zen hence the Z. expression "Kill the Buddha!" MATTHIESSEN, PETER, 10
The freedom and poverty of Z. WATTS, ALAN, 3
Z. and the Art of Motorcycle Maintenance PIRSIG, ROBERT T., 13
Z. dispenses with all forms of theorization WATTS, ALAN, 8
Z. does not attempt to be intelligible WATTS, ALAN, 5
Z. spirituality is...to peel the potatoes WATTS, ALAN, 10
zero *we* discovered that z.—an unknown Indian RAY, SATYAJIT, 5
Zionism Z....a moral, lawful, humanitarian movement HERZL, THEODOR, 1
Z. is our return to Judaism HERZL, THEODOR, 4
Z. that recognizes...homeland of two peoples OZ, AMOS, 6
Zionist The Z. enterprise has no other...justification OZ, AMOS, 5
Zulus Z. know Chaplin better than Arkansas knows Garbo CHAPLIN, CHARLIE, 2

THEMATIC INDEX

Thematic Index

11; Harris, George, 1; James, Henry, 12; Johnson, Samuel, 63; Kirkland, Lane, 2; Lagrange, Joseph Louis, 2; La Rochefoucauld, François, 18; Loesser, Frank, 5; Loos, Anita, 7; Macaulay, Thomas Babington, 12; McCormack, Mark, 7; Mallaby, George, 1; Mansfield, Katherine, 6; Marcus Aurelius, 2, 10, 11; Marquis, Don, 12; Marshall, Thomas R., 1; Martial, 1; Massinger, Philip, 3; Miller, Henry, 13; Milne, A. A., 13; Milner, Alfred, 1; Niven, Larry, 1; Proverbs, Modern, 3; Reade, Charles, 1; Renard, Jules, 17; Rogers, Will, 14; Satie, Erik, 2; Schein, Edgar H., 2; Seneca, "the Younger," 6; Sévigné, Madame de, 2; Steinbeck, John, 13; Sullivan, Anne, 1; Teresa of Ávila, Saint, 3; Thoreau, Henry David, 36; West, Nathanael, 1; Whistler, James Abbott McNeill, 12

Aesthetics Key, Ellen, 1; Marinetti, Filippo Tommaso, 2, 3, 4; Mayakovsky, Vladimir, 6; Olson, Charles, 8, 9; Stalin, Joseph, 5; Williams, William Carlos, 15, 16

Afterlife Allen, Woody, 13; al-Mufid, Abu Abdullah Muhammad al-Harithi al-Baghdadi, 1, 10; Browne, Thomas, 37; Bunyan, John, 25; Byron, Lord, 21; Chandra, Vikram, 2, 3, 4; Chaucer, Geoffrey, 36; Coward, Noel, 9; Dillon, Wentworth, 3; FitzGerald, Edward, 18; Forster, E. M., 2; Freud, Sigmund, 49; Hawthorne, Nathaniel, 4; Hill, Joe, 1; Kant, Immanuel, 1; Keats, John (1795–1821), 29; Koran, 43; Rabelais, François, 18; Schopenhauer, Arthur, 6; Shakespeare, William, 177, 329; Swinburne, Algernon Charles, 8; Tennyson, Alfred, 6, 23; Thoreau, Henry David, 48; Wordsworth, William, 55

Afternoon Sartre, Jean-Paul, 14

Age Adenauer, Konrad, 5; Astor, Nancy, 7, 11; Bacall, Lauren, 1; Bacon, Francis (1561–1626), 3, 53; Bai Juyi, 1; Bainville, Jacques, 2; Barnes, Julian, 4; Bastard, Thomas, 1; Bellamy, Edward, 1; Blunden, Edmund, 1; Browning, Robert, 3, 33, 34; Buck, Pearl, 4; Burke, Edmund, 6; Burns, Robert, 22; Butlin, Billy, 1; Byron, Lord, 15, 71; Calment, Jeanne, 1; Camus, Albert, 8; Carew, Thomas, 1; Cary, Joyce, 3; Chamfort, Nicolas, 1; Chapman, George, 1; Chevalier, Maurice, 1; Christie, Agatha, 2, 8; Churchill, Charles, 3; Colette, 5, 6; Confucius, 31; Cosby, Bill, 6; Delany, Annie Elizabeth "Bessie," 1; Diane de Poitiers, 1; Dickens, Charles, 29; Disraeli, Benjamin, 24; Dylan, Bob, 26; Ebner-Eschenbach, Marie von, 10; Eliot, George, 4; Estienne, Henri, 1; Faulkner, William, 19; Feiffer, Jules, 1; Fellini, Federico, 1; Franklin, Benjamin, 24; Gilbert, W. S., 16, 42; Gogol, Nikolay, 7; Hall, Peter, 1; Hawn, Goldie, 1; Ibsen, Henrik, 17; Inge, William Ralph, 8; Irving, Washington, 2; James, Alice, 3; Johnson, James Weldon, 3; Johnson, Samuel, 124; Jung, Carl Gustav, 18; Lennon & McCartney, 16; Linkletter, Art, 2; London, Jack, 11; Lowell, Robert, 27; McMurtry, Larry, 2; Makeba, Miriam, 1; Martin, Agnes, 1; Meir, Golda, 4; Middleton, Thomas, 8; Milton, John, 125; Molière, 14; Montagu, Mary Wortley, 5; Moreau, Jeanne, 2; Mozart, Wolfgang Amadeus, 5; Navratilova, Martina, 1; Oates, Joyce Carol, 2; Orwell, George, 2, 42; Pitt the Elder, William, 4, 7; Prior, Matthew, 8; Prochnow, Herbert V., 1; Rexford, Eben, 1; Roth, Philip, 10; Rubin, Jerry, 2; Saki, 5; Satie, Erik, 1; Saunders, Jennifer, 2; Shakespeare, William, 450, 632; Shaw, George Bernard, 25, 53; Spark, Muriel, 2, 9; Steinem, Gloria, 4, 6; Streep, Meryl, 1; Swift, Jonathan, 25; Tree, Herbert Beerbohm, 3; Updike, John, 12; Virgil, 21; Wilde, Oscar, 56; Woolf, Virginia, 3; Zhang Jie, 1

Aggression Brecht, Bertolt, 26; Bunyan, John, 12; Gilbert, W. S., 38; Watts, Isaac, 3

Agnosticism Darrow, Clarence, 2; Hofstadter, Douglas R., 2

Agreement Bacon, Francis (1561–1626), 75; Bismarck, Prince Otto von, 23; Browne, Thomas, 12; Disraeli, Benjamin, 26; Milton, John, 97; Spaak, Paul Henri, 1; Wilde, Oscar, 21

Agriculture Bible, 114; Dyson, Freeman, 2; Hoover, Herbert, 9; Jerrold, Douglas, 4; Lease, Mary Elizabeth, 1; Reagan, Ronald, 4; Roosevelt, Franklin D., 8

AIDS Diana, Princess, 3; Everett, Kenny, 1; Fierstein, Harvey, 2; Gunn, Thom, 2; Johnson, Adam, 1; Koch, Ed, 1; McGinley, Robert, 1; McKellen, Ian, 3; Mottos and Slogans, 13; Sontag, Susan, 11; White, Edmund, 1

Airplanes Hamel, Gary, 8; Harvey-Jones, John, 5; Wright, Orville, 2

Alabama Hughes, Langston, 9

Alaska Kirkup, James, 2; London, Jack, 8

Alchemy Jonson, Ben, 15

Alcohol Æ, 1; Aga Khan III, Sir, 1; Ai Qing, 3; Aldrich, Henry, 1; Belloc, Hilaire, 30; Benchley, Robert, 12; Bible, 207; Booth, Charles, 1; Bukowski, Charles, 5; Byron, Lord, 47; Calverley, C. S., 1; Cervantes, Miguel de, 41; Chandler, Raymond, 4; Chaucer, Geoffrey, 11; Constitution of the United States, 5; Dibdin, Charles, 4; Dickens, Charles, 66, 77, 90; Farquhar, George, 4; Faulkner, William, 18; Fields, W. C., 2; FitzGerald, Edward, 17; Fitzgerald, F. Scott, 23; Fleming, Alexander, 4; Fletcher, John, 2, 3; Folk Verse, 48; Goldsmith, Oliver, 10; Harris, Joel Chandler, 4; Herbert, George, 1; Hoover, Herbert, 5; Horace, 26; James, William, 32; Jerome, Jerome K., 6; Johnson, Samuel, 58, 126; Kerr, Jean, 5; La Bruyère, Jean de, 7; Leacock, Stephen, 14; Lewis, Joe E., 1; Lewis, Sinclair, 1; Lowell, Robert, 3; Lyly, John, 8; MacNeice, Louis, 17; Magee, William Connor, 1; Map, Walter, 1; Mencken, H. L., 9; Milton, John, 3, 16, 114; Nash, Ogden, 15; O'Brien, Flann, 2; Oldys, William, 1; O'Sullivan, John L., 3; Parker, Dorothy, 36; Peacock, Thomas Love, 8; Persius, 4; Rabelais, François, 2, 3; Rockne, Knute, 2; Saki, 7; Selden, John, 7; Shakespeare, William, 482; Shaw, George Bernard, 23, 76; Sitwell, Edith, 3; Stanshall, Vivian, 1; Swift, Jonathan, 23; Tarkington, Booth, 2; Thomas, Dylan, 31, 34; Wodehouse, P. G., 23; Young, George W., 1

Alibis and Excuses Eliot, T. S., 23

Alternative Therapies Hahnemann, Samuel, 1; Holmes, Oliver Wendell, 11

Ambition Adams, Henry, 19; Aeschylus, 6; Bailey, Pearl, 1; Bond, Alan, 3; Browning, Robert, 44; Campbell, Thomas, 3; Carter, Angela, 11; Churchill, Jennie, 1; Congreve, William, 23; Cromwell, Oliver, 1; Einstein, Albert, 55; Elizabeth I, 23; Emerson, Ralph Waldo, 41; Felker, Clay S., 1; Fisher, Marve, 1; Gilman, Charlotte Perkins, 1; Grossart, Angus, 1; Gutfreund, John, 1; Hammerstein, Oscar, II, 16; Hitler, Adolf, 30; Homer, 8; Hurston, Zora Neale, 5; Iacocca, Lee, 9; Jackson, Jesse, 10; Jefferson, Thomas, 1; Johnson, Lyndon Baines, 12; Johnson, Samuel, 173; Keats, John (1795–1821), 47; Kelly, Patrick C., 2; Kennedy, Edward M., 1; La Bruyère, Jean de, 3; Laozi, 18; Liotta, Ray, 1; Longfellow, Henry Wadsworth, 5; Luciano, Lucky, 1; Macaulay, Thomas Babington, 2; Mallory, George, 1; Mann, Horace, 1; Marley, Bob, 3; Massinger, Philip, 1; Midler, Bette, 1; Miller, Jonathan, 3; Milton, John, 64; Mottos and Slogans, 2, 19; Murdoch, Rupert, 5; Peters, Tom, 6; Powys, John Cowper, 1; Raleigh, Walter, 11; Riley, James Whitcomb, 1; Shakespeare, William, 161, 301, 314, 390, 394, 402, 494; Spenser, Edmund, 10, 11; Stevenson, Robert Louis, 11; Swift, Jonathan, 12, 42; Thatcher, Margaret, 33; Trump, Donald, 4; Turner, Ted, 4; Webster, Daniel, 9; Webster, John, 1; White, Patrick, 4; Wilde, Oscar, 70; William II, 4

American Revolution Adams, John, 3, 4; Adams, Samuel, 1; Allen, Ethan, 1; Bangs, Edward, 1; Burgoyne, John, 1; Clark, Abraham, 1; Franklin, Benjamin, 28; George III, 1; Hancock, John, 1; Henry, Patrick, 1, 2; Jefferson, Thomas, 33, 34, 35; Longfellow, Henry Wadsworth, 7; Morison, Samuel Eliot, 3; Washington, George, 7, 10

Americans Appleton, Thomas Gold, 1; Arnold, Matthew, 17; Bailey, Thomas A., 5; Barry, Dave, 2; Barzun, Jacques, 7; Beerbohm, Max, 13; Bombeck, Erma, 2; Boorstin, Daniel J., 2; Carter, Jimmy, 5; Chesterton, G. K., 23; Clark, Mark, 1; Cleaver, Eldridge, 7; Clinton, Bill, 10; Cooper, James Fenimore, 1, 18; Eco, Umberto, 16; Fuller, Margaret, 3; Geldof, Bob, 3; Goodman, Paul, 5; Jarrell, Randall, 3; Johnson, Samuel, 90; Keats, John (b.1920), 1; Keynes, John Maynard, 2; King, Martin Luther, Jr., 6; Linklater, Eric, 3; London, Jack, 14; Lucas, E. V., 1; Maugham, Somerset, 1; Maurois, André, 4; O'Rourke, P. J., 7; Pynchon, Thomas, 9; Reed, Ishmael, 2; Rice, Grantland, 1; Russell, Bertrand, 52; Said, Edward W., 1; Sartre, Jean-Paul, 20; Simon, Paul, 1; Snyder, Gary, 6, 11; Soyinka, Wole, 5; Springsteen, Bruce, 2; Stapledon, Olaf, 1; Steinbeck, John, 3, 22; Twain, Mark, 48; Updike, John, 2; Verona, Virginia, 1; Vonnegut, Kurt, 1, 4, 5; Webster, Daniel,

Arrogance Bai Juyi, 3; Beefheart, Captain, 2; Brown, James, 1; Emerson, Ralph Waldo, 2; Fenton, James, 2; Feynman, Richard Phillips, 1; Gregory, Dick, 7; Henry VIII, 2; Leacock, Stephen, 15; Louis XIV, 3; Luther, Martin, 2; Morrissey, 4; Toscanini, Arturo, 1; Weidman, Jerome, 2; Yeats, W. B., 3

Art Abakanowicz, Magdalena, 1; Adamov, Arthur, 1; Agathon, 2; Anderson, Laurie, 1; Arp, Jean, 1, 2, 3; Auden, W. H., 53; Baldwin, James, 14; Beerbohm, Max, 10; Beethoven, Ludwig van, 6; Behrman, S. N., 1; Bell, Clive, 1; Berenson, Bernard, 3; Bonheur, Rosa, 1; Bourgeois, Louise, 1; Bowen, Elizabeth, 4; Braque, Georges, 1; Bukowski, Charles, 7; Buren, Daniel, 1; Carducho, Vicente, 2; Cézanne, Paul, 1; Chagall, Marc, 1; Chesterton, G. K., 21; Chicago, Judy, 1; Cousin, Victor, 1; cummings, e. e., 10; Davy, Humphry, 2; Degas, Edgar, 1, 2, 4; DeVoto, Bernard, 1; de Wyzewa, Téodor, 1; Diderot, Denis, 9; Disney, Walt, 1; Dreiser, Theodore, 2; Duchamp, Marcel, 1; Du Fresnoy, Charles-Alphonse, 1; Duncan, Isadora, 7; Dürer, Albrecht, 2; Eliot, T. S., 46; Emerson, Ralph Waldo, 56, 61, 62; Epstein, Jacob, 2; Fischl, Eric, 1; Flack, Audrey, 1; Frankenthaler, Helen, 3; García Lorca, Federico, 6; Giacometti, Alberto, 1; Goethe, Johann Wolfgang von, 28; Guston, Philip, 1; Haring, Keith, 1; Haydon, Benjamin Robert, 1; Henri, Robert, 2, 3; Hepworth, Barbara, 2; Hirschfeld, Al, 1; Hirst, Damien, 1; Hockney, David, 1; Ingres, Jean-Auguste Dominique, 1; James, C. L. R., 12; Kael, Pauline, 4; Kennedy, John Fitzgerald, 3; Kiesler, Frederick, 1; Kipling, Rudyard, 25; Kosuth, Joseph, 1; Kounellis, Jannis, 1; Kruger, Barbara, 1; Langer, Susanne K., 1; Leonardo da Vinci, 3, 14; Lethaby, W. R., 1; LeWitt, Sol, 1; Lowell, Robert, 4; MacCarthy, Desmond, 2; MacInnes, Colin, 3; Mailer, Norman, 26; Malraux, André, 9; Man Ray, 3; Matisse, Henri, 2, 3, 4; Mayakovsky, Vladimir, 10; Meier-Graefe, Julius, 1; Meyer, Melissa, 1; Michelangelo, 1; Miller, Henry, 3; Miró, Joan, 2, 3, 10; Mitchell, Joni, 6; Moore, George, 7; Moore, Marianne, 6; Morrison, Toni, 20; Morris, William, 5, 6; Murdoch, Iris, 6; Mussorgsky, Modest, 2; Nathan, G. J., 1; Ngugi wa Thiongo, 1; Oldenburg, Claes, 1, 2; Olmsted, Frederick Law, 2; Paglia, Camille, 2; Pasternak, Boris, 2; Pater, Walter, 1; Picasso, Pablo, 7, 9, 12, 13, 15; Plato, 5; Pliny the Elder, 12; Plotinus, 1; Pollock, Jackson, 3; Rauschenberg, Robert, 1; Reinhardt, Ad, 1, 2, 3; Renoir, Pierre Auguste, 3; Reynolds, Sir Joshua, 3, 4; Robbe-Grillet, Alain, 2; Rodin, Auguste, 1, 2; Ross, Harold W., 2; Ruskin, John, 3, 5, 22; Sagan, Françoise, 3; Sargent, John Singer, 1; Schiller, Friedrich von, 3, 14; Schnabel, Julian, 1; Schoenberg, Arnold, 1; Seneca, "the Elder," 2; Serrano, Andres, 1; Shaw, George Bernard, 103; Singer, Isaac Bashevis, 4; Smithson, Robert, 1; Sontag, Susan, 1, 2; Speicher, Eugene, 1; Stevens, Wallace, 22; Titian, 1; Uccello, Paolo, 1; Voltaire, 29, 33; Warhol, Andy, 6; Welles, Orson, 7; West, Rebecca, 4; Whistler, James Abbott McNeill, 6; Whitehead, A. N., 9; Yevtushenko, Yevgeny, 1; Zhang Yimou, 1; Zhuangzi, 7

Artists Anderson, Sherwood, 2; Anonymous, 47; Armah, Ayi Kwei, 2; Baker, Josephine, 1; Barker, Howard, 2; Bellori, Giovanni Pietro, 1; Carducho, Vicente, 1; Cary, Joyce, 2; Cervantes, Miguel de, 4; Cézanne, Paul, 2, 3; Chesterton, G. K., 27; Clark, Kenneth (1903–83), 6; Dalí, Salvador, 2; David, Jacques-Louis, 1; Duchamp, Marcel, 2; Durand, Asher B., 1; Faulkner, William, 9, 11; Fitzgerald, F. Scott, 21; Gainsborough, Thomas, 1; García Lorca, Federico, 3; Garland, Hamlin, 1; Gunn, Thom, 1; Hesse, Eva, 1; Hockney, David, 2; Joyce, James, 9; Liyong, Taban Lo, 4; Mamet, David, 15; Man Ray, 2; Manzoni, Piero, 1; Marden, Brice, 1; Marinetti, Filippo Tommaso, 1; Matisse, Henri, 1; Miró, Joan, 1, 11, 12; Morrison, Toni, 10; Murdoch, Iris, 14; Musset, Alfred de, 4; Nietzsche, Friedrich Wilhelm, 13; Ortega y Gasset, José, 17; Pearce, Lord, 1; Péguy, Charles Pierre, 15; Pérez Galdós, Benito, 2; Picasso, Pablo, 1, 2, 3, 8; Renoir, Pierre Auguste, 1; Richter, Gerhard, 1; Rosenberg, Harold, 1; Tàpies, Antoni, 1, 2; Thomas, Dylan, 32; Turner, J. M. W., 1, 2; Ustinov, Peter, 8; Valéry, Paul, 2; Walker, Alice, 4; Warhol, Andy, 2, 9; Whistler, James Abbott McNeill, 13; Wilder, Thornton, 2

Arts, The Berdyaev, Nikolai, 1; Bishop, Elizabeth, 3; Bradford, Bobby, 1; Butler, Samuel (1835–1902), 10; Céline, Louis-Ferdinand, 1; Churchill, Sarah, 1; Cole, Thomas, 1; Graham, Martha, 4; Hopper, Edward, 1; Horace, 38; Jong, Erica, 8; Keats, John (1795–1821), 44; Malraux, André, 4, 7; Mao Zedong, 19; Miller, Henry, 16; Nietzsche, Friedrich Wilhelm, 19; Paleotti, Gabriele, 1; Pliny the Elder, 13; Reynolds, Sir Joshua, 1; Roosevelt, Franklin D., 17; Ruskin, John, 20; Tarkovsky, Andrey, 1; Tolstoy, Leo, 15; Zhou Yang, 1

Asia Kipling, Rudyard, 38

Assassination Booth, John Wilkes, 1; Charles II, 12; De Gaulle, Charles, 18; Disraeli, Benjamin, 18; Gandhi, Mahatma, 3; Kaye, Danny, 1; Kennedy, Robert, 8; Lincoln, Abraham, 2, 6; Mountbatten, Lord, 3; Murphy, Eddy, 1; Palme, Olof, 1; Reagan, Ronald, 36; Shaw, George Bernard, 92; Thatcher, Margaret, 12; Vonnegut, Kurt, 11

Astrology Nairn, Tom, 2; Narayan, R. K., 1, 2; Prior, Matthew, 3

Astronomy Clarke, Arthur C., 1, 2; France, Anatole, 7; Galileo, 3, 6; Leacock, Stephen, 10; Wheeler, John Archibald, 1, 2

Atheism Beauvoir, Simone de, 3; Büchner, Georg, 4; Buñuel, Luis, 4; Fosdick, Henry Emerson, 1; Ingersoll, Robert G., 3, 5; Jowett, Benjamin, 7; Marshall, Paule, 6; Orwell, George, 13; Otway, Thomas, 1; Proust, Marcel, 16; Russell, Bertrand, 41; Sartre, Jean-Paul, 30; Updike, John, 20; Young, Edward, 8

Atoms Nerval, Gérard de, 2; O'Brien, Flann, 9; Updike, John, 23

Audiences Agate, James, 1; Barrymore, John, 1; Bernard, Tristan, 1; Brice, Fanny, 1; Cash, Johnny, 1; Coward, Noel, 4; Fosse, Bob, 1; Hitchcock, Alfred, 6; Hope, Bob, 3; Jouvet, Louis, 1; Lennon, John, 7; May, Brian, 1; Osborne, John, 7, 10; Reed, Lou, 5; Rogers, Will, 1; Schnabel, Artur, 3, 4; Simone, Nina, 3; Spielberg, Steven, 7; Wilde, Oscar, 81; Wilder, Billy, 2

Aunts Wodehouse, P. G., 20

Australia Banks, Joseph, 1; Packer, Kerry, 1; Paterson, A. B., 1

Authoritarianism Catherine the Great, 2; Thatcher, Margaret, 30; Ustinov, Peter, 11

Autobiography Bunyan, John, 3; Carver, Raymond, 10; Crisp, Quentin, 4; Lowry, Malcolm, 1; Pétain, Henri Philippe, 2; Shostakovich, Dmitri, 2

Automobiles Barthes, Roland, 2; Bierce, Ambrose, 8; Grahame, Kenneth, 4; Joplin, Janis, 2; Keller, Maryann, 3; Lowell, Robert, 9; McLuhan, Marshall, 12; Morton, J. C., 3; Norris, Steven, 1; O'Rourke, P. J., 2; Siple, Paul Allman, 1

Awards Benny, Jack, 4; Buñuel, Luis, 6; Field, Sally, 1; Jackson, Glenda, 1; Melbourne, Lord, 3; Milligan, Spike, 1; Thompson, Emma, 1

Babies Bagnold, Enid, 1; Bible, 369; Diana, Princess, 4; Dickens, Charles, 63, 64; Elizabeth II, 3; Freud, Sigmund, 14; Herbert, A. P., 1; Knox, Ronald, 3; Marryat, Frederick, 1; Maugham, Somerset, 14; Mistral, Gabriela, 5; Pliny the Elder, 7; Runyon, Damon, 8; Stanton, Frank L., 1; Thomas, Dylan, 25

Ballet Baryshnikov, Mikhail, 1; Fonteyn, Margot, 1, 3; Kirstein, Lincoln, 4; Noverre, Jean Georges, 1; Pavlova, Anna, 3, 4; Rambert, Dame Marie, 1, 2, 3

Banks and Bankers Benchley, Robert, 9; Hope, Bob, 2; Hutton, Will, 2; Kelly, Patrick C., 1; Proxmire, William, 1; Sarnoff, Robert W., 1; Volcker, Paul A., 2; Wriston, Walter B., 3

Baseball Aaron, Hank, 1; Anonymous, 32, 74; Banks, Ernie, 1, 2; Benny, Jack, 2; Berra, Yogi, 2, 3, 4, 5; Blue, Vida, 1; Brooke, Rupert, 8; Cobb, Ty, 1, 2, 3; Cooke, Alistair, 3; Coolidge, Calvin, 14; DiMaggio, Joe, 1, 2, 3; Edison, Thomas Alva, 2; Eisenhower, Dwight D., 27; Eliot, Charles William, 1; Fitzgerald, F. Scott, 25; Frost, Robert, 25; Garvey, Steve, 1; Giamatti, A. Bartlett, 1, 2; Halberstam, David, 1; Hemingway, Ernest, 17; Hoagland, Edward, 1; Hoover, Herbert, 2, 11; Jackson, Bo, 1; Jackson, Reggie, 1; Jackson, Shoeless Joe, 1; Keeler, William, 1; Kennedy, John Fitzgerald, 37; Kennedy, Terry, 1; Kissinger, Henry, 16; Lardner, Ring, 4; McLuhan, Marshall, 1; Mays, Willie, 1; Mitchell, Liz, 1; Moore, Marianne, 3; Nash, Ogden, 18; Newspapers, 22; Odom, Jim, 1; Rizzuto, Phil, 1; Robinson, Frank, 1, 2; Robinson, Jackie, 1, 2, 3; Roosevelt, Franklin D., 29, 33; Roth, Philip, 4; Ruth,

Babe, 1, 2, 3; Saroyan, William, 1; Shaw, George Bernard, 109; Steinberg, Saul, 1; Stengel, Casey, 1, 2; Thayer, Ernest Lawrence, 1; Thurber, James, 19; Twain, Mark, 6, 7; Williams, Dick, 1; Williams, William Carlos, 12

Bathos Colman, George, 4; Ford, John (1586–1640?), 1

Battles Benét, Stephen Vincent, 2; Corneille, Pierre, 7; Drake, Francis, 1, 3, 4; Drayton, Michael, 6; Edward III, 2; Foch, Ferdinand, 2; McGonagall, William, 3; Napoleon I, 15, 32; Nelson, Horatio, 2; Virgil, 8; Wellington, Duke of, 5, 6

Beauty Aimée, Anouk, 1; Antar, 1; Avedon, Richard, 1; Bacon, Francis (1561–1626), 15; Barnes, William, 1; Baudelaire, Charles, 15; Beerbohm, Max, 15, 20; Betjeman, John, 6; Bible, 131; Blake, William, 46; Bonner, Marita, 3; Boucicault, Dion, 2; Browning, Robert, 55; Bryant, William Cullen, 1; Bunyan, John, 5; Burke, Edmund, 33; Byron, Lord, 13; Campbell, Naomi, 1; Césaire, Aimé, 4; Chandler, Raymond, 2; Cher, 1; Coleridge, Samuel Taylor, 21; Congreve, William, 22; Constable, John, 2; Debussy, Claude, 6; Donne, John, 19; Dryden, John, 28; Dunbar, William, 2; Dürer, Albrecht, 3; Fitzgerald, F. Scott, 18; Folk Verse, 38; Gay, John, 1; Goldsmith, James, 2; Gray, Thomas, 8; Hume, David, 31; Hungerford, Margaret Wolfe, 1; Hunt, Leigh, 5; Keats, John (1795–1821), 14, 31, 56, 83; Kerouac, Jack, 13; Kincaid, Jamaica, 3; Lamarr, Hedy, 1; Loos, Anita, 3; Lyly, John, 4; MacNally, Leonard, 1; Malory, Thomas, 6; Marlowe, Christopher, 7, 8; Mayakovsky, Vladimir, 8; Milman, Henry Hart, 2; Milton, John, 20, 62, 79, 87, 100; Morrison, Toni, 22; Paglia, Camille, 11; Peacock, Thomas Love, 5; Philips, Ambrose, 1; Plato, 7, 14; Poe, Edgar Allan, 8, 14; Pope, Alexander, 94; Pound, Ezra, 11; Poussin, Nicolas, 3; Prior, Matthew, 5; Raphael, 1; Rowe, Nicholas, 2; Runyon, Damon, 4; Ruskin, John, 15; Savonarola, Girolamo, 2; Schiller, Friedrich von, 13, 15; Sévigné, Madame de, 5; Shakespeare, William, 74, 75, 200, 538, 560, 564, 633, 668; Shelley, Percy Bysshe, 39; Sontag, Susan, 9; Suckling, John, 1; Tennyson, Alfred, 64, 72; Toomer, Jean, 1; Venning, Ralph, 2; Virgil, 4; Weatherly, Frederic Edward, 1; Wilde, Oscar, 65; Williams, William Carlos, 5; Wolf, Naomi, 3; Wordsworth, William, 27; Yeats, W. B., 48

Bed Anonymous, 88; Hood, Thomas, 19; Pepys, Samuel, 15

Beginning Anonymous, 60; Aristotle, 20; Bible, 101, 266, 501; Branson, Richard, 7; Deffand, Marie du, 1; Euripides, 2; Fleming, Peter, 2; Harvey, William, 2; Horace, 18; Hume, David, 24; Kerouac, Jack, 2; Salinger, J. D., 14; Ussher, James, 1

Behavior Berryman, John, 9; Bible, 314, 410; Browning, Robert, 30; Gide, André, 6; Goldsmith, Oliver, 27; Hare, R. M., 2; Hazlitt, William, 14; Hitler, Adolf, 14; Holloway, David, 1; McCormack, Mark, 16; MacLeod, Sheila, 1; Madonna, 3; Nation, Carry, 2; Pavese, Cesare, 3; Pirandello, Luigi, 15; Sima Qian, 1; Sophocles, 7; Stern, Richard G., 1; Stevenson, Robert Louis, 2; Swift, Jonathan, 17; Szasz, Thomas, 5; Thackeray, William Makepeace, 11; Thomas, Dylan, 27

Beijing Lo, Kenneth H., 1; Lu Xun, 11

Being Descartes, René, 11; Dewey, John, 8, 15; Heidegger, Martin, 3; Jiménez, Juan Ramón, 13; Lacan, Jacques, 1; Marcus Aurelius, 1; Prévert, Jacques, 1; Quine, Willard V., 1, 2

Belief Allen, Woody, 16; Ammons, A. R., 2; Bible, 277, 279, 282, 304, 360, 399; Browning, Robert, 35; Bryan, William Jennings, 5; Burke, Edmund, 55; Carroll, Lewis, 46; Clough, Arthur Hugh, 7; Einstein, Albert, 11; Freud, Sigmund, 47; García Márquez, Gabriel, 7; Goddard, Robert, 1; Jefferson, Thomas, 9; Koran, 2; Kronenberger, Louis, 1; Lawrence, D. H., 44; Loyola, Ignatius of, 4; Luther, Martin, 4; Machado de Assis, Joaquim Maria, 4; Marquis, Don, 9; Martin, Graham Dunstan, 1; Orwell, George, 22; Paine, Thomas, 3; Powell, John Wesley, 1; Russell, Bertrand, 66; Sartre, Jean-Paul, 3; Thackeray, William Makepeace, 4; Toynbee, Arnold, 5; Turgenev, Ivan, 3; Virgil, 14; Watts, Alan, 9; Weyer, Johann, 1; Wittgenstein, Ludwig, 11

Bequests Rabelais, François, 20; Voltaire, 8

Bereavement Donne, John, 9; Milton, John, 119, 121; O'Connell, Eibhlin Dubh, 1; Ray, Satyajit, 2; Tennyson, Alfred, 40, 41; Wilde, Oscar, 84

Betrayal Attlee, Clement, 5; Auden, W. H., 15; Bible, 3, 433, 434, 438; Burns, Robert, 36; Caesar, Julius, 6; Congreve, William, 15; Coward, Noel, 19; Elizabeth I, 8; Goldsmith, Oliver, 33; Nixon, Richard, 29; Renoir, Jean, 1; Sancho, Ignatius, 3; Scott, Sir Walter, 20; Shakespeare, William, 237, 305, 675; Windebank, Francis, 1

Bible Arnold, Matthew, 7; Belloc, Hilaire, 36; Bible, 49, 197, 222, 306, 311, 313, 378, 447; Blake, William, 35; Chapman, John Jay, 1; De Mille, Cecil B., 2; Ellington, Duke, 1; Fields, W. C., 11; French, Marilyn, 1; Frye, Northrop, 5; Galbraith, J. K., 6; Henry VIII, 11; Macaulay, Thomas Babington, 11; Tate, Nahum, 1; Voltaire, 5; Wesley, John, 4; West, Mae, 5; Whitehead, A. N., 1

Bigotry Hague, Frank, 1; Parker, Dorothy, 32; Swift, Jonathan, 49; Watts, Isaac, 5

Biography Anthony, Susan B., 1; Bentley, Edmund Clerihew, 2; Bunin, Ivan, 1; Byron, Lord, 62; Carlyle, Thomas, 11, 13; Coleridge, Samuel Taylor, 7; Disraeli, Benjamin, 11; Lu Xun, 6; Lyndhurst, John Singleton Copley, 1; Malamud, Bernard, 2; Map, Walter, 2; Milton, John, 2; Ortega y Gasset, José, 9; Russell, Bertrand, 3; West, Rebecca, 8

Birth Ackerley, J. R., 1; Coleridge, Samuel Taylor, 63; Congreve, William, 3; Fromm, Erich, 3, 4; Leboyer, Frédérick, 1; Lillie, Beatrice, 1; Milton, John, 128; Molière, 2; Parker, Dorothy, 6; Pliny the Elder, 6; Quarles, Francis, 6; Shakespeare, William, 423; Stowe, Harriet Beecher, 6; Tertullian, 1; Vallejo, César, 2; Wordsworth, William, 52; Yankwich, Léon R., 1

Bitterness Bennett, Lerone, Jr., 1; Bhutto, Benazir, 2; Bontemps, Arna, 1; Hazlitt, William, 27; Kerouac, Jack, 3; Shakespeare, William, 640; Tennyson, Alfred, 53

Blessing Bible, 169, 362, 375, 435, 448; Blake, William, 45; Book of Common Prayer, 1, 10; Cobain, Kurt, 2; Dickens, Charles, 2; Field, Eugene, 1; Folk Verse, 10, 53; Hervey, James, 1

Blindness Carriera, Rosalba, 1; Lindsay, Vachel, 1; Milton, John, 94, 95, 99, 108, 126, 131; Vidal, Gore, 1; Wonder, Stevie, 2

Boasts Alexander the Great, 5; Ali, Muhammad, 1; Bible, 462; Brien, Alan, 1; Bunting, Basil, 1; Gilbert, W. S., 3, 5, 37; Grade, Lew, 1; Grahame, Kenneth, 5; Hardy, Thomas, 7; Maxwell, Robert, 3; Stein, Gertrude, 11; Wilhelmina, 1; Young, Brigham, 3

Boats Grahame, Kenneth, 3; London, Jack, 13; Munro, Neil, 1; Murphy, Richard, 1; Rimbaud, Arthur, 8; Savile, Sir George, 1

Body Bible, 154; Billings, Josh, 4; Cannon, Walter Bradford, 1; Drabble, Margaret, 2; Freud, Sigmund, 32; Heller, Joseph, 12; Hildegarde of Bingen, 1; Hoffer, Eric, 4; La Mettrie, Julien Offroy de, 1, 2; Linkletter, Art, 1; Melville, Herman, 9; Miller, Jonathan, 4; Proulx, E. Annie, 1; Proust, Marcel, 17; Shaw, Henry Wheeler, 1; Stopes, Marie, 5; Tolstoy, Leo, 13; Whitman, Walt, 25; Wittig, Monique, 1

Boldness Brecht, Bertolt, 11; Danton, Georges Jacques, 1; Hitler, Adolf, 23; Koestler, Arthur, 3; Spenser, Edmund, 3

Books Akhmatova, Anna, 8; Alembert, Jean le Rond d', 2; Ampère, Jean-Jaques, 1; Auden, W. H., 30; Bacon, Francis (1561–1626), 65; Belloc, Hilaire, 33; Benchley, Robert, 3; Brontë, Charlotte, 2; Browning, Robert, 54; Bunyan, John, 11; Burgess, Anthony, 7; Burns, Robert, 14; Butler, Samuel (1835–1902), 8; Byron, Lord, 85; Capote, Truman, 1; Carlyle, Thomas, 26, 44; Chesterfield, Lord, 9; Cooper, James Fenimore, 8; Crabbe, George, 5; De Quincey, Thomas, 7; Dillon, Wentworth, 1; Disraeli, Benjamin, 58; Doyle, Arthur Conan, 19; Eco, Umberto, 9; Eliot, T. S., 56; Fitzgerald, F. Scott, 4, 32; Flaubert, Gustave, 1; Folk Verse, 42; Grahame, Kenneth, 1; Graves, Robert, 2; Hemingway, Ernest, 12; Hugo, Victor, 4; Hume, David, 2; Huxley, Aldous, 18; Johnson, Samuel, 49, 76, 83; Joyce, James, 1; Kazin, Alfred, 1; Laing, R. D., 12; Larkin, Philip, 1; Lawrence, D. H., 1, 5, 33; Lebowitz, Fran, 4; Lichtenberg, Georg Christoph, 7; Macaulay, Rose, 3; Mackenzie, Compton, 2; Mao Zedong, 2; Maupin, Armistead, 3; Miller, Henry, 2;

Milton, John, 11, 13; Mitchell, Julian, 1; Molière, 20; Mortimer, John, 2; O'Brien, Flann, 10; Pamuk, Orhan, 7, 8; Parker, Dorothy, 33; Porter, Peter, 5; Remarque, Erich Maria, 1; Rogers, Samuel, 11; Roosevelt, Franklin D., 10; Ruskin, John, 8, 9, 11; Samuel, Herbert, 2; Smith, Logan Pearsall, 4; Smith, Sydney, 15, 23; Steinbeck, John, 33; Steiner, George, 2; Sterne, Laurence, 13; Stevenson, Robert Louis, 21, 28; Sylvester, Robert, 2; Tupper, Martin Farquhar, 1; Ustinov, Peter, 9; Vidal, Gore, 7; Wharton, Edith, 10; Wilde, Oscar, 67; Williams, William Carlos, 7; Woolf, Virginia, 16; Zhuangzi, 6

Boredom Beckett, Samuel, 21; Bierce, Ambrose, 9; Boileau, Nicolas, 1; Bryson, Bill, 9; Byron, Lord, 79; Churchill, Winston, 63; Edward VIII, 7; Ertz, Susan, 1; Foote, Samuel, 4; Fromm, Erich, 5; Hailsham, Lord, 4; Mandelstam, Osip, 13; Mumford, Lewis, 2; Nietzsche, Friedrich Wilhelm, 4; Pope, Alexander, 85; Prévert, Jacques, 3; Rhys, Jean, 4; Russell, Bertrand, 47; Saint Laurent, Yves, 1; Sanders, George, 1; Seth, Vikram, 2; Shakespeare, William, 326; Sitwell, Osbert, 1; Somerville, Edith, 1; Soyinka, Wole, 7; Valenzuela, Luisa, 2; Whitehead, A. N., 2

Bores Leonardo da Vinci, 2; Rhodes, William Barnes, 1; Taylor, Bert Leston, 1; Thomas, Dylan, 30; Updike, John, 3

Borrowing Baudelaire, Charles, 3; Franklin, Benjamin, 16; James, Henry, 23; Lamb, Charles, 17, 18; Nash, Ogden, 19; Rabelais, François, 17; Sheridan, Richard Brinsley, 2; Townsend, Robert, 14; Ward, Artemus, 3

Bosses Adams, Scott, 3; Ashcroft, John, 4; Carnegie, Andrew, 3; Hamel, Gary, 9; Icahn, Carl, 1

Boston Aldrich, Thomas Bailey, 2; Allen, Fred, 1; Appleton, Thomas Gold, 2; Emerson, Ralph Waldo, 57

Boxing Ali, Muhammad, 2, 4, 10, 11, 12, 13; Bruno, Frank, 1; Cosell, Howard, 1; Dempsey, Jack, 2; Fitzsimmons, Bob, 1; Foreman, George, 2; Johnson, Jack, 1; Leonard, Sugar Ray, 1, 2; Louis, Joe, 1, 2, 3; Robinson, Sugar Ray, 3; Tyson, Mike, 3, 4

Boys Carroll, Lewis, 1; Connolly, Cyril, 8; Lamb, Charles, 15; Morley, Robert, 3

Brevity Coolidge, Calvin, 19; Gracián, Baltasar, 1; Hugo, Victor, 3; James, Henry, 15; La Fontaine, Jean de, 12; Shakespeare, William, 172

Bribery Butler, Samuel (1612–80), 21; Greene, Graham, 4; Khasoggi, Adnan, 3; Penn, William, 10; Shakespeare, William, 669

Brides Bierce, Ambrose, 11; Whitman, Walt, 38

Britain Acheson, Dean, 1; Adams, Samuel, 3; Balladur, Edouard, 1; Betjeman, John, 10; Braithwaite, Edward R., 2; Bryson, Bill, 1, 4; Bullock, Alan, 1; Burke, Edmund, 15; Callaghan, Jim, 5; Casson, Hugh, 1; Chesterfield, Lord, 13; Chesterton, G. K., 7; Churchill, Winston, 17, 75; Cooper, James Fenimore, 13; Cope, Wendy, 1; Cowper, William, 3; Dibdin, Charles, 5; Hamilton, William (b.1917), 1; Heath, Edward, 1; Holmes, Oliver Wendell, 27; Joseph, Keith, 3; Lodge, David, 1; Macaulay, Thomas Babington, 7; Muldoon, Paul, 2; Paisley, Ian, 3; Pitt the Elder, William, 11; Rifkind, Malcolm, 1

British Empire, The Anonymous, 15; Burke, Edmund, 24; Carson, George Nathaniel, 1; Churchill, Winston, 20; Curzon, George Nathaniel, 1; Foster, George E., 1; Leacock, Stephen, 23; Macdonald, John A., 2; Mosley, Oswald, 1; Newspapers, 19; North, Christopher, 2; Riddell, William Renwick, 1; Smith, Adam, 9; Trollope, Joanna, 1; Webster, Daniel, 6

Brothers Bible, 129

Buddhism Buddha, 1, 2, 3, 4, 5; Kerouac, Jack, 24; Matthiessen, Peter, 10; Strindberg, August, 8; Tillich, Paul, 7, 8; Watts, Alan, 3, 4, 5, 8, 10

Budgets Dickens, Charles, 20; Hopper, Grace Murray, 1

Bureaucracy Bennis, Warren, 14, 17; Bulgakov, Mikhail, 11; Carter, Jimmy, 7; Dickens, Charles, 40; Foot, Michael, 1; Ionesco, Eugène, 9; Marsh, Richard, 4; Proverbs, Modern, 24; Reagan, Ronald, 46; Schumpeter, Joseph Alois, 1; Weber, Max, 1, 6; Williams, Shirley, 2

Business Adams, Scott, 1; Adams, William, 1; Aguilar, Francis J., 1; Ansoff, Igor, 1; Archer, Jeffrey, 1, 2; Armstrong, Michael, 2; Augustine, Norman R., 1; Ayala, Francisco, 1; Baker, Russell, 1; Bartlett, Christopher A., 1, 3; Baudrillard, Jean, 1; Bernbach, William, 8; Betjeman, John, 12; Bierce, Ambrose, 2, 7; Bird, Frederick Bruce, 1, 2; Blair, Tony, 4; Boesky, Ivan, 3; Branson, Richard, 2, 3, 4; Buffett, Warren, 5; Carnegie, Andrew, 1; Carroll, Lewis, 7; Charles II, 5; Clarke, Kenneth, 3; Clausen, A. W., 1; Clinton, Bill, 12, 15; Cohen, Jack, 1; Coolidge, Calvin, 10; Covey, Stephen R., 1; Cronin, Mary J., 2, 3; Davis, Clive, 1; Defoe, Daniel, 14; de Geus, Arie, 1, 3, 4, 5; Dell, Michael, 1, 2, 3; Dickens, Charles, 49; Dos Passos, John, 8; Drucker, Peter, 9, 13, 17; Edelman, Robert, 1; Eisner, Michael, 3, 5, 6; Elkington, John, 1, 2; Fanon, Frantz, 12; Fayol, Henri, 1; Ford, Henry, 11, 12; Fox, Harrison W., Jr., 2, 4, 6; Fox, Muriel, 1; Franklin, Benjamin, 6; Friedman, Milton, 10; Fukuyama, Francis, 1, 2, 3, 4, 10; Fuller, Thomas (1654–1734), 2; Gates, Bill, 1, 3, 6; Geneen, Harold, 3; Gerstner, Louis, Jr., 1, 2; Geschke, Chuck, 1; Getty, J. Paul, 10; Gilbert, Daniel J., Jr., 1; Goizueta, Roberto, 3; Goldsmith, James, 1, 4, 5, 7; Goldsmith, Oliver, 25; Goleman, Daniel, 2, 4, 5; Goncourt, Edmond de, 3; Green, Hetty, 1; Grove, Andrew S., 1, 2, 3, 4, 5; Haas, Robert, 1, 5; Haeckel, Steve H., 1; Hailey, Arthur, 1; Hamel, Gary, 1; Hammer, Armand, 2; Hammer, Michael, 2; Handy, Charles, 1, 2, 3, 4; Harvey-Jones, John, 1, 7; Hawken, Paul, 1, 2, 4, 5; Hickman, Craig R., 4, 5, 7; Holmes à Court, Robert, 2; Hopper, Grace Murray, 2; Hubbard, Elbert, 5; Hutcheson, Dan, 1; Iacocca, Lee, 3, 7; Icahn, Carl, 2; Ihara Saikaku, 1; Imparato, Nicholas, 2; Iverson, Ken, 1, 3; Jackson, Janet, 1; Jenrette, Richard, 3; Jobs, Steve, 2, 5; Jones, Chris, 1; Kanter, Rosabeth Moss, 3, 5; Keen, Peter, 1, 2, 4, 5; Keynes, John Maynard, 9; Khrushchev, Nikita, 8; Kinsley, Michael, 1; Kline, Nancy, 2, 3, 5, 6, 7; Kline, Stephen, 1; Knight, Frank Hyneman, 3; Kotler, Philip, 1; Kotter, John P., 2, 4, 5, 6; Kroc, Ray, 1, 2, 3; Lauder, Estée, 1, 2, 3; Lebed, Alexander, 1; Long, Clarisa, 1; Luce, Henry R., 3, 4; Lynch, Peter, 2, 3, 7; McCormack, Mark, 6, 12; Maclachlan, Jim, 1; McNealy, Scott, 1; Mahoney, Richard J., 2; Makihara, Minoru, 1; Malamud, Bernard, 3; Marcus, Bernie, 1, 2; Marshall, Alfred, 1; Meyers, John, 1; Michael, George, 1; Micklethwait, John, 1; Miller, Steven E., 1, 2, 3, 4, 5; Morgan, John Pierpont, 1; Mougayar, Walid, 1, 2, 3, 4; Mulgan, Geoff, 2, 3, 6; Murdoch, Rupert, 1, 6; Myhrvold, Nathan, 1, 2; Negroponte, Nicholas, 7; Ogilvy, David, 4; O'Hara, Theodore, 3; Ohmae, Kenichi, 2, 8; Onassis, Aristotle, 1; Parker, Sir Peter, 1; Perlman, Lawrence, 3; Peters, Tom, 1, 3; Petzinger, Thomas, Jr., 1; Platt, Lewis, 2; Proverbs, Modern, 30; Revson, Charles, 1; Rockefeller, John D., 3; Rodgers, T. J., 1; Rodin, Robert, 1; Romer, Paul M., 1; Roszak, Theodore, 1, 6; Samuelson, P. A., 1; Sanford, Charles, Jr., 3; Schwerin, David A., 1; Scott, William, 1; Senge, Peter M., 1, 3, 4, 5, 6; Shapiro, Robert B., 2; Sieger, Robin, 2; Sloan, Alfred P., Jr., 1; Smith, Adam, 3; Smith, Raymond W., 1; Solomon, Robert C., 2, 3, 4, 6; Stalin, Joseph, 13; Sugar, Alan, 3; Taylor, James, 1; Teeter, Robert M., 1; Terry, Jesse A., 1; Thornton, Charles, 1; Tichy, Noel M., 1, 2, 3; Tobias, Randall L., 1; Toffler, Alvin, 5; Townley, Preston, 1; Veblen, Thorstein Bunde, 1; Walton, Sam, 1, 2; Warhol, Andy, 8; Watson, Thomas, Jr., 1; Welch, Jack, 2, 3, 6, 8, 9, 10; White, E. B., 13; Whitehorn, Katharine, 8, 10, 11; White, Theodore H., 1; Winfrey, Oprah, 4; Wrigley, William, Jr., 1; Yoxen, Edward, 2; Zeldin, Theodore, 2, 7, 8

Byzantine Empire Mandelstam, Osip, 12

Calcutta Banerjee, Sudhansu Mohan, 1

California Allen, Fred, 9; Berryman, John, 2; Bryce, James, 2; Carter, Jimmy, 8; Chandler, Raymond, 5, 7; Didion, Joan, 6; Frost, Robert, 14; Hammett, Dashiell, 1; Isherwood, Christopher, 2; Kerouac, Jack, 14; Lindsay, Vachel, 3; Steinbeck, John, 4; Stevenson, Robert Louis, 14; Twain, Mark, 33

Camping Sackville-West, Vita, 6

Canada Brown, George, 1; Call, Frank Oliver, 1; Cartier, George-Étienne, 1; Cartwright, Richard, 1; Clark, Joe, 1; Frye, Northrop, 9; Howe, Joseph, 2; Hutton,

Maurice, 1; Laurier, Wilfrid, 4, 7, 8, 9, 11; Leacock, Stephen, 1, 7; Lower, A. R. M., 1; Macdonald, John A., 1; McGee, Thomas D'Arcy, 1, 2; MacMechan, Archibald, 1; Martin, Chester Bailey, 1; Moodie, Susanna, 1; Newspapers, 31; Papineau, Louis Joseph, 1; Parkman, Francis, 1; Smith, Goldwin, 2; Trotter, Reginald George, 1; Trudeau, Pierre, 2; Underhill, Frank H., 1; Whelan, Eugene, 1; Wilson, Edmund, 4; Wrong, George M., 1, 4

Cancer Haldane, J. B. S., 1; O'Hare, Dean, 3; Reich, Wilhelm, 3; Zaharias, Babe, 1

Capitalism Baraka, Imamu Amiri, 12; Barnevik, Percy, 2; Bellow, Saul, 13, 22; Berger, John, 2; Bookchin, Murray, 1; Borman, Frank, 1; Brooks, Gwendolyn, 3; Bruyn, Severyn, 2; Burroughs, William S., 10; Clark, John Bates, 2; Connolly, Cyril, 12; Davis, Angela, 3; Day, Graham, 2; Dimma, William, 1; Eco, Umberto, 15; Eisenhower, Dwight D., 2; Friedman, Milton, 4; Fry, Elizabeth, 1; Gandhi, Mahatma, 8; Gorbachev, Mikhail, 10; Hampton, Christopher, 1; Hutton, Will, 1; Huxley, Aldous, 21; Ignatieff, Michael, 1; Illich, Ivan, 7; Ingersoll, Robert G., 1; Kaunda, Kenneth David, 6; Keegan, William, 1, 2; Keller, Helen, 7; Keynes, John Maynard, 5, 18; Khrushchev, Nikita, 2; Kinnock, Neil, 9; Lekachman, Robert, 1; Lenin, Vladimir Ilyich, 4; Malcolm X, 11; Marcuse, Herbert, 1; Marx, Karl, 6, 13, 14; Mulgan, Geoff, 1; Norberg-Hodge, Helena, 2; O'Connor, Frank, 3; Paglia, Camille, 12; Pankhurst, Sylvia, 3; Proverbs, Modern, 8; Ricardo, David, 1, 2; Rockefeller, John D., 4; Schell, Jonathan, 6; Schumpeter, Joseph Alois, 3; Shaw, George Bernard, 41; Twain, Mark, 59; Waugh, Evelyn, 27; Weber, Max, 3, 5; Wilson, Charles E., 1; Wriston, Walter B., 1; Yeltsin, Boris, 2

Careers Buchwald, Art, 1; Curie, Irène, 1; Figes, Eva, 1; Jobs, Steve, 4; Kotter, John P., 3; Perlman, Lawrence, 1; Riley, Janet Mary, 1; Welles, Orson, 12; Whistler, James Abbott McNeill, 8; Whitehorn, Katharine, 7

Caribbean Carew, Jan, 2; Lamming, George, 3

Catchphrases Blackwell, Otis, 1; Candid Camera, 1; Doyle, Arthur Conan, 12; Dragnet, 1; Dr. Who, 1; Durante, Jimmy, 1; Fleming, Ian, 4; Flintstones, The, 1; Hardy, Oliver, 1; Johnson, Lyndon Baines, 11; Monty Python's Flying Circus, 2, 4; Reith, Lord, 2; Savalas, Telly, 1; Schwarzenegger, Arnold, 2; Scooby Doo, 1; South Park, 1; Star Trek, 1; Wacky Races, 1; West, Mae, 17; Williams, Robin, 1, 2

Catholicism Butz, Earl, 1; Gogarty, Oliver St. John, 5; Gregory VII, 1; Innocent III, 5; Johnson, Samuel, 125; Lawrence, D. H., 13; McCarthy, Mary, 5, 10; MacNeice, Louis, 26; Newman, John Henry, 4; O'Neill, Terence, 1; Orwell, George, 11; Waugh, Evelyn, 2; Wilson, Angus, 3; Wotton, Henry, 6

Caution Adams, Douglas, 11; Aesop, 6; Anonymous, 7; Cornford, F. M., 1; Hare, Julius, 1; Horace, 15; Ingres, Jean-Auguste Dominique, 2; La Fontaine, Jean de, 13; McCormack, Mark, 18; Nyerere, Julius Kambarage, 7; Pope, Alexander, 87; Proverbs, 312; Shakespeare, William, 178, 212, 279, 549; Thoreau, Henry David, 35

Celebrity Astor, Brooke, 1; Beethoven, Ludwig van, 10; Boorstin, Daniel J., 3; Huxley, Aldous, 53; Presley, Elvis, 4; Salinger, J. D., 16

Celibacy Bacon, Francis (1561–1626), 42; Behan, Brendan, 18; Hume, Basil, 2; Marvell, Andrew, 6; Peacock, Thomas Love, 9

Censorship Anonymous, 87; Bellow, Saul, 24; Black, Hugo LaFayette, 1; Brophy, Brigid, 1; Bulgakov, Mikhail, 2, 10; Dickens, Charles, 72; Eccles, David McAdam, 2; Eisenhower, Dwight D., 22; Freud, Sigmund, 22; Goodman, Paul, 6; Herbert, A. P., 2; Huston, John, 4; Marquis, Don, 11; Maupin, Armistead, 8; Mayakovsky, Vladimir, 4; Monroe, Marilyn, 11; Rushdie, Salman, 1; Shakespeare, William, 4; Smythe, Tony, 1; West, Rebecca, 7; White, E. B., 1; Wong Kar Wai, 1; Zamyatin, Yevgeny, 1

Certainty Barnes, Julian, 3; Bierce, Ambrose, 41; Drabble, Margaret, 5; Guy, Rosa, 2; Lyly, John, 9; Peirce, C. S., 3; Waugh, Evelyn, 5

Chance Betti, Ugo, 5; Boethius, 2; Burns, Robert, 49; Burton, Robert, 9; Longfellow, Henry Wadsworth, 8; Marquis, Don, 5; Procter, Adelaide Ann, 1; Ridge, William Pett, 1; Shakespeare, William, 536, 631; Southwell, Robert, 2

Change Arendt, Hannah, 18; Barton, Bruce, 3; Behn, Aphra, 10; Carver, Raymond, 6; Casely-Hayford, Joseph Ephraim, 1; Cervantes, Miguel de, 50; Chesterton, G. K., 29; Churchill, Winston, 39; Confucius, 10, 22; Dylan, Bob, 14, 15; Falkland, Lucius Cary, 1; France, Anatole, 13; Frisch, Max, 2; Frost, Robert, 18; Gay, John, 2; Gordimer, Nadine, 1; Guy, Rosa, 5; Handy, Charles, 7, 9; Head, Bessie, 2; Heraclitus, 1, 2; James, C. L. R., 3; Jiménez, Juan Ramón, 8; Kerouac, Jack, 11; Koran, 16; Lee, Laurie, 2; Macaulay, Thomas Babington, 16, 17; Machiavelli, Niccolò, 12; Marx, Karl, 24, 25; Milton, John, 83, 107, 120, 124; Oppenheimer, J. Robert, 7; Osborne, John, 4; Prahalad, C. K., 2; Rabin, Yitzhak, 2; Reagan, Ronald, 19; Roosevelt, Franklin D., 25; Roosevelt, Theodore, 20; Shakespeare, William, 642; Steinbeck, John, 20; Tate, Nahum, 2; Tennyson, Alfred, 57; Updike, John, 11; Waugh, Evelyn, 14; Webb, Sidney, 1; Yeats, W. B., 20

Character Adams, Franklin P., 3; Adams, John Quincy, 2; Aesop, 5; Astor, Nancy, 5; Austen, Jane, 19, 29; Barrie, J. M., 19; Beaumont & Fletcher, 5; Behan, Brendan, 8; Bible, 166; Blyden, Edward Wilmot, 2; Burke, Thomas, 1; Cervantes, Miguel de, 30, 38; Crèvecoeur, Jean de, 2; Dickens, Charles, 74; Dostoyevsky, Anna, 1; Drayton, Michael, 5; Dryden, John, 7, 16, 44; Durocher, Leo, 1, 2; Eliot, George, 21; Elizabeth I, 5; Emerson, Ralph Waldo, 16, 27; Frank, Anne, 4; Goethe, Johann Wolfgang von, 26; Greene, Robert, 1; Han Yu, 1, 2; Hardy, Thomas, 8; Irving, Washington, 6; James, Henry, 13, 36; Johnson, Samuel, 149, 151; La Rochefoucauld, François, 8; Leacock, Stephen, 11; Lloyd-George, David, 6; McGovern, George, 2; Miller, Arthur, 5; Miller, Henry, 29; Milton, John, 77, 106; Newman, John Henry, 6; Overbury, Thomas, 1; Pamuk, Orhan, 3; Reagan, Ronald, 15, 34; Reuther, Walter, 1; Richard I, 2; Shakespeare, William, 654; Simon, Neil, 2; Simpson, O. J., 2; Snow, C. P., 2; Spencer, Herbert, 7; Wells, H. G., 12; Wilde, Oscar, 60; Wilder, Billy, 1; Williams, Tennessee, 4; Williams, William Carlos, 8

Charity Abernethy, John, 2; Arnold, George, 2; Bacon, Francis (1561–1626), 33; Bailey, Pearl, 2; Bâ, Mariama, 3; Bankhead, Tallulah, 11; Beaumont & Fletcher, 18; Bible, 181, 380, 397; Book of Common Prayer, 8; Brooks, Gwendolyn, 6, 7; Browne, Thomas, 31; Carnegie, Andrew, 12; Cervantes, Miguel de, 23; Dickens, Charles, 97; Geldof, Bob, 1; Jerome, Saint, 1; Khomeini, Ruhollah, 5; Perón, Eva, 3; Pestalozzi, Johann Heinrich, 2; Pope, Alexander, 36; Shakespeare, William, 646; Sheppard, Dick, 1; Sitting Bull, 1

Charm Barrie, J. M., 17; Connolly, Cyril, 7; Joyce, James, 39; Lee, Spike, 2; Lerner, Alan Jay, 8; Martí, José, 1; Pope, Alexander, 97; Wilde, Oscar, 29

Chastity Augustine of Hippo, Saint, 3; Bonhoeffer, Dietrich, 4; Byron, Lord, 87; de Jars, Marie, 1; Qurtubiyya, 'Aisha bint Ahmad al-, 1; Shakespeare, William, 126; Tennyson, Alfred, 44; Waller, Edmund, 5; Wycherley, William, 1

Chess Byron, Henry James, 1; Duchamp, Marcel, 3; Mandelstam, Osip, 6

Chicago Algren, Nelson, 2; Anonymous, 64; Capone, Al, 3; Gregory, Dick, 1; Norris, Frank, 4; Sandburg, Carl, 3, 4, 5, 11; Twain, Mark, 22

Childhood Auden, W. H., 9; Bainbridge, Beryl, 3; Behan, Brendan, 9; Belloc, Hilaire, 6, 29; Betjeman, John, 18; Bible, 321; Bierce, Ambrose, 14, 29; Blackmore, R. D., 4; Blake, William, 31; Box-Car Bertha, 1; Hoyle, Fred, 3; Jarrell, Randall, 4; Joyce, James, 4; Keane, Molly, 1; Key, Ellen, 3; Lamb, Charles, 9; Longfellow, Henry Wadsworth, 31; Macaulay, Thomas Babington, 27; MacNeice, Louis, 11; Merrill, James, 1; Millay, Edna St. Vincent, 1; Milne, A. A., 8, 9, 11, 12, 14, 16, 21; Mistral, Gabriela, 3; Orwell, George, 4; Pavese, Cesare, 5; Piaget, Jean, 5, 7; Praed, Winthrop, 1; Rose, Billy, 2; Wordsworth, William, 35, 49, 51, 69

Children Amis, Kingsley, 6; Auden, W. H., 39; Bacon, Francis (1561–1626), 51; Baldwin, James, 1; Beckett, Samuel, 17; Bertolucci, Bernardo, 2; Bible, 26, 63, 411; Bismarck, Prince Otto von, 24; Blake, William, 20; Book of Common Prayer, 18; Breton, Nicholas, 2; Browning, Elizabeth Barrett, 1; Calvino, Italo, 5; Carter,

Lillian, 1, 2; Cisneros, Sandra, 1; Connolly, Cyril, 6; Cosby, Bill, 1; Coward, Noel, 28; Democritus, 1; Dumas, Alexandre, 6; Edelman, Marian Wright, 1; Fields, W. C., 3; Fleming, Marjory, 1; Gandhi, Indira, 8; García Márquez, Gabriel, 9; Gibran, Kahlil, 4; Gómez de la Serna, Ramón, 5; Hoffman, Heinrich, 3, 4, 5; Hoffmann, Amadeus, 1; Hughes, Langston, 17; John Paul II, 5; John XXIII, 3; Juvenal, 19; Kemble, John Philip, 1; Kerr, Jean, 4; Krutch, Joseph Wood, 1; Lamb, Charles, 19; Lamb, Mary Ann, 1; Larkin, Philip, 12; Leach, Penelope, 1; Lindgren, Astrid, 1; Longfellow, Henry Wadsworth, 18, 34; Lowry, Malcolm, 2; Marryat, Frederick, 3; Mitford, Nancy, 7; Nash, Ogden, 13; Nwapa, Flora, 1; Penn, William, 9; Perón, Eva, 2; Piaget, Jean, 6; Pinker, Steven, 1, 4; Plato, 6; Richard, Cliff, 1; Saki, 23; Salinger, J. D., 12; Scott, Hazel, 2; Singer, Isaac Bashevis, 1; Skelton, John, 1; Spock, Benjamin, 2; Strindberg, August, 6; Szasz, Thomas, 6; Venning, Ralph, 1; Vidal, Gore, 13; West, Nathanael, 3; Whitehorn, Katharine, 1; Williams, Sherley Anne, 1; Woolf, Virginia, 12

Chile Zurita, Raul, 1

China Bing Xin, 1; Buck, Pearl, 3; Chen Duxiu, 2, 3; Chow, Selina, 1; Cixi, 1; Clinton, Bill, 18; Deng Xiaoping, 4, 5, 6, 7, 8, 10, 11, 15, 16, 17, 19, 20; Du Ma, 1; Hua Guofeng, 1; Hu Shi, 2; Jiang Zemin, 1; Jin Guantao, 1; Jung Chang, 2, 3; Kang Youwei, 1; Kingston, Maxine Hong, 3; Kissinger, Henry, 9; Levy, Paul, 1; Liang Qichao, 1; Lin Biao, 1; Lin Yutang, 1; Li Peng, 1, 4; Loesser, Frank, 1; Lo, Vivienne, 1; Lu Xun, 8, 12, 15, 16; Mao Zedong, 7, 27, 28, 29, 30, 31, 32, 33, 37; Mottos and Slogans, 6, 7; Mu Dan, 1; Newspapers, 15, 16; Saki, 8; Soros, George, 8; Sun Yat-sen, 3; Wang Tao, 1; Woodhatch, Alex, 1, 2; Wu, Harry, 1, 2, 3; Xu Wenli, 3; Yu Jie, 1

Chinese Empire Guo Moruo, 1

Chivalry Adler, Freda, 1; Benchley, Robert, 1; Chaucer, Geoffrey, 9, 15; Clough, Arthur Hugh, 8; Kingsley, Charles, 8; Sidney, Philip, 5; Spenser, Edmund, 5; Tennyson, Alfred, 70; Wellington, Duke of, 9; West, Mae, 23

Choice Attalah, Naim, 1; Bayly, Thomas Haynes, 6; Beaumont & Fletcher, 14; Beerbohm, Max, 3; Bible, 420; Browning, Robert, 74; Chen Yi, 1; Dewey, George, 1; Ford, Henry, 7; Frost, Robert, 12; Jaspers, Karl, 4; Kalashnikov, Mikhail, 1; Kempis, Thomas à, 9; Mead, Margaret, 4; Milton, John, 55; Peacock, Thomas Love, 13; Prior, Matthew, 13; Steinbeck, John, 6; Tucholsky, Kurt, 2, 5; Yeats, W. B., 61; Zhuangzi, 5

Christianity Addison, Joseph, 22; Agobard, Saint, 1; Alexander, C. F., 4; Augustine of Hippo, Saint, 2; Bacon, Francis (1561–1626), 11; Baring-Gould, Sabine, 1; Barton, Bruce, 2; Bernard of Clairvaux, Saint, 2, 3; Bible, 1, 4, 8, 9, 11, 13, 14, 24, 147, 151, 267, 268, 272, 278, 291, 292, 296, 300, 301, 302, 343, 351, 361, 364, 366, 374, 394, 398, 408, 412, 422, 432; Bierce, Ambrose, 15; Blake, William, 24; Book of Common Prayer, 13, 15, 20; Bradley, F. H., 1; Browne, Thomas, 10; Browning, Robert, 8; Bruce, Lenny, 2; Bunyan, John, 23; Burton, Robert, 8; Butler, Samuel (1835–1902), 20; Castillejo, José, 1; Charlemagne, 1; Chesterton, G. K., 47; Child, Lydia Maria, 1; Coleridge, Samuel Taylor, 25; Cranmer, Thomas, 2; Ernst, Max, 1; Galileo, 5; Graham, Billy, 1; Hammon, Jupiter, 1; Hardy, Thomas, 25; Harris, Frank, 2; Heine, Heinrich, 11; Hood, Thomas, 10; Hume, David, 3; Hutchinson, Anne, 1; Huxley, Aldous, 30; Jenkins, David, 1; John Paul II, 7; Jung, Carl Gustav, 7, 8; Kierkegaard, Søren, 2, 3; Laud, William, 1; Lawrence, D. H., 6; Linacre, Thomas, 1; Logau, Friedrich von, 2; Lucian, 1; McPherson, Aimee Semple, 2; Maximilian I, 1; Melville, Herman, 8; Montesquieu, 6; Newton, John, 1; Nietzsche, Friedrich Wilhelm, 27, 30, 36; Ouida, 2; Patrick, Saint, 1; Pius II, 1; Pope, Alexander, 53; Renan, Ernest, 11; Russell, Bertrand, 54; Salinger, J. D., 11; Sitwell, Edith, 11; Speght, Rachel, 1; Temple, William, 2; Tennyson, Alfred, 29; Tertullian, 2; Toplady, Augustus Montague, 1; Wilberforce, Samuel, 3; Wotton, Henry, 3; Zell, Katharina, 1

Christmas Addison, Joseph, 16; Alexander, C. F., 3; Berlin, Irving, 5; Betjeman, John, 1, 7; Bible, 201, 323, 324, 367, 368; Brooks, Phillips, 1; Children's Verse, 22; Fisher, M. F. K., 1; Folk Verse, 20, 29, 35; Milligan, Spike, 9; Moore, Clement, 1, 2; Neale, John Mason, 2; Oakeley, Frederick, 1; Sears, E. H., 1; Tate, Nahum, 3; Tusser, Thomas, 4; White, E. B., 10

Church Augustine of Hippo, Saint, 11; Barth, Karl, 2; Bible, 407; Blythe, Ronald, 1; Bossuet, Jacques-Bénigne, 2; Carey, George, 2, 3; Daly, Mary, 2; Damian, Peter, 1; Defoe, Daniel, 10, 12; Dowler, Harold, 1; Doyle, Francis, 1; Draper, John, 2; Fielding, Henry, 9; James I, 7; Johnson, Samuel, 75; Laud, William, 2, 3; Machiavelli, Niccolò, 3; Macmillan, Harold, 8; Miller, Arthur, 15; Royden, Maud, 1; Smith, Sydney, 12; Temple, William, 4; Waugh, Evelyn, 17; Winterson, Jeanette, 3; Wright, Richard, 3

Cities Anonymous, 42; Beecham, Thomas, 4; Bible, 219; Cowley, Abraham, 4; Cowper, William, 26; Dickens, Charles, 6; Fields, W. C., 7; Goytisolo, Juan, 3; Hart, Moss, 2; Hillman, James, 4; Hoagland, Edward, 9; Huxtable, Ada Louise, 1; Jacobs, Jane, 1; Jiménez, Juan Ramón, 7; Kerouac, Jack, 12, 21; Lemmon, Jack, 1; Mandelstam, Osip, 2; Mead, Margaret, 11, 13; Mitchell, Margaret, 6, 9, 10; Morris, Desmond, 4; Morrison, Toni, 8, 13; Olmsted, Frederick Law, 3; Perelman, S. J., 1; Pynchon, Thomas, 4; Rivers, Joan, 2; Sandburg, Carl, 6, 7; Shakespeare, William, 123; Thompson, Hunter S., 4, 12; Trollope, Frances, 2; Twain, Mark, 45; Varro, Marcus Terentius, 1; Voinovich, Vladimir, 4; Ward, Artemus, 1; Wodehouse, P. G., 13; Wright, Frank Lloyd, 3

Civilization Addams, Jane, 3; Asimov, Isaac, 2; Auden, W. H., 44; Barbey d'Aurevilly, Jules-Amédée, 1; Beard, Charles, 4; Carlyle, Thomas, 15; Césaire, Aimé, 1, 2; Chesnutt, Charles W., 2; Chesterton, G. K., 9; Coolidge, Calvin, 9; Duhamel, Georges, 2; Durant, Will, 2; Epstein, Jacob, 1; Erasmus, Desiderius, 1; Gandhi, Mahatma, 26; Hillary, Edmund, 3; James, William, 29; Johnson, Lyndon Baines, 19; Kane, Cheikh Hamidou, 1; Knox, Ronald, 1; Laozi, 7; Lovell, Bernard, 2; Luther, Martin, 1; Macaulay, Thomas Babington, 13; Mann, Thomas, 17; Mansfield, Katherine, 1; Marcuse, Herbert, 2; Maugham, Somerset, 20; Needham, Joseph, 1; Ortega y Gasset, José, 22; Park, Mungo, 1; Rand, Ayn, 3; Roosevelt, Theodore, 14; Rousseau, Jean-Jacques, 3, 19; Rowse, A. L., 1; Russell, Bertrand, 16; Sandburg, Carl, 10; Snyder, Gary, 1; Toynbee, Arnold, 8; Trevelyan, G. M., 3; Twain, Mark, 41; Whitehead, A. N., 4

Civil Rights Cleaver, Eldridge, 1; Harlan, John Marshall, 1; Humphrey, Hubert H., 2; La Follette, Suzanne, 1; Marshall, Thurgood, 2; Pitt the Elder, William, 3; Touré, Kwame, 1; Twain, Mark, 17; Tyler, Wat, 1; Young, Whitney M., Jr., 1

Civil War (American) Armistead, Lewis Addison, 1; Bee, Barnard, 1; Crane, Stephen, 12, 13; Grant, Ulysses S., 1, 3, 6, 8; Jackson, Stonewall, 1, 2; Johnson, Andrew, 1; Lincoln, Abraham, 14, 21; McClellan, George, 1; Scott, Winfield, 1; Tate, Allen, 2

Clarity Burton, Robert, 18; Giraudoux, Jean, 4; Greenspan, Alan, 2; Horace, 2; Renard, Jules, 3; Rivarol, Antoine de, 3; Wesley, John, 7

Class Alexander, C. F., 2; Alfonso XIII, 1; Andersen, Hans Christian, 3; Bellamy, Edward, 4; Bleasdale, Alan, 1; Bonham-Carter, Lady Violet, 1; Brecht, Bertolt, 15; Brougham, Henry Peter, 1; Burgess, Anthony, 8; Cambridge, Godfrey, 1; Carter, Angela, 15; Cartland, Barbara, 6; Charles II, 3; Colette, 7; Confucius, 34; Coward, Noel, 18; Curzon, George Nathaniel, 4; Defoe, Daniel, 4; Dickens, Charles, 88; Disraeli, Benjamin, 31; Douglas-Home, Caroline, 1; Ehrenreich, Barbara, 1; Engels, Friedrich, 5; Fitzgerald, F. Scott, 19; Forster, E. M., 4; France, Anatole, 10; Friedenberg, Edgar Z., 1; Hope, Anthony, 5; James, C. L. R., 10; Johnson, Samuel, 135; Kipling, Rudyard, 48; Lawrence, D. H., 30; Lenin, Vladimir Ilyich, 18; Lennon, John, 8; Lewis, John L., 2; Livingstone, Ken, 2; Lytton, Bulwer, 1; Mao Zedong, 15, 25; Marx, Karl, 18, 19; Maugham, Somerset, 15; Mikes, George, 1; Milligan, Spike, 2; Monty Python's Flying Circus, 1; Mortimer, John, 3; Nixon, Richard, 20; Ortega y Gasset, José, 31; Orwell, George, 39; Pasolini, Pier Paolo, 2; Pérez Galdós, Benito, 3; Peter, Laurence J., 7; Renard, Jules, 12; Roy, Arundhati, 1; Scott, Paul, 1; Shaw, George Bernard, 52, 69, 77, 80; Stanton, Elizabeth Cady, 5; Theroux, Paul, 11; Voltaire, 11; Whitehorn, Katharine, 3; Wilde, Oscar, 45; Willkie, Wendell Lewis, 1; Wolfe, Tom, 20

Classical Era Byron, Lord, 51; Horace, 27; Iphicrates, 1

Classical Music Beethoven, Ludwig van, 7

Classics Fry, Christopher, 1; Goncourt, Edmond de, 2; Leacock, Stephen, 2; Miller, Henry, 24; Twain, Mark, 3, 23

Classification Waugh, Evelyn, 20

Clichés Anonymous, 76; Brenan, Gerald, 8; Fletcher, John, 8; Goldwyn, Samuel, 4

Clients and Customers Deming, W. Edwards, 4; Iacocca, Lee, 4; McCormack, Mark, 11; Popcorn, Faith, 1; Robens, Alfred, 2

Climate Martineau, Harriet, 2

Clocks Work, Henry Clay, 2, 3

Clothes Alcott, Louisa May, 6; Anonymous, 93; Astaire, Fred, 11; Bainbridge, Beryl, 1; Barney, Sydney D., 1; Beaton, Cecil, 2; Buchanan, Robert Williams, 1; Clinton, Bill, 8; Darrow, Clarence, 6; Dekker, Thomas, 3; De Wolfe, Elsie, 3; Dior, Christian, 2; Ebner-Eschenbach, Marie von, 3; Etherington-Smith, Meredith, 1; Fawconer, Samuel, 1, 2; Fischer-Mirkin, Toby, 1, 2; Flügel, J. C., 1; Forbes, Miss C. F., 1; Gascoigne, George, 1; Gaultier, Jean Paul, 2; Harragan, Betty Lehan, 1; Hilfiger, Tommy, 1; Hunter, Anne, 1; Jaeger, Gustav, 1, 2; Julia, 1; Kalendarian, Tom, 1; Lacroix, Christian, 1; Leacock, Stephen, 24; Louis IX, 1; Machado de Assis, Joaquim Maria, 19; Miyake, Issey, 1; Napoleon I, 25; Parker, Dorothy, 35; Poiret, Paul, 2; Schiaparelli, Elsa, 1; Vionnet, Madeleine, 1; Westwood, Vivienne, 3; Whitehorn, Katharine, 12, 13; Yeats, W. B., 57

Coasts Douglas, Norman, 1

Cold War Antall, Jozsef, 1; Barton, Bruce, 1; Baruch, Bernard Mannes, 2; Carrington, Lord, 1; Churchill, Winston, 8; De Gaulle, Charles, 13; Gaitskell, Hugh, 2; Goldwater, Barry, 4; Kennedy, John Fitzgerald, 20; Khrushchev, Nikita, 1; Lie, Trygve, 1; Troubridge, T. St Vincent, 1; Yeltsin, Boris, 4

Colleagues Lennon, John, 2

Colonialism Berry, Wendell, 1; Brathwaite, Edward Kamau, 1; Columbus, Christopher, 2; Gambetta, Léon, 2; Gandhi, Indira, 4; Gandhi, Mahatma, 23; Garvey, Marcus, 3, 8, 10; Harrington, James, 1; Jhabvala, Ruth Prawer, 1; Kipling, Rudyard, 12, 53; Lessing, Doris, 4, 5; Ngugi wa Thiongo, 5; Palmerston, Lord, 2; Senghor, Léopold, 2; Tacitus, 3; Tewodros II, 1; Van der Post, Laurens, 6; Vespucci, Amerigo, 1; Vittachi, Varindra Tarzie, 1; Walpole, Horace, 4

Color Davies, W. H., 3; Davis, Angela, 5; Douglass, Frederick, 8; Killens, John Oliver, 2; Malcolm X, 1; Senghor, Léopold, 1; Shange, Ntozake, 2; Walker, David, 1; Washington, Booker T., 8; Wheatley, Phillis, 1

Comfort Adams, Richard, 1; Barrie, J. M., 15; de la Mare, Walter, 10; Dickens, Charles, 26; Hesse, Hermann, 3; Russell, Bertrand, 32; Scott, Sir Walter, 12; Shakespeare, William, 139, 330

Commercialism Ascherson, Neal, 1; Bierce, Ambrose, 16; Bowie, David, 2; Carey, George, 1; Connolly, Billy, 1; Doyle, Roddy, 3; Fromm, Erich, 19; Iacocca, Lee, 2; Morris, William, 7; Paz, Octavio, 2; Peake, Mervyn, 4; Simon, Neil, 13; Streisand, Barbra, 3; Taubman, Alfred, 1

Commitment Bevan, Aneurin, 7; Bible, 58; Clinton, Bill, 6; Flammarion, Camille, 1; Greene, Graham, 5; Kaunda, Kenneth David, 4; McCormack, Mark, 4; Morgan, Robin, 1; Spark, Muriel, 13; Walesa, Lech, 1; Whitman, Walt, 34

Communication Acheson, Dean, 3; Bacon, Francis (1561–1626), 21, 48, 98; Belli, Melvin, 1; Bernbach, William, 1; Bible, 122; Charles V, 4; Coate, John, 2; Coppola, Francis Ford, 3; Cronin, Mary J., 4; E. T., 1; Forster, E. M., 15; Gates, Bill, 5; Handy, Charles, 10; Kraus, Karl, 14; McLuhan, Marshall, 7, 11; Nixon, Richard, 21; Ozick, Cynthia, 5; Pynchon, Thomas, 10; Randolph, A. Philip, 2; Rendall, Montague John, 1; Saki, 14; Schein, Edgar H., 1; Sheridan, Richard Brinsley, 13; Thoreau, Henry David, 46; Wolfe, Tom, 8; Zeldin, Theodore, 6

Communism Behan, Brendan, 11; Brezhnev, Leonid, 1; Castro, Fidel, 2; Césaire, Aimé, 5; Comte, Auguste, 2; Davis, Angela, 4; Deng Xiaoping, 1; Dulles, John Foster, 5; Engels, Friedrich, 4, 7; Herzen, Aleksandr Ivanovich, 1; Keegan, William, 3; Keynes, John Maynard, 7; Khrushchev, Nikita, 4, 12; King, Martin Luther, Jr., 31; Lenin, Vladimir Ilyich, 5, 15; Li Peng, 2, 3; McCarthy, Joseph (1909–57), 3; Mao Zedong, 13, 17; Marx, Karl, 20, 22; Morris, William, 2; Nehru, Jawaharlal, 3; Padmore, George, 7; Platonov, Andrei, 1; Rogers, Will, 11; Smith, F. E., 4; Sobukwe, Robert Mangaliso, 3; Solzhenitsyn, Alexander, 10; Steffens, Lincoln, 2; Stevenson, Adlai, 6; Trotsky, Leon, 9; Wright, Richard, 6; Zamyatin, Yevgeny, 2

Competition Berra, Yogi, 1; Galvin, Robert W., 1; Heller, Robert, 4, 7; Hughes, Howard, 1; Kanter, Rosabeth Moss, 2; Klein, Allen, 1; Kotter, John P., 1; Laker, Freddie, 3; Morita Akio, 2; Ross, Diana, 1; Sloan, Alfred P., Jr., 3, 4; Stewart, Thomas A., 4

Complaints Adams, Douglas, 8; Eden, Emily, 1; Galsworthy, John, 2; Jagger, Mick, 2; Johnson, Samuel, 138; Lawrence, D. H., 31; Marx, Groucho, 24; Priestley, J. B., 5; Saki, 22; Shakespeare, William, 192

Compliments Chekhov, Anton, 20; Coward, Noel, 36; Maugham, Somerset, 5; Porter, Cole, 3; Roosevelt, Eleanor, 1; Seacole, Mary, 2; Whittington, Robert, 1

Composers Barber, Samuel, 1; Berlin, Irving, 1; Cage, John, 2, 10; Casals, Pablo, 5; Copland, Aaron, 7; Dorati, Antal, 1; Foss, Lukas, 1; Gershwin, George, 2, 3, 4; Honegger, Arthur, 1; Morton, J. C., 8; Mozart, Wolfgang Amadeus, 3, 7; Rachmaninov, Sergei Vasilyevich, 1; Stravinsky, Igor, 1, 6, 8; Wagner, Richard, 1, 3

Compromise Chesterton, G. K., 45; Clay, Henry, 1; Day-Lewis, Cecil, 1; Follett, Mary Parker, 2; Massinger, Philip, 4; Montaigne, Michel de, 31; Shakespeare, William, 121

Computers Agre, Philip A., 1; DeLillo, Don, 7; Dudley Edwards, Ruth, 1; Eco, Umberto, 1; Ellis, Bill, 1; Hoff, Ted, 1; Hopper, Grace Murray, 3; Negroponte, Nicholas, 3; Newspapers, 4, 9; Rose, Frank, 1, 2, 3; Roszak, Theodore, 2; Schuler, Douglas, 1, 2; Sinclair, Clive, 2, 4, 5, 7; Stewart, Thomas A., 9; Stoll, Clifford, 1, 2, 3, 4; Townsend, Robert, 1; Tucker, Laurie, 1; Ullman, Ellen, 1; Watson, Thomas J., 1

Conceit Bacon, Francis (1561–1626), 76; Beerbohm, Max, 23; Conrad, Joseph, 6; Eliot, George, 7; Jerome, Jerome K., 1; Smith, Sydney, 2; Tree, Herbert Beerbohm, 5; Trollope, Anthony, 5; Welles, Orson, 2; Whistler, James Abbott McNeill, 9, 10, 11

Conflict Adams, Gerry, 1; Bible, 383; Castro, Fidel, 1; Cooper, James Fenimore, 11; Gandhi, Indira, 3; Hampshire, Stuart, 1; Heaney, Seamus, 3; Milton, John, 37, 70; Morrison, Danny, 1; Okri, Ben, 1; Saki, 17; Salvandy, Comte de, 1; Schwarzkopf, Norman, 1, 2

Conformity Ambrose, Saint, 1; Auden, W. H., 17; Beerbohm, Max, 21; Burton, Robert, 23; Butler, Samuel (1612–80), 23; Caesar, Julius, 1; Chesterfield, Lord, 14; Dobie, J. Frank, 1; Getty, J. Paul, 3, 4, 7; Hartley, L. P., 2; Proverbs, Modern, 14; Seth, Vikram, 3

Confusion Anonymous, 89; Arnold, Matthew, 2; Bible, 96; Kerouac, Jack, 19; Lloyd, Marie, 1; Miller, Henry, 28; Milton, John, 44; Mondale, Walter, 2; More, Thomas, 8; O'Casey, Sean, 4; Peters, Tom, 10

Conscience Browne, Thomas, 7; Butler, Joseph, 1; Butler, Samuel (1612–80), 19; Conrad, Joseph, 10; Droste-Hülshoff, Annette Elisabeth von, 2; Einstein, Albert, 41; Farmer, James, 1; Freud, Sigmund, 51; Fromm, Erich, 2; Gladstone, William Ewart, 6; Goldsmith, Oliver, 30; Hellman, Lillian, 5; Henry IV, 2; Lee, Harper, 4; Melville, Herman, 14; Mencken, H. L., 2; Ossietzky, Carl von, 1; Pirandello, Luigi, 1; Racine, Jean, 2; Reich, Wilhelm, 2; Schopenhauer, Arthur, 1; Shakespeare, William, 157, 281, 534; Twain, Mark, 40; Washington, George, 6; Waugh, Evelyn, 19; Webster, Daniel, 8

Consequences Bible, 100, 402; Liu Binyan, 1; Liu Shahe, 2; Shakespeare, William, 395, 511, 590; Skinner, B. F., 1

Conservation Channon, Paul, 1; Cousteau, Jacques, 1; Leopold, Aldo, 1; Morris, George Pope, 1; Morrison, Jim, 3; Nyerere, Julius Kambarage, 2; Pavese, Cesare, 7; Philip, Prince, 4; Roosevelt, Franklin D., 38; Strong, Maurice F., 1; Teale, Edwin Way, 1, 2; Thoreau, Henry David, 9; Wallace, Henry A., 2

Conservatism Beerbohm, Max, 26; Bierce, Ambrose, 17; Croker, John Wilson, 2; Keynes, John Maynard, 15; Lincoln, Abraham, 27; Mailer, Norman, 13; Mumford, Lewis, 4

Constancy Ibsen, Henrik, 8; Keats, John (1795–1821), 10; Laozi, 10; Shakespeare, William, 543, 657; Spinoza, Baruch, 7; Wordsworth, William, 91; Yan Yi, 1

Constitution Ames, Fisher, 1; Black, Hugo LaFayette, 3; Blackstone, William, 1, 2; Brandeis, Louis D., 6; Bryce, James, 3; Burke, Edmund, 4; Chase, Salmon P., 1; Garfield, James A., 4; Gibbon, Edward, 4; Hill, Benjamin H., 1; Hoffman, Abbie, 2; Jefferson, Thomas, 27, 36; Madison, James, 3; Marshall, John, 1; Marshall, Thurgood, 1; Mary of Teck, 1; Seward, William Henry, 2

Contempt Anonymous, 72; Bible, 17; Bickerstaffe, Isaac, 5; Greene, Graham, 7; Retz, Cardinal de, 2; Shakespeare, William, 453, 526, 528

Contentment Burns, Robert, 15; Davies, W. H., 5; Dyer, Edward, 1; FitzGerald, Edward, 5; Gershwin, Ira, 2; Graham, Katharine, 2; Horace, 40; James, Alice, 2; Mallet, David, 1; Marcus Aurelius, 5, 12; Milton, John, 113; Powell, Adam Clayton, Jr., 4; Shakespeare, William, 112, 374; Spenser, Edmund, 6; Surrey, Henry Howard, 1

Continuity Wordsworth, William, 48

Contraception Adler, Larry, 1; Allen, Woody, 24; Bird, Caroline, 2; Hume, Basil, 3; Inge, William Ralph, 6; Lynch, Jack, 1; Mencken, H. L., 12; Paintin, David, 1, 2; Paul VI, 1; Proverbs, Modern, 23; Russell, Dora, 1; Sanger, Margaret, 1; Stopes, Marie, 2; Teresa of Calcutta, Mother, 10; Thomas, Irene, 1; Virchow, Rudolf, 3

Conversation Austen, Jane, 26; Bambara, Toni Cade, 2; Bellow, Saul, 8; Bramah, Ernest, 3; Eliot, T. S., 32; Frank, Anne, 6; Goncourt, Edmond de, 1; Johnson, Samuel, 36, 119; Kipling, Rudyard, 15; Longworth, Alice Lee, 1; Maupassant, Guy de, 3; Mikes, George, 4; Milton, John, 58; Morley, Christopher Darlington, 8; Morley, Robert, 1; Pepys, Samuel, 5; Post, Emily, 1; Seneca, "the Younger," 3; Shakespeare, William, 440, 446; Shelley, Percy Bysshe, 12; Smith, Sydney, 18; Southey, Robert, 7; West, Rebecca, 5; Whitehorn, Katharine, 16; Wodehouse, P. G., 6

Cooking Apicius, Marcus Gavius, 1; Berryman, John, 8; Child, Julia, 1, 2, 3; Glasse, Hannah, 1; Melville, Herman, 7; Plato, 3; Saki, 6; Schiaparelli, Elsa, 2; Shakespeare, William, 557; Spry, Constance, 1; Ude, Louis Eustache, 1, 2

Correspondence Adams, Abigail, 2; Donne, John, 8; Hemingway, Ernest, 6; Wilde, Oscar, 7

Corruption Acton, Lord, 2; Attali, Jacques, 2; Awolowo, Obafemi, 2; Bible, 196, 247; Blake, William, 8; Carlyle, Thomas, 38; Chaucer, Geoffrey, 13; Dean, John, 1; Emerson, Ralph Waldo, 47; Gibbon, Edward, 6; Greene, Graham, 6; Jeffers, Robinson, 1; Kipling, Rudyard, 60; Matthiessen, Peter, 2; Merton, Thomas, 1; Mohamad, Mahathir bin, 4; Nixon, Richard, 16, 24; Ovid, 12; Roosevelt, Theodore, 18; Shakespeare, William, 153, 579; Somoza Debayle, Anastasio, 1; Walker, Jimmy, 1

Cosmetics Jong, Erica, 4; Walker, Alice, 23

Cosmopolitanism James, Henry, 3

Countryside Doyle, Arthur Conan, 6; Goldsmith, Oliver, 15; Hanson, Lord, 2; Hazlitt, William, 28; Housman, A. E., 10, 17; Joad, C. E. M., 1; Meredith, George, 12; Scott, Sir Walter, 17; Smith, Sydney, 4; White, E. B., 4

Courage Akhmatova, Anna, 5; Awolowo, Obafemi, 1; Bible, 215; Blair, Robert, 1; Brontë, Emily, 1; Brown, Sterling, 1; Burns, Robert, 34; Cheever, John, 2; Childers, Erskine, 1; Churchill, Winston, 34; Crane, Stephen, 7; Davis, Elmer, 1; Deschamps, Eustache, 1; Douglas, Archibald, 1; Earhart, Amelia, 3; Eco, Umberto, 8; Fanon, Frantz, 1; Ferber, Edna, 1; Harold II, 1; Hemans, Felicia, 1; Hemingway, Ernest, 7, 21; Henley, William Ernest, 2; Henry IV, 1; Hill, Aaron, 2; Horace, 42; Ibárruri, Dolores, 4, 6; Kennedy, John Fitzgerald, 34; Laski, Harold, 1; Lincoln, Abraham, 39; Luthuli, Albert, 2; Macaulay, Thomas Babington, 22; Mamet, David, 7; Marie-Antoinette, 1; Milne, A. A., 23; Miró, Joan, 5; Mitchell, Margaret, 4; Napoleon I, 20; Nimitz, Chester, 1; Paine, Thomas, 5; Raleigh, Walter, 10; Schiller, Friedrich von, 23; Scott, Captain, 1; Semiramis, 1; Shakespeare, William, 321, 424, 439; Smith, Logan Pearsall, 18; Solzhenitsyn, Alexander, 7; Tennyson, Alfred, 37, 38, 76; Virgil, 22, 23; Walpole, Hugh, 1

Courtesy Bacon, Francis (1561–1626), 32; Belloc, Hilaire, 31; Duhamel, Georges, 4; Montagu, Mary Wortley, 3; Montesquieu, 9

Courtship Bayly, Thomas Haynes, 7; Congreve, William, 18; Dickens, Charles, 83; Folk Verse, 32; Lowell, Robert, 20; O'Hara, Geoffrey, 1; Shakespeare, William, 286; Wells, H. G., 4

Cowardice Bible, 436; Carroll, Lewis, 39; Coward, Noel, 1; Duvalier, François, 1; Fletcher, Phineas, 2; Foch, Ferdinand, 3; Gilbert, W. S., 22; Granville, George, 1; Johnson, Samuel, 95; Madhubuti, Haki R., 1; Milligan, Spike, 5; O'Brien, Edna, 1; O'Connor, Frank, 2; Shakespeare, William, 302; Twain, Mark, 19; Wycherley, William, 4

Creativity Achebe, Chinua, 2; Azikiwe, Nnamdi, 1; Barthelme, Donald, 3; Beethoven, Ludwig van, 4; Bernbach, William, 3; Bible, 102; Brackett, Anna C., 1; Brancusi, Constantin, 1; Bronowski, Jacob, 1; Burns, Robert, 16; Chisholm, Shirley, 3; Clark, Septima Poinsette, 1; Conran, Terence, 3; Dagerman, Stig, 1; Dillard, Annie, 8; Doctorow, E. L., 6; Dryden, John, 5; FitzGerald, Edward, 14; Fitz-Gibbon, Bernice, 1; Gautier, Théophile, 1; Goodman, Paul, 2; Horace, 7; Hughes, Ted, 7; Kao, John J., 1; Kilmer, Joyce, 2; King, Martin Luther, Jr., 12; Kroc, Ray, 4; Lyttelton, Humphrey, 3; Mailer, Norman, 28; Mao Zedong, 34; Marley, Bob, 4; Milton, John, 74; Morrison, Jim, 8; Munch, Edvard, 3; Ortega y Gasset, José, 30; Peters, Tom, 9; Pope, Alexander, 49; Proust, Marcel, 1, 19; Rand, Ayn, 4; Shapiro, Robert B., 4; Sitting Bull, 2; Walcott, Derek, 3; Watson, James Dewey, 3; Wordsworth, William, 23; Zeeman, E.C., 1

Credit Franklin, Benjamin, 5; Hurst, Gerald, 1; Johnson, Samuel, 22; Rabelais, François, 9, 10, 11, 12; Seneca, "the Elder," 1

Cricket Botham, Ian, 1; Brathwaite, Edward Kamau, 2; Grace, W. G., 2; Hughes, Thomas, 2; James, C. L. R., 4, 5; Newbolt, Henry, 3; Pinter, Harold, 4; Wilde, Oscar, 80; Williams, Eric, 1

Crime Alfieri, Vittorio, 1; Allen, Woody, 11; Arendt, Hannah, 11, 13; Bellow, Saul, 7; Chandler, Raymond, 10; Doctorow, E. L., 3; Doyle, Arthur Conan, 10; Dryden, John, 46; Du Bois, W. E. B., 14; Emerson, Ralph Waldo, 25; Garvey, Marcus, 4; Genet, Jean, 1, 2; Hawthorne, Nathaniel, 13; Juvenal, 1, 2; Leacock, Stephen, 19; Lee, Kuan Yew, 5; Machado de Assis, Joaquim Maria, 15; Mezzrow, Mezz, 2; Miller, Henry, 11; More, Hannah, 1; Publilius Syrus, 15; Puzo, Mario, 2; Quételet, Lambert Adolphe Jacques, 1; Racine, Jean, 20; Ross, Nick, 1; Runciman of Doxford, Lady, 1; Seneca, "the Younger," 13; Shakespeare, William, 263; Virgil, 11; Waugh, Evelyn, 18

Criticism Arnold, Matthew, 18; Bankhead, Tallulah, 7; Benchley, Robert, 10; Browne, Thomas, 4; Browning, Robert, 4; Brown, John Mason, 2; Buchanan, Robert Williams, 2; Burke, Edmund, 35; Cagney, James, 1; Cervantes, Miguel de, 44; Chesterton, G. K., 10; Coward, Noel, 35; Crosby, David, 1; Debussy, Claude, 1; Dickens, Charles, 31; Dryden, John, 2, 10; Durbin, Karen, 1; Field, Eugene, 5; Frye, Northrop, 2, 3; Gray, Thomas, 1; Heine, Heinrich, 2; Holloway, Joseph, 1; Hood, Thomas, 18; Jarrell, Randall, 2; Johnson, Samuel, 28, 158, 166, 175; La Bruyère, Jean de, 13; MacNeice, Louis, 3; Mao Zedong, 26; Marx, Groucho, 30; Maugham, Somerset, 17; Morrison, Toni, 15; O'Brien, Flann, 5; Poe, Edgar Allan,

25; Vidal, Gore, 16; Waugh, Evelyn, 8, 10, 12; Wilde, Oscar, 76; Woodson, Carter G., 1

Effort Chesterton, G. K., 46; Clough, Arthur Hugh, 13; Kennedy, Florynce R., 1; Land, Edwin Herbert, 1; Longfellow, Henry Wadsworth, 23; Plutarch, 8; Rorty, Richard, 3; Wilde, Oscar, 73

Egotism Adler, Alfred, 10; Amis, Martin, 2; Barnes, Djuna, 4; Bierce, Ambrose, 22; Chamfort, Nicolas, 2; Frye, Northrop, 8; Heifetz, Jascha, 1; Hiatt, Arnold, 1; Hughes, Ted, 4; Leahy, Frank, 1; Lester, Julius, 3; Miller, Henry, 25; Powell, Colin, 4; Shakespeare, William, 596; Stoppard, Tom, 7; Wilde, Oscar, 14, 30; Wordsworth, William, 6

Egypt Husayn, Taha, 1; Mahfouz, Naguib, 9; Nasser, Gamal Abdel, 1, 3; Ross, Ronald, 1; Sadat, Anwar al-, 4; Shakespeare, William, 69; Shawqi, Ahmad, 1

Elation Shakespeare, William, 651

Elections Bush, George, 4; Clinton, Bill, 1, 4; Denisova, Galina, 1; Eliot, George, 14; Henry II, 4; Kinnock, Neil, 1; McGovern, George, 1; Major, John, 6; Malcolm X, 7; Mandela, Nelson, 9; Maura, Antonio, 1; Mondale, Walter, 1; Reagan, Ronald, 21; Sherman, William Tecumseh, 2; Thatcher, Margaret, 21; Wilson, Woodrow, 4

Electricity Hawthorne, Nathaniel, 5; Thurber, James, 8

Elitism Jenkins, Roy, 2; Pareto, Vilfredo, 1; Voltaire, 19

Embarrassment Astaire, Fred, 7; Congreve, William, 20; Grossmith, George, 2; Parker, Dorothy, 40; Philip, Prince, 5

Emigration Büchner, Georg, 3; Wilkins, James, 1

Emotion Barnard, Charlotte Alington, 1; Byron, Lord, 33, 76; Calvino, Italo, 2; Chesterton, G. K., 36; Crisp, Quentin, 9; Crompton, Richmal, 1; Dickens, Charles, 12, 102; Epicurus, 3; Hume, David, 13; Jung, Carl Gustav, 15; Keats, John (1795–1821), 59; Kunitz, Stanley, 3; Laing, R. D., 16; Leary, Timothy, 7; Lyly, John, 12; Miller, Henry, 15; Paisiello, Giovanni, 1; Parker, Dorothy, 2; Porchia, Antonio, 5; Rogers, Samuel, 9; Schopenhauer, Arthur, 10; Sharp, William, 1; Sibelius, Jean, 1; Soyinka, Wole, 11; Susruta, 1; Walker, Alice, 2; Watson, John B., 2; Williams, Tennessee, 16

Empiricism Chomsky, Noam, 5

Employees Carnegie, Andrew, 8; Morita Akio, 5; Peters, Tom, 14; Semler, Ricardo, 6; Stewart, Thomas A., 1

Ending Browning, Robert, 45; Forché, Carolyn, 1; Moore, Thomas, 8; O'Connor, Edwin, 1; Porter, Cole, 12; Shakespeare, William, 59; Wolstenholme, Kenneth, 1

Endurance Acheson, Dean, 5; Angelou, Maya, 3; Baring-Gould, Sabine, 3; Clough, Arthur Hugh, 2; Cotter, Joseph Seamon, Jr., 1; Dickinson, Emily, 15; Keller, Helen, 3; Longfellow, Henry Wadsworth, 26; Orczy, Baroness, 2; Roth, Philip, 1; Seferis, George, 1; Shakespeare, William, 100, 351, 366, 599; Virgil, 3, 6

Enemies Breton, Nicholas, 1; Campbell, Thomas, 11; Coward, Noel, 30; Hoover, J. Edgar, 2; James, C. L. R., 7; Kennedy, Robert, 7; Linklater, Eric, 1; Mao Zedong, 36; Napier, Charles James, 2; Narváez, Ramón María, 2; Rossetti, Dante Gabriel, 1; Rushdie, Salman, 10; Shakespeare, William, 114

England Battiscombe, Georgina, 1; Bede, 2, 3; Blake, William, 18; Bossuet, Jacques-Bénigne, 3; Bradbury, Malcolm, 2; Browning, Robert, 24; Byron, Lord, 8, 78; Carey, Henry, 2; Churchill, Charles, 5, 6; Collingbourne, William, 1; Crisp, Quentin, 5; Davy, Humphry, 1; Defoe, Daniel, 11; Delaney, Shelagh, 3; Denning, Lord, 2; Dickens, Charles, 91; Drayton, Michael, 7; Durrell, Gerald, 2; Elizabeth I, 3; Ellis, Alice Thomas, 1; Empson, William, 1; Fielding, Henry, 14; Florio, John, 2; Forster, E. M., 5; Fuller, Margaret, 4; Hale, Matthew, 1; Halsey, Margaret, 1, 2, 3, 5; Hatton, Christopher, 1; Hazlitt, William, 18; Hegel, G. W. F., 4; Henley, William Ernest, 4; Henry V, 1; Herbert, A. P., 10; Hitchcock, Alfred, 4; Inge, William Ralph, 4; Irving, Washington, 3; James, Henry, 28; Jerrold, Douglas, 9; Johnson, Linton Kwesi, 1; Kipling, Rudyard, 6; Kureishi, Hanif, 1; Lerner, Alan Jay, 5; Macaulay, Thomas Babington, 5; MacInnes, Colin, 2; MacNeice, Louis, 2; Malory, Thomas, 1; Martineau, Harriet, 6; Mikes, George, 6, 8; Mitchell, Adrian, 2; Montesquieu, 10; Moritz, Karl Philipp, 1; Muggeridge, Malcolm, 6; Napoleon I, 26; Nash, Ogden, 9; Novalis, 4; Orwell, George, 31, 36; Osborne, John, 1; Pepys, Samuel, 1; Philip II (1527–98), 1; Pitt the Elder, William, 2; Porter, Peter, 4; Richard II, 1; Santayana, George, 7; Seacole, Mary, 1; Shaw, George Bernard, 51; Smith, Stevie, 2; Smith, Sydney, 25; Sully, Maximilien de Béthune, 1; Swift, Jonathan, 19; Verne, Jules, 2; Wilde, Oscar, 4, 5; Ximénèz, Augustin, 1

Entertainment Berlin, Irving, 2; Cobb, Irvin S., 2; Cohn, Nik, 1; Cook, Peter, 2; Dangerfield, Rodney, 1; Disney, Walt, 2; Dunbar-Nelson, Alice, 1; Eliot, T. S., 1; George, Nelson, 1; Liberace, 1; Madonna, 6; Pop, Iggy, 1; Warhol, Andy, 12; Wonder, Stevie, 4

Enthusiasm Alcuin, 3; Balfour, Arthur, 2; Emerson, Ralph Waldo, 7; Goldwyn, Samuel, 12; Hammer, Michael, 1; Hemingway, Ernest, 4; Lytton, Bulwer, 5; Shakespeare, William, 78

Entrepreneurs Anderson, Kye, 1; Blair, Tony, 2; Bloomberg, Michael, 1; Forbes, Malcolm S., 1; Greene, Hunt, 1; Iverson, Ken, 5; Keen, Peter, 3; Peters, Tom, 16; Taubman, Alfred, 2; Thatcher, Margaret, 3; Travis, Dempsey J., 1

Environment Arbuthnot, John, 1; Beckett, Samuel, 6; Betjeman, John, 14; Brautigan, Richard, 5; Carson, Rachel, 1, 2, 3; Cecil, Robert, 2; Chekhov, Anton, 19; Gummer, John Selwyn, 1; Hoagland, Edward, 5; Ingersoll, Robert G., 4; Krutch, Joseph Wood, 2; Leopold, Aldo, 2, 3; Marquis, Don, 7; Mead, Margaret, 12, 17; Mitchell, Joni, 2; Newspapers, 20; Parmenter, Ross, 1; Peattie, Donald Culross, 1; Porter, George, 2; Raymond, Lee R., 1, 2; Rowland, Sherwood, 1; Santayana, George, 18; Saro-Wiwa, Ken, 2; Simak, Clifford D., 1; Summers, Lawrence H., 1; Thoreau, Henry David, 23, 41; Udall, Stewart L., 3, 4; Vidal, Gore, 3; Wiener, Norbert, 6

Envy Aesop, 3; Beerbohm, Max, 14; Byron, Lord, 67; Flynn, Errol, 1; Gay, John, 8; Roethke, Theodore, 7; Shaw, George Bernard, 46; Swift, Jonathan, 50; Vidal, Gore, 9

Epigrams Coleridge, Samuel Taylor, 11; Flaubert, Gustave, 6, 7; Harington, John, 1; Retz, Cardinal de, 8

Epitaphs Africanus, Scipio, 1; Atkinson, E. L., 1; Belloc, Hilaire, 18; Binyon, Laurence, 2; Browne, William, 1; Busta, Christine, 1; Byron, Lord, 34; Camden, William, 1; Coleridge, Samuel Taylor, 12; Davis, Thomas, 3; Donne, John, 1, 3; Elizabeth I, 22; Emmet, Robert, 1; Epitaphs, 1, 2, 3, 4, 5, 6, 7, 8, 9, 10, 11, 12, 13, 14; Fitzgerald, F. Scott, 2; Folk Verse, 64; Franklin, Benjamin, 4, 7; Gandhi, Mahatma, 5; Garrick, David, 1; Goldsmith, Oliver, 1, 3; Gray, Thomas, 12, 13; Hardy, Thomas, 16; Johnson, Samuel, 97; Jonson, Ben, 3; Jowett, Benjamin, 2; Kaufman, George S., 2; Keats, John (1795–1821), 92; Knox, John, 1; La Bruyère, Jean de, 17; Leonidas, 1; Mencken, H. L., 39; Parker, Dorothy, 22, 42; Pope, Alexander, 46; Pound, Ezra, 14, 15; Robinson, Jackie, 4; Rochester, 2nd Earl of, 1; Scott, Sir Walter, 7; Shakespeare, William, 14, 27, 28, 220; Stevenson, Robert Louis, 4; Sturges, Preston, 1; Swanson, Gloria, 2; Swift, Jonathan, 7; Voltaire, 52; Wilson, Woodrow, 3; Yeats, W. B., 18

Equality Adams, Abigail, 5; Anthony, Susan B., 3, 5, 6; Ball, John, 2; Balzac, Honoré de, 4; Barbey d'Aurevilly, Jules-Amédée, 3; Barnes, Ernest William, 1; Barrie, J. M., 14; Becque, Henry, 1; Bentham, Jeremy, 5; Berlin, Isaiah, 1; Bible, 15; Burns, Robert, 18; Congreve, William, 11; Defoe, Daniel, 6; Du Bois, W. E. B., 3, 11; Fallaci, Oriana, 1; Forster, E. M., 13; France, Anatole, 8; Froude, J. A., 1; Gandhi, Indira, 5; Garnet, Henry Highland, 3; Giroud, Françoise, 3; Gould, Stephen Jay, 12; Harper, Frances E. W., 4; Heide, Wilma Scott, 1; Huxley, Aldous, 46; Jackson, Jesse, 3; Johnson, Samuel, 100; Joseph, Chief, 2; Kennedy, Florynce R., 3; Kennedy, John Fitzgerald, 12; Kent, Corita, 1; King, Martin Luther, Jr., 8, 11, 26; Livermore, Mary Ashton, 2; Long, Huey, 2; Macleod, Iain, 4; Mancroft, Stormont Samuel, 2; Mansfield, William Murray, 1; Martineau, Harriet, 7; Mill, John Stuart, 15; Mott, Lucretia, 1; Murdoch, Iris, 5; Nixon, Richard, 30; Orwell,

George, 10; Pankhurst, Emmeline, 5; Paz, Octavio, 1; Peake, Mervyn, 5; Rawls, John, 1; Ruskin, John, 26; Shakespeare, William, 132, 205, 208, 670; Shaw, George Bernard, 62; Stanton, Elizabeth Cady, 9; Stone, Lucy, 1; Sun, Madame, 1; Tracy, Spencer, 2; Truth, Sojourner, 1; Wilson, Harold, 3; Wood, Victoria, 1; Wordsworth, William, 90

Eternity Bible, 426, 442; Brontë, Emily, 4; Browne, Thomas, 14; Büchner, Georg, 5; Campbell, Thomas, 9; Congreve, William, 16; Dionysius the Areopagite, 1; Leacock, Stephen, 13; Marcus Aurelius, 3; Roethke, Theodore, 6; Stoppard, Tom, 10; Vaughan, Henry, 5; Walker, Alice, 13

Ethics Beauvoir, Simone de, 6; Bennis, Warren, 1; Byron, Lord, 4; Cleaver, Eldridge, 3; Einstein, Albert, 9, 28; Goldman, Emma, 2; King, Martin Luther, Jr., 13, 16; Ramsey, Frank, 2; Russell, Bertrand, 26, 33, 61; Service, Robert W., 3; Spencer, Herbert, 3; Trotsky, Leon, 12

Etiquette Betjeman, John, 3; Calverley, C. S., 2; Carter, Jimmy, 1; De Wolfe, Elsie, 2; Gaskell, Elizabeth, 3; Herbert, A. P., 7; John Paul II, 8; Johnson, Samuel, 111; Joyce, James, 22; Mankiewicz, Herman J., 3; Maugham, Somerset, 2; Mikes, George, 2; Post, Emily, 2, 3

Euphemisms Eden, Anthony, 2; McCarthy, Mary, 12; Smith, Sydney, 5

Europe Adenauer, Konrad, 2; Armah, Ayi Kwei, 4; Bismarck, Prince Otto von, 4, 5; Brandt, Willy, 5; Burke, Edmund, 38; Churchill, Winston, 37; De Gaulle, Charles, 4; DeLillo, Don, 3; Delors, Jacques, 2, 5, 6; Enzensberger, Hans, 2; Gaitskell, Hugh, 1; Goldsmith, James, 3; Kohl, Helmut, 1; Lothian, Lord, 1; Mead, Walter Russell, 1; Metternich, 2, 3; Mosley, Walter, 4; Thatcher, Margaret, 14; Weidman, Jerome, 1; Williams, Tennessee, 9

Evening Baring-Gould, Sabine, 2; Baudelaire, Charles, 14; Eliot, T. S., 33; Ellerton, John, 1; Gray, Thomas, 4; Lauder, Harry, 1; Milton, John, 57, 89; Wordsworth, William, 42

Evil Anouilh, Jean, 2; Arendt, Hannah, 9; Bible, 64, 111, 355; Boethius, 4; Boileau, Nicolas, 4; Brecht, Bertolt, 23; Chesterton, G. K., 40; Conrad, Joseph, 12; Corneille, Pierre, 3; Einstein, Albert, 45; Faulkner, William, 10; Hesiod, 1; Hood, Thomas, 12; Hume, David, 27; International Military Tribunal of the Nuremberg Trials, 1; Joyce, James, 34; Jung, Carl Gustav, 1, 11; King, Martin Luther, Jr., 20; La Rochefoucauld, François, 24; Mahfouz, Naguib, 4; Milton, John, 98; Montaigne, Michel de, 25; Morrison, Toni, 21, 24; Muhammad, 13; Poe, Edgar Allan, 15; Roosevelt, Theodore, 25; Seaborg, Glenn, 1; Shakespeare, William, 227, 381, 679; Shelley, Percy Bysshe, 37; Soyinka, Wole, 12; Spenser, Edmund, 7; Steiner, George, 5; Taylor, Ron, 1; West, Mae, 10

Evolution Bryan, William Jennings, 4; Butler, Samuel (1835–1902), 7; Congreve, William, 1; Cuppy, Will, 1; Darwin, Charles, 4, 5, 8, 9, 10, 12; Darwin, Charles Galton, 1; Disraeli, Benjamin, 44; Ennius, Quintus, 3; Gould, Stephen Jay, 4; Hoagland, Edward, 8; Hubbard, Elbert, 3; Huxley, T. H., 2; Kipling, Rudyard, 30; Lorenz, Konrad, 8; Lucretius, 5; Luther, Martin, 18; Pauling, Linus, 1; Queneau, Raymond, 1; Sagan, Carl, 8, 19; Santayana, George, 5; Spencer, Herbert, 1, 5; Stevenson, Robert Louis, 42; Teilhard de Chardin, Pierre, 1; Wallace, Alfred Russel, 3; Wilberforce, Samuel, 2; Wilson, Edward O., 1, 5

Examinations Colton, Charles, 1; Sellar, W. C., 7

Example Milton, John, 7; Selden, John, 13

Excellence Chesterfield, Lord, 17; Churchill, Charles, 1, 2; Fitzgerald, F. Scott, 16; Peters, Tom, 2; Schopenhauer, Arthur, 3; Shakespeare, William, 145

Excess Allainval, Abbé d', 1; Anouilh, Jean, 7; Blake, William, 39; Disraeli, Benjamin, 47; MacDougall, Donald, 1; Shakespeare, William, 96, 328; Wilde, Oscar, 20; William of Malmesbury, 1

Execution Bible, 346; Charles I, 1, 5; Cromwell, Oliver, 4; Fairfax, Lord, 1; Farquhar, George, 13; Gilbert, W. S., 29, 33; Hawthorne, Nathaniel, 20; Housman, A. E., 13, 14; Jonson, Ben, 6; Karr, Alphonse, 1; Kipling, Rudyard, 62; Lu Xun, 10; Molière, 23; Monmouth, James Scott, 1; Montpensier, Duchesse de, 1; More, Thomas, 2, 3, 7; Pepys, Samuel, 4; Plath, Sylvia, 8; Sartre, Jean-Paul, 21; Shakespeare, William, 218, 225; Socrates, 7; Stevenson, Robert Louis, 16; Voltaire, 17

Exercise Depew, Chauncey, 1; Ford, Henry, 14; Hutchins, Robert M., 3; Jefferson, Thomas, 2; Kelvin, William Thomson, 1; Xu Zhimo, 3

Exile Charles II, 7; Fry, Christopher, 10; Mitchell, John, 1; Payne, John Howard, 1; Shakespeare, William, 514

Existence Adonis, 1; Anselm, Saint, 4; Aristotle, 5; Beckett, Samuel, 29; Berkeley, Bishop, 2; Betti, Ugo, 11; Clement XIII, 1; Descartes, René, 6, 8, 12; Éluard, Paul, 2; Hawking, Stephen, 4; Hooker, Richard, 3; Ionesco, Eugène, 2; Jung, Carl Gustav, 16; Keats, John (1795–1821), 79; London, Jack, 3; MacNeice, Louis, 9, 23; Merleau-Ponty, Maurice, 3, 13; Millay, Edna St. Vincent, 2; Monod, Jacques Lucien, 1; Naipaul, V. S., 1; Pascal, Blaise, 11; Renard, Jules, 19; Sartre, Jean-Paul, 11; Schopenhauer, Arthur, 7, 13; Spender, Stephen, 9; Updike, John, 21; Wesker, Arnold, 1

Expectation Aquinas, Thomas, 1; Beckett, Samuel, 3; Chesterton, G. K., 8; Connolly, Cyril, 5; Hofstadter, Douglas R., 1; Jolson, Al, 2; La Fontaine, Jean de, 3; Lincoln, Abraham, 16; Scott, Sir Walter, 16; White, Patrick, 1

Expediency Bible, 294; Disraeli, Benjamin, 4, 60; Goldsmith, Oliver, 13; Khasoggi, Adnan, 2; Shakespeare, William, 313, 593; Waugh, Evelyn, 9

Experience Antrim, Minna, 2; Arnold, Matthew, 3; Baruch, Bernard Mannes, 5; Bax, Arnold, 1; Bowen, Elizabeth, 2; Chekhov, Anton, 6; Dillard, Annie, 7; Dylan, Bob, 13; Emerson, Ralph Waldo, 10; Fanon, Frantz, 11; Froude, J. A., 3; Fry, Christopher, 3; Gibson, Althea, 1; Gillespie, Dizzy, 1; Guthrie, Woody, 2; Holmes, Oliver Wendell, 32; James, Henry, 10; Joyce, James, 6; Keats, John (1795–1821), 39, 91; Lonsdale, Kathleen, 1; Lord, Betty Bao, 1; McCarthy, Joseph (1885–1943), 1; MacNeice, Louis, 18; Meredith, George, 5, 6; Proverbs, 209; Renard, Jules, 18; Shakespeare, William, 368; Stevenson, Robert Louis, 26; Virgil, 24; Weil, Simone, 4; Wilde, Oscar, 33; Wilder, Thornton, 9; Young, Edward, 9

Experts Bierce, Ambrose, 48; Bohr, Niels, 1; Butler, Nicholas Murray, 2; Fischer, Martin H., 21; Fisher, Geoffrey, 1; Heisenberg, Werner, 1; Hubbard, Elbert, 16; Lec, Stanislaw, 4; Morgan, Elaine, 1; Peter, Laurence J., 6; Peters, Tom, 12; Wright, Frank Lloyd, 5

Explanations Adams, Douglas, 1, 13; Beresford, Charles William de la Poer, 1; Carroll, Lewis, 42; Coleridge, Samuel Taylor, 2; Coward, Noel, 27; Grange, Red, 1; Grayson, Victor, 1; Ionesco, Eugène, 1; Kerouac, Jack, 27; Morrison, Jim, 6; Shakespeare, William, 276

Exploitation Byron, Lord, 97; Cliff, Michelle, 2; Cowper, William, 19; Diddley, Bo, 1; Fromm, Erich, 6; Horney, Karen, 5; Joel, Billy, 1; Malcolm X, 6; Nyerere, Julius Kambarage, 3; Stanton, Elizabeth Cady, 2; Waters, Muddy, 2; Weber, Max, 2

Exploration Boone, Daniel, 1; Bradford, William, 1; Columbus, Christopher, 4; Peary, Robert Edwin, 1, 7; Thomson, Joseph, 1

Extravagance Churchill, Jennie, 4; Grade, Lew, 2; Hayes, Helen, 2; Julia, 2; Polo, Marco, 5; Portland, Duke of, 1

Extremes Man Ray, 1; Paine, Thomas, 4; Roach, Stephen S., 3; Sontag, Susan, 16; Spark, Muriel, 5; Voltaire, 36

Eyes Beerbohm, Max, 17; Mercer, Johnny, 1; Middleton, Thomas, 4; Morrison, Jim, 7; Reagan, Ronald, 3

Facts Banks, Russell, 1; Browning, Robert, 71; Carr, John Dickson, 1; Darwin, Charles, 3; Dickens, Charles, 38; Fischer, Martin H., 6; Huxley, Aldous, 45, 54; Mailer, Norman, 18; Olson, Charles, 6; Pirandello, Luigi, 6, 19; Putnam, Hilary, 1; Salinger, J. D., 10; Shea, Michael, 1; Smith, Logan Pearsall, 16; Streatfield, Geoffrey, 1; Taylor, A. J. P., 6; Thoreau, Henry David, 14

Failure Arno, Peter, 2; Bronowski, Jacob, 5; Cervantes, Miguel de, 42; Chekhov,

2; Emecheta, Buchi, 2; French, Marilyn, 2; Fuller, Margaret, 7, 9; Golden, Marita, 3; Goldman, Emma, 3; Greer, Germaine, 1, 8; Huffington, Arianna, 2; Johnson, Sonia, 1; Jones, Amanda Theodosia, 1; Loos, Anita, 8; Luce, Clare Boothe, 3; Mead, Margaret, 16; Meir, Golda, 2; Mitchell, Joni, 7; Morgan, Elaine, 2; Morgan, Robin, 2; Nasreen, Taslima, 3; Norton, Caroline, 2; Norton, Eleanor Holmes, 1, 3; Paglia, Camille, 9; Ramey, Estelle, 1; Richardson, Dorothy M., 1; Rover, Constance, 1; Saadawi, Nawal el-, 1; Stanton, Elizabeth Cady, 6, 7; Steinem, Gloria, 3, 7, 10, 13, 16; Stopes, Marie, 7; Thatcher, Margaret, 7, 24; West, Rebecca, 9; Wolfard, Mary, 1; Wolf, Naomi, 2, 4

Festivals Jonson, Ben, 5; Tennyson, Alfred, 77

Fiction Barbour, John, 1; Brontë, Charlotte, 6; Doctorow, E. L., 4; Forster, E. M., 10; Fowles, John, 1; Kincaid, Jamaica, 4; Smith, Logan Pearsall, 11; Stendhal, 5; Trollope, Anthony, 9; White, Patrick, 2; Woolf, Virginia, 1

Fighting Browning, Robert, 19; Clough, Arthur Hugh, 1; Malraux, André, 8; Marlowe, Christopher, 21; Mitchell, Margaret, 5; Shakespeare, William, 79, 468

Fire Evelyn, John, 4; Francis de Sales, Saint, 1; Luo Guanzhong, 2; Sheridan, Richard Brinsley, 16

First Impressions Louis XIV, 8

First Lines du Maurier, Daphne, 1; Orwell, George, 19; Tolkien, J. R. R., 2

Fishing Bishop, Elizabeth, 7, 8; Brautigan, Richard, 4; Chalkhill, John, 1; Johnson, Samuel, 53; Lawrence, D. H., 14; Walton, Izaak, 2, 5, 6

Flattery Austen, Jane, 33; Chesterfield, Lord, 10; Colton, Charles, 2; Congreve, William, 2; Cowper, William, 13; Cromwell, Oliver, 7; Disraeli, Benjamin, 52; Johnson, Samuel, 51; Jonson, Ben, 22; La Fontaine, Jean de, 6; Marx, Groucho, 29; Milton, John, 8; Monroe, James, 3; Nwapa, Flora, 3; Shakespeare, William, 333, 673; Spinoza, Baruch, 3; Stevenson, Adlai, 7; Swift, Jonathan, 6

Flirtation Bacall, Lauren, 2; Browning, Robert, 41; Burns, Robert, 13, 20; Byron, Lord, 22, 74; Gay, John, 14; Hoffman, Dustin, 1; Marx, Groucho, 2; Smith, Sydney, 13; Smith, Will, 1; Sterne, Laurence, 6; Wilde, Oscar, 58

Florida Bishop, Elizabeth, 6; Ozick, Cynthia, 3; Rawlings, Marjorie, 1; Steinbeck, John, 19

Flowers Brooke, Rupert, 6; Browning, Robert, 70; de la Mare, Walter, 9; Herrick, Robert, 7; Keats, John (1795–1821), 72; Marlowe, Christopher, 2; Muir, John, 4; Scott, Sir Walter, 5; Stein, Gertrude, 8; Wordsworth, William, 73

Flying Amis, Martin, 3; Greene, Graham, 13; Jiles, Paulette, 1; Johnson, Amy, 1; Kerr, Jean, 7; Leonardo da Vinci, 7; Magee, John Gillespie, 1; Matthiessen, Peter, 4; Thoreau, Henry David, 15; Welles, Orson, 6; Wright, Wilbur, 1

Food Anonymous, 49; Barlow, Joel, 1; Beard, James, 1; Bible, 236; Brillat-Savarin, Anthelme, 1; Caracciolo, Francesco, 1; Cobbett, William, 4; Dahl, Roald, 1; De Wolfe, Elsie, 1; Dickens, Charles, 4; Disraeli, Benjamin, 38; Douglas, Norman, 2; du Bartas, Guillaume, 13; Dunn, Douglas, 2; Farb, Peter, 1; Farmer, Fannie, 2; Fern, Fanny, 1; Feuerbach, Ludwig Andreas, 2; Fischer, Martin H., 7; Franklin, Benjamin, 11; Gandhi, Mahatma, 9; Grappelli, Stephane, 1; Hawthorne, Nathaniel, 10; Higgins, Andrew, 1; Hubbard, Frank McKinney, 2; James, Clive, 2; Jefferies, Richard, 2; Johnson, Samuel, 13, 59, 136; Joyce, James, 27; Keillor, Garrison, 12; Kipling, Rudyard, 65; Koran, 13, 40; Lebowitz, Fran, 1; Louis XIV, 1; Lo, Vivienne, 2; Mercier, Louis-Sébastien, 2; Milne, A. A., 3, 17; Moreau, Jeanne, 3; Morley, Robert, 2; Muir, Frank, 3; Norberg-Hodge, Helena, 1; O'Brien, Flann, 7; Peary, Robert Edwin, 4; Pepys, Samuel, 9; Pliny the Younger, 1; Pynchon, Thomas, 2; Roden, Claudia, 1; Shaw, George Bernard, 102, 107; Simon, Neil, 7; Smith, Delia, 1; Smith, Sydney, 19; Spry, Constance, 3; Stevens, Wallace, 6; Swift, Jonathan, 32; Twain, Mark, 32; Tyler, Anne, 1; Voltaire, 53; Welty, Eudora, 2; Wesker, Arnold, 2; White, E. B., 7; Winfrey, Oprah, 2; Young, Mary Evans, 1

Foolishness Aidoo, Ama Ata, 4; Bible, 461; Boileau, Nicolas, 2; Buckingham, Duke of, 1; Cervantes, Miguel de, 34, 54; Donne, John, 45, 46; Gilbert, W. S., 24; Halifax, George Savile, 3; Horace, 54; Ibsen, Henrik, 4; Kinnock, Neil, 8; Lee, Laurie, 1; Molière, 19; Pliny the Elder, 15; Plutarch, 6; Pope, Alexander, 16; Rowland, Helen, 3, 4; Selden, John, 12; Shakespeare, William, 60, 207, 335; Shenstone, William, 1; Townsend, Robert, 11; Updike, John, 18; Wilder, Thornton, 5

Football Eisner, Michael, 1; Reagan, Ronald, 44

Force Annan, Kofi, 1; Bright, John, 2; Burke, Edmund, 28

Foreboding Auden, W. H., 18; Dickinson, Emily, 20; Powell, Enoch, 1; Townsend, Robert, 9

Foreigners Bradbury, Malcolm, 1; Browne, Thomas, 30; Kipling, Rudyard, 21, 59; Mitford, Nancy, 5; Trollope, Anthony, 4

Foreign Lands Keillor, Garrison, 10; Kipling, Rudyard, 39

Forgiveness Anonymous, 53; Arendt, Hannah, 20; Beckett, Samuel, 11; Bible, 62, 212, 244, 281, 347, 353, 413; Blake, William, 41; Browning, Robert, 72; Dryden, John, 37, 40; Elizabeth I, 17; Euripides, 4; Holmes, Oliver Wendell, 4; Kennedy, William, 1; Meredith, George, 4; Naimbanna, John Henry, 1; Pope, Alexander, 14; Richard I, 5; Shakespeare, William, 470, 661; Shaw, George Bernard, 55; Szasz, Thomas, 10; Waugh, Evelyn, 7; West, Jessamyn, 1

Fortune Bacon, Francis (1561–1626), 27; Bloomberg, Michael, 2; Boethius, 3; Disraeli, Benjamin, 13; Gay, John, 6; Jonson, Ben, 11, 16; La Rochefoucauld, François, 6; Publilius Syrus, 3; Shakespeare, William, 551; Terence, 2

France Aron, Raymond, 2; Baker, Josephine, 5; Baudelaire, Charles, 6; Bellow, Saul, 14; Bossuet, Jacques-Bénigne, 1; Carlyle, Thomas, 37; Chevalier, Michel, 2; Clemenceau, Georges, 6; Coren, Alan, 3; De Gaulle, Charles, 3, 5, 6, 8, 9; du Bartas, Guillaume, 6; du Bellay, Joachim, 1; Lamartine, Alphonse de, 2; Louis XVI, 2; Mazarin, Jules, 1; Moore, Thomas, 3; Napoleon III, 5; Nelson, Horatio, 3; Rivarol, Antoine de, 2; Rolland, Romain, 2; Rouget de Lisle, Claude-Joseph, 1; Rowland, Edward, 1; Sterne, Laurence, 1; Twain, Mark, 46; Voltaire, 10; Wharton, Edith, 4; Wilder, Billy, 3; Williams, John A., 2; Zeldin, Theodore, 9

Frankness Cooper, James Fenimore, 5; Johnson, Samuel, 91; Jonson, Ben, 19; Joyce, James, 33; Pascal, Blaise, 3; Voltaire, 7; Wilde, Oscar, 51

Fraud Bacon, Francis (1561–1626), 7; Law, Bonar, 1; Matos Guerra, Gregório de, 1; Napoleon I, 11; Vargas Llosa, Mario, 10

Freedom Abrahams, Peter, 2; Ahrends, Martin, 1, 2; Arendt, Hannah, 15; Baldwin, James, 12; Baraka, Imamu Amiri, 10; Barbour, John, 2; Beaumont, Francis, 2; Beethoven, Ludwig van, 5; Bible, 21; Bowles, William Lisle, 1; Brown, H. Rap, 3; Byron, Lord, 26, 60; Cavour, Camillo Benso, 1; Child, Lydia Maria, 5; Claudel, Paul, 2; Cobden, Richard, 2; Coleridge, Hartley, 1; Dalai Lama, 10; de Geus, Arie, 2; Dickens, Charles, 16; Diderot, Denis, 2; Diefenbaker, John, 1; Douglas, William Orville, 1; Einstein, Albert, 10; Eisenhower, Dwight D., 9, 13, 14; Engels, Friedrich, 2; Evers, Medgar, 1; Fonda, Jane, 2; Forten, James, 1; Fraser, Antonia, 2; Friedman, Milton, 5; Grossman, Vasily, 2; Hallam, Arthur Henry, 3; Hayden, Robert E., 1; Herbert, George, 17; Horace, 1; Howe, Edgar Watson, 3; Ibsen, Henrik, 7; Inge, William Ralph, 17; Jaspers, Karl, 2; Jordan, June, 5; Kafka, Franz, 5; Kelman, James, 1; Kennedy, John Fitzgerald, 26; Kenyatta, Jomo, 2; King, Martin Luther, Jr., 7, 9; Klein, Yves, 2; Kristofferson, Kris, 1; Lenin, Vladimir Ilyich, 19; Lincoln, Abraham, 12, 18, 24; Lippmann, Walter, 5; Locke, John, 7; Lovelace, Richard, 3; Luthuli, Albert, 1; Luxemburg, Rosa, 1; McCarthy, John, 1; Mandela, Nelson, 3, 7, 21, 22, 24, 25; Mann, Thomas, 1; Mao Yushi, 1; Marley, Bob, 5; Martí, José, 2; Mason, George, 3; Miller, Henry, 5; Miró, Joan, 7; Mistral, Gabriela, 6; Muir, John, 3; Murdoch, Iris, 11; Murrow, Ed, 1; Mussolini, Benito, 3; Nkomo, Joshua, 1, 2; Nkrumah, Kwame, 5, 8; Nyerere, Julius Kambarage, 4, 5, 6; Orwell, George, 32; Padmore, George, 5; Palme, Olof, 2; Parker, Theodore, 1; Pasternak, Boris, 9; Pitt the Younger, William, 2; Popper, Karl, 7; Powys, John Cowper, 2; Robeson, Paul, 5, 6; Roosevelt, Franklin D., 26; Rousseau, Jean-Jacques, 17; Ruskin, John, 23; Sartre, Jean-Paul, 8; Schiller, Friedrich von, 6; Scott, Hazel, 3; Singer, Isaac Bashevis, 7;

Solzhenitsyn, Alexander, 13; Soyinka, Wole, 3; Spivak, Gayatri, 1; Staël, Madame de, 3; Stravinsky, Igor, 5; Touré, Sékou, 1; Toussaint L'Ouverture, 2; Tramp, The, 1; Tubman, Harriet, 1; Tutuola, Amos, 1; U2, 2; Ustinov, Peter, 12; Valenzuela, Luisa, 1; Voltaire, 25; Washington, Booker T., 3; Westwood, Vivienne, 4; Whitman, Walt, 44; Wilkins, Roy, 1; Williams, Tennessee, 5; Willkie, Wendell Lewis, 3; Wilson, Woodrow, 5, 16; Winstanley, Gerrard, 1; Xu Wenli, 2; Zappa, Frank, 4

Free Speech Beaverbrook, Max Aitken, Lord, 6; Holmes, Oliver Wendell, Jr., 2; Johnson, Samuel, 96; Milton, John, 129; Suharto, 1; Swaffer, Hannen, 1

French Revolution Babeuf, François Noël, 1; Burke, Edmund, 42, 44, 45; Chamfort, Nicolas, 14; Dickens, Charles, 9; Fox, Charles James, 1; Jefferson, Thomas, 22; Louis XVI, 1, 3; Marat, Jean Paul, 2; Orczy, Baroness, 1; Pitt the Younger, William, 4; Robespierre, Maximilien, 2; Rousseau, Jean-Jacques, 2; Sieyès, Abbé, 1; Trevelyan, G. M., 1; Vergniaud, Pierre-Victurnien, 1; Wordsworth, William, 87

Friends Bacon, Francis (1561–1626), 103; Confucius, 6; Delille, Jacques, 1; Emerson, Ralph Waldo, 8; Farquhar, George, 10; Housman, A. E., 24; Kierkegaard, Søren, 6; Kingsmill, Hugh, 2; Montgomery, James, 1; Morrison, Toni, 3; Plautus, 4; Pope, Alexander, 71; Selden, John, 5; Taleb, Ali ben Abi, 1; Twain, Mark, 20; Voltaire, 23; Walker, Margaret, 1; Weldon, Fay, 1; Welles, Orson, 5; Whitman, Walt, 19

Friendship Aristotle, 8, 15; Bacon, Francis (1561–1626), 4, 28, 29; Bâ, Mariama, 2; Beerbohm, Max, 25; Bible, 40, 175; Bogart, Humphrey, 6; Bradbury, Malcolm, 9; Brecht, Bertolt, 9; Burns, Robert, 9, 10, 11; Byron, Lord, 53; Canning, George, 3; Cather, Willa, 5; Catherwood, Mary, 1; Dante Alighieri, 3; De Gaulle, Charles, 23; Eliot, George, 13; Epicurus, 7; Everyman, 2; Golden, Marita, 7; Grimald, Nicholas, 1; Hesiod, 2; Hope, Bob, 1; Howell, James, 1; Hurston, Zora Neale, 2; Johnson, Samuel, 71, 89, 93, 114; King, Carole, 1; Lennon & McCartney, 4; Levant, Oscar, 2; Lewis, C. S., 4; Lindbergh, Anne Morrow, 2; Logau, Friedrich von, 4; Lytton, Bulwer, 4; Malory, Thomas, 5; Mamet, David, 3; Montagu, Elizabeth, 1; Moore, Thomas Sturge, 1; Morris, Desmond, 3; Napoleon I, 2; Naylor, Gloria, 6; Nin, Anaïs, 3; O'Casey, Sean, 2; Peacock, Thomas Love, 1; Péguy, Charles Pierre, 7; Plutarch, 28; Pope, Alexander, 72; Sallust, 1; Shakespeare, William, 58, 228, 315, 447, 513; Shelley, Percy Bysshe, 29; Sickert, Walter, 1; Smith, Logan Pearsall, 1; Stevenson, Robert Louis, 6; Swift, Jonathan, 22; Waugh, Evelyn, 39; Weil, Simone, 3; Whitman, Walt, 45; Wodehouse, P. G., 16; Yeats, W. B., 23

Frugality Plutarch, 19

Fruit Alison, Richard, 1; Bible, 493; Zayyad, Tawfiq, 1

Funerals al-Fayed, Mohamed, 2; Andersen, Hans Christian, 5; Auden, W. H., 22; Bainbridge, Beryl, 6; Brenan, Gerald, 5; Day, Clarence Shepard, 2; Dillingham, Charles Bancroft, 1; Donleavy, J. P., 5; Everett, Edward, 1; Heaney, Seamus, 2, 6; Jonson, Ben, 29; Keats, John (1795–1821), 26; Keillor, Garrison, 4; Mitford, Jessica, 1; Mphahlele, Es'kia, 3; Shakespeare, William, 146; Wolfe, Charles, 1, 2

Futility Darrow, Clarence, 1; Eliot, George, 8; Miller, Henry, 17; O'Neill, Eugene, 2; Pyrrhus, 1

Future, The Ampère, Jean-Jaques, 2; Aquinas, Thomas, 5; Baldwin, James, 10; Bierce, Ambrose, 23; Burgess, Anthony, 3; Céline, Louis-Ferdinand, 2; Coolidge, Calvin, 13; Dix, Dorothy, 2; Einstein, Albert, 20; Farmer, James, 2; Gladstone, William Ewart, 8; Goethe, Johann Wolfgang von, 34; Handy, Charles, 6; Harding, Warren G., 5; Hawthorne, Nathaniel, 6; Henry, Patrick, 3; Ionesco, Eugène, 6; Jefferson, Thomas, 43; Johnson, Lyndon Baines, 6; Lamming, George, 1; Levi, Primo, 1; Lewis, C. S., 6; Mandela, Nelson, 18; Milton, John, 90; Mosley, Walter, 1; O'Brien, Conor Cruise, 1; Story, Jack Trevor, 1; Tennyson, Alfred, 22; Toffler, Alvin, 1; Wiener, Norbert, 3

Gambling Fields, W. C., 4; Foster, Stephen, 1; Johnson, Samuel, 62; Simon, Neil, 9; Thompson, Hunter S., 3; Williams, Tennessee, 1

Gardens Bacon, Francis (1561–1626), 31; Bible, 495; Brown, Thomas Edward, 1; Charles, Prince, 4; Cowper, William, 31; Frost, Robert, 2; Kipling, Rudyard, 7; Landor, Walter Savage, 5; Marvell, Andrew, 5, 9; Meynell, Alice, 2; Plath, Sylvia, 13; Tao Qian, 4; Warner, Charles Dudley, 2

Generosity Bible, 165; Brown, Thomas, 3; Dylan, Bob, 5; Hope, Anthony, 6; La Bruyère, Jean de, 8; La Fontaine, Jean de, 8; Lennon & McCartney, 8; Peterborough, 3rd Earl of, 1; Pope, Alexander, 83; Retz, Cardinal de, 11; Saki, 21; Schweitzer, Albert, 4; Sembène, Ousmane, 3; Shakespeare, William, 340; Sidney, Philip, 1; Turner, Ted, 3

Genetics Dawkins, Richard, 1; Huxley, Aldous, 29; Proverbs, Modern, 25; Thomas, Lewis, 2; Wilson, Edward O., 3, 4

Genius Alcott, Louisa May, 5; Aragon, Louis, 2; Beethoven, Ludwig van, 2; Browning, Elizabeth Barrett, 4; Buffon, Comte de, 2; Carlyle, Thomas, 19; Child, Lydia Maria, 6; Churchill, Charles, 9; Dalí, Salvador, 3; Debussy, Claude, 5; Disraeli, Benjamin, 1; Doyle, Arthur Conan, 13; Edison, Thomas Alva, 4; Einstein, Albert, 5; FitzGerald, Edward, 1; Hubbard, Elbert, 1, 2; Johnson, Samuel, 26; Liyong, Taban Lo, 2; Owen, Meredith, 1; Pankhurst, Emmeline, 1; Pope, Alexander, 17; Pynchon, Thomas, 6; Reid, Thomas, 1; Seneca, "the Younger," 2; Simone, Nina, 1; Stein, Gertrude, 5; Swift, Jonathan, 53; Wilde, Oscar, 86

Genocide Newspapers, 27

Georgia Charles, Ray, 2; Gunther, John, 1; Lanier, Sidney, 1; Mitchell, Margaret, 2; Work, Henry Clay, 4

Germany Adenauer, Konrad, 1; Adorno, Theodor, 1; Bismarck, Prince Otto von, 1, 9, 15, 17, 18; Celtis, Conrad, 1; Collier, Price, 1; Dumas, Roland, 1; Enzensberger, Hans, 5; Frederick I, 1; Frederick William IV, 1; Gay, Peter, 1; Genscher, Hans-Dietrich, 1, 2; Goethe, Johann Wolfgang von, 3; Grass, Günter, 2, 3, 5; Grey, Edward, 1; Hamilton, Alexander, 5; Havel, Vaclav, 1; Heine, Heinrich, 3, 4; Hitler, Adolf, 15, 35; Hölderlin, Friedrich, 2; Hütter, Ralf, 1; Huxley, Aldous, 55; Jaspers, Karl, 1; Kant, Immanuel, 25; Kohl, Helmut, 2, 3, 4; Lewis, Flora, 1; Mann, Golo, 1; Mann, Heinrich, 1; Mann, Thomas, 2, 5, 6; Moltke, Helmuth Johannes von, 3; O'Rourke, P. J., 6; Ossietzky, Carl von, 3, 4, 5; Scheidemann, Philipp, 1; Schneckenburger, Max, 1; Stalin, Joseph, 9; Wolf, Christa, 7

Gifts Corneille, Pierre, 8; Euripides, 11; Morell, Thomas, 2; Parker, Dorothy, 13; Porchia, Antonio, 4; Tennyson, Alfred, 8

Girlfriends Dubin, Al, 1

Girls Alcott, Louisa May, 4; Austen, Jane, 17; Belloc, Hilaire, 10; Gilbert, W. S., 27; Hope, Anthony, 4

Glory Anderson, Maxwell, 2; Chateaubriand, René, 3; Chaucer, Geoffrey, 24; Hugo, Victor, 13; Marvell, Andrew, 4; Tennyson, Alfred, 27; Unamuno y Jugo, Miguel de, 7

God Addison, Joseph, 19; Albo, Joseph, 1; al-Ghazali, 1, 2; Allen, Woody, 5; Anonymous, 30, 56; Anouilh, Jean, 9; Aquinas, Thomas, 7, 8; Athenagoras, 1, 2; Auden, W. H., 43; Augustine of Hippo, Saint, 4, 5; Ayer, A. J., 2; Bacon, Francis (1561–1626), 13, 68; Bakunin, Mikhail, 2; Baldwin, James, 21; Baraka, Imamu Amiri, 8; Baudelaire, Charles, 4; Bergman, Ingmar, 8; Bible, 16, 18, 19, 22, 35, 39, 70, 77, 79, 88, 116, 141, 143, 152, 153, 159, 160, 190, 214, 320, 482, 484; Biko, Stephen, 3; Blake, William, 27, 28; Bonhoeffer, Dietrich, 1, 6; Borrow, George Henry, 5; Browne, Thomas, 17; Browning, Elizabeth Barrett, 7; Browning, Robert, 64, 67, 69; Buber, Martin, 1, 4; Burnet, Gilbert, 1; Camus, Albert, 14, 17; Channing, William Ellery, 3; Cleveland, Grover, 1; Clough, Arthur Hugh, 5, 11; Cosby, Bill, 3; Cowper, William, 24; Crisp, Quentin, 3; Dante Alighieri, 5; Day, Clarence Shepard, 1; De Vries, Peter, 7, 8; Dillard, Annie, 10; Dirac, Paul, 1; Donne, John, 17, 18, 47; Eberhart, Richard, 1; Einstein, Albert, 12, 46, 50; Freud, Sigmund, 25, 42; Frost, Robert, 11; Fuller, R. Buckminster, 2; Gandhi, Mahatma,

George, 4; Doyle, Arthur Conan, 8; Hubbard, Elbert, 14; MacNeice, Louis, 16; Miller, Jonathan, 1; Ovid, 10; Publilius Syrus, 4; Pushkin, Alexander, 1; Radiguet, Raymond, 2; Tolstoy, Leo, 6

Happiness Anouilh, Jean, 6; Ayckbourn, Alan, 7; Bainbridge, Beryl, 4; Barbey d'Aurevilly, Jules-Amédée, 2; Barnes, Julian, 1; Beauvoir, Simone de, 4; Beckett, Samuel, 8; Beethoven, Ludwig van, 8; Bible, 341; Bradley, F. H., 5; Browning, Robert, 68; Burns, George, 1; Byron, Lord, 48; Cather, Willa, 7; Chesterton, G. K., 17; Coleridge, Samuel Taylor, 23; Cowper, William, 32; Dillard, Annie, 1; Dryden, John, 49; Éluard, Paul, 1; Fitzgerald, F. Scott, 12; Frank, Anne, 5; Freud, Sigmund, 58; Horace, 21, 24, 53; Hugo, Victor, 10; Husain, 1; Huxley, Aldous, 33, 44; Jefferson, Thomas, 19; Jerome, Jerome K., 2; John, Elton, 3; Johnson, Samuel, 34, 118, 130; Joyce, James, 13; Kant, Immanuel, 19; Keats, John (1795–1821), 58; La Bruyère, Jean de, 9; Landor, Walter Savage, 2; La Rochefoucauld, François, 10; Lennon & McCartney, 17; London, Jack, 12; Machado de Assis, Joaquim Maria, 9; Mata Hari, 1; Melly, George, 1; Miller, Henry, 18, 20; Mill, John Stuart, 5; Milton, John, 60, 116, 117; Montesquieu, 11; Pavlova, Anna, 5; Peters, Tom, 11; Pope, Alexander, 51; Porter, Cole, 9; Publilius Syrus, 8; Purim, Flora, 1; Racine, Jean, 6; Renan, Ernest, 6; Roosevelt, Franklin D., 6; Rose, Billy, 3; Rousseau, Jean-Jacques, 22; Russell, Bertrand, 18, 29, 60, 65; Sand, George, 1, 2; Santayana, George, 13; Shakespeare, William, 119, 448; Shaw, George Bernard, 47; Sigismund, 1; Simone, Nina, 4; Smith, Logan Pearsall, 10; Smith, Sydney, 6; Solzhenitsyn, Alexander, 4; Stevenson, Robert Louis, 30; Szasz, Thomas, 9; Vian, Boris, 1; Waugh, Evelyn, 11; Webster, John, 13; Whately, Richard, 1; Yeats, W. B., 46, 62; Yevtushenko, Yevgeny, 4

Haste Augustus, 2; Confucius, 3; Fitzgerald, Ella, 2; Jiménez, Juan Ramón, 11; Rowley, William, 1; Shadwell, Thomas, 2; Stevenson, Robert Louis, 29; Wesley, John, 1

Hate Brontë, Charlotte, 9; Butler, Samuel (1835–1902), 23; Crossman, Richard, 1; Enzensberger, Hans, 3; Hazlitt, William, 19; Hesse, Hermann, 1; Jiménez, Juan Ramón, 12; La Rochefoucauld, François, 12; Loyola, Ignatius of, 5; Ortega y Gasset, José, 1; Racine, Jean, 1; Savile, Sir George, 3; Walker, Alice, 8; Walker, Margaret, 2; Yeats, W. B., 36

Hawaii London, Jack, 6

Health and Healthy Living Addison, Joseph, 17; Amiel, Henri Frédéric, 1; Anonymous, 43; Armstrong, John, 2; Bacon, Francis (1561–1626), 54; Burton, Robert, 13; Canetti, Elias, 4; Cartland, Barbara, 2; Cicero, 13; Cleobulus, 1; Coué, Émile, 1; Currie, Edwina, 5; Davis, Adelle, 1; Disraeli, Benjamin, 3; Emerson, Ralph Waldo, 38, 59; Flaubert, Gustave, 5; Folk Verse, 31; Foreman, George, 1; Hurdis, James, 1; Hutchison, Robert, 2, 3; Ingersoll, Robert G., 7; Jefferson, Thomas, 6; Jonson, Ben, 25; Juvenal, 17; La Rochefoucauld, François, 21; Locke, John, 10; Logau, Friedrich von, 1; Loyola, Ignatius of, 1; Martial, 2; Mayo, Charles Horace, 5; Montaigne, Michel de, 10; Morton, J. C., 2; Osler, William, 10; Plato, 32; Pope, Alexander, 30; Proverbs, Modern, 13; Rabelais, François, 14; Reagan, Ronald, 25; Scott, Sir Walter, 3; Shaw, George Bernard, 91; Shenstone, William, 2; Smith, Sydney, 1; Spencer, Herbert, 9; Swift, Jonathan, 36; Szent-Györgyi, Albert, 1; Thoreau, Henry David, 47; Toynbee, Arnold, 9; Voltaire, 26; Walton, Izaak, 8; Wilcox, Ella Wheeler, 5

Hearing Charles, Ray, 3; Spark, Muriel, 14

Heart, The Byron, Lord, 66; Harvey, William, 1; Hawthorne, Nathaniel, 8; Wordsworth, William, 57; Yeats, W. B., 45

Heaven Aristotle, 3; Baldwin, James, 9; Bible, 271, 290, 418; Butler, Samuel (1835–1902), 29; Dylan, Bob, 7; Hardy, Thomas, 6; Lichtenberg, Georg Christoph, 4; Melville, Herman, 19; Milton, John, 53, 67; Petrarch, 4; Robbins, Tom, 2; Rushdie, Salman, 5; Sedgwick, Catharine Maria, 1; Shaw, George Bernard, 60, 70; Spring-Rice, Cecil Arthur, 1; Swift, Jonathan, 51; Taylor, Jane, 2; Thomas, R. S., 1; Twain, Mark, 15; Watts, Isaac, 8

Hedonism Dowson, Ernest, 2; Jonson, Ben, 9

Hell Beckett, Samuel, 1; Bernanos, Georges, 1; Bhagavad-Gita, 1; Browne, Thomas, 23; Brown, Thomas, 2; Eliot, T. S., 40; Kemal, Yasar, 1; Lewis, C. S., 8; Lewis, Jerry Lee, 1; Malraux, André, 2; Marlowe, Christopher, 5; Milton, John, 26, 39; Naylor, Gloria, 3; Paris, Matthew, 1; Rimbaud, Arthur, 11; Sartre, Jean-Paul, 9; Shelley, Percy Bysshe, 13; Virgil, 17, 19

Help Brecht, Bertolt, 19; Galbraith, J. K., 5; Gilbert, W. S., 18; Hügel, Friedrich, 1; La Fontaine, Jean de, 5; Newman, Ernest, 2; Young, Brigham, 2

Heroism Anonymous, 22; Bible, 226; Brecht, Bertolt, 20; Brown, John, 3; Butler, Samuel (1612–80), 8; Byron, Lord, 20; Carlyle, Thomas, 27; Crane, Stephen, 10, 11; Daly, Daniel, 1; Daudet, Alphonse, 2; Fitzgerald, F. Scott, 9; Folk Verse, 1; Goytisolo, Juan, 4; Hardwick, Elizabeth, 1; Kipling, Rudyard, 26, 27; Kollwitz, Käthe, 3; Mailer, Norman, 19; Malcolm X, 3; Mamet, David, 4; Mencken, H. L., 28; Nightingale, Florence, 2; Pope, Alexander, 77, 86; Renan, Ernest, 2; Rogers, Will, 3; Rolland, Romain, 1; Ruskin, John, 16; Shakespeare, William, 25; Shostakovich, Dmitri, 1; Siegel, Jerry, 1; Virgil, 5; Wordsworth, William, 76

Historians Adams, Henry, 13, 17, 18; Bailey, Thomas A., 3, 4, 6; Bailyn, Bernard, 2, 4; Balfour, Arthur, 6; Beard, Charles, 7; Beck, Earl R., 3; Becker, Carl, 5, 7, 9; Bennett, Edward W., 3; Benson, Lee, 1; Berkhofer, Robert Frederick, Jr., 1; Birrell, Augustine, 1; Commager, Henry Steele, 7; Darnton, Robert, 1; Davies, Norman, 3; Degler, Carl N., 5; Du Bois, W. E. B., 9; Duhamel, Georges, 1; Franklin, Benjamin, 17; Guedalla, Philip, 3; Handlin, Oscar, 1; Herodotus, 1; Himmelfarb, Gertrude, 1; Hofstadter, Richard, 2; James, Henry, 18; Johnson, Samuel, 86; Macleod, Iain, 2; Schlegel, Friedrich von, 1; Taylor, A. J. P., 2; Tolstoy, Leo, 17; Truman, Harry S., 4

History Adams, Henry, 1, 7, 8, 9, 14, 20; Adams, James, 1; Adams, John Quincy, 4, 7; Adenauer, Konrad, 4; Andersch, Alfred, 1; Angelou, Maya, 1; Aptheker, Herbert, 1; Arendt, Hannah, 1, 12; Auden, W. H., 28; Bailey, Thomas A., 1; Bailyn, Bernard, 1, 3; Bainville, Jacques, 1; Baldwin, James, 17, 28; Barzun, Jacques, 1, 2, 3, 4, 5, 6; Bayle, Pierre, 1; Beard, Charles, 1, 2, 3, 5, 6; Beard, Mary Ritter, 2; Beck, Earl R., 1, 2; Becker, Carl, 1, 2, 3, 4, 8, 11; Bede, 1; Beecher, Henry Ward, 3; Bennett, Edward W., 1, 2; Bhutto, Benazir, 1; Bierce, Ambrose, 25; Binchy, Maeve, 1; Blair, Tony, 7; Bolingbroke, Henry St. John, 3; Boorstin, Daniel J., 5; Bourne, Randolph S., 1; Bowen, Elizabeth, 1; Bradford, William, 5, 6; Brandeis, Louis D., 5; Brandt, Willy, 4; Brinton, Crane, 1; Brittain, Vera, 1; Brown, Norman O., 1, 3; Burns, Ken, 1; Bush, George, 8; Byron, Lord, 27; Calhoun, John C., 2; Callcott, George H., 1, 2; Canby, Henry S., 1; Canetti, Elias, 7, 9; Carlyle, Thomas, 23, 40; Carter, Jimmy, 4; Choate, Rufus, 1; Clarke, John Henrik, 5; Cleaver, Eldridge, 2; Cohen, Leonard, 1; Coleridge, Samuel Taylor, 54; Commager, Henry Steele, 1, 2, 3, 4, 5, 6; Confucius, 18; Cook, Samuel D., 1, 4; Cooper, James Fenimore, 2, 9; Cousins, Norman, 1, 2; Craig, Gordon A., 1; Craven, Avery O., 1, 2; Creighton, Donald, 1; Croce, Benedetto, 1; Dacier, Anne Lefevre, 1; Darrow, Clarence, 8; Day, Clarence Shepard, 6; DeLillo, Don, 6; Dewey, John, 7; Diderot, Denis, 7; Diggins, John P., 1, 2; Dionysius of Halicarnassus, 1, 2; Dunne, Finley Peter, 6, 7, 8; Dunning, William A., 1; Durant, Will, 3, 4, 5, 6, 9, 10, 11, 14, 15; Durrell, Lawrence, 4; Eban, Abba, 1; Eggleston, Edward, 1; Eisenhower, Dwight D., 30; Emerson, Ralph Waldo, 4, 9, 11, 12, 13, 17, 29, 30, 35, 55; Fabre, Jean Henri, 4; Ford, Henry, 1, 2, 8; Fortune, Timothy Thomas, 1; Frankfurter, Felix, 1; Franklin, Benjamin, 14; Franklin, John Hope, 1; Gardner, John W., 2; Garfield, James A., 5, 6; Gould, Stephen Jay, 9, 10, 11; Grass, Günter, 1, 4; Guare, John, 2; Haley, Alex, 2; Hamerow, Theodore S., 1, 2; Handlin, Oscar, 2; Hansen, Karl-Heinz, 1; Harris, Frank, 4; Hegel, G. W. F., 1, 6; Hitler, Adolf, 24; Holmes, Oliver Wendell, Jr., 3; Hook, Sidney, 1; Hoover, Herbert, 10; Hubbard, Elbert, 11, 12; Hughes-Hallett, Lucy, 1; Humphrey, Hubert H., 5; Inge, William Ralph, 5, 18; Irving, Washington, 1; James, C. L. R., 8; James, William, 5; Jefferson, Thomas, 16, 42; Jordan, Neil, 1; Joyce, James, 23; Kavanagh, Patrick, 2; Kennedy, Robert, 2; Kissinger, Henry, 5, 6; Lerner, Gerda, 1; Lévi-Strauss, Claude, 2; Lincoln, Abraham, 15; Liu Binyan, 3; Lloyd, Cecil Francis, 1; Lower, A. R. M., 3; Macaulay, Rose, 6; Macaulay, Thomas Babington,

4, 10; Mailer, Norman, 12; Marx, Karl, 2; Mary I, 2; Maupassant, Guy de, 4; Michelet, Jules, 3; Miller, Henry, 27; Monterroso, Augusto, 1; Morgan, Edwin, 1; Mumford, James Gregory, 3; Murphy, Richard, 3; Napoleon I, 18; O'Connor, Joseph, 3; Ortega y Gasset, José, 29; Paglia, Camille, 5; Pearse, Patrick, 1; Péguy, Charles Pierre, 10; Popper, Karl, 5; Priestley, J. B., 10; Qutb, Sayyid, 1; Ranke, Leopold von, 1; Repington, Charles à Court, 1; Roy, Arundhati, 2, 3; Ryan, Desmond, 1; Schiller, Friedrich von, 11; Sellar, W. C., 1, 3, 5; Smith, Goldwin, 1; Sontag, Susan, 10; Taylor, A. J. P., 4; Tolson, Melvin, 4; Truman, Harry S., 16; Voltaire, 32, 35; Walpole, Sir Robert, 2; Webster, Daniel, 3; Whitelaw, William, 2; Wideman, John Edgar, 2; Wilder, Billy, 4; Wrong, George M., 2, 3, 5, 6; Yan Fu, 1

Holiness Hume, Basil, 1; Laozi, 2

Holistic Medicine Cicero, 9; Plato, 2; Plautus, 3; Schick, Béla, 6; Sigerist, Henry E., 9

Holland Coren, Alan, 4; Hood, Thomas, 20

Hollywood Allen, Fred, 4; Barrymore, Ethel, 1; Barrymore, Lionel, 1; Burke, Billie, 1; Chandler, Raymond, 12, 14; Diana, Princess, 2; Doyle, Roddy, 1; Gable, Clark, 3; Ginsberg, Allen, 3; Goldwyn, Samuel, 1, 16; Hitchcock, Alfred, 10; Konchalovsky, Andrei, 1; Lahr, Bert, 2; Lancaster, Burt, 1; Mamet, David, 14; Mizner, Wilson, 1; Reagan, Ronald, 39; Von Sternberg, Josef, 2; Welles, Orson, 3; Wilson, Edmund, 3

Holocaust, The Himmler, Heinrich, 2; Hitler, Adolf, 39; Malraux, André, 3; Mottos and Slogans, 26; Oz, Amos, 7; Vonnegut, Kurt, 8; Wiesel, Elie, 2, 3

Home Adler, Polly, 1; Anonymous, 46; Barry, Dave, 3, 4; Bohn, Henry George, 1; Bryson, Bill, 8; Catullus, 3; Clarke, John, 1; Cullen, Countee, 1; Douglas, Norman, 3; Frost, Robert, 19; Grossmith, George, 3; Guest, Edgar A., 1; Haliburton, Thomas Chandler, 1; Harris, Joel Chandler, 1; Larkin, Philip, 2; Lennon & McCartney, 15; Lewis, Sinclair, 3; Marshall, Paule, 5; Montgomery, Robert, 1; Morgenstern, Christian, 2; Nash, Ogden, 22; Naylor, Gloria, 4; Payne, John Howard, 2; Peake, Mervyn, 2; Thatcher, Margaret, 34; Tusser, Thomas, 3; Walcott, Derek, 1; Young, Brigham, 5

Homeopathy Bierce, Ambrose, 26

Homesickness Bland, James A., 1; Burns, Robert, 28; Cheever, John, 1; Donleavy, J. P., 2; Evans, Mari, 3; Foster, Stephen, 2, 5; García Márquez, Gabriel, 1; Gellhorn, Martha, 2; Higley, Brewster, 1; La Rochefoucauld, François, 27; Stacpoole, Henry de Vere, 1; Tsvetaeva, Marina, 4, 5; Wordsworth, William, 44

Homosexuality Amis, Kingsley, 7; Balzac, Honoré de, 1; Barnfield, Richard, 3, 6, 7; Benkert, Karoly Maria, 1; Cavafy, Constantine, 1; Clinton, Bill, 9; Core, Philip, 1; Crisp, Quentin, 10; Crowley, Mart, 1; Cunard, Lady "Emerald," 1; Douglas, Alfred, 2; Drayton, Michael, 1; Dryden, John, 26; Fierstein, Harvey, 3; Fitzgerald, F. Scott, 30; Flecker, James Elroy, 5; Forster, E. M., 1; Ginsberg, Allen, 1; Hervey, John, 2; Hollinghurst, Alan, 1; Housman, A. E., 29; Isherwood, Christopher, 1; Juvenal, 8; Lambert, Kit, 1; Lancaster, Osbert, 1; Lewis, Wyndham, 3; Liverpool, Lord, 1; Loyden, Eddie, 1; McKellen, Ian, 1, 2, 4; Marlowe, Christopher, 17; Martial, 3; Matlovich, Leonard, 1; Maupin, Armistead, 1, 2, 5, 6, 7; Melville, Herman, 16; Montgomery of Alamein, Sir Bernard Law, 2; Nilsen, Dennis, 1; Norse, Harold, 1; Orton, Joe, 11; Otway, Thomas, 4; Plomer, William, 1; Reagan, Ronald, 22; Rossetti, Christina, 4; Stead, W. T., 1; Thatcher, Margaret, 16; Thompson, Clara, 1; Tyler, Robin, 1; Village People, 1; Whitman, Walt, 1, 29; Wilde, Oscar, 1, 10, 11; Williams, Tennessee, 17

Honesty Bennis, Warren, 11; Browne, Thomas, 21; Burns, Robert, 17, 38; Cabral, Amilcar, 1; Carnegie, Andrew, 10; Cobain, Kurt, 4; Douglass, Frederick, 10; Dylan, Bob, 18, 25; Garvey, Marcus, 9; Hemingway, Ernest, 20; James, Henry, 21; Johnson, Samuel, 139; Larkin, Philip, 6; Lincoln, Abraham, 37; Middleton, Thomas, 9; Murphy, Dervla, 1; Péguy, Charles Pierre, 1, 5, 8; Pope, Alexander, 31; Prior, Matthew, 14; Quintilian, 2; Roosevelt, Theodore, 28; Sanford, Charles, Jr., 2; Shakespeare, William, 115, 169, 457, 485, 665, 667; Skelton, John, 6; Vieira, António, 1; Washington, George, 8; Whately, Richard, 2

Honor Auden, W. H., 47; Bible, 403; Jonson, Ben, 27; Juvenal, 13; Lovelace, Richard, 4; Marlowe, Christopher, 23; Pagnol, Marcel, 4; Racine, Jean, 15; Shakespeare, William, 211, 240, 297, 312; Tennyson, Alfred, 12; Teresa of Calcutta, Mother, 3; Thoreau, Henry David, 45

Hope Adamson, Harold, 1; Aidoo, Ama Ata, 3; Ai Qing, 2; Bacon, Francis (1561–1626), 5; Beckett, Samuel, 27; Chesterton, G. K., 19; Cowper, William, 22; Dickinson, Emily, 5; Franklin, Benjamin, 27; García Lorca, Federico, 5; Gay, John, 10; Golden, Marita, 5; Harburg, E. Y., 4, 5; Harper, Frances E. W., 5; Jackson, Mahalia, 1; Johnson, Samuel, 39, 42; Kerr, Jean, 6; King, Martin Luther, Jr., 2; Longfellow, Henry Wadsworth, 3; Lu Xun, 2; McPherson, Aimee Semple, 1; Mahon, Derek, 4; Mapanje, Jack, 1; Marley, Bob, 6; Menninger, Karl, 1; Milton, John, 85; Mitchell, Margaret, 8; Montgomery, James, 2; Okri, Ben, 5; Paré, Ambroise, 1; Plautus, 5; Pope, Alexander, 25; Prior, Matthew, 10, 15; Shakespeare, William, 434; Smith, Sydney, 10; Sophocles, 4; Tutu, Desmond, 6; Verlaine, Paul, 4; Wolf, Christa, 8

Horror Hopkins, Anthony, 4; Poe, Edgar Allan, 7

Horses Betjeman, John, 8; Chaucer, Geoffrey, 12; Folk Verse, 21; Martial, 4; Muir, Edwin, 3; Somerville, Edith, 2

Hospitality Beerbohm, Max, 7; Dickens, Charles, 3; Macaulay, Thomas Babington, 1; Spry, Constance, 2

Hospitals Billings, John Shaw, 2; Kerr, Jean, 2; Lee, Hannah Farnham, 2; Mayo, Charles Horace, 6; Nightingale, Florence, 4; Parker, Dorothy, 26

Houses Cibber, Colley, 4; Momaday, N. Scott, 1; Morris, William, 4

Housework Alcott, Louisa May, 2; Conran, Shirley, 1; Crisp, Quentin, 11; Diller, Phyllis, 1; Hale, Sarah Josepha, 1; Hardy, Thomas, 22; Hood, Thomas, 13; Loud, Pat, 1; Post, Emily, 4; Simon, Neil, 6

Human Condition Angelus Silesius, 2, 3; Arendt, Hannah, 21; Aristotle, 11; Arnold, Matthew, 11; Auden, W. H., 42, 50; Auerbach, Berthold, 1; Bacon, Francis (1561–1626), 93; Barnes, Djuna, 2; Beaumarchais, Pierre-Augustin Caron de, 1; Becker, Carl, 12; Beckett, Samuel, 24, 28; Berdyaev, Nikolai, 2, 3; Berlin, Isaiah, 2; Bernard of Chartres, 1; Bible, 43, 48, 113, 140, 238, 259; Böll, Heinrich, 1; Born, Max, 2; Breton, Nicholas, 3; Brodsky, Joseph, 3; Browning, Robert, 43; Bulgakov, Mikhail, 12; Burns, Robert, 25, 43, 44; Burroughs, William S., 8; Calderón de la Barca, Pedro, 1; Campbell, Thomas, 7; Camus, Albert, 9, 15; Canning, George, 2; Carlyle, Thomas, 31; Carter, Angela, 4, 7; Charles, Prince, 7; Chekhov, Anton, 15; Chesterton, G. K., 6; Cocteau, Jean, 6; Conrad, Joseph, 9; cummings, e. e., 18; Dante Alighieri, 4; Degler, Carl N., 1; Dickens, Charles, 8, 34; Disney, Walt, 6; Disraeli, Benjamin, 9; Donne, John, 12; Dos Passos, John, 7; Dostoyevsky, Fyodor, 1, 3; Edwin, John, 1; Eliot, T. S., 21, 30, 38, 44, 52; Emerson, Ralph Waldo, 23; Empson, William, 3; Enzensberger, Hans, 1; Erasmus, Desiderius, 3; Faulkner, William, 16; Ferlinghetti, Lawrence, 5; Fromm, Erich, 12, 16; Goethe, Johann Wolfgang von, 27; Goodman, Paul, 7; Greene, Graham, 14; Greville, Fulke, 2; Gurdjieff, G. I., 1; Hallam, Arthur Henry, 9; Hecht, Ben, 1; Heilbroner, Robert, 1; Hemingway, Ernest, 8; Henry, O., 3; Herzberg, Frederick, 1; Hoagland, Edward, 2; Hobbes, Thomas, 9, 13; Hoffer, Eric, 3; Horace, 16, 39; Housman, A. E., 3; Inge, William Ralph, 12; Jackson, Andrew, 1; Jefferson, Thomas, 28; Johnson, Samuel, 29; Jung, Carl Gustav, 5, 13; Kraus, Karl, 22; Laforgue, Jules, 1; Laozi, 5; Laplace, Pierre Simon, 1; Lawrence, D. H., 23; Lessing, Gotthold Ephraim, 5; London, Jack, 17; Lumumba, Patrice, 2; Machado, Antonio, 3; Mamet, David, 2; Mann, Thomas, 3, 12; Melville, Herman, 15; Mill, John Stuart, 18; Mirren, Helen, 1; Mitterrand, François, 2; Monod, Jacques Lucien, 3; Montaigne, Michel de, 27; Moravia, Alberto, 2; Morgenstern, Christian, 1; Morton, Thomas, 1; Neel, Alice, 1; Nietzsche, Friedrich Wilhelm, 6, 39; O'Casey, Sean, 3; O'Neill, Eugene, 1; Orwell, George, 25; Parker, Dorothy, 37; Pomfret, John, 1; Protagoras, 2; Radhakrishnan, Sarvepalli, 2; Renan, Ernest, 7; Robert, Yves, 1; Rosewarne, V. A., 1; Saint-Exupéry, Antoine de, 6; Santayana,

Infidelity Austen, Jane, 11; Koran, 3; Marx, Chico, 1; Plessis, Armand-Emmanuel du, 1

Infinity Blake, William, 3; Frost, Robert, 5; Jefferies, Richard, 1; Musset, Alfred de, 2; Roethke, Theodore, 2; Zhuangzi, 1

Influence Astor, Nancy, 1; Burbank, Luther, 3; Carnegie, Dale, 3; Hypatia, 1; Ibsen, Henrik, 10; Inge, William Ralph, 9; Keynes, John Maynard, 13; Mingus, Charles, 2; Nietzsche, Friedrich Wilhelm, 14; Pope, Alexander, 23; Porchia, Antonio, 6; Shakespeare, William, 292; Shea, Michael, 2; Smith, Sydney, 11; Stalin, Joseph, 15

Information Colman, George, 2; de Bono, Edward, 1, 2; Dickens, Charles, 23; Kline, Nancy, 9; Krugman, Paul, 1; Roszak, Theodore, 3, 7; Semler, Ricardo, 5; Smith, Raymond W., 3; Stewart, Thomas A., 3; Wriston, Walter B., 5

Ingratitude Anonymous, 73; Burke, Edmund, 52; Schwarzenberg, Felix zu, 1; Shakespeare, William, 108, 336, 337, 710

Injustice Auden, W. H., 46; Burke, Edmund, 17, 48; Carlyle, Jane, 3; Cicero, 7; Darling, Charles John, 6; Debs, Eugene Victor, 3; France, Anatole, 1, 2; Gladstone, William Ewart, 7; Guan Hanqing, 1; Hayes, Rutherford B., 2; Hoffer, Eric, 1; Junius, 1; King, Martin Luther, Jr., 4, 23; Lec, Stanislaw, 2; Pope, Alexander, 73; Racine, Jean, 13; Seeger, Pete, 2; Shakespeare, William, 343, 490; Terence, 8; Tolstoy, Leo, 16; Ulpian, 1; Vanzetti, Bartolomeo, 2; Warren, Mercy, 1; Wright, Richard, 2

In-Laws Foch, Ferdinand, 4; Malcolm X, 15

Innocence Adorno, Theodor, 5; Baldwin, James, 18; Bowen, Elizabeth, 8; Burney, Fanny, 3; Das, Kamala, 1; Dunne, Finley Peter, 3; Golding, William, 1; Hill, Geoffrey, 1; Jackson, George, 5; Kipling, Rudyard, 42; Li Bai, 4; Morrison, Toni, 23; Newton, Isaac, 9; Orton, Joe, 1; Péguy, Charles Pierre, 2; Pope, Alexander, 60; Sand, George, 5; Shakespeare, William, 488, 619; Simpson, O. J., 1; Thomas, Dylan, 15; Thomas, R. S., 2; Voltaire, 9; Walton, Izaak, 4

Innovation Bacon, Francis (1561–1626), 37; Burke, Edmund, 3; Hamel, Gary, 7; Long, Clarisa, 2; Muhammad, 11; Peters, Tom, 5, 7; Rogers, Everett, 1; Sculley, John, 3, 4; Semler, Ricardo, 7

Innuendo Barker, Ronnie, 1; Benchley, Robert, 11; Butler, Samuel (1612–80), 20; Milligan, Spike, 7; Monty Python's Flying Circus, 3

Insensitivity Herbert, George, 22; Rousseau, Jean-Jacques, 7

Insignificance Parker, Dorothy, 17; Pirsig, Robert T., 11

Insincerity Charles II, 2; Dickens, Charles, 46; Donne, John, 36; Fadiman, Clifton, 2; Johnson, Samuel, 88; La Bruyère, Jean de, 2; McEnroe, John, 2; McGahern, John, 1; Shakespeare, William, 109

Insomnia Fitzgerald, F. Scott, 11; Horne, Marilyn, 2; Hubbard, Elbert, 9; Mandelstam, Osip, 14; Waugh, Evelyn, 16; Wolfe, Tom, 13

Inspiration Beethoven, Ludwig van, 9; Brooks, Gwendolyn, 8; Coleridge, Samuel Taylor, 6; James, Henry, 17; Keats, John (1795–1821), 60; Milton, John, 24; Naylor, Gloria, 5; Peter the Great, 3; Reynolds, Sir Joshua, 6; Sidney, Philip, 2; Smith, Patti, 1; Williams, Robin, 6; Wordsworth, Dorothy, 1; Wordsworth, William, 7

Insults Anonymous, 11; Arlen, Michael, 1; Asquith, Margot, 1, 4; Bevan, Aneurin, 1, 2; Brahms, Johannes, 3; Brown, Thomas, 1; Bryan, William Jennings, 1; Byron, Lord, 88; Capote, Truman, 7; Carter, Jimmy, 2; Chesterfield, Lord, 1, 2, 6; Churchill, Winston, 67, 82, 83; Clemenceau, Georges, 9; Coleridge, Samuel Taylor, 1; Coward, Noel, 26; De Gaulle, Charles, 1; Dickens, Charles, 55; Eisenhower, Dwight D., 6; Eliot, T. S., 2; Elizabeth I, 21; Freud, Clement, 1; Gibbon, Edward, 1; Hone, William, 1; James, Henry, 2; Jerrold, Douglas, 10; Johnson, Samuel, 140; Jordan, June, 10; Kipling, Rudyard, 2; Laing, Dilys, 1; Landowska, Wanda, 1; Levant, Oscar, 1, 4; Lloyd-George, David, 9; Lutyens, Edwin Landseer, 1; McEnroe, John, 3; Marx, Groucho, 12, 14, 17, 19; Milne, A. A., 10; Moore, Edward, 1; Murray, Bill, 1; Parker, Dorothy, 27, 38; Perón, Eva, 1; Reagan, Ronald, 13; Reeves, Keanu, 1; Shakespeare, William, 338, 356; Shaw, George Bernard, 10, 104; Thoreau, Henry David, 2; Turing, Alan, 1; Wodehouse, P. G., 8; Wordsworth, William, 3, 4

Insurance Bierce, Ambrose, 30; Coren, Alan, 2; Keller, Maryann, 2

Integrity Anonymous, 59; Bai Fengxi, 2; Bible, 255; Buffalo Bill, 1; Faraday, Michael, 2; Johnson, Samuel, 31; Kipling, Rudyard, 49; Meir, Golda, 7; O'Hare, Dean, 1; Shakespeare, William, 152, 331; Tennyson, Alfred, 10, 15

Intellect Adorno, Theodor, 3; Aristotle, 12; Benda, Julien, 1; Browning, Robert, 75; Christie, Agatha, 4; Einstein, Albert, 35; Erasmus, Desiderius, 5; Euripides, 6; Freud, Sigmund, 39; James, William, 33; Johnson, Samuel, 27; Malone, Michael S., 1; Mead, Margaret, 2; Montaigne, Michel de, 2; Schopenhauer, Arthur, 2; Tucholsky, Kurt, 4; Tuwim, Julian, 2; Watts, Alan, 7; Wordsworth, William, 22; Yeats, W. B., 19

Intellectuals Agnew, Spiro T., 4, 5; Auden, W. H., 16; Bankhead, Tallulah, 4; Barzun, Jacques, 8; Brenan, Gerald, 6; Bukowski, Charles, 3; Burroughs, William S., 12; Camus, Albert, 1; Davies, Robertson, 5; Einstein, Albert, 27; Elizabeth I, 7; Flanagan, Oliver J., 2; Hofstadter, Richard, 1; Ngugi wa Thiongo, 2; Sherwood, Robert E., 1; Socrates, 8

Intelligence al-Mufid, Abu Abdullah Muhammad al-Harithi al-Baghdadi, 3; Barney, Natalie Clifford, 1; Baroja, Pío, 1; Baruch, Bernard Mannes, 3; Bergson, Henri-Louis, 2; Carlyle, Thomas, 4; Carrel, Alexis, 1; Coleridge, Samuel Taylor, 64; De Vries, Peter, 1; Dewey, John, 11; Dickens, Charles, 103; Dryden, John, 14; Finch, Anne, 2; Fitzgerald, F. Scott, 27; Goleman, Daniel, 1, 3; Harper, Frances E. W., 2; Kettering, Charles, 3; Leigh, Vivien, 1; Luce, Clare Boothe, 2; Mencken, H. L., 49; Montesquieu, 3; Ohmae, Kenichi, 6, 7; Smith, F. E., 1; Stevenson, Robert Louis, 24

Interruptions León, Luis Ponce de, 1

Intrigue Charles II, 1; Coward, Noel, 12; Louis XIV, 5

Introductions George IV, 3; Lee, Harper, 1; Marx, Groucho, 23; Star Wars, 1

Intuition Shakespeare, William, 655

Inventions Bell, Alexander Graham, 1; Edison, Thomas Alva, 1; Emerson, Ralph Waldo, 66; Franklin, Benjamin, 30; Fuller, R. Buckminster, 6; Gómez de la Serna, Ramón, 2; Sinclair, Clive, 1; Weiner, Norbert, 1

Investment Boesky, Ivan, 4; Buffett, Warren, 1; Carnegie, Andrew, 2, 4; Dickens, Charles, 35, 50; Goizueta, Roberto, 5; Hamel, Gary, 3; Heller, Robert, 5; Keynes, John Maynard, 10; Knight, Frank Hyneman, 4; Lynch, Peter, 1; Rose, Billy, 1; Sachs, Jeffrey, 1; Soros, George, 1, 4; Walesa, Lech, 3

Invitations Boyer, Charles, 1; Pliny the Younger, 2; West, Mae, 14

Iowa Bryson, Bill, 5, 7

Iran Khomeini, Ruhollah, 13

Iraq Ahmed, Akbar, 2

Ireland Adams, Gerry, 5; Anonymous, 12; Auden, W. H., 12; Beckett, Samuel, 7; Behan, Brendan, 4, 14; Boucicault, Dion, 4; Brugha, Cathal, 1; Casement, Roger, 4; Chesterton, G. K., 5; Child, Lydia Maria, 2; Churchill, Winston, 6; Collins, Michael, 1; Davis, Thomas, 2; de Valera, Eamon, 2, 6, 7; Devlin, Polly, 1; Disraeli, Benjamin, 16; Donleavy, J. P., 4; Drennan, William, 1; Folk Verse, 5, 7; Griffith, Arthur, 1; Hume, John, 1; Johnson, Samuel, 121; Joyce, James, 7, 26; Littlewood, Sydney, 1; McCourt, Frank, 1; MacNeice, Louis, 10; Major, John, 1; Mangan, James Clarence, 1; Maudling, Reginald, 1; Merriman, Brian, 1; Moore, George, 2, 3; Moore, Marianne, 5; Moore, Thomas, 6; Newspapers, 21, 28; O'Brien, Flann, 11; O'Casey, Sean, 6; O'Connell, Daniel, 3; O'Connor, Joseph, 1, 2; Ó'Faoláin, Sean, 1; O'Neill, Hugh, 1; Parnell, Charles Stewart, 2, 3, 4, 5; Rice, Stephen, 1; Robinson, Mary, 1; Rogers, Will, 7; Roosevelt, Franklin D., 9; Sarsfield, Patrick, 1; Sellar, W. C., 6; Tone, Wolfe, 1; Victoria, 3; Wentworth, Thomas, 4; Yeats, W. B., 60

Rudolf, 1; Carroll, Lewis, 13, 35, 40; Chaucer, Geoffrey, 17; Chesterton, G. K., 41; Dunsany, Lord, 1; Heller, Joseph, 4; Jowett, Benjamin, 4; Kline, Morris, 2; Piaget, Jean, 1; Wallas, Graham, 1; Wilson, Woodrow, 14; Wittgenstein, Ludwig, 6, 8, 20

London Akhmatova, Anna, 6; Austen, Jane, 13; Bateman, Edgar, 1; Blücher, Gebhard Leberecht von, 1; Cobbett, William, 5; Colman, George, 3; Disraeli, Benjamin, 23, 37; Doyle, Arthur Conan, 1; Dunbar, William, 3; Eliot, T. S., 51; Furber, Douglas, 1; George VI, 1; James, Henry, 24; Johnson, James Weldon, 1, 8; Johnson, Samuel, 4, 99, 132; Joyce, James, 15; Pepys, Samuel, 13; Pitt the Elder, William, 1; Richard I, 6; Wordsworth, William, 40, 41

Loneliness Arnold, Matthew, 12; Coleridge, Samuel Taylor, 42; Corry, John, 1; Du Fu, 1; Ferrier, Susan Edmonstone, 1; Fromm, Erich, 20; Gilbert, W. S., 35; Golden, Marita, 4; Hammarskjöld, Dag, 7; Hammerstein, Oscar, II, 1; Harrison, Jim, 1; Hopper, Edward, 2; Joplin, Janis, 4; Komachi, 2; Lamartine, Alphonse de, 5; Lennon & McCartney, 1, 9; Li Bai, 3; Li Qingzhao, 2; Llewellyn, Richard, 1; McCaig, Norman, 2; McCullers, Carson, 2; Milne, A. A., 24; Nannakaiyar, Kaccipettu, 1; Pasternak, Boris, 11; Shaw, George Bernard, 82; Smith, Sydney, 14; Teresa of Calcutta, Mother, 5; Tillich, Paul, 11; Whitman, Walt, 37; Wolfe, Thomas, 2

Longevity Bible, 115; Bierce, Ambrose, 33; Blake, Eubie, 1; Connolly, Cyril, 11; Folk Verse, 50; Johnson, Samuel, 6; Kennedy, John Fitzgerald, 17; Leacock, Stephen, 12; Stone, I. F., 1; Tucker, Sophie, 1; Waugh, Evelyn, 6

Los Angeles Caine, Michael, 1; Campbell, Glen, 1; Didion, Joan, 2; Ford, Harrison, 1; Isherwood, Christopher, 3; Jacobs, Jane, 2; Kerouac, Jack, 16, 17; Mencken, H. L., 7

Losing Connors, Jimmy, 1; McEnroe, John, 1; Navratilova, Martina, 6

Loss Adams, Gerry, 3; Aiken, Conrad, 2; Bishop, Elizabeth, 5; Folk Verse, 11, 40; Keats, John (1795–1821), 13; Levertov, Denise, 2; Lindbergh, Anne Morrow, 1; Li Qingzhao, 5; Mann, Horace, 2; Mitchell, Margaret, 1; Plautus, 2; Rossetti, Dante Gabriel, 5; Seeger, Pete, 1; Shakespeare, William, 85, 606; Sitwell, Edith, 1; Synge, J. M., 2; Tolkien, J. R. R., 6; Walton, Izaak, 7; Wordsworth, William, 32, 39, 50; Yeats, W. B., 16

Love Abrahams, Peter, 1; Amichai, Yehuda, 5; Angelou, Maya, 8; Anonymous, 1; Anouilh, Jean, 3, 4; Arendt, Hannah, 19; Atwood, Margaret, 1; Auden, W. H., 14, 23, 24, 35, 38, 41; Austen, Jane, 28, 34; Bacon, Francis (1561–1626), 40, 41; Baldwin, James, 30; Bâ, Mariama, 1; Barnes, Julian, 5; Barnfield, Richard, 2, 8; Beaumont & Fletcher, 10; Beckett, Samuel, 13; Beerbohm, Max, 18; Behn, Aphra, 7; Bible, 65, 161, 182, 289, 305, 431, 486, 489, 490, 491, 494, 496, 497, 498; Bickerstaffe, Isaac, 1, 3; Billings, Josh, 3; Bingen, Hildegard of, 1; Blake, William, 22, 23; Boccaccio, Giovanni, 3; Bogart, Humphrey, 4, 7; Bolingbroke, Henry St. John, 1; Bourdillon, Francis William, 1; Bradley, F. H., 3; Brecht, Bertolt, 3, 18; Brontë, Emily, 3; Brown, George Mackay, 1; Browning, Elizabeth Barrett, 6, 9; Browning, Robert, 29, 63; Bukowski, Charles, 1; Bulgakov, Mikhail, 4, 7; Burns, Robert, 6, 8; Butler, Samuel (1612–80), 18; Butler, Samuel (1835–1902), 15, 21; Byron, Lord, 16, 17, 36, 45, 54, 75; Campion, Thomas, 5; Cantor, Eddie, 1; Carey, Henry, 4; Catullus, 5, 6, 8; Chamfort, Nicolas, 4, 11; Charles, Prince, 10; Chevalier, Albert, 1; Chevalier, Maurice, 2; Child, Lydia Maria, 3; Cibber, Colley, 6; Coleridge, Samuel Taylor, 18, 19; Colum, Padraig, 1; Confucius, 25; Congreve, William, 14, 21; Cope, Wendy, 2; Coward, Noel, 5; Cowley, Abraham, 2, 3; Crashaw, Richard, 1; Cullen, Countee, 6, 7; cummings, e. e., 2, 4; Dalai Lama, 8; Diderot, Denis, 5; Dipoko, Mbella Sonne, 1; Donne, John, 7, 20, 29, 30, 33, 34, 38, 40, 43; Dryden, John, 43; du Bartas, Guillaume, 9; Ebner-Eschenbach, Marie von, 2; Edward VIII, 6; Egbuna, Obi, 1; Ekelöf, Gunnar, 2; English, Thomas Dunn, 1; Farah, Nuruddin, 6; Fielding, Henry, 8; Fitzgerald, Zelda, 1; Fletcher, Phineas, 1; Florian, Jean-Pierre Claris de, 1; Folk Verse, 8, 28, 30, 37, 46, 47; Formby, George, 1; Gay, John, 16, 19; Gershwin, Ira, 7, 8; Gibran, Kahlil, 2, 6; Ginsberg, Allen, 4, 5; Golden, Marita, 1; Gorky, Maksim, 5; Gower, John, 2; Graves, Robert, 5; Greer, Germaine, 10; Grossmith, George, 1; Hallam, Arthur Henry, 4; Halm, Friedrich, 1; Hammerstein, Oscar, II, 3, 6, 8, 9, 11, 15; Handy, W. C., 2; Hansberry, Lorraine, 1; Hart, Lorenz, 1, 3, 4; Heath-Stubbs, John, 1; Hepburn, Katharine, 2; Herbert, George, 11; Herrick, Robert, 9; hooks, bell, 1; Housman, A. E., 6, 7, 28; Hubbard, Elbert, 7; Hughes, Langston, 13; Hurston, Zora Neale, 4, 12; Hu Shi, 1; Jackson, George, 10; Jepson, Edgar, 1; Jerome, Jerome K., 5; Jerrold, Douglas, 3, 5; Johnson, Samuel, 57; Jonson, Ben, 2, 26; Kahn, Gus, 1; Keats, John (1795–1821), 16, 33, 49, 55; Kempis, Thomas à, 8; Labé, Louise, 1; Lamb, Caroline, 1; Larkin, Philip, 3, 20; La Rochefoucauld, François, 1; Lauder, Harry, 2; Lawrence, D. H., 8, 49; Leboyer, Frédérick, 2; Leibniz, Gottfried Wilhelm, 5; Lennon & McCartney, 3, 6, 7; Loesser, Frank, 6; Lovell, Maria, 1; Lowry, Malcolm, 3; McCarthy, Mary, 3; MacDiarmid, Hugh, 2; McGough, Roger, 2; McKinney, Joyce, 1; MacNeice, Louis, 8; Mahfouz, Naguib, 5; Ma Lihua, 1; Malory, Thomas, 4; Marlowe, Christopher, 1; Martineau, Harriet, 4, 5; Marvell, Andrew, 3, 15; Marx, Groucho, 10; Maugham, Somerset, 4, 25, 33; Mencken, H. L., 48; Meredith, George, 8; Meynell, Alice, 1; Millay, Edna St. Vincent, 5; Milton, John, 14, 54, 56, 59, 88, 122; Montrose, Percy, 1; Moore, Thomas, 1, 4; Motherwell, William, 1; Muir, Edwin, 1; Murdoch, Iris, 3, 4; Navarre, Margaret of, 3; Nietzsche, Friedrich Wilhelm, 25; Norman, Barry, 1; Norton, Caroline, 1; Norworth, Jack, 1; Parker, Dorothy, 8, 24, 45; Patmore, Coventry, 1, 3, 4; Patten, Brian, 2; Pavese, Cesare, 2; Peele, George, 2, 3; Penn, William, 4; Perelman, S. J., 9; Pestalozzi, Johann Heinrich, 4; Philostratus, 1; Poe, Edgar Allan, 4, 10, 13; Porter, Cole, 4, 5, 15, 17, 19; Pound, Ezra, 19; Proust, Marcel, 7, 8, 12; Pynchon, Thomas, 8; Qabbani, Nizar, 3, 4, 5; Raleigh, Walter, 2, 5, 7; Rawlings, Marjorie, 2; Redding, Otis, 1; Reed, Lou, 10; Reik, Theodor, 1; Robinson, Edwin Arlington, 3; Rochester, 2nd Earl of, 3; Rogers, Samuel, 1, 7; Rossetti, Christina, 1, 2; Rossetti, Dante Gabriel, 3, 4; Russell, Bertrand, 15, 40, 49; Sagan, Françoise, 1; Saint-Exupéry, Antoine de, 8; Salinger, J. D., 8; Sand, George, 4; Schiller, Friedrich von, 10; Scott, Sir Walter, 10, 24; Sedley, Charles, 1; Segal, Erich, 1; Sembène, Ousmane, 2; Service, Robert W., 5; Shakespeare, William, 56, 70, 102, 191, 216, 444, 452, 458, 475, 479, 492, 541, 542, 544, 545, 546, 547, 554, 568, 574, 581, 582, 584, 586, 604, 628, 678, 681, 685, 687, 693, 699, 701, 704, 713; Shange, Ntozake, 4; Shelley, Percy Bysshe, 5, 6, 22, 31; Simon, Paul, 3; Simpson, Wallis, 1; Spenser, Edmund, 2, 4, 8; Staël, Madame de, 5; Sterne, Laurence, 5; Stevens, Wallace, 13; Strindberg, August, 3; Suckling, John, 2; Taylor, Bayard, 1; Tennyson, Alfred, 24, 28, 47, 52, 61, 63, 82; Teresa of Ávila, Saint, 2; Teresa of Calcutta, Mother, 4; Tertullian, 7; Thackeray, William Makepeace, 3, 5; Tolstoy, Leo, 7; Trollope, Anthony, 7; Tsvetaeva, Marina, 6, 7, 8; Tutu, Desmond, 10; Virgil, 30, 31, 34; Voltaire, 12; Walker, Alice, 1; Waller, Edmund, 2; Wavell, Archibald Percival, 1; Weil, Simone, 9; West, Mae, 24; Whitman, Walt, 28, 46; Wilcox, Ella Wheeler, 1; Wittgenstein, Ludwig, 12; Wodehouse, P. G., 15; Wordsworth, William, 28, 36, 92; Wyatt, Thomas, 2, 3; Yeats, W. B., 32, 34, 44, 54, 56; Zamyatin, Yevgeny, 3

Love and Friendship Belloc, Hilaire, 32; Bussy-Rabutin, 2; Byron, Lord, 10; Gibran, Kahlil, 3; Goldsmith, Oliver, 19; Housman, A. E., 27; Montherlant, Henri de, 4; Rilke, Rainer Maria, 4; Steele, Richard, 5; Thoreau, Henry David, 1

Love and Hate Akhtar-ul-Iman, 1; Antrim, Minna, 4; Barnes, Djuna, 5; Cleaver, Eldridge, 6; Frost, Robert, 10; Gabor, Zsa Zsa, 3; Melbourne, Lord, 6; Moore, Thomas, 10; Navarre, Margaret of, 2; Stoddard, Elizabeth, 1

Love and Marriage Burton, Robert, 17; Byron, Lord, 55; Callas, Maria, 1; Carver, Raymond, 9; Clark, Kenneth (1903–83), 4; Dacre, Harry, 1; Ding Ling, 1; Dryden, John, 22; Herrick, Robert, 14; Jerrold, Douglas, 3; Leacock, Stephen, 9; Meredith, George, 1

Love at First Sight Burns, Robert, 12

Love: First Love Shakespeare, William, 539

Lovers Beckett, Samuel, 5; Bellow, Saul, 4; Berryman, John, 1; Browning,

Heath, Roy A. K., 1; Hecht, Ben, 2; Henry VIII, 9; Herbert, A. P., 5, 12; Herrick, Robert, 17; Hesiod, 4; Holiday, Billie, 3; Howe, Edgar Watson, 1; Hughes, Langston, 10; Johnson, Samuel, 30, 157; Joyce, James, 18; Keith of Kinkel, Lord, 1; Kerr, Jean, 8; Key, Ellen, 5; Koran, 27; Kunitz, Stanley, 1; Laclos, Pierre Choderlos de, 2, 3; Lamb, Charles, 11; Lampton, William James, 1; Lane, Geoffrey Dawson, 1; Larkin, Philip, 5; Lawrence, D. H., 2; Longfellow, Henry Wadsworth, 6, 32, 33; Lowry, L. S., 1; McGonagall, William, 5; McMillan, Terry, 4, 8; Mailer, Norman, 11; Mandela, Nelson, 2; Martineau, Harriet, 1; Marx, Groucho, 35; Maugham, Somerset, 28; Mencken, H. L., 32; Meredith, George, 13; Miller, Arthur, 1; Montaigne, Michel de, 20; Montefiore, Hugh, 1; Mosley, Walter, 11; Mossell, Mrs. N. F., 1; Mozart, Wolfgang Amadeus, 2; Msham, Mwana Kupona Binti, 1, 2, 3; Muir, Frank, 2; Murdoch, Iris, 1; Murray, Jenni, 1; Newspapers, 1; Niven, David, 2; Parkinson, Cyril Northcote, 5; Pepys, Samuel, 8; Philip, Prince, 8; Plath, Sylvia, 15; Plutarch, 22; Priestley, J. B., 9; Rogers, Samuel, 10; Roosevelt, Edith Carow, 1; Roosevelt, Franklin D., 5; Rostand, Jean, 2; Rowland, Helen, 5; Russell, Bertrand, 13; Saki, 24; Samuel, Herbert, 3; Selden, John, 9; Shaffer, Peter, 2; Shakespeare, William, 52, 117, 451, 624, 637, 641, 647, 695, 700; Shaw, George Bernard, 48, 63; Sheridan, Richard Brinsley, 9, 14; Simpson, Wallis, 2; Smith, Logan Pearsall, 13; Smith, Sydney, 17; Stevenson, Robert Louis, 25, 33, 34, 35, 36, 37, 39; Swift, Jonathan, 10; Thackeray, William Makepeace, 6, 8; Thatcher, Denis, 1; Thomas, Dylan, 22; Thorndike, Sybil, 1; Thurber, James, 14; Tolkien, J. R. R., 1; Tolson, Melvin, 1; Tooke, Horne, 1; Updike, John, 5; Vidor, King, 1; Webb, Sidney, 2; West, Mae, 26; Wilder, Thornton, 3, 6; Wodehouse, P. G., 4, 7, 17, 27; Wycherley, William, 5; Wyndham, John, 2; Young, Brigham, 1

Martyrdom Borges, Jorge Luis, 4; Brown, John, 1, 5; Darwish, Mahmoud, 1; Eco, Umberto, 11; Edgeworth de Firmont, Abbé, 1; Masefield, John, 5; Romero, Oscar, 3; Shakespeare, William, 660; Tertullian, 3

Marxism Didion, Joan, 9; Foot, Michael, 3; Keynes, John Maynard, 16; Logue, Christopher, 1; Macmillan, Harold, 4; Marx, Karl, 1, 3, 7, 8, 28; Orwell, George, 6; Schumpeter, Joseph Alois, 4; Stalin, Joseph, 6

Maryland Whittier, John Greenleaf, 2

Masculinity Austin, Mary, 1, 10; Beauvoir, Simone de, 16; Brando, Marlon, 6; Gibbons, Stella, 3; Hellman, Lillian, 6; Lawrence, D. H., 47; Marshall, Paule, 2; Melville, Herman, 3; Middleton, Thomas, 3; Pater, Walter, 3; Updike, John, 16; Whitman, Walt, 23

Massachusetts James, Henry, 22; Lowell, Robert, 21, 23

Masturbation Allen, Woody, 2, 6; Bible, 135; David, Larry, 1; Elton, Ben, 2; Hampton, Christopher, 3; Szasz, Thomas, 14

Materialism Anderson, Sherwood, 1; Auster, Paul, 2; Barney, Natalie Clifford, 2; Emecheta, Buchi, 7; Holiday, Billie, 1; Huxley, Aldous, 15; Illich, Ivan, 2; Juvenal, 16; Loos, Anita, 5, 6; McCarthy, Mary, 14; McMillan, Terry, 1; Marx, Karl, 15; Miller, Arthur, 19; Russell, Bertrand, 7; Sadat, Anwar al-, 2; Vanbrugh, John, 1; Veblen, Thorstein Bunde, 3

Mathematics Adler, Alfred, 8, 9; Alembert, Jean le Rond d', 1, 3; Arbuthnot, John, 2; Ascham, Roger, 3; Augustine of Hippo, Saint, 9; Bacon, Roger, 3, 4; Barrie, J. M., 12; Bell, Eric Temple, 1; Bolyai, Farkas, 1; Bolyai, János, 1; Buck, Pearl, 7; Butler, Samuel (1612–80), 6; Cayley, Arthur, 1; Chekhov, Anton, 22; Churchill, Randolph (1849–95), 3; Darwin, Charles, 13; Dürer, Albrecht, 4; Eddington, Arthur, 4; Einstein, Albert, 40, 42, 54; Ellis, Havelock, 5, 9; Euclid, 1, 2; Fermat, Pierre de, 1; Gauss, Carl Friedrich, 1, 4, 5; Gilbert, W. S., 34; Haldane, J. B. S., 2; Hardy, Godfrey Harold, 2, 3, 4; Hermite, Charles, 1; Hesse, Hermann, 5; Ibn Khaldun, 1; Jacobi, Karl Gustav Jakob, 1, 2; Keller, Helen, 8; Kepler, Johannes, 2; Kronecker, Leopold, 1; Laozi, 1; Leonardo da Vinci, 8; Littlewood, John, 1; Lobachevsky, Nikolay, 1; Mann, Thomas, 11; Nash, Ogden, 10; Nicely, Thomas R., 1; Oppenheimer, J. Robert, 2; Peirce, Benjamin, 1; Plato, 30; Poincaré, Jules Henri, 6; Poisson, Siméon-Denis, 1; Ray, Satyajit, 5; Rossi, Hugo, 1; Russell, Bertrand, 1, 17, 25, 28, 30, 51; Sayers, Dorothy L., 4; Smith, Anthony, 1; Smith, Henry John Stephen, 1; Spinoza, Baruch, 1; Stendhal, 3; Voltaire, 45; Von Neumann, John, 1; Weil, André, 1; Weil, Simone, 8; West, Nathanael, 4; Weyl, Hermann, 1; Whitehead, A. N., 13, 16

Meaning Burroughs, William S., 11; Carroll, Lewis, 12, 18, 28, 44; Dylan, Bob, 27; Hay, Ian, 1; Johns, Jasper, 1; Jung, Carl Gustav, 20, 21; Milton, John, 110; Pound, Ezra, 3; Schiller, Friedrich von, 16; Szasz, Thomas, 16; Tillich, Paul, 9; Tolstoy, Leo, 8; Wideman, John Edgar, 3

Meanness Burns, George, 4; Marx, Groucho, 7

Media Agnew, Spiro T., 3; Barker, Howard, 3; Benn, Tony, 2; Calvino, Italo, 7; Einstein, Albert, 15; Farah, Nuruddin, 2; Greene, Graham, 15; Harris, Janet, 2; Hoffman, Abbie, 3; Longford, Lord, 2; Murdoch, Rupert, 3; Negroponte, Nicholas, 5; Nicolson, Harold, 1; O'Rourke, P. J., 1; Scott, C. P., 2; Stoppard, Tom, 6; Teresa of Calcutta, Mother, 9

Medicine Abernethy, John, 1; Al-Razi, 1, 2; Anderson, Elizabeth Garrett, 1; Anonymous, 70; Armstrong, John, 1; Avicenna, 1; Ayres, Pam, 1; Bacon, Francis (1561–1626), 60, 85, 96; Barnard, Christiaan, 1; Baruch, Bernard Mannes, 1; Beaumont, William, 1; Bierce, Ambrose, 20; Bryce, James, 1; Buckle, Henry Thomas, 1; Butler, Samuel (1835–1902), 36; Chamfort, Nicolas, 15; Chrysostom, Saint John, 1; Cobb, Irvin S., 1; Cohen, Henry, 1; Cooper, Astley, 1, 2; Corvisart des Marets, Jean Nicolas, 1; Edgeworth, Maria, 3; Eliot, T. S., 19; Emerson, Ralph Waldo, 24, 64, 65; Fischer, Martin H., 26; Florio, John, 1; Fuller, Thomas (1654–1734), 3; Galen, 2, 3, 4; Goethe, Johann Wolfgang von, 38; Gourmont, Rémy de, 1; Gull, William Withey, 2; Hendrick, Burton J., 2; Hippocrates, 2, 8; Holmes, Oliver Wendell, 5, 7, 8, 10, 15, 16; Howard, Russell John, 1, 3, 4; Hutchison, Robert, 1; Illich, Ivan, 4; Inge, William Ralph, 11; Jefferson, Thomas, 12; Johnson, Luke, 1; Kennedy, John Fitzgerald, 4; Kenny, Elizabeth, 1; Kübler-Ross, Elisabeth, 3; Kuhn, Maggie, 1; Latham, Peter Mere, 1, 2; Lettsom, John Coakley, 1; Liebig, Justus, 1; Lister, Joseph, 2; Maimonides, 1; Maudsley, Henry, 2; Mayo, Charles Horace, 7; Mayo, William James, 5; Meltzer, Samuel J., 1; Mencken, H. L., 34; Merck, George, 1; Molière, 10; Morris, Robert Tuttle, 3, 4; Nash, Ogden, 17; Osler, William, 4, 5; Ovid, 7, 11, 13; Paget, Stephen, 1, 2; Paracelsus, 1, 2; Payne, Frank, 1; Pickering, George White, 1; Plato, 4, 10; Plutarch, 21; Proverbs, 335; Proverbs, Modern, 11, 27, 31; Quintilian, 3; Rolleston, Humphrey, 2; Ross, Ronald, 3; Runyon, Damon, 12; Schick, Béla, 3; Schweitzer, Albert, 2; Seneca, "the Younger," 4, 15; Shakespeare, William, 137; Sigerist, Henry E., 1, 7; Simon, Neil, 4; Sophocles, 11; Spence, James Calvert, 1; Sydenham, Thomas, 2, 3, 4; Szasz, Thomas, 13; Welch, William H., 1; Wodehouse, P. G., 9

Mediocrity Agate, James, 3; Anderson, Eric, 1; Beerbohm, Max, 22; Disraeli, Benjamin, 28; Doyle, Arthur Conan, 18; Giraudoux, Jean, 6; Heller, Joseph, 7; Mailer, Norman, 21; Mead, Margaret, 10; Newspapers, 2; Plomer, William, 3; Reynolds, Sir Joshua, 2; Rorem, Ned, 1; Shakespeare, William, 199; Vanbrugh, John, 3

Meditation Browning, Robert, 26; Cather, Willa, 6; Krishnamurti, Jiddu, 3; Yeats, W. B., 41

Meetings Allen, Fred, 7; Dickens, Charles, 98; McCormack, Mark, 5; Parkinson, Cyril Northcote, 1; Perot, H. Ross, 2; Platt, Lewis, 1; Shakespeare, William, 379; Townsend, Robert, 13; Voinovich, Vladimir, 6; Wagner, Jane, 1

Melancholy Beaumont, Francis, 8; Burton, Robert, 1, 25; Ford, John (1586–1640?), 4; Gilbert, W. S., 31; Herbert, George, 4; Keats, John (1795–1821), 57; Luther, Martin, 8, 12; Lyly, John, 7; Musset, Alfred de, 5; Nerval, Gérard de, 3; Tennyson, Alfred, 93

Memorials Akhmatova, Anna, 1; Alexander the Great, 2; Anonymous, 4; Fields, W. C., 10; Gray, Thomas, 9; Joyce, James, 37; Macmillan, Harold, 7; Sassoon, Siegfried, 3; Scharping, Rudolf, 1; Shakespeare, William, 309; Williams, William Carlos, 4, 17; Wu Yingtao, 1

Memory Amichai, Yehuda, 4; Armah, Ayi Kwei, 3; Auster, Paul, 4; Barrie, J. M., 1; Baudelaire, Charles, 16; Betti, Ugo, 1; Bible, 44; Bogart, Humphrey, 3;

Brautigan, Richard, 3; Chateaubriand, René, 5; Chaucer, Geoffrey, 39; Chesterton, G. K., 49; Clifton, Lucille, 2; Dai Wangshu, 1; Degas, Edgar, 6; Doyle, Arthur Conan, 7; Eliot, T. S., 13; Faulkner, William, 7; Gogol, Nikolay, 6; Grandma Moses, 2; Hofstadter, Richard, 3; Ignatieff, Michael, 2; James, William, 14, 18, 20; Jarry, Alfred, 2; Kempis, Thomas à, 6; Kipling, Rudyard, 22; La Bruyère, Jean de, 19; Lerner, Alan Jay, 2; Lincoln, Abraham, 9, 10; Machado de Assis, Joaquim Maria, 14; Masefield, John, 7; Maugham, Somerset, 22; Moore, Marianne, 9; Moore, Thomas, 11; Newspapers, 34; Nietzsche, Friedrich Wilhelm, 2; Olson, Charles, 3; Pamuk, Orhan, 4; Pavese, Cesare, 4; Pinter, Harold, 5; Proust, Marcel, 9; Quintilian, 1; Robin, Leo, 1; Rogers, Samuel, 8; Rossetti, Christina, 7, 8; Rossetti, Dante Gabriel, 2; Scott, Sir Walter, 22; Shakespeare, William, 54, 215, 274; Shelley, Percy Bysshe, 25; Stevenson, Robert Louis, 9; Stevens, Wallace, 3; Svevo, Italo, 1; Swinburne, Algernon Charles, 2; Thales, 2; Thomas, Dylan, 9; Thomas, Edward, 1; Thurber, James, 7; Trevor, William, 2; Williams, Tennessee, 13; Wodehouse, P. G., 5; Wordsworth, William, 46, 54; Yeats, W. B., 31

Men Abrahams, Peter, 4; Astor, Nancy, 3, 6; Austen, Jane, 35; Cope, Wendy, 4; Crystal, Billy, 1; Davis, Bette, 6; Dietrich, Marlene, 4; Eliot, George, 19; Ford, Anna, 2; Gaskell, Elizabeth, 2; Glasgow, Ellen, 1; Greer, Germaine, 11; Hearne, John, 2; James, C. L. R., 9; John Paul II, 2; Keillor, Garrison, 11; Lawrence, D. H., 40; Lerner, Alan Jay, 10; Lu Xun, 9; McMillan, Terry, 10; Morley, Christopher Darlington, 6; Naylor, Gloria, 7; Paglia, Camille, 7, 15; Porter, Cole, 14; Routsong, Alma, 1; Sévigné, Madame de, 4; Shepard, Sam, 3; Somerville, Edith, 3; Steinem, Gloria, 1; Tsvetaeva, Marina, 1; Voltaire, 20; Walker, Alice, 28; Waters, John, 3; Whately, Richard, 3; Wilde, Oscar, 3

Mercy Bible, 309, 310, 337; Blake, William, 33; Book of Common Prayer, 7; Coleridge, Samuel Taylor, 46; Henry V, 2; Marvell, Andrew, 11; Medici, Catherine de', 1; Shakespeare, William, 617; Sterne, Laurence, 3; Thorpe, Rose Hartwick, 1; Whittier, John Greenleaf, 4

Merit Book of Lord Shang, 1; Jefferson, Thomas, 31; Laozi, 3; Molière, 22; Washington, Booker T., 6; Young, Michael, 1

Merrymaking Kaufman, George S., 1; Shakespeare, William, 697, 698

Metaphysics Bowen, Charles, 2; Bradley, F. H., 6; Chamfort, Nicolas, 12; Comte, Auguste, 1, 3; Democritus, 2, 3; Fichte, Johann, 1, 3; Heidegger, Martin, 4; Heraclitus, 3; Krutch, Joseph Wood, 5; MacNeice, Louis, 24; Mencken, H. L., 15; Rorty, Richard, 1; Stevens, Wallace, 17; Wordsworth, William, 2

Mexico Díaz, Porfirio, 1

Michigan Bryson, Bill, 15

Middle Age Adams, Franklin P., 2; Arnold, Matthew, 4; Defoe, Daniel, 16; Depardieu, Gérard, 2; Eliot, T. S., 55; Gorky, Maksim, 4; Hughes, Richard, 2; Nash, Ogden, 26; Proverbs, Modern, 12, 33; White, E. B., 11; Wolfe, Tom, 10

Middle East Alhegelan, Nouha, 1; al-Takriti, Barzan, 1; Arafat, Yasir, 1; Ashrawi, Hanan, 1; Bevan, Aneurin, 4; Bush, George, 11, 14; Faisal, 1; Kabbani, Rana, 1; Macaulay, Rose, 7; Nyerere, Julius Kambarage, 8; Qabbani, Nizar, 1; Rabin, Yitzhak, 1, 4; Said, Edward W., 5; Shaykh, Hanan al-, 1; Tuqan, Fadwa, 1; Waite, Terry, 3; Yehoshua, A. B., 2, 3

Military Leaders Alba, Duke of, 1; Churchill, Winston, 62; Eisenhower, Dwight D., 5; Haig, Douglas, 1; MacArthur, Douglas, 2, 3; Napoleon I, 5; Nelson, Horatio, 1; Newbolt, Henry, 1, 2; Orwell, George, 40; Tennyson, Alfred, 31, 32, 33; Tuchman, Barbara, 1

Mind Agate, James, 2; Anaxagoras, 1; Arnauld, Antoine, 1; Bacon, Francis (1561–1626), 14; Barnes, Djuna, 3; Bellow, Saul, 6; Bierce, Ambrose, 10; Blok, Aleksandr, 5; Browning, Robert, 65; Coleridge, Samuel Taylor, 56; Colton, Charles, 6; Davies, Scrope, 1; Descartes, René, 3, 5, 13; Dewey, John, 3, 10, 12, 18; Freud, Anna, 4; Freud, Sigmund, 52, 53, 56; Hawkes, Jacquetta, 1; Hegel, G. W. F., 10, 11, 12, 14, 16, 17; Hippocrates, 5, 6; Holmes, Oliver Wendell, 33; Hopkins, Gerard Manley, 4; Horace, 17, 37; Huxley, Aldous, 36; James, William, 10, 11, 13, 26; Jefferson, Thomas, 18; Jung, Carl Gustav, 14; Juvenal, 14; Laing, R. D., 15; La Rochefoucauld, François, 30; Lawrence, D. H., 22; Leary, Timothy, 3; Locke, John, 1, 3; Lovecraft, H. P., 1; Lucretius, 6; McCaig, Norman, 4; Milton, John, 30; Molière, 11; Moore, Marianne, 2, 8; Ovid, 4, 8; Pirsig, Robert T., 12; Plato, 8; Plutarch, 15; Pope, Alexander, 42; Ramón y Cajal, Santiago, 1; Ross, Harold W., 3; Russell, Bertrand, 2; Sartre, Jean-Paul, 24; Simon, Paul, 2; Snyder, Gary, 7; Stevens, Anthony, 4; Stevens, Wallace, 21, 28; Teresa of Ávila, Saint, 4; Ustinov, Peter, 7; Watts, Alan, 6; Wordsworth, William, 11, 80

Minnesota Keillor, Garrison, 3

Minority Mailer, Norman, 7; Watt, James G., 1

Misanthropy Bentham, Jeremy, 7; Byron, Lord, 32; Wilde, Oscar, 13

Misfortune Ai Qing, 5; Barnfield, Richard, 4; Beaumont & Fletcher, 2; Bierce, Ambrose, 12; Delaney, Lucy A., 1; Drayton, Michael, 4; Dryden, John, 6; Hammarskjöld, Dag, 11; Johnson, Samuel, 82; La Rochefoucauld, François, 4, 17; Marias, Javier, 2; Rogers, Will, 10; Shakespeare, William, 214; Smith, Sydney, 7; Tennyson, Alfred, 78; Wilde, Oscar, 52

Misogyny Amagat, Emile Hilaire, 1; Lerner, Alan Jay, 7; Lin Yutang, 3; Miller, Kelly, 1; Nogarola, Isotta, 1; Tertullian, 5

Misquotations Harburg, E. Y., 1; Hillingdon, Alice, 1; Pearson, Hesketh, 1, 2; Strunsky, Simeon, 1

Mississippi Bryson, Bill, 11

Missouri Sterling, Andrew B., 1

Mistakes Bankhead, Tallulah, 10; Boulay de La Meurthe, Antoine, 1; Confucius, 1, 24; Cromwell, Oliver, 3; Curzon, George Nathaniel, 3; Edgeworth, Maria, 1; Lichtenberg, Georg Christoph, 1; Malesherbes, Chrétien de, 1; Morton, J. C., 5; O'Donoghue, Bernard, 1; Phelps, Edward John, 1; Plutarch, 17; Pope, Alexander, 52; Retz, Cardinal de, 9; Smith, Stevie, 1; Thurber, James, 11; Trotsky, Leon, 6

Mistrust Mosley, Walter, 2; Shakespeare, William, 264; Wallace, Michele, 1

Mixed Metaphors Goldwyn, Samuel, 11, 17

Moderation Burke, Edmund, 9; Butler, Samuel (1835–1902), 9; Clive, Robert, 2; Dryden, John, 25; Franklin, Benjamin, 29; Kissinger, Henry, 11; Lamb, Charles, 8; La Rochefoucauld, François, 32; Shakespeare, William, 550; Solon, 1; Talleyrand, Charles Maurice de, 4; Thurber, James, 4

Modern Art Bourgeois, Louise, 2; Ciardi, John, 1; Kandinsky, Wassily, 1; Mills, Hugh, 1; Mitchell, Joni, 1; Warhol, Andy, 14

Modesty Charlemagne, 2; Chesterfield, Lord, 7; Fielding, Henry, 12; Kissinger, Henry, 17; Montaigne, Michel de, 3; Renard, Jules, 1, 15; Russell, Bertrand, 42; Sitwell, Edith, 5; Theano, 1; Valois, Ninette de, 1

Monarchy Alcuin, 1; Asser, 2; Bagehot, Walter, 3, 6, 7, 8; Bible, 184, 189, 227; Bismarck, Prince Otto von, 7; Blackstone, William, 4; Byron, Lord, 99; Charles I, 6; Charles V, 1; Chomsky, Noam, 1; Dee, John, 1; Diderot, Denis, 1; Dryden, John, 29; Dunning, John, 1; Edward VIII, 5; Erasmus, Desiderius, 4; Farouk I, 1; Francis Joseph I, 2; George II, 1; Hamilton, William (b.1917), 2; Henry I, 2; Henry V, 3; Henry VIII, 7, 8; Ivan IV, 1, 2; James I, 2; Leopold II, 1; Locke, John, 9; Louis XIV, 2; Louis XVIII, 1; Marlowe, Christopher, 15; Napoleon I, 8; Nicholas II, 2; Peter the Great, 2; Philip, Prince, 7; Pitt the Elder, William, 9; Polo, Marco, 3; Pope, Alexander, 65; Prior, Matthew, 16; Richard I, 1; Rudolf I, 1; Schiller, Friedrich von, 12; Shakespeare, William, 197, 213, 255, 270, 271, 280, 515, 516; William of Newburgh, 1

Money Allen, Woody, 14; Anderson, Marian, 2; Anonymous, 85; Armour, Philip D., 1; Austen, Jane, 16; Bacon, Francis (1561–1626), 58; Baldwin, James, 4; Baring, Maurice, 1; Beauvoir, Simone de, 9; Behn, Aphra, 14; Bellamy, Edward, 3; Belloc, Hilaire, 1; Bellow, Saul, 20; Berry, Chuck, 1; Bible, 57, 239; Bloom, Allan, 1; Branson, Richard, 6; Brecht, Bertolt, 22; Browne, Thomas, 40; Burton, Robert, 7, 28; Butler, Samuel (1835–1902), 4, 17; Camus, Albert, 3; Carver,

Dylan, 1, 2, 3, 4, 5; Trilling, Lionel, 1; Villon, François, 1; Waller, Edmund, 4; Whitman, Walt, 3, 51; Woolf, Virginia, 19; Wordsworth, William, 1, 5, 8, 9, 47; Yeats, W. B., 1, 40

Poland Alexander II, 1; Hitler, Adolf, 21, 22; Molotov, Vyacheslav Mikhailovich, 1

Police Behan, Brendan, 16; Daley, Richard, 1; Gilbert, W. S., 39; Hitchcock, Alfred, 9; McCaig, Norman, 6; Mailer, Norman, 15; Mamet, David, 19; Marnoch, Alex, 1; Mosley, Walter, 3; O'Brien, Flann, 8; Orton, Joe, 7, 8; Peel, Arthur Wellesley, 1; Philippe, Charles-Louis, 1

Politeness Bradbury, Malcolm, 5; Chesterfield, Lord, 8; Churchill, Winston, 50; Johnson, Samuel, 24; Kerr, Jean, 1; Lu Xun, 1; Van der Post, Laurens, 7

Political Correctness Alibhai-Brown, Yasmin, 1; Fenton, James, 1

Politicians Adams, Henry, 4; Adams, John Quincy, 1, 8; Adams, Samuel, 2; Agnew, Spiro T., 2; Archer, Gilbert, 1; Asquith, Margot, 5; Attlee, Clement, 1; Auden, W. H., 48; Baker, Josephine, 2; Baldwin, Stanley, 1; Barrès, Maurice, 1; Belloc, Hilaire, 3, 19; Bennett, Arnold, 9; Benn, Tony, 6; Benton, Thomas Hart, 1; Briand, Aristide, 1; Bryan, William Jennings, 2; Bulmer-Thomas, Ivor, 1; Burke, Edmund, 13; Butler, Rab, 1; Camus, Albert, 4; Chamberlain, Neville, 1; Chesterfield, Lord, 3; Churchill, Randolph (1911–68), 2; Churchill, Winston, 1, 2, 4, 7, 22, 55; Clarendon, Edward Hyde, 2; Clarke, Kenneth, 1; Clinton, Bill, 3; Coolidge, Calvin, 7; Critchley, Julian, 1; cummings, e. e., 5; Darrow, Clarence, 7; De Gaulle, Charles, 2, 15, 16, 21; de Valera, Eamon, 3; Disraeli, Benjamin, 19; Douglas-Home, Alec, 3; Dryden, John, 13, 19; Dylan, Bob, 19; Eden, Anthony, 1; Ford, Gerald, 3; Gandhi, Mahatma, 1, 4; Garner, John Nance, 1; George V, 1; Gilbert, W. S., 4, 15; Gladstone, William Ewart, 1; Gorbachev, Mikhail, 1, 2; Hale, Edward Everett, 1; Hamilton, Alexander, 1; Harrington, James, 2; Hearst, William Randolph, 2; Hughes, Richard, 1; Humphrey, Hubert H., 1; Huxley, Aldous, 14; Jackson, Andrew, 2; Johnson, Lady Bird, 1, 3; Johnson, Samuel, 129; Khrushchev, Nikita, 3; Kinnock, Neil, 5; Kissinger, Henry, 1; Lenin, Vladimir Ilyich, 2; Lincoln, Abraham, 1; Lippmann, Walter, 2; Livingstone, Ken, 1; Long, Huey, 1; McCarthy, Joseph (1909–57), 2; MacDonald, Ramsay, 1, 2; Macmillan, Harold, 1, 5; Mailer, Norman, 9; Metternich, 1; Morley, John, 2; Morley, Lord, 1; Morris, Charles, 1; Mottos and Slogans, 39; Muggeridge, Malcolm, 9; Nixon, Richard, 2, 3, 6, 7, 8, 11, 12, 13, 22, 34; O'Brien, Flann, 12; Owen, David, 1; Parnell, Charles Stewart, 1; Pitt the Younger, William, 1; Plunkitt, George Washington, 1; Profumo, John, 1; Quayle, Dan, 1, 2; Quinton, Sir John, 1; Qu Yuan, 3; Reagan, Ronald, 8, 11, 35; Roosevelt, Franklin D., 1, 2, 3, 30; Roosevelt, Theodore, 4, 5; Russell, Bertrand, 20, 57; Russell, Lord, 1; Shaw, George Bernard, 37; Sheridan, Richard Brinsley, 17; Stalin, Joseph, 1, 3; Stevenson, Adlai, 10; Stockdale, James B., 1; Swift, Jonathan, 20; Thatcher, Margaret, 1, 2, 4, 5, 8, 9; Thompson, Hunter S., 5; Truman, Harry S., 10; Voltaire, 49; Walpole, Sir Robert, 3; Waugh, Auberon, 2; Webster, John, 3; Whitehorn, Katharine, 6; Whitman, Walt, 43; Wilberforce, William, 2; Wilson, Harold, 1

Politics Acheson, Dean, 6; Adams, Franklin P., 1; Adams, Henry, 10, 11; Anonymous, 92; Arbuthnot, John, 3; Aristotle, 27, 29; Arnim-Boytzenburg, Adolf Heinrich von, 1; Baldwin, Stanley, 2, 11; Barker, Howard, 1; Bell, Martin, 1; Belloc, Hilaire, 17; Bell, Ronald, 1; Benn, Ernest, 1; Benn, Tony, 1; Berkeley, Bishop, 4; Berlin, Isaiah, 4; Bevan, Aneurin, 11; Bevin, Ernest, 3; Bierce, Ambrose, 45; Bismarck, Prince Otto von, 6, 10, 13, 19, 21; Blair, Tony, 5, 9; Bolingbroke, Henry St. John, 4; Brennan, William J., 3; Brittain, Vera, 5; Burke, Edmund, 1, 22, 37; Bush, George, 5, 7, 10, 16; Butler, Samuel (1835–1902), 33, 34; Byron, Lord, 73; Calhoun, John C., 3; Camus, Albert, 21; Carlyle, Thomas, 33; Chekhov, Anton, 1; Churchill, Winston, 13, 14, 26, 41, 70; Cleveland, Grover, 2; Clinton, Bill, 2, 7, 20; Connell, James, 2; Coolidge, Calvin, 5; Cranmer, Thomas, 1; Crossman, Richard, 2; Culbertson, Ely, 1; Cuomo, Mario, 1; Davis, Jefferson, 1; Disraeli, Benjamin, 12, 17, 36, 42; Eden, Anthony, 4; Eden, Clarissa, 1; Eisenhower, Dwight D., 16; Erhard, Ludwig, 1; Ford, Gerald, 5; Fox, Charles James, 2; Fox, Harrison W., Jr., 1, 8; Gaitskell, Dora, 1; Galbraith, J. K., 3, 7, 15; Galsworthy, John, 1; Gandhi, Mahatma, 7, 11; Gilbert, W. S., 14; Gladstone, William Ewart, 10; Glasgow, Ellen, 2; Gogarty, Oliver St. John, 2; Goldman, Emma, 4; Goldwater, Barry, 1; Gorbachev, Mikhail, 3, 5; Gore, Al, 1; Hailsham, Lord, 1; Harrison, William Henry, 2; Hayes, Rutherford B., 1; Healey, Denis, 3; Hearne, John, 1; Hegel, G. W. F., 3; Hitler, Adolf, 4; Hooker, Richard, 1; Howe, Louis McHenry, 1; Icke, David, 1; Jackson, Jesse, 1, 4; James, C. L. R., 11; Johnson, James Weldon, 2; Johnson, Lyndon Baines, 23; Johnson, Samuel, 110, 134; Joseph, Keith, 2; Kennedy, Robert, 4; Keynes, John Maynard, 14; Khrushchev, Nikita, 6; Kinnock, Neil, 3; Kirkpatrick, Jeane Jordan, 1; Kissinger, Henry, 3; La Bruyère, Jean de, 10; La Guardia, Fiorello, 2; Laurier, Wilfrid, 5, 6; Leacock, Stephen, 21; Lefèvre, Théo, 1; Le Guin, Ursula, 1; Long, Huey, 3; Lowell, Robert, 13; Machado de Assis, Joaquim Maria, 16; Mackintosh, James, 2; Major, John, 2; Manley, Michael, 1; Mann, Thomas, 9, 10; Mao Zedong, 20; Maura, Antonio, 3; Menon, V. K. Krishna, 1; Mill, John Stuart, 7; Mohamad, Mahathir bin, 1; Morgan, Edwin, 3; Morrow, Dwight Whitney, 2; Morton, Rogers, 1; Mosley, Oswald, 2; Mottos and Slogans, 8; Mountbatten, Lord, 4; Moyers, Bill, 1, 2; Mussolini, Benito, 13; Napoleon I, 9, 17, 31; Nixon, Richard, 14, 18, 19, 23, 33, 38; Nkomo, Joshua, 3; Nkrumah, Kwame, 2, 7; Ortega y Gasset, José, 27; Orwell, George, 26; Padmore, George, 1, 3, 4; Paine, Thomas, 6; Palmerston, Lord, 5; Pankhurst, Christabel, 5; Picasso, Pablo, 11; Powell, Enoch, 3; Priestley, J. B., 1; Quayle, Dan, 6, 7; Randolph, A. Philip, 1; Reagan, Ronald, 2, 43, 45; Retz, Cardinal de, 12; Richler, Mordecai, 1; Riney, Hal, 1; Rogers, Will, 5, 9; Roosevelt, Franklin D., 11, 13, 22, 39; Roosevelt, Theodore, 19; Roszak, Theodore, 9; Rusk, Dean, 1; Sanford, Charles, Jr., 4; Smith, Al, 2; Soros, George, 6; Stalin, Joseph, 10; Stanley, Edward Geoffrey Smith, 2; Stevenson, Adlai, 4; Stevenson, Robert Louis, 8; Taaffe, Eduard von, 1; Tocqueville, Alexis de, 1; Trotsky, Leon, 10; Tweed, Boss, 1; Updike, John, 15; Valéry, Paul, 8; Vidal, Gore, 8, 20; Waite, Terry, 2; Washington, George, 3; Wilson, Harold, 5; Wolfe, Tom, 4; Yeats, W. B., 13

Pollution Clarke, Gillian, 1; Cortez, Jayne, 1; Cousteau, Jacques, 2; Lewis, Drew, 1; Newspapers, 23; Summers, Lawrence H., 2; Udall, Stewart L., 2; Young, Brigham, 4

Pope, The Hobbes, Thomas, 17; Innocent III, 2, 3, 4; Leo X, 2; Martin IV, 1

Popularity Ant, Adam, 1; Bernstein, Leonard, 1; De Vries, Peter, 11; Halifax, George Savile, 2; Kennedy, John Fitzgerald, 38; Lennon, John, 9; Mizner, Wilson, 5, 7; Shakespeare, William, 39, 443; Washington, George, 1

Popular Music Anka, Paul, 2; Beefheart, Captain, 1; Burgess, Anthony, 1; Coker, Cheo Hodari, 1; Costello, Elvis, 2; D, Chuck, 1, 2; Diddley, Bo, 2; Donovan, 1; Gaye, Marvin, 1, 2; George, Nelson, 2; Gunn, Thom, 4; Harry, Deborah, 3; Jagger, Mick, 7; Leiber, Jerry, 2; Lennon, John, 12; MacInnes, Colin, 4; Mama Cass, 1; Marks, Johnny, 1; Marley, Bob, 7; Marsh, Richard, 2; Newman, Randy, 1; Pound, Ezra, 22; Prince, 1; Roth, David Lee, 1, 3; Schneider, Florian, 1; Shakespeare, William, 37; Simon, Paul, 5; Spector, Phil, 1; Swartley, Ariel, 1; Wexler, Jerry, 1; Yetnikoff, Walter, 1

Population Akhter, Farida, 1; Daniel, Samuel, 3; Heller, Joseph, 13; Malthus, Thomas, 1; Shapiro, Robert B., 1

Pornography Albee, Edward, 2; Barnes, Clive, 1; Coward, Noel, 15; Dworkin, Andrea, 4, 5; English, Deirdre, 1; Hefner, Hugh, 1; Lawrence, D. H., 34; Sontag, Susan, 17; Steinem, Gloria, 5; Steiner, George, 7

Possibility Browning, Robert, 49; Dostoyevsky, Fyodor, 2; Hallam, Arthur Henry, 14; Kennedy, Robert, 3; Sheridan, Richard Brinsley, 7

Posterity Addison, Joseph, 21; Broun, Heywood, 1; Butler, Samuel (1835–1902), 37; Hardy, Thomas, 17; Hatshepsut, 1; Horace, 49; Lamb, Charles, 5; Porchia, Antonio, 8; Roche, Boyle, 1; Weill, Kurt, 1

Poverty Agnew, Spiro T., 1; Bagehot, Walter, 12; Baldwin, James, 11; Behn, Aphra, 12; Bible, 334; Biko, Stephen, 5; Büchner, Georg, 10; Caird, Edward, 1; Caldwell, Erskine, 1; Chamfort, Nicolas, 13; Cleaver, Eldridge, 8; Cobbett, William, 2; Compton-Burnett, Ivy, 1; Confucius, 8; Cowper, William, 4; Davis,

Robert, 62; Burke, Edmund, 10; Carlyle, Thomas, 10; Charcot, Jean Martin, 1; Chesterton, G. K., 16, 53; cummings, e. e., 7; Darwin, Erasmus, 3; Davis, Bob, 1; Deng Xiaoping, 9; Disraeli, Benjamin, 46; Douglass, Frederick, 5; Ellis, Havelock, 3; Farmer, Fannie, 1; Goldsmith, Oliver, 8; Gyllenhammar, Pehr G., 1; Harvey-Jones, John, 3; Hawthorne, Nathaniel, 12; Humphrey, Hubert H., 3; Huxley, T. H., 15; Imparato, Nicholas, 1; Kennedy, John Fitzgerald, 18; Kettering, Charles, 1; Keynes, John Maynard, 1; King, Martin Luther, Jr., 15; Krugman, Paul, 3; Lenin, Vladimir Ilyich, 13; Lennon & McCartney, 12; Liyong, Taban Lo, 1; McLuhan, Marshall, 9; Pankhurst, Emmeline, 4; Reagan, Ronald, 16; Renan, Ernest, 9; Russell, Bertrand, 19; Stalin, Joseph, 14; Teller, Edward, 2; Whittier, John Greenleaf, 6; Winkler, Paul, 1

Promiscuity Davis, Bette, 4; Dibdin, Charles, 3; Doyle, Arthur Conan, 15; Lawrence, D. H., 12; Marlowe, Christopher, 25; Orton, Joe, 10; Raphael, Frederic, 1; Simenon, Georges, 2

Promises Arendt, Hannah, 4; Baden-Powell, Robert, 4; Beaumont & Fletcher, 16; Bible, 119, 138, 177, 192, 252, 265, 286, 404; Butler, Samuel (1612–80), 17; Henry III, 2; Hobbes, Thomas, 14; Johnson, Lyndon Baines, 3; Ogilvy, David, 1; Publilius Syrus, 7; Robeson, Paul, 2; Spenser, Edmund, 13; Swift, Jonathan, 30

Promotion Gilbert, W. S., 7; Halifax, George Savile, 1; Louis XIV, 6; Shakespeare, William, 384

Pronunciation Shaw, George Bernard, 121; Twain, Mark, 43

Proof La Fontaine, Jean de, 14; Mill, John Stuart, 19

Propaganda Byron, Lord, 61; Cornford, F. M., 2; Huxley, Aldous, 52; Joyce, William, 1; Lec, Stanislaw, 1; Manley, Michael, 2; Mao Zedong, 3; Moravia, Alberto, 1; Solzhenitsyn, Alexander, 11; Steiner, George, 6; Thatcher, Margaret, 17

Prophecy Bible, 41, 89, 93, 94, 95, 123, 198, 199, 200, 202, 203, 211, 213, 223, 349, 370, 373, 386, 444, 467, 474, 476, 477; Calderón de la Barca, Pedro, 6; Churchill, Winston, 23; Coleridge, Samuel Taylor, 16; Davis, Bette, 2; Disraeli, Benjamin, 15; Edward VIII, 2; Eliot, George, 16; Folk Verse, 12; Krugman, Paul, 6; MacArthur, Douglas, 5; Mead, Margaret, 6; Momaday, N. Scott, 3; Nostradamus, 1, 2; Pompadour, Madame de, 1; Shakespeare, William, 299, 409; Symonds, John Addington, 1; Tennyson, Alfred, 54, 67; Thatcher, Margaret, 15; Wellington, Duke of, 4; Weygand, Maxime, 1; William II, 3

Prose Churchill, Winston, 9; Little, A. G., 1; Maugham, Somerset, 37

Prostitution De Niro, Robert, 1; Heller, Joseph, 11; Tristan, Flora, 1

Protest Arendt, Hannah, 5; Mottos and Slogans, 16, 21; Newspapers, 8; Norton, Charles Eliot, 2; Odets, Clifford, 1; Pankhurst, Emmeline, 2; Powell, Adam Clayton, Jr., 5; Thompson, Hunter S., 6

Protestantism Brathwaite, Richard, 1; Disraeli, Benjamin, 22; Henry IV, 3; Luther, Martin, 3, 7; Mailer, Norman, 5; Mencken, H. L., 17

Proverbs Proverbs, 1–513

Provocation Pope, Alexander, 37

Prudence Belloc, Hilaire, 13; Butler, Samuel (1612–80), 24; Crowther, Geoffrey, 2; Dickens, Charles, 92, 93; Emerson, Ralph Waldo, 15; Folk Verse, 39; Mizner, Wilson, 3; Wentworth, Thomas, 1

Prudery Stendhal, 1

Psychiatry Adler, Alfred, 6; Asher, Richard, 1; Berenson, Bernard, 2; Bettelheim, Bruno, 2; Breggin, Peter R., 2, 3; Brown, Norman O., 2; Cicero, 5, 17; Frame, Janet, 1; Freud, Anna, 1, 3, 5; Freud, Sigmund, 1, 4, 5, 7, 9, 12, 13, 17, 18, 21, 29, 59; Fromm, Erich, 11; Gardner, John W., 3; Gellner, Ernest, 1; Goethe, Johann Wolfgang von, 2; Greer, Germaine, 12; H. D., 2; Horney, Karen, 6, 7, 10, 15; Klein, Melanie, 2, 6, 7, 8, 9; Kraus, Karl, 3; Laing, R. D., 2, 3, 4, 6, 9, 13, 14; Leary, Timothy, 6; Lindner, Robert, 1, 3; McLuhan, Marshall, 13; Merleau-Ponty, Maurice, 7, 8, 11, 15; Miller, Henry, 8; Mingus, Charles, 3; Mitchell, Alexander, 1; Muir, Edwin, 2; Nakhla, Fayed, 1; Piaget, Jean, 4; Pirsig, Robert T., 1; Proverbs, Modern, 6, 26, 28; Reich, Wilhelm, 4, 5, 6, 8; Sartre, Jean-Paul, 26; Stockwood, Mervyn, 1; Storr, Anthony, 1; Szasz, Thomas, 1, 2, 3, 4, 12, 17; Williams, Tennessee, 19; Winnicott, Donald W., 1; Wittgenstein, Ludwig, 17; Wodehouse, P. G., 21

Psychology Auden, W. H., 2, 19; Beerbohm, Max, 24; Berne, Eric, 2; Chesterton, G. K., 54; Connell, James, 1; Dewey, John, 16, 17, 20; Ebbinghaus, Hermann, 1; Erikson, Erik, 1; Foucault, Michel, 4; Freud, Sigmund, 10, 11, 19, 20, 24, 28, 33, 34, 35, 36, 37, 57, 61; Fromm, Erich, 15; James, William, 2, 16, 19, 21; Jung, Carl Gustav, 12, 19, 22; Kierkegaard, Søren, 11, 12, 14; Koffka, Kurt, 1; Leary, Timothy, 2, 4, 8; Maslow, Abraham, 3; Maugham, Somerset, 31; Medawar, Peter, 3; Merleau-Ponty, Maurice, 9, 10; Moore, Marianne, 1; Nietzsche, Friedrich Wilhelm, 34; Piaget, Jean, 3; Proverbs, Modern, 5; Quine, Willard V., 4; Sartre, Jean-Paul, 10, 33; Sontag, Susan, 13; Storr, Anthony, 4; Szasz, Thomas, 11; Townsend, Robert, 15; Valéry, Paul, 9; Van Buren, Abigail, 1; Vidal, Gore, 6; Voltaire, 6; Watson, John B., 1; Wittgenstein, Ludwig, 18

Public Carlyle, Thomas, 20; Cohn, Harry, 1; Hazlitt, William, 22; Northcliffe, Lord, 2; Vanderbilt, William Henry, 2; Weill, Kurt, 3

Publishing Acland, Richard, 1; Barrie, J. M., 4; Byron, Lord, 84; Campbell, Thomas, 10; Caxton, William, 1; Chaucer, Geoffrey, 3; Connolly, Cyril, 3; Horace, 10; Knopf, Alfred A., 1; Montherlant, Henri de, 1; Pauli, Wolfgang, 1; Soyinka, Wole, 13

Punctuality Haliburton, Thomas Chandler, 2; Louis XVIII, 2; Mayakovsky, Vladimir, 7; Mitford, Nancy, 1; Monroe, Marilyn, 9; Waugh, Evelyn, 35

Punishment Arnold, Thomas, 1; Bentham, Jeremy, 3; Bible, 118, 126, 174, 221, 457; Brennan, William J., 2; Bunyan, John, 7; Byron, Lord, 14; Carey, Michael S., 1; Coleridge, Samuel Taylor, 47; Cook, Eliza, 1; Cooper, James Fenimore, 12; Cranmer, Thomas, 3; Darrow, Clarence, 4; Foucault, Michel, 6; Fry, Elizabeth, 2; Gilbert, W. S., 23, 32; Hood, Thomas, 11; Horace, 44; Howe, Edgar Watson, 2; Johnson, Samuel, 32; Justin Martyr, Saint, 1; Kipling, Rudyard, 16; Lawrence, D. H., 18; Luther, Martin, 5; Russell, Lord, 4; Shakespeare, William, 427; Vidal, Gore, 19; Wolf, L. J., 1; Yeo, George, 2

Puns Austen, Jane, 21; Burke, Johnny, 2; Dennis, John, 1; Fry, Christopher, 7; Herford, Oliver, 1; Hood, Thomas, 4; Joyce, James, 17, 21; Mackenzie, Compton, 1; Perelman, S. J., 8; Tynan, Kenneth, 6; Vidal, Gore, 21; Wallach, Eli, 1

Puritanism Austin, Mary, 7; Bradford, William, 4; Butler, Samuel (1612–80), 10; Hume, David, 34; Jordan, Thomas, 1; Lawrence, D. H., 17; Macaulay, Thomas Babington, 19; Mencken, H. L., 4; Robinson, Edwin Arlington, 4

Purity Bible, 499; Campion, Thomas, 1, 3; Dante Alighieri, 8; Khomeini, Ruhollah, 1; Shakespeare, William, 666; Tennyson, Alfred, 59

Purpose Allen, James, 1; Aristotle, 19; Carroll, Lewis, 16; Jackson, Michael, 2; Leonard, Graham, 1; Raglan, Lord, 1; Schiller, Friedrich von, 20; Shakespeare, William, 696; White, William Allen, 1

Quotations Burgess, Gelett, 1; Chamfort, Nicolas, 9; Churchill, Winston, 43; de Botton, Alain, 1; France, Anatole, 11; Johnson, Samuel, 20, 81; Montague, C. E., 1; Saki, 18; Sayers, Dorothy L., 3; Talmud, 1; Waugh, Evelyn, 28; Wilde, Oscar, 6

Race Alegre, Costa, 1; Anonymous, 55; Archer, John Richard, 1; Baldwin, James, 15, 20, 25; Baraka, Imamu Amiri, 13; Campbell, Naomi, 3; Césaire, Aimé, 3; Cosby, Bill, 4; Cullen, Countee, 4; Du Bois, W. E. B., 13; Forster, E. M., 8; Garvey, Marcus, 5; Gillespie, Dizzy, 2; Goldberg, Whoopi, 1; Gregory, Dick, 5; Harding, Vincent, 1; Holiday, Billie, 5; Hughes, Langston, 8, 16; Jackson, Jesse, 11; Killens, John Oliver, 3; McWilliams, Carey, 1; Malcolm X, 9, 12, 17; Meredith, James, 2; Morrison, Toni, 11, 12, 29; Mottos and Slogans, 28; Muhammad, Elijah, 1;

Pickens, William, 2; Powell, Colin, 1; Shange, Ntozake, 7; Terrell, Mary Church, 1; Washington, Booker T., 10; Wideman, John Edgar, 1; Winfrey, Oprah, 3; Wonder, Stevie, 3; Young, Whitney M., Jr., 2

Racism Abrahams, Peter, 3; Abse, Dannie, 1; Aggrey, James Emman Kwegyir, 2, 3; Anderson, Marian, 1; Angelou, Maya, 2; Baldwin, James, 22; Benedict, Ruth, 4; Benjamin, Judah, 2; Beveridge, Albert J., 1; Bryson, Bill, 10; Collins, Merle, 1; Constitution of the United States, 7; Cooper, James Fenimore, 3; Covey, Donna, 1; cummings, e. e., 23; Davis, Sammy, Jr., 1; Du Bois, W. E. B., 1, 6, 16; Dumas, Henry, 2; Ellison, Ralph, 5; Fanon, Frantz, 6; Gregory, Dick, 2, 3, 4, 6; Hansberry, Lorraine, 2; Herzl, Theodor, 7; Himes, Chester, 1; Hughes, Langston, 4; Hurston, Zora Neale, 17; Jackson, Jesse, 12; Johnson, Paul, 1; Kaunda, Kenneth David, 5; Kennedy, Florynce R., 4; Kennedy, John Fitzgerald, 11; King, Don, 1; King, Martin Luther, Jr., 3, 28; Kingston, Maxine Hong, 2; Larsen, Nella, 1; Lawrence, George, 2; Lowell, Robert, 11; McKay, Claude, 1; McKinley, William, 2; McMillan, Terry, 5; Malcolm X, 13; Mandela, Nelson, 4; Marshall, Thurgood, 3; Mather, Cotton, 1; Mencken, H. L., 16; Mohamad, Mahathir bin, 2; Mosley, Walter, 7; Naylor, Gloria, 2; Newspapers, 12; Norton, Eleanor Holmes, 2; Oppenheimer, Harry, 1; Parker, Dorothy, 7; Remond, Charles Lenox, 2; Rustin, Bayard, 2; Smith, Ian, 1; Thomas, Clarence, 1; Twain, Mark, 38; Walker, Alice, 7; Wallace, George, 1; Washington, Booker T., 1

Radicalism Bierce, Ambrose, 44; Mphahlele, Es'kia, 2; Twain, Mark, 27

Rape Adler, Freda, 2; Cambridge Rape Crisis Centre, 1; Griffin, Susan, 1; Ovid, 2

Rationalism Deane, Seamus, 2

Reading Addison, Joseph, 11; Bacon, Francis (1561–1626), 64; Balfour, Arthur, 5; Baudelaire, Charles, 11; Berryman, John, 10; Chekhov, Anton, 3; Descartes, René, 9; Flaubert, Gustave, 3; Ford, Richard, 2; Franklin, Benjamin, 32; Greene, Graham, 2; Hamerton, Philip Gilbert, 1; Hemingway, Ernest, 2; James, William, 1; Johnson, Samuel, 72; Joyce, James, 12; Keillor, Garrison, 13; Kraus, Karl, 15; Lamb, Charles, 20; Manguel, Alberto, 2; Mao Zedong, 12; Mitford, Nancy, 3; Nabokov, Vladimir, 14; O'Connor, Flannery, 2; Russell, Bertrand, 46; Shakespeare, William, 9; Shange, Ntozake, 6; Snyder, Gary, 10; Steele, Richard, 6; Unamuno y Jugo, Miguel de, 4; White, E. B., 9

Realism Doyle, Roddy, 6; Fields, W. C., 6; France, Anatole, 4; Illich, Ivan, 3; Novalis, 2; Parker, Dorothy, 11, 12; Shakespeare, William, 585; Washington, Booker T., 7

Reality Angelus Silesius, 1; Barthes, Roland, 1; Bohm, David, 1; Brookner, Anita, 3; Calderón de la Barca, Pedro, 4; Dick, Philip K., 2; Dürrenmatt, Friedrich, 1; Eliot, T. S., 14; Ellison, Ralph, 6; Fichte, Johann, 2; Fitzgerald, F. Scott, 24; Fry, Christopher, 4; James, William, 4; Jiménez, Juan Ramón, 4; Keller, Helen, 6; Kipling, Rudyard, 63; Koestler, Arthur, 5; L'Estrange, Roger, 1; Marechera, Dambudzo, 1; Miller, Henry, 26; Minnelli, Liza, 1; Mosley, Walter, 5; Murdoch, Iris, 13; Peirce, C. S., 4; Pinter, Harold, 7; Pirandello, Luigi, 14; Sartre, Jean-Paul, 23; Shakespeare, William, 385; Stevens, Wallace, 30; Vitruvius, Marcus, 1; Winterson, Jeanette, 4; Xu Yunuo, 1; Zhuangzi, 9

Reason Bacon, Roger, 2; Beckett, Samuel, 9; Bettelheim, Bruno, 1; Burke, Edmund, 7; Calderón de la Barca, Pedro, 2; Chesterton, G. K., 28; Collins, Wilkie, 1; Connolly, Cyril, 22; Crescas, Hasdai ben Abraham, 1; Engels, Friedrich, 3; Hegel, G. W. F., 7, 9, 19, 21; Horney, Karen, 9; Hume, David, 16, 18, 20, 22; James, William, 17; Johnson, Lyndon Baines, 26; Kyd, Thomas, 1; Lessing, Gotthold Ephraim, 1; Marinetti, Filippo Tommaso, 5; Paisley, Ian, 2; Pascal, Blaise, 13; Pope, Alexander, 40; Reid, Thomas, 3; Rochester, 2nd Earl of, 2; Schell, Jonathan, 2; Voltaire, 38

Rebellion Anglo-Saxon Chronicle, 1; Bible, 92; Birrell, Augustine, 2; Brown, John, 6; Byron, Lord, 95; Camus, Albert, 19, 23, 26; Carlos I, Juan, 1; Castlereagh, Lord, 2; Djilas, Milovan, 1; Fairfield, John, 1; Fawkes, Guy, 2; Gunn, Thom, 6; James II, 3; Jefferson, Thomas, 15; King, Martin Luther, Jr., 27; Mandela, Nelson, 16; Parkes, Francis Ernest Kobina, 1; Parks, Rosa, 1; Paul, Leslie, 1; Pearse, Patrick, 2, 3; Seeckt, Hans von, 1; Steinem, Gloria, 15; Vesey, Denmark, 1; Wilde, Oscar, 15

Recession Callaghan, Jim, 3; Friedman, Milton, 3; Johnson, Richard W., 1, 2, 3, 4, 5; Pankin, Boris, 1; Reagan, Ronald, 42

Reformation, The Saki, 9

Regret Bible, 256, 340, 440; Book of Common Prayer, 14; Cowper, William, 18; Drummond, William, 3; Du Mu, 1; Hallam, Arthur Henry, 16; Landon, Letitia Elizabeth, 1, 3; Li Shangyin, 1; Longfellow, Henry Wadsworth, 20; Machado de Assis, Joaquim Maria, 11; Marquis, Don, 4; Montrose, Percy, 2; Moore, G. E., 3; Nash, Ogden, 5; Patil, Chandrashekhara, 1; Porter, Cole, 7; Reed, Lou, 2; Robinson, Edwin Arlington, 7; Rousseau, Jean-Jacques, 6; Scott, Sir Walter, 15; Shakespeare, William, 284, 307, 417, 471, 502, 519, 524, 570; Stowe, Harriet Beecher, 3; Suetonius, 3; Vaucaire, Michel, 1; Whittier, John Greenleaf, 3; Wordsworth, William, 67

Regulation Beckett, Terence, 1; Lloyd, Henry Demarest, 1

Relationships Austen, Jane, 7; Brodsky, Joseph, 1; Churchill, Winston, 33; Dietrich, Marlene, 1; Eliot, George, 12; Forché, Carolyn, 3; Forster, E. M., 14; Gibran, Kahlil, 8; Goldsmith, Oliver, 20; Hay, John, 1; Hillman, James, 2; Ionesco, Eugène, 7; Kanter, Rosabeth Moss, 4; Proust, Marcel, 10; Simon, Neil, 11, 12; Strindberg, August, 2; Swift, Jonathan, 24; Trompenaars, Fons, 1; Updike, John, 6

Relatives Dickens, Charles, 18

Religion Ali, Muhammad, 15; Amis, Kingsley, 5; Armstrong, Louis, 10; Arnold, Matthew, 21; Auster, Paul, 7; Bacon, Francis (1561–1626), 78; Bambara, Toni Cade, 1; Bancroft, George, 2; Barnes, Julian, 2; Barrie, J. M., 16; Baxter, Richard, 1; Beckford, William, 1; Behan, Brendan, 17; Belloc, Hilaire, 2; Bernard of Clairvaux, Saint, 1; Bible, 6, 149, 210, 224, 356, 392, 395, 465; Blake, William, 14; Bliss, Philip Paul, 1; Brontë, Charlotte, 7; Browne, Thomas, 36; Bruce, Lenny, 1; Buber, Martin, 5; Burbank, Luther, 1, 2, 5; Burroughs, William S., 2; Burton, Robert, 21; Bushnell, Horace, 1; Butler, Joseph, 5; Butler, Samuel (1612–80), 22; Butler, Samuel (1835–1902), 6; Calvin, John, 1; Cervantes, Miguel de, 31; Chaplin, Charlie, 4; Charles II, 10; Chesterfield, Lord, 4, 20; Chesterton, G. K., 3, 31; Colton, Charles, 5; Corso, Gregory, 2; Dalai Lama, 1, 9; Diderot, Denis, 3, 12; Dix, Gregory, 1; Ducas, 1; Durant, Will, 12; Eco, Umberto, 10; Eddy, Mary Baker, 1, 3; Ellis, Havelock, 2; Emerson, Ralph Waldo, 21; Erasmus, Desiderius, 6; Feuerbach, Ludwig Andreas, 1; Fielding, Henry, 17; Fortunatus, 1; Franco, Francisco, 5; Freud, Sigmund, 31, 40, 41, 43, 44, 45, 46, 48, 54, 55; Fry, Christopher, 5; Gambetta, Léon, 1; Goldsmith, Oliver, 34; Greene, Graham, 1; Hare, David, 2; Hölderlin, Friedrich, 1; Huxley, Aldous, 17; Hypatia, 3; Inge, William Ralph, 2, 7; Jaurès, Jean, 2; Jerrold, Douglas, 2; John of Lancaster, 1; Johnson, Samuel, 160; John XXII, 1; Kabbani, Rana, 4; Keillor, Garrison, 8; Kempe, Margery, 1; King, Martin Luther, Jr., 18; Krishnamurti, Jiddu, 2; Kumin, Maxine, 1; Larsen, Nella, 2; Lowell, Robert, 8; Lucretius, 2; Machado, Antonio, 4; Mackenzie, Compton, 5, 8; Margaret of Valois, 1; Marlowe, Christopher, 26; Marx, Karl, 9, 12; Matthiessen, Peter, 11; Melbourne, Lord, 1; Melville, Herman, 20; Mencken, H. L., 11; Montesquieu, 5; Morley, John, 3; Mottos and Slogans, 18; Newman, John Henry, 2; Nietzsche, Friedrich Wilhelm, 29; O'Casey, Sean, 5; Parnell, Thomas, 1; Pascal, Blaise, 8; Peacock, Thomas Love, 6; Penn, William, 1; Plato, 23; Potter, Dennis, 1; Prince, Mary, 1; Protagoras, 1; Radhakrishnan, Sarvepalli, 1, 3, 4, 6; Renan, Ernest, 5; Rockefeller, Nelson A., 1; Roth, Philip, 6; Rushdie, Salman, 3, 4, 9; Sacks, Jonathan, 9; Sancho, Ignatius, 1; Selden, John, 4; Shaw, George Bernard, 15, 36; Smith, Joseph, 1, 2; Teresa of Ávila, Saint, 6; Theroux, Paul, 13; Tillich, Paul, 1, 2, 3, 5, 6; Toynbee, Arnold, 2, 4; Tutu, Desmond, 8; Updike, John, 1; Van Buren, Abigail, 2; Van der Post, Laurens, 2; Walker, Alice, 20; Wantling, William, 1; Waugh, Evelyn, 15, 30; Webb, Beatrice, 1; Wesley, John, 2; West, Nathanael, 5; Whitman, Walt, 12; Wilcox, Ella Wheeler, 4; Wollaston, William, 1; Xenophanes, 1

Religious Leaders Bacon, Francis (1561–1626), 18; Bible, 235; Disraeli, Benjamin, 55; Durcan, Paul, 3; Folk Verse, 51; Fox, George, 2; Moore, George, 6; Otto of Freising, 1; Sacks, Jonathan, 8; Swift, Jonathan, 43; Tennyson, Alfred, 42

Remedies Amiel, Henri Frédéric, 2; Butler, Samuel (1612–80), 1; Chekhov, Anton, 9; Cooper, Astley, 3; Corneille, Pierre, 1; Disraeli, Benjamin, 21; du Bartas, Guillaume, 7; Emerson, Ralph Waldo, 50; Hippocrates, 1; Jefferson, Thomas, 8, 10; Leonardo da Vinci, 10; Mangipan, Theodore, 1; Molière, 9; Moore, J. Earle, 1; Pindar, 1; Proverbs, 446; Shakespeare, William, 462; Sigerist, Henry E., 4

Renunciation Bunyan, John, 16; Goethe, Johann Wolfgang von, 16; Lorenz, Konrad, 7

Repartee Beecher, Henry Ward, 6; Brien, Alan, 2; Broun, Heywood, 3; Charles II, 11; Cook, Peter, 3; Diderot, Denis, 6; Dylan, Bob, 22; Grant, Cary, 2; Hewart, Gordon, 2; Holberg, Ludvig, 1; Kinnock, Neil, 2; Menzies, Robert, 1, 2; Parker, Dorothy, 5, 48; Shakespeare, William, 249; Shaw, George Bernard, 5; Smith, F. E., 3, 5; Toscanini, Arturo, 7; Twain, Mark, 61; Wilde, Oscar, 8

Republics Mariana, Juan de, 1; Martínez de la Mata, Don, 1; Tocqueville, Alexis de, 2

Republicans Burchard, Samuel Dickinson, 1; McLaurin, A. J., 1

Reputation Anne, Princess, 2; Bacon, Francis (1561–1626), 81, 88; Beaumont, Francis, 9; Beaverbrook, Max Aitken, Lord, 3; Benn, Tony, 4; Bergman, Ingrid, 2; Buffett, Warren, 6; Bunner, Henry Cuyler, 1; Cervantes, Miguel de, 39; Cockburn, Catherine, 1; Colette, 3; Dickens, Charles, 76; Du Fu, 2; Dulles, John Foster, 1; Eames, Emma, 1; Henry VIII, 3; Horace, 52; Keynes, John Maynard, 11; Laurier, Wilfrid, 2; Marx, Groucho, 22; Mitchell, Margaret, 3; Pope, Alexander, 1; Publilius Syrus, 1; Shakespeare, William, 481, 483, 508; Shaw, George Bernard, 96; Soros, George, 3; Washington, George, 5; Webster, Daniel, 7; West, Mae, 28

Research Aldrich, Thomas Bailey, 1; Anderson, Poul, 1; Aristotle, 2; Bernard, Claude, 1; Dalton, John, 1; Darwin, Charles, 2; Darwin, Erasmus, 4; Donatus, Aelius, 1; Einstein, Albert, 51, 57; Fischer, Martin H., 5, 17; Hurston, Zora Neale, 8; Jowett, Benjamin, 5; Morton, J. C., 1; Pattison, Mark, 1; Pavlov, Ivan Petrovich, 2; Routh, Martin Joseph, 1; Rutherford, Ernest, 1; Schick, Béla, 2, 5; Smith, Theobald, 1; Veblen, Thorstein Bunde, 2; Whitehead, A. N., 12

Resentment Confucius, 7; Kirstein, Lincoln, 2; Newman, John Henry, 3

Respect Baudelaire, Charles, 9; Bible, 478; Harper, Frances E. W., 3; Koran, 28; Maslow, Abraham, 4; Mays, Benjamin E., 1; Pascal, Blaise, 2; Plutarch, 27; Rand, Ayn, 6; Salinger, J. D., 6; Twain, Mark, 21; Voltaire, 37

Respectability Burns, Robert, 40; Dos Passos, John, 11; Graham, Martha, 3; Huston, John, 2; Rogers, Will, 15; Shaw, George Bernard, 93

Responsibility Armstrong, Michael, 4; Bonhoeffer, Dietrich, 5; Churchill, Winston, 10; Clinton, Hillary, 3; Doctorow, E. L., 1; Gladstone, William Ewart, 4; Golding, William, 4; Iacocca, Lee, 8; John XXIII, 4; Kanter, Rosabeth Moss, 1; Keenan, Brian, 1; Kennedy, John Fitzgerald, 40; Mandelstam, Nadezhda, 1; Morita Akio, 4; Murdoch, Iris, 2; Newman, John Henry, 1; Saint-Exupéry, Antoine de, 5; Shakespeare, William, 272; Sieff, Marcus, 2; Tennyson, Alfred, 16; Yeats, W. B., 25

Rest Bible, 106; Coleridge, Samuel Taylor, 65; Shakespeare, William, 81; Shaw, George Bernard, 19

Restaurants Kaufman, George S., 3; Raphael, Frederic, 2

Results Hesiod, 5

Retribution Bible, 150, 208, 218, 390, 439, 446; Child, Lydia Maria, 4; Euripides, 13; Geddes, Eric, 1; Hammurabi, 1; La Rochefoucauld, François, 3; Mussorgsky, Modest, 1; Shakespeare, William, 608, 618

Return Armah, Ayi Kwei, 1; Scott, Sir Walter, 25; Southey, Robert, 9

Revenge Ayckbourn, Alan, 3; Bacon, Francis (1561–1626), 55, 56; Bible, 81; Byron, Lord, 43; Charles V, 5; Cowper, William, 2; Cyrano de Bergerac, Savinien, 1; Hazlewood, Lee, 1; Juvenal, 18; Kennedy, Joseph, 1; Mary, Queen of Scots, 2; Maurras, Charles, 1; Milton, John, 82; Shakespeare, William, 341, 711, 712; Toussaint L'Ouverture, 1; Vanderbilt, Cornelius, 1; Whittier, John Greenleaf, 5

Revolution Aristotle, 30; Baldwin, Stanley, 3; Bloch, Marc, 1; Bo Yang, 1; Büchner, Georg, 1, 2, 11; Cabellero, Francisco Largo, 1; Carlyle, Thomas, 39; Channing, William Ellery, 2; Conrad, Joseph, 13; cummings, e. e., 15; Deng Xiaoping, 3; Douglas, William Orville, 2; Fonda, Jane, 1; Golding, William, 2; Guevara, Che, 1, 2; Huxley, Aldous, 9, 25; Ibárruri, Dolores, 5; Khrushchev, Nikita, 5, 11; Lawrence, D. H., 37; Mao Zedong, 5, 23, 24, 35; Mirabeau, Comte de, 1; Mottos and Slogans, 22; Nasser, Gamal Abdel, 6; Newspapers, 14; Nichols, Grace, 1; Nkrumah, Kwame, 1; Ortega y Gasset, José, 24; Osborne, John, 6; Perón, Juan Domingo, 2; Pestalozzi, Johann Heinrich, 7; Phillips, Wendell, 3, 4; Pi y Margall, Francisco, 2; Richelieu, Cardinal, 3; Rubin, Jerry, 1; Sankara, Thomas, 1; Schama, Simon, 1; Seale, Bobby, 2; Stalin, Joseph, 4; Trotsky, Leon, 2, 4, 5; Weiss, Peter, 2; Welch, Jack, 7; Winstanley, Gerrard, 2, 3; Wolf, Christa, 1; Wriston, Walter B., 4; Yang Ping, 1

Reward Austin, Mary, 8; Bible, 99; Galbraith, J. K., 4; Handy, Charles, 5; Loesser, Frank, 3

Rhetoric Butler, Samuel (1612–80), 4; Johnson, Samuel, 104; Sobukwe, Robert Mangaliso, 1

Ridicule Renard, Jules, 10; Scott, Sir Walter, 14

Right Faber, Frederick William, 1; Pickens, William, 1; Pliny the Younger, 3; Thurber, James, 17; Twain, Mark, 5

Righteousness Arnold, Matthew, 22; Bevan, Aneurin, 10; Bible, 243, 473; Chesterton, G. K., 51; Hammarskjöld, Dag, 2; La Chaussée, Nivelle de, 1; Orton, Joe, 4; Zhanguo Ce, 1

Ripostes Diogenes, 4; Disraeli, Benjamin, 63; Goethe, Johann Wolfgang von, 18; Hearst, William Randolph, 1; Milligan, Spike, 10; Whistler, James Abbott McNeill, 3, 15, 18; Wilson, Harriette, 1

Ritual Koran, 4

Rivers Burns, Robert, 7; Douglas, William, 2; Hammerstein, Oscar, II, 7; Joyce, James, 16; Spenser, Edmund, 1; Su Dongpo, 1; Su Xiaokang, 1

Rock Music Anonymous, 57; Cobain, Kurt, 3; Costello, Elvis, 3; Dury, Ian, 1; Dylan, Bob, 24; Hell, Richard, 1; Hynde, Chrissie, 1; Jagger, Mick, 1; Jones, Mablen, 1; Kaye, Lenny, 1; Lennon, John, 1, 10; Little Richard, 2; McLaren, Malcolm, 1; Mitchell, Joni, 4; Morrison, Jim, 1; Morrison, Van, 1; Morrissey, 2; Newspapers, 32; Reed, Lou, 3; Roth, David Lee, 2; Sinatra, Frank, 2; Springsteen, Bruce, 1; Stipe, Michael, 1; Troup, Bobby, 1; Vicious, Sid, 1; Waters, Muddy, 1

Romance Betjeman, John, 5; Blackmore, R. D., 2; Jones, David, 3; Lennon & McCartney, 18; Ouida, 3; Tennyson, Alfred, 60

Romanticism Mailer, Norman, 27; Stendhal, 4

Rome Augustus, 1; Byron, Lord, 35; Cavour, Camillo Benso, 2; Cervantes, Miguel de, 45; Otto III, 1; Plutarch, 29; Shakespeare, William, 7

Royalty Alexandra, Empress, 1; Amin, Idi, 1; Anonymous, 5, 6, 33, 79, 84; Armstrong, Louis, 3; Bagehot, Walter, 4, 9; Bentley, Edmund Clerihew, 5; Bierce, Ambrose, 31; Boleyn, Anne, 1; Brinton, Thomas, 1; Burke, Edmund, 12; Carey, Robert, 1; Catherine the Great, 3, 4; Charles I, 1; Charles II, 4; Charles, Prince, 1, 11; Charles X, 1; Defoe, Daniel, 13; Edward VII, 1; Edward VIII, 1, 9; Elizabeth I, 2, 9, 10, 12, 13, 16, 18; Elizabeth II, 1, 2, 4; Evelyn, John, 3, 5; Frederick II (1712–86), 4, 7; George IV, 2; George VI, 2; Gray, Lord Patrick, 1; Henry VIII, 1, 4, 5, 6; Hentzner, Paul, 1; James I, 1; Jefferson, Thomas, 29; John of Gaunt, 1; Johnson, Samuel, 85; Landor, Walter Savage, 4; Langton, Thomas, 1; Louis XIV, 7; Marlowe, Christopher, 22; Milne, A. A., 5; More, Thomas, 4; Mountbatten, Lord, 2; Nairne, Carolina, 1, 2; Nicholas II, 1; Orléans, Duchess of, 1; Pegler, Westbrook, 1; Pepys, Samuel, 2, 3; Richard, Duke of York, 1; Richelieu, Cardinal,

Michael, 1, 2, 3, 4, 5; McCaig, Norman, 9; McGonagall, William, 1; Morgan, Edwin, 2; Nairn, Tom, 1, 3; Ramsay, Allan, 1

Sculpture Bourgeois, Louise, 3; Goncharova, Natalia, 1; Hepworth, Barbara, 1; Hirschfeld, Al, 2; Jáuregui, Juan de, 1; Moore, Henry, 1, 2; Plomer, William, 5; Shaw, George Bernard, 98

Sea Carson, Rachel, 5; Chopin, Kate, 1; Coleridge, Samuel Taylor, 40, 41, 42; Conrad, Joseph, 2; Crane, Stephen, 4, 5; Flecker, James Elroy, 1, 2; Hardy, Thomas, 20; Jiménez, Juan Ramón, 3; Johnson, Samuel, 133; Joyce, James, 32; Kingston, Maxine Hong, 1; Lowell, Robert, 10, 22, 24; Masefield, John, 1, 2, 4; Michelet, Jules, 2; Pound, Ezra, 21; Procter, Bryan Waller, 1, 2; Proulx, E. Annie, 2; Radcliffe, Ann, 1; Rimbaud, Arthur, 6; Sargent, Epes, 1; Synge, J. M., 1; Xenophon, 1; Yeats, W. B., 53

Seasons Blake, William, 38; Hood, Thomas, 9; Keats, John (1795–1821), 76, 77; Loesser, Frank, 2; Shelley, Percy Bysshe, 8, 9; Swinburne, Algernon Charles, 4; Verlaine, Paul, 3

Secrecy Bible, 456; Billings, Josh, 1; Cervantes, Miguel de, 11, 48; Colman, George, 1; Congreve, William, 5; Crabbe, George, 3; DeLillo, Don, 1; Dickens, Charles, 81; Dryden, John, 36; Franklin, Benjamin, 23; Franks, Oliver, 1; Kipling, Rudyard, 43; Pirandello, Luigi, 7; Townsend, Robert, 8

Seduction Byron, Lord, 42; Homer, 9; Joyce, James, 38; Marvell, Andrew, 12; Muir, Frank, 6; Perelman, S. J., 5; Pushkin, Alexander, 2; Shakespeare, William, 529

Self Browne, Thomas, 15; Browning, Robert, 52; Emerson, Ralph Waldo, 28; Fichte, Johann, 4; Fitzgerald, F. Scott, 28; Hammett, Dashiell, 5; Keats, John (1795–1821), 65; Kierkegaard, Søren, 17; Lamming, George, 4; Montaigne, Michel de, 18; Montale, Eugenio, 1; Ortega y Gasset, José, 3; Rimbaud, Arthur, 2; Shaw, George Bernard, 65; Strindberg, August, 4; Theobald, Lewis, 1; Tyson, Mike, 2; Whitman, Walt, 30; Whittemore, Reed, 1

Self-Confidence al-Fayed, Mohamed, 1; Barrie, J. M., 6; Becker, Boris, 1; Bethune, Mary McLeod, 3; Bristow, Alan, 1; Butler, Samuel (1835–1902), 14; Dulles, John Foster, 6; Huxley, Aldous, 47; Keats, John (1795–1821), 38; Melbourne, Lord, 4; Napoleon I, 14; Shakespeare, William, 415, 418; Temple, William, 3; Trump, Donald, 1; Webb, Beatrice, 2; West, Mae, 25; Westwood, Vivienne, 1

Self-Control Darwin, Charles, 11; Herbert, George, 15; Koestler, Arthur, 2; Massinger, Philip, 2; Pestalozzi, Johann Heinrich, 8; Pinero, Arthur, 2; Pope, Walter, 1; Powell, Colin, 5

Self-Denial Shaw, George Bernard, 64

Self-Help Aesop, 1; La Fontaine, Jean de, 1; Pestalozzi, Johann Heinrich, 10

Self-Interest Angelou, Maya, 4; Cervantes, Miguel de, 25; De Vries, Peter, 6; Hazlitt, William, 6; Kingsmill, Hugh, 1; Laozi, 17; La Rochefoucauld, François, 9, 19, 20; Machiavelli, Niccolò, 1; Milton, John, 75; Pope, Alexander, 59; Proverbs, Modern, 18; Shakespeare, William, 466; Shaw, George Bernard, 58; Smith, Adam, 4; Toynbee, Arnold, 1; Walker, Alice, 19; Wallace, Lew, 2

Selfishness Bickerstaffe, Isaac, 2; Bierce, Ambrose, 47; Blake, William, 11, 16; Eliot, George, 9; Emerson, Ralph Waldo, 53; La Fontaine, Jean de, 11; Warren, Earl, 1

Self-Knowledge Adams, John Quincy, 3; Ammons, A. R., 1; Arnold, Matthew, 9; Auden, W. H., 21; Bacon, Francis (1561–1626), 79; Ball, Lucille, 2; Behan, Brendan, 15; Browne, Thomas, 27; Burns, Robert, 47; Carver, Raymond, 5, 8; Confucius, 29, 30; Connolly, Cyril, 9; Cormac mac Airt, 1; De Gaulle, Charles, 10; Dillard, Annie, 6; Donne, John, 11; Du Bois, W. E. B., 17; Garvey, Marcus, 1, 2, 7; Gautier, Théophile, 2; Goethe, Johann Wolfgang von, 17, 30, 33; Golden, Marita, 8; Gracián, Baltasar, 2; Green, Al, 1; Heaney, Seamus, 5; Huxley, Aldous, 57; Jaspers, Karl, 3; King, Stephen, 3; Lerner, Alan Jay, 12; Liyong, Taban Lo, 3; McCaig, Norman, 11; McCarthy, Mary, 8; Mandelstam, Osip, 8; Marshall, Paule, 4; Marx, Groucho, 18; Maxwell, Robert, 2; Merleau-Ponty, Maurice, 6; Molière, 15; Pagnol, Marcel, 1; Plutarch, 3; Pope, Alexander, 27, 28, 32; Shakespeare, William, 50, 198, 239, 441; Shapiro, Karl, 1; Soyinka, Wole, 2; Thales, 1; Thoreau, Henry David, 30; Villon, François, 2; Walker, Alice, 11; Watts, Alan, 1; Whitman, Walt, 35, 36; Wilde, Oscar, 54; Woolf, Virginia, 10

Selflessness Bible, 293; Bulgakov, Mikhail, 9; Hutcheson, Francis, 1; Jowett, Benjamin, 6; Lewis, C. S., 7; Smith, Adam, 1

Self-Preservation Ali, Muhammad, 3; Bonner, Marita, 1; Burke, Edmund, 51; Dempsey, Jack, 1; Dryden, John, 48; Fall, Aminata Sow, 1; Gwyn, Nell, 1; Heller, Joseph, 5; Hoover, J. Edgar, 1; Johnson, Samuel, 92; Juvenal, 15; Meir, Golda, 5; Meredith, George, 15; Mérimée, Prosper, 1; Perelman, S. J., 10; Plath, Sylvia, 12; Rousseau, Jean-Jacques, 16; Shakespeare, William, 245; Sieyès, Abbé, 2; Szasz, Thomas, 7; Voltaire, 51; Waugh, Evelyn, 24

Self-Reliance Baden-Powell, Robert, 2; Beaverbrook, Max Aitken, Lord, 5; Browne, Thomas, 5; Cervantes, Miguel de, 12; Charles V, 2; Crockett, Davy, 1; Elizabeth I, 11; Emerson, Ralph Waldo, 19; Hammarskjöld, Dag, 9; Ibsen, Henrik, 3; Marryat, Frederick, 2; Montaigne, Michel de, 4; O'Casey, Sean, 7; Shakespeare, William, 300; Stokes, Donald Gresham, 1; Young, David Ivor, 2

Self-Respect Baudelaire, Charles, 10; Bethune, Mary McLeod, 4; Browning, Robert, 47; Du Bois, W. E. B., 15; Emecheta, Buchi, 8; Gwyn, Nell, 2; Ibárruri, Dolores, 3; Mencken, H. L., 6; Nietzsche, Friedrich Wilhelm, 11; Perry, Eleanor, 1; Thoreau, Henry David, 24, 25; Tresckow, Henning von, 1; Washington, Booker T., 4; Whitman, Walt, 31; Wotton, Henry, 1

Sensation Chekhov, Anton, 18; Keats, John (1795–1821), 27; Laozi, 15; Muhammad, 15; Shakespeare, William, 136

Sensuality Pérez Galdós, Benito, 1; Vargas Llosa, Mario, 1; Wharton, Edith, 12

Sentimentality de Valera, Eamon, 5; Jung, Carl Gustav, 23; Mailer, Norman, 8; Maugham, Somerset, 8

Separation Cowper, William, 9; Li Shangyin, 2; Mandela, Winnie, 3; Muir, John, 9; Quincy, Josiah, 1

Seriousness Abzug, Bella, 1; Chateaubriand, René, 8; O'Brien, Flann, 6; Thiers, Adolphe, 1

Sermons Shaw, George Bernard, 116; Smith, Sydney, 21; Wellington, Duke of, 11; Winthrop, John, 1

Service Betjeman, John, 2; Bible, 288; Chisholm, Shirley, 5; Cornuel, Anne-Marie Bigot de, 1; Defoe, Daniel, 5; Fry, Christopher, 2; Keynes, John Maynard, 20; Kipling, Rudyard, 20; Lowell, A. Lawrence, 1; Loyola, Ignatius of, 3; Luce, Henry R., 2; O'Connell, Daniel, 1; Selfridge, H. Gordon, 1; Wells, H. G., 3; Wordsworth, William, 10

Servility Casely-Hayford, Joseph Ephraim, 2; Delany, Martin Robinson, 2; Rhodes, Cecil, 3; Thackeray, William Makepeace, 9

Sex Allen, Woody, 3, 4, 10, 25; al-Nawawi, Muhyid-Din Abu Zakariyya ibn Sharaf, 3; Amis, Martin, 1; Armstrong, Louis, 8; Austin, Mary, 6; Axelrod, George, 1; Ayckbourn, Alan, 2; Baden-Powell, Robert, 3; Bankhead, Tallulah, 8; Barham, Richard Harris, 1; Baudelaire, Charles, 2; Beauvoir, Simone de, 10; Beckett, Samuel, 15; Beerbohm, Max, 16; Bellow, Saul, 16; Bible, 171; Black, Hugo LaFayette, 2; Blackwell, Elizabeth, 2, 3; Bradbury, Malcolm, 10; Burgess, Anthony, 5; Burns, Robert, 51; Burroughs, William S., 4; Byron, Lord, 40; Calderone, Mary, 1; Campbell, Mrs. Patrick, 2; Campion, Thomas, 7; Cartland, Barbara, 3, 4; Catullus, 2; Chandler, Raymond, 3; Chekhov, Anton, 2; Chesterfield, Lord, 19; Cope, Wendy, 3; Costello, Lou, 1; Cullen, Countee, 2; Curzon, George Nathaniel, 5; Degler, Carl N., 3; Drabble, Margaret, 3; Durrell, Lawrence, 6; Dworkin, Andrea, 1, 2, 3; Eliot, T. S., 53; Escrivá de Balaguer y Albas, José María, 1; Fichte, Johann, 5; Figes, Eva, 2; Flanagan, Oliver J., 1, 3; Fleming, Ian, 1, 6; Folk Verse, 22, 26; Foot, Michael, 4; Forster, E. M., 3; Freud, Sigmund, 3, 16, 27, 50; Fuller, Margaret, 1; Grant, Cary, 1; Greer, Germaine, 2, 14; Harris, Frank, 1; Harris, Janet, 4; Hemingway, Ernest, 13; Housman, A. E.,

11; Hughes, Langston, 12; Huxley, Aldous, 27, 32; Jagger, Mick, 8; Jong, Erica, 3; Jonson, Ben, 14; Jung, Carl Gustav, 29; Kahn, Gus, 2; Kinsey, Alfred, 1; Landers, Ann, 1; Larkin, Philip, 11; Lawrence, D. H., 25, 26, 28; Lehrer, Tom, 1; Lennon & McCartney, 20; Lipman, Maureen, 1; Lodge, David, 2; Longford, Lord, 1; Loos, Anita, 1; McLuhan, Marshall, 4; MacNeice, Louis, 6; Marx, Groucho, 34; Midler, Bette, 2; Mikes, George, 3; Miller, Henry, 6; Miller, Max, 1; Milligan, Spike, 8; Mitford, Nancy, 4; Morrison, Toni, 26; Muggeridge, Malcolm, 3, 4, 5, 7; O'Casey, Sean, 8; O'Keeffe, John, 1; Ortega y Gasset, José, 6; Orton, Joe, 3; Osborne, John, 13; Paglia, Camille, 16; Parker, Dorothy, 28; Pasolini, Pier Paolo, 1; Payne, Cynthia, 1; Prior, Matthew, 2; Pryor, Richard, 3; Reuben, David, 1; Roethke, Theodore, 11; Rowland, Helen, 6; Sade, Marquis de, 2; Salinger, J. D., 15; Sankara, Thomas, 2; Scharlieb, Dame Mary Ann Dacomb, 2; Shakespeare, William, 254, 360, 401, 465, 467; Sharpe, Tom, 1; Sigerist, Henry E., 3; Spark, Muriel, 6; Stopes, Marie, 6; Swift, Jonathan, 4; Szasz, Thomas, 15; Thomas, Dylan, 17, 21; Updike, John, 7; Vail, Amanda, 1; Voltaire, 55; Walker, Alice, 16; Warhol, Andy, 11; Waugh, Evelyn, 33; Welch, Raquel, 1; West, Mae, 3, 7, 8, 22; White, E. B., 12; Wilde, Oscar, 16; Williams, Tennessee, 14; Wilson, Harriette, 2; Winn, Mary Day, 1; Yeats, W. B., 50; Young, Brigham, 7; Zucker, David, 1

Sexes Adams, Abigail, 8; Austin, Mary, 5; Ayckbourn, Alan, 6; Balzac, Honoré de, 9; Bashkirtseff, Marie, 1; Beauvoir, Simone de, 15; Behan, Brendan, 1; Behn, Aphra, 4; Bellow, Saul, 5; Blackwell, Antoinette Louisa, 2; Cao Xueqin, 1; Chamfort, Nicolas, 3; Chisholm, Shirley, 2; Compton-Burnett, Ivy, 3; Connolly, Cyril, 15; Cope, Wendy, 5; Crummell, Alexander, 1; Darwin, Charles, 7; Dickens, Charles, 42; Dors, Diana, 1; Douglass, Frederick, 23; Dunne, Finley Peter, 2; Gassman, Vittorio, 1; Gingold, Hermione, 1; Golden, Marita, 6; Greer, Germaine, 9; Head, Bessie, 6; Johnson, Georgia Douglas, 2; Koran, 12; Lebowitz, Fran, 2; Lee-Potter, Linda, 1; Loos, Anita, 4; Mackenzie, Compton, 6; Mead, Margaret, 7; Mencken, H. L., 50; Mill, John Stuart, 14; Nicholson, Jack, 1; Plath, Sylvia, 9; Pope, Alexander, 39; Proverbs, Modern, 17; Pynchon, Thomas, 5; Smith, Adam, 2; Solanas, Valerie, 1; Spice Girls, The, 1; Steinem, Gloria, 2, 8; Sterne, Laurence, 7; Stevenson, Robert Louis, 38; Tennyson, Alfred, 86, 87; Thurber, James, 10; Tuke, Samuel, 1; Turnbull, Margaret, 2; Wallace, Naomi, 1; Woolf, Virginia, 7

Sexism Boccaccio, Giovanni, 1; Constitution of the United States, 6; Greer, Germaine, 7; Jordan, June, 6; Madonna, 2; Mitchell, Margaret, 11; Thomas, Irene, 2; Walker, Alice, 24; Whitehorn, Katharine, 5

Sexuality Adler, Alfred, 4; Bara, Theda, 1; Bergman, Ingmar, 5; Bowie, David, 3; Harris, Janet, 3; Huxley, Aldous, 13; Kollwitz, Käthe, 1; Lawrence, D. H., 21; Nietzsche, Friedrich Wilhelm, 7; Polanski, Roman, 1; Springfield, Dusty, 1; Stopes, Marie, 4; Wax, Ruby, 1; William III, 3; Young, Allen, 1

Shame Canetti, Elias, 2; Shakespeare, William, 605; Twain, Mark, 39; Whittier, John Greenleaf, 1

Shops Selfridge, H. Gordon, 2

Shortness Richards, Gordon, 1

Shyness Allen, Woody, 9; Darling, Charles John, 1; Herrick, Robert, 15; Keith, Penelope, 1; Marlowe, Christopher, 27; Taylor, Elizabeth, 4; Wordsworth, William, 31

Sight Addison, Joseph, 18; Larkin, Philip, 8; McCaig, Norman, 15

Signatures Joyce, James, 25

Silence Beckett, Samuel, 18; Bowen, Elizabeth, 6; Cage, John, 8; Coleridge, Samuel Taylor, 49; Columbus, Christopher, 8; Durant, Will, 17; Goldsmith, Oliver, 23; Hardy, Thomas, 31; Harris, Joel Chandler, 2; Heaney, Seamus, 7; Hurston, Zora Neale, 9; Huxley, Aldous, 41; Kübler-Ross, Elisabeth, 1; La Rochefoucauld, François, 14; Lawrence, D. H., 41; Lu Xun, 4; Mahon, Derek, 5; Olson, Charles, 5; Pinter, Harold, 2; Plath, Sylvia, 6; Plutarch, 1; Proverbs, 266; Sartre, Jean-Paul, 15; Shakespeare, William, 567; Shaw, George Bernard, 20; Simon, Paul, 4; Sitwell, Edith, 12; Tennyson, Alfred, 13; Teresa of Ávila, Saint, 8; Teresa of Calcutta, Mother, 8; Vega, Lope de, 1; Vigny, Alfred de, 2; Wither, George, 1; Yeats, W. B., 12

Similarity Forster, E. M., 7; Lyly, John, 5; Van Buren, Abigail, 3; Van der Post, Laurens, 1

Simplicity Addison, Joseph, 6; Berlin, Irving, 3; Fischer, Martin H., 12; Freeman, Richard Austin, 1; Hofmann, Hans, 1; Huss, John, 1; James, Henry, 41; Jerome, Saint, 2; Laozi, 20; Reid, Thomas, 2; Shakespeare, William, 531; Victoria, 2; Whitehead, A. N., 18

Sin Auden, W. H., 20; Beecham, Thomas, 10; Bible, 124, 180, 195, 234, 245, 276, 280, 357, 481; Bunyan, John, 19; Byron, Lord, 9; Campbell, Thomas, 8; Cao Yu, 1; Cervantes, Miguel de, 36; Cliff, Michelle, 1; Coolidge, Calvin, 18; Crane, Stephen, 1; Dos Passos, John, 12; Durant, Will, 7; Eddy, Mary Baker, 4; Elaw, Zilpha, 1; Folk Verse, 41; France, Anatole, 6; Garbo, Greta, 2; Hellman, Lillian, 4; Henry, Matthew, 2; Huxley, Aldous, 49; Kierkegaard, Søren, 8, 9; Lawrence, D. H., 45; Lee, Harper, 3; McGinley, Phyllis, 2; Machado de Assis, Joaquim Maria, 2; Milton, John, 23; Morley, Christopher Darlington, 5; Napier, Charles James, 1; Nash, Ogden, 4; Plomer, William, 4; Quevedo y Villegas, Francisco Gómez de, 1; Schiller, Friedrich von, 7; Shakespeare, William, 176, 196, 260; Talmud, 7; Teresa of Ávila, Saint, 9; West, Mae, 11, 21; Wilde, Oscar, 26

Sincerity Bryan, William Jennings, 3; Coleridge, Samuel Taylor, 59; Donne, John, 39; Driberg, Tom, 1; Hailsham, Lord, 3; Ortega y Gasset, José, 28; Renard, Jules, 7; Shaw, George Bernard, 44; Vauvenargues, Marquis de, 1; Wilde, Oscar, 22

Singapore Lee, Kuan Yew, 1, 4

Singers and Singing Brel, Jacques, 1; Charles, Ray, 1; Coleridge, Samuel Taylor, 61; Gershwin, George, 1; Gilbert, W. S., 41; Harry, Deborah, 1; Holiday, Billie, 2, 4; Horne, Marilyn, 1; Joplin, Janis, 5; King, B. B., 1; Melba, Nellie, 4; Newman, Ernest, 3; Presley, Elvis, 1; Reeves, Martha, 1; Stipe, Michael, 2; Tennyson, Alfred, 69; Tucker, Sophie, 3; Williams, Hank, 1

Sinners Bible, 258, 284, 339; Runyon, Damon, 7

Sisters Rossetti, Christina, 3

Slavery Alexander II, 2; al-Mufid, Abu Abdullah Muhammad al-Harithi al-Baghdadi, 8; Aptheker, Herbert, 3; Aristotle, 25; Baldwin, James, 5; Ball, John, 1; Baraka, Imamu Amiri, 14; Behn, Aphra, 2; Brown, John, 2; Constantine, Learie, 1, 3; Constitution of the United States, 4; Cugoano, Ottobah, 1, 2; Delany, Martin Robinson, 1; Douglass, Frederick, 1, 4, 11, 12, 13, 15, 16, 17, 18, 19, 20, 22, 25; Douglas, Stephen A., 1; Drumgoold, Kate, 1; Dunbar, Paul Laurence, 4; Equiano, Olaudah, 3; Evans, Mari, 2; Fanon, Frantz, 5; Folk Verse, 61; Garnet, Henry Highland, 2; Garrison, William Lloyd, 1, 2, 3; Giovanni, Nikki, 1; Grimké, Angelina Emily, 2; Harper, Frances E. W., 7; Horton, George Moses, 1; Jackson, Mattie J., 1; Jacobs, Harriet Ann, 1; Jefferson, Thomas, 39, 40; Lincoln, Abraham, 28, 31; Marley, Bob, 1; Northup, Solomon, 1, 2; Paul, Nathaniel, 1; Pope, Alexander, 92; Remond, Charles Lenox, 1; Sadat, Anwar al-, 1; Sembène, Ousmane, 4; Sewall, Samuel, 1; Seward, William Henry, 1; Thoreau, Henry David, 3; Toussaint L'Ouverture, 3; Twain, Mark, 37; Walker, Alice, 29; Washington, Booker T., 9; Wedderburn, Robert, 1; Wheatley, Phillis, 2

Sleep Achebe, Chinua, 3; Bowles, Paul, 1; Browne, Thomas, 2, 33; Burgess, Anthony, 6; Cervantes, Miguel de, 49; Chamfort, Nicolas, 10; Dekker, Thomas, 2, 4; Dove, Rita, 2; Emerson, Ralph Waldo, 63; Heraclitus, 8; Holmes, Oliver Wendell, 17; Jennings, Elizabeth, 2; Keats, John (1795–1821), 68, 73; Lebowitz, Fran, 3; Matthiessen, Peter, 8; O'Brien, Edna, 3; Parker, Dorothy, 16; Phaer, Thomas, 1; Priestley, J. B., 2; Proverbs, Modern, 22; Shakespeare, William, 256; Sidney, Philip, 3; Steinbeck, John, 34; Sterne, Laurence, 17; Stevens, Anthony, 5; Thomas, Edward, 3; Twain, Mark, 44; Virgil, 15

Slogans Advertisements, 1, 4, 7, 8, 11, 14, 17, 20, 22, 25; Allen, William, 1; Arafat, Yasir, 2; Lenin, Vladimir Ilyich, 11; Mottos and Slogans, 1, 3, 4, 9, 14,

24, 27, 29, 30, 31, 33, 34, 35, 36, 37, 38; Mussolini, Benito, 1; O'Keefe, Patrick, 1; Sloan, Alfred P., Jr., 6

Smallness Maupassant, Guy de, 2; Woolf, Virginia, 18

Smoking Anonymous, 28; Barrie, J. M., 5; Beecham, Thomas, 12; Buñuel, Luis, 5; Burton, Robert, 10; Colette, 2; Elizabeth I, 20; Field, Eugene, 4; Freneau, Philip, 4; Helps, Arthur, 1; Hoban, Russell, 2; James I, 3, 4; Johnson, Samuel, 64; Jonson, Ben, 4, 12; Kellogg, John Harvey, 1; Kipling, Rudyard, 32; Lamb, Charles, 6, 10, 26; Morris, Desmond, 1; Napoleon III, 6; Shields, Brooke, 1; Sylvester, Robert, 1; Toscanini, Arturo, 3; Twain, Mark, 60; Venner, Tobias, 1; Wilde, Oscar, 64

Snobbery Beardsley, Aubrey, 1; Belloc, Hilaire, 12; Bossidy, John Collins, 1; Dickens, Charles, 32; Douglas-Home, Alec, 1; Farjeon, Herbert, 1; Farquhar, George, 2; Gandhi, Indira, 1; Gogarty, Oliver St. John, 4; Hardy, Thomas, 28; Hoagland, Edward, 10; Morgan, John Pierpont, 3; Proust, Marcel, 15; Sitwell, Edith, 9; Smith, Adam, 6; Strindberg, August, 5; Thackeray, William Makepeace, 2; Waugh, Evelyn, 1; Wilde, Oscar, 48, 55; Wilson, Angus, 2

Soccer Marsh, Rodney, 1; Stubbes, Philip, 2

Socialism Bennett, Alan, 2; Bevan, Aneurin, 8; Buber, Martin, 10; Dubček, Alexander, 1, 2; Durant, Will, 18; Engels, Friedrich, 6; Gorbachev, Mikhail, 9, 14; Heym, Stefan, 1; Jaurès, Jean, 1, 3; Lenin, Vladimir Ilyich, 7, 8, 20; MacDonald, Ramsay, 3; Marsh, Richard, 1; Marx, Karl, 4, 10; Orwell, George, 37, 38

Social Mobility Brando, Marlon, 4; Thatcher, Margaret, 27

Society Arendt, Hannah, 16; Bacon, Francis (1561–1626), 94; Ballard, J. G., 1; Blackstone, William, 6; Blackwell, Elizabeth, 1; Bramah, Ernest, 2; Brontë, Charlotte, 8; Butler, Nicholas Murray, 1; Cavafy, Constantine, 2; Chaplin, Charlie, 9; Cicero, 6, 12; Clinton, Hillary, 1; Coate, John, 1; Delors, Jacques, 3; Gandhi, Mahatma, 22; George, Henry, 3; Howells, William Dean, 1; Illich, Ivan, 1; Kennedy, John Fitzgerald, 15; Keynes, John Maynard, 12; Lu Xun, 13; Major, John, 5; Malcolm X, 8; Mead, Margaret, 3; Montale, Eugenio, 3; Mumford, Lewis, 1; Napoleon III, 1; Olson, Charles, 2; Perlman, Lawrence, 4; Pirenne, Henri, 1; Popper, Karl, 4; Priestley, J. B., 4; Robespierre, Maximilien, 3; Roosevelt, Theodore, 12; Schell, Jonathan, 4, 5; Shakespeare, William, 133; Shaw, George Bernard, 27; Sinclair, Clive, 6; Solon, 2; Stevenson, Adlai, 2; Stowe, Harriet Beecher, 2; Temple, William, 1; Thatcher, Margaret, 35; Walker, Margaret, 4; White, E. B., 3; Wilde, Oscar, 72

Sociology Chomsky, Noam, 2; Knight, Frank Hyneman, 6; Merton, Robert K., 1; Poincaré, Jules Henri, 5

Soldiers Anna Comnena, 1; Browning, Robert, 12, 13; Davenant, William, 1; Ewer, William Norman, 1; Freneau, Philip, 3; Hippolytus of Rome, 1; Hood, Thomas, 21; Kipling, Rudyard, 17, 28; O'Brien, Tim, 2, 4, 5; O'Hara, Theodore, 1; Owen, Wilfred, 1, 2, 8, 9; Rosten, Norman, 1; Saint-Exupéry, Antoine de, 1; Scott, Sir Walter, 6; Shaw, George Bernard, 17, 86, 119; Tolstoy, Leo, 11; Trinder, Tommy, 1; Ustinov, Peter, 4

Solidarity Bible, 50, 51; Meredith, James, 1

Solitude Bacon, Francis (1561–1626), 9, 30; Cowper, William, 23; De Gaulle, Charles, 12; Dickens, Charles, 104; Dickinson, Emily, 21; Donne, John, 49; Garbo, Greta, 5; Gibbon, Edward, 2; Hazlitt, William, 20; Jia Dao, 1; Jiménez, Juan Ramón, 6; Jong, Erica, 2; Kilvert, Francis, 2; Milton, John, 78; Mitchell, Adrian, 1; Montaigne, Michel de, 8; Nabokov, Vladimir, 2; Sacks, Jonathan, 4; Stendhal, 2; Tennyson, Alfred, 50; Thoreau, Henry David, 39, 40; Wordsworth, William, 30, 65, 86; Yeats, W. B., 30

Songs Children's Verse, 63; Cohn, Nik, 2; Costello, Elvis, 1; Dubin, Al, 2; Dylan, Bob, 23; Emmett, Daniel Decatur, 1; Hall, Charles Sprague, 1; Herrick, Robert, 4; Heywood, John, 1; Hill, Rowland, 1; Joyce, James, 24; Maugham, Somerset, 6; Murphy, C. W., 1; Nelson, Willie, 1; Parra, Violeta, 1; Pope, Alexander, 50; Porter, Cole, 1; Robin, Leo, 2; Shelley, Percy Bysshe, 23, 24; Sondheim, Stephen, 1, 2; Travis, Merle, 1; Watson, William, 1; Wyatt, Thomas, 1

Sons Bible, 132; Kyd, Thomas, 2; Shakespeare, William, 187

Sorrow Aidoo, Ama Ata, 2; Al-Khansa, 1; Bennett, Gwendolyn, 1; Bible, 287; Brathwaite, Edward Kamau, 3; Faulkner, William, 15; Ferguson, Samuel, 1; Folk Verse, 55; Gide, André, 3; Goethe, Johann Wolfgang von, 12; Hallam, Arthur Henry, 5, 11; Hardy, Thomas, 24; Harper, Frances E. W., 6; Joyce, James, 11; Longfellow, Henry Wadsworth, 21; McMurtry, Larry, 3; Milton, John, 36; Moore, Thomas, 16; O'Connell, Eibhlin Dubh, 2; Parker, Dorothy, 15; Pope, Alexander, 96; Rhys, Jean, 1; Saint-Exupéry, Antoine de, 4; Shakespeare, William, 141, 339, 503, 558, 671; Tennyson, Alfred, 26; Tolstoy, Leo, 14; Verlaine, Paul, 5; Virgil, 9; West, Rebecca, 2

Soul Aristotle, 4; Bible, 246, 359; Boyle, Robert, 1; Brontë, Charlotte, 5; Browning, Robert, 42; Buber, Martin, 9; Cicero, 16; Gu Cheng, 1; Hadrian, 1; Himes, Chester, 2; Hume, David, 14; James, William, 15; Jiménez, Juan Ramón, 2; Leibniz, Gottfried Wilhelm, 10; Lewis, Alun, 1; Lowell, Robert, 17; Machado, Antonio, 13; Mistral, Gabriela, 4; Ortega y Gasset, José, 12; Pliny the Younger, 4; Pope, Alexander, 54; Raleigh, Walter, 4; Smart, Christopher, 7; Soyinka, Wole, 1; Sterne, Laurence, 4; Vaughan, Henry, 2; Wilbur, Richard, 1; Wittgenstein, Ludwig, 2; Wordsworth, William, 14, 38; Ye Si, 1

South Africa Botha, P. W., 2, 3; Campbell, Roy, 1; Cullen, Countee, 3; de Blank, Joost, 1; de Klerk, F. W., 1, 2; Mandela, Nelson, 11; Tambo, Oliver, 1; Tutu, Desmond, 11

South America Dietrich, Marlene, 2

South Carolina Timrod, Henry, 1

Southeast Asia Conrad, Joseph, 14

Soviet Union, The Attlee, Clement, 2; Bukovsky, Vladimir, 2; Bulgakov, Mikhail, 3; Gorbachev, Mikhail, 6; Hurd, Douglas, 1; Nabokov, Vladimir, 11; Solzhenitsyn, Alexander, 1; Zoshchenko, Mikhail, 2

Space Adams, Douglas, 7; Armstrong, Neil, 1, 3; Asimov, Isaac, 3; Dillard, Annie, 3; Hoyle, Fred, 2; Lovell, James, 1; Milton, John, 80; Nixon, Richard, 37; Taupin, Bernie, 3; Tomlinson, Rick, 1; Vidal, Gore, 14; von Braun, Wernher, 1; Wolfe, Tom, 22

Spain Alcala Galiano, Juan Valera, 1; Brenan, Gerald, 1; Calvo Sotelo, José, 1; Cambó, Francisco, 1, 2; Cánovas del Castillo, Antonio, 1, 2; Franco, Francisco, 6; Ibárruri, Dolores, 1; Machado, Antonio, 1; Maragall, Joan, 1; Narváez, Ramón María, 1; Orwell, George, 14; Pérez Galdós, Benito, 7, 8; Vallejo, César, 1

Speculation Baruch, Bernard Mannes, 6; Hanson, Lord, 1; Hazlitt, William, 5; Kennedy, Joseph, 2

Speech Aragon, Louis, 1; Bible, 27; Cervantes, Miguel de, 27; Darwin, Erasmus, 1; Dickens, Charles, 44; Goldsmith, Oliver, 6; Hammett, Dashiell, 2; Hobbes, Thomas, 10; James, Henry, 37; James, William, 25; Johnson, Samuel, 68; Jonson, Ben, 21; Langland, William, 6; Meredith, George, 14; Molière, 6; Moore, Thomas, 15; Plutarch, 13; Richardson, Ralph, 2; Shaw, George Bernard, 2, 78

Speeches Anonymous, 75; Attlee, Clement, 7; Brabazon, Derek, 1; Cavendish, Spencer Compton, 1; Churchill, Winston, 5, 23, 65, 81; Emerson, Ralph Waldo, 42, 67; Hubbard, Frank McKinney, 3; Johnson, Samuel, 2; Macaulay, Thomas Babington, 26; Mancroft, Stormont Samuel, 3; Meyer, Lawrence H., 1; Montesquieu, 13; Roosevelt, Franklin D., 37; Shakespeare, William, 308; Twain, Mark, 53; Wilson, Woodrow, 28

Splitting Up Andersson, Benny, 1; Koehler, Ted, 1; Lennon, John, 3; Spector, Phil, 2

Spontaneity Addison, Joseph, 8; Cantona, Eric, 1; Lawrence, D. H., 35; Sartre, Jean-Paul, 19; Talleyrand, Charles Maurice de, 8

Spoonerisms Spooner, William Archibald, 1, 2, 3, 4, 5

Sports and Games Addison, Joseph, 24; Austen, Jane, 23; Bernhardt, Sarah, 2; Blanchflower, Danny, 1; Bradley, Bill, 1; Christie, Linford, 2, 3; Coe, Sebastian,